To
Read
Literature
Fiction
Poetry
Drama

Donald Hall

Also by Donald Hall

Poetry

Exiles and Marriages
The Dark Houses
A Roof of Tiger Lilies
The Alligator Bride: Poems New and Selected
The Yellow Room
The Town of Hill
Kicking the Leaves

Prose

String Too Short to Be Saved
Henry Moore
Writing Well
Playing Around (with G. McCauley et al.)
Dock Ellis in the Country of Baseball
Goatfoot Milktongue Twinbird
Remembering Poets
Ox Cart Man

Editions

New Poets of England and America (with R. Pack and L. Simpson)
The Poetry Sampler
New Poets of England and America (Second Selection) (with R. Pack)
Contemporary American Poets
A Concise Encyclopedia of English and American Poetry and Poets
 (with Stephen Spender)
Poetry in English (with Warren Taylor)
The Modern Stylists
A Choice of Whitman's Verse
Man and Boy
American Poetry
A Writer's Reader (with D. L. Emblen)

To
Read
Literature
Fiction
Poetry
Drama

Donald Hall

Holt, Rinehart and Winston

New York   Chicago   San Francisco   Atlanta
Dallas   Montreal   Toronto   London   Sydney

To Ralph and Mary Lou

Library of Congress Cataloging in Publication Data
Hall, Donald, 1928–
  To read literature: fiction, poetry, drama.

  Includes index.

  1. Literature—History and criticism. 2. Literature
—Collections. I. Title.

PN524.H25   808.8   80–19971

ISBN 0–03–021006–2

1 2 3 4 5 6 7 8 9   032   9 8 7 6 5 4 3 2 1

Acknowledgments of copyright ownership and permission to reproduce works included in this
volume begin on page 1477.

Special projects editor: Pamela Forcey
Project editor and copy editor: H. L. Kirk
Editorial assistant: Anita Baskin
Production manager: Nancy J. Myers
Art director: Louis Scardino
Typography and cover design: Ben Kann
Cover photo: J. D. Brown/Taurus Photos

To the Student

To read literature

This book introduces the three principal types or genres of literature: fiction, poetry, and drama. When we learn to read literature, we acquire a pleasure and a resource we never lose. Although literary study is impractical in one sense— few people make their living reading books—in another sense it is almost as practical as breathing. Literature records and embodies centuries of human thought and feeling, preserving for us the minds of people who lived before us, who were like us and unlike us, against whom we can measure our common humanity and our historical difference. And when we read the stories, poems, and plays of our contemporaries they illuminate the world all of us share.

When we read great literature, something changes in us that stays changed. Literature remembered becomes material to think with. No one who has read *Hamlet* well is quite the same again. Reading adds tools by which we observe, measure, and judge the people and the properties of our universe; we understand the actions and motives of others and of ourselves.

In the fable of the ant and the grasshopper, the wise ant builds his storehouse against winter and prospers; the foolish grasshopper saves nothing and perishes. Anyone who dismisses the study of literature on the ground that it will not be useful—to a chemist or an engineer, to a foreman or an X-ray technician—imitates the grasshopper. When we shut from our lives everything except food and shelter, part of us starves to death. Food for this hunger is music, painting, film, plays, poems, stories, and novels. Much writing in newspapers, magazines, and popular novels is not literature, if we reserve that word for work of high quality. This reading gives us as little nourishment as most television and most fast food. For the long winters and energetic summers of our lives, we require the sustenance of literature.

Reading literature old and new—taking into ourselves the work of nineteenth-century Russian storytellers, sixteenth-century English dramatists, and contemporary American poets—we build a storehouse of knowledge and we entertain ourselves as well. But to take pleasure and understanding from literature we have to learn how to read it. No one expects to walk up to a computer and be able to program it without first learning something about computers. For some reason—perhaps because we are familiar with words from childhood and take them for granted—we tend to think that a quick glance at the written word should reward us, and that if we do not take instant satisfaction the work is beyond us, or not worth it, or irrelevant or boring. But all our lives, in other skills, we have needed instruction and practice—to be able to ride a bicycle, drive a car, play guitar, shoot baskets, typewrite, dance.

The knowledge we derive from literature can seem confusing. Equally great works may contradict each other in the generalizations we derive from them. One work may recommend solitude, another society. One may advise us to seize the moment, another to live a life of contemplation. Or, two good readers may disagree about the implication of a work and each argue convincingly, with detailed references to the writing, in support of contrary interpretations. A complex work of literature cannot be reduced to a simple, correct meaning. In an elementary arithmetic text, the answers may be printed in the back of the book. There are no answers to be printed in the back of this book or any collection of literature.

Such nebulousness, or ambiguity, disturbs some students. After an hour's class discussion of a short story, with varying interpretations offered, they want to know "But what *does* it mean?" We must admit that literature is inexact, and its truth is not easily verifiable. Probably the story means several things at once, and not one thing at all. This is not to say, however, that it means anything that anybody finds in it. Although differing, equally defensible opinions are common, error is even more common.

When we speak of truth in the modern world, we usually mean something scientific or tautological. Arithmetic contains the truth of tautology; two and two make four because our definitions of *two* and *four* say so. In laboratories we encounter the truth of statistics and the truth of observation. If we smoke cigarettes heavily, it is true that we have one chance in four to develop lung cancer. When we heat copper wire over a Bunsen burner, the flame turns blue.

But there is an older sense of truth, in which statements apparently opposite can both be valid. In this older tradition, truth is dependent on context and circumstance, on the agreement of sensible men and women—like the "Guilty" or "Not guilty" verdict of a jury. Because this literary (or philosophical, or legal, or historical) truth is inexact, changeable, and subject to argument, literature can seem nebulous to minds accustomed to arithmetical certainty.

Let me argue this: If literature is nebulous or inexact; if it is impossible to determine, with scientific precision, the value or the meaning of a work of art, *this inexactness is the price literature pays for representing whole human beings.* Human beings themselves, in their feelings and thoughts, in the wanderings of their short lives, are ambiguous and ambivalent, shifting mixtures of permanence and change, direction and disorder. Because literature is true to life, true to the complexities of human feeling, different people will read the same work with different responses. And literary art will sometimes affirm that opposite things are both true *because they are.* Such a condition is not tidy; it is perhaps regrettable—but it is human nature.

The words themselves

I have talked as if literature were the feelings and thoughts we derive from reading. Whatever literature accomplishes in us, it accomplishes by words. As paint and canvas form the medium of painting, as sequences and combinations of sound different in pitch, duration, and quality form the medium of music, so the right words in the right order make literature.

A Japanese named Basho wrote this haiku about three hundred years ago:

> The morning glory—
> another thing
> that will never be my friend.

Basho reminds us that the natural world is separate from us, that we may not shoulder our way into it, like invading troops of the imagination, and assume that we are intimate with everything. The American poet Robert Bly translated these lines. Here are three other versions:

A. The morning glory
   is a separate being
   and I can never know it intimately.

B. The morning glory
   is yet another object
   with which I will never become closely acquainted.

C. The morning glory—
   something else
   that won't call me companion.

To understand and appreciate how these four versions differ from one another is to become sensitive to the words that make literature. In a general way, they all mean the same thing. After the identical first lines, the translations differ in diction, which is the kinds of words chosen, and in rhythm, which is the pace and tempo of the words. Versions A and B are dry, stiff, and unnatural. *Separate being* sounds pretentious compared to *another thing. Yet another object* is finicky with its *yet another,* and *object* is more scientific-sounding than the casual *thing.* "With which I will never become closely acquainted" is formal and distant, rhythmically slow. "And I can never know it intimately" lacks interest or surprise in its words. The simplicity of "that will never be my friend," coming to rest on the surprise of the last word, makes Bly's translation blossom in its final word. In version C, on the other hand, we have a translation nearly as pleasing as the original one. *Something else* has its own casual simplicity, and the little action of *call me companion*—where the morning glory is imagined capable of speech—has some of the surprise that the original translation found in *friend*.

The difference is the words and their order.

What's good, what's bad

The claims I make for literature are large: that it alters and enlarges our minds, our connections with each other past and present, our understanding of our own feelings. These claims apply to excellent literature only. This introduction to literature suggests that some literature is better than other literature, and that some writing is not literature at all. Even if judgments are always subject to reversal, even if there is no way we can be certain of being correct, evaluation lives at the center of literary study.

When I was nineteen, I liked to read everything: science fiction, Russian novels, mystery stories, great poems, adventure magazines. Then for six months after an accident, sentenced to a hospital bed and a body cast, I set myself a reading list, all serious books I had been thinking about getting to. Of course there was a background to this choice: I had been taught by a good teacher who had directed and encouraged and stimulated my reading. I read through Shakespeare, the Bible in the King James version, novels by Henry James and Ernest Hemingway and William Faulkner. Toward the end of six months, taking physical therapy, I hurried to finish the books I had assigned myself; I looked forward to taking a vacation among private detectives and adventurers of the twenty-fourth century. I thought I would take a holiday of light reading.

When I tried to read the light things, I experienced one of those "turning points in life" we are asked to describe in freshman composition. I remember the dismay, the abject melancholy that crept over me as I realized—restless, turning from book to book in search of entertainment—that these books bored me; that I was ruined for life, that I would never again lose myself to stick-figure characters and artificial suspense. Literature ruined me for light reading.

To you who begin this book, I give fair warning. If you read these stories and poems and plays with attention, you may lose any taste you have for television sit-coms, for Gothic novels, for Rod McKuen. Something happens.

I don't mean to say that I was able to give reasons why Fyodor Dostoyevsky's novel about a murder was better than Agatha Christie's or why Aldous Huxley's view of the future, though less exciting, was more satisfying than *Astounding Science Fiction*'s. But I began a lifetime of trying to figure out why. What *is* it that makes Shakespeare so valuable to us? The struggle to name reasons for value—to evaluate works of art—is lifelong, and although we may never arrive at satisfactory explanations, the struggle makes the mind more sensitive, more receptive to the next work of literature it encounters. And as the mind becomes more sensitive and receptive to literature, it may become more sensitive and receptive to all sorts of things.

. . . and to the Instructor

In making selections and in writing the text for this collection, I have tried to serve one purpose: to help students read literature with intelligence, gusto, and discrimination.

This book begins the study of fiction and poetry by examining whole examples, emphasizing that the goal of reading is not the analysis of parts, but the understanding of wholes. For fuller definition of literature's components, later chapters concentrate on parts: on characterization in fiction, for example, and on images in poetry.

Selections are frequently modern or contemporary; students best begin literary study without the distraction of an unfamiliar vocabulary. Of course it would be silly to let this principle cheat us of Shakespeare; *Othello* and *Hamlet* are both included, *Hamlet* paired with Tom Stoppard's absurdist comedy *Rosencrantz and Guildenstern Are Dead*. The drama section begins with a new translation of Sophocles' *Oedipus the King,* and ends with a section on film that includes the script of a classic American movie, Orson Welles' *Citizen Kane.*

I intend the text to be readable and entertaining while it remains serious. Because everyone is curious about the lives of authors we read (whether we ought to be or not), there are biographical notes on all the writers. My emphasis is nevertheless neither biographical nor historical but aesthetic: I mean to examine the way literature works. Discussing characterization, I wish to find the writer's practical means toward characterization—in his choice of words, in his dialogue and description.

Footnotes and glosses translate foreign-language material, provide essential identifications, and define words not available in many dictionaries, or words used in archaic sense. The Appendix, "Writing on Writing," should provide guidance for students preparing papers on literature.

I've taken advice from several hundred American teachers of literature. When this book was only a notion, several years back, many people answered a questionnaire about what it should include. I am grateful; I have followed many suggestions.

Other professors read portions of the manuscript and commented in detail. I should like especially to thank Sylvan Barnet, R. S. Beal, Gary Blake, John Boni, Larry Champion, Barbara J. Cicardo, Paul Davis, R. H. Deutsch, Richard Dietrich, Donald Drury, John L. Fell, Art Goldsher, Randolph Goodman, William J. Gracie, Jr., Barnett Guttenberg, Nancy J. Hazelton, Michael Hogan, Woodrow L. Holbein, John Huxhold, Henry E. Jacobs, Robert C. Johnson, John J. Keenan, Mike Keene, X. J. Kennedy, Hannah Laipson, Bette B. Lansdown, James MacKillop, James Moody, William W. Nolte II, Anne Pidgeon, Doris Powers, Jules Ryckebusch, H. Miller Solomon, Joe Sperry, William Stull, Cathy Turner, Martha Weathers, and James D. Welch.

Collaboration and help at Holt, Rinehart and Winston began with Harriett Prentiss and continued with Kenney Withers and Susan Katz, editors to whom I am especially grateful. Pamela Forcey was masterful at production and H. L. Kirk a superb copy editor. Anita Baskin handled permissions and many other matters.

Finally, let me thank my own helpers in New Hampshire, in Ann Arbor, and in Santa Monica: Lois Fierro, Sharon Giannotta, Dorothy Foster, Pat Wykes, and Frank Barham—not to mention Jane Kenyon.

D. H.

Contents

TO READ A POEM   383

TO READ A PLAY   731

To Read Literature
Fiction
Poetry
Drama

Donald Hall

TO READ A STORY

Chapter 1 **One Modern Short Story**

People are story-telling animals. The Bible is full of stories—the history of a people, moral tales, magical tales, parables. An epic like the *Odyssey* is one big story made up of hundreds of little ones, passed from generation to generation by storytellers before there was a written language. These are tales from the youth of our civilization. In our own early youth, we listen to stories and we learn to tell them. On television and movie screens we watch stories develop before our eyes, as we do in the panels of a comic strip. As we grow up, we read narratives of contemporary events in newspapers. In novels we read long imaginary narratives. Stories accompany us through our lives.

A story need not be literature, but most literature begins as story or includes story. It thus makes sense to start studying literature by reading one good modern short story as a gateway to others. To begin investigating fiction, we will ask twenty questions about the story—and then try to answer them. Writing about "A Rose for Emily," we will touch on critical terms treated at greater length in later chapters. Chapter 4 concentrates on plot, Chapter 5 on character, and Chapter 6 on setting. In this chapter we will speak briefly about each of these elements of fiction as they appear in "A Rose for Emily."

William Faulkner
A Rose for Emily

William Faulkner (1897–1962) remains one of America's great novelists and storywriters. A chronicler of the South, he was born and raised in Oxford, Mississippi, where he lived most of his life and where he died. Although Faulkner traveled to New York to see his publishers, to Hollywood to write screenplays, and late in his life to the University of Virginia to teach, Oxford was the main locus of his life and his fiction. As a young man he attended Ole Miss (The University of Mississippi in Oxford), where he was considered both uppity and shiftless, a combination that earned him the nickname Count No 'Count. He wrote poems without great success and then turned to storytelling, for which he had great talent. His novels began with *Soldier's Pay* (1926) and *Mosquitoes* (1927), which won him attention and little else. With *Sartoris* (1929) he found his great theme, the history of a mythical Southern county called Yoknapatawpha. Faulkner chronicled Yoknapatawpha's inhabitants from its original Indians to its rich, plantation-owning families—Compson and Sartoris—then on through rebellion and Reconstruction to a modern era dominated by the shrewd and ignoble Snopes clan. In 1929 he also published *The Sound and the Fury,* which many critics find his best work. The year 1930 brought *As I Lay Dying*; *Light in August* followed in 1932, *Absalom, Absalom* in 1936. His best later work is comic: *The Hamlet* (1940), *The Town* (1957), and *The Mansion* (1960) further chronicle the unscrupulous Snopeses.

In 1931 *Sanctuary* sold well, but for the most part Faulkner's novels earned him little, and for his living he had to look elsewhere. Even after being awarded the Nobel Prize in 1950, Faulkner needed money from universities and from Hollywood. Earlier, he had supported himself by writing well-crafted short stories for popular magazines. "A Rose for Emily" appeared in *Forum* in 1930.

1

When Miss Emily Grierson died, our whole town went to her funeral: the men through a sort of respectful affection for a fallen monument, the women mostly out of curiosity to see the inside of her house, which no one save an old manservant—a combined gardener and cook—had seen in at least ten years.

It was a big, squarish frame house that had once been white, decorated with cupolas and spires and scrolled balconies in the heavily lightsome style of the seventies, set on what had once been our most select street. But garages and cotton gins had encroached and obliterated even the august names of that neighborhood; only Miss Emily's house was left, lifting its stubborn and coquettish decay above the cotton wagons and the gasoline pumps—an eyesore among eyesores. And now Miss Emily had gone to join the representatives of those august

a civic voice in narrator

4

names where they lay in the cedar-bemused cemetery among the ranked and anonymous graves of Union and Confederate soldiers who fell at the battle of Jefferson.

Alive, Miss Emily had been a tradition, a duty and a care; a sort of hereditary obligation upon the town, dating from that day in 1894 when Colonel Sartoris, the mayor—he who fathered the edict that no Negro woman should appear on the streets without an apron—remitted her taxes, the dispensation dating from the death of her father on into perpetuity. Not that Miss Emily would have accepted charity. Colonel Sartoris invented an involved tale to the effect that Miss Emily's father had loaned money to the town, which the town, as a matter of business, preferred this way of repaying. Only a man of Colonel Sartoris' generation and thought could have invented it, and only a woman could have believed it.

When the next generation, with its more modern ideas, became mayors and aldermen, this arrangement created some little dissatisfaction. On the first of the year they mailed her a tax notice. February came, and there was no reply. They wrote her a formal letter, asking her to call at the sheriff's office at her convenience. A week later the mayor wrote her himself, offering to call or send his car for her and received in reply a note on paper of an archaic shape, in a thin flowing calligraphy in faded ink, to the effect that she no longer went out at all. The tax notice was also enclosed, without comment.

They called a special meeting of the Board of Aldermen. A deputation waited upon her, knocked at the door through which no visitor had passed since she ceased giving china-painting lessons eight or ten years earlier. They were admitted by the old Negro into a dim hall from which a stairway mounted into still more shadow. It smelled of dust and disuse—a close, dank smell. The Negro led them into the parlor. It was furnished in heavy, leather-covered furniture. When the Negro opened the blinds of one window, they could see that the leather was cracked; and when they sat down, a faint dust rose sluggishly about their thighs, spinning with slow motes in the single sun-ray. On a tarnished gilt easel before the fireplace stood a crayon portrait of Miss Emily's father.

They rose when she entered—a small, fat woman in black, with a thin gold chain descending to her waist and vanishing into her belt, leaning on an ebony cane with a tarnished gold head. Her skeleton was small and spare; perhaps that was why what would have been merely plumpness in another was obesity in her. She looked bloated, like a body long submerged in motionless water, and of that pallid hue. Her eyes, lost in the fatty ridges of her face, looked like two small pieces of coal pressed into a lump of dough as they moved from one face to another while the visitors stated their errand.

She did not ask them to sit. She just stood in the door and listened quietly until the spokesman came to a stumbling halt. Then they could hear the invisible watch ticking at the end of the gold chain.

Her voice was dry and cold. "I have no taxes in Jefferson. Colonel Sartoris explained it to me. Perhaps one of you can gain access to the city records and satisfy yourselves."

"But we have. We are the city authorities, Miss Emily. Didn't you get a notice from the sheriff, signed by him?"

"I received a paper, yes," Miss Emily said. "Perhaps he considers himself the sheriff . . . I have no taxes in Jefferson."

"But there is nothing on the books to show that, you see. We must go by the—"

"See Colonel Sartoris. I have no taxes in Jefferson."

"But, Miss Emily—"

"See Colonel Sartoris." (Colonel Sartoris had been dead almost ten years.) "I have no taxes in Jefferson. Tobe!" The Negro appeared. "Show these gentlemen out."

2

15   So she vanquished them, horse and foot, just as she had vanquished their fathers thirty years before about the smell. That was two years after her father's death and a short time after her sweetheart—the one we believed would marry her—had deserted her. After her father's death she went out very little; after her sweetheart went away, people hardly saw her at all. A few of the ladies had the temerity to call, but were not received, and the only sign of life about the place was the Negro man—a young man then—going in and out with a market basket.

"Just as if a man—any man—could keep a kitchen properly," the ladies said; so they were not surprised when the smell developed. It was another link between the gross, teeming world and the high and mighty Griersons.

A neighbor, a woman, complained to the mayor, Judge Stevens, eighty years old.

"But what will you have me do about it, madam?" he said.

"Why, send her word to stop it," the woman said. "Isn't there a law?"

20   "I'm sure that won't be necessary," Judge Stevens said. "It's probably just a snake or a rat that nigger of hers killed in the yard. I'll speak to him about it."

The next day he received two more complaints, one from a man who came in diffident deprecation. "We really must do something about it, Judge. I'd be the last one in the world to bother Miss Emily, but we've got to do something." That night the Board of Aldermen met—three graybeards and one younger man, a member of the rising generation.

"It's simple enough," he said. "Send her word to have her place cleaned up. Give her a certain time to do it in, and if she don't . . ."

"Dammit, sir," Judge Stevens said, "will you accuse a lady to her face of smelling bad?"

So the next night, after midnight, four men crossed Miss Emily's lawn and slunk about the house like burglars, sniffing along the base of the brickwork and at the cellar openings while one of them performed a regular sowing motion with his hand out of a sack slung from his shoulder. They broke open the cellar door and sprinkled lime there, and in all the outbuildings. As they recrossed the lawn, a window that had been dark was lighted and Miss Emily sat in it, the light behind her, and her upright torso motionless as that of an idol. They crept quietly across the lawn and into the shadow of the locusts that lined the street. After a week or two the smell went away.

25   That was when people had begun to feel really sorry for her. People in our town, remembering how old lady Wyatt, her great-aunt, had gone completely crazy at last, believed that the Griersons held themselves a little too high for what they really were. None of the young men were quite good enough for Miss Emily and such. We had long thought of them as a tableau, Miss Emily a slender figure in white in the background, her father a spraddled silhouette in the foreground, his back to her and clutching a horsewhip, the two of them framed by the back-flung front door. So when she got to be thirty and was still single, we were not pleased exactly, but vindicated; even with insanity in the family she wouldn't have turned down all of her chances if they had really materialized.

When her father died, it got about that the house was all that was left to her;

and in a way, people were glad. At last they could pity Miss Emily. Being left alone, and a pauper, she had become humanized. Now she too would know the old thrill and the old despair of a penny more or less.

The day after his death all the ladies prepared to call at the house and offer condolence and aid, as is our custom. Miss Emily met them at the door, dressed as usual and with no trace of grief on her face. She told them that her father was not dead. She did that for three days, with the ministers calling on her, and the doctors, trying to persuade her to let them dispose of the body. Just as they were about to resort to law and force, she broke down, and they buried her father quickly.

We did not say she was crazy then. We believed she had to do that. We remembered all the young men her father had driven away, and we knew that with nothing left, she would have to cling to that which had robbed her, as people will.

3

She was sick for a long time. When we saw her again, her hair was cut short, making her look like a girl, with a vague resemblance to those angels in colored church windows—sort of tragic and serene.

30 The town had just let the contracts for paving the sidewalks, and in the summer after her father's death they began the work. The construction company came with niggers and mules and machinery, and a foreman named Homer Barron, a Yankee—a big, dark, ready man, with a big voice and eyes lighter than his face. The little boys would follow in groups to hear him cuss the niggers, and the niggers singing in time to the rise and fall of picks. Pretty soon he knew everybody in town. Whenever you heard a lot of laughing anywhere about the square, Homer Barron would be in the center of the group. Presently we began to see him and Miss Emily on Sunday afternoons driving in the yellow-wheeled buggy and the matched team of bays from the livery stable.

At first we were glad that Miss Emily would have an interest, because the ladies all said, "Of course a Grierson would not think seriously of a Northerner, a day laborer." But there were still others, older people, who said that even grief could not cause a real lady to forget *noblesse oblige*[1]—without calling it *noblesse oblige*. They just said, "Poor Emily. Her kinsfolk should come to her." She had some kin in Alabama; but years ago her father had fallen out with them over the estate of old lady Wyatt, the crazy woman, and there was no communication between the two families. They had not even been represented at the funeral.

And as soon as the old people said, "Poor Emily," the whispering began. "Do you suppose it's really so?" they said to one another. "Of course it is. What else could . . ." This behind their hands; rustling of craned silk and satin behind jalousies closed upon the sun of Sunday afternoon as the thin, swift clop-clop-clop of the matched team passed: "Poor Emily."

She carried her head high enough—even when we believed that she was fallen. It was as if she demanded more than ever the recognition of her dignity as the last Grierson; as if it had wanted that touch of earthiness to reaffirm her imperviousness. Like when she bought the rat poison, the arsenic. That was over a year after they had begun to say "Poor Emily," and while the two female cousins were visiting her.

"I want some poison," she said to the druggist. She was over thirty then, still

[1] Duty of the well-born

a slight woman, though thinner than usual, with cold, haughty black eyes in a face the flesh of which was strained across the temples and about the eye-sockets as you imagine a lighthouse-keeper's face ought to look. "I want some poison," she said.

35   "Yes, Miss Emily. What kind? For rats and such? I'd recom—"

"I want the best you have. I don't care what kind."

The druggist named several. "They'll kill anything up to an elephant. But what you want is—"

"Arsenic," Miss Emily said. "Is that a good one?"

"Is . . . arsenic? Yes, ma'am. But what you want—"

40   "I want arsenic."

The druggist looked down at her. She looked back at him, erect, her face like a strained flag. "Why, of course," the druggist said. "If that's what you want. But the law requires you to tell what you are going to use it for."

Miss Emily just stared at him, her head tilted back in order to look him eye for eye, until he looked away and went and got the arsenic and wrapped it up. The Negro delivery boy brought her the package; the druggist didn't come back. When she opened the package at home there was written on the box, under the skull and bones: "For rats."

humor

4

So the next day we all said, "She will kill herself"; and we said it would be the best thing. When she had first begun to be seen with Homer Barron, we had said, "She will marry him." Then we said, "She will persuade him yet," because Homer himself had remarked—he liked men, and it was known that he drank with the younger men in the Elks' Club—that he was not a marrying man. Later we said, "Poor Emily" behind the jalousies as they passed on Sunday afternoon in the glittering buggy, Miss Emily with her head high and Homer Barron with his hat cocked and a cigar in his teeth, reins and whip in a yellow glove.

Then some of the ladies began to say that it was a disgrace to the town, and a bad example to the young people. The men did not want to interfere, but at last the ladies forced the Baptist minister—Miss Emily's people were Episcopal—to call upon her. He would never divulge what happened during that interview, but he refused to go back again. The next Sunday they again drove about the streets, and the following day the minister's wife wrote to Miss Emily's relations in Alabama.

45   So she had blood-kin under her roof again and we sat back to watch developments. At first nothing happened. Then we were sure they were to be married. We learned that Miss Emily had been to the jeweler's and ordered a man's toilet set in silver, with the letters H.B. on each piece. Two days later we learned that she had bought a complete outfit of men's clothing, including a nightshirt, and we said, "They are married." We were really glad. We were glad because the two female cousins were even more Grierson than Miss Emily had ever been.

So we were not surprised when Homer Barron—the streets had been finished some time since—was gone. We were a little disappointed that there was not a public blowing-off, but we believed that he had gone on to prepare for Miss Emily's coming, or to give her a chance to get rid of the cousins. (By that time it was a cabal, and we were all Miss Emily's allies to help circumvent the cousins.) Sure enough, after another week they departed. And, as we had expected all along, within three days Homer Barron was back in town. A neighbor saw the Negro man admit him at the kitchen door at dusk one evening.

And that was the last we saw of Homer Barron. And of Miss Emily for some time. The Negro man went in and out with the market basket, but the front door remained closed. Now and then we would see her at a window for a moment, as the men did that night when they sprinkled the lime, but for almost six months she did not appear on the streets. Then we knew that this was to be expected too; as if that quality of her father which had thwarted her woman's life so many times had been too virulent and too furious to die.

When we next saw Miss Emily, she had grown fat and her hair was turning gray. During the next few years it grew grayer and grayer until it attained an even pepper-and-salt iron-gray, when it ceased turning. Up to the day of her death at seventy-four it was still that vigorous iron-gray, like the hair of an active man.

From that time on her front door remained closed, save for a period of six or seven years, when she was about forty, during which she gave lessons in china-painting. She fitted up a studio in one of the downstairs rooms, where the daughters and grand-daughters of Colonel Sartoris' contemporaries were sent to her with the same regularity and in the same spirit that they were sent to church on Sundays, with a twenty-five cent piece for the collection plate. Meanwhile her taxes had been remitted.

50   The newer generation became the backbone and the spirit of the town, and the painting pupils grew up and fell away and did not send their children to her with boxes of color and tedious brushes and pictures cut from the ladies' magazines. The front door closed upon the last one and remained closed for good. When the town got free postal delivery, Miss Emily alone refused to let them fasten the metal numbers above her door and attach a mailbox to it. She would not listen to them.

Daily, monthly, yearly we watched the Negro grow grayer and more stooped, going in and out with the market basket. Each December we sent her a tax notice, which would be returned by the post office a week later, unclaimed. Now and then we would see her in one of the downstairs windows—she had evidently shut up the top floor of the house—like the carven torso of an idol in a niche, looking or not looking at us, we could never tell which. Thus she passed from generation to generation—dear, inescapable, impervious, tranquil, and perverse.

And so she died. Fell ill in the house filled with dust and shadows, with only a doddering Negro man to wait on her. We did not even know she was sick; we had long since given up trying to get any information from the Negro. He talked to no one, probably not even to her, for his voice had grown harsh and rusty, as if from disuse.

She died in one of the downstairs rooms, in a heavy walnut bed with a curtain, her gray head propped on a pillow yellow and moldy with age and lack of sunlight.

5

The Negro met the first of the ladies at the front door and let them in, with their hushed, sibilant voices and their quick, curious glances, and then he disappeared. He walked right through the house and out the back and was not seen again.

55   The two female cousins came at once. They held the funeral on the second day, with the town coming to look at Miss Emily beneath a mass of bought flowers, with the crayon face of her father musing profoundly above the bier and the ladies sibilant and macabre; and the very old men—some in their brushed Confederate

uniforms—on the porch and the lawn, talking of Miss Emily as if she had been a contemporary of theirs, believing that they had danced with her and courted her perhaps, confusing time with its mathematical progression, as the old do, to whom all the past is not a diminishing road but, instead, a huge meadow which no winter ever quite touches, divided from them now by the narrow bottleneck of the most recent decade of years.

Already we knew that there was one room in that region above stairs which no one had seen in forty years, and which would have to be forced. They waited until Miss Emily was decently in the ground before they opened it.

The violence of breaking down the door seemed to fill this room with pervading dust. A thin, acrid pall as of the tomb seemed to lie everywhere upon this room decked and furnished as for a bridal: upon the valance curtains of faded rose color, upon the rose-shaded lights, upon the dressing table, upon the delicate array of crystal and the man's toilet things backed with tarnished silver, silver so tarnished that the monogram was obscured. Among them lay a collar and tie, as if they had just been removed, which, lifted, left upon the surface a pale crescent in the dust. Upon a chair hung the suit, carefully folded; beneath it the two mute shoes and the discarded socks.

The man himself lay in the bed.

For a long while we just stood there, looking down at the profound and fleshless grin. The body had apparently once lain in the attitude of an embrace, but now the long sleep that outlasts love, that conquers even the grimace of love, had cuckolded him. What was left of him, rotted beneath what was left of the nightshirt, had become inextricable from the bed in which he lay; and upon him and upon the pillow beside him lay that even coating of the patient and biding dust.

60   Then we noticed that in the second pillow was the indentation of a head. One of us lifted something from it, and leaning forward, that faint and invisible dust dry and acrid in the nostrils, we saw a long strand of iron-gray hair.

Questions for rereading

1. What happens? Look back at the story and construct the exact sequence of events. When did Homer Barron die? How did he die? Point out the sentences and the paragraphs that let you know what happened.

2. When you first read the story, did you guess how it would end? Were there clues you did not understand? Would you have understood more quickly if the anecdote about buying poison had preceded the anecdote of the odor?

   When you first read about the odor and about buying poison, did the incidents seem told for a purpose? What purpose?

3. People who talk about fiction claim that a story must include **conflict**—some clash between **protagonist** (hero or character in the forefront) and **antagonist** (some character or force that acts against the protagonist, denying his or her desires). If Miss Emily is the protagonist, who is her antagonist? What is the conflict in the story?

   If you are tempted to think of Homer Barron as antagonist, does it matter that the story continues thirty years after his death? (Remember that a conflict is not necessarily between individuals.)

4. Notice references to the Civil War in this story. Does that war play a role in this story? Where is it first mentioned? When last? Why is it in the story?

5. In paragraphs 1 and 2 the author speaks of buildings and structures, beginning with an image of Miss Emily herself as a fallen monument. Look through the story for mention of buildings and structures, and comment on Miss Emily as a statue. If she is indeed a fallen monument, what is she a monument *to*?

6. In the plot of the story, an aristocratic Southerner murders a Yankee carpetbagger. Is the story about the triumph of a defeated South over a supposedly triumphant North? What is this story about?

7. Who tells us this story? What sort of person? What kind of knowledge does the storyteller have? Can the storyteller see into people's minds? Does the storyteller represent any one character in the story? A place? A theme?

8. At the outset, Miss Emily receives a deputation from the Board of Aldermen. We already know her attitude toward taxes. The anecdote does not therefore advance the plot; it offers no clue to the eventual story of Emily and her lover. Does it nonetheless have a function in the story?

9. How many scenes would you need to turn this story into a play or a film? List the scenes and title them. Is their order essential to Faulkner's telling? Why does he choose this order?

10. In paragraph 15, what does *horse and foot* mean? To what or to whom does this phrase compare Miss Emily?

11. In retrospect, what hint about the plot occurs in paragraph 27?

12. Why *sidewalks* in paragraph 30?

13. What do you think happened when the Baptist minister called on Miss Emily (paragraph 44)? Why do you think you understand what happened? Is it important that you think you understand?

14. In paragraph 46, why are we not surprised when Homer disappears? How does the storyteller insure that we are not surprised?

15. It has been said of this story that "Miss Emily has a shadow, and by this shadow we tell the time of her life." What is her shadow?

16. In paragraph 48, why do we need to know about Miss Emily's hair changing color?

17. In paragraph 51, had she really shut up the top floor of her house? Why *evidently*?

18. In paragraph 54, what purpose is served by telling us that the Negro "walked right through the house and out the back and was not seen again"?

19. The end of paragraph 55 is a lyrical and metaphorical account of the old people's sense of the past, a poetic kind of prose with which a self-indulgent author will sometimes pad out a story or tease us by delaying the resolution of our suspense. Does Faulkner perform this last trick upon us? Does he do anything else as well? Does this image present an alternative or a parallel to anything else in the story?

20. Paragraph 56: Why did they wait until after the funeral to open the closed room? What word in the story informs you about the reasons for this delay? Is the delay consistent with the world of this story?

Plot

In "A Rose for Emily," plot—the events that make up the story, linked together in a chain of cause and effect—is of first importance. We feel called upon to examine the plot because the story surprises us. In the last three paragraphs, we learn that Miss Emily murdered Homer Barron and that she slept in bed next to his corpse long after his death. Actually, we receive this shocking information not from the last three paragraphs alone but from these paragraphs together with hints we picked up earlier—long before we suspected murder and necrophilia (an attraction to corpses). For example, we learn that Miss Emily's hair did not begin to turn gray until after Homer Barron's disappearance (paragraph 48) and that it took several years before it turned iron-gray. In the final phrase of the story, "we" discover, on the pillow beside the decayed corpse, "a long strand of iron-gray hair."

Someone legally inclined, reading the paragraph above, might object "But you cannot *say* that the hair is Miss Emily's; lots of people have iron-gray hair. And how do you know she murdered Barron? Yes, she bought arsenic, and he disappeared, and there was the smell, and here is the corpse—but your evidence is merely circumstantial!" *Yes,* we must answer, we do not know beyond all reasonable doubt, as a court of law would have it, that Miss Emily killed Homer Barron. But fiction works with probabilities, and the story creates a network of probabilities. We *know* that Barron died thirty years ago, before the tax anecdote that ends the first section; we know as readers, if not as jurors, that he died from the arsenic Miss Emily bought and administered.

Consider Faulkner's skill in telling this story. He constructs each of the first three sections around one anecdote that furthers the plot. Yet each section contains more than the single incident and advances more than the plot. The opening section foreshadows Miss Emily's death and includes references to the Civil War, a contrast of past and present, and summary narrative—but all these details lead to the action that closes the section. This first section gives us no special clues about the climax, but it sets the story's place and proposes the theme of historical change. And in its main incident it advances character. It is also in the first section that we come under the spell of the narrator's point of view.

This first section advances the plot insofar as it establishes character and setting. And it accomplishes one other goal. In a mystery story, an author often tries to outwit readers while remaining fair; the writer gives us clues veiled so that we do not know that they are clues. The first anecdote of Miss Emily reveals character in a way that amuses us, yet gives us no clues about murder and necrophilia. When in the next two sections we learn of two more incidents, bizarre and entertaining in themselves, we are led to suspect that each of them is as innocent as the first. But the next two anecdotes—about the smell and about the purchase of rat poison—are essential to our understanding of plot. Because the first incident included nothing sinister, it lightened the later anecdotes—which, had we understood them, would have suggested murder and a decaying corpse.

It is essential in literature that every part perform several functions at once, though the reader may not perceive these simultaneous functions on first reading. In a poem a word at once contributes to rhythm, to image, to metaphor, to meaning, to overall coherence, to pleasure—making its contribution all at once. In "A Rose for Emily" Faulkner early gives us (incidents two and three) information about Miss Emily's character, about how the other townspeople see her and react to her, about her changing society, about the setting of her life—and at the same time, like every wily storyteller, he gives us clues to a mystery.

Notice that the story of the smell comes earlier than the story of the rat poison, whereas in the real sequence it came afterward. If we first heard that Miss Emily bought rat poison and then heard that her house smelled of rotting flesh, we might smell a rat. By reversing the order, Faulkner gives us the same information but makes it harder for us to connect the two facts. Most likely, we accept these details as random notes on an eccentric character. At the same time, the unchronological order seems natural enough. From the start, the narration has zipped back and forth in time, as if we were not so much hearing a sequential story as listening to someone's free recollections.

The fourth section of the story covers many years. It begins with a suggestion that Miss Emily might have chosen to commit suicide, presumably because she felt disgraced by her episode with Homer Barron. Yet we accept Homer's disappearance without connecting it to rat poison or bad smells because the narrator has conditioned us to think of Barron as someone who might run away under the threat of marriage. Of course it is also true (it is the foundation of the story) that we do not consider Miss Emily the murdering kind.

We do not know exactly why Miss Emily murders Homer, even when we have finished the story. We know that she prizes her independence, her dignity, and her status. We know that she does not want to lose anything. (Remember that she wanted to keep her father's body—in itself a foreshadowing of her keeping Homer Barron's.) We know that Homer is not the marrying kind. Worse, he is a vulgar Northerner. Miss Emily's pride drove her to him in the first place, along with the minister's remonstrances and her cousins'. Perhaps we can say that she killed him out of pride, for the sake of her dignity. But we do not know if Homer finally agreed to marry her or not.

There is no answer to these questions raised in the last paragraph, and the argument cannot be won. It is useful to argue about probabilities when we stick to information supplied to us by the author, because by arguing we concentrate on the story. But it is useless to argue Miss Emily's motives by reference to anything outside the story—like our sense of human nature or our memory of a weekend in a small Mississippi town—because Miss Emily does not exist outside the story.

No probability is conclusive; we are left with mystery, with puzzlement over human behavior. If this dissatisfies us, we should ask ourselves if it would have been a more honest story, or more true to life, if we had finished it knowing exactly why Miss Emily acted as she did. Are human motives for significant actions usually clear and distinct?

Character

In speaking about plot we had to mention character, because character is revealed by actions. Surely the character of Miss Emily, which we gradually discover through her bizarre actions, is central to the story, and at the beginning it is almost Faulkner's whole focus. Notice the different devices with which the storyteller renders character. Take the first sentence: that the whole town went to her funeral tells us that she was important; that to the men she seemed a fallen monument makes her distant, grand, and ruined; and the women's curiosity points up Miss Emily's eccentricity. At the beginning we learn her character from the outside, through reactions to her death. In this second paragraph, Miss Emily's house is described as coquettish in a metaphor that compares a house to a flirtatious woman, perhaps a woman of the Old South. We hear of a grand past and present decay. We learn still more of Miss Emily's character, and of the theme of historical change, from details of architecture and through metaphor.

The third paragraph is a summary; it gives us a brief account of Miss Emily's past, her present sorry circumstances, and her intact if eccentric dignity. Subsequent paragraphs contrast Colonel Sartoris with the town's new governors, and paragraph 5 creates character by describing the interior of the house. That the easel is tarnished confirms one notion; that the sketch is of her father confirms another. In paragraph 6, Miss Emily's physical appearance repels: bloated obesity over a small skeleton. These images of death subliminally prepare us for our eventual discovery. In the next paragraphs, we finally observe Miss Emily for ourselves and watch her win a battle. From the general opinion of others, from summary, from description and setting, from action and speech we gain a strong sense of her character.

Point of view

In reading a story, we must consider the **point of view** from which the story is told. Sometimes the author's point of view allows us knowledge of everything, everywhere, all the time, inside brains as well as through walls. Sometimes a story is told by "I," someone who may be a character in the story, or by a narrator who speaks of "he" or "she" and sees everything through one character's eyes. "A Rose for Emily" is told by a narrator who appears in the story only as a citizen of Jefferson. The narrator is not somebody named "I" but a representative "we": "We did not say she was crazy then. We believed she had to do that." This point of view is a collective consensus of townspeople. At the end of the story, the "we" becomes so obviously a substitute for "I" that its use is awkward: "For a long while we just stood there, looking down at the profound and fleshless grin. . . . Then we noticed that in the second pillow was the indentation of a head." At this point a single individual must perform an act for the sake of the plot; Faulkner might have shifted his point of view from plural to singular and used *I*, but he did not; he used an awkward locution to reduce plural to singular and preserved the tone he had taken pains to create: "One of us lifted something from it. . . ." This is awkward because it requires us to believe that the narrator doesn't care to name the person who lifted the strand of hair. But this awkwardness preserves the anonymous and multiple *we* of the Jefferson citizenry.

Setting

All elements of fiction affect each other. Because the point of view identifiably belongs to the townspeople of Jefferson, point of view and setting affect each other. The setting of Jefferson, over years when memory of the Civil War declines, underscores the historical theme of the story. "A Rose for Emily" (and Faulkner's work in general) is saturated with the heroism, defeat, dignity, and degradation of the Civil War. Like many authors, Faulkner is obsessed with a single subject and takes his power from his obsession. Miss Emily Grierson is the last representative of a family ruined by the war. At the beginning of the story, in the second paragraph, we learn that her house stood in a decaying neighborhood. "And now

> Miss Emily had gone to join the representatives of those august names where they lay in the cedar-bemused cemetery among the ranked and anonymous graves of Union and Confederate soldiers who fell at the battle of Jefferson.

For Faulkner, such a setting provided a strong emotional background against which to narrate his tale. And such a setting led him directly into his theme.

Theme

Thus, setting is described in terms of conflict. Now consider the content of the story, its meaning or theme by way of the particular conflicts suggested and portrayed in it. Reading a story, we are justified in asking "What is it *for*? Does this story leave us with anything beside a moment's entertainment?" (Entertainment is, of course, its own excuse for being. Some stories entertain us *and* instruct us at the same time.) Conflict in "A Rose for Emily" arises between the doomed survivor of the Old South and citizens of the new city that grows out of Reconstruction. Miss Emily's personal conflict with Homer Barron exemplifies the conflict, because Barron is a Northerner, a carpetbagger come south for work and gain, employed to build Jefferson's first sidewalks, themselves signs of urbanization. Colonel Sartoris, who protected Miss Emily, represented the Old South, as did the later alderman Judge Stevens when he was outraged at the suggestion that a "lady" be told that her house smelled bad. In the changing habits of the governors, we see a changing Jefferson; in Miss Emily we see the decadent past attempting to withstand change. Finally, in the story's outrageous climax, Miss Emily's necrophilia is a metaphor of her refusal to change. The Emily-world is graceful, dignified, honorable—quaint and decayed, finally morbid. The Barron-world is vital, vulgar, and inevitable. In the story one feels a conflict within the narrator, perhaps between a heart that loves the old ways and a head that knows them doomed. If the head speaks warning to the heart, it might want to say "Although the past was attractive, it is sentimental and useless to love the departed past. It is worse than sentimental and useless. It is as if you paid love and devotion, not to a living spouse, but to a corpse."

We find the ultimate lesson of "A Rose for Emily" in Miss Emily's real denial of death, her holding onto the dead—first her father, then Homer Barron. Homer alive was part of the new and progressive society; Miss Emily's retention of his corpse wrests him from one world to another. By using necrophilia as his metaphor Faulkner chastises the surviving South's wish to hold onto the dead past.

Symbolism

We have not yet mentioned one important character. Miss Emily could not have survived so long as she did without the help of her servant, who grows old along with her, almost as if he were her visible black shadow, aging in public while she stays out of sight. He represents the exploited underclass on whom the aristocratic, impoverished survivor depends. After Emily's death, "The Negro met the first of the ladies at the front door and let them in . . . [and] walked right through the house and out the back and was not seen again." This disappearance is a convenience for the storyteller, who need not deal with another presence who might be party to morbid knowledge (and might not). However, the disappearance is not improbable—and it is highly appropriate to Faulkner's theme, where Miss Emily and her necrophilia become a **symbol** of the Old South. A symbol is a sign, something that stands for more than itself. The Negro stands for Miss Emily's connection to the outside world; when Miss Emily ceases to exist, her servant no longer has a connection to this world. It is reasonable that he vanish.

Chapter 2 **From Parable to Sketch**

Fiction has developed over thousands of years—from early stories of heroes, from moral parables and supernatural tales; it has adapted to fit changing religious and secular beliefs, to explain new phenomena, and to record history; it has accommodated fantasy and provided mnemonics for genealogies. Now that we have studied one contemporary story, let's glance backward over fiction's long history.

Stories began before writing, in oral traditions that continue today. Narrative is as old as the first hunter, separated from his tribe, who returned to speak of being treed by lions. He told a *story*; we need not trouble ourselves whether he told the facts. If the telling is proper we trust the tale. The *griot* Alex Haley consulted in Africa for the story of Kunta Kinte was the tribe's oral historian, its collective memory. The Old Testament collects stories remembered by the tribes of Israel, written down after centuries of oral transmission, recording the heroes and the history of the tribe—the stories of Moses leading his people out of Egypt, of Abraham and Isaac, of Joseph and his brothers. In Greece the great stories were preserved in epic poems. Homer's stories centered on the war with Troy and its aftermath, recording the encounter of Hector and Achilles, Odysseus and the Sirens.

The parable

Homer's *Odyssey* teaches the virtues of shrewdness and endurance—and incidentally passes along good tips on shipbuilding and seamanship, good manners, politics, piety, cooking, and morals. When Jesus wished to impress a moral point upon his disciples he told them a story. In these moral stories, or parables, natural objects often stand for ideas. Thus Mark tells us:

> Again he began to teach beside the sea. And a very large crowd gathered about him, so that he got into a boat and sat in it on the sea; and the whole crowd was beside the sea on the land. And he taught them many things in parables, and in his teaching he said to them: "Listen! A sower went out to sow. And as he sowed, some seed fell along the path, and the birds came and devoured it. Other seed fell on rocky ground, where it had not much soil, and immediately it sprang up, since it had no depth of soil; and when the sun rose it was scorched, and since it had no root it withered away. Other seed fell among thorns and the thorns grew up and choked it, and it yielded no grain. And other seeds fell into good soil and brought forth grain, growing up and increasing and yielding thirtyfold and sixtyfold and a hundredfold." And he said, "He who has ears to hear, let him hear."

As so often in the New Testament, the disciples confess their puzzlement. Mark continues:

> And when he was alone, those who were about him with the twelve asked him concerning the parables. And he said to them, "To you has been given the secret of the kingdom of God, but for those outside everything is in parables; so that they may indeed see but not perceive, and may indeed hear but not understand; lest they should turn again, and be forgiven." And he said to them, "Do you not understand this parable? How then will you understand all the parables? The sower sows the word. And these are the ones along the path, where the word is sown; when they hear, Satan immediately comes and takes away the word which is sown in them. And these in like manner are the ones sown upon rocky ground, who, when they hear the word, immediately receive it with joy; and they have no root in themselves, but endure for a while; then, when tribulation or persecution arises on account of the word, immediately they fall away. And others are the ones sown among thorns; they are those who hear the word, but the cares of the world, and the delight in riches, and the desire for other things, enter in and choke the word, and it proves unfruitful. But those that were sown upon the good soil are the ones who hear the word and accept it and bear fruit, thirtyfold and sixtyfold and a hundredfold."

Although the parable tells a story, our interest is not in what will happen next but in interpretation. What *are* the seeds? What do they *stand for*? Mark tells us that the seeds in Jesus' parable stand for words, and shows us Jesus interpreting the different fates of the seeds as different responses to the Word of God.

The fable

Many old stories teach us how to live. A **fable** is a tale that sums up an observation of human character in narrative form and leads to a lesson to live by called a *moral*. A Greek named Aesop is credited with many fables that teach behavior to the young. We say someone cried wolf, often not knowing that we quote Aesop. Probably few of us read the fable, but at some point in our young lives, if we complained or raised an alarm when we didn't need to, some adult told us this tale invented by a slave in ancient Greece: a boy tricks his elders by warning about wolves when there are no wolves; when a wolf really threatens no one believes his warning. The fable illustrates an idea and makes a lesson concrete. And when we remember the fox and the sour grapes, we have learned from Aesop another useful generalization about human character.

The fairy tale

Another ancient form of narration is the fairy tale, which describes adventures of a hero or heroine who usually encounters magic or the supernatural. Charms, spells, and riddles are common to fairy tales, some of which also include moral lessons or observations. Often these tales reverse a character's fortunes—like "Cinderella," in which the last becomes the first. Many fairy stories code human secrets into plots that resemble dreams; psychologists study them for clues to human behavior. "Rumpelstiltskin" is a story that occurs in various forms and with changes of the magic name all over Europe. The brothers Jacob and Wilhelm Grimm found four different versions in one area of Germany alone and produced a composite. (This translation was published in England in 1823.)

Rumpelstiltskin

In a certain kingdom once lived a poor miller who had a very beautiful daughter. She was moreover exceedingly shrewd and clever; and the miller was so vain and proud of her, that he one day told the king of the land that his daughter could spin gold out of straw. Now this king was very fond of money; and when he heard the miller's boast, his avarice was excited, and he ordered the girl to be brought before him. Then he led her to a chamber where there was a great quantity of straw, gave her a spinning-wheel, and said, "All this must be spun into gold before morning, as you value your life." It was in vain that the poor maiden declared that she could do no such thing, the chamber was locked and she remained alone.

She sat down in one corner of the room and began to lament over her hard fate, when on a sudden the door opened, and a droll-looking little man hobbled in, and said "Good morrow to you, my good lass, what are you weeping for?" "Alas!" answered she, "I must spin this straw into gold and I know not how." "What will you give me," said the little man, "to do it for you?" "My necklace," replied the maiden. He took her at her word, and set himself down to the wheel; round about it went merrily, and presently the work was done and the gold all spun.

When the king came and saw this, he was greatly astonished and pleased; but his heart grew still more greedy of gain, and he shut up the poor miller's daughter again with a fresh task. Then she knew not what to do, and sat down once more to weep; but the little man presently opened the door, and said "What will you give me to do your task?" "The ring on my finger," replied she. So her little friend took the ring, and began to work at the wheel, till by the morning all was finished again.

The king was vastly delighted to see all this glittering treasure; but still he was not satisfied, and took the miller's daughter into a yet larger room, and said, "All this must be spun to-night; and if you succeed, you shall be my queen." As soon as she was alone the dwarf came in, and said "What will you give me to spin gold for you this third time?" "I have nothing left," said she. "Then promise me," said the little man, "your first little child when you are queen." "That may never be," thought the miller's daughter; and as she knew no other way to get her task done, she promised him what he asked, and he spun once more the whole heap of gold. The king came in the morning, and finding all he wanted, married her, and so the miller's daughter really became queen.

5   At the birth of her first little child the queen rejoiced very much, and forgot the little man and her promise; but one day he came into her chamber and reminded her of it. Then she grieved sorely at her misfortune, and offered him all the treasures of the kingdom in exchange; but in vain, till at last her tears softened him, and he said "I will give you three days' grace, and if during that time you tell me my name, you shall keep your child."

Now the queen lay awake all night, thinking of all the odd names that she had ever heard, and dispatched messengers all over the land to inquire after new ones. The next day the little man came, and she began with Timothy, Benjamin, Jeremiah, and all the names she could remember; but to all of them he said, "That's not my name."

The second day she began with all the comical names she could hear of, Bandylegs, Hunch-back, Crook-shanks, and so on, but the little gentleman still said to every one of them, "That's not my name."

The third day came back one of the messengers, and said "I can hear of no one other name; but yesterday, as I was climbing a high hill among the trees of the forest where the fox and the hare bid each other good night, I saw a little hut, and before the hut burnt a fire, and round the fire danced a funny little man upon one leg, and sung

'Merrily the feast I'll make,
To-day I'll brew, to-morrow bake;
Merrily I'll dance and sing,
For next day will a stranger bring:
Little does my lady dream
Rumpelstiltskin is my name!' "

When the queen heard this, she jumped for joy, and as soon as her little visitor came, and said "Now, lady, what is my name?" "It is John?" asked she. "No!" "Is it Tom?" "No!"

10   "Can your name be Rumpelstiltskin?"

"Some witch told you that! Some witch told you that!" cried the little man, and dashed his right foot in a rage so deep into the floor, that he was forced to lay hold of it with both hands to pull it out. Then he made the best of his way off, while everybody laughed at him for having had all his trouble for nothing.

This text comes from *The Classic Fairy Tales,* edited by Iona and Peter Opie, who say:

It is a moral tale in that it shows the perils of boasting, though this aspect is not stressed. It is a fairy tale in that the heroine receives supernatural assistance. It is a properly constructed dramatic tale in that to obtain such assistance the heroine has to make the most terrible of pledges, the life of her first-born child. And it is a primitive tale in that it hinges on the belief of the interdependence of name and identity: the dwarf's power is only to be broken if his name can be discovered. It is also a tale possessing genuine folk appeal in that a supernatural creature is outwitted by human cleverness.

"Rumpelstiltskin" is not, then, like Aesop's story about the boy who cried wolf; "Rumpelstiltskin" rouses first our delight in the gnome's outrage and then our fear for the daughter with her two enemies: child-stealing gnome and greedy king. (Note that the greedy king becomes her husband, and consider for a moment woman's relationship to man in this story.) Notice the economy of the fairy tale, how much information is given in the first two sentences. Notice also how qualities of character are fixed, constant, and openly stated. The miller was *vain,* his daughter was *shrewd and clever.* We learn the latter two qualities in the story's course, but the miller's vanity is a given fact; told, not shown. Accident, magic, coincidence mark the fairy story (and the folk tale, the fable, the epic) and separate it from much modern fiction. And although this tale has its moral (don't brag about your daughter), as a whole it is curiously amoral. We hear that the king is greedy, but he is not judged wrong or wicked or evil. He is as greedy as the miller is vain—as a given fact of character—and because he is king he has the power to kill the miller's daughter if she does not do what he wishes.

In this primitive form, narrative takes precedence over other elements of fiction—narrative without development of character, without complexity of motive, without specified place or setting, without intricacies of time sequence or point of view. Story is everything.

Folk tales

Another ancient form of story is the joke. My grandfather used to tell the tragic tale of the death of his horse Nellie. One summer, the hottest August in history, he put ears of popcorn on the barn roof for drying, right along the window of Nellie's stall. The day the thermometer hit 112 degrees the corn got so hot it popped right off the cob, slid down the roof, and fell to the ground past Nellie's window. Poor Nellie thought it was a blizzard and froze to death.

Even this joke tells a story, with characters, props, setting, and action.

A joke is a very short narration, usually anonymous in its authorship and oral in its transmission. Most cultures have folk stories, longer than jokes but often humorous, also anonymous and oral. The tall story is a common type of folk tale. In the northern Midwest, and in the Pacific Northwest, Paul Bunyan and his big blue ox Babe were heroes. *Bigness* was the real hero, as in this story Constance Rourke heard and wrote down (if you have trouble reading it, try saying it aloud).

Paul Bunyan's Big Griddle

Once the king of Sweden drove all the good farmers out of the country and a senator from North Dakota he wanted all the fine upstanding timber cleared off the whole state so as to make room for them, so he asked Paul Bunyan for to do the job, and Paul he took the contract. Paul cut lumber out in North Dakota at the rate of a million foot a hour, and he didn't hardly know how to feed his men, he had so many in the camp. The worst trouble was with his hot-cake griddle. It weren't near big enough though it were a pretty good size. The cookees used to grease it with telephone poles with bunches of gunny sacks on the end, but it weren't near big enough. Paul knew where he could get a bigger griddle but he didn't hardly know how to get it to the camp. When it was got up on one aidge it made a track as wide as a wagon road and it were pretty hard to lift. So Paul he thought, and finally he hitched up his mule team. That mule team could travel so fast when they had their regular feed of seven bushels of wheat apiece that nobody couldn't hold them, and Paul had to drive them to a flat-bottomed wagon without no wheels. This time Paul hitched a couple of these here electromagnets on the back, and he drove off to where the griddle was, and he swung them magnets round till he got the griddle on its aidge, and then he drove off lippity-cut to the camp, and he got the griddle a-goin' round so fast he didn't hardly know how to stop it, but he got her near the place where he wanted it, and then he let her go by herself, and she went round and round and round and round, gittin' nearer and nearer the center, and finally she gouged out a hole big enough for a furnace and settled down on top. Then Paul he built a corral around the griddle and put a diamond-shaped roof over it, and built some grain elevators alongside, and put in eight of the biggest concrete mixers he could find. Long in the afternoon every day they'd begin to fill the elevators and start the mixers, and then the cookees would grease the griddle. They all had slabs of bacon on their feet, and they each had their routes. Paul he fixed up a fence of chicken wire round the aidge, in case some cookees didn't get off quick enough when the batter began to roll down, so's they'd have some place to climb to. When the batter was all ready somebody on the aidge used to blow a whistle, and it took four minutes for the sound to get across. Then they'd trip the chute, and out would roll a wave of hot-cake batter four feet high, and any poor cookee that was overtook was kinda out of luck.

Paul's cook shanty was so big that he had to have lunch counters all along the wall so's the hands could stop and get something to eat before they found their places or else they'd get faint a-lookin' for them. Paul he had the tables arranged in three decks, with the oldest hands on the top; and the men on the second deck wore tin hats like a fireman's, with little spouts up the back, and away from the third deck Paul ran a V-flume to the pigpen, for Paul he did hate waste. The problem was how to get the grub to the crew fast enough, because the cookees had so far to go from the cook shanty that it all got cold before they could get it onto the table. So Paul he put up a stop-clock ten foot across the face so as he could see it any place in the eatin' shanty, and he got in one of these here efficiency experts, and they got it all timed down to the plumb limit how long it ought to take to get that food hot to the table. Then Paul he decided to put in some Shetland ponies on roller skates for to draw the food around, and everything seemed fine. But them ponies was trotters, and they couldn't take the corners with any speed, and Paul he had to learn 'em how to pace, and a whole lot of victuals was wasted while he was a-learnin' of them, and Paul was losin' time and he knowed it. So finally he done away with the ponies and put in a train of grub cars with switches and double track and a loop at the end back to the main line, so that when the cars got started proper they came back by themselves. And Paul put in a steel tank especial for the soup, with an air-compressor cupola, six hundred pounds to the square inch, and they used to run the soup down to the men through a four-inch fire hose which the feller on top used to open up as he came through.

Here is the sort of story people tell and retell, embellishing it so that authorship becomes collaborative. Notice how much background information turns up in the first sentence or two, as in "Rumpelstiltskin." This exaggeration, *a million foot an hour,* announces the genre of the tall tale as if it were a signpost. When we learn that Paul's old skillet was greased by telephone poles with gunny sacks tied on the end, we could continue the tale ourselves: *we get the idea.* The basis of this genre is outrageous exaggeration. Applying 1980 notions to 1890 scenes, we could drop two-ton butter pats from 747s equipped with bomb bays onto a griddle laid across the Grand Canyon with all of Texas's natural gas piped into it for flame.

The sketch

Parable, fable, fairy story, and folk tale are the ancestors of modern fiction. The **sketch** is modern and resembles the short story. It is a short prose work that may include narrative, description, dialogue, or characterization but lacks the conflict of a short story. Some sketches, like Ivan Turgenev's great *A Sportsman's Sketches,* may be long and richly textured. Others are more modest, merely capturing the precise tone and atmosphere of a setting; others use psychological observation to form the **character sketch**. Ernest Hemingway printed brief sketches between the short stories of his first collection, *In Our Time.* Here is one:

> They shot the six cabinet ministers at half-past six in the morning against the wall of a hospital. There were pools of water in the courtyard. There were wet dead leaves on the paving of the courtyard. It rained hard. All the shutters of the hospital were nailed shut. One of the ministers was sick with typhoid. Two soldiers carried him downstairs and out into the rain. They tried to hold him up against the wall but he sat down in a puddle of water. The other five stood very quietly against the wall. Finally the officer told the soldiers it was no good trying to make him stand up. When they fired the first volley he was sitting down in the water with his head on his knees.

Hemingway offers no conflict here, only an unblinking and exact rendering of the scene. Although brief, a sketch can be powerful.

Before we pay closer attention to the elements of fiction like plot and conflict, let us look briefly at some of the criteria for excellence in fiction, the ways we discriminate between good fiction and bad, between good and better.

Chapter 3 **Telling Good Fiction from Bad**

Like most television, most film, most poetry, and most drama, most fiction is not "great literature." Much popular fiction is good entertainment without artistic goals or pretensions. There is nothing evil about entertainment, but our education should reveal the values of literature—which include entertainment and much more. Some people ascribe literary value to a piece of writing in inverse proportion to its popularity; this is snobbery. Anyone who equates popularity with failure will be hard put to explain Dickens and Shakespeare, who were massively popular during their lifetime.

But popularity does not make a writer good, either. Here are the first paragraphs of *Dare to Love* by Jennifer Wilde:

> They still stared and whispered to themselves as I walked down the street. Three years had passed since I was home last, but the village hadn't changed at all, nor had the people. At eighteen, I was no longer a child, but to the villagers I was still the Lawrence girl, the subject of scandal. It pleased me to find that I was not affected by the stares, the whispers. What these people thought simply didn't matter any more. They would never again be able to cause the anger, the pain, the resentment that had marred my childhood.
>
> My blue-black hair fell to my shoulders in waves, and I wore a dusty rose cotton frock trimmed with lace. My manner of dress shocked the villagers, as did my cool, self-possessed attitude.

And here is the end of the same novel:

> "I've never stopped loving you," I whispered.
> Pulling me into his arms, he held me loosely for a moment and looked into my eyes. Then he smiled and kissed me with incredible tenderness, murmuring my name as his lips touched mine. This was the way it was meant to be. This was the destiny Inez had foretold for me so many years ago in the gypsy camp. As I put my arms around him, I knew at last that dreams can come true.

If you almost feel that you could write the 548 intervening pages, you are calling this writing predictable. Such excess predictability gives us a place to start. Inferior art pleases, in a mild way, by fulfilling expectations; there are no surprises: the bad will be punished, the detective will get his man. If details are not wholly predictable in *Dare to Love* (we don't know whether there will be a shipwreck in Corsica or a mysterious letter from the Azores), we can be sure that nothing will happen to tax our understanding. Literature, on the other hand, entertains us while it enlarges our awareness of unpredictable human experience.

Popular conventions reveal the state of society and the popular mind. But while literary study does not neglect history, society, or the human psyche, it looks also at form and theme in a work of art. The literary form in most best sellers is simple, repetitive, and secondhand. Original form takes original reading, which most readers are unprepared to offer. And theme in most best sellers is conventional daydream, to beguile our time away and to provide a setting for reverie, which is sometimes about our blue-black hair and sometimes about violence. For example, Mickey Spillane's *Kiss Me, Deadly* begins with this little daydream:

> All I saw was the dame standing there in the glare of the headlights waving her arms like a huge puppet and the curse I spit out filled the car and my own ears. I wrenched the wheel over, felt the rear end start to slide, brought it out with a splash of power and almost ran up the side of the cliff as the car fishtailed. The brakes bit in, gouging a furrow in the shoulder, then jumped to the pavement and held.

Spillane's universe is sexual exploitation and masculine violence. (In Jennifer Wilde everything in the world is implicitly sexual, but nothing is explicit; in Mickey Spillane sex is a form of violence.) Here is the ending of the same book:

> She laughed and I heard the insanity in it. The gun pressed into my belt as she kneeled forward, bringing the revulsion with her. "You're going to die now . . . but first you can do it. Deadly . . . deadly . . . kiss me."
> The smile never left her mouth and before it was on me I thumbed the lighter and in the moment of time before the scream blossoms into the wild cry of terror she was a mass of flame tumbling on the floor with the blue flames of alcohol turning the white of her hair into black char and her body convulsing under the

agony of it. The flames were teeth that ate, ripping and tearing, into scars of other flames and her voice the shrill sound of death on the loose.

I looked, looked away. The door was closed and maybe I had enough left to make it.

Sadism and sentimentality are equally predictable.

Like *Kiss Me, Deadly,* "A Rose for Emily" ends with horror. Then why is "A Rose for Emily" good and *Kiss Me, Deadly* bad? There are many partial answers, beginning with originality, but in the end we must look to theme or content. *Kiss Me, Deadly* has nothing to say beyond affirming its sadism; it is solemn but it is not serious. On the other hand, "A Rose for Emily" says something— about the South, about people who cling to the dead past—that is not commonplace. It records observations that are not trite, in language fresh enough to awaken the reader's mind and emotions. We are not speaking of Spillane's intention or purpose, nor of Faulkner's. After all, if Mickey Spillane asserted on a stack of Bibles that his intention was high art, it would not change the value of one word he has written. And if the ghost of William Faulkner rose before us to protest that he wrote "A Rose for Emily" in haste, for money, to meet a mortgage payment, it would not change the value of that story either.

We call some fiction bad when it fails through want of skill; badness like Spillane's or Wilde's derives from the nature of the product. To be good, a thing has to worth making. One argument for reading good literature is that it educates us to our sensibilities, makes us more sensitive, wiser, broader in understanding and empathy, and more sophisticated. Reading Flannery O'Connor or James Joyce, we see how literature can refine our perceptions. Reading Mickey Spillane, we see something contrary: how writing can equally serve to brutalize and desensitize, to exercise our latent sadism rather than to awaken sensitivity to the suffering of others. If good literature aims to enlarge and enhance our sensibilities, Spillane is bad; *bad* becomes a moral term and not merely a technical one.

Chapter 4 **Plot**

Plot is what happens in a story, the story's organized development, usually a chain linking cause and effect. Plot is the first and most obvious quality of a story. When we agree on what happened in a story, we can go on to discuss its significance. To introduce plot, then, let us rehearse some common terms.

Plot first requires **conflict**. Conflict may arise between characters; if Sam and Bill are in love with the same woman, their conflict can engender a thousand plots. Conflict may arise between a person and an idea, or a person and an event. A dying protagonist may conflict with antagonist death. Or an old-fashioned Southern spinster may conflict with the modern world. Such conflict often continues throughout a story, frequently to be resolved at the story's end.

Second, the reader needs to know where and when the story happens, and other information germane to plot. **Exposition** is the presentation of needed facts; it can occur at any point in the story, but it is usually most necessary at the beginning. An old storyteller might begin:

> On the morning of February 10, 18—, a stranger alighted from the coach in the square of the town of M——. It was a frosty morning, and the stranger appeared ill-dressed for the climate where she chose to take herself, for . . .

To the modern reader, such overt exposition seems too slow, not subtle enough. In "A Rose for Emily," early description of Miss Emily's house and surroundings gives us social and historical background we need to have while it pretends only to paint a picture.

After exposition, the conflict between protagonist and antagonist unfolds and grows more intense, in a **rising action** of increasing intensity, until the **climax** of the story when we reach the conflict's outcome. Then we have the **dé-nouement** (French for untying a knot) that elucidates and concludes the story. At the climax, one of the conflicting forces usually wins out over the other. The dénouement is almost the counterpart of exposition—bookends of the story— as it accounts for loose ends, backing us out of the story as the exposition edged us in. With dénouement as with exposition, it is elegant to avoid the obvious. In "A Rose for Emily" the climax occurs when the townspeople break into the locked room; the grisly discovery provides the dénouement.

Some stories lack an obvious climax. It is a writer's joke that to turn an ordinary short story into a story for *The New Yorker,* all you need to do is throw away the last two pages. Sketches lack conflict and climax. Other stories (thrill-ers, adventure stories) may provide climax after climax, a rising action of peaks with brief valleys.

A story's plot stimulates our wish to know what happens next; **suspense** keeps us turning the page to find out who killed whom, or who marries whom, or why a character behaves in a bizarre fashion. On the other hand, many writers find it useful to **foreshadow**, hinting what will happen next. Foreshad-owing creates the sense of necessity, inevitability, fate. Many plots use **flash-back**, an ancient and honorable device. In films and novels, in stories and in modern plays, we many times enter someone's mind and watch how a present event recalls a past one, which often serves to reveal the character's motives.

A similar device is the **frame**: a story begins and ends in the same moment, while the story's middle recalls a past that explains the present. Obviously a frame can accommodate foreshadowing; it can present us with a character in a situation—say, on Death Row waiting for execution—and then flash back to childhood to show us the character's progress to condemnation. A frame may create suspense as well as a sense of doom. "A Rose for Emily" begins and ends just after Miss Emily's death, and it is her death that raises the question of her life.

Using terms like plot, we isolate a story's parts. It is worth keeping in mind, however, that a good story is an organic whole: one sentence, or one phrase within a sentence, may advance the plot, indicate character, represent point of view, describe setting, and promote theme or meaning. In literature, everything happens at once.

James Thurber
The Catbird Seat

James Thurber (1894–1961) is associated for most of us with *The New Yorker,* which he helped edit, for which he wrote stories and drew cartoons. Thurber was a comic writer. But, as with many humorists (like Woody Allen, pages 173–177), Thurber's mind has a dark and obsessive side. (Readers interested in pursuing the difficult man behind the stories and cartoons may appreciate Burton Bernstein's biography, *Thurber.*) James Thurber grew up in Columbus, Ohio, and worked for newspapers in Ohio, France, and New York. But not until he joined *The New Yorker*'s staff, when he observed the stylistic devices of E. B. White—with whom he collaborated on *Is Sex Necessary?* (1929)—did he discover and develop the wry manner we cherish.

Mr. Martin bought the pack of Camels on Monday night in the most crowded cigar store on Broadway. It was theater time and seven or eight men were buying cigarettes. The clerk didn't even glance at Mr. Martin, who put the pack in his overcoat pocket and went out. If any of the staff at F & S had seen him buy the cigarettes, they would have been astonished, for it was generally known that Mr. Martin did not smoke, and never had. No one saw him.

It was just a week to the day since Mr. Martin had decided to rub out Mrs. Ulgine Barrows. The term "rub out" pleased him because it suggested nothing more than the correction of an error—in this case an error of Mr. Fitweiler. Mr. Martin had spent each night of the past week working out his plan and examining it. As he walked home now he went over it again. For the hundredth time he resented the element of imprecision, the margin of guesswork that entered into the business. The project as he had worked it out was casual and bold, the risks were considerable. Something might go wrong anywhere along the line. And therein lay the cunning of his scheme. No one would ever see in it the cautious, painstaking hand of Erwin Martin, head of the filing department at F & S, of whom Mr. Fitweiler had once said, "Man is fallible but Martin isn't." No one would see his hand, that is, unless it were caught in the act.

Sitting in his apartment, drinking a glass of milk, Mr. Martin reviewed his case against Mrs. Ulgine Barrows, as he had every night for seven nights. He began at the beginning. Her quacking voice and braying laugh had first profaned the halls of F & S on March 7, 1941 (Mr. Martin had a head for dates). Old Roberts, the personnel chief, had introduced her as the newly appointed special adviser to the president of the firm, Mr. Fitweiler. The woman had appalled Mr. Martin instantly, but he hadn't shown it. He had given her his dry hand, a look of studious concentration, and a faint smile. "Well," she had said, looking at the papers on his desk, "are you lifting the oxcart out of the ditch?" As Mr. Martin recalled that moment, over his milk, he squirmed slightly. He must keep his mind on her crimes as a special adviser, not on her peccadillos as a personality. This he found difficult to do, in spite of entering an objection and sustaining it. The faults of the woman as a woman kept chattering on in his mind like an unruly witness. She had, for almost two years now, baited him. In the halls, in the elevator, even in his own office, into which she romped now and then like a circus horse, she was constantly shouting these silly questions at him. "Are you lifting the oxcart out of the ditch? Are you tearing up the pea patch? Are you hollering down the rain barrel? Are you scraping around the bottom of the pickle barrel? Are you sitting in the catbird seat?"

It was Joey Hart, one of Mr. Martin's two assistants, who had explained what the gibberish meant. "She must be a Dodger fan," he had said. "Red Barber announces the Dodger games over the radio and he uses those expressions—picked 'em up down South." Joey had gone on to explain one or two. "Tearing up the pea patch" meant going on a rampage; "sitting in the catbird seat" meant sitting pretty, like a batter with three balls and no strikes on him. Mr. Martin dismissed all this with an effort. It had been annoying, it had driven him near to distraction, but he was too solid a man to be moved to murder by anything so childish. It was fortunate, he reflected as he passed on to the important charges against Mrs. Barrows, that he had stood up under it so well. He had maintained always an outward appearance of polite tolerance. "Why, I even believe you like the woman," Miss Paird, his other assistant, had once said to him. He had simply smiled.

5 A gavel rapped in Mr. Martin's mind and the case proper was resumed. Mrs. Ulgine Barrows stood charged with willful, blatant, and persistent attempts to destroy the efficiency and system of F & S. It was competent, material, and relevant to review her advent and rise to power. Mr. Martin had got the story from Miss Paird, who seemed always able to find things out. According to her, Mrs. Barrows had met Mr. Fitweiler at a party, where she had rescued him from the embraces of a powerfully built drunken man who had mistaken the president of F & S for a famous retired Middle Western football coach. She had led him to a sofa and somehow worked upon him a monstrous magic. The aging gentleman had jumped to the conclusion there and then that this was a woman of singular attainments, equipped to bring out the best in him and in the firm. A week later he had introduced her into F & S as his special adviser. On that day confusion got its foot in the door. After Miss Tyson, Mr. Brundage, and Mr. Bartlett had been fired and Mr. Munson had taken his hat and stalked out, mailing in his resignation later, old Roberts had been emboldened to speak to Mr. Fitweiler. He mentioned that Mr. Munson's department had been "a little disrupted" and hadn't they perhaps better resume the old system there? Mr. Fitweiler had said certainly not. He had the greatest faith in Mrs. Barrows' ideas. "They require a little seasoning, a little seasoning, is all," he had added. Mr. Roberts had given it up. Mr. Martin reviewed in detail all the changes wrought by Mrs. Barrows. She had begun chipping at the cornices of the firm's edifice and now she was swinging at the foundation stones with a pickaxe.

Mr. Martin came now, in his summing up, to the afternoon of Monday, November 2, 1942—just one week ago. On that day, at 3 P.M., Mrs. Barrows had bounced into his office. "Boo!" she had yelled. "Are you scraping around the bottom of the pickle barrel?" Mr. Martin had looked at her from under his green eyeshade, saying nothing. She had begun to wander about the office, taking it in with her great, popping eyes. "Do you really need *all* these filing cabinets?" she had demanded suddenly. Mr. Martin's heart had jumped. "Each of these files," he had said, keeping his voice even, "plays an indispensable part in the system of F & S." She had brayed at him, "Well, don't tear up the pea patch!" and gone to the door. From there she had bawled, "But you sure have got a lot of fine scrap in here!" Mr. Martin could no longer doubt that the finger was on his beloved department. Her pickaxe was on the upswing, poised for the first blow. It had not come yet; he had received no blue memo from the enchanted Mr. Fitweiler bearing nonsensical instructions deriving from the obscene woman. But there was no doubt in Mr. Martin's mind that one would be forthcoming. He must act quickly. Already a precious week had gone by. Mr. Martin stood up in his living room, still holding his milk glass. "Gentlemen of the jury," he said to himself, "I demand the death penalty for this horrible person."

The next day Mr. Martin followed his routine, as usual. He polished his glasses more often and once sharpened an already sharp pencil, but not even Miss Paird noticed. Only once did he catch sight of his victim; she swept past him in the hall with a patronizing "Hi!" At five-thirty he walked home, as usual, and had a glass of milk, as usual. He had never drunk anything stronger in his life—unless you could count ginger ale. The late Sam Schlosser, the S of F & S, had praised Mr. Martin at a staff meeting several years before for his temperate habits. "Our most efficient worker neither drinks nor smokes," he had said. "The results speak for themselves." Mr. Fitweiler had sat by, nodding approval.

Mr. Martin was still thinking about that red-letter day as he walked over to the Schrafft's on Fifth Avenue near Forty-sixth Street. He got there, as he always did, at eight o'clock. He finished his dinner and the financial page of the *Sun* at a quarter to nine, as he always did. It was his custom after dinner to take a walk. This time he walked down Fifth Avenue at a casual pace. His gloved hands felt moist and warm, his forehead cold. He transferred the Camels from his overcoat to a jacket pocket. He wondered, as he did so, if they did not represent an unnecessary note of strain. Mrs. Barrows smoked only Luckies. It was his idea to puff a few puffs on a Camel (after the rubbing-out), stub it out in the ashtray holding her lipstick-stained Luckies, and thus drag a small red herring across the trail. Perhaps it was not a good idea. It would take time. He might even choke, too loudly.

Mr. Martin had never seen the house on West Twelfth Street where Mrs. Barrows lived, but he had a clear enough picture of it. Fortunately, she had bragged to everybody about her ducky first-floor apartment in the perfectly darling three-story redbrick. There would be no doorman or other attendants; just the tenants on the second and third floors. As he walked along, Mr. Martin realized that he would get there before nine-thirty. He had considered walking north on Fifth Avenue from Schrafft's to a point from which it would take him until ten o'clock to reach the house. At that hour people were less likely to be coming in or going out. But the procedure would have made an awkward loop in the straight thread of his casualness, and he had abandoned it. It was impossible to figure when people would be entering or leaving the house, anyway. There was a great risk at any hour. If he ran into anybody, he would simply have to place the rubbing-out of Ulgine Barrows in the inactive file forever. The same thing would hold true if there were someone in her apartment. In that case he would just say that he had been passing by, recognized her charming house and thought to drop in.

10   It was eighteen minutes after nine when Mr. Martin turned into Twelfth Street. A man passed him, and a man and a woman talking. There was no one within fifty paces when he came to the house, halfway down the block. He was up the steps and in the small vestibule in no time, pressing the bell under the card that said "Mrs. Ulgine Barrows." When the clicking in the lock started, he jumped forward against the door. He got inside fast, closing the door behind him. A bulb in a lantern hung from the hall ceiling on a chain seemed to give a monstrously bright light. There was nobody on the stair, which went up ahead of him along the left wall. A door opened down the hall in the wall on the right. He went toward it swiftly, on tiptoe.

"Well, for God's sake, look who's here!" bawled Mrs. Barrows, and her braying laugh rang out like the report of a shotgun. He rushed past her like a football tackle, bumping her. "Hey, quit shoving!" she said, closing the door behind them. They were in her living room, which seemed to Mr. Martin to be lighted by a hundred lamps. "What's after you?" she said. "You're as jumpy as a goat." He found he was unable to speak. His heart was wheezing in his throat. "I—yes," he finally brought out. She was jabbering and laughing as she started to help him off with his coat. "No, no," he said. "I'll put it here." He took it off and put it on a chair near the door. "Your hat and gloves, too," she said. "You're in a lady's house." He put his hat on top of the coat. Mrs. Barrows seemed larger than he had thought. He kept his gloves on. "I was passing by," he said. "I recognized— is there anyone here?" She laughed louder than ever. "No," she said, "we're all alone. You're as white as a sheet, you funny man. Whatever *has* come over you? I'll mix you a toddy." She started towards a door across the room. "Scotch-and- soda be all right? But say, you don't drink, do you?" She turned and gave him her amused look. Mr. Martin pulled himself together. "Scotch-and-soda will be all right," he heard himself say. He could hear her laughing in the kitchen.

Mr. Martin looked quickly around the living room for the weapon. He had counted on finding one there. There were andirons and a poker and something in a corner that looked like an Indian club. None of them would do. It couldn't be that way. He began to pace around. He came to a desk. On it lay a metal paper knife with an ornate handle. Would it be sharp enough? He reached for it and knocked over a small brass jar. Stamps spilled out of it and it fell to the floor with a clatter. "Hey," Mrs. Barrows yelled from the kitchen, "are you tearing up the pea patch?" Mr. Martin gave a strange laugh. Picking up the knife, he tried its point against his left wrist. It was blunt. It wouldn't do.

When Mrs. Barrows reappeared, carrying two highballs, Mr. Martin, standing there with his gloves on, became acutely conscious of the fantasy he had wrought. Cigarettes in his pocket, a drink prepared for him—it was all too grossly improb- able. It was more than that; it was impossible. Somewhere in the back of his mind a vague idea stirred, sprouted. "For heaven's sake, take off those gloves," said Mrs. Barrows. "I always wear them in the house," said Mr. Martin. The idea began to bloom, strange and wonderful. She put the glasses on a coffee table in front of a sofa and sat on the sofa. "Come over here, you odd little man," she said. Mr. Martin went over and sat beside her. It was difficult getting a cigarette out of the pack of Camels, but he managed it. She held a match for him, laughing. "Well," she said, handing him his drink, "this is perfectly marvelous. You with a drink and a cigarette."

Mr. Martin puffed, not too awkwardly, and took a gulp of the highball. "I drink and smoke all the time," he said. He clinked his glass against hers. "Here's nuts to that old windbag, Fitweiler," he said, and gulped again. The stuff tasted awful, but he made no grimace. "Really, Mr. Martin," she said, her voice and posture changing, "you are insulting our employer." Mrs. Barrows was now all special adviser to the president. "I am preparing a bomb," said Mr. Martin, "which will blow the old goat higher than hell." He had only had a little of the drink, which was not strong. It couldn't be that. "Do you take dope or something?" Mrs. Bar- rows asked coldly. "Heroin," said Mr. Martin. "I'll be coked to the gills when I bump that old buzzard off." "Mr. Martin!" she shouted, getting to her feet. "That will be all of that. You must go at once." Mr. Martin took another swallow of his drink. He tapped his cigarette out in the ashtray and put the pack of Camels on the coffee table. Then he got up. She stood glaring at him. He walked over and put on his hat and coat. "Not a word about this," he said, and laid an index finger against his lips. All Mrs. Barrows could bring out was "Really!" Mr. Martin put his hand on the doorknob. "I'm sitting in the catbird seat," he said. He stuck his tongue out at her and left. Nobody saw him go.

15   Mr. Martin got to his apartment, walking, well before eleven. No one saw him go in. He had two glasses of milk after brushing his teeth, and he felt elated. It wasn't tipsiness, because he hadn't been tipsy. Anyway, the walk had worn off all effects of the whisky. He got in bed and read a magazine for a while. He was asleep before midnight.

Mr. Martin got to the office at eight-thirty the next morning, as usual. At a quarter to nine, Ulgine Barrows, who had never before arrived at work before ten, swept into his office. "I'm reporting to Mr. Fitweiler now!" she shouted. "If he turns you over to the police, it's no more than you deserve!" Mr. Martin gave her a look of shocked surprise. "I beg your pardon?" he said. Mrs. Barrows snorted and bounced out of the room, leaving Miss Paird and Joey Hart staring after her. "What's the matter with that old devil now?" asked Miss Paird. "I have no idea," said Mr. Martin, resuming his work. The other two looked at him and then at each other. Miss Paird got up and went out. She walked slowly past the closed door of Mr. Fitweiler's office. Mrs. Barrows was yelling inside, but she was not braying. Miss Paird could not hear what the woman was saying. She went back to her desk.

Forty-five minutes later, Mrs. Barrows left the president's office and went into her own, shutting the door. It wasn't until half an hour later that Mr. Fitweiler sent for Mr. Martin. The head of the filing department, neat, quiet, attentive, stood in front of the old man's desk. Mr. Fitweiler was pale and nervous. He took his glasses off and twiddled them. He made a small, bruffing sound in his throat. "Martin," he said, "you have been with us more than twenty years." "Twenty-two, sir," said Mr. Martin. "In that time," pursued the president, "your work and your— uh—manner have been exemplary." "I trust so, sir," said Mr. Martin. "I have understood, Martin," said Mr. Fitweiler, "that you have never taken a drink or smoked." "That is correct, sir," said Mr. Martin. "Ah, yes." Mr. Fitweiler polished his glasses. "You may describe what you did after leaving the office yesterday, Martin," he said. Mr. Martin allowed less than a second for his bewildered pause. "Certainly, sir," he said. "I walked home. Then I went to Schrafft's for dinner. Afterward I walked home again. I went to bed early, sir, and read a magazine for a while. I was asleep before eleven." "Ah, yes," said Mr. Fitweiler again. He was silent for a moment, searching for the proper words to say to the head of the filing department. "Mrs. Barrows," he said finally, "Mrs. Barrows has worked hard, Martin, very hard. It grieves me to report that she has suffered a severe breakdown. It has taken the form of a persecution complex accompanied by distressing hal- lucinations." "I am very sorry, sir," said Mr. Martin. "Mrs. Barrows is under the delusion," continued Mr. Fitweiler, "that you visited her last evening and behaved yourself in an—ah—unseemly manner." He raised his hand to silence Mr. Martin's little pained outcry. "It is the nature of these psychological diseases," Mr. Fitweiler said, "to fix upon the least likely and most innocent party as the—uh—source of persecution. These matters are not for the lay mind to grasp, Martin. I've just had my psychiatrist, Dr. Fitch, on the phone. He would not, of course, commit him- self, but he made enough generalizations to substantiate my suspicions. I sug- gested to Mrs. Barrows when she had completed her—uh—story to me this morning, that she visit Dr. Fitch, for I suspected a condition at once. She flew, I regret to say, into a rage, and demanded—uh—requested that I call you on the carpet. You may not know, Martin, but Mrs. Barrows had planned a reorganization of your department—subject to my approval, of course, subject to my approval. This brought you, rather than anyone else, to her mind—but again that is a phenomenon for Dr. Fitch and not for us. So, Martin, I am afraid Mrs. Barrows' usefulness here is at an end." "I am dreadfully sorry, sir," said Mr. Martin.

It was at this point that the door to the office blew open with the suddenness of a gas-main explosion and Mrs. Barrows catapulted through it. "Is the little rat denying it?" she screamed. "He can't get away with that!" Mr. Martin got up and moved discreetly to a point beside Mr. Fitweiler's chair. "You drank and smoked at my apartment," she bawled at Mr. Martin, "and you know it! You called Mr. Fitweiler an old windbag and said you were going to blow him up when you got coked to the gills on your heroin!" She stopped yelling to catch her breath and a new glint came into her popping eyes. "If you weren't such a drab, ordinary little man," she said, "I'd think you'd planned it all. Sticking your tongue out, saying you were sitting in the catbird seat, because you thought no one would believe me when I told it! My God, it's really perfect!" She brayed loudly and hysterically, and the fury was on her again. She glared at Mr. Fitweiler. "Can't you see how he has tricked us, you old fool? Can't you see his little game?" But Mr. Fitweiler had been surreptitiously pressing all the buttons under the top of his desk and employees of F & S began pouring into the room. "Stockton," said Mr. Fitweiler, "you and Fishbein will take Mrs. Barrows to her home. Mrs. Powell, you will go with them." Stockton, who had played a little football in high school, blocked Mrs. Barrows as she made for Mr. Martin. It took him and Fishbein together to force her out of the door into the hall, crowded with stenographers and office boys. She was still screaming imprecations at Mr. Martin, tangled and contradictory imprecations. The hubbub finally died out down the corridor.

"I regret that this has happened," said Mr. Fitweiler. "I shall ask you to dismiss it from your mind, Martin." "Yes, sir," said Mr. Martin, anticipating his chief's "That will be all" by moving to the door. "I will dismiss it." He went out and shut the door, and his step was light and quick in the hall. When he entered his department he had slowed down to his customary gait, and he walked quietly across the room to the W20 file, wearing a look of studious concentration.

Questions on plot

1. In the opening paragraph there are details that may seem pointless when you first read them. In retrospect, do these details serve the plot? At what point does Thurber allow you to see their purpose?
2. The last sentence of the first paragraph is brief. What do these four words do for the plot of the story?
3. We learn at the start that Mr. Martin has a plan of action. Later we learn his motives. What does Thurber gain by organizing his plot backward? Why didn't he start at the beginning and let us see Mr. Martin being provoked into revenge, then developing a plan of action?
4. Where does Thurber's exposition begin? Is it subtle? Is it obvious? Is it necessary?
5. Describe the rising action in Thurber's summary of past events. What is the final straw?

6. Describe Thurber's use of a glass of milk early in the story. Is this detail useful for creating character? Plot?
7. When do we return to the time of the opening paragraph?
8. What is the story's climax? If the story's dénouement is long, is there a reason?
9. Describe the various means Thurber uses in the first three paragraphs to establish Mr. Martin's character.
10. Is this story implicitly sexist?

Flannery O'Connor
A Good Man Is Hard to Find

Flannery O'Connor (1925–1964) is another great storyteller from the American South. In her brief life she completed two novels (*Wise Blood,* 1952; *The Violent Bear It Away,* 1960) and two books of stories, collected with others in *The Complete Stories* (1971). Born in Georgia, she attended the Writers Workshop at the University of Iowa and returned to Georgia to write. She was affected early by the rare disease of lupus and was dying during the years of her mature writing. Flannery O'Connor's stories are often called Gothic—in the old sense of exotic and horrifying. She was a Roman Catholic with strong convictions that often inform or direct the themes of her stories. A collection of her letters, *The Habit of Being,* appeared in 1979.

The grandmother didn't want to go to Florida. She wanted to visit some of her connections in east Tennessee and she was seizing at every chance to change Bailey's mind. Bailey was the son she lived with, her only boy. He was sitting on the edge of his chair at the table, bent over the orange sports section of the *Journal.* "Now look here, Bailey," she said, "see here, read this," and she stood with one hand on her thin hip and the other rattling the newspaper at his bald head. "Here this fellow that calls himself The Misfit is aloose from the Federal Pen and headed toward Florida and you read here what it says he did to these people. Just you read it. I wouldn't take my children in any direction with a criminal like that aloose in it. I couldn't answer to my conscience if I did."

Bailey didn't look up from his reading so she wheeled around then and faced the children's mother, a young woman in slacks, whose face was as broad and innocent as a cabbage and was tied round with a green head-kerchief that had two points on the top like rabbit's ears. She was sitting on the sofa, feeding the baby his apricots out of a jar. "The children have been to Florida before," the old lady said. "You all ought to take them somewhere else for a change so they would see different parts of the world and be broad. They never have been to east Tennessee."

The children's mother didn't seem to hear her but the eight-year-old boy, John Wesley, a stocky child with glasses, said, "If you don't want to go to Florida, why dontcha stay at home?" He and the little girl, June Star, were reading the funny papers on the floor.

"She wouldn't stay at home to be queen for a day," June Star said without raising her yellow head.

5   "Yes, and what would you do if this fellow, The Misfit, caught you?" the grand-mother asked.

"I'd smack his face," John Wesley said.

"She wouldn't stay at home for a million bucks," June Star said. "Afraid she'd miss something. She has to go everywhere we go."

"All right, Miss," the grandmother said. "Just remember that the next time you want me to curl your hair."

June Star said her hair was naturally curly.

10   The next morning the grandmother was the first one in the car, ready to go. She had her big black valise that looked like the head of a hippopotamus in one corner, and underneath it she was hiding a basket with Pitty Sing, the cat, in it. She didn't intend for the cat to be left alone in the house for three days because he would miss her too much and she was afraid he might brush against one of the gas burners and accidentally asphyxiate himself. Her son, Bailey, didn't like to arrive at a motel with a cat.

She sat in the middle of the back seat with John Wesley and June Star on either side of her. Bailey and the children's mother and the baby sat in front and they left Atlanta at eight forty-five with the mileage on the car at 55890. The grand-mother wrote this down because she thought it would be interesting to say how many miles they had been when they got back. It took them twenty minutes to reach the outskirts of the city.

The old lady settled herself comfortably, removing her white cotton gloves and putting them up with her purse on the shelf in front of the back window. The children's mother still had on slacks and still had her head tied up in a green kerchief, but the grandmother had on a navy blue straw sailor hat with a bunch of white violets on the brim and a navy blue dress with a small white dot in the print. Her collars and cuffs were white organdy trimmed with lace and at her neckline she had pinned a purple spray of cloth violets containing a sachet. In case of an accident, anyone seeing her dead on the highway would know at once that she was a lady.

She said she thought it was going to be a good day for driving, neither too hot nor too cold, and she cautioned Bailey that the speed limit was fifty-five miles an hour and that the patrolmen hid themselves behind billboards and small clumps of trees and sped out after you before you had a chance to slow down. She pointed out interesting details of the scenery: Stone Mountain; the blue granite that in some places came up to both sides of the highway; the brilliant red clay banks slightly streaked with purple; and the various crops that made rows of green lace-work on the ground. The trees were full of silver-white sunlight and the meanest of them sparkled. The children were reading comic magazines and their mother had gone back to sleep.

"Let's go through Georgia fast so we won't have to look at it much," John Wesley said.

15   "If I were a little boy," said the grandmother, "I wouldn't talk about my native state that way. Tennessee has the mountains and Georgia has the hills."

"Tennessee is just a hillbilly dumping ground," John Wesley said, "and Georgia is a lousy state too."

"You said it," June Star said.

"In my time," said the grandmother, folding her thin veined fingers, "children were more respectful of their native states and their parents and everything else. People did right then. Oh look at the cute little pickaninny!" she said and pointed to a Negro child standing in the door of a shack. "Wouldn't that make a picture, now?" she asked and they all turned and looked at the little Negro out of the back window. He waved.

"He didn't have any britches on," June Star said.

20   "He probably didn't have any," the grandmother explained. "Little niggers in the country don't have things like we do. If I could paint, I'd paint that picture," she said.

The children exchanged comic books.

The grandmother offered to hold the baby and the children's mother passed him over the front seat to her. She set him on her knee and bounced him and told him about the things they were passing. She rolled her eyes and screwed up her mouth and stuck her leathery thin face into his smooth bland one. Occasionally he gave her a faraway smile. They passed a large cotton field with five or six graves fenced in the middle of it, like a small island. "Look at the graveyard!" the grandmother said, pointing it out. "That was the old family burying ground. That belonged to the plantation."

"Where's the plantation?" John Wesley asked.

"Gone With the Wind," said the grandmother. "Ha. Ha."

25   When the children finished all the comic books they had brought, they opened the lunch and ate it. The grandmother ate a peanut butter sandwich and an olive and would not let the children throw the box and the paper napkins out the window. When there was nothing else to do they played a game by choosing a cloud and making the other two guess what shape it suggested. John Wesley took one the shape of a cow and June Star guessed a cow and John Wesley said, no, an automobile, and June Star said he didn't play fair, and they began to slap each other over the grandmother.

The grandmother said she would tell them a story if they would keep quiet. When she told a story, she rolled her eyes and waved her head and was very dramatic. She said once when she was a maiden lady she had been courted by a Mr. Edgar Atkins Teagarden from Jasper, Georgia. She said he was a very good-looking man and a gentleman and that he brought her a watermelon every Saturday afternoon with his initials cut in it, E.A.T. Well, one Saturday, she said, Mr. Teagarden brought the watermelon and there was nobody at home and he left it on the front porch and returned in his buggy to Jasper, but she never got the watermelon, she said, because a nigger boy ate it when he saw the initials, E.A.T.! This story tickled John Wesley's funny bone and he giggled and giggled but June Star didn't think it was any good. She said she wouldn't marry a man that just brought her a watermelon on Saturday. The grandmother said she would have done well to marry Mr. Teagarden because he was a gentleman and had bought Coca-Cola stock when it first came out and that he had died only a few years ago, a very wealthy man.

They stopped at The Tower for barbecued sandwiches. The Tower was a part stucco and part wood filling station and dance hall set in a clearing outside of Timothy. A fat man named Red Sammy Butts ran it and there were signs stuck here and there on the building and for miles up and down the highway saying, TRY RED SAMMY'S FAMOUS BARBEQUE. NONE LIKE FAMOUS RED SAMMY'S! RED SAM! THE FAT BOY WITH THE HAPPY LAUGH. A VETERAN! RED SAMMY'S YOUR MAN!

Red Sammy was lying on the bare ground outside The Tower with his head under a truck while a gray monkey about a foot high, chained to a small chinaberry tree, chattered nearby. The monkey sprang back into the tree and got on the highest limb as soon as he saw the children jump out of the car and run toward him.

Inside, The Tower was a long dark room with a counter at one end and tables at the other and dancing space in the middle. They all sat down at a board table next to the nickelodeon and Red Sam's wife, a tall burnt-brown woman with hair and eyes lighter than her skin, came and took their order. The children's mother put a dime in the machine and played "The Tennessee Waltz," and the grandmother said that tune always made her want to dance. She asked Bailey if he would like to dance but he only glared at her. He didn't have a naturally sunny disposition like she did and trips made him nervous. The grandmother's brown eyes were very bright. She swayed her head from side to side and pretended she was dancing in her chair. June Star said play something she could tap to so the children's mother put in another dime and played a fast number and June Star stepped out onto the dance floor and did her tap routine.

30 "Ain't she cute?" Red Sam's wife said, leaning over the counter. "Would you like to come be my little girl?"

"No I certainly wouldn't," June Star said. "I wouldn't live in a broken-down place like this for a million bucks!" and she ran back to the table.

"Ain't she cute?" the woman repeated, stretching her mouth politely.

"Aren't you ashamed?" hissed the grandmother.

Red Sam came in and told his wife to quit lounging on the counter and hurry with these people's order. His khaki trousers reached just to his hip bones and his stomach hung over them like a sack of meal swaying under his shirt. He came over and sat down at a table nearby and let out a combination sigh and yodel. "You can't win," he said. "You can't win," and he wiped his sweating red face off with a gray handkerchief. "These days you don't know who to trust," he said. "Ain't that the truth?"

35 "People are certainly not nice like they used to be," said the grandmother.

"Two fellers come in here last week," Red Sammy said, "driving a Chrysler. It was a old beat-up car but it was a good one and these boys looked all right to me. Said they worked at the mill and you know I let them fellers charge the gas they bought? Now why did I do that?"

"Because you're a good man!" the grandmother said at once.

"Yes'm, I suppose so," Red Sam said as if he were struck with the answer.

His wife brought the orders, carrying the five plates all at once without a tray, two in each hand and one balanced on her arm. "It isn't a soul in this green world of God's that you can trust," she said. "And I don't count nobody out of that, not nobody," she repeated, looking at Red Sammy.

40 "Did you read about that criminal, The Misfit, that's escaped?" asked the grandmother.

"I wouldn't be a bit surprised if he didn't attack this place right here," said the woman. "If he hears about it being here, I wouldn't be none surprised to see him. If he hears it's two cent in the cash register, I wouldn't be a tall surprised if he . . ."

"That'll do," Red Sam said. "Go bring these people their Co'Colas," and the woman went off to get the rest of the order.

"A good man is hard to find," Red Sammy said. "Everything is getting terrible. I remember the day you could go off and leave your screen door unlatched. Not no more."

He and the grandmother discussed better times. The old lady said that in her opinion Europe was entirely to blame for the way things were now. She said the way Europe acted you would think we were made of money and Red Sam said it was no use talking about it, she was exactly right. The children ran outside into the white sunlight and looked at the monkey in the lacy chinaberry tree. He was busy catching fleas on himself and biting each one carefully between his teeth as if it were a delicacy.

45   They drove off again into the hot afternoon. The grandmother took cat naps and woke up every few minutes with her own snoring. Outside of Toombsboro she woke up and recalled an old plantation that she had visited in this neighborhood once when she was a young lady. She said the house had six white columns across the front and that there was an avenue of oaks leading up to it and two little wooden trellis arbors on either side in front where you sat down with your suitor after a stroll in the garden. She recalled exactly which road to turn off to get to it. She knew that Bailey would not be willing to lose any time looking at an old house, but the more she talked about it, the more she wanted to see it once again and find out if the little twin arbors were still standing. "There was a secret panel in this house," she said craftily, not telling the truth but wishing that she were, "and the story went that all the family silver was hidden in it when Sherman came through but it was never found . . ."

"Hey!" John Wesley said. "Let's go see it! We'll find it! We'll poke all the wood-work and find it! Who lives there? Where do you turn off at? Hey Pop, can't we turn off there?"

"We never have seen a house with a secret panel!" June Star shrieked. "Let's go to the house with the secret panel! Hey Pop, can't we go see the house with the secret panel!"

"It's not far from here, I know," the grandmother said. "It wouldn't take over twenty minutes."

Bailey was looking straight ahead. His jaw was as rigid as a horseshoe. "No," he said.

50   The children began to yell and scream that they wanted to see the house with the secret panel. John Wesley kicked the back of the front seat and June Star hung over her mother's shoulder and whined desperately into her ear that they never had any fun even on their vacation, that they could never do what THEY wanted to do. The baby began to scream and John Wesley kicked the back of the seat so hard that his father could feel the blows in his kidney.

"All right!" he shouted and drew the car to a stop at the side of the road. "Will you all shut up? Will you all just shut up for one second? If you don't shut up, we won't go anywhere."

"It would be very educational for them," the grandmother murmured.

"All right," Bailey said, "but get this: this is the only time we're going to stop for anything like this. This is the one and only time."

"The dirt road that you have to turn down is about a mile back," the grandmother directed. "I marked it when we passed."

55 "A dirt road," Bailey groaned.

After they had turned around and were headed toward the dirt road, the grandmother recalled other points about the house, the beautiful glass over the front doorway and the candle-lamp in the hall. John Wesley said that the secret panel was probably in the fireplace.

"You can't go inside this house," Bailey said. "You don't know who lives there."

"While you all talk to the people in front, I'll run around behind and get in a window," John Wesley suggested.

"We'll all stay in the car," his mother said.

60 They turned onto the dirt road and the car raced roughly along in a swirl of pink dust. The grandmother recalled the times when there were no paved roads and thirty miles was a day's journey. The dirt road was hilly and there were sudden washes in it and sharp curves on dangerous embankments. All at once they would be on a hill, looking down over the blue tops of trees for miles around, then the next minute, they would be in a red depression with the dust-coated trees looking down on them.

"This place had better turn up in a minute," Bailey said, "or I'm going to turn around."

The road looked as if no one had traveled on it in months.

"It's not much farther," the grandmother said and just as she said it, a horrible thought came to her. The thought was so embarrassing that she turned red in the face and her eyes dilated and her feet jumped up, upsetting her valise in the corner. The instant the valise moved, the newspaper top she had over the basket under it rose with a snarl and Pitty Sing, the cat, sprang onto Bailey's shoulder.

The children were thrown to the floor and their mother, clutching the baby, was thrown out the door onto the ground; the old lady was thrown into the front seat. The car turned over once and landed right-side-up in a gulch on the side of the road. Bailey remained in the driver's seat with the cat—gray-striped with a broad white face and an orange nose—clinging to his neck like a caterpillar.

65 As soon as the children saw they could move their arms and legs, they scrambled out of the car, shouting, "We've had an ACCIDENT!" The grandmother was curled up under the dashboard, hoping she was injured so that Bailey's wrath would not come down on her all at once. The horrible thought she had had before the accident was that the house she had remembered so vividly was not in Georgia but in Tennessee.

Bailey removed the cat from his neck with both hands and flung it out the window against the side of a pine tree. Then he got out of the car and started looking for the children's mother. She was sitting against the side of the red gutted ditch, holding the screaming baby, but she only had a cut down her face and a broken shoulder. "We've had an ACCIDENT!" the children screamed in a frenzy of delight.

"But nobody's killed," June Star said with disappointment as the grandmother limped out of the car, her hat still pinned to her head but the broken front brim standing up at a jaunty angle and the violet spray hanging off the side. They all sat down in the ditch, except the children, to recover from the shock. They were all shaking.

"Maybe a car will come along," said the children's mother hoarsely.

"I believe I have an injured organ," said the grandmother, pressing her side, but no one answered her. Bailey's teeth were clattering. He had on a yellow sport shirt with bright blue parrots designed on it and his face was as yellow as the shirt. The grandmother decided that she would not mention that the house was in Tennessee.

70 The road was about ten feet above and they could see only the tops of the trees on the other side of it. Behind the ditch they were sitting in there were more woods, tall and dark and deep. In a few minutes they saw a car some distance away on top of a hill, coming slowly as if the occupants were watching them. The grandmother stood up and waved both arms dramatically to attract their attention. The car continued to come on slowly, disappeared around a bend and appeared again, moving even slower, on top of the hill they had gone over. It was a big black battered hearse-like automobile. There were three men in it.

It came to a stop just over them and for some minutes, the driver looked down with a steady expressionless gaze to where they were sitting, and didn't speak. Then he turned his head and muttered something to the other two and they got out. One was a fat boy in black trousers and a red sweat shirt with a silver stallion embossed on the front of it. He moved around on the right side of them and stood staring, his mouth partly open in a kind of loose grin. The other had on khaki pants and a blue striped coat and a gray hat pulled down very low, hiding most of his face. He came around slowly on the left side. Neither spoke.

The driver got out of the car and stood by the side of it, looking down at them. He was an older man than the other two. His hair was just beginning to gray and he wore silver-rimmed spectacles that gave him a scholarly look. He had a long creased face and didn't have on any shirt or undershirt. He had on blue jeans that were too tight for him and was holding a black hat and a gun. The two boys also had guns.

"We've had an ACCIDENT!" the children screamed.

The grandmother had the peculiar feeling that the bespectacled man was someone she knew. His face was as familiar to her as if she had known him all her life but she could not recall who he was. He moved away from the car and began to come down the embankment, placing his feet carefully so that he wouldn't slip. He had on tan and white shoes and no socks, and his ankles were red and thin. "Good afternoon," he said. "I see you all had you a little spill."

75 "We turned over twice!" said the grandmother.

"Oncet," he corrected. "We seen it happen. Try their car and see will it run, Hiram," he said quietly to the boy with the gray hat.

"What you got that gun for?" John Wesley asked. "Whatcha gonna do with that gun?"

"Lady," the man said to the children's mother, "would you mind calling them children to sit down by you? Children make me nervous. I want all you all to sit down right together there where you're at."

"What are you telling US what to do for?" June Star asked.

80 Behind them the line of woods gaped like a dark open mouth. "Come here," said their mother.

"Look here now," Bailey began suddenly, "we're in a predicament! We're in . . ."

The grandmother shrieked. She scrambled to her feet and stood staring. "You're The Misfit!" she said. "I recognized you at once!"

"Yes'm," the man said, smiling slightly as if he were pleased in spite of himself to be known, "but it would have been better for all of you, lady, if you hadn't of reckernized me."

Bailey turned his head sharply and said something to his mother that shocked even the children. The old lady began to cry and The Misfit reddened.

85   "Lady," he said, "don't you get upset. Sometimes a man says things he don't mean. I don't reckon he meant to talk to you thataway."

"You wouldn't shoot a lady, would you?" the grandmother said and removed a clean handkerchief from her cuff and began to slap at her eyes with it.

The Misfit pointed the toe of his shoe into the ground and made a little hole and then covered it up again. "I would hate to have to," he said.

"Listen," the grandmother almost screamed, "I know you're a good man. You don't look a bit like you have common blood. I know you must come from nice people!"

"Yes mam," he said, "finest people in the world." When he smiled he showed a row of strong white teeth. "God never made a finer woman than my mother and my daddy's heart was pure gold," he said. The boy with the red sweat shirt had come around behind them and was standing with his gun at his hip. The Misfit squatted down on the ground. "Watch them children, Bobby Lee," he said. "You know they make me nervous." He looked at the six of them huddled together in front of him and he seemed to be embarrassed as if he couldn't think of anything to say. "Ain't a cloud in the sky," he remarked, looking up at it. "Don't see no sun but don't see no cloud neither."

90   "Yes, it's a beautiful day," said the grandmother. "Listen," she said, "you shouldn't call yourself The Misfit because I know you're a good man at heart. I can just look at you and tell."

"Hush!" Bailey yelled. "Hush! Everybody shut up and let me handle this!" He was squatting in the position of a runner about to sprint forward but he didn't move.

"I pre-chate that, lady," The Misfit said and drew a little circle in the ground with the butt of his gun.

"It'll take a half a hour to fix this here car," Hiram called, looking over the raised hood of it.

"Well, first you and Bobby Lee get him and that little boy to step over yonder with you," The Misfit said, pointing to Bailey and John Wesley. "The boys want to ask you something," he said to Bailey. "Would you mind stepping back in them woods there with them?"

95   "Listen," Bailey began, "we're in a terrible predicament! Nobody realizes what this is," and his voice cracked. His eyes were as blue and intense as the parrots on his shirt and he remained perfectly still.

The grandmother reached up to adjust her hat brim as if she were going to the woods with him but it came off in her hand. She stood staring at it and after a second she let it fall on the ground. Hiram pulled Bailey up by the arm as if he were assisting an old man. John Wesley caught hold of his father's hand and Bobby Lee followed. They went off toward the woods and just as they reached the dark edge, Bailey turned and supporting himself against a gray naked pine trunk, he shouted, "I'll be back in a minute, Mamma, wait on me!"

"Come back this instant!" his mother shrilled but they all disappeared into the woods.

"Bailey Boy!" the grandmother called in a tragic voice but she found she was looking at The Misfit squatting on the ground in front of her. "I just know you're a good man," she said desperately. "You're not a bit common!"

"Nome, I ain't a good man," The Misfit said after a second as if he had considered her statement carefully, "but I ain't the worst in the world neither. My daddy said I was different breed of dog from my brothers and sisters. 'You know,' Daddy said, 'it's some that can live their whole life out without asking about it and it's others has to know why it is, and this boy is one of the latters. He's going to be into everything!' " He put on his black hat and looked up suddenly and then away deep into the woods as if he were embarrassed again. "I'm sorry I don't have on a shirt before you ladies," he said, hunching his shoulders slightly. "We buried our clothes that we had on when we escaped and we're just making do until we can get better. We borrowed these from some folks we met," he explained.

100   "That's perfectly all right," the grandmother said. "Maybe Bailey has an extra shirt in his suitcase."

"I'll look and see terrectly," The Misfit said.

"Where are they taking him?" the children's mother screamed.

"Daddy was a card himself," The Misfit said. "You couldn't put anything over on him. He never got in trouble with the Authorities though. Just had the knack of handling them."

"You could be honest too if you'd only try," said the grandmother. "Think how wonderful it would be to settle down and live a comfortable life and not have to think about somebody chasing you all the time."

105   The Misfit kept scratching in the ground with the butt of his gun as if he were thinking about it. "Yes'm, somebody is always after you," he murmured.

The grandmother noticed how thin his shoulder blades were just behind his hat because she was standing up looking down on him. "Do you ever pray?" she asked.

He shook his head. All she saw was the black hat wiggle between his shoulder blades. "Nome," he said.

There was a pistol shot from the woods, followed closely by another. Then silence. The old lady's head jerked around. She could hear the wind move through the tree tops like a long satisfied insuck of breath. "Bailey Boy!" she called.

"I was a gospel singer for a while," The Misfit said. "I been most everything. Been in the arm service, both land and sea, at home and abroad, been twict married, been an undertaker, been with the railroads, plowed Mother Earth, been in a tornado, seen a man burnt alive oncet," and he looked up at the children's mother and the little girl who were sitting close together, their faces white and their eyes glassy; "I even seen a woman flogged," he said.

110   "Pray, pray," the grandmother began, "pray, pray . . ."

"I never was a bad boy that I remember of," The Misfit said in an almost dreamy voice, "but somewheres along the line I done something wrong and got sent to the penitentiary. I was buried alive," and he looked up and held her attention to him by a steady stare.

"That's when you should have started to pray," she said. "What did you do to get sent to the penitentiary that first time?"

"Turn to the right, it was a wall," The Misfit said, looking up again at the cloudless sky. "Turn to the left, it was a wall. Look up it was a ceiling, look down it was a floor. I forgot what I done, lady. I set there and set there, trying to remember what it was I done and I ain't recalled it to this day. Oncet in a while, I would think it was coming to me, but it never come."

"Maybe they put you in by mistake," the old lady said vaguely.

115 "Nome," he said. "It wasn't no mistake. They had the papers on me."

"You must have stolen something," she said.

The Misfit sneered slightly. "Nobody had nothing I wanted," he said. "It was a head-doctor at the penitentiary said what I had done was kill my daddy but I known that for a lie. My daddy died in nineteen ought nineteen of the epidemic flu and I never had a thing to do with it. He was buried in the Mount Hopewell Baptist churchyard and you can go there and see for yourself."

"If you would pray," the old lady said, "Jesus would help you."

"That's right," The Misfit said.

120 "Well then, why don't you pray?" she asked trembling with delight suddenly.

"I don't want no help," he said. "I'm doing all right by myself."

Bobby Lee and Hiram came ambling back from the woods. Bobby Lee was dragging a yellow shirt with bright blue parrots in it.

"Throw me that shirt, Bobby Lee," The Misfit said. The shirt came flying at him and landed on his shoulder and he put it on. The grandmother couldn't name what the shirt reminded her of. "No, lady," The Misfit said while he was buttoning it up, "I found out the crime don't matter. You can do one thing or you can do another, kill a man or take a tire off his car, because sooner or later you're going to forget what it was you done and just be punished for it."

The children's mother had begun to making heaving noises as if she couldn't get her breath. "Lady," he asked, "would you and that little girl like to step off yonder with Bobby Lee and Hiram and join your husband?"

125 "Yes, thank you," the mother said faintly. Her left arm dangled helplessly and she was holding the baby, who had gone to sleep, in the other. "Hep that lady up, Hiram," The Misfit said as she struggled to climb out of the ditch, "and Bobby Lee, you hold onto that little girl's hand."

"I don't want to hold hands with him," June Star said. "He reminds me of a pig."

The fat boy blushed and laughed and caught her by the arm and pulled her off into the woods after Hiram and her mother.

Alone with The Misfit, the grandmother found that she had lost her voice. There was not a cloud in the sky nor any sun. There was nothing around her but woods. She wanted to tell him that he must pray. She opened and closed her mouth several times before anything came out. Finally she found herself saying, "Jesus, Jesus," meaning Jesus will help you, but the way she was saying it, it sounded as if she might be cursing.

"Yes'm," The Misfit said as if he agreed. "Jesus thown everything off balance. It was the same case with Him as with me except He hadn't committed any crime and they could prove I had committed one because they had the papers on me. Of course," he said, "they never shown me my papers. That's why I sign myself now. I said long ago, you get you a signature and sign everything you do and keep a copy of it. Then you'll know what you done and you can hold up the crime to the punishment and see do they match and in the end you'll have something to prove you ain't been treated right. I call myself The Misfit," he said, "because I can't make what all I done wrong fit what all I gone through in punishment."

130 There was a piercing scream from the woods, followed closely by a pistol report. "Does it seem right to you, lady, that one is punished a heap and another ain't punished at all?"

"Jesus!" the old lady cried. "You've got good blood! I know you wouldn't shoot a lady! I know you come from nice people! Pray! Jesus, you ought not to shoot a lady. I'll give you all the money I've got!"

"Lady," The Misfit said, looking beyond her far into the woods, "there never was a body that give the undertaker a tip."

There were two more pistol reports and the gra.. . other raised her head like a parched old turkey hen crying for water and called, "Bailey Boy, Bailey Boy!" as if her heart would break.

"Jesus was the only One that ever raised the dead," The Misfit continued, "and He shouldn't have done it. He thown everything off balance. If He did what He said, then it's nothing for you to do but thow away everything and follow Him, and if He didn't, then it's nothing for you to do but enjoy the few minutes you got left the best way you can—by killing somebody or burning down his house or doing some other meanness to him. No pleasure but meanness," he said and his voice had become almost a snarl.

135   "Maybe He didn't raise the dead," the old lady mumbled, not knowing what she was saying and feeling so dizzy that she sank down in the ditch with her legs twisted under her.

"I wasn't there so I can't say He didn't," The Misfit said. "I wisht I had of been there," he said, hitting the ground with his fist. "It ain't right I wasn't there because if I had of been there I would of known. Listen lady," he said in a high voice, "if I had of been there I would of known and I wouldn't be like I am now." His voice seemed about to crack and the grandmother's head cleared for an instant. She saw the man's face twisted close to her own as if he were going to cry and she murmured, "Why you're one of my babies. You're one of my own children!" She reached out and touched him on the shoulder. The Misfit sprang back as if a snake had bitten him and shot her three times through the chest. Then he put his gun down on the ground and took off his glasses and began to clean them.

Hiram and Bobby Lee returned from the woods and stood over the ditch, looking down at the grandmother who half sat and half lay in a puddle of blood and with her legs crossed under her like a child's and her face smiling up at the cloudless sky.

Without his glasses, The Misfit's eyes were red-rimmed and pale and defenseless-looking. "Take her off and thow her where you thown the others," he said, picking up the cat that was rubbing itself against his leg.

"She was a talker, wasn't she?" Bobby Lee said, sliding down the ditch with a yodel.

140   "She would of been a good woman," The Misfit said, "if it had been somebody there to shoot her every minute of her life."

"Some fun!" Bobby Lee said.

"Shut up, Bobby Lee," The Misfit said. "It's no real pleasure in life."

Questions on plot . . .

1. When you first hear of The Misfit, do you expect to meet him? How does this early mention affect the plot?
2. How many different tasks does paragraph 10 perform for this story?
3. What does the conversation with Red Sammy contribute to the plot? Is it part of the complication or the conflict?
4. A lie takes the family onto the dirt road. A lie and an error thus combine to advance the plot. Are these coincidences? Do they arise from character?

5. Notice the *horrible thought* at the start of paragraph 63, completed at the end of paragraph 65. What is accomplished by interrupting this horrible thought with action?

6. How soon do you know that the man we meet is actually The Misfit? Does the lapsed time, before the grandmother names him, further the story's interest?

7. During the conversation between the grandmother and The Misfit, events take place offstage. What is the relationship between the dialogue and the action? What is the effect on the story?

8. Where is the climax of the story?

. . . and other elements

9. Who is the deepest thinker among the characters? Does the story emphasize an idea?

10. The protagonist is first identified as the grandmother, not by a proper name. Does this general name characterize her?

11. Do you ever understand anything in this story before a character does? What is the effect of this device?

12. Remembering the title, look over the grandmother's conversation with Red Sammy and her conversation with The Misfit. Is this story about good and evil? What does it say about good and evil?

13. Do any of the characters change or develop?

14. Who is most morally responsible for the five deaths of this family?

Chapter 5 **Character**

A **character** is an imagined person in a story, whom we know from the words we read on the page.

Plot shows character; character causes plot. In most stories you cannot speak of the one without evoking the other. In "A Good Man Is Hard to Find," the grandmother's hiding the cat is essential to the plot, yet if her character did not make the act probable, the plot of the story would be flawed. In some stories characterization is minimal and plot is the all; "action-packed" the advertisers call them, and for characterization we may learn little more than that the cowboy is lean-jawed and the heiress raven-haired. Such descriptions make for stereotypes, thoroughly predictable characters.

Characterization

Fiction writers have many ways to present character, beginning with the names they bestow on characters. When Henry James shows us *May* Bartram in love with John *Marcher,* we may fear that his frosts will chill her flowers. Charles Dickens is a resourceful namer: Mr. Gradgrind, Uriah Heep. But of course characterization requires more than a name. Let us start with a broad division. If in conversation with friends we try to describe an absent person whom they have never met, we can describe the person directly: the absent friend is five foot ten inches tall, black-haired, stammers, is Irish in ancestry and interested in politics, goes to law school, is loyal, decent, and brave. This method is **exposition of character.** On the other hand, we may prefer to reveal the person indirectly, by showing action. We then have the choice of *telling* what he is, or of *showing* what he is like. Thus, we can characterize our old friend by telling about a day we went to the roller skating rink to recruit donors for the blood drive, and all of a sudden. . . . This is **characterization by action** or anecdote.

A slogan of the creative writing class: "Don't tell 'em, show 'em." Writers characterize mostly by *showing* a character in action, but they do both. In "A Rose for Emily," for instance, Miss Emily is characterized first in a summary, a *telling,* and then by a series of anecdotes, a *showing*. This organization—brief telling followed by considerable showing—is common in fiction.

Indirect presentation takes various forms. Describing the character's house or clothes or furniture with the objectivity of a camera provides indirect characterization. When some characters talk about others, they help to characterize them—not only by what they say, at its face value, but by what they don't say. For instance, if one character is known to be a sneak and a liar, and praises another character, we are apt to take that praise ironically. And of course we know a character best from what that character *does*. Thus Miss Emily's independence, eccentricity, and doughtiness show in the way she deals with the aldermen and the pharmacist.

In reading most fiction, we make three related demands on the author's characterization. First, we demand that his characters be *consistent*. We do not demand that they be unchanging; but if characters change, they must change for a reason. Our second demand: we must understand that the characters' change is *motivated;* it is usual in the psychology of fiction that characters act from known motives. This psychology serves to make characters *plausible* to us—which is our third requirement: that they be credible, realistic, probable.

These doctrines of realistic characterization do not apply to all fiction but do to most fiction. Stories that differ—with unmotivated acts and implausible or unrealistic characters—often declare themselves deliberate exceptions from the norms of literature.

Characters round and flat, dynamic and static

The English novelist E. M. Forster, in his book *Aspects of the Novel* (1927), distinguished between "round" characters and "flat" ones. Sometimes we make much the same metaphor by calling characters "three-dimensional" or "two-dimensional." The round or three-dimensional character in fiction seems more real and more whole than the flat character, the character abstracted into two dimensions. The round character is complex, the flat character simple; the round character can surprise us, remaining unpredictable but probable; the flat character remains predictable, summed up in a few traits. In a novel we regularly find several round characters and a backdrop of flat ones. In a story we often find one or two round characters among flat ones. It takes time to develop a round character. In second-rate fiction (and drama, film, and television) all characters are flat, and no one has the complexity Forster describes as round.

The absence of round characters, or the dominance of flat ones, is therefore often, but not always, a clear indication of fiction's failure or inferiority. Sometimes flat characters are exactly what a story requires. Some stories concentrate so much on matters *outside* characterization that flat characters do the job. In Thurber's "The Catbird Seat," the characters are two-dimensional, yet the story emphasizes ideas and plot above all; the characterization is adequate to the story's purposes. Some novelists (like Dickens) show genius in constructing flat characters, dominated by a few traits, with such a richness that we remember them forever.

Sometimes flat or two-dimensional characters are **stereotypes**. Much television drama relies on stereotypes: the tough, street-wise detective and his sidekick the idealistic rookie. Everyone recognizes stereotypes and sums them up in clichés: the whore with the heart of gold; the dumb jock; the pompous bank president; the hillbilly. But not all flat characters are stereotypes. In "A Good Man Is Hard to Find," both the grandmother and The Misfit are round; once met, we would know them anywhere. The other characters—The Misfit's henchman, the father and mother—are flat without dwindling into stereotype. Unlike mere clichés, they are recognizably individual, even though they lack the detail and depth of the round characters.

Usually a round character is **dynamic** or changing. It is common but not invariable that a short story recount a crisis in a protagonist's life and a subsequent change. Some important event takes place, something is decided or understood: a life alters. If a character's life alters—and we find the change convincing—that character must almost certainly be round. Usually such change occurs within the character, but sometimes the change occurs within someone observing the action, and we grow to understand a character as more complex than we had believed. (Consider "A Rose for Emily.") Other characters remain **static** or unchanging. Two stories strong in the portrayal of character follow.

James Joyce
Counterparts

James Joyce (1882–1941) was born in Dublin and spent most of his adult life in Paris and Zürich. His long, innovative novel *Ulysses* (1922) is widely considered a major work of our literature. Earlier, Joyce wrote an autobiographical novel, *A Portrait of the Artist as a Young Man* (1916), as well as poems and a play. "Counterparts" comes from *Dubliners,* a collection of short stories that, taken together, makes a portrait of the Dubliner in different guises: male and female, young and old, married and single. Farrington is the Dubliner as an adult, married man.

The bell rang furiously and, when Miss Parker went to the tube, a furious voice called out in a piercing North of Ireland accent:

—Send Farrington here!

Miss Parker returned to her machine, saying to a man who was writing at a desk:

—Mr Alleyne wants you upstairs.

5   The man muttered *Blast him!* under his breath and pushed back his chair to

stand up. When he stood up he was tall and of great bulk. He had a hanging face, dark wine-coloured, with fair eyebrows and moustache: his eyes bulged forward slightly and the whites of them were dirty. He lifted up the counter and, passing by the clients, went out of the office with a heavy step.

He went heavily upstairs until he came to the second landing, where a door bore a brass plate with the inscription *Mr Alleyne*. Here he halted, puffing with labour and vexation, and knocked. The shrill voice cried:

—Come in!

The man entered Mr Alleyne's room. Simultaneously Mr Alleyne, a little man wearing gold-rimmed glasses on a clean-shaven face, shot his head up over a pile of documents. The head itself was so pink and hairless that it seemed like a large egg reposing on the papers. Mr Alleyne did not lose a moment:

—Farrington? What is the meaning of this? Why have I always to complain of you? May I ask you why you haven't made a copy of that contract between Bodley and Kirwan? I told you it must be ready by four o'clock.

10   —But Mr Shelley said, sir—

—*Mr Shelley said, sir.* . . . Kindly attend to what I say and not to what *Mr Shelley says, sir.* You have always some excuse or another for shirking work. Let me tell you that if the contract is not copied before this evening I'll lay the matter before Mr Crosbie. . . . Do you hear me now?

—Yes, sir.

—Do you hear me now? . . . Ay and another little matter! I might as well be talking to the wall as talking to you. Understand once for all that you get a half an hour for your lunch and not an hour and a half. How many courses do you want, I'd like to know. . . . Do you mind me, now?

—Yes, sir.

15   Mr Alleyne bent his head again upon his pile of papers. The man stared fixedly at the polished skull which directed the affairs of Crosbie & Alleyne, gauging its fragility. A spasm of rage gripped his throat for a few moments and then passed, leaving after it a sharp sensation of thirst. The man recognized the sensation and felt that he must have a good night's drinking. The middle of the month was passed and, if he could get the copy done in time, Mr Alleyne might give him an order on the cashier. He stood still, gazing fixedly at the head upon the pile of papers. Suddenly Mr Alleyne began to upset all the papers, searching for something. Then, as if he had been unaware of the man's presence till that moment, he shot up his head again, saying:

—Eh? Are you going to stand there all day? Upon my word, Farrington, you take things easy!

—I was waiting to see . . .

—Very good, you needn't wait to see. Go downstairs and do your work.

The man walked heavily towards the door and, as he went out of the room, he heard Mr Alleyne cry after him that if the contract was not copied by evening Mr Crosbie would hear of the matter.

20   He returned to his desk in the lower office and counted the sheets which remained to be copied. He took up his pen and dipped it in the ink but he continued to stare stupidly at the last words he had written: *In no case shall the said Bernard Bodley be* . . . The evening was falling and in a few minutes they would be lighting the gas: then he could write. He felt that he must slake the thirst in his throat. He stood up from his desk and, lifting the counter as before, passed out of the office. As he was passing out the chief clerk looked at him inquiringly.

—It's all right, Mr Shelley, said the man, pointing with his finger to indicate the objective of his journey.

The chief clerk glanced at the hat-rack but, seeing the row complete, offered no remark. As soon as he was on the landing the man pulled a shepherd's plaid cap out of his pocket, put it on his head and ran quickly down the rickety stairs. From the street door he walked on furtively on the inner side of the path towards the corner and all at once dived into a doorway. He was now safe in the dark snug of O'Neill's shop, and, filling up the little window that looked into the bar with his inflamed face, the colour of dark wine or dark meat, he called out:

—Here, Pat, give us a g.p.,[1] like a good fellow.

The curate[2] brought him a glass of plain porter. The man drank it at a gulp and asked for a caraway seed. He put his penny on the counter and, leaving the curate to grope for it in the gloom, retreated out of the snug as furtively as he had entered it.

25 Darkness, accompanied by a thick fog, was gaining upon the dusk of February and the lamps in Eustace Street had been lit. The man went up by the houses until he reached the door of the office, wondering whether he could finish his copy in time. On the stairs a moist pungent odour of perfumes saluted his nose: evidently Miss Delacour had come while he was out in O'Neill's. He crammed his cap back again into his pocket and re-entered the office, assuming an air of absent-mindedness.

—Mr Alleyne has been calling for you, said the chief clerk severely. Where were you?

The man glanced at the two clients who were standing at the counter as if to intimate that their presence prevented him from answering. As the clients were both male the chief clerk allowed himself a laugh.

—I know that game, he said. Five times in one day is a little bit. . . . Well, you better look sharp and get a copy of our correspondence in the Delacour case for Mr Alleyne.

This address in the presence of the public, his run upstairs and the porter he had gulped down so hastily confused the man and, as he sat down at his desk to get what was required, he realized how hopeless was the task of finishing his copy of the contract before half past five. The dark damp night was coming and he longed to spend it in the bars, drinking with his friends amid the glare of gas and the clatter of glasses. He got out the Delacour correspondence and passed out of the office. He hoped Mr Alleyne would not discover that the last two letters were missing.

30 The moist pungent perfume lay all the way up to Mr Alleyne's room. Miss Delacour was a middle-aged woman of Jewish appearance. Mr Alleyne was said to be sweet on her or on her money. She came to the office often and stayed a long time when she came. She was sitting beside his desk now in an aroma of perfumes, smoothing the handle of her umbrella and nodding the great black feather in her hat. Mr Alleyne had swivelled his chair round to face her and thrown his right foot jauntily upon his left knee. The man put the correspondence on the desk and bowed respectfully but neither Mr Alleyne nor Miss Delacour took any notice of his bow. Mr Alleyne tapped a finger on the correspondence and then flicked it towards him as if to say: *That's all right: you can go.*

---

[1]Glass of porter (dark beer, or light stout)
[2]Bartender; ironic reference to an assistant parish priest

The man returned to the lower office and sat down again at his desk. He stared intently at the incomplete phrase: *In no case shall the said Bernard Bodley be* . . . and thought how strange it was that the last three words began with the same letter. The chief clerk began to hurry Miss Parker, saying she would never have the letters typed in time for post. The man listened to the clicking of the machine for a few minutes and then set to work to finish his copy. But his head was not clear and his mind wandered away to the glare and rattle of the public-house. It was a night for hot punches. He struggled on with his copy, but when the clock struck five he had still fourteen pages to write. Blast it! He couldn't finish it in time. He longed to execrate aloud, to bring his fist down on something violently. He was so enraged that he wrote *Bernard Bernard* instead of *Bernard Bodley* and had to begin again on a clean sheet.

He felt strong enough to clear out the whole office single-handed. His body ached to do something, to rush out and revel in violence. All the indignities of his life enraged him. . . . Could he ask the cashier privately for an advance? No, the cashier was no good, no damn good: he wouldn't give an advance. . . . He knew where he would meet the boys: Leonard and O'Halloran and Nosey Flynn. The barometer of his emotional nature was set for a spell of riot.

His imagination had so abstracted him that his name was called twice before he answered. Mr Alleyne and Miss Delacour were standing outside the counter and all the clerks had turned round in anticipation of something. The man got up from his desk. Mr Alleyne began a tirade of abuse, saying that two letters were missing. The man answered that he knew nothing about them, that he had made a faithful copy. The tirade continued: it was so bitter and violent that the man could hardly restrain his fist from descending upon the head of the manikin before him.

—I know nothing about any other two letters, he said stupidly.

35   —*You—know—nothing.* Of course you know nothing, said Mr Alleyne. Tell me, he added, glancing first for approval to the lady beside him, do you take me for a fool? Do you think me an utter fool?

The man glanced from the lady's face to the little egg-shaped head and back again; and, almost before he was aware of it, his tongue had found a felicitous moment:

—I don't think, sir, he said, that that's a fair question to put to me.

There was a pause in the very breathing of the clerks. Everyone was astounded (the author of the witticism no less than his neighbours) and Miss Delacour, who was a stout amiable person, began to smile broadly. Mr Alleyne flushed to the hue of a wild rose and his mouth twitched with a dwarf's passion. He shook his fist in the man's face till it seemed to vibrate like the knob of some electric machine:

—You impertinent ruffian! You impertinent ruffian! I'll make short work of you! Wait till you see! You'll apologize to me for your impertinence or you'll quit the office instanter! You'll quit this, I'm telling you, or you'll apologize to me!

•   •   •   •   •   •

40   He stood in a doorway opposite the office watching to see if the cashier would come out alone. All the clerks passed out and finally the cashier came out with the chief clerk. It was no use trying to say a word to him when he was with the chief clerk. The man felt that his position was bad enough. He had been obliged to offer an abject apology to Mr Alleyne for his impertinence but he knew what a hornet's nest the office would be for him. He could remember the way in which Mr Alleyne had hounded little Peake out of the office in order to make room for his own nephew. He felt savage and thirsty and revengeful, annoyed with himself

and with everyone else. Mr Alleyne would never give him an hour's rest; his life would be a hell to him. He had made a proper fool of himself this time. Could he not keep his tongue in his cheek? But they had never pulled together from the first, he and Mr Alleyne, ever since the day Mr Alleyne had overheard him mimicking his North of Ireland accent to amuse Higgins and Miss Parker: that had been the beginning of it. He might have tried Higgins for the money, but sure Higgins never had anything for himself. A man with two establishments to keep up, of course he couldn't. . . .

He felt his great body again aching for the comfort of the public-house. The fog had begun to chill him and he wondered could he touch Pat in O'Neill's. He could not touch him for more than a bob—and a bob was no use. Yet he must get money somewhere or other: he had spent his last penny for the g.p. and soon it would be too late for getting money anywhere. Suddenly, as he was fingering his watch-chain, he thought of Terry Kelly's pawn-office in Fleet Street. That was the dart! Why didn't he think of it sooner?

He went through the narrow alley of Temple Bar quickly, muttering to himself that they could all go to hell because he was going to have a good night of it. The clerk in Terry Kelly's said *A crown!* but the consignor held out for six shillings; and in the end the six shillings was allowed him literally. He came out of the pawn-office joyfully, making a little cylinder of the coins between his thumb and fingers. In Westmoreland Street the footpaths were crowded with young men and women returning from business and ragged urchins ran here and there yelling out the names of the evening editions. The man passed through the crowd, looking on the spectacle generally with proud satisfaction and staring masterfully at the office-girls. His head was full of the noises of tram-gongs and swishing trolleys and his nose already sniffed the curling fumes of punch. As he walked on he preconsidered the terms in which he would narrate the incident to the boys:

—So, I just looked at him—coolly, you know, and looked at her. Then I looked back at him again—taking my time, you know. *I don't think that that's a fair question to put to me,* says I.

Nosey Flynn was sitting up in his usual corner of Davy Bryne's and, when he heard the story, he stood Farrington a half-one, saying it was as smart a thing as ever he heard. Farrington stood a drink in his turn. After a while O'Halloran and Paddy Leonard came in and the story was repeated to them. O'Halloran stood tailors of malt, hot, all round and told the story of the retort he had made to the chief clerk when he was in Callan's of Fownes's Street; but, as the retort was after the manner of the liberal shepherds in the eclogues,[1] he had to admit that it was not so clever as Farrington's retort. At this Farrington told the boys to polish off that and have another.

Just as they were naming their poisons who should come in but Higgins! Of course he had to join in with the others. The men asked him to give his version of it, and he did so with great vivacity for the sight of five small hot whiskies was very exhilarating. Everyone roared laughing when he showed the way in which Mr Alleyne shook his fist in Farrington's face. Then he imitated Farrington, saying, *And here was my nabs, as cool as you please,* while Farrington looked at the company out of his heavy dirty eyes, smiling and at times drawing forth stray drops of liquor from his moustache with the aid of his lower lip.

[1]In the Roman poet Vergil's *Eclogues,* ten short poems idealizing rural life, the shepherds are gentle and hospitable.

When that round was over there was a pause. O'Halloran had money but neither of the other two seemed to have any; so the whole party left the shop somewhat regretfully. At the corner of Duke Street Higgins and Nosey Flynn bevelled off to the left while the other three turned back towards the city. Rain was drizzling down on the cold streets and, when they reached the Ballast Office, Farrington suggested the Scotch House. The bar was full of men and loud with the noise of tongues and glasses. The three men pushed past the whining match-sellers at the door and formed a little party at the corner of the counter. They began to exchange stories. Leonard introduced them to a young fellow named Weathers who was performing at the Tivoli as an acrobat and knock-about *artiste*. Farrington stood a drink all round. Weathers said he would take a small Irish[1] and Apollinaris.[2] Farrington, who had definite notions of what was what, asked the boys would they have an Apollinaris too; but the boys told Tim to make theirs hot. The talk became theatrical. O'Halloran stood a round and then Farrington stood another round, Weathers protesting that the hospitality was too Irish. He promised to get them in behind the scenes and introduce them to some nice girls. O'Halloran said that he and Leonard would go but that Farrington wouldn't go because he was a married man; and Farrington's heavy dirty eyes leered at the company in token that he understood he was being chaffed. Weathers made them all have just one little tincture at his expense and promised to meet them later on at Mulligan's in Poolbeg Street.

When the Scotch House closed they went round to Mulligan's. They went into the parlour at the back and O'Halloran ordered small hot specials all round. They were all beginning to feel mellow. Farrington was just standing another round when Weathers came back. Much to Farrington's relief he drank a glass of bitter[3] this time. Funds were running low but they had enough to keep them going. Presently two young women with big hats and a young man in a check suit came in and sat at a table close by. Weathers saluted them and told the company that they were out of the Tivoli. Farrington's eyes wandered at every moment in the direction of one of the young women. There was something striking in her appearance. An immense scarf of peacock-blue muslin was wound round her hat and knotted in a great bow under her chin; and she wore bright yellow gloves, reaching to the elbow. Farrington gazed admiringly at the plump arm which she moved very often and with much grace; and when, after a little time, she answered his gaze he admired still more her large dark brown eyes. The oblique staring expression in them fascinated him. She glanced at him once or twice and, when the party was leaving the room, she brushed against his chair and said *O, pardon!* in a London accent. He watched her leave the room in the hope that she would look back at him, but he was disappointed. He cursed his want of money and cursed all the rounds he had stood, particularly all the whiskies and Apollinaris which he had stood to Weathers. If there was one thing that he hated it was a sponge. He was so angry that he lost count of the conversation of his friends.

When Paddy Leonard called him he found that they were talking about feats of strength. Weathers was showing his biceps muscle to the company and boasting so much that the other two had called on Farrington to uphold the national honour. Farrington pulled up his sleeve accordingly and showed his biceps muscle to the company. The two arms were examined and compared and finally it was agreed

[1] Irish whiskey [2] A German mineral water [3] Ale

to have a trial of strength. The table was cleared and the two men rested their elbows on it, clasping hands. When Paddy Leonard said *Go!* each was to try to bring down the other's hand on to the table. Farrington looked very serious and determined.

The trial began. After about thirty seconds, Weathers brought his opponent's hand slowly down on to the table. Farrington's dark wine-coloured face flushed darker still with anger and humiliation at having been defeated by such a stripling.

—You're not to put the weight of your body behind it. Play fair, he said.

50 —Who's not playing fair? said the other.

—Come on again. The two best out of three.

The trial began again. The veins stood out on Farrington's forehead, and the pallor of Weathers' complexion changed to peony. Their hands and arms trembled under the stress. After a long struggle Weathers again brought his opponent's hand slowly on to the table. There was a murmur of applause from the spectators. The curate, who was standing beside the table, nodded his red head toward the victor and said with loutish familiarity:

—Ah! that's the knack!

—What the hell do you know about it? said Farrington fiercely, turning on the man. What do you put in your gab for?

55 —Sh, sh! said O'Halloran, observing the violent expression of Farrington's face. Pony up, boys. We'll have just one little smahan[1] more and then we'll be off.

A very sullen-faced man stood at the corner of O'Connell Bridge waiting for the little Sandymount tram to take him home. He was full of smouldering anger and revengefulness. He felt humiliated and discontented; he did not even feel drunk; and he had only twopence in his pocket. He cursed everything. He had done for himself in the office, pawned his watch, spent all his money; and he had not even got drunk. He began to feel thirsty again and he longed to be back again in the hot reeking public-house. He had lost his reputation as a strong man, having been defeated twice by a mere boy. His heart swelled with fury and, when he thought of the woman in the big hat who had brushed against him and said *Pardon!* his fury nearly choked him.

His tram let him down at Shelbourne Road and he steered his great body along in the shadow of the wall of the barracks. He loathed returning to his home. When he went in by the side-door he found the kitchen empty and the kitchen fire nearly out. He bawled upstairs:

—Ada! Ada!

His wife was a little sharp-faced woman who bullied her husband when he was sober and was bullied by him when he was drunk. They had five children. A little boy came running down the stairs.

60 —Who is that? said the man, peering through the darkness.

—Me, pa.

—Who are you? Charlie?

—No, pa. Tom.

—Where's your mother?

65 —She's out at the chapel.

—That's right. . . . Did she think of leaving any dinner for me?

---

[1]An Irish dialect word for *taste*; a smidgeon

—Yes, pa. I—

—Light the lamp. What do you mean by having the place in darkness? Are the other children in bed?

The man sat down heavily on one of the chairs while the little boy lit the lamp. He began to mimic his son's flat accent, saying half to himself: *At the chapel. At the chapel, if you please!* When the lamp was lit he banged his fist on the table and shouted:

70   —What's for my dinner?

—I'm going . . . to cook it, pa, said the little boy.

The man jumped up furiously and pointed to the fire.

—On that fire! You let the fire out! By God, I'll teach you to do that again!

He took a step to the door and seized the walking-stick which was standing behind it.

75   —I'll teach you to let the fire out! he said, rolling up his sleeve in order to give his arm free play.

The little boy cried *O, pa!* and ran whimpering round the table, but the man followed him and caught him by the coat. The little boy looked about him wildly but, seeing no way of escape, fell upon his knees.

—Now, you'll let the fire out the next time! said the man, striking at him viciously with the stick. Take that, you little whelp!

The boy uttered a squeal of pain as the stick cut his thigh. He clasped his hands together in the air and his voice shook with fright.

—O, pa! he cried. Don't beat me, pa! And I'll . . . I'll say a *Hail Mary* for you. . . . I'll say a *Hail Mary* for you, pa, if you don't beat me. . . . I'll say a *Hail Mary.* . . .

Questions on character . . .

1. Go through this story, noting Joyce's different methods of conveying Farrington's character. List the methods of characterization you find.
2. Point of view affects characterization. From whose point of view is this story told? When *furiously* and *furious* both turn up in the first paragraph, is this the author's contribution? Or does the character contribute the idea of furiousness?
3. In paragraph 3, how do we know who *a man* is? How does this introduction help the characterization?
4. When do we find the first physical description of Farrington? How does it help characterize him? Is *a heavy step* description of gesture or action? Does it characterize Farrington?
5. In paragraph 8, does the last sentence characterize Mr. Alleyne? Farrington? Both? How could it characterize both?
6. Is Farrington a dynamic character? Is he static? Does anything change in the story? Will Farrington be different tomorrow? Do you know more about his character than he does? How can this be so? How do we get this impression?
7. Does Miss Delacour's presence help establish or develop Farrington's character?
8. Farrington makes a witticism. Is it consistent with his character? Contrast Farrington's different reactions to his own witticism. Does this variety indicate a round character?
9. In paragraph 45, is the first sentence the author's way of expressing himself? Who says it? What does it do?

10. How do we begin to understand Weathers's character? Do we observe it objectively? Through Farrington's eyes? Both?

11. Later in the story we learn a little about Farrington's wife. How much? Does this information contribute to Farrington's characterization?

12. Is Farrington's last action the final touch in his characterization? Is it a climax to the story? Does it resemble other scenes in the story?

13. On the basis of what you know, construct these scenes:
    a. Ada returns and finds Farrington beating her child.
    b. Farrington has breakfast with Ada and the children.
    c. Farrington is summoned to Mr. Alleyne's office the next morning.

. . . and other elements

14. What does the title mean?

15. In Farrington's mind, two places are in conflict. Could you describe this story as a conflict of settings?

Eudora Welty
A Worn Path

Eudora Welty (1909–   ) was born and lives in Jackson, Mississippi, having lived elsewhere only briefly. Her novels include *The Robber Bridegroom* (1942), *Delta Wedding* (1946), *The Ponder Heart* (1954), and *Losing Battles* (1970). This story comes from her first book, a collection of stories called *A Curtain of Green* (1941), which was followed by *The Wide Net* (1943), *The Golden Apple* (1949), and *The Bride of the Innisfallen* (1954). Miss Welty has also published a collection of essays called *The Eye of the Story* (1978), in which she comments on "A Worn Path."

It was December—a bright frozen day in the early morning. Far out in the country there was an old Negro woman with her head tied in a red rag, coming along a path through the pinewoods. Her name was Phoenix Jackson. She was very old and small and she walked slowly in the dark pine shadows, moving a little from side to side in her steps, with the balanced heaviness and lightness of a pendulum in a grandfather clock. She carried a thin, small cane made from an umbrella, and with this she kept tapping the frozen earth in front of her. This made a grave and persistent noise in the still air, that seemed meditative like the chirping of a solitary little bird.

She wore a dark striped dress reaching down to her shoe tops, and an equally long apron of bleached sugar sacks, with a full pocket: all neat and tidy, but every time she took a step she might have fallen over her shoelaces, which dragged from her unlaced shoes. She looked straight ahead. Her eyes were blue with age. Her skin had a pattern all its own of numberless branching wrinkles and as though a whole little tree stood in the middle of her forehead, but a golden color ran underneath, and the two knobs of her cheeks were illumined by a yellow burning under the dark. Under the red rag her hair came down on her neck in the frailest of ringlets, still black, and with an odor like copper.

Now and then there was a quivering in the thicket. Old Phoenix said, "Out of my way, all you foxes, owls, beetles, jack rabbits, coons and wild animals! . . . Keep out from under these feet, little bob-whites. . . . Keep the big wild hogs out of my path. Don't let none of those come running my direction. I got a long way." Under her small black-freckled hand her cane, limber as a buggy whip, would switch at the brush as if to rouse up any hiding things.

On she went. The woods were deep and still. The sun made the pine needles almost too bright to look at, up where the wind rocked. The cones dropped as light as feathers. Down in the hollow was the mourning dove—it was not too late for him.

5   The path ran up a hill. "Seem like there is chains about my feet, time I get this far," she said, in the voice of argument old people keep to use with themselves. "Something always take a hold of me on this hill—pleads I should stay."

After she got to the top she turned and gave a full, severe look behind her where she had come. "Up through pines," she said at length. "Now down through oaks."

Her eyes opened their widest, and she started down gently. But before she got to the bottom of the hill a bush caught her dress.

Her fingers were busy and intent, but her skirts were full and long, so that before she could pull them free in one place they were caught in another. It was not possible to allow the dress to tear. "I in the thorny bush," she said. "Thorns, you doing your appointed work. Never want to let folks pass, no sir. Old eyes thought you was a pretty little *green* bush."

Finally, trembling all over, she stood free, and after a moment dared to stoop for her cane.

10   "Sun so high!" she cried, leaning back and looking, while the thick tears went over her eyes. "The time getting all gone here."

At the foot of this hill was a place where a log was laid across the creek.

"Now comes the trial," said Phoenix.

Putting her right foot out, she mounted the log and shut her eyes. Lifting her skirt, leveling her cane fiercely before her, like a festival figure in some parade, she began to march across. Then she opened her eyes and she was safe on the other side.

"I wasn't as old as I thought," she said.

15   But she sat down to rest. She spread her skirts on the bank around her and folded her hands over her knees. Up above her was a tree in a pearly cloud of mistletoe. She did not dare to close her eyes, and when a little boy brought her a plate with a slice of marble-cake on it she spoke to him. "That would be acceptable," she said. But when she went to take it there was just her own hand in the air.

So she left that tree, and had to go through a barbed-wire fence. There she had to creep and crawl, spreading her knees and stretching her fingers like a baby trying to climb the steps. But she talked loudly to herself: she could not let her dress be torn now, so late in the day, and she could not pay for having her arm or her leg sawed off if she got caught fast where she was.

At last she was safe through the fence and risen up out in the clearing. Big dead trees, like black men with one arm, were standing in the purple stalks of the withered cotton field. There sat a buzzard.

"Who you watching?"

In the furrow she made her way along.

20 "Glad this not the season for bulls," she said, looking sideways, "and the good Lord made his snakes to curl up and sleep in the winter. A pleasure I don't see no two-headed snake coming around that tree, where it come once. It took a while to get by him, back in the summer."

She passed through the old cotton and went into a field of dead corn. It whispered and shook and was taller than her head. "Through the maze now," she said, for there was no path.

Then there was something tall, black, and skinny there, moving before her.

At first she took it for a man. It could have been a man dancing in the field. But she stood still and listened, and it did not make a sound. It was as silent as a ghost.

"Ghost," she said sharply, "who be you the ghost of? For I have heard of nary death close by."

25 But there was no answer—only the ragged dancing in the wind.

She shut her eyes, reached out her hand, and touched a sleeve. She found a coat and inside that an emptiness, cold as ice.

"You scarecrow," she said. Her face lighted. "I ought to be shut up for good," she said with laughter. "My senses is gone. I too old. I the oldest people I ever know. Dance, old scarecrow," she said, "while I dancing with you."

She kicked her foot over the furrow, and with mouth drawn down, shook her head once or twice in a little strutting way. Some husks blew down and whirled in streamers about her skirts.

Then she went on, parting her way from side to side with the cane, through the whispering field. At last she came to the end, to a wagon track where the silver grass blew between the red ruts. The quail were walking around like pullets, seeming all dainty and unseen.

30 "Walk pretty," she said. "This the easy place. This the easy going."

She followed the track, swaying through the quiet bare fields, through the little strings of trees silver in their dead leaves, past cabins silver from weather, with the doors and windows boarded shut, all like old women under a spell sitting there. "I walking in their sleep," she said, nodding her head vigorously.

In a ravine she went where a spring was silently flowing through a hollow log. Old Phoenix bent and drank. "Sweet-gum makes the water sweet," she said, and drank more. "Nobody know who made this well, for it was here when I was born."

The track crossed a swampy part where the moss hung as white as lace from every limb. "Sleep on, alligators, and blow your bubbles." Then the track went into the road.

Deep, deep the road went down between the high green-colored banks. Overhead the live-oaks met, and it was as dark as a cave.

35 A black dog with a lolling tongue came up out of the weeds by the ditch. She was meditating, and not ready, and when he came at her she only hit him a little with her cane. Over she went in the ditch, like a little puff of milkweed.

Down there, her senses drifted away. A dream visited her, and she reached her hand up, but nothing reached down and gave her a pull. So she lay there and presently went to talking. "Old woman," she said to herself, "that black dog come up out of the weeds to stall you off, and now there he sitting on his fine tail, smiling at you."

A white man finally came along and found her—a hunter, a young man, with his dog on a chain.

"Well, Granny!" he laughed. "What are you doing there?"

"Lying on my back like a June-bug waiting to be turned over, mister," she said, reaching up her hand.

40   He lifted her up, gave her a swing in the air, and set her down. "Anything broken, Granny?"

"No sir, them old dead weeds is springy enough," said Phoenix, when she had got her breath. "I thank you for your trouble."

"Where do you live, Granny?" he asked, while the two dogs were growling at each other.

"Away back yonder, sir, behind the ridge. You can't even see it from here."

"On your way home?"

45   "No sir, I going to town."

"Why, that's too far! That's as far as I walk when I come out myself, and I get something for my trouble." He patted the stuffed bag he carried, and there hung down a little closed claw. It was one of the bob-whites, with its beak hooked bitterly to show it was dead. "Now you go on home, Granny!"

"I bound to go to town, mister," said Phoenix. "The time come around."

He gave another laugh, filling the whole landscape. "I know you old colored people! Wouldn't miss going to town to see Santa Claus!"

But something held old Phoenix very still. The deep lines in her face went into a fierce and different radiation. Without warning, she had seen with her own eyes a flashing nickel fall out of the man's pocket onto the ground.

50   "How old are you, Granny?" he was saying.

"There is no telling, mister," she said, "no telling."

Then she gave a little cry and clapped her hands and said, "Git on away from here, dog! Look! Look at that dog!" She laughed as if in admiration. "He ain't scared of nobody. He a big black dog." She whispered, "Sic him!"

"Watch me get rid of that cur," said the man. "Sic him, Pete! Sic him!"

Phoenix heard the dogs fighting, and heard the man running and throwing sticks. She even heard a gunshot. But she was slowly bending forward by that time, further and further forward, the lid stretched down over her eyes, as if she were doing this in her sleep. Her chin was lowered almost to her knees. The yellow palm of her hand came out from the fold of her apron. Her fingers slid down and along the ground under the piece of money with the grace and care they would have in lifting an egg from under a setting hen. Then she slowly straightened up, she stood erect, and the nickel was in her apron pocket. A bird flew by. Her lips moved. "God watching me the whole time. I come to stealing."

55   The man came back, and his own dog panted about them. "Well, I scared him off that time," he said, and then he laughed and lifted his gun and pointed it at Phoenix.

She stood straight and faced him.

"Doesn't the gun scare you?" he said, still pointing it.

"No, sir, I seen plenty go off closer by, in my day, and for less than what I done," she said, holding utterly still.

60   He smiled, and shouldered the gun. "Well, Granny," he said, "you must be a hundred years old, and scared of nothing. I'd give you a dime if I had any money with me. But you take my advice and stay home, and nothing will happen to you."

"I bound to go on my way, mister," said Phoenix. She inclined her head in the red rag. Then they went in different directions, but she could hear the gun shooting again and again over the hill.

She walked on. The shadows hung from the oak trees to the road like curtains. Then she smelled wood-smoke, and smelled the river, and she saw a steeple and the cabins on their steep steps. Dozens of little black children whirled around her. There ahead was Natchez shining. Bells were ringing. She walked on.

In the paved city it was Christmas time. There were red and green electric lights strung and crisscrossed everywhere, and all turned on in the daytime. Old Phoenix would have been lost if she had not distrusted her eyesight and depended on her feet to know where to take her.

She paused quietly on the sidewalk where people were passing by. A lady came along in the crowd, carrying an armful of red-, green- and silver-wrapped presents; she gave off perfume like the red roses in hot summer, and Phoenix stopped her.

65   "Please, missy, will you lace up my shoe?" She held up her foot.

"What do you want, Grandma?"

"See my shoe," said Phoenix. "Do all right for out in the country, but wouldn't look right to go in a big building."

"Stand still then, Grandma," said the lady. She put her packages down on the sidewalk beside her and laced and tied both shoes tightly.

"Can't lace 'em with a cane," said Phoenix. "Thank you, missy. I doesn't mind asking a nice lady to tie up my shoe, when I gets out on the street."

70   Moving slowly and from side to side, she went into the big building, and into a tower of steps, where she walked up and around and around until her feet knew to stop.

She entered a door, and there she saw nailed up on the wall the document that had been stamped with the gold seal and framed in the gold frame, which matched the dream that was hung up in her head.

"Here I be," she said. There was a fixed and ceremonial stiffness over her body.

"A charity case, I suppose," said an attendant who sat at the desk before her.

But Phoenix only looked above her head. There was sweat on her face, the wrinkles in her skin shone like a bright net.

75   "Speak up, Grandma," the woman said. "What's your name? We must have your history, you know. Have you been here before? What seems to be the trouble with you?"

Old Phoenix only gave a twitch to her face as if a fly were bothering her.

"Are you deaf?" cried the attendant.

But then the nurse came in.

"Oh, that's just old Aunt Phoenix," she said. "She doesn't come for herself— she has a little grandson. She makes these trips just as regular as clockwork. She lives away back off the Old Natchez Trace." She bent down. "Well, Aunt Phoenix, why don't you just take a seat? We won't keep you standing after your long trip." She pointed.

80   The old woman sat down, bolt upright in the chair.

"Now, how is the boy?" asked the nurse.

Old Phoenix did not speak.

"I said, how is the boy?"

But Phoenix only waited and stared straight ahead, her face very solemn and withdrawn into rigidity.

85   "Is his throat any better?" asked the nurse. "Aunt Phoenix, don't you hear me? Is your grandson's throat any better since the last time you came for the medicine?"

With her hands on her knees, the old woman waited, silent, erect and motionless, just as if she were in armor.

"You mustn't take up our time this way, Aunt Phoenix," the nurse said. "Tell us quickly about your grandson, and get it over. He isn't dead, is he?"

At last there came a flicker and then a flame of comprehension across her face, and she spoke.

"My grandson. It was my memory had left me. There I sat and forgot why I made my long trip."

90   "Forgot?" The nurse frowned. "After you came so far?"

Then Phoenix was like an old woman begging a dignified forgiveness for waking up frightened in the night. "I never did go to school, I was too old at the Surrender," she said in a soft voice. "I'm an old woman without an education. It was my memory fail me. My little grandson, he is just the same, and I forgot it in the coming."

"Throat never heals, does it?" said the nurse, speaking in a loud, sure voice to old Phoenix. By now she had a card with something written on it, a little list. "Yes. Swallowed lye. When was it?—January—two-three years ago—"

Phoenix spoke unasked now. "No, missy, he not dead, he just the same. Every little while his throat begin to close up again, and he not able to swallow. He not get his breath. He not able to help himself. So the time come around, and I go on another trip for the soothing medicine."

"All right. The doctor said as long as you came to get it, you could have it," said the nurse. "But it's an obstinate case."

95   "My little grandson, he sit up there in the house all wrapped up waiting by himself," Phoenix went on. "We is the only two left in the world. He suffer and it don't seem to put him back at all. He got a sweet look. He going to last. He wear a little patch quilt and peep out holding his mouth open like a little bird. I remembers so plain now. I not going to forget him again, no, the whole enduring time. I could tell him from all the others in creation."

"All right." The nurse was trying to hush her now. She brought her a bottle of medicine. "Charity," she said, making a check mark in a book.

Old Phoenix held the bottle close to her eyes, and then carefully put it into her pocket.

"I thank you," she said.

"It's Christmas time, Grandma," said the attendant. "Could I give you a few pennies out of my purse?"

100   "Five pennies is a nickel," said Phoenix stiffly.

"Here's a nickel," said the attendant.

Phoenix rose carefully and held out her hand. She received the nickel and then fished the other nickel out of her pocket and laid it beside the new one. She stared at her palm closely, with her head on one side.

Then she gave a tap with her cane on the floor.

"This is what come to me to do," she said. "I going to the store and buy my child a little windmill they sells, made out of paper. He going to find it hard to believe there such a thing in the world. I'll march myself back where he waiting, holding it straight up in this hand."

105   She lifted her free hand, gave a little nod, turned around, and walked out of the doctor's office. Then her slow step began on the stairs, going down.

Questions on character . . .

1. In the first paragraph, notice how the narrative moves from naming into description and beyond description into metaphor. Do you begin to find characterization in this description? How do the metaphors give you notions of Phoenix's character?

2. Throughout the story, what categories of characterization does Welty use for Phoenix?

3. Most people revise their estimate of Phoenix's age upward as they read the story. What details suggest her age?

4. Why does Phoenix talk to herself? How much do you learn from this one-way conversation? Do you learn different things from her out-loud talk and from her silent thoughts?

5. Pick out the thoughts by which Phoenix reveals most about her character. Do you feel that you know something of Phoenix's past life? Find instances of Phoenix's sense of humor when she is alone.

6. What do you learn of Phoenix's character when she first meets another person?

7. In the hospital, Phoenix forgets everything. Does anything in the story earlier—we could call it plot or character—prepare you for this forgetting? Is it another *hill*?

8. In paragraph 78 we learn about Phoenix from another character. Does it hurt the story that this information comes so late? Would it have been better for the story if we had known earlier? Why?

9. In paragraph 100, why does Phoenix define a nickel? What does this add to her character?

10. Comment on the last sentence of the story. Relate it to the title.

. . . and other elements

11. In paragraph 2 we hear about Phoenix's shoelaces; in paragraph 65, we hear of them again. Why repeat this one detail? Does it tell us something about Phoenix, about her character or her situation?

12. What happens to Phoenix in paragraph 15?

13. The plot is a journey and a task. If you were going to make it into a film, how many scenes would you need?

14. In the hospital we meet a nurse who knows Phoenix and remembers her grandson. Would it be correct to say that the nurse's speeches make the story's climax?

15. In paragraph 96: " 'Charity,' she said, making a checkmark in a book." Comment on the theme of the story.

Chapter 6 **Setting**

Setting is the place or time of a story—its geography, era, season, and society. In many stories, setting is only the air characters breathe, vital and taken for granted. In others, setting is basic to the theme of a story. Some stories need no background at all. Fables live in a timeless present where crickets talk; usually fantasy happens anywhere and nowhere. But most writers invoke particular places and particular times, and their stories establish these settings precisely. Precise setting helps to establish the truth of the story, to persuade the reader of the validity of the tale.

Setting can give us information vital to plot and theme. The two leading characters of Thurber's "The Catbird Seat" grow out of their generalized office life. Faulkner's Miss Emily is shaped by the social details of her changing town. Without these specific historical and social settings, the story would be melodrama; its theme arises from its setting. In "A Good Man Is Hard to Find" the three settings (home, Red Sammy's, the scene of the accident) contrast sordid reality with would-be elevated talk to ironic effect. In "A Worn Path" the setting is the path itself.

In this last type of setting landscape fits a subjective mood, and description becomes symbolic. Edgar Allan Poe's "The Fall of the House of Usher" begins with such a description, where physical details represent mental traits:

> Shaking off from my spirit what *must* have been a dream, I scanned more narrowly the real aspect of the building. Its principal feature seemed to be that of an excessive antiquity. The discoloration of ages had been great. Minute fungi overspread the whole exterior, hanging in a fine tangled web-work from the eaves. Yet

all this was apart from any extraordinary dilapidation. No portion of the masonry had fallen; and there appeared to be a wild inconsistency between its still perfect adaptation of parts, and the crumbling condition of the individual stones. In this there was much that reminded me of the specious totality of old woodwork which has rotted for long years in some neglected vault, with no disturbance from the breath of the external air. Beyond this indication of extensive decay, however, the fabric gave little token of instability. Perhaps the eye of a scrutinizing observer might have discovered a barely perceptible fissure, which, extending from the roof of the building in front, made its way down the wall in a zig-zag direction, until it became lost in the sullen waters of the tarn.

The *fissure* is subjective, a representation of the psyche of Roderick Usher, the story's main character and the owner of the house.

Finally, we should not forget that we read to entertain ourselves, among other reasons, and that we are entertained by the exotic and the unusual. For the same reasons we travel to strange places, we read about strange places.

Mary Lavin
The Green Grave and the Black Grave

Mary Lavin (1912–   ) was born in Massachusetts to Irish parents, emigrants who migrated back when she was ten years old. She has lived in Ireland ever since, and now divides her time between a house in Dublin and a farm in County Meath. Her *Collected Stories* appeared in the United States in 1971, *The Shrine and Other Stories* in 1977.

It was a body all right. It was hard to see in the dark, and the scaly black sea was heaving up between them and the place where they saw the thing floating. But it was a body all right.

"I knew it was a shout I heard," said the taller of the two tall men in the black boat that was out fishing for mackerel. He was Tadg Mor and he was the father of the less tall man, that was blacker in the hair than him and broader in the chest than him, but was called Tadg Og because he was son to him. *Mor* means "big" and *Og* means "son."

"I knew it was a shout I heard," said Tadg Mor.

"I knew it was a boat I saw and I dragging in the second net," said Tadg Og.

5 "I said the sound I heard was a kittiwake, crying in the dark."

"And I said the boat I saw was a black wave blown up on the wind."

"It was a shout all right."

"It was a boat all right."

"It was a body all right."

10 "But where is the black boat?" Tadg Og asked.

"It must be that the black boat capsized," said Tadg Mor, "and went down into the green sea."

"Whose boat was it, would you venture for to say?" Tadg Og asked, pulling stroke for stroke at the sea.

"I'd venture for to say it was the boat of Eamon Buidhe," said Tadg Mor, pulling with his oar against the sharp up-pointing waves of the scaly, scurvy sea. The tall men rowed hard toward the clumsy thing that tossed on the tips of the deft green waves.

"Eamon Buidhe Murnane!" said Tadg Mor, lifting clear his silver-dropping oar.

15   "Eamon Buidhe Murnane!" said Tadg Og lifting his clear, dripless, yellow oar.

It was a hard drag, dragging him over the arching sides of the boat. His clothes logged him down to the water and the jutting waves jottled him back against the boat. His yellow hair slipped from their fingers like floss, and the loose fibers of his island-spun clothes broke free from their grip. But they got him up over the edge of the boat, at the end of a black hour that was only lit by the whiteness of the breaking wave. They laid him down on the boards of the floor on their haul of glittering mackerel, and they spread the nets out over him. But the scales of the fish glittered up through the net and so, too, the eyes of Eamon Buidhe Murnane glittered up through the net. And the live glitter of the dead eyes put a strain on Tadg Mor and he turned the body over on its face among the fish; and when they had looked a time at the black corpse with yellow hair, set in the silver and opal casket of fishes, they turned the oar blades out again into the scurvy seas, and pulled toward the land.

"How did you know it was Eamon Buidhe Murnane, and we forty pointed waves away from him at the time of your naming his name?" Tadg Og asked Tadg Mor.

"Whenever it is a thing that a man is pulled under by the sea," said Tadg Mor, "think around in your mind until you think out which man of all the men it might be that would be the man most missed, and that man, that you think out in your mind, will be the man that will be cast up on the shingle."

20   "This is a man that will be missed mightily," said Tadg Og.

"He is a man that will be mightily bemoaned," said Tadg Mor.

"He is a man that will never be replaced."

"He is a man that will be prayed for bitterly and mightily."

"Many a night, forgetful, his wife will set out food for him," said Tadg Og.

"The Brightest and the Bravest!" said Tadg Mor. "Those are the words that will be read over him—the Brightest and the Bravest."

25   The boat rose up on the points of the waves and cleft down again between the points, and the oars of Tadg Mor and the oars of Tadg Og split the points of many waves.

"How is it the green sea always greeds after the Brightest and the Bravest?" Tadg Og asked Tadg Mor.

"And for the only son?" Tadg Mor said.

"And the widows' sons?"

"And the men with one-year wives. The one-year wife that's getting this corpse tonight"—Tadg Mor pointed down with his eyes—"will have a black sorrow this night."

30   "And every night after this night," said Tadg Og, because he was a young man and knew about such things.

"It's a great thing that he was not dragged down to the green grave, and that is a thing will lighten the nights of the one-year wife," said Tadg Mor.

"It isn't many are saved out of the green grave," said Tadg Og.

"Mairtin Mor wasn't got," said Tadg Mor.

"And Muiris Fada wasn't got."

35   "Lorcan Og wasn't got."

"Ruairi Dubh wasn't got."

"It was three weeks and the best part of a night before the Frenchman with the leather coat was got, and five boats out looking for him."

"It was seven weeks before Maolshaughlin O'Dalaigh was got, and his eye sockets emptied by the gulls and the gannies."

"And by the waves. The waves are great people to lick out your eyeballs!" said Tadg Mor.

40 "It was a good thing, this man to be got," said Tadg Og, "and his eyes bright in his head."

"Like he was looking up at the sky!"

"Like he was thinking to smile next thing he'd do."

"He was a great man to smile, this man," said Tadg Mor. "He was ever and always smiling."

"He was a great man to laugh too," said Tadg Og. "He was ever and always laughing."

45 "Times he was laughing and times he was not laughing," said Tadg Mor.

"Times all men stop from laughing," said Tadg Og.

"Times I saw this man and he not laughing. Times I saw him and he putting out in the black boat looking back at the inland woman where she'd be standing on the shore and her hair weaving the wind, and there wouldn't be any laugh on his face those times."

"An island man should take an island wife," said Tadg Og.

"An inland woman should take an inland man."

50 "The inland woman that took this man had a dreadful dread on her of the sea and the boats that put out in it."

"Times I saw this woman from the inlands standing on the shore, from his putting out with the dry black boat to his coming back with the shivering silver-belly boat."

"He got it hard to go from her every night."

"He got it harder than iron to go from her if there was a streak of storm gold in the sky at time of putting out."

"An island man should not be held down to a woman from the silent inlands."

55 "It was love-talk and love-looks that held down this man," said Tadg Mor.

"The island women give love-words and love-talk too," said Tadg Og.

"But not the love-words and the love-looks of this woman," said Tadg Mor. "Times I saw her wetting her feet in the waves and wetting her fingers in the waves and you'd see she was a kind of lovering the waves so they'd bring him back to her. Times he told me himself she had a dreadful dread of the green grave. 'There dies as many men in the inlands as in the islands,' I said. 'Tell her that,' I said. 'I told her that,' said he.

" ' "But they get the black grave burial," she said. "They get the black grave burial in clay that's blessed by two priests and they get the speeding of the green sods thrown down on them by their kinsmen." 'Tell her there's no worms in the green grave,' I said to him. 'I did,' said he. 'What did she say to that?' said I. 'She said, "The bone waits for the bone," said he. 'What does she mean by that?' said I. 'She gave another saying as her meaning to that saying,' said he. 'She said, "There's no sorrow in death when two go down together into the one black grave. Clay binds closer than love," she said, "but the green grave binds nothing," she said. "The green grave scatters," she said. "The green grave is for sons," she said, "and for brothers," she said, "but the black grave is for lovers," she said, "and for husbands in the faithful clay under the jealous sods." ' "

"She must be a great woman to make sayings," said Tadg Og.

60   "She made great sayings for that man every hour of the day, and she stitching the nets for him on the step while he'd be salting fish or blading oars."

"She'll be glad us to have saved him from the salt green grave. It's a great wonder but he was dragged down before he was got."

"She is the kind of woman that always has great wonders happening round her," said Tadg Mor. "If she is a woman from the inlands itself, she has a great power in herself. She has a great power over the sea. Times—and she on the cliff shore and her hair weaving the wind, like I told you—I'd point my eyes through the wind across at where Éamon Buidhe would be in the waves back of me, and there wouldn't be as much as one white tongue of spite rising out of the waves around his boat, and my black boat would be splattered over every board of it with white sea-spittle."

"I heard tell of women like that. She took the fury out of the sea and burned it out to white salt in her own heart."

The talk about the inland woman who fought the seas in her heart was slow talk and heavy talk, and slow and heavy talk was fit talk as the scurvy waves crawled over one another, scale by scale, and brought the bitter boat back to the shore.

65   Sometimes a spiteful tongue of foam forked up in the dark by the side of the boat and reached for the netted corpse on the boards. When this happened Tadg Og picked up the loose end of the raggy net and lashed out with it at the sea.

"Get down, you scaly-belly serpent," he said, "and let the corpse dry out in his dead-clothes."

"Take heed to your words, Tadg Og," Tadg Mor would say. "We have the point to round yet. Take heed to your words!"

"Here's a man took heed to his words and that didn't save him," said Tadg Og. "Here was a man was always singing back song for song to the singing sea, and look at him now lying there."

They looked at him lying on his face under the brown web of the nets in his casket of fish scales, silver and opal. And as they looked, another venomous tongue of the sea licked up the side of the boat and strained in toward the body. Tadg Og beat at it with the raggy net.

70   "Keep your strength for the loud knocking you'll have to give on the wooden door," said Tadg Mor. And Tadg Og understood that he was the one would walk up the shingle and bring the death news to the one-year wife, who was so strange among the island women with her hair weaving the wind at evening and her white feet wetted in the sea by day.

"Is it not a thing that she'll be, likely, out on the shore?" he asked, in a bright hope, pointing his eyes to where the white edge of the shore-wash shone by its own light in the dark.

"Is there a storm tonight?" said Tadg Mor. "Is there a great wind tonight? Is there a rain spate? Are there any signs of danger on the sea?"

"No," said Tadg Og, "there are none of those things that you mention."

"I will tell you the reason you asked that question," said Tadg Mor. "You asked that question because that question is the answer that you'd like to get."

75   "It's a hard thing to bring news to a one-year wife and she one that has a dreadful dread of the sea," said Tadg Og.

"It's good news you're bringing to the one-year wife when you bring news that her man is got safe, to go down like any inlander into a black grave blessed by a priest and tramped down by the feet of his kinsmen on the sod."

"It's a queer thing to be caught by the sea on a fine night with no wind blowing," said Tadg Og.

"On a fine night the women lie down to sleep, and if any woman has a power over the sea, with her white feet in the water and her black hair in the wind and a bright fire in her heart, the sea can only wait until that woman's spirit is out of her body, likely back home in the inlands, and then the sea serpent gives a slow turnover on his scales, one that you wouldn't heed to yourself, maybe, and you standing up with no hold on the oars; and before there's time for more than the first shout out of you the boat is logging down to the depths of the water. And all the time the woman that would have saved you, with her willing and wishing for you, is in the deep bed of a dark sleep, having no knowledge of the thing that has happened until she hears the loud-handed knocking of the neighbor on the door outside."

Tadg Og knocked with his knuckles on the sideboards of the boat.

80 "Louder than that," Tadg Mor said.

Tadg Og knocked another, louder knock on the boat side.

"Have you no more knowledge than that of how to knock at a door in the fastness of the night and the people inside the house buried in sleep and the corpse down on the shore getting covered with sand and the fish scales drying into him so tight that the fingernails of the washing women will be broken and split peeling them off him? Have you no more knowledge than that of how to knock with your knucklebones?"

Tadg Mor gave a loud knocking on the wet seat of the boat.

"That is the knock of a man that you might say knows how to knock at a door, daytime or nighttime," he said, and he knocked again. And he knocked again, louder, if it could be that any knock could be louder than the first knock.

85 Tadg Og listened and then he spoke, not looking at Tadg Mor, but looking at the oar he was rolling in the water. "Two people knocking would make a loud knocking entirely," he said.

"One has to stay with the dead," said Tadg Mor.

Tadg Og drew a long stroke on the oar and he drew a long breath out of his lungs, and he took a long look at the nearing shore.

"What will I say," he asked, "when she comes to my knocking?"

"When she comes to the knocking, step back a bit from the door, so's she'll see the wet shining on you and smell the salt water off you, and say in a loud voice that the sea is queer and rough this night."

90 "She'll be down with her to the shore if that's what I say."

"Say then," said Tadg Mor, pulling in the oar to slow the boat a bit, "say there's news come in that a boat went down beyond the point."

"If I say that, she'll be down with her to the shore without waiting to hear more, and her hair flying and her white feet freezing on the shingle."

"If that is so," said Tadg Mor, "then you'll have to stand back bold from the door and call out loudly in the night, 'The Brightest and the Bravest!' "

"What will she say to that?"

95 "She'll say, 'God bless them!' "

"And what will I say to that?"

"You'll say, 'God rest them!' "

"And what will she say to that?"

"She'll say, 'Is it in the black grave or the green grave?' "

100 "And what will I say to that?"

"You say, 'God rest Eamon Buidhe, in the black grave in the holy ground, blessed by the priest and sodded by the people.' "

"And what will she say to that?"

"She'll say, likely, 'Bring him in to me, Tadg Og!' "

"And what will I say to that?"

105 "Whatever you say after that, let it be loud and raising echoes under the rafters, so she won't hear the sound of the corpse being dragged up on the shingle. And when he's lifted up on to the scoured table, let whatever you say be loud then too, so's she won't be listening for the sound of the water drabbling down off his clothes on the floor!

There was only the noise of the oars then, till a shoaly sound stole in between the oar strokes. It was the shoaly sound of the pebbles dragged back from the shore by the tide.

A few strokes more and they beached, and stepped out among the sprawling waves and dragged the boat after them till it cleft its depth in the damp shingle.

"See that you give a loud knocking, Tadg Og," said Tadg Mor, and Tadg Og set his head against the darkness, and his feet were heard for a good time grinding down the shifting shingle as he made for the house of the one-year wife. The house was set in a shrifty sea-field, and his steps did not sound down to the shore once he got to the dune grass of the shrifty sea-field. But in another little while there was a sound of a fist knocking upon wood, stroke after stroke of a strong hand coming down on hard wood. Tadg Mor, waiting with the body in the boat, recalled to himself all the times he went knocking on the island doors bringing news to the women of the death of their men. But island wives were the daughters of island widows. The sea gave food. The sea gave death. Life or death, it was all one in the end. The sea never lost its scabs. The sea was there before the coming of man. Island women had that knowledge. But what knowledge of the sea and its place in the world since the beginning of time had a woman from the inlands? No knowledge. An inland woman had no knowledge when the loud knocking came on her door in the night. Tadg Mor listened to the loud, hard knocking of his son Tadg Og on the door of the one-year wife of Eamon Buidhe that was lying in the silver casket of fishes on the floor of the boat, cleft fast in the shingle sand. The night was cold. The fish scales glittered even though it was dark. They glittered in the whiteness made by the breaking waves breaking on the shore. The sound of the sea was sadder than the sight of the yellow-haired corpse, but still Tadg Mor was gladder to be down on the shore than up in the dune grass knocking at the one-night widow's door.

The knocking sound of Tadg Og's knuckles on the wooden door was a human sound and it sounded good in the ears of Tadg Mor for a time; but, like all sounds that continue too long, it sounded soon to be as inhuman as the washing of the waves tiding in on the shingle. Tadg Mor put up his rounded palms to his mouth and shouted out to Tadg Og to come back to the boat. Tadg Og came back running over the shore, and the air was grained with sounds of sliding shingle.

110 "There's no one in the house where you were knocking," said Tadg Mor.

"I knocked louder on the door than you knocked on the boat boards," said Tadg Og.

"I heard how you knocked," said Tadg Mor; "you knocked well. But let you knock better when you go to the neighbor's house to find out where the one-night widow is from her own house this night."

"If I got no answer at one door is it likely I'll get an answer at another door?" said Tadg Og. "It was you yourself I heard to say one time that the man that knows how a thing is to be done is the man should do that thing when that thing is to be done."

"How is a man to get knowledge of how to do a thing if that man doesn't do that thing when that thing is to be done?" said Tadg Mor.

115   Tadg Og got into the boat again and they sat there in the dark. After four or maybe five waves had broken by their side, Tadg Og lifted the net and felt the clothes of Eamon Buidhe.

"The clothes are drying into him," he said.

"If I was to go up with you to the house of Seana Bhride, who would there be to watch the dead?" said Tadg Mor, and then Tadg Og knew that Tadg Mor was going with him and he had no need to put great heed on the answer he gave to him.

"Let the sea watch him," he said, putting a leg out over the boat after the wave went back with its fistful of little complaining pebbles.

"We must take him out of the boat first," said Tadg Mor. "Take hold of him there by the feet," he said as he rolled back the net, putting it over the oar with each roll so it would not ravel and knot.

120   They lifted Eamon Buidhe out of the boat and the mackerel slipped about their feet into the place where he had left his shape. They dragged him up a boat length from the sprawling waves, and they faced his feet to the shore, but when they saw that that left his head lower than his feet, because the shingle shelved greatly at that point, they faced him about again toward the waves that were clashing their sharp, pointy scales together and sending up spits of white spray in the air. The dead man glittered with the silver and verdigris scales of the mackerel that were clinging to his clothing over every part.

Tadg Mor went up the sliding shingle in front of Tadg Og, and Tadg Og put his feet in the shelves that were made in the shingle by Tadg Mor because the length of the step they took was the same length. The sea sounded in their ears as they went through the shingle, but by the time the first coarse dune grass scratched at their clothing the only sound they could hear was the sound of the other's breathing.

The first cottage that rose out blacker than the night in their path was the cottage where Tadg Og made the empty knocking. Tadg Mor stopped in front of the door as if he might be thinking of trying his hand at knocking, but he thought better of it and went on after Tadg Og to the house that was next to that house, and that was the house of Seana Bhride, a woman that would know anything that eye or ear could know about those that lived within three islands of her. Tadg Mor hit the door of Seana Bhride's house with a knock of his knuckles, and although it was a less loud knock than the echo of the knock that came down to the shore when Tadg Og struck the first knock on the door of the wife of Eamon Buidhe, there was a foot to the floor before he could raise his knuckle off the wood for another knock.

A candle lit up and a shadow fell across the windowpane and a face came whitening at the door gap.

"You came to the wrong house this dark night," said Seana Bhride. "The sea took all the men was ever in this house twelve years ago and two months and seventeen days."

125 "It may be that we have no corpse for this house, but we came to the right house for all that," said Tadg Mor. "We came to this house for knowledge of the house across two sea-fields from this house, where we got no answer to our knocking with our knuckles."

"And I knocked with a stone up out of the ground, as well," said Tadg Og, coming closer.

The woman with the candle-flame blowing drew back into the dark.

"Is it for the inland woman, the one-year wife, you're bringing the corpse you have below in the boat this night?" she said.

"It is, God help us," said Tadg Mor.

130 "It is, God help us," said Tadg Og.

"The Brightest and the Bravest," said Tadg Mor.

"Is it a thing that you got no answer to your knocking?" said the old woman, bending out again with the blowing candle-flame.

"No answer," said Tadg Og, "and sturdy knocking."

"Knocking to be heard above the sound of the sea," said Tadg Mor.

135 "They sleep deep, the people from the inland?" said Tadg Og, asking a question.

"The people of the inland sleep deep in the cottage in the middle of the fields," said Seana Bhride, "but when they're rooted up and set down by the sea their spirit never passes out of hearing of the step on the shingle. It's a queer thing entirely that you got no answer to your knocking."

"We got no answer to our knocking," said Tadg Mor and Tadg Og, bringing their words together like two oars striking the one wave, one on this side of the boat and one on that.

"When the inland woman puts her face down on the feather pillow," said Seana Bhride, "that pillow is like the seashells children put against their ears, that pillow has in it the sad crying voices of the sea."

"Is it that you think she is from home this night?" said Tadg Mor.

140 "It must be a thing that she is," said the old woman.

"Is it back to her people in the inlands she'd be gone?" said Tadg Og, who had more than the curiosity of the one night in him.

"Step into the kitchen," said the old woman, "while I ask Bríd Og if she saw the wife of Eamon Buidhe go from her house this night."

While she went into the room that was back from the kitchen, Tadg Og put a foot inside the kitchen door, but Tadg Mor stayed looking down to the shore.

"If it is a thing the inland woman is from home this night, where will we put Eamon Buidhe, that we have below on the shore, with his face and no sheet on it, and his eyes and no lids drawn down tight over them, and the fish scales sticking to him faster than they stuck to the mackerels when they swam beyond the nets, blue and silver and green?"

145 "Listen to Bríd Og," said Tadg Og, and he stepped a bit farther into the kitchen of Seana Bhride.

"Bríd Og," the old woman asked, "is it a thing that the inland woman from two fields over went from her house this night?"

"It is a thing that she went," said Bríd Og.

Tadg Og spoke to Tadg Mor: "Bríd Og talks soft in the day, but she talks as soft as the sea in summer when she talks in the night in the dark."

"Listen to what she says," said Tadg Mor, coming in a step after Tadg Og.

150 "Is it that she went to her people in the inlands?" Seana Bhride asked.

"The wife of Eamon Buidhe never stirred a foot to her people in the inlands since the first day she came to the islands, in her blue dress with the beads," said the voice of Bríd Og.

"Where did she go then?" said the old woman. "If it is a thing that she didn't go to her people in the inlands?"

"Where else but where she said she'd go," said the voice of Bríd Og, "out in the boat with her one-year husband?"

There was sound of rusty springs creaking in the room where Bríd Og slept, back behind the kitchen, and her voice was clearer and stronger like as if she was sitting up in the bed looking out at the black sea and the white points rising in it, lit by the light of their own brightness.

155 "She said the sea would never drag Eamon Buidhe down to the green grave and leave her to lie lonely in the black grave on the shore, in the black clay that held tight, under the weighty sods. She said a man and woman should lie in the one grave. She said a night never passed without her heart being burnt out to a cold white salt. She said that this night, and every night after, she'd go out with Eamon in the black boat over the scabby back of the sea. She said if he got the green grave, she'd get the green grave too, and her arms would be stronger than the weeds of the sea, to bind them together forever. She said the island women never fought the sea. She said the sea needed taming and besting. She said there was a curse on the black clay for women that lay alone in it while their men washed to and fro in the caves of the sea. She said the black clay was all right for inland women. She said the black clay was all right for sisters and mothers. She said the black clay was all right for girls that died at seven years. But the green grave was the grave for wives, she said, and she went out in the black boat this night and she's going out every night after," said Bríd Og.

"Tell Bríd Og there will be no night after," said Tadg Mor.

"Let her sleep till day," said Tadg Og. "Time enough to tell her in the day," and he strained his eyes past the flutter-flame candle as the old woman came out from Bríd Og's room.

"You heard what she said?" said the old woman.

"It's a bad thing he was got," said Tadg Og.

160 "That's a thing was never said on this island before this night," said Tadg Mor.

"There was a fire on every point of the cliff shore to light home the men who were dragging for Mairtin Mor," the old woman said.

"And he never was got," said Tadg Mor.

"There was a shroud spun for Ruairi Dubh between the time of the putting-out of the island boats to look for him and their coming back with the empty news in the green daylight," said the old woman.

"Ruairi Dubh was never got."

165 "Mairtin Mor was never got."

"Lorcan Og was never got."

"Muiris Fada was never got."

"My four sons were never got," said the old woman.

"The father of Bríd Og was never got," said Tadg Og, and he was looking at the shut door of the room where Bríd Og was lying in the dark; the candle shadows were running their hands over that door.

170 "The father of Bríd Og was never got," said Tadg Og again, forgetting what he was saying.

"Of all the men that had yellow coffins standing up on their ends by the gable, and all the men that had brown shrouds hanging up on the wall with the iron nail eating out through the yarn, it had to be the one man that should have never been got that was got," said Tadg Og, opening the top half of the door and letting in the deeper sound of the tide.

"That is the way," said Tadg Mor.

"That is ever and always the way," said the old woman.

"The sea is stronger than any man," said Tadg Mor.

175 "The sea is stronger than any woman," said Tadg Og.

"The sea is stronger than women from the inland fields," said Tadg Mor, going to the door.

"The sea is stronger than talk of love," said Tadg Og, going out after him into the dark. It was so dark, he could not see where the window of Bríd Og's room was, but he was looking where it might be while he buttoned over his jacket.

Tadg Mor and Tadg Og went back to the shore, keeping their feet well on the shelving shingle, as they went toward the sprawling waves. The waves were up to the sea-break in the graywacke wall.

The boat was floating free. It was gone from the cleft in the shingle. And the body of Eamon Bui, that had glittered with fish scales of opal and silver and verdigris, was gone from the shore. It was gone from the black land that was scored crisscross with gravecuts by spade and shovel. It was gone and would never be got. The men spoke together.

180 "Mairtin Mor wasn't got."

"Muiris Fada wasn't got."

"Lorcan Og wasn't got."

"Ruairi Dubh wasn't got."

"The four sons of Seana Bhride were never got."

185 "The father of Bríd Og wasn't got."

The men of the island were caught down in the sea by the tight weeds of the sea. They were held in the tendrils of the sea anemone and by the pricks of the sallow thorn, by the green sea-grasses and the green sea-reeds and the winding stems of the green sea-daffodil. But Eamon Buidhe Murnane would be held fast in the white arms of his one-year wife, who came from the inlands where women have no knowledge of the sea but only a knowledge of love.

Questions on setting . . .

1. Does this story's title suggest the importance of setting to this story? If you were the writer, what phrase or bit of information (overheard on a visit to the west of Ireland, say) might have started you off inventing this story?
2. Do these characters react to death as you would react? Are their feelings implausible? Does setting affect plausibility of character and feeling?

. . . and other elements

3. Do you have trouble telling the two men apart at first? Could this difficulty be deliberate?

4. What is the conflict in this story? The climax? The dénouement?
5. Can you identify a narrative in this story? From whose point of view is the story told?
6. Do you find this story realistic? Do you start out feeling one way about its realism and end up feeling another way? Why?
7. Midway through the story, Tadg Mor and Tagd Og anticipate a conversation. Does this anticipated conversation figure in the plot? How?
8. Rewrite any strong passage of description—say, the last third of paragraph 108—in plain American. What have you lost?

Peter Taylor
A Spinster's Tale

Peter Taylor (1917–   ) was born in Tennessee and now teaches at the University of Virginia and lives in Charlottesville. He has written plays and novels but is principally a writer of short stories, which are gathered in *The Collected Stories of Peter Taylor* (1969) and in *In the Miro District* (1977).

My brother would often get drunk when I was a little girl, but that put a different sort of fear into me from what Mr. Speed did. With Brother it was a spiritual thing. And though it was frightening to know that he would have to burn for all that giggling and bouncing around on the stair at night, the truth was that he only seemed jollier to me when I would stick my head out of the hall door. It made him seem almost my age for him to act so silly, putting his white forefinger all over his flushed face and finally over his lips to say, "Sh-sh-sh-sh!" But the really frightening thing about seeing Brother drunk was what I always heard when I had slid back into bed. I could always recall my mother's words to him when he was sixteen, the year before she died, spoken in her greatest sincerity, in her most religious tone: "Son, I'd rather see you in your grave."

Yet those nights put a scaredness into me that was clearly distinguishable from the terror that Mr. Speed instilled by stumbling past our house two or three afternoons a week. The most that I knew about Mr. Speed was his name. And this I considered that I had somewhat fabricated—by allowing him the "Mr."—in my effort to humanize and soften the monster that was forever passing our house on Church Street. My father would point him out through the wide parlor window in soberness and severity to my brother with: "There goes Old Speed, again." Or on Saturday when Brother was with the Benton boys and my two uncles were over having toddies with Father in the parlor, Father would refer to Mr. Speed's passing with a similar speech, but in a blustering tone of merry tolerance: "There goes Old Speed, again. The rascal!" These designations were equally awful, both spoken in tones that were foreign to my father's manner of addressing me; and not unconsciously I prepared the euphemism, Mister Speed, against the inevitable day when I should have to speak of him to someone.

I was named Elizabeth, for my mother. My mother had died in the spring before Mr. Speed first came to my notice on that late afternoon in October. I had bathed at four with the aid of Lucy, who had been my nurse and who was now the upstairs maid; and Lucy was upstairs turning back the covers of the beds in the rooms with their color schemes of blue and green and rose. I wandered into the shadowy parlor and sat first on one chair, then on another. I tried lying down on the settee that went with the parlor set, but my legs had got too long this summer to stretch out straight on the settee. And my feet looked long in their pumps against the wicker arm. I looked at the pictures around the room blankly and at the stained-glass windows on either side of the fireplace; and the winter light coming through them was hardly bright enough to show the colors. I struck a match on the mosaic hearth and lit the gas logs.

Kneeling on the hearth I watched the flames till my face felt hot. I stood up then and turned directly to one of the full-length mirror panels that were on each side of the front window. This one was just to the right of the broad window and my reflection in it stood out strangely from the rest of the room in the dull light that did not penetrate beyond my figure. I leaned closer to the mirror trying to discover a resemblance between myself and the wondrous Alice who walked through a looking glass. But that resemblance I was seeking I could not find in my sharp features, or in my heavy, dark curls hanging like fragments of hosepipe to my shoulders.

5   I propped my hands on the borders of the narrow mirror and put my face close to watch my lips say, "Away." I would hardly open them for the "a"; and then I would contort my face by the great opening I made for the "way." I whispered, "Away, away." I whispered it over and over, faster and faster, watching myself in the mirror: "A-way—a-way—away-away-awayaway." Suddenly I burst into tears and turned from the gloomy mirror to the daylight at the wide parlor window. Gazing tearfully through the expanse of plate glass there, I beheld Mr. Speed walking like a cripple with one foot on the curb and one in the street. And faintly I could hear him cursing the trees as he passed them, giving each a lick with his heavy walking cane.

Presently I was dry-eyed in my fright. My breath came short, and I clasped the black bow at the neck of my middy blouse.

When he had passed from view, I stumbled back from the window. I hadn't heard the houseboy enter the parlor, and he must not have noticed me there, I made no move of recognition as he drew the draperies across the wide front window for the night. I stood cold and silent before the gas logs with a sudden inexplicable memory of my mother's cheek and a vision of her in her bedroom on a spring day.

That April day when spring had seemed to crowd itself through the windows into the bright upstairs rooms, the old-fashioned mahogany sick-chair had been brought down from the attic to my mother's room. Three days before, a quiet service had been held there for the stillborn baby, and I had accompanied my father and brother to our lot in the gray cemetery to see the box (large for so tiny a parcel) lowered and covered with mud. But in the parlor now by the gas logs I remembered the day that my mother had sent for the sick-chair and for me.

The practical nurse, sitting in a straight chair busy at her needlework, looked over her glasses to give me some little instruction in the arrangement of my mother's pillows in the chair. A few minutes before, this practical nurse had lifted my sick mother bodily from the bed, and I had the privilege of rolling my mother to the big bay window that looked out ideally over the new foliage of small trees in our side yard.

10   I stood self-consciously straight, close by my mother, a maturing little girl awkward in my curls and long-waisted dress. My pale mother, in her silk bed jacket, with a smile leaned her cheek against the cheek of her daughter. Outside it was

spring. The furnishings of the great blue room seemed to partake for that one moment of nature's life. And my mother's cheek was warm on mine. This I remembered when I sat before the gas logs trying to put Mr. Speed out of my mind; but that a few moments later my mother beckoned to the practical nurse and sent me suddenly from the room, my memory did not dwell upon. I remembered only the warmth of the cheek and the comfort of that other moment.

I sat near the blue burning logs and waited for my father and my brother to come in. When they came saying the same things about office and school that they said every day, turning on lights beside chairs that they liked to flop into, I realized not that I was ready or unready for them but that there had been, within me, an attempt at a preparation for such readiness.

They sat so customarily in their chairs at first and the talk ran so easily that I thought that Mr. Speed could be forgotten as quickly and painlessly as a doubting of Jesus or a fear of death from the measles. But the conversation took insinuating and malicious twists this afternoon. My father talked about the possibilities of a general war and recalled opinions that people had had just before the Spanish-American. He talked about the hundreds of men in the Union Depot. Thinking of all those men there, that close together, was something like meeting Mr. Speed in the front hall. I asked my father not to talk about war, which seemed to him a natural enough request for a young lady to make.

"How is your school, my dear?" he asked me. "How are Miss Hood and Miss Herron? Have they found who's stealing the boarders' things, my dear?"

All of those little girls safely in Belmont School being called for by gentle ladies or warm-breasted Negro women were a pitiable sight beside the beastly vision of Mr. Speed which even they somehow conjured.

15   At dinner, with Lucy serving and sometimes helping my plate (because she had done so for so many years), Brother teased me first one way and then another. My father joined in on each point until I began to take the teasing very seriously, and then he told Brother that he was forever carrying things too far.

Once at dinner I was convinced that my preposterous fears that Brother knew what had happened to me by the window in the afternoon were not at all preposterous. He had been talking quietly. It was something about the meeting that he and the Benton boys were going to attend after dinner. But quickly, without reason, he turned his eyes on me across the table and fairly shouted in his new deep voice: "I saw three horses running away out on Harding Road today! They were just like the mules we saw at the mines in the mountains! They were running to beat hell and with little girls riding them!"

The first week after I had the glimpse of Mr. Speed through the parlor window, I spent the afternoon dusting the bureau and mantel and bedside table in my room, arranging on the chaise longue the dolls which at this age I never played with and rarely even talked to; or I would absent-mindedly assist Lucy in turning down the beds and maybe watch the houseboy set the dinner table. I went to the parlor only when Father came or when Brother came earlier and called me in to show me a shin bruise or a box of cigarettes which a girl had given him.

Finally, I put my hand on the parlor doorknob just at four one afternoon and entered the parlor, walking stiffly as I might have done with my hands in a muff going into church. The big room with its heavy furniture and pictures showed no change since the last afternoon that I had spent there, unless possibly there were fresh antimacassars on the chairs. I confidently pushed an odd chair over to the window and took my seat and sat erect and waited.

My heart would beat hard when, from the corner of my eye, I caught sight of some figure moving up Church Street. And as it drew nearer, showing the form of some Negro or neighbor or drummer, I would sigh from relief and from regret. I was ready for Mr. Speed. And I knew that he would come again and again, that he had been passing our house for inconceivable numbers of years. I knew that if he did not appear today, he would pass tomorrow. Not because I had had accidental, unavoidable glimpses of him from upstairs windows during the past week, nor because there were indistinct memories of such a figure, hardly noticed, seen on afternoons that preceded that day when I had seen him stumbling like a cripple along the curb and beating and cursing the trees did I know that Mr. Speed was a permanent and formidable figure in my life which I would be called upon to deal with; my knowledge, I was certain, was purely intuitive.

20   I was ready now not to face him with his drunken rage directed at me, but to look at him far off in the street and to appraise him. He didn't come that afternoon, but he came the next. I sat prim and straight before the window. I turned my head neither to the right to anticipate the sight of him nor to the left to follow his figure when it had passed. But when he was passing before my window, I put my eyes full on him and looked though my teeth chattered in my head. And now I saw his face heavy, red, fierce like his body. He walked with an awkward, stomping sort of stagger, carrying his gray topcoat over one arm; and with his other hand he kept poking his walnut cane into the soft sod along the sidewalk. When he was gone, I recalled my mother's cheek again, but the recollection this time, though more deliberate, was dwelt less upon; and I could only think of watching Mr. Speed again and again.

There was snow on the ground the third time that I watched Mr. Speed pass our house. Mr. Speed spat on the snow, and with his cane he aimed at the brown spot that his tobacco made there. And I could see that he missed his aim. The fourth time that I sat watching for him from the window, snow was actually falling outside; and I felt a sort of anxiety to know what would ever drive him into my own house. For a moment I doubted that he would really come to my door; but I prodded myself with the thought of his coming and finding me unprepared. And I continued to keep my secret watch for him two or three times a week during the rest of the winter.

Meanwhile my life with my father and brother and the servants in the shadowy house went on from day to day. On week nights the evening meal usually ended with petulant arguing between the two men, the atlas or the encyclopedia usually drawing them from the table to read out the statistics. Often Brother was accused of having looked-them-up-previously and of maneuvering the conversation toward the particular subject, for topics were very easily introduced and dismissed by the two. Once I, sent to the library to fetch a cigar, returned to find the discourse shifted in two minutes' time from the Kentucky Derby winners to the languages in which the Bible was first written. Once I actually heard the conversation slip, in the course of a small dessert, from the comparative advantages of urban and agrarian life for boys between the ages of fifteen and twenty to the probable origin and age of the Icelandic parliament and then to the doctrines of the Campbellite Church.

That night I followed them to the library and beheld them fingering the pages of the flimsy old atlas in the light from the beaded lampshade. They paid no attention to me and little to one another, each trying to turn the pages of the book and mumbling references to newspaper articles and to statements of persons of responsibility. I slipped from the library to the front parlor across the hall where I could hear the contentious hum. And I lit the gas logs, trying to warm my long legs before them as I examined my own response to the unguided and remorseless bickering of the masculine voices.

It was, I thought, their indifferent shifting from topic to topic that most disturbed me. Then I decided that it was the tremendous gaps that there seemed to be between the subjects that was bewildering to me. Still again, I thought that it was the equal interest which they displayed for each subject that was dismaying. All things in the world were equally at home in their arguments. They exhibited equal indifference to the horrors that each topic might suggest; and I wondered whether or not their imperturbability was a thing that they had achieved.

I knew that I had got myself so accustomed to the sight of Mr. Speed's peregrinations, persistent yet, withal, seemingly without destination, that I could view his passing with perfect equanimity. And from this I knew that I must extend my preparation for the day when I should have to view him at closer range. When the day would come, I knew that it must involve my father and my brother and that his existence therefore must not remain an unmentionable thing, the secrecy of which to explode at the moment of crisis, only adding to its confusion.

Now, the door to my room was the first at the top of the long red-carpeted stairway. A wall light beside it was left burning on nights when Brother was out, and, when he came in, he turned it off. The light shining through my transom was a comforting sight when I had gone to bed in the big room; and in the summertime I could see the reflection of light bugs on it, and often one would plop against it. Sometimes I would wake up in the night with a start and would be frightened in the dark, not knowing what had awakened me until I realized that Brother had just turned out the light. On other nights, however, I would hear him close the front door and hear him bouncing up the steps. When I then stuck my head out the door, usually he would toss me a piece of candy and he always signaled to me to be quiet.

I had never intentionally stayed awake till he came in until one night toward the end of February of that year, and I hadn't been certain then that I should be able to do it. Indeed, when finally the front door closed, I had dozed several times sitting up in the dark bed. But I was standing with my door half open before he had come a third of the way up the stair. When he saw me, he stopped still on the stairway resting his hand on the banister. I realized that purposefulness must be showing on my face, and so I smiled at him and beckoned. His red face broke into a fine grin, and he took the next few steps two at a time. But he stumbled on the carpeted steps. He was on his knees, yet with his hand still on the banister. He was motionless there for a moment with his head cocked to one side, listening. The house was quiet and still. He smiled again, sheepishly this time, and kept putting his white forefinger to his red face as he ascended on tiptoe the last third of the flight of steps.

At the head of the stair he paused, breathing hard. He reached his hand into his coat pocket and smiled confidently as he shook his head at me. I stepped backward into my room.

"Oh," he whispered. "Your candy."

I stood straight in my white nightgown with my black hair hanging over my shoulders, knowing that he could see me only indistinctly. I beckoned to him again. He looked suspiciously about the hall, then stepped into the room and closed the door behind him.

"What's the matter, Betsy?" he said.

I turned and ran and climbed between the covers of my bed.

"What's the matter, Betsy?" he said. He crossed to my bed and sat down beside me on it.

I told him that I didn't know what was the matter.

35   "Have you been reading something you shouldn't, Betsy?" he asked.

I was silent.

"Are you lonely, Betsy?" he said. "Are you a lonely little girl?"

I sat up on the bed and threw my arms about his neck. And as I sobbed on his shoulder I smelled for the first time the fierce odor of his cheap whiskey.

"Yes, I'm always lonely," I said with directness, and I was then silent with my eyes open and my cheek on the shoulder of his overcoat which was yet cold from the February night air.

40   He kept his face turned away from me and finally spoke, out of the other corner of his mouth, I thought, "I'll come home earlier some afternoons and we'll talk and play."

"Tomorrow."

When I had said this distinctly, I fell away from him back on the bed. He stood up and looked at me curiously, as though in some way repelled by my settling so comfortably in the covers. And I could see his eighteen-year-old head cocked to one side as though trying to see my face in the dark. He leaned over me, and I smelled his whiskey breath. It was not repugnant to me. It was blended with the odor that he always had. I thought that he was going to strike me. He didn't, however, and in a moment was opening the door to the lighted hall. Before he went out, again I said: "Tomorrow."

The hall light dark and the sound of Brother's footsteps gone, I naturally repeated the whole scene in my mind and upon examination found strange elements present. One was something like a longing for my brother to strike me when he was leaning over me. Another was his bewilderment at my procedure. On the whole I was amazed at the way I had carried the thing off. It was the first incident that I had ever actively carried off. Now I only wished that in the darkness when he was leaning over me I had said languidly, "Oh, Brother," had said it in a tone indicating that we had in common some unmentionable trouble. Then I should have been certain of his presence next day. As it was, though, I had little doubt of his coming home early.

I would not let myself reflect further on my feelings for my brother—my desire for him to strike me and my delight in his natural odor. I had got myself in the habit of postponing such elucidations until after I had completely settled with Mr. Speed. But, as after all such meetings with my brother, I reflected upon the posthumous punishments in store for him for his carousing and drinking, and remembered my mother's saying that she had rather see him in his grave.

45   The next afternoon at four I had the chessboard on the tea table before the front parlor window. I waited for my brother, knowing pretty well that he would come and feeling certain that Mr. Speed would pass. (For this was a Thursday afternoon; and during the winter months I had found that there were two days of the week

on which Mr. Speed never failed to pass our house. These were Thursday and Saturday.) I led my brother into that dismal parlor chattering about the places where I had found the chessmen long in disuse. When I paused a minute, slipping into my seat by the chessboard, he picked up with talk of the senior class play and his chances for being chosen valedictorian. Apparently I no longer seemed an enigma to him. I thought that he must have concluded that I was just a lonely little girl named Betsy. But I doubted that his nature was so different from my own that he could sustain objective sympathy for another child, particularly a younger sister, from one day to another. And since I saw no favors that he could ask from me at this time, my conclusion was that he believed that he had never exhibited his drunkenness to me with all his bouncing about on the stair at night; but that he was not certain that talking from the other corner of his mouth had been precaution enough against his whiskey breath.

We faced each other over the chessboard and set the men in order. There were only a few days before it would be March, and the light through the window was first bright and then dull. During my brother's moves, I stared out the window at the clouds that passed before the sun and watched pieces of newspaper that blew about the yard. I was calm beyond my own credulity. I found myself responding to my brother's little jokes and showing real interest in the game. I tried to terrorize myself by imagining Mr. Speed's coming up to the very window this day. I even had him shaking his cane and his derby hat at us. But the frenzy which I expected at this step of my preparation did not come. And some part of Mr. Speed's formidability seemed to have vanished. I realized that by not hiding my face in my mother's bosom and by looking at him so regularly for so many months, I had come to accept his existence as a natural part of my life on Church Street, though something to be guarded against, or, as I had put it before, to be thoroughly prepared for when it came to my door.

The problem then, in relation to my brother, had suddenly resolved itself in something much simpler than the conquest of my fear of looking upon Mr. Speed alone had been. This would be only a matter of how I should act and of what words I should use. And from the incident of the night before, I had some notion that I'd find a suitable way of procedure in our household.

Mr. Speed appeared in the street without his overcoat but with one hand holding the turned-up lapels and collar of his gray suit coat. He followed his cane, stomping like an enraged blind man with his head bowed against the March wind. I squeezed from between my chair and the table and stood right at the great plate glass window, looking out. From the corner of my eye I saw that Brother was intent upon his play. Presently, in the wind, Mr. Speed's derby went back on his head, and his hand grabbed at it, pulled it back in place, then returned to hold his lapels. I took a sharp breath, and Brother looked up. And just as he looked out the window, Mr. Speed's derby did blow off and across the sidewalk, over the lawn. Mr. Speed turned, holding his lapels with his tremendous hand, shouting oaths that I could hear ever so faintly, and tried to stumble after his hat.

Then I realized that my brother was gone from the room; and he was outside the window with Mr. Speed chasing Mr. Speed's hat in the wind.

50   I sat back in my chair, breathless; one elbow went down on the chessboard disordering the black and white pawns and kings and castles. And through the window I watched Brother handing Mr. Speed his derby. I saw his apparent indifference to the drunk man's oaths and curses. I saw him coming back to the

house while the old man yet stood railing at him. I pushed the table aside and ran to the front door lest Brother be locked outside. He met me in the hall smiling blandly.

I said, "That's Mr. Speed."

He sat down on the bottom step of the stairway, leaning backward and looking at me inquisitively.

"He's drunk, Brother," I said. "Always."

My brother looked frankly into the eyes of this half-grown sister of his but said nothing for a while.

55   I pushed myself up on the console table and sat swinging my legs and looking seriously about the walls of the cavernous hallway at the expanse of oak paneling, at the inset canvas of the sixteenth-century Frenchman making love to his lady, at the hat rack, and at the grandfather's clock in the darkest corner. I waited for Brother to speak.

"You don't like people who get drunk?" he said.

I saw that he was taking the whole thing as a thrust at his own behavior.

"I just think Mr. Speed is very ugly, Brother."

From the detached expression of his eyes I knew that he was not convinced.

60   "I wouldn't mind him less if he were sober," I said. "Mr Speed's like—a loose horse."

This analogy convinced him. He knew then what I meant.

"You mustn't waste your time being afraid of such things," he said in great earnestness. "In two or three years there'll be things that you'll have to be afraid of. Things you really can't avoid."

"What did he say to you?" I asked.

"He cussed and threatened to hit me with that stick."

65   "For no reason?"

"Old Mr. Speed's burned out his reason with whiskey."

"Tell me about him." I was almost imploring him.

"Everybody knows about him. He just wanders around town, drunk. Sometimes downtown they take him off in the Black Maria."

I pictured him on the main streets that I knew downtown and in the big department stores. I could see him in that formal neighborhood where my grandmother used to live. In the neighborhood of Miss Hood and Miss Herron's school. Around the little houses out where my father's secretary lived. Even in nigger town.

70   "You'll get used to him, for all his ugliness," Brother said. Then we sat there till my father came in, talking almost gaily about things that were particularly ugly in Mr. Speed's clothes and face and in his way of walking.

Since the day that I watched myself say "away" in the mirror, I had spent painful hours trying to know once more that experience which I now regarded as something like mystical. But the stringent course that I, motherless and lonely in our big house, had brought myself to follow while only thirteen had given me certain mature habits of thought. Idle and unrestrained daydreaming I eliminated almost entirely from my experience, though I delighted myself with fantasies that I quite consciously worked out and which, when concluded, I usually considered carefully, trying to fix them with some sort of childish symbolism.

Even idleness in my nightly dreams disturbed me. And sometimes as I tossed half awake in my big bed I would try to piece together my dreams into at least a form of logic. Sometimes I would complete an unfinished dream and wouldn't know in the morning what part I had dreamed and what part pieced out. I would often smile over the ends that I had plotted in half-wakeful moments but found pride in dreams that were complete in themselves and easy to fix with allegory, which I called "meaning." I found that a dream could start for no discoverable reason, with the sight of a printed page on which the first line was, "Once upon a time"; and soon could have me a character in a strange story. Once upon a time there was a little girl whose hands began to get very large. Grown men came for miles around to look at the giant hands and to shake them, but the little girl was ashamed of them and hid them under her skirt. It seemed that the little girl lived in the stable behind my grandmother's old house, and I watched her from the top of the loft ladder. Whenever there was the sound of footsteps, she trembled and wept; so I would beat on the floor above her and laugh uproariously at her fear. But presently I was the little girl listening to the noise. At first I trembled and called out for my father, but then I recollected that it was I who had made the noises and I felt that I had made a very considerable discovery for myself.

I awoke one Saturday morning in early March at the sound of my father's voice in the downstairs hall. He was talking to the servants, ordering the carriage I think. I believe that I awoke at the sound of the carriage horses' names. I went to my door and called "Goodbye" to him. He was twisting his mustache before the hall mirror, and he looked up the stairway at me and smiled. He was always abashed to be caught before a looking glass, and he called out self-consciously and affectionately that he would be home at noon.

I closed my door and went to the little dressing table that he had had put in my room on my birthday. The card with his handwriting on it was still stuck in the corner of the mirror: "For my young lady daughter." I was so thoroughly aware of the gentleness in his nature this morning that any childish timidity before him would, I thought, seem an injustice, and I determined that I should sit with him and my uncles in the parlor that afternoon and perhaps tell them all of my fear of the habitually drunken Mr. Speed and with them watch him pass before the parlor window. That morning I sat before the mirror of my dressing table and put up my hair in a knot on the back of my head for the first time.

75   Before Father came home at noon, however, I had taken my hair down, and I was not now certain that he would be unoffended by my mention of the neighborhood drunkard. But I was resolute in my purpose, and when my two uncles came after lunch, and the three men shut themselves up in the parlor for the afternoon, I took my seat across the hall in the little library, or den, as my mother had called it, and spent the first of the afternoon skimming over the familiar pages of *Tales of Ol' Virginny,* by Thomas Nelson Page.

My father had seemed tired at lunch. He talked very little and drank only half his cup of coffee. He asked Brother matter-of-fact questions about his plans for college in the fall and told me once to try cutting my meat instead of pulling it to pieces. And as I sat in the library afterward, I wondered if he had been thinking of my mother. Indeed, I wondered whether or not he ever thought of her. He never mentioned her to us; and in a year I had forgotten exactly how he treated her when she had been alive.

It was not only the fate of my brother's soul that I had given thought to since my mother's death. Father had always had his toddy on Saturday afternoon with his two bachelor brothers. But there was more than one round of toddies served in the parlor on Saturday now. Throughout the early part of this afternoon I could hear the tinkle of the bell in the kitchen, and presently the houseboy would appear at the door of the parlor with a tray of ice-filled glasses.

As he entered the parlor each time, I would catch a glimpse over my book of the three men. One was usually standing, whichever one was leading the conver- sation. Once they were laughing heartily; and as the Negro boy came out with the tray of empty glasses, there was a smile on his face.

As their voices grew louder and merrier, my courage slackened. It was then I first put into words the thought that in my brother and father I saw something of Mr. Speed. And I knew that it was more than a taste for whiskey they had in common.

80   At four o'clock I heard Brother's voice mixed with those of the Benton boys outside the front door. They came into the hall, and their voices were high and excited. First one, then another would demand to be heard with: "No, listen now; let me tell you what." In a moment I heard Brother on the stairs. Then two of the Benton brothers appeared in the doorway of the library. Even the youngest, who was not a year older than I and whose name was Henry, wore long pants, and each carried a cap in hand and a linen duster over his arm. I stood up and smiled at them, and with my right forefinger I pushed the black locks which hung loosely about my shoulders behind my ears.

"We're going motoring in the Carltons' machine," Henry said.

I stammered my surprise and asked if Brother were going to ride in it. One of them said that he was upstairs getting his hunting cap, since he had no motoring cap. The older brother, Gary Benton, went back into the hall. I walked toward Henry, who was standing in the doorway.

"But does Father know you're going?" I asked.

As I tried to go through the doorway, Henry stretched his arm across it and looked at me with a critical frown on his face.

85   "Why don't you put up your hair?" he said.

I looked at him seriously, and I felt the heat of the blush that came over my face. I felt it on the back of my neck. I stooped with what I thought considerable grace and slid under his arm and passed into the hall. There were the other two Benton boys listening to the voices of my uncles and my father through the parlor door. I stepped between them and threw open the door. Just as I did so, Henry Benton commanded, "Elizabeth, don't do that!" And I, swinging the door open, turned and smiled at him.

I stood for a moment looking blandly at my father and my uncles. I was con- sidering what had made me burst in upon them in this manner. It was not merely that I had perceived the opportunity of creating this little disturbance and slipping in under its noise, though I was not unaware of the advantage. I was frightened by the boys' impending adventure in the horseless carriage but surely not so much as I normally should have been at breaking into the parlor at this forbidden hour. The immediate cause could only be the attention which Henry Benton had shown me. His insinuation had been that I remained too much a little girl, and I had shown him that at any rate I was a bold, or at least a naughty, little girl.

My father was on his feet. He put his glass on the mantelpiece. And it seemed to me that from the three men came in rapid succession all possible arrangements of the words, Boys-come-in. Come-in-boys. Well-boys-come-in. Come-on-in. Boys-come-in-the-parlor. The boys went in, rather showing off their breeding and poise, I thought. The three men moved and talked clumsily before them, as the three Benton brothers went each to each of the men carefully distinguishing between my uncles' titles: doctor and colonel. I thought how awkward all of the members of my own family appeared on occasions that called for grace. Brother strode into the room with his hunting cap sideways on his head, and he announced their plans, which the tactful Bentons, uncertain of our family's prejudices regarding machines, had not mentioned. Father and my uncles had a great deal to say about who was going-to-do-the-driving, and Henry Benton without giving an answer gave a polite invitation to the men to join them. To my chagrin, both my uncles accepted with-the-greatest-of-pleasure what really had not been an invitation at all. And they persisted in accepting it even after Brother in his rudeness raised the question of room in the five-passenger vehicle.

Father said, "Sure. The more, the merrier." But he declined to go himself and declined for me Henry's invitation.

90 The plan was, then, as finally outlined by the oldest of the Benton brothers, that the boys should proceed to the Carltons' and that Brother should return with the driver to take our uncles out to the Carltons' house which was one of the new residences across from Centennial Park, where the excursions in the machine were to be made.

The four slender youths took their leave from the heavy men with the gold watch chains across their stomachs, and I had to shake hands with each of the Benton brothers. To each I expressed my regret that Father would not let me ride with them, emulating their poise with all my art. Henry Benton was the last, and he smiled as though he knew what I was up to. In answer to his smile I said, "Games are *so* much fun."

I stood by the window watching the four boys in the street until they were out of sight. My father and his brothers had taken their seats in silence, and I was aware of just how unwelcome I was in the room. Finally, my uncle, who had been a colonel in the Spanish War and who wore bushy blond sideburns, whistled under his breath and said, "Well, there's no doubt about it, no doubt about it."

He winked at my father, and my father looked at me and then at my uncle. Then quickly in a ridiculously overserious tone he asked, "What, sir? No doubt about what, sir?"

"Why, there's no doubt that this daughter of yours was flirting with the youngest of the Messrs. Benton."

95 My father looked at me and twisted his mustache and said with the same pomp that he didn't know what he'd do with me if I started that sort of thing. My two uncles threw back their heads, each giving a short laugh. My uncle the doctor took off his pince-nez and shook them at me and spoke in the same mock-serious tone of his brothers: "Young lady, if you spend your time in such pursuits you'll only bring upon yourself and upon the young men about Nashville the greatest unhappiness. I, as a bachelor, must plead the cause of the young Bentons!"

I turned to my father in indignation that approached rage.

"Father," I shouted, "there's Mr. Speed out there!"

Father sprang from his chair and quickly stepped up beside me at the window. Then, seeing the old man staggering harmlessly along the sidewalk, he said in, I thought, affected easiness: "Yes. Yes, dear."

"He's drunk," I said. My lips quivered, and I think I must have blushed at this first mention of the unmentionable to my father.

100 "Poor Old Speed," he said. I looked at my uncles, and they were shaking their heads, echoing my father's tone.

"What ever did happen to Speed's old-maid sister?" my uncle the doctor said.

"She's still with him," Father said.

Mr. Speed appeared soberer today than I had ever seen him. He carried no overcoat to drag on the ground, and his stagger was barely noticeable. The movement of his lips and an occasional gesture were the only evidence of intoxication. I was enraged by the irony that his good behavior on this of all days presented. Had I been a little younger I might have suspected conspiracy on the part of all men against me, but I was old enough to suspect no person's being even interested enough in me to plot against my understanding, unless it be some vague personification of life itself.

The course which I took, I thought afterward, was the proper one. I do not think that it was because I was then really conscious that when one is determined to follow some course rigidly and is blockaded one must fire furiously, if blindly, into the blockade, but rather because I was frightened and in my fear forgot all logic of attack. At any rate, I fired furiously at the three immutable creatures.

105   "I'm afraid of him," I broke out tearfully. I shouted at them, "He's always drunk! He's always going by our house drunk!"

My father put his arms about me, but I continued talking as I wept on his shirt front. I heard the barking sound of the machine horn out in front, and I felt my father move one hand from my back to motion my uncles to go. And as they shut the parlor door after them, I felt that I had let them escape me.

I heard the sound of the motor fading out up Church Street, and Father led me to the settee. We sat there together for a long while, and neither of us spoke until my tears had dried.

I was eager to tell him just exactly how fearful I was of Mr. Speed's coming into our house. But he only allowed me to tell him that I *was* afraid; for when I had barely suggested that much, he said that I had no business watching Mr. Speed, that I must shut my eyes to some things. "After all," he said, nonsensically I thought, "you're a young lady now." And in several curiously twisted sentences he told me that I mustn't seek things to fear in this world. He said that it was most unlikely, besides, that Speed would ever have business at our house. He punched at his left side several times, gave a prolonged belch, settled a pillow behind his head, and soon was sprawled beside me on the settee, snoring.

But Mr. Speed did come to our house, and it was in less than two months after this dreary twilight. And he came as I had feared he might come, in his most extreme state of drunkenness and at a time when I was alone in the house with the maid Lucy. But I had done everything that a little girl, now fourteen, could do in preparation for such an eventuality. And the sort of preparation that I had been able to make, the clearance of all restraints and inhibitions regarding Mr. Speed in my own mind and in my relationship with my world, had necessarily, I think, given me a maturer view of my own limited experiences; though, too, my very age must be held to account for a natural step toward maturity.

110   In the two months following the day that I first faced Mr. Speed's existence with my father, I came to look at every phase of our household life with a more direct and more discerning eye. As I wandered about that shadowy and somehow brutally elegant house, sometimes now with a knot of hair on the back of my head, events and customs there that had repelled or frightened me I gave the closest scrutiny. In the daytime I ventured into such forbidden spots as the servants' and the men's bathrooms. The filth of the former became a matter of interest in the study of the

servants' natures, instead of the object of ineffable disgust. The other became a fascinating place of wet shaving brushes and leather straps and red rubber bags.

There was an anonymous little Negro boy that I had seen many mornings hurrying away from our back door with a pail. I discovered that he was toting buttermilk from our icebox with the permission of our cook. And I sprang at him from behind a corner of the house one morning and scared him so that he spilled the buttermilk and never returned for more.

Another morning I heard the cook threatening to slash the houseboy with her butcher knife, and I made myself burst in upon them; and before Lucy and the houseboy I told her that if she didn't leave our house that day, I'd call my father and, hardly knowing what I was saying, I added, "And the police." She was gone, and Lucy had got a new cook before dinnertime. In this way, from day to day, I began to take my place as mistress in our motherless household.

I could no longer be frightened by my brother with a mention of runaway horses. And instead of terrorized I felt only depressed by his long and curious arguments with my father. I was depressed by the number of the subjects to and from which they oscillated. The world as a whole still seemed unconscionably larger than anything I could comprehend. But I had learned not to concern myself with so general and so unreal a problem until I had cleared up more particular and real ones.

It was during these two months that I noticed the difference between the manner in which my father spoke before my uncles of Mr. Speed when he passed and that in which he spoke of him before my brother. To my brother it was the condemning, "There goes Old Speed, again." But to my uncles it was, "There goes Old Speed," with the sympathetic addition, "the rascal." Though my father and his brothers obviously found me more agreeable because a pleasant spirit had replaced my old timidity, they yet considered me a child; and my father little dreamed that I discerned such traits in his character, or that I understood, if I even listened to, their anecdotes and their long funny stories, and it was an interest in the peculiar choice of subject and in the way that the men told their stories.

115   When Mr. Speed came, I was accustomed to thinking that there was something in my brother's and in my father's natures that was fully in sympathy with the very brutality of his drunkenness. And I knew that they would not consider my hatred for him and for that part of him which I saw in them. For that alone I was glad that it was on a Thursday afternoon, when I was in the house alone with Lucy, that one of the heavy sort of rains that come toward the end of May drove Mr. Speed onto our porch for shelter.

Otherwise I wished for nothing more than the sound of my father's strong voice when I stood trembling before the parlor window and watched Mr. Speed stumbling across our lawn in the flaying rain. I only knew to keep at the window and make sure that he was actually coming into our house. I believe that he was drunker than I had ever before seen him, and his usual ire seemed to be doubled by the raging weather.

Despite the aid of his cane, Mr. Speed fell to his knees once in the muddy sod. He remained kneeling there for a time with his face cast in resignation. Then once more he struggled to his feet in the rain. Though I was ever conscious that I was entering into young womanhood at that age, I can only think of myself as a child at that moment; for it was the helpless fear of a child that I felt as I watched Mr. Speed approaching our door. Perhaps it was the last time I ever experienced the inconsolable desperation of childhood.

Next, I could hear his cane beating on the boarding of the little porch before our door. I knew that he must be walking up and down in that little shelter. Then I heard Lucy's exasperated voice as she came down the steps. I knew immediately, what she confirmed afterward, that she thought it Brother, eager to get into the house, beating on the door.

I, aghast, opened the parlor door just as she pulled open the great front door. Her black skin ashened as she beheld Mr. Speed—his face crimson, his eyes bleary, and his gray clothes dripping water. He shuffled through the doorway and threw his stick on the hall floor. Between his oaths and profanities he shouted over and over in his broken, old man's voice, "Nigger, nigger." I could understand little of his rapid and slurred speech, but I knew his rage went round and round a man in the rain and the shelter of a neighbor's house.

120   Lucy fled up the long flight of steps and was on her knees at the head of the stair, in the dark upstairs hall, begging me to come up to her. I only stared, as though paralyzed and dumb, at him and then up the steps at her. The front door was still open; the hall was half in light; and I could hear the rain on the roof of the porch and the wind blowing the trees which were in full green foliage.

At last I moved. I acted. I slid along the wall past the hat rack and the console table, my eyes on the drunken old man who was swearing up the steps at Lucy. I reached for the telephone; and when I had rung for central, I called for the police station. I knew what they did with Mr. Speed downtown, and I knew with what I had threatened the cook. There was a part of me that was crouching on the top step with Lucy, vaguely longing to hide my face from this in my own mother's bosom. But there was another part which was making me deal with Mr. Speed, however wrongly, myself. Innocently I asked the voice to send "the Black Maria" to our house number on Church Street.

Mr. Speed had heard me make the call. He was still and silent for just one moment. Then he broke into tears, and he seemed to be chanting his words. He repeated the word "child" so many times that I felt I had acted wrongly, with courage but without wisdom. I saw myself as a little beast adding to the injury that what was bestial in man had already done him. He picked up his cane and didn't seem to be talking either to Lucy or to me, but to the cane. He started out the doorway, and I heard Lucy come running down the stairs. She fairly glided around the newel post and past me to the telephone. She wasn't certain that I had made the call. She asked if I had called my father. I simply told her that I had not.

As she rang the telephone, I watched Mr. Speed cross the porch. He turned to us at the edge of the porch and shouted one more oath. But his foot touched the wet porch step, and he slid and fell unconscious on the steps.

He lay there with the rain beating upon him and with Lucy and myself watching him, motionless from our place by the telephone. I was frightened by the thought of the cruelty which I found I was capable of, a cruelty which seemed inextricably mixed with what I had called courage. I looked at him lying out there in the rain and despised and pitied him at the same time, and I was afraid to go minister to the helpless old Mr. Speed.

125   Lucy had her arms about me and kept them there until two gray horses pulling their black coach had galloped up in front of the house and two policemen had carried the limp body through the rain to the dreadful vehicle.

Just as the policemen closed the doors in the back of the coach, my father rode up in a closed cab. He jumped out and stood in the rain for several minutes arguing with the policemen. Lucy and I went to the door and waited for him to come in.

When he came, he looked at neither of us. He walked past us saying only, "I regret that the bluecoats were called." And he went into the parlor and closed the door.

I never discussed the events of that day with my father, and I never saw Mr. Speed again. But, despite the surge of pity I felt for the old man on our porch that afternoon, my hatred and fear of what he had stood for in my eyes has never left me. And since the day that I watched myself say "away" in the mirror, not a week has passed but that he has been brought to my mind by one thing or another. It was only the other night that I dreamed I was a little girl on Church Street again and that there was a drunk horse in our yard.

Questions on setting . . .

1. How does the author, using a first-person narrator who takes her own place for granted, let us know about setting? Reading the first dozen paragraphs, list all the words that tell you about place and era.
2. As if you were making a play from this story, describe rooms so that a designer might draw a stage setting.
3. Are clothes part of setting in this story? When? How?
4. Does setting help to explain why the narrator's father is displeased that she called the police?

. . . and other elements

5. Does the title contribute to the story? How?
6. How do you feel about a male author writing a first-person story of a woman?
7. Does the first paragraph associate or disassociate the narrator's brother and Mr. Speed?
8. How many characters do you meet in the first paragraph?
9. In paragraph 2, why does the author use *scaredness* instead of the more common *fear*?
10. Does Mr. Speed's name matter?
11. In paragraph 16, what does the narrator mean? What do the horses have to do with Mr. Speed?
12. What do the brother and Mr. Speed have in common besides drink?
13. Consider the mirrors in this story. Do all the characters encounter mirrors?
14. Do you sense that the narrator unconsciously desires something from her father or brother that they will not give her, that she does not know she wants?

Chapter 7 **Point of View and Irony**

A story's point of view is our window on its fictional world and gives us our angle of vision. Often we watch through the viewpoint of one character, but not always. In fiction, the window's angle makes all the difference.

Suppose I met you on the street, having just witnessed a bank robbery and a police shootout with the criminal. I could tell you about it from my position as an observer. On the other hand, suppose I met you having just been mugged and having chased and caught my assailant. I could tell you about it as protagonist of the story. Next, suppose that you continued walking, met someone else you know, and repeated what I told you. You would make one essential change in the telling. No longer would the story be told in the first person (*I* and *we* are first-person pronouns). Because it had not happened to you, you would change *I* to the third-person *he*. "Then he saw a policeman vault over a Porsche, firing his revolver. . . ." If I had told you my thoughts or feelings, you could recount them: "He was scared."

Storytellers use three principal points of view. The first uses an *I* who is an observer or peripheral character. The second uses an *I* who is central to the story either as protagonist or participant. The third (and most common) uses the third person *he, she,* or *they*—and the storyteller conveys only that one person's thoughts and feelings. We call this point of view **limited omniscience**—omniscient because it can read minds, limited because it cannot read all minds.

Another point of view is **unlimited omniscience**. Suppose that, when you repeated the story I told you, you imagined what the bank robbers and the police were thinking and feeling. You would continue to use the third person, but you would assert your own unlimited omniscience into the minds of others.

Of course there are other variations and combinations, and there are still more possible points of view. On rare occasions, an author may use the second person: "Suppose that *you* continued walking. . . ," but this point of view is rare. More common is the **objective point of view**, which narrates action but does not report on anyone's ideas or feelings. The reteller of the mugging story, for instance, could tell what happened without speaking of anybody's fear. In the objective point of view the narrator appears to acknowledge that no one can know what anyone else is thinking. Ernest Hemingway wrote some stories with an objective point of view, never reporting on thoughts or feelings, but he wrote many others that are *largely* objective (reticent about violating privacy) but at a crucial moment indicate, in an adverb perhaps, something about a character's feelings. It should be noted that *objective* is a technical term for a device of fiction, not a critical compliment to an author's disinterest.

We have considered these possibilities:

> First-person observer
> First-person participant or protagonist
> Third person with limited omniscience
> Unlimited omniscience
> Objective point of view

Now we must look into the distinctive features of each point of view:

The first person grants a sense of immediacy. Sometimes the point-of-view character speaks in the first person as an observer of the action and narrates a story about *him, her,* or *them*—like a narrator either objective or with limited omniscience. In "A Rose for Emily" the narrator is an observer, a collective bystander who speaks as a plural *we*. The citizenry-as-narrator is rare but not unique to this story; it exemplifies the point of view of first person as observer.

In Tillie Olsen's "I Stand Here Ironing," the *I* is at the center of the story, the mother in a story about mother and daughter. Here we have an *I* narrator who is a protagonist rather than an observer. We watch everything from her angle of vision. She is our eyes and ears, she is our interpreting brain; we must decide whether we trust her or not. The character of the narrator qualifies the narration. If you distrust the *I*'s honesty, for instance, you will look behind the words.

Be cautious. Never assume that the *I* of a story is the author. In "I Stand Here Ironing," *I* is not Tillie Olsen; *I* is a character invented by Tillie Olsen.

With the point of view called limited omniscience, everyone except the narrator is presented objectively, without access to thoughts and feelings. We enter only one person's head, and that character may be first- or third-person. The viewpoint character may have *opinions* about somebody else's feelings ("George *looked* terrified"), but does not have *knowledge* ("George *felt* terrified").

The third-person narrator with limited omniscience is the most common point of view in the modern short story. In John Cheever's "The Chaste Clarissa," we know what we know by way of Baxter's thoughts and feelings. Clarissa comes to us through him, and if we think we understand her, we understand her through Baxter's observations. If we think we understand Baxter himself, it is because the author has given us a window on Baxter's skull through which we watch his thoughts.

Finally, let us consider unlimited omniscience, in which the narrator has total access to knowledge, thoughts, and feelings. This point of view was common when the novel was new, in the eighteenth century. Novelists then seemed conscious of creating their worlds and felt free to tell us not only what groups of people were saying but what they were thinking at the same time. Authors were apt to enter their stories not only as all-knowing voices but also as all-judging moralists. As the novel developed, unlimited omniscience began to seem gross to many novelists. Many preferred the limited omniscience of the third-person narrator. Others switched points of view from chapter to chapter. A common device in both novels and stories keeps *almost* entirely to limited omniscience but switches subtly and almost imperceptibly to unlimited omniscience when the point-of-view character is not on the scene.

With this subtle exception, the short story usually works best with a single and limited point of view. We can read a story (unlike a novel) in one sitting and comprehend it whole. In the short story, unlimited omniscience can seem formally clumsy, untethered, and unsettling—as when, settled into one vantage for observation, we are jerked away to another place by a single sentence. Think of how disturbing it would have been in "A Rose for Emily" if the *we* narrating the story had suddenly claimed to know what *we* couldn't know, saying "But Miss Emily in her heart never intended to marry Homer Barron." It is not to exaggerate to say that it would ruin the story, and the ruin is not only a ruin in *form*. Limited omniscience owes its popularity neither to form nor to fashion but to human nature; from our own experience we find *real* the notion that one consciousness and only one consciousness—whether it be represented as *he* or as *I*—observes and interprets the world.

About the objective point of view there is less to observe. Often it carries an air of careful reticence, as if the narrator were too noble to gossip or too cool to care. Of course the author must somehow embody feelings in descriptions of gesture and action so that we know how a character feels or responds or changes. The objective point of view is the acme of showing-without-telling. For an objective story, see Raymond Carver's "The Father," pages 376–377.

Deliberately shifting points of view can provide authors opportunities for effects like light and shade, bright sun and dark shadow. Joseph Conrad uses a narrator named Marlowe in a number of stories in which Marlowe speaks in a modern present about the past (for one contrast) to a group of rich Londoners about savages in a jungle (for another contrast) with his own observant (*I*) character sharply contrasted with a (*he*) protagonist. Marlowe may tell his story for many pages as if he were an author writing from a limited-omniscient third-person point of view. Then one of his listeners may interrupt him, and the reader is jolted back into the first-person present. The effect gives depth and perspective to a series of contrasts, one scene or time or circumstance illuminated by its opposite.

We have not yet mentioned the ultimate subjectivity, which is **stream of consciousness**. Here the author gives us not only the viewpoint character's relevant thought or feeling but also imitates the whole flow of mind from observation to reverie. In his novel *Ulysses,* James Joyce gives us Leopold Bloom's stream of consciousness:

> Nice kind of evening feeling. No more wandering about. Just loll there: quiet dusk: let everything rip. Forget. Tell about places you have been, strange customs. The other one, jar on her head, was getting the supper: fruit, olives, lovely cool water out of the well stonecold like the hole in the wall at Ashtown. Must carry a paper goblet next time I go to the trottingmatches. She listens with big dark soft eyes. Tell her: more and more: all. Then a sigh: silence. Long long long rest.

In "Counterparts," an earlier work, Joyce's acquaintance with Farrington's mind does not extend so far.

Joyce is expert at another device bearing on point of view. He will narrate using style, jargon, or lingo appropriate to the subject of his narration. In "Counterparts" he introduces a narrative passage "Just as they were naming their poisons who should come in but Higgins!" This sentence is *not* James Joyce's own voice—with its cliché for ordering drinks—and it is not a sentence actually spoken. It uses language appropriate to the scene to characterize both the scene and the people in it. If in the future Farrington or one of his barfly friends recounts this pointless evening, he will use this sort of language.

Irony and the unreliable narrator

Point of view often contributes to a short story's irony. **Irony** is the perception of incongruity or discrepancy—between words and meanings, between actions and reality, between appearances and reality. If I tell you that breaking my leg in three places was enjoyable, I am either ironic or very sick; you perceive the incongruity between statement and meaning. In "The Catbird Seat," it is ironic that a villain gets her comeuppance by being considered a liar when she is telling the truth. In "A Good Man Is Hard to Find," ironic discrepancies between overt statement and implicit meaning color the dialogue between the grandmother and The Misfit. Dramatic irony occurs when a character says more than he means, or when he proclaims as false something that the reader later discovers to be true.

Some ironic effects arise from situations rather than from words; we distinguish **verbal irony** from **situational irony**. An old burlesque act featured a violinist performing a solo at the front of the stage while a stripper performed behind him, fully visible to the audience. Cooperating, the audience would applaud the stripper, while the violinist pretended to accept the applause as a reward for his own efforts. In literature, of course, we learn situational irony from the narrator's words. But we can distinguish between irony that arises from the author's language and irony implicit in the situation. Sometimes we have both at once. In Flannery O'Connor's "A Good Man Is Hard to Find," the grandmother praises The Misfit, in a desperate attempt at placating him, while it is obvious that other members of the family are being executed. This irony is situational, but the grandmother's pious language adds verbal irony to the irony of situation.

A common ironic device uses a narrator who is dishonest or stupid, who gives the reader an interpretation of the action which the writer expects the reader to distrust. In Joyce's "Counterparts," Farrington is obtuse and unreliable. He thinks it appropriate to pawn his watch for a night's drinking; we know better. He thinks he beats his son because his son let the fire go out; we know better. Because of the writer's skill the reader sees through the narrator, or sees more than the narrator sees. This device—the "unreliable narrator"—can work with first person or third. William Faulkner narrated a large portion of *The Sound and the Fury* in the first person, through the mind of an idiot. Henry James achieved some of his finest effects through an obtuse narrator. In "The Beast in the Jungle," John Marcher is cold and reticent, unable to connect with energetic life outside him. In this long story, we see him with his friend May Bartram, and we see her fall in love with him, offer him in effect a chance to join humanity. We see everything through the third-person point of view of John Marcher. We realize that he is drying up for want of love, and we see love offered—but we see as well that he does not see it. The effect is extraordinary: *our mountaineering guide cannot see the mountain he walks on;* we want to reach into the book, shake John Marcher by the shoulder, and say *Look!*

For practice in thinking about point of view, identify the following examples made up for the occasion:

1. Hopeless and forlorn, the shepherd regarded his prize sheep covered with mud. Meantime the sheep was thinking of nothing but supper.
2. Harry knew that Gloria was stingy, but this topless convertible was worse than he had expected. He kissed her. She spat into the wind.
   a. I guess she's annoyed, thought Harry.
   b. She was annoyed.
   c. She looked annoyed.
   d. Annoyance crept over her features like a swarm of bees.
3. The grass turned blue in front of Angelique as she stumbled in the hot wind. Black cattle swung their long heads to stare, then bent to graze again. In the distance a speck of dust grew larger.
4. As I watched, the Mexican reached under the porch and retrieved his pistol. I wondered what Maravich would do under such provocation. Before I could imagine the next moment, I heard a shot from somewhere deep in the house and watched Maravich's body twist in the air.
5. I broke the walls myself, and it took a long time. Let me tell you the story from the beginning.
6. While Henry sat at the table, Marge pretended to read comic books. He was praising Verdi's *Otello*, as it happened, when Marge flicked her gum in his hair. Smiling at her youthful exuberance, Henry. . . .

John Cheever
The Chaste Clarissa

John Cheever (1912–   ) is a novelist (*The Wapshot Chronicle*, 1957; *The Wapshot Scandal*, 1964; *Bullet Park*, 1969; *Falconer*, 1976) who has published many volumes of short stories, collected in *The Stories of John Cheever* (1978). Born in Quincy, Massachusetts, he has lived in the East all his life and has first published most of his stories in *The New Yorker*.

The evening boat for Vineyard Haven was loading freight. In a little while, the warning whistle would separate the sheep from the goats—that's the way Baxter thought of it—the islanders from the tourists wandering through the streets of Woods Hole. His car, like all the others ticketed for the ferry, was parked near the wharf. He sat on the front bumper, smoking. The noise and movement of the small port seemed to signify that the spring had ended and that the shores of West Chop, across the Sound, were the shores of summer, but the implications of the hour and the voyage made no impression on Baxter at all. The delay bored and irritated him. When someone called his name, he got to his feet with relief.

It was old Mrs. Ryan. She called to him from a dusty station wagon, and he went over to speak to her. "I knew it," she said. "I knew that I'd see someone here from Holly Cove. I had that feeling in my bones. We've been traveling since nine this morning. We had trouble with the brakes outside Worcester. Now I'm wondering if Mrs. Talbot will have cleaned the house. She wanted seventy-five dollars for opening it last summer and I told her I wouldn't pay her that again, and I wouldn't be surprised if she's thrown all my letters away. Oh, I hate to have a journey end in a dirty house, but if worse comes to worst, we can clean it ourselves. Can't we, Clarissa?" she asked, turning to a young woman who sat beside her on the front seat. "Oh, excuse me, Baxter!" she exclaimed. "You haven't met Clarissa, have you? This is Bob's wife, Clarissa Ryan."

Baxter's first thought was that a girl like that shouldn't have to ride in a dusty station wagon; she should have done much better. She was young. He guessed that she was about twenty-five. Red-headed, deep-breasted, slender, and indolent, she seemed to belong to a different species from old Mrs. Ryan and her large-boned, forthright daughters. " 'The Cape Cod girls, they have no combs. They comb their hair with codfish bones,' " he said to himself but Clarissa's hair was well groomed. Her bare arms were perfectly white. Woods Hole and the activity on the wharf seemed to bore her and she was not interested in Mrs. Ryan's insular gossip. She lighted a cigarette.

At a pause in the old lady's monologue, Baxter spoke to her daughter-in-law. "When is Bob coming down, Mrs. Ryan?" he asked.

5 "He isn't coming at all," the beautiful Clarissa said. "He's in France. He's—"

"He's gone there for the government," old Mrs. Ryan interrupted, as if her daughter-in-law could not be entrusted with this simple explanation. "He's working on this terribly interesting project. He won't be back until autumn. I'm going abroad myself. I'm leaving Clarissa alone. Of course," she added forcefully, "I expect that she will *love* the island. Everyone does. I expect that she will be kept very busy. I expect that she—"

The warning signal from the ferry cut her off. Baxter said goodbye. One by one, the cars drove aboard, and the boat started to cross the shoal water from the mainland to the resort. Baxter drank a beer in the cabin and watched Clarissa and old Mrs. Ryan, who were sitting on deck. Since he had never seen Clarissa before, he supposed that Bob Ryan must have married her during the past winter. He did not understand how this beauty had ended up with the Ryans. They were a family of passionate amateur geologists and bird-watchers. "We're all terribly keen about birds and rocks," they said when they were introduced to strangers. Their cottage was a couple of miles from any other and had, as Mrs. Ryan often said, "been thrown together out of a barn in 1922." They sailed, hiked, swam in the surf, and organized expeditions to Cuttyhunk and Tarpaulin Cove. They were people who emphasized *corpore sano* unduly, Baxter thought, and they shouldn't leave Clarissa alone in the cottage. The wind had blown a strand of her flame-colored hair across her cheek. Her long legs were crossed. As the ferry entered the harbor, she stood up and made her way down the deck against the light salt wind, and Baxter, who had returned to the island indifferently, felt that the summer had begun.

Baxter knew that in trying to get some information about Clarissa Ryan he had to be careful. He was accepted in Holly Cove because he had summered there all his life. He could be pleasant and he was a good-looking man, but his two divorces, his promiscuity, his stinginess, and his Latin complexion had left with his neighbors a vague feeling that he was unsavory. He learned that Clarissa had married Bob Ryan in November and that she was from Chicago. He heard people say that she was beautiful and stupid. That was all he did find out about her.

He looked for Clarissa on the tennis courts and the beaches. He didn't see her. He went several times to the beach nearest the Ryans' cottage. She wasn't there. When he had been on the island only a short time, he received from Mrs. Ryan, in the mail, an invitation to tea. It was an invitation that he would not ordinarily have accepted, but he drove eagerly that afternoon over to the Ryans' cottage. He was late. The cars of most of his friends and neighbors were parked in Mrs. Ryan's field. Their voices drifted out of the open windows into the garden, where Mrs. Ryan's climbing roses were in bloom. "Welcome aboard!" Mrs. Ryan shouted when he crossed the porch. "This is my farewell party. I'm going to Norway." She led him into a crowded room.

10   Clarissa sat behind the teacups. Against the wall at her back was a glass cabinet that held the Ryans' geological specimens. Her arms were bare. Baxter watched them while she poured his tea. "Hot? . . . Cold? Lemon? . . . Cream?" seemed to be all she had to say, but her red hair and her white arms dominated that end of the room. Baxter ate a sandwich. He hung around the table.

"Have you ever been to the island before, Clarissa?" he asked.

"Yes."

"Do you swim at the beach at Holly Cove?"

"It's too far away."

15   "When your mother-in-law leaves," Baxter said, "you must let me drive you there in the mornings. I go down at eleven."

"Well, thank you." Clarissa lowered her green eyes. She seemed uncomfortable, and the thought that she might be susceptible crossed Baxter's mind exuberantly. "Well, thank you," she repeated, "but I have a car of my own and—well, I don't know, I don't—"

"What are *you* two talking about?" Mrs. Ryan asked, coming between them and smiling wildly in an effort to conceal some of the force of her interference. "I know it isn't geology," she went on, "and I know that it isn't birds, and I know that it can't be books or music, because those are all things that Clarissa doesn't like, aren't they, Clarissa? Come with me, Baxter," and she led him to the other side of the room and talked to him about sheep raising. When the conversation had ended, the party itself was nearly over. Clarissa's chair was empty. She was not in the room. Stopping at the door to thank Mrs. Ryan and say goodbye, Baxter said that he hoped she wasn't leaving for Europe immediately.

"Oh, but I am," Mrs. Ryan said. "I'm going to the mainland on the six-o'clock boat and sailing from Boston at noon tomorrow."

At half past ten the next morning, Baxter drove up to the Ryans' cottage. Mrs. Talbot, the local woman who helped the Ryans with their housework, answered the door. She said that young Mrs. Ryan was home, and let him in. Clarissa came downstairs. She looked more beautiful than ever, although she seemed put out at finding him there. She accepted his invitation to go swimming, but she accepted it unenthusiastically. "Oh, all right," she said.

20   When she came downstairs again, she had on a bathrobe over her bathing suit, and a broad-brimmed hat. On the drive to Holly Cove, he asked about her plans for the summer. She was noncommittal. She seemed preoccupied and unwilling to talk. They parked the car and walked side by side over the dunes to the beach, where she lay in the sand with her eyes closed. A few of Baxter's friends and neighbors stopped to pass the time, but they didn't stop for long, Baxter noticed. Clarissa's unresponsiveness made it difficult to talk. He didn't care.

He went swimming. Clarissa remained on the sand, bundled in her wrap. When he came out of the water, he lay down near her. He watched his neighbors and their children. The weather had been fair. The women were tanned. They were all married women and, unlike Clarissa, women with children, but the rigors of marriage and childbirth had left them all pretty, agile, and contented. While he was admiring them, Clarissa stood up and took off her bathrobe.

Here was something else, and it took his breath away. Some of the inescapable power of her beauty lay in the whiteness of her skin, some of it in the fact that, unlike the other women, who were at ease in bathing suits, Clarissa seemed humiliated and ashamed to find herself wearing so little. She walked down toward the water as if she were naked. When she first felt the water, she stopped short, for, again unlike the others, who were sporting around the pier like seals, Clarissa didn't like the cold. Then, caught for a second between nakedness and the cold, Clarissa waded in and swam a few feet. She came out of the water, hastily wrapped herself in the robe, and lay down in the sand. Then she spoke, for the first time that morning—for the first time in Baxter's experience—with warmth and feeling.

"You know, those stones on the point have grown a lot since I was here last," she said.

"What?" Baxter said.

25   "Those stones on the point," Clarissa said. "They've grown a lot."

"Stones don't grow," Baxter said.

"Oh yes they do," Clarissa said. "Didn't you know that? Stones grow. There's a stone in Mother's rose garden that's grown a foot in the last few years."

"I didn't know that stones grew," Baxter said.

"Well, they do," Clarissa said. She yawned; she shut her eyes. She seemed to fall asleep. When she opened her eyes again, she asked Baxter the time.

30   "Twelve o'clock," he said.

"I have to go home," she said. "I'm expecting guests."

Baxter could not contest this. He drove her home. She was unresponsive on the ride, and when he asked her if he could drive her to the beach again, she said no. It was a hot, fair day and most of the doors on the island stood open, but when Clarissa said goodbye to Baxter, she closed the door in his face.

Baxter got Clarissa's mail and newspapers from the post office the next day, but when he called with them at the cottage, Mrs. Talbot said that Mrs. Ryan was busy. He went that week to two large parties that she might have attended, but she was not at either. On Saturday night, he went to a barn dance, and late in the evening—they were dancing "Lady of the Lake"—he noticed Clarissa, sitting against the wall.

She was a striking wallflower. She was much more beautiful than any other woman there, but her beauty seemed to have intimidated the men. Baxter dropped out of the dance when he could and went to her. She was sitting on a packing case. It was the first thing she complained about. "There isn't even anything to sit on," she said.

35   "Don't you want to dance?" Baxter asked.

"Oh, I love to dance," she said. "I could dance all night, but I don't think *that's* dancing." She winced at the music of the fiddle and the piano. "I came with the Hortons. They just told me there was going to be a dance. They didn't tell me it was going to be this kind of a dance. I don't like all that skipping and hopping."

"Have your guests left?" Baxter asked.

"What guests?" Clarissa said.

"You told me you were expecting guests on Tuesday. When we were at the beach."

40   "I didn't say they were coming on Tuesday, did I?" Clarissa asked. "They're coming tomorrow."

"Can't I take you home?" Baxter asked.

"All right."

He brought the car around to the barn and turned on the radio. She got in and slammed the door with spirit. He raced the car over the back roads, and when he brought it up to the Ryans' cottage, he turned off the lights. He watched her hands. She folded them on her purse. "Well, thank you very much," she said. "I was having an awful time and you saved my life. I just don't understand this place, I guess. I've always had plenty of partners, but I sat on that hard box for nearly an hour and nobody even spoke to me. You saved my life."

"You're lovely, Clarissa," Baxter said.

45   "Well," Clarissa said, and she sighed. "That's just my outward self. Nobody knows the real me."

That was it, Baxter thought, and if he could only adjust his flattery to what she believed herself to be her scruples would dissolve. Did she think of herself as an actress, he wondered, a Channel swimmer, an heiress? The intimations of susceptibility that came from her in the summer night were so powerful, so heady, that they convinced Baxter that here was a woman whose chastity hung by a thread.

"I think I know the real you," Baxter said.

"Oh no you don't," Clarissa said. "Nobody does."

The radio played some lovelorn music from a Boston hotel. By the calendar, it was still early in the summer, but it seemed, from the stillness and the hugeness of the dark trees, to be much later. Baxter put his arms around Clarissa and planted a kiss on her lips.

50   She pushed him away violently and reached for the door. "Oh, now you've spoiled everything," she said as she got out of the car. "Now you've spoiled everything. I know what you've been thinking. I know you've been thinking it all along." She slammed the door and spoke to him across the window. "Well, you needn't come around here any more, Baxter," she said. "My girl friends are coming down from New York tomorrow on the morning plane and I'll be too busy to see you for the rest of the summer. Good night."

Baxter was aware that he had only himself to blame; he had moved too quickly. He knew better. He went to bed feeling angry and sad, and slept poorly. He was depressed when he woke, and his depression was deepened by the noise of a sea rain, blowing in from the northeast. He lay in bed listening to the rain and the surf. The storm would metamorphose the island. The beaches would be empty. Drawers would stick. Suddenly he got out of bed, went to the telephone, called the airport. The New York plane had been unable to land, they told him, and no more planes were expected that day. The storm seemed to be playing directly into his hands. At noon, he drove in to the village and bought a Sunday paper and a box of candy. The candy was for Clarissa, but he was in no hurry to give it to her.

She would have stocked the icebox, put out the towels, and planned the picnic, but now the arrival of her friends had been postponed, and the lively day that she had anticipated had turned out to be rainy and idle. There were ways, of course, for her to overcome her disappointment, but on the evidence of the barn dance he felt that she was lost without her husband or her mother-in-law, and that there were few, if any, people on the island who would pay her a chance call or ask her over for a drink. It was likely that she would spend the day listening to the radio and the rain and that by the end of it she would be ready to welcome anyone, including Baxter. But as long as the forces of loneliness and idleness were working on his side, it was shrewder, Baxter knew, to wait. It would be best to come just before dark, and he waited until then. He drove to the Ryans' with his box of candy. The windows were lighted. Clarissa opened the door.

"I wanted to welcome your friends to the island," Baxter said. "I—"

"They didn't come," Clarissa said. "The plane couldn't land. They went back to New York. They telephoned me. I had planned such a nice visit. Now everything's changed."

55   "I'm sorry, Clarissa," Baxter said. "I've brought you a present."

"Oh!" She took the box of candy. "What a beautiful box! What a lovely present! What—" Her face and her voice were, for a minute, ingenuous and yielding, and then he saw the force of resistance transform them. "You shouldn't have done it," she said.

"May I come in?" Baxter asked.

"Well, I don't know," she said. "You can't come in if you're just going to sit around."

"We could play cards," Baxter said.

60   "I don't know how," she said.

"I'll teach you," Baxter said.

"No," she said. "No, Baxter, you'll have to go. You just don't understand the kind of woman I am. I spent all day writing a letter to Bob. I wrote and told him that you kissed me last night. I can't let you come in." She closed the door.

From the look on Clarissa's face when he gave her the box of candy, Baxter judged that she liked to get presents. An inexpensive gold bracelet or even a bunch of flowers might do it, he knew, but Baxter was an extremely stingy man, and while he saw the usefulness of a present, he could not bring himself to buy one. He decided to wait.

The storm blew all Monday and Tuesday. It cleared on Tuesday night, and by Wednesday afternoon the tennis courts were dry and Baxter played. He played until late. Then, when he had bathed and changed his clothes, he stopped at a cocktail party to pick up a drink. Here one of his neighbors, a married woman with four children, sat down beside him and began a general discussion of the nature of married love.

65   It was a conversation, with its glances and innuendoes, that Baxter had been through many times, and he knew roughly what it promised. His neighbor was one of the pretty mothers that Baxter had admired on the beach. Her hair was brown. Her arms were thin and tanned. Her teeth were sound. But while he appeared to be deeply concerned with her opinions on love, the white image of Clarissa loomed up in his mind, and he broke off the conversation and left the party. He drove to the Ryans'.

From a distance, the cottage looked shut. The house and the garden were perfectly still. He knocked and then rang. Clarissa spoke to him from an upstairs window.

"Oh, hello, Baxter," she said.

"I've come to say goodbye, Clarissa," Baxter said. He couldn't think of anything better.

"Oh, dear," Clarissa said. "Well, wait just a minute. I'll be down."

70   "I'm going away, Clarissa," Baxter said when she opened the door. "I've come to say goodbye."

"Where are you going?"

"I don't know." He said this sadly.

"Well, come in, then," she said hesitantly. "Come in for a minute. This is the last time that I'll see you, I guess, isn't it? Please excuse the way the place looks. Mr. Talbot got sick on Monday and Mrs. Talbot had to take him to the hospital on the mainland, and I haven't had anybody to help me. I've been all alone."

He followed her into the living room and sat down. She was more beautiful than ever. She talked about the problems that had been presented by Mrs. Talbot's departure. The fire in the stove that heated the water had died. There was a mouse in the kitchen. The bathtub wouldn't drain. She hadn't been able to get the car started.

75   In the quiet house, Baxter heard the sound of a leaky water tap and a clock pendulum. The sheet of glass that protected the Ryans' geological specimens reflected the fading sky outside the window. The cottage was near the water, and he could hear the surf. He noted these details dispassionately and for what they were worth. When Clarissa finished her remarks about Mrs. Talbot, he waited a full minute before he spoke.

"The sun is in your hair," he said.

"What?"

"The sun is in your hair. It's a beautiful color."

"Well, it isn't as pretty as it used to be," she said. "Hair like mine gets dark. But I'm not going to dye it. I don't think that women should dye their hair."

80   "You're so intelligent," he murmured.

"You don't mean that?"

"Mean what?"

"Mean that I'm intelligent."

"Oh, but I do," he said. "You're intelligent. You're beautiful. I'll never forget that night I met you at the boat. I hadn't wanted to come to the island. I'd made plans to go out West."

85 "I can't be intelligent," Clarissa said miserably. "I must be stupid. Mother Ryan says that I'm stupid, and Bob says that I'm stupid, and even Mrs. Talbot says that I'm stupid, and—" She began to cry. She went to a mirror and dried her eyes. Baxter followed. He put his arms around her. "Don't put your arms around me," she said, more in despair than in anger. "Nobody ever takes me seriously until they get their arms around me." She sat down again and Baxter sat near her. "But you're not stupid, Clarissa," he said. "You have a wonderful intelligence, a wonderful mind. I've often thought so. I've often felt that you must have a lot of very interesting opinions."

"Well, that's funny," she said, "because I do have a lot of opinions. Of course, I never dare say them to anyone, and Bob and Mother Ryan don't ever let me speak. They always interrupt me, as if they were ashamed of me. But I do have these opinions. I mean, I think we're like cogs in a wheel. I've concluded that we're like cogs in a wheel. Do you think we're like cogs in a wheel?"

"Oh, yes," he said. "Oh, yes, I do!"

"I think we're like cogs in a wheel," she said. "For instance, do you think that women should work? I've given that a lot of thought. My opinion is that I don't think married women should work. I mean, unless they have a lot of money, of course, but even then I think it's a full-time job to take care of a man. Or do you think that women should work?"

"What do you think?" he asked. "I'm terribly interested in knowing what you think."

90 "Well, my opinion is," she said timidly, "that you just have to hoe your row. I don't think that working or joining the church is going to change everything, or special diets, either. I don't put much stock in fancy diets. We have a friend who eats a quarter of a pound of meat at every meal. He has a scales right on the table and he weighs the meat. It makes the table look awful and I don't see what good it's going to do him. I buy what's reasonable. If ham is reasonable, I buy ham. If lamb is reasonable, I buy lamb. Don't you think that's intelligent?"

"I think that's very intelligent."

"And progressive education," she said. "I don't have a good opinion of progressive education. When we go to the Howards' for dinner, the children ride their tricycles around the table all the time, and it's my opinion that they get this way from progressive schools, and that children ought to be told what's nice and what isn't."

The sun that had lighted her hair was gone, but there was still enough light in the room for Baxter to see that as she aired her opinions, her face suffused with color and her pupils dilated. Baxter listened patiently, for he knew by then that she merely wanted to be taken for something that she was not—that the poor girl was lost. "You're very intelligent," he said, now and then. "You're so intelligent."

It was as simple as that.

Questions on point of view . . .

1. From whose point of view is this story told? Are there any exceptions?
2. Do we miss being told Clarissa's thoughts?

3. Imagine what would happen if the story were told from Clarissa's point of view. Rewrite a paragraph from Clarissa's point of view.
4. What difference would it make if this story were told in the first person?
5. If you feel that you know what Clarissa thinks, how did you acquire your knowledge?
6. Could this story be told from an objective point of view? What kind of problem would arise?

. . . and other elements

7. What is the conflict in this story? The climax? The dénouement?
8. What is the author's attitude toward his characters?
9. Divide the story into scenes to determine the function of each scene to the story as a whole.
10. Is Baxter a round character?

Tillie Olsen
I Stand Here Ironing

Tillie Olsen (1913–   ) has lived most of her life in San Francisco. Mother of four children, she had little time for her writing when she was young, and did not publish her first book, *Tell Me a Riddle*, until 1962. *Yonnondio* appeared in 1974, and in 1978 *Silences,* which investigates the problems of writers, especially women, who have written little or stopped writing. "I Stand Here Ironing" comes from *Tell Me a Riddle.*

I stand here ironing, and what you asked me moves tormented back and forth with the iron.

"I wish you would manage the time to come in and talk with me about your daughter. I'm sure you can help me understand her. She's a youngster who needs help and whom I'm deeply interested in helping."

"Who needs help." . . . Even if I came, what good would it do? You think because I am her mother I have a key, or that in some way you could use me as a key? She has lived for nineteen years. There is all that life that has happened outside of me, beyond me.

And when is there time to remember, to sift, to weigh, to estimate, to total? I will start and there will be an interruption and I will have to gather it all together again. Or I will become engulfed with all I did or did not do, with what should have been and what cannot be helped.

5   She was a beautiful baby. The first and only one of our five that was beautiful at birth. You do not guess how new and uneasy her tenancy in her now-loveliness. You did not know her all those years she was thought homely, or see her poring over her baby pictures, making me tell her over and over how beautiful she had been—and would be, I would tell her—and was now, to the seeing eye. But the seeing eyes were few or non-existent. Including mine.

I nursed her. They feel that's important nowadays. I nursed all the children, but with her, with all the fierce rigidity of first motherhood, I did like the books then said. Though her cries battered me to trembling and my breasts ached with swollenness, I waited till the clock decreed.

Why do I put that first? I do not even know if it matters, or if it explains anything.

She was a beautiful baby. She blew shining bubbles of sound. She loved motion, loved light, loved color and music and textures. She would lie on the floor in her blue overalls patting the surface so hard in ecstasy her hands and feet would blur. She was a miracle to me, but when she was eight months old I had to leave her daytimes with the woman downstairs to whom she was no miracle at all, for I worked or looked for work and for Emily's father, who "could no longer endure" (he wrote in his good-bye note) "sharing want with us."

I was nineteen, it was the pre-relief, pre-WPA world of the depression. I would start running as soon as I got off the streetcar, running up the stairs, the place smelling sour, and awake or asleep to startle awake, when she saw me she would break into a clogged weeping that could not be comforted, a weeping I can hear yet.

10   After a while I found a job hashing at night so I could be with her days, and it was better. But it came to where I had to bring her to his family and leave her.

It took a long time to raise the money for her fare back. Then she got chicken pox and I had to wait longer. When she finally came, I hardly knew her, walking quick and nervous like her father, looking like her father, thin, and dressed in a shoddy red that yellowed her skin and glared at the pockmarks. All the baby loveliness gone.

She was two. Old enough for nursery school they said, and I did not know then what I know now—the fatigue of the long day, and the lacerations of group life in the kinds of nurseries that are only parking places for children.

Except that it would have made no difference if I had known. It was the only place there was. It was the only way we could be together, the only way I could hold a job.

And even without knowing, I knew. I knew the teacher that was evil because all these years it has curdled into my memory, the little boy hunched in the corner, her rasp, "why aren't you outside, because Alvin hits you? that's no reason, go out, scaredy." I knew Emily hated it even if she did not clutch and implore "don't go Mommy" like the other children, mornings.

15   She always had a reason why we should stay home. Momma, you look sick, Momma, I feel sick. Momma, the teachers aren't there today, they're sick. Momma, we can't go, there was a fire there last night. Momma, it's a holiday today, no school, they told me.

But never a direct protest, never rebellious. I think of our others in their three, four-year-oldness—the explosions, the tempers, the denunciations, the demands—and I feel suddenly ill. I put the iron down. What in me demanded that goodness in her? And what was the cost, the cost to her of such goodness?

The old man living in the back once said in his gentle way: "You should smile at Emily more when you look at her." What was in my face when I looked at her? I loved her. There were all the acts of love.

It was only with the others I remembered what he said, and it was the face of joy, and not of care or tightness or worry I turned to them—too late for Emily. She does not smile easily, let alone almost always as her brothers and sisters do. Her face is closed and sombre, but when she wants, how fluid. You must have seen it in her pantomimes, you spoke of her rare gift for comedy on the stage that rouses a laughter out of the audience so dear they applaud and applaud and do not want to let her go.

Where does it come from, that comedy? There was none of it in her when she came back to me that second time, after I had had to send her away again. She had a new daddy now to learn to love, and I think perhaps it was a better time.

20   Except when we left her alone nights, telling ourselves she was old enough.

"Can't you go some other time, Mommy, like tomorrow?" she would ask. "Will it be just a little while you'll be gone? Do you promise?"

The time we came back, the front door open, the clock on the floor in the hall. She rigid awake. "It wasn't just a little while. I didn't cry. Three times I called you, just three times, and then I ran downstairs to open the door so you could come faster. The clock talked loud. I threw it away, it scared me what it talked."

She said the clock talked loud again that night I went to the hospital to have Susan. She was delirious with the fever that comes before red measles but she was fully conscious all the week I was gone and the week after we were home when she could not come near the new baby or me.

She did not get well. She stayed skeleton thin, not wanting to eat, and night after night she had nightmares. She would call for me, and I would rouse from exhaustion to sleepily call back: "You're all right, darling, go to sleep, it's just a dream," and if she still called, in a sterner voice, "now go to sleep, Emily, there's nothing to hurt you." Twice, only twice, when I had to get up for Susan anyhow, I went in to sit with her.

25   Now when it is too late (as if she would let me hold and comfort her like I do the others) I get up and go to her at once at her moan or restless stirring. "Are you awake, Emily? Can I get you something?" And the answer is always the same: "No, I'm all right, go back to sleep, Mother."

They persuaded me at the clinic to send her away to a convalescent home in the country where "she can have the kind of food and care you can't manage for her, and you'll be free to concentrate on the new baby." They still send children to that place. I see pictures on the society page of sleek young women planning affairs to raise money for it, or dancing at the affairs, or decorating Easter eggs or filling Christmas stockings for the children.

They never have a picture of the children so I do not know if the girls still wear those gigantic red bows and the ravaged looks on the every other Sunday when parents can come to visit "unless otherwise notified"—as we were notified the first six weeks.

Oh it is a handsome place, green lawns and tall trees and fluted flower beds. High up on the balconies of each cottage the children stand, the girls in their red bows and white dresses, the boys in white suits and giant red ties. The parents stand below shrieking up to be heard and the children shriek down to be heard, and between them the invisible wall "Not To Be Contaminated by Parental Germs or Physical Affection."

There was a tiny girl who always stood hand in hand with Emily. Her parents never came. One visit she was gone. "They moved her to Rose Cottage," Emily shouted in explanation. "They don't like you to love anybody here."

30   She wrote once a week, the labored writing of a seven-year-old. "I am fine. How is the baby. If I write my leter nicly I will have a star. Love." There never was a star. We wrote every other day, letters she could never hold or keep but only hear read—once. "We simply do not have room for children to keep any personal possessions," they patiently explained when we pieced one Sunday's shrieking together to plead how much it would mean to Emily, who loved so to keep things, to be allowed to keep her letters and cards.

Each visit she looked frailer. "She isn't eating," they told us.

(They had runny eggs for breakfast or mush with lumps, Emily said later, I'd hold it in my mouth and not swallow. Nothing ever tasted good, just when they had chicken.)

It took us eight months to get her released home, and only the fact that she gained back so little of her seven lost pounds convinced the social worker.

I used to try to hold and love her after she came back, but her body would stay stiff, and after a while she'd push away. She ate little. Food sickened her, and I think much of life too. Oh she had physical lightness and brightness, twinkling by on skates, bouncing like a ball up and down up and down over the jump rope, skimming over the hill; but these were momentary.

She fretted about her appearance, thin and dark and foreign-looking at a time when every little girl was supposed to look or thought she should look a chubby blonde replica of Shirley Temple. The doorbell sometimes rang for her, but no one seemed to come and play in the house or be a best friend. Maybe because we moved so much.

There was a boy she loved painfully through two school semesters. Months later she told me how she had taken pennies from my purse to buy him candy. "Licorice was his favorite and I brought him some every day, but he still liked Jennifer better'n me. Why, Mommy?" The kind of question for which there is no answer.

School was a worry to her. She was not glib or quick in a world where glibness and quickness were easily confused with ability to learn. To her overworked and exasperated teachers she was an overconscientious "slow learner" who kept trying to catch up and was absent entirely too often.

I let her be absent, though sometimes the illness was imaginary. How different from my now-strictness about attendance with the others. I wasn't working. We had a new baby, I was home anyhow. Sometimes, after Susan grew old enough, I would keep her home from school, too, to have them all together.

Mostly Emily had asthma, and her breathing, harsh and labored, would fill the house with a curiously tranquil sound. I would bring the two old dresser mirrors and her boxes of collections to her bed. She would select beads and single earrings, bottle tops and shells, dried flowers and pebbles, old postcards and scraps, all sorts of oddments; then she and Susan would play Kingdom, setting up landscapes and furniture, peopling them with action.

Those were the only times of peaceful companionship between her and Susan. I have edged away from it, that poisonous feeling between them, the terrible balancing of hurts and needs I had to do between the two, and did so badly, those earlier years.

Oh there are conflicts between the others too, each one human, needing, demanding, hurting, taking—but only between Emily and Susan, no, Emily toward Susan that corroding resentment. It seems so obvious on the surface yet it is not obvious. Susan, the second child, Susan, golden- and curly-haired and chubby, quick and articulate and assured, everything in appearance and manner Emily was not; Susan, not able to resist Emily's precious things, losing or sometimes clumsily breaking them; Susan telling jokes and riddles to company for applause while Emily sat silent (to say to me later that was *my* riddle, Mother, I told it to Susan); Susan, who for all the five years' difference in age was just a year behind Emily in developing physically.

I am glad for that slow physical development that widened the difference between her and her contemporaries, though she suffered over it. She was too vulnerable for that terrible world of youthful competition, of preening and parading, of constant measuring of yourself against every other, of envy. "If I had that copper hair," "If I had that skin. . . ." She tormented herself enough about not looking like the others, there was enough of the unsureness, the having to be conscious of words before you speak, the constant caring—what are they thinking of me? without having it all magnified by the merciless physical drives.

Ronnie is calling. He is wet and I change him. It is rare there is such a cry now. That time of motherhood is almost behind me when the ear is not one's own but must always be racked and listening for the child cry, the child call. We sit for a while and I hold him, looking out over the city spread in charcoal with its soft aisles of light. *"Shoogily,"* he breathes and curls closer. I carry him back to bed, asleep. *Shoogily.* A funny word, a family word, inherited from Emily, invented by her to say: *comfort.*

In this and other ways she leaves her seal, I say aloud. And startle at my saying it. What do I mean? What did I start to gather together, to try and make coherent? I was at the terrible, growing years. War years. I do not remember them well. I was working, there were four smaller ones now, there was not time for her. She had to help be a mother, and housekeeper, and shopper. She had to set her seal. Mornings of crisis and near hysteria trying to get lunches packed, hair combed, coats and shoes found, everyone to school or Child Care on time, the baby ready for transportation. And always the paper scribbled on by a smaller one, the book looked at by Susan then mislaid, the homework not done. Running out to that huge school where she was one, she was lost, she was a drop; suffering over the unpreparedness, stammering and unsure in her classes.

45   There was so little time left at night after the kids were bedded down. She would struggle over books, always eating (it was in those years she developed her enormous appetite that is legendary in our family) and I would be ironing, or preparing food for the next day, or writing V-mail to Bill, or tending the baby. Sometimes, to make me laugh, or out of her despair, she would imitate happenings or types at school.

I think I said once: "Why don't you do something like this in the school amateur show?" One morning she phoned me at work, hardly understandable through the weeping: "Mother, I did it. I won, I won; they gave me first prize; they clapped and clapped and wouldn't let me go."

Now suddenly she was Somebody, and as imprisoned in her difference as she had been in anonymity.

She began to be asked to perform at other high schools, even in colleges, then at city and statewide affairs. The first one we went to, I only recognized her that first moment when thin, shy, she almost drowned herself into the curtains. Then: Was this Emily? The control, the command, the convulsing and deadly clowning, the spell, then the roaring, stamping audience, unwilling to let this rare and precious laughter out of their lives.

Afterwards: You ought to do something about her with a gift like that—but without money or knowing how, what does one do? We have left it all to her, and the gift has as often eddied inside, clogged and clotted, as been used and growing.

50   She is coming. She runs up the stairs two at a time with her light graceful step, and I know she is happy tonight. Whatever it was that occasioned your call did not happen today.

"Aren't you ever going to finish the ironing, Mother? Whistler painted his mother in a rocker. I'd have to paint mine standing over an ironing board." This is one of her communicative nights and she tells me everything and nothing as she fixes herself a plate of food out of the icebox.

She is so lovely. Why did you want me to come in at all? Why were you concerned? She will find her way.

She starts up the stairs to bed. "Don't get me up with the rest in the morning." "But I thought you were having midterms." "Oh, those," she comes back in, kisses me, and says quite lightly, "in a couple of years when we'll all be atom-dead they won't matter a bit."

She has said it before. She *believes* it. But because I have been dredging the past, and all that compounds a human being is so heavy and meaningful in me, I cannot endure it tonight.

55   I will never total it all. I will never come in to say: She was a child seldom smiled at. Her father left me before she was a year old. I had to work her first six years when there was work, or I sent her home and to his relatives. There were years she had care she hated. She was dark and thin and foreign-looking in a world where the prestige went to blondeness and curly hair and dimples, she was slow where glibness was prized. She was a child of anxious, not proud, love. We were poor and could not afford for her the soil of easy growth. I was a young mother, I was a distracted mother. There were the other children pushing up, demanding. Her younger sister seemed all that she was not. There were years she did not want me to touch her. She kept too much in herself, her life was such she had to keep too much in herself. My wisdom came too late. She has much to her and probably nothing will come of it. She is a child of her age, of depression, of war, of fear.

Let her be. So all that is in her will not bloom—but in how many does it? There is still enough left to live by. Only help her to know—help make it so there is cause for her to know—that she is more than this dress on the ironing-board, helpless before the iron.

Questions on point of view . . .

1. What is the point of view in this story? Is it consistent?
2. Who is *you* in the first line? Does the reader know exactly? Does the reader know approximately? Does Olsen's story require that the reader know no more than the reader knows?
3. What kind of speech is this story? Is it spoken out loud? Is the narrator speaking to anyone in particular? When? Why is the story told as it is?
4. The narrator supplies important information in paragraph 18. Did you know it at the time?
5. What do we learn about *you* in paragraph 50?
6. Who speaks in paragraph 51?
7. What does the verb tense tell us in paragraph 52?
8. Does paragraph 53 offer information lacking since paragraph 1? Would this story be better if you had known it before?

. . . and other elements

9. How is Emily characterized?
10. How much do we know of Emily's father? Reconstruct the major events of the mother's life in sequence.

11. How does the final image of the mother ironing, given prominence by the title, bear on the structure and the theme of the story?

Anton Chekhov
Gooseberries

Translated by Avrahm Yarmolinsky

Anton Chekhov (1860–1904) trained to be a doctor but abandoned medicine to write stories. Later he became a playwright (see pages 956–958 for a further note on Chekhov and for the text of *The Cherry Orchard*). His grandfather began life as a serf and died a wealthy merchant. Although his father was born to the middle class, he lost his money while Chekhov was in school. If his social and family background was thus confused, Chekhov learned from the confusion. In stories written during the last decades of the Czarist regime, he reached out to all levels of society. Although tuberculosis shortened his life, he virtually invented the modern short story, leaving behind hundreds.

The sky had been overcast since early morning; it was a still day, not hot, but tedious, as it usually is when the weather is gray and dull, when clouds have been hanging over the fields for a long time, and you wait for the rain that does not come. Ivan Ivanych, a veterinary, and Burkin, a high school teacher, were already tired with walking, and the plain seemed endless to them. Far ahead were the scarcely visible windmills of the village of Mironositzkoe; to the right lay a range of hills that disappeared in the distance beyond the village, and both of them knew that over there were the river, and fields, green willows, homesteads, and if you stood on one of the hills, you could see from there another vast plain, telegraph poles, and a train that from afar looked like a caterpillar crawling, and in clear weather you could even see the town. Now, when it was still and when nature seemed mild and pensive, Ivan Ivanych and Burkin were filled with love for this plain, and both of them thought what a beautiful land it was.

"Last time when we were in Elder Prokofy's barn," said Burkin, "you were going to tell me a story."

"Yes; I wanted to tell you about my brother."

Ivan Ivanych heaved a slow sigh and lit his pipe before beginning his story, but just then it began to rain. And five minutes later there was a downpour, and it was hard to tell when it would be over. The two men halted, at a loss; the dogs, already wet, stood with their tails between their legs and looked at them feelingly.

5   "We must find shelter somewhere," said Burkin. "Let's go to Alyohin's; it's quite near."

"Let's."

They turned aside and walked across a mown meadow, now going straight ahead, now bearing to the right, until they reached the road. Soon poplars came into view, a garden, then the red roofs of barns; the river gleamed, and the view opened on a broad expanse of water with a mill and a white bathing-cabin. That was Sofyino, Alyohin's place.

The mill was going, drowning out the sound of the rain; the dam was shaking. Wet horses stood near the carts, their heads drooping, and men were walking about, their heads covered with sacks. It was damp, muddy, dreary; and the water looked cold and unkind. Ivan Ivanych and Burkin felt cold and messy and uncomfortable through and through; their feet were heavy with mud and when, having crossed the dam, they climbed up to the barns, they were silent as though they were cross with each other.

The noise of a winnowing-machine came from one of the barns, the door was open, and clouds of dust were pouring from within. On the threshold stood Alyohin himself, a man of forty, tall and rotund, with long hair, looking more like a professor or an artist than a gentleman farmer. He was wearing a white blouse, badly in need of washing, that was belted with a rope, and drawers, and his high boots were plastered with mud and straw. His eyes and nose were black with dust. He recognized Ivan Ivanych and Burkin and was apparently very glad to see them.

10   "Please go up to the house, gentlemen," he said, smiling; "I'll be there directly, in a moment."

It was a large structure of two stories. Alyohin lived downstairs in what was formerly the stewards' quarters: two rooms that had arched ceilings and small windows; the furniture was plain, and the place smelled of rye bread, cheap vodka, and harness. He went into the showy rooms upstairs only rarely, when he had guests. Once in the house, the two visitors were met by a chambermaid, a young woman so beautiful that both of them stood still at the same moment and glanced at each other.

"You can't imagine how glad I am to see you, gentlemen," said Alyohin, joining them in the hall. "What a surprise! Pelageya," he said, turning to the chambermaid, "give the guests a change of clothes. And, come to think of it, I will change, too. But I must go and bathe first, I don't think I've had a wash since spring. Don't you want to go into the bathing-cabin? In the meanwhile things will be got ready here."

The beautiful Pelageya, with her soft, delicate air, brought them bath towels and soap, and Alyohin went to the bathing-cabin with his guests.

"Yes, it's a long time since I've bathed," he said, as he undressed. "I've an excellent bathing-cabin, as you see—it was put up by my father—but somehow I never find time to use it." He sat down on the steps and lathered his long hair and neck, and the water around him turned brown.

15   "I say—" observed Ivan Ivanych significantly, looking at his head.

"I haven't had a good wash for a long time," repeated Alyohin, embarrassed, and soaped himself once more; the water about him turned dark-blue, the color of ink.

Ivan Ivanych came out of the cabin, plunged into the water with a splash and swam in the rain, thrusting his arms out wide; he raised waves on which white lilies swayed. He swam out to the middle of the river and dived and a minute later came up in another spot and swam on and kept diving, trying to touch bottom. "By God!" he kept repeating delightedly, "by God!" He swam to the mill, spoke to the peasants there, and turned back and in the middle of the river lay floating, exposing his face to the rain. Burkin and Alyohin were already dressed and ready to leave, but he kept on swimming and diving. <u>"By God!" he kept exclaiming.</u> <u>"Lord, have mercy on me."</u>

"You've had enough!" Burkin shouted to him.

They returned to the house. And only when the lamp was lit in the big drawing room upstairs, and the two guests, in silk dressing-gowns and warm slippers, were lounging in armchairs, and Alyohin himself, washed and combed, wearing a new jacket, was walking about the room, evidently savoring the warmth, the cleanliness, the dry clothes and light footwear, and when pretty Pelageya, stepping noiselessly across the carpet and smiling softly, brought in a tray with tea and jam, only then did Ivan Ivanych begin his story, and it was as though not only Burkin and Alyohin were listening, but also the ladies, old and young, and the military men who looked down upon them, calmly and severely, from their gold frames.

20   "We are two brothers," he began, "I, Ivan Ivanych, and my brother, Nikolay Ivanych, who is two years my junior. I went in for a learned profession and became a veterinary; Nikolay at nineteen began to clerk in a provincial branch of the Treasury. Our father was a *kantonist*,[1] but he rose to be an officer and so a nobleman, a rank that he bequeathed to us together with a small estate. After his death there was a lawsuit and we lost the estate to creditors, but be that as it may, we spent our childhood in the country. Just like peasant children we passed days and nights in the fields and the woods, herded horses, stripped bast from the trees, fished, and so on. And, you know, whoever even once in his life has caught a perch or seen thrushes migrate in the autumn, when on clear, cool days they sweep in flocks over the village, will never really be a townsman and to the day of his death will have a longing for the open. My brother was unhappy in the government office. Years passed, but he went on warming the same seat, scratching away at the same papers, and thinking of one and the same thing: how to get away to the country. And little by little this vague longing turned into a definite desire, into a dream of buying a little property somewhere on the banks of a river or a lake.

"He was a kind and gentle soul and I loved him, but I never sympathized with his desire to shut himself up for the rest of his life on a little property of his own. It is a common saying that a man needs only six feet of earth. But six feet is what a corpse needs, not a man. It is also asserted that if our educated class is drawn to the land and seeks to settle on farms, that's a good thing. But these farms amount to the same six feet of earth. To retire from the city, from the struggle, from the hubbub, to go off and hide on one's own farm—that's not life, it is selfishness, sloth, it is a kind of monasticism, but monasticism without works. Man needs not six feet of earth, not a farm, but the whole globe, all of Nature, where unhindered he can display all the capacities and peculiarities of his free spirit.

"My brother Nikolay, sitting in his office, dreamed of eating his own *shchi,* which would fill the whole farmyard with a delicious aroma, of picnicking on the green grass, of sleeping in the sun, of sitting for hours on the seat by the gate gazing at field and forest. Books on agriculture and the farming items in almanacs were his joy, the delight of his soul. He liked newspapers too, but the only things he read in them were advertisements of land for sale, so many acres of tillable land and pasture, with house, garden, river, mill, and millpond. And he pictured to himself garden paths, flowers, fruit, birdhouses with starlings in them, crucians in the pond, and all that sort of thing, you know. These imaginary pictures varied with the advertisements he came upon, but somehow gooseberry bushes figured in every one of them. He could not picture to himself a single country-house, a single rustic nook, without gooseberries.

" 'Country life has its advantages,' he used to say. 'You sit on the veranda having tea, and your ducks swim in the pond, and everything smells delicious and—the gooseberries are ripening.'

---

[1]The son of a low-ranking soldier, enrolled in a military school

"He would draw a plan of his estate and invariably it would contain the following features: a) the master's house; b) servants' quarters; c) kitchen-garden; d) a gooseberry patch. He lived meagerly: he deprived himself of food and drink; he dressed God knows how, like a beggar, but he kept on saving and salting money away in the bank. He was terribly stingy. It was painful for me to see it, and I used to give him small sums and send him something on holidays, but he would put that away too. Once a man is possessed by an idea, there is no doing anything with him.

25   "Years passed. He was transferred to another province, he was already past forty, yet he was still reading newspaper advertisements and saving up money. Then I heard that he was married. Still for the sake of buying a property with a gooseberry patch he married an elderly, homely widow, without a trace of affection for her, but simply because she had money. After marrying her, he went on living parsimoniously, keeping her half-starved, and he put her money in the bank in his own name. She had previously been the wife of a postmaster, who had got her used to pies and cordials. This second husband did not even give her enough black bread. She began to sicken, and some three years later gave up the ghost. And, of course, it never for a moment occurred to my brother that he was to blame for her death. Money, like vodka, can do queer things to a man. Once in our town a merchant lay on his deathbed; before he died, he ordered a plateful of honey and he ate up all his money and lottery tickets with the honey, so that no one should get it. One day when I was inspecting a drove of cattle at a railway station, a cattle dealer fell under a locomotive and it sliced off his leg. We carried him in to the infirmary, the blood was gushing from the wound—a terrible business, but he kept begging us to find his leg and was very anxious about it: he had twenty rubles in the boot that was on that leg, and he was afraid they would be lost."

"That's a tune from another opera," said Burkin.

Ivan Ivanych paused a moment and then continued:

"After his wife's death, my brother began to look around for a property. Of course, you may scout about for five years and in the end make a mistake, and buy something quite different from what you have been dreaming of. Through an agent my brother bought a mortgaged estate of three hundred acres with a house, servants' quarters, a park, but with no orchard, no gooseberry patch, no duckpond. There was a stream, but the water in it was the color of coffee, for on one of its banks there was a brickyard and on the other a glue factory. But my brother was not at all disconcerted: he ordered a score of gooseberry bushes, planted them, and settled down to the life of a country gentleman.

"Last year I paid him a visit. I thought I would go and see how things were with him. In his letter to me my brother called his estate 'Chumbaroklov Waste, or Himalaiskoe' (our surname was Chimsha-Himalaisky). I reached the place in the afternoon. It was hot. Everywhere there were ditches, fences, hedges, rows of fir trees, and I was at a loss as to how to get to the yard and where to leave my horse. I made my way to the house and was met by a fat dog with reddish hair that looked like a pig. It wanted to bark, but was too lazy. The cook, a fat, barelegged woman, who also looked like a pig, came out of the kitchen and said that the master was resting after dinner. I went in to see my brother, and found him sitting up in bed, with a quilt over his knees. He had grown older, stouter, flabby; his cheeks, his nose, his lips jutted out: it looked as though he might grunt into the quilt at any moment.

30   "We embraced and dropped tears of joy and also of sadness at the thought that

the two of us had once been young, but were now gray and nearing death. He got dressed and took me out to show me his estate.

" 'Well, how are you getting on here?' I asked.

" 'Oh, all right, thank God. I am doing very well.'

"He was no longer the poor, timid clerk he used to be but a real landowner, a gentleman. He had already grown used to his new manner of living and developed a taste for it. He ate a great deal, steamed himself in the bathhouse, was growing stout, was already having a lawsuit with the village commune and the two factories and was very much offended when the peasants failed to address him as 'Your Honor.' And he concerned himself with his soul's welfare too in a substantial, upper-class manner, and performed good deeds not simply, but pompously. And what good works! He dosed the peasants with bicarbonate and castor oil for all their ailments and on his name day he had a thanksgiving service celebrated in the center of the village, and then treated the villagers to a gallon of vodka, which he thought was the thing to do. Oh, those horrible gallons of vodka! One day a fat landowner hauls the peasants up before the rural police officer for trespassing, and the next, to mark a feast day, treats them to a gallon of vodka, and they drink and shout 'Hurrah' and when they are drunk bow down at his feet. A higher standard of living, overeating and idleness develop the most insolent self-conceit in a Russian. Nikolay Ivanych, who when he was a petty official was afraid to have opinions of his own even if he kept them to himself, now uttered nothing but incontrovertible truths and did so in the tone of a minister of state: 'Education is necessary, but the masses are not ready for it; corporal punishment is generally harmful, but in some cases it is useful and nothing else will serve.'

" 'I know the common people, and I know how to deal with them,' he would say. 'They love me. I only have to raise my little finger, and they will do anything I want.'

35   "And all this, mark you, would be said with a smile that bespoke kindness and intelligence. Twenty times over he repeated: 'We, of the gentry,' 'I, as a member of the gentry.' Apparently he no longer remembered that our grandfather had been a peasant and our father just a private. Even our surname, 'Chimsha-Himalaisky,' which in reality is grotesque, seemed to him sonorous, distinguished, and delightful.

"But I am concerned now not with him, but with me. I want to tell you about the change that took place in me during the few hours that I spent on his estate. In the evening when we were having tea, the cook served a plateful of gooseberries. They were not bought, they were his own gooseberries, the first ones picked since the bushes were planted. My brother gave a laugh and for a minute looked at the gooseberries in silence, with tears in his eyes—he could not speak for excitement. Then he put one berry in his mouth, glanced at me with the triumph of a child who has at last been given a toy he was longing for and said: 'How tasty!' And he ate the gooseberries greedily, and kept repeating: 'Ah, how delicious! Do taste them!'

"They were hard and sour, but as Pushkin has it,

> The falsehood that exalts we cherish more
> Than meaner truths that are a thousand strong.

I saw a happy man, one whose cherished dream had so obviously come true, who had attained his goal in life, who had got what he wanted, who was satisfied with his lot and with himself. For some reason an element of sadness had always mingled with my thoughts of human happiness, and now at the sight of a happy man I was assailed by an oppressive feeling bordering on despair. It weighed on me particularly at night. A bed was made up for me in a room next to my brother's bedroom, and I could hear that he was wakeful, and that he would get up again and again, go to the plate of gooseberries and eat one after another. I said to myself: how many contented, happy people there really are! What an overwhelming force they are! Look at life: the insolence and idleness of the strong, the ignorance and brutishness of the weak, horrible poverty everywhere, overcrowding, degeneration, drunkenness, hypocrisy, lying— Yet in all the houses and on all the streets there is peace and quiet; of the fifty thousand people who live in our town there is not one who would cry out, who would vent his indignation aloud. We see the people who go to market, eat by day, sleep by night, who babble nonsense, marry, grow old, good-naturedly drag their dead to the cemetery, but we do not see or hear those who suffer, and what is terrible in life goes on somewhere behind the scenes. Everything is peaceful and quiet and only mute statistics protest: so many people gone out of their minds, so many gallons of vodka drunk, so many children dead from malnutrition— And such a state of things is evidently necessary; obviously the happy man is at ease only because the unhappy ones bear their burdens in silence, and if there were not this silence, happiness would be impossible. It is a general hypnosis. Behind the door of every contented, happy man there ought to be someone standing with a little hammer and continually reminding him with a knock that there are unhappy people, that however happy he may be, life will sooner or later show him its claws, and trouble will come to him—illness, poverty, losses, and then no one will see or hear him, just as now he neither sees nor hears others. But there is no man with a hammer. The happy man lives at his ease, faintly fluttered by small daily cares, like an aspen in the wind—and all is well."

"That night I came to understand that I too had been contented and happy," Ivan Ivanych continued, getting up. "I too over the dinner table or out hunting would hold forth on how to live, what to believe, the right way to govern the people. I too would say that learning was the enemy of darkness, that education was necessary but that for the common people the three R's were sufficient for the time being. Freedom is a boon, I used to say, it is as essential as air, but we must wait awhile. Yes, that's what I used to say, and now I ask: Why must we wait?" said Ivan Ivanych, looking wrathfully at Burkin. "Why must we wait, I ask you? For what reason? I am told that nothing can be done all at once, that every idea is realized gradually, in its own time. But who is it that says so? Where is the proof that it is just? You cite the natural order of things, the law governing all phenomena, but is there law, is there order in the fact that I, a living, thinking man, stand beside a ditch and wait for it to close up of itself or fill up with silt, when I could jump over it or throw a bridge across it? And again, why must we wait? Wait, until we have no strength to live, and yet we have to live and are eager to live!

"I left my brother's place early in the morning, and ever since then it has become intolerable for me to stay in town. I am oppressed by the peace and the quiet, I am afraid to look at the windows, for there is nothing that pains me more than the spectacle of a happy family sitting at table having tea. I am an old man now and unfit for combat, I am not even capable of hating. I can only grieve inwardly, get irritated, worked up, and at night my head is ablaze with the rush of ideas and I cannot sleep. Oh, if I were young!"

40   Ivan Ivanych paced up and down the room excitedly and repeated, "If I were young!"

He suddenly walked up to Alyohin and began to press now one of his hands, now the other.

"Pavel Konstantinych," he said imploringly, "don't quiet down, don't let yourself be lulled to sleep! As long as you are young, strong, alert, do not cease to do good! There is no happiness and there should be none, and if life has a meaning and a purpose, that meaning and purpose is not our happiness but something greater and more rational. Do good!"

All this Ivan Ivanych said with a pitiful, imploring smile, as though he were asking a personal favor.

Afterwards all three of them sat in armchairs in different corners of the drawing room and were silent. Ivan Ivanych's story satisfied neither Burkin nor Alyohin. With the ladies and generals looking down from the golden frames, seeming alive in the dim light, it was tedious to listen to the story of the poor devil of a clerk who ate gooseberries. One felt like talking about elegant people, about women. And the fact that they were sitting in a drawing room where everything—the chandelier under its cover, the armchairs, the carpets underfoot—testified that the very people who were now looking down from the frames had once moved about here, sat and had tea, and the fact that lovely Pelageya was noiselessly moving about—that was better than any story.

45   Alyohin was very sleepy; he had gotten up early, before three o'clock in the morning, to get some work done, and now he could hardly keep his eyes open, but he was afraid his visitors might tell an interesting story in his absence, and he would not leave. He did not trouble to ask himself if what Ivan Ivanych had just said was intelligent or right. The guests were not talking about groats, or hay, or tar, but about something that had no direct bearing on his life, and he was glad of it and wanted them to go on.

"However, it's bedtime," said Burkin, rising. "Allow me to wish you good night."

Alyohin took leave of his guests and went downstairs to his own quarters, while they remained upstairs. They were installed for the night in a big room in which stood two old wooden beds decorated with carvings and in the corner was an ivory crucifix. The wide cool beds which had been made by the lovely Pelageya gave off a pleasant smell of clean linen.

Ivan Ivanych undressed silently and got into bed.

"Lord forgive us sinners!" he murmured, and drew the bedclothes over his head.

50   His pipe, which lay on the table, smelled strongly of burnt tobacco, and Burkin, who could not sleep for a long time, kept wondering where the unpleasant odor came from.

The rain beat against the window panes all night.

Questions on point of view . . .

1. What point of view do we find in the first paragraph? How long does this last? When does a different point of view take over? In paragraph 9, how does the word *apparently* enforce a point of view? In paragraph 15, can you feel the point of view shifting? Can the story accommodate the change? Why? How? In paragraph 20, how does point of view change? Name the different points of view.

2. Ivan is a judgmental narrator. Do you take his judgments as valid?

3. In paragraphs 26 and 27, Ivan is interrogated. What happens to the point of view? Does this interrogation further the plot?

4. In paragraph 29 Ivan says that he was "met by a fat dog with reddish hair that looked like a pig . . ." and so on. What would the brother's point of view be?

   How much of Chekhov's theme is accomplished by his strategy in writing "Gooseberries" from different points of view?

5. Summarize Chekhov's use of point of view in "Gooseberries." Connect the story's structure with the story's theme or meaning.

. . . and other elements

6. Is the first paragraph's description ironic?

7. Explicate the title.

8. "Once a man is possessed by an idea, there is no doing anything with him." How far will this go as a summary of "Gooseberries"?

9. Does it make sense to speak of "framing" in the plot of this story? How does the story-within-a-story reflect upon the outer story?

10. Before Ivan begins his story, do you know enough of his character to trust him as a storyteller? Do you learn more of his character later? How do you find out about him?

11. In his story, Ivan continually contrasts reality and pretense. Make two columns and see how many contrasts you can find. You could start with "delicious gooseberries" under *Pretense,* and "sour tasting" under *Reality.*

12. Summarize Ivan's opinion of happiness. Are you inclined to accept his ideas? Are you inclined to skepticism? Why?

13. Discuss smells in this story. Does Ivan's pipe stand in for anything else? Does the rain?

Chapter 8 **Style and Tone**

Literary **style** means at least three different things. We speak of a writer's personal style as a particular way of putting things. Some writers are more distinctive than others—more individual or more identifiable—without necessarily being better writers. Some writers, good and bad, show a style as distinctive as a fingerprint, the result of diction, syntax, rhythm, imagery, and metaphor. But we also speak of style as belonging to a period, like Elizabethan style—a set of characteristics peculiar to a historical era. In yet another sense, *style* is a word of praise, and a stylist is a writer we honor for meticulous care.

We can begin by identifying distinctive voices. Here is the beginning of a short story by Ernest Hemingway:

> In the fall the war was always there, but we did not go to it any more. It was cold in the fall in Milan and the dark came very early. Then the electric lights came on, and it was pleasant along the streets looking in the windows. There was much game hanging outside the shops, and the snow powdered in the fur of the foxes and the wind blew their tails. The deer hung stiff and heavy and empty, and small birds blew in the wind and the wind turned their feathers.

This distinctive style announces itself as Ernest Hemingway's—with its short sentences, its simplicity of grammar and diction, and its scarcity of adjectives. Here is the very different style of William Faulkner:

> It had not coiled yet and the buzzer had not sounded either, only one thick rapid contraction, one loop cast sideways as though merely for purchase from which the raised head might start slightly backward, not in fright either, not in threat quite

yet, more than six feet of it, the head raised higher than his knee and less than his knee's length away, and old, the once-bright markings of its youth dulled now to a monotone concordant too with the wilderness it crawled and lurked: the old one, the ancient and accursed about the earth, fatal and solitary and he could smell it now: the thin sick smell of rotting cucumbers and something else which had no name, evocative of all knowledge and an old weariness and of pariah-hood and of death.

Notice the long and complicated sentences, the abundance of clauses and modifiers. Notice how different are the distinctive styles of Hemingway and Faulkner, writers who flourished in the same decades. For style of the same period, less distinctive but used with equal skill, see Katherine Anne Porter, for instance.

Both a distinctive style and an excellent but general period style will contrast with unskilled writing. Good style connects right word to right word to make the right sentence. Bad style either uses the wrong word ("In the fall the fights were still there . . .") or the wrong level of diction for its subject matter ("In the autumn of the year the hostilities continued to ensue . . ."). **Diction** refers to the writer's choice of an individual word: war, fights, hostilities. Diction characterizes the speaker. In Peter Taylor's "A Spinster's Tale," when the protagonist speaks of her scaredness instead of her fear, a word choice helps fix her youth and naïveté without the author's statement of age. **Syntax** is grammar or sentence structure, and is as characteristic of style as word-choice is. Where Hemingway uses short words in short sentences, or makes long compound sentences by saying *and,* Faulkner writes sentences elongated with dependent clauses.

Using both syntax and diction, Eudora Welty characterizes Phoenix by her style in "A Worn Path" when she says to herself "Seems like there is chains about my feet . . ." Tillie Olsen's unnamed protagonist says to herself "She blew shining bubbles of sound." Their different speech styles—embodied in diction, syntax, idiom, and metaphor—help establish their characters. Stream of consciousness, like monologue, can also capture a character for us. Third-person narration often characterizes even if it does not report thoughts. When Joyce wrote "Just as they were naming their poisons . . . ," he characterized not only Farrington but also the whole ambience of Farrington's bar-culture. The grandmother in Flannery O'Connor's "A Good Man Is Hard to Find" speaks clichés of speech and thought that indicate her petty manipulations and little dishonesties. Even her cat's name—Pitty Sing—helps to indicate character by its baby-talk cuteness; the difference between "Pretty Thing" and "Pitty Sing" is style.

It is style that creates **tone**. Tone is the value that style or gesture gives to words. We can say almost anything, in spoken language, and hang varying tones on it by intonation or gesture. If two of us are eating together, one can say "Please pass the salt" so that it is ironic, tender, sarcastic, loving, angry, bored, depressed, joyous, or indifferent. Tone, then, has no simple relation to content. You can imagine a scene—with eye contact, gesture, and context—in which "I hate you" translates as "I love you" or "I love you" as "I hate you."

One can speak in an ironic tone, which calls attention to incongruity by saying words that indicate one thing and reveal another. One can exaggerate irony to the point of sarcasm—another word describing tone. One's tone can be genteel; when a character speaks of someone as wealthy, avoiding the word *rich* because it seems vulgar, that character's tone is genteel. The same genteel character is apt to say that he builds a new home rather than a house, because the word *home* has a comfy tone to it. Both *house* and *home* may denote the same wooden frame or brick structure, but the connotations or associations of the two words differ. We speak of words as having **denotations** or dictionary meanings, by which *rich* and *wealthy* are synonyms. But a good writer, careful of style, uses **connotations** or associations to characterize; connotations are like gestures of social tone: someone using the word *wealthy* wishes to sound genteel; someone saying *rich* is plain-spoken.

When we read good fiction, we understand the tone by the author's manipulation of language, which is why we speak of tone in connection with style. An unskilled author might use an adverb ("He said, sarcastically") but the best writers seldom need such obvious signposts. We understand the tone, as it were, by gesture—but it is a gesture the author makes in words. When Peter Taylor's spinster says of spring that it "had seemed to crowd itself through the windows . . ." we understand by her style that she is reticent, fearful of energy outside herself; her choice of metaphors tells us. Metaphors indicate a character's feelings, ideas, and background. A happy farmer may feel like the cow let out of the barn after winter; a consumer character may feel as if he had free run of Tiffany's.

Style can convey an author's judgment of a character. Instead of saying "For Miss Simmons was vain and silly, unable to tell the difference between . . ." the author can make Miss Simmons reveal her vanity and silliness in the style and tone of her speech.

John Updike
Ace in the Hole

John Updike (1932–   ) grew up in Pennsylvania, attended Harvard and Oxford, and worked for a while at *The New Yorker,* where his stories and poems first appeared. He writes articles and reviews, stories and poems, and he is best known as a novelist. Some of his many novels are *Rabbit Run* (1960), *The Centaur* (1963), *Couples* (1968), *Rabbit Redux* (1971), and *The Coup* (1978). Updike's fiction is detailed, observant, and exactly constructed. "Ace in the Hole" comes from his earliest collection of stories, *The Same Door* (1959), and gives us an early version of the character Updike developed under another name in *Rabbit Run* and *Rabbit Redux.*

No sooner did his car touch the boulevard heading home than Ace flicked on the radio. He needed the radio, especially today. In the seconds before the tubes warmed up, he said aloud, doing it just to hear a human voice, "Jesus. She'll pop her lid." His voice, though familiar, irked him; it sounded thin and scratchy, as if the bones in his head were picking up static. In a deeper register Ace added,

"She'll murder me." Then the radio came on, warm and strong, so he stopped worrying. The Five Kings were doing "Blueberry Hill"; to hear them made Ace feel so sure inside that from the pack pinched between the car roof and the sun shield he plucked a cigarette, hung it on his lower lip, snapped a match across the rusty place on the dash, held the flame in the instinctive spot near the tip of his nose, dragged, and blew out the match, all in time to the music. He rolled down the window and snapped the match so it spun end-over-end into the gutter. "Two points," he said, and cocked the cigarette toward the roof of the car, sucked powerfully, and exhaled two plumes through his nostrils. He was beginning to feel like himself, Ace Anderson, for the first time that whole day, a bad day. He beat time on the accelerator. The car jerked crazily. "On Blueberry Hill," he sang, "my heart stood still. The wind in the wil-low tree"—he braked for a red light—"played love's suh-*weet* melodee—"

"Go, Dad, bust your lungs!" a kid's voice blared. The kid was riding in a '52 Pontiac that had pulled up beside Ace at the light. The profile of the driver, another kid, was dark over his shoulder.

Ace looked over at him and smiled slowly, just letting one side of his mouth lift a little. "Shove it," he said, good-naturedly, across the little gap of years that separated them. He knew how they felt, young and mean and shy.

But the kid, who looked Greek, lifted his thick upper lip and spat out the window. The spit gleamed on the asphalt like a half-dollar.

5   "Now isn't that pretty?" Ace said, keeping one eye on the light. "You miserable wop. You are *mis*erable." While the kid was trying to think of some smart comeback, the light changed. Ace dug out so hard he smelled burned rubber. In his rear-view mirror he saw the Pontiac lurch forward a few yards, then stop dead, right in the middle of the intersection.

The idea of them stalling their fat tin Pontiac kept him in a good humor all the way home. He decided to stop at his mother's place and pick up the baby, instead of waiting for Evey to do it. His mother must have seen him drive up. She came out on the porch holding a plastic spoon and smelling of cake.

"You're out early," she told him.

"Friedman fired me," Ace told her.

"Good for you," his mother said. "I always said he never treated you right." She brought a cigarette out of her apron pocket and tucked it deep into one corner of her mouth, the way she did when something pleased her.

10   Ace lighted it for her. "Friedman was O.K. personally," he said. "He just wanted too much for his money. I didn't mind working Saturdays, but until eleven, twelve Friday nights was too much. Everybody has a right to some leisure."

"Well, I don't dare think what Evey will say, but I, for one, thank dear God you had the brains to get out of it. I always said that job had no future to it—no future of any kind, Freddy."

"I guess," Ace admitted. "But I wanted to keep at it, for the family's sake."

"Now, I know I shouldn't be saying this, but any time Evey—this is just between us—any time Evey thinks she can do better, there's room for you *and* Bonnie right in your father's house." She pinched her lips together. He could almost hear the old lady think, *There, I've said it.*

"Look, Mom, Evey tries awfully hard, and anyway you know she can't work that way. Not that *that*—I mean, she's a realist, too . . ." He let the rest of the thought fade as he watched a kid across the street dribbling a basketball around a telephone pole that had a backboard and net nailed on it.

15   "Evey's a wonderful girl of her own kind. But I've always said, and your father agrees, Roman Catholics ought to marry among themselves. Now I know I've said it before, but when they get out in the greater world—"

"*No,* Mom."

She frowned, smoothed herself, and said, "Your name was in the paper today."

Ace chose to let that go by. He kept watching the kid with the basketball. It was funny how, though the whole point was to get the ball up into the air, kids grabbed it by the sides and squeezed. Kids just didn't think.

"Did you hear?" his mother asked.

20   "Sure, but so what?" Ace said. His mother's lower lip was coming at him, so he changed the subject. "I guess I'll take Bonnie."

His mother went into the house and brought back his daughter, wrapped in a blue blanket. The baby looked dopey. "She fussed all day," his mother complained. "I said to your father, 'Bonnie is a dear little girl, but without a doubt she's her mother's daughter.' You were the best-natured boy."

"Well I *had* everything." Ace said with an impatience that made his mother blink. He nicely dropped his cigarette into a brown flowerpot on the edge of the porch and took his daughter into his arms. She was getting heavier, solid. When he reached the end of the cement walk, his mother was still on the porch, waving to him. He was so close he could see the fat around her elbow jiggle, and he only lived a half block up the street, yet here she was, waving to him as if he was going to Japan.

At the door of his car, it seemed stupid to him to drive the measly half block home. His old coach, Bob Behn, used to say never to ride where you could walk. Cars were the death of legs. Ace left the ignition keys in his pocket and ran along the pavement with Bonnie laughing and bouncing at his chest. He slammed the door of his landlady's house open and shut, pounded up the two flights of stairs, and was panting so hard when he reached the door of his apartment that it took him a couple of seconds to fit the key into the lock.

The run must have tuned Bonnie up. As soon as he lowered her into the crib, she began to shout and wave her arms. He didn't want to play with her. He tossed some blocks and a rattle into the crib and walked into the bathroom, where he turned on the hot water and began to comb his hair. Holding the comb under the faucet before every stroke, he combed his hair forward. It was so long, one strand curled under his nose and touched his lips. He whipped the whole mass back with a single pull. He tucked in the tufts around his ears, and ran the comb straight back on both sides of his head. With his fingers he felt for the little ridge at the back where the two sides met. It was there, as it should have been. Finally, he mussed the hair in front enough for one little lock to droop over his forehead, like Alan Ladd. It made the temple seem lower than it was. Every day, his hairline looked higher. He had observed all around him how blond men went bald first. He remembered reading somewhere, though, that baldness shows virility.

25   On his way to the kitchen he flipped the left-hand knob of the television. Bonnie was always quieter with the set on. Ace didn't see how she could understand much of it, but it seemed to mean something to her. He found a can of beer in the refrigerator behind some brownish lettuce and those hot dogs Evey never got around to cooking. She'd be home any time. The clock said 5:12. She'd pop her lid.

Ace didn't see what he could do but try and reason with her. "Evey," he'd say, "you ought to thank God I got out of it. It had no future to it at all." He hoped she wouldn't get too mad, because when she was mad he wondered if he should have married her, and doubting that made him feel crowded. It was bad enough, his mother always crowding him. He punched the two triangles in the top of the beer can, the little triangle first, and then the big one, the one he drank from. He hoped Evey wouldn't say anything that couldn't be forgotten. What women didn't seem to realize was that there were things you knew but shouldn't say.

He felt sorry he had called the kid in the car a wop.

Ace balanced the beer on a corner where two rails of the crib met and looked under the chairs for the morning paper. He had trouble finding his name, because it was at the bottom of a column on an inside sports page, in a small article about the county basketball statistics:

> "Dusty" Tremwick, Grosvenor Park's sure-fingered center, copped the individual scoring honors with a season's grand (and we do mean grand) total of 376 points. This is within eighteen points of the all-time record of 394 racked up in the 1949–1950 season by Olinger High's Fred Anderson.

Ace angrily sailed the paper into an armchair. Now it was Fred Anderson; it used to be Ace. He hated being called Fred, especially in print, but then the sportswriters were all office boys anyway, Behn used to say.

30 "Do not just ask for shoe polish," a man on television said, "but ask for *Emu Shoe Gloss,* the *only* polish that absolutely *guarantees* to make your shoes look shinier than new." Ace turned the sound off, so that the man moved his mouth like a fish blowing bubbles. Right away, Bonnie howled, so Ace turned it up loud enough to drown her out and went into the kitchen, without knowing what he wanted there. He wasn't hungry; his stomach was tight. It used to be like that when he walked to the gymnasium alone in the dark before a game and could see the people from town, kids and parents, crowding in at the lighted doors. But once he was inside, the locker room would be bright and hot, and the other guys would be there, laughing it up and towel-slapping, and the tight feeling would leave. Now there were whole days when it didn't leave.

A key scratched at the door lock. Ace decided to stay in the kitchen. Let *her* find *him.* Her heels clicked on the floor for a step or two; then the television set went off. Bonnie began to cry. "Shut up, honey," Evey said. There was a silence.

"I'm home," Ace called.

"No kidding. I thought Bonnie got the beer by herself."

Ace laughed. She was in a sarcastic mood, thinking she was Lauren Bacall. That was all right, just so she kept funny. Still smiling, Ace eased into the living room and got hit with, "What are *you* smirking about? Another question: What's the idea running up the street with Bonnie like she was a football?"

35 "You saw that?"

"Your mother told me."

"You saw her?"

"Of course I saw her. I dropped by to pick up Bonnie. What the hell do you think?—I read her tiny mind?"

"Take it easy," Ace said, wondering if Mom had told her about Friedman.

40 "Take it easy? Don't coach *me.* Another question: Why's the car out in front of her place? You give the car to her?"

"Look, I parked it there to pick up Bonnie, and I thought I'd leave it there."

"Why?"

"Whaddeya mean, why? I just did. I just thought I'd walk. It's not that far, you know."

"No, I don't know. If you'd be on your feet all day a block would look like one hell of a long way."

45   "Okay. I'm sorry."

She hung up her coat and stepped out of her shoes and walked around the room picking up things. She stuck the newspaper in the wastebasket.

Ace said, "My name was in the paper today."

"They spell it right?" She shoved the paper deep into the basket with her foot. There was no doubt; she knew about Friedman.

"They called me Fred."

50   "Isn't that your name? What *is* your name anyway? Hero J. Great?"

There wasn't any answer, so Ace didn't try any. He sat down on the sofa, lighted a cigarette, and waited.

Evey picked up Bonnie. "Poor thing stinks. What does your mother do, scrub out the toilet with her?"

"Can't you take it easy? I know you're tired."

"You should. I'm always tired."

55   Evey and Bonnie went into the bathroom; when they came out, Bonnie was clean and Evey was calm. Evey sat down in an easy chair beside Ace and rested her stocking feet on his knees. "Hit me," she said, twiddling her fingers for the cigarette.

The baby crawled up to her chair and tried to stand, to see what he gave her. Leaning over close to Bonnie's nose, Evey grinned, smoke leaking through her teeth, and said, "Only for grownups, honey."

"Eve," Ace began, "there was no future in that job. Working all Saturday, and then Friday nights on top of it."

"I know. Your mother told *me* all that, too. All I want from you is what happened."

She was going to take it like a sport, then. He tried to remember how it *did* happen. "It wasn't my fault," he said. "Friedman told me to back this '51 Chevy into the line that faces Church Street. He just bought it from an old guy this morning who said it only had thirteen thousand on it. So in I jump and start her up. There was a knock in the engine like a machine gun. I almost told Friedman he'd bought a squirrel, but you know I cut that smart stuff out ever since Palotta laid me off."

60   "You told me that story. What happens in this one?"

"Look, Eve. I *am* telling ya. Do you want me to go out to a movie or something?"

"Suit yourself."

"So I jump in the Chevy and snap it back in line, and there was a kind of scrape and thump. I get out and look and Friedman's running over, his arms going like *this*"—Ace whirled his own arms and laughed—"and here was the whole back fender of a '49 Merc mashed in. Just looked like somebody took a planer and shaved off the bulge, you know, there at the back." He tried to show her with his hands. "The Chevy, though, didn't have a dent. It even gained some paint. But *Friedman,* to hear *him*—Boy, they can rave when their pocketbook's hit. He said"—Ace laughed again—"never mind."

Evey said, "You're proud of yourself."

65   "No, listen. I'm not happy about it. But there wasn't a thing I could *do*. It wasn't

my driving at all. I looked over on the other side, and there was just two or three inches between the Chevvy and a Buick. *Nobody* could have gotten into that hole. Even if it had hair on it." He thought this was pretty good.

She didn't. "You could have looked."

"There just wasn't the *space*. Friedman said stick it in; I stuck it in."

"But you could have looked and moved the other cars to make more room."

"I guess that would have been the smart thing."

70   "I guess, too. Now what?"

"What do you mean?"

"I mean now what? Are you going to give up? Go back to the Army? Your mother? Be a basketball pro? What?"

"You know I'm not tall enough. Anybody under six-six they don't want."

"Is that so? Six-six? Well, please listen to this, Mr. Six-Foot-Five-and-a-Half: I'm fed up. I'm ready as Christ to let you run." She stabbed her cigarette into an ashtray on the arm of the chair so hard the ashtray jumped to the floor. Evey flushed and shut up.

75   What Ace hated most in their arguments was these silences after Evey had said something so ugly she wanted to take it back. "Better ask the priest first," he murmured.

She sat right up. "If there's one thing I don't want to hear about from you it's priests. You let the priests to me. You don't know a damn thing about it. Not a damn thing."

"Hey, look at Bonnie," he said, trying to make a fresh start with his tone.

Evey didn't hear him. "If you think," she went on, "if for one rotten moment you think, Mr. Fred, that the be-all and end-all of my life is you and your hot-shot stunts—"

"Look, Mother," Ace pleaded, pointing at Bonnie. The baby had picked up the ashtray and put it on her head for a hat and was waiting for praise.

80   Evey glanced down sharply at the child. "Cute," she said. "Cute as her daddy."

The ashtray slid from Bonnie's head and she patted where it had been and looked around puzzled.

"Yeah, but watch," Ace said. "Watch her hands. They're really terrific hands."

"You're nuts," Evey said.

"No, honest. Bonnie's great. She's a natural. Get the rattle for her. Never mind, I'll get it." In two steps, Ace was at Bonnie's crib, picking the rattle out of the mess of blocks and plastic rings and beanbags. He extended the rattle toward his daughter, shaking it delicately. Made wary by this burst of attention, Bonnie reached with both hands; like two separate animals they approached from opposite sides and touched the smooth rattle simultaneously. A smile bubbled up on her face. Ace tugged weakly. She held on, and then tugged back. "She's a natural," Ace said, "and it won't do her any good because she's a girl. Baby, we got to have a boy."

85   "I'm not your baby," Evey said, closing her eyes.

Saying "Baby" over and over again, Ace backed up to the radio and, without turning around, switched on the volume knob. In the moment before the tubes warmed up, Evey had time to say, "Wise up, Freddy. What shall we do?"

The radio came in on something slow: dinner music. Ace picked Bonnie up and set her in the crib. "Shall we dance?" he asked his wife, bowing.

"I want to talk."

"Baby. It's the cocktail hour."

90   "This is getting us no place," she said, rising from her chair, though.

"Fred Junior. I can see him now," he said, seeing nothing.

"We will have no Juniors."

In her crib, Bonnie whimpered at the sight of her mother being seized. Ace fitted his hand into the natural place on Evey's back and she shuffled stiffly into his lead. When, with a sudden injection of saxophones, the tempo quickened, he spun her out carefully, keeping the beat with his shoulders. Her hair brushed his lips as she minced in, then swung away, to the end of his arm; he could feel her toes dig into the carpet. He flipped his own hair back from his eyes. The music ate through his skin and mixed with the nerves and small veins; he seemed to be great again, and all the other kids were around them, in a ring, clapping time.

Questions on style . . .

1. There are two verbs in the first sentence. Which of them characterizes Ace? If you substituted *turned* for *flicked,* would you lose anything?
2. Characterize Ace's personal style in both diction and syntax.
3. Looking at the first paragraph alone, list all the details that define Ace's character. How many of these details depend on style?
4. Note the adverb in paragraph 3. Is it an example of too much telling?
5. Discuss the simile in paragraph 4. Whose character does it indicate?
6. When Ace speaks, does he ever sound as if he is quoting something he picked up, say, from a television ad? Look at paragraph 10. Is this a matter of style?
7. How much of Ace's mother's character do you learn from her speech? Her gestures? Ace's interpretations?
8. In paragraph 24, do we see Ace comb his hair as he would describe it? Does Updike's style characterize Ace here?
9. In paragraph 30, does the author's style change when Ace remembers something from the past? Does this change happen again in the story? What does it mean in the story?
10. Discuss Evey's style. What words characterize her tone?

. . . and other elements

11. When do you realize the point of view in the story? What tells you?
12. How much attention does Updike pay to setting?

Ernest Hemingway
In Another Country

Ernest Hemingway (1898–1961) is a great American novelist who began as a poet and short-story writer. Many critics prefer his stories to his novels, even the celebrated *The Sun Also Rises* (1926) and *A Farewell to Arms* (1929). *In Our Time* (1925) alternated short stories with italicized sketches (see page 23). Later novels included *To Have and Have Not* (1937), *For Whom the Bell Tolls* (1940), *Across the River and into the Trees* (1950), *The Old Man and the Sea* (1952), and the posthumous *Islands in the Stream* (1970). During the First World War, Hemingway was an ambulance driver on the Italian front, where he was wounded and hospitalized, an experience presumably behind "In Another Country." Hemingway's individual style colors the world he inhabited: a place of melancholy where codes of behavior protect the hero from madness and dissolution.

In the fall the war was always there, but we did not go to it any more. It was cold in the fall in Milan and the dark came very early. Then the electric lights came on, and it was pleasant along the streets looking in the windows. There was much game hanging outside the shops, and the snow powdered in the fur of the foxes and the wind blew their tails. The deer hung stiff and heavy and empty, and small birds blew in the wind and the wind turned their feathers. It was a cold fall and the wind came down from the mountains.

We were all at the hospital every afternoon, and there were different ways of walking across the town through the dusk to the hospital. Two of the ways were alongside canals, but they were long. Always, though, you crossed a bridge across a canal to enter the hospital. There was a choice of three bridges. On one of them a woman sold roasted chestnuts. It was warm, standing in front of her charcoal fire, and the chestnuts were warm afterward in your pocket. The hospital was very old and very beautiful, and you entered through a gate and walked across a courtyard and out a gate on the other side. There were usually funerals starting from the courtyard. Beyond the old hospital were the new brick pavilions, and there we met every afternoon and were all very polite and interested in what was the matter, and sat in the machines that were to make so much difference.

The doctor came up to the machine where I was sitting and said: "What did you like best to do before the war? Did you practice a sport?"

I said: "Yes, football."

5   "Good," he said. "You will be able to play football again better than ever."

My knee did not bend and the leg dropped straight from the knee to the ankle without a calf, and the machine was to bend the knee and make it move as in riding a tricycle. But it did not bend yet, and instead the machine lurched when it came to the bending part. The doctor said: "That will all pass. You are a fortunate young man. You will play football again like a champion."

In the next machine was a major who had a little hand like a baby's. He winked at me when the doctor examined his hand, which was between two leather straps that bounced up and down and flapped the stiff fingers, and said: "And will I, too, play football, captain-doctor?" He had been a very great fencer, and before the war the greatest fencer in Italy.

The doctor went to his office in a back room and brought a photograph which showed a hand that had been withered almost as small as the major's, before it had taken a machine course, and after was a little larger. The major held the photograph with his good hand and looked at it very carefully. "A wound?" he asked.

"An industrial accident," the doctor said.

"Very interesting, very interesting," the major said, and handed it back to the doctor.

"You have confidence?"

"No," said the major.

There were three boys who came each day who were about the same age I was. They were all three from Milan, and one of them was to be a lawyer, and one was to be a painter, and one had intended to be a soldier, and after we were finished with the machines, sometimes we walked back together to the Café Cova, which was next door to the Scala. We walked the short way through the Communist quarter because we were four together. The people hated us because we were officers, and from a wineshop someone would call out, *"A basso gli ufficiali!"* as we passed. Another boy who walked with us sometimes and made five wore a black silk handkerchief across his face because he had no nose then and his face was to be rebuilt. He had gone out to the front from the military academy and been wounded within an hour after he had gone into the front line for the first time. They rebuilt his face, but he came from a very old family and they could never get the nose exactly right. He went to South America and worked in a bank. But this was a long time ago, and then we did not any of us know how it was going to be afterward. We only knew then that there was always the war, but that we were not going to it any more.

We all had the same medals, except the boy with the black silk bandage across his face, and he had not been at the front long enough to get any medals. The tall boy with a very pale face who was to be a lawyer had been a lieutenant of Arditi and had three medals of the sort we each had only one of. He had lived a very long time with death and was a little detached. We were all a little detached, and there was nothing that held us together except that we met every afternoon at the hospital. Although, as we walked to the Cova through the tough part of town, walking in the dark, with light and singing coming out of the wineshops, and sometimes having to walk into the street when the men and women would crowd together on the sidewalk so that we would have had to jostle them to get by, we felt held together by there being something that had happened that they, the people who disliked us, did not understand.

We ourselves all understood the Cova, where it was rich and warm and not too brightly lighted, and noisy and smoky at certain hours, and there were always girls at the tables and the illustrated papers on a rack on the wall. The girls at the Cova were very patriotic, and I found that the most patriotic people in Italy were the café girls—and I believe they are still patriotic.

The boys at first were very polite about my medals and asked me what I had done to get them. I showed them the papers, which were written in very beautiful language and full of *fratellanza* and *abnegazione,* but which really said, with the adjectives removed, that I had been given the medals because I was an American. After that their manner changed a little toward me, although I was their friend against outsiders. I was a friend, but I was never really one of them after they had read the citations, because it had been different with them and they had done very different things to get their medals. I had been wounded, it was true; but we all knew that being wounded, after all, was really an accident. I was never ashamed of the ribbons, though, and sometimes, after the cocktail hour, I would imagine myself having done all the things they had done to get their medals; but walking home at night through the empty streets with the cold wind and all the shops closed, trying to keep near the streetlights, I knew that I would never have done such things, and I was very much afraid to die, and often lay in bed at night by myself, afraid to die and wondering how I would be when I went back to the front again.

The three with the medals were like hunting-hawks; and I was not a hawk, although I might seem a hawk to those who had never hunted; they, the three, knew better and so we drifted apart. But I stayed good friends with the boy who had been wounded his first day at the front, because he would never know now how he would have turned out; so he could never be accepted either, and I liked him because I thought perhaps he would not have turned out to be a hawk either.

The major, who had been the great fencer, did not believe in bravery and spent much time while we sat in the machines correcting my grammar. He had complimented me on how I spoke Italian, and we talked together very easily. One day I had said that Italian seemed such an easy language to me that I could not take a great interest in it; everything was so easy to say. "Ah, yes," the major said. "Why, then, do you not take up the use of grammar?" So we took up the use of grammar, and soon Italian was such a difficult language that I was afraid to talk to him until I had the grammar straight in my mind.

The major came very regularly to the hospital. I do not think he ever missed a day, although I am sure he did not believe in the machines. There was a time when none of us believed in the machines, and one day the major said it was all nonsense. The machines were new then and it was we who were to prove them. It was an idiotic idea, he said, "a theory, like another." I had not learned my grammar, and he said I was a stupid impossible disgrace, and he was a fool to have bothered with me. He was a small man and he sat straight up in his chair with his right hand thrust into the machine and looked straight ahead at the wall while the straps thumped up and down with his fingers in them.

20   "What will you do when the war is over if it is over?" he asked me. "Speak grammatically!"

"I will go to the States."

"Are you married?"

"No, but I hope to be."

"The more of a fool you are," he said. He seemed very angry. "A man must not marry."

25   "Why, Signor Maggiore?"

"Don't call me 'Signor Maggiore.' "

"Why must not a man marry?"

"He cannot marry. He cannot marry," he said angrily. "If he is to lose everything, he should not place himself in a position to lose that. He should not place himself in a position to lose. He should find things he cannot lose."

He spoke very angrily and bitterly, and looked straight ahead while he talked.

30   "But why should he necessarily lose it?"

"He'll lose it," the major said. He was looking at the wall. Then he looked down at the machine and jerked his little hand out from between the straps and slapped it hard against his thigh. "He'll lose it," he almost shouted. "Don't argue with me!" Then he called to the attendant who ran the machines. "Come and turn this damned thing off."

He went back into the other room for the light treatment and the massage. Then

I heard him ask the doctor if he might use his telephone and he shut the door. When he came back into the room, I was sitting in another machine. He was wearing his cape and had his cap on, and he came directly toward my machine and put his arm on my shoulder.

"I am so sorry," he said, and patted me on the shoulder with his good hand. "I would not be rude. My wife has just died. You must forgive me."

"Oh—" I said, feeling sick for him. "I am so sorry."

He stood there, biting his lower lip. "It is very difficult," he said. "I cannot resign myself."

He looked straight past me and out through the window. Then he began to cry. "I am utterly unable to resign myself," he said and choked. And then crying, his head up looking at nothing, carrying himself straight and soldierly, with tears on both his cheeks and biting his lips, he walked past the machines and out the door.

The doctor told me that the major's wife, who was very young and whom he had not married until he was definitely invalided out of the war, had died of pneumonia. She had been sick only a few days. No one expected her to die. The major did not come to the hospital for three days. Then he came at the usual hour, wearing a black band on the sleeve of his uniform. When he came back, there were large framed photographs around the wall, of all sorts of wounds before and after they had been cured by the machines. In front of the machine the major used were three photographs of hands like his that were completely restored. I do not know where the doctor got them. I always understood we were the first to use the machines. The photographs did not make much difference to the major because he only looked out of the window.

Questions on style . . .

1. Does the first sentence indicate an attitude toward the war? Try rewriting it to give the same information but by style to alter the tone.
2. In the first paragraph, there is no first-person speaker. Do the sentences, however, seem to indicate a single character's feelings? If you have this impression, try to find out how you get it.
3. What is the doctor up to in paragraphs 3 through 6? How do you know?
4. In the last sentence of paragraph 7, Hemingway almost says the same thing twice. What happens in the second half of the sentence to warrant the repetition? What is the effect of this redundancy?
5. Paragraph 13 echoes an earlier sentence. Is this stylistic trait realistic?
6. In paragraph 15 the narrator thinks of patriotism. He does not tell us what he thinks of it. Does the style show you what the narrator thinks of patriotism?
7. The narrator speaks of hawks in paragraph 17. What is he thinking about? How do you know?
8. In paragraph 18 and following, how do you learn about the major's mind and character? How much do you know from the narrator's comments? How much do you know from the objective description and dialogue?
9. How much does Hemingway's way of telling this story contribute to the theme of the story?

. . . and other elements

10. Describe the point of view in this story.

11. How important is setting to this story? How does Hemingway indicate the setting?
12. How do we know what the first-person character thinks? Distinguish between degrees of objective and subjective narration in this story.
13. If the narrator told us his feelings about the wounds he describes, would the story be more effective?
14. In paragraph 13 there is a flash forward in time, the opposite of the usual flashback. What does it do to the plot?
15. Why does the major care about grammar? Do you have the sense that he treats grammar as a symbol of something else?

Chapter 9 **Theme**

The **theme** of a story is the implicit generality the story supports. Often we consider that a story's theme is its reason for being. When we speak of a story's theme, we suggest that a tale implies a central insight into human experience. We express the theme of a story not by summarizing its plot but by a sentence or two of generalization. Thus we might sum up Chekhov's "Gooseberries": people deceive themselves, and their overriding purposes distort their perceptions of reality; we might sum up Joyce's "Counterparts": people when bullied by someone more powerful than themselves express their anger by bullying someone weaker than themselves.

Of course these simple summaries of theme are not adequate to describe great short stories. The story is not a problem to which thematic summary provides an answer. But summaries of plot and of theme can reassure us that we are all reading the same story. Such summaries are always arguable. One of the weaknesses and one of the strengths of literature is that interpretation is never final, always subject to refinement and alteration. But at the same time, one interpretation is *not* as good as another; literature does not resemble clouds in which we can freely imagine shapes. Interpretations will vary, but we must be able to support them by reference to the story. When we compare varying interpretations, they will often both be true and both be limited. By comparing them we can enlarge our response to the story. And it is possible— even commonplace—for interpretations to be wrong. Reading "Counterparts" after a session in sociology, we might feel that its theme connected drunkenness with child abuse. We would be wrong. Reading "Gooseberries" without full attention, we might take Ivan Ivanych's theme—that happiness is nothing, that only altruism is important—as a theme propounded by the author himself. Again we would be wrong. All in all, theme is harder to argue about than technical matters like plot, character, point of view, and setting. But, difficult or not, theme requires our attention because it is a story's reason for being.

Not all stories have themes. When Edgar Allan Poe embarks on "The Murders in the Rue Morgue," the purpose of the story is suspense and mystery. It will not lead to an insight into human character. Generally, stories without themes are inferior art. They can be entertaining, they can be well-written and pleasing, but they lack seriousness. On the other hand, not all stories with themes are serious works of art. Many popular stories develop commonplace or trite themes. Finishing such stories, we say to ourselves, with satisfaction in our wisdom, "How true! It *does* take all kinds to make a world, just as I always said."

There is also the propaganda story, whose theme has designs on us. The author wants to manipulate us into a particular view of the world or into a particular political position. Everyone is familiar with stories about how evil Communists are; in Communist countries, people read the same stories with capitalist villains. Themes and meanings are clear and sharp: hate the wicked ———— and love the noble ————. But in a political propaganda story (or a didactic tale in the *Sunday School Weekly,* for that matter) we find no subtle characterization, no overview, no genuine insight. Propaganda characters have the simple-mindedness we associate with comic books, whether the cause be good (ours) or bad (theirs). When you read a propaganda story, be wary of approving the fiction just because you agree with the politics. Don't swallow bad art for the sake of worthy ideas.

Looking for themes

It helps, when we investigate stories for their themes, to keep several matters in mind:

1. In looking for a theme, pay attention to the story's title. It may help, as it does in "Counterparts." In "Gooseberries," the title helps as long as we already have some notion of the theme; most of us have our own gooseberries. In "A Good Man Is Hard to Find," the title's irony leads us toward the theme. In "A Spinster's Tale," the title points toward a generalization; like many titles it works as a hint.

2. Remember to state a theme as a complete sentence. "Old people" is not a theme; it's a topic. "Old people continually find the young neglectful" could be a theme.

3. Remember to state a theme as a generalization. "Farrington is bullied, gets drunk, and beats his son" is a plot summary, not a theme.

4. If in the course of a story you come to understand a character, or a character comes to understand herself or himself, the discovery probably suggests the story's theme. Joyce constructed his stories to contain **epiphanies**, sudden moments of revelation—either to character or to reader or to both. In

"Counterparts," the epiphany occurs to us as readers when we understand the title, which leads us to the theme.

5. When you write down the generality that is the theme, double-check: does it encompass all the major events of the story? If it doesn't, the theme is probably incomplete. Does anything in the story contradict the generality? If anything does, start over again. Do you find your generality in the story, or do you bring to the story some expectation from outside?

6. If you are baffled in finding the theme of a story, reread it one more time, paying special attention to those parts of the story that seem not to make sense or seem irrelevant or seem odd. If, for instance, at the end of "The Spinster's Tale," her dream of a drunk horse puzzles you, you are missing some of the theme.

Katherine Anne Porter
Rope

Katherine Anne Porter (1890–1980) was novelist, essayist, and short-story writer. She grew up in Texas, an independent young woman determined to write. She worked for newspapers, traveled widely, lived in Europe and Mexico, and did not publish a volume until she collected short stories into *Flowering Judas* (1930). Further collections are *Pale Horse, Pale Rider* (1939) and *The Leaning Tower* (1944), followed by her only novel, *Ship of Fools* (1962). Her *Collected Essays* and *Collected Stories* are available in paperback.

On the third day after they moved to the country he came walking back from the village carrying a basket of groceries and a twenty-four-yard coil of rope. She came out to meet him, wiping her hands on her green smock. Her hair was tumbled, her nose was scarlet with sunburn; he told her that already she looked like a born country woman. His gray flannel shirt stuck to him, his heavy shoes were dusty. She assured him he looked like a rural character in a play.

Had he brought the coffee? She had been waiting all day long for coffee. They had forgot it when they ordered at the store the first day.

Gosh, no, he hadn't. Lord, now he'd have to go back. Yes, he would if it killed him. He thought, though, he had everything else. She reminded him it was only because he didn't drink coffee himself. If he did he would remember it quick enough. Suppose they ran out of cigarettes? Then she saw the rope. What was that for? Well, he thought it might do to hang clothes on, or something. Naturally she asked him if he thought they were going to run a laundry? They already had a fifty-foot line hanging right before his eyes? Why, hadn't he noticed it, really? It was a blot on the landscape to her.

He thought there were a lot of things a rope might come in handy for. She wanted to know what, for instance. He thought a few seconds, but nothing occurred. They could wait and see, couldn't they? You need all sorts of strange odds and ends around a place in the country. She said, yes, that was so; but she thought just at that time when every penny counted, it seemed funny to buy more rope. That was all. She hadn't meant anything else. She hadn't just seen, not at first, why he felt it was necessary.

5   Well, thunder, he had bought it because he wanted to, and that was all there

was to it. She thought that was reason enough, and couldn't understand why he hadn't said so, at first. Undoubtedly it would be useful, twenty-four yards of rope, there were hundreds of things, she couldn't think of any at the moment, but it would come in. Of course. As he had said, things always did in the country.

But she was a little disappointed about the coffee, and oh, look, look, look at the eggs! Oh, my, they're all running! What had he put on top of them? Hadn't he known eggs mustn't be squeezed? Squeezed, who had squeezed them, he wanted to know. What a silly thing to say. He had simply brought them along in the basket with the other things. If they got broke it was the grocer's fault. He should know better than to put heavy things on top of eggs.

She believed it was the rope. That was the heaviest thing in the pack, she saw him plainly when he came in from the road, the rope was a big package on top of everything. He desired the whole wide world to witness that this was not a fact. He had carried the rope in one hand and the basket in the other, and what was the use of her having eyes if that was the best they could do for her?

Well, anyhow, she could see one thing plain: no eggs for breakfast. They'd have to scramble them now, for supper. It was too damned bad. She had planned to have steak for supper. No ice, meat wouldn't keep. He wanted to know why she couldn't finish breaking the eggs in a bowl and set them in a cool place.

Cool place! if he could find one for her, she'd be glad to set them there. Well, then, it seemed to him they might very well cook the meat at the same time they cooked the eggs and then warm up the meat for tomorrow. The idea simply choked her. Warmed-over meat, when they might as well have had it fresh. Second best and scraps and makeshifts, even to the meat! He rubbed her shoulder a little. It doesn't really matter so much, does it, darling? Sometimes when they were playful, he would rub her shoulder and she would arch and purr. This time she hissed and almost clawed. He was getting ready to say that they could surely manage somehow when she turned on him and said, if he told her they could manage somehow she would certainly slap his face.

He swallowed the words red hot, his face burned. He picked up the rope and started to put it on the top shelf. She would not have it on the top shelf, the jars and tins belonged there; positively she would not have the top shelf cluttered up with a lot of rope. She had borne all the clutter she meant to bear in the flat in town, there was space here at least and she meant to keep things in order.

Well, in that case, he wanted to know what the hammer and nails were doing up there? And why had she put them there when she knew very well he needed that hammer and those nails upstairs to fix the window sashes? She simply slowed down everything and made double work on the place with her insane habit of changing things around and hiding them.

She was sure she begged his pardon, and if she had had any reason to believe he was going to fix the sashes this summer she would have left the hammer and nails right where he put them; in the middle of the bedroom floor where they could step on them in the dark. And now if he didn't clear the whole mess out of there she would throw them down the well.

Oh, all right, all right—could he put them in the closet? Naturally not, there were brooms and mops and dustpans in the closet, and why couldn't he find a place for his rope outside her kitchen? Had he stopped to consider there were seven God-forsaken rooms in the house, and only one kitchen?

He wanted to know what of it? And did she realize she was making a complete fool of herself? And what did she take him for, a three-year-old-idiot? The whole trouble with her was she needed something weaker than she was to heckle and tyrannize over. He wished to God now they had a couple of children she could take it out on. Maybe he'd get some rest.

15   Her face changed at this, she reminded him he had forgot the coffee and had bought a worthless piece of rope. And when she thought of all the things they actually needed to make the place even decently fit to live in, well, she could cry, that was all. She looked so forlorn, so lost and despairing he couldn't believe it was only a piece of rope that was causing all the racket. What *was* the matter, for God's sake?

Oh, would he please hush and go away, and *stay* away, if he could, for five minutes? By all means, yes, he would. He'd stay away indefinitely if she wished. Lord, yes, there was nothing he'd like better than to clear out and never come back. She couldn't for the life of her see what was holding him, then. It was a swell time. Here she was, stuck, miles from a railroad, with a half-empty house on her hands, and not a penny in her pocket, and everything on earth to do; it seemed the God-sent moment for him to get out from under. She was surprised he hadn't stayed in town as it was until she had come out and done the work and got things straightened out. It was his usual trick.

It appeared to him that this was going a little far. Just a touch out of bounds, if she didn't mind his saying so. Why the hell had he stayed in town the summer before? To do a half-dozen extra jobs to get the money he had sent her. That was it. She knew perfectly well they couldn't have done it otherwise. She had agreed with him at the time. And that was the only time so help him he had ever left her to do anything by herself.

Oh, he could tell that to his great-grandmother. She had her notion of what had kept him in town. Considerably more than a notion, if he wanted to know. So, she was going to bring all that up again, was she? Well, she could just think what she pleased. He was tired of explaining. It may have looked funny but he had simply got hooked in, and what could he do? It was impossible to believe that she was going to take it seriously. Yes, yes, she knew how it was with a man: if he was left by himself a minute, some woman was certain to kidnap him. And naturally he couldn't hurt her feelings by refusing!

Well, what was she raving about? Did she forget she had told him those two weeks alone in the country were the happiest she had known for four years? And how long had they been married when she said that? All right, shut up! If she thought that hadn't stuck in his craw.

20   She hadn't meant she was happy because she was away from him. She meant she was happy getting the devilish house nice and ready for him. That was what she had meant, and now look! Bringing up something she had said a year ago simply to justify himself for forgetting her coffee and breaking the eggs and buying a wretched piece of rope they couldn't afford. She really thought it was time to drop the subject, and now she wanted only two things in the world. She wanted him to get that rope from underfoot, and go back to the village and get her coffee, and if he could remember it, he might bring a metal mitt for the skillets, and two more curtain rods, and if there were any rubber gloves in the village, her hands were simply raw, and a bottle of milk of magnesia from the drugstore.

He looked out at the dark blue afternoon sweltering on the slopes, and mopped his forehead and sighed heavily and said, if only she could wait a minute for *anything,* he was going back. He had said so, hadn't he, the very instant they found he had overlooked it?

Oh, yes, well . . . run along. She was going to wash windows. The country was so beautiful! She doubted they'd have a moment to enjoy it. He meant to go, but he could not until he had said that if she wasn't such a hopeless melancholiac she might see that this was only for a few days. Couldn't she remember anything pleasant about the other summers? Hadn't they ever had any fun? She hadn't time to talk about it, and now would he please not leave that rope lying around for her to trip on? He picked it up, somehow it had toppled off the table, and walked out with it under his arm.

Was he going this minute? He certainly was. She thought so. Sometimes it seemed to her he had second sight about the precisely perfect moment to leave her ditched. She had meant to put the mattresses out to sun, if they put them out this minute they would get at least three hours, he must have heard her say that morning she meant to put them out. So of course he would walk off and leave her to it. She supposed he thought the exercise would do her good.

Well, he was merely going to get her coffee. A four-mile walk for two pounds of coffee was ridiculous, but he was perfectly willing to do it. The habit was making a wreck of her, but if she wanted to wreck herself there was nothing he could do about it. If he thought it was coffee that was making a wreck of her, she congratulated him: he must have a damned easy conscience.

25 Conscience or no conscience, he didn't see why the mattresses couldn't very well wait until tomorrow. And anyhow, for God's sake, were they living *in* the house, or were they going to let the house ride them to death? She paled at this, her face grew livid about the mouth, she looked quite dangerous, and reminded him that housekeeping was no more her work than it was his: she had other work to do as well, and when did he think she was going to find time to do it at this rate?

Was she going to start on that again? She knew as well as he did that his work brought in the regular money, hers was only occasional, if they depended on what *she* made—and she might as well get straight on this question once for all!

That was positively not the point. The question was, when both of them were working on their own time, was there going to be a division of the housework, or wasn't there? She merely wanted to know, she had to make her plans. Why, he thought that was all arranged. It was understood that he was to help. Hadn't he always, in summers?

Hadn't he, though? Oh, just hadn't he? And when, and where, and doing what? Lord, what an uproarious joke!

It was such a very uproarious joke that her face turned slightly purple, and she screamed with laughter. She laughed so hard she had to sit down, and finally a rush of tears spurted from her eyes and poured down into the lifted corners of her mouth. He dashed towards her and dragged her up to her feet and tried to pour water on her head. The dipper hung by a string on a nail and he broke it loose. Then he tried to pump water with one hand while she struggled in the other. So he gave it up and shook her instead.

30 She wrenched away, crying out for him to take his rope and go to hell, she had simply given him up: and ran. He heard her high-heeled bedroom slippers clattering and stumbling on the stairs.

He went out around the house and into the lane; he suddenly realized he had a blister on his heel and his shirt felt as if it were on fire. Things broke so suddenly you didn't know where you were. She could work herself into a fury about simply nothing. She was terrible, damn it: not an ounce of reason. You might as well talk to a sieve as that woman when she got going. Damned if he'd spend his life humoring her! Well, what to do now? He would take back the rope and exchange it for something else. Things accumulated, things were mountainous, you couldn't move them or sort them out or get rid of them. They just lay and rotted around. He'd take it back. Hell, why should he? He wanted it. What was it anyhow? A piece of rope. Imagine anybody caring more about a piece of rope than about a man's feelings. What earthly right had she to say a word about it? He remembered all the useless, meaningless things she bought for herself: Why? because I wanted it, that's why! He stopped and selected a large stone by the road. He would put the rope behind it. He would put it in the tool-box when he got back. He'd heard enough about it to last him a life-time.

When he came back she was leaning against the post box beside the road waiting. It was pretty late, the smell of broiled steak floated nose high in the cooling air. Her face was young and smooth and fresh-looking. Her unmanageable funny black hair was all on end. She waved to him from a distance, and he speeded up. She called out that supper was ready and waiting, was he starved?

You bet he was starved. Here was the coffee. He waved it at her. She looked at his other hand. What was that he had there?

Well, it was the rope again. He stopped short. He had meant to exchange it but forgot. She wanted to know why he should exchange it, if it was something he really wanted. Wasn't the air sweet now, and wasn't it fine to be here?

35   She walked beside him with one hand hooked into his leather belt. She pulled and jostled him a little as he walked, and leaned against him. He put his arm clear around her and patted her stomach. They exchanged wary smiles. Coffee, coffee for the Ootsum-Wootsums! He felt as if he were bringing her a beautiful present.

He was a love, she firmly believed, and if she had had her coffee in the morning, she wouldn't have behaved so funny. . . . There was a whippoorwill still coming back, imagine, clear out of season, sitting in the crab-apple tree calling all by himself. Maybe his girl stood him up. Maybe she did. She hoped to hear him once more, she loved whippoorwills . . . He knew how she was, didn't he?

Sure, he knew how she was.

Questions on theme

1. State the theme of the story. Remember to make it a whole sentence of generalization, not a plot summary.
2. Does the title "Rope" work like Chekhov's title "Gooseberries"? Does it help define theme? Does the title comment on the story?
3. Does the author present a moral or give us a lesson? What is the story's purpose?

. . . and other elements

4. What is the point of view of this story?
5. This story is almost entirely dialogue without direct quotation. What is the effect?
6. Try putting part of this story into direct quotation. How does it change? Try rewriting a portion of the story as a play, with stage directions. How is it different?
7. Does the first sentence present us with information important to the characters' motives?

8. Are these characters flat or round?
9. How much setting do you have in the story? Would you like to have more?

Richard Wilbur
A Game of Catch

Richard Wilbur (1921–   ) was born in New York, attended Amherst, and fought in Europe during World War II, when he began to write poems. (There are a number of his poems in this text, some with commentary—check the index.) He has translated into English verse three plays by Molière, including *Tartuffe*, which begins on page 905. Richard Wilbur has taught at several universities, has a house in Massachusetts, and winters in Key West.

Monk and Glennie were playing catch on the side lawn of the firehouse when Scho caught sight of them. They were good at it, for seventh-graders, as anyone could see right away. Monk, wearing a catcher's mitt, would lean easily sidewise and back, with one leg lifted and his throwing hand almost down to the grass, and then lob the white ball straight up into the sunlight. Glennie would shield his eyes with his left hand and, just as the ball fell past him, snag it with a little dart of his glove. Then he would burn the ball straight toward Monk, and it would spank into the round mitt and sit, like a still-life apple on a plate, until Monk flipped it over into his right hand and, with a negligent flick of his hanging arm, gave Glennie a fast grounder.

They were going on and on like that, in a kind of slow, mannered, luxurious dance in the sun, their faces perfectly blank and entranced, when Glennie noticed Scho dawdling along the other side of the street and called hello to him. Scho crossed over and stood at the front edge of the lawn, near an apple tree, watching.

"Got your glove?" asked Glennie after a time. Scho obviously hadn't.

"You could give me some easy grounders," said Scho. "But don't burn 'em."

5   "All right," Glennie said. He moved off a little, so the three of them formed a triangle, and they passed the ball around for about five minutes, Monk tossing easy grounders to Scho, Scho throwing to Glennie, and Glennie burning them in to Monk. After a while, Monk began to throw them back to Glennie once or twice before he let Scho have his grounder, and finally Monk gave Scho a fast, bumpy grounder that hopped over his shoulder and went into the brake on the other side of the street.

"Not so hard," called Scho as he ran across to get it.

"You should've had it," Monk shouted.

It took Scho a little while to find the ball among the ferns and dead leaves, and when he saw it, he grabbed it up and threw it toward Glennie. It struck the trunk of the apple tree, bounced back at an angle, and rolled steadily and stupidly onto the cement apron in front of the firehouse, where one of the trucks was parked. Scho ran hard and stopped it just before it rolled under the truck, and this time he carried it back to his former position on the lawn and threw it carefully to Glennie.

"I got an idea," said Glennie. "Why don't Monk and I catch for five minutes more, and then you can borrow one of our gloves?"

10   "That's all right with me," said Monk. He socked his fist into his mitt, and Glennie burned one in.

"All right," Scho said, and went over and sat under the tree. There in the shade he watched them resume their skillful play. They threw lazily fast or lazily slow— high, low, or wide—and always handsomely, their expressions serene, changeless, and forgetful. When Monk missed a low backhand catch, he walked indolently after the ball and, hardly even looking, flung it sidearm for an imaginary put-out. After a good while of this, Scho said, "Isn't it five minutes yet?"

"One minute to go," said Monk with a fraction of a grin.

Scho stood up and watched the ball slap back and forth for several minutes more, and then he turned and pulled himself up into the crotch of the tree.

"Where you going?" Monk asked.

15   "Just up the tree," Scho said.

"I guess he doesn't want to catch," said Monk.

Scho went up and up through the fat light-gray branches until they grew slender and bright and gave under him. He found a place where several supple branches were knit to make a dangerous chair, and sat there with his head coming out of the leaves into the sunlight. He could see the two other boys down below, the ball going back and forth between them as if they were bowling on the grass, and Glennie's crew-cut head looking like a sea urchin.

"I found a wonderful seat up here," Scho said loudly. "If I don't fall out." Monk and Glennie didn't look up or comment, and so he began jouncing gently in his chair of branches and singing. "Yo-ho, heave ho" in an exaggerated way.

"Do you know what, Monk?" he announced in a few moments. "I can make you two guys do anything I want. Catch that ball, Monk! Now you catch it, Glennie!"

20   "I was going to catch it anyway," Monk suddenly said. "You're not making anybody do anything when they're already going to do it anyway."

"I made you say what you just said," Scho replied joyfully.

"No, you didn't," said Monk, still throwing and catching but now less serenely absorbed in the game.

"That's what I wanted you to say," Scho said.

The ball bounced off the rim of Monk's mitt and plowed into a gladiolus bed beside the firehouse, and Monk ran to get it while Scho jounced in his treetop and sang, "I wanted you to miss that. Anything you do is what I wanted you to do."

25   "Let's quit for a minute," Glennie suggested.

"We might as well, until the peanut gallery shuts up," Monk said.

They went over and sat cross-legged in the shade of the tree. Scho looked down between his legs and saw them on the dim, spotty ground, saying nothing to one another. Glennie soon began abstractedly spinning his glove between his palms; Monk pulled his nose and stared out across the lawn.

"I want you to mess around with your nose, Monk," said Scho, giggling. Monk withdrew his hand from his face.

"Do that with your glove, Glennie," Scho persisted. "Monk, I want you to pull up hunks of grass and chew on it."

30   Glennie looked up and saw a self-delighted, intense face staring down at him through the leaves. "Stop being a dope and come down and we'll catch for a few minutes," he said.

Scho hesitated, and then said, in a tentatively mocking voice, "That's what I wanted you to say."

"All right, then, nuts to you," said Glennie.

"Why don't you keep quiet and stop bothering people?" Monk asked.

"I made you say that," Scho replied, softly.

35   "Shut up," Monk said.

"I made you say that, and I want you to be standing there looking sore. And I want you to climb the tree. I'm making you do it!"

Monk was scrambling up through the branches, awkward in his haste, and getting snagged on twigs. His face was furious and foolish, and he kept telling Scho to shut up, shut up, shut up, while the other's exuberant and panicky voice poured down upon his head.

"*Now* you shut up or you'll be sorry," Monk said, breathing hard as he reached up and threatened to shake the cradle of slight branches in which Scho was sitting.

"I *want*—" Scho screamed as he fell. Two lower branches broke his rustling, crackling fall, but he landed on his back with a deep thud and lay still, with a strangled look on his face and his eyes clenched. Glennie knelt down and asked breathlessly, "Are you O.K., Scho? Are you O.K.?," while Monk swung down through the leaves crying that honestly he hadn't even touched him, the crazy guy just let go. Scho doubled up and turned over on his right side, and now both the other boys knelt beside him, pawing at his shoulder and begging to know how he was.

40   Then Scho rolled away from them and sat partly up, still struggling to get his wind but forcing a species of smile onto his face.

"I'm sorry, Scho," Monk said. "I didn't mean to make you fall."

Scho's voice came out weak and gravelly, in gasps. "I meant—you to do it. You—had to. You can't do—anything—unless I want—you to."

Glennie and Monk looked helplessly at him as he sat there, breathing a bit more easily and smiling fixedly, with tears in his eyes. Then they picked up their gloves and the ball, walked over to the street, and went slowly away down the sidewalk, Monk punching his fist into the mitt, Glennie juggling the ball between glove and hand.

From under the apple tree, Scho, still bent over a little for lack of breath, croaked after them in triumph and misery, "I want you to do whatever you're going to do for the whole rest of your life!"

Questions on theme . . .

1. What is the theme of this story? How do you derive it? From action? From character?
2. Wilbur has written a book of poetry for children called *Opposites*. Might he have called this story by the same title?

    Is the title, "A Game of Catch," as ordinary as it sounds? After you think about the theme, does the title mean more than it did at first? Explain.
3. Is it possible that Wilbur agrees with Scho's sense of omnipotence? How do you know he does not?
4. When Monk climbs the tree and the story moves to its climax, Wilbur uses some adverbs that are important to the story. Find them.

. . . and other elements

5. Describe point of view. Does it change to fit the plot?
6. How much characterization can you find in the description of playing catch?
7. How can anybody speak at once "in triumph and misery"?

Chapter 10 **Symbolism**

A symbol is something that remains itself while it stands for something besides itself—the way a piece of red, white, and blue cloth is literally fabric while symbolically it stands for our country. The word *symbol* begins by meaning a sign, like a circle containing a cigarette crossed out by a diagonal line. Everybody knows that this sign is a symbol for NO SMOKING. We speak of **conventional symbols** like these signs, like national flags, or like the logos of sports teams. We also speak of **natural symbols**, which occur in literature but veer toward the cliché: night is a natural symbol of death, and so is autumn. Shakespeare and other geniuses have made great literature using natural symbols; Hallmark makes greeting cards out of them.

In a story a symbol usually stands for or suggests something *more* than it is—for a *class* of events or relationships. In "Gooseberries," the fruit literally grows on Ivan Ivanych's brother's estate. As Ivan Ivanych describes the gooseberries, they become a symbol of how a person's dreams promote self-deceit; as Chekhov manipulates his story, we understand that Ivan Ivanych has "gooseberries" of his own—as most of us do. Chekhov uses gooseberries to stand in for something else; he uses gooseberries as a symbol.

Chekhov's gooseberries make a **literary symbol**, a term that needs defining. Let us begin by saying what a literary symbol is not. It is *not* a type; Farrington is not a symbol of middle-aged Irish drunkards; Farrington is a *type*. He is typical, but he does not stand for anything. A literary symbol signifies something of another class—the way gooseberries stand in for dreaming and deception. Also, a literary symbol is *not* a translation of an abstract idea into a concrete image. This device is **allegory**, not symbolism. In the medieval allegorical play called *Everyman,* the hero of the title has acquaintances called Fellowship, Kindred, Goods, Knowledge, Beauty, and Strength. Summoned by Death, Everyman finds only Good Deeds willing to accompany him to the grave. In "A Worn Path," Phoenix is another character who undertakes a journey, but Phoenix's journey is not allegorical. A good case might be made, however, for taking Phoenix's journey as a symbol of the human ability to endure and survive.

It remains to say what a literary symbol *is*. It is characteristic of the literary symbol, as opposed to the allegorical device, that it is difficult to name what the symbol stands for. If it were not difficult, the author could name it without troubling himself to invent a literary symbol; the French poet Stéphane Mallarmé called the symbol "the new word," suggesting that the writer creates in symbols new concepts previously unexpressed. Perhaps we would call "Gooseberries" a "new word." In the context of his story, Chekhov makes gooseberries *stand* for something. The attempt to *name* the symbol of "Gooseberries" feels awkward and inadequate, but the image of gooseberries remains when we have finished the story, resonant in our memories like a figure from a dream.

When we read a story, certain clues suggest the presence of symbolism; we discover a symbol in a story by its aura of import, its obsessive presence, its inexplicability. Often but not always the presence of fantasy suggests symbolism. Here are two symbolic stories that—unlike "A Worn Path" or "Gooseberries"—are dreamlike and fantastic.

Nathaniel Hawthorne
Young Goodman Brown

Nathaniel Hawthorne (1804–1864) is the first great author of American literature. One of his ancestors was a judge at the Salem witch trials, and Hawthorne throughout his life expressed ambivalence toward his Puritan past. His father was a sea captain who died on a voyage when Nathaniel was four. Growing up in a small town in Maine, he attended Bowdoin College as a classmate of Longfellow and roommate of Franklin Pierce, who became president. After college he began to write, mixing his literary pursuits with various government posts. President Pierce made him American consul at Liverpool in 1853, after which he spent some time in Italy. Next to his novels *The Scarlet Letter* (1848) and *The House of the Seven Gables* (1851), Hawthorne's short stories are his best work.

Young Goodman Brown came forth at sunset into the street at Salem village;[1] but put his head back, after crossing the threshold, to exchange a parting kiss with his young wife. And Faith, as the wife was aptly named, thrust her own pretty head into the street, letting the wind play with the pink ribbons of her cap while she called to Goodman Brown.

"Dearest heart," whispered she, softly and rather sadly, when her lips were close to his ear, "prithee put off your journey until sunrise and sleep in your own bed to-night. A lone woman is troubled with such dreams and such thoughts that

---

[1]In 1692 nineteen people were executed in Salem, Massachusetts, after being convicted of witchcraft.

she's afeared of herself sometimes. Pray tarry with me this night, dear husband, of all nights in the year."

"My love and my Faith," replied young Goodman Brown, "of all nights in the year, this one night must I tarry away from thee. My journey, as thou callest it, forth and back again, must needs be done 'twixt now and sunrise. What, my sweet, pretty wife, dost thou doubt me already, and we but three months married?"

"Then God bless you!" said Faith, with the pink ribbons; "and may you find all well when you come back."

5   "Amen!" cried Goodman Brown. "Say thy prayers, dear Faith, and go to bed at dusk, and no harm will come to thee."

So they parted; and the young man pursued his way until, being about to turn the corner by the meeting-house, he looked back and saw the head of Faith still peeping after him with a melancholy air in spite of her pink ribbons.

"Poor little Faith!" thought he, for his heart smote him. "What a wretch am I to leave her on such an errand! She talks of dreams, too. Methought as she spoke there was trouble in her face, as if a dream had warned her what work is to be done to-night. But no, no; 'twould kill her to think it. Well, she's a blessed angel on earth; and after this one night I'll cling to her skirts and follow her to heaven."

With this excellent resolve for the future, Goodman Brown felt himself justified in making more haste on his present evil purpose. He had taken a dreary road, darkened by all the gloomiest trees of the forest, which barely stood aside to let the narrow path creep through, and closed immediately behind. It was all as lonely as could be; and there is this peculiarity in such a solitude, that the traveller knows not who may be concealed by the innumerable trunks and the thick boughs over-head; so that with lonely footsteps he may yet be passing through an unseen multitude.

"There may be a devilish Indian behind every tree," said Goodman Brown to himself; and he glanced fearfully behind him as he added, "What if the devil himself should be at my very elbow!"

10   His head being turned back, he passed a crook of the road, and, looking forward again, beheld the figure of a man, in grave and decent attire, seated at the foot of an old tree. He arose at Goodman Brown's approach and walked onward side by side with him.

"You are late, Goodman Brown," said he. "The clock of the Old South was striking as I came through Boston, and that is full fifteen minutes agone."

"Faith kept me back a while," replied the young man, with a tremor in his voice, caused by the sudden appearance of his companion, though not wholly unex-pected.

It was now deep dusk in the forest, and deepest in that part of it where these two were journeying. As nearly as could be discerned, the second traveller was about fifty years old, apparently in the same rank of life as Goodman Brown, and bearing a considerable resemblance to him, though perhaps more in expression than features. Still they might have been taken for father and son. And yet, though the elder person was as simply clad as the younger, and as simple in manner too, he had an indescribable air of one who knew the world, and who would not have felt abashed at the governor's dinner table or in King William's court, were it possible that his affairs should call him thither. But the only thing about him that could be fixed upon as remarkable was his staff, which bore the likeness of a great black snake, so curiously wrought that it might almost be seen to twist and wriggle itself like a living serpent. This, of course, must have been an ocular deception, assisted by the uncertain light.

"Come, Goodman Brown," cried his fellow-traveller, "this is a dull place for the beginning of a journey. Take my staff, if you are so soon weary."

15   "Friend," said the other, exchanging his slow pace for a full stop, "having kept covenant by meeting thee here, it is my purpose now to return whence I came. I have scruples touching the matter thou wot'st of."

"Sayest thou so?" replied he of the serpent, smiling apart. "Let us walk on, nevertheless, reasoning as we go; and if I convince thee not thou shalt turn back. We are but a little way in the forest yet."

"Too far! too far!" exclaimed the goodman, unconsciously resuming his walk. "My father never went into the woods on such an errand, nor his father before him. We have been a race of honest men and good Christians since the days of the martyrs; and shall I be the first of the name of Brown that ever took this path and kept—"

"Such company, thou wouldst say," observed the elder person, interpreting his pause. "Well said, Goodman Brown! I have been as well acquainted with your family as with ever a one among the Puritans; and that's no trifle to say. I helped your grandfather, the constable, when he lashed the Quaker woman so smartly through the streets of Salem; and it was I that brought your father a pitch-pine knot, kindled at my own hearth, to set fire to an Indian village, in King Philip's war.[1] They were my good friends, both; and many a pleasant walk have we had along this path, and returned merrily after midnight. I would fain be friends with you for their sake."

"If it be as thou sayest," replied Goodman Brown, "I marvel they never spoke of these matters; or, verily, I marvel not, seeing that the least rumor of the sort would have driven them from New England. We are a people of prayer, and good works to boot, and abide no such wickedness."

20   "Wickedness or not," said the traveller with the twisted staff, "I have a very general acquaintance here in New England. The deacons of many a church have drunk the communion wine with me; the selectmen of divers towns make me their chairman; and a majority of the Great and General Court[2] are firm supporters of my interest. The governor and I, too—But these are state secrets."

"Can this be so?" cried Goodman Brown, with a stare of amazement at his undisturbed companion. "Howbeit, I have nothing to do with the govenor and council; they have their own ways, and are no rule for a simple husbandman like me. But, were I to go on with thee, how should I meet the eye of that good old man, or minister, at Salem village? Oh, his voice would make me tremble both Sabbath day and lecture[3] day."

Thus far the elder traveller had listened with due gravity; but now burst into a fit of irrepressible mirth, shaking himself so violently that his snakelike staff actually seemed to wriggle in sympathy.

"Ha! ha! ha!" shouted he again and again; then composing himself, "Well, go on, Goodman Brown, go on; but, prithee, don't kill me with laughing."

---

[1]The last Indian uprising against the Puritan colonists (1675—1676). King Philip was also known as Metacomet.   [2]The colonial legislature of Massachusetts Colony   [3]A midweek sermon, often delivered on Thursday

"Well, then, to end the matter at once," said Goodman Brown, considerably nettled, "there is my wife, Faith. It would break her dear little heart; and I'd rather break my own."

25 "Nay, if that be the case," answered the other, "e'en go thy ways, Goodman Brown. I would not for twenty old women like the one hobbling before us that Faith should come to any harm."

As he spoke he pointed his staff at a female figure on the path, in whom Goodman Brown recognized a very pious and exemplary dame, who had taught him his catechism in youth, and was still his moral and spiritual adviser, jointly with the minister and Deacon Gookin.

"A marvel, truly, that Goody Cloyse[1] should be so far in the wilderness at night-fall," said he. "But with your leave, friend, I shall take a cut through the woods until we have left this Christian woman behind. Being a stranger to you, she might ask whom I was consorting with and whither I was going."

"Be it so," said his fellow-traveller. "Betake you the woods, and let me keep the path."

Accordingly the young man turned aside, but took care to watch his companion, who advanced softly along the road until he had come within a staff's length of the old dame. She, meanwhile, was making the best of her way, with singular speed for so aged a woman, and mumbling some indistinct words—a prayer, doubtless—as she went. The traveller put forth his staff and touched her withered neck with what seemed the serpent's tail.

30 "The devil!" screamed the pious old lady.

"Then Goody Cloyse knows her old friend?" observed the traveller, confronting her and leaning on his writhing stick.

"Ah, forsooth, and is it your worship indeed?" cried the good dame. "Yea, truly it is, and in the very image of my old gossip,[2] Goodman Brown, the grandfather of the silly fellow that now is. But—would your worship believe it?—my broom-stick hath strangely disappeared, stolen, as I suspect, by that unhanged witch, Goody Cory, and that, too, when I was all anointed with the juice of smallage, and cinquefoil, and wolf's bane—"

"Mingled with fine wheat and the fat of a new-born babe," said the shape of old Goodman Brown.

"Ah, your worship knows the recipe," cried the old lady, cackling aloud. "So, as I was saying, being all ready for the meeting, and no horse to ride on, I made up my mind to foot it; for they tell me there is a nice young man to be taken into communion to-night. But now your good worship will lend me your arm, and we shall be there in a twinkling."

35 "That can hardly be," answered her friend. "I may not spare you my arm, Goody Cloyse; but here is my staff, if you will."

So saying, he threw it down at her feet, where, perhaps, it assumed life, being one of the rods which its owner had formerly lent to the Egyptian magi.[3] Of this fact, however, Goodman Brown could not take cognizance. He had cast up his eyes in astonishment, and, looking down again, beheld neither Goody Cloyse nor the serpentine staff, but his fellow-traveller alone, who waited for him as calmly as if nothing had happened.

---

[1]The real name of a woman condemned in 1692. *Goody* is a contraction of Goodwife, which like Goodman was an epithet for a married person.   [2]Friend   [3]Exodus 7

"That old woman taught me my catechism," said the young man; and there was a world of meaning in this simple comment.

They continued to walk onward, while the elder traveller exhorted his companion to make good speed and persevere in the path, discoursing so aptly that his arguments seemed rather to spring up in the bosom of his auditor than to be suggested by himself. As they went, he plucked a branch of maple to serve for a walking stick, and began to strip it of the twigs and little boughs, which were wet with evening dew. The moment his fingers touched them they became strangely withered and dried up as with a week's sunshine. Thus the pair proceeded, at a good free pace, until suddenly, in a gloomy hollow of the road, Goodman Brown sat himself down on the stump of a tree and refused to go any farther.

"Friend," said he, stubbornly, "my mind is made up. Not another step will I budge on this errand. What if a wretched old woman do choose to go to the devil when I thought she was going to heaven: is that any reason why I should quit my dear Faith and go after her?"

40   "You will think better of this by and by," said his acquaintance, composedly. "Sit here and rest yourself a while; and when you feel like moving again, there is my staff to help you along."

Without more words, he threw his companion the maple stick, and was as speedily out of sight as if he had vanished into the deepening gloom. The young man sat a few moments by the roadside, applauding himself greatly, and thinking with how clear a conscience he should meet the minister in his morning walk, nor shrink from the eye of good old Deacon Gookin. And what calm sleep would be his that very night, which was to have been spent so wickedly, but so purely and sweetly now, in the arms of Faith! Amidst these pleasant and praiseworthy meditations, Goodman Brown heard the tramp of horses along the road, and deemed it advisable to conceal himself within the verge of the forest, conscious of the guilty purpose that had brought him thither, though now so happily turned from it.

On came the hoof tramps and the voices of the riders, two grave old voices, conversing soberly as they drew near. These mingled sounds appeared to pass along the road, within a few yards of the young man's hiding-place; but, owing doubtless to the depth of the gloom at that particular spot, neither the travellers nor their steeds were visible. Though their figures brushed the small boughs by the wayside, it could not be seen that they intercepted, even for a moment, the faint gleam from the strip of bright sky athwart which they must have passed. Goodman Brown alternately crouched and stood on tiptoe, pulling aside the branches and thrusting forth his head as far as he durst without discerning so much as a shadow. It vexed him the more, because he could have sworn, were such a thing possible, that he recognized the voices of the minister and Deacon Gookin, jogging along quietly, as they were wont to do, when bound to some ordination or ecclesiastical council. While yet within hearing, one of the riders stopped to pluck a switch.

"Of the two, reverend sir," said the voice like the deacon's, "I had rather miss an ordination dinner than to-night's meeting. They tell me that some of our community are to be here from Falmouth and beyond, and others from Connecticut and Rhode Island, besides several of the Indian powwows,[1] who, after their fash-

---

[1]Medicine men

ion, know almost as much deviltry as the best of us. Moreover, there is a goodly young woman to be taken into communion."

"Mighty well, Deacon Gookin!" replied the solemn old tones of the minister. "Spur up, or we shall be late. Nothing can be done, you know, until I get on the ground."

45 The hoofs clattered again; and the voices talking so strangely in the empty air, passed on through the forest, where no church had ever been gathered or solitary Christian prayed. Whither, then, could these holy men be journeying so deep into the heathen wilderness? Young Goodman Brown caught hold of a tree for support, being ready to sink down on the ground, faint and overburdened with the heavy sickness of his heart. He looked up to the sky, doubting whether there really was a heaven above him. Yet there was the blue arch, and the stars brightening in it.

"With heaven above and Faith below, I will stand firm against the devil!" cried Goodman Brown.

While he still gazed upward into the deep arch of the firmament and had lifted his hands to pray, a cloud, though no wind was stirring, hurried across the zenith and hid the brightening stars. The blue sky was still visible, except directly over-head, where this black mass of cloud was sweeping swiftly northward. Aloft in the air, as if from the depths of the cloud, came a confused and doubtful sound of voices. Once the listener fancied that he could distinguish the accents of towns-people of his own, men and women, both pious and ungodly, many of whom he had met at the communion table, and had seen others rioting at the tavern. The next moment, so indistinct were the sounds, he doubted whether he had heard aught but the murmur of the old forest, whispering without a wind. Then came a stronger swell of those familiar tones, heard daily in the sunshine at Salem village, but never until now from a cloud of night. There was one voice, of a young woman, uttering lamentations, yet with an uncertain sorrow, and entreating for some favor, which, perhaps, it would grieve her to obtain; and all the unseen multitude, both saints and sinners, seemed to encourage her onward.

"Faith!" shouted Goodman Brown, in a voice of agony and desperation; and the echoes of the forest mocked him, crying, "Faith! Faith!" as if bewildered wretches were seeking her all through the wilderness.

The cry of grief, rage, and terror was yet piercing the night, when the unhappy husband held his breath for a response. There was a scream, drowned immediately in a louder murmur of voices, fading into far-off laughter, as the dark cloud swept away, leaving the clear and silent sky above Goodman Brown. But something fluttered lightly down through the air and caught on the branch of a tree. The young man seized it, and beheld a pink ribbon.

50 "My Faith is gone!" cried he, after one stupefied moment. "There is no good on earth; and sin is but a name. Come, devil; for to thee is this world given."

And, maddened with despair, so that he laughed loud and long, did Goodman Brown grasp his staff and set forth again, at such a rate that he seemed to fly along the forest path rather than to walk or run. The road grew wilder and drearier and more faintly traced, and vanished at length, leaving him in the heart of the dark wilderness, still rushing onward with the instinct that guides mortal man to evil. The whole forest was peopled with frightful sounds—the creaking of the trees, the howling of wild beasts, and the yell of Indians; while sometimes the wind tolled like a distant church bell, and sometimes gave a broad roar around the traveller, as if all Nature were laughing him to scorn. But he was himself the chief horror of the scene, and shrank not from its other horrors.

"Ha! ha! ha!" roared Goodman Brown when the wind laughed at him. "Let us hear which will laugh loudest. Think not to frighten me with your deviltry. Come witch, come wizard, come Indian powwow, come devil himself, and here comes Goodman Brown. You may as well fear him as he fear you."

In truth, all through the haunted forest there could be nothing more frightful than the figure of Goodman Brown. On he flew among the black pines, brandishing his staff with frenzied gestures, now giving vent to an inspiration of horrid blasphemy, and now shouting forth such laughter as set all the echoes of the forest laughing like demons around him. The fiend in his own shape is less hideous than when he rages in the breast of man. Thus sped the demoniac on his course, until, quivering among the trees, he saw a red light before him, as when the felled trunks and branches of a clearing have been set on fire, and throw up their lurid blaze against the sky, at the hour of midnight. He paused, in a lull the of tempest that had driven him onward, and heard the swell of what seemed a hymn, rolling solemnly from a distance with the weight of many voices. He knew the tune; it was a familiar one in the choir of the village meeting-house. The verse died heavily away, and was lengthened by a chorus, not of human voice, but of all the sounds of the benighted wilderness pealing in awful harmony together. Goodman Brown cried out, and his cry was lost to his own ear by its unison with the cry of the desert.

In the interval of silence he stole forward until the light glared full upon his eyes. At one extremity of an open space, hemmed in by the dark wall of the forest, arose a rock, bearing some rude, natural resemblance either to an altar or a pulpit, and surrounded by four blazing pines, their tops aflame, their stems untouched, like candles at an evening meeting. The mass of foliage that had overgrown the summit of the rock was all on fire, blazing high into the night and fitfully illuminating the whole field. Each pendent twig and leafy festoon was in a blaze. As the red light arose and fell, a numerous congregation alternately shone forth, then disappeared in shadow, and again grew, as it were, out of the darkness, peopling the heart of the solitary woods at once.

55 "A grave and dark-clad company," quoth Goodman Brown.

In truth they were such. Among them, quivering to and fro between gloom and splendor, appeared faces that would be seen next day at the council board of the province, and others which, Sabbath after Sabbath, looked devoutly heavenward, and benignantly over the crowded pews, from the holiest pulpits in the land. Some affirm that the lady of the governor was there. At least there were high dames well known to her, and wives of honored husbands, and widows, a great multitude, and ancient maidens, all of excellent repute, and fair young girls, who trembled lest their mothers should espy them. Either the sudden gleams of light flashing over the obscure field bedazzled Goodman Brown, or he recognized a score of the church members of Salem village famous for their especial sanctity. Good old Deacon Gookin had arrived, and waited at the skirts of that venerable saint, his revered pastor. But, irreverently consorting with these grave, reputable, and pious people, these elders of the church, these chaste dames and dewy virgins, there were men of dissolute lives and women of spotted fame, wretches given over to all mean and filthy vice, and suspected even of horrid crimes. It was strange to see that the good shrank not from the wicked, nor were the sinners abashed by the saints. Scattered also among their pale-faced enemies were the Indian priests, or powwows, who had often scared their native forest with more hideous incantations than any known to English witchcraft.

"But where is Faith?" thought Goodman Brown; and, as hope came into his heart, he trembled.

Another verse of the hymn arose, a slow and mournful strain, such as the pious love, but joined to words which expressed all that our nature can conceive of sin, and darkly hinted at far more. Unfathomable to mere mortals is the lore of fiends. Verse after verse was sung; and still the chorus of the desert swelled between like the deepest tone of a mighty organ; and with the final peal of that dreadful anthem there came a sound, as if the roaring wind, the rushing streams, the howling beasts, and every other voice of the unconcerted wilderness were mingling and according with the voice of guilty man in homage to the prince of all. The four blazing pines threw up a loftier flame, and obscurely discovered shapes and visages of horror on the smoke wreaths above the impious assembly. At the same moment the fire on the rock shot redly forth and formed a glowing arch above its base, where now appeared a figure. With reverence be it spoken, the figure bore no slight similitude, both in garb and manner, to some grave divine of the New England churches.

"Bring forth the converts!" cried a voice that echoed through the field and rolled into the forest.

60   At the word, Goodman Brown stepped forth from the shadow of the trees and approached the congregation, with whom he felt a loathful brotherhood by the sympathy of all that was wicked in his heart. He could have well-nigh sworn that the shape of his own dead father beckoned him to advance, looking downward from a smoke wreath, while a woman, with dim features of despair, threw out her hand to warn him back. Was it his mother? But he had no power to retreat one step, nor to resist, even in thought, when the minister and good old Deacon Gookin seized his arms and led him to the blazing rock. Thither came also the slender form of a veiled female, led between Goody Cloyse, that pious teacher of the catechism, and Martha Carrier, who had received the devil's promise to be queen of hell. A rampant hag was she. And there stood the proselytes beneath the canopy of fire.

"Welcome, my children" said the dark figure, "to the communion of your race. Ye have found thus young your nature and your destiny. My children, look behind you!"

They turned; and flashing forth, as it were, in a sheet of flame, the fiend worshippers were seen; the smile of welcome gleamed darkly on every visage.

"There," resumed the sable form, "are all whom ye have reverenced from youth. Ye deemed them holier than yourselves, and shrank from your own sin, contrasting it with their lives of righteousness and prayerful aspirations heavenward. Yet here are they all in my worshipping assembly. This night it shall be granted you to know their secret deeds: how hoary-bearded elders of the church have whispered wanton words to the young maids of their households; how many a woman, eager for widows' weeds, has given her husband a drink at bedtime and let him sleep his last sleep in her bosom; how beardless youths have made haste to inherit their fathers' wealth; and how fair damsels—blush not, sweet ones—have dug little graves in the garden, and bidden me, the sole guest, to an infant's funeral. By the sympathy of your human hearts for sin ye shall scent out all the places—whether in church, bed-chamber, street, field, or forest—where crime has been committed, and shall exult to behold the whole earth one stain of guilt, one mighty blood spot. Far more than this. It shall be yours to penetrate, in every bosom, the deep mystery of sin, the fountain of all wicked arts, and which inexhaustibly supplies more evil impulses than human power—than my power at its utmost—can make manifest in deeds. And now, my children, look upon each other."

They did so; and, by the blaze of the hell-kindled torches, the wretched man beheld his Faith, and the wife her husband, trembling before that unhallowed altar.

65   "Lo, there ye stand, my children," said the figure, in a deep and solemn tone, almost sad with its despairing awfulness, as if his once angelic nature could yet mourn for our miserable race. "Depending upon one another's hearts, ye had still hoped that virtue were not all a dream. Now are ye undeceived. Evil is the nature of mankind. Evil must be your only happiness. Welcome again, my children, to the communion of your race."

"Welcome," repeated the fiend worshippers, in one cry of despair and triumph.

And there they stood, the only pair, as it seemed, who were yet hesitating on the verge of wickedness in this dark world. A basin was hallowed, naturally, in the rock. Did it contain water, reddened by the lurid light! or was it blood? or, perchance, a liquid flame? Herein did the shape of evil dip his hand and prepare to lay the mark of baptism upon their foreheads, that they might be partakers of the mystery of sin, more conscious of the secret guilt of others, both in deed and thought, than they could now be of their own. The husband cast one look at his pale wife, and Faith at him. What polluted wretches would the next glance show them to each other, shuddering alike at what they disclosed and what they saw!

"Faith! Faith!" cried the husband, "look up to heaven, and resist the wicked one."

Whether Faith obeyed he knew not. Hardly had he spoken when he found himself amid calm night and solitude, listening to a roar of the wind which died heavily away through the forest. He staggered against the rock, and felt it chill and damp; while a hanging twig, that had been all on fire, besprinkled his cheek with the coldest dew.

70   The next morning young Goodman Brown came slowly into the street of Salem village, staring around him like a bewildered man. The good old minister was taking a walk along the graveyard to get an appetite for breakfast and meditate his sermon, and bestowed a blessing, as he passed, on Goodman Brown. He shrank from the venerable saint as if to avoid anathema. Old Deacon Gookin was at domestic worship, and the holy words of his prayer were heard through the open window. "What God doth the wizard pray to?" quoth Goodman Brown. Goody Cloyse, that excellent old Christian, stood in the early sunshine at her own lattice, catechizing a little girl who had brought her a pint of morning's milk. Goodman Brown snatched away the child as from the grasp of the fiend himself. Turning the corner by the meeting-house, he spied the head of Faith, with the pink ribbons, gazing anxiously forth, and bursting into such joy at sight of him that she skipped along the street and almost kissed her husband before the whole village. But Goodman Brown looked sternly and sadly into her face, and passed on without a greeting.

Had Goodman Brown fallen asleep in the forest and only dreamed a wild dream of a witch-meeting?

Be it so if you will; but, alas! it was a dream of evil omen for young Goodman Brown. A stern, a sad, a darkly meditative, a distrustful, if not a desperate man did he become from the night of that fearful dream. On the Sabbath day, when the congregation were singing a holy psalm, he could not listen because an anthem of sin rushed loudly upon his ear and drowned all the blessed strain. When the minister spoke from the pulpit with power and fervid eloquence, and, with his hand on the open Bible, of the sacred truths of our religion, and of saint-like lives and triumphant deaths, and of future bliss or misery unutterable, then did Goodman Brown turn pale, dreading lest the roof should thunder down upon the gray blasphemer and his hearers. Often, awaking suddenly at midnight, he shrank from the bosom of Faith; and at morning or eventide, when the family knelt down at prayer, he scowled and muttered to himself, and gazed sternly at his wife, and turned away. And when he had lived long, and was borne to his grave a hoary corpse, followed by Faith, an aged woman, and children and grandchildren, a goodly procession, besides neighbors not a few, they carved no hopeful verse upon his tombstone, for his dying hour was gloom.

Questions on symbolism . . .

1. Is Goodman an allegorical name like Everyman? What sort of a name is Brown? Can names be symbolic? Ironic?
2. Is this tale an allegory? Why?
3. Who is it that Young Goodman Brown meets in the forest? Discuss the staff the man carries. Why does Hawthorne suggest a reasonable explanation for its appearance?
4. Why do Young Goodman Brown and his companion look alike?
5. Is the forest itself a symbol? Is it conventional, natural, traditional, or literary?
6. Does symbolism enhance the theme of this story?

. . . and other elements

7. What is the point of view? Who thinks that Faith is aptly named?
8. What happened before the beginning of this story? How do you know about it?
9. Can you find a motif of reversals in this story? List all the reversals you can find.
10. Was it all a dream? What kind of experience has Young Goodman Brown undergone?

Franz Kafka
A Hunger Artist

Translated by Edwin and Willa Muir

Franz Kafka (1883–1924) made fantastic and symbolic fictions. In "The Metamorphosis" the hero is transformed into a gigantic insect. His *Amerika* (1927) is a symbolic country, and *The Castle* (1926) is a symbolic structure. Kafka was an insurance clerk who published little in his lifetime and who, when he died of tuberculosis, requested that his manuscripts be burned. Fortunately for us his best friend ignored his request.

During these last decades the interest in professional fasting has markedly diminished. It used to pay very well to stage such great performances under one's own management, but today that is quite impossible. We live in a different world now. At one time the whole town took a lively interest in the hunger artist; from day to day of his fast the excitement mounted; everybody wanted to see him at least once a day; there were people who bought season tickets for the last few days and sat from morning till night in front of his small barred cage; even in the nighttime there were visiting hours, when the whole effect was heightened by torch flares; on fine days the cage was sent out in the open air, and then it was the children's special treat to see the hunger artist; for their elders he was often just a joke that happened to be in fashion, but the children stood open-mouthed, holding each other's hands for greater security, marveling at him as he sat there pallid in black tights, with his ribs sticking out so prominently, not even on a seat but down among straw on the ground, sometimes giving a courteous nod, answering questions with a constrained smile, or perhaps stretching an arm through the bars so that one might feel how thin it was, and then again withdrawing deep into himself, paying no attention to anyone or anything, not even to the all-important striking of the clock that was the only piece of furniture in his cage, but merely staring into vacancy with half-shut eyes, now and then taking a sip from a tiny glass of water to moisten his lips.

Besides casual onlookers there were also relays of permanent watchers selected by the public, usually butchers, strangely enough, and it was their task to watch the hunger artist day and night, three of them at a time, in case he should have some secret recourse to nourishment. This was nothing but a formality, instituted to reassure the masses, for the initiates knew well enough that during his fast the artist would never in any circumstances, not even under forcible compulsion, swallow the smallest morsel of food; the honor of his profession forbade it. Not every watcher, of course, was capable of understanding this, there were often groups of night watchers who were very lax in carrying out their duties and deliberately huddled together in a retired corner to play cards with great absorption, obviously intending to give the hunger artist the chance of a little refreshment, which they supposed he could draw from some private hoard. Nothing annoyed the artist more than such watchers; they made him miserable; they made his fast seem unendurable; sometimes he mastered his feebleness sufficiently to sing during their watch for as long as he could keep going, to show them how unjust their suspicions were. But that was of little use; they only wondered at his cleverness in being able to fill his mouth even while singing. Much more to his taste were the watchers who sat close up to the bars, who were not content with the dim night lighting of the hall but focused him in the full glare of the electric pocket torch given them by the impresario. The harsh light did not trouble him at all. In any case he could never sleep properly, and he could always drowse a little, whatever the light, at any hour, even when the hall was thronged with noisy onlookers. He was quite happy at the prospect of spending a sleepless night with such watchers; he was ready to exchange jokes with them, to tell them stories out of his nomadic life, anything at all to keep them awake and demonstrate to them again that he had no eatables in his cage and that he was fasting as not one of them could fast. But his happiest moment was when the morning came and an enormous breakfast was brought them, at his expense, on which they flung themselves with the keen appetite of healthy men after a weary night of wakefulness. Of course there were people who argued that this breakfast was an unfair attempt to bribe the watchers, but that was going rather too far, and when they were invited to take on a night's vigil without a breakfast, merely for the sake of the cause, they made themselves scarce, although they stuck stubbornly to their suspicions.

Such suspicions, anyhow, were a necessary accompaniment to the profession of fasting. No one could possibly watch the hunger artist continuously, day and night, and so no one could produce first-hand evidence that the fast had really been rigorous and continuous; only the artist himself could know that; he was therefore bound to be the sole completely satisfied spectator of his own fast. Yet for other reasons he was never satisfied; it was not perhaps mere fasting that had brought him to such skeleton thinness that many people had regretfully to keep away from his exhibitions, because the sight of him was too much for them, perhaps it was dissatisfaction with himself that had worn him down. For he alone knew, what no other initiate knew, how easy it was to fast. It was the easiest thing in the world. He made no secret of this, yet people did not believe him; at the best they set him down as modest, most of them, however, thought he was out for publicity or else was some kind of cheat who found it easy to fast because he had discovered a way of making it easy, and then had the impudence to admit the fact, more or less. He had to put up with all that, and in the course of time had got used to it, but his inner dissatisfaction always rankled, and never yet, after any term of fasting—this must be granted to his credit—had he left the cage of his own free will. The longest period of fasting was fixed by his impresario at forty days, beyond that term he was not allowed to go, not even in great cities, and there was good reason for it, too. Experience had proved that for about forty days the interest of the public could be stimulated by a steadily increasing pressure of advertisement, but after that the town began to lose interest, sympathetic support began notably to fall off; there were of course local variations as between one town and another or one country and another, but as a general rule forty days marked the limit. So on the fortieth day the flower-bedecked cage was opened, enthusiastic spectators filled the hall, a military band played, two doctors entered the cage to measure the results of the fast, which were announced through a megaphone, and finally two young ladies appeared, blissful at having been selected for the honor, to help the hunger artist down the few steps leading to a small table on which was spread a carefully chosen invalid repast. And at this very moment the artist always turned stubborn. True, he would entrust his bony arms to the outstretched helping hands of the ladies bending over him, but stand up he would not. Why stop fasting at this particular moment, after forty days of it? He had held out for a long time, an illimitably long time; why stop now, when he was in his best fasting form, or rather, not yet quite in his best fasting form? Why should he be cheated of the fame he would get for fasting longer, for being not only the record hunger artist of all time, which presumably he was already, but for beating his own record by a performance beyond human imagination, since he felt that there were no limits to his capacity for fasting? His public pretended to admire him so much, why should it have so little patience with him; he could endure fasting longer, why shouldn't the public endure it? Besides, he was tired, he was comfortable sitting in the straw, and now he was supposed to lift himself to his full height and go down to a meal the very thought of which gave him a nausea that only the presence of the ladies kept him from betraying, and even that with an effort. And he looked up into the eyes of the ladies who were apparently so friendly and in reality so cruel, and shook his head, which felt too heavy on its strengthless neck. But then there happened yet again what always happened. The impresario came forward, without a word—for the band made speech impossible—lifted his arms in the air above the artist, as if inviting Heaven to look down upon its creature here in the straw, this suffering martyr, which indeed he was, although in quite another sense, grasped him round the emaciated waist, with exaggerated caution, so that the frail condition he was in might be appreciated; and committed him to the care of the blench-ing ladies, not without secretly giving him a shaking so that his legs and body tottered and swayed. The artist now submitted completely; his head lolled on his breast as if it had landed there by chance; his body was hollowed out; his legs in a spasm of self-preservation clung close to each other at the knees, yet scraped on the ground as if it were not really solid ground, as if they were only trying to find solid ground; and the whole weight of his body, a feather-weight after all, relapsed onto one of the ladies, who, looking round for help and panting a little— this post of honor was not at all what she had expected it to be—first stretched her neck as far as she could to keep her face at least free from contact with the artist, then finding this impossible, and her more fortunate companion not coming to her aid but merely holding extended on her own trembling hand the little bunch of knucklebones that was the artist's, to the great delight of the spectators burst into tears and had to be replaced by an attendant who had long been stationed in readiness. Then came the food, a little of which the impresario managed to get between the artist's lips, while he sat in a kind of half-fainting trance, to the accompaniment of cheerful patter designed to distract the public's attention from the artist's condition; after that, a toast was drunk to the public, supposedly prompted by a whisper from the artist in the impresario's ear; the band confirmed it with a mighty flourish, the spectators melted away, and no one had any cause to be dissatisfied with the proceedings, no one except the hunger artist himself, he only, as always.

So he lived for many years, with small regular intervals of recuperation, in visible glory, honored by the world, yet in spite of that troubled in spirit, and all the more troubled because no one would take his trouble seriously. What comfort could he possibly need? What more could he possibly wish for? And if some good-natured person, feeling sorry for him, tried to console him by pointing out that his melancholy was probably caused by fasting, it could happen, especially when he had been fasting for some time, that he reacted with an outburst of fury and to the general alarm began to shake the bars of his cage like a wild animal. Yet the impresario had a way of punishing these outbreaks which he rather enjoyed putting into operation. He would apologize publicly for the artist's behavior, which was only to be excused, he admitted, because of the irritability caused by fasting; a condition hardly to be understood by well-fed people; then by natural transition he went on to mention the artist's equally incomprehensible boast that he could fast for much longer than he was doing; he praised the high ambition, the good will, the great self-denial undoubtedly implicit in such a statement; and then quite simply countered it by bringing out photographs, which were also on sale to the public, showing the artist on the fortieth day of a fast lying in bed almost dead from exhaustion. This perversion of the truth, familiar to the artist though it was, always unnerved him afresh and proved too much for him. What was a consequence of the premature ending of his fast was here presented as the cause of it! To fight against this lack of understanding, against a whole world of nonunderstanding, was impossible. Time and again in good faith he stood by the bars listening to the impresario, but as soon as the photographs appeared he always let go and sank with a groan back on to his straw, and the reassured public could once more come close and gaze at him.

5   A few years later when the witnesses of such scenes called them to mind, they often failed to understand themselves at all. For meanwhile the aforementioned change in public interest had set in; it seemed to happen almost overnight; there may have been profound causes for it, but who was going to bother about that; at any rate the pampered hunger artist suddenly found himself deserted one fine day

by the amusement seekers, who went streaming past him to other more favored attractions. For the last time the impresario hurried him over half Europe to discover whether the old interest might still survive here and there; all in vain; everywhere, as if by secret agreement, a positive revulsion from professional fasting was in evidence. Of course it could not really have sprung up so suddenly as all that, and many premonitory symptoms which had not been sufficiently remarked or suppressed during the rush and glitter of success now came retrospectively to mind, but it was now too late to take any counter-measures. Fasting would surely come into fashion again at some future date, yet that was no comfort for those living in the present. What, then, was the hunger artist to do? He had been applauded by thousands in his time and could hardly come down to showing himself in a street booth at village fairs, and as for adopting another profession, he was not only too old for that but too fanatically devoted to fasting. So he took leave of the impresario, his partner in an unparalleled career, and hired himself to a large circus; in order to spare his own feelings he avoided reading the conditions of his contract.

A large circus with its enormous traffic in replacing and recruiting men, animals and apparatus can always find a use for people at any time, even for a hunger artist, provided of course that he does not ask too much, and in this particular case anyhow it was not only the artist who was taken on but his famous and long-known name as well; indeed considering the peculiar nature of his performance, which was not impaired by advancing age, it could not be objected that here was an artist past his prime, no longer at the height of his professional skill, seeking a refuge in some quiet corner of a circus; on the contrary, the hunger artist averred that he could fast as well as ever, which was entirely credible; he even alleged that if he were allowed to fast as he liked, and this was at once promised him without more ado, he could astound the world by establishing a record never yet achieved, a statement which certainly provoked a smile among the other professionals, since it left out of account the change in public opinion, which the hunger artist in his zeal conveniently forgot.

He had not, however, actually lost his sense of the real situation and took it as a matter of course that he and his cage should be stationed, not in the middle of the ring as a main attraction, but outside, near the animal cages, on a site that was after all easily accessible. Large and gaily painted placards made a frame for the cage and announced what was to be seen inside it. When the public came thronging out in the intervals to see the animals, they could hardly avoid passing the hunger artist's cage and stopping there for a moment, perhaps they might even have stayed longer had not those pressing behind them in the narrow gangway, who did not understand why they should be held up on their way towards the excitements of the menagerie, made it impossible for anyone to stand gazing quietly for any length of time. And that was the reason why the hunger artist, who had of course been looking forward to these visiting hours as the main achievement of his life, began instead to shrink from them. At first he could hardly wait for the intervals; it was exhilarating to watch the crowds come streaming his way, until only too soon—not even the most obstinate self-deception, clung to almost consciously, could hold out against the fact—the conviction was borne in upon him that these people, most of them, to judge from their actions, again and again, without exception, were all on their way to the menagerie. And the first sight of them from the distance remained the best. For when they reached his cage he was at once deafened by the storm of shouting and abuse that arose from the two contending factions, which renewed themselves continuously, of those who wanted to stop and stare at him—he soon began to dislike them more than the others—not out of real interest but only out of obstinate self-assertiveness, and those who wanted to go straight on to the animals. When the first great rush was past, the stragglers came along, and these, whom nothing could have prevented from stopping to look at him as long as they had breath, raced past with long strides, hardly even glancing at him, in their haste to get to the menagerie in time. And all too rarely did it happen that he had a stroke of luck, when some father of a family fetched up before him with his children, pointed a finger at the hunger artist and explained at length what the phenomenon meant, telling stories of earlier years when he himself had watched similar but much more thrilling performances, and the children, still rather uncomprehending, since neither inside nor outside school had they been sufficiently prepared for this lesson—what did they care about fasting?—yet showed by the brightness of their intent eyes that new and better times might be coming. Perhaps, said the hunger artist to himself many a time, things would be a little better if his cage were set not quite so near the menagerie. That made it too easy for people to make their choice, to say nothing of what he suffered from the stench of the menagerie, the animals' restlessness by night, the carrying past of raw lumps of flesh for the beasts of prey, the roaring at feeding times, which depressed him continually. But he did not dare to lodge a complaint with the management; after all, he had the animals to thank for the troops of people who passed his cage, among whom there might always be one here and there to take an interest in him, and who could tell where they might seclude him if he called attention to his existence and thereby to the fact that, strictly speaking, he was only an impediment on the way to the menagerie.

A small impediment, to be sure, one that grew steadily less. People grew familiar with the strange idea that they could be expected, in times like these, to take an interest in a hunger artist, and with this familiarity the verdict went out against him. He might fast as much as he could, and he did so; but nothing could save him now, people passed him by. Just try to explain to anyone the art of fasting! Anyone who has no feeling for it cannot be made to understand it. The fine placards grew dirty and illegible, they were torn down; the little notice board telling the number of fast days achieved, which at first was changed carefully every day, had long stayed at the same figure, for after the first few weeks even this small task seemed pointless to the staff; and so the artist simply fasted on and on, as he had once dreamed of doing, and it was no trouble to him, just as he had always foretold, but no one counted the days, no one, not even the artist himself, knew what records he was already breaking, and his heart grew heavy. And when once in a time some leisurely passer-by stopped, made merry over the old figure on the board and spoke of swindling, that was in its way the stupidest lie ever invented by indifference and inborn malice, since it was not the hunger artist who was cheating; he was working honestly, but the world was cheating him of his record.

Many more days went by, however, and that too came to an end. An overseer's eye fell on the cage one day and he asked the attendants why this perfectly good stage should be left standing there unused with dirty straw inside it; nobody knew, until one man, helped out by the notice board, remembered about the hunger artist. They poked into the straw with sticks and found him in it. "Are you still fasting?" asked the overseer. "When on earth do you mean to stop?" "Forgive me, everybody," whispered the hunger artist; only the overseer, who had his ear to the bars, understood him. "Of course," said the overseer, and tapped his forehead with a finger to let the attendants know what state the man was in, "we forgive you." "I always wanted you to admire my fasting," said the hunger artist. "We do admire it," said the overseer, affably. "But you shouldn't admire it," said the hunger artist. "Well, then we don't admire it," said the overseer, "but why shouldn't we admire it?" "Because I have to fast, I can't help it," said the hunger artist. "What a fellow you are," said the overseer, "and why can't you help it?" "Because," said the hunger artist, lifting his head a little and speaking, with his lips pursed, as if for a kiss, right into the overseer's ear, so that no syllable might be lost, "because I couldn't find the food I liked. If I had found it, believe me, I should have made no fuss and stuffed myself like you or anyone else." These were his last words, but in his dimming eyes remained the firm though no longer proud persuasion that he was still continuing to fast.

10   "Well, clear this out now!" said the overseer, and they buried the hunger artist, straw and all. Into the cage they put a young panther. Even the most insensitive felt it refreshing to see this wild creature leaping around the cage that had so long been dreary. The panther was all right. The food he liked was brought him without hesitation by the attendants; he seemed not even to miss his freedom; his noble body, furnished almost to the bursting point with all that it needed, seemed to carry freedom around with it too; somewhere in his jaws it seemed to lurk; and the joy of life streamed with such ardent passion from his throat that for the onlookers it was not easy to stand the shock of it. But they braced themselves, crowded round the cage, and did not want ever to move away.

Questions on symbolism . . .

1. Is the hunger artist an allegorical figure? What idea would he stand in for?
2. Do you find the hunger artist symbolic? Of what? Is he a "new word"? Do you know anyone who is a hunger artist in matters not related to food and nourishment?
3. Could a writer tell a story of a flagpole sitter or a person who remained in a dark closet for three months and still convey Kafka's theme?
4. What is the relationship between symbol and theme?
5. Is the panther symbolic?
6. What is the point of view of this story? How does the point of view affect the symbolism of the story?

. . . and other elements

7. How does the first sentence set the tone for the whole story? Do you suspect irony when you read the first sentence? What word tells you the most?
8. What is the function of the minor characters here?

Chapter 11 **Three Modes of Contemporary Fiction**

In the preceding chapter we concluded our introduction to the elements of fiction. Now it remains to provide further examples of fiction, with a few notes on particular categories. First we will look at stories of fantasy and absurdity, then at humorous stories, and finally at examples of science fiction—which might have been printed as further examples of fantasy, except that the mode is so pervasive it calls out for special treatment.

Fantasy and absurdity

The fiction of **fantasy** describes an imagined world where everyday reality is distorted. In literature, works of fantasy are as various as the two stories in the preceding chapter, as J. R. R. Tolkien's *Lord of the Rings,* and as Jonathan Swift's *Gulliver's Travels;* science fiction is fantasy, along with Shakespeare's *The Tempest,* Lewis Carroll's *Alice's Adventures in Wonderland,* and most of the horror stories of Edgar Allan Poe. The only thing these works have in common is negative: the world they describe does not duplicate our common-sense reality.

Fantastic fiction begins with an improbable basis or *given* (like an imaginary hypothesis in mathematics) and then becomes probable in terms of that given. It is unlikely that any of us will walk like Alice through a mirror into a land peopled with fantastic creatures, but we demand that Alice behave appropriately under her fantastic circumstances. Alice of course is human, and many works mix the human into a fantastic world. But even when all the creatures of fiction are fantastic, they behave according to the character given them by the author.

Often an author uses the unhuman behavior of a fantastic folk—Tolkien's Middle Earthlings—to comment on actual human life and on human character.

Only recently have critics spoken of the absurd in fiction; absurd literature is modern but, like fantasy, its antecedents go back as far as literature does. To the absurdist vision, the ordinary world seems insane and purposeless. In one of his novels, Samuel Beckett spends page after page describing how his protagonist sucks on pebbles and the scheme he develops to switch pebbles among his pockets in order to give them equal attention. We understand that, pointless as his behavior is, it is no sillier than anything else; we understand that the world's habits—its nations and laws and institutions and schools and businesses and customs and morals—are as arbitrary as pebble-sucking. In Albert Camus's novel *The Stranger* we understand the irrelevance of all behavior, until finally there is no reason for doing anything at all, or for not doing anything at all.

Despite the grimness of the vision—a purposeless world without destiny or divinity—absurdist literature is often comic. If comedy lies in the perception of incongruity, an absurdist vision, where everything in the world is incongruous, would therefore naturally be comical. Thus, when describing the absurd in literature, critics have spoken of **black comedy**, a combination of despair and laughter that seems peculiarly modern.

In America, Donald Barthelme creates a world in his short stories where everything is arbitrary, fantastic, absurd, dark, and usually funny. Other writers—Philip Roth has a man turn into a woman's breast, Robert Coover has the Cat in the Hat run for President, Max Apple imagines a Mr. Howard Johnson—also write in this modern tradition.

Donald Barthelme
The Indian Uprising

Donald Barthelme (1933–   ) has published two novels, *Snow White* (1967) and *The Dead Father* (1975), and many collections of short fiction. Born in Texas, living now in New York City, he writes from a comic, surreal vision of American life and fragments his perceptions as if he looked at the world through a verbal kaleidoscope. Yet he is one of our most careful and conscious stylists, gathering his fragments into fine sentences.

We defended the city as best we could. The arrows of the Comanches came in clouds. The war clubs of the Comanches clattered on the soft, yellow pavements. There were earthworks along the Boulevard Mark Clark and the hedges had been laced with sparkling wire. People were trying to understand. I spoke to Sylvia. "Do you think this is a good life?" The table held apples, books, long-playing records. She looked up. "No."

Patrols of paras and volunteers with armbands guarded the tall, flat buildings. We interrogated the captured Comanche. Two of us forced his head back while another poured water into his nostrils. His body jerked, he choked and wept. Not believing a hurried, careless, and exaggerated report of the number of casualties in the outer districts where trees, lamps, swans had been reduced to clear fields of fire we issued entrenching tools to those who seemed trustworthy and turned the heavy-weapons companies so that we could not be surprised from that direction. And I sat there getting drunker and more in love and more in love. We talked.

"Do you know Fauré's 'Dolly'?"

"Would that be Gabriel Fauré?"

"It would."

"Then I know it," she said. "May I say that I play it at certain times, when I am sad, or happy, although it requires four hands."

"How is that managed?"

"I accelerate," she said, "ignoring the time signature."

And when they shot the scene in the bed I wondered how you felt under the eyes of the cameramen, grips, juicers, men in the mixing booth: excited? stimulated? And when they shot the scene in the shower I sanded a hollow-core door working carefully against the illustrations in texts and whispered instructions from one who had already solved the problem. I had made after all other tables, one while living with Nancy, one while living with Alice, one while living with Eunice, one while living with Marianne.

Red men in waves like people scattering in a square startled by something tragic or a sudden, loud noise accumulated against the barricades we had made of window dummies, silk, thoughtfully planned job descriptions (including scales for the orderly progress of other colors), wine in demijohns, and robes. I analyzed the composition of the barricade nearest me and found two ashtrays, ceramic, one dark brown and one dark brown with an orange blur at the lip; a tin frying pan; two-litre bottles of red wine; three-quarter-litre bottles of Black & White, aquavit, cognac, vodka, gin, Fad #6 sherry; a hollow-core door in birch veneer on black wrought-iron legs; a blanket, red-orange with faint blue stripes; a red pillow and a blue pillow; a woven straw wastebasket; two glass jars for flowers; corkscrews and can openers; two plates and two cups, ceramic, dark brown; a yellow-and-purple poster; a Yugoslavian carved flute, wood, dark brown; and other items. I decided I knew nothing.

The hospitals dusted wounds with powders the worth of which was not quite established, other supplies having been exhausted early in the first day. I decided I knew nothing. Friends put me in touch with a Miss R., a teacher, unorthodox they said, excellent they said, successful with difficult cases, steel shutters on the windows made the house safe. I had just learned via an International Distress Coupon that Jane had been beaten up by a dwarf in a bar on Tenerife but Miss R. did not allow me to speak of it. "You know nothing," she said, "you feel nothing, you are locked in a most savage and terrible ignorance, I despise you, my boy, *mon cher, my* heart. You may attend but you must not attend now, you must attend later, a day or a week or an hour, you are making me ill. . . ." I nonevaluated these remarks as Korzybski instructed. But it was difficult. Then they pulled back in a feint near the river and we rushed into that sector with a reinforced battalion hastily formed among the Zouaves and cabdrivers. This unit was crushed in the afternoon of a day that began with spoons and letters in hallways and under windows where men tested the history of the heart, cone-shaped muscular organ that maintains *circulation of the blood.*

But it is you I want now, here in the middle of this Uprising, with the streets yellow and threatening, short, ugly lances with fur at the throat and inexplicable shell money lying in the grass. It is when I am with you that I am happiest, and it is for you that I am making this hollow-core door table with black wrought-iron legs. I held Sylvia by her bear-claw necklace. "Call off your braves," I said. "We have many years left to live." There was a sort of muck running in the gutters, yellowish, filthy stream suggesting excrement, or nervousness, a city that does not know what it has done to deserve baldness, errors, infidelity. "With luck you will survive until matins," Sylvia said. She ran off down the Rue Chester Nimitz, uttering shrill cries.

Then it was learned that they had infiltrated our ghetto and that the people of the ghetto instead of resisting had joined the smooth, well-coordinated attack with zipguns, telegrams, lockets, causing that portion of the line held by the I.R.A. to swell and collapse. We sent more heroin into the ghetto, and hyacinths, ordering another hundred thousand of the pale, delicate flowers. On the map we considered the situation with its strung-out inhabitants and merely personal emotions. Our parts were blue and their parts were green. I showed the blue-and-green map to Sylvia. "Your parts are green," I said. "You gave me heroin first a year ago," Sylvia said. She ran off down George C. Marshall Allée, uttering shrill cries. Miss R. pushed me into a large room painted white (jolting and dancing in the soft light, and I was excited! and there were people watching!) in which there were two chairs. I sat in one chair and Miss R. sat in the other. She wore a blue dress containing a red figure. There was nothing exceptional about her. I was disappointed by her plainness, by the bareness of the room, by the absence of books.

The girls of my quarter wore long blue mufflers that reached to their knees. Sometimes the girls hid Comanches in their rooms, the blue mufflers together in a room creating a great blue fog. Block opened the door. He was carrying weapons, flowers, loaves of bread. And he was friendly, kind, enthusiastic, so I related a little of the history of torture, reviewing the technical literature quoting the best modern sources, French, German, and American, and pointing out the flies which had gathered in anticipation of some new, cool color.

15　　"What is the situation?" I asked.

"The situation is liquid," he said. "We hold the south quarter and they hold the north quarter. The rest is silence."

"And Kenneth?"

"That girl is not in love with Kenneth," Block said frankly. "She is in love with his coat. When she is not wearing it she is huddling under it. Once I caught it going down the stairs by itself. I looked inside. Sylvia."

Once I caught Kenneth's coat going down the stairs by itself but the coat was a trap and inside a Comanche who made a thrust with his short, ugly knife at my leg which buckled and tossed me over the balustrade through a window and into another situation. Not believing that your body brilliant as it was and your fat, liquid spirit distinguished and angry as it was were stable quantities to which one could return on wires more than once, twice, or another number of times I said: "See the table?"

20　　In Skinny Wainwright Square the forces of green and blue swayed and struggled. The referees ran out on the field trailing chains. And then the blue part would be enlarged, the green diminished. Miss R. began to speak. "A former king of Spain, a Bonaparte, lived for a time in Bordentown, New Jersey. But that's no good." She paused. "The ardor aroused in men by the beauty of women can only be satisfied by God. That is *very* good (it is Valéry) but it is not what I have to teach you, goat, muck, filth, heart of my heart." I showed the table to Nancy. "See the table?" She stuck out her tongue red as a cardinal's hat. "I made such a table once," Block said frankly. "People all over America have made such tables. I doubt very much whether one can enter an American home without finding at least one such table, or traces of its having been there, such as faded places in the carpet." And afterward in the garden the men of the 7th Cavalry played Gabrieli, Albinoni, Marcello, Vivaldi, Boccherini. I saw Sylvia. She wore a yellow ribbon, under a long blue muffler. "Which side are you on," I cried, "after all?"

"The only form of discourse of which I approve," Miss R. said in her dry, tense voice, "is the litany. I believe our masters and teachers as well as plain citizens should confine themselves to what can safely be said. Thus when I hear the words *pewter, snake, tea, Fad #6 sherry, serviette, fenestration, crown, blue* coming from the mouth of some public official, or some raw youth, I am not disappointed. Vertical organization is also possible," Miss R. said, "as in

 pewter
 snake
 tea
 Fad #6 sherry
 serviette
 fenestration
 crown
 blue.

I run to liquids and colors," she said, "but you, you may run to something else, my virgin, my darling, my thistle, my poppet, my own. Young people," Miss R. said, "run to more and more unpleasant combinations as they sense the nature of our society. Some people," Miss R. said, "run to conceits or wisdom but I hold to the hard, brown, nutlike word. I might point out that there is enough aesthetic excitement here to satisfy anyone but a damned fool." I sat in solemn silence.

Fire arrows lit my way to the post office in Patton Place where members of the Abraham Lincoln Brigade offered their last, exhausted letters, postcards, calendars. I opened a letter but inside was a Comanche flint arrowhead play by Frank Wedekind in an elegant gold chain and congratulations. Your earring rattled against my spectacles when I leaned forward to touch the soft, ruined place where the hearing aid had been. "Pack it in! Pack it in!" I urged, but the men in charge of the Uprising refused to listen to reason or to understand that it was real and that our water supply had evaporated and that our credit was no longer what it had been, once.

We attached wires to the testicles of the captured Comanche. And I sat there getting drunker and drunker and more in love and more in love. When we threw the switch he spoke. His name, he said, was Gustave Aschenbach. He was born at L—, a country town in the province of Silesia. He was the son of an upper official in the judicature, and his forebears had all been officers, judges, departmental functionaries. . . . And you can never touch a girl in the same way more than once, twice, or another number of times however much you may wish to hold, wrap, or otherwise fix her hand, or look, or some other quality, or incident, known to you previously. In Sweden the little Swedish children cheered when we managed nothing more remarkable than getting off a bus burdened with packages, bread and liver-paste and beer. We went to an old church and sat in the royal box. The organist was practicing. And then into the graveyard next to the church. *Here lies Anna Pedersen, a good woman.* I threw a mushroom on the grave. The officer commanding the garbage dump reported by radio that the garbage had begun to move.

Jane! I heard via an International Distress Coupon that you were beaten up by a dwarf in a bar on Tenerife. That doesn't sound like you, Jane. Mostly you kick the dwarf in his little dwarf groin before he can get his teeth into your tasty and nice-looking leg, don't you, Jane? Your affair with Harold is reprehensible, you know that, don't you, Jane? Harold is married to Nancy. And there is Paula to think about (Harold's kid), and Billy (Harold's other kid). I think your values are peculiar, Jane! Strings of language extend in every direction to bind the world into a rushing, ribald whole.

25   And you can never return to felicities in the same way, the brilliant body, the distinguished spirit recapitulating moments that occur once, twice, or another number of times in rebellions, or water. The rolling consensus of the Comanche nation smashed our inner defenses on three sides. Block was firing a greasegun from the upper floor of a building designed by Emery Roth & Sons. "See the table?" "Oh, pack it in with your bloody table!" The city officials were tied to trees. Dusky warriors padded with their forest tread into the mouth of the mayor. "Who do you want to be?" I asked Kenneth and he said he wanted to be Jean-Luc Godard but later when time permitted conversations in large lighted rooms, whispering galleries with black-and-white Spanish rugs and problematic sculpture on calm, red catafalques. The sickness of the quarrel lay thick in the bed. I touched your back, the white, raised scars.

We killed a great many in the south suddenly with helicopters and rockets but we found that those we had killed were children and more came from the north and from the east and from other places where there are children preparing to live. "Skin," Miss R. said softly in the white, yellow room. "This is the Clemency Committee. And would you remove your belt and shoelaces." I removed my belt and shoelaces and looked (rain shattering from a great height the prospects of silence and clear, neat rows of houses in the subdivisions) into their savage black eyes, paint; feathers, beads.

Questions

1. After reading this story through, you may well feel bewildered; most people do the first time. Ask yourself, in a general way, what the story is about. What sort of *feeling,* what sort of *world,* is Barthelme describing or embodying? Looking back at the story, try to discover what happens in it. For instance, what happens at the very end?

    What do you learn about the speaker? Do you like him? Are you supposed to like him?
2. How soon do you realize that these Comanches are not the Comanches of history? When do you begin to realize their identity, or their *sort* of identity?
3. Its date of composition sometimes affects the meaning of a work of art. This story appeared in *The New Yorker* in 1967, while the Vietnam war flourished and young Americans took to the streets in protest.

    Have I just hinted that the Comanches are the Viet Cong? The Yippies?
4. Why are the public places named as they are?
5. Find places Barthelme seems to comment, not on the world outside, but on the form of fiction itself, or on language. Can you relate this interest to other concerns in the story?
6. Some of Barthelme's sentences end by disappointing an expectation set up in

the first part of the sentence. Find examples. Does this technique remind you of James Thurber?

7. Why the motif of the tables? Is there social commentary here? Social satire?
8. What is the point of view here? Who is *you*?
9. What is the Clemency Committee and what is it going to do?
10. What is fantastic in this story? What is absurd?

Max Apple
The Oranging of America

Max Apple (1941–   ) was born in Grand Rapids and studied at the University of Michigan, where he won awards for his writing. He published a collection of short stories, *The Oranging of America,* in 1976, and a novel— *Zip*—in 1978. He teaches English at Rice University in Houston.

I

From the outside it looked like any ordinary 1964 Cadillac limousine. In the expensive space between the driver and passengers, where some installed bars or even bathrooms, Mr. Howard Johnson kept a tidy ice-cream freezer in which there were always at least eighteen flavors on hand, though Mr. Johnson ate only vanilla. The freezer's power came from the battery with an independent auxiliary generator as a back-up system. Although now Howard Johnson means primarily motels, Millie, Mr. HJ, and Otis Brighton, the chauffeur, had not forgotten that ice cream was the cornerstone of their empire. Some of the important tasting was still done in the car. Mr. HJ might have reports in his pocket from sales executives and marketing analysts, from home economists and chemists, but not until Mr. Johnson reached over the lowered Plexiglas to spoon a taste or two into the expert waiting mouth of Otis Brighton did he make any final flavor decision. He might go ahead with butterfly shrimp, with candy kisses, and with packaged chocolate-chip cookies on the opinion of the specialists, but in ice cream he trusted only Otis. From the back seat Howard Johnson would keep his eye on the rearview mirror, where the reflection of pleasure or disgust showed itself in the dark eyes of Otis Brighton no matter what the driving conditions. He could be stalled in a commuter rush with the engine overheating and a dripping oil pan, and still a taste of the right kind never went unappreciated.

When Otis finally said, "Mr. Howard, that shore is sumpin, that one is um-hum. That is it, my man, that is it." Then and not until then did Mr. HJ finally decide to go ahead with something like banana-fudge-ripple royale.

Mildred rarely tasted and Mr. HJ was addicted to one scoop of vanilla every afternoon at three, eaten from his aluminum dish with a disposable plastic spoon. The duties of Otis, Millie, and Mr. Johnson were so divided that they rarely infringed upon one another in the car, which was their office. Neither Mr. HJ nor Millie knew how to drive, Millie and Otis understood little of financing and leasing, and Mr. HJ left the compiling of the "Traveling Reports" and "The Howard Johnson Newsletter" strictly to the literary style of his longtime associate, Miss Mildred Bryce. It was an ideal division of labor, which, in one form or another, had been in continuous operation for well over a quarter of a century.

While Otis listened to the radio behind his soundproof Plexiglas, while Millie in her small, neat hand compiled data for the newsletter, Mr. HJ liked to lean back into the spongy leather seat looking through his specially tinted windshield at the fleeting land. Occasionally, lulled by the hum of the freezer, he might doze off, his large pink head lolling toward the shoulder of his blue suit, but there was not too much that Mr. Johnson missed, even in advanced age.

Along with Millie he planned their continuous itinerary as they traveled. Mildred would tape a large green relief map of the United States to the Plexiglas separating them from Otis. The mountains on the map were light brown and seemed to melt toward the valleys like the crust of a fresh apple pie settling into cinnamon surroundings. The existing HJ houses (Millie called the restaurants and motels houses) were marked by orange dots, while projected future sites bore white dots. The deep green map with its brown mountains and colorful dots seemed much more alive than the miles that twinkled past Mr. Johnson's gaze, and nothing gave the ice-cream king greater pleasure than watching Mildred with her fine touch, and using the original crayon, turn an empty white dot into an orange fulfillment.

"It's like a seed grown into a tree, Millie," Mr. HJ liked to say at such moments when he contemplated the map and saw that it was good.

They had started traveling together in 1925: Mildred, then a secretary to Mr. Johnson, a young man with two restaurants and a dream of hospitality, and Otis, a twenty-year-old busboy and former driver of a Louisiana mule. When Mildred graduated from college, her father, a Michigan doctor who kept his money in a blue steel box under the examining table, encouraged her to try the big city. He sent her a monthly allowance. In those early days she always had more than Mr. Johnson, who paid her $16.50 a week and meals. In the first decade they traveled only on weekends, but every year since 1936 they had spent at least six months on the road, and it might have gone on much longer if Mildred's pain and the trouble in New York with Howard Jr. had not come so close together.

They were all stoical at the Los Angeles International Airport. Otis waited at the car for what might be his last job while Miss Bryce and Mr. Johnson traveled toward the New York plane along a silent moving floor. Millie stood beside Howard while they passed a mural of a Mexican landscape and some Christmas drawings by fourth graders from Watts. For forty years they had been together in spite of Sonny and the others, but at this most recent appeal from New York Millie urged him to go back. Sonny had cabled, "My God, Dad, you're sixty-nine years old, haven't you been a gypsy long enough? Board meeting December third with or without you. Policy changes imminent."

Normally, they ignored Sonny's cables, but this time Millie wanted him to go, wanted to be alone with the pain that had recently come to her. She had left Howard holding the new canvas suitcase in which she had packed her three notebooks of regional reports along with his aluminum dish, and in a moment of real despair she had even packed the orange crayon. When Howard boarded Flight 965 he looked old to Millie. His feet dragged in the wing-tipped shoes, the hand she shook was moist, the lip felt dry, and as he passed from her sight down the entry ramp Mildred Bryce felt a fresh new ache that sent her hobbling toward the car. Otis had unplugged the freezer, and the silence caused by the missing hum was as intense to Millie as her abdominal pain.

It had come quite suddenly in Albuquerque, New Mexico, at the grand opening of a 210-unit house. She did not make a fuss. Mildred Bryce had never caused trouble to anyone, except perhaps to Mrs. HJ. Millie's quick precise actions, angular face, and thin body made her seem birdlike, especially next to Mr. HJ, six three with splendid white hair accenting his dark blue gabardine suits. Howard was slow and sure. He could sit in the same position for hours while Millie fidgeted on the seat, wrote memos, and field reports in the small gray cabinet that sat in front of her and parallel to the ice-cream freezer. Her health had always been good, so at first she tried to ignore the pain. It was gas: it was perhaps the New Mexico water or the cooking oil in the fish dinner. But she could not convince away the pain. It stayed like a match burning around in her belly, etching itself into her as the round HJ emblem was so symmetrically embroidered into the bedspread, which she had kicked off in the flush that accompanied the pain. She felt as if her sweat would engulf the foam mattress and crisp percale sheet. Finally, Millie brought up her knees and made a ball of herself as if being as small as possible might make her misery disappear. It worked for everything except the pain. The little circle of hot torment was all that remained of her, and when finally at some-time in the early morning it left, it occurred to her that perhaps she had struggled with a demon and been suddenly relieved by the coming of daylight. She stepped lightly into the bathroom and before a full-length mirror (new in HJ motels exclu-sively) saw herself whole and unmarked, but sign enough to Mildred was her smell, damp and musty, sign enough that something had begun and that some-thing else would therefore necessarily end.

II

Before she had the report from her doctor, Howard Jr.'s message had given her the excuse she needed. There was no reason why Millie could not tell Howard she was sick, but telling him would be admitting too much to herself. Along with Howard Johnson Millie had grown rich beyond dreams. Her inheritance, the $100,000 from her father's steel box in 1939, went directly to Mr. Johnson, who desperately needed it, and the results of that investment brought Millie enough capital to employ two people at the Chase Manhattan with the management of her finances. With money beyond the hope of use, she had vacationed all over the world and spent some time in the company of celebrities, but the reality of her life, like his, was in the back seat of the limousine, waiting for that point at which the needs of the automobile and the human body met the undeviating purpose of the highway and momentarily conquered it.

Her life was measured in rest stops. She, Howard, and Otis had found them out before they existed. They knew the places to stop between Buffalo and Albany, Chicago and Milwaukee, Toledo and Columbus, Des Moines and Minneapolis, they knew through their own bodies, measured in hunger and discomfort in the '30s and '40s when they would stop at remote places to buy land and borrow money, sensing in themselves the hunger that would one day be upon the place. People were wary and Howard had trouble borrowing (her $100,000 had perhaps been the key) but invariably he was right. Howard knew the land, Mildred thought, the way the Indians must have known it. There were even spots along the way where the earth itself seemed to make men stop. Howard had a sixth sense that would sometimes lead them from the main roads to, say, a dark green field in Iowa or Kansas. Howard, who might have seemed asleep, would rap with his knuckles on the Plexiglas, causing the knowing Otis to bring the car to such a quick stop that Millie almost flew into her filing cabinet. And before the emergency brake had settled into its final prong, Howard Johnson was into the field and after the scent. While Millie and Otis waited, he would walk it out slowly. Sometimes he would sit down, disappearing in a field of long and tangled weeds, or he might find a large smooth rock to sit on while he felt some secret vibration from the place. Turning his back to Millie, he would mark the spot with his urine or break some of the clayey earth in his strong pink hands, sifting it like flour for a delicate recipe. She had actually seen him chew the grass, getting down on all fours like an animal and biting the tops without pulling the entire blade from the soil. At times he ran in a slow jog as far as his aging legs would carry him. Whenever he slipped out of sight behind the uneven terrain, Millie felt him in danger, felt that something alien might be there to resist the civilizing instinct of Howard Johnson. Once when Howard had been out of sight for more than an hour and did not respond to their frantic calls, Mille sent Otis into the field and in desperation flagged a passing car.

"Howard Johnson is lost in that field," she told the surprised driver. "He went in to look for a new location and we can't find him now."

"The restaurant Howard Johnson?" the man asked.

15 "Yes. Help us please."

The man drove off, leaving Millie to taste in his exhaust fumes the barbarism of an ungrateful public. Otis found Howard asleep in a field of light blue wild flowers. He had collapsed from the exertion of his run. Millie brought water to him, and when he felt better, right there in the field, he ate his scoop of vanilla on the very spot where three years later they opened the first fully air-conditioned motel in the world. When she stopped to think about it, Millie knew they were more than businessmen, they were pioneers. And once, while on her own, she had the feeling too. In 1951 when she visited the Holy Land there was an inkling of what Howard must have felt all the time. It happened without any warning on a bus crowded with tourists and resident Arabs on their way to the Dead Sea. Past ancient Sodom the bus creaked and bumped, down, down, toward the lowest point on earth, when suddenly in the midst of the crowd and her stomach queasy with the motion of the bus, Mildred Bryce experienced an overwhelming calm. A light brown patch of earth surrounded by a few pale desert rocks overwhelmed her perception, seemed closer to her than the Arab lady in the black flowered dress pushing her basket against Millie at that very moment. She wanted to stop the bus. Had she been near the door she might have actually jumped, so strong was her sensitivity to that barren spot in the endless desert. Her whole body ached for it as if in unison, bone by bone. Her limbs tingled, her breath came in short gasps, the sky rolled out of the bus windows and obliterated her view. The Arab lady spat on the floor and moved a suspicious eye over a squirming Mildred.

When the bus stopped at the Dead Sea, the Arabs and tourists rushed to the soupy brine clutching damaged limbs, while Millie pressed twenty dollars American into the dirty palm of a cab-driver who took her back to the very place where the music of her body began once more as sweetly as the first time. While the incredulous driver waited, Millie walked about the place wishing Howard were there to understand her new understanding of his kind of process. There was nothing there, absolutely nothing but pure bliss. The sun beat on her like a wish, the air was hot and stale as a Viennese bathhouse, and yet Mildred felt peace and rest there, and as her cab bill mounted she actually did rest in the miserable barren desert of an altogether unsatisfactory land. When the driver, wiping the sweat from his neck, asked, "Meesez . . . pleeze. Why American woman wants Old Jericho in such kind of heat?" When he said "Jericho," she understood that this was a place where men had always stopped. In dim antiquity Jacob had perhaps watered a flock here, and not far away Lot's wife paused to scan for the last time the city of her youth. Perhaps Mildred now stood where Abraham had been visited by a vision and, making a rock his pillow, had first put the ease into the earth. Whatever it was, Millie knew from her own experience that rest was created here by historical precedent. She tried to buy that piece of land, going as far as King Hussein's secretary of the interior. She imagined a Palestinian HJ with an orange roof angling toward Sodom, a seafood restaurant, and an oasis of fresh fruit. But the land was in dispute between Israel and Jordan, and even King Hussein, who expressed admiration for Howard Johnson, could not sell to Millie the place of her comfort.

That was her single visionary moment, but sharing them with Howard was almost as good. And to end all this, to finally stay in her eighteenth-floor Santa Monica penthouse, where the Pacific dived into California, this seemed to Mildred a paltry conclusion to an adventurous life. Her doctor said it was not so serious, she had a bleeding ulcer and must watch her diet. The prognosis was, in fact, excellent. But Mildred, fifty-six and alone in California, found the doctor less comforting than most of the rest stops she had experienced.

III

California, right after the Second War, was hardly a civilized place for travelers. Millie, HJ, and Otis had a twelve-cylinder '47 Lincoln and snaked along five days between Sacramento and Los Angeles. "Comfort, comfort," said HJ as he surveyed the redwood forest and the bubbly surf while it slipped away from Otis, who had rolled his trousers to chase the ocean away during a stop near San Francisco. Howard Johnson was contemplative in California. They had never been in the West before. Their route, always slightly new, was yet bound by Canada, where a person couldn't get a tax break, and roughly by the Mississippi as a western frontier. Their journeys took them up the eastern seaboard and through New England to the early reaches of the Midwest, stopping at the plains of Wisconsin and the cool crisp edge of Chicago where two HJ lodges twinkled at the lake.

20 One day in 1947 while on the way from Chicago to Cairo, Illinois, HJ looked long at the green relief maps. While Millie kept busy with her filing, HJ loosened the tape and placed the map across his soft round knees. The map jiggled and sagged, the Mid- and Southwest hanging between his legs. When Mildred finally noticed that look, he had been staring at the map for perhaps fifteen minutes, brooding over it, and Millie knew something was in the air.

HJ looked at that map the way some people looked down from an airplane trying to pick out the familiar from the colorful mass receding beneath them. Howard Johnson's eye flew over the land—over the Tetons, over the Sierra Nevada, over the long thin gouge of the Canyon flew his gaze—charting his course by rest stops the way an antique mariner might have gazed at the stars.

"Millie," he said just north of Carbondale, "Millie . . ." He looked toward her, saw her fingers engaged and her thumbs circling each other in anticipation. He looked at Millie and saw that she saw what he saw. "Millie"—HJ raised his right arm and its shadow spread across the continent like a prophecy—"Millie, what if we turn right at Cairo and go that way?" California, already peeling on the green map, balanced on HJ's left knee like a happy child.

Twenty years later Mildred settled in her eighteenth-floor apartment in the building owned by Lawrence Welk. Howard was in New York, Otis and the car waited in Arizona. The pain did not return as powerfully as it had appeared that night in

Albuquerque, but it hurt with dull regularity and an occasional streak of dark blood from her bowels kept her mind on it even on painless days.

Directly beneath her gaze were the organized activities of the golden-age groups, tiny figures playing bridge or shuffleboard or looking out at the water from their benches as she sat on her sofa and looked out at them and the fluffy ocean. Mildred did not regret family life. The HJ houses were her offspring. She had watched them blossom from the rough youngsters of the '40s with steam heat and even occasional kitchenettes into cool mature adults with king-sized beds, color TVs, and room service. Her late years were spent comfortably in the modern houses just as one might enjoy in age the benefits of a child's prosperity. She regretted only that it was probably over.

25   But she did not give up completely until she received a personal letter one day telling her that she was eligible for burial insurance until age eighty. A $1000 policy would guarantee a complete and dignified service. Millie crumpled the advertisement, but a few hours later called her Los Angeles lawyer. As she suspected, there were no plans, but as the executor of the estate he would assume full responsibility, subject of course to her approval.

"I'll do it myself," Millie had said, but she could not bring herself to do it. The idea was too alien. In more than forty years Mildred had not gone a day without a shower and change of underclothing. Everything about her suggested order and precision. Her fingernails were shaped so that the soft meat of the tips could stroke a typewriter without damaging the apex of a nail, her arch slid over a 6B shoe like an egg in a shell, and never in her adult life did Mildred recall having vomited. It did not seem right to suddenly let all this sink into the dark green earth of Forest Lawn because some organ or other developed a hole as big as a nickel. It was not right and she wouldn't do it. Her first idea was to stay in the apartment, to write it into the lease if necessary. She had the lawyer make an appointment for her with Mr. Welk's management firm, but canceled it the day before. "They will just think I'm crazy," she said aloud to herself, "and they'll bury me anyway."

She thought of cryonics while reading a biography of William Chesebrough, the man who invented petroleum jelly. Howard had known him and often mentioned that his own daily ritual of the scoop of vanilla was like old Chesebrough's two teaspoons of Vaseline every day. Chesebrough lived to be ninety. In the biography it said that after taking the daily dose of Vaseline, he drank three cups of green tea to melt everything down, rested for twelve minutes, and then felt fit as a young man, even in his late eighties. When he died they froze his body and Millie had her idea. The Vaseline people kept him in a secret laboratory somewhere near Cleveland and claimed he was in better condition than Lenin, whom the Russians kept hermetically sealed, but at room temperature.

In the phone book she found the Los Angeles Cryonic Society and asked it to send her information. It all seemed very clean. The cost was $200 a year for maintaining the cold. She sent the pamphlet to her lawyer to be sure that the society was legitimate. It wasn't much money, but, still, if they were charlatans, she didn't want them to take advantage of her even if she would never know about it. They were aboveboard, the lawyer said. "The interest on a ten-thousand-dollar trust fund would pay about five hundred a year," the lawyer said, "and they only charge two hundred dollars. Still, who knows what the cost might be in say two hundred years?" To be extra safe, they put $25,000 in trust for eternal maintenance, to be eternally overseen by Longstreet, Williams, and their eternal heirs. When it was arranged, Mildred felt better than she had in weeks.

IV

Four months to the day after she had left Howard at the Los Angeles International Airport, he returned for Mildred without the slightest warning. She was in her housecoat and had not even washed the night cream from her cheeks when she saw through the viewing space in her door the familiar long pink jowls, even longer in the distorted glass.

30   "Howard," she gasped fumbling with the door, and in an instant he was there picking her up as he might a child or an ice-cream cone while her tears fell like dandruff on his blue suit. While Millie sobbed into his soft padded shoulder, HJ told her the good news. "I'm chairman emeritus of the board now. That means no more New York responsibilities. They still have to listen to me because we hold the majority of the stock, but Howard Junior and Keyes will take care of the business. Our main job is new home-owned franchises. And, Millie, guess where we're going first?"

So overcome was Mildred that she could not hold back her sobs even to guess. Howard Johnson put her down, beaming pleasure through his old bright eyes. "Florida," HJ said, then slowly repeated it, "Flor-idda, and guess what we're going to do?"

"Howard," Millie said, swiping at her tears with the filmy lace cuffs of her dressing gown, "I'm so surprised I don't know what to say. You could tell me we're going to the moon and I'd believe you. Just seeing you again has brought back all my hope." They came out of the hallway and sat on the sofa that looked out over the Pacific. HJ, all pink, kept his hands on his knees like paperweights.

"Millie, you're almost right. I can't fool you about anything and never could. We're going down near where they launch the rockets from. I've heard . . ." HJ leaned toward the kitchen as if to check for spies. He looked at the stainless-steel-and-glass table, at the built-in avocado appliances, then leaned his large moist lips toward Mildred's ear. "Walt Disney is planning right this minute a new Disneyland down there. They're trying to keep it a secret, but his brother Roy bought options on thousands of acres. We're going down to buy as much as we can as close in as we can." Howard sparkled. "Millie, don't you see, it's a sure thing."

After her emotional outburst at seeing Howard again, a calmer Millie felt a slight twitch in her upper stomach and in the midst of her joy was reminded of another sure thing.

35   They would be a few weeks in Los Angeles anyway. Howard wanted to thoroughly scout out the existing Disneyland, so Millie had some time to think it out. She could go, as her heart directed her, with HJ to Florida and points beyond. She could take the future as it happened like a Disneyland ride or she could listen to the dismal eloquence of her ulcer and try to make the best arrangements she could. Howard and Otis would take care of her to the end, there were no doubts about that, and the end would be the end. But if she stayed in this apartment, sure of the arrangements for later, she would miss whatever might still be left before the end. Mildred wished there were some clergyman she could consult, but she had never attended a church and believed in no religious doctrine. Her father had been a firm atheist to the very moment of his office suicide, and she remained a passive nonbeliever. Her theology was the order of her own life. Millie had never

deceived herself; in spite of her riches all she truly owned was her life, a pocket of habits in the burning universe. But the habits were careful and clean and they were best represented in the body that was she. Freezing her remains was the closest image she could conjure of eternal life. It might not be eternal and it surely would not be life, but that damp, musty feel, that odor she smelled on herself after the pain, that could be avoided, and who knew what else might be saved from the void for a small initial investment and $200 a year. And if you did not believe in a soul, was there not every reason to preserve a body?

Mrs. Albert of the Cryonic Society welcomed Mildred to a tour of the premises. "See it while you can," she cheerfully told the group (Millie, two men, and a boy with notebook and Polaroid camera). Mrs. Albert, a big woman perhaps in her mid-sixties, carried a face heavy in flesh. Perhaps once the skin had been tight around her long chin and pointed cheekbones, but having lost its spring, the skin merely hung at her neck like a patient animal waiting for the rest of her to join in the decline. From the way she took the concrete stairs down to the vault, it looked as if the wait would be long. "I'm not ready for the freezer yet. I tell every group I take down here, it's gonna be a long time until they get me." Millie believed her. "I may not be the world's smartest cookie"—Mrs. Albert looked directly at Millie— "but a bird in the hand is the only bird I know, huh? That's why when it does come . . . Mrs. A. is going to be right here in this facility, and you better believe it. Now, Mr. King on your left"—she pointed to a capsule that looked like a large bullet to Millie—"Mr. King is the gentleman who took me on my first tour, cancer finally but had everything perfectly ready and I would say he was in prime cooling state within seconds and I believe that if they ever cure cancer, and you know they will the way they do most everything nowadays, old Mr. King may be back yet. If anyone got down to low-enough temperature immediately it would be Mr. King." Mildred saw the boy write "Return of the King" in his notebook. "Over here is Mr. and Mizz Winkleman, married sixty years, and went off within a month of each other, a lovely, lovely couple."

While Mrs. Albert continued her necrology and posed for a photo beside the Winklemans, Millie took careful note of the neon-lit room filled with bulletlike capsules. She watched the cool breaths of the group gather like flowers on the steel and vanish without dimming the bright surface. The capsules stood in straight lines with ample walking space between them. To Mrs. Albert they were friends, to Millie it seemed as if she were in a furniture store of the Scandinavian type where elegance is suggested by the absence of material, where straight lines of steel, wood, and glass indicate that relaxation too requires some taste and is not an indifferent sprawl across any soft object that happens to be nearby.

Cemeteries always bothered Millie, but here she felt none of the dread she had expected. She averted her eyes from the cluttered graveyards they always used to pass at the tips of cities in the early days. Fortunately, the superhighways twisted traffic into the city and away from those desolate marking places where used-car lots and the names of famous hotels inscribed on barns often neighbored the dead. Howard had once commented that never in all his experience did he have an intuition of a good location near a cemetery. You could put a lot of things there, you could put up a bowling alley, or maybe even a theater, but never a motel, and Millie knew he was right. He knew where to put his houses but it was Millie who knew how. From that first orange roof angling toward the east, the HJ design and the idea had been Millie's. She had not invented the motel, she had changed it from a place where you had to be to a place where you wanted to be. Perhaps, she thought, the Cryonic Society was trying to do the same for cemeteries.

When she and Howard had started their travels, the old motel courts huddled like so many dark graves around the stone marking of the highway. And what traveler coming into one of those dingy cabins could watch the watery rust dripping from his faucet without thinking of everything he was missing by being a traveler . . . his two-stall garage, his wife small in the half-empty bed, his children with hair the color of that rust. Under the orange Howard Johnson roof all this changed. For about the same price you were redeemed from the road. Headlights did not dazzle you on the foam mattress and percale sheets, your sanitized glasses and toilet appliances sparkled like the mirror behind them. The room was not just there, it awaited you, courted your pleasure, sat like a young bride outside the walls of the city wanting only to please you, you only you on the smoothly pressed sheets, your friend, your one-night destiny.

40   As if it were yesterday, Millie recalled right there in the cryonic vault the moment when she had first thought the thought that made Howard Johnson Howard Johnson's. And when she told Howard her decision that evening after cooking a cheese soufflé and risking a taste of wine, it was that memory she invoked for both of them, the memory of a cool autumn day in the '30s when a break in their schedule found Millie with a free afternoon in New Hampshire, an afternoon she had spent at the farm of a man who had once been her teacher and remembered her after ten years. Otis drove her out to Robert Frost's farm, where the poet made for her a lunch of scrambled eggs and 7 Up. Millie and Robert Frost talked mostly about the farm, about the cold winter he was expecting and the autumn apples they picked from the trees. He was not so famous then, his hair was only streaked with gray as Howard's was, and she told the poet about what she and Howard were doing, about what she felt about being on the road in America, and Robert Frost said he hadn't been that much but she sounded like she knew and he believed she might be able to accomplish something. He did not remember the poem she wrote in his class but that didn't matter.

"Do you remember, Howard, how I introduced you to him? Mr. Frost, this is Mr. Johnson. I can still see the two of you shaking hands there beside the car. I've always been proud that I introduced you to one another." Howard Johnson nodded his head at the memory, seemed as nostalgic as Millie while he sat in her apartment learning why she would not go to Florida to help bring Howard Johnson's to the new Disneyland.

"And after we left his farm, Howard, remember? Otis took the car in for servicing and left us with some sandwiches on the top of a hill overlooking a town, I don't even remember which one, maybe we never knew the name of it. And we stayed on that hilltop while the sun began to set in New Hampshire. I felt so full of poetry and"—she looked at Howard—"of love, Howard, only about an hour's drive from Robert Frost's farmhouse. Maybe it was just the way we felt then, but I think the sun set differently that night, filtering through the clouds like a big paintbrush making the top of the town all orange. And suddenly I thought what if the tops of our houses were that kind of orange, what a world it would be, Howard, and my God, that orange stayed until the last drop of light was left in it. I didn't feel the cold up there even though it took Otis so long to get back to us. The feeling we had about that orange, Howard, that was ours and that's what I've tried to bring to every house, the way we felt that night. Oh, it makes me sick to think of Colonel Sanders, and Big Boy, and Holiday Inn, and Best Western . . ."

"It's all right, Millie, it's all right." Howard patted her heaving back. Now that he knew about her ulcer and why she wanted to stay behind, the mind that had conjured butterfly shrimp and twenty-eight flavors set himself a new project. He contemplated Millie sobbing in his lap the way he contemplated prime acreage. There was so little of her, less than one hundred pounds, yet without her Howard Johnson felt himself no match for the wily Disneys gathering near the moonport.

He left her in all her sad resignation that evening, left her thinking she had to give up what remained here to be sure of the proper freezing. But Howard Johnson had other ideas. He did not cancel the advance reservations made for Mildred Bryce along the route to Florida, nor did he remove her filing cabinet from the limousine. The man who hosted a nation and already kept one freezer in his car ordered another, this one designed according to cryonic specifications and presented to Mildred housed in a twelve-foot orange U-Haul trailer connected to the rear bumper of the limousine.

45   "Everything's here," he told the astonished Millie, who thought Howard had left the week before, "everything is here and you'll never have to be more than seconds away from it. It's exactly like a refrigerated truck." Howard Johnson opened the rear door of the U-Haul as proudly as he had ever dedicated a motel. Millie's steel capsule shone within, surrounded by an array of chemicals stored on heavily padded rubber shelves. The California sun was on her back, but her cold breath hovered visibly within the U-Haul. No tears came to Mildred now; she felt relief much as she had felt it that afternoon near ancient Jericho. On Santa Monica Boulevard, in front of Lawrence Welk's apartment building, Mildred Bryce confronted her immortality, a gift from the ice-cream king, another companion for the remainder of her travels. Howard Johnson had turned away, looking toward the ocean. To his blue back and patriarchal white hairs, Mildred said, "Howard, you can do anything," and closing the doors of the U-Haul, she joined the host of the highways, a man with two portable freezers, ready now for the challenge of Disney World.

Questions

1. How soon do you suspect that this is not about the real founder of the Howard Johnson restaurants and motels, but someone made up?

    Is it fantasy for Max Apple to remake Howard Johnson according to his imagination? Is this an absurdist story? How?

2. Is this story satirical? Does it have a theme?

3. Discuss this story in terms of point of view, characterization round and flat, plot structure, and setting.

4. Take this sentence: "It was an ideal division of labor, which, in one form or another, had been in continuous operation for well over a quarter of a century." Discuss the style of this sentence—its diction, syntax, and familiarity of phrase.

5. ". . . he contemplated the map and saw that it was good." Who is Howard Johnson compared to by this allusion?

6. A book called *The Greening of America* prophesied a new nonmaterialistic culture in our country, growing from the 1960s of flower people and Woodstock. Apple's "The Oranging of America" came afterward. Does this suggest a theme?

7. Does Apple use many clichés in this story? Might he intend to? Why?

8. If Apple is a satirist, does he feel affection for what he satirizes? How do you know?

9. Is cryonics essential to the theme of this story? Would another technological fad have done as well?

10. What is Robert Frost doing in this story? Does he belong in it?

The comic story

Thurber's "The Catbird Seat" and Apple's "The Oranging of America" are stories that make us laugh. Several of the writers here represented by unfunny stories—William Faulkner, Eudora Welty, James Joyce—have written literature that is also comic. Great writing often includes scenes or moments of humor: Dickens is a superb comedian; Shakespeare makes humor not only in his comedies but also in his tragedies; Mark Twain's fiction makes him a great American humorist. We must not allow our perception of literature's seriousness to prevent us from seeing its humor, for literature may be serious and comic at the same time.

Woody Allen
The Whore of Mensa

Woody Allen (1935–   ) is an actor, playwright, screenwriter, and film director as well as author of short stories and parodies usually printed in *The New Yorker*. His two collections of prose are *Getting Even* (1971) and *Without Feathers* (1975). "The Whore of Mensa" parodies detective fiction, like Raymond Chandler's novels about a hard-boiled private eye. Mensa (an organization for people with high scores on IQ tests) is irrelevant to hard-boiled private detective stories, except insofar as contrast makes irony and comedy.

One thing about being a private investigator, you've got to learn to go with your hunches. That's why when a quivering pat of butter named Word Babcock walked into my office and laid his cards on the table, I should have trusted the cold chill that shot up my spine.

"Kaiser?" he said, "Kaiser Lupowitz?"

"That's what it says on my license," I owned up.

"You've got to help me. I'm being blackmailed. Please!"

5 He was shaking like the lead singer in a rumba band. I pushed a glass across the desk top and a bottle of rye I keep handy for nonmedicinal purposes. "Suppose you relax and tell me all about it."

"You . . . you won't tell my wife?"

"Level with me, Word. I can't make any promises."

He tried pouring a drink, but you could hear the clicking sound across the street, and most of the stuff wound up in his shoes.

"I'm a working guy," he said. "Mechanical maintenance. I build and service joy buzzers. You know—those little fun gimmicks that give people a shock when they shake hands?"

10 "So?"

"A lot of your executives like 'em. Particularly down on Wall Street."

"Get to the point."

"I'm on the road a lot. You know how it is—lonely. Oh, not what you're thinking. See, Kaiser, I'm basically an intellectual. Sure, a guy can meet all the bimbos he wants. But the really brainy women—they're not so easy to find on short notice."

"Keep talking."

15   "Well, I heard of this young girl. Eighteen years old. A Yassar student. For a price, she'll come over and discuss any subject—Proust, Yeats, anthropology. Exchange of ideas. You see what I'm driving at?"

"Not exactly."

"I mean, my wife is great, don't get me wrong. But she won't discuss Pound with me. Or Eliot. I didn't know that when I married her. See, I need a woman who's mentally stimulating, Kaiser. And I'm willing to pay for it. I don't want an involvement—I want a quick intellectual experience, then I want the girl to leave. Christ, Kaiser, I'm a happily married man."

"How long has this been going on?"

"Six months. Whenever I have that craving, I call Flossie. She's a madam, with a master's in comparative lit. She sends me over an intellectual, see?"

20   So he was one of those guys whose weakness was really bright women. I felt sorry for the poor sap. I figured there must be a lot of jokers in his position, who were starved for a little intellectual communication with the opposite sex and would pay through the nose for it.

"Now she's threatening to tell my wife," he said.

"Who is?"

"Flossie. They bugged the motel room. They got tapes of me discussing *The Waste Land* and *Styles of Radical Will,* and, well, really getting into some issues. They want ten grand or they go to Carla. Kaiser, you've got to help me! Carla would die if she knew she didn't turn me on up here."

The old call-girl racket. I had heard rumors that the boys at headquarters were on to something involving a group of educated women, but so far they were stymied.

25   "Get Flossie on the phone for me."

"What?"

"I'll take your case, Word. But I get fifty dollars a day, plus expenses. You'll have to repair a lot of joy buzzers."

"It won't be ten Gs' worth, I'm sure of that," he said with a grin, and picked up the phone and dialed a number. I took it from him and winked. I was beginning to like him.

Seconds later, a silky voice answered, and I told her what was on my mind. "I understand you can help me set up an hour of good chat," I said.

30   "Sure, honey, What do you have in mind?"

"I'd like to discuss Melville."

"*Moby Dick* or the shorter novels?"

"What's the difference?"

"The price. That's all. Symbolism's extra."

35   "What'll it run me?"

"Fifty, maybe a hundred for *Moby Dick*. You want a comparative discussion—Melville and Hawthorne? That could be arranged for a hundred."

"The dough's fine," I told her and gave her the number of a room at the Plaza.

"You want a blonde or a brunette?"

"Surprise me," I said, and hung up.

40   I shaved and grabbed some black coffee while I checked over the Monarch College Outline series. Hardly an hour had passed before there was a knock on my door. I opened it, and standing there was a young redhead who was packed into her slacks like two big scoops of vanilla ice cream.

"Hi, I'm Sherry."

They really knew how to appeal to your fantasies. Long straight hair, leather bag, silver earrings, no make-up.

"I'm surprised you weren't stopped, walking into the hotel dressed like that," I said. "The house dick can usually spot an intellectual."

"A five-spot cools him."

45   "Shall we begin?" I said, motioning her to the couch.

She lit a cigarette and got right to it. "I think we could start by approaching *Billy Budd* as Melville's justification of the ways of God to man, *n'est-ce pas?*"

"Interestingly, though, not in a Miltonian sense." I was bluffing. I wanted to see if she'd go for it.

"No. *Paradise Lost* lacked the substructure of pessimism." She did.

"Right, right. God, you're right," I murmured.

50   "I think Melville reaffirmed the virtues of innocence in a naïve yet sophisticated sense—don't you agree?"

I let her go on. She was barely nineteen years old, but already she had developed the hardened facility of the pseudo-intellectual. She rattled off her ideas glibly, but it was all mechanical. Whenever I offered an insight, she faked a response: "Oh, yes, Kaiser. Yes, baby, that's deep. A platonic comprehension of Christianity—why didn't I see it before?"

We talked for about an hour and then she said she had to go. She stood up and I laid a C-note on her.

"Thanks, honey."

"There's plenty more where that came from."

55   "What are you trying to say?"

I had piqued her curiosity. She sat down again.

"Suppose I wanted to—have a party?" I said.

"Like, what kind of party?"

"Suppose I wanted Noam Chomsky explained to me by two girls?"

60   "Oh, wow."

"If you'd rather forget it . . ."

"You'd have to speak with Flossie," she said. "It'd cost you."

Now was the time to tighten the screws. I flashed my private-investigator's badge and informed her it was a bust.

"What!"

65   "I'm fuzz, sugar, and discussing Melville for money is an 802. You can do time."

"You louse!"

"Better come clean, baby. Unless you want to tell your story down at Alfred Kazin's office, and I don't think he'd be too happy to hear it."

She began to cry. "Don't turn me in, Kaiser," she said. "I needed the money to complete my master's. I've been turned down for a grant. *Twice*. Oh, Christ."

It all poured out—the whole story. Central Park West upbringing. Socialist summer camps, Brandeis. She was every dame you saw waiting in line at the Elgin or the Thalia, or penciling the words "Yes, very true" into the margin of some book on Kant. Only somewhere along the line she had made a wrong turn.

70 "I needed cash. A girl friend said she knew a married guy whose wife wasn't very profound. He was into Blake. She couldn't hack it. I said sure, for a price I'd talk Blake with him. I was nervous at first. I faked a lot of it. He didn't care. My friend said there were others. Oh, I've been busted before. I got caught reading *Commentary* in a parked car, and I was once stopped and frisked at Tanglewood. Once more and I'm a three-time loser."

"Then take me to Flossie."

She bit her lip and said, "The Hunter College Book Store is a front."

"Yes?"

"Like those bookie joints that have barbershops outside for show. You'll see."

75 I made a quick call to headquarters and then said to her, "Okay, sugar. You're off the hook. But don't leave town."

She tilted her face up toward mine gratefully. "I can get you photographs of Dwight Macdonald reading," she said.

"Some other time."

I walked into the Hunter College Book Store. The salesman, a young man with sensitive eyes, came up to me. "Can I help you?" he said.

"I'm looking for a special edition of *Advertisements for Myself.* I understand the author had several thousand gold-leaf copies printed up for friends."

80 "I'll have to check," he said. "We have a WATS line to Mailer's house."

I fixed him with a look. "Sherry sent me," I said.

"Oh, in that case, go on back," he said. He pressed a button. A wall of books opened, and I walked like a lamb into that bustling pleasure palace known as Flossie's.

Red flocked wallpaper and a Victorian décor set the tone. Pale, nervous girls with black-rimmed glasses and blunt-cut hair lolled around on sofas, riffling Penguin Classics provocatively. A blonde with a big smile winked at me, nodded toward a room upstairs, and said, "Wallace Stevens, eh?" But it wasn't just intellectual experiences—they were peddling emotional ones, too. For fifty bucks, I learned, you could "relate without getting close." For a hundred, a girl would lend you her Bartók records, have dinner, and then let you watch while she had an anxiety attack. For one-fifty, you could listen to FM radio with twins. For three bills, you got the works: A thin Jewish brunette would pretend to pick you up at the Museum of Modern Art, let you read her master's, get you involved in a screaming quarrel at Elaine's over Freud's conception of women, and then fake a suicide of your choosing—the perfect evening, for some guys. Nice racket. Great town, New York.

"Like what you see?" a voice said behind me. I turned and suddenly found myself standing face to face with the business end of a .38. I'm a guy with a strong stomach, but this time it did a back flip. It was Flossie, all right. The voice was the same, but Flossie was a man. His face was hidden by a mask.

85 "You'll never believe this," he said, "but I don't even have a college degree. I was thrown out for low grades."

"Is that why you wear that mask?"

"I devised a complicated scheme to take over *The New York Review of Books,* but it meant I had to pass for Lionel Trilling. I went to Mexico for an operation. There's a doctor in Juarez who gives people Trilling's features—for a price. Something went wrong. I came out looking like Auden, with Mary McCarthy's voice. That's when I started working on the other side of the law."

Quickly, before he could tighten his finger on the trigger, I went into action.

Heaving forward, I snapped my elbow across his jaw and grabbed the gun as he fell back. He hit the ground like a ton of bricks. He was still whimpering when the police showed up.

"Nice work, Kaiser," Sergeant Holmes said. "When we're through with this guy, the F.B.I. wants to have a talk with him. A little matter involving some gamblers and an annotated copy of Dante's *Inferno.* Take him away, boys."

90   Later that night, I looked up an old account of mine named Gloria. She was blond. She had graduated *cum laude.* The difference was she majored in physical education. It felt good.

Questions

1. Which details of Allen's style are accurate imitations of a detective story? What details of his style make parody? How does he turn these details into humor?
2. Who wrote *Styles of Radical Will?* Does Allen make up any titles or names in this story?
3. A highlight of Allen's parody is the inappropriate metaphor or simile. Find some funny ones.
4. Is this story serious? Satirical?
5. Sergeant *Holmes*? See the next story.

Spencer Holst
The Case of the Giant Rat of Sumatra

Spencer Holst (1926–   ) grew up in Detroit and Toledo and now lives in Greenwich Village in New York. He is a storyteller who lists his influences as Hans Christian Andersen, Baudelaire, Martin Buber, and Edgar Allan Poe. In addition to one book of poetry, he has published two collections of short stories: *The Language of Cats* (1971) and *Spencer Holst Stories* (1976).

In Arthur Conan Doyle's Sherlock Holmes story "The Adventure of the Sussex Vampire," Holmes mentions "the giant rat of Sumatra, a story for which the world is not yet prepared."

1

A jar of olives in pitch darkness on the shelf of the restaurant kitchen in the small hours of the morning . . . the place closed and everyone gone. . . .

A large rat, fat and round as an olive, sat on its haunches on top of the jar.

It sniffed intently, and listened to the shrieking wind blowing a blinding blizzard into huge drifts. A 50-mile-an-hour wind in fifteen-below-zero weather boded death for the Traveler, and made even the restaurant kitchen unusually chilly, the water pipes having frozen, and there was ice in the sink.

High North Atlantic tides and the weather had forced the huge wharf rat to abandon its usual haunts—its nest was soaking wet—and seek shelter in this kitchen. He was a ten-year-old male from Sumatra three months off the ship from Rangoon and it was his first experience of the Norwegian winter.

5   He sat on the olive jar and twitched his whiskers, and listened long, for surrounding him and coming at him from every direction was the odor of . . . cat. Two cats guarded this kitchen. For an hour the rat sat there in the dark, relatively

warm, waiting quietly, and the rat heard no sound . . . except the wind, and in the distance the sloshing surf that had flooded his nest in the warehouse that faced the fjord.

A number of hours later the owner of the restaurant with his wife entered the building. They discovered the kitchen in chaos, evidence that a fantastic fight had taken place, blood all over the place, and small bones in the middle of the floor that had been eaten clean.

"What's wrong with this cat?" asked the wife who had found one of her cats huddled in a dark corner trembling and mewing softly, whimpering in a state of shock. The old lady sensed that the cat was not even aware of her presence. "What could have frightened her so?" inquired the old lady.

"Whatever it was," answered the husband, kneeling and examining the pile of bones, "it ate the other cat."

2

Large tropical wharf rats are noted for their uncanny intelligence, there are many stories of a fabled cleverness at avoiding traps, and this rat was quite bright.

10   During his entire stay in Norway he was not seen by a single human being.

And one is tempted to assume it was his wharf-rat intelligence that caused him soon to climb a cable of a ship about to set to sea, no doubt with a notion to return to Sumatra and warm sunshine.

The rat obviously couldn't understand Norwegian or he would have heard the sailors talking, and known that this ship—it was the ill-fated *Matilda Briggs*—housed an Arctic expedition.

Shortly thereafter the ship entered the pack ice, the ship became frozen in the ice, and the men huddled in the icy boat barely clinging to life as hopeless months passed and their provisions eventually gave out.

The rat's whiskers quivered with cold, and his eyebrows froze.

15   The leader of the expedition with three others set off on foot across the pack ice with the intention of bringing back help for those who stayed inside the meager shelter of the ship; and of course they succeeded, they brought back help, and a number of those who had waited, suffering in the ship, survived.

Among those who survived was an old English seaman, not an officer or any-thing—an old salt. On his first day in a civilized port, as he sat in a fancy tavern eating kidney pie, he was interviewed by an English journalist, a lady.

"Did the men pray?" asked the journalist.

"God *answered* my prayer!" said the seaman seriously. "It was a bloody miracle . . . about the rat!"

"What do you mean?" asked the journalist.

20   "There was a tropical wharf rat aboard, and I was determined to catch it. Many, many months I tried. I'm handy with tools, and I built a half-a-dozen traps, each more ingenious than the last. The men said I was mad, they said I was obsessed with catching the rat . . . but in the end they admitted I wasn't crazy. You see, it saved our lives. I'll never forget it was in the middle of an endless night, the party had left on foot four months before . . . finally in desperation I got up on the kitchen table so that the other sailors could see me, and I kneeled and clasped my hands, and I said out loud so that all could hear—I prayed to God that I catch the rat. And at that moment . . . so that all could hear it, there was a loud click, the sound of my trap snapping shut. I had caught the rat alive. If ever there was one of God's creatures who was at the right place at the right time, it was that rat in

my trap. After that we all knew that God was with us, was with us in the very room."

"You caught the rat . . . I see . . ." said the bewildered lady. And then she added, frowning heavily, "But what did you do with the rat?"

"We ate it," said the seaman. "Tasted like Chinese food. He was a remarkably healthy animal. Can't figure out what he ever found to eat on the ship, but he was round and fat as an olive."

"Did you like the taste?" asked the lady.

He looked sharply at her, for how could she know how many traps he had contrived, what a battle of wits it had become, the wharf-rat intelligence at avoiding traps pitted against the human intelligence of the animal trapper. But the trapper, the human, had finally won out; after many months in an endless night the human brain surpassed the wharf-rat brain . . . with a little help from God . . . and how could this poor lady understand that satisfaction? Grinning broadly he said, "Like Chinese food—it was delicious!"

3

25   Yet what does an old sailor know of the world?

What can he know of the life of the English journalist? Would it surprise him that a journalist would think nothing of eating a few mice on an afternoon?

Let us follow this lady as she leaves the restaurant and notice how, at the nearest garbage can, she disposes of her notes, and now as she enters a rather shabby deserted street along the waterfront she removes her pearls and rings, throwing these, along with her pocketbook, into another refuse can. Now her journey takes an unexpected turn as she slips between two abandoned buildings, and in those darkest shadows—is she taking off her clothes?

Now out of the darkest shadows comes a cat.

A skinny tomcat all sinew and bone.

30   He pauses a moment and goes beneath a fence and now down deserted passageways, now through a broken basement window into what some might call a cozy apartment, though somewhat messy, and smelling strongly of pipe tobacco and chemicals.

A rather large, comfortable old gray cat who had been napping, stirred and said, "Eh! What! Is that you Holmes? Where the devil have you been?"

"Watson, my good fellow! Don't bother getting up! I've been disguised as a lady journalist and I've had an enlightening conversation with a sailor, and he told me everything I wanted to know. Watson, do you recall several years ago in a Norwegian port there was a brutal murder and that I said I would not rest until I knew the fiend had gotten his just deserts?"

"You mean the waterfront restaurant murder! Two cats, sisters, I believe . . . lived alone in the restaurant. One found brutally murdered, and *eaten,* and the other left a raving lunatic! A hideous business!"

"And do you recall, Watson, that I found at the scene of the crime a hair from a large wharf rat that had lived in Sumatra and come to Norway via a ship from Rangoon. I learned that here in my laboratory from studying the hair. I could find no witness, neither cat nor human, who had seen such a rat in the vicinity. Yet I knew he had been there, and after awhile I realised he had escaped. I studied the shipping lists and the only boat he could have left on was the *Matilda Briggs,* Arctic bound. Well at long last, Watson, the ship has returned, and today I got positive proof that a rat fitting that description was indeed aboard, and was caught alive, and then eaten by the crew. So though no one in Norway ever once laid eyes on the murderer, even so, he is discovered and dead; he got his just deserts. Justice was served. I think we can call that case closed."

4

35   The gray cat fumbled with a key held awkwardly in his paw trying to open his desk.

"Watson, allow me to assist you with that," said Holmes, easily opening the recalcitrant drawer which held the famous files kept by Dr. Watson on the cases of Sherlock Holmes. "Watson, sometimes I think you're ambisinistrous," chided the great detective.

Watson blushed. "I was thinking of something else! Damnation about the key— I had an idea! The title! Imagine this in large letters in my Table of Contents: The Case of the GIANT RAT OF SUMATRA . . . What do you think?"

"Watson, old friend, the world is not ready for this tale. You must not publish it."

"What's that you say! Not publish it! Tosh! Certainly I'll publish it, it's one of your greatest triumphs!"

40   "Confound it, Watson! Don't you see? You'll be revealing the Secret of Literature, and the world isn't ready for it, especially the publishing world isn't ready for the Secret of Literature. There is no way you can tell the story without revealing that you and I are Conan Doyle's cats. When an author's cat wishes to dress-up and act like a man he becomes a character in a book, and in fiction no one can discern that we are not regular people. But it must remain secret! The publishing world— those editors, those critics, those literary agents of whom I know you are so fond— would be dismayed, Watson, *deeply* dismayed to learn you are a cat, that Lady Chatterley, Bloom, Scrooge, Robinson Crusoe, and Moby Dick himself were all cats! Cats all! And your friends . . . unquestionably . . . would grow to feel queer about their work. . . ."

"Good Doctor Watson, don't you see? The Case of the GIANT RAT OF SU-MATRA must never be published . . . ever. I, Sherlock Holmes, forbid it!"

Questions

1. Discuss point of view in this story.
2. Is Holst fair in his storytelling? Does the construction of this story play havoc with your expectations of short fiction? Does this havoc seem intentional?
3. Is this story absurd? Fantastic?
4. Many assert that every detail in a story must point toward a certain effect, so that there are no loose ends. Does Holst abide by this rule? What do you make of the last paragraphs of the second section?
5. Do you notice any punning in this story? Look at the last few lines of the third section.
6. What does Holst say about the nature of fiction in the next-to-last paragraph of the story?

Science fiction

Science fiction is popular art, giving us movies (*Star Wars*) and television shows (*Star Trek, Battlestar Galactica*) as well as magazines and racks of paperbacks. Historically, science fiction begins in the nineteenth century as a variety of the horror story that combines fantasy with science. When Mary Shelley wrote *Frankenstein,* she made a horror story in which a body was constructed by the scientific Dr. Frankenstein. When Robert Louis Stevenson wrote *Doctor Jekyll and Mr. Hyde,* the transformation was accomplished by a chemical potion.

As science and technology developed, they readily entered fiction. During the last forty or fifty years, science fiction has thrived, from thrillers in pulp magazines to ambitious novels. Some writers have constructed ideal future worlds combining leisure with ethics, Utopias of technology. A Utopia is an imagined ideal country, a way of arguing politics and morals by the fantasy of a perfect model. But more important in recent decades has been the anti-Utopia, an inverted ideal describing a world where everything has gone rotten. Writers have set this bad world in the future, making science fiction that is *against* science, or against the uses technology serves. Two famous examples are Aldous Huxley's *Brave New World* and George Orwell's *1984.* Many of the stories published in science-fiction magazines like *Analog* present small anti-Utopias, as does some of the best work of Kurt Vonnegut and Ray Bradbury.

Many reasons have been offered for the popularity of science fiction. One source is our perennial love for the exotic—and for adventure. Some science fiction resembles the old travel books, which told of dragons guarding the ocean's edge. When the Western American frontier still retained its myth, we made it a place for daydream adventures. Now science fiction imagines a new frontier of the stars.

But some sources are more profound. In religious societies of the past, much popular attention focused on death and the afterlife, on hell and on heaven. In recent secular times, people have looked to the future instead of the afterlife. Now we read in newspapers and magazines projections of a golden future of leisure, people served by machines and relieved of drudgery. Where people used to imagine a golden age of the past or project a golden heaven, consumer-readers now daydream a golden age of gadgets. Writers imagine for us a house automatically cleaned, with its food automatically cooked according to a program punched into a keyboard. If this daydream seems paradisal, it finds its dark side in the nightmarish anti-Utopia, for our love of machines is also fear of machines. The (mad) scientist need not consult the devil in his laboratory—but if he goes too far, he oversteps the bounds, and all of us are punished. With this fear—of going too far, of being enslaved by our own slave-machines—come a dread and a hope that are virtually religious. It is not fanciful to say that in much science fiction we exercise our old religious fears and religious desires, our serious intercourse with the unknown.

Kurt Vonnegut, Jr.
Harrison Bergeron

Kurt Vonnegut, Jr. (1922–   ) was a prisoner of war in Germany during the Second World War. In recent years he has combined writing with university teaching. He writes science fiction, fantasy, and political satire. His works include *The Sirens of Titan* (1961), *Cat's Cradle* (1963), *Slaughterhouse Five* (1969), *Breakfast of Champions* (1972), *Slapstick* (1976), and *Jailbird* (1979).

The year was 2081, and everybody was finally equal. They weren't only equal before God and the law. They were equal every which way. Nobody was smarter than anybody else. Nobody was better looking than anybody else. Nobody was stronger or quicker than anybody else. All this equality was due to the 211th, 212th, and 213th Amendments to the Constitution, and to the unceasing vigilance of agents of the United States Handicapper General.

Some things about living still weren't quite right, though. April, for instance, still drove people crazy by not being springtime. And it was in that clammy month that the H-G men took George and Hazel Bergeron's fourteen-year-old son, Harrison, away.

It was tragic, all right, but George and Hazel couldn't think about it very hard. Hazel had a perfectly average intelligence, which meant she couldn't think about anything except in short bursts. And George, while his intelligence was way above normal, had a little mental handicap radio in his ear. He was required by law to wear it at all times. He was tuned to a government transmitter. Every twenty seconds or so, the transmitter would send out some sharp noise to keep people like George from taking unfair advantage of their brains.

George and Hazel were watching television. There were tears on Hazel's cheeks, but she'd forgotten for the moment what they were about.

5   On the television screen were ballerinas.

A buzzer sounded in George's head. His thoughts fled in panic, like bandits from a burglar alarm.

"That was a really pretty dance, that dance they just did," said Hazel.

"Huh?" said George.

"That dance—it was nice," said Hazel.

10   "Yup," said George. He tried to think a little about the ballerinas. They weren't really very good—no better than anybody else would have been, anyway. They were burdened with sash-weights and bags of birdshot, and their faces were masked, so that no one, seeing a free and graceful gesture or a pretty face, would feel like something the cat drug in. George was toying with the vague notion that maybe dancers shouldn't be handicapped. But he didn't get very far with it before another noise in his ear radio scattered his thoughts.

George winced. So did two out of the eight ballerinas.

Hazel saw him wince. Having no mental handicap herself, she had to ask George what the latest sound had been.

"Sounded like somebody hitting a milk bottle with a ball peen hammer," said George.

"I'd think it would be real interesting, hearing all the different sounds," said Hazel, a little envious. "All the things they think up."

15   "Um," said George.

182

"Only, if I was Handicapper General, you know what I would do?" said Hazel. Hazel, as a matter of fact, bore a strong resemblance to the Handicapper General, a woman named Diana Moon Glampers. "If I was Diana Moon Glampers," said Hazel, "I'd have chimes on Sunday—fast chimes. Kind of in honor of religion."

"I could think, if it was just chimes," said George.

"Well—maybe make 'em real loud," said Hazel. "I think I'd make a good Handicapper General."

"Good as anybody else," said George.

20   "Who knows better'n I do what normal is?" said Hazel.

"Right," said George. He began to think glimmeringly about his abnormal son who was now in jail, about Harrison, but a twenty-one-gun salute in his head stopped that.

"Boy!" said Hazel, "that was a doozy, wasn't it?"

It was such a doozy that George was white and trembling, and tears stood on the rims of his red eyes. Two of the eight ballerinas had collapsed to the studio floor, were holding their temples.

"All of a sudden you look so tired," said Hazel. "Why don't you stretch out on the sofa, so's you can rest your handicap bag on the pillows, honeybunch." She was referring to the forty-seven pounds of birdshot in a canvas bag, which was padlocked around George's neck. "Go on and rest the bag for a little while," she said. "I don't care if you're not equal to me for a while."

25   George weighed the bag with his hands. "I don't mind it," he said. "I don't notice it any more. It's just a part of me."

"You been so tired lately—kind of wore out," said Hazel. "If there was just some way we could make a little hole in the bottom of the bag, and just take out a few of them lead balls. Just a few."

"Two years in prison and two thousand dollars fine for every ball I took out," said George. "I don't call that a bargain."

"If you could just take a few out when you came home from work," said Hazel. "I mean—you don't compete with anybody around here. You just set around."

"If I tried to get away with it," said George, "then other people'd get away with it—and pretty soon we'd be right back to the dark ages again, with everybody competing against everybody else. You wouldn't like that, would you?"

30   "I'd hate it," said Hazel.

"There you are," said George. "The minute people start cheating on laws, what do you think happens to society?"

If Hazel hadn't been able to come up with an answer to this question, George couldn't have supplied one. A siren was going off in his head.

"Reckon it'd fall all apart," said Hazel.

"What would?" said George blankly.

35   "Society," said Hazel uncertainly. "Wasn't that what you just said?"

"Who knows?" said George.

The television program was suddenly interrupted for a news bulletin. It wasn't clear at first as to what the bulletin was about, since the announcer, like all announcers, had a serious speech impediment. For about half a minute, and in a state of high excitement, the announcer tried to say, "Ladies and gentlemen—"

He finally gave up, handed the bulletin to a ballerina to read.

"That's all right—" Hazel said of the announcer, "he tried. That's the big thing. He tried to do the best he could with what God gave him. He should get a nice raise for trying so hard."

40   "Ladies and gentlemen—" said the ballerina, reading the bulletin. She must have been extraordinarily beautiful, because the mask she wore was hideous. And it was easy to see that she was the strongest and most graceful of all the dancers, for her handicap bags were as big as those worn by two-hundred-pound men.

And she had to apologize at once for her voice, which was a very unfair voice for a woman to use. Her voice was a warm, luminous, timeless melody. "Excuse me—" she said, and she began again, making her voice absolutely uncompetitive.

"Harrison Bergeron, age fourteen," she said in a grackle squawk, "has just escaped from jail, where he was held on suspicion of plotting to overthrow the government. He is a genius and an athlete, is under-handicapped, and should be regarded as extremely dangerous."

A police photograph of Harrison Bergeron was flashed on the screen upside down, then sideways, upside down again, then right side up. The picture showed the full length of Harrison against a background calibrated in feet and inches. He was exactly seven feet tall.

The rest of Harrison's appearance was Halloween and hardware. Nobody had ever borne heavier handicaps. He had outgrown hindrances faster than the H-G men could think them up. Instead of a little ear radio for a mental handicap, he wore a tremendous pair of earphones, and spectacles with thick wavy lenses. The spectacles were intended to make him not only half blind, but to give him whanging headaches besides.

45   Scrap metal was hung all over him. Ordinarily, there was a certain symmetry, a military neatness to the handicaps issued to strong people, but Harrison looked like a walking junkyard. In the race of life, Harrison carried three hundred pounds.

And to offset his good looks, the H-G men required that he wear at all times a red rubber ball for a nose, keep his eyebrows shaved off, and cover his even white teeth with black caps at snaggle-tooth random.

"If you see this boy," said the ballerina, "do not—I repeat, do not—try to reason with him."

There was the shriek of a door being torn from its hinges.

Screams and barking cries of consternation came from the television set. The photograph of Harrison Bergeron on the screen jumped again and again, as though dancing to the tune of an earthquake.

50   George Bergeron correctly identified the earthquake, and well he might have— for many was the time his own home had danced to the same crashing tune. "My God—" said George, "that must be Harrison!"

The realization was blasted from his mind instantly by the sound of an automobile collision in his head.

When George could open his eyes again, the photograph of Harrison was gone. A living, breathing Harrison filled the screen.

Clanking, clownish, and huge, Harrison stood in the center of the studio. The knob of the uprooted studio door was still in his hand. Ballerinas, technicians, musicians, and announcers cowered on their knees before him, expecting to die.

"I am the Emperor!" cried Harrison. "Do you hear? I am the Emperor! Everybody must do what I say at once!" He stamped his foot and the studio shook.

55   "Even as I stand here—" he bellowed, "crippled, hobbled, sickened—I am a greater ruler than any man who ever lived! Now watch me become what I *can* become!"

Harrison tore the straps of his handicap harness like wet tissue paper, tore straps guaranteed to support five thousand pounds.

Harrison's scrap-iron handicaps crashed to the floor.

Harrison thrust his thumbs under the bar of the padlock that secured his head harness. The bar snapped like celery. Harrison smashed his headphones and spectacles against the wall.

He flung away his rubber-ball nose, revealed a man that would have awed Thor, the god of thunder.

60   "I shall now select my Empress!" he said, looking down on the cowering people. "Let the first woman who dares rise to her feet claim her mate and her throne!"

A moment passed, and then a ballerina arose, swaying like a willow.

Harrison plucked the mental handicap from her ear, snapped off her physical handicaps with marvelous delicacy. Last of all, he removed her mask.

She was blindingly beautiful.

"Now—" said Harrison, taking her hand, "shall we show the people the meaning of the word dance? Music!" he commanded.

65   The musicians scrambled back into their chairs, and Harrison stripped them of their handicaps, too. "Play your best," he told them, "and I'll make you barons and dukes and earls."

The music began. It was normal at first—cheap, silly, false. But Harrison snatched two musicians from their chairs, waved them like batons as he sang the music as he wanted it played. He slammed them back into their chairs.

The music began again and was much improved.

Harrison and his Empress merely listened to the music for a while—listened gravely, as though synchronizing their heartbeats with it.

They shifted their weights to their toes.

70   Harrison placed his big hands on the girl's tiny waist, letting her sense the weightlessness that would soon be hers.

And then, in an explosion of joy and grace, into the air they sprang!

Not only were the laws of the land abandoned, but the law of gravity and the laws of motion as well.

They reeled, whirled, swiveled, flounced, capered, gamboled, and spun.

They leaped like deer on the moon.

75   The studio ceiling was thirty feet high, but each leap brought the dancers nearer to it.

It became their obvious intention to kiss the ceiling.

They kissed it.

And then, neutralizing gravity with love and pure will, they remained suspended in air inches below the ceiling, and they kissed each other for a long, long time.

It was then that Diana Moon Glampers, the Handicapper General, came into the studio with a double-barreled ten-gauge shotgun. She fired twice, and the Emperor and the Empress were dead before they hit the floor.

80   Diana Moon Glampers loaded the gun again. She aimed it at the musicians and told them they had ten seconds to get their handicaps back on.

It was then that the Bergerons' television tube burned out.

Hazel turned to comment about the blackout to George. But George had gone out into the kitchen for a can of beer.

George came back in with a beer, paused while a handicap signal shook him up. And then he sat down again. "You been crying?" he said to Hazel.

"Yup," she said.

85   "What about?" he said.

"I forget," she said. "Something real sad on television."

"What was it?" he said.

"It's all kind of mixed up in my mind," said Hazel.

"Forget sad things," said George.

90　"I always do," said Hagel.

"That's my girl," said George. He winced. There was the sound of a rivetting gun in his head.

"Gee—I could tell that one was a doozy," said Hazel.

"You can say that again," said George.

"Gee—" said Hazel, "I could tell that one was a doozy."

Questions

1. What does the first paragraph tell you about this story? If it is exposition, do you learn only facts? Do you learn an attitude toward these facts? Do you catch a tone?

2. George's mind is distracted by certain sounds. In choosing and naming these sounds, does the author reveal a satirical purpose?

3. Discuss point of view in this story. What difference would it have made if you had the story from Harrison's point of view?

4. Do George and Hazel remind you of anybody you know? Despite all the invented hardware they live among, do they seem ordinary? Does their commonness contribute to the story's theme?

5. The story ends with a very old joke. Why?

Stanislaw Lem
How Erg the Self-Inducting Slew a Paleface

Stanislaw Lem (1921–　　) was born in Lvov, now a part of the Soviet Union, when it was still a Polish city. He trained in medicine, spent the Nazi occupation as a garage mechanic, and began to publish fiction after World War II. He has written more than thirty books, most of them science fiction, including *The Invincible, Memoirs Found in a Bathtub, The Futurological Congress, The Cyberiad,* and *The Star Diaries.* He lives in the Polish city of Cracow.

The mighty King Boludar loved curiosities and devoted himself wholly to the collecting of them, often forgetting about important affairs of state. He had a collection of clocks, and among them were dancing clocks, sunrise clocks and clock-clouds. He also had stuffed monsters from all four corners of the Universe, and in a special room, under a bell glass, the rarest of creatures—the Homos Anthropos, most wonderfully pale, two-legged, and it even had eyes, though empty. The King ordered two lovely rubies set in them, giving the Homos a red stare. Whenever he grew mellow with drink, Boludar would invite his favorite guests to this room and show them the frightful thing.

One day there came to the King's court an electrosage so old that the crystals of his mind had grown somewhat confused with age; nevertheless this electrosage, named Halazon, possessed the wisdom of a galaxy. It was said that he knew ways of threading photons on a string, producing thereby necklaces of light, and even that he knew how to capture a living Anthropos. Aware of the old one's weakness, the King ordered the wine cellars opened immediately: the electrosage, having taken one pull too many from the Leyden jug, when the pleasant currents were coursing through his limbs, betrayed a terrible secret to the King and promised to obtain for him an Anthropos, which was the ruler of a certain interstellar tribe. The price he set was high—the weight of the Anthropos in fist-sized diamonds—but the King didn't blink at it.

Halazon then set off on his journey. The King meanwhile began to boast before the royal council of his expected acquisition, which he could not in any case conceal, having already ordered a cage of heavy iron bars to be built in the castle park, where the most magnificent crystals grew. The court was thrown into great consternation. Seeing that the King would not give in, the advisors summoned to the castle two erudite homologists, whom the King received warmly, for he was curious as to what these much-knowledged ones, Salamid and Thaladon, could tell him that he did not already know about the pale being.

"Is it true," he asked, as soon as they had risen from their knees, rendering him obeisance, "that the Homos is softer than wax?"

5   "It is, Your Luminositude," both replied.

"And is it also true that the aperture it has at the bottom of its face can produce a number of different sounds?"

"Yes, Your Royal Highness, and in addition, into this same opening the Homos stuffs various objects, then moves the lower portion of the head, which is fastened by hinges to the upper portion, wherewith the objects are broken up and it draws them into its interior."

"A peculiar custom, of which I've heard," said the King. "But tell me, my wise ones, for what purpose does it do this?"

"On that particular subject there are four theories, Your Royal Highness," replied the homologists. "The first, that it does this to rid itself of excess venom (for it is venomous to an extreme). The second, that this act is performed for the sake of destruction, which it places above all other pleasures. The third—out of greed, for it would consume everything if it were able, and the fourth, that . . ."

10   "Fine, fine!" said the King. "Is it true the thing is made of water, and yet non-transparent, like that puppet of mine?"

"This too is true! It has, Sire, a multitude of slimy tubes inside, through which waters circulate; some are yellow, some pearl gray, but most are red—the red carry a dreadful poison called phlogiston or oxygen, which gas turns everything it touches instantly to rust or else to flame. The Homos itself therefore changes color, pearly, yellow, and pink. Nevertheless, Your Royal Highness, we humbly beseech you to abandon your idea of bringing here a live Homos, for it is a powerful creature and malicious as no other. . . ."

"This you must explain to me more fully," said the King, as though he were ready to accede to the wise ones. In reality, however, he only wished to feed his enormous curiosity.

"The beings to which the Homos belongs are called miasmals, Sire. To these belong the silicites and the proteids; the first are of thicker consistency, thus we call them gelatinoids or aspics; the others, more rare, are given different names by different authors—as, for example, gummids or mucilids by Pollomender; quag-backed pasties or bogheads by Tricephalos of Arboran; and finally, Analcymander the Brazen dubbed them fenny-eyed slubber-yucks. . . ."

"Is it true, then, that even their eyes are full of scum?" King Boludar asked eagerly.

15   "It is, Sire. These creatures, outwardly weak and frail, so that a drop of sixty feet is all it takes to make one splat into a liquid red, by their native cunning represent a danger worse than all the whirlpools and reefs of the Great Asteroid Noose together! And so we beg of you, Sire, for the good of the kingdom . . ."

"Yes, yes, fine," interrupted the King. "You may go now, my dears, and we shall arrive at our decision with all due deliberation."

The wise homologists bowed low and departed, uneasy in their minds, fearing that King Boludar had not forsaken his dangerous plan.

By and by a stellar vessel came in the night and brought enormous crates. These were conveyed immediately to the royal garden. Before long the gold gates were opened wide for all the royal subjects; there among the diamond groves, the gazebos of carved jasper and the marble prodigies, they saw an iron cage, and in it a pale thing, and flabby, that sat upon a small barrel before a saucer filled with something strange—true, the substance did give off the smell of oil, but of oil burnt over a flame, therefore spoiled and totally unfit for use. Yet the creature calmly dipped a kind of shovel in the saucer and, lifting up the oily goo, deposited it into its facial opening.

The spectators were speechless with horror when they read the sign on the cage, which said that they had before them an Anthropos, Homos, a living paleface. The mob began to taunt it, but then the Homos rose, scooped up something from the barrel on which it had been sitting, and sprayed the gaping crowd with a lethal water. Some fled, others seized stones to smite the abomination, but the guards dispersed everyone at once.

20   These events reached the ear of the King's daughter, Electrina. It would seem she had inherited her father's curiosity, for she was not afraid to approach the cage in which the monster spent its time scratching itself or imbibing enough water and rancid oil to kill a hundred royal subjects on the spot.

The Homos quickly learned intelligent speech and was so bold as to engage Electrina in conversation.

The Princess asked it once what that white stuff was which glittered in its maw.

"That I call teeth," it said.

"Oh, let me have one!" requested the Princess.

25   "And what will you give me for it?" it asked.

"I'll give you my little golden key, but only for a moment."

"What kind of key is it?"

"My personal key. I use it every evening to wind up my mind. You must have one too."

"My key is different from yours," it answered evasively. "And where do you keep it?"

30   "Here, on my breast, beneath this little golden lid."

"Hand it over. . . ."

"And you'll give me teeth?"

"Sure."

The princess turned a little golden screw, opened the lid, took out a little golden key and passed it through the bars. The paleface grabbed it greedily and, chuckling with glee, retreated to the center of the cage. The Princess implored and pleaded with it to return the key, but all in vain. Afraid to let anyone find out what she had done, Electrina went back to her palace chambers with a heavy heart. She had acted foolishly, perhaps, but then she was still practically a child. The next day her servants found her senseless in her crystal bed. The King and Queen came running, and the whole court after them. She lay as if asleep, but it was not possible to waken her. The King summoned the court physicians-electricians, his medics, techs and mechanicians, and these, examining the princess, discovered that her lid was open—no little screw, no little key! The alarm was sounded in the castle; pandemonium reigned; everyone rushed here and there looking for the little key, but to no avail. The next day the King, deep in despair, was informed that his paleface wished to speak with him on the matter of the missing key. The King went himself to the park without delay, and the monstrosity told him that it knew where the Princess had lost her key, but would reveal this only when the King had given his royal word to restore to it its freedom, and moreover, supply a spacefaring vessel so it could return to its own kind. The King stubbornly refused, ordering the park searched up and down, but at last agreed to these terms. Thus a spacecraft was readied for flight, and guards escorted the paleface from its cage. The King was waiting by the ship; the Anthropos, however, promised to tell him where the key lay as soon as it was on board and not before.

35   But once on board, it stuck its head out a vent hole and, holding up the bright key in its hand, shouted:

"Here is the key! I'm taking it with me, King, so that your daughter will never wake again, because I crave revenge, in that you humiliated me, keeping me in an iron cage as a laughingstock!!"

Flame shot from under the sterm of the spacecraft and the vessel rose into the sky while everyone stood dumbfounded. The King sent his fastest steel cloud-scorchers and whirlyprops in pursuit, but their crews all came back empty-handed, for the wily paleface had covered its tracks and given its pursuers the slip.

King Boludar now understood how wrong it had been of him not to heed the wise homologists, but the damage had been done. The foremost electrical locksmiths worked to fashion a duplicate key, the Great Assembler to the Throne, royal artisans, armorers and artefactotums, Lord High steelwrights and master goldforgers, and cybercounts and dynamargraves—all came to try their skill, but in vain. The King realized he would have to recover the key taken by the paleface; otherwise darkness would forever lie upon the sense and senses of the Princess.

He proclaimed therefore throughout the realm that this, that and the other had taken place, the anthropic paleface Homos had absconded with the golden key, and whosoever captured it, or retrieved the life-giving jewel and woke the Princess, would have her hand in marriage and ascend the throne.

40   Straightaway there appeared in droves daredevils of various cuts and sizes. Among these were electroknights of great renown as well as charlatan-swindlers, astrothieves, star drifters. To the castle came Demetricus Megawatt, the celebrated fencer-oscillator, possessing such feedback and speedback that no one could hold the field against him in single combat; and self-motes came from distant lands—the two Automatts, vector-victors in a hundred battles, and Prostheseus, constructionist *par excellence,* who never went anywhere without two spark absorbers, one black, the other silver. And there was Arbitron Cosmoski, all built of protocrystals and svelte as a spire; and Cyfer of Agrym the intellectrician, who on forty andromedaries in eighty boxes brought with him an old digital computer, rusted from much thinking yet still mighty of mind. Three champions from the race of the Selectivitites arrived: Diodius, Triodius and Heptodius, who possessed such a perfect vacuum in their heads that their black thought was like the starless

night. And Perpetuan came too, all in Leyden armor, with his commutator covered with verdigris from three hundred encounters; and Matrix Perforatem, who never went a day that he did not integrate someone. The latter brought to the palace his invincible cybersteed, a supercharger he called Megasus. They all assembled, and when the court was full, a barrel rolled up to the threshold and out of it spilled, in the shape of mercury, Erg the Self-inducting, who could assume whatever aspect he desired.

The heroes banqueted, lighting up the castle halls so that the marble of the ceilings glowed pink like a cloud at sunset. Then off they set, each his separate way, to seek out the paleface, challenge it to mortal combat and regain the key, and thereby win the Princess and the throne of Boludar. The first, Demetricus Megawatt, flew to Koldlea, where live the Jellyclabbers, for he thought to find out something there. And thus he dove into their ooze, carving out the way with blows from his remote-control saber, but nothing did he achieve; for when he waxed too warm his cooling system went, and the incomparable warrior found his grave on foreign soil, and the unclean ooze of the Jellyclabbers closed over his dauntless cathodes forever.

The two Automatts Vectorian reached the land of the Radomants, who raise up edifices out of luminescent gas, dabbling in radioactivity, and are such misers that each evening they count the atoms on their planet. Ill was the reception the grasping Radomants gave the Automatts, for they showed them a chasm full of onyxes, chrysolites, chalcedonies and spinels, and when the electroknights yielded to the temptation of the jewels, the Radomants stoned them to death, setting off from above an avalanche of precious stones, which, as it moved, blazed like a falling comet of a hundred colors. For the Radomants were allied to the palefaces by a secret pact, about which no one knew.

The third, Prostheseus the Constructionist, arrived after a long voyage through the interstellar dark at the land of the Algoncs. There meteors move in blizzards of rock. The schooner of Prostheseus ran into their inexorable wall. With a broken rudder he drifted through the deep; and when at last he neared some distant suns, their light played across that poor adventurer's sightless eyes.

The fourth, Arbitron Cosmoski, had better luck at first. He made it through the Andromeda straits, crossed the four spiral whirlpools of the Hunting Dogs, and after that came out into quiet space favorable for photon sailing. Like a nimble beam he took the helm and, leaving a trail of sweeping fire, reached the shores of the planet Maestricia, where amid meteorite boulders he spied the shattered wreck of the schooner on which Prostheseus had embarked. The body of the constructionist, powerful, shiny and cold as in life, he buried beneath a basalt heap, but took from him both spark-absorbers, the silver and the black, to serve as shields, and proceeded on his way. Wild and craggy was Maestricia; avalanches of stone roared across it, with a silver tangle of lightning in the clouds above the precipices. The knight came to a region of ravines and there the Palindromides fell upon him in a canyon of malachite, all green. With thunderbolts they lashed him from above, but he parried these with his spark-absorbing buckler till they moved up a volcano, set the crater on its side and, taking aim, belched fire at him. The knight fell and bubbling lava entered his skull, from which flowed all the silver.

45   The fifth, Cyfer of Agrym the intellectrician, went nowhere. Instead, halting right outside the borders of Boludar's kingdom, he released his andromedaries to graze in stellar pastures, and himself connected the machine, adjusted it, programmed it, bustled about its eighty boxes, and when all were brimming with current so

that it swelled with intelligence, he began putting to it precisely formulated questions: Where did the paleface live? How could one find the way? How could it be tricked? Trapped? How forced to give up the key? The answers, when they came, were vague and noncommittal. In a fury he whipped the machine until it began to smell of heated copper, and he continued to belabor it, crying, "The truth now, out with it, you blasted old digital computer!"—until at last its joints melted, tin trickled from them in silvery tears, the overheated pipes split open with a bang, and he was left standing incensed over a fused junkheap with a cudgel in his hand.

Shamefaced, he had to return home. He ordered a new machine, but did not see it until four hundred years later.

Sixth was the sally of the Selectivitites. Diodius, Triodius and Heptodius set about things differently. They had an inexhaustible supply of tritium, lithium and deuterium, and decided with explosions of heavy hydrogen to force open all the roads leading to the land of the palefaces. It was not known, however, where those roads began. They sought to ask the Pyropods, but the latter locked themselves behind the gold walls of their capital and hurled flame; the valiant-valent Selectivitites stormed the bastion, using both deuterium and tritium without stint till an inferno of stripped atoms looked the sky boldly in its starry eye. The walls of the citadel shone gold, but in the fire they betrayed their true nature, turning into yellow clouds of sulfuric smoke, for they had been built of pyrites-marcasites. There Diodius fell, trampled by the Pyropods, and his mind burst like a bouquet of colored crystals, spraying his armor. In a tomb of black olivine they buried him, then pressed on to the borders of the kingdom of Char, where the starkiller King Astrocida reigned. This king had a treasure house full of fiery nuclei plucked from white dwarfs, which were so heavy that only the terrible force of the palace magnets kept them from tearing through to the planet's core. Whoever stepped upon its ground could move neither arms nor legs, for the prodigious gravitation clamped down stronger than bolts or chains. Triodius and Heptodius were hard set here; for Astrocida, catching sight of them beneath the castle ramparts, rolled out one white dwarf after another and loosed the fire-spouting masses in their faces. They defeated him, however, and he revealed to them the way that led to the palefaces, wherein he deceived them, for he did not know the way, but wished only to be rid of the fearsome warriors. So they delved into the black heart of the void, where Triodius was shot by someone with an antimatter blunderbuss—it might have been one of the hunter-Cyberneers, or possibly a mine set for a tailless comet. In any case, Triodius vanished, with barely time to shout, "Tikcuff!!," his favorite word and the battle cry of his race. Heptodius stubbornly forged ahead, but a bitter end was in store for him as well. His vessel found itself between two vortices of gravitation called Bakhrida and Scintilla; Bakhrida speeds up time, Scintilla on the other hand slows it down, and between them lies a zone of stagnation in which the present, becalmed, flows neither backward nor forward. There Heptodius froze alive, and remains to this day, along with the countless frigates and galleons of other astromariners, pirates and spaceswashers, not aging in the least, suspended in the silence and excruciating boredom that is Eternity.

When thus had concluded the campaign of the three Selectivitites, Perpetuan, cybercount of Fud, who as the seventh was next to go, did not set forth for the longest time. Instead that electroknight made lengthy preparations for war, fitting himself with ever sharper conductors, with more and more striking spark plugs, mortars and tractors. Full of caution, he decided he would go at the head of a loyal retinue. Under his banner flocked conquistadors, also many rejects, robots who having nothing else to do wished to try their hand at soldiering. Out of these Perpetuan formed a galactic light cavalry and an infantry, heavy, ironclad and bullion-headed, plus several platoons of polydragoons and palladins. However, at the thought that now he must go and meet his fate in some unknown land, and that in any puddle he might rust away utterly, the iron shanks buckled under him, he was seized with a terrible regret—and immediately headed home, in shame and sorrow shedding tears of topaz, for he was a mighty lord with a soul full of jewels.

As for the next to the last, Matrix Perforatem, he approached the matter sensibly. He had heard of the land of the Pygmelliants, robot gnomes whose race originated thus: their constructor's pencil had slipped on the drawing board, whereupon from the master mold they all came out, every last one of them, as hunchbacked deformities. Alteration didn't pay and thus they remained. These dwarfs amass knowledge as others do treasure; for this reason they are called Hoarders of the Absolute. Their wisdom lies in the fact that they collect knowledge but never use it. To them went Perforatem, not in a military way but on galleons whose decks sagged beneath magnificent gifts; he intended to win the Pygmelliants over with garments aglitter with positrons and lashed by a rain of neutrons; he brought them atoms of gold as big as seven fists, and flagons swirling with the rarest ionospheres. But the Pygmelliants scorned even the noble vacuum embroidered with waves in exquisite astral spectra. In vain too did he rage and threaten to set upon them his snorting electricourser Megasus. They offered him at last a guide, but the guide was a myriaphalangeal thousand-hander who always pointed in all directions at once.

50   Perforatem sent him packing and spurred Megasus on the trail of the palefaces; but the trail turned out to be false, for a comet of calcium hydroxide was wont to pass that way, and the simple-minded steed confused this with calcium phosphate, which is the basic ingredient of the paleface skeleton: Megasus mistook the lime for slime. Perforatem roamed long among suns that grew increasingly dim, for he had entered into a very ancient section of the Cosmos.

He traveled past a row of purple giants until he noticed that his ship along with the silent pageant of stars was being reflected in a spiral mirror, a silver-surfaced speculum; he was surprised at this and, just in case, drew his supernova extinguisher, which he had purchased from the Pygmelliants in order to protect himself against excessive heat along the Milky Way. He knew not what it was he saw— actually it was a knot in space, the continuum's most contiguous factorial, unknown even to the Monoasterists of that place. All they say is that whoever encounters it never returns. To this day no one knows what happened to Matrix in that stellar mill. His faithful Megasus sped home alone, whimpering softly in the void, and its sapphire eyes were pools of such horror that no one could look into them without a shudder. Neither vessel, nor extinguishers, nor Matrix was ever seen again.

And so the last, Erg the Self-inducting, rode forth alone. He was gone a year and fortnights three. When he returned, he told of lands unknown to anyone, such as that of the Periscones, who build hot sluices of corruption; of the planet of the Epoxy-eyed, who merged before him into rows of black billows, for that is what they do in time of war. He hewed them in two, laying bare the limstone that was their bone; but after he overcame their slaughterfalls, he found himself face to face with one that took up half the sky. When he fell upon it to demand the way, its skin split open beneath the blade of his firesword and exposed white, writhing forests of nerves. And he spoke of the transparent ice planet Aberrabia, which like a diamond lens holds the image of the entire Universe within itself. There Erg copied down the way to palefaceland. He told of a region of eternal silence. Alumnium Cryotrica, where he saw only the reflections of the stars in the surfaces of hanging glaciers; and of the kingdom of the molten Marmaloids, who fashion boiling baubles out of lava; and of the Electropneumaticists, who in mists of methane, ozone, chlorine and volcano smoke are able to kindle the spark of intelligence, and who continually wrestle with the problem of how to put into a gas the quality of genius. He told them that in order to reach the realm of the palefaces he had to force open the door of a sun called Caput Medusae; how after lifting this door off its chromatic hinges, he ran through the star's interior, a long succession of purple and light-blue flames, till his armor curled from the heat. How for thirty days he tried to guess the word that would activate the hatch of Astroprocyonum, since only through it can one enter the cold hell of miasmal beings; how finally he found himself among the palefaces, and they tried to catch him in their sticky, lipid snares, knock the mercury from his head or short-circuit him; how they deluded him, pointing to mis-shapen stars, but that was a counterfeit sky, the real one they had hidden in their sneaking way; how with torture they sought to pry from him his algorithm and then, when he withstood everything, threw him into a pit and dropped a slab of magnetite over the opening. Inside, however, he immediately multiplied himself into thousands of Ergs the Self-inducting, pushed aside the iron lid, emerged on the surface and wreaked his retribution upon the palefaces for one full month and five days. How then the monsters, in a last attempt, attacked on trackers they called casterpillars; but that availed them nothing, for, never slackening in his zeal for battle, but hacking, stabbing and slashing away, he brought them to such a pass that they threw the dastardly paleface key thief at his feet, whereupon Erg lopped off its loathsome head and disemboweled the carcass. In it he found a stone known as a trichobezoar, and on it was carved an inscription in the scrofulous paleface tongue, revealing where the key was. The Self-inducting cut open sixty-seven suns—white, blue and ruby red—before, pulling apart the right one, he found the key.

The adventures he met with, the battles he was forced to wage on the journey back—of these he did not even wish to think, so great now was his yearning for the Princess, and great too his impatience for the wedding and the coronation. With joy the King and Queen led him to the chamber of their daughter, who was silent as the grave, plunged in sleep. Erg leaned over her, fiddled a little near the open lid, inserted something, gave a turn, and instantly the Princess—to the delight of her mother and the King and the entire court—lifted her eyes and smiled at her deliverer. Erg closed the little lid, sealed it with a bit of plaster to keep it closed, and explained that the little screw, which he had also found, had been dropped during a fight with Poleander Partabon, emperor of all Jatapurgovia. But no one gave this any thought, and a pity too, for both the King and Queen would have quickly realized that he never sallied forth at all, because even as a child Erg the Self-inducting had possessed the ability to open any lock, and thanks to this he had wound up the Princess Electrina. In reality, then, he had met with not a single one of the adventures he described, but simply waited out a year and fortnights three in order that it not appear suspicious, his returning too soon with the missing object. Also he wanted to make sure that none of his rivals would come back. Only then did he show up at the court of King Boludar and restore the

Princess to life, and so married her and reigned long and happily on the throne of Boludar. His subterfuge was never discovered. From which one can see straight-away that we have told the truth and not a fairy tale, for in fairy tales virtue always triumphs.

Questions:

1. What is the point of view in this story? Does it resemble the point of view in anything else you have read? Why does the author end the story as he does?
2. When you come on a word like *electrosage*—which was not a word until Stan-islaw Lem made it up, a *neologism*—how do you decide what it means?
3. Discuss exposition in the first two paragraphs. What do you know of these people, and how do you know what you know? Does every sentence contribute some item of knowledge or background?
4. Do you find irony in this story? In what does it consist? Find examples.
5. Does this story have a theme? Many people have found it entertaining, and some have found it entertaining and wise.

Chapter 12 **Longer Fiction: The Short Novel**

The difference between a short story and a novel, as the wise tell us, is that the novel is longer. This difference is as much qualitative as quantitative. With its greater space and time in which to develop, the novel tends to take on shapes and purposes different from the short story's. Length allows (and perhaps requires) multiple structures. A typical story follows a main protagonist through a brief conflict to a conclusion that is also a discovery; it will have space to develop only one or two round characters. In the novel, we usually have several protagonists and more characters, both round and flat. We come to know a novelist's main protagonist well, possibly following him or her throughout life. Or we may follow whole generations of a family. Either way, we are likely to follow the course of many conflicts, conflicts in sequence and simultaneous conflicts, some not resolved for decades. The plot will take many ups and downs, moving toward a single climax by way of many small climaxes. There may be counterplots and subplots, stories outside the main story, often arranged for contrast or ironic comment. We will not likely find a single change or discovery, but a development through many changes leading to many discoveries. In the novel we have room for more social and historical complexity, more richness of character, motive, and choice, along with a setting so particular we can draw a map. Finally, in a novel we usually find not the short story's single theme but a woven fabric of themes, complex and interrelated.

The short novel falls between the typical story and the typical novel. In both *The Death of Ivan Ilych* and *Bartleby the Scrivener,* we come to know a single protagonist, as in a story, and in each we concentrate on a single theme. But in each of these short works the narrative develops character and theme fully, as in a novel.

Herman Melville
Bartleby the Scrivener

A Story of Wall Street

Herman Melville (1819–1891) wrote *Moby-Dick,* the great American novel
about the pursuit of a white whale. He grew up in New York and
Massachusetts, taking jobs as a sailor when he was young. Returning to dry
land, he lived in Boston and then Pittsfield, Massachusetts, where he wrote a
series of novels out of his sailing experience, beginning with *Typee* in 1846.
Mardi and *Redburn* followed in 1849, *White Jacket* in 1850. In Pittsfield he was
neighbor to the older novelist Nathaniel Hawthorne (see pages 141–150). Like
most of Melville's work, *Moby-Dick* (1851) was not a public success. Afterward
he wrote *Pierre* (1852), *The Confidence Man* (1857), some great short novels,
and little else although he lived long. When he died in obscurity he left his last
great short novel, *Billy Budd,* among his papers—and it was not published until
1922. Some of his best work outside *Moby-Dick* takes the form of the short
novel: *Benito Cereno, The Encantadas, Billy Budd,* and *Bartleby the Scrivener.* (A
scrivener was a copier—like Farrington in "Counterparts"—in the days before
typewriters and Xerox machines.)

I am a rather elderly man. The nature of my avocations, for the last thirty years,
has brought me into more than ordinary contact with what would seem an interesting and somewhat singular set of men, of whom, as yet, nothing, that I know
of, has ever been written—I mean, the law-copyists, or scriveners. I have known
very many of them, professionally and privately, and, if I pleased, could relate
divers histories, at which good-natured gentlemen might smile, and sentimental
souls might weep. But I waive the biographies of all other scriveners, for a few
passages in the life of Bartleby, who was a scrivener, the strangest I ever saw, or
heard of. While, of other law-copyists, I might write the complete life, of Bartleby
nothing of that sort can be done. I believe that no materials exist, for a full and
satisfactory biography of this man. It is an irreparable loss to literature. Bartleby
was one of those beings of whom nothing is ascertainable except from the original
sources, and, in his case, those are very small. What my own astonished eyes saw
of Bartleby, *that* is all I know of him, except, indeed, one vague report, which will
appear in the sequel.

Ere introducing the scrivener, as he first appeared to me, it is fit I make some
mention of myself, my *employés,* my business, my chambers and general surroundings; because some such description is indispensable to an adequate understanding of the chief character about to be presented. Imprimis:[1] I am a man
who, from his youth upwards, has been filled with a profound conviction that the
easiest way of life is the best. Hence, though I belong to a profession proverbially
energetic and nervous, even to turbulence, at times, yet nothing of that sort have
I ever suffered to invade my peace. I am one of those unambitious lawyers who
never addresses a jury, or in any way draws down public applause; but, in the cool
tranquility of a snug retreat, do a snug business among rich men's bonds, and
mortgages, and title-deeds. All who know me, consider me an eminently *safe* man.
The late John Jacob Astor,[2] a personage little given to poetic enthusiasm, had no

---

[1]In the first place

[2]The richest American of his era, Astor (1763–1843) amassed his fortune first from the fur trade
and then from real estate.

hesitation in pronouncing my first grand point to be prudence; my next, method. I do not speak it in vanity, but simply record the fact, that I was not unemployed in my profession by the late John Jacob Astor; a name which, I admit, I love to repeat; for it hath a rounded and orbicular sound to it, and rings like unto bullion. I will freely add, that I was not insensible to the late John Jacob Astor's good opinion.

Some time prior to the period at which this little history begins, my avocations had been largely increased. The good old office, now extinct in the State of New York, of a Master in Chancery,[1] had been conferred upon me. It was not a very arduous office, but very pleasantly remunerative. I seldom lose my temper; much more seldom indulge in dangerous indignation at wrongs and outrages; but I must be permitted to be rash here and declare, that I consider the sudden and violent abrogation of the office of Master in Chancery, by the new Constitution, as a ————premature act; inasmuch as I had counted upon a life-lease of the profits, whereas I only received those of a few short years. But this is by the way.

My chambers were up stairs, at No.——Wall Street. At one end, they looked upon the white wall of the interior of a spacious skylight shaft, penetrating the building from top to bottom.

This view might have been considered rather tame than otherwise, deficient in what landscape painters call "life." But, if so, the view from the other end of my chambers offered, at least, a contrast, if nothing more. In that direction, my windows commanded an unobstructed view of a lofty brick wall, black by age and everlasting shade; which wall required no spy-glass to bring out its lurking beauties, but, for the benefit of all near-sighted spectators, was pushed up to within ten feet of my window panes. Owing to the great height of the surrounding buildings, and my chambers being on the second floor, the interval between this wall and mine not a little resembled a huge square cistern.

At the period just preceding the advent of Bartleby, I had two persons as copyists in my employment, and a promising lad as an office-boy. First, Turkey; second, Nippers; third, Ginger Nut. These may seem names, the like of which are not usually found in the Directory.[2] In truth, they were nicknames, mutually conferred upon each other by my three clerks, and were deemed expressive of their respective persons or characters. Turkey was a short, pursy Englishman, of about my age—that is, somewhere not far from sixty. In the morning, one might say, his face was of a fine florid hue, but after twelve o'clock, meridian—his dinner hour—it blazed like a grate full of Christmas coals; and continued blazing—but, as it were, with a gradual wane—till six o'clock, P.M., or thereabouts; after which, I saw no more of the proprietor of the face, which, gaining its meridian with the sun, seemed to set with it, to rise, culminate, and decline the following day, with the like regularity and undiminished glory. There are many singular coincidences I have known in the course of my life, not the least among which was the fact, that, exactly when Turkey displayed his fullest beams from his red and radiant countenance, just then, too, at that critical moment, began the daily period when I considered his business capacities as seriously disturbed for the remainder of the twenty-four hours. Not that he was absolutely idle, or averse to business, then; far from it. The difficulty was, he was apt to be altogether too energetic. There was a strange, inflamed, flurried, flighty recklessness of activity about him.

---

[1]An officer of a law court; the office was abolished in 1846.
[2]Post-office directory

He would be incautious in dipping his pen into his inkstand. All his blots upon my documents were dropped there after twelve o'clock, meridian. Indeed, not only would he be reckless, and sadly given to making blots in the afternoon, but, some days, he went further, and was rather noisy. At such times, too, his face flamed with augmented blazonry, as if cannel coal had been heaped on anthracite. He made an unpleasant racket with his chair; spilled his sand-box,[1] in mending his pens, impatiently split them all to pieces, and threw them on the floor in a sudden passion; stood up, and leaned over his table, boxing his papers about in a most indecorous manner, very sad to behold in an elderly man like him. Nevertheless, as he was in many ways a most valuable person to me, and all the time before twelve o'clock meridian, was the quickest, steadiest creature, too, accomplishing a great deal of work in a style not easily to be matched—for these reasons, I was willing to overlook his eccentricities, though, indeed, occasionally, I remonstrated with him. I did this very gently, however, because, though the civilest, nay, the blandest and most reverential of men in the morning, yet, in the afternoon, he was disposed upon provocation, to be slightly rash with his tongue—in fact, insolent. Now, valuing his morning services as I did, and resolved not to lose them—yet, at the same time, made uncomfortable by his inflamed ways after twelve o'clock— and being a man of peace, unwilling by my admonitions to call forth unseemly retorts from him, I took upon me, one Saturday noon (he was always worse on Saturdays) to hint to him, very kindly, that, perhaps, now that he was growing old, it might be well to abridge his labors; in short, he need not come to my chambers after twelve o'clock, but, dinner over, had best go home to his lodgings, and rest himself till tea-time. But no; he insisted upon his afternoon devotions. His countenance became intolerably fervid, as he oratorically assured me—gesti- culating with a long ruler at the other end of the room—that if his services in the morning were useful, how indispensable, then, in the afternoon?

"With submission, sir," said Turkey, on this occasion, "I consider myself your right-hand man. In the morning I but marshal and deploy my columns; but in the afternoon I put myself at their head, and gallantly charge the foe, thus"—and he made a violent thrust with the ruler.

"But the blots, Turkey," intimated I.

"True; but, with submission, sir, behold these hairs! I am getting old. Surely, sir, a blot or two of a warm afternoon is not to be severely urged against gray hairs. Old age—even if it blot the page—is honorable. With submission, sir, we *both* are getting old."

10   This appeal to my fellow-feeling was hardly to be resisted. At all events, I saw that go he would not. So I made up my mind to let him stay, resolving, neverthe- less, to see to it that, during the afternoon, he had to do with my less important papers.

Nippers, the second on my list, was a whiskered, sallow, and upon the whole, rather piratical-looking young man, of about five-and-twenty. I always deemed him the victim of two evil powers—ambition and indigestion. The ambition was evinced by a certain impatience of the duties of a mere copyist, and unwarrantable usur- pation of strictly professional affairs, such as the original drawing up of legal doc- uments. The indigestion seemed betokened in an occasional nervous testiness and grinning irritability, causing the teeth to audibly grind together over mistakes committed in copying; unnecessary maledictions, hissed, rather than spoken, in

[1]Container for sand that was sprinkled over a sheet of paper to absorb wet ink

the heat of business; and especially by a continual discontent with the height of the table where he worked. Though of a very ingenious mechanical turn, Nippers could never get this table to suit him. He put chips under it, blocks of various sorts, bits of pasteboard, and at last went so far as to attempt an exquisite adjustment, by final pieces of folded blotting-paper. But no invention would answer. If, for the sake of easing his back, he brought the table-lid at a sharp angle well up towards his chin, and wrote there like a man using the steep roof of a Dutch house for his desk, then he declared that it stopped the circulation in his arms. If now he lowered the table to his waistbands, and stooped over it in writing, then there was a sore aching in his back. In short, the truth of the matter was, Nippers knew not what he wanted. Or, if he wanted anything, it was to be rid of a scrivener's table altogether. Among the manifestations of his diseased ambition was a fondness he had for receiving visits from certain ambiguous-looking fellows in seedy coats, whom he called his clients. Indeed, I was aware that not only was he, at times, considerable of a ward-politician, but he occasionally did a little business at the Justices' courts, and was not unknown on the steps of the Tombs.[1] I have good reason to believe, however, that one individual who called upon him at my chambers, and who, with a grand air, he insisted was his client, was no other than a dun, and the alleged title-deed, a bill. But, with all his failings, and the annoyances he caused me, Nippers, like his compatriot Turkey, was a very useful man to me; wrote a neat, swift hand; and, when he chose, was not deficient in a gentlemanly sort of deportment. Added to this, he always dressed in a gentlemanly sort of way; and so, incidentally, reflected credit upon my chambers. Whereas, with respect to Turkey, I had much ado to keep him from being a reproach to me. His clothes were apt to look oily, and smell of eating-houses. He wore his pantaloons very loose and baggy in summer. His coats were execrable; his hat not to be handled. But while the hat was a thing of indifference to me, inasmuch as his natural civility and deference, as a dependent Englishman, always led him to doff it the moment he entered the room, yet his coat was another matter. Concerning his coats, I reasoned with him; but with no effect. The truth was, I suppose, that a man with so small an income could not afford to sport such a lustrous face and a lustrous coat at one and the same time. As Nippers once observed, Turkey's money went chiefly for red ink. One winter day, I presented Turkey with a highly respectable-looking coat of my own—a padded gray coat, of a most comfortable warmth, and which buttoned straight up from the knee to the neck. I thought Turkey would appreciate the favor, and abate his rashness and obstreperousness of afternoons. But no; I verily believe that buttoning himself up in so downy and blanketlike a coat had a pernicious effect upon him—upon the same principle that too much oats are bad for horses. In fact, precisely as a rash, restive horse is said to feel his oats, so Turkey felt his coat. It made him insolent. He was a man whom prosperity harmed.

Though, concerning the self-indulgent habits of Turkey, I had my own private surmises, yet, touching Nippers, I was well persuaded that, whatever might be his faults in other respects, he was, at least, a temperate young man. But, indeed, nature herself seemed to have been his vintner, and, at his birth, charged him so thoroughly with an irritable, brandy-like disposition, that all subsequent potations were needless. When I consider how, amid the stillness of my chambers, Nippers would sometimes impatiently rise from his seat, and stooping over his table,

[1] A New York City jail.

spread his arms wide apart, seize the whole desk, and move it, and jerk it, with a grim, grinding motion on the floor, as if the table were a perverse voluntary agent, intent on thwarting and vexing him, I plainly perceive that, for Nippers, brandy-and-water were altogether superfluous.

It was fortunate for me that, owing to its peculiar cause—indigestion—the irritability and consequent nervousness of Nippers were mainly observable in the morning, while in the afternoon he was comparatively mild. So that, Turkey's paroxysms only coming on about twelve o'clock, I never had to do with their eccentricities at one time. Their fits relieved each other, like guards. When Nippers's was on, Turkey's was off; and *vice versa*. This was a good natural arrangement, under the circumstances.

Ginger Nut, the third on my list, was a lad, some twelve years old. His father was a carman, ambitious of seeing his son on the bench instead of a cart, before he died. So he sent him to my office, as student at law, errand-boy, cleaner and sweeper, at the rate of one dollar a week. He had a little desk to himself, but he did not use it much. Upon inspection, the drawer exhibited a great array of the shells of various sorts of nuts. Indeed, to this quick-witted youth, the whole noble science of the law was contained in a nutshell. Not the least among the employments of Giner Nut, as well as one which he discharged with the most alacrity, was his duty as cake and apple purveyor for Turkey and Nippers. Copying law-papers being proverbially a dry, husky sort of business, my two scriveners were fain to moisten their mouths very often with Spitzenbergs,[1] to be had at the numerous stalls nigh the Custom House and Post Office. Also, they sent Ginger Nut very frequently for that peculiar cake—small, flat, round, and very spicy—after which he had been named by them. Of a cold morning, when business was but dull, Turkey would gobble up scores of these cakes, as if they were mere wafers—indeed, they sell them at the rate of six or eight for a penny—the scrape of his pen blending with the crunching of the crisp particles in his mouth. Rashest of all the fiery afternoon blunders and flurried rashnesses of Turkey, was his once moistening a gingercake between his lips, and clapping it on to a mortgage, for a seal. I came within an ace of dismissing him then. But he mollified me by making an oriental bow, and saying—

15 "With submission, sir, it was generous of me to find you in stationery on my own account."

Now my original business—that of a conveyancer[2] and title hunter, and drawer-up of recondite documents of all sorts—was considerably increased by receiving the master's office. There was now great work for scriveners. Not only must I push the clerks already with me, but I must have additional help.

In answer to my advertisement, a motionless young man one morning stood upon my office threshold, the door being open, for it was summer. I can see that figure now—pallidly neat, pitiably respectable, incurably forlorn! It was Bartleby.

After a few words touching his qualifications, I engaged him, glad to have among my corps of copyists a man of so singularly sedate an aspect, which I thought might operate beneficially upon the flighty temper of Turkey, and the fiery one of Nippers.

I should have stated before that ground-glass folding-doors divided my premises into two parts, one of which was occupied by my scriveners, the other by myself. According to my humor, I threw open these doors, or closed them. I resolved to

[1]A kind of apple   [2]A lawyer who assists in transfer of ownership of mortgages and deeds

assign Bartleby a corner by the folding-doors, but on my side of them, so as to have this quiet man within easy call, in case any trifling thing was to be done. I placed his desk close up to a small side-window in that part of the room, a window which originally had afforded a lateral view of certain grimy back-yards and bricks, but which, owing to subsequent erections, commanded at present no view at all, though it gave some light. Within three feet of the panes was a wall, and the light came down from far above, between two lofty buildings, as from a very small opening in a dome. Still further to a satisfactory arrangement, I procured a high green folding screen, which might entirely isolate Bartleby from my sight, though not remove him from my voice. And thus, in a manner, privacy and society were conjoined.

20   At first, Bartleby did an extraordinary quantity of writing. As if long famishing for something to copy, he seemed to gorge himself on my documents. There was no pause for digestion. He ran a day and night line, copying by sunlight and by candle-light. I should have been quite delighted with his application, had he been cheerfully industrious. But he wrote on silently, palely, mechanically.

It is, of course, an indispensable part of a scrivener's business to verify the accuracy of his copy, word by word. Where there are two or more scriveners in an office, they assist each other in this examination, one reading from the copy, the other holding the original. It is a very dull, wearisome, and lethargic affair. I can readily imagine that, to some sanguine temperaments, it would be altogether intolerable. For example, I cannot credit that the mettlesome poet, Byron, would have contentedly sat down with Bartleby to examine a law document, of, say five hundred pages, closely written in a crimpy hand.

Now and then, in the haste of business, it had been my habit to assist in comparing some brief document myself, calling Turkey or Nippers for this purpose. One object I had, in placing Bartleby so handy to me behind the screen, was, to avail myself of his services on such trivial occasions. It was on the third day, I think, of his being with me, and before any necessity had arisen for having his own writing examined, that, being much hurried to complete a small affair I had in hand, I abruptly called to Bartleby. In my haste and natural expectancy of instant compliance, I sat with my head bent over the original on my desk, and my right hand sideways, and somewhat nervously extended with the copy, so that, immediately upon emerging from his retreat, Bartleby might snatch it and proceed to business without the least delay.

In this very attitude did I sit when I called to him, rapidly stating what it was I wanted him to do—namely, to examine a small paper with me. Imagine my surprise, nay, my consternation, when, without moving from his privacy, Bartleby, in a singularly mild, firm voice, replied, "I would prefer not to."

I sat awhile in perfect silence, rallying my stunned faculties. Immediately it occurred to me that my ears had deceived me, or Bartleby had entirely misunderstood my meaning. I repeated my request in the clearest tone I could assume; but in quite as clear a one came the previous reply, "I would prefer not to."

25   "Prefer not to," echoed I, rising in high excitement, and crossing the room with a stride. "What do you mean? Are you moon-struck? I want you to help me compare this sheet here—take it," and I thrust it towards him.

"I would prefer not to," said he.

I looked at him steadfastly. His face was leanly composed; his gray eye dimly calm. Not a wrinkle of agitation rippled him. Had there been the least uneasiness, anger, impatience or impertinence in his manner; in other words, had there been anything ordinarily human about him, doubtless I should have violently dismissed him from the premises. But as it was, I should have as soon thought of turning my pale plaster-of-paris bust of Cicero[1] out of doors. I stood gazing at him awhile, as he went on with his own writing, and then reseated myself at my desk. This is very strange, thought I. What had one best do? But my business hurried me. I concluded to forget the matter for the present, reserving it for my future leisure. So, calling Nippers from the other room, the paper was speedily examined.

A few days after this, Bartleby concluded four lengthy documents, being quad-ruplicates of a week's testimony taken before me in my High Court of Chancery. It became necessary to examine them. It was an important suit, and great accuracy was imperative. Having all things arranged, I called Turkey, Nippers and Ginger Nut, from the next room, meaning to place the four copies in the hands of my four clerks, while I should read from the original. Accordingly, Turkey, Nippers, and Ginger Nut had taken their seats in a row, each with his document in his hand, when I called to Bartleby to join this interesting group.

"Bartleby! quick, I am waiting."

30   I heard a slow scrape of his chair legs on the uncarpeted floor, and soon he appeared standing at the entrance of his hermitage.

"What is wanted?" said he, mildly.

"The copies, the copies," said I, hurriedly. "We are going to examine them. There"—and I held towards him the fourth quadruplicate.

"I would prefer not to," he said, and gently disappeared behind the screen.

For a few moments I was turned into a pillar of salt,[2] standing at the head of my seated column of clerks. Recovering myself, I advanced towards the screen, and demanded the reason for such extraordinary conduct.

35   "*Why* do you refuse?"

"I would prefer not to."

With any other man I should have flown outright into a dreadful passion, scorned all further words, and thrust him ignominiously from my presence. But there was something about Bartleby that not only strangely disarmed me, but, in a wonderful manner, touched and disconcerted me. I began to reason with him.

"These are your own copies we are about to examine. It is labor saving to you, because one examination will answer for your four papers. It is common usage. Every copyist is bound to help examine his copy. Is it not so? Will you not speak? Answer!"

"I prefer not to," he replied in a flute-like tone. It seemed to me that, while I had been addressing him, he carefully revolved every statement that I made; fully comprehended the meaning; could not gainsay the irresistible conclusion; but at the same time, some paramount consideration prevailed with him to reply as he did.

40   "You are decided, then, not to comply with my request—a request made ac-cording to common usage and common sense?"

He briefly gave me to understand, that on that point my judgment was sound. Yes: his decision was irreversible.

It is not seldom the case that, when a man is browbeaten in some unprecedented and violently unreasonably way, he begins to stagger in his own plainest faith. He begins, as it were, vaguely to surmise that, wonderful as it may be, all the justice

[1]Marcus Tullius Cicero, Roman politician, orator, and essayist (106–43 B.C.)
[2]See Genesis 19:26

and all the reason is on the other side. Accordingly, if any disinterested persons are present, he turns to them for some reinforcement for his own faltering mind.

"Turkey," said I, "what do you think of this? Am I not right?"

"With submission, sir," said Turkey, in his blandest tone, "I think that you are."

45 "Nippers," said I, "what do *you* think of it?"

"I think I should kick him out of the office."

(The reader of nice perceptions will here perceive that, it being morning, Turkey's answer is couched in polite and tranquil terms, but Nippers replies in ill-tempered ones. Or, to repeat a previous sentence, Nipper's ugly mood was on duty, and Turkey's off.)

"Ginger Nut," said I, willing to enlist the smallest suffrage in my behalf, "what do *you* think of it?"

"I think, sir, he's a little *luny,*" replied Ginger Nut, with a grin.

50 "You hear what they say," said I, turning towards the screen, "come forth and do your duty."

But he vouchsafed no reply. I pondered a moment in sore perplexity. But once more business hurried me. I determined again to postpone the consideration of this dilemma to my future leisure. With a little trouble we made out to examine the papers without Bartleby, though at every page or two Turkey deferentially dropped his opinion, that this proceeding was quite out of the common; while Nippers, twitching in his chair with a dyspeptic nervousness, ground out, between his set teeth, occasional hissing maledictions against the stubborn oaf behind the screen. And for his (Nipper's) part, this was the first and the last time he would do another man's business without pay.

Meanwhile Bartleby sat in his hermitage, oblivious to everything but his own peculiar business there.

Some days passed, the scrivener being employed upon another lengthy work. His late remarkable conduct led me to regard his ways narrowly. I observed that he never went to dinner; indeed, that he never went anywhere. As yet I had never, of my personal knowledge, known him to be outside of my office. He was a perpetual sentry in the corner. At about eleven o'clock though, in the morning, I noticed Ginger Nut would advance toward the opening in Bartleby's screen, as if silently beckoned thither by a gesture invisible to me where I sat. The boy would then leave the office, jingling a few pence, and reappear with a handful of ginger-nuts which he delivered in the hermitage, receiving two of the cakes for his trouble.

He lives, then, on ginger-nuts thought I; never eats a dinner, properly speaking; he must be a vegetarian, then, but no; he never eats even vegetables, he eats nothing but ginger-nuts. My mind then ran on in reveries concerning the probable effects upon the human constitution of living entirely on ginger-nuts. Ginger-nuts are so called, because they contain ginger as one of the peculiar constituents, and the final flavoring one. Now, what was ginger? A hot, spicy thing. Was Bartleby hot and spicy? Not at all. Ginger then, had no effect upon Bartleby. Probably he preferred it should have none.

55 Nothing so aggravates an earnest person as a passive resistance. If the individual so resisted be of a not inhumane temper, and the resisting one perfectly harmless in his passivity, then, in the better moods of the former, he will endeavor charitably to construe to his imagination what proves impossible to be solved by his judgment. Even so, for the most part, I regarded Bartleby and his ways. Poor fellow! thought I, he means no mischief; it is plain he intends no insolence; his aspect sufficiently evinces that his eccentricities are involuntary. He is useful to me. I

can get along with him. If I turn him away, the chances are he will fall in with some less-indulgent employer, and then he will be rudely treated, and perhaps driven forth miserably to starve. Yes. Here I can cheaply purchase a delicious self-approval. To befriend Bartleby; to humor him in his strange willfulness, will cost me little or nothing, while I lay up in my soul what will eventually prove a sweet morsel for my conscience. But this mood was not invariable with me. The passiveness of Bartleby sometimes irritated me. I felt strangely goaded on to encounter him in new opposition—to elicit some angry spark from him answerable to my own. But, indeed, I might as well have essayed to strike fire with my knuckles against a bit of Windsor soap. But one afternoon the evil impulse in me mastered me, and the following little scene ensued:

"Bartleby," said I, "when those papers are all copied, I will compare them with you."

"I would prefer not to."

"How? Surely you do not mean to persist in that mulish vagary?"

No answer.

60   I threw open the folding-doors near by, and, turning upon Turkey and Nippers, exclaimed:

"Bartleby a second time says, he won't examine his papers. What do you think of it, Turkey?"

It was afternoon, be it remembered. Turkey sat glowing like a brass boiler; his bald head steaming; his hands reeling among his blotted papers.

"Think of it?" roared Turkey. "I think I'll just step behind his screen, and black his eyes for him!"

So saying, Turkey rose to his feet and threw his arms into a pugilistic position. He was hurrying away to make good his promise, when I detained him, alarmed at the effect of incautiously rousing Turkey's combativeness after dinner.

65   "Sit down, Turkey," said I, "and hear what Nippers has to say. What do you think of it, Nippers? Would I not be justified in immediately dismissing Bartleby?"

"Excuse me, that is for you to decide, sir. I think his conduct quite unusual, and, indeed, unjust, as regards Turkey and myself. But it may only be a passing whim."

"Ah," exclaimed I, "you have strangely changed your mind, then—you speak very gently of him now."

"All beer," cried Turkey; "gentleness is effects of beer—Nippers and I dined together to-day. You see how gentle *I* am, sir. Shall I go and black his eyes?"

"You refer to Bartleby, I suppose. No, not to-day, Turkey," I replied; "pray, put up your fists."

70   I closed the doors, and again advanced towards Bartleby. I felt additional incentives tempting me to my fate. I burned to be rebelled against again. I remembered that Bartleby never left the office.

"Bartleby," said I, "Ginger Nut is away; just step around to the Post Office, won't you?" (it was but a three minutes' walk) "and see if there is anything for me."

"I would prefer not to."

"You *will* not?"

"I *prefer* not."

75   I staggered to my desk, and sat there in a deep study. My blind inveteracy returned. Was there any other thing in which I could procure myself to be igno-

miniously repulsed by this lean, penniless wight?[1]—my hired clerk? What added thing is there, perfectly reasonable, that he will be sure to refuse to do?

"Bartleby!"

No answer.

"Bartleby," in a louder tone.

No answer.

80 "Bartleby," I roared.

Like a very ghost, agreeably to the laws of magical invocation, at the third summons, he appeared at the entrance of his hermitage.

"Go to the next room, and tell Nippers to come to me."

"I prefer not to," he respectfully and slowly said, and mildly disappeared.

"Very good, Bartleby," said I, in a quiet sort of serenely-severe self-possessed tone, intimating the unalterable purpose of some terrible retribution very close at hand. At the moment I half intended something of the kind. But upon the whole, as it was drawing towards my dinner-hour, I thought it best to put on my hat and walk home for the day, suffering much from perplexity and distress of mind.

85 Shall I acknowledge it? The conclusion of this whole business was, that it soon became a fixed fact of my chambers, that a pale young scrivener, by the name of Bartleby, had a desk there; that he copied for me at the usual rate of four cents a folio (one hundred words); but he was permanently exempt from examining the work done by him, that duty being transferred to Turkey and Nippers, out of compliment, doubtless, to their superior acuteness; moreover, said Bartleby was never, on any account, to be dispatched on the most trivial errand of any sort; and that even if entreated to take upon him such a matter, it was generally understood that he would "prefer not to"—in other words, that he would refuse point-blank.

As days passed on, I became considerably reconciled to Bartleby. His steadiness, his freedom from all dissipation, his incessant industry (except when he chose to throw himself into a standing revery behind his screen), his great stillness, his unalterableness of demeanor under all circumstances, made him a valuable acquisition. One prime thing was this—*he was always there*—first in the morning, continually through the day, and the last at night. I had a singular confidence in his honesty. I felt my most precious papers perfectly safe in his hands. Sometimes, to be sure, I could not, for the very soul of me, avoid falling into sudden spasmodic passions with him. For it was exceeding difficult to bear in mind all the time those strange peculiarities, privileges, and unheard-of-exemptions, forming the tacit stipulations on Bartleby's part under which he remained in my office. Now and then, in the eagerness of dispatching pressing business, I would inadvertently summon Bartleby, in a short, rapid tone, to put his finger, say, on the incipient tie of a bit of red tape with which I was about compressing some papers. Of course, from behind the screen the usual answer, "I prefer not to," was sure to come; and then, how could a human creature, with the common infirmities of our nature, refrain from bitterly exclaiming upon such perverseness—such unreasonableness? However, every added repulse of this sort which I received only tended to lessen the probability of my repeating the inadvertence.

Here it must be said, that, according to the custom of most legal gentlemen occupying chambers in densely-populated law buildings, there were several keys to my door. One was kept by a woman residing in the attic, which person weekly

[1]Person

scrubbed and daily swept and dusted my apartments. Another was kept by Turkey for convenience sake. The third I sometimes carried in my own pocket. The fourth I knew not who had.

Now, one Sunday morning I happened to go to Trinity Church, to hear a celebrated preacher, and finding myself rather early on the ground I thought I would walk round to my chambers for a while. Luckily I had my key with me; but upon applying it to the lock, I found it resisted by something inserted from the inside. Quite surprised, I called out; when to my consternation a key was turned from within; and thrusting his lean visage at me, and holding the door ajar, the apparition of Bartleby appeared, in his shirtsleeves, and otherwise in a strangely tattered *déshabillé*,[1] saying quietly that he was sorry, but he was deeply engaged just then, and—preferred not admitting me at present. In a brief word or two, he moreover added, that perhaps I had better walk round the block two or three times, and by that time he would probably have concluded his affairs.

Now, the utterly unsurmised appearance of Bartleby, tenanting my law-chambers of a Sunday morning, with his cadaverously gentlemanly *nonchalance,* yet withal firm and self-possessed, had such a strange effect upon me, that incontinently I slunk away from my own door, and did as desired. But not without sundry twinges of impotent rebellion against the mild effrontery of this unaccountable scrivener. Indeed, it was his wonderful mildness chiefly, which not only disarmed me, but unmanned me as it were. For I consider that one, for the time, is sort of unmanned when he tranquilly permits his hired clerk to dictate to him, and order him away from his own premises. Furthermore, I was full of uneasiness as to what Bartleby could possibly be doing in my office in his shirt sleeves, and in an otherwise dismantled condition of a Sunday morning. Was anything amiss going on? Nay, that was out of the question. It was not to be thought of for a moment that Bartleby was an immoral person. But what could he be doing there?—copying? Nay again, whatever might be his eccentricities, Bartleby was an eminently decorous person. He would be the last man to sit down to his desk in any state approaching to nudity. Besides, it was Sunday; and there was something about Bartleby that forbade the supposition that he would by any secular occupation violate the proprieties of the day.

90   Nevertheless, my mind was not pacified; and full of restless curiosity, at last I returned to the door. Without hindrance I inserted my key, opened it, and entered. Bartleby was not to be seen. I looked around anxiously, peeped behind his screen; but it was very plain that he was gone. Upon more closely examining the place, I surmised that for an indefinite period Bartleby must have eaten, dressed, and slept in my office, and that too without plate, mirror, or bed. The cushioned seat of a ricketty old sofa in one corner bore the faint impress of a lean, reclining form. Rolled away under his desk, I found a blanket; under the empty grate, a blacking box[2] and brush; on a chair, a tin basin, with soap and a ragged towel; in a newspaper a few crumbs of ginger-nuts and a morsel of cheese. Yes, thought I, it is evident enough that Bartleby has been making his home here, keeping bachelor's hall all by himself. Immediately then the thought came sweeping across me, what miserable friendlessness and loneliness are here revealed! His poverty is great; but his solitude, how horrible! Think of it. Of a Sunday, Wall Street is deserted as Petra,[3] and every night of every day it is an emptiness. This building, too, which

---

[1]Careless undress   [2]Shoe polish   [3]A ruined Palestinian city rediscovered in 1812

of week-days hums with industry and life, at nightfall echoes with sheer vacancy, and all through Sunday is forlorn. And here Bartleby makes his home; sole spectator of a solitude which he has seen all populous—a sort of innocent and transformed Marius brooding among the ruins of Carthage![1]

For the first time in my life a feeling of overpowering stinging melancholy seized me. Before, I had never experienced aught but a not unpleasing sadness. The bond of a common humanity now drew me irresistibly to gloom. A fraternal melancholy! For both I and Bartleby were sons of Adam. I remembered the bright silks and sparkling faces I had seen that day, in gala trim, swan-like sailing down the Mississippi of Broadway; and I contrasted them with the pallid copyist, and thought to myself, Ah, happiness courts the light, so we deem the world is gay; but misery hides aloof, so we deem that misery there is none. These sad fancyings—chimeras, doubtless, of a sick and silly brain—led on to other and more special thoughts, concerning the eccentricities of Bartleby. Presentiments of strange discoveries hovered round me. The scrivener's pale form appeared to me laid out, among uncaring strangers, in its shivering winding-sheet.[2]

Suddenly I was attracted by Bartleby's closed desk, the key in open sight left in the lock.

I mean no mischief, seek the gratification of no heartless curiosity, thought I; besides, the desk is mine, and its contents, too, so I will make bold to look within. Everything was methodically arranged, the papers smoothly placed. The pigeon holes were deep, and removing the files of documents, I groped into their recesses. Presently I felt something there, and dragged it out. It was an old bandana handkerchief heavy and knotted. I opened it, and saw it was a savings' bank.

I now recalled all the quiet mysteries which I had noted in the man. I remembered that he never spoke but to answer; that, though at intervals he had considerable time to himself, yet I had never seen him reading—no, not even a newspaper; that for long periods he would stand looking out, at his pale window behind the screen, upon the dead brick wall; I was quite sure he never visited any refectory or eating house; while his pale face clearly indicated that he never drank beer like Turkey, or tea and coffee even, like other men; that he never went anywhere in particular that I could learn; never went out for a walk, unless, indeed, that was the case at present; that he had declined telling who he was, or whence he came, or whether he had any relatives in the world; that though so thin and pale, he never complained of ill health. And more than all, I remembered a certain unconscious air of pallid—how shall I call it?—of pallid haughtiness, say, or rather an austere reserve about him, which had positively awed me into my tame compliance with his eccentricities, when I had feared to ask him to do the slightest incidental thing for me, even though I might know, from his long-continued motionlessness, that behind his screen he must be standing in one of those dead-wall reveries of his.

95 Revolving all these things, and coupling them with the recently discovered fact, that he made my office his constant abiding place and home, and not forgetful of his morbid moodiness; revolving all these things, a prudential feeling began to steal over me. My first emotions had been those of pure melancholy and sincerest pity; but just in proportion as the forlornness of Bartleby grew and grew to my

[1]Gaius Marius, a Roman general exiled from his homeland, is sometimes portrayed sitting among the ruins of the north-African city destroyed by Roman forces in the third Punic War.   [2]Shroud

imagination, did that same melancholy merge into fear, that pity into repulsion. So true it is, and so terrible, too, that up to a certain point the thought or sight of misery enlists our best affections; but, in certain special cases, beyond that point it does not. They err who would assert that invariably this is owing to the inherent selfishness of the human heart. It rather proceeds from a certain hopelessness of remedying excessive and organic ill. To a sensitive being, pity is not seldom pain. And when at last it is perceived that such pity cannot lead to effectual succor, common sense bids the soul be rid of it. What I saw that morning persuaded me that the scrivener was the victim of innate and incurable disorder. I might give alms to his body; but his body did not pain him; it was his soul that suffered, and his soul I could not reach.

I did not accomplish the purpose of going to Trinity Church that morning. Somehow, the things I had seen disqualified me for the time from church-going. I walked homeward, thinking what I would do with Bartleby. Finally, I resolved upon this—I would put certain calm questions to him the next morning, touching his history, etc., and if he declined to answer them openly and unreservedly (and I supposed he would prefer not), then to give him a twenty dollar bill over and above whatever I might owe him, and tell him his services were no longer required; but that if any other way I could assist him, I would be happy to do so, especially if he desired to return to his native place, wherever that might be, I would willingly help to defray the expenses. Moreover, if, after reaching home, he found himself at any time in want of aid, a letter from him would be sure of a reply.

The next morning came.

"Bartleby," said I, gently calling to him behind his screen.

No reply.

100   "Bartleby," said I, in a still gentler tone, "come here; I am not going to ask you to do anything you would prefer not to do—I simply wish to speak to you."

Upon this he noiselessly slid into view.

"Will you tell me, Bartleby, where you were born?"

"I would prefer not to."

"Will you tell me *anything* about yourself?"

105   "I would prefer not to."

"But what reasonable objection can you have to speak to me? I feel friendly towards you."

He did not look at me while I spoke, but kept his glance fixed upon my bust of Cicero, which, as I then sat, was directly behind me, some six inches above my head.

"What is your answer, Bartleby?" said I, after waiting a considerable time for a reply, during which his countenance remained immovable, only there was the faintest conceivable tremor of the white attenuated mouth.

"At present I prefer to give no answer," he said, and retired into his hermitage.

110   It was rather weak in me I confess, but his manner, on this occasion, nettled me. Not only did there seem to lurk in it a certain calm disdain, but his perverseness seemed ungrateful, considering the undeniable good usage and indulgence he had received from me.

Again I sat ruminating what I should do. Mortified as I was at his behavior, and resolved as I had been to dismiss him when I entered my office, nevertheless I strangely felt something superstitious knocking at my heart, and forbidding me to carry out my purpose, and denouncing me for a villain if I dared to breathe one bitter word against this forlornest of mankind. At last, familiarly drawing my chair

behind his screen, I sat down and said: "Bartleby, never mind, then, about revealing your history; but let me entreat you, as a friend, to comply as far as may
be with the usages of this office. Say now, you will help to examine papers tomorrow or next day: in short, say now, that in a day or two you will begin to be
a little reasonable:—say so, Bartleby."

"At present I would prefer not to be a little reasonable," was his mildly cadaverous reply.

Just then the folding-doors opened, and Nippers approached. He seemed suffering from an unusually bad night's rest, induced by severer indigestion than
common. He overheard those final words of Bartleby.

"*Prefer not*, eh?" gritted Nippers—"I'd *prefer* him, if I were you, sir," addressing
me—"I'd *prefer* him; I'd give him preferences, the stubborn mule! What is it, sir,
pray, that he *prefers* not to do now?"

115   Bartleby moved not a limb.

"Mr. Nippers," said I, "I'd prefer that you would withdraw for the present."

Somehow, of late, I had got into the way of involuntarily using this word "prefer"
upon all sorts of not exactly suitable occasions. And I trembled to think that my
contact with the scrivener had already and seriously affected me in a mental way.
And what further and deeper aberration might it not yet produce? This apprehension had not been without efficacy in determining me to summary measures.

As Nippers, looking very sour and sulky, was departing, Turkey blandly and
deferentially approached.

"With submission, sir," said he, "yesterday I was thinking about Bartleby here,
and I think that if he would but prefer to take a quart of good ale every day, it
would do much towards mending him, and enabling him to assist in examining
his papers."

120   "So you have got the word, too," said I, slightly excited.

"With submission, what word sir?" asked Turkey, respectfully crowding himself
into the contracted space behind the screen, and by so doing, making me jostle
the scrivener. "What word, sir?"

"I would prefer to be left alone here," said Bartleby, as if offended at being
mobbed in his privacy.

"*That's* the word, Turkey," said I—"*that's* it."

"Oh, *prefer?* oh yes—queer word. I never use it myself. But, sir, as I was saying,
if he would but prefer—"

125   "Turkey," interrupted I, "you will please withdraw."

"Oh certainly, sir, if you prefer that I should."

As he opened the folding-door to retire, Nippers at his desk caught a glimpse of
me, and asked whether I would prefer to have a certain paper copied on blue paper
or white. He did not in the least roguishly accent the word "prefer." It was plain
that it involuntarily rolled from his tongue. I thought to myself, surely I must get
rid of a demented man, who already has in some degree turned the tongues, if not
the heads, of myself and clerks. But I thought it prudent not to break the dismis-
sion at once.

The next day I noticed that Bartleby did nothing but stand at his window in his
dead-wall revery. Upon asking him why he did not write he said that he had decided
upon doing no more writing.

"Why, how now? what next?" exclaimed I, "do no more writing?"

130   "No more."

"And what is the reason?"

"Do you not see the reason for yourself?" he indifferently replied.

I looked steadfastly at him and perceived that his eyes looked dull and glazed. Instantly it occurred to me, that his unexampled diligence in copying by his dim window for the first few weeks of his stay with me might have temporarily impaired his vision.

I was touched. I said something in condolence with him. I hinted that of course he did wisely in abstaining from writing for a while; and urged him to embrace that opportunity of taking wholesome exercise in the open air. This, however, he did not do. A few days after this, my other clerks being absent, and being in a great hurry to dispatch certain letters by the mail, I thought that, having nothing else earthly to do, Bartleby would surely be less inflexible than usual, and carry these letters to the post-office. But he blankly declined. So, much to my inconvenience, I went myself.

135   Still added days went by. Whether Bartleby's eyes improved or not, I could not say. To all appearance, I thought they did. But when I asked him if they did, he vouchsafed no answer. At all events, he would do no copying. At last, in reply to my urgings, he informed me that he had permanently given up copying.

"What!" exclaimed I; "suppose your eyes should get entirely well—better than ever before—would you not copy then?"

"I have given up copying," he answered, and slid aside.

He remained as ever, a fixture in my chamber. Nay—if that were possible—he became still more of a fixture than before. What was to be done? He would do nothing in the office; why should he stay there? In plain fact, he had now become a millstone to me, not only useless as a necklace, but afflictive to bear. Yet I was sorry for him. I speak less than truth when I say that, on his own account, he occasioned me uneasiness. If he would but have named a single relative or friend, I would instantly have written, and urged their taking the poor fellow away to some convenient retreat. But he seemed alone, absolutely alone in the universe. A bit of wreck in the mid Atlantic. At length, necessities connected with my business tyrannized over all other considerations. Decently as I could, I told Bartleby that in six days' time he must unconditionally leave the office. I warned him to take measures, in the interval, for procuring some other abode. I offered to assist him in this endeavor, if he himself would but take the first step towards a removal. "And when you finally quit me, Bartleby," added I, "I shall see that you go not away entirely unprovided. Six days from this hour, remember."

At the expiration of that period, I peeped behind the screen, and lo! Bartleby was there.

140   I buttoned up my coat, balanced myself; advanced slowly towards him, touched his shoulder, and said, "The time has come; you must quit this place; I am sorry for you; here is money; but you must go."

"I would prefer not," he replied, with his back still towards me.

"You *must*."

He remained silent.

Now I had an unbounded confidence in this man's common honesty. He had frequently restored to me sixpences and shillings carelessly dropped upon the floor, for I am apt to be very reckless in such shirt-button affairs. The proceeding, then, which followed will not be deemed extraordinary.

145   "Bartleby," said I, "I owe you twelve dollars on account; here are thirty-two; the odd twenty are yours—Will you take it?" and I handed the bills towards him.

But he made no motion.

"I will leave them here, then," putting them under a weight on the table. Then taking my hat and cane and going to the door, I tranquilly turned and added— "After you have removed your things from these offices, Bartleby, you will of course lock the door—since every one is now gone for the day but you——and if you please, slip your key underneath the mat, so that I may have it in the morning. I shall not see you again; so good-by to you. If, hereafter, in your new place of abode, I can be of any service to you, do not fail to advise me by letter. Good-by, Bartleby, and fare you well."

But he answered not a word; like the last column of some ruined temple, he remained standing mute and solitary in the middle of the otherwise deserted room.

As I walked home in a pensive mood, my vanity got the better of my pity. I could not but highly plume myself on my masterly management in getting rid of Bartleby. Masterly I call it, and such it must appear to any dispassionate thinker. The beauty of my procedure seemed to consist in its perfect quietness. There was no vulgar bullying, no bravado of any sort, no choleric hectoring, and striding to and fro across the apartment, jerking out vehement commands for Bartleby to bundle himself off with his beggarly traps.[1] Nothing of the kind. Without loudly bidding Bartleby depart—as an inferior genius might have done—I *assumed* the ground that depart he must; and upon that assumption built all I had to say. The more I thought over my procedure, the more I was charmed with it. Nevertheless, next morning, upon awakening, I had my doubts—I had somehow slept off the fumes of vanity. One of the coolest and wisest hours a man has, is just after he awakes in the morning. My procedure seemed as sagacious as ever—but only in theory. How it would prove in practice—there was the rub. It was truly a beautiful thought to have assumed Bartleby's departure; but, after all, that assumption was simply my own, and none of Bartleby's. The great point was, not whether I had assumed that he would quit me, but whether he would prefer so to do. He was more a man of preferences than assumptions.

150 After breakfast, I walked down town, arguing the probabilities *pro* and *con*. One moment I thought it would prove a miserable failure, and Bartleby would be found all alive at my office as usual; the next moment it seemed certain that I should find his chair empty. And so I kept veering about. At the corner of Broadway and Canal Street, I saw quite an excited group of people standing in earnest conversation.

"I'll take odds he doesn't," said a voice as I passed.

"Doesn't go?—done!" said I, "put up your money."

I was instinctively putting my hand in my pocket to produce my own, when I remembered that this was an election day. The words I had overheard bore no reference to Bartleby, but to the success or non-success of some candidate for the mayorality. In my intent frame of mind, I had, as it were, imagined that all Broadway shared in my excitement, and were debating the same question with me. I passed on, very thankful that the uproar of the street screened my momentary absent-mindedness.

As I had intended, I was earlier than usual at my office door. I stood listening for a moment. All was still. He must be gone. I tried the knob. The door was locked. Yes, my procedure had worked to a charm; he indeed must be vanished. Yet a certain melancholy mixed with this: I was almost sorry for my brilliant success. I was fumbling under the door mat for the key, which Bartleby was to

[1]Belongings, personal gear

have left there for me, when accidentally my knee knocked against a panel, producing a summoning sound, and in response a voice came to me from within—
"Not yet ; I am occupied."

155   It was Bartleby.

I was thunderstruck. For an instant I stood like the man who, pipe in mouth,
was killed one cloudless afternoon long ago in Virginia, by summer lightning; at
his own warm open window he was killed, and remained leaning out there upon
the dreamy afternoon, till some one touched him, when he fell.

"Not gone!" I murmured at last. But again obeying that wondrous ascendancy
which the inscrutable scrivener had over me, and from which ascendancy, for all
my chafing, I could not completely escape, I slowly went downstairs and out into
the street, and while walking round the block, considered what I should next do
in this unheard-of perplexity. Turn the man out by an actual thrusting I could not;
to drive away by calling him hard names would not do; calling in the police was
an unpleasant idea; and yet, permit him to enjoy his cadaverous triumph over
me—this, too, I could not think of. What was to be done? or, if nothing could be
done, was there anything further that I could *assume* in the matter? Yes, as before
I had prospectively assumed that Bartleby would depart, so now I might retrospectively assume that departed he was. In legitimate carrying out of this assumption, I might enter my office in a great hurry, and pretending not to see
Bartleby at all, walk straight against him as if he were air. Such a proceeding would
in a singular degree have the appearance of a home-thrust. It was hardly possible
that Bartleby could withstand such an application of the doctrine of assumptions.
But upon second thoughts the success of the plan seemed rather dubious. I resolved to argue the matter over with him.

"Bartleby," said I, entering the office, with a quietly severe expression, "I am
seriously displeased. I am pained, Bartleby. I had thought better of you. I had
imagined you of such a gentlemanly organization, that in any delicate dilemma a
slight hint would suffice—in short, an assumption. But it appears I am deceived.
Why," I added, unaffectedly starting, "you have not even touched that money yet,"
pointing to it, just where I had left it the evening previous.

He answered nothing.

160   "Will you, or will you not, quit me?" I now demanded in a sudden passion,
advancing close to him.

"I would prefer *not* to quit you," he replied, gently emphasizing the *not*.

"What earthly right have you to stay here? Do you pay any rent? Do you pay my
taxes? Or is this property yours?"

He answered nothing.

"Are you ready to go on and write now? Are your eyes recovered? Could you
copy a small paper for me this morning? or help examine a few lines? or step
round to the post-office? In a word, will you do anything at all, to give a coloring
to your refusal to depart the premises?"

165   He silently retired into his hermitage.

I was now in such a state of nervous resentment that I thought it but prudent
to check myself at present from further demonstrations. Bartleby and I were alone.
I remembered the tragedy of the unfortunate Adams and the still more unfortunate
Colt[1] in the solitary office of the latter; and how poor Colt, being dreadfully in-

---

[1]In 1842 John C. Colt inadvertently killed Samuel Adams by striking him during a quarrel.
Sentenced to death, he killed himself before the state could hang him.

censed by Adams, and imprudently permitting himself to get wildly excited, was at unawares hurried into his fatal act—an act which certainly no man could possibly deplore more than the actor himself. Often it had occurred to me in my ponderings upon the subject that had that altercation taken place in the public street, or at a private residence, it would not have terminated as it did. It was the circumstance of being alone in a solitary office, up stairs, of a building entirely unhallowed by humanizing domestic associations—an uncarpeted office, doubtless, of a dusty, haggard sort of appearance—this it must have been, which greatly helped to enhance the irritable desperation of the hapless Colt.

But when this old Adam of resentment rose in me and tempted me concerning Bartleby, I grappled him and threw him. How? Why, simply by recalling the divine injunction: "A new commandment give I unto you, that ye love one another."[1] Yes, this it was that saved me. Aside from higher considerations, charity often operates as a vastly wise and prudent principle—a great safeguard to its possessor. Men have committed murder for jealousy's sake, and anger's sake, and hatred's sake, and selfishness' sake, and spiritual pride's sake; but no man, that ever I heard of, ever committed a diabolical murder for sweet charity's sake. Mere self-interest, then, if no better motive can be enlisted, should, especially with high-tempered men, prompt all beings to charity and philanthropy. At any rate, upon the occasion in question, I strove to drown my exasperated feelings towards the scrivener by benevolently construing his conduct. Poor fellow, poor fellow! thought I, he don't mean anything; and besides, he has seen hard times, and ought to be indulged.

I endeavored, also, immediately to occupy myself, and at the same time to comfort my despondency. I tried to fancy, that in the course of the morning, at such time as might prove agreeable to him, Bartleby, of his own free accord, would emerge from his hermitage and take up some decided line of march in the direction of the door. But no. Half-past twelve o'clock came; Turkey began to glow in the face, overturn his inkstand, and become generally obstreperous; Nippers abated down into quietude and courtesy; Ginger Nut munched his noon apple; and Bartleby remained standing at his window in one of his profoundest dead-wall reveries. Will it be credited? Ought I to acknowledge it? That afternoon I left the office without saying one further word to him.

Some days now passed, during which, at leisure intervals I looked a little into "Edwards on the Will," and "Priestley on Necessity."[2] Under the circumstances, those books induced a salutary feeling. Gradually I slid into the persuasion that these troubles of mine, touching the scrivener, had been all predestinated from eternity, and Bartleby was billeted upon me for some mysterious purpose of an allwise Providence, which it was not for a mere mortal like me to fathom. Yes, Bartleby, stay there behind your screen, thought I; I shall persecute you no more; you are harmless and noiseless as any of these old chairs; in short, I never feel so private as when I know you are here. At last I see it, I feel it; I penetrate to the predestinated purpose of my life. I am content. Others may have loftier parts to enact; but my mission in this world, Bartleby, is to furnish you with office-room for such period as you may see fit to remain.

170   I believe that this wise and blessed frame of mind would have continued with

[1]John 13:34   [2]Both Jonathan Edwards (1703–1758), a prominent American Calvinist divine, and Joseph Priestley (1733–1804), an English philosopher, argued against the existence of free will.

me, had it not been for the unsolicited and uncharitable remarks obtruded upon me by my professional friends who visited the rooms. But thus it often is, that the constant friction of illiberal minds wears out at last the best resolves of the more generous. Though to be sure, when I reflected upon it, it was not strange that people entering my office should be struck by the peculiar aspect of the unaccountable Bartleby, and so be tempted to throw out some sinister observations concerning him. Sometimes an attorney, having business with me, and calling at my office, and finding no one but the scrivener there, would undertake to obtain some sort of precise information from him touching my whereabouts; but without heeding his idle talk, Bartleby would remain standing immovable in the middle of the room. So after contemplating him in that position for a time, the attorney would depart, no wiser than he came.

Also, when a Reference[1] was going on, and the room full of lawyers and witnesses, and business driving fast, some deeply-occupied legal gentleman present, seeing Bartleby wholly unemployed, would request him to run round to his (the legal gentleman's) office and fetch some papers for him. Thereupon, Bartleby would tranquilly decline, and yet remain idle as before. Then the lawyer would give a great stare, and turn to me. And what could I say? At last I was made aware that all through the circle of my professional acquaintance, a whisper of wonder was running round, having reference to the strange creature I kept at my office. This worried me very much. And as the idea came upon me of his possibly turning out a long-lived man, and keep occupying my chambers, and denying my authority; and perplexing my visitors; and scandalizing my professional reputation; and casting a general gloom over the premises; keeping soul and body together to the last upon his savings (for doubtless he spent but half a dime a day), and in the end perhaps outlive me, and claim possession of my office by right of his perpetual occupancy: as all these dark anticipations crowded upon me more and more, and my friends continually intruded their relentless remarks upon the apparition in my room; a great change was wrought in me. I resolved to gather all my faculties together, and forever rid me of this intolerable incubus.

Ere revolving any complicated project, however, adapted to this end, I first simply suggested to Bartleby the propriety of his permanent departure. In a calm and serious tone, I commended the idea to his careful and mature consideration. But, having taken three days to meditate upon it, he apprised me, that his original determination remained the same; in short, that he still preferred to abide with me.

What shall I do? I now said to myself, buttoning up my coat to the last button. What shall I do? what ought I to do? what does conscience say I *should* do with this man, or, rather, ghost. Rid myself of him, I must; go, he shall. But how? You will not thrust him, the poor, pale, passive mortal—you will not thrust such a helpless creature out of your door? you will not dishonor yourself by such cruelty? No, I will not, I cannot do that. Rather would I let him live and die here, and then mason up his remains in the wall. What, then, will you do? For all your coaxing, he will not budge. Bribes he leaves under your own paperweight on your table; in short, it is quite plain that he prefers to cling to you.

Then something severe, something unusual must be done. What! surely you will not have him collared by a constable, and commit his innocent pallor to the common jail? And upon what ground could you procure such a thing to be done?—

---

[1]A session of the Court of Chancery

a vagrant, is he? What! he a vagrant, a wanderer, who refuses to budge? It is because he will *not* be a vagrant, then, that you seek to count him *as* a vagrant. That is too absurd. No visible means of support: there I have him. Wrong again: for indubitably he *does* support himself, and that is the only unanswerable proof that any man can show of his possessing the means so to do. No more, then. Since he will not quit me, I must quit him. I will change my offices; I will move elsewhere, and give him fair notice, that if I find him on my new premises I will then proceed against him as a common trespasser.

175 Acting accordingly, next day I thus addressed him: 'I find these chambers too far from the City Hall; the air is unwholesome. In a word, I propose to remove my offices next week, and shall no longer require your services. I tell you this now, in order that you may seek another place."

He made no reply, and nothing more was said.

On the appointed day I engaged carts and men, proceeded to my chambers, and, having but little furniture, everything was removed in a few hours. Throughout, the scrivener remained standing behind the screen, which I directed to be removed the last thing. It was withdrawn; and, being folded up like a huge folio, left him the motionless occupant of a naked room. I stood in the entry watching him a moment, while something from within me upbraided me.

I re-entered, with my hand in my pocket—and—and my heart in my mouth.

"Good-by, Bartleby; I am going—good-by, and God some way bless you; and take that," slipping something in his hand. But it dropped upon the floor, and then—strange to say—I tore myself from him whom I had so longed to be rid of.

180 Established in my new quarters, for a day or two I kept the door locked, and started at every footfall in the passages. When I returned to my rooms, after any little absence, I would pause at the threshold for an instant, and attentively listen, ere applying my key. But these fears were needless. Bartleby never came nigh me.

I thought all was going well, when a perturbed-looking stranger visited me, inquiring whether I was the person who had recently occupied rooms at No.— Wall Street.

Full of forebodings, I replied that I was.

"Then, sir," said the stranger, who proved a lawyer, "you are responsible for the man you left there. He refuses to do any copying; he refuses to do anything; he says he prefers not to; and he refuses to quit the premises."

"I am very sorry, sir," said I, with assumed tranquillity, but an inward tremor, "but, really, the man you allude to is nothing to me—he is no relation or apprentice of mine, that you should hold me responsible for him."

185 "In mercy's name, who is he?"

"I certainly cannot inform you. I know nothing about him. Formerly I employed him as a copyist; but he has done nothing for me now for some time past."

"I shall settle him, then—good morning, sir."

Several days passed, and I heard nothing more; and, though I often felt a charitable prompting to call at the place and see poor Bartleby, yet a certain squeamishness, of I know not what, withheld me.

All is over with him, by this time, thought I, at last, when, through another week, no further intelligence reached me. But, coming to my room the day after, I found several persons waiting at my door in a high state of nervous excitement.

190 "That's the man—here he comes," cried the foremost one, whom I recognized as the lawyer who had previously called upon me alone.

"You must take him away, sir, at once," cried a portly person among them, advancing upon me, and whom I knew to be the landlord of No.—Wall Street. "These gentlemen, my tenants, cannot stand it any longer; Mr. B—," pointing to the lawyer, "has turned him out of his room, and he now persists in haunting the building generally, sitting upon the banisters of the stairs by day, and sleeping in the entry by night. Everybody is concerned; clients are leaving the offices; some fears are entertained of a mob; something you must do, and that without delay."

Aghast at this torrent, I fell back before it, and would fain have locked myself in my new quarters. In vain I persisted that Bartleby was nothing to me—no more than to any one else. In vain—I was the last person known to have anything to do with him, and they held me to the terrible account. Fearful, then, of being exposed in the papers (as one person present obscurely threatened), I considered the matter, and, at length, said, that if the lawyer would give me a confidential interview with the scrivener, in his (the lawyer's) own room, I would, that afternoon, strive my best to rid them of the nuisance they complained of.

Going up stairs to my old haunt, there was Bartleby silently sitting upon the banister at the landing.

"What are you doing here, Bartleby?" said I.

195 "Sitting upon the banister," he mildly replied.

I motioned him into the lawyer's room, who then left us.

"Bartleby," said I, "are you aware that you are the cause of great tribulation to me, by persisting in occupying the entry after being dismissed from the office?"

No answer.

"Now one of two things must take place. Either you must do something, or something must be done to you. Now what sort of business would you like to engage in? Would you like to re-engage in copying for some one?"

200 "No; I would prefer not to make any change."

"Would you like a clerkship in a dry-goods store?"

"There is too much confinement about that. No, I would not like a clerkship; but I am not particular."

"Too much confinement," I cried, "why, you keep yourself confined all the time!"

"I would prefer not to take a clerkship," he rejoined, as if to settle that little item at once.

205 "How would a bar-tender's business suit you? There is no trying of the eyesight in that."

"I would not like it at all; though, as I said before, I am not particular."

His unwonted wordiness inspirited me. I returned to the charge.

"Well, then, would you like to travel through the country collecting bills for the merchants? That would improve your health."

"No, I would prefer to do something else."

210 "How, then, would going as a companion to Europe, to entertain some young gentleman with your conversation—how would that suit you?"

"Not at all. It does not strike me that there is anything definite about that. I like to be stationary. But I am not particular."

"Stationary you shall be, then," I cried, now losing all patience, and, for the first time in all my exasperating connection with him, fairly flying into a passion. "If you do not go away from these premises before night, I shall feel bound—indeed, I *am* bound—to—to—to quit the premises myself!" I rather absurdly concluded, knowing not with what possible threat to try to frighten his immobility into compliance. Despairing of all further efforts, I was precipitately leaving him, when a final thought occurred to me—one which had not been wholly unindulged before.

"Bartleby," said I, in the kindest tone I could assume under such exciting circumstances, "will you go home with me now—not to my office, but my dwelling—and remain there till we can conclude upon some convenient arrangement for you at our leisure? Come, let us start now, right away."

"No: at present I would prefer not to make any change at all."

215   I answered nothing; but, effectually dodging every one by the suddenness and rapidity of my flight, rushed from the building, ran up Wall Street towards Broadway, and, jumping into the first omnibus, was soon removed from pursuit. As soon as tranquillity returned, I distinctly perceived that I had now done all that I possibly could, both in respect to the demands of the landlord and his tenants, and with regard to my own desire and sense of duty, to benefit Bartleby, and shield him from rude persecution. I now strove to be entirely care-free and quiescent; and my conscience justified me in the attempt; though, indeed, it was not so successful as I could have wished. So fearful was I of being again hunted out by the incensed landlord and his exasperated tenants, that, surrendering my business to Nippers, for a few days, I drove about the upper part of the town and through the suburbs, in my rockaway;[1] crossed over to Jersey City and Hoboken, and paid fugitive visits to Manhattanville and Astoria. In fact, I almost lived in my rockaway for the time.

When again I entered my office, lo, a note from the landlord lay upon the desk. I opened it with trembling hands. It informed me that the writer had sent to the police, and had Bartleby removed to the Tombs as a vagrant. Moreover, since I knew more about him than any one else, he wished me to appear at the place, and make a suitable statement of the facts. These tidings had a conflicting effect upon me. At first I was indignant; but, at last, almost approved. The landlord's energetic, summary disposition, had led him to adopt a procedure which I do not think I would have decided upon myself; and yet, as a last resort, under such peculiar circumstances, it seemed the only plan.

As I afterwards learned, the poor scrivener, when told that he must be conducted to the Tombs, offered not the slightest obstacle, but, in his pale, unmoving way, silently acquiesced.

Some of the compassionate and curious bystanders joined the party; and headed by one of the constables arm-in-arm with Bartleby, the silent procession filed its way through all the noise, and heat, and joy of the roaring thoroughfares at noon.

The same day I received the note, I went to the Tombs, or, to speak more properly, the Halls of Justice. Seeking the right officer, I stated the purpose of my call, and was informed that the individual I described was, indeed, within. I then assured the functionary that Bartleby was a perfectly honest man, and greatly to be compassionated, however unaccountably eccentric. I narrated all I knew, and closed by suggesting the idea of letting him remain in as indulgent confinement as possible, till something less harsh might be done—though, indeed, I hardly knew what. At all events, if nothing else could be decided upon, the alms-house must receive him. I then begged to have an interview.

220   Being under no disgraceful charge, and quite serene and harmless in all his ways, they had permitted him freely to wander about the prison, and, especially,

---

[1]A fast-moving buggy

in the inclosed grass-platted yards thereof. And so I found him there, standing all alone in the quietest of the yards, his face towards a high wall, while all around, from the narrow slits of the jail windows, I thought I saw peering out upon him the eyes of murderers and thieves.

"Bartleby!"

"I know you," he said, without looking round—"and I want nothing to say to you."

"It was not I that brought you here, Bartleby," said I, keenly pained at his implied suspicion. "And to you, this should not be so vile a place. Nothing reproachful attaches to you being here. And see, it is not so sad a place as one might think. Look, there is the sky, and here is the grass."

"I know where I am," he replied, but would say nothing more, and so I left him.

225   As I entered the corridor again, a broad meat-like man, in an apron, accosted me, and, jerking his thumb over his shoulder, said—"Is that your friend?"

"Yes."

"Does he want to starve? If he does, let him live on the prison fare, that's all."

"Who are you?" asked I, not knowing what to make of such an unofficially speaking person in such a place.

"I am the grub-man. Such gentlemen as have friends here, hire me to provide them with something good to eat."

230   "Is this so?" said I, turning to the turnkey.

He said it was.

"Well, then," said I, slipping some silver into the grub-man's hands (for so they called him), "I want you to give particular attention to my friend there; let him have the best dinner you can get. And you must be as polite to him as possible."

"Introduce me, will you?" said the grub-man, looking at me with an expression which seemed to say he was all impatience for an opportunity to give a specimen of his breeding.

Thinking it would prove of benefit to the scrivener, I acquiesced; and, asking the grub-man his name; went up with him to Bartleby.

235   "Bartleby, this is a friend; you will find him very useful to you."

"Your sarvant, sir, your sarvant," said the grub-man, making a low salutation behind his apron. "Hope you find it pleasant here, sir; nice grounds—cool apartments—hope you'll stay with us some time—try to make it agreeable. What will you have for dinner today?"

"I prefer not to dine to-day," said Bartleby, turning away. "It would disagree with me; I am unused to dinners." So saying, he slowly moved to the other side of the inclosure, and took up a position fronting the dead-wall.

"How's this?" said the grub-man, addressing me with a stare of astonishment. "He's odd, ain't he?"

"I think he is a little deranged," said I, sadly.

240   "Deranged? deranged is it? Well, now, upon my word, I thought that friend of yourn was a gentleman forger; they are always pale and genteel-like, them forgers. I can't help pity 'em—can't help it, sir. Did you know Monroe Edwards?" he added, touchingly, and paused. Then, laying his hand piteously on my shoulder, sighed, "he died of consumption at Sing-Sing. So you weren't acquainted with Monroe?"

"No, I was never socially acquainted with any forgers. But I cannot stop longer. Look to my friend yonder. You will not lose by it. I will see you again."

Some few days after this, I again obtained admission to the Tombs, and went through the corridors in quest of Bartleby; but without finding him.

"I saw him coming from his cell not long ago," said a turnkey, "may be he's gone to loiter in the yards."

So I went in that direction.

245 "Are you looking for the silent man?" said another turnkey, passing me. "Yonder he lies—sleeping in the yard there. 'Tis not twenty minutes since I saw him lie down."

The yard was entirely quiet. It was not accessible to the common prisoners. The surrounding walls, of amazing thickness, kept off all sounds behind them. The Egyptian character of the masonry weighed upon me with its gloom. But a soft imprisoned turf grew under foot. The heart of the eternal pyramids, it seemed, wherein, by some stange magic, through the clefts, grass-seed, dropped by birds, had sprung.

Strangely huddled at the base of the wall, his knees drawn up, and lying on his side, his head touching the cold stones, I saw the wasted Bartleby. But nothing stirred. I paused; then went close up to him; stooped over, and saw that his dim eyes were open; otherwise he seemed profoundly sleeping. Something prompted me to touch him. I felt his hand, when a tingling shiver ran up my arm and down my spine to my feet.

The round face of the grub-man peered upon me now. "His dinner is ready. Won't he dine to-day, either? Or does he live without dining?"

"Lives without dining," said I, and closed the eyes.

250 "Eh!—He's asleep, ain't he?"

"With kings and counselors,"[1] murmured I.

There would seem little need for proceeding further in this history. Imagination will readily supply the meagre recital of poor Bartleby's interment. But, ere parting with the reader, let me say, that if this little narrative has sufficiently interested him, to awaken curiosity as to who Bartleby was, and what manner of life he led prior to the present narrator's making his acquaintance, I can only reply, that in such curiosity I fully share, but am wholly unable to gratify it. Yet here I hardly know whether I should divulge one little item of rumor, which came to my ear a few months after the scrivener's decease. Upon what basis it rested, I could never ascertain; and hence, how true it is I cannot now tell. But, inasmuch as this vague report has not been without a certain suggestive interest to me, however sad, it may prove the same with some others; and so I will briefly mention it. The report was this: that Bartleby had been a subordinate clerk in the Dead Letter Office at Washington, from which he had been suddenly removed by a change in the administration. When I think over this rumor, hardly can I express the emotions which seize me. Dead letters! does it not sound like dead men? Conceive a man by nature and misfortune prone to a pallid hopelessness, can any business seem more fitted to heighten it than that of continually handling these dead letters, and assorting them for the flames? For by the cartload they are annually burned. Sometimes from out the folded paper the pale clerk takes a ring—the finger it was meant for, perhaps, moulders in the grave; a bank-note sent in swiftest charity—he whom it would relieve, nor eats nor hungers any more; pardon for those who died despairing; hope for those who died unhoping; good tidings for those who died stifled by unrelieved calamities. On errands of life, these letters speed to death.

Ah, Bartleby! Ah, humanity!

---

[1] Job 3:13–14

Questions

1. Melville published this short novel in 1856. Does the story give you problems because it is more than a hundred years old? How do you use historical imagination to read *Bartleby the Scrivener*? What is a *ginger nut*? Have you ever eaten one? Could this story be told in a modern setting and remain intact?

2. We are told that Lucifer, who was originally an angel, thought "I will not serve," which brought about his fall from heaven, and in time the fall of all of us. Does Bartleby resemble the devil?

3. Melville chooses to tell this story by means of a character who speaks in the first person. Is the point of view obtuse or unreliable? Is the point of view consistent?

    What would happen if you tried to tell the story from Bartleby's limited omniscient third-person point of view? In Bartleby's first-person?

4. How much setting do we have or need?

5. How much do we know of the narrator? Of Turkey? Nippers? Ginger Nut? Why are all these characters here?

6. Chart the events of the plot. How do they move the action? Do they embody a theme?

7. Discuss Bartleby's effects on others.

8. Discuss theme, meaning, and purpose in this story. Is this a symbolic story?

Leo Tolstoy
The Death of Ivan Ilych

Translated by Louise Aylmer Maude

Leo Tolstoy (1828–1910) is the author of *War and Peace* (1869), *Anna Karenina* (1877), and the less successful *Resurrection* (1899), novels that place him among the greatest of writers. He also wrote autobiography, drama, and philosophical and religious works—and many stories and short novels, like *The Death of Ivan Ilych* (1886). As he grew older his religious ideas took possession of his life. An aristocrat, he dressed like a peasant and worked in the fields. He renounced his earlier fiction as too worldly, gave up his royalties, divided his property, and tried to live his conception of the Christian life.

I

During an interval in the Melvinski trial in the large building of the Law Courts, the members and public prosecutor met in Ivan Egorovich Shebek's private room, where the conversation turned on the celebrated Krasovski case. Fëdor Vasilievich warmly maintained that it was not subject to their jurisdiction. Ivan Egorovich maintained the contrary, while Peter Ivanovich, not having entered into the discussion at the start, took no part in it but looked through the *Gazette* which had just been handed in.

"Gentlemen," he said, "Ivan Ilych[1] has died!"

"You don't say so!"

"Here, read it yourself," replied Peter Ivanovich, handing Fëdor Vasilievich the paper still damp from the press. Surrounded by a black border were the words: "Praskovya Fëdorovna Golovina, with profound sorrow, informs relatives and friends of the demise of her beloved husband Ivan Ilych Golovin, Member of the Court of Justice, which occurred on February the 4th of this year 1882. The funeral will take place on Friday at one o'clock in the afternoon."

5   Ivan Ilych had been a colleague of the gentlemen present and was liked by them all. He had been ill for some weeks with an illness said to be incurable. His post had been kept open for him, but there had been conjectures that in case of his death Alexeev might receive his appointment, and that either Vinnikov or Shtabel would succeed Alexeev. So on receiving the news of Ivan Ilych's death the first thought of each of the gentlemen in that private room was of the changes and promotions it might occasion among themselves or their acquaintances.

[1]It was customary in Russia for friends to refer to one another by the first two of their three names. Ivan Ilych Golovin would have been known among his peers as Ivan Ilych.

"I shall be sure to get Shtabel's place or Vinnikov's," thought Fëdor Vasilievich. "I was promised that long ago, and the promotion means an extra eight hundred rubles[1] a year for me beside the allowance."

"Now I must apply for my brother-in-law's transfer from Kaluga," thought Peter Ivanovich. "My wife will be very glad, and then she won't be able to say that I never do anything for her relations."

"I thought he would never leave his bed again," said Peter Ivanovich aloud. "It's very sad."

"But what really was the matter with him?"

10   "The doctors couldn't say—at least they could, but each of them said something different. When last I saw him I thought he was getting better."

"And I haven't been to see him since the holidays. I always meant to go."

"Had he any property?"

"I think his wife has a little—but something quite trifling."

"We shall have to go to see her, but they live so terribly far away."

15   "Far away from you, you mean. Everything's far away from your place."

"You see, he never can forgive my living on the other side of the river," said Peter Ivanovich, smiling at Shebek. Then, still talking of the distances between different parts of the city, they returned to the Court.

Besides considerations as to the possible transfers and promotions likely to result from Ivan Ilych's death, the mere fact of the death of a near acquaintance aroused, as usual, in all who heard of it the complacent feeling that, "it is he who is dead and not I."

Each one thought or felt, "Well, he's dead but I'm alive!" But the more intimate of Ivan Ilych's acquaintances, his so-called friends, could not help thinking also that they would now have to fulfil the very tiresome demands of propriety by attending the funeral service and paying a visit of condolence to the widow.

Fëdor Vasilievich and Peter Ivanovich had been his nearest acquaintances. Peter Ivanovich had studied law with Ivan Ilych and had considered himself to be under obligations to him.

20   Having told his wife at dinner-time of Ivan Ilych's death and of his conjecture that it might be possible to get her brother transferred to their circuit, Peter Ivanovich sacrificed his usual nap, put on his evening clothes, and drove to Ivan Ilych's house.

At the entrance stood a carriage and two cabs. Leaning against the wall in the hall downstairs near the cloak-stand was a coffin-lid covered with cloth of gold, ornamented with gold cord and tassels, that had been polished up with metal powder. Two ladies in black were taking off their fur cloaks. Peter Ivanovich recognized one of them as Ivan Ilych's sister, but the other was a stranger to him. His colleague Schwartz was just coming downstairs, but on seeing Peter Ivanovich enter he stopped and winked at him, as if to say: "Ivan Ilych has made a mess of things—not like you and me."

Schwartz's face with his Piccadilly whiskers and his slim figure in evening dress, had as usual an air of elegant solemnity which contrasted with the playfulness of his character and had a special piquancy here, or so it seemed to Peter Ivanovich.

Peter Ivanovich allowed the ladies to precede him and slowly followed them upstairs. Schwartz did not come down but remained where he was, and Peter

---

[1] A considerable sum in the 1880s

Ivanovich understood that he wanted to arrange where they should play bridge that evening. The ladies went upstairs to the widow's room, and Schwartz with seriously compressed lips but a playful look in his eyes, indicated by a twist of his eyebrows the room to the right where the body lay.

Peter Ivanovich, like everyone else on such occasions, entered feeling uncertain what he would have to do. All he knew was that at such times it is always safe to cross oneself. But he was not quite sure whether one should make obeisances while doing so. He therefore adopted a middle course. On entering the room he began crossing himself and made a slight movement resembling a bow. At the same time, as far as the motion of his head and arm allowed, he surveyed the room. Two young men—apparently nephews, one of whom was a high-school pupil—were leaving the room, crossing themselves as they did so. An old woman was standing motionless, and a lady with strangely arched eyebrows was saying something to her in a whisper. A vigorous, resolute Church Reader, in a frock-coat, was reading something in a loud voice with an expression that precluded any contradiction. The butler's assistant, Gerasim, stepping lightly in front of Peter Ivanovich, was strewing something on the floor. Noticing this, Peter Ivanovich was immediately aware of a faint odour of a decomposing body.

25 The last time he had called on Ivan Ilych, Peter Ivanovich had seen Gerasim in the study. Ivan Ilych had been particularly fond of him and he was performing the duty of a sick nurse.

Peter Ivanovich continued to make the sign of the cross slightly inclining his head in an intermediate direction between the coffin, the Reader, and the icons on the table in a corner of the room. Afterwards, when it seemed to him that this movement of his arm in crossing himself had gone on too long, he stopped and began to look at the corpse.

The dead man lay, as dead men always lie, in a specially heavy way, his rigid limbs sunk in the soft cushions of the coffin, with the head forever bowed on the pillow. His yellow waxen brow with bald patches over his sunken temples was thrust up in the way peculiar to the dead, the protruding nose seeming to press on the upper lip. He was much changed and had grown even thinner since Peter Ivanovich had last seen him, but, as is always the case with the dead, his face was handsomer and above all more dignified than when he was alive. The expression on the face said that what was necessary had been accomplished, and accomplished rightly. Besides this there was in that expression a reproach and a warning to the living. This warning seemed to Peter Ivanovich out of place, or at least not applicable to him. He felt a certain discomfort and so he hurriedly crossed himself once more and turned and went out of the door—too hurriedly and too regardless of propriety, as he himself was aware.

Schwartz was waiting for him in the adjoining room with legs spread wide apart and both hands toying with his top-hat behind his back. The mere sight of that playful, well-groomed, and elegant figure refreshed Peter Ivanovich. He felt that Schwartz was above all these happenings and would not surrender to any depressing influences. His very look said that this incident of a church service for Ivan Ilych could not be a sufficient reason for infringing the order of the session—in other words, that it would certainly not prevent his unwrapping a new pack of cards and shuffling them that evening while a footman placed four fresh candles on the table: in fact, that there was no reason for supposing that this incident would hinder their spending the evening agreeably. Indeed he said this in a whisper as Peter Ivanovich passed him, proposing that they should meet for a game at

Fëdor Vasilievich's. But apparently Peter Ivanovich was not destined to play bridge that evening. Praskovya Fëdorovna (a short, fat woman who despite all efforts to the contrary had continued to broaden steadily from her shoulders downwards and who had the same extraordinarily arched eyebrows as the lady who had been standing by the coffin), dressed all in black, her head covered with lace, came out of her own room with some other ladies, conducted them to the room where the dead body lay, and said: "The service will begin immediately. Please go in."

Schwartz, making an indefinite bow, stood still, evidently neither accepting nor declining this invitation. Praskovya Fëdorovna, recognizing Peter Ivanovich, sighed, went close up to him, took his hand, and said: "I know you were a true friend to Ivan Ilych . . ." and looked at him awaiting some suitable response. And Peter Ivanovich knew that, just as it had been the right thing to cross himself in that room, so what he had to do here was to press her hand, sigh, and say, "Believe me. . . ." So he did all this and as he did it felt that the desired result had been achieved: that both he and she were touched.

30   "Come with me. I want to speak to you before it begins," said the widow. "Give me your arm."

Peter Ivanovich gave her his arm and they went to the inner rooms, passing Schwartz, who winked at Peter Ivanovich compassionately.

"That does for our bridge! Don't object if we find another player. Perhaps you can cut in when you do escape," said his playful look.

Peter Ivanovich sighed still more deeply and despondently, and Praskovya Fëdorovna pressed his arm gratefully. When they reached the drawing-room, up-holstered in pink cretonne and lighted by a dim lamp, they sat down at the table—she on a sofa and Peter Ivanovich on a low pouffe,[1] the springs of which yielded spasmodically under his weight. Praskovya Fëdorovna had been on the point of warning him to take another seat, but felt that such a warning was out of keeping with her present condition and so changed her mind. As he sat down on the pouffe Peter Ivanovich recalled how Ivan Ilych had arranged this room and had consulted him regarding this pink cretonne with green leaves. The whole room was full of furniture and knickknacks, and on her way to the sofa the lace of the widow's black shawl caught on the carved edge of the table. Peter Ivanovich rose to detach it, and the springs of the pouffe, relieved of his weight, rose also and gave him a push. The widow began detaching her shawl herself, and Peter Ivanovich again sat down, suppressing the rebellious springs of the pouffe under him. But the widow had not quite freed herself and Peter Ivanovich got up again, and again the pouffe rebelled and even creaked. When this was all over she took out a clean cambric handkerchief and began to weep. The episode with the shawl and the struggle with the pouffe had cooled Peter Ivanovich's emotions and he sat there with a sullen look on his face. This awkward situation was interrupted by Sokolov, Ivan Ilych's butler, who came to report that the plot in the cemetery that Praskovya Fëdorovna had chosen would cost two hundred rubles. She stopped weeping and, looking at Peter Ivanovich with the air of a victim, remarked in French that it was very hard for her. Peter Ivanovich made a silent gesture signifying his full convic-tion that it must indeed be so.

"Please smoke," she said in a magnanimous yet crushed voice, and turned to discuss with Sokolov the price of the plot for the grave.

35   Peter Ivanovich while lighting his cigarette heard her inquiring very circumstan-

[1]Ottoman or hassock

tially into the prices of different plots in the cemetery and finally decide which she would take. When that was done she gave instructions about engaging the choir. Sokolov then left the room.

"I look after everything myself," she told Peter Ivanovich, shifting the albums that lay on the table; and noticing that the table was endangered by his cigarette-ash, she immediately passed him an ash-tray, saying as she did so: "I consider it an affectation to say that my grief prevents my attending to practical affairs. On the contrary, if anything can—I won't say console me, but—distract me, it is seeing to everything concerning him." She again took out her handkerchief as if preparing to cry, but suddenly, as if mastering her feeling, she shook herself and began to speak calmly. "But there is something I want to talk to you about."

Peter Ivanovich bowed, keeping control of the springs of the pouffe, which immediately began quivering under him.

"He suffered terribly the last few days."

"Did he?" said Peter Ivanovich.

40 "Oh, terribly! He screamed unceasingly, not for minutes but for hours. For the last three days he screamed incessantly. It was unendurable. I cannot understand how I bore it; you could hear him three rooms off. Oh, what I have suffered!"

"Is it possible that he was conscious all that time?" asked Peter Ivanovich.

"Yes," she whispered. "To the last moment. He took leave of us a quarter of an hour before he died, and asked us to take Volodya away."

The thought of the sufferings of this man he had known so intimately, first as a merry little boy, then as a school-mate, and later as a grown-up colleague, suddenly struck Peter Ivanovich with horror, despite an unpleasant consciousness of his own and this woman's dissimulation. He again saw that brow, and that nose pressing down on the lip, and felt afraid for himself.

"Three days of frightful suffering and then death! Why, that might suddenly, at any time, happen to me," he thought, and for a moment felt terrified. But—he did not himself know how—the customary reflection at once occurred to him that this had happened to Ivan Ilych and not to him, and that it should not and could not happen to him, and to think that it could would be yielding to depression which he ought not to do, as Schwartz's expression plainly showed. After which reflection Peter Ivanovich felt reassured, and began to ask with interest about the details of Ivan Ilych's death, as though death was an accident natural to Ivan Ilych but certainly not to himself.

45 After many details of the really dreadful physical sufferings Ivan Ilych had endured (which details he learnt only from the effect those sufferings had produced on Praskovya Fëdorovna's nerves) the widow apparently found it necessary to get to business.

"Oh, Peter Ivanovich, how hard it is! How terribly, terribly hard!" and she again began to weep.

Peter Ivanovich sighed and waited for her to finish blowing her nose. When she had done so he said, "Believe me . . ." and she again began talking and brought out what was evidently her chief concern with him—namely, to question him as to how she could obtain a grant of money from the government on the occasion of her husband's death. She made it appear that she was asking Peter Ivanovich's advice about her pension, but he soon saw that she already knew about that to the minutest detail, more even than he did himself. She knew how much could be got out of the government in consequence of her husband's death, but wanted to find out whether she could not possibly extract something more. Peter Ivanovich tried to think of some means of doing so, but after reflecting for a while and, out of propriety, condemning the government for its niggardliness, he said he thought that nothing more could be got. Then she sighed and evidently began to devise means of getting rid of her visitor. Noticing this, he put out his cigarette, rose, pressed her hand, and went out into the anteroom.

In the dining-room where the clock stood that Ivan Ilych had liked so much and had bought at an antique shop, Peter Ivanovich met a priest and a few acquaintances who had come to attend the service, and he recognized Ivan Ilych's daughter, a handsome young woman. She was in black and her slim figure appeared slimmer than ever. She had a gloomy, determined, almost angry expression, and bowed to Peter Ivanovich as though he were in some way to blame. Behind her, with the same offended look, stood a wealthy young man, an examining magistrate, whom Peter Ivanovich also knew and who was her fiancé, as he had heard. He bowed mournfully to them and was about to pass into the death-chamber, when from under the stairs appeared the figure of Ivan Ilych's schoolboy son, who was extremely like his father. He seemed a little Ivan Ilych, such as Peter Ivanovich remembered when they studied law together. His tear-stained eyes had in them the look that is seen in the eyes of boys of thirteen or fourteen who are not pureminded. When he saw Peter Ivanovich he scowled morosely and shamefacedly. Peter Ivanovich nodded to him and entered the death-chamber. The service began: candles, groans, incense, tears, and sobs. Peter Ivanovich stood looking gloomily down at his feet. He did not look once at the dead man, did not yield to any depressing influence, and was one of the first to leave the room. There was no one in the anteroom, but Gerasim darted out of the dead man's room, rummaged with his strong hands among the fur coats to find Peter Ivanovich's and helped him on with it.

"Well, friend Gerasim," said Peter Ivanovich, so as to say something. "It's a sad affair, isn't it?"

50   "It's God's will. We shall all come to it some day," said Gerasim, displaying his teeth—the even, white teeth of a healthy peasant—and, like a man in the thick of urgent work, he briskly opened the front door, called the coachman, helped Peter Ivanovich into the sledge, and sprang back to the porch as if in readiness for what he had to do next.

Peter Ivanovich found the fresh air particularly pleasant after the smell of incense, the dead body, and carbolic acid.

"Where to, sir?" asked the coachman.

"It's not too late even now. . . . I'll call round on Fëdor Vasilievich."

He accordingly drove there and found them just finishing the first rubber, so that it was quite convenient for him to cut in.

II

55   Ivan Ilych's life had been most simple and most ordinary and therefore most terrible.

He had been a member of the Court of Justice, and died at the age of forty-five. His father had been an official who after serving in various ministries and departments in Petersburg had made the sort of career which brings men to positions from which by reason of their long service they cannot be dismissed, though they are obviously unfit to hold any responsible position, and for whom therefore posts are especially created, which though fictitious carry salaries of from six to ten thousand rubles that are not fictitious, and in receipt of which they live on to a great age.

Such was the Privy Councillor and superfluous member of various superfluous institutions, Ilya Epimovich Golovin.

He had three sons, of whom Ivan Ilych was the second. The eldest son was following in his father's footsteps only in another department, and was already approaching that stage in the service at which a similar sinecure would be reached. The third son was a failure. He had ruined his prospects in a number of positions and was now serving in the railway department. His father and brothers, and still more their wives, not merely disliked meeting him, but avoided remembering his existence unless compelled to do so. His sister had married Baron Greff, a Petersburg official of her father's type. Ivan Ilych was *le phénix de la famille*[1] as people said. He was neither as cold and formal as his elder brother nor as wild as the younger, but was a happy mean between them—an intelligent, polished, lively and agreeable man. He had studied with his younger brother at the School of Law, but the latter had failed to complete the course and was expelled when he was in the fifth class. Ivan Ilych finished the course well. Even when he was at the School of Law he was just what he remained for the rest of his life: a capable, cheerful, good-natured, and sociable man, though strict in the fulfilment of what he considered to be his duty: and he considered his duty to be what was so considered by those in authority. Neither as a boy nor as a man was he a toady, but from early youth was by nature attracted to people of high station as a fly is drawn to the light, assimilating their ways and views of life and establishing friendly relations with them. All the enthusiasms of childhood and youth passed without leaving much trace on him; he succumbed to sensuality, to vanity, and latterly among the highest classes to liberalism, but always within limits which his instinct unfailingly indicated to him as correct.

At school he had done things which had formerly seemed to him very horrid and made him feel disgusted with himself when he did them; but when later on he saw that such actions were done by people of good position and that they did not regard them as wrong, he was able not exactly to regard them as right, but to forget about them entirely or not be at all troubled at remembering them.

60 Having graduated from the School of Law and qualified for the tenth rank of the civil service,[2] and having received money from his father for his equipment, Ivan Ilych ordered himself clothes at Scharmer's, the fashionable tailor, hung a medallion inscribed *respice finem*[3] on his watch-chain, took leave of his professor and the prince who was patron of the school, had a farewell dinner with his comrades at Donon's first-class restaurant, and with his new and fashionable portmanteau, linen, clothes, shaving and other toilet appliances, and a travelling rug, all purchased at the best shops, he set off for one of the provinces where, through his father's influence, he had been attached to the Governor as an official for special service.

In the province Ivan Ilych soon arranged as easy and agreeable a position for himself as he had had at the School of Law. He performed his official tasks, made his career, and at the same time amused himself pleasantly and decorously. Occasionally he paid official visits to country districts, where he behaved with dignity both to his superiors and inferiors, and performed the duties entrusted to him,

---

[1]His family's darling   [2]A good status in the hierarchy at the time   [3]Consider the end

which related chiefly to the sectarians,[1] with an exactness and incorruptible honesty of which he could not but feel proud.

In official matters, despite his youth and taste for frivolous gaiety, he was exceedingly reserved, punctilious, and even severe; but in society he was often amusing and witty, and always good-natured, correct in his manner, and *bon enfant*,[2] as the governor and his wife—with whom he was like one of the family—used to say of him.

In the province he had an affair with a lady who made advances to the elegant young lawyer, and there was also a milliner; and there were carousals with aides-de-camp who visited the district, and after-supper visits to a certain outlying street of doubtful reputation; and there was too some obsequiousness to his chief and even to his chief's wife, but all this was done with such a tone of good breeding that no hard names could be applied to it. It all came under the heading of the French saying: *"Il faut que jeunesse se passe."*[3] It was all done with clean hands, in clean linen, with French phrases, and above all among people of the best society and consequently with the approval of people of rank.

So Ivan Ilych served for five years and then came a change in his official life. The new and reformed judicial institutions were introduced, and new men were needed. Ivan Ilych became such a new man. He was offered the post of examining magistrate, and he accepted it though the post was in another province and obliged him to give up the connexions he had formed and to make new ones. His friends met to give him a send-off; they had a group-photograph taken and presented him with a silver cigarette-case, and he set off to his new post.

As examining magistrate Ivan Ilych was just as *comme il faut*[4] and decorous a man, inspiring general respect and capable of separating his official duties from his private life, as he had been when acting as an official on special service. His duties now as examining magistrate were far more interesting and attractive than before. In his former position it had been pleasant to wear an undress uniform made by Scharmer, and to pass through the crowd of petitioners and officials who were timorously awaiting an audience with the governor, and who envied him as with free and easy gait he went straight into his chief's private room to have a cup of tea and cigarette with him. But not many people had then been directly dependent on him—only police officials and the sectarians when he went on special missions—and he liked to treat them politely, almost as comrades, as if he were letting them feel that he who had the power to crush them was treating them in this simple, friendly way. There were then but few such people. But now, as an examining magistrate, Ivan Ilych felt that everyone without exception, even the most important and self-satisfied, was in his power, and that he need only write a few words on a sheet of paper with a certain heading, and this or that important, self-satisfied person would be brought before him in the role of an accused person or a witness, and if he did not choose to allow him to sit down, would have to stand before him and answer his questions. Ivan Ilych never abused his power; he tried on the contrary to soften its expression, but the consciousness of it and of the possibility of softening its effect, supplied the chief interest and attraction of his office. In his work itself, especially in his examinations, he very soon acquired a method of eliminating all considerations irrelevant to the legal aspect of the case, and reducing even the most complicated case to a form in which it would

---

[1]"Old Believers," who dissented from the modern Russian Orthodox Church
[2]Good fellow   [3]Youth must have its fling   [4]Proper

be presented on paper only in its externals, completely excluding his personal opinion of the matter, while above all observing every prescribed formality. The work was new and Ivan Ilych was one of the first men to apply the new Code of 1864.[1]

On taking up the post of examining magistrate in a new town, he made new acquaintances and connexions, placed himself on a new footing, and assumed a somewhat different tone. He took up an attitude of rather dignified aloofness towards the provincial authorities, but picked out the best circle of legal gentlemen and wealthy gentry living in the town and assumed a tone of slight dissatisfaction with the government, of moderate liberalism, and of enlightened citizenship. At the same time, without at all altering the elegance of his toilet, he ceased shaving his chin and allowed his beard to grow as it pleased.

Ivan Ilych settled down very pleasantly in this new town. The society there, which inclined towards opposition to the Governor, was friendly, his salary was larger, and he began to play *vint*,[2] which he found added not a little to the pleasure of life, for he had a capacity for cards, played good-humouredly, and calculated rapidly and astutely, so that he usually won.

After living there for two years he met his future wife, Praskovya Fëdorovna Mikhel, who was the most attractive, clever, and brilliant girl of the set in which he moved, and among other amusements and relaxations from his labours as examining magistrate, Ivan Ilych established light and playful relations with her.

While he had been an official on special service he had been accustomed to dance, but now as an examining magistrate it was exceptional for him to do so. If he danced now, he did it as if to show that though he served under the reformed order of things, and had reached the fifth official rank, yet when it came to dancing he could do it better than most people. So at the end of an evening he sometimes danced with Praskovya Fëdorovna, and it was chiefly during these dances that he captivated her. She fell in love with him. Ivan Ilych had at first no definite intention of marrying, but when the girl fell in love with him he said to himself: "Really, why shouldn't I marry?"

70   Praskovya Fëdorovna came of a good family, was not bad looking, and had some little property. Ivan Ilych might have aspired to a more brilliant match, but even this was good. He had his salary, and she, he hoped, would have an equal income. She was well connected, and was a sweet, pretty, and thoroughly correct young woman. To say that Ivan Ilych married because he fell in love with Praskovya Fëdorovna and found that she sympathized with his views of life would be as incorrect as to say that he married because his social circle approved of the match. He was swayed by both these considerations: the marriage gave him personal satisfaction, and at the same time it was considered the right thing by the most highly placed of his associates.

So Ivan Ilych got married.

The preparations for marriage and the beginning of married life, with its conjugal caresses, the new furniture, new crockery, and new linen, were very pleasant until his wife became pregnant—so that Ivan Ilych had begun to think that marriage would not impair the easy, agreeable, gay and always decorous character of his life, approved of by society and regarded by himself as natural, but would even improve it. But from the first months of his wife's pregnancy, something new,

[1]I.e., appropriately progressive; the new Code followed the 1861 emancipation of the serfs
[2]A card game somewhat similar to both whist and bridge

unpleasant, depressing, and unseemly, and from which there was no way of escape, unexpectedly showed itself.

His wife, without any reason—*de gaieté de coeur*[1] as Ivan Ilych expressed it to himself—began to disturb the pleasure and propriety of their life. She began to be jealous without any cause, expected him to devote his whole attention to her, found fault with everything, and made coarse and ill-mannered scenes.

At first Ivan Ilych hoped to escape from the unpleasantness of this state of affairs by the same easy and decorous relation to life that had served him heretofore: he tried to ignore his wife's disagreeable moods, continued to live in his usual easy and pleasant way, invited friends to his house for a game of cards, and also tried going out to his club or spending his evenings with friends. But one day his wife began upbraiding him so vigorously, using such coarse words, and continued to abuse him every time he did not fulfil her demands, so resolutely and with such evident determination not to give way till he submitted—that is, till he stayed at home and was bored just as she was—that he became alarmed. He now realized that matrimony—at any rate with Praskovya Fëdorovna—was not always conducive to the pleasures and amenities of life, but on the contrary often infringed both comfort and propriety, and that he must therefore entrench himself against such infringement. And Ivan Ilych began to seek for means of doing so. His official duties were the one thing that imposed upon Praskovya Fëdorovna, and by means of his official work and the duties attached to it he began struggling with his wife to secure his own independence.

75   With the birth of their child, the attempts to feed it and the various failures in doing so, and with the real and imaginary illnesses of mother and child, in which Ivan Ilych's sympathy was demanded but about which he understood nothing, the need of securing for himself an existence outside his family life became still more imperative.

As his wife grew more irritable and exacting and Ivan Ilych transferred the centre of gravity of his life more and more to his official work, so did he grow to like his work better and became more ambitious than before.

Very soon, within a year of his wedding, Ivan Ilych had realized that marriage, though it may add some comforts to life, is in fact a very intricate and difficult affair towards which in order to perform one's duty, that is, to lead a decorous life approved of by society, one must adopt a definite attitude just as towards one's official duties.

And Ivan Ilych evolved such an attitude towards married life. He only required of it those conveniences—dinner at home, housewife, and bed—which it could give him, and above all that propriety of external forms required by public opinion. For the rest he looked for light-hearted pleasure and propriety, and was very thankful when he found them, but if he met with antagonism and querulousness he at once retired into his separate fenced-off world of official duties, where he found satisfaction.

Ivan Ilych was esteemed a good official, and after three years was made Assistant Public Prosecutor. His new duties, their importance, the possibility of indicting and imprisoning anyone he chose, the publicity his speeches received, and the success he had in all these things, made his work still more attractive.

80   More children came. His wife became more and more querulous and ill-tem-

[1]Lightheartedly

pered, but the attitude Ivan Ilych had adopted towards his home life rendered him almost impervious to her grumbling.

After seven years' service in that town he was transferred to another province as Public Prosecutor. They moved, but were short of money and his wife did not like the place they moved to. Though the salary was higher the cost of living was greater, besides which two of their children died and family life became still more unpleasant for him.

Praskovya Fëdorovna blamed her husband for every inconvenience they encountered in their new home. Most of the conversations between husband and wife, especially as to the children's education, led to topics which recalled former disputes, and those disputes were apt to flare up again at any moment. There remained only those rare periods of amorousness which still came to them at times but did not last long. These were islets at which they anchored for a while and then again set out upon that ocean of veiled hostility which showed itself in their aloofness from one another. This aloofness might have grieved Ivan Ilych had he considered that it ought not to exist, but he now regarded the position as normal, and even made it the goal at which he aimed in family life. His aim was to free himself more and more from those unpleasantnesses and to give them a semblance of harmlessness and propriety. He attained this by spending less and less time with his family, and when obliged to be at home he tried to safeguard his position by the presence of outsiders. The chief thing however was that he had his official duties. The whole interest of his life now centered in the official world and that interest absorbed him. The consciousness of his power, being able to ruin anybody he wished to ruin, the importance, even the external dignity of his entry into court, or meetings with his subordinates, his success with superiors and inferiors, and above all his masterly handling of cases, of which he was conscious—all this gave him pleasure and filled his life, together with chats with his colleagues, dinners, and bridge. So that on the whole Ivan Ilych's life continued to flow as he considered it should do—pleasantly and properly.

So things continued for another seven years. His eldest daughter was already sixteen, another child had died, and only one son was left, a schoolboy and a subject of dissension. Ivan Ilych wanted to put him in the School of Law, but to spite him Praskovya Fëdorovna entered him at the High School. The daughter had been educated at home and had turned out well: the boy did not learn badly either.

III

So Ivan Ilych lived for seventeen years after his marriage. He was already a Public Prosecutor of long standing, and had declined several proposed transfers while awaiting a more desirable post, when an unanticipated and unpleasant occurrence quite upset the peaceful course of his life. He was expecting to be offered the post of presiding judge in a University town, but Happe somehow came to the front and obtained the appointment instead. Ivan Ilych became irritable, reproached Happe, and quarrelled both with him and with his immediate superiors—who became colder to him and again passed him over when other appointments were made.

85

This was in 1880, the hardest year of Ivan Ilych's life. It was then that it became evident on the one hand that his salary was insufficient for them to live on, and on the other hand that he had been forgotten, and not only this, but that what was for him the greatest and most cruel injustice appeared to others a quite ordinary occurrence. Even his father did not consider it his duty to help him. Ivan

Ilych felt himself abandoned by everyone, and that they regarded his position with a salary of 3,500 rubles as quite normal and even fortunate. He alone knew that with the consciousness of the injustices done him, with his wife's incessant nagging, and with the debts he had contracted by living beyond his means, his position was far from normal.

In order to save money that summer he obtained leave of absence and went with his wife to live in the country at her brother's place.

In the country, without his work, he experienced *ennui*[1] for the first time in his life, and not only *ennui* but intolerable depression, and he decided that it was impossible to go on living like that, and that it was necessary to take energetic measures.

Having passed a sleepless night pacing up and down the veranda, he decided to go to Petersburg and bestir himself, in order to punish those who had failed to appreciate him and to get transferred to another ministry.

Next day, despite many protests from his wife and her brother, he started for Petersburg with the sole object of obtaining a post with a salary of five thousand rubles a year. He was no longer bent on any particular department or tendency, or kind of activity. All he now wanted was an appointment to another post with a salary of five thousand rubles, either in the administration, in the banks, with the railways, in one of the Empress Marya's Institutions,[2] or even in the customs— but it had to carry with it a salary of five thousand rubles and be in a ministry other than that in which they had failed to appreciate him.

90   And this quest of Ivan Ilych's was crowned with remarkable and unexpected success. At Kursk an acquaintance of his, F. I. Ilyin, got into the first-class carriage, sat down beside Ivan Ilych, and told him of a telegram just received by the Governor of Kursk announcing that a change was about to take place in the ministry: Peter Ivanovich was to be superseded by Ivan Seménovich.

The proposed change, apart from its significance for Russia, had a special significance for Ivan Ilych, because by bringing forward a new man, Peter Petrovich, and consequently his friend Zachar Ivanovich, it was highly favourable for Ivan Ilych, since Zachar Ivanovich was a friend and colleague of his.

In Moscow this news was confirmed, and on reaching Petersburg Ivan Ilych found Zachar Ivanovich and received a definite promise of an appointment in his former department of Justice.

A week later he telegraphed to his wife: "Zachar in Miller's place. I shall receive appointment on presentation of report."

Thanks to this change of personnel, Ivan Ilych had unexpectedly obtained an appointment in his former ministry which placed him two stages above his former colleagues besides giving him five thousand rubles salary and three thousand five hundred rubles for expenses connected with his removal. All his ill humour towards his former enemies and the whole department vanished, and Ivan Ilych was completely happy.

95   He returned to the country more cheerful and contented than he had been for a long time. Praskovya Fëdorovna also cheered up and a truce was arranged between them. Ivan Ilych told of how he had been fêted by everybody in Petersburg, how all those who had been his enemies were put to shame and now fawned on him, how envious they were of his appointment, and how much everybody in Petersburg had liked him.

---

[1]Boredom   [2]A ministry of charitable works

Praskovya Fëdorovna listened to all this and appeared to believe it. She did not contradict anything, but only made plans for their life in the town to which they were going. Ivan Ilych saw with delight that these plans were his plans, that he and his wife agreed, and that, after a stumble, his life was regaining its due and natural character of pleasant lightheartedness and decorum.

Ivan Ilych had come back for a short time only, for he had to take up his new duties on the 10th of September. Moreover, he needed time to settle into the new place, to move all his belongings from the province, and to buy and order many additional things: in a word, to make such arrangements as he had resolved on, which were almost exactly what Praskovya Fëdorovna too had decided on.

Now that everything had happened so fortunately, and that he and his wife were at one in their aims and moreover saw so little of one another, they got on together better than they had done since the first years of marriage. Ivan Ilych had thought of taking his family away with him at once, but the insistence of his wife's brother and her sister-in-law, who had suddenly become particularly amiable and friendly to him and his family, induced him to depart alone.

So he departed, and the cheerful state of mind induced by his success and by the harmony between his wife and himself, the one intensifying the other, did not leave him. He found a delightful house, just the thing both he and his wife had dreamt of. Spacious, lofty reception rooms in the old style, a convenient and dignified study, rooms for his wife and daughter, a study for his son—it might have been specially built for them. Ivan Ilych himself superintended the arrangements, chose the wallpapers, supplemented the furniture (preferably with antiques which he considered particularly *comme il faut*), and supervised the upholstering. Everything progressed and progressed and approached the ideal he had set himself: even when things were only half completed they exceeded his expectations. He saw what a refined and elegant character, free from vulgarity, it would all have when it was ready. On falling asleep he pictured to himself how the reception-room would look. Looking at the yet unfinished drawing-room he could see the fireplace, the screen, the what-not, the little chairs dotted here and there, the dishes and plates on the walls, and the bronzes, as they would be when everything was in place. He was pleased by the thought of how his wife and daughter, who shared his taste in this matter, would be impressed by it. They were certainly not expecting as much. He had been particularly successful in finding, and buying cheaply, antiques which gave a particularly aristocratic character to the whole place. But in his letters he intentionally understated everything in order to be able to surprise them. All this so absorbed him that his new duties—though he liked his official work—interested him less than he had expected. Sometimes he even had moments of absentmindedness during the Court Sessions, and would consider whether he should have straight or curved cornices for his curtains. He was so interested in it all that he often did things himself, rearranging the furniture, or rehanging the curtains. Once when mounting a step-ladder to show the upholsterer, who did not understand, how he wanted the hangings draped, he made a false step and slipped, but being a strong and agile man he clung on and only knocked his side against the knob of the window frame. The bruised place was painful but the pain soon passed, and he felt particularly bright and well just then. He wrote: "I feel fifteen years younger." He thought he would have everything ready by September, but it dragged on till mid-October. But the result was charming not only in his eyes but to everyone who saw it.

100 In reality it was just what is usually seen in the houses of people of moderate

means who want to appear rich, and therefore succeed only in resembling others like themselves: there were damasks, dark wood, plants, rugs, and dull and polished bronzes—all the things people of a certain class have in order to resemble other people of that class. His house was so like the others that it would never have been noticed, but to him it all seemed to be quite exceptional. He was very happy when he met his family at the station and brought them to the newly furnished house all lit up, where a footman in a white tie opened the door into the hall decorated with plants, and when they went on into the drawing-room and the study uttering exclamations of delight. He conducted them everywhere, drank in their praises eagerly, and beamed with pleasure. At tea that evening, when Praskovya Fëdorovna among other things asked him about his fall, he laughed and showed them how he had gone flying and had frightened the upholsterer.

"It's a good thing I'm a bit of an athlete. Another man might have been killed, but I merely knocked myself, just here; it hurts when it's touched, but it's passing off already—it's only a bruise."

So they began living in their new home—in which, as always happens, when they got thoroughly settled in they found they were just one room short—and with the increased income, which as always was just a little (some five hundred rubles) too little, but it was all very nice.

Things went particularly well at first, before everything was finally arranged and while something had still to be done: this thing bought, that thing ordered, another thing moved, and something else adjusted. Though there were some disputes between husband and wife, they were both so well satisfied and had so much to do that it all passed off without any serious quarrels. When nothing was left to arrange it became rather dull and something seemed to be lacking, but they were then making acquaintances, forming habits, and life was growing fuller.

Ivan Ilych spent his mornings at the law court and came home to dinner, and at first he was generally in a good humour, though he occasionally became irritable just on account of his house. (Every spot on the tablecloth or the upholstery, and every broken window-blind string, irritated him. He had devoted so much trouble to arranging it all that every disturbance of it distressed him.) But on the whole his life ran its course as he believed life should do: easily, pleasantly, and decorously.

105   He got up at nine, drank his coffee, read the paper, and then put on his undress uniform and went to the law courts. There the harness in which he worked had already been stretched to fit him and he donned it without a hitch: petitioners, inquiries at the chancery, the chancery itself, and the sittings public and administrative. In all this the thing was to exclude everything fresh and vital, which always disturbs the regular course of official business, and to admit only official relations with people, and then only on official grounds. A man would come, for instance, wanting some information. Ivan Ilych, as one in whose sphere the matter did not lie, would have nothing to do with him: but if the man had some business with him in his official capacity, something that could be expressed on officially stamped paper, he would do everything, positively everything he could within the limits of such relations, and in doing so would maintain the semblance of friendly human relations, that is, would observe the courtesies of life. As soon as the official relations ended, so did everything else. Ivan Ilych possessed this capacity to separate his real life from the official side of affairs and not mix the two, in the highest degree, and by long practice and natural aptitude had brought it to such a pitch that sometimes, in the manner of a virtuoso, he would even allow himself

to let the human and official relations mingle. He let himself do this just because he felt that he could at any time he chose resume the strictly official attitude again and drop the human relation. And he did it all easily, pleasantly, correctly, and even artistically. In the intervals between the sessions he smoked, drank tea, chatted a little about politics, a little about general topics, a little about cards, but most of all about official appointments. Tired, but with the feelings of a virtuoso— one of the first violins who has played his part in an orchestra with precision—he would return home to find that his wife and daughter had been out paying calls, or had a visitor, and that his son had been to school, had done his homework with the tutor, and was duly learning what is taught at High Schools. Everything was as it should be. After dinner, if they had no visitors, Ivan Ilych sometimes read a book that was being much discussed at the time, and in the evening settled down to work, that is, read official papers, compared the depositions of witnesses, and noted paragraphs of the Code applying to them. This was neither dull nor amusing. It was dull when he might have been playing bridge but if no bridge was available it was at any rate better than doing nothing or sitting with his wife. Ivan Ilych's chief pleasure was giving little dinners to which he invited men and women of good social position, and just as his drawing-room resembled all other drawing-rooms so did his enjoyable little parties resemble all other such parties.

Once they even gave a dance. Ivan Ilych enjoyed it and everything went off well, except that it led to a violent quarrel with his wife about the cakes and sweets. Praskovya Fëdorovna had made her own plans, but Ivan Ilych insisted on getting everything from an expensive confectioner and ordered too many cakes, and the quarrel occurred because some of those cakes were left over and the confectioner's bill came to forty-five rubles. It was a great and disagreeable quarrel. Praskovya Fëdorovna called him "a fool and an imbecile," and he clutched at his head and made angry allusions to divorce.

But the dance itself had been enjoyable. The best people were there, and Ivan Ilych had danced with Princess Trufonova, a sister of the distinguished founder of the Society "Bear my Burden."

The pleasures connected with his work were pleasures of ambition; his social pleasures were those of vanity; but Ivan Ilych's greatest pleasure was playing bridge. He acknowledged that whatever disagreeable incident happened in his life, the pleasure that beamed like a ray of light above everything else was to sit down to bridge with good players, not noisy partners, and of course to four-handed bridge (with five players its was annoying to have to stand out, though one pretended not to mind), to play a clever and serious game (when the cards allowed it) and then to have supper and drink a glass of wine. After a game of bridge, especially if he had won a little (to win a large sum was unpleasant), Ivan Ilych went to bed in specially good humour.

So they lived. They formed a circle of acquaintances among the best people and were visited by people of importance and by young folk. In their views as to their acquaintances, husband, wife and daughter were entirely agreed, and tacitly and unanimously kept at arm's length and shook off the shabby friends and relations who, with much show of affection, gushed into the drawing-room with its Japanese plates on the walls. Soon these shabby friends ceased to obtrude themselves and only the best people remained in the Golovins' set.

110 Young men made up to Lisa, and Petrishchev, an examining magistrate and Dmitri Ivanovich Petrischev's son and sole heir, began to be so attentive to her that Ivan Ilych had already spoken to Praskovya Fëdorovna about it, and consid-

ered whether they should not arrange a party for them, or get up some private theatricals.

So they lived, and all went well, without change, and life flowed pleasantly.

IV

They were all in good health. It could not be called ill health if Ivan Ilych sometimes said that he had a queer taste in his mouth and felt some discomfort in his left side.

But this discomfort increased and, though not exactly painful, grew into a sense of pressure in his side accompanied by ill humour. And his irritability became worse and worse and began to mar the agreeable, easy, and correct life that had established itself in the Golovin family. Quarrels between husband and wife became more and more frequent, and soon the ease and amenity disappeared and even the decorum was barely maintained. Scenes again became frequent, and very few of those islets remained on which husband and wife could meet without an explosion. Praskovya Fëdorovna now had good reason to say that her husband's temper was trying. With characteristic exaggeration she said he had always had a dreadful temper, and that it had needed all her good nature to put up with it for twenty years. It was true that now the quarrels were started by him. His bursts of temper always came just before dinner, often just as he began to eat his soup. Sometimes he noticed that a plate or dish was chipped, or the food was not right, or his son put his elbow on the table, or his daughter's hair was not done as he liked it, and for all this he blamed Praskovya Fëdorovna. At first she retorted and said disagreeable things to him, but once or twice he fell into such a rage at the beginning of dinner that she realized it was due to some physical derangement brought on by taking food, and so she restrained herself and did not answer, but only hurried to get the dinner over. She regarded this self-restraint as highly praiseworthy. Having come to the conclusion that her husband had a dreadful temper and made her life miserable, she began to feel sorry for herself, and the more she pitied herself the more she hated her husband. She began to wish he would die; yet she did not want him to die because then his salary would cease. And this irritated her against him still more. She considered herself dreadfully unhappy just because not even his death could save her, and though she concealed her exasperation, that hidden exasperation of hers increased his irritation also.

After one scene in which Ivan Ilych had been particularly unfair and after which he had said in explanation that he certainly was irritable but that it was due to his not being well, she said that if he was ill it should be attended to, and insisted on his going to see a celebrated doctor.

115   He went. Everything took place as he had expected and as it always does. There was the usual waiting and the important air assumed by the doctor, with which he was so familiar (resembling that which he himself assumed in court), and the sounding and listening, and the questions which called for answers that were foregone conclusions and were evidently unnecessary, and the look of importance which implied that "if only you put yourself in our hands we will arrange everything—we know indubitably how it has to be done, always in the same way for everybody alike." It was all just as it was in the law courts. The doctor put on just the same air towards him as he himself put on towards an accused person.

The doctor said that so-and-so indicated there was so-and-so inside the patient, but if the investigation of so-and-so did not confirm this, then he must assume that and that. If he assumed that and that, then . . . and so on. To Ivan Ilych only one question was important: was his case serious or not? But the doctor ignored that inappropriate question. From his point of view it was not the one under consideration, the real question was to decide between a floating kidney, chronic catarrh, or appendicitis. It was not a question of Ivan Ilych's life or death, but one between a floating kidney and appendicitis. And that question the doctor solved brilliantly, as it seemed to Ivan Ilych, in favour of the appendix, with the reservation that should an examination of the urine give fresh indications the matter would be reconsidered. All this was just what Ivan Ilych had himself brilliantly accomplished a thousand times in dealing with men on trial. The doctor summed up just as brilliantly, looking over his spectacles triumphantly and even gaily at the accused. From the doctor's summing up Ivan Ilych concluded that things were bad, but that for the doctor, and perhaps for everybody else, it was a matter of indifference, though for him it was bad. And this conclusion struck him painfully, arousing in him a great feeling of pity for himself and of bitterness towards the doctor's indifference to a matter of such importance.

He said nothing of this, but rose, placed the doctor's fee on the table, and remarked with a sigh: "We sick people probably often put inappropriate questions. But tell me, in general, is this complaint dangerous, or not? . . ."

The doctor looked at him sternly over his spectacles with one eye, as if to say: "Prisoner, if you will not keep to the questions put to you, I shall be obliged to have you removed from the court."

"I have already told you what I consider necessary and proper. The analysis may show something more." And the doctor bowed.

120   Ivan Ilych went out slowly, seated himself disconsolately in his sledge, and drove home. All the way home he was going over what the doctor had said, trying to translate those complicated, obscure, scientific phrases into plain language and find in them an answer to the question: "Is my condition bad? Is it very bad? Or is there as yet nothing much wrong?" And it seemed to him that the meaning of what the doctor had said was that it was very bad. Everything in the streets seemed depressing. The cabmen, the houses, the passers-by, and the shops, were dismal. His ache, this dull gnawing ache that never ceased for a moment, seemed to have acquired a new and more serious significance from the doctor's dubious remarks. Ivan Ilych now watched it with a new and oppressive feeling.

He reached home and began to tell his wife about it. She listened, but in the middle of his account his daughter came in with her hat on, ready to go out with her mother. She sat down reluctantly to listen to this tedious story, but could not stand it long, and her mother too did not hear him to the end.

"Well, I am very glad," she said. "Mind now to take your medicine regularly. Give me the prescription and I'll send Gerasim to the chemist's." And she went to get ready to go out.

While she was in the room Ivan Ilych had hardly taken time to breathe, but he sighed deeply when she left it.

"Well," he thought, "perhaps it isn't so bad after all."

125   He began taking his medicine and following the doctor's directions, which had been altered after the examination of the urine. But then it happened that there was a contradiction between the indications drawn from the examination of the urine and the symptoms that showed themselves. It turned out that what was happening differed from what the doctor had told him, and that he had either

forgotten, or blundered, or hidden something from him. He could not, however, be blamed for that, and Ivan Ilych still obeyed his orders implicitly and at first derived some comfort from doing so.

From the time of his visit to the doctor, Ivan Ilych's chief occupation was the exact fulfillment of the doctor's instructions regarding hygiene and the taking of medicine, and the observation of his pain and his excretions. His chief interests came to be people's ailments and people's health. When sickness, deaths, or recoveries were mentioned in his presence, especially when the illness resembled his own, he listened with agitation which he tried to hide, asked questions, and applied what he heard to his own case.

The pain did not grow less, but Ivan Ilych made efforts to force himself to think that he was better. And he could do this so long as nothing agitated him. But as soon as he had any unpleasantness with his wife, or a lack of success in his official work, or held bad cards at bridge, he was at once acutely sensible of his disease. He had formerly borne such mischances, hoping soon to adjust what was wrong, to master it and attain success, or make a grand slam. But now every mischance upset him and plunged him into despair. He would say to himself: "There now, just as I was beginning to get better and the medicine had begun to take effect, comes this accursed misfortune, or unpleasantness . . ." And he was furious with the mishap, or with the people who were causing the unpleasantness and killing him, for he felt that this fury was killing him but could not restrain it. One would have thought that it should have been clear to him that this exasperation with circumstances and people aggravated his illness, and that he ought therefore to ignore unpleasant occurrences. But he drew the very opposite conclusion: he said that he needed peace, and he watched for everything that might disturb it and became irritable at the slightest infringement of it. His condition was rendered worse by the fact that he read medical books and consulted doctors. The progress of his disease was so gradual that he could deceive himself when comparing one day with another—the difference was so slight. But when he consulted the doctors it seemed to him that he was getting worse, and even very rapidly. Yet despite this he was continually consulting them.

That month he went to see another celebrity, who told him almost the same as the first had done but put his questions rather differently, and the interview with this celebrity only increased Ivan Ilych's doubts and fears. A friend of a friend of his, a very good doctor, diagnosed his illness again quite differently from the others, and though he predicted recovery, his questions and suppositions bewildered Ivan Ilych still more and increased his doubts. A homeopathist diagnosed the disease in yet another way, and prescribed medicine which Ivan Ilych took secretly for a week. But after a week, not feeling any improvement and having lost confidence both in the former doctor's treatment and in this one's, he became still more despondent. One day a lady acquaintance mentioned a cure effected by a wonder-working icon. Ivan Ilych caught himself listening attentively and beginning to believe that it had occurred. This incident alarmed him. "Has my mind really weakened to such an extent?" he asked himself. "Nonsense! It's all rubbish. I mustn't give way to nervous fears but having chosen a doctor must keep strictly to his treatment. That is what I will do. Now it's all settled. I won't think about it, but will follow the treatment seriously till summer, and then we shall see. From now there must be no more of this wavering!" This was easy to say but impossible to carry out. The pain in his side oppressed him and seemed to grow worse and more incessant, while the taste in his mouth grew stranger and stranger. It seemed to him that his breath had a disgusting smell, and he was conscious of a loss of appetite and strength. There was no deceiving himself: something terrible, new, and more important than anything before in his life, was taking place within him of which he alone was aware. Those about him did not understand or would not understand it, but thought everything in the world was going on as usual. That tormented Ivan Ilych more than anything. He saw that his household, especially his wife and daughter who were in a perfect whirl of visiting, did not understand anything of it and were annoyed that he was so depressed and so exacting, as if he were to blame for it. Though they tried to disguise it he saw that he was an obstacle in their path, and that his wife had adopted a definite line in regard to his illness and kept to it regardless of anything he said or did. Her attitude was this: "You know," she would say to her friends, "Ivan Ilych can't do as other people do, and keep to the treatment prescribed for him. One day he'll take his drops and keep strictly to his diet and go to bed in good time, but the next day unless I watch him he'll suddenly forget his medicine, eat sturgeon—which is forbidden—and sit up playing cards till one o'clock in the morning."

"Oh, come, when was that?" Ivan Ilych would ask in vexation. "Only once at Peter Ivanovich's."

130 "And yesterday with Shebek."

"Well, even if I hadn't stayed up, this pain would have kept me awake."

"Be that as it may you'll never get well like that, but will always make us wretched."

Praskovya Fëdorovna's attitude to Ivan Ilych's illness, as she expressed it both to others and to him, was that it was his own fault and was another of the annoyances he caused her. Ivan Ilych felt that this opinion escaped her involuntarily—but that did not make it easier for him.

At the law courts too, Ivan Ilych noticed, or thought he noticed, a strange attitude towards himself. It sometimes seemed to him that people were watching him inquisitively as a man whose place might soon be vacant. Then again, his friends would suddenly begin to chaff him in a friendly way about his low spirits, as if the awful, horrible, and unheard-of thing that was going on within him, incessantly gnawing at him and irresistibly drawing him away, was a very agreeable subject for jests. Schwartz in particular irritated him by his jocularity, vivacity, and *savoir-faire*,[1] which reminded him of what he himself had been ten years ago.

135 Friends came to make up a set and they sat down to cards. They dealt, bending the new cards to soften them, and he sorted the diamonds in his hand and found he had seven. His partner said "No trumps" and supported him with two diamonds. What more could be wished for? It ought to be jolly and lively. They would make a grand slam. But suddenly Ivan Ilych was conscious of that gnawing pain, that taste in his mouth, and it seemed ridiculous that in such circumstances he should be pleased to make a grand slam.

He looked at his partner Mikhail Mikhaylovich, who rapped the table with his strong hand and instead of snatching up the tricks pushed the cards courteously and indulgently towards Ivan Ilych that he might have the pleasure of gathering them up without the trouble of stretching out his hand for them. "Does he think I am too weak to stretch out my arm?" thought Ivan Ilych, and forgetting what he was doing he over-trumped his partner, missing the grand slam by three tricks. And what was most awful of all was that he saw how upset Mikhail Mikhaylovich

[1]Tact; social grace

was about it but did not himself care. And it was dreadful to realize why he did not care.

They all saw that he was suffering and said: "We can stop if you are tired. Take a rest." Lie down? No, he was not at all tired, and he finished the rubber. All were gloomy and silent. Ivan Ilych felt that he had diffused this gloom over them and could not dispel it. They had supper and went away, and Ivan Ilych was left alone with the consciousness that his life was poisoned and was poisoning the lives of others, and that this poison did not weaken but penetrated more and more deeply into his whole being.

With this consciousness, and with physical pain besides that terror, he must go to bed, often to lie awake the greater part of the night. Next morning he had to get up again, dress, go to the law courts, speak, and write; or if he did not go out, spend at home those twenty-four hours a day each of which was a torture. And he had to live thus all alone on the brink of an abyss, with no one who understood or pitied him.

V

So one month passed and then another. Just before the New Year his brother-in-law came to town and stayed at their house. Ivan Ilych was at the law courts and Praskovya Fëdorovna had gone shopping. When Ivan Ilych came home and entered his study he found his brother-in-law there—a healthy, florid man—unpacking his portmanteau himself. He raised his head on hearing Ivan Ilych's footsteps and looked up at him for a moment without a word. That stare told Ivan Ilych everything. His brother-in-law opened his mouth to utter an exclamation of surprise but checked himself, and that action confirmed it all.

140   "I have changed, eh?"

"Yes, there is a change."

And after that, try as he would to get his brother-in-law to return to the subject of his looks, the latter would say nothing about it. Praskovya Fëdorovna came home and her brother went out to her. Ivan Ilych locked the door and began to examine himself in the glass, first full face, then in profile. He took up a portrait of himself taken with his wife, and compared it with what he saw in the glass. The change in him was immense. Then he bared his arms to the elbow, looked at them, drew the sleeves down again, sat down on an ottoman, and grew blacker than night.

"No, no, this won't do!" he said to himself, and jumped up, went to the table, took up some law papers and began to read them, but could not continue. He unlocked the door and went into the reception-room. The door leading to the drawing-room was shut. He approached it on tiptoe and listened.

"No, you are exaggerating!" Praskovya Fëdorovna was saying.

145   "Exaggerating! Don't you see it? Why, he's a dead man! Look at his eyes—there's no light in them. But what is it that is wrong with him?"

"No one knows. Nikolaevich [that was another doctor] said something, but I don't know what. And Leshchetitsky [this was the celebrated specialist] said quite the contrary . . ."

Ivan Ilych walked away, went to his own room, lay down, and began musing: "The kidney, a floating kidney." He recalled all the doctors had told him of how it detached itself and swayed about. And by an effort of imagination he tried to catch that kidney and arrest it and support it. So little was needed for this, it seemed to him. "No, I'll go to see Peter Ivanovich again." [That was the friend whose friend was a doctor.] He rang, ordered the carriage and got ready to go.

"Where are you going, Jean?" asked his wife, with a specially sad and exceptionally kind look.

This exceptionally kind look irritated him. He looked morosely at her.

150   "I must go to see Peter Ivanovich."

He went to see Peter Ivanovich, and together they went to see his friend, the doctor. He was in, and Ivan Ilych had a long talk with him.

Reviewing the anatomical and physiological details of what in the doctor's opinion was going on inside him, he understood it all.

There was something, a small thing, in the vermiform appendix. It might all come right. Only stimulate the energy of one organ and check the activity of another, then absorption would take place and everything would come right. He got home rather late for dinner, ate his dinner, conversed cheerfully, but could not for a long time bring himself to go back to work in his room. At last, however, he went to his study and did what was necessary, but the consciousness that he had put something aside—an important, intimate matter which he would revert to when his work was done—never left him. When he had finished his work he remembered that this intimate matter was the thought of his vermiform appendix. But he did not give himself up to it, and went to the drawing-room for tea. There were callers there, including the examining magistrate who was a desirable match for his daughter, and they were conversing, playing the piano, and singing. Ivan Ilych, as Praskovya Fëdorovna remarked, spent that evening more cheerfully than usual, but he never for a moment forgot that he had postponed the important matter of the appendix. At eleven o'clock he said good-night and went to his bedroom. Since his illness he had slept alone in a small room next to his study. He undressed and took up a novel by Zola,[1] but instead of reading it fell into thought, and in his imagination that desired improvement in the vermiform appendix occurred. There was the absorption and evacuation and the re-establishment of normal activity. "Yes, that's it!" he said to himself. "One need only assist nature, that's all." He remembered his medicine, rose, took it, and lay down on his back watching for the beneficent action of the medicine and for it to lessen the pain. "I need only take it regularly and avoid all injurious influences. I am already feeling better, much better." He began touching his side: it was not painful to the touch. "There, I really don't feel it. It's much better already." He put out the light and turned on his side . . . "The appendix is getting better, absorption is occurring." Suddenly he felt the old, familiar, dull, gnawing pain, stubborn and serious. There was the same familiar loathsome taste in his mouth. His heart sank and he felt dazed. "My God! My God!" he muttered. "Again, again! and it will never cease." And suddenly the matter presented itself in a quite different aspect. "Vermiform appendix! Kidney!" he said to himself. "It's not a question of appendix or kidney, but of life and . . . death. Yes, life was there and now it is going, going and I cannot stop it. Yes. Why deceive myself? Isn't it obvious to everyone but me that I'm dying, and that it's only a question of weeks, days . . . it may happen this moment. There was light and now there is darkness. I was here and now I'm going there! Where?" A chill came over him, his breathing ceased, and he felt only the throbbing of his heart.

[1]The realistic French novelist (1840–1902)

"When I am not, what will there be? There will be nothing. Then where shall I be when I am no more? Can this be dying? No, I don't want to!" He jumped up and tried to light the candle, felt for it with trembling hands, dropped candle and candlestick on the floor, and fell back on his pillow.

155 "What's the use? It makes no difference," he said to himself, staring with wide-open eyes into the darkness. "Death, Yes, death. And none of them know or wish to know it, and they have no pity for me. Now they are playing." (He heard through the door the distant sound of a song and its accompaniment.) "It's all the same to them, but they will die too! Fools! I first, and they later, but it will be the same for them. And now they are merry . . . . the beasts!"

Anger choked him and he was agonizingly, unbearably, miserable. "It is impossible that all men have been doomed to suffer this awful horror!" He raised himself.

"Something must be wrong. I must calm myself—must think it all over from the beginning." And he again began thinking. "Yes, the beginning of my illness: I knocked my side, but I was quite well that day and the next. It hurt a little, then rather more. I saw the doctor, then followed despondency and anguish, more doctors, and I drew nearer to the abyss. My strength grew less and I kept coming nearer and nearer, and now I have wasted away and there is no light in my eyes. I think of the appendix—but this is death! I think of mending the appendix, and all the while here is death! Can it really be death?" Again terror seized him and he gasped for breath. He leant down and began feeling for the matches, pressing with his elbow on the stand beside the bed. It was in the way and hurt him, he grew furious with it, pressed on it still harder, and upset it. Breathless and in despair he fell on his back, expecting death to come immediately.

Meanwhile the visitors were leaving. Praskovya Fëdorovna was seeing them off. She heard something fall and came in.

"What has happened?"

160 "Nothing, I knocked it over accidentally."

She went out and returned with a candle. He lay there panting heavily, like a man who has run a thousand yards, and stared upwards at her with a fixed look.

"What is it, Jean?"

"No . . . o . . . thing. I upset it." ("Why speak of it? She won't understand," he thought.)

And in truth she did not understand. She picked up the stand, lit his candle, and hurried away to see another visitor off. When she came back he still lay on his back, looking upwards.

165 "What is it? Do you feel worse?"

"Yes."

She shook her head and sat down.

"Do you know, Jean, I think we must ask Leshchetitsky to come and see you here."

This meant calling in the famous specialist, regardless of expense. He smiled malignantly and said "No." She remained a little longer and then went up to him and kissed his forehead.

170 While she was kissing him he hated her from the bottom of his soul and with difficulty refrained from pushing her away.

"Good-night. Please God you'll sleep."

"Yes."

VI

Ivan Ilych saw that he was dying, and he was in continual despair.

In the depth of his heart he knew he was dying, but not only was he not accustomed to the thought, he simply did not and could not grasp it.

175 The syllogism he had learnt from Kiezewetter's Logic. "Caius is a man, men are mortal, therefore Caius is mortal," had always seemed to him correct as applied to Caius, but certainly not as applied to himself. That Caius—man in the abstract—was mortal, was perfectly correct, but he was not Caius, not an abstract man, but a creature quite, quite separate from all others. He had been little Vanya, with a mamma and papa, with Mitya and Volodya, with the toys, a coachman and a nurse, afterwards with Katenka and with all the joys, griefs, and delights of childhood, boyhood, and youth. What did Caius know of the smell of that striped leather ball Vanya had been so fond of? Had Caius kissed his mother's hand like that, and did the silk of her dress rustle so for Caius? Had he rioted like that at school when the pastry was bad? Had Caius been in love like that? Could Caius preside at a session as he did? "Caius really was mortal, and it was right for him to die; but for me, little Vanya, Ivan Ilych, with all my thoughts and emotions, it's altogether a different matter. It cannot be that I ought to die. That would be too terrible."

Such was his feeling.

"If I had to die like Caius, I should have known it was so. An inner voice would have told me so, but there was nothing of the sort in me and I and all my friends felt that our case was quite different from that of Caius. And now here it is!" he said to himself. "It can't be. It's impossible! But here it is. How is this? How is one to understand it?"

He could not understand it, and tried to drive this false, incorrect, morbid thought away and to replace it by other proper and healthy thoughts. But that thought, and not the thought only but the reality itself, seemed to come and confront him.

And to replace that thought he called up a succession of others, hoping to find in them some support. He tried to get back into the former current of thoughts that had once screened the thought of death from him. But strange to say, all that had formerly shut off, hidden, and destroyed, his consciousness of death, no longer had that effect. Ivan Ilych now spent most of his time in attempting to re-establish that old current. He would say to himself: "I will take up my duties again—after all I used to live by them." And banishing all doubts he would go to the law courts, enter into conversation with his colleagues, and sit carelessly as was his wont, scanning the crowd with a thoughtful look and leaning both his emaciated arms on the arms of his oak chair; bending over as usual to a colleague and drawing his papers nearer he would interchange whispers with him, and then suddenly raising his eyes and sitting erect would pronounce certain words and open the proceedings. But suddenly in the midst of those proceedings the pain in his side, regardless of the stage the proceedings had reached, would begin its own gnawing work. Ivan Ilych would turn his attention to it and try to drive the thought of it away, but without success. *It* would come and stand before him and look at him, and he would be petrified and the light would die out of his eyes, and he would again begin asking himself whether *It* alone was true. And his colleagues and subordinates would see with surprise and distress that he, the brilliant and subtle judge, was becoming confused and making mistakes. He would shake himself, try to pull himself together, manage somehow to bring the sitting to a close, and return home with the sorrowful consciousness that his judicial labours could not as formerly hide from him what he wanted them to hide, and could not deliver him from *It*. And what was worst of all was that *It* drew his attention to itself not in order to make him take some action but only that he should look at *It*, look it straight in the face: look at it and without doing anything, suffer inexpressibly.

180   And to save himself from this condition Ivan Ilych looked for consolations—new screens—and new screens were found and for a while seemed to save him, but then they immediately fell to pieces or rather became transparent as if *It* penetrated them and nothing could veil *It*.

In these latter days he would go into the drawing-room he had arranged—that drawing-room where he had fallen and for the sake of which (how bitterly ridiculous it seemed) he had sacrificed his life—for he knew that his illness originated with that knock. He would enter and see that something had scratched the polished table. He would look for the cause of this and find that it was the bronze ornamentation of an album, that had got bent. He would take up the expensive album which he had lovingly arranged, and feel vexed with his daughter and her friends for their untidiness—for the album was torn here and there and some of the photographs turned upside down. He would put it carefully in order and bend the ornamentation back into position. Then it would occur to him to place all those things in another corner of the room, near the plants. He would call the footman, but his daughter or wife would come to help him. They would not agree, and his wife would contradict him, and he would dispute and grow angry. But that was all right, for then he did not think about *It*. *It* was invisible.

But then, when he was moving something himself, his wife would say: "Let the servants do it. You will hurt yourself again." And suddenly *It* would flash through the screen and he would see it. It was just a flash, and he hoped it would disappear, but he would involuntarily pay attention to his side. "It sits there as before, gnawing just the same!" And he could no longer forget *It,* but could distinctly see it looking at him from behind the flowers. "What is it all for?"

"It really is so! I lost my life over that curtain as I might have done when storming a fort. Is that possible? How terrible and how stupid. It can't be true! It can't, but it is."

He would go to his study, lie down, and again be alone with *It:* face to face with *It*. And nothing could be done with *It* except to look at it and shudder.

VII

185   How it happened it is impossible to say because it came about step by step, unnoticed, but in the third month of Ivan Ilych's illness, his wife, his daughter, his son, his acquaintances, the doctors, the servants, and above all he himself, were aware that the whole interest he had for other people was whether he would soon vacate his place, and at last release the living from the discomfort caused by his presence and be himself released from his sufferings.

He slept less and less. He was given opium and hypodermic injections of morphine, but this did not relieve him. The dull depression he experienced in a somnolent condition at first gave him a little relief, but only as something new, afterwards it became as distressing as the pain itself or even more so.

Special foods were prepared for him by the doctors' orders, but all those foods became increasingly distasteful and disgusting to him.

For his excretions also special arrangements had to be made, and this was a torment to him every time—a torment from the uncleanliness, the unseemliness, and the smell, and from knowing that another person had to take part in it.

But just through this most unpleasant matter, Ivan Ilych obtained comfort. Gerasim, the butler's young assistant, always came in to carry the things out. Gerasim was a clean, fresh peasant lad, grown stout on town food and always cheerful and bright. At first the sight of him, in his clean Russian peasant costume, engaged in that disgusting task embarrassed Ivan Ilych.

190   Once when he got up from the commode too weak to draw up his trousers, he dropped into a soft armchair and looked with horror at his bare, enfeebled thighs with the muscles so sharply marked on them.

Gerasim with a firm light tread, his heavy boots emitting a pleasant smell of tar and fresh winter air, came in wearing a clean Hessian apron, the sleeves of his print shirt tucked up over his strong bare young arms; and refraining from looking at his sick master out of consideration for his feelings, and restraining the joy of life that beamed from his face, he went up to the commode.

"Gerasim!" said Ivan Ilych in a weak voice.

Gerasim started, evidently afraid he might have committed some blunder, and with a rapid movement turned his fresh, kind, simple young face which just showed the first downy signs of a beard.

"Yes, sir?"

195   "That must be very unpleasant for you. You must forgive me. I am helpless."

"Oh, why, sir," and Gerasim's eyes beamed and he showed his glistening white teeth, "what's a little trouble? It's a case of illness with you, sir."

And his deft strong hands did their accustomed task, and he went out of the room stepping lightly. Five minutes later he as lightly returned.

Ivan Ilych was still sitting in the same position in the armchair.

"Gerasim," he said when the latter had replaced the freshly-washed utensil. "Please come here and help me." Gerasim went up to him. "Lift me up. It is hard for me to get up, and I have sent Dmitri away."

200   Gerasim went up to him, grasped his master with his strong arms deftly but gently, in the same way that he stepped—lifted him, supported him with one hand, and with the other drew up his trousers and would have set him down again, but Ivan Ilych asked to be led to the sofa. Gerasim, without an effort and without apparent pressure, led him, almost lifting him, to the sofa and placed him on it.

"Thank you. How easily and well you do it all!"

Gerasim smiled again and turned to leave the room. But Ivan Ilych felt his presence such a comfort that he did not want to let him go.

"One thing more, please move up that chair. No, the other one—under my feet. It is easier for me when my feet are raised."

Gerasim brought the chair, set it down gently in place, and raised Ivan Ilych's legs on to it. It seemed to Ivan Ilych that he felt better while Gerasim was holding up his legs.

205   "It's better when my legs are higher," he said. "Place that cushion under them."

Gerasim did so. He again lifted his legs and placed them, and again Ivan Ilych felt better while Gerasim held his legs. When he set them down Ivan Ilych fancied he felt worse.

"Gerasim," he said. "Are you busy now?"

"Not at all, sir," said Gerasim, who had learnt from the townfolk how to speak to gentlefolk.

"What have you still to do?"

210   "What have I to do? I've done everything except chopping the logs for tomorrow."

"Then hold my legs up a bit higher, can you?"

"Of course I can. Why not?" And Gerasim raised his master's legs higher and Ivan Ilych thought that in that position he did not feel any pain at all.

"And how about the logs?"

"Don't trouble about that, sir. There's plenty of time."

215   Ivan Ilych told Gerasim to sit down and hold his legs, and began to talk to him. And strange to say it seemed to him that he felt better while Gerasim held his legs up.

After that Ivan Ilych would sometimes call Gerasim and get him to hold his legs on his shoulders, and he liked talking to him. Gerasim did it all easily, willingly, simply, and with a good nature that touched Ivan Ilych. Health, strength, and vitality in other people were offensive to him, but Gerasim's strength and vitality did not mortify but soothed him.

What tormented Ivan Ilych most was the deception, the lie, which for some reason they all accepted, that he was not dying but was simply ill, and that he only need keep quiet and undergo a treatment and then something very good would result. He however knew that do what they would nothing would come of it, only still more agonizing suffering and death. This deception tortured him—their not wishing to admit what they all knew and what he knew, but wanting to lie to him concerning his terrible condition, and wishing and forcing him to participate in that lie. Those lies—lies enacted over him on the eve of his death and destined to degrade this awful, solemn act to the level of their visitings, their curtains, their sturgeon for dinner—were a terrible agony for Ivan Ilych. And strangely enough, many times when they were going through their antics over him he had been within a hairbreadth of calling out to them: "Stop lying! You know and I know that I am dying. Then at least stop lying about it!" But he had never had the spirit to do it. The awful, terrible act of his dying was, as he could see, reduced by those about him to the level of a casual, unpleasant, and almost indecorous incident (as if someone entered a drawing room diffusing an unpleasant odour) and this was done by that very decorum which he had served all his life long. He saw that no one felt for him, because no one even wished to grasp his position. Only Gerasim recognized it and pitied him. And so Ivan Ilych felt at ease only with him. He felt comforted when Gerasim supported his legs (sometimes all night long) and refused to go to bed, saying: "Don't you worry, Ivan Ilych. I'll get sleep enough later on," or when he suddenly became familiar and exclaimed: "If you weren't sick it would be another matter, but as it is, why should I grudge a little trouble?" Gerasim alone did not lie; everything showed that he alone understood the facts of the case and did not consider it necessary to disguise them, but simply felt sorry for his emaciated and enfeebled master. Once when Ivan Ilych was sending him away he even said straight out: "We shall all of us die, so why should I grudge a little trouble?"—expressing the fact that he did not think his work burdensome, because he was doing it for a dying man and hoped someone would do the same for him when his time came.

Apart from this lying, or because of it, what most tormented Ivan Ilych was that no one pitied him as he wished to be pitied. At certain moments after prolonged suffering he wished most of all (though he would have been ashamed to confess it) for someone to pity him as a sick child is pitied. He longed to be petted and comforted. He knew he was an important functionary, that he had a beard turning grey, and that therefore what he longed for was impossible, but still he longed for it. And in Gerasim's attitude towards him there was something akin to what he wished for, and so that attitude comforted him. Ivan Ilych wanted to weep, wanted to be petted and cried over, and then his colleague Shebek would come, and instead of weeping and being petted, Ivan Ilych would assume a serious, severe, and profound air, and by force of habit would express his opinion on a decision of the Court of Cassation[1] and would stubbornly insist on that view. This falsity around him and within him did more than anything else to poison his last days.

VIII

It was morning. He knew it was morning because Gerasim had gone, and Peter the footman had come and put out the candles, drawn back one of the curtains, and begun quietly to tidy up. Whether it was morning or evening, Friday or Sunday, made no difference, it was all just the same: the gnawing, unmitigated, agonizing pain, never ceasing for an instant, the consciousness of life inexorably waning but not yet extinguished, the approach of that ever dreadful and hateful Death which was the only reality, and always the same falsity. What were days, weeks, hours, in such a case?

220   "Will you have some tea, sir?"

"He wants things to be regular, and wishes the gentlefolk to drink tea in the morning," thought Ivan Ilych, and only said "No."

"Wouldn't you like to move onto the sofa, sir?"

"He wants to tidy up the room, and I'm in the way. I am uncleanliness and disorder," he thought, and said only:

"No, leave me alone."

225   The man went on bustling about. Ivan Ilych stretched out his hand. Peter came up, ready to help.

"What is it, sir?"

"My watch."

Peter took the watch which was close at hand and gave it to his master.

"Half-past eight. Are they up?"

230   "No, sir, except Vladimir Ivanich" (the son) "who has gone to school. Praskovya Fëdorovna ordered me to wake her if you asked for her. Shall I do so?"

"No, there's no need to." "Perhaps I'd better have some tea," he thought, and added aloud: "Yes, bring me some tea."

Peter went to the door, but Ivan Ilych dreaded being left alone. "How can I keep him here? Oh yes, my medicine." "Peter, give me my medicine." "Why not? Perhaps it may still do me some good." He took a spoonful and swallowed it." "No, it won't help. It's all tomfoolery, all deception," he decided as soon as he became aware of the familiar, sickly, hopeless taste. "No, I can't believe in it any longer. But the pain, why this pain? If it would only cease just for a moment!" And he moaned. Peter turned towards him. "It's all right. Go and fetch me some tea."

Peter went out. Left alone Ivan Ilych groaned not so much with pain, terrible though that was, as from mental anguish. Always and for ever the same, always these endless days and nights. If only it would come quicker! If only *what* would come quicker? Death, darkness? . . . No, no! Anything rather than death!

When Peter returned with the tea on a tray, Ivan Ilych stared at him for a time in perplexity, not realizing who and what he was. Peter was disconcerted by that look and his embarrassment brought Ivan Ilych to himself.

---

[1]The highest court of appeals

235   "Oh, tea! All right, put it down. Only help me to wash and put on a clean shirt."

And Ivan Ilych began to wash. With pauses for rest, he washed his hands and then his face, cleaned his teeth, brushed his hair, and looked in the glass. He was terrified by what he saw, especially by the limp way in which his hair clung to his pallid forehead.

While his shirt was being changed he knew that he would be still more frightened at the sight of his body, so he avoided looking at it. Finally he was ready. He drew on a dressing-gown, wrapped himself in a plaid, and sat down in the armchair to take his tea. For a moment he felt refreshed, but as soon as he began to drink the tea he was again aware of the same taste, and the pain also returned. He finished it with an effort, and then lay down stretching out his legs, and dismissed Peter.

Always the same. Now a spark of hope flashes up, then a sea of despair rages, and always pain; always pain, always despair, and always the same. When alone he had a dreadful and distressing desire to call someone, but he knew beforehand that with others present it would be still worse. "Another dose of morphine—to lose consciousness. I will tell him, the doctor, that he must think of something else. It's impossible, impossible, to go on like this."

An hour and another pass like that. But now there is a ring at the door bell. Perhaps it's the doctor? It is. He comes in fresh, hearty, plump, and cheerful, with that look on his face that seems to say: "There now, you're in a panic about something, but we'll arrange it all for you directly!" The doctor knows this expression is out of place here, but he has put it on once for all and can't take it off—like a man who has put on a frock-coat in the morning to pay a round of calls.

240   The doctor rubs his hands vigorously and reassuringly.

"Brr! How cold it is! There's such a sharp frost; just let me warm myself!" he says, as if it were only a matter of waiting till he was warm, and then he would put everything right.

"Well now, how are you?"

Ivan Ilych feels that the doctor would like to say: "Well, how are your affairs?" but that even he feels that this would not do, and says instead: "What sort of a night have you had?"

Ivan Ilych looks at him as much as to say: "Are you really never ashamed of lying?" But the doctor does not wish to understand this question, and Ivan Ilych says: "Just as terrible as ever. The pain never leaves me and never subsides. If only something . . ."

245   "Yes, you sick people are always like that . . . There, now I think I am warm enough. Even Praskovya Fëdorovna, who is so particular, could find no fault with my temperature. Well, now I can say good-morning," and the doctor presses his patient's hand.

Then, dropping his former playfulness, he begins with a most serious face to examine the patient, feeling his pulse and taking his temperature, and then begins the sounding and auscultation.

Ivan Ilych knows quite well and definitely that all this is nonsense and pure deception, but when the doctor, getting down on his knee, leans over him, putting the ear first higher then lower, and performs various gymnastic movements over him with a significant expression on his face, Ivan Ilych submits to it all as he used to submit to the speeches of the lawyers, though he knew very well that they were all lying and why they were lying.

The doctor, kneeling on the sofa, is still sounding him when Praskovya

Fëdorovna's silk dress rustles at the door and she is heard scolding Peter for not having let her know of the doctor's arrival.

She comes in, kisses her husband, and at once proceeds to prove that she has been up a long time already, and only owing to a misunderstanding failed to be there when the doctor arrived.

Ivan Ilych looks at her, scans her all over, sets against her the whiteness and plumpness and cleanness of her hands and neck, the gloss of her hair, and the sparkle of her vivacious eyes. He hates her with his whole soul. And the thrill of hatred he feels for her makes him suffer from her touch.

Her attitude towards him and his disease is still the same. Just as the doctor had adopted a certain relation to his patient which he could not abandon, so had she formed one towards him—that he was not doing something he ought to do and was himself to blame, and that she reproached him lovingly for this—and she could not now change that attitude.

"You see he doesn't listen to me and doesn't take his medicine at the proper time. And above all he lies in a position that is no doubt bad for him—with his legs up."

She described how he made Gerasim hold his legs up.

The doctor smiled with a contemptuous affability that said: "What's to be done? These sick people do have foolish fancies of that kind, but we must forgive them."

When the examination was over the doctor looked at his watch, and then Praskovya Fëdorovna announced to Ivan Ilych that it was of course as he pleased, but she had sent today for a celebrated specialist who would examine him and have a consultation with Michael Danilovich (their regular doctor).

"Please don't raise any objections. I am doing this for my own sake," she said ironically, letting it be felt that she was doing it all for his sake and only said this to leave him no right to refuse. He remained silent, knitting his brows. He felt that he was so surrounded and involved in a mesh of falsity that it was hard to unravel anything.

Everything she did for him was entirely for her own sake, and she told him she was doing for herself what she actually was doing for herself, as if that was so incredible that he must understand the opposite.

At half-past eleven the celebrated specialist arrived. Again the sounding began and the significant conversations in his presence and in another room, about the kidneys and the appendix, and the questions and answers, with such an air of importance that again, instead of the real question of life and death which now alone confronted him, the question arose of the kidney and appendix which were not behaving as they ought to and would now be attacked by Michael Danilovich and the specialist and forced to mend their ways.

The celebrated specialist took leave of him with a serious though not hopeless look, and in reply to the timid question Ivan Ilych, with eyes glistening with fear and hope, put to him as to whether there was a chance of recovery, said that he could not vouch for it but there was a possibility. The look of hope with which Ivan Ilych watched the doctor out was so pathetic that Praskovya Fëdorovna, seeing it, even wept as she left the room to hand the doctor his fee.

The gleam of hope kindled by the doctor's encouragement did not last long. The same room, the same pictures, curtains, wall-paper, medicine bottles, were all there, and the same aching suffering body, and Ivan Ilych began to moan. They gave him a subcutaneous injection and he sank into oblivion.

It was twilight when he came to. They brought him his dinner and he swallowed some beef tea with difficulty, and then everything was the same again and night was coming on.

After dinner, at seven o'clock, Praskovya Fëdorovna came into the room in evening dress, her full bosom pushed up by her corset, and with traces of powder on her face. She had reminded him in the morning that they were going to the theatre. Sarah Bernhardt[1] was visiting the town and they had a box, which he had insisted on their taking. Now he had forgotten about it and her toilet offended him, but he concealed his vexation when he remembered that he had himself insisted on their securing a box and going because it would be an instructive and aesthetic pleasure for the children.

Praskovya Fëdorovna came in, self-satisfied but yet with a rather guilty air. She sat down and asked how he was, but, as he saw, only for the sake of asking and not in order to learn about it, knowing that there was nothing to learn—and then went on to what she really wanted to say: that she would not on any account have gone but that the box had been taken and Helen and their daughter were going, as well as Petrishchev (the examining magistrate, their daughter's fiancé) and that it was out of the question to let them go alone; but that she would have much preferred to sit with him for a while; and he must be sure to follow the doctor's orders while she was away.

"Oh, and Fëdor Petrovich" (the fiancé) "would like to come in. May he? And Lisa?"

265 "All right."

Their daughter came in in full evening dress, her fresh young flesh exposed (making a show of that very flesh which in his own case caused so much suffering), strong, healthy, evidently in love, and impatient with illness, suffering, and death, because they interfered with her happiness.

Fëdor Petrovich came in too, in evening dress, his hair curled *á la Capoul*,[2] a tight stiff collar round his long sinewy neck, an enormous white shirt-front and narrow black trousers tightly stretched over his strong thighs. He had one white glove tightly drawn on, and was holding his opera hat in his hand.

Following him the schoolboy crept in unnoticed, in a new uniform, poor little fellow, and wearing gloves. Terribly dark shadows showed under his eyes, the meaning of which Ivan Ilych knew well.

His son had always seemed pathetic to him, and now it was dreadful to see the boy's frightened look of pity. It seemed to Ivan Ilych that Vasya was the only one besides Gerasim who understood and pitied him.

270 They all sat down and again asked how he was. A silence followed. Lisa asked her mother about the opera-glasses, and there was an altercation between mother and daughter as to who had taken them and where they had been put. This occasioned some unpleasantness.

Fëdor Petrovich inquired of Ivan Ilych whether he had ever seen Sarah Bernhardt. Ivan Ilych did not at first catch the question, but then replied: "No, have you seen her before?"

"Yes, in *Adrienne Lecouvreur*."[3]

---

[1]The celebrated French actress (1844–1923), who performed throughout the world, received great acclaim in St. Petersburg in 1882.   [2]Hairstyle named for French operatic tenor Victor Capoul (1839–1924)   [3]By French playwrights Eugène Scribe (1791–1861) and Ernest Legouvé (1807–1903).

Praskovya Fëdorovna mentioned some rôles in which Sarah Bernhardt was particularly good. Her daughter disagreed. Conversation sprang up as to the elegance and realism of her acting—the sort of conversation that is always repeated and is always the same.

In the midst of the conversation Fëdor Petrovich glanced at Ivan Ilych and became silent. Ivan Ilych was staring with glittering eyes straight before him, evidently indignant with them. This had to be rectified, but it was impossible to do so. The silence had to be broken, but for a time no one dared to break it and they all became afraid that the conventional deception would suddenly become obvious and the truth become plain to all. Lisa was the first to pluck up courage and break that silence, but by trying to hide what everybody was feeling, she betrayed it.

275 "Well, if we are going it's time to start," she said, looking at her watch, a present from her father, and with a faint and significant smile at Fëdor Petrovich relating to something known only to them. She got up with a rustle of her dress.

They all rose, said good-night, and went away.

When they had gone it seemed to Ivan Ilych that he felt better; the falsity had gone with them. But the pain remained—that same pain and that same fear that made everything monotonously alike, nothing harder and nothing easier. Everything was worse.

Again minute followed minute and hour followed hour. Everything remained the same and there was no cessation. And the inevitable end of it all became more and more terrible.

"Yes, send Gerasim here," he replied to a question Peter asked.

IX

280 His wife returned late at night. She came in on tiptoe, but he heard her, opened his eyes, and made haste to close them again. She wished to send Gerasim away and sit with him herself, but he opened his eyes and said: "No, go away."

"Are you in great pain?"

"Always the same."

"Take some opium."

He agreed and took some. She went away.

285 Till about three in the morning he was in a state of stupefied misery. It seemed to him that he and his pain were being thrust into a narrow, deep black sack, but though they were pushed further and further in they could not be pushed to the bottom. And this, terrible enough in itself, was accompanied by suffering. He struggled but yet cooperated. And suddenly he broke through, fell, and regained consciousness. Gerasim was sitting at the foot of the bed dozing quietly, while he himself lay with his emaciated stockinged legs resting on Gerasim's shoulders; the same shaded candle was there and the same unceasing pain.

"Go away, Gerasim," he whispered.

"It's all right, sir. I'll stay a while."

"No. Go away."

He removed his legs from Gerasim's shoulders, turned sideways onto his arm, and felt sorry for himself. He only waited till Gerasim had gone into the next room and then restrained himself no longer but wept like a child. He wept on account of his helplessness, his terrible loneliness, the cruelty of man, the cruelty of God, and the absence of God.

290   "Why hast Thou done all this? Why hast Thou brought me here? Why, why dost Thou torment me so terribly?"

He did not expect an answer and yet wept because there was no answer and could be none. The pain again grew more acute, but he did not stir and did not call. He said to himself: "Go on! Strike me! But what is it for? What have I done to Thee? What is it for?"

Then he grew quiet and not only ceased weeping but even held his breath and became all attention. It was as though he were listening not to an audible voice but to the voice of his soul, to the current of thoughts arising within him.

"What is it you want?" was the first clear conception capable of expression in words, that he heard.

"What do you want? What do you want?" he repeated to himself.

295   "What do I want? To live and not to suffer," he answered.

And again he listened with such concentrated attention that even his pain did not distract him.

"To live? How?" asked the inner voice.

"Why, to live as I used to—well and pleasantly."

"As you lived before, well and pleasantly?" the voice repeated.

300   And in imagination he began to recall the best moments of his pleasant life. But strange to say none of those best moments of his pleasant life now seemed at all what they had then seemed—none of them except the first recollections of childhood. There, in childhood, there had been something really pleasant with which it would be possible to live if it could return. But the child who had experienced that happiness existed no longer, it was like a reminiscence of somebody else.

As soon as the period began which had produced the present Ivan Ilych, all that had then seemed joys now melted before his sight and turned into something trivial and often nasty.

And the further he departed from childhood and the nearer he came to the present the more worthless and doubtful were the joys. This began with the School of Law. A little that was really good was still found there—there was light-heartedness, friendship, and hope. But in the upper classes there had already been fewer of such good moments. Then during the first years of his official career, when he was in the service of the Governor, some pleasant moments again occurred: they were the memories of love for a woman. Then all became confused and there was still less of what was good; later on again there was still less that was good, and the further he went the less there was. His marriage, a mere accident, then the disenchantment that followed it, his wife's bad breath and the sensuality and hypocrisy: then that deadly official life and those preoccupations about money, a year of it, and two, and ten, and twenty, and always the same thing. And the longer it lasted the more deadly it became. "It is as if I had been going downhill while I imagined I was going up. And that is really what it was. I was going up in public opinion, but to the same extent life was ebbing away from me. And now it is all done and there is only death."

"Then what does it mean? Why? It can't be that life is so senseless and horrible. But if it really has been so horrible and senseless, why must I die and die in agony? There is something wrong!"

"Maybe I did not live as I ought to have done," it suddenly occurred to him. "But how could that be, when I did everything properly?" he replied, and immediately dismissed from his mind this, the sole solution of all the riddles of life and death, as something quite impossible.

305   "Then what do you want now? To live? Live how? Live as you lived in the law courts when the usher proclaimed 'The judge is coming!' The judge is coming, the judge!" he repeated to himself. "Here he is, the judge. But I am not guilty!" he exclaimed angrily. "What is it for?" And he ceased crying, but turning his face to the wall continued to ponder on the same question: Why, and for what purpose, is there all this horror? But however much he pondered he found no answer. And whenever the thought occurred to him, as it often did, that it all resulted from his not having lived as he ought to have done, he at once recalled the correctness of his whole life and dismissed so strange an idea.

X

Another fortnight passed. Ivan Ilych now no longer left his sofa. He would not lie in bed but lay on the sofa, facing the wall nearly all the time. He suffered ever the same unceasing agonies and in his loneliness pondered always on the same insoluble question: "What is this? Can it be that it is Death?" And the inner voice answered: "Yes, it is Death."

"Why these sufferings?" And the voice answered, "For no reason—they just are so." Beyond and besides this there was nothing.

From the very beginning of his illness, ever since he had first been to see the doctor, Ivan Ilych's life had been divided between two contrary and alternating moods: now it was despair and the expectation of this uncomprehended and terrible death, and now hope and an intently interested observation of the functioning of his organs. Now before his eyes there was only a kidney or an intestine that temporarily evaded its duty, and now only that incomprehensible and dreadful death from which it was impossible to escape.

These two states of mind had alternated from the very beginning of his illness, but the further it progressed the more doubtful and fantastic became the conception of the kidney, and the more real the sense of impending death.

310   He had but to call to mind what he had been three months before and what he was now, to call to mind with what regularity he had been going downhill, for every possibility of hope to be shattered.

Latterly during that loneliness in which he found himself as he lay facing the back of the sofa, a loneliness in the midst of a populous town and surrounded by numerous acquaintances and relations but that yet could not have been more complete anywhere—either at the bottom of the sea or under the earth—during that terrible loneliness Ivan Ilych had lived only in memories of the past. Pictures of his past rose before him one after another. They always began with what was nearest in time and then went back to what was the most remote—to his childhood—and rested there. If he thought of the stewed prunes that had been offered him that day, his mind went back to the raw shrivelled French plums of his childhood, their peculiar flavour and the flow of saliva when he sucked their stones, and along with the memory of that taste came a whole series of memories of those days: his nurse, his brother, and their toys. "No, I mustn't think of that . . . It is too painful," Ivan Ilych said to himself, and brought himself back to the present—to the button on the back of the sofa and the creases in its morocco. "Morocco is expensive, but it does not wear well: there had been a quarrel about it. It was a different kind of quarrel and a different kind of morocco that time when we tore father's portfolio and were punished, and Mamma brought us some tarts . . ." And again his thoughts dwelt on his childhood, and again it was painful and he tried to banish them and fix his mind on something else.

Then again together with that chain of memories another series passed through his mind—of how his illness had progressed and grown worse. There also the further back he looked the more life there had been. There had been more of what was good life and more of life itself. The two merged together. "Just as the pain went on getting worse and worse, so my life grew worse and worse," he thought. "There is one bright spot there at the back, at the beginning of life, and afterwards all becomes blacker and blacker and proceeds more and more rapidly—in inverse ratio to the square of the distance from death," thought Ivan Ilych. And the example of a stone falling downwards with increasing velocity entered his mind. Life, a series of increasing sufferings, flies further and further towards its end—the most terrible suffering. "I am flying . . ." He shuddered, shifted himself, and tried to resist, but was already aware that resistance was impossible, and again with eyes weary of gazing but unable to cease seeing what was before them, he stared at the back of the sofa and waited—awaiting that dreadful fall and shock and destruction.

"Resistance is impossible!" he said to himself. "If I could only understand what it is all for! But that too is impossible. An explanation would be possible if it could be said that I have not lived as I ought to. But it is impossible to say that," and he remembered all the legality, correctitude, and propriety of his life. "That at any rate can certainly not be admitted," he thought, and his lips smiled ironically as if someone could see that smile and be taken in by it. "There is no explanation! Agony, death . . . What for?"

XI

Another two weeks went by in this way and during that fortnight an event occurred that Ivan Ilych and his wife had desired. Petrishchev formally proposed. It happened in the evening. The next day Praskovya Fëdorovna came into her husband's room considering how best to inform him of it, but that very night there had been a fresh change for the worse in his condition. She found him still lying on the sofa but in a different position. He lay on his back, groaning and staring fixedly in front of him.

315   She began to remind him of his medicines, but he turned his eyes towards her with such a look that she did not finish what she was saying; so great an animosity, to her in particular, did that look express.

"For Christ's sake let me die in peace!" he said.

She would have gone away, but just then their daughter came in and went up to say good morning. He looked at her as he had done at his wife, and in reply to her inquiry about his health said dryly that he would soon free them all of himself. They were both silent and after sitting with him for a while went away.

"Is it our fault?" Lisa said to her mother. "It's as if we were to blame! I am sorry for papa, but why should we be tortured?"

The doctor came at his usual time. Ivan Ilych answered "Yes" and "No," never taking his angry eyes from him, and at last said: "You know you can do nothing for me, so leave me alone."

320   "We can ease your sufferings."

The doctor went into the drawing-room and told Praskovya Fëdorovna that the case was very serious and that the only resource left was opium to allay her husband's sufferings, which must be terrible.

It was true, as the doctor said, that Ivan Ilych's physical sufferings were terrible, but worse than the physical sufferings were his mental sufferings, which were his chief torture.

His mental sufferings were due to the fact that that night, as he looked at Gerasim's sleepy, good-natured face with its prominent cheek-bones, the question suddenly occurred to him: "What if my whole life has really been wrong?"

It occurred to him that what had appeared perfectly impossible before, namely that he had not spent his life as he should have done, might after all be true. It occurred to him that his scarcely perceptible attempts to struggle against what was considered good by the most highly placed people, those scarcely noticeable impulses which he had immediately suppressed, might have been the real thing, and all the rest false. And his professional duties and the whole arrangement of his life and of his family, and all his social and official interests, might all have been false. He tried to defend all those things to himself and suddenly felt the weakness of what he was defending. There was nothing to defend.

325 "But if that is so," he said to himself, "and I am leaving this life with the consciousness that I have lost all that was given me and it is impossible to rectify it— what then?"

He lay on his back and began to pass his life in review in quite a new way. In the morning when he saw first his footman, then his wife, then his daughter, and then the doctor, their every word and movement confirmed to him the awful truth that had been revealed to him during the night. In them he saw himself—all that for which he had lived—and saw clearly that it was not real at all, but a terrible and huge deception which had hidden both life and death. This consciousness intensified his physical suffering tenfold. He groaned and tossed about, and pulled at his clothing which choked and stifled him. And he hated them on that account.

He was given a large dose of opium and became unconscious, but at noon his sufferings began again. He drove everybody away and tossed from side to side.

His wife came to him and said:

"Jean, my dear, do this for me. It can't do any harm and often helps. Healthy people often do it."

330 He opened his eyes wide.

"What? Take communion? Why? It's unnecessary! However . . ." She began to cry.

"Yes, do, my dear. I'll send for our priest. He is such a nice man."

"All right. Very well," he muttered.

When the priest came and heard his confession, Ivan Ilych was softened and seemed to feel a relief from his doubts and consequently from his sufferings, and for a moment there came a ray of hope. He again began to think of the vermiform appendix and the possibility of correcting it. He received the sacrament with tears in his eyes.

335 When they laid him down again afterwards he felt a moment's ease, and the hope that he might live awoke in him again. He began to think of the operation that had been suggested to him. "To live! I want to live!" he said to himself.

His wife came to congraulate him after his communion, and when uttering the usual conventional words she added:

"You feel better, don't you?"

Without looking at her he said "Yes."

Her dress, her figure, the expression of her face, the tone of her voice, all revealed the same thing. "This is wrong, it is not as it should be. All you have lived for and still live for is falsehood and deception, hiding life and death from you." And as soon as he admitted that thought, his hatred and his agonizing physical suffering again sprang up, and with that suffering a consciousness of the unavoidable, approaching end. And to this was added a new sensation of grinding shooting pain and a feeling of suffocation.

340   The expression of his face when he uttered that "yes" was dreadful. Having uttered it, he looked her straight in the eyes, turned on his face with a rapidity extraordinary in his weak state and shouted:

"Go away! Go away and leave me alone!"

XII

From that moment the screaming began that continued for three days, and was so terrible that one could not hear it through two closed doors without horror. At the moment he answered his wife he realized that he was lost, that there was no return, that the end had come, the very end, and his doubts were still unsolved and remained doubts.

"Oh! Oh! Oh!" he cried in various intonations. He had begun by screaming "I won't!" and continued screaming on the letter *O*.

For three whole days, during which time did not exist for him, he struggled in that black sack into which he was being thrust by an invisible resistless force. He struggled as a man condemned to death struggles in the hands of the executioner, knowing that he cannot save himself. And every moment he felt that despite all his efforts he was drawing nearer and nearer to what terrified him. He felt that his agony was due to his being thrust into that black hole and still more to his not being able to get right into it. He was hindered from getting into it by his conviction that his life had been a good one. That very justification of his life held him fast and prevented his moving forward, and it caused him most torment of all.

345   Suddenly some force struck him in the chest and side, making it still harder to breathe, and he fell through the hole and there at the bottom was a light. What had happened to him was like the sensation one sometimes experiences in a railway carriage when one thinks one is going backwards while one is really going forwards and suddenly becomes aware of the real direction.

"Yes, it was all not the right thing," he said to himself, "but that's no matter. It can be done. But what *is* the right thing?" he asked himself, and suddenly grew quiet.

This occurred at the end of the third day, two hours before his death. Just then his schoolboy son had crept softly in and gone up to the bedside. The dying man was still screaming and waving his arms. His hand fell on the boy's head, and the boy caught it, pressed it to his lips, and began to cry.

At that very moment Ivan Ilych fell through and caught sight of the light, and it was revealed to him that though his life had not been what it should have been, this could still be rectified. He asked himself, "What *is* the right thing?" and grew still, listening. Then he felt that someone was kissing his hand. He opened his eyes, looked at his son, and felt sorry for him. His wife came up to him and he glanced at her. She was gazing at him openmouthed, with undried tears on her nose and cheek and a despairing look on her face. He felt sorry for her too.

"Yes, I am making them wretched," he thought. "They are sorry, but it will be better for them when I die." He wished to say this but had not the strength to utter it. "Besides, why speak? I must act," he thought. With a look at his wife he indicated his son and said: "Take him away . . . sorry for him . . . sorry for you too . . ." He tried to add, "forgive me," but said "forgo" and waved his hand, knowing that He whose understanding mattered would understand.

350 And suddenly it grew clear to him that what had been oppressing him and would not leave him was dropping away at once from two sides, from ten sides, and from all sides. He was sorry for them, he must act so as not to hurt them and free himself from these sufferings. "How good and how simple!" he thought. "And the pain?" he asked himself. "What has become of it? Where are you, pain?"

He turned his attention to it.

"Yes, here it is. Well, what of it? Let the pain be."

"And death . . . where is it?"

He sought his former accustomed fear of death and did not find it. "Where is it? What death?" There was no fear because there was no death.

355 In place of death there was light.

"So that's what it is!" he suddenly exclaimed aloud. "What joy!"

To him all this happened in a single instant, and the meaning of that instant did not change. For those present his agony continued for another two hours. Something rattled in his throat, his emaciated body twitched, then the gasping and rattle became less and less frequent.

"It is finished!" said someone near him.

He heard these words and repeated them in his soul.

360 "Death is finished," he said to himself. "It is no more!"

He drew in a breath, stopped in the midst of a sigh, stretched out, and died.

Questions

1. Consider the point of view in the first section of this short novel. Is it necessary at the start? Why? When and why does the point of view change? Is it consistent thereafter?
2. Discuss the chronological sequence. We know from the start that Ivan Ilych will die. Why does Tolstoy remove the suspense? If we moved the first section to the end, how would it affect Tolstoy's theme?
3. From reading the story, what do you know of upper-middle-class life in Czarist Russia? How important is the setting of this story? Do you need to know as much as you know?
4. Ivan Ilych's house-fixing gets much attention. It seems to him that he dies because of it. Why does Tolstoy make it so important?
5. Do you feel the author present in this story, offering his own ideas and judgments, his morality? Discuss.
6. How many characters do you feel you know well in this story? Are the characters particularized? Could you imagine a reason that (to a given author and a given story) individual character could seem unimportant?
7. What is Tolstoy's theme in *Ivan Ilych*? Do you agree with the commentator who compared this story to the book of Job, calling it "an exploration of the problem of undeserved suffering"? Is this story symbolic?
8. Find ironies in this story. Is the story generally ironic?
9. The name "Ivan Ilych" is like "John Smith" in the United States. Can a character's name help to characterize him? Does Ivan Ilych himself resemble any Americans you know, despite the obvious differences of time and place?
10. Is this story ever funny?
11. What is Gerasim's function in this story?

Stories for Further Reading

Edgar Allan Poe
The Murders in the Rue Morgue

Edgar Allan Poe (1809–1849) is known for his macabre, grotesque, and mysterious stories and poems. He invented the detective story with tales like "The Purloined Letter" and "The Murders in the Rue Morgue." Poe's short life was unsettled and tempestuous. He attended the University of Virginia for a few months, leaving when he quarreled with his grandfather over gambling debts he had contracted. He was expelled from West Point for breaking rules, married his thirteen-year-old cousin, and struggled to earn enough money by his writing to support himself and his family. He is one of the first great American authors, and his literary criticism is as original as his stories and poems.

What song the Syrens sang, or what name Achilles assumed when he hid himself among women, although puzzling questions, are not beyond *all* conjecture.

—*Sir Thomas Browne,* Urn-Burial

The mental features discoursed of as the analytical, are, in themselves, but little susceptible of analysis. We appreciate them only in their effects. We know of them, among other things, that they are always to their possessor, when inordinately possessed, a source of the liveliest enjoyment. As the strong man exults in his physical ability, delighting in such exercises as call his muscles into action, so glories the analyst in that moral activity which *disentangles*. He derives pleasure from even the most trivial occupations bringing his talents into play. He is fond of enigmas, of conundrums, of hieroglyphics; exhibiting in his solutions of each a degree of *acumen* which appears to the ordinary apprehension preternatural. His results, brought about by the very soul and essence of method, have, in truth, the whole air of intuition. The faculty of re-solution is possibly much invigorated by mathematical study, and especially by that highest branch of it which, unjustly, and merely on account of its retrograde operations, has been called, as if *par excellence*, analysis. Yet to calculate is not in itself to analyze. A chess-player, for example, does the one without effort at the other. It follows that the game of chess, in its effects upon mental character, is greatly misunderstood. I am not now writing a treatise, but simply prefacing a somewhat peculiar narrative by observations very much at random; I will, therefore, take occasion to assert that the higher powers of the reflective intellect are more decidedly and more usefully tasked by the unostentatious game of draughts than by all the elaborate frivolity of chess. In this latter, where the pieces have different and *bizarre* motions, with various and variable values, what is only complex is mistaken (a not unusual error) for what is profound. The *attention* is here called powerfully into play. If it flag for an instant, an oversight is committed, resulting in injury or defeat. The possible moves being not only manifold but involute, the chances of such oversights are multiplied; and in nine cases out of ten it is the more concentrative rather than the more acute player who conquers. In draughts, on the contrary, where the moves are *unique* and have but little variation, the probabilities of inadvertence are diminished, and the mere attention being left comparatively unemployed, what advantages are obtained by either party are obtained by superior *acumen*. To be less abstract—Let us suppose a game of draughts where the pieces are reduced to four kings, and where, of course, no oversight is to be expected. It is obvious that here the victory can be decided (the players being at all equal) only by some *recherché* movement, the result of some strong exertion of the intellect. Deprived of ordinary resources, the analyst throws himself into the spirit of his opponent, identifies himself therewith, and not unfrequently sees thus, at a glance, the sole methods (sometimes indeed absurdly simple ones) by which he may seduce into error or hurry into miscalculation.

Whist has long been noted for its influence upon what is termed the calculating power; and men of the highest order of intellect have been known to take an apparently unaccountable delight in it, while eschewing chess as frivolous. Beyond doubt there is nothing of a similar nature so greatly tasking the faculty of analysis. The best chess-player in Christendom *may* be little more than the best player of chess; but proficiency in whist implies capacity for success in all these more important undertakings where mind struggles with mind. When I say proficiency, I mean that perfection in the game which includes a comprehension of *all* the sources whence legitimate advantage may be derived. These are not only manifold but multiform, and lie frequently among recesses of thought altogether inaccessible to the ordinary understanding. To observe attentively is to remember distinctly; and, so far, the concentrative chess-player will do very well at whist; while the rules of Hoyle (themselves based upon the mere mechanism of the game) are sufficiently and generally comprehensible. Thus to have a retentive memory, and to proceed by "the book," are points commonly regarded as the sum total of good playing. But it is in matters beyond the limits of mere rule that the skill of the analyst is evinced. He makes, in silence, a host of observations and inferences. So, perhaps, do his companions; and the difference in the extent of the information obtained, lies not so much in the validity of the inference as in the quality of the observation. The necessary knowledge is that of *what* to observe. Our player confines himself not at all; nor, because the game is the object, does he reject deductions from things external to the game. He examines the countenance of his partner, comparing it carefully with that of each of his opponents. He considers the mode of assorting the cards in each hand; often counting trump by trump, and honor by honor, through the glances bestowed by their holders upon each. He notes every variation of face as the play progresses, gathering a fund of thought from the differences in the expression of certainty, of surprise, of triumph, or chagrin. From the manner of gathering up a trick he judges whether the person taking it can make another in the suit. He recognizes what is played through feint, by the air with which it is thrown upon the table. A casual or inadvertent word; the accidental dropping or turning of a card, with the accompanying anxiety or carelessness in regard to its concealment; the counting of the tricks, with the order of their arrangement; embarrassment, hesitation, eagerness or trepidation— all afford, to his apparently intuitive perception, indications of the true state of affairs. The first two or three rounds having been played, he is in full possession of the contents of each hand, and thenceforward puts down his cards with as absolute a precision of purpose as if the rest of the party had turned outward the faces of their own.

The analytical power should not be confounded with simple ingenuity; for while the analyst is necessarily ingenious, the ingenious man is often remarkably incapable of analysis. The consecutive or combining power, by which ingenuity is usually manifested, and to which the phrenologists (I believe erroneously) have assigned a separate organ, supposing it a primitive faculty, has been so frequently seen in those whose intellect bordered otherwise upon idiocy, as to have attracted general observation among writers on morals. Between ingenuity and the analytic ability there exists a difference far greater, indeed, than that between the fancy and the imagination, but of a character very strictly analogous. It will be found, in fact, that the ingenious are always fanciful, and the *truly* imaginative never otherwise than analytic.

The narrative which follows will appear to the reader somewhat in the light of a commentary upon the propositions just advanced.

5   Residing in Paris during the spring and part of the summer of 18——, I there became acquainted with a Monsieur C. Auguste Dupin. This young gentleman was of an excellent—indeed of an illustrious family, but, by a variety of untoward events, had been reduced to such poverty that the energy of his character succumbed beneath it, and he ceased to bestir himself in the world, or to care for the retrieval of his fortunes. By courtesy of his creditors, there still remained in his possession a small remnant of his patrimony; and, upon the income arising from this, he managed, by means of a rigorous economy, to procure the necessaries of life, without troubling himself about its superfluities. Books, indeed, were his sole luxuries, and in Paris these are easily obtained.

Our first meeting was at an obscure library in the Rue Montmartre, where the accident of our both being in search of the same very rare and very remarkable volume, brought us into closer communion. We saw each other again and again. I was deeply interested in the little family history which he detailed to me with all that candor which a Frenchman indulges whenever mere self is the theme. I was astonished, too, at the vast extent of his reading; and, above all, I felt my soul enkindled within me by the wild fervor, and the vivid freshness of his imagination. Seeking in Paris the objects I then sought, I felt that the society of such a man would be to me a treasure beyond price; and this feeling I frankly confided to him.

It was at length arranged that we should live together during my stay in the city; and as my worldly circumstances were somewhat less embarrassed than his own, I was permitted to be at the expense of renting, and furnishing in a style which suited the rather fantastic gloom of our common temper, a time-eaten and grotesque mansion, long deserted through superstitions into which we did not inquire, and tottering to its fall in a retired and desolate portion of the Faubourg St. Germain.

Had the routine of our life at this place been known to the world, we should have been regarded as madmen—although, perhaps, as madmen of a harmless nature. Our seclusion was perfect. We admitted no visitors. Indeed the locality of our retirement had been carefully kept a secret from my own former associates; and it had been many years since Dupin had ceased to know or be known in Paris. We existed within ourselves alone.

It was a freak of fancy in my friend (for what else shall I call it?) to be enamored of the Night, for her own sake; and into this *bizarrerie,* as into all his others, I quietly fell; giving myself up to his wild whims with a perfect *abandon.* The sable divinity would not herself dwell with us always; but we could counterfeit her presence. At the first dawn of the morning we closed all the massy shutters of our old building; lighted a couple of tapers which, strongly perfumed, threw out only the ghastliest and feeblest of rays. By the aid of these we then busied our souls in dreams—reading, writing, or conversing; until warned by the clock of the advent of the true Darkness. Then we sallied forth into the streets, arm and arm, continuing the topics of the day, or roaming far and wide until a late hour, seeking, amid the wild lights and shadows of the populous city, that infinity of mental excitement which quiet observation can afford.

At such times I could not help remarking and admiring (although from his rich ideality I had been prepared to expect it) a peculiar analytic ability in Dupin. He seemed, too, to take an eager delight in this exercise—if not exactly in its display—and did not hesitate to confess the pleasure thus derived. He boasted to me, with a low chuckling laugh, that most men, in respect to himself, wore windows in their bosoms, and was wont to follow up such assertions by direct and very startling proof of his intimate knowledge of my own. His manner at these moments was frigid and abstract; his eyes were vacant in expression; while his voice, usually a rich tenor, rose into a treble which would have sounded petulantly but for the deliberateness and entire distinctness of the enunciation. Observing him in these moods, I often dwelt meditatively upon the old philosophy of the Bi-Part Soul, and amused myself with the fancy of a double Dupin—the creative and the resolvent.

10   Let it not be supposed, from what I have just said, that I am detailing any mystery, or penning any romance. What I have described in the Frenchman was merely the result of an excited, or perhaps of a diseased, intelligence. But of the character of his remarks at the periods in question an example will best convey the idea.

We were strolling one night down a long dirty street, in the vicinity of the Palais Royal. Being both, apparently, occupied with thought, neither of us had spoken a syllable for fifteen minutes at least. All at once Dupin broke forth with these words:

"He is a very little fellow, that's true, and would do better for the *Théâtre des Variétés.*"

"There can be no doubt of that," I replied unwittingly, and not at first observing (so much had I been absorbed in reflection) the extraordinary manner in which the speaker had chimed in with my meditations. In an instant afterwards I recollected myself, and my astonishment was profound.

"Dupin," said I, gravely, "this is beyond my comprehension. I do not hesitate to say that I am amazed, and can scarcely credit my senses. How was it possible you should know I was thinking of ——?" Here I paused, to ascertain beyond a doubt whether he really knew of whom I thought.

15 —— "of Chantilly," said he, "why do you pause? You were remarking to yourself that his diminutive figure unfitted him for tragedy."

This was precisely what had formed the subject of my reflections. Chantilly was a *quondam*[1] cobbler of the Rue St. Denis, who, becoming stage-mad, had attempted the *rôle* of Xerxes, in Crébillon's tragedy so called, and been notoriously Pasquinaded[2] for his pains.

"Tell me, for Heaven's sake," I exclaimed, "the method—if method there is—by which you have been enabled to fathom my soul in this matter." In fact I was even more startled than I would have been willing to express.

"It was the fruiterer," replied my friend, "who brought you to the conclusion that the mender of soles was not of sufficient height for Xerxes *et id genus omne*."[3]

"The fruiterer!—you astonish me—I know no fruiterer whomsoever."

20 "The man who ran up against you as we entered the street—it may have been fifteen minutes ago."

I now remembered that, in fact, a fruiterer, carrying upon his head a large basket of apples, had nearly thrown me down, by accident, as we passed from the Rue C—— into the thoroughfare where we stood; but what this had to do with Chantilly I could not possibly understand.

There was not a particle of *charlatanerie* about Dupin. "I will explain," he said, "and that you may comprehend all clearly, we will first retrace the course of your meditations, from the moment in which I spoke to you until that of the *rencontre*[4] with the fruiterer in question. The larger links of the chain run thus—Chantilly, Orion, Dr. Nichols, Epicurus, Stereotomy, the street stones, the fruiterer."

There are few persons who have not, at some period of their lives, amused themselves in retracing the steps by which particular conclusions of their own minds have been attained. The occupation is often full of interest; and he who attempts it for the first time is astonished by the apparently illimitable distance and incoherence between the starting-point and the goal. What, then, must have been my amazement when I heard the Frenchman speak what he had just spoken, and when I could not help acknowledging that he had spoken the truth. He continued:

"We had been talking of horses, if I remember aright, just before leaving the Rue C——. This was the last subject we discussed. As we crossed into the street, a fruiterer, with a large basket upon his head, brushing quickly past us, thrust you upon a pile of paving-stones collected at a spot where the causeway is undergoing repair. You stepped upon one of the loose fragments, slipped, slightly strained your ankle, appeared vexed or sulky, muttered a few words, turned to look at the pile, and then proceeded in silence. I was not particularly attentive to what you did; but observation has become with me, of late, a species of necessity.

[1]Former   [2]Mocked, ridiculed   [3]And everything of this kind   [4]Meeting, encounter

25 "You kept your eyes upon the ground—glancing, with a petulant expression, at the holes and ruts in the pavement (so that I saw you were still thinking of the stones), until we reached the little alley called Lamartine, which has been paved, by way of experiment, with the overlapping and riveted blocks. Here your countenance brightened up, and, perceiving your lips move, I could not doubt that you murmured the word 'stereotomy,' a term very affectedly applied to this species of pavement. I knew that you could not say to yourself 'stereotomy' without being brought to think of atomies, and thus of the theories of Epicurus; and since, when we discussed this subject not very long ago, I mentioned to you how singularly, yet with how little notice, the vague guesses of that noble Greek had met with confirmation in the late nebular cosmogony, I felt that you could not avoid casting your eyes upwards to the great *nebula* in Orion, and I certainly expected that you would do so. You did look up; and I was now assured that I had correctly followed your steps. But in that bitter *tirade* upon Chantilly, which appeared in yesterday's *'Musée,'* the satirist, making some disgraceful allusions to the cobbler's change of name upon assuming the buskin, quoted a Latin line about which we have often conversed, I mean the line

Perdidit antiquum litera prima sonum[1]

I had told you that this was in reference to Orion, formerly written Urion; and, from certain pungencies connected with this explanation, I was aware that you could not have forgotten it. It was clear, therefore, that you would not fail to combine the two ideas of Orion and Chantilly. That you did combine them I saw by the character of the smile which passed over your lips. You thought of the poor cobbler's immolation. So far, you had been stooping in your gait; but now I saw you draw yourself up to your full height. I was then sure that you reflected upon the diminutive figure of Chantilly. At this point I interrupted your meditations to remark that as, in fact, he *was* a very little fellow—that Chantilly—he would do better at the *Théâtre des Variétés.*"

Not long after this, we were looking over an evening edition of the "Gazette des Tribunaux," when the following paragraphs arrested our attention.

"EXTRAORDINARY MURDERS.—This morning, about three o'clock, the inhabitants of the Quartier St. Roch were aroused from sleep by a succession of terrific shrieks, issuing, apparently, from the fourth story of a house in the Rue Morgue, known to be in the sole occupancy of one Madame L'Espanaye, and her daughter, Mademoiselle Camille L'Espanaye. After some delay, occasioned by a fruitless attempt to procure admission in the usual manner, the gateway was broken in with a crowbar, and eight or ten of the neighbors entered, accompanied by two *gendarmes.* By this time the cries had ceased; but, as the party rushed up the first flight of stairs, two or more rough voices, in angry contention, were distinguished, and seemed to proceed from the upper part of the house. As the second landing was reached, these sounds, also, had ceased, and everything remained perfectly quiet. The party spread themselves, and hurried from room to room. Upon arriving at a large back chamber in the fourth story (the door of which, being found locked, with the key inside, was forced open), a spectacle presented itself which struck every one present not less with horror than with astonishment.

"The apartment was in the wildest disorder—the furniture broken and thrown about in all directions. There was only one bedstead; and from this the bed had

---

[1]"The first letter has lost its original sound."

been removed, and thrown into the middle of the floor. On a chair lay a razor, besmeared with blood. On the hearth were two or three long and thick tresses of gray human hair, also dabbled in blood, and seeming to have been pulled out by the roots. Upon the floor were found four Napoleons,[1] an earring of topaz, three large silver spoons, three smaller of *métal d'Alger*,[2] and two bags, containing nearly four thousand francs in gold. The drawers of a *bureau*, which stood in one corner, were open, and had been, apparently, rifled, although many articles still remained in them. A small iron safe was discovered under the *bed* (not under the bedstead). It was open, with the key still in the door. It had no contents beyond a few old letters, and other papers of little consequence.

"Of Madame L'Espanaye no traces were here seen; but an unusual quantity of soot being observed in the fireplace, a search was made in the chimney, and (horrible to relate!) the corpse of the daughter, head downwards, was dragged therefrom; it having been thus forced up the narrow aperture for a considerable distance. The body was quite warm. Upon examining it, many excoriations were perceived, no doubt occasioned by the violence with which it had been thrust up and disengaged. Upon the face were many severe scratches, and, upon the throat, dark bruises, and deep indentations of finger-nails, as if the deceased had been throttled to death.

30   "After a thorough investigation of every portion of the house, without farther discovery, the party made its way into a small paved yard in the rear of the building, where lay the corpse of the old lady, with her throat so entirely cut that, upon an attempt to raise her, the head fell off. The body, as well as the head, was fearfully mutilated—the former so much so as scarcely to retain any semblance of humanity.

"To this horrible mystery there is not as yet, we believe, the slightest clue."

The next day's paper had these additional particulars.

"*The Tragedy in the Rue Morgue.* Many individuals have been examined in relation to this most extraordinary and frightful affair" (the word *'affaire'* has not yet, in France, that levity of import which it conveys with us), "but nothing whatever has transpired to throw light upon it. We give below all the material testimony elicited.

"*Pauline Dubourg*, laundress, deposes that she has known both the deceased for three years, having washed for them during that period. The old lady and her daughter seemed on good terms—very affectionate towards each other. They were excellent pay. Could not speak in regard to their mode or means of living. Believed that Madame L. told fortunes for a living. Was reputed to have money put by. Never met any persons in the house when she called for the clothes or took them home. Was sure that they had no servant in employ. There appeared to be no furniture in any part of the building except in the fourth story.

35   "*Pierre Moreau*, tobacconist, deposes that he has been in the habit of selling small quantities of tobacco and snuff to Madame L'Espanaye for nearly four years. Was born in the neighborhood, and has always resided there. The deceased and her daughter had occupied the house in which the corpses were found, for more than six years. It was formerly occupied by a jeweler, who under-let the upper rooms to various persons. The house was the property of Madame L. She became dissatisfied with the abuse of the premises by her tenant, and moved into them

[1] A twenty-franc piece bearing Napoleon's image   [2] A silvered-colored alloy of tin, lead, and antimony

herself, refusing to let any portion. The old lady was childish. Witness had seen the daughter some five or six times during the six years. The two lived an exceedingly retired life—were reputed to have money. Had heard it said among the neighbors that Madame L. told fortunes—did not believe it. Had never seen any person enter the door except the old lady and her daughter, porter once or twice, and a physician some eight or ten times.

"Many other persons, neighbors, gave evidence to the same effect. No one was spoken of as frequenting the house. It was not known whether there were any living connections of Madame L. and her daughter. The shutters of the front windows were seldom opened. Those in the rear were always closed, with the exception of the large back room, fourth story. The house was a good house—not very old.

"*Isidore Musèt, gendarme*, deposes that he was called to the house about three o'clock in the morning, and found some twenty or thirty persons at the gateway, endeavoring to gain admittance. Forced it open, at length, with a bayonet—not with a crowbar. Had but little difficulty in getting it open, on account of its being a double or folding gate, and bolted neither at bottom nor top. The shrieks were continued until the gate was forced—and then suddenly ceased. They seemed to be screams of some person (or persons) in great agony—were loud and drawn out, not short and quick. Witness led the way upstairs. Upon reaching the first landing, heard two voices in loud and angry contention—the one a gruff voice, the other much shriller—a very strange voice. Could distinguish some words of the former, which was that of a Frenchman. Was positive that it was not a woman's voice. Could distinguish the words '*sacré*' and '*diable.*' The shrill voice was that of a foreigner. Could not be sure whether it was the voice of a man or of a woman. Could not make out what was said, but believed the language to be Spanish. The state of the room and of the bodies was described by this witness as we described them yesterday.

"*Henri Duval*, a neighbor, and by trade a silversmith, deposes that he was one of the party who first entered the house. Corroborates the testimony of Musèt in general. As soon as they forced an entrance, they reclosed the door, to keep out the crowd, which collected very fast, notwithstanding the lateness of the hour. The shrill voice, the witness thinks, was that of an Italian. Was certain it was not French. Could not be sure that it was a man's voice. It might have been a woman's. Was not acquainted with the Italian language. Could not distinguish the words, but was convinced by the intonation that the speaker was an Italian. Knew Madame L. and her daughter. Had conversed with both frequently. Was sure that the shrill voice was not that of either of the deceased.

"——— *Odenheimer, restaurateur*. This witness volunteered his testimony. Not speaking French, was examined through an interpreter. Is a native of Amsterdam. Was passing the house at the time of the shrieks. They lasted for several minutes—probably ten. They were long and loud—very awful and distressing. Was one of those who entered the building. Corroborated the previous evidence in every respect but one. Was sure that the shrill voice was that of a man—of a Frenchman. Could not distinguish the words uttered. They were loud and quick—unequal—spoken apparently in fear as well as in anger. The voice was harsh—not so much shrill as harsh. Could not call it a shrill voice. The gruff voice said repeatedly '*sacré*,' '*diable*' and once '*mon Dieu.*'

40   "*Jules Mignaud*, banker, of the firm of Mignaud et Fils, Rue Deloraine. Is the elder Mignaud. Madame L'Espanaye had some property. Had opened an account

with his banking house in the spring of the year —— (eight years previously). Made frequent deposits in small sums. Had checked for nothing until the third day before her death, when she took out in person the sum of 4000 francs. This sum was paid in gold, and a clerk sent home with the money.

"*Adolphe Le Bon*, clerk to Mignaud et Fils, deposes that on the day in question, about noon, he accompanied Madame L'Espanaye to her residence with the 4000 francs, put up in two bags. Upon the door being opened, Mademoiselle L. appeared and took from his hands one of the bags, while the old lady relieved him of the other. He then bowed and departed. Did not see any person in the street at the time. It is a bye-street—very lonely.

"*William Bird*, tailor, deposes that he was one of the party who entered the house. Is an Englishman. Has lived in Paris two years. Was one of the first to ascend the stairs. Heard the voices in contention. The gruff voice was that of a Frenchman. Could make out several words, but cannot now remember all. Heard distinctly '*sacré*' and '*mon Dieu.*' There was a sound at the moment as if of several persons struggling—a scraping and scuffling sound. The shrill voice was very loud—louder than the gruff one. Is sure that it was not the voice of an Englishman. Appeared to be that of a German. Might have been a woman's voice. Does not understand German.

"Four of the above-named witnesses, being recalled, deposed that the door of the chamber in which was found the body of Mademoiselle L. was locked on the inside when the party reached it. Everything was perfectly silent—no groans or noises of any kind. Upon forcing the door no person was seen. The windows, both of the back and front room, were down and firmly fastened from within. A door between the two rooms was closed, but not locked. The door leading from the front room into the passage was locked, with the key on the inside. A small room in the front of the house, on the fourth story, at the head of the passage, was open, the door being ajar. This room was crowded with old beds, boxes, and so forth. These were carefully removed and searched. There was not an inch of any portion of the house which was not carefully searched. Sweeps were sent up and down the chimneys. The house was a four-story one, with garrets (*man-sardes*). A trap-door on the roof was nailed down very securely—did not appear to have been opened for years. The time elapsing between the hearing of the voices in contention and the breaking open of the room door, was variously stated by the witnesses. Some made it as short as three minutes—some as long as five. The door was opened with difficulty.

"*Alfonzo Garcio*, undertaker, deposes that he resides in the Rue Morgue. Is a native of Spain. Was one of the party who entered the house. Did not proceed upstairs. Is nervous, and was apprehensive of the consequences of agitation. Heard the voices in contention. The gruff voice was that of a Frenchman. Could not distinguish what was said. The shrill voice was that of an Englishman—is sure of this. Does not understand the English language, but judges by the intonation.

45   "*Alberto Montani*, confectioner, deposes that he was among the first to ascend the stairs. Heard the voices in question. The gruff voice was that of a Frenchman. Distinguished several words. The speaker appeared to be expostulating. Could not make out the words of the shrill voice. Spoke quick and unevenly. Thinks it the voice of a Russian. Corroborates the general testimony. Is an Italian. Never conversed with a native of Russia.

"Several witnesses, recalled, here testified that the chimneys of all the rooms on the fourth story were too narrow to admit the passage of a human being. By 'sweeps' were meant cylindrical sweeping-brushes, such as are employed by those who clean chimneys. These brushes were passed up and down every flue in the house. There is no back passage by which any one could have descended while the party proceeded upstairs. The body of Mademoiselle L'Espanaye was so firmly wedged in the chimney that it could not be got down until four or five of the party united their strength.

"*Paul Dumas*, physician, deposes that he was called to view the bodies about daybreak. They were both then lying on the sacking of the bedstead in the chamber where Mademoiselle L. was found. The corpse of the young lady was much bruised and excoriated. The fact that it had been thrust up the chimney would sufficiently account for these appearances. The throat was greatly chafed. There were several deep scratches just below the chin, together with a series of livid spots which were evidently the impression of fingers. The face was fearfully discolored, and the eyeballs protruded. The tongue had been partially bitten through. A large bruise was discovered upon the pit of the stomach, produced, apparently, by the pressure of a knee. In the opinion of M. Dumas, Mademoiselle L'Espanaye had been throttled to death by some person or persons unknown. The corpse of the mother was horribly mutilated. All the bones of the right leg and arm were more or less shattered. The left *tibia* much splintered, as well as all the ribs of the left side. Whole body dreadfully bruised and discolored. It was not possible to say how the injuries had been inflicted. A heavy club of wood, or a broad bar of iron—a chair—any large, heavy, and obtuse weapon would have produced such results, if wielded by the hands of a very powerful man. No woman could have inflicted the blows with any weapon. The head of the deceased, when seen by witness, was entirely separated from the body, and was also greatly shattered. The throat had evidently been cut with some very sharp instrument—probably with a razor.

"*Alexandre Etienne*, surgeon, was called with M. Dumas to view the bodies. Corroborated the testimony, and the opinions of M. Dumas.

"Nothing farther of importance was elicited, although several other persons were examined. A murder so mysterious, and so perplexing in all its particulars, was never before committed in Paris—if indeed a murder has been committed at all. The police are entirely at fault—an unusual occurrence in affairs of this nature. There is not, however, the shadow of a clue apparent."

50   The evening edition of the paper stated that the greatest excitement still continued in the Quartier St. Roch—that the premises in question had been carefully researched, and fresh examinations of witnesses instituted, but all to no purpose. A postscript, however, mentioned that Adolphe Le Bon had been arrested and imprisoned—although nothing appeared to criminate him, beyond the facts already detailed.

Dupin seemed singularly interested in the progress of this affair—at least so I judged from his manner, for he made no comments. It was only after the announcement that Le Bon had been imprisoned, that he asked me my opinion respecting the murders.

I could merely agree with all Paris in considering them an insoluble mystery. I saw no means by which it would be possible to trace the murderer.

"We must not judge of the means," said Dupin, "by this shell of an examination. The Parisian police, so much extolled for *acumen*, are cunning, but no more. There is no method in their proceedings, beyond the method of the moment. They make a vast parade of measures; but, not unfrequently, these are so ill adapted to the objects proposed, as to put us in mind of Monsieur Jourdain's calling for his *robe-de-chambre—pour mieux entendre la musique.*[1] The results attained by them are not unfrequently surprising, but, for the most part, are brought about by simple diligence and activity. When these qualities are unavailing, their schemes fail. Vidocq, for example, was a good guesser, and a persevering man. But, without educated thought, he erred continually by the very intensity of his investigations. He impaired his vision by holding the object too close. He might see, perhaps, one or two points with unusual clearness, but in so doing he, necessarily, lost sight of the matter as a whole. Thus there is such a thing as being too profound. Truth is not always in a well. In fact, as regards the more important knowledge, I do believe that she is invariably superficial. The depth lies in the valleys where we seek her, and not upon the mountain-tops where she is found. The modes and sources of this kind of error are well typified in the contemplation of the heavenly bodies. To look at a star by glances—to view it in a side-long way, by turning towards it the exterior portions of the *retina* (more susceptible of feeble impressions of light than the interior), is to behold the star distinctly—is to have the best appreciation of its luster—a luster which grows dim just in proportion as we turn our vision *fully* upon it. A greater number of rays actually fall upon the eye in the latter case, but in the former, there is the more refined capacity for comprehension. By undue profundity we perplex and enfeeble thought; and it is possible to make even Venus herself vanish from the firmament by a scrutiny too sustained, too concentrated, or too direct.

"As for these murders, let us enter into some examinations for ourselves, before we make up an opinion respecting them. An inquiry will afford us amusement" (I thought this an odd term, so applied, but said nothing), "and, besides, Le Bon once rendered me a service for which I am not ungrateful. We will go and see the premises with our own eyes. I know G———, the Prefect of Police, and shall have no difficulty in obtaining the necessary permission."

55   The permission was obtained, and we proceeded at once to the Rue Morgue. This is one of those miserable thoroughfares, which intervene between the Rue Richelieu and the Rue St. Roch. It was late in the afternoon when we reached it; as this quarter is at a great distance from that in which we resided. The house was readily found; for there were still many persons gazing up at the closed shutters, with an objectless curiosity, from the opposite side of the way. It was an ordinary Parisian house, with a gateway, on one side of which was a glazed watchbox, with a sliding panel in the window, indicating a *loge de concierge.* Before going in we walked up the street, turned down an alley, and then, again turning, passed in the rear of the building—Dupin, meanwhile, examining the whole neighborhood, as well as the house, with a minuteness of attention for which I could see no possible object.

Retracing our steps, we came again to the front of the dwelling, rang, and, having shown our credentials, were admitted by the agents in charge. We went upstairs—into the chamber where the body of Mademoiselle L'Espanaye had been found, and where both the deceased still lay. The disorders of the room had, as usual, been suffered to exist. I saw nothing beyond what had been stated in the "Gazette des Tribunaux." Dupin scrutinized everything—not excepting the bodies of the

---

[1]In Molière's comedy *The Bourgeois Gentleman*, M. Jourdain believes he can hear music better when he wears his bathrobe.

victims. We then went into the other rooms, and into the yard: a *gendarme* accompanying us throughout. The examination occupied us until dark, when we took our departure. On our way home my companion stopped in for a moment at the office of the daily papers.

I have said that the whims of my friend were manifold, and that *Je les ménageais:*—for this phrase there is no English equivalent. It was his humor, now, to decline all conversation on the subject of the murder, until about noon the next day. He then asked me, suddenly, if I had observed anything *peculiar* at the scene of the atrocity.

There was something in his manner of emphasizing the word "peculiar," which caused me to shudder, without knowing why.

"No, nothing *peculiar*," I said; "nothing more, at least, than we both saw stated in the paper."

60 "The 'Gazette,' " he replied, "has not entered, I fear, into the unusual horror of the thing. But dismiss the idle opinions of this print. It appears to me that this mystery is considered insoluble, for the very reason which should cause it to be regarded as easy of solution—I mean for the *outré* character of its features. The police are confounded by the seeming absence of motive—not for the murder itself—but for the atrocity of the murder. They are puzzled, too, by the seeming impossibility of reconciling the voices heard in contention, with the facts that no one was discovered upstairs but the assassinated Mademoiselle L'Espanaye, and that there were no means of egress without the notice of the party ascending. The wild disorder of the room; the corpse thrust, with the head downwards, up the chimney; the frightful mutilation of the body of the old lady; these considerations, with those just mentioned, and others which I need not mention, have sufficed to paralyze the powers, by putting completely at fault the boasted *acumen*, of the government agents. They have fallen into the gross but common error of confounding the unusual with the abstruse. But it is by these deviations from the plane of the ordinary, that reason feels its way, if at all, in its search for the true. In investigations such as we are now pursuing, it should not be so much asked 'what has occurred,' as 'what has occurred that has never occurred before.' In fact, the facility with which I shall arrive, or have arrived, at the solution of this mystery, is in the direct ratio of its apparent insolubility in the eyes of the police."

I stared at the speaker in mute astonishment.

"I am now awaiting," continued he, looking towards the door of our apartment— "I am now awaiting a person who, although perhaps not the perpetrator of these butcheries, must have been in some measure implicated in their perpetration. Of the worst portion of the crimes committed, it is probable that he is innocent. I hope that I am right in this supposition; for upon it I build my expectation of reading the entire riddle. I look for the man here—in this room—every moment. It is true that he may not arrive; but the probability is that he will. Should he come, it will be necessary to detain him. Here are pistols; and we both know how to use them when occasion demands their use."

I took the pistols, scarcely knowing what I did, or believing what I heard, while Dupin went on, very much as if in a soliloquy. I have already spoken of his abstract manner at such times. His discourse was addressed to myself; but his voice, although by no means loud, had that intonation which is commonly employed in speaking to some one at a great distance. His eyes, vacant in expression, regarded only the wall.

"That the voices heard in contention," he said, "by the party upon the stairs, were not the voices of the women themselves, was fully proved by the evidence. This relieves us of all doubt upon the question whether the old lady could have first destroyed the daughter, and afterward have committed suicide, I speak of this point chiefly for the sake of method; for the strength of Madame L'Espanaye would have been utterly unequal to the task of thrusting her daughter's corpse up the chimney as it was found; and the nature of the wounds upon her own person entirely preclude the idea of self-destruction. Murder, then, has been committed by some third party; and the voices of this third party were those heard in contention. Let me now advert—not to the whole testimony respecting these voices— but to what was *peculiar* in that testimony. Did you observe anything peculiar about it?"

65   I remarked that, while all the witnesses agreed in supposing the gruff voice to be that of a Frenchman, there was much disagreement in regard to the shrill, or, as one individual termed it, the harsh voice.

"That was the evidence iself," said Dupin, "but it was not the peculiarity of the evidence. You have observed nothing distinctive. Yet there *was* something to be observed. The witnesses, as you remark, agreed about the gruff voice; they were here unanimous. But in regard to the shrill voice, the peculiarity is—not that they disagreed—but that, while an Italian, an Englishman, a Spaniard, a Hollander, and a Frenchman attempted to describe it, each one spoke of it as that *of a foreigner*. Each is sure that it was not the voice of one of his own countrymen. Each likens it—not to the voice of an individual of any nation with whose language he is conversant—but the converse. The Frenchman supposes it the voice of a Spaniard, and 'might have distinguished some words *had he been acquainted with the Spanish.*' The Dutchman maintains it to have been that of a Frenchman; but we find it stated that '*not understanding French this witness was examined through an interpreter.*' The Englishman thinks it the voice of a German, and '*does not understand German.*' The Spaniard 'is sure' that it was that of an Englishman, but 'judges by the intonation' altogether, '*as he has no knowledge of the English.*' The Italian believes it the voice of a Russian, but '*has never conversed with a native of Russia.*' A second Frenchman differs, moreover, with the first, and is positive that the voice was that of an Italian; but, *not being cognizant of that tongue*, is, like the Spaniard, 'convinced by the intonation.' Now, how strangely unusual must that voice have really been, about which such testimony as this *could* have been elicited!—in whose *tones*, even, denizens of the five great divisions of Europe could recognize nothing familiar! You will say that it might have been the voice of an Asiatic—of an African. Neither Asiatics nor Africans abound in Paris; but, without denying the inference, I will now merely call your attention to three points. The voice is termed by one witness 'harsh rather than shrill.' It is represented by two others to have been 'quick and *unequal.*' No words—no sounds resembling words—were by any witness mentioned as distinguishable.

"I know not," continued Dupin, "what impression I may have made, so far, upon your own understanding; but I do not hesitate to say that legitimate deductions even from this portion of the testimony—the portion respecting the gruff and shrill voices—are in themselves sufficient to engender a suspicion which should give direction to all farther progress in the investigation of the mystery. I said 'legitimate deductions'; but my meaning is not thus fully expressed. I designed to imply that the deductions are the *sole* proper ones, and that the suspicion arises *inevitably* from them as the single result. What the suspicion is, however, I will not say just yet. I merely wish you to bear in mind that, with myself, it was sufficiently forcible to give a definite form—a certain tendency—to my inquiries in the chamber.

"Let us now transport ourselves, in fancy, to this chamber. What shall we first seek here? The means of egress employed by the murderers. It is not too much to say that neither of us believe in præternatural events. Madame and Mademoiselle L'Espanaye were not destroyed by spirits. The doers of the deed were material, and escaped materially. Then how? Fortunately, there is but one mode of reasoning upon the point, and that mode *must* lead us to a definite decision.—Let us examine, each by each, the possible means of egress. It is clear that the assassins were in the room where Mademoiselle L'Espanaye was found, or at least in the room adjoining, when the party ascended the stairs. It is then only from these two apartments that we have to seek issues. The police have laid bare the floors, the ceilings, and the masonry of the walls, in every direction. No *secret* issues could have escaped their vigilance. But not trusting to *their* eyes, I examined with my own. There were, then, *no* secret issues. Both doors leading from the rooms into the passage were securely locked, with the keys inside. Let us turn to the chimneys. These, although of ordinary width for some eight or ten feet above the hearths, will not admit, throughout their extent, the body of a large cat. The impossibility of egress, by means already stated, being thus absolute, we are reduced to the windows. Through those of the front room no one could have escaped without notice from the crowd in the street. The murderers *must* have passed, then, through those of the back room. Now, brought to this conclusion in so unequivocal a manner as we are, it is not our part, as reasoners, to reject it on account of apparent impossibilities. It is only left for us to prove that these apparent 'impossibilities' are, in reality, not such.

"There are two windows in the chamber. One of them is unobstructed by furniture, and is wholly visible. The lower portion of the other is hidden from view by the head of the unwieldy bedstead which is thrust close up against it. The former was found securely fastened from within. It resisted the utmost force of those who endeavored to raise it. A large gimlet-hole had been pierced in its frame to the left, and a very stout nail was found fitted therein, nearly to the head. Upon examining the other window, a similar nail was seen similarly fitted in it; and a vigorous attempt to raise this sash, failed also. The police were now entirely satisfied that egress had not been in these directions. And, *therefore*, it was thought a matter of supererogation to withdraw the nails and open the windows.

70   "My own examination was somewhat more particular, and was so for the reason I have just given—because here it was, I knew, that all apparent impossibilities *must* be proved to be not such in reality.

"I proceeded to think thus—*à posteriori.*[1] The murderers *did* escape from one of these windows. This being so, they could not have refastened the sashes from the inside, as they were found fastened;—the consideration which put a stop, through its obviousness, to the scrutiny of the police in this quarter. Yet the sashes *were* fastened. They *must*, then, have the power of fastening themselves. There was no escape from this conclusion. I stepped to the unobstructed casement, withdrew the nail with some difficulty, and attempted to raise the sash. It resisted all my efforts, as I had anticipated. A concealed spring must, I now knew, exist; and this corroboration of my idea convinced me that my premises, at least, were correct, however mysterious still appeared the circumstances attending the

---

[1]Reasoning from effect back to cause

nails. A careful search soon brought to light the hidden spring. I pressed it, and, satisfied with the discovery, forbore to upraise the sash.

"I now replaced the nail and regarded it attentively. A person passing out through this window might have reclosed it, and the spring would have caught—but the nail could not have been replaced. The conclusion was plain, and again narrowed in the field of my investigations. The assassins *must* have escaped through the other window. Supposing, then, the springs upon each sash to be the same, as was probable, there *must* be found a difference between the nails, or at least between the modes of their fixture. Getting upon the sacking of the bedstead, I looked over the head-board minutely at the second casement. Passing my hand down behind the board, I readily discovered and pressed the spring, which was, as I had supposed, identical in character with its neighbor. I now looked at the nail. It was as stout as the other, and apparently fitted in the same manner— driven in nearly up to the head.

"You will say that I was puzzled; but, if you think so, you must have misunderstood the nature of the inductions. To use a sporting phrase, I had not been once 'at fault.' The scent had never for an instant been lost. There was no flaw in any link of the chain. I had traced the secret to its ultimate result,—and that result was *the nail*. It had, I say, in every respect, the appearance of its fellow in the other window; but this fact was an absolute nullity (conclusive as it might seem to be) when compared with the consideration that here, at this point, terminated the clue. 'There *must* be something wrong,' I said, 'about the nail.' I touched it; and the head, with about a quarter of an inch of the shank, came off in my fingers. The rest of the shank was in the gimlet-hole, where it had been broken off. The fracture was an old one (for its edges were incrusted with rust), and had apparently been accomplished by the blow of a hammer, which had partially imbedded, in the top of the bottom sash, the head portion of the nail, I now carefully replaced this head portion in the indentation whence I had taken it, and the resemblance to a perfect nail was complete—the fissure was invisible. Pressing the spring, I gently raised the sash for a few inches; the head went up with it, remaining firm in its bed. I closed the window, and the semblance of the whole nail was again perfect.

"The riddle, so far, was now unriddled. The assassin had escaped through the window which looked upon the bed. Dropping of its own accord upon his exit (or perhaps purposely closed), it had become fastened by the spring; and it was the retention of this spring which had been mistaken by the police for that of the nail,—farther inquiry being thus considered unnecessary.

75 "The next question is that of the mode of descent. Upon this point I had been satisfied in my walk with you around the building. About five feet and a half from the casement in question there runs a lightning-rod. From this rod it would have been impossible for any one to reach the window itself, to say nothing of entering it. I observed, however, that the shutters of the fourth story were of the peculiar kind called by Parisian carpenters *ferrades*—a kind rarely employed at the present day, but frequently seen upon very old mansions at Lyons and Bordeaux. They are in the form of an ordinary door (a single, not a folding door), except that the upper half is latticed or worked in open trellis—thus affording an excellent hold for the hands. In the present instance these shutters are fully three feet and a half broad. When we saw them from the rear of the house, they were both about half open—that is to say, they stood off at right angles from the wall. It is possible that the police, as well as myself, examined the back of the tenement; but, if so, in looking at these *ferrades* in the line of their breadth (as they must have done),

they did not perceive this great breadth itself, or, at all events, failed to take it into due consideration. In fact, having once satisfied themselves that no egress could have been made in this quarter, they would naturally bestow here a very cursory examination. It was clear to me, however, that the shutter belonging to the window at the head of the bed, would, if swung fully back to the wall, reach to within two feet of the lightning-rod. It was also evident that, by exertion of a very unusual degree of activity and courage, an entrance into the window, from the rod, might have been thus effected.—By reaching to the distance of two feet and a half (we now suppose the shutter open to its whole extent) a robber might have taken a firm grasp upon the trellis-work. Letting go, then, his hold upon the rod, placing his feet securely against the wall, and springing boldly from it, he might have swung the shutter so as to close it, and, if we imagine the window open at the time, might even have swung himself into the room.

"I wish you to bear especially in mind that I have spoken of a *very* unusual degree of activity as requisite to success in so hazardous and so difficult a feat. It is my design to show you, first, that the thing might possibly have been accomplished:—but, secondly and *chiefly*, I wish to impress upon your understanding the *very extraordinary*—the almost præternatural character of that agility which could have accomplished it.

"You will say, no doubt, using the language of the law, that 'to make out my case' I should rather undervalue, than insist upon a full estimation of the activity required in this matter. This may be the practice in law, but it is not the usage of reason. My ultimate object is only the truth. My immediate purpose is to lead you to place in juxtaposition that *very unusual* activity of which I have just spoken, with that *very peculiar* shrill (or harsh) and *unequal* voice, about whose nationality no two persons could be found to agree, and in whose utterance no syllabification could be detected."

At these words a vague and half-formed conception of the meaning of Dupin flitted over my mind. I seemed to be upon the verge of comprehension, without power to comprehend—as men, at times, find themselves upon the brink of rememberance, without being able, in the end, to remember. My friend went on with his discourse.

"You will see," he said, "that I have shifted the question from the mode of egress to that of ingress. It was my design to suggest that both were effected in the same manner, at the same point. Let us now revert to the interior of the room. Let us survey the appearances here. The drawers of the bureau, it is said, had been rifled, although many articles of apparel still remained within them. The conclusion here is absurd. It is a mere guess—a very silly one—and no more. How are we to know that the articles found in the drawers were not all these drawers had originally contained? Madame L'Espanaye and her daughter lived an exceedingly retired life—saw no company—seldom went out—had little use for numerous changes of habiliment. Those found were at least of as good quality as any likely to be possessed by these ladies. If a thief had taken any, why did he not take the best— why did he not take all? In a word, why did he abandon four thousand francs in gold to encumber himself with a bundle of linen? The gold *was* abandoned. Nearly the whole sum mentioned by Monsieur Mignaud, the banker, was discovered, in bags, upon the floor. I wish you, therefore, to discard from your thoughts the blundering idea of *motive*, engendered in the brains of the police by that portion of the evidence which speaks of money delivered at the door of the house. Coincidences ten times as remarkable as this (the delivery of the money, and murder committed within three days upon the party receiving it), happen to all of us every hour of our lives, without attracting even momentary notice. Coincidences, in general, are great stumbling-blocks in the way of that class of thinkers who have been educated to know nothing of the theory of probabilities—that theory to which the most glorious objects of human research are indebted for the most glorious of illustration. In the present instance, had the gold been gone, the fact of its delivery three days before would have formed something more than a coincidence. It would have been corroborative of this idea of motive. But, under the real circumstances of the case, if we are to suppose gold the motive of this outrage, we must also imagine the perpetrator so vacillating an idiot as to have abandoned his gold and his motive together.

80   "Keeping now steadily in mind the points to which I have drawn your attention— that peculiar voice, that unusual agility, and that startling absence of motive in a murder so singularly atrocious as this—let us glance at the butchery itself. Here is a woman strangled to death by manual strength, and thrust up a chimney, head downwards. Ordinary assassins employ no such modes of murder as this. Least of all, do they thus dispose of the murdered. In the manner of thrusting the corpse up the chimney, you will admit that there was something *excessively outré*—something altogether irreconcilable with our common notions of human action, even when we suppose the actors the most depraved of men. Think, too, how great must have been that strength which could have thrust the body *up* such an aperture so forcibly that the united vigor of several persons was found barely sufficient to drag it *down!*

"Turn, now, to other indications of the employment of a vigor most marvelous. On the hearth were thick tresses—very thick tresses—of gray human hair. These had been torn out by the roots. You are aware of the great force necessary in tearing thus from the head even twenty or thirty hairs together. You saw the locks in question as well as myself. Their roots (a hideous sight!) were clotted with fragments of the flesh of the scalp—sure token of the prodigious power which had been exerted in uprooting perhaps half a million of hairs at a time. The throat of the old lady was not merely cut, but the head absolutely severed from the body: the instrument was a mere razor. I wish you also to look at the *brutal* ferocity of these deeds. Of the bruises upon the body of Madame L'Espanaye I do not speak. Monsieur Dumas, and his worthy coadjutor Monsieur Etienne, have pronounced that they were inflicted by some obtuse instrument; and so far these gentlemen are very correct. The obtuse instrument was clearly the stone pavement in the yard, upon which the victim had fallen from the window which looked in upon the bed. This idea, however simple it may now seem, escaped the police for the same reason that the breadth of the shutters escaped them—because, by the affair of the nails, their perceptions had been hermetically sealed against the possibility of the windows having ever been opened at all.

"If now, in addition to all these things, you have properly reflected upon the odd disorder of the chamber, we have gone so far as to combine the ideas of an agility astounding, a strength superhuman, a ferocity brutal, a butchery without motive, a *grotesquerie* in horror absolutely alien from humanity, and a voice foreign in tone to the ears of men of many nations, and devoid of all distinct or intelligible syllabification. What result, then, has ensued? What impression have I made upon your fancy?"

I felt a creeping of the flesh as Dupin asked me the question. "A madman," I said, "has done this deed—some raving maniac, escaped from a neighboring *Maison de Santé.*"

"In some respects," he replied, "your idea is not irrelevant. But the voices of madmen, even in their wildest paroxysms, are never found to tally with that peculiar voice heard upon the stairs. Madmen are of some nation, and their language, however incoherent in its words, has always the coherence of syllabification. Besides, the hair of a madman is not such as I now hold in my hand. I disentangled this little tuft from the rigidly clutched fingers of Madame L'Espanaye. Tell me what you can make of it."

85 "Dupin!" I said, completely unnerved; "this hair is most unusual—this is no *human* hair."

"I have not asserted that it is," said he; "but, before we decide this point, I wish you to glance at the little sketch I have here traced upon this paper. It is a *facsimile* drawing of what has been described in one portion of the testimony as 'dark bruises, and deep indentations of fingernails,' upon the throat of Mademoiselle L'Espanaye, and in another (by Messrs. Dumas and Etienne), as a 'series of livid spots, evidently the impression of fingers.'

"You will perceive," continued my friend, spreading out the paper upon the table before us, "that this drawing gives the idea of a firm and fixed hold. There is no *slipping* apparent. Each finger has retained—possibly until the death of the victim—the fearful grasp by which it originally imbedded itself. Attempt, now, to place all your fingers, at the same time, in the respective impressions as you see them."

I made the attempt in vain.

"We are possibly not giving this matter a fair trial," he said. "The paper is spread out upon a plane surface; but the human throat is cylindrical. Here is a billet of wood, the circumference of which is about that of the throat. Wrap the drawing around it, and try the experiment again."

90 I did so; but the difficulty was even more obvious than before.

"This," I said, "is the mark of no human hand."

"Read now," replied Dupin, "this passage from Cuvier."

It was a minute anatomical and generally descriptive account of the large fulvous Orang-Outang of the East Indian Islands. The gigantic stature, the prodigious strength and activity, the wild ferocity, and the imitative propensities of these mammalia are sufficiently well known to all. I understood the full horrors of the murder at once.

"The description of the digits," said I, as I made an end of reading, "is in exact accordance with this drawing. I see that no animal but an Orang-Outang, of the species here mentioned, could have impressed the indentations as you have traced them. This tuft of tawny hair, too, is identical in character with that of the beast of Cuvier. But I cannot possibly comprehend the particulars of this frightful mystery. Besides, there were *two* voices heard in contention, and one of them was unquestionably the voice of a Frenchman."

95 "True; and you will remember an expression attributed almost unanimously, by the evidence, to this voice,—the expression, '*mon Dieu!*' This, under the circumstances, has been justly characterized by one of the witnesses (Montani, the confectioner), as an expression of remonstrance or expostulation. Upon these two words, therefore, I have mainly built my hopes of a full solution of the riddle. A Frenchman was cognizant of the murder. It is possible—indeed it is far more than probable—that he was innocent of all participation in the bloody transactions

which took place. The Orang-Outang may have escaped from him. He may have traced it to the chamber; but, under the agitating circumstances which ensued, he could never have recaptured it. It is still at large. I will not pursue these guesses—for I have no right to call them more—since the shades of reflection upon which they are based are scarcely of sufficient depth to be appreciable by my own intellect, and since I could not pretend to make them intelligible to the understanding of another. We will call them guesses then, and speak of them as such. If the Frenchman in question is indeed, as I suppose, innocent of this atrocity, this advertisement, which I left last night, upon our return home, at the office of 'Le Monde' (a paper devoted to the shipping interest, and much sought by sailors), will bring him to our residence."

He handed me a paper, and I read thus:

CAUGHT—*In the Bois de Boulogne, early in the morning of the —— inst. (the morning of the murder), a very large tawny Orang-Outang of the Bornese species. The owner (who is ascertained to be a sailor, belonging to a Maltese vessel), may have the animal again, upon identifying it satisfactorily, and paying a few charges arising from its capture and keeping. Call at No. ——, Rue ——, Faubourg St. Germain—au troisième.*

"How was it possible," I asked, "that you should know the man to be a sailor, and belonging to a Maltese vessel?"

"I do *not* know it," said Dupin. "I am not *sure* of it. Here, however, is a small piece of ribbon, which from its form, and from its greasy appearance, has evidently been used in tying the hair in one of those long *queues* of which sailors are so fond. Moreover, this knot is one which few besides sailors can tie, and is peculiar to the Maltese. I picked the ribbon up at the foot of the lightning-rod. It could not have belonged to either of the deceased. Now if, after all, I am wrong in my induction from this ribbon, that the Frenchman was a sailor belonging to a Maltese vessel, still I can have done no harm in saying what I did in the advertisement. If I am in error, he will merely suppose that I have been misled by some circumstance into which he will not take the trouble to inquire. But if I am right, a great point is gained. Cognizant although innocent of the murder, the Frenchman will naturally hesitate about replying to the advertisement—about demanding the Orang-Outang. He will reason thus:—'I am innocent; I am poor; my Orang-Outang is of great value—to one in my circumstances a fortune of itself—why should I lose it through idle apprehensions of danger? Here it is, within my grasp. It was found in the Bois de Boulogne—at a vast distance from the scene of that butchery. How can it ever be suspected that a brute beast should have done the deed? The police are at fault—they have failed to procure the slightest clue. Should they even trace the animal, it would be impossible to prove me cognizant of the murder, or to implicate me in guilt on account of that cognizance. Above all, *I am known.* The advertiser designates me as the possessor of the beast. I am not sure to what limit his knowledge may extend. Should I avoid claiming a property of so great value, which it is known that I possess, I will render the animal, at least, liable to suspicion. It is not my policy to attract attention either to myself or to the beast. I will answer the advertisement, get the Orang-Outang, and keep it close until this matter has blown over.' "

100   At this moment we heard a step upon the stairs.

"Be ready," said Dupin, "with your pistols, but neither use them nor show them until at a signal from myself."

The front door of the house had been left open, and the visitor had entered, without ringing, and advanced several steps upon the staircase. Now, however, he seemed to hesitate. Presently we heard him descending. Dupin was moving quickly to the door, when we again heard him coming up. He did not turn back a second time, but stepped up with decision and rapped at the door of our chamber.

"Come in," said Dupin, in a cheerful and hearty tone.

A man entered. He was a sailor, evidently,—a tall, stout, and muscular-looking person, with a certain dare-devil expression of countenance, not altogether un-prepossessing. His face, greatly sunburnt, was more than half hidden by whisker and *mustachio*. He had with him a huge oaken cudgel, but appeared to be other-wise unarmed. He bowed awkwardly, and bade us "good evening," in French accents, which, although somewhat Neufchatelish, were still sufficiently indicative of a Parisian origin.

105   "Sit down, my friend," said Dupin. "I suppose you have called about the Orang-Outang. Upon my word, I almost envy you the possession of him; a remarkably fine, and no doubt a very valuable animal. How old do you suppose him to be?"

The sailor drew a long breath, with the air of a man relieved of some intolerable burthen, and then replied, in an assured tone:

"I have no way of telling—but he can't be more than four or five years old. Have you got him here?"

"Oh no; we had no conveniences for keeping him here. He is at a livery stable in the Rue Dubourg, just by. You can get him in the morning. Of course you are prepared to identify the property?"

"To be sure I am, sir."

110   "I shall be sorry to part with him," said Dupin.

"I don't mean that you should be at all this trouble for nothing, sir," said the man. "Couldn't expect it. Am very willing to pay a reward for the finding of the animal—that is to say, anything in reason."

"Well," replied my friend, "that is all very fair, to be sure. Let me think!—what should I have? Oh! I will tell you. My reward shall be this. You shall give me all the information in your power about these murders in the Rue Morgue."

Dupin said the last words in a very low tone, and very quietly. Just as quietly, too, he walked towards the door, locked it, and put the key in his pocket. He then drew a pistol from his bosom and placed it, without the least flurry, upon the table.

The sailor's face flushed up as if he were struggling with suffocation. He started to his feet and grasped his cudgel; but the next moment he fell back into his seat, trembling violently, and with the countenance of death itself. He spoke not a word. I pitied him from the bottom of my heart.

115   "My friend," said Dupin, in a kind tone, "you are alarming yourself unneces-sarily—you are indeed. We mean you no harm whatever. I pledge you the honor of a gentleman, and of a Frenchman, that we intend you no injury. I perfectly well know that you are innocent of the atrocities in the Rue Morgue. It will not do, however, to deny that you are in some measure implicated in them. From what I have already said, you must know that I have had means of information about this matter—means of which you could never have dreamed. Now the thing stands thus. You have done nothing which you could have avoided—nothing, certainly, which renders you culpable. You were not even guilty of robbery, when you might have robbed with impunity. You have nothing to conceal. You have no reason for concealment. On the other hand, you are bound by every principle of honor to

confess all you know. An innocent man is now imprisoned, charged with that crime of which you can point out the perpetrator."

The sailor had recovered his presence of mind, in a great measure, while Dupin uttered these words; but his original boldness of bearing was all gone.

"So help me God," said he, after a brief pause, "I *will* tell you all I know about this affair;—but I do not expect you to believe one half I say—I would be a fool indeed if I did. Still, I *am* innocent, and I will make a clean breast if I die for it."

What he stated was, in substance, this. He had lately made a voyage to the Indian Archipelago. A party, of which he formed one, landed at Borneo, and passed into the interior on an excursion of pleasure. Himself and a companion had captured the Orang-Outang. This companion dying, the animal fell into his own exclusive possession. After great trouble, occasioned by the intractable ferocity of his captive during the home voyage, he at length succeeded in lodging it safely at his own residence in Paris, where, not to attract towards himself the unpleasant curiosity of his neighbors, he kept it carefully secluded, until such time as it should recover from a wound in the foot, received from a splinter on board ship. His ultimate design was to sell it.

Returning home from some sailors' frolic on the night, or rather in the morning of the murder, he found the beast occupying his own bedroom, into which it had broken from a closet adjoining, where it had been, as was thought, securely confined. Razor in hand, and fully lathered, it was sitting before a looking-glass, attempting the operation of shaving, in which it had no doubt previously watched its master through the keyhole of the closet. Terrified at the sight of so dangerous a weapon in the possession of an animal so ferocious, and so well able to use it, the man, for some moments, was at a loss what to do. He had been accustomed, however, to quiet the creature, even in its fiercest moods, by the use of a whip, and to this he now resorted. Upon sight of it, the Orang-Outang sprang at once through the door of the chamber, down the stairs, and thence, through a window, unfortunately open, into the street.

120   The Frenchman followed in despair; the ape, razor still in hand, occasionally stopping to look back and gesticulate at its pursuer, until the latter had nearly come up with it. It then again made off. In this manner the chase continued for a long time. The streets were profoundly quiet, as it was nearly three o'clock in the morning. In passing down an alley in the rear of the Rue Morgue, the fugitive's attention was arrested by a light gleaming from the open window of Madame L'Espanaye's chamber, in the fourth story of her house. Rushing to the building, it perceived the lightning-rod, chambered up with inconceivable agility, grasped the shutter, which was thrown fully back against the wall, and, by its means, swung itself directly upon the headboard of the bed. The whole feat did not occupy a minute. The shutter was kicked open again by the Orang-Outang as it entered the room.

The sailor, in the meantime, was both rejoiced and perplexed. He had strong hopes of now recapturing the brute, as it could scarcely escape from the trap into which it had ventured, except by the rod, where it might be intercepted as it came down. On the other hand, there was much cause for anxiety as to what it might do in the house. This latter reflection urged the man still to follow the fugitive. A lightning-rod is ascended without difficulty, especially by a sailor; but, when he had arrived as high as the window, which lay far to his left, his career was stopped; the most that he could accomplish was to reach over so as to obtain a glimpse of the interior of the room. At this glimpse he nearly fell from his hold through excess of horror. Now it was that those hideous shrieks arose upon the night, which had startled from slumber the inmates of the Rue Morgue. Madame L'Espanaye and her daughter, habited in their night clothes, had apparently been arranging some papers in the iron chest already mentioned, which had been wheeled into the middle of the room. It was open, and its contents lay beside it on the floor. The victims must have been sitting with their backs toward the window; and, from the time elapsing between the ingress of the beast and the screams, it seems probable that it was not immediately perceived. The flapping-to of the shutter would naturally have been attributed to the wind.

As the sailor looked in, the gigantic animal had seized Madame L'Espanaye by the hair (which was loose, as she had been combing it), and was flourishing the razor about her face, in imitation of the motions of a barber. The daughter lay prostrate and motionless; she had swooned. The screams and struggles of the old lady (during which the hair was torn from her head) had the effect of changing the probably pacific purposes of the Orang-Outang into those of wrath. With one determined sweep of its muscular arm it nearly severed her head from her body. The sight of blood inflamed its anger into frenzy. Gnashing its teeth, and flashing fire from its eyes, it flew upon the body of the girl, and imbedded its fearful talons in her throat, retaining its grasp until she expired. Its wandering and wild glances fell at this moment upon the head of the bed, over which the face of its master, rigid with horror, was just discernible. The fury of the beast, who no doubt bore still in mind the dreaded whip, was instantly converted into fear. Conscious of having deserved punishment, it seemed desirous of concealing its bloody deeds, and skipped about the chamber in an agony of nervous agitation; throwing down and breaking the furniture as it moved, and dragging the bed from the bedstead. In conclusion, it seized first the corpse of the daughter, and thrust it up the chimney, as it was found; then that of the old lady, which it immediately hurled through the window headlong.

As the ape approached the casement with its mutilated burthen, the sailor shrank aghast to the rod, and, rather gliding than clambering down it, hurried at once home—dreading the consequences of the butchery, and gladly abandoning, in his terror, all solicitude about the fate of the Orang-Outang. The words heard by the party upon the staircase were the Frenchman's exclamations of horror and affright, comingled with the fiendish jabberings of the brute.

I have scarcely anything to add. The Orang-Outang must have escaped from the chamber, by the rod, just before the breaking of the door. It must have closed the window as it passed through it. It was subsequently caught by the owner himself, who obtained for it a very large sum at the *Jardin des Plantes*. Le Bon was instantly released, upon our narration of the circumstances (with some comments from Dupin) at the *bureau* of the Prefect of Police. This functionary, however well disposed to my friend, could not altogether conceal his chagrin at the turn which affairs had taken, and was fain to indulge in a sarcasm or two, about the propriety of every person minding his own business.

125 "Let them talk," said Dupin, who had not thought it necessary to reply. "Let him discourse; it will ease his conscience. I am satisfied with having defeated him in his own castle. Nevertheless, that he failed in the solution of this mystery, is by no means that matter for wonder which he supposes it; for, in truth, our friend the Prefect is somewhat too cunning to be profound. In his wisdom is no *stamen*. It is all head and no body, like the pictures of the Goddess Laverna,—or, at best, all head and shoulders, like a codfish. But he is a good creature after all. I like

him especially for one master stroke of cant, by which he has attained his reputation for ingenuity. I mean the way he had *'de nier ce qui est, et d'expliquer ce
qui n'est pas.'* "[1]

[1]"To deny the existence of what is, and to explain the notion of what isn't."—Rousseau, *Nouvelle
Héloïse*

Joseph Conrad
Youth

Joseph Conrad (1857–1924) was born in Poland and learned English as a
second language. He went to sea in 1874, joined the British Merchant Marine,
and eventually became an English citizen. The sea forms the background of
many of his novels and stories. In 1894, Conrad retired from the Merchant
Marine in order to write. His novels are among the best works of modern
English fiction, all the more extraordinary because he became a superb stylist
in a language he learned as an adult.

This could have occurred nowhere but in England, where men and sea inter-
penetrate, so to speak—the sea entering into the life of most men, and the men
knowing something or everything about the sea, in the way of amusement, of
travel, or of bread-winning.

We were sitting round a mahogany table that reflected the bottle, the claret-
glasses, and our faces as we leaned on our elbows. There was a director of companies, an accountant, a lawyer, Marlow, and myself. The director had been a
Conway boy,[1] the accountant had served four years at sea, the lawyer—a fine
crusted Tory, High Churchman, the best of old fellows, the soul of honor—had
been chief officer in the P. & O.[2] service in the good old days when mail-boats
were square-rigged at least on two masts, and used to come down the China Sea
before a fair monsoon with stun'-sails set alow and aloft. We all began life in the
merchant service. Between the five of us there was the strong bond of the sea,
and also the fellowship of the craft, which no amount of enthusiasm for yachting,
cruising, and so on can give, since one is only the amusement of life and the other
is life itself.

Marlow (at least I think that is how he spelt his name) told the story, or rather
the chronicle, of a voyage:—

"Yes, I have seen a little of the Eastern seas; but what I remember best is my
first voyage there. You fellows know there are those voyages that seem ordered
for the illustration of life, that might stand for a symbol of existence. You fight,
work, sweat, nearly kill yourself, trying to accomplish something—and you can't.
Not from any fault of yours. You simply can do nothing, neither great nor little—
not a thing in the world—not even marry an old maid, or get a wretched 600-ton
cargo of coal to its port of destination.

5   "It was altogether a memorable affair. It was my first voyage to the East, and
my first voyage as second mate; it was also my skipper's first command. You'll
admit it was time. He was sixty if a day; a little man, with a broad, not very straight
back, with bowed shoulders and one leg more bandy than the other, he had that
queer twisted-about appearance you see so often in men who work in the fields.
He had a nutcracker face—chin and nose trying to come together over a sunken

[1]The frigate *Conway* was a training ship.   [2]Peninsular and Oriental, a shipping company

mouth—and it was framed in iron-gray fluffy hair, that looked like a chin strap of cotton-wool sprinkled with coal dust. And he had blue eyes in that old face of his, which were amazingly like a boy's, with that candid expression some quite common men preserve to the end of their days by a rare internal gift of simplicity of heart and rectitude of soul. What induced him to accept me was a wonder. I had come out of a crack Australian clipper, where I had been third officer, and he seemed to have a prejudice against crack clippers as aristocratic and high-toned. He said to me, 'You know, in this ship you will have to work.' I said I had to work in every ship I had ever been in. 'Ah, but this is different, and you gentlemen out of them big ships; . . . but there! I dare say you will do. Join tomorrow.'

"I joined tomorrow. It was twenty-two years ago; and I was just twenty. How time passes! It was one of the happiest days of my life. Fancy! Second mate for the first time—a really responsible officer! I wouldn't have thrown up my new billet for a fortune. The mate looked me over carefully. He was also an old chap, but of another stamp. He had a Roman nose, a snow-white, long beard, and his name was Mahon, but he insisted that it should be pronounced Mann. He was well connected; yet there was something wrong with his luck, and he had never got on.

"As to the captain, he had been for years in coasters, then in the Mediterranean, and last in the West Indian trade. He had never been round the Capes. He could just write a kind of sketchy hand, and didn't care for writing at all. Both were thorough good seamen of course, and between those two old chaps I felt like a small boy between two grandfathers.

"The ship also was old. Her name was the *Judea*. Queer name, isn't it? She belonged to a man Wilmer, Wilcox—some name like that; but he has been bankrupt and dead these twenty years or more, and his name don't matter. She had been laid up in Shadwell basin for ever so long. You can imagine her state. She was all rust, dust, grime—soot aloft, dirt on deck. To me it was like coming out of a palace into a ruined cottage. She was about 400 tons, had a primitive windlass, wooden latches on the doors, not a bit of brass about her, and a big square stern. There was on it, below her name in big letters, a lot of scroll work, with the gilt off, and some sort of a coat of arms, with the motto 'Do or Die' underneath. I remember it took my fancy immediately. There was a touch of romance in it, something that made me love the old thing—something that appealed to my youth!

"We left London in ballast—sand ballast—to load a cargo of coal in a northern port for Bankok. Bankok! I thrilled. I had been six years at sea, but had only seen Melbourne and Sydney, very good places, charming places in their way—but Bankok!

10 "We worked out of the Thames under canvas, with a North Sea pilot on board. His name was Jermyn, and he dodged all day long about the galley drying his handkerchief before the stove. Apparently he never slept. He was a dismal man, with a perpetual tear sparkling at the end of his nose, who either had been in trouble, or was in trouble, or expected to be in trouble—couldn't be happy unless something went wrong. He mistrusted my youth, my common sense, and my seamanship, and made a point of showing it in a hundred little ways. I dare say he was right. It seems to me I knew very little then, and I know not much more now; but I cherish a hate for that Jermyn to this day.

"We were a week working up as far as Yarmouth Roads, and then we got into a gale—the famous October gale of twenty-two years ago. It was wind, lightning, sleet, snow, and a terrific sea. We were flying light, and you may imagine how bad it was when I tell you we had smashed bulwarks and a flooded deck. On the second night she shifted her ballast into the lee bow, and by that time we had been blown off somewhere on the Dogger Bank. There was nothing for it but go below with shovels and try to right her, and there we were in that vast hold, gloomy like a cavern, the tallow dips stuck and flickering on the beams, the gale howling above, the ship tossing about like mad on her side; there we all were, Jermyn, the captain, everyone, hardly able to keep our feet, engaged on that gravedigger's work, and trying to toss shovelfuls of wet sand up to windward. At every tumble of the ship you could see vaguely in the dim light men falling down with a great flourish of shovels. One of the ship's boys (we had two), impressed by the weirdness of the scene, wept as if his heart would break. We could hear him blubbering somewhere in the shadows.

"On the third day the gale died out, and by-and-by a north-country tug picked us up. We took sixteen days in all to get from London to the Tyne! When we got into dock we had lost our turn for loading, and they hauled us off to a pier where we remained for a month. Mrs. Beard (the captain's name was Beard) came from Colchester to see the old man. She lived on board. The crew of runners had left, and there remained only the officers, one boy, and the steward, a mulatto who answered to the name of Abraham. Mrs. Beard was an old woman, with a face all wrinkled and ruddy like a winter apple, and the figure of a young girl. She caught sight of me once, sewing on a button, and insisted on having my shirts to repair. This was something different from the captains' wives I had known on board crack clippers. When I brought her the shirts, she said: 'And the socks? They want mending, I am sure, and John's—Captain Beard's—things are all in order now. I would be glad of something to do.' Bless the old woman. She overhauled my outfit for me, and meantime I read for the first time *Sartor Resartus*[1] and Burnaby's *Ride to Khiva*.[2] I didn't understand much of the first then; but I remember I preferred the soldier to the philosopher at the time; a preference which life has only confirmed. One was a man, and the other was either more—or less. However, they are both dead and Mrs. Beard is dead, and youth, strength, genius, thoughts, achievements, simple hearts—all die. . . . No matter.

"They loaded us at last. We shipped a crew. Eight able seamen and two boys. We hauled off one evening to the buoys at the dockgates, ready to go out, and with a fair prospect of beginning the voyage next day. Mrs. Beard was to start for home by a late train. When the ship was fast we went to tea. We sat rather silent through the meal—Mahon, the old couple, and I. I finished first, and slipped away for a smoke, my cabin being in a deck-house just against the poop. It was high water, blowing fresh with a drizzle; the double dock-gates were opened, and the steam-colliers were going in and out in the darkness with their lights burning bright, a great plashing of propellers, rattling of winches, and a lot of hailing on the pier-heads. I watched the procession of head-lights gliding high and of green lights gliding low in the night, when suddenly a red gleam flashed at me, vanished, came into view again, and remained. The fore-end of a steamer loomed up close. I shouted down the cabin, 'Come up, quick!' and then heard a startled voice saying afar in the dark, 'Stop her, sir.' A bell jingled. Another voice cried warningly, 'We are going right into that barque, sir.' The answer to this was a gruff 'All right,' and

---

[1]Philosophical work by Thomas Carlyle (1795–1881); the title translated roughly "Tailor Repatched"   [2]Frederick Gustavus Burnaby (1842–1885) was a soldier who also wrote.

the next thing was a heavy crash as the steamer struck a glancing blow with the bluff of her bow about our fore-rigging. There was a moment of confusion, yelling, and running about. Steam roared. Then somebody was heard saying, 'All clear, sir.' . . . 'Are you all right?' asked the gruff voice. I had jumped forward to see the damage, and hailed back, 'I think so.' 'Easy astern,' said the gruff voice. A bell jingled. 'What steamer is that?' screamed Mahon. By that time she was no more to us than a bulky shadow maneuvering a little way off. They shouted at us some name—a woman's name, Miranda or Melissa—or some such thing. 'This means another month in this beastly hole,' said Mahon to me, as we peered with lamps about the splintered bulwarks and broken braces. 'But where's the captain?'

"We had not heard or seen anything of him all that time. We went aft to look. A doleful voice arose hailing somewhere in the middle of the dark, '*Judea* ahoy!' . . . How the devil did he get there? . . . 'Hallo!' we shouted. 'I am adrift in our boat without oars,' he cried. A belated water-man offered his services, and Mahon struck a bargain with him for half-a-crown to tow our skipper alongside; but it was Mrs. Beard that came up the ladder first. They had been floating about the dock in that mizzly cold rain for nearly an hour. I was never so surprised in my life.

15 "It appears that when he heard my shout 'Come up' he understood at once what was the matter, caught up his wife, ran on deck, and across, and down into our boat, which was fast to the ladder. Not bad for a sixty-year old. Just imagine that old fellow saving heroically in his arms that old woman—the woman of his life. He set her down on a thwart, and was ready to climb back on board when the painter came adrift somehow, and away they went together. Of course in the confusion we did not hear him shouting. He looked abashed. She said cheerfully, 'I suppose it does not matter my losing the train now?' 'No, Jenny—you go below and get warm,' he growled. Then to us: 'A sailor has no business with a wife—I say. There I was, out of the ship. Well, no harm done this time. Let's go and look at what that fool of a steamer smashed.'

"It wasn't much, but it delayed us three weeks. At the end of that time, the captain being engaged with his agents, I carried Mrs. Beard's bag to the railway-station and put her all comfy into a third-class carriage. She lowered the window to say, 'You are a good young man. If you see—John—Captain Beard—without his muffler at night, just remind him from me to keep his throat well wrapped up.' 'Certainly, Mrs. Beard,' I said. 'You are a good young man; I noticed how attentive you are to John—to Captain—' The train pulled out suddenly; I took my cap off to the old woman: I never saw her again. . . . Pass the bottle.

"We went to sea next day. When we made that start for Bangkok we had been already three months out of London. We had expected to be a fortnight or so—at the outside.

"It was January, and the weather was beautiful—the beautiful sunny winter weather that has more charm than in the summertime, because it is unexpected, and crisp, and you know it won't, it can't, last long. It's like a windfall, like a godsend, like an unexpected piece of luck.

"It lasted all down the North Sea, all down Channel; and it lasted till we were three hundred miles or so to the westward of the Lizards:[1] then the wind went round to the sou'west and began to pipe up. In two days it blew a gale. The *Judea,* hove to, wallowed on the Atlantic like an old candle-box. It blew day after day: it blew with spite, without interval, without mercy, without rest. The world was

---

[1]In southwest Cornwall

nothing but an immensity of great foaming waves rushing at us, under a sky low enough to touch with the hand and dirty like a smoked ceiling. In the stormy space surrounding us there was as much flying spray as air. Day after day and night after night there was nothing round the ship but the howl of the wind, the tumult of the sea, the noise of water pouring over her deck. There was no rest for her and no rest for us. She tossed, she pitched, she stood on her head, she sat on her tail, she rolled, she groaned, and we had to hold on while on deck and cling to our bunks when below, in a constant effort of body and worry of mind.

20   "One night Mahon spoke through the small window of my berth. It opened right into my bed, and I was lying there sleepless, in my boots, feeling as though I had not slept for years, and could not if I tried. He said excitedly—

   " 'You got the sounding-rod in here, Marlow? I can't get the pumps to suck. By God! it's no child's play.'

   "I gave him the sounding-rod and lay down again, trying to think of various things—but I thought only of the pumps. When I came on deck they were still at it, and my watch relieved at the pumps. By the light of the lantern brought on deck to examine the sounding-rod I caught a glimpse of their weary, serious faces. We pumped all the four hours. We pumped all night, all day, all the week—watch and watch. She was working herself loose, and leaked badly—not enough to drown us at once, but enough to kill us with the work at the pumps. And while we pumped the ship was going from us piecemeal: the bulwarks went, the stanchions were torn out, the ventilators smashed, the cabin-door burst in. There was not a dry spot in the ship. She was being gutted bit by bit. The long-boat changed, as if by magic, into matchwood where she stood in her gripes. I had lashed her myself, and was rather proud of my handiwork, which had withstood so long the malice of the sea. And we pumped. And there was no break in the weather. The sea was white like a sheet of foam, like a caldron of boiling milk; there was not a break in the clouds, no—not the size of a man's hand—no, not for so much as ten seconds. There was for us no sky, there were for us no stars, no sun, no universe—nothing but angry clouds and an infuriated sea. We pumped watch and watch, for dear life; and it seemed to last for months, for years, for all eternity, as though we had been dead and gone to a hell for sailors. We forgot the day of the week, the name of the month, what year it was, and whether we had ever been ashore. The sails blew away, she lay broadside on under a weather-cloth, the ocean poured over her, and we did not care. We turned those handles, and had the eyes of idiots. As soon as we had crawled on deck I used to take a round turn with a rope about the men, the pumps, the mainmast, and we turned, we turned incessantly, with the water to our waists, to our necks, over our heads. It was all one. We had forgotten how it felt to be dry.

   "And there was somewhere in me the thought: By Jove! this is the deuce of an adventure—something you read about; and it is my first voyage as second mate— and I am only twenty—and here I am lasting it out as well as any of these men, and keeping my chaps up to the mark. I was pleased. I would not have given up the experience for worlds. I had moments of exultation. Whenever the old dismantled craft pitched heavily with her counter high in the air, she seemed to me to throw up, like an appeal, like a defiance, like a cry to the clouds without mercy, the words written on her stern: '*Judea,* London. Do or Die.'

   "O youth! The strength of it, the faith of it, the imagination of it! To me she was not an old rattletrap carting about the world a lot of coal for a freight—to me she was the endeavor, the test, the trial of life. I think of her with pleasure, with affection, with regret—as you would think of someone dead you have loved. I shall never forget her. . . . Pass the bottle.

25   "One night when tied to the mast, as I explained, we were pumping on, deafened with the wind, and without spirit enough in us to wish ourselves dead, a heavy sea crashed aboard and swept clean over us. As soon as I got my breath I shouted, as in duty bound, 'Keep on, boys!' when suddenly I felt something hard floating on deck strike the calf of my leg. I made a grab at it and missed. It was so dark we could not see each other's faces within a foot—you understand.

"After that thump the ship kept quiet for a while, and the thing, whatever it was, struck my leg again. This time I caught it—and it was a saucepan. At first, being stupid with fatigue and thinking of nothing but the pumps, I did not understand what I had in my hand. Suddenly it dawned upon me, and I shouted, 'Boys, the house on deck is gone. Leave this, and let's look for the cook.'

"There was a deck-house forward, which contained the galley, the cook's berth, and the quarters of the crew. As we had expected for days to see it swept away, the hands had been ordered to sleep in the cabin—the only safe place in the ship. The steward, Abraham, however, persisted in clinging to his berth, stupidly, like a mule—from sheer fright I believe, like an animal that won't leave a stable falling in an earthquake. So we went to look for him. It was chancing death, since once out of our lashings we were exposed as if on a raft. But we went. The house was shattered as if a shell had exploded inside. Most of it had gone overboard—stove, men's quarters, and their property, all was gone; but two posts, holding a portion of the bulkhead to which Abraham's bunk was attached, remained as if by a miracle. We groped in the ruins and came upon this, and there he was, sitting in his bunk, surrounded by foam and wreckage, jabbering cheerfully to himself. He was out of his mind; completely and forever mad, with this sudden shock coming upon the fag-end of his endurance. We snatched him up, lugged him aft, and pitched him headfirst down the cabin companion. You understand there was no time to carry him down with infinite precautions and wait to see how he got on. Those below would pick him up at the bottom of the stairs all right. We were in a hurry to go back to the pumps. That business could not wait. A bad leak is an inhuman thing.

"One would think that the sole purpose of that fiendish gale had been to make a lunatic of that poor devil of a mulatto. It eased before morning, and the next day the sky cleared, and as the sea went down the leak took up. When it came to bending a fresh set of sails the crew demanded to put back—and really there was nothing else to do. Boats gone, decks swept clean, cabin gutted, men without a stitch but what they stood in, stores spoiled, ship strained. We put her head for home, and—would you believe it? The wind came east right in our teeth. It blew fresh, it blew continuously. We had to beat up every inch of the way, but she did not leak so badly, the water keeping comparatively smooth. Two hours' pumping in every four is no joke—but it kept her afloat as far as Falmouth.

"The good people there live on casualties of the sea, and no doubt were glad to see us. A hungry crowd of shipwrights sharpened their chisels at the sight of that carcass of a ship. And, by Jove! they had pretty pickings off us before they were done. I fancy the owner was already in a tight place. There were delays. Then it was decided to take part of the cargo out and caulk her topsides. This was done, the repairs finished, cargo reshipped; a new crew came on board, and we went out—for Bangkok. At the end of a week we were back again. The crew said they weren't going to Bangkok—a hundred and fifty days' passage—in a something hooker that wanted pumping eight hours out of the twenty-four; and the nautical papers inserted again the little paragraph: '*Judea*. Bark. Tyne to Bangkok; coals; put back to Falmouth leaky and with crew refusing duty.'

30   "There were more delays—more tinkering. The owner came down for a day, and said she was as right as a fiddle. Poor old Captain Beard looked like the ghost of a Geordie[1] skipper—through the worry and humiliation of it. Remember he was sixty, and it was his first command. Mahon said it was a foolish business, and would end badly. I loved the ship more than ever, and wanted awfully to get to Bangkok. To Bangkok! Magic name, blessed name. Mesopotamia wasn't a patch on it. Remember I was twenty, and it was my first second-mate's billet, and the East was waiting for me.

"We went out and anchored in the outer roads with a fresh crew—the third. She leaked worse than ever. It was as if those confounded shipwrights had actually made a hole in her. This time we did not even go outside. The crew simply refused to man the windlass.

"They towed us back to the inner harbor, and we became a fixture, a feature, an institution of the place. People pointed us out to visitors as 'That 'ere barque that's going to Bangkok—has been here six months—put back three times.' On holidays the small boys pulling about in boats would hail, '*Judea*, ahoy!' and if a head showed above the rail shouted, 'Where you bound to?—Bangkok?' and jeered. We were only three on board. The poor old skipper mooned in the cabin. Mahon undertook the cooking, and unexpectedly developed all a Frenchman's genius for preparing nice little messes. I looked languidly after the rigging. We became citizens of Falmouth. Every shopkeeper knew us. At the barber's or to-bacconist's they asked familiarly, 'Do you think you will ever get to Bangkok?' Meantime the owner, the underwriters, and the charterers squabbled amongst themselves in London, and our pay went on. . . . Pass the bottle.

"It was horrid. Morally it was worse than pumping for life. It seemed as though we had been forgotten by the world, belonged to nobody, would get nowhere; it seemed that, as if bewitched, we would have to live for ever and ever in that inner harbor, a derision and a byword to generations of long-shore loafers and dishonest boatmen. I obtained three months' pay and a five days' leave, and made a rush for London. It took me a day to get there and pretty well another to come back—but three months' pay went all the same. I don't know what I did with it. I went to a music-hall, I believe, lunched, dined, and supped in a swell place in Regent Street, and was back in time, with nothing but a complete set of Byron's works and a new railway rug to show for three months' work. The boat-man who pulled me off to the ship said: 'Hallo! I thought you had left the old thing. *She* will never get to Bangkok.' 'That's all *you* know about it,' I said scornfully—but I didn't like that prophecy at all.

"Suddenly a man, some kind of agent to somebody, appeared with full powers. He had grog-blossoms all over his face, an indomitable energy, and was a jolly soul. We leaped into life again. A hulk came alongside, took our cargo, and then we went into dry dock to get our copper stripped. No wonder she leaked. The poor thing, strained beyond endurance by the gale, had, as if in disgust, spat out all the oakum of her lower seams. She was recaulked, new coppered, and made as tight as a bottle. We went back to the hulk and reshipped our cargo.

35   "Then, on a fine moonlight night, all the rats left the ship.

---

[1]Boat for carrying coal—a collier

"We had been infested with them. They had destroyed our sails, consumed more stores than the crew, affably shared our beds and our dangers, and now, when the ship was made seaworthy, concluded to clear out. I called Mahon to enjoy the spectacle. Rat after rat appeared on our rail, took a last look over his shoulder, and leaped with a hollow thud into the empty hulk. We tried to count them, but soon lost the tale. Mahon said: 'Well, well! don't talk to me about the intelligence of rats. They ought to have left before, when we had that narrow squeak from foundering. There you have the proof how silly is the superstition about them. They leave a good ship for an old rotten hulk, where there is nothing to eat, too, the fools! . . . I don't believe they know what is safe or what is good for them, any more than you or I.'

"And after some more talk we agreed that the wisdom of rats had been grossly overrated, being in fact no greater than that of men.

"The story of the ship was known, by this, all up the Channel from Land's End to the Forelands, and we could get no crew on the south coast. They sent us one all complete from Liverpool, and we left once more—for Bangkok.

"We had fair breezes, smooth water right into the tropics, and the old *Judea* lumbered along in the sunshine. When she went eight knots everything cracked aloft, and we tied our caps to our heads; but mostly she strolled on at the rate of three miles an hour. What could you expect. She was tired—that old ship. Her youth was where mine is—where yours is—you fellows who listen to this yarn; and what friend would throw your years and your weariness in your face? We didn't grumble at her. To us aft, at least, it seemed as though we had been born in her, reared in her, had lived in her for ages, had never known any other ship. I would just as soon have abused the old village church at home for not being a cathedral.

40   "And for me there was also my youth to make me patient. There was all the East before me, and all life, and the thought that I had been tried in that ship and had come out pretty well. And I thought of men of old who, centuries ago, went that road in ships that sailed no better, to the land of palms, and spices, and yellow sands, and of brown nations ruled by kings more cruel than Nero the Roman, and more splendid than Solomon the Jew. The old bark lumbered on, heavy with her age and the burden of her cargo, while I lived the life of youth in ignorance and hope. She lumbered on through an interminable procession of days; and the fresh gilding flashed back at the setting sun, seemed to cry out over the darkening sea the words painted on her stern, '*Judea*, London. Do or Die.'

"Then we entered the Indian Ocean and steered northerly for Java Head. The winds were light. Weeks slipped by. She crawled on, do or die, and people at home began to think of posting us as overdue.

"One Saturday evening, I being off duty, the men asked me to give them an extra bucket of water or so—for washing clothes. As I did not wish to screw on the fresh-water pump so late, I went forward whistling, and with a key in my hand to unlock the forepeak scuttle, intending to serve the water out of a spare tank we kept there.

"The smell down below was as unexpected as it was frightful. One would have thought hundreds of paraffin-lamps had been flaring and smoking in that hole for days. I was glad to get out. The man with me coughed and said, 'Funny smell, sir.' I answered negligently, 'It's good for the health they say,' and walked aft.

"The first thing I did was to put my head down the square of the midship ventilator. As I lifted the lid a visible breath, something like a thin fog, a puff of faint haze, rose from the opening. The ascending air was hot, and had a heavy, sooty, paraffiny smell. I gave one sniff, and put down the lid gently. It was no use choking myself. The cargo was on fire.

45   "Next day she began to smoke in earnest. You see it was to be expected, for though the coal was of a safe kind, that cargo had been so handled, so broken up with handling, that it looked more like smithy coal than anything else. Then it had been wetted—more than once. It rained all the time we were taking it back from the hulk, and now with this long passage it got heated, and there was another case of spontaneous combustion.

"The captain called us into the cabin. He had a chart spread on the table, and looked unhappy. He said, 'The coast of West Australia is near, but I mean to proceed to our destination. It is the hurricane month, too; but we will just keep her head for Bangkok, and fight the fire. No more putting back anywhere, if we all get roasted. We will try first to stifle this 'ere damned combustion by want of air.'

"We tried. We battened down everything, and still she smoked. The smoke kept coming out through imperceptible crevices; it forced itself through bulkheads and covers; it oozed here and there and everywhere in slender threads, in an invisible film, in an incomprehensible manner. It made its way into the cabin, into the forecastle; it poisoned the sheltered places on the deck, it could be sniffed as high as the mainyard. It was clear that if the smoke came out the air came in. This was disheartening. This combustion refused to be stifled.

"We resolved to try water, and took the hatches off. Enormous volumes of smoke, whitish, yellowish, thick, greasy, misty, choking, ascended as high as the trucks. All hands cleared out aft. Then the poisonous cloud blew away, and we went back to work in a smoke that was no thicker now than that of an ordinary factory chimney.

"We rigged the force-pump, got the hose along, and by and by it burst. Well, it was as old as the ship—a prehistoric hose, and past repair. Then we pumped with the feeble head-pump, drew water with buckets, and in this way managed in time to pour lots of Indian Ocean into the main hatch. The bright stream flashed in sunshine, fell into a layer of white crawling smoke, and vanished on the black surface of coal. Steam ascended mingling with the smoke. We poured salt water as into a barrel without a bottom. It was our fate to pump in that ship, to pump out of her, to pump into her; and after keeping water out of her to save ourselves from being drowned, we frantically poured water into her to save ourselves from being burned.

50   "And she crawled on, do or die, in the serene weather. The sky was a miracle of purity, a miracle of azure. The sea was polished, was blue, was pellucid, was sparkling like a precious stone, extending on all sides, all round to the horizon— as if the whole terrestrial globe had been one jewel, one colossal sapphire, a single gem fashioned into a planet. And on the luster of the great calm waters the *Judea* glided imperceptibly, enveloped in languid and unclean vapors, in a lazy cloud that drifted to leeward, light and slow; a pestiferous cloud defiling the splendor of sea and sky.

"All this time of course we saw no fire. The cargo smoldered at the bottom somewhere. Once Mahon, as we were working side by side, said to me with a queer smile: 'Now, if she only would spring a tidy leak—like that time when we first left the Channel—it would put a stopper on this fire. Wouldn't it?' I remarked irrelevantly, 'Do you remember the rats?'

"We fought the fire and sailed the ship too as carefully as though nothing had been the matter. The steward cooked and attended on us. Of the other twelve men, eight worked while four rested. Everyone took his turn, captain included. There was equality, and if not exactly fraternity, then a deal of good feeling. Sometimes a man, as he dashed a bucketful of water down the hatchway, would yell out, 'Hurrah for Bangkok!' and the rest laughed. But generally we were taciturn and serious—and thirsty. Oh! how thirsty! And we had to be careful with the water. Strict allowance. The ship smoked, the sun blazed. . . . Pass the bottle.

"We tried everything. We even made an attempt to dig down to the fire. No good, of course. No man could remain more than a minute below. Mahon, who went first, fainted there, and the man who went to fetch him out did likewise. We lugged them out on deck. Then I leaped down to show how easily it could be done. They had learned wisdom by that time, and contented themselves by fishing for me with a chain-hook tied to a broom-handle, I believe. I did not offer to go and fetch up my shovel, which was left down below.

"Things began to look bad. We put the long-boat into the water. The second boat was ready to swing out. We had also another, a 14-foot thing, on davits aft, where it was quite safe.

"Then, behold, the smoke suddenly decreased. We redoubled our efforts to flood the bottom of the ship. In two days there was no smoke at all. Everybody was on the broad grin. This was on a Friday. On Saturday no work, but sailing the ship of course, was done. The men washed their clothes and their faces for the first time in a fortnight, and had a special dinner given them. They spoke of spontaneous combustion with contempt, and implied *they* were the boys to put out combustions. Somehow we all felt as though we each had inherited a large fortune. But a beastly smell of burning hung about the ship. Captain Beard had hollow eyes and sunken cheeks. I had never noticed so much before how twisted and bowed he was. He and Mahon prowled soberly about hatches and ventilators, sniffing. It struck me suddenly poor Mahon was a very, very old chap. As to me, I was as pleased and proud as though I had helped to win a great naval battle. O! Youth!

"The night was fine. In the morning a homeward-bound ship passed us hull down—the first we had seen for months; but we were nearing the land at last, Java Head being about 190 miles off, and nearly due north.

"Next day it was my watch on deck from eight to twelve. At breakfast the captain observed, 'It's wonderful how that smell hangs about the cabin.' About ten, the mate being on the poop, I stepped down on the main-deck for a moment. The carpenter's bench stood abaft the mainmast: I leaned against it sucking at my pipe, and the carpenter, a young chap, came to talk to me. He remarked, 'I think we have done very well, haven't we?' and then I perceived with annoyance the fool was trying to tilt the bench. I said curtly, 'Don't, Chips,' and immediately became aware of a queer sensation, of an absurd delusion,—I seemed somehow to be in the air. I heard all round me like a pent-up breath released—as if a thousand giants simultaneously had said Phoo!—and felt a dull concussion which made my ribs ache suddenly. No doubt about it—I was in the air, and my body was describing a short parabola. But short as it was, I had the time to think several thoughts in, as far as I can remember, the following order: 'This can't be the carpenter—What is it?—Some accident—Submarine volcano?—Coals, gas!—By Jove! we are being blown up—Everybody's dead—I am falling into the afterhatch—I see fire in it.'

"The coal-dust suspended in the air of the hold had glowed dull-red at the moment of the explosion. In the twinkling of an eye, in an infinitesimal fraction of a second since the first tilt of the bench, I was sprawling full length on the cargo. I picked myself up and scrambled out. It was quick like a rebound. The deck was a wilderness of smashed timber, lying crosswise like trees in a wood after a hurricane; an immense curtain of soiled rags waved gently before me—it was the mainsail blown to strips. I thought, The masts will be toppling over directly; and to get out of the way bolted on all-fours towards the poop-ladder. The first person I saw was Mahon, with eyes like saucers, his mouth open, and the long white hair standing straight on end round his head like a silver halo. He was just about to go down when the sight of the main-deck stirring, heaving up, and changing into splinters before his eyes, petrified him on the top step. I stared at him in unbelief, and he stared at me with a queer kind of shocked curiosity. I did not know that I had no hair, no eyebrows, no eyelashes, that my young moustache was burnt off, that my face was black, one cheek laid open, my nose cut, and my chin bleeding. I had lost my cap, one of my slippers, and my shirt was torn to rags. Of all this I was not aware. I was amazed to see the ship still afloat, the poop-deck whole—and, most of all, to see anybody alive. Also the peace of the sky and the serenity of the sea were distinctly surprising. I suppose I expected to see them convulsed with horror. . . . Pass the bottle.

"There was a voice hailing the ship from somewhere—in the air, in the sky—I couldn't tell. Presently I saw the captain—and he was mad. He asked me eagerly, 'Where's the cabin-table?' and to hear such a question was a frightful shock. I had just been blown up, you understand, and vibrated with that experience,—I wasn't quite sure whether I was alive. Mahon began to stamp with both feet and yelled at him, 'Good God! don't you see the deck's blown out of her?' I found my voice, and stammered out as if conscious of some gross neglect of duty, 'I don't know where the cabin-table is.' It was like an absurd dream.

60   "Do you know what he wanted next? Well, he wanted to trim the yards. Very placidly, and as if lost in thought, he insisted on having the foreyard squared. 'I don't know if there's anybody alive,' said Mahon, almost tearfully. 'Surely,' he said, gently, 'there will be enough left to square the foreyard.'

"The old chap, it seems, was in his own berth winding up the chronometers, when the shock sent him spinning. Immediately it occurred to him—as he said afterwards—that the ship had struck something, and he ran out into the cabin. There, he saw, the cabin-table had vanished somewhere. The deck being blown up, it had fallen down into the lazarette[1] of course. Where we had our breakfast that morning he saw only a great hole in the floor. This appeared to him so awfully mysterious, and impressed him so immensely, that what he saw and heard after he got on deck were mere trifles in comparison. And, mark, he noticed directly the wheel deserted and his bark off her course—and his only thought was to get that miserable, stripped, undecked, smoldering shell of a ship back again with her head pointing at her port of destination. Bangkok! That's what he was after. I tell you this quiet, bowed, bandy-legged, almost deformed little man was immense in the singleness of his idea and in his placid ignorance of our agitation. He motioned us forward with a commanding gesture, and went to take the wheel himself.

"Yes; that was the first thing we did—trim the yards of that wreck! No one was killed, or even disabled, but everyone was more or less hurt. You should have

_____
[1]A storeroom, in between decks

seen them! Some were in rags, with black faces, like coal-heavers, like sweeps, and had bullet heads that seemed closely cropped, but were in fact singed to the skin. Others, of the watch below, awakened by being shot out from their collapsing bunks, shivered incessantly, and kept on groaning even as we went about our work. But they all worked. That crew of Liverpool hard cases had in them the right stuff. It's my experience they always have. It is the sea that gives it—the vastness, the loneliness surrounding their dark stolid souls. Ah! Well! we stumbled, we crept, we fell, we barked our shins on the wreckage, we hauled. The masts stood, but we did not know how much they might be charred down below. It was nearly calm, but a long swell ran from the west and made her roll. They might go at any moment. We looked at them with apprehension. One could not foresee which way they would fall.

"Then we retreated aft and looked about us. The deck was a tangle of planks on edge, of planks on end, of splinters, of ruined woodwork. The masts rose from that chaos like big trees above a matted undergrowth. The interstices of that mass of wreckage were full of something whitish, sluggish, stirring—of something that was like a greasy fog. The smoke of the invisible fire was coming up again, was trailing, like a poisonous thick mist in some valley choked with dead wood. Already lazy wisps were beginning to curl upwards amongst the mass of splinters. Here and there a piece of timber, stuck upright, resembled a post. Half of a fiferail had been shot through the foresail, and the sky made a patch of glorious blue in the ignobly soiled canvas. A portion of several boards holding together had fallen across the rail, and one end protruded overboard, like a gangway leading upon nothing, like a gangway leading over the deep sea, leading to death—as if inviting us to walk the plank at once and be done with our ridiculous troubles. And still the air, the sky—a ghost, something invisible was hailing the ship.

"Someone had the sense to look over, and there was the helmsman, who had impulsively jumped overboard, anxious to come back. He yelled and swam lustily like a merman, keeping up with the ship. We threw him a rope, and presently he stood amongst us streaming with water and very crestfallen. The captain had surrendered the wheel, and apart, elbow on rail and chin in hand, gazed at the sea wistfully. We asked ourselves, What next? I thought, Now, this is something like. This is great. I wonder what will happen. O youth!

65

"Suddenly Mahon sighted a steamer far astern. Captain Beard said, 'We may do something with her yet.' We hoisted two flags, which said in the international language of the sea, 'On fire. Want immediate assistance.' The steamer grew bigger rapidly, and by and by spoke with two flags on her foremast, 'I am coming to your assistance.'

"In half an hour she was abreast, to windward, within hail, and rolling slightly, with her engines stopped. We lost our composure, and yelled all together with excitement, 'We've been blown up!' A man in a white helmet, on the bridge, cried, 'Yes! All right! all right!' and he nodded his head, and smiled, and made soothing motions with his hand as though at a lot of frightened children. One of the boats dropped in the water, and walked towards us upon the sea with her long oars. Four Calashes pulled a swinging stroke. This was my first sight of Malay seamen. I've known them since, but what struck me then was their unconcern: they came alongside, and even the bowman standing up and holding to our mainchains with the boat-hook did not deign to lift his head for a glance. I thought people who had been blown up deserved more attention.

"A little man, dry like a chip and agile like a monkey, clambered up. It was the mate of the steamer. He gave one look, and cried, 'O boys—you had better quit.'

"We were silent. He talked apart with the captain for a time,—seemed to argue with him. Then they went away together to the steamer.

"When our skipper came back we learned that the steamer was the *Somerville,* Captain Nash, from West Australia to Singapore *via* Batavia with mails, and that the agreement was she should tow us to Anjer or Batavia, if possible, where we could extinguish the fire by scuttling, and then proceed on our voyage—to Bangkok! The old man seemed excited. 'We will do it yet,' he said to Mahon, fiercely. He shook his fist at the sky. Nobody else said a word.

70   "At noon the steamer began to tow. She went ahead slim and high, and what was left of the *Judea* followed at the end of seventy fathom of tow-rope,—followed her swiftly like a cloud of smoke with mast-heads protruding above. We went aloft to furl the sails. We coughed on the yards, and were careful about the bunts. Do you see the lot of us there, putting a neat furl on the sails of that ship doomed to arrive nowhere? There was not a man who didn't think that at any moment the masts would topple over. From aloft we could not see the ship for smoke, and they worked carefully, passing the gaskets with even turns. 'Harbor furl—aloft there!' cried Mahon from below.

"You understand this? I don't think one of those chaps expected to get down in the usual way. When we did I heard them saying to each other, 'Well, I thought we would come down overboard, in a lump—sticks and all—blame me if I didn't.' 'That's what I was thinking to myself,' would answer wearily another battered and bandaged scarecrow. And, mind, these were men without the drilled-in habit of obedience. To an onlooker they would be a lot of profane scallywags without a redeeming point. What made them do it—what made them obey me when I, thinking consciously how fine it was, made them drop the bunt of the forsail twice to try and do it better? What? They had no professional reputation—no examples, no praise. It wasn't a sense of duty; they all knew well enough how to shirk, and laze, and dodge—when they had a mind to it—and mostly they had. Was it the two pounds ten a-month that sent them there? They didn't think their pay half good enough. No; it was something in them, something inborn and subtle and everlasting. I don't say positively that the crew of a French or German merchantman wouldn't have done it, but I doubt whether it would have been done in the same way. There was a completeness in it, something solid like a principle, and masterful like an instinct—a disclosure of something secret—of that hidden something, that gift of good or evil that makes racial difference, that shapes the fate of nations.

"It was that night at ten that, for the first time since we had been fighting it, we saw the fire. The speed of the towing had fanned the smoldering destruction. A blue gleam appeared forward, shining below the wreck of the deck. It wavered in patches, it seemed to stir and creep like the light of a glowworm. I saw it first, and told Mahon. 'Then the game's up,' he said. 'We had better stop this towing, or she will burst out suddenly fore and aft before we can clear out.' We set up a yell; rang bells to attract their attention; they towed on. At last Mahon and I had to crawl forward and cut the rope with an axe. There was no time to cast off the lashings. Red tongues could be seen licking the wilderness of splinters under our feet as we made our way back to the poop.

"Of course they very soon found out in the steamer that the rope was gone. She gave a loud blast of her whistle, her lights were seen sweeping in a wide circle, she came up ranging close alongside, and stopped. We were all in a tight group on the poop looking at her. Every man had saved a little bundle or a bag. Suddenly a conical flame with a twisted top shot up forward and threw upon the black sea a circle of light, with two vessels side by side and heaving gently in its centre. Captain Beard had been sitting on the gratings still and mute for hours, but now he rose slowly and advanced in front of us, to the mizzen-shrouds. Captain Nash hailed: 'Come along! Look sharp. I have mail-bags on board. I will take you and your boats to Singapore.'

" 'Thank you! No!' said our skipper. 'We must see the last of the ship.'

75   " 'I can't stand by any longer,' shouted the other. 'Mails—you know.'

" 'Ay! ay! We are all right.'

" 'Very well! I'll report you in Singapore. . . . Good-bye!'

"He waved his hand. Our men dropped their bundles quietly. The steamer moved ahead, and pasing out of the circle of light, vanished at once from our sight, dazzled by the fire which burned fiercely. And then I knew that I would see the East first as commander of a small boat. I thought it fine; and the fidelity to the old ship was fine. We should see the last of her. Oh, the glamor of youth! Oh! the fire of it, more dazzling than the flames of the burning ship, throwing a magic light on the wide earth, leaping audaciously to the sky, presently to be quenched by time, more cruel, more pitiless, more bitter than the sea—and like the flames of the burning ship surrounded by an impenetrable night.

"The old man warned us in his gentle and inflexible way that it was part of our duty to save for the underwriters as much as we could of the ship's gear. Accordingly we went to work aft, while she blazed forward to give us plenty of light. We lugged out a lot of rubbish. What didn't we save? An old barometer fixed with an absurd quantity of screws nearly cost me my life: a sudden rush of smoke came upon me, and I just got away in time. There were various stores, bolts of canvas, coils of rope; the poop looked like a marine bazaar, and the boats were lumbered to the gunwales. One would have thought the old man wanted to take as much as he could of his first command with him. He was very, very quiet, but off his balance evidently. Would you believe it? He wanted to take a length of old stream-cable and a kedge-anchor with him in the long-boat. We said, 'Ay, ay, sir,' deferentially, and on the quiet let the things slip overboard. The heavy medicine-chest went that way, two bags of green coffee, tins of paint—fancy, paint!—a whole lot of things. Then I was ordered with two hands into the boats to make a stowage and get them ready against the time it would be proper for us to leave the ship.

80   "We put everything straight, stepped the long-boat's mast for our skipper, who was to take charge of her, and I was not sorry to sit down for a moment. My face felt raw, every limb ached as if broken, I was aware of all my ribs, and would have sworn to a twist in the backbone. The boats, fast astern, lay in a deep shadow, and all around I could see the circle of the sea lighted by the fire. A gigantic flame arose forward straight and clear. It flared fierce, with noises like the whirr of wings, with rumbles as of thunder. There were cracks, detonations, and from the cone of flame the sparks flew upwards, as man is born to trouble, to leaky ships, and to ships that burn.

"What bothered me was that the ship, lying broadside to the swell and to such wind as there was—a mere breath—the boats would not keep astern where they were safe, but persisted, in a pig-headed way boats have, in getting under the counter and then swinging alongside. They were knocking about dangerously and coming near the flame, while the ship rolled on them, and, of course, there was always the danger of the masts going over the side at any moment. I and my two boat-keepers kept them off as best we could, with oars and boat-hooks; but to be constantly at it became exasperating, since there was no reason why we should not leave at once. We could not see those on board, nor could we imagine what caused the delay. The boat-keepers were swearing feebly, and I had not only my share of the work but also had to keep at it two men who showed a constant inclination to lay themselves down and let things slide.

"At last I hailed, 'On deck there,' and someone looked over. 'We're ready here,' I said. The head disappeared, and very soon popped up again. 'The captain says, All right, sir, and to keep the boats well clear of the ship.'

"Half an hour passed. Suddenly there was a frightful racket, rattle, clanking of chain, hiss of water, and millions of sparks flew up into the shivering column of smoke that stood leaning slightly above the ship. The cat-heads had burned away, and the two red-hot anchors had gone to the bottom, tearing out after them two hundred fathom of red-hot chain. The ship trembled, the mass of flame swayed as if ready to collapse, and the fore top-gallant-mast fell. It darted down like an arrow of fire, shot under, and instantly leaping up within an oar's-length of the boats, floated quietly, very black on the luminous sea. I hailed the deck again. After some time a man in an unexpectedly cheerful but also muffled tone, as though he had been trying to speak with his mouth shut, informed me, 'Coming directly, sir,' and vanished. For a long time I heard nothing but the whirr and roar of the fire. There were also whistling sounds. The boats jumped, tugged at the painters, ran at each other playfully, knocked their sides together, or, do what we would, swung in a bunch against the ship's side. I couldn't stand it any longer, and swarming up a rope, clambered aboard over the stern.

"It was as bright as day. Coming up like this, the sheet of fire facing me was a terrifying sight, and the heat seemed hardly bearable at first. On a settee cushion dragged out of the cabin Captain Beard, his legs drawn up and one arm under his head, slept with the light playing on him. Do you know what the rest were busy about? They were sitting on deck right aft, round an open case, eating bread and cheese and drinking bottled stout.

85   "On the background of flames twisting in fierce tongues above their heads they seemed at home like salamanders,[1] and looked like a band of desperate pirates. The fire sparkled in the whites of their eyes, gleamed on patches of white skin seen through the torn shirts. Each had the marks as of a battle about him— bandaged heads, tied-up arms, a strip of dirty rag round a knee—and each man had a bottle between his legs and a chunk of cheese in his hand. Mahon got up. With his handsome and disreputable head, his hooked profile, his long white beard, and with an uncorked bottle in his hand, he resembled one of those reckless sea-robbers of old, making merry amidst violence and disaster. 'The last meal on board,' he explained solemnly. 'We had nothing to eat all day, and it was no use leaving all this.' He flourished the bottle and indicated the sleeping skipper. 'He said he couldn't swallow anything, so I got him to lie down,' he went on; and as I stared, 'I don't know whether you are aware, young fellow, the man had no sleep to speak of for days—and there will be dam' little sleep in the boats.' 'There will be no boats by-and-by if you fool about much longer,' I said, indignantly. I walked

---

[1] In mythology salamanders can live in fire without being burned

up to the skipper and shook him by the shoulder. At last he opened his eyes, but did not move. 'Time to leave her, sir,' I said quietly.

"He got up painfully, looked at the flames, at the sea sparkling round the ship, and black, black as ink farther away; he looked at the stars shining dim through a thin veil of smoke in a sky black, black as Erebus.[1]

" 'Youngest first,' he said.

"And the ordinary seaman, wiping his mouth with the back of his hand, got up, clambered over the taffrail, and vanished. Others followed. One, on the point of going over, stopped short to drain his bottle, and with a great swing of his arm flung it at the fire. 'Take this!' he cried.

"The skipper lingered disconsolately, and we left him to commune alone for a while with his first command. Then I went up again and brought him away at last. It was time. The ironwork on the poop was hot to the touch.

90

"Then the painter of the long-boat was cut, and the three boats, tied together, drifted clear of the ship. It was just sixteen hours after the explosion when we abandoned her. Mahon had charge of the second boat, and I had the smallest— the 14-foot thing. The long-boat would have taken the lot of us; but the skipper said we must save as much property as we could—for the underwriters—and so I got my first command. I had two men with me, a bag of biscuits, a few tins of meat, and a breaker of water. I was ordered to keep close to the long-boat, that in case of bad weather we might be taken into her.

"And do you know what I thought? I thought I would part company as soon as I could. I wanted to have my first command all to myself. I wasn't going to sail in a squadron if there were a chance for independent cruising. I would make land by myself. I would beat the other boats. Youth! All youth! The silly, charming, beautiful youth.

"But we did not make a start at once. We must see the last of the ship. And so the boats drifted about that night, heaving and setting on the swell. The men dozed, waked, sighed, groaned. I looked at the burning ship.

"Between the darkness of earth and heaven she was burning fiercely upon a disc of purple sea shot by the blood-red play of gleams; upon a disc of water glittering and sinister. A high, clear flame, an immense and lonely flame, ascended from the ocean, and from its summit the black smoke poured continuously at the sky. She burned furiously; mournful and imposing like a funeral pile kindled in the night, surrounded by the sea, watched over by the stars. A magnificent death had come like a grace, like a gift, like a reward to that old ship at the end of her laborious days. The surrender of her weary ghost to the keeping of stars and sea was stirring like the sight of a glorious triumph. The masts fell just before daybreak, and for a moment there was a burst and turmoil of sparks that seemed to fill with flying fire the night patient and watchful, the vast night lying silent upon the sea. At daylight she was only a charred shell, floating still under a cloud of smoke and bearing a glowing mass of coal within.

"Then the oars were got out, and the boats forming in a line moved round her remains as if in procession—the long-boat leading. As we pulled across her stern a slim dart of fire shot out viciously at us, and suddenly she went down, head first, in a great hiss of steam. The unconsumed stern was the last to sink; but the paint had gone, had cracked, had peeled off, and there were no letters, there was

[1]The outskirts of Hades

no word, no stubborn device that was like her soul, to flash at the rising sun her creed and her name.

95 "We made our way north. A breeze sprang up, and about noon all the boats came together for the last time. I had no mast or sail in mine, but I made a mast out of a space oar and hoisted a boat-awning for a sail, with a boat-hook for a yard. She was certainly over-masted, but I had the satisfaction of knowing that with the wind aft I could beat the other two. I had to wait for them. Then we all had a look at the captain's chart, and, after a sociable meal of hard bread and water, got our last instructions. They were simple: steer north, and keep together as much as possible. 'Be careful with that jury-rig, Marlow,' said the captain; and Mahon, as I sailed proudly past his boat, wrinkled his curved nose and hailed, 'You will sail that ship of yours under water, if you don't look out, young fellow.' He was a malicious old man—and may the deep sea where he sleeps now rock him gently, rock him tenderly to the end of time!

"Before sunset a thick rain-squall passed over the two boats, which were far astern, and that was the last I saw of them for a time. Next day I sat steering my cockle-shell—my first command—with nothing but water and sky around me. I did sight in the afternoon the upper sails of a ship far away, but said nothing, and my men did not notice her. You see I was afraid she might be homeward bound, and I had no mind to turn back from the portals of the East. I was steering for Java—another blessed name—like Bangkok, you know. I steered many days.

"I need not tell you what it is to be knocking about in an open boat. I remember nights and days of calm, when we pulled, we pulled, and the boat seemed to stand still, as if bewitched within the circle of the sea horizon. I remember the heat, the deluge of rain-squalls that kept us bailing for dear life (but filled our water cask), and I remember sixteen hours on end with a mouth dry as a cinder and a steering-oar over the stern to keep my first command head on to a breaking sea. I did not know how good a man I was till then. I remember the drawn faces, the dejected figures of my two men, and I remember my youth and the feeling that will never come back any more—the feeling that I could last for ever, outlast the sea, the earth, and all men; the deceitful feeling that lures us on to joys, to perils, to love, to vain effort—to death; the triumphant conviction of strength, the heat of life in the handful of dust, the glow in the heart that with every year grows dim, grows cold, grows small, and expires—and expires, too soon, too soon—before life itself.

"And this is how I see the East. I have seen its secret places and have looked into its very soul; but now I see it always from a small boat, a high outline of mountains, blue and afar in the morning; like faint mist at noon; a jagged wall of purple at sunset. I have the feel of the oar in my hand, the vision of a scorching blue sea in my eyes. And I see a bay, a wide bay, smooth as glass and polished like ice, shimmering in the dark. A red light burns far off upon the gloom of the land, and the night is soft and warm. We drag at the oars with aching arms, and suddenly a puff of wind, a puff faint and tepid and laden with strange odors of blossoms, of aromatic wood, comes out of the still night—the first sigh of the East on my face. That I can never forget. It was impalpable and enslaving, like a charm, like a whispered promise of mysterious delight.

"We had been pulling this finishing spell for eleven hours. Two pulled, and he whose turn it was to rest sat at the tiller. We had made out the red light in that bay and steered for it, guessing it must mark some small coasting port. We passed two vessels, outlandish and high-sterned, sleeping at anchor, and, approaching the light, now very dim, ran the boat's nose against the end of a jutting wharf. We were blind with fatigue. My men dropped the oars and fell off the thwarts as if dead. I made fast to a pile. A current rippled softly. The scented obscurity of the shore was grouped into vast masses, a density of colossal clumps of vegetation, probably—mute and fantastic shapes. And at their foot the semi-circle of a beach gleamed faintly, like an illusion. There was not a light, not a stir, not a sound. The mysterious East faced me, perfumed like a flower, silent like death, dark like a grave.

100   "And I sat weary beyond expression, exulting like a conqueror, sleepless and entranced as if before a profound, a fateful enigma.

"A splashing of oars, a measured dip reverberating on the level of water, inten-sified by the silence of the shore into loud claps, made me jump up. A boat, a European boat, was coming in. I invoked the name of the dead; I hailed: *Judea* ahoy! A thin shout answered.

"It was the captain. I had beaten the flagship by three hours, and I was glad to hear the old man's voice again, tremulous and tired. 'Is it you, Marlow?' 'Mind the end of that jetty, sir,' I cried.

"He approached cautiously, and brought up with the deep-sea lead-line which we had saved—for the underwriters. I eased my painter and fell along-side. He sat, a broken figure at the stern, wet with dew, his hands clasped in his lap. His men were asleep already. 'I had a terrible time of it,' he murmured. 'Mahon is behind—not very far.' We conversed in whispers, in low whispers, as if afraid to wake up the land. Guns, thunder, earthquakes would not have awakened the men just then.

"Looking round as we talked, I saw away at sea a bright light traveling in the night. 'There's a steamer passing the bay,' I said. She was not passing, she was entering, and she even came close and anchored. 'I wish,' said the old man, 'you would find out whether she is English. Perhaps they could give us a passage somewhere.' He seemed nervously anxious. So by dint of punching and kicking I started one of my men into a state of somnambulism, and giving him an oar, took another and pulled towards the lights of the steamer.

105   "There was a murmur of voices in her, metallic hollow clangs of the engineroom, footsteps on the deck. Her ports shone, round like dilated eyes. Shapes moved about, and there was a shadowy man high up on the bridge. He heard my oars.

"And then, before I could open my lips, the East spoke to me, but it was in a Western voice. A torrent of words was poured into the enigmatical, the fateful silence; outlandish, angry words, mixed with words and even whole sentences of good English, less strange but even more surprising. The voice swore and cursed violently; it riddled the solemn peace of the bay by a volley of abuse. It began by calling me Pig, and from that went crescendo into unmentionable adjectives—in English. The man up there raged aloud in two languages, and with a sincerity in his fury that almost convinced me I had, in some way, sinned against the harmony of the universe. I could hardly see him, but began to think he would work himself into a fit.

"Suddenly he ceased, and I could hear him snorting and blowing like a porpoise. I said—

" 'What steamer is this, pray?'

" 'Eh? What's this? And who are you?'

110   " 'Castaway crew of an English bark burnt at sea. We came here to-night. I am the second mate. The captain is in the long-boat, and wishes to know if you would give us a passage somewhere.'

" 'Oh, my goodness! I say. . . . This is the *Celestial* from Singapore on her return trip. I'll arrange with your captain in the morning, . . . and, . . . I say, . . . did you hear me just now?'

" 'I should think the whole bay heard you.'

" 'I thought you were a shore-boat. Now, look here—this infernal lazy scoundrel of a caretaker has gone to sleep again—curse him. The light is out, and I nearly ran foul of the end of this damned jetty. This is the third time he plays me this trick. Now, I ask you, can anybody stand this kind of thing? It's enough to drive a man out of his mind. I'll report him. . . . I'll get the Assistant Resident to give him the sack, by . . . ! See—there's no light. It's out, isn't it? I take you to witness the light's out. There should be a light, you know. A red light on the—'

" 'There was a light,' I said, mildly.

115   " 'But it's out, man! What's the use of talking like this? You can see for yourself it's out—don't you? If you had to take a valuable steamer along this God-forsaken coast you would want a light, too. I'll kick him from end to end of his miserable wharf. You'll see if I don't. I will—'

" 'So I may tell my captain you'll take us?' I broke in.

" 'Yes, I'll take you. Good-night,' he said, brusquely.

"I pulled back, made fast again to the jetty, and then went to sleep at last. I had faced the silence of the East. I had heard some of its language. But when I opened my eyes again the silence was as complete as though it had never been broken. I was lying in a flood of light, and the sky had never looked so far, so high, before. I opened my eyes and lay without moving.

"And then I saw the men of the East—they were looking at me. The whole length of the jetty was full of people. I saw brown, bronze, yellow faces, the black eyes, the glitter, the color of an Eastern crowd. And all these beings stared without a murmur, without a sigh, without a movement. They stared down at the boats, at the sleeping men who at night had come to them from the sea. Nothing moved. The fronds of palms stood still against the sky. Not a branch stirred along the shore, and the brown roofs of hidden houses peeped through the green foliage, through the big leaves that hung shining and still like leaves forged of heavy metal. This was the East of the ancient navigators, so old, so mysterious, resplendent and somber, living and unchanged, full of danger and promise. And these were the men. I sat up suddenly. A wave of movement passed through the crowd from end to end, passed along the heads, swayed the bodies, ran along the jetty like a ripple on the water, like a breath of wind on a field—and all was still again. I see it now—the wide sweep of the bay, the glittering sands, the wealth of green infinite and varied, the sea blue like the sea of a dream, the crowd of attentive faces, the blaze of vivid color—the water reflecting it all, the curve of the shore, the jetty, the high-sterned outlandish craft floating still, and the three boats with the tired men from the West sleeping, unconscious of the land and the people and of the violence of sunshine. They slept thrown across the thwarts, curled on bottom-boards, in the careless attitudes of death. The head of the old skipper, leaning back in the stern of the long-boat, had fallen on his breast, and he looked as though he would never wake. Farther out old Mahon's face was upturned to the sky, with the long white beard spread out on his breast, as though he had been shot where he sat at the tiller; and a man, all in a heap in the bows of the boat, slept with both arms embracing the stem-head and with his cheek laid on the gunwale. The East looked at them without a sound.

120   "I have known its fascination since; I have seen the mysterious shores, the still

water, the lands of brown nations, where a stealthy Nemesis lies in wait, pursues, overtakes so many of the conquering race, who are proud of their wisdom, of their knowledge, of their strength. But for me all the East is contained in that vision of my youth. It is all in that moment when I opened my young eyes on it. I came upon it from a tussle with the sea—and I was young—and I saw it looking at me. And this is all that is left of it! Only a moment; a moment of strength, of romance, of glamor—of youth! . . . A flick of sunshine upon a strange shore, the time to remember, the time for a sigh, and—good-bye!—Night—Good-bye . . . !"

He drank.

"Ah! The good old time—the good old time. Youth and the sea. Glamor and the sea! The good, strong sea, the salt, bitter sea, that could whisper to you and roar at you and knock your breath out of you."

He drank again.

"By all that's wonderful it is the sea, I believe, the sea itself—or is it youth alone? Who can tell? But you here—you all had something out of life: money, love—whatever one gets on shore—and, tell me, wasn't that the best time, that time when we were young at sea; young and had nothing, on the sea that gives nothing, except hard knocks—and sometimes a chance to feel your strength—that only—what you all regret?"

125   And we all nodded at him: the man of finance, the man of accounts, the man of law, we all nodded at him over the polished table that like a still sheet of brown water reflected our faces, lined, wrinkled; our faces marked by toil, by deceptions, by success, by love; our weary eyes looking still, looking always, looking anxiously for something out of life, that while it is expected is already gone—has passed unseen, in a sigh, in a flash—together with the youth, with the strength, with the romance of illusions.

Virginia Woolf
A Haunted House

Virginia Woolf (1882–1941) is best known as a novelist, but she made much of her living by writing essays for periodicals. She was educated at home; she married Leonard Woolf in 1912. The two writers established the Hogarth Press in 1917, publishing early work of T. S. Eliot, among others. The Woolfs were at the center of the influential Bloomsbury group of artists and writers in England during the twenties and thirties. Virginia suffered nervous breakdowns on more than one occasion, and drowned herself in 1941. She wrote feminist essays, biography, critical essays, and short stories as well as novels: *The Voyage Out* (1915), *Night and Day* (1919), *Jacob's Room* (1922), *Mrs. Dalloway* (1925), *To the Lighthouse* (1927), *Orlando* (1928), *The Waves* (1931), and *The Years* (1937).

Whatever hour you woke there was a door shutting. From room to room they went, hand in hand, lifting here, opening there, making sure—a ghostly couple.

"Here we left it," she said. And he added, "Oh, but here too!" "It's upstairs," she murmured. "And in the garden," he whispered. "Quietly," they said, "or we shall wake them."

But it wasn't that you woke us. Oh, no. "They're looking for it; they're drawing the curtain," one might say, and so read on a page or two. "Now they've found it," one would be certain, stopping the pencil on the margin. And then, tired of reading, one might rise and see for oneself, the house all empty, the doors standing open, only the wood pigeons bubbling with content and the hum of the threshing machine sounding from the farm. "What did I come in here for? What did I want to find?" My hands were empty. "Perhaps it's upstairs then?" The apples were in the loft. And so down again, the garden still as ever, only the book had slipped into the grass.

But they had found it in the drawing-room. Not that one could ever see them. The window panes reflected apples, reflected roses; all the leaves were green in the glass. If they moved in the drawing-room, the apple only turned its yellow side. Yet, the moment after, if the door was opened, spread about the floor, hung upon the walls, pendant from the ceiling—what? My hands were empty. The shadow of a thrush crossed the carpet; from the deepest wells of silence the wood pigeon drew its bubble of sound. "Safe, safe, safe," the pulse of the house beat softly. "The treasure buried; the room . . ." the pulse stopped short. Oh, was that the buried treasure?

5   A moment later the light had faded. Out in the garden then? But the trees spun darkness for a wandering beam of sun. So fine, so rare, coolly sunk beneath the surface the beam I sought always burnt behind the glass. Death was the glass; death was between us; coming to the woman first, hundreds of years ago, leaving the house, sealing all the windows; the rooms were darkened. He left it, left her, went North, went East, saw the stars turned in the Southern sky; sought the house, found it dropped beneath the Downs. "Safe, safe, safe," the pulse of the house beat gladly. "The Treasure yours."

The wind roars up the avenue. Trees stoop and bend this way and that. Moonbeams splash and spill wildly in the rain. But the beam of the lamp falls straight from the window. The candle burns stiff and still. Wandering through the house, opening the windows, whispering not to wake us, the ghostly couple seek their joy.

"Here we slept," she says. And he adds, "Kisses without number." "Waking in the morning—" "Silver between the trees—" "Upstairs—" "In the garden—" "When summer came—" "In winter snowtime—" The doors go shutting far in the distance, gently knocking like the pulse of a heart.

Nearer they come; cease at the doorway. The wind falls, the rain slides silver down the glass. Our eyes darken; we hear no steps beside us; we see no lady spread her ghostly cloak. His hands shield the lantern. "Look," he breathes. "Sound asleep. Love upon their lips."

Stooping, holding their silver lamp above us, long they look and deeply. Long they pause. The wind drives straightly; the flame stoops slightly. Wild beams of moonlight cross both floor and wall, and, meeting, stain the faces bent; the faces pondering; the faces that search the sleepers and seek their hidden joy.

10   "Safe, safe, safe," the heart of the house beats proudly. "Long years—" he sighs. "Again you found me." "Here," she murmurs, "sleeping; in the garden reading; laughing, rolling apples in the loft. Here we left our treasure—" Stooping, their light lifts the lids upon my eyes. "Safe! safe! safe!" the pulse of the house beats wildly. Waking, I cry "Oh, is this *your* buried treasure? The light in the heart."

D. H. Lawrence
The Rocking-Horse Winner

D. H. (David Herbert) Lawrence (1885–1930) was the son of a coalminer. He graduated from a teachers' college, taught school for a time, and wrote poems and novels with a prolific energy. In 1912, he began living with a German noblewoman, Frieda von Richthofen Weekley. Married two years later, they were objects of suspicion during the First World War in England because of Frieda's nationality and Lawrence's pacifism. After the war they moved restlessly around the world: Italy, Ceylon, Australia, New Mexico, Mexico. Lawrence excelled at writing travel literature—together with criticism, philosophical essays, and almost every literary form. Examples of his poems are printed in this volume on pages 618–619. Among his most famous novels are *Sons and Lovers* (1913), *The Rainbow* (1915), *Women in Love* (1921), and *Lady Chatterley's Lover* (1928).

There was a woman who was beautiful, who started with all the advantages, yet she had no luck. She married for love, and the love turned to dust. She had bonny children, yet she felt they had been thrust upon her, and she could not love them. They looked at her coldly, as if they were finding fault with her. And hurriedly she felt she must cover up some fault in herself. Yet what it was that she must cover up she never knew. Nevertheless, when her children were present, she always felt the centre of her heart go hard. This troubled her, and in her manner she was all the more gentle and anxious for her children, as if she loved them very much. Only she herself knew that at the centre of her heart was a hard little place that could not feel love, no, not for anybody. Everybody else said of her: "She is such a good mother. She adores her children." Only she herself, and her children themselves, knew it was not so. They read it in each other's eyes.

There were a boy and two little girls. They lived in a pleasant house, with a garden, and they had discreet servants, and felt themselves superior to anyone in the neighbourhood.

Although they lived in style, they felt always an anxiety in the house. There was never enough money. The mother had a small income, and the father had a small income, but not nearly enough for the social position which they had to keep up. The father went into town to some office. But though he had good prospects, these prospects never materialized. There was always the grinding sense of the shortage of money, though the style was always kept up.

At last the mother said: "I will see if I can't make something." But she did not know where to begin. She racked her brains, and tried this thing and the other, but could not find anything successful. The failure made deep lines come into her face. Her children were growing up, they would have to go to school. There must be more money, there must be more money. The father, who was always very handsome and expensive in his tastes, seemed as if he never would be able to do anything worth doing. And the mother, who had a great belief in herself, did not succeed any better, and her tastes were just as expensive.

5   And so the house came to be haunted by the unspoken phrase: There must be more money! There must be more money! The children could hear it all the time, though nobody said it aloud. They heard it at Christmas, when the expensive and splendid toys filled the nursery. Behind the shining modern rocking horse, behind the smart doll's-house, a voice would start whispering: "There must be more

money! There must be more money!" And the children would stop playing, to listen for a moment. They would look into each other's eyes, to see if they had all heard. And each one saw in the eyes of the other two that they too had heard. "There must be more money! There must be more money!"

It came whispering from the springs of the still-swaying rocking horse, and even the horse, bending his wooden, champing head, heard it. The big doll, sitting so pink and smirking in her new pram, could hear it quite plainly, and seemed to be smirking all the more self-consciously because of it. The foolish puppy, too, that took the place of the Teddy bear, he was looking so extraordinarily foolish for no other reason but that he heard the secret whisper all over the house: "There must be more money!"

Yet nobody ever said it aloud. The whisper was everywhere, and therefore no one spoke it. Just as no one ever says: "We are breathing!" in spite of the fact that breath is coming and going all the time.

"Mother," said the boy Paul one day, "why don't we keep a car of our own? Why do we always use uncle's, or else a taxi?"

"Because we're the poor members of the family," said the mother.

10 "But why are we, mother?"

"Well—I suppose," she said slowly and bitterly, "it's because your father has no luck."

The boy was silent for some time.

"Is luck money, mother?" he asked, rather timidly.

"No, Paul. Not quite. It's what causes you to have money."

15 "Oh!" said Paul vaguely. "I thought when Uncle Oscar said filthy lucker, it meant money."

"Filthy lucre does mean money," said the mother. "But it's lucre, not luck."

"Oh!" said the boy. "Then what is luck, mother?"

"It's what causes you to have money. If you're lucky you have money. That's why it's better to be born lucky than rich. If you're rich, you may lose your money. But if you're lucky, you will always get more money."

"Oh! Will you? And is father not lucky?"

20 "Very unlucky, I should say," she said bitterly.

The boy watched her with unsure eyes.

"Why?" he asked.

"I don't know. Nobody ever knows why one person is lucky and another unlucky."

"Don't they? Nobody at all? Does nobody know?"

25 "Perhaps God. But He never tells."

"He ought to, then. And aren't you lucky either, mother?"

"I can't be, if I married an unlucky husband."

"But by yourself, aren't you?"

"I used to think I was, before I married. Now I think I am very unlucky indeed."

30 "Why?"

"Well—never mind! Perhaps I'm not really," she said.

The child looked at her, to see if she meant it. But he saw, by the lines of her mouth, that she was only trying to hide something from him.

"Well, anyhow," he said stoutly, "I'm a lucky person."

"Why?" said his mother, with a sudden laugh.

35 He stared at her. He didn't even know why he had said it.

"God told me," he asserted, brazening it out.

"I hope He did, dear!" she said, again with a laugh, but rather bitter.

"He did, mother!"

"Excellent!" said the mother, using one of her husband's exclamations.

40 The boy saw she did not believe him; or, rather, that she paid no attention to his assertion. This angered him somewhat, and made him want to compel her attention.

He went off by himself, vaguely, in a childish way, seeking for the clue to "luck." Absorbed, taking no heed of other people, he went about with a sort of stealth, seeking inwardly for luck. He wanted luck, he wanted it, he wanted it. When the two girls were playing dolls in the nursery, he would sit on his big rocking horse, charging madly into space, with a frenzy that made the little girls peer at him uneasily. Wildly the horse careered, the waving dark hair of the boy tossed, his eyes had a strange glare in them. The little girls dared not speak to him.

When he had ridden to the end of his mad little journey, he climbed down and stood in front of his rocking horse, staring fixedly into its lowered face. Its red mouth was slightly open, its big eye was wide and glassy-bright.

"Now!" he would silently command the snorting steed. "Now, take me to where there is luck! Now take me!"

And he would slash the horse on the neck with the little whip he had asked Uncle Oscar for. He knew the horse could take him to where there was luck, if only he forced it. So he would mount again, and start on his furious ride, hoping at last to get there. He knew he could get there.

45 "You'll break your horse, Paul!" said the nurse.

"He's always riding like that! I wish he'd leave off!" said his elder sister Joan.

But he only glared down on them in silence. Nurse gave him up. She could make nothing of him. Anyhow he was growing beyond her.

One day his mother and his Uncle Oscar came in when he was on one of his furious rides. He did not speak to them.

"Hallo, you young jockey! Riding a winner?" said his uncle.

50 "Aren't you growing too big for a rocking horse? You're not a very little boy any longer, you know," said his mother.

But Paul only gave a blue glare from his big, rather close-set eyes. He would speak to nobody when he was in full tilt. His mother watched him with an anxious expression on her face.

At last he suddenly stopped forcing his horse into the mechanical gallop, and slid down.

"Well, I got there!" he announced fiercely, his blue eyes still flaring, and his sturdy long legs straddling apart.

"Where did you get to?" asked his mother.

55 "Where I wanted to go," he flared back at her.

"That's right, son!" said Uncle Oscar. "Don't you stop till you get there. What's the horse's name?"

"He doesn't have a name," said the boy.

"Gets on without all right?" asked the uncle.

"Well, he has different names. He was called Sansovino last week."

60 "Sansovino, eh? Won the Ascot. How did you know his name?"

"He always talks about horse races with Bassett," said Joan.

The uncle was delighted to find that his small nephew was posted with all the racing news. Bassett, the young gardener, who had been wounded in the left foot in the war and had got his present job through Oscar Cresswell, whose batman he had been, was a perfect blade of the "turf." He lived in the racing events, and the small boy lived with him.

Oscar Cresswell got it all from Bassett.

"Master Paul comes and asks me, so I can't do more than tell him, sir," said Bassett, his face terribly serious, as if he were speaking of religious matters.

"And does he ever put anything on a horse he fancies?"

"Well—I don't want to give him away—he's a young sport, a fine sport, sir. Would you mind asking him yourself? He sort of takes a pleasure in it, and perhaps he'd feel I was giving him away, sir, if you don't mind."

Bassett was serious as a church.

The uncle went back to his nephew, and took him off for a ride in the car.

"Say, Paul, old man, do you ever put anything on a horse?" the uncle asked.

The boy watched the handsome man closely.

"Why, do you think I oughtn't to?" he parried.

"Not a bit of it! I thought perhaps you might give me a tip for the Lincoln."

The car sped on into the country, going down to Uncle Oscar's place in Hampshire.

"Honour bright?" said the nephew.

"Honour bright, son!" said the uncle.

"Well, then, Daffodil."

"Daffodil! I doubt it, sonny. What about Mirza?"

"I only know the winner," said the boy. "That's Daffodil."

"Daffodil, eh?"

There was a pause. Daffodil was an obscure horse comparatively.

"Uncle!"

"Yes, son?"

"You won't let it go any further, will you? I promised Bassett."

"Bassett be damned, old man! What's he got to do with it?"

"We're partners. We've been partners from the first. Uncle, he lent me my first five shillings, which I lost. I promised him, honour bright, it was only between me and him; only you gave me that ten-shilling note I started winning with, so I thought you were lucky. You won't let it go any further, will you?"

The boy gazed at his uncle from those big, hot, blue eyes, set rather close together. The uncle stirred and laughed uneasily.

"Right you are, son! I'll keep your tip private. Daffodil, eh? How much are you putting on him?"

"All except twenty pounds," said the boy. "I keep that in reserve."

The uncle thought it a good joke.

"You keep twenty pounds in reserve, do you, you young romancer. What are you betting, then?"

"I'm betting three hundred," said the boy gravely. "But it's between you and me, Uncle Oscar! Honour bright?"

The uncle burst into a roar of laughter.

"It's between you and me all right, you young Nat Gould," he said, laughing. "But where's your three hundred?"

"Bassett keeps it for me. We're partners."

"You are, are you! And what is Bassett putting on Daffodil?"

"He won't go quite as high as I do, I expect. Perhaps he'll go a hundred and fifty."

"What, pennies?" laughed the uncle.

"Pounds," said the child, with a surprised look at his uncle. "Bassett keeps a bigger reserve than I do."

Between wonder and amusement Uncle Oscar was silent. He pursued the matter no further, but he determined to take his nephew with him to the Lincoln races.

"Now, son," he said, "I'm putting twenty on Mizra, and I'll put five for you on any horse you fancy. What's your pick?"

"Daffodil, uncle."

"No, not the fiver on Daffodil!"

"I should if it was my own fiver," said the child.

"Good! Good! Right you are! A fiver for me and a fiver for you on Daffodil."

The child had never been to a race meeting before, and his eyes were blue fire. He pursed his mouth tight, and watched. A Frenchman just in front had put his money on Lancelot. Wild with excitement, he flayed his arms up and down, yelling "Lancelot! Lancelot!" in his French accent.

Daffodil came in first, Lancelot second, Mizra third. The child, flushed and with eyes blazing, was curiously serene. His uncle brought him four five-pound notes, four to one.

"What am I to do with these?" he cried, waving them before the boy's eyes.

"I suppose we'll talk to Bassett," said the boy. "I expect I have fifteen hundred now; and twenty in reserve; and this twenty."

His uncle studied him for some moments.

"Look here, son!" he said. "You're not serious about Bassett and that fifteen hundred, are you?"

"Yes, I am. But it's between you and me, uncle. Honour bright!"

"Honour bright all right, son! But I must talk to Bassett."

"If you'd like to be a partner, uncle, with Bassett and me, we could all be partners. Only, you'd have to promise, honour bright, uncle, not to let it go beyond us three. Bassett and I are lucky, and you must be lucky, because it was your ten shillings I started winning with. . . ."

Uncle Oscar took both Bassett and Paul into Richmond Park for an afternoon, and there they talked.

"It's like this, you see, sir," Bassett said. "Master Paul would get me talking about racing events, spinning yarns, you know, sir. And he was always keen on knowing if I'd made or if I'd lost. It's about a year since, now, that I put five shillings on Blush of Dawn for him—and we lost. Then the luck turned, with that ten shillings he had from you, that we put on Singhalese. And since that time, it's been pretty steady, all things considering. What do you say, Master Paul?"

"We're all right when we're sure," said Paul. "It's when we're not quite sure that we go down."

"Oh, but we're careful then," said Bassett.

"But when are you sure?" smiled Uncle Oscar.

"It's Master Paul, sir," said Bassett, in a secret, religious voice. "It's as if he had it from heaven. Like Daffodil, now, for the Lincoln. That was as sure as eggs."

"Did you put anything on Daffodil?" asked Oscar Cresswell.

"Yes, sir, I made my bit."

"And my nephew?"

Bassett was obstinately silent, looking at Paul.

"I made twelve hundred, didn't I, Bassett? I told uncle I was putting three hundred on Daffodil."

125 "That's right," said Bassett, nodding.

"But where's the money?" asked the uncle.

"I keep it safe locked up, sir. Master Paul he can have it any minute he likes to ask for it."

"What, fifteen hundred pounds?"

"And twenty! and forty, that is, with the twenty he made on the course."

130 "It's amazing!" said the uncle.

"If Master Paul offers you to be partners, sir, I would, if I were you; if you'll excuse me," said Bassett.

Oscar Cresswell thought about it.

"I'll see the money," he said.

They drove home again, and sure enough, Bassett came round to the garden-house with fifteen hundred pounds in notes. The twenty pounds reserve was left with Joe Glee, in the Turf Commission deposit.

135 "You see, it's all right, uncle, when I'm sure! Then we go strong, for all we're worth. Don't we, Bassett?"

"We do at that, Master Paul."

"And when are you sure?" said the uncle, laughing.

"Oh, well, sometimes I'm absolutely sure, like about Daffodil," said the boy; "and sometimes I have an idea; and sometimes I haven't even an idea, have I, Bassett? Then we're careful, because we mostly go down."

"You do, do you? And when you're sure, like about Daffodil, what makes you sure, sonny?"

140 "Oh, well, I don't know," said the boy uneasily. "I'm sure, you know, uncle; that's all."

"It's as if he had it from heaven, sir," Bassett reiterated.

"I should say so!" said the uncle.

But he became a partner. And when the Leger was coming on, Paul was "sure" about Lively Spark, which was a quite inconsiderable horse. The boy insisted on putting a thousand on the horse, Bassett went for five hundred, and Oscar Cresswell two hundred. Lively Spark came in first, and the betting had been ten to one against him. Paul had made ten thousand.

"You see," he said, "I was absolutely sure of him."

145 Even Oscar Cresswell had cleared two thousand.

"Look here, son," he said, "this sort of thing makes me nervous."

"It needn't, uncle! Perhaps I shan't be sure again for a long time."

"But what are you going to do with your money?" asked the uncle.

"Of course," said the boy, "I started it for mother. She said she had no luck, because father is unlucky, so I thought if I was lucky, it might stop whispering."

150 "What might stop whispering?"

"Our house. I hate our house for whispering."

"What does it whisper?"

"Why—why"—the boy fidgeted—"why, I don't know. But it's always short of money, you know, uncle."

"I know it, son, I know it."

155 "You know people send mother writs, don't you, uncle?"

"I'm afraid I do," said the uncle.

"And then the house whispers, like people laughing at you behind your back, it's awful, that is! I thought if I was lucky. . . ."

"You might stop it," added the uncle.

The boy watched him with big blue eyes that had an uncanny cold fire in them, and he said never a word.

160   "Well, then!" said the uncle. "What are we doing?"

"I shouldn't like mother to know I was lucky," said the boy.

"Why not, son?"

"She'd stop me."

"I don't think she would."

165   "Oh!"—and the boy writhed in an odd way—"I don't want her to know, uncle."

"All right, son! We'll manage it without her knowing."

They managed it very easily. Paul, at the other's suggestion, handed over five thousand pounds to his uncle, who deposited it with the family lawyer, who was then to inform Paul's mother that a relative had put five thousand pounds into his hands, which sum was to be paid out a thousand pounds at a time, on the mother's birthday, for the next five years.

"So she'll have a birthday present of a thousand pounds for five successive years," said Uncle Oscar. "I hope it won't make it all the harder for her later."

Paul's mother had her birthday in November. The house had been "whispering" worse than ever lately, and, even in spite of his luck, Paul could not bear up against it. He was very anxious to see the effect of the birthday letter, telling his mother about the thousand pounds.

170   When there were no visitors, Paul now took his meals with his parents, as he was beyond the nursery control. His mother went into town nearly every day. She had discovered that she had an odd knack of sketching furs and dress materials, so she worked secretly in the studio of a friend who was the chief "artist" for the leading drapers. She drew the figures of ladies in furs and ladies in silk and sequins for the newspaper advertisements. This young woman artist earned several thousand pounds a year, but Paul's mother only made several hundreds, and she was again dissatisfied. She so wanted to be first in something, and she did not succeed, even in making sketches for drapery advertisements.

She was down to breakfast on the morning of her birthday. Paul watched her face as she read her letters. He knew the lawyer's letter. As his mother read it, her face hardened and became more expressionless. Then a cold, determined look came on her mouth. She hid the letter under the pile of others and said not a word about it.

"Didn't you have anything nice in the post for your birthday, mother?" said Paul.

"Quite moderately nice," she said, her voice cold and absent.

She went away to town without saying more.

175   But in the afternoon Uncle Oscar appeared. He said Paul's mother had had a long interview with the lawyer, asking if the whole five thousand could be advanced at once, as she was in debt.

"What do you think, uncle?" said the boy.

"I leave it to you, son."

"Oh, let her have it, then! We can get some more with the other," said the boy.

"A bird in the hand is worth two in the bush, laddie!" said Uncle Oscar.

180   "But I'm sure to know for the Grand National; or the Lincolnshire; or else the Derby. I'm sure to know for one of them," said Paul.

So Uncle Oscar signed the agreement, and Paul's mother touched the whole five thousand. Then something very curious happened. The voice in the house suddenly went mad, like a chorus of frogs on a spring evening. There were certain new furnishings, and Paul had a tutor. He was really going to Eton, his father's school, in the following autumn. There were flowers in the winter, and a blossoming of the luxury Paul's mother had been used to. And yet the voices in the house, behind the sprays of mimosa and almond blossom, and from under the piles of iridescent cushions, simply trilled and screamed in a sort of ecstasy: "There must be more money! Oh-h, there must be more money. Oh, now, now-w! Now-w-w—there must be more money!—more than ever! More than ever!"

It frightened Paul terribly. He studied away at his Latin and Greek with his tutors. But his intense hours were spent with Bassett. The Grand National had gone by: he had not "known," and had lost a hundred pounds. Summer was at hand. He was in agony for the Lincoln. But even for the Lincoln he didn't "know" and he lost fifty pounds. He became wild-eyed and strange, as if something were going to explode in him.

"Let it alone, son! Don't you bother about it!" urged Uncle Oscar. But it was as if the boy couldn't really hear what his uncle was saying.

"I've got to know for the Derby! I've got to know for the Derby!" the child reiterated, his big eyes blazing with a sort of madness.

185   His mother noticed how overwrought he was.

"You'd better go to the seaside. Wouldn't you like to go now to the seaside, instead of waiting? I think you'd better," she said, looking down at him anxiously, her heart curiously heavy because of him.

But the child lifted his uncanny blue eyes.

"I couldn't possibly go before the Derby, mother!" he said. "I couldn't possibly!"

"Why not?" she said, her voice becoming heavy when she was opposed. "Why not? You can still go from the seaside to see the Derby with your Uncle Oscar, if that's what you wish. No need for you to wait here. Besides, I think you care too much about these races. It's a bad sign. My family has been a gambling family, and you won't know till you grow up how much damage it has done. But it has done damage. I shall have to send Bassett away, and ask Uncle Oscar not to talk racing to you, unless you promise to be reasonable about it; go away to the seaside and forget it. You're all nerves!"

190   "I'll do what you like, mother, so long as you don't send me away till after the Derby," the boy said.

"Send you away from where? Just from this house?"

"Yes," he said, gazing at her.

"Why, you curious child, what makes you care about this house so much, suddenly? I never knew you loved it."

He gazed at her without speaking. He had a secret within a secret, something he had not divulged, even to Bassett or to his Uncle Oscar.

195   But his mother, after standing undecided and a little bit sullen for some moments, said:

"Very well, then! Don't go to the seaside till after the Derby, if you don't wish it. But promise me you won't let your nerves go to pieces. Promise you won't think so much about horse racing and events, as you call them!"

"Oh, no," said the boy casually. "I won't think much about them, mother. You needn't worry. I wouldn't worry, mother, if I were you."

"If you were me and I were you," said his mother, "I wonder what we should do!"

"But you know you needn't worry, mother, don't you?" the boy repeated.

200   "I should be awfully glad to know it," she said wearily.

"Oh, well, you can, you know. I mean, you ought to know you needn't worry," he insisted.

"Ought I? Then I'll see about it," she said.

Paul's secret of secrets was his wooden horse, that which had no name. Since he was emancipated from a nurse and a nursery-governess, he had had his rocking horse removed to his own bedroom at the top of the house.

"Surely, you're too big for a rocking horse!" his mother had remonstrated.

205 "Well, you see, mother, till I can have a real horse, I like to have some sort of animal about," had been his quaint answer.

"Do you feel he keeps you company?" she laughed.

"Oh, yes! He's very good, he always keeps me company, when I'm there," said Paul.

So the horse, rather shabby, stood in an arrested prance in the boy's bedroom.

The Derby was drawing near, and the boy grew more and more tense. He hardly heard what was spoken to him, he was very frail, and his eyes were really uncanny. His mother had sudden seizures of uneasiness about him. Sometimes, for half-an-hour, she would feel a sudden anxiety about him that was almost anguish. She wanted to rush to him at once, and know he was safe.

210 Two nights before the Derby, she was at a big party in town, when one of her rushes of anxiety about her boy, her first-born, gripped her heart till she could hardly speak. She fought with the feeling, might and main, for she believed in common sense. But it was too strong. She had to leave the dance and go down-stairs to telephone to the country. The children's nursery-governess was terribly surprised and startled at being rung up in the night.

"Are the children all right, Miss Wilmot?"

"Oh, yes, they are quite all right."

"Master Paul? Is he all right?"

"He went to bed as right as a trivet. Shall I run up and look at him?"

215 "No," said Paul's mother reluctantly. "No! Don't trouble. It's all right. Don't sit up. We shall be home fairly soon." She did not want her son's privacy intruded upon.

"Very good," said the governess.

It was about one o'clock when Paul's mother and father drove up to their house. All was still. Paul's mother went to her room and slipped off her white fur coat. She had told her maid not to wait up for her. She heard her husband downstairs, mixing a whisky-and-soda.

And then, because of the strange anxiety at her heart, she stole upstairs to her son's room. Noiselessly she went along the upper corridor. Was there a faint noise? What was it?

She stood, with arrested muscles, outside his door, listening. There was a strange, heavy, and yet not loud noise. Her heart stood still. It was a soundless noise, yet rushing and powerful. Something huge, in violent, hushed motion. What was it? What in God's name was it? She ought to know. She felt that she knew the noise. She knew what it was.

220 Yet she could not place it. She couldn't say what it was. And on and on it went, like a madness.

Softly, frozen with anxiety and fear, she turned the door handle.

The room was dark. Yet in the space near the window, she heard and saw something plunging to and fro. She gazed in fear and amazement.

Then suddenly she switched on the light, and saw her son, in his green pyjamas, madly surging on the rocking horse. The blaze of light suddenly lit him up, as he urged the wooden horse, and lit her up, as she stood, blonde, in her dress of pale green and crystal, in the doorway.

"Paul!" she cried. "Whatever are you doing?"

225   "It's Malabar!" he screamed, in a powerful, strange voice. "It's Malabar."

His eyes blazed at her for one strange and senseless second, as he ceased urging his wooden horse. Then he fell with a crash to the ground, and she, all her tormented motherhood flooding upon her, rushed to gather him up.

But he was unconscious, and unconscious he remained, with some brain-fever. He talked and tossed, and his mother sat stonily by his side.

"Malabar! It's Malabar! Bassett, Bassett, I know! It's Malabar!"

So the child cried, trying to get up and urge the rocking horse that gave him his inspiration.

230   "What does he mean by Malabar?" asked the heart-frozen mother.

"I don't know," said the father stonily.

"What does he mean by Malabar?" she asked her brother Oscar.

"It's one of the horses running for the Derby," was the answer.

And, in spite of himself, Oscar Cresswell spoke to Bassett, and himself put a thousand on Malabar: at fourteen to one.

235   The third day of the illness was critical: they were waiting for a change. The boy, with his rather long, curly hair, was tossing ceaselessly on the pillow. He neither slept nor regained consciousness, and his eyes were like blue stones. His mother sat, feeling her heart had gone, turned actually into stone.

In the evening, Oscar Cresswell did not come, but Bassett sent a message, saying could he come up for one moment, just one moment? Paul's mother was very angry at the intrusion, but on second thought she agreed. The boy was the same. Perhaps Bassett might bring him to consciousness.

The gardener, a shortish fellow with a little brown moustache, and sharp little brown eyes, tiptoed into the room, touched his imaginary cap to Paul's mother, and stole to the bedside, staring with glittering, smallish eyes, at the tossing, dying child.

"Master Paul!" he whispered. "Master Paul! Malabar came in first all right, a clean win. I did as you told me. You've made over seventy thousand pounds, you have; you've got over eighty thousand. Malabar came in all right, Master Paul."

"Malabar! Malabar! Did I say Malabar, mother? Did I say Malabar? Do you think I'm lucky, mother? I knew Malabar, didn't I? Over eighty thousand pounds! I call that lucky, don't you, mother? Over eighty thousand pounds! I knew, didn't I know I knew? Malabar came in all right. If I ride my horse till I'm sure, then I tell you, Bassett, you can go as high as you like. Did you go for all you were worth, Bassett?"

240   "I went a thousand on it, Master Paul."

"I never told you, mother, that if I can ride my horse, and get there, then I'm absolutely sure—oh, absolutely! Mother, did I ever tell you? I am lucky."

"No, you never did," said the mother.

But the boy died in the night.

And even as he lay dead, his mother heard her brother's voice saying to her: "My God, Hester, you're eighty-odd thousand to the good and a poor devil of a son to the bad. But, poor devil, poor devil, he's best gone out of a life where he rides his rocking horse to find a winner."

Jorge Luis Borges
The Secret Miracle

Translated by Harriet de Onís

Jorge Luis Borges (1899–   ) was born and lives in Buenos Aires, Argentina.
At a time when Spanish-American literature is extraordinarily rich and lively,
Borges is perhaps the foremost Spanish-American writer. Enigmatic and
fantastic, his work has influenced writers all over the world.

And God had him die for a hundred years and then revived him and said:
 "How long have you been here?"
 "A day or a part of a day," he answered.
—Koran, II, 261

The night of March 14, 1943, in an apartment in the Zeltnergasse of Prague,
Jaromir Hladik, the author of the unfinished drama entitled *The Enemies*, of *Vindication of Eternity* and of a study of the indirect Jewish sources of Jakob Böhme,[1]
had a dream of a long game of chess. The players were not two persons, but two
illustrious families; the game had been going on for centuries. Nobody could remember what the stakes were, but it was rumored that they were enormous,
perhaps infinite; the chessmen and the board were in a secret tower. Jaromir (in
his dream) was the first-born of one of the contending families. The clock struck
the hour for the game, which could not be postponed. The dreamer raced over the
sands of a rainy desert, and was unable to recall either the pieces or the rules of
chess. At that moment he awoke. The clangor of the rain and of the terrible clocks
ceased. A rhythmic, unanimous noise, punctuated by shouts of command, arose
from the Zeltnergasse. It was dawn, and the armored vanguard of the Third Reich[2]
was entering Prague.

On the nineteenth the authorities received a denunciation; that same nineteenth,
toward evening, Jaromir Hladik was arrested. He was taken to an aseptic, white
barracks on the opposite bank of the Moldau. He was unable to refute a single
one of the Gestapo's charges; his mother's family name was Jaroslavski, he was
of Jewish blood, his study on Böhme had a marked Jewish emphasis, his signature had been one more on the protest against the *Anschluss*. In 1928 he had
translated the *Sepher Yezirah*[3] for the publishing house of Hermann Barsdorf.
The fulsome catalogue of the firm had exaggerated, for publicity purposes, the
translator's reputation, and the catalogue had been examined by Julius Rothe, one
of the officials who held Hladik's fate in his hands. There is not a person who,
except in the field of his own specialization, is not credulous; two or three adjectives in Gothic type were enough to persuade Julius Rothe of Hladik's importance,
and he ordered him sentenced to death *pour encourager les autres*.[4] The execution
was set for March 29th, at 9:00 A.M. This delay (whose importance the reader will
grasp later) was owing to the desire on the authorities' part to proceed impersonally
and slowly, after the manner of vegetables and plants.

---

[1]German mystic and philosopher (1575–1624)   [2]Hitler's Germany. On 15 March 1939 German armies took over Prague, in Czechoslovakia, by *Anschluss* (annexation); the Gestapo was the
secret police.   [3]Ancient Jewish mystical writings   [4]To encourage others

Hladik's first reaction was mere terror. He felt he would not have shrunk from the gallows, the block, or the knife, but that death by a firing squad was unbearable. In vain he tried to convince himself that the plain, unvarnished fact of dying was the fearsome thing, not the attendant circumstances. He never wearied of conjuring up these circumstances, senselessly trying to exhaust all their possible variations. He infinitely anticipated the process of his dying, from the sleepless dawn to the mysterious volley. Before the day set by Julius Rothe he died hundreds of deaths in courtyards whose forms and angles strained geometrical probabilities, machine-gunned by variable soldiers in changing numbers, who at times killed him from a distance, at others from close by. He faced these imaginary executions with real terror (perhaps with real bravery); each simulacrum lasted a few seconds. When the circle was closed, Jaromir returned once more and interminably to the tremulous vespers of his death. Then he reflected that reality does not usually coincide with our anticipation of it; with a logic of his own he inferred that to foresee a circumstantial detail is to prevent its happening. Trusting in this weak magic, he invented, *so that they would not happen*, the most gruesome details. Finally, as was natural, he came to fear that they were prophetic. Miserable in the night, he endeavored to find some way to hold fast to the fleeting substance of time. He knew that it was rushing headlong toward the dawn of the twenty-ninth. He reasoned aloud: "I am now in the night of the twenty-second; while this night lasts (and for six nights more), I am invulnerable, immortal." The nights of sleep seemed to him deep, dark pools in which he could submerge himself. There were moments when he longed impatiently for the final burst of fire that would free him, for better or for worse, from the vain compulsion of his imaginings. On the twenth-eighth, as the last sunset was reverberating from the high barred windows, the thought of his drama, *The Enemies*, deflected him from these abject considerations.

Hladik had rounded forty. Aside from a few friendships and many habits, the problematic exercise of literature constituted his life. Like all writers, he measured the achievements of others by what they had accomplished, asking of them that they measure him by what he envisaged or planned. All the books he had published had left him with a complex feeling of repentance. His studies of the work of Böhme, of Ibn Erza,[1] and of Fludd[2] had been characterized essentially by mere application; his translation of the *Sepher Yezirah*, by carelessness, fatigue, and conjecture. *Vindication of Eternity* perhaps had fewer shortcomings. The first volume gave a history of man's various concepts of eternity, from the immutable Being of Parmenides[3] to the modifiable Past of Hinton[4] The second denied (with Francis Bradley)[5] that all the events of the universe make up a temporal series, arguing that the number of man's possible experiences is not infinite, and that a single "repetition" suffices to prove that time is a fallacy . . . Unfortunately, the arguments that demonstrate this fallacy are equally fallacious. Hladik was in the habit of going over them with a kind of contemptuous perplexity. He had also composed a series of Expressionist poems; to the poet's chagrin they had been

---

[1]Jewish philosopher (1090?–1164) born in Spain   [2]Sir Robert Fludd (1574–1637), English mystical philosopher and physician   [3]Greek philosopher who lived six centuries before the birth of Christ   [4]James Hinton (1822–1875), English philosopher and physician   [5]Francis H. Bradley (1846–1924), English philosopher and logician

included in an anthology published in 1924, and no subsequent anthology but inherited them. From all this equivocal, uninspired past Hladik had hoped to redeem himself with his drama in verse, *The Enemies*. (Hladik felt the verse form to be essential because it makes it impossible for the spectators to lose sight of irreality, one of art's requisites.)

5

The drama observed the unities of time, place, and action. The scene was laid in Hradčany, in the library of Baron von Roemerstadt, on one of the last afternoons of the nineteenth century. In the first scene of the first act a strange man visits Roemerstadt. (A clock was striking seven, the vehemence of the setting sun's rays glorified the windows, a passionate, familiar Hungarian music floated in the air.) This visit is followed by others; Roemerstadt does not know the people who are importuning him, but he has the uncomfortable feeling that he has seen them somewhere, perhaps in a dream. They all fawn upon him, but it is apparent—first to the audience and then to the Baron—that they are secret enemies, in league to ruin him. Roemerstadt succeeds in checking or evading their involved schemings. In the dialogue mention is made of his sweetheart, Julia von Weidenau, and a certain Jaroslav Kubin, who at one time pressed his attentions on her. Kubin has now lost his mind, and believes himself to be Roemerstadt. The dangers increase; Roemerstadt, at the end of the second act, is forced to kill one of the conspirators. The third and final act opens. The incoherencies gradually increase; actors who had seemed out of the play reappear; the man Roemerstadt killed returns for a moment. Someone points out that evening has not fallen; the clock strikes seven, the high windows reverberate in the western sun, the air carries an impassioned Hungarian melody. The first actor comes on and repeats the lines he had spoken in the first scene of the first act. Roemerstadt speaks to him without surprise; the audience understands that Roemerstadt is the miserable Jaroslav Kubin. The drama has never taken place; it is the circular delirium that Kubin lives and relives endlessly.

Hladik had never asked himself whether this tragicomedy of errors was preposterous or admirable, well thought out or slipshod. He felt that the plot I have just sketched was best contrived to cover up his defects and point up his abilities and held the possibility of allowing him to redeem (symbolically) the meaning of his life. He had finished the first act and one or two scenes of the third; the metrical mixture of the work made it possible for him to keep working it over, changing the hexameters, without the manuscript in front of him. He thought how he still had two acts to do, and that he was going to die very soon. He spoke with God in the darkness: "If in some fashion I exist, if I am not one of Your repetitions and mistakes, I exist as the author of *The Enemies*. To finish this drama, which can justify me and justify You, I need another year. Grant me these days, You to whom the centuries and time belong." This was the last night, the most dreadful of all, but ten minutes later sleep flooded over him like a dark water.

Toward dawn he dreamed that he had concealed himself in one of the naves of the Clementine Library. A librarian wearing dark glasses asked him: "What are you looking for?" Hladik answered: "I am looking for God." The librarian said to him: "God is in one of the letters on one of the pages of one of the four hundred thousand volumes of the Clementine. My fathers and the fathers of my fathers have searched for this letter; I have grown blind seeking it." He removed his glasses, and Hladik saw his eyes, which were dead. A reader came in to return an atlas. "This atlas is worthless," he said, and handed it to Hladik, who opened it at random. He saw a map of India as in a daze. Suddenly sure of himself, he touched one of the tiniest letters. A ubiquitous voice said to him: "The time of your labor has been granted." At this point Hladik awoke.

He remembered that men's dreams belong to God, and that Maimonides[1] had written that the words heard in a dream are divine when they are distinct and clear and the person uttering them cannot be seen. He dressed: two soldiers came into the cell and ordered him to follow them.

From behind the door, Hladik had envisaged a labyrinth of passageways, stairs, and separate buildings. The reality was less spectacular: they descended to an inner court by a narrow iron stairway. Several soldiers—some with uniform unbuttoned—were examining a motorcycle and discussing it. The sergeant looked at the clock; it was 8:44. They had to wait until it struck nine. Hladik, more insignificant than pitiable, sat down on a pile of wood. He noticed that the soldiers' eyes avoided his. To ease his wait, the sergeant handed him a cigarette. Hladik did not smoke; he accepted it out of politeness or humility. As he lighted it, he noticed that his hands were shaking. The day was clouding over; the soldiers spoke in a low voice as though he were already dead. Vainly he tried to recall the woman of whom Julia von Weidenau was the symbol.

10   The squad formed and stood at attention. Hladik, standing against the barracks wall, waited for the volley. Someone pointed out that the wall was going to be stained with blood; the victim was ordered to step forward a few paces. Incongruously, this reminded Hladik of the fumbling preparations of photographers. A big drop of rain struck one of Hladik's temples and rolled slowly down his cheek; the sergeant shouted the final order.

The physical universe came to a halt.

The guns converged on Hladik, but the men who were to kill him stood motionless. The sergeant's arm eternized an unfinished gesture. On a paving stone of the courtyard a bee cast an unchanging shadow. The wind had ceased, as in a picture. Hladik attempted a cry, a word, a movement of the hand. He realized that he was paralyzed. Not a sound reached him from the halted world. He thought: "I am in hell, I am dead." He thought: "I am mad." He thought: "Time has stopped." Then he reflected that if that was the case, his mind would have stopped too. He wanted to test this; he repeated (without moving his lips) Vergil's mysterious fourth Eclogue.[2] He imagined that the now remote soldiers must be sharing his anxiety; he longed to be able to communicate with them. It astonished him not to feel the least fatigue, not even the numbness of his protracted immobility. After an indeterminate time he fell asleep. When he awoke the world continued motionless and mute. The drop of water still clung to his cheek, the shadow of the bee to the stone. The smoke from the cigarette he had thrown away had not dispersed. Another "day" went by before Hladik understood.

He had asked God for a whole year to finish his work; His omnipotence had granted it. God had worked a secret miracle for him; German lead would kill him at the set hour, but in his mind a year would go by between the order and its execution. From perplexity he passed to stupor, from stupor to resignation, from resignation to sudden gratitude.

---

[1]Moses Maimonides (1135–1204), a philosopher born in Spain, collected Jewish oral law into a written code.   [2]The fourth Eclogue (see note on page 53) of the Roman epic poet Publius Vergilius Maro (70–19 B.C.) is sometimes called messianic.

He had no document but his memory; the training he had acquired with each added hexameter gave him a discipline unsuspected by those who set down and forget temporary, incomplete paragraphs. He was not working for posterity or even for God, whose literary tastes were unknown to him. Meticulously, motionlessly, secretly, he wrought in time his lofty, invisible labyrinth. He worked the third act over twice. He eliminated certain symbols as over-obvious, such as the repeated striking of the clock, the music. Nothing hurried him. He omitted, he condensed, he amplified. In certain instances he came back to the original version. He came to feel an affection for the courtyard, the barracks; one of the faces before him modified his conception of Roemerstadt's character. He discovered that the wearying cacophonies that bothered Flaubert[1] so much are mere visual superstitions, weakness and limitation of the written word, not the spoken. . . . He concluded his drama. He had only the problem of a single phrase. He found it. The drop of water slid down his cheek. He opened his mouth in a maddened cry, moved his face, dropped under the quadruple blast.

15   Jaromir Hladik died on March 29, at 9:02 A.M.

Langston Hughes
On the Road

Langston Hughes (1902–1967) was born in Joplin, Missouri. He came to New York, where he was a leading spirit in the Harlem renaissance of black American writers in the twenties and thirties. Best known as a poet—*Shakespeare in Harlem* (1942), *One Way Ticket* (1949), *Selected Poems* (1959)—he also wrote children's books, plays, and novels. See also page 640.

He was not interested in the snow. When he got off the freight, one early evening during the depression, Sargeant never even noticed the snow. But he must have felt it seeping down his neck, cold, wet, sopping in his shoes. But if you had asked him, he wouldn't have known it was snowing. Sargeant didn't see the snow, not even under the bright lights of the main street, falling white and flaky against the night. He was too hungry, too sleepy, too tired.

The Reverend Mr. Dorset, however, saw the snow when he switched on his porch light, opened the front door of his parsonage, and found standing there before him a big black man with snow on his face, a human piece of night with snow on his face—obviously unemployed.

Said the Reverend Mr. Dorset before Sargeant even realized he'd opened his mouth: "I'm sorry. No! Go right on down this street four blocks and turn to your left, walk up seven and you'll see the Relief Shelter. I'm sorry. No!" He shut the door.

Sargeant wanted to tell the holy man that he had already been to the Relief Shelter, been to hundreds of relief shelters during the depression years, the beds were always gone and supper was over, the place was full, and they drew the color line anyhow. But the minister said, "No," and shut the door. Evidently he didn't want to hear about it. And he *had* a door to shut.

5   The big black man turned away. And even yet he didn't see the snow, walking

---

[1]The novelist Gustave Flaubert (1821–1880), a magnificent stylist of the French language, contended that every word in a piece of fiction must have precision and harmony.

right into it. Maybe he sensed it, cold, wet, sticking to his jaws, wet on his black hands, sopping in his shoes. He stopped and stood on the sidewalk hunched over—hungry, sleepy, cold—looking up and down. Then he looked right where he was—in front of a church. Of course! A church! Sure, right next to a parsonage, certainly a church.

It had *two* doors.

Broad white steps in the night all snowy white. Two high arched doors with slender stone pillars on either side. And way up, a round lacy window with a stone crucifix in the middle and Christ on the crucifix in stone. All this was pale in the street lights, solid and stony pale in the snow.

Sargeant blinked. When he looked up, the snow fell into his eyes. For the first time that night he *saw* the snow. He shook his head. He shook the snow from his coat sleeves, felt hungry, felt lost, felt not lost, felt cold. He walked up the steps of the church. He knocked at the door. No answer. He tried the handle. Locked. He put his shoulder against the door and his long black body slanted like a ramrod. He pushed. With loud rhythmic grunts, like the grunts in a chain-gang song, he pushed against the door.

"I'm tired . . . Huh! . . . Hongry . . . Uh! . . . I'm sleepy . . . Huh! I'm cold . . . I got to sleep somewheres," Sargeant said. "This here is a church, ain't it? Well, uh!"

10   He pushed against the door.

Suddenly, with an undue cracking and screaking, the door began to give way to the tall black Negro who pushed ferociously against it.

By now two or three white people had stopped in the street, and Sargeant was vaguely aware of some of them yelling at him concerning the door. Three or four more came running, yelling at him.

"Hey!" they said. "Hey!"

"Uh-huh," answered the big tall Negro, "I know it's a white folks' church, but I got to sleep somewhere." He gave another lunge at the door. "Huh!"

15   And the door broke open.

But just when the door gave way, two white cops arrived in a car, ran up the steps with their clubs, and grabbed Sargeant. But Sargeant for once had no intention of being pulled or pushed away from the door.

Sargeant grabbed, but not for anything so weak as a broken door. He grabbed for one of the tall stone pillars beside the door, grabbed at it and caught it. And held it. The cops pulled and Sargeant pulled. Most of the people in the street got behind the cops and helped them pull.

"A big black unemployed Negro holding onto our church!" thought the people. "The idea!"

The cops began to beat Sargeant over the head, and nobody protested. But he held on.

20   And then the church fell down.

Gradually, the big stone front of the church fell down, the walls and the rafters, the crucifix and the Christ. Then the whole thing fell down, covering the cops and the people with bricks and stones and debris. The whole church fell down in the snow.

Sargeant got out from under the church and went walking on up the street with the stone pillar on his shoulder. He was under the impression that he had buried the parsonage and the Reverend Mr. Dorset who said, "No!" So he laughed, and threw the pillar six blocks up the street and went on.

Sargeant thought he was alone, but listening to the *crunch, crunch, crunch* on the snow of his own footsteps, he heard other footsteps, too, doubling his own. He looked around, and there was Christ walking along beside him, the same Christ that had been on the cross on the church—still stone with a rough stone surface, walking along beside him just like he was broken off the cross when the church fell down.

"Well, I'll be dogged," said Sargeant. "This here's the first time I ever seed you off the cross."

"Yes," said Christ, crunching his feet in the snow. "You had to pull the church down to get me off the cross."

"You glad?" said Sargeant.

"I sure am," said Christ.

They both laughed.

"I'm a hell of a fellow, ain't I?" said Sargeant. "Done pulled the church down!"

"You did a good job," said Christ. "They have kept me nailed on a cross for nearly two thousand years."

"Whee-ee-e!" said Sargeant. "I know you are glad to get off."

"I sure am," said Christ.

They walked on in the snow. Sargeant looked at the man of stone.

"And you have been up there two thousand years?"

"I sure have," Christ said.

"Well, if I had a little cash," said Sargeant, "I'd show you around a bit."

"I been around," said Christ.

"Yeah, but that was a long time ago."

"All the same," said Christ, "I've been around."

They walked on in the snow until they came to the railroad yards. Sargeant was tired, sweating and tired.

"Where you goin'?" Sargeant said, stopping by the tracks. He looked at Christ. Sargeant said, "I'm just a bum on the road. How about you? Where you goin'?"

"God knows," Christ said, "but I'm leavin' here."

They saw the red and green lights of the railroad yard half veiled by the snow that fell out of the night. Away down the track they saw a fire in a hobo jungle.

"I can go there and sleep," Sargeant said.

"You can?"

"Sure," said Sargeant. "That place ain't got no doors."

Outside the town, along the tracks, there were barren trees and bushes below the embankment, snow-gray in the dark. And down among the trees and bushes there were makeshift houses made out of boxes and tin and old pieces of wood and canvas. You couldn't see them in the dark, but you knew they were there if you'd ever been on the road, if you had ever lived with the homeless and hungry in a depression.

"I'm side-tracking," Sargeant said. "I'm tired."

"I'm gonna make it on to Kansas City," said Christ.

"O.K.," Sargeant said. "So long!"

He went down into the hobo jungle and found himself a place to sleep. He never did see Christ no more. About 6:00 A.M. a freight came by. Sargeant scrambled out of the jungle with a dozen or so more hobos and ran along the track, grabbing at the freight. It was dawn, early dawn, cold and gray.

"Wonder where Christ is by now?" Sargeant thought. "He musta gone on way on down the road. He didn't sleep in this jungle."

Sargeant grabbed the train and started to pull himself up into a moving coal car, over the edge of a wheeling coal car. But strangely enough, the car was full of cops. The nearest cop rapped Sargeant soundly across the knuckles with his night stick. Wham! Rapped his big black hands for clinging to the top of the car. Wham! But Sargeant did not turn loose. He clung on and tried to pull himself into the car. He hollered at the top of his voice, "Damn it, lemme in this car!"

"Shut up," barked the cop. "You crazy coon!" He rapped Sargeant across the knuckles and punched him in the stomach. "You ain't out in no jungle now. This ain't no train. You in jail."

55   Wham! across his bare black fingers clinging to the bars of his cell. Wham! between the steel bars low down against his shins.

Suddenly Sargeant realized that he really was in jail. He wasn't on no train. The blood of the night before had dried on his face, his head hurt terribly, and a cop outside in the corridor was hitting him across the knuckles for holding onto the door, yelling and shaking the cell door.

"They musta took me to jail for breaking down the door last night," Sargeant thought, "that church door."

Sargeant went over and sat on a wooden bench against the cold stone wall. He was emptier than ever. His clothes were wet, clammy cold wet, and shoes sloppy with snow water. It was just about dawn. There he was, locked up behind a cell door, nursing his bruised fingers.

The bruised fingers were his, but not the *door*.

60   Not the *club*, but the fingers.

"You wait," mumbled Sargeant, black against the jail wall. "I'm gonna break down this door, too."

"Shut up—or I'll paste you one," said the cop.

"I'm gonna break down this door," yelled Sargeant as he stood up in his cell.

Then he must have been talking to himself because he said, "I wonder where Christ's gone? I wonder if he's gone to Kansas City?"

John Steinbeck
The Chrysanthemums

John Steinbeck (1902–1968) was a Californian, born in Salinas, who studied at Stanford University. *The Grapes of Wrath* (1939), probably his best-known novel, describes the migrant workers who fled the Dust Bowl for the fields of California. In *Tortilla Flat* (1935) his characters are Mexican-Americans in Monterey. Steinbeck wrote many novels, stories, screenplays, and travelogues. In 1962 he was awarded the Nobel Prize for Literature.

The high grey-flannel fog of winter closed off the Salinas Valley from the sky and from all the rest of the world. On every side it sat like a lid on the mountains and made of the great valley a closed pot. On the broad, level land floor the gang ploughs bit deep and left the black earth shining like metal where the shares had cut. On the foot-hill ranches across the Salinas River, the yellow stubble fields seemed to be bathed in pale cold sunshine, but there was no sunshine in the valley now in December. The thick willow scrub along the river flamed with sharp and positive yellow leaves.

It was a time of quiet and of waiting. The air was cold and tender. A light wind blew up from the southwest so that the farmers were mildly hopeful of a good rain before long; but fog and rain do not go together.

Across the river, on Henry Allen's foot-hill ranch there was little work to be done, for the hay was cut and stored and the orchards were ploughed up to receive the rain deeply when it should come. The cattle on the higher slopes were becoming shaggy and rough-coated.

Elisa Allen, working in her flower garden, looked down across the yard and saw Henry, her husband, talking to two men in business suits. The three of them stood by the tractor-shed, each man with one foot on the side of the little Fordson. They smoked cigarettes and studied the machine as they talked.

5 Elisa watched them for a moment and then went back to her work. She was thirty-five. Her face was lean and strong and her eyes were as clear as water. Her figure looked blocked and heavy in her gardening costume, a man's black hat pulled low down over her eyes, clod-hopper shoes, a figured print dress almost completely covered by a big corduroy apron with four big pockets to hold the snips, the trowel and scratcher, the seeds and the knife she worked with. She wore heavy leather gloves to protect her hands while she worked.

She was cutting down the old year's chrysanthemum stalks with a pair of short and powerful scissors. She looked down toward the men by the tractor-shed now and then. Her face was eager and mature and handsome; even her work with the scissors was over-eager, over-powerful. The chrysanthemum stems seemed too small and easy for her energy.

She brushed a cloud of hair out of her eyes with the back of her glove, and left a smudge of earth on her cheek in doing it. Behind her stood the neat white farmhouse with red geraniums close-banked around it as high as the windows. It was a hard-swept-looking little house, with hard-polished windows, and a clean mud-mat on the front steps.

Elisa cast another glance toward the tractor-shed. The strangers were getting into their Ford coupé. She took off a glove and put her strong fingers down into the forest of new green chrysanthemum sprouts that were growing around the old roots. She spread the leaves and looked down among the close-growing stems. No aphids were there, no sow bugs or snails or cutworms. Her terrier fingers destroyed such pests before they could get started.

Elisa started at the sound of her husband's voice. He had come near quietly, and he leaned over the wire fence that protected her flower garden from cattle and dogs and chickens.

10 "At it again," he said. "You've got a strong new crop coming."

Elisa straightened her back and pulled on the gardening glove again. "Yes. They'll be strong this coming year." In her tone and on her face there was a little smugness.

"You've got a gift with things," Henry observed. "Some of those yellow chrysanthemums you had this year were ten inches across. I wish you'd work out in the orchard and raise some apples that big."

Her eyes sharpened. "Maybe I could do it, too. I've a gift with things, all right. My mother had it. She could stick anything in the ground and make it grow. She said it was having planters' hands that knew how to do it."

"Well, it sure works with flowers," he said.

15 "Henry, who were those men you were talking to?"

"Why, sure, that's what I came to tell you. They were from the Western Meat

Company. I sold those thirty head of three-year-old steers. Got nearly my own price, too."

"Good," she said. "Good for you."

"And I thought," he continued, "I thought how it's Saturday afternoon, and we might go into Salinas for dinner at a restaurant, and then to a picture show—to celebrate, you see."

"Good," she repeated. "Oh, yes. That will be good."

20   Henry put on his joking tone. "There's fights tonight. How'd you like to go to the fights?"

"Oh, no," she said breathlessly. "No, I wouldn't like fights."

"Just fooling, Elisa. We'll go to a movie. Let's see. It's two now. I'm going to take Scotty and bring down those steers from the hill. It'll take us maybe two hours. We'll go in town about five and have a dinner at the Cominos Hotel. Like that?"

"Of course I'll like it. It's good to eat away from home."

"All right, then. I'll go get up a couple of horses."

25   She said: "I'll have plenty of time to transplant some of these sets, I guess."

She heard her husband calling Scotty down by the barn. And a little later she saw the two men ride up the pale yellow hillside in search of the steers.

There was a little square sandy bed kept for rooting the chrysanthemums. With her trowel she turned the soil over and over, and smoothed it and patted it firm. Then she dug ten parallel trenches to receive the sets. Back at the chrysanthemum bed she pulled out the little crisp shoots, trimmed off the leaves of each one with her scissors and laid it on a small orderly pile.

A squeak of wheels and plod of hoofs came from the road. Elisa looked up. The country road ran along the dense bank of willows and cottonwoods that bordered the river, and up this road came a curious vehicle, curiously drawn. It was an old spring-wagon, with a round canvas top on it like the cover of a prairie schooner. It was drawn by an old bay horse and a little grey-and-white burro. A big stubble-bearded man sat between the cover flaps and drove the crawling team. Underneath the wagon, between the hind wheels, a lean and rangy mongrel dog walked sedately. Words were painted on the canvas, in clumsy, crooked letters. "Pots, pans, knives, sisors, lawn mores, Fixed." Two rows of articles, and the triumphantly definitive "Fixed" below. The black paint had run down in little sharp points beneath each letter.

Elisa, squatting on the ground, watched to see the crazy, loose-jointed wagon pass by. But it didn't pass. It turned into the farm road in front of her house, crooked old wheels skirling and squeaking. The rangy dog darted from between the wheels and ran ahead. Instantly the two ranch shepherds flew out at him. Then all three stopped, and with stiff and quivering tails, with taut straight legs, with ambassadorial dignity, they slowly circled, sniffing daintily. The caravan pulled up to Elisa's wire fence and stopped. Now the newcomer dog, feeling outnumbered, lowered his tail and retired under the wagon with raised hackles and bared teeth.

30   The man on the wagon seat called out: "That's a bad dog in a fight when he gets started."

Elisa laughed. "I see he is. How soon does he generally get started?"

The man caught up her laughter and echoed it heartily. "Sometimes not for weeks and weeks," he said. He climbed stiffly down, over the wheel. The horse and the donkey drooped like unwatered flowers.

Elisa saw that he was a very big man. Although his hair and beard were greying, he did not look old. His worn black suit was wrinkled and spotted with grease. The laughter had disappeared from his face and eyes the moment his laughing voice ceased. His eyes were dark, and they were full of the brooding that gets in the eyes of teamsters and of sailors. The calloused hands he rested on the wire fence were cracked, and every crack was a black line. He took off his battered hat.

"I'm off my general road, ma'am," he said. "Does this dirt road cut over across the river to the Los Angeles highway?"

35   Elisa stood up and shoved the thick scissors in her apron pocket. "Well, yes, it does, but it winds around and then fords the river. I don't think your team could pull through the sand."

He replied with some asperity: "It might surprise you what them beasts can pull through."

"When they get started?" she asked.

He smiled for a second. "Yes. When they get started."

"Well," said Elisa, "I think you'll save time if you go back to the Salinas road and pick up the highway there."

40   He drew a big finger down the chicken wire and made it sing. "I ain't in any hurry, ma'am. I go from Seattle to San Diego and back every year. Takes all my time. About six months each way. I aim to follow nice weather."

Elisa took off her gloves and stuffed them in the apron pocket with the scissors. She touched the under edge of her man's hat, searching for fugitive hairs. "That sounds like a nice kind of way to live," she said.

He leaned confidentially over the fence. "Maybe you noticed the writing on my wagon. I mend pots and sharpen knives and scissors. You got any of them things to do?"

"Oh, no," she said quickly. "Nothing like that." Her eyes hardened with resistance.

"Scissors is the worst thing," he explained. "Most people just ruin scissors trying to sharpen 'em, but I know how. I got a special tool. It's a little bobbit kind of thing, and patented. But it sure does the trick."

45   "No. My scissors are all sharp."

"All right, then. Take a pot," he continued earnestly, "a bent pot, or a pot with a hole. I can make it like new so you don't have to buy no new ones. That's a saving for you."

"No," she said shortly. "I tell you I have nothing like that for you to do."

His face fell to an exaggerated sadness. His voice took on a whining undertone. "I ain't had a thing to do today. Maybe I won't have no supper tonight. You see I'm off my regular road. I know folks on the highway clear from Seattle to San Diego. They save their things for me to sharpen up because they know I do it so good and save them money."

"I'm sorry," Elisa said irritably. "I haven't anything for you to do."

50   His eyes left her face and fell to searching the ground. They roamed about until they came to the chrysanthemum bed where she had been working. "What's them plants, ma'am?"

The irritation and resistance melted from Elisa's face. "Oh, those are chrysanthemums, giant whites and yellows. I raise them every year, bigger than anybody around here."

"Kind of a long-stemmed flower? Looks like a quick puff of colored smoke?" he asked.

"That's it. What a nice way to describe them."

"They smell kind of nasty till you get used to them," he said.

55 "It's a good bitter smell," she retorted, "not nasty at all."

He changed his tone quickly. "I like the smell myself."

"I had ten-inch blooms this year," she said.

The man leaned farther over the fence. "Look. I know a lady down the road a piece, has got the nicest garden you ever seen. Got nearly every kind of flower but no chrysanthemums. Last time I was mending a copper-bottom washtub for her (that's a hard job but I do it good), she said to me: 'If you ever run acrost some nice chrysanthemums I wish you'd try to get me a few seeds.' That's what she told me."

Elisa's eyes grew alert and eager. "She couldn't have known much about chrysanthemums. You can raise them from seed, but it's much easier to root the little sprouts you see there."

60 "Oh," he said. "I s'pose I can take none to her, then."

"Why yes you can," Elisa cried. "I can put some in damp sand, and you can carry them right along with you. They'll take root in the pot if you keep them damp. And then she can transplant them."

"She'd sure like to have some, ma'am. You say they're nice ones?"

"Beautiful," she said. "Oh, beautiful." Her eyes shone. She tore off the battered hat and shook out her dark pretty hair. "I'll put them in a flowerpot, and you can take them right with you. Come into the yard."

While the man came through the picket gate Elisa ran excitedly along the geranium-bordered path to the back of the house. And she returned carrying a big red flowerpot. The gloves were forgotten now. She kneeled on the ground by the starting bed and dug up the sandy soil with her fingers and scooped it into the bright new flowerpot. Then she picked up the little pile of shoots she had prepared. With her strong fingers she pressed them into the sand and tamped around them with her knuckles. The man stood over her. "I'll tell you what to do," she said. "You remember so you can tell the lady."

65 "Yes, I'll try to remember."

"Well, look. These will take root in about a month. Then she must set them out, about a foot apart in good rich earth like this, see?" She lifted a handful of dark soil for him to look at. "They'll grow fast and tall. Now remember this: In July tell her to cut them down, about eight inches from the ground."

"Before they bloom?" he asked.

"Yes, before they bloom." Her face was tight with eagerness. "They'll grow right up again. About the last of September the buds will start."

She stopped and seemed perplexed. "It's the budding that takes the most care," she said hesitantly. "I don't know how to tell you." She looked deep into his eyes, searchingly. Her mouth opened a little, and she seemed to be listening. "I'll try to tell you," she said. "Did you ever hear of planting hands?"

70 "Can't say I have, ma'am."

"Well, I can only tell you what it feels like. It's when you're picking off the buds you don't want. Everything goes right down into your fingertips. You watch your fingers work. They do it themselves. You can feel how it is. They pick and pick the buds. They never make a mistake. They're with the plant. Do you see? Your fingers and the plant. You can feel that, right up your arm. They know. They never make a mistake. You can feel it. When you're like that you can't do anything wrong. Do you see that? Can you understand that?"

She was kneeling on the ground looking up at him. Her breast swelled passionately.

The man's eyes narrowed. He looked away self-consciously. "Maybe I know," he said. "Sometimes in the night in the wagon there——"

Elisa's voice grew husky. She broke in on him: "I've never lived as you do, but I know what you mean. When the night is dark—why, the stars are sharp-pointed, and there's quiet. Why, you rise up and up! Every pointed star gets driven into your body. It's like that. Hot and sharp and—lovely."

75   Kneeling there, her hand went out toward his legs in the greasy black trousers. Her hesitant fingers almost touched the cloth. Then her hand dropped to the ground. She crouched low like a fawning dog.

He said: "It's nice, just like you say. Only when you don't have no dinner, it ain't."

She stood up then, very straight, and her face was ashamed. She held the flowerpot out to him and placed it gently in his arms. "Here. Put it in your wagon, on the seat, where you can watch it. Maybe I can find something for you to do."

At the back of the house she dug in the can pile and found two old and battered aluminum saucepans. She carried them back and gave them to him. "Here, maybe you can fix these."

His manner changed. He became professional. "Good as new I can fix them." At the back of his wagon he set a little anvil, and out of an oily toolbox dug a small machine hammer. Elisa came through the gate to watch him while he pounded out the dents in the kettles. His mouth grew sure and knowing. At a difficult part of the work he sucked his underlip.

80   "You sleep right in the wagon?" Elisa asked.

"Right in the wagon, ma'am. Rain or shine. I'm dry as a cow in there."

"It must be nice," she said. "It must be very nice. I wish women could do such things."

"It ain't the right kind of a life for a woman."

Her upper lip raised a little, showing her teeth. "How do you know? How can you tell?" she said.

85   "I don't know, ma'am," he protested. "Of course I don't know. Now here's your kettles, done. You don't have to buy no new ones."

"How much?"

"Oh, fifty cents'll do. I keep my prices down and my work good. That's why I have all them satisfied customers up and down the highway."

Elisa brought him a fifty-cent piece from the house and dropped it in his hand. "You might be surprised to have a rival some time. I can sharpen scissors, too. And I can beat the dents out of little pots. I could show you what a woman might do."

He put his hammer back in the oily box and shoved the little anvil out of sight. "It would be a lonely life for a woman, ma'am, and a scarey life, too, with animals creeping under the wagon all night." He climbed over the single-tree, steadying himself with a hand on the burro's white rump. He settled himself in the seat, picked up the lines. "Thank you kindly ma'am," he said. "I'll do like you told me; I'll go back and catch the Salinas road."

90   "Mind," she called, "if you're long in getting there, keep the sand damp."

"Sand, ma'am? . . . Sand? Oh, sure. You mean around the chrysanthemums. Sure I will." He clucked his tongue. The beasts leaned luxuriously into their collars. The mongrel dog took his place between the back wheels. The wagon turned and crawled out the entrance road and back the way it had come, along the river.

Elisa stood in front of her wire fence watching the slow progress of the caravan. Her shoulders were straight, her head thrown back, her eyes half-closed, so that the scene came vaguely into them. Her lips moved silently, forming the words "Good-bye—good-bye." Then she whispered: "That's a bright direction. There's a glowing there." The sound of her whisper startled her. She shook herself free and looked about to see whether anyone had been listening. Only the dogs had heard. They lifted their heads toward her from their sleeping in the dust, and then stretched out their chins and settled asleep again. Elisa turned and ran hurriedly into the house.

In the kitchen she reached behind the stove and felt the water tank. It was full of hot water from the noonday cooking. In the bathroom she tore off her soiled clothes and flung them into the corner. And then she scrubbed herself with a little block of pumice, legs and thighs, loins and chest and arms, until her skin was scratched and red. When she had dried herself she stood in front of a mirror in her bedroom and looked at her body. She tightened her stomach and threw out her chest. She turned and looked over her shoulder at her back.

After a while she began to dress, slowly. She put on her newest underclothing and her nicest stockings and the dress which was the symbol of her prettiness. She worked carefully on her hair, pencilled her eyebrows and rouged her lips.

95   Before she was finished she heard the little thunder of hoofs and the shouts of Henry and his helper as they drove the red steers into the corral. She heard the gate bang shut and set herself for Henry's arrival.

His step sounded on the porch. He entered the house calling: "Elisa, where are you?"

"In my room, dressing. I'm not ready. There's hot water for your bath. Hurry up. It's getting late."

When she heard him splashing in the tub, Elisa laid his dark suit on the bed, and shirt and socks and tie beside it. She stood his polished shoes on the floor beside the bed. Then she went to the porch and sat primly and stiffly down. She looked toward the river road where the willow-line was still yellow with frosted leaves so that under the high grey fog they seemed a thin band of sunshine. This was the only color in the grey afternoon. She sat unmoving for a long time. Her eyes blinked rarely.

Henry came banging out of the door, shoving his tie inside his vest as he came. Elisa stiffened and her face grew tight. Henry stopped short and looked at her. "Why—why, Elisa. You look so nice!"

100   "Nice? You think I look nice? What do you mean by 'nice'?"

Henry blundered on. "I don't know. I mean you look different, strong and happy."

"I am strong? Yes, strong. What do you mean 'strong'?"

He looked bewildered. "You're playing some kind of a game," he said helplessly. "It's a kind of a play. You look strong enough to break a calf over your knee, happy enough to eat it like a watermelon."

For a second she lost her rigidity. "Henry! Don't talk like that. You didn't know what you said." She grew complete again. "I'm strong," she boasted. "I never knew before how strong."

105   Henry looked down toward the tractor-shed, and when he brought his eyes back

to her, they were his own again. "I'll get out the car. You can put on your coat while I'm starting."

Elisa went into the house. She heard him drive to the gate and idle down his motor, and then she took a long time to put on her hat. She pulled it here and pressed it there. When Henry turned the motor off she slipped into her coat and went out.

The little roadster bounced along on the dirt road by the river, raising the birds and driving the rabbits into the brush. Two cranes flapped heavily over the willow-line and dropped into the river-bed.

Far ahead on the road Elisa saw a dark speck. She knew.

She tried not to look as they passed it, but her eyes would not obey. She whispered to herself sadly: "He might have thrown them off the road. That wouldn't have been much trouble, not very much. But he kept the pot," she explained. "He had to keep the pot. That's why he couldn't get them off the road."

110 The roadster turned a bend and she saw the caravan ahead. She swung full around toward her husband so she could not see the little covered wagon and the mis-matched team as the car passed them.

In a moment it was over. The thing was done. She did not look back.

She said loudly, to be heard above the motor: "It will be good, tonight, a good dinner."

"Now you've changed again," Henry complained. He took one hand from the wheel and patted her knee. "I ought to take you in to dinner oftener. It would be good for both of us. We get so heavy out on the ranch."

"Henry," she asked, "could we have wine at dinner?"

115 "Sure we could. Say! That will be fine."

She was silent for a while; then she said: "Henry, at those prizefights, do the men hurt each other very much?"

"Sometimes a little, not often. Why?"

"Well, I've read how they break noses, and blood runs down their chests. I've read how the fighting gloves get heavy and soggy with blood."

He looked around at her. "What's the matter, Elisa? I didn't know you read things like that." He brought the car to a stop, then turned to the right over the Salinas River bridge.

120 "Do any women ever go to the fights?" she asked.

"Oh, sure, some. What's the matter, Elisa? Do you want to go? I don't think you'd like it, but I'll take you if you really want to go."

She relaxed limply in the seat. "Oh, no. No. I don't want to go. I'm sure I don't." Her face was turned away from him. "It will be enough if we can have wine. It will be plenty." She turned up her coat collar so he could not see that she was crying weakly—like an old woman.

Isaac Bashevis Singer
Gimpel the Fool

Isaac Bashevis Singer (1904–   ) was born in Poland and came to the United
States in 1935, becoming a U.S. citizen in 1943. He writes in Yiddish, from
which his work is then translated into English. He lives in Manhattan and
draws frequently on the remembered past of Jewish communities in Poland.
His novels include *The Family Moskat*, which appeared in England in 1950,
Satan in Goray (1955), *The Magician of Lublin* (1960), and *Sosha* (1979). He
has collected his short stories, which are probably his best work, in *Gimpel the
Fool* (1957), *The Spinoza of Market Street* (1961), *Short Friday* (1964), and *The
Seance and Other Stories* (1968). In 1978 he was awarded the Nobel Prize for
Literature.

I

I am Gimpel the fool. I don't think myself a fool. On the contrary. But that's what
folks call me. They gave me the name while I was still in school. I had seven
names in all: imbecile, donkey, flax-head, dope, glump, ninny, and fool. The last
name stuck. What did my foolishness consist of? I was easy to take in. They said,
"Gimpel, you know the rabbi's wife has been brought to childbed?" So I skipped
school. Well, it turned out to be a lie. How was I supposed to know? She hadn't
had a big belly. But I never looked at her belly. Was that really so foolish? The
gang laughed and hee-hawed, stomped and danced and chanted a good-night
prayer. And instead of the raisins they give when a woman's lying in, they stuffed
my hand full of goat turds. I was no weakling. If I slapped someone he'd see all
the way to Cracow. But I'm really not a slugger by nature. I think to myself: Let
it pass. So they take advantage of me.

I was coming home from school and heard a dog barking. I'm not afraid of dogs,
but of course I never want to start up with them. One of them may be mad, and
if he bites there's not a Tartar in the world who can help you. So I made tracks.
Then I looked around and saw the whole market-place wild with laughter. It was
no dog at all but Wolf-Leib the Thief. How was I supposed to know it was he? It
sounded like a howling bitch.

When the pranksters and leg-pullers found that I was easy to fool, every one of
them tried his luck with me. "Gimpel, the Czar is coming to Frampol; Gimpel, the
moon fell down in Turbeen; Gimpel, little Hodel Furpiece found a treasure behind
the bathhouse." And I like a golem[1] believed everyone. In the first place, everything
is possible, as it is written in the Wisdom of the Fathers, I've forgotten just how.
Second, I had to believe when the whole town came down on me! If I ever dared
to say, "Ah, you're kidding!" there was trouble. People got angry. "What do you
mean! You want to call everyone a liar?" What was I to do? I believed them, and
I hope at least that did them some good.

I am an orphan. My grandfather who brought me up was already bent toward
the grave. So they turned me over to a baker, and what a time they gave me there!
Every woman or girl who came to bake a batch of noodles had to fool me at least
once. "Gimpel, there's a fair in heaven; Gimpel, the rabbi gave birth to a calf in
the seventh month; Gimpel, a cow flew over the roof and laid brass eggs." A
student from the yeshiva[2] came once to buy a roll, and he said, "You, Gimpel,

---

[1]Stupid person   [2]School of Jewish thought and tradition

while you stand here scraping with your baker's shovel the Messiah has come. The dead have arisen." "What do you mean?" I said. "I heard no one blowing the ram's horn!" He said, "Are you deaf?" And all began to cry, "We heard it, we heard!" Then in came Rietze the Candle-dipper and called out in her hoarse voice, "Gimpel, your father and mother have stood up from the grave. They're looking for you."

5   To tell the truth, I knew very well that nothing of the sort had happened, but all the same, as folks were talking, I threw on my wool vest and went out. Maybe something had happened. What did I stand to lose by looking? Well, what a cat music went up! And then I took a vow to believe nothing more. But that was no go either. They confused me so that I didn't know the big end from the small.

I went to the rabbi to get some advice. He said, "It is written, better to be a fool all your days than for one hour to be evil. You are not a fool. They are the fools. For he who causes his neighbor to feel shame loses Paradise himself." Nevertheless the rabbi's daughter took me in. As I left the rabbinical court she said, "Have you kissed the wall yet?" I said, "No, what for?" She answered, "It's the law; you've got to do it after every visit." Well, there didn't seem to be any harm in it. And she burst out laughing. It was a fine trick. She put one over on me all right.

I wanted to go off to another town, but then everyone got busy matchmaking, and they were after me so they nearly tore my coat tails off. They talked at me and talked until I got water on the ear. She was no chaste maiden, but they told me she was a virgin pure. She had a limp, and they said it was deliberate, from coyness. She had a bastard, and they told me the child was her little brother. I cried, "You're wasting your time. I'll never marry that whore." But they said indignantly, "What a way to talk! Aren't you ashamed of yourself? We can take you to the rabbi and have you fined for giving her a bad name." I saw then that I wouldn't escape them so easily and I thought: They're set on making me their butt. But when you're married the husband's the master, and if that's all right with her it's agreeable to me too. Besides, you can't pass through life unscathed, nor expect to.

I went to her clay house, which was built on the sand, and the whole gang, hollering and chorusing, came after me. They acted like bear-baiters. When we came to the well they stopped all the same. They were afraid to start anything with Elka. Her mouth would open as if it were on a hinge, and she had a fierce tongue. I entered the house. Lines were strung from wall to wall and clothes were drying. Barefoot she stood by the tub, doing the wash. She was dressed in a worn hand-me-down gown of plush. She had her hair up in braids and pinned across her head. It took my breath away, almost, the reek of it all.

Evidently she knew who I was. She took a look at me and said, "Look who's here! He's come, the drip. Grab a seat."

10   I told her all; I denied nothing. "Tell me the truth," I said, "are you really a virgin, and is that mischievous Yechiel actually your little brother? Don't be deceitful with me, for I'm an orphan."

"I'm an orphan myself," she answered, "and whoever tries to twist you up, may the end of his nose take a twist. But don't let them think they can take advantage of me. I want a dowry of fifty guilders, and let them take up a collection besides. Otherwise they can kiss my you-know-what." She was very plainspoken. I said, "It's the bride and not the groom who gives a dowry." Then she said, "Don't bargain with me. Either a flat 'yes' or a flat 'no'—Go back where you came from."

I thought: No bread will ever be baked from *this* dough. But ours is not a poor town. They consented to everything and proceeded with the wedding. It so happened that there was a dysentery epidemic at the time. The ceremony was held at the cemetery gates, near the little corpse-washing hut. The fellows got drunk. While the marriage contract was being drawn up I heard the most pious high rabbi ask, "Is the bride a widow or a divorced woman?" And the sexton's wife answered for her, "Both a widow and divorced." It was a black moment for me. But what was I to do, run away from under the marriage canopy?

There was singing and dancing. An old granny danced opposite men, hugging a braided white *chalah*.[1] The master of revels made a "God 'a mercy" in memory of the bride's parents. The schoolboys threw burrs, as on Tishe b'Av[2] fast day. There were a lot of gifts after the sermon: a noodle board, a kneading trough, a bucket, brooms, ladles, household articles galore. Then I took a look and saw two strapping young men carrying a crib. "What do we need this for?" I asked. So they said, "Don't rack your brains about it. It's all right, it'll come in handy." I realized I was going to be rooked. Take it another way though, what did I stand to lose? I reflected: I'll see what comes of it. A whole town can't go altogether crazy.

II

At night I came where my wife lay, but she wouldn't let me in. "Say, look here, is this what they married us for?" I said. And she said, "My monthly has come." "But yesterday they took you to the ritual bath, and that's afterward, isn't it supposed to be?" "Today isn't yesterday," said she, "and yesterday's not today. You can beat it if you don't like it." In short, I waited.

15   Not four months later she was in childbed. The townsfolk hid their laughter with their knuckles. But what could I do? She suffered intolerable pains and clawed at the walls. "Gimpel," she cried, "I'm going. Forgive me!" The house filled with women. They were boiling pans of water. The screams rose to the welkin.

The thing to do was to go to the House of Prayer to repeat Psalms, and that was what I did.

The townsfolk liked that, all right. I stood in a corner saying Psalms and prayers, and they shook their heads at me. "Pray, pray!" they told me. "Prayer never made any woman pregnant." One of the congregation put a straw to my mouth and said, "Hay for the cows." There was something to that too, by God!

She gave birth to a boy. Friday at the synagogue the sexton stood up before the Ark,[3] pounded on the reading table, and announced, "The wealthy Reb Gimpel invites the congregation to a feast in honor of the birth of a son." The whole House of Prayer rang with laughter. My face was flaming. But there was nothing I could do. After all, I *was* the one responsible for the circumcision honors and rituals.

Half the town came running. You couldn't wedge another soul in. Women brought peppered chick-peas, and there was a keg of beer from the tavern. I ate and drank as much as anyone, and they all congratulated me. Then there was a circumcision, and I named the boy after my father, may he rest in peace. When all were gone and I was left with my wife alone, she thrust her head through the bed-curtain and called me to her.

20   "Gimpel," said she, "why are you silent? Has your ship gone and sunk?"

"What shall I say?" I answered. "A fine thing you've done to me! If my mother had known of it she'd have died a second time."

---

[1] Loaf of bread eaten on the Sabbath and other holidays   [2] A day of fasting and deep mourning
[3] Container of the holy books of the Torah

She said, "Are you crazy, or what?"

"How can you make such a fool," I said, "of one who should be the lord and master?"

"What's the matter with you?" she said. "What have you taken it into your head to imagine?"

I saw that I must speak bluntly and openly. "Do you think this the way to use an orphan?" I said. "You have borne a bastard."

She answered, "Drive this foolishness out of your head. The child is yours."

"How can he be mine?" I argued. "He was born seventeen weeks after the wedding."

She told me then that he was premature. I said, "Isn't he a little too premature?" She said she had had a grandmother who carried just as short a time and she resembled this grandmother of hers as one drop of water does another. She swore to it with such oaths that you would have believed a peasant at the fair if he had used them. To tell the plain truth, I didn't believe her; but when I talked it over next day with the schoolmaster he told me that the very same thing had happened to Adam and Eve. Two they went up to bed, and four they descended.

"There isn't a woman in the world who is not the granddaughter of Eve," he said.

That was how it was; they argued me dumb. But then, who really knows how such things are?

I began to forget my sorrow. I loved the child madly, and he loved me too. As soon as he saw me he'd wave his little hands and want me to pick him up, and when he was colicky I was the only one who could pacify him. I bought him a little bone teething ring and a little gilded cap. He was forever catching the evil eye from someone, and then I had to run to get one of those abracadabras for him that would get him out of it. I worked like an ox. You know how expenses go up when there's an infant in the house. I don't want to lie about it; I didn't dislike Elka either, for that matter. She swore at me and cursed, and I couldn't get enough of her. What strength she had! One of her looks could rob you of the power of speech. And her orations! Pitch and sulphur, that's what they were full of, and yet somehow also full of charm. I adored her every word. She gave me bloody wounds though.

In the evening I brought her a white loaf as well as a dark one, and also poppyseed rolls I baked myself. I thieved because of her and swiped everything I could lay hands on: macaroons, raisins, almonds, cakes. I hope I may be forgiven for stealing from the Saturday pots the women left to warm in the baker's oven. I would take out scraps of meat, a chunk of pudding, a chicken leg or head, a piece of tripe, whatever I could nip quickly. She ate and became fat and handsome.

I had to sleep away from home all during the week, at the bakery. On Friday nights when I got home she always made an excuse of some sort. Either she had heartburn, or a stitch in the side or hiccups, or headaches. You know what women's excuses are. I had a bitter time of it. It was rough. To add to it, this little brother of hers, the bastard, was growing bigger. He'd put lumps on me, and when I wanted to hit back she'd open her mouth and curse so powerfully I saw a green haze floating before my eyes. Ten times a day she threatened to divorce me. Another man in my place would have taken French leave and disappeared. But I'm the type that bears it and says nothing. What's one to do? Shoulders are from God, and burdens too.

One night there was a calamity in the bakery; the oven burst, and we almost had a fire. There was nothing to do but go home, so I went home. Let me, I thought, also taste the joy of sleeping in bed in mid-week. I didn't want to wake the sleeping mite and tiptoed into the house. Coming in, it seemed to me that I heard not the snoring of one but, as it were, a double snore, one a thin enough snore and the other like the snoring of a slaughtered ox. Oh, I didn't like that! I didn't like it at all. I went up to the bed, and things suddenly turned black. Next to Elka lay a man's form. Another in my place would have made an uproar, and enough noise to rouse the whole town, but the thought occurred to me that I might wake the child. A little thing like that—why frighten a little swallow, I thought. All right then, I went back to the bakery and stretched out on a sack of flour and till morning I never shut an eye. I shivered as if I had malaria. "Enough of being a donkey," I said to myself. "Gimpel isn't going to be a sucker all his life. There's a limit even to the foolishness of a fool like Gimpel."

35   In the morning I went to the rabbi to get advice, and it made a great commotion in the town. They sent the beadle for Elka right away. She came, carrying the child. And what do you think she did? She denied it, denied everything, bone and stone! "He's out of his head," she said. "I know nothing of dreams or divinations." They yelled at her, warned her, hammered on the table, but she stuck to her guns: it was a false accusation, she said.

The butchers and the horse-traders took her part. One of the lads from the slaughterhouse came by and said to me, "We've got our eye on you, you're a marked man." Meanwhile the child started to bear down and soiled itself. In the rabbinical court there was an Ark of the Covenant,[1] and they couldn't allow that, so they sent Elka away.

I said to the rabbi, "What shall I do?"

"You must divorce her at once." said he.

"And what if she refuses?" I asked.

40   He said, "You must serve the divorce. That's all you have to do."

I said, "Well, all right, Rabbi. Let me think about it."

"There's nothing to think about," said he. "You mustn't remain under the same roof with her."

"And if I want to see the child?" I asked.

"Let her go, the harlot," said he, "and her brood of bastards with her."

45   The verdict he gave was that I mustn't even cross her threshold—never again, as long as I should live.

During the day it didn't bother me so much. I thought: It was bound to happen, the abscess had to burst. But at night when I stretched out upon the sacks I felt it all very bitterly. A longing took me, for her and for the child. I wanted to be angry, but that's my misfortune exactly, I don't have it in me to be really angry. In the first place—this was how my thoughts went—there's bound to be a slip sometimes. You can't live without errors. Probably that lad who was with her led her on and gave her presents and what not, and women are often long on hair and short on sense, and so he got around her. And then since she denies it so, maybe I was only seeing things? Hallucinations do happen. You see a figure or a mannikin or something, but when you come up closer it's nothing, there's not a thing there. And if that's so, I'm doing her an injustice. And when I got so far in my thoughts I started to weep. I sobbed so that I wet the flour where I lay. In the morning I

[1]Box holding the Ten Commandments

went to the rabbi and told him that I had made a mistake. The rabbi wrote on with his quill, and he said that if that were so he would have to reconsider the whole case. Until he had finished I wasn't to go near my wife, but I might send her bread and money by messenger.

III

Nine months passed before all the rabbis could come to an agreement. Letters went back and forth. I hadn't realized that there could be so much erudition about a matter like this.

Meanwhile Elka gave birth to still another child, a girl this time. On the Sabbath I went to the synagogue and invoked a blessing on her. They called me up to the Torah, and I named the child for my mother-in-law—may she rest in peace. The louts and loudmouths of the town who came into the bakery gave me a going over. All Frampol refreshed its spirits because of my trouble and grief. However, I re-solved that I would always believe what I was told. What's the good of *not* be-lieving? Today it's your wife you don't believe; tomorrow it's God Himself you won't take stock in.

By an apprentice who was her neighbor I sent daily a corn or a wheat loaf, or a piece of pastry, rolls or bagels, or, when I got the chance, a slab of pudding, a slice of honeycake, or wedding strudel—whatever came my way. The apprentice was a goodhearted lad, and more than once he added something on his own. He had formerly annoyed me a lot, plucking my nose and digging me in the ribs, but when he started to be a visitor to my house he became kind and friendly. "Hey, you, Gimpel," he said to me, "you have a very decent little wife and two fine kids. You don't deserve them."

"But the things people say about her," I said.

"Well, they have long tongues," he said, "and nothing to do with them but babble. Ignore it as you ignore the cold of last winter."

One day the rabbi sent for me and said, "Are you certain, Gimpel, that you were wrong about your wife?"

I said, "I'm certain."

"Why, but look here! You yourself saw it."

55   "It must have been a shadow," I said.

"The shadow of what?"

"Just one of the beams, I think."

"You can go home then. You owe thanks to the Yanover rabbi. He found an obscure reference in Maimonides[1] that favored you."

I seized the rabbi's hand and kissed it.

60   I wanted to run home immediately. It's no small thing to be separated for so long a time from wife and child. Then I reflected: I'd better go back to work now, and go home in the evening. I said nothing to anyone, although as far as my heart was concerned it was like one of the Holy Days. The women teased and twitted me as they did every day, but my thought was: Go on, with your loose talk. The truth is out, like the oil upon the water. Maimonides says it's right, and therefore it is right!

At night, when I had covered the dough to let it rise, I took my share of bread and a little sack of flour and started homeward. The moon was full and the stars

[1]See note 1, page 314.

were glistening, something to terrify the soul. I hurried onward, and before me darted a long shadow. It was winter, and a fresh snow had fallen. I had a mind to sing, but it was growing late and I didn't want to wake the householders. Then I felt like whistling, but I remembered that you don't whistle at night because it brings the demons out. So I was silent and walked as fast as I could.

Dogs in the Christian yards barked at me when I passed, but I thought: Bark your teeth out! What are you but mere dogs? Whereas I am a man, the husband of a fine wife, the father of promising children.

As I approached the house my heart started to pound as though it were the heart of a criminal. I felt no fear, but my heart went thump! thump! Well, no drawing back. I quietly lifted the latch and went in. Elka was asleep. I looked at the infant's cradle. The shutter was closed, but the moon forced its way through the cracks. I saw the newborn child's face and loved it as soon as I saw it— immediately—each tiny bone.

Then I came nearer to the bed. And what did I see but the apprentice lying there beside Elka. The moon went out all at once. It was utterly black, and I trembled. My teeth chattered. The bread fell from my hands, and my wife waked and said, "Who is that, ah?"

65   I muttered, "It's me."

"Gimpel?" she asked. "How come you're here? I thought it was forbidden."

"The rabbi said," I answered and shook as with a fever.

"Listen to me, Gimpel," she said, "go out to the shed and see if the goat's all right. It seems she's been sick." I have forgotten to say that we had a goat. When I heard she was unwell I went into the yard. The nannygoat was a good little creature. I had a nearly human feeling for her.

With hesitant steps I went up to the shed and opened the door. The goat stood there on her four feet. I felt her everywhere, drew her by the horns, examined her udders, and found nothing wrong. She had probably eaten too much bark. "Good night, little goat," I said. "Keep well." And the little beast answered with a "Maa" as though to thank me for the good will.

70   I went back. The apprentice had vanished.

"Where," I asked, "is the lad?"

"What lad?" my wife answered.

"What do you mean?" I said. "The apprentice. You were sleeping with him."

"The things I have dreamed this night and the night before," she said, "may they come true and lay you low, body and soul! An evil spirit has taken root in you and dazzles your sight." She screamed out, "You hateful creature! You moon calf! You spook! You uncouth man! Get out, or I'll scream all Frampol out of bed!"

75   Before I could move, her brother sprang out from behind the oven and struck me a blow on the back of the head. I thought he had broken my neck. I felt that something about me was deeply wrong, and I said, "Don't make a scandal. All that's needed now is that people should accuse me of raising spooks and *dybbuks*."[1] For that was what she had meant. "No one will touch bread of my baking."

In short, I somehow calmed her.

"Well," she said, "that's enough. Lie down, and be shattered by wheels."

Next morning I called the apprentice aside. "Listen here, brother!" I said. And so on and so forth. "What do you say?" He stared at me as though I had dropped from the roof or something.

---

[1]Evil spirits

"I swear," he said, "you'd better go to an herb doctor or some healer. I'm afraid you have a screw loose, but I'll hush it up for you." And that's how the thing stood.

80   To make a long story short, I lived twenty years with my wife. She bore me six children, four daughters and two sons. All kinds of things happened, but I neither saw nor heard. I believed, and that's all. The rabbi recently said to me, "Belief in itself is beneficial. It is written that a good man lives by his faith."

Suddenly my wife took sick. It began with a trifle, a little growth upon the breast. But she evidently was not destined to live long; she had no years. I spent a fortune on her. I have fogotten to say that by this time I had a bakery of my own and in Frampol was considered to be something of a rich man. Daily the healer came, and every witch doctor in the neighborhood was brought. They decided to use leeches, and after that to try cupping. They even called a doctor from Lublin, but it was too late. Before she died she called me to her bed and said, "Forgive me, Gimpel."

I said, "What is there to forgive? You have been a good and faithful wife."

"Woe, Gimpel!" she said. "It was ugly how I deceived you all these years. I want to go clean to my Maker, and so I have to tell you that the children are not yours."

If I had been clouted on the head with a piece of wood it couldn't have bewildered me more.

85   "Whose are they?" I asked.

"I don't know," she said. "There were a lot . . . but they're not yours." And as she spoke she tossed her head to the side, her eyes turned glassy, and it was all up with Elka. On her whitened lips there remained a smile.

I imagined that, dead as she was, she was saying, "I deceived Gimpel. That was the meaning of my brief life."

IV

One night, when the period of mourning was done, as I lay dreaming on the flour sacks, there came the Spirit of Evil himself and said to me, "Gimpel, why do you sleep?"

I said, "What should I be doing? Eating *kreplach*?"[1]

90   "The whole world deceives you," he said, "and you ought to deceive the world in your turn."

"How can I deceive all the world?" I asked him.

He answered, "You might accumulate a bucket of urine every day and at night pour it into the dough. Let the sages of Frampol eat filth."

"What about the judgment in the world to come?" I said.

"There is no world to come," he said. "They've sold you a bill of goods and talked you into believing you carried a cat in your belly. What nonsense!"

95   "Well then," I said, "and is there a God?"

He answered, "There is no God either."

"What," I said, "*is* there, then?"

"A thick mire."

He stood before my eyes with a goatish beard and horn, long-toothed, and with a tail. Hearing such words, I wanted to snatch him by the tail, but I tumbled from the flour sacks and nearly broke a rib. Then it happened that I had to answer the

[1]A dumpling filled with cheese or meat

call of nature, and, passing, I saw the risen dough, which seemed to say to me, "Do it." In brief, I let myself be persuaded.

100   At dawn the apprentice came. We kneaded the bread, scattered caraway seeds on it, and set it to bake. Then the apprentice went away, and I was left sitting in the little trench by the oven on a pile of rags. Well, Gimpel, I thought, you've revenged yourself on them for all the shame they've put on you. Outside the frost glittered, but it was warm beside the oven. The flames heated my face. I bent my head and fell into a doze.

I saw in a dream at once, Elka in her shroud. She called to me, "What have you done, Gimpel?"

I said to her, "It's all your fault," and started to cry.

"You fool!" she said. "You fool! Because I was false is everything false too? I never deceived anyone but myself. I'm paying for it all, Gimpel. They spare you nothing here."

I looked at her face. It was black; I was startled and waked, and remained sitting dumb. I sensed that everything hung in the balance. A false step now and I'd lose Eternal Life. But God gave me His help. I seized the long shovel and took out the loaves, carried them into the yard, and started to dig a hole in the frozen earth.

105   My apprentice came back as I was doing it. "What are you doing boss?" he said, and grew pale as a corpse.

"I know what I'm doing," I said and I buried it all before his very eyes.

Then I went home, and took my hoard from its hiding place, and divided it among the children. "I saw your mother tonight," I said. "She's turning black, poor thing."

They were so astounded they couldn't speak a word.

"Be well," I said, "and forget that such a one as Gimpel ever existed." I put on my short coat, a pair of boots, took the bag that held my prayer shawl in one hand, my stock in the other, and kissed the *mezzuzah*.[1] When people saw me in the street they were greatly surprised.

110   "Where are you going?" they said.

I answered, "Into the world." And so I departed from Frampol.

I wandered over the land, and good people did not neglect me. After many years I became old and white; I heard a great deal, many lies and falsehoods, but the longer I lived the more I understood that there were really no lies. Whatever doesn't really happen is dreamed at night. It happens to one if it doesn't happen to another, tomorrow if not today, or a century hence if not next year. What difference can it make? Often I heard tales of which I said, "Now this is a thing that cannot happen." But before a year had elapsed I heard that it actually had come to pass somewhere.

Going from place to place, eating at strange tables, it oftens happens that I spin yarns—improbable things that could never have happened—about devils, magicians, windmills, and the like. The children run after me, calling, "Grandfather, tell us a story." Sometimes they ask for particular stories, and I try to please them. A fat young boy once said to me, "Grandfather, it's the same story you told us before." The little rogue, he was right.

So it is with dreams too. It is many years since I left Frampol, but as soon as I shut my eyes I am there again. And whom do you think I see? Elka. She is standing by the washtub, as at our first encounter, but her face is shining and her

[1] A container for texts from Deuteronomy (6:4–9, 11:13–21) that is affixed to doorposts by Orthodox Jews

eyes are as radiant as the eyes of a saint, and she speaks outlandish words to me, strange things. When I wake I have forgotten it all. But while the dream lasts I am comforted. She answers all my queries, and what comes out is that all is right. I weep and implore, "Let me be with you." And she consoles me and tells me to be patient. The time is nearer than it is far. Sometimes she strokes and kisses me and weeps upon my face. When I awaken I feel her lips and taste the salt of her tears.

115   No doubt the world is entirely an imaginary world, but it is only once removed from the true world. At the door of the hovel where I lie, there stands the plank on which the dead are taken away. The gravedigger Jew has his spade ready. The grave waits and the worms are hungry; the shrouds are prepared—I carry them in my beggar's sack. Another *shnorrer*[1] is waiting to inherit my bed of straw. When the time comes I will go joyfully. Whatever may be there, it will be real, without complication, without ridicule, without deception. God be praised: there even Gimpel cannot be deceived.

[1]Beggar

Ralph Ellison
Battle Royal

Ralph Ellison (1914–   ) was born in Oklahoma and has lived in recent years in New York City. His one novel, *The Invisible Man* (1952), won him immediate recognition as a leading black American writer. In 1964 he published a collection of essays, *Shadow and Act.*

It goes a long way back, some twenty years. All my life I had been looking for something, and everywhere I turned someone tried to tell me what it was. I accepted their answers too, though they were often in contradiction and even self-contradictory. I was naïve. I was looking for myself and asking everyone except myself questions which I, and only I, could answer. It took me a long time and much painful boomeranging of my expectations to achieve a realization everyone else appears to have been born with: That I am nobody but myself. But first I had to discover that I am an invisible man!

And yet I am no freak of nature, nor of history. I was in the cards, other things having been equal (or unequal) eighty-five years ago. I am not ashamed of my grandparents for having been slaves. I am only ashamed of myself for having at one time been ashamed. About eighty-five years ago they were told that they were free, united with others of our country in everything pertaining to the common good, and, in everything social, separate like the fingers of the hand. And they believed it. They exulted in it. They stayed in their place, worked hard, and brought up my father to do the same. But my grandfather is the one. He was an odd old guy, my grandfather, and I am told I take after him. It was he who caused the trouble. On his deathbed he called my father to him and said, "Son, after I'm gone I want you to keep up the fight. I never told you, but our life is a war and I have been a traitor all my born days, a spy in the enemy's country ever since I give up my gun back in the Reconstruction. Live with your head in the. lion's mouth. I want you to overcome 'em with yeses, undermine 'em with grins, agree 'em to death and destruction, let 'em swoller you till they vomit or bust wide open." They thought the old man had gone out of his mind. He had been the meekest of men. The younger children were rushed from the room, the shades drawn and the flame of the lamp turned so low that it sputtered on the wick like the old man's breathing. "Learn it to the younguns," he whispered fiercely; then he died.

But my folks were more alarmed over his last words than over his dying. It was as though he had not died at all, his words caused so much anxiety. I was warned emphatically to forget what he had said and, indeed, this is the first time it has been mentioned outside the family circle. It had a tremendous effect upon me, however. I could never be sure of what he meant. Grandfather had been a quiet old man who never made any trouble, yet on his deathbed he had called himself a traitor and a spy, and he had spoken of his meekness as a dangerous activity. It became a constant puzzle which lay unanswered in the back of my mind. And whenever things went well for me I remembered my grandfather and felt guilty and uncomfortable. It was as though I was carrying out his advice in spite of myself. And to make it worse, everyone loved me for it. I was praised by the most lily-white men of the town. I was considered an example of desirable conduct—just as my grandfather had been. And what puzzled me was that the old man had defined it as *treachery*. When I was praised for my conduct I felt a guilt that in some way I was doing something that was really against the wishes of the white folks, that if they had understood they would have desired me to act just the opposite, that I should have been sulky and mean, and that that really would have been what they wanted, even though they were fooled and thought they wanted me to act as I did. It made me afraid that some day they would look upon me as a traitor and I would be lost. Still I was more afraid to act any other way because they didn't like that at all. The old man's words were like a curse. On my graduation day I delivered an oration in which I showed that humility was the secret, indeed, the very essence of progress. (Not that I believed this—how could I, remembering my grandfather?—I only believed that it worked.) It was a great success. Everyone praised me and I was invited to give the speech at a gathering of the town's leading white citizens. It was a triumph for our whole community.

It was in the main ballroom of the leading hotel. When I got there I discovered that it was on the occasion of a smoker, and I was told that since I was to be there anyway I might as well take part in the battle royal to be fought by some of my schoolmates as part of the entertainment. The battle royal came first.

5   All of the town's big shots were there in their tuxedos, wolfing down the buffet foods, drinking beer and whiskey and smoking black cigars. It was a large room with a high ceiling. Chairs were arranged in neat rows around three sides of a portable boxing ring. The fourth side was clear, revealing a gleaming space of polished floor. I had some misgivings over the battle royal,. by the way. Not from

a distaste for fighting, but because I didn't care too much for the other fellows who were to take part. They were tough guys who seemed to have no grandfather's curse worrying their minds. No one could mistake their toughness. And besides, I suspected that fighting a battle royal might detract from the dignity of my speech. In those pre-invisible days I visualized myself as a potential Booker T. Washington.[1] But the other fellows didn't care too much for me either, and there were nine of them. I felt superior to them in my way, and I didn't like the manner in which we were all crowded together into the servants' elevator. Nor did they like my being there. In fact, as the warmly lighted floors flashed past the elevator we had words over the fact that I, by taking part in the fight, had knocked one of their friends out of a night's work.

We were led out of the elevator through a rococo hall into an anteroom and told to get into our fighting togs. Each of us was issued a pair of boxing gloves and ushered out into the big mirrored hall, which we entered looking cautiously about us and whispering, lest we might accidentally be heard above the noise of the room. It was foggy with cigar smoke. And already the whiskey was taking effect. I was shocked to see some of the most important men of the town quite tipsy. They were all there—bankers, lawyers, judges, doctors, fire chiefs, teachers, merchants. Even one of the more fashionable pastors. Something we could not see was going on up front. A clarinet was vibrating sensuously and the men were standing up and moving eagerly forward. We were a small tight group, clustered together, our bare upper bodies touching and shining with anticipatory sweat; while up front the big shots were becoming increasingly excited over something we still could not see. Suddenly I heard the school superintendent, who had told me to come, yell, "Bring up the shines, gentlemen! Bring up the little shines!"

We were rushed up to the front of the ballroom, where it smelled even more strongly of tobacco and whiskey. Then we were pushed into place. I almost wet my pants. A sea of faces, some hostile, some amused, ringed around us, and in the center, facing us, stood a magnificent blonde—stark naked. There was a dead silence. I felt a blast of cold air chill me. I tried to back away, but they were behind me and around me. Some of the boys stood with lowered heads, trembling. I felt a wave of irrational guilt and fear. My teeth chattered, my skin turned to goose flesh, my knees knocked. Yet I was strongly attracted and looked in spite of myself. Had the price of looking been blindness, I would have looked. The hair was yellow like that of a circus kewpie doll, the face heavily powdered and rouged, as though to form an abstract mask, the eyes hollow and smeared a cool blue, the color of a baboon's butt. I felt a desire to spit upon her as my eyes brushed slowly over her body. Her breasts were firm and round as the domes of East Indian temples, and I stood so close as to see the fine skin texture and beads of pearly perspiration glistening like dew around the pink and erected buds of her nipples. I wanted at one and the same time to run from the room, to sink through the floor, or go to her and cover her from my eyes and the eyes of the others with my body; to feel the soft thighs, to caress her and destroy her, to love her and murder her, to hide from her, and yet to stroke where below the small American flag tattooed upon her belly her thighs formed a capital V. I had a notion that of all in the room she saw only me with her impersonal eyes.

And then she began to dance, a slow sensuous movement; the smoke of a hundred cigars clinging to her like the thinnest of veils. She seemed like a fair

[1]Black American teacher and leader (1856–1915)

bird-girl girdled in veils calling to me from the angry surface of some gray and threatening sea. I was transported. Then I became aware of the clarinet playing and the big shots yelling at us. Some threatened us if we looked and others if we did not. On my right I saw one boy faint. And now a man grabbed a silver pitcher from a table and stepped close as he dashed ice water upon him and stood him up and forced two of us to support him as his head hung and moans issued from his thick bluish lips. Another boy began to plead to go home. He was the largest of the group, wearing dark red fighting trunks much too small to conceal the erection which projected from him as though in answer to the insinuating low-registered moaning of the clarinet. He tried to hide himself with his boxing gloves.

And all the while the blonde continued dancing, smiling faintly at the big shots who watched her with fascination, and faintly smiling at our fear. I noticed a certain merchant who followed her hungrily, his lips loose and drooling. He was a large man who wore diamond studs in a shirtfront which swelled with the ample paunch underneath, and each time the blonde swayed her undulating hips he ran his hand through the thin hair of his bald head and, with his arms upheld, his posture clumsy like that of an intoxicated panda, wound his belly in a slow and obscene grind. This creature was completely hypnotized. The music had quickened. As the dancer flung herself about with a detached expression on her face, the men began reaching out to touch her. I could see their beefy fingers sink into the soft flesh. Some of the others tried to stop them and she began to move around the floor in graceful circles, as they gave chase, slipping and sliding over the polished floor. It was mad. Chairs went crashing, drinks were spilt, as they ran laughing and howling after her. They caught her just as she reached a door, raised her from the floor, and tossed her as college boys are tossed at a hazing, and above her red, fixed-smiling lips I saw the terror and disgust in her eyes, almost like my own terror and that which I saw in some of the other boys. As I watched, they tossed her twice and her soft breasts seemed to flatten against the air and her legs flung wildly as she spun. Some of the more sober ones helped her to escape. And I started off the floor, heading for the anteroom with the rest of the boys.

10   Some were still crying and in hysteria. But as we tried to leave we were stopped and ordered to get into the ring. There was nothing to do but what we were told. All ten of us climbed under the ropes and allowed ourselves to be blindfolded with broad bands of white cloth. One of the men seemed to feel a bit sympathetic and tried to cheer us up as we stood with our backs against the ropes. Some of us tried to grin. "See that boy over there?" one of the men said. "I want you to run across at the bell and give it to him right in the belly. If you don't get him, I'm going to get you. I don't like his looks." Each of us was told the same. The blindfolds were put on. Yet even then I had been going over my speech. In my mind each word was as bright as flame. I felt the cloth pressed into place, and frowned so that it would be loosened when I relaxed.

But now I felt a sudden fit of blind terror. I was unused to darkness. It was as though I had suddenly found myself in a dark room filled with poisonous cottonmouths. I could hear the bleary voices yelling insistently for the battle royal to begin.

"Get going in there!"

"Let me at the big nigger!"

I strained to pick up the school superintendent's voice, as though to squeeze some security out of that slightly more familiar sound.

15   "Let me at those black sonsabitches!" someone yelled.

"No, Jackson, no!" another voice yelled. "Here, somebody, help me hold Jack."

"I want to get at that ginger-colored nigger. Tear him limb from limb," the first voice yelled.

I stood against the ropes trembling. For in those days I was what they called ginger-colored, and he sounded as though he might crunch me between his teeth like a crisp ginger cookie.

Quite a struggle was going on. Chairs were being kicked about and I could hear voices grunting as with a terrific effort. I wanted to see, to see more desperately than ever before. But the blindfold was as tight as a thick skin-puckering scab and when I raised my gloved hands to push the layers of white aside a voice yelled, "Oh, no you don't, black bastard! Leave that alone!"

20   "Ring the bell before Jackson kills him a coon!" someone boomed in the sudden silence. And I heard the bell clang and the sound of feet scuffling forward.

A glove smacked against my head. I pivoted, striking out stiffly as someone went past, and felt the jar ripple along the length of my arm to my shoulder. Then it seemed as though all nine of the boys had turned upon me at once. Blows pounded me from all sides while I struck out as best I could. So many blows landed upon me that I wondered if I were not the only blindfolded fighter in the ring, or if the man called Jackson hadn't succeeded in getting me after all.

Blindfolded, I could no longer control my motions. I had no dignity. I stumbled about like a baby or a drunken man. The smoke had become thicker and with each new blow it seemed to sear and further restrict my lungs. My saliva became like hot bitter glue. A glove connected with my head, filling my mouth with warm blood. It was everywhere. I could not tell if the moisture I felt upon my body was sweat or blood. A blow landed hard against the nape of my neck. I felt myself going over, my head hitting the floor. Streaks of blue light filled the black world behind the blindfold. I lay prone, pretending that I was knocked out, but felt myself seized by hands and yanked to my feet. "Get going, black boy! Mix it up!" My arms were like lead, my head smarting from blows. I managed to feel my way to the ropes and held on, trying to catch my breath. A glove landed in my midsection and I went over again, feeling as though the smoke had become a knife jabbed into my guts. Pushed this way and that by the legs milling around me, I finally pulled erect and discovered that I could see the black, sweat-washed forms weaving in the smoky-blue atmosphere like drunken dancers weaving to the rapid drumlike thuds of blows.

Everyone fought hysterically. It was complete anarchy. Everybody fought everybody else. No group fought together for long. Two, three, four, fought one, then turned to fight each other, were themselves attacked. Blows landed below the belt and in the kidney, with the gloves open as well as closed, and with my eye partly opened now there was not so much terror. I moved carefully, avoiding blows, although not too many to attract attention, fighting from group to group. The boys groped about like blind, cautious crabs crouching to protect their mid-sections, their heads pulled in short against their shoulders, their arms stretched nervously before them, with their fists testing the smoke-filled air like the knobbed feelers of hypersensitive snails. In the corner I glimpsed a boy violently punching the air and heard him scream in pain as he smashed his hand against a ring post. For a second I saw him bent over holding his hand, then going down as a blow caught his unprotected head. I played one group against the other, slipping in and throwing a punch then stepping out of range while pushing the others into the melee to take the blows blindly aimed at me. The smoke was agonizing and there were no rounds, no bells at three minute intervals to relieve our exhaustion. The room spun around me, a swirl of lights, smoke, sweating bodies surrounded by tense white faces. I bled from both nose and mouth, the blood spattering upon my chest.

The men kept yelling, "Slug him, black boy! Knock his guts out!"

25   "Uppercut him! Kill him! Kill that big boy!"

Taking a fake fall, I saw a boy going down heavily beside me as though we were felled by a single blow, saw a sneaker-clad foot shoot into his groin as the two who had knocked him down stumbled upon him. I rolled out of range, feeling a twinge of nausea.

The harder we fought the more threatening the men became. And yet, I had begun to worry about my speech again. How would it go? Would they recognize my ability? What would they give me?

I was fighting automatically when suddenly I noticed that one after another of the boys was leaving the ring. I was surprised, filled with panic, as though I had been left alone with an unknown danger. Then I understood. The boys had arranged it among themselves. It was custom for the two men left in the ring to slug it out for the winner's prize. I discovered this too late. When the bell sounded two men in tuxedos leaped into the ring and removed the blindfold. I found myself facing Tatlock, the biggest of the gang. I felt sick at my stomach. Hardly had the bell stopped ringing in my ears than it clanged again and I saw him moving swiftly toward me. Thinking of nothing else to do I hit him smash on the nose. He kept coming, bringing the rank sharp violence of stale sweat. His face was a black blank of a face, only his eyes alive—with hate of me and aglow with a feverish terror from what had happened to us all. I became anxious. I wanted to deliver my speech and he came at me as though he meant to beat it out of me. I smashed him again and again, taking his blows as they came. Then on a sudden impulse I struck him lightly and as we clinched, I whispered, "Fake like I knocked you out, you can have the prize."

"I'll break your behind," he whispered hoarsely.

30   "For *them?*"

"For *me,* sonofabitch."

They were yelling for us to break it up and Tatlock spun me half around with a blow, and as a joggled camera sweeps in a reeling scene, I saw the howling red faces crouching tense beneath the cloud of blue-gray smoke. For a moment the world wavered, unraveled, flowed, then my head cleared and Tatlock bounced before me. The fluttering shadow before my eyes was his jabbing left hand. Then falling forward, my head against his damp shoulder, I whispered.

"I'll make it five dollars more."

"Go to hell!"

35   But his muscles relaxed a trifle beneath my pressure and I breathed, "Seven?"

"Give it to your ma," he said, ripping me beneath the heart.

And while I still held him I butted him and moved away. I felt myself bombarded with punches. I fought back with hopeless desperation. I wanted to deliver my speech more than anything else in the world, because I felt only these men could judge truly my ability, and now this stupid clown was ruining my chances. I began fighting carefully now, moving in to punch him and out again with my greater speed. A lucky blow to his chin and I had him going too—until I heard a loud voice yell, "I got my money on the big boy."

Hearing this, I almost dropped my guard. I was confused: Should I try to win against the voice out there? Would not this go against my speech, and was not this a moment for humility, for nonresistance? A blow to my head as I danced about sent my right eye popping like a jack-in-the-box and settled my dilemma. The room went red as I fell. It was a dream fall, my body languid and fastidious as to where to land, until the floor became impatient and smashed up to meet me. A moment later I came to. An hypnotic voice said FIVE emphatically. And I lay there, hazily watching a dark red spot of my own blood shaping itself into a butterfly, glistening and soaking into the soiled gray world of the canvas.

When the voice drawled TEN I was lifted up and dragged to a chair. I sat dazed. My eye pained and swelled with each throb of my poundiing heart and I wondered if now I would be allowed to speak. I was wringing wet, my mouth still bleeding. We were grouped along the wall now. The other boys ignored me as they congratulated Tatlock and speculated as to how much they would be paid. One boy whimpered over his smashed hand. Looking up front, I saw attendants in white jackets rolling the portable ring away and placing a small square rug in the vacant space surrounded by chairs. Perhaps, I thought, I will stand on the rug to deliver my speech.

40   Then the M.C. called to us, "Come on up here boys and get your money."

We ran forward to where the men laughed and talked in their chairs, waiting. Everyone seemed friendly now.

"There it is on the rug," the man said. I saw the rug covered with coins of all dimensions and a few crumpled bills. But what excited me, scattered here and there, were the gold pieces.

"Boys, it's all yours," the man said. "You get all you grab."

"That's right, Sambo," a blond man said, winking at me confidentially.

45   I trembled with excitement, forgetting my pain. I would get the gold and the bills, I thought. I would use both hands. I would throw my body against the boys nearest me to block them from the gold.

"Get down around the rug now," the man commanded, "and don't anyone touch it until I give the signal."

"This ought to be good," I heard.

As told, we got around the square rug on our knees. Slowly the man raised his freckled hand as we followed it upward with our eyes.

I heard, "These niggers look like they're about to pray!"

50   Then, "Ready," the man said. "Go!"

I lunged for a yellow coin lying on the blue design on the carpet, touching it and sending a surprised shriek to join those rising around me. I tried frantically to remove my hand but could not let go. A hot, violent force tore through my body, shaking me like a wet rat. The rug was electrified. The hair bristled up on my head as I shook myself free. My muscles jumped, my nerves jangled, writhed. But I saw that this was not stopping the other boys. Laughing in fear and embarrassment, some were holding back and scooping up the coins knocked off by the painful contortions of the others. The men roared above us as we struggled.

"Pick it up, goddamnit, pick it up!" someone called like a bass-voiced parrot. "Go on, get it!"

I crawled rapidly around the floor, picking up the coins, trying to avoid the coppers and to get greenbacks and the gold. Ignoring the shock by laughing, as I brushed the coins off quickly, I discovered that I could contain the electricity— a contradiction, but it works. Then the men began to push us onto the rug. Laughing embarrassedly, we struggled out of their hands and kept after the coins. We were all wet and slippery and hard to hold. Suddenly I saw a boy lifted into the air, glistening with sweat like a circus seal, and dropped, his wet back landing flush upon the charged rug, heard him yell and saw him literally dance upon his back, his elbows beating a frenzied tattoo upon the floor, his muscles twitching like the flesh of a horse stung by many flies. When he finally rolled off, his face was gray and no one stopped him when he ran from the floor amid booming laughter.

"Get the money," the M.C. called. "That's good hard American cash!"

55   And we snatched and grabbed, snatched and grabbed. I was careful not to come too close to the rug now, and when I felt the hot whiskey breath descend upon me like a cloud of foul air I reached out and grabbed the leg of a chair. It was occupied and I held on desperately.

"Leggo nigger! Leggo!"

The huge face wavered down to mine as he tried to push me free. But my body was slippery and he was too drunk. It was Mr. Colcord, who owned a chain of movie houses and "entertainment palaces." Each time he grabbed me I slipped out of his hands. It became a real struggle. I feared the rug more than I did the drunk, so I held on, surprising myself for a moment by trying to topple *him* upon the rug. It was such an enormous idea that I found myself actually carrying it out. I tried not to be obvious, yet when I grabbed his leg, trying to tumble him out of the chair, he raised up roaring with laughter, and, looking at me with soberness dead in the eye, kicked me viciously in the chest. The chair leg flew out of my hand and I felt myself going and rolled. It was as though I had rolled through a bed of hot coals. It seemed a whole century would pass before I would roll free, a century in which I was seared through the deepest levels of my body to the fearful breath within me and the breath seared and heated to the point of explosion. It'll all be over in a flash, I thought as I rolled clear. It'll all be over in a flash.

But not yet, the men on the other side were waiting, red faces swollen as though from apoplexy as they bent forward in their chairs. Seeing their fingers coming toward me I rolled away as a fumbled football rolls off the receiver's fingertips, back into the coals. That time I luckily sent the rug sliding out of place and heard the coins ringing against the floor and the boys scuffling to pick them up and the M.C. calling, "All right, boys, that's all. Go get dressed and get your money."

I was limp as a dish rag. My back felt as though it had been beaten with wires.

60   When we had dressed the M.C. came in and gave us each five dollars, except Tatlock, who got ten for being last in the ring. Then he told us to leave. I was not to get a chance to deliver my speech, I thought. I was going out into the dim alley in despair when I was stopped and told to go back. I returned to the ballroom, where the men were pushing back their chairs and gathering in groups to talk.

The M.C. knocked on a table for quiet. "Gentlemen," he said, "we almost forgot an important part of the program. A most serious part, gentlemen. This boy was brought here to deliver a speech which he made at his graduation yesterday. . ."

"Bravo!"

"I'm told that he is the smartest boy we've got out there in Greenwood. I'm told that he knows more big words than a pocket-sized dictionary."

Much applause and laughter.

65   "So now, gentlemen, I want you to give him your attention."

There was still laughter as I faced them, my mouth dry, my eye throbbing. I began slowly, but evidently my throat was tense, because they began shouting, "Louder! Louder!"

"We of the younger generation extol the wisdom of that great leader and educator," I shouted, "who first spoke these flaming words of wisdom. 'A ship lost at sea for many days suddenly sighted a friendly vessel. From the mast of the unfortunate vessel was seen a signal: "Water, water; we die of thirst!" The answer from the friendly vessel came back: "Cast down your bucket where you are." The captain of the distressed vessel, at last heeding the injunction, cast down his bucket, and it came up full of fresh sparkling water from the mouth of the Amazon River.' And like him I say, and in his words, 'To those of my race who depend upon bettering their condition in a foreign land, or who underestimate the importance of cultivating friendly relations with the Southern white man, who is his next-door neighbor, I would say: "Cast down your bucket where you are"—cast it down in making friends in every manly way of the people of all races by whom we are surrounded. . . .' "

I spoke automatically and with such fervor that I did not realize that the men were still talking and laughing until my dry mouth, filling up with blood from the cut, almost strangled me. I coughed, wanting to stop and go to one of the tall brass, sand-filled spittoons to relieve myself, but a few of the men, especially the superintendent, were listening and I was afraid. So I gulped it down, blood, saliva, and all, and continued. (What powers of endurance I had during those days! What enthusiasm! What a belief in the rightness of things!) I spoke even louder in spite of the pain. But still they talked and still they laughed, as though deaf with cotton in dirty ears. So I spoke with greater emotional emphasis. I closed my ears and swallowed blood until I was nauseated. The speech seemed a hundred times as long as before, but I could not leave out a single word. All had to be said, each memorized nuance considered, rendered. Nor was that all. Whenever I uttered a word of three or more syllables a group of voices would yell for me to repeat it. I used the phrase "social responsibility" and they yelled:

"What's that word you say, boy?"

70 "Social responsibility," I said.

"What?"

"Social . . ."

"Louder."

". . . responsibility."

75 "More!"

"Respon—"

"Repeat!"

"—sibility."

The room filled with the uproar of laughter until, no doubt, distracted by having to gulp down my blood, I made a mistake and yelled a phrase I had often seen denounced with newspaper editorials, heard debated in private.

80 "Social . . ."

"What?" they yelled.

". . . equality—"

The laughter hung smokelike in the sudden stillness. I opened my eyes, puzzled. Sounds of displeasure filled the room. The M.C. rushed forward. They shouted hostile phrases at me. But I did not understand.

A small dry mustached man in the front row blared out, "Say that slowly, son!"

"What sir?"

"What you just said!"

"Social responsibility, sir," I said.

"You weren't being smart, were you, boy?" he said, not unkindly.

"No, sir!"

"You sure that about 'equality' was a mistake?"

"Oh, yes, sir," I said. "I was swallowing blood."

"Well, you had better speak more slowly so we can understand. We mean to do right by you, but you've got to know your place at all times. All right, now, go on with your speech."

I was afraid. I wanted to leave but I wanted also to speak and I was afraid they'd snatch me down.

"Thank you, sir," I said, beginning where I had left off, and having them ignore me as before.

Yet when I finished there was a thunderous applause. I was surprised to see the superintendent come forth with a package wrapped in white tissue paper, and, gesturing for quiet, address the men.

"Gentlemen, you see that I did not overpraise this boy. He makes a good speech and some day he'll lead his people in the proper paths. And I don't have to tell you that that is important in these days and times. This is a good, smart boy, and so to encourage him in the right direction, in the name of the Board of Education I wish to present him a prize in the form of this . . ."

He paused, removing the tissue paper and revealing a gleaming calfskin brief case.

". . . in the form of this first-class article from Shad Whitmore's shop."

"Boy," he said, addressing me, "take this prize and keep it well. Consider it a badge of office. Prize it. Keep developing as you are and some day it will be filled with important papers that will help shape the destiny of your people."

I was so moved that I could hardly express my thanks. A rope of bloody saliva forming a shape like an undiscovered continent drooled upon the leather and I wiped it quickly away. I felt an importance that I had never dreamed.

"Open it and see what's inside," I was told.

My fingers a-tremble, I complied, smelling the fresh leather and finding an official-looking document inside. It was a scholarship to the state college for Negroes. My eyes filled with tears and I ran awkwardly off the floor.

I was so overjoyed; I did not even mind when I discovered that the gold pieces I had scrambled for were brass pocket tokens advertising a certain make of automobile.

When I reached home everyone was excited. Next day the neighbors came to congratulate me. I even felt safe from grandfather, whose deathbed curse usually spoiled my triumphs. I stood beneath his photograph with my brief case in hand and smiled triumphantly into his stolid black peasant's face. It was a face that fascinated me. The eyes seemed to follow everywhere I went.

That night I dreamed I was at a circus with him and that he refused to laugh at the clowns no matter what they did. Then later he told me to open my brief case and read what was inside and I did, finding an official envelope stamped with the state seal; and inside the envelope I found another and another, endlessly, and I thought I would fall of weariness. "Them's years," he said. "Now open that one."

And I did and in it I found an engraved document containing a short message in letters of gold. "Read it," my grandfather said. "Out loud."

"To Whom It May Concern," I intoned. "Keep This Nigger-Boy Running."

I awoke with the old man's laughter ringing in my ears.

(It was a dream I was to remember and dream again for many years after. But at that time I had no insight into its meaning. First I had to attend college.)

Bernard Malamud
The Magic Barrel

Bernard Malamud (1914–   ) was born in Brooklyn and attended City College and Columbia University. His novels include *The Natural* (1952), *The Assistant* (1957), *A New Life* (1961), *The Fixer* (1966), *The Tenants* (1971), and *Dubin's Lives* (1979). His collections of short stories are *The Magic Barrel* (1958), *Idiots First* (1963), *Pictures of Fidelman: An Exhibition* (1969), and *Rembrandt's Hat* (1973).

Not long ago there lived in uptown New York, in a small, almost meager room, though crowded with books, Leo Finkle, a rabbinical student in the Yeshivah University. Finkle, after six years of study, was to be ordained in June and had been advised by an acquaintance that he might find it easier to win himself a congregation if he were married. Since he had no present prospects of marriage, after two tormented days of turning it over in his mind, he called Pinye Salzman, a marriage broker whose two-line advertisement he had read in the *Forward*.

The matchmaker appeared one night out of the dark fourth-floor hallway of the graystone rooming house where Finkle lived, grasping a black, strapped portfolio that had been worn thin with use. Salzman, who had been long in the business, was of slight but dignified build, wearing an old hat, and an overcoat too short and tight for him. He smelled frankly of fish, which he loved to eat, and although he was missing a few teeth, his presence was not displeasing, because of an amiable manner curiously contrasted with mournful eyes. His voice, his lips, his wisp of beard, his bony fingers were animated, but give him a moment of repose and his mild blue eyes revealed a depth of sadness, a characteristic that put Leo a little at ease although the situation, for him, was inherently tense.

He at once informed Salzman why he had asked him to come, explaining that his home was in Cleveland, and that but for his parents, who had married comparatively late in life, he was alone in the world. He had for six years devoted himself almost entirely to his studies, as a result of which, understandably, he had found himself without time for a social life and the company of young women. Therefore he thought it the better part of trial and error—of embarrassing fumbling—to call in an experienced person to advise him on these matters. He remarked in passing that the function of the marriage broker was ancient and honorable, highly approved in the Jewish community, because it made practical the necessary without hindering joy. Moreover, his own parents had been brought together by a matchmaker. They had made, if not a financially profitable marriage—since neither had possessed any wordly goods to speak of—at least a successful one in the sense of their everlasting devotion to each other. Salzman listened in embarrassed surprise, sensing a sort of apology. Later, however, he experienced a glow of pride in his work, an emotion that had left him years ago, and he heartily approved of Finkle.

The two went to their business. Leo had led Salzman to the only clear place in the room, a table near a window that overlooked the lamp-lit city. He seated himself at the matchmaker's side but facing him, attempting by an act of will to suppress the unpleasant tickle in his throat. Salzman eagerly unstrapped his portfolio and removed a loose rubber band from a thin packet of much-handled cards. As he flipped through them, a gesture and sound that physically hurt Leo, the student pretended not to see and gazed steadfastly out the window. Although it was still February, winter was on its last legs, signs of which he had for the first time in years begun to notice. He now observed the round white moon, moving high in the sky through a cloud menagerie, and watched with half-open mouth as it penetrated a huge hen, and dropped out of her like an egg laying itself. Salzman, though pretending through eyeglasses he had just slipped on to be engaged in scanning the writing on the cards, stole occasional glances at the young man's distinguished face, noting with pleasure the long, severe scholar's nose, brown eyes heavy with learning, sensitive yet ascetic lips, and a certain, almost hollow quality of the dark cheeks. He gazed around at shelves upon shelves of books and let out a soft, contented sigh.

5   When Leo's eyes fell upon the cards, he counted six spread out in Salzman's hand.

"So few?" he asked in disappointment.

"You wouldn't believe me how much cards I got in my office," Salzman replied. "The drawers are already filled to the top, so I keep them now in a barrel, but is every girl good for a new rabbi?"

Leo blushed at this, regretting all he had revealed of himself in a curriculum vitae he had sent to Salzman. He had thought it best to acquaint him with his strict standards and specifications, but in having done so, felt he had told the marriage broker more than was absolutely necessary.

He hesitantly inquired, "Do you keep photographs of your clients on file?"

10   "First comes family, amount of dowry, also what kind promises," Salzman replied, unbuttoning his tight coat and settling himself in the chair. "After comes pictures, rabbi."

"Call me Mr. Finkle, I'm not yet a rabbi."

Salzman said he would, but instead called him doctor, which he changed to rabbi when Leo was not listening too attentively.

Salzman adjusted his horn-rimmed spectacles, gently cleared his throat and read in an eager voice the contents of the top card:

"Sophie P. Twenty-four years. Widow one year. No children. Educated high school and two years college. Father promises eight thousand dollars. Has wonderful wholesale business. Also real estate. On the mother's side comes teachers, also one actor. Well known on Second Avenue."

15   Leo gazed up in surprise. "Did you say a widow?"

"A widow don't mean spoiled, rabbi. She lived with her husband maybe four months. He was a sick boy she made a mistake to marry him."

"Marrying a widow has never entered my mind."

"This is because you have no experience. A widow, especially if she is young and healthy like this girl, is a wonderful person to marry. She will be thankful to you the rest of her life. Believe me, if I was looking now for a bride, I would marry a widow."

Leo reflected, then shook his head.

20 Salzman hunched his shoulders in an almost imperceptible gesture of disappointment. He placed the card down on the wooden table and began to read another:

"Lily H. High school teacher. Regular. Not a substitute. Has savings and new Dodge car. Lived in Paris one year. Father is successful dentist thirty-five years. Interested in professional man. Well Americanized family. Wonderful opportunity."

"I knew her personally," said Salzman. "I wish you could see this girl. She is a doll. Also very intelligent. All day you could talk to her about books and theater and what not. She also knows current events."

"I don't believe you mentioned her age?"

"Her age?" Salzman said, raising his brows. "Her age is thirty-two years."

25 Leo said after a while, "I'm afraid that seems a little too old."

Salzman let out a laugh. "So how old are you, rabbi?"

"Twenty-seven."

"So what is the difference, tell me, between twenty-seven and thirty-two? My own wife is seven years older than me. So what did I suffer?—Nothing. If Rothschild's daughter wants to marry you, would you say on account her age, no?"

"Yes," Leo said dryly.

30 Salzman shook off the no in the yes. "Five years don't mean a thing I give you my word that when you will live with her for one week you will forget her age. What does it mean five years—that she lived more and knows more than somebody who is younger? On this girl, God bless her, years are not wasted. Each one that it comes makes better the bargain."

"What subject does she teach in high sccool?"

"Languages. If you heard the way she speaks French, you will think it is music. I am in the business twenty-five years, and I recommend her with my whole heart. Believe me, I know what I'm talking, rabbi."

"What's on the next card?" Leo said abruptly.

Salzman reluctantly turned up the third card:

35 "Ruth K. Nineteen years. Honor student. Father offers thirteen thousand cash to the right bridegroom. He is a medical doctor. Stomach specialist with marvelous practice. Brother-in-law owns own garment business. Particular people."

Salzman looked as if he had read his trump card.

"Did you say nineteen?" Leo asked with interest.

"On the dot."

"Is she attractive?" He blushed. "Pretty?"

40 Salzman kissed his finger tips. "A little doll. On this I give you my word. Let me call the father tonight and you will see what means pretty."

But Leo was troubled. "You're sure she's that young?"

"This I am positive. The father will show you the birth certificate."

"Are you positive there isn't something wrong with her?" Leo insisted.

"Who says there is wrong?"

45 "I don't understand why an American girl her age should go to a marriage broker."

A smile spread over Salzman's face.

"So for the same reason you went, she comes."

Leo flushed. "I am pressed for time."

Salzman, realizing he had been tactless, quickly explained. "The father came, not her. He wants she should have the best, so he looks around himself. When we will locate the right boy he will introduce him and encourage. This makes a better marriage than if a young girl without experience takes for herself. I don't have to tell you this."

50   "But don't you think this young girl believes in love?" Leo spoke uneasily.

Salzman was about to guffaw but caught himself and said soberly, "Love comes with the right person, not before."

Leo parted dry lips but did not speak. Noticing that Salzman had snatched a glance at the next card, he cleverly asked. "How is her health?"

"Perfect," Salzman said, breathing with difficulty. "Of course, she is a little lame on her right foot from an auto accident that it happened to her when she was twelve years, but nobody notices on account she is so brilliant and also beautiful."

Leo got up heavily and went to the window. He felt curiously bitter and upbraided himself for having called in the marriage broker. Finally, he shook his head.

55   "Why not?" Salzman persisted, the pitch of his voice rising.

"Because I detest stomach specialists."

"So what do you care what is his business? After you marry her do you need him? Who says he must come every Friday night in your house?"

Ashamed of the way the talk was going, Leo dismissed Salzman, who went home with heavy, melancholy eyes.

Though he had felt only relief at the marriage broker's departure, Leo was in low spirits the next day. He explained it as arising from Salzman's failure to produce a suitable bride for him. He did not care for his type of clientele. But when Leo found himself hesitating whether to seek out another matchmaker, one more polished than Pinye, he wondered if it could be—his protestations to the contrary, and although he honored his father and mother—that he did not, in essence, care for the match-making institution? This thought he quickly put out of mind yet found himself still upset. All day he ran around in the woods—missed an important appointment, forgot to give out his laundry, walked out of a Broadway cafeteria without paying and had to run back with the ticket in his hand; had even not recognized his landlady in the street when she passed with a friend and courteously called out, "A good evening to you, Doctor Finkle." By nightfall, however, he had regained sufficient calm to sink his nose into a book and there found peace from his thoughts.

60   Almost at once there came a knock on the door. Before Leo could say enter, Salzman, commercial cupid, was standing in the room. His face was gray and meager, his expression hungry, and he looked as if he would expire on his feet. Yet the marriage broker managed, by some trick of the muscles, to display a broad smile.

"So good evening. I am invited?"

Leo nodded, disturbed to see him again, yet unwilling to ask the man to leave.

Beaming still, Salzman laid his portfolio on the table. "Rabbi, I got for you tonight good news."

"I've asked you not to call me rabbi. I'm still a student."

65   "Your worries are finished. I have for you a first-class bride."

"Leave me in peace concerning this subject." Leo pretended lack of interest.

"The world will dance at your wedding."

"Please, Mr. Salzman, no more."

"But first must come back my strength," Salzman said weakly. He fumbled with the portfolio straps and took out of the leather case an oily paper bag, from which he extracted a hard, seeded roll and a small, smoked white fish. With a quick motion of his hand he stripped the fish out of its skin and began ravenously to chew. "All day in a rush," he muttered.

70   Leo watched him eat.

"A sliced tomato you have maybe?" Salzman hesitantly inquired.

"No."

The marriage broker shut his eyes and ate. When he had finished he carefully cleaned up the crumbs and rolled up the remains of the fish, in the paper bag. His spectacled eyes roamed the room until he discovered, amid some piles of books, a one-burner gas stove. Lifting his hat he humbly asked, "A glass of tea you got, rabbi?"

Conscience-stricken, Leo rose and brewed the tea. He served it with a chunk of lemon and two cubes of lump sugar, delighting Salzman.

75   After he had drunk his tea, Salzman's strength and good spirits were restored.

"So tell me, rabbi," he said amiably, "you considered some more the three clients I mentioned yesterday?"

"There was no need to consider."

"Why not?"

"None of them suits me."

80   "What then suits you?"

Leo let it pass because he could give only a confused answer.

Without waiting for a reply, Salzman asked, "You remember this girl I talked to you—the high school teacher?"

"Age thirty-two?"

But, surprisingly, Salzman's face lit in a smile. "Age twenty-nine."

85   Leo shot him a look. "Reduced from thirty-two?"

"A mistake," Salzman avowed. "I talked today with the dentist. He took me to his safety deposit box and showed me the birth certificate. She was twenty-nine years last August. They made her a party in the mountains where she went for her vacation. When her father spoke to me the first time I forgot to write the age and I told you thirty-two, but now I remember this was a different client, a widow."

"The same one you told me about? I thought she was twenty-four?"

"A different. Am I responsible that the world is filled with widows?"

"No, but I'm not interested in them, nor for that matter, in school teachers."

90   Salzman pulled his clasped hands to his breast. Looking at the ceiling he devoutly exclaimed, "Yiddishe kinder, what can I say to somebody that is not interested in high school teachers? So what then you are interested?"

Leo flushed but controlled himself.

"In what else will you be interested," Salzman went on, "if you not interested in this fine girl that she speaks four languages and has personally in the bank ten thousand dollars? Also her father guarantees further twelve thousand. Also, she has a new car, wonderful clothes, talks on all subjects, and she will give you a first-class home and children. How near do we come in our life to paradise?"

"If she's so wonderful, why wasn't she married ten years ago?"

"Why?" said Salzman with a heavy laugh. "—Why? Because she is *partikiler*. This is why. She wants the *best*."

95   Leo was silent, amused at how he had entangled himself. But Salzman had aroused his interest in Lily H., and he began seriously to consider calling on her. When the marriage broker observed how intently Leo's mind was at work on the facts he had supplied, he felt certain they would soon come to an agreement.

Late Saturday afternoon, conscious of Salzman, Leo Finkle walked with Lily Hir-schorn along Riverside Drive. He walked briskly and erectly, wearing with distinction the black fedora he had that morning taken with trepidation out of the dusty hat box on his closet shelf, and the heavy black Saturday coat he had thoroughly whisked clean. Leo also owned a walking stick, a present from a distant relative, but quickly put temptation aside and did not use it. Lily, petite and not unpretty, had on something signifying the approach of spring. She was au courant, animatedly, with all sorts of subjects, and he weighed her words and found her surprisingly sound—score another for Salzman, whom he uneasily sensed to be somewhere around, hiding perhaps high in a tree along the street, flashing the lady signals with a pocket mirror; or perhaps a cloven-hoofed Pan, piping nuptial ditties as he danced his invisible way before them, strewing wild buds on the walk and purple grapes in their path, symbolizing fruit of a union, though there was of course still none.

Lily startled Leo by remarking, "I was thinking of Mr. Salzman, a curious figure, wouldn't you say?"

Not certain what to answer, he nodded.

She bravely went on, blushing, "I for one am grateful for his introducing us. Aren't you?"

100   He courteously replied, "I am."

"I mean," she said with a little laugh—and it was all in good taste, or at least gave the effect of being not in bad—"do you mind that we came together so?"

He was not displeased with her honesty, recognizing that she meant to set the relationship aright, and understanding that it took a certain amount of experience in life, and courage, to want to do it quite that way. One had to have some sort of past to make that kind of beginning.

He said that he did not mind. Salzman's function was traditional and honorable—valuable for what it might achieve, which, he pointed out, was frequently nothing.

Lily agreed with a sigh. They walked on for a while and she said after a long silence, again with a nervous laugh, "Would you mind if I asked you something a little bit personal? Frankly, I find the subject fascinating." Although Leo shrugged, she went on half embarrassedly, "How was it that you came to your calling? I mean was it a sudden passionate inspiration?"

105   Leo, after a time, slowly replied, "I was always interested in the Law."

"You saw revealed in it the presence of the Highest?"

He nodded and changed the subject. "I understand that you spent a little time in Paris, Miss Hirschorn?"

"Oh, did Mr. Salzman tell you, Rabbi Finkle?" Leo winced but she went on, "It was ages ago and almost forgotten. I remember I had to return for my sister's wedding."

And Lily would not be put off. "When," she asked in a trembly voice, "did you become enamored of God?"

110   He stared at her. Then it came to him that she was talking not about Leo Finkle, but of a total stranger, some mystical figure, perhaps even passionate prophet that Salzman had dreamed up for her—no relation to the living or dead. Leo trembled with rage and weakness. The trickster had obviously sold her a bill of goods, just as he had him, who'd expected to become acquainted with a young lady of twenty-nine, only to behold, the moment he laid eyes upon her strained and anxious face,

a woman past thirty-five and aging rapidly. Only his self-control had kept him this long in her presence.

"I am not," he said gravely, "a talented religious person," and in seeking words to go on, found himself possessed by shame and fear. "I think," he said in a strained manner, "that I came to God not because I loved Him, but because I did not."

This confession he spoke harshly because its unexpectedness shook him.

Lily wilted. Leo saw a profusion of loaves of bread go flying like ducks high over his head, not unlike the winged loaves by which he had counted himself to sleep last night. Mercifully, then, it snowed, which he would not put past Salzman's machinations.

He was infuriated with the marriage broker and swore he would throw him out of the room the minute he reappeared. But Salzman did not come that night, and when Leo's anger had subsided, an unaccountable despair grew in its place. At first he thought this was caused by his disappointment in Lily, but before long it became evident that he had involved himself with Salzman without a true knowledge of his own intent. He gradually realized—with an emptiness that seized him with six hands—that he had called in the broker to find him a bride because he was incapable of doing it himself. This terrifying insight he had derived as a result of his meeting and conversation with Lily Hirschorn. Her probing questions had somehow irritated him into revealing—to himself more than her—the true nature of his relationship to God, and from that it had come upon him, with shocking force, that apart from his parents, he had never loved anyone. Or perhaps it went the other way, that he did not love God so well as he might, because he had not loved man. It seemed to Leo that his whole life stood starkly revealed and he saw himself for the first time as he truly was—unloved and loveless. This bitter but somehow not fully unexpected revelation brought him to a point of panic, controlled only by extraordinary effort. He covered his face with his hands and cried.

115   The week that followed was the worst of his life. He did not eat and lost weight. His beard darkened and grew ragged. He stopped attending seminars and almost never opened a book. He seriously considered leaving the Yeshivah, although he was deeply troubled at the thought of the loss of all his years of study—saw them like pages torn from a book, strewn over the city—and at the devastating effect of this decision upon his parents. But he had lived without knowledge of himself, and never in the Five Books and all the Commentaries—mea culpa—had the truth been revealed to him. He did not know where to turn, and in all this desolating loneliness there was no *to whom,* although he often thought of Lily but not once could bring himself to go downstairs and make the call. He became touchy and irritable, especially with his landlady, who asked him all manner of personal questions; on the other hand, sensing his own disagreeableness, he waylaid her on the stairs and apologized abjectly, until mortified, she ran from him. Out of this, however, he drew the consolation that he was a Jew and that a Jew suffered. But gradually, as the long and terrible week drew to a close, he regained his composure and some idea of purpose in life: to go on as planned. Although he was imperfect, the idea was not. As for his quest of a bride, the thought of continuing afflicted him with anxiety and heartburn, yet perhaps with this new knowledge of himself he would be more successful than in the past. Perhaps love would now come to him and a bride to that love. And for this sanctified seeking who needed a Salzman?

The marriage broker, a skeleton with haunted eyes, returned that very night. He looked, withal, the picture of frustrated expectancy—as if he had steadfastly waited the week at Miss Lily Hirschorn's side for a telephone call that never came.

Casually coughing, Salzman came immediately to the point: "So how did you like her?"

Leo's anger rose and he could not refrain from chiding the matchmaker: "Why did you lie to me, Salzman?"

Salzman's pale face went dead white, the world had snowed on him.

120   "Did you not state that she was twenty-nine?" Leo insisted.

"I give you my word—"

"She was thirty-five, if a day. *At least* thirty-five."

"Of this don't be too sure. Her father told me—".

"Never mind. The worst of it was that you lied to her."

125   "How did I lie to her, tell me?"

"You told her things about me that weren't true. You made me out to be more, consequently less than I am. She had in mind a totally different person, a sort of semi-mystical Wonder Rabbi."

"All I said, you was a religious man."

"I can imagine."

Salzman sighed. "This is my weakness that I have," he confessed. "My wife says to me I shouldn't be a salesman, but when I have two fine people that they would be wonderful to be married, I am so happy that I talk too much." He smiled wanly. "This is why Salzman is a poor man."

130   Leo's anger left him. "Well, Salzman, I'm afraid that's all."

The marriage broker fastened hungry eyes on him.

"You don't want any more a bride?"

"I do," said Leo, "but I have decided to seek her in a different way. I am no longer interested in an arranged marriage. To be frank, I now admit the necessity of premarital love. That is, I want to be in love with the one I marry."

"Love?" said Salzman, astounded. After a moment he remarked, "For us, our love is our life, not for the ladies. In the ghetto they—"

135   "I know, I know," said Leo. "I've thought of it often. Love, I have said to myself, should be a by-product of living and worship rather than its own end. Yet for myself I find it necessary to establish the level of my need and fulfill it."

Salzman shrugged but answered, "Listen, rabbi, if you want love, this I can find for you also. I have such beautiful clients that you will love them the minute your eyes will see them."

Leo smiled unhappily. "I'm afraid you don't understand."

But Salzman hastily unstrapped his portfolio and withdrew a manila packet from it.

"Pictures," he said, quickly laying the envelope on the table.

140   Leo called after him to take the pictures away, but as if on the wings of the wind, Salzman had disappeared.

March came. Leo had returned to his regular routine. Although he felt not quite himself yet—lacked energy—he was making plans for a more active social life. Of course it would cost something, but he was an expert in cutting corners; and when there were no corners left he would make circles rounder. All the while Salzman's pictures had lain on the table, gathering dust. Occasionally as Leo sat studying, or enjoying a cup of tea, his eyes fell on the manila envelope, but he never opened it.

The days went by and no social life to speak of developed with a member of the opposite sex—it was difficult, given the circumstances of his situation. One morning Leo toiled up the stairs to his room and stared out the window at the city. Although the day was bright his view of it was dark. For some time he watched the people in the street below hurrying along and then turned with a heavy heart to his little room. On the table was the packet. With a sudden relentless gesture he tore it open. For a half-hour he stood by the table in a state of excitement, examining the photographs of the ladies Salzman had included. Finally, with a deep sigh he put them down. There were six, of varying degrees of attractiveness, but look at them long enough and they all become Lily Hirschorn: all past their prime, all starved behind bright smiles, not a true personality in the lot. Life, despite their frantic yoohooings, had passed them by; they were pictures in a briefcase that stank of fish. After a while, however, as Leo attempted to return the photographs into the envelope, he found in it another, a snapshot of the type taken by a machine for a quarter. He gazed at it a moment and let out a cry.

Her face deeply moved him. Why, he could at first not say. It gave him the impression of youth—spring flowers, yet age—a sense of having been used to the bone, wasted; this came from the eyes, which were hauntingly familiar, yet absolutely strange. He had a vivid impression that he had met her before, but try as he might he could not place her although he could almost recall her name, as if he had read it in her own handwriting. No, this couldn't be; he would have remembered her. It was not, he affirmed, that she had an extraordinary beauty—no, though her face was attractive enough; it was that *something* about her moved him. Feature for feature, even some of the ladies of the photographs could do better; but she leaped forth to his heart—had *lived,* or wanted to—more than just wanted, perhaps regretted how she had lived—had somehow deeply suffered: it could be seen in the depths of those reluctant eyes, from the way the light enclosed and shone from her, and within her, opening realms of possibility: this was her own. Her he desired. His head ached and eyes narrowed with the intensity of his gazing, then as if an obscure fog had blown up in the mind, he experienced fear of her and was aware that he had received an impression, somehow, of evil. He shuddered, saying softly, it is thus with us all. Leo brewed some tea in a small pot and sat sipping it without sugar, to calm himself. But before he had finished drinking, again with excitement he examined the face and found it good: good for Leo Finkle. Only such a one could understand him and help him seek whatever he was seeking. She might, perhaps, love him. How she had happened to be among the discards in Salzman's barrel he could never guess, but he knew he must urgently go find her.

Leo rushed downstairs, grabbed up the Bronx telephone book, and searched for Salzman's home address. He was not listed nor was his office. Neither was he in the Manhattan book. But Leo remembered having written down the address on a slip of paper after he had read Salzman's advertisement in the "personals" column of the *Forward*. He ran up to his room and tore through his papers, without luck. It was exasperating. Just when he needed the matchmaker he was nowhere to be found. Fortunately Leo remembered to look in his wallet. There on a card he found his name written and a Bronx address. No phone number was listed, the reason— Leo now recalled—he had originally communicated with Salzman by letter. He got on his coat, put a hat on over his skull cap and hurried to the subway station. All the way to the far end of the Bronx he sat on the edge of his seat. He was more than once tempted to take out the picture and see if the girl's face was as he remembered it, but he refrained, allowing the snapshot to remain in his inside coat pocket, content to have her so close. When the train pulled into the station he was waiting at the door and bolted out. He quickly located the street Salzman had advertised.

145   The building he sought was less than a block from the subway, but it was not an office building, nor even a loft, nor a store in which one could rent office space. It was a very old tenement house. Leo found Salzman's name in pencil on a soiled tag under the bell and climbed three dark flights to his apartment. When he knocked, the door was opened by a thin, asthmatic, gray-haired woman, in felt slippers.

"Yes?" she said, expecting nothing. She listened without listening. He could have sworn he had seen her, too, before but knew it was an illusion.

"Salzman—does he live here? Pinye Salzman," he said, "the matchmaker?"

She stared at him a long minute. "Of course."

He felt embarrassed. "Is he in?"

150   "No." Her mouth, though left open, offered nothing more.

"The matter is urgent. Can you tell me where his office is?"

"In the air." She pointed upward.

"You mean he has no office?" Leo asked.

"In his socks."

155   He peered into the apartment. It was sunless and dingy, one large room divided by a half-open curtain, beyond which he could see a sagging metal bed. The near side of the room was crowded with rickety chairs, old bureaus, a three-legged table, racks of cooking utensils, and all the apparatus of a kitchen. But there was no sign of Salzman or his magic barrel, probably also a figment of the imagination. An odor of frying fish made Leo weak to the knees.

"Where is he?" he insisted. "I've got to see your husband."

At length she answered. "So who knows where he is? Every time he thinks a new thought he runs to a different place. Go home, he will find you."

"Tell him Leo Finkle."

She gave no sign she had heard.

160   He walked downstairs, depressed.

But Salzman, breathless, stood waiting at his door.

Leo was astounded and overjoyed. "How did you get here before me?"

"I rushed."

"Come inside."

165   They entered. Leo fixed tea, and a sardine sandwich for Salzman. As they were drinking he reached behind him for the packet of pictures and handed them to the marriage broker.

Salzman put down his glass and said expectantly, "You found somebody you like?"

"Not among these."

The marriage broker turned away.

"Here is the one I want." Leo held forth the snapshot.

170   Salzman slipped on his glasses and took the picture into his trembling hand. He turned ghastly and let out a groan.

"What's the matter?" cried Leo.

"Excuse me. Was an accident this picture. She isn't for you."

Salzman frantically shoved the manila packet into his portfolio. He thrust the snapshot into his pocket and fled down the stairs.

Leo, after momentary paralysis, gave chase and cornered the marriage broker in the vestibule. The landlady made hysterical outcries but neither of them listened.

175 "Give me back the picture, Salzman."

"No." The pain in his eyes was terrible.

"Tell me who she is then."

"This I can't tell you. Excuse me."

He made to depart, but Leo, forgetting himself, seized the matchmaker by his tight coat and shook him frenziedly.

180 "Please," sighed Salzman. "*Please*."

Leo ashamedly let him go. "Tell me who she is," he begged. "It's very important for me to know."

"She is not for you. She is a wild one—wild, without shame. This is not a bride for a rabbi."

"What do you mean wild?"

"Like an animal. Like a dog. For her to be poor was a sin. This is why to me she is dead now."

185 "In God's name, what do you mean?"

"Her I can't introduce to you," Salzman cried.

"Why are you so excited?"

"Why, he asks," Salzman said, bursting into tears. "This is my baby, my Stella, she should burn in hell."

Leo hurried up to bed and hid under the covers. Under the covers he thought his life through. Although he soon fell asleep he could not sleep her out of his mind. He woke, beating his breast. Though he prayed to be rid of her, his prayers were unanswered. Through days of torment he endlessly struggled not to love her; fearing success, he escaped it. He then concluded to convert her to goodness, himself to God. The idea alternately nauseated and exalted him.

190 He perhaps did not know that he had come to a final decision until he encountered Salzman in a Broadway cafeteria. He was sitting alone at a rear table, sucking the bony remains of a fish. The marriage broker appeared haggard, and transparent to the point of vanishing.

Salzman looked up at first without recognizing him. Leo had grown a pointed beard and his eyes were weighted with wisdom.

"Salzman," he said, "love has at last come to my heart."

"Who can love from a picture?" mocked the marriage broker.

"It is not impossible."

195 "If you can love her, then you can love anybody. Let me show you some new clients that they just sent me their photographs. One is a little doll."

"Just her I want," Leo murmured.

"Don't be a fool, doctor. Don't bother with her."

"Put me in touch with her, Salzman," Leo said humbly. "Perhaps I can be of service."

Salzman had stoₚppd eating and Leo understood with emotion that it was now arranged.

200 Leaving the cafeteria, he was, however, afflicted by a tormenting suspicion that Salzman had planned it all to happen this way.

Leo was informed by letter that she would meet him on a certain corner, and she was there one spring night, waiting under a street lamp. He appeared, carrying a small bouquet of violets and rosebuds. Stella stood by the lamp post, smoking. She wore white with red shoes, which fitted his expectations, although in a troubled moment he had imagined the dress red, and only the shoes white. She waited uneasily and shyly. From afar he saw that her eyes—clearly her father's—were filled with desperate innocence. He pictured, in her, his own redemption. Violins and lit candles revolved in the sky. Leo ran forward with flowers outthrust.

Around the corner, Salzman, leaning against a wall, chanted prayers for the dead.

Sylvia Plath
Johnny Panic and the Bible of Dreams

Sylvia Plath (1932–1963) was born in Boston and published prose and poetry from an early age. She graduated from Smith College and attended Cambridge University in England. Her novel, *The Bell Jar*, appeared under a pen name in England and was not published in the United States until 1971. It describes the nervous breakdown she suffered while she was in college, an experience that lies behind this short story. Her disciplined, intense poems are collected in *The Colossus* (1960) and in the three posthumous volumes *Ariel* (1965), *Crossing the Water* (1971), and *Winter Trees* (1972). (See also pages 718–721.) Plath was married to the poet Ted Hughes and was survived by two children when she killed herself in London in 1963. *Johnny Panic and the Bible of Dreams* (1978) collected short fiction, articles, and passages from her notebooks.

Every day from nine to five I sit at my desk facing the door of the office and type up other people's dreams. Not just dreams. That wouldn't be practical enough for my bosses. I type up also people's daytime complaints: trouble with mother, trouble with father, trouble with the bottle, the bed, the headache that bangs home and blacks out the sweet world for no known reason. Nobody comes to our office unless they have troubles. Troubles that can't be pinpointed by Wassermanns or Wechsler-Bellevues alone.

Maybe a mouse gets to thinking pretty early on how the whole world is run by these enormous feet. Well, from where I sit, I figure the world is run by one thing and this one thing only. Panic with a dog-face, devil-face, hag-face, whore-face, panic in capital letters with no face at all—it's the same Johnny Panic, awake or asleep.

When people ask me where I work, I tell them I'm Assistant to the Secretary in one of the Out-Patient Departments of the Clinics Building of the City Hospital. This sounds so be-all end-all they seldom get around to asking me more than what I do, and what I do is mainly type up records. On my own hook though, and completely under cover, I am pursuing a vocation that would set these doctors on their ears. In the privacy of my one-room apartment I call myself secretary to none other than Johnny Panic himself.

Dream by dream I am educating myself to become that rare character, rarer, in truth, than any member of the Psychoanalytic Institute, a dream connoisseur. Not a dream stopper, a dream explainer, an exploiter of dreams for the crass practical ends of health and happiness, but an unsordid collector of dreams for themselves alone. A lover of dreams for Johnny Panic's sake, the Maker of them all.

5   There isn't a dream I've typed up in our record books that I don't know by heart.

There isn't a dream I haven't copied out at home into Johnny Panic's Bible of Dreams.

This is my real calling.

Some nights I take the elevator up to the roof of my apartment building. Some nights, about three A.M. Over the trees at the far side of the park the United Fund torch flare flattens and recovers under some witchy invisible push and here and there in the hunks of stone and brick I see a light. Most of all, though, I feel the city sleeping. Sleeping from the river on the west to the ocean on the east, like some rootless island rockabying itself on nothing at all.

I can be tight and nervy as the top string on a violin, and yet by the time the sky begins to blue I'm ready for sleep. It's the thought of all those dreamers and what they're dreaming wears me down till I sleep the sleep of fever. Monday to Friday what do I do but type up those same dreams. Sure, I don't touch a fraction of them the city over, but page by page, dream by dream, my Intake books fatten and weigh down the bookshelves of the cabinet in the narrow passage running parallel to the main hall, off which passage the doors to all the doctors' little interviewing cubicles open.

I've got a funny habit of identifying the people who come in by their dreams. As far as I'm concerned, the dreams single them out more than any Christian name. This one guy, for example, who works for a ball-bearing company in town, dreams every night how he's lying on his back with a grain of sand on his chest. Bit by bit this grain of sand grows bigger and bigger till it's big as a fair-sized house and he can't draw breath. Another fellow I know of has had a certain dream ever since they gave him ether and cut out his tonsils and adenoids when he was a kid. In this dream he's caught in the rollers of a cotton mill, fighting for his life. Oh, he's not alone, although he thinks he is. A lot of people these days dream they're being run over or eaten by machines. They're the cagey ones who won't go on the subway or the elevators. Coming back from my lunch hour in the hospital cafeteria I often pass them, puffing up the unswept stone stairs to our office on the fourth floor. I wonder, now and then, what dreams people had before ball bearings and cotton mills were invented.

10   I've a dream of my own. My one dream. A dream of dreams.

In this dream there's a great half-transparent lake stretching away in every direction, too big for me to see the shores of it, if there are any shores, and I'm hanging over it, looking down from the glass belly of some helicopter. At the bottom of the lake—so deep I can only guess at the dark masses moving and heaving—are the real dragons. The ones that were around before men started living in caves and cooking meat over fires and figuring out the wheel and the alphabet. Enormous isn't the word for them; they've got more wrinkles than Johnny Panic himself. Dream about these long enough and your feet and hands shrivel away when you look at them too closely. The sun shrinks to the size of an orange, only chillier, and you've been living in Roxbury since the last ice age. No place for you but a room padded soft as the first room you knew of, where you can dream and float, float and dream, till at last you actually are back among those great originals and there's no point in any dreams at all.

It's into this lake people's minds run at night, brooks and gutter trickles to one borderless common reservoir. It bears no resemblance to those pure sparkling-blue sources of drinking water the suburbs guard more jealously than the Hope diamond in the middle of pine woods and barbed fences.

It's the sewage farm of the ages, transparence aside.

Now the water in this lake naturally stinks and smokes from what dreams have been left sogging around in it over the centuries. When you think how much room one night of dream props would take up for one person in one city, and that city a mere pinprick on a map of the world, and when you start multiplying this space by the population of the world, and that space by the number of nights there have been since the apes took to chipping axes out of stone and losing their hair, you have some idea what I mean. I'm not the mathematical type: my head starts splitting when I get only as far as the number of dreams going on during one night in the State of Massachusetts.

15   By this time, I already see the surface of the lake swarming with snakes, dead bodies puffed as blowfish, human embryos bobbing around in laboratory bottles like so many unfinished messages from the great I Am. I see whole storehouses of hardware: knives, paper cutters, pistons and cogs and nutcrackers; the shiny fronts of cars looming up, glass-eyed and evil-toothed. Then there's the spider-man and the webfooted man from Mars, and the simple, lugubrious vision of a human face turning aside forever, in spite of rings and vows, to the last lover of all.

One of the most frequent shapes in this backwash is so commonplace it seems silly to mention it. It's a grain of dirt. The water is thick with these grains. They seep in among everything else and revolve under some queer power of their own, opaque, ubiquitous. Call the water what you will, Lake Nightmare, Bog of Madness, it's here the sleeping people lie and toss together among the props of their worst dreams, one great brotherhood, though each of them, waking, thinks himself singular, utterly apart.

This is my dream. You won't find it written up in any casebook. Now the routine in our office is very different from the routine in Skin Clinic, for example, or in Tumor. The other clinics have strong similarities to each other; none are like ours. In our clinic, treatment doesn't get prescribed. It is invisible. It goes right on in those little cubicles, each with its desk, its two chairs, its window and its door with the opaque glass rectangle set in the wood. There is a certain spiritual purity about this kind of doctoring. I can't help feeling the special privilege of my position as Assistant Secretary in the Adult Psychiatric Clinic. My sense of pride is borne out by the rude invasions of other clinics into our cubicles on certain days of the week for lack of space elsewhere: our building is a very old one, and the facilities have not expanded with the expanding needs of the time. On these days of overlap the contrast between us and the other clinics is marked.

On Tuesdays and Thursdays, for instance, we have lumbar punctures in one of our offices in the morning. If the practical nurse chances to leave the door of the cubicle open, as she usually does, I can glimpse the end of the white cot and the dirty yellow-soled bare feet of the patient sticking out from under the sheet. In spite of my distaste at this sight, I can't keep my eyes away from the bare feet, and I find myself glancing back from my typing every few minutes to see if they are still there, if they have changed their position at all. You can understand what a distraction this is in the middle of my work. I often have to reread what I have typed several times, under the pretense of careful proofreading, in order to memorize the dreams I have copied down from the doctor's voice over the audiograph.

Nerve Clinic next door, which tends to the grosser, more unimaginative end of our business, also disturbs us in the mornings. We use their offices for therapy in the afternoon, as they are only a morning clinic, but to have their people crying, or singing, or chattering loudly in Italian or Chinese, as they often do, without break for four hours at a stretch every morning, is distracting to say the least.

20   In spite of such interruptions by other clinics, my own work is advancing at a great rate. By now I am far beyond copying only what comes after the patient's saying: "I have this dream, Doctor." I am at the point of re-creating dreams that are not even written down at all. Dreams that shadow themselves forth in the vaguest way, but are themselves hid, like a statue under red velvet before the grand unveiling.

To illustrate. This woman came in with her tongue swollen and stuck out so far she had to leave a party she was giving for twenty friends of her French-Canadian mother-in-law and be rushed to our Emergency Ward. She thought she didn't want her tongue to stick out and, to tell the truth, it was an exceedingly embarrassing affair for her, but she hated that French-Canadian mother-in-law worse than pigs, and her tongue was true to her opinion, even if the rest of her wasn't. Now she didn't lay claim to any dreams. I have only the bare facts above to begin with, yet behind them I detect the bulge and promise of a dream.

So I set myself to uprooting this dream from its comfortable purchase under her tongue.

Whatever the dream I unearth, by work, taxing work, and even by a kind of prayer, I am sure to find a thumbprint in the corner, a malicious detail to the right of center, a bodiless midair Cheshire cat grin, which shows the whole work to be gotten up by the genius of Johnny Panic, and him alone. He's sly, he's subtle, he's sudden as thunder, but he gives himself away only too often. He simply can't resist melodrama. Melodrama of the oldest, most obvious variety.

I remember one guy, a stocky fellow in a nail-studded black leather jacket, running straight into us from a boxing match at Mechanics Hall, Johnny Panic hot at his heels. This guy, good Catholic though he was, young and upright and all, had one mean fear of death. He was actually scared blue he'd go to hell. He was a pieceworker at a fluorescent light plant. I remember this detail because I thought it funny he should work there, him being so afraid of the dark as it turned out. Johnny Panic injects a poetic element in this business you don't often find elsewhere. And for that he has my eternal gratitude.

25   I also remember quite clearly the scenario of the dream I had worked out for this guy: a gothic interior in some monastery cellar, going on and on as far as you could see, one of those endless perspectives between two mirrors, and the pillars and walls were made of nothing but human skulls and bones, and in every niche there was a body laid out, and it was the Hall of Time, with the bodies in the foreground still warm, discoloring and starting to rot in the middle distance, and the bones emerging, clean as a whistle, in a kind of white futuristic glow at the end of the line. As I recall, I had the whole scene lighted, for the sake of accuracy, not with candles, but with the ice-bright fluorescence that makes skin look green and all the pink and red flushes dead black-purple.

You ask, how do I know this was the dream of the guy in the black leather jacket. I don't know. I only believe this was his dream, and I work at belief with more energy and tears and entreaties than I work at re-creating the dream itself.

My office, of course, has its limitations. The lady with her tongue stuck out, the guy from Mechanics Hall—these are our wildest ones. The people who have really gone floating down toward the bottom of that boggy lake come in only once, and are then referred to a place more permanent than our office which receives the public from nine to five, five days a week only. Even those people who are barely able to walk about the streets and keep working, who aren't yet halfway down in the lake, get sent to the Out-Patient Department at another hospital specializing in severer cases. Or they may stay a month or so in our own Observation Ward in the central hospital which I've never seen.

I've seen the secretary of that ward, though. Something about her merely smoking and drinking her coffee in the cafeteria at the ten o'clock break put me off so I never went to sit next to her again. She has a funny name I don't ever quite remember correctly, something really odd, like Miss Milleravage. One of those names that seem more like a pun mixing up Milltown and Ravage than anything in the city phone directory. But not so odd a name, after all, if you've ever read through the phone directory, with its Hyman Diddlebockers and Sasparilla Green-leafs. I read through the phone book once, never mind when, and it satisfied a deep need in me to realize how many people aren't called Smith.

Anyhow, this Miss Milleravage is a large woman, not fat, but all sturdy muscle and tall on top of it. She wears a gray suit over her hard bulk that reminds me vaguely of some kind of uniform, without the details of cut having anything strikingly military about them. Her face, hefty as a bullock's, is covered with a remarkable number of tiny maculae, as if she'd been lying under water for some time and little algae had latched on to her skin, smutching it over with tobacco-browns and greens. These moles are noticeable mainly because the skin around them is so pallid. I sometimes wonder if Miss Milleravage has ever seen the wholesome light of day. I wouldn't be a bit surprised if she'd been brought up from the cradle with the sole benefit of artificial lighting.

30   Byrna, the secretary in Alcoholic Clinic just across the hall from us, introduced me to Miss Milleravage with the gambit that I'd "been in England too."

Miss Milleravage, it turned out, had spent the best years of her life in London hospitals.

"Had a friend," she boomed in her queer, doggish basso, not favoring me with a direct look, "a nurse at Bart's. Tried to get in touch with her after the war, but the head of the nurses had changed, everybody'd changed, nobody'd heard of her. She must've gone down with the old head nurse, rubbish and all, in the bombings." She followed this with a large grin.

Now I've seen medical students cutting up cadavers, four stiffs to a classroom, about as recognizably human as Moby Dick, and the students playing catch with the dead men's livers. I've heard guys joke about sewing a woman up wrong after a delivery at the charity ward of the Lying-In. But I wouldn't want to see what Miss Milleravage would write off as the biggest laugh of all time. No thanks and then some. You could scratch her eyes with a pin and swear you'd struck solid quartz.

My boss has a sense of humor too, only it's gentle. Generous as Santa on Christmas Eve.

35   I work for a middle-aged lady named Miss Taylor who is the Head Secretary of the clinic and has been since the clinic started thirty-three years ago—the year of my birth, oddly enough. Miss Taylor knows every doctor, every patient, every outmoded appointment slip, referral slip and billing procedure the hospital has ever used or thought of using. She plans to stick with the clinic until she's farmed out in the green pastures of Social Security checks. A woman more dedicated to

her work I never saw. She's the same way about statistics as I am about dreams: if the building caught fire she would throw every last one of those books of statistics to the firemen below at the serious risk of her own skin.

I get along extremely well with Miss Taylor. The one thing I never let her catch me doing is reading the old record books. I have actually very little time for this. Our office is busier than the stock exchange with the staff of twenty-five doctors in and out, medical students in training, patients, patients' relatives, and visiting officials from other clinics referring patients to us, so even when I'm covering the office alone, during Miss Taylor's coffee break and lunch hour, I seldom get to dash down more than a note or two.

This kind of catch-as-catch-can is nerve-racking, to say the least. A lot of the best dreamers are in the old books, the dreamers that come in to us only once or twice for evaluation before they're sent elsewhere. For copying out these dreams I need time, a lot of time. My circumstances are hardly ideal for the unhurried pursuit of my art. There is, of course, a certain derring-do in working under such hazards, but I long for the rich leisure of the true connoisseur who indulges his nostrils above the brandy snifter for an hour before his tongue reaches out for the first taste.

I find myself all too often lately imagining what a relief it would be to bring a briefcase into work, big enough to hold one of those thick, blue, cloth-bound record books full of dreams. At Miss Taylor's lunch time, in the lull before the doctors and students crowd in to take their afternoon patients, I could simply slip one of the books, dated ten or fifteen years back, into my briefcase, and leave the briefcase under my desk till five o'clock struck. Of course, odd-looking bundles are inspected by the doorman of the Clinics Building and the hospital has its own staff of police to check up on the multiple varieties of thievery that go on, but for heaven's sake, I'm not thinking of making off with typewriters or heroin. I'd only borrow the book overnight and slip it back on the shelf first thing the next day before anybody else came in. Still, being caught taking a book out of the hospital would probably mean losing my job and all my source material with it.

This idea of mulling over a record book in the privacy and comfort of my own apartment, even if I have to stay up night after night for this purpose, attracts me so much I become more and more impatient with my usual method of snatching minutes to look up dreams in Miss Taylor's half-hours out of the office.

40   The trouble is, I can never tell exactly when Miss Taylor will come back to the office. She is so conscientious about her job she'd be likely to cut her half hour at lunch short and her twenty minutes at coffee shorter, if it weren't for her lame left leg. The distinct sound of this lame leg in the corridor warns me of her approach in time for me to whip the record book I'm reading into my drawer out of sight and pretend to be putting down the final flourishes on a phone message or some such alibi. The only catch, as far as my nerves are concerned, is that Amputee Clinic is around the corner from us in the opposite direction from Nerve Clinic and I've gotten really jumpy due to a lot of false alarms where I've mistaken some pegleg's hitching step for the step of Miss Taylor herself returning early to the office.

On the blackest days, when I've scarcely time to squeeze one dream out of the old books and my copywork is nothing but weepy college sophomores who can't get a lead in *Camino Real*, I feel Johnny Panic turn his back, stony as Everest, higher than Orion, and the motto of the great Bible of Dreams, "Perfect fear casteth out all else," is ash and lemon water on my lips. I'm a wormy hermit in a country of prize pigs so corn-happy they can't see the slaughterhouse at the end of the track. I'm Jeremiah vision-bitten in the Land of Cockaigne.

What's worse: day by day I see these psyche-doctors studying to win Johnny Panic's converts from him by hook, crook, and talk, talk, talk. Those deep-eyed, bush-bearded dream collectors who preceded me in history, and their contemporary inheritors with their white jackets and knotty-pine-paneled offices and leather couches, practiced and still practice their dream-gathering for worldly ends: health and money, money and health. To be a true member of Johnny Panic's congregation one must forget the dreamer and remember the dream: the dreamer is merely a flimsy vehicle for the great Dream Maker himself. This they will not do. Johnny Panic is gold in the bowels, and they try to root him out by spiritual stomach pumps.

Take what happened to Harry Bilbo. Mr. Bilbo came into our office with the hand of Johnny Panic heavy as a lead coffin on his shoulder. He had an interesting notion about the filth in this world. I figured him for a prominent part in Johnny Panic's Bible of Dreams, Third Book of Fear, Chapter Nine on Dirt, Disease and General Decay. A friend of Harry's blew a trumpet in the Boy Scout band when they were kids. Harry Bilbo'd also blown on this friend's trumpet. Years later the friend got cancer and died. Then, one day not so long ago, a cancer doctor came into Harry's house, sat down in a chair, passed the top of the morning with Harry's mother and, on leaving, shook her hand and opened the door for himself. Suddenly Harry Bilbo wouldn't blow trumpets or sit down on chairs or shake hands if all the cardinals of Rome took to blessing him twenty-four hours around the clock for fear of catching cancer. His mother had to go turning the TV knobs and water faucets on and off and opening doors for him. Pretty soon Harry stopped going to work because of the spit and dog turds in the street. First that stuff gets on your shoes and then when you take your shoes off it gets on your hands and then at dinner it's a quick trip into your mouth and not a hundred Hail Marys can keep you from the chain reaction.

The last straw was, Harry quit weight lifting at the public gym when he saw this cripple exercising with the dumbbells. You can never tell what germs cripples carry behind their ears and under their fingernails. Day and night Harry Bilbo lived in holy worship of Johnny Panic, devout as any priest among censers and sacraments. He had a beauty all his own.

45   Well, these white-coated tinkerers managed, the lot of them, to talk Harry into turning on the TV himself, and the water faucets, and to opening closet doors, front doors, bar doors. Before they were through with him, he was sitting down on movie-house chairs, and benches all over the Public Garden, and weight lifting every day of the week at the gym in spite of the fact another cripple took to using the rowing machine. At the end of his treatment he came in to shake hands with the Clinic Director. In Harry Bilbo's own words, he was "a changed man." The pure Panic-light had left his face. He went out of the office doomed to the crass fate these doctors call health and happiness.

About the time of Harry Bilbo's cure a new idea starts nudging at the bottom of my brain. I find it hard to ignore as those bare feet sticking out of the lumbar puncture room. If I don't want to risk carrying a record book out of the hospital in case I get discovered and fired and have to end my research forever, I can really speed up work by staying in the Clinics Building overnight. I am nowhere near exhausting the clinic's resources and the piddling amount of cases I am able to read in Miss Taylor's brief absences during the day are nothing to what I could get through in a few nights of steady copying. I need to accelerate my work if only to counteract those doctors.

Before I know it, I am putting on my coat at five and saying goodnight to Miss Taylor, who usually stays a few minutes' overtime to clear up the day's statistics, and sneaking around the corner into the ladies' room. It is empty. I slip into the patients' john, lock the door from the inside, and wait. For all I know, one of the clinic cleaning ladies may try to knock the door down, thinking some patient's passed out on the seat. My fingers are crossed. About twenty minutes later the door of the lavatory opens and someone limps over the threshold like a chicken favoring a bad leg. It is Miss Taylor, I can tell by the resigned sigh as she meets the jaundiced eye of the lavatory mirror. I hear the click-cluck of various touch-up equipment in the bowl, water sloshing, the scritch of a comb in frizzed hair, and then the door is closing with a slow-hinged wheeze behind her.

I am lucky. When I come out of the ladies' room at six o'clock the corridor lights are off and the fourth-floor hall is as empty as church on Monday. I have my own key to our office; I come in first every morning, so that's no trouble. The type-writers are folded back into the desks, the locks are on the dial phones, all's right with the world.

Outside the window the last of the winter light is fading. Yet I do not forget myself and turn on the overhead bulb. I don't want to be spotted by any hawk-eyed doctor or janitor in the hospital buildings across the little courtyard. The cabinet with the record books is in the windowless passage opening onto the doctors' cubicles, which have windows overlooking the courtyard. I make sure the doors to all the cubicles are shut. Then I switch on the passage light, a sallow twenty-five-watt affair blackening at the top. Better than an altarful of candles to me at this point, though. I didn't think to bring a sandwich. There is an apple in my desk drawer left over from lunch, so I reserve that for whatever pangs I may feel about one o'clock in the morning, and get out my pocket notebook. At home every evening it is my habit to tear out the notebook pages I've written on at the office during the day and pile them up to be copied in my manuscript. In this way I cover my tracks so no one idly picking up my notebook at the office could ever guess the type or scope of my work.

50   I begin systematically by opening the oldest book on the bottom shelf. The once-blue cover is no-color now, the pages are thumbed and blurry carbons, but I'm humming from foot to topknot: this dream book was spanking new the day I was born. When I really get organized I'll have hot soup in a thermos for the dead-of-winter nights, turkey pies and chocolate éclairs. I'll bring hair curlers and four changes of blouse to work in my biggest handbag on Monday mornings so no one will notice me going downhill in looks and start suspecting unhappy love affairs or pink affiliations or my working on dream books in the clinic four nights a week.

Eleven hours later. I am down to apple core and seeds and in the month of May, 1931, with a private nurse who has just opened a laundry bag in her patient's closet and found five severed heads in it, including her mother's.

A chill air touches the nape of my neck. From where I am sitting cross-legged on the floor in front of the cabinet, the record book heavy on my lap, I notice out of the corner of my eye that the door of the cubicle beside me is letting in a little crack of blue light. Not only along the floor, but up the side of the door too. This is odd since I made sure from the first that all the doors were shut tight. The crack of blue light is widening and my eyes are fastened to two motionless shoes in the doorway, toes pointing toward me.

They are brown leather shoes of a foreign make, with thick elevator soles. Above the shoes are black silk socks through which shows a pallor of flesh. I get as far as the gray pinstriped trouser cuffs.

"Tch, tch," chides an infinitely gentle voice from the cloudy regions above my head. "Such an uncomfortable position! Your legs must be asleep by now. Let me help you up. The sun will be rising shortly."

55   Two hands slip under my arms from behind and I am raised, wobbly as an unset custard, to my feet, which I cannot feel because my legs are, in fact, asleep. The record book slumps to the floor, pages splayed.

"Stand still a minute." The Clinic Director's voice fans the lobe of my right ear. "Then the circulation will revive."

The blood in my not-there legs starts pinging under a million sewing-machine needles and a vision of the Clinic Director acid-etches itself on my brain. I don't even need to look around: fat pot-belly buttoned into his gray pinstriped waistcoat, woodchuck teeth yellow and buck, every-color eyes behind the thick-lensed glasses quick as minnows.

I clutch my notebook. The last floating timber of the *Titanic*.

What does he know, what does he know?

60   Everything.

"I know where there is a nice hot bowl of chicken noodle soup." His voice rustles, dust under the bed, mice in straw. His hand welds onto my left upper arm in fatherly love. The record book of all the dreams going on in the city of my birth at my first yawp in this world's air he nudges under the bookcase with a polished toe.

We meet nobody in the dawn-dark hall. Nobody on the chill stone stair down to the basement corridors where Billy the Record Room Boy cracked his head skipping steps one night on a rush errand.

I begin to double-quickstep so he won't think it's me he's hustling. "You can't fire me," I say calmly. "I quit."

The Clinic Director's laugh wheezes up from his accordian-pleated bottom gut. "We mustn't lose you so soon." His whisper snakes off down the whitewashed basement passages, echoing among the elbow pipes, the wheelchairs and stretchers beached for the night along the steam-stained walls. "Why, we need you more than you know."

65   We wind and double and my legs keep time with his until we come, somewhere in those barren rat tunnels, to an all-night elevator run by a one-armed Negro. We get on, and the door grinds shut like the door on a cattle car, and we go up and up. It is a freight elevator, crude and clanky, a far cry from the plush passenger lifts I am used to in the Clinics Building.

We get off at an indeterminate floor. The Clinic Director leads me down a bare corridor lit at intervals by socketed bulbs in little wire cages on the ceiling. Locked doors set with screened windows line the hall on either hand. I plan to part company with the Clinic Director at the first red Exit sign, but on our journey there are none. I am in alien territory, coat on the hanger in the office, handbag and money in my top desk drawer, notebook in my hand, and only Johnny Panic to warm me against the ice age outside.

Ahead a light gathers, brightens. The Clinic Director, puffing slightly at the walk, brisk and long, to which he is obviously unaccustomed, propels me around a bend and into a square, brilliantly lit room.

"Here she is."

"The little witch!"

70 Miss Milleravage hoists her tonnage up from behind the steel desk facing the door.

The walls and the ceiling of the room are riveted metal battleship plates. There are no windows.

From small, barred cells lining the sides and back of the room I see Johnny Panic's top priests staring out at me, arms swaddled behind their backs in the white Ward nightshirts, eyes redder than coals and hungry-hot.

They welcome me with queer croaks and grunts, as if their tongues were locked in their jaws. They have no doubt heard of my work by way of Johnny Panic's grapevine and want to know how his apostles thrive in the world.

I lift my hands to reassure them, holding up my notebook, my voice loud as Johnny Panic's organ with all stops out.

75 "Peace! I bring to you . . ."

The Book.

"None of that old stuff, sweetie." Miss Milleravage is dancing out at me from behind her desk like a trick elephant.

The Clinic Director closes the door to the room.

The minute Miss Milleravage moves I notice what her hulk has been hiding from view behind the desk—a white cot high as a man's waist with a single sheet stretched over the mattress, spotless and drumskin tight. At the head of the cot is a table on which sits a metal box covered with dials and gauges.

80 The box seems to be eyeing me, copperhead-ugly, from its coil of electric wires, the latest model in Johnny-Panic-Killers.

I get ready to dodge to one side. When Miss Milleravage grabs, her fat hand comes away with a fist full of nothing. She starts for me again, her smile heavy as dogdays in August.

"None of that. None of that. I'll have that little black book."

Fast as I run around the high white cot, Miss Milleravage is so fast you'd think she wore rollerskates. She grabs and gets. Against her great bulk I beat my fists, and against her whopping milkless breasts, until her hands on my wrists are iron hoops and her breath hushabyes me with a love-stink fouler than Undertaker's Basement.

"My baby, my own baby's come back to me . . ."

85 "She," says the Clinic Director, sad and stern, "has been making time with Johnny Panic again."

"Naughty naughty."

The white cot is ready. With a terrible gentleness Miss Milleravage takes the watch from my wrist, the rings from my fingers, the hairpins from my hair. She begins to undress me. When I am bare, I am anointed on the temples and robed in sheets virginal as the first snow.

Then, from the four corners of the room and from the door behind me come five false priests in white surgical gowns and masks whose one lifework is to unseat Johnny Panic from his own throne. They extend me full-length on my back on the cot. The crown of wire is placed on my head, the wafer of forgetfulness on my tongue.The masked priests move to their posts and take hold: one of my left leg, one of my right, one of my right arm, one of my left. One behind my head at the metal box where I can't see.

From their cramped niches along the wall, the votaries raise their voices in protest. They begin the devotional chant:

> The only thing to love is Fear itself.
> Love of Fear is the beginning of wisdom.
> The only thing to love is Fear itself.
> May Fear and Fear and Fear be everywhere.

90   There is no time for Miss Milleravage or the Clinic Director or the priests to muzzle them.

The signal is given.

The machine betrays them.

At the moment when I think I am most lost the face of Johnny Panic appears in a nimbus of arc lights on the ceiling overhead. I am shaken like a leaf in the teeth of glory. His beard is lightning. Lightning is in his eye. His Word charges and illumines the universe.

The air crackles with his blue-tongued lightning-haloed angels.

95   His love is the twenty-story leap, the rope at the throat, the knife at the heart. He forgets not his own.

Joyce Carol Oates
How I Contemplated the World from the Detroit House of Correction and Began My Life Over Again

Joyce Carol Oates (1938–   ) grew up in New York, went to the University of Wisconsin, and studied creative writing at Syracuse University. A prolific author, Oates creates characters who are ordinary people inhabiting a Gothic world. She writes short stories, literary criticism, and poetry, but her best-known volumes are novels: *With Shuddering Fall* (1964), *A Garden of Earthly Delights* (1967), *Expensive People* (1968), *them* (1969), *Wonderland* (1971), and *Do with Me What You Will* (1973).

Notes for an essay for an English class at Baldwin Country Day School; poking around in debris; disgust and curiosity; a revelation of the meaning of life; a happy ending. . . .

I. Events

1. The girl (myself) is walking through Branden's, that excellent store. Suburb of a large famous city that is a symbol for large famous American cities. The event sneaks up on the girl, who believes she is herding it along with a small fixed smile, a girl of fifteen, innocently experienced. She dawdles in a certain style by a counter of costume jewelry. Rings, earrings, necklaces. Prices from $5 to $50, all within reach. All ugly. She eases over to the glove counter, where everything is ugly too. In her close-fitted coat with its black fur collar she contemplates the luxury of Branden's, which she has known for many years: its many mild pale lights, easy

on the eye and the soul, its elaborate tinkly decorations, its women shoppers with their excellent shoes and coats and hairdos, all dawdling gracefully, in no hurry.

Who was ever in a hurry here?

2. The girl seated at home. A small library, paneled walls of oak. Someone is talking to me. An earnest husky female voice drives itself against my ears, nervous, frightened, groping around my heart, saying, "If you wanted gloves why didn't you say so? Why didn't you ask for them?" That store, Branden's, is owned by Raymond Forrest who lives on DuMaurier Drive. We live on Sioux Drive. Raymond Forrest. A handsome man? An ugly man? A man of fifty or sixty, with gray hair, or a man of forty with earnest courteous eyes, a good golf game, who is Raymond Forrest, this man who is my salvation? Father has been talking to him. Father is not his physician; Dr. Berg is his physician. Father and Dr. Berg refer patients to each other. There is a connection. Mother plays bridge with. . . . On Mondays and Wednesdays our maid Billie works at. . . . The strings draw together in a cat's cradle, making a net to save you when you fall. . . .

3. *Harriet Arnold's.* A small shop, better than Branden's. Mother in her black coat, I in my close-fitted blue coat. Shopping. Now look at this, isn't this cute, do you want this, why don't you want this, try this on, take this with you to the fitting room, take this also, what's wrong with you, what can I do for you, why are you so strange . . .? "I wanted to steal but not to buy," I don't tell her. The girl droops along in her coat and gloves and leather boots, her eyes scan the horizon which is pastel pink and decorated like Branden's, tasteful walls and modern ceilings with graceful glimmering lights.

5   4. Weeks later, the girl at a bus-stop. Two o'clock in the afternoon, a Tuesday, obviously she has walked out of school.

5. The girl stepping down from a bus. Afternoon, weather changing to colder. Detroit. Pavement and closed-up stores; grill work over the windows of a pawn-shop. What is a pawnshop, exactly?

II. Characters

1. The girl stands five feet five inches tall. An ordinary height. Baldwin Country Day School draws them up to that height. She dreams along the corridors and presses her face against the Thermoplex Glass. No frost or steam can ever form on that glass. A smudge of grease from her forehead . . . could she be boiled down to grease? She wears her hair loose and long and straight in suburban teenage style, 1968. Eyes smudged with pencil, dark brown. Brown hair. Vague green eyes. A pretty girl? An ugly girl? She sings to herself under her breath, idling in the corridor, thinking of her many secrets (the thirty dollars she once took from the purse of a friend's mother, just for fun, the basement window she smashed in her own house just for fun) and thinking of her brother who is at Susquehanna Boys' Academy, an excellent preparatory school in Maine, remembering him unclearly . . . he has long manic hair and a squeaking voice and he looks like one of the popular teenage singers of 1968, one of those in a group, *The Certain Forces, The Way Out, The Maniacs Responsible.* The girl in her turn looks like one of those fieldsful of girls who listen to the boys' singing, dreaming and mooning restlessly, breaking into high sullen laughter, innocently experienced.

2. The mother. A midwestern woman of Detroit and suburbs. Belongs to the Detroit Athletic Club. Also the Detroit Golf Club. Also the Bloomfield Hills Country Club. The Village Women's Club at which lectures are given each winter on Genet and Sartre and James Baldwin, by the Director of the Adult Education Program at Wayne State University. . . . The Bloomfield Art Association. Also the Founders Society of the Detroit Institute of Arts. Also. . . . Oh, she is in perpetual motion, this lady, hair like blown-up gold and finer than gold, hair and fingers and body of inestimable grace. Heavy weighs the gold on the back of her hairbrush and hand mirror. Heavy heavy the candlesticks in the dining room. Very heavy is the big car, a Lincoln, long, and black, that on one cool autumn day split a squirrel's body in two unequal parts.

3. The father, Dr. ———. He belongs to the same clubs as # 2. A player of squash and golf; he has a golfer's umbrella of stripes. Candy stripes. In his mouth nothing turns to sugar, however, saliva works no miracles here. His doctoring is of the slightly sick. The sick are sent elsewhere (to Dr. Berg?), the deathly sick are sent back for more tests and their bills are sent to their homes, the unsick are sent to Dr. Coronet (Isabel, a lady), an excellent psychiatrist for unsick people who angrily believe they are sick and want to do something about it. If they demand a male psychiatrist, the unsick are sent by Dr. ——— (my father) to Dr. Lowenstein, a male psychiatrist, excellent and expensive, with a limited practice.

10   4. Clarita. She is twenty, twenty-five, she is thirty or more? Pretty, ugly, what? She is a woman lounging by the side of a road, in jeans and a sweater, hitch-hiking, or she is slouched on a stool at a counter in some roadside diner. A hard line of jaw. Curious eyes. Amused eyes. Behind her eyes processions move, funeral pageants, cartoons. She says, "I never can figure out why girls like you bum around down here. What are you looking for anyway?" An odor of tobacco about her. Unwashed underclothes, or no underclothes, unwashed skin, gritty toes, hair long and falling into strands, not recently washed.

5. Simon. In this city the weather changes abruptly, so Simon's weather changes abruptly. He sleeps through the afternoon. He sleeps through the morning. Rising he gropes around for something to get him going, for a cigarette or a pill to drive him out to the street, where the temperature is hovering around 35°. Why doesn't it drop? Why, why doesn't the cold clean air come down from Canada, will he have to go up into Canada to get it, will he have to leave the Country of his Birth and sink into Canada's frosty fields . . .? Will the F.B.I. (which he dreams about constantly) chase him over the Canadian border on foot, hounded out in a blizzard of broken glass and horns . . .?

"Once I was Huckleberry Finn," Simon says, "but now I am Roderick Usher." Beset by frenzies and fears, this man who makes my spine go cold, he takes green pills, yellow pills, pills of white and capsules of dark blue and green . . . he takes other things I may not mention, for what if Simon seeks me out and climbs into my girl's bedroom here in Bloomfield Hills and strangles me, what then . . .? (As I write this I begin to shiver. Why do I shiver? I am now sixteen and sixteen is not an age for shivering.) It comes from Simon, who is always cold.

III. World Events
Nothing.

IV. People and Circumstances Contributing to This Delinquency

Nothing.

V. Sioux Drive

15 George, Clyde G. 240 Sioux. A manufacturer's representative; children, a dog; a wife. Georgian with the usual columns. You think of the White House, then of Thomas Jefferson, then your mind goes blank on the white pillars and you think of nothing. Norris, Ralph W. 246 Sioux. Public relations. Colonial. Bay window, brick, stone, concrete, wood, green shutters, sidewalk, lantern, grass, trees, black-top drive, two children, one of them my classmate Esther (Esther Norris) at Baldwin. Wife, cars. Ramsey, Michael D. 250 Sioux. Colonial. Big living room, thirty by twenty-five, fireplaces in living room library recreation room, paneled walls wet bar five bathrooms five bedrooms two lavatories central air conditioning automatic sprinkler automatic garage door three children one wife two cars a breakfast room a patio a large fenced lot fourteen trees a front door with a brass knocker never knocked. Next is our house. Classic contemporary. Traditional modern. Attached garage, attached Florida room, attached patio, attached pool and cabana, attached roof. A front door mailslot through which pour *Time Magazine, Fortune, Life, Business Week, The Wall Street Journal, The New York Times, The New Yorker, The Saturday Review, M.D., Modern Medicine, Disease of the Month* . . . and also. . . . And in addition to all this a quiet sealed letter from Baldwin saying: *Your daughter is not doing work compatible with her performance on the Stanford-Binet.* . . . And your son is not doing well, not well at all, very sad. Where is your son anyway? Once he stole trick-and-treat candy from some six-year-old kids, he himself being a robust ten. The beginning. Now your daughter steals. In the Village Pharmacy she made off with, yes she did, don't deny it, she made off with a copy of *Pageant Magazine* for no reason, she swiped a roll of lifesavers in a green wrapper and was in no need of saving her life or even in need of sucking candy, when she was no more than eight years old she stole, don't blush, she stole a package of *Tums* only because it was out on the counter and available, and the nice lady behind the counter (now dead) said nothing. . . . Sioux Drive. Maples, oaks, elms. Diseased elms cut down. Sioux Drive runs into Roosevelt Drive. Slow turning lanes, not streets, all drives and lanes and ways and passes. A private police force. Quiet private police, in unmarked cars. Cruising on Saturday evenings with paternal smiles for the residents who are streaming in and out of houses, going to and from parties, a thousand parties, slightly staggering, the women in their furs alighting from automobiles bought of Ford and General Motors and Chrysler, very heavy automobiles. No foreign cars. Detroit. In 275 Sioux, down the block, in that magnificent French Normandy mansion, lives ———— ———— himself, who has the C——— account itself, imagine that! Look at where he lives and look at the enormous trees and chimneys, imagine his many fireplaces, imagine his wife and children, imagine his wife's hair, imagine her fingernails, imagine her bathtub of smooth clean glowing pink, imagine their embraces, his trouser pockets filled with odd coins and keys and dust and peanuts, imagine their ecstasy on Sioux Drive, imagine their income tax returns, imagine their little boy's pride in his experimental car, a scaled-down C———, as he roars around the neighborhood on the sidewalks frightening dogs and Negro maids, oh imagine all these things, imagine everything, let your mind roar out all over Sioux Drive and DuMaurier Drive and Roosevelt Drive and Ticonderoga Pass and Burning Bush Way and Lincolnshire Pass and Lois Lane.

When spring comes its winds blow nothing to Sioux Drive, no odors of holly-hocks or forsythia, nothing Sioux Drive doesn't already possess, everything is planted and performing. The weather vanes, had they weather vanes, don't have to turn with the wind, don't have to contend with the weather. There is no weather.

VI. Detroit

There is always weather in Detroit. Detroit's temperature is always 32°. Fast falling temperatures. Slow rising temperatures. Wind from the north northeast four to forty miles an hour, small craft warnings, partly cloudy today and Wednesday changing to partly sunny through Thursday . . . small warnings of frost, soot warnings, traffic warnings, hazardous lake conditions for small craft and swim-mers, restless Negro gangs, restless cloud formations, restless temperatures ach-ing to fall out the very bottom of the thermometer or shoot up over the top and boil everything over in red mercury.

Detroit's temperature is 32°. Fast falling temperatures. Slow rising temperatures. Wind from the north northeast four to forty miles an hour. . . .

VII. Events

1. The girl's heart is pounding. In her pocket is a pair of gloves! In a plastic bag! Airproof breathproof plastic bag, gloves selling for twenty-five dollars on Branden's counter! In her pocket! Shoplifted! . . . In her purse is a blue comb, not very clean. In her purse is a leather billfold (a birthday present from her grandmother in Philadelphia) with snapshots of the family in clean plastic windows, in the billfold are bills, she doesn't know how many bills. . . . In her purse is an ominous note from her friend Tykie *What's this about Joe H. and the kids hanging around at Louise's Sat. night? You heard anything?* . . . passed in French class. In her purse is a lot of dirty yellow Kleenex, her mother's heart would break to see such very dirty Kleenex, and at the bottom of her purse are brown hairpins and safety pins and a broken pencil and a ballpoint pen (blue) stolen from somewhere for-gotten and a purse-size compact of Cover Girl Make-Up, Ivory Rose. . . . Her lipstick is Broken Heart, a corrupt pink; her fingers are trembling like crazy; her teeth are beginning to chatter; her insides are alive; her eyes glow in her head; she is saying to her mother's astonished face *I want to steal but not to buy.*

20   2. At Clarita's. Day or night? What room is this? A bed, a regular bed, and a mattress on the floor nearby. Wallpaper hanging in strips. Clarita says she tore it like that with her teeth. She was fighting a barbaric tribe that night, high from some pills she was battling for her life with men wearing helmets of heavy iron and their faces no more than Christian crosses to breathe through, every one of those bastards looking like her lover Simon, who seems to breathe with great difficulty through the slits of mouth and nostrils in his face. Clarita has never heard of Sioux Drive. Raymond Forrest cuts no ice with her, nor does the C——— account and its millions; Harvard Business School could be at the corner of Vernor and 12th Street for all she cares, and Vietnam might have sunk by now into the Dead Sea under its tons of debris, for all the amazement she could show . . . her face is overworked, overwrought, at the age of twenty (thirty?) it is already exhausted but fanciful and ready for a laugh. Clarita says mournfully to me *Honey somebody is going to turn you out let me give you warning.* In a movie shown on late television Clarita is not a mess like this but a nurse, with short neat hair and

a dedicated look, in love with her doctor and her doctor's patients and their diseases, enamored of needles and sponges and rubbing alcohol. . . . Or no: she is a private secretary. Robert Cummings is her boss. She helps him with fantastic plots, the canned audience laughs, no, the audience doesn't laugh because nothing is funny, instead her boss is Robert Taylor and they are not boss and secretary but husband and wife, she is threatened by a young starlet, she is grim, handsome, wifely, a good companion for a good man. . . . She is Claudette Colbert. Her sister too is Claudette Colbert. They are twins, identical. Her husband Charles Boyer is a very rich handsome man and her sister, Claudette Colbert, is plotting her death in order to take her place as the rich man's wife, no one will know because they are *twins*. . . . All these marvelous lives Clarita might have lived, but she fell out the bottom at the age of thirteen. At the age when I was packing my overnight case for a slumber party at Toni Deshield's she was tearing filthy sheets off a bed and scratching up a rash on her arms. . . . Thirteen is uncommonly young for a white girl in Detroit, Miss Brook of the Detroit House of Correction said in a sad newspaper interview for the *Detroit News*; fifteen and sixteen are more likely. Eleven, twelve, thirteen are not surprising in colored . . . they are more precocious. What can we do? Taxes are rising and the tax base is falling. The temperature rises slowly but falls rapidly. Everything is falling out the bottom, Woodward Avenue is filthy, Livernois Avenue filthy! Scraps of paper flutter in the air like pigeons, dirt flies up and hits you right in the eye, oh Detroit is breaking up into dangerous bits of newspaper and dirt, watch out. . . .

Clarita's apartment is over a restaurant. Simon her lover emerges from the cracks at dark. Mrs. Olesko, a neighbor of Clarita's, an aged white whisp of a woman, doesn't complain but sniffs with contentment at Clarita's noisy life and doesn't tell the cops, hating cops, when the cops arrive. I should give more fake names, more blanks, instead of telling all these secrets. I myself am a secret; I am a minor.

3. My father reads a paper at a medical convention in Los Angeles. There he is, on the edge of the North American continent, when the unmarked detective put his hand so gently on my arm in the aisle of Branden's and said, "Miss, would you like to step over here for a minute?"

And where was he when Clarita put her hand on my arm, that wintry dark sulphurous aching day in Detroit, in the company of closed-down barber shops, closed-down diners, closed-down movie houses, homes, windows, basements, faces . . . she put her hand on my arm and said, "Honey, are you looking for somebody down here?"

And was he home worrying about me, gone for two weeks solid, when they carried me off . . .? It took three of them to get me in the police cruiser, so they said, and they put more than their hands on my arm.

25 4. I worked on this lesson. My English teacher is Mr. Forest, who is from Michigan State. Not handsome, Mr. Forest, and his name is plain unlike Raymond Forrest's, but he is sweet and rodent-like, he has conferred with the principal and my parents, and everything is fixed . . . treat her as if nothing has happened, a new start, begin again, only sixteen years old, what a shame, how did it happen?—nothing happened, nothing could have happened, a slight physiological modification known only to a gynecologist or to Dr. Coronet. I work on my lesson. I sit in my pink room. I look around the room with my sad pink eyes. I sigh, I dawdle, I

pause, I eat up time, I am limp and happy to be home, I am sixteen years old suddenly, my head hangs heavy as a pumpkin on my shoulders, and my hair has just been cut by Mr. Faye at the Crystal Salon and is said to be very becoming.

(Simon too put his hand on my arm and said, "Honey, you have got to come with me," and in his six-by-six room we got to know each other. Would I go back to Simon again? Would I lie down with him in all that filth and craziness? Over and over again.

a Clarita is being betrayed as in front of a Cunningham Drug Store she is nervously eyeing a colored man who may or may not have money, or a nervous white boy of twenty with sideburns and an Appalachian look, who may or may not have a knife hidden in his jacket pocket, or a husky red-faced man of friendly countenance who may or may not be a member of the Vice Squad out for an early twilight walk.)

I work on my lesson for Mr. Forest. I have filled up eleven pages. Words pour out of me and won't stop. I want to tell everything . . . what was the song Simon was always humming, and who was Simon's friend in a very new trench coat with an old high school graduation ring on his finger . . .? Simon's bearded friend? When I was down too low for him Simon kicked me out and gave me to him for three days, I think, on Fourteenth Street in Detroit, an airy room of cold cruel drafts with newspapers on the floor. . . . Do I really remember that or am I piecing it together from what they told me? Did they tell the truth? Did they know much of the truth?

VIII. Characters

1. Wednesdays after school, at four; Saturday mornings at ten. Mother drives me to Dr. Coronet. Ferns in the office, plastic or real, they look the same. Dr. Coronet is queenly, an elegant nicotine-stained lady, who would have studied with Freud had circumstances not prevented it, a bit of a Catholic, ready to offer you some mystery if your teeth will ache too much without it. Highly recommended by Father! Forty dollars an hour, Father's forty dollars! Progress! Looking up! Looking better! That new haircut is so becoming, says Dr. Coronet herself, showing how normal she is for a woman with an I.Q. of 180 and many advanced degrees.

30   2. Mother. A lady in a brown suede coat. Boots of shiny black material, black gloves, a black fur hat. She would be humiliated could she know that of all the people in the world it is my ex-lover Simon who walks most like her . . . self-conscious and unreal, listening to distant music, a little bowlegged with craft-iness. . .

3. Father. Tying a necktie. In a hurry. On my first evening home he put his hand on my arm and said, "Honey, we're going to forget all about this."

4. Simon. Outside a plane is crossing the sky, in here we're in a hurry. Morning. It must be morning. The girl is half out of her mind, whimpering and vague, Simon her dear friend is wretched this morning . . . he is wretched with morning itself . . . he forces her to give him an injection, with that needle she knows is filthy, she has a dread of needles and surgical instruments and the odor of things that are to be sent into the blood, thinking somehow of her father. . . . This is a bad morning, Simon says that his mind is being twisted out of shape, and so he submits to the needle which he usually scorns and bites his lip with his yellowish

teeth, his face going very pale. *Ah baby!* he says in his soft mocking voice, which with all women is a mockery of love, *do it like this—Slowly—*And the girl, terrified, almost drops the precious needle but manages to turn it up to the light from the window . . . it is an extension of herself, then? She can give him this gift, then? *I wish you wouldn't do this to me,* she says, wise in her terror, because it seems to her that Simon's danger—in a few minutes he might be dead—is a way of pressing her against him that is more powerful than any other embrace. She has to work over his arm, the knotted corded veins of his arm, her forehead wet with perspiration as she pushes and releases the needle, staring at that mixture of liquid now stained with Simon's bright blood. . . . When the drug hits him she can feel it herself, she feels that magic that is more than any woman can give him, striking the back of his head and making his face stretch as if with the impact of a terrible sun. . . . She tries to embrace him but he pushes her aside and stumbles to his feet, *Jesus Christ,* he says. . . .

5. Princess, a Negro girl of eighteen. What is her charge? She is closemouthed about it, shrewd and silent, you know that no one had to wrestle her to the sidewalk to get her in here; she came with dignity. In the recreation room she sits reading *Nancy Drew and the Jewel Box Mystery,* which inspires in her face tiny wrinkles of alarm and interest: what a face! Light brown skin, heavy shaded eyes, heavy eyelashes, a serious sinister dark brow, graceful fingers, graceful wrist-bones, graceful legs, lips, tongue, a sugarsweet voice, a leggy stride more masculine than Simon's and my mother's, decked out in a dirty white blouse and dirty white slacks; vaguely nautical is Princess's style. . . . At breakfast she is in charge of clearing the table and leans over me, saying, *Honey you sure you ate enough?*

6. The girl lies sleepless, wondering. Why here, why not there? Why Bloomfield Hills and not jail? Why jail and not her pink room? Why downtown Detroit and not Sioux Drive? What is the difference? Is Simon all the difference? The girl's head is a parade of wonders. She is nearly sixteen, her breath is marvelous with wonders, not long ago she was coloring with crayons and now she is smearing the landscape with paints that won't come off and won't come off her fingers either. She says to the matron *I am not talking about anything,* not because everyone has warned her not to talk but because, because she will not talk, because she won't say anything about Simon who is her secret. And she says to the matron *I won't go home* up until that night in the lavatory when everything was changed. . . . "No, I won't go home I want to stay here," she says, listening to her own words with amazement, thinking that weeds might climb everywhere over that marvelous $86,000 house and dinosaurs might return to muddy the beige carpeting, but never will she reconcile four o'clock in the morning in Detroit with eight o'clock breakfasts in Bloomfield Hills . . . oh, she aches still for Simon's hands and his caressing breath, though he gave her little pleasure, he took everything from her (five-dollar bills, ten-dollar bills, passed into her numb hands by men and taken out of her hands by Simon) until she herself was passed into the hands of other men, police, when Simon evidently got tired of her and her hysteria. . . . *No, I won't go home, I don't want to be bailed out,* the girl thinks as a *Stubborn and Wayward Child* (one of several charges lodged against her) and the matron understands her crazy white-rimmed eyes that are seeking out some new violence that will keep her in jail, should someone threaten to let her out. Such children try to strangle the matrons, the attendants, or one another . . . they want the locks

locked forever, the doors nailed shut . . . and this girl is no different up until that night her mind is changed for her. . . .

IX. That Night

35   Princess and Dolly, a little white girl of maybe fifteen, hardy however as a sergeant and in the House of Correction for armed robbery, corner her in the lavatory at the farthest sink and the other girls look away and file out to bed, leaving her. God how she is beaten up! Why is she beaten up? Why do they pound her, why such hatred? Princess vents all the hatred of a thousand silent Detroit winters on her body, this girl whose body belongs to me, fiercely she rides across the midwestern plains on this girl's tender bruised body . . . revenge on the oppressed minorities of America! revenge on the slaughtered Indians! revenge on the female sex, on the male sex, revenge on Bloomfield Hills, revenge revenge. . . .

X. Detroit

In Detroit weather weighs heavily upon everyone. The sky looms large. The horizon shimmers in smoke. Downtown the buildings are imprecise in the haze. Perpetual haze. Perpetual motion inside the haze. Across the choppy river is the city of Windsor, in Canada. Part of the continent has bunched up here and is bulging outward, at the tip of Detroit, a cold hard rain is forever falling on the expressway . . . shoppers shop grimly, their cars are not parked in safe places, their windshields may be smashed and graceful ebony hands may drag them out through their shatterproof smashed windshields crying *Revenge for the Indians!* Ah, they all fear leaving Hudson's and being dragged to the very tip of the city and thrown off the parking roof of Cobo Hall, that expensive tomb, into the river. . . .

XI. Characters We Are Forever Entwined With

1. Simon drew me into his tender rotting arms and breathed gravity into me. Then I came to earth, weighted down. He said *You are such a little girl,* and he weighed me down with his delight. In the palms of his hands were teeth marks from his previous life experiences. He was thirty-five, they said. Imagine Simon in this room, in my pink room: he is about six feet tall and stoops slightly, in a feline cautious way, always thinking, always on guard, with his scuffed light suede shoes and his clothes which are anyone's clothes, slightly rumpled ordinary clothes that ordinary men might wear to not-bad jobs. Simon has fair, long hair, curly hair, spent languid curls that are like . . . exactly like the curls of wood shavings to the touch, I am trying to be exact . . . and he smells of unheated mornings and coffee and too many pills coating his tongue with a faint green-white scum. . . . Dear Simon, who would be panicked in this room and in this house (right now Billie is vacuuming next door in my parents' room: a vacuum cleaner's roar is a sign of all good things), Simon who is said to have come from a home not much different from this, years ago, fleeing all the carpeting and the polished banisters . . . Simon has a deathly face, only desperate people fall in love with it. His face is bony and cautious, the bones of his cheeks prominent as if with the rigidity of his ceaseless thinking, plotting, for he has to make money out of girls to whom money means nothing, they're so far gone they can hardly count it, and in a sense money means nothing to him either except as a way of keeping on with his life. *Each Day's Proud Struggle,* the title of a novel we could read at jail. . . . Each day he needs a certain amount of money. He devours it. It wasn't love he uncoiled in me with

his hollowed-out eyes and his courteous smile, that remnant of a prosperous past, but a dark terror that needed to press itself flat against him, or against another man . . . but he was the first, he came over to me and took my arm, a claim. We struggled on the stairs and I said, "Let me loose, you're hurting my neck, my face," it was such a surprise that my skin hurt where he rubbed it, and afterward we lay face to face and he breathed everything into me. In the end I think he turned me in.

2. Raymond Forrest. I just read this morning that Raymond Forrest's father, the chairman of the board at ————, died of a heart attack on a plane bound for London. I would like to write Raymond Forrest a note of sympathy. I would like to thank him for not pressing charges against me one hundred years ago, saving me, being so generous . . . well, men like Raymond Forrest are generous men, not like Simon. I would like to write him a letter telling of my love, or of some other emotion that is positive and healthy. Not like Simon and his poetry, which he scrawled down when he was high and never changed a word . . . but when I try to think of something to say it is Simon's language that comes back to me, caught in my head like a bad song, it is always Simon's language:

> There is no reality only dreams
> Your neck may get snapped when you wake
> My love is drawn to some violent end
> She keeps wanting to get away
> My love is heading downward
> And I am heading upward
> She is going to crash on the sidewalk
> And I am going to dissolve into the clouds

XII. Events

1. Out of the hospital, bruised and saddened and converted, with Princess's grunts still tangled in my hair . . . and Father in his overcoat looking like a Prince himself, come to carry me off. Up the expressway and out north to home. Jesus Christ but the air is thinner and cleaner here. Monumental houses. Heartbreaking side-walks, so clean.

40 2. Weeping in the living room. The ceiling is two storeys high and two chandeliers hang from it. Weeping, weeping, though Billie the maid is *probably listening*. I will never leave home again. Never. Never leave home. Never leave this home again, never.

3. Sugar doughnuts for breakfast. The toaster is very shiny and my face is distorted in it. Is that my face?

4. The car is turning in the driveway. Father brings me home. Mother embraces me. Sunlight breaks in movieland patches on the roof of our traditional contemporary home, which was designed for the famous automotive stylist whose identity, if I told you the name of the famous car he designed, you would all know, so I can't tell you because my teeth chatter at the thought of being sued . . . or having someone climb into my bedroom window with a rope to strangle me. . . . The car turns up the black-top drive. The house opens to me like a doll's house, so lovely in the sunlight, the big living room beckons to me with its walls falling away in a

delirium of joy at my return, Billie the maid is *no doubt* listening from the kitchen as I burst into tears and the hysteria Simon got so sick of. Convulsed in Father's arms I say I will never leave again, never, why did I leave, where did I go, what happened, my mind is gone wrong, my body is one big bruise, my backbone was sucked dry, it wasn't the men who hurt me and Simon never hurt me but only those girls . . . my God how they hurt me . . . I will never leave home again. . . . The car is perpetually turning up the drive and I am perpetually breaking down in the living room and we are perpetually taking the right exit from the expressway (Lahser Road) and the wall of the restroom is perpetually banging against my head and perpetually are Simon's hands moving across my body and adding everything up and so too are Father's hands on my shaking bruised back, far from the surface of my skin on the surface of my good blue cashmere coat (drycleaned for my release). . . . I weep for all the money here, for God in gold and beige carpeting, for the beauty of chandeliers and the miracle of a clean polished gleaming toaster and faucets that run both hot and cold water, and I tell them *I will never leave home, this is my home, I love everything here, I am in love with everything here.* . . .

I am home.

Raymond Carver
The Father

Raymond Carver (1938–   ) was born in Oregon, went to California State College at Humboldt, and has lived most of his life in California. His poems have been collected in three small volumes and his stories in two collections: *Will You Please Be Quiet, Please?* (1976) and *Furious Seasons* (1977). He lives in Tucson, Arizona.

The baby lay in a basket beside the bed, dressed in a white bonnet and sleeper. The basket had been newly painted and tied with ice blue ribbons and padded with blue quilts. The three little sisters and the mother, who had just gotten out of bed and was still not herself, and the grandmother all stood around the baby, watching it stare and sometimes raise its fist to its mouth. He did not smile or laugh, but now and then he blinked his eyes and flicked his tongue back and forth through his lips when one of the girls rubbed his chin.

The father was in the kitchen and could hear them playing with the baby.

"Who do you love, baby?" Phyllis said and tickled his chin.

"He loves us all," Phyllis said, "but he really loves Daddy because Daddy's a boy too!"

5   The grandmother sat down on the edge of the bed and said, "Look at its little arm! So fat. And those little fingers! Just like its mother."

"Isn't he sweet?" the mother said. "So healthy, my little baby." And bending over, she kissed the baby on its forehead and touched the cover over its arm. "We love him too."

"But who does he look like, who does he look like?" Alice cried, and they all moved up closer around the basket to see who the baby looked like.

"He has pretty eyes," Carol said.

"*All* babies have pretty eyes," Phyllis said.

10   "He has his grandfather's lips," the grandmother said. "Look at those lips."

"I don't know . . ." the mother said. "I wouldn't say."

"The nose! The nose!" Alice cried.

"What about his nose?" the mother asked.

"It looks like somebody's nose," the girl answered.

15   "No, I don't know," the mother said. "I don't think so."

"Those lips . . ." the grandmother murmured. "Those little fingers . . ." she said, uncovering the baby's hand and spreading out its fingers.

"Who does the baby look like?"

"He doesn't look like anybody," Phyllis said. And they moved even closer.

"*I* know! *I* know!" Carol said. "He looks like *Daddy!*" Then they looked closer at the baby.

20   "But who does Daddy *look* like?" Phyllis asked.

"Who does Daddy *look* like?" Alice repeated, and they all at once looked through to the kitchen where the father was sitting at the table with his back to them.

"Why, nobody!" Phyllis said and began to cry a little.

"Hush," the grandmother said and looked away and then back at the baby.

"Daddy doesn't look like *anybody!*" Alice said.

25   "But he has to look like *somebody*," Phyllis said, wiping her eyes with one of the ribbons. And all of them except the grandmother looked at the father, sitting at the table.

He had turned around in his chair and his face was white and without expression.

Gayl Jones
White Rat

Gayl Jones (1949–   ) was born in Lexington, Kentucky, graduated from
Connecticut College, and did graduate work at Brown University. She published
two novels, *Corregidora* (1975) and *Eva's Man* (1976), and a book of short
stories, *White Rat* (1977), by the age of twenty-seven. She teaches at the
University of Michigan.

I learned where she was when Cousin Willie come down home and said Maggie sent for her but told her not to tell nobody where she was, especially me, but Cousin Willie come and told me anyway cause she said I was the lessen two evils and she didn't like to see Maggie stuck up in the room up there like she was. I asked her what she mean like she was. Willie said that she was pregnant by J. T. J. T. the man she run off with because she said I treat her like dirt. And now Willie say J. T. run off and left her after he got her knocked up. I asked Willie where she was. Willie said she was up in that room over Babe Lawson's. She told me not to be surprised when I saw her looking real bad. I said I wouldn't be least surprised. I asked Willie she think Maggie come back. Willie say she better.

The room was dirty and Maggie looked worser than Willie say she going to look. I knocked on the door but there weren't no answer so I just opened the door and went in and saw Maggie laying on the bed turned up against the wall. She turnt around when I come in but she didn't say nothing. I said Maggie we getting out a here. So I got the bag she brung when she run away and put all her loose things in it and just took her by the arm and brung her on home. You couldn't tell nothing was in her belly though.

I been taking care of little Henry since she been gone but he 3½ years old and ain't no trouble since he can play hisself and know what it mean when you hit him on the ass when he do something wrong.

Maggie don't say nothing when we get in the house. She just go over to little Henry. He sleeping in the front room on the couch. She go over to little Henry and bend down an kiss him on the cheek and then she ask me have I had supper and when I say Naw she go back in the kitchen and start fixing it. We sitting at the table and nobody saying nothing but I feel I got to say something.

5 "You can go head and have the baby," I say. "I give him my name."

I say it meaner than I want to. She just look up at me and don't say nothing. Then she say, "He ain't yours."

I say, "I know he ain't mine. But don't nobody else have to know. Even the baby. He don't even never have to know."

She just keep looking at me with her big eyes that don't say nothing, and then she say, "You know. I know."

She look down at her plate and go on eating. We don't say nothing no more and then when she get through she clear up the dishes and I just go round front and sit out on the front porch. She don't come out like she used to before she start saying I treat her like dirt, and then when I go on in the house to go to bed, she hunched up on her side, with her back to me, so I just take my clothes off and get on in the bed on my side.

10 Maggie a light yeller woman with chicken scratch hair. That what my mama used to call it chicken scratch hair cause she say there weren't enough hair for a chicken to scratch around in. If it weren't for her hair she look like she was a white woman, a light yeller white woman though. Anyway, when we was coming up somebody say, "Woman cover you hair if you ain't go'n' straightin' it. Look like chicken scratch." Sometime they say look like chicken shit, but they don't tell them to cover it no more, so they wear it like it is. Maggie wear hers like it is.

Me, I come from a family of white-looking niggers, some of 'em, my mama, my daddy musta been, my half daddy he weren't. Come down from the hills round Hazard, Kentucky most of them and claimed nigger cause somebody grandmammy way back there was. First people I know ever claim nigger, 'cept my mama say my daddy hate hoogies (up North I hear they call em honkies) worser than anybody. She say cause he look like he one hisself and then she laugh. I laugh too but I didn't know why she laugh. She say when I come, I look just like a little white rat, so tha's why some a the people I hang aroun with call me "White Rat." When little Henry come he look just like a little white rabbit, but don't nobody call him "White Rabbit" they just call him little Henry. I guess the other jus' ain't took. I tried to get them to call him little White Rabbit, but Maggie say naw, cause she say when he grow up he develop a complex, what with the problem he got already. I say what you come at me for with this a complex and then she say, Nothin, jus' something I heard on the radio on one of them edgecation morning shows. And then I say Aw. And then she say Anyway by the time he get seven or eight he probably get the pigment and be dark, cause some of her family was. So I say where I heard somewhere where the chil'ren couldn't be no darker'n the darkest of the two parent and bout the best he could do would be high yeller like she was. And then she say how her sister Lucky got the pigment when she was bout seven and come out real dark. I tell her Well y'all's daddy was dark. And she say, "Yeah."

Anyway, I guess well she still think little Henry gonna get the pigment when he get to be seven or eight, and told me about all these people come out lighter'n I was and got the pigment fore they growed up.

Like I told you my relatives come down out of the hills and claimed nigger, but only people that believe 'em is people that got to know 'em and people that know 'em, so I usually just stay around with people I know and go in some joint over to Versailles or up to Lexington or down over in Midway where they know me cause I don't like to walk in no place where they say, "What's that white man doing in here." They probably say "yap"—that the Kentucky word for honky. Or "What that yap doing in here with that nigger woman." So I jus' keep to the places where they know me. I member when I was young me and the other niggers used to ride around in these cars and when we go to some town where they don't know "White Rat" everybody look at me like I'm some hoogie, but I don't pay them no mind. 'Cept sometime it hard not to pay em no mind cause I hate the hoogie much as they do, much as my daddy did. I drove up to this filling station one time and these other niggers drove up at the same time, they mighta even drove up a little ahead of me, but this filling station man come up to me first and bent down and said, "I wait on you first, 'fore I wait on them niggers," and then he laugh. And then I laugh and say, "You can wait on them first. I'm a nigger too." He don't say nothing. He just look at me like he thought I was crazy. I don't remember who he wait on first. But I guess he be careful next time who he say nigger to, even somebody got blonde hair like me, most which done passed over anyhow. That, or the way things been go'n, go'n be trying to pass back. I member once all us was riding around one Saturday night, I must a been bout twenty-five then, close to forty now, but we was driving around, all us drunk cause it was Saturday, and Shotgun, he was driving and probably drunker'n a shunk and drunken the rest of us hit up on this police car and the police got out and by that time Shotgun done stop, and the police come over and told all us to get out the car, and he looked us over, he didn't have to do much looking because he probably smell it before he got there but he looked us all over and say he gonna haul us all in for being drunk and disord'ly. He say, "I'm gone haul all y'all in." And I say, "Haul y'all all." Everybody laugh, but he don't hear me cause he over to his car ringing up the police station to have them send the wagon out. He turn his back to us cause he know we wasn goin nowhere. Didn't have to call but one man cause the only people in the whole Midway police station is Fat Dick and Skinny Dick, Buster Crab and Mr. Willie. Sometime we call Buster, Crab Face too, and Mr. Willie is John Willie, but everybody call him Mr. Willie cause the name just took. So Skinny Dick come out with the wagon and hauled us all in. So they didn't know me well as I knew them. Thought I was some hoogie jus' run around with the niggers instead of be one of them. So they put my cousin Covington, cause he dark, in the cell with Shotgun and the other niggers and they put me in the cell with the white men. So I'm drunkern a skunk and I'm yellin' let me outa here I'm a nigger too. And Crab Face say, "If you a nigger I'm a Chinee." And I keep rattling the bars and saying "Cov', they got me in here with the white men. Tell 'em I'm a nigger too," and Cov' yell back, "He a nigger too," and then they all laugh, all the niggers laugh, the hoogies they laugh too, but for a different reason and Cov' say, "Tha's what you get for being drunk and orderly." And I say, "Put me in there with the niggers too, I'm a nigger too." And then one of the white men, he's sitting over in his corner say, "I ain't never heard of a white man want to be a nigger. 'Cept maybe for the nigger women." So I look around at him and haul off cause I'm goin hit him and then some man grab me and say, "He keep a blade," but that don't make me no difrent and I say, "A spade don't need a blade." But then he get his friend to help hole me and then he call Crab Face to come get me out a the cage. So Crab Face come and get me out a the cage and put me in a cage by myself and say, "When you get out a here you can run around with the niggers all you want, but while you in here you ain't getting no niggers." By now I'm more sober so I jus' say, "My cousin's a nigger." And he say, "My cousin a monkey's uncle."

By that time Grandy come. Cause Cov' took his free call but didn't nobody else. Grandy's Cov's grandmama. She my grandmama too on my stepdaddy's side. Anyway, Grandy come and she say, "I want my *two* sons." And he take her over to the nigger cage and say, "Which two?" and she say, "There one of them," and points to Cov'ton. "But I don't see t'other one." And Crab Face say, "Well, if you don't see him I don't see him." Cov'ton just standing there grinning, and don't say nothing. I don't say nothing. I'm just waiting. Grandy ask, "Cov, where Rat?" Sometime she just call me Rat and leave the "White" off. Cov' say, "They put him in the cage with the white men." Crab Face standing there looking funny now. His back to me, but I figure he looking funny now. Grandy says, "Take me to my other boy, I want to see my other boy." I don't think Crab Face want her to know he thought I was white so he don't say nothing. She just standing there looking up at him cause he tall and fat and she short and fat. Crab Face finally say, "I put him in a cell by hisself cause he started a rucus." He point over to me, and she turn and see me and frown. I'm just sitting there. She look back at Crab Face and say, "I want them both out." "That be about five dollars a piece for the both of them for disturbing the peace." That what Crab Face say. I'm sitting there thinking he a poet and don't know it. He a bad poet and don't know it. Grandy say she pay it if it take all her money, which it probably did. So the police let Cov' and me out. And Shotgun waving. Some of the others already settled. Didn't care if they got out the next day. I wouldn't a cared neither, but Grandy say she didn like to see nobody in a cage, specially her own. I say I pay her back. Cov' say he pay her back too. She say we can both pay her back if we just stay out a trouble. So we got together and pay her next week's grocery bill.

Well, that was one 'sperience. I had others, but like I said, now I jus' about keep to the people I know and that know me. The ony other big sperience was when me and Maggie tried to get married. We went down to the courthouse and 'fore I even said a word, the man behind the glass cage look up at us and say, "Round here nigger don't marry white." I don't say nothing just standing up there looking at him and he looking like a white toad, and I'm wondering if they call him "white toad" more likely "white turd." But I just keep looking at him. Then he the one get tired a looking first and he say, "Next." I'm thinking I want to reach in that little winder and pull him right out of that little glass cage. But I don't. He say again, "Around here nigger don't marry white." I say, "I'm a nigger. Nigger marry nigger, don't they?" He just look at me like he think I'm crazy. I say, "I got rel'tives blacker'n your shit. Ain't you never heard a niggers what look like they white." He just look at me like I'm a nigger too, and tell me where to sign.

15   Then we get married and I bring her over here to live in this house in Huntertown ain't got but three rooms and a outhouse that's where we always lived, seems like to me, all us Hawks, cept the ones come down from the mountains way back yonder, cept they don't count no more anyway. I keep telling Maggie it get harder and harder to be a white nigger now specially since it don't count no more how much white blood you got in you, in fact, it make you worser for it. I said nowadays

sted a walking around like you something special people look at you, after they find out what you are if you like me, like you some kind a bad news that you had something to do with. I tell em I ain't had nothing to do with the way I come out. They ack like they like you better if you go on ahead and try to pass, cause, least then they know how to feel about you. Cept nowadays everybody want to be a nigger, or it getting that way. I tell Maggie she got it made, cause at least she got that chicken shit hair, but all she answer is, "That why you treat me like chicken shit." But tha's only since we been having our troubles.

Little Henry the cause a our troubles. I tell Maggie I ain't changed since he was borned, but she say I have. I always say I been a hard man, kind of quick-tempered. A hard man to crack like one of them walnuts. She say all it take to crack a walnut is your teeth. She say she put a walnut between her teeth and it crack not even need a hammer. So I say I'm a nigger toe nut then. I ask her if she ever seen one of them nigger toe nuts they the toughest nuts to crack. She say, "A nigger toe nut is black. A white nigger toe nut be easy to crack." Then I don't say nothing and she keep saying I changed cause I took to drink. I tell her I drink before I married her. She say then I start up again. She say she don't like it when I drink cause I'm quicker tempered than when I ain't drunk. She say I come home drunk and say things and then go sleep and then the next morning forget what I say. She won't tell me what I say. I say, "You a woman scart of words. Won't do nothing." She say she ain't scart of words. She say one of these times I might not jus' say something. I might *do* something. Short time after she say that was when she run off with J. T.

Reason I took to drink again was because little Henry was borned club-footed. I tell the truth in the beginning I blamed Maggie, cause I herited all those hill man's superstitions and nigger superstitions too, and I said she didn't do something right when she was carrying him or she did something she shouldn't oughta did or looked at something she shouldn't oughta looked at like some cows fucking or something. I'm serious. I blamed her. Little Henry come out looking like a little club-footed rabbit. Or some rabbits being birthed or something. I said there weren't never nothing like that in my family ever since we been living on this earth. And they must have come from her side. And then I said cause she had more of whatever it was in her than I had in me. And then she said that brought it all out. All that stuff I been hiding up inside me cause she said I didn't hated them hoogies like my daddy did and I just been feeling I had to live up to something he set and the onliest reason I married her was because she was the lightest and brightest nigger woman I could get and still be nigger. Once that nigger start to lay it on me she jus' kept it up till I didn't feel nothing but start to feeling what she say, and then I even told her I was leaving and she say, "What about little Henry?" And I say, "He's your nigger." And then it was like I didn't know no other word but nigger when I was going out that door.

I found some joint and went in it and just start pouring the stuff down. It weren't no nigger joint neither, it was a hoogie joint. First time in my life I ever been in a hoogie joint too, and I kept thinking a nigger woman did it. I wasn't drunk enough *not* to know what I was saying neither. I was sitting up to the bar talking to the tender. He just standing up there, wasn nothing special to him, he probably weren't even lisen cept but with one ear. I say, "I know this nigger. You know I know the niggers (He just nod but don't say nothing.) Know them close. You know what I mean. Know them like they was my own. Know them where you s'pose to know them." I grinned at him like he was s'pose to know them too. "You know my family came down out of the hills, like they was some kind of rain gods, you know, miss'ology. What they teached you bout the Juicifer. Anyway, I knew this nigger what made hisself a priest, you know turned his white color I mean turned his white collar backwards and dressed up in a monkey suit—you get it?" He didn't get it. "Well, he made hisself a priest, but after a while he didn't want to be no priest, so he pronounced hisself." The bartender said, "Renounced." "So he 'nounced hisself and took off his turned back collar and went back to just being a plain old every day chi'lins and downhome and hamhocks and corn pone nigger. And you know what else he did? He got married. Yeah the nigger what once was a priest got married. Once took all them vows of cel'bacy come and got married. Got married so he could come." I laugh. He don't. I got evil. "Well, he come awright. He come and she come too. She come and had a baby. And you know what else? The baby come too. Ha. No ha? The baby come out club-footed. So you know what he did? He didn't blame his wife. He blamed hisself. The nigger blamed hisself cause he said the God put a curse on him for goin' agin his vows. He said the God put a curse on him cause he took his vows of cel'bacy, which mean no fuckin', cept everybody know what *they* do, and went agin his vows of cel'bacy and married a nigger woman so he could do what every ord'narry onery person was doing and the Lord didn't just put a curse on him. He said he could a stood that. But the Lord carried the curse clear over to the next gen'ration and put a curse on his little baby boy who didn do nothing in his whole life . . . cept come." I laugh and laugh. Then when I quit laughing I drink some more, and then when I quit drinking I talk some more. "And you know something else?" I say. This time he say, "No." I say, "I knew another priest what took the vows, only this priest was white. You wanta know what happen to him. He broke his vows same as the nigger and got married same as the nigger. And they had a baby too. Want to know what happen to him?" "What?" "He come out a nigger."

Then I get so drunk I can't go no place but home. I'm thinking it's the Hawk's house, not hers. If anybody get throwed out it's her. She the nigger. I'm goin' fool her. Throw her right *out* the bed if she in it. But then when I get home I'm the one that's fool. Cause she gone *and* little Henry gone. So I guess I just badmouthed the walls like the devil till I jus' layed down and went to sleep. The next morning little Henry come back with a neighbor woman but Maggie don't come. The woman hand over little Henry, and I ask her, "Where Maggie?" She looked at me like she think I'm the devil and say, "I don't know, but she lef' me this note to give to you." So she jus' give me the note and went. I open the note and read. She write like a chicken too, I'm thinking, chicken scratch. I read: "I run off with J. T. cause he been wanting me to run off with him and I ain't been wanting to tell now. I'm send litle Henry back cause I just took him away last night cause I didn't want you to be doing nothing you regrit in the morning." So I figured she figured I got to stay sober if I got to take care of myself and little Henry. Little Henry didn't say nothing and I didn't say nothing. I just put him on in the house and let him play with hisself.

20   That was two months ago. I ain't take a drop since. But last night Cousin Willie come and say where Maggie was and now she moving around in the kitchen and feeding little Henry and I guess when I get up she feed me. I get up and get dressed and go in the kitchen. She say when the new baby come we see whose fault it was. J. T. blacker'n a lump of coal. Maggie keep saying "When the baby come we see who fault it was." It's two more months now that I been look at her, but I still don't see no belly change.

TO READ A POEM

To read a poem, we must concentrate on its particular words and on the way its words connect with each other. To read a story, we fix our attention on character and plot, conflict and resolution. Poems often use plots and characters, but in reading a poem we must first respond to poetry's basic elements: images and metaphors, for instance, tones of voice and allusions.

When we pay close attention to words we understand poems and take pleasure in them. For the sake of that ultimate pleasure, most of the next chapters explore the elements, types, and forms of poetry. Then we collect many poems by three Americans—Emily Dickinson, Robert Frost, and Theodore Roethke—so that we can look at a few poets in depth; and then we gather a few poems by many poets, for further reading in the poetry of our language.

But before we look into the elements of poetry one at a time we will discuss poems as a whole, the way "To Read a Story" began with William Faulkner's "A Rose for Emily." Because poems are shorter, we can look at more than one and we can also take the time to learn from a little bad poetry.

Chapter 1 **Good Poems and Bad**

Robert Frost, "Stopping by Woods on a Snowy Evening"

Here is a detailed reading of a poem by Robert Frost, "Stopping by Woods on a Snowy Evening." A close reading is called an **explication**, which someone has defined as "an explanation with complications." A pure explanation might first paraphrase the poem, turning its lines into words of prose; an explication goes further, tries to account for the whole poem in its sounds, in its minute suggestions of meaning, in its shapeliness. No explication will equal the poem itself, but in a good explication we can feel that we have come close to noticing and naming everything in the poem that affects us.

Stopping by Woods on a Snowy Evening

Whose woods these are I think I know.
His house is in the village though;
He will not see me stopping here
To watch his woods fill up with snow.

My little horse must think it queer
To stop without a farmhouse near
Between the woods and frozen lake
The darkest evening of the year.

He gives his harness bells a shake
10 To ask if there is some mistake.
The only other sound's the sweep
Of easy wind and downy flake.

The woods are lovely, dark and deep,
But I have promises to keep,
And miles to go before I sleep,
And miles to go before I sleep.

Read this poem aloud, separating the lines with slight pauses but keeping your sense of whole sentences. The different lengths of pause between the lines affect a poem's rhythm. The pause you make at the end of the first line, where Frost ends the sentence with a period, should be longer than the pauses between lines in the second stanza, where there is no punctuation until the end. When we say or hear a poem, we encounter its body. Unless we feel a poem in our own bodies, we are apt to consider it merely an idea; we are apt to confuse a poem with its paraphrase.

But a good way to begin talking about a poem is to paraphrase or summarize it, to see if we are discussing the same poem. (A **paraphrase** finds different words for each of the poem's phrases. A **summary** is shorter, a simple report of the plot, the way *TV Guide* describes a television show.) Once we have paraphrased or summarized the poem, we can talk about its body and its soul. Here, summary is easy: *A man driving a horse pauses beside a forest to watch the snow falling on it; his horse seems to want to keep moving, and the man decides he ought to move on although the scene is pretty, and even inviting.*

Frost used to define poetry as what gets left out in a translation. You might as well say what gets left out in a summary; there's a gap the size of New Hampshire between Frost's sixteen lines and my forty-one words. But summary helps at the start of an explication. When you've read a poem two or three times—slowly and quickly, silently and out loud, and when you have arrived at a tentative paraphrase—you are ready to go back to the poem and look at it bit by bit, as if you were taking apart a machine in order to understand how it works.

Start with the title; sometimes it gives us information we need to understand a poem's wholeness. This title, "Stopping by Woods on a Snowy Evening," is a description or label; it tells us what we're going to see, and then we see it. This particular title requires little work on the reader's part.

In his first line—"Whose woods these are I think I know"—Frost turns normal word order around. Ordinary word order would have us say something like "I think I know whose woods these are." By moving *woods* to the start of the sentence, Frost gives it more prominence or power. We might say "What *nerve* you've got, heaven only knows!" for a similar emphasis.

In the second line, "His house is in the village though," the last word makes no logical sense; *though* or *although* should make some sort of contradiction or qualification to the statement that *I* know who owns this woodlot. But Frost writes as we usually speak—and the *though* qualifies something left out. To understand *though,* we might paraphrase the whole statement, bracketing what is implicit: "I know who owns this land [and I would feel self-conscious if the owner saw me standing and staring into space this way] but he doesn't live out here, and therefore he won't see me pausing to gaze idly." The word *though* implies more than its one syllable would seem able to contain.

At the same time *though* implies something, it rhymes with the word that ends the first line. A rhyme word must feel natural or the poet will seem to have chosen it for the sake of rhyming. Looking to the rest of the stanza, we see that Frost doesn't rhyme the next line with anything nearby but that the fourth line rhymes with the first and the second, tying the stanza together. Because we have the word *snowy* in the title, the idea of snow is important to this poem before we start reading it. Then the word *snow* ends a three-line sentence that makes snow the object of our attention. The last two lines of the stanza are a natural, inevitable journey to the culminating word *snow*. As soon as we get there, we realize that this is where we had to go, all the time. This inevitability is underlined by the rhyme, where *know* and *though* build up a sound-expectancy to culminate in *snow*.

Maybe the speaker's self-consciousness is the most important element in the first stanza. (I say "the speaker"—though it feels awkward—because I don't want to say "Robert Frost" and make the mistake of thinking that *I* in a poem necessarily means the poet.) To sense his embarrassment is to catch the tone of voice,* the way we all learn to catch the tone of people talking, when we understand by hundreds of small signals whether the person's tone is ironic or straightforward, conniving or sincere.

As the stanza ends we learn something besides the speaker's embarrassment; we learn his motive for stopping: "To watch his woods fill up with snow." Frost's language here is plain, but it could be plainer or flatter still; *I* could have said "to see it snow in his trees" or "to look at the snow falling on his forest." Saying *fill up* contributes to the image* or picture made by the poet; *his woods* becomes a container—empty or partly empty—which *snow* can fill.

As mentioned before, *here* doesn't rhyme with anything around it. If we hold the sound of the word in our ears, however, we are rewarded when we read the first line of the second stanza. We experience the pleasure of completing something begun earlier, like the moment in a piece of music that a theme (or a phrase or a chord) returns. Rhyme in this poem holds parts together, linking stanzas more firmly than many poems try to do. The third line of each stanza, unrhymed to the lines near it, rhymes with three of the lines in the stanza following. The four stanzas together are like four groups of four dancers doing the same dance, with one member of each foursome holding hands with the group beyond it.

If it's a dance, it must move to a tune. **Rhythm** is an approximate recurrence or repetition in the pacing of sound; rhythm is fast or slow, staccato or flowing. **Meter**, which is a measure or count of something, puts its own mark on certain rhythms. "Stopping by Woods" is written in meter, and this meter helps define the rhythm of the poem. Counting *evening* as two syllables, in every line the even-numbered syllables (two, four, six, and eight) are louder than the odd-numbered syllables. Not all the even syllables are loud, but they are louder; in *promises, prom-* is louder than the *have* before it, and *-ses* is louder than the *-i-*—just barely louder; you cannot say *prom*–IH–*ses*. This alternation of louder and softer syllables is the meter of the poem. Other matters besides meter contribute to differing lengths of pause at lines' ends. A poet can manipulate punctuation to speed or slow rhythm. In prose, if we said that we stopped between the woods and a frozen lake, the darkest evening of the year we would

---

*Tone and image as elements of poetry are subjects of later chapters.

put a comma after lake, as I do in this sentence. But Frost uses the line's pause and avoids a comma, which would slow the stanza down more than he wants it slowed. On the other hand, in prose he wouldn't need a comma if he were telling us that he had promises to keep and miles to go before he slept—but here the poet slows his rhythm at the measured ending of the poem, and he puts a comma after *keep*. Notice that Frost manipulates commas only where commas in prose would be optional.

The second stanza, picking up the *here* rhyme, tells us that the *little* horse (*little* sounds affectionate; this person seems to care about his horse's feelings) *must think it queer*. Consider the word *must* as we use it in speech. If we know that it's raining, we say "It's raining"; if we only think so—because of forecasts or the distant sound of falling water—we say "It *must* be raining." We only claim that something must be true if we don't know it for certain. When Frost writes "My little horse must think it queer," he uses the doubtful *must* because he knows a human cannot mindread his horse. The speaker in the poem attributes doubts to his horse because he himself believes it weird or eccentric to stop one's horse for no good reason out in the middle of nowhere to watch snow falling in the darkness. This man's uneasiness shows in his self-mockery: even his horse *must* think he's crazy.

As this stanza continues, ostensibly telling what the horse must think queer, the poet gives us more information, and he gives us information in images that carry feeling on their backs. The road, we learn, passes between *the woods*— which are like a container filling with snow—and the *frozen lake*. Sometimes an image informs us by what it omits. While *frozen* adds cold to the poem (an image records not just pictures but *any* experience of the senses, like cold), the line also increases the solitude of the scene: the lane runs between wood and lake only, no houses or factories here, no inns or filling stations, just these cold and natural things, on "The darkest evening of the year."

This last detail (if we read clearly enough, looking for the implications of words) is strange; it is strange if we take it literally, and when we read a poem we ought to try at first to take it literally. We cannot take it literally that this man has determined scientifically, using some instrument that measures light, that this clouded—moonless, starless—night contains fewer candlepower units than any other night in the preceding twelve months. We could take it, in a roundabout way, that tonight is December 22, the longest night of the year, and insist with some logic that the length of its darkness aggregates more darkness and that therefore this is indeed the "darkest evening in the year." But poetry usually works by common sense, not on riddles that ingenuity must solve. It's just too complicated to explain this line as telling us that tonight is the winter solstice. Probably we do best to take the line as an expressive exaggeration, the way people always talk about the weather: "There's enough snow out there to bury the barn." "It hasn't rained so much since Noah." "It's the darkest night of the whole damned year."

In the third stanza, the little horse does what horses do; he shudders or shakes, standing still in the cold night, and to the driver who still feels foolish pausing to gaze at snow in the woods, the horse's jingling harness bells seem like the horse's reproach. The jingling is another image—so far we've had images of sight (*to watch*), of touch (*frozen lake*), and of sound (*bells*)—and now the sound images multiply: "the sweep / Of easy wind and downy flake." Notice that images often appeal to more than one sense. If *frozen* is an image of cold in *frozen lake,* it is an image of sight also, because we know what a frozen lake looks like. And *the sweep* is a swooshing sound, but it's also (at least distantly) a visual broom moving.

The phrase *easy wind* is not an image at all. We could not draw (or play on an instrument, or hear) an easy wind as opposed to a difficult wind or an uneasy one. Does it mean anything at all to call the wind easy? First let us paraphrase, using alternative words. Perhaps this wind is light and gentle—*easy* as "full of ease," like the softness of *downy* that *easy* is parallel to. If this paraphrase is accurate, someone might ask why the poet doesn't call the wind "light and gentle" or, to keep line length the same, just "gentle." Because *gentle* is not the same as *easy* and *easy* does it better; the paraphrase is only intellectual, and *easy* says it better because of its sound. It is a long and luxuriant word. That long e stretches itself out like a big cat on a sofa, and then the z-sound (spelled with an *s*) slinks sensuously and stretches again into a shorter *e,* spelled *y* this time. These two syllables take longer to say than half a line elsewhere in the poem.

I would not argue that "sound imitates sense" in this word the way the sound of *drop* or *squish* is similar to the meanings of the words. (When sound imitates sense, we call it **onomatopoeia**.) I am not sure that a light wind speaks in long *es* and in *z*s. But I am sure that the grateful tongue delights in this word, picking up the long *e* of *sweep,* looking ahead to the long *e* that ends *downy,* and that these words, giving us in our minds qualities of the scene, at the same time give us a sound-pleasure. We have two pleasures at once, one in our minds as we assent to a description, the other in our mouths as the poet arranges vowels and consonants, much as a chef arranges flavors for our pleasure.

We have concentrated on *easy. Downy* gives pleasure also. The *y* picks up the *e* sound earlier in the line; the *ow* picks up a vowel from *sounds* in the line before. (This repetition of vowel sounds is called **assonance**.) If you don't know the word *downy,* look it up. Always look up words you are not certain of. *Down* means a good many things; among others it means goosefeathers, soft and white, and *downy* is an adjective made from the noun *down.* Because down is soft (touch) and white (vision), it gives us two kinds of image at once, and perhaps also distantly gives us an image of the snow as a great white bird. It is also a rural image, connected with barnyard and countryside. If Frost had tried comparing the whiteness of the snow to the whiteness of a sailboat's sails, his comparison would have gone far from the poem's world. Finally, the word *down* works its power on us for at least one more reason: it reminds us of the direction in which, relentlessly, snow must fall.

By the end of the third stanza the poem has erected a dramatic conflict, like a story or a play. The conflict lives in the mind of the speaker, who attributes one side of his feeling to his horse; of course, it is the speaker who thinks it queer to pause where he pauses; at the same time it is the speaker who stops to gaze into the lovely beauty of the wood, exercising the other side of his feeling. He is "of two minds about it," in the old expression. In the final stanza, mind 1 writes the first line and mind 2 answers with the second, third, and fourth; the mind with the most lines has the last word.

In our daily lives, we are often ambivalent—of two minds, sometimes of three or four—about what we do. Often simply two desires are in conflict; the woods are lovely, but I have duties; the scoop of ice cream will taste good, but I will get fat; I want to see this movie, but I want to pass that test. Human beings are ambivalent by nature: we often find ourselves headed in two directions at the same time. In our deepest selves we are never one-hundred percent *any-thing,* neither loving nor hating, and if we tell ourselves we are pure, we fool ourselves.

Poetry expresses human ambivalence. That's one reason poetry is complicated—because people are complicated, and because poetry is true to people. Bad poems are often bad—lying, distorted, phony, sentimental—exactly because they deny ambivalent feeling. This poem is excellent (here is one criterion for excellence in poetry) because it embodies with honest clarity true human ambivalence. This poem is almost *about* ambivalence and its conflicts; at least it acts out a particular ambivalence with so much clarity that the poem in the reader's mind can stand for other conflicts. What for Frost's speaker was a quarrel between woods and duties can translate, in our lives, into the quarrel between birdwatching or writing a letter. When one set of particulars can stand in for another set of relationships, we have a **symbol**.

Symbols raise another subject: in interpreting a poem, where does the reader stop? Many people find further complexities—"levels," "meanings"—in this poem. Some readers have found this poem suicidal and claimed that it contains a wish to die. People have often tended to look for a death wish in Frost because in his lifetime Frost spoke about suicidal feelings. But should we *therefore* consider that when Frost's speaker looks into the woods he takes the woods as a symbol for death and longs for the darkness of his own death? Not *therefore,* at any rate, for then we would be leaping from life to poem as if it were always possible to make equations between the facts of the life and the facts of the poem.

What can we say, finally, about the meaning of this poem—looking only at the poem itself? Meaning is not paraphrase, nor is it singling out words for their special effects, nor is it accounting for rhythm and form. It is all these things, and it is more. Meaning is what we try to explicate: the whole impression of a poem on our minds, our emotions, and our bodies. We can never wholly explicate a poem any more than we can explicate ourselves, or another person—but we can try to come close. The only way to stretch and exercise our ability to read a poem is to try to understand and to name our whole response.

Then how shall we understand this last stanza, and the implications of the whole poem? Implication is the word I want to use. Although I may understand what is said on the surface, another voice speaks from underneath the poem—not a "hidden meaning," implying that the poet is a riddler or an Easter-egg-hider, but a second language of the poem, which exists underneath the first language. This is the quiet voice of implication, the poet's psyche speaking to the reader's psyche in a language just underneath the commonsense words, a language only these words in this order could manage to imply.

A poem makes a contract with the reader: I agree to use words as thoroughly as I can; you agree to read them the same way. Because this is a poem, we shall do well to examine even the simplest words. First, we have the bald statement of attraction: "These woods are lovely, dark and deep." The word *lovely* has the word *love* in it, as *downy* included *down*. So the woods pertain somehow to love. *Dark* and *deep* go together, not just for their **alliteration** (the repetition of initial consonants). The woods are dark in this evening, filling up with snow that by definition is white; and they are deep, like a vessel with room for the filling. The woods are mysterious, perhaps a place suitable for hiding, and this sensation of mystery has an attraction like the attraction people feel for each other; so the woods are *lovely*. *Dark and deep* work together as a double adjective, explaining the *kind* of "lovely." How different the line would be if Frost had punctuated it differently and used a comma after *dark*. "The woods are lovely, dark, and deep"—pronounced as punctuated—makes a different sound, and even a different *meaning*: the extra comma makes the three adjectives enumerate separate qualities of the wood; in the line as Frost wrote it, instead of enumerated qualities we have a rush of feeling. Such difference a comma makes!

Apparently the feelings in this poem are universal, and all of us find in ourselves on occasion a desire to abandon the track of duty, the track of the everyday, and to embrace the peace of nothingness. But perhaps I go too far—in trying to name the unnameable—when in my paraphrase I say "the peace of nothingness." My naming is not so good as Frost's naming, and some readers will prefer their own different naming. "The peace of nothingness" attempts to paraphrase a feeling that for some people apparently sounds suicidal—and for others merely sleepy. My inadequate phrase attempts to bring together the two sides.

Different readings can be valid—but *not all readings*. There are limits to the validity of interpretations, limits set by the poem. One reader tells me that the poem indicates a desire to put a bullet through one's head. Another says the poem implies that Frost wants to move to Arizona and escape the winter. The suicidal reading is only a little askew. If all of us sometimes desire what we might call peace or oblivion, such feeling is not entirely alien to the desire to die. Perhaps sleep—"death's second self," as Shakespeare called it—will satisfy the desire. The speaker in this poem expresses a taste for darkness that resembles the wish to die but does not duplicate it; to find a death wish in this poem is only an exaggeration, like calling the pain of a stubbed toe "excruciating agony." On the other hand, the reader who finds Frost on his way to Arizona simply misreads; there is nothing like it in the poem. Presumably the cold of the poem made the reader think of a warm climate and then attribute the thought to Frost's poem. To avoid misinterpretation, always take care to distinguish the source of a notion: does Phoenix happen in the poem or in your own head?

After talking about one poem for so many pages, I think of Whitman's little poem about listening to the "Learn'd Astronomer," who spoke in scientific terms about astronomical data. Whitman's response is to go outside the lecture hall and look up "in perfect silence at the stars." Read again Robert Frost's simple, pleasurable, universal poem:

Stopping by Woods on a Snowy Evening

Whose woods these are I think I know.
His house is in the village though;
He will not see me stopping here
To watch his woods fill up with snow.

My little horse must think it queer
To stop without a farmhouse near
Between the woods and frozen lake
The darkest evening of the year.

He gives his harness bells a shake
10   To ask if there is some mistake.
The only other sound's the sweep
Of easy wind and downy flake.

The woods are lovely, dark and deep,
But I have promises to keep,
And miles to go before I sleep,
And miles to go before I sleep.

Questions and exercises

1. What happens when Frost repeats a line?

2. Whose feet these are I think I know.
   His head's beneath a T-shirt though.
   He will not mind an ice cube here . . .

   Complete a fourth line.

3. Rewrite the poem, staying as close to the original as you can, but change all the important words. Use a thesaurus or a dictionary of synonyms, if you like. Let *whose* and *I* and *his* remain; change *woods, know, horse,* and so forth. You could begin "Whose forest this is, I recognize . . ." Compare different versions in class, deciding which is closest to the original, and which most ingenious. Compare the class versions with Frost's original. (Sometimes it works best to concentrate on one stanza only or to divide the class into four sections, each doing one stanza.)

William Carlos Williams, "so much depends"

Robert Frost was a traditional poet, writing in rhyme and meter. During Frost's lifetime, the slightly younger William Carlos Williams made a different sort of poem. Williams was born in Rutherford, New Jersey, where he practiced medicine for more than forty years after education in Switzerland, at the University of Pennsylvania, and in Germany. He wrote **free verse**, lines of poetry strong in rhythm but free of the regular repetitions of meter. He is another good poet whose poems force us to acknowledge kinds of excellence foreign to Frost's excellence. Williams in his poems invents original shapes and forces us to become aware of the poem as a made object. He was a poet of images, of the *eye*; but as we will see, he wrote also for the *ear* and placed his words for our maximum pleasure in their sound.

> So much depends upon a red wheelbarrow, glazed with rainwater, beside the white chickens.

This sentence is unlikely to elicit much response. It seems nonsensical, unworthy of attention. In a way, attention is exactly the problem. This poem by William Carlos Williams is printed above not as a poem but as a one-sentence paragraph in which the words have not been *attended to*. *Attention,* which Williams brings to bear by his use of *lines,* is exactly what we miss.

When someone asks the difference between poetry and prose, I like to answer: "Poetry is jagged on the right-hand side of the page." Poetry is written in lines, and lines make a big difference. Lines act like a musician's notation, telling us how to say a poem aloud, or how to hear it. Yet most beginning readers of poetry either read as if lines didn't exist at all or as if the sense always stopped at the lines' ends.

Knowing that the wheelbarrow sentence is really a poem, let us try putting it into lines, starting with the most obvious arrangment:

> So much depends upon
> a red wheelbarrow
> glazed with rainwater
> beside the white chickens.

I call this arrangement obvious because the lines break where the phrases pause. If you were saying the prose sentence aloud and had to pause three times because you were out of breath, you would pause where these lines end. As it happens, these linebreaks are not the poet's—but if they were, let us see what we could find in them. Putting the sentence into these lines must affect the meaning of the sentence, if we take "meaning" to be the words' total impact on the reader. In search of meaning, let us first try paraphrase: "These things are really important: a small red cart with wheels on it, with water on it from a rainshower, next to the poultry." (I cannot paraphrase the simplicities of *red* and *white*.) When I asserted that meaning must be changed by the line arrangement, my claim was not grand; putting these clauses into lines slows down the sentence, adding pauses greater than the pauses we would make if we spoke the sentence as prose. The pauses isolate the clauses within white brackets of time, made visible on poetry's page by the white spaces around the poem. The result is focus, intensity, concentration, emphasis.

In the lines quoted, the last three make visual images, and the first line insists on the importance of what follows, therefore on the importance of the visual. To isolate these lines—by pauses and spaces—is to emphasize the singularity of each unit and to draw closer attention to the redness of the wheelbarrow, to the wetness of the rain, to the whiteness of the chickens. The greater emphasis of these lines *intensifies* meaning.

But not sufficiently for William Carlos Williams. Here is the poem as he actually wrote it:

> so much depends
> upon
>
> a red wheel
> barrow
>
> glazed with rain
> water
>
> beside the white
> chickens

By this arrangement meaning is further enhanced, sound released, and the poem made exact, fixed, permanent—like a carving. The prose sentence from page 393 is repeated exactly, but by breaking the words into these lines Williams makes an object; and his object enforces a meaning.

First, *look* at the poem William Carlos Williams wrote. Looking at shape on the page, without reading or understanding a word, the poem already begins to make a statement, saying "I am orderly; I am arranged on purpose; there is nothing sloppy or careless or inadvertent in me; I will reward careful reading." The visual statement of a poem on the page may be the least of poetry's sensuous qualities; but it exists.

The visual shape suggests an audible performance, behaving like musical notation. In its true form, the poem has more pauses than it had in the four-line version, and more variety in the pauses; generally, the pause between the lines of each two-line stanza is short—like the pause between *wheel* and *barrow*—while the pause that leaps the larger white space between stanzas is longer. But there are degrees of difference within this generalization. Syntax and sense require that the pause between *rain* and *water* be shorter than the pause between *white* and *chickens*. With seven places for pauses at line-ends, the poem calls for seven different degrees of pause.

More pause creates still more emphasis, focus. We see this most clearly in *wheelbarrow: wheel / barrow,* where a linebreak gives us two nouns for one, shows us the original parts of a compound word, and makes a statement about the importance of observing the physical world. This linebreak gives us twice as much *thingness,* making us recognize wheels as separate, barrow as separate, and wheelbarrow as a synthesis of the two, which is also a third thing. In *rainwater,* we see the same act repeated. The first line's *depend / upon* splits a verb phrase into its parts (like the later splitting of compound nouns) and hangs the preposition from a verb that originally meant "hang from." In the last stanza, splitting *white* from *chickens* gives us at least a little more attention to the quality of the color than we get if *white chickens* is printed on one line.

But the poem's arrangement does more than intensify meaning and more than make a pretty shape. It releases varied sounds, two assonances in particular, that grant the reader a pleasure equivalent to the eye's pleasure in seeing *red, rain,* and *white.* In the four-line arrangement, the third line was "glazed with rainwater." When the poet did it his way, the fifth line of the poem becomes "glazed with rain," and the long diphthong *āi* bursts twice into bloom. The flowering of the diphthong alters the pace of the line, for when the reader comes to *rain* and tastes the pleasure of the repeated sound, he or she stretches it a little; the *n* of "rain" allows the sound to be held on the tongue and savored.

And the next pair of lines gives the same pleasure to the mouth alerted to assonance. The long-*i* diphthong in the second syllable of *beside* finds itself mirrored and repeated in the vowel of *white,* buried midline in the earlier version. Both times the word stretched and exalted is a sensuous and meaningful word, *rain* describing the sources of *water, white* the color of chickens; insofar as sound specifies more attention given to a word, assonance impinges upon our understanding, and the coincidence of vowel sounds contributes to meaning.

This little poem by William Carlos Williams is not a vessel loaded with philosophical or intellectual content; it does not resemble the works of Plato or Thomas Jefferson. The poem does have meaning, but its statement belongs more to the area of sensation than to the area of thought.

Feelings and ideas happen at the same time, ideas carry feelings with them, and feelings imply ideas. If Williams's poem insists on the importance of the physical world, the *insistence* is an emotional value placed on a philosophical idea. And the poem makes its statement not by generalizing but by giving a particular example—something of the world, visible, stared at and held to. The visual details are perceived with passion and necessity, as if they were rails on a narrow bridge onto which we hold in order not to fall into the chasm below. The intensity of this experience, which makes the poem valuable, derives largely from the poet's skill in manipulating sounds. Here it is again:

> so much depends
> upon
>
> a red wheel
> barrow
>
> glazed with rain
> water
>
> beside the white
> chickens

Exercise

Using different words, imitate the shape and sound of Williams's poem.

A form is anything done a second time. The first time somebody wrote a sonnet, it was not a sonnet; the second time somebody wrote one, and the third—then we began to call them sonnets. So consider that you are writing a newly discovered form of poetry called a wheelbarrow. You can define a wheelbarrow as four two-line stanzas; each first line has three words, each second line has one word; each one-word second line has two syllables; each three-word first line has either three or four syllables.

Here's one student's wheelbarrow:

it is extremely
serious

to watch the
teacher

writing long words
in chalk

on blackboards
all morning

Which lines fit the form? Which don't?

Wallace Stevens, "Disillusionment of Ten O'Clock"

A third example of a good poem is one by Wallace Stevens, who was a friend of William Carlos Williams when they were both young and who met Robert Frost in Florida winters when both poets were old. After graduation from Harvard and the New York University Law School Stevens practiced law in New York City; he lived in Greenwich Village and spent much time with other writers who gathered there. In his late thirties he became associated with the Hartford Accident and Indemnity Company, serving as a vice-president for the last decade of his life.

Disillusionment of Ten O'Clock

The houses are haunted
By white night-gowns.
None are green,
Or purple with green rings,
Or green with yellow rings,
Or yellow with blue rings.
None of them are strange,
With socks of lace
And beaded ceintures.
10 People are not going
To dream of baboons and periwinkles.
Only, here and there, an old sailor,
Drunk and asleep in his boots,
Catches tigers
In red weather.

With this poem I will not provide an explication; instead, I will ask questions, hoping to suggest ways of arriving at an explication. Read the poem several times, slowly, before you begin to read the questions.

Questions

1. In the title, is *ten o'clock* A.M. or P.M.? What in the poem suggests one or the other?
2. Think of the word *disillusionment*. Take it apart. What might this word have to do with the hour of ten o'clock? Are there illusions or disillusions in the body of the poem?
3. Does *haunted* tell you anything about the title? How?
4. There is a ghost in the word *haunted*. Ordinarily there would be no ghost in the word *night-gown*. What word makes *haunted* go with *night-gown*?
5. Do you know whether there are bodies inside these nightgowns?
6. In lines 3 through 6 the poet presents images in the negative. Can we learn anything from being told that something does *not* exist? What do these negatives imply? What is missing from these houses?
7. In line 7 *strange* can be a vague and imprecise word; in this context, do other words define *strange* and make it less vague?
8. A ceinture is a belt, and the word was already unusual when Stevens published the poem in 1915. Why would a poet use a word most readers would have to look up? Can a poet mean something simply by using an outlandish word?
9. In line 10 we finally hear of people. Are these the people whose houses are haunted by white nightgowns? How can you tell?
10. Stevens could have broken his lines differently:

    People are not
    Going to dream of baboons . . .

    or:

    People are not going to dream
    Of baboons . . .

    Can you think of why it was a good idea to break the line where Stevens broke it?
11. In this poem, baboons and periwinkles are examples that are parallel to other examples. What words in this poem are they parallel to? Why?
12. What is the relationship of the last four lines of the poem to the lines that came earlier?
13. Why is the sailor drunk? What is he doing? How do these details contrast with the main scene of the poem?
14. Someone has said that in this poem Stevens was eating his cake and having it too. Comment.
15. Frost's poem was written in metrical four-line stanzas. Williams's poem was tightly structured free verse. Characterize sound and rhythm in this poem, pointing out particular effects. Can you find assonance? Alliteration?

To find other poems by these poets, check the index.

Some bad poems

Before undertaking chapters that investigate the elements of poetry, let us move from studying good poems to glancing at two bad ones. Bad poems outnumber good poems. Poems can fail for technical reasons—trite language, boring rhythms, dull sounds, clumsy metaphors, sloppy images—but most bad poetry fails when technical ineptness combines with emotional dishonesty or senti-mentality. To be good, a poem must tell the truth of feeling, and it must tell the whole of a complex feeling, not just a part of it. In Robert Frost's "Stopping by Woods on a Snowy Evening," the poet acknowledged contrary emotions: he wants to stay, he feels foolish staying, he must go on. The sentimental poet, denying the ambivalence of his feelings and wishing to strike a grand pose, might have declared to us that he would remain sitting in his wagon staring into these woods forever and ever and ever.

In asserting badness, as in asserting goodness, the critic cannot prove him-self right as he might in a laboratory, by measurement. There is an older sense of "proof" that operates outside laboratories, the proof of argument or discus-sion leading to the agreement of reasonable people. This sort of proof begins with premises and proceeds to demonstrate whether a poem fulfills these prem-ises. We begin with a premise that poems should tell the complex truth of feeling. Then we add another premise; we demand also that the poem be shapely and whole—a formal premise all good poems satisfy, whether metrical or free. Earlier in this chapter, we emphasized the first premise in discussing Frost, the second in discussing Williams.

In every age since the invention of the printing press there have been popular poets who outsold the best poets of their day, and who a generation later have gone unread. Although the poet Alfred, Lord Tennyson was enormously pop-ular in Victorian England, he was outsold in his own lifetime by a pious rhyme-ster named Martin Tupper. Robert Frost, the most popular *good* poet in Amer-ican history, won the Pulitzer Prize four times, and supported himself by his successful poetry readings, but the best-selling poet in the United States during most of Frost's lifetime was Edgar A. Guest, whose most famous poem begins "It takes a heap o' livin' in a house t' make it home."

Here is the kind of poem that made Edgar Guest the most popular of Amer-ican poets a couple of generations back:

The Rough Little Rascal

A smudge on his nose and a smear on his cheek
And knees that might not have been washed in a week;
A bump on his forehead, a scar on his lip,
A relic of many a tumble and trip:
A rough little, tough little rascal, but sweet,
Is he that each evening I'm eager to meet.

A brow that is beady with jewels of sweat;
A face that's as black as a visage can get;
A suit that at noon was a garment of white,

10   Now one that his mother declares is a fright:
A fun-loving, sun-loving rascal, and fine,
Is he that comes placing his black fist in mine.

A crop of brown hair that is tousled and tossed;
A waist from which two of the buttons are lost;
A smile that shines out through the dirt and the grime,
And eyes that are flashing delight all the time:
All these are the joys that I'm eager to meet
And look for the moment I get to my street.

Rascal is a cuddly sort of word that sets off a chain of **stock responses** (substitute emotions, which *resemble* emotions but cause neither thought nor true feeling; they stand in for true responses the way plastic sometimes stands in for wood). Guest uses clichés to elicit stock responses. A rough little rascal, we could know before we read a line, would have a smudge on his nose. *Tumble* is a cuddly word for fall—the kind of fall that never ruptures a spleen. The notion of sweet is already contained in the connotation of *rascal*, at least when *little* is added. The combination is sentimental, and the poem never approaches an emotion—only the stock imitation of emotion, which is what some readers want: the naïve reader finds his tritest associations fulfilled by the poem.

Rod McKuen tomorrow will look like Edgar A. Guest today. In *Listen to the Warm,* a volume of poems, the title poem is a series of poems addressed to a lover. Here is the first of the series:

This is the way it was
while I was waiting for your eyes
              to find me.
I was drifting
       going no place.
Hypnotized by sunshine
         maybe,
barking back at seals along the beach.
Skipping flat stones on the water,
10   but much too wise for sand castles.
My castles were across the sea
or still within my mind.

There were the beach bars
and the other beach people
sometimes little bedrooms were my beach,
        but I was drifting.

I must have thought the night could save me
as I went down into pillows
        looked up through dirty windows
20   smiled back from broken mattresses
turned in Thunderbirds
       and kissed in elevators.

I cried too sometimes.
      For me.

I loved every face I thought looked pretty
and every kindred eye I caught in crowds.
      But I was drifting,
          before you.

The first line is a cliché, *the way it was,* commonplace enough to be the title of a television series. Then, "I was drifting," says the poet. This word, *drifting,* was once a useful metaphor; if something drifts, it is compared to a boat set loose without the direction of a rudder. In poems we use words efficiently, and if the poet mentions drifting, a good reader knows that the poet refers to a boat. But "I was drifting" has become another cliché. If somehow the poet was able to identify himself as a boat in his poem—fulfilling the metaphor, using other boat words to make *drift* come alive again—"Cut loose from my pier, I drifted / without oars or rudder . . ."—the poet would *establish* himself as a boat, and *continue* the metaphor. A good poet fulfills his metaphors so that the comparison flows with feeling, develops and grows. A bad poet, on the other hand, using a **cliché** or **dead metaphor** (a dead metaphor has lost its power to make a comparison because of triteness or overuse) like "I was drifting" without knowing what he is doing, quickly uses another dead metaphor that cancels out the first—the way McKuen uses *hypnotized.* This next metaphor requires two people: *I,* the subject of hypnosis, and the hypnotist, who is identified here as sunshine. If we read the whole of the word, we are treated to the spectacle of sunshine dressed up in a hypnotist suit, speaking in soothing tones to a rowboat. Then the rowboat barks at seals from the middle of its trance.

Because we cannot take the words seriously, we have less a mixed metaphor than mere slackness of language—the kind of language that will speak of being "haunted by a memory" without realizing that it has spoken of ghosts or "the key to the problem" without understanding that keys need keyholes and that keys lock doors.

McKuen's poem goes on to talk about skipping stones on water, which is plain enough, and waits for another line before it becomes poetical again. The poet is, he tells us, "much too wise for sand castles." We are meant to understand *much* as self-mockery, the poet gently chiding himself for believing that he is not a child. This mild self-mockery is self-love, the poet looking with affection at his small foibles. And *sand castles* is another cliché, a trite symbol for daydreams.

There are many failures in this poem that the attentive reader can notice: clichés, slack rhythms, confused or unresolved metaphors, words that do not go together, and emotional deceit. See what you can find.

Chapter 2 **Poems Are Made of Words**

A poem is single, whole, and seamless, but to discuss it we need to treat it as if we could take it apart and examine elements as we can examine elements of a machine: this is a carburetor, which mixes air and fuel; this is a spark plug. . . . The parts of an internal-combustion engine, however, are genuinely separate; in a poem, you cannot detach rhythm from imagery except by paying attention to the one element rather than to the other; within the poem, rhythm and imagery are properties of the same words.

But before we concentrate on the elements of poetry, let us look at the medium of poetry, which is words. Many people assume that poetry's medium is emotions and ideas. Emotions and ideas exist *in* poems or *through* poems, and we must account for them in paraphrase when we explicate, but they are not poetry's medium. If we argued that emotions and ideas are poetry's medium, we would have to claim that trees and mountains are the medium of landscape painting. Canvas and paint make the painter's medium, and poems are made of words.

Reading poetry, we read words used with the greatest *energy* and *fixity*.

Fixity is the unique correctness and immovability of a word in its place. If you change almost any word in a long novel, you change the novel very little; if you change a word in a good poem, you change the poem considerably: "His house is in the hamlet though" would change Frost's poem by substituting *hamlet* for *village*. This fixity is partly a function of size, but not entirely; it is a measure of relative exactness in use. Poetry does not acknowledge synonyms.

Roget's Thesaurus and any other dictionary of synonyms list words that resemble each other in their meaning, but a poet makes poems by manipulating the small differences in meaning between synonyms; think of the differences between *hamlet* and *village,* or the many differences among *hide, conceal, cover up, secrete, screen, obscure, suppress, veil, disguise, camouflage, shroud.* . . .

Energy comes from the efficiency with which the poet uses language, and to repeat: Poems are made of words used efficiently. When I write this sentence, I sound like an engineer—and I want to. An efficient machine turns energy received into a nearly equal amount of energy put out. Sloppy language wastes energy, often by failing to say what it means; at best it uses more words than are necessary, three vague words in place of the precise one; "glazed with rain / water" is better than "covered all over with dampness as a result of precipitation." *Good poetry is the perfect machine of language.*

To use words most efficiently, the writer must be aware of their wholeness, aware of the dictionary senses of words or **denotations**, and of **connotations**— the associations you do not usually get from a dictionary. The poet uses the history of a word, its family, its origins, its associations. *Snow* carries "whiteness" with it, a connotation. Other connotations for snow include cold and winter. Further associations can become less universal and more particular. For a Northerner *snow* may include "skiing"; for a Sun Belt resident, *snow* may include the notion of travel. If the associations of *snow* include not only travel but a three-day drive in a Plymouth that uses too much oil, we have passed connotation to make a private association. Much connotation is public enough for use not only by poets and not only for literature. Real estate agents do not sell houses; they sell *homes,* which denotes the same buildings *houses* denotes but connotes comfort, warmth, and a dog sleeping in front of the fireplace. A *sanitation engineer* may do the same work a plumber used to do, but the title sounds more impressive. If poets use connotations to tell us honest feelings, politicians and lobbyists can use connotations for deceit. *Honorarium* sounds better than *payment, payment* better than *bribe.* All three words are heavy with connotation.

Concepts of denotation and connotation are useful, but we need to understand that they don't tell us everything. The *connotation* of *wheelbarrow* does not include its compoundness, revealed only when a poet splits it back into two words: *wheel barrow.* And when a word has different *denotations,* different dictionary meanings, the peripheral definitions of the word in the poem hover around the central ones.

Poets do not always use every potential meaning of a word. By their context they can employ some connotations or unused denotations and shut off others. Thomas Hardy's poem "During Wind and Rain" includes the line

How the sick leaves reel down in throngs.

A dictionary may tell us that to reel is to be thrown off balance, to stagger, to move in a circle, to dance a reel, or to pull in a fishing line. In the context of the poem, not every meaning becomes active. When the word before *leaves* is *sick,* then *reel* as in "stagger"—like a sick person too weak to walk—becomes strengthened by context. Earlier in this poem, the poet speaks of music: "They sing their dearest songs . . . / Treble and tenor and bass / And one to play . . . ," and although the songs may be hymns or folk songs, the "dance" part of *reel* shows signs of life. (All of these meanings are related: *reel* started by meaning a kind of spool and evolved into all sorts of circular motions.) Connotations interweave, and peripheral denotations act like connotations. In this poem's context, the stagger-meaning is foremost, the dance-meaning acts like a strong connotation, and the fishing-meaning hovers unused in the distance. If a reader on first glancing at this line thought of *reel* as fishing reel, the line would remain obscure until the reader looked for another denotation of *reel*.

When leaves are compared to dancers, the poet has made a metaphor. And here we should mention one other matter connecting word and metaphor. Many readers leap to interpret a word as metaphor when the poet has used it literally. The insistence on the fanciful, at the expense of the plain, is a common source of misreading. Edwin Arlington Robinson begins a stanza about a dying man

> Blind, with but a wandering hour to live . . .

Many readers see the word *blind* and think that Robinson means "obtuse" in the common metaphorical use of the word—as in "Egad, sir, are you *blind?*" But the rest of the stanza reveals that the man is sightless. Readers who hold onto the "obtuse" meaning find the poem highly obscure. It is wise to remember a rule of thumb: take poems literally until they make you take them figuratively. "Sightless" is the denotation of the word *blind*. *Blind* has meant "sightless" for a long time; the first citation in the *Oxford English Dictionary* (that wonderful, enormous dictionary that quotes words in contexts as they change over history) is dated A.D. 1000. And the first citation of *blind* as "obtuse" is also A.D. 1000, the metaphorical use as ancient as the literal.

Reading old poems, we need the *OED* to let us know how poets used words—efficiently, with energy and fixity—in their own times, for words change. When the eighteenth-century poet Alexander Pope spoke of *science* he did not mean physics or chemistry but knowledge in general; our word *science* comes from *scio,* Latin for "I know," which becomes a part of the participle *knowing* and then the noun *knowledge.*

Reading new poems, we can use the *OED* also, because many poets—seeking the energy that comes from using words in their wholeness—refer by their context to a word's history, its old or original meanings. Richard Wilbur is a contemporary American who likes to play with **etymology,** the study of word origins and history. In his poem "Lamarck Elaborated" he pretends to believe genetic theories which say that genes transmit acquired characteristics.* The theory is untrue, but with his imagination Wilbur tries out a world where the

---

*French naturalist Jean Baptiste Pierre Antoine de Monet, Chevalier de Lamarck (1744–1829). His flawed theory of evolution was nevertheless an important forerunner of the work of Charles Darwin.

things of the world created our bodies. The sun, for instance, made our eyes. Wilbur writes a stanza of complicated wordplay:

> The yielding water, the repugnant stone,
> The poisoned berry and the flaring rose
> Attired in sense the tactless finger-bone
> And set the taste-buds and inspired the nose.

Paraphrased, the stanza says that we acquired touch, taste, and smell by acts of touching, tasting, and smelling. Water, which gives to the touch, and stone, which doesn't—which pushes it back, which is what *repugnant* means—*attired* (clothed) *in sense* (in our senses) *the finger-bone,* which had formerly been clumsy or without tact; *tact* comes from the word for "touch," as in *tactile,* so *tactless* by etymology means "untouching": before it was clothed in sensation, the finger-bone was without touch. The *berry* that poisons us, which we distinguish by taste, *sets* our taste buds, the way a gardener sets out plants. The flaring rose (flared like a nostril to smell) *inspired* our noses. *Inspired* in one common usage means "invented"—"Monday Night Football was the inspiration of Roone Arledge"—but actually comes from a Latin word that means "to breathe in."

Here are a few poems—with questions intended to sharpen your sensitivity to the manipulation of words.

Hogwash

> The tongue that mothered such a metaphor
> Only the purest purist could despair of.
>
> Nobody ever called swill sweet but isn't
> Hogwash a daisy in a field of daisies?
>
> What beside sports and flowers could you find
> To praise better than the American language?
>
> Bruised by American foreign policy
> What shall I soothe me, what defend me with
>
> But a handful of clean unmistakable words—
> Daisies, daisies, in a field of daisies?
>   —*Robert Francis**

10

---

*See page 639 for a note about Robert Francis. Brief biographical notes on poets whose work is included in this book precede their poems in "A Gathering of Poems," which begins on page 535. For rapid location of dates and other information about any author represented in this volume, look for the italicized page number following the entry for his or her name in the index.

Questions

1. In the first line,what happens if you remove *mothered* and substitute "fathered?" "conjured"? "created"? "gathered"? "mounted"? "built up"? "constructed"? What are the associations of *mothered* and of the substitute words?
2. How does the word *swill* find its way into this poem? Would "junk" be just as good? "Garbage"?
3. Look up the word *daisy* to check on its ancestry. What are the insides of *daisy*? If you used "tulip," how would its different history match the rest of the poem? Is *daisy* better for this poem, or just different? If the word were "flower," would the poem be less than it is?
4. Does *defend*, in its associations, relate to other words in this poem?
5. In the last stanza, what sort of *handful* would you have if your hand were full of words? A handful of swill? What does the poet compare words to?

During Wind and Rain

They sing their dearest songs—
He, she, all of them—yea,
Treble and tenor and bass,
    And one to play;
With the candles mooning each face. . . .
    Ah, no; the years O!
How the sick leaves reel down in throngs!

They clear the creeping moss—
Elders and juniors—aye,
Making the pathway neat
    And the garden gay;
And they build a shady seat. . . .
    Ah, no; the years, the years;
See, the white storm-birds wing across!

They are blithely breakfasting all—
Men and maidens—yea,
Under the summer tree,
    With a glimpse of the bay,
While pet fowl come to the knee. . . .
    Ah, no; the years O!
And the rotten rose is ript from the wall.

They change to a high new house,
He, she, all of them—aye,
Clocks and carpets and chairs
    On the lawn all day,
And brightest things that are theirs. . . .
    Ah, no; the years, the years;
Down their carved names the rain-drop ploughs.
                —*Thomas Hardy*

Questions

1. Consider the associations of *creeping*. Which are used? Which unused? Does the word make a comparison?
2. In line 21, Hardy uses the word *ript*. Substitute *pulled* and consider the differences. Substitute "descends" for *is ript*. Discuss the differing associations of the words. Discuss the differing grammar.
3. In line 22, try these substitutes for *high*: "tall," "white," "brand," "dark," and "low." Is difference in image a difference in value?
4. The last word of the poem is *ploughs*. How do its denotation, connotations, sound, and grammar—the whole word, family associations and all—contribute to this poem? Does the whole word *conclude* the poem?

Silence

My father used to say,
"Superior people never make long visits,
have to be shown Longfellow's grave
or the glass flowers at Harvard.
Self-reliant like the cat—
that takes its prey to privacy,
the mouse's limp tail hanging like a shoelace from its mouth—
they sometimes enjoy solitude,
and can be robbed of speech
10 by speech which has delighted them.
The deepest feeling always shows itself in silence;
not in silence, but restraint."
Nor was he insincere in saying, "Make my house your inn."
Inns are not residences.

—*Marianne Moore*

Questions

1. In the second line, the poet uses the word *superior*. Make a list of words that might be considered synonyms and that would make sense in this context. Discuss the difference each substitution would make to the poem.
2. Longfellow's grave is in Cambridge, Massachusetts, a city that also contains Harvard University, which shows in a museum some remarkably realistic glass reproductions of flowers—a favorite stop for tourists. What is the connection of the sentence containing these objects with the sentences that make the rest of this poem? In lines 3 and 4, what words provide the implicit connection?
3. In this poem, where does the idea of silence enter, after the title?
4. What do you make of this cat? Have you known cats who liked to show off their prey, who are not reticent at all? If you have, does the knowledge bother you in reading this poem? Do you feel that the cat somehow seems more important to the poem than its use as an illustrative simile could warrant? How?
5. How does the author show that although *Superior people* enjoy being by themselves, they are equipped to encounter others?

6. "Not in silence, but restraint." What is the difference? Why does the author say one thing and then correct it? What is the effect of using two words instead of one?
7. The last two lines make a distinction by means of definitions. How does this verbal contrast grow out of earlier lines of the poem?

When President John F. Kennedy was inaugurated in 1961, he invited Robert Frost to read a poem as part of the ceremony. Frost recited this poem, which he had written years before.

The Gift Outright

The land was ours before we were the land's.
She was our land more than a hundred years
Before we were her people. She was ours
In Massachusetts, in Virginia,
But we were England's, still colonials,
Possessing what we still were unpossessed by,
Possessed by what we now no more possessed.
Something we were withholding made us weak
Until we found out that it was ourselves
10   We were withholding from our land of living,
And forthwith found salvation in surrender.
Such as we were we gave ourselves outright
(The deed of gift was many deeds of war)
To the land vaguely realizing westward,
But still unstoried, artless, unenhanced,
Such as she was, such as she would become.

Questions

1. Or Frost almost recited it. For the next to last word he said *will* instead of *would*. How did this alter the meaning of the poem?
2. Distinguish different sorts of possession. Why does Frost use the same word when the reader must learn to distinguish different meanings for it? What allows you to find different meanings for one word in a single poem?
3. What sort of a phrase is *salvation in surrender*?
4. Does *realize* usually take an object? Does it here? How does the grammar help to define this use of the word?
5. Notice the many balances throughout the poem. List them.

Here's an old poem, written during Queen Elizabeth's reign, with its spelling modernized. Ben Jonson was a great playwright, a rival and friend of Shakespeare. He wrote on the death of his firstborn son.

On My First Son

Farewell, thou child of my right hand, and joy;
My sin was too much hope of thee, loved boy.
Seven years thou wert lent to me, and I thee pay,
Exacted by thy fate, on the just day.
O, could I lose all father now. For why
Will man lament the state he should envy?
To have so soon 'scaped° world's, and flesh's, rage,   escaped
And if no other misery, yet age?
Rest in soft peace, and, asked, say here doth lie
10 Ben Jonson, his° best piece of poetry.   Jonson's
For whose sake, henceforth, all his vows be such,
As what he loves may never like too much.

Questions

1. In the third line Jonson's word order puts *I* next to *thee*, which we would not do. *Thee* is the object of *pay*, and we would say "And I pay thee" or "And I pay you." In what sense is *pay* used?
2. How can Jonson call the day *just*? What other words—or what ideas carried by what words—support *just*?
3. How would you paraphrase *all father*?
4. Look up the word *poetry* in an etymological dictionary. How can Jonson use the word to stand in for his son?
5. The poem works by a series of contrasted words. What does *lament* contrast with? *rage*? *world's*?
6. Describe the contrast in the last line.

Chapter 3 **Images**

An **image** is language that speaks to our senses, recording a sensuous experience. Poetry abounds in visual images, directed to the sense of sight, like "white chickens" or ". . . woods fill up with snow." Poetry also includes images of touch, taste, smell, and hearing. Hot-and-cold is tactile, a form of touch; here is a poem made of images for heat:

Heat

    O wind, rend open the heat,
    cut apart the heat,
    rend it to tatters.

    Fruit cannot drop
    through this thick air—
    fruit cannot fall into heat
    that presses up and blunts
    the points of pears
    and rounds the grapes.

10   Cut the heat—
    plough through it,
    turning it on either side
    of your path.
                —H.D.

The American poet H.D. (Hilda Doolittle) was one of the Imagist poets, a group dedicated to writing vivid and precise natural description. When H.D. asks the wind to *rend open the heat*, she gives the invisible heat a bulk that can be *cut apart*, therefore making an image of heat as something thick, substantial. Then she tells us how bulky it is: "Fruit cannot drop / through this thick air." These lines imply a natural scene with fruit trees, and air so heavy that even a falling apple cannot penetrate it. H.D. communicates feeling through exaggeration; she does not merely render like a snapshot. She describes the heat not as an inert thing but as a pressure, antigravitational and upward, blunting the pears that would otherwise be sharp-angled; heat acts by its constant pressure to make grapes round. Then the poet ends her poem by returning implicitly to the wind for help—meteorological reality, because breezes blow away hot air—and when she asks the wind to become a plow, she again evokes the thickness, weight, and density of the heat, comparing it to earth a plow turns.

Images of touch like H.D.'s are not as common as visual images. Here's an old poem in which a male poet describes the appearance of a woman:

Upon Julia's Clothes

Whenas in silks my Julia goes,
Then, then, methinks, how sweetly flows
That liquefaction of her clothes.

Next, when I cast mine eyes, and see
That brave vibration, each way free,
O, how that glittering taketh me!
                    —*Robert Herrick*

Herrick describes something seen, and his images are visual. We are invited to *see* Julia in motion wearing a silk dress. We don't know the color of the silk, and we know nothing of Julia's appearance except for her dress. We have the watery image of *flows* and *liquefaction*, and later her sway from side to side and the silk's glitter. The poem gives us only a partial picture of Julia, but we feel Herrick's whole delight: the visual images embody Herrick's feeling.

Poets use images to embody feelings; they use images instead of abstract explanations. Here's a poem by Allen Ginsberg:

First Party at Ken Kesey's with Hell's Angels

Cool black night thru redwoods
cars parked outside in shade
behind the gate, stars dim above
the ravine, a fire burning by the side
porch and a few tired souls hunched over
in black leather jackets. In the huge
wooden house, a yellow chandelier
at 3 a.m. the blast of loudspeakers
hi-fi Rolling Stones Ray Charles Beatles

10   Jumping Joe Jackson and twenty youths
        dancing to the vibration thru the floor,
        a little weed in the bathroom, girls in scarlet
        tights, one muscular smooth skinned man
        sweating dancing for hours, beer cans
        bent littering the yard, a hanged man
        sculpture dangling from a high creek branch,
        children sleeping softly in bedroom bunks,
        And 4 police cars parked outside the painted
        gate, red lights revolving in the leaves.

The poem starts with a word of skin-feelings, *cool*, and ends with a compelling visual image. With the phrases *cool black, shade, stars dim*, and *fire burning*, Ginsberg sets a scene of contrasts. Then the poet speaks of *souls hunched over*, and we feel a tiredness. Next in the poem we have an image of sound, then dancing; the dancing comes as a visual image, but the word's associations contain muscular feeling as well. Then the poem leads us through everything seen, in a list of images—litter, a sculpture, children sleeping—with a cinematic effect, as if a camera panned slowly over a static scene, recording frame after frame of reality. Finally the camera settles on the ominous image of the police cars with lights revolving. The poem's effect comes entirely from its images; there is no commentary at all.

The reader is *shown*: he is not *told*. Modern poets usually avoid abstract language, using concrete details instead. At the end of this poem, Ginsberg might have written about fear or apprehensiveness or dread or ominousness. Using instead the images *police cars parked* and *red lights revolving*, he communicates feeling directly; abstractions would have communicated the *names* of feelings, or *ideas* about feelings, not the feelings themselves.

H.D.'s heat was tactile, using images of touch. Ginsberg's poem is mostly visual but also uses images of touch and hearing. When Robert Frost, in "Stopping by Woods on a Snowy Evening," wrote about "the sweep / Of easy wind . . ." he used an image of sound. Poets use images of smell more rarely—"the acrid odor of maple"—and also images of taste: when Keats longs for wine, he calls it "a draught of vintage that hath been / Cool'd a long time . . ."; he appeals to the touch-sense of the tongue, or taste.

All these images describe real things, and these poems come from the world we live in. Here are more poems of our world, with questions that mostly call attention to their images.

Nantucket

Flowers through the window
lavender and yellow

changed by white curtains—
Smell of cleanliness—

Sunshine of late afternoon—
On the glass tray

a glass pitcher, the tumbler
turned down, by which

a key is lying—And the
10   immaculate white bed
    —*William Carlos Williams*

Questions

1. Most of these images are visual. Is there an exception?
2. Is *changed* an image? Is it an idea?
3. Do these images carry feeling? Can you name the feeling?
4. Can you paraphrase this poem for its ideas?

Gary Soto is a young Chicano poet who grew up working in the fields of the San Joaquin Valley in California. He uses images from his experience as a farm worker. This poem comes from a sequence called "The Elements of San Joaquin":

Sun

In June the sun is a bonnet of light
Coming up,
Little by little,
From behind a skyline of pine.

The pastures sway with fiddle-neck
Tassels of foxtail.

At Piedra
A couple fish on the river's edge,
Their shadows deep against the water.
10   Above, in the stubbled slopes,
Cows climb down
As the heat rises
In a mist of blond locusts,
Returning to the valley.

Questions

1. Compare this poem with H.D.'s "Heat," p. 409.
2. Distinguish the different senses Soto's images appeal to.
3. What kind of action lies behind *sway* and connects it with *fiddle-neck*? What does the poet compare the foxtail to?

Denise Levertov is an American poet who takes great pleasure in observation of the world outside. Sight and sound, coolness and soot from chimneys.

The World Outside

i

On the kitchen wall a flash
of shadow:
        swift pilgrimage
of pigeons, a spiral
celebration of air, of sky-deserts.
And on tenement windows
a blaze
      of lustred watermelon:
stain of the sun
10   westering somewhere back of Hoboken.

ii

The goatherd upstairs! Music
from his sweet flute
roves from summer to summer
in the dusty air of airshafts
and among the flakes
of soot that float
in a daze from chimney
to chimney—notes
remote, cool, speaking of slender
20   shadows under olive-leaves. A silence.

iii

Groans, sighs, in profusion,
with coughing, muttering, orchestrate
solitary grief; the crash of glass, a low voice
repeating over and over, 'No.
   No. I want my key. No you did not.
   No.'—a commonplace.
And in counterpoint, from other windows,
the effort to be merry—ay, maracas!
—sibilant, intricate—the voices wailing pleasure,
30   arriving perhaps at joy, late, after sets
have been switched off, and silences
are dark windows?

Questions

1. How many images can you find in this poem, appealing to how many senses?
2. When the poet says *pilgrimage*, what world does she enter? Is it figurative or literal? What other words go with *pilgrimage*?
3. Is there any sort of connection between "a blaze / of . . . watermelon" and "notes / remote, cool . . ."?

We have been reading poems that describe realities. Allen Ginsberg's dancers and police cars are really there—we accept his word for it. Herrick's Julia wears silk clothing. H.D.'s poem exaggerates, but it does not invent a bizarre world. William Carlos Williams, Gary Soto, and Denise Levertov describe an objective world in language that specifies the way they take it in.

But some poems use fantastic images to create worlds previously uncreated, as if the poet were recounting a dream. Here's a dreamy poem by Gregory Orr called "Washing My Face":

> Last night's dreams disappear.
> They are like the sink draining:
> a transparent rose swallowed by its stem.

The last image conjures up something imaginary—*a transparent rose*. Because we know what roses look like, and because we know what transparency means, we can assemble these words into an image of a transparent rose. Then we understand that the transparent rose resembles the water in the washstand, when we wash our faces at waking, making a swirling shape like petals as it disappears down the drain. The tenuousness of last night's dreams makes *transparent* feel right; the pleasant word *rose* implies that these disappearing dreams were happy ones.

Many contemporary Americans write poems that include realistic as well as fantastic images. These poems may move back and forth from one sort of concrete detail to another, from the seen to the dreamed and back again. James Wright wrote many poems that combined the two ways of seeing—looking out and looking in. Here is one:

Lying in a Hammock at William Duffy's Farm in Pine Island, Minnesota

> Over my head, I see the bronze butterfly,
> Asleep on the black trunk,
> Blowing like a leaf in green shadow.
> Down the ravine behind the empty house,
> The cowbells follow one another
> Into the distances of the afternoon.
> To my right,
> In a field of sunlight between two pines,
> The droppings of last year's horses
10   Blaze up into golden stones.
> I lean back, as the evening darkens and comes on.
> A chicken hawk floats over, looking for home.
> I have wasted my life.

The first time one reads the poem, the last line is a shock. Some people feel that the last line is not earned, that it comes out of nowhere, that the poem fails because of a trick ending. Other readers report that although they are shocked by the ending, it feels right. The issue is whether the last line grows naturally out of what goes before. Granted that it is a surprise, is it a cheap surprise or is it a surprise that leads to clear understanding?

Look back at what the poet sees, as he lies in the hammock at William Duffy's farm in Pine Island, Minnesota. Notice the lethargy and passivity, not only of lying in a hammock but also of the many enclosures of space—in a hammock, which is on a farm, which is in a town, which is named after an island, which is in a state. There are many layers to this cocoon.

First the poet sees a butterfly colored bronze. But bronze is not only a color; it is a metal, and if a butterfly were bronze it would be permanent and inorganic. One of the connotations of *butterfly*, on the other hand, is the fragility of a brief life. In the phrase *bronze butterfly*, fantastic when we think of the metal bronze, we find the paradox of evanescence and solidity, change and permanence. We also see the color of bronze in contrast to the tree trunk's color, and then we see the butterfly move, "Blowing like a leaf in green shadow," as if its fragility returned quickly and the vision of permanence were brief. In the dream world images can change quickly. The first three lines give us an extended image of clear contrasting colors—and contrasting senses of permanence and change. In the next three lines we cannot see the cows but, hearing the cowbells, we can visualize the ravine where they walk. Some of these words carry feeling without carrying images. "Into the distances of the afternoon" is not a visual image, nor is it addressed to any other sense, but the line takes the cows away from us, and the increasing distance—together with the emptiness of the house in the line before—introduces loneliness. The next four lines give us another scene and an absence of horses. We begin to realize that most things in this poem are gone. The horses have left behind only their manure.

In this poem, nothing goes down but what it must come up; nothing comes up but what it must go down. Any perception calls forth its opposite; if a butterfly is bronze it is also moving in the wind. Even when the poet talks of the cowbells (more frail and distant than cows) he has them *follow one another* (which is warm and companionable) *into the distances*, which is far, lonely, and separate. Now, like a playwright keeping our attention with dramatic contrast, the poet has built to something glorious—and shocks us with horse manure; then he shocks us again by making horse manure glorious: it blazes up "into golden stones," an image of fantasy. The more we look at these words, the more we realize the complications of feeling that control them. The poem is not intellectually complex; it is complex in feeling, an emotional density embodied in images.

In the next line, the poet at first departs from imaging the world around him, and says *I lean back* as if in passive withdrawal. Then he observes the world again, *as the evening darkens and comes on*. This is not the absence of light but the gathering of darkness, something coming close to him as everything else leaves. Loneliness slides toward something more desperate, and the poet writes the line that brings everything together. The next-to-last line is the climax of the poem and the skeleton key to the feelings of the poem: "A chicken hawk floats over, looking for home." In the mind of this lonely speaker, the bird is going home; even this predator, killer of the homely chicken, has a home to look for. By implication of the whole poem, and especially of the last line, the speaker does not have a home to go to. Instead, he lies in a hammock on somebody else's farm, and everything he looks at reminds him of his solitude and his unworthiness. We sense that wherever the poet looks in the landscape, he cannot help but see his own troubles.

Once you have understood the psychological state of the poem's speaker, its images make their melancholy point. At first sight, the butterfly was transformed into solidity and value—the speaker *wants* his life to change—then it becomes fragile and transitory again; but it remains beautiful in its sleep, as he does not in his passivity. The *empty house* is the home the speaker is exiled from, as he is exiled from cows' company. Wherever the cowbells move, we know that eventually in the afternoon the cows will go home to be milked; the bells remind us of a destination. While the speaker remains static, passive, unchanging, even horse droppings are glorified! All the speaker can think to do, under the ominous pressure of darkness, is give up.

Try reading another poem by James Wright and following the track of its different images.

A Blessing

Just off the highway to Rochester, Minnesota,
Twilight bounds softly forth on the grass.
And the eyes of those two Indian ponies
Darken with kindness.
They have come gladly out of the willows
To welcome my friend and me.
We step over the barbed wire into the pasture
Where they have been grazing all day, alone.
They ripple tensely, they can hardly contain their happiness
10   That we have come.
They bow shyly as wet swans. They love each other.
There is no loneliness like theirs.
At home once more,
They begin munching the young tufts of spring in the darkness.
I would like to hold the slenderer one in my arms,
For she has walked over to me
And nuzzled my left hand.
She is black and white,
Her mane falls wild on her forehead,
20   And the light breeze moves me to caress her long ear
That is delicate as the skin over a girl's wrist.
Suddenly I realize
That if I stepped out of my body I would break
Into blossom.

Questions

1. Which images describe a real world? Which are fantastic? Interpret the fantastic images.

2. Why is it appropriate that there be two ponies, instead of one or three?
3. In the second line, is the verb *bounds* an image? What sense does it bring you?
4. The poet puts together two sentences—"They love each other. There is no loneliness like theirs"—that would not normally seem to go together. Can you defend the juxtaposition?
5. Analyze the image *young tufts of spring*.

Other poetry goes further into fantasy than James Wright's. Sometimes a poet will use wholly bizarre images—without even the connection of rose to washbasin, or horse droppings to gold—to tell the truth of feeling. Chilean poet Pablo Neruda received the gift of a pair of socks hand-knitted by a peasant woman. He was pleased at this tribute, and wrote a poem that embodied his pleasure. Robert Bly translated it from the Spanish.

Ode to My Socks

    Maru Mori brought me
    a pair
    of socks
    which she knitted herself
    with her sheep-herder's hands,
    two socks as soft
    as rabbits.
    I slipped my feet
    into them
10   as though into
    two
    cases
    knitted
    with threads of
    twilight
    and goatskin.
    Violent socks,
    my feet were
    two fish made
20   of wool,
    two long sharks
    seablue, shot
    through
    by one golden thread,
    two immense blackbirds,
    two cannons,
    my feet
    were honored
    in this way
30   by
    these

heavenly
socks.
They were
so handsome
for the first time
my feet seemed to me
unacceptable
like two decrepit
40   firemen, firemen
unworthy
of that woven
fire,
of those glowing
socks.

Nevertheless
I resisted
the sharp temptation
to save them somewhere
50   as schoolboys
keep
fireflies,
as learned men
collect
sacred texts,
I resisted
the mad impulse
to put them
in a golden
60   cage
and each day give them
birdseed
and pieces of pink melon.
Like explorers
in the jungle who hand
over the very rare
green deer
to the spit
and eat it
70   with remorse,
I stretched out
my feet
and pulled on
the magnificent
socks
and then my shoes.

The moral
of my ode is this:
beauty is twice
80   beauty

and what is good is doubly
good
when it is a matter of two socks
made of wool
in winter.

Questions

1. When Neruda writes that he "resisted / the mad impulse / to put them / in a golden / cage . . . ," is he using an image to describe the socks? Did this help you know what they look like? If an image does not describe an object, what else can it describe?
2. In rapid succession, Neruda says that his feet were "two fish made / of wool," "two long sharks," "two immense blackbirds," and "two cannons." What does this do to advice about trying to take poems literally?
3. Find other examples of the fantastic image in this poem and interpret them.
4. Contrast:

Dear Maru Mori,

   Thank you ever so much for your kind gift of a pair of socks. They are very pretty. They are warm. They fit me perfectly. I will wear them all the time. Mrs. Neruda likes them too. Thank you again.

Yours truly,
Pablo Neruda

Chapter 4 **Figures of Speech, Especially Metaphors**

Figures of speech are extraordinary, original, nonliteral uses of language, common to lively speech and literature. It would be literal to say "She walked slowly across the field." To say "She walked across the field as slowly as a snail with a pulled muscle" uses a figure of speech; this figure is **simile**, which makes an explicit comparison using *like* or *as* or a verb like *seems* or *appears*. A **metaphor** resembles a simile by talking about one thing in terms of another, but a metaphor's comparison is implicit; it does not use *like* or *as, seems* or *appears:* "She snailed her painful way across the field." Poems abound in metaphors. This chapter deals mainly with metaphors and similes; at the end we will mention a few other figures of speech.

Here is another poem by Gregory Orr that uses simile:

All Morning

All morning the dream lingers.
I am like thick grass
in a meadow, still
soaked with dew at noon.

The poet compares himself to grass, declaring that he shares a quality with it. The simile works through a visual image—we *see* grass soaked with dew—but it is not the picture that does the comparing: a set of relationships makes the comparison work. This simile, like many, can be expressed as an equation: dew is to grass as dreams are to me. The comparison *states* that my dreams remain with me for a while, the way dew clings to a blade of grass. Besides this statement there are two implications to the simile: eventually the dream/dew will vanish/evaporate; because dew brings nourishment to grass, dreaming has value for me.

If we omitted *like* from Orr's poem, we would have:

> All morning the dream lingers.
> I am thick grass
> in a meadow, still
> soaked with dew at noon.

The last three lines would make not a simile but a metaphor. The terms compared—*I* to *thick grass,* dreams to persistent dew—would remain the same, but the manner of the comparison would change. The reader is led by the simile: "I am *like* thick grass"; when the line becomes "I am thick grass," the guiding hand disappears and the reader may not know where to go.

Often metaphor is more powerful than simile. Apparently it is older and more primitive, and derives from "primary process thinking," as psychologists describe it, in which dissimilar things are perceived as identical. Metaphor is the poetic mode of thought, flying across barriers of logic to assert identities. When a small child speaks of the leg of a table or the hand of a clock, he or she perceives a flesh-and-blood leg and a hand; the table in his language has power to walk, the clock to gesture and to point. For the child, such metaphors are alive; for the adult they are dead. When the adult mind thinks in metaphor, it regains lost power misplaced in the pursuit of maturity.

All language began as metaphor, and in many of our words is buried an image that unites dissimilar things: a daisy was once a day's eye. In casual speech we use continual **personification** (a figure of speech by which we humanize the nonhuman): clouds frown, fires rage, distant mountains glower, meadows look cheerful, zippers prove recalcitrant, the sun smiles, and the horizon looks inviting.

Metaphors in poems often happen quickly; we are moved without knowing what has touched us; unless we are explicating, we do not even notice that the poet has used metaphor. One of Robert Frost's best poems, "To Earthward" (p. 515), begins by saying that when he was young feelings came easily; a tiny stimulus produced a strong response: "The petal of the rose," he says, "It was that stung." We understand *stung* as "gave pain" with the consciousness that this pain derives from pleasure too exquisite; the pang of beauty is overwhelming and therefore painful. If we think about it, *stung* is a metaphor, because a rose does not ordinarily sting anything. What stings us? A thorn pricks, but it does not sting. When Frost writes "The petal of the rose / It was that stung," he compares the soft petal of a flower to the harsh sting of a bee. Metaphors work by contrast as well as by comparison; things compared in a metaphor must be unlike, and the poet makes them alike. Usually difference affects us more than similarity; when a poet compares the seemingly incomparable he wins us with energy of resolved contrast.

It is easy to see how *sting* and *petal* contrast. But how do they come together? A bee—never named, yet part of the connotations of *sting*—belongs in a garden. A poem often finds its metaphors within an area, and Frost's poem moves among flowers and gardens for its images and metaphors. Bees work in gardens for pollen. If Frost had substituted for *stung* an image of a dentist's office— "The petal of the rose / It was that drilled"—we would not have been able to follow him in his feeling. Coherence of metaphor makes Frost's words operate upon us, even if we do not know that we are operated upon. Coherence of *rose* and *stung,* by way of an unstated bee, develops the metaphor.

Many metaphors in poetry work almost subliminally, like Frost's *stung,* but we also find extended metaphors. In the following poem, William Shakespeare starts by asking if he might make a comparison:

> Shall I compare thee to a summer's day?
> Thou art more lovely and more temperate:
> Rough winds do shake the darling buds of May,
> And summer's lease hath all too short a date.
> Sometime too hot the eye of heaven shines,
> And often is his gold complexion dimm'd;
> And every fair° from fair sometime declines,   beautiful thing
> By chance or nature's changing course untrimm'd.
> But thy eternal summer shall not fade
> 10   Nor lose possession of that fair thou ow'st.°   ownest: possess
> Nor shall Death brag thou wand'rest in his shade,
> When in eternal lines to time thou grow'st;
>   So long as men can breathe or eyes can see,
>   So long lives this and this gives life to thee.

This poem follows the common poetic form of the **sonnet**, fourteen lines of rhymed iambic pentameter (see pages 459, 472–474). In the course of his fourteen lines, Shakespeare compares relentlessly, always to the effect that A is greater than B. No, you are not like a summer's day, you are better. To prove his conclusion, he compares parts of wholes. He breaks a summer's day down into weather, temperature, and temperament. Weather is more changeable than you are; you remain the same as the weather does not. Even in May, when blossoms begin to show, the weather can be unpleasant—but not you. Summer is a tenant who has rented an estate for a short time only (Shakespeare's sonnets and plays are full of legal and financial metaphor) but your tenancy of beauty is longer than a mere summer. Notice that by the fourth line Shakespeare has established his comparison of *thee* and *summer* so thoroughly that he can introduce the further metaphor of tenancy without confusion.

If summer leases, summer resembles a human being. The fifth line introduces another personification, when we hear of *the eye of heaven,* and we identify the *eye* with the sun when we hear that this eye *shines.* Having established the sun, without speaking of it directly, Shakespeare describes *his gold complexion,* as if the yellow sun had skin, and makes a cloudy day the sun's loss. In contrast his love is never lessened or dimmed. Notice how the connotations of precious metal work to flatter the day, and thus flatter the love that is greater than the day.

The first eight lines of the poem—the **octave** of a sonnet—carry out its implications. The **sestet**—the sonnet's last six lines—expands upon the unchanging quality of the love and ends by praising itself. Death shall not brag of keeping this person-summer's day in shade, because these lines of poetry give eternal life. Shakespeare is able to bring Death into his metaphor, because shade treats sun as death treats life.

Shakespeare's poem extends a series of linked metaphors through fourteen lines. Here is another example of a single-word metaphor, like Frost's *stung*, which I use in order to move on to another subject. At the end of "During Wind and Rain" (page 405), Thomas Hardy writes:

> Down their carved names the rain-drop ploughs.

A plow is a natural object in the rural scene of this poem—and thus belongs in this poem's metaphorical area—but this is not a literal plow; metaphor turns a raindrop into an agricultural implement: raindrop is to gravestone as plow is to earth. The metaphor of *ploughs* has implications central to the poem: if raindrop acts on granite as plow on meadow, by implication many years have passed. If, however, we read the line lazily, taking *ploughs* as if it meant "moves vigorously forward"—as in a dead metaphor like "the fullback plows through the line" or "the tugboat plows through the waves"—nothing happens at all.

We constantly use figures of speech that once enjoyed freshness and vitality but that we no longer hear as figures of speech. Declaring we feel immovable, we say "I am glued to my chair." If we picture what we have said, we have a comical scene. But with dead metaphors, neither speaker nor hearer pictures anything at all. In a dead metaphor, the old comparison or assertion of identity is what is dead. If we did not say that we were glued to the chair, we might have said that we were anchored to the spot and no one would see the old schooner in the harbor, its anchor played out behind it, caught in the coral of the harbor bottom. For that matter, "dead metaphor" is a dead metaphor; and if I say that the old comparison is buried, I make the same morbid assertion. Once these metaphors were alive; now they are decayed corpses. The first time anyone used the metaphor of "dead metaphor," he implied that a hole had been dug—six feet deep, six feet long, three feet across—in the dirt of the phrase, and that somebody had placed the body of a comparison in this hole and heaped dirt over the body.

Live metaphors embody feelings. Dead metaphors embody stock responses, clichés, and lethargy. Bad poetry uses dead metaphors as commonly as we do in speech. Good poetry invents new metaphors, making vivid comparisons.

People often even mix their dead metaphors. "Then the hand of God stepped in . . . " makes a wonderful anatomical mixture. Of course *the hand of God* was used as if it meant "fortuitous circumstance," and *stepped in* as if it meant "happened next." When I first taught writing, one of my students wrote in a poem "The door yawned and beckoned." By *yawned* she meant that it opened, by *beckoned* that it looked inviting. But the two dead metaphors together made an impossible anatomy again, in which a door was an open mouth from which a hand suddenly extended. (Journalists as well as poets are experts at mixing dead metaphors. Take this example: "Mushrooming insurance and energy costs represent a double-barreled shotgun pointed at New England's ski areas." The writer of this sentence developed the ability *not* to see, or the writer could not have turned a soft vegetable into a steel weapon.)

Forming the habit of taking things literally, a reader becomes increasingly sensitive to language. Reading literally, we do not read the word *blind* automatically as if it meant "obtuse"—which is to use *blind* as a dead metaphor. When we read *blind*, we take it to mean "sightless" until we find out otherwise. Then we do not write a sentence like this one recently printed in a country weekly: " 'American optometrists are blind to the advantages of small town living,' said Dr. Harvey Bagnold to the Rotary Club last Tuesday."

Taking words as literally as possible—until the poem forces us to understand that we are reading a metaphor—we read the metaphor that is there. When Hamlet talks about his problems, he says that one possibility is to "take arms against a sea of troubles." The *Encyclopaedia Britannica*, in an otherwise sensible entry on "Metaphor," cites this figure as a mixed metaphor because people do not bear weapons against the ocean. It is not a mixed metaphor. It is visual metaphor embodying an idea and the emotions appropriate to that idea. Hamlet acknowledges that his problems are as soluble as the sea is vulnerable to his assault. The image expresses his feelings of futility. Shakespeare has Hamlet reveal his feelings by making a metaphor that provides an image of someone taking arms—in the context of the play, a sword or dagger—against an ocean.

Besides personification, a subdivision of metaphor mentioned on page 421, and **hyperbole**, or extreme exaggeration ("That room was two miles wide!"), we need mention only two other forms of figurative language, not quite so common as metaphor and simile. In **synechdoche** we speak of something by naming only a part of it. A poet might refer to a naval fleet as "two hundred keels," for instance, and his audience would understand that *keel* stood for boat. It is a way of referring to boats without using the word, which has perhaps lost freshness through overuse. We use synechdoche in everyday speech if we say that, during the summer, Gloria acquired wheels—she bought a used Oldsmobile. The part of the car stands in for the whole of the car.

In **metonomy** we speak of the object in terms of something closely connected with it, not a part of it as in synechdoche but a thing closely and legitimately associated with it. Thus we can refer to a stove as its heat, for heat is not a part of the stove but a quality of it, or an association. Charles Reznikoff writes:

> Holding the stem of the
> beauty she had
> as if it were still
> a rose.

The poet first uses *beauty* by metonomy, as a quality of flowers; then he makes the flower particular.

Here are some poems followed by questions about metaphor and other figures of speech.

> That time of year thou mayst in me behold
> When yellow leaves, or none, or few, do hang
> Upon those boughs which shake against the cold,
> Bare ruin'd choirs[1] where late the sweet birds sang.
> In me thou seest the twilight of such day
> As after sunset fadeth in the west,
> Which by and by black night doth take away,
> Death's second self, that seals up all in rest.
> In me thou seest the glowing of such fire
> That on the ashes of his youth doth lie,
> As the death-bed whereon it must expire,
> Consumed with that which it was nourish'd by.
> >   This thou perceiv'st which makes thy love more strong,
> >   To love that well which thou must leave ere long.
> > —*William Shakespeare*

10

[1]Choir lofts, the part of the church building where the choirboys sang during religious services.

Questions

1. Paraphrase the poem, summarize the content, and discern the structure.
2. Where do you find the first figure of speech? What sort of figure is it?
3. How are the three quatrains linked in idea? Is there metaphorical coherence? Imagistic coherence?
4. In the fourth line, are the birds literal or figurative or both?
5. In the eleventh and twelfth lines, does the analogy make a complex idea simpler? Or does it make a simple idea more difficult?
6. List and name all figures of speech in this sonnet.

Orchids

> They lean over the path,
> Adder-mouthed,
> Swaying close to the face,
> Coming out, soft and deceptive,
> Limp and damp, delicate as a young bird's tongue;
> Their fluttery fledgling lips
> Move slowly,
> Drawing in the warm air.
>
> And at night,
> The faint moon falling through whitewashed glass,
> The heat going down
> So their musky smell comes even stronger,

10

Drifting down from their mossy cradles:
So many devouring infants!
Soft luminescent fingers,
Lips neither dead nor alive,
Loose ghostly mouths
Breathing.

—*Theodore Roethke*

Questions

1. List the different things the orchids are compared to.
2. The poem moves from one metaphoric area to another. What are the areas? Does the poem cohere? What keeps its different parts together?

The Hill

It is sometime since I have been
to what it was had once turned me backwards,
and made my head into
a cruel instrument.

It is simple
to confess. Then done,
to walk away, walk away,
to come again.

But that form, I must answer,
10   is dead in me, completely,
and I will not allow it
to reappear—

Saith perversity, the willful,
the magnanimous cruelty,
which is in me
like a hill.

—*Robert Creeley*

Questions

1. What are the connotations of *instrument*? Is the word a metaphor?
2. Note all the metaphors in this poem. Is there a dead metaphor here? A personification?
3. Note other figures of speech.
4. Does the final figure of speech have impact on the earlier word *me*?

Chapter 5 **Tone, with a Note on Intentions**

A poem's **tone**, in common definition, reveals the writer's attitude toward subject, an attitude that could include sarcasm or irony or awe. In conversation we indicate tone by our manner of speaking or by our facial expression: "Great!" can be pronounced so that it is a compliment or an insult. When we discuss a poem's tone, we discuss the value we attribute to its statements. In Wallace Stevens's "Disillusionment of Ten O'Clock," he wrote:

> People are not going
> To dream of baboons and periwinkles.

In the context of this poem, which has already told us about "houses . . . haunted / By white night-gowns," we hear the speaker's tone as ironic. **Irony** is the perception of incongruity or discrepancy—between statement and meaning, for instance. Because we know that these unimaginative people will dream colorless dreams, it is ironic to name the exotic *baboons and periwinkles* as possible subjects of their dreams. Other poems are explosive and angry in tone, like John Donne's line beginning "The Canonization":

> For Godsake hold your tongue and let me love!

Other poems reveal sarcasm, as in E. E. Cummings's lines from "Poem, or Beauty Hurts Mr. Vinal":

take it from me kiddo
believe me
my country, 'tis of

you, land of the Cluett
Shirt Boston Garter and Spearmint
Girl With The Wrigley Eyes (of you
land of the Arrow Ide
and Earl &
Wilson
10   Collars) of you i
sing:land of Abraham Lincoln and Lydia E. Pinkham,
land above all of Just Add Hot Water and Serve—
from every B. V. D.

let freedom ring

These examples are relatively simple. As most poems are complex, many-sided, and ambivalent, so the tone of many poems is hard to name and easy to mistake.

When we speak of a poem's tone we make a metaphor, speaking of a poem as if it were a person and voiced its own words. It can help, studying tone in poetry, to try out the analogy of poems-as-people. If we sometimes misunderstand tone in poems, it is also true that we can misunderstand personal tones of voice, even when we have body and pitch, gesture and eyebrows to help us understand. In everyday life, we interpret people's tones every hour of the day, without noticing that we do it. When we are offended by someone, or when we are touched or pleased, it is often the tone that does the offending or the pleasing. Perhaps we live with someone, and after dinner one night someone says "I'll do the dishes." These four words, depending on their tone, could mean a great many things. They could mean "Of course I'm getting stuck with doing the dishes, you slob, the way I always do, and the way I get stuck with taking out the garbage and picking up the biology notes from Gerry and standing in line for the football tickets." Or they could mean "I want to do the dishes because you look so tired, and I'm always happy to take on a little work on your behalf, because you do so much for me, and I'm grateful for you getting that book from the library." Or they could mean "I'm about to ask a favor," or "I think you're mad at me," or "I'll get points this way," or "Here is something I can do in order to avoid doing homework," or "When you wash the dishes they never get clean."

Usually we can decode the tone of somebody's voice. For that matter, we decode the way someone crosses a room or closes a door or drinks a Coke. Decoding a roommate, we use a glossary of behavior that we have been learning since birth. Door slams mean anger, says this dictionary; deep sighs mean frustration. We receive signals through gestures and through words, and we respond in kind; we communicate by tones.

Readers of poetry learn a system of signals by which they understand the tone of a poem, just as everybody learns the tones of personal pitch and gesture. One of the contracts that poet makes with reader stipulates that tone shall be ascertainable: an assured tone is another criterion of excellence in poetry. Sometimes poems fail by not making tone clear enough. For instance, here is a portion of a poem by a talented student:

> . . . on sour air, the bells
> chimed season's greetings
> to the departed host
> of Christmas . . .

If you cannot decode the tone of this fragment, you are not alone. What is the author's attitude toward the subject? The poet intended *season's greetings* to be highly ironic, even sarcastic, but reading it one could not be certain; a potential irony floated, unanchored, two inches above the page. The poet might have anchored irony any number of ways, but it is worth saying that ironic clichés are difficult to control; sometimes a context that demands irony provides control, sometimes a structure that repeats and varies the same irony. This fragment fails to make the irony seem intentional.

A note on intentions

When most of us speak about poetry, we refer to an author's intentions without even noticing that we do it. Speaking of diction and idiom, metaphor and image, we couch our discoveries in terms of the poet's presumed wishes and endeavors. Interpreting meaning, we say "This is what the poet was trying to say." The last phrase is especially common—and it is unfortunate: it promotes a picture of the poet as a fumbling, inarticulate slob, unable to say what is meant. The expression suggests that we will help out the dolt standing there with mouth open; let us inform the grateful poet of what he or she was trying and failing to say.

Whenever we begin to speak of a poet's intentions, we ought to consider what we are *really* talking about. Surely no one is so presumptuous as to believe that he or she *really* knows what was in Milton's mind before he wrote *Paradise Lost*—or what was in Robert Frost's mind before he wrote "Stopping by Woods on a Snowy Evening," for that matter. Common sense reveals our ignorance; we need no degrees in psychology. Everything that ever happened to Robert Frost—every poem he ever read, every conversation he ever took part in, every winter he ever lived through, every horse he ever drove—entered his poem. Or so I am free to suppose.

We never know, with anything like certainty, why we make important decisions in our own lives. If ignorance prevails about our own intentions, how can we possibly presume to know someone else's? The formula What was he trying to do? How well did he accomplish his purposes? presupposes a sort of knowledge we cannot claim. It is true that some poets have revealed their intentions to us—in autobiography, in letters to editors or to friends, and in answer to questions. I suggest that we should not believe them. We should *listen* to what they say—if the poem is good, the poet's talk about it is bound to be interesting, even if only for what the poet leaves out. But we should listen skeptically, with our minds alert for falsity; we should not listen naïvely, as if we were getting the words from the horse's mouth. Often the most sophisticated people become naïve when artists claim to explain their work. When politicians explain that their motives are noble and selfless, nobody believes them. When poets do the same, people nod their heads. Really, there is every reason for artists to lie to us when they tell us about their work—because they have every reason to lie to themselves. Good poems by their nature reveal many sides of a person, including sides poets may wish to conceal. Robert Frost, for instance, revealed a dark side in many poems—fears of madness, longings for oblivion, notions of evil, intimations of meaninglessness—which was not the self he chose to reveal on the lecture platform. In speaking about his poems, he denied their darkness.

Some poets have the illusion that they intend whatever takes place in their poems. They are like people who, in an argument, defend the rightness of everything they have ever said or done. Other poets admit that they wrote this phrase, or that whole poem, without knowing exactly what they were saying. T. S. Eliot, for instance, proclaimed his innocence of intention in much of "The Waste Land." Probably more often, a writer will consciously intend something on the surface—and write something else as well, underneath the surface, that the writer is not aware of until later, when somebody points it out, or that, sometimes, the writer denies even after it is pointed out. Some students and teachers talk in classrooms about "hidden meanings" in a poem, an unfortunate phrase that makes reading poems sound like detective work. If we must speak of "hidden meanings," we ought to acknowledge that poets frequently hide meanings from themselves, and not just from readers.

Maybe the word *intention* should be stricken from our critical vocabulary; for we begin to speak sometimes of "unconscious intentions," a phrase in which the noun contradicts the adjective. In our lives we tend to judge by actions or results rather than intentions; if someone breaks our jaw while "only trying to help," we are smarter to remember the broken jaw than to warm ourselves over the avowed intention. Thus with poems: we must pay no attention to intentions, or even to the idea of intentions, but to actions and results. We must attend to what is there, *really there on the page*, and to the impingements of those words upon us.

Tone is easy to miss or misinterpret. Many readers seize on one notion of tone, a quick reading, and ignore or cannot see alternative readings. Assuming one tone, we eliminate the possibility of others, or of tonal variation. Here is a short poem, alive with tone, requiring thoughtful reading.

Transformations

Portion of this yew
Is a man my grandsire knew,
Bosomed here at its foot:

This branch may be his wife,
A ruddy human life
Now turned to a green shoot.

These grasses must be made
Of her who often prayed,
Last century, for repose;
10   And the fair girl long ago
Whom I often tried to know
May be entering this rose.

So, they are not underground,
But as nerves and veins abound
In the growths of upper air,
And they feel the sun and rain,
And the energy again
That made them what they were!
                            —*Thomas Hardy*

First, let us see if we can agree on a summary. A man walks among the graves of people he has heard about or has known in life. He observes that all these bodies endure, at least as particles in graveyard plants.

This summary is as pale as a government bulletin because I am trying to sanitize the tone of it. What, then, is the tone of Hardy's poem? Is he melancholy? Is he happy in the graveyard? Does he announce molecular immortality as a discovery of vast scientific and spiritual importance? At first glance, he may seem to do the last. One student writing about this poem said, at the end of a paper, "So after this depression about everybody dying Thos. Hardy shakes himself out of it. He decides to look on the bright side of things so he notices that everybody really lives and nobody really dies because the roses etcetera go on blooming year after year after year after year." These sentences run into trouble as a parphrase, and describe a poem which, if Hardy had written it, would have been dishonest; this student has Hardy turn himself away from sadness by lying to himself and to his readers. And this poem is *almost* the one Hardy wrote; I don't think that this student's interpretation is far off, but that it mistook Hardy's tone.

"Transformations" begins with a physical scene. An old man—many clues, like his acquaintance with someone "last century," hint that the speaker is getting on—walks musing in a graveyard. At the beginning, he thinks of deaths remote from him, and the tone is quiet and contemplative. As the old man moves forward in time, closer to his own end, the tone shifts.

Notice that Hardy begins by implying that he is certain, and modifies his tone of certainty as the poem develops. The change in the degree and in the type of assertion makes the change in tone. The first two lines are plain statement: "Portion of this yew / Is a man my grandsire knew. . . ." Obviously, the speaker knows the truth of what he says, and we believe him; the yew tree must be adjacent to the grave, and we can accept this assertion scientifically. If someone is buried next to a tree, after a number of years it must be true that some of the tree's molecules contain atoms that were earlier part of that person's body. When the speaker goes on "Bosomed here at its foot," he moves into metaphor. The metaphor has resonance and secondary implication, but it also carries information: the man my grandsire knew is buried (his burial compared to a baby snuggled up to a breast) at the base of the tree.

When the speaker continues, he has taken his certainty as a starting point and added fancy: "This branch *may be* his wife . . ." He plays straight with us: he *admits* that when he begins to think of a particular part of the tree as composed of a particular person, he is *playing* with the possibilities of his scientific commonplace. If the wife (as we can assume) is buried beside her husband "here at its foot," it is common sense to assume that she also participates in the tree's molecules, but it is fanciful to think of her as a special new branch. (That she's thought of as a *green shoot* implies that she died more recently than her husband.) The speaker modestly admits his lack of knowledge or certainty, admits his playful fancy, by using the verb form *may be*.

The first line of the second stanza appears at first glance to make a definite assertion: "These grasses must be made . . ." If *must be* in our usage meant "absolutely, incontrovertibly has to be," we would have a statement of certainty. But, with the typical oddity of our speech, *must be* encodes a lack of certainty. When Hardy writes "These grasses must be made," he uses *must be* the way we do when we say "It must be six o'clock." (Robert Frost, as we have seen, used the same idiom when he wrote "My little horse must think it queer . . .") In Hardy's poem, we are allowed to understand that a woman (who "prayed / Last century for repose") is buried hereabouts, so her remains may well be part of the grasses here; on the other hand, the lines say, possibly they are not (because of the length of time? because of possible error about the gravesite?). In the second part of this stanza Hardy reverts to the *may be* form of possibility, making the metaphor that is the high point of the poem: "the fair girl . . . / May be entering this rose." Her molecules promenade through the stem to the blossom. In the metaphor, the rose has doors or portals, like house or church, and the pretty young woman in the shape of her molecules walks through the door.

So far the tone has been simple. Hardy told us a certainty followed by fancies and probabilities. We walk beside an old man through a churchyard, where he ruminates on the persistence of matter translated from one organism to another. In the third stanza tone changes entirely. We can perceive the change in the poem's grammar. In his verb forms, Hardy reverts from *must be* and *may be* to direct assertion. "So," the poem tells us, as a result of what has just been said, "they [the dead] *are* not underground."

But they are. Yes, some molecules of decay may have escaped, but the dead are not *really* "as nerves or veins" abounding "In the growths of upper air." We know that the poem tells us false when it says that they *abound* and that "they *feel* the sun and rain / And the energy again / That made them what they were!" The *tone* of this assertion is made loud by the exclamation point, a triumphant, almost ecstatic assertion of the survival of the dead. It is the *tone* of the exclamation that must concern the reader. The poem seems to argue that it has proved survival after death by what it has observed of plant life. The poem began by winning our trust with its scrupulous use of verbs moving from *is* to *may be* and *must be*. Now it seems to violate that trust, by asserting *are* when we must be aware that the idea depends on speculation, on fantasy, and on a scientific notion that deals with particles of human flesh, not with whole human beings.

Because the leap to assertion is such a grand leap, because we have learned to trust the implicit reasonableness of the speaker, the leap to false assertion creates a tone of strong and urgent feeling, which speaks to us like unwritten lines of poetry, saying "I know this assertion to be false; I make it only because I must, because the mortality of bodies is unacceptable to me!" The poem, through its tone—tone accomplished mostly by variations in verbs—speaks to us eloquently of the dread and fear of death.

Hardy's intention, in writing the poem, is not known to the reader—not to me, not to you, not to Hardy's most devoted student or scholar. But his poem in its own words, in its slow and steady motion down the page, makes its shape inevitable—if we read with a steady care, with attention, and with the same sensitivity we use interpreting the gesture and pitch of a person we love.

Here are some poems to read for their tone.

Museum Piece

The good grey guardians of art
Patrol the halls on spongy shoes,
Impartially protective, though
Perhaps suspicious of Toulouse.[1]

Here dozes one against the wall,
Disposed upon a funeral chair.
A Degas[2] dancer pirouettes
Upon the parting of his hair.

See how she spins! The grace is there,
10   But strain as well is plain to see.
Degas loved the two together:
Beauty joined to energy.

Edgar Degas purchased once
A fine El Greco,[3] which he kept
Against the wall beside his bed
To hang his pants on while he slept.
                    —*Richard Wilbur*

[1] Henri de Toulouse-Lautrec Monfa (1864–1901) made notable paintings of Parisian life and characters but is best known for his posters of nightclubs and entertainers.

[2] Edgar Degas (1834–1917), one of the important French impressionists, is best known for his paintings and pastels of ballerinas.

[3] El Greco (1548?–1614? or 1625?), native of Crete and student of the Venetian master Titian, lived in Toledo from his late twenties and was the leading sixteenth-century mystical Spanish painter. His work often distorts the human form by elongating it.

Questions

1. In the first line, what is the tone of the word *good*?
2. Alliteration is the repetition of consonant sounds, as in *good gray guardians*. Does alliteration in the first line contribute to the tone of the line?
3. Notice the rhyme in the first stanza. Can a rhyme contribute to tone? Does this rhyme?
4. Does the first stanza introduce a tone that remains the same throughout the poem? Where does the poem's tone change? How do you know?
5. What is the tone of the last line of the poem? Does it resolve the differing tones earlier in the poem?

Hay for the Horses

He had driven half the night
From far down San Joaquin
Through Mariposa, up the
Dangerous mountain roads,
And pulled in at eight a.m.
With his big truckload of hay behind the barn.
With winch and ropes and hooks
We stacked the bales up clean
To splintery redwood rafters
10   High in the dark, flecks of alfalfa
Whirling through shingle-cracks of light,
Itch of haydust in the sweaty shirt and shoes.
At lunchtime under Black oak
Out in the hot corral,
—The old mare nosing lunchpails,
Grasshoppers crackling in the weeds—
'I'm sixty-eight,' he said,
'I first bucked hay when I was seventeen.
I thought, that day I started,
20   I sure would hate to do this all my life.
And dammit, that's just what
I've gone and done.'

               —*Gary Snyder*

Questions

1. How would you characterize the tone of the first stanza of this poem? Do you trust it to be straightforward? Why?
2. In the poem's middle, does the tone change at all? Do you sense any change in the speaker's attitude toward the subject?
3. In the last part of the poem, the poet quotes another speaker. Does this new speaker have a characteristic tone? What do you know of him from his tone? What does the poet do to reveal his tone?

Ends

Loud talk in the overlighted house
That made us stumble past.
Oh, there had once been night the first,
But this was night the last.

Of all the things he might have said,
Sincere or insincere,
He never said she wasn't young,
And hadn't been his dear.

Oh, some as soon would throw it all
10   As throw a part away.
And some will say all sorts of things,
But some mean what they say.

                              —*Robert Frost*

Questions

1. Who is *us*?
2. What is overheard?
3. Do any overheard words have a tone to them that you trust? distrust? What words give you your impressions?
4. What do you feel you know about the overheard people? Try to discover everything you can about them, and then decide how you know what you know.
5. What are these people arguing about? Do you know? Or do you only know the tone of the argument? Which is more important, the subject of an argument or its tone?

Chapter 6 **Symbols and Allusions**

In "To Read a Story," a symbol was defined as a person, object, place, or event that comes to stand for something other than it is, usually something more than it is, and for a class of events or relationships. This definition can serve as a starter here. Again, we must make distinctions among kinds of symbolism: the **conventional** (or **traditional**) **symbol**, the **natural symbol**, and the **literary symbol**. And we must speak as well about allusion and reference in poetry, devices that overlap when a poet refers or alludes to a traditional symbol and that resemble each other in the difficulty they cause for students.

It is easiest to speak first of *natural symbols*, which occur in literature but which tend toward cliché: night is a natural symbol of death, and so is autumn. Shakespeare and other geniuses have made great literature using natural symbols; remember "That time of year thou mayst in me behold . . ." (page 425), where both night and autumn are symbols of death. Because natural symbols tend to be trite, modern writers seldom use them, or use them in the negative, setting up the expectation of a stock response, and then disappointing it. The great modern poet T. S. Eliot began one of his first poems, "The Love Song of J. Alfred Prufrock," with

> Let us go then, you and I,
> When the evening is spread out against the sky . . .

appealing to stock responses, and to the natural symbolism of sunset as beauty or fulfillment. His audience, when he wrote the poem in 1911, might have expected him to go on:

> Like veils of painted gossamer on high . . .

Instead, he turned this expectation upside down with his actual third line:

> Like a patient etherized upon a table.

A natural symbol underwent a radical alteration.

The word *symbol* begins by meaning a simple sign, like a circle containing a cigarette, with a diagonal line crossing out the cigarette; everybody knows the sign of the symbol for NO SMOKING. We speak of *conventional symbols* like these signs and like national flags or the logos of sports teams. Another sort of conventional symbol (it would be better perhaps to speak of these as *traditional symbols*) are images or phrases that have acquired meaning over centuries of history or association, like the cross and the Star of David. When a poet uses an image of a cross, he can hardly avoid reference to Christ, Christianity, and to suffering. Therefore **reference** allies itself to traditional (and conventional) symbolism. We speak of conventional and traditional symbols together because the distinction between them is quantitative; "conventional" symbols are simple signs; "traditional" symbols are signs with long and complex associations.

Finally, there is the *literary symbol*, of which a fictional example was Chekhov's "Gooseberries." Here is a poem by William Blake:

The Sick Rose

> O Rose, thou art sick!
> The invisible worm
> That flies in the night,
> In the howling storm,
>
> Has found out thy bed
> Of crimson joy,
> And his dark secret love
> Does thy life destroy.

Reading this poem, let us as always first try the literal. A sick rose could suffer from a plant bacterium. But the second line of the poem reveals that we cannot continue to read on a literal level, because invisible worms fly only in the imagination. Back to the first line, then. *Rose* is capitalized, which may give us the sense that this flower is more than a flower, or that a real flower is addressed as if it embodied something beyond itself. To connect this flower with the notion of sickness seems a violation of the natural, as if we said that a mountain squeaked like a mouse. The contrast between *rose* and *sick* occurs at the levels of both sound and idea, as the full *os* of the first two syllables dwindle into the quick short *is* of *sick* and *invisible*.

"The Sick Rose" makes a literary symbol. When we ask what it is a symbol *of*, we ask the wrong sort of question. A literary symbol is not a figure or a riddle to which there exists a simple answer, or a correct interpretation. Instead, it is a series of words—creating image or event or character or fantasy or plot or scene—that is irreducible, that in itself is a formula for a complex set of feelings and ideas never before rendered in the same way. *The literary symbol cannot be translated or identified.* We can talk about it and we can talk around it, but the symbol will always sit in the center of our words, smiling enigmatically, content to be itself. A great French symbolist poet, Stéphane Mallarmé, made a metaphor for the symbol: he said it was "the new word." We can find the metaphor useful to our thinking about the literary symbol, because it cannot be defined or named by anything except itself. It resembles, then, a "new word" as if the poet invented the word *chair* for the first time, and there were no other word for chair but *chair*.

William Blake makes a symbol for a new thing. *The invisible worm* is not described in terms of horns and claws; it is a general "worm," with the particular attribute of invisibility—and with other attributes as well that associate feelings with this *new word*. This is a worm gifted with flight like a dragon, and gifted especially to fly in a darkness (night as a natural symbol is frightening, possibly the place of evil) and through a storm (destruction, possibly divine wrath) that makes a noise like the cries of someone in pain. The sick rose and its worm live in a place of terror and fear, are themselves instruments and victims of terror and fear. Syntax of subject and object, predator and victim, locates a scene in the second stanza. The worm has found "thy bed / Of crimson joy . . ." The word *joy* seems unambivalent, but it is not: crimson is blood-color, one of sin's colors, and dangerous; at least violent and extreme. One would expect malice from such a worm, and one hears instead of *love*; but it is a *dark, secret* love, and it is a love that rhymes *joy* with *destroy*. When love is both dark and secret, adjectives like crimson complicate the wholeness of the noun; if they do not reverse love into hate, or joy into pain, or fondness into malice, they introduce elements of the negative into the positive; they make by their complexity a wholeness. It is a wholeness that is also a new, single thing: symbolist poem or "new word."

Many poems speak of roses, in many different ways—sometimes as traditional or literary symbols and sometimes not. Theodore Roethke's great contemporary poem, "The Rose" (page 530), makes a literary symbol, another new word like William Blake's. But in Charles Reznikoff's four-line poem,

> Holding the stem of the
> beauty she had
> as if it were still
> a rose.

rose is not a symbol but a type, "a thing of beauty." When Shakespeare says "A rose by any other name would smell as sweet," or when Gertrude Stein tells us "A rose is a rose is a rose," these writers do not make new words, but like Reznikoff use the rose as a type: a flower beautiful in its odor; a thing of this world.

The problem of allusion

Blake's "The Sick Rose" carries countless associations for the student of literature. If a contemporary poet wrote now about "the rose's worm"—he would make an **allusion** to "The Sick Rose," almost a quotation. Allusion works with ideas as well as with words. One critic reading Blake's "The Sick Rose" believed that he found an allusion to Shakespeare's line "Lilies that fester smell far worse than weeds." It is now time for us to focus on allusion. Poems can allude to other poems and to history, to ideas, to fact, and to myth. All poems retelling old stories are allusive; a new version of "Casey at the Bat" would be an allusion to the old ballad; a new poem that tells about Oedipus or Hamlet must be based on allusions to the old plays.

Allusion has become a problem for modern readers, because people no longer share the same backgrounds. A century ago, an allusion to the Bible supposed no special knowledge; a century ago, among literate people, it was not obscure to speak of Greek deities like Apollo or Aphrodite; a century ago, even scientific knowledge was commonly held, partly because there was relatively little of it. Now we not only specialize in fields; we find specialties within specialties. The high-energy physicist cannot understand the physicist who studies the behavior of particles at low temperatures.

Allusion is common in poetry, and acts as a barrier to understanding. Sensitivity to allusion in poetry can only grow with extended reading. It is not an element of poetry that can be studied by exercise and thought; it is an element of poetry that can be named and introduced—but then it must be learned and practiced by much reading. No short cut will solve the problem of allusion.

But one short cut, obvious enough, will *help* with certain poems. Here is an **epigram** (a short, pithy poem; see pages 479–480) by Louise Bogan:

To an Artist, to Take Heart

> Slipping in blood, by his own hand, through pride,
> Hamlet, Othello, Coriolanus fall.
> Upon his bed, however, Shakespeare died,
> Having endured them all.

Bogan alludes to three Shakespearean heroes. The names of Hamlet and Othello will be familiar to most American students, though not always the stories that their names allude to. The name of Coriolanus will be new to most.

Reading this poem, the student is forced to a dictionary or a reference book.*
The problem of allusion is often a problem of vocabulary, especially when it is
a matter of proper names. To know that Hamlet is the hero of a play by Shakespeare called *Hamlet*—as a dictionary might tell us—would not help, even with
this brief poem. But if we know enough of the story to remember that Hamlet
died young and by violence, we can begin to understand the allusion and the
poem. We cannot understand the poem without understanding the allusions.

Checking allusions in Louise Bogan's four lines, we learn that Coriolanus's
tragic flaw was pride; we add this fact to Othello's suicide and Hamlet's death
in a duel. We notice that the three phrases of Bogan's first line follow the order
of the three heroes' names in the second line. We understand that the playwright who conceived them lived longer than they did, even if he suffered (*endured* has the connotation of survival with difficulty) and ended by dying in
bed—which is viewed as preferable to violent death.

Because of the difficulties of allusion, certain great and allusive poets are
under-represented in this book, among them Milton, Dryden, and Pope. For
the same reason, it is hard to choose poems that can give fair exercise in
uncovering allusions. The poems that follow, and the questions that go with
them, raise issues largely of symbolism. But not entirely.

Proust's Madeleine

> Somebody has given my
> Baby daughter a box of
> Old poker chips to play with.
> Today she hands me one while
> I am sitting with my tired
> Brain at my desk. It is red.
> On it is a picture of
> An elk's head and the letters
> B.P.O.E.—a chip from
> 10 A small town Elks' Club. I flip
> It idly in the air and
> Catch it and do a coin trick
> To amuse my little girl.

*Earlier this book urged the use of the *Oxford English Dictionary* (page 403). In the pursuit of
allusions, the student can use the whole reference room. For help with the proper names in Bogan's
poem, the *Oxford Companion to English Literature* would perhaps be the best resource, in which
entries for these names summarize plots and tell the tragic flaws of heroes. Oxford also prints a
Companion to American Literature, and *Companions* to the literatures of other languages. The
Oxford Classical Dictionary is very good on mythology, and there are classical dictionaries and
companions from other publishers. The *Readers' Encyclopedia* is a useful volume, as are more
specialized volumes of reference: the *Encyclopedia of American Biography, Webster's Biographical
Dictionary, An Encyclopedia of World History,* and of course the *Encyclopaedia Britannica.* The
New Columbia Encyclopedia is an excellent resource in one volume. Reference librarians will often
point you in the right direction. With certain poets, especially highly allusive poets of the eighteenth
century who refer to their own contemporaries by name and by pseudonym, it is useful to consult the notes of a scholarly edition of the poet's work, where the research has been done
for us.

Suddenly everything slips aside.
I see my father
Doing the very same thing,
Whistling "Beautiful Dreamer,"
His breath smelling richly
Of whiskey and cigars. I can
20   Hear him coming home drunk
From the Elks' Club in Elkhart
Indiana, bumping the
Chairs in the dark. I can see
Him dying of cirrhosis
Of the liver and stomach
Ulcers and pneumonia,
Or, as he said on his deathbed, of
Crooked cards and straight whiskey,
Slow horses and fast women.
                  —Kenneth Rexroth

Questions

1. Where does allusion begin in this poem? List and explain its allusions.
2. Does this poem use any sort of symbol?

Taking the hands of someone you love

Taking the hands of someone you love,
You see they are delicate cages . . .
Tiny birds are singing
In the secluded prairies
And in the deep valleys of the hand.
                  —Robert Bly

Question

Compare this poem with the poem above by Kenneth Rexroth. Does this one invite you to look for symbolism? What sort of symbolism? Why?

The Draft Horse

With a lantern that wouldn't burn
In too frail a buggy we drove
Behind too heavy a horse
Through a pitch-dark limitless grove.

And a man came out of the trees
And took our horse by the head
And reaching back to his ribs
Deliberately stabbed him dead.

The ponderous beast went down
10   With a crack of a broken shaft.

And the night drew through the trees
In one long invidious draft.

The most unquestioning pair
That ever accepted fate
And the least disposed to ascribe
Any more than we had to to hate,

We assumed that the man himself
Or someone he had to obey
Wanted us to get down
20   And walk the rest of the way.
              —*Robert Frost*

Questions

1. Do you take this action literally?
2. Are there natural symbols here? Traditional or conventional symbols?
3. Does this poem make a "new word"? What in this poem gives you the suggestion that it might be symbolic?

The Monument

Now can you see the monument? It is of wood
built somewhat like a box. No. Built
like several boxes in descending sizes
one above the other.
Each is turned half-way round so that
its corners point toward the sides
of the one below and the angles alternate.
Then on the topmost cube is set
a sort of fleur-de-lys of weathered wood,
10   long petals of board, pierced with odd holes,
four-sided, stiff, ecclesiastical.
From it four thin, warped poles spring out,
(slanted like fishing-poles or flag-poles)
and from them jig-saw work hangs down,
four lines of vaguely whittled ornament
over the edges of the boxes
to the ground.
The monument is one-third set against
a sea; two-thirds against a sky.
20   The view is geared
(that is, the view's perspective)
so low there is no "far away,"
and we are far away within the view.
A sea of narrow, horizontal boards
lies out behind our lonely monument,
its long grains alternating right and left
like floor-boards—spotted, swarming-still,

and motionless. A sky runs parallel,
and it is palings, coarser than the sea's:
30   splintery sunlight and long-fibred clouds.
"Why does that strange sea make no sound?
Is it because we're far away?
Where are we? Are we in Asia Minor,
or in Mongolia?"
                              An ancient promontory,
an ancient principality whose artist-prince
might have wanted to build a monument
to mark a tomb or boundary, or make
a melancholy or romantic scene of it . . .
40   "But that queer sea looks made of wood,
half-shining, like a driftwood sea.
And the sky looks wooden, grained with cloud.
It's like a stage-set; it is all so flat!
Those clouds are full of glistening splinters!
What is that?"
                              It is the monument.
"It's piled-up boxes,
outlined with shoddy fret-work, half-fallen off,
cracked and unpainted. It looks old."
50   —The strong sunlight, the wind from the sea,
all the conditions of its existence,
may have flaked off the paint, if ever it was painted,
and made it homelier than it was.
"Why did you bring me here to see it?
A temple of crates in cramped and crated scenery,
what can it prove?
I am tired of breathing this eroded air,
this dryness in which the monument is cracking."

It is an artifact
60   of wood. Wood holds together better
than sea or cloud or sand could by itself,
much better than real sea or sand or cloud.
It chose that way to grow and not to move.
The monument's an object, yet those decorations,
carelessly nailed, looking like nothing at all,
give it away as having life, and wishing;
wanting to be a monument, to cherish something.
The crudest scroll-work says "commemorate,"
while once each day the light goes around it
70   like a prowling animal,
or the rain falls on it, or the wind blows into it.
It may be solid, may be hollow.
The bones of the artist-prince may be inside
or far away on even drier soil.
But roughly but adequately it can shelter

what is within (which after all
cannot have been intended to be seen).
It is the beginning of a painting,
a piece of sculpture, or poem, or monument,
80   and all of wood. Watch it closely.
                              —*Elizabeth Bishop*

Questions

1. Is this a symbolist poem? What lines or words help you decide?
2. What sorts of symbol can you discover in this poem?

The Apparitions

Because there is safety in derision
I talked about an apparition,
I took no trouble to convince,
Or seem plausible to a man of sense,
Distrustful of that popular eye
Whether it be bold or sly.
Fifteen apparitions have I seen;
The worst a coat upon a coat-hanger.

I have found nothing half so good
10   As my long-planned half solitude,
Where I can sit up half the night
With some friend that has the wit
Not to allow his looks to tell
When I am unintelligible.
Fifteen apparitions have I seen;
The worst a coat upon a coat-hanger.

When a man grows old his joy
Grows more deep day after day,
His empty heart is full at length,
20   But he has need of all that strength
Because of the increasing Night
That opens her mystery and fright.
Fifteen apparitions have I seen;
The worst a coat upon a coat-hanger.
                              —*William Butler Yeats*

Questions

1. Note any use of conventional or traditional symbols.
2. Does the image of *a coat upon a coat-hanger* change its implications as it is repeated?
3. Does the poem make a literary symbol?

The Return

See, they return; ah, see the tentative
        Movements, and the slow feet,
        The trouble in the pace and the uncertain
        Wavering!

See they return, one, and by one,
With fear, as half-awakened;
As if the snow should hesitate
And murmur in the wind,
        and half turn back;
10   These were the 'Wing'd-with-Awe,'
        Inviolable.

Gods of the wingèd shoe!
With them the silver hounds,
        sniffing the trace of air!

Haie! Haie!
        These were the swift to harry;
These the keen-scented;
These were the souls of blood.

Slow on the leash,
20   pallid the leash-men!
             —Ezra Pound

Questions

1. Can you find any allusions in this poem?
2. Can you identify *they* in this poem? If you cannot name a definite identity, can you name a kind of action that *they* embody?
3. If the poem is symbolic, what kind of a symbol does it make?

Chapter 7 **The Sound of Poems**

When we explicate a poem, we investigate its sound as well as its symbol, its shape and architecture as well as its paraphrase and implication. Talking about William Carlos Williams's wheelbarrow poem, we looked at the poem as artifact, as made object. This chapter concentrates on the pleasures poems make by their sound.

There are at least two distinct pleasures we derive from the sound of language in poetry. One is the pleasure of *rhythm*, of words in motion, uncoiling in sentences from poetic line to line. Here is the beginning of *Paradise Lost* by John Milton:

> Of man's first disobedience, and the fruit
> Of that forbidden tree, whose mortal taste
> Brought death into the world, and all our woe,
> With loss of Eden, till one greater Man
> Restore us, and regain the blissful seat,
> Sing, Heavenly Muse . . .

The pleasure of rhythm is like the pleasure of dancing, or of tapping our feet to keep time with music, and it recalls primitive origins of poetry where song and poem and dance happened together. This rhythm-pleasure of poetry's sound connects with our pleasure in bodily motion.

The other pleasure is the delight that we take in adjacent sounds rubbing together, vowels held and savored, consonants clicking together. Here are some lines from "To Autumn" by John Keats:

Then in a wailful choir the small gnats mourn
  Among the river sallows,° borne aloft   willows
    Or sinking as the light wind lives or dies; . . .

Rhythm and linebreak

First, let us look at rhythm. The lines of a poem are essential to its signature and its identity. Milton broke some of his lines where the meaning paused, as with

Brought death into the world, and all our woe . . .

When the sense pauses or stops at the end of a line we call it **end-stopped**. Most of the time, Milton broke his lines in the middle of a phrase, so that the sense of the sentence ran over into the line following, as with

With loss of Eden, till one greater Man
Restore us . . .

When the sense runs over the end of a line we call the line enjambed, and the practice **enjambment**.

Even when a line is enjambed, it retains its identity as a line of poetry, and reading it aloud we make a slight pause at the end. Or we show the line-end in another way, by raising our voice perhaps, or by holding onto the last syllable. We do not pause evenly—we pause longer when the line is end-stopped—but we find some means to show with our voices that we have come to the end of a line. If we do not, we might as well be reading prose. One eighteenth-century critic with no ear suggested that we print Milton as prose or that we re-break his lines according to phrases or sense, which could make the first lines of *Paradise Lost* look like this:

Of man's first disobedience
and the fruit
of that forbidden tree
whose mortal taste
brought death
into the world
and all our woe,
with loss of Eden,
till one greater Man
restore us,
and regain
the blissful seat,
sing
Heavenly Muse . . .

How boring and flat the lines become! There can be little attention to pauses within lines, because the critic would break the line wherever there might be a pause. There is no tension; music and sense become identical, which results in the disappearance of music.

We must develop a sense of the poetic line if we are to take pleasure in poetry. Here are lines by Louis Simpson:

> Caesar Augustus
> In his time lay
> Dying, and just as
> Cold as they,
> On the cold morning
> Of a cold day.

These lines lose their pleasure, as well as their dance and their power, if we space them according to the phrases of their sense:

> Caesar Augustus
> In his time lay dying
> And just as cold as they
> On the cold morning
> Of a cold day.

And as prose it disappears completely: "Caear Augustus in his time lay dying and just as cold as they on the cold morning of a cold day."
(The complete poem is on pages 467–468.)

The examples we have looked at use rhyme and meter, subjects of the next chapter. With free verse, which lacks any regular beat, the line becomes the major way of organizing sound. Here is a stanza from a free-verse poem by John Haines, "And When the Green Man Comes," revised into phrase-unit lines:

> His eyes are blind with April,
> his breath distilled
> of butterflies and bees,
> and in his beard the maggot sings.

Here it is with the lines broken arbitrarily, *not* as the poet broke them in his finished poem:

> His eyes are
> blind with April, his
> breath
> distilled of
> butterflies and
> bees, and in
> his beard the
> maggot sings.

The first version is boring, the second jagged or nervous. Here is the stanza as Haines actually wrote it:

> His eyes are blind
> with April,
> his breath distilled
> of butterflies
> and bees, and in his beard
> the maggot sings.

Notice how the organized rhythm of the last version calls attention to sound; putting *eyes* and *blind* together in a short line, for instance, repeats the long *ais*. Notice as well the repetition of *l*s, in the last syllable of each of the first four lines.

Sounds can exist for their own sakes—and because they can, sounds organize emphasis. *blind / with April* and *distilled / of butterflies* share a syntactic structure, but instead of ending at the same place, one of the two clauses continues *of butterflies / and bees*. Syntax and linebreak combine to isolate, in the last line of the stanza, the significant conclusion: *the maggot sings.* My earlier linebreaks, falsifying the poem, obscured or invalidated these possibilities.

Some free-verse poems use a long line in which the linebreak seldom interrupts the sense. They are all end-stopped. Take these lines by Walt Whitman, from "Song of Myself":

> I think I could turn and live with animals, they're so placid and self-contain'd,
> I stand and look at them long and long.
>
> They do not sweat and whine about their condition,
> They do not lie awake in the dark and weep for their sins,
> They do not make me sick discussing their duty to God,
> Not one is dissatisfied, not one is demented with the mania of owning things,
> Not one kneels to another, nor to his kind that lived thousands of years ago,
> Not one is respectable or unhappy over the whole earth.

If one printed these lines as prose, in paragraph form, one would lose the slow pace that the long lines give. On the other hand, one could slow the pace into absolute boredom by breaking the lines at the commas, making them shorter:

> I think I could turn and live
> with animals,
> they're so placid
> and self-contain'd.
> I stand and look at them
> long and long.
>
> They do not sweat and whine
> about their condition.

They do not lie awake in the dark
and weep for their sins.
They do not make me sick
discussing their duty to God.
Not one is dissatisfied.
Not one is demented
with the mania
of owning things.
Not one kneels to another
nor to his kind
that lived thousands of years ago.
Not one is respectable
or unhappy
over the whole earth.

In this mistreatment, I have reduced the various pauses—commas, shorter pauses between whole phrases, lone line-end pauses—into one sort of pause. We should be grateful for Whitman's generous line, which makes a satisfying rhythm within itself—and not only by its motion from line to line. A pause within the line is called a **caesura**, and is shown by a pair of vertical lines ||. Whitman's lines include many pauses or caesuras. In a shorter line like Milton's we do not have so many, but we can often find an obvious place to pause, sometimes shown by punctuation:

Of man's first disobedience, || and the fruit

and sometimes not, as in Keats's line:

Or sinking || as the light wind lifts or dies . . .

Poets work with a variety of pauses, at the ends of lines and inside them, which contribute to the rhythm of the poetic line.

Here are some exercises possibly suited for out-loud performance in the classroom.

Exercises

1. Following is a passage from *Antony and Cleopatra*, done Shakespeare's way and as two actors with differing interpretations might have done it. Notice which lines are enjambed, which end-stopped, in the first passage. Discuss the difference the linebreaks make in the three versions.

   a. The barge she sat in, like a burnished throne,
   Burned on the water: the poop was beaten gold;
   Purple the sails, and so perfumèd that
   The winds were love-sick with them; the oars were silver,
   Which to the tune of flutes kept stroke, and made
   The water which they beat to follow faster.

b.   The barge she sat in
     like a burnished throne
     burned on the water.
     The poop was beaten gold,
     purple the sails,
     and so perfumèd
     that the winds
     were love-sick with them.
     The oars were silver,
     which to the flutes kept stroke
     and made the water
     which they beat
     to follow faster.

c.   The barge
     she sat in like
     a burnished throne burned on the
     water the poop was
     beaten
     gold purple the
     sails and so perfumèd that the winds
     were love-

     . . .

     sick
     with
     them
     the oars were silver which to the tune of flutes kept stroke and made the water
     which they beat to
     follow
     faster.

2. Here are three versions of a free-verse poem by William Carlos Williams. Which is the poet's? Which is the least pleasing lineation?

a.   As the cat climbed
     over the top of

     the jamcloset first
     the right forefoot

     carefully then the
     hind stepped down

     into the pit of the
     empty flower pot

b.   As the cat
     climbed over
     the top of

     the jamcloset
     first the right
     forefoot

     carefully
     then the hind
     stepped down

into the pit of
the empty
flowerpot

c. As the cat climbed
over the top
of the jamcloset
first the right
forefoot carefully
then the hind
stepped down
into the pit
of the empty
flower pot

Vowels and consonants

To enjoy the intimate sounds of poems, we take pleasure in savoring words and parts of words. This pleasure does not exclude meanings but it can exist for its own sake. Sometimes we enjoy tripping along with nonsense sounds, as when Yeats makes a line of "fol, de rol, de rolly o," or Shakespeare mixes words and sounds: "With a hey, ho, the wind and the rain."

Alliteration is the repetition of consonant sounds, especially at the beginning of words. When Wallace Stevens writes "In kitchen cups concupiscent curds," he keeps our tongues flicking at the roofs of our mouths.

Assonance is the repetition of vowel sounds—"beside the white"; "glazed with rain." We take pleasure in holding onto vowels which remind us of each other. The last line of Hardy's "During Wind and Rain" shows interlocking assonance and alliteration:

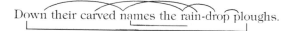

Down their carved names the rain-drop ploughs.

The two syllables at the beginning and end of the line contain the same *ow* vowel sound; in the middle of the line, there is the long *a* of *names* and the long *a* of *rain*. In addition, the lines repeat the *n* of *down*, *names*, and *rain*; the *r* of *carved*, *rain*, and *drop*; the *p* of *drop* and *ploughs*.

Poets typically ascend to assonance, holding long vowels, when their poems are most exalted, as when Hardy ends his lyric. When Keats wrote his odes— more than in his other poems—he especially delighted in repeating vowels and consonants. This stanza is from "Ode to a Nightingale":

I cannot see what flowers are at my feet,
    Nor what soft incense hangs upon the boughs,
But, in embalmèd darkness, guess each sweet
    Wherewith the seasonable month endows
The grass, the thicket, and the fruit-tree wild—

> White hawthorn, and the pastoral eglantine;
>   Fast-fading violets covered up in leaves;
>   And mid-May's eldest child,
>   The coming musk-rose, full of dewy wine,
> 10   The murmurous haunt of flies on summer eves.

In the first line Keats mixes assonance and alliteration. The vowels of *see* and *feet* are identical, while *flowers* and *feet* begin with the same consonant. The consonant sound of *th* repeats softly through lines 4 to 6: *Wherewith, the* (four times), *month, thicket,* and *hawthorn.* Two of the sets of rhyme words have the same long *ai*: wild, eglantine, child, wine. The identical **diphthong** (a double vowel, this one composed of *ah* and *ee*) occurs elsewhere within the lines: *White, violets, flies.*

It is not a requirement of great poetry that sounds be so gorgeous. Frost is *never* so ornate, in his alliteration or his assonance, as Keats in the odes. Frost's attention dotes on rhythm, linebreak, on the happy and continuous tension between sentence and line. Here are poems for sound study.

New Year's Day

> Again and then again . . . the year is born
>
> To ice and death, and it will never do
>
> To skulk behind storm-windows by the stove
>
> To hear the postgirl sounding her French horn
>
> When the thin tidal ice is wearing through.
>
> Here is the understanding not to love
>
> Each other, or tomorrow that will sieve
>
> Our resolutions. While we live, we live
>
> To snuff the smoke of victims. In the snow
>
> 10 The kitten heaved its hindlegs, as if fouled,
>
> And died. We bent it in a Christmas box
>
> And scattered blazing weeds to scare the crow
>
> Until the snake-tailed sea-winds coughed and howled
>
> For alms outside the church whose double locks
>
> Wait for St. Peter, the distorted key.
>
> Under St. Peter's bell the parish sea

Swells with its smelt into the burlap shack

Where Joseph plucks his hand-lines like a harp,

And hears the fearful *Puer natus est*[1]

20   Of Circumcision, and relives the wrack

And howls of Jesus whom he holds. How sharp

The burden of the Law before the beast:

Time and the grindstone and the knife of God.

The Child is born in blood, O child of blood.

—*Robert Lowell*

[1]The Child is born

Questions

1. At the end of each line, write either S (for end-stopped) or E (for enjambed).
2. What one consonant is most often repeated at the beginnings of words in this poem? Can you discover further alliteration?
3. In the next-to-last line, what vowel sound dominates?

I Wake and Feel the Fell of Dark

I wake and feel the fell of dark, not day.

What hours, O what black hours we have spent

This night! what sights you, heart, saw; ways you went!

And more must, in yet longer light's delay.

With witness I speak this. But where I say

Hours I mean years, mean life. And my lament

Is cries countless, cries like dead letters sent

To dearest him that lives alas! away.

I am gall, I am heartburn. God's most deep decree

10   Bitter would have me taste: my taste was me;

Bones built in me, flesh filled, blood brimmed the curse.

Selfyeast of spirit a dull dough sours. I see

The lost are like this, and their scourge to be

As I am mine, their sweating selves; but worse.

—*Gerard Manley Hopkins*

Questions

1. Underline the alliteration in this poem.
2. Letter each line as end-stopped (S) or enjambed (E).

The Dalliance of the Eagles

Skirting the river road, (my forenoon walk, my rest,)

Skyward in air a sudden muffled sound, the dalliance of the eagles,

The rushing amorous contact high in space together,

The clinching interlocking claws, a living, fierce, gyrating wheel,

Four beating wings, two beaks, a swirling mass tight grappling,

In tumbling turning clustering loops, straight downward falling,

Till o'er the river pois'd, the twain yet one, a moment's lull,

A motionless still balance in the air, then parting, talons loosing,

Upward again on slow-firm pinions slanting, their separate diverse flight,

10   She hers, he his, pursuing.

—*Walt Whitman*

Questions

1. In this poem, mark the pauses within the line (caesuras) with a double line.
2. Note any alliteration or assonance.

To Autumn

I

Season of mists and mellow fruitfulness,

   Close bosom friend of the maturing sun,

Conspiring with him how to load and bless

   With fruit the vines that round the thatch-eaves run:

To bend with apples the mossed cottage-trees,

   And fill all fruit with ripeness to the core;

      To swell the gourd, and plump the hazel shells

   With a sweet kernel; to set budding more,

And still more, later flowers for the bees,

10   Until they think warm days will never cease,

      For summer has o'er-brimmed their clammy cells.

II

Who hath not seen thee oft amid thy store?

   Sometimes whoever seeks abroad may find

Thee sitting careless on a granary floor,

   Thy hair soft-lifted by the winnowing wind;

Or on a half-reaped furrow sound asleep,

   Drowsed with the fume of poppies, while thy hook

      Spares the next swath and all its twinèd flowers;

And sometimes like a gleaner thou dost keep

20   Steady thy laden head across a brook;

Or by a cider-press, with patient look,

   Thou watchest the last oozings, hours by hours.

III

Where are the songs of spring? Ay, where are they?

   Think not of them, thou hast thy music too—

While barrèd clouds bloom the soft-dying day,

   And touch the stubble-plains with rosy hue.

Then in a wailful choir the small gnats mourn

   Among the river sallows,° borne aloft   willows

      Or sinking as the light wind lives or dies;

30 And full-grown lambs loud bleat from hilly bourn;

   Hedge-crickets sing; and now with treble soft

The redbreast whistles from a garden-croft;

   And gathering swallows twitter in the skies.

                                        —*John Keats*

Question

Make curved marks over the lines showing the interconnections of alliteration; underneath the lines, make angular marks to connect assonances. (See the markings on a line by Thomas Hardy, page 452.)

Chapter 8 **Meter and Rhyme**

"Meter and Rhyme" is examined separately from "The Sound of Poetry" to make a point. From all poems we demand pleasing sound. All good poems are formal: the poem's words, and their order and arrangement, must seem inevitable and immovable. In some poems, meter and rhyme provide specialized means toward these ends. Now we must define meter, distinguishing it from rhythm, and exemplifying its use by poets in the English tradition. Because rhyme is a separate device, and because meter and rhyme can each occur without the other, we will treat rhyme separately later in the chapter.

Meter

English meter is a count of syllables, usually syllables in pairs of which one is louder than the other.

Meter is not the same as rhythm. Meter is numbers or counting; rhythm is a vaguer word, implying an approximate recurrence or repetition in the pacing of sound; rhythm is fast or slow, staccato or flowing. Words describing rhythm are imprecise, because rhythm cannot accept precise description. We compare rhythm to a liquid when we call it flowing, or to a broken solid when we call it jagged. The last chapter devoted space to rhythm in the poetic line, and contrasted the rhythm of Milton's metrical line with the rhythm of the same words broken into different lines; then it made the same contrast with free verse, using poems by John Haines and Walt Whitman (pages 448–450). In each example the poet's rhythms, deployed in lines, were pleasing to the ear. The same words, broken into other lines, made monotonous or unpleasing rhythms. When we read poems, we invariably perceive rhythm: in a good poem, the rhythm is pleasurable—and from time to time it is even expressive. In a bad poem, the rhythm tends to be weak, prosaic, boring, and without expressive function. Poems in free verse and poems in meter both have rhythm; in either metrical verse or free verse, rhythms may be good or bad.

Meter is numbers, or counting, as we have noted already. The word comes from a Greek word, *metron*, which means "measure"—like a yardstick or the metric system. Meter is a count of something we can hear.

Each language has its own genius, and in English the common meter (known by various names) counts relative loudness and softness of syllables.

Relative stress

In order to hear English meter, you must be able to distinguish relative loudness, which is also called *stress* or *accent*. Within a word that has more than one syllable, one syllable is louder than the rest. We speak of proNOUNcing a word, not of PROnouncing or of pronounCING it. In pronouncing the words of our own language, we have memorized a pattern of loudness. When we say conTENT our listeners know we are not speaking of CONtent, because we make two different words depending on which of the syllables we pronounce more loudly.

Practice your sense of relative loudness. Everyone knows how to pronounce the words that follow; everyone saying them aloud will put the **accent** at the right place. (Accent means prominence; in our language, accent is mostly achieved by relative volume. Sometimes greater length or pitch variation is *added* to volume for the sake of accentuation.) But not everyone, in his head, can name what it is he is doing when he pronounces correctly. Pronounce each of these words; then decide which of the two syllables is louder.

depict	necktie
hammer	destroy
cowbell	dispatch
rampart	debris
nugget	dental
neglect	

Try these words of three and more syllables:

memory	implement
rambunctious	implementation
amaryllis	compliment
reputation	comprehend
dangerous	

Three-syllable words which take their major accent on the first or the third syllable carry a minor accent on the syllable at the word's other end. In MEM-or-y, *mem* is the accentuated syllable, but the little *-y* at the end is louder, at least, than the *-or-* in the middle. The opposite arrangement works with com-pre-HEND. A word like ar-RANGE-ment, with the accent in the middle, shows no minor accent. (Minor accent is sometimes called secondary stress.) These habits of three-syllable words become important in metrical poems.

Iambic pentameter: the foot

For examples, let's start with the English ten-syllable line, arranged as **iambic pentameter**, the most common meter in great English poems. An **iambic foot** in English is a softer syllable followed by a louder one. *Pentameter* translates as "five-measure." Therefore, typical iambic pentameter is five groups of two syllables, the second syllable in each group louder than the first. When we scan—or put marks to indicate the meter of a line—we put bars to separate the feet of the line, making the typical line ⌣⁄ | ⌣⁄ | ⌣⁄ | ⌣⁄ | ⌣⁄ | : these bars erect a figurative barrier between the feet to emphasize that stress is relative (and relevant) *only within the foot.*

The ⌣⁄ | ⌣⁄ | ⌣⁄ | ⌣⁄ | ⌣⁄ | shows the counting which remains constant, which assures that the verse remains metrical. But while the counting, or **scansion**, stays the same, the rhythm can vary considerably. After all, ⌣⁄ | ⌣⁄ | ⌣⁄ | ⌣⁄ | ⌣⁄ | could contain ten monosyllables or two polysyllables; it could be fast, it could be slow; it could contain a period, the end of one sentence and the start of another; it could contain many commas, caesuras slowing the line, or it could contain no punctuation at all and move more quickly. The ⌣⁄ | ⌣⁄ | ⌣⁄ | ⌣⁄ | ⌣⁄ | tells us very little of what the line will sound like; it shows meter, not rhythm, five relative hills and five relative valleys. The hills at one point in the line may be lower in elevation than the valleys in another part of the line. "Bang *bang*, bang *bang*, bang *bang*, bang *bang*, bang *bang*" fulfills the pattern. (We can bang this out on the desk top, every even bang louder than every odd one.) But "The University of Michigan" also fulfills the pattern. Say it slowly, exaggerating a little, and you can hear it: "The U-ni-VER-sit-Y of MICH-i-GAN." If you try saying "THE u-NI-ver-SI-ty OF Mich-I-gan," you do not pronounce our language.

The scansion ⌣⁄ | ⌣⁄ | ⌣⁄ | ⌣⁄ | ⌣⁄ |, common to many lines different in rhythm, describes an expectation the mind develops from reading thousands of lines of poetry—iambic pentameter means, or translates, "the only thing which *all* these lines have in common."

Terms for feet and for length of line

In the examples we shall continue to concentrate on the iambic foot, most often in the pentameter line. Because we occasionally encounter other meters it is useful to know terms for the most common feet and lengths of lines.

Some types of feet:

Iambic: a softer syllable followed by a louder: *des*PAIR   ⌣⁄
Trochaic: a louder syllable followed by a softer: HAPPy   ⁄⌣
Dactylic: a louder syllable followed by two softer ones: CHANGE*able*   ⁄⌣⌣
Anapestic: two softer syllables followed by a louder one: *in the* HOUSE   ⌣⌣⁄

Some lengths of lines:

Monometer: one foot
Dimeter: two feet
Trimeter: three feet
Tetrameter: four feet
Pentameter: five feet
Hexameter (or the Alexandrine): six feet

Rhythmical variety within metrical regularity

Within absolute metrical regularity, every line scanning ˘ / | ˘ / | ˘ / | ˘ / | ˘ / |, iambic pentameter can find all the variety it wants or needs. It need never depart from this scheme for variety's sake. Iambic pentameter finds most of its variety in playing upon the relativity of stress. Seldom in our literature do you find a line as evenly stressed as bang *bang*, or as "The man who stole the bread was making toast." "The University of Michigan," which has only two really loud noises, is more typical of iambic pentameter. Here is the beginning of Keats's "The Eve of St. Agnes":

St. Ăg | nĕs Eve— | Ah, bĭt | tĕr chĭll | ĭt wăs . . .

The first line scans exactly as our example does, ˘ / | ˘ / | ˘ / | ˘ / | ˘ / |. There is a pause after the fourth syllable, a rhythmical fact the meter does not count. All the even-numbered syllables are louder than all the odd-numbered syllables in this line, and in this particular line, the "louder" sounds are almost equal to each other. The last syllable, *was*, is probably a little softer than the second, fourth, sixth, or eighth syllables—a fact that is part of the rhythm of the line but is irrelevant to its meter. The second line reads:

Thĕ owl, | fŏr all | hĭs feath | ĕrs, was | ă-cold;

which again scans like the pattern. Two caesuras after the second and the seventh syllables contribute rhythmical variation. Of the five relatively loud syllables, creating the five feet, three are *quite* loud; two are not so loud as the other three, but still louder than their proximate neighbors *all* and *was*. So the variations in true loudness, small as they are, make rhythmical variety, while the sameness of relative loudness makes metrical identity. In the third line,

Thĕ hare | lĭmp'd tremb | lĭng through | thĕ fro | zĕn grass,

we have another line that scans typically—but this line varies considerably in rhythm from the earlier two. For instance, *through* is louder than the *-ing* of *trembling*, and thus *-ing through* makes a regular foot of relative stress, but *through* is not truly loud at all; its softness—which remains louder than its neighbor—is *metrically* irrelevant, and *rhythmically* pleasing by providing variety. In the first half of this line, the second, third, and fourth syllables are all quite loud. Bang, bang, bang. I do not mean that they are *equally* loud; it would be absurd to suggest that they were each pronounced with an equal number of decibels. But they are all louder than the *through* that takes metrical stress later in the line.

But they cannot be louder than each other. English meter uses *relative* stress, and we can expect that the first loud syllable (the second syllable in the line) is louder than the first soft syllable; the line begins with a regular iamb. Then we have two loud syllables together, *limp'd tremb-*, and in English we would expect that one of the two—the second, if the poem appears iambic— can easily and naturally be spoken more loudly than the first. And so it can.

The order of these four syllables, as a reader says them, may climb four steps of increasing volume, each syllable a little louder than the one before it. If that is so, then *limp'd*—a softer syllable in the meter of the line—would in fact be louder than *hare*—a louder syllable in the meter of the whole line. *Because an invisible foot-separator comes between the two syllables, the relative loudness of* hare *and* limp'd *is metrically irrelevant.*

Keats's fourth line is more like his second line:

And si | lent was | the flock | in wool | ly fold . . .

Was is not very loud, but it is relatively loud. Nowhere else in the line is there metrical ambiguity or a rhythmical variation.

Thus English meter, by shrewd use of relativity, can find rhythmical variation without changing the number of syllables in a line, and without changing the order of louder and softer syllables. Once we have read a few thousand lines with a typical swing of louder and softer, we have an expectation in our heads through which we perceive and sort out the syllables on the page. Meter is what lines have in common. If you were asked to scan the single line:

Rocks, caves, lakes, fens, bogs, dens, and shades of death

you would be right to refuse. But if you came upon this line deep in Milton's *Paradise Lost*, when you had learned to step to the tune of iambic pentameter, you would sort it by twos, giving a sharp beat like a foot tap to the even-numbered syllables:

Rocks, *caves*, lakes, *fens*, bogs, *dens*, and *shades* of *death* . . .

You would not sort it (as you could have done if the words had turned up in a prose paragraph) by threes, for instance:

Rocks, caves, *lakes*, bogs, fens, *dens*, and *shades* of *death* . . .

The reading dictated by meter allows large latitude—there can be different heights to these peaks and valleys—but meter imposes limits to its latitude: a peak remains peakish, relative to an adjacent valley.

The Miltonic line gives us an example of iambic pentameter which finds rhythmic variation by adding more volume. It has *more* loud noises in the line than we expect, though it retains only five relative stresses. More commonly, lines like "The University of Michigan" contain *fewer* loud noises than five. Scholars tell us that Shakespeare's pentameter averages about three loud noises a line—and, *not by average but always*, five relative stresses. In *Macbeth*

> Tomorrow and tomorrow and tomorrow . . .

makes a typical Shakespearean line. The three -*mor*-s, middles of three *tomorrows*, make three loud noises, each louder than the syllable in front of it, the three *to*s. The two *and*s are not loud, but they are louder than the -*ow*s which come before them, thus adding up to the five iambics of the pentameter.

Metrical variations

There are several common departures from the ˘′ | ˘′ | ˘′ | ˘′ | ˘′ | scheme, departures that are not irregularities; we call them metrical variations—they are variations *within* meter, not outside it—and we will talk about them in the order of their frequency. As they are used, they contribute to the variety of metrical verse.

Initial inversion   By far the most common metrical variation is reversal of the order of louder and softer syllables in one foot. This happens most frequently in the first foot in the line and is called **initial inversion.**

Suppose you have read a hundred lines that share ˘′ | ˘′ | ˘′ | ˘′ | ˘′ | . Then you come on a line beginning with a loud syllable—maybe a two-syllable word that can only be pronounced with the louder syllable first, like *studies*. The beginning of this line reverses for one second the order of louder and softer, only to return immediately to the old and expected order. This line with initial inversion scans ′˘ | ˘′ | ˘′ | ˘′ | ˘′ | . Look at this sample:

> Thĕ Ú | nĭvér | sĭtý | ŏf Mĭch | ĭgán
> Stúdiĕs | thĕ pó | ĕtrý | ŏf Keáts | ănd Fróst.

The little rhythmical turn at the beginning of the second line becomes a familiar dance step in the motion of metrical poetry in English: a little whirl, a sudden tipping-over and recovery, *bang* bang-bang *bang*. The movement can remind us of one of those large dolls children play with, weighted on the round bottom, which a child will push over and which will then immediately right itself. When Macbeth has said "Tomorrow and tomorrow and tomorrow," he continues,

> Creéps ĭn | thĭs pét | tў páce | frŏm dáy | tŏ dáy . . .

and it is clear that *in* is softer than *Creeps*. Although the remainder of this line scans like the pattern, the first foot is inverted—and the expectation that this foot *may* be inverted lurks in the head of the reader. Shakespeare, Milton, Keats, Frost—metrical poets use initial variation frequently. After Keats wrote

"And silent was the flock in woolly fold," his next line made the dance-step of initial inversion:

> Numb wĕre | thĕ beáds | man's fíng | ĕrs, whíle | hĕ tóld . . .

and the next lines returned to regular motion:

> His rosary, and while his frosted breath
> Like pious incense from a censor old . . .

Medial inversion Less frequent than initial inversion is inversion elsewhere in the line, which is called **medial inversion** wherever it comes. Medial inversion makes its own pause, wherever it happens in the line; most medial inversions therefore take place after natural caesuras, often indicated by commas or other marks of punctuation:

> She said to me: open your book and read!

Open your book is that little dance-step of inversion again, now in the middle of the line. In "The Eve of St. Agnes," Keats makes this line:

> Frŏm húr | rў tó | and fró. | Soón, ŭp | ălóft . . .

Soon is louder than its neighboring *up*. After the pause for the end of the preceding sentence, Keats has started a new thought with a medial inversion.

Even if the line lacks a natural caesura, medial inversion will make a pause. In Theodore Roethke's "My Papa's Waltz," the poet makes a sudden medial inversion (with an iambic trimeter line, three feet, not five):

> Yŏu béat | tíme ŏn | mў heád . . .

The slight awkwardness of the enforced pause between *beat* and *time* sounds just right for someone beating time on a small boy's head.

Feminine endings After inversion, the most common metrical variation is the extra syllable. Shakespeare's line

> Tomorrow and tomorrow and tomorrow . . .

is regular iambic. But it has eleven syllables, with an extra syllable at the end of the line, called a **feminine ending.** The extra syllable dangles into the pause at the end of the line. It does not feel like a variation, although it varies in fact from the basic scheme. We scan it ˘′ | ˘′ | ˘′ | ˘′ | ˘′˘ |. Robert Frost's blank verse has many feminine endings, as in "The Death of the Hired Man":

> Hĕ búnd | lĕs év | erў fórk | fŭl ín | tŏ pláce
> And tágs | and númb | ĕrs ít | fŏr fúr | thĕr réferĕnce
> Sŏ hé | căn fínd | and eás | ĭlў | dislódge ĭt.

The last two lines have feminine endings, providing you pronounce *reference* with two syllables, as Frost did.

Extra syllables   An extra syllable elsewhere in the line—or in the final foot *before* the last stress—is a palpable metrical variation. The extra syllable makes a second softer syllable, a foot of three syllables, which scans ⌣⌣′. Again in "The Death of the Hired Man," Frost writes:

> You never see him standing on the hay
> He's trying to lift, straining to lift himself.

Practice scanning these lines. In the second line, the meter begins easily enough with an iambic, *He's trý-*; the line ends with three feet that start with a medial inversion: *stráining | to líft | himsélf*. In between these two clumps we have the three syllables of an extra-syllabic foot: *-ing to líft*. You may notice that these three syllables are quick to say, occupying no more elapsed time than two syllables elsewhere in the line. Three-syllable feet in an iambic poem tend to be quick to say.

When metrical poetry sounds most conversational and speechlike (in later Shakespeare, in Robert Frost) we find most extra syllables and feminine endings.

Exercises

1. To mark the meter of a line, as we have done in the text, is to *scan*—the result called *scansion*, as we have seen. Scan the following poems, drawing vertical lines to separate the feet, and showing which syllables are louder, which softer.

from *Richard II*

> Let's talk of graves, of worms, and epitaphs,
>
> Make dust our paper, and with rainy eyes
>
> Write sorrow on the bosom of the earth . . .
>
> For God's sake, let us sit upon the ground,
>
> And tell sad stories of the death of kings:
>
> How some have been deposed; some slain in war;
>
> Some haunted by the ghosts they have deposed;
>
> Some poisoned by their wives; some sleeping killed;
>
> All murdered: for within the hollow crown
>
> 10   That rounds the mortal temples of a king
>
> Keeps Death his court; and there the antick sits,

Scoffing his state, and grinning at his pomp;

Allowing him a breath, a little scene,

To monarchize, be feared, and kill with looks;

Infusing him with self and vain conceit—

As if this flesh which walls about our life,

Were brass impregnable; and humoured thus,

Comes at the last, and with a little pin

Bores through his castle-wall, and—farewell king!

—William Shakespeare

To the Western World

A siren sang, and Europe turned away

From the high castle and the shepherd's crook.

Three caravels went sailing to Cathay

On the strange ocean, and the captains shook

Their banners out across the Mexique Bay.

And in our early days we did the same.

Remembering our fathers in their wreck

We crossed the sea from Palos where they came

And saw, enormous to the little deck,

10   A shore in silence waiting for a name.

The treasures of Cathay were never found.

In this America, this wilderness

Where the axe echoes with a lonely sound,

The generations labor to possess

And grave by grave we civilize the ground.

—Louis Simpson

2. The following examples, fabricated for this text, include metrical errors. Assume that they come from poems which have established themselves as iambic pentameter.

a. Ridiculous impoverishments of gold
   Adorn her throat, where jealousy was often told.

b. The dance of death, begun in August air,
   Regales the Autumn and the fair.

c. Harsh moments fail the resplendent flesh of
   Doorjambs heavy, gilt, worn, and repulsive.

Rhyme

Rhyme is a feature common to many metrical poems, not to all. **Blank verse** is iambic pentameter without rhyme; rhyme is what it is blank of. (Do not confuse blank verse with free verse. Free verse, which is free of meters, occasionally has rhyme.) The most common rhyme is the exact repetition, in two or more words, of the final vowel and consonants of a word. *Love*, as we all know, rhymes with *dove*. Here *-ove* is the unity, *l* and *d* the variety.

Direct rhyme

Look at a rhyming dictionary, and you may be astonished at the variety of rhymes available. Suppose I am writing a rhymed poem and am stuck for a rhyme with the word *decrease*. Probably I would find the right word in my head, but if I didn't I could look in *The Complete Rhyming Dictionary and Poet's Craft Book*, edited by Clement Wood, and find under the sound *ees* fifty-nine possible words, beginning: afterpiece/ambergris/battlepiece/Bereneice/Bernice/cantatrice/caprice/cease/surrice/chimney-piece/Clarisse/coulease/crease . . . If I were rhyming on two or more syllables, **feminine rhyme**, I would find in another list: accretion/completion/concretion/deletion; for three-syllable rhyme, I would go to another list: credulous/sedulous. These examples are **direct rhyme**.

Indirect rhyme

Sometimes poets use **indirect rhyme** or **off-rhyme**, almost-but-not-quite directly rhyming. Rhyme/line, for instance, is indirect because the consonants though similar are not the same. In rhyme/spice, the vowels rhyme but the consonants differ; this example is also indirect rhyme, but the degree of indirectness is greater. Another poet might rhyme consonants and let the vowels fend for themselves: rhyme/lame/: goat/bleet. Emily Dickinson used indirect rhyme on many occasions, often rhyming open vowels together, vowels similar but not the same:

> The Silence condescended—
> Creation stopped—for Me—
> But awed beyond my errand—
> I worshipped—did not "pray"—

If you hold on to the vowel ending *pray*, its diphthong separates out into an *a* and an *e*. The *e* you end by holding rhymes with *Me*. Dickinson also rhymes consonants:

I cannot live with You—
It would be Life—
And Life is over there—
Behind the Shelf.

Cliché rhyme

When poets rhyme *love* with *dove*, they make a **cliché rhyme**. Other cliché rhymes include fire/desire, breath/death, and womb/tomb. Occasionally good poets get away with cliché rhyme, because their syntax or sense makes the second of the cliché rhymes somehow unexpected. Most times a cliché rhyme is a flaw in a poem. This is not an important tool in evaluating poems, but a way to look at what happens in rhyming. These rhymes are cliché not only because they have been used so often, but also because the words resemble each other: in the list above, each of the examples can be a noun, and all but one are monosyllables. Each belongs to the same level of diction. Most important, each recalls its mate by similarity or opposition of meaning. Fire is a symbol of desire. Breath is ended by death. What begins in the womb ends in the tomb. For all these reasons, the first word of each pair leads one to expect the second, and when expectation is exactly fulfilled, the result is boredom. A poem must balance the predictable with the unpredictable, expectation with surprise, unity with variety.

Original rhyme

In a rhyme, the unity is the repetition of sound; the variety is all the other differences two words can muster. For instance, words can differ in length, and we can rhyme a monosyllable with a polysyllable, like *tracks* with *haversacks*. We can rhyme words spelled differently, like *tracks* with *axe*. We can rhyme different parts of speech, a verb *hacks* with a noun *jacks*. We can rhyme words of different backgrounds, like *egomaniacs* with *humpbacks*,or *kleptomaniacs* with *packs*. We can rhyme combinations of alien words: Jack's/hypochondriacs/ kayaks/quacks. In feminine rhyme, we can pair two words with one, rhyming *pluck it* with *Nantucket*.

The further apart the words are, the more original the rhyme. At extremes, rhyme can be witty or comic. In one of his poems Ogden Nash uses a *boom-erang* for hunting in order to cook a *kangaroo meringue*. Witty rhyme would be inappropriate to many poems, in which neither poet nor reader would want rhyme to stand out and be noticeable apart from the poem's other qualities. Highly original rhyme is appropriate in this poem:

Early in the Morning

Early in the morning
The dark Queen said,
"The trumpets are warning
There's trouble ahead."
Spent with carousing,

With wine-soaked wits,
Antony drowsing
Whispered, "It's
Too cold a morning
10   To get out of bed."

The army's retreating,
The fleet has fled,
Caesar is beating
His drums through the dead.
"Antony, horses!
We'll get away,
Gather our forces
For another day . . ."
"It's a cold morning,"
20   Antony said.

Caesar Augustus
Cleared his phlegm.
"Corpses disgust us.
Cover them."
Caesar Augustus
In his time lay
Dying, and just as
Cold as they,
On the cold morning
30   Of a cold day.
             —*Louis Simpson*

Line length contributes to the wit of rhyming here; with only two feet to a line, rhyming becomes a stunt. Who would have expected *drowsing* to rhyme with *carousing*, or *Augustus* with *just as* and *disgust us*?

Natural rhyme

On the other hand, here is a poem by Thomas Hardy in which rhyme is neither cliché nor witty, but through the skill of the poet appears natural in the poem while it adds its particular music.

The Oxen

Christmas Eve, and twelve of the clock.
    "Now they are all on their knees,"
An elder said as we sat in a flock
    By the embers in hearthside ease.

We pictured the meek mild creatures where
    They dwelt in their strawy pen,
Nor did it occur to one of us there
    To doubt they were kneeling then.

So fair a fancy few would weave
10   In these years! Yet, I feel,
If someone said on Christmas Eve,
   "Come; see the oxen kneel

"In the lonely barton° by yonder coomb°   farmyard; a hollow
   Our childhood used to know,"
I should go with him in the gloom,
   Hoping it might be so.
                    —*Thomas Hardy*

This rhyme helps fix the poem's form, click the lid of its box; it neither stands out as a stunt of wit nor bores us with the overly predictable.

Rhymed stanzas

"The Oxen" is written in **stanzas**; a stanza is an arrangement of metrical lines, sometimes different in length, with a repeated order of rhyme, a **rhyme-scheme**. Here, the first and third lines rhyme, and the second and fourth; we indicate rhyme-schemes by letters; this scheme is ABAB. (First and third lines are iambic tetrameter, second and fourth iambic trimeter.) Sometimes poets invent stanzas and rhyme schemes of great complexity, varying line length and the arrangements of rhyme.

Exercises

Look at the rhyming of these poems.

1. Mark the rhyme-schemes and stanza patterns in each poem.
2. Find three direct rhymes. Can you find indirect or off-rhymes of different sorts? Discuss the difference.
3. Can you find examples of cliché rhyme? Original rhyme? Natural rhyme?

Tywater

Death of Sir Nihil, book the *nth*,
Upon the charred and clotted sward,
Lacking the lily of our Lord,
Alases of the hyacinth.

Could flicker from behind his ear
A whistling silver throwing knife
And with a holler punch the life
Out of a swallow in the air.

Behind the lariat's butterfly
10   Shuttled his white and gritted grin,
And cuts of sky would roll within
The noose-hole, when he spun it high.

The violent, neat and practised skill
Was all he loved and all he learned;
When he was hit, his body turned
To clumsy dirt before it fell.

And what to say of him, God knows.
Such violence. And such repose.
                    —*Richard Wilbur*

Samuel Sewall

Samuel Sewall, in a world of wigs,
Flouted opinion in his personal hair;
For foppery he gave not any figs,
But in his right and honor took the air.

Thus in his naked style, though well attired,
He went forth in the city, or paid court
To Madam Winthrop, whom he much admired,
Most godly, but yet liberal with the port.

And all the town admired for two full years
His excellent address, his gifts of fruit,
Her gracious ways and delicate white ears,
And held the course of nature absolute.

But yet she bade him suffer a peruke,
'That One be not distinguished from the All';
Delivered of herself this stern rebuke
Framed in the resonant language of St. Paul.

'Madam,' he answered her, 'I have a Friend
Furnishes me with hair out of His strength,
And He requires only I attend
Unto His charity and to its length.'

And all the town was witness to his trust:
On Monday he walked out with the Widow Gibbs,
A pious lady of charm and notable bust,
Whose heart beat tolerably beneath her ribs.

On Saturday he wrote proposing marriage,
And closed, imploring that she be not cruel,
'Your favorable answer will oblige,
Madam, your humble servant, Samuel Sewall.'
                    —*Anthony Hecht*

Chapter 9 **Forms and Types of Poetry**

Poetic forms are traditional arrangements of line and rhyme-scheme, like the sonnet. (If we use the word *forms* for these arrangements, we are not calling other poetry—like free verse or blank verse—formless. *Form* is merely a traditional word for this sort of arrangement.)

By types of poetry we mean distinctions between narrative and dramatic poetry on the one hand and on the other subdivisions like the epigram and the prose poem.

Poetic forms

The limerick

Each form of poetry demands a particular number of lines, of certain length, rhyming in a certain way. In a *limerick*, for instance, two trimeter lines rhyme, followed by two dimeter lines which also rhyme, and then a fifth trimeter line which rhymes with the first two. The rhyme-scheme is AABBA, and the BB lines are often indented. A limerick's feet are usually three syllables long, each an **anapest:** softer, softer, louder, or ˘˘´. (Authors of limericks sometimes substitute iambs for anapests.) Here is an example by a modern master of the form, Edward Gorey (born 1925):

> Each night Father fills me with dread
> When he sits on the foot of my bed;
> 　I'd not mind that he speaks
> 　In gibbers and squeaks,
> But for seventeen years he's been dead.

These anonymous limericks can provide a refresher course in meter:

> There was a young man of Japan
> Whose verses would never scan.
>   When he was asked why
>   He would reply,
> Well, I simply try to get as many syllables into the last line as I possibly can.

> There was a young man of China
> Whose aesthetic was somewhat fina.
>   It was his design
>   To make the last line
> Short.

So much for limericks, which can serve as an example of many forms.*

The haiku

Many American students have written haikus in school. When the English haiku-writer follows the Japanese syllable count, he uses lines of five, seven, and five syllables. The **haiku** is an imagistic poem, usually including two images, of which the second is a surprise, a leap from the first; or at least the two images conflict. Here is a translation from a sixteenth-century Japanese poet named Moritaki:

> A falling petal
> drops upward, back to the branch;
> it's a butterfly.

Many poets writing haikus in English, aware of differences between English and Japanese, ignore syllable count and concentrate on images.

The sonnet

Important for us to know is a poetic form that has remained at the center of English poetry from the sixteenth century onward. English poets from Thomas Wyatt (1503–1542) to the present have found the sonnet a congenial form, mostly for emotional statement. In one of his own sonnets, Wordsworth spoke of the sonnet as the key with which Shakespeare unlocked his heart. Shakespeare wrote a sequence of sonnets, as did many other poets in the sixteenth and seventeenth centuries. Even when it is a part of a sequence, a sonnet is a whole and individual poem, a certain length with several possible internal structures whereby a poet can entertain and conclude a whole, small subject. Early sonnets and sonnet sequences were mostly concerned with love. John Donne's "Holy Sonnets" are religious, as are many of Milton's sonnets. More recently, sonnets have extended themselves to all sorts of feelings.

---

*Readers interested in the many poetic forms not mentioned here may consult Lewis Turco's *A Book of Forms*, which defines and exemplifies widely among special forms. Or look at the pages about poetic forms in Clement Wood's *Complete Rhyming Dictionary*.

The sonnet is fourteen lines long, and written in iambic pentameter. (We can find poems called sonnets that are exceptions to these rules; the word originally meant "little song" and some poets have interpreted the word broadly.) There are three main traditional structures and rhyme schemes. One is the **Italian** or **Petrarchan sonnet**, which is divided into two parts. The octave is the first eight lines, and it uses only two rhymes: ABBAABBA. The sestet in an Italian or Petrarchan sonnet can rhyme in several ways—CDECDE is common; so is CDCDCD—so long as it does not end in a couplet. Many English poets have practiced the Italian sonnet with success, notably Milton and Wordsworth.

The English language, however, is noted for the paucity of its rhyme, especially compared to the Italian richness in rhyme-words. Therefore the octave of the Italian sonnet can make trouble for the English poet because it uses only two rhyme-sounds for eight words. The **English sonnet**, more commonly called the **Shakespearean sonnet**, began a little earlier than Shakespeare—it was first used by Henry Howard, Earl of Surrey (1517–1547)—and uses a rhyme scheme more adapted to the English language: ABAB CDCD EFEF GG. Edmund Spenser, finding the Italian sonnet not suited to English but the English sonnet too loose, invented a third rhyme scheme that is a compromise between the two: ABAB BCBC CDCD EE. This arrangement makes the **Spenserian sonnet**.

Rhyme-schemes are probably less important to sonnets than structures of thought, but rhyme-schemes seem to suggest such structures. In the Italian sonnet, the octave and the sestet usually make a two-part structure not further subdivided. Frequently an octave will set forth a problem, or tell a story, to which the sestet may provide a solution, a counterdirection, a commentary, or a surprise. Of course there are exceptions; some Italian sonnets feature no division at all but make an indivisible fourteen-line poem.

On the other hand, the English or Shakespearean sonnet, which often breaks down into eight and six, may also break in other places. It may further subdivide into four and four, plus four and two, or it may break down into four, four, four, and two; or it may break down into eight, four, and two. If the Shakespearean sonnet is structurally more adaptable, it is for the same reason a less precise form.

Quoted throughout this text are sonnets by Shakespeare (see pages 422 and 425). Here is another:

Let me not to the marriage of true minds

> Let me not to the marriage of true minds
> Admit impediments. Love is not love
> Which alters when it alteration finds,
> Or bends with the remover to remove.
> O no, it is an ever-fixèd mark
> That looks on tempests and is never shaken;
> It is the star to every wand'ring bark,
> Whose worth's unknown, although his height be taken.

Love's not Time's fool, though rosy lips and cheeks
10   Within his bending sickle's compass come;
Love alters not with his brief hours and weeks,
But bears it out even to the edge of doom.
    If this be error and upon me proved,
    I never writ, nor no man ever loved.

Here is a sonnet by John Milton. Notice the rhyme scheme:

On the Late Massacre in Piedmont[1]

Avenge, O Lord, thy slaughtered saints, whose bones
Lie scattered on the Alpine mountains cold;
Ev'n them who kept thy truth so pure of old,
When all our fathers worshipped stocks and stones,
Forget not: in thy book record their groans
Who were thy sheep, and in their ancient fold
Slain by the bloody Piedmontese, that rolled
Mother with infant down the rocks. Their moans
The vales redoubled to the hills, and they
10   To heav'n. Their martyred blood and ashes sow
O'er all th' Italian fields, where still doth sway
The triple[2] Tyrant that from these may grow
A hundredfold, who, having learnt thy way,
Early may fly the Babylonian woe.[3]

[1]In 1655 the Protestant Waldenses of southern France were suppressed for refusing to adhere to Roman Catholicism.   [2]A reference to the papal crown.   [3]See Revelation 27:8.

Wordsworth, Keats, Tennyson, Frost—most great poets have turned to the sonnet during their lives. Examples of the sonnet may be found throughout this book. See, for instance, pages 454, 538, 541, 545, 546, 549, and 574.

Poetic types

Ballad

A ballad is almost a form; at least, there are typical stanzas, and even ballads we can call typical; but the word *ballad* does not represent a form as codified as sonnet. Although ballads tell stories, we separate them from the later category of narrative poetry because they form a great body of anonymous literature; and there is also the later, sophisticated imitation of the ballad. Here is an anonymous Scots ballad, with some old Scottish words footnoted.

Edward

"Why dois[1] your brand[2] sae[3] drap[4] wi bluid,[5]
    Edward, Edward,
Why dois your brand sae drap wi bluid,
    And why sae sad gang[6] yee O?"
"O I hae[7] killed my hauke[8] sae guid,[9]
    Mither, mither,
O I hae killed my hauke sae guid,
    And I had nae mair[10] but hee O."

"Your haukis bluid was nevir sae reid,[11]
10   Edward, Edward,
Your haukis bluid was nevir sae reid,
    My deir son I tell thee O."
"O I hae killed my reid roan steid,[12]
    Mither, mither,
O I hae killed my reid roan steid,
    That erst[13] was sae fair and free O."

"Your steid was auld,[14] and ye hae gat mair,
    Edward, Edward,
Your steid was auld, and ye hae gat mair,
20   Sum other dule[15] ye drie[16] O."
"O I hae killed my fadir[17] deir,
    Mither, mither,
O I hae killed my fadir deir,
    Alas, and wae[18] is mee O!"

"And whatten penance wul[19] ye drie for that,
    Edward, Edward?
And whatten penance wul ye drie for that?
    My deir son, now tell me O."
"Ile set my feet in yonder boat,
30   Mither, mither,
Ile set me feet in yonder boat,
    And Ile fare ovir the sea O."

"And what wul ye doe wi your towirs and your ha,[20]
    Edward, Edward?
And what wul ye doe wi your towirs and your ha,
    That were sae fair to see O?"
"Ile let thame stand tul they doun fa,
    Mither, mither,
Ile let thame stand tul they doun fa,
40   For here nevir mair maun[21] I bee O."

"And what wul ye leive to your bairns[22] and your wife,
    Edward, Edward?
And what wul ye leive to your bairns and your wife,
    Whan ye gang ovir the sea O?"
"The warldis[23] room, let them beg thrae[24] life,
    Mither, mither,

[1]does   [2]sword   [3]so   [4]drip   [5]blood   [6]go   [7]have   [8]hawk   [9]good   [10]more   [11]red
[12]steed   [13]formerly   [14]old   [15]grief   [16]suffer   [17]father   [18]woe   [19]will   [20]hall   [21]must
[22]children   [23]world's   [24]through

The warldis room, let them beg thrae life,
    For thame nevir mair wul I see O."

"And what wul ye leive to your ain[25] mither deir?
50   Edward, Edward?
And what wul ye leive to your ain mither deir?
    My deir son, now tell me O."
"The curse of hell frae[26] me sall[27] ye beir,[28]
    Mither, mither,
The curse of hell frae me sall ye beir,
    Sic[29] counseils ye gave to me O."

                                  —Anonymous

[25]own   [26]from   [27]shall   [28]bear   [29]such

A ballad tells a story. In "Edward," the story is told in dialogue, as if the poem were a tiny play, the speeches organized into stanzas. In the tight and musical stanzas of this ballad, we hear a son reluctantly telling his mother that he has killed his father, and finally cursing his mother for having urged him to patricide. When a harrowing story is told in rhymed and delicate verses, the tension between form and content, story and music makes a dreadful energy.

See page 536 for another ballad.

Later poets imitated old ballad forms in writing narrative poems. One of the most famous literary ballads in English is by John Keats.

La Belle Dame sans Merci[1]

Oh, what can ail thee, knight-at-arms,
    Alone and palely loitering?
The sedge has withered from the lake,
    And no birds sing!

Oh, what can ail thee, knight-at-arms,
    So haggard and so woe-begone?
The squirrel's granary is full,
    And the harvest's done.

I see a lily on thy brow,
10   With anguish moist and fever-dew,
And on thy cheek a fading rose
    Fast withereth too.

I met a lady in the meads
    Full beautiful, a fairy's child.
Her hair was long, her foot was light,
    And her eyes were wild.

I made a garland for her head,
    And bracelets too, and fragrant zone;

[1]The beautiful, pitiless woman

She looked at me as she did love,
20   And made sweet moan.

I set her on my pacing steed,
    And nothing else saw all day long;
For sidelong would she bend, and sing
    A fairy's song.

She found me roots of relish sweet,
    And honey wild, and manna dew;
And sure in language strange she said,
    "I love thee true."

She took me to her elfin grot,
30   And there she wept, and sighed full sore,
And there I shut her wild wild eyes
    With kisses four.

And there she lullèd me asleep
    And there I dreamed—Ah! woe betide!—
The latest dream I ever dreamed
    On the cold hill side.

I saw pale kings and princes too,
    Pale warriors, death-pale were they all;
They cried—"La belle Dame sans merci
40   Hath thee in thrall!"

I saw their starved lips in the gloam
    With horrid warning gapèd wide,
And I awoke and found me here,
    On the cold hill side.

And this is why I sojourn here,
    Alone and palely loitering,
Though the sedge is withered from the lake,
    And no birds sing.

(On page 489 are examples of Keats's revisions of this poem.) The verse is smoother and more literary than the old ballads, and the language is closer to our own, but the poem makes its ancestry clear.

Narrative, epic, dramatic

Many poems, including ballads, tell stories, and are therefore narrative. The earliest surviving poetry is narrative, ancient epics originally chanted or sung to a form of musical accompaniment. *Gilgamesh* is the oldest surviving poem, composed in Sumeria about five thousand years ago; Homer's *Iliad* and *Odyssey* are a mere three thousand years old. These epics were composed orally, before the invention of writing; they were memorized, and changed ("revised") by generations of reciter-poets. (There was no single, innovative, sole-author Homer; though it is possible that one blind bard assembled and organized the *Iliad* and the *Odyssey* more thoroughly than any of his predecessors.)

Prehistoric Greeks remembered and celebrated their past by memorizing Homer. Epics are historical records of the heroes of the tribe, combining fact and legend. Centuries after these oral epics were composed, professional poets made sophisticated epics in imitation of the old collective style. The Roman Vergil, wishing to write a patriotic poem to flatter the emperor Augustus, followed the pattern of Homer when he composed *The Aeneid.*

In the Christian era, Dante's *Divine Comedy* is a sophisticated epic. Its embodiment of Christian theology makes it a vast departure from classical forms, but the ghost who guides Dante through hell to purgatory is Vergil himself. In English, the great epic is Milton's seventeenth-century account of creation, and the war between good and evil, in *Paradise Lost.*

Many poems are narrative tales, comic or tragic, without being epic. The great narrative poet in English is Geoffrey Chaucer. His language is archaic, and best saved for advanced study, but there is a sample of his poetry on page 535. *The Canterbury Tales* is a lengthy series of different stories told by and about ordinary people—not, like an epic, tales of gods and heroes making history.

After Chaucer, to the present time, many poets have written stories in rhyme and meter (less often in free verse). Sometimes the stories take dramatic form, most often as monologues by a speaker who reveals himself as he tells his story (see Robert Browning's "My Last Duchess," page 589). One example of modern narrative is a story poem by Robert Frost:

"Out, Out—"

The buzz saw snarled and rattled in the yard
And made dust and dropped stove-length sticks of wood.
Sweet-scented stuff when the breeze drew across it.
And from there those that lifted eyes could count
Five mountain ranges one behind the other
Under the sunset far into Vermont.
And the saw snarled and rattled, snarled and rattled,
As it ran light, or had to bear a load.
And nothing happened: day was all but done.
10 Call it a day, I wish they might have said
To please the boy by giving him the half hour
That a boy counts so much when saved from work.
His sister stood beside them in her apron
To tell them "Supper." At the word, the saw,
As if to prove saws knew what supper meant,
Leaped out at the boy's hand, or seemed to leap—
He must have given the hand. However it was,
Neither refused the meeting. But the hand!
The boy's first outcry was a rueful laugh,
20 As he swung toward them holding up the hand
Half in appeal, but half as if to keep
The life from spilling. Then the boy saw all—

Since he was old enough to know, big boy
Doing a man's work, though a child at heart—
He saw all spoiled. "Don't let him cut my hand off—
The doctor, when he comes. Don't let him, sister!"
So. But the hand was gone already.
The doctor put him in the dark of ether.
He lay and puffed his lips out with his breath.
30   And then—the watcher at his pulse took fright.
No one believed. They listened at his heart.
Little—less—nothing!—and that ended it.
No more to build on there. And they, since they
Were not the one dead, turned to their affairs.

Lyric and song

We have come to use **lyric** to mean a short poem, usually emotional or descriptive. The term is perhaps too general to be useful. Originally derived from the word for lyre (a musical instrument) the word indicated a poem composed for singing. Many old poems were originally written as songs. Here is one of Shakespeare's songs, from *Love's Labour's Lost*:

Winter

When icicles hang by the wall,
    And Dick the shepherd blows his nail,
And Tom bears logs into the hall,
    And milk comes frozen home in pail,
When blood is nipp'd, and ways be foul,
Then nightly sings the staring owl,
                     Tu-who;
Tu-whit, tu-who—a merry note,
While greasy Joan doth keel the pot.

10   When all aloud the wind doth blow,
    And coughing drowns the parson's saw,
And birds sit brooding in the snow,
    And Marian's nose looks red and raw,
When roasted crabs hiss in the bowl,
Then nightly sings the staring owl,
                     Tu-who;
Tu-whit, tu-who—a merry note,
While greasy Joan doth keel the pot.

Epigrams

An epigram is short, pithy, witty, and conclusive. Here is one by Thomas Hardy:

Epitaph on a Pessimist

I'm Smith of Stoke, aged sixty-odd,
    I've lived without a dame
From youth-time on; and would to God
    My Dad had done the same.

(An **epitaph** is an inscription for a gravestone; some epitaphs are also epigrams. Note that there is a third word sometimes confused with epigram and epitaph; an **epigraph** is a quotation an author places at the start of a work.) Walter Savage Landor wrote many epigrams, among them this one:

I strove with none, for none was worth my strife.
    Nature I loved and, next to Nature, Art:
I warmed both hands before the fire of life;
    It sinks, and I am ready to depart.

The modern American J. V. Cunningham has written most of his work in epigrammatic form, some of it very funny:

Naked I came, naked I leave the scene,
And naked was my pastime in between.

some not:

On a cold night I came through the cold rain
And false snow to the wind shrill on your pane
With no hope and no anger and no fear:
Who are you? and with whom do you sleep here?

Most epigrams rhyme. We call a short free-verse poem an epigram only when brevity combines with wit:

The Bath Tub

As a bathtub lined with white porcelain,
When the hot water gives out or goes tepid,
So is the slow cooling of our chivalrous passion,
O my much praised but-not-altogether-satisfactory lady.
                        —Ezra Pound

Visual poetry

While most poetry appeals to the ear, some poetry arranges itself for the pleasure of the eye. Early in the seventeenth century, George Herbert wrote "Easter Wings."

Lord, who createdst man in wealth and store,
Though foolishly he lost the same,
Decaying more and more
Till he became
Most poor:
With thee
O let me rise
As larks, harmoniously,
And sing this day thy victories:
10   Then shall the fall further the flight in me.

My tender age in sorrow did begin;
And still with sicknesses and shame
Thou didst so punish sin,
That I became
Most thin.
With thee
Let me combine,
And feel this day thy victory;
For, if I imp my wing on thine,
20   Affliction shall advance the flight in me.

This poem is a pleasure both to ear and to eye. If you heard the poem read aloud, you would be aware of lines becoming shorter, then longer again—a closing in, an opening up—but you would not be aware that the poem created on the page the visual shape of an angel's wings. Reading and seeing the poem are separate pleasures. Herbert's "Easter Wings" is a concrete poem because a portion of its creation is visual.

Modern poems sometimes exist to the eye and not to the ear. When E. E. Cummings makes

l(a

le
af
fa

ll

s)
one
l

iness

there is no way to pronounce the poem except by spelling it and indicating marks of punctuation. (Even then the voicing will detract from the poem; the voice will have to decide whether the first character is *ell* or *one*. (It is *ell*, in terms of the words *loneliness* and *a leaf falls*, but the meaning of the poem is underscored by the visual pun on *ell* and *one*.) The poem exists, not to the eye and ear together, nor to both eye and ear separately, but to the eye alone.

Concrete poetry is a blend of poetry and painting, or visual art. Ian Hamilton Finlay is a contemporary leader among concretists. Here is his "Homage to Malevich"—the painter who tilted a white square on a white background in "White on White":

lackblockblackb
lockblackblockb
lackblockblackb
lockblackblockb
lackblockblackb
lockblackblockb
lackblockblackb
lockblackblockb

lackblockblackb   lackblockblackb   lackblockblackb
lockblackblockb   lockblackblockb   lockblackblockb
lackblockblackb   lackblockblackb   lackblockblackb
lockblackblockb   lockblackblockb   lockblackblockb
lackblockblackb   lackblockblackb   lackblockblackb
lockblackblockb   lockblackblockb   lockblackblockb
lackblockblackb   lackblockblackb   lackblockblackb
lockblackblockb   lockblackblockb   lockblackblockb

lackblockblackb
lockblackblockb
lackblockblackb
lockblackblockb
lackblockblackb
lockblackblockb
lackblockblackb
lockblackblockb

Some poems assembled as concrete are less like pictures and more like collections of letters for the mind to dwell on—like the French movement *lettrism*. Thus Aram Saroyan has composed poems of a single word like *oxygen*, or a single nonword like *blod* (immortalized by the *Guinness Book of Records* as the world's shortest poem). These poems are not so interesting in their own sensuous shape as they are in the thoughts they lead to. Thus they resemble conceptual sculpture, like Yoko Ono's row of empty flowerpots titled "Imagining Flowers."

Prose poems

Poems written in paragraphs have been a part of literature for more than a hundred years. Usually a prose poem shares most of the qualities we associate with poetry—images, metaphor, figures, controlled rhythm, and fantasy—except for lines and linebreaks. Most poets who make prose poems write lined poems also. Robert Bly's lined poems appear on pages 441 and 681.

The Dead Seal near McClure's Beach

1

Walking north toward the point, I came on a dead seal. From a few feet away, he looks like a brown log. The body is on its back, dead only a few hours. I stand and look at him. There's a quiver in the dead flesh. My God he is still alive. A shock goes through me, as if a wall of my room had fallen away.

His head is arched back, the small eyes closed, the whiskers sometimes rise and fall. He is dying. This is the oil. Here on its back is the oil that heats our houses so efficiently. Wind blows fine sand back toward the ocean. The flipper near me lies folded over the stomach, looking like an unfinished arm, lightly glazed with sand at the edges. The other flipper lies half underneath. The seal's skin looks like an old overcoat, scratched here and there, by sharp mussel-shells maybe. . . .

I reach out and touch him. Suddenly he rears up, turns over, gives three cries, Awaark! Awaark! Awaark!—like the cries from Christmas toys. He lunges toward me. I am terrified and leap back, although I know there can be no teeth in that jaw. He starts flopping toward the sea. But he falls over, on his face. He does not want to go back to the sea. He looks up at the sky, and he looks like an old lady who has lost her hair.

He puts his chin back on the sand, rearranges his flippers, and waits for me to go. I go.

2

Today I go back to say goodbye: he's dead now. But he's not—he's a quarter mile farther up the shore. Today he is thinner, squatting on his stomach, head out. The ribs show more—each vertebra on the back under the coat is now visible, shiny. He breathes in and out.

He raises himself up, and tucks his flippers under, as if to keep them warm. A wave comes in, touches his nose. He turns and looks at me—the eyes slanted, the crown of his head is like a black leather jacket. He is taking a long time to die. The whiskers white as porcupine quills, the forehead slopes . . . goodbye brother, die in the sound of waves, forgive us if we have killed you, long live your race, your inner-tube race, so uncomfortable on land, so comfortable in the ocean. Be comfortable in death then, where the sand will be out of your nostrils, and you can swim in long loops through the pure death, ducking under as assassinations break above you. You don't want to be touched by me. I climb the cliff and go home the other way.

Notice how in the form of prose Bly uses the details of the world and yet (as in a poem) leaps across spaces of thought to see inside things.

Russell Edson is another contemporary American who writes prose poems. He writes tiny narratives—which might be called fables, or novels to read through a microscope—that other people call prose poems. When it becomes difficult to decide whether a piece of writing is a story, a poem, a play, or an essay, then by and large the task is useless. Here is a prose poem—I'll call it—by Russell Edson:

Bringing a Dead Man Back into Life

The dead man is introduced back into life. They take him
to a country fair, to a French restaurant, a round of late
night parties . . .He's beginning to smell.

They give him a few days off in bed.

He's taken to a country fair again; a second engagement
at the French restaurant; another round of late night parties
. . . No response . . . They brush the maggots away . . .
That terrible smell! . . . No use . . .

What's wrong with you?

10   . . . No use . . .

They slap his face. His cheek comes off; bone underneath, jaws and teeth . . .

Another round of late night parties . . . Dropping his
fingers . . . An ear falls off . . . Loses a foot in a taxi . . .
No use . . . The smell . . . Maggots everywhere!

Another round of late night parties. His head comes off,
rolls on the floor. A woman stumbles on it, an eye rolls
out. She screams.

No use . . . Under his jacket nothing but maggots and
20   ribs . . . No use . . .

Chapter 10 **Versions of the Same**

This chapter gathers different versions of the same texts: poets' revisions of their own work, variant translations of one original, and a pedagogic paraphrase. Saying that different words express the same content, we beg questions; when two texts differ in their wording, by definition nothing is truly the same. Still, revisions and variant translations can give us multiple examples of phrases that resemble each other and are *not* the same, thus providing opportunity to examine differences of diction, rhythm, image, metaphor, sound, and (often) meter. By noticing these differences, we can review the study of poetry and sharpen our ability to tell better from good, best from better.

Poets' revisions

William Butler Yeats revised his poems every chance he got. He published his first volume in 1885, and by 1895 he had revised some of these poems in a new collection of his work. When he was in his sixties he rewrote some poems he had written in his twenties. When people objected, he made an answer:

> The friends that have it I do wrong
> Whenever I remake a song,
> Should know what issue is at stake:
> It is myself that I remake.

With his early revisions, he remade style, not self. He changed:

> In three days' time he stood up with a moan
> And he went down to the long sands alone.

to:

> In three days' time, Cuchulain* with a moan
> Stood up, and came to the long sands alone.

In this revision a proper name replaces a pronoun, and a boring rhythm becomes varied and expressive: *Stood up*, with a pause after it, then eight syllables of walking, seems to imitate in its rhythm the action it describes.

In 1892, in the first version of a famous poem called "When You Are Old," Yeats wrote the couplet:

> Murmur, a little sad, "From us fled Love.
> He paced upon the mountains far above . . ."

The adjective *sad* goes strangely with the verb *murmur*, and the normal word order at the end of the first line would have been *Love fled from us*. Dissatisfied six years later, Yeats rewrote the lines to read:

> Murmur, a little sadly, how Love fled
> And paced upon the mountains overhead . . .

Now this line approaches natural speech, without affectation or awkwardness.

Four versions of the last stanza of "Cradle Song" show Yeats growing in simplicity and directness:

1889

> My darling I kiss you,
>   With arms round my own.
> Ah, how I shall miss you
>   When heavy and grown.

1892

> I kiss you and kiss you
>   With arms round my own.
> Ah, how I shall miss you
>   When, dear, you have grown.

1901

> I kiss you and kiss you
> My pigeon, my own.
> Ah, how I shall miss you,
> When you have grown.

*Cuchulain is pronounced cuh-HULL-an.

1925

I sigh that kiss you
For I must own
That I shall miss you
When you have grown.

In the 1889 stanza, the first line lacks the energy it picked up later when Yeats packed the line with two verbs. In the last line, the word *heavy* is unfortunate—the kind of error any writer can make, where a word brings in an irrelevant association the writer is blind to; *heavy* for Yeats probably implied ponderous and slow-moving, an end to youth; unfortunately it is a euphemism for obesity. In 1892, he improved the first line and in the fourth line got rid of *heavy* but added the rhythmically awkward apostrophe to *dear*, chopping the line up with commas. In 1901 he repaired the fourth line—finally—but left behind the decorative *pigeon* and the decorative *Ah*. By 1925 he was all for spareness. In judging among these "versions of the same" there is room for difference of opinion, but I like the last version best. This 1925 change comes closer to remaking the self, like these two versions of "The Lamentation of the Old Pensioner" (original title "The Old Pensioner"):

1890

I had a chair at every hearth,
When no one turned to see
With "Look at that old fellow there;
And who may he be?"
And therefore do I wander on,
And the fret is on me.

The road-side trees keep murmuring—
Ah, wherefore murmur ye
As in the old days long gone by,
10   Green oak and poplar tree!
The well-known faces are all gone,
And the fret is on me.

1939

Although I shelter from the rain
Under a broken tree
My chair was nearest to the fire
In every company
That talked of love or politics,
Ere Time transfigured me.

Though lads are making pikes again
For some conspiracy,
And crazy rascals rage their fill
10   At human tyranny,
My contemplations are of Time
That has transfigured me.

There's not a woman turns her face
Upon a broken tree,
And yet the beauties that I loved
Are in my memory;
I spit into the face of Time
That has transfigured me.

Exercises

1. The two poems use a different sort of sound, for different effect. Pick out the characteristic sounds of each poem.

2. It is often said that Yeats's poems became more speechlike as he matured. Could you use these poems to support this assertion?

Here are more examples of Yeats's revisions. Those labeled A are the earlier versions, B the later. See if you can decide why Yeats changed the lines.

A

"My father," made he smiling answer then,
"Still treads the world amid his armed men."

B

"My father dwells among the sea-worn bands,
And breaks the ridge of battle with his hands."

A

The oldest hound with mournful din
  Lifts slow his wintery head:—
The servants bear the body in—
  The hounds keen for the dead.

B

The blind hound with a mournful din
  Lifts slow his wintery head;—
The servants bear the body in—
  The hounds wail for the dead.

Yeats was not the only great poet to revise his work. William Blake in "London" (page 566), originally wrote:

But most the midnight harlot's curse
From every dismal street I hear,
Weaves around the marriage hearse
And blasts the new born infant's tear.

A year later, he revised these lines into:

> But most through midnight streets I hear
> How the youthful harlot's curse
> Blasts the new-born infant's tear
> And blights with plagues the marriage hearse.

Notice that the elements of the first stanza—midnight, harlot's curse, street, infant, marriage hearse, blasts, tear—turn up again in the later stanza. We lose *dismal* and we gain another adjective, *youthful*, in exchange. We lose the pretty word *weave*—to weave is to create, to turn thread into cloth; in this context the pretty word is oddly used for destructive purpose—and we have in return the far more powerful *blights with plagues*, combining diseases of plants and animals. Although the first stanza was powerful, the revision increases the poem's power, the intensity, and the density, adding a new area of meaning in the metaphor of diseases. Before, death entered with *hearse*, but we lacked the cause of death. The order of things is changed in the second version, and the order itself makes the poetry more powerful. It moves from the innocent streets to the prostitute and her oath, to the damnation of the infant's weeping, and finally to the disease and death of the institution of marriage.

Exercise

In "La Belle Dame sans Merci," Keats originally wrote the stanza:

> She took me to her elfin grot,
>   And there she wept, and sighed full sore,
> And there I shut her wild wild eyes
>   With kisses four.

He changed these lines—three out of four—into:

> She took me to her elfin grot,
>   And there she gazed and sighèd deep,
> And there I shut her wild sad eyes—
>   So kissed to sleep.

Many critics feel that Keat's revision is inferior to the original. What do you think, and why?

Robert Frost kept most of his variant versions from the public. He liked to give the impression that he revised little. Still, he published a number of poems in an early version, tinkered with them, and published them in revised form. His most remarkable printed revision is that of "Design," one of his greatest poems. In 1912 he included in a letter this poem:

In White

> A dented spider like a snowdrop white
> On a white Heal-all,[1] holding up a moth
> Like a white piece of lifeless satin cloth—
> Saw ever curious eye so strange a sight?

[1] A flower, normally blue, reported to have healing qualities

Portent in little, assorted death and blight
Like the ingredients of a witches' broth?
The beady spider, the flower like a froth,
And the moth carried like a paper kite.

What had that flower to do with being white,
10   The blue Brunella,[2] every child's delight?
What brought the kindred spider to that height?
(Make we no thesis of the miller's° plight.)   moth
What but design of darkness and of night?
Design, design! Do I use the word aright?

[2]Another name for the healall

Not until 1922 did "In White" turn up again:

Design

I found a dimpled spider, fat and white,
On a white heal-all, holding up a moth
Like a white piece of rigid satin cloth—
Assorted characters of death and blight
Mixed ready to begin the morning right,
Like the ingredients of a witches' broth—
A snow-drop spider, a flower like a froth,
And dead wings carried like a paper kite.

What had that flower to do with being white,
10   The wayside blue and innocent heal-all?
What brought the kindred spider to that height,
Then steered the white moth thither in the night?
What but design of darkness to appall?—
If design govern in a thing so small.

It is useful with this poem, or these two poems, to compare them line by line. Here "In White" is in roman type, "Design" in italic.

1. A dented spider like a snowdrop white
   1. I found a dimpled spider, fat and white,
2. On a white Heal-all, holding up a moth
   2. On a white heal-all, holding up a moth
3. Like a white piece of lifeless satin cloth—
   3. Like a white piece of rigid satin cloth—
4. Saw ever curious eye so strange a sight?
   4. Assorted characters of death and blight
5. Portent in little, assorted death and blight
   5. Mixed ready to begin the morning right,
6. Like the ingredients of a witches' broth?
   6. Like the ingredients of a witches' broth—
7. The beady spider, the flower like a froth,
   7. A snow-drop spider, a flower like a froth,

8. And the moth carried like a paper kite.
   8. And dead wings carried like a paper kite.

9. What had that flower to do with being white,
   9. What had that flower to do with being white,
10. The blue Brunella every child's delight?
   10. The wayside blue and innocent heal-all?
11. What brought the kindred spider to that height?
   11. What brought the kindred spider to that height,
12. (Make we no thesis of the miller's plight.)
   12. Then steered the white moth thither in the night?
13. What the design of darkness and of night?
   13. What but design of darkness to appall?—
14. Design, design! Do I use the word aright?
   14. If design govern in a thing so small.

Exercises

1. In 1/1, compare *dented* with *dimpled*. What kind of object do you associate with *dented*? What kind with *dimpled*? Is either association preferable to the other in the context of the whole poem?
2. In 3/3, could you defend *lifeless* against *rigid*? Is either of these adjectives more specific than the other? More physical?
3. Paraphrase 3/4. How does the sentence work? Does 3/4 say something similar? Different? Does the grammar help the later poem?
4. In 7/7, compare *beady* and *snow-drop*.
5. In 8/8, compare the rhythms of the two lines at the beginning. What are the changes? Do you like the change? Can you say why?
6. The second stanzas or sestets of these two versions differ in a number of ways. List all the differences you can see. Decide whether you approve of the changes made. Imagine why Robert Frost might have wanted to make them. Look up the history of *appall* and decide how it is used in this poem. Which of the two poems is clearer? Which of the two poems is better? Why?

Different translations

Different translations of the same poem can offer us an opportunity to compare style, rhythm, and diction—even when we do not know the original. We can turn translations to our purposes by deciding which version we prefer, and why. We can sharpen our wits by defining our choices. Here is the Twenty-third Psalm, translated from the Hebrew of the Old Testament, in the seventeenth-century King James version:

   The Lord is my shepherd;
I shall not want.
He maketh me to lie down in green pastures: he leadeth me beside the still
   waters.

He restoreth my soul: he leadeth me in the paths of righteousness for his
    name's sake.
Yea, though I walk through the valley of the shadow of death, I will fear
no evil: for thou art with me; thy rod and thy staff they comfort me.
    Thou preparest a table before me in the presence of mine enemies:
Thou annointest my head with oil; my cup runneth over.
    Surely goodness and mercy shall follow me all the days of my life:
10   And I will dwell in the house of the Lord forever.

Here is the Revised Standard Version, which came out first in 1952—very
close, but not the same:

The Lord is my shepherd, I shall not want;
    he makes me lie down in green pastures.
He leads me beside still waters;
    he restores my soul.
He leads me in paths of righteousness
    for his name's sake.

Even though I walk through the valley of the shadow of death,
    I fear no evil; for thou art with me;
    thy rod and thy staff,
10   they comfort me.

Thou preparest a table before me
in the presence of my enemies;
thou anointest my head with oil,
    my cup overflows.
Surely goodness and mercy shall follow me
    all the days of my life;
and I shall dwell in the house of the Lord
    for ever.

Here is the same Psalm in a version from *The Psalms for Modern Man*,
copyrighted by the American Bible Society in 1970:

The Lord is my shepherd;
    I have everything I need.
He lets me rest in fields of green grass
    and leads me to quiet pools of fresh water.
He gives me new strength.

He guides me in the right way,
    as he has promised.
Even if that way goes through deepest darkness,
    I will not be afraid, Lord,
10   because you are with me!
Your shepherd's rod and staff keep me safe.

You prepare a banquet for me,
    where all my enemies can see me;

You welcome me by pouring ointment on my head
    and filling my cup to the brim.
Certainly your goodness and love will be with me as long as I live;
    and your house will be my home forever.

Finally, here is a version by a young American poet named David Rosenberg who is translating "A Poet's Bible" book by book; this modern version is taken from *Blues of the Sky*, Rosenberg's selection from the Psalms:

The Lord is my shepherd
and keeps me from wanting
what I can't have

lush green grass is set
around me and crystal water
to graze by

there I revive with my soul
find the way that love makes
for his name

10   and though I pass through cities of pain, through death's living shadow
I'm not afraid to touch
to know what I am

your shepherd's staff is always there
to keep me calm
in my body

you set a table before me
in the presence of my enemies
you give me grace to speak

to quiet them
20   to be full with humanness
to be warm in my soul's lightness

to feel contact every day
in my hand and in my belly
love coming down to me

in the air of your name, Lord
in your house
in my life

Here is a poem in Pablo Neruda's Spanish, followed by four American translations:

Entierro en el Este

Yo trabajo de noche, rodeado de ciudad,
de pescadores, de alfareros, de difuntos quemados
con azafrán y frutas, envueltos en muselina escarlata:

bajo mi balcón esos muertos terribles
pasan sonando cadenas y flautas de cobre,
estridentes y finas y lúgubres silban
entre el color de las pesadas flores envenenadas
y el grito de los cenicientos danzarines
y el creciente monótono de los tamtam
10   y el humo de las maderas que arden y huelen.

Porque una vez doblado el camino, junto al turbio río,
sus corazones, detenidos o iniciando un mayor movimiento,
rodarán quemados, con la pierna y el pie hechos fuego,
y la trémula ceniza caerá sobre el agua,
flotará como ramo de flores calcinadas
o como extinto fuego dejado por tan poderosos viajeros
que hicieron arder algo sobre las negras aguas, y devoraron
un aliento desaparecido y un licor extremo.

Burial in the East

I work nights, in the ring of the city,
among fisherfolk, potters, cadavers, cremations
of saffron and fruits shrouded into red muslin.
Under my balcony pass the terrible dead
sounding their coppery flutes and their chains,
strident and mournful and delicate—they hiss
in a blazon of poisoned and ponderous flowers,
through the cries of the smoldering dancers,
the tom-tom's augmented monotony,
10   in the crackle and fume of the woodsmoke.

One turn in the road, by the ooze of the river,
and their hearts, clogging up or preparing some monstrous exertion,
will whirl away burning, their legs and their feet incandescent;
the tremulous ash will descend on the water
and float like a branching of carbonized flowers—
a bonfire put out by the might of some wayfarer
who lighted the black of the water and devoured some part
of a vanished subsistence, a consummate libation.

—Ben Bellitt

Burial in the East

I work at night, surrounded by city,
by fishermen, by potters, by the dead burned
with saffron and fruits, wrapped in red muslin:
under my balcony these terrible corpses
go past playing chains and copper flutes,
strident and thin and lugubrious they whistle
amidst the colour of the heavy poisoned flowers
and the cry of the holy fire-dancers

and the growing monotony of the tom-toms
10   and the smoke of the different woods burning and giving off odours.

Because once around the corner, by the muddy river,
their hearts, held in check or beginning a major motion,
will roll, burning, their legs and feet will be fire
and the tremulous ash will fall over the water,
will float like a branch of calcined flowers
or like an extinct fire left by such mighty voyagers
as forced to burn something over the black waters, and devoured
a vanished breath and an extreme liquor.

—W. S. Merwin

Burial in the East

I work at night, surrounded by city,
by fishermen, by potters, by corpses burned
with saffron and fruit, wrapped in scarlet muslin:
underneath my balcony those terrible dead
go by, sounding their chains and copper flutes,
strident and clear and lugubrious they pipe
amid the colour of heavy poisoned flowers
and the cry of the ash-coloured dancers
and the mounting monotony of the drums
10   and smoke from logs that burn and smell.

For, once they reach the turn in the road, near the turbid river,
their hearts unmoving, or in greater movement,
they will roll burning, leg and foot made flame,
and the tremulous ashes will fall upon the water,
will float like a cluster of calcined flowers
or a quenched fire left by travelers so powerful
that they burned something over the black waters, and devoured
a vanished food, an utter liquor.

—Angel Flores

Funeral in the East

I work at night, the city all around me,
fishermen, and potters, and corpses that are burned
with saffron and fruit, rolled in scarlet muslin:
those terrifying corpses go past under my balcony,
making their chains and copper flutes give off noise,
whistling sounds, harsh and pure and mournful,
among the brightness of the flowers heavy and poisoned,
and the cries of the dancers covered with ashes,
and the constantly rising monotony of the drum,
10   and the smoke from the logs scented and burning.

For once around the corner, near the muddy river,
their hearts, either stopping or starting off at a greater speed,

will roll over, burned, the leg and the foot turned to fire,
and the fluttering ashes will settle down on the water
and float like a branch of chalky flowers,
or like an extinct fire left by travellers with such great powers
they made something blaze up on the black waters, and bolted down
a food no longer found, and one finishing drink.

—Robert Bly

Shakespeare in paraphrase

Let us end with a gross example of paraphrase. Recently a publisher issued four Shakespearean tragedies with the original lines on the left-hand page and line-by-line paraphrases on the right. The editors—or translators—intended to provide pedagogical help for contemporary students, changing archaic words into modern synonyms. At the same time, they often turned Shakespeare's metaphors into plain speech. At the beginning of *Hamlet*, when the guards challenge each other, one of them says "Stand and unfold yourself." In the paraphrase the sentence reads "Stand still and tell me who you are."

When we remove metaphor in favor of plain speech, we remove images—and often we remove images that carry feelings on their backs. When Francisco asked Bernardo "Stand and unfold yourself," he thought of Bernardo physically opening up his body like a bird or like a butterfly expanding vulnerable wings or perhaps like a flag unfurling. But when Francisco asks Bernardo in the paraphrase "Stand still and tell me who you are," we have a mere request for identification. We have no picture, no image, no sense of something vulnerable, no sense of something formerly closed in on itself, now opening up.

Here is a well-known speech, with Shakespeare's text in roman type. Indented, in italic, after each Shakespearean line, is the modern paraphrase. You can read each speech as a whole or read one line at a time, first the original and then the paraphrase.

1. To be, or not to be: that is the question:
   1. To be, or not to be: that is what really matters.
2. Whether 'tis nobler in the mind to suffer
   2. Is it nobler to accept passively
3. The slings and arrows of outrageous fortune,
   3. the trials and tribulations that unjust fate sends,
4. Or to take arms against a sea of troubles,
   4. or to resist an ocean of troubles,
5. And by opposing end them. To die, to sleep—
   5. and, by our own effort, defeat them? To die, to fall asleep—
6. No more—and by a sleep to say we end
   6. perhaps that's all there is to it—and by that sleep suppose we put an end to
7. The heartache, and the thousand natural shocks
   7. the heartache and the thousands of pains and worries
8. That flesh is heir to! 'Tis a consummation

8. *that are a part of being human! That's an end*

9. Devoutly to be wished. To die, to sleep—
   9. *we could all look forward to. To die, to sleep—*

10. To sleep—perchance to dream: ay, there's the rub,
    10. *to sleep—maybe to dream: yes, that's the catch.*

11. For in that sleep of death what dreams may come
    11. *For in that sleep of death the nightmares that may come*

12. When we have shuffled off this mortal coil,
    12. *when we have freed ourselves from the turmoil of this mortal life*

13. Must give us pause. There's the respect
    13. *must make us hesitate. There's the thought*

14. That makes calamity of so long life:
    14. *that makes a disaster out of living to a ripe old age.*

15. For who would bear the whips and scorns of time,
    15. *After all, who wants to put up with the lashes and insults of this world,*

16. Th' oppressor's wrong, the proud man's contumely,
    16. *the tyrant's injustice and contempt of arrogant men,*

17. The pangs of despised love, the law's delay,
    17. *the pains of rejected love, the law's frustrating slowness,*

18. The insolence of office, and the spurns
    18. *insults from our superiors, and the snubs*

19. That patient merit of th' unworthy takes,
    19. *that deserving and hopeful people have to take from powerful inferiors,*

20. When he himself might his quietus make
    20. *when he could end the whole process by killing himself*

21. With a bare bodkin? . . .
    21. *with a bare dagger? . . .*

In Shakespeare's first line he speaks of *the question*, which as Hamlet thinks out loud becomes a true, unanswerable question—not a question in the abstracted sense of problem, like "the Middle East question." Instead of using *question*, the paraphraser speaks of *what really matters*, which is empty language. The difference is small, because Shakespeare's *question* is not a word of great importance in Hamlet's speech. Yet the difference in the two words is typical: *question* is concrete, in the form of a real question; *what really matters* has neither "reality" nor "matter" in its syllabic bones.

When the paraphraser substitutes *to accept passively* for *in the mind to suffer*, one wants to argue. Shakespeare distinguishes between inaction, which includes mental suffering, and external action against huge forces. The paraphraser includes the notion of passivity but excludes mental suffering; Shakespeare seems mistranslated. In *trials and tribulations* we find a cliché to substitute for an image of weapons. Although the *slings and arrows* may be abstracted into *trials and tribulations* in our minds—almost like calling them "nuisances and annoyances"—the cliché is pale; we lose the implication of pain and death carried in *slings and arrows*. Paraphrasing *outrageous* as *unjust* is another diminishment. *Outrageous* retains in modern speech most of its old character, especially when we denounce something with the noun an *outrage*. *Unjust* is less emotional, more intellectual. We begin to see that the paraphrase, by draining the language of particularity in metaphor and image, drains the poetry of feeling.

So much for the first five lines. The rest of this speech, and another famous one, can bear more attention.

Exercises

1. In 7/7 discuss the removal of *natural*. Is anything missing that Shakespeare may have felt essential?
2. In 8/8, what is the first metaphor removed? Does the missing metaphor have any general relevance to this play?
3. In 9/9, is *devoutly* paraphrased?
4. 12/12. Using a large dictionary (the *Oxford English Dictionary*, usually in a college library, would be the best) consider the metaphor of *shuffle . . . coil*. Does *the turmoil of this mortal life* paraphrase parts of Shakespeare's line? Does it paraphrase the whole?
5. In 14/*14*, find a new metaphor added by the paraphraser. Is it good poetry?
6. 15/*15*, are the substitute words examples of the occasional usefulness of paraphrases in reading older authors? Do you find other good examples of paraphrase in this passage from *Hamlet*?

A paraphrase from *Macbeth*

22. Tomorrow, and tomorrow, and tomorrow
    22. Tomorrow follows tomorrow and is followed by tomorrow,
23. Creeps in this petty pace from day to day,
    23. feebly creeping from day to day
24. To the last syllable of recorded time;
    24. to the last syllable of written history,
25. And all our yesterdays have lighted fools
    25.and our entire past has lighted the way for fools
26. The way to dusty death. Out, out, brief candle!
    26. down the path to dusty death. Burn out, burn out, you short candle of life.
27. Life's but a walking shadow, a poor player
    27. A man's life is only a walking shadow, a poor actor
28. That struts and frets his hour upon the stage
    28. who swaggers and paces about the stage for an hour
29. And then is heard no more. It is a tale
    29. and then is never heard from again. Life is a tale
30. Told by an idiot, full of sound and fury
    30. told by an idiot, full of noise and rage,
31. Signifying nothing . . .
    31. but meaning nothing . . .

Exercises

1. In 22–23/*22–23*, notice the change in grammatical mood and syntactic structure. Does Shakespeare's syntax enforce Shakespeare's meaning? Is the paraphrased syntax equal in energy?

2. In 25/25, discuss the difference between *all our yesterdays* and *our entire past.* Is it accurate paraphrase? Is it equal in forcefulness? Why?

3. In 25–26, readers have noticed that Macbeth's image of a candle derived from his earlier notion of *yesterday* that *lighted* people on a path or *way.* When *candle* becomes *candle of life,* what happens to the notion of the passage?

4. No one expects paraphrase to equal the sound and rhythm of the original; however, one may *use* a paraphrase's relative deficiency in sound as a way to notice the sound of the poet's original language. Analyze the rhythmic distinction between lines 27–31 and *27–31.*

Three Poets

After studying elements of poetry, where examples are as brief as a line and as long as a single poem, it will be useful to concentrate next on a group of poems by a single poet. Here are selections from the poems of three American poets, each represented by poems characteristic of their range and development. Here we have a woman and two men; an Easterner who lived most of her life in one town, a Californian who became the great poet of New England, and a Midwesterner who ended his life as a poet of the Pacific Northwest, one born in 1830, another in 1874, the third in 1908.

Emily Dickinson

Emily Dickinson (1830–1886) grew up in Amherst, Massachusetts, where her family was associated with Amherst College. She attended school with other young women, but as she grew older became reclusive, until she rarely left her own room. When she was young she made attempts to print her poems and she placed a few in obscure publications. Then she apparently renounced this notion of fame and wrote, so far as we know, for herself. Her eccentricities of punctuation, not to mention the strangeness of her metaphors and rhymes, may derive from her sense that she was her own and only audience. Yet power and insight accumulated in her isolation. She is probably the greatest female poet of our language, and every year her audience grows wider.

He put the Belt around my life—

He put the Belt around my life—
I heard the Buckle snap—
And turned away, imperial,
My Lifetime folding up—
Deliberate, as a Duke would do
A Kingdom's Title Deed—
Henceforth, a Dedicated sort—
A Member of the Cloud.

Yet not too far to come at call—
10 And do the little Toils
That make the Circuit of the Rest—
And deal occasional smiles
To lives that stoop to notice mine—
And kindly ask it in—
Whose invitation, know you not
For Whom I must decline?

He fumbles at your Soul

He fumbles at your Soul
As Players at the Keys
Before they drop full Music on—
He stuns you by degrees—
Prepares your brittle Nature
For the Ethereal Blow
By fainter Hammers—further heard—
Then nearer—Then so slow
Your Breath has time to straighten—
10 Your Brain—to bubble Cool—
Deals—One—imperial—Thunderbolt—
That scalps your naked Soul—

When Winds take Forests in their Paws—
The Universe—is still—

After great pain, a formal feeling comes—

After great pain, a formal feeling comes—
The Nerves sit ceremonious, like Tombs—
The stiff Heart questions was it He, that bore,
And Yesterday, or Centuries before?

The Feet, mechanical, go round—
Of Ground, or Air, or Ought—
A Wooden way
Regardless grown,
A Quartz contentment, like a stone—

10 This is the Hour of Lead—
Remembered, if outlived,
As Freezing persons, recollect the Snow—
First—Chill—then Stupor—then the letting go—

The first Day's Night had come—

The first Day's Night had come—
And grateful that a thing
So terrible—had been endured—
I told my Soul to sing—

She said her Strings were snapt—
Her Bow—to Atoms blown—
And so to mend her—gave me work
Until another Morn—

And then—a Day as huge
10   As Yesterdays in pairs,
Unrolled its horror in my face—
Until it blocked my eyes—

My Brain—begun to laugh—
I mumbled—like a fool—
And tho' 'tis Years ago—that Day—
My Brain keeps giggling—still.

And Something's odd—within—
That person that I was—
And this One—do not feel the same—
20   Could it be Madness—this?

Much Madness is divinest Sense—

Much Madness is divinest Sense—
To a discerning Eye—
Much Sense—the starkest Madness—
'Tis the Majority
In this, as All, prevail—
Assent—and you are sane—
Demur—you're straightway dangerous—
And handled with a Chain—

I heard a Fly buzz—when I died—

I heard a Fly buzz—when I died—
The Stillness in the Room
Was like the Stillness in the Air—
Between the Heaves of Storm—

The Eyes around—had wrung them dry—
And Breaths were gathering firm
For that last Onset—when the King
Be witnessed—in the Room—

I willed my Keepsakes—Signed away
10   What portion of me be
Assignable—and then it was
There interposed a Fly—

With Blue—uncertain stumbling Buzz—
Between the light—and me—
And then the Windows failed—and then
I could not see to see—

I would not paint—a picture—

I would not paint—a picture—
I'd rather be the One
Its bright impossibility
To dwell—delicious—on—
And wonder how the fingers feel
Whose rare—celestial—stir—
Evokes so sweet a Torment—
Such sumptuous—Despair—

I would not talk, like Cornets—
10   I'd rather be the One
Raised softly to the Ceilings—
And out, and easy on—
Through Villages of Ether—
Myself endued Balloon
By but a lip of Metal—
The pier to my Pontoon—

Nor would I be a Poet—
It's finer—own the Ear—
Enamored—impotent—content—
20   The License to revere,
A privilege so awful
What would the Dower be,
Had I the Art to stun myself
With Bolts of Melody!

I'm ceded—I've stopped being Theirs—

I'm ceded—I've stopped being Theirs—
The name They dropped upon my face
With water, in the country church
Is finished using, now,
And They can put it with my Dolls,
My childhood, and the string of spools,
I've finished threading—too—

Baptized, before, without the choice,
But this time, consciously, of Grace—
10   Unto supremest name—
Called to my Full—The Crescent dropped—
Existence's whole Arc, filled up,
With one small Diadem.

My second Rank—too small the first—
Crowned—Crowing—on my Father's breast—
A half unconscious Queen—
But this time—Adequate—Erect,
With Will to choose, or to reject,
And I choose, just a Crown—

The Soul has Bandaged moments—

The Soul has Bandaged moments—
When too appalled to stir—
She feels some ghastly Fright come up
And stop to look at her—

Salute her—with long fingers—
Caress her freezing hair—
Sip, Goblin, from the very lips
The Lover—hovered—o'er—
Unworthy, that a thought so mean
10   Accost a Theme—so—fair—

The soul has moments of Escape—
When bursting all the doors—
She dances like a Bomb, abroad,
And swings upon the Hours,

As do the Bee—delirious borne—
Long Dungeoned from his Rose—
Touch Liberty—then know no more,
But Noon, and Paradise—

The Soul's retaken moments—
20   When, Felon led along,
With shackles on the plumed feet,
And staples, in the Song,

The Horror welcomes her, again,
These, are not brayed of Tongue—

The Province of the Saved

The Province of the Saved
Should be the Art—To save—
Through Skill obtained in Themselves—
The Science of the Grave

No Man can understand
But He that hath endured
The Dissolution—in Himself—
That Man—be qualified

To qualify Despair
10   To Those who failing new—
Mistake Defeat for Death—Each time—
Till acclimated—to—

A still—Volcano—Life—

A still—Volcano—Life—
That flickered in the night—

When it was dark enough to do
Without erasing sight—

A quiet—Earthquake Style—
Too subtle to suspect
By natures this side Naples—
The North cannot detect

The Solemn—Torrid—Symbol—
10   The lips that never lie—
Whose hissing Corals part—and shut—
And Cities—ooze away—

I cannot live with You—

I cannot live with You—
It would be Life—
And Life is over there—
Behind the Shelf

The Sexton keeps the Key to—
Putting up
Our Life—His Porcelain—
Like a Cup—

Discarded of the Housewife—
10   Quaint—or Broke—
A newer Sevres pleases—
Old Ones crack—

I could not die—with You—
For One must wait
To shut the Other's Gaze down—
You—could not—

And I—Could I stand by
And see You—freeze—
Without my Right of Frost—
20   Death's privilege?

Nor could I rise—with You—
Because Your Face
Would put out Jesus'—
That New Grace

Glow plain—and foreign
On my homesick Eye—
Except that You than He
Shone closer by—

They'd judge Us—How—
30   For You—served Heaven—You know,
Or sought to—
I could not—

Because You saturated Sight—
And I had no more Eyes
For sordid excellence
As Paradise

And were You lost, I would be—
Though My Name
Rang loudest
40   On the Heavenly fame—

And were You—saved—
And I—condemned to be
Where You were not—
That self—were Hell to Me—

So We must meet apart—
You there—I—here—
With just the Door ajar
That Oceans are—and Prayer—
And that White Sustenance—
50   Despair—

Me from Myself—to banish—

Me from Myself—to banish—
Had I Art—
Impregnable my Fortress
Unto All Heart—

But since Myself—assault Me—
How have I peace
Except by subjugating
Consciousness?

And since We're mutual Monarch
10   How this be
Except by Abdication—
Me—of Me?

Because I could not stop for Death—

Because I could not stop for Death—
He kindly stopped for me—
The Carriage held but just Ourselves—
And Immortality.

We slowly drove—He knew no haste
And I had put away
My labor and my leisure too,
For His Civility—

We passed the School, where Children strove
10   At Recess—in the Ring—
We passed the Fields of Gazing Grain—
We passed the Setting Sun—

Or rather   He passed Us—
The Dews drew quivering and chill—
For only Gossamer, my Gown—
My Tippet—only Tulle—

We paused before a House that seemed
A Swelling of the Ground—
The Roof was scarcely visible—
20   The Cornice—in the Ground—

Since then—'tis Centuries—and yet
Feels shorter than the Day
I first surmised the Horses' Heads
Were toward Eternity—

My Life had stood—a Loaded Gun—

My Life had stood—a Loaded Gun—
In Corners—till a Day
The Owner passed—identified—
And carried Me away—

And now We roam in Sovereign Woods—
And now We hunt the Doe—
And every time I speak for Him—
The Mountains straight reply—

And do I smile, such cordial light
10   Upon the Valley glow—
It is as a Vesuvian face
Had let its pleasure through—

And when at Night—Our good Day done—
I guard My Master's Head—
'Tis better than the Eider-Duck's
Deep Pillow—to have shared—

To foe of His—I'm deadly foe—
None stir the second time—
On whom I lay a Yellow Eye—
20   Or an emphatic Thumb—

Though I than He—may longer live
He longer must—than I—

For I have but the power to kill,
Without—the power to die—

Severer Service of myself

Severer Service of myself
I—hastened to demand
To fill the awful Vacuum
Your life had left behind—

I worried Nature with my Wheels
When Hers had ceased to run—
When she had put away Her Work
My own had just begun.

I strove to weary Brain and Bone—
10　To harass to fatigue
The glittering Retinue of nerves—
Vitality to clog

To some dull comfort Those obtain
Who put a Head away
They knew the Hair to—
And forget the color of the Day—

Affliction would not be appeased—
The Darkness braced as firm
As all my stratagem had been
20　The Midnight to confirm—

No Drug for Consciousness—can be—
Alternative to die
Is Nature's only Pharmacy
For Being's Malady—

I felt a Cleaving in my Mind—

I felt a Cleaving in my Mind—
As if my Brain had split—
I tried to match it—Seam by Seam—
But could not make them fit.

The thought behind, I strove to join
Unto the thought before—
But Sequence ravelled out of Sound
Like Balls—upon a Floor.

A narrow Fellow in the Grass

A narrow Fellow in the Grass
Occasionally rides—
You may have met Him—did you not
His notice sudden is—

The Grass divides as with a Comb—
A spotted shaft is seen—

And then it closes at your feet
And opens further on—

He likes a Boggy Acre
10 A Floor too cool for Corn—
Yet when a Boy, and Barefoot—
I more than once at Noon
Have passed, I thought, a Whip lash
Unbraiding in the Sun
When stooping to secure it
It wrinkled, and was gone—

Several of Nature's People
I know, and they know me—
I feel for them a transport
20 Of cordiality—

But never met this Fellow
Attended, or alone
Without a tighter breathing
And Zero at the Bone—

Robert Frost

Robert Frost (1874–1963) was born in California and died in New England at the age of eighty-eight. The New England countryside, its people, and their speech take center stage in his poems. Frost's father died when he was ten, and his mother took him back East. He attended high school in Massachusetts, went to Dartmouth briefly, worked in mills, and after marriage spent two years at Harvard without taking a degree. He tried his hand at farming while he wrote poems, but his poems did not win acceptance from American editors. In 1912 he took his family to England, where a London publisher recognized the quality of the work; *A Boy's Will* appeared in 1913. When Frost returned to the United States in 1915, he found America ready for him. He won the Pulitzer Prize four times, and two years before he died read a poem at the inauguration of President John F. Kennedy.

The Pasture

I'm going out to clean the pasture spring;
I'll only stop to rake the leaves away
(And wait to watch the water clear, I may)
I sha'n't be gone long.—You come too.

I'm going out to fetch the little calf
That's standing by the mother. It's so young
It totters when she licks it with her tongue.
I sha'n't be gone long.—You come too.

Mowing

There was never a sound beside the wood but one,
And that was my long scythe whispering to the ground.
What was it it whispered? I knew not well myself;
Perhaps it was something about the heat of the sun,
Something, perhaps, about the lack of sound—
And that was why it whispered and did not speak.
It was no dream of the gift of idle hours,
Or easy gold at the hand of fay or elf:
Anything more than the truth would have seemed too weak
10   To the earnest love that laid the swale in rows,
Not without feeble-pointed spikes of flowers
(Pale orchises), and scared a bright green snake.
The fact is the sweetest dream that labor knows.
My long scythe whispered and left the hay to make.

Home Burial

He saw her from the bottom of the stairs
Before she saw him. She was starting down,
Looking back over her shoulder at some fear.
She took a doubtful step and then undid it
To raise herself and look again. He spoke
Advancing toward her: 'What is it you see
From up there always—for I want to know.'
She turned and sank upon her skirts at that,
And her face changed from terrified to dull.
10   He said to gain time: 'What is it you see,'
Mounting until she cowered under him.
'I will find out now—you must tell me, dear.'
She, in her place, refused him any help
With the least stiffening of her neck and silence.
She let him look, sure that he wouldn't see,
Blind creature; and awhile he didn't see.
But at last he murmured, 'Oh,' and again, 'Oh.'

'What is it—what?' she said.

                    'Just that I see.'

20   'You don't,' she challenged. 'Tell me what it is.'

'The wonder is I didn't see at once.
I never noticed it from here before.
I must be wonted to it—that's the reason.
The little graveyard where my people are!
So small the window frames the whole of it.
Not so much larger than a bedroom, is it?
There are three stones of slate and one of marble,
Broad-shouldered little slabs there in the sunlight
On the sidehill. We haven't to mind *those*.
30   But I understand: it is not the stones,
But the child's mound—'

                    'Don't, don't, don't, don't,' she cried.

She withdrew shrinking from beneath his arm
That rested on the bannister, and slid downstairs;
And turned on him with such a daunting look,
He said twice over before he knew himself:
'Can't a man speak of his own child he's lost?'

'Not you! Oh, where's my hat? Oh, I don't need it!
I must get out of here. I must get air.
40   I don't know rightly whether any man can.'

'Amy! Don't go to someone else this time.
Listen to me. I won't come down the stairs.'
He sat and fixed his chin between his fists.
'There's something I should like to ask you, dear.'

'You don't know how to ask it.'

                                'Help me, then.'

Her fingers moved the latch for all reply.

'My words are nearly always an offense.
I don't know how to speak of anything
50   So as to please you. But I might be taught
I should suppose. I can't say I see how.
A man must partly give up being a man
With women-folk. We could have some arrangement
By which I'd bind myself to keep hands off
Anything special you're a-mind to name.
Though I don't like such things 'twixt those that love
Two that don't love can't live together without them.
But two that do can't live together with them.'
She moved the latch a little. 'Don't—don't go.
60   Don't carry it to someone else this time.
Tell me about it if it's something human.
Let me into your grief. I'm not so much
Unlike other folks as your standing there
Apart would make me out. Give me my chance.

I do think, though, you overdo it a little.
What was it brought you up to think it the thing
To take your mother-loss of a first child
So inconsolably—in the face of love.
You'd think his memory might be satisfied—'

70   'There you go sneering now!'

                              'I'm not, I'm not!
You make me angry. I'll come down to you.
God, what a woman! And it's come to this,
A man can't speak of his own child that's dead.'

'You can't because you don't know how to speak.
If you had any feelings, you that dug
With your own hand—how could you?—his little grave;
I saw you from that very window there,
Making the gravel leap and leap in air,
80   Leap up, like that, like that, and land so lightly
And roll back down the mound beside the hole.
I thought, Who is that man? I didn't know you.
And I crept down the stairs and up the stairs
To look again, and still your spade kept lifting.
Then you came in. I heard your rumbling voice
Out in the kitchen, and I don't know why,
But I went near to see with my own eyes.
You could sit there with the stains on your shoes
Of the fresh earth from your own baby's grave
90   And talk about your everyday concerns.
You had stood the spade up against the wall
Outside there in the entry, for I saw it.'

'I shall laugh the worst laugh I ever laughed.
I'm cursed. God, if I don't believe I'm cursed.'

'I can repeat the very words you were saying.
"Three foggy mornings and one rainy day
Will rot the best birch fence a man can build."
Think of it, talk like that at such a time!
What had how long it takes a birch to rot
100   To do with what was in the darkened parlor.
You *couldn't* care! The nearest friends can go
With anyone to death, comes so far short
They might as well not try to go at all.
No, from the time when one is sick to death,
One is alone, and he dies more alone.
Friends make pretense of following to the grave,
But before one is in it, their minds are turned
And making the best of their way back to life
And living people, and things they understand.
110   But the world's evil. I won't have grief so
If I can change it. Oh, I won't, I won't!'

'There, you have said it all and you feel better.
You won't go now. You're crying. Close the door.

The heart's gone out of it: why keep it up.
Amy! There's someone coming down the road!'

'*You*—oh, you think the talk is all. I must go—
Somewhere out of this house. How can I make you—'

'If—you—do!' She was opening the door wider.
'Where do you mean to go? First tell me that.
120   I'll follow and bring you back by force. I *will!*—'

After Apple-Picking

My long two-pointed ladder's sticking through a tree
Toward heaven still,
And there's a barrel that I didn't fill
Beside it, and there may be two or three
Apples I didn't pick upon some bough.
But I am done with apple-picking now.
Essence of winter sleep is on the night,
The scent of apples: I am drowsing off.
I cannot rub the strangeness from my sight
10   I got from looking through a pane of glass
I skimmed this morning from the drinking trough
And held against the world of hoary grass.
It melted, and I let it fall and break.
But I was well
Upon my way to sleep before it fell,
And I could tell
What form my dreaming was about to take.
Magnified apples appear and disappear,
Stem end and blossom end,
20   And every fleck of russet showing clear.
My instep arch not only keeps the ache,
It keeps the pressure of a ladder round.
I feel the ladder sway as the boughs bend.
And I keep hearing from the cellar bin
The rumbling sound
Of load on load of apples coming in.
For I have had too much
Of apple-picking: I am overtired
Of the great harvest I myself desired.
30   There were ten thousand thousand fruit to touch,
Cherish in hand, lift down, and not let fall.
For all
That struck the earth,
No matter if not bruised or spiked with stubble,
Went surely to the cider-apple heap
As of no worth.

One can see what will trouble
This sleep of mine, whatever sleep it is.
Were he not gone,
40   The woodchuck could say whether it's like his
Long sleep, as I describe its coming on,
Or just some human sleep.

The Road Not Taken

Two roads diverged in a yellow wood,
And sorry I could not travel both
And be one traveler, long I stood
And looked down one as far as I could
To where it bent in the undergrowth;

Then took the other, as just as fair,
And having perhaps the better claim,
Because it was grassy and wanted wear;
Though as for that the passing there
10   Had worn them really about the same,

And both that morning equally lay
In leaves no step had trodden black.
Oh, I kept the first for another day!
Yet knowing how way leads on to way,
I doubted if I should ever come back.

I shall be telling this with a sigh
Somewhere ages and ages hence:
Two roads diverged in a wood, and I—
I took the one less traveled by,
20   And that has made all the difference.

Birches

When I see birches bend to left and right
Across the lines of straighter darker trees,
I like to think some boy's been swinging them.
But swinging doesn't bend them down to stay
As ice-storms do. Often you must have seen them
Loaded with ice a sunny winter morning
After a rain. They click upon themselves
As the breeze rises, and turn many-colored
As the stir cracks and crazes their enamel.
10   Soon the sun's warmth makes them shed crystal shells
Shattering and avalanching on the snow-crust—
Such heaps of broken glass to sweep away
You'd think the inner dome of heaven had fallen.
They are dragged to the withered bracken by the load,
And they seem not to break; though once they are bowed
So low for long, they never right themselves:

You may see their trunks arching in the woods
Years afterwards, trailing their leaves on the ground
Like girls on hands and knees that throw their hair
20   Before them over their heads to dry in the sun.
But I was going to say when Truth broke in
With all her matter-of-fact about the ice-storm
I should prefer to have some boy bend them
As he went out and in to fetch the cows—
Some boy too far from town to learn baseball,
Whose only play was what he found himself,
Summer or winter, and could play alone.
One by one he subdued his father's trees
By riding them down over and over again
30   Until he took the stiffness out of them,
And not one but hung limp, not one was left
For him to conquer. He learned all there was
To learn about not launching out too soon
And so not carrying the tree away
Clear to the ground. He always kept his poise
To the top branches, climbing carefully
With the same pains you use to fill a cup
Up to the brim, and even above the brim.
Then he flung outward, feet first, with a swish,
40   Kicking his way down through the air to the ground.
So was I once myself a swinger of birches.
And so I dream of going back to be.
It's when I'm weary of considerations,
And life is too much like a pathless wood
Where your face burns and tickles with the cobwebs
Broken across it, and one eye is weeping
From a twig's having lashed across it open.
I'd like to get away from earth awhile
And then come back to it and begin over.
50   May no fate willfully misunderstand me
And half grant what I wish and snatch me away
Not to return. Earth's the right place for love:
I don't know where it's likely to go better.
I'd like to go by climbing a birch tree,
And climb black branches up a snow-white trunk
Toward heaven, till the tree could bear no more,
But dipped its top and set me down again.
That would be good both going and coming back.
One could do worse than be a swinger of birches.

To Earthward

Love at the lips was touch
As sweet as I could bear;
And once that seemed too much;
I lived on air

That crossed me from sweet things
The flow of—was it musk
From hidden grapevine springs
Down hill at dusk?

I had the swirl and ache
10   From sprays of honeysuckle
That when they're gathered shake
Dew on the knuckle.

I craved strong sweets, but those
Seemed strong when I was young;
The petal of the rose
It was that stung.

Now no joy but lacks salt
That is not dashed with pain
And weariness and fault;
20   I crave the stain

Of tears, the aftermark
Of almost too much love,
The sweet of bitter bark
And burning clove.

When stiff and sore and scarred
I take away my hand
From leaning on it hard
In grass and sand,

The hurt is not enough:
30   I long for weight and strength
To feel the earth as rough
To all my length.

The Need of Being Versed in Country Things

The house had gone to bring again
To the midnight sky a sunset glow.
Now the chimney was all of the house that stood,
Like a pistil after the petals go.

The barn opposed across the way,
That would have joined the house in flame
Had it been the will of the wind, was left
To bear forsaken the place's name.

No more it opened with all one end
10   For teams that came by the stony road
To drum on the floor with scurrying hoofs
And brush the mow with the summer load.

The birds that came to it through the air
At broken windows flew out and in,
Their murmur more like the sigh we sigh
From too much dwelling on what has been.

Yet for them the lilac renewed its leaf,
And the aged elm, though touched with fire;
And the dry pump flung up an awkward arm;
20   And the fence post carried a strand of wire.

For them there was really nothing sad.
But though they rejoiced in the nest they kept,
One had to be versed in country things
Not to believe the phoebes wept.

Once by the Pacific

The shattered water made a misty din.
Great waves looked over others coming in,
And thought of doing something to the shore
That water never did to land before.
The clouds were low and hairy in the skies,
Like locks blown forward in the gleam of eyes.
You could not tell, and yet it looked as if
The shore was lucky in being backed by cliff,
The cliff in being backed by continent;
10   It looked as if a night of dark intent
Was coming, and not only a night, an age.
Someone had better be prepared for rage.
There would be more than ocean-water broken
Before God's last *Put out the Light* was spoken.

Acquainted with the Night

I have been one acquainted with the night.
I have walked out in rain—and back in rain.
I have outwalked the furthest city light.

I have looked down the saddest city lane.
I have passed by the watchman on his beat
And dropped my eyes, unwilling to explain.

I have stood still and stopped the sound of feet
When far away an interrupted cry
Came over houses from another street,

10   But not to call me back or say good-by;
And further still at an unearthly height,
One luminary clock against the sky

Proclaimed the time was neither wrong nor right.
I have been one acquainted with the night.

Desert Places

Snow falling and night falling fast, oh, fast
In a field I looked into going past,
And the ground almost covered smooth in snow,
But a few weeds and stubble showing last.

The woods around it have it—it is theirs.
All animals are smothered in their lairs.
I am too absent-spirited to count;
The loneliness includes me unawares.

And lonely as it is that loneliness
10   Will be more lonely ere it will be less—
A blanker whiteness of benighted snow
With no expression, nothing to express.

They cannot scare me with their empty spaces
Between stars—on stars where no human race is.
I have it in me so much nearer home
To scare myself with my own desert places.

Neither Out Far Nor In Deep

The people along the sand
All turn and look one way.
They turn their back on the land.
They look at the sea all day.

As long as it takes to pass
A ship keeps raising its hull;
The wetter ground like glass
Reflects a standing gull.

The land may vary more;
10   But wherever the truth may be—
The water comes ashore,
And the people look at the sea.

They cannot look out far.
They cannot look in deep.
But when was that ever a bar
To any watch they keep?

The Silken Tent

She is as in a field a silken tent
At midday when a sunny summer breeze
Has dried the dew and all its ropes relent,
So that in guys it gently sways at ease,
And its supporting central cedar pole,

That is its pinnacle to heavenward
And signifies the sureness of the soul,
Seems to owe naught to any single cord,
But strictly held by none, is loosely bound
10   By countless silken ties of love and thought
To everything on earth the compass round,
And only by one's going slightly taut
In the capriciousness of summer air
Is of the slightest bondage made aware.

Come In

As I came to the edge of the woods,
Thrush music—hark!
Now if it was dusk outside,
Inside it was dark.

Too dark in the woods for a bird
By sleight of wing
To better its perch for the night,
Though it still could sing.

The last of the light of the sun
10   That had died in the west
Still lived for one song more
In a thrush's breast.

Far in the pillared dark
Thrush music went—
Almost like a call to come in
To the dark and lament.

But no, I was out for stars:
I would not come in.
I meant not even if asked,
20   And I hadn't been.

The Most of It

He thought he kept the universe alone;
For all the voice in answer he could wake
Was but the mocking echo of his own
From some tree-hidden cliff across the lake.
Some morning from the boulder-broken beach
He would cry out on life, that what it wants
Is not its own love back in copy speech,
But counter-love, original response.
And nothing ever came of what he cried

10 Unless it was the embodiment that crashed
In the cliff's talus on the other side,
And then in the far distant water splashed.
But after a time allowed for it to swim,
Instead of proving human when it neared
And someone else additional to him,
As a great buck it powerfully appeared,
Pushing the crumpled water up ahead,
And landed pouring like a waterfall,
And stumbled through the rocks with horny tread,
20 And forced the underbrush—and that was all.

Other poems by Robert Frost will be found on pages 385, 407, 435, 441,
478, and 489–490.

Theodore Roethke

Theodore Roethke (1908–1963) was born in Saginaw, Michigan, where his
father kept the greenhouse that figures so prominently in his poems. He
attended the University of Michigan and spent his last sixteen years in Seattle,
where he was a professor at the University of Washington. He began by writing
tight, formal stanzas and later broadened his repertoire to include a wide
variety of tones and manners. Possibly no other major poet has traveled so
widely in the realms of style. When he died he had recently written his best
work, notably "The Rose." See also page 425.

Cuttings
(later)

This urge, wrestle, resurrection of dry sticks,
Cut stems struggling to put down feet,
What saint strained so much,
Rose on such lopped limbs to a new life?

I can hear, underground, that sucking and sobbing,
In my veins, in my bones I feel it,—
The small waters seeping upward,

The tight grains parting at last.
When sprouts break out,
10   Slippery as fish,
I quail, lean to beginnings, sheath-wet.

Big Wind

Where were the greenhouses going,
Lunging into the lashing
Wind driving water
So far down the river
All the faucets stopped?—
So we drained the manure-machine
For the steam plant,
Pumping the stale mixture
Into the rusty boilers,
10   Watching the pressure gauge
Waver over to red,
As the seams hissed
And the live steam
Drove to the far
End of the rose-house,
Where the worst wind was,
Creaking the cypress window-frames,
Cracking so much thin glass
We stayed all night,
20   Stuffing the holes with burlap;
But she rode it out,
That old rose-house,
She hove into the teeth of it,
The core and pith of that ugly storm,
Ploughing with her stiff prow,
Bucking into the wind-waves
That broke over the whole of her,
Flailing her sides with spray,
Flinging long strings of wet across the roof-top,
30   Finally veering, wearing themselves out, merely
Whistling thinly under the wind-vents;
She sailed until the calm morning,
Carrying her full cargo of roses.

Dolor

I have known the inexorable sadness of pencils,
Neat in their boxes, dolor of pad and paper-weight,
All the misery of manilla folders and mucilage,
Desolation in immaculate public places,
Lonely reception room, lavatory, switchboard,
The unalterable pathos of basin and pitcher,

Ritual of multigraph, paper-clip, comma,
Endless duplication of lives and objects.
And I have seen dust from the walls of institutions,
10 Finer than flour, alive, more dangerous than silica,
Sift, almost invisible, through long afternoons of tedium,
Dropping a fine film on nails and delicate eyebrows,
Glazing the pale hair, the duplicate grey standard faces.

My Papa's Waltz

The whiskey on your breath
Could make a small boy dizzy;
But I hung on like death:
Such waltzing was not easy.

We romped until the pans
Slid from the kitchen shelf;
My mother's countenance
Could not unfrown itself.

The hand that held my wrist
10 Was battered on one knuckle;
At every step you missed
My right ear scraped a buckle.

You beat time on my head
With a palm caked hard by dirt,
Then waltzed me off to bed
Still clinging to your shirt.

The Lost Son

1. The Flight
At Woodlawn I heard the dead cry:
I was lulled by the slamming of iron,
A slow drip over stones,
Toads brooding wells.
All the leaves stuck out their tongues;
I shook the softening chalk of my bones,
Saying,
Snail, snail, glister me forward,
Bird, soft-sigh me home,
10 Worm, be with me.
This is my hard time.

Fished in an old wound,
The soft pond of repose;
Nothing nibbled my line,
Not even the minnows came.

Sat in an empty house
Watching shadows crawl,

Scratching.
There was one fly.

20   Voice, come out of the silence.
Say something.
Appear in the form of a spider
Or a moth beating the curtain.

Tell me:
Which is the way I take;
Out of what door do I go,
Where and to whom?

 Dark hollows said, lee to the wind,
 The moon said, back of an eel,
30 The salt said, look by the sea,
 Your tears are not enough praise,
 You will find no comfort here,
 In the kingdom of bang and blab.

 Running lightly over spongy ground,
 Past the pasture of flat stones,
 The three elms,
 The sheep strewn on a field,
 Over a rickety bridge
 Toward the quick-water, wrinkling and rippling.

40 Hunting along the river,
 Down among the rubbish, the bug-riddled foliage,
 By the muddy pond-edge, by the bog-holes,
 By the shrunken lake, hunting, in the heat of summer.

The shape of a rat?
  It's bigger than that.
  It's less than a leg
  And more than a nose,
  Just under the water
  It usually goes.

50 Is it soft like a mouse?
 Can it wrinkle its nose?
 Could it come in the house
 On the tips of its toes?

  Take the skin of a cat
  And the back of an eel,
  Then roll them in grease,—
  That's the way it would feel.

  It's sleek as an otter
  With wide webby toes
60 Just under the water
  It usually goes.

2. The Pit

Where do the roots go?
 Look down under the leaves.
Who put the moss there?
 These stones have been here too long.
Who stunned the dirt into noise?
 Ask the mole, he knows.
I feel the slime of a wet nest.
 Beware Mother Mildew.
70 Nibble again, fish nerves.

3. The Gibber

At the wood's mouth,
By the cave's door,
I listened to something
I had heard before.

Dogs of the groin
Barked and howled,
The sun was against me,
The moon would not have me.

The weeds whined,
80 The snakes cried,
The cows and briars
Said to me: Die.

What a small song. What slow clouds. What dark water.
Hath the rain a father? All the caves are ice. Only the snow's here.
I'm cold. I'm cold all over. Rub me in father and mother.
Fear was my father, Father Fear.
His look drained the stones.

 What gliding shape
 Beckoning through halls,
90 Stood poised on the stair,
 Fell dreamily down?

 From the mouths of jugs
 Perched on many shelves,
 I saw substance flowing
 That cold morning.

 Like a slither of eels
 That watery cheek
 As my own tongue kissed
 My lips awake.

100 Is this the storm's heart? The ground is unstilling itself.
My veins are running nowhere. Do the bones cast out their fire?
Is the seed leaving the old bed? These buds are live as birds.
Where, where are the tears of the world?
Let the kisses resound, flat like a butcher's palm;

Let the gestures freeze; our doom is already decided.
All the windows are burning! What's left of my life?
I want the old rage, the lash of primordial milk!
Goodbye, goodbye, old stones, the time-order is going,
I have married my hands to perpetual agitation,
110   I run, I run to the whistle of money.

> Money money money
> Water water water

> How cool the grass is.
> Has the bird left?
> The stalk still sways.
> Has the worm a shadow?
> What do the clouds say?

These sweeps of light undo me.
Look, look, the ditch is running white!
120   I've more veins than a tree!
Kiss me, ashes, I'm falling through a dark swirl.

4. The Return

> The way to the boiler was dark,
> Dark all the way,
> Over slippery cinders
> Through the long greenhouse.

> The roses kept breathing in the dark.
> They had many mouths to breathe with.
> My knees made little winds underneath
> Where the weeds slept.

130   There was always a single light
> Swinging by the fire-pit,
> Where the fireman pulled out roses,
> The big roses, the big bloody clinkers.

> Once I stayed all night.
> The light in the morning came slowly over the white
> Snow.
> There were many kinds of cool
> Air.
> Then came steam.

140   Pipe-knock.

Scurry of warm over small plants.
Ordnung! ordnung!
Papa is coming!

> A fine haze moved off the leaves;
> Frost melted on far panes;
> The rose, the chrysanthemum turned toward the light.
> Even the hushed forms, the bent yellowy weeds
> Moved in a slow up-sway.

5. "It was beginning winter"

It was beginning winter,
150   An in-between time,
The landscape still partly brown:
The bones of weeds kept swinging in the wind,
Above the blue snow.

It was beginning winter,
The light moved slowly over the frozen field,
Over the dry seed-crowns,
The beautiful surviving bones
Swinging in the wind.

Light traveled over the wide field;
160   Stayed.
The weeds stopped swinging.
The mind moved, not alone,
Through the clear air, in the silence.

Was it light?
Was it light within?
Was it light within light?
Stillness becoming alive,
Yet still?

A lively understandable spirit
170   Once entertained you.
It will come again.
Be still.
Wait.

Elegy for Jane
My Student, Thrown by a Horse

I remember the neckcurls, limp and damp as tendrils;
And her quick look, a sidelong pickerel smile;
And how, once startled into talk, the light syllables leaped for her,
And she balanced in the delight of her thought,
A wren, happy, tail into the wind,
Her song trembling the twigs and small branches.
The shade sang with her;
The leaves, their whispers turned to kissing;
And the mold sang in the bleached valleys under the rose.

10   Oh, when she was sad, she cast herself down into such a pure depth,
Even a father could not find her:
Scraping her cheek against straw;
Stirring the clearest water.

My sparrow, you are not here,
Waiting like a fern, making a spiny shadow.

The sides of wet stones cannot console me,
Nor the moss, wound with the last light.

If only I could nudge you from this sleep,
My maimed darling, my skittery pigeon.
20 Over this damp grave I speak the words of my love:
I, with no rights in this matter,
Neither father nor lover.

The Sloth

In moving-slow he has no Peer.
You ask him something in his Ear,
He thinks about it for a Year;

And, then, before he says a Word
There, upside down (unlike a Bird),
He will assume that you have Heard—

A most Ex-as-per-at-ing Lug.
But should you call his manner Smug,
He'll sigh and give his Branch a Hug;

10 Then off again to Sleep he goes,
Still swaying gently by his Toes,
And you just *know* he knows he knows.

I Knew a Woman

I knew a woman, lovely in her bones,
When small birds sighed, she would sigh back at them;
Ah, when she moved, she moved more ways than one:
The shapes a bright container can contain!
Of her choice virtues only gods should speak,
Or English poets who grew up on Greek
(I'd have them sing in chorus, cheek to cheek).

How well her wishes went! She stroked my chin,
She taught me Turn, and Counter-turn, and Stand;
10 She taught me Touch, that undulant white skin;
I nibbled meekly from her proffered hand;
She was the sickle; I, poor I, the rake,
Coming behind her for her pretty sake
(But what prodigious mowing we did make).

Love likes a gander, and adores a goose:
Her full lips pursed, the errant note to seize;
She played it quick, she played it light and loose;
My eyes, they dazzled at her flowing knees;
Her several parts could keep a pure repose,
20 Or one hip quiver with a mobile nose
(She moved in circles, and those circles moved).

Let seed be grass, and grass turn into hay:
I'm martyr to a motion not my own;
What's freedom for? To know eternity.
I swear she cast a shadow white as stone.
But who would count eternity in days?
These old bones live to learn her wanton ways:
(I measure time by how a body sways).

The Visitant

1

A cloud moved close. The bulk of the wind shifted.
A tree swayed over water.
A voice said:
Stay. Stay by the slip-ooze. Stay.

Dearest tree, I said, may I rest here?
A ripple made a soft reply.
I waited, alert as a dog.
The leech clinging to a stone waited;
And the crab, the quiet breather.

2

10   Slow, slow as a fish she came,
Slow as a fish coming forward,
Swaying in a long wave;
Her skirts not touching a leaf,
Her white arms reaching towards me.

She came without sound,
Without brushing the wet stones;

In the soft dark of early evening,
She came,
The wind in her hair,
20   The moon beginning.

3

I woke in the first of morning.
Staring at a tree, I felt the pulse of a stone.
Where's she now, I kept saying.
Where's she now, the mountain's downy girl?
But the bright day had no answer.
A wind stirred in a web of appleworms;
The tree, the close willow, swayed.

Journey to the Interior

1

In the long journey out of the self,
There are many detours, washed-out interrupted raw places

Where the shale slides dangerously
And the back wheels hang almost over the edge
At the sudden veering, the moment of turning.
Better to hug close, wary of rubble and falling stones.
The arroyo cracking the road, the wind-bitten buttes, the canyons,
Creeks swollen in midsummer from the flash-flood roaring into the narrow
    valley.
Reeds beaten flat by wind and rain,
10   Grey from the long winter, burnt at the base in late summer.
—Or the path narrowing,
Winding upward toward the stream with its sharp stones,
The upland of alder and birchtrees,
Through the swamp alive with quicksand,
The way blocked at last by a fallen fir-tree,
The thickets darkening,
The ravines ugly.

2

I remember how it was to drive in gravel,
Watching for dangerous down-hill places, where the wheels whined beyond
    eighty—
20   When you hit the deep pit at the bottom of the swale,
The trick was to throw the car sideways and charge over the hill, full of the
    throttle.
Grinding up and over the narrow road, spitting and roaring.
A chance? Perhaps. But the road was part of me, and its ditches,
And the dust lay thick on my eyelids,—Who ever wore goggles?—
Always a sharp turn to the left past a barn close to the roadside,
To a scurry of small dogs and a shriek of children,
The highway ribboning out in a straight thrust to the North,
To the sand dunes and fish flies, hanging, thicker than moths,
Dying brightly under the street lights sunk in coarse concrete,
30   The towns with their high pitted road-crowns and deep gutters,
Their wooden stores of silvery pine and weather-beaten red courthouses,
An old bridge below with a buckled iron railing, broken by some idiot plunger;
Underneath, the sluggish water running between weeds, broken wheels, tires,
    stones.
And all flows past—
The cemetery with two scrubby trees in the middle of the prairie,
The dead snakes and muskrats, the turtles gasping in the rubble,
The spikey purple bushes in the winding dry creek bed—
The floating hawks, the jackrabbits, the grazing cattle—
I am not moving but they are,
40   And the sun comes out of a blue cloud over the Tetons,
While, farther away, the heat-lightning flashes.
I rise and fall in the slow sea of a grassy plain,
The wind veering the car slightly to the right,
Whipping the line of white laundry, bending the cottonwoods apart,
The scraggly wind-break of a dusty ranch-house.

I rise and fall, and time folds
Into a long moment;
And I hear the lichen speak,
And the ivy advance with its white lizard feet—
50   On the shimmering road,
On the dusty detour.

3

I see the flower of all water, above and below me, the never receding,
Moving, unmoving in a parched land, white in the moonlight:
The soul at a still-stand,
At ease after rocking the flesh to sleep,
Petals and reflections of petals mixed on the surface of a glassy pool,
And the waves flattening out when the fishermen drag their nets over the
        stones.

In the moment of time when the small drop forms, but does not fall,
I have known the heart of the sun,—
60   In the dark and light of a dry place,
In a flicker of fire brisked by a dusty wind.
I have heard, in a drip of leaves,
A slight song,
After the midnight cries.
I rehearse myself for this:
The stand at the stretch in the face of death,
Delighting in surface change, the glitter of light on waves,
And I roam elsewhere, my body thinking,
Turning toward the other side of light,
70   In a tower of wind, a tree idling in air,
Beyond my own echo,
Neither forward nor backward,
Unperplexed, in a place leading nowhere.

As a blind man, lifting a curtain, knows it is morning,
I know this change:
On one side of silence there is no smile;
But when I breathe with the birds,
The spirit of wrath becomes the spirit of blessing,
And the dead begin from their dark to sing in my sleep.

The Rose

1

There are those to whom place is unimportant,
But this place, where sea and fresh water meet,
Is important—
Where the hawks sway out into the wind,
Without a single wingbeat,
And the eagles sail low over the fir trees,
And the gulls cry against the crows

In the curved harbors,
And the tide rises up against the grass
10   Nibbled by sheep and rabbits.

A time for watching the tide,
For the heron's hieratic fishing,
For the sleepy cries of the towhee,
The morning birds gone, the twittering finches,
But still the flash of the kingfisher, the wingbeat of the scoter,
The sun a ball of fire coming down over the water,
The last geese crossing against the reflected afterlight,
The moon retreating into a vague cloud-shape
To the cries of the owl, the eerie whooper.
20   The old log subsides with the lessening waves,
And there is silence.

I sway outside myself
Into the darkening currents,
Into the small spillage of driftwood,
The waters swirling past the tiny headlands.
Was it here I wore a crown of birds for a moment
While on a far point of the rocks
The light heightened,
And below, in a mist out of nowhere,
30   The first rain gathered?

2

As when a ship sails with a light wind—
The waves less than the ripples made by rising fish,
The lacelike wrinkles of the wake widening, thinning out,
Sliding away from the traveler's eye,
The prow pitching easily up and down,
The whole ship rolling slightly sideways,
The stern high, dipping like a child's boat in a pond—
Our motion continues.

But this rose, this rose in the sea-wind,
40   Stays,
Stays in its true place,
Flowering out of the dark,
Widening at high noon, face upward,
A single wild rose, struggling out of the white embrace of the morning-glory,
Out of the briary hedge, the tangle of matted underbrush,
Beyond the clover, the ragged hay,
Beyond the sea pine, the oak, the wind-tipped madrona,
Moving with the waves, the undulating driftwood,
Where the slow creek winds down to the black sand of the shore
50   With its thick grassy scum and crabs scuttling back into their glistening craters.

And I think of roses, roses,
White and red, in the wide six-hundred-foot greenhouses,
And my father standing astride the cement benches,

Lifting me high over the four-foot stems, the Mrs. Russells, and his own
    elaborate hybrids.
And how those flowerheads seemed to flow toward me, to beckon me, only a
    child, out of myself.

What need for heaven, then,
With that man, and those roses?

3

What do they tell us, sound and silence?
I think of American sounds in this silence:
On the banks of the Tombstone, the wind-harps having their say,
The thrush singing alone, that easy bird,
The killdeer whistling away from me,
The mimetic chortling of the catbird
Down in the corner of the garden, among the raggedy lilacs,
The bobolink skirring from a broken fencepost,
The bluebird, lover of holes in old wood, lilting its light song,
And that thin cry, like a needle piercing the ear, the insistent cicada,
And the ticking of snow around oil drums in the Dakotas,
The thin whine of telephone wires in the wind of a Michigan winter,
The shriek of nails as old shingles are ripped from the top of a roof,
The bulldozer backing away, the hiss of the sandblaster,
And the deep chorus of horns coming up from the streets in early morning.
I return to the twittering of swallows above water,
And that sound, that single sound,
When the mind remembers all,
And gently the light enters the sleeping soul,
A sound so thin it could not woo a bird,

Beautiful my desire, and the place of my desire.

I think of the rock singing, and light making its own silence,
At the edge of a ripening meadow, in early summer,
The moon lolling in the close elm, a shimmer of silver,
Or that lonely time before the breaking of morning
When the slow freight winds along the edge of the ravaged hillside,
And the wind tries the shape of a tree,
While the moon lingers,
And a drop of rain water hangs at the tip of a leaf
Shifting in the wakening sunlight
Like the eye of a new-caught fish.

4

I live with the rocks, their weeds,
Their filmy fringes of green, their harsh
Edges, their holes
Cut by the sea-slime, far from the crash
Of the long swell,
The oily, tar-laden walls
Of the toppling waves,

Where the salmon ease their way into the kelp beds,
And the sea rearranges itself among the small islands.

Near this rose, in this grove of sun-parched, wind-warped madronas,
Among the half-dead trees, I came upon the true ease of myself,
100   As if another man appeared out of the depths of my being,
And I stood outside myself,
Beyond becoming and perishing,
A something wholly other,
As if I swayed out on the wildest wave alive,
And yet was still.
And I rejoiced in being what I was:
In the lilac change, the white reptilian calm,
In the bird beyond the bough, the single one
With all the air to greet him as he flies,
110   The dolphin rising from the darkening waves;

And in this rose, this rose in the sea-wind,
Rooted in stone, keeping the whole of light,
Gathering to itself sound and silence—
Mine and the sea-wind's.

The Meadow Mouse

1

In a shoe box stuffed in an old nylon stocking
Sleeps the baby mouse I found in the meadow,
Where he trembled and shook beneath a stick
Till I caught him up by the tail and brought him in,
Cradled in my hand,
A little quaker, the whole body of him trembling,
His absurd whiskers sticking out like a cartoon-mouse,
His feet like small leaves,
Little lizard-feet,
10   Whitish and spread wide when he tried to struggle away,
Wriggling like a miniscule puppy.

Now he's eaten his three kinds of cheese and drunk from his bottle-cap
        watering-trough—
So much he just lies in one corner,
His tail curled under him, his belly big
As his head: his bat-like ears
Twitching, tilting toward the least sound.

Do I imagine he no longer trembles
When I come close to him?
He seems no longer to tremble.

2

20   But this morning the shoe-box house on the back porch is empty.
Where has he gone, my meadow mouse,

My thumb of a child that nuzzled in my palm?—
To run under the hawk's wing,
Under the eye of the great owl watching from the elm-tree,
To live by courtesy of the shrike, the snake, the tom-cat.

I think of the nestling fallen into the deep grass,
The turtle gasping in the dusty rubble of the highway,
The paralytic stunned in the tub, and the water rising,—
All things innocent, hapless, forsaken.

Another poem by Theodore Roethke may be found on page 425.

A Gathering of Poems

Geoffrey Chaucer

Geoffrey Chaucer (1340?–1400) grew up in London, son of a man who made wine. He fought for England in France, and later worked for his king as a diplomat on foreign service. During his busy public life, he wrote poems, most notably *The Canterbury Tales*, a loose assemblage of stories told by pilgrims traveling to the shrine in Kent. He is the first great poet of England, and remains the funniest. Because the Middle English that was his language requires special study, this selection is small—only a hint of the sound that Chaucer makes.

from the Prologue to *The Canterbury Tales*

Whan that Aprill with his shoures soote[1]
The droghte[2] of March hath perced[3] to the roote,
And bathed every veyne[4] in swich licour,[5]
Of which vertu[6] engendred is the flour;[7]
Whan Zephyrus eek[8] with his sweete breeth
Inspired hath in every holt and heeth
The tendre croppes,[9] and the yonge sonne
Hath in the Ram his halfe cours yronne,
And smale foweles[10] maken melodye
10   That slepen al the nyght with open yë[11]—
So priketh hem Nature in hir corages[12]—
Thanne longen folk to goon on pilgrimages,

[1]sweet showers   [2]drought   [3]pierced   [4]vein   [5]such liquid   [6]power   [7]flower   [8]also
[9]shoots   [10]birds   [11]eye   [12]hearts

And palmeres for to seken straunge strondes[13]
To ferne halwes,[14] kouthe[15] in sondry londes;
And specially from every shires ende
Of Engelond to Caunterbury[16] they wende,
The holy blisful martir for to seke
That hem[17] hath holpen[18] whan that they were seeke.[19]

[13]shores   [14]distant shrines   [15]known   [16]shrine of Thomas à Becket (1118?–1170), English martyr   [17]them   [18]helped   [19]sick

Anonymous ballads and songs

For a few words about ballads, see pages 446–447. Anonymous songs made up the best poetry between Chaucer's time and the great explosion of poetry that happened under the Tudor monarchs.

Anonymous

Lord Randal

"O where hae° ye been, Lord Randal, my son?   have
O where hae ye been, my handsome young man?"
"I hae been to the wild wood; mother, make my bed soon,
For I'm weary wi hunting, and fain wald° lie down."   would

"Where gat ye your dinner, Lord Randal, my son?
Where gat ye your dinner, my handsome young man?"
"I din'd wi my true-love; mother, make my bed soon,
For I'm weary wi hunting, and fain wald lie down."

"What gat ye to your dinner, Lord Randal, my son?
10   What gat ye to your dinner, my handsome young man?"
"I gat eels boiled in broo,° mother, make my bed soon,   broth
For I'm weary wi hunting, and fain wald lie down."

"What became of your bloodhounds, Lord Randal, my son?
What became of your bloodhounds, my handsome young man?"
"O they swelld and they died; mother, make my bed soon,
For I'm weary wi hunting, and fain wald lie down."

"O I fear ye are poisond, Lord Randal, my son!
O I fear ye are poisond, my handsome young man!"
"O yes! I am poisond; mother, make my bed soon,
20   For I'm sick at the heart, and I fain wald lie down."

Adam Lay I-Bowndyn

Adam lay i-bowndyn,
   Bowndyn in a bond—
Fowre thousand wynter
   Thoght he not too long;

And al was for an appil,
  An appil that he tok,
As clerkes° fynden,   scholars
  Writen in here° book.   their

Ne hadde the appil takë ben,[1]
10   The appil taken ben,
Ne haddë never our lady
  A ben° hevenë quene.   have been
Blyssid be the tyme
  That appil takë was,
Ther fore we mown° syngyn   must
  Deo Gracias.[2]

[1] If the apple had not been taken   [2] Thanks be to God

Thomas Wyatt

Sir Thomas Wyatt (1503–1542) was ambassador for Henry VIII—and several times imprisoned by him in the Tower of London for alleged offenses. Wyatt brought the sonnet to England, imitating the form used by Italian poets. When the music of English verse had vanished for a hundred years after Chaucer's death, Wyatt's lyrics and sonnets began its restoration.

They Flee from Me

They flee from me, that sometime did me seek,
With naked foot, stalking in my chamber.
I have seen them, gentle, tame, and meek,
That now are wild, and do not remember
That sometime they put themselves in danger
To take bread at my hand, and now they range,
Busily seeking with a continual change.

Thankèd be fortune, it hath been otherwise
Twenty times better; but once, in special,
10   In thin array, after a pleasant guise,
When her loose gown from her shoulders did fall,
And she me caught in her arms long and small,
Therewithal sweetly did me kiss,
And softly said, "Dear heart, how like you this?"

It was no dream; I lay broad waking.
But all is turned, thorough my gentleness,
Into a strange fashion of forsaking;
And I have leave to go, of her goodness,
And she also to use new-fangledness.
20   But since that I so kindely° am served,   naturally
I would fain know what she hath deserved.

Sir Walter Ralegh

Sir Walter Ralegh (1552?–1618) is the same man who was alleged to have spread his cloak over a puddle that his queen might walk dry-shod. More reliably, we know of Ralegh as adventurer, explorer, and prisoner. He was a man of action who fought in France and who led several voyages to the New World. Three times, on various charges, he was committed to the Tower, where he probably wrote most of his poetry. After a failed expedition to the Orinoco, during which a Spanish colony was raised, Ralegh was executed (a major cause of death among Elizabethan poets).

Verses Written the Night Before His Execution

Even such is time, that takes in trust
Our youth, our joys, our all we have,
And pays us but with age and dust;
Who in the dark and silent grave,
When we have wandered all our ways,
Shuts up the story of our days:
But from this earth, this grave, this dust,
My God shall raise me up, I trust.

Sir Philip Sidney

Sir Philip Sidney (1554–1586) died fighting for England against Spain, and none of his considerable work appeared until after his death. In his generation he was widely admired and became the subject of several elegies, most notably Spenser's. He was loved not only for his talent and his intelligence but also for the nobility of his character. According to legend, while he was dying he refused a cup of water, sending it to the wounded man beside him, claiming "Thy necessity is greater than mine."

from Astrophel and Stella

With how sad steps, O Moon! thou climb'st the skies!
How silently, and with how wan a face!
What! may it be, that even in heavenly place
That busy archer° his sharp arrows tries?   Cupid
Sure, if that long-with-love-acquainted eyes
Can judge of love, thou feel'st a lover's case;
I read it in thy looks; thy languish'd grace,
To me that feel the like, thy state descries.
Then, even of fellowship, O Moon, tell me,
10   Is constant love deem'd there but want of wit?
Are beauties there as proud as here they be?
Do they above love to be loved, and yet
   Those lovers scorn whom that love doth possess?
   Do they call virtue there ungratefulness?

Robert Southwell

Robert Southwell (1561?–1595), a Catholic, wrote most of his devotional poetry in prison, where he was tortured and finally executed.

The Burning Babe

As I in hoary winter's night stood shivering in the snow,
Surprised I was with sudden heat, which made my heart to glow;
And lifting up a fearful eye to view what fire was near,
A pretty Babe all burning bright, did in the air appear,
Who scorched with excessive heat, such floods of tears did shed,
As though His floods should quench His flames which with His tears were fed;
Alas! quoth He, but newly born, in fiery heats I fry,
Yet none approach to warm their hearts or feel my fire but I!
My faultless breast the furnace is, the fuel wounding thorns,
10 Love is the fire, and sighs the smoke, the ashes shame and scorns;
The fuel Justice layeth on, and Mercy blows the coals,
The metal in this furnace wrought are men's defilèd souls,
For which, as now on fire I am to work them to their good,
So will I melt into a bath to wash them in My blood:
With this He vanished out of sight, and swiftly shrank away,
And straight I callèd unto mind that it was Christmas-day.

Christopher Marlowe

Christopher Marlowe (1564–1593) was a great playwright, slightly younger than Shakespeare, who helped establish English poetry upon the stage. Two of his best plays were his *Tragedy of Doctor Faustus* and *Edward II*. He was murdered in a tavern at Deptford by a man named Ingram Frisar.

The Passionate Shepherd to His Love

Come live with me and be my love,
And we will all the pleasures prove
That hills and valleys, dale and field,
And all the craggy mountains yield!

There will we sit upon the rocks
And see the shepherds feed their flocks,
By shallow rivers, to whose falls
Melodious birds sing madrigals.

There will I make thee beds of roses
10 With a thousand fragrant posies;
A cap of flowers, and a kirtle
Embroider'd all with leaves of myrtle;

A gown made of the finest wool
Which from our pretty lambs we pull;
Fair lined slippers for the cold,
With buckles of the purest gold;

A belt of straw and ivy buds,
With coral clasps and amber studs:
And if these pleasures may thee move,
20   Come live with me and be my love!

Thy silver dishes, for thy meat
As precious as the gods do eat,
Shall on an ivory table be
Prepared each day for thee and me.

The shepherd swains shall dance and sing
For thy delight each May morning.
If these delights thy mind may move,
Then live with me and be my love!

Sir Walter Ralegh wrote an answer for the Nymph to address to the Shepherd:

The Nymph's Reply to the Shepherd

If all the world and love were young,
And truth in every shepherd's tongue,
These pretty pleasures might me move
To live with thee and be thy love.

Time drives the flocks from field to fold
When rivers rage and rocks grow cold,
And Philomel° becometh dumb;   the nightingale
The rest complains of care to come.

The flowers do fade, and wanton fields
10   To wayward winter reckoning yields;
A honey tongue, a heart of gall,
Is fancy's spring, but sorrow's fall.

Thy gowns, thy shoes, thy beds of roses,
Thy cap, thy kirtle,° and thy posies   underdress
Soon break, soon wither, soon forgotten—
In folly ripe, in reason rotten.

Thy belt of straw and ivy buds,
Thy coral clasps and amber studs,
All these in me no means can move
20   To come to thee and be thy love.

But could youth last and love still breed,
Had joys no date nor age no need,
Then these delights my mind might move
To live with thee and be thy love.

William Shakespeare

William Shakespeare (1564–1616) left Stratford in 1585, three years after he married, and arrived a year later in London, where he became an actor. He was in the original cast of two of Ben Jonson's plays. He began writing for the stage in about 1591, and his last finished work was *The Tempest*, 1611–1612. He spent the last years of his life largely in retirement at New Place, which he built in Stratford with his London earnings. His sonnets appeared during his lifetime (1609); scholars conjecture that they were written earlier, most of them between 1593 and 1596. He also wrote three long poems, but the best of his poetry is spoken by characters in his plays; his finest lyrics are sung by the same characters. See pages 422, 425, 473, 479, and 496–499.

When, in disgrace with fortune and men's eyes

When, in disgrace with fortune and men's eyes,
I all alone beweep my outcast state
And trouble deaf heaven with my bootless° cries   useless
And look upon myself and curse my fate,
Wishing me like to one more rich in hope,
Featured like him, like him with friends possess'd,
Desiring this man's art and that man's scope,
With what I most enjoy contented least;
Yet in these thoughts myself almost despising
10 Haply I think on thee, and then my state,
Like to the lark at break of day arising
From sullen earth, sings hymns at heaven's gate;
    For thy sweet love remember'd such wealth brings
    That then I scorn to change my state with kings.

They that have power to hurt and will do none

They that have power to hurt and will do none,
That do not do the thing they most do show,
Who, moving others, are themselves as stone,
Unmovèd, cold, and to temptation slow,—
They rightly do inherit heaven's graces
And husband nature's riches from expense;
They are the lords and owners of their faces,
Others but stewards of their excellence.
The summer's flower is to the summer sweet,
10 Though to itself it only live and die:
But if that flower with base infection meet,
The basest weed outbraves his dignity:
    For sweetest things turn sourest by their deeds;
    Lilies that fester smell far worse than weeds.

Not mine own fears, nor the prophetic soul

Not mine own fears, nor the prophetic soul
Of the wide world dreaming on things to come,
Can yet the lease of my true love control,
Supposed as forfeit to a confined doom.

The mortal moon hath her eclipse endured,
And the sad augurs mock their own presage;
Incertainties now crown themselves assured,
And peace proclaims olives of endless age.
Now with the drops of this most balmy time
10   My love looks fresh, and Death to me subscribes,
Since, spite of him, I'll live in this poor rhyme,
While he insults o'er dull and speechless tribes.
   And thou in this shalt find thy monument,
   When tyrants' crests and tombs of brass are spent.

from *Twelfth Night*

When that I was and a little tiny boy,
   With hey, ho, the wind and the rain,
A foolish thing was but a toy,
   For the rain it raineth every day.

But when I came to man's estate
   With hey, ho, the wind and the rain,
'Gainst knaves and thieves men shut their gate,
   For the rain it raineth every day.

But when I came, alas! to wive,
10   With hey, ho, the wind and the rain,
By swaggering could I never thrive,
   For the rain it raineth every day.

But when I came unto my beds,
   With hey, ho, the wind and the rain,
With toss-pots still had drunken heads,
   For the rain it raineth every day.

A great while ago the world begun,
   With hey, ho, the wind and the rain,
But that's all one, our play is done,
20   And we'll strive to please you every day.

Thomas Campion

Thomas Campion (1567–1620) composed music for his lyrics, one of the few artists to become master of two arts. Although he could rhyme well enough when he wanted to, he despised English rhyming as vulgar, and argued for the establishment of Greek and Roman meters in English verse.

Rose-Cheeked Laura

Rose-cheeked Laura, come,
Sing thou smoothly with thy beauty's
Silent music, either other
   Sweetly gracing.

Lovely forms do flow
From concent° divinely framèd;   sounds in harmony
Heaven is music, and thy beauty's
   Birth is heavenly.

These dull notes we sing
10 Discords need for helps to grace them;
Only beauty purely loving
   Knows no discord,

But still moves delight,
Like clear springs renewed by flowing,
Ever perfect, ever in them-
   Selves eternal.

Thomas Nashe

Thomas Nashe (1567–1601) was a literary jack-of-all-trades—pamphleteer,
playwright, poet, and author of the first adventure novel in English. Ever
contentious, he wrote a comedy called "The Isle of Dogs" which attacked the
government so thoroughly that Nashe spent some months in jail. This poem is
said to have been written during the Plague that afflicted London from 1592
to 1594.

Adieu! Farewell Earth's Bliss!

Adieu! farewell earth's bliss!
This world uncertain is:
Fond are life's lustful joys,
Death proves them all but toys,
None from his darts can fly:
I am sick, I must die.
   Lord, have mercy on us!

Rich men, trust not in wealth!
Gold cannot buy you health;
10 Physic himself must fade,
All things to end are made,
The plague full swift goes by:
I am sick, I must die.
   Lord, have mercy on us!

Beauty is but a flower
Which wrinkles will devour;
Brightness falls from the air,
Queens have died young and fair,
Dust hath closed Helen's eye:
20 I am sick, I must die.
   Lord, have mercy on us!

Strength stoops unto the grave:
Worms feed on Hector brave;
Swords may not fight with fate;

Earth still holds ope her gate;
'Come! come!' the bells do cry.
I am sick, I must die.
   Lord, have mercy on us!

Wit with his wantonness
30 Tasteth death's bitterness;
Hell's executioner
Hath no ears for to hear
What vain art can reply:
I am sick, I must die.
   Lord, have mercy on us!

Haste, therefore, each degree,
To welcome destiny:
Heaven is our heritage,
Earth but a player's stage,
40 Mount we unto the sky:
I am sick, I must die.
   Lord, have mercy on us!

John Donne

John Donne (1572–1631) was chief of the "Metaphysical Poets." It was his wit, and that of other metaphysicals, to speak of one thing in terms of another far removed, as when the parting of husband and wife is compared to the two feet of a geometric compass. In youth he wrote playful and complex erotic poetry; after he became an Anglican priest in 1615, his poetry became increasingly religious, thus providing literary observers with a division into two poets, Jack Donne and Dr. Donne. His devotional prose, including his sermons, ranks among the best English prose of the seventeenth century. From 1621 until he died, he was Dean of St. Paul's in London, and he preached his final sermon wearing a shroud.

The Canonization

For Godsake hold your tongue, and let me love,
  Or chide my palsy, or my gout,
My five grey hairs, or ruined fortune flout;
  With wealth your state, your mind with arts improve,
    Take you a course, get you a place,
    Observe his Honor, or his Grace;
Or the king's real, or his stampèd face[1]
  Contemplate; what you will, approve,
So you will let me love.

10 Alas, alas, who's injured by my love?
  What merchant's ships have my sighs drowned?
Who says my tears have overflowed his ground?
  When did my colds a forward spring remove?

[1]On coins

When did the heats which my veins fill
   Add one more to the plaguy bill?[2]
Soldiers find wars, and lawyers find out still
   Litigious men, which quarrels move,
   Though she and I do love.

Call us what you will, we are made such by love;
20   Call her one, me another fly,
We're tapers too, and at our own cost die,
   And we in us find the eagle and the dove.
      The phoenix riddle hath more wit
      By us; we two being one are it.
So to one neutral thing both sexes fit,
   We die and rise the same, and prove
   Mysterious by this love.

We can die by it, if not live by love,
   And if unfit for tombs and hearse
30   Our legend be, it will be fit for verse;
   And if no piece of chronicle we prove,
      We'll build in sonnets pretty rooms;
      As well a well-wrought urn becomes
The greatest ashes, as half-acre tombs,
   And by these hymns all shall approve
   Us canonized for love:

And thus invoke us; You, whom reverend love
   Made one another's hermitage;
You, to whom love was peace, that now is rage;
40   Who did the whole world's soul contract, and drove
      Into the glasses of your eyes—
      So made such mirrors, and such spies,
That they did all to you epitomize,
   Countries, towns, courts: beg from above
   A pattern of your love!

[2]List of those dead of plague

Death, Be Not Proud

Death, be not proud, though some have callèd thee
Mighty and dreadful, for thou are not so;
For those whom thou think'st thou dost overthrow
Die not, poor Death; nor yet canst thou kill me.
From rest and sleep, which but thy pictures be,
Much pleasure; then from thee much more must flow;
And soonest our best men with thee do go—
Rest of their bones and souls' delivery!
Thou'rt slave to fate, chance, kings, and desperate men,
10   And dost with poison, war, and sickness dwell;
And poppy or charms can make us sleep as well

And better than thy stroke. Why swell'st thou then?
One short sleep past, we wake eternally,
And Death shall be no more: Death, thou shalt die.

Batter My Heart

Batter my heart, three-personed God; for you
As yet but knock, breathe, shine, and seek to mend.
That I may rise and stand, o'erthrow me and bend
Your force to break, blow, burn, and make me new.
I, like an usurped town, to another due,
Labor to admit you, but, oh, to no end;
Reason, your viceroy in me, me should defend,
But is captived and proves weak or untrue.
Yet dearly I love you and would be lovèd fain,
10   But am betrothed unto your enemy:
Divorce me, untie or break that knot again,
Take me to you, imprison me, for I,
Except you enthrall me, never shall be free,
Nor ever chaste, except you ravish me.

Ben Jonson

Ben Jonson (1572–1637) was actor as well as playwright, and his great plays
rank second only to Shakespeare's. In 1598 he killed another actor in a duel
but avoided execution by pleading benefit of clergy—at least he spoke Latin.
Although his plays remain at the center of his work, he mastered the art of
poetry in all forms, and his works are voluminous and superb in range and in
accomplishment. See also page 408.

To Heaven

Good and great God! can I not think of Thee,
    But it must straight my melancholy be?
Is it interpreted in me disease,
    That, laden with my sins, I seek for ease?
O be Thou witness, that the reins dost know
    And hearts of all, if I be sad for show;
And judge me after, if I dare pretend
    To aught but grace, or aim at other end.
As Thou art all, so be Thou all to me,
10   First, midst, and last, converted One and Three!
My faith, my hope, my love; and, in this state,
    My judge, my witness, and my advocate!
Where have I been this while exiled from Thee,
    And whither rapt, now Thou but stoop'st to me?
Dwell, dwell here still! O, being everywhere,
    How can I doubt to find Thee ever here?
I know my state, both full of shame and scorn,
    Conceived in sin, and unto labor born,

Standing with fear, and must with horror fall,
20   And destined unto judgment, after all.
I feel my griefs too, and there scarce is ground
     Upon my flesh t'inflict another wound;
Yet dare I not complain or wish for death
     With holy Paul, lest it be thought the breath
Of discontent; or that these prayers be
     For weariness of life, not love of Thee.

Robert Herrick

Robert Herrick (1591–1674) is among the most playful of English poets. An admirer of Ben Jonson, he wrote short poems, sacred and profane, in a variety of forms. See also page 410.

Delight in Disorder

A sweet disorder in the dress
Kindles in clothes a wantonness:
A lawn° about the shoulders thrown   a thin fabric
Into a fine distraction;
An erring lace, which here and there
Enthralls the crimson stomacher;°   decorative garment,
A cuff neglectful, and thereby   often embroidered
Ribands to flow confusedly;
A winning wave, deserving note,
10   In the tempestuous petticoat;
A careless shoe-string, in whose tie
I see a wild civility,—
Do more bewitch me, than when art
Is too precise in every part.

George Herbert

George Herbert (1593–1633) was a priest and author of great religious poetry. He attended Cambridge University and died as a country parson. See also page 481.

The Pulley

When God at first made Man,
Having a glass of blessings standing by;
Let us (said He) pour on him all we can:
Let the world's riches, which disperséd lie,
     Contract into a span.

So strength first made a way;
Then beauty flow'd, then wisdom, honour, pleasure:
When almost all was out, God made a stay,
Perceiving that alone, of all His treasure,
10   Rest in the bottom lay.

For if I should (said He)
Bestow this jewel also on My creature,
He would adore My gifts instead of Me,
And rest in Nature, not the God of Nature:
    So both should losers be.

    Yet let him keep the rest,
But keep them with repining restlessness:
Let him be rich and weary, that at least,
If goodness lead him not, yet weariness
20   May toss him to My breast.

Church Monuments

While that my soul repairs to her devotion,
Here I intomb my flesh, that it betimes
May take acquaintance of this heap of dust;
To which the blast of death's incessant motion,
Fed with the exhalation of our crimes,
Drives all at last. Therefore I gladly trust

My body to this school, that it may learn
To spell his elements, and find his birth
Written in dusty heraldry and lines;
10   Which dissolution sure doth best discern,
Comparing dust with dust, and earth with earth.
These laugh at jet and marble, put for signs,

To sever the good fellowship of dust,
And spoil the meeting. What shall point out them
When they shall bow, and kneel, and fall down flat
To kiss those heaps, which now they have in trust?
Dear flesh, while I do pray, learn here thy stem
And true descent, that when thou shalt grow fat,

And wanton in thy cravings, thou mayst know,
20   That flesh is but the glass which holds the dust
That measures all our time; which also shall
Be crumbled into dust. Mark here below
How tame these ashes are, how free from lust—
That thou mayst fit thyself against thy fall.

John Milton

John Milton (1608–1674) was a precocious poet. He prepared himself
assiduously for his poetic vocation, and in 1637 wrote the remarkable elegy
"Lycidas" for a young man he had known at Cambridge. During the next twenty
years he wrote a few sonnets—excellent poems—but largely he substituted
politics and political action for poetry, working as Cromwell's Latin secretary.
His first marriage was tempestuous, and he wrote prose works advocating
divorce, which earned him considerable denunciation. He became blind while
he was still Cromwell's secretary, and was assisted by several helpers, notably
Andrew Marvell. After Cromwell's death and the restoration of the monarchy,
he was imprisoned, released, and lived in poverty. He had begun his great
work, the religious epic *Paradise Lost*, while he was chiefly engaged in politics,
but he completed it in blindness and poverty. Afterward he wrote "Paradise
Regained" and "Samson Agonistes." In prose, his "Areopagitica" (on freedom of
the press) is his most celebrated work. See also page 474.

On His Blindness

When I consider how my light is spent
Ere half my days in this dark world and wide,
And that one talent which is death to hide
Lodged with me useless, though my soul more bent
To serve therewith my Maker, and present
My true account, lest He returning chide,
"Doth God exact day-labor, light denied?"
I fondly ask. But Patience, to prevent
That murmur, soon replies, "God doth not need
10   Either man's work or his own gifts. Who best
Bear His mild yoke, they serve Him best. His state
Is kingly: thousands at His bidding speed,
And post o'er land and ocean without rest;
They also serve who only stand and wait."

Andrew Marvell

Andrew Marvell (1621–1678) was a poet in youth who, as he grew older,
became increasingly more political than poetical. A defender of Cromwell and
Milton, after the restoration of the monarchy he joined Parliament and
represented his birthplace, Hull, attacking the king and his ministers with
considerable vigor.

The Garden

How vainly men themselves amaze
To win the palm, the oak, or bays;[1]
And their incessant labours see
Crowned from some single herb or tree,
Whose short and narrow-vergèd shade
Does prudently their toils upbraid;
While all flowers and all trees do close
To weave the garlands of repose.

[1]Laurel wreaths, symbolizing achievement in sport, politics, and poetry

Fair Quiet, have I found thee here,
10 And Innocence, thy sister dear!
Mistaken long, I sought you then
In busy companies of men.
Your sacred plants, if here below,
Only among the plants will grow:
Society is all but rude
To this delicious solitude.

No white nor red was ever seen
So amorous as this lovely green.
Fond lovers, cruel as their flame,
20 Cut in these trees their mistress' name:
Little, alas, they know or heed,
How far these beauties hers exceed!
Fair trees! wheres'e'er your barks I wound,
No name shall but your own be found.

When we have run our passion's heat,
Love hither makes his best retreat.
The gods, that mortal beauty chase,
Still in a tree did end their race.
Apollo hunted Daphne so,
30 Only that she might laurel grow;
And Pan did after Syrinx speed,
Not as a nymph, but for a reed.

What wondrous life in this I lead!
Ripe apples drop about my head;
The luscious clusters of the vine
Upon my mouth do crush their wine;
The nectarine, and curious peach,
Into my hands themselves do reach;
Stumbling on melons, as I pass,
40 Ensnared with flowers, I fall on grass.

Meanwhile the mind, from pleasure less,
Withdraws into its happiness:
The mind, that ocean where each kind
Does straight its own resemblance find;
Yet it creates, transcending these,
Far other worlds, and other seas;
Annihilating all that's made
To a green thought in a green shade.

Here at the fountain's sliding foot,
50 Or at some fruit-tree's mossy root,
Casting the body's vest aside,
My soul into the boughs does glide:
There like a bird it sits and sings,
Then whets, and combs its silver wings;
And, till prepared for longer flight,
Waves in its plumes the various light.

Such was that happy garden-state,
While man there walked without a mate:
After a place so pure and sweet,
60   What other help could yet be meet?
But 'twas beyond a mortal's share
To wander solitary there:
Two Paradises 'twere in one,
To live in Paradise alone.

How well the skilful gardener drew
Of flowers and herbs this dial new!
Where, from above, the milder sun
Does through a fragrant zodiac run;
And, as it works, the industrious bee
70   Computes its time as well as we
How could such sweet and wholesome hours
Be reckoned but with herbs and flowers?

To His Coy Mistress

Had we but world enough, and time,
This coyness, Lady, were no crime.
We would sit down, and think which way
To walk, and pass our long love's day.
Thou by the Indian Ganges' side
Shouldst rubies find; I by the tide
Of Humber would complain. I would
Love you ten years before the Flood;
And you should, if you please, refuse
10   Till the conversion of the Jews.
My vegetable° love should grow   vegetative
Vaster than empires, and more slow.
An hundred years should go to praise
Thine eyes, and on thy forehead gaze;
Two hundred to adore each breast;
But thirty thousand to the rest:
An age, at least, to every part,
And the last age should show your heart.
For, Lady, you deserve this state,
20   Nor would I love at lower rate.
But, at my back, I always hear
Time's wingèd chariot hurrying near:
And yonder, all before us lie
Deserts of vast eternity.
Thy beauty shall no more be found;
Nor, in thy marble vault, shall sound
My echoing song. Then worms shall try
That long preserved virginity:
And your quaint honour turn to dust;
30   And into ashes all my lust.
The grave's a fine and private place,
But none, I think, do there embrace.

Now, therefore, while the youthful hue
Sits on thy skin like morning dew,
And while thy willing soul transpires
At every pore with instant fires,
Now let us sport us while we may;
And now, like amorous birds of prey,
Rather at once our time devour,
40 Than languish in his slow-chapt° power.   slow-jawed
Let us roll all our strength, and all
Our sweetness, up into one ball;
And tear our pleasures, with rough strife,
Thorough° the iron gates of life.   through
Thus, though we cannot make our sun
Stand still, yet we will make him run.

Henry Vaughan

Henry Vaughan (1622–1695), a great religious poet, was an admirer of George
Herbert.

The World

I saw Eternity the other night,
Like a great ring of pure and endless light,
All calm, as it was bright;
And round beneath it, Time in hours, days, years,
Driven by the spheres
Like a vast shadow moved; in which the world
And all her train were hurled.
The doting lover in his quaintest strain
Did there complain;
10 Near him, his lute, his fancy, and his flights,
Wit's sour delights;
With gloves, and knots, the silly snares of pleasure,
Yet his dear treasure,
All scattered lay, while he his eyes did pour
Upon a flower.

The darksome statesman, hung with weights and woe,
Like a thick midnight-fog, moved there so slow,
He did not stay, nor go;
Condemning thoughts—like sad eclipses—scowl
20 Upon his soul,
And clouds of crying witnesses without
Pursued him with one shout.
Yet digged the mole, and lest his ways be found,
Worked underground,
Where he did clutch his prey; but one did see
That policy.
Churches and altars fed him; perjuries
Were gnats and flies;

It rained about him blood and tears, but he
30   Drank them as free.

The fearful miser on a heap of rust
Sat pining all his life there, did scarce trust
          His own hands with the dust,
Yet would not place one piece above, but lives
          In fear of thieves.
Thousands there were as frantic as himself
          And hugged each one his pelf;
The downright epicure placed heav'n in sense,
          And scorned pretence;
40   While others, slipped into a wide excess,
          Said little less;
The weaker sort slight, trivial wares enslave,
          Who think them brave;
And poor, despisèd Truth sat counting by
          Their victory.

Yet some, who all this while did weep and sing,
And sing and weep, soared up into the ring;
          But most would use no wing.
Oh, fools—said I—thus to prefer dark night
50   Before true light!
To live in grots and caves, and hate the day
          Because it shows the way;
The way, which from this dead and dark abode
          Leads up to God;
A way where you might tread the sun, and be
          More bright than he!
But as I did their madness so discuss,
          One whispered thus,
'This ring the Bridegroom did for none provide,
60   But for His bride.'

John Dryden

John Dryden (1631–1700) was a prolific writer, a great literary man, Milton's
successor and Pope's predecessor—without being quite so great a poet as
either of them. He wrote many of his plays in rhymed couplets. The heroic
couplet is Dryden's particular measure: pairs of end-stopped pentameter lines,
rhymed directly, usually forming a complete two-line unit of thought or
narrative; Dryden codified the form. Chaucer had written in couplets, as had
Ben Jonson. Dryden made the form more rigid while retaining great vigor and
force. Pope, with unprecedented dexterity and skill, carried it even further,
and some feel that Dryden's verse is more vigorous than Pope's. Most of his
best work is in long poems, philosophical or satirical, allusive, difficult to read
without study of the age. This short poem shows Dryden's finish and his energy.

To the Memory of Mr. Oldham

Farewell, too little and too lately known,
Whom I began to think and call my own;

For sure our souls were near allied, and thine
Cast in the same poetic mold with mine.
One common note on either lyre did strike,
And knaves and fools we both abhorred alike.
To the same goal did both our studies drive:
The last set out the soonest did arrive.
Thus Nisus[1] fell upon the slippery place,
10   Whilst his young friend performed and won the race.
O early ripe! to thy abundant store
What could advancing age have added more?
It might (what nature never gives the young)
Have taught the numbers° of thy native tongue.   poetic meters
But satire needs not those, and wit will shine
Through the harsh cadence of a rugged line.
A noble error, and but seldom made,
When poets are by too much force betrayed.
Thy gen'rous fruits, though gathered ere their prime,
20   Still shewed a quickness; and maturing time
But mellows what we write to the dull sweets of rhyme.
Once more, hail, and farewell! farewell, thou young,
But ah! too short, Marcellus[2] of our tongue!
Thy brows with ivy and with laurels bound;
But fate and gloomy night encompass thee around.

[1]In Vergil's *Aeneid* Nisus is beaten in a race by a younger friend.   [2]Marcus Claudius Marcellus, nephew and adopted son of Augustus Caesar, died at twenty and is lamented by Vergil in the sixth book of the *Aeneid*.

Alexander Pope

Alexander Pope (1688–1744), crippled by a childhood disease, was unusually small. He was precocious, beginning to write with considerable excellence at sixteen. The "Essay on Criticism," from which this poem is excerpted, appeared when he was only twenty-three. Much of the later and greater work is highly allusive. Although the poetry becomes more subtle and wise, the wit-work of the young Pope was never surpassed. Pope was so proficient at the couplet that he was able to translate the entire *Iliad* and *Odyssey* into these twenty-syllable units.

Part II *of* An Essay on Criticism

Of all the Causes which conspire to blind
Man's erring judgment, and misguide the mind,
What the weak head with strongest bias rules,
Is *Pride*, the never-failing vice of fools.
Whatever Nature has in worth denied,
She gives in large recruits of needful Pride:
For as in bodies, thus in souls, we find
What wants in blood and spirits, swelled with wind:
Pride, where Wit fails, steps in to our defence,
10   And fills up all the mighty Void of sense.

If once right reason drives that cloud away,
Truth breaks upon us with resistless day.
Trust not yourself; but your defects to know,
Make use of every friend—and every foe.
    A *little learning* is a dangerous thing;
Drink deep, or taste not the Pierian spring:[1]
There shallow draughts intoxicate the brain,
And drinking largely sobers us again.
Fired at first sight with what the Muse imparts,
20   In fearless youth we tempt the heights of Arts,
While from the bounded level of our mind,
Short views we take, nor see the lengths behind;
But more advanced, behold with strange surprise
New distant scenes of endless science° rise!   knowledge
So pleased at first the towering Alps we try,
Mount o'er the vales, and seem to tread the sky,
Th' eternal snows appear already past,
And the first clouds and mountains seem the last:
But, those attained, we tremble to survey
30   The growing labours of the lengthened way;
Th' increasing prospect tires our wandering eyes,
Hills peep o'er hills, and Alps on Alps arise!
    A perfect Judge will read each work of Wit
With the same spirit that its author writ:
Survey the WHOLE, nor seek slight faults to find
Where nature moves, and rapture warms the mind;
Nor lose, for that malignant dull delight,
The generous pleasure to be charmed with wit.
But in such lays as neither ebb, nor flow,
40   Correctly cold, and regularly low,
That shunning faults, one quiet tenour keep;
We cannot blame indeed——but we may sleep.
In Wit, as Nature, what affects our hearts
Is not th' exactness of peculiar parts;
'Tis not a lip, or eye, we beauty call,
But the joint force and full result of all.
Thus when we view some well-proportioned dome,
(The world's just wonder, and even thine, O Rome!)
No single parts unequally surprise,
50   All comes united to th' admiring eyes;
No monstrous height, or breadth, or length appear;
The Whole at once is bold, and regular.
    Whoever thinks a faultless piece to see,
Thinks what ne'er was, nor is, nor e'er shall be.
In every work regard the writer's End,
Since none can compass more than they intend;
And if the means be just, the conduct true,
Applause, in spite of trivial faults, is due.

---

[1]In Greek mythology, a spring sacred to the Muses

As men of breeding, sometimes men of wit,
60   T' avoid great errors, must the less commit:
Neglect the rules each verbal Critic lays,
For not to know some trifles is a praise.
Most Critics, fond of some subservient art,
Still make the Whole depend upon a Part:
They talk of principles, but notions prize,
And all to one loved Folly sacrifice.
 Once on a time, La Mancha's Knight,° they say,   Don Quixote
A certain Bard encountering on the way,
Discoursed in tems as just, with looks as sage,
70   As e'er could Dennis[2] of the Grecian stage;
Concluding all were desperate sots and fools,
Who durst depart from Aristotle's rules.
Our Author, happy in a judge so nice,
Produced his Play, and begged the Knight's advice;
Made him observe the subject, and the plot,
The manners, passions, unities; what not?
All which, exact to rule, were brought about,
Were but a Combat in the lists left out.
"What! leave the Combat out?" exclaims the Knight;
80   "Yes, or we must renounce the Stagirite."°   Aristotle
"Not so by Heaven!" (he answers in a rage)
"Knights, squires, and steeds, must enter on the stage."
"So vast a throng the stage can ne'er contain."
"Then build a new, or act it in a plain."
 Thus Critics, of less judgment than caprice,
Curious not knowing, not exact but nice,
Form short Ideas; and offend in arts
(As most in manners) by a love to parts.
 Some to *Conceit* alone their taste confine,
90   And glittering thoughts struck out at every line;
Pleased with a work where nothing's just or fit;
One glaring Chaos and wild heap of wit.
Poets like painters, thus, unskilled to trace
The naked nature and the living grace,
With gold and jewels cover every part,
And hide with ornaments their want of art.
True Wit is Nature to advantage dressed,
What oft was thought, but ne'er so well expressed;
Something, whose truth convinced at sight we find,
100   That gives us back the image of our mind.
As shades more sweetly recommend the light,
So modest plainness sets off sprightly wit.
For works may have more wit than does 'em good,
As bodies perish through excess of blood.
 Others for *Language* all their care express,
And value books, as women men, for Dress:

[2]John Dennis (1657–1734), an author Pope satirizes

Their praise is still,—the Style is excellent:
The Sense, they humbly take upon content.
Words are like leaves; and where they most abound,
110 Much fruit of sense beneath is rarely found.
False Eloquence, like the prismatic glass,
Its gaudy colours spreads on every place;
The face of Nature we no more survey,
All glares alike, without distinction gay:
But true Expression, like th' unchanging Sun,
Clears, and improves whate'er it shines upon,
It gilds all objects, but it alters none.
Expression is the dress of thought, and still
Appears more decent, as more suitable;
120 A vile conceit in pompous words expressed,
Is like a clown in regal purple dressed:
For different styles with different subjects sort,
As several garbs with country, town, and court.
Some by old words to fame have made pretence,
Ancients in phrase, mere moderns in their sense;
Such laboured nothings, in so strange a style,
Amaze th' unlearned, and make the learnèd smile.
Unlucky, as Fungoso in the Play,[3]
These sparks with awkward vanity display
130 What the fine gentleman wore yesterday;
And but so mimic ancient wits at best,
As apes our grandsires, in their doublets drest.
In words, as fashions, the same rule will hold;
Alike fantastic, if too new, or old:
Be not the first by whom the new are tried,
Nor yet the last to lay the old aside.
  But most by Numbers° judge a Poet's song;   poetic meters
And smooth or rough, with them is right or wrong:
In the bright Muse though thousand charms conspire,
140 Her Voice is all these tuneful fools admire;
Who haunt Parnassus[4] but to please their ear,
Not mend their minds; as some to Church repair,
Not for the doctrine, but the music there.
These equal syllables alone require,
Though oft the ear the open vowels tire;
While expletives their feeble aid do join;
And ten low words oft creep in one dull line:
While they ring round the same unvaried chimes,
With sure returns of still expected rhymes;
150 Where'er you find "the cooling western breeze,"
In the next line, it "whispers through the trees:"
If crystal streams "with pleasing murmurs creep,"
The reader's threatened (not in vain) with "sleep:"
Then, at the last and only couplet, fraught

[3]Ben Jonson's *Every Man Out of His Humour*   [4]Mountain home of the Muses

With some unmeaning thing they call a thought,
A needless Alexandrine ends the song,
That, like a wounded snake, drags its slow length along.
Leave such to tune their own dull rhymes, and know
What's roundly smooth, or languishingly slow;
160   And praise the easy vigour of a line,
Where Denham's strength, and Waller's⁵ sweetness join.
True ease in writing comes from art, not chance,
As those move easiest who have learned to dance.
'Tis not enough no harshness gives offence,
The sound must seem an Echo to the sense:
Soft is the strain when Zephyr⁶ gently blows,
And the smooth stream in smoother numbers flows;
But when loud surges lash the sounding shore,
The hoarse, rough verse should like the torrent roar:
170   When Ajax⁷ strives some rock's vast weight to throw,
The line too labours, and the words move slow;
Not so, when swift Camilla⁸ scours the plain,
Flies o'er th' unbending corn, and skims along the main.
Hear how Timotheus'⁹ varied lays surprise,
And bid alternate passions fall and rise!
While, at each change, the son of Libyan Jove¹⁰
Now burns with glory, and then melts with love;
Now his fierce eyes with sparkling fury glow,
Now sighs steal out, and tears begin to flow:
180   Persians and Greeks like turns of nature found,
And the World's victor stood subdued by Sound!
The power of Music all our hearts allow,
And what Timotheus was, is DRYDEN now.
   Avoid Extremes; and shun the fault of such,
Who still are pleased too little or too much.
At every trifle scorn to take offence,
That always shows great pride, or little sense;
Those heads, as stomachs, are not sure the best,
Which nauseate all, and nothing can digest.
190   Yet let not each gay Turn thy rapture move;
For fools admire,° but men of sense approve: wonder at
As things seem large which we through mists descry,
Dulness is ever apt to magnify.
   Some foreign writers, some our own despise;
The Ancients only, or the Moderns prize.
Thus Wit, like Faith, by each man is applied
To one small sect, and all are damned beside.
Meanly they seek the blessing to confine,
And force that sun but on a part to shine,
200   Which not alone the southern wit sublimes,

⁵Sir John Denham (1615–1669) and Edmund Waller (1606–1687) were poets Pope admired.   ⁶The West Wind   ⁷A strong warrior in Homer's *Iliad*   ⁸A maiden warrior in Vergil's *Aeneid*   ⁹A Greek musician   ¹⁰A reference to Dryden's poem in praise of music, "Alexander's Feast" ·

But ripens spirits in cold northern climes;
Which from the first has shone on ages past,
Enlights the present, and shall warm the last;
Though each may feel increases and decays,
And see now clearer and now darker days.
Regard not then if Wit be old or new,
But blame the false, and value still the true.
    Some ne'er advance a Judgment of their own,
But catch the spreading notion of the Town;
210   They reason and conclude by precedent,
And own stale nonsense which they ne'er invent.
Some judge of authors' names, not works, and then
Nor praise nor blame the writings, but the men.
Of all this servile herd, the worst is he
That in proud dulness joins with Quality.
A constant Critic at the great man's board,
To fetch and carry nonsense for my Lord.
What woeful stuff this madrigal would be,
In some starved hackney sonneteer, or me?
220   But let a Lord once own the happy lines,
How the wit brightens! how the style refines!
Before his sacred name flies every fault,
And each exalted stanza teems with thought!
    The Vulgar thus through Imitation err;
As oft the Learned by being singular;
So much they scorn the crowd, that if the throng
By chance go right, they purposely go wrong:
So Schismatics the plain believers quit,
And are but damned for having too much wit.
230   Some praise at morning what they blame at night;
But always think the last opinion right.
A Muse by these is like a mistress used,
This hour she's idolized, the next abused;
While their weak heads like towns unfortified,
Twixt sense and nonsense daily change their side.
Ask them the cause; they're wiser still, they say;
And still tomorrow's wiser than today.
We think our fathers fools, so wise we grow;
Our wiser sons, no doubt, will think us so.
240   Once School divines this zealous isle o'erspread;
Who knew most Sentences, was deepest read;
Faith, Gospel, all, seemed made to be disputed,
And none had sense enough to be confuted:
Scotists and Thomists,[11] now, in peace remain,
Amidst their kindred cobwebs in Duck Lane.[12]
If Faith itself has different dresses worn,
What wonder modes in Wit should take their turn?

---

[11]Followers of the differing theologians Duns Scotus (1265?–1308) and Thomas Aquinas (1225?–1274) [12]A London street known for dealers in old books

Oft, leaving what is natural and fit,
The current folly proves the ready wit;
250 And authors think their reputation safe,
Which lives as long as fools are pleased to laugh.
    Some valuing those of their own side or mind,
Still make themselves the measure of mankind:
Fondly we think we honour merit then,
When we but praise ourselves in other men.
Parties in Wit attend on those of State,
And public faction doubles private hate.
Pride, Malice, Folly, against Dryden rose,
In various shapes of Parsons, Critics, Beaus;
260 But sense survived, when merry jests were past;
For rising merit will buoy up at last.
Might he return, and bless once more our eyes,
New Blackmores and new Milbourns[13] must arise:
Nay should great Homer lift his awful head,
Zoilus[14] again would start up from the dead.
Envy will merit, as its shade, pursue;
But like a shadow, proves the substance true;
For envied Wit, like Sol eclipsed, makes known
Th' opposing body's grossness, not its own.
270 When first that sun too powerful beams displays,
It draws up vapours which obscure its rays;
But even those clouds at last adorn its way,
Reflect new glories, and augment the day.
    Be thou the first true merit to befriend;
His praise is lost, who stays till all commend.
Short is the date, alas, of modern rhymes,
And 'tis but just to let them live betimes.
No longer now that golden age appears,
When Patriarch wits survived a thousand years:
280 Now length of Fame (our second life) is lost,
And bare threescore is all even that can boast;
Our sons their fathers' failing language see,
And such as Chaucer is, shall Dryden be.
So when the faithful pencil has designed
Some bright Idea of the master's mind,
Where a new world leaps out at his command,
And ready Nature waits upon his hand;
When the ripe colours soften and unite,
And sweetly melt into just shade and light;
290 When mellowing years their full perfection give,
And each bold figure just begins to live,
The treacherous colours the fair art betray,
And all the bright creation fades away!
    Unhappy Wit, like most mistaken things,

---

[13]Richard Blackmore (1652–1729) and Luke Milbourn (1649–1720) attacked Dryden.   [14]Critic of Homer, fourth century B.C.

Atones not for that envy which it brings.
In youth alone its empty praise we boast,
But soon the short-lived vanity is lost:
Like some fair flower the early spring supplies,
That gaily blooms, but even in blooming dies.
300 What is this Wit, which must our cares employ?
The owner's wife, that other men enjoy;
Then most our trouble still when most admired,
And still the more we give, the more required;
Whose fame with pains we guard, but lose with ease,
Sure some to vex, but never all to please;
'Tis what the vicious fear, the virtuous shun,
By fools 'tis hated, and by knaves undone!
      If Wit so much from Ignorance undergo,
Ah let not Learning too commence its foe!
310 Of old, those met rewards who could excel,
And such were praised who but endeavoured well:
Though triumphs were to generals only due,
Crowns were reserved to grace the soldiers too.
Now, they who reach Parnassus' lofty crown,
Employ their pains to spurn some others down;
And while self-love each jealous writer rules,
Contending wits become the sport of fools:
But still the worst with most regret commend,
For each ill Author is as bad a Friend.
320 To what base ends, and by what abject ways,
Are mortals urged through sacred lust of praise!
Ah ne'er so dire a thirst of glory boast,
Nor in the Critic let the Man be lost.
Good nature and good sense must ever join;
To err is human, to forgive, divine.
      But if in noble minds some dregs remain
Not yet purged off, of spleen and sour disdain;
Discharge that rage on more provoking crimes,
Nor fear a dearth in these flagitious° times.   vicious
330 No pardon vile Obscenity should find,
Though wit and art conspire to move your mind;
But Dulness with Obscenity must prove
As shameful sure as Impotence in love.
In the fat age of pleasure, wealth and ease,
Sprung the rank weed, and thrived with large increase:
When love was all an easy Monarch's care;
Seldom at council, never in a war:
Jilts ruled the state, and statesmen farces writ;
Nay wits had pensions, and young Lords had wit:
340 The Fair sat panting at a Courtier's play,
And not a Mask went unimproved away:
The modest fan was lifted up no more,
And Virgins smiled at what they blushed before.
The following license of a Foreign reign

Did all the dregs of bold Socinus[15] drain;
Then unbelieving Priests reformed the nation,
And taught more pleasant methods of salvation;
Where Heaven's free subjects might their rights dispute,
Lest God himself should seem too absolute:
350   Pulpits their sacred satire learned to spare,
And Vice admired to find a flatterer there!
Encouraged thus, Wit's Titans braved the skies,
And the press groaned with licensed blasphemies.
These monsters, Critics! with your darts engage,
Here point your thunder, and exhaust your rage!
Yet shun their fault, who, scandalously nice,
Will needs mistake an author into vice;
All seems infected that th' infected spy,
As all looks yellow to the jaundiced eye.

[15]Author of the Socinian heresy condemned by the Inquisition

Christopher Smart

Christopher Smart (1722–1771) wrote the long poem excerpted below when he was insane. It was his habit, in his madness, to go down on his knees in a crowded street and ask other people to pray with him. Samuel Johnson, apprised of Smart's eccentricities, avowed that he would as soon pray with Kit Smart as with any man.

from Jubilate Agno[1]

For I will consider my Cat Jeoffry.
For he is the servant of the Living God, duly and daily serving him.
For at the first glance of the glory of God in the East he worships in his way.
For is this done by wreathing his body seven times round with elegant
    quickness.
For then he leaps up to catch the musk,° which is the blessing of   catnip (?)
    God upon his prayer.
For he rolls upon prank to work it in.
For having done duty and received blessing he begins to consider himself.
For this he performs in ten degrees.
For first he looks upon his fore-paws to see if they are clean.
10   For secondly he kicks up behind to clear away there.
For thirdly he works it upon stretch with the fore-paws extended.
For fourthly he sharpens his paws by wood.
For fifthly he washes himself.
For sixthly he rolls upon wash.
For seventhly he fleas himself, that he may not be interrupted upon the beat.
For eighthly he rubs himself against a post.
For ninthly he looks up for his instructions.
For tenthly he goes in quest of food.

[1]Rejoice in the Lamb

For having considered God and himself he will consider his neighbor.
20   For if he meets another cat he will kiss her in kindness.
For when he takes his prey he plays with it to give it chance.
For one mouse in seven escapes by his dallying.
For when his day's work is done his business more properly begins.
For he keeps the Lord's watch in the night against the adversary.
For he counteracts the powers of darkness by his electrical skin and glaring
     eyes.
For he counteracts the Devil, who is death, by brisking about the life.
For in his morning orisons he loves the sun and the sun loves him.
For he is of the tribe of Tiger.
For the Cherub Cat is a term of the Angel Tiger.
For he has the subtlety and hissing of a serpent, which in goodness he
30   suppresses.
For he will not do destruction if he is well-fed, neither will he spit without
     provocation.
For he purrs in thankfulness, when God tells him he's a good Cat.
For he is an instrument for the children to learn benevolence upon.
For every house is incomplete without him and a blessing is lacking in the
     spirit.
For the Lord commanded Moses concerning the cats at the departure of the
     Children of Israel from Egypt.
For every family had one cat at least in the bag.
For the English Cats are the best in Europe.

William Cowper

William Cowper (1731–1800) suffered from fits of depression and was suicidal.
His temporary insanity was influenced, in its particular shape, by his
Calvinism, whereby he was convinced that he was one of the damned. His
metaphor for damnation is "The Castaway." If Elizabethan poets suffered from
a malady of executions, many eighteenth-century poets seem to have
specialized in insanity.

The Castaway

Obscurest night involved the sky,
   The Atlantic billows roared,
When such a destined wretch as I,
   Washed headlong from on board,
Of friends, of hope, of all bereft,
His floating home forever left.

No braver chief could Albion° boast   England
   Than he with whom he went,[1]
Nor ever ship left Albion's coast,
10   With warmer wishes sent.
He loved them both, but both in vain,
Nor him beheld, nor her again.

[1]"He" is George, Lord Anson (1697–1762), from whose *Voyage Round the World* Cowper took
this story.

Not long beneath the whelming brine,
    Expert to swim, he lay;
Nor soon he felt his strength decline,
    Or courage die away;
But waged with death a lasting strife,
Supported by despair of life.

He shouted; nor his friends had failed
20   To check the vessel's course,
But so the furious blast prevailed,
    That, pitiless perforce,
They left their outcast mate behind,
And scudded still before the wind.

Some succor yet they could afford;
    And, such as storms allow,
The cask, the coop, the floated cord,
    Delayed not to bestow.
But he (they knew) nor ship, nor shore,
30   Whate'er they gave, should visit more.

Nor, cruel as it seemed, could he
    Their haste himself condemn,
Aware that flight, in such a sea,
    Alone could rescue them;
Yet bitter felt it still to die
Deserted, and his friends so nigh.

He long survives, who lives an hour
    In ocean, self-upheld;
And so long he, with unspent power,
40   His destiny repelled;
And ever, as the minutes flew,
Entreated help, or cried, "Adieu!"

At length, his transient respite past,
    His comrades, who before
Had heard his voice in every blast,
    Could catch the sound no more.
For then, by toil subdued, he drank
The stifling wave, and then he sank.

No poet wept him; but the page
50   Of narrative sincere,
That tells his name, his worth, his age,
    Is wet with Anson's tear.
And tears by bards or heroes shed
Alike immortalize the dead.

I therefore purpose not, or dream,
    Descanting on his fate,
To give the melancholy theme
    A more enduring date:

But misery still delights to trace
60 Its semblance in another's case.

No voice divine the storm allayed,
 No light propitious shone,
When, snatched from all effectual aid,
 We perished, each alone;
But I beneath a rougher sea,
And whelmed in deeper gulfs than he.

William Blake

William Blake (1757–1827) called his first major work *Songs of Innocence and Experience*. This sequence included many pairings of poems, the one viewed under the aspect of innocence and the other under the aspect of experience. So we have paired poems which follow under the same names; and we have on the one hand the lamb, and on the other the tiger. His later work is obscure, difficult—and superbly rewarding. He was an engraver by trade, and executed his own etchings and engravings. Like Campion, Blake was master of two arts. He was a mystic, and told how some of his poems were dictated to him by voices. See also pages 437 and 488–489.

The Lamb

 Little Lamb, who made thee?
 Dost thou know who made thee;
Gave thee life and bid thee feed
By the stream and o'er the mead;
Gave thee clothing of delight,
Softest clothing, woolly, bright;
Gave thee such a tender voice
Making all the vales rejoice?
 Little Lamb, who made thee?
10 Dost thou know who made thee?

 Little Lamb, I'll tell thee,
 Little Lamb, I'll tell thee:
He is callèd by thy name,
For He calls Himself a Lamb.
He is meek and He is mild:
He became a little child.
I a child and thou a lamb,
We are callèd by His name.
 Little Lamb, God bless thee.
20 Little Lamb, God bless thee.

The Tyger

Tyger! Tyger! burning bright
In the forests of the night,
What immortal hand or eye
Could frame thy fearful symmetry?

In what distant deeps or skies
Burnt the fire of thine eyes?
On what wings dare he aspire?
What the hand dare seize the fire?

And what shoulder, and what art,
10   Could twist the sinews of thy heart?
And when thy heart began to beat,
What dread hand? and what dread feet?

What the hammer? what the chain?
In what furnace was thy brain?
What the anvil? what dread grasp
Dare its deadly terrors clasp?

When the stars threw down their spears
And watered heaven with their tears,
Did he smile his work to see?
20   Did he who made the Lamb make thee?

Tyger! Tyger! burning bright
In the forests of the night,
What immortal hand or eye
Dare frame thy fearful symmetry?

The Garden of Love

I went to the Garden of Love,
And saw what I never had seen:
A Chapel was built in the midst,
Where I used to play on the green.

And the gates of this Chapel were shut,
And "Thou shalt not" writ over the door;
So I turned to the Garden of Love
That so many sweet flowers bore;

And I saw it was filled with graves,
10   And tomb-stones where flowers should be,
And Priests in black gowns were walking their rounds,
And binding with briars my joys and desires.

London

I wander thro' each chartered street,
Near where the chartered Thames does flow,
And mark in every face I meet
Marks of weakness, marks of woe.

In every cry of every Man,
In every Infant's cry of fear,

In every voice, in every ban,
The mind-forged manacles I hear.

How the Chimney-sweeper's cry
10   Every black'ning Church appalls;
And the hapless Soldier's sigh
Runs in blood down Palace walls.

But most thro' midnight streets I hear
How the youthful Harlot's curse
Blasts the new-born Infant's tear,
And blights with plagues the Marriage hearse.

Mock On, Mock On, Voltaire, Rousseau

Mock on, mock on, Voltaire, Rousseau,
   Mock on, mock on, 'tis all in vain;
You throw the sand against the wind
   And the wind blows it back again.

And every sand becomes a gem
   Reflected in the beams divine;
Blown back, they blind the mocking eye,
   But still in Israel's paths they shine.

The atoms of Democritus
10   And Newton's particles of light
Are sands upon the Red Sea shore,
   Where Israel's tents do shine so bright.

from Milton

And did those feet in ancient time
Walk upon England's mountains green?
And was the Holy Lamb of God
On England's pleasant pastures seen?

And did the countenance divine
Shine forth upon our clouded hills?
And was Jerusalem builded here
Among these dark satanic mills?

Bring me my bow of burning gold!
10   Bring me my arrows of desire!
Bring me my spear! O clouds, unfold!
Bring me my chariot of fire!

I will not cease from mental fight,
Nor shall my sword sleep in my hand,
Till we have built Jerusalem
In England's green and pleasant land.

Robert Burns

Robert Burns (1759–1796), after the medieval poets, is the great poet of Scotland. He is one of the few British poets to arise from the working classes, having begun life as a farm laborer. Much of his work derives from a folk tradition and from anonymous Scots songs.

Green Grow the Rashes, O

Chorus

Green grow the rashes, O;
Green grow the rashes, O;
The sweetest hours that e'er I spend,
Are spent among the lasses, O!

There's nought but care on ev'ry han',
     In ev'ry hour that passes, O:
What signifies the life o' man,
     An' 'twere na for the lasses, O.

The war'ly° race may riches chase,   worldly
10   An' riches still may fly them, O;
An' tho' at last they catch them fast,
     Their hearts can ne'er enjoy them, O.

But gie me a canny° hour at e'en   quiet
     My arms about my dearie, O,
An' war'ly cares, an' war'ly men
     May a' gae tapsalteerie,° O!   topsy-turvy

For you sae douce,° ye sneer at this;   sedate
     Ye're nought but senseless asses, O;
The wisest man the warl' e'er saw,
20   He dearly lov'd the lasses, O.

Auld Nature swears, the lovely dears
     Her noblest work she classes, O:
Her prentice han' she try'd on man,
     An' then she made the lasses, O.

John Anderson My Jo

John Anderson my jo,° John,   darling
     When we were first acquent,
Your locks were like the raven,
     Your bonnie brow was brent;°   straight, steep
But now your brow is beld,° John,   bald
     Your locks are like the snaw,
But blessings on your frosty pow,°   head
     John Anderson, my jo.

John Anderson my jo, John,
10   We clamb° the hill thegither,   climbed
And monie a cantie° day, John,   merry

We've had wi' ane anither
Now we maun° totter down, John,   must
   And hand in hand we'll go,
And sleep thegither at the foot,
   John Anderson my jo.

William Wordsworth

William Wordsworth (1770–1850) attended Cambridge, afterward touring
Europe on foot and living for a year in France when the revolutionary society
was at its most exciting. Back in England, he continued to write poems, and in
1795 began his long and close friendship with Samuel Taylor Coleridge. The
two poets, with Wordsworth's sister Dorothy and with Coleridge's wife, lived
near each other for a time, and Wordsworth and Coleridge published *Lyrical
Ballads* in 1798, a collection of poetry by both of them, including Coleridge's
"Rime of the Ancient Mariner" and Wordsworth's "Lines Written Above Tintern
Abbey." The year of publication provides as good a date as any for the
beginning of the romantic movement in English literature. Two years later,
reprinting the volume, Wordsworth added prose "observations" in which he
defended his own theory of poetry, deriving his language from rustic life. His
imagery also derived from rustic life, and his poems were at first denounced as
obscure and meaningless. Later, he became one of the most popular poets of
the English tradition. In his long life he wrote prolifically; most of his best work
is early.

Ode: Intimations of Immortality
from Recollections of Early Childhood

   The Child is father of the Man;
   And I could wish my days to be
   Bound each to each by natural piety.

I

There was a time when meadow, grove, and stream,
The earth, and every common sight,
    To me did seem
   Apparelled in celestial light,
The glory and the freshness of a dream.
It is not now as it hath been of yore;—
    Turn whereso'er I may,
     By night or day,
The things which I have seen I now can see no more.

II

10   The Rainbow comes and goes,
     And lovely is the Rose,
     The Moon doth with delight
Look round her when the heavens are bare,
     Waters on a starry night
     Are beautiful and fair;
  The sunshine is a glorious birth;
  But yet I know, where'er I go,
That there hath past away a glory from the earth.

III

Now, while the birds thus sing a joyous song,
20   And while the young lambs bound
              As to the tabor's sound.
To me alone there came a thought of grief:
A timely utterance gave that thought relief,
              And I again am strong:
The cataracts blow their trumpets from the steep;
No more shall grief of mine the season wrong;
I hear the Echoes through the mountains throng,
The Winds come to me from the fields of sleep,
              And all the earth is gay;
30   Land and sea
         Give themselves up to jollity,
              And with the heart of May
         Doth every Beast keep holiday;—
              Thou Child of Joy,
Shout round me, let me hear thy shouts, thou happy
              Shepherd-boy!

IV

Ye blessèd Creatures, I have heard the call
         Ye to each other make; I see
The heavens laugh with you in your jubilee;
40   My heart is at your festival,
              My head hath its coronal,
The fulness of your bliss, I feel—I feel it all.
              Oh evil day! if I were sullen
              While Earth herself is adorning,
                 This sweet May-morning,
              And the Children are culling
                 On every side,
              In a thousand valleys far and wide,
              Fresh flowers; while the sun shines warm,
50   And the Babe leaps up on his Mother's arm:—
              I hear, I hear, with joy I hear!
              —But there's a Tree, of many, one,
A single Field which I have looked upon,
Both of them speak of something that is gone:
              The Pansy at my feet
              Doth the same tale repeat:
Whither is fled the visionary gleam?
Where is it now, the glory and the dream?

V

Our birth is but a sleep and a forgetting:
60   The Soul that rises with us, our life's Star,
              Hath had elsewhere its setting,
                 And cometh from afar:

Not in entire forgetfulness,
And not in utter nakedness,
But trailing clouds of glory do we come
From God, who is our home:
Heaven lies about us in our infancy!
Shades of the prison-house begin to close
Upon the growing Boy,
70 But He beholds the light, and whence it flows,
He sees it in his joy;
The Youth, who daily farther from the east
Must travel, still is Nature's Priest,
And by the vision splendid
Is on his way attended;
At length the Man perceives it die away,
And fade into the light of common day.

VI

Earth fills her lap with pleasures of her own;
Yearnings she hath in her own natural kind,
80 And, even with something of a Mother's mind,
And no unworthy aim,
The homely Nurse doth all she can
To make her Foster-child, her Inmate Man,
Forget the glories he hath known,
And that imperial palace whence he came.

VII

Behold the Child among his new-born blisses,
A six years' Darling of a pigmy size!
See, where 'mid work of his own hand he lies,
Fretted by sallies of his mother's kisses,
90 With light upon him from his father's eyes!
See, at his feet, some little plan or chart,
Some fragment from his dream of human life,
Shaped by himself with newly-learned art;
A wedding or a festival,
A mourning or a funeral;
And this hath now his heart,
And unto this he frames his song.
Then will he fit his tongue
To dialogues of business, love, or strife;
100 But it will not be long
Ere this be thrown aside,
And with new joy and pride
The little Actor cons another part;
Filling from time to time his "humorous stage"
With all the Persons, down to palsied Age,
That Life brings with her in her equipage;
As if his whole vocation
Were endless imitation.

VIII

Thou, whose exterior semblance doth belie
110   Thy Soul's immensity;
Thou best Philosopher, who yet dost keep
Thy heritage, thou Eye among the blind,
That, deaf and silent, read'st the eternal deep,
Haunted for ever by the eternal mind,—
    Mighty Prophet! Seer blest!
    On whom those truths do rest,
Which we are toiling all our lives to find,
In darkness lost, the darkness of the grave,
Thou, over whom thy Immortality
120 Broods like the Day, a Master o'er a Slave,
A Presence which is not to be put by;
Thou little Child, yet glorious in the might
Of heaven-born freedom on thy being's height,
Why with such earnest pains dost thou provoke
The years to bring the inevitable yoke,
Thus blindly with thy blessedness at strife?
Full soon thy Soul shall have her earthly freight,
And custom lie upon thee with a weight,
Heavy as frost, and deep almost as life!

IX

130   O joy! that in our embers
    Is something that doth live,
    That nature yet remembers
    What was so fugitive!
The thought of our past years in me doth breed
Perpetual benediction: not indeed
For that which is most worthy to be blest;
Delight and liberty, the simple creed
Of Childhood, whether busy or at rest,
With new-fledged hope still fluttering in his breast:—
140   Not for these I raise
    The song of thanks and praise;
    But for those obstinate questionings
    Of sense and outward things,
    Fallings from us, vanishings;
    Blank misgivings of a Creature
Moving about in worlds not realised,
High instincts before which our mortal Nature
Did tremble like a guilty Thing surprised:
    But for those first affections,
150   Those shadowy recollections,
    Which, be they what they may,
Are yet the fountain-light of all our day,
Are yet a master-light of all our seeing;
    Uphold us, cherish, and have power to make
Our noisy years seem moments in the being

Of the eternal Silence: truths that wake,
  To perish never:
Which neither listlessness, nor mad endeavour,
  Nor Man nor Boy,
160 Nor all that is at enmity with joy,
Can utterly abolish or destroy!
    Hence in a season of calm weather
      Though inland far we be,
Our Souls have sight of that immortal sea
      Which brought us hither,
    Can in a moment travel thither,
And see the Children sport upon the shore,
And hear the mighty waters rolling evermore.

X

Then sing, ye Birds, sing, sing a joyous song!
170   And let the young Lambs bound
      As to the tabor's sound!
We in thought will join your throng,
      Ye that pipe and ye that play,
      Ye that through your hearts today
      Feel the gladness of the May!
What though the radiance which was once so bright
Be now for ever taken from my sight,
    Though nothing can bring back the hour
Of splendour in the grass, of glory in the flower;
180   We will grieve not, rather find
      Strength in what remains behind;
      In the primal sympathy
      Which having been must ever be;
      In the soothing thoughts that spring
      Out of human suffering;
      In the faith that looks through death,
In years that bring the philosophic mind.

XI

And O, ye Fountains, Meadows, Hills, and Groves,
Forebode not any severing of our loves!
190 Yet in my heart of hearts I feel your might;
I only have relinquished one delight
To live beneath your more habitual sway.
I love the Brooks which down their channels fret,
Even more than when I tripped lightly as they;
The innocent brightness of a new-born Day
      Is lovely yet;
The Clouds that gather round the setting sun
Do take a sober colouring from an eye
That hath kept watch o'er man's mortality;
200 Another race hath been, and other palms are won.
Thanks to the human heart by which we live,

Thanks to its tenderness, its joys, and fears,
To me the meanest flower that blows can give
Thoughts that do often lie too deep for tears.

The World Is Too Much with Us

The world is too much with us; late and soon,
Getting and spending, we lay waste our powers:
Little we see in Nature that is ours;
We have given our hearts away, a sordid boon!
The sea that bares her bosom to the moon;
The winds that will be howling at all hours,
And are up-gathered now like sleeping flowers;
For this, for everything, we are out of tune;
It moves us not.—Great God! I'd rather be
10 A pagan suckled in a creed outworn;
So might I, standing on this pleasant lea,
Have glimpses that would make me less forlorn;
Have sight of Proteus rising from the sea;
Or hear old Triton blow his wreathèd horn.

It Is a Beauteous Evening

It is a beauteous evening, calm and free;
The holy time is quiet as a nun
Breathless with adoration; the broad sun
Is sinking down in its tranquillity;
The gentleness of heaven broods o'er the sea:
Listen! the mighty Being is awake,
And doth with his eternal motion make
A sound like thunder—everlastingly.
Dear child! dear girl! that walkest with me here,
10 If thou appear untouched by solemn thought,
Thy nature is not therefore less divine:
Thou liest in Abraham's bosom all the year,
And worship'st at the Temple's inner shrine,
God being with thee when we know it not.

Samuel Taylor Coleridge

Samuel Taylor Coleridge (1772–1834), thinker, talker, and preacher as well as
poet, was a man of enormous promise. His failure to live up to the extent of
his promise has obscured his real accomplishment. After he collaborated with
Wordsworth on *Lyrical Ballads*, the volume of his poetry declined considerably,
though the quality of an occasional poem remained high. His literary
autobiography, called *Biographia Literaria*, adds to the valuable critical work
English poets have contributed to the language.

Kubla Khan

In Xanadu did Kubla Khan
A stately pleasure-dome decree:
Where Alph, the sacred river, ran
Through caverns measureless to man
   Down to a sunless sea.
So twice five miles of fertile ground
With walls and towers were girdled round:
And there were gardens bright with sinuous rills,
Where blossomed many an incense-bearing tree;
10   And here were forests ancient as the hills,
Enfolding sunny spots of greenery.

But oh! that deep romantic chasm which slanted
Down the green hill athwart a cedarn cover!
A savage place! as holy and enchanted
As e'er beneath a waning moon was haunted
By woman wailing for her demon-lover!
And from this chasm, with ceaseless turmoil seething,
As if this earth in fast thick pants were breathing,
A mighty fountain momently was forced:
20   Amid whose swift half-intermitted burst
Huge fragments vaulted like rebounding hail,
Or chaffy grain beneath the thresher's flail:
And 'mid these dancing rocks at once and ever
It flung up momently the sacred river
Five miles meandering with a mazy motion
Through wood and dale the sacred river ran,
Then reached the caverns measureless to man,
And sank in tumult to a lifeless ocean:
And 'mid this tumult Kubla heard from far
30   Ancestral voices prophesying war!
     The shadow of the dome of pleasure
     Floated midway on the waves;
     Where was heard the mingled measure
     From the fountain and the caves.
It was a miracle of rare device,
A sunny pleasure-dome with caves of ice!

     A damsel with a dulcimer
     In a vision once I saw:
     It was an Abyssinian maid,
40   And on her dulcimer she played,
     Singing of Mount Abora.
     Could I revive within me
     Her symphony and song,
     To such a deep delight 'twould win me,
That with music loud and long,
I would build that dome in air,

That sunny dome! those caves of ice!
And all who heard should see them there,
And all should cry, Beware! Beware!
50   His flashing eyes, his floating hair!
Weave a circle round him thrice,
And close your eyes with holy dread,
For he on honey-dew hath fed,
And drunk the milk of Paradise.

Walter Savage Landor

Walter Savage Landor (1775–1864) wrote short poems over a long life. He was
famous for his violent temper; according to one often-repeated anecdote, he
took out his anger on a servant by throwing her through a window onto a
garden. He was best at the epigram and short, pointed verse. See also page
480.

I Strove with None

I strove with none, for none was worth my strife.
   Nature I loved and, next to Nature, Art:
I warmed both hands before the fire of life;
   It sinks, and I am ready to depart.

George Gordon, Lord Byron

George Gordon, Lord Byron (1788–1824) in his life was the stereotype of the
romantic poet—handsome, promiscuous, daring. His most romantic poems,
valuing emotion above all things, were not his best work, which was satirical
and comic and shared attitudes, though not form or diction, with the poets of
the eighteenth century. In 1823 Byron joined a Greek revolutionary movement
striving to establish freedom for the Greek people; he died of a fever at
Missolonghi in April 1824.

So We'll Go No More A-Roving

So we'll go no more a-roving
   So late into the night,
Though the heart be still as loving,
   And the moon be still as bright.

For the sword outwears its sheath,
   And the soul wears out the breast,
And the heart must pause to breathe,
   And Love itself have rest.

Though the night was made for loving,
10   And the day returns too soon,
Yet we'll go no more a-roving
   By the light of the moon.

Stanzas
(When a man hath no freedom to fight for at home)

When a man hath no freedom to fight for at home,
   Let him combat for that of his neighbors;
Let him think of the glories of Greece and of Rome,
   And get knocked on the head for his labors.

To do good to mankind is the chivalrous plan,
   And is always as nobly requited;
Then battle for freedom wherever you can,
   And, if not shot or hanged, you'll get knighted.

Percy Bysshe Shelley

Percy Bysshe Shelley (1792–1822) was expelled from Oxford in 1811 for writing a pamphlet in defense of atheism. That year he married his first wife, who was sixteen, from whom he separated three years later. She killed herself. He married Mary Wollstonecraft—author of *Frankenstein*—in 1814 and spent much of the rest of his life in Italy. He was friendly with Byron and acquainted with Keats. In Italy, in the last three years of his life, he wrote his best poems, including "Ode to the West Wind." On July 8, 1822, he was shipwrecked in a storm while sailing off the Italian coast and drowned.

Ode to the West Wind

1

O wild West Wind, thou breath of Autumn's being,
Thou, from whose unseen presence the leaves dead
Are driven, like ghosts from an enchanter fleeing,

Yellow, and black, and pale, and hectic red,
Pestilence-stricken multitudes: O thou,
Who chariotest to their dark wintry bed

The wingéd seeds, where they lie cold and low,
Each like a corpse within its grave, until
Thine azure sister of the Spring shall blow

10   Her clarion o'er the dreaming earth, and fill
(Driving sweet buds like flocks to feed in air)
With living hues and odours plain and hill:

Wild Spirit, which art moving everywhere;
Destroyer and preserver; hear, oh, hear!

2

Thou on whose stream, 'mid the steep sky's commotion,
Loose clouds like earth's decaying leaves are shed,
Shook from the tangled boughs of Heaven and Ocean,

Angels of rain and lightning: there are spread
On the blue surface of thine airy surge,
20   Like the bright hair uplifted from the head

Of some fierce Mænad, even from the dim verge
Of the horizon to the zenith's height,
The locks of the approaching storm. Thou dirge

Of the dying year, to which this closing night
Will be the dome of a vast sepulchre,
Vaulted with all thy congregated might

Of vapours, from whose solid atmosphere
Black rain, and fire, and hail will burst: oh, hear!

3

Thou who didst waken from his summer dreams
30   The blue Mediterranean, where he lay,
Lulled by the coil of his crystálline streams,

Beside a pumice isle in Baiæ's bay,
And saw in sleep old palaces and towers
Quivering within the wave's intenser day,

All overgrown with azure moss and flowers
So sweet, the sense faints picturing them! Thou
For whose path the Atlantic's level powers

Cleave themselves into chasms, while far below
The sea-blooms and the oozy woods which wear
40   The sapless foliage of the ocean, know

Thy voice, and suddenly grow gray with fear,
And tremble and despoil themselves: oh, hear!

4

If I were a dead leaf thou mightest bear;
If I were a swift cloud to fly with thee;
A wave to pant beneath thy power, and share

The impulse of thy strength, only less free
Than thou, O uncontrollable! If even
I were as in my boyhood, and could be

The comrade of thy wanderings over Heaven,
50   As then, when to outstrip thy skyey speed
Scarce seemed a vision; I would ne'er have striven

As thus with thee in prayer in my sore need.
Oh, lift me as a wave, a leaf, a cloud!
I fall upon the thorns of life! I bleed!

A heavy weight of hours has chained and bowed
One too like thee: tameless, and swift, and proud.

5

Make me thy lyre, even as the forest is:
What if my leaves are falling like its own!
The tumult of thy mighty harmonies

60   Will take from both a deep, autumnal tone,
Sweet though in sadness. Be thou, Spirit fierce,
My spirit! Be thou me, impetuous one!

Drive my dead thoughts over the universe
Like withered leaves to quicken a new birth!
And, by the incantation of this verse,

Scatter, as from an unextinguished hearth
Ashes and sparks, my words among mankind!
Be through my lips to unawakened earth

The trumpet of a prophecy! O, wind,
70   If Winter comes, can Spring be far behind?

John Clare

John Clare (1793–1864) was an agricultural laborer who went insane in 1837 but continued to write poems in the asylum.

I Am

I am: yet what I am none cares or knows,
    My friends forsake me like a memory lost;
I am the self-consumer of my woes,
    They rise and vanish in oblivious host,
Like shades in love and death's oblivion lost;
And yet I am, and live with shadows tost

Into the nothingness of scorn and noise,
    Into the living sea of waking dreams,
Where there is neither sense of life nor joys,
10   But the vast shipwreck of my life's esteems;
And e'en the dearest—that I loved the best—
Are strange—nay, rather stranger than the rest.

I long for scenes where man has never trod,
    A place where woman never smiled or wept;
There to abide with my Creator, God,
    And sleep as I in childhood sweetly slept:
Untroubling and untroubled where I lie,
The grass below—above the vaulted sky.

John Keats

John Keats (1795–1821) trained to become a pharmacist, then abandoned that career to learn medicine, then gave up his medical studies to devote himself to poetry. Among his friends were the critic William Hazlitt and the older poet Leigh Hunt. It was at Hunt's house that Keats met Shelley, who helped him publish his first book of poems in 1817. In the nineteenth century, literary criticism was frequently affected by political beliefs or associations, and Keats's poems were attacked viciously because of his associations with the liberal thinkers of his day. He developed tuberculosis early. In the space of a few months he wrote the greatest of his poems, among the greatest in English literature, his odes: on a Grecian Urn, to a Nightingale, to Autumn. He went to Italy for his health in September 1820 but died on February 23 of the next year. Carved on his tomb at his request were the words "Here lies one whose name was writ in water." Keats's letters contain superb suggestions about the nature of poetry. See also pages 455, 476.

Ode to a Nightingale

I

My heart aches, and a drowsy numbness pains
   My sense, as though of hemlock[1] I had drunk,
Or emptied some dull opiate to the drains
   One minute past, and Lethe-wards[2] had sunk.
'Tis not through envy of thy happy lot,
   But being too happy in thine happiness,—
     That thou, light-wingèd Dryad° of the trees,   *nymph*
       In some melodious plot
Of beechen green, and shadows numberless,
10   Singest of summer in full-throated ease.

II

O for a draught of vintage that hath been
   Cooled a long age in the deep-delvèd earth,
Tasting of Flora[3] and the country green,
   Dance, and Provençal song,[4] and sunburnt mirth!
O for a beaker full of the warm South,
   Full of the true, the blushful Hippocrene,[5]
     With beaded bubbles winking at the brim,
       And purple-stainèd mouth,
That I might drink, and leave the world unseen,
20   And with thee fade away into the forest dim.

III

Fade far away, dissolve, and quite forget
   What thou among the leaves hast never known,

---

[1]Poison hemlock, a lethally poisonous herb of the carrot family, was used in ancient Greece to execute criminals.   [2]In Greek mythology, Lethe was the river in the underworld from which the shades of the dead drank to obtain forgetfulness of the past.   [3]Roman goddess of flowers and spring   [4]Provence, the South of France, was famous for the songs of love and adventure constructed or repeated by its medieval troubadors.   [5]The "Fountain of the Horse" on Mount Helicon, sacred to the Muses

The weariness, the fever, and the fret
   Here, where men sit and hear each other groan;
Where palsy shakes a few, sad, last gray hairs,
    Where youth grows pale, and spectre-thin, and dies;
      Where but to think is to be full of sorrow
         And leaden-eyed despairs;
   Where Beauty cannot keep her lustrous eyes,
30   Or new Love pine at them beyond to-morrow.

IV

Away! away! for I will fly to thee,
   Not charioted by Bacchus and his pards,[6]
But on the viewless° wings of Poesy,   *invisible*
   Though the dull brain perplexes and retards.
Already with thee! tender is the night,
   And haply the Queen-Moon is on her throne,
     Clustered around by all her starry fays;°   *fairies*
       But here there is no light,
  Save what from heaven is with the breezes blown
40   Through verdurous glooms and winding mossy ways.

V

I cannot see what flowers are at my feet,
   Nor what soft incense hangs upon the boughs,
But, in embalmèd° darkness, guess each sweet   *fragrant*
   Wherewith the seasonable month endows
The grass, the thicket, and the fruit-tree wild—
   White hawthorn, and the pastoral eglantine;
     Fast-fading violets covered up in leaves;
       And mid-May's eldest child,
   The coming musk-rose, full of dewy wine,
50   The murmurous haunt of flies on summer eves.

VI

Darkling° I listen, and for many a time   *In darkness*
   I have been half in love with easeful Death,
Called him soft names in many a musèd rhyme,
   To take into the air my quiet breath;
Now more than ever seems it rich to die,
   To cease upon the midnight with no pain,
     While thou art pouring forth thy soul abroad
       In such an ecstasy.
   Still wouldst thou sing, and I have ears in vain—
60   To thy high requiem become a sod.

[6]Bacchus, the Roman god of wine, was sometimes portrayed riding in a chariot drawn by leopards.

VII

Thou wast not born for death, immortal bird!
  No hungry generations tread thee down;
The voice I hear this passing night was heard
  In ancient days by emperor and clown:
Perhaps the self-same song that found a path
    Through the sad heart of Ruth,[7] when, sick for home,
      She stood in tears amid the alien corn;°   wheat
        The same that oft-times hath
    Charmed magic casements, opening on the foam
70   Of perilous seas, in faery lands forlorn.

VIII

Forlorn! the very word is like a bell
  To toll me back from thee to my sole self!
Adieu! the fancy cannot cheat so well
  As she is famed to do, deceiving elf.
Adieu! adieu! thy plaintive anthem fades
    Past the near meadows, over the still stream,
      Up the hill-side; and now 'tis buried deep
        In the next valley-glades:
    Was it a vision, or a waking dream?
80   Fled is that music . . . Do I wake or sleep?

[7]A reference to the Moabite widow whose story is told in the Old Testament book of Ruth

Ode on a Grecian Urn

I

Thou still unravished bride of quietness,
  Thou foster-child of silence and slow time,
Sylvan historian, who canst thus express
  A flowery tale more sweetly than our rhyme!
What leaf-fringed legend haunts about thy shape
    Of deities or mortals, or of both,
      In Tempe or the dales of Arcady?[1]
    What men or gods are these? What maidens loth?
What mad pursuit? What struggle to escape?
10   What pipes and timbrels? What wild ecstasy?

II

Heard melodies are sweet, but those unheard
  Are sweeter; therefore, ye soft pipes, play on;
Not to the sensual° ear, but, more endeared,   sensuous
  Pipe to the spirit ditties of no tone.
Fair youth beneath the trees, thou canst not leave
  Thy song, nor ever can those trees be bare;

[1]Tempe and the glens of Arcady are landscapes of legendary beauty.

Bold lover, never, never canst thou kiss,
Though winning near the goal—yet do not grieve:
 She cannot fade, though thou hast not thy bliss,
20   For ever wilt thou love, and she be fair!

III

Ah, happy, happy boughs, that cannot shed
 Your leaves, nor ever bid the spring adieu;
And, happy melodist, unwearièd,
 For ever piping songs for ever new!
More happy love, more happy, happy love!
 For ever warm and still to be enjoyed,
  For ever panting, and for ever young—
All breathing human passion far above,
 That leaves a heart high-sorrowful and cloyed,
30   A burning forehead, and a parching tongue.

IV

Who are these coming to the sacrifice?
 To what green altar, O mysterious priest,
Lead'st thou that heifer lowing at the skies,
 And all her silken flanks with garlands drest?
What little town by river or sea shore,
 Or mountain built with peaceful citadel,
  Is emptied of this folk, this pious morn?
And, little town, thy streets for evermore
 Will silent be; and not a soul to tell
40   Why thou art desolate can e'er return.

V

O Attic² shape! Fair attitude! With brede°   pattern, design
 Of marble men and maidens overwrought,
With forest branches and the trodden weed—
 Thou, silent form, dost tease us out of thought
As doth eternity. Cold pastoral!
 When old age shall this generation waste,
  Thou shalt remain, in midst of other woe
Than ours, a friend to man, to whom thou say'st,
 "Beauty is truth, truth beauty"—that is all
50   Ye know on earth, and all ye need to know.

This Living Hand

This living hand, now warm and capable
Of earnest grasping, would, if it were cold
And in the icy silence of the tomb,
So haunt thy days and chill thy dreaming nights

---

²Attic equals Athenian and therefore classic grace and simplicity.

That thou would wish thine own heart dry of blood
So in my veins red life might stream again,
And thou be conscience-calmed. See here it is—
I hold it towards you.

Edward Fitzgerald

Edward Fitzgerald (1809–1883) first translated the *Rubáiyát* of Omar Khayyám
in 1859 and continued to revise it the rest of his life. His other poems and
translations have attracted little attention, but this translation—more
adaptation than translation—has endured like no other foreign poem done into
English.

from The Rubáiyát of Omar Khayyám

1

Wake! for the Sun, who scattered into flight
The Stars before him from the Field of Night,
   Drives Night along with them from Heav'n, and strikes
The Sultán's Turret with a Shaft of Light.

7

Come, fill the Cup, and in the fire of Spring
Your Winter-garment of Repentance fling:
   The Bird of Time has but a little way
To flutter—and the Bird is on the Wing.

12

A Book of Verses underneath the Bough,
A jug of Wine, a Loaf of Bread—and Thou
   Beside me singing in the Wilderness—
Oh, Wilderness were Paradise enow!

13

Some for the Glories of This World; and some
Sigh for the Prophet's Paradise to come;
   Ah, take the Cash, and let the Credit go,
Nor heed the rumble of a distant Drum!

19

I sometimes think that never blows so red
The Rose as where some buried Cæsar bled;
   That every Hyacinth the Garden wears
Dropt in her Lap from some once lovely Head.

22

For some we loved, the loveliest and the best
That from his Vintage rolling Time hath prest,
   Have drunk their Cup a Round or two before,
And one by one crept silently to rest.

27
Myself when young did eagerly frequent
Doctor and Saint, and heard great argument
    About it and about: but evermore
Came out by the same door where in I went.

71
The Moving Finger writes; and, having writ,
Moves on: nor all your Piety nor Wit
    Shall lure it back to cancel half a Line,
Nor all your Tears wash out a Word of it.

100
Yon rising Moon that looks for us again—
How oft hereafter will she wax and wane;
    How oft hereafter rising look for us
Through this same Garden—and for *one* in vain!

101
And when like her, oh Sákí, you shall pass
Among the Guests Star-scatter'd on the Grass,
    And in your joyous errand reach the spot
Where I made One—turn down an empty Glass!

Edgar Allan Poe

Edgar Allan Poe (1809–1849) may be the strangest of all major American
authors—in a literature whose greatest artists often seem to specialize in
eccentricity. He attended West Point briefly, the University of Virginia
inconclusively, and began early to explore the exotic, necrophiliac geography of
his stories and poems. He died in Baltimore on election day, apparently victim
of alcohol passed out to potential voters. See also his short story "The Murders
in the Rue Morgue" on pages 258–280.

The City in the Sea

Lo! Death has reared himself a throne
In a strange city lying alone
Far down within the dim West,
Where the good and the bad and the worst and the best
Have gone to their eternal rest.
There shrines and palaces and towers
(Time-eaten towers that tremble not!)
Resemble nothing that is ours.
Around, by lifting winds forgot,
10 Resignedly beneath the sky
The melancholy waters lie.

No rays from the holy heaven come down
On the long night-time of that town;
But light from out the lurid sea

Streams up the turrets silently—
Gleams up the pinnacles far and free—
Up domes—up spires—up kingly halls—
Up fanes—up Babylon-like walls—
Up shadowy long-forgotten bowers
20   Of sculptured ivy and stone flowers—
Up many and many a marvellous shrine
Whose wreathéd friezes intertwine
The viol, the violet, and the vine.

Resignedly beneath the sky
The melancholy waters lie.
So blend the turrets and shadows there
That all seem pendulous in air,
While from a proud tower in the town
Death looks gigantically down.

30   There open fanes and gaping graves
Yawn level with the luminous waves;
But not the riches there that lie
In each idol's diamond eye—
Not the gaily-jewelled dead
Tempt the waters from their bed;
For no ripples curl, alas!
Along that wilderness of glass—
No swellings tell that winds may be
Upon some far-off happier sea—
40   No heavings hint that winds have been
On seas less hideously serene.

But lo, a stir is in the air!
The wave—there is a movement there!
As if the towers had thrust aside,
In slightly sinking, the dull tide—
As if their tops had feebly given
A void within the filmy Heaven.
The waves have now a redder glow—
The hours are breathing faint and low—
50   And when, amid no earthly moans,
Down, down that town shall settle hence,
Hell, rising from a thousand thrones,
Shall do it reverence.

Alfred, Lord Tennyson

Alfred, Lord Tennyson (1809–1892), who began to publish poems before he was twenty, matured in technical accomplishment early. After his great friend Arthur Hallam died in 1833, Tennyson matured in other ways, beginning his long, elegiac "In Memoriam." In Tennyson's character there was a quarrel between a personal predilection for melancholy and the Victorian duty to be optimistic and progressive. For much of his life, Victorian optimism won out; he is the poet of his age. When he speaks the philosophy of imperialism, as in "Ulysses," he speaks it with eloquence and vigor. In his more private poems, sweetness and fire remain as public gusto vanishes.

Ulysses

It little profits that an idle king,
By this still hearth, among these barren crags,
Matched with an agèd wife, I mete and dole
Unequal laws unto a savage race,
That hoard, and sleep, and feed, and know not me.
I cannot rest from travel: I will drink
Life to the lees: all times I have enjoyed
Greatly, have suffered greatly, both with those
That loved me, and alone; on shore, and when
10   Through scudding drifts the rainy Hyades
Vext the dim sea: I am become a name;
For always roaming with a hungry heart
Much have I seen and known; cities of men
And manners, climates, councils, governments,
Myself not least, but honored of them all;
And drunk delight of battle with my peers,
Far on the ringing plains of windy Troy.
I am a part of all that I have met;
Yet all experience is an arch wherethro'
20   Gleams that untraveled world, whose margin fades
For ever and for ever when I move.
How dull it is to pause, to make an end,
To rust unburnished, not to shine in use!
As though to breathe were life. Life piled on life
Were all too little, and of one to me
Little remains: but every hour is saved
From that eternal silence, something more,
A bringer of new things; and vile it were
For some three suns to store and hoard myself,
30   And this gray spirit yearning in desire
To follow knowledge like a sinking star,
Beyond the utmost bound of human thought.

This is my son, mine own Telemachus,
To whom I leave the scepter and the isle—
Well-loved of me, discerning to fulfill
This labor, by slow prudence to make mild
A rugged people, and through soft degrees

Subdue them to the useful and the good.
Most blameless is he, centered in the sphere
40   Of common duties, decent not to fail
In offices of tenderness, and pay
Meet adoration to my household gods,
When I am gone. He works his work, I mine.

There lies the port; the vessel puffs her sail:
There gloom the dark broad seas. My mariners,
Souls that have toiled, and wrought, and thought with me—
That ever with a frolic welcome took
The thunder and the sunshine, and opposed
Free hearts, free foreheads—you and I are old;
50   Old age hath yet his honor and his toil;
Death closes all: but something ere the end,
Some work of noble note, may yet be done,
Not unbecoming men that strove with Gods.
The lights begin to twinkle from the rocks:
The long day wanes: the slow moon climbs: the deep
Moans round with many voices. Come, my friends,
'Tis not too late to seek a newer world.
Push off, and sitting well in order smite
The sounding furrows; for my purpose holds
60   To sail beyond the sunset, and the baths
Of all the western stars, until I die.
It may be that the gulfs will wash us down:
It may be we shall touch the Happy Isles,
And see the great Achilles, whom we knew.
Though much is taken, much abides; and though
We are not now that strength which in old days
Moved earth and heaven; that which we are, we are;
One equal temper of heroic hearts,
Made weak by time and fate, but strong in will
70   To strive, to seek, to find, and not to yield.

Tears, Idle Tears

Tears, idle tears, I know not what they mean,
Tears from the depth of some divine despair
Rise in the heart, and gather to the eyes,
In looking on the happy Autumn-fields,
And thinking of the days that are no more.

Fresh as the first beam glittering on a sail,
That brings our friends up from the underworld,
Sad as the last which reddens over one
That sinks with all we love below the verge;
10   So sad, so fresh, the days that are no more.

Ah, sad and strange as in dark summer dawns
The earliest pipe of half-awakened birds

To dying ears, when unto dying eyes
The casement slowly grows a glimmering square;
So sad, so strange, the days that are no more.

Dear as remembered kisses after death,
And sweet as those by hopeless fancy feigned
On lips that are for others; deep as love,
Deep as first love, and wild with all regret;
20   O Death in Life, the days that are no more.

The Eagle

He clasps the crag with crooked hands;
Close to the sun in lonely lands,
Ringed with the azure world, he stands.

The wrinkled sea beneath him crawls;
He watches from his mountain walls,
And like a thunderbolt he falls.

Robert Browning

Robert Browning (1812–1889) was three years younger than Tennyson and
shared with him first rank among Victorian poets. In 1846 he and Elizabeth
Barrett were married and wrote poems together for fifteen years, until she died
in 1861. He is most celebrated for his dramatic monologues. He is buried in
Westminster Abbey.

My Last Duchess

FERRARA

That's my last Duchess painted on the wall,
Looking as if she were alive. I call
That piece a wonder, now: Frà Pandolf's hands
Worked busily a day, and there she stands.
Will't please you sit and look at her? I said
"Frà Pandolf" by design, for never read
Strangers like you that pictured countenance,
The depth and passion of its earnest glance,
But to myself they turned (since none puts by
10   The curtain I have drawn for you, but I)
And seemed as they would ask me, if they durst,
How such a glance came there; so, not the first
Are you to turn and ask thus. Sir, 'twas not
Her husband's presence only, called that spot
Of joy into the Duchess' cheek: perhaps
Frà Pandolf chanced to say, "Her mantle laps
Over my lady's wrist too much," or "Paint
Must never hope to reproduce the faint
Half-flush that dies along her throat." Such stuff
20   Was courtesy, she thought, and cause enough

For calling up that spot of joy. She had
A heart—how shall I say?—too soon made glad,
Too easily impressed; she liked whate'er
She looked on, and her looks went everywhere.
Sir, 'twas all one! My favour at her breast,
The dropping of the daylight in the West,
The bough of cherries some officious fool
Broke in the orchard for her, the white mule
She rode with round the terrace—all and each
30   Would draw from her alike the approving speech,
Or blush, at least. She thanked men,—good! but thanked
Somehow—I know not how—as if she ranked
My gift of a nine-hundred-years-old name
With anybody's gift. Who'd stoop to blame
This sort of trifling? Even had you skill
In speech—(which I have not)—to make your will
Quite clear to such an one, and say, "Just this
"Or that in you disgusts me; here you miss,
"Or there exceed the mark"—and if she let
40   Herself be lessoned so, nor plainly set
Her wits to yours, forsooth, and made excuse,
—E'en then would be some stooping; and I choose
Never to stoop. Oh sir, she smiled, no doubt,
Whene'er I passed her; but who passed without
Much the same smile? This grew; I gave commands;
Then all smiles stopped together. There she stands
As if alive. Will't please you rise? We'll meet
The company below, then. I repeat,
The Count your master's known munificence
50   Is ample warrant that no just pretense
Of mine for dowry will be disallowed;
Though his fair daughter's self, as I avowed
At starting, is my object. Nay, we'll go
Together down, sir. Notice Neptune, though,
Taming a sea-horse, thought a rarity,
Which Claus of Innsbruck cast in bronze for me!

Emily Brontë

Emily Brontë (1818–1848) was sister of Charlotte and Anne; all novelists, all
poets in their youths. Emily wrote *Wuthering Heights*.

No Coward Soul Is Mine

No coward soul is mine,
No trembler in the world's storm-troubled sphere:
I see Heaven's glories shine,
And faith shines equal, arming me from fear.

O God within my breast,
Almighty, ever-present Deity!
Life, that in me hast rest
As I, undying life, have power in Thee!

Vain are the thousand creeds

10   That move men's hearts: unutterably vain;
Worthless as withered weeds,
Or idlest froth amid the boundless main,

To waken doubt in one
Holding so fast by Thy infinity,
So surely anchored on
The steadfast rock of immortality.

With wide embracing love
Thy spirit animates eternal years,
Pervades and broods above,

20   Changes, sustains, dissolves, creates, and rears.

Though earth and moon were gone,
And suns and universes cease to be,
And Thou wert left alone,
Every existence would exist in Thee.

There is not room for death,
Nor atom that his might could render void:
Since Thou art Being and Breath
And what Thou art may never be destroyed.

Walt Whitman

Walt Whitman (1819–1892) is the first great American poet. He is also one
of the greatest innovators in the history of the art. His long, loose rhythms
derive in part from the King James version of the Bible and in part from the
expansive gestures of nineteenth-century political oratory. But largely they
seem Whitman's own creation.

Born on Long Island, son of a carpenter who was also a farmer, Whitman was
sporadically educated, became a newspaper editor, and created himself as a
poet. The first edition of *Leaves of Grass*, which through subsequent editions
became a collection of his life's work, appeared in 1855. Emerson praised him,
but few other early readers had the imagination to understand that his writing
was poetry at all. Not only was his work innovative; in its broad sensuality and
in its hints at homoeroticism, it was shocking. Emily Dickinson's comment,
in a letter to Thomas Wentworth Higginson, tells the tale: "You speak of Mr.
Whitman—I never read his Book—but was told that he was disgraceful—" See
also page 455.

Out of the Cradle Endlessly Rocking

Out of the cradle endlessly rocking,
Out of the mocking-bird's throat, the musical shuttle,
Out of the Ninth-month midnight,
Over the sterile sands and the fields beyond, where the child leaving his bed
        wandered alone, bareheaded, barefoot,

Down from the showered halo,
Up from the mystic play of shadows twining and twisting as if they were alive,
Out from the patches of briers and blackberries,
From the memories of the bird that chanted to me,
From your memories sad brother, from the fitful risings and fallings I heard,
10   From under that yellow half-moon late-risen and swollen as if with tears,
From those beginning notes of yearning and love there in the mist,
From the thousand responses of my heart never to cease,
From the myriad thence-aroused words,
From the word stronger and more delicious than any,
From such as now they start the scene revisiting,
As a flock, twittering, rising, or overhead passing,
Borne hither, ere all eludes me, hurriedly,
A man, yet by these tears a little boy again,
Throwing myself on the sand, confronting the waves,
20   I, chanter of pains and joys, uniter of here and hereafter,
Taking all hints to use them, but swiftly leaping beyond them,
A reminiscence sing.

Once Paumanok,
When the lilac-scent was in the air and Fifth-month grass was growing,
Up this seashore in some briers,
Two feathered guests from Alabama, two together,
And their nest, and four light-green eggs spotted with brown,
And every day the he-bird to and fro near at hand,
And every day the she-bird crouched on her nest, silent, with bright eyes,
30   And every day I, a curious boy, never too close, never disturbing them,
Cautiously peering, absorbing, translating.

Shine! shine! shine!
Pour down your warmth, great sun!
While we bask, we two together.

Two together!
Winds blow south, or winds blow north,
Day come white, or night come black,
Home, or rivers and mountains from home,
Singing all time, minding no time,
40   *While we two keep together.*

Till of a sudden,
May-be killed, unknown to her mate,
One forenoon the she-bird crouched not on the nest,
Nor returned that afternoon, nor the next,
Nor ever appeared again.

And thenceforward all summer in the sound of the sea,
And at night under the full of the moon in calmer weather,
Over the hoarse surging of the sea,
Or flitting from brier to brier by day,
50   I saw, I heard at intervals the remaining one, the he-bird,
The solitary guest from Alabama.

Blow! blow! blow!
Blow up sea-winds along Paumanok's shore;
I wait and I wait till you blow my mate to me.

Yes, when the stars glistened,
All night long on the prong of a moss-scalloped stake,
Down almost amid the slapping waves,
Sat the lone singer wonderful causing tears.

He called on his mate,
60   He poured forth the meanings which I of all men know.

Yes my brother I know,
The rest might not, but I have treasured every note,
For more than once dimly down to the beach gliding,
Silent, avoiding the moonbeams, blending myself with the shadows,
Recalling now the obscure shapes, the echoes, the sounds and sights after their
        sorts,
The white arms out in the breakers tirelessly tossing,
I, with bare feet, a child, the wind wafting my hair,
Listened long and long.

Listened to keep, to sing, now translating the notes,
70   Following you my brother.

Soothe! soothe! soothe!
Close on its wave soothes the wave behind,
And again another behind embracing and lapping, every one close,
But my love soothes not me, not me.

Low hangs the moon, it rose late,
It is lagging—O I think it is heavy with love, with love.

O madly the sea pushes upon the land,
With love, with love.

O night! do I not see my love fluttering out among the breakers?
80   *What is that little black thing I see there in the white?*

Loud! loud! loud!
Loud I call to you, my love!

High and clear I shoot my voice over the waves,
Surely you must know who is here, is here,
You must know who I am, my love.

Low-hanging moon!
What is that dusky spot in your brown yellow?
O it is the shape, the shape of my mate!
O moon do not keep her from me any longer.

90   *Land! land! O land!*
Whichever way I turn, O I think you could give me my mate back again if you
        only would,
For I am almost sure I see her dimly whichever way I look.

O rising stars!
Perhaps the one I want so much will rise, will rise with some of you.

O throat! O trembling throat!
Sound clearer through the atmosphere!
Pierce the woods, the earth,
Somewhere listening to catch you must be the one I want.

Shake out carols!
100   *Solitary here, the night's carols!*
Carols of lonesome love! death's carols!
Carols under that lagging, yellow, waning moon!
O under that moon where she droops almost down into the sea!
O reckless despairing carols.

But soft! sink low!
Soft! let me just murmur,
And do you wait a moment you husky-noised sea,
For somewhere I believe I heard my mate responding to me,
So faint, I must be still, be still to listen,
110   *But not altogether still, for then she might not come immediately to me.*

Hither my love!
Here I am! Here!
With this just-sustained note I announce myself to you,
This gentle call is for you my love, for you.

Do not be decoyed elsewhere,
That is the whistle of the wind, it is not my voice,
That is the fluttering, the fluttering of the spray,
Those are the shadows of leaves.

O darkness! O in vain!
120   *O I am very sick and sorrowful.*

O brown halo in the sky near the moon, drooping upon the sea!
O troubled reflection in the sea!
O throat! O throbbing heart!
And I singing uselessly, uselessly all the night.

O past! O happy life! O songs of joy!
In the air, in the woods, over fields,
Loved! loved! loved! loved! loved!
But my mate no more, no more with me!
We two together no more.

130   The aria sinking,
All else continuing, the stars shining,
The winds blowing, the notes of the bird continuous echoing,
With angry moans the fierce old mother incessantly moaning,
On the sands of Paumanok's shore gray and rustling,
The yellow half-moon enlarged, sagging down, drooping, the face of the sea
        almost touching,

The boy ecstatic, with his bare feet the waves, with his hair the atmosphere
     dallying,
The love in the heart long pent, now loose, now at last tumultuously bursting,
The aria's meaning, the ears, the soul, swiftly depositing,
The strange tears down the cheeks coursing,
140   The colloquy there, the trio, each uttering,
The undertone, the savage old mother incessantly crying,
To the boy's soul's questions sullenly timing, some drowned secret hissing,
To the outsetting bard.

Demon or bird! (said the boy's soul,)
Is it indeed toward your mate you sing? or is it really to me?
For I, that was a child, my tongue's use sleeping, now I have heard you,
Now in a moment I know what I am for, I awake,
And already a thousand singers, a thousand songs, clearer, louder and more
     sorrowful than yours,
A thousand warbling echoes have started to life within me, never to die.

150   O you singer solitary, singing by yourself, projecting me,
O solitary me listening, never more shall I cease perpetuating you,
Never more shall I escape, never more the reverberations,
Never more the cries of unsatisfied love be absent from me,
Never again leave me to be the peaceful child I was before what there in the
     night,
By the sea under the yellow and sagging moon,
The messenger there aroused, the fire, the sweet hell within,
The unknown want, the destiny of me.

O give me the clue! (it lurks in the night here somewhere,)
O if I am to have so much, let me have more!

160   A word then, (for I will conquer it,)
The word final, superior to all,
Subtle, sent up—what is it?—I listen;
Are you whispering it, and have been all the time, you sea-waves?
Is that it from your liquid rims and wet sands?

Whereto answering, the sea,
Delaying not, hurrying not,
Whispered me through the night, and very plainly before daybreak,
Lisped to me the low and delicious word death,
And again death, death, death, death,
170   Hissing melodious, neither like the bird nor like my aroused child's heart,
But edging near as privately for me rustling at my feet,
Creeping thence steadily up to my ears and laving me softly all over,
Death, death, death, death, death.

Which I do not forget,
But fuse the song of my dusky demon and brother,
That he sang to me in the moonlight on Paumanok's gray beach,
With the thousand responsive songs at random,
My own songs awaked from that hour,

And with them the key, the word up from the waves,
180   The word of the sweetest song and all songs,
That strong and delicious word which, creeping to my feet,
(Or like some old crone rocking the cradle, swathed in sweet garments, bending
          aside,)
The sea whispered me.

A Farm Picture

Through the ample open door of the peaceful country barn,
A sunlit pasture field with cattle and horses feeding,
And haze and vista, and the far horizon fading away.

Cavalry Crossing a Ford

A line in long array where they wind betwixt green islands,
They take a serpentine course, their arms flash in the sun—hark to the musical
          clank,
Behold the silvery river, in it the splashing horses loitering stop to drink,
Behold the brown-faced men, each group, each person a picture, the negligent
          rest on the saddles,
Some emerge on the opposite bank, others are just entering the ford—while,
Scarlet and blue and snowy white,
The guidon flags flutter gayly in the wind.

Matthew Arnold

Matthew Arnold (1822–1888) comes after Tennyson and Browning as a poet of
the Victorian age, but as a man of letters he comes after no one. His father was
headmaster of Rugby, and Arnold was educated at Rugby, at Winchester, and
at Oxford, where he won the Newdigate Prize for Poetry. For many years he
inspected schools for the government. He lectured on poetry at Oxford. He
wrote his poems mostly in early life; as he grew older, he concentrated on the
essay.

Dover Beach

The sea is calm tonight,
The tide is full, the moon lies fair
Upon the straits;—on the French coast the light
Gleams and is gone; the cliffs of England stand,
Glimmering and vast, out in the tranquil bay.
Come to the window, sweet is the night-air!
Only, from the long line of spray
Where the sea meets the moon-blanched land,
Listen! you hear the grating roar
10   Of pebbles which the waves draw back, and fling,
At their return, up the high strand,
Begin and cease, and then again begin,
With tremulous cadence slow, and bring
The eternal note of sadness in.

Sophocles long ago
Heard it on the Aegean, and it brought
Into his mind the turbid ebb and flow
Of human misery; we
Find also in the sound a thought,
20   Hearing it by this distant northern sea.

The Sea of Faith
Was once, too, at the full, and round earth's shore
Lay like the folds of a bright girdle furled.
But now I only hear
Its melancholy, long, withdrawing roar,
Retreating, to the breath
Of the night-wind, down the vast edges drear
And naked shingles of the world.

Ah, love, let us be true
30   To one another! for the world, which seems
To lie before us like a land of dreams,
So various, so beautiful, so new,
Hath really neither joy, nor love, nor light,
Nor certitude, nor peace, nor help for pain;
And we are here as on a darkling plain
Swept with confused alarms of struggle and flight,
Where ignorant armies clash by night.

(See also "The Dover Bitch," page 675.)

Emily Dickinson (1830–1886)

See pages 500–509.

Lewis Carroll

Lewis Carroll was the pen name of Charles Lutwidge Dodgson (1832–1898), a distinguished mathematician, when he wrote *Alice's Adventures in Wonderland* and other works of fantasy and nonsense. On the faculty at Oxford, amateur photographer as well as writer, Carroll made up numerous words when he composed "Jabberwocky"; some of them have taken their place in language.

Jabberwocky

'Twas brillig, and the slithy toves
    Did gyre and gimble in the wabe:
All mimsy were the borogoves,
    And the mome raths outgrabe.

"Beware the Jabberwock, my son!
    The jaws that bite, the claws that catch!
Beware the Jubjub bird, and shun
    The frumious Bandersnatch!"

He took his vorpal sword in hand;
10   Long time the manxome foe he sought—
So rested he by the Tumtum tree,
      And stood awhile in thought.

And, as in uffish thought he stood,
      The Jabberwock, with eyes of flame,
Came whiffling through the tulgey wood,
      And burbled as it came!

One, two! One, two! And through and through
      The vorpal blade went snicker-snack!
He left it dead, and with its head
20   He went galumphing back.

"And hast thou slain the Jabberwock?
      Come to my arms, my beamish boy!
O frabjous day! Callooh, Callay!"
      He chortled in his joy.

'Twas brillig, and the slithy toves
      Did gyre and gimble in the wabe:
All mimsy were the borogoves,
      And the mome raths outgrabe.

Thomas Hardy

Thomas Hardy (1840–1928) is better known as a novelist than as a poet, but many devoted readers find the poetry even better than the fiction. He began life as an architect and published his first novel when he was thirty-two. For many years Hardy wrote few poems and concentrated on novels, of which the best-known are *The Return of the Native, The Mayor of Casterbridge, Tess of the D'Urbervilles,* and *Jude the Obscure. Jude* appeared in 1896, and was denounced as obscene. Perhaps using that denunciation as an excuse, Hardy renounced fiction, and—now freed by the success of his fiction from the necessity to make money—devoted himself to poetry, as he had always wanted to do. He was almost sixty when his first book of poems appeared. Between 1898 and his death at eighty-eight in 1928 he published the fifteen hundred poems that appear in his *Collected Poems.* He is a poet admired by other poets. See also pages 405, 430, 468, and 480.

The Man He Killed

"Had he and I but met
      By some old ancient inn,
We should have sat us down to wet
      Right many a nipperkin!°   half-pint cup

"But ranged as infantry,
      And staring face to face,
I shot at him as he at me,
      And killed him in his place.

"I shot him dead because—
10   Because he was my foe,
     Just so: my foe of course he was;
         That's clear enough; although

     "He thought he'd 'list,° perhaps,   enlist
     Off-hand like—just as I—
     Was out of work—had sold his traps°—   possessions
         No other reason why.

     "Yes; quaint and curious war is!
     You shoot a fellow down
     You'd treat if met where any bar is,
20   Or help to half-a-crown."°   two and a half shillings

The Ruined Maid

     "O'Melia, my dear, this does everything crown!
     Who could have supposed I should meet you in Town?
     And whence such fair garments, such prosperi-ty?"—
     "O didn't you know I'd been ruined?" said she.

     —"You left us in tatters, without shoes or socks,
     Tired of digging potatoes, and spudding up docks;°   digging weeds
     And now you've gay bracelets and bright feathers three!"—
     "Yes: that's how we dress when we're ruined," said she.

     —"At home in the barton° you said 'thee' and 'thou,'   farmyard
10   And 'thik oon,' and 'theäs oon,' and 't'other'; but now
     Your talking quite fits 'ee for high compa-ny!"—
     "Some polish is gained with one's ruin," said she.

     —"Your hands were like paws then, your face blue and bleak
     But now I'm bewitched by your delicate cheek,
     And your little gloves fit as on any la-dy!"—
     "We never do work when we're ruined," said she.

     —"You used to call home-life a hag-ridden dream,
     And you'd sigh, and you'd sock; but at present you seem
     To know not of megrims° or melancho-ly!"—   depressions
20   "True. One's pretty lively when ruined," said she.

     —"I wish I had feathers, a fine sweeping gown,
     And a delicate face, and could strut about Town!"—
     "My dear—a raw country girl, such as you be,
     Cannot quite expect that. You ain't ruined," said she.

Gerard Manley Hopkins

Gerard Manley Hopkins (1844–1889) attended Oxford, and in his early twenties converted to Roman Catholicism, becoming a Jesuit in 1868. He corresponded with Robert Bridges and Coventry Patmore and devoted himself considerably to his poetry insofar as such devotion was consistent with his calling. But he did not publish, and he was not known until Robert Bridges collected his poems after Hopkins's death and edited and published them. He has been a major influence on modern poets. See also page 454.

Spring and Fall
To a Young Child

Márgarét, are you gríeving
Over Goldengrove unleaving?
Leáves, líke the things of man, you
With your fresh thoughts care for, can you?
Áh! ás the heart grows older
It will come to such sights colder
By and by, nor spare a sigh
Though worlds of wanwood leafmeal lie;
And yet you wíll weep and know why.
10   Now no matter, child, the name:
Sórrow's spríngs áre the same.
Nor mouth had, no nor mind, expressed
What heart heard of, ghost guessed:
It ís the blight man was born for,
It is Margaret you mourn for.

The Windhover
To Christ Our Lord

I caught this morning morning's minion, king-
   dom of daylight's dauphin, dapple-dawn-drawn Falcon, in his riding
     Of the rolling level underneath him steady air, and striding
High there, how he rung upon the rein of a wimpling wing
In his ecstacy! then off, off forth on swing,
   As a skate's heel sweeps smooth on a bow-bend; the hurl and gliding
   Rebuffed the big wind. My heart in hiding
Stirred for a bird,—the achieve of, the mastery of the thing!

Brute beauty and valor and act, oh, air, pride, plume, here
10   Buckle! AND the fire that breaks from thee then, a billion
Times told lovelier, more dangerous, O my chevalier!

   No wonder of it: shéer plód makes plough down sillion
Shine, and blue-bleak embers, ah my dear,
   Fall, gall themselves, and gash gold-vermilion.

Carrion Comfort

Not, I'll not, carrion comfort, Despair, not feast on thee;
Not untwist—slack they may be—these last strands of man
In me ór, most weary, cry *I can no more.* I can;
Can something, hope, wish day come, not choose not to be.
But ah, but O thou terrible, why wouldst thou rude on me
Thy wring-world right foot rock? lay a lionlimb against me? scan
With darksome devouring eyes my bruisèd bones? and fan,
O in turns of tempest, me heaped there; me frantic to avoid thee and flee?

    Why? That my chaff might fly; my grain lie, sheer and clear.
10 Nay in all that toil, that coil, since (seems) I kissed the rod,
Hand rather, my heart lo! lapped strength, stole joy, would laugh, chéer.
Cheer whom though? the hero whose heaven-handling flung me, foót tród
Me? or me that fought him? O which one? is it each one? That night, that year
Of now done darkness I wretch lay wrestling with (my God!) my God.

A. E. Housman

Alfred Edward Housman (1859–1936) was a classical scholar and professor of
Latin at Cambridge University. He wrote little poetry, notably *A Shropshire Lad*
in 1896 and *Last Poems* in 1922, but what he wrote was extraordinarily fine
and finished, if lacking in range and depth.

Eight O'Clock

He stood, and heard the steeple
    Sprinkle the quarters on the morning town.
One, two, three, four, to market-place and people
    It tossed them down.

Strapped, noosed, nighing his hour,
    He stood and counted them and cursed his luck;
And then the clock collected in the tower
    Its strength, and struck.

To an Athlete Dying Young

The time you won your town the race
We chaired you through the market-place;
Man and boy stood cheering by,
And home we brought you shoulder-high.

To-day, the road all runners come,
Shoulder-high we bring you home,
And set you at your threshold down,
Townsman of a stiller town.

Smart lad, to slip betimes away
10   From fields where glory does not stay
And early though the laurel grows
It withers quicker than the rose.

Eyes the shady night has shut
Cannot see the record cut,
And silence sounds no worse than cheers
After earth has stopped the ears:

Now you will not swell the rout
Of lads that wore their honors out,
Runners whom renown outran
20   And the name died before the man.

So set, before its echoes fade,
The fleet foot on the sill of shade,
And hold to the low lintel up
The still-defended challenge-cup.

And round that early-laurelled head
Will flock to gaze the strengthless dead,
And find unwithered on its curls
The garland briefer than a girl's.

William Butler Yeats

William Butler Yeats (1865–1939), born in Dublin, grew up largely in Ireland
in an Anglo-Irish family. Both his father and his brother were well-known
artists. Yeats published his first collection of poetry when he was twenty-four
and wrote continually until his death fifty years later. Considered by many the
greatest of modern poets, Yeats was a leader in the Irish renaissance,
playwright and a founder of the Abbey Theatre, an Irish patriot and a
denouncer of nationalism, mystic and skeptic—a man of passion and conflict
whose poetry derived from passionate conflict. He married in 1917, and his
wife's automatic writing helped him explore mystical theories, which
culminated in a prose work called *A Vision*, published in 1925. In 1919 he
acquired Thoor Ballylee, an ancient Norman tower in the west of Ireland that
became a feature and a fixture in his poetry. He became a senator of
independent Ireland and was awarded the Nobel Prize for literature in 1923.
He made his best books of poems after receiving the prize: *The Tower* in 1928
and the posthumous *Last Poems* in 1940. See also page 444.

Who Goes with Fergus?

Who will go drive with Fergus[1] now,
And pierce the deep wood's woven shade,
And dance upon the level shore?
Young man, lift up your russet brow,
And lift your tender eyelids, maid,
And brood on hopes and fear no more.

[1]Legendary king who renounced his throne to become an itinerant poet

And no more turn aside and brood
Upon love's bitter mystery;
For Fergus rules the brazen cars,
10   And rules the shadows of the wood,
And the white breast of the dim sea
And all dishevelled wandering stars.

The Magi

Now as at all times I can see in the mind's eye,
In their stiff, painted clothes, the pale unsatisfied ones
Appear and disappear in the blue depth of the sky
With all their ancient faces like rain-beaten stones,
And all their helms of silver hovering side by side,
And all their eyes still fixed, hoping to find once more,
Being by Calvary's turbulence unsatisfied,
The uncontrollable mystery on the bestial floor.

The Second Coming

Turning and turning in the widening gyre°   spiral
The falcon cannot hear the falconer;
Things fall apart; the centre cannot hold;
Mere anarchy is loosed upon the world,
The blood-dimmed tide is loosed, and everywhere
The ceremony of innocence is drowned;
The best lack all conviction, while the worst
Are full of passionate intensity.

Surely some revelation is at hand;
10   Surely the Second Coming is at hand.
The Second Coming! Hardly are those words out
When a vast image out of *Spiritus Mundi*°   soul of the world
Troubles my sight: somewhere in sands of the desert
A shape with lion body and the head of a man,
A gaze blank and pitiless as the sun,
Is moving its slow thighs, while all about it
Reel shadows of the indignant desert birds.
The darkness drops again; but now I know
That twenty centuries of stony sleep
20   Were vexed to nightmare by a rocking cradle,
And what rough beast, its hour come round at last,
Slouches towards Bethlehem to be born?

Sailing to Byzantium

I

That is no country for old men. The young
In one another's arms, birds in the trees
—Those dying generations—at their song,

The salmon-falls, the mackerel-crowded seas,
Fish, flesh, or fowl, commend all summer long
Whatever is begotten, born, and dies.
Caught in that sensual music all neglect
Monuments of unageing intellect.

II

An aged man is but a paltry thing,
10   A tattered coat upon a stick, unless
Soul clap its hands and sing, and louder sing
For every tatter in its mortal dress,
Nor is there singing school but studying
Monuments of its own magnificence;
And therefore I have sailed the seas and come
To the holy city of Byzantium.

III

O sages standing in God's holy fire
As in the gold mosaic of a wall,
Come from the holy fire, perne° in a gyre,   *wind or unwind*
20   And be the singing-masters of my soul.
Consume my heart away; sick with desire
And fastened to a dying animal
It knows not what it is; and gather me
Into the artifice of eternity.

IV

Once out of nature I shall never take
My bodily form from any natural thing,
But such a form as Grecian goldsmiths make
Of hammered gold and gold enamelling
To keep a drowsy Emperor awake;
30   Or set upon a golden bough to sing
To lords and ladies of Byzantium
Of what is past, or passing, or to come.

Leda and the Swan

A sudden blow: the great wings beating still
Above the staggering girl, her thighs caressed
By the dark webs, her nape caught in his bill,
He holds her helpless breast upon his breast.

How can those terrified vague fingers push
The feathered glory from her loosening thighs?
And how can body, laid in that white rush,
But feel the strange heart beating where it lies?

A shudder in the loins engenders there
10   The broken wall, the burning roof and tower

And Agamemnon dead.
                    Being so caught up,
So mastered by the brute blood of the air,
Did she put on his knowledge with his power
Before the indifferent beak could let her drop?

Among School Children

I

I walk through the long schoolroom questioning;
A kind old nun in a white hood replies;
The children learn to cipher and to sing,
To study reading-books and history,
To cut and sew, be neat in everything
In the best modern way—the children's eyes
In momentary wonder stare upon
A sixty-year-old smiling public man.

II

I dream of a Ledaean body, bent
10   Above a sinking fire, a tale that she
Told of a harsh reproof, or trivial event
That changed some childish day to tragedy—
Told, and it seemed that our two natures blent
Into a sphere from youthful sympathy,
Or else, to alter Plato's parable,
Into the yolk and white of the one shell.

III

And thinking of that fit of grief or rage
I look upon one child or t'other there
And wonder if she stood so at that age—
20   For even daughters of the swan can share
Something of every paddler's heritage—
And had that color upon cheek or hair,
And thereupon my heart is driven wild:
She stands before me as a living child.

IV

Her present image floats into the mind—
Did Quattrocento finger fashion it
Hollow of cheek as though it drank the wind
And took a mess of shadows for its meat?
And I though never of Ledaean kind
30   Had pretty plumage once—enough of that,
Better to smile on all that smile, and show
There is a comfortable kind of old scarecrow.

V

What youthful mother, a shape upon her lap
Honey of generation had betrayed,
And that must sleep, shriek, struggle to escape
As recollection or the drug decide,
Would think her son, did she but see that shape
With sixty or more winters on its head,
A compensation for the pang of his birth,
40   Or the uncertainty of his setting forth?

VI

Plato thought nature but a spume that plays
Upon a ghostly paradigm of things;
Solider Aristotle played the taws
Upon the bottom of a king of kings;[1]
World-famous golden-thighed Pythagoras
Fingered upon a fiddle-stick or strings
What a star sang and careless Muses heard:
Old clothes upon old sticks to scare a bird.

VII

Both nuns and mothers worship images,
50   But those the candles light are not as those
That animate a mother's reveries,
But keep a marble or a bronze repose.
And yet they too break hearts—O Presences
That passion, piety or affection knows,
And that all heavenly glory symbolize—
O self-born mockers of man's enterprise;

VIII

Labor is blossoming or dancing where
The body is not bruised to pleasure soul,
Nor beauty born out of its own despair,
60   Nor blear-eyed wisdom out of midnight oil.
O chestnut-tree, great-rooted blossomer,
Are you the leaf, the blossom or the bole?
O body swayed to music, O brightening glance,
How can we know the dancer from the dance?

[1]Aristotle tutored Alexander the Great.

Crazy Jane Talks with the Bishop

I met the Bishop on the road
And much said he and I.
'Those breasts are flat and fallen now,
Those veins must soon be dry;
Live in a heavenly mansion,
Not in some foul sty.'

'Fair and foul are near of kin,
And fair needs foul,' I cried.
'My friends are gone, but that's a truth
10   Nor grave nor bed denied,
Learned in bodily lowliness
And in the heart's pride.

'A woman can be proud and stiff
When on love intent;
But Love has pitched his mansion in
The place of excrement;
For nothing can be sole or whole
That has not been rent.'

Edwin Arlington Robinson

Edwin Arlington Robinson (1869–1935) was born in Maine, and many of his poems use the background of small towns in New England. Most of his adult life, he spent the summers in New Hampshire at the MacDowell Colony and the rest of the year in a New York apartment. He wrote many book-length poems, some of them on subjects like *Merlin* and *Lancelot*. For most readers, the best of his work is the shorter poems of character and narrative.

Eros Turannos[1]

She fears him, and will always ask
      What fated her to choose him;
She meets in his engaging mask
      All reasons to refuse him;
But what she meets and what she fears
Are less than are the downward years,
Drawn slowly to the foamless weirs
      Of age, were she to lose him.

Between a blurred sagacity
10   That once had power to sound him,
And Love, that will not let him be
      The Judas that she found him,
Her pride assuages her almost,
As if it were alone the cost.—
He sees that he will not be lost,
      And waits and looks around him.

A sense of ocean and old trees
      Envelops and allures him;
Tradition, touching all he sees,
20   Beguiles and reassures him;
And all her doubts of what he says
Are dimmed with what she knows of days—
Till even prejudice delays
      And fades, and she secures him.

[1]Love, the Tyrant

The falling leaf inaugurates
   The reign of her confusion:
The pounding wave reverberates
   The dirge of her illusion;
And home, where passion lived and died,
30   Becomes a place where she can hide,
While all the town and harbor side
   Vibrate with her seclusion.

We tell you, tapping on our brows,
   The story as it should be,—
As if the story of a house
   Were told, or ever could be;
We'll have no kindly veil between
Her visions and those we have seen,—
As if we guessed what hers have been,
40   Or what they are or would be.

Meanwhile we do no harm; for they
   That with a god have striven,
Not hearing much of what we say,
   Take what the god has given;
Though like waves breaking it may be,
Or like a changed familiar tree,
Or like a stairway to the sea
   Where down the blind are driven.

Mr. Flood's Party

Old Eben Flood, climbing alone one night
Over the hill between the town below
And the forsaken upland hermitage
That held as much as he should ever know
On earth again of home, paused warily.
The road was his with not a native near;
And Eben, having leisure, said aloud,
For no man else in Tilbury Town to hear:

"Well, Mr. Flood, we have the harvest moon
10   Again, and we may not have many more;
The bird is on the wing, the poet says,
And you and I have said it here before.
Drink to the bird." He raised up to the light
The jug that he had gone so far to fill,
And answered huskily: "Well, Mr. Flood,
Since you propose it, I believe I will."

Alone, as if enduring to the end
A valiant armor of scarred hopes outworn,
He stood there in the middle of the road
20   Like Roland's[1] ghost winding a silent horn.

[1]A hero of French medieval romances who died, ambushed by Saracens, after summoning help by blowing his famous horn

Below him, in the town among the trees,
Where friends of other days had honored him,
A phantom salutation of the dead
Rang thinly till old Eben's eyes were dim.

Then, as a mother lays her sleeping child
Down tenderly, fearing it may awake,
He set the jug down slowly at his feet
With trembling care, knowing that most things break;
And only when assured that on firm earth
30   It stood, as the uncertain lives of men
Assuredly did not, he paced away,
And with his hand extended paused again:

"Well, Mr. Flood, we have not met like this
In a long time; and many a change has come
To both of us, I fear, since last it was
We had a drop together. Welcome home!"
Convivially returning with himself,
Again he raised the jug up to the light;
And with an acquiescent quaver said:
40   "Well, Mr. Flood, if you insist, I might.

"Only a very little, Mr. Flood—
For auld lang syne. No more, sir; that will do."
So, for the time, apparently it did,
And Eben evidently thought so too;
For soon amid the silver loneliness
Of night he lifted up his voice and sang,
Secure, with only two moons listening,
Until the whole harmonious landscape rang—

"For auld lang syne." The weary throat gave out,
50   The last word wavered, and the song was done.
He raised again the jug regretfully
And shook his head, and was again alone.
There was not much that was ahead of him,
And there was nothing in the town below—
Where strangers would have shut the many doors
That many friends had opened long ago.

Hillcrest

(To Mrs. Edward MacDowell)[1]

No sound of any storm that shakes
Old island walls with older seas
Comes here where now September makes
An island in a sea of trees.

[1]Marian Nevins MacDowell, widow of the important American composer Edward MacDowell (1861–1908), founded the MacDowell Colony in Peterborough, New Hampshire, and was its moving force until her death in 1956 at ninety-nine.

Between the sunlight and the shade
A man may learn till he forgets
The roaring of a world remade,
And all his ruins and regrets;

And if he still remembers here
10 Poor fights he may have won or lost,—
If he be ridden with the fear
Of what some other fight may cost,—

If, eager to confuse too soon,
What he has known with what may be,
He reads a planet out of tune
For cause of his jarred harmony,—

If here he venture to unroll
His index of adagios,
And he be given to console
20 Humanity with what he knows,—

He may by contemplation learn
A little more than what he knew,
And even see great oaks return
To acorns out of which they grew.

He may, if he but listen well,
Through twilight and the silence here,
Be told what there are none may tell
To vanity's impatient ear;

And he may never dare again
30 Say what awaits him, or be sure
What sunlit labyrinth of pain
He may not enter and endure.

Who knows to-day from yesterday
May learn to count no thing too strange:
Love builds of what Time takes away,
Till Death itself is less than Change.

Who sees enough in his duress
May go as far as dreams have gone;
Who sees a little may do less
40 Than many who are blind have done;

Who sees unchastened here the soul
Triumphant has no other sight
Than has a child who sees the whole
World radiant with his own delight.

Far journeys and hard wandering
Await him in whose crude surmise
Peace, like a mask, hides everything
That is and has been from his eyes;

And all his wisdom is unfound,
50   Or like a web that error weaves
On airy looms that have a sound
No louder now than falling leaves.

Robert Frost (1874–1963)

See pages 509–520.

Carl Sandburg

Carl Sandburg (1878–1967) became known as a poet in 1914, when *Poetry*
published "Chicago," later reprinted in *Chicago Poems*. Deriving from Whitman,
populist, a celebrator of the commonplace, Sandburg was a popular poet who
became the biographer of Abraham Lincoln (six volumes, awarded a Pulitzer
Prize in 1939) and toward the end of his life the author of a long novel called
Remembrance Rock.

Chicago

Hog Butcher for the World,
Tool Maker, Stacker of Wheat,
Player with Railroads and the Nation's Freight Handler;
Stormy, husky, brawling,
City of the Big Shoulders:
They tell me you are wicked and I believe them, for I have seen your painted
women under the gas lamps luring the farm boys.
And they tell me you are crooked and I answer: Yes, it is true I have seen the
gunman kill and go free to kill again.
And they tell me you are brutal and my reply is: On the faces of women and
children I have seen the marks of wanton hunger.
And having answered so I turn once more to those who sneer at this my city,
and I give them back the sneer and say to them:
10   Come and show me another city with lifted head singing so proud to be alive
and coarse and strong and cunning.
Flinging magnetic curses amid the toil of piling job on job, here is a tall bold
slugger set vivid against the little soft cities;
Fierce as a dog with tongue lapping for action, cunning as a savage pitted
against the wilderness,
Bareheaded,
Shoveling,
Wrecking,
Planning,
Building, breaking, rebuilding,
Under the smoke, dust all over his mouth, laughing with white teeth,
Under the terrible burden of destiny laughing as a young man laughs,
20   Laughing even as an ignorant fighter laughs who has never lost a battle,

Bragging and laughing that under his wrist is the pulse, and under his ribs the
    heart of the people,
                       Laughing!
Laughing the stormy, husky, brawling laughter of Youth, half-naked, sweating,
    proud to be Hog Butcher, Tool Maker, Stacker of Wheat, Player with
    Railroads and Freight Handler to the Nation.

Edward Thomas

Edward Thomas (1878 –1917) was Robert Frost's great English friend, a
freelance writer of prose whom Frost teased and encouraged into poetry.
Thomas came to poetry late, wrote furiously in his brief poetic life, and was
killed in World War I.

The Owl

Downhill I came, hungry, and yet not starved;
Cold, yet had heat within me that was proof
Against the North wind; tired, yet so that rest
Had seemed the sweetest thing under a roof.

Then at the inn I had food, fire, and rest,
Knowing how hungry, cold, and tired was I.
All of the night was quite barred out except
An owl's cry, a most melancholy cry

Shaken out long and clear upon the hill,
No merry note, nor cause of merriment,
But one telling me plain what I escaped
And others could not, that night, as in I went.

And salted was my food, and my repose,
Salted and sobered, too, by the bird's voice
Speaking for all who lay under the stars,
Soldiers and poor, unable to rejoice.

Vachel Lindsay

Vachel Lindsay (1879–1931) is best known for the long poems—like "General
William Booth Enters into Heaven" and "The Congo"—which he recited on
platforms with energy, showmanship, and pizzaz. His readings were popular,
his poetry successful for many years. Toward the end of his life, during the
Great Depression, he found it difficult to make a living. He had perhaps
published too much, too uncritically.

The Flower-Fed Buffaloes

The flower-fed buffaloes of the spring
In the days of long ago,
Ranged where the locomotives sing
And the prairie flowers lie low:—

The tossing, blooming, perfumed grass
Is swept away by the wheat,
Wheels and wheels and wheels spin by
In the spring that still is sweet.
But the flower-fed buffaloes of the spring
10   Left us, long ago.
They gore no more, they bellow no more,
They trundle around the hills no more:—
With the Blackfeet, lying low,
With the Pawnees, lying low,
Lying low.

Wallace Stevens

Wallace Stevens (1879–1955) is one of the finest of American poets. He
attended Harvard, tried his luck as a journalist, and went to New York
University Law School. After practicing some years in New York City, he took a
job with the legal department of Hartford Accident and Indemnity, an
insurance company, and eventually moved to Hartford, thus becoming known
as "the insurance man who is a poet." His poetry has a delicacy, a Frenchified
elegance, and a nice concern for matters epistemological. There seemed to
be a clear and sustained break between the poetry he wrote and the life he
lived. Perhaps they came together in Florida, which like many Connecticut
businessmen he visited every winter and which entered his poems as a place of
unsurpassable bright lushness. See also page 396.

The Emperor of Ice-Cream

Call the roller of big cigars,
The muscular one, and bid him whip
In kitchen cups concupiscent curds.
Let the wenches dawdle in such dress
As they are used to wear, and let the boys
Bring flowers in last month's newspapers.
Let be be finale of seem.
The only emperor is the emperor of ice-cream.

Take from the dresser of deal,
10   Lacking the three glass knobs, that sheet
On which she embroidered fantails once
And spread it so as to cover her face.
If her horny feet protrude, they come
To show how cold she is, and dumb.
Let the lamp affix its beam.
The only emperor is the emperor of ice-cream.

The Snow Man

One must have a mind of winter
To regard the frost and the boughs
Of the pine-trees crusted with snow;

And have been cold a long time
To behold the junipers shagged with ice,
The spruces rough in the distant glitter

Of the January sun; and not to think
Of any misery in the sound of the wind,
In the sound of a few leaves,

10   Which is the sound of the land
Full of the same wind
That is blowing in the same bare place

For the listener, who listens in the snow,
And, nothing himself, beholds
Nothing that is not there and the nothing that is.

Sunday Morning

I

Complacencies of the peignoir, and late
Coffee and oranges in a sunny chair,
And the green freedom of a cockatoo
Upon a rug mingle to dissipate
The holy hush of ancient sacrifice.
She dreams a little, and she feels the dark
Encroachment of that old catastrophe,
As a calm darkens among water-lights.
The pungent oranges and bright, green wings
10   Seem things in some procession of the dead,
Winding across wide water, without sound.
The day is like wide water, without sound,
Stilled for the passing of her dreaming feet
Over the seas, to silent Palestine,
Dominion of the blood and sepulchre.

II

Why should she give her bounty to the dead?
What is divinity if it can come
Only in silent shadows and in dreams?
Shall she not find in comforts of the sun,
20   In pungent fruit and bright, green wings, or else
In any balm or beauty of the earth,
Things to be cherished like the thought of heaven?
Divinity must live within herself:
Passions of rain, or moods in falling snow;
Grievings in loneliness, or unsubdued
Elations when the forest blooms; gusty
Emotions on wet roads on autumn nights;
All pleasures and all pains, remembering
The bough of summer and the winter branch.
30   These are the measures destined for her soul.

III

Jove in the clouds had his inhuman birth.
No mother suckled him, no sweet land gave
Large-mannered motions to his mythy mind
He moved among us, as a muttering king,
Magnificent, would move among his hinds,
Until our blood, commingling, virginal,
With heaven, brought such requital to desire
The very hinds discerned it, in a star.
Shall our blood fail? Or shall it come to be
40   The blood of paradise? And shall the earth
Seem all of paradise that we shall know?
The sky will be much friendlier then than now,
A part of labor and a part of pain,
And next in glory to enduring love,
Not this dividing and indifferent blue.

IV

She says, "I am content when wakened birds,
Before they fly, test the reality
Of misty fields, by their sweet questionings;
But when the birds are gone, and their warm fields
50   Return no more, where, then, is paradise?"
There is not any haunt of prophecy,
Nor any old chimera of the grave,
Neither the golden underground, nor isle
Melodious, where spirits gat them home,
Nor visionary south, nor cloudy palm
Remote on heaven's hill, that has endured
As April's green endures; or will endure
Like her remembrance of awakened birds,
Or her desire for June and evening, tipped
60   By the consummation of the swallow's wings.

V

She says, "But in contentment I still feel
The need of some imperishable bliss."
Death is the mother of beauty; hence from her,
Alone, shall come fulfilment to our dreams
And our desires. Although she strews the leaves
Of sure obliteration on our paths,
The path sick sorrow took, the many paths
Where triumph rang its brassy phrase, or love
Whispered a little out of tenderness,
70   She makes the willow shiver in the sun
For maidens who were wont to sit and gaze
Upon the grass, relinquished to their feet.
She causes boys to pile new plums and pears
On disregarded plate. The maidens taste
And stray impassioned in the littering leaves.

VI

Is there no change of death in paradise?
Does ripe fruit never fall? Or do the boughs
Hang always heavy in that perfect sky,
Unchanging, yet so like our perishing earth,
80   With rivers like our own that seek for seas
They never find, the same receding shores
That never touch with inarticulate pang?
Why set the pear upon those river-banks
Or spice the shores with odors of the plum?
Alas, that they should wear our colors there,
The silken weavings of our afternoons,
And pick the strings of our insipid lutes!
Death is the mother of beauty, mystical,
Within whose burning bosom we devise
90   Our earthly mothers waiting, sleeplessly.

VII

Supple and turbulent, a ring of men
Shall chant in orgy on a summer morn
Their boisterous devotion to the sun,
Not as a god, but as a god might be,
Naked among them, like a savage source
Their chant shall be a chant of paradise,
Out of their blood, returning to the sky;
And in their chant shall enter, voice by voice,
The windy lake wherein their lord delights,
100   The trees, like serafin, and echoing hills,
That choir among themselves long afterward.
They shall know well the heavenly fellowship
Of men that perish and of summer morn.
And whence they came and whither they shall go
The dew upon their feet shall manifest.

VIII

She hears, upon that water without sound,
A voice that cries, "The tomb in Palestine
Is not the porch of spirits lingering.
It is the grave of Jesus, where he lay."
110   We live in an old chaos of the sun,
Or old dependency of day and night,
Or island solitude, unsponsored, free,
Of that wide water, inescapable.
Deer walk upon our mountains, and the quail
Whistle about us their spontaneous cries;
Sweet berries ripen in the wilderness;
And, in the isolation of the sky,
At evening, casual flocks of pigeons make
Ambiguous undulations as they sink,
120   Downward to darkness, on extended wings.

William Carlos Williams

William Carlos Williams (1883–1963) knew Ezra Pound at the University of Pennsylvania when they were students. Williams went on to become a medical doctor, living most of his life in suburban Rutherford, New Jersey, where he practiced medicine, specializing in obstetrics. His poetry was resolute in its use of the American idiom. Followers have turned his theory and his practice into one of the main schools of contemporary American poetry. See also pages 393, 411, and 451.

This Is Just to Say

I have eaten
the plums
that were in
the icebox

and which
you were probably
saving
for breakfast

Forgive me
10   they were delicious
so sweet
and so cold

Spring and All

By the road to the contagious hospital
under the surge of the blue
mottled clouds driven from the
northeast—a cold wind. Beyond, the
waste of broad, muddy fields
brown with dried weeds, standing and fallen

patches of standing water
the scattering of tall trees

All along the road the reddish
10   purplish, forked, upstanding, twiggy
stuff of bushes and small trees
with dead, brown leaves under them
leafless vines—

Lifeless in appearance, sluggish
dazed spring approaches—

They enter the new world naked,
cold, uncertain of all
save that they enter. All about them
the cold, familiar wind—

20   Now the grass, tomorrow
the stiff curl of wildcarrot leaf

One by one objects are defined—
It quickens: clarity, outline of leaf

But now the stark dignity of
entrance—Still, the profound change
has come upon them: rooted they
grip down and begin to awaken

D. H. Lawrence

David Herbert Lawrence (1885–1930) was the son of a coalminer, born in a
working-class district of England. He wrote from an early age, and with the aid
of scholarships wrested himself away from his background to become a writer.
Best known as a novelist, especially for *The Rainbow, Women in Love,* and *Lady
Chatterley's Lover,* he was a great essayist, literary critic, writer of travel books,
letter-writer—and to some critics best of all as a poet. He died of tuberculosis,
having accomplished an enormous volume of work, before he turned forty-five.

The Song of a Man Who Has Come Through

Not I, not I, but the wind that blows through me!
A fine wind is blowing the new direction of Time.
If only I let it bear me, carry me, if only it carry me!
If only I am sensitive, subtle, oh, delicate, a winged gift!
If only, most lovely of all, I yield myself and am borrowed
By the fine, fine wind that takes its course through the chaos of the world
Like a fine, an exquisite chisel, a wedge-blade inserted;
If only I am keen and hard like the sheer tip of a wedge
Driven by invisible blows,
10   The rock will split, we shall come at the wonder, we shall find the Hesperides.[1]

Oh, for the wonder that bubbles into my soul,
I would be a good fountain, a good well-head,
Would blur no whisper, spoil no expression.

What is the knocking?
What is the knocking at the door in the night?
It is somebody wants to do us harm.

No, no, it is the three strange angels.
Admit them, admit them.

[1]In Greek mythology, sisters who protected a garden in which grew a tree bearing golden apples

Bavarian Gentians

Not every man has gentians in his house
In soft September, at slow, sad Michaelmas.

Bavarian gentians, tall and dark, but dark
darkening the daytime torch-like with the smoking blueness of Pluto's gloom,
ribbed hellish flowers erect, with their blaze of darkness spread blue,
blown flat into points, by the heavy white draught of the day.

Torch-flowers of the blue-smoking darkness, Pluto's dark-blue blaze
black lamps from the halls of Dis,[1] smoking dark blue
giving off darkness, blue darkness, upon Demeter's yellow-pale day
10 whom have you come for, here in the white-cast day?

Reach me a gentian, give me a torch!
let me guide myself with the blue, forked torch of a flower
down the darker and darker stairs, where blue is darkened on blueness
down the way Persephone goes, just now, in first-frosted September.
to the sightless realm where darkness is married to dark
and Persephone herself is but a voice, as a bride,
a gloom invisible enfolded in the deeper dark
of the arms of Pluto as he ravishes her once again
and pierces her once more with his passion of the utter dark
among the splendour of black-blue torches, shedding fathomless darkness on
20   the nuptials.

Give me a flower on a tall stem, and three dark flames,
for I will go to the wedding, and be wedding-guest
at the marriage of the living dark.

[1]Dis, Dispater, the Roman name for a deity who was the same as the Greek Pluto, god of the underworld

Ezra Pound

Ezra Pound (1885–1972) was born in Idaho, but left as an infant and grew up
in the suburbs of Philadelphia. From an early age he determined to become
a great poet and set out to educate himself to that end. After graduate work
at the University of Pennsylvania he taught briefly at Wabash College in
Crawfordsville, Indiana. He was fired when he afforded a night's shelter to a
homeless dancing girl and left almost immediately for Europe, where he spent
most of the rest of his life. A young man of extraordinary generosity, he
discovered or promoted writers as diverse as Lawrence, Eliot, Joyce, and Frost.
And as a young man he was determinedly esthetic. After the First World War
killed off many friends—young artists of great promise—he became increasingly
embittered about social matters and turned paranoid. This development led
to his admiration for Benito Mussolini, the Italian dictator, and to the act of
broadcasting on Italian radio to American troops during the Second World War.
After the war, he was accused of treason but was judged mentally unfit to stand
trial. After many years in St. Elizabeth's Hospital in Washington, D.C., under
guard, he was released as an old man to return to Italy, where he lived out his
long life. See also pages 445 and 480.

The River-Merchant's Wife: A Letter

While my hair was still cut straight across my forehead
I played about the front gate, pulling flowers.
You came by on bamboo stilts, playing horse,
You walked about my seat, playing with blue plums.
And we went on living in the village of Chokan:
Two small people, without dislike or suspicion.

At fourteen I married My Lord you.
I never laughed, being bashful.

Lowering my head, I looked at the wall.
10   Called to, a thousand times, I never looked back.

At fifteen I stopped scowling,
I desired my dust to be mingled with yours
For ever and for ever and for ever.
Why should I climb the look out?

At sixteen you departed,
You went into far Ku-to-yen, by the river of swirling eddies,
And you have been gone five months.
The monkeys make sorrowful noise overhead.

You dragged your feet when you went out.
20   By the gate now, the moss is grown, the different mosses,
Too deep to clear them away!
The leaves fall early this autumn, in wind.
The paired butterflies are already yellow with August
Over the grass in the West garden;
They hurt me. I grow older.
If you are coming down through the narrows of the river Kiang,
Please let me know beforehand,
And I will come out to meet you
                    As far as Cho-fu-Sa.   *(By Rihaku)*[1]

[1]The Japanese name for Chinese poet Li Po, who wrote the original

from Hugh Selwyn Mauberley

IV

These fought in any case,
and some believing,
              pro domo,[1] in any case . . .

Some quick to arm,
some for adventure,
some from fear of weakness,
some from fear of censure,
some for love of slaughter, in imagination,
learning later . . .
10   some in fear, learning love of slaughter;

Died some, pro patria,[1]
              non 'dulce' non 'et decor'[1] . . .
walked eye-deep in hell
believing in old men's lies, then unbelieving
came home, home to a lie,
home to many deceits,
home to old lies and new infamy;

[1]In Latin *pro domo* means "for home." Pound is alluding to a poem by the Roman poet Horace, whom he quotes (and later contradicts), who wrote that it is "sweet and fitting" (*dulce et decor* [*um*]) to die "for one's country" (*pro patria*). Compare Wilfred Owen's poem on page 632.

usury age-old and age-thick
and liars in public places.

20 Daring as never before, wastage as never before.
Young blood and high blood,
fair cheeks, and fine bodies;

fortitude as never before

frankness as never before,
disillusions as never told in the old days,
hysterias, trench confessions,
laughter out of dead bellies.

V

There died a myriad,
And of the best, among them,
30 For an old bitch gone in the teeth,
For a botched civilization,

Charm, smiling at the good mouth,
Quick eyes gone under earth's lid,

For two gross of broken statues,
For a few thousand battered books.

H.D. (Hilda Doolittle)

Hilda Doolittle (1886–1961) attended Bryn Mawr College and knew William
Carlos Williams and Ezra Pound when all three poets were young. (It was at
Pound's suggestion that she began signing her poems with her initials only.)
She began as an imagist poet; later in life she wrote long philosophic poems.
See also page 409.

Sea Rose

Rose, harsh rose,
marred and with stint of petals,
meagre flower, thin,
sparse of leaf,

more precious
than a wet rose,
single on a stem—
you are caught in the drift.

Stunted, with small leaf,
10 you are flung on the sand,
you are lifted
in the crisp sand
that drives in the wind.

Can the spice-rose
drip such acrid fragrance
hardened in a leaf?

Robinson Jeffers

Robinson Jeffers (1887–1962) settled with his family in California when he was sixteen years old. His third book, *Tamar and Other Poems* (1924), brought him to readers' attention. As he grew older he became progressively more misanthropic, with a passionate and romantic love for the natural world, which found man pathetic and inadequate in comparison to its natural grandeurs. He built his own house out of stone in Carmel.

Hurt Hawks

I

The broken pillar of the wing jags from the clotted shoulder,
The wing trails like a banner in defeat,
No more to use the sky forever but live with famine
And pain a few days: cat nor coyote
Will shorten the week of waiting for death, there is game without talons
He stands under the oak-bush and waits
The lame feet of salvation; at night he remembers freedom
And flies in a dream, the dawns ruin it.
He is strong and pain is worse to the strong, incapacity is worse.
10   The curs of the day come and torment him
At distance, no one but death the redeemer will humble that head,
The intrepid readiness, the terrible eyes.
The wild God of the world is sometimes merciful to those
That ask mercy, not often to the arrogant,
You do not know him, you communal people, or you have forgotten him;
Intemperate and savage, the hawk remembers him;
Beautiful and wild, the hawks, and men that are dying, remember him.

II

I'd sooner, except the penalties, kill a man than a hawk; but the great redtail[1]
Had nothing left but unable misery
From the bone too shattered for mending, the wing that trailed under his talons
20   when he moved.
We had fed him six weeks, I gave him freedom,
He wandered over the foreland hill and returned in the evening, asking for death,
Not like a beggar, still eyed with the old
Implacable arrogance. I gave him the lead gift in the twilight. What fell was relaxed,
Owl-downy, soft feminine feathers; but what
Soared: the fierce rush: the night-herons by the flooded river cried fear at its rising
Before it was quite unsheathed from reality.

[1]Red-tailed hawk

Marianne Moore

Marianne Moore (1887–1972) was born in St. Louis, graduated from Bryn Mawr, and taught school in Pennsylvania, but lived most of her life in Brooklyn. As editor of *The Dial* from 1925 to 1929 she published many of the best modern poets. Her own poems are original and even eccentric. Her intricate descriptions are scrupulous in detail, shaped into prosaic lines that achieve a singular music. See also page 406.

A Grave

Man looking into the sea,
taking the view from those who have as much right to it as you have to it
    yourself,
it is human nature to stand in the middle of a thing,
but you cannot stand in the middle of this;
the sea has nothing to give but a well excavated grave.
The firs stand in a procession, each with an emerald turkey foot at the top,
reserved as their contours, saying nothing;
repression, however, is not the most obvious characteristic of the sea;
the sea is a collector, quick to return a rapacious look.
10   There are others besides you who have worn that look—
whose expression is no longer a protest; the fish no longer investigate them
for their bones have not lasted:
men lower nets, unconscious of the fact that they are desecrating a grave,
and row quickly away—the blades of the oars
moving together like the feet of water spiders as if there were no such thing as
    death.
The wrinkles progress among themselves in a phalanx—beautiful under
    networks of foam,
and fade breathlessly while the sea rustles in and out of the seaweed;
the birds swim through the air at top speed, emitting catcalls as heretofore—
the tortoise shell scourges about the feet of the cliffs, in motion beneath them;
20   and the ocean, under the pulsation of lighthouses and noise of bell buoys,
advances as usual, looking as if it were not that ocean in which dropped things
    are bound to sink—
in which if they turn and twist, it is neither with volition nor consciousness.

Edwin Muir

Edwin Muir (1887–1959) was born in the Orkneys, off the coast of Scotland. After his father was evicted from an island farm, young Muir grew up in the slums of Glasgow. His poetry built upon the contrast between the pastoral and the industrial. He and his wife Willa lived by their wits most of their lives, and are Kafka's translators. Muir is author of an excellent *Autobiography* as well as the neglected *Collected Poems*.

The Horses

Barely a twelvemonth after
The seven days war that put the world to sleep,
Late in the evening the strange horses came.

By then we had made our covenant with silence,
But in the first few days it was so still
We listened to our breathing and were afraid.
On the second day
The radios failed; we turned the knobs; no answer.
On the third day a warship passed us, heading north,
10   Dead bodies piled on the deck. On the sixth day
A plane plunged over us into the sea. Thereafter
Nothing. The radios dumb;
And still they stand in corners of our kitchens,
And stand, perhaps, turned on, in a million rooms
All over the world. But now if they should speak,
If on a sudden they should speak again,
If on the stroke of noon a voice should speak,
We would not listen, we would not let it bring
That old bad world that swallowed its children quick
20   At one great gulp. We would not have it again.
Sometimes we think of the nations lying asleep,
Curled blindly in impenetrable sorrow,
And then the thought confounds us with its strangeness.
The tractors lie about our fields; at evening
They look like dank sea-monsters couched and waiting.
We leave them where they are and let them rust:
'They'll moulder away and be like other loam.'
We make our oxen drag our rusty ploughs,
Long laid aside. We have gone back
30   Far past our fathers' land.
                              And then, that evening
Late in the summer the strange horses came.
We heard a distant tapping on the road,
A deepening drumming; it stopped, went on again
And at the corner changed to hollow thunder.
We saw the heads
Like a wild wave charging and were afraid.
We had sold our horses in our fathers' time
To buy new tractors. Now they were strange to us
40   As fabulous steeds set on an ancient shield
Or illustrations in a book of knights.
We did not dare go near them. Yet they waited,
Stubborn and shy, as if they had been sent
By an old command to find our whereabouts
And that long-lost archaic companionship.
In the first moment we had never a thought
That they were creatures to be owned and used.
Among them were some half-a-dozen colts
Dropped in some wilderness of the broken world,
50   Yet new as if they had come from their own Eden.
Since then they have pulled our ploughs and borne our loads
But that free servitude still can pierce our hearts.
Our life is changed; their coming our beginning.

T. S. Eliot

Thomas Stearns Eliot (1888–1965) was born in St. Louis, Missouri, into a family two generations removed from Boston that had created its own small Boston in St. Louis. Eliot went to prep school in Massachusetts, to Harvard, and then abroad. After some time in Europe on fellowships (he expected to finish a doctorate in philosophy at Harvard) he married an Englishwoman and settled in England, dedicating himself to the life of a poet. For a time he taught school, for a longer time he worked in a bank, and finally he became a publisher, overseer of the best poetry list in England, at Faber & Faber. His early work, derived largely from French sources, was notable for its irony and for the desolation of its landscape. This work culminated in the great modernist poem *The Waste Land* in 1922. Toward the end of that decade, Eliot converted to Anglo-Catholicism and most of the rest of his poetry was dedicated to exploring the implications of conversion. "Journey of the Magi" is one record. *The Four Quartets* is the last of his great work in poetry, though he wrote verse plays for the West End and Broadway afterward, with success more commercial than poetical. He was awarded the Nobel Prize in 1948, was widely celebrated as a critic, and was the leading literary figure of the English-speaking world during the first half of the twentieth century.

The Love Song of J. Alfred Prufrock

S'io credesse che mia risposta fosse
A persona che mai tornasse al mondo,
Questa fiamma staria senza piu scosse.
Ma perciocche giammai di questo fondo
Non torno vivo alcun, s'i'odo il vero,
Senza tema d'infamia ti rispondo.[1]

Let us go then, you and I,
When the evening is spread out against the sky
Like a patient etherized upon a table;
Let us go, through certain half-deserted streets,
The muttering retreats
Of restless nights in one-night cheap hotels
And sawdust restaurants with oyster-shells:
Streets that follow like a tedious argument
Of insidious intent
10   To lead you to an overwhelming question . . .
Oh, do not ask, "What is it?"
Let us go and make our visit.

   In the room the women come and go
Talking of Michelangelo.

   The yellow fog that rubs its back upon the window-panes,
The yellow smoke that rubs its muzzle on the window-panes
Licked its tongue into the corners of the evening,

---

[1]The Italian epigraph, from Dante's *Inferno*, is the speech of one who is dead and damned, whose punishment is to be wrapped in a constantly burning flame. He believes his hearer also will remain in Hell and thus says: "If I thought my reply were to someone who could ever return to the world, this flame would waver no more [i.e., I would speak no more]. But since, I'm told, nobody ever escapes from this pit, I'll tell you without fear of ill fame."

Lingered upon the pools that stand in drains,
Let fall upon its back the soot that falls from chimneys,
20 Slipped by the terrace, made a sudden leap,
And seeing that it was a soft October night,
Curled once about the house, and fell asleep.

   And indeed there will be time
For the yellow smoke that slides along the street,
Rubbing its back upon the window-panes;
There will be time, there will be time
To prepare a face to meet the faces that you meet;
There will be time to murder and create,
And time for all the works and days of hands
30 That lift and drop a question on your plate;
Time for you and time for me,
And time yet for a hundred indecisions,
And for a hundred visions and revisions,
Before the taking of a toast and tea.

   In the room the women come and go
Talking of Michelangelo.

   And indeed there will be time
To wonder, "Do I dare?" and, "Do I dare?"
Time to turn back and descend the stair,
40 With a bald spot in the middle of my hair—
[They will say: "How his hair is growing thin!"]
My morning coat, my collar mounting firmly to the chin,
My necktie rich and modest, but asserted by a simple pin—
[They will say: "But how his arms and legs are thin!"]
Do I dare
Disturb the universe?
In a minute there is time
For decisions and revisions which a minute will reverse.

   For I have known them all already, known them all:—
50 Have known the evenings, mornings, afternoons,
I have measured out my life with coffee spoons;
I know the voices dying with a dying fall
Beneath the music from a farther room.
   So how should I presume?

   And I have known the eyes already, known them all—
The eyes that fix you in a formulated phrase,
And when I am formulated, sprawling on a pin,
When I am pinned and wriggling on the wall,
Then how should I begin
60 To spit out all the butt-ends of my days and ways?
   And how should I presume?

   And I have known the arms already, known them all—
Arms that are braceleted and white and bare
[But in the lamplight, downed with light brown hair!]

Is it perfume from a dress
That makes me so digress?
Arms that lie along a table, or wrap about a shawl.
    And should I then presume?
    And how should I begin?

       . . . . .

70   Shall I say, I have gone at dusk through narrow streets
And watched the smoke that rises from the pipes
Of lonely men in shirt-sleeves, leaning out of windows? . . .

    I should have been a pair of ragged claws
Scuttling across the floors of silent seas.

       . . . . .

And the afternoon, the evening, sleeps so peacefully!
Smoothed by long fingers,
Asleep . . . tired . . . or it malingers,
Stretched on the floor, here beside you and me.
Should I, after tea and cakes and ices,
80   Have the strength to force the moment to its crisis?
But though I have wept and fasted, wept and prayed,
Though I have seen my head [grown slightly bald] brought in upon a platter,
I am no prophet—and here's no great matter;
I have seen the moment of my greatness flicker,
And I have seen the eternal Footman hold my coat, and snicker,
And in short, I was afraid.

    And would it have been worth it, after all,
After the cups, the marmalade, the tea,
Among the porcelain, among some talk of you and me,
90   Would it have been worth while,
To have bitten off the matter with a smile,
To have squeezed the universe into a ball
To roll it toward some overwhelming question,
To say: "I am Lazarus, come from the dead,
Come back to tell you all, I shall tell you all"—
If one, settling a pillow by her head,
    Should say: "That is not what I meant at all.
    That is not it, at all."

    And would it have been worth it, after all,
100   Would it have been worth while,
After the sunsets and the dooryards and the sprinkled streets,
After the novels, after the teacups, after the skirts that trail along the floor—
And this, and so much more?—
It is impossible to say just what I mean!
But as if a magic lantern threw the nerves in patterns on a screen:
Would it have been worth while
If one, settling a pillow or throwing off a shawl,
And turning toward the window, should say:
    "That is not it at all,
110   That is not what I meant, at all."

. . . . .

No! I am not Prince Hamlet, nor was meant to be;
Am an attendant lord, one that will do
To swell a progress, start a scene or two,
Advise the prince; no doubt, an easy tool,
Deferential, glad to be of use,
Politic, cautious, and meticulous;
Full of high sentence, but a bit obtuse;
At times, indeed, almost ridiculous—
Almost, at times, the Fool.

120   I grow old . . . I grow old . . .
I shall wear the bottoms of my trousers rolled.

Shall I part my hair behind? Do I dare to eat a peach?
I shall wear white flannel trousers, and walk upon the beach.
I have heard the mermaids singing, each to each.

I do not think that they will sing to me.

I have seen them riding seaward on the waves
Combing the white hair of the waves blown back
When the wind blows the water white and black.

We have lingered in the chambers of the sea
130   By sea-girls wreathed with seaweed red and brown
Till human voices wake us, and we drown.

Journey of the Magi

'A cold coming we had of it,
Just the worst time of the year
For a journey, and such a long journey:
The ways deep and the weather sharp,
The very dead of winter.'
And the camels galled, sore-footed, refractory,
Lying down in the melting snow.
There were times we regretted
The summer palaces on slopes, the terraces,
10   And the silken girls bringing sherbet.
Then the camel men cursing and grumbling
And running away, and wanting their liquor and women,
And the night-fires going out, and the lack of shelters,
And the cities hostile and the towns unfriendly
And the villages dirty and charging high prices:
A hard time we had of it.
At the end we preferred to travel all night,
Sleeping in snatches,
With the voices singing in our ears, saying
20   That this was all folly.

Then at dawn we came down to a temperate valley,
Wet, below the snow line, smelling of vegetation;
With a running stream and a water-mill beating the darkness,

And three trees on the low sky,
And an old white horse galloped away in the meadow.
Then we came to a tavern with vine-leaves over the lintel,
Six hands at an open door dicing for pieces of silver,
And feet kicking the empty wine-skins.
But there was no information, and so we continued
30 And arrived at evening, not a moment too soon
Finding the place; it was (you may say) satisfactory.

    All this was a long time ago, I remember,
And I would do it again, but set down
This set down
This: were we led all that way for
Birth or Death? There was a Birth, certainly,
We had evidence and no doubt. I had seen birth and death,
But had thought they were different; this Birth was
Hard and bitter agony for us, like Death, our death.
40 We returned to our places, these Kingdoms,
But no longer at ease here, in the old dispensation,
With an alien people clutching their gods.
I should be glad of another death.

John Crowe Ransom

John Crowe Ransom (1888–1974) grew up in Tennessee and was a Rhodes
scholar at Oxford. A leader in the Agrarian movement (a group of Southern
writers in the late 1920s and the 1930s) he went to Kenyon College as a
professor in 1937, edited the highly successful *Kenyon Review*, and wrote
criticism as well as poetry.

Captain Carpenter

Captain Carpenter rose up in his prime
Put on his pistols and went riding out
But had got wellnigh nowhere at that time
Till he fell in with ladies in a rout.

It was a pretty lady and all her train
That played with him so sweetly but before
An hour she'd taken a sword with all her main
And twined him of his nose for evermore.

Captain Carpenter mounted up one day
10 And rode straightway into a stranger rogue
That looked unchristian but be that as may
The Captain did not wait upon prologue.

But drew upon him out of his great heart
The other swung against him with a club
And cracked his two legs at the shinny part
And let him roll and stick like any tub.

Captain Carpenter rode many a time
From male and female took he sundry harms
He met the wife of Satan crying "I'm
20   The she-wolf bids you shall bear no more arms."

Their strokes and counters whistled in the wind
I wish he had delivered half his blows
But where she should have made off like a hind
The bitch bit off his arms at the elbows.

And Captain Carpenter parted with his ears
To a black devil that used him in this wise
O Jesus ere his threescore and ten years
Another had plucked out his sweet blue eyes.

Captain Carpenter got up on his roan
30   And sallied from the gate in hell's despite
I heard him asking in the grimmest tone
If any enemy yet there was to fight?

"To any adversary it is fame
If he risk to be wounded by my tongue
Or burnt in two beneath my red heart's flame
Such are the perils he is cast among.

"But if he can he has a pretty choice
From an anatomy with little to lose
Whether he cut my tongue and take my voice
40   Or whether it be my round red heart he choose."

It was the neatest knave that ever was seen
Stepping in perfume from his lady's bower
Who at this word put in his merry mien
And fell on Captain Carpenter like a tower.

I would not knock old fellows in the dust
But there lay Captain Carpenter on his back
His weapons were the old heart in his bust
And a blade shook between rotten teeth alack.

The rogue in scarlet and grey soon knew his mind
50   He wished to get his trophy and depart
With gentle apology and touch refined
He pierced him and produced the Captain's heart.

God's mercy rest on Captain Carpenter now
I thought him Sirs an honest gentlemen
Citizen husband soldier and scholar enow
Let jangling kites eat of him if they can.

But God's deep curses follow after those
That shore him of his goodly nose and ears
His legs and strong arms at the two elbows
60   And eyes that had not watered seventy years.

The curse of hell upon the sleek upstart
That got the Captain finally on his back
And took the red red vitals of his heart
And made the kites to whet their beaks clack clack.

Archibald MacLeish

Archibald MacLeish (1892–   ) attended Yale, went to law school at Harvard, practiced law briefly, and then moved to France as an American expatriate in the 1920s. When the Depression hit the United States he returned to this country, where he became increasingly political. He worked for *Fortune*, wrote on political subjects, and eventually allied himself with President Franklin D. Roosevelt. He was Librarian of Congress, and toward the end of Roosevelt's life became an Assistant Secretary of State. When Roosevelt died, MacLeish left government. He taught at Harvard for some years, beginning in 1949, and returned to the writing of poetry.

You, Andrew Marvell

And here face down beneath the sun
And here upon earth's noonward height
To feel the always coming on
The always rising of the night:

To feel creep up the curving east
The earthy chill of dusk and slow
Upon those under lands the vast
And ever climbing shadow grow

10   And strange at Ecbatan the trees
Take leaf by leaf the evening strange
The flooding dark about their knees
The mountains over Persia change

And now at Kermanshah the gate
Dark empty and the withered grass
And through the twilight now the late
Few travelers in the westward pass

And Baghdad darken and the bridge
Across the silent river gone
And through Arabia the edge
20   Of evening widen and steal on

And deepen on Palmyra's street
The wheel rut in the ruined stone
And Lebanon fade out and Crete
High through the clouds and overblown

And over Sicily the air
Still flashing with the landward gulls
And loom and slowly disappear
The sails above the shadowy hulls

And Spain go under and the shore
30   Of Africa the gilded sand
And evening vanish and no more
The low pale light across that land

Nor now the long light on the sea:

And here face downward in the sun
To feel how swift how secretly
The shadow of the night comes on . . .

Wilfred Owen

Wilfred Owen (1893–1918) was a poet of the First World War. Like most young
Englishmen in 1914, he had cherished a romantic notion of battle. He lived
long enough—before the war killed him, just a few days before the armistice—
to write bitter and antiromantic poems of real modern war.

Dulce et Decorum Est[1]

Bent double, like old beggars under sacks,
Knock-kneed, coughing like hags, we cursed through sludge,
Till on the haunting flares we turned our backs,
And towards our distant rest began to trudge.
Men marched asleep. Many had lost their boots,
But limped on, blood-shod. All went lame, all blind;
Drunk with fatigue; deaf even to the hoots
Of gas-shells dropping softly behind.

Gas! Gas! Quick, boys!—An ecstasy of fumbling,
10   Fitting the clumsy helmets just in time,
But someone still was yelling out and stumbling
And floundering like a man in fire or lime.—
Dim through the misty panes and thick green light,
As under a green sea, I saw him drowning.

In all my dreams before my helpless sight
He plunges at me, guttering, choking, drowning.

If in some smothering dreams, you too could pace
Behind the wagon that we flung him in,
And watch the white eyes writhing in his face,
20   His hanging face, like a devil's sick of sin;
If you could hear, at every jolt, the blood
Come gargling from the froth-corrupted lungs,
Bitter as the cud
Of vile, incurable sores on innocent tongues,—
My friend, you would not tell with such high zest
To children ardent for some desperate glory,
The old Lie: Dulce et decorum est
Pro patria mori.[1]

[1]The Roman poet Horace wrote that it "is sweet and fitting" (*dulce et decorum est*) "to die for
one's country" (*pro patria mori*). Compare Pound's poem on page 620.

E. E. Cummings

Edward Estlin Cummings (1894–1962) grew up in Cambridge, Massachusetts, and attended Harvard before becoming a volunteer ambulance driver in the First World War. He wrote a prose book about this experience, *The Enormous Room*, and began to publish books of poems in 1923. His typographical innovations tended to conceal a diction which, much of the time, was traditional and romantic. The bitter humor of his satires proved his best work in poetry. See also pages 427 and 481.

Poem, or Beauty Hurts Mr. Vinal

take it from me kiddo
believe me
my country, 'tis of

you, land of the Cluett
Shirt Boston Garter and Spearmint
Girl With The Wrigley Eyes(of you
land of the Arrow Ide
and Earl &
Wilson
10   Collars) of you i
sing:land of Abraham Lincoln and Lydia E. Pinkham,
land above all of Just Add Hot Water And Serve—
from every B.V.D.

let freedom ring

amen. i do however protest, anent the un
-spontaneous and otherwise scented merde which
greets one (Everywhere Why) as divine poesy per
that and this radically defunct periodical. i would
suggest that certain ideas gestures
20   rhymes, like Gillette Razor Blades
having been used and reused
to the mystical moment of dullness emphatically are
Not To Be Resharpened.(Case in point

if we are to believe these gently O sweetly
melancholy trillers amid the thrillers
these crepuscular violinists among my and your
skyscrapers—Helen & Cleopatra were Just Too Lovely,
The Snail's On The Thorn enter Morn and God's
In His andsoforth

30   do you get me?)according
to such supposedly indigenous
throstles Art is O World O Life
a formula:example, Turn Your Shirttails Into
Drawers and If It Isn't An Eastman It Isn't A
Kodak therefore my friends let
us now sing each and all fortissimo A-
mer
i

ca, I
40 love,
You. And there're a
hun-dred-mil-lion-oth-ers, like
all of you successfully if
delicately gelded(or spaded)
gentlemen(and ladies)—pretty

littleliverpill-
hearted-Nujolneeding-There's-A-Reason
americans(who tensetendoned and with
upward vacant eyes, painfully
50 perpetually crouched, quivering, upon the
sternly allotted sandpile
—how silently
emit a tiny violetflavored nuisance:Odor?

ono.
comes out like a ribbon lies flat on the brush

next to of course god america i

"next to of course god america i
love you land of the pilgrims' and so forth oh
say can you see by the dawn's early my
country 'tis of centuries come and go
and are no more what of it we should worry
in every language even deafanddumb
thy sons acclaim your glorious name by gorry
by jingo by gee by gosh by gum
why talk of beauty what could be more beaut-
10 iful than these heroic happy dead
who rushed like lions to the roaring slaughter
they did not stop to think they died instead
then shall the voices of liberty be mute?"

He spoke. And drank rapidly a glass of water

Charles Reznikoff

Charles Reznikoff (1894–1975), a leading Objectivist poet, was born in New York City, where he lived most of his life. He wrote poems about the people he observed in the place where he lived. He also wrote some excellent poems out of his reading about American labor history, about the holocaust, and about biblical subjects. See also page 438.

A Deserter

Their new landlord was a handsome man. On his rounds to collect rent she
    became friendly
Finally, she asked him in to have a cup of tea. After that he came often.

Once his mouth jerked, and turning, she saw her husband in the doorway.
She thought, One of the neighbors must have told him.
She smiled and opened her mouth to speak, but could say nothing.
Her husband stood looking at the floor. He turned and went away.

She lay awake all night waiting for him.
In the morning she went to his store. It was closed.
She sent for his brothers and told them he had not been home.
10   They went to the police. Hospitals and morgues were
        searched. For weeks they were called to identify drowned men.

His business had been prosperous; bank account and all were untouched. She
        and their baby girl were provided for.
In a few years they heard of him. He was dead.
He had been making a poor living in a far off city. One day he stepped in front of
        a street-car and was killed.
She married again. Her daughter married and had children. She named none
        after her father.

Jean Toomer

Jean Toomer (1894–1967) wrote in *Cane* a combination of poetry and prose
that was an early contribution to the literature of the black American.

Reapers

Black reapers with the sound of steel on stones
Are sharpening scythes. I see them place the hones
In their hip-pockets as a thing that's done,
And start their silent swinging, one by one.
Black horses drive a mower through the weeds,
And there, a field rat, startled, squealing bleeds,
His belly close to ground. I see the blade,
Blood-stained, continue cutting weeds and shade.

Robert Graves

Robert Graves (1895–   ) fought in the First World War directly upon
graduation from English public school. He was one of the survivors, and later
wrote, in his autobiographical *Good-Bye to All That,* one of the great accounts of
that war. He has written many novels, including *I, Claudius,* and collections
of essays and humor, but he has been first and foremost a poet throughout a
long and prolific career. His mythic system, concerned with the muse of poetry,
was described in *The White Goddess,* and he has remained faithful to his Muse
through many poems, revised many times, in the many volumes of his *Collected
Poems.*

In Broken Images

He is quick, thinking in clear images;
I am slow, thinking in broken images.

He becomes dull, trusting to his clear images;
I become sharp, mistrusting my broken images.

Trusting his images, he assumes their relevance;
Mistrusting my images, I question their relevance.

Assuming their relevance, he assumes the fact;
Questioning their relevance, I question the fact.

When the fact fails him, he questions his senses;
10   When the fact fails me, I approve my senses.

He continues quick and dull in his clear images;
I continue slow and sharp in my broken images.

He in a new confusion of his understanding;
I in a new understanding of my confusion.

To Juan at the Winter Solstice

There is one story and one story only
That will prove worth your telling,
Whether as learned bard or gifted child;
To it all lines or lesser gauds belong
That startle with their shining
Such common stories as they stray into.

Is it of trees you tell, their months and virtues,
Or strange beasts that beset you,
Of birds that croak at you the Triple will?
10   Or of the Zodiac and how slow it turns
Below the Boreal Crown,
Prison of all true kings that ever reigned?

Water to water, ark again to ark,
From woman back to woman:
So each new victim treads unfalteringly
The never altered circuit of his fate,
Bringing twelve peers as witness
Both to his starry rise and starry fall.

Or is it of the Virgin's silver beauty,
20   All fish below the thighs?
She in her left hand bears a leafy quince;
When with her right she crooks a finger, smiling,
How may the King hold back?
Royally then he barters life for love.

Or of the undying snake from chaos hatched,
Whose coils contain the ocean,
Into whose chops with naked sword he springs,
Then in black water, tangled by the reeds,
Battles three days and nights,
30   To be spewed up beside her scalloped shore?

Much snow is falling, winds roar hollowly,
The owl hoots from the elder,
Fear in your heart cries to the loving-cup:

Sorrow to sorrow as the sparks fly upward.
The log groans and confesses:
There is one story and one story only.

Dwell on her graciousness, dwell on her smiling,
Do not forget what flowers
The great boar trampled down in ivy time.
40   Her brow was creamy as the crested wave,
Her sea-grey eyes were wild
But nothing promised that is not performed.

Louise Bogan

Louise Bogan (1897–1970) was born in Maine and lived most of her life in New York City. She was an excellent critic, her letters and journals extraordinary— and her poems were few, spare, and perfect. See also page 439.

Cartography

As you lay in sleep
I saw the chart
Of artery and vein
Running from your heart,

Plain as the strength
Marked upon the leaf
Along the length,
Mortal and brief,

Of your gaunt hand.
10   I saw it clear:
The wiry brand
Of the life we bear

Mapped like the great
Rivers that rise
Beyond our fate
And distant from our eyes.

Hart Crane

Hart Crane (1899–1932) published his first book of poems, *White Buildings,* in 1926. *The Bridge* (1930), a long poem centering on the Brooklyn Bridge, was an attempt to provide a myth of America. Alcoholic and homosexual, prone to binges and fights, Crane lived a short and turbulent life, ended by suicide when he jumped from a ship taking him from Mexico back to New York in 1932.

from The Bridge
To Brooklyn Bridge

How many dawns, chill from his rippling rest
The seagull's wings shall dip and pivot him,
Shedding white rings of tumult, building high
Over the chained bay waters Liberty—

Then, with inviolate curve, forsake our eyes
As apparitional as sails that cross
Some page of figures to be filed away;
—Till elevators drop us from our day . . .

I think of cinemas, panoramic sleights
10   With multitudes bent toward some flashing scene
Never disclosed, but hastened to again,
Foretold to other eyes on the same screen;

And Thee, across the harbor, silver-paced
As though the sun took step of thee, yet left
Some motion ever unspent in thy stride,—
Implicitly thy freedom staying thee!

Out of some subway scuttle, cell or loft
A bedlamite speeds to thy parapets,
Tilting there momently, shrill shirt ballooning,
20   A jest falls from the speechless caravan.

Down Wall, from girder into street noon leaks,
A rip-tooth of the sky's acetylene;
All afternoon the cloud-flown derricks turn . . .
Thy cables breathe the North Atlantic still.

And obscure as that heaven of the Jews,
Thy guerdon . . . Accolade thou dost bestow
Of anonymity time cannot raise:
Vibrant reprieve and pardon thou dost show.

O harp and altar, of the fury fused,
30   (How could mere toil align thy choiring strings!)
Terrific threshold of the prophet's pledge,
Prayer of pariah, and the lover's cry,—

Again the traffic lights that skim thy swift
Unfractioned idiom, immaculate sigh of stars,
Beading thy path—condense eternity:
And we have seen night lifted in thine arms.

Under thy shadow by the piers I waited;
Only in darkness is thy shadow clear.
The City's fiery parcels all undone,
40   Already snow submerges an iron year . . .

O Sleepless as the river under thee,
Vaulting the sea, the prairies' dreaming sod,
Unto us lowliest sometime sweep, descend
And of the curveship lend a myth to God.

from Voyages

II

And yet this great wink of eternity,
Of rimless floods, unfettered leewardings,

Samite sheeted and processioned where
Her undinal vast belly moonward bends,
Laughing the wrapt inflections of our love;

Take this Sea, whose diapason knells
On scrolls of silver snowy sentences,
The sceptred terror of whose sessions rends
As her demeanors motion well or ill,
10   All but the pieties of lovers' hands.

And onward, as bells off San Salvador
Salute the crocus lustres of the stars,
In these poinsettia meadows of her tides,—
Adagios of islands, O my Prodigal,
Complete the dark confessions her veins spell.

Mark how her turning shoulders wind the hours,
And hasten while her penniless rich palms
Pass superscription of bent foam and wave,—
Hasten, while they are true,—sleep, death, desire,
20   Close round one instant in one floating flower.

Bind us in time, O Seasons clear, and awe.
O minstrel galleons of Carib fire,
Bequeath us to no earthly shore until
Is answered in the vortex of our grave
The seal's wide spindrift gaze toward paradise.

Robert Francis

Robert Francis (1901–   ) has lived most of his life in Massachusetts, mostly
in a house called Fort Juniper in the countryside outside Amherst. He has
written an autobiography, some fiction, and some satirical prose. A poet of
reticence and quiet, he has lived without much attention from critics and
prizegivers, writing his finished poems one at a time. See also page 404.

Three Woodchoppers

Three woodchoppers walk up the road.
Day after day it is the same.
The short man always takes the lead
Limping like one a trifle lame.

And number two leans as he goes
And number three walks very straight.
I do not time them but I know
They're never early, never late.

So I have seen them for a week,
10   Have seen them but have heard no sound.
I never saw one turn to speak.
I never saw one look around.

Out of a window to the south
I watch them come against the light.
I cross the room and to the north
I watch till they are out of sight.

Langston Hughes

Langston Hughes (1902–1967) was leader of the Harlem renaissance of black American literature and often used folk sources in his poetry, especially the forms, diction, and rhythm of blues. He also wrote fiction, essays, and drama.

Hope

Sometimes when I'm lonely,
Don't know why,
Keep thinkin' I won't be lonely
By and by.

Bad Luck Card

Cause you don't love me
Is awful, awful hard.
Gypsy done showed me
My bad luck card.

There ain't no good left
In this world for me.
Gypsy done tole me—
Unlucky as can be.

I don't know what
10   Po' weary me can do.
Gypsy says I'd kill my self
If I was you.

Homecoming

I went back in the alley
And I opened up my door.
All her clothes was gone:
She wasn't home no more.

I pulled back the covers,
I made down the bed.
A *whole* lot of room
Was the only thing I had.

Richard Eberhart

Richard Eberhart (1904–   ) attended Dartmouth College in New Hampshire and went from there to Cambridge University in England, where he first published. He taught at a preparatory school, served in the Navy (some of his poems of the Second World War are deservedly famous), and for many years taught at Dartmouth.

The Groundhog

In June, amid the golden fields,
I saw a groundhog lying dead.
Dead lay he; my senses shook,
And mind outshot our naked frailty.
There lowly in the vigorous summer
His form began its senseless change,
And made my senses waver dim
Seeing nature ferocious in him.
Inspecting close his maggots' might
10   And seething cauldron of his being,
Half with loathing, half with a strange love,
I poked him with an angry stick.
The fever arose, became a flame
And Vigour circumscribed the skies,
Immense energy in the sun,
And through my frame a sunless trembling.
My stick had done nor good nor harm.
Then stood I silent in the day
Watching the object, as before;
20   And kept my reverence for knowledge
Trying for control, to be still,
To quell the passion of the blood;
Until I had bent down on my knees
Praying for joy in the sight of decay.
And so I left; and I returned
In Autumn strict of eye, to see
The sap gone out of the groundhog,
But the bony sodden hulk remained.
But the year had lost its meaning,
30   And in intellectual chains
I lost both love and loathing,
Mured up in the wall of wisdom.
Another summer took the fields again
Massive and burning, full of life,
But when I chanced upon the spot
There was only a little hair left,
And bones bleaching in the sunlight
Beautiful as architecture;
I watched them like a geometer,

40   And cut a walking stick from a birch.
It has been three years, now.
There is no sign of the groundhog.
I stood there in the whirling summer,
My hand capped a withered heart,
And thought of China and of Greece,
Of Alexander in his tent;
Of Montaigne in his tower,
Of Saint Theresa in her wild lament.

Louis Zukovsky

Louis Zukovsky (1904–   ) is one of the founders of Objectivism, a school of
poets that declared the poem itself an object, and natural objects the material
of poetry. He began as a follower of Ezra Pound, published widely in the 1930s,
and then survived in obscurity until a group of younger poets, following a
similar esthetic, rediscovered him in the 1960s.

"In Arizona"

In Arizona
         (how many years in the mountains)
The small stumped bark of a tree
Looks up
         in the shape of an adored pup

The indians do not approach it
The round indian tents
                remain where they are
The tanned whites
10   are never seen by it
And one can imagine its imploring eyes

The skies
         it seems to look up to
                blue
The same sun that warms the desert
Warms what one
         can imagine to be its ears.

Kenneth Rexroth

Kenneth Rexroth (1905–   ) was born in Indiana and has lived for many years
in San Francisco, where he was an elder figure behind the Beat Generation.
Anarchist in politics, broad in learning, he has published essays and
translations as well as original poems. See also page 440.

The Signature of All Things

My head and shoulders, and my book
In the cool shade, and my body
Stretched bathing in the sun, I lie

Reading beside the waterfall—
Boehme's "Signature of all Things."[1]
Through the deep July day the leaves
Of the laurel, all the colors
Of gold, spin down through the moving
Deep laurel shade all day. They float
10   On the mirrored sky and forest
For a while, and then, still slowly
Spinning, sink through the crystal deep
Of the pool to its leaf gold floor.
The saint saw the world as streaming
In the electrolysis of love.
I put him by and gaze through shade
Folded into shade of slender
Laurel trunks and leaves filled with sun.
The wren broods in her moss domed nest.
20   A newt struggles with a white moth
Drowning in the pool. The hawks scream,
Playing together on the ceiling
Of heaven. The long hours go by.
I think of those who have loved me,
Of all the mountains I have climbed,
Of all the seas I have swum in.
The evil of the world sinks.
My own sin and trouble fall away
Like Christian's bundle, and I watch
30   My forty summers fall like falling
Leaves and falling water held
Eternally in summer air.

———————————

Deer are stamping in the glades,
Under the full July moon.
There is a smell of dry grass
In the air, and more faintly,
The scent of a far off skunk.
As I stand at the wood's edge,
Watching the darkness, listening
40   To the stillness, a small owl
Comes to the branch above me,
On wings more still than my breath.
When I turn my light on him,
His eyes glow like drops of iron,
And he perks his head at me,
Like a curious kitten.
The meadow is bright as snow.
My dog prowls the grass, a dark

[1]*The Signature of All Things* is one of the major works of German religious mystic writer Jakob Boehme (1575–1624), whose thought influenced such later philosophers as Hegel and Schopenhauer.

Blur in the blur of brightness.
50   I walk to the oak grove where
The Indian village was once.
There, in blotched and cobwebbed light
And dark, dim in the blue haze,
Are twenty Holstein heifers,
Black and white, all lying down,
Quietly together, under
The huge trees rooted in the graves.

When I dragged the rotten log
From the bottom of the pool,
60   It seemed heavy as stone.
I let it lie in the sun
For a month; and then chopped it
Into sections, and split them
For kindling, and spread them out
To dry some more. Late that night,
After reading for hours,
While moths rattled at the lamp—
The saints and the philosophers
On the destiny of man—
70   I went out on my cabin porch,
And looked up through the black forest
At the swaying islands of stars.
Suddenly I saw at my feet,
Spread on the floor of night, ingots
Of quivering phosphorescence,
And all about were scattered chips
Of pale cold light that was alive.

William Empson

William Empson (1906–   ) is known for his criticism, especially *Seven Types of Ambiguity* (1930), and for his ambiguous poems. He taught in China for many years, now lives and teaches in Sheffield, England.

Villanelle

It is the pain, it is the pain, endures.
Your chemic beauty burned my muscles through.
Poise of my hands reminded me of yours.

What later purge from this deep toxin cures?
What kindness now could the old salve renew?
It is the pain, it is the pain, endures.

The infection slept (custom or change inures)
And when pain's secondary phase was due
Poise of my hands reminded me of yours.

10 How safe I felt, whom memory assures,
Rich that your grace safely by heart I knew.
It is the pain, it is the pain, endures.

My stare drank deep beauty that still allures.
My heart pumps yet the poison draught of you.
Poise of my hands reminded me of yours.

You are still kind whom the same shape immures.
Kind and beyond adieu. We miss our cue.
It is the pain, it is the pain, endures.
Poise of my hands reminded me of yours.

W. H. Auden

Wystan Hugh Auden (1907–1973) began to publish at the end of the 1920s
and in the next decade became the spokesman of a generation. Marxist,
psychological, he wrote a poetry of ideas; then his ideas changed. Just before
the Second World War he emigrated to America and lived in New York for most
of the remainder of his life, becoming an Anglo-Catholic and altering his old
political concepts.

Musée des Beaux Arts[1]

About suffering they were never wrong,
The Old Masters: how well they understood
Its human position; how it takes place
While someone else is eating or opening a window or just walking dully along;
How, when the aged are reverently, passionately waiting
For the miraculous birth, there always must be
Children who did not specially want it to happen, skating
On a pond at the edge of the wood:
They never forgot
10 That even the dreadful martyrdom must run its course
Anyhow in a corner, some untidy spot
Where the dogs go on with their doggy life and the torturer's horse
Scratches its innocent behind on a tree.

In Brueghel's *Icarus*,[2] for instance: how everything turns away
Quite leisurely from the disaster; the ploughman may
Have heard the splash, the forsaken cry,
But for him it was not an important failure; the sun shone
As it had to on the white legs disappearing into the green
Water; and the expensive delicate ship that must have seen
20 Something amazing, a boy falling out of the sky,
Had somewhere to get to and sailed calmly on.

---

[1]Museum of Fine Arts   [2]Pieter Brueghel the Elder (1520?–1569) was a major sixteenth-century
Flemish painter. His *The Fall of Icarus,* to which Auden alludes here, is in the Musée des Beaux
Arts in Brussels.

In Memory of W. B. Yeats

(d. Jan. 1939)

1

He disappeared in the dead of winter:
The brooks were frozen, the airports almost deserted,
And snow disfigured the public statues;
The mercury sank in the mouth of the dying day.
O all the instruments agree
The day of his death was a dark cold day.

Far from his illness
The wolves ran on through the evergreen forests,
The peasant river was untempted by the fashionable quays;
10   By mourning tongues
The death of the poet was kept from his poems.

But for him it was his last afternoon as himself,
An afternoon of nurses and rumors;
The provinces of his body revolted,
The squares of his mind were empty,
Silence invaded the suburbs,
The current of his feeling failed: he became his admirers.

Now he is scattered among a hundred cities
And wholly given over to unfamiliar affections;
20   To find his happiness in another kind of wood
And be punished under a foreign code of conscience.
The words of a dead man
Are modified in the guts of the living.

But in the importance and noise of tomorrow
When the brokers are roaring like beasts on the floor of the Bourse,
And the poor have the sufferings to which they are fairly accustomed,
And each in the cell of himself is almost convinced of his freedom;
A few thousand will think of this day
As one thinks of a day when one did something slightly unusual.

30   O all the instruments agree
The day of his death was a dark cold day.

2

You were silly like us: your gift survived it all;
The parish of rich women, physical decay,
Yourself; mad Ireland hurt you into poetry.
Now Ireland has her madness and her weather still,
For poetry makes nothing happen: it survives
In the valley of its saying where executives
Would never want to tamper; it flows south
From ranches of isolation and the busy griefs,

40   Raw towns that we believe and die in; it survives,
      A way of happening, a mouth.

      3

      Earth, receive an honored guest;
      William Yeats is laid to rest:
      Let the Irish vessel lie
      Emptied of its poetry.

      Time that is intolerant
      Of the brave and innocent,
      And indifferent in a week
      To a beautiful physique,

50   Worships language and forgives
      Everyone by whom it lives;
      Pardons cowardice, conceit,
      Lays its honors at their feet.

      Time that with this strange excuse
      Pardoned Kipling[1] and his views,
      And will pardon Paul Claudel,[2]
      Pardons him for writing well.

      In the nightmare of the dark
      All the dogs of Europe bark,
60   And the living nations wait,
      Each sequestered in its hate;

      Intellectual disgrace
      Stares from every human face,
      And the seas of pity lie
      Locked and frozen in each eye.

      Follow, poet, follow right
      To the bottom of the night,
      With your unconstraining voice
      Still persuade us to rejoice;

70   With the farming of a verse
      Make a vineyard of the curse,
      Sing of human unsuccess
      In a rapture of distress;

      In the deserts of the heart
      Let the healing fountain start,
      In the prison of his days
      Teach the free man how to praise.

[1]Rudyard Kipling (1865–1936), British writer born in Bombay and author of the *Jungle Books, Kim,* novels, short stories, and many poems, wrote much about the British Empire.   [2]Paul Claudel (1868–1955), French dramatist, poet, and diplomat, produced works that were highly mystical and often symbolist.

Louis MacNeice

Louis MacNeice (1907–1963) was an English poet of the 1930s associated with W. H. Auden, who collaborated with him on *Letters from Iceland*. Born in Ireland, he lived most of his life in London, where he was a producer for the BBC.

The Sunlight on the Garden

The sunlight on the garden
Hardens and grows cold,
We cannot cage the minute
Within its nets of gold,
When all is told
We cannot beg for pardon.

Our freedom as free lances
Advances towards its end;
The earth compels, upon it
10   Sonnets and birds descend;
And soon, my friend,
We shall have no time for dances.

The sky was good for flying
Defying the church bells
And every evil iron
Siren and what it tells:
The earth compels,
We are dying, Egypt, dying

And not expecting pardon,
20   Hardened in heart anew,
But glad to have sat under
Thunder and rain with you,
And grateful too
For sunlight on the garden.

Theodore Roethke (1908–1963)

See pages 520–534.

Stephen Spender

Stephen Spender (1909–   ) is the survivor of the 1930s group of English poets. He met Auden at Oxford and was influenced by him. Like Auden, he sympathized with the Loyalist side in Spain, which he visited during the Spanish Civil War. Unlike Auden, Spender remained largely in England, and made fewer poems as time passed, writing essays and representing a liberal literary consensus. He edited *Encounter* from 1953 to 1965.

What I Expected, Was

What I expected, was
Thunder, fighting,
Long struggles with men
And climbing.

After continual straining
I should grow strong;
Then the rocks would shake,
And I rest long.

10   What I had not foreseen
Was the gradual day
Weakening the will
Leaking the brightness away,
The lack of good to touch,
The fading of body and soul
—Smoke before wind,
Corrupt, unsubstantial.

The wearing of Time,
And the watching of cripples pass
With limbs shaped like questions
20   In their odd twist,
The pulverous grief
Melting the bones with pity,
The sick falling from earth—
These, I could not foresee.

Expecting always
Some brightness to hold in trust,
Some final innocence
Exempt from dust,
That, hanging solid,
30   Would dangle through all,
Like the created poem,
Or faceted crystal.

Charles Olson

Charles Olson (1910–1970) was highly influential as poet and literary thinker.
His first publication was critical, a book about *Moby-Dick* called *Call Me
Ishmael*. He wrote an essay on "Projective Verse" which may be regarded as the
manifesto of the Black Mountain School of American poets, loosely derived
from Pound and from Zukovsky's Objectivism. His long series of *Maximus
Poems* is his major poetic work.

Maximus, to Gloucester, Sunday, July 19

and they stopped before that bad sculpture of a fisherman

—"as if one were to talk to a man's house,
knowing not what gods or heroes are"—

not knowing what a fisherman is
instead of going straight to the Bridge
and doing no more than—saying no more than—
in the Charybdises of the
Cut waters the flowers tear off
the wreathes

10 the flowers
turn
the character of the sea The sea jumps
the fate of the flower The drowned men are undrowned
in the eddies
      of the eyes
      of the flowers
      opening
      the sea's eyes

The disaster
20 is undone
What was received as alien
—the flower
on the water, that a man drowns
that he dies in water as he dies on earth, the impossible
     that this gross fact can return to us
        in this upset
on a summer day
of a particular tide

that the sensation is true,
that the transformations of fire are, first of all, sea—
30   "as gold for wares wares for gold"

    Let them be told who stopped first
    by a bronze idol

    A fisherman is not a successful man,
    he is not a famous man he is not a man
    of power, these are the damned by God

whose surface bubbles
with these gimlets
which screw-in like

potholes, caustic
40 caked earth of painted
pools, Yellowstone

Park of holes
is death the diseased
presence on us, the spilling lesion

of the brilliance
it is to be alive: to walk onto it,
as Jim Bridger the first into it,

it is more true a scabious
field than it is a pretty
50 meadow

    When a man's coffin is the sea
    the whole of creation shall come to his funeral,

it turns out; the globe
is below, all lapis

and its blue surface golded
by what happened

this afternoon: there are eyes
in this water

the flowers
60   from the shore,

awakened
the sea

      Men are so sure they know very many things,
      they don't even know night and day are one

      A fisherman works without reference to
      that difference. It is possible he also

      by lying there when he does lie, jowl
      to the sea, has another advantage: it is said,

'You rectify what can be rectified,' and when a man's heart
70   cannot see this, the door of his divine intelligence is shut

      let you who paraded to the Cut today
      to hold memorial services to all fishermen
      who have been lost at sea in a year
      when for the first time not one life was lost

            radar sonar radio telephone good engines
            bed-check seaplanes goodness over and under us

no difference
when men come back

Elizabeth Bishop

Elizabeth Bishop (1911–1979) was born in Massachusetts, attended Vassar, and lived for many years in Brazil. Critics noticed the influence of Marianne Moore on her first book of poems, *North and South* (1946). She won a Pulitzer Prize in 1956 for *Poems* and later published *Questions of Travel* (1965), *Collected Poems* (1969), and *Geography III* (1977). See also page 442.

The Fish

I caught a tremendous fish
and held him beside the boat
half out of water, with my hook
fast in a corner of his mouth.
He didn't fight.
He hadn't fought at all.
He hung a grunting weight,

battered and venerable
and homely. Here and there
10   his brown skin hung in strips
like ancient wallpaper,
and its pattern of darker brown
was like wallpaper:
shapes like full-blown roses
stained and lost through age.
He was speckled with barnacles,
fine rosettes of lime,
and infested
with tiny white sea-lice,
20   and underneath two or three
rags of green weed hung down.
While his gills were breathing in
the terrible oxygen
—the frightening gills,
fresh and crisp with blood,
that can cut so badly—
I thought of the coarse white flesh
packed in like feathers,
the big bones and the little bones,
30   the dramatic reds and blacks
of his shiny entrails,
and the pink swim-bladder
like a big peony.
I looked into his eyes
which were far larger than mine
but shallower, and yellowed,
the irises backed and packed
with tarnished tinfoil
seen through the lenses
40   of old scratched isinglass.
They shifted a little, but not
to return my stare.
—It was more like the tipping
of an object toward the light.
I admired his sullen face,
the mechanism of his jaw,
and then I saw
that from his lower lip
—if you could call it a lip—
50   grim, wet, and weaponlike,
hung five old pieces of fish-line,
or four and a wire leader
with the swivel still attached,
with all their five big hooks
grown firmly in his mouth.
A green line, frayed at the end
where he broke it, two heavier lines,

and a fine black thread
still crimped from the strain and snap
60   when it broke and he got away.
Like medals with their ribbons
frayed and wavering,
a five-haired beard of wisdom
trailing from his aching jaw.
I stared and stared
and victory filled up
the little rented boat,
from the pool of bilge
where oil had spread a rainbow
70   around the rusted engine
to the bailer rusted orange,
the sun-cracked thwarts,
the oarlocks on their strings,
the gunnels—until everything
was rainbow, rainbow, rainbow!
And I let the fish go.

Robert Hayden

Robert Hayden (1913–1980) grew up in Detroit, where he attended Wayne
State University, later studying at the University of Michigan. He taught at Fisk
in Nashville for many years and then returned to teach at Michigan. In 1976
he went to Washington as Poetry Consultant at the Library of Congress. His
poems explored areas of the black American experience, and in a time of
militancy Hayden avoided militancy. He became an adherent of the Bahai faith
when he was a young man and remained true to it.

Middle Passage

I

Jesús, Estrella, Esperanza, Mercy:

    Sails flashing to the wind like weapons,
    sharks following the moans the fever and the dying;
    horror the corposant and compass rose.

Middle Passage:
    voyage through death
        to life upon these shores.

    "10 April 1800—
    Blacks rebellious. Crew uneasy. Our linguist says
10   their moaning is a prayer for death,
    ours and their own. Some try to starve themselves.
    Lost three this morning leaped with crazy laughter
    to the waiting sharks, sang as they went under."

Desire, Adventure, Tartar, Ann:

    Standing to America, bringing home
    black gold, black ivory, black seed.

Deep in the festering hold thy father lies,
of his bones New England pews are made,
those are altar lights that were his eyes.

20 Jesus   Saviour   Pilot   Me
    Over   Life's   Tempestuous   Sea

We pray that Thou wilt grant, O Lord,
safe passage to our vessels bringing
heathen souls unto Thy chastening.

Jesus   Saviour
          "8 bells. I cannot sleep, for I am sick
          with fear, but writing eases fear a little
          since still my eyes can see these words take shape
          upon the page & so I write, as one
30   would turn to exorcism. 4 days scudding,
          but now the sea is calm again. Misfortune
          follows in our wake like sharks (our grinning
          tutelary gods). Which one of us
          has killed an albatross? A plague among
          our blacks—Ophthalmia: blindness—& we
          have jettisoned the blind to no avail.
          It spreads, the terrifying sickness spreads.
          Its claws have scratched sight from the Capt.'s eyes
          & there is blindness in the fo'c'sle
40   & we must sail 3 weeks before we come
          to port."

          What port awaits us, Davy Jones'
          or home? I've heard of slavers drifting, drifting,
          playthings of wind and storm and chance, their crews
          gone blind, the jungle hatred
          crawling up on deck.

    Thou   Who   Walked   On   Galilee

          "Deponent further sayeth *The Bella J*
          left the Guinea Coast
50   with cargo of five hundred blacks and odd
          for the barracoons of Florida:

          "That there was hardly room 'tween-decks for half
          the sweltering cattle stowed spoon-fashion there;
          that some went mad of thirst and tore their flesh
          and sucked the blood:

          "That Crew and Captain lusted with the comeliest
          of the savage girls kept naked in the cabins;
          that there was one they called The Guinea Rose
          and they cast lots and fought to lie with her:

60   "That when the Bo's'n piped all hands, the flames
          spreading from starboard already were beyond

control, the negroes howling and their chains
entangled with the flames:

"That the burning blacks could not be reached,
that the Crew abandoned ship,
leaving their shrieking negresses behind,
that the Captain perished drunken with the wenches:

"Further Deponent sayeth not."

Pilot   Oh   Pilot   Me

II

70   Aye, lad, and I have seen those factories,
Gambia, Rio Pongo, Calabar;
have watched the artful mongos baiting traps
of war wherein the victor and the vanquished

Were caught as prizes for our barracoons.
Have seen the nigger kings whose vanity
and greed turned wild black hides of Fellatah,
Mandingo, Ibo, Kru to gold for us.

And there was one—King Anthracite we named him—
fetish face beneath French parasols
80   of brass and orange velvet, impudent mouth
whose cups were carven skulls of enemies:

He'd honor us with drum and feast and conjo
and palm-oil-glistening wenches deft in love,
and for tin crowns that shone with paste,
red calico and German-silver trinkets

Would have the drums talk war and send
his warriors to burn the sleeping villages
and kill the sick and old and lead the young
in coffles to our factories.

90   Twenty years a trader, twenty years,
for there was wealth aplenty to be harvested
from those black fields, and I'd be trading still
but for the fevers melting down my bones.

III

Shuttles in the rocking loom of history,
the dark ships move, the dark ships move,
their bright ironical names
like jests of kindness on a murderer's mouth;
plough through thrashing glister toward
fata morgana's lucent melting shore,
100   weave toward New World littorals that are
mirage and myth and actual shore.

Voyage through death,

voyage whose chartings are unlove.

A charnel stench, effluvium of living death
spreads outward from the hold,
where the living and the dead, the horribly dying,
lie interlocked, lie foul with blood and excrement.

Deep in the festering hold thy father lies,
the corpse of mercy rots with him,
110   *rats eat love's rotten gelid eyes.*

But, oh, the living look at you
with human eyes whose suffering accuses you,
whose hatred reaches through the swill of dark
to strike you like a leper's claw.

You cannot stare that hatred down
or chain the fear that stalks the watches
and breathes on you its fetid scorching breath;
cannot kill the deep immortal human wish,
the timeless will.

120   "But for the storm that flung up barriers
of wind and wave, *The Amistad*, señores,
would have reached the port of Príncipe in two,
three days at most; but for the storm we should
have been prepared for what befell.
Swift as the puma's leap it came. There was
that interval of moonless calm filled only
with the water's and the rigging's usual sounds,
then sudden movement, blows and snarling cries
and they had fallen on us with machete
130   and marlinspike. It was as though the very
air, the night itself were striking us.
Exhausted by the rigors of the storm,
we were no match for them. Our men went down
before the murderous Africans. Our loyal
Celestino ran from below with gun
and lantern and I saw, before the cane-
knife's wounding flash, Cinquez,
that surly brute who calls himself a prince,
directing, urging on the ghastly work.
140   He hacked the poor mulatto down, and then
he turned on me. The decks were slippery
when daylight finally came. It sickens me
to think of what I saw, of how these apes
threw overboard the butchered bodies of
our men, true Christians all, like so much jetsam.
Enough, enough. The rest is quickly told:
Cinquez was forced to spare the two of us
you see to steer the ship to Africa,

150 and we like phantoms doomed to rove the sea
voyaged east by day and west by night,
deceiving them, hoping for rescue,
prisoners on our own vessel, till
at length we drifted to the shores of this
your land, America, where we were freed
from our unspeakable misery. Now we
demand, good sirs, the extradition of
Cinquez and his accomplices to La
Havana. And it distresses us to know
there are so many here who seem inclined
160 to justify the mutiny of these blacks.
We find it paradoxical indeed
that you whose wealth, whose tree of liberty
are rooted in the labor of your slaves
should suffer the august John Quincy Adams
to speak with so much passion of the right
of chattel slaves to kill their lawful masters
and with his Roman rhetoric weave a hero's
garland for Cinquez. I tell you that
we are determined to return to Cuba
170 with our slaves and there see justice done. Cinquez—
or let us say 'the Prince'—Cinquez shall die."

The deep immortal human wish,
the timeless will:

Cinquez its deathless primaveral image,
life that transfigures many lives.

Voyage through death
to life upon these shores.

Delmore Schwartz

Delmore Schwartz (1913–1966) was a member of a generation of American poets unusually talented and unusually cursed in their private lives. Schwartz had periods of madness, and when he died in a New York hotel in 1966 he was alone and friendless; his body went unclaimed for three days. In early years his poetry carried great promise, and he published as well some exemplary fiction and criticism.

In the Naked Bed, in Plato's Cave

In the naked bed, in Plato's cave,
Reflected headlights slowly slid the wall,
Carpenters hammered under the shaded window,
Wind troubled the window curtains all night long,
A fleet of trucks strained uphill, grinding,
Their freights covered, as usual.
The ceiling lightened again, the slanting diagram

Slid slowly forth.
                    Hearing the milkman's chop,
10   His striving up the stair, the bottle's chink,
I rose from bed, lit a cigarette,
And walked to the window. The stony street
Displayed the stillness in which buildings stand,
The street-lamp's vigil and the horse's patience.
The winter sky's pure capital
Turned me back to bed with exhausted eyes.

Strangeness grew in the motionless air. The loose
Film grayed. Shaking wagons, hooves' waterfalls,
Sounded far off, increasing, louder and nearer.
20   A car coughed, starting. Morning, softly
Melting the air, lifted the half-covered chair
From underseas, kindled the looking-glass,
Distinguished the dresser and the white wall.
The bird called tentatively, whistled, called,
Bubbled and whistled, so! Perplexed, still wet
With sleep, affectionate, hungry and cold. So, so,
O son of man, the ignorant night, the travail
Of early morning, the mystery of beginning
Again and again,
                    while History is unforgiven.

John Berryman

John Berryman (1914–1972) wrote with great ambition and intensity (fiction and essays as well as poetry) and is best known for *Homage to Mistress Bradstreet* (1954) and *The Dream Songs* (1969).

from The Dream Songs

14

Life, friends, is boring. We must not say so.
After all, the sky flashes, the great sea yearns,
we ourselves flash and yearn,
and moreover my mother told me as a boy
(repeatedly) 'Ever to confess you're bored
means you have no

Inner Resources.' I conclude now I have no
inner resources, because I am heavy bored.
Peoples bore me,
10   literature bores me, especially great literature,
Henry bores me, with his plights & gripes
as bad as achilles,

who loves people and valiant art, which bores me.
And the tranquil hills, & gin, look like a drag

and somehow a dog
has taken itself & its tail considerably away
into mountains or sea or sky, leaving
behind: me, wag.

16

Henry's pelt was put on sundry walls
20 where it did much resemble Henry and
them persons was delighted.
Especially his long & glowing tail
by all them was admired, and visitors.
They whistled: This is *it*!

Golden, whilst your frozen daiquiris
whir at midnight, gleams on you his fur
& silky & black.
Mission accomplished, pal.
My molten yellow & moonless bag,
30 drained, hangs at rest.

Collect in the cold depths barracuda. Ay,
In Sealdah Station some possessionless
children survive to die.
The Chinese communes hum. Two daiquiris
withdrew into a corner of the gorgeous room
and one told the other a lie.

312

I have moved to Dublin to have it out with you,
majestic Shade,[1] You whom I read so well
so many years ago,
40 did I read your lesson right? did I see through
your phases to the real? your heaven, your hell
did I enquire properly into?

For years then I forgot you, I put you down,
ingratitude is the necessary curse
of making things new:
I brought my family to see me through,
I brought my homage & my soft remorse,
I brought a book or two

only, including in the end your last
50 strange poems made under the shadow of death
Your high figures float
again across my mind and all your past
fills my walled garden with your honey breath
wherein I move, a mote.

---

[1]A reference to William Butler Yeats

David Ignatow

David Ignatow (1914–   ) was born in Brooklyn, New York, and worked for many years in business. Since the mid-1960s he has taught at numerous universities while continuing to publish books of poems including *Facing the Tree* and *Selected Poems*, edited by Robert Bly, both in 1975. Living most of his life in the environs of New York City, Ignatow is a poet of the city.

Rescue the Dead

Finally, to forgo love is to kiss a leaf,
is to let rain fall nakedly upon your head,
is to respect fire,
is to study man's eyes and his gestures
as he talks,
is to set bread upon the table
and a knife discreetly by,
is to pass through crowds
like a crowd of oneself.
10 Not to love is to live.

To love is to be led away
into a forest where the secret grave
is dug, singing, praising darkness
under the trees.

To live is to sign your name,
is to ignore the dead,
is to carry a wallet
and shake hands.

To love is to be a fish.
20 My boat wallows in the sea.
You who are free,
rescue the dead.

Randall Jarrell

Randall Jarrell (1914–1965) was born in Tennessee and studied at Vanderbilt. He taught at Kenyon College as a young man, along with John Crowe Ransom. Robert Lowell and Peter Taylor were students there, and from this concentration of literary men emerged much American literature. Jarrell served in the Second World War and wrote about it. In the last decades of his life he lived in North Carolina, where he taught, and he wrote criticism that was possibly better known during his lifetime than his poetry.

Eighth Air Force[1]

If, in an odd angle of the hutment,
A puppy laps the water from a can
Of flowers, and the drunk sergeant shaving

[1] In World War II, the U.S. Eighth Air Force bombed Germany and occupied Europe from bases in England.

660

Whistles *O Paradiso!*[2]—shall I say that man
Is not as men have said: a wolf to man?

The other murderers troop in yawning;
Three of them play Pitch, one sleeps, and one
Lies counting missions, lies there sweating
Till even his heart beats: One; One; One.
10   *O murderers!* . . . Still, this is how it's done:

This is war. . . . But since these play, before they die,
Like puppies with their puppy; since, a man,
I did as these have done, but did not die—
I will content the people as I can
And give up these to them: Behold the man![3]

I have suffered, in a dream, because of him,
Many things;[4] for this last saviour, man,
I have lied as I lie now. But what is lying?
Men wash their hands, in blood, as best they can:
20   I find no fault in this just man.

[2]An aria from Meyerbeer's *L'Africaine*   [3]John 19:4–5   [4]Matthew 27:19

William Stafford

William Stafford (1914–   ) was born in Kansas and has lived most of his life
in the Pacific Northwest. His *Poems New and Collected* appeared in 1977, only
fifteen years after his first collection, *Travelling Through the Dark*, won the
National Book Award. His poetry is quiet, reticent, reserved, compassionate,
and ultimately happy.

Travelling Through the Dark

Travelling through the dark I found a deer
dead on the edge of the Wilson River road.
It is usually best to roll them into the canyon:
that road is narrow; to swerve might make more dead.

By glow of the tail-light I stumbled back of the car
and stood by the heap, a doe, a recent killing;
she had stiffened already, almost cold.
I dragged her off; she was large in the belly.

My fingers touching her side brought me the reason—
10   her side was warm; her fawn lay there waiting,
alive, still, never to be born.
Beside that mountain road I hesitated.

The car aimed ahead its lowered parking lights;
under the hood purred the steady engine.
I stood in the glare of the warm exhaust turning red;
around our group I could hear the wilderness listen.

I thought hard for us all—my only swerving—,
then pushed her over the edge into the river.

Returned to Say

When I face north a lost Cree
on some new shore puts a moccasin down,
rock in the light and noon for seeing,
he in a hurry and I beside him.

It will be a long trip; he will be a new chief;
we have drunk new water from an unnamed stream;
under little dark trees he is to find a path
we both must travel because we have met.

Henceforth we gesture even by waiting;
10   there is a grain of sand on his knifeblade
so small he blows it and while his breathing
darkens the steel his eyes become set

And start a new vision: the rest of his life.
We will mean what he does. Back of this page
the path turns north. We are looking for a sign.
Our moccasins do not mark the ground.

Dylan Thomas

Dylan Thomas (1914–1953) grew up in Wales and wrote prose and poetry about his childhood. He began early to write excellent lyrical poetry, and published his first book when he was only nineteen. At least half of his *Collected Poems* was written or drafted before he was twenty-two. Continually in debt, alcoholic, he lived a life with less and less poetry in it. The sparse later work remained high in quality, like the play *Under Milk Wood*, finished just as he died at the age of thirty-nine.

This Bread I Break

This bread I break was once the oat,
This wine upon a foreign tree
Plunged in its fruit;
Man in the day or wind at night
Laid the crops low, broke the grape's joy.

Once in this wind the summer blood
Knocked in the flesh that decked the vine,
Once in this bread
The oat was merry in the wind;
10   Man broke the sun, pulled the wind down.

This flesh you break, this blood you let
Make desolation in the vein,
Were oat and grape
Born of the sensual root and sap;
My wine you drink, my bread you snap.

A Refusal to Mourn the Death, by Fire, of a Child in London

Never until the mankind making
Bird beast and flower
Fathering and all humbling darkness
Tells with silence the last light breaking
And the still hour
Is come of the sea tumbling in harness

And I must enter again the round
Zion of the water bead
And the synagogue of the ear of corn
10   Shall I let pray the shadow of a sound
Or sow my salt seed
In the least valley of sackcloth to mourn

The majesty and burning of the child's death.
I shall not murder
The mankind of her going with a grave truth
Nor blaspheme down the stations of the breath
With any further
Elegy of innocence and youth.

Deep with the first dead lies London's daughter,
20   Robed in the long friends,
The grains beyond age, the dark veins of her mother,
Secret by the unmourning water
Of the riding Thames.
After the first death, there is no other.

Fern Hill

Now as I was young and easy under the apple boughs
About the lilting house and happy as the grass was green,
  The night above the dingle starry,
   Time let me hail and climb
  Golden in the heydays of his eyes,
And honoured among wagons I was prince of the apple towns
And once below a time I lordly had the trees and leaves
   Trail with daisies and barley
  Down the rivers of the windfall light.

10   And as I was green and carefree, famous among the barns
About the happy yard and singing as the farm was home,
  In the sun that is young once only,
   Time let me play and be
  Golden in the mercy of his means,
And green and golden I was huntsman and herdsman, the calves
Sang to my horn, the foxes on the hills barked clear and cold,
   And the sabbath rang slowly
  In the pebbles of the holy streams.

All the sun long it was running, it was lovely, the hay
20   Fields high as the house, the tunes from the chimneys, it was air
            And playing, lovely and watery
                  And fire green as grass.
            And nightly under the simple stars
      As I rode to sleep the owls were bearing the farm away,
      All the moon long I heard, blessed among stables, the night-jars
            Flying with the ricks, and the horses
                  Flashing into the dark.

      And then to awake, and the farm, like a wanderer white
      With the dew, come back, the cock on his shoulder: it was all
30   Shining, it was Adam and maiden,
                  The sky gathered again
            And the sun grew round that very day.
      So it must have been after the birth of the simple light
      In the first, spinning place, the spellbound horses walking warm
            Out of the whinnying green stable
                  On to the fields of praise.

      And honoured among foxes and pheasants by the gay house
      Under the new made clouds and happy as the heart was long,
            In the sun born over and over,
40   I ran my heedless ways,
            My wishes raced through the house high hay
      And nothing I cared, at my sky blue trades, that time allows
      In all his tuneful turning so few and such morning songs
            Before the children green and golden
                  Follow him out of grace,

      Nothing I cared, in the lamb white days, that time would take me
      Up to the swallow thronged loft by the shadow of my hand,
            In the moon that is always rising,
                  Nor that riding to sleep
50   I should hear him fly with the high fields
      And wake to the farm forever fled from the childless land.
      Oh as I was young and easy in the mercy of his means,
            Time held me green and dying
            Though I sang in my chains like the sea.

Gwendolyn Brooks

Gwendolyn Brooks (1917–   ) is a leading black American poet, born in
Kansas, who began publishing with *A Street in Bronzeville* in 1945. *Annie Allen*,
published in 1949, received a Pulitzer Prize. Brooks took a new life from the
vitality of the black movement of the 1960s.

The Bean Eaters

They eat beans mostly, this old yellow pair.
Dinner is a casual affair.

Plain chipware on a plain and creaking wood,
Tin flatware.

Two who are Mostly Good.
Two who have lived their day,
But keep on putting on their clothes
And putting things away.

And remembering . . .
10   Remembering, with twinklings and twinges,
As they lean over the beans in their rented back room that is full of beads
   and receipts and dolls and cloths, tobacco crumbs, vases and fringes.

We Real Cool

   The Pool Players.
Seven at the Golden Shovel.

We real cool. We
Left school. We

Lurk late. We
Strike straight. We

Sing sin. We
Thin gin. We

Jazz June. We
Die soon.

Robert Lowell

Robert Lowell (1917–1977) was born in Massachusetts into the eminent
literary and academic family of the Lowells, related to the poets Amy and
James Russell Lowell and to a president of Harvard. After attending Harvard
for several terms, he transferred to Kenyon College in Ohio, where he studied
with John Crowe Ransom and made the acquaintance of Allen Tate and
Randall Jarrell. His first book, *Land of Unlikeness*, was published in a small
edition in 1944, followed by *Lord Weary's Castle* in 1947, which won the
Pulitzer Prize. With *Life Studies* in 1959 his work took an abrupt turn away
from the formal stanzas and couplets of his early poetry into the painful
confessional verse that came to characterize him. In his last years he wrote
with a prolixity he had lacked as a young man and perhaps with less success,
publishing nine volumes in the last twelve years of his life, before he died of a
heart attack at the age of sixty. See also page 453.

After the Surprising Conversions

September twenty-second, Sir: today
I answer. In the latter part of May,
Hard on our Lord's Ascension, it began
To be more sensible. A gentleman
Of more than common understanding, strict
In morals, pious in behavior, kicked

Against our goad. A man of some renown,
An useful, honored person in the town,
He came of melancholy parents; prone
10   To secret spells, for years they kept alone—
His uncle, I believe, was killed of it:
Good people, but of too much or little wit.
I preached one Sabbath on a text from Kings;
He showed concernment for his soul. Some things
In his experience were hopeful. He
Would sit and watch the wind knocking a tree
And praise this countryside our Lord has made.
Once when a poor man's heifer died, he laid
A shilling on the doorsill; though a thirst
20   For loving shook him like a snake, he durst
Not entertain much hope of his estate
In heaven. Once we saw him sitting late
Behind his attic window by a light
That guttered on his Bible; through that night
He meditated terror, and he seemed
Beyond advice or reason, for he dreamed
That he was called to trumpet Judgment Day
To Concord. In the latter part of May
He cut his throat. And though the coroner
30   Judged him delirious, soon a noisome stir
Palsied our village. At Jehovah's nod
Satan seemed more let loose amongst us: God
Abandoned us to Satan, and he pressed
Us hard, until we thought we could not rest
Till we had done with life. Content was gone.
All the good work was quashed. We were undone.
The breath of God had carried out a planned
And sensible withdrawal from this land;
The multitude, once unconcerned with doubt,
40   Once neither callous, curious nor devout,
Jumped at broad noon, as though some peddler groaned
At it in its familiar twang: "My friend,
Cut your own throat. Cut your own throat. Now! Now!"
September twenty-second, Sir, the bough
Cracks with the unpicked apples, and at dawn
The small-mouth bass breaks water, gorged with spawn.

Skunk Hour

(For Elizabeth Bishop)

Nautilus Island's hermit
heiress still lives through winter in her Spartan cottage;
her sheep still graze above the sea.
Her son's a bishop. Her farmer

is first selectman in our village;
she's in her dotage.

Thirsting for
the hierarchic privacy
of Queen Victoria's century,
10   she buys up all
the eyesores facing her shore,
and lets them fall.

The season's ill—
we've lost our summer millionaire,
who seemed to leap from an L. L. Bean[1]
catalogue. His nine-knot yawl
was auctioned off to lobstermen.
A red fox stain covers Blue Hill.

And now our fairy
20   decorator brightens his shop for fall;
his fishnet's filled with orange cork,
orange, his cobbler's bench and awl;
there is no money in his work,
he'd rather marry.

One dark night,
my Tudor Ford climbed the hill's skull;
I watched for love-cars. Lights turned down,
they lay together, hull to hull,
where the graveyard shelves on the town. . . .
30   My mind's not right.

A car radio bleats,
"Love, O careless Love. . . ." I hear
my ill-spirit sob in each blood cell,
as if my hand were at its throat. . . .
I myself am hell;
nobody's here—

only skunks, that search
in the moonlight for a bite to eat.
They march on their soles up Main Street:
40   white stripes, moonstruck eyes' red fire
under the chalk-dry and spar spire
of the Trinitarian Church.

I stand on top
of our back steps and breathe the rich air—
a mother skunk with her column of kittens swills the garbage pail.
She jabs her wedge-head in a cup
of sour cream, drops her ostrich tail,
and will not scare.

---

[1]A Maine store that specializes in outdoor gear and country clothing; its label is popular among
affluent city people who summer in the country.

For the Union Dead

"Relinquunt Omnia Servare Rem Publicam."[1]

The old South Boston Aquarium stands
in a Sahara of snow now. Its broken windows are boarded.
The bronze weathervane cod has lost half its scales.
The airy tanks are dry.

Once my nose crawled like a snail on the glass;
my hand tingled
to burst the bubbles
drifting from the noses of the cowed, compliant fish.

My hand draws back. I often sigh still
10   for the dark downward and vegetating kingdom
of the fish and reptile. One morning last March,
I pressed against the new barbed and galvanized

fence on the Boston Common. Behind their cage,
yellow dinosaur steamshovels were grunting
as they cropped up tons of mush and grass
to gouge their underworld garage.

Parking spaces luxuriate like civic
sandpiles in the heart of Boston.
A girdle of orange, Puritan-pumpkin colored girders
20   braces the tingling Statehouse,

shaking over the excavations, as it faces Colonel Shaw
and his bell-cheeked Negro infantry
on St. Gaudens'[2] shaking Civil War relief,
propped by a plank splint against the garage's earthquake.

Two months after marching through Boston,
half the regiment was dead;
at the dedication,
William James[3] could almost hear the bronze Negroes breathe.

Their monument sticks like a fishbone
30   in the city's throat.
Its Colonel is as lean
as a compass-needle.

He has an angry wrenlike vigilance,
a greyhound's gentle tautness;
he seems to wince at pleasure,
and suffocate for privacy.

[1]"They sacrifice everything to serve the republic."
[2]Sculptor Augustus Saint-Gaudens (1848–1907) made a bronze relief of Colonel Robert Shaw (1837–1863), who led a black regiment during the Civil War.
[3]William James (1842–1910), American psychologist and philosopher, professor at Harvard

He is out of bounds now. He rejoices in man's lovely,
peculiar power to choose life and die—
when he leads his black soldiers to death,
40   he cannot bend his back.

On a thousand small town New England greens,
the old white churches hold their air
of sparse, sincere rebellion; frayed flags
quilt the graveyards of the Grand Army of the Republic.

The stone statues of the abstract Union Soldier
grow slimmer and younger each year—
wasp-waisted, they doze over muskets
and muse through their sideburns . . .

Shaw's father wanted no monument
50   except the ditch,
where his son's body was thrown
and lost with his "niggers."

The ditch is nearer.
There are no statues for the last war here;
on Boylston Street, a commercial photograph
shows Hiroshima boiling

over a Mosler Safe, the "Rock of Ages"
that survived the blast. Space is nearer.
When I crouch to my television set,
60   the drained faces of Negro school-children rise like balloons.

Colonel Shaw
is riding on his bubble,
he waits
for the blessèd break.

The Aquarium is gone. Everywhere,
giant finned cars nose forward like fish;
a savage servility
slides by on grease.

Robert Duncan

Robert Duncan (1919–   ) born in Oakland, has been a San Francisco poet
for most of his life, associated with the Black Mountain group of poets. Erudite
and prolific, Duncan has been a source of energy for other poets, especially in
the Bay Area, in ideas and example.

Poetry, a Natural Thing

Neither our vices nor our virtues
further the poem. "They came up
    and died
just like they do every year
    on the rocks."

The poem
feeds upon thought, feeling, impulse,
    to breed   itself,
a spiritual urgency at the dark ladders leaping.

10   This beauty is an inner persistence
        toward the source
    striving against (within) down-rushet of the river,
        a call we heard and answer
    in the lateness of the world
        primordial bellowings
    from which the youngest world might spring,

    salmon not in the well where the
        hazelnut falls
    but at the falls battling, inarticulate,
20   blindly making it.

    This is one picture apt for the mind.

    A second: a moose painted by Stubbs,[1]
    where last year's extravagant antlers
        lie on the ground.
    The forlorn moosey-faced poem wears
        new antler-buds,
        the same,

    "a little heavy, a little contrived,"

    his only beauty to be
30   all moose.

[1]George Stubbs (1724–1806), an English artist, is best known for his animal paintings.

Howard Nemerov

Howard Nemerov (1920–   ) attended Harvard before serving in the Royal
Canadian Air Force and the United States Air Force in the Second World War.
He has taught at various American universities, currently at Washington
University in St. Louis. Over the years, he has written steadily, with
considerable skill, without drawing great attention. His *Collected Poems*
appeared in 1977.

Brainstorm

The house was shaken by a rising wind
That rattled window and door. He sat alone
In an upstairs room and heard these things: a blind
Ran up with a bang, a door slammed, a groan
Came from some hidden joist, and a leaky tap,
At any silence of the wind walked like
A blind man through the house. Timber and sap
Revolt, he thought, from washer, baulk and spike.
Bent to his book, continued unafraid

10   Until the crows came down from their loud flight
To walk along the rooftree overhead.
Their horny feet, so near but out of sight,
Scratched on the slate; when they were blown away
He heard their wings beat till they came again,
While the wind rose, and the house seemed to sway,
And window panes began to blind with rain.
The house was talking, not to him, he thought,
But to the crows; the crows were talking back
In their black voices. The secret might be out:
20   Houses are only trees stretched on the rack.
And once the crows knew, all nature would know.
Fur, leaf and feather would invade the form,
Nail rust with rain and shingle warp with snow,
Vine tear the wall, till any straw-borne storm
Could rip both roof and rooftree off and show
Naked to nature what they had kept warm.

He came to feel the crows walk on his head
As if he were the house, their crooked feet
Scratched, through the hair, his scalp. He might be dead
30   It seemed, and all the noises underneath
Be but the cooling of the sinews, veins,
Juices, and sodden sacks suddenly let go;
While in his ruins of wiring, his burst mains,
The rainy wind had been set free to blow
Until the green uprising and mob rule
That ran the world had taken over him,
Split him like seed, and set him in the school
Where any crutch can learn to be a limb.

Inside his head he heard the stormy crows.

Richard Wilbur

Richard Wilbur (1921–   ) was born in New Jersey and has lived in the
eastern United States. During the Second World War he fought in Italy and
France; he began writing poems in the Army. His work is decorative, skillful,
aimed to please and to enlighten rather than to shock or to overwhelm. He is
one of the few poets of his generation who has not undergone violent change, in
work and private life, which has earned him the disapproval of critics. See also
pages 433 and 469.

Still, Citizen Sparrow

Still, citizen sparrow, this vulture which you call
Unnatural, let him but lumber again to air
Over the rotten office, let him bear
The carrion ballast up, and at the tall

Tip of the sky lie cruising. Then you'll see
That no more beautiful bird is in heaven's height,
No wider more placid wings, no watchfuller flight;
He shoulders nature there, the frightfully free,

The naked-headed one. Pardon him, you
10   Who dart in the orchard aisles, for it is he
Devours death, mocks mutability,
Has heart to make an end, keeps nature new.

Thinking of Noah, childheart, try to forget
How for so many bedlam hours his saw
Soured the song of birds with its wheezy gnaw,
And the slam of his hammer all the day beset

The people's ears. Forget that he could bear
To see the towns like coral under the keel,
And the fields so dismal deep. Try rather to feel
20   How high and weary it was, on the waters where

He rocked his only world, and everyone's.
Forgive the hero, you who would have died
Gladly with all you knew; he rode that tide
To Ararat;[1] all men are Noah's sons.

[1]The mountain on which Noah's Ark landed

Mind

Mind in its purest play is like some bat
That beats about in caverns all alone,
Contriving by a kind of senseless wit
Not to conclude against a wall of stone.

It has no need to falter or explore;
Darkly it knows what obstacles are there,
And so may weave and flitter, dip and soar
In perfect courses through the blackest air.

And has this simile a like perfection?
10   The mind is like a bat. Precisely. Save
That in the very happiest intellection
A graceful error may correct the cave.

Philip Larkin

Philip Larkin (1922–   ) attended Oxford, wrote two early novels, and chose
the life of a professional librarian. He has written little, but his work has been
finished and fine. In the eyes of most observers, he is the best English poet
of his time. He is librarian of the University at Hull. His volumes are *The Less
Deceived* (1955), *The Whitsun Weddings* (1964), and *High Windows* (1974).

Mr. Bleaney

'This was Mr. Bleaney's room. He stayed
The whole time he was at the Bodies, till
They moved him.' Flowered curtains, thin and frayed,
Fall to within five inches of the sill,

Whose window shows a strip of building land,
Tussocky, littered. 'Mr. Bleaney took
My bit of garden properly in hand.'
Bed, upright chair, sixty-watt bulb, no hook

10   Behind the door, no room for books or bags—
'I'll take it.' So it happens that I lie
Where Mr. Bleaney lay, and stub my fags
On the same saucer-souvenir, and try

Stuffing my ears with cotton-wool, to drown
The jabbering set he egged her on to buy.
I know his habits—what time he came down,
His preference for sauce to gravy, why

He kept on plugging at the four aways[1]—
Likewise their yearly frame: the Frinton folk
Who put him up for summer holidays,
20   And Christmas at his sister's house in Stoke.

But if he stood and watched the frigid wind
Tousling the clouds, lay on the fusty bed
Telling himself that this was home, and grinned,
And shivered, without shaking off the dread

That how we live measures our own nature,
And at his age having no more to show
Than one hired box should make him pretty sure
He warranted no better, I don't know.

[1]A form of betting on English professional soccer games

Aubade

I work all day, and get half drunk at night.
Waking at four to soundless dark, I stare.
In time the curtain-edges will grow light.
Till then I see what's really always there:
Unresting death, a whole day nearer now,
Making all thought impossible but how
And where and when I shall myself die.
Arid interrogation: yet the dread
Of dying, and being dead,
10   Flashes afresh to hold and horrify.

The mind blanks at the glare. Not in remorse
—The good not done, the love not given, time
Torn off unused—nor wretchedly because
An only life can take so long to climb
Clear of its wrong beginnings, and may never;
But at the total emptiness for ever,
The sure extinction that we travel to

And shall be lost in always. Not to be here,
Not to be anywhere,
20   And soon; nothing more terrible, nothing more true.

This is a special way of being afraid
No trick dispels. Religion used to try,
That vast moth-eaten musical brocade
Created to pretend we never die,
And specious stuff that says *No rational being*
Can fear a thing it will not feel, not seeing
That this is what we fear—no sight, no sound,
No touch or taste to smell, nothing to think with,
Nothing to love or link with,
30   The anaesthetic from which none come round.

And so it stays just on the edge of vision,
A small unfocused blur, a standing chill
That slows each impulse down to indecision.
Most things may never happen: this one will,
And realisation of it rages out
In furnace-fear when we are caught without
People or drink. Courage is no good:
It means not scaring others. Being brave
Lets no one off the grave.
40   Death is no different whined at than withstood.

Slowly light strengthens, and the room takes shape.
It stands plain as a wardrobe, what we know,
Have always known, know that we can't escape,
Yet can't accept. One side will have to go.
Meanwhile telephones crouch, getting ready to ring
In locked-up offices, and all the uncaring
Intricate rented world begins to rouse.
The sky is white as clay, with no sun.
Work has to be done.
50   Postmen like doctors go from house to house.

James Dickey

James Dickey (1923–   ) was an All-Southern halfback as a young man and
then a fighter pilot during the Second World War and the Korean War. He tried
teaching and advertising and after publishing volumes of poetry returned to
teaching again. His *Collected Poems* won the National Book Award in 1966. His
novel *Deliverance* became a successful motion picture.

The Heaven of Animals

Here they are. The soft eyes open.
If they have lived in a wood
It is a wood.
If they have lived on plains
It is grass rolling
Under their feet forever.

Having no souls, they have come,
Anyway, beyond their knowing.
Their instincts wholly bloom
10   And they rise.
The soft eyes open.

To match them, the landscape flowers,
Outdoing, desperately
Outdoing what is required:
The richest wood,
The deepest field.

For some of these,
It could not be the place
It is, without blood.
20   These hunt, as they have done,
But with claws and teeth grown perfect,

More deadly than they can believe.
They stalk more silently,
And crouch on the limbs of trees,
And their descent
Upon the bright backs of their prey

May take years
In a sovereign floating of joy.
And those that are hunted
30   Know this as their life,
Their reward: to walk

Under such trees in full knowledge
Of what is in glory above them,
And to feel no fear,
But acceptance, compliance.
Fulfilling themselves without pain

At the cycle's center,
They tremble, they walk
Under the tree,
40   They fall, they are torn,
They rise, they walk again.

Anthony Hecht

Anthony Hecht (1923–   ) fought in the infantry in the Second World War and
has taught at American universities for most of his life. He is not prolific,
finishes few poems, and finishes them with an extraordinarily high gloss. *The
Hard Hours* (1967) includes a selection of early poems. See also page 470.

The Dover Bitch: A Criticism of Life

(for Andrews Wanning)

So there stood Matthew Arnold and this girl
With the cliffs of England crumbling away behind them,
And he said to her, "Try to be true to me,

And I'll do the same for you, for things are bad
All over, etc., etc."
Well now, I knew this girl. It's true she had read
Sophocles in a fairly good translation
And caught that bitter allusion to the sea,
But all the time he was talking she had in mind
10   The notion of what his whiskers would feel like
On the back of her neck. She told me later on
That after a while she got to looking out
At the lights across the channel, and really felt sad,
Thinking of all the wine and enormous beds
And blandishments in French and the perfumes.
And then she got really angry. To have been brought
All the way down from London, and then be addressed
As a sort of mournful cosmic last resort
Is really tough on a girl, and she was pretty.
20   Anyway, she watched him pace the room
And finger his watch-chain and seem to sweat a bit,
And then she said one or two unprintable things.
But you mustn't judge her by that. What I mean to say is,
She's really all right. I still see her once in a while
And she always treats me right. We have a drink
And I give her a good time, and perhaps it's a year
Before I see her again, but there she is,
Running to fat, but dependable as they come.
And sometimes I bring her a bottle of *Nuit d'Amour.*

Denise Levertov

Denise Levertov (1923–   ), who was born in England, came to the United
States when she married an American soldier. Her early poems were collected
in England. After her move to the United States, she became affiliated with
the Black Mountain group of poets and her style changed considerably. She was
a leader in the antiwar movement during the Vietnam years. See also page 413.

October

Certain branches cut
certain leaves fallen
the grapes
              cooked and put up
for winter

mountains without one
shrug of cloud
no feint of blurred
wind-willow leaf-light

10   their chins up
in blue of the eastern sky
their red cloaks
wrapped tight to the bone

John Logan

John Logan (1923–   ) was born in Red Oak, Iowa and went to school in the
Midwest. In more recent years he has lived in California, in upstate New York,
and in Hawaii, writing his poems and editing *Choice*.

The Picnic

It is the picnic with Ruth in the spring.
Ruth was third on my list of seven girls
But the first two were gone (Betty) or else
Had someone (Ellen has accepted Doug).
Indian Gully the last day of school;
Girls make the lunches for the boys too.
I wrote a note to Ruth in algebra class
Day before the test. She smiled, and nodded.
We left the cars and walked through the young corn
10   The shoots green as paint and the leaves like tongues
Trembling. Beyond the fence where we stood
Some wild strawberry flowered by an elm tree
And Jack-in-the-pulpit was olive ripe.
A blackbird fled as I crossed, and showed
A spot of gold or red under its quick wing.
I held the wire for Ruth and watched the whip
Of her long, striped skirt as she followed.
Three freckles blossomed on her thin, white back
Underneath the loop where the blouse buttoned.
20   We went for our lunch away from the rest,
Stretched in the new grass, our heads close
Over unknown things wrapped up in wax papers.
Ruth tried for the same, I forget what it was,
And our hands were together. She laughed,
And a breeze caught the edge of her little
Collar and the edge of her brown, loose hair
That touched my cheek. I turned my face in-
to the gentle fall. I saw how sweet it smelled.
She didn't move her head or take her hand.
30   I felt a soft caving in my stomach
As at the top of the highest slide
When I had been a child, but was not afraid,
And did not know why my eyes moved with wet
As I brushed her cheek with my lips and brushed
Her lips with my own lips. She said to me
Jack, Jack, different than I had ever heard,
Because she wasn't calling me, I think,
Or telling me. She used my name to
Talk in another way I wanted to know.
40   She laughed again and then she took her hand;
I gave her what we both had touched—can't
Remember what it was, and we ate the lunch.
Afterward we walked in the small, cool creek

Our shoes off, her skirt hitched, and she smiling,
My pants rolled, and then we climbed up the high
Side of Indian Gully and looked
Where we had been, our hands together again.
It was then some bright thing came in my eyes,
Starting at the back of them and flowing
50   Suddenly through my head and down my arms
And stomach and my bare legs that seemed not
To stop in feet, not to feel the red earth
Of the Gully, as though we hung in a
Touch of birds. There was a word in my throat
With the feeling and I knew the first time
What it meant and I said, it's beautiful.
Yes, she said, and I felt the sound and word
In my hand join the sound and word in hers
As in one name said, or in one cupped hand.
60   We put back on our shoes and socks and we
Sat in the grass awhile, crosslegged, under
A blowing tree, not saying anything.
And Ruth played with shells she found in the creek,
As I watched. Her small wrist which was so sweet
To me turned by her breast and the shells dropped
Green, white, blue, easily into her lap,
Passing light through themselves. She gave the pale
Shells to me, and got up and touched her hips
With her light hands, and we walked down slowly
70   To play the school games with the others.

Louis Simpson

Louis Simpson (1923–   ) was born in Jamaica and grew up there, coming to
the United States when he was seventeen. He left Columbia College to enter
the U.S. Army during the Second World War and received his citizenship at
Berchtesgaden. He has published a novel, a textbook, two books of criticism,
and numerous books of poems. *At the End of the Open Road* (1963) won a
Pulitzer Prize. See also page 467.

Walt Whitman at Bear Mountain

". . . life which does not give the preference to any other life, of any
previous period, which therefore prefers its own existence . . ."
                                                    —*Ortega y Gasset*

Neither on horseback nor seated,
But like himself, squarely on two feet,
The poet of death and lilacs
Loafs by the footpath. Even the bronze looks alive
Where it is folded like cloth. And he seems friendly.

'Where is the Mississippi panorama
And the girl who played the piano?

Where are you, Walt?
The Open Road goes to the used-car lot.

10   'Where is the nation you promised?
These houses built of wood sustain
Colossal snows,
And the light above the street is sick to death.

'As for the people—see how they neglect you!
Only a poet pauses to read the inscription.'

'I am here,' he answered.
'It seems you have found me out.
Yet, did I not warn you that it was Myself
I advertised? Were my words not sufficiently plain?

20   'I gave no prescriptions,
And those who have taken my moods for prophecies
Mistake the matter.'
Then, vastly amused—'Why do you reproach me?
I freely confess I am wholly disreputable.
Yet I am happy, because you have found me out.'

A crocodile in wrinkled metal loafing . . .

Then all the realtors,
Pickpockets, salesmen, and the actors peforming
Official scenarios,
30   Turned a deaf ear, for they had contracted
American dreams.

But the man who keeps a store on a lonely road,
And the housewife who knows she's dumb,
And the earth, are relieved.

All that grave weight of America
Cancelled! Like Greece and Rome.
The future in ruins!
The castles, the prisons, the cathedrals
Unbuilding, and roses
40   Blossoming from the stones that are not there . . .

The clouds are lifting from the high Sierras,
The Bay mists clearing;
And the angel in the gate, the flowering plum,
Dances like Italy, imagining red.

In the Suburbs

There's no way out.
You were born to waste your life.
You were born to this middleclass life

As others before you
Were born to walk in procession
To the temple, singing.

John Haines

John Haines (1924–   ) was a homesteader in Alaska for fifteen years and now divides his time between Alaska and the continental United States. See also page 448.

To Turn Back

The grass people bow
their heads before the wind.

How would it be
to stand among them, bending
our heads like that . . . ?

Yes . . . and no . . . perhaps . . .
lifting our dusty faces
as if we were waiting for
the rain . . . ?

10 The grass people stand
all year, patient and obedient—

to be among them
is to have only simple
and friendly thoughts,

and not be afraid.

Donald Justice

Donald Justice (1925–   ) grew up in Florida and attended the Writers Workshop at Iowa, where he now teaches. His *Selected Poems* appeared in 1979.

Counting the Mad

This one was put in a jacket,
This one was sent home,
This one was given bread and meat
But would eat none,
And this one cried No No No No
All day long.

This one looked at the window
As thought it were a wall,
This one saw things that were not there,
10 This one things that were,
And this one cried No No No No
All day long.

This one thought himself a bird,
This one a dog,
And this one thought himself a man,
An ordinary man,
And cried and cried No No No No
All day long.

A. R. Ammons

Archie Randolph Ammons (1926–   ) worked in business for many years before he became a professor of English. He teaches at Cornell.

Working with Tools

I make a simple assertion
like a nice piece of stone
and you
alert to presence and entrance
man your pick and hammer

and by chip and deflection
distract simplicity
and cut my assertion
back to mangles, little heaps:

10   well, baby, that's the way
you get along: it's all right,
I understand such
ways of being afraid:
sometimes you want my come-on

hard, something to
take in and be around:
sometimes you want
a vaguer touch: I understand
and won't give assertion up.

Robert Bly

Robert Bly (1926–   ) comes from a farm in western Minnesota, and after some time in the Navy attended Harvard, from which he graduated in 1950. Editor of an influential literary magazine—variously called *The Fifties, The Sixties,* and *The Seventies*—he has championed modernist poets of other literatures and has extended great influence on a younger generation of American poets. His own poems have been collected in *Silence in the Snowy Fields* (1962), *The Light Around the Body* (1967)—which won a National Book Award—and in seven other collections. See also page 441 and, for Bly's translations, pages 417 and 495.

Hunting Pheasants in a Cornfield

I

What is so strange about a tree alone in an open field?
It is a willow tree. I walk around and around it.
The body is strangely torn, and cannot leave it.
At last I sit down beneath it.

II

It is a willow tree alone in acres of dry corn.
Its leaves are scattered around its trunk, and around me,

Brown now, and speckled with delicate black.
Only the cornstalks now can make a noise.

III

The sun is cold, burning through the frosty distances of space.
10   The weeds are frozen to death long ago.
Why then do I love to watch
The sun moving on the chill skin of the branches?

IV

The mind has shed leaves alone for years.
It stands apart with small creatures near its roots.
I am happy in this ancient place,
A spot easily caught sight of above the corn,
If I were a young animal ready to turn home at dusk.

A Man Writes to a Part of Himself

What cave are you in, hiding, rained on?
Like a wife, starving, without care,
Water dripping from your head, bent
Over ground corn . . .

     You raise your face into the rain
That drives over the valley—
Forgive me, your husband,
On the streets of a distant city, laughing,
With many appointments,
10   Though at night going also
To a bare room, a room of poverty,
To sleep among a bare pitcher and basin
In a room with no heat—

     Which of us two then is the worse off?
And how did this separation come about?

Robert Creeley

Robert Creeley (1926–   ) grew up in New England, and attended Harvard,
after which he tried chicken farming in New Hampshire, then lived on the
Spanish island of Majorca. Most recently he has alternated between Placitas,
New Mexico, and the University of Buffalo in New York. Creeley taught at Black
Mountain College and edited the *Black Mountain Review*, and as much as
anyone else formed the Black Mountain school of poetry. His *Selected Poems*
appeared in 1977. See also page 426.

The Rain

All night the sound had
come back again,
and again falls
this quiet, persistent rain.

What am I to myself
that must be remembered,
insisted upon
so often? Is it

10   that never the ease,
even the hardness,
of rain falling
will have for me

something other than this,
something not so insistent—
am I to be locked in this
final uneasiness.

Love, if you love me,
lie next to me.
Be for me, like rain,
20   the getting out

of the tiredness, the fatuousness, the semi-
lust of intentional indifference.
Be wet
with a decent happiness.

For My Mother: Genevieve Jules Creeley

(April 8, 1887—October 7, 1972)

Tender, semi-
articulate flickers
of your

presence, all
those years
past

now, eighty-
five, impossible to
count them

10   one by one, like
addition, sub-
traction, missing

not one. The last
curled up, in
on yourself,

position you take
in the bed, hair
wisped up

on your head, a
20   top knot, body
skeletal, eyes

closed against,
it must be,
further disturbance—

breathing a skim
of time, lightly
kicks the intervals—

days, days and
years of it,
30   work, changes,

sweet flesh caught
at the edges,
dignity's faded

dilemma. It
is *your* life, oh
no one's

forgotten anything
ever. They want
to make you

40   happy when
they remember. Walk
a little, get

up, now, die
safely,
easily, into

singleness, too
tired with it
to keep

on and on.
50   Waves break at
the darkness

under the road, sounds
in the faint
night's softness. Look

at them, catching
the light, white
edge as they turn—

always again
and again. Dead
60   one, two,

three hours—
all these minutes
pass. Is it,

was it, ever
you alone
again, how

long you kept
at it, your
pride, your

70   lovely, confusing
discretion. Mother, I
love you—for

whatever that
means,
meant—more

than I know, body
gave me my
own, generous,

inexorable place
80   of you. I feel
the mouth's sluggish-

ness, slips on
turns of things
said, to you,

too soon, too late,
wants to
go back to beginning,

smells of the hospital
room, the doctor
90   she responds

to now, the
order—get me
there. "Death's

let you out—"
comes true,
this, that,

endlessly circular
life, and we
came back

100   to see you one
last
time, this

time? Your head
shuddered,
it seemed, your

eyes wanted,
I thought,
to see

who it was.
110   I am here,
and will follow.

Allen Ginsberg

Allen Ginsberg (1926–   ) was born in New Jersey and attended Columbia in
New York City, but became known as a San Francisco poet with the publication
of *Howl* in 1956. At the forefront of the Beat Generation (he appears in several
novels by Jack Kerouac, under different names), Ginsberg has been a leader,
spiritual and political as well as poetic. See also page 410.

America

America I've given you all and now I'm nothing.
American two dollars and twentyseven cents January 17, 1956.
I can't stand on my own mind.
America when will we end the human war?
Go fuck yourself with your atom bomb.
I don't feel good don't bother me.
I won't write my poem till I'm in my right mind.
America when will you be angelic?
When will you take off your clothes?
10   When will you look at yourself through the grave?
When will you be worthy of your million Trotskyites?
America why are your libraries full of tears?
America when will you send your eggs to India?
I'm sick of your insane demands.
When can I go into the supermarket and buy what I need with my good looks?
American after all it is you and I who are perfect not the next world.
Your machinery is too much for me.
You made me want to be a saint.
There must be some other way to settle this argument.
20   Burroughs is in Tangiers I don't think he'll come back it's sinister.
Are you being sinister or is this some form of practical joke?
I'm trying to come to the point.
I refuse to give up my obsession.
America stop pushing I know what I'm doing.
America the plum blossoms are falling.
I haven't read the newspapers for months, everyday somebody goes on trial for
     murder.
America I feel sentimental about the Wobblies.
America I used to be a communist when I was a kid I'm not sorry.

I smoke marijuana every chance I get.
30   I sit in my house for days on end and stare at the roses in the closet.
When I go to Chinatown I get drunk and never get laid.
My mind is made up there's going to be trouble.
You should have seen me reading Marx.
My psychoanalyst thinks I'm perfectly right.
I won't say the Lord's Prayer.
I have mystical visions and cosmic vibrations.
America I still haven't told you what you did to Uncle Max after he came over
      from Russia.

I'm addressing you.
Are you going to let your emotional life be run by Time Magazine?
40   I'm obsessed by Time Magazine.
I read it every week.
Its cover stares at me every time I slink past the corner candystore.
I read it in the basement of the Berkeley Public Library.
It's always telling me about responsibility. Businessmen are serious.
      Movie producers are serious. Everybody's serious but me.
It occurs to me that I am America.
I am talking to myself again.

Asia is rising against me.
I haven't got a chinaman's chance.
50   I'd better consider my national resources.
My national resources consist of two joints of marijuana millions of genitals an
      unpublishable private literature that goes 1400 miles an hour and
      twentyfive-thousand mental institutions.
I say nothing about my prisons nor the millions of underprivileged who live in
      my flowerpots under the light of five hundred suns.
I have abolished the whorehouses of France, Tangiers is the next to go.
My ambition is to be President despite the fact that I'm a Catholic.

American how can I write a holy litany in your silly mood?
I will continue like Henry Ford my strophes are as individual as his automobiles
      more so they're all different sexes.
America I will sell you strophes $2500 apiece $500 down on your old strophe
America free Tom Mooney
America save the Spanish Loyalists
60   America Sacco & Vanzetti must not die
America I am the Scottsboro boys.
America when I was seven momma took me to Communist Cell meetings they
      sold us garbanzos a handful per ticket a ticket costs a nickel and the
      speeches were free everybody was angelic and sentimental about the
      workers it was all so sincere you have no idea what a good thing the party
      was in 1835 Scott Nearing was a grand old man a real mensch Mother
      Bloor made me cry I once saw Israel Amter plain. Everybody must have
      been a spy.
America you don't really want to go to war.
America it's them bad Russians.
Them Russians them Russians and them Chinamen. And them Russians.

The Russia wants to eat us alive. The Russia's power mad. She wants to take
    our cars from out our garages.
Her wants to grab Chicago. Her needs a Red Readers' Digest. Her wants our
    auto plants in Siberia. Him big bureaucracy running our fillingstations.
That no good. Ugh. Him make Indians learn read. Him need big black niggers.
    Hah. Her make us all work sixteen hours a day. Help.
America this is quite serious.
70   America this is the impression I get from looking in the television set.
America is this correct?
I'd better get right down to the job.
It's true I don't want to join the Army or turn lathes in precision parts factories,
    I'm nearsighted and psychopathic anyway.
America I'm putting my queer shoulder to the wheel.

James Merrill

James Merrill (1926–   ) attended Amherst and now alternates between a
house in Greece and a house in Connecticut. He has published two novels; his
books of poems have twice won the National Book Award.

After Greece

Light into the olive entered
And was oil. Rain made the huge pale stones
Shine from within. The moon turned his hair white
Who next stepped from between the columns,
Shielding his eyes. All through
The countryside were old ideas
Found lying open to the elements.
Of the gods' houses only
A minor premise here and there
10   Would be balancing the heaven of fixed stars
Upon a Doric capital. The rest
Lay spilled, their fluted drums half sunk in cyclamen
Or deep in water's biting clarity
Which just barely upheld me
The next week, when I sailed for home.
But where is home—these walls?
These limbs? The very spaniel underfoot
Races in sleep, toward what?
It is autumn. I did not invite
20   Those guests, windy and brittle, who drink my liquor.
Returning from a walk I find
The bottles filled with spleen, my room itself
Smeared by reflection on to the far hemlocks.
I some days flee in dream
Back to the exposed porch of the maidens
Only to find my great-great-grandmothers
Erect there, peering
Into a globe of red Bohemian glass.
As it swells and sinks, I call up

30   Graces, Furies, Fates, removed
    To my country's warm, lit halls, with rivets forced
    Through drapery, and nothing left to bear.
    They seem anxious to know
    What holds up heaven nowadays.
    I start explaining how in that vast fire
    Were other irons—well, Art, Public Spirit,
    Ignorance, Economics, Love of Self,
    Hatred of Self, a hundred more,
    Each burning to be felt, each dedicated
40   To sparing us the worst; how I distrust them
    As I should have done those ladies; how I want
    Essentials: salt, wine, olive, the light, the scream—
    No! I have scarcely named you,
    And look, in a flash you stand full-grown before me,
    Row upon row, Essentials,
    Dressed like your sister caryatids
    Or tombstone angels jealous of their dead,
    With undulant coiffures, lips weathered, cracked by grime,
    And faultless eyes gone blank beneath the immense
50   Zinc and gunmetal northern sky . . .
    Stay then. Perhaps the system
    Calls for spirits. This first glass I down
    To the last time
    I ate and drank in that old world. May I
    Also survive its meanings, and my own.

Frank O'Hara

Frank O'Hara (1926–1966) was a poet of vast influence; the naturalness of O'Hara's language has earned him many followers. He attended Harvard and then worked at the Museum of Modern Art in New York, where he held an important position at the time of his accidental death in 1966. His *Collected Poems* came out in 1971.

The Day Lady Died

It is 12:20 in New York a Friday
three days after Bastille day, yes
it is 1959 and I go get a shoeshine
because I will get off the 4:19 in Easthampton
at 7:15 and then go straight to dinner
and I don't know the people who will feed me

I walk up the muggy street beginning to sun
and have a hamburger and a malted and buy
an ugly NEW WORLD WRITING to see what the poets
10   in Ghana are doing these days
                       I go on to the bank
and Miss Stillwagon (first name Linda I once heard)
doesn't even look up my balance for once in her life
and in the GOLDEN GRIFFIN I get a little Verlaine

for Patsy with drawings by Bonnard although I do
think of Hesiod, trans. Richmond Lattimore or
Brendan Behan's new play or *Le Balcon* or *Les Nègres*

of Genet, but I don't, I stick with Verlaine
after practically going to sleep with quandariness

20   and for Mike I just stroll into the PARK LANE
Liquor Store and ask for a bottle of Strega and
then I go back where I came from to 6th Avenue
and the tobacconist in the Ziegfeld Theatre and
casually ask for a carton of Gauloises and a carton
of Picayunes, and a NEW YORK POST with her face on it

and I am sweating a lot by now and thinking of
leaning on the john door in the 5 SPOT
while she whispered a song along the keyboard
to Mal Waldron and everyone and I stopped breathing

Why I Am Not a Painter

I am not a painter, I am a poet.
Why? I think I would rather be
a painter, but I am not. Well,

for instance, Mike Goldberg[1]
is starting a painting. I drop in.
"Sit down and have a drink" he
says. I drink; we drink. I look
up. "You have SARDINES in it."
"Yes, it needed something there."
10   "Oh," I go and the days go by
and I drop in again. The painting
is going on, and I go, and the days
go by. I drop in. The painting is
finished. "Where's SARDINES?"
All that's left is just
letters, "It was too much," Mike says.

But me? One day I am thinking of
a color: orange. I write a line
about orange. Pretty soon it is a
20   whole page of words, not lines.
Then another page. There should be
so much more, not of orange, of
words, of how terrible orange is
and life. Days go by. It is even in
prose, I am a real poet. My poem
is finished and I haven't mentioned
orange yet. It's twelve poems, I call
it ORANGES. And one day in a gallery
I see Mike's painting, called SARDINES.

[1]A contemporary American painter

W. D. Snodgrass

William DeWitt Snodgrass (1926–   ), born in Pennsylvania, attended the
Writers Workshop at Iowa, where he wrote his first book, *Heart's Needle*.
Credited by Robert Lowell with the invention of confessional verse, Snodgrass
in his own work has moved on to the use of dramatic monologue.

April Inventory

The green catalpa tree has turned
All white; the cherry blooms once more.
In one whole year I haven't learned
A blessed thing they pay you for.
The blossoms snow down in my hair;
The trees and I will soon be bare.

The trees have more than I to spare.
The sleek, expensive girls I teach,
Younger and pinker every year,
10   Bloom gradually out of reach.
The pear tree lets its petals drop
Like dandruff on a tabletop.

The girls have grown so young by now
I have to nudge myself to stare.
This year they smile and mind me how
My teeth are falling with my hair.
In thirty years I may not get
Younger, shrewder, or out of debt.

The tenth time, just a year ago,
20   I made myself a little list
Of all the things I'd ought to know,
Then told my parents, analyst,
And everyone who's trusted me
I'd be substantial, presently.

I haven't read one book about
A book or memorized one plot.
Or found a mind I did not doubt.
I learned one date. And then forgot.
And one by one the solid scholars
30   Get the degrees, the jobs, the dollars.

And smile above their starchy collars.
I taught my classes Whitehead's[1] notions;
One lovely girl, a song of Mahler's.[2]
Lacking a source-book or promotions,
I showed one child the colors of
A luna moth and how to love.

---

[1]Alfred North Whitehead (1861–1947), English philosopher and mathematician   [2]Gustav Mahler (1860–1911), Austrian composer and conductor, wrote several songs and song cycles in addition to nine monumental symphonies.

I taught myself to name my name,
To bark back, loosen love and crying;
To ease my woman so she came,
40   To ease an old man who was dying.
I have not learned how often I
Can win, can love, but choose to die.

I have not learned there is a lie
Love shall be blonder, slimmer, younger;
That my equivocating eye
Loves only by my body's hunger;
That I have forces, true to feel,
Or that the lovely world is real.

While scholars speak authority
50   And wear their ulcers on their sleeves,
My eyes in spectacles shall see
These trees procure and spend their leaves.
There is a value underneath
The gold and silver in my teeth.

Though trees turn bare and girls turn wives,
We shall afford our costly seasons;
There is a gentleness survives
That will outspeak and has its reasons.
There is a loveliness exists,
60   Preserves us, not for specialists.

Lobsters in the Window

First, you think they are dead.
Then you are almost sure
One is beginning to stir.
Out of the crushed ice, slow
As the hands of a schoolroom clock,
He lifts his one great claw
And holds it over his head;
Now, he is trying to walk.

But like a run-down toy;
10   Like the backward crabs we boys
Splashed after in the creek,
Trapped in jars or a net,
And then took home to keep.
Overgrown, retarded, weak,
He is fumbling yet
From the deep chill of his sleep

As if, in a glacial thaw,
Some ancient thing might wake
Sore and cold and stiff
20   Struggling to raise one claw
Like a defiant fist;

Yet wavering, as if
Starting to swell and ache
With that thick peg in the wrist.

I should wave back, I guess.
But still in his permanent clench
He's fallen back with the mass
Heaped in their common trench
Who stir, but do not look out
30   Through the rainstreaming glass,
Hear what the newsboys shout,
Or see the raincoats pass.

John Ashbery

John Ashbery (1927–   ) attended Harvard, overlapping with Robert Creeley,
Robert Bly, Adrienne Rich, and Frank O'Hara. He spent ten years in Paris,
writing for an American newspaper there, and later worked for *Art News* in
New York. For many years his poetry has attracted a small but enthusiastic
group of readers. In 1975, his latest volume won the Pulitzer Prize, the
National Book Award, and the award of the National Book Critics Circle.

Rivers and Mountains

On the secret map the assassins
Cloistered, the Moon River was marked
Near the eighteen peaks and the city
Of humiliation and defeat—wan ending
Of the trail among dry, papery leaves
Gray-brown quills like thoughts
In the melodious but vast mass of today's
Writing through fields and swamps
Marked, on the map, with little bunches of weeds.
10   Certainly squirrels lived in the woods
But devastation and dull sleep still
Hung over the land, quelled
The rioters turned out of sleep in the peace of prisons
Singing on marble factory walls
Deaf consolation of minor tunes that pack
The air with heavy invisible rods
Pent in some sand valley from
Which only quiet walking ever instructs.
The bird flew over and
20   Sat—there was nothing else to do.
Do not mistake its silence for pride or strength
Or the waterfall for a harbor
Full of light boats that is there
Performing for thousands of people
In clothes some with places to go
Or games. Sometimes over the pillar
Of square stones its impact
Makes a light print.

So going around cities
30   To get to other places you found
It all on paper but the land
Was made of paper processed
To look like ferns, mud or other
Whose sea unrolled its magic
Distances and then rolled them up
Its secret was only a pocket
After all but some corners are darker
Than these moonless nights spent as on a raft
In the seclusion of a melody heard
40   As though through trees
And you can never ignite their touch
Long but there were homes
Flung far out near the asperities
Of a sharp, rocky pinnacle
And other collective places
Shadows of vineyards whose wine
Tasted of the forest floor
Fisheries and oyster beds
Tides under the pole
50   Seminaries of instruction, public
Places for electric light
And the major tax assessment area
Wrinkled on the plan
Of election to public office
Sixty-two years old bath and breakfast
The formal traffic, shadows
To make it not worth joining
After the ox had pulled away the cart.

Your plan was to separate the enemy into two groups
60   With the razor-edged mountains between.
It worked well on paper
But their camp had grown
To be the mountains and the map
Carefully peeled away and not torn
Was the light, a tender but tough bark
On everything. Fortunately the war was solved
In another way by isolating the two sections
Of the enemy's navy so that the mainland
Warded away the big floating ships.
70   Light bounced off the ends
Of the small gray waves to tell
Them in the observatory
About the great drama that was being won
To turn off the machinery
And quietly move among the rustic landscape
Scooping snow off the mountains rinsing
The coarser ones that love had

Slowly risen in the night to overflow
Wetting pillow and petal
80   Determined to place the letter
On the unassassinated president's desk
So that a stamp could reproduce all this
In detail, down to the last autumn leaf
And the affliction of June ride
Slowly out into the sun-blackened landscape.

Galway Kinnell

Galway Kinnell (1927–   ) grew up in Rhode Island and attended Princeton
University. For many years he supported himself by teaching correspondence
courses, spending a year teaching in Iran and an occasional term at an
American university while he devoted himself to literary work. He has
published one novel, and translations of Villon and the contemporary French
poet Yves Bonnefoy. The *Book of Nightmares*, probably his best-known book of
poems, appeared in 1971.

The Bear

1

In late winter
I sometimes glimpse bits of steam
coming up from
some fault in the old snow
and bend close and see it is lung-colored
and put down my nose
and know
the chilly, enduring odor of bear.

2

I take a wolf's rib and whittle
10   it sharp at both ends
and coil it up
and freeze it in blubber and place it out
on the fairway of the bears.

And when it has vanished
I move out on the bear tracks,
roaming in circles
until I come to the first, tentative, dark
splash on the earth.

And I set out
20   running, following the splashes
of blood wandering over the world.
At the cut, gashed resting places
I stop and rest,
at the crawl-marks
where he lay out on his belly

to overpass some stretch of bauchy ice
I lie out
dragging myself forward with bear-knives in my fists.

3

On the third day I begin to starve,
30   at nightfall I bend down as I knew I would
at a turd sopped in blood,
and hesitate, and pick it up,
and thrust it in my mouth, and gnash it down,
and rise
and go on running.

4

On the seventh day,
living by now on bear blood alone,
I can see his upturned carcass far out ahead, a scraggled,
steamy hulk,
40   the heavy fur riffling in the wind.

I come up to him
and stare at the narrow-spaced, petty eyes,
the dismayed
face laid back on the shoulder, the nostrils
flared, catching
perhaps the first taint of me as he
died.

I hack
a ravine in his thigh, and eat and drink,
50   and tear him down his whole length
and open him and climb in
and close him up after me, against the wind
and sleep.

5

And dream
of lumbering flatfooted
over the tundra,
stabbed twice from within,
splattering a trail behind me,
splattering it out no matter which way I lurch,
60   no matter which parabola of bear-transcendence,
which dance of solitude I attempt,
which gravity-clutched leap,
which trudge, which groan.

6

Until one day I totter and fall—
fall on this

stomach that has tried so hard to keep up,
to digest the blood as it leaked in,
to break up
and digest the bone itself: and now the breeze
70   blows over me, blows off
the hideous belches of ill-digested bear blood
and rotted stomach
and the ordinary, wretched odor of bear,

blows across
my sore, lolled tongue a song
or screech, until I think I must rise up
and dance. And I lie still.

7

I awaken I think. Marshlights
reappear, geese
80   come trailing again up the flyway.
In her ravine under old snow the dam-bear
lies, licking
lumps of smeared fur
and drizzly eyes into shapes

with her tongue. And one
hairy-soled trudge stuck out before me,
the next groaned out,
the next,
the next,
90   the rest of my days I spend
wandering: wondering
what, anyway,
was that sticky infusion, that rank flavor of blood, that poetry, by which I lived?

W. S. Merwin

William Stanley Merwin (1927–   ) attended Princeton with Galway Kinnell
and lived for some years in Spain, where for a while he tutored Robert Graves's
children. He has translated from French and from Spanish especially. In recent
years he has written short, symbolic prose, collected into two volumes. He has
published eight books of his poems.

Something I've Not Done

Something I've not done
is following me
I haven't done it again and again
so it has many footsteps
like a drumstick that's grown old and never been used

In late afternoon I hear it come closer
at times it climbs out of a sea
onto my shoulders
and I shrug it off
10   losing one more chance

Every morning
it's drunk up part of my breath for the day
and knows which way
I'm going
and already it's not done there

But once more I say I'll lay hands on it
tomorrow
and add its footsteps to my heart
and its story to my regrets
20   and its silence to my compass

Charles Tomlinson

Charles Tomlinson (1927–   ) was born in an industrial English town and
attended Cambridge. He teaches at Bristol and is a painter as well as a poet.
In some of his poetry he has learned from American sources, especially Wallace
Stevens and the Black Mountain poets.

Paring the Apple

There are portraits and still-lifes.

And there is paring the apple.

And then? Paring it slowly,
From under cool-yellow
Cold-white emerging. And . . .?

The spring of concentric peel
Unwinding off white,
The blade hidden, dividing.

There are portraits and still-lifes
10   And the first, because 'human'
Does not excel the second, and
Neither is less weighted
With a human gesture, than paring the apple
With a human stillness.

The cool blade
Severs between coolness, apple-rind
Compelling a recognition.

James Wright

James Wright (1927–1980) grew up among the coal mines and steel mills of Ohio and attended Kenyon College, where he studied with John Crowe Ransom. His first book was *The Green Wall*, which made him the Yale Younger Poet in 1957. *To a Blossoming Pear Tree*, his eighth book, appeared in 1977. See also pages 414 and 416.

The First Days

Optima dies prima fugit[1]

The first thing I saw in the morning
Was a huge golden bee ploughing
His burly right shoulder into the belly
Of a sleek yellow pear
Low on a bough.
Before he could find that sudden black honey
That squirms around in there
Inside the seed, the tree could not bear any more.
The pear fell to the ground
10   With the bee still half alive
Inside its body.
He would have died if I hadn't knelt down
And sliced the pear gently
A little more open.
The bee shuddered, and returned.
Maybe I should have left him alone there,
Drowning in his own delight.
The best days are the first
To flee, sang the lovely
20   Musician born in this town
So like my own.
I let the bee go
Among the gasworks at the edge of Mantua.

[1]"The best day is the first to flee," a line from the Roman poet Vergil, who was born near Mantua

Philip Levine

Philip Levine (1928–   ) grew up in Detroit and attended the Writers Workshop at Iowa. His work was formal at the beginning, restrained and delicate, and has acquired strength and vitality as he has grown older. His volumes include *They Feed They Lion* (1972) and *1933: Poems* (1974).

Salami

Stomach of goat, crushed
sheep balls, soft full
pearls of pig eyes,
snout gristle, fresh earth,

worn iron of trotter, slate
of Zaragoza, dried cat heart,
cock claws. She grinds
them with one hand and
with the other fists
10   mountain thyme, basil,
paprika, and knobs of garlic.
And if a tooth of stink thistle
pulls blood from the round
blue marbled hand
all the better for
this ruby of Pamplona,
this bright jewel of Vich,
this stained crown
of Solsona, this
20   salami.
           The daughter
of mismatched eyes,
36 year old infant smelling
of milk. Mama, she cries, mama,
but mama is gone,
and the old stone cutter
must wipe the drool
from her jumper. His puffed fingers
unbutton and point her
30   to toilet. Ten, twelve hours
a day, as long as the winter sun
holds up he rebuilds
the unvisited church
of San Martin. Cheep cheep
of the hammer high above
the town, sparrow cries
lost in the wind or lost
in the mind. At dusk he leans
to the coal dull wooden Virgin
40   and asks for blessings on
the slow one and peace
on his grizzled head, asks
finally and each night
for the forbidden, for
the knowledge of every
mysterious stone, and
the words go out on
the overwhelming incense
of salami.
50   A single crow
passed high over the house,
I wakened out of nightmare.
The winds had changed,
the Tremontana was tearing

out of the Holy Mountains
to meet the sea winds
in my yard, burning and
scaring the young pines.
The single poplar wailed
60   in terror. With salt,
with guilt, with the need
to die, the vestments
of my life flared, I
was on fire, a stranger
staggering through my house
butting walls and falling
over furniture, looking
for a way out. In the last room
where moonlight slanted
70   through a broken shutter
I found my smallest son
asleep or dead, floating
on a bed of colorless light.
When I leaned closer
I could smell the small breaths
going and coming, and each
bore its prayer for me,
the true and earthy prayer
of salami.

Anne Sexton

Anne Sexton (1928–1974) did not begin to write poems until she was in her
late twenties, attending poetry workshops. Then she wrote prolifically and with
great energy for many years, combating psychosis and an urge to suicide. Her
books include *To Bedlam and Part Way Back* (1960), *Live or Die* (1967), and
The Awful Rowing Towards God (1975).

Wanting to Die

Since you ask, most days I cannot remember.
I walk in my clothing, unmarked by that voyage.
Then the almost unnameable lust returns.

Even then I have nothing against life.
I know well the grass blades you mention,
the furniture you have placed under the sun.

But suicides have a special language.
Like carpenters they want to know *which tools*.
They never ask *why build*.

10   Twice I have so simply declared myself,
have possessed the enemy, eaten the enemy,
have taken on his craft, his magic.

In this way, heavy and thoughtful,
warmer than oil or water,
I have rested, drooling at the mouth-hole.

I did not think of my body at needle point.
Even the cornea and the leftover urine were gone.
Suicides have already betrayed the body.

Still-born, they don't always die,
20   but dazzled, they can't forget a drug so sweet
that even children would look on and smile.

To thrust all that life under your tongue!—
that, all by itself, becomes a passion.
Death's a sad bone; bruised, you'd say,

and yet she waits for me, year after year,
to so delicately undo an old wound,
to empty my breath from its bad prison.

Balanced there, suicides sometimes meet,
raging at the fruit, a pumped-up moon,
30   leaving the bread they mistook for a kiss,

leaving the page of the book carelessly open,
something unsaid, the phone off the hook
and the love, whatever it was, an infection.

Edward Dorn

Edward Dorn (1929–   ) attended Black Mountain College and studied with
Robert Creeley and Charles Olson. One of Olson's didactic pamphlets is a
bibliography addressed to Ed Dorn. Perhaps his best work is the long poem
originally called *Gunslinger*, now shortened to *Slinger*.

On the Debt My Mother Owed to Sears Roebuck

Summer was dry, dry the garden
our beating hearts, on that farm, dry
with the rows of corn the grasshoppers
came happily to strip, in hordes, the first
thing I knew about locust was they came
dry under the foot like the breaking of
a mechanical bare heart which collapses
from an unkind an incessant word whispered
in the house of the major farmer
10   and the catalogue company,
from no fault of anyone
my father coming home tired
and grinning down the road, turning in
is the tank full? thinking of the horse
and my lazy arms thinking of the water
so far below the well platform.

On the debt my mother owed to sears roebuck
we brooded, she in the house, a little heavy
from too much corn meal, she
20   a little melancholy from the dust of the fields
in her eye, the only title she ever had to lands—
and man's ways winged their way to her through the mail
saying so much per month
so many months, this is yours, take it
take it, take it, take it
and in the corncrib, like her lives in that house
the mouse nibbled away at the cob's yellow grain
until six o'clock when her sorrows grew less
and my father came home

30   On the debt my mother owed to sears roebuck?
I have nothing to say, it gave me clothes to
wear to school,
and my mother brooded
in the rooms of the house, the kitchen, waiting
for the men she knew, her husband, her son
from work, from school, from the air of locusts
and dust masking the hedges of fields she knew
in her eye as a vague land where she lived,
boundaries, whose tractors chugged pulling harrows
40   pulling discs, pulling great yields from the earth
pulse for the armies in two hemispheres, 1943
and she was part of that *stay at home army* to keep
things going, owing that debt.

Thom Gunn

Thom Gunn (1929–   ) grew up in England, son of a successful journalist,
attended Cambridge, and came to California in 1954. He lives in San
Francisco, where he has spent most of the time since leaving England.

On the Move

'Man, you gotta Go.'

The blue jay scuffling in the bushes follows
Some hidden purpose, and the gust of birds
That spurts across the field, the wheeling swallows,
Have nested in the trees and undergrowth.
Seeking their instinct, or their poise, or both,
One moves with an uncertain violence
Under the dust thrown by a baffled sense
Or the dull thunder of approximate words.

On motorcycles, up the road, they come:
10   Small, black, as flies hanging in heat, the Boys,
Until the distance throws them forth, their hum
Bulges to thunder held by calf and thigh.

In goggles, donned impersonality,
In gleaming jackets trophied with the dust,
They strap in doubt—by hiding it, robust—
And almost hear a meaning in their noise.

Exact conclusion of their hardiness
Has no shape yet, but from known whereabouts
They ride, direction where the tires press.
20 They scare a flight of birds across the field:
Much that is natural, to the will must yield.
Men manufacture both machine and soul,
And use what they imperfectly control
To dare a future from the taken routes.

It is a part solution, after all.
One is not necessarily discord
On earth; or damned because, half animal,
One lacks direct instinct, because one wakes
Afloat on movement that divides and breaks.
30 One joins the movement in a valueless world,
Choosing it, till, both hurler and the hurled,
One moves as well, always toward, toward.

A minute holds them, who have come to go:
The self-defined, astride the created will
They burst away; the towns they travel through
Are home for neither bird nor holiness,
For birds and saints complete their purposes.
At worst, one is in motion; and at best,
Reaching no absolute, in which to rest,
40 One is always nearer by not keeping still.

X. J. Kennedy

X. J. Kennedy (1929–   ) is the only poet in this book with a pen-initial. His name is Joseph Kennedy, but he felt that there had been enough Joseph Kennedys in the news. He is the author of poems for children, successful textbooks, and two books of poems.

In a Prominent Bar in Secaucus One Day

(To the tune of 'The Old Orange Flute' or the tune of 'Sweet Betsy from Pike')

In a prominent bar in Secaucus one day
Rose a lady in skunk with a topheavy sway,
Raised a knobby red finger—all turned from their beer—
While with eyes bright as snowcrust she sang high and clear:

'Now who of you'd think from an eyeload of me
That I once was a lady as proud as could be?
Oh I'd never sit down by a tumbledown drunk
If it wasn't, my dears, for the high cost of junk.

'All the gents used to swear that the white of my calf
10 Beat the down of the swan by a length and a half.
In the kerchief of linen I caught to my nose
Ah, there never fell snot, but a little gold rose.

'I had seven gold teeth and a toothpick of gold,
My Virginia cheroot was a leaf of it rolled
And I'd light it each time with a thousand in cash—
Why the bums used to fight if I flicked them an ash.

'Once the toast of the Biltmore, the belle of the Taft,
I would drink bottle beer at the Drake, never draught,
And dine at the Astor on Salisbury steak
20 With a clean tablecloth for each bite I did take.

'In a car like the Roxy I'd roll to the track,
A steel-guitar trio, a bar in the back,
And the wheels made no noise, they turned over so fast,
Still it took you ten minutes to see me go past.

'When the horses bowed down to me that I might choose,
I bet on them all, for I hated to lose.
Now I'm saddled each night for my butter and eggs
And the broken threads race down the backs of my legs.

'Let you hold in mind, girls, that your beauty must pass
30 Like a lovely white clover that rusts with its grass.
Keep your bottoms off bar stools and marry you young
Or be left—an old barrel with many a bung.

'For when time takes you out for a spin in his car
You'll be hard-pressed to stop him from going too far
And be left by the roadside, for all your good deeds,
Two toadstools for tits and a face full of weeds.'

All the house raised a cheer, but the man at the bar
Made a phonecall and up pulled a red patrol car
And she blew us a kiss as they copped her away
40 From that prominent bar in Secaucus, N.J.

Adrienne Rich

Adrienne Rich (1929–   ) grew up in Baltimore and attended Radcliffe
College. She was Yale Younger Poet in her senior year at college and two years
later received a Guggenheim Fellowship. Her second volume—*The Diamond
Cutters*—followed in 1955 and then there was a gap of some years, while she
had three sons in rapid succession. Her work has changed considerably, losing
its decorativeness, becoming starker, tighter, tougher, and more emotional.
Her prose book, *Of Woman Born* (1977), is a monument of the feminist
movement.

From an Old House in America

1.

Deliberately, long ago
the carcasses

of old bugs crumbled
into the rut of the window

and we started sleeping here
Fresh June bugs batter this June's

screens, June-lightning batters
the spiderweb

I sweep the wood-dust
10   from the wood-box

the snout of the vacuum cleaner
sucks the past away

2.

Other lives were lived here:
mostly un-articulate

yet someone left her creamy signature
in the trail of rusticated

narcissus straggling up
through meadowgrass and vetch

Families breathed close
20   boxed-in from the cold

hard times, short growing season
the old rainwater cistern

hulks in the cellar

3.

Like turning through the contents of a drawer:
these rusted screws, this empty vial

useless, this box of watercolor paints
dried to insolubility—

but this—
this pack of cards with no card missing

30   still playable
and three good fuses

and this toy: a little truck
scarred red, yet all its wheels still turn

The humble tenacity of things
waiting for people, waiting for months, for years

4.

Often rebuked, yet always back returning
I place my hand on the hand

of the dead, invisible palm-print
on the doorframe

40   spiked with daylilies, green leaves
      catching in the screen door

      or I read the backs of old postcards
      curling from thumbtacks, winter and summer

      fading through cobweb-tinted panes—
      white church in Norway

      Dutch hyacinths bleeding azure
      red beach on Corsica

      set-pieces of the world
      stuck to this house of plank

50   I flash on wife and husband
      embattled, in the years

      that dried, dim ink was wet
      those signatures

      5.
      If they call me man-hater, you
      would have known it for a lie

      but the *you* I want to speak to
      has become your death

      If I dream of you these days
      I know my dreams are mine and not of you

60   yet something hangs between us
      older and stranger than ourselves

      like a translucent curtain, a sheet of water
      a dusty window

      the irreducible, incomplete connection
      between the dead and living

      or between man and woman in this
      savagely fathered and unmothered world

      6.
      The other side of a translucent
      curtain, a sheet of water

70   a dusty window, Non-being
      utters its flat tones

      the speech of an actor learning his lines
      phonetically

      the final autistic statement
      of the self-destroyer

      All my energy reaches out tonight
      to comprehend a miracle beyond

raising the dead: the undead to watch
back on the road of birth

7.

80 I am an American woman:
I turn that over

like a leaf pressed in a book
I stop and look up from

into the coals of the stove
or the black square of the window

Foot-slogging through the Bering Strait
jumping from the *Arbella* to my death

chained to the corpse beside me
I feel my pains begin

90 I am washed up on this continent
shipped here to be fruitful

my body a hollow ship
bearing sons to the wilderness

sons who ride away
on horseback, daughters

whose juices drain like mine
into the *arroyo* of stillbirths, massacres

Hanged as witches, sold as breeding-wenches
my sisters leave me

100 I am not the wheatfield
nor the virgin forest

I never chose this place
yet I am of it now

In my decent collar, in the daguerrotype
I pierce its legend with my look

my hands wring the necks of prairie chickens
I am used to blood

When the men hit the hobo track
I stay on with the children

110 my power is brief and local
but I know my power

I have lived in isolation
from other women, so much

in the mining camps, the first cities
the Great Plains winters

Most of the time, in my sex, I was alone

8.

Tonight in this northeast kingdom
striated iris stand in a jar with daisies

120 the porcupine gnaws in the shed
fireflies beat and simmer

caterpillars begin again
their long, innocent climb

the length of leaves of burdock
or webbing of a garden chair

plain and ordinary things
speak softly

the light square on old wallpaper
where a poster has fallen down

Robert Indiana's LOVE
130 leftover of a decade

9.

I do not want to simplify
Or: I would simplify

by naming the complexity
It was made over-simple all along

the separation of powers
the allotment of sufferings

her spine cracking in labor
his plow driving across the Indian graves

her hand unconscious on the cradle, her mind
140 with the wild geese

his mother-hatred driving him
into exile from the earth

the refugee couple with their cardboard luggage
standing on the ramshackle landing-stage

he with fingers frozen around his Law
she with her down quilt sewn through iron nights

—the weight of the old world, plucked
drags after them, a random feather-bed

10.

Her children dead of diphtheria, she
150 set herself on fire with kerosene

(O Lord I was unworthy
Thou didst find me out)

she left the kitchen scrubbed
down to the marrow of its boards

"The penalty for barrenness
is emptiness

my punishment is my crime
what I have failed to do, is me . . ."

—Another month without a show
160   and this the seventh year

O Father let this thing pass out of me
I swear to You

I will live for the others, asking nothing
I will ask nothing, ever, for myself

11.

Out back of this old house
datura tangles with a gentler weed

its spiked pods smelling
of bad dreams and death

I reach through the dark, groping
170   past spines of nightmare

to brush the leaves of sensuality
A dream of tenderness

wrestles with all I know of history
I cannot now lie down

with a man who fears my power
or reaches for me as for death

or with a lover who imagines
we are not in danger

12.

If it was lust that had defined us—
180   their lust and fear of our deep places

we have done our time
as faceless torsos licked by fire

we are in the open, on our way—
our counterparts

the pinyon jay, the small
gilt-winged insect

the Cessna throbbing level
the raven floating in the gorge

the rose and violet vulva of the earth
190   filling with darkness

yet deep within a single sparkle
of red, a human fire

and near and yet above the western planet
calmly biding her time

13.
They were the distractions, lust and fear
but are

themselves a key
Everything that can be used, will be:

the fathers in their ceremonies
200   the genital contests

the cleansing of blood from pubic hair
the placenta buried and guarded

their terror of blinding
by the look of her who bore them

If you do not believe
that fear and hatred

read the lesson again
in the old dialect

14.
But can't you see me as a human being
210   he said

What is a human being
she said

I try to understand
he said

what will you undertake
she said

will you punish me for history
he said

what will you undertake
220   she said

do you believe in collective guilt
he said

let me look in your eyes
she said

15.

Who is here. The Erinyes.[1]
One to sit in judgment.

One to speak tenderness.
One to inscribe the verdict on the canyon wall.

If you have not confessed
230   the damage

if you have not recognized
the Mother of reparations

if you have not come to terms
with the women in the mirror

if you have not come to terms
with the inscription

the terms of the ordeal
the discipline   the verdict

if still you are on your way
240   still She awaits your coming

16.

"Such women are dangerous
to the order of things"

and yes, we will be dangerous
to ourselves

groping through spines of nightmare
(*datura* tangling with a simpler herb)

because the line dividing
lucidity from darkness

is yet to be marked out

250   Isolation, the dream
of the frontier woman

leveling her rifle along
the homestead fence

still snares our pride
—a suicidal leaf

laid under the burning-glass
in the sun's eye

Any woman's death diminishes me

---

[1]The Furies; in Greek mythology, terrible winged goddesses who avenge unpunished crime.

Gregory Corso

Gregory Corso (1930–   ), born in New York, has worked as a manual
laborer, a merchant seaman, and a teacher. Two of his early books were
published by City Lights Books in San Francisco, where he belonged to the
Beat Generation.

Marriage

Should I get married? Should I be good?
Astound the girl next door with my velvet suit and faustus hood?
Don't take her to movies but to cemeteries
tell all about werewolf bathtubs and forked clarinets
then desire her and kiss her and all the preliminaries
and she going just so far and I understanding why
not getting angry saying You must feel! It's beautiful to feel!
Instead take her in my arms lean against an old crooked tombstone
and woo her the entire night the constellations in the sky—

10 When she introduces me to her parents
back straightened, hair finally combed, strangled by a tie,
should I sit knees together on their 3rd degree sofa
and not ask Where's the bathroom?
How else to feel other than I am,
often thinking Flash Gordon soap—
O how terrible it must be for a young man
seated before a family and the family thinking
We never saw him before! He wants our Mary Lou!
After tea and homemade cookies they ask What do you do for a living?
20 Should I tell them? Would they like me then?
Say All right get married, we're losing a daughter
but we're gaining a son—
And should I then ask Where's the bathroom?

O God, and the wedding! All her family and her friends
and only a handful of mine all scroungy and bearded
just wait to get at the drinks and food—
And the priest! he looking at me as if I masturbated
asking me Do you take this woman for your lawful wedded wife?
And I trembling what to say say Pie Glue!
30 I kiss the bride all those corny men slapping me on the back
She's all yours, boy! Ha-ha-ha!
And in their eyes you could see some obscene honeymoon going on—
Then all that absurd rice and clanky cans and shoes
Niagara Falls! Hordes of us! Husbands! Wives! Flowers! Chocolates!
All streaming into cozy hotels
All going to do the same thing tonight
The indifferent clerk he knowing what was going to happen
The lobby zombies they knowing what
The whistling elevator man he knowing
40 The winking bellboy knowing
Everybody knowing! I'd be almost inclined not to do anything!

Stay up all night! Stare that hotel clerk in the eye!
Screaming: I deny honeymoon! I deny honeymoon!
running rampant into those almost climactic suites
yelling Radio belly! Cat shovel!
O I'd live in Niagara forever! in a dark cave beneath the Falls
I'd sit there the Mad Honeymooner
devising ways to break marriages, a scourge of bigamy
a saint of divorce—

50   But I should get married I should be good
How nice it'd be to come home to her
and sit by the fireplace and she in the kitchen
aproned young and lovely wanting my baby
and so happy about me she burns the roast beef
and comes crying to me and I get up from my big papa chair
saying Christmas teeth! Radiant brains! Apple deaf!
God what a husband I'd make! Yes, I should get married!
So much to do! like sneaking into Mr Jones' house late at night
and cover his golf clubs with 1920 Norwegian books
60   Like hanging a picture of Rimbaud on the lawnmower
like pasting Tannu Tuva postage stamps all over the picket fence
like when Mrs Kindhead comes to collect for the Community Chest
grab her and tell her There are unfavorable omens in the sky!
And when the mayor comes to get my vote tell him
When are you going to stop people killing whales!
And when the milkman comes leave him a note in the bottle
Penguin dust, bring me penguin dust, I want penguin dust—

Yet if I should get married and it's Connecticut and snow
and she gives birth to a child and I am sleepless, worn,
70   up for nights, head bowed against a quiet window, the past behind me,
finding myself in the most common of situations a trembling man
knowledged with responsibility not twig-smear nor Roman coin soup—
O what would that be like!
Surely I'd give it for a nipple a rubber Tacitus
For a rattle a bag of broken Bach records
Tack Della Francesca all over its crib
Sew the Greek alphabet on its bib
And build for its playpen a roofless Parthenon

No, I doubt I'd be that kind of father
80   not rural not snow no quiet window
but hot smelly tight New York City
seven flights up, roaches and rats in the walls
a fat Reichian wife screeching over potatoes Get a job!
And five nose running brats in love with Batman
And the neighbors all toothless and dry haired
like those hag masses of the 18th century
all wanting to come in and watch TV
The landlord wants his rent
Grocery store Blue Cross & Electric Knights of Columbus

90   Impossible to lie back and dream Telephone snow, ghost parking—
No! I should not get married I should never get married!
But—imagine If I were married to a beautiful sophisticated woman
tall and pale wearing an elegant black dress and long black gloves
holding a cigarette holder in one hand and a highball in the other
and we lived high up in a penthouse with a huge window
from which we could see all of New York and ever farther on clearer days
No, can't imagine myself married to that pleasant prison dream—

O but what about love? I forget love
not that I am incapable of love
100   it's just that I see love as odd as wearing shoes—
I never wanted to marry a girl who was like my mother
And Ingrid Bergman was always impossible
And there's maybe a girl now but she's already married
And I don't like men and—
but there's got to be somebody!
Because what if I'm 60 years old and not married,
all alone in a furnished room with pee stains on my underwear
and everybody else is married! All the universe married but me!

Ah, yet well I know that were a woman possible as I am possible
110   then marriage would be possible—
Like SHE in her lonely alien gaud waiting her Egyptian lover
so I wait—bereft of 2,000 years and the bath of life.

Ted Hughes

Ted Hughes (1930–   ) attended Cambridge University, where he met and
married Sylvia Plath. His poems have been continually difficult, obdurate, and
violent, often about animals—real or mythical. He is concerned to discover and
explore instinctual life.

Thrushes

Terrifying are the attent sleek thrushes on the lawn,
More coiled steel than living—a poised
Dark deadly eye, those delicate legs
Triggered to stirrings beyond sense—with a start, a bounce, a stab
Overtake the instant and drag out some writhing thing.
No indolent procrastinations and no yawning stares,
No sighs or head-scratchings. Nothing but bounce and stab
And a ravening second.

Is it their single-mind-sized skulls, or a trained
10   Body, or genius, or a nestful of brats
Gives their days this bullet and automatic
Purpose? Mozart's brain had it, and the shark's mouth
That hungers down the blood-smell even to a leak of its own

Side and devouring of itself: efficiency which
Strikes too streamlined for any doubt to pluck at it
Or obstruction deflect.

With a man it is otherwise. Heroisms on horseback,
Outstripping his desk-diary at a broad desk,
Carving at a tiny ivory ornament
20   For years: his act worships itself—while for him,
Though he bends to be blent in the prayer, how loud and above what
Furious spaces of fire do the distracting devils
Orgy and hosannah, under what wilderness
Of black silent waters weep.

Gary Snyder

Gary Snyder (1930–   ) grew up on the West Coast and attended Reed
College. He did graduate work in Oriental languages at Berkeley and has lived
many years in Japan, studying Zen Buddhism in Kyoto. Now he lives in a house
of his own construction called Kitkitdizze, north of Sacramento, and practices
the life he preaches. See also page 434.

Above Pate Valley

We finished clearing the last
Section of trail by noon,
High on the ridge-side
Two thousand feet above the creek—
Reached the pass, went on
Beyond the white pine groves,
Granite shoulders, to a small
Green meadow watered by the snow,
Edged with Aspen—sun
10   Straight high and blazing
But the air was cool.
Ate a cold fried trout in the
Trembling shadows. I spied
A glitter, and found a flake
Black volcanic glass—obsidian—
By a flower. Hands and knees
Pushing the Bear grass, thousands
Of arrowhead leavings over a
Hundred yards. Not one good
20   Head, just razor flakes
On a hill snowed all but summer,
A land of fat summer deer,
They came to camp. On their
Own trails. I followed my own
Trail here. Picked up the cold-drill,
Pick, singlejack, and sack
Of dynamite.
Ten thousand years.

Geoffrey Hill

Geoffrey Hill (1932–   ) grew up in a Midlands English town, where his
father was the local policeman. He attended Oxford, and after earning two
degrees there went to Leeds, where he has become a professor. He writes his
poems slowly and produces little, but his work has great power and originality.

Merlin

I will consider the outnumbering dead:
For they are the husks of what was rich seed.
Now, should they come together to be fed,
They would outstrip the locusts' covering tide.

Arthur, Elaine, Mordred; they are all gone
Among the raftered galleries of bone.
By the long barrows of Logres they are made one,
And over their city stands the pinnacled corn.

Orpheus and Eurydice

Though there are wild dogs
    Infesting the roads
We have recitals, catalogues
    Of protected birds;

And the rare pale sun
    To water our days.
Men turn to savagery now or turn
    To the laws'

Immutable black and red.
10   To be judged for his song,
Traversing the still-moist dead,
    The newly-stung,

Love goes, carrying compassion
    To the rawly-difficult;
His countenance, his hands' motion,
    Serene even to a fault.

Sylvia Plath

Sylvia Plath (1932–1963) attended Smith College, and wrote with a professional skill from an early age. She attended Cambridge University on a fellowship, where she met and married the English poet Ted Hughes. After the birth of their second child, when Plath and Hughes were separated, her work abandoned its skillful surfaces and became profoundly emotional, angry, brilliant, and disturbing. There was a brief moment of great poetry, ended by her suicide. The posthumous *Ariel* (1965) collects her best poetry.

Poppies in October

Even the sun-clouds this morning cannot manage such skirts.
Nor the woman in the ambulance
Whose red heart blooms through her coat so astoundingly—

A gift, a love gift
Utterly unasked for
By a sky

Palely and flamily
Igniting its carbon monoxides, by eyes
Dulled to a halt under bowlers.

10   O my God, what am I
That these late mouths should cry open
In a forest of frost, in a dawn of cornflowers.

Lady Lazarus

I have done it again.
One year in every ten
I manage it—

A sort of walking miracle, my skin
Bright as a Nazi lampshade,
My right foot

A paperweight,
My face a featureless, fine
Jew linen.

10   Peel off the napkin
O my enemy.
Do I terrify?—

The nose, the eye pits, the full set of teeth?
The sour breath
Will vanish in a day.

Soon, soon the flesh
The grave cave ate will be
At home on me

And I a smiling woman.
20 I am only thirty.
And like the cat I have nine times to die.

This is Number Three.
What a trash
To annihilate each decade.

What a million filaments.
The peanut-crunching crowd
Shoves in to see

Them unwrap me hand and foot—
The big strip tease.
30 Gentleman, ladies,

These are my hands,
My knees.
I may be skin and bone,

Nevertheless, I am the same, identical woman.
The first time it happened I was ten.
It was an accident.

The second time I meant
To last it out and not come back at all.
I rocked shut

40 As a seashell.
They had to call and call
And pick the worms off me like sticky pearls.

Dying
Is an art, like everything else.
I do it exceptionally well.

I do it so it feels like hell.
I do it so it feels real.
I guess you could say I've a call.

It's easy enough to do it in a cell.
50 It's easy enough to do it and stay put.
It's the theatrical

Comeback in broad day
To the same place, the same face, the same brute
Amused shout:

"A miracle!"
That knocks me out.
There is a charge

For the eyeing of my scars, there is a charge
For the hearing of my heart—
60 It really goes.

And there is a charge, a very large charge,
For a word or a touch
Or a bit of blood

Or a piece of my hair or my clothes.
So, so, Herr Doktor.
So, Herr Enemy.

I am your opus,
I am your valuable,
The pure gold baby

70   That melts to a shriek.
I turn and burn.
Do not think I underestimate your great concern.

Ash, ash—
You poke and stir.
Flesh, bone, there is nothing there—

A cake of soap,
A wedding ring,
A gold filling.

Herr God, Herr Lucifer,
80   Beware
Beware.

Out of the ash
I rise with my red hair
And I eat men like air.

Death & Co.

Two, of course there are two.
It seems perfectly natural now—
The one who never looks up, whose eyes are lidded
And balled, like Blake's,
Who exhibits

The birthmarks that are his trademark—
The scald scar of water,
The nude
Verdigris of the condor.
10   I am red meat. His beak

Claps sidewise: I am not his yet.
He tells me how badly I photograph.
He tells me how sweet
The babies look in their hospital
Icebox, a simple

Frill at the neck,
Then the flutings of their Ionian
Death-gowns,

Then two little feet.
20   He does not smile or smoke.

The other does that,
His hair long and plausive.
Bastard
Masturbating a glitter,
He wants to be loved.

I do not stir.
The frost makes a flower,
The dew makes a star,
The dead bell,
30   The dead bell.

Somebody's done for.

Etheridge Knight

Etheridge Knight (1933–   ) was wounded in Korea and later became addicted to heroin. He supported his habit by stealing, which left him in the Indiana State Prison. He began to write poems in prison, where Gwendolyn Brooks visited and encouraged him. His first volume was called *Poems from Prison*. Since his release he has taught poetry at various colleges and conducted workshops all over the United States.

Hard Rock Returns to Prison from the Hospital for the Criminal Insane

Hard Rock was "known not to take no shit
From nobody," and he had the scars to prove it:
Split purple lips, lumped ears, welts above
His yellow eyes, and one long scar that cut
Across his temple and plowed through a thick
Canopy of kinky hair.

The WORD was that Hard Rock wasn't a mean nigger
Anymore, that the doctors had bored a hole in his head,
Cut out part of his brain, and shot electricity
10   Through the rest. When they brought Hard Rock back,
Handcuffed and chained, he was turned loose,
Like a freshly gelded stallion, to try his new status.
And we all waited and watched, like indians at a corral,
To see if the WORD was true.

As we waited we wrapped ourselves in the cloak
Of his exploits: "Man, the last time, it took eight
Screws to put him in the Hole." "Yeah, remember when he
Smacked the captain with his dinner tray?" "He set
The record for time in the Hole—67 straight days!"
20   "Ol Hard Rock! man, that's one crazy nigger."
And then the jewel of a myth that Hard Rock had once bit
A screw on the thumb and poisoned him with syphilitic spit.

The testing came, to see if Hard Rock was really tame.
A hillbilly called him a black son of a bitch
And didn't lose his teeth, a screw who knew Hard Rock
From before shook him down and barked in his face.
And Hard Rock did *nothing*. Just grinned and looked silly,
His eyes empty like knot holes in a fence.

30
And even after we discovered that it took Hard Rock
Exactly 3 minutes to tell you his first name,
We told ourselves that he had just wised up,
Was being cool; but we could not fool ourselves for long,
And we turned away, our eyes on the ground. Crushed.
He had been our Destroyer, the doer of things
We dreamed of doing but could not bring ourselves to do,
The fears of years, like a biting whip,
Had cut grooves too deeply across our backs.

2 Poems for Black Relocation Centers

I

Flukum couldn't stand the strain. Flukum
wanted inner and outer order, so
he joined the army where U.S. Manuals made
everything plain—even how to button his shirt,
and how to kill the yellow men. (If Flukum
ever felt hurt or doubt about who his enemy
was, the Troop Information Officer or the Stars
and Stripes[1] straightened him out.)
Plus, we must not forget
10
that Flukum was paid well to let the Red
Blood. And sin? If Flukum ever thought about sin
or Hell for squashing the yellow men, the good Chaplain
(Holy by God and by Congress) pointed out with
Devilish skill that to kill the colored men was not
altogether a sin.

Flukum marched back from the war, straight and tall,
and with presents for all: a water pipe for daddy,
teeny tea cups for mama, sheer silk for tittee, and
a jade inlaid dagger for me. But, with a smile
20
on his face in a place just across the bay,
Flukum, the patriot, got shot that same day,
got shot in his great wide chest, bedecked with good
conduct ribbons. He died surprised, he had thought
the enemy far away on the other side of the sea.

(When we received his belongings they took away my dagger.)

[1]Newspaper published for U.S. service personnel overseas

II
Dead. He died in Detroit, his beard
was filled with lice; his halo glowed
and his white robe flowed magnificently
over the charred beams and splintered glass;
30   his stern blue eyes were rimmed with red,
and full of reproach; and the stench: roasted rats
and fat baby rumps swept up his nose that
had lost its arch of triumph. He died outraged,
and indecently, shouting impieties and betrayals.
And he arose out of his own ashes. Stripped.
A faggot in steel boots.

Imamu Amiri Baraka

Imamu Amiri Baraka (LeRoi Jones) (1934–   ) is a leading black playwright
and poet. He has also published short stories and polemical prose. He began
publishing as an integrated black writer and edited a magazine in collaboration
with white editors. In later years his politics have moved from black
separatism to Marxism-Leninism.

Watergate

"Dead Crow" is an ol ugly
eagle
i know
run a "eagle
laundry"
wash
eagles
over & over
this eagle wash
10   hisself
like lady macbeth
blood mad & sterile
hooked teeth
pulled
out
in a flag costume
just stripes
no stars

Careers

What is the life
of the old lady
standing
on the stair
print flowered
housedress

gray and orange
hair
bent
10 on a rail
eyes open for
jr.
bobby
jb, somebody
to come, and carry her
wish
slow
cripple woman, still does
white folks work
20 in the mornings she get up
creeps into a cadillac
up into the florient lilac titty valleys
of blind ugliness, you think the woman loves
the younger white woman
the woman she ladles soup for
the radio she turns on when the white lady nods
she carries them in her bowed back hunched face
my grandmother workd the same
but stole things for jesus' sake
30 we wore boss rags in grammar school
straight off the backs of straight up americans
used but groovy and my grandmother when she returned at night
with mason jars and hat boxes full of goods
probably asked for forgiveness on the bus
i think the lady across from me must do the same
though she comes back in a cab, so times, it seems,
have changed.

Wendell Berry

Wendell Berry (1934–   ) was born in Kentucky, lived in New York briefly,
and returned to Kentucky, where for a time he taught at the University.
Increasingly Berry has turned to farming his own land and to writing about
"culture and agriculture." He has written novels and books of essays as well as
poems. With Gary Synder, he is a poet whose work and life serve to preserve
the planet.

The Wild Geese

Horseback on Sunday morning,
harvest over, we taste persimmon
and wild grape, sharp sweet
of summer's end. In time's maze
over the fall fields, we name names
that went west from here, names
that rest on graves. We open

a persimmon seed to find the tree
that stands in promise,
10 pale, in the seed's marrow.
Geese appear high over us,
pass, and the sky closes. Abandon,
as in love or sleep, holds
them to their way, clear,
in the ancient faith: what we need
is here. And we pray, not
for new earth or heaven, but to be
quiet in heart, and in eye
clear. What we need is here.

Mark Strand

Mark Strand (1934–   ) was born in Canada and attended colleges in the
United States, where he has settled. He lives in New York City.

Pot Roast

I gaze upon the roast,
that is sliced and laid out
on my plate
and over it
I spoon the juices
of carrot and onion.
And for once I do not regret
the passage of time.

I sit by a window
10 that looks
on the soot-stained brick of buildings
and do not care that I see
no living thing—not a bird,
not a branch in bloom,
not a soul moving
in the rooms
behind the dark panes.
These days when there is little
to love or to praise
20 one could do worse
than yield
to the power of food.
So I bend

to inhale
the steam that rises
from my plate, and I think
of the first time
I tasted a roast
like this.

30   It was years ago
        in Seabright,
        Nova Scotia;
        my mother leaned
        over my dish and filled it
        and when I finished
        filled it again.
        I remember the gravy,
        its odor of garlic and celery,
        and sopping it up
40   with pieces of bread.

        And now
        I taste it again.
        The meat of memory.
        The meat of no change.
        I raise my fork in praise,
        and I eat.

Charles Wright

Charles Wright (1935–   ) comes from Virginia and lives in California, where he teaches at the University of California at Irvine.

Virgo Descending

        Through the viridian (and black of the burnt match),
        Through ox-blood and ochre, the ham colored clay,
        Through plate after plate, down
        Where the worm and the mole will not go,
        Through ore-seam and fire-seam,
        My grandmother, senile and 89, crimpbacked, stands
        Like a door ajar on her soft bed,
        The open beams and bare studs of the hall
        Pink as an infant's skin in the floating dark;
10   Shavings and curls swing down like snowflakes across her face.

        My aunt and I walk past. As always, my father
        Is planning rooms, dragging his lame leg,
        Stroke-straightened and foreign, behind him,
        An aberrant 2-by-4 he can't fit snug.
        I lay my head on my aunt's shoulder, feeling
        At home, and walk on.
        Through arches and door jambs, the spidery wires
        And coiled cables, the blueprint takes shape:
        My mother's room to the left, the door closed;
20   My father's room to the left, the door closed—

        Ahead, my brother's room, unfinished;
        Behind, my sister's room, also unfinished.
        Buttresses, winches, block-and-tackle: the scale of everything

Is enormous. We keep on walking. And pass
My aunt's room, almost complete, the curtains up,
The lamp and the medicine arranged
In their proper places, in arm's reach of where the bed will go . . .
The next one is mine, now more than half done,
Cloyed by the scent of jasmine
30 White-gummed and anxious, their mouths sucking the air dry.

Home is what you lie in, or hang above, the house
Your father made, or keeps on making,
The dirt you moisten, the sap you push up and nourish . . .
I enter the living room, it, too, unfinished, its far wall
Not there, opening on to a radiance
I can't begin to imagine, a light
My father walks from, approaching me,
Dragging his right leg, rolling his plans into a perfect curl.
That light, he mutters, that damned light.
40 We can't keep it out. It keeps on filling your room.

Charles Simic

Charles Simic (1938–   ) was born in Yugoslavia and came to the United
States in 1949. He lives in New Hampshire and has published three books of
poems.

Fork

This strange thing must have crept
Right out of hell.
It resembles a bird's foot
Worn around the cannibal's neck.

As you hold it in your hand,
As you stab with it into a piece of meat,
It is possible to imagine the rest of the bird:
Its head which like your fist
Is large, bald, beakless and blind.

Tom Clark

Tom Clark (1941–   ) was born in Illinois, attended the University of
Michigan, and studied at Cambridge University in England. He writes books on
baseball: *Champagne and Baloney* about Charles Finley, *No Big Deal* about Mark
Fidrych.

Poem

Like musical instruments
Abandoned in a field
The parts of your feelings

Are starting to know a quiet
The pure conversion of your
Life into art seems destined

Never to occur
You don't mind
You feel spiritual and alert

10   As the air must feel
Turning into sky aloft and blue
You feel like

You'll never feel like touching anything or anyone
Again
And then you do

Louise Glück

Louise Glück (1943–   ) lives in Vermont and has published two collections
of her poems, the latest *The House on the Marshland* (1975).

Gratitude

Do not think I am not grateful for your small
kindness to me.
I like small kindnesses.
In fact I actually prefer them to the more
substantial kindness, that is always eying you,
like a large animal on a rug,
until your whole life reduces
to nothing but waking up morning after morning
cramped, and the bright sun shining on its tusks.

Gregory Orr

Gregory Orr (1947–   ) published two books of poems, *Burning the Empty
Nests* and *Gathering the Bones Together,* while still in his twenties. He was born
in upper New York state and attended Antioch College and Columbia
University. He teaches at the University of Virginia. See also pages 414 and
420.

The Sweater

I will lose you. It is written
into this poem the way
the fisherman's wife knits
his death into the sweater.

Joyce Peseroff

Joyce Peseroff (1948–   ) grew up in New York City, studied writing at the University of California at Irvine, and lives outside Boston.

The Hardness Scale

Diamonds are forever so I gave you quartz
which is #7 on the hardness scale
and it's hard enough to get to know anybody these days
if only to scratch the surface
and quartz will scratch six other mineral surfaces:
it will scratch glass
it will scratch gold
it will even
scratch your eyes out one morning—you can't be
10   too careful.
Diamonds are industrial so I bought
a ring of topaz
which is #8 on the hardness scale.
I wear it on my right hand, the way it was
supposed to be, right? No tears and fewer regrets
for reasons smooth and clear as glass. Topaz will scratch glass,
it will scratch your quartz,
and all your radio crystals. You'll have to be silent
the rest of your days
20   not to mention your nights. Not to mention
the night you ran away very drunk very
very drunk and you tried to cross the border
but couldn't make it across the lake.
Stirring up geysers with the oars you drove the red canoe
in circles, tried to pole it but
your left hand didn't know
what the right hand was doing.
You fell asleep
and let everyone know it when you woke up.
30   In a gin-soaked morning (hair of the dog) you went
hunting for geese,
shot three lake trout in violation of the game laws,
told me to clean them and that
my eyes were bright as sapphires
which is #9 on the hardness scale.
A sapphire will cut a pearl
it will cut stainless steel
it will cut vinyl and mylar and will probably
cut a record this fall
40   to be released on an obscure label known only to aficionados.
I will buy a copy.
I may buy you a copy
depending on how your tastes have changed.
I will buy copies for my friends

we'll get a new needle,
a diamond needle,
which is #10 on the hardness scale
and will cut anything.
It will cut wood and mortar,
50 plaster and iron,
it will cut the sapphires in my eyes and I will bleed
blind as 4 A.M. in the subways when even degenerates
are dreaming, blind as the time
you shot up the room with a new hunting rifle
blind drunk
as you were.
You were #11 on the hardness scale
later that night
apologetic as
60 you worked your way up
slowly from the knees
and you worked your way down
from the open-throated blouse.
Diamonds are forever so I give you softer things.

TO READ A PLAY

Chapter 1 **The Mental Theater**

Each genre of literature suggests its own style of reading. We usually read fiction and poetry silently, in private. When we read plays, privacy and silence impoverish the genre, for a play comes alive only when it is performed before an audience. In a theater, actors' voices may sink to a whisper, rise to a shout, or tremble with emotion: bodies gesture, eyes weep; flowing robes sweep beneath elegant wigs in front of painted mountains, while a bird sings offstage. Characters with names like Hamlet and Hedda Gabler walk, leap, wheel about; others dance, strut, collapse on a stage that (we are instructed) is a castle in Denmark or a drawing room in Norway. Characters hold objects in their hands: the skull of an old jester, a philosopher's manuscript. When we read drama* in silence and in private, we must make up for the absence of sight and sound.

The playwright,* the poet, and the novelist have different powers at their disposal. Neither playwright nor novelist can expect focused attention on particular words as the poet can. Nor can the playwright declaim onstage his own psychological analysis of character the way the novelist sometimes does. The play we read is a **script** (dialogue and stage directions) in which the playwright provides the means for a production that will *show* characters in action, and in this showing drama discovers its power: the dramatist has the advantage of

---

****Drama** can mean several things. It means the entire genre of plays, as in "An Introduction to Drama." It means a historical segment of the genre, as in "Greek drama." Yet *a* drama is a single play—"*Hamlet* is Shakespeare's greatest drama." We also use the word as a metaphor to describe exciting events: "a real-life drama." A **playwright** writes plays, as a wheelwright makes wheels. (Do not spell the word *playwrite*.)

employing actual bodies and voices of skilled actors, costumed by expert designers, directed and coached and rehearsed for performance. With the movements of bodies, occupying space, surrounded by objects, the playwright's words engage the playwright's audience.

The biggest distinguishing fact about the genre of drama is that to experience it fully we must experience it communally. An audience responds to language, spectacle, motion, and gesture as a community, and each of us is affected by the responses—laughter, tears, coughs, intaken breaths—of people around us. Actors are aware of audience too, and partly because no audience is identical to another, no two performances of a play are ever quite the same—even when the same actors perform the same drama twice in one day. The uniqueness of each performance is product of the interaction of actors and watchers.

Reading drama in private, we can to a degree supply what is missing by making a mental theater as we read. We can supply the missing voice, gesture, motion, and spectacle. The more we have experienced theater, the more vividly we can populate the brain's stage with imagined actors.

Sometimes, knowing what we are doing, we may turn off the lights of the mental stage and read plays as if they were stories or poems. Shakespeare's plays *are* poetry as well as drama, and they reward the close attention to language that poetry demands of us. Chekhov's plays, with their psychological curiosities, and Shaw's with their psychological stage directions, invite us to investigate and understand character, as if we were reading Katherine Anne Porter's or Joseph Conrad's fiction. When we read **closet drama**—works written in the form of plays but intended for reading rather than for production—of course we read as if we were reading fiction or poetry.

But we do not read drama fully without knowing particularities of staging and performance. To prepare the way for reading plays, let us start by listing Aristotle's classic components of drama and then the common features of the theater like direction, acting, costuming, blocking, and lighting.

Chapter 2 **Elements of Drama**

The first critic to analyze plays was the Greek philosopher Aristotle, in his *Poetics*. While Aristotle based his analysis only on Greek plays, his description of drama's elements remains useful. He discussed them in an order of importance: plot, character, thought, diction, spectacle, and song. Of course, many modern playwrights and directors depart from Aristotle's sequence. Some elevate character over plot, others put thought above both plot and character; still others emphasize one or two qualities to the exclusion of others. **Melodramas**, for instance, are plays in which action and suspense dominate the stage at the expense of thought, character, and all other qualities; musicals like *A Chorus Line* emphasize spectacle and song.

Plot

Plot is the sequence of events in narration, the structure of action and incident by which the playwright tells a story. Usually a play's plot divides into **acts**, which are the main divisions of plays, traditionally signaled by the lowering of the curtain if one is used and raising of the house lights, followed by an intermission. Modern plays are usually divided into three or two acts; older plays often have five. Both the Greeks and the Elizabethans performed plays without interruption, like today's films, but modern editors and directors have divided old plays into acts for modern audiences and readers. Acts are often subdivided into **scenes**, separate episodes of dialogue among groups of characters.

Acts and scenes are the blocks out of which the playwright constructs the plot. A commonplace example of plot is "Boy meets girl, boy loses girl, boy gets girl" (the sexes are reversible). The cliché describes a brief union, then a crisis or conflict of separation, and finally a resolution of conflict joining girl and boy. It makes a stick-figure story, which exemplifies the **unified** or **symmetrical plot**. In a unified plot, the audience finds formal satisfaction in the raising and resolution of **suspense** and expectation. If an issue is raised or a problem is stated early in the play, we know that the plot will return to this issue or problem. Suspense raises **tension** when it asks if something desired or feared will happen. In a **conflict** (often between characters, sometimes between character and circumstance or idea or fate) we need to discover who will prevail and how. When the play's end answers the questions suspense had raised, our tension is resolved. As audience we are first excited, then we are relaxed. Along with our emotional response, we take esthetic pleasure in resolution of tension, as we do in the tension and release of a piece of music when we enjoy a theme's return.

All plays include conflict, tension, suspense, resolution. But plots need not be unified or symmetrical. Sometimes a plot is **linear** or **episodic**, thrusting a narrative forward scene by scene. The episodic plot emphasizes time and sequence, and it can be seen mainly in the pageants or panoramas by which townspeople sometimes present the history of their town at its centennial. Such linear plots proceed chronologically without attention to symmetries or balances. Of course they may retain conflict, tension, resolution: they tend to proceed by a series of conflicts resolved and new conflicts encountered; the township survives a flood only to be ravaged by cholera. An episodic play in this volume is Shaw's *Saint Joan,* where a life unfolds through chosen episodes; the film *Citizen Kane* is also episodic. Both play and movie are unified in ways besides plot—by character, by idea, in *Citizen Kane* by a thematic device—but the plots are largely linear and episodic.

Oedipus the King, Hamlet, Tartuffe, Hedda Gabler, and *Death of a Salesman* are all plays with a unified or symmetrical plot. For familiar examples of each plot type at its extreme we need look no further than a television play. A soap opera is episodic, interweaving different plot lines like braided hair. On the other hand, a half-hour situation comedy is unified, even predictable in shape— with a goal (raise money for the school band) and a conflict (against the school board's rules) and a crisis (a student ruse is defeated) and a resolution (alternate funding discovered).

In many plays, more than one plot occupies the stage; if one plot dominates, anything else is considered a **subplot**. In an episodic play, a subplot may be a story told and completed in one episode; in a unified play it is likely to be ongoing; in either case, the subplot tells a story in tandem with the main story (often plots touch each other, as characters meet or overlap from one plot to another) that usually acts as commentary on the main story. In the heroic plays of the eighteenth century, the main plot was often a highly serious tale of love and honor; yet underneath the story of lords and ladies, servants or commoners played out a love story, less honorable and more funny, that cast an ironic reflection on the main plot. In Shakespeare's *A Midsummer Night's Dream,* the love-quarrels of the nobility and the love-quarrels of the fairy king and queen interweave to our delight; the workers' stage company, rehearsing a play about tragic lovers, makes a third set of characters interwoven with the other two.

It is helpful to know certain terms used in discussing plot. Often at the beginning of a play, the author needs to present information on which the plot is based. In *Saint Joan,* Shaw must let us know about the military and political situation of the French before he can show us Joan trying to rectify matters. **Exposition** is the presentation of necessary background information. We find exposition in fiction and in poetry also, but on the stage it gives the playwright a particular problem; poet or storyteller can speak as narrator, but the playwright cannot speak so directly. (Occasionally plays use narrators. Shakespeare occasionally used a **prologue**—lines spoken by an actor to introduce a play— and Thornton Wilder's Stage Manager in *Our Town* narrates background and provides commentary, but the device is uncommon.) A skillful playwright gives us necessary information through the dialogue of his characters—so cleverly that we are not aware that we are being informed. A less experienced writer may begin a play with the butler and the maid, otherwise unimportant to the story, letting us know that Lord and Lady Redesworth are expected home soon from the bridge tournament, that their spendthrift nephew will arrive for supper, and that the murder trial of Sir Humphrey's niece begins in the morning.

Clumsy exposition is faulty plotting. Plays without conflict or tension bore us; so do plays in which the motives for action seem arbitrary; many a poor playwright has killed an innocent character merely to lower the first-act curtain. On the other hand, some second-rate theater is skillful in plotting—and we associate its inferiority with the slickness of its skill. Of course skillful construction is essential to the theater, but if a play shows nothing but formal skill we belittle it with the label **well-made play**. The expression refers to a type of theater piece developed by the French playwright Eugène Scribe (1791–1861) and his followers, a play constructed on an ingenious pattern, sure to satisfy the box office—often rather shallow in situation and character. Ibsen (who directed nearly a hundred light French plays as an apprentice) broke away from the formula but kept elements like the "obligatory scene"—as when Hedda Gabler's idealistic illusions are destroyed. Bernard Shaw inverted the tricks of the well-made play to disguise his satire of Victorian complacency.

If exposition tells us what has already happened or can be expected to happen, **foreshadowing** predicts, hints, warns, or threatens what *may* happen. Oedipus warns what will happen to the guilty party (whom the audience knows to be Oedipus himself, thus contributing to the play's tension). As the complexities and complications build, we speak of **rising action**—as if it toiled uphill through small conflicts and minor crises toward a supreme crisis, a final conflict. This is the play's climax, answer to the **dramatic question** posed by the conflict: Will Hamlet avenge his father's murder? After the climax, there are often smaller questions left to be answered, problems to be solved; the play's conclusion, a **falling action** generally swifter than its rising action, may be called its **resolution**, or its **conclusion**, or its **dénouement**—from a French word that means the untying of a knot. If the dénouement drags on too long, though, we grow displeased or frustrated and call it **anticlimax**.

Character

A **character** is an imagined person, created by the playwright in dialogue and stage direction, made particular by director and by actor. A character begins in the script—a potential, an outline, a series of possibilities noted in dialogue— and can be realized in different ways (and with different degrees of success) by different directors and actors.

We may divide characters, as we find them in reading drama, as realistic, nonrealistic, and stereotyped. A realistic character is a human being presented with background or history that discloses motivation for actions and feelings. Usually in the realistic drama we **empathize** with the character; empathy allows us to *feel* ourselves *into* a character, imaginatively to become that character. A nonrealistic character, on the other hand, may be nonhuman, a talking fish or a leprechaun. When medieval playwrights wrote allegory for the theater, characters on the stage would take the roles of abstractions like Christian or Lust. In contemporary pageants we sometimes find allegorical figures standing in for abstractions like Liberty or Totalitarianism. But allegory is only one form of nonrealism. William Butler Yeats in his modern poetic drama uses characters called The Fool and The Blind Man. They cannot be reduced to abstractions, the way allegorical figures can, but neither are they realistic human beings with histories and motives.

The **stereotype** is a familiar kind of character. When we use the word *stereotype* about modern drama, we are usually being critical, as when we criticize a poet for using clichés or stock language. In a television show about a police department, we often find stereotypes like the old street-wise detective paired with the young idealistic detective. In the classic American western movie, we expect the figure of the hero's loyal sidekick.

In earlier times, many dramatists wrote parts for characters their audience expected. When we speak of such characters as stereotypes, we speak of expected features of a kind of drama; we are not being critical. In Roman comedy audiences laughed at a bragging, vainglorious military man; English comedy from Shakespeare's time onward invented variants on the stereotype of the fop—generally overdressed peacocks with pretentions to valor and to success with women—whose lies and stratagems are comically exposed. A stereotype is a collection of characteristics. While a fully drawn character may be expected to change within a play, a stereotype remains a sum of qualities unchanged and unchanging. Even exposed, the fop will remain a fop.

In great drama, we find characters who enter as stereotypes but soon transcend their expected roles. One stereotype is the **ingénue**—the innocent or naïve young woman—but to call *Hamlet*'s Ophelia an ingenue, while true enough, tells us little about her. Shakespeare creates Ophelia's character with Ophelia's distinctive language, and she becomes a fully realized character, as when she says, observing Hamlet when he appears insane:

> O, what a noble mind is here o'erthrown!
> The courtier's, soldier's, scholar's, eye, tongue, sword,
> Th'expectancy and rose of the fair state,

The glass of fashion, and the mould of form,
Th'observed of all observers, quite quite down,
And I of ladies most deject and wretched,
That sucked the honey of his music vows,
Now see that noble and most sovereign reason
Like sweet bells jangled, out of tune and harsh,
That unmatched form and feature of blown youth,
Blasted with ecstasy!

No essayist could *tell* of devotion and grief more eloquently than Shakespeare *shows* us in Ophelia's words.

Frequently conflict, mentioned in discussing plot, flares up between the characters of a play. We call the hero of a play, especially a tragedy, the play's **protagonist**, and sometimes he finds himself in conflict with an enemy or **antagonist** who seeks to thwart his purpose. Not all plays are so neat in their opposition of characters. If Oedipus is clearly the protagonist of the play bearing his name, his early conflict with Kreon would seem to name Kreon an antagonist; but surely Oedipus's ultimate antagonist is Fate. In *Hamlet* the villain is Claudius, but Hamlet's conflict is largely internal.

In a modern play, the playwright may indicate character by writing **stage directions** in the script, lines describing character or scene or action. At the beginning of *Saint Joan,* Shaw has the violent Captain Robert seize his steward *by the scruff of his neck.* After a few words of dialogue, Shaw's stage directions tell us *Robert has to let him drop. He* [the steward] *squats on his knees on the floor, contemplating his own master resignedly.* Shaw gives the actor something to do on the stage; with the last word of stage direction he specifies a facial expression.

Stage business is the gesture or nonverbal action of actors on the stage; stage business contributes to characterization. Although the modern playwright supplies business in his stage directions, no author describes every minute action or expression of every character. In any production of a play, characterization is developed by further stage business, facial expression, gesture, and movement—hundreds of particulars not specified in any script. These expressions of the text are the province of the play's **director**—the person who oversees the play's performance, controlling interpretations, movement, pacing, lighting, scenery, and integrating all the dramatic ingredients. When we stage a play in our mental theater, we are our own director.

With the director we pass from characterization as a quality of the script to characterization as a product of performance. Stage business, in practice, is partly the playwright's doing and partly the director's. At least this division of labor holds true for the modern theater; until the eighteenth century, authors did not supply stage directions, and directors as such were unknown. Plays were produced under somebody's leadership—perhaps the chief actor of the company, perhaps the playwright, perhaps the stage manager. When the modern director takes on an old play, he feels free to invent his own staging. For that matter, many directors feel considerable freedom to make new interpreta-

tions of a modern play, even to departing from the playwright's indicated interpretation.

If the director is the emperor of characterization in the play's world, actors
are the lieutenants who control the realm. The actor's skills, acquired over
years of training and experience, cover the range of feelings that voice and body
can express. Volume, pitch, timbre, and accent of voice combine with the vocabulary of body language in gesture, gait, and posture. But actors' skills must
work in service to the whole production, and it is the director's job to set the
overall tone and to make the production cohere. A simple text is subject to
many interpretations. Readers and critics of *Hamlet* differ widely in their understanding of the play, and different productions reflect these differences.
Laurence Olivier's film production of *Hamlet* (1948) has been called a psychoanalytic interpretation, dwelling on the young prince's attachment to his
mother as the motive for his actions. On the other hand, a few decades back
the American actor Maurice Evans directed a fast-moving and decisive *Hamlet,*
the prince less meditative than he is in Olivier's production. To fit these varying
interpretations of the protagonist, each production required a different Gertrude, a different Ophelia.

The director begins production with a script from which he or she derives a
notion of character. Under ideal circumstances, the director chooses actors
who fulfill the requirements of the interpretation. One director might want a
muscular, vigorous lead actor; another might want someone lean and ascetic.

Director and actor are also subject to the **theatrical conventions** of their day.
Stereotypes are conventions of theater. In the Greek theater it was a convention
that the players speak from behind masks; women's parts in Elizabethan theater
were taken by boys. The usual realism of the modern play is itself a series of
conventions; in most modern plays we take it as realistic that a drawing room
or a bedroom should have one open side, through which we can view the
proceedings, and that most of the actors face that open side as they speak to
each other. Although it is easy enough to notice conventions alien to our own,
like masks, we seldom notice the conventions we are used to.

Perhaps nothing dates so quickly as theatrical styles and conventions. For
example, on the Elizabethan stage, where boys played women's roles, love
scenes were understandably stylized. When in the late seventeenth century
women began to play women's roles, love scenes became more realistic; yet
from the Restoration until recent times, an actor and actress in a passionate
love scene would wait for applause after an eloquent embrace, as if they had
just sung an operatic duet. Only in the late nineteenth century and the early
twentieth did actors begin to imitate feeling, not from the gesture book but from
their own psyches and their director's ideas of human character.

Some actors are highly technical, learning by study what to do with body,
voice, and expression, and they reproduce feeling by expertise. Others draw
from their own feelings, improvising dramatic movement and gesture out of
private emotion. Konstantin Stanislavsky (1865–1938) proposed in his book
An Actor Prepares (1926) that actors perform by summoning their own feelings. In his Moscow Art Theater, he trained his actors to search their own

psyches for their characters' emotions, and then to act on stage as the character would.

Language

Aristotle's fourth element of drama is usually translated "diction." In the *Poetics* Aristotle defines the style appropriate to Greek drama, writing from a theatrical tradition other than ours. The importance he grants to language may serve to remind us that plays are language first, that they begin as dialogue, and that great dialogue is words arranged in the best order. (Exceptions like the **one-actor play**—Samuel Beckett's *Krapp's Last Tape,* for instance—give us theatrical language without dialogue, although Krapp converses with his own taped voice. Wordless **mime theater**, sometimes one-actor performances like Marcel Marceau's, remain a portion of theater strictly speaking outside literature.) The greatest playwrights are great writers: Shakespeare and Sophocles poets, Chekhov and Shaw masters of prose. It is no coincidence that Shakespeare's sonnets and long poems would earn him prominence in the history of literature if he had written no plays or that Chekhov is often considered literature's greatest master of the short story.

The "best words" for a particular play depend on the subject undertaken. If we did not feel that the characters in *Death of a Salesman* speak in an American idiom, we would not believe in them. If the poetic language of Yeats's *Cat and the Moon* were attributed to the salesman Willy Loman, we would find the play intolerably confusing. Good plays range wide in their language, from the poetic choruses of Sophocles to the natural non sequiturs of Chekhov's characters in *The Cherry Orchard*. In comedy, characters often speak with a wit—balanced phrases, paradox, epigram—few of us can manage in everyday life; and as their language is, so is their witty construction of plot.

For a quick look at the difference language makes, glance at Shakespeare and Shakespearean paraphrase, pages 496–498. On page 904 are two translations of the same passage from Molière's *Tartuffe*.

Thought

For most readers, the thought of a play, its theme, its ideas, will take precedence over other elements. Thought is drama's summation, what remains in the mind when the theater is dark or the book is closed. Aristotle placed thought third, recognizing it as product of plot and character. For Aristotle, thought is the statement about human life that the play's action exemplifies. It resides largely in dialogue, Aristotle tells us, and can be subsumed under three headings: first, "proof and refutation"; second, "the excitation of the feelings, such as pity, fear, anger . . ."; third, "the suggestion of importance or its opposite."

These three categories suggest different sorts of thought in drama, or different uses of thought. If a play offers "proof or refutation" the play is argumentative, and its design is **didactic.** To be didactic is to teach. There is a long tradition of plays which teach, which have a design on our thoughts and actions. Shaw's plays are almost always didactic as well as entertaining; they make persuasive statements about politics and society. Of course if a didactic play does not otherwise engage us, it will not convince us by its arguments or persuade us by its teaching; finding it *merely* didactic, we will dismiss it as propaganda.

Aristotle's second category of thought implies a response to script and production observable in the audience: "the excitation of the feelings. . . ." Aristotle does not separate idea from feeling: he includes emotions *within* his category of thought or theme. Finally Aristotle speaks of values—"importance and its opposite." Thought ascribes value—or lack of value—to a drama's action. Sophocles' subject in *Oedipus*—the welfare of a people, the fated guilt of their king, his punishment—has a magnitude to which his characters in their speech and actions are adequate. The "opposite of importance," on the other hand, can result from the triviality of a subject or from the inadequate treatment of a serious subject. The themes of popular dramatic art can often be justly summarized by a cliché: "It takes all kinds to make a world" or "There's a little bit of good in just about everybody."

In most plays, the protagonist's conflicts embody the play's thought. In *Saint Joan* Shaw uses the life of his protagonist as a vehicle for thought about politics, the state, and the individual. Although we cannot reduce *Hamlet*'s themes to an easy paraphrase, we can observe Shakespeare's thought in his protagonist's crises: first as Hamlet strives to establish his uncle's guilt, second as he struggles within himself to act upon his knowledge. We understand that the thought of the play centers on the question of Hamlet's *action* and on the conflicts within him that prevent or impede action.

But the reader does well to observe the minor characters as well as major ones, for in theater everything coalesces to create the play's thought. Thinking about a play, we should draw back from the emotional crises of the plot to ask ourselves, for instance, about Horatio's *function* in *Hamlet*: What does his presence mean to the play's ideas, as well as to its structure? If Lopahin were not onstage in *The Cherry Orchard,* what would be lacking in Chekhov's play? What use is Cléante in *Tartuffe*? By analyzing the intellectual function of a play's characters, we analyze the content of the play.

Sometimes a play or a film includes physical objects important to its thought. If a playwright continually reminds us of a place or a thing, onstage or off, we should consider its function and meaning in the play with as much attention as if it were another character. The cherry orchard itself in Chekhov's play is not listed among the performers and remains invisible to the audience, but it is essential to the play's theme and thought; Chekhov suggests as much by taking it for his title. In the film script of *Citizen Kane,* one word runs through the plot, a mysterious unidentified *Rosebud,* its nature revealed visually to the cinema audience in a late frame of film. Rosebud is a clue to Kane's character, and to the "importance and its opposite" of the life the film portrays.

Spectacle

The physical stage

Spectacle is what the audience sees, the play as it exists to the eye, the visual theater. The first element of spectacle is the theater itself and its physical stage. When we read *Oedipus the King* and *Hamlet,* it helps to know about the actual theaters Sophocles and Shakespeare wrote for. Beginning with the mid-seventeenth century, the most common western theater shape (almost universal until recent years) has been the **proscenium stage.** The stage with which modern Americans are most familiar is a slight variant, which we will call the **picture stage**: at the front of an auditorium is a framed, rectangular space—the proscenium arch—across which we may draw a **stage curtain.** At the bottom of the stage's front there are **footlights** for low illumination; at the top of the frame are further lights to cast illumination downward. This framed rectangular lighted space is the box within which the actors act, and it extends to various depths from the **stage front** to **stage rear.**

The original proscenium stages of the seventeenth century featured a **fore-stage**, a platform thrust into the audience before the proscenium arch. Most of the acting was done on this forward deck, but gradually in the eighteenth and in the earlier nineteenth centuries, the forestage grew smaller, and acting tended to concentrate itself behind the proscenium arch, where lighting could be better controlled, where scenery could be varied, where **stage machinery** could raise and lower painted scenes on pulleys, for instance, or slide them on rails laterally from the wings.

Although most theaters and auditoriums, from high schools to Broadway, still feature the picture stage, many vary in shape. In the later nineteenth century some theatrical producers began to experiment with the return of the forestage, often building a platform over the **orchestra pit**—a sunken area, below the level of the audience, between picture stage and the first row of seats, where musicians play their instruments in productions of musical plays and opera. Some more modern theaters, especially those built for the production of Shakespearean plays, extend a narrowing forestage (sometimes called the **thrust stage**) into the audience, with rows of seats on three sides. Some theatrical spaces are constructed with the audience seated on all sides—called the **arena stage**, or **theater in the round**. For this physical theater, plays must be directed to be seen on all sides and must do largely without scenery. Still other experimental theaters feature actors who wander among the spectators.

Scenery, set, and props

A director typically relies on a **set** or **scenic designer**; the **set** is the scenery and furniture the audience sees. The setting for a play may include a realistic painted **backdrop** of forest or castle, or the back of the set may be the wall of a room, with real wallpaper and a real window in it. The designer submits sketches to the director; carpenters and painters turn these designs into furniture and scenery. In the most realistic interpretations of plays, rooms look like rooms we live in and forests as much like forests as a designer's skills can make them. This sort of production may require many changes of scene as the play's plot moves from battleground to commander's tent to king's palace. Often the curtain is drawn while the set is changed. A production may use backdrops painted on sliding wings, stored out of sight to left and right until they are needed. Or sets may be lifted to hang above the stage, lowered by stage machinery when they are needed. Stage machinery needed for such equipment is expensive and bulky. Some modern stages are equipped with a **revolving stage**, a circular platform cut into the stage floor, moved by hand or by machine; this revolving stage is divided into segments, and each segment can be rotated to face the audience with a different set.

On the other hand, many modern directors use a nonrealistic set, even for scripts and productions with realistic characters. On a relatively bare stage, the designer may create a **unit set**, perhaps a platform with steps leading to it, and a few black boxes; as the script requires, a box may become a throne or a tree trunk, the platform a balcony or a bedroom. Such staging requires imagination from director and audience; it is cheaper in production and it allows the play to move faster because no set changes are required.

In nonrealistic modern theater, like Yeats's *The Cat and the Moon,* a non-realistic setting is often specified in stage directions: a curtain, a rug, a screen. Samuel Beckett's nonrealistic *Waiting for Godot* specifies only "A Country Road. A tree"; few designers have been tempted to realism. Taking the play-wright's general indication, the designer makes the set particular.

Props are properties, or portable pieces of scenery, not attached to walls or screens, which may include sofas and chairs or objects characters carry in their hands.

Costume

Only in the last century and a half has costuming attempted realism. When Elizabethans took on the roles of Romans, they dressed in high Elizabethan fashion (a practice used as an argument for performing old plays in the dress of our own day). Actors tended to strut the stage in their greatest finery and thus their clothing contributed to theatrical spectacle. In the middle of the nineteenth century, as the theater moved further toward the illusion of reality, actors began to wear clothes considered appropriate to the historical time of the script, and Romans looked as we believe Romans to have looked.

The play's director collaborates with the **costume designer** or **costumer** as he does with the set designer, and for many productions both settings and costumes are created by a single designer.

Makeup

On the Greek stage actors wore masks that made their faces look larger, more powerful from the distant perspective of the Greek auditorium. In the modern realistic stage, makeup is a portion of spectacle—and frequently it uses artifice to appear natural. The bright lighting of most stage productions can give a healthy actor the pallor of a corpse unless the actor first applies a ruddy base makeup, lightly rouges lips, and emphasizes eyes. Made-up eyes look larger; eyes tend to disappear without it, especially from the rear of the second balcony.

Lighting

The ancient stage, from the Greeks to the Elizabethans, used no light but the sun. The only variations of light occurred when an actor entered a shaded area of the stage, as when an Elizabethan hid or conspired under the small balcony at stage rear. When the theater moved indoors in the seventeenth century, only candles illuminated the stage, casting a dim and fitful light even when massed in candelabra. Successive technological innovations gradually improved stage lighting. Oil lamps afforded more control than candles and could cast bright light on a single part of the stage by the use of reflecting mirrors; colored glass in front of the flame could cast tinted light to imitate sunlight or fire. Then early in the nineteenth century came the gas light—still brighter than oil lamps and still more controllable. Late in the nineteenth century theaters began to use electric lights, which could go and off without the use of matches—a miracle.

Today's directors planning productions write **light cues** into their texts and work with lighting engineers to realize their intentions.* Options are many: light can be general and uniform all over the stage; light can illuminate one character or one group of characters, keeping the rest of the stage dark or dim; lights can emphasize the finality of a scene by turning off all at once (a **black-out**); lights can shine on an actor from the theater ceiling in front of the stage, or from a balcony, or from banks of lights at the theater's side; light can come from below (footlights) or behind (backlighting) or beside (from the wings.)

Lighting can further the plot as in the weird contrasts of melodrama, or the thought when it delineates part of the stage as a dream area or a reality area. Lights can be used for character; one actor can wear a virtual halo of **follow spots**. Lights can turn one character sallow and another ruddy. They can indicate the lapse of time by suggesting twilight or dawn. The rear of the stage may be occupied by a **cyclorama**—a curved white surface that readily accepts lighting, useful for sunrises, sunsets, rainbows, or the abstract play of color and shadow. With actors positioned behind gauze or **scrim**, a sidelight will render the gauze opaque and the actors invisible; a front light will reverse the vision—actors visible and gauze transparent; still another arrangement of lights will show the actors as shadows against the scrim.

Because light can create illusions of movement—when actors move out of light into dimness, for instance, they appear to move farther than they do— lighting is integral to the planning of the play's movement and gesture. The more subtle the play, the more subtle the lighting it calls for. Melodramas tend to be higher in contrast of dark and light, and musicals more bright, than *Hamlet* or *Saint Joan*. In the didactic theater of Brecht and others, the playwright may specify an even light—like the light in a classroom or lecture hall.

---

*A **lighting designer** is sometimes one of a three-part design team (with scenic and costume designers) who work with each other and with the director to mount a theater production.

Blocking

When directors plan a production, they plan the movement of players on the stage: this control of movement is called **blocking**. The audience looks at actors placed on stage in relationship to one another, and the director's blocking creates and continually recreates the relationships the audience perceives. Moving or standing still, bodies in relationship to each other can express character and further plot or contribute to the expression of idea. If character A walks nervously up and down during an interview with character B, who sits still, we observe in spectacle an enactment of character and conflict. Nowhere are directors more active or are their presences more felt than in this spectacle of bodies in relation.

Dance

A final element of spectacle is dance. In a musical play its presence is obvious and necessitates the use of a **choreographer** or dance director. These plays are entertainment, and spectacle remains spectacle. But in other plays, like Peter Shaffer's *Equus* or like Sean O'Casey's *Juno and the Paycock,* with its actor impersonating a bird, dance or dancelike movement is essential to plot, character, and thought.

Music and sound

When Aristotle incorporated music in his list of drama's components, he was writing about an ancient theater in which speech was probably sung or chanted. In theater as we know it, sound is part of the total effect: first as spoken dialogue, in its manner of speaking; then as nonverbal utterance by actors—laughs and grunts and cries of pain; then as noises made by props, like a chair scraping or a radio turned on, or Hedda Gabler's piano-playing; then as silence; then as sound effects, like train whistles and a mysterious snapping sound in *The Cherry Orchard* or a telephone ringing or an offstage gunshot.

Assembling the elements

Theatrical genius can be defined as the ability to make all these elements of theater work at once. Though the proportions of responsibility differ—playwright largely responsible for language and director largely responsible for spectacle—the results are interdependent. In good productions plot is not sacrificed to spectacle or sound to character, but all cohere to make the single masterpiece. In the plays that follow, we must gauge the possibilities of coherence in a script. Thinking of Aristotle's six categories, we can observe their potential interaction or integration. When Laertes and Ophelia talk with their father Polonius in *Hamlet*, the language provides us with plot, character, thought, and language; but the playwright has also allowed us, by his power of imaginative seeing, to make a mental theater.

Some suggestions for studying drama

Reading the plays that follow, students may study characterization and interpretation by reading scenes aloud in class, different students using the same words for different ideas of character. In discussion a class may simulate a production, down to details of gesture, costuming, and lighting. Still, it is good to practice not only at directing but at our most familiar role—at being an audience. If a class is able to attend a performance of any drama on any level of competence, it can profit by discussing the production in the terms used in this chapter. Excerpts from a recorded play heard in the classroom will provide no examples of spectacle but for that very reason may prove useful to consideration of plot, character, thought, voice-acting, and sound. A film will allow discussion of spectacle. Or the class may agree to watch the same television show (a half-hour dramatic show would be best) for discussions of dramatic ingredients. Some profit may even be discovered in analysis of the plot structure of a thirty-second commercial.

Chapter 3 **Greek Drama, Tragedy, and Sophocles**

History

About the origins of Greek theater we can only speculate; by the time we are able to speak of probable fact we are only a century away from Sophocles' *Oedipus the King,* which was first produced about 430 or 425 B.C. Apparently by 535 B.C. the citizens of Athens watched tragedies during the festival of Dionysus—a Greek fertility god and the god of wine, worshiped in late winter and early spring at ceremonies called the **Dionysia**. One part of the Dionysia was a contest among playwrights, in which three authors each entered a tragic **trilogy** (three plays) accompanied by a short comedy or satire.

Drama seems to have evolved from religious worship in which a chorus of voices spoke hymns to Dionysus. We are told that a man named Thespis added to the chorus the figure of a single speaker who addressed the group and thus invented drama. Although further speakers or characters were added, the **chorus** always remained part of Greek drama, speaking as the collective voice of a people. In some plays the chorus leader detaches himself from the group, almost becoming another individual character, to engage in dialogue.

The great playwright Aeschylus (ca. 524–456 B.C.) wrote the earliest plays that survive. According to Aristotle, it was Aeschylus who added a second speaker to Thespis's first, and Sophocles (ca. 496–406 B.C.) who added the third actor and fixed the fluctuating size of the chorus at fifteen speakers. The surviving plays of Aeschylus are great works of the ancient world, notably the *Oresteia* trilogy (*Agamemnon, Choephoroe,* and *Eumenides*) and *Seven Against Thebes*. It is testimony to drama's ritual origins that Aeschylus was accused of revealing in his plays religious secrets he had learned in a private initiation. Among the Greek gods, only Dionysus took possession of his worshipers; the actors at the Dionysia, shedding their personal identities to act, could be regarded as possessed by Dionysus.

The classic Greek theater at Epidaurus, constructed in the fourth century B.C., seated fourteen thousand spectators on fifty-five tiers. Today, as in Hellenistic times, audiences throng there for performances of the tragedies of Sophocles and other masterworks.

We do know a little about the staging of Greek drama. At the back of the stage was a row of decorative columns, suggestive of a palace, before which the play took place. Behind this façade stood a small room where the actors could retire. The front of this room, visible between the columns, was probably decorated with scenery; this façade was called the *skene,* ancestor of our word *scene.* In front of the *skene* and the columns, the actors spoke their roles. As a voice of the citizenry, the chorus occupied an intermediary place in the *orchestron,* an area for dancing and choral speaking midway between actors and audience.

Greek theater thus placed distance between actors and audience, perhaps because of the drama's religious nature. Actors were magnified, their faces enlarged and made rigid by masks that apparently also functioned as megaphones, enlarging voice as well as face. The voice needed amplification because Greek theaters were huge: at Epidaurus the amphitheater seated fourteen thousand people. Each stage was built below a small hill, the audience seated in tiers rising in horseshoe shape uphill from the stage. Actors' voices boomed from the wall of the *skene* and rose up the hillside.

Aristotle's *Poetics*

The Greek philosopher Aristotle (384–322 B.C.), writing shortly after the great age of the playwrights, investigated their work in his *Poetics,* which remains history's most influential work of literary criticism. Earlier we noted his six elements of drama. Here we need to touch on Aristotle's larger idea of art as imitation of nature, on his definition of tragedy, on his notions of the psychological functions of tragedy, and on a few of his formal observations.

For us today, the word *imitation* sounds negative; an imitation is inferior, secondhand, derivative. But the Greeks attached no negative connotation to *mimesis* or imitation: to imitate nature meant to be true to life. Truth was not defined historically as what *really* happened, or morally as what *ought* to happen, but philosophically as what *would happen according to the laws of probability and human nature*. If Sophocles' Oedipus howls with anguish when he learns his dreadful secret, it is probable or true to nature that he would do so. If his mother-wife hangs herself when she learns the horrid truth, it is probable or true to nature that she would do so.

Aristotle tells us *Literature is more probable than history*. Historical fact gives us the actions of one person on one day under the accidental conditions of that day. If a reporter were recording the events of a historic Thebes, maybe we would learn that it was raining or that a messenger fell asleep in a ditch and was late or that Kreon pulled a muscle and needed help climbing stairs. These historical particulars would be irrelevant to the general truth to nature that Greek playwrights imitated.

This notion of probability helps explain the clear line of plot in Greek drama. If the playwright's task is to imitate nature's probability, the playwright may dispense with local particulars and concentrate on essences. This directness helps account for the inevitability we sense in Greek tragedy as events follow each other, not at random or by accident but because one event leads to the next by inexorable laws.

Aristotle defined tragedy not as a theorist saying what it ought to be but as a critic telling us what it had been. He described the features of tragedy as he observed them, like a naturalist describing a species of fish. "Tragedy, then," he summarizes "is the imitation of an action that is serious, complete, and of a certain magnitude . . . in the form of action, not of narrative; through pity and fear effecting the proper purgation of these emotions." Defining terms within this famous definition, he tells us that "an action implies personal agents, who necessarily possess certain distinctive qualities both of character and thought . . . the two natural causes from which accidents spring. . . . But most important of all is the structure of the incident. For Tragedy is an imitation, not of men, but of an action and of life. . . ." Thus Aristotle places plot foremost in his hierarchy of elements. Probability of the plot, built on causation rather than accident, becomes a requirement of form—for it leads to the clarity with which we perceive the whole "complete" and "serious" action.

Becoming more particular, Aristotle tells us that a tragedy by its nature must tell of a *downfall,* and that the hero must be a virtuous man of some eminence, brought down by "some error or frailty." The unmerited fall of someone perfectly virtuous would merely shock us. On the other hand, the fall of a villain "would inspire neither pity nor fear." For the Greek words usually translated "fear" and "pity" commentators have suggested that we might better understand Aristotle's ideas if we read *dread* and *compassion.* Dread is the emotion that confronts inevitable evil; if pity seems to elevate and separate the audience from the character of the drama, compassion identifies the audience with the protagonist in his downfall; without some manner of empathy or identification it is difficult to argue for the presence of dread.

Aristotle asserts that the audience—as a result of experiencing these emotions in witnessing tragedy—undergoes an emotional purging or **catharsis**. This idea has puzzled commentators for hundreds of years. The notion of catharsis, most people agree, is Aristotle's defense of drama's social value and therefore a reply to Plato, who banned poets from his ideal Republic for promoting irrationality. Catharsis does not simply imply that tragedy is a safety valve for dangerous feelings, the way American football is sometimes defended as relieving spectators of their aggression. Aristotle's idea implies that art first arouses emotions and then directs and controls them, not removing them but shaping them. Plato's complaint that poetry "feeds and waters the passions instead of starving them" is countered by the notion that the emotions need not be (perhaps *can*not be) starved, but that they may be directed by intelligence and by the formal control of the dramatic artist.

A few other points from Aristotle's *Poetics:* The protagonist is "of high estate" and is frequently a king. Remember that a Greek king was not a symbolic monarch but a leader and protector of his people. We should think of Greek kings in terms of power and the state. When the dramatic protagonist is royal, like Oedipus, his downfall is a calamity for his people. And tragedy deals not with *any* king, but with kings who have displayed special courage or nobility or intelligence. Oedipus came to Thebes a stranger without title or wealth, then by his wit he solved the riddle of the Sphinx and saved the city.

People commonly speak of the tragic protagonist as possessed of a "tragic flaw"—like a flaw in a diamond. Aristotle himself speaks of the tragic hero's "error or frailty." In later tragedies we can often speak of flaws like Macbeth's ambition or Hamlet's indecisiveness—though one-word summations remain superficial. If we look for such a fatal weakness in Oedipus, we might point to his violent temper, his killing a stranger at a crossroads. But *Oedipus the King* is clearly more than a play about someone who should have controlled his temper. It is a play about someone of whom it was prophesied at birth that he would kill his father—and who killed his father, despite everybody's attempts to keep it from happening. *Oedipus* is a play about fate or inevitability. Although some tragic heroes possess a moral Achilles' heel, it is more correct to understand Oedipus' frailty as being intrinsic to all human beings, not avoidable by exercise of will to virtue. These errors or frailties are fated and ineluctable; the dread with which we watch them work their way to the hero's downfall is a religious dread. Greek tragedies are saturated with awe for the gods, with a sense of the distinction between mortals and the divine. Remember that Dionysus was a god of fertility. We rely for the food we eat on the fated, necessary, ineluctable death and rebirth of the year. Nature must die in the autumn in order to be born again in the spring. Many primitive peoples felt that, unless they enacted the ritual of dying, using their king as a sacrifice or scapegoat, some year the spring would not return.

In discussing the plots of Greek tragedies, Aristotle emphasized formal features: **reversal of intention** and **recognition**. These features are usually interrelated; Aristotle says that they must "form the internal structure of the plot, so that what follows should be the necessary or probable result. . . ." In reversal of intention, the audience watches a character take an action intended to accomplish one thing, and as the audience watches, this action accomplishes the opposite of what the character intends. "Thus in the *Oedipus* a messenger came to cheer Oedipus and free him from his alarms about his mother, but by revealing who he is, he produces the opposite effect." Recognition is revelation, something previously unknown coming to light. The messenger's reversal, in the paragraph above, affords Oedipus a terrible recognition: his wife Jocasta is also his mother.

Many critics have noticed that an almost pervasive concern of the theater is to question appearance and reality, perhaps because in watching a drama we are aware that the stage is occupied by actors who pretend to be what they are not. Central to the theater as we know it is the act of unmasking—a form of recognition—and we should notice that the mask itself was a property of the Greek stage. While tragic recognition is shocking or painful, comic recognition is often funny and satirical, as when, in *Tartuffe,* a villain's hypocrisy is publicly unmasked.

More terms of tragedy

Later critics have named other features of tragedy. **Dramatic irony** is sometimes called **tragic irony** because it is so common to tragedy. It often results from reversal of intention. Dramatic irony runs throughout *Oedipus the King,* where the hero unwittingly denounces himself when he denounces the evildoer. In dramatic irony the audience understands the consequences of the character's speech or act, but the character understands nothing until too late. We may want to rise in our chairs like the naïve watcher of a melodrama, to shout at the hero "Look out! Behind you!" We may want to say "Oedipus, *think* about what you're saying!" But no matter what we wish to say, the story will act itself out, as it has acted itself out over the centuries. Dramatic irony supports a sense of tragic inevitability and therefore supports and intensifies our dread and our awe.

Inevitable and inexorable is our sense of our own death and the deaths of people close to us—and possibly the deaths of our country, culture, or kind. The Sphinx's riddle that Oedipus solved was the identity of the creature that had four legs in morning, two legs at noon, and three at nightfall. Oedipus answered: Humankind, that crawls as a baby, stands up as an adult, and hobbles with a cane in old age. Moreover, the riddle prefigures the play. Although we see nothing of baby Oedipus on stage, the plot relies on accounts of Oedipus's infancy; the play starts with a strong, upright, powerful, two-legged king of his country; it ends with Oedipus a pitiful wreck, self-aged by his self-blinding, being led off the stage in disgrace, impotence, and exile. The hero's downfall has moved him from noon to night.

If catharsis is an idea difficult to understand, we know it is Aristotle's attempt to explain the exaltation or relief with which audiences and readers have responded to tragedy over the centuries. Why does a spectacle so depressing exalt us, or leave us better than we were? People have put forward all sorts of explanations. In a poem he called "Lapis Lazuli" William Butler Yeats suggests something that may help us understand Aristotle's catharsis. The poet describes a world in which civilization may be destroyed at any moment, and then asserts that every human figure acts out a tragic role; he describes the world as if it were a play. Moving back from individual to group, he says that every culture or civilization *will* die, as we all know. Finally, he imagines people carved in lapis lazuli (a hard stone known for its long endurance) who regard the world's scene from a distance while they listen to a skilled artist performing tragic art. When we see the characters of the world through the spectacles of tragedy, he tells us, our deaths and downfalls become acceptable; Yeats even claims that we may accept the tragic world with gaiety if we view human life and death through the form of tragedy. He answers Plato firmly. We may regard catharsis as tragic art's ability to reconcile us, through its inevitable form, to the dread of our own ending.

Sophocles

Sophocles was born at Colonus about 496 B.C. As a young man he was musician, dancer, poet, and actor—roles the Greeks did not differentiate so much as we do. Like Shakespeare and Molière, he learned stagecraft by performing as an actor. We are told that he wrote 123 plays by which he won twenty-four victories in the playwrights' contest at the Dionysia. Only seven of his plays survive entire: after *Oedipus the King* the best known are *Antigone* and *Oedipus at Colonus*—Sophocles' final play, performed after his death at the age of ninety.

When the first audience witnessed the first production of *Oedipus the King*, around 430 to 425 B.C., they already knew the myth of Oedipus, which Homer recounted briefly in the *Odyssey*. Born to the king and queen of Thebes, Oedipus was sent to be exposed on a hillside because a prophecy warned that he would kill his father. By a series of believable events, the baby was not killed, and Oedipus was raised in another city thinking himself the true son of another couple. Traveling as a stranger, he killed a man at a crossroads; coming to Thebes thereafter he saved the city from the scourge of the Sphinx by answering the Sphinx's riddle. He then married the widowed queen. At the beginning of the play many years have passed since the encounter at the crossroads, the triumph over the Sphinx, and the marriage, but a plague has infested the city, the result of an impious act at first unknown. In the course of the play Oedipus discovers that he killed his father and married his mother.

Sophocles
Oedipus the King

Translated by Stephen Berg and Diskin Clay*

Characters

OEDIPUS, king of Thebes
PRIEST of Zeus
KREON, Oedipus' brother-in-law
CHORUS of Theban elders
LEADER of the chorus
TEIRESIAS, prophet, servant to Apollo

JOCASTA, wife of Oedipus
MESSENGER from Corinth
SHEPHERD, member of Laios'
  household
SERVANT, household slave of Oedipus

Delegation of Thebans, servants to lead Teiresias and Oedipus; attendants to Oedipus, Kreon, Jocasta; and Antigone and Ismene, the daughters of Oedipus.

Dawn. Silence. The royal palace of Thebes. The altar of Apollo to the left of the central palace. A delegation of Thebans—old men, boys, young children—enters the orchestra by the steps below the altar, assembles, and waits. They carry suppliant boughs—olive branches tied with strips of wool. Some climb the steps between the orchestra and the altar, place their branches on the altar, and return to the orchestra. A PRIEST stands apart from the suppliants at the foot of one of the two stairs. Silence. Waiting. The central doors open. From inside the palace, limping, OEDIPUS comes through the palace doors and stands at the top of the steps leading down into the orchestra. He is dressed in gold and wears a golden crown.

OEDIPUS Why, children,
  why are you here, why
  are you holding those branches tied with wool,[1]
  begging me for help? Children,
5 the whole city smolders with incense.
  Wherever I go I hear sobbing, praying. Groans fill the air.

*Our text of *Oedipus the King* is a new translation by the poet Stephen Berg and the classical scholar Diskin Clay, under the general editorship of William Arrowsmith, published in 1978 by Oxford University Press. In his introduction, Arrowsmith writes: "To my perhaps prejudiced eye, the special achievements of this new translation of *Oedipus the King* are, first, the functional precision and power of its poetry; and, second, its pervasive metaphysical suggestiveness. Again and again the play, but also the translation, evokes the sense of another, larger world, of an eternally recurring reality looming behind, sometimes violently erupting into, the immediate foreground, here and now, of the dramatic situation."

[1]Wool was an offering to Apollo, god of healing as well as a source of oracles.

Rumors, news from messengers, they are not enough for me.
Others cannot tell me what you need.
I am king, I had to come. As king,
10   I had to know. Know for myself, know for me.
Everybody everywhere knows who I am: Oedipus. King.
Priest of Zeus, we respect your age, your high office.
Speak.
Why are you kneeling? Are you afraid, old man?
15   What can I give you?
How can I help? Ask.
Ask me anything. Anything at all.
My heart would be a stone
if I felt no pity for these poor shattered people of mine
20   kneeling here, at my feet.
PRIEST Oedipus, lord of Thebes, you see us, the people of Thebes, your
        people,
crowding in prayer around your altar,
these small children here, old men bent with age, priests, and I, the priest of
        Zeus,
and our noblest young men, the pride and strength of Thebes.
25   And there are more of us, lord Oedipus, more—gathered in the city, stunned,
kneeling, offering their branches, praying before the two great temples of
        Athena[1]
or staring into the ashes of burnt offerings, staring,
waiting, waiting for the god to speak.
Look,
30   look at it,
lord Oedipus—right there,
in front of your eyes—this city—
it reels under a wild storm of blood, wave after wave battering Thebes.
We cannot breathe or stand.
35   We hunger, our world shivers with hunger. A disease hungers,
nothing grows, wheat, fruit, nothing grows bigger than a seed.
Our women bear
dead things,
all they can do is grieve,
40   our cattle wither, stumble, drop to the ground,
flies simmer on their bloated tongues,
the plague spreads everywhere, a stain seeping through our streets, our fields,
        our houses,
look—god's fire eating everyone, everything,
stroke after stroke of lightning, the god stabbing it alive—
45   it can't be put out, it can't be stopped,
its heat thickens the air, it glows like smoking metal,
this god of plague guts our city and fills the black world under us.where the
        dead go
with the shrieks of women,

---

[1]Pallas Athena, goddess of wisdom and protector of Athens. The original audience was aware of
her two temples on the city's Acropolis.

living women, wailing.

50   You are a man, not a god—I know.
We all know this, the young kneeling here before you know it, too,
but we know how great you are, Oedipus, greater than any man.
When crisis struck, you saved us here in Thebes,
you faced the mysterious, strange disasters hammered against us by the gods.

55   This is our history—
we paid our own flesh to the Sphinx[1] until you set us free.
You knew no more than anyone, but you knew.
There was a god in it, a god in you.

[*The* PRIEST *kneels.*]

Help us. Oedipus, we beg you, we all turn to you, kneeling to your greatness.
Advice from the gods or advice from human beings—you will know which is

60   needed.
But help us. Power and experience are yours, all yours.
Between thought and action, between
our plans and their results a distance opens.
Only a man like you, Oedipus, tested by experience,

65   can make them one. That much I know.
Oedipus, more like a god than any man alive,
deliver us, raise us to our feet. Remember who you are.
Remember your love for Thebes. Your skill was our salvation once before.
For this Thebes calls you savior.

70   Don't let us remember you as the king—godlike in power—
who gave us back our life, then let us die.
Steady us forever. You broke the riddle for us then.
It was a sign. A god was in it. Be the man you were—
rule now as you ruled before.

75   Oh Oedipus,
how much better to rule a city of men than be king of empty earth.
A city is nothing, a ship is nothing
where no men live together, where no men work together.
OEDIPUS   Children, poor helpless children,

80   I know what brings you here, I know.
You suffer, this plague is agony for each of you,
but none of you, not one suffers as I do.
Each of you suffers for himself, only himself.
My whole being wails and breaks

85   for this city, for myself, for all of you,
old man, all of you.
Everything ends here, with me. I am the man.
You have not wakened me from some kind of sleep.
I have wept, struggled, wandered in this maze of thought,

90   tried every road, searched hard—

---

[1]When the young Oedipus arrived at Thebes the monster Sphinx (lion's body, bird's wings, woman's face) controlled the city. He saved Thebes by answering the Sphinx's riddle (see page 752) and was made king.

finally I found one cure, only one:
I sent my wife's brother, Kreon, to great Apollo's shrine at Delphi;[1]
I sent him to learn what I must say or do to save Thebes.
But his long absence troubles me. Why isn't he here? Where is he?
95   When he returns, what kind of man would I be
if I failed to do everything the god reveals?

Some of the suppliants by the steps to the orchestra stand to announce KREON's *arrival to the* PRIEST. KREON *comes in by the entrance to the audience's left with a garland on his head.*

PRIEST   You speak of Kreon, and Kreon is here.
OEDIPUS [*turning to the altar of Apollo, then to* KREON]   Lord Apollo, look at
    him—his head is crowned with laurel, his eyes glitter.
Let his words blaze, blaze like his eyes, and save us.
PRIEST   He looks calm, radiant, like a god. If he brought bad news,
100   would he be wearing that crown of sparkling leaves?
OEDIPUS   At last we will know.
Lord Kreon, what did the god Apollo say?
KREON   His words are hopeful.
105   Once everything is clear, exposed to the light,
we will see our suffering is blessing. All we need is luck.
OEDIPUS   What do you mean? What did Apollo say? What should we do?
Speak.
KREON   Here? Now? In front of all these people?
110   Or inside, privately?

[KREON *moves toward the palace.*]

OEDIPUS   Stop. Say it. Say it to the whole city.
I grieve for them, for their sorrow and loss, far more than I grieve for myself.
KREON   This is what I heard—there was no mistaking the god's meaning—
Apollo commands us:
115   Cleanse the city of Thebes, cleanse the plague from that city,
destroy the black stain spreading everywhere, spreading,
poisoning the earth, touching each house, each citizen,
sickening the hearts of the people of Thebes!
Cure this disease that wastes all of you, spreading, spreading,
120   before it grows so vast nothing can cure it
OEDIPUS   What is this plague?
How can we purify the city?
KREON   A man must be banished. Banished or killed.
Blood for blood. The plague is blood,
125   blood, breaking over Thebes.
OEDIPUS   *Who* is the man? *Who* is Apollo's victim?
KREON   My lord, before you came to Thebes, before you came to power,
Laios was our king.
OEDIPUS   I know. But I never saw Laios.

---

[1]Where an oracle revealed the future and uncovered past secrets

130 KREON Laios was murdered. Apollo's command was very clear:
       Avenge the murderers of Laios. Whoever they are.
     OEDIPUS But where *are* his murderers?
       The crime is old. How will we find their tracks?
       The killers could be anywhere.
135 KREON Apollo said the killers are still here, here in Thebes.
       Pursue a thing, and you may catch it;
       ignored, it slips away.
     OEDIPUS And Laios—where was he murdered?
       At home? Or was he away from Thebes?
140 KREON He told us before he left—he was on a mission to Delphi,
       his last trip away from Thebes. He never returned.
     OEDIPUS Wasn't there a witness, someone with Laios who saw what
         happened?
     KREON They were all killed, except for one man. He escaped.
       But he was so terrified he remembered only one thing.
145 OEDIPUS What was it? One small clue might lead to others.
     KREON This is what he said: bandits ambushed Laios, not one man.
       They attacked him like hail crushing a stalk of wheat.
     OEDIPUS How could a single bandit dare attack a king
       unless he had supporters, people with money, here,
150   here in Thebes?
     KREON There were suspicions. But after Laios died we had no leader, no king.
       Our life was turmoil, uncertainty.
     OEDIPUS But once the throne was empty,
       what threw you off the track, what kept you from searching
155   until you uncovered everything, knew every detail?
     KREON The intricate, hard song of the Sphinx
       persuaded us the crime was not important, not then.
       It seemed to say we should focus on what lay at our feet, in front of us,
       ignore what we could not see.
160 OEDIPUS Now *I* am here.
       I will begin the search again, I
       will reveal the truth, expose everything, let it all be seen.
       Apollo and you were right to make us wonder about the dead man.
       Like Apollo, I am your ally.
165   Justice and vengeance are what I want,
       for Thebes, for the god.
       Family, friends—I won't rid myself of this stain, this disease, for them—
       they're far from here. I'll do it for myself, for me.
       The man who killed Laios might take revenge on me
170   just as violently.
       So by avenging Laios' death, I protect myself.
       [*Turning to the suppliants*] Rise, children,
       pick up your branches,
       let someone announce my decision to the whole city of Thebes.
175   [*To the* PRIEST] I will do everything. Everything.
       And, with the god's help, we will be saved.
       Bright Apollo, let your light help us see.
       Our happiness is yours to give, our failure and ruin yours.

PRIEST   Rise. We have the help we came for, children.
180   The king himself has promised.
May Apollo, who gave these oracles, come as our savior now.
Apollo, heal us, save us from this plague!

OEDIPUS *enters the palace. Its doors close.* KREON *leaves by a door to the right on the wing of the stage. The* PRIEST *and suppliants go down into the orchestra and leave by the entrance to the left as a chorus of fifteen Theban elders files into the orchestra by the entrance on the right, preceded by a flute player.*

CHORUS   voice   voice   voice
voice who knows everything o god
185   glorious voice of Zeus
how have you come from Delphi bathed in gold
what are you telling our bright city Thebes
what are you bringing me
health death fear
190   I know nothing
so frightened rooted here
awed by you
healer what have you sent
is it the sudden doom of grief
195   or the old curse the darkness
looming in the turning season

o holy immortal voice
hope golden seed of the future
listen be with me speak
200   these cries of mine rise
tell me
I call to you reach out to you first
holy Athena god's daughter who lives forever
and your sister Artemis
205   who cradles the earth our earth
who sits on her great throne at the hub of the market place
and I call to Apollo who hurls light
from deep in the sky
o gods be with us now
210   shine on us your three' shields
blazing against the darkness
come in our suffering as you came once before
to Thebes o bright divinities
and threw your saving light against the god of grief
215   o gods
be with us now

pain pain my sorrows have no sound
no name no word no pain like this
plague sears my people everywhere
220   everyone army citizens no one escapes
no spear of strong anxious thought protects us

          great Thebes grows nothing
          seeds rot in the ground
          our women when they labor
225   cry Apollo Apollo but their children die
          and lives one after another split the air
          birds taking off
          wingrush hungrier than fire
          souls leaping away they fly
230   to the shore
          of the cold god of evening
          west

          the death stain spreads
          so many corpses lie in the streets everywhere
235   nobody grieves for them
          the city dies and young wives
          and mothers gray-haired mothers wail
          sob on the altar steps
          they come from the city everywhere mourning their bitter days
240   prayers blaze to the Healer
          grief cries a flute mingling
          daughter of Zeus o shining daughter show us
          the warm bright face of peace of help
          of our salvation

                              [*The doors of the palace open.* OEDIPUS *enters.*]

245   and turn back the huge raging jaws of the death god Ares
          drive him back drive him away
          his flames lash at me
          this is his war these are his shields
          shouts pierce us on all sides
250   turn him back lift him on a strong wind
          rush him away
          to the two seas at the world's edge
          the sea where the waters boil
          the sea where no traveler can land
255   because if night leaves anything alive
          day destroys it
          o Zeus
          god beyond all other gods
          handler of the fire
260   father
          make the god of our sickness
          ashes

          Apollo
          great bowman of light draw back your bow
265   fire arrow after arrow
          make them a wall circling us
          shoot into our enemy's eyes

draw the string twined with gold
come goddess
270   who dances on the mountains
sowing light where your feet brush the ground
blind our enemy come
god of golden hair
piled under your golden cap Bacchus[1]
275   your face blazing like the sea when the sun falls on it
like sunlight on wine
god whose name is our name Bacchus
god of joy god of terror
be with us now your bright face
280   like a pine torch roaring
thrust into the face of the slaughtering war god
blind him
drive him down from Olympos
drive him away from Thebes
285   forever
   OEDIPUS Every word of your prayers has touched me.
Listen. Follow me. Join me in fighting this sickness, this plague,
and all your suffering may end, like a dark sky,
clear suddenly, blue, after a week of storms,
290   soothing the torn face of the sea,
soothing our fears.
Your fate looms in my words—
I heard nothing about Laios' death,
I know nothing about the murder,
295   I was alone, how could I have tracked the killer, without a clue,
I came to Thebes after the crime was done,
I was made a Theban after Laios' death. Listen carefully—
these words come from an innocent man.

[Addressing the CHORUS*]*

One of *you* knows who killed Laios.
300   Where is that man?
Speak.
I command it. Fear is no excuse.
He must clear himself of the dangerous charge.
Who did this thing?
305   Was it a stranger?
Speak.
I will not harm him. The worst he will suffer is exile.
I will pay him well. He will have a king's thanks.
But if he will not speak because he fears me,
310   if he fears what I will do to him or to those he loves,
if he will not obey me,

[1]"So Thebes, the site of the oriental Dionysos' vindication of his claim to power over Greece, is called 'Bacchic.' . . ." [Translator's note]

I say to him:
My power is absolute in Thebes, my rule reaches everywhere,
my words will drive the guilty man, the man who knows,
315   out of this city, away from Thebes, forever.
Nothing.
My word for him is nothing.
Let him *be* nothing.
Give him nothing.
320   Let him touch nothing of yours, he is nothing to you.
Lock your doors when he approaches.
Say nothing to him, do not speak.
No prayers with him, no offerings with him.
No purifying water.
325   Nothing.
Drive him from your homes. Let him have no home, nothing.
No words, no food, shelter, warmth of hand, shared worship.
Let him have nothing. Drive him out, let him die.
He is our disease.
330   I know.
                     Apollo has made it clear.
Nothing can stop me, nothing can change my words.
I fight for Apollo, I fight for the dead man.
You see me, you hear me, moving against the killer.
335   My words are his doom.
Whether he did it alone, and escaped unseen,
whether others helped him kill, it makes no difference—
let my hatred burn out his life, hatred, always.
Make him an ember of suffering.
340   Make all his happiness
ashes.
If he eats at my side, sits at my sacred hearth, and I know these things,
let every curse I spit out against him find *me,*
come home to *me.*
345   Carry out my orders. You must,
for me, for Apollo, and for Thebes, Thebes,
this poor wasted city,
deserted by its gods.
350   I know—the gods have given us this disease.
That makes no difference. You should have acted,
you should have done something long ago to purge our guilt.
The victim was noble, a king—
you should have done everything to track his murderer down.
355   And so,
because I rule now where he ruled;
because I share his bed, his wife;
because the same woman who mothered my children might have mothered
     his;
because fate swooped out of nowhere and cut him down;
360   because of all these things
I will fight for him as I would fight for my own murdered father.

Nothing will stop me.
No man, no place, nothing will escape my gaze. I will not stop
until I know it all, all, until everything is clear.
365   For every king, every king's son and his sons,
for every royal generation of Thebes, *my* Thebes,
I will expose the killer, I will reveal him
to the light.
Oh gods, gods,
370   destroy all those who will not listen, will not obey.
Freeze the ground until they starve.
Make their wives barren as stone.
Let this disease that shakes Thebes to its roots—
or any worse disease, if there is any worse than this—waste them,
375   crush everything they have, everything they are.
But you men of Thebes—
you, who know my words are right, who obey me—
may justice and the gods defend you, bless you,
graciously, forever.
380   LEADER Your curse forces me to speak, Master.
I cannot escape it.
I did not murder the king, I cannot show you the man who did.
Apollo told us to search for the killer.
Apollo must name him.
385   OEDIPUS No man can force the gods to speak.
LEADER Then I will say the next best thing.
OEDIPUS If there's a third best thing, say that too.
LEADER Teiresias sees what the god Apollo sees.
Truth, truth.
390   If you heard the god speaking, heard his voice,
you might see more, more, and more.
OEDIPUS Teiresias? I have seen to that already.
Kreon spoke of Teiresias, and I sent for him. Twice.
I find it strange he still hasn't come.
395   LEADER And there's an old story, almost forgotten,
a dark, faded rumor.
OEDIPUS What rumor? I must sift each story,
see it, understand it.
LEADER Laios was killed by bandits.
OEDIPUS I have heard that story: but who can show me the man who saw the
400   murderer?
Has anyone seen him?
LEADER If he knows the meaning of fear,
if he heard those curses you spoke against him,
those words still scorching the air,
405   you won't find him now, not in Thebes.
OEDIPUS The man *murdered*. Why would words frighten him?

TEIRESIAS *has appeared from the stage entrance to the right of the audience. He
walks with a staff and is helped by a slave boy and attendants. He stops at some
distance from center stage.*

LEADER Here is the man who can catch the criminal.
　　They're bringing him now—
　　the godlike prophet who speaks with the voice of god.
410　　He, only he, knows truth.
　　The truth is rooted in his soul.
OEDIPUS Teiresias, you understand all things,
　　what can be taught, what is locked in silence,
　　the distant things of heaven, and things that crawl the earth.
415　　You cannot see, yet you know the nature of this plague infesting our city.
　　Only you, my lord, can save us, only you can defend us.
　　Apollo told our messenger—did you hear?—
　　that we could be saved only by tracking down Laios' killers,
　　only by killing them, or sending them into exile.
420　　Help us, Teiresias.
　　Study the cries of birds, study their wild paths,
　　ponder the signs of fire, use all your skills of prophecy.
　　Rescue us, preserve us.
　　Rescue yourself, rescue Thebes, rescue me.
425　　Cleanse every trace of the growing stain left by the dead man's blood.
　　We are in your hands, Teiresias.
　　No work is more nobly human than helping others,
　　helping with all the strength and skill we possess.
TEIRESIAS Wisdom is a curse
430　　when wisdom does nothing for the man who has it.
　　Once I knew this well, but I forgot.
　　I never should have come.
OEDIPUS Never should have come? Why this reluctance, prophet?
TEIRESIAS Let me go home.
435　　That way is best, for you, for me.
　　Let me live my life, and you live yours.
OEDIPUS Strange words, Teiresias, cruel to the city that gave you life.
　　Your holy knowledge could save Thebes. How can you keep silent?
TEIRESIAS What have *you* said that helps Thebes? Your words are wasted.
440　　I would rather be silent than waste my words.
OEDIPUS Look at us,　　　　　　　　　　[OEDIPUS *stands, the* CHORUS *kneel*]
　　kneeling to you, Teiresias, imploring you.
　　In the name of the gods, if you know—
　　help us, tell us what you know.
445　TEIRESIAS You kneel because you do not understand.
　　But I will never let you see my grief. Never.
　　My grief is yours.
OEDIPUS What? You know and won't speak?
　　You'd betray us all, you'd destroy the city of Thebes?
450　TEIRESIAS I will do nothing to hurt myself, or you. Why insist?
　　I will not speak.
OEDIPUS Stubborn old fool, you'd make a rock angry!
　　Tell me what you know! Say it!
　　Where are your feelings? Won't you ever speak?
455　TEIRESIAS You call me cold, stubborn, unfeeling, you insult me. But *you,*
　　Oedipus, what do you know about yourself,

about your real feelings?
You don't see how much alike we are.
OEDIPUS   How can *I* restrain my anger when I see how little you care for
Thebes.
460   TEIRESIAS   The truth will come, by itself,
the truth will come
no matter how I shroud it in silence.
OEDIPUS   All the more reason why you should speak.
TEIRESIAS   Not another word.
465   Rage away. You will never make me speak.
OEDIPUS   I'll rage, prophet, I'll give you all my anger.
I'll say it all—
Listen: I think you were involved in the murder of Laios,
you helped plan it, I think you
470   did everything in your power to kill Laios,
everything but strike him with your own hands,
and if you weren't blind, if you still had eyes to see with,
I'd say you, and *you* alone, did it all.
TEIRESIAS   Do you think so? Then obey your own words, obey
475   the curse everyone heard break from your own lips:
Never speak again to these men of Thebes,
never speak again to me.
            You, it's
you.
480   What plagues the city is *you.*
The plague is *you.*
OEDIPUS   Do you know what you're saying?
Do you think I'll let you get away with these vile accusations?
TEIRESIAS   I am safe.
485   Truth lives in me, and the truth is strong.
OEDIPUS   Who taught you this truth of yours? Not your prophet's craft.
TEIRESIAS   *You* taught me. You forced me to speak.
OEDIPUS   Speak what? Explain. Teach me.
TEIRESIAS   Didn't you understand?
490   Are you trying to make me say the word?
OEDIPUS   What word? Say it. Spit it out.
TEIRESIAS   Murderer.
I say *you,*
you are the killer you're searching for.
495   OEDIPUS   You won't say *that* again to me and get away with it.
TEIRESIAS   Do you want more? Shall I make you really angry?
OEDIPUS   Say anything you like. Your words are wasted.
TEIRESIAS   I say you live in shame, and you do not know it,
do not know that you
500   and those you love most
wallow in shame,
you do not know
in what shame you live.
OEDIPUS   You'll pay for these insults, I swear it.
505   TEIRESIAS   Not if the truth is strong.

OEDIPUS The truth *is* strong, but not your truth.
You have no truth. You're blind.
Blind in your eyes. Blind in your ears. Blind in your mind.
TEIRESIAS And I pity you for mocking my blindness.
510   Soon everyone in Thebes will mock you, Oedipus. They'll mock you
as you have mocked me.
OEDIPUS One endless night swaddles you in its unbroken black sky.
You can't hurt me, you can't hurt anyone who sees the light of day.
TEIRESIAS True. Nothing I do will harm you. You, you
515   and your fate belong to Apollo.
Apollo will see to you.
OEDIPUS Are these your own lies, prophet—or Kreon's?
TEIRESIAS Kreon? Your plague is *you,* not Kreon.
OEDIPUS Money, power, one great skill surpassing another,
520   if a man has these things, other men's envy grows and grows,
their greed and hunger are insatiable.
Most men would lust for a life like mine—but I did not demand my life,
Thebes gave me my life, and from the beginning, my good friend Kreon,
loyal, trusted Kreon,
was reaching for my power, wanted to ambush me, get rid of me by hiring this
525   cheap wizard,
this crass, conniving priest, who sees nothing but profit,
whose prophecy is simple profit. *You,*
what did *you* ever do that proves you a real seer? What did you ever *see,*
prophet?
530   And when the Sphinx who sang mysteriously
imprisoned us
why didn't you speak and set us free?
No ordinary man could have solved her riddle,
it took prophecy, prophecy and skill you clearly never had.
535   Even the paths of birds, even the gods' voices were useless.
But I showed up, I, Oedipus,
stupid, untutored Oedipus,
I silenced her, I destroyed her, I used my wits, not omens,
to sift the meaning of her song.
540   And this is the man you want to kill so you can get close to King Kreon,
weigh his affairs for him, advise him, influence him.
No, I think you and your master, Kreon, who contrived this plot,
will be whipped out of Thebes.
Look at you.
545   If you weren't so old, and weak, oh
I'd make you pay
for this conspiracy of yours.
LEADER Oedipus, both of you spoke in anger.
Anger is not what we need.
550   We need all our wits, all our energy to interpret Apollo's words.
Then we will know what to do.
TEIRESIAS Oedipus, you are king, but you must hear my reply.
My right to speak is just as valid as yours.
I am not your slave. Kreon is not my patron.

555   My master is Apollo. I can say what I please.
      You insulted me. You mocked me. You called me blind.
      Now hear *me* speak, Oedipus.
      You have eyes to see with,
      but you do not see yourself, you do not see
560   the horror shadowing every step of your life,
      the blind shame in which you live,
      you do not see where you live and who lives with you,
      lives always at your side.
      Tell me, Oedipus, who are your parents?
565   Do you know?
      You do not even know
      the shame and grief you have brought your family,
      those still alive, those buried beneath the earth.
      But the curse of your mother, the curse of your father
570   will whip you, whip you again and again, wherever you turn,
      it will whip you out of Thebes forever,
      your clear eyes flooded with darkness.
      That day will come.
      And then what scoured, homeless plain, what leafless tree,
575   what place on Kithairon,
      where no other humans are or ever will be,
      where the wind is the only thing that moves,
      what raw track of thorns and stones, what rock, gulley,
      or blind hill won't echo your screams, your howls of anguish
580   when you find out that the marriage song,
      sung when you came to Thebes, heard in your house,
      guided you to *this* shore, this wilderness
      you thought was home, *your* home?
      And you do not see
585   all the other awful things
      that will show you who you really are, show you
      to your children, face to face.
      Go ahead! Call me quack, abuse Kreon, insult Apollo, the god
      who speaks through me, whose words move on my lips.
590   No man will ever know worse suffering than you,
      your life, your flesh, your happiness an ember of pain. Ashes.
      OEDIPUS [*to the* CHORUS]   Must I stand here and listen to these attacks?
      TEIRESIAS [*beginning to move away*]   I am here, Oedipus, because you sent for
         me.
      OEDIPUS   You old fool,
595   I'd have thought twice before asking you to come
        if I had known you'd spew out such idiocy.
      TEIRESIAS   Call me fool, if you like, but your parents,
        who gave you life, they respected my judgment.
      OEDIPUS   Parents?
600   What do you mean?
                                        Who are my mother and father?
      TEIRESIAS   This day is your mother and father—this day will give you your
         birth,

it will destroy you too.

OEDIPUS How you love mysterious, twisted words.

605 TEIRESIAS Aren't you the great solver of riddles?
 Aren't you Oedipus?

OEDIPUS Taunt me for the gift of my brilliant mind.
 That gift is what makes me great.

TEIRESIAS That gift is your destiny. It made you everything you are,
610 and it has ruined you.

OEDIPUS But if this gift of mine saved Thebes, who cares what happens to me?

TEIRESIAS I'm leaving. Boy, take me home.

OEDIPUS Good. Take him home. Here
 I keep stumbling over you, here you're in my way.
615 Scuttle home, and leave us in peace!

TEIRESIAS I'm going. I said what I came to say,
 and that scowl, darkening your face, doesn't frighten me. How can you hurt
  me?
 I tell you again:
 the man you've been trying to expose—
620 with all your threats, with your inquest into Laios' murder—
 that man is here, in Thebes.
 Now people think he comes from Corinth, but later
 they will see he was born in Thebes.
 When they know, he'll have no pleasure in that news.
625 Now he has eyes to see with, but they will be slashed out;
 rich and powerful now, he will be a beggar,
 poking his way with a stick, feeling his way to a strange country.
 And his children—the children he lives with—
 will see him at last, see what he is, see who he really is:
630 their brother and their father; his wife's son, his mother's husband;
 the lover who slept with his father's wife; the man who murdered his father—
 the man whose hands still drip with his father's blood.
 These truths will be revealed.

 Go inside and ponder *that* riddle, and if you find I've lied,
635 then call me a prophet who cannot see.

OEDIPUS *turns and enters the palace.* TEIRESIAS *is led out through the stage
entrance on the right.*

CHORUS who did crimes unnameable things
 things words cringe at
 which man did the rock of prophecy at Delphi say
 did these things
640 his hands dripping with blood
 he should run now flee
 his strong feet swallowing the air
 stronger than the horses of storm winds
 their hooves slicing the air
645 now in his armor
 Apollo lunges at him
 his infinite branching fire reaches out

and the steady dread death-hungry Fates follow and never stop
their quick scissors seeking the cloth of his life

650　just now
from high snowy Parnassus
the god's voice exploded its blazing message
follow his track find the man
no one knows
655　a bull loose under wild bushes and trees
among caves and gray rocks
cut from the herd he runs and runs but runs nowhere
zigzagging desperate to get away
birds of prophecy birds of death circling his head
660　forever
voices forged at the white stone core of the earth
they go where he goes always

terror's in me flooding me
how can I judge
665　what the god Apollo says
trapped hoping confused
I do not see what is here now
when I look to the past I see nothing
I know nothing about a feud
670　wounding the families of Laios or Oedipus
no clue to the truth then or now
nothing to blacken his golden fame in Thebes
and help Laios' family
solve the mystery of his death

675　Zeus and Apollo know
they understand
only they see
the dark threads crossing beneath our life
but no man can say a prophet sees more than I
680　one man surpasses another
wisdom against wisdom skill against skill
but I will not blame Oedipus
whatever anyone says
until words are as real as things

685　one thing is clear
years back the Sphinx tested him
his answer was true
he was wise and sweet to the city
so he can never be evil
690　not to me

KREON *enters through the stage entrance at right, and addresses the* CHORUS.

KREON　Men of Thebes, I hear Oedipus, our king and master,
has brought terrible charges against me.

I have come to face those charges. I resent them bitterly.
If he imagines I have hurt him, spoken or acted against him
695   while our city dies, believe me—I have nothing left to live for.
His accusations pierce me, wound me mortally—
nothing they touch is trivial, private—
if you, my family and friends,
think I'm a traitor, if all Thebes believes it, says it.
700   LEADER Perhaps he spoke in anger, without thinking,
perhaps his anger made him accuse you.
KREON Did he really say I persuaded Teiresias to lie?
LEADER I heard him say these things,
but I don't know what they mean.
705   KREON Did he look you in the eyes when he accused me?
Was he in his right mind?
LEADER I do not know or see what great men do.

[*Turning to* OEDIPUS, *who has emerged from the palace*]

But here he is—Oedipus.
OEDIPUS What? *You* here? Murderer!
710   You dare come here, to my palace, when it's clear
you've been plotting to murder me and seize the throne of Thebes?
You're the bandit, *you're* the killer.
                              Answer me—
Did you think I was cowardly or stupid?
715   Is that why you betrayed me?
Did you really think I wouldn't see what you were plotting,
how you crept up on me like a cloud inching across the sun?
Did you think I wouldn't defend myself against you?
You thought I was a fool, but the fool was *you,* Kreon.
720   Thrones are won with money and men, you fool!
KREON You have said enough, Oedipus. Now let me reply.
Weigh my words against your charges, then judge for yourself.
OEDIPUS Eloquent, Kreon. But you won't convince me now.
Now that I know your hatred, your malice.
725   KREON Let me explain.
OEDIPUS Explain?
What could explain your treachery?
KREON If you think this stubborn anger of yours, this perversity,
is something to be proud of, you're mad.
730   OEDIPUS And if you think you can injure your sister's husband,
and not pay for it, *you're* mad.
KREON I would be mad to hurt you. How have I hurt you?
OEDIPUS Was it you who advised me to send for that great holy prophet?
KREON Yes, and I'd do it again.
735   OEDIPUS How long has it been since Laios disappeared?
KREON Disappeared?
OEDIPUS Died. Was murdered. . . .
KREON Many, many years.
OEDIPUS And this prophet of yours—was he practicing his trade at the time?

740   KREON With as much skill, wisdom and honor as ever.

       OEDIPUS Did he ever mention my name?

       KREON Not in my presence.

       OEDIPUS Was there an inquest? A formal inquiry?

       KREON Of course. Nothing was ever discovered.

745   OEDIPUS Then why didn't our wonderful prophet, our Theban wizard,
          denounce me as the murderer then?

       KREON I don't know. And when I don't know, I don't speak.

       OEDIPUS But you know this. You know it with perfect certainty.

       KREON What do you mean?

750   OEDIPUS This: if you and Teiresias were not conspiring against me,
          Teiresias would never have charged *me* with Laios' murder.

       KREON If he said that, you should know.
          But now, Oedipus, it's my right, my turn to question you.

       OEDIPUS Ask anything. You'll never prove I killed Laios.

755   KREON Did you marry my sister, Jocasta?

       OEDIPUS I married Jocasta.

       KREON And you gave her an equal share of the power in Thebes?

       OEDIPUS Whatever she wants is hers.

       KREON And I share that power equally with you and her?

760   OEDIPUS Equally.
          And that's precisely why it's clear you're false, treacherous.

       KREON No, Oedipus.
          Consider it rationally, as I have. Reflect:
          What man, what sane man, would prefer a king's power

765   with all its dangers and anxieties,
          when he could enjoy the same power, without its cares,
          and sleep in peace each night? Power?
          I have no instinct for power, no hunger for it either.
          It isn't royal power I want, but its advantages.

770   And any sensible man would want the same.
          Look at the life I lead. Whatever I want, I get from you,
          with your goodwill and blessing. I have nothing to fear.
          If I were king, my life would be constant duty and constraint.
          Why would I want your power or the throne of Thebes

775   more than what I enjoy now—the privilege of power
          without its dangers? I would be a fool to want more
          than what I have—the substance, not the show, of power.
          As matters stand, no man envies me, I am courted
          and admired by all. Men wear no smiling masks for Kreon.

780   And those who want something from you come to me
          because the way to royal favor lies through me.
          Tell me, Oedipus, why should I give these blessings up
          to seize your throne and all the dangers it confers?
          A man like me, who knows his mortal limits and accepts them,

785   cannot be vicious or treacherous by nature.
          The love of power is not my nature, nor is treason
          or the thoughts of treason that go with love of power.
          I would never dare conspire against your life.

Do you want to test the truth of what I say?
790   Go to Delphi, put the question to the oracle,
        ask if I have told you exactly what Apollo said.
        Then if you find that Teiresias and I have plotted against you,
        seize me and put me to death. Convict me
        not by one vote alone, but two—yours *and* mine, Oedipus.
795   But don't convict me on the strength of your suspicions,
        don't confuse friends with traitors, traitors with friends.
        There's no justice in that.
        To throw away a good and loyal friend
        is to destroy what you love most—
800   your own life, and what makes life worth living.
        Someday you will know the truth:
        time, only time reveals the good man;
        one day's light reveals the evil man.
        LEADER   Good words
805   for someone careful, afraid he'll fall.
        But a mind like lightning
        stumbles.
        OEDIPUS   When a clever man plots against me and moves swiftly
        I must move just as swiftly, I must plan.
810   But if I wait, if I do nothing, he will win, win everything,
        and I will lose.
        KREON   What do you want? My exile?
        OEDIPUS   No. Your death.
        KREON   You won't change your mind? You won't believe me?
815   OEDIPUS   I'll believe you when you teach me the meaning of envy.
        KREON   Envy? You talk about envy. You don't even know what sense is.
          Can't you listen to me?
        OEDIPUS   I *am* listening. To my own good sense.
        KREON   Listen to me. I have sense on my side too.
820   OEDIPUS   You? You were born devious.
        KREON   And if you're wrong?
        OEDIPUS   I still must govern.
        KREON   Not if you govern badly.
        OEDIPUS   Oh Thebes, Thebes . . .
825   KREON   Thebes is mine too.
        LEADER [*turning to* JOCASTA, *who has entered from the palace, accompanied by
          a woman attendant*]
        Stop. I see
        Jocasta coming from the palace
        just in time, my lords, to help you
        settle this deep, bitter feud raging between you.
830   Listen to what she says
        JOCASTA   Oedipus! Kreon! Why this insane quarreling?
        You should be ashamed, both of you. Forget yourselves.
        This is no time for petty personal bickering.
        Thebes is sick, dying.
835   —Come inside, Oedipus.
        —And you, Kreon, leave us.

Must you create all this misery over nothing, nothing?
KREON Jocasta,
Oedipus has given me two impossible choices:
840 Either I must be banished from Thebes, my city, my home,
or be arrested and put to death.
OEDIPUS That's right.
I caught him plotting against me, Jocasta.
Viciously, cunningly plotting against the king of Thebes.
845 KREON Take every pleasure I have in life, curse me, let me die,
if I've done what you accuse me of, let the gods
destroy everything I have, let them do anything to me.
I stand here, exposed to their infinite power.
JOCASTA Oedipus, in the name of the gods, believe him.
850 His prayer has made him holy, naked to the mysterious
whims of the gods, has taken him beyond what is human.
Respect his words, respect me, respect these men standing at your side.
CHORUS [*beginning a dirgelike appeal to* OEDIPUS]
listen to her
think yield
855 we implore you
OEDIPUS What do you want?
CHORUS be generous to Kreon give him respect
he was never foolish before
now his prayer to the gods has made him great
860 great and frightening
OEDIPUS Do you know what you're asking?
CHORUS I know
OEDIPUS Then say it.
CHORUS don't ever cut him off
865 without rights or honor
blood binds you both
his prayer has made him sacred
don't accuse him
because some blind suspicion hounds you
870 OEDIPUS Understand me:
when you ask for these things
you ask for my death or exile.
CHORUS no
by the sun
875 the god who bathes us in his light
who sees all
I will die godless no family no friends
if what I ask means that
it is Thebes
880 Thebes dying wasting away life by life
this is the misery
that breaks my heart
and now this quarrel raging between you and Kreon
is more more than I can bear
885 OEDIPUS Then let him go, even if it means I must die

or be forced out of Thebes forever, stripped of all my rights, all my honors.
Your grief, *your* words touch me. Not his.
I pity you. But him,
my hatred will reach him wherever he goes.

890   KREON   It's clear you hate to yield, clear
you yield only under pressure, only
when you've worn out the fierceness of your anger.
Then all you can do is sit, and brood.
Natures like yours are a torment to themselves.

895   OEDIPUS   Leave. Go!
KREON   I'm going. Now I know
you do not know me.
But these men know I am the man I seem to be, a just man,
not devious, not a traitor.

[KREON *leaves*]

900   CHORUS   woman why are you waiting
lead him inside comfort him
JOCASTA   Not before I know what has happened here.
CHORUS   blind ignorant words suspicion without proof
the injustice of it
905   gnaws at us
JOCASTA   From both men?
CHORUS   yes
JOCASTA   What caused it?
CHORUS   enough enough
910   no more words
Thebes is so tormented now
let it rest where it ended
OEDIPUS   Look where cooling my rage,
where all your decent, practical thoughts have led you.
915   CHORUS   Oedipus I have said this many times
I would be mad helpless to give advice
if I turned against you now
once
you took our city in her storm of pain
920   straightened her course found fair weather
o lead her to safety now
if you can
JOCASTA   If you love the gods, tell me, too, Oedipus—I implore you—
why are you still so angry, why can't you let it go?
925   OEDIPUS   I will tell you, Jocasta.
You mean more, far more to me than these men here.
Jocasta, it is Kreon—Kreon and his plots against me.
JOCASTA   What started your quarrel?
OEDIPUS   He said I murdered Laios.
930   JOCASTA   Does he know something? Or is it pure hearsay?
OEDIPUS   He sent me a vicious, trouble-making prophet
to avoid implicating himself. He did not say it to my face.

JOCASTA   Oedipus, forget all this. Listen to me:
no mortal can practice the art of prophecy, no man can see the future.
935   One experience of mine will show you why.
Long ago an oracle came to Laios.
It came not from Apollo himself but from his priests.
It said Laios was doomed to be murdered by a son, his son and mine.
But Laios, from what we heard, was murdered by bandits from a foreign
country,
940   cut down at a crossroads. My poor baby
was only three days old when Laios had his feet pierced together behind the
ankles
and gave orders to abandon our child on a mountain, leave him alone to die
in a wilderness of rocks and bare gray trees
where there were no roads, no people.
945   So you see—Apollo didn't make that child his father's killer,
Laios wasn't murdered by his son. That dreadful act which so terrified
Laios—
it never happened.

All those oracular voices meant was nothing, nothing.
Ignore them.
950   Apollo creates. Apollo reveals. He needs no help from men.
OEDIPUS [*who has been very still*]
While you were speaking, Jocasta, it flashed through my mind
like wind suddenly ruffling a stretch of calm sea.
It stuns me. I can almost see it—some memory, some image.
My heart races and swells—
955   JOCASTA   Why are you so strangely excited, Oedipus?
OEDIPUS   You said Laios was cut down *near* a crossroads?
JOCASTA   That was the story. It hasn't changed.
OEDIPUS   Where did it happen? Tell me. Where?
JOCASTA   In Phokis. Where the roads from Delphi and Daulia meet.
960   OEDIPUS   When?
JOCASTA   Just before you came to Thebes and assumed power.
Just before you were proclaimed King.
OEDIPUS   O Zeus, Zeus,
what are you doing with my life?
965   JOCASTA   Why are you so disturbed, Oedipus?
OEDIPUS   Don't ask me. Not yet.
Tell me about Laios.
How old was he? What did he look like?
JOCASTA   Streaks of gray were beginning to show in his black hair.
970   He was tall, strong—built something like you.
OEDIPUS   No! O gods, o
it seems each hard, arrogant curse
I spit out
was meant for me, and I
975   didn't
know it!
JOCASTA   Oedipus, what do you mean? Your face is so strange.
You frighten me.

OEDIPUS It *is* frightening—can the blind prophet see, can he really see?
980   I would know if you told me . . .
JOCASTA I'm afraid to ask, Oedipus.
  Told you what?
OEDIPUS Was Laios traveling with a small escort
  or with many armed men, like a king?
985   JOCASTA There were five, including a herald.
  Laios was riding in his chariot.
OEDIPUS Light, o light, light
  now everything, everything is clear. All of it.
  Who told you this? Who was it?
990   JOCASTA A household slave. The only survivor.
OEDIPUS Is he here, in Thebes?
JOCASTA No. When he returned and saw that you were king
  and learned Laios was dead, he came to me and clutched my hand,
  begged me to send him to the mountains
995   where shepherds graze their flocks, far from the city,
  so he could never see Thebes again.
  I sent him, of course. He deserved that much, for a slave, and more.
OEDIPUS Can he be called back? Now?
JOCASTA Easily. But why?
1000   OEDIPUS I am afraid I may have said too much—
  I *must* see him.
  Now.
JOCASTA Then he will come.
  But surely I have a right to know what disturbs you, Oedipus.
1005   OEDIPUS Now that I've come this far, Jocasta,
  hope torturing me, each step of mine heavy with fear,
  I won't keep anything from you.
  Wandering through the mazes of a fate like this,
  how could I confide in anyone but you?

1010   My father was Polybos, of Corinth.
  My mother, Merope, was Dorian.
  Everyone in Corinth saw me as its first citizen,
  but one day something happened,
  something strange, puzzling. Puzzling, but nothing more.
1015   Still, it worried me.
  One night, I was at a banquet,
  and a man—he was very drunk—said I wasn't my father's son,
  called me "bastard." That stung me, I was shocked.
  I could barely control my anger, I lay awake all night.
1020   The next day I went to my father and mother,
  I questioned them about the man and what he said.
  They were furious with him, outraged by his insult,
  and I was reassured. But I kept hearing the word "bastard" "bastard"—
  I couldn't get it out of my head.
1025   Without my parents' knowledge, I went to Delphi: I wanted the truth,
  but Apollo refused to answer me.

And yet he did reveal other things, he did show me
a future dark with torment, evil, horror,
he made me *see*—
1030   see myself, doomed to sleep with my own mother, doomed
to bring children into this world where the sun pours down,
children no one could bear to see, doomed
to murder the man who gave me life, whose blood is *my* blood. My father.
And after I heard all this, I fled Corinth,
1035   measuring my progress by the stars, searching for a place
where I would never see those words, those dreadful predictions
come true. And on my way
I came to the place where you say King Laios was murdered.

Jocasta, the story I'm about to tell you is the truth:
1040   I was on the road, near the crossroads you mentioned,
when I met a herald, with an old man, just as you described him.
The man was riding in a chariot
and his driver tried to push me off the road
and when he shoved me I hit him. I hit him.
1045   The old man stood quiet in the chariot until I passed under him,
then he leaned out and caught me on the head with an ugly goad—
its two teeth wounded me—and with this hand of mine,
this hand clenched around my staff,
I struck him back even harder—so hard, so quick he couldn't dodge it,
1050   and he toppled out of the chariot and hit the ground, face up.
I killed them. Every one of them. I still see them.

[*To the* CHORUS]

If this stranger and Laios
are somehow linked by blood,
tell me what man's torment equals mine?

1055   Citizens, hear my curse again—
Give this man nothing. Let him touch nothing of yours.
Lock your doors when he approaches.
Say nothing to him when he approaches.
                                                And these, these curses,
1060   with my own mouth I
spoke these monstrous curses against myself.

[OEDIPUS *turns back to* JOCASTA]

These hands, these bloodstained hands made love to you in your dead
    husband's bed,
these hands murdered him.

If I must be exiled, never to see my family,
1065   never to walk the soil of my country
so I will not sleep with my mother

and kill Polybos, my father, who raised me—his son!—
wasn't I born evil—answer me!—isn't every part of me
unclean? Oh
1070   some unknown god, some savage venomous demon must have done this,
raging, swollen with hatred. Hatred
for me.

Holiness, pure, radiant powers, o gods
don't let me see that day,
1075   don't let it come, take me away
from men, men with their eyes, hide me
before I see
the filthy black stain reaching down over me, into me.

[*The* CHORUS *have moved away from the stage*]

LEADER   Your words make us shudder, Oedipus,
1080   but hope, hope
until you hear more from the man who witnessed the murder.
OEDIPUS   That is the only hope I have. Waiting.
Waiting for that man to come from the pastures.
JOCASTA   And when he finally comes, what do you hope to learn?
1085   OEDIPUS   If his story matches yours, I am saved.
JOCASTA   What makes you say that?
OEDIPUS   Bandits—you said he told you bandits killed Laios.
So if he still talks about bandits,
more than one, I couldn't have killed Laios.
1090   One man is not the same as many men.
But if he speaks of one man, traveling alone,
then all the evidence points to me.
JOCASTA   Believe me, Oedipus, those were his words.
And he can't take them back: the whole city heard him, not only me.
1095   And if he changes only the smallest detail of his story,
that still won't prove Laios was murdered as the oracle foretold.
Apollo was clear—it was Laios' fate to be killed by my son.
but my poor child died before his father died.
The future has no shape. The shapes of prophecy lie.
1100   I see nothing in them, they are all illusions.
OEDIPUS   Even so, I want that shepherd summoned here.
Now. Do it now.
JOCASTA   I'll send for him immediately. But come inside.
My only wish is to please you.

[JOCASTA *dispatches a servant*]

1105   CHORUS   fate
be here let what I say be pure
let all my acts be pure
laws forged in the huge clear fields of heaven
rove the sky
1110   shaping my words limiting what I do

Olympos made those laws not men who live and die
nothing lulls those laws to sleep
they cannot die
and the infinite god in them never ages

1115   arrogance insatiable pride
breed the tyrant
feed him on thing after thing blindly
at the wrong time uselessly
and he grows reaches so high
1120   nothing can stop his fall
his feet thrashing the air standing on nothing
and nowhere to stand he plunges down
o god shatter the tyrant
but let men complete let self-perfection grow
1125   let men sharpen their skills
soldiers citizens building the good city
Apollo
protect me always
always the god I will honor
1130   if a man walks through his life arrogant
strutting proud
says anything does anything
does not fear justice
fear the gods bow to their shining presences
1135   let fate make him stumble in his tracks
for all his lecheries and headlong greed
if he takes whatever he wants right or wrong
if he touches forbidden things
what man who acts like this would boast
1140   he can escape the anger of the gods
why should I join these sacred public dances
if such acts are honored

no
I will never go to the holy untouchable stone
1145   navel of the earth at Delphi
never again
go to the temples at Olympia at Abai[1]
if all these things are not joined
if past present future are not made one
1150   made clear to mortal eyes
o Zeus if that is your name
power above all immortal king
see these things look
those great prophecies are fading
1155   men say they're nothing
nobody prays to the god of light no one believes
nothing of the gods stays

---

[1]Like Delphi, the site of an oracle

JOCASTA *enters from the palace, carrying a branch tied with strands of wool, and a jar of incense. She is accompanied by a servant woman. She addresses the* CHORUS.

JOCASTA Lords of Thebes, I come to the temples of the god
with offerings—this incense and this branch.
1160 So many thoughts torture Oedipus. He never rests.
He acts without reason. He is like a man
who has lost everything he knows—the past
is useless to him; strange, new things baffle him.
And if someone talks disaster, it stuns him: he listens, he is afraid.
1165 I have tried to reassure him, but nothing helps.
So I have come to you—
Apollo, close to my life, close to this house,
listen to my prayers: [*She kneels*]
                              help us purify ourselves of this disease,
1170 help us survive the long night of our suffering,
protect us. We are afraid when we see Oedipus confused
and frightened—Oedipus, the only man who can pilot Thebes
to safety.

A MESSENGER *from Corinth has arrived by the entrance to the orchestra on the audience's left. He sees* JOCASTA *praying, then turns to address the* CHORUS.

MESSENGER Friends,
1175 can you tell me where King Oedipus lives
or better still, where I can find him?
LEADER Here, in this house.
This lady is his wife and mother
of his children.
1180 MESSENGER May you and your family prosper.
May you be happy always under this great roof.
JOCASTA Happiness and prosperity to you, too, for your kind words.
But why are you here? Do you bring news?
MESSENGER Good news for your house, good news for King Oedipus.
1185 JOCASTA What is your news? Who sent you?
MESSENGER I come from Corinth, and what I have to say I know will bring
    you joy.
And pain perhaps. . . . I do not know.
JOCASTA Both joy and pain? What news could do that?
MESSENGER The people of Corinth want Oedipus as their king.
1190 That's what they're saying.
JOCASTA But isn't old Polybos still king of Corinth?
MESSENGER His kingdom is his grave.
JOCASTA Polybos is *dead?*
MESSENGER If I'm lying, my lady, let me die for it.
1195 JOCASTA You. [*To a servant*] Go in and tell Oedipus.
O oracles of the gods, where are you now!
This man, the man Oedipus was afraid he would murder,

the man he feared, the man he fled from has died a natural death.
Oedipus didn't kill him, it was luck, luck.

[*She turns to greet* OEDIPUS *as he comes out of the palace*]

1200 OEDIPUS Jocasta, why did you send for me? [*Taking her gently by the arm*]
JOCASTA Oedipus,
   listen to this man, see what those ominous, holy predictions of Apollo mean
      now.
OEDIPUS Who is this man? What does he say?
JOCASTA He comes from Corinth.
1205   Your father is dead. Polybos is dead!
OEDIPUS What?
   Let me hear those words from your own mouth, stranger.
   Tell me yourself, in your own words.
MESSENGER If that's what you want to hear first, then I'll say it:
1210   Polybos is dead.
OEDIPUS How did he die? Assassination? Illness? How?
MESSENGER An old man's life hangs by a fragile thread. Anything can snap it.
OEDIPUS That poor old man. It was illness then?
MESSENGER Illness and old age.
1215 OEDIPUS Why, Jocasta,
   why should men look to the great hearth at Delphi
   or listen to birds shrieking and wheeling overhead—
   cries meaning I was doomed to kill my father?
   He is dead, gone, covered by the earth.
1220   And here I am—my hands never even touched a spear—
   I did not kill him,
   unless he died from wanting me to come home.
   No. Polybos has bundled up all these oracles
   and taken them with him to the world below.
1225   They are only words now, lost in the air.
JOCASTA Isn't that what I predicted?
OEDIPUS You were right. My fears confused me.
JOCASTA You have nothing to fear. Not now. Not ever.
OEDIPUS But the oracle said I am doomed to sleep with my mother.
1230   How can I live with that and not be afraid?
JOCASTA Why should men be afraid of anything? Fortune rules our lives.
   Luck is everything. Things happen. The future is darkness.
   No human mind can know it.
   It's best to live in the moment, live for today, Oedipus.
1235   Why should the thought of marrying your mother make you so afraid?
   Many men have slept with their mothers in their dreams.
   Why worry? See your dreams for what they are—nothing, nothing at all.
   Be happy, Oedipus.
OEDIPUS All that you say is right, Jocasta. I know it.
1240   I should be happy,
   but my mother is still living. As long as she's alive,
   I live in fear. This fear is necessary.

I have no choice.
JOCASTA But Oedipus, your father's death is a sign, a great sign—
1245   the sky has cleared, the sun's gaze holds us in its warm, hopeful light.
OEDIPUS A great sign, I agree. But so long as my mother is alive,
my fear lives too.
MESSENGER Who is this woman you fear so much?
OEDIPUS Merope, King Polybos' wife.
1250   MESSENGER Why does Merope frighten you so much?
OEDIPUS A harrowing oracle hurled down upon us by some great god.
MESSENGER Can you tell me? Or did the god seal your lips?
OEDIPUS I can.
Long ago, Apollo told me I was doomed to sleep with my mother
1255   and spill my father's blood, murder him
with these two hands of mine.
That's why I never returned to Corinth. Luckily, it would seem.
Still, nothing on earth is sweeter to a man's eyes
than the sight of his father and mother.
1260   MESSENGER And you left Corinth because of this prophecy?
OEDIPUS Yes. And because of my father. To avoid killing my father.
MESSENGER But didn't my news prove you have nothing to fear?
I brought good news.
OEDIPUS And I will reward you for your kindness.
1265   MESSENGER That's why I came, my lord. I knew you'd remember me
when you returned to Corinth.
OEDIPUS I will never return, never live with my parents again.
MESSENGER Son, it's clear you don't know what you're doing.
OEDIPUS What do you mean? In the name of the gods, speak.
1270   MESSENGER If you're afraid to go home because of your parents.
OEDIPUS I *am* afraid, afraid
Apollo's prediction will come true, all of it,
as god's sunlight grows brighter on a man's face at dawn
when he's in bed, still sleeping,
1275   and reaches into his eyes and wakes him.
MESSENGER Afraid of murdering your father, of having his blood on your
hands?
OEDIPUS Yes. His blood. The stain of his blood. That terror never leaves me.
MESSENGER But Oedipus, then you have no reason to be afraid.
OEDIPUS I'm their son, they're my parents, aren't they?
1280   MESSENGER Polybos is nothing to you.
OEDIPUS Polybos is not my father?
MESSENGER No more than I am.
OEDIPUS But you are nothing to me. Nothing.
MESSENGER And Polybos is nothing to you either.
1285   OEDIPUS Then why did he call me his son?
MESSENGER Because I gave you to him. With these hands
I gave you to him.
OEDIPUS How could he have loved me like a father if I am not his son?
MESSENGER He had no children. That opened his heart.
1290   OEDIPUS And what about you?
Did you buy me from someone? Or did you find me?

MESSENGER I found you squawling, left alone to die in the thickets of
    Kithairon.
OEDIPUS Kithairon? What were you doing on Kithairon?
MESSENGER Herding sheep in the high summer pastures.
1295 OEDIPUS You were a shepherd, a drifter looking for work?
MESSENGER A drifter, yes, but it was I who saved you.
OEDIPUS Saved me? Was I hurt when you picked me up?
MESSENGER Ask your feet.
OEDIPUS Why,
1300   why did you bring up that childhood pain?
MESSENGER I cut you free. Your feet were pierced, tied together at the ankles
    with leather thongs strung between the tendons and the bone.
OEDIPUS That mark of my shame—I've worn it from the cradle.
MESSENGER That mark is the meaning of your name:
1305   Oedipus, Swollenfoot, Oedipus.
OEDIPUS Oh gods
    who did this to me?
    My mother?
    My father?
1310 MESSENGER I don't know. The man I took you from—he would know.
OEDIPUS So you didn't find me? Somebody else gave me to you?
MESSENGER I got you from another shepherd.
OEDIPUS What shepherd? Who was he? Do you know?
MESSENGER As I recall, he worked for Laios.
1315 OEDIPUS The same Laios who was king of Thebes?
MESSENGER The same Laios. The man was one of Laios' shepherds.
OEDIPUS Is he still alive? I want to see this man.
MESSENGER [pointing to the CHORUS] These people would know that better
    than I do.
OEDIPUS Do any of you know this shepherd he's talking about?
1320   Have you ever noticed him in the fields or in the city?
    Answer, if you have.
    It is time everything came out, time everything was made clear.
    Everything.
LEADER I think he's the shepherd you sent for.
1325   But Jocasta, she would know.
OEDIPUS [to JOCASTA]
    Jocasta, do you know this man?
    Is he the man this shepherd here says worked for Laios?
JOCASTA What man? Forget about him. Forget what was said.
1330   It's not worth talking about.
OEDIPUS How can I forget
    with clues like these in my hands?
    With the secret of my birth staring me in the face?
JOCASTA No, Oedipus!
1335   No more questions.
    For god's sake, for the sake of your own life!
    Isn't my anguish enough—more than enough?
OEDIPUS You have nothing to fear, Jocasta.
    Even if my mother

1340　　and her mother before her were both slaves,
　　　　that doesn't make *you* the daughter of slaves.
　　JOCASTA　Oedipus, you *must* stop.
　　　　　　　　　　　　　　　　　I beg you—stop!
　　OEDIPUS　Nothing can stop me now. I must know everything.
1345　　Everything!
　　JOCASTA　I implore you, Oedipus. For your own good.
　　OEDIPUS　Damn my own good!
　　JOCASTA　Oh, Oedipus, Oedipus,
　　　　I pray to god you never see who you are!
1350　OEDIPUS [*to one of the attendants, who hurries off through the exit stage left*]
　　　　You there, go find that shepherd, bring him here.
　　　　Let that woman bask in the glory of her noble birth.
　　JOCASTA　God help you, Oedipus—
　　　　you were born to suffer, born
1355　　to misery and grief.
　　　　These are the last last words I will ever speak, ever
　　　　Oedipus.

　　JOCASTA *rushes offstage into the palace. Long silence.*

　　LEADER　Why did Jocasta rush away,
　　　　Oedipus, fleeing in such pain?
1360　　I fear disaster, or worse,
　　　　will break from this silence of hers.
　　OEDIPUS　Let it break! Let everything break!
　　　　I must discover who I am, know the secret of my birth,
　　　　no matter how humble, how vile.
1365　　Perhaps Jocasta is ashamed of my low birth, ashamed to be my wife.
　　　　Like all women she's proud.
　　　　But Luck, goddess who gives men all that is good, made *me*,
　　　　and I won't be cheated of what is mine, nothing can dishonor me, ever.
　　　　I am like the months, my brothers the months—they shaped me
1370　　when I was a baby in the cold hills of Kithairon,
　　　　they guided me, carved out my times of greatness,
　　　　and they still move their hands over my life.
　　　　I am the man I am. I will not stop
　　　　until I discover who my parents are.
1375　CHORUS　if I know if I see
　　　　if the dark force of prophecy is mine
　　　　Kithairon
　　　　when the full moon
　　　　rides over us tomorrow
1380　　listen listen to us sing to you
　　　　dance worship praise you
　　　　mountain where Oedipus was found
　　　　know Oedipus will praise you
　　　　praise his nurse country and mother
1385　　who blessed our king

I call on you Apollo
let these visions please you
god Apollo
healer

1390   Oedipus son
who was your mother
which of the deathless mountain nymphs who lay
with the great god Pan
on the high peaks he runs across
1395   or with Apollo
who loves the high green pastures above
which one bore you
did the god of the bare windy peaks Hermes
or the wild, dervish Dionysos
1400   living in the cool air of the hills
take you
a foundling
from one of the nymphs he plays with
joyously lift you hold you in his arms
1405   OEDIPUS   Old men, I think the man coming toward us now
must be the shepherd we are looking for.
I have never seen him, but the years, chalking his face and hair, tell me
he's the man. And my men are with him. But you probably know him.
LEADER   I do know him. If Laios ever had a man he trusted,
1410   this was the man.
OEDIPUS [*to the* MESSENGER]
You—is this the man you told me about?
MESSENGER   That's him. You're looking at the man.
OEDIPUS [*to the* SHEPHERD *who has been waiting, hanging back*]
1415   You there, come closer.
                              Answer me, old man.
Did you work for Laios?
SHEPHERD   I was born his slave, and grew up in his household.
OEDIPUS   What was your work?
1420   SHEPHERD   Herding sheep, all my life.
OEDIPUS   Where?
SHEPHERD   Kithairon, mostly. And the country around Kithairon.
OEDIPUS   Do you remember ever seeing this man?
MESSENGER   Which man?
1425   OEDIPUS [*pointing to the* MESSENGER]
This man standing here. Have you ever seen him before?
SHEPHERD   Not that I remember.
MESSENGER   No wonder, master. But I'll make him remember.
He knows who I am. We used to graze our flocks together
1430   in the pastures around Kithairon.
Every year, for six whole months, three years running.
From March until September, when the Dipper rose, signaling the harvest.
I had one flock, he had two.

And when the frost came, I drove my sheep back to their winter pens
1435   and he drove his back to Laios' fold.
Remember, old man? Isn't that how it was?
SHEPHERD   Yes. But it was all so long ago.
MESSENGER   And do you remember giving me a baby boy at the time—
to raise as my own son?
1440   SHEPHERD   What if I do? Why all these questions?
MESSENGER   That boy became King Oedipus, friend.
SHEPHERD   Damn you, can't you keep quiet.
OEDIPUS   Don't scold him, old man.
It's you who deserve to be punished, not him.
1445   SHEPHERD   What did I say, good master?
OEDIPUS   You haven't answered his question about the boy.
SHEPHERD   He's making trouble, master. He doesn't know a thing.

[OEDIPUS *takes the* SHEPHERD *by the cloak*]

OEDIPUS   Tell me or you'll be sorry.
SHEPHERD   For god's sake, don't hurt me, I'm an old man.
1450   OEDIPUS [*to one of his men*]   You there, hold him. We'll make him talk.

The attendant pins the SHEPHERD's arms behind his back

SHEPHERD   Oedipus, Oedipus,
god knows I pity you.
What more do you want to know?
OEDIPUS   Did you give the child to this man?
1455
                                        Speak.   Yes or no?
SHEPHERD   Yes.
And I wish to god I'd died that day.
OEDIPUS   You *will* be dead unless you tell me the whole truth.
SHEPHERD   And worse than dead, if I do.
1460   OEDIPUS   It seems our man won't answer.
SHEPHERD   No. I told you already. I gave him the boy.
OEDIPUS   Where did you get him? From Laios' household? Or where?
SHEPHERD   He wasn't *my* child. He was given to me.
OEDIPUS [*turning to the* CHORUS *and the audience*]   By whom? Someone here
in Thebes?
1465   SHEPHERD   Master, please, in god's name, no more questions.
OEDIPUS   You're a dead man if I have to ask you once more.
SHEPHERD   He was one
of the children
from Laios'
1470   household.
OEDIPUS   A slave child? Or Laios' own?
SHEPHERD   I can't say it . . . it's
awful, the words
are awful . . . awful.
1475   OEDIPUS   And I,
I am afraid to hear them . . .

　　　　　but I must.
　　　　SHEPHERD He was Laios' own child.
　　　　　Your wife, inside the palace, she can explain it all.
1480　　OEDIPUS *She* gave you the child?
　　　　SHEPHERD My lord . . . yes.
　　　　OEDIPUS Why?
　　　　SHEPHERD She wanted me to abandon the child on a mountain.
　　　　OEDIPUS His own mother?
1485　　SHEPHERD Yes. There were prophecies, horrible oracles. She was afraid.
　　　　OEDIPUS What oracles?
　　　　SHEPHERD Oracles predicting he would murder his own father.
　　　　OEDIPUS But why did you give the boy to this old man?
　　　　SHEPHERD Because I pitied him, master, because I
1490　　　thought the man would take the child away, take him to another country.
　　　　　Instead he saved him. Saved him for—oh gods,
　　　　　a fate so horrible, so awful, words can't describe it.
　　　　　If you were the baby that man took from me, Oedipus,
　　　　　what misery, what grief is yours!
　　　　OEDIPUS [*looking up at the sun*]
1495　　　LIGHT   LIGHT   LIGHT
　　　　　never again flood these eyes with your white radiance, oh gods, my eyes. All, all
　　　　　the oracles have proven true. I, Oedipus, I
　　　　　am the child
1500　　　of parents who should never have been mine—doomed, doomed!
　　　　　Now everything is clear—I
　　　　　lived with a woman, she was my mother, I slept in my mother's bed, and I
　　　　　murdered, murdered my father,
　　　　　the man whose blood flows in these veins of mine,
1505　　　whose blood stains these two hands red.

OEDIPUS *raises his hands to the sun, then turns and walks into the palace.*

　　　　CHORUS   man after man after man
　　　　　o mortal generations
　　　　　here once
　　　　　almost not here
1510　　　what are we
　　　　　dust ghosts images a rustling of air
　　　　　nothing nothing
　　　　　we breathe on the abyss
　　　　　we are the abyss
1515　　　our happiness no more than traces of a dream
　　　　　the high noon sun sinking into the sea
　　　　　the red spume of its wake raining behind it
　　　　　we are you
　　　　　we are you Oedipus
1520　　　dragging your maimed foot
　　　　　in agony
　　　　　and now that I see your life finally revealed

your life fused with the god
blazing out of the black nothingness of all we know
1525   I say
no happiness lasts nothing human lasts

wherever you aimed you hit
no archer had your skill
you grew rich powerful great
1530   everything came falling to your feet
o Zeus
after he killed the Sphinx
whose claws curled under
whose weird song of the future baffled and destroyed
1535   he stood like a tower high above our country
warding off death
and from then on Oedipus we called you
king our king
draped you in gold
1540   our highest honors were yours
and you ruled this shining city
Thebes   Thebes
now
your story is pain pity no story is worse
1545   than yours Oedipus
ruined savage blind
as you struggle with your life
as your life changes
and breaks and shows you who you are
1550   Oedipus   Oedipus
son father you harbored in the selfsame place
the same place sheltered you both
bridegroom
how could the furrow your father plowed
1555   not have cried out all this time
while you lay there unknowing
and saw the truth too late

time like the sun sees all things
and it sees you
1560   you cannot hide from that light
your own life opening itself to you
to all
married unmarried father son
for so long
1565   justice comes like the dawn
always
and it shows the world your marriage now

I wish
o child of Laios
1570   I wish I had never seen you

I grieve for you
wail after wail fills me and pours out
because of you my breath came flowing back
but now
1575 the darkness of your life
floods my eyes

The palace doors open. A SERVANT *enters and approaches the* CHORUS *and*
audience.

SERVANT Noble citizens, honored above all others in Thebes,
if you still care for the house of Laios,
if you still can feel the spirit of those who ruled before, now
1580 the horrors you will hear, the horrors you will see, will shake your hearts and
shatter you with grief beyond enduring.
Not even the waters of those great rivers Ister and Phasis
could wash away the blood
that now darkens every stone of this shining house,
this house that will reveal, soon, soon
1585 the misery and evil two mortals,
both masters of this house, have brought upon themselves.

The griefs we cause ourselves cut deepest of all.
LEADER What we already know
has hurt us enough,
1590 has made us cry out in pain.
What more can you say?
SERVANT This:
Jocasta is dead. The queen is dead.
LEADER Ah, poor
1595 unhappy Jocasta,
how did she die?
SERVANT She killed herself. She did it.
But you did not see what happened there,
you were not there, in the palace. You did not see it.
1600 I did.
I will tell you how Queen Jocasta died,
the whole story, all of it. All I can remember.
After her last words to Oedipus
she rushed past us through the entrance hall, screaming,
1605 raking her hair with both hands, and flew into the bedroom, *their* bedroom,
and slammed the doors shut as she lunged at her bridal bed,
crying "Laios" "Laios"—dead all these years—
remembering Laios—how his own son years ago
grew up and then killed him, leaving her to
1610 sleep with her own son, to have his children, *their* children,
children—not sons, not daughters, something else, monsters. . . .
Then she collapsed, sobbing, cursing the bed where she held both men in her
arms,
got husband from husband, children from her child.

We heard it all, but suddenly, I couldn't tell what was happening.

1615 Oedipus came crashing in, he was howling,
stalking up and down—we couldn't take our eyes off him—
and we stopped listening to her pitiful cries.
We stood there, watching him move like a bull, lurching, charging,
shouting at each of us to give him a sword, demanding we tell him

1620 where his wife was, that woman whose womb carried him,
him and his children, that wife who gave him birth.
Some god, some demon, led him to her, and he knew—
none of us showed him—
suddenly a mad, inhuman cry burst from his mouth

1625 as if the wind rushed through his tortured body,
and he heaved against those bedroom doors so the hinges whined
and bent from their sockets and the bolts snapped,
and he stood in the room.
There she was—

1630 we could see her—his wife
dangling by her neck from a noose of braided, silken cords
tied to a rafter, still swaying.
And when he saw her he bellowed and stretched up and loosened the rope,
cradling her in one arm,

1635 and slowly laid her body on the ground.

That's when it happened—he
ripped off the gold
brooches she was wearing—one on each shoulder of her gown—
and raised them over his head—you could see them flashing—

1640 and tilted his face up and
brought them right down into his eyes
and the long pins sank deep, all the way back into the sockets,
and he shouted at his eyes:
"Now you won't see me, you won't see

1645 my agonies or my crimes,
but in endless darkness, always, there you'll see
those I never should have seen.
And those I should have known were my parents, father and mother—
these eyes will never see their faces in the light.

1650 These eyes will never see the light again, never."
Cursing his two blind eyes over and over, he
lifted the brooches again and drove their pins through his eyeballs up
to the hilts until they were pulp, until the blood streamed out
soaking his beard and cheeks,

1655 a black storm splashing its hail across his face.

Two mortals acted. Now grief tears their lives apart
as if that pain sprang from a single, sorrowing root
to curse each one, man and wife. For all those years
their happiness was truly happiness, but now, now

1660 wailing, madness, shame and death,
every evil men have given a name,

everything criminal and vile
that mankind suffers they suffer. Not one evil is missing.
LEADER But now

1665   does this torn, anguished man
have any rest from his pain?
SERVANT No, no—
then he shouted at us to open the doors and show everyone in Thebes
his father's killer, his mother's—I cannot say it.

1670   Once we have seen him as he is
he will leave Thebes, lift the curse from his city—
banish himself, cursed by his own curses.
But his strength is gone, his whole life is pain,
more pain than any man can bear.

1675   He needs help, someone to guide him.
He is alone, and blind. Look,
look—the palace doors are opening—now
a thing
so horrible will stand before you

1680   you will shudder with disgust and try to turn away
while your hearts will swell with pity for what you see.

The central doors open. OEDIPUS *enters, led by his household servants. His mask is covered with blood. The* CHORUS *begin a dirge to which* OEDIPUS *responds antiphonally.*

CHORUS   horror horror o what suffering
men see
but none is worse than this

1685   Oedipus o
how could you have slashed out your eyes
what god leaped on you
from beyond the last border of space
what madness entered you

1690   clawing even more misery into you
I cannot look at you

but there are questions
so much I would know
so much that I would see

1695   no   no
the shape of your life makes me shudder
OEDIPUS I   I
this voice of agony
I am   what place am I

1700   where? Not here, nowhere I know!
What force, what tide breaks over my life?
Pain, demon stabbing into me
leaving nothing, nothing, no man I know, not human,
fate howling out of nowhere   what am I

1705   fire   a voice   where   where
is it being taken?

LEADER   Beyond everything to a place
   so terrible nothing is seen there, nothing is heard.
OEDIPUS [*reaching out, groping*]
1710   Thing   thing   darkness
   spilling into me, my
   black cloud smothering me forever,
   nothing can stop you, nothing can escape,
   I cannot push you away.

1715   I am
   nothing but my own cries breaking
   again and again
   the agony of those gold pins
   the memory of what I did
1720   stab me
   again
   again.
LEADER   What can you feel but pain.
   It all comes back, pain in remorse,
1725   remorse in pain, to tear you apart with grief.
OEDIPUS   Dear, loyal friend
   you, only you, are still here with me, still care
   for this blind, tortured man.
   Oh,
1730   I know you are there, I know you, friend,
   even in this darkness, friend, touched by your voice.
LEADER   What you did was horrible,
   but how could you quench the fire of your eyes,
   what demon lifted your hands?
1735 OEDIPUS   Apollo   Apollo
   it was Apollo, always Apollo,
   who brought each of my agonies to birth,
   but I,
   nobody else, *I,*
1740   I raised these two hands of mine, held them above my head,
   and plunged them down,
   I stabbed out these eyes.
   Why should I have eyes? Why,
   when nothing I saw was worth seeing?
1745   Nothing.
LEADER   Nothing. Nothing.
OEDIPUS   Oh friends. Nothing.
   No one to see, no one to love,
   no one to speak to, no one to hear!
1750   Friends, friends, lead me away now.
   Lead me away from Thebes—Oedipus,
   destroyer and destroyed,
   the man whose life is hell
   for others and for himself, the man
1755   more hated by the gods than any other man, ever.

LEADER   Oh I pity you,
   I weep for your fate
   and for your mind,
   for what it is to be you, Oedipus.
1760   I wish you had never seen the man you are.
OEDIPUS   I hate
   the man who found me, cut the thongs from my feet,
   snatched me from death, cared for me—
   I wish he were dead!
1765   I should have died up there on those wild, desolate slopes of Kithairon.
   Then my pain and the pain
   those I love suffer now
   never would have been.
LEADER   These are my wishes too.
1770 OEDIPUS   Then I never would have murdered my father,
   never heard men call me my mother's husband.

   Now
   I am
   Oedipus!
1775   Oedipus, who lay in that loathsome bed, made love there in that bed,
   his father's and mother's bed, the bed
   where he was born.

   No gods anywhere now, not for me, now,
   unholy, broken man.
1780   What man ever suffered grief like this?
LEADER   How can I say that what you did was right?
   Better to be dead than live blind.
OEDIPUS   I did what I had to do. No more advice.
   How could *my* eyes,
1785   when I went down into that black, sightless place beneath the earth,
   the place where the dead go down, how,
   how could I have looked at anything,
   with what human eyes could I have gazed
   on my father, on my mother—
1790   oh gods, my mother!
   What I did against those two
   not even strangling could punish.
   And my children, how would the sight of them, born as they were born,
   be sweet? Not to these eyes of mine, never to these eyes.
1795   Nothing, nothing is left me now—no city with its high walls,
   no shining statues of the gods. I stripped all these things from myself—
   I, Oedipus, fallen lower than any man now, born nobler than the best,
   born the king of Thebes! Cursed with my own curses, I
   commanded Thebes to drive out the killer.
1800   I banished the royal son of Laios, the man the gods revealed
   is stained with the awful stain. The secret stain
   that I myself revealed is *my* stain. And now, revealed at last,
   how could I ever look men in the eyes?
   Never. Never.

1805   If I could, I would have walled my ears so they heard nothing,
        I would have made this body of mine a wall.
        I would have heard nothing, tasted nothing, smelled nothing, seen
        nothing.
                No thought. No feeling. Nothing. Nothing.
1810   So pain would never reach me any more.

        O Kithairon,
        why did you shelter me and take me in?
        Why did you let me live? Better to have died on that bare slope of yours
        where no man would ever have seen me or known the secret of my birth!

1815   Polybos, Corinth, that house I thought was my father's home,
        how beautiful I was when you sheltered me as a child
        and oh what disease festered beneath that beauty.
        Now everyone knows the secret of my birth, knows
        how vile I am.

1820   O roads, secret valley, cluster of oaks,
        O narrow place where two roads join a third,
        roads that drank my blood as it streamed from my hands,
        flowing from my dead father's body,
        do you remember me now?
1825   Do you remember what I did with my own two hands, there in your presence,
        and what I did after that, when I came here to Thebes?
        O marriage, marriage, you gave me my life, and then
        from the same seed, *my* seed, spewed out
        fathers, brothers, sisters, children, brides, wives—
1830   nothing, no words can express the shame.
        No more words. Men should not name what men should never do.

                                                    [*To the* CHORUS]

        Gods, oh gods, gods,
        hide me, hide me
        now
1835   far away from Thebes,
        kill me,
        cast me into the sea,
        drive me where you will never see me—never again.

                        [*Reaching out to the* CHORUS, *who back away*]

        Touch this poor man, touch me,
1840   don't be afraid to touch me. Believe me, nobody,
        nobody but me can bear
        this fire of anguish.
        It is mine. Mine.
    LEADER   Kreon has come.
1845   Now he, not you, is the sole guardian of Thebes,
        and only he can grant you what you ask.

OEDIPUS [*turning toward the palace*]
    What can I say to him, how can anything I say
    make him listen now?
1850   I wronged him. I accused him, and now everything I said
    proves I am vile.
KREON [*enters from the entrance to the right. He is accompanied by men who
    gather around* OEDIPUS]
    I have not come to mock you, Oedipus; I have not come to blame you for the
    past.

                                                 [*To attendants*]

    You men, standing there, if you have no respect for human dignity,
    at least revere the master of life,
1855   the all-seeing sun whose light nourishes
    every living thing on earth.
    Come, cover this cursed, naked, holy thing, hide him
    from the earth and the sacred rain and the light,
    you powers who cringe from his touch.
1860   Take him. Do it now. Be reverent.
    Only his family should see and hear his grief.
    Their grief.
OEDIPUS I beg you, Kreon, if you love the gods,
    grant me what I ask.
1865   I have been vile to you, worse than vile.
    I have hurt you, terribly, and yet
    you have treated me with kindness, with nobility.
    You have calmed my fear, you did not turn away from me.
    Do what I ask. Do it for yourself, not for me.
1870 KREON What do you want from me, Oedipus?
OEDIPUS Drive me out of Thebes, do it now, now—
    drive me someplace where no man can speak to me,
    where no man can see me anymore.
KREON Believe me, Oedipus, I would have done it long ago.
1875   But I refuse to act until I know precisely what the god desires.
OEDIPUS Apollo has revealed what he desires. Everything is clear.
    I killed my father, I am polluted and unclean.
    I must die.
KREON That is what the god commanded, Oedipus.
1880   But there are no precedents for what has happened.
    We need to *know* before we act.
OEDIPUS Do you care so much for me, enough to ask Apollo?
    For *me,* Oedipus?
KREON Now even you will trust the god, I think.
1885 OEDIPUS I will. And I turn to you, I implore you, Kreon—
    the woman lying dead inside, your sister,
    give her whatever burial you think best.
                         As for me,
    never let this city of my fathers see me here in Thebes.

1890   Let me go and live on the mountains, on Kithairon—the mountain
my parents intended for my grave.
Let me die the way they wanted me to die: slowly, alone—
die *their* way.
And yet this much I know—

1895   no sickness,
no ordinary, natural death is mine.
I have been saved, preserved, kept alive
for some strange fate, for something far more awful still.
When that thing comes, let it take me
1900   where it will.

                          [OEDIPUS *turns, looking for something, waiting*]

As for my sons, Kreon,
they are grown men, they can look out for themselves.
But my daughters, those two poor girls of mine,
who have never left their home before, never left their father's side,
1905   who ate at my side every day, who shared whatever was mine,
I beg you, Kreon,
care for them, love them.
But more than anything, Kreon,
I want to touch them,

                              [*He begins to lift his hands*]

1910   let me touch them with these hands of mine,
let them come to me so we can grieve together.
My noble lord, if only I could touch them with my hands,
they would still be mine just as they were
when I had eyes that could still see.

               [*Oedipus' two small daughters are brought out of the palace*]

1915   O gods, gods, is it possible? Do I hear
my two daughters crying? Has Kreon pitied me and brought me
what I love more than my life—
my daughters?
KREON   I brought them to you, knowing how much you love them, Oedipus,
1920   knowing the joy you would feel if they were here.
OEDIPUS   May the gods who watch over the path of your life, Kreon,
prove kinder to you than they were to me.
Where are you, children?
Come, come to your brother's hands—

                              [*Taking his daughters into his arms*]

1925   his mother was your mother, too,
come to these hands which made these eyes, bright clear eyes once,
sockets seeing nothing, the eyes

of the man who fathered you. Look . . . your father's eyes,
your father—
1930 who knew nothing until now, saw nothing until now, and became
the husband of the woman who gave him birth.
                                    I weep for you
when I think how men will treat you, how bitter your lives will be.
What festivals will you attend, whose homes will you visit
1935 and not be assailed by whispers, and people's stares?
Where will you go and not leave in tears?
And when the time comes for you to marry,
what men will take you as their brides, and risk the shame of marrying
the daughters of Oedipus?
1940 What sorrow will not be yours?
Your father killed his father, made love
to the woman who gave birth to him. And he fathered you
in the same place where he was fathered.
That is what you will hear; that is what they will say.
1945 Who will marry you then? You will never marry,
but grow hard and dry like wheat so far beyond harvest
that the wind blows its white flakes into the winter sky.
Oh Kreon,
now you are the only father my daughters have.
1950 Jocasta and I, their parents, are lost to them forever.
These poor girls are yours. Your blood.
Don't let them wander all their lives,
begging, alone, unmarried, helpless.
Don't let them suffer as their father has. Pity them, Kreon,
1955 pity these girls, so young and helpless except for you.
Promise me this. Noble Kreon,
touch me with your hand, give me a sign.

                                    [KREON *takes his hands*]

                                    Daughters,
daughters, if you were older, if you could understand,
1960 there is so much more I would say to you.
But for now, I give you this prayer—
                              Live,
live your lives, live each day as best you can,
may your lives be happier than your father's was.
1965 KREON No more grief. Come in.
OEDIPUS I must. But obedience comes hard.
KREON Everything has its time.
OEDIPUS First, promise me this.
KREON Name it.
1970 OEDIPUS Banish me from Thebes.
KREON I cannot.   Ask the gods for that.
OEDIPUS The gods hate me.
KREON Then you will have your wish.
OEDIPUS You promise?

1975   KREON   I say only what I mean.
OEDIPUS   Then lead me in.

OEDIPUS *reaches out and touches his daughters, trying to take them with him.*

KREON   Oedipus, come with me. Let your daughters go. Come.
OEDIPUS   No. You will not take my daughters. I forbid it.
KREON   You *forbid* me?
1980   You have no power any more.
         All the great power you once had is gone,
         gone forever.

The CHORUS *turn to face the audience.* KREON *leads* OEDIPUS *toward the palace.*
His daughters follow. He moves slowly, and disappears into the palace as the
CHORUS *ends.*

CHORUS   O citizens of Thebes, this is Oedipus,
         who solved the famous riddle, who held more power than any mortal.
1985   See what he is: all men gazed on his fortunate life,
         all men envied him, but look at him, look.
         All he had, all this man was,
         pulled down and swallowed by the storm of his own life,
         and by the god.
1990   Keep your eyes on that last day, on your dying.
         Happiness and peace, they were not yours
         unless at death you can look back on your life and say
         I lived, I did not suffer.

Questions

1. On a sheet of paper, outline the plot of *Oedipus the King* by summarizing what
   happens in each exchange of dialogue between two or more characters. (Count
   the chorus or the leader of the chorus as a character.) For instance:

   Chorus complains about plague; Oedipus consults oracle . . .

   Using your outline, summarize the conflicts and crises of the play.
2. How many reversals of intention can you discover? Recognitions? Moments
   of dramatic irony? (See definitions, page 752.)
3. After Teiresias first reveals Oedipus' guilt (to the audience if not to Oedipus),
   there is a moment of dialogue when it seems that Teiresias must be mistaken.
   Where is it? What purpose does this misdirection serve in the shape of the
   play?
4. Discuss coincidence and probability in *Oedipus the King*. What is the effect of
   the accumulation of coincidence?
5. Does Jocasta understand what happened before Oedipus does? What does
   she know? How do we know that she knows?
6. After the guilt and the punishment of this tragic hero, what will happen to
   Thebes? Does Sophocles prepare us for an enduring society? (You might like
   to know that *Kreon* means "ruler" or "king.")

7. A servant describes Jocasta's hanging and Oedipus' self-mutilation. Would the play be better if these actions took place onstage?

8. How does Sophocles give us the character of Oedipus? How much do we learn from other characters when Oedipus is not on the stage? From other characters in the way they speak to Oedipus? From his own speech? From his gestures? From his actions?

9. How does the chorus represent the citizenry of Thebes? When is it most like a group, and when is it most like a particular person? How does it serve the action of the play?

10. After Oedipus' discovery and downfall, does his character change? How? Is there development? After his downfall, how is it possible to continue to speak of his greatness?

11. Why does Oedipus blind himself as he does? What instruments does he use and why?

12. The last three lines of the play, uttered by the chorus, give a warning to the audience—which now includes you. Do you take this warning?

13. Discuss in class possible stagings of *Oedipus the King*.

    If you performed the play in what you understand of the ancient Greek manner, how would you stage it? To answer the question, choose two or three pages of the play and consider the blocking and the entrances and exits for them. Remember that you are dealing with an all-male cast, wearing masks, in daylight, with limited scenery.

    How would you stage the same two or three pages in a contemporary theater with a picture stage? How would you use lighting? How realistic would you want to be, in costuming, make-up, properties?

    Discuss the differences in the productions.

14. To watch the play with understanding, how much would a contemporary audience need to know that an ancient audience would already have known? Could we make up for ignorance by staging? By other means?

15. Is this play out of date? Can you apply its thought to yourself, to your own life, to other twentieth-century American lives? Can you apply it to all people everywhere at any time?

Chapter 4 **Elizabethan Drama and Shakespeare**

In England during the reign of Elizabeth I (1558–1603), theater flourished as it had not for some centuries. Roman theater had followed and imitated the Greek, producing the great comedies of Plautus and Terence, who wrote in the third and second centuries B.C. In the Middle Ages elements of theater survived in church ritual and in popular festivals. In tenth-century England, for example, we find the *Quem Quaeritis* (Latin: "Whom do you seek?"), a dialogue in which priests representing the three Marys, as part of a church service, approach another priest dressed in white, playing the role of an angel at the tomb of Jesus. The angel speaks from the tomb: "Whom do you seek?"; the three answer that they seek Jesus; the angel tells them "He has risen as He foretold," and the three Marys announce the Resurrection to the world—the worshipers in the church.

In this small enactment, theater had its rebirth. But six centuries elapsed between the *Quem Quaeritis* and the Elizabethan age. We are aware of the gradual growth of theater, and some medieval plays survive. A few old secular plays chronicle the adventures of Robin Hood, but most plays from the Middle Ages to the time of Elizabeth are religious. Perhaps the best known is the *Second Shepherds' Play*; although it is a drama that enacts Christ's birth, the anonymous playwright makes broad and bawdy comedy before he shows the birth in the manger. In the Renaissance a revival of classical learning added the remains of ancient drama to existing religious plays. Drama expanded into the universities, aristocratic houses, the court, the law schools, and the inn yards. This same period saw the development of short secular plays called interludes and the beginning of professional acting companies. Drama gradually became a popular form of entertainment, and permanent theaters were built in the suburbs of London. The first generation of Elizabethan playwrights included Christopher Marlowe, Thomas Kyd, John Lyly, Robert Greene, and George Peele.

Christopher Marlowe (1564–1593), author of *The Tragical History of Doctor Faustus,* is the first great Elizabethan playwright. He developed for dramatic use the poetic line of iambic pentameter, or blank verse, that Shakespeare perfected. (For a discussion of blank verse, see page 466.) Ben Jonson (1572–1637) was Shakespeare's greatest contemporary, author of great comedies, *Volpone* (1606) and *The Alchemist* (1610) for example. (There is a poem by Christopher Marlowe on page 539; for two of Ben Jonson's poems see pages 408 and 546.) Along with many other playwrights, Jonson lived from Elizabeth's time into the reign of James I. But when Oliver Cromwell's Puritan revolution overthrew James's son Charles I, Cromwell, like a good Puritan, closed the theaters. About twenty years later, when Cromwell had died and the monarchy had been returned, the Restoration began a new era in English theater.

The Globe Playhouse— Shakespeare's theater—stood on the Bankside, across the Thames from the walled city of London. Constructed in 1599, it burned during the performance of a play in June 1613. (This is a model reconstruction by John Cranford Adams.)

Elizabethan theater was a secular, popular art played by traveling troupes like the wandering players in *Hamlet* and by resident companies in London playhouses. The Globe was Shakespeare's theater, located across the Thames from London proper. It was many-sided, almost round—the "wooden O" which Shakespeare describes in *Henry V.* Going inside, an Elizabethan could stand on the ground before the stage for a fee of one penny. Or with more money he could sit in one of the galleries that ran for three stories around three-quarters of the building. Perhaps eight hundred people stood in the unroofed center—where they might be rained on—while fifteen hundred sat in the sheltered galleries. The stage itself thrust from a rear wall, with entrances and exits at the sides and rear, where characters might hide or where they might be revealed by an opening curtain. (It was from behind this curtain that Polonius spied on Hamlet.) Over the alcove actors could perform on a balcony or gallery. At the front of the stage, a trapdoor allowed a ghost to rise or a damned soul to drop screaming into hell.

Elizabethan theater used little scenery and few props; an Elizabethan diary lists some of the props one company owned, including swords, pikes, daggers, scepters, broken staffs, scrolls, and torches. Gravediggers might carry shovels. Servants might bring tables and chairs on stage. For the most part, speeches described where the characters were and what they carried. Instead of lights rising pink to show us dawn, a character described the light of dawn in a poetic image. (In the first scene of *Hamlet,* Horatio points: "But look, the morn in russet mantle clad / Walks o'er the dew. . . .") Lacking scenery, the staging required neither blackout nor curtain for changing scenery, and stage action for the Elizabethans was continuous, like the action of a modern film. Actors walked off, actors walked on—and we learned by their dialogue that the scene had shifted. Stimulated by language, the audience made a seacoast of a bare stage or by imagination turned the bare stage into the opulent dining hall of a great king. Modern editors have added stage directions to our texts of Shakespeare.

As we study the drama of the Greeks and the Elizabethans, one of the greatest differences appears to be the audience played to. Elizabethan society and theater were more secular and more diverse than the Greek. Both societies were prosperous, expanding, energetic, adventurous, imperialistic, but the society of Athens was more cohesive, more unified by religion and by social order. Elizabethan England was colorful, chaotic, and relatively lawless. Elizabethan tragedy is more diverse, various, and inclusive than Greek; less singular and uncompromising in its shape and purpose. An Elizabethan came to the theater expecting to be lifted from his seat by surprise, shock, shouting, outrage, and murder; he would be cajoled by fools, he would hear songs, he would laugh at puns and leer at sexual innuendoes. He probably knew how the story went, just as the Greeks did. (*Hamlet* is an old story, apparently the subject of an earlier play now lost.) Although Hamlet and Oedipus derive from similar psychic sources (we have been told, for the last seventy-five years, that Hamlet suffered from an Oedipus complex), the details of the plays suggest wide differences in the two eras. Sophocles would never have invented Rosencrantz and Guildenstern, that hapless pair from Wittenberg. Nor would Hamlet's bawdy remarks to Ophelia find their way to Thebes, or his jokes to the players, or the extraordinary number of crude bits of reality—like the discovery of Yorick's skull. Elizabethan drama was superabundant in energy and language and life; Greek drama found its magnificence not so much in abundance as in starkness. The Elizabethans were less interested in probability, more in particular color; the Greeks were more obsessed by the sense of inevitability.

Two terms need special definition in connection with Elizabethan drama. Sometimes a character on the Elizabethan stage will speak an **aside** directed to the audience, which by convention the other characters on the stage are unable to hear. Its ironic utility is clear: the audience learns something from character A that character B knows nothing of—although the audience can see that A and B occupy the same stage. As an aside provides access to a character's mind, to his concealed or private thoughts, so does the **soliloquy**—a speech by an actor alone on the stage, like Hamlet's meditation on suicide beginning "To be or not to be. . . ." When playwrights have their characters think aloud on the stage, in asides or in soliloquies, they show not only a character's actions but a character's inward thoughts.

William Shakespeare

About William Shakespeare (1564–1616) we do not know as much as we would like. He was born in Stratford-upon-Avon, son of a glovemaker who became mayor of his town. Apparently Shakespeare attended school in Stratford, and in 1582 married Anne Hathaway, who was eight years his senior. They had three children; one son named Hamnet died in childhood. At some point in the decade after his marriage, Shakespeare moved to London alone and became an actor. (He continued acting after becoming a playwright; tradition has him playing Hamlet's father's ghost.) He began writing for the stage about 1590. He acted and wrote for the Lord Chamberlain's Men, later called the King's Men, which was the best company of his time and starred the great actor Richard Burbage, who took the original lead in Hamlet.

Other great Shakespearean tragedies include *Julius Caesar, Macbeth, King Lear,* and *Othello.* He excelled not only in tragedy but also in comedy: *Love's Labour's Lost, The Taming of the Shrew, A Midsummer Night's Dream, The Tempest, Measure for Measure, Twelfth Night,* and many others. He excelled as well in writing the history play, a form of drama that recounted English history—reigns, rebellions, and wars. Over the centuries, however, when readers have looked for literature's highest moments, they have found them in tragedy, and in no tragedian more than in William Shakespeare. Although a given reader may prefer *King Lear* or *Othello, Hamlet, Prince of Denmark* is the most intriguing of tragedies—combining nobility and power with an unusual psychological subtlety.

William Shakespeare
Hamlet, Prince of Denmark

Dramatis Personae

CLAUDIUS, King of Denmark
HAMLET, son to the late, and nephew to
  the present, King
POLONIUS, Lord Chamberlain
HORATIO, friend to Hamlet
LAERTES, son to Polonius
VOLTEMAND ⎫
CORNELIUS ⎪
ROSENCRANTZ ⎬ courtiers
GUILDENSTERN ⎪
OSRIC ⎪
A GENTLEMAN ⎭
A PRIEST
MARCELLUS ⎫ officers
BARNARDO ⎭

FRANCISCO, a soldier
REYNALDO, servant to Polonius
PLAYERS
TWO CLOWNS, gravediggers
FORTINBRAS, Prince of Norway
A NORWEGIAN CAPTAIN
ENGLISH AMBASSADORS
GERTRUDE, Queen of Denmark, mother
  to Hamlet
OPHELIA, daughter to Polonius
GHOST of Hamlet's father
LORDS, LADIES, OFFICERS, SOLDIERS,
    SAILORS, MESSENGERS, ATTENDANTS

Scene: Elsinore

Act I, Scene I. *A guard platform of the castle.*

Enter BARNARDO *and* FRANCISCO, *two sentinels.*

BARNARDO Who's there?
FRANCISCO Nay, answer me. Stand and unfold[1] yourself.
BARNARDO Long live the King![2]
FRANCISCO Barnardo?
5   BARNARDO He.
FRANCISCO You come most carefully upon your hour.
BARNARDO 'Tis now struck twelve. Get thee to bed, Francisco.
FRANCISCO For this relief much thanks. 'Tis bitter cold,
  And I am sick at heart.
BARNARDO Have you had quiet guard?
10 FRANCISCO   Not a mouse stirring.
BARNARDO Well, good night.
  If you do meet Horatio and Marcellus,
  The rivals[3] of my watch, bid them make haste.

Enter HORATIO *and* MARCELLUS.

FRANCISCO I think I hear them. Stand, ho! Who is there?
HORATIO Friends to this ground.

This text of *Hamlet, Prince of Denmark,* edited by Edward Hubler, includes his explanatory notations. Footnotes that gloss or translate a single word are in roman type. When the explanation covers more than one word, the relevant passage in Shakespeare precedes the explanation, in *italic* type.

[1]disclose   [2]*Long live the King* (perhaps a password, perhaps a greeting)   [3]partners

15   MARCELLUS   And liegemen to the Dane.[1]
    FRANCISCO Give you[2] good night.
    MARCELLUS   O, farewell, honest soldier.
      Who hath relieved you?
    FRANCISCO   Barnardo hath my place.
      Give you good night.   *Exit* FRANCISCO.
    MARCELLUS   Holla, Barnardo!
    BARNARDO   Say——
      What, is Horatio there?
    HORATIO   A piece of him.
20   BARNARDO Welcome, Horatio. Welcome, good Marcellus.
    MARCELLUS What, has this thing appeared again tonight?
    BARNARDO I have seen nothing.
    MARCELLUS Horatio says 'tis but our fantasy,
      And will not let belief take hold of him
25   Touching this dreaded sight twice seen of us;
      Therefore I have entreated him along
      With us to watch the minutes of this night,
      That, if again this apparition come,
      He may approve[3] our eyes and speak to it.
    HORATIO Tush, tush, 'twill not appear.
30   BARNARDO   Sit down awhile,
      And let us once again assail your ears,
      That are so fortified against our story,
      What we have two nights seen.
    HORATIO   Well, sit we down,
      And let us hear Barnardo speak of this.
35   BARNARDO Last night of all,
      When yond same star that's westward from the pole[4]
      Had made his course t' illume that part of heaven
      Where now it burns, Marcellus and myself,
      The bell then beating one——

    Enter GHOST.

40   MARCELLUS Peace, break thee off. Look where it comes again.
    BARNARDO In the same figure like the king that's dead.
    MARCELLUS Thou art a scholar; speak to it, Horatio.
    BARNARDO Look 'a not like the king? Mark it, Horatio.
    HORATIO Most like: it harrows me with fear and wonder.
    BARNARDO It would be spoke to.
45   MARCELLUS   Speak to it, Horatio.
    HORATIO What art thou that usurp'st this time of night,
      Together with that fair and warlike form
      In which the majesty of buried Denmark[5]
      Did sometimes march? By heaven I charge thee, speak.
    MARCELLUS It is offended.
50   BARNARDO   See, it stalks away.

---

[1]*liegemen to the Dane* loyal subjects to the King of Denmark   [2]*Give you* God give you
[3]confirm   [4]*polestar*   [5]*buried Denmark* the buried King of Denmark

HORATIO Stay! Speak, speak. I charge thee, speak.

Exit GHOST.

MARCELLUS 'Tis gone and will not answer.
BARNARDO How now, Horatio? You tremble and look pale.
Is not this something more than fantasy?
55 What think you on't?
HORATIO Before my God, I might not this believe
Without the sensible and true avouch[1]
Of mine own eyes.
MARCELLUS   Is it not like the King?
HORATIO As thou art to thyself.
60 Such was the very armor he had on
When he the ambitious Norway[2] combated:
So frowned he once, when, in an angry parle,[3]
He smote the sledded Polacks[4] on the ice.
'Tis strange.
65 MARCELLUS Thus twice before, and jump[5] at this dead hour,
With martial stalk hath he gone by our watch.
HORATIO In what particular thought to work I know not;
But, in the gross and scope[6] of my opinion,
This bodes some strange eruption to our state.
70 MARCELLUS Good now, sit down, and tell me he that knows,
Why this same strict and most observant watch
So nightly toils the subject[7] of the land,
And why such daily cast of brazen cannon
And foreign mart[8] for implements of war,
75 Why such impress[9] of shipwrights, whose sore task
Does not divide the Sunday from the week,
What might be toward[10] that this sweaty haste
Doth make the night joint-laborer with the day?
Who is't that can inform me?
HORATIO   That can I.
80 At least the whisper goes so: our last king,
Whose image even but now appeared to us,
Was, as you know, by Fortinbras of Norway,
Thereto pricked on by a most emulate pride,
Dared to the combat; in which our valiant Hamlet
85 (For so this side of our known world esteemed him)
Did slay this Fortinbras, who, by a sealed compact
Well ratified by law and heraldry,[11]
Did forfeit, with his life, all those his lands
Which he stood seized[12] of, to the conqueror;
90 Against the which a moiety competent[13]
Was gagèd[14] by our King, which had returned

---

[1]*sensible and true avouch* sensory and true proof   [2]*King of Norway*   [3]parley   [4]*sledded Po-lacks* Poles in sledges   [5]*just*   [6]*gross and scope* general drift   [7]*toils the subject* makes the subjects toil   [8]trading   [9]forced service   [10]in preparation   [11]*law and heraldry* heraldic law (governing the combat)   [12]possessed   [13]*moiety competent* equal portion   [14]engaged, pledged

To the inheritance of Fortinbras,
Had he been vanquisher, as, by the same comart[1]
And carriage of the article designed,[2]
His fell to Hamlet. Now, sir, young Fortinbras,
Of unimprovèd[3] mettle hot and full,
Hath in the skirts[4] of Norway here and there
Sharked up[5] a list of lawless resolutes,[6]
For food and diet, to some enterprise
That hath a stomach in't;[7] which is no other,
As it doth well appear unto our state,
But to recover of us by strong hand
And terms compulsatory, those foresaid lands
So by his father lost; and this, I take it,
Is the main motive of our preparations,
The source of this our watch, and the chief head[8]
Of this posthaste and romage[9] in the land.
BARNARDO   I think it be no other but e'en so;
Well may it sort[10] that this portentous figure
Comes armèd through our watch so like the King
That was and is the question of these wars.
HORATIO   A mote it is to trouble the mind's eye:
In the most high and palmy state of Rome,
A little ere the mightiest Julius fell,
The graves stood tenantless, and the sheeted dead
Did squeak and gibber in the Roman streets;[11]
As stars with trains of fire and dews of blood,
Disasters[12] in the sun; and the moist star,[13]
Upon whose influence Neptune's empire stands,
Was sick almost to doomsday with eclipse.
And even the like precurse[14] of feared events,
As harbingers[15] preceding still[16] the fates
And prologue to the omen[17] coming on,
Have heaven and earth together demonstrated
Unto our climatures[18] and countrymen.

   Enter GHOST.

But soft, behold, lo, where it comes again!
I'll cross it,[19] though it blast me.—Stay, illusion.

                                    It spreads his[20] arms.

---

[1]agreement   [2]*carriage of the article designed* import of the agreement drawn up   [3]untried
[4]borders   [5]*Sharked up* collected indiscriminately (as a shark gulps its prey)   [6]desperadoes
[7]*hath a stomach in't* i.e., requires courage   [8]fountainhead, origin   [9]bustle   [10]befit   [11]*Did squeak . . . Roman streets* (the break in the sense which follows this line suggests that a line has dropped out)   [12]threatening signs   [13]*moist star* moon   [14]precursor, foreshadowing
[15]forerunners   [16]always   [17]calamity   [18]regions   [19]*cross it* (1) cross its path, confront it (2) make the sign of the cross in front of it   [20]its, the ghost's (though possibly what is meant is that Horatio spreads his own arms, making a cross of himself)

If thou hast any sound or use of voice,
Speak to me.
130   If there be any good thing to be done
That may to thee do ease and grace to me,
Speak to me.
If thou art privy to thy country's fate,
Which happily[1] foreknowing may avoid,
135   O, speak!
Or if thou hast uphoarded in thy life
Extorted[2] treasure in the womb of earth,
For which, they say, you spirits oft walk in death,

The cock crows.

Speak of it. Stay and speak. Stop it, Marcellus.
140   MARCELLUS   Shall I strike at it with my partisan?[3]
HORATIO   Do, if it will not stand.
BARNARDO   'Tis here.
HORATIO   'Tis here.
MARCELLUS   'Tis gone.

Exit GHOST.

We do it wrong, being so majestical,
To offer it the show of violence,
145   For it is as the air, invulnerable,
And our vain blows malicious mockery.
BARNARDO   It was about to speak when the cock crew.
HORATIO   And then it started, like a guilty thing
Upon a fearful summons. I have heard,
150   The cock, that is the trumpet to the morn,
Doth with his lofty and shrill-sounding throat
Awake the god of day, and at his warning,
Whether in sea or fire, in earth or air,
Th' extravagant and erring[4] spirit hies
155   To his confine; and of the truth herein
This present object made probation.[5]
MARCELLUS   It faded on the crowing of the cock.
Some say that ever 'gainst[6] that season, comes
Wherein our Savior's birth is celebrated,
160   This bird of dawning singeth all night long,
And then, they say, no spirit dare stir abroad,
The nights are wholesome, then no planets strike,[7]
No fairy takes,[8] nor witch hath power to charm:
So hallowed and so gracious is that time.
165   HORATIO   So have I heard and do in part believe it.
But look, the morn in russet mantle clad
Walks o'er the dew of yon high eastward hill.
Break we our watch up, and by my advice

---

[1]haply, perhaps   [2]ill-won   [3]pike (a long-handled weapon)   [4]*extravagant and erring* out of
bounds and wandering   [5]proof   [6]just before   [7]exert an evil influence   [8]bewitches

Let us impart what we have seen tonight
170   Unto young Hamlet, for upon my life
This spirit, dumb to us, will speak to him.
Do you consent we shall acquaint him with it,
As needful in our loves, fitting our duty?
MARCELLUS   Let's do't, I pray, and I this morning know
175   Where we shall find him most convenient.   *Exeunt.*

Scene II. *The castle.*

Flourish.[1] *Enter* CLAUDIUS, *King of Denmark,* GERTRUDE *the Queen,* COUN-
CILORS, POLONIUS *and his son* LAERTES, HAMLET, *cum aliis*[2] *including* VOL-
TEMAND *and* CORNELIUS.

KING   Though yet of Hamlet our dear brother's death
The memory be green, and that it us befitted
To bear our hearts in grief, and our whole kingdom
To be contracted in one brow of woe,
5   Yet so far hath discretion fought with nature
That we with wisest sorrow think on him
Together with remembrance of ourselves.
Therefore our sometime sister,[3] now our Queen,
Th' imperial jointress[4] to this warlike state,
10   Have we, as 'twere, with a defeated joy,
With an auspicious[5] and a dropping eye,
With mirth in funeral, and with dirge in marriage,
In equal scale weighing delight and dole,
Taken to wife. Nor have we herein barred
15   Your better wisdoms, which have freely gone
With this affair along. For all, our thanks.
Now follows that you know young Fortinbras,
Holding a weak supposal of our worth,
Or thinking by our late dear brother's death
20   Our state to be disjoint and out of frame,[6]
Colleaguèd with this dream of his advantage,[7]
He hath not failed to pester us with message,
Importing the surrender of those lands
Lost by his father, with all bands of law,
25   To our most valiant brother. So much for him.
Now for ourself and for this time of meeting.
Thus much the business is: we have here writ
To Norway, uncle of young Fortinbras—
Who, impotent and bedrid, scarcely hears
30   Of this his nephew's purpose—to suppress
His further gait[8] herein, in that the levies,

---

[1]fanfare of trumpets   [2]*cum aliis* with others   [3]*our sometime sister* my (the royal "we") former
sister-in-law   [4]joint tenant, partner   [5]joyful   [6]order   [7]superiority   [8]proceeding

The lists, and full proportions[1] are all made
Out of his subject;[2] and we here dispatch
You, good Cornelius, and you, Voltemand,
35   For bearers of this greeting to old Norway,
Giving to you no further personal power
To business with the King, more than the scope
Of these delated articles[3] allow.
Farewell, and let your haste commend your duty.
40   CORNELIUS, VOLTEMAND   In that, and all things, will we show our duty.
     KING   We doubt it nothing. Heartily farewell.

Exit VOLTEMAND *and* CORNELIUS.

And now, Laertes, what's the news with you?
You told us of some of it. What is't, Laertes?
You cannot speak of reason to the Dane
45   And lose your voice.[4] What wouldst thou beg, Laertes,
That shall not be my offer, not thy asking?
The head is not more native[5] to the heart,
The hand more instrumental to the mouth,
Than is the throne of Denmark to thy father.
What wouldst thou have, Laertes?
50   LAERTES   My dread lord,
Your leave and favor to return to France,
From whence, though willingly I came to Denmark
To show my duty in your coronation,
Yet now I must confess, that duty done,
55   My thoughts and wishes bend again toward France
And bow them to your gracious leave and pardon.
     KING   Have you your father's leave? What says Polonius?
     POLONIUS   He hath, my lord, wrung from me my slow leave
By laborsome petition, and at last
60   Upon his will I sealed my hard consent.[6]
I do beseech you give him leave to go.
     KING   Take thy fair hour, Laertes. Time be thine,
And thy best graces spend it at thy will.
But now, my cousin[7] Hamlet, and my son—
65   HAMLET [*Aside*]   A little more than kin, and less than kind![8]
     KING   How is it that the clouds still hang on you?
     HAMLET   Not so, my lord. I am too much in the sun.[9]
     QUEEN   Good Hamlet, cast thy nighted color off,
And let thine eye look like a friend on Denmark.
70   Do not forever with thy vailèd[10] lids

---

[1]supplies for war   [2]*Out of his subject* out of old Norway's subjects and realm   [3]*delated articles* detailed documents   [4]*lose your voice* waste your breath   [5]related   [6]*Upon his . . . hard consent* to his desire I gave my reluctant consent   [7]kinsman   [8]pun on the meanings "kindly" and "natural"; though doubly related—*more than kin*—Hamlet asserts that he neither resembles Claudius in nature nor feels kindly toward him   [9]sunshine of royal favor (with a pun on "son")   [10]lowered

Seek for thy noble father in the dust.
Thou know'st 'tis common; all that lives must die,
Passing through nature to eternity.
HAMLET Ay, madam, it is common.[1]
QUEEN   If it be,
75   Why seems it so particular with thee?
HAMLET Seems, madam? Nay, it is. I know not "seems."
'Tis not alone my inky cloak, good mother,
Nor customary suits of solemn black,
Nor windy suspiration[2] of forced breath,
80   No, nor the fruitful river in the eye,
Nor the dejected havior of the visage,
Together with all forms, moods, shapes of grief,
That can denote me truly. These indeed seem,
For they are actions that a man might play,
85   But I have that within which passes show;
These but the trappings and the suits of woe.
KING 'Tis sweet and commendable in your nature, Hamlet,
To give these mourning duties to your father,
But you must know your father lost a father,
90   That father lost, lost his, and the survivor bound
In filial obligation for some term
To do obsequious[3] sorrow. But to persever
In obstinate condolement[4] is a course
Of impious stubbornness. 'Tis unmanly grief.
95   It shows a will most incorrect to heaven,
A heart unfortified, a mind impatient,
An understanding simple and unschooled.
For what we know must be and is as common
As any the most vulgar[5] thing to sense,
100   Why should we in our peevish opposition
Take it to heart? Fie, 'tis a fault to heaven,
A fault against the dead, a fault to nature,
To reason most absurd, whose common theme
Is death of fathers, and who still hath cried,
105   From the first corse[6] till he that died today,
"This must be so." We pray you throw to earth
This unprevailing[7] woe, and think of us
As of a father, for let the world take note
You are the most immediate to our throne,
110   And with no less nobility of love
Than that which dearest father bears his son
Do I impart toward you. For your intent
In going back to school in Wittenberg,
It is most retrograde[8] to our desire,
115   And we beseech you, bend you[9] to remain

---

[1] (1) universal (2) vulgar   [2] *windy suspiration* heavy sighing   [3] suitable to obsequies (funerals)
[4] mourning   [5] common   [6] corpse   [7] unavailing   [8] contrary   [9] *bend you* incline

Here in the cheer and comfort of our eye,
Our chiefest courtier, cousin, and our son.
QUEEN   Let not thy mother lose her prayers, Hamlet.
I pray thee stay with us, go not to Wittenberg.
120   HAMLET   I shall in all my best obey you, madam.
KING   Why, 'tis a loving and a fair reply.
Be as ourself in Denmark. Madam, come.
This gentle and unforced accord of Hamlet
Sits smiling to my heart, in grace whereof
125   No jocund health that Denmark drinks today,
But the great cannon to the clouds shall tell,
And the King's rouse[1] the heaven shall bruit[2] again,
Respeaking earthly thunder. Come away.

Flourish. Exeunt all but HAMLET.

HAMLET   O that this too too sullied[3] flesh would melt,
130   Thaw, and resolve itself into a dew,
Or that the Everlasting had not fixed
His canon[4] 'gainst self-slaughter. O God, God,
How weary, stale, flat, and unprofitable
Seem to me all the uses of this world!
135   Fie on't, ah, fie, 'tis an unweeded garden
That grows to seed. Things rank and gross in nature
Possess it merely.[5] That it should come to this:
But two months dead, nay, not so much, not two,
So excellent a king, that was to this
140   Hyperion[6] to a satyr, so loving to my mother
That he might not beteem[7] the winds of heaven
Visit her face too roughly. Heaven and earth,
Must I remember? Why, she would hang on him
As if increase of appetite had grown
145   By what it fed on; and yet within a month—
Let me not think on't; frailty, thy name is woman—
A little month, or ere those shoes were old
With which she followed my poor father's body
Like Niobe,[8] all tears, why she, even she—
150   O God, a beast that wants discourse of reason[9]
Would have mourned longer—married with my uncle,
My father's brother, but no more like my father
Than I to Hercules. Within a month,
Ere yet the salt of most unrighteous tears
155   Had left the flushing[10] in her gallèd eyes,
She married. O, most wicked speed, to post[11]

---

[1]deep drink   [2]announce noisily   [3](The Second Quarto has *sallied,* here modernized to *sullied,*
which makes sense and is therefore given; but the Folio reading, *solid,* which fits better with *melt,*
is quite possibly correct)   [4]law   [5]entirely   [6]the sun god, a model of beauty   [7]allow   [8]a
mother who wept profusely at the death of her children   [9]*wants discourse of reason* lacks reasoning power   [10]*left the flushing* stopped reddening   [11]hasten

With such dexterity to incestuous[1] sheets!
It is not, nor it cannot come to good.
But break my heart for I must hold my tongue.

Enter HORATIO, MARCELLUS, *and* BARNARDO.

HORATIO   Hail to your lordship!

160   HAMLET   I am glad to see you well.
   Horatio—or I do forget myself.

HORATIO   The same, my lord, and your poor servant ever.

HAMLET   Sir, my good friend, I'll change[2] that name with you.
   And what make you from Wittenberg, Horatio?

165   Marcellus.

MARCELLUS   My good lord!

HAMLET   I am very glad to see you. [*To* BARNARDO] Good even, sir.
   But what, in faith, make you from Wittenberg?

HORATIO   A truant disposition, good my lord.

170   HAMLET   I would not hear your enemy say so,
   Nor shall you do my ear that violence
   To make it truster[3] of your own report
   Against yourself. I know you are no truant.
   But what is your affair in Elsinore?

175   We'll teach you to drink deep ere you depart.

HORATIO   My lord, I came to see your father's funeral.

HAMLET   I prithee do not mock me, fellow student.
   I think it was to see my mother's wedding.

HORATIO   Indeed, my lord, it followed hard upon.

180   HAMLET   Thrift, thrift, Horatio. The funeral baked meats
   Did coldly furnish forth the marriage tables.
   Would I had met my dearest[4] foe in heaven
   Or ever I had seen that day, Horatio!
   My father, methinks I see my father.

HORATIO   Where, my lord?

185   HAMLET   In my mind's eye, Horatio

HORATIO   I saw him once. 'A[5] was a goodly king.

HAMLET   'A was a man, take him for all in all,
   I shall not look upon his like again.

HORATIO   My lord, I think I saw him yesternight.

190   HAMLET   Saw? Who?

HORATIO   My lord, the King your father.

HAMLET   The King my father?

HORATIO   Season your admiration[6] for a while
   With an attent ear till I may deliver
   Upon the witness of these gentlemen
   This marvel to you.

195   HAMLET   For God's love let me hear!

---

[1]canon law considered marriage with a deceased brother's widow to be incestuous   [2]exchange
[3]believer   [4]most intensely felt   [5]he   [6]*Season your admiration* control your wonder

HORATIO Two nights together had these gentlemen,
　　　Marcellus and Barnardo, on their watch
　　　In the dead waste and middle of the night
　　　Been thus encountered. A figure like your father,
200　Armèd at point exactly, cap-a-pe,[1]
　　　Appears before them, and with solemn march
　　　Goes slow and stately by them. Thrice he walked
　　　By their oppressed and fear-surprisèd eyes,
　　　Within his truncheon's length,[2] whilst they, distilled[3]
205　Almost to jelly with the act[4] of fear,
　　　Stand dumb and speak not to him. This to me
　　　In dreadful[5] secrecy impart they did,
　　　And I with them the third night kept the watch,
　　　Where, as they had delivered, both in time,
210　Form of the thing, each word made true and good,
　　　The apparition comes. I knew your father.
　　　These hands are not more like.
HAMLET   But where was this?
MARCELLUS My lord, upon the platform where we watched.
HAMLET Did you not speak to it?
HORATIO   My lord, I did;
215　But answer made it none. Yet once methought
　　　It lifted up it[6] head and did address
　　　Itself to motion like as it would speak:
　　　But even then the morning cock crew loud,
　　　And at the sound it shrunk in haste away
　　　And vanished from our sight.
220　HAMLET   'Tis very strange.
HORATIO As I do live, my honored lord, 'tis true,
　　　And we did think it writ down in our duty
　　　To let you know of it.
HAMLET Indeed, indeed, sirs, but this troubles me.
　　　Hold you the watch tonight?
225　ALL   We do, my lord.
HAMLET Armed, say you?
ALL Armed, my lord.
HAMLET From top to toe?
ALL   My lord, from head to foot.
HAMLET Then saw you not his face.
230　HORATIO O, yes, my lord. He wore his beaver[7] up.
HAMLET What, looked he frowningly?
HORATIO A countenance more in sorrow than in anger.
HAMLET Pale or red?
HORATIO Nay, very pale.
HAMLET   And fixed his eyes upon you?
HORATIO Most constantly.

---

[1]head to foot   [2]*truncheon's length* space of a short staff   [3]reduced   [4]action   [5]terrified
[6]its   [7]visor, face guard

235   HAMLET   I would I had been there.
       HORATIO It would have much amazed you.
       HAMLET Very like, very like. Stayed it long?
       HORATIO While one with moderate haste might tell[1] a hundred.
       BOTH Longer, longer.
       HORATIO Not when I saw't.
240   HAMLET   His beard was grizzled,[2] no?
       HORATIO It was as I have seen it in his life,
         A sable-silvered.[3]
       HAMLET   I will watch tonight.
         Perchance 'twill walk again.
       HORATIO   I warr'nt it will.
       HAMLET If it assume my noble father's person,
245   I'll speak to it though hell itself should gape
        And bid me hold my peace. I pray you all,
        If you have hitherto concealed this sight,
        Let it be tenable[4] in your silence still,
        And whatsomever else shall hap tonight,
250   Give it an understanding but no tongue;
        I will requite your loves. So fare you well.
        Upon the platform 'twixt eleven and twelve
        I'll visit you.
       ALL   Our duty to your honor.
       HAMLET Your loves, as mine to you. Farewell.

Exeunt [all but HAMLET].

255   My father's spirit—in arms? All is not well.
        I doubt[5] some foul play. Would the night were come!
        Till then sit still, my soul. Foul deeds will rise,
        Though all the earth o'erwhelm them, to men's eyes.

Exit.

Scene III. *A room.*

Enter LAERTES *and* OPHELIA, *his sister.*

       LAERTES My necessaries are embarked. Farewell.
         And, sister, as the winds give benefit
        And convoy[6] is assistant, do not sleep,
        But let me hear from you.
       OPHELIA   Do you doubt that?
5   LAERTES For Hamlet, and the trifling of his favor,
        Hold it a fashion and a toy[7] in blood,
        A violet in the youth of primy[8] nature,
        Forward,[9] not permanent, sweet, not lasting,
        The perfume and suppliance[10] of a minute,
        No more.

[1]count   [2]gray   [3]*sable-silvered* black mingled with white   [4]held   [5]suspect   [6]convey-ance   [7]idle fancy   [8]springlike   [9]premature   [10]diversion

OPHELIA   No more but so?

10   LAERTES   Think it no more.
For nature crescent[1] does not grow alone
In thews[2] and bulk, but as this temple[3] waxes,
The inward service of the mind and soul
Grows wide withal. Perhaps he loves you now,
15   And now no soil nor cautel[4] doth besmirch
The virtue of his will; but you must fear,
His greatness weighed,[5] his will is not his own.
For he himself is subject to his birth.
He may not, as unvalued[6] persons do,
20   Carve for himself; for on his choice depends
The safety and health of this whole state;
And therefore must his choice be circumscribed
Unto the voice and yielding of that body
Whereof he is the head. Then if he says he loves you,
25   It fits your wisdom so far to believe it
As he in his particular act and place
May give his saying deed, which is no further
Than the main voice of Denmark goes withal.
Then weigh what loss your honor may sustain
30   If with too credent[7] ear you list his songs,
Or lose your heart, or your chaste treasure open
To his unmastered importunity.
Fear it, Ophelia, fear it, my dear sister,
And keep you in the rear of your affection,
35   Out of the shot and danger of desire.
The chariest maid is prodigal enough
If she unmask her beauty to the moon.
Virtue itself scapes not calumnious strokes.
The canker[8] galls the infants of the spring
40   Too oft before their buttons[9] be disclosed,
And in the morn and liquid dew of youth
Contagious blastments are most imminent.
Be wary then; best safety lies in fear;
Youth to itself rebels, though none else near.
45   OPHELIA   I shall the effect of this good lesson keep
As watchman to my heart, but, good my brother,
Do not, as some ungracious[10] pastors do,
Show me the steep and thorny way to heaven,
Whiles, like a puffed and reckless libertine,
50   Himself the primrose path of dalliance treads
And recks not his own rede.[11]

Enter POLONIUS.

LAERTES   O, fear me not.
I stay too long. But here my father comes.

[1]growing   [2]muscles and sinews   [3]i.e., the body   [4]deceit   [5]*greatness weighed* high rank
considered   [6]of low rank   [7]credulous   [8]cankerworm   [9]buds   [10]lacking grace   [11]*recks
not his own rede* does not heed his own advice

A double blessing is a double grace;
Occasion smiles upon a second leave.

55 POLONIUS Yet here, Laertes? Aboard, aboard, for shame!
The wind sits in the shoulder of your sail,
And you are stayed for. There—my blessing with thee,
And these few precepts in thy memory
Look thou character.[1] Give thy thoughts no tongue,
60 Nor any unproportioned[2] thought his act.
Be thou familiar, but by no means vulgar.
Those friends thou hast, and their adoption tried,
Grapple them unto thy soul with hoops of steel,
But do not dull thy palm with entertainment
65 Of each new-hatched, unfledged courage.[3] Beware
Of entrance to a quarrel; but being in,
Bear't that th' opposèd may beware of thee.
Give every man thine ear, but few thy voice;
Take each man's censure,[4] but reserve thy judgment.
70 Costly thy habit as thy purse can buy,
But not expressed in fancy; rich, not gaudy,
For the apparel oft proclaims the man,
And they in France of the best rank and station
Are of a most select and generous, chief in that.[5]
75 Neither a borrower nor a lender be,
For loan oft loses both itself and friend,
And borrowing dulleth edge of husbandry.[6]
This above all, to thine own self be true,
And it must follow, as the night the day,
80 Thou canst not then be false to any man.
Farewell. My blessing season this[7] in thee!
LAERTES Most humbly do I take my leave, my lord.
POLONIUS The time invites you. Go, your servants tend.[8]
LAERTES Farewell, Ophelia, and remember well
What I have said to you.
85 OPHELIA   'Tis in my memory locked,
And you yourself shall keep the key of it.
LAERTES Farewell.   *Exit* LAERTES.
POLONIUS What is't, Ophelia, he hath said to you?
OPHELIA So please you, something touching the Lord Hamlet.
90 POLONIUS Marry,[9] well bethought.
'Tis told me he hath very oft of late
Given private time to you, and you yourself
Have of your audience been most free and bounteous.
If it be so—as so 'tis put on me,

---

[1]inscribe [2]unbalanced [3]gallant youth [4]opinion [5]*Are of . . . in that* show their fine taste
and their gentlemanly instincts more in that than in any other point of manners (Kittredge)
[6]thrift [7]*season this* make fruitful this (advice) [8]attend [9](a light oath, from "By the Virgin
Mary")

95   And that in way of caution—I must tell you
        You do not understand yourself so clearly
        As it behooves my daughter and your honor.
        What is between you? Give me up the truth.
        OPHELIA   He hath, my lord, of late made many tenders[1]
100   Of his affection to me.
        POLONIUS   Affection pooh! You speak like a green girl,
        Unsifted[2] in such perilous circumstance.
        Do you believe his tenders, as you call them?
        OPHELIA   I do not know, my lord, what I should think.
105   POLONIUS   Marry, I will teach you. Think yourself a baby
        That you have ta'en these tenders for true pay
        Which are not sterling. Tender yourself more dearly,
        Or (not to crack the wind of the poor phase)
        Tend'ring it thus you'll tender me a fool.[3]
110   OPHELIA   My lord, he hath importuned me with love
        In honorable fashion.
        POLONIUS   Ay, fashion you may call it. Go to, go to.
        OPHELIA   And hath given countenance to his speech, my lord,
        With almost all the holy vows of heaven.
115   POLONIUS   Ay, springes to catch woodcocks.[4] I do know,
        When the blood burns, how prodigal the soul
        Lends the tongue vows. These blazes, daughter,
        Giving more light than heat, extinct in both,
        Even in their promise, as it is a-making,
120   You must not take for fire. From this time
        Be something scanter of your maiden presence.
        Set your entreatments[5] at a higher rate
        Than a command to parley. For Lord Hamlet,
        Believe so much in him that he is young,
125   And with a larger tether may he walk
        Than may be given you. In few, Ophelia,
        Do not believe his vows, for they are brokers,[6]
        Not of that dye[7] which their investments[8] show,
        But mere implorators[9] of unholy suits,
130   Breathing like sanctified and pious bonds,[10]
        The better to beguile. This is for all:
        I would not, in plain terms, from this time forth
        Have you so slander[11] any moment leisure
        As to give words or talk with the Lord Hamlet.
135   Look to't, I charge you. Come your ways.
        OPHELIA   I shall obey, my lord.   *Exeunt.*

---

[1]offers (in line 103 it has the same meaning, but in line 106 Polonius speaks of *tenders* in the sense of counters or chips; in line 109 *Tend'ring* means "holding," and *tender* means "give," "present")   [2]untried   [3]*tender me a fool* (1) present me with a fool (2) present me with a baby   [4]*springes to catch woodcocks* snares to catch stupid birds   [5]interviews   [6]procurers   [7]i.e., kind   [8]garments   [9]solicitors   [10]pledges   [11]disgrace

Scene IV. *A guard platform.*

Enter HAMLET, HORATIO, *and* MARCELLUS.

HAMLET   The air bites shrewdly;[1] it is very cold.
HORATIO   It is a nipping and an eager[2] air.
HAMLET   What hour now?
HORATIO   I think it lacks of twelve.
MARCELLUS   No, it is struck.
5   HORATIO   Indeed? I heard it not. It then draws near the season
     Wherein the spirit held his wont to walk.

                    A flourish of trumpets, and two pieces go off.

     What does this mean, my lord?
HAMLET   The King doth wake[3] tonight and takes his rouse,[4]
     Keeps wassail, and the swagg'ring upspring[5] reels,
10   And as he drains his draughts of Rhenish[6] down
     The kettledrum and trumpet thus bray out
     The triumph of his pledge.[7]
HORATIO   Is it a custom?
HAMLET   Ay, marry, is't,
     But to my mind, though I am native here
15   And to the manner born, it is a custom
     More honored in the breach than the observance.
     This heavy-headed revel east and west
     Makes us traduced and taxed of[8] other nations.
     They clepe[9] us drunkards and with swinish phrase
20   Soil our addition,[10] and indeed it takes
     From our achievements, though performed at height,
     The pith and marrow of our attribute.[11]
     So oft it chances in particular men
     That for some vicious mole[12] of nature in them,
25   As in their birth, wherein they are not guilty,
     (Since nature cannot choose his origin)
     By the o'ergrowth of some complexion,[13]
     Oft breaking down the pales[14] and forts of reason,
     Or by some habit that too much o'erleavens[15]
30   The form of plausive[16] manners, that (these men,
     Carrying, I say, the stamp of one defect,
     Being nature's livery, or fortune's star[17])
     Their virtues else, be they as pure as grace,
     As infinite as man may undergo,
35   Shall in the general censure[18] take corruption
     From that particular fault. The dram of evil

---

[1]bitterly   [2]sharp   [3]hold a revel by night   [4]*takes his rouse* carouses   [5]a dance   [6]Rhine wine   [7]*The triumph of his pledge* the achievement (of drinking a wine cup in one draught) of his toast   [8]*taxed of* blamed by   [9]call   [10]reputation (literally, "title of honor")   [11]reputation   [12]blemish   [13]natural disposition   [14]enclosures   [15]mixes with, corrupts   [16]pleasing   [17]*nature's livery, or fortune's star* nature's equipment (i.e., "innate"), or a person's destiny determined by the stars   [18]*general censure* popular judgment

Doth all the noble substance of a doubt,
To his own scandal.[1]

Enter GHOST.

HORATIO   Look, my lord, it comes.
HAMLET Angels and masters of grace defend us!
40   Be thou a spirit of health[2] or goblin damned,
        Bring with thee airs from heaven or blasts from hell,
        Be thy intents wicked or charitable,
        Thou com'st in such a questionable[3] shape
        That I will speak to thee. I'll call thee Hamlet,
45   King, father, royal Dane. O, answer me!
        Let me not burst in ignorance, but tell
        Why thy canonized[4] bones, hearsèd in death,
        Have burst their cerements,[5] why the sepulcher
        Wherein we saw thee quietly interred
50   Hath oped his ponderous and marble jaws
        To cast thee up again. What may this mean
        That thou, dead corse, again in complete steel,
        Revisits thus the glimpses of the moon,
        Making night hideous, and we fools of nature
55   So horridly to shake our disposition[6]
        With thoughts beyond the reaches of our souls?
        Say, why is this? Wherefore? What should we do?

GHOST *beckons* HAMLET.

HORATIO It beckons you to go away with it,
        As if it some impartment[7] did desire
        To you alone.
60   MARCELLUS   Look with what courteous action
        It waves you to a more removèd ground.
        But do not go with it.
HORATIO   No, by no means.
HAMLET It will not speak. Then I will follow it.
HORATIO Do not, my lord.
HAMLET   Why, what should be the fear?
65   I do not set my life at a pin's fee,
        And for my soul, what can it do to that,
        Being a thing immortal as itself?
        It waves me forth again. I'll follow it.
HORATIO What if it tempt you toward the flood, my lord,
70   Or to the dreadful summit of the cliff
        That beetles[8] o'er his base into the sea,
        And there assume some other horrible form,
        Which might deprive your sovereignty of reason[9]

[1]*The dram ... own scandal* (though the drift is clear, there is no agreement as to the exact meaning of these lines)   [2]*spirit of health* good spirit   [3](1) capable of discourse (2) dubious   [4]buried according to the canon or ordinance of the church   [5]waxed linen shroud   [6]*shake our disposition* disturb us   [7]communication   [8]juts out   [9]*deprive your sovereignty of reason* destroy the sovereignty of your reason

And draw you into madness? Think of it.
75   The very place puts toys[1] of desperation,
Without more motive, into every brain
That looks so many fathoms to the sea
And hears it roar beneath.
HAMLET   It waves me still.
  Go on; I'll follow thee.
MARCELLUS You shall not go, my lord.
80   HAMLET   Hold off your hands.
HORATIO Be ruled. You shall not go.
HAMLET   My fate cries out
  And makes each petty artere[2] in this body
  As hardy as the Nemean lion's nerve.[3]
  Still am I called! Unhand me, gentlemen.
85   By heaven, I'll make a ghost of him that lets[4] me!
  I say, away! Go on. I'll follow thee.

Exit GHOST *and* HAMLET.

HORATIO He waxes desperate with imagination.
MARCELLUS Let's follow. 'Tis not fit thus to obey him.
HORATIO Have after! To what issue will this come?
90   MARCELLUS Something is rotten in the state of Denmark.
HORATIO Heaven will direct it.
MARCELLUS   Nay, let's follow him.   *Exeunt.*

Scene V. *The battlements.*

Enter GHOST *and* HAMLET.

HAMLET Whither wilt thou lead me? Speak; I'll go no further.
GHOST Mark me.
HAMLET   I will.
GHOST   My hour is almost come,
  When I to sulf'rous and tormenting flames
  Must render up myself.
HAMLET   Alas, poor ghost.
5   GHOST Pity me not, but lend thy serious hearing
  To what I shall unfold.
HAMLET   Speak. I am bound to hear.
GHOST So art thou to revenge, when thou shalt hear.
HAMLET What?
GHOST I am thy father's spirit,
10   Doomed for a certain term to walk the night,
  And for the day confined to fast in fires,
  Till the foul crimes[5] done in my days of nature
  Are burnt and purged away. But that I am forbid
  To tell the secrets of my prison house,

---

[1]whims, fancies   [2]artery   [3]*Nemean lion's nerve* sinews of the mythical lion slain by Hercules   [4]hinders   [5]sins

15 I could a tale unfold whose lightest word
 Would harrow up thy soul, freeze thy young blood,
 Make thy two eyes like stars start from their spheres,[1]
 Thy knotted and combinèd locks to part,
 And each particular hair to stand an end
20 Like quills upon the fearful porpentine.[2]
 But this eternal blazon[3] must not be
 To ears of flesh and blood. List, list, O, list!
 If thou didst ever thy dear father love——
HAMLET O God!
25 GHOST Revenge his foul and most unnatural murder.
HAMLET Murder?
GHOST Murder most foul, as in the best it is,
 But this most foul, strange, and unnatural.
HAMLET Haste me to know't, that I, with wings as swift
30 As meditation[4] or the thoughts of love,
 May sweep to my revenge.
GHOST   I find thee apt,
 And duller shouldst thou be than the fat weed
 That roots itself in ease on Lethe wharf,[5]
 Wouldst thou not stir in this. Now, Hamlet, hear.
35 'Tis given out that, sleeping in my orchard,
 A serpent stung me. So the whole ear of Denmark
 Is by a forgèd process[6] of my death
 Rankly abused. But know, thou noble youth,
 The serpent that did sting thy father's life
 Now wears his crown.
40 HAMLET   O my prophetic soul!
 My uncle?
GHOST Ay, that incestuous, that adulterate[7] beast,
 With witchcraft of his wits, with traitorous gifts—
 O wicked wit and gifts, that have the power
45 So to seduce!—won to his shameful lust
 The will of my most seeming-virtuous queen.
 O Hamlet, what a falling-off was there,
 From me, whose love was of that dignity
 That it went hand in hand even with the vow
50 I made to her in marriage, and to decline
 Upon a wretch whose natural gifts were poor
 To those of mine.
 But virtue, as it never will be moved,
 Though lewdness[8] court it in a shape of heaven,
55 So lust, though to a radiant angel linked,
 Will sate itself in a celestial bed
 And prey on garbage.

---

[1]In Ptolemaic astronomy, each planet was fixed in a hollow transparent shell concentric with the earth [2]*fearful porpentine* timid porcupine [3]*eternal blazon* revelation of eternity [4]thought [5]*Lethe wharf* bank of the river of forgetfulness in Hades [6]*forgèd process* false account [7]adulterous [8]lust

But soft, methinks I scent the morning air;
Brief let me be. Sleeping within my orchard,
60   My custom always of the afternoon,
Upon my secure[1] hour thy uncle stole
With juice of cursed hebona[2] in a vial,
And in the porches of my ears did pour
The leperous distillment, whose effect
65   Holds such an enmity with blood of man
That swift as quicksilver it courses through
The natural gates and alleys of the body,
And with a sudden vigor it doth posset[3]
And curd, like eager[4] droppings into milk,
70   The thin and wholesome blood. So did it mine,
And a most instant tetter[5] barked about
Most lazarlike[6] with vile and loathsome crust
All my smooth body.
Thus was I, sleeping, by a brother's hand
75   Of life, of crown, of queen at once dispatched,
Cut off even in the blossoms of my sin,
Unhouseled, disappointed, unaneled,[7]
No reck'ning made, but sent to my account
With all my imperfections on my head.
80   O, horrible! O, horrible! Most horrible!
If thou hast nature in thee, bear it not.
Let not the royal bed of Denmark be
A couch for luxury[8] and damnèd incest.
But howsomever thou pursues this act,
85   Taint not thy mind, nor let thy soul contrive
Against thy mother aught. Leave her to heaven
And to those thorns that in her bosom lodge
To prick and sting her. Fare thee well at once.
The glowworm shows the matin[9] to be near
90   And 'gins to pale his uneffectual fire.
Adieu, adieu, adieu. Remember me.   *Exit.*
HAMLET   O all you host of heaven! O earth! What else?
And shall I couple hell? O fie! Hold, hold, my heart,
And you, my sinews, grow not instant old,
95   But bear me stiffly up. Remember thee?
Ay, thou poor ghost, whiles memory holds a seat
In this distracted globe.[10] Remember thee?
Yea, from the table[11] of my memory
I'll wipe away all trivial fond[12] records,
100   All saws[13] of books, all forms, all pressures[14] past
That youth and observation copied there,
And thy commandment all alone shall live
Within the book and volume of my brain,

[1]unsuspecting   [2]a poisonous plant   [3]curdle   [4]acid   [5]scab   [6]leperlike   [7]*Unhouseled, disappointed, unaneled* without the sacrament of communion, unabsolved, without extreme unction   [8]lust   [9]morning   [10]i.e., his head   [11]tablet, notebook   [12]foolish   [13]maxims   [14]impressions

Unmixed with baser matter. Yes, by heaven!
105 O most pernicious woman!
O villain, villain, smiling, damnèd villain!
My tables—meet it is I set it down
That one may smile, and smile, and be a villain.
At least I am sure it may be so in Denmark. [*Writes.*]
110 So, uncle, there you are. Now to my word:
It is "Adieu, adieu, remember me."
I have sworn't.
HORATIO AND MARCELLUS [*Within*] My lord, my lord!

Enter HORATIO *and* MARCELLUS.

MARCELLUS   Lord Hamlet!
HORATIO   Heavens secure him!
HAMLET So be it!
115 MARCELLUS Illo, ho, ho,[1] my lord!
HAMLET Hillo, ho, ho, boy! Come, bird, come.
MARCELLUS How is't, my noble lord?
HORATIO   What news, my lord?
HAMLET O, wonderful!
HORATIO Good my lord, tell it.
HAMLET   No, you will reveal it.
HORATIO Not I, my lord, by heaven.
120 MARCELLUS   Nor I, my lord.
HAMLET How say you then? Would heart of man once think it?
But you'll be secret?
BOTH   Ay, by heaven, my lord.
HAMLET There's never a villain dwelling in all Denmark
But he's an arrant knave.
125 HORATIO There needs no ghost, my lord, come from the grave
To tell us this.
HAMLET   Why, right, you are in the right;
And so, without more circumstance[2] at all,
I hold it fit that we shake hands and part:
You, as your business and desire shall point you,
130 For every man hath business and desire
Such as it is, and for my own poor part,
Look you, I'll go pray.
HORATIO These are but wild and whirling words, my lord.
HAMLET I am sorry they offend you, heartily;
Yes, faith, heartily.
135 HORATIO   There's no offense, my lord.
HAMLET Yes, by Saint Patrick, but there is, Horatio,
And much offense too. Touching this vision here,
It is an honest ghost,[3] that let me tell you.
For your desire to know what is between us,

---

[1]*Illo, ho, ho* (falconer's call to his hawk)   [2]details   [3]*honest ghost* i.e., not a demon in his father's shape

140   O'ermaster't as you may. And now, good friends,
        As you are friends, scholars, and soldiers,
        Give me one poor request.
        HORATIO What is't, my lord? We will.
        HAMLET Never make known what you have seen tonight.
        BOTH My lord, we will not.
        HAMLET   Nay, but swear't.
145   HORATIO   In faith,
        My lord, not I.
        MARCELLUS   Nor I, my lord—in faith.
        HAMLET Upon my sword.
        MARCELLUS   We have sworn, my lord, already.
        HAMLET Indeed, upon my sword, indeed.

                                      GHOST *cries under the stage.*

        GHOST Swear.
150   HAMLET Ha, ha, boy, say'st thou so? Art thou there, truepenny?[1]
        Come on. You hear this fellow in the cellarage.
        Consent to swear.
        HORATIO   Propose the oath, my lord.
        HAMLET Never to speak of this that you have seen.
        Swear by my sword.
155   GHOST [*Beneath*] Swear.
        HAMLET *Hic et ubique?*[2] Then we'll shift our ground;
        Come hither, gentlemen,
        And lay your hands again upon my sword.
        Swear by my sword
160   Never to speak of this that you have heard.
        GHOST [*Beneath*] Swear by his sword.
        HAMLET Well said, old mole! Canst work i' th' earth so fast?
        A worthy pioner![3] Once more remove, good friends.
        HORATIO O day and night, but this is wondrous strange!
165   HAMLET And therefore as a stranger give it welcome.
        There are more things in heaven and earth, Horatio,
        Than are dreamt of in your philosophy.
        But come:
        Here as before, never, so help you mercy,
170   How strange or odd some'er I bear myself
        (As I perchance hereafter shall think meet
        To put an antic disposition[4] on),
        That you, at such times seeing me, never shall
        With arms encumb'red[5] thus, or this headshake,
175   Or by pronouncing of some doubtful phrase,
        As "Well, well, we know," or "We could, an if we would,"
        Or "If we list to speak," or "There be, an if they might,"
        Or such ambiguous giving out, to note

---

[1]honest fellow   [2]*Hic et ubique* here and everywhere (Latin)   [3]digger of mines   [4]*antic dis-*
position fantastic behavior   [5]folded

That you know aught of me—this do swear,
180   So grace and mercy at your most need help you.
        GHOST [*Beneath*] Swear.   [*They swear.*]
        HAMLET   Rest, rest, perturbèd spirit. So, gentlemen,
            With all my love I do commend me¹ to you,
            And what so poor a man as Hamlet is
185   May do t' express his love and friending to you,
            God willing, shall not lack. Let us go in together,
            And still your fingers on your lips, I pray.
            The time is out of joint. O cursèd spite,
            That ever I was born to set it right!
190   Nay, come, let's go together.   *Exeunt.*

        Act II, Scene I. *A room.*

        Enter old POLONIUS, *with his man* REYNALDO.

        POLONIUS   Give him this money and these notes, Reynaldo.
        REYNALDO   I will, my lord.
        POLONIUS   You shall do marvell's² wisely, good Reynaldo,
            Before you visit him, to make inquire
            Of his behavior.
5   REYNALDO   My lord, I did intend it.
        POLONIUS   Marry, well said, very well said. Look you sir,
            Inquire me first what Danskers³ are in Paris,
            And how, and who, what means, and where they keep,⁴
            What company, at what expense; and finding
10   By this encompassment⁵ and drift of question
            That they do know my son, come you more nearer
            Than your particular demands⁶ will touch it.
            Take you as 'twere some distant knowledge of him,
            As thus, "I know his father and his friends,
15   And in part him." Do you mark this, Reynaldo?
        REYNALDO   Ay, very well, my lord.
        POLONIUS   "And in part him, but," you may say, "not well,
            But if't be he I mean, he's very wild,
            Addicted so and so." And there put on him
20   What forgeries⁷ you please; marry, none so rank
            As may dishonor him—take heed of that—
            But, sir, such wanton, wild, and usual slips
            As are companions noted and most known
            To youth and liberty.
        REYNALDO   As gaming, my lord.
25   POLONIUS   Ay, or drinking, fencing, swearing, quarreling,
            Drabbing.⁸ You may go so far.

---

¹*commend me* entrust myself   ²marvelous(ly)   ³Danes   ⁴dwell   ⁵circling   ⁶questions
⁷inventions   ⁸wenching

REYNALDO My lord, that would dishonor him.
POLONIUS Faith, no, as you may season it in the charge.
　　You must not put another scandal on him,
30　　That he is open to incontinency.[1]
　　That's not my meaning. But breathe his faults so quaintly[2]
　　That they may seem the taints of liberty,
　　The flash and outbreak of a fiery mind,
　　A savageness in unreclaimèd blood,
　　Of general assault.[3]
35 REYNALDO　　　　　　　But, my good lord—
POLONIUS Wherefore should you do this?
REYNALDO　　　　　　　　　　　Ay, my lord,
　　I would know that.
POLONIUS　　　　　Marry, sir, here's my drift,
　　And I believe it is a fetch of warrant.[4]
　　You laying these slight sullies on my son
40　　As 'twere a thing a little solid i' th' working,
　　Mark you,
　　Your party in converse, him you would sound,
　　Having ever seen in the prenominate crimes[5]
　　The youth you breathe of guilty, be assured
45　　He closes with you in this consequence:[6]
　　"Good sir," or so, or "friend," or "gentleman"—
　　According to the phrase or the addition[7]
　　Of man and country—
REYNALDO　　　　　　　Very good, my lord.
POLONIUS And then, sir, does 'a[8] this—'a does—
50　　What was I about to say? By the mass, I was about
　　to say something! Where did I leave?
REYNALDO At "closes in the consequence," at "friend
　　or so," and "gentleman."
POLONIUS At "closes in the consequence"—Ay, marry!
55　　He closes thus: "I know the gentleman;
　　I saw him yesterday, or t'other day,
　　Or then, or then, with such or such, and, as you say,
　　There was 'a gaming, there o'ertook in 's rouse,
　　There falling out at tennis"; or perchance,
60　　"I saw him enter such a house of sale,"
　　Videlicet,[9] a brothel, or so forth.
　　See you now—
　　Your bait of falsehood take this carp of truth,
　　And thus do we of wisdom and of reach,[10]
65　　With windlasses[11] and with assays of bias,[12]

---

[1]habitual licentiousness   [2]ingeniously, delicately   [3]*Of general assault* common to all men   [4]*fetch of warrant* justifiable device   [5]*Having ... crimes* if he has ever been seen in the aforementioned crimes   [6]*He closes ... this consequence* he falls in with you in this conclusion   [7]title   [8]he   [9]namely   [10]far-reaching awareness(?)   [11]circuitous courses   [12]*assays of bias* indirect attempts (metaphor from bowling; *bias* = curved course)

By indirections find directions out.
So, by my former lecture and advice,
Shall you my son. You have me, have you not?
REYNALDO   My lord, I have.
POLONIUS   God bye ye, fare ye well.
REYNALDO   Good my lord.
70   POLONIUS   Observe his inclination in yourself.[1]
REYNALDO   I shall, my lord.
POLONIUS   And let him ply his music.
REYNALDO   Well, my lord.
POLONIUS   Farewell.   *Exit* REYNALDO.

Enter OPHELIA.
                             How now, Ophelia, what's the matter?
75   OPHELIA   O my lord, my lord, I have been so affrighted!
POLONIUS   With what, i' th' name of God?
OPHELIA   My lord, as I was sewing in my closet,[2]
     Lord Hamlet, with his doublet all unbraced,[3]
     No hat upon his head, his stockings fouled,
80   Ungartered, and down-gyvèd[4] to his ankle,
     Pale as his shirt, his knees knocking each other,
     And with a look so piteous in purport,[5]
     As if he had been loosèd out of hell
     To speak of horrors—he comes before me.
POLONIUS   Mad for thy love?
85   OPHELIA   My lord, I do not know,
     But truly I do fear it.
POLONIUS   What said he?
OPHELIA   He took me by the wrist and held me hard;
     Then goes he to the length of all his arm,
     And with his other hand thus o'er his brow
90   He falls to such perusal of my face
     As 'a would draw it. Long stayed he so.
     At last, a little shaking of mine arm,
     And thrice his head thus waving up and down,
     He raised a sigh so piteous and profound
95   As it did seem to shatter all his bulk
     And end his being. That done, he lets me go,
     And, with his head over his shoulder turned,
     He seemed to find his way without his eyes,
     For out o' doors he went without their helps,
100   And to the last bended their light on me.
POLONIUS   Come, go with me. I will go seek the King.
     This is the very ecstasy[6] of love,
     Whose violent property fordoes[7] itself
     And leads the will to desperate undertakings

---

[1]*in yourself* for yourself   [2]private room   [3]*doublet all unbraced* jacket entirely unlaced
[4]*down-gyvèd* hanging down like fetters   [5]expression   [6]madness   [7]*property fordoes* quality
destroys

105   As oft as any passions under heaven
         That does afflict our natures. I am sorry.
         What, have you given him any hard words of late?
     OPHELIA No, my good lord; but as you did command,
         I did repel his letters and denied
         His access to me.
110 POLONIUS   That hath made him mad.
         I am sorry that with better heed and judgment
         I had not quoted[1] him. I feared he did but trifle
         And meant to wrack thee; but beshrew my jealousy.[2]
         By heaven, it is as proper[3] to our age
115   To cast beyond ourselves[4] in our opinions
         As it is common for the younger sort
         To lack discretion. Come, go we to the King.
         This must be known, which, being kept close, might move
         More grief to hide than hate to utter love.[5]
120   Come.   *Exeunt.*

Scene II. *The castle.*

Flourish. Enter KING *and* QUEEN, ROSENCRANTZ, *and* GUILDENSTERN [*with others*].

     KING Welcome, dear Rosencrantz and Guildenstern.
         Moreover that[6] we much did long to see you,
         The need we have to use you did provoke
         Our hasty sending. Something have you heard
5   Of Hamlet's transformation: so call it,
         Sith[7] nor th' exterior nor the inward man
         Resembles that it was. What it should be,
         More than his father's death, that thus hath put him
         So much from th' understanding of himself,
10   I cannot dream of. I entreat you both
         That, being of so[8] young days brought up with him,
         And sith so neighbored to his youth and havior,[9]
         That you vouchsafe your rest[10] here in our court
         Some little time, so by your companies
15   To draw him on to pleasures, and to gather
         So much as from occasion you may glean,
         Whether aught to us unknown afflicts him thus,
         That opened[11] lies within our remedy.
     QUEEN Good gentlemen, he hath much talked of you,
20   And sure I am, two men there is not living
         To whom he more adheres. If it will please you

---

[1]noted   [2]*beshrew my jealousy* curse on my suspicions   [3]natural   [4]*To cast beyond ourselves* to be overcalculating   [5]*Come, go . . . utter love* (the general meaning is that while telling the King of Hamlet's love may anger the King, more grief would come from keeping it secret)   [6]*Moreover that* beside the fact that   [7]since   [8]*of so* from such   [9]*youth and havior* behavior in his youth   [10]*vouchsafe your rest* consent to remain   [11]revealed

To show us so much gentry[1] and good will
As to expend your time with us awhile
For the supply and profit of our hope,
25   Your visitation shall receive such thanks
As fits a king's remembrance.
ROSENCRANTZ   Both your Majesties
Might, by the sovereign power you have of us,
Put your dread pleasures more into command
Than to entreaty.
GUILDENSTERN   But we both obey,
30   And here give up ourselves in the full bent[2]
To lay our service freely at your feet,
To be commanded.
KING   Thanks, Rosencrantz and gentle Guildenstern.
QUEEN   Thanks, Guildenstern and gentle Rosencrantz.
35   And I beseech you instantly to visit
My too much changèd son. Go, some of you,
And bring these gentlemen where Hamlet is.
GUILDENSTERN   Heavens make our presence and our practices
Pleasant and helpful to him!
QUEEN   Ay, amen!

Exeunt ROSENCRANTZ *and* GUILDENSTERN [*with some* ATTENDANTS].

Enter POLONIUS.

40   POLONIUS   Th' ambassadors from Norway, my good lord,
Are joyfully returned.
KING   Thou still[3] hast been the father of good news.
POLONIUS   Have I, my lord? Assure you, my good liege,
I hold my duty, as I hold my soul,
45   Both to my God and to my gracious king;
And I do think, or else this brain of mine
Hunts not the trial of policy so sure[4]
As it hath used to do, that I have found
The very cause of Hamlet's lunacy.
50   KING   O, speak of that! That do I long to hear.
POLONIUS   Give first admittance to th' ambassadors.
My news shall be the fruit to that great feast.
KING   Thyself do grace to them and bring them in.

[*Exit* POLONIUS.]

He tells me, my dear Gertrude, he hath found
55   The head and source of all your son's distemper.
QUEEN   I doubt[5] it is no other but the main,[6]
His father's death and our o'erhasty marriage.
KING   Well, we shall sift him.

---

[1]courtesy   [2]*in the full bent* entirely (the figure is of a bow bent to its capacity)   [3]always
[4]*Hunts not ... so sure* does not follow clues of political doings with such sureness   [5]suspect
[6]principal point

Enter POLONIUS, VOLTEMAND, *and* CORNELIUS.

                                    Welcome, my good friends.
              Say, Voltemand, what from our brother Norway?
60   VOLTEMAND   Most fair return of greetings and desires.
              Upon our first,[1] he sent out to suppress
              His nephew's levies, which to him appeared
              To be a preparation 'gainst the Polack;
              But better looked into, he truly found
65   It was against your Highness, whereat grieved,
              That so his sickness, age, and impotence
              Was falsely borne in hand,[2] sends out arrests
              On Fortinbras; which he, in brief, obeys,
              Receives rebuke from Norway, and in fine,[3]
70   Makes vow before his uncle never more
              To give th' assay[4] of arms against your Majesty.
              Whereon old Norway, overcome with joy,
              Gives him threescore thousand crowns in annual fee
              And his commission to employ those soldiers,
75   So levied as before, against the Polack,
              With an entreaty, herein further shown,

                                                    [*Gives a paper.*]

              That it might please you to give quiet pass
              Through your dominions for this enterprise,
              On such regards of safety and allowance[5]
              As therein are set down.
80   KING   It likes us well;
              And at our more considered time[6] we'll read,
              Answer, and think upon this business.
              Meantime, we thank you for your well-took labor.
              Go to your rest; at night we'll feast together.
              Most welcome home!   *Exeunt Ambassadors.*
85   POLONIUS   This business is well ended.
              My liege and madam, to expostulate[7]
              What majesty should be, what duty is,
              Why day is day, night night, and time is time,
              Were nothing but to waste night, day, and time.
90   Therefore, since brevity is the soul of wit,[8]
              And tediousness the limbs and outward flourishes,
              I will be brief. Your noble son is mad.
              Mad call I it, for, to define true madness,
              What is't but to be nothing else but mad?
              But let that go.
95   QUEEN   More matter, with less art.
        POLONIUS   Madam, I swear I use no art at all.
              That he's mad, 'tis true: 'tis true 'tis pity,

---

[1]first audience   [2]*borne in hand* deceived   [3]*in fine* finally   [4]trial   [5]*regards of safety and allowance* i.e., conditions   [6]*considered time* time proper for considering   [7]discuss   [8]wisdom, understanding

And pity 'tis true—a foolish figure.[1]
But farewell it, for I will use no art.
100 Mad let us grant him then; and now remains
That we find out the cause of this effect,
Or rather say, the cause of this defect,
For this effect defective comes by cause.
Thus it remains, and the remainder thus.
105 Perpend.[2]
I have a daughter: have, while she is mine,
Who in her duty and obedience, mark,
Hath given me this. Now gather, and surmise.

                                        [*Reads*] *the letter.*

"To the celestial, and my soul's idol, the most
110 beautified Ophelia"—
That's an ill phrase, a vile phrase; "beautified" is a
vile phrase. But you shall hear. Thus:
"In her excellent white bosom, these, &c."
QUEEN Came this from Hamlet to her?
115 POLONIUS Good madam, stay awhile. I will be faithful.
                "Doubt thou the stars are fire,
                    Doubt that the sun doth move;
                Doubt[3] truth to be a liar,
                    But never doubt I love.
120 O dear Ophelia, I am ill at these numbers.[4] I have
not art to reckon my groans; but that I love thee
best, O most best, believe it. Adieu.
        Thine evermore, most dear lady, whilst this machine[5] is to him, HAMLET."
125 This in obedience hath my daughter shown me,
And more above[6] hath his solicitings,
As they fell out by time, by means, and place,
All given to mine ear.
KING   But how hath she
Received his love?
POLONIUS   What do you think of me?
130 KING As a man faithful and honorable.
POLONIUS I would fain prove so. But what might you think,
When I had seen this hot love on the wing
(As I perceived it, I must tell you that,
Before my daughter told me), what might you,
135 Or my dear Majesty your Queen here, think,
If I played the desk or table book,[7]
Or given my heart a winking,[8] mute and dumb,
Or looked upon this love with idle sight?
What might you think? No, I went round to work

---

[1]figure of rhetoric   [2]consider carefully   [3]suspect   [4]*ill at these numbers* unskilled in
verses   [5]complex device (here, his body)   [6]*more above* in addition   [7]*played the desk or table
book* i.e., been a passive recipient of secrets   [8]closing of the eyes

140   And my young mistress thus I did bespeak:
        "Lord Hamlet is a prince, out of thy star.[1]
        This must not be." And then I prescripts gave her,
        That she should lock herself from his resort,
        Admit no messengers, receive no tokens.
145   Which done, she took the fruits of my advice,
        And he, repellèd, a short tale to make,
        Fell into a sadness, then into a fast,
        Thence to a watch,[2] thence into a weakness,
        Thence to a lightness,[3] and, by this declension,
150   Into the madness wherein now he raves,
        And all we mourn for.
KING   Do you think 'tis this?
QUEEN   It may be, very like.
POLONIUS   Hath there been such a time, I would fain know that,
        That I have positively said "Tis so,"
        When it proved otherwise?
155   KING   Not that I know.
POLONIUS [*Pointing to his head and shoulder*]   Take this from this, if this be
        otherwise.
        If circumstances lead me, I will find
        Where truth is hid, though it were hid indeed
        Within the center.[4]
KING   How may we try it further?
160   POLONIUS   You know sometimes he walks four hours together
    Here in the lobby.
QUEEN   So he does indeed.
POLONIUS   At such a time. I'll loose my daughter to him.
    Be you and I behind an arras[5] then.
    Mark the encounter. If he love her not,
165   And be not from his reason fall'n thereon,
    Let me be no assistant for a state
    But keep a farm and carters.
KING   We will try it.

Enter HAMLET *reading on a book.*

QUEEN   But look where sadly the poor wretch comes reading.
POLONIUS   Away, I do beseech you both, away.

                             Exit KING *and* QUEEN.

170   I'll board him presently.[6] O, give me leave.
    How does my good Lord Hamlet?
HAMLET   Well, God-a-mercy.
POLONIUS   Do you know me, my lord?
HAMLET   Excellent well. You are a fishmonger.[7]

---

[1]sphere   [2]wakefulness   [3]mental derangement   [4]center of the earth   [5]tapestry hanging in front of a wall   [6]*board him presently* accost him at once   [7]dealer in fish (slang for a procurer)

175 POLONIUS Not I, my lord.
     HAMLET Then I would you were so honest a man.
     POLONIUS Honest, my lord?
     HAMLET Ay, sir. To be honest, as this world goes, is to be one man picked out
        of ten thousand.
180 POLONIUS That's very true, my lord.
     HAMLET For if the sun breed maggots in a dead dog, being a good kissing car-
        rion[1]——Have you a daughter?
     POLONIUS I have, my lord.
185 HAMLET Let her not walk i' th' sun. Conception[2] is a blessing, but as your daugh-
        ter may conceive, friend, look to't.
     POLONIUS [Aside] How say you by that? Still harping on my daughter. Yet he
        knew me not at first. 'A said I was a fishmonger. 'A is far gone, far gone. And
        truly in my youth I suffered much extremity for love, very near this. I'll speak
        to him again—What do you read, my lord?
190 HAMLET Words, words, words.
     POLONIUS What is the matter, my lord?
     HAMLET Between who?
     POLONIUS I mean the matter[3] that you read, my lord.
     HAMLET Slanders, sir; for the satirical rogue says here that old men have gray
195   beards, that their faces are wrinkled, their eyes purging thick amber and plum-
        tree gum, and that they have a plentiful lack of wit, together with most weak
        hams. All which, sir, though I most powerfully and potently believe, yet I hold
        it not honesty[4] to have it thus set down; for you yourself, sir, should be old as
        I am if, like a crab, you could go backward.
200 POLONIUS [Aside] Though this be madness, yet there is method in 't. Will you
        walk out of the air, my lord?
     HAMLET Into my grave.
     POLONIUS Indeed, that's out of the air. [Aside] How pregnant[5] sometimes his
        replies are! A happiness[6] that often madness hits on, which reason and sanity
205   could not so prosperously be delivered of. I will leave him and suddenly contrive
        the means of meeting between him and my daughter.—My lord, I will take my
        leave of you.
     HAMLET You cannot take from me anything that I will more willingly part withal—
        except my life, except my life, except my life.

     Enter GUILDENSTERN *and* ROSENCRANTZ.

210 POLONIUS Fare you well, my lord.
     HAMLET These tedious old fools!
     POLONIUS You go to seek the Lord Hamlet? There he is.
     ROSENCRANTZ [*To* POLONIUS] God save you, sir!

                                                              [*Exit* POLONIUS.]

     GUILDENSTERN My honored lord!
215 ROSENCRANTZ My most dear lord!

---

[1]*a good kissing carrion* (perhaps the meaning is "a good piece of flesh to kiss," but many editors
emend *good to god,* taking the word to refer to the sun)   [2](1) understanding (2) becoming pregnant   [3]Polonius means "subject matter," but Hamlet pretends to take the word in the sense of
"quarrel"   [4]decency   [5]meaningful   [6]apt turn of phrase

HAMLET My excellent good friends! How dost thou, Guildenstern? Ah, Rosencrantz! Good lads, how do you both?

ROSENCRANTZ As the indifferent[1] children of the earth.

GUILDENSTERN Happy in that we are not overhappy.
220 On Fortune's cap we are not the very button.

HAMLET Nor the soles of her shoe?

ROSENCRANTZ Neither, my lord.

HAMLET Then you live about her waist, or in the middle of her favors?

GUILDENSTERN Faith, her privates[2] we.

225 HAMLET In the secret parts of Fortune? O, most true!
She is a strumpet. What news?

ROSENCRANTZ None, my lord, but that the world's grown honest.

HAMLET Then is doomsday near. But your news is not true. Let me question
more in particular. What have you, my good friends, deserved at the hands of
230 Fortune that she sends you to prison hither?

GUILDENSTERN Prison, my lord?

HAMLET Denmark's a prison.

ROSENCRANTZ Then is the world one.

HAMLET A goodly one, in which there are many confines, wards,[3] and dungeons,
235 Denmark being one o' th' worst.

ROSENCRANTZ We think not so, my lord.

HAMLET Why, then 'tis none to you, for there is nothing good or bad but thinking
makes it so. To me it is a prison.

ROSENCRANTZ Why then your ambition makes it one. 'Tis too narrow for your
240 mind.

HAMLET O God, I could be bounded in a nutshell and count myself a king of
infinite space, were it not that I have bad dreams.

GUILDENSTERN Which dreams indeed are ambition, for the very substance of the
ambitious is merely the shadow of a dream.

245 HAMLET A dream itself is but a shadow.

ROSENCRANTZ Truly, and I hold ambition of so airy and light a quality that it is
but a shadow's shadow.

HAMLET Then are our beggars bodies, and our monarchs and outstretched heroes
the beggars' shadows.[4] Shall we to th' court? For, by my fay,[5] I cannot reason.

250 BOTH We'll wait upon you.

HAMLET No such matter. I will not sort you with the rest of my servants, for, to
speak to you like an honest man, I am most dreadfully attended. But in the
beaten way of friendship, what make you at Elsinore?

ROSENCRANTZ To visit you, my lord; no other occasion.

255 HAMLET Beggar that I am, I am even poor in thanks, but I thank you; and sure,
dear friends, my thanks are too dear a halfpenny.[6] Were you not sent for? Is it
your own inclining? Is it a free visitation? Come, come, deal justly with me.
Come, come; nay, speak.

GUILDENSTERN What should we say, my lord?

260 HAMLET Why anything—but to th' purpose. You were sent for, and there is a

---

[1]ordinary   [2]ordinary men (with a pun on "private parts")   [3]cells   [4]*Then are ... beggars'
shadows* i.e., by your logic, beggars (lacking ambition) are substantial, and great men are elongated
shadows   [5]faith   [6]*too dear a halfpenny* i.e., not worth a halfpenny

kind of confession in your looks, which your modesties have not craft enough
to color. I know the good King and Queen have sent for you.

ROSENCRANTZ To what end, my lord?

HAMLET That you must teach me. But let me conjure you by the rights of our
265   fellowship, by the consonancy of our youth, by the obligation of our ever-pre-
served love, and by what more dear a better proposer can charge you withal, be
even and direct with me, whether you were sent for or no.

ROSENCRANTZ [*Aside to* GUILDENSTERN] What say you?

HAMLET [*Aside*] Nay then, I have an eye of you.—If you love me, hold not off.
270   GUILDENSTERN My lord, we were sent for.

HAMLET I will tell you why; so shall my anticipation prevent your discovery,[1] and
your secrecy to the King and Queen molt no feather. I have of late, but wherefore
I know not, lost all my mirth, forgone all custom of exercises; and indeed, it
goes so heavily with my disposition that this goodly frame, the earth, seems to
275   me a sterile promontory; this most excellent canopy, the air, look you, this brave
o'erhanging firmament, this majestical roof fretted[2] with golden fire: why, it
appeareth nothing to me but a foul and pestilent congregation of vapors. What
a piece of work is a man, how noble in reason, how infinite in faculties, in form
and moving how express[3] and admirable, in action how like an angel, in appre-
280   hension how like a god: the beauty of the world, the paragon of animals; and
yet to me, what is this quintessence of dust? Man delights not me; nor woman
neither, though by your smiling you seem to say so.

ROSENCRANTZ My lord, there was no such stuff in my thoughts.

HAMLET Why did ye laugh then, when I said "Man delights not me"?
285   ROSENCRANTZ To think, my lord, if you delight not in man, what lenten[4] entertainment the players shall receive from you. We coted[5] them on the way, and
hither are they coming to offer you service.

HAMLET He that plays the king shall be welcome; his Majesty shall have tribute
290   of me; the adventurous knight shall use his foil and target;[6] the lover shall not
sigh gratis; the humorous man[7] shall end his part in peace; the clown shall
make those laugh whose lungs are tickle o' th' sere;[8] and the lady shall say her
mind freely, or[9] the blank verse shall halt[10] for't. What players are they?

ROSENCRANTZ Even those you were wont to take such delight in, the tragedians
295   of the city.

HAMLET How chances it they travel? Their residence, both in reputation and
profit, was better both ways.

ROSENCRANTZ I think their inhibition[11] comes by the means of the late innovation.[12]

300   HAMLET Do they hold the same estimation they did when I was in the city? Are
they so followed?

ROSENCRANTZ No indeed, are they not.

HAMLET How comes it? Do they grow rusty?

ROSENCRANTZ Nay, their endeavor keeps in the wonted pace, but there is, sir,

---

[1]*prevent your discovery* forestall your disclosure   [2]adorned   [3]exact   [4]meager   [5]overtook
[6]shield   [7]*humorous man* i.e., eccentric (among stock characters in dramas were men dominated
by a "humor" or odd trait)   [8]*tickle o' th' sere* on hair trigger (*sere* = part of the gunlock)
[9]else   [10]limp   [11]hindrance   [12]probably an allusion to the companies of child actors that had
become popular and were offering serious competition to the adult actors

305   an eyrie[1] of children, little eyases, that cry out on the top of question[2] and are
      most tyrannically[3] clapped for't. These are now the fashion, and so berattle the
      common stages[4] (so they call them) that many wearing rapiers are afraid of
      goosequills[5] and dare scarce come thither.
      HAMLET What, are they children? Who maintains 'em? How are they escoted?[6]
310   Will they pursue the quality[7] no longer than they can sing? Will they not say
      afterwards, if they should grow themselves to common players (as it is most
      like, if their means are no better), their writers do them wrong to make them
      exclaim against their own succession?[8]
      ROSENCRANTZ Faith, there has been much to-do on both sides, and the nation
315   holds it no sin to tarre[9] them to controversy. There was, for a while, no money
      bid for argument[10] unless the poet and the player went to cuffs in the question.
      HAMLET Is't possible?
      GUILDENSTERN O, there has been much throwing about of brains.
      HAMLET Do the boys carry it away?
320   ROSENCRANTZ Ay, that they do, my lord—Hercules and his load[11] too.
      HAMLET It is not very strange, for my uncle is King of Denmark, and those that
      would make mouths at him while my father lived give twenty, forty, fifty, a
      hundred ducats apiece for his picture in little. 'Sblood,[12] there is something in
      this more than natural, if philosophy could find it out.

                                                          A flourish.

325   GUILDENSTERN There are the players.
      HAMLET Gentlemen, you are welcome to Elsinore. Your hands, come then. Th'
      appurtenance of welcome is fashion and ceremony. Let me comply[13] with you
      in this garb,[14] lest my extent[15] to the players (which I tell you must show fairly
      outwards) should more appear like entertainment than yours. You are welcome.
330   But my uncle-father and aunt-mother are deceived.
      GUILDENSTERN In what, my dear lord?
      HAMLET I am but mad north-northwest:[16] when the wind is southerly I know a
      hawk from a handsaw.[17]

      Enter POLONIUS.

      POLONIUS Well be with you, gentlemen.
335   HAMLET Hark you, Guildenstern, and you too; at each ear a hearer. That great
      baby you see there is not yet out of his swaddling clouts.
      ROSENCRANTZ Happily[18] he is the second time come to them, for they say an old
      man is twice a child.
      HAMLET I will prophesy he comes to tell me of the players. Mark it.—You say
340   right, sir; a Monday morning, 'twas then indeed.

---

[1]nest   [2]*eyases, that . . . of question* unfledged hawks that cry shrilly above others in matters of
debate   [3]violently   [4]*berattle the common stages* cry down the public theaters (with the adult
acting companies)   [5]pens (of satirists who ridicule the public theaters and their audiences)
[6]financially supported   [7]profession of acting   [8]future   [9]incite   [10]plot of a play   [11]*Hercules
and his load* i.e., the whole world (with a reference to the Globe Theatre, which had a sign that
represented Hercules bearing the globe)   [12]by God's blood   [13]be courteous   [14]outward
show   [15]behavior   [16]i.e., on one point of the compass only   [17]*hawk from a handsaw* (*hawk*
can refer not only to a bird but to a kind of pickax; *handsaw*—a carpenter's tool—may involve a
similar pun on "hernshaw," a heron)   [18]perhaps

POLONIUS My lord, I have news to tell you.

HAMLET My lord, I have news to tell you. When Roscius[1] was an actor in Rome—

POLONIUS The actors are come hither, my lord.

HAMLET Buzz, buzz.[2]

345 POLONIUS Upon my honor—

HAMLET Then came each actor on his ass—

POLONIUS The best actors in the world, either for tragedy, comedy, history, pastoral, pastoral-comical, historical-pastoral, tragical-historical, tragical-comical-
historical-pastoral; scene individable,[3] or poem unlimited.[4] Seneca[5] cannot be

350 too heavy, nor Plautus[6] too light. For the law of writ and the liberty,[7] these are
the only men.

HAMLET O Jeptha, judge of Israel,[8] what a treasure hadst thou!

POLONIUS What a treasure had he, my lord?

HAMLET Why,

355   "One fair daughter, and no more,
                      The which he lovèd passing well."

POLONIUS [Aside] Still on my daughter.

HAMLET Am I not i' th' right, old Jeptha?

POLONIUS If you call me Jeptha, my lord, I have a daughter that I love passing

360 well.

HAMLET Nay, that follows not.

POLONIUS What follows then, my lord?

HAMLET Why,

                    "As by lot, God wot,"

365 and then, you know,

                    "It came to pass, as most like it was."

The first row of the pious chanson[9] will show you more, for look where my
abridgment[10] comes.

Enter the PLAYERS.

You are welcome, masters, welcome, all. I am glad to see thee well. Welcome,

370 good friends. O, old friend, why, thy face is valanced[11] since I saw thee last.
Com'st thou to beard me in Denmark? What, my young lady[12] and mistress?
By'r Lady, your ladyship is nearer to heaven than when I saw you last by the
altitude of a chopine.[13] Pray God your voice, like a piece of uncurrent gold, be
not cracked within the ring.[14]—Masters, you are all welcome. We'll e'en to't like

375 French falconers, fly at anything we see. We'll have a speech straight. Come,
give us a taste of your quality. Come, a passionate speech.

PLAYER What speech, my good lord?

---

[1]*a famous Roman comic actor*   [2]*Buzz, buzz* (an interjection perhaps indicating that the news
is old)   [3]*scene individable* plays observing the unities of time, place, and action   [4]*poem unlimited* plays not restricted by the tenets of criticism   [5]Roman tragic dramatist   [6]Roman comic
dramatist   [7]*For the law of writ and the liberty* (perhaps "for sticking to the text and for improvising"; perhaps "for classical plays and for modern loosely written plays")   [8]*Jeptha, judge of
Israel* (the title of a ballad on the Hebrew judge who sacrificed his daughter; see Judges 11)   [9]*row
of the pious chanson* stanza of the scriptural song   [10](1) i.e., entertainers, who abridge the time
(2) interrupters   [11]fringed (with a beard)   [12]*young lady* i.e., boy for female roles   [13]thick-soled
shoe   [14]*like a piece . . . the ring* (a coin was unfit for legal tender if a crack extended from the
edge through the ring enclosing the monarch's head. Hamlet, punning on *ring,* refers to the change
of voice that the boy actor will undergo)

HAMLET I heard thee speak me a speech once, but it was never acted, or if it
was, not above once, for the play, I remember, pleased not the million; 'twas
380   caviary to the general,[1] but it was (as I received it, and others, whose judgments
in such matters cried in the top of[2] mine) an excellent play, well digested in the
scenes, set down with as much modesty as cunning.[3] I remember one said there
were no sallets[4] in the lines to make the matter savory; nor no matter in the
phrase that might indict the author of affectation, but called it an honest method,
385   as wholesome as sweet, and by very much more handsome than fine.[5] One
speech in't I chiefly loved. 'Twas Aeneas' tale to Dido, and thereabout of it
especially when he speaks of Priam's slaughter. If it live in your memory, begin
at this line—let me see, let me see:
       "The rugged Pyrrhus, like th' Hyrcanian beast[6]—"
390   'Tis not so; it begins with Pyrrhus:
       "The rugged Pyrrhus, he whose sable[7] arms,
       Black as his purpose, did the night resemble
       When he lay couchèd in th' ominous horse,[8]
       Hath now this dread and black complexion smeared
395   With heraldry more dismal.[9] Head to foot
       Now is he total gules, horridly tricked[10]
       With blood of fathers, mothers, daughters, sons,
       Baked and impasted[11] with the parching streets,
       That lend a tyrannous and a damnèd light
400   To their lord's murder. Roasted in wrath and fire,
       And thus o'ersizèd[12] with coagulate gore,
       With eyes like carbuncles, the hellish Pyrrhus
       Old grandsire Priam seeks."
       So, proceed you.
405   POLONIUS Fore God, my lord, well spoken, with good accent and good
discretion.
PLAYER   "Anon he finds him,
       Striking too short at Greeks. His antique sword,
       Rebellious to his arm, lies where it falls,
410   Repugnant to command.[13] Unequal matched,
       Pyrrhus at Priam drives, in rage strikes wide,
       But with the whiff and wind of his fell sword
       Th' unnervèd father falls. Then senseless Ilium,[14]
       Seeming to feel this blow, with flaming top
415   Stoops to his base,[15] and with a hideous crash
       Takes prisoner Pyrrhus' ear. For lo, his sword,
       Which was declining on the milky head
       Of reverend Priam, seemed i' th' air to stick.
       So as a painted tyrant[16] Pyrrhus stood,
420   And like a neutral to his will and matter[17]

[1]caviary to the general i.e., too choice for the multitude   [2]in the top of overtopping   [3]modesty
as cunning restraint as art   [4]salads, spicy jests   [5]more handsome than fine well-proportioned
rather than ornamented   [6]Hyrcanian beast i.e., tiger (Hyrcania was in Asia)   [7]black   [8]ominous
horse i.e., wooden horse at the siege of Troy   [9]ill-omened   [10]total gules, horridly tricked all
red, horridly adorned   [11]encrusted   [12]smeared over   [13]Repugnant to command disobedient
[14]senseless Ilium insensate Troy   [15]Stoops to his base collapses (his = its)   [16]painted tyrant tyrant in a picture   [17]task

                   Did nothing.
                   But as we often see, against[1] some storm,
                   A silence in the heavens, the rack[2] stand still,
                   The bold winds speechless, and the orb below
425   As hush as death, anon the dreadful thunder
                   Doth rend the region, so after Pyrrhus' pause,
                   A rousèd vengeance sets him new awork,
                   And never did the Cyclops' hammers fall
                   On Mars's armor, forged for proof eterne,[3]
430   With less remorse than Pyrrhus' bleeding sword
                   Now falls on Priam.
                   Out, out, thou strumpet Fortune! All you gods,
                   In general synod[4] take away her power,
                   Break all the spokes and fellies[5] from her wheel,
435   And bowl the round nave[6] down the hill of heaven,
                   As low as to the fiends."

POLONIUS This is too long.

HAMLET It shall to the barber's, with your beard.—Prithee say on. He's for a jig
or a tale of bawdry, or he sleeps. Say on; come to Hecuba.

440   PLAYER "But who (ah woe!) had seen the mobled[7] queen—"

HAMLET "The mobled queen"?

POLONIUS That's good, "Mobled queen" is good.

PLAYER "Run barefoot up and down, threat'ning the flames
                   With bisson rheum;[8] a clout[9] upon that head
445   Where late the diadem stood, and for a robe,
                   About her lank and all o'erteemèd[10] loins,
                   A blanket in the alarm of fear caught up—
                   Who this had seen, with tongue in venom steeped
                   'Gainst Fortune's state would treason have pronounced.
450   But if the gods themselves did see her then,
                   When she saw Pyrrhus make malicious sport
                   In mincing with his sword her husband's limbs,
                   The instant burst of clamor that she made
                   (Unless things mortal move them not at all)
455   Would have made milch[11] the burning eyes of heaven
                   And passion in the gods."

POLONIUS Look, whe'r[12] he has not turned his color, and has tears in's eyes.
Prithee no more.

HAMLET 'Tis well. I'll have thee speak out the rest of this soon. Good my lord,
460   will you see the players well bestowed?[13] Do you hear? Let them be well used,
for they are the abstract and brief chronicles of the time. After your death you
were better have a bad epitaph than their ill report while you live.

POLONIUS My lord, I will use them according to their desert.

HAMLET God's bodkin,[14] man, much better! Use every man after his desert, and
465   who shall scape whipping? Use them after your own honor and dignity. The less
they deserve, the more merit is in your bounty. Take them in.

---

[1]just before   [2]clouds   [3]*proof eterne* eternal endurance   [4]council   [5]rims   [6]hub
[7]muffled   [8]*bisson rheum* blinding tears   [9]rag   [10]exhausted with childbearing   [11]moist
(literally, "milk-giving")   [12]whether   [13]housed   [14]*God's bodkin* by God's little body

POLONIUS Come, sirs.

HAMLET Follow him, friends. We'll hear a play tomorrow. [*Aside to* PLAYER] Dost thou hear me, old friend? Can you play *The Murder of Gonzago?*

470   PLAYER Ay, my lord.

HAMLET We'll ha't tomorrow night. You could for a need study a speech of some dozen or sixteen lines which I would set down and insert in't, could you not?

PLAYER Ay, my lord.

HAMLET Very well. Follow that lord, and look you mock him not. My good

475   friends, I'll leave you till night. You are welcome to Elsinore.

Exeunt POLONIUS *and* PLAYERS.

ROSENCRANTZ Good my lord.

Exeunt [ROSENCRANTZ *and* GUILDENSTERN].

HAMLET Ay, so, God bye to you.—Now I am alone.
O, what a rogue and peasant slave am I!
Is it not monstrous that this player here,
480   But in a fiction, in a dream of passion,[1]
Could force his soul so to his own conceit[2]
That from her working all his visage wanned,
Tears in his eyes, distraction in his aspect,
A broken voice, and his whole function[3] suiting
485   With forms[4] to his conceit? And all for nothing!
For Hecuba!
What's Hecuba to him, or he to Hecuba,
That he should weep for her? What would he do
Had he the motive and the cue for passion
490   That I have? He would drown the stage with tears
And cleave the general ear with horrid speech,
Make mad the guilty and appall the free,[5]
Confound the ignorant, and amaze indeed
The very faculties of eyes and ears.
495   Yet I,
A dull and muddy-mettled[6] rascal, peak
Like John-a-dreams,[7] unpregnant of[8] my cause,
And can say nothing. No, not for a king,
Upon whose property and most dear life
500   A damned defeat was made. Am I a coward?
Who calls me villain? Breaks my pate across?
Plucks off my beard and blows it in my face?
Tweaks me by the nose? Gives me the lie i' th' throat
As deep as to the lungs? Who does me this?
505   Ha, 'swounds,[9] I should take it, for it cannot be
But I am pigeon-livered[10] and lack gall

---

[1]*dream of passion* imaginary emotion   [2]*imagination*   [3]*action*   [4]*bodily expressions*
[5]*appall the free* terrify (make pale?) the guiltless.   [6]*muddy-mettled* weak-spirited   [7]*peak/Like John-a-dreams* mope like a dreamer   [8]*unpregnant of* unquickened by   [9] by God's wounds
[10]gentle as a dove

To make oppression bitter, or ere this
I should ha' fatted all the region kites[1]
With this slave's offal. Bloody, bawdy villain!
510 Remorseless, treacherous, lecherous, kindless[2] villain!
O, vengeance!
Why, what an ass am I! This is most brave,[3]
That I, the son of a dear father murdered,
Prompted to my revenge by heaven and hell,
515 Must, like a whore, unpack my heart with words
And fall a-cursing like a very drab,[4]
A stallion![5] Fie upon't, foh! About,[6] my brains.
Hum—
I have heard that guilty creatures sitting at a play
520 Have by the very cunning of the scene
Been struck so to the soul that presently[7]
They have proclaimed their malefactions.
For murder, though it have no tongue, will speak
With most miraculous organ. I'll have these players
525 Play something like the murder of my father
Before mine uncle. I'll observe his looks,
I'll tent[8] him to the quick. If 'a do blench,[9]
I know my course. The spirit that I have seen
May be a devil, and the devil hath power
530 T' assume a pleasing shape, yea, and perhaps
Out of my weakness and my melancholy,
As he is very potent with such spirits,
Abuses me to damn me. I'll have grounds
More relative[10] than this. The play's the thing
535 Wherein I'll catch the conscience of the King.   *Exit.*

Act III, Scene I. *The castle.*

Enter KING, QUEEN, POLONIUS, OPHELIA, ROSENCRANTZ, GUILDENSTERN, LORDS.

KING And can you by no drift of conference[11]
Get from him why he puts on this confusion,
Grating so harshly all his days of quiet
With turbulent and dangerous lunacy?
5 ROSENCRANTZ He does confess he feels himself distracted,
But from what cause 'a will by no means speak.
GUILDENSTERN Nor do we find him forward to be sounded,[12]
But with a crafty madness keeps aloof

---

[1] *region kites* kites (scavenger birds) of the sky   [2] unnatural   [3] fine   [4] prostitute   [5] male prostitute (perhaps one should adopt the Folio reading, *scullion* = kitchen wench)   [6] to work   [7] immediately   [8] probe   [9] flinch   [10] probably "pertinent," but possibly "able to be related plausibly"   [11] *drift of conference* management of conversation   [12] *forward to be sounded* willing to be questioned

When we would bring him on to some confession
Of his true state.
10   QUEEN   Did he receive you well?
ROSENCRANTZ Most like a gentleman.
GUILDENSTERN But with much forcing of his disposition.[1]
ROSENCRANTZ Niggard of question,[2] but of our demands
    Most free in his reply.
QUEEN   Did you assay[3] him
15   To any pastime?
ROSENCRANTZ Madam, it so fell out that certain players
    We o'erraught[4] on the way; of these we told him,
    And there did seem in him a kind of joy
    To hear of it. They are here about the court,
20   And, as I think, they have already order
    This night to play before him.
POLONIUS   'Tis most true,
    And he beseeched me to entreat your Majesties
    To hear and see the matter.
KING With all my heart, and it doth much content me
25   To hear him so inclined.
    Good gentlemen, give him a further edge
    And drive his purpose into these delights.
ROSENCRANTZ We shall, my lord.

                    Exeunt ROSENCRANTZ *and* GUILDENSTERN.

KING   Sweet Gertrude, leave us too,
    For we have closely[5] sent for Hamlet hither,
30   That he, as 'twere by accident, may here
    Affront[6] Ophelia.
    Her father and myself (lawful espials)[7]
    Will so bestow ourselves that, seeing unseen,
    We may of their encounter frankly judge
35   And gather by him, as he is behaved,
    If't be th' affliction of his love or no
    That thus he suffers for.
QUEEN   I shall obey you.
    And for your part, Ophelia, I do wish
    That your good beauties be the happy cause
40   Of Hamlet's wildness. So shall I hope your virtues
    Will bring him to his wonted way again,
    To both your honors.
OPHELIA   Madam, I wish it may.

                    Exit QUEEN.

POLONIUS Ophelia, walk you here.—Gracious, so please you,
    We will bestow ourselves. [*To* OPHELIA] Read on this book,

---

[1]*forcing of his disposition* effort   [2]*Niggard of question* uninclined to talk   [3]tempt
[4]overtook   [5]secretly   [6]meet face to face   [7]spies

45   That show of such an exercise may color[1]
        Your loneliness. We are oft to blame in this,
        'Tis too much proved, that with devotion's visage
        And pious action we do sugar o'er
        The devil himself.
        KING   [*Aside*] O, 'tis too true.
50   How smart a lash that speech doth give my conscience!
        The harlot's cheek, beautied with plast'ring art,
        Is not more ugly to the thing that helps it
        Than is my deed to my most painted word.
        O heavy burden!
55   POLONIUS I hear him coming. Let's withdraw, my lord.

                                Exeunt KING *and* POLONIUS.

        Enter HAMLET.

        HAMLET To be, or not to be: that is the question:
        Whether 'tis nobler in the mind to suffer
        The slings and arrows of outrageous fortune,
        Or to take arms against a sea of troubles,
60   And by opposing end them. To die, to sleep—
        No more—and by a sleep to say we end
        The heartache, and the thousand natural shocks
        That flesh is heir to! 'Tis a consummation
        Devoutly to be wished. To die, to sleep—
65   To sleep—perchance to dream: ay, there's the rub,[2]
        For in that sleep of death what dreams may come
        When we have shuffled off this mortal coil,[3]
        Must give us pause. There's the respect[4]
        That makes calamity of so long life:[5]
70   For who would bear the whips and scorns of time,
        Th' oppressor's wrong, the proud man's contumely,
        The pangs of despised love, the law's delay,
        The insolence of office, and the spurns
        That patient merit of th' unworthy takes,
75   When he himself might his quietus[6] make
        With a bare bodkin?[7] Who would fardels[8] bear,
        To grunt and sweat under a weary life,
        But that the dread of something after death,
        The undiscovered country, from whose bourn[9]
80   No traveler returns, puzzles the will,
        And makes us rather bear those ills we have,
        Than fly to others that we know not of?
        Thus conscience[10] does make cowards of us all,

[1]*exercise may color* act of devotion may give a plausible hue to (the book is one of devotion)
[2]*impediment* (obstruction to a bowler's ball)   [3](1) turmoil (2) a ring of rope (here the flesh encircling the soul)   [4]consideration   [5]*makes calamity of so long life* (1) makes calamity so long-lived (2) makes living so long a calamity   [6]full discharge (a legal term)   [7]dagger   [8]burdens   [9] region   [10]self-consciousness, introspection

And thus the native hue of resolution
85   Is sicklied o'er with the pale cast[1] of thought,
And enterprises of great pitch[2] and moment,
With this regard[3] their currents turn awry,
And lose the name of action.—Soft you now,
The fair Ophelia!—Nymph, in thy orisons[4]
Be all my sins remembered.

90   OPHELIA   Good my lord,
How does your honor for this many a day?

HAMLET I humbly thank you; well, well, well.

OPHELIA My lord, I have remembrances of yours
That I have longèd long to redeliver.
I pray you now, receive them.

95   HAMLET   No, not I,
I never gave you aught.

OPHELIA My honored lord, you know right well you did,
And with them words of so sweet breath composed
As made these things more rich. Their perfume lost,
100 Take these again, for to the noble mind
Rich gifts wax poor when givers prove unkind.
There, my lord.

HAMLET Ha, ha! Are you honest?[5]

OPHELIA My lord?

105 HAMLET Are you fair?

OPHELIA What means your lordship?

HAMLET That if you be honest and fair, your honesty should admit no discourse
to your beauty.[6]

OPHELIA Could beauty, my lord, have better commerce than with honesty?

110 HAMLET Ay, truly; for the power of beauty will sooner transform honesty from
what it is to a bawd[7] than the force of honesty can translate beauty into his
likeness. This was sometime a paradox, but now the time gives it proof. I did
love you once.

OPHELIA Indeed, my lord, you made me believe so.

115 HAMLET You should not have believed me, for virtue cannot so inoculate[8] our
old stock but we shall relish of it.[9] I loved you not.

OPHELIA I was the more deceived.

HAMLET Get thee to a nunnery. Why wouldst thou be a breeder of sinners? I am
myself indifferent honest,[10] but yet I could accuse me of such things that it were
120 better my mother had not borne me: I am very proud, revengeful, ambitious,
with more offenses at my beck[11] than I have thoughts to put them in, imagination
to give them shape, or time to act them in. What should such fellows as I do
crawling between earth and heaven? We are arrant knaves all; believe none of
us. Go thy ways to a nunnery. Where's your father?

125 OPHELIA At home, my lord.

---

[1]color   [2]height (a term from falconry)   [3]consideration   [4]prayers   [5]*Are you honest* (1) are
you modest (2) are you chaste (3) have you integrity   [6]*your honesty . . . to your beauty* your
modesty should permit no approach to your beauty   [7]procurer   [8]graft   [9]*relish of it* smack of
it (our old sinful nature)   [10]*indifferent honest* moderately virtuous   [11]call

HAMLET Let the doors be shut upon him, that he may play the fool nowhere but
in's own house. Farewell.

OPHELIA O help him, you sweet heavens!

HAMLET If thou dost marry, I'll give thee this plague for thy dowry: be thou as
130 chaste as ice, as pure as snow, thou shalt not escape calumny. Get thee to a
nunnery. Go, farewell. Or if thou wilt needs marry, marry a fool, for wise men
know well enough what monsters[1] you make of them. To a nunnery, go, and
quickly too. Farewell.

OPHELIA Heavenly powers, restore him!

135 HAMLET I have heard of your paintings, well enough. God hath given you one
face, and you make yourselves another. You jig and amble, and you lisp; you
nickname God's creatures and make your wantonness your ignorance.[2] Go to,
I'll no more on't; it hath made me mad. I say we will have no moe[3] marriage.
Those that are married already—all but one—shall live. The rest shall keep as
140 they are. To a nunnery, go.   *Exit.*

OPHELIA O what a noble mind is here o'erthrown!
The courtier's, soldier's, scholar's, eye, tongue, sword,
Th' expectancy and rose[4] of the fair state,
The glass of fashion, and the mold of form,[5]
145 Th' observed of all observers, quite, quite down!
And I, of ladies most deject and wretched,
That sucked the honey of his musicked vows,
Now see that noble and most sovereign reason
Like sweet bells jangled, out of time and harsh,
150 That unmatched form and feature of blown[6] youth
Blasted with ecstasy.[7] O, woe is me
T' have seen what I have seen, see what I see!

Enter KING *and* POLONIUS.

KING Love? His affections[8] do not that way tend,
Nor what he spake, though it lacked form a little,
155 Was not like madness. There's something in his soul
O'er which his melancholy sits on brood,
And I do doubt[9] the hatch and the disclose
Will be some danger; which for to prevent,
I have in quick determination
160 Thus set it down: he shall with speed to England
For the demand of our neglected tribute.
Haply the seas, and countries different,
With variable objects, shall expel
This something-settled[10] matter in his heart,
165 Whereon his brains still beating puts him thus
From fashion of himself. What think you on't?

POLONIUS It shall do well. But yet do I believe

---

[1]horned beasts, cuckolds   [2]*make your wantonness your ignorance* excuse your wanton
speech by pretending ignorance   [3]more   [4]*expectancy and rose* i.e., fair hope   [5]*The glass . . .
of form* the mirror of fashion, and the pattern of excellent behavior   [6]blooming   [7]madness
[8]inclinations   [9]fear   [10]somewhat settled

The origin and commencement of his grief
Sprung from neglected love. How now, Ophelia?
170   You need not tell us what Lord Hamlet said;
We heard it all. My lord, do as you please,
But if you hold it fit, after the play,
Let his queen mother all alone entreat him
To show his grief. Let her be round[1] with him,
175   And I'll be placed, so please you, in the ear
Of all their conference. If she find him not,[2]
To England send him, or confine him where
Your wisdom best shall think.
KING   It shall be so.
Madness in great ones must not unwatched go.

Exeunt.

Scene II. *The castle.*

Enter HAMLET *and three of the* PLAYERS.

180   HAMLET Speak the speech, I pray you, as I pronounced it to you, trippingly on
the tongue. But if you mouth it, as many of our players do, I had as lief the town
crier spoke my lines. Nor do not saw the air too much with your hand, thus,
but use all gently, for in the very torrent, tempest, and (as I may say) whirlwind
of your passion, you must acquire and beget a temperance that may give it
185   smoothness. O, it offends me to the soul to hear a robustious periwig-pated[3]
fellow tear a passion to tatters, to very rags, to split the ears of the groundlings,[4]
who for the most part are capable of[5] nothing but inexplicable dumb shows[6] and
noise. I would have such a fellow whipped for o'erdoing Termagant. It out-
herods Herod.[7] Pray you avoid it.
190   PLAYER I warrant your honor.
HAMLET Be not too tame neither, but let your own discretion be your tutor. Suit
the action to the word, the word to the action, with this special observance, that
you o'erstep not the modesty of nature. For anything so o'erdone is from[8] the
purpose of playing, whose end, both at the first and now, was and is, to hold,
195   as 'twere, the mirror up to nature; to show virtue her own feature, scorn her
own image, and the very age and body of the time his form and pressure.[9] Now,
this overdone, or come tardy off, though it makes the unskillful laugh, cannot
but make the judicious grieve, the censure of the which one must in your allowance o'erweigh a whole theater of others. O, there be players that I have
200   seen play, and heard others praise, and that highly (not to speak it profanely),
that neither having th' accent of Christians, nor the gait of Christian, pagan, nor
man, have so strutted and bellowed that I have thought some of Nature's jour-
neymen[10] had made men, and not made them well, they imitated humanity so
abominably.

[1]blunt   [2]*find him not* does not find him out   [3]*robustious periwig-pated* boisterous wig-
headed   [4]those who stood in the pit of the theater (the poorest and presumably most ignorant of
the audience)   [5]*are capable of* are able to understand   [6]*dumb shows* (it had been the fashion
for actors to preface plays or parts of plays with silent mime)   [7]*Termagant . . . Herod* (boisterous
characters in the old mystery plays)   [8]contrary to   [9]image, impress   [10]workers not yet masters
of their craft

205 PLAYER I hope we have reformed that indifferently[1] with us, sir.
HAMLET O, reform it altogether! And let those that play your clowns speak no
more than is set down for them, for there be of them that will themselves laugh,
to set on some quantity of barren spectators to laugh too, though in the meantime some necessary question of the play be then to be considered. That's vil-
210 lainous and shows a most pitiful ambition in the fool that uses it. Go make you
ready.

Exit PLAYERS.

Enter POLONIUS, GUILDENSTERN, *and* ROSENCRANTZ.

How now, my lord? Will the King hear this piece of work?
POLONIUS And the Queen too, and that presently.
HAMLET Bid the players make haste.   *Exit* POLONIUS.
215 Will you two help to hasten them?
ROSENCRANTZ Ay, my lord.

Exeunt they two.

HAMLET What, ho, Horatio!

Enter HORATIO.

HORATIO Here, sweet lord, at your service.
HAMLET Horatio, thou art e'en as just a man
220 As e'er my conversation coped withal.[2]
HORATIO O, my dear lord—
HAMLET   Nay, do not think I flatter.
For what advancement[3] may I hope from thee,
That no revenue hast but thy good spirits
225 To feed and clothe thee? Why should the poor be flattered?
No, let the candied[4] tongue lick absurd pomp,
And crook the pregnant[5] hinges of the knee
Where thrift[6] may follow fawning. Dost thou hear?
Since my dear soul was mistress of her choice
230 And could of men distinguish her election,
S' hath sealed thee[7] for herself, for thou hast been
As one, in suff'ring all, that suffers nothing,
A man that Fortune's buffets and rewards
Hast ta'en with equal thanks; and blest are those
235 Whose blood[8] and judgment are so well commeddled[9]
That they are not a pipe for Fortune's finger
To sound what stop she please. Give me that man
That is not passion's slave, and I will wear him
In my heart's core, ay, in my heart of heart,
240 As I do thee. Something too much of this—
There is a play tonight before the King.
One scene of it comes near the circumstance
Which I have told thee, of my father's death.
I prithee, when thou seest that act afoot,

[1]tolerably [2]*coped withal* met with [3]promotion [4]sugared, flattering [5](1) pliant
(2) full of promise of good fortune [6]profit [7]*S' hath sealed thee* she (the soul) has set
a mark on you [8]passion [9]blended

245   Even with the very comment[1] of thy soul
        Observe my uncle. If his occulted[2] guilt
        Do not itself unkennel in one speech,
        It is a damnèd ghost that we have seen,
        And my imaginations are as foul
250   As Vulcan's stithy.[3] Give him heedful note,
        For I mine eyes will rivet to his face,
        And after we will both our judgments join
        In censure of his seeming.[4]

HORATIO   Well, my lord.
255   If 'a steal aught the whilst this play is playing,
        And scape detecting, I will pay the theft.

Enter Trumpets and Kettledrums, KING, QUEEN, POLONIUS, OPHELIA, ROSEN-
CRANTZ, GUILDERSTERN, *and other* LORDS *attendant with his Guard carrying
torches. Danish March. Sound a Flourish.*

HAMLET   They are coming to the play: I must be idle;[5] Get you a place.

KING   How fares our cousin Hamlet?

HAMLET   Excellent, i' faith, of the chameleon's dish;[6] I eat the air, promise-
260   crammed; you cannot feed capons so.

KING   I have nothing with this answer, Hamlet; these words are not mine.

HAMLET   No, nor mine now. [*To* POLONIUS] My lord, you played once i' th' uni-
    versity, you say?

POLONIUS   That did I, my lord, and was accounted a good actor.

265   HAMLET   What did you enact?

POLONIUS   I did enact Julius Caesar. I was killed i' th' Capitol; Brutus killed me.

HAMLET   It was a brute part of him to kill so capital a calf there. Be the players
    ready?

ROSENCRANTZ   Ay, my lord. They stay upon your patience.

270   QUEEN   Come hither, my dear Hamlet, sit by me.

HAMLET   No, good mother. Here's metal and more attractive.[7]

POLONIUS   [*To the* KING] O ho! Do you mark that?

HAMLET   Lady, shall I lie in your lap?

                                    He lies at OPHELIA'*s feet.*

OPHELIA   No, my lord.

275   HAMLET   I mean, my head upon your lap?

OPHELIA   Ay, my lord.

HAMLET   Do you think I meant country matters?[8]

OPHELIA   I think nothing, my lord.

HAMLET   That's a fair thought to lie between maids' legs.

280   OPHELIA   What is, my lord?

HAMLET   Nothing.

OPHELIA   You are merry, my lord.

HAMLET   Who, I?

---

[1]*very comment* deepest wisdom   [2]hidden   [3]forge, smithy   [4]*censure of his seeming* judgment
on his looks   [5]*be idle* play the fool   [6]*the chameleon's dish* air (on which chameleons were
thought to live)   [7]magnetic   [8]*country matters* rustic doings (with a pun on the vulgar word for
the pudendum)

OPHELIA   Ay, my lord.

285   HAMLET   O God, your only jig-maker![1] What should a man do but be merry? For look you how cheerfully my mother looks, and my father died within's two hours.

OPHELIA   Nay, 'tis twice two months, my lord.

HAMLET   So long? Nay then, let the devil wear black, for I'll have a suit of sables.[2]

290   O heavens! Die two months ago, and not forgotten yet? Then there's hope a great man's memory may outlive his life half a year. But, by'r Lady, 'a must build churches then, or else shall 'a suffer not thinking on, with the hobby-horse,[3] whose epitaph is "For O, for O, the hobby-horse is forgot!"

The trumpets sound. Dumb show follows:
Enter a King and a Queen very lovingly, the Queen embracing him, and he her. She kneels; and makes show of protestation unto him. He takes her up, and declines his head upon her neck. He lies him down upon a bank of flowers. She, seeing him asleep, leaves him. Anon come in another man: takes off his crown, kisses it, pours poison in the sleeper's ears, and leaves him. The Queen returns, finds the King dead, makes passionate action. The poisoner, with some three or four, come in again, seem to condole with her. The dead body is carried away. The poisoner woos the Queen with gifts; she seems harsh awhile, but in the end accepts love.

Exeunt.

OPHELIA   What means this, my lord?

295   HAMLET   Marry, this is miching mallecho;[4] it means mischief.

OPHELIA   Belike this show imports the argument[5] of the play.

Enter PROLOGUE.

HAMLET   We shall know by this fellow. The players cannot keep counsel; they'll tell all.

OPHELIA   Will 'a tell us what this show meant?

300   HAMLET   Ay, or any show that you will show him. Be not you ashamed to show, he'll not shame to tell you what it means.

OPHELIA   You are naught,[6] you are naught; I'll mark the play.

PROLOGUE   For us, and for our tragedy,
             Here stooping to your clemency,
305   We beg your hearing patiently.   [*Exit.*]

HAMLET   Is this a prologue, or the posy of a ring?[7]

OPHELIA   'Tis brief, my lord.

HAMLET   As woman's love.

Enter [two PLAYERS *as] King and Queen.*

PLAYER KING   Full thirty times hath Phoebus' cart[8] gone round
310   Neptune's salt wash[9] and Tellus'[10] orbèd ground,

---

[1]composer of songs and dances (often a Fool, who performed them)   [2]pun on "black" and "luxurious furs"   [3]mock horse worn by a performer in the morris dance   [4]*miching mallecho* sneaking mischief   [5]plot   [6]wicked, improper   [7]*posy of a ring* motto inscribed in a ring   [8]*Phoebus' cart* the sun's chariot   [9]*Neptune's salt wash* the sea   [10]Roman goddess of the earth

And thirty dozen moons with borrowed sheen
About the world have times twelve thirties been,
Since love our hearts, and Hymen did our hands,
Unite commutual in most sacred bands.
315   PLAYER QUEEN So many journeys may the sun and moon
Make us again count o'er ere love be done!
But woe is me, you are so sick of late,
So far from cheer and from your former state,
That I distrust[1] you. Yet, though I distrust,
320   Discomfort you, my lord, it nothing must.
For women fear too much, even as they love,
And women's fear and love hold quantity,
In neither aught, or in extremity.[2]
Now what my love is, proof[3] hath made you know,
325   And as my love is sized, my fear is so.
Where love is great, the littlest doubts are fear;
Where little fears grow great, great love grows there.
PLAYER KING Faith, I must leave thee, love, and shortly too;
My operant[4] powers their functions leave to do:
330   And thou shalt live in this fair world behind,
Honored, beloved, and haply one as kind
For husband shalt thou—
PLAYER QUEEN   O, confound the rest!
Such love must needs be treason in my breast.
335   In second husband let me be accurst!
None wed the second but who killed the first.
HAMLET [Aside] That's wormwood.[5]
PLAYER QUEEN The instances[6] that second marriage move[7]
Are base respects of thrift,[8] but none of love.
340   A second time I kill my husband dead
When second husband kisses me in bed.
PLAYER KING I do believe you think what now you speak,
But what we do determine oft we break.
Purpose is but the slave to memory,
345   Of violent birth, but poor validity,[9]
Which now like fruit unripe sticks on the tree,
But fall unshaken when they mellow be.
Most necessary 'tis that we forget
To pay ourselves what to ourselves is debt.
350   What to ourselves in passion we propose,
The passion ending, doth the purpose lose.
The violence of either grief or joy
Their own enactures[10] with themselves destroy:
Where joy most revels, grief doth most lament;
355   Grief joys, joy grieves, on slender accident.

---

[1]am anxious about   [2]And women's . . . in extremity (perhaps the idea is that women's
anxiety is great or little in proportion to their love. The previous line, unrhymed, may be a false
start that Shakespeare neglected to delete)   [3]experience   [4]active   [5]a bitter herb   [6]motives
[7]induce   [8]respects of thrift considerations of profit   [9]strength   [10]acts

This world is not for aye, nor 'tis not strange
That even our loves should with our fortunes change,
For 'tis a question left us yet to prove,
Whether love lead fortune, or else fortune love.
360 The great man down, you mark his favorite flies;
The poor advanced makes friends of enemies;
And hitherto doth love on fortune tend,
For who not needs shall never lack a friend;
And who in want a hollow friend doth try,
365 Directly seasons him¹ his enemy.
But, orderly to end where I begun,
Our wills and fates do so contrary run
That our devices still are overthrown;
Our thoughts are ours, their ends none of our own.
370 So think thou wilt no second husband wed,
But die thy thoughts when thy first lord is dead.
PLAYER QUEEN   Nor earth to me give food, nor heaven light,
Sport and repose lock from me day and night,
To desperation turn my trust and hope,
375 An anchor's² cheer in prison be my scope,
Each opposite that blanks³ the face of joy
Meet what I would have well, and it destroy:
Both here and hence pursue me lasting strife,
If, once a widow, ever I be wife!
380 HAMLET If she should break it now!
PLAYER KING 'Tis deeply sworn. Sweet, leave me here awhile;
My spirits grow dull, and fain I would beguile
The tedious day with sleep.
PLAYER QUEEN   Sleep rock thy brain,

[He] sleeps.

385 And never come mischance between us twain!   *Exit.*
HAMLET Madam, how like you this play?
QUEEN The lady doth protest too much, methinks.
HAMLET O, but she'll keep her word.
KING Have you heard the argument?⁴ Is there no offense in't?
390 HAMLET No, no, they do but jest, poison in jest; no offense i' th' world.
KING What do you call the play?
HAMLET *The Mousetrap.* Marry, how? Tropically.⁵ This play is the image of a
murder done in Vienna: Gonzago is the Duke's name; his wife, Baptista. You
shall see anon. 'Tis a knavish piece of work, but what of that? Your Majesty,
395 and we that have free⁶ souls, it touches us not. Let the galled jade winch;⁷ our
withers are unwrung.

Enter LUCIANUS.

This is one Lucianus, nephew to the King.

---

¹*seasons him* ripens him into   ²*anchorite's, hermit's*   ³*opposite that blanks* adverse thing
that blanches   ⁴plot   ⁵figuratively (with a pun on "trap")   ⁶innocent   ⁷*galled jade winch* chafed
horse wince

OPHELIA   You are as good as a chorus, my lord.

HAMLET   I could interpret[1] between you and your love, if I could see the puppets
400   dallying.

OPHELIA   You are keen,[2] my lord, you are keen.

HAMLET   It would cost you a groaning to take off mine edge.

OPHELIA   Still better, and worse.

HAMLET   So you mistake[3] your husbands.—Begin, murderer. Leave thy damnable
405   faces and begin. Come, the croaking raven doth bellow for revenge.

LUCIANUS   Thoughts black, hands apt, drugs fit, and time agreeing,
         Confederate season,[4] else no creature seeing,
         Thou mixture rank of midnight weeds collected,
         With Hecate's ban[5] thrice blasted, thrice infected,
410   Thy natural magic and dire property[6]
         On wholesome life usurps immediately.

                                              Pours the poison in his ears.

HAMLET   'A poisons him i' th' garden for his estate. His name's Gonzago. The
         story is extant, and written in very choice Italian. You shall see anon how the
         murderer gets the love of Gonzago's wife.
415   OPHELIA   The King rises.

HAMLET   What, frighted with false fire?[7]

QUEEN   How fares my lord?

POLONIUS   Give o'er the play.

KING   Give me some light. Away!
420   POLONIUS   Lights, lights, lights!

                                              Exeunt all but HAMLET *and* HORATIO.

HAMLET   Why, let the strucken deer go weep,
             The hart ungallèd play:
         For some must watch, while some must sleep;
             Thus runs the world away.
425   Would not this, sir, and a forest of feathers[8]—if the rest of my fortunes turn
      Turk[9] with me—with two Provincial roses[10] on my razed[11] shoes, get me a
      fellowship in a cry[12] of players?

HORATIO   Half a share.

HAMLET   A whole one, I.
430   For thou dost know, O Damon dear,
             This realm dismantled was
         Of Jove himself; and now reigns here
             A very, very—pajock.[13]

HORATIO   You might have rhymed.[14]
435   HAMLET   O good Horatio, I'll take the ghost's word for a thousand pound. Didst
      perceive?

---

[1]like a showman explaining the action of puppets   [2](1) sharp (2) sexually aroused   [3]err in
taking   [4]*Confederate season* the opportunity allied with me   [5]*Hecate's ban* the curse of the
goddess of sorcery   [6]nature   [7]*false fire* blank discharge of firearms   [8]plumes were sometimes
part of a costume   [9]*turn Turk* i.e., go bad, treat me badly   [10]*Provincial roses* rosettes like the
roses of Provence (?)   [11]ornamented with slashes   [12]pack, company   [13]peacock   [14]*You
might have rhymed* i.e., rhymed "was" with "ass"

HORATIO Very well, my lord.

HAMLET Upon the talk of poisoning?

HORATIO I did very well note him.

440 HAMLET Ah ha! Come, some music! Come, the recorders![1]
　　　　　　　For if the King like not the comedy,
　　　　　　　Why then, belike he likes it not, perdy.[2]
　　　　Come, some music!

Enter ROSENCRANTZ *and* GUILDENSTERN.

GUILDENSTERN Good my lord, vouchsafe me a word with you.

445 HAMLET Sir, a whole history.

GUILDENSTERN The King, sir—

HAMLET Ay, sir, what of him?

GUILDENSTERN Is in his retirement marvelous distemp'red.

HAMLET With drink, sir?

450 GUILDENSTERN No, my lord, with choler.[3]

HAMLET Your wisdom should show itself more richer to signify this to the doctor,
　　　for for me to put him to his purgation would perhaps plunge him into more
　　　choler.

GUILDENSTERN Good my lord, put your discourse into some frame,[4] and start

455 　　not so wildly from my affair.

HAMLET I am tame, sir; pronounce.

GUILDENSTERN The Queen, your mother, in most great affliction of spirit hath
　　　sent me to you.

HAMLET You are welcome.

460 GUILDENSTERN Nay, good my lord, this courtesy is not of the right breed. If it
　　　shall please you to make me a wholesome answer, I will do your mother's
　　　commandment: if not, your pardon and my return shall be the end of my busi-
　　　ness.

HAMLET Sir, I cannot.

465 ROSENCRANTZ What, my lord?

HAMLET Make you a wholesome[5] answer; my wit's diseased. But, sir, such an-
　　　swer as I can make, you shall command, or rather, as you say, my mother.
　　　Therefore no more, but to the matter. My mother, you say—

ROSENCRANTZ Then thus she says: your behavior hath struck her into amaze-

470 　　ment and admiration.[6]

HAMLET O wonderful son, that can so stonish a mother! But is there no sequel
　　　at the heels of this mother's admiration? Impart.

ROSENCRANTZ She desires to speak with you in her closet ere you go to bed.

HAMLET We shall obey, were she ten times our mother. Have you any further

475 　　trade with us?

ROSENCRANTZ My lord, you once did love me.

HAMLET And do still, by these pickers and stealers.[7]

ROSENCRANTZ Good my lord, what is your cause of distemper? You do surely
　　　bar the door upon your own liberty, if you deny your griefs to your friend.

480 HAMLET Sir, I lack advancement.[8]

[1]flutelike instruments   [2]by God (French : *par dieu*)   [3]anger (but Hamlet pretends to take the
word in its sense of "biliousness")   [4]*frame* order, control   [5]sane   [6]wonder   [7]*pickers and
stealers* i.e., hands (with reference to the prayer "Keep my hands from picking and
stealing")   [8]promotion

ROSENCRANTZ How can that be, when you have the voice of the King himself for your succession in Denmark?

Enter the PLAYERS *with recorders.*

HAMLET Ay, sir, but "while the grass grows"—the proverb[1] is something musty. O, the recorders. Let me see one. To withdraw[2] with you—why do you go about
485 to recover the wind[3] of me as if you would drive me into a toil?[4]
GUILDENSTERN O my lord, if my duty be too bold, my love is too unmannerly.[5]
HAMLET I do not well understand that. Will you play upon this pipe?
GUILDENSTERN My lord, I cannot.
HAMLET I pray you.
490 GUILDENSTERN Believe me, I cannot.
HAMLET I pray you.
GUILDENSTERN Believe me, I cannot.
HAMLET I do beseech you.
GUILDENSTERN I know no touch of it, my lord.
495 HAMLET It is as easy as lying. Govern these ventages[6] with your fingers and thumb, give it breath with your mouth, and it will discourse most eloquent music. Look you, these are the stops.
GUILDENSTERN But these cannot I command to any utt'rance of harmony; I have not the skill.
500 HAMLET Why, look you now, how unworthy a thing you make of me! You would play upon me; you would seem to know my stops; you would pluck out the heart of my mystery; you would sound me from my lowest note to the top of my compass;[7] and there is much music, excellent voice, in this little organ,[8] yet cannot you make it speak. 'Sblood, do you think I am easier to be played on
505 than a pipe? Call me what instrument you will, though you can fret[9] me, you cannot play upon me.

Enter POLONIUS.

God bless you, sir!
POLONIUS My lord, the Queen would speak with you, and presently.
HAMLET Do you see yonder cloud that's almost in shape of a camel?
510 POLONIUS By th' mass and 'tis, like a camel indeed.
HAMLET Methinks it is like a weasel.
POLONIUS It is backed like a weasel.
HAMLET Or like a whale.
POLONIUS Very like a whale.
515 HAMLET Then I will come to my mother by and by. [*Aside*] They fool me to the top of my bent.[10]—I will come by and by.[11]
POLONIUS I will say so.   *Exit.*
HAMLET "By and by" is easily said. Leave me, friends.

[*Exeunt all but* HAMLET.]

---

[1]"While the grass groweth, the horse starveth"   [2]speak in private   [3]*recover the wind* get on the windward side (as in hunting)   [4]snare   [5]*if my duty . . . too unmannerly* i.e., if these questions seem rude, it is because my love for you leads me beyond good manners.   [6]vents, stops on a recorder   [7]range of voice   [8]i.e., the recorder   [9]vex (with a pun alluding to the frets, or ridges, that guide the fingering on some instruments)   [10]*They fool . . . my bent* they compel me to play the fool to the limit of my capacity   [11]*by and by* very soon

'Tis now the very witching time of night,
520   When churchyards yawn, and hell itself breathes out
Contagion to this world. Now could I drink hot blood
And do such bitter business as the day
Would quake to look on. Soft, now to my mother.
O heart, lose not thy nature; let not ever
525   The soul of Nero[1] enter this firm bosom.
Let me be cruel, not unnatural;
I will speak daggers to her, but use none.
My tongue and soul in this be hypocrites:
How in my words somever she be shent,[2]
530   To give them seals[3] never, my soul, consent!   *Exit.*

Scene III. *The castle.*

Enter KING, ROSENCRANTZ, *and* GUILDENSTERN.

KING I like him not, nor stands it safe with us
To let his madness range. Therefore prepare you.
I your commission will forthwith dispatch,
And he to England shall along with you.
5   The terms[4] of our estate may not endure
Hazard so near's[5] as doth hourly grow
Out of his brows.
GUILDENSTERN   We will ourselves provide.
Most holy and religious fear it is
To keep those many many bodies safe
10   That live and feed upon your Majesty.
ROSENCRANTZ The single and peculiar[6] life is bound
With all the strength and armor of the mind
To keep itself from noyance,[7] but much more
That spirit upon whose weal depends and rests
15   The lives of many. The cess of majesty[8]
Dies not alone, but like a gulf[9] doth draw
What's near it with it; or it is a massy wheel
Fixed on the summit of the highest mount,
To whose huge spokes ten thousand lesser things
20   Are mortised and adjoined, which when it falls,
Each small annexment, petty consequence,
Attends[10] the boist'rous ruin. Never alone
Did the King sigh, but with a general groan.
KING Arm[11] you, I pray you, to this speedy voyage,
25   For we will fetters put about this fear,
Which now goes too free-footed.
ROSENCRANTZ   We will haste us.

                                                    Exeunt GENTLEMEN.

[1]Roman emperor who had his mother murdered   [2]rebuked   [3]*give them seals* confirm them
with deeds   [4]conditions   [5]near us   [6]individual, private   [7]injury   [8]*cess of majesty* cessation
(death) of a king   [9]whirlpool   [10]waits on, participates in   [11]prepare

Enter POLONIUS.

POLONIUS My lord, he's going to his mother's closet.
    Behind the arras I'll convey myself
    To hear the process.[1] I'll warrant she'll tax him home,[2]
30   And, as you said, and wisely was it said,
    'Tis meet that some more audience than a mother,
    Since nature makes them partial, should o'erhear
    The speech of vantage.[3] Fare you well, my liege.
    I'll call upon you ere you go to bed
    And tell you what I know.
35 KING   Thanks, dear my lord.

Exit [POLONIUS].

    O, my offense is rank, it smells to heaven;
    It hath the primal eldest curse[4] upon't,
    A brother's murder. Pray can I not,
    Though inclination be as sharp as will.
40   My stronger guilt defeats my strong intent,
    And like a man to double business bound
    I stand in pause where I shall first begin,
    And both neglect. What if this cursèd hand
    Were thicker than itself with brother's blood,
45   Is there not rain enough in the sweet heavens
    To wash it white as snow? Whereto serves mercy
    But to confront[5] the visage of offense?
    And what's in prayer but this twofold force,
    To be forestallèd ere we come to fall,
50   Or pardoned being down? Then I'll look up.
    My fault is past. But, O, what form of prayer
    Can serve my turn? "Forgive me my foul murder"?
    That cannot be, since I am still possessed
    Of those effects[6] for which I did the murder,
55   My crown, mine own ambition, and my queen.
    May one be pardoned and retain th' offense?
    In the corrupted currents of this world
    Offense's gilded hand may shove by justice,
    And oft 'tis seen the wicked prize itself
60   Buys out the law. But 'tis not so above.
    There is no shuffling;[7] there the action lies
    In his true nature, and we ourselves compelled
    Even to the teeth and forehead of our faults,
    To give in evidence. What then? What rests?[8]
65   Try what repentance can. What can it not?
    Yet what can it when one cannot repent?
    O wretched state! O bosom black as death!
    O limèd[9] soul, that struggling to be free

[1]proceedings   [2]*tax him home* censure him sharply   [3]*of vantage* from an advantageous place   [4]*primal eldest curse* curse of Cain, who killed Abel   [5]oppose   [6]things gained   [7]trickery   [8]remains   [9]caught (as with birdlime, a sticky substance spread on boughs to snare birds)

Art more engaged![1] Help, angels! Make assay.[2]
70   Bow, stubborn knees, and, heart with strings of steel,
Be soft as sinews of the newborn babe.
All may be well.   *He kneels.*

Enter HAMLET.

HAMLET   Now might I do it pat, now 'a is a-praying,
And now I'll do 't. And so 'a goes to heaven,
75   And so am I revenged. That would be scanned.[3]
A villain kills my father, and for that
I, his sole son, do this same villain send
To heaven.
Why, this is hire and salary, not revenge.
80   'A took my father grossly, full of bread,[4]
With all his crimes broad blown,[5] as flush[6] as May;
And how his audit[7] stands, who knows save heaven?
But in our circumstance and course of thought,
'Tis heavy with him; and am I then revenged,
85   To take him in the purging of his soul,
When he is fit and seasoned for his passage?
No.
Up, sword, and know thou a more horrid hent.[8]
When he is drunk asleep, or in his rage,
90   Or in th' incestuous pleasure of his bed,
At game a-swearing, or about some act
That has no relish[9] of salvation in 't—
Then trip him, that his heels may kick at heaven,
And that his soul may be as damned and black
95   As hell, whereto it goes. My mother stays.
This physic[10] but prolongs thy sickly days.   *Exit.*
KING [*Rises*]   My words fly up, my thoughts remain below.
Words without thoughts never to heaven go.   *Exit.*

Scene IV. *The Queen's closet.*

Enter [QUEEN] GERTRUDE *and* POLONIUS.

POLONIUS   'A will come straight. Look you lay home[11] to him.
Tell him his pranks have been too broad[12] to bear with,
And that your Grace hath screened and stood between
Much heat and him. I'll silence me even here.
5   Pray you be round with him.
HAMLET [*Within*]   Mother, Mother, Mother!
QUEEN   I'll warrant you; fear me not. Withdraw; I hear him coming.

POLONIUS *hides behind the arras.*

---

[1]ensnared   [2]an attempt   [3]*would be scanned* ought to be looked into   [4]i.e., worldly gratification   [5]*crimes broad blown* sins in full bloom   [6]vigorous   [7]account   [8]grasp (here, occasion
for seizing)   [9]flavor   [10]Claudius' purgation by prayer, as Hamlet thinks in line 85   [11]*lay
home* thrust (rebuke) him sharply   [12]unrestrained

Enter HAMLET.

HAMLET Now, Mother, what's the matter?
10 QUEEN Hamlet, thou hast thy father much offended.
HAMLET Mother, you have my father much offended.
QUEEN Come, come, you answer with an idle[1] tongue.
HAMLET Go, go, you question with a wicked tongue.
QUEEN Why, how now, Hamlet?
HAMLET   What's the matter now?
QUEEN Have you forgot me?
15 HAMLET   No, by the rood,[2] not so!
    You are the Queen, your husband's brother's wife,
    And would it were not so, you are my mother.
QUEEN Nay, then I'll set those to you that can speak.
HAMLET Come, come, and sit you down. You shall not budge.
20   You go not till I set you up a glass[3]
    Where you may see the inmost part of you!
QUEEN What wilt thou do? Thou wilt not murder me?
    Help, ho!
POLONIUS [*Behind*] What, ho! Help!
25 HAMLET [*Draws*] How now? A rat? Dead for a ducat, dead!

    [*Makes a pass through the arras and*] *kills* POLONIUS.

POLONIUS [*Behind*] O, I am slain!
QUEEN   O me, what hast thou done?
HAMLET Nay, I know not. Is it the King?
QUEEN O, what a rash and bloody deed is this!
HAMLET A bloody deed—almost as bad, good Mother,
30   As kill a king, and marry with his brother.
QUEEN As kill a king?
HAMLET   Ay, lady, it was my word.

                          [*Lifts up the arras and sees* POLONIUS.]

    Thou wretched, rash, intruding fool, farewell!
    I took thee for thy better. Take thy fortune.
    Thou find'st to be too busy is some danger.—
35   Leave wringing of your hands. Peace, sit you down
    And let me wring your heart, for so I shall
    If it be made of penetrable stuff,
    If damnèd custom have not brazed[4] it so
    That it be proof[5] and bulwark against sense.[6]
40 QUEEN What have I done that thou dar'st wag thy tongue
    In noise so rude against me?
HAMLET   Such an act
    That blurs the grace and blush of modesty,
    Calls virtue hypocrite, takes off the rose
    From the fair forehead of an innocent love,

---

[1]foolish [2]cross [3]mirror [4]hardened like brass [5]armor [6]feeling

45   And sets a blister[1] there, makes marriage vows
        As false as dicers' oaths. O, such a deed
        As from the body of contraction[2] plucks
        The very soul, and sweet religion makes
        A rhapsody[3] of words! Heaven's face does glow
50   O'er this solidity and compound mass
        With heated visage, as against the doom
        Is thoughtsick at the act.[4]
        QUEEN   Ay me, what act,
        That roars so loud and thunders in the index?[5]
        HAMLET Look here upon this picture, and on this,
55   The counterfeit presentment[6] of two brothers.
        See what a grace was seated on this brow:
        Hyperion's curls, the front[7] of Jove himself,
        An eye like Mars, to threaten and command,
        A station[8] like the herald Mercury
60   New lighted on a heaven-kissing hill—
        A combination and a form indeed
        Where every god did seem to set his seal
        To give the world assurance of a man.
        This was your husband. Look you now what follows.
65   Here is your husband, like a mildewed ear
        Blasting his wholesome brother. Have you eyes?
        Could you on this fair mountain leave to feed,
        And batten[9] on this moor? Ha! Have you eyes?
        You cannot call it love, for at your age
70   The heyday[10] in the blood is tame, it's humble,
        And waits upon the judgment, and what judgment
        Would step from this to this? Sense[11] sure you have,
        Else could you not have motion, but sure that sense
        Is apoplexed,[12] for madness would not err,
75   Nor sense to ecstasy[13] was ne'er so thralled
        But it reserved some quantity of choice
        To serve in such a difference. What devil was't
        That thus hath cozened you at hoodman-blind?[14]
        Eyes without feeling, feeling without sight,
80   Ears without hands or eyes, smelling sans[15] all,
        Or but a sickly part of one true sense
        Could not so mope.[16]
        O shame, where is thy blush? Rebellious hell,
        If thou canst mutine in a matron's bones,
85   To flaming youth let virtue be as wax
        And melt in her own fire. Proclaim no shame

[1]*sets a blister* brands (as a harlot)   [2]marriage contract   [3]senseless string   [4]*Heaven's face
. . . the act* i.e., the face of heaven blushes over this earth (compounded of four elements), the face
hot, as if Judgment Day were near, and it is thoughtsick at the act   [5]prologue   [6]*counterfeit
presentment* represented image   [7]forehead   [8]bearing   [9]feed gluttonously   [10]excitement
[11]feeling   [12]paralyzed   [13]madness   [14]*cozened you at hoodman-blind* cheated you at blindman's
buff   [15]without   [16]be stupid

When the compulsive ardor[1] gives the charge,
Since frost itself as actively doth burn,
And reason panders will.[2]
QUEEN   O Hamlet, speak no more.
90   Thou turn'st mine eyes into my very soul,
And there I see such black and grainèd[3] spots
As will not leave their tinct.[4]
HAMLET   Nay, but to live
In the rank sweat of an enseamèd[5] bed,
Stewed in corruption, honeying and making love
Over the nasty sty—
95   QUEEN   O, speak to me no more.
These words like daggers enter in my ears.
No more, sweet Hamlet.
HAMLET   A murderer and a villain,
A slave that is not twentieth part the tithe[6]
Of your precedent lord, a vice[7] of kings,
100   A cutpurse of the empire and the rule,
That from a shelf the precious diadem stole
And put it in his pocket—
QUEEN   No more.

Enter GHOST.

HAMLET   A king of shreds and patches—
Save me and hover o'er me with your wings,
105   You heavenly guards! What would your gracious figure?
QUEEN   Alas, he's mad.
HAMLET   Do you not come your tardy son to chide,
That, lapsed in time and passion, lets go by
Th' important acting of your dread command?
110   O, say!
GHOST   Do not forget. This visitation
Is but to whet thy almost blunted purpose.
But look, amazement on thy mother sits.
O, step between her and her fighting soul!
115   Conceit[8] in weakest bodies strongest works.
Speak to her, Hamlet.
HAMLET   How is it with you, lady?
QUEEN   Alas, how is't with you,
That you do bend your eye on vacancy,
And with th' incorporal[9] air do hold discourse?
120   Forth at your eyes your spirits wildly peep,
And as the sleeping soldiers in th' alarm

---

[1]*compulsive ardor* compelling passion   [2]*reason panders will* reason acts as a procurer for desire   [3]dyed in grain (fast dyed)   [4]color   [5]perhaps "soaked in grease," i.e., sweaty; perhaps "much wrinkled"   [6]tenth part   [7]like the Vice, a fool and mischief-maker in the old morality plays   [8]imagination   [9]bodiless

Your bedded hair[1] like life in excrements[2]
Start up and stand an end.[3] O gentle son,
Upon the heat and flame of thy distemper
125 Sprinkle cool patience. Whereon do you look?
HAMLET On him, on him! Look you, how pale he glares!
His form and cause conjoined, preaching to stones,
Would make them capable.[4]—Do not look upon me,
Lest with this piteous action you convert
130 My stern effects.[5] Then what I have to do
Will want true color; tears perchance for blood.
QUEEN To whom do you speak this?
HAMLET   Do you see nothing there?
QUEEN Nothing at all; yet all that is I see.
HAMLET Nor did you nothing hear?
QUEEN   No, nothing but ourselves.
135 HAMLET Why, look you there! Look how it steals away!
My father, in his habit[6] as he lived!
Look where he goes even now out at the portal!

Exit GHOST.

QUEEN This is the very coinage of your brain.
This bodiless creation ecstasy
Is very cunning in.
140 HAMLET   Ecstasy?
My pulse as yours doth temperately keep time
And makes as healthful music. It is not madness
That I have uttered. Bring me to the test,
And I the matter will reword, which madness
145 Would gambol[7] from. Mother, for love of grace,
Lay not that flattering unction[8] to your soul,
That not your trespass but my madness speaks.
It will but skin and film the ulcerous place
Whiles rank corruption, mining[9] all within,
150 Infects unseen. Confess yourself to heaven,
Repent what's past, avoid what is to come,
And do not spread the compost[10] on the weeds
To make them ranker. Forgive me this my virtue.
For in the fatness of these pursy[11] times
155 Virtue itself of vice must pardon beg,
Yea, curb[12] and woo for leave to do him good.
QUEEN O Hamlet, thou hast cleft my heart in twain.
HAMLET O, throw away the worser part of it,
And live the purer with the other half.
160 Good night—but go not to my uncle's bed.

---

[1]*bedded hair* hairs laid flat   [2]outgrowths (here, the hair)   [3]*an end* on end   [4]receptive
[5]*convert/My stern effects* divert my stern deeds   [6]garment (the First Quarto is probably correct in
saying that at line 102 the ghost enters "in his nightgown," i.e., dressing gown)   [7]start
away   [8]ointment   [9]undermining   [10]fertilizing substance   [11]bloated   [12]bow low

Assume a virtue, if you have it not.
That monster custom, who all sense doth eat,
Of habits devil, is angel yet in this,
That to the use[1] of actions fair and good

165   He likewise gives a frock or livery[2]
That aptly is put on. Refrain tonight,
And that shall lend a kind of easiness
To the next abstinence; the next more easy;
For use almost can change the stamp of nature,

170   And either[3] the devil, or throw him out
With wondrous potency. Once more, good night,
And when you are desirous to be blest,
I'll blessing beg of you.—For this same lord,
I do repent; but heaven hath pleased it so,

175   To punish me with this, and this with me,
That I must be their[4] scourge and minister.
I will bestow[5] him and will answer well
The death I gave him. So again, good night.
I must be cruel only to be kind.

180   Thus bad begins, and worse remains behind.
One word more, good lady.
QUEEN   What shall I do?
HAMLET Not this, by no means, that I bid you do:
Let the bloat King tempt you again to bed,
Pinch wanton on your cheek, call you his mouse,

185   And let him, for a pair of reechy[6] kisses,
Or paddling in your neck with his damned fingers,
Make you to ravel[7] all this matter out,
That I essentially am not in madness,
But mad in craft. 'Twere good you let him know,

190   For who that's but a queen, fair, sober, wise,
Would from a paddock,[8] from a bat, a gib,[9]
Such dear concernings hide? Who would do so?
No, in despite of sense and secrecy,
Unpeg the basket on the house's top,

195   Let the birds fly, and like the famous ape,
To try conclusions,[10] in the basket creep
And break your own neck down.
QUEEN Be thou assured, if words be made of breath,
And breath of life, I have no life to breathe

200   What thou hast said to me.
HAMLET I must to England; you know that?
QUEEN   Alack,
I had forgot. 'Tis so concluded on.
HAMLET There's letters sealed, and my two schoolfellows,

---

[1]practice   [2]characteristic garment (punning on "habits" in line 163)   [3]probably a word is missing after *either;* among suggestions are "master," "curb," and "house"; but possibly *either* is a verb meaning "make easier"   [4]i.e., the heavens'   [5]stow, lodge   [6]foul (literally "smoky")   [7]unravel, reveal   [8]toad   [9]tomcat   [10]*To try conclusions* to make experiments

Whom I will trust as I will adders fanged,
205   They bear the mandate;[1] they must sweep my way
And marshal me to knavery. Let it work;
For 'tis the sport to have the enginer
Hoist with his own petar,[2] and 't shall go hard
But I will delve one yard below their mines
210   And blow them at the moon. O, 'tis most sweet
When in one line two crafts[3] directly meet.
This man shall set me packing:
I'll lug the guts into the neighbor room.
Mother, good night. Indeed, this counselor
215   Is now most still, most secret, and most grave,
Who was in life a foolish prating knave.
Come, sir, to draw toward an end with you.
Good night, Mother.

                [*Exit the* QUEEN. *Then*] exit HAMLET, *tugging in* POLONIUS.

Act IV, Scene I. *The castle.*

Enter KING *and* QUEEN, *with* ROSENCRANTZ *and* GUILDENSTERN.

KING There's matter in these sighs. These profound heaves
    You must translate; 'tis fit we understand them.
    Where is your son?
QUEEN Bestow this place on us a little while.

                [*Exeunt* ROSENCRANTZ *and* GUILDENSTERN.]

5   Ah, mine own lord, what have I seen tonight!
KING What, Gertrude? How does Hamlet?
QUEEN Mad as the sea and wind when both contend
    Which is the mightier. In his lawless fit,
    Behind the arras hearing something stir,
10   Whips out his rapier, cries, "A rat, a rat!"
    And in this brainish apprehension[4] kills
    The unseen good old man.
KING   O heavy deed!
    It had been so with us, had we been there.
    His liberty is full of threats to all,
15   To you yourself, to us, to every one.
    Alas, how shall this bloody deed be answered?
    It will be laid to us, whose providence[5]
    Should have kept short, restrained, and out of haunt[6]
    This mad young man. But so much was our love
20   We would not understand what was most fit,
    But, like the owner of a foul disease,
    To keep it from divulging, let it feed

---

[1]command   [2]bomb   [3](1) boats (2) acts of guile, crafty schemes   [4]*brainish apprehension* mad
imagination   [5]foresight   [6]*out of haunt* away from association with others

Even on the pith of life. Where is he gone?
QUEEN   To draw apart the body he hath killed;
25   O'er whom his very madness, like some ore
        Among a mineral[1] of metals base,
        Shows itself pure. 'A weeps for what is done.
      KING   O Gertrude, come away!
        The sun no sooner shall the mountains touch
30   But we will ship him hence, and this vile deed
        We must with all our majesty and skill
        Both countenance and excuse. Ho, Guildenstern!

        Enter ROSENCRANTZ *and* GUILDENSTERN.

        Friends both, go join you with some further aid:
        Hamlet in madness hath Polonius slain,
35   And from his mother's closet hath he dragged him.
        Go seek him out; speak fair, and bring the body
        Into the chapel. I pray you haste in this.

                                [*Exeunt* ROSENCRANTZ *and* GUILDENSTERN.]

        Come, Gertrude, we'll call up our wisest friends
        And let them know both what we mean to do
40   And what's untimely done . . .[2]
        Whose whisper o'er the world's diameter,
        As level as the cannon to his blank[3]
        Transports his poisoned shot, may miss our name
        And hit the woundless[4] air. O, come away!
45   My soul is full of discord and dismay.   *Exeunt.*

Scene II. *The castle.*

        Enter HAMLET.

HAMLET   Safely stowed.
GENTLEMEN [*Within*]   Hamlet! Lord Hamlet!
HAMLET   But soft, what noise? Who calls on Hamlet?
        O, here they come.

        Enter ROSENCRANTZ *and* GUILDENSTERN.

5   ROSENCRANTZ   What have you done, my lord, with the dead body?
      HAMLET   Compounded it with dust, whereto 'tis kin.
      ROSENCRANTZ   Tell us where 'tis, that we may take it thence
        And bear it to the chapel.
      HAMLET   Do not believe it.
10   ROSENCRANTZ   Believe what?

---

[1]*ore/Among a mineral* vein of gold in a mine   [2]*done* . . . (evidently something has dropped out of the text. Capell's conjecture, "So, haply slander," is usually printed)   [3]white center of a target   [4]invulnerable

HAMLET That I can keep your counsel and not mine own. Besides, to be demanded of[1] a sponge, what replication[2] should be made by the son of a king?

ROSENCRANTZ Take you me for a sponge, my lord?

HAMLET Ay, sir, that soaks up the King's countenance,[3] his rewards, his au-
15   thorities. But such officers do the King best service in the end. He keeps them,
like an ape, in the corner of his jaw, first mouthed, to be last swallowed. When
he needs what you have gleaned, it is but squeezing you and, sponge, you shall
be dry again.

ROSENCRANTZ I understand you not, my lord.

20 HAMLET I am glad of it: a knavish speech sleeps in a foolish ear.

ROSENCRANTZ My lord, you must tell us where the body is and go with us to the
King.

HAMLET The body is with the King, but the King is not with the body. The King
is a thing—

25 GUILDENSTERN A thing, my lord?

HAMLET Of nothing. Bring me to him. Hide fox, and all after.[4]   *Exeunt.*

Scene III. *The castle.*

Enter KING, and two or three.

KING I have sent to seek him and to find the body:
How dangerous is it that this man goes loose!
Yet must not we put the strong law on him:
He's loved of the distracted[5] multitude,
5 Who like not in their judgment, but their eyes,
And where 'tis so, th' offender's scourge is weighed,
But never the offense. To bear[6] all smooth and even,
This sudden sending him away must seem
Deliberate pause.[7] Diseases desperate grown
10 By desperate appliance are relieved,
Or not at all.

Enter ROSENCRANTZ, [GUILDENSTERN,] and all the rest.

         How now? What hath befall'n?

ROSENCRANTZ Where the dead body is bestowed, my lord,
We cannot get from him.

KING   But where is he?

ROSENCRANTZ Without, my lord; guarded, to know your pleasure.

KING Bring him before us.

15 ROSENCRANTZ   Ho! Bring in the lord.

    They enter.

KING Now, Hamlet, where's Polonius?

---

[1]*demanded of* questioned by   [2]reply   [3]favor   [4]*Hide fox, and all after* (a cry in a game such
as hide-and-seek; Hamlet runs from the stage)   [5]bewildered, senseless   [6]carry out   [7]planning

HAMLET At supper.

KING At supper? Where?

HAMLET Not where he eats, but where 'a is eaten. A certain convocation of
20   politic[1] worms are e'en at him. Your worm is your only emperor for diet. We fat
        all creatures else to fat us, and we fat ouselves for maggots. Your fat king and
        your lean beggar is but variable service[2]—two dishes, but to one table. That's
        the end.

KING Alas, alas!

25 HAMLET A man may fish with the worm that hath eat of a king, and eat of the
        fish that hath fed of that worm.

KING What dost thou mean by this?

HAMLET Nothing but to show you how a king may go a progress[3] through the
        guts of a beggar.

30 KING Where is Polonius?

HAMLET In heaven. Send thither to see. If your messenger find him not there,
        seek him i' th' other place yourself. But if indeed you find him not within this
        month, you shall nose him as you go up the stairs into the lobby.

KING [to ATTENDANTS] Go seek him there.

35 HAMLET 'A will stay till you come.

[Exeunt ATTENDANTS.]

KING Hamlet, this deed, for thine especial safety,
        Which we do tender[4] as we dearly grieve
        For that which thou hast done, must send thee hence
        With fiery quickness. Therefore prepare thyself.
40   The bark is ready and the wind at help,
        Th' associates tend,[5] and everything is bent
        For England.

HAMLET   For England?

KING   Ay, Hamlet.

HAMLET   Good.

KING So is it, if thou knew'st our purposes.

HAMLET I see a cherub[6] that sees them. But come, for England! Farewell, dear
45   Mother.

KING Thy loving father, Hamlet.

HAMLET My mother—father and mother is man and wife, man and wife is one
        flesh, and so, my mother. Come, for England!   Exit.

KING Follow him at foot;[7] tempt him with speed aboard.
50   Delay it not; I'll have him hence tonight.
        Away! For everything is sealed and done
        That else leans[8] on th' affair. Pray you make haste.

[Exeunt all but the KING.]

And, England, if my love thou hold'st at aught—
        As my great power thereof may give thee sense,
55   Since yet thy cicatrice[9] looks raw and red

---

[1]statesmanlike, shrewd   [2]*variable service* different courses   [3]royal journey   [4]hold dear
[5]wait   [6]angel of knowledge   [7]*at foot* closely   [8]depends   [9]scar

After the Danish sword, and thy free awe[1]
Pays homage to us—thou mayst not coldly set
Our sovereign process,[2] which imports at full
By letters congruing to that effect
60   The present[3] death of Hamlet. Do it, England,
For like the hectic[4] in my blood he rages,
And thou must cure me. Till I know 'tis done,
Howe'er my haps,[5] my joys were ne'er begun.

                                                                                        Exit.

Scene IV. *A plain in Denmark.*

Enter FORTINBRAS *with his Army over the stage.*

FORTINBRAS   Go, Captain, from me greet the Danish king.
Tell him that by his license Fortinbras
Craves the conveyance of[6] a promised march
Over his kingdom. You know the rendezvous.
5   If that his Majesty would aught with us,
We shall express our duty in his eye;[7]
And let him know so.
CAPTAIN   I will do't, my lord.
FORTINBRAS   Go softly[8] on.

                                         [*Exeunt all but the* CAPTAIN.]

Enter HAMLET, ROSENCRANTZ, &c.

HAMLET   Good sir, whose powers[9] are these?
10   CAPTAIN   They are of Norway, sir.
HAMLET   How purposed, sir, I pray you?
CAPTAIN   Against some part of Poland.
HAMLET   Who commands them, sir?
CAPTAIN   The nephew to old Norway, Fortinbras.
15   HAMLET   Goes it against the main[10] of Poland, sir,
Or for some frontier?
CAPTAIN   Truly to speak, and with no addition,[11]
We go to gain a little patch of ground
That hath in it no profit but the name.
20   To pay five ducats, five, I would not farm it,
Nor will it yield to Norway or the Pole
A ranker[12] rate, should it be sold in fee.[13]
HAMLET   Why, then the Polack never will defend it.
CAPTAIN   Yes, it is already garrisoned.
25   HAMLET   Two thousand souls and twenty thousand ducats

---

[1]*free awe* uncompelled submission   [2]*coldly set/Our sovereign process* regard slightly our royal command   [3]instant   [4]fever   [5]chances, fortunes   [6]*conveyance of* escort for   [7]*in his eye* before his eyes (i.e., in his presence)   [8]slowly   [9]forces   [10]main part   [11]*with no addition* plainly   [12]higher   [13]*in fee* outright

Will not debate[1] the question of this straw.
This is th' imposthume[2] of much wealth and peace,
That inward breaks, and shows no cause without
Why the man dies. I humbly thank you, sir.
CAPTAIN   God bye you, sir.   *Exit.*
30   ROSENCRANTZ   Will't please you go, my lord?
HAMLET   I'll be with you straight. Go a little before.

                                             [*Exeunt all but* HAMLET.]

How all occasions do inform against me
And spur my dull revenge! What is a man,
If his chief good and market[3] of his time
35   Be but to sleep and feed? A beast, no more.
Sure he that made us with such large discourse,[4]
Looking before and after, gave us not
That capability and godlike reason
To fust[5] in us unused. Now, whether it be
40   Bestial oblivion,[6] or some craven scruple
Of thinking too precisely on th' event[7]—
A thought which, quartered, hath but one part wisdom
And ever three parts coward—I do not know
Why yet I live to say, "This thing's to do,"
45   Sith I have cause, and will, and strength, and means
To do't. Examples gross[8] as earth exhort me.
Witness this army of such mass and charge,[9]
Led by a delicate and tender prince,
Whose spirit, with divine ambition puffed,
50   Makes mouths at the invisible event,[10]
Exposing what is mortal and unsure
To all that fortune, death, and danger dare,
Even for an eggshell. Rightly to be great
Is not[11] to stir without great argument,[12]
55   But greatly[13] to find quarrel in a straw
When honor's at the stake. How stand I then,
That have a father killed, a mother stained,
Excitements[14] of my reason and my blood,
And let all sleep, while to my shame I see
60   The imminent death of twenty thousand men
That for a fantasy and trick of fame[15]
Go to their graves like beds, fight for a plot
Whereon the numbers cannot try the cause,
Which is not tomb enough and continent[16]
65   To hide the slain? O, from this time forth,
My thoughts be bloody, or be nothing worth!   *Exit.*

[1]settle   [2]abscess, ulcer   [3]profit   [4]understanding   [5]grow moldy   [6]forgetfulness
[7]outcome   [8]large, obvious   [9]expense   [10]*Makes mouths at the invisible event* makes
scornful faces (is contemptuous of) the unseen outcome   [11]the sense seems to require "not
not"   [12]reason   [13]i.e., nobly   [14]incentives   [15]*fantasy and trick of fame* illusion and trifle of
reputation   [16]receptacle, container

Scene V. *The castle.*

Enter HORATIO, [QUEEN] GERTRUDE, *and a* GENTLEMAN.

QUEEN   I will not speak with her.
GENTLEMAN   She is importunate, indeed distract.
  Her mood will needs be pitied.
QUEEN   What would she have?
GENTLEMAN   She speaks much of her father, says she hears
5   There's tricks i' th' world, and hems, and beats her heart,
     Spurns enviously at straws,¹ speaks things in doubt²
     That carry but half sense. Her speech is nothing,
     Yet the unshapèd use of it doth move
     The hearers to collection;³ they yawn⁴ at it,
10   And botch the words up fit to their own thoughts,
     Which, as her winks and nods and gestures yield them,
     Indeed would make one think there might be thought,
     Though nothing sure, yet much unhappily.
HORATIO   'Twere good she were spoken with, for she may strew
15   Dangerous conjectures in ill-breeding minds.
QUEEN   Let her come in.   [*Exit* GENTLEMAN.]
     [*Aside*] To my sick soul (as sin's true nature is)
     Each toy seems prologue to some great amiss;⁵
     So full of artless jealousy⁶ is guilt
20   It spills⁷ itself in fearing to be spilt.

     Enter OPHELIA [*distracted.*]

OPHELIA   Where is the beauteous majesty of Denmark?
QUEEN   How now, Ophelia?
OPHELIA *(She sings.)*   How should I your truelove know
      From another one?
25   By his cockle hat⁸ and staff
      And his sandal shoon.⁹
QUEEN   Alas, sweet lady, what imports this song?
OPHELIA   Say you? Nay, pray you mark.
     He is dead and gone, lady,   *(Song)*
30   He is dead and gone;
     At his head a grass-green turf,
      At his heels a stone.
     O, ho!
QUEEN   Nay, but Ophelia—
35   OPHELIA   Pray you mark.
     [*Sings.*] White his shroud as the mountain snow—

---

¹*Spurns enviously at straws* objects spitefully to insignificant matters   ²*in doubt*
uncertainly   ³*Yet the . . . to collection* i.e., yet the formless manner of it moves her listeners to
gather up some sort of meaning   ⁴gape (?)   ⁵misfortune   ⁶*artless jealousy* crude suspicion
⁷destroys   ⁸*cockle hat* (a cockleshell on the hat was the sign of a pilgrim who had journeyed
to shrines overseas. The association of lovers and pilgrims was a common one.)   ⁹shoes

Enter KING.

QUEEN Alas, look here, my lord.
OPHELIA Larded[1] all with sweet flowers   *(Song)*
    Which bewept to the grave did not go
40   With truelove showers.
KING How do you, pretty lady?
OPHELIA Well, God dild[2] you! They say the owl was a baker's daughter.[3] Lord,
    we know what we are, but know not what we may be. God be at your table!
KING Conceit[4] upon her father.
45 OPHELIA Pray let's have no words of this, but when they ask you what it means,
    say you this:
      Tomorrow is Saint Valentine's day.[5]   *(Song)*
        All in the morning betime,
    And I a maid at your window,
50   To be your Valentine.

    Then up he rose and donned his clothes
      And dupped[6] the chamber door,
    Let in the maid, that out a maid
      Never departed more.
55 KING Pretty Ophelia
OPHELIA Indeed, la, without an oath, I'll make an end on't:
    [*Sings.*] By Gis[7] and by Saint Charity,
        Alack, and fie for shame!
      Young men will do't if they come to't,
60   By Cock,[8] they are to blame.
      Quoth she, "Before you tumbled me,
        You promised me to wed."
    He answers:
      "So would I 'a' done, by yonder sun,
65   An thou hadst not come to my bed."
KING How long hath she been thus?
OPHELIA I hope all will be well. We must be patient, but I cannot choose but
    weep to think they would lay him i' th' cold ground. My brother shall know of
    it; and so I thank you for your good counsel. Come, my coach! Good night,
70   ladies, good night. Sweet ladies, good night, good night.   *Exit.*
KING Follow her close; give her good watch, I pray you.   [*Exit* HORATIO.]
    O, this is the poison of deep grief; it springs
    All from her father's death—and now behold!
    O Gertrude, Gertrude,
75   When sorrows come, they come not single spies,
    But in battalions: first, her father slain;
    Next, your son gone, and he most violent author
    Of his own just remove; the people muddied,[9]
    Thick and unwholesome in their thoughts and whispers

---

[1]decorated   [2]yield, i.e., reward   [3]*baker's daughter* (an allusion to a tale of a baker's daughter
who begrudged bread to Christ and was turned into an owl)   [4]brooding   [5]*Saint Valentine's
day* Feb. 14 (the notion was that a bachelor would become the truelove of the first girl he saw on
this day)   [6]opened (did up)   [7]contraction of "Jesus"   [8](1) God (2) phallus   [9]muddled

80   For good Polonius' death, and we have done but greenly[1]
      In huggermugger[2] to inter him; poor Ophelia
      Divided from herself and her fair judgment,
      Without the which we are pictures or mere beasts;
      Last, and as much containing as all these,
85   Her brother is in secret come from France,
      Feeds on his wonder,[3] keeps himself in clouds,
      And wants not buzzers[4] to infect his ear
      With pestilent speeches of his father's death,
      Wherein necessity, of matter beggared,[5]
90   Will nothing stick[6] our person to arraign
      In ear and ear. O my dear Gertrude, this,
      Like to a murd'ring piece,[7] in many places
      Gives me superfluous death.   *A noise within.*

      Enter a MESSENGER.

      QUEEN   Alack, what noise is this?
95   KING   Attend, where are my Switzers?[8] Let them guard the door.
      What is the matter?
      MESSENGER   Save yourself, my lord.
      The ocean, overpeering of his list,[9]
      Eats not the flats with more impiteous haste
      Than young Laertes, in a riotous head,[10]
100   O'erbears your officers. The rabble call him lord,
      And, as the world were now but to begin,
      Antiquity forgot, custom not known,
      The ratifiers and props of every word,
      They cry, "Choose we! Laertes shall be king!"
105   Caps, hands, and tongues applaud it to the clouds
      "Laertes shall be king! Laertes king!"   *A noise within.*
      QUEEN   How cheerfully on the false trail they cry!
      O, this is counter,[11] you false Danish dogs!

      Enter LAERTES *with others.*

      KING   The doors are broke.
110   LAERTES   Where is this king?—Sirs, stand you all without.
      ALL   No, let's come in.
      LAERTES   I pray you give me leave.
      ALL.   We will, we will.
      LAERTES   I thank you. Keep the door. [*Exeunt his Followers.*] O thou vile King,
      Give me my father.
115   QUEEN   Calmly, good Laertes.
      LAERTES   That drop of blood that's calm proclaims me bastard,
      Cries cuckold[12] to my father, brands the harlot

---

[1]foolishly   [2]secret haste   [3]suspicion   [4]*wants not buzzers* does not lack talebearers   [5]*of matter beggared* unprovided with facts   [6]*Will nothing stick* will not hesitate   [7]*murd'ring piece* (a cannon that shot a kind of shrapnel)   [8]Swiss guards   [9]shore   [10]*in a riotous head* with a rebellious force   [11]a hound runs counter when he follows the scent backward from the prey   [12]man whose wife is unfaithful

Even here between the chaste unsmirchèd brow
Of my true mother.

120   KING   What is the cause, Laertes,
That thy rebellion looks so giantlike?
Let him go, Gertrude. Do not fear[1] our person.
There's such divinity doth hedge a king
That treason can but peep to[2] what it would,

125   Acts little of his will. Tell me, Laertes,
Why thou art thus incensed. Let him go, Gertrude.
Speak, man.

LAERTES   Where is my father?

KING   Dead.

QUEEN   But not by him.

KING   Let him demand his fill.

130   LAERTES   How came he dead? I'll not be juggled with.
To hell allegiance, vows to the blackest devil,
Conscience and grace to the profound pit!
I dare damnation. To this point I stand,
That both the worlds I give to negligence,[3]

135   Let come what comes, only I'll be revenged
Most throughly for my father.

KING   Who shall stay you?

LAERTES   My will, not all the world's.
And for my means, I'll husband them[4] so well
They shall go far with little.

KING   Good Laertes,

140   If you desire to know the certainty
Of your dear father, is't writ in your revenge
That swoopstake[5] you will draw both friend and foe,
Winner and loser?

LAERTES   None but his enemies.

KING   Will you know them then?

145   LAERTES   To his good friends thus wide I'll ope my arms
And like the kind life-rend'ring pelican[6]
Repast[7] them with my blood.

KING   Why, now you speak
Like a good child and a true gentleman.
That I am guiltless of your father's death,

150   And am most sensibly[8] in grief for it,
It shall as level to your judgment 'pear
As day does to your eye.

A noise within: "Let her come in."

LAERTES   How now? What noise is that?

Enter OPHELIA.

---

[1]fear for   [2]*peep to* i.e., look at from a distance   [3]*That both . . . to negligence* i.e., I care not what may happen (to me) in this world or the next   [4]*husband them* use them economically   [5]in a clean sweep   [6]thought to feed its young with its own blood   [7]feed   [8]acutely

O heat, dry up my brains; tears seven times salt
155   Burn out the sense and virtue[1] of mine eye!
By heaven, thy madness shall be paid with weight
Till our scale turn the beam.[2] O rose of May,
Dear maid, kind sister, sweet Ophelia!
O heavens, is't possible a young maid's wits
160   Should be as mortal as an old man's life?
Nature is fine[3] in love, and where 'tis fine,
It sends some precious instance[4] of itself
After the thing it loves.
OPHELIA   They bore him barefaced on the bier   *(Song)*
165   Hey non nony, nony, hey nony
                    And in his grave rained many a tear—
Fare you well, my dove!
LAERTES   Hadst thou thy wits, and didst persuade revenge,
It could not move thus.
170   OPHELIA   You must sing "A-down a-down, and you call him a-down-a." O, how
        the wheel[5] becomes it! It is the false steward, that stole his master's daughter.
LAERTES   This nothing's more than matter.[6]
OPHELIA   There's rosemary, that's for remembrance. Pray you, love, remember.
And there is pansies, that's for thoughts.
175   LAERTES   A document[7] in madness, thoughts and remembrance fitted.
OPHELIA   There's fennel[8] for you, and columbines. There's rue for you, and here's
        some for me. We may call it herb of grace o' Sundays. O, you must wear your
        rue with a difference. There's a daisy. I would give you some violets, but they
        withered all when my father died. They say 'a made a good end. [*Sings*] For
180   bonny sweet Robin is all my joy.
LAERTES   Thought and affliction, passion, hell itself,
She turns to favor[9] and to prettiness.
OPHELIA   And will 'a not come again?   *(Song)*
                    And will 'a not come again?
185   No, no, he is dead,
                    Go to thy deathbed,
                    He never will come again.

                    His beard was as white as snow,
190   All flaxen was his poll.[10]
                    He is gone, he is gone,
                    And we cast away moan.
                    God 'a' mercy on his soul!
And of all Christian souls, I pray God, God bye you.

                                                                Exit.

[1]power   [2]*turn the beam* weigh down the bar (of the balance)   [3]refined, delicate   [4]sample
[5]of uncertain meaning, but probably a turn or dance of Ophelia's, rather than Fortune's wheel
[6]*This nothing's more than matter* this nonsense has more meaning than matters of consequence
[7]lesson   [8]The distribution of flowers in the ensuing lines has symbolic meaning, but the
meaning is disputed. Perhaps *fennel,* flattery; *columbines,* cuckoldry; *rue,* sorrow for Ophelia
and repentance for the Queen; *daisy,* dissembling; *violets,* faithfulness. For other interpretations,
see J. W. Lever in *Review of English Studies,* New Series 3 [1952], pp. 123-29.
[9]charm, beauty   [10]*All flaxen was his poll* white as flax was his head

LAERTES Do you see this, O God?

195 KING Laertes, I must commune with your grief,
Or you deny me right. Go but apart,
Make choice of whom your wisest friends you will,
And they shall hear and judge 'twixt you and me.
If by direct or by collateral[1] hand
200 They find us touched,[2] we will our kingdom give,
Our crown, our life, and all that we call ours,
To you in satisfaction; but if not,
Be you content to lend your patience to us,
And we shall jointly labor with your soul
205 To give it due content.

LAERTES   Let this be so.
His means of death, his obscure funeral—
No trophy, sword, nor hatchment[3] o'er his bones,
No noble rite nor formal ostentation[4]—
Cry to be heard, as 'twere from heaven to earth,
210 That I must call't in question.

KING   So you shall;
And where th' offense is, let the great ax fall.
I pray you go with me.   *Exeunt.*

Scene VI. *The castle.*

Enter HORATIO *and others.*

HORATIO What are they that would speak with me?
GENTLEMAN Seafaring men, sir. They say they have letters for you.
HORATIO Let them come in.   [*Exit* ATTENDANT.]
5 I do not know from what part of the world
I should be greeted, if not from Lord Hamlet.

Enter SAILORS.

SAILOR God bless you, sir.
HORATIO Let Him bless thee too.
SAILOR 'A shall, sir, an't please Him. There's a letter for you, sir—it came from
10 th' ambassador that was bound for England—if your name be Horatio, as I am
let to know it is.
HORATIO [*Reads the letter.*] "Horatio, when thou shalt have overlooked[5] this,
give these fellows some means to the King. They have letters for him. Ere we
were two days old at sea, a pirate of very warlike appointment[6] gave us chase.
15 Finding ourselves too slow of sail, we put on a compelled valor, and in the
grapple I boarded them. On the instant they got clear of our ship; so I alone
became their prisoner. They have dealt with me like thieves of mercy, but they
knew what they did: I am to do a good turn for them. Let the King have the
letters I have sent, and repair thou to me with as much speed as thou wouldst

---

[1]indirect [2]implicated [3]tablet bearing the coat of arms of the dead [4]ceremony
[5]surveyed [6]equipment

20   fly death. I have words to speak in thine ear will make thee dumb; yet are they
        much too light for the bore[1] of the matter. These good fellows will bring thee
        where I am. Rosencrantz and Guildenstern hold their course for England. Of
        them I have much to tell thee. Farewell.

                                    He that thou knowest thine, HAMLET."

25   Come, I will give you way for these letters,
        And do't the speedier that you may direct me
        To him from whom you brought them.   *Exeunt.*

        Scene VII. *The castle.*

        Enter KING *and* LAERTES.

        KING Now must your conscience my acquittance seal,
            And you must put me in your heart for friend,
            Sith you have heard, and with a knowing ear,
            That he which hath your noble father slain
            Pursued my life.
5   LAERTES   It well appears. But tell me
            Why you proceeded not against these feats
            So criminal and so capital[2] in nature,
            As by your safety, greatness, wisdom, all things else,
            You mainly[3] were stirred up.
        KING   O, for two special reasons,
10   Which may to you perhaps seem much unsinewed,[4]
            But yet to me they're strong. The Queen his mother
            Lives almost by his looks, and for myself—
            My virtue or my plague, be it either which—
            She is so conjunctive[5] to my life and soul,
15   That, as the star moves not but in his sphere,
            I could not but by her. The other motive
            Why to a public count[6] I might not go
            Is the great love the general gender[7] bear him,
            Who, dipping all his faults in their affection,
20   Would, like the spring that turneth wood to stone,[8]
            Convert his gyves[9] to graces; so that my arrows,
            Too slightly timbered[10] for so loud a wind,
            Would have reverted to my bow again,
            And not where I had aimed them.
25   LAERTES And so have I a noble father lost,
            A sister driven into desp'rate terms,[11]
            Whose worth, if praises may go back again,[12]
            Stood challenger on mount of all the age

---

[1]caliber (here, "importance")   [2]deserving death   [3]powerfully   [4]weak   [5]closely united
[6]reckoning   [7]*general gender* common people   [8]*spring that turneth wood to stone* (a spring in
Shakespeare's county was so charged with lime that it would petrify wood placed in
it)   [9]fetters   [10]shafted   [11]conditions   [12]*go back again* revert to what is past

   For her perfections. But my revenge will come.
30 KING Break not your sleeps for that. You must not think
   That we are made of stuff so flat and dull
   That we can let our beard be shook with danger,
   And think it pastime. You shortly shall hear more.
   I loved your father, and we love ourself,
35   And that, I hope, will teach you to imagine—

   Enter a MESSENGER *with letters.*

   How now? What news?
  MESSENGER   Letters, my lord, from Hamlet:
   These to your Majesty; this to the Queen.
  KING From Hamlet? Who brought them?
  MESSENGER Sailors, my lord, they say; I saw them not.
40   They were given me by Claudio; he received them
   Of him that brought them.
  KING   Laertes, you shall hear them.—
   Leave us.
                [*Exit* MESSENGER.]

   [*Reads.*] "High and mighty, you shall know I am set naked[1] on your kingdom.
   Tomorrow shall I beg leave to see your kingly eyes; when I shall (first asking
45   your pardon thereunto) recount the occasion of my sudden and more strange
   return.

                  HAMLET."

   What should this mean? Are all the rest come back?
   Or is it some abuse,[2] and no such thing?
50 LAERTES Know you the hand?
  KING   'Tis Hamlet's character.[3] "Naked"!
   And in a postscript here, he says "alone."
   Can you devise[4] me?
  LAERTES I am lost in it, my lord. But let him come.
   It warms the very sickness in my heart
55   That I shall live and tell him to his teeth,
   "Thus did'st thou."
  KING   If it be so, Laertes
   (As how should it be so? How otherwise?),
   Will you be ruled by me?
  LAERTES   Ay, my lord,
60   So you will not o'errule me to a peace.
  KING To thine own peace. If he be now returned,
   As checking at[5] his voyage, and that he means
   No more to undertake it, I will work him
   To an exploit now ripe in my device,
65   Under the which he shall not choose but fall;
   And for his death no wind of blame shall breathe,

---

[1]destitute [2]deception [3]handwriting [4]advise [5]*checking at* turning away from (a term in falconry)

But even his mother shall uncharge the practice[1]
And call it accident.
LAERTES   My lord, I will be ruled;
The rather if you could devise it so
70   That I might be the organ.
KING   It falls right.
You have been talked of since your travel much,
And that in Hamlet's hearing, for a quality
Wherein they say you shine. Your sum of parts
Did not together pluck such envy from him
75   As did that one, and that, in my regard,
Of the unworthiest siege.[2]
LAERTES   What part is that, my lord?
KING   A very riband in the cap of youth,
Yet needful too, for youth no less becomes
The light and careless livery that it wears
80   Than settled age his sables and his weeds,[3]
Importing health and graveness. Two months since
Here was a gentleman of Normandy.
I have seen myself, and served against, the French,
And they can[4] well on horseback, but this gallant
85   Had witchcraft in't. He grew unto his seat,
And to such wondrous doing brought his horse
As had he been incorpsed and deminatured
With the brave beast. So far he topped my thought
That I, in forgery[5] of shapes and tricks,
90   Come short of what he did.
LAERTES   A Norman was't?
KING   A Norman.
LAERTES   Upon my life, Lamord.
KING   The very same.
LAERTES   I know him well. He is the brooch[6] indeed
And gem of all the nation.
KING   He made confession[7] of you,
95   And gave you such a masterly report,
For art and exercise in your defense,
And for your rapier most especial,
That he cried out 'twould be a sight indeed
If one could match you. The scrimers[8] of their nation
100   He swore had neither motion, guard, nor eye,
If you opposed them. Sir, this report of his
Did Hamlet to envenom with his envy
That he could nothing do but wish and beg
Your sudden coming o'er to play with you.
105   Now, out of this—
LAERTES   What out of this, my lord?
KING   Laertes, was your father dear to you?

---

[1]*uncharge the practice* not charge the device with treachery   [2]rank   [3]*sables and his weeds*
i.e., sober attire   [4]do   [5]invention   [6]ornament   [7]report   [8]fencers

Or are you like the painting of a sorrow,
A face without a heart?
LAERTES   Why ask you this?
KING   Not that I think you did not love your father,
110   But that I know love is begun by time,
And that I see, in passages of proof,[1]
Time qualifies[2] the spark and fire of it.
There lives within the very flame of love
A kind of wick or snuff[3] that will abate it,
115   And nothing is at a like goodness still,[4]
For goodness, growing to a plurisy,[5]
Dies in his own too-much. That we would do
We should do when we would, for this "would" changes,
And hath abatements and delays as many
120   As there are tongues, are hands, are accidents,
And then this "should" is like a spendthrift sigh,[6]
That hurts by easing. But to the quick[7] of th' ulcer—
Hamlet comes back; what would you undertake
To show yourself in deed your father's son
125   More than in words?
LAERTES   To cut his throat i' th' church!
KING   No place indeed should murder sanctuarize;[8]
Revenge should have no bounds. But, good Laertes,
Will you do this? Keep close within your chamber.
Hamlet returned shall know you are come home.
130   We'll put on those[9] shall praise your excellence
And set a double varnish on the fame
The Frenchman gave you, bring you in fine[10] together
And wager on your heads. He, being remiss,
Most generous, and free from all contriving,
135   Will not peruse the foils, so that with ease,
Or with a little shuffling, you may choose
A sword unbated,[11] and, in a pass of practice,[12]
Requite him for your father.
LAERTES   I will do't,
And for that purpose I'll anoint my sword.
140   I bought an unction of a mountebank,[13]
So mortal that, but dip a knife in it,
Where it draws blood, no cataplasm[14] so rare,
Collected from all simples[15] that have virtue[16]
Under the moon, can save the thing from death
145   That is but scratched withal. I'll touch my point
With this contagion that, if I gall him slightly,
It may be death.

[1]*passages of proof* proved cases   [2]diminishes   [3]residue of burnt wick (which dims the light)   [4]always   [5]fullness, excess   [6]*spendthrift sigh* (sighing provides ease, but because it was thought to thin the blood and so shorten life it was spendthrift)   [7]sensitive flesh [8]protect   [9]*We'll put on those* we'll incite persons who   [10]*in fine* finally   [11]not blunted [12]*pass of practice* treacherous thrust   [13]quack   [14]poultice   [15]medicinal herbs   [16]*virtue* power (to heal)

KING   Let's further think of this,
    Weigh what convenience both of time and means
    May fit us to our shape.[1] If this should fail,
150   And that our drift look through[2] our bad performance,
    'Twere better not assayed. Therefore this project
    Should have a back or second, that might hold
    If this did blast in proof.[3] Soft, let me see.
    We'll make a solemn wager on your cunnings—
155   I ha't!
    When in your motion you are hot and dry—
    As make your bouts more violent to that end—
    And that he calls for drink, I'll have prepared him
    A chalice for the nonce,[4] whereon but sipping,
160   If he by chance escape your venomed stuck,[5]
    Our purpose may hold there.—But stay, what noise?

    Enter QUEEN.

QUEEN One woe doth tread upon another's heel.
    So fast they follow. Your sister's drowned, Laertes.
LAERTES Drowned! O, where?
165 QUEEN There is a willow grows askant[6] the brook,
    That shows his hoar[7] leaves in the glassy stream:
    Therewith[8] fantastic garlands did she make
    Of crowflowers, nettles, daisies, and long purples,
    That liberal[9] shepherds give a grosser name,
170   But our cold maids do dead men's fingers call them.
    There on the pendent boughs her crownet[10] weeds
    Clamb'ring to hang, an envious sliver[11] broke,
    When down her weedy trophies and herself
    Fell in the weeping brook. Her clothes spread wide,
175   And mermaidlike awhile they bore her up,
    Which time she chanted snatches of old lauds,[12]
    As one incapable[13] of her own distress,
    Or like a creature native and indued[14]
    Unto that element. But long it could not be
180   Till that her garments, heavy with their drink,
    Pulled the poor wretch from her melodious lay
    To muddy death.
LAERTES   Alas, then she is drowned?
QUEEN Drowned, drowned.
LAERTES Too much of water hast thou, poor Ophelia,
185   And therefore I forbid my tears; but yet
    It is our trick;[15] nature her custom holds,
    Let shame say what it will: when these are gone,
    The woman[16] will be out. Adieu, my lord.

[1]role   [2]*drift look through* purpose show through   [3]*blast in proof* burst (fail) in performance
[4]occasion   [5]thrust   [6]aslant   [7]silver-gray   [8]i.e., with willow twigs   [9]free-spoken, coarse-
mouthed   [10]coronet   [11]*envious sliver* malicious branch   [12]hymns   [13]unaware   [14]in harmony with   [15]trait, way   [16]i.e., womanly part of me

190   I have a speech o' fire, that fain would blaze,
     But that this folly drowns it.   *Exit.*
KING   Let's follow, Gertrude.
     How much I had to do to calm his rage!
     Now fear I this will give it start again;
     Therefore let's follow.   *Exeunt.*

Act V, Scene I. *A churchyard.*

Enter two CLOWNS.[1]

CLOWN   Is she to be buried in Christian burial when she willfully seeks her own
    salvation?
OTHER   I tell thee she is. Therefore make her grave straight.[2] The crowner[3] hath
    sate on her, and finds it Christian burial.
5   CLOWN   How can that be, unless she drowned herself in her own defense?
OTHER   Why, 'tis found so.
CLOWN   It must be *se offendendo*;[4] it cannot be else. For here lies the point: if I
    drown myself wittingly, it argues an act, and an act hath three branches—it is
    to act, to do, to perform. Argal,[5] she drowned herself wittingly.
10   OTHER   Nay, but hear you, Goodman Delver.
CLOWN   Give me leave. Here lies the water—good. Here stands the man—good.
    If the man go to this water and drown himself, it is, will he nill he,[6] he goes;
    mark you that. But if the water come to him and drown him, he drowns not
    himself. Argal, he that is not guilty of his own death, shortens not his own life.
15   OTHER   But is this law?
CLOWN   Ay marry, is't—crowner's quest[7] law.
OTHER   Will you ha' the truth on't? If this had not been a gentlewoman, she
    should have been buried out o' Christian burial.
CLOWN   Why, there thou say'st. And the more pity that great folk should have
20   count'nance[8] in this world to drown or hang themselves more than their even-
    Christen.[9] Come, my spade. There is not ancient gentlemen but gard'ners, ditch-
    ers, and gravemakers. They hold up[10] Adam's profession.
OTHER   Was he a gentleman?
CLOWN   'A was the first that ever bore arms.[11]
25   OTHER   Why, he had none.
CLOWN   What, art a heathen? How dost thou understand the Scripture? The Scrip-
    ture says Adam digged. Could he dig without arms? I'll put another question to
    thee. If thou answerest me not to the purpose, confess thyself—
OTHER   Go to.
30   CLOWN   What is he that builds stronger than either the mason, the shipwright, or
    the carpenter?
OTHER   The gallowsmaker, for that frame outlives a thousand tenants.
CLOWN   I like thy wit well, in good faith. The gallows does well. But how does it
    well? It does well to those that do ill. Now thou dost ill to say the gallows is
35   built stronger than the church. Argal, the gallows may do well to thee. To't
    again, come.

---

[1]rustics   [2]straightway   [3]coroner   [4]*se offendendo* (blunder for *se defendendo,* a legal term
meaning "in self-defense")   [5]blunder for Latin *ergo,* "therefore"   [6]*will he nill he* will he or will
he not (whether he will or will not)   [7]inquest   [8]privilege   [9]fellow Christian   [10]*hold up* keep
up   [11]*bore arms* had a coat of arms (the sign of a gentleman)

OTHER   Who builds stronger than a mason, a shipwright, or a carpenter?

CLOWN   Ay, tell me that, and unyoke.[1]

OTHER   Marry, now I can tell.

40 CLOWN   To't.

OTHER   Mass,[2] I cannot tell.

Enter HAMLET *and* HORATIO *afar off.*

CLOWN   Cudgel thy brains no more about it, for your dull ass will not mend his pace with beating. And when you are asked this question next, say "a grave-maker." The houses he makes lasts till doomsday. Go, get thee in, and fetch

45 me a stoup[3] of liquor.

[*Exit* OTHER CLOWN.]

In youth when I did love, did love,   *(Song)*
   Methought it was very sweet
To contract—O—the time for—a—my behove,[4]
   O, methought there—a—was nothing—a—meet.

50 HAMLET   Has this fellow no feeling of his business? 'A sings in gravemaking.

HORATIO   Custom hath made it in him a property of easiness.[5]

HAMLET   'Tis e'en so. The hand of little employment hath the daintier sense.[6]

CLOWN   But age with his stealing steps   *(Song)*
   Hath clawed me in his clutch,
55   And hath shipped me into the land,
   As if I had never been such.

[*Throws up a skull.*]

HAMLET   That skull had a tongue in it, and could sing once. How the knave jowls[7] it to the ground, as if 'twere Cain's jawbone, that did the first murder! This might be the pate of a politician, which this ass now o'erreaches,[8] one that

60 would circumvent God, might it not?

HORATIO   It might, my lord.

HAMLET   Or of a courtier, which could say "Good morrow, sweet lord! How dost thou, sweet lord?" This might be my Lord Such-a-one, that praised my Lord Such-a-one's horse when 'a went to beg it, might it not?

65 HORATIO   Ay, my lord.

HAMLET   Why, e'en so, and now my Lady Worm's, chapless,[9] and knocked about the mazzard[10] with a sexton's spade. Here's fine revolution, an we had the trick to see't. Did these bones cost no more the breeding but to play at loggets[11] with them? Mine ache to think on't.

70 CLOWN   A pickax and a spade, a spade,   *(Song)*
   For and a shrouding sheet;
   O, a pit of clay for to be made
   For such a guest is meet.

[*Throws up another skull.*]

[1]i.e., stop work for the day   [2]by the mass   [3]tankard   [4]advantage   [5]*in him a property of easiness* easy for him   [6]*hath the daintier sense* is more sensitive (because it is not calloused)   [7]hurls   [8](1) reaches over (2) has the advantage over   [9]lacking the lower jaw   [10]head   [11]a game in which small pieces of wood were thrown at an object

HAMLET There's another. Why may not that be the skull of a lawyer? Where be
his quiddities[1] now, his quillities,[2] his cases, his tenures,[3] and his tricks? Why
does he suffer this mad knave now to knock him about the sconce[4] with a dirty
shovel, and will not tell him of his action of battery? Hum! This fellow might be
in's time a great buyer of land, with his statutes, his recognizances, his fines,[5]
his double vouchers, his recoveries. Is this the fine[6] of his fines, and the recovery of his recoveries, to have his fine pate full of fine dirt? Will his vouchers
vouch him not more of his purchases, and double ones too, than the length and
breadth of a pair of indentures?[7] The very conveyances[8] of his lands will scarcely
lie in this box, and must th' inheritor himself have no more, ha?

HORATIO Not a jot more, my lord.

HAMLET Is not parchment made of sheepskins?

HORATIO Ay, my lord, and of calveskins too.

HAMLET They are sheep and calves which seek out assurance[9] in that. I will
speak to this fellow. Whose grave's this, sirrah?

CLOWN Mine, sir.

[*Sings.*] O, a pit of clay for to be made
              For such a guest is meet.

HAMLET I think it be thine indeed, for thou liest in't.

CLOWN You lie out on't, sir, and therefore 'tis not yours. For my part, I do not
lie in't, yet it is mine.

HAMLET Thou dost lie in't, to be in't and say it is thine. 'Tis for the dead, not for
the quick;[10] therefore thou liest.

CLOWN 'Tis a quick lie, sir; 'twill away again from me to you.

HAMLET What man dost thou dig it for?

CLOWN For no man, sir.

HAMLET What woman then?

CLOWN For none neither.

HAMLET Who is to be buried in't?

CLOWN One that was a woman, sir; but, rest her soul, she's dead.

HAMLET How absolute[11] the knave is! We must speak by the card,[12] or equivocation[13] will undo us. By the Lord, Horatio, this three years I have took note
of it, the age is grown so picked[14] that the toe of the peasant comes so near the
heel of the courtier he galls his kibe.[15] How long hast thou been a gravemaker?

CLOWN Of all the days i' th' year, I came to't that day that our last king Hamlet
overcame Fortinbras.

HAMLET How long is that since?

CLOWN Cannot you tell that? Every fool can tell that. It was that very day that
young Hamlet was born—he that is mad, and sent into England.

HAMLET Ay, marry, why was he sent into England?

CLOWN Why, because 'a was mad. 'A shall recover his wits there; or, if 'a do not,
'tis no great matter there.

HAMLET Why?

---

[1]subtle arguments (from Latin *quidditas*, "whatness")   [2]fine distinctions   [3]legal means of
holding land   [4]head   [5]*his statutes, his recognizances, his fines* his documents giving a creditor
control of a debtor's land, his bonds of surety, his documents changing an entailed estate into fee
simple (unrestricted ownership)   [6]end   [7]contracts   [8]legal documents for the transference of
land   [9]safety   [10]living   [11]positive, decided   [12]*by the card* by the compass card, i.e., exactly   [13]ambiguity   [14]refined   [15]sore on the back of the heel

CLOWN 'Twill not be seen in him there. There the men are as mad as he.

HAMLET How came he mad?

CLOWN Very strangely, they say.

120 HAMLET How strangely?

CLOWN Faith, e'en with losing his wits.

HAMLET Upon what ground?

CLOWN Why, here in Denmark. I have been sexton here, man and boy, thirty years.

125 HAMLET How long will a man lie i' th' earth ere he rot?

CLOWN Faith, if 'a be not rotten before 'a die (as we have many pocky corses[1] nowadays that will scarce hold the laying in), 'a will last you some eight year or nine year. A tanner will last you nine year.

HAMLET Why he, more than another?

130 CLOWN Why, sir, his hide is so tanned with his trade that 'a will keep out water a great while, and your water is a sore decayer of your whoreson dead body. Here's a skull now hath lien you i' th' earth three and twenty years.

HAMLET Whose was it?

CLOWN A whoreson mad fellow's it was. Whose do you think it was?

135 HAMLET Nay, I know not.

CLOWN A pestilence on him for a mad rogue! 'A poured a flagon of Rhenish on my head once. This same skull, sir, was, sir, Yorick's skull, the King's jester.

HAMLET This?

CLOWN E'en that.

140 HAMLET Let me see. [*Takes the skull.*] Alas, poor Yorick! I knew him, Horatio, a fellow of infinite jest, of most excellent fancy. He hath borne me on his back a thousand times. And now how abhorred in my imagination it is! My gorge rises at it. Here hung those lips that I have kissed I know not how oft. Where be your gibes now? Your gambols, your songs, your flashes of merriment that

145 were wont to set the table on a roar? Not one now to mock your own grinning? Quite chapfall'n?[2] Now get you to my lady's chamber, and tell her, let her paint an inch thick, to this favor[3] she must come. Make her laugh at that. Prithee, Horatio, tell me one thing.

HORATIO What's that, my lord?

150 HAMLET Dost thou think Alexander looked o' this fashion i' th' earth?

HORATIO E'en so.

HAMLET And smelt so? Pah!   *Puts down the skull.*

HORATIO E'en so, my lord.

HAMLET To what base uses we may return, Horatio! Why may not imagination

155 trace the noble dust of Alexander till 'a find it stopping a bunghole?

HORATIO 'Twere to consider too curiously,[4] to consider so.

HAMLET No, faith, not a jot, but to follow him thither with modesty enough,[5] and likelihood to lead it; as thus: Alexander died, Alexander was buried, Alexander returneth to dust; the dust is earth; of earth we make loam; and why of that

160 loam whereto he was converted might they not stop a beer barrel? Imperious Caesar, dead and turned to clay,

---

[1]*pocky corses* bodies of persons who had been infected with the pox (syphilis)   [2](1) down in the mouth (2) jawless   [3]facial appearance   [4]minutely   [5]*with modesty enough* without exaggeration

Might stop a hole to keep the wind away.
O, that that earth which kept the world in awe
Should patch a wall t' expel the winter's flaw![1]
165   But soft, but soft awhile! Here comes the King.

Enter KING, QUEEN, LAERTES, *and a coffin, with* LORDS *attendant* [*and a Doctor of Divinity*].

The Queen, the courtiers. Who is this they follow?
And with such maimèd[2] rites? This doth betoken
The corse they follow did with desp'rate hand
Fordo it[3] own life. 'Twas of some estate.[4]
170   Couch[5] we awhile, and mark. [*Retires with* HORATIO.]
LAERTES   What ceremony else?
HAMLET   That is Laertes,
  A very noble youth. Mark.
LAERTES   What ceremony else?
DOCTOR   Her obsequies have been as far enlarged
175   As we have warranty. Her death was doubtful,[6]
  And, but that great command o'ersways the order,
  She should in ground unsanctified been lodged
  Till the last trumpet. For charitable prayers,
  Shards,[7] flints, and pebbles should be thrown on her.
180   Yet here she is allowed her virgin crants,[8]
  Her maiden strewments,[9] and the bringing home
  Of bell and burial.
LAERTES   Must there no more be done?
DOCTOR   No more be done.
  We should profane the service of the dead
185   To sing a requiem and such rest to her
  As to peace-parted souls.
LAERTES   Lay her i' th' earth,
  And from her fair and unpolluted flesh
  May violets spring! I tell thee, churlish priest,
  A minist'ring angel shall my sister be
190   When thou liest howling!
HAMLET   What, the fair Ophelia?
QUEEN   Sweets to the sweet! Farewell.

                                        [*Scatters flowers.*]

I hoped thou shouldst have been my Hamlet's wife.
I thought thy bride bed to have decked, sweet maid,
And not have strewed thy grave.
LAERTES   O, treble woe
195   Fall ten times treble on that cursèd head
  Whose wicked deed thy most ingenious sense[10]
  Deprived thee of! Hold off the earth awhile,
  Till I have caught her once more in mine arms.

---

[1]gust   [2]incomplete   [3]*Fordo it* destroy its   [4]high rank   [5]hide   [6]suspicious   [7]broken
pieces of pottery   [8]garlands   [9]i.e., of flowers   [10]*most ingenious sense* finely endowed mind

Leaps in the grave.

Now pile your dust upon the quick and dead
200   Till of this flat a mountain you have made
T'o'ertop old Pelion[1] on the skyish head
Of blue Olympus.
HAMLET   [*Coming forward*] What is he whose grief
Bears such an emphasis, whose phrase of sorrow
Conjures the wand'ring stars,[2] and makes them stand
205   Like wonder-wounded hearers? This is I,
Hamlet the Dane.
LAERTES   The devil take thy soul!

[*Grapples with him.*][3]

HAMLET Thou pray'st not well.
I prithee take thy fingers from my throat,
For, though I am not splenitive[4] and rash,
210   Yet have I in me something dangerous,
Which let thy wisdom fear. Hold off thy hand.
KING   Pluck them asunder.
QUEEN   Hamlet, Hamlet!
ALL   Gentlemen!
HORATIO   Good my lord, be quiet.

[ATTENDANTS *part them.*]

HAMLET Why, I will fight with him upon this theme
215   Until my eyelids will no longer wag.
QUEEN O my son, what theme?
HAMLET I love Ophelia. Forty thousand brothers
Could not with all their quantity of love
Make up my sum. What wilt thou do for her?
220   KING O, he is mad, Laertes.
QUEEN For love of God forbear him.
HAMLET 'Swounds, show me what thou't do.
Woo't weep? Woo't fight? Woo't fast? Woo't tear thyself?
Woo't drink up eisel?[5] Eat a crocodile?
225   I'll do't. Dost thou come here to whine?
To outface me with leaping in her grave?
Be buried quick with her, and so will I.
And if thou prate of mountains, let them throw
Millions of acres on us, till our ground,
230   Singeing his pate against the burning zone,[6]

[1]According to classical legend, giants in their fight with the gods sought to reach heaven by piling Mount Pelion and Mount Ossa on Mount Olympus   [2]*wand'ring stars* planets   [3]*Grapples with him* (the First Quarto, a bad quarto, presumably reporting a version that toured, has a previous direction saying "Hamlet leaps in after Laertes." Possibly he does so, somewhat hysterically. But such a direction—absent from the two good texts, Quarto 2 and Folio—makes Hamlet the aggressor, somewhat contradicting his next speech. Perhaps Laertes leaps out of the grave to attack Hamlet)   [4]fiery (the spleen was thought to be the seat of anger)   [5]vinegar   [6]*burning zone* sun's orbit

Make Ossa like a wart! Nay, an thou'lt mouth,
I'll rant as well as thou.
QUEEN   This is mere madness;
And thus a while the fit will work on him.
Anon, as patient as the female dove
235   When that her golden couplets are disclosed,[1]
His silence will sit drooping.
HAMLET   Hear you, sir.
What is the reason that you use me thus?
I loved you ever. But it is no matter.
Let Hercules himself do what he may,
240   The cat will mew, and dog will have his day.
KING   I pray thee, good Horatio, wait upon him.

[Exit HAMLET *and* HORATIO.]

[*To Laertes*] Strengthen your patience in our last night's speech.
We'll put the matter to the present push.[2]
Good Gertrude, set some watch over your son.
245   This grave shall have a living[3] monument.
An hour of quiet shortly shall we see;
Till then in patience our proceeding be.   *Exeunt.*

Scene II. *The castle.*

Enter HAMLET *and* HORATIO.

HAMLET   So much for this, sir; now shall you see the other.
You do remember all the circumstance?
HORATIO   Remember it, my lord!
HAMLET   Sir, in my heart there was a kind of fighting
5   That would not let me sleep. Methought I lay
Worse than the mutines in the bilboes.[4] Rashly
(And praised be rashness for it) let us know,
Our indiscretion sometimes serves us well
When our deep plots do pall,[5] and that should learn us
10   There's a divinity that shapes our ends,
Rough-hew them how we will.
HORATIO   That is most certain.
HAMLET   Up from my cabin,
My sea gown scarfed about me, in the dark
Groped I to find out them, had my desire,
15   Fingered[6] their packet, and in fine[7] withdrew
To mine own room again, making so bold,
My fears forgetting manners, to unseal

---

[1]*golden couplets are disclosed* (the dove lays two eggs, and the newly hatched [*disclosed*] young
are covered with golden down)   [2]*present push* immediate test   [3]lasting (with perhaps also a
reference to the plot against Hamlet's life)   [4]*mutines in the bilboes* mutineers in fetters
[5]fail   [6]stole   [7]*in fine* finally

Their grand commission; where I found, Horatio—
Ah, royal knavery!—an exact command,
20   Larded[1] with many several sorts of reasons,
Importing Denmark's health, and England's too,
With, ho, such bugs and goblins in my life,[2]
That on the supervise,[3] no leisure bated,[4]
No, not to stay the grinding of the ax,
My head should be struck off.
25   HORATIO   Is't possible?
HAMLET   Here's the commission; read it at more leisure.
But wilt thou hear now how I did proceed?
HORATIO   I beseech you.
HAMLET   Being thus benetted round with villains,
30   Or[5] I could make a prologue to my brains,
They had begun the play. I sat me down,
Devised a new commission, wrote it fair.
I once did hold it, as our statists[6] do,
A baseness to write fair,[7] and labored much
35   How to forget that learning, but, sir, now
It did me yeoman's service. Wilt thou know
Th' effect[8] of what I wrote?
HORATIO   Ay, good my lord.
HAMLET   An earnest conjuration from the King,
As England was his faithful tributary,
40   As love between them like the palm might flourish,
As peace should still her wheaten garland wear
And stand a comma[9] 'tween their amities,
And many suchlike as's of great charge,[10]
That on the view and knowing of these contents,
45   Without debatement further, more or less,
He should those bearers put to sudden death,
Not shriving[11] time allowed.
HORATIO   How was this sealed?
HAMLET   Why, even in that was heaven ordinant.[12]
I had my father's signet in my purse,
50   Which was the model[13] of that Danish seal,
Folded the writ up in the form of th' other,
Subscribed it, gave't th' impression, placed it safely,
The changeling never known. Now, the next day
Was our sea fight, and what to this was sequent
55   Thou knowest already.
HORATIO   So Guildenstern and Rosencrantz go to't.
HAMLET   Why, man, they did make love to this employment.
They are not near my conscience; their defeat
Does by their own insinuation[14] grow.

---

[1]enriched   [2]*such bugs and goblins in my life*   such bugbears and imagined terrors if I were
allowed to live   [3]reading   [4]*leisure bated* delay allowed   [5]ere   [6]statesmen   [7]clearly
[8]purport   [9]link   [10]*great charge* (1) serious exhortation (2) heavy burden (punning on
as's and "asses")   [11]absolution   [12]ruling   [13]counterpart   [14]meddling

60   'Tis dangerous when the baser nature comes
   Between the pass[1] and fell[2] incensèd points
   Of mighty opposites.
  HORATIO   Why, what a king is this!
  HAMLET Does it not, think thee, stand me now upon[3]—
   He that hath killed my king, and whored my mother,
65   Popped in between th' election[4] and my hopes,
   Thrown out his angle[5] for my proper life,[6]
   And with such coz'nage[7]—is't not perfect conscience
   To quit[8] him with this arm? And is't not to be damned
   To let this canker of our nature come
70   In further evil?
  HORATIO It must be shortly known to him from England
   What is the issue of the business there.
  HAMLET It will be short; the interim's mine,
   And a man's life's no more than to say "one."
75   But I am very sorry, good Horatio,
   That to Laertes I forgot myself,
   For by the image of my cause I see
   The portraiture of his. I'll court his favors.
   But sure the bravery[9] of his grief did put me
   Into a tow'ring passion.
80   HORATIO   Peace, who comes here?

  Enter young OSRIC, *a courtier.*

  OSRIC Your lordship is right welcome back to Denmark.
  HAMLET I humbly thank you, sir. [*Aside to* HORATIO]
  Dost know this waterfly?
  HORATIO [*Aside to* HAMLET] No, my good lord.
85   HAMLET [*Aside to* HORATIO] Thy state is the more gracious, for 'tis a vice to
  know him. He hath much land, and fertile. Let a beast be lord of beasts, and
  his crib shall stand at the king's mess.[10] 'Tis a chough,[11] but, as I say, spacious[12]
  in the possession of dirt.
  OSRIC Sweet lord, if your lordship were at leisure, I should impart a thing to you
90   from his Majesty.
  HAMLET I will receive it, sir, with all diligence of spirit.
  Put your bonnet to his right use. 'Tis for the head.
  OSRIC I thank your lordship, it is very hot.
  HAMLET No, believe me, 'tis very cold; the wind is northerly.
95   OSRIC It is indifferent cold, my lord, indeed.
  HAMLET But yet methinks it is very sultry and hot for my complexion.[13]
  OSRIC Exceedingly, my lord; it is very sultry, as 'twere—I cannot tell how. But,
  my lord, his Majesty bade me signify to you that 'a has laid a great wager on
  your head. Sir, this is the matter—
100   HAMLET I beseech you remember.

           HAMLET *moves him to put on his hat.*

[1]thrust [2]cruel [3]*stand me now upon* become incumbent upon me [4]the Danish
monarchy was elective [5]fishing line [6]*my proper life* my own life [7]trickery [8]pay back
[9]bravado [10]table [11]jackdaw (here, chatterer) [12]well off [13]temperament

OSRIC Nay, good my lord; for my ease, in good faith. Sir, here is newly come to court Laertes—believe me, an absolute gentleman, full of most excellent differences,[1] of very soft society and great showing. Indeed, to speak feelingly[2] of him, he is the card[3] or calendar of gentry; for you shall find in him the continent[4]

105 of what part a gentleman would see.

HAMLET Sir, his definement[5] suffers no perdition[6] in you, though, I know, to divide him inventorially would dozy[7] th' arithmetic of memory, and yet but yaw neither in respect of his quick sail.[8] But, in the verity of extolment, I take him to be a soul of great article,[9] and his infusion[10] of such dearth and rareness as,

110 to make true diction[11] of him, his semblable[12] is his mirror, and who else would trace him, his umbrage,[13] nothing more.

OSRIC Your lordship speaks most infallibly of him.

HAMLET The concernancy,[14] sir? Why do we wrap the gentleman in our more rawer breath?

115 OSRIC Sir?

HORATIO Is't not possible to understand in another tongue? You will to't,[15] sir, really.

HAMLET What imports the nomination of this gentleman?

OSRIC Of Laertes?

120 HORATIO [*Aside to* HAMLET] His purse is empty already. All's golden words are spent.

HAMLET Of him, sir.

OSRIC I know you are not ignorant—

HAMLET I would you did, sir; yet, in faith, if you did, it would not much approve[16]

125 me. Well, sir?

OSRIC You are not ignorant of what excellence Laertes is—

HAMLET I dare not confess that, lest I should compare with him in excellence; but to know a man well were to know himself.

OSRIC I mean, sir, for his weapon; but in the imputation[17] laid on him by them,

130 in his meed[18] he's unfellowed.

HAMLET What's his weapon?

OSRIC Rapier and dagger.

HAMLET That's two of his weapons—but well.

OSRIC The King, sir, hath wagered with him six Barbary horses, against the

135 which he has impawned,[19] as I take it, six French rapiers and poniards, with their assigns,[20] as girdle, hangers,[21] and so. Three of the carriages,[22] in faith, are very dear to fancy, very responsive[23] to the hilts, most delicate carriages, and of very liberal conceit.[24]

HAMLET What call you the carriages?

HORATIO [*Aside to* HAMLET] I knew you must be edified by the margent[25] ere

140 you had done.

OSRIC The carriages, sir, are the hangers.

HAMLET The phrase would be more germane to the matter if we could carry a

---

[1]distinguishing characteristics   [2]justly   [3]chart   [4]summary   [5]description   [6]loss   [7]dizzy
[8]*and yet . . . quick sail* i.e., and yet only stagger despite all (*yaw neither*) in trying to overtake his virtues   [9]literally, "item," but here perhaps "traits" or "importance"   [10]essential quality
[11]description   [12]likeness   [13]shadow   [14]meaning   [15]*will to't* will get there   [16]commend
[17]reputation   [18]merit   [19]wagered   [20]accompaniments   [21]straps hanging the sword to the belt
[22]an affected word for hangers   [23]corresponding   [24]*liberal conceit* elaborate design   [25]i.e., marginal (explanatory) comment

145　cannon by our sides. I would it might be hangers till then. But on! Six Barbary horses against six French swords, their assigns, and three liberal-conceited carriages—that's the French bet against the Danish. Why is this all impawned, as you call it?

OSRIC　The King, sir, hath laid, sir, that in a dozen passes between yourself and him he shall not exceed you three hits; he hath laid on twelve for nine, and it
150　would come to immediate trial if your lordship would vouchsafe the answer.

HAMLET　How if I answer no?

OSRIC　I mean, my lord, the opposition of your person in trial.

HAMLET　Sir, I will walk here in the hall. If it please his Majesty, it is the breathing time of day with me.[1] Let the foils be brought, the gentleman willing, and the
155　King hold his purpose, I will win for him an I can; if not, I will gain nothing but my shame and the odd hits.

OSRIC　Shall I deliver you e'en so?

HAMLET　To this effect, sir, after what flourish your nature will.

OSRIC　I commend my duty to your lordship.

160　HAMLET　Yours, yours. [*Exit* OSRIC.] He does well to commend it himself; there are no tongues else for's turn.

HORATIO　This lapwing[2] runs away with the shell on his head.

HAMLET　'A did comply, sir, with his dug[3] before 'a sucked it. Thus has he, and many more of the same breed that I know the drossy age dotes on, only got the
165　tune of the time and, out of an habit of encounter,[4] a kind of yeasty[5] collection, which carries them through and through the most fanned and winnowed opinions; and do but blow them to their trial, the bubbles are out.[6]

Enter a LORD.

LORD　My lord, his Majesty commended him to you by young Osric, who brings back to him that you attend him in the hall. He sends to know if your pleasure
170　hold to play with Laertes, or that you will take longer time.

HAMLET　I am constant to my purposes; they follow the King's pleasure. If his fitness speaks, mine is ready; now or whensoever, provided I be so able as now.

LORD　The King and Queen and all are coming down.

HAMLET　In happy time.

175　LORD　The Queen desires you to use some gentle entertainment[7] to Laertes before you fall to play.

HAMLET　She well instructs me.　　　　　　　　　　　　　　　　　*Exit* LORD.

HORATIO　You will lose this wager, my lord.

HAMLET　I do not think so. Since he went into France I have been in continual
180　practice. I shall win at the odds. But thou wouldst not think how ill all's here about my heart. But it is no matter.

HORATIO　Nay, good my lord—

HAMLET　It is but foolery, but it is such a kind of gain-giving[8] as would perhaps trouble a woman.

---

[1]*breathing time of day with me* time when I take exercise　　[2]the new-hatched lapwing was thought to run around with half its shell on its head　　[3]*A did comply, sir, with his dug* he was ceremoniously polite to his mother's breast　　[4]*out of an habit of encounter* out of his own superficial way of meeting and conversing with people　　[5]frothy　　[6]*the bubbles are out* i.e., they are blown away (the reference is to the "yeasty collection")　　[7]*to use some gentle entertainment* to be courteous　　[8]misgiving

185   HORATIO If your mind dislike anything, obey it. I will forestall their repair hither
      and say you are not fit.
      HAMLET Not a whit, we defy augury. There is special providence in the fall of a
      sparrow.[1] If it be now, 'tis not to come; if it be not to come, it will be now; if it
      be not now, yet it will come. The readiness is all. Since no man of aught he
190   leaves knows, what is't to leave betimes?[2] Let be.

      A table prepared. [*Enter*] *Trumpets, Drums, and* OFFICERS *with cushions;*
      KING, QUEEN, [OSRIC,] *and all the State,* [*with*] *foils, daggers,* [*and stoups of*
      wine borne in]; *and* LAERTES.

      KING Come, Hamlet, come, and take this hand from me.

      [*The* KING *puts* LAERTES' *hand into* HAMLET's.]

      HAMLET Give me your pardon, sir. I have done you wrong,
      But pardon't, as you are a gentleman.
      This presence[3] knows, and you must needs have heard,
195   How I am punished with a sore distraction.
      What I have done
      That might your nature, honor, and exception[4]
      Roughly awake, I here proclaim was madness.
      Was't Hamlet wronged Laertes? Never Hamlet.
200   If Hamlet from himself be ta'en away,
      And when he's not himself does wrong Laertes,
      Then Hamlet does it not, Hamlet denies it.
      Who does it then? His madness. If't be so,
      Hamlet is of the faction[5] that is wronged;
205   His madness is poor Hamlet's enemy.
      Sir, in this audience,
      Let my disclaiming from a purposed evil
      Free me so far in your most generous thoughts
      That I have shot my arrow o'er the house
210   And hurt my brother.
      LAERTES   I am satisfied in nature,
      Whose motive in this case should stir me most
      To my revenge. But in my terms of honor
      I stand aloof, and will no reconcilement
      Till by some elder masters of known honor
215   I have a voice and precedent[6] of peace
      To keep my name ungored. But till that time
      I do receive your offered love like love,
      And will not wrong it.
      HAMLET   I embrace it freely,
      And will this brother's wager frankly play.
220   Give us the foils. Come on.
      LAERTES   Come, one for me.
      HAMLET I'll be your foil,[7] Laertes. In mine ignorance

---

[1]*the fall of a sparrow* (cf. Matthew 10:29 "Are not two sparrows sold for a farthing? and one
of them shall not fall on the ground without your Father")   [2]early   [3]royal assembly
[4]disapproval   [5]party, side   [6]*voice and precedent* authoritative opinion justified by precedent
[7](1) blunt sword (2) background (of metallic leaf) for a jewel

       Your skill shall, like a star i' th' darkest night,
       Stick fiery off[1] indeed.
LAERTES   You mock me, sir.
HAMLET No, by this hand.
225   KING Give them the foils, young Osric. Cousin Hamlet,
       You know the wager?
HAMLET   Very well, my lord.
       Your grace has laid the odds o' th' weaker side.
       KING I do not fear it, I have seen you both;
       But since he is bettered,[2] we have therefore odds.
230   LAERTES This is too heavy; let me see another.
       HAMLET This likes me well. These foils have all a length?

Prepare to play.

OSRIC Ay, my good lord.
KING Set me the stoups of wine upon that table.
       If Hamlet give the first or second hit,
235   Or quit[3] in answer of the third exchange,
       Let all the battlements their ordnance fire.
       The King shall drink to Hamlet's better breath,
       And in the cup an union[4] shall he throw
       Richer than that which four successive kings
240   In Denmark's crown have worn. Give me the cups,
       And let the kettle[5] to the trumpet speak,
       The trumpet to the cannoneer without,
       The cannons to the heavens, the heaven to earth,
       "Now the King drinks to Hamlet." Come, begin.

Trumpets the while.

245   And you, the judges, bear a wary eye.
       HAMLET Come on, sir
       LAERTES   Come, my lord.

They play.

HAMLET   One.
LAERTES   No.
HAMLET   Judgment?
OSRIC A hit, a very palpable hit.

Drum, trumpets, and shot. Flourish; a piece goes off.

LAERTES   Well, again.
KING Stay, give me drink. Hamlet, this pearl is thine.
       Here's to thy health. Give him the cup.
250   HAMLET I'll play this bout first; set it by awhile.
       Come. [*They play.*] Another hit. What say you?
       LAERTES A touch, a touch; I do confess't.
       KING Our son shall win.

---

[1]*Stick fiery off* stand out brilliantly   [2]has improved (in France)   [3]repay, hit back   [4]pearl
[5]kettledrum

QUEEN   He's fat,[1] and scant of breath.
255   Here, Hamlet, take my napkin, rub thy brows.
       The Queen carouses to thy fortune, Hamlet.
HAMLET   Good madam!
KING   Gertrude, do not drink.
QUEEN   I will, my lord; I pray you pardon me. [*Drinks.*]
KING [*Aside*]   It is the poisoned cup; it is too late.
260   HAMLET   I dare not drink yet, madam—by and by.
QUEEN   Come, let me wipe thy face.
LAERTES   My lord, I'll hit him now.
KING   I do not think't.
LAERTES [*Aside*]   And yet it is almost against my conscience.
HAMLET   Come for the third, Laertes. You do but dally.
265   I pray you pass with your best violence;
       I am sure you make a wanton[2] of me.
LAERTES   Say you so? Come on.   [*They*] *play.*
OSRIC   Nothing neither way.
LAERTES   Have at you now!

In scuffling they change rapiers, [*and both are wounded*].

KING   Part them. They are incensed.
270   HAMLET   Nay, come—again!   [*The* QUEEN *falls.*]
OSRIC   Look to the Queen there, ho!
HORATIO   They bleed on both sides. How is it, my lord?
OSRIC   How is't, Laertes?
LAERTES   Why, as a woodcock to mine own springe,[3] Osric.
       I am justly killed with mine own treachery.
275   HAMLET   How does the Queen?
KING   She sounds[4] to see them bleed.
QUEEN   No, no, the drink, the drink! O my dear Hamlet!
       The drink, the drink! I am poisoned.   [*Dies.*]
HAMLET   O villainy! Ho! Let the door be locked.
       Treachery! Seek it out.   [LAERTES *falls.*]
280   LAERTES   It is here, Hamlet. Hamlet, thou art slain;
       No med'cine in the world can do thee good.
       In thee there is not half an hour's life.
       The treacherous instrument is in thy hand,
       Unbated and envenomed. The foul practice[5]
285   Hath turned itself on me. Lo, here I lie,
       Never to rise again. Thy mother's poisoned.
       I can no more. The King, the King's to blame.
HAMLET   The point envenomed too?
       Then, venom, to thy work.   *Hurts the* KING.
ALL   Treason! Treason!
290   KING   O, yet defend me, friends. I am but hurt.
HAMLET   Here, thou incestuous, murd'rous, damnèd Dane,
       Drink off this potion. Is thy union here?
       Follow my mother.   KING *dies.*

---

[1](1) sweaty (2) out of training   [2]spoiled child   [3]snare   [4]swoons   [5]deception

LAERTES   He is justly served.
It is a poison tempered[1] by himself.
295   Exchange forgiveness with me, noble Hamlet.
Mine and my father's death come not upon thee,
Nor thine on me!   *Dies.*
HAMLET Heaven make thee free of it! I follow thee.
I am dead, Horatio. Wretched Queen, adieu!
300   You that look pale and tremble at this chance,
That are but mutes[2] or audience to this act,
Had I but time (as this fell sergeant,[3] Death,
Is strict in his arrest) O, I could tell you—
But let it be. Horatio, I am dead;
305   Thou livest; report me and my cause aright
To the unsatisfied.[4]
HORATIO   Never believe it.
I am more an antique Roman[5] than a Dane.
Here's yet some liquor left.
HAMLET   As th' art a man,
Give me the cup. Let go. By heaven, I'll ha't!
310   O God, Horatio, what a wounded name,
Things standing thus unknown, shall live behind me!
If thou didst ever hold me in thy heart,
Absent thee from felicity[6] awhile,
And in this harsh world draw thy breath in pain,
315   To tell my story.   *A march afar off.* [*Exit* OSRIC.]
What warlike noise is this?

Enter OSRIC.

OSRIC Young Fortinbras, with conquest come from Poland,
To th' ambassadors of England gives
This warlike volley.
HAMLET   O, I die, Horatio!
The potent poison quite o'ercrows[7] my spirit.
320   I cannot live to hear the news from England,
But I do prophesy th' election lights
On Fortinbras. He has my dying voice.
So tell him, with th' occurrents,[8] more and less,
Which have solicited[9]—the rest is silence.   *Dies.*
325 HORATIO Now cracks a noble heart. Good night, sweet Prince,
And flights of angels sing thee to thy rest.
Why does the drum come hither?   [*March within.*]

Enter FORTINBRAS, *with the* AMBASSADORS *with Drum, Colors, and* ATTEND-
ANTS.
FORTINBRAS Where is this sight?
HORATIO   What is it you would see?
If aught of woe or wonder, cease your search.

[1]mixed   [2]performers who have no words to speak   [3]*fell sergeant* dread sheriff's officer
[4]uninformed   [5]*antique Roman* (with reference to the old Roman fashion of suicide)
[6]i.e., the felicity of death   [7]overpowers (as a triumphant cock crows over its weak opponent)
[8]occurrences   [9]incited

FORTINBRAS This quarry[1] cries on havoc.[2] O proud Death,
330 What feast is toward[3] in thine eternal cell
That thou so many princes at a shot
So bloodily hast struck?
AMBASSADOR   The sight is dismal;
And our affairs from England come too late.
The ears are senseless that should give us hearing
335 To tell him his commandment is fulfilled,
That Rosencrantz and Guildenstern are dead.
Where should we have our thanks?
HORATIO   Not from his[4] mouth,
Had it th' ability of life to thank you.
He never gave commandment for their death.
340 But since, so jump[5] upon this bloody question,
You from the Polack wars, and you from England,
Are here arrived, give order that these bodies
High on a stage[6] be placèd to the view,
And let me speak to th' yet unknowing world
345 How these things came about. So shall you hear
Of carnal, bloody, and unnatural acts,
Of accidental judgments, casual[7] slaughters,
Of deaths put on by cunning and forced cause,
And, in this upshot, purposes mistook
350 Fall'n on th' inventors' heads. All this can I
Truly deliver.
FORTINBRAS   Let us haste to hear it,
And call the noblest to the audience.
For me, with sorrow I embrace my fortune.
I have some rights of memory[8] in this kingdom,
355 Which now to claim my vantage doth invite me.
HORATIO Of that I shall have also cause to speak,
And from his mouth whose voice will draw on[9] more.
But let this same be presently performed,
Even while men's minds are wild, lest more mischance
360 On[10] plots and errors happen.
FORTINBRAS   Let four captains
Bear Hamlet like a soldier to the stage,
For he was likely, had he been put on,[11]
To have proved most royal; and for his passage[12]
The soldiers' music and the rite of war
365 Speak loudly for him.
Take up the bodies. Such a sight as this
Becomes the field,[13] but here shows much amiss.
Go, bid the soldiers shoot.

Exeunt marching; after the which a peal of ordnance are shot off.

[1]heap of slain bodies   [2]*cries on havoc* proclaims general slaughter   [3]in preparation
[4]Claudius'   [5]precisely   [6]platform   [7]not humanly planned, chance   [8]*rights of memory*
remembered claims   [9]*voice will draw on* vote will influence   [10]on top of   [11]*put
on* advanced (to the throne)   [12]death   [13]battlefield

Questions

1. Write a brief description of the purposes of plot served by each scene in the first act. From this outline, determine the crises and conflicts that begin *Hamlet*.

2. Make a list of the comic scenes in the play. How are they placed in relation to the rest of the action? Does their position in the plot suggest a function?

3. Discuss conflict in the character of Hamlet—conflict with other people, with himself, with fate. Could you argue that all small conflicts combine to become one major conflict in the uncoiling of the play?

4. We know Hamlet's motives in constructing the play within the play. We as audience watch the play within the play, and we watch Claudius watch. Consider the dramatic purposes of the play within the play.

5. *Hamlet* is a long play, and often when producers mount a new production, they cut scenes out of it. If you had to cut one scene from the play, which would you cut? Why? Would you lose anything? A class discussion can raise many issues about the construction of *Hamlet*.

6. When do you become certain that Claudius murdered Hamlet's father? What are the stages by which you become certain?

7. *Hamlet* has been called a subjective play: "We perceive all action through Hamlet's mind." Is this statement exaggerated?

8. Hamlet treats the play's women badly. Does anything justify his treatment of his mother? Of Ophelia? Does he love Ophelia? Is he ambivalent?

9. Is Hamlet crazy? Is Ophelia? Does Shakespeare in the language of their speeches indicate a difference in their mental conditions?

10. "Purely evil characters are uninteresting because purity is inhuman." Does Claudius seem purely evil?

11. Aristotle required that a tragic hero be a great man. Is Hamlet great? What supports the notion of Hamlet's greatness? What detracts from these notions?

12. Where did innocent Ophelia learn such nasty language? Is it unrealistic that Ophelia speaks as she does? On the other hand, could you use Ophelia's bawdy speeches as an argument for Shakespeare's greatness?

13. Compare the poetic originals with the prose paraphrases quoted on pages 496 through 498. Does Shakespeare's own language advance the action as well as the modern paraphrase does?

14. In a famous essay, "Hamlet and His Problems," T. S. Eliot wrote:

> Hamlet (the man) is dominated by an emotion which is inexpressible, because it is in *excess* of the facts as they appear. And the supposed identity of Hamlet with his author is genuine to this point: that Hamlet's bafflement at the absence of objective equivalent to his feelings is a prolongation of the bafflement of his creator in the face of his artistic problem. Hamlet is up against the difficulty that his disgust is occasioned by his mother, but that his mother is not an adequate equivalent for it; his disgust envelops and exceeds her. It is thus a feeling which he cannot understand; he cannot objectify it, and it therefore remains to poison life and obstruct action. None of the possible actions can satisfy it; and nothing that Shakespeare can do with the plot can express Hamlet for him.

Discuss

15. Taking a brief scene—the dialogue between Hamlet and his mother, for instance, before he kills Polonius (Act III, Scene IV)—describe how you would

stage it in the Globe Theater. Remember that you can use the balcony, different exits, and the alcove at the rear of the stage. Remember when you do your blocking that the audience stands on three sides of the thrust stage. Remember that you have no lighting, that your sound effects are limited, that costuming is contemporary, and that you may use only simple props.

Write another staging of the same scene using the picture stage and features available to a modern theater.

16. Is there a role in *Hamlet* like Kreon's in *Oedipus the King?*

17. Someone has suggested that the ghost in *Hamlet* functions like the plague in *Oedipus.* To what extent does this suggestion make sense?

18. Do you feel in *Hamlet,* as much as you do in *Oedipus,* the inevitability of what must happen? If you do, notice what elements of each play produce this result; discover if the plays use different methods to achieve the same end. If you do not believe that *Hamlet's* plot seems so inevitable as *Oedipus the King's,* search out and explain the reasons why.

Chapter 5 **Comedy, Neoclassicism, and Molière**

Comedy makes us laugh and leaves us smiling, but that is not all it does. The tragic mask in Greek theater shows the downturned mouth, fitted to the role of the protagonist whose downfall is fated. If the comic mask shows a perpetual smile, we should not imagine that comedy is evenly comic or does not provoke tears and sober thoughts. Comedy is various in its mixture of feelings, frequently frightening in its crises, frequently satiric and cruel—but by definition in a comedy *things come out all right in the end*.

Like tragedy, comedy derived from the worship of Dionysus, the wine god of ancient Greece. Although the year must die each autumn into winter, passing inexorably underground, the year will be born again in spring—just as necessarily. The Greek word that becomes *comedy* means *revelry* and suggests the celebration of triumph over adversity. In tragedy adversity overcomes a king. In comedy at its most typical, someone socially a little lower than a king faces adversity, overcomes it by good luck—and gets married. The hero's adversity may take the form of a villain, whose overthrow may be comic or satiric, or adversity may be a trick of fate, like a mixed-up set of identical twins and a shipwreck. In the ritual that lies behind comedy, adversity was winter and triumph was the green shoots of spring. Both comedy and the year's cycle lead to fruition: from the marriage that brings down the final curtain we can expect a green crop of children.

Aristotle's elements of theater can be applied to comedy as well as to tragedy. Comic plots move through conflicts and crises as the protagonist works to overcome adversity. Coincidence and improbable good luck aid the protagonist; scenes of recognition make our happy ending: long-lost wives and sons sold into slavery miraculously reappear; the beggar inherits a great fortune; the villain proves to be the heir's double and an imposter. Improbability of resolution, rather than displeasing us, seems essential to the comic view of the world. The counterpart to tragedy's unavoidable doom, comedy's happy ending is unavoidable. Improbability emphasizes the comic understanding: no matter how bad things look, something will turn up to save the day.

Characters in comedy tend to be types, as tragic characters tend to be individuals. Titles of comedies often name a characteristic, as in Molière's *The Misanthrope*; titles of tragedies like *Oedipus the King* and *Hamlet* tend to be the names of tragic heroes. (Molière's *Tartuffe* is an exception, named after the play's villain; although at one point Molière called it *The Imposter*.) It is common for a comic character to embody one human trait with a monstrous consistency: the miser is always and only a miser, the fop nothing but a fop. The ancient idea of **humours** portrayed human character according to the mixture of four bodily fluids, or humours: blood, phlegm, yellow bile, black bile—and a dominance of any one determined a person's character: sanguine, phlegmatic, choleric, or melancholy. In the comedy of humours, a character is wholly dominated by one characteristic trait or humour—rather like Dopey or Grumpy among Disney's Seven Dwarfs.

Exaggeration, of course, is a device of humor. By multiplying or expanding a trait to monstrosity, we expose it to laughter. Comedies use exaggerated stock characters to expose social foolishness as well as the foolishness of individuals. With types, and exaggerated types, we approach stereotypes (see page 738), which are common to comedy, less common in tragedy. Thus we have the classic stereotypes of the braggart and the artful slave. Even in Shakespearean comedy, and comedies of the modern theater, we find many expected roles: the young lovers, the scheming (for good or evil) servant, the kind parent and the wicked guardian, the drunk, the greedy landlord.

Thought in comedy runs the gamut from profundity to fatuousness. **Satiric comedy** is moral, and exposes foolishness to ridicule. As such, it can be said to benefit society by providing moral guidelines and allowing us to correct ourselves. Tartuffe's hypocritical mask of pious morality in the endeavor to enrich himself is condemned by being revealed. Because Tartuffe is thoroughly evil, he himself provides an audience no moral lesson. We know that we do not resemble this man. But the dupe of his wickedness is Orgon, who believes the most outrageous of Tartuffe's lies. It is Orgon's eyes that must be opened, his foolishness that the play's satire condemns, exposes, and holds up to ridicule.

Even in satiric comedies we usually find blameless young lovers to admire. Not all comedies, however, are satiric. Shakespeare's early comedies, like *As You Like It,* or *Love's Labour's Lost,* while they include obvious silliness obviously corrected, entertain us first—and seldom bother to persuade us of moral ideas. We take from these plays a delight in their shape, their wit, their resolution: we are entertained. This is the **romantic comedy**, at which Shakespeare excelled; his rival Ben Jonson wrote satiric comedy. While the satiric comedy takes a sharp view of human foibles, a romantic comedy is good-natured, optimistic, or accepting.

Language provides us another means for distinguishing types of comedy. In **high comedy** the characters speak with verbal wit. Shakespeare's fools may tease puns for lines, his heroes sum up a scene in an epigram; on Broadway characters wisecrack at each other. In **low comedy** we laugh at situations and pratfalls. A **farce** is low comedy usually without pretention to satire or to profound thought, in which plotting makes situations which are inherently absurd. The variant **bedroom farce** may show us a woman stuffing one lover after another into closets, under beds, and onto balconies. In **slapstick**, the laughter comes from physical movement more than from situation, as characters slip and fall down, bang their heads on closet doors, and hit each other with anything handy.

There are many theories of laughter and its sources, and no consensus. The poet Baudelaire, the philosopher Bergson, the novelist George Meredith, and the psychologist Freud have all written famous essays on humor. Reading comedy, attending to its thoughts, action, and language, we find incongruity a comic constant. Perhaps we laugh feeling superior to characters on the stage, perceiving an incongruity between what we would do and what they have done. Perhaps we laugh because we see our suppressed desires acted out on the stage, our alienated characteristics exhibited, an incongruity between desire and performance. Perhaps we laugh to see our wishes fulfilled.

Tragicomedy and mixed forms

We have treated tragedy and comedy as if these forms of drama never touched upon each other. But few great plays are so pure: in Shakespeare's great tragedies, we have noticed comic routines and considerable laughter; in Shakespeare's comedy we have tears; and in a late comedy like *Measure for Measure* we have tragic figures and possible tragedy, turned aside into comedy. In modern theater the mixture of laughter and tears has become the rule rather than the exception. Chekhov's comedies are funny and melancholy at once. In retrospect, modern readers have found that even the later Greek drama admitted some mixture; in Euripides' comedy *Alcestis* we see a tragedy averted by a comic turn of plot.

When in Shakespeare's *Macbeth,* after a dreadful murder a drunken porter delivers a comic, bawdy soliloquy, some critics have spoken of **comic relief**. Perhaps we feel in laughter a release of the tension that mounts as we witness evil. Other critics find the dramatic effect greater than mere relief; a conflict of modes in the play's form, they claim, adds to the play's complexity by providing dramatic contrast: while our hearts are still swollen with horror at the murder of an innocent and generous king, we are wrenched aside by a description of the effects of alcohol on sexual desire and potency. Presumably a similar conflict has similar effects when a serious element enters a play that is mostly funny: our laughter and our lightness stand out against a black background.

Neoclassic drama

Because the Renaissance brought about a revival of classical learning, it was natural that the new theater should model itself on the classic plays of Greece and Rome. **Neoclassic** (*neo* means new) drama began in Italy, and spread to France to influence the great French drama of the seventeenth century, dominated by the tragedians Pierre Corneille (1606–1684) and Jean Baptiste Racine (1639–1699) and by the comic playwright Molière (1622–1673.) In neoclassic theory and practice, comedy and tragedy are kept distinct, any mixture considered barbarous. (The playwright and philosopher Voltaire [1694–1778] dismissed Shakespeare as "a drunken savage.") Neoclassic drama further insisted on the three **unities** of time, place, and action. The time elapsed in the plot should take no more than twenty-four hours; the place of the action should remain the same; the action must be unified and integral, one plot in one tone of voice. Italian critics of the Renaissance claimed to derive the three unities from Aristotle's *Poetics,* although Aristotle never mentioned time and place, only unity of action: a beginning and a middle and an end. Wherever the three unities came from, they dominated the neoclassic stage with their formal demands, and *Tartuffe* obeys them. *Tartuffe* uses one stage set, depicting one room; its events take place on one day; and it tells a simple and unified story, to which only the lovers' quarrel makes something like a brief subplot.

French neoclassic staging

The architecture of the neoclassic theater was like our own common stage. The theater was indoors—with a proscenium arch, a curtain, and a box stage: the room with the missing wall. Scenery was painted, and illuminated by the light of candles and lanterns. Actors wore makeup. Women played women's roles, with the exception of the role of a grotesque woman like Mme. Pernell in *Tartuffe,* whose part could be played by a man.

Molière

Molière (Jean-Baptiste Poquelin, 1622–1673) gave up the study of law when he was a young man to join a theatrical company. The company failed and Molière was jailed for debt; but as soon as he emerged from prison he returned to the stage, and after a few years of touring the provinces began to produce plays he had written. After an apprenticeship as the author of farces, he turned his hand to satirical comedy. Besides *Tartuffe,* his famous plays include *The School for Wives* (1662), *The Misanthrope* (1666), *The Doctor in Spite of Himself* (1666), *The Miser* (1668), *The Would-Be Gentleman* (1671), and *The Imaginary Invalid* (1673). During a performance of this last play—like Shakespeare, he continued to act—Molière became fatally ill onstage.

In *Tartuffe* he played Orgon. We know something of the cast of his company, and it is amusing to note that his Tartuffe (an actor named Du Croisy) was a big healthy fellow with a florid complexion. Part of the humor for Molière's audience was to see this burly man brag of wearing hair shirts and going without food; casting made Tartuffe's deception part of the play's spectacle.

When *Tartuffe* was first produced in 1664 it was suppressed by forces that considered it an attack on religion. In 1667, Molière presented it in altered form, but opposition persisted. Not until 1669 was the play allowed free production. Reading the play now, it is hard to see how it could have been considered an attack on religion. No one is so far from religious feeling as Tartuffe; he merely uses the piety of gullible people in his ruthless pursuit of wealth.

Like *Oedipus the King* and *Hamlet, Tartuffe* is written in verse. Molière's form is the hexameter couplet, each pair of twelve-syllable lines (called Alexandrines) rhyming. Molière wrote some of his plays in prose, and *Tartuffe* has been well translated into English prose, but we will use a verse translation by the contemporary American poet Richard Wilbur. It may be interesting to look at the difference between the same speech in prose and in verse. Here is the play's opening—its exposition—as translated by John Wood:

MADAME PERNELLE Come, Flipote, come along. Let me be getting away from them.
ELMIRE You walk so fast one can hardly keep up with you.
MADAME PERNELLE Never mind, my dear, never mind! Don't come any further. I can do without all this politeness.
ELMIRE We are only paying you the respect that is due to you. Why must you be in such a hurry to go, mother?
MADAME PERNELLE Because I can't bear to see the goings-on in this house and because there's no consideration shown to me at all. I have had a very unedifying visit indeed! All my advice goes for nothing here. There's no respect paid to anything. Everybody airs his opinions—the place is a veritable Bedlam!
DORINE If . . .

We catch the bustle, the abruptness of interchange; we absorb the subtlety of exposition. Here is Wilbur's verse translation of the same speeches:

MADAME PERNELLE Come, come, Flipote; it's time I left this place.
ELMIRE I can't keep up, you walk at such a pace.
MADAME PERNELLE Don't trouble child; no need to show me out.
It's not your manners I'm concerned about.
ELMIRE We merely pay you the respect we owe.
But, Mother, why this hurry? Must you go?
MADAME PERNELLE I must. This house appals me. No one in it
Will pay attention for a single minute.
Children, I take my leave much vexed in spirit.
I offer good advice, but you won't hear it.
You all break in and chatter on and on.
It's like a madhouse with the keeper gone.
DORINE If . . .

We have the same qualities of character in the speeches, but in Wilbur we also find the rhythm and resolution of the rhymed ten-syllable line.*

---

*Neither *a madhouse with the keeper gone* nor *a veritable Bedlam* translates Molière's French precisely, yet each phrase adequately renders the gesture of his meaning. For anyone who has studied some French it may be interesting to read these speeches in the original:

MADAME PERNELLE Allons, Flipote, allons, que d'eux je me délivre.
ELMIRE Vous marchez d'un tel pas qu'on a peine à vous suivre.
MADAME PERNELLE Laissez, ma bru, laissez; ne venez pas plus loin;
Ce sont toutes façons dont je n'ai pas besoin.
ELMIRE De ce que l'on vous doit envers vous on s'acquitte.
Mais ma mère, d'où vient que vous sortez si vite?
MADAME PERNELLE C'est que je ne puis voir tout ce ménage-ci
Et que de me complaire on ne prend nul souci
Oui, je sors de chez vous fort mal èdifiée;
Dans toutes mes leçons j'y suis contrariée:
On n'y respecte rien, chacun y parle haut,
Et c'est tout justement la cour du roi Pétaud.
DORINE Si . . .

Molière
Tartuffe

Translated by Richard Wilbur

Characters

MME PERNELLE, Orgon's mother
ORGON, Elmire's husband
ELMIRE, Orgon's wife
DAMIS, Orgon's son, Elmire's stepson
MARIANE, Orgon's daughter, Elmire's
   stepdaughter, in love with Valère
VALÈRE, in love with Mariane

CLÉANTE, Orgon's brother-in-law
TARTUFFE, a hypocrite
DORINE, Mariane's lady's-maid
M. LOYAL, a bailiff
A POLICE OFFICER
FLIPOTE, Mme Pernelle's maid

The scene throughout: ORGON's *house in Paris*

Act I
Scene 1

MADAME PERNELLE *and* FLIPOTE, *her maid*
ELMIRE   DORINE   CLÉANTE   MARIANE   DAMIS

MADAME PERNELLE Come, come, Flipote; it's time I left this place.
ELMIRE I can't keep up, you walk at such a pace.
MADAME PERNELLE Don't trouble, child; no need to show me out.
   It's not your manners I'm concerned about.
5   ELMIRE We merely pay you the respect we owe.
   But, Mother, why this hurry? Must you go?
MADAME PERNELLE I must. This house appalls me. No one in it
   Will pay attention for a single minute.
   Children, I take my leave much vexed in spirit.
10   I offer good advice, but you won't hear it.
   You all break in and chatter on and on.
   It's like a madhouse with the keeper gone.
DORINE If . . .
MADAME PERNELLE Girl, you talk too much, and I'm afraid
   You're far too saucy for a lady's maid.
15   You push in everywhere and have your say.
DAMIS But . . .
MADAME PERNELLE You, boy, grow more foolish every day.
   To think my grandson should be such a dunce!
   I've said a hundred times, if I've said it once,
   That if you keep the course on which you've started,
20   You'll leave your worthy father broken-hearted.
MARIANE I think . . .
MADAME PERNELLE And you, his sister, seem so pure,
   So shy, so innocent, and so demure.

But you know what they say about still waters.
I pity parents with secretive daughters.
ELMIRE   Now, Mother . . .
25   MADAME PERNELLE   And as for you, child, let me add
That your behavior is extremely bad,
And a poor example for these children, too.
Their dear, dead mother did far better than you.
You're much too free with money, and I'm distressed
30   To see you so elaborately dressed.
When it's one's husband that one aims to please,
One has no need of costly fripperies.
CLÉANTE   Oh, Madam, really . . .
MADAME PERNELLE   You are her brother, Sir,
And I respect and love you; yet if I were
35   My son, this lady's good and pious spouse,
I wouldn't make you welcome in my house.
You're full of worldly counsels which, I fear,
Aren't suitable for decent folk to hear.
I've spoken bluntly, Sir; but it behooves us
40   Not to mince words when righteous fervor moves us.
DAMIS   Your man Tartuffe is full of holy speeches . . .
MADAME PERNELLE   And practises precisely what he preaches.
He's a fine man, and should be listened to.
I will not hear him mocked by fools like you.
45   DAMIS   Good God! Do you expect me to submit
To the tyranny of that carping hypocrite?
Must we forgo all joys and satisfactions
Because that bigot censures all our actions?
DORINE   To hear him talk—and he talks all the time—
50   There's nothing one can do that's not a crime.
He rails at everything, your dear Tartuffe.
MADAME PERNELLE   Whatever he reproves deserves reproof.
He's out to save your souls, and all of you
Must love him, as my son would have you do.
55   DAMIS   Ah no, Grandmother, I could never take
To such a rascal, even for my father's sake.
That's how I feel, and I shall not dissemble.
His every action makes me seethe and tremble
With helpless anger, and I have no doubt
60   That he and I will shortly have it out.
DORINE   Surely it is a shame and a disgrace
To see this man usurp the master's place—
To see this beggar who, when first he came,
Had not a shoe or shoestring to his name
65   So far forget himself that he behaves
As if the house were his, and we his slaves.
MADAME PERNELLE   Well, mark my words, your souls would fare far better
If you obeyed his precepts to the letter.
DORINE   You see him as a saint. I'm far less awed;
70   In fact, I see right through him. He's a fraud.

MADAME PERNELLE   Nonsense!

DORINE   His man Laurent's the same, or worse;
   I'd not trust either with a penny purse.

MADAME PERNELLE   I can't say what his servant's morals may be;
   His own great goodness I can guarantee.

75   You all regard him with distaste and fear
   Because he tells you what you're loath to hear,
   Condemns your sins, points out your moral flaws,
   And humbly strives to further Heaven's cause.

DORINE   If sin is all that bothers him, why is it

80   He's so upset when folk drop in to visit?
   Is Heaven so outraged by a social call
   That he must prophesy against us all?
   I'll tell you what I think: if you ask me
   He's jealous of my mistress' company.

MADAME PERNELLE   Rubbish! [*To* ELMIRE] He's not alone, child, in

85   complaining
   Of all your promiscuous entertaining.
   Why, the whole neighborhood's upset, I know,
   By all these carriages that come and go,
   With crowds of guests parading in and out

90   And noisy servants loitering about.
   In all of this, I'm sure there's nothing vicious;
   But why give people cause to be suspicious?

CLÉANTE   They need no cause; they'll talk in any case.
   Madam, this world would be a joyless place

95   If, fearing what malicious tongues might say,
   We locked our doors and turned our friends away.
   And even if one did so dreary a thing,
   D'you think those tongues would cease their chattering?
   One can't fight slander; it's a losing battle;

100   Let us instead ignore their tittle-tattle.
   Let's strive to live by conscience' clear decrees,
   And let the gossips gossip as they please.

DORINE   If there is talk against us, I know the source:
   It's Daphne and her little husband, of course.

105   Those who have greatest cause for guilt and shame
   Are quickest to besmirch a neighbor's name.
   When there's a chance for libel, they never miss it;
   When something can be made to seem illicit
   They're off at once to spread the joyous news,

110   Adding to fact what fantasies they choose.
   By talking up their neighbor's indiscretions
   They seek to camouflage their own transgressions,
   Hoping that others' innocent affairs
   Will lend a hue of innocence to theirs,

115   Or that their own black guilt will come to seem
   Part of a general shady color-scheme.

MADAME PERNELLE   All that is quite irrelevant. I doubt
   That anyone's more virtuous and devout

Than dear Orante; and I'm informed that she
120   Condemns your mode of life most vehemently.
    DORINE   Oh, yes, she's strict, devout, and has no taint
        Of worldliness; in short, she seems a saint.
        But it was time which taught her that disguise;
        She's thus because she can't be otherwise.
125   So long as her attractions could enthrall,
        She flounced and flirted and enjoyed it all,
        But now that they're no longer what they were
        She quits a world which fast is quitting her,
        And wears a veil of virtue to conceal
130   Her bankrupt beauty and her lost appeal.
        That's what becomes of old coquettes today:
        Distressed when all their lovers fall away,
        They see no recourse but to play the prude,
        And so confer a style on solitude.
135   Thereafter, they're severe with everyone,
        Condemning all our actions, pardoning none,
        And claiming to be pure, austere, and zealous
        When, if the truth were known, they're merely jealous,
        And cannot bear to see another know
140   The pleasures time has forced them to forgo.
    MADAME PERNELLE [*initially to* ELMIRE]   That sort of talk is what you like to
            hear;
        Therefore you'd have us all keep still, my dear,
        While Madam rattles on the livelong day.
        Nevertheless, I mean to have my say.
145   I tell you that you're blest to have Tartuffe
        Dwelling, as my son's guest, beneath this roof;
        That Heaven has sent him to forestall its wrath
        By leading you, once more, to the true path;
        That all he reprehends its reprehensible,
150   And that you'd better heed him, and be sensible.
        These visits, balls, and parties in which you revel
        Are nothing but inventions of the Devil.
        One never hears a word that's edifying:
        Nothing but chaff and foolishness and lying,
155   As well as vicious gossip in which one's neighbor
        Is cut to bits with epee, foil, and saber.
        People of sense are driven half-insane
        At such affairs, where noise and folly reign
        And reputations perish thick and fast.
160   As a wise preacher said on Sunday last,
        Parties are Towers of Babylon, because
        The guests all babble on with never a pause;
        And then he told a story which, I think . . .
        [*To* CLÉANTE] I heard that laugh, Sir, and I saw that wink!
165   Go find your silly friends and laugh some more!
        Enough; I'm going; don't show me to the door.

I leave this household much dismayed and vexed;
I cannot say when I shall see you next.
[*Slapping* FLIPOTE] Wake up, don't stand there gaping into space!
170   I'll slap some sense into that stupid face.
Move, move, you slut.

Scene 2

CLÉANTE   DORINE

CLÉANTE   I think I'll stay behind;
I want no further pieces of her mind.
How that old lady . . .
DORINE   Oh, what wouldn't she say
If she could hear you speak of her that way!
5   She'd thank you for the *lady,* but I'm sure
She'd find the *old* a little premature.
CLÉANTE   My, what a scene she made, and what a din!
And how this man Tartuffe has taken her in!
DORINE   Yes, but her son is even worse deceived;
10   His folly must be seen to be believed.
In the late troubles, he played an able part
And served his king with wise and loyal heart,
But he's quite lost his senses since he fell
Beneath Tartuffe's infatuating spell.
15   He calls him brother, and loves him as his life,
Preferring him to mother, child, or wife.
In him and him alone will he confide;
He's made him his confessor and his guide;
He pets and pampers him with love more tender
20   Than any pretty mistress could engender,
Gives him the place of honor when they dine,
Delights to see him gorging like a swine,
Stuffs him with dainties till his guts distend,
And when he belches, cries "God bless you, friend!"
25   In short, he's mad; he worships him; he dotes;
His deeds he marvels at, his words he quotes,
Thinking each act a miracle, each word
Oracular as those that Moses heard.
Tartuffe, much pleased to find so easy a victim,
30   Has in a hundred ways beguiled and tricked him,
Milked him of money, and with his permission
Established here a sort of Inquisition.
Even Laurent, his lackey, dares to give
Us arrogant advice on how to live;
35   He sermonizes us in thundering tones
And confiscates our ribbons and colognes.
Last week he tore a kerchief into pieces

Because he found it pressed in a *Life of Jesus*:
He said it was a sin to juxtapose
40   Unholy vanities and holy prose.

Scene 3

ELMIRE   DAMIS   DORINE   MARIANE   CLÉANTE

ELMIRE [*to* CLÉANTE]   You did well not to follow; she stood in the door
   And said *verbatim* all she'd said before.
   I saw my husband coming. I think I'd best
   Go upstairs now, and take a little rest.
5   CLÉANTE   I'll wait and greet him here; then I must go.
   I've really only time to say hello.
DAMIS   Sound him about my sister's wedding, please.
   I think Tartuffe's against it, and that he's
   Been urging Father to withdraw his blessing.
10   As you well know, I'd find that most distressing.
   Unless my sister and Valère can marry,
   My hopes to wed *his* sister will miscarry,
   And I'm determined . . .
DORINE   He's coming.

Scene 4

ORGON   CLÉANTE   DORINE

ORGON   Ah, Brother, good-day.
CLÉANTE   Well, welcome back. I'm sorry I can't stay.
   How was the country? Blooming, I trust, and green?
ORGON   Excuse me, Brother; just one moment.
   [*To* DORINE]   Dorine . . .
   [*To* CLÉANTE]
5   To put my mind at rest, I always learn
   The household news the moment I return.
   [*To* DORINE] Has all been well, these two days I've been gone?
   How are the family? What's been going on?
DORINE   Your wife, two days ago, had a bad fever,
10   And a fierce headache which refused to leave her.
ORGON   Ah. And Tartuffe?
DORINE   Tartuffe? Why, he's round and red,
   Bursting with health, and excellently fed.
ORGON   Poor fellow!
DORINE   That night, the mistress was unable
   To take a single bite at the dinner-table.
15   Her headache-pains, she said, were simply hellish.
ORGON   Ah. And Tartuffe?
DORINE   He ate his meal with relish,

And zealously devoured in her presence
A leg of mutton and a brace of pheasants.
ORGON Poor fellow!
DORINE   Well, the pains continued strong,
20   And so she tossed and tossed the whole night long,
Now icy-cold, now burning like a flame.
We sat beside her till morning came.
ORGON Ah. And Tartuffe?
DORINE   Why, having eaten, he rose
And sought his room, already in a doze,
25   Got into his warm bed, and snored away
In perfect peace until the break of day.
ORGON Poor fellow!
DORINE   After much ado, we talked her
Into dispatching someone for the doctor.
He bled her, and the fever quickly fell.
ORGON Ah. And Tartuffe?
30   DORINE   He bore it very well.
To keep his cheerfulness at any cost,
And make up for the blood *Madame* had lost,
He drank, at lunch, four beakers full of port.
ORGON Poor fellow!
DORINE   Both are doing well, in short.
35   I'll go and tell *Madame* that you've expressed
Keen sympathy and anxious interest.

Scene 5

ORGON CLÉANTE

CLÉANTE That girl was laughing in your face, and though
I've no wish to offend you, even so
I'm bound to say that she had some excuse.
How can you possibly be such a goose?
5   Are you so dazed by this man's hocus-pocus
That all the world, save him, is out of focus?
You've given him clothing, shelter, food, and care;
Why must you also . . .
ORGON   Brother, stop right there.
You do not know the man of whom you speak.
10   CLÉANTE I grant you that. But my judgment's not so weak
That I can't tell, by his effect on others . . .
ORGON Ah, when you meet him, you two will be like brothers!
There's been no loftier soul since time began.
He is a man who . . . a man who . . . an excellent man.
15   To keep his precepts is to be reborn,
And view this dunghill of a world with scorn.
Yes, thanks to him I'm a changed man indeed.
Under his tutelage my soul's been freed
From earthly loves, and every human tie:

20   My mother, children, brother, and wife could die,
      And I'd not feel a single moment's pain.
    CLÉANTE   That's a fine sentiment, Brother; most humane.
    ORGON   Oh, had you seen Tartuffe as I first knew him,
      Your heart, like mine, would have surrendered to him.
25   He used to come into our church each day
      And humbly kneel nearby, and start to pray.
      He'd draw the eyes of everybody there
      By the deep fervor of his heartfelt prayer;
      He'd sigh and weep, and sometimes with a sound
30   Of rapture he would bend and kiss the ground;
      And when I rose to go, he'd run before
      To offer me holy-water at the door.
      His serving-man, no less devout than he,
      Informed me of his master's poverty;
35   I gave him gifts, but in his humbleness
      He'd beg me every time to give him less.
      "Oh, that's too much," he'd cry, "too much by twice!
      I don't deserve it. The half, Sir, would suffice."
      And when I wouldn't take it back, he'd share
40   Half of it with the poor, right then and there.
      At length, Heaven prompted me to take him in
      To dwell with us, and free our souls from sin.
      He guides our lives, and to protect my honor
      Stays by my wife, and keeps an eye on her;
45   He tells me whom she sees, and all she does,
      And seems more jealous than I ever was!
      And how austere he is! Why, he can detect
      A mortal sin where you would least suspect;
      In smallest trifles, he's extremely strict.
50   Last week, his conscience was severely pricked
      Because, while praying, he had caught a flea
      And killed it, so he felt, too wrathfully.
    CLÉANTE   Good God, man! Have you lost your common sense—
      Or is this all some joke at my expense?
55   How can you stand there and in all sobriety . . .
    ORGON   Brother, your language savors of impiety.
      Too much free-thinking's made your faith unsteady,
      And as I've warned you many times already,
      'Twill get you into trouble before you're through.
60   CLÉANTE   So I've been told before by dupes like you:
      Being blind, you'd have all others blind as well;
      The clear-eyed man you call an infidel,
      And he who sees through humbug and pretense
      Is charged, by you, with want of reverence.
65   Spare me your warnings, Brother; I have no fear
      Of speaking out, for you and Heaven to hear,
      Against affected zeal and pious knavery.
      There's true and false in piety, as in bravery,
      And just as those whose courage shines the most

70   In battle, are the least inclined to boast,
        So those whose hearts are truly pure and lowly
        Don't make a flashy show of being holy.
        There's a vast difference, so it seems to me,
        Between true piety and hypocrisy:
75   How do you fail to see it, may I ask?
        Is not a face quite different from a mask?
        Cannot sincerity and cunning art,
        Reality and semblance, be told apart?
        Are scarecrows just like men, and do you hold
80   That a false coin is just as good as gold?
        Ah, Brother, man's a strangely fashioned creature
        Who seldom is content to follow Nature,
        But recklessly pursues his inclination
        Beyond the narrow bounds of moderation,
85   And often, by transgressing Reason's laws,
        Perverts a lofty aim or noble cause.
        A passing observation, but it applies.
    ORGON   I see, dear Brother, that you're profoundly wise;
        You harbor all the insight of the age.
90   You are our one clear mind, our only sage,
        The era's oracle, its Cato too,
        And all mankind are fools compared to you.
    CLÉANTE   Brother, I don't pretend to be a sage,
        Nor have I all the wisdom of the age.
95   There's just one insight I would dare to claim:
        I know that true and false are not the same;
        And just as there is nothing I more revere
        Than a soul whose faith is steadfast and sincere,
        Nothing that I more cherish and admire
100   Than honest zeal and true religious fire,
        So there is nothing that I find more base
        Than specious piety's dishonest face—
        Than these bold mountebanks, these histrios
        Whose impious mummeries and hollow shows
105   Exploit our love of Heaven, and make a jest
        Of all that men think holiest and best;
        These calculating souls who offer prayers
        Not to their Maker, but as public wares,
        And seek to buy respect and reputation
110   With lifted eyes and sighs of exaltation;
        These charlatans, I say, whose pilgrim souls
        Proceed, by way of Heaven, toward earthly goals,
        Who weep and pray and swindle and extort,
        Who preach the monkish life, but haunt the court,
115   Who make their zeal the partner of their vice—
        Such men are vengeful, sly, and cold as ice,
        And when there is an enemy to defame
        They cloak their spite in fair religion's name,
        Their private spleen and malice being made

120   To seem a high and virtuous crusade,
         Until, to mankind's reverent applause,
         They crucify their foe in Heaven's cause.
         Such knaves are all too common; yet, for the wise,
         True piety isn't hard to recognize,
125   And, happily, these present times provide us
         With bright examples to instruct and guide us.
         Consider Ariston and Périandre;
         Look at Oronte, Alcidamas, Clitandre;
         Their virtue is acknowledged; who could doubt it?
130   But you won't hear them beat the drum about it.
         They're never ostentatious, never vain,
         And their religion's moderate and humane;
         It's not their way to criticize and chide:
         They think censoriousness a mark of pride,
135   And therefore, letting others preach and rave,
         They show, by deeds, how Christians should behave.
         They think no evil of their fellow man,
         But judge of him as kindly as they can.
         They don't intrigue and wangle and conspire;
140   To lead a good life is their one desire;
         The sinner wakes no rancorous hate in them;
         It is the sin alone which they condemn;
         Nor do they try to show a fiercer zeal
         For Heaven's cause than Heaven itself could feel.
145   These men I honor, these men I advocate
         As models for us all to emulate.
         Your man is not their sort at all, I fear:
         And, while your praise of him is quite sincere,
         I think that you've been dreadfully deluded.
150 ORGON   Now then, dear Brother, is your speech concluded?
     CLÉANTE   Why, yes.
     ORGON   Your servant, Sir.   [*He turns to go.*]
     CLÉANTE   No, Brother; wait.
         There's one more matter. You agreed of late
         That young Valère might have your daughter's hand.
     ORGON   I did.
     CLÉANTE   And set the date, I understand.
     ORGON   Quite so.
155 CLÉANTE   You've now postponed it; is that true?
     ORGON   No doubt.
     CLÉANTE   The match no longer pleases you?
     ORGON   Who knows?
     CLÉANTE   D'you mean to go back on your word?
     ORGON   I won't say that.
     CLÉANTE   Has anything occurred
         Which might entitle you to break your pledge?
     ORGON   Perhaps.
160 CLÉANTE   Why must you hem, and haw, and hedge?
         The boy asked me to sound you in this affair . . .

ORGON   It's been a pleasure.
CLÉANTE   But what shall I tell Valère?
ORGON   Whatever you like.
CLÉANTE   But what have you decided?
   What are your plans?
ORGON   I plan, Sir, to be guided
   By Heaven's will.
165   CLÉANTE   Come, Brother, don't talk rot.
   You've given Valère your word; will you keep it, or not?
ORGON   Good day.
CLÉANTE   This looks like poor Valère's undoing;
   I'll go and warn him that there's trouble brewing.

Act II

Scene 1

ORGON   MARIANE

ORGON   Mariane.
MARIANE   Yes, Father?
ORGON   A word with you; come here.
MARIANE   What are you looking for?
ORGON [*peering into a small closet*]   Eavesdroppers, dear.
   I'm making sure we shan't be overheard.
   Someone in there could catch our every word.
5   Ah, good, we're safe. Now, Mariane, my child,
   You're a sweet girl who's tractable and mild,
   Whom I hold dear, and think most highly of.
MARIANE   I'm deeply grateful, Father, for your love.
ORGON   That's well said, Daughter; and you can repay me
10   If, in all things, you'll cheerfully obey me.
MARIANE   To please you, Sir, is what delights me best.
ORGON   Good, good. Now, what d'you think of Tartuffe, our guest?
MARIANE   I, sir?
ORGON   Yes. Weigh your answer; think it through.
MARIANE   Oh, dear. I'll say whatever you wish me to.
15   ORGON   That's wisely said, my Daughter. Say of him, then,
   That he's the very worthiest of men,
   And that you're fond of him, and would rejoice
   In being his wife, if that should be my choice.
   Well?
MARIANE   What?
ORGON   What's that?
MARIANE   I . . .
ORGON   Well?
MARIANE   Forgive me, pray.
ORGON   Did you not hear me?
20   MARIANE   Of *whom,* Sir, must I say
   That I am fond of him, and would rejoice
   In being his wife, if that should be your choice?

ORGON   Why, of Tartuffe.
MARIANE   But, Father, that's false, you know.
   Why would you have me say what isn't so?
25   ORGON   Because I am resolved it shall be true.
   That it's my wish should be enough for you.
MARIANE   You can't mean, Father . . .
ORGON   Yes, Tartuffe shall be
   Allied by marriage to this family,
   And he's to be your husband, is that clear?
30   It's a father's privilege . . .

Scene 2

DORINE   ORGON   MARIANE

ORGON [*to* DORINE]   What are you doing in here?
   Is curiosity so fierce a passion
   With you, that you must eavesdrop in this fashion?
DORINE   There's lately been a rumor going about—
5   Based on some hunch or chance remark, no doubt—
   That you mean Mariane to wed Tartuffe.
   I've laughed it off, of course, as just a spoof.
ORGON   You find it so incredible?
DORINE   Yes, I do.
   I won't accept that story, even from you.
10   ORGON   Well, you'll believe it when the thing is done.
DORINE   Yes, yes, of course. Go on and have your fun.
ORGON   I've never been more serious in my life.
DORINE   Ha!
ORGON   Daughter, I mean it; you're to be his wife.
DORINE   No, don't believe your father; it's all a hoax.
ORGON   See here, young woman . . .
15   DORINE   Come, Sir, no more jokes;
   You can't fool us,
ORGON   How dare you talk that way?
DORINE   All right, then: we believe you, sad to say.
   But how a man like you, who looks so wise
   And wears a moustache of such splendid size,
   Can be so foolish as to . . .
20   ORGON   Silence, please!
   My girl, you take too many liberties.
   I'm master here, as you must not forget.
DORINE   Do let's discuss this calmly; don't be upset.
   You can't be serious, Sir, about this plan.
25   What should that bigot want with Mariane?
   Praying and fasting ought to keep him busy.
   And then, in terms of wealth and rank, what is he?
   Why should a man of property like you
   Pick out a beggar son-in-law?

ORGON   That will do.
30   Speak of his poverty with reverence.
     His is a pure and saintly indigence
     Which far transcends all worldly pride and pelf.
     He lost his fortune, as he says himself,
     Because he cared for Heaven alone, and so
35   Was careless of his interests here below.
     I mean to get him out of his present straits
     And help him to recover his estates—
     Which, in his part of the world, have no small fame.
     Poor though he is, he's a gentleman just the same.
40   DORINE   Yes, so he tells us; and, Sir, it seems to me
     Such pride goes very ill with piety.
     A man whose spirit spurns this dungy earth
     Ought not to brag of lands and noble birth;
     Such worldly arrogance will hardly square
45   With meek devotion and the life of prayer.
     . . . But this approach, I see, has drawn a blank;
     Let's speak, then, of his person, not his rank.
     Doesn't it seem to you a trifle grim
     To give a girl like her to a man like him?
50   When two are so ill-suited, can't you see
     What the sad consequence is bound to be?
     A young girl's virtue is imperilled, Sir,
     When such a marriage is imposed on her;
     For if one's bridegroom isn't to one's taste,
55   It's hardly an inducement to be chaste,
     And many a man with horns upon his brow
     Has made his wife the thing that she is now.
     It's hard to be a faithful wife, in short,
     To certain husbands of a certain sort,
60   And he who gives his daughter to a man she hates
     Must answer for her sins at Heaven's gates.
     Think, Sir, before you play so risky a role.
     ORGON   This servant-girl presumes to save my soul!
     DORINE   You would do well to ponder what I've said.
65   ORGON   Daughter, we'll disregard this dunderhead.
     Just trust your father's judgment. Oh, I'm aware
     That I once promised you to young Valère;
     But now I hear he gambles, which greatly shocks me;
     What's more, I've doubts about his orthodoxy.
70   His visits to church, I note, are very few.
     DORINE   Would you have him go at the same hours as you,
     And kneel nearby, to be sure of being seen?
     ORGON   I can dispense with such remarks, Dorine.
     [To MARIANE] Tartuffe, however, is sure of Heaven's blessing,
75   And that's the only treasure worth possessing.
     This match will bring you joys beyond all measure;
     Your cup will overflow with every pleasure;
     You two will interchange your faithful loves

Like two sweet cherubs, or two turtle-doves.
80   No harsh word shall be heard, no frown be seen,
        And he shall make you happy as a queen.
    DORINE   And she'll make him a cuckold, just wait and see.
    ORGON   What language!
    DORINE   Oh, he's a man of destiny;
        He's *made* for horns, and what the stars demand
85   Your daughter's virtue surely can't withstand.
    ORGON   Don't interrupt me further. Why can't you learn
        That certain things are none of your concern?
    DORINE   It's for your own sake that I interfere.

She repeatedly interrupts ORGON *just as he is turning to speak to his daughter.*

    ORGON   Most kind of you. Now, hold your tongue, d'you hear?
    DORINE   If I didn't love you . . .
90   ORGON   Spare me your affection.
    DORINE   I love you, Sir, in spite of your objection.
    ORGON   Blast!
    DORINE   I can't bear, Sir, for your honor's sake,
        To let you make this ludicrous mistake.
    ORGON   You mean to go on talking?
    DORINE   If I didn't protest
95   This sinful marriage, my conscience couldn't rest.
    ORGON   If you don't hold your tongue, you little shrew . . .
    DORINE   What, lost your temper? A pious man like you?
    ORGON   Yes! Yes! You talk and talk. I'm maddened by it.
        Once and for all, I tell you to be quiet.
100   DORINE   Well, I'll be quiet. But I'll be thinking hard.
    ORGON   Think all you like, but you had better guard
        That saucy tongue of yours, or I'll . . .
        [*Turning back to* MARIANE]   Now, child,
        I've weighed this matter fully.
    DORINE [*aside*]   It drives me wild
        That I can't speak.

ORGON *turns his head, and she is silent.*

    ORGON   Tartuffe is no young dandy,
        But, still, his person . . .
105   DORINE [*aside*]   Is as sweet as candy.
    ORGON   Is such that, even if you shouldn't care
        For his other merits . . .

He turns and stands facing DORINE, *arms crossed.*

    DORINE [*aside*]   They'll make a lovely pair.
        If I were she, no man would marry me
        Against my inclination, and go scot-free.
110   He'd learn, before the wedding day was over,

How readily a wife can find a lover.
ORGON [*to* DORINE]   It seems you treat my orders as a joke.
DORINE   Why, what's the matter? 'Twas not to you I spoke.
ORGON   What *were* you doing?
DORINE   Talking to myself, that's all.
115   ORGON   Ah! [*Aside*] One more bit of impudence and gall,
And I shall give her a good slap in the face.

[*He puts himself in position to slap her;* DORINE, *whenever he glances at her,
stands immobile and silent.*]

Daughter, you shall accept, and with good grace,
The husband I've selected . . . Your wedding-day . . .
[*To* DORINE] Why don't you talk to yourself?
DORINE   I've nothing to say.
ORGON   Come, just one word.
120   DORINE   No thank you, Sir. I pass.
ORGON   Come, speak; I'm waiting.
DORINE   I'd not be such an ass.
ORGON [*turning to* MARIANE]   In short, dear Daughter, I mean to be obeyed,
And you must bow to the sound choice I've made.
DORINE [*moving away*]   I'd not wed such a monster, even in jest.

ORGON *attempts to slap her, but misses.*

125   ORGON   Daughter, that maid of yours is a thorough pest;
She makes me sinfully annoyed and nettled.
I can't speak further; my nerves are too unsettled.
She's so upset me by her insolent talk,
I'll calm myself by going for a walk.

Scene 3

DORINE   MARIANE

DORINE [*returning*]   Well, have you lost your tongue, girl? Must I play
Your part, and say the lines you ought to say?
Faced with a fate so hideous and absurd,
Can you not utter one dissenting word?
5   MARIANE   What good would it do? A father's power is great.
DORINE   Resist him now, or it will be too late.
MARIANE   But . . .
DORINE   Tell him one cannot love at a father's whim;
That you shall marry for yourself, not him;
That since it's you who are to be the bride,
10   It's you, not he, who must be satisfied;
And that if his Tartuffe is so sublime,
He's free to marry him at any time.
MARIANE   I've bowed so long to Father's strict control,
I couldn't oppose him now, to save my soul.

15 DORINE Come, come, Mariane. Do listen to reason, won't you?
Valère has asked your hand. Do you love him, or don't you?
MARIANE Oh, how unjust of you! What can you mean
By asking such a question, dear Dorine?
You know the depth of my affection for him;
20 I've told you a hundred times how I adore him.
DORINE I don't believe in everything I hear;
Who knows if your professions were sincere?
MARIANE They were, Dorine, and you do me wrong to doubt it;
Heaven knows that I've been all too frank about it.
DORINE You love him, then?
25 MARIANE   Oh, more than I can express.
DORINE And he, I take it, cares for you no less?
MARIANE I think so.
DORINE   And you both, with equal fire,
Burn to be married?
MARIANE   That is our one desire.
DORINE What of Tartuffe, then? What of your father's plan?
30 MARIANE I'll kill myself, if I'm forced to wed that man.
DORINE I hadn't thought of that recourse. How splendid!
Just die, and all your troubles will be ended!
A fine solution. Oh, it maddens me
To hear you talk in that self-pitying key.
35 MARIANE Dorine, how harsh you are! It's most unfair.
You have no sympathy for my despair.
DORINE I've none at all for people who talk drivel
And, faced with difficulties, whine and snivel.
MARIANE No doubt I'm timid, but it would be wrong . . .
40 DORINE True love requires a heart that's firm and strong.
MARIANE I'm strong in my affection for Valère,
But coping with my father is his affair.
DORINE But if your father's brain has grown so cracked
Over his dear Tartuffe that he can retract
45 His blessing, though your wedding-day was named,
It's surely not Valère who's to be blamed.
MARIANE If I defied my father, as you suggest,
Would it not seem unmaidenly, at best?
Shall I defend my love at the expense
50 Of brazenness and disobedience?
Shall I parade my heart's desires, and flaunt . . .
DORINE No, I ask nothing of you. Clearly you want
To be Madame Tartuffe, and I feel bound
Not to oppose a wish so very sound.
55 What right have I to criticize the match?
Indeed, my dear, the man's a brilliant catch.
Monsieur Tartuffe! Now, there's a man of weight!
Yes, yes, Monsieur Tartuffe, I'm bound to state,
Is quite a person; that's not to be denied;
60 'Twill be no little thing to be his bride.

The world already rings with his renown;
He's a great noble—in his native town;
His ears are red, he has a pink complexion,
And all in all, he'll suit you to perfection.
MARIANE   Dear God!
65   DORINE   Oh, how triumphant you will feel
At having caught a husband so ideal!
MARIANE   Oh, do stop teasing, and use your cleverness
To get me out of this appalling mess.
Advise me, and I'll do whatever you say.
70   DORINE   Ah no, a dutiful daughter must obey
Her father, even if he weds her to an ape.
You've a bright future; why struggle to escape?
Tartuffe will take you back where his family lives,
To a small town aswarm with relatives—
75   Uncles and cousins whom you'll be charmed to meet.
You'll be received at once by the elite,
Calling upon the bailiff's wife, no less—
Even, perhaps, upon the mayoress,
Who'll sit you down in the *best* kitchen chair.
80   Then, once a year, you'll dance at the village fair
To the drone of bagpipes—two of them, in fact—
And see a puppet-show, or an animal act.
Your husband . . .
MARIANE   Oh, you turn my blood to ice!
Stop torturing me, and give me your advice.
DORINE [*threatening to go*]   Your servant, Madam.
85   MARIANE   Dorine, I beg of you . . .
DORINE   No, you deserve it; this marriage must go through.
MARIANE   Dorine!
DORINE   No.
MARIANE   Not Tartuffe! You know I think him . . .
DORINE   Tartuffe's your cup of tea, and you shall drink him.
MARIANE   I've always told you everything, and relied . . .
90   DORINE   No. You deserve to be tartuffified.
MARIANE   Well, since you mock me and refuse to care,
I'll henceforth seek my solace in despair:
Despair shall be my counsellor and friend,
And help me bring my sorrows to an end.

She starts to leave.

95   DORINE   There now, come back; my anger has subsided.
You do deserve some pity, I've decided.
MARIANE   Dorine, if Father makes me undergo
This dreadful martyrdom, I'll die, I know.
DORINE   Don't fret; it won't be difficult to discover
100   Some plan of action . . . But here's Valère, your lover.

Scene 4

VALÈRE   MARIANE   DORINE

VALÈRE   Madam, I've just received some wondrous news
 Regarding which I'd like to hear your views.
MARIANE   What news?
VALÈRE   You're marrying Tartuffe.
MARIANE   I find
 That Father does have such a match in mind.
VALÈRE   Your father, Madam . . .
5   MARIANE   . . . has just this minute said
 That it's Tartuffe he wishes me to wed.
VALÈRE   Can he be serious?
MARIANE   Oh, indeed he can;
 He's clearly set his heart upon the plan.
VALÈRE   And what position do you propose to take,
 Madam?
MARIANE   Why—I don't know.
10   VALÈRE   For heaven's sake—
 You don't know?
MARIANE   No.
VALÈRE   Well, well!
MARIANE   Advise me, do.
VALÈRE   Marry the man. That's my advice to you.
MARIANE   That's your advice?
VALÈRE   Yes.
MARIANE   Truly?
VALÈRE   Oh, absolutely.
 You couldn't choose more wisely, more astutely.
15   MARIANE   Thanks for this counsel; I'll follow it, of course.
VALÈRE   Do, do; I'm sure 'twill cost you no remorse.
MARIANE   To give it didn't cause your heart to break.
VALÈRE   I gave it, Madam, only for your sake.
MARIANE   And it's for your sake that I take it, Sir.
DORINE [*withdrawing to the rear of the stage*]   Let's see which fool will prove
20   the stubborner.
VALÈRE   So! I am nothing to you, and it was flat
 Deception when you . . .
MARIANE   Please, enough of that.
 You've told me plainly that I should agree
 To wed the man my father's chosen for me,
25   And since you've designed to counsel me so wisely,
 I promise, Sir, to do as you advise me.
VALÈRE   Ah, no, 'twas not by me that you were swayed.
 No, your decision was already made;
 Though now, to save appearances, you protest
30   That you're betraying me at my behest.
MARIANE   Just as you say.

VALÈRE   Quite so. And I now see
  That you were never truly in love with me.
MARIANE   Alas, you're free to think so if you choose.
VALÈRE   I choose to think so, and here's a bit of news:
35   You've spurned my hand, but I know where to turn
  For kinder treatment, as you shall quickly learn.
MARIANE   I'm sure you do. Your noble qualities
  Inspire affection . . .
VALÈRE   Forget my qualities, please.
  They don't inspire you overmuch, I find.
40   But there's another lady I have in mind
  Whose sweet and generous nature will not scorn
  To compensate me for the loss I've borne.
MARIANE   I'm no great loss, and I'm sure that you'll transfer
  Your heart quite painlessly from me to her.
45 VALÈRE   I'll do my best to take it in my stride.
  The pain I feel at being cast aside
  Time and forgetfulness may put an end to.
  Or if I can't forget, I shall pretend to.
  No self-respecting person is expected
50   To go on loving once he's been rejected.
MARIANE   Now, that's a fine, high-minded sentiment.
VALÈRE   One to which any sane man would assent.
  Would you prefer it if I pined away
  In hopeless passion till my dying day?
55   Am I to yield you to a rival's arms
  And not console myself with other charms?
MARIANE   Go then: console yourself; don't hesitate.
  I wish you to; indeed, I cannot wait.
VALÈRE   You wish me to?
MARIANE   Yes.
VALÈRE   That's the final straw.
60   Madam, farewell. Your wish shall be my law.

He starts to leave, and then returns: this repeatedly.

MARIANE   Splendid.
VALÈRE [*coming back again*]
                    This breach, remember, is of your making;
  It's you who've driven me to the step I'm taking.
MARIANE   Of course.
VALÈRE [*coming back again*]
                      Remember, too, that I am merely
  Following your example.
MARIANE   I see that clearly.
65 VALÈRE   Enough, I'll go and do your bidding, then.
MARIANE   Good.
VALÈRE [*coming back again*]
                    You shall never see my face again.

MARIANE Excellent.
VALÈRE [*walking to the door, then turning about*]
                    Yes?
MARIANE   What?
VALÈRE   What's that? What did you say?
MARIANE Nothing. You're dreaming.
VALÈRE   Ah. Well, I'm on my way.
    Farewell, *Madame*.

He moves slowly away.
MARIANE   Farewell.
DORINE [*to* MARIANE]   If you ask me,
70   Both of you are as mad as mad can be.
    Do stop this nonsense, now. I've only let you
    Squabble so long to see where it would get you.
    Whoa there, Monsieur Valère!

She goes and seizes VALÈRE *by the arm; he makes a great show of resistance.*

VALÈRE   What's this, Dorine?
DORINE Come here.
VALÈRE   No, no, my heart's too full of spleen.
75   Don't hold me back; her wish must be obeyed.
DORINE Stop!
VALÈRE   It's too late now; my decision's made.
DORINE Oh, pooh!
MARIANE [*aside*] He hates the sight of me, that's plain.
    I'll go, and so deliver him from pain.
DORINE [*leaving* VALÈRE, *running after* MARIANE]
    And now *you* run away! Come back.
MARIANE   No, No.
80   Nothing you say will keep me here. Let go!
VALÈRE [*aside*] She cannot bear my presence, I perceive.
    To spare her further torment, I shall leave.
DORINE [*leaving* MARIANE, *running after* VALÈRE] Again! You'll not escape,
        Sir; don't you try it.
    Come here, you two. Stop fussing, and be quiet.

She takes VALÈRE *by the hand, then* MARIANE, *and draws them together.*

VALÈRE [*to* DORINE] What do you want of me?
85   MARIANE [*to* DORINE]   What is the point of this?
DORINE We're going to have a little armistice.
    [*To* VALÈRE] Now weren't you silly to get so overheated?
VALÈRE Didn't you see how badly I was treated?
DORINE [*to* MARIANE] Aren't you a simpleton, to have lost your head?
90   MARIANE Didn't you hear the hateful things he said?
DORINE [*to* VALÈRE] You're both great fools. Her sole desire, Valère,
    Is to be yours in marriage. To that I'll swear.

[*To* MARIANE] He loves you only, and he wants no wife
But you, Mariane. On that I'll stake my life.
95   MARIANE [*to* VALÈRE]   Then why you advised me so, I cannot see.
VALÈRE [*to* MARIANE]   On such a question, why ask advice of *me?*
DORINE   Oh, you're impossible. Give me your hands, you two.
     [*To* VALÈRE]   Yours first.
VALÈRE [*giving* DORINE *his hand*]   But why?
DORINE [*to* MARIANE]   And now a hand from you.
MARIANE [*also giving* DORINE *her hand*]
     What are you doing?
DORINE   There: a perfect fit.
100   You suit each other better than you'll admit.

VALÈRE *and* MARIANE *hold hands for some time without looking at each other.*

VALÈRE [*turning toward* MARIANE]   Ah, come, don't be so haughty. Give a man
     A look of kindness, won't you, Mariane?

MARIANE *turns toward* VALÈRE *and smiles.*

DORINE   I tell you, lovers are completely mad!
VALÈRE [*to* MARIANE]   Now come, confess that you were very bad
105   To hurt my feelings as you did just now.
     I have a just complaint, you must allow.
MARIANE   *You* must allow that you were most unpleasant . . .
DORINE   Let's table that discussion for the present;
     Your father has a plan which must be stopped.
110   MARIANE   Advise us, then; what means must we adopt?
DORINE   We'll use all manner of means, and all at once.
     [*To* MARIANE] Your father's addled; he's acting like a dunce.
     Therefore you'd better humor the old fossil.
     Pretend to yield to him, be sweet and docile,
115   And then postpone, as often as necessary,
     The day on which you have agreed to marry.
     You'll thus gain time, and time will turn the trick.
     Sometimes, for instance, you'll be taken sick,
     And that will seem good reason for delay;
120   Or some bad omen will make you change the day—
     You'll dream of muddy water, or you'll pass
     A dead man's hearse, or break a looking-glass.
     If all else fails, no man can marry you
     Unless you take his ring and say "I do."
125   But now, let's separate. If they should find
     Us talking here, our plot might be divined.
     [*To* VALÈRE] Go to your friends, and tell them what's occurred,
     And have them urge her father to keep his word.
     Meanwhile, we'll stir her brother into action,
130   And get Elmire, as well, to join our faction.

Good-bye.
VALÈRE [*to* MARIANE]
             Though each of us will do his best,
   It's your true heart on which my hopes shall rest.
MARIANE [*to* VALÈRE] Regardless of what Father may decide,
   None but Valère shall claim me as his bride.
135   VALÈRE Oh, how those words content me! Come what will . . .
   DORINE Oh, lovers, lovers! Their tongues are never still.
   Be off, now.
VALÈRE [*turning to go, then turning back*]
             One last word . . .
   DORINE   No time to chat:
      You leave by this door; and *you* leave by that.

   DORINE *pushes them, by the shoulders, toward opposing doors.*

Act III

   Scene 1

   DAMIS   DORINE

   DAMIS   May lightning strike me even as I speak,
      May all men call me cowardly and weak,
      If any fear or scruple holds me back
      From settling things, at once, with that great quack!
5   DORINE   Now, don't give way to violent emotion.
      Your father's merely talked about this notion,
      And words and deeds are far from being one.
      Much that is talked about is left undone.
   DAMIS   No, I must stop that scoundrel's machinations;
10   I'll go and tell him off; I'm out of patience.
   DORINE   Do calm down and be practical. I had rather
      My mistress dealt with him—and with your father.
      She has some influence with Tartuffe, I've noted.
      He hangs upon her words, seems most devoted,
15   And may, indeed, be smitten by her charm.
      Pray Heaven it's true! 'Twould do our cause no harm.
      She sent for him, just now, to sound him out
      On this affair you're so incensed about;
      She'll find out where he stands, and tell him, too,
20   What dreadful strife and trouble will ensue
      If he lends countenance to your father's plan.
      I couldn't get in to see him, but his man
      Says that he's almost finished with his prayers.
      Go, now. I'll catch him when he comes downstairs.
25   DAMIS   I want to hear this conference, and I will.
   DORINE   No, they must be alone.
   DAMIS   Oh, I'll keep still.
   DORINE   Not you. I know your temper. You'd start a brawl,
      And shout and stamp your foot and spoil it all.

Go on.
DAMIS   I won't; I have a perfect right . . .
30   DORINE   Lord, you're a nuisance! He's coming; get out of sight.

DAMIS *conceals himself in a closet at the rear of the stage.*

Scene 2

TARTUFFE   DORINE

TARTUFFE [*observing* DORINE*, and calling to his manservant offstage*
   Hang up my hair-shirt, put my scourge in place,
   And pray, Laurent, for Heaven's perpetual grace.
   I'm going to the prison now, to share
   My last few coins with the poor wretches there.
5   DORINE [*aside*]   Dear God, what affectation! What a fake!
   TARTUFFE   You wished to see me?
   DORINE   Yes . . .
   TARTUFFE [*taking a handkerchief from his pocket*]
                                   For mercy's sake,
   Please take this handkerchief, before you speak.
   DORINE   What?
   TARTUFFE   Cover that bosom, girl. The flesh is weak,
   And unclean thoughts are difficult to control.
10   Such sights as that can undermine the soul.
   DORINE   Your soul, it seems, has very poor defenses,
   And flesh makes quite an impact on your senses.
   It's strange that you're so easily excited;
   My own desires are not so soon ignited,
15   And if I saw you naked as a beast,
   Not all your hide would tempt me in the least.
   TARTUFFE   Girl, speak more modestly; unless you do,
   I shall be forced to take my leave of you.
   DORINE   Oh, no, it's I who must be on my way;
20   I've just one little message to convey.
   Madame is coming down, and begs you, Sir,
   To wait and have a word or two with her.
   TARTUFFE   Gladly.
   DORINE [*aside*]   *That* had a softening effect!
   I think my guess about him was correct.
   TARTUFFE   Will she be long?
25   DORINE   No: that's her step I hear.
   Ah, here she is, and I shall disappear.

Scene 3

ELMIRE   TARTUFFE

TARTUFFE   May Heaven, whose infinite goodness we adore,
   Preserve your body and soul forevermore,
   And bless your days, and answer thus the plea

Of one who is its humblest votary.

5 ELMIRE I thank you for that pious wish. But please,
Do take a chair and let's be more at ease.

They sit down.

TARTUFFE I trust that you are once more well and strong?
ELMIRE Oh, yes: the fever didn't last for long.
TARTUFFE My prayers are too unworthy, I am sure,
10   To have gained from Heaven this most gracious cure;
But lately, Madam, my every supplication
Has had for object your recuperation.
ELMIRE You shouldn't have troubled so. I don't deserve it.
TARTUFFE Your health is priceless, Madam, and to preserve it
15   I'd gladly give my own, in all sincerity.
ELMIRE Sir, you outdo us all in Christian charity.
You've been most kind. I count myself your debtor.
TARTUFFE 'Twas nothing, Madam. I long to serve you better.
ELMIRE There's a private matter I'm anxious to discuss.
20   I'm glad there's no one here to hinder us.
TARTUFFE I too am glad; it floods my heart with bliss
To find myself alone with you like this.
For just this chance I've prayed with all my power—
But prayed in vain, until this happy hour.
25 ELMIRE This won't take long, Sir, and I hope you'll be
Entirely frank and unconstrained with me.
TARTUFFE Indeed, there's nothing I had rather do
Than bare my inmost heart and soul to you.
First, let me say that what remarks I've made
30   About the constant visits you are paid
Were prompted not by any mean emotion,
But rather by a pure and deep devotion,
A fervent zeal . . .
ELMIRE   No need for explanation.
Your sole concern, I'm sure, was my salvation.
TARTUFFE [*taking* ELMIRE's *hand and pressing her fingertips*] Quite so; and
35   such great fervor do I feel . . .
ELMIRE Ooh! Please! You're pinching!
TARTUFFE   'Twas from excess of zeal.
I never meant to cause you pain, I swear.
I'd rather . . .

He places his hand on ELMIRE's *knee.*

ELMIRE   What can your hand be doing there?
40 TARTUFFE Feeling your gown; what soft, fine-woven stuff!
ELMIRE Please, I'm extremely ticklish. That's enough.

She draws her chair away; TARTUFFE *pulls his after her.*

TARTUFFE [*fondling the lace collar of her gown*]   My, my, what lovely lacework
    on your dress!
  The workmanship's miraculous, no less.
  I've not seen anything to equal it.
ELMIRE   Yes, quite. But let's talk business for a bit.
45   They say my husband means to break his word
  And give his daughter to you, Sir. Had you heard?
TARTUFFE   He did once mention it. But I confess
  I dream of quite a different happiness.
  It's elsewhere, Madam, that my eyes discern
50   The promise of that bliss for which I yearn.
ELMIRE   I see: you care for nothing here below.
TARTUFFE   Ah, well—my heart's not made of stone, you know.
ELMIRE   All your desires mount heavenward, I'm sure,
  In scorn of all that's earthly and impure.
55 TARTUFFE   A love of heavenly beauty does not preclude
  A proper love for earthly pulchritude;
  Our senses are quite rightly captivated
  By perfect works our Master has created.
  Some glory clings to all that Heaven has made;
60   In you, all Heaven's marvels are displayed.
  On that fair face, such beauties have been lavished,
  The eyes are dazzled and the heart is ravished;
  How could I look on you, O flawless creature,
  And not adore the Author of all Nature,
65   Feeling a love both passionate and pure
  For you, his triumph of self-portraiture?
  At first, I trembled lest that love should be
  A subtle snare that Hell had laid for me;
  I vowed to flee the sight of you, eschewing
70   A rapture that might prove my soul's undoing;
  But soon, fair being, I became aware
  That my deep passion could be made to square
  With rectitude, and with my bounden duty.
  I thereupon surrendered to your beauty.
75   It is, I know, presumptuous on my part
  To bring you this poor offering of my heart,
  And it is not my merit, Heaven knows,
  But your compassion on which my hopes repose.
  You are my peace, my solace, my salvation;
80   On you depends my bliss—or desolation;
  I bide your judgment and, as you think best,
  I shall be either miserable or blest.
ELMIRE   Your declaration is most gallant, Sir,
  But don't you think it's out of character?
85   You'd have done better to restrain your passion
  And think before you spoke in such a fashion.
  It ill becomes a pious man like you . . .
TARTUFFE   I may be pious, but I'm human too:
  With your celestial charms before his eyes,

90   A man has not the power to be wise.
        I know such words sound strangely, coming from me,
        But I'm no angel, nor was meant to be,
        And if you blame my passion, you must needs
        Reproach as well the charms on which it feeds.
95   Your loveliness I had no sooner seen
        Than you became my soul's unrivalled queen;
        Before your seraph glance, divinely sweet,
        My heart's defenses crumbled in defeat,
        And nothing fasting, prayer, or tears might do
100   Could stay my spirit from adoring you.
        My eyes, my sighs have told you in the past
        What now my lips make bold to say at last,
        And if, in your great goodness, you will deign
        To look upon your slave, and ease his pain,—
105   If, in compassion for my soul's distress,
        You'll stoop to comfort my unworthiness,
        I'll raise to you, in thanks for that sweet manna,
        An endless hymn, an infinite hosanna.
        With me, of course, there need be no anxiety,
110   No fear of scandal or of notoriety.
        These young court gallants, whom all the ladies fancy,
        Are vain in speech, in action rash and chancy;
        When they succeed in love, the world soon knows it;
        No favor's granted them but they disclose it
115   And by the looseness of their tongues profane
        The very altar where their hearts have lain.
        Men of my sort, however, love discreetly,
        And one may trust our reticence completely.
        My keen concern for my good name insures
120   The absolute security of yours;
        In short, I offer you, my dear Elmire,
        Love without scandal, pleasure without fear.
    ELMIRE   I've heard your well-turned speeches to the end,
        And what you urge I clearly apprehend.
125   Aren't you afraid that I may take a notion
        To tell my husband of your warm devotion,
        And that, supposing he were duly told,
        His feelings toward you might grow rather cold?
    TARTUFFE   I know, dear lady, that your exceeding charity
130   Will lead your heart to pardon my temerity;
        That you'll excuse my violent affection
        As human weakness, human imperfection;
        And that—O fairest!—you will bear in mind
        That I'm but flesh and blood, and am not blind.
135 ELMIRE   Some women might do otherwise, perhaps,
        But I shall be discreet about your lapse;
        I'll tell my husband nothing of what's occurred
        If, in return, you'll give your solemn word
        To advocate as forcefully as you can

140   The marriage of Valère and Mariane,
           Renouncing all desire to dispossess
           Another of his rightful happiness,
           And . . .

Scene 4

DAMIS ELMIRE TARTUFFE

DAMIS [*emerging from the closet where he has been hiding*]
               No! We'll not hush up this vile affair;
       I heard it all inside that closet there,
       Where Heaven, in order to confound the pride
       Of this great rascal prompted me to hide.
5   Ah, now I have my long-awaited chance
       To punish his deceit and arrogance,
       And give my father clear and shocking proof
       Of the black character of his dear Tartuffe.
     ELMIRE Ah, no, Damis; I'll be content if he
10   Will study to deserve my leniency.
       I've promised silence—don't make me break my word;
       To make a scandal would be too absurd.
       Good wives laugh off such trifles, and forget them;
       Why should they tell their husbands, and upset them?
15   DAMIS You have your reasons for taking such a course,
       And I have reasons, too, of equal force.
       To spare him now would be insanely wrong.
       I've swallowed my just wrath for far too long
       And watched this insolent bigot bringing strife
20   And bitterness into our family life.
       Too long he's meddled in my father's affairs,
       Thwarting my marriage-hopes, and poor Valère's.
       It's high time that my father was undeceived,
       And now I've proof that can't be disbelieved—
25   Proof that was furnished me by Heaven above.
       It's too good not to take advantage of.
       This is my chance, and I deserve to lose it
       If, for one moment, I hesitate to use it.
     ELMIRE Damis . . .
     DAMIS   No, I must do what I think right.
30   Madam, my heart is bursting with delight,
       And, say whatever you will, I'll not consent
       To lose the sweet revenge on which I'm bent.
       I'll settle matters without more ado;
       And here, most opportunely, is my cue.

Scene 5

ORGON TARTUFFE DAMIS ELMIRE

DAMIS Father, I'm glad you've joined us. Let us advise you
     Of some fresh news which doubtless will surprise you.

You've just now been repaid with interest
For all your loving-kindness to our guest.
5   He's proved his warm and grateful feelings toward you;
It's with a pair of horns he would reward you.
Yes, I surprised him with your wife, and heard
His whole adulterous offer, every word.
She, with her all too gentle disposition,
10   Would not have told you of his proposition;
But I shall not make terms with brazen lechery,
And feel that not to tell you would be treachery.
ELMIRE And I hold that one's husband's peace of mind
Should not be spoilt by tattle of this kind.
15   One's honor doesn't require it: to be proficient
In keeping men at bay is quite sufficient.
These are my sentiments, and I wish, Damis,
That you had heeded me and held your peace.

Scene 6

ORGON DAMIS TARTUFFE

ORGON Can it be true, this dreadful thing I hear?
TARTUFFE Yes, Brother, I'm a wicked man, I fear:
A wretched sinner, all depraved and twisted,
The greatest villain that has ever existed.
5   My life's one heap of crimes, which grows each minute;
There's naught but foulness and corruption in it;
And I perceive that Heaven, outraged by me,
Has chosen this occasion to mortify me.
Charge me with any deed you wish to name;
10   I'll not defend myself, but take the blame.
Believe what you are told, and drive Tartuffe
Like some base criminal from beneath your roof;
Yes, drive me hence, and with a parting curse:
I shan't protest, for I deserve far worse.
15   ORGON [to DAMIS] Ah, you deceitful boy, how dare you try
To stain his purity with so foul a lie?
DAMIS What! Are you taken in by such a bluff?
Did you not hear . . .
ORGON   Enough, you rogue, enough!
TARTUFFE Ah, Brother, let him speak: you're being unjust.
20   Believe his story; the boy deserves your trust.
Why, after all, should you have faith in me?
How can you know what I might do, or be?
Is it on my good actions that you base
Your favor? Do you trust my pious face?
25   Ah, no, don't be deceived by hollow shows;
I'm far, alas, from being what men suppose;
Though the world takes me for a man of worth,
I'm truly the most worthless man on earth.
[To DAMIS] Yes, my dear son, speak out now: call me the chief

30 Of sinners, a wretch, a murderer, a thief;
    Load me with all the names men most abhor;
    I'll not complain; I've earned them all, and more;
    I'll kneel here while you pour them on my head
    As a just punishment for the life I've led.
    ORGON [*to* TARTUFFE]   This is too much, dear Brother.
35   [*To* DAMIS]   Have you no heart?
    DAMIS Are you so hoodwinked by this rascal's art . . . ?
    ORGON Be still, you monster.
       [*To* TARTUFFE]   Brother, I pray you, rise.
       [*To* DAMIS] Villain!
    DAMIS   But . . .
    ORGON   Silence!
    DAMIS   Can't you realize . . . ?
    ORGON Just one word more, and I'll tear you limb from limb.
40 TARTUFFE In God's name, Brother, don't be harsh with him.
       I'd rather far be tortured at the stake
       Than see him bear one scratch for my poor sake.
    ORGON [*to* DAMIS] Ingrate!
    TARTUFFE   If I must beg you, on bended knee,
       To pardon him . . .
    ORGON [*falling to his kness, addressing* TARTUFFE]
                   Such goodness cannot be!
       [*To* DAMIS] Now, *there's* true charity!
    DAMIS   What, you . . . ?
45 ORGON   Villain, be still!
       I know your motives; I know you wish him ill:
       Yes, all of you—wife, children, servants, all—
       Conspire against him and desire his fall,
       Employing every shameful trick you can
50   To alienate me from this saintly man.
       Ah, but the more you seek to drive him away,
       The more I'll do to keep him. Without delay,
       I'll spite this household and confound its pride
       By giving him my daughter as his bride.
55 DAMIS You're going to force her to accept his hand?
    ORGON Yes, and this very night, d'you understand?
       I shall defy you all, and make it clear
       That I'm the one who gives the orders here.
       Come, wretch, kneel down and clasp his blessed feet,
60   And ask his pardon for your black deceit.
    DAMIS I ask that swindler's pardon? Why, I'd rather . . .
    ORGON So! You insult him, and defy your father!
       A stick! A stick! [*To* TARTUFFE] No, no—release me, do.
       [*To* DAMIS] Out of my house this minute! Be off with you,
65   And never dare set foot in it again.
    DAMIS Well, I shall go, but . . .
    ORGON   Well, go quickly, then.
       I disinherit you; an empty purse
       Is all you'll get from me—except my curse!

Scene 7

ORGON   TARTUFFE

ORGON   How he blasphemed your goodness! What a son!
TARTUFFE   Forgive him, Lord, as I've already done.
   [*To* ORGON] You can't know how it hurts when someone tries
   To blacken me in my dear Brother's eyes.
ORGON   Ahh!
5   TARTUFFE   The mere thought of such ingratitude
   Plunges my soul into so dark a mood . . .
   Such horror grips my heart . . . I gasp for breath,
   And cannot speak, and feel myself near death.
ORGON [*He runs, in tears, to the door through which he has just driven his*
      son]   You blackguard! Why did I spare you? Why did I not
10   Break you in little pieces on the spot?
   Compose yourself, and don't be hurt, dear friend.
TARTUFFE   These scenes, these dreadful quarrels, have got to end.
   I've much upset your household, and I perceive
   That the best thing will be for me to leave.
ORGON   What are you saying!
15   TARTUFFE   They're all against me here;
   They'd have you think me false and insincere.
ORGON   Ah, what of that? Have I ceased believing in you?
TARTUFFE   Their adverse talk will certainly continue,
   And charges which you now repudiate
20   You may find credible at a later date.
ORGON   No, Brother, never.
TARTUFFE   Brother, a wife can sway
   Her husband's mind in many a subtle way.
ORGON   No, no.
TARTUFFE   To leave at once is the solution;
   Thus only can I end their persecution.
25   ORGON   No, no, I'll not allow it; you shall remain.
TARTUFFE   Ah, well; 'twill mean much martyrdom and pain,
   But if you wish it . . .
ORGON   Ah!
TARTUFFE   Enough; so be it.
   But one thing must be settled, as I see it.
   For your dear honor, and for our friendship's sake,
30   There's one precaution I feel bound to take.
   I shall avoid your wife, and keep away . . .
ORGON   No, you shall not, whatever they may say.
   It pleases me to vex them, and for spite
   I'd have them see you with her day and night.
35   What's more, I'm going to drive them to despair
   By making you my only son and heir;
   This very day, I'll give to you alone
   Clear deed and title to everything I own.
   A dear, good friend and son-in-law-to-be
40   Is more than wife, or child, or kin to me.

Will you accept my offer, dearest son?
TARTUFFE   In all things, let the will of Heaven be done.
ORGON   Poor fellow! Come, we'll go draw up the deed.
Then let them burst with disappointed greed!

Act IV

Scene 1

CLÉANTE   TARTUFFE

CLÉANTE   Yes, all the town's discussing it, and truly,
Their comments do not flatter you unduly.
I'm glad we've met, Sir, and I'll give my view
Of this sad matter in a word or two.
5   As for who's guilty, that I shan't discuss;
Let's say it was Damis who caused the fuss;
Assuming, then, that you have been ill-used
By young Damis, and groundlessly accused,
Ought not a Christian to forgive, and ought
10   He not to stifle every vengeful thought?
Should you stand by and watch a father make
His only son an exile for your sake?
Again I tell you frankly, be advised:
The whole town, high and low, is scandalized;
15   This quarrel must be mended, and my advice is
Not to push matters to a further crisis.
No, sacrifice your wrath to God above,
And help Damis regain his father's love.
TARTUFFE   Alas, for my part I should take great joy
20   In doing so. I've nothing against the boy.
I pardon all, I harbor no resentment;
To serve him would afford me much contentment.
But Heaven's interest will not have it so:
If he comes back, then I shall have to go.
25   After his conduct—so extreme, so vicious—
Our further intercourse would look suspicious.
God knows what people would think! Why, they'd describe
My goodness to him as a sort of bribe;
They'd say that out of guilt I made pretense
30   Of loving-kindness and benevolence—
That, fearing my accuser's tongue, I strove
To buy his silence with a show of love.
CLÉANTE   Your reasoning is badly warped and stretched,
And these excuses, Sir, are most far-fetched.
35   Why put yourself in charge of Heaven's cause?
Does Heaven need our help to enforce its laws?
Leave vengeance to the Lord, Sir; while we live,
Our duty's not to punish, but forgive;
And what the Lord commands, we should obey
40   Without regard to what the world may say.

What! Shall the fear of being misunderstood
Prevent our doing what is right and good?
No, no; let's simply do what Heaven ordains,
And let no other thoughts perplex our brains.

45 TARTUFFE   Again, Sir, let me say that I've forgiven
Damis, and thus obeyed the laws of Heaven;
But I am not commanded by the Bible
To live with one who smears my name with libel.

CLÉANTE   Were you commanded, Sir, to indulge the whim
50 Of poor Orgon, and to encourage him
In suddenly transferring to your name
A large estate to which you have no claim?

TARTUFFE   'Twould never occur to those who know me best
To think I acted from self-interest.
55 The treasures of this world I quite despise;
Their specious glitter does not charm my eyes;
And if I have resigned myself to taking
The gift which my dear Brother insists on making,
I do so only, as he well understands,
60 Lest so much wealth fall into wicked hands,
Lest those to whom it might descend in time
Turn it to purposes of sin and crime,
And not, as I shall do, make use of it
For Heaven's glory and mankind's benefit.

65 CLÉANTE   Forget these trumped-up fears. Your argument
Is one the rightful heir might well resent;
It *is* a moral burden to inherit
Such wealth, but give Damis a chance to bear it.
And would it not be worse to be accused
70 Of swindling, than to see that wealth misused?
I'm shocked that you allowed Orgon to broach
This matter, and that you feel no self-reproach;
Does true religion teach that lawful heirs
May freely be deprived of what is theirs?
75 And if the Lord has told you in your heart
That you and young Damis must dwell apart,
Would it not be the decent thing to beat
A generous and honorable retreat,
Rather than let the son of the house be sent,
80 For your convenience, into banishment?
Sir, if you wish to prove the honesty
Of your intentions . . .

TARTUFFE   Sir, it is half-past three.
I've certain pious duties to attend to,
And hope my prompt departure won't offend you.

CLÉANTE [*alone*]   Damn.

Scene 2

ELMIRE   CLÉANTE   MARIANE   DORINE

DORINE   Stay, Sir, and help Mariane, for Heaven's sake!

She's suffering so, I fear her heart will break.
Her father's plan to marry her off tonight
Has put the poor child in a desperate plight.
5   I hear him coming. Let's stand together, now,
And see if we can't change his mind, somehow,
About this match we all deplore and fear.

Scene 3

ORGON   MARIANE   DORINE   ELMIRE   CLÉANTE

ORGON   Hah! Glad to find you all assembled here.
   [*To* MARIANE] This contract, child, contains your happiness,
   And what it says I think your heart can guess.
MARIANE [*falling to her kness*]   Sir, by that Heaven which sees me here
      distressed,
5   And by whatever else can move your breast,
   Do not employ a father's power, I pray you,
   To crush my heart and force it to obey you,
   Nor by your harsh commands, oppress me so
   That I'll begrudge the duty which I owe—
10   And do not so embitter and enslave me
   That I shall hate the very life you gave me.
   If my sweet hopes must perish, if you refuse
   To give me to the one I've dared to choose,
   Spare me at least—I beg you, I implore—
15   The pain of wedding one whom I abhor;
   And do not, by a heartless use of force,
   Drive me to contemplate some desperate course.
ORGON [*feeling himself touched by her*]   Be firm, my soul. No human
      weakness, now.
MARIANE   I don't resent your love for him. Allow
20   Your heart free rein, Sir; give him your property,
   And if that's not enough, take mine from me;
   He's most welcome to my money; take it, do,
   But don't, I pray, include my person too.
   Spare me, I beg you; and let me end the tale
25   Of my sad days behind a convent veil.
ORGON   A convent! Hah! When crossed in their amours,
   All lovesick girls have the same thought as yours.
   Get up! The more you loathe the man, and dread him,
   The more ennobling it will be to wed him.
30   Marry Tartuffe, and mortify your flesh!
   Enough; don't start that whimpering afresh.
DORINE   But why . . . ?
ORGON   Be still, there. Speak when you're spoken to.
   Not one more bit of impudence out of you.
CLÉANTE   If I may offer a word of counsel here . . .
35   ORGON   Brother, in counseling you have no peer;
   All your advice is forceful, sound, and clever;
   I don't propose to follow it, however.

ELMIRE [*to* ORGON]   I am amazed, and don't know what to say;
    Your blindness simply takes my breath away.
40   You are indeed bewitched, to take no warning
    From our account of what occurred this morning.
ORGON   Madam, I know a few plain facts, and one
    Is that you're partial to my rascal son;
    Hence, when he sought to make Tartuffe the victim
45   Of a base lie, you dared not contradict him.
    Ah, but you underplayed your part, my pet;
    You should have looked more angry, more upset.
ELMIRE   When men make overtures, must we reply
    With righteous anger and a battle-cry?
50   Must we turn back their amorous advances
    With sharp reproaches and with fiery glances?
    Myself, I find such offers merely amusing,
    And make no scenes and fusses in refusing;
    My taste is for good-natured rectitude,
55   And I dislike the savage sort of prude
    Who guards her virtue with her teeth and claws,
    And tears men's eyes out for the slightest cause:
    The Lord preserve me from such honor as that,
    Which bites and scratches like an alley-cat!
60   I've found that a polite and cool rebuff
    Discourages a lover quite enough.
ORGON   I know the facts, and I shall not be shaken.
ELMIRE   I marvel at your power to be mistaken.
    Would it, I wonder, carry weight with you
65   If I could *show* you that our tale was true?
ORGON   Show me?
ELMIRE   Yes.
ORGON   Rot.
ELMIRE   Come, what if I found a way
    To make you see the facts as plain as day?
ORGON   Nonsense.
ELMIRE   Do answer me; don't be absurd.
    I'm not now asking you to trust our word.
70   Suppose that from some hiding-place in here
    You learned the whole sad truth by eye and ear—
    What would you say of your good friend, after that?
ORGON   Why, I'd say . . . nothing, by Jehoshaphat!
    It can't be true.
ELMIRE   You've been too long deceived,
75   And I'm quite tired of being disbelieved.
    Come now: let's put my statements to the test,
    And you shall see the truth made manifest.
ORGON   I'll take that challenge. Now do your uttermost.
    We'll see how you make good your empty boast.
ELMIRE [*to* DORINE]   Send him to me.
80 DORINE   He's crafty; it may be hard
    To catch the cunning scoundrel off his guard.

ELMIRE   No, amorous men are gullible. Their conceit
　　　So blinds them that they're never hard to cheat.
　　　Have him come down. [*To* CLÉANTE *and* MARIANE] Please leave us, for a bit.

Scene 4

ELMIRE   ORGON

ELMIRE   Pull up this table, and get under it.
ORGON   What?
ELMIRE　　　　　It's essential that you be well-hidden.
ORGON   Why there?
ELMIRE　　　　　　　Oh, Heavens! Just do as you are bidden.
　　　I have my plans; we'll soon see how they fare.
5　　　Under the table, now; and once you're there,
　　　Take care that you are neither seen nor heard.
ORGON   Well, I'll indulge you, since I gave my word
　　　To see you through this infantile charade.
ELMIRE   Once it is over, you'll be glad we played.
　　　[*To her husband, who is now under the table*] I'm going to act quite
10　　　　strangely, now, and you
　　　Must not be shocked at anything I do.
　　　Whatever I may say, you must excuse
　　　As part of that deceit I'm forced to use.
　　　I shall employ sweet speeches in the task
15　　　Of making that impostor drop his mask;
　　　I'll give encouragement to his bold desires,
　　　And furnish fuel to his amorous fires.
　　　Since it's for your sake, and for his destruction,
　　　That I shall seem to yield to his seduction,
20　　　I'll gladly stop whenever you decide
　　　That all your doubts are fully satisfied.
　　　I'll count on you, as soon as you have seen
　　　What sort of man he is, to intervene,
　　　And not expose me to his odious lust
25　　　One moment longer than you feel you must.
　　　Remember: you're to save me from my plight
　　　Whenever . . . He's coming! Hush! Keep out of sight!

Scene 5

TARTUFFE   ELMIRE   ORGON

TARTUFFE   You wish to have a word with me, I'm told.
ELMIRE   Yes. I've a little secret to unfold.
　　　Before I speak, however, it would be wise
　　　To close that door, and look about for spies.

[TARTUFFE *goes to the door, closes it, and returns.*]

5　　　The very last thing that must happen now

Is a repetition of this morning's row.
I've never been so badly caught off guard.
Oh, how I feared for you! You saw how hard
I tried to make that troublesome Damis
10   Control his dreadful temper, and hold his peace.
In my confusion, I didn't have the sense
Simply to contradict his evidence;
But as it happened, that was for the best,
And all has worked out in our interest.
15   This storm has only bettered your position;
My husband doesn't have the least suspicion,
And now, in mockery of those who do,
He bids me be continually with you.
And that is why, quite fearless of reproof,
20   I now can be alone with my Tartuffe,
And why my heart—perhaps too quick to yield—
Feels free to let its passion be revealed.
     TARTUFFE   Madam, your words confuse me. Not long ago,
You spoke in quite a different style, you know.
25   ELMIRE   Ah, Sir, if that refusal made you smart,
It's little that you know of woman's heart,
Or what that heart is trying to convey
When it resists in such a feeble way!
Always, at first, our modesty prevents
30   The frank avowal of tender sentiments;
However high the passion which inflames us,
Still, to confess its power somehow shames us.
Thus we reluct, at first, yet in a tone
Which tells you that our heart is overthrown,
35   That what our lips deny, our pulse confesses,
And that, in time, all noes will turn to yesses.
I fear my words are all too frank and free,
And a poor proof of woman's modesty;
But since I'm started, tell me, if you will—
40   Would I have tried to make Damis be still,
Would I have listened, calm and unoffended,
Until your lengthy offer of love was ended,
And been so very mild in my reaction,
Had your sweet words not given me satisfaction?
45   And when I tried to force you to undo
The marriage-plans my husband has in view,
What did my urgent pleading signify
If not that I admired you, and that I
Deplored the thought that someone else might own
50   Part of a heart I wished for mine alone?
     TARTUFFE   Madam, no happiness is so complete
As when, from lips we love, come words so sweet;
Their nectar floods my every sense, and drains
In honeyed rivulets through all my veins.
55   To please you is my joy, my only goal;
Your love is the restorer of my soul;

And yet I must beg leave, now, to confess
Some lingering doubts as to my happiness.
Might this not be a trick? Might not the catch
60   Be that you wish me to break off the match
With Mariane, and so have feigned to love me?
I shan't quite trust your fond opinion of me
Until the feelings you've expressed so sweetly
Are demonstrated somewhat more concretely,
65   And you have shown, by certain kind concessions,
That I may put my faith in your professions.
ELMIRE [*She coughs, to warn her husband*]   Why be in such a hurry? Must my heart
Exhaust its bounty at the very start?
To make that sweet admission cost me dear,
70   But you'll not be content, it would appear,
Unless my store of favors is disbursed
To the last farthing, and at the very first.
TARTUFFE The less we merit, the less we dare to hope,
And with our doubts, mere words can never cope.
75   We trust no promised bliss till we receive it;
Not till a joy is ours can we believe it.
I, who so little merit your esteem,
Can't credit this fulfillment of my dream,
And shan't believe it, Madam, until I savor
80   Some palpable assurance of your favor.
ELMIRE My, how tyrannical your love can be,
And how it flusters and perplexes me!
How furiously you take one's heart in hand,
And make your every wish a fierce command!
85   Come, must you hound and harry me to death?
Will you not give me time to catch my breath?
Can it be right to press me with such force,
Give me no quarter, show me no remorse,
And take advantage, by your stern insistence,
90   Of the fond feelings which weaken my resistance?
TARTUFFE Well, if you look with favor upon my love,
Why, then, begrudge me some clear proof thereof?
ELMIRE But how can I consent without offense
To Heaven, toward which you feel such reverence?
95 TARTUFFE If Heaven is all that holds you back, don't worry.
I can remove that hindrance in a hurry.
Nothing of that sort need obstruct our path.
ELMIRE Must one not be afraid of Heaven's wrath?
TARTUFFE Madam, forget such fears, and be my pupil,
100   And I shall teach you how to conquer scruple.
Some joys, it's true, are wrong in Heaven's eyes;
Yet Heaven is not averse to compromise;
There is a science, lately formulated,
Whereby one's conscience may be liberated,
105   And any wrongful act you care to mention
May be redeemed by purity of intention.

I'll teach you, Madam, the secrets of that science;
Meanwhile, just place on me your full reliance.
Assuage my keen desires, and feel no dread:
110   The sin, if any, shall be on my head.

[ELMIRE *coughs, this time more loudly.*]

You've a bad cough.
ELMIRE   Yes, yes. It's bad indeed.
TARTUFFE [*producing a little paper bag*]   A bit of licorice may be what you
    need.
ELMIRE   No, I've a stubborn cold, it seems. I'm sure it
    Will take much more than licorice to cure it.
TARTUFFE   How aggravating.
115   ELMIRE   Oh, more than I can say.
TARTUFFE   If you're still troubled, think of things this way:
    No one shall know our joys, save us alone,
    And there's no evil till the act is known;
    It's scandal, Madam, which makes it an offense,
120   And it's no sin to sin in confidence.
ELMIRE [*having coughed once more*]   Well, clearly I must do as you require,
    And yield to your importunate desire.
    It is apparent, now, that nothing less
    Will satisfy you, and so I acquiesce.
125   To go so far is much against my will;
    I'm vexed that it should come to this; but still,
    Since you are so determined on it, since you
    Will not allow mere language to convince you,
    And since you ask for concrete evidence, I
130   See nothing for it, now, but to comply.
    If this is sinful, if I'm wrong to do it,
    So much the worse for him who drove me to it.
    The fault can surely not be charged to me.
TARTUFFE   Madam, the fault is mine, if fault there be,
    And
135   ELMIRE   Open the door a little, and peek out;
    I wouldn't want my husband poking about.
TARTUFFE   Why worry about the man? Each day he grows
    More gullible; one can lead him by the nose.
    To find us here would fill him with delight,
140   And if he saw the worst, he'd doubt his sight.
ELMIRE   Nevertheless, do step out for a minute
    Into the hall, and see that no one's in it.

Scene 6

ORGON   ELMIRE

ORGON [*coming out from under the table*]   That man's a perfect monster, I
    must admit!

I'm simply stunned. I can't get over it.
ELMIRE   What, coming out so soon? How premature!
Get back in hiding, and wait until you're sure.
5   Stay till the end, and be convinced completely;
We mustn't stop till things are proved concretely.
ORGON   Hell never harbored anything so vicious!
ELMIRE   Tut, don't be hasty. Try to be judicious.
Wait, and be certain that there's no mistake.
10   No jumping to conclusions, for Heaven's sake!

She places ORGON *behind her, as* TARTUFFE *re-enters.*

Scene 7

TARTUFFE   ELMIRE   ORGON

TARTUFFE [*not seeing* ORGON]   Madam, all things have worked out to
perfection;
I've given the neighboring rooms a full inspection;
No one's about; and now I may at last . . .
ORGON [*intercepting him*]   Hold on, my passionate fellow, not so fast!
5   I should advise a little more restraint.
Well, so you thought you'd fool me, my dear saint!
How soon you wearied of the saintly life—
Wedding my daughter, and coveting my wife!
I've long suspected you, and had a feeling
10   That soon I'd catch you at your double-dealing.
Just now, you've given me evidence galore;
It's quite enough; I have no wish for more.
ELMIRE [*to* TARTUFFE]   I'm sorry to have treated you so slyly,
But circumstances forced me to be wily.
TARTUFFE   Brother, you can't think . . .
15   ORGON   No more talk from you;
Just leave this household, without more ado.
TARTUFFE   What I intended . . .
ORGON   That seems fairly clear.
Spare me your falsehoods and get out of here.
TARTUFFE   No, I'm the master, and you're the one to go!
20   This house belongs to me, I'll have you know,
And I shall show you that you can't hurt *me*
By this contemptible conspiracy,
That those who cross me know not what they do,
And that I've means to expose and punish you,
25   Avenge offended Heaven, and make you grieve
That ever you dared order me to leave.

Scene 8

ELMIRE   ORGON

ELMIRE   What was the point of all that angry chatter?

ORGON   Dear God, I'm worried. This is no laughing matter.
ELMIRE   How so?
ORGON   I fear I understood his drift.
   I'm much disturbed about that deed of gift.
ELMIRE   You gave him . . . ?
5   ORGON   Yes, it's all been drawn and signed.
   But one thing more is weighing on my mind.
ELMIRE   What's that?
ORGON   I'll tell you; but first let's see if there's
   A certain strong-box in his room upstairs.

Act V

Scene 1

ORGON   CLÉANTE

CLÉANTE   Where are you going so fast?
ORGON   God knows!
CLÉANTE   Then wait;
   Let's have a conference, and deliberate
   On how this situation's to be met.
ORGON   That strong-box has me utterly upset;
5   This is the worst of many, many shocks.
CLÉANTE   Is there some fearful mystery in that box?
ORGON   My poor friend Argas brought that box to me
   With his own hands, in utmost secrecy;
   'Twas on the very morning of his flight.
10   It's full of papers which, if they came to light,
   Would ruin him—or such is my impression.
CLÉANTE   Then why did you let it out of your possession?
ORGON   Those papers vexed my conscience, and it seemed best
   To ask the counsel of my pious guest.
15   The cunning scoundrel got me to agree
   To leave the strong-box in his custody,
   So that, in case of an investigation,
   I could employ a slight equivocation
   And swear I didn't have it, and thereby,
20   At no expense to conscience, tell a lie.
CLÉANTE   It looks to me as if you're out on a limb.
   Trusting him with that box, and offering him
   That deed of gift, were actions of a kind
   Which scarcely indicate a prudent mind.
25   With two such weapons, he has the upper hand,
   And since you're vulnerable, as matters stand,
   You erred once more in bringing him to bay.
   You should have acted in some subtler way.
ORGON   Just think of it: behind that fervent face,
30   A heart so wicked, and a soul so base!
   I took him in, a hungry beggar, and then . . .
   Enough, by God! I'm through with pious men:

Henceforth I'll hate the whole false brotherhood,
And persecute them worse than Satan could.
35   CLÉANTE   Ah, there you go—extravagant as ever!
Why can you not be rational? You never
Manage to take the middle course, it seems,
But jump, instead, between absurd extremes.
You've recognized your recent grave mistake
40   In falling victim to a pious fake;
Now, to correct that error, must you embrace
An even greater error in its place,
And judge our worthy neighbors as a whole
By what you've learned of one corrupted soul?
45   Come, just because one rascal made you swallow
A show of zeal which turned out to be hollow,
Shall you conclude that all men are deceivers,
And that, today, there are no true believers?
Let atheists make that foolish inference;
50   Learn to distinguish virtue from pretense,
Be cautious in bestowing admiration,
And cultivate a sober moderation.
Don't humor fraud, but also don't asperse
True piety; the latter fault is worse,
55   And it is best to err, if err one must,
As you have done, upon the side of trust.

Scene 2

DAMIS   ORGON   CLÉANTE

DAMIS   Father, I hear that scoundrel's uttered threats
Against you; that he pridefully forgets
How, in his need, he was befriended by you,
And means to use your gifts to crucify you.
5   ORGON   It's true, my boy. I'm too distressed for tears.
DAMIS   Leave it to me, Sir; let me trim his ears.
Faced with such insolence, we must not waver.
I shall rejoice in doing you the favor
Of cutting short his life, and your distress.
10   CLÉANTE   What a display of young hotheadedness!
Do learn to moderate your fits of rage.
In this just kingdom, this enlightened age,
One does not settle things by violence.

Scene 3

MADAME PERNELLE   DORINE   ORGON   MARIANE   DAMIS   CLÉANTE   ELMIRE

MADAME PERNELLE   I hear strange tales of very strange events.
ORGON   Yes, strange events which these two eyes beheld.

The man's ingratitude is unparalleled.
I save a wretched pauper from starvation,
5   House him, and treat him like a blood relation,
Shower him every day with my largesse,
Give him my daughter, and all that I possess;
And meanwhile the unconscionable knave
Tries to induce my wife to misbehave;
10   And not content with such extreme rascality,
Now threatens me with my own liberality,
And aims, by taking base advantage of
The gifts I gave him out of Christian love,
To drive me from my house, a ruined man,
15   And make me end a pauper, as he began.
DORINE   Poor fellow!
MADAME PERNELLE   No, my son, I'll never bring
Myself to think him guilty of such a thing.
ORGON   How's that?
MADAME PERNELLE   The righteous always were maligned.
ORGON   Speak clearly, Mother. Say what's on your mind.
20   MADAME PERNELLE   I mean that I can smell a rat, my dear.
You know how everybody hates him, here.
ORGON   That has no bearing on the case at all.
MADAME PERNELLE   I told you a hundred times, when you were small,
That virtue in this world is hated ever;
25   Malicious men may die, but malice never.
ORGON   No doubt that's true, but how does it apply?
MADAME PERNELLE   They've turned you against him by a clever lie.
ORGON   I've told you, I was there and saw it done.
MADAME PERNELLE   Ah, slanderers will stop at nothing, Son.
30   ORGON   Mother, I'll lose my temper . . . For the last time,
I tell you I was witness to the crime.
MADAME PERNELLE   The tongues of spite are busy night and noon,
And to their venom no man is immune.
ORGON   You're talking nonsense. Can't you realize
35   I saw it; saw it; saw it with my eyes?
Saw, do you understand me? Must I shout it
Into your ears before you'll cease to doubt it?
MADAME PERNELLE   Appearances can deceive, my son. Dear me,
We cannot always judge by what we see.
ORGON   Drat! Drat!
40   MADAME PERNELLE   One often interprets things awry;
Good can seem evil to a suspicious eye.
ORGON   Was I to see his pawing at Elmire
As an act of charity?
MADAME PERNELLE   Till his guilt is clear,
A man deserves the benefit of the doubt.
45   You should have waited, to see how things turned out.
ORGON   Great God in Heaven, what more proof did I need?
Was I to sit there, watching, until he'd . . .
You drive me to the brink of impropriety.

MADAME PERNELLE No, no, a man of such surpassing piety
50   Could not do such a thing. You cannot shake me.
        I don't believe it, and you shall not make me.
ORGON You vex me so that, if you weren't my mother,
        I'd say to you . . . some dreadful thing or other.
DORINE It's your turn now, Sir, not to be listened to;
55   You'd not trust us, and now she won't trust you.
CLÉANTE My friends, we're wasting time which should be spent
        In facing up to our predicament.
        I fear that scoundrel's threats weren't made in sport.
DAMIS Do you think he'd have the nerve to go to court?
60 ELMIRE I'm sure he won't: they'd find it all too crude
        A case of swindling and ingratitude.
CLÉANTE Don't be too sure. He won't be at a loss
        To give his claims a high and righteous gloss;
        And clever rogues with far less valid cause
65   Have trapped their victims in a web of laws.
        I say again that to antagonize
        A man so strongly armed was most unwise.
ORGON I know it; but the man's appalling cheek
        Outraged me so, I couldn't control my pique.
70 CLÉANTE I wish to Heaven that we could devise
        Some truce between you, or some compromise.
ELMIRE If I had known what cards he held, I'd not
        Have roused his anger by my little plot.
ORGON [to DORINE, as M. LOYAL enters] What is that fellow looking for? Who
        is he?
75   Go talk to him—and tell him that I'm busy.

Scene 4

MONSIEUR LOYAL DAMIS ELMIRE MADAME PERNELLE
MARIANE CLÉANTE ORGON DORINE

MONSIEUR LOYAL Good day, dear sister. Kindly let me see
        Your master.
DORINE   He's involved with company,
        And cannot be disturbed just now, I fear.
MONSIEUR LOYAL I hate to intrude; but what has brought me here
5   Will not disturb your master, in any event.
        Indeed, my news will make him most content.
DORINE   He's involved with company,
MONSIEUR LOYAL   Just say that I bring greetings from
        Monsieur Tartuffe, on whose behalf I've come.
DORINE [to ORGON] Sir, he's a very gracious man, and bears
10   A message from Tartuffe, which, he declares,
        Will make you most content.
CLÉANTE   Upon my word,
        I think this man had best be seen, and heard.
ORGON Perhaps he has some settlement to suggest.

How shall I treat him? What manner would be best?

15   CLÉANTE Control your anger, and if he should mention
      Some fair adjustment, give him your full attention.

  MONSIEUR LOYAL Good health to you, good Sir. May Heaven confound
      Your enemies, and may your joys abound.

  ORGON [*aside, to* CLÉANTE] A gentle salutation: it confirms

20   My guess that he is here to offer terms.

  MONSIEUR LOYAL I've always held your family most dear;
      I served your father, Sir, for many a year.

  ORGON Sir, I must ask your pardon; to my shame,
      I cannot now recall your face or name.

25   MONSIEUR LOYAL Loyal's my name; I come from Normandy,
      And I'm a bailiff, in all modesty.
      For forty years, praise God, it's been my boast
      To serve with honor in that vital post,
      And I am here, Sir, if you will permit

30   The liberty, to serve you with this writ . . .

  ORGON To—*what?*

  MONSIEUR LOYAL Now, please, Sir, let us have no friction:
      It's nothing but an order of eviction.
      You are to move your goods and family out
      And make way for new occupants, without

35   Deferment or delay, and give the keys . . .

  ORGON I? Leave this house?

  MONSIEUR LOYAL   Why yes, Sir, if you please.
      This house, Sir, from the cellar to the roof,
      Belongs now to the good Monsieur Tartuffe,
      And he is lord and master of your estate

40   By virtue of a deed of present date,
      Drawn in due form, with clearest legal phrasing . . .

  DAMIS Your insolence is utterly amazing!

  MONSIEUR LOYAL Young man, my business here is not with you,
      But with your wise and temperate father, who,

45   Like every worthy citizen, stands in awe
      Of justice, and would never obstruct the law.

  ORGON But . . .

  MONSIEUR LOYAL Not for a million, Sir, would you rebel
      Against authority; I know that well.
      You'll not make trouble, Sir, or interfere

50   With the execution of my duties here.

  DAMIS Someone may execute a smart tattoo
      On that black jacket of yours, before you're through.

  MONSIEUR LOYAL Sir, bid your son be silent. I'd much regret
      Having to mention such a nasty threat

55   Of violence, in writing my report.

  DORINE [*aside*] This man Loyal's a most disloyal sort!

  MONSIEUR LOYAL I love all men of upright character,
      And when I agreed to serve these papers, Sir,
      It was your feelings that I had in mind.

60   I couldn't bear to see the case assigned

To someone else, who might esteem you less
And so subject you to unpleasantness.
ORGON   What's more unpleasant than telling a man to leave
His house and home?
MONSIEUR LOYAL   You'd like a short reprieve?
65   If you desire it, Sir, I shall not press you,
But wait until tomorrow to dispossess you.
Splendid. I'll come and spend the night here, then,
Most quietly, with half a score of men.
For form's sake, you might bring me, just before
70   You go to bed, the keys to the front door.
My men, I promise, will be on their best
Behavior, and will not disturb your rest.
But bright and early, Sir, you must be quick
And move out all your furniture, every stick:
75   The men I've chosen are both young and strong,
And with their help it shouldn't take you long.
In short, I'll make things pleasant and convenient,
And since I'm being so extremely lenient,
Please show me, Sir, a like consideration,
80   And give me your entire cooperation.
ORGON [aside]   I may be all but bankrupt, but I vow
I'd give a hundred louis, here and now,
Just for the pleasure of landing one good clout
Right on the end of that complacent snout.
CLÉANTE   Careful; don't make things worse.
85   DAMIS   My bootsole itches
To give that beggar a good kick in the breeches.
DORINE   Monsieur Loyal, I'd love to hear the whack
Of a stout stick across your fine broad back.
MONSIEUR LOYAL   Take care: a woman too may go to jail if
90   She uses threatening language to a bailiff.
CLÉANTE   Enough, enough, Sir. This must not go on.
Give me that paper, please, and then begone.
MONSIEUR LOYAL   Well, *au revoir*. God give you all good cheer!
ORGON   May God confound you, and him who sent you here!

Scene 5

ORGON   ELMIRE   DORINE   CLÉANTE   MADAME PERNELLE   DAMIS   MARIANE

ORGON   Now, Mother, was I right or not? This writ
Should change your notion of Tartuffe a bit.
Do you perceive his villainy at last?
MADAME PERNELLE   I'm thunderstruck. I'm utterly aghast.
5   DORINE   Oh, come, be fair. You mustn't take offense
At this new proof of his benevolence.
He's acting out of selfless love, I know.
Material things enslave the soul, and so
He kindly has arranged your liberation

10   From all that might endanger your salvation.
        ORGON Will you not ever hold your tongue, you dunce?
        CLÉANTE Come, you must take some action, and at once.
        ELMIRE Go tell the world of the low trick he's tried.
           The deed of gift is surely nullified
15   By such behavior, and public rage will not
           Permit the wretch to carry out his plot.

Scene 6

VALÈRE ELMIRE DAMIS ORGON MARIANE DORINE CLÉANTE
MADAME PERNELLE

        VALÈRE Sir, though I hate to bring you more bad news,
           Such is the danger that I cannot choose.
           A friend who is extremely close to me
           And knows my interest in your family
5   Has, for my sake, presumed to violate
           The secrecy that's due to things of state,
           And sends me word that you are in a plight
           From which your one salvation lies in flight.
           That scoundrel who's imposed upon you so
10   Denounced you to the King an hour ago
           And, as supporting evidence, displayed
           The strong-box of a certain renegade
           Whose secret papers, so he testified,
           You had disloyally agreed to hide.
15   I don't know just what charges may be pressed,
           But there's a warrant out for your arrest;
           Tartuffe has been instructed, furthermore,
           To guide the arresting officer to your door.
        CLÉANTE He's clearly done this to facilitate
20   His seizure of your house and your estate.
        ORGON That man, I must say, is a vicious beast!
        VALÈRE Quick, Sir; you mustn't tarry in the least.
           My carriage is outside, to take you hence;
           This thousand louis should cover all expense.
25   Let's lose no time, or you shall be undone;
           The sole defense, in this case, is to run.
           I shall go with you all the way, and place you
           In a safe refuge to which they'll never trace you.
        ORGON Alas, dear boy, I wish that I could show you
30   My gratitude for everything I owe you.
           But now is not the time; I pray the Lord
           That I may live to give you your reward.
           Farewell, my dears; be careful . . .
        CLÉANTE   Brother, hurry.
           We shall take care of things; you needn't worry.

Scene 7

THE OFFICER ELMIRE DORINE TARTUFFE MARIANE CLÉANTE VALÈRE
MADAME PERNELLE DAMIS ORGON

TARTUFFE Gently, Sir, gently; stay right where you are.
    No need for haste; your lodging isn't far.
    You're off to prison, by order of the Prince.
ORGON This is the crowning blow, you wretch; and since
5   It means my total ruin and defeat,
    Your villainy is now at last complete.
TARTUFFE You needn't try to provoke me; it's no use.
    Those who serve Heaven must expect abuse.
CLÉANTE You are indeed most patient, sweet, and blameless.
10   DORINE How he exploits the name of Heaven! It's shameless.
TARTUFFE Your taunts and mockeries are all for naught;
    To do my duty is my only thought.
MARIANE Your love of duty is most meritorious,
    And what you've done is little short of glorious.
15   TARTUFFE All deeds are glorious, Madam, which obey
    The sovereign prince who sent me here today.
ORGON I rescued you when you were destitute;
    Have you forgotten that, you thankless brute?
TARTUFFE No, no, I well remember everything;
20   But my first duty is to serve my King.
    That obligation is so paramount
    That other claims, beside it, do not count;
    And for it I would sacrifice my wife,
    My family, my friend, or my own life.
ELMIRE Hypocrite!
25   DORINE   All that we most revere, he uses
    To cloak his plots and camouflage his ruses.
CLÉANTE If it is true that you are animated
    By pure and loyal zeal, as you have stated,
    Why was this zeal not roused until you'd sought
30   To make Orgon a cuckold, and been caught?
    Why weren't you moved to give your evidence
    Until your outraged host had driven you hence?
    I shan't say that the gift of all his treasure
    Ought to have damped your zeal in any measure;
35   But if he is a traitor, as you declare,
    How could you condescend to be his heir?
TARTUFFE [to the OFFICER] Sir, spare me all this clamor; it's growing shrill.
    Please carry out your orders, if you will.
OFFICER Yes, I've delayed too long, Sir. Thank you kindly.
40   You're just the proper person to remind me.
    Come, you are off to join the other boarders
    In the King's prison, according to his orders.
TARTUFFE Who I, Sir?
OFFICER   Yes,

TARTUFFE   To prison? This can't be true!
OFFICER   I owe an explanation, but not to you.
45   [*To* ORGON] Sir, all is well; rest easy, and be grateful.
        We serve a Prince to whom all sham is hateful,
        A Prince who sees into our inmost hearts,
        And can't be fooled by any trickster's arts.
        His royal soul, though generous and human,
50   Views all things with discernment and acumen;
        His sovereign reason is not lightly swayed,
        And all his judgments are discreetly weighed.
        He honors righteous men of every kind,
        And yet his zeal for virtue is not blind,
55   Nor does his love of piety numb his wits
        And make him tolerant of hypocrites.
        'Twas hardly likely that this man could cozen
        A King who's foiled such liars by the dozen.
        With one keen glance, the King perceived the whole
60   Perverseness and corruption of his soul,
        And thus high Heaven's justice was displayed:
        Betraying you, the rogue stood self-betrayed.
        The King soon recognized Tartuffe as one
        Notorious by another name, who'd done
65   So many vicious crimes that one could fill
        Ten volumes with them, and be writing still.
        But to be brief: our sovereign was appalled
        By this man's treachery toward you, which he called
        The last, worst villainy of a vile career,
70   And bade me follow the imposter here
        To see how gross his impudence could be,
        And force him to restore your property.
        Your private papers, by the King's command,
        I hereby seize and give into your hand.
75   The King, by royal order, invalidates
        The deed which gave this rascal your estates,
        And pardons, furthermore, your grave offense
        In harboring an exile's documents.
        By these decrees, our Prince rewards you for
80   Your loyal deeds in the late civil war,
        And shows how heartfelt is his satisfaction
        In recompensing any worthy action,
        How much he prizes merit, and how he makes
        More of men's virtues than of their mistakes.
DORINE   Heaven be praised!
85   MADAME PERNELLE   I breathe again, at last.
ELMIRE   We're safe.
MARIANE   I can't believe the danger's past.
ORGON [*to* TARTUFFE]   Well, traitor, now you see . . .
CLÉANTE   Ah, Brother, please,
        Let's not descend to such indignities.
        Leave the poor wretch to his unhappy fate,

90   And don't say anything to aggravate
        His present woes; but rather hope that he
        Will soon embrace an honest piety,
        And mend his ways, and by a true repentance
        Move our just King to moderate his sentence.
95   Meanwhile, go kneel before your sovereign's throne
        And thank him for the mercies he has shown.
     ORGON   Well said: let's go at once and, gladly kneeling,
        Express the gratitude which all are feeling.
        Then, when that first great duty has been done,
100   We'll turn with pleasure to a second one,
        And give Valère, whose love has proven so true,
        The wedded happiness which is his due.

Questions

foreshadowing
characterization
how the author moves the plot
Dorine
Orgon

1. Molière has been criticized for delaying Tartuffe's entrance: although Tartuffe's character runs away with the play and steals its title, he does not make
   his entrance until the third act. Molière himself wrote: "I have employed
   . . . two entire acts to prepare for the entrance of my scoundrel. He does not
   fool the auditor for a single moment . . . from one end to the other he says
   not a word and performs not an action which does not paint for the spectators
   the character of an evil man." Does this statement justify Tartuffe's late entrance? Or is it a flaw in the play's structure? Explain.
2. How does earlier dialogue prepare us for Tartuffe's entrance? In the first
   three or four minutes of Tartuffe's presence on the stage, what earlier
   speeches are illustrated or explained?
3. Describe in a few words what Cléante's character supplies to the plot of *Tartuffe*. Is a character of this sort necessary to the unfolding of the plot?
4. Define Dorine's function in the plot, especially early in the play. Have you
   noticed other characters who perform in other plays as she does? Some people
   have found her like a playwright or a play's director; what do they mean by
   such a suggestion?
5. "When Damis denounces Tartuffe to his father as Elmire's would-be seducer,
   Tartuffe readily admits his sinfulness in such sweeping terms of self-abase-
   ment that Orgon becomes only further convinced of his Christian humility."
   What is the term for such a twist of plot?
6. The translator writes: "We gather from the maid Dorine that Orgon has until
   lately seemed a good and sensible man, but the Orgon whom we meet in Act
   I, Scene IV, has become a fool. What has happened to him?" What do you
   think?
7. "While the Tartuffes of the world are dangerous, they can exist only because
   of the Orgons, for the prosperity of the wicked depends on the gullibility of
   the foolish." Could you defend the assertion that Tartuffe, who is merely a
   criminal, is not genuinely the villain of this play?
8. Is this play about religious hypocrisy? If religious hypocrisy is not the major
   topic of this play, what is? Did Molière want to convince his audience of
   anything in particular? Is this play didactic? Satiric?
9. Using a desk or a table and a screen or a large map, stage in the classroom

one of the scenes in which characters overhear other characters. Discuss possibilities of blocking, gesture (including facial expression), and lighting.

10. In other plays you have read, how often does someone hide and overhear something? It happens twice in *Tartuffe*. Often it is a comic device, but it happens in tragedy also; Polonius hides behind a curtain in *Hamlet* with results that are not funny. Is overhearing dramatic or theatrical by its nature? Why? In real life, if a crook like Tartuffe is exposed—perhaps a politician who has taken bribes or an embezzling banker—a newspaper will often declare that the culprit has been "unmasked." Is there anything inherently theatrical about unmasking? Is Tartuffe unmasked? Was Oedipus unmasked?

11. Richard Wilbur writes: "*Tartuffe* is only incidentally satiric; what we experience in reading or seeing it, as several modern critics have argued, is not a satire, but a 'deep' comedy in which (1) a knave tries to control life by cold chicanery, (2) a fool tries to oppress life by unconscious misuse of the highest values, and (3) Life, happily, will not have it." Does this summation omit anything of importance?

Chapter 6 **Modern Drama, Realism, and Chekhov**

The idea of realism

We call modern drama realistic when it uses theatrical conventions we accept as representing the world we live in. In realistic modern drama we look at actors imitating actual people, speaking dialogue constructed to resemble people talking, among sets that resemble rooms or gardens. To understand why we call this theater realistic we must look at it from the other side of history, and understand **realism** in the context of earlier drama. We must understand what modern realistic drama is *not*: people do not speak in rhymed couplets; people do not converse with ghosts or address the audience in asides or speak eloquent blank-verse meditations on empty stages; people are not kings fated to marry widowed queens who are their secret mothers. On the modern realistic stage, instead of kings, characters are salesmen, landowners, nurses, society matrons, politicians, real-estate developers. Instead of poetry they speak prose, and they interrupt and misunderstand each other. Their problems lie not in mysterious plagues but in diseases like tuberculosis. Instead of needing to avenge a king-father's murder, realistic heroes struggle to prevail over petty envy or to love and be loved, find a job or keep a pension.

If we contrast *Oedipus the King* with *Death of a Salesman,* the difference seems to justify the word *realistic*. Yet the term is treacherous. After all, when we praise *Oedipus the King* as true to nature, or *Hamlet* as psychologically profound, we are calling each of the plays *real*—if not realistic drama.

The movement toward realism on the stage began earlier than the mid-nineteenth century and arose from social and historical causes. Even on the stage of the Jacobean period, which succeeded the Elizabethan era in England, mid-

955

dle-class characters took over subplots; gradually middle-class subplots weighed heavier than noble main plots. A rising middle class required mirrors of itself on the stage it patronized. Realism necessitated improved technology in lighting, stage machinery, sets, and sound effects. The same capitalist industrialism that enriched the middle class invented the phonograph and the electric light. By the late nineteenth century a materialistic world view, which substituted neurosis for witchcraft and syphillis for fate, demanded from the theater plain talk and sophisticated technology.

For the great playwrights of the modern stage, drama was no mere plaything of the middle class or an entertainment for tired capitalists. Their art was a representation of life as it actually was lived, viewed with attitudes ranging from indictment to affection. Henrik Ibsen (1828–1906) wrote realistic drama in the great middle period of his long artistic life (see "Henrik Ibsen and *Hedda Gabler*," page 1150). A great British realist was George Bernard Shaw (1856–1950), represented in this volume by his historical play *Saint Joan* (page 1208). Among many playwrights of the realistic stage, August Strindberg (1849–1912) in his early work carried realism on to **naturalism**—a variant that is concerned with the most sordid parts of reality, or, to use the title of a naturalist play by Maxim Gorki (1868–1936), *The Lower Depths*.

Chekhov and *The Cherry Orchard*

One of the masters of dramatic realism was the Russian Anton Chekhov (1864–1904), a master as well of the short story (his "Gooseberries" appears on pages 108–114). Chekhov emerged from the rising merchant class in the late years of Tzarist Russia; his grandfather had been a serf and his father was a small shopkeeper. Chekhov trained to be a doctor, and while he was studying medicine wrote humorous short stories to make money. Ultimately literature won out over medicine. Yet when he turned to the theater after success in fiction, the first production of *The Sea Gull* was a disaster. Only when Konstantin Stanislavsky (see page 740), the great director of the Moscow Art Theater, produced *The Sea Gull* in 1898 did the play succeed. In the brief time

Act 1 of the first production of *The Cherry Orchard* at the Moscow Art Theater, January 1904.

remaining to him, Chekhov wrote *Uncle Vanya* (1899), *The Three Sisters* (1901), and *The Cherry Orchard* (1904).

Contemporary Americans should understand the social background of Chekhov's plays, perhaps most particularly of *The Cherry Orchard*. In fiction and in drama alike, Chekhov presents peasants and merchants and aristocrats with equal clarity, compassion, and humor. Reading *The Cherry Orchard,* we must realize that the serfs, who had been virtual slaves, had been only recently liberated; it became legal for landowners to free serfs in 1803, compulsory in 1861. Old Fiers therefore acts as if he were still a serf. On the other hand, Lopahin like Chekhov comes from a family of liberated serfs—and Lopahin belongs to a rising class of entrepreneurs. We might expect Chekhov with his background to make class war on Madame Ranevskaya and her brother, but Chekhov's temperament is gentle and ironic, his artistic attitude objective. In *The Cherry Orchard* liberated serfs and impoverished landowners associate with one another, and younger Russians of various backgrounds attempt to adjust to the new Russia. Many of the characters seem left over from an old life; others are visionaries of the future. Yet if the play is dense with the texture of society, it is by no means a social document. The historical context of *The Cherry Orchard* merely provides particulars for a view of the world—as human comedy—Chekhov was able to discover.

The Cherry Orchard has survived seventy years of melancholy productions. Chekhov considered it a comedy almost as broad as farce, and recently the play has been acted for its humor. The best productions are nevertheless funny and sad at the same time. *The Cherry Orchard* varies emotional pitch continually, is by turns euphoric and miserable. Its realism lies not in its social particularity so much as in its psychological exactness; here is a silly, vain, affectionate woman; here is her ineffectual, optimistic, doomed brother; here is a shrewd, opportunistic peasant, at the same time shy, diffident; here are lovers, here are fools: *and each is unique.* Chekhov's stage is large enough to suggest the universe.

Anton Chekhov
The Cherry Orchard

Translated by Stark Young

Characters

LYUBOFF ANDREEVNA RANEVSKAYA, a
  landowner
ANYA, her daughter, seventeen years old
VARYA, her adopted daughter, twenty-
  four years old
LEONID ANDREEVICH GAYEFF, brother
  of Ranevskaya
YERMOLAY ALEXEEVICH LOPAHIN, a
  merchant
PYOTR SERGEEVICH TROFIMOFF, a
  student
BORIS BORISOVICH SEMYONOFF-
  PISHTCHIK, a landowner

CHARLOTTA IVANOVNA, a governess
SEMYON PANTELEEVICH EPIHODOFF, a
  clerk
DUNYASHA, a maid
FIERS, a valet, an old man of eighty-
  seven
YASHA, a young valet
A PASSERBY or STRANGER
THE STATIONMASTER
A POST-OFFICE CLERK
VISITORS, SERVANTS

The action takes place on the estate of L. A. Ranevskaya.

Act I

A room that is still called the nursery. One of the doors leads into ANYA's *room. Dawn, the sun will soon be rising. It is May, the cherry trees are in blossom but in the orchard it is cold, with a morning frost. The windows in the room are closed. Enter* DUNYASHA *with a candle and* LOPAHIN *with a book in his hand.*

LOPAHIN   The train got in, thank God! What time is it?

DUNYASHA   It's nearly two. [*Blows out his candle*] It's already daylight.

LOPAHIN   But how late was the train? Two hours at least. [*Yawning and stretching*] I'm a fine one, I am, look what a fool thing I did! I drove here on purpose just to meet them at the station, and then all of a sudden I'd overslept myself! Fell asleep in my chair. How provoking!—You could have waked me up.

DUNYASHA   I thought you had gone. [*Listening*] Listen, I think they are coming now.

LOPAHIN [*listening*]   No—No, there's the luggage and one thing and another. [*A pause*] Lyuboff Andreevna has been living abroad five years. I don't know what she is like now—She is a good woman. An easy-going, simple woman. I remember when I was a boy about fifteen, my father, who is at rest—in those days he ran a shop here in the village—hit me in the face with his fist, my nose was bleeding— We'd come to the yard together for something or other, and he was a little drunk.

Lyuboff Andreevna, I can see her now, still so young, so slim, led me to the washbasin here in this very room, in the nursery. "Don't cry," she says, "little peasant, it will be well in time for your wedding"—[*A pause*] Yes, little peasant— My father was a peasant truly, and here I am in a white waistcoat and yellow shoes. Like a pig rooting in a pastry shop—I've got this rich, lots of money, but if you really stop and think of it, I'm just a peasant—[*Turning the pages of a book*] Here I was reading a book and didn't get a thing out of it. Reading and went to sleep. [*A pause*]

DUNYASHA   And all night long the dogs were not asleep, they know their masters are coming.

LOPAHIN   What is it, Dunyasha, you're so—

DUNYASHA   My hands are shaking. I'm going to faint.

LOPAHIN   You're just so delicate, Dunyasha. And all dressed up like a lady, and your hair all done up! Mustn't do that. Must know your place.

Enter EPIHODOFF, *with a bouquet: he wears a jacket and highly polished boots with a loud squeak. As he enters he drops the bouquet.*

EPIHODOFF [*picking up the bouquet*]   Look, the gardener sent these, he says to put them in the dining room. [*Giving the bouquet to* DUNYASHA]

LOPAHIN   And bring me some kvass.

DUNYASHA   Yes, sir. [*Goes out.*]

EPIHODOFF   There is a morning frost now, three degrees of frost [*Sighing*] and the cherries all in bloom. I cannot approve of our climate—I cannot. Our climate can never quite rise to the occasion. Listen, Yermolay Alexeevich, allow me to subtend. I bought myself, day before yesterday, some boots and they, I venture to assure you, squeak so that it is impossible. What could I grease them with?

LOPAHIN   Go on. You annoy me.

EPIHODOFF   Every day some misfortune happens to me. But I don't complain, I am used to it and I even smile.

DUNYASHA *enters, serves* LOPAHIN *the kvass.*

I'm going. [*Stumbling over a chair and upsetting it.*] There. [*As if triumphant.*] There, you see, pardon the expression, a circumstance like that, among others— It is simply quite remarkable. [*Goes out.*]

DUNYASHA   And I must tell you, Yermolay Alexeevich, that Epihodoff has proposed to me.

LOPAHIN   Ah!

DUNYASHA   I don't know really what to—He is a quiet man but sometimes when he starts talking, you can't understand a thing he means. It's all very nice, and full of feeling, but just doesn't make any sense. I sort of like him. He loves me madly. He's a man that's unfortunate, every day there's something or other. They tease him around here, call him twenty-two misfortunes—

LOPAHIN [*Cocking his ear*]   Listen, I think they are coming—

DUNYASHA   They are coming! But what's the matter with me—I'm cold all over.

LOPAHIN   They're really coming. Let's go meet them. Will she recognize me? It's five years we haven't seen each other.

DUNYASHA [*Excitedly*]   I'm going to faint this very minute. Ah, I'm going to faint!

Two carriages can be heard driving up to the house. LOPAHIN *and* DUNYASHA *hurry out. The stage is empty. In the adjoining rooms a noise begins.* FIERS *hurries across the stage, leaning on a stick; he has been to meet* LYUBOFF ANDREEVNA, *and wears an old-fashioned livery and a high hat; he mutters something to himself, but you cannot understand a word of it. The noise offstage gets louder and louder. A voice: "Look! Let's go through here—"* LYUBOFF ANDREEVNA, ANYA *and* CHARLOTTA IVANOVNA, *with a little dog on a chain, all of them dressed for traveling,* VARYA, *in a coat and kerchief,* GAYEFF, SEMYONOFF-PISHTCHIK, LOPAHIN, DUNYASHA, *with a bundle and an umbrella, servants with pieces of luggage—all pass through the room.*

ANYA   Let's go through here. Mama, do you remember what room this is?

LYUBOFF ANDREEVNA [*happily, through her tears*]   The nursery!

VARYA   How cold it is, my hands are stiff. [*To* LYUBOFF ANDREEVNA.] Your rooms, the white one and the violet, are just the same as ever, Mama.

LYUBOFF ANDREEVNA   The nursery, my dear beautiful room—I slept here when I was little—[*Crying*] And now I am like a child—[*Kisses her brother and* VARYA, *then her brother again*] And Varya is just the same as ever, looks like a nun. And I knew Dunyasha—[*Kisses* DUNYASHA.]

GAYEFF   The train was two hours late. How's that? How's that for good management?

CHARLOTTA [*to* PISHTCHIK.]   My dog he eats nuts too.

PISHTCHIK [*astonished*] Think of that!

Everybody goes out except ANYA *and* DUNYASHA.

DUNYASHA   We waited so long—[*Taking off* ANYA's *coat and hat.*]

ANYA   I didn't sleep all four nights on the way. And now I feel so chilly.

DUNYASHA   It was Lent when you left, there was some snow then, there was frost, and now? My darling [*Laughing and kissing her*], I waited so long for you, my joy, my life—I'm telling you now, I can't keep from it another minute.

ANYA [*wearily*]   There we go again—

DUNYASHA   The clerk Epihodoff proposed to me after Holy Week.

ANYA   You're always talking about the same thing—[*Arranging her hair*] I've lost all my hairpins—[*She is tired to the point of staggering.*]

DUNYASHA   I just don't know what to think. He loves me, loves me so!

ANYA [*looks in through her door, tenderly.*]   My room, my windows, it's just as if I had never been away. I'm home! Tomorrow morning I'll get up, I'll run into the orchard—Oh, if I only could go to sleep! I haven't slept all the way, I was tormented by anxiety.

DUNYASHA   Day before yesterday, Pyotr Sergeevich arrived.

ANYA [*joyfully*]   Petya!

DUNYASHA   He's asleep in the bathhouse, he lives there. I am afraid, he says, of being in the way. [*Taking her watch from her pocket and looking at it.*] Somebody ought to wake him up. It's only that Varvara Mikhailovna told us not to. Don't you wake him up, she said.

Enter VARYA *with a bunch of keys at her belt.*

VARYA   Dunyasha, coffee, quick—Mama is asking for coffee.

DUNYASHA   This minute. [*Goes out.*]

VARYA   Well, thank goodness, you've come back. You are home again. [*Caressingly*] My darling is back! My precious is back!

ANYA   I've had such a time.

VARYA   I can imagine!

ANYA   I left during Holy Week, it was cold then. Charlotta talked all the way and did her tricks. Why did you fasten Charlotta on to me—?

VARYA   But you couldn't have traveled alone, darling: not at seventeen!

ANYA   We arrived in Paris, it was cold there and snowing. I speak terrible French. Mama lived on the fifth floor; I went to see her; there were some French people in her room, ladies, an old priest with his prayer book, and the place was full of tobacco smoke—very dreary. Suddenly I began to feel sorry for Mama, so sorry, I drew her to me, held her close and couldn't let her go. Then Mama kept hugging me, crying—yes—

VARYA [*tearfully*]   Don't—oh, don't—

ANYA   Her villa near Mentone she had already sold, she had nothing left, nothing. And I didn't have a kopeck left. It was all we could do to get here. And Mama doesn't understand! We sit down to dinner at a station and she orders, insists on the most expensive things and gives the waiters rouble tips. Charlotta does the same. Yasha too demands his share; it's simply dreadful. Mama has her butler, Yasha, we've brought him here—

VARYA   I saw the wretch.

ANYA   Well, how are things? Has the interest on the mortgage been paid?

VARYA   How could we?

ANYA   Oh, my God, my God—!

VARYA   In August the estate is to be sold—

ANYA   My God—!

LOPAHIN [*looking in through the door and mooing like a cow.*]   Moo-o-o— [*Goes away.*]

VARYA [*tearfully*]   I'd land him one like that— [*Shaking her fist*]

ANYA [*embracing* VARYA *gently*]   Varya, has he proposed? [*Varya shakes her head.*] But he loves you—Why don't you have it out with him, what are you waiting for?

VARYA   I don't think anything will come of it for us. He is very busy, he hasn't any time for me—And doesn't notice me. God knows, it's painful for me to see him—Everybody talks about our marriage, everybody congratulates us, and the truth is, there's nothing to it—it's all like a dream— [*In a different tone*] You have a brooch looks like a bee.

ANYA [*sadly*]   Mama bought it. [*Going toward her room, speaking gaily, like a child*] And in Paris I went up in a balloon!

VARYA   My darling is back! My precious is back! [DUNYASHA *has returned with the coffee pot and is making coffee.* VARYA *is standing by the door.*] Darling, I'm busy all day long with the house and I go around thinking things. If only you could be married to a rich man, I'd be more at peace too, I would go all by myself to a hermitage—then to Kiev—to Moscow, and I'd keep going like that from one holy place to another—I would go on and on. Heavenly!

ANYA   The birds are singing in the orchard. What time is it now?

VARYA   It must be after two. It's time you were asleep, darling. [*Going into* ANYA's *room*] Heavenly!

YASHA *enters with a lap robe and a traveling bag.*

YASHA [*crossing the stage airily*]   May I go through here?

DUNYASHA   We'd hardly recognize you, Yasha; you've changed so abroad!

YASHA   Hm— And who are you?

DUNYASHA   When you left here, I was like that—[*Her hand so high from the floor*] I'm Dunyasha, Fyodor Kozoyedoff's daughter. You don't remember!

YASHA   Hm— You little peach!

Looking around before he embraces her; she shrieks and drops a saucer; YASHA *hurries out.*

VARYA [*at the door, in a vexed tone*]   And what's going on here?

DUNYASHA [*tearfully*]   I broke a saucer—

VARYA   That's good luck.

ANYA [*emerging from her room*]   We ought to tell Mama beforehand: Petya is here—

VARYA   I told them not to wake him up.

ANYA [*pensively*]   Six years ago our father died, a month later our brother Grisha was drowned in the river, such a pretty little boy, just seven. Mama couldn't bear it, she went away, went away without ever looking back—[*Shuddering*] How I understand her, if she only knew I did. [*A pause*] And Petya Trofimoff was Grisha's tutor, he might remind—

Enter FIERS; *he is in a jacket and white waistcoat. Goes to the coffee urn, busy with it.*

FIERS   The mistress will have her breakfast here— [*Putting on white gloves*] Is the coffee ready? [*To* DUNYASHA, *sternly*] You! What about the cream?

DUNYASHA   Oh, my God— [*Hurrying out*]

FIERS [*busy at the coffee urn*]   Oh, you good-for-nothing—! [*Muttering to himself.*] Come back from Paris—And the master used to go to Paris by coach— [*Laughing*]

VARYA   Fiers, what are you—?

FIERS   At your service. [*Joyfully*] My mistress is back! It's what I've been waiting for! Now I'm ready to die— [*Crying for joy*]

LYUBOFF ANDREEVNA, GAYEFF and SEMYONOFF-PISHTCHIK *enter;* SEMYONOFF-PISHTCHIK *is in a podyovka*[1] *of fine cloth and sharovary.*[2] GAYEFF *enters; he makes gestures with his hands and body as if he were playing billiards.*

LYUBOFF ANDREEVNA   How is it? Let me remember—Yellow into the corner! Duplicate in the middle!

GAYEFF   I cut into the corner. Sister, you and I slept here in this very room once, and now I am fifty-one years old, strange as that may seem—

LOPAHIN   Yes, time passes.

GAYEFF   What?

LOPAHIN   Time, I say, passes.

GAYEFF   And it smells like patchouli here.

ANYA   I'm going to bed. Good night, Mama. [*Kissing her mother*]

---

[1]The traditional Russian long jacket   [2]Loose trousers bloused over the boots

LYUBOFF ANDREEVNA   My sweet little child. [*Kissing her hands*] You're glad you are home? I still can't get myself together.

ANYA   Good-by, Uncle.

GAYEFF [*kissing her face and hands*] God be with you. How like your mother you are! [*To his sister*] Lyuba, at her age you were exactly like her.

ANYA *shakes hands with* LOPAHIN *and* PISHTCHIK, *goes out and closes the door behind her.*

LYUBOFF ANDREEVNA   She's very tired.

PISHTCHIK   It is a long trip, I imagine.

VARYA [*to* LOPAHIN *and* PISHTCHIK]   Well, then, sirs? It's going on three o'clock, time for gentlemen to be going.

LYUBOFF ANDREEVNA [*Laughing*]   The same old Varya. [*Drawing her to her and kissing her*] There, I'll drink my coffee, then we'll all go. [FIERS *puts a small cushion under her feet.*] Thank you, my dear. I am used to coffee. Drink it day and night. Thank you, my dear old soul.

Kissing FIERS.

VARYA   I'll go see if all the things have come. [*Goes out.*]

LYUBOFF ANDREEVNA   Is it really me sitting here? [*Laughing*] I'd like to jump around and wave my arms. [*Covering her face with her hands.*] But I may be dreaming! God knows I love my country, love it deeply, I couldn't look out of the car window, I just kept crying. [*Tearfully*] However, I must drink my coffee. Thank you, Fiers, thank you, my dear old friend. I'm so glad you're still alive.

FIERS   Day before yesterday.

GAYEFF   He doesn't hear well.

LOPAHIN   And I must leave right now. It's nearly five o'clock in the morning, for Harkoff. What a nuisance! I wanted to look at you—talk— You are as beautiful as ever.

PISHTCHIK [*breathing heavily*]   Even more beautiful— In your Paris clothes —It's a feast for the eyes—

LOPAHIN   Your brother, Leonid Andreevich here, says I'm a boor, a peasant money grubber, but that's all the same to me, absolutely. Let him say it. All I wish is you'd trust me as you used to, and your wonderful, touching eyes would look at me as they did. Merciful God! My father was a serf; belonged to your grandfather and your father; but you, your own self, you did so much for me once that I've forgotten all that and love you like my own kin—more than my kin.

LYUBOFF ANDREEVNA   I can't sit still—I can't. [*Jumping up and walking about in great excitement.*] I'll never live through this happiness— Laugh at me, I'm silly—My own little bookcase—! [*Kissing the bookcase.*] My little table!

GAYEFF   And in your absence the nurse here died.

LYUBOFF ANDREEVNA [*sitting down and drinking coffee.*]   Yes, may she rest in Heaven! They wrote me.

GAYEFF   And Anastasy died. Cross-eyes Petrushka left me and lives in town now at the police officer's. [*Taking out of his pocket a box of hard candy and sucking a piece.*]

PISHTCHIK   My daughter, Dashenka—sends you her greetings—

LOPAHIN   I want to tell you something very pleasant, cheerful. [*Glancing at his watch*] I'm going right away. There's no time for talking. Well, I'll make it two or three words. As you know, your cherry orchard is to be sold for your debts; the auction is set for August 22nd, but don't you worry, my dear, you just sleep in peace, there's a way out of it. Here's my plan. Please listen to me. Your estate is only thirteen miles from town. They've run the railroad by it. Now if the cherry orchard and the land along the river were cut up into building lots and leased for summer cottages, you'd have at the very lowest twenty-five thousand roubles per year income.

GAYEFF Excuse me, what rot!

LYUBOFF ANDREEVNA I don't quite understand you, Yermolay Alexeevich.

LOPAHIN At the very least you will get from the summer residents twenty-five roubles per year for a two-and-a-half acre lot and if you post a notice right off, I'll bet you anything that by autumn you won't have a single patch of land free, everything will be taken. In a word, my congratulations, you are saved. The location is wonderful, the river's so deep. Except, of course, it all needs to be tidied up, cleared— For instance, let's say, tear all the old buildings down and this house, which is no good any more, and cut down the old cherry orchard—

LYUBOFF ANDREEVNA Cut down? My dear, forgive me, you don't understand at all. If there's one thing in the whole province that's interesting—not to say remarkable—it's our cherry orchard.

LOPAHIN The only remarkable thing about this cherry orchard is that it's very big. There's a crop of cherries once every two years and even that's hard to get rid of. Nobody buys them.

GAYEFF This orchard is even mentioned in the encyclopedia.

LOPAHIN [*glancing at his watch*] If we don't cook up something and don't get somewhere, the cherry orchard and the entire estate will be sold at auction on the twenty-second of August. Do get it settled then! I swear there is no other way out. Not a one!

FIERS There was a time, forty-fifty years ago when the cherries were dried, soaked, pickled, cooked into jam and it used to be—

GAYEFF Keep quiet, Fiers.

FIERS And it used to be that the dried cherries were shipped by the wagon-load to Moscow and to Kharkov. And the money there was! And the dried cherries were soft then, juicy, sweet, fragrant— They had a way of treating them then—

LYUBOFF ANDREEVNA And where is that way now?

FIERS They have forgotten it. Nobody remembers it.

PISHTCHIK [*to* LYUBOFF ANDREEVNA] What's happening in Paris? How is everything? Did you eat frogs?

LYUBOFF ANDREEVNA I ate crocodiles.

PISHTCHIK Think of it—!

LOPAHIN Up to now in the country there have been only the gentry and the peasants, but now in summer the villa people too are coming in. All the towns, even the least big ones, are surrounded with cottages. In about twenty years very likely the summer resident will multiply enormously. He merely drinks tea on the porch now, but it might well happen that on this two-and-a-half acre lot of his, he'll go in for farming, and then your cherry orchard would be happy, rich, splendid—

GAYEFF [*getting hot*] What rot!

Enter VARYA *and* YASHA.

VARYA   Here, Mama. Two telegrams for you. [*Choosing a key and opening the old bookcase noisily*] Here they are.

LYUBOFF ANDREEVNA   From Paris. [*Tearing up the telegrams without reading them*] Paris, that's all over—

GAYEFF   Do you know how old this bookcase is, Lyuba? A week ago I pulled out the bottom drawer and looked, and there the figures were burned on it. The bookcase was made exactly a hundred years ago. How's that? Eh? You might celebrate its jubilee. It's an inanimate object, but all the same, be that as it may, it's a bookcase.

PISHTCHIK [*in astonishment*]   A hundred years—! Think of it—!

GAYEFF   Yes—quite something— [*Shaking the bookcase*] Dear, honored bookcase! I salute your existence, which for more than a hundred years has been directed toward the clear ideals of goodness and justice; your silent appeal to fruitful endeavor has not flagged in all the course of a hundred years, sustaining [*Tearfully*] through the generations of our family, our courage and our faith in a better future and nurturing in us ideals of goodness and of a social consciousness.

A pause.

LOPAHIN   Yes.

LYUBOFF ANDREEVNA   You're the same as ever, Lenya.

GAYEFF [*slightly embarrassed*]   Carom to the right into the corner pocket. I cut into the side pocket!

LOPAHIN [*glancing at his watch*]   Well, it's time for me to go.

YASHA [*handing medicine to* LYUBOFF ANDREEVNA]   Perhaps you'll take the pills now—

PISHTCHIK   You should never take medicaments, dear madam— They do neither harm nor good— Hand them here, dearest lady. [*He takes the pillbox, shakes the pills out into his palm, blows on them, puts them in his mouth and washes them down with kvass.*] There! Now!

LYUBOFF ANDREEVNA [*startled*]   Why, you've lost your mind!

PISHTCHIK   I took all the pills.

LOPAHIN   Such a glutton!

Everyone laughs.

FIERS   The gentleman stayed with us during Holy Week, he ate half a bucket of pickles— [*Muttering*]

LYUBOFF ANDREEVNA   What is he muttering about?

VARYA   He's been muttering like that for three years. We're used to it.

YASHA   In his dotage.

CHARLOTTA IVANOVNA *in a white dress—she is very thin, her corset laced very tight—with a lorgnette at her belt, crosses the stage.*

LOPAHIN   Excuse me, Charlotta Ivanovna, I haven't had a chance yet to welcome you. [*Trying to kiss her hand*]

CHARLOTTA [*drawing her hand away*]   If I let you kiss my hand, 'twould be my elbow next, then my shoulder—

LOPAHIN   No luck for me today. [*Everyone laughs.*] Charlotta Ivanovna, show us a trick!

CHARLOTTA   No. I want to go to bed. [*Exit*]

LOPAHIN   In three weeks we shall see each other. [*Kissing* LYUBOFF AN-DREEVNA's *hand*] Till then, good-by. It's time. [*To* GAYEFF] See you soon. (Kissing PISHTCHIK] See you soon. [*Shaking* VARYA's *hand, then* FIER's *and* YASHA's] I don't feel like going. [*To* LYUBOFF ANDREEVNA] If you think it over and make up your mind about the summer cottages, let me know and I'll arrange a loan of something like fifty thousand roubles. Think it over seriously.

VARYA [*angrily*]   Do go on, anyhow, will you!

LOPAHIN   I'm going, I'm going— [*Exit*]

GAYEFF   Boor. However, pardon—Varya is going to marry him, it's Varya's little fiancé.

VARYA   Don't talk too much, Uncle.

LYUBOFF ANDREEVNA   Well, Varya, I should be very glad. He's a good man.

PISHTCHIK   A man, one must say truthfully—A most worthy—And my Dash-enka—says also that—she says all sorts of things— [*Snoring but immediately waking up*] Nevertheless, dearest lady, oblige me—With a loan of two hundred and forty roubles—Tomorrow the interest on my mortgage has got to be paid—

VARYA [*startled*]   There's not any money, none at all.

LYUBOFF ANDREEVNA   Really, I haven't got anything.

PISHTCHIK   I'll find it, somehow. [*Laughing*] I never give up hope. There, I think to myself, all is lost, I am ruined and lo and behold—a railroad is put through my land and—they paid me. And then, just watch, something else will turn up—if not today, then tomorrow—Dashenka will win two hundred thousand— She has a ticket.

LYUBOFF ANDREEVNA   We've finished the coffee, now we can go to bed.

FIERS [*brushing* GAYEFF's *clothes, reprovingly*]   You put on the wrong trousers again. What am I going to do with you!

VARYA [*softly*]   Anya is asleep. [*Opening the window softly*] Already the sun's rising—it's not cold. Look, Mama! What beautiful trees! My Lord, what air! The starlings are singing!

GAYEFF [*opening another window*]   The orchard is all white. You haven't for-gotten, Lyuba? That long lane there runs straight—as a strap stretched out. It glistens on moonlight nights. Do you remember? You haven't forgotten it?

LYUBOFF ANDREEVNA [*looking out of the window on to the orchard*]   Oh, my childhood, my innocence! I slept in this nursery and looked out on the orchard from here, every morning happiness awoke with me, it was just as it is now, then, nothing has changed. [*Laughing with joy*] All, all white! Oh, my orchard! After a dark, rainy autumn and cold winter, you are young again and full of happiness. The heavenly angels have not deserted you—If I only could lift the weight from my breast, from my shoulders, if I could only forget my past!

GAYEFF   Yes, and the orchard will be sold for debt, strange as that may seem.

LYUBOFF ANDREEVNA   Look, our dear mother is walking through the orchard—In a white dress! [*Laughing happily*] It's she.

GAYEFF   Where?

VARYA   God be with you, Mama!

LYUBOFF ANDREEVNA   There's not anybody, it only seemed so. To the right, as you turn to the summerhouse, a little white tree is leaning there, looks like a woman—

Enter TROFIMOFF, *in a student's uniform, well worn, and glasses.*

What a wonderful orchard! The white masses of blossoms, the sky all blue.

TROFIMOFF   Lyuboff Andreevna! [*She looks around at him.*] I will just greet you and go immediately. [*Kissing her hand warmly*] I was told to wait until morning, but I hadn't the patience—

LYUBOFF ANDREEVNA *looks at him puzzled.*

VARYA [*tearfully*]   This is Petya Trofimoff—

TROFIMOFF   Petya Trofimoff, the former tutor of your Grisha— Have I really changed so?

LYUBOFF ANDREEVNA *embraces him; and crying quietly.*

GAYEFF [*embarrassed*]   There, there, Lyuba.

VARYA [*crying*]   I told you, Petya, to wait till tomorrow.

LYUBOFF ANDREEVNA   My Grisha—My boy—Grisha—Son—

VARYA   What can we do, Mama? It's God's will.

TROFIMOFF [*in a low voice tearfully*]   There, there—

LYUBOFF ANDREEVNA [*weeping softly*]   My boy was lost, drowned— Why? Why, my friend? [*More quietly*] Anya is asleep there, and I am talking so loud— Making so much noise— But why, Petya? Why have you lost your looks? Why do you look so much older?

TROFIMOFF   A peasant woman on the train called me a mangy-looking gentleman.

LYUBOFF ANDREEVNA   You were a mere boy then, a charming young student, and now your hair's not very thick any more and you wear glasses. Are you really a student still? [*Going to the door.*]

TROFIMOFF   Very likely I'll be a perennial student.

LYUBOFF ANDREEVNA [*kissing her brother, then* VARYA]   Well, go to bed— You've grown older too, Leonid.

PISHTCHIK [*following her*]   So that's it, we are going to bed now. Oh, my gout! I'm staying here— I'd like, Lyuboff Andreevna, my soul, tomorrow morning—Two hundred and forty roubles—

GAYEFF   He's still at it.

PISHTCHIK   Two hundred and forty roubles— To pay interest on the mortgage.

LYUBOFF ANDREEVNA   I haven't any money, my dove.

PISHTCHIK   I'll pay it back, my dear— It's a trifling sum—

LYUBOFF ANDREEVNA   Oh, very well, Leonid will give—You give it to him, Leonid.

GAYEFF   Oh, certainly, I'll give it to him. Hold out your pockets.

LYUBOFF ANDREEVNA   What can we do, give it, he needs it— He'll pay it back.

LYUBOFF ANDREEVNA, TROFIMOFF, PISHTCHIK *and* FIERS *go out.* GAYEFF, VARYA *and* YASHA *remain.*

GAYEFF   My sister hasn't yet lost her habit of throwing money away. [*To* YASHA] Get away, my good fellow, you smell like hens.

YASHA [*with a grin*]   And you are just the same as you used to be, Leonid Andreevich.

GAYEFF   What? [*To* VARYA] What did he say?

VARYA [*to* YASHA] Your mother has come from the village, she's been sitting in the servants' hall ever since yesterday, she wants to see you—

YASHA The devil take her!

VARYA Ach, shameless creature!

YASHA A lot I need her! She might have come tomorrow.

Goes out.

VARYA Mama is just the same as she was, she hasn't changed at all. If she could, she'd give away everything she has.

GAYEFF Yes— If many remedies are prescribed for an illness, you may know the illness is incurable. I keep thinking, I wrack my brains, I have many remedies, a great many, and that means, really, I haven't any at all. It would be fine to inherit a fortune from somebody, it would be fine to marry off our Anya to a very rich man, it would be fine to go to Yaroslavl and try our luck with our old aunt, the Countess. Auntie is very, very rich.

VARYA [*crying*] If God would only help us!

GAYEFF Don't bawl! Auntie is very rich but she doesn't like us. To begin with, Sister married a lawyer, not a nobleman— [ANYA *appears at the door.*] Married not a nobleman and behaved herself, you could say, not very virtuously. She is good, kind, nice, I love her very much, but no matter how much you allow for the extenuating circumstances, you must admit she's a depraved woman. You feel it in her slightest movement.

VARYA [*whispering*] Anya is standing in the door there.

GAYEFF What? [*A pause*] It's amazing, something got in my right eye. I am beginning to see poorly. And on Thursday, when I was in the District Court—

ANYA *enters.*

VARYA But why aren't you asleep, Anya?

ANYA I don't feel like sleeping. I can't.

GAYEFF My little girl— [*Kissing* ANYA's *face and hands*] My child— [*Tearfully*] You are not my niece, you are my angel, you are everything to me. Believe me, believe—

ANYA I believe you, Uncle. Everybody loves you, respects you— But dear Uncle, you must keep quiet, just keep quiet— What were you saying, just now, about my mother, about your own sister? What did you say that for?

GAYEFF Yes, yes— [*Putting her hand up over his face*] Really, it's terrible! My God! Oh, God, save me! And today I made a speech to the bookcase— So silly! And it was only when I finished it that I could see it was silly.

VARYA It's true. Uncle, you ought to keep quiet. Just keep quiet. That's all.

ANYA If you kept quiet, you'd have more peace.

GAYEFF I'll keep quiet. [*Kissing* ANYA's *and* VARYA's *hands*] I'll keep quiet. Only this, it's about business. On Thursday I was in the District Court; well, a few of us gathered around and a conversation began about this and that, about lots of things; apparently it will be possible to arrange a loan on a promissory note to pay the bank the interest due.

VARYA If the Lord would only help us!

GAYEFF Tuesday I shall go and talk it over again. [*To* VARYA] Don't bawl! [*To* ANYA] Your mother will talk to Lopahin; of course, he won't refuse her . . . And as soon as you rest up, you will go to Yaroslavl to your great-aunt, the Countess. There, that's how we will move from three directions, and the business is in the bag. We'll pay the interest. I am convinced of that— [*Putting a hard candy in his mouth*] On my honor I'll swear, by anything you like, that the estate shall not be sold! [*Excitedly*] By my happiness, I swear! Here's my hand, call me a worthless, dishonorable man, if I allow it to come up for auction! With all my soul I swear it!

ANYA [*a quieter mood returns to her; she is happy.*]   How good you are, Uncle, how clever! [*Embracing her uncle*] I feel easy now! I feel easy! I'm happy!

FIERS *enters.*

FIERS [*reproachfully*]   Leonid Andreevich, have you no fear of God! When are you going to bed?

GAYEFF   Right away, right away. You may go, Fiers. For this once I'll undress myself. Well, children, beddy bye— More details tomorrow, and now, go to bed. [*Kissing* ANYA *and* VARYA] I am a man of the eighties— It is a period that's not admired, but I can say, nevertheless, that I've suffered no little for my convictions in the course of my life. It is not for nothing that the peasant loves me. One must know the peasant! One must know from what—

ANYA   Again, Uncle!

VARYA   You, Uncle dear, keep quiet.

FIERS [*angrily*]   Leonid Andreevich!

GAYEFF   I'm coming, I'm coming— Go to bed. A double bank into the side pocket! A clean shot—

Goes out, FIERS *hobbling after him.*

ANYA   I feel easy now. I don't feel like going to Yaroslavl; I don't like Great-aunt, but still I feel easy. Thanks to Uncle. [*Sits down.*]

VARYA   I must get to sleep. I'm going. And there was unpleasantness here during your absence. In the old servants' quarters, as you know, live only the old servants: Yephemushka, Polya, Yevstignay, well, and Karp. They began to let every sort of creature spend the night with them—I didn't say anything. But then I hear they've spread the rumor that I'd given orders to feed them nothing but beans. Out of stinginess, you see— And all that from Yevstignay— Very well, I think to myself. If that's the way it is, I think to myself, then you just wait. I call in Yevstignay— [*Yawning*] He comes— How is it, I say, that you, Yevstignay— You're such a fool!— [*Glancing at* ANYA] Anitchka!—[*A pause*] Asleep! [*Takes* ANYA *by her arm*] Let's go to bed— Come on!— [*Leading her*] My little darling fell asleep! Come on—

[*They go. Far away beyond the orchard a shepherd is playing on a pipe.* TROFI-MOFF *walks across the stage and, seeing* VARYA *and* ANYA, *stops.*]

Shh—She is asleep—asleep—Let's go, dear.

ANYA [*softly, half dreaming*]   I'm so tired— All the bells!—Uncle—dear— And Mama and Uncle—Varya.

VARYA   Come on, my dear, come on.

They go into ANYA's *room.*

TROFIMOFF [*tenderly*]   My little sun! My spring!

Act II

A field. An old chapel, long abandoned, with crooked walls, near it a well, big stones that apparently were once tombstones, and an old bench. A road to the estate of GAYEFF *can be seen. On one side poplars rise, casting their shadows, the cherry orchard begins there. In the distance a row of telegraph poles; and far, far away, faintly traced on the horizon, is a large town, visible only in the clearest weather. The sun will soon be down.* CHARLOTTA, YASHA *and* DUNYASHA *are sitting on the bench;* EPIHODOFF *is standing near and playing the guitar; everyone sits lost in thought.* CHARLOTTA *wears an old peak cap* (fourrage); *she has taken a rifle from off her shoulders and is adjusting the buckle on the strap.*

CHARLOTTA [*pensively*]   I have no proper passport, I don't know how old I am—it always seems to me I'm very young. When I was a little girl, my father and mother traveled from fair to fair and gave performances, very good ones. And I did *salto mortale* and different tricks. And when Papa and Mama died, a German lady took me to live with her and began teaching me. Good. I grew up. And became a governess. But where I came from and who I am I don't know— Who my parents were, perhaps they weren't even married—I don't know. [*Taking a cucumber out of her pocket and beginning to eat it*] I don't know a thing. [*A pause*] I'd like so much to talk but there's not anybody. I haven't anybody.

EPIHODOFF [*playing the guitar and singing*]   "What care I for the noisy world, what care I for friends and foes."—How pleasant it is to play the mandolin!

DUNYASHA   That's a guitar, not a mandolin. [*Looking into a little mirror and powdering her face.*]

EPIHODOFF   For a madman who is in love this is a mandolin— [*Singing*] "If only my heart were warm with the fire of requited love."

YASHA *sings with him.*

CHARLOTTA   How dreadfully these people sing— Phooey! Like jackals.

DUNYASHA [*to* YASHA]   All the same what happiness to have been abroad.

YASHA   Yes, of course. I cannot disagree with you.

Yawning and then lighting a cigar.

EPIHODOFF   That's easily understood. Abroad everything long since attained its complete development.

YASHA   That's obvious.

EPIHODOFF   I am a cultured man. I read all kinds of remarkable books, but the trouble is I cannot discover my own inclinations, whether to live or to shoot myself, but nevertheless, I always carry a revolver on me. Here it is— [*Showing a revolver*]

CHARLOTTA   That's done. Now I am going. [*Slinging the rifle over her shoulder*] You are a very clever man, Epihodoff, and a very terrible one; the women must love you madly. Brrrr-r-r-r! [*Going*] These clever people are all so silly, I haven't anybody to talk with. I'm always alone, alone, I have nobody and— Who I am, why I am, is unknown— [*Goes out without hurrying*]

EPIHODOFF   Strictly speaking, not touching on other subjects, I must state about myself, in passing, that fate treats me mercilessly, as a storm does a small ship. If, let us suppose, I am mistaken, then why, to mention one instance, do I wake up this morning, look and there on my chest is a spider of terrific size— There, like that. [*Showing the size with both hands*] And also I take some kvass to drink and in it I find something in the highest degree indecent, such as a cockroach. [*A pause*] Have you read Buckle? [*A pause*] I desire to trouble you, Avdotya Feodorovna, with a couple of words.

DUNYASHA   Speak.

EPIHODOFF   I have a desire to speak with you alone—

Sighing.

DUNYASHA [*embarrassed*]   Very well— But bring me my cape first—by the cupboard— It's rather damp here—

EPIHODOFF   Very well—I'll fetch it— Now I know what I should do with my revolver—[*Takes the guitar and goes out playing*]

YASHA   Twenty-two misfortunes! Between us he's a stupid man, it must be said. [*Yawning*]

DUNYASHA   God forbid he should shoot himself. [*A pause*] I've grown so uneasy, I'm always fretting. I was only a girl when I was taken into the master's house, and now I've lost the habit of simple living—and here are my hands white, white as a lady's. I've become so delicate, fragile, ladylike, afraid of everything— Frightfully so. And, Yasha, if you deceive me, I don't know what will happen to my nerves.

YASHA [*kissing her*]   You little cucumber! Of course every girl must behave properly. What I dislike above everything is for a girl to conduct herself badly.

DUNYASHA   I have come to love you passionately, you are educated, you can discuss anything. [*A pause*]

YASHA [*Yawning*]   Yes, sir—To my mind it is like this: If a girl loves someone, it means she is immoral. [*A pause*] It is pleasant to smoke a cigar in the clear air—[*Listening*] They are coming here— It is the ladies and gentlemen—

DUNYASHA *impulsively embraces him.*

YASHA   Go to the house, as though you had been to bathe in the river, go by this path, otherwise, they might meet you and suspect me of making a rendezvous with you. That I cannot tolerate.

DUNYASHA [*with a little cough*]   Your cigar has given me the headache. [*Goes out*]

YASHA *remains, sitting near the chapel.* LYUBOFF ANDREEVNA, GAYEFF *and* LOPAHIN *enter.*

LOPAHIN   We must decide definitely, time doesn't wait. Why, the matter's quite simple. Are you willing to lease your land for summer cottages or are you not? Answer in one word, yes or no? Just one word!

LYUBOFF ANDREEVNA   Who is it smokes those disgusting cigars out here—? [*Sitting down*]

GAYEFF   The railroad running so near is a great convenience. [*Sitting down*] We made a trip to town and lunched there— Yellow in the side pocket! Perhaps I should go in the house first and play one game—

LYUBOFF ANDREEVNA   You'll have time.

LOPAHIN   Just one word! [*Imploringly*] Do give me your answer!

GAYEFF [*Yawning*]   What?

LYUBOFF ANDREEVNA [*looking in her purse*]   Yesterday there was lots of money in it. Today there's very little. My poor Varya! For the sake of economy she feeds everybody milk soup, and in the kitchen the old people get nothing but beans, and here I spend money—senselessly— [*Dropping her purse and scattering gold coins*] There they go scattering! [*She is vexed.*]

YASHA   Allow me, I'll pick them up in a second. [*Picking up the coins*]

LYUBOFF ANDREEVNA   If you will, Yasha. And why did I go in town for lunch—? Your restaurant with its music is trashy, the tablecloths smell of soap— Why drink so much, Lyonya? Why eat so much? Why talk so much? Today in the restaurant you were talking a lot again, and all of it beside the point. About the seventies, about the decadents. And to whom? Talking to waiters about the decadents!

LOPAHIN   Yes.

GAYEFF [*waving his hand*]   I am incorrigible, that's evident— [*To* YASHA *irritably*] What is it?—You are forever swirling around in front of us.

YASHA [*laughing*]   I cannot hear your voice without laughing.

GAYEFF [*to his sister*]   Either I or he—

LYUBOFF ANDREEVNA   Go away, Yasha. Go on—

YASHA [*giving* LYUBOFF ANDREEVNA *her purse*]   I am going right away. [*Barely suppressing his laughter*] This minute. [*Goes out*]

LOPAHIN   The rich Deriganoff intends to buy your estate. They say he is coming personally to the auction.

LYUBOFF ANDREEVNA   And where did you hear that?

LOPAHIN   In town they are saying it.

GAYEFF   Our Yaroslavl aunt promised to send us something, but when and how much she will send, nobody knows—

LOPAHIN   How much will she send? A hundred thousand? Two hundred?

LYUBOFF ANDREEVNA   Well—maybe ten, fifteen thousand—we'd be thankful for that.

LOPAHIN   Excuse me, but such light-minded people as you are, such odd, unbusinesslike people, I never saw. You are told in plain Russian that your estate is being sold up and you just don't seem to take it in.

LYUBOFF ANDREEVNA   But what are we to do? Tell us what?

LOPAHIN   I tell you every day. Every day I tell you the same thing. Both the cherry orchard and the land have got to be leased for summer cottages, it has to be done right now, quick— The auction is right under your noses. Do understand! Once you finally decide that there are to be summer cottages, you will get all the money you want, and then you'll be saved.

LYUBOFF ANDREEVNA   Summer cottages and summer residents—it is so trivial, excuse me.

GAYEFF   I absolutely agree with you.

LOPAHIN   I'll either burst out crying, or scream, or faint. I can't bear it! You are torturing me! [*To* GAYEFF] You're a perfect old woman!

GAYEFF   What?

LOPAHIN   A perfect old woman! [*About to go*]

LYUBOFF ANDREEVNA [*alarmed*]   No, don't go, stay, my lamb, I beg you. Perhaps we will think of something!

LOPAHIN   What is there to think about?

LYUBOFF ANDREEVNA   Don't go, I beg you. With you here it is more cheerful anyhow— [*A pause*] I keep waiting for something, as if the house were about to tumble down on our heads.

GAYEFF [*deep in thought*]   Double into the corner pocket— Bank into the wide pocket—

LYUBOFF ANDREEVNA   We have sinned so much—

LOPAHIN   What sins have you—?

GAYEFF [*puts a hard candy into his mouth*]   They say I've eaten my fortune up in hard candies— [*Laughing*]

LYUBOFF ANDREEVNA   Oh, my sins—I've always thrown money around like mad, recklessly, and I married a man who accumulated nothing but debts. My husband died from champagne—he drank fearfully—and to my misfortune I fell in love with another man. I lived with him, and just at that time—it was my first punishment—a blow over the head: right here in the river my boy was drowned and I went abroad—went away for good, never to return, never to see this river again—I shut my eyes, ran away, beside myself, and he after me—mercilessly, brutally. I bought a villa near Mentone, because he fell ill there, and for three years I knew no rest day or night, the sick man exhausted me, my soul dried up. And last year when the villa was sold for debts, I went to Paris and there he robbed me of everything, threw me over, took up with another woman; I tried to poison myself—so stupid, so shameful— And suddenly I was seized with longing for Russia, for my own country, for my little girl— [*Wiping away her tears*] Lord, Lord, have mercy, forgive me my sins! Don't punish me any more! [*Getting a telegram out of her pocket*] I got this today from Paris, he asks forgiveness, begs me to return— [*Tears up the telegram*] That sounds like music somewhere.

Listening.

GAYEFF   It is our famous Jewish orchestra. You remember, four violins, a flute and double bass.

LYUBOFF ANDREEVNA   Does it still exist? We ought to get hold of it sometime and give a party.

LOPAHIN [*listening*]   Can't hear it— [*Singing softly*] "And for money the Germans will frenchify a Russian." [*Laughing*] What a play I saw yesterday at the theatre, very funny!

LYUBOFF ANDREEVNA   And most likely there was nothing funny about it. You shouldn't look at plays, but look oftener at yourselves. How gray all your lives are, what a lot of idle things you say!

LOPAHIN   That's true. It must be said frankly this life of ours is idiotic— [*A pause*] My father was a peasant, an idiot, he understood nothing, he taught me nothing, he just beat me in his drunken fits and always with a stick. At bottom I am just as big a dolt and idiot as he was. I wasn't taught anything, my handwriting is vile, I write like a pig—I am ashamed for people to see it.

LYUBOFF ANDREEVNA   You ought to get married, my friend.

LOPAHIN   Yes—That's true.

LYUBOFF ANDREEVNA   To our Varya, perhaps. She is a good girl.

LOPAHIN   Yes.

LYUBOFF ANDREEVNA   She comes from simple people, and she works all day long, but the main thing is she loves you. And you, too, have liked her a long time.

LOPAHIN   Why not? I am not against it— She's a good girl. [*A pause*]

GAYEFF   They are offering me a position in a bank. Six thousand a year—Have you heard that?

LYUBOFF ANDREEVNA   Not you! You stay where you are—

FIERS enters, bringing an overcoat.

FIERS [*to* GAYEFF]   Pray, Sir, put this on, it's damp.

GAYEFF [*putting on the overcoat*]   You're a pest, old man.

FIERS   That's all right— This morning you went off without letting me know. [*Looking him over*]

LYUBOFF ANDREEVNA   How old you've grown, Fiers!

FIERS   At your service.

LOPAHIN   She says you've grown very old!

FIERS   I've lived a long time. They were planning to marry me off before your papa was born. [*Laughing*] And at the time the serfs were freed I was already the head footman. I didn't want to be freed then, I stayed with the masters—[*A pause*] And I remember, everybody was happy, but what they were happy about they didn't know themselves.

LOPAHIN   In the old days it was fine. At least they flogged.

FIERS [*not hearing*]   But, of course. The peasants stuck to the masters, the masters stuck to the peasants, and now everything is all smashed up, you can't tell about anything.

GAYEFF   Keep still, Fiers. Tomorrow I must go to town. They have promised to introduce me to a certain general who might make us a loan.

LOPAHIN   Nothing will come of it. And you can rest assured you won't pay the interest.

LYUBOFF ANDREEVNA   He's just raving on. There aren't any such generals.

TROFIMOFF, ANYA and VARYA enter.

GAYEFF   Here they come.

ANYA   There is Mama sitting there.

LYUBOFF ANDREEVNA [*tenderly*]   Come, come—My darlings—[*Embracing ANYA and VARYA*] If you only knew how I love you both! Come sit by me—there—like that.

Everybody sits down.

LOPAHIN   Our perennial student is always strolling with the young ladies.

TROFIMOFF   It's none of your business.

LOPAHIN   He will soon be fifty and he's still a student.

TROFIMOFF   Stop your stupid jokes.

LOPAHIN   But why are you so peevish, you queer duck?

TROFIMOFF   Don't you pester me.

LOPAHIN [*laughing*]   Permit me to ask you, what do you make of me?

TROFIMOFF   Yermolay Alexeevich, I make this of you: you are a rich man, you'll soon be a millionaire. Just as it is in the metabolism of nature, a wild beast is needed to eat up everything that comes his way; so you too are needed.

Everyone laughs.

VARYA   Petya, you'd better tell us about the planets.

LYUBOFF ANDREEVNA   No, let's go on with yesterday's conversation.

TROFIMOFF   What was it about?

GAYEFF   About the proud man.

TROFIMOFF   We talked a long time yesterday, but didn't get anywhere. In a proud man, in your sense of the word, there is something mystical. Maybe you are right, from your standpoint, but if we are to discuss it in simple terms, without whimsy, then what pride can there be, is there any sense in it, if man physiologically is poorly constructed, if in the great majority he is crude, unintelligent, profoundly miserable. One must stop admiring oneself. One must only work.

GAYEFF   All the same, you will die.

TROFIMOFF   Who knows? And what does it mean—you will die? Man may have a hundred senses, and when he dies only the five that are known to us may perish, and the remaining ninety-five go on living.   .

LYUBOFF ANDREEVNA   How clever you are, Petya!

LOPAHIN [*ironically.*]   Terribly!

TROFIMOFF   Humanity goes forward, perfecting its powers. Everything that's unattainable now will some day become familiar, understandable; it is only that one must work and must help with all one's might those who seek the truth. With us in Russia so far only a very few work. The great majority of the intelligentsia that I know are looking for nothing, doing nothing, and as yet have no capacity for work. They call themselves intelligentsia, are free and easy with the servants, treat the peasants like animals, educate themselves poorly, read nothing seriously, do absolutely nothing; about science they just talk and about art they understand very little. Every one of them is serious, all have stern faces; they all talk of nothing but important things, philosophize, and all the time everybody can see that the workmen eat abominably, sleep without any pillows, thirty or forty to a room, and everywhere there are bedbugs, stench, dampness, moral uncleanness— And apparently with us, all the fine talk is only to divert the attention of ourselves and of others. Show me where we have the day nurseries they are always talking so much about, where are the reading rooms? They only write of these in novels, for the truth is there are not any at all. There is only filth, vulgarity, orientalism— I am afraid of very serious faces and dislike them. I'm afraid of serious conversations. Rather than that let's just keep still.

LOPAHIN   You know I get up before five o'clock in the morning and work from morning till night. Well, I always have money, my own and other people's, on hand, and I see what the people around me are. One has only to start doing something to find out how few honest and decent people there are. At times when I can't go to sleep, I think: Lord, thou gavest us immense forests, unbounded fields and the widest horizons, and living in the midst of them we should indeed be giants—

LYUBOFF ANDREEVNA   You feel the need for giants— They are good only in fairy tales, anywhere else they only frighten us.

At the back of the stage EPIHODOFF *passes by, playing the guitar.* [LYUBOFF AN-DREEVNA, *lost in thought, says:*]

Epihodoff is coming—
   ANYA [*lost in thought*]   Epihodoff is coming.
   GAYEFF   The sun has set, ladies and gentlemen.
   TROFIMOFF   Yes.
   GAYEFF [*not loud and as if he were declaiming*]   Oh, Nature, wonderful, you gleam with eternal radiance, beautiful and indifferent, you, whom we call Mother, combine in yourself both life and death, you give life and you take it away.
   VARYA [*Beseechingly*]   Uncle!
   ANYA   Uncle, you're doing it again!
   TROFIMOFF   You'd better bank the yellow into the side pocket.
   GAYEFF   I'll be quiet, quiet.

All sit absorbed in their thoughts. There is only the silence. FIERS *is heard muttering to himself softly. Suddenly a distant sound is heard, as if from the sky, like the sound of a snapped string, dying away, mournful.*

   LYUBOFF ANDREEVNA   What's that?
   LOPAHIN   I don't know. Somewhere far off in a mine shaft a bucket fell. But somewhere very far off.
   GAYEFF   And it may be some bird—like a heron.
   TROFIMOFF   Or an owl—
   LYUBOFF ANDREEVNA [*shivering*]   It's unpleasant, somehow. [*A pause*]
   FIERS   Before the disaster it was like that. The owl hooted and the samovar hummed without stopping, both.
   GAYEFF   Before what disaster?
   FIERS   Before the emancipation.

A pause.

   LYUBOFF ANDREEVNA   You know, my friends, let's go. Twilight is falling. [*To* ANYA] You have tears in your eyes— What is it, my dear little girl? [*Embracing her*]
   ANYA   It's just that, Mama. It's nothing.
   TROFIMOFF   Somebody is coming.

A STRANGER *appears in a shabby white cap, and an overcoat; he is a little drunk.*

   THE STRANGER   Allow me to ask you, can I go straight through here to the station?
   GAYEFF   You can. Go by that road.
   THE STRANGER   I am heartily grateful to you. [*Coughing*] The weather is splendid— [*Declaiming*] Brother of mine, suffering brother— Go out to the Volga, whose moans— [*To* VARYA] Mademoiselle, grant a hungry Russian man some thirty kopecks—

VARYA *is frightened and gives a shriek.*

LOPAHIN [*angrily*]   There's a limit to everything.

LYUBOFF ANDREEVNA [*flustered*]   Take this— Here's this for you— [*Searching in her purse*] No silver—It's all the same, here's a gold piece for you—

THE STRANGER   I am heartily grateful to you. [*Goes out. Laughter.*]

VARYA [*frightened*]   I'm going—I'm going— Oh, Mama, you poor little Mama! There's nothing in the house for people to eat, and you gave him a gold piece.

LYUBOFF ANDREEVNA   What is to be done with me, so silly? I shall give you all I have in the house. Yermolay Alexeevich, you will lend me some this once more!—

LOPAHIN   Agreed.

LYUBOFF ANDREEVNA   Let's go, ladies and gentlemen, it's time. And here, Varya, we have definitely made a match for you, I congratulate you.

VARYA [*through her tears*]   Mama, that's not something to joke about.

LOPAHIN   Achmelia, get thee to a nunnery.

GAYEFF   And my hands are trembling; it is a long time since I have played billiards.

LOPAHIN   Achmelia, Oh nymph, in thine orisons be all my sins remember'd—

LYUBOFF ANDREEVNA   Let's go, my dear friends, it will soon be suppertime.

VARYA   He frightened me. My heart is thumping so!

LOPAHIN   I remind you, ladies and gentleman: August 22nd the cherry orchard will be auctioned off. Think about that!—Think!—

All go out except TROFIMOFF *and* ANYA.

ANYA [*laughing*]   My thanks to the stranger, he frightened Varya, now we are alone.

TROFIMOFF   Varya is afraid we might begin to love each other and all day long she won't leave us to ourselves. With her narrow mind she cannot understand that we are above love. To sidestep the petty and illusory, which prevent our being free and happy, that is the aim and meaning of our life. Forward! We march on irresistibly toward the bright star that burns there in the distance. Forward! Do not fall behind, friends!

ANYA [*extending her arms upward*]   How well you talk! [*A pause*] It's wonderful here today!

TROFIMOFF   Yes, the weather is marvelous.

ANYA   What have you done to me, Petya, why don't I love the cherry orchard any longer the way I used to? I loved it so tenderly, it seemed to me there was not a better place on earth than our orchard.

TROFIMOFF   All Russia is our orchard. The earth is immense and beautiful, and on it are many wonderful places. [*A pause*] Just think, Anya: your grandfather, great-grandfather and all your ancestors were slave owners, in possession of living souls, and can you doubt that from every cherry in the orchard, from every leaf, from every trunk, human beings are looking at you, can it be that you don't hear their voices? To possess living souls, well, that depraved all of you who lived before and who are living now, so that your mother and you, and your uncle no longer notice that you live by debt, at somebody else's expense, at the expense of those very people whom you wouldn't let past your front door— We are at least two hundred years behind the times, we have as yet absolutely nothing, we have no definite attitude toward the past, we only philosophize, complain of our sadness or drink vodka. Why, it is quite clear that to begin to live in the present we must first atone for our past, must be done with it; and we can atone for it only through suffering, only through uncommon, incessant labor. Understand that, Anya.

ANYA   The house we live in ceased to be ours long ago, and I'll go away, I give you my word.

TROFIMOFF   If you have the household keys, throw them in the well and go away. Be free as the wind.

ANYA [*transported*]   How well you said that!

TROFIMOFF   Believe me, Anya, believe me! I am not thirty yet, I am young, I am still a student, but I have already borne so much! Every winter I am hungry, sick, anxious, poor as a beggar, and—where has destiny not chased me, where haven't I been! And yet, my soul has always, every minute, day and night, been full of inexplicable premonitions. I have a premonition of happiness, Anya, I see it already—

ANYA [*pensively*]   The moon is rising.

EPIHODOFF *is heard playing on the guitar, always the same sad song. The moon rises. Somewhere near the poplars* VARYA *is looking for* ANYA *and calling: "Anya! Where are you?"*

TROFIMOFF   Yes, the moon is rising. [*A pause*] Here is happiness, here it comes, comes always nearer and nearer, I hear its footsteps now. And if we shall not see it, shall not come to know it, what does that matter? Others will see it!

VARYA [*off*]   Anya! Where are you?

TROFIMOFF   Again, that Varya! [*Angrily*] It's scandalous!

ANYA   Well, let's go to the river. It's lovely there.

TROFIMOFF   Let's go. [*They go out.*]

VARYA [*off*]   Anya! Anya!

Act III

The drawing room, separated by an arch from the ballroom. A chandelier is lighted. A Jewish orchestra is playing—the same that was mentioned in Act II. Evening. In the ballroom they are dancing grand rond. The voice of SEMYONOFF-PISHTCHIK: *"Promenade à une paire!" They enter the drawing room; in the first couple are* PISHTCHIK *and* CHARLOTTA IVANOVNA; *in the second,* TROFIMOFF *and* LYUBOFF ANDREEVNA; *in the third,* ANYA *with the* POST-OFFICE CLERK; *in the fourth,* VARYA *with the* STATIONMASTER, *et cetera—*VARYA *is crying softly and wipes away her tears while she is dancing.* DUNYASHA *is in the last couple through the drawing room,* PISHTCHIK *shouts: "Grand rond, balancez!" and "Les Cavaliers à genoux et remerciez vos dames!"* FIERS *in a frock coat goes by with seltzer water on a tray.* PISHTCHIK *and* TROFIMOFF *come into the drawing room.*

PISHTCHIK   I am full-blooded, I have had two strokes already, and dancing is hard for me, but as they say, if you are in a pack of dogs, you may bark and bark, but you must still wag your tail. At that, I have the health of a horse. My dear father—he was a great joker—may he dwell in Heaven—used to talk as if our ancient line, the Semyonoff-Pishtchiks, were descended from the very horse that Caligula made a Senator—[*Sitting down*] But here's my trouble: I haven't any money. A hungry dog believes in nothing but meat—[*Snoring but waking at once*] And the same way with me—I can't talk about anything but money.

TROFIMOFF   Well, to tell you the truth, there is something of a horse about your figure.

PISHTCHIK   Well—a horse is a fine animal— You can sell a horse—

The sound of playing billiards comes from the next room. VARYA *appears under the arch to the ballroom.*

TROFIMOFF [*teasing*]   Madam Lopahin! Madam Lopahin!

VARYA [*angrily*]   A mangy-looking gentleman!

TROFIMOFF   Yes, I am a mangy-looking gentleman, and proud of it!

VARYA [*In bitter thought*]   Here we have gone and hired musicians and what are we going to pay them with?

Goes out.

TROFIMOFF [*to* PISHTCHIK]   If the energy you have wasted in the course of your life trying to find money to pay the interest had gone into something else, you could very likely have turned the world upside down before you were done with it.

PISHTCHIK   Nietzsche—the philosopher—the greatest—the most celebrated—a man of tremendous mind—says in his works that one may make counterfeit money.

TROFIMOFF   And have you read Nietzsche?

PISHTCHIK   Well—Dashenka told me. And I'm in such a state now that I could make counterfeit money myself— Day after tomorrow three hundred and ten roubles must be paid—one hundred and thirty I've on hand— [*Feeling in his pockets, alarmed*] The money is gone! I have lost the money! [*Tearfully*] Where is the money? [*Joyfully*] Here it is, inside the lining— I was in quite a sweat—

LYUBOFF ANDREEVNA *and* CHARLOTTA IVANOVNA *come in.*

LYUBOFF ANDREEVNA [*humming lazginka, a Georgian dance*]   Why does Leonid take so long? What's he doing in town? [*To* DUNYASHA] Dunyasha, offer the musicians some tea—

TROFIMOFF   In all probability the auction did not take place.

LYUBOFF ANDREEVNA   And the musicians came at an unfortunate moment and we planned the ball at an unfortunate moment—Well, it doesn't matter. [*Sitting down and singing softly*]

CHARLOTTA [*gives* PISHTCHIK *a deck of cards.*]   Here is a deck of cards for you, think of some one card.

PISHTCHIK   I have thought of one.

CHARLOTTA   Now, shuffle the deck. Very good. Hand it here; oh, my dear Monsieur Pishtchik. *Eins, zwei, drei!* Now look for it, it's in your coat pocket—

PISHTCHIK [*getting a card out of his coat pocket*]   The eight of spades, that's absolutely right! [*Amazed*] Fancy that!

CHARLOTTA [*Holding a deck of cards in her palm; to* TROFIMOFF]   Tell me quick now, which card is on top?

TROFIMOFF   What is it? Well—the Queen of Spades.

CHARLOTTA   Right! [*to* PISHTCHIK] Well? Which card's on top?

PISHTCHIK   The Ace of Hearts.

CHARLOTTA   Right! [*Strikes the deck against her palm; the deck of cards disappears.*] And what beautiful weather we are having today!

A mysterious feminine voice answers her, as if from under the floor: "Oh, yes. The weather is splendid, madame." "You are so nice, you're my ideal—" The voice: "Madame, you too please me greatly."

THE STATIONMASTER [*applauding*]   Madam Ventriloquist, bravo!

PISHTCHIK [*amazed*]   Fancy that! Most charming Charlotta Ivanovna—I am simply in love with you.

CHARLOTTA   In love? [*Shrugging her shoulders*] Is it possible that you can love? *Guter Mensch aber schlechter Musikant.*

TROFIMOFF [*slapping* PISHTCHIK *on the shoulder*]   You horse, you—

CHARLOTTA   I beg your attention, one more trick. [*Taking a lap robe from the chair*] Here is a very fine lap robe—I want to sell it— [*Shaking it out*] Wouldn't somebody like to buy it?

PISHTCHIK [*amazed*]   Fancy that!

CHARLOTTA   *Eins, zwei, drei!*

She quickly raises the lowered robe, behind it stands ANYA, *who curtseys, runs to her mother, embraces her and runs back into the ballroom amid the general delight.*

LYUBOFF ANDREEVNA [*applauding*]   Bravo, bravo—!

CHARLOTTA   Now again! *Eins, zwei, drei!*

Lifting the robe: behind it stands VARYA, *she bows.*

PISHTCHIK [*amazed*]   Fancy that!

CHARLOTTA   That's all.

Throwing the robe at PISHTCHIK, *curtseying and running into the ballroom.*

PISHTCHIK [*hurrying after her*]   You little rascal—What a girl! What a girl! [*Goes out.*]

LYUBOFF ANDREEVNA   And Leonid is not here yet. What he's doing in town so long, I don't understand! Everything is finished there, either the estate is sold by now, or the auction didn't take place. Why keep it from us so long?

VARYA [*trying to comfort her*]   Uncle has bought it, I am sure of that.

TROFIMOFF [*mockingly*]   Yes.

VARYA   Great-aunt sent him power of attorney to buy it in her name and transfer the debt. She did this for Anya. And I feel certain, God willing, that Uncle will buy it.

LYUBOFF ANDREEVNA   Our Yaroslavl great-aunt has sent fifteen thousand to buy the estate in her name— She doesn't trust us, but that wouldn't be enough to pay the interest even— [*Covering her face with her hands*] Today my fate will be decided, my fate—

TROFIMOFF [*teasing* VARYA]   Madam Lopahin!

VARYA [*angrily*]   Perennial student! You have already been expelled from the University twice.

LYUBOFF ANDREEVNA   But why are you angry, Varya? He teases you about Lopahin, what of it? Marry Lopahin if you want to, he is a good man, interesting. If you don't want to, don't marry him; darling, nobody is making you do it.

VARYA   I look at this matter seriously, Mama, one must speak straight out. He's a good man, I like him.

LYUBOFF ANDREEVNA   Then marry him. What there is to wait for I don't understand!

VARYA   But I can't propose to him myself, Mama. It's two years now; everyone has been talking to me about him, everyone talks, and he either remains silent or jokes. I understand. He's getting rich, he's busy with his own affairs, and has no time for me. If there were money, ever so little, even a hundred roubles, I would drop everything, and go far away. I'd go to a nunnery.

TROFIMOFF   How saintly!

VARYA [*to* TROFIMOFF]   A student should be intelligent! [*In a low voice, tearfully*] How homely you have grown, Petya, how old you've got. [*To* LYUBOFF ANDREEVNA, *no longer crying*] It is just that I can't live without working, Mama. I must be doing something every minute.

YASHA *enters.*

YASHA [*barely restraining his laughter*]   Epihodoff has broken a billiard cue!— [*Goes out*]

VARYA   But why is Epihodoff here? Who allowed him to play billiards? I don't understand these people—[*Goes out*]

LYUBOFF ANDREEVNA   Don't tease her, Petya; you can see she has troubles enough without that.

TROFIMOFF   She is just too zealous. Sticking her nose into things that are none of her business. All summer she gave us no peace, neither me nor Anya; she was afraid a romance would spring up between us. What business is that of hers? And besides I haven't shown any signs of it. I am so remote from triviality. We are above love!

LYUBOFF ANDREEVNA   Well, then, I must be beneath love. [*Very anxiously*] Why isn't Leonid here? Just to tell us whether the estate is sold or not? Calamity seems to me so incredible that I don't know what to think, I'm lost—I could scream this minute—I could do something insane. Save me, Petya. Say something, do say. . . .

TROFIMOFF   Whether the estate is sold today or is not sold—is it not the same? There is no turning back, the path is all grown over. Calm yourself, my dear, all that was over long ago. One mustn't deceive oneself, one must for once at least in one's life look truth straight in the eye.

LYUBOFF ANDREEVNA   What truth? You see where the truth is and where the untruth is, but as for me, it's as if I had lost my sight, I see nothing. You boldly decide all important questions, but tell me, my dear boy, isn't that because you are young and haven't had time yet to suffer through any one of your problems? You look boldly ahead, and isn't that because you don't see and don't expect anything terrible, since life is still hidden from your young eyes? You are braver, more honest, more profound than we are, but stop and think, be magnanimous, have a little mercy on me, just a little. Why, I was born here. My father and mother lived here and my grandfather. I love this house, I can't imagine my life without the cherry orchard and if it is very necessary to sell it, then sell me along with the orchard—[*Embracing* TROFIMOFF *and kissing him on the forehead*] Why, my son was drowned here—[*Crying*] Have mercy on me, good, kind man.

TROFIMOFF   You know I sympathize with you from the bottom of my heart.

LYUBOFF ANDREEVNA   But that should be said differently, differently—[*Taking out her handkerchief; a telegram falls on the floor.*] My heart is heavy today, you can't imagine how heavy. It is too noisy for me here, my soul trembles at every sound, I tremble all over and yet I can't go off to myself, when I am alone the silence frightens me. Don't blame me, Petya—I love you as one of my own. I should gladly have given you Anya's hand, I assure you, only, my dear, you must study and finish your course. You do nothing. Fate simply flings you about from place to place, and that's so strange—Isn't that so? Yes? And you must do something about your beard, to make it grow somehow—[*Laughing*] You look funny!

TROFIMOFF [*picking up the telegram*]   I do not desire to be beautiful.

LYUBOFF ANDREEVNA   This telegram is from Paris. I get one every day. Yesterday and today too. That wild man has fallen ill again, something is wrong again with him—He asks forgiveness, begs me to come, and really I ought to make a trip to Paris and stay awhile near him. Your face looks stern, Petya, but what is there to do, my dear, what am I to do, he is ill, he is alone, unhappy and who will look after him there, who will keep him from doing the wrong thing, who will give him his medicine on time? And what is there to hide or keep still about? I love him, that's plain. I love him, love him—It's a stone about my neck, I'm sinking to the bottom with it, but I love that stone and live without it I cannot. [*Pressing* TROFIMOFF'*s hand*] Don't think harshly of me, Petya, don't say anything to me, don't—

TROFIMOFF [*tearfully*]   Forgive my frankness, for God's sake! Why, he picked your bones.

LYUBOFF ANDREEVNA   No, no, no, you must not talk like that. [*Stopping her ears*]

TROFIMOFF   But he is a scoundrel, only you, you are the only one that doesn't know it. He is a petty scoundrel, a nonentity—

LYUBOFF ANDREEVNA [*angry but controlling herself*]   You are twenty-six years old or twenty-seven, but you are still a schoolboy in the second grade!

TROFIMOFF   Very well!

LYUBOFF ANDREEVNA   You should be a man—at your age you should understand people who love. And you yourself should love someone—you should fall in love! [*Angrily*] Yes, yes! And there is no purity in you; you are simply smug, a ridiculous crank, a freak—

TROFIMOFF [*Horrified*]   What is she saying!

LYUBOFF ANDREEVNA   "I am above love!" You are not above love, Petya, you are, as our Fiers would say, just a good-for-nothing. Imagine, at your age, not having a mistress—!

TROFIMOFF [*horrified*]   This is terrible! What is she saying! [*Goes quickly into the ballroom, clutching his head*] This is horrible—I can't bear it, I am going—[*Goes out but immediately returns*] All is over between us. [*Goes out into the hall*]

LYUBOFF ANDREEVNA [*shouting after him*]   Petya, wait! You funny creature, I was joking! Petya!

[*In the hall you hear someone running up the stairs and suddenly falling back down with a crash. You hear* ANYA *and* VARYA *scream but immediately you hear laughter.*]

What's that?

ANYA *runs in.*

> ANYA [*laughing*]   Petya fell down the stairs! [*Runs out.*]
> LYUBOFF ANDREEVNA   What a funny boy that Petya is—!

[*The* STATIONMASTER *stops in the center of the ballroom and begins to recite "The Sinner" by A. Tolstoi. They listen to him but he has recited only a few lines when the strains of a waltz are heard from the hall and the recitation is broken off. They all dance.* TROFIMOFF, ANYA, VARYA *and* LYUBOFF ANDREEVNA *come in from the hall.*]

But, Petya—but, dear soul—I beg your forgiveness— Let's go dance.

She dances with TROFIMOFF. ANYA *and* VARYA *dance.* FIERS *enters, leaving his stick by the side door.* YASHA *also comes into the drawing room and watches the dancers.*

> YASHA   What is it, Grandpa?
> FIERS   I don't feel very well. In the old days there were generals, barons, admirals dancing at our parties, and now we send for the post-office clerk and the stationmaster, and even they are none too anxious to come. Somehow I've grown feeble. The old master, the grandfather, treated everybody with sealing-wax for all sickness. I take sealing-wax every day, have done so for twenty-odd years or more; it may be due to that that I'm alive.
> YASHA   You are tiresome, Grandpa. [*Yawning*] Why don't you go off and die?
> FIERS   Aw, you—good-for-nothing!— [*Muttering*]

TROFIMOFF *and* LYUBOFF ANDREEVNA *dance in the ballroom and then in the drawing room.*

> LYUBOFF ANDREEVNA   *Merci.* I'll sit down awhile— [*Sitting down*] I'm tired.

ANYA *enters.*

> ANYA [*agitated*]   And just now in the kitchen some man was saying that the cherry orchard had been sold today.
> LYUBOFF ANDREEVNA   Sold to whom?
> ANYA   He didn't say who to. He's gone.

Dancing with TROFIMOFF, *they pass into the ballroom.*

> YASHA   It was some old man babbling there. A stranger.
> FIERS   And Leonid Andreevich is still not here, he has not arrived. The overcoat he has on is light, mid-season—let's hope he won't catch cold. Ach, these young things!
> LYUBOFF ANDREEVNA   I shall die this minute. Go, Yasha, find out who it was sold to.
> YASHA   But he's been gone a long time, the old fellow.

Laughing.

LYUBOFF ANDREEVNA [*with some annoyance*]   Well, what are you laughing at? What are you so amused at?

YASHA   Epihodoff is just too funny. An empty-headed man. Twenty-two misfortunes!

LYUBOFF ANDREEVNA   Fiers, if the estate is sold, where will you go?

FIERS   Wherever you say, there I'll go.

LYUBOFF ANDREEVNA   Why do you look like that? Aren't you well? You know you ought to go to bed—

FIERS   Yes—[*With a sneer*] I go to bed and without me who's going to serve, who'll take care of things? I'm the only one in the whole house.

YASHA [*to* LYUBOFF ANDREEVNA]   Lyuboff Andreevna, let me ask a favor of you, do be so kind! If you ever go back to Paris, take me with you, please do! It's impossible for me to stay here. [*Looking around him, and speaking in a low voice.*] Why talk about it? You can see for yourself it's an uncivilized country, an immoral people and not only that, there's the boredom of it. The food they give us in that kitchen is abominable and there's that Fiers, too, walking about and muttering all kinds of words that are out of place. Take me with you, be so kind!

PISHTCHIK *enters.*

PISHTCHIK   Allow me to ask you—for a little waltz, most beautiful lady— [LYUBOFF ANDREEVNA *goes with him.*] Charming lady, I must borrow a hundred and eighty roubles from you—will borrow— [*Dancing*] a hundred and eighty roubles— [*They pass into the ballroom.*]

YASHA [*singing low*]   "Wilt thou know the unrest in my soul!"

In the ballroom a figure in a gray top hat and checked trousers waves both hands and jumps about; there are shouts of "Bravo, Charlotta Ivanovna!"

DUNYASHA [*stopping to powder her face*]   The young lady orders me to dance—there are a lot of gentlemen and very few ladies—but dancing makes my head swim and my heart thump. Fiers Nikolaevich, the post-office clerk said something to me just now that took my breath away.

The music plays more softly.

FIERS   What did he say to you?

DUNYASHA   You are like a flower, he says.

YASHA [*yawning*]   What ignorance—! [*Goes out*]

DUNYASHA   Like a flower—I am such a sensitive girl, I love tender words awfully.

FIERS   You'll be getting your head turned.

EPIHODOFF *enters.*

EPIHODOFF   Avdotya Feodorovna, you don't want to see me— It's as if I were some sort of insect. [*Sighing*] Ach, life!

DUNYASHA   What do you want?

EPIHODOFF   Undoubtedly you may be right. [*Sighing*] But of course, if one considers it from a given point of view, then you, I will allow myself so to express it, forgive my frankness, absolutely led me into a state of mind. I know my fate, every day some misfortune happens to me, but I have long since become accustomed to that, and so I look on my misfortunes with a smile. You gave me your word and, although I—

DUNYASHA   I beg you, we'll talk later on, but leave me now in peace. I'm in a dream now. [*Playing with her fan*]

EPIHODOFF   I have a something wrong happens every day—I will allow myself so to express it—I just smile, I even laugh.

VARYA *enters from the ballroom.*

VARYA   You are not gone yet, Semyon? What a really disrespectful man you are! [*To* DUNYASHA] Get out of here, Dunyasha. [*To* EPIHODOFF] You either play billiards and break a cue or you walk about the drawing room like a guest.

EPIHODOFF   Allow me to tell you, you cannot make any demands on me.

VARYA   I'm not making any demands on you, I'm talking to you. All you know is to walk from place to place but not do any work. We keep a clerk, but what for, nobody knows.

EPIHODOFF [*offended*]   Whether I work, whether I walk, whether I eat, or whether I play billiards are matters to be discussed only by people of understanding and my seniors.

VARYA   You dare to say that to me! [*Flying into a temper*] You dare? So I don't understand anything? Get out of here! This minute!

EPIHODOFF [*alarmed*]   I beg you to express yourself in a delicate manner.

VARYA [*beside herself*]   This very minute, get out of here! Get out [*He goes to the door; she follows him.*] Twenty-two misfortunes! Don't you dare breathe in here! Don't let me set eyes on you!

EPIHODOFF *has gone out, but his voice comes from outside the door: "I shall complain about you."*

Ah, you are coming back? [*Grabbing the stick that* FIERS *put by the door*] Come on, come—come on, I'll show you— Ah, you are coming? You are coming? Take that then—!

She swings the stick, at the very moment when LOPAHIN *is coming in.*

LOPAHIN   Most humbly, I thank you.

VARYA [*angrily and ironically*]   I beg your pardon!

LOPAHIN   It's nothing at all. I humbly thank you for the pleasant treat.

VARYA   It isn't worth your thanks. [*Moving away, then looking back and asking gently*] I haven't hurt you?

LOPAHIN   No, it's nothing. There's a great bump coming though.

Voices in the ballroom: "Lopahin has come back." "Yermolay Alexeevich!"
PISHTCHIK *enters.*

PISHTCHIK   See what we see, hear what we hear—! [*He and* LOPAHIN *kiss one another.*] You smell slightly of cognac, my dear, my good old chap. And we are amusing ourselves here too.

LYUBOFF ANDREEVNA *enters.*

LYUBOFF ANDREEVNA   Is that you, Yermolay Alexeevich? Why were you so long? Where is Leonid?
LOPAHIN   Leonid Andreevich got back when I did, he's coming.
LYUBOFF ANDREEVNA [*agitated*]   Well, what? Was there an auction? Do speak!
LOPAHIN [*embarrassed, afraid of showing the joy he feels*]   The auction was over by four o'clock— We were late for the train, had to wait till half-past nine. [*Sighing heavily*] Ugh, my head's swimming a bit!

GAYEFF *enters; with his right hand he carries his purchases, with his left he wipes away his tears.*

LYUBOFF ANDREEVNA   Lyona, what? Lyona, eh? [*Impatiently, with tears in her eyes*] Quick, for God's sake—
GAYEFF [*not answering her, merely waving his hand; to* FIERS, *crying*]   Here, take it— There are anchovies, some Kertch herrings— I haven't eaten anything all day—What I have suffered!

[*The door into the billiard room is open; you hear the balls clicking and* YASHA's *voice: "Seven and eighteen!"* GAYEFF's *expression changes, he is no longer crying.*]

I'm terribly tired. You help me change, Fiers.

Goes to his room through the ballroom, FIERS *behind him.*

PISHTCHIK   What happened at the auction? Go on, tell us!
LYUBOFF ANDREEVNA   Is the cherry orchard sold?
LOPAHIN   It's sold.
LYUBOFF ANDREEVNA   Who bought it?
LOPAHIN   I bought it.

[*A pause.* LYUBOFF ANDREEVNA *is overcome. She would have fallen had she not been standing near the chair and table.* VARYA *takes the keys from her belt, throws them on the floor in the middle of the drawing room and goes out.*]

I bought it. Kindly wait a moment, ladies and gentlemen, everything is muddled up in my head, I can't speak—[*Laughing*] We arrived at the auction, Deriganoff was already there. Leonid Andreevich had only fifteen thousand and Deriganoff right off bids thirty over and above indebtedness. I see how things are, I match him with forty thousand. He forty-five. I fifty-five. That is to say he raises it by fives, I by tens.—So it ended. Over and above the indebtedness, I bid up to ninety thousand, it was knocked down to me. The cherry orchard is mine now. Mine! [*Guffawing*] My God, Lord, the cherry orchard is mine! Tell me I'm drunk, out of my head, that I'm imagining all this— [*Stamps his feet*] Don't laugh at me! If only my father and grandfather could rise from their graves and see this whole business, see how their Yermolay, beaten, half-illiterate Yermolay, who used to run around barefoot in winter, how that very Yermolay has bought an estate that nothing in the world can beat. I bought the estate where grandfather and father were slaves, where you wouldn't even let me in the kitchen. I am asleep, it's only some dream of mine, it only seems so to me— That's nothing but the fruit of your imagination, covered with the darkness of the unknown—[*Picking up the keys, with a gentle smile*] She threw down the keys, wants to show she is not mistress any more— [*Jingling the keys*] Well, it's all the same. [*The orchestra is heard tuning up.*] Hey, musicians, play, I want to hear you! Come on everybody, and see how Yermolay Lopahin will swing the ax in the cherry orchard, how the trees will fall to the ground! We are going to build villas and our grandsons and great-grandsons will see a new life here— Music, play! [*The music is playing.* LYUBOFF ANDREEVNA *has sunk into a chair, crying bitterly.* LOPAHIN, *reproachfully*] Why, then, didn't you listen to me? My poor dear, it can't be undone now. [*With tears*] Oh, if this could all be over soon, if somehow our awkward, unhappy life would be changed!

PISHTCHIK [*taking him by the arm, in a low voice*]   She is crying. Come on in the ballroom, let her be by herself—Come on— [*Taking him by the arm and leading him into the ballroom*]

LOPAHIN   What's the matter? Music, there, play up! [*Sarcastically*] Everything is to be as I want it! Here comes the new squire, the owner of the cherry orchard. [*Quite accidentally, he bumps into the little table, and very nearly upsets the candelabra.*] I can pay for everything!

Goes out with PISHTCHIK. *There is nobody left either in the ballroom or the drawing room but* LYUBOFF ANDREEVNA, *who sits all huddled up and crying bitterly. The music plays softly.* ANYA *and* TROFIMOFF *enter hurriedly.* ANYA *comes up to her mother and kneels in front of her.* TROFIMOFF *remains at the ballroom door.*

ANYA   Mama—! Mama, you are crying? My dear, kind, good Mama, my beautiful, I love you—I bless you. The cherry orchard is sold, it's not ours any more, that's true, true; but don't cry, Mama, you've your life still left you, you've your good, pure heart ahead of you— Come with me, come on, darling, away from here, come on— We will plant a new orchard, finer than this one, you'll see it, you'll understand; and joy, quiet, deep joy will sink into your heart, like the sun at evening, and you'll smile, Mama! Come, darling, come on!

Act IV

The same setting as in Act I. There are neither curtains on the windows nor are there any pictures on the walls. Only a little furniture remains piled up in one corner as if for sale. A sense of emptiness is felt. Near the outer door, at the rear of the stage, is a pile of suitcases, traveling bags, and so on. The door on the left is open, and through it VARYA's *and* ANYA's *voices are heard.* LOPAHIN *is standing waiting.* YASHA *is holding a tray with glasses of champagne. In the hall* EPIHODOFF *is tying up a box, offstage at the rear there is a hum. It is the peasants who have come to say good-by.* GAYEFF's *voice: "Thanks, brothers, thank you."*

YASHA   The simple folk have come to say good-by. I am of the opinion, Yermolay Alexeevich, that the people are kind enough but don't understand anything.

The hum subsides. LYUBOFF ANDREEVNA *enters through the hall with* GAYEFF; *she is not crying, but is pale, her face quivers, she is not able to speak.*

GAYEFF You gave them your purse, Lyuba. Mustn't do that! Mustn't do that!
LYUBOFF ANDREEVNA I couldn't help it! I couldn't help it!

Both go out.

LOPAHIN [*calling through the door after them*] Please, I humbly beg you! A little glass at parting. I didn't think to bring some from town, and at the station I found just one bottle. Please! [*A pause*] Well, then, ladies and gentlemen! You don't want it? [*Moving away from the door*] If I'd known that, I wouldn't have bought it. Well, then I won't drink any either. [YASHA *carefully sets the tray down on a chair.*] At least, you have some, Yasha.
YASHA To those who are departing! Pleasant days to those who stay behind! [*Drinking*] This champagne is not the real stuff, I can assure you.
LOPAHIN Eight roubles a bottle. [*A pause*] It's devilish cold in here.
YASHA They didn't heat up today, we are leaving anyway. [*Laughing*]
LOPAHIN What are you laughing about?
YASHA For joy.
LOPAHIN Outside it's October, but it's sunny and still, like summer. Good for building. [*Looking at his watch, then through the door*] Ladies and gentlemen, bear in mind we have forty-six minutes in all till train time! Which means you have to go to the station in twenty minutes. Hurry up a little.
TROFIMOFF [*in an overcoat, entering from outside*] Seems to me it is time to go. The carriages are ready. The devil knows where my rubbers are. They've disappeared. [*In the door*] Anya, my rubbers are not here! I can't find them.
LOPAHIN And I have to go to Harkoff. I'm going on the same train with you. I'm going to live in Harkoff all winter. I've been dilly-dallying along with you, I'm tired of doing nothing. I can't be without work, look, I don't know what to do with my hands here, see, they are dangling somehow, as if they didn't belong to me.
TROFIMOFF We are leaving right away, and you'll set about your useful labors again.
LOPAHIN Here, drink a glass.
TROFIMOFF I shan't.
LOPAHIN It's to Moscow now?
TROFIMOFF Yes. I'll see them off to town, and tomorrow to Moscow.
LOPAHIN Yes— Maybe the professors are not giving their lectures. I imagine they are waiting till you arrive.
TROFIMOFF That's none of your business.
LOPAHIN How many years is it you've been studying at the University?
TROFIMOFF Think of something newer. This is old and flat. [*Looking for his rubbers*] You know, perhaps, we shall not see each other again; therefore, permit me to give you one piece of advice at parting! Don't wave your arms! Cure yourself of that habit—of arm waving. And also of building summer cottages, figuring that the summer residents will in time become individual landowners; figuring like that is arm waving too— Just the same, however, I like you. You have delicate soft fingers like an artist, you have a delicate soft heart—
LOPAHIN [*embracing him*] Good-by, my dear boy. Thanks for everything. If you need it, take some money from me for the trip.

TROFIMOFF   Why should I? There's no need for it.

LOPAHIN   But you haven't any!

TROFIMOFF   I have. Thank you. I got some for a translation. Here it is in my pocket. [*Anxiously*] But my rubbers are gone.

VARYA [*from another room*]   Take your nasty things! [*Throws a pair of rubbers on to the stage*]

TROFIMOFF   But what are you angry about, Varya? Hm— Why, these are not my rubbers.

LOPAHIN   In the spring I planted twenty-seven hundred acres of poppies and now I've made forty thousand clear. And when my poppies were in bloom, what a picture it was! So look, as I say, I've made forty thousand, which means I'm offering you a loan because I can afford to. Why turn up your nose? I'm a peasant— I speak straight out.

TROFIMOFF   Your father was a peasant, mine—an apothecary—and from that absolutely nothing follows. [LOPAHIN *takes out his wallet.*] Leave it alone, leave it alone—If you gave me two hundred thousand even, I wouldn't take it. I am a free man. And everything that you all value so highly and dearly, both rich man and beggars, has not the slightest power over me, it's like a mere feather floating in the air. I can get along without you. I can pass you by, I am strong and proud. Humanity is moving toward the loftiest truth, toward the loftiest happiness that is possible on earth and I am in the front ranks.

LOPAHIN   Will you get there?

TROFIMOFF   I'll get there. [*A pause*] I'll get there, or I'll show the others the way to get there.

In the distance is heard the sound of an ax on a tree.

LOPAHIN   Well, good-by, my dear boy. It's time to go. We turn up our noses at one another, but life keeps on passing. When I work a long time without stopping, my thoughts are clearer, and it seems as if I, too, know what I exist for, and, brother, how many people are there in Russia who exist, nobody knows for what! Well, all the same, it's not that that keeps things circulating. Leonid Andreevich, they say, has accepted a position—he'll be in a bank, six thousand a year—the only thing is he won't stay there, he's very lazy—

ANYA [*in the doorway*]   Mama begs of you until she's gone, not to cut down the orchard.

TROFIMOFF   Honestly, haven't you enough tact to—

Goes out through the hall.

LOPAHIN   Right away, right away— What people, really!

Goes out after him.

ANYA   Has Fiers been sent to the hospital?

YASHA   I told them to this morning. They must have sent him.

ANYA [*to* EPIHODOFF, *who is passing through the room*]   Semyon Panteleevich, please inquire whether or not they have taken Fiers to the hospital.

YASHA [*huffily*]   This morning, I told Igor. Why ask ten times over!

EPIHODOFF   The venerable Fiers, according to my conclusive opinion, is not worth mending, he ought to join his forefathers. And I can only envy him. [*Putting a suitcase on a hatbox and crushing it*] Well, there you are, of course. I knew it. [*Goes out*]

YASHA [*mockingly*] Twenty-two misfortunes—

VARYA [*on the other side of the door*] Have they taken Fiers to the hospital?

ANYA They have.

VARYA Then why didn't they take the letter to the doctor?

ANYA We must send it on after them— [*Goes out*]

VARYA [*from the next room*] Where is Yasha? Tell him his mother has come, she wants to say good-by to him.

YASHA [*waving his hand*] They merely try my patience.

DUNYASHA *has been busying herself with the luggage; now when* YASHA *is left alone, she goes up to him.*

DUNYASHA If you'd only look at me once, Yasha. You are going away—leaving me—[*Crying and throwing herself on his neck*]

YASHA Why are you crying? [*Drinking champagne*] In six days I'll be in Paris again. Tomorrow we will board the express train and dash off out of sight; somehow, I can't believe it. *Vive la France!* It doesn't suit me here—I can't live here— Can't help that. I've seen enough ignorance—enough for me. [*Drinking champagne*] Why do you cry? Behave yourself properly, then you won't be crying.

DUNYASHA [*Powdering her face, looking into a small mirror*] Send me a letter from Paris. I loved you, Yasha, you know, loved you so! I am a tender creature, Yasha!

YASHA They are coming here. [*Bustling about near the suitcases, humming low*]

LYUBOFF ANDREEVNA, GAYEFF, ANYA *and* CHARLOTTA IVANOVNA *enter.*

GAYEFF We should be going. There is very little time left. [*Looking at* YASHA] Who is it smells like herring!

LYUBOFF ANDREEVNA In about ten minutes let's be in the carriage—[*Glancing around the room*] Good-by, dear house, old Grandfather. Winter will pass, spring will be here, but you won't be here any longer, they'll tear you down. How much these walls have seen! [*Kissing her daughter warmly*] My treasure, you are beaming, your eyes are dancing like two diamonds. Are you happy? Very?

ANYA Very! It's the beginning of a new life, Mama!

GAYEFF [*gaily*] Yes, indeed, everything is fine now. Before the sale of the cherry orchard, we all were troubled, distressed, and then when the question was settled definitely, irrevocably, we all calmed down and were even cheerful— I'm a bank official. I am a financier now— Yellow ball into the side pocket, anyway, Lyuba, you look better, no doubt about that.

LYUBOFF ANDREEVNA Yes. My nerves are better, that's true. [*They hand her her hat and coat.*] I sleep well. Carry out my things, Yasha. It's time. [*To* ANYA] My little girl, we shall see each other again soon— I am going to Paris, I shall live there on the money your Yaroslavl great-aunt sent for the purchase of the estate— long live Great-aunt! But that money won't last long.

ANYA Mama, you'll come back soon, soon— Isn't that so? I'll prepare myself, pass the examination at high school, and then I'll work, I will help you. We'll read all sorts of books together. Mama, isn't that so? [*Kissing her mother's hands*] We'll read in the autumn evenings, read lots of books, and a new, wonderful world will open up before us—[*Daydreaming*] Mama, do come—

LYUBOFF ANDREEVNA   I'll come, my precious. [*Embracing her daughter*]

LOPAHIN *enters with* CHARLOTTA, *who is softly humming a song.*

GAYEFF   Lucky Charlotta: she's singing!

CHARLOTTA [*taking a bundle that looks like a baby wrapped up*]   My baby, bye, bye—[*A baby's cry is heard: Ooah, ooah—!*] Hush, my darling, my dear little boy. [*Ooah, ooah—!*] I am so sorry for you! [*Throwing the bundle back*] Will you please find me a position? I cannot go on like this.

LOPAHIN   We will find something, Charlotta Ivanovna, don't worry.

GAYEFF   Everybody is dropping us, Varya is going away.—All of a sudden we are not needed.

CHARLOTTA   I have no place in town to live. I must go away. [*Humming*] It's all the same—

PISHTCHIK *enters.*

LOPAHIN   The freak of nature—!

PISHTCHIK [*Out of breath*]   Ugh, let me catch my breath—I'm exhausted— My honored friends— Give me some water—

GAYEFF   After money, I suppose? This humble servant will flee from sin!

Goes out.

PISHTCHIK   It's a long time since I was here— Most beautiful lady— [*To* LO-PAHIN] You here—? Glad to see you—a man of the greatest intellect—Here— Take it— [*Giving* LOPAHIN *some money*] Four hundred roubles— That leaves eight hundred and forty I still owe you—

LOPAHIN [*With astonishment, shrugging his shoulders*]   I must be dreaming. But where did you get it?

PISHTCHIK   Wait—I'm hot— Most extraordinary event. Some Englishmen came and found on my land some kind of white clay— [*To* LYUBOFF ANDREEVNA] And four hundred for you—Beautiful lady—Wonderful lady— [*Handing over the money*] The rest later. [*Taking a drink of water*] Just now a young man was saying on the train that some great philosopher recommends jumping off roofs— "Jump!" he says, and "therein lies the whole problem." [*With astonishment*] You don't say! Water!

LOPAHIN   And what Englishmen were they?

PISHTCHIK   I leased them the parcel of land with the clay for twenty-four years— And now, excuse me, I haven't time—I must run along—I'm going to Znoykoff's—To Kardamonoff's—I owe everybody—[*Drinking*] I wish you well— I'll drop in on Thursday—

LYUBOFF ANDREEVNA   We are moving to town right away, and tomorrow I'm going abroad—

PISHTCHIK   What? [*Alarmed*] Why to town? That's why I see furniture— Suitcases—Well, no matter—[*Tearfully*] No matter— Men of the greatest minds— those Englishmen— No matter— Good luck! God will help you— No matter— Everything in this world comes to an end—[*Kissing* LYUBOFF ANDREEVNA's *hand*] And should the report reach you that my end has come, think of that well-known horse and say: "There was once on earth a so and so— Semyonoff Pishtchik— The Kingdom of Heaven be his." Most remarkable weather—yes— [*Going out greatly disconcerted, but immediately returning and speaking from the door*] Dashenka sends her greetings!

Goes out.

   LYUBOFF ANDREEVNA   And now we can go. I am leaving with two worries. First, that Fiers is sick. [*Glancing at her watch*] We still have five minutes—
   ANYA   Mama, Fiers has already been sent to the hospital. Yasha sent him off this morning.
   LYUBOFF ANDREEVNA   My second worry—is Varya. She is used to getting up early and working, and now without any work she is like a fish out of water. She has grown thin, pale and cries all the time, poor thing— [*A pause*] You know this, Yermolay Alexeevich: I dreamed— of marrying her to you. And there was every sign of your getting married.

Whispering to ANYA, *who beckons to* CHARLOTTA; *both go out.*

She loves you, you are fond of her, and I don't know, don't know why it is you seem to avoid each other—I don't understand it!
   LOPAHIN   I don't understand it either, I must confess. It's all strange some-how— If there's still time, I am ready right now even— Let's finish it up—and *basta,* but without you I feel I won't propose.
   LYUBOFF ANDREEVNA   But that's excellent. Surely it takes only a minute. I'll call her at once.
   LOPAHIN   And to fit the occasion there's the champagne. [*Looking at the glasses*] Empty, somebody has already drunk them. [YASHA *coughs.*] That's what's called lapping it up—
   LYUBOFF ANDREEVNA [*vivaciously*]   Splendid! We'll go out— Yasha, *allez!* I'll call her— [*Through the door*] Varya, drop everything and come here. Come on!

Goes out with YASHA.

   LOPAHIN [*looking at his watch*]   Yes—

A pause. Behind the door you hear smothered laughter, whispering, finally VARYA *enters.*

   VARYA [*looking at the luggage a long time*]   That's strange, I just can't find it—
   LOPAHIN   What are you looking for?
   VARYA   I packed it myself and don't remember where.

A pause.

LOPAHIN   Where do you expect to go now, Varvara Mikhailovna?

VARYA   I? To Regulin's. I agreed to go there to look after the house— As a sort of housekeeper.

LOPAHIN   That's in Yashnevo? It's nigh on to seventy miles. [*A pause*] And here ends life in this house—

VARYA [*examining the luggage*]   But where is it? Either I put it in the trunk, perhaps— Yes, life in this house is ended—it won't be any more—

LOPAHIN   And I am going to Harkoff now— By the next train. I've a lot to do. And I am leaving Epihodoff—on the ground here—I've hired him.

VARYA   Well!

LOPAHIN   Last year at this time it had already been snowing, if you remember, and now it's quiet, it's sunny. It's only that it's cold, about three degrees of frost.

VARYA   I haven't noticed. [*A pause*] And besides our thermometer is broken—
[*A pause. A voice from the yard through the door: "Yermolay Alexevich—"*]

LOPAHIN [*As if he had been expecting this call for a long time*]   This minute!
[*Goes out quickly*]

VARYA, *sitting on the floor, putting her head on a bundle of clothes, sobs quietly. The door opens,* LYUBOFF ANDREEVNA *enters cautiously.*

VARYA [*she is not crying any longer, and has wiped her eyes.*]   Yes, it's time, Mama. I can get to Regulin's today, if we are just not too late for the train— [*Through the door*] Anya, put your things on!

[ANYA, *then* GAYEFF *and* CHARLOTTA IVANOVNA *enter.* GAYEFF *has on a warm overcoat, with a hood. The servants gather, also the drivers.* EPIHODOFF *busies himself with the luggage.*]

Now we can be on our way.

ANYA [*joyfully*]   On our way!

GAYEFF   My friends, my dear, kind friends! leaving this house forever, can I remain silent, can I restrain myself from expressing, as we say, farewell, those feelings that fill now my whole being—

ANYA [*beseechingly*]   Uncle!

VARYA   Dear Uncle, don't!

GAYEFF [*dejectedly*]   Bank the yellow into the side pocket— I am silent—

TROFIMOFF *and then* LOPAHIN *enter.*

TROFIMOFF   Well, ladies and gentlemen, it's time to go!

LOPAHIN   Epihodoff, my coat!

LYUBOFF ANDREEVNA   I'll sit here just a minute more. It's as if I had never seen before what the walls in this house are like, what kind of ceilings, and now I look at them greedily, with such tender love—

GAYEFF   I remember when I was six years old, on Trinity Day, I sat in this window and watched my father going to Church—

LYUBOFF ANDREEVNA   Are all the things taken out?

LOPAHIN   Everything, I think. [*Putting on his overcoat. To* EPIHODOFF]   Epihodoff, you see that everything is in order.

EPIHODOFF [*talking in a hoarse voice*]   Don't worry, Yermolay Alexeevich!

LOPAHIN   Why is your voice like that?

EPIHODOFF   Just drank some water, swallowed something.

YASHA [*with contempt*]   The ignorance—

LYUBOFF ANDREEVNA   We are going and there won't be a soul left here—

LOPAHIN   Till spring.

VARYA [*She pulls an umbrella out from a bundle, it looks as if she were going to hit someone;* LOPAHIN *pretends to be frightened.*]   What do you, what do you— I never thought of it.

TROFIMOFF   Ladies and gentlemen, let's get in the carriages— It's time! The train is coming any minute.

VARYA   Petya, here they are, your rubbers, by the suitcase. [*Tearfully*] And how dirty yours are, how old—!

TROFIMOFF [*putting on the rubbers*]   Let's go, ladies and gentlemen!

GAYEFF [*greatly embarrassed, afraid he will cry*]   The train— The station— Cross into the side, combination off the white into the corner—

LYUBOFF ANDREEVNA   Let's go!

LOPAHIN   Everybody here? Nobody there? [*Locking the side door on the left*] Things are stored here, it must be locked up, let's go!

ANYA   Good-by, house! Good-by, the old life!

TROFIMOFF   Long live the new life!

Goes out with ANYA. VARYA *casts a glance around the room and, without hurrying, goes out.* YASHA *and* CHARLOTTA, *with her dog, go out.*

LOPAHIN   And so, till spring. Out, ladies and gentlemen— Till we meet. [*Goes out*]

LYUBOFF ANDREEVNA *and* GAYEFF *are left alone. As if they had been waiting for this, they throw themselves on one another's necks sobbing, but smothering their sobs as if afraid of being heard.*

GAYEFF [*in despair*]   Oh, Sister, Sister—

LYUBOFF ANDREEVNA   Oh, my dear, my lovely, beautiful orchard! My life, my youth, my happiness, good-by!

ANYA [ANYA's *voice, gaily, appealingly*]   Mama—!

TROFIMOFF [TROFIMOFF's *voice, gaily, excitedly*]   Aaooch!

LYUBOFF ANDREEVNA   For the last time, just to look at the walls, at the window—My dear mother used to love to walk around in this room—

GAYEFF   Oh, Sister, Sister—!

ANYA [ANYA's *voice*]   Mama—!

TROFIMOFF [TROFIMOFF's *voice*]   Aaooch—!

LYUBOFF ANDREEVNA   We are coming! [*They go out.*]

The stage is empty. You hear the keys locking all the doors, then the carriages drive off. It grows quiet. In the silence you hear the dull thud of an ax on a tree, a lonely, mournful sound. Footsteps are heard. From the door on the right FIERS *appears. He is dressed as usual, in a jacket and a white waistcoat, slippers on his feet. He is sick.*

FIERS [*going to the door and trying the knob*]   Locked. They've gone. [*Sitting down on the sofa*] They forgot about me— No matter— I'll sit here awhile— And Leonid Andreevich, for sure, didn't put on his fur coat, he went off with his top-coat—[*Sighing anxiously*] And I didn't see to it— The young saplings! [*He mutters something that cannot be understood.*] Life has gone by, as if I hadn't lived at all— [*Lying down*] I'll lie down awhile— You haven't got any strength, nothing is left, nothing— Ach, you—good-for-nothing— [*He lies still.*]

There is a far-off sound as if out of the sky, the sound of a snapped string, dying away, sad. A stillness falls, and there is only the thud of an ax on a tree, far away in the orchard.

Curtain

Questions

1. Is there a villain in this play? If so, is Lopahin the villain? Explain.
2. Chekhov's stage directions require the sound effects of trains. What other sound effects does the author specify? Follow sounds through *The Cherry Orchard* and see how they contribute to plot or character. How do these stage directions separate *The Cherry Orchard* from older drama?
3. Is Lopahin a practical, decisive character? In what matters is he indecisive?
4. We think of masks as worn to delude other people. Do any of these characters wear masks to delude themselves? Describe them.
5. The cherry orchard itself has been called the tragic hero of this play. Comment. Discuss each character in terms of what the cherry orchard means to him or her.
6. Is it funny that Fiers is locked in a deserted house at the end of the play? Could one argue that Fiers's death would make this play a tragedy? Discuss.
7. Do you sense that Chekhov's characters are not speaking to each other? Aren't hearing each other? Find an example. How would you block the scene you find so that spectacle reflected incomplete dialogue?
8. Look up *non sequitur* in the dictionary, if you do not know it. Are there non sequiturs in Chekhov's dialogue? Are there non sequiturs in the plot? Comment on this description of the play: "A monument to disconnectedness."
9. Try turning *The Cherry Orchard* into a California play, with *The Tomato Patch* threatened by a condominium developer. What problems do you encounter?
10. When the dying Chekhov saw *The Cherry Orchard* performed for the first time he was disappointed. He considered it broad comedy, and Stanislavsky had directed it as a melancholy play. Chekhov protested when he attended rehearsals but was too ill to press his arguments. "Stanislavsky has ruined my play," said the author.

    Write a dialogue between playwright and director on the subject of this play. Stanislavsky came from the landowning class; Chekhov did not.
11. Is it possible to imagine a tragic production of *Tartuffe*? A comic production of *Hamlet*? *Oedipus*? Compare with Chekhov.
12. Chekhov wrote "The artist should be, not the judge of his characters and their conversations, but only an unbiased witness." Does Chekhov practice what he preaches in *The Cherry Orchard*?

13. Compare "Gooseberries" (pages 108–114) with *The Cherry Orchard*. Is Chekhov an "unbiased witness" in "Gooseberries"? In *The Cherry Orchard?* How do the two works remind you of each other?

   Compare point of view in the short story with dramatic form in the play. What can plays do that stories cannot? What can stories do that plays cannot? If you turned "Gooseberries" into a play, what would you lose? What might you gain?

Chapter 7 **Nonrealistic Modern Drama, Theater of the Absurd, and Tom Stoppard**

Most contemporary among varieties of nonrealistic drama is **theater of the absurd**, which Luigi Pirandello anticipated with his public doubts about reality and identity. To define absurdity in the theater, we must first mention **existentialism**, a modern philosophic doctrine that derives from the philosophy of Søren Kierkegaard (1813–1855). Kierkegaard was a religious thinker who felt that God and humanity were utterly distinct, and human life inherently absurd. Kierkegaard himself made "a leap of faith" to Christianity, but the later German philosopher Martin Heidegger (1889–1976) and the French philosopher, novelist, and playwright Jean Paul Sartre (1905–1980) affirmed absurdity while they denied divinity. Another French philosopher, novelist, and playwright, Albert Camus (1913–1960), wrote a collection of essays called *The Myth of Sisyphus* (1942) that set forth literary existentialist notions of absurdity. In existentialist thought, humans are distinguished from the rest of nature by their consciousness and their will. Human character has no innate form, but is self-created against the nothingness and meaninglessness out of which people are born and into which they die.

Absurdist playwrights need not subscribe to existentialist philosophy, but they share the notions that human life lacks discernible meaning or purpose, that we make up our own characters as we go along, that we act without rules or with rules which make no sense, that our consciousness is dominated only by certain death, that our existence in a word is *absurd.* If absurdity makes for comedy, it is hardly happy; the smile on the comic mask of absurdist theater is sometimes sardonic, sometimes wild with graveyard gaiety; it is never placid. When we speak of absurdist plays as tragicomedies, we speak of a mixture of laughter and anxiety, melancholy and farce—not of elements found in the classic definitions of either tragedy or comedy.

Human beings have always been prone to visions of life's absurdity, and we can point to pre-absurdist writers from Aristophanes to Oscar Wilde who anticipate these later playwrights. In France the playwright Alfred Jarry

(1873–1907) wrote in *Ubu Roi* (1898) a zany, meaningless, very funny play that anticipated both surrealism and absurdity. But the true originator of absurdism is surely Samuel Beckett (1906–   ), an Irishman living in Paris and writing in French. In his *Waiting for Godot* (1953), which inaugurated absurdist theater, two tramps who resemble clowns occupy the stage, attended by a servant or a slave who is worse off than they are. They wait for the mysterious and powerful Godot who will come and set things right—and who never arrives. These two tramps are **antiheroes**, far from the noble souls of high estate that Aristotle prescribed for tragedy. Beckett subtitles his play a tragicomedy, and the comedy is indeed broad and farcical, featuring bits of slapstick that may remind us of The Three Stooges. We laugh, we feel dread, we sympathize and emphathize—and we laugh again. Among other Beckett dramas, *Endgame* (1957) sums up humanity in a blind, paralyzed hero who lives like his father and mother in a garbage can. In *Krapp's Last Tape* (1958), a single actor playing an old man talks to himself, and listens to tape recordings made in years past. Other leading playwrights of the absurd include Eugène Ionesco, who was born in Romania in 1912 and writes in French; the Englishman Harold Pinter (1930–   ); and the American Edward Albee (1928–   ).

Tom Stoppard and *Rosencrantz and Guildenstern Are Dead*

Tom Stoppard was born in Czechoslovakia in 1937 to parents named Straussler who fled Hitler and settled in Singapore, then fled the Japanese to India. After the war, his widowed mother married an Englishman from whom Stoppard took his name and they settled in England, where Stoppard was educated. He worked for a time as a journalist and reviewed plays in the city of Bristol, which had an excellent repertory company in the Bristol Old Vic. He wrote fiction; he tried his hand at plays. Stoppard's first success was *Rosencrantz and Guildenstern Are Dead* (1967), his absurdist encounter with Shakespeare's *Hamlet*. The playwright has followed *Rosencrantz* with an almost unbroken series of commercial and literary successes, many of them based on earlier theater. *The Real Inspector Hound* (1968) parodies the stage thriller, especially Agatha Christie's highly successful contributions to the genre. *Jumpers* (1972) is a witty and learned encounter not with theater but with modern English linguistic philosophy. *Travesties* (1974) is set in Zürich and makes reference to Oscar Wilde's *The Importance of Being Earnest*, as *Rosencrantz* does to *Hamlet*. *Night and Day* opened in London in 1978 and in New York in 1979, as did *Dogg's Hamlet, Cahoot's Macbeth*.

Plays have been written out of plays before. Shakespeare's *Hamlet* was based on an earlier play; many seventeenth-century plays had classical sources. But recent literature has especially delighted in recalling earlier literature, and not only in drama. James Joyce's great novel *Ulysses* bases itself on Homer's *Odyssey*, with an antiheroic Odysseus in the Irish Jew Leopold Bloom. Ezra Pound's epic *Cantos* used Dante's *Divine Comedy* as a structural scaffold. Each of T. S. Eliot's plays, from *The Family Reunion* on, used a Greek model.

In *Rosencrantz and Guildenstern Are Dead, Hamlet* is not a model but a context. In modern antiheroic fashion, Stoppard focuses on Hamlet's feckless fellow students from Wittenberg.

In Shakespeare's *Hamlet* these characters are so peripheral that in some productions directors remove them in order to shorten the play. Yet for Stoppard, their very inconsequence makes them consequential. The world Stoppard's Rosencrantz and Guildenstern inhabit is existential; from the opening scene, where chance is abolished, there is no certainty for Rosencrantz and Guildenstern except the certainty that the title foreshadows.

Tom Stoppard
Rosencrantz and Guildenstern Are Dead

Characters

ROSENCRANTZ	GERTRUDE
GUILDENSTERN	POLONIUS
THE PLAYER	SOLDIER
ALFRED	HORATIO
TRAGEDIANS	COURTIERS, AMBASSADORS, SOLDIERS,
HAMLET	AND ATTENDANTS
OPHELIA	MUSICIANS
CLAUDIUS	

Act I

Two ELIZABETHANS *passing the time in a place without any visible character.*

They are well dressed—hats, cloaks, sticks and all.

Each of them has a large leather money bag.

GUILDENSTERN's *bag is nearly empty.*

ROSENCRANTZ's *bag is nearly full.*

The reason being: they are betting on the toss of a coin, in the following manner: GUILDENSTERN *(hereafter "GUIL") takes a coin out of his bag, spins it, letting it fall.* ROSENCRANTZ *(hereafter "ROS") studies it, announces it as "heads" (as it happens) and puts it into his own bag. Then they repeat the process. They have apparently been doing this for some time.*

The run of "heads" is impossible, yet ROS *betrays no surprise at all—he feels none. However, he is nice enough to feel a little embarrassed at taking so much money off his friend. Let that be his character note.*

GUIL *is well alive to the oddity of it. He is not worried about the money, but he is worried by the implications; aware but not going to panic about it—his character note.*

GUIL *sits.* ROS *stands (he does the moving, retrieving coins).* GUIL *spins.* ROS *studies coin.*

ROS   Heads.

[*He picks it up and puts it in his bag. The process is repeated.*]

Heads.

[*Again*]

Heads.

[*Again*]

Heads.

[*Again*]

Heads.
  GUIL [*flipping a coin*]   There is an art to the building up of suspense.
  ROS   Heads.
  GUIL [*flipping another*]   Though it can be done by luck alone.
  ROS   Heads.
  GUIL   If that's the word I'm after.
  ROS [*raises his head at* GUIL]   Seventy-six—love.

GUIL *gets up but has nowhere to go. He spins another coin over his shoulder without looking at it, his attention being directed at his environment or lack of it.*

Heads.
  GUIL   A weaker man might be moved to re-examine his faith, if in nothing else at least in the law of probability. [*He slips a coin over his shoulder as he goes to look upstage.*]
  ROS   Heads.

GUIL, *examining the confines of the stage, flips over two more coins as he does so, one by one of course.* ROS *announces each of them as "heads."*

  GUIL [*musing*]   The law of probability, it has been oddly asserted, is something to do with the proposition that if six monkeys [*he has surprised himself*] . . . if six monkeys were . . .
  ROS   Game?
  GUIL   Were they?

ROS   Are you?

GUIL [*understanding*]   Game. [*Flips a coin.*] The law of averages, if I have got this right, means that if six monkeys were thrown up in the air for long enough they would land on their tails about as often as they would land on their—

ROS   Heads. [*He picks up the coin.*]

GUIL   Which even at first glance does not strike one as a particularly rewarding speculation, in either sense, even without the monkeys. I mean you wouldn't *bet* on it. I mean *I* would, but *you* wouldn't. . . . [*As he flips a coin.*]

ROS   Heads.

GUIL   Would you? [*Flips a coin.*]

ROS   Heads.

[*Repeat*]

Heads. [*He looks up at* GUIL—*embarrassed laugh.*] Getting a bit of a bore, isn't it?

GUIL [*coldly*]   A bore?

ROS   Well . . .

GUIL   What about the suspense?

ROS [*innocently*]   What suspense?

Small pause.

GUIL   It must be the law of diminishing returns. . . . I feel the spell about to be broken. [*Energizing himself somewhat. He takes out a coin, spins it high, catches it, turns it over on to the back of his other hand, studies the coin—and tosses it to* ROS. *His energy deflates and he sits.*]

Well, it was an even chance . . . if my calculations are correct.

ROS   Eighty-five in a row—beaten the record!

GUIL   Don't be absurd.

ROS   Easily!

GUIL [*angry*]   Is that *it,* then? Is that all?

ROS   What?

GUIL   A new record? Is that as far as you are prepared to go?

ROS   Well . . .

GUIL   No questions? Not even a pause?

ROS   You spun them yourself.

GUIL   Not a flicker of doubt?

ROS [*aggrieved, aggressive*]   Well, I won—didn't I?

GUIL [*approaches him—quieter*]   And if you'd lost? If they'd come down against you, eighty-five times, one after another, just like that?

ROS [*dumbly*]   Eighty-five in a row? *Tails?*

GUIL   Yes! What would you think?

ROS [*doubtfully*]   Well . . . [*Jocularly.*] Well, I'd have a good look at your coins for a start!

GUIL [*retiring*]   I'm relieved. At least we can still count on self-interest as a predictable factor. . . . I suppose it's the last to go. Your capacity for trust made me wonder if perhaps . . . you, alone . . . [*He turns on him suddenly, reaches out a hand.*] Touch.

ROS *clasps his hand.* GUIL *pulls him up to him.*

GUIL [*more intensely*] We have been spinning coins together since— [*He re-leases him almost as violently.*] This is not the first time we have spun coins!
ROS   Oh no—we've been spinning coins for as long as I remember.
GUIL   How long is that?
ROS   I forget. Mind you—eighty-five times!
GUIL   Yes?
ROS   It'll take some beating, I imagine.
GUIL   Is *that* what you imagine? Is that it? No *fear?*
ROS   Fear?
GUIL [*in fury—flings a coin on the ground*] Fear! The crack that might flood your brain with light!
ROS   Heads. . . . [*He puts it in his bag.*]

GUIL *sits despondently. He takes a coin, spins it, lets it fall between his feet. He looks at it, picks it up, throws it to* ROS, *who puts it in his bag.*

GUIL *takes another coin, spins it, catches it, turns it over on to his other hand, looks at it, and throws it to* ROS, *who puts it in his bag.*

GUIL *takes a third coin, spins it, catches it in his right hand, turns it over onto his left wrist, lobs it in the air, catches it with his left hand, raises his left leg, throws the coin up under it, catches it and turns it over on the top of his head, where it sits.* ROS *comes, looks at it, puts it in his bag.*
ROS   I'm afraid—
GUIL   So am I.
ROS   I'm afraid it isn't your day.
GUIL   I'm afraid it is.

Small pause.

ROS   Eighty-nine.
GUIL   It must be indicative of something, besides the redistribution of wealth. [*He muses.*] List of possible explanations. One: I'm willing it. Inside where nothing shows, I am the essence of a man spinning double-headed coins, and betting against himself in private atonement for an unremembered past. [*He spins a coin at* ROS.]
ROS   Heads.
GUIL   Two: time has stopped dead, and the single experience of one coin being spun once has been repeated ninety times. . . . [*He flips a coin, looks at it, tosses it to* ROS.] On the whole, doubtful. Three: divine intervention, that is to say, a good turn from above concerning him, cf. children of Israel, or retribution from above concerning me, cf. Lot's wife. Four: a spectacular vindication of the principle that each individual coin spun individually [*he spins one*] is as likely to come down heads as tails and therefore should cause no surprise each individual time it does. [*It does. He tosses it to* ROS.]
ROS   I've never known anything like it!
GUIL   And a syllogism: One, he has never known anything like it. Two, he has never known anything to write home about. Three, it is nothing to write home about. . . . Home . . . What's the first thing you remember?

ROS   Oh, let's see. . . . The first thing that comes into my head, you mean?

GUIL   No—the first thing you remember.

ROS   Ah. [*Pause.*] No, it's no good, it's gone. It was a long time ago.

GUIL [*patient but edged*]   You don't get my meaning. What is the first thing after all the things you've forgotten?

ROS   Oh I see. [*Pause.*] I've forgotten the question.

GUIL *leaps up and paces.*

GUIL   Are you happy?

ROS   What?

GUIL   Content? At ease?

ROS   I suppose so.

GUIL   What are you going to do now?

ROS   I don't know. What do you want to do?

GUIL   I have no desires. None. [*He stops pacing dead.*] There was a messenger . . . that's right. We were sent for. [*He wheels at* ROS *and raps out*] Syllogism the second: One, probability is a factor which operates within natural forces. Two, probability is not operating as a factor. Three, we are now within un-, sub- or supernatural forces. Discuss. [ROS *is suitably startled. Acidly.*] Not too heatedly.

ROS   I'm sorry I—What's the matter with you?

GUIL   The scientific approach to the examination of phenomena is a defence against the pure emotion of fear. Keep tight hold and continue while there's time. Now—counter to the previous syllogism: tricky one, follow me carefully, it may prove a comfort. If we postulate, and we just have, that within un-, sub- or supernatural forces *the probability is* that the law of probability will not operate as a factor, then we must accept that the probability of the *first* part will not operate as a factor, in which case the law of probability *will* operate as a factor within un-, sub- or supernatural forces. And since it obviously hasn't been doing so, we can take it that we are not held within un-, sub- or supernatural forces after all; in all probability, that is. Which is a great relief to me personally. [*Small pause.*] Which is all very well, except that—[*He continues with tight hysteria, under control.*] We have been spinning coins together since I don't know when, and in all that time (if it *is* all that time) I don't suppose either of us was more than a couple of gold pieces up or down. I hope that doesn't sound surprising because its very unsurprisingness is something I am trying to keep hold of. The equanimity of your average tosser of coins depends upon a law, or rather a tendency, or let us say a probability, or at any rate a mathematically calculable chance, which ensures that he will not upset himself by losing too much nor upset his opponent by winning too often. This made for a kind of harmony and a kind of confidence. It related the fortuitous and the ordained into a reassuring union which we recognized as nature. The sun came up about as often as it went down, in the long run, and a coin showed heads about as often as it showed tails. Then a messenger arrived. We had been sent for. Nothing else happened. Ninety-two coins spun consecutively have come down heads ninety-two consecutive times . . . and for the last three minutes on the wind of a windless day I have heard the sound of drums and flute. . . .

ROS [*cutting his fingernails*]   Another curious scientific phenomenon is the fact that the fingernails grow after death, as does the beard.

GUIL   What?

ROS [*loud*] Beard!

GUIL But you're not dead.

ROS [*irritated*] I didn't say they *started* to grow after death! [*Pause, calmer.*] The fingernails also grow before birth, though *not* the beard.

GUIL *What?*

ROS [*shouts*] Beard! What's the matter with you? [*Reflectively.*] The toenails, on the other hand, never grow at all.

GUIL [*bemused*] The toenails never grow at all?

ROS Do they? It's a funny thing—I cut my fingernails all the time, and every time I think to cut them, they need cutting. Now, for instance. And yet, I never, to the best of my knowledge, cut my toenails. They ought to be curled under my feet by now, but it doesn't happen. I never think about them. Perhaps I cut them absent-mindedly, when I'm thinking of something else.

GUIL [*tensed up by this rambling*] Do you remember the first thing that happened today?

ROS [*promptly*] I woke up, I suppose. [*Triggered.*] Oh—I've got it now—that man, a foreigner, he woke us up—

GUIL A messenger. [*He relaxes, sits.*]

ROS That's it—pale sky before dawn, a man standing on his saddle to bang on the shutters—shouts—What's all the row about?! Clear off!—But then he called our names. You remember that—this man woke us up.

GUIL Yes.

ROS We were sent for.

GUIL Yes.

ROS That's why we're here. [*He looks round, seems doubtful, then the explanation.*] Travelling.

GUIL Yes.

ROS [*dramatically*] It was urgent—a matter of extreme urgency, a royal summons, his very words: official business and no questions asked—lights in the stable-yard, saddle up and off headlong and hotfoot across the land, our guides outstripped in breakneck pursuit of our duty! Fearful lest we come too late!!

Small pause.

GUIL Too late for what?

ROS How do I know? We haven't got there yet.

GUIL Then what are we doing here, I ask myself.

ROS You might well ask.

GUIL We better get on.

ROS You might well think.

GUIL We better get on.

ROS [*actively*] Right! [*Pause.*] On where?

GUIL Forward.

ROS [*forward to footlights*] Ah. [*Hesitates.*] Which way do we——[*He turns round.*] Which way did we——?

GUIL Practically starting from scratch. . . . An awakening, a man standing on his saddle to bang on the shutters, our names shouted in a certain dawn, a message, a summons . . . A new record for heads and tails. We have not been . . . picked out . . . simply to be abandoned . . . set loose to find our own way. . . . We are entitled to some direction. . . . I would have thought.

ROS [*alert, listening*] I say——! I say——

GUIL Yes?

ROS I can hear—I thought I heard—music.

GUIL *raises himself.*

GUIL Yes?

ROS Like a band. [*He looks around, laughs embarrassedly, expiating himself.*] It sounded like—a band. Drums.

GUIL Yes.

ROS [*relaxes*] It couldn't have been real.

GUIL "The colours red, blue and green are real. The colour yellow is a mystical experience shared by everybody"—demolish.

ROS [*at edge of stage*] It must have been thunder. Like drums . . .

By the end of the next speech, the band is faintly audible.

GUIL A man breaking his journey between one place and another at a third place of no name, character, population or significance, sees a unicorn cross his path and disappear. That in itself is startling, but there are precedents for mystical encounters of various kinds, or to be less extreme, a choice of persuasions to put it down to fancy; until—"My God," says a second man, "I must be dreaming, I thought I saw a unicorn." At which point, a dimension is added that makes the experience as alarming as it will ever be. A third witness, you understand, adds no further dimension but only spreads it thinner, and a fourth thinner still, and the more witnesses there are the thinner it gets and the more reasonable it becomes until it is as thin as reality, the name we give to the common experience. . . . "Look, look!" recites the crowd. "A horse with an arrow in its forehead! It must have been mistaken for a deer."

ROS [*eagerly*] I knew all along it was a band.

GUIL [*tiredly*] He knew all along it was a band.

ROS Here they come!

GUIL [*at the last moment before they enter—wistfully*] I'm sorry it wasn't a unicorn. It would have been nice to have unicorns.

The TRAGEDIANS *are six in number, including a small* BOY [ALFRED]. *Two pull and push a cart piled with props and belongings. There is also a* DRUMMER, *a* HORN-PLAYER *and a* FLAUTIST. *The* SPOKESMAN ["*the* PLAYER"] *has no instrument. He brings up the rear and is the first to notice them.*

PLAYER Halt!

The group turns and halts.

[*Joyously*] An audience!

[ROS *and* GUIL *half rise*]

Don't move!

[*They sink back. He regards them fondly.*]

Perfect! A lucky thing we came along.
   ROS   For us?
   PLAYER   Let us hope so. But to meet two gentlemen on the road—we would
not hope to meet them off it.
   ROS   No?
   PLAYER   Well met, in fact, and just in time.
   ROS   Why's that?
   PLAYER   Why, we grow rusty and you catch us at the very point of decadence—
by this time tomorrow we might have forgotten everything we ever knew. That's
a thought, isn't it? [*He laughs generously.*] We'd be back where we started—im-
provising.
   ROS   Tumblers, are you?
   PLAYER   We can give you a tumble if that's your taste, and times being what
they are. . . . Otherwise, for a jingle of coin we can do you a selection of gory
romances, full of fine cadence and corpses, pirated from the Italian; and it doesn't
take much to make a jingle—even a single coin has music in it.

[*They all flourish and bow, raggedly.*]

Tragedians, at your command.

ROS *and* GUIL *have got to their feet.*

   ROS   My name is Guildenstern, and this is Rosencrantz.

[GUIL *confers briefly with him.*]

[*Without embarrassment*] I'm sorry—*his* name's Guildenstern, and *I'm* Rosencrantz.

   PLAYER   A pleasure. We've played to bigger, of course, but quality counts for
something. I recognized you at once——
   ROS   And who are we?
   PLAYER   —as fellow artists.
   ROS   I thought we were gentlemen.
   PLAYER   For some of us it is performance, for others, patronage. They are two
sides of the same coin, or, let us say, being as there are so many of us, the same
side of two coins. [*Bows again.*] Don't clap too loudly—it's a very old world.
   ROS   What is your line?
   PLAYER   Tragedy, sir. Deaths and disclosures, universal and particular, de-
nouements both unexpected and inexorable, transvestite melodrama on all levels
including the suggestive. We transport you into a world of intrigue and illusion
. . . clowns, if you like, murderers—we can do you ghosts and battles, on the
skirmish level, heroes, villains, tormented lovers—set pieces in the poetic vein;
we can do you rapiers or rape or both, by all means, faithless wives and ravished
virgins—*flagrante delicto* at a price, but that comes under realism for which there
are special terms. Getting warm, am I?
   ROS [*doubtfully*]   Well, I don't know. . . .

PLAYER   It costs little to watch, and little more if you happen to get caught up in the action, if that's your taste and times being what they are.

ROS   What are they?

PLAYER   Indifferent.

ROS   Bad?

PLAYER   Wicked. Now what precisely is your pleasure? [*He turns to the* TRA-GEDIANS.] Gentlemen, disport yourselves.

[*The* TRAGEDIANS *shuffle into some kind of line.*]

There! See anything you like?

ROS [*doubtful, innocent*]   What do they do?

PLAYER   Let your imagination run riot. They are beyond surprise.

ROS   And how much?

PLAYER   To take part?

ROS   To watch.

PLAYER   Watch what?

ROS   A private performance.

PLAYER   How private?

ROS   Well, there are only two of us. Is that enough?

PLAYER   For an audience, disappointing. For voyeurs, about average.

ROS   What's the difference?

PLAYER   Ten guilders.

ROS [*horrified*]   Ten *guilders!*

PLAYER   I mean eight.

ROS   Together?

PLAYER   Each. I don't think you understand—

ROS   What are you *saying?*

PLAYER   What am I saying—seven.

ROS   Where have you *been?*

PLAYER   Roundabout. A nest of children carries the custom of the town. Juvenile companies, they are the fashion. But they cannot match our repertoire . . . we'll stoop to anything if that's your bent. . . .

He regards ROS *meaningfully but* ROS *returns the stare blankly.*

ROS   They'll grow up.

PLAYER [*giving up*]   There's one born every minute. [*To* TRAGEDIANS] Onward!

The TRAGEDIANS *start to resume their burdens and their journey.* GUIL *stirs himself at last.*

GUIL   Where are you going?

PLAYER   Ha-alt!

[*They halt and turn.*]

Home, sir.

GUIL   Where from?

PLAYER   Home. We're travelling people. We take our chances where we find
them.
GUIL   It was chance, then?
PLAYER   Chance?
GUIL   You found us.
PLAYER   Oh, yes.
GUIL   You were looking?
PLAYER   Oh no.
GUIL   Chance, then.
PLAYER   Or fate.
GUIL   Yours or ours?
PLAYER   It could hardly be one without the other.
GUIL   Fate, then.
PLAYER   Oh, yes. We have no control. Tonight we play to the court. Or the
night after. Or to the tavern. Or not.
GUIL   Perhaps I can use my influence.
PLAYER   At the tavern?
GUIL   At the court. I would say I have some influence.
PLAYER   Would you say so?
GUIL   I have influence yet.
PLAYER   Yet what?

GUIL *seizes the* PLAYER *violently.*

GUIL   I have influence!

[*The* PLAYER *does not resist.* GUIL *loosens his hold.*]

[*More calmly.*] You said something—about getting caught up in the action——
PLAYER [*gaily freeing himself*]   I did!—I did!—You're quicker than your
friend. . . . [*Confidently.*] Now for a handful of guilders I happen to have a private
and uncut performance of *The Rape of the Sabine Women*—or rather woman, or
rather Alfred——[*Over his shoulder.*] Get your skirt on, Alfred——

[*The* BOY *starts struggling into a female robe.*]
. . . and for eight you can participate.

[GUIL *backs,* PLAYER *follows.*]

. . . taking either part.

[GUIL *backs.*]

. . . or both for ten.

[GUIL *tries to turn away,* PLAYER *holds his sleeve.*]

. . . with encores——

[GUIL *smashes the* PLAYER *across the face. The* PLAYER *recoils.* GUIL *stands trembling.*]

[*Resigned and quiet*]. Get your skirt off, Alfred. . .

ALFRED *struggles out of his half-on robe.*

GUIL [*shaking with rage and fright*] It could have been—it didn't have to be *obscene*. . . . It could have been—a bird out of season, dropping bright-feathered on my shoulder. . . . It could have been a tongueless dwarf standing by the road to point the way. . . . I was *prepared*. But it's this, is it? No enigma, no dignity, nothing classical, portentous, only this—a comic pornographer and a rabble of prostitutes. . . .

PLAYER [*acknowledging the description with a sweep of his hat, bowing; sadly*] You should have caught us in better times. We were purists then. [*Straightens up.*] On-ward.

The PLAYERS *make to leave.*

ROS [*his voice has changed: he has caught on*] Excuse me!
PLAYER: Ha-alt!

[*They halt.*]

A-al-l-fred!

ALFRED *resumes the struggle. The* PLAYER *comes forward.*

ROS   You're not—ah—exclusively players, then?
PLAYER   We're inclusively players, sir.
ROS   So you give—exhibitions?
PLAYER   Performances, sir.
ROS   Yes, of course. There's more money in that, is there?
PLAYER   There's more trade, sir.
ROS   Times being what they are.
PLAYER   Yes.
ROS   Indifferent.
PLAYER   Completely.
ROS   You know I'd no idea——
PLAYER   No——
ROS   I mean, I've *heard* of—but I've never actually——
PLAYER   No.
ROS   I mean, what exactly do you *do?*
PLAYER   We keep to our usual stuff, more or less, only inside out. We do on stage the things that are supposed to happen off. Which is a kind of integrity, if you look on every exit being an entrance somewhere else.
ROS [*nervy, loud*] Well, I'm not really the type of man who—no, but don't hurry off—sit down and tell us about some of the things people ask you to do——

The PLAYER *turns away.*

PLAYER   On-ward!
ROS   Just a minute!

[*They turn and look at him without expression.*]

Well, all right—I wouldn't mind seeing—just an idea of the kind of—[*Bravely.*] What will you do for that? [*And tosses a single coin on the ground between them.*]

[*The* PLAYER *spits at the coin, from where he stands.*

The TRAGEDIANS *demur, trying to get at the coin. He kicks and cuffs them back.*]

On!

[ALFRED *is still half in and out of his robe. The* PLAYER *cuffs him.*]

[*To* ALFRED] What are you playing at?

ROS *is shamed into fury.*

> ROS   Filth! Disgusting—I'll report you to the authorities—*perverts!* I know your game all right, it's all filth!

The PLAYERS *are about to leave.* GUIL *has remained detached.*

> GUIL [*casually*]   Do you like a bet?

The TRAGEDIANS *turn and look interested. The* PLAYER *comes forward.*

> PLAYER   What kind of bet did you have in mind?

GUIL *walks half the distance towards the* PLAYER, *stops with his foot over the coin.*

> GUIL   Double or quits.
> PLAYER   Well . . . heads.

GUIL *raises his foot. The* PLAYER *bends. The* TRAGEDIANS *crowd round. Relief and congratulations. The* PLAYER *picks up the coin.* GUIL *throws him a second coin.*

> GUIL   Again?

Some of the TRAGEDIANS *are for it, others against.*

> GUIL   Evens.

The PLAYER *nods and tosses the coin.*

> GUIL   Heads.

[*It is. He picks it up.*]

Again.

GUIL *spins coin.*

PLAYER   Heads.

It is. PLAYER *picks up coin. He has two coins again. He spins one.*

GUIL   Heads.

It is. GUIL *picks it up. Then tosses it immediately.*

PLAYER [*fractional hesitation*]   Tails.

But it's heads. GUIL *picks it up.* PLAYER *tosses down his last coin by way of paying up, and turns away.* GUIL *doesn't pick it up; he puts his foot on it.*

GUIL   Heads.
PLAYER   No!

[*Pause. The* TRAGEDIANS *are against this.*]

[*Apologetically.*] They don't like the odds.
    GUIL [*lifts his foot, squats; picks up the coin still squatting; looks up*]   You were right—heads. [*Spins it, slaps his hand on it, on the floor.*] Heads I win.
    PLAYER   No.
    GUIL [*uncovers coin*]   Right again. [*Repeat.*] Heads I win.
    PLAYER   No.
    GUIL [*uncovers coin*]   And right again. [*Repeat.*] Heads I win.
    PLAYER   *No!*

He turns away, the TRAGEDIANS *with him.* GUIL *stands up, comes close.*

GUIL   Would you believe it? [*Stands back, relaxes, smiles.*] Bet me the year of my birth doubled is an odd number.
    PLAYER   *Your* birth——!
    GUIL   If you don't trust me don't bet with me.
    PLAYER   Would you trust *me?*
    GUIL   *Bet* me then.
    PLAYER   My birth?
    GUIL   Odd numbers you win.
    PLAYER   You're on——

The TRAGEDIANS *have come forward, wide awake.*

GUIL   Good. Year of your birth. Double it. Even numbers I win, odd numbers I lose.

Silence. An awful sigh as the TRAGEDIANS *realize that any number doubled is even. Then a terrible row as they object. Then a terrible silence.*

PLAYER   We have no money.

GUIL *turns to him.*

GUIL   Ah. Then what *have* you got?

[*The* PLAYER *silently brings* ALFRED *forward.* GUIL *regards* ALFRED *sadly.*]

Was it for this?
    PLAYER   It's the best we've got.
    GUIL [*looking up and around*]   Then the times are bad indeed.

[*The* PLAYER *starts to speak, protestation, but* GUIL *turns on him viciously.*]

The very *air* stinks.

[*The* PLAYER *moves back.* GUIL *moves down to the footlights and turns.*]

Come here, Alfred.

[ALFRED *moves down and stands, frightened and small.*]

[*Gently.*] Do you lose often?
    ALFRED   Yes, sir.
    GUIL   Then what could you have left to lose?
    ALFRED   Nothing, sir.

Pause. GUIL *regards him.*

    GUIL   Do you like being . . . an actor?
    ALFRED   No, sir.

GUIL *looks around, at the audience.*

    GUIL   You and I, Alfred—we could create a dramatic precedent here.

[*And* ALFRED, *who has been near tears, starts to sniffle.*]

Come, come, Alfred, this is no way to fill the theatres of Europe.

[*The* PLAYER *has moved down, to remonstrate with* ALFRED. GUIL *cuts him off again.*]

[*Viciously.*] Do you know any good plays?
    PLAYER   Plays?
    ROS [*coming forward, faltering shyly*]   Exhibitions. . . .
    GUIL   I thought you said you were actors.
    PLAYER [*dawning*]   Oh. Oh well, we *are*. We are. But there hasn't been much call——
    GUIL   You lost. Well then—one of the Greeks, perhaps? You're familiar with the tragedies of antiquity, are you? The great homicidal classics? Matri, patri, fratri, sorrori, uxori and it goes without saying——

ROS Saucy——
GUIL —Suicidal—hm? Maidens aspiring to godheads——
ROS And vice versa——
GUIL Your kind of thing, is it?
PLAYER Well, no, I can't say it is, really. We're more of the blood, love and rhetoric school.
GUIL Well, I'll leave the choice to you, if there is anything to choose between them.
PLAYER They're hardly divisible, sir—well, I can do you blood and love without the rhetoric, and I can do you blood and rhetoric without the love, and I can do you all three concurrent or consecutive, but I can't do you love and rhetoric without the blood. Blood is compulsory—they're all blood, you see.
GUIL Is that what people want?
PLAYER It's what we do. [*Small pause. He turns away.*]

GUIL *touches* ALFRED *on the shoulder.*

GUIL [*wry, gentle*] Thank you; we'll let you know.

The PLAYER *has moved upstage.* ALFRED *follows.*

PLAYER [*to* TRAGEDIANS] Thirty-eight!
ROS [*moving across, fascinated and hopeful*] Position?
PLAYER Sir?
ROS One of your—tableaux?
PLAYER No, sir.
ROS Oh.
PLAYER [*to the* TRAGEDIANS, *now departing with their cart, already taking various props off it*] Entrances there and there [*indicating upstage*].

The PLAYER *has not moved his position for his last four lines. He does not move now.* GUIL *waits.*

GUIL Well . . . aren't you going to change into your costume?
PLAYER I never change out of it, sir.
GUIL Always in character.
PLAYER That's it.

Pause.

GUIL Aren't you going to—come *on?*
PLAYER I *am* on.
GUIL But if you *are* on, you can't *come* on. *Can* you?
PLAYER I *start* on.
GUIL But it hasn't *started.* Go on. We'll look out for you.
PLAYER I'll give you a wave.

He does not move. His immobility is now pointed, and getting awkward. Pause.
ROS *walks up to him till they are face to face.*

ROS   Excuse me.

[*Pause. The* PLAYER *lifts his downstage foot. It was covering* GUIL'S *coin.* ROS *puts his foot on the coin. Smiles.*]

Thank you.

The PLAYER *turns and goes.* ROS *has bent for the coin.*

GUIL [*moving out*]   Come on.
ROS   I say—that was lucky.
GUIL [*turning*]   What?
ROS   It was tails.

He tosses the coin to GUIL *who catches it. Simultaneously—a lighting change sufficient to alter the exterior mood into interior, but nothing violent.*

And OPHELIA *runs on in some alarm, holding up her skirts—followed by* HAMLET.

OPHELIA *has been sewing and she holds the garment. They are both mute.* HAMLET, *with his doublet all unbraced, no hat upon his head, his stockings fouled, ungartered and downgyved to his ankle, pale as his shirt, his knees knocking each other . . . and with a look so piteous, he takes her by the wrist and holds her hard, then he goes to the length of his arm, and with his other hand over his brow, falls to such perusal of her face as he would draw it. . . . At last, with a little shaking of his arm, and thrice his head waving up and down, he raises a sigh so piteous and profound that it does seem to shatter all his bulk and end his being. That done he lets her go, and with his head over his shoulder turned, he goes out backwards without taking his eyes off her . . . she runs off in the opposite direction.*

ROS *and* GUIL *have frozen.* GUIL *unfreezes first. He jumps at* ROS.

GUIL   Come on!

But a flourish—enter CLAUDIUS *and* GERTRUDE, *attended.*

CLAUDIUS   Welcome, dear Rosencrantz . . . [*he raises a hand at* GUIL *while* ROS *bows—*GUIL *bows late and hurriedly*] . . . and Guildenstern.

[*He raises a hand at* ROS *while* GUIL *bows to him—*ROS *is still straightening up from his previous bow and halfway up he bows down again. With his head down, he twists to look at* GUIL, *who is on the way up.*]

Moreover that we did much long to see you,
The need we have to use you did provoke
Our hasty sending.

[ROS *and* GUIL *still adjusting their clothing for* CLAUDIUS's *presence.*]

Something have you heard
Of Hamlet's transformation, so call it,

Sith nor th'exterior nor the inward man
Resembles that it was. What it should be,
More than his father's death, that thus hath put him,
So much from th'understanding of himself,
I cannot dream of. I entreat you both
That, being of so young days brought up with him
And sith so neighboured to his youth and haviour
That you vouchsafe your rest here in our court
Some little time, so by your companies
To draw him on to pleasures, and to gather
So much as from occasion you may glean,
Whether aught to us unknown afflicts him thus,
That opened lies within our remedy.
    GERTRUDE   Good [*fractional suspense*] gentlemen . . .

[*They both bow.*]

He hath much talked of you,
And sure I am, two men there is not living
To whom he more adheres. If it will please you
To show us so much gentry and goodwill
As to expand your time with us awhile
For the supply and profit of our hope,
Your visitation shall receive such thanks
As fits a king's remembrance.
    ROS   Both your majesties
Might, by the sovereign power you have of us,
Put your dread pleasures more into command
Than to entreaty.
    GUIL   But we both obey,
And here give up ourselves in the full bent
To lay our service freely at your feet,
To be commanded.
    CLAUDIUS   Thanks, Rosencrantz [*turning to* ROS *who is caught unprepared, while* GUIL *bows*] and gentle Guildenstern [*turning to* GUIL *who is bent double*].
    GERTRUDE [*correcting*]   Thanks Guildenstern [*turning to* ROS, *who bows as* GUIL *checks upward movement to bow too—both bent double, squinting at each other*] . . . and gentle Rosencrantz [*turning to* GUIL, *both straightening up—*GUIL *checks again and bows again*].

And I beseech you instantly to visit
My too much changed son. Go, some of you,
And bring these gentlemen where Hamlet is.

Two ATTENDANTS *exit backwards, indicating that* ROS *and* GUIL *should follow.*

    GUIL   Heaven make our presence and our practices
Pleasant and helpful to him.
    GERTRUDE   Ay, amen!

ROS *and* GUIL *move towards a downstage wing. Before they get there,* POLONIUS *enters. They stop and bow to him. He nods and hurries upstage to* CLAUDIUS. *They turn to look at him.*

POLONIUS   The ambassadors from Norway, my good lord, are joyfully returned.
CLAUDIUS   Thou still hast been the father of good news.
POLONIUS   Have I, my lord? Assure you, my good liege,
I hold my duty as I hold my soul,
Both to my God and to my gracious King;
And I do think, or else this brain of mine
Hunts not the trail of policy so sure
As it hath used to do, that I have found
The very cause of Hamlet's lunacy. . . .

Exeunt—leaving ROS *and* GUIL.

ROS   I want to go home.
GUIL   Don't let them confuse you.
ROS   I'm out of my step here——
GUIL   We'll soon be home and high—dry and home—I'll——
ROS   It's all over my *depth*——
GUIL   —I'll hie you home and——
ROS   —out of my head——
GUIL   —dry you high and——
ROS [*cracking, high*]   —over my step over my head body!—I tell you it's all stopping to a death, it's boding to a depth, stepping to a head, it's all heading to a dead stop——
GUIL [*the nursemaid*]   There! . . . and we'll soon be home and dry . . . and *high* and dry. . . . [*Rapidly.*] Has it ever happened to you that all of a sudden and for no reason at all you haven't the faintest idea how to spell the word—"wife"—or "house"—because when you write it down you just can't remember ever having seen those letters in that order before . . . ?
ROS   I remember——
GUIL   Yes?
ROS   I remember when there were no questions.
GUIL   There were always questions. To exchange one set for another is no great matter.
ROS   Answers, yes. There were answers to everything.
GUIL   You've forgotten.
ROS [*flaring*]   I haven't forgotten—how I used to remember my own name—and yours, oh *yes!* There were answers everywhere you *looked.* There was no question about it—people knew who I was and if they didn't they asked and I told them.
GUIL   You did, the trouble is, each of them is . . . plausible, without being instinctive. All your life you live so close to truth, it becomes a permanent blur in the corner of your eye, and when something nudges it into outline it is like being ambushed by a grotesque. A man standing in his saddle in the half-lit half-alive dawn banged on the shutters and called two names. He was just a hat and a cloak levitating in the grey plume of his own breath, but when he called we came. That much is certain—we came.
ROS   Well I can tell you I'm sick to death of it. I don't care one way or another, so why don't you make up your mind.

GUIL   We can't afford anything quite so arbitrary. Nor did we come all this way for a christening. All *that*—preceded us. But we are comparatively fortunate; we might have been left to sift the whole field of human nomenclature, like two blind men looting a bazaar for their own portraits. . . . At least we are presented with alternatives.

ROS   Well as from now——

GUIL   —But not choice.

ROS   You made me look ridiculous in there.

GUIL   I looked just as ridiculous as you did.

ROS [*an anguished cry*]   Consistency is all I ask!

GUIL [*low, wry rhetoric*]   Give us this day our daily mask.

ROS [*a dying fall*]   I want to go home. [*Moves*] Which way did we come in? I've lost my sense of direction.

GUIL   The only beginning is birth and the only end is death—if you can't count on that, what can you count on?

They connect again.

ROS   We don't owe anything to anyone.

GUIL   We've been caught up. Your smallest action sets off another somewhere else, and is set off by it. Keep an eye open, an ear cocked. Tread warily, follow instructions. We'll be all right.

ROS   For how long?

GUIL   Till events have played themselves out. There's a logic at work—it's all done for you, don't worry. Enjoy it. Relax. To be taken in hand and led, like being a child again, even without the innocence, a child—it's like being given a prize, an extra slice of childhood when you least expect it, as a prize for being good, or compensation for never having had one. . . . Do I contradict myself?

ROS   I can't remember. . . . What have we got to go on?

GUIL   We have been briefed. Hamlet's transformation. What do you recollect?

ROS   Well, he's changed, hasn't he? The exterior and inward man fails to re-semble——

GUIL   Draw him on to pleasures—glean what afflicts him.

ROS   Something more than his father's death——

GUIL   He's always talking about us—there aren't two people living whom he dotes on more than us.

ROS   We cheer him up—find out what's the matter——

GUIL   Exactly, it's a matter of asking the right questions and giving away as little as we can. It's a game.

ROS   And then we can go?

GUIL   And receive such thanks as fits a king's remembrance.

ROS   I like the sound of that. What do you think he means by remembrance?

GUIL   He doesn't forget his friends.

ROS   Would you care to estimate?

GUIL   Difficult to say, really—some kings tend to be amnesiac, others I sup-pose—the opposite, whatever that is. . . .

ROS   Yes—but——

GUIL   Elephantine . . . ?

ROS   Not how long—how much?

GUIL   *Retentive*—he's a very retentive king, a royal retainer. . . .

ROS What are you playing at?
GUIL Words, words. They're all we have to go on.

Pause.

ROS Shouldn't we be doing something—constructive?
GUIL What did you have in mind? . . . A short, blunt human pyramid . . . ?
ROS We could go.
GUIL Where?
ROS After him.
GUIL Why? They've got us placed now—if we start moving around, we'll all be chasing each other all night.

Hiatus.

ROS [*at footlights*] How very intriguing! [*Turns*] I feel like a spectator—an appalling business. The only thing that makes it bearable is the irrational belief that somebody interesting will come on in a minute. . . .
GUIL See anyone?
ROS No. You?
GUIL No. [*At footlights*] What a fine persecution—to be kept intrigued without ever quite being enlightened. . . . [*Pause*] We've had no practice.
ROS We could play at questions.
GUIL What good would that do?
ROS Practice!
GUIL Statement! One—love.
ROS Cheating!
GUIL How?
ROS I hadn't started yet.
GUIL Statement. Two—love.
ROS Are you counting that?
GUIL What?
ROS Are you counting that?
GUIL Foul! No repetitions. Three—love. First game to . . .
ROS I'm not going to play if you're going to be like that.
GUIL Whose serve?
ROS Hah?
GUIL Foul! No grunts. Love—one.
ROS Whose go?
GUIL Why?
ROS Why not?
GUIL What for?
ROS Foul! No synonyms! One—all.
GUIL What in God's name is going on?
ROS Foul! No rhetoric. Two—one.
GUIL What does it all add up to?
ROS Can't you guess?
GUIL Were you addressing me?
ROS Is there anyone else?
GUIL Who?

ROS How would I know?
GUIL Why do you ask?
ROS Are you serious?
GUIL Was that rhetoric?
ROS No.
GUIL Statement! Two—all. Game point.
ROS What's the matter with you today?
GUIL When?
ROS What?
GUIL Are you deaf?
ROS Am I dead?
GUIL Yes or no?
ROSR Is there a choice?
GUIL Is there a God?
ROS Foul! No *non sequiturs*, three—two, one game all.
GUIL [*seriously*] What's your name?
ROS What's yours?
GUIL I asked you first.
ROS Statement. One—love.
GUIL What's your name when you're at home?
ROS What's yours?
GUIL When I'm at home?
ROS Is it different at home?
GUIL What home?
ROS Haven't you got one?
GUIL Why do you ask?
ROS What are you driving at?
GUIL [*with emphasis*] What's your name?!
ROS Repetition. Two—love. Match point to me.
GUIL [*seizing him violently*] WHO DO YOU THINK YOU ARE?
ROS Rhetoric! Game and match! [*Pause*] Where's it going to end?
GUIL That's the question.
ROS It's *all* questions.
GUIL Do you think it matters?
ROS Doesn't it matter to you?
GUIL Why should it matter?
ROS What does it matter why?
GUIL [*teasing gently*] Doesn't it *matter* why it matters?
ROS [*rounding on him*] What's the *matter* with you?

Pause.

GUIL It doesn't matter.
ROS [*voice in the wilderness*] . . . What's the game?
GUIL What are the rules?

Enter HAMLET *behind, crossing the stage, reading a book—as he is about to disappear* GUIL *notices him.*

GUIL [*sharply*] Rosencrantz!

ROS [*jumps*] What!

HAMLET *goes. Triumph dawns on them, they smile.*

GUIL There! How was that?
ROS Clever!
GUIL Natural?
ROS Instinctive.
GUIL Got it in your head?
ROS I take my hat off to you.
GUIL Shake hands.

They do.

ROS Now I'll try you—Guil—!
GUIL —Not yet—catch me unawares.
ROS Right.

[*They separate. Pause. Aside to* GUIL.]

Ready?
GUIL [*explodes*] Don't be stupid.
ROS Sorry.

Pause.

GUIL [*snaps*] Guildenstern!
ROS [*jumps*] What?

He is immediately crestfallen, GUIL *is disgusted.*

GUIL Consistency is all I ask!
ROS [*quietly*] Immortality is all I seek. . . .
GUIL [*dying fall*] Give us this day our daily week. . . .

Beat.

ROS Who was that?
GUIL Didn't you know him?
ROS He didn't know me.
GUIL He didn't see you.
ROS I didn't see him.
GUIL We shall see. I *hardly* knew him, he's changed.
ROS You could see that?
GUIL Transformed.
ROS How do you know?
GUIL Inside and out.
ROS I see.
GUIL He's not himself.

ROS   He's changed.
GUIL   I could see that.

[*Beat.*]

Glean what afflicts him.
ROS   Me?
GUIL   Him.
ROS   How?
GUIL   Question and answer. Old ways are the best ways.
ROS   He's afflicted.
GUIL   You question, I'll answer.
ROS   He's not himself, you know.
GUIL   I'm him, you see.

Beat.

ROS   Who am I then?
GUIL   You're yourself.
ROS   And he's you?
GUIL   Not a bit of it.
ROS   Are you afflicted?
GUIL   That's the idea. Are you ready?
ROS   Let's go back a bit.
GUIL   I'm afflicted.
ROS   I see.
GUIL   Glean what afflicts me.
ROS   Right.
GUIL   Question and answer.
ROS   How should I begin?
GUIL   Address me.
ROS   My dear Guildenstern!
GUIL [*quietly*]   You've forgotten—haven't you?
ROS   My dear Rosencrantz!
GUIL [*great control*]   I don't think you quite understand. What we are attempting is a hypothesis in which *I* answer for *him,* while *you* ask me questions.
ROS   Ah! Ready?
GUIL   You know what to do?
ROS   What?
GUIL   Are you stupid?
ROS   Pardon?
GUIL   Are you deaf?
ROS   Did you speak?
GUIL [*admonishing*]   Not now——
ROS   Statement.
GUIL [*shouts*]   Not now! [*Pause*] If I had any doubts, or rather hopes, they are dispelled. What could we possibly have in common except our situation? [*They separate and sit.*] Perhaps he'll come back this way.
ROS   Should we go?
GUIL   Why?

Pause.

ROS [*starts up. Snaps fingers*]   Oh! You mean—you pretend to be *him*, and *I* ask you questions!
   GUIL [*dry*]   Very good.
   ROS   You had me confused.
   GUIL   I could see I had.
   ROS   How should I begin?
   GUIL   Address me.

They stand and face each other, posing.

ROS   My honoured Lord!
   GUIL   My dear Rosencrantz!

Pause.

ROS   Am I pretending to be you, then?
   GUIL   Certainly not. If you like. Shall we continue?
   ROS   Question and answer.
   GUIL   Right.
   ROS   Right. My honoured lord!
   GUIL   My dear fellow!
   ROS   How are you?
   GUIL   Afflicted!
   ROS   Really? In what way?
   GUIL   Transformed.
   ROS   Inside or out?
   GUIL   Both.
   ROS   I see. [*Pause*] Not much new there.
   GUIL   Go into details. *Delve.* Probe the background, establish the situation.
   ROS   So—so your uncle is the king of Denmark?!
   GUIL   And my father before him.
   ROS   His father before him?
   GUIL   No, my father before him.
   ROS   But surely——
   GUIL   You might well ask.
   ROS   Let me get it straight. Your father was king. You were his only son. Your father dies. You are of age. Your uncle becomes king.
   GUIL   Yes.
   ROS   Unorthodox.
   GUIL   Undid me.
   ROS   Undeniable. Where were you?
   GUIL   In Germany.
   ROS   Usurpation, then.
   GUIL   He slipped in.
   ROS   Which reminds me.
   GUIL   Well, it would.
   ROS   I don't want to be personal.
   GUIL   It's common knowledge.

ROS   Your mother's marriage.
GUIL   He slipped in.

Beat.

ROS [*lugubriously*]   His body was still warm.
GUIL   So was hers.
ROS   Extraordinary.
GUIL   Indecent.
ROS   Hasty.
GUIL   Suspicious.
ROS   It makes you think.
GUIL   Don't think I haven't thought of it.
ROS   And with her husband's brother.
GUIL   They were close.
ROS   She went to him——
GUIL   —Too close——
ROS   —for comfort.
GUIL   It looks bad.
ROS   It adds up.
GUIL   Incest to adultery.
ROS   Would you go so far?
GUIL   Never.
ROS   To sum up: your father, whom you love, dies, you are his heir, you come back to find that hardly was the corpse cold before his young brother popped onto his throne and into his sheets, thereby offending both legal and natural practice. Now why exactly are you behaving in this extraordinary manner?
GUIL   I can't imagine! [*Pause*] But all that is well known, common property. Yet he sent for us. And we did come.
ROS [*alert, ear cocked*]   I say! I heard music——
GUIL   We're here.
ROS   —Like a band—I thought I heard a band.
GUIL   Rosencrantz . . .
ROS [*absently, still listening*]   What?

Pause, short.

GUIL [*gently wry*]   Guildenstern . . .
ROS [*irritated by the repetition*]   What?
GUIL   Don't you discriminate at all?
ROS [*turning dumbly*]   Wha'?

Pause.

GUIL   Go and see if he's there.
ROS   Who?
GUIL   There.

ROS *goes to an upstage wing, looks, returns, formally making his report.*

ROS   Yes.
GUIL   What is he doing?

ROS *repeats movement.*

ROS   Talking.
GUIL   To himself?

[ROS *starts to move.* GUIL *cuts in impatiently.*]

Is he alone?

ROS   No.
GUIL   Then he's not talking to himself, is he?
ROS   Not *by* himself. . . . Coming this way, I think. [*Shiftily*] Should we go?
GUIL   Why? We're marked now.

HAMLET *enters, backwards, talking, followed by* POLONIUS, *upstage,* ROS *and* GUIL *occupy the two downstage corners looking upstage.*

HAMLET   . . . for you yourself, sir, should be as old as I am if like a crab you could go backward.
POLONIUS [*aside*]   Though this be madness, yet there is method in it. Will you walk out of the air, my lord?
HAMLET   Into my grave.
POLONIUS   Indeed, that's out of the air.

[HAMLET *crosses to upstage exit,* POLONIUS *asiding unintelligibly until——*]

My lord, I will take my leave of you.
HAMLET   You cannot take from me anything that I will more willingly part withal—except my life, except my life, except my life. . . .
POLONIUS [*crossing downstage*]   Fare you well, my lord. [*To* ROS] You go to seek Lord Hamlet? There he is.
ROS [*to* POLONIUS]   God save you sir.

POLONIUS *goes*
GUIL [*calls upstage to* HAMLET]   My honoured lord!
ROS   My most dear lord!

HAMLET *centred upstage, turns to them.*

HAMLET   My excellent good friends! How dost thou Guildenstern? [*Coming downstage with an arm raised to* ROS, GUIL *meanwhile bowing to no greeting.* HAMLET *corrects himself. Still to* ROS] Ah Rosencrantz!

They laugh good-naturedly at the mistake. They all meet midstage, turn upstage to walk, HAMLET *in the middle, arm over each shoulder.*

HAMLET   Good lads how do you both?

BLACKOUT

Act II

HAMLET, ROS *and* GUIL *talking, the continuation of the previous scene. Their conversation, on the move, is indecipherable at first. The first intelligible line is* HAMLET's, *coming at the end of a short speech—see Shakespeare Act II, scene ii.*

HAMLET   S'blood, there is something in this more than natural, if philosophy could find it out.

A flourish from the TRAGEDIANS' *band.*

GUIL   There are the players.
HAMLET   Gentlemen, you are welcome to Elsinore. Your hands, come then. [*He takes their hands.*] The appurtenance of welcome is fashion and ceremony. Let me comply with you in this garb, lest my extent to the players (which I tell you must show fairly outwards) should more appear like entertainment than yours. You are welcome. [*About to leave.*] But my uncle-father and aunt-mother are deceived.
GUIL   In what, my dear lord?
HAMLET   I am but mad north north-west; when the wind is southerly I know a hawk from a handsaw.

POLONIUS *enters as* GUIL *turns away.*

POLONIUS   Well be with you gentlemen.
HAMLET [*to* ROS]   Mark you, Guildenstern [*uncertainly to* GUIL] and you too; at each ear a hearer. That great baby you see there is not yet out of his swaddling clouts. . . . [*He takes* ROS *upstage with him, talking together.*]
POLONIUS   My Lord! I have news to tell you.
HAMLET [*releasing* ROS *and mimicking*]   My lord, I have news to tell you. . . . When Roscius was an actor in Rome . . .

ROS *comes downstage to rejoin* GUIL.

POLONIUS [*as he follows* HAMLET *out*]   The actors are come hither my lord.
HAMLET   Buzz, buzz.

Exeunt HAMLET *and* POLONIUS.

ROS *and* GUIL *ponder. Each reluctant to speak first.*

GUIL   Hm?
ROS   Yes?
GUIL   What?
ROS   I thought you . . .
GUIL   No.
ROS   Ah.

Pause.

GUIL   I think we can say we made some headway.
ROS   You think so?
GUIL   I think we can say that.

ROS   I think we can say he made us look ridiculous.

GUIL   We played it close to the chest of course.

ROS [*derisively*]   "Question and answer. Old ways are the best ways"! He was scoring off us all down the line.

GUIL   He caught us on the wrong foot once or twice, perhaps, but I thought we gained some ground.

ROS [*simply*]   He murdered us.

GUIL   He might have had the edge.

ROS [*roused*]   Twenty-seven—three, and you think he might have had the edge?! He *murdered* us.

GUIL   What about our evasions?

ROS   Oh, our evasions were lovely. "Were you sent for?" he says. "My lord, we were sent for. . . ." I didn't know where to put myself.

GUIL   He had six rheticals——

ROS   It was question and answer, all right. Twenty-seven questions he got out in ten minutes, and answered three. I was waiting for you to *delve*. "When is he going to start *delving*?" I asked myself.

GUIL   —And two repetitions.

ROS   Hardly a leading question between us.

GUIL   We got his *symptoms,* didn't we?

ROS   Half of what he said meant something else, and the other half didn't mean anything at all.

GUIL   Thwarted ambition—a sense of grievance, that's my diagnosis.

ROS   Six rhetorical and two repetition, leaving nineteen, of which we answered fifteen. And what did we get in return? He's depressed! . . . Denmark's a prison and he'd rather live in a nutshell; some shadow-play about the nature of ambition, which never got down to cases, and finally one direct question which might have led somewhere, and led in fact to his illuminating claim to tell a hawk from a handsaw.

Pause.

GUIL   When the wind is southerly.

ROS   And the weather's clear.

GUIL   And when it isn't he can't.

ROS   He's at the mercy of the elements. [*Licks his finger and holds it up— facing audience*] Is that southerly?

They stare at audience.

GUIL   It doesn't *look* southerly. What made you think so?

ROS   I didn't *say* I think so. It could be northerly for all I know.

GUIL   I wouldn't have thought so.

ROS   Well, if you're going to be dogmatic.

GUIL   Wait a minute—we came from roughly south according to a rough map.

ROS   I see. Well, which way did we come in? [GUIL *looks round vaguely.*] Roughly.

GUIL [*clears his throat*]   In the morning the sun would be easterly. I think we can assume that.

ROS   That it's morning?

GUIL   If it is, and the sun is over *there* [*his right as he faces the audience*] for instance, *that* [*front*] would be northerly. On the other hand, if it is not morning and the sun is over *there* [*his left*] . . . *that* . . . [*lamely*] would *still* be northerly. [*Picking up*] To put it another way, if we came from down there [*front*] and it is morning, the sun would be up there [*his left*], and if it is actually over *there* [*his right*] and it's still morning, we must have come from up *there* [*behind him*], and if *that* is southerly [*his left*] and the sun is really over *there* [*front*], then it's the afternoon. However, if none of these is the case——

ROS   Why don't you go and have a look?

GUIL   Pragmatism?!—is that all you have to offer? You seem to have no conception of where we stand! You won't find the answer written down for you in the bowl of a compass—I can tell you that. [*Pause*] Besides, you can never tell this far north—it's probably dark out there.

ROS   I merely suggest that the position of the sun, if it is out, would give you a rough idea of the time; alternatively, the clock, if it is going, would give you a rough idea of the position of the sun. I forget which you're trying to establish.

GUIL   I'm trying to establish the direction of the wind.

ROS   There isn't any wind. *Draught,* yes.

GUIL   In that case, the origin. Trace it to its source and it might give us a rough idea of the way we came in—which might give us a rough idea of south, for further reference.

ROS   It's coming up through the floor. [*He studies the floor.*] That can't be south, can it?

GUIL   That's not a direction. Lick your toe and wave it around a bit.

ROS *considers the distance of his foot.*

ROS   No, I think you'd have to lick it for me.

Pause.

GUIL   I'm prepared to let the whole matter drop.

ROS   Or I could lick yours, of course.

GUIL   No thank you.

ROS   I'll even wave it around for you.

GUIL [*down* ROS*'s throat*]   What in God's name is the matter with you?

ROS   Just being friendly.

GUIL [*retiring*]   Somebody might come in. It's what we're counting on, after all. Ultimately.

Good pause.

ROS   Perhaps they've all trampled each other to death in the rush. . . . Give them a shout. Something provocative. *Intrigue* them.

GUIL   Wheels have been set in motion, and they have their own pace, to which we are . . . condemned. Each move is dictated by the previous one—that is the meaning of order. If we start being arbitrary it'll just be a shambles: at least, let us hope so. Because if we happened, just happened to discover, or even suspect, that our spontaneity was part of their order, we'd know that we were lost. [*He sits.*] A Chinaman of the Tang Dynasty—and, by which definition, a philosopher—

dreamed he was a butterfly, and from that moment he was never quite sure that he was not a butterfly dreaming it was a Chinese philosopher. Envy him; in his two-fold security.

A good pause. ROS *leaps up and bellows at the audience.*

    ROS   Fire!

GUIL *jumps up.*

    GUIL   Where?
    ROS   It's all right—I'm demonstrating the misuse of free speech. To prove that it exists. [*He regards the audience, that is the direction, with contempt—and other directions, then front again.*] Not a move. They should burn to death in their shoes. [*He takes out one of his coins. Spins it. Catches it. Looks at it. Replaces it.*]
    GUIL   What was it?
    ROS   What?
    GUIL   Heads or tails?
    ROS   Oh. I didn't look.
    GUIL   Yes you did.
    ROS   Oh, did I? [*He takes out a coin, studies it.*] Quite right—it rings a bell.
    GUIL   What's the last thing you remember?
    ROS   I don't wish to be reminded of it.
    GUIL   We cross our bridges when we come to them and burn them behind us, with nothing to show for our progress except a memory of the smell of smoke, and a presumption that once our eyes watered.

ROS *approaches him brightly, holding a coin between finger and thumb. He covers it with his other hand, draws his fists apart and holds them for* GUIL. GUIL *considers them. Indicates the left hand,* ROS *opens it to show it empty.*

    ROS   No.

[*Repeat process.* GUIL *indicates left hand again.* ROS *shows it empty.*]

Double bluff!

Repeat process—GUIL *taps one hand, then the other hand, quickly.* ROS *inadvertently shows that both are empty.* ROS *laughs as* GUIL *turns upstage.* ROS *stops laughing, looks around his feet, pats his clothes, puzzled.*

POLONIUS *breaks that up by entering upstage followed by the* TRAGEDIANS *and* HAMLET.

    POLONIUS [*entering*]   Come sirs.
    HAMLET   Follow him, friends. We'll hear a play tomorrow. [*Aside to the* PLAYER, *who is the last of the* TRAGEDIANS:] Dost thou hear me, old friend? Can you play *The Murder of Gonzago?*
    PLAYER   Ay, my lord.

HAMLET We'll ha't tomorrow night. You could for a need study a speech of some dozen or sixteen lines which I would set down and insert in't, could you not?

PLAYER Ay, my lord.

HAMLET Very well. Follow that lord, and look you mock him not.

The PLAYER *crossing downstage, notes* ROS *and* GUIL. *Stops.* HAMLET *crossing downstage addresses them without pause.*

HAMLET My good friends, I'll leave you till tonight. You are welcome to Elsinore.

ROS Good, my lord.

HAMLET *goes.*

GUIL So you've caught up.

PLAYER [*coldly*] Not yet, sir.

GUIL Now mind your tongue, or we'll have it out and throw the rest of you away, like a nightingale at a Roman feast.

ROS Took the very words out of my mouth.

GUIL You'd be *lost* for words.

ROS You'd be tongue-tied.

GUIL Like a mute in a monologue.

ROS Like a nightingale at a Roman feast.

GUIL Your diction will go to pieces.

ROS Your lines will be cut.

GUIL To dumbshows.

ROS And dramatic pauses.

GUIL You'll never *find* your tongue.

ROS Lick your lips.

GUIL Taste your tears.

ROS Your breakfast.

GUIL You won't know the difference.

ROS There won't be any.

GUIL We'll take the very words out of your mouth.

ROS So you've caught on.

GUIL So you've caught up.

PLAYER [*tops*] Not yet! [*Bitterly*] You left us.

GUIL Ah! I'd forgotten—you performed a dramatic spectacle on the way. Yes, I'm sorry we had to miss it.

PLAYER [*bursts out*] We can't look each other in the face! [*Pause, more in control*] You don't understand the humiliation of it—to be tricked out of the single assumption which makes our existence viable—that somebody is *watching*. . . . The plot was two corpses gone before we caught sight of ourselves, stripped naked in the middle of nowhere and pouring ourselves down a bottomless well.

ROS Is *that* thirty-eight?

PLAYER [*lost*] There we were—demented children mincing about in clothes that no one ever wore, speaking as no man ever spoke, swearing love in wigs and rhymed couplets, killing each other with wooden swords, hollow protestations of faith hurled after empty promises of vengeance—and every gesture, every pose, vanishing into the thin unpopulated air. We ransomed our dignity to the clouds, and the uncomprehending birds listened. [*He rounds on them.*] Don't you see?! We're *actors*—we're the opposite of people! [*They recoil nonplussed, his voice calms.*] Think, in your head, *now,* think of the most . . . *private* . . . *secret* . . . *intimate* thing you have ever done secure in the knowledge of its privacy. . . . [*He gives them—and the audience—a good pause.* ROS *takes on a shifty look.*] Are you thinking of it? [*He strikes with his voice and his head.*] *Well, I saw you do it!*

ROS *leaps up, dissembling madly.*

ROS   You never! It's a lie! [*He catches himself with a giggle in a vacuum and sits down again.*]

PLAYER   We're actors. . . . We pledged our identities, secure in the conventions of our trade, that someone would be watching. And then, gradually, no one was. We were caught, high and dry. It was not until the murderer's long soliloquy that we were able to look around; frozen as we were in profile, our eyes searched you out, first confidently, then hesitantly, then desperately as each patch of turf, each log, every exposed corner in every direction proved uninhabited, and all the while the murderous King addressed the horizon with his dreary interminable guilt. . . . Our heads began to move, wary as lizards, the corpse of unsullied Rosalinda peeped through his fingers, and the King faltered. Even then, habit and a stubborn trust that our audience spied upon us from behind the nearest bush, forced our bodies to blunder on long after they had emptied of meaning, until like runaway carts they dragged to a halt. No one came forward. No one shouted at us. The silence was unbreakable, it imposed itself upon us; it was obscene. We took off our crowns and swords and cloth of gold and moved silent on the road to Elsinore.

Silence. Then GUIL *claps solo with slow measured irony.*

GUIL   Brilliantly re-created—if these eyes could weep! . . . Rather strong on metaphor, mind you. No criticism—only a matter of taste. And so here you are—with a vengeance. That's a figure of speech . . . isn't it? Well let's say we're made up for it, for you may have no doubt whom to thank for your performance at the court.

ROS   We are counting on you to take him out of himself. You are the pleasures which we draw him on to—[*he escapes a fractional giggle but recovers immediately*] and by that I don't mean your usual filth; you can't treat royalty like people with normal perverted desires. They know nothing of that and you know nothing of them, to your mutual survival. So give him a good clean show suitable for all the family, or you can rest assured you'll be playing the tavern tonight.

GUIL   Or the night after.

ROS   Or not.

PLAYER   We already have an entry here. And always have had.

GUIL   You've played for him before?

PLAYER   Yes, sir.

ROS   And what's *his* bent?

PLAYER   Classical.

ROS   Saucy!

GUIL   What will you play?

PLAYER   *The Murder of Gonzago.*

GUIL   Full of fine cadence and corpses.
PLAYER   Pirated from the Italian. . . .
ROS   What is it about?
PLAYER   It's about a King and Queen. . . .
GUIL   Escapism! What else?
PLAYER   Blood——
GUIL   —Love and rhetoric.
PLAYER   Yes. [*Going*]
GUIL   Where are you going?
PLAYER   I can come and go as I please.
GUIL   You're evidently a man who knows his way around.
PLAYER   I've been here before.
GUIL   We're still finding our feet.
PLAYER   I should concentrate on not losing your heads.
GUIL   Do you speak from knowledge?
PLAYER   Precedent.
GUIL   You've been here before.
PLAYER   And I know which way the wind is blowing.
GUIL   Operating on two levels, are we?! How clever! I expect it comes naturally to you, being in the business so to speak.

[*The* PLAYER's *grave face does not change. He makes to move off again.* GUIL *for the second time cuts him off.*]

The truth is, we value your company, for want of any other. We have been left so much to our own devices—after a while one welcomes the uncertainty of being left to other people's.
PLAYER   Uncertainty is the normal state. You're nobody special.

He makes to leave again. GUIL *loses his cool.*

GUIL   But for God's sake what are we supposed to *do?!*
PLAYER   Relax. Respond. That's what people do. You can't go through life questioning your situation at every turn.
GUIL   But we don't know what's going on, or what to do with ourselves. We don't know how to *act.*
PLAYER   Act natural. You know why you're here at least.
GUIL   We only know what we're told, and that's little enough. And for all we know it isn't even true.
PLAYER   For all anyone knows, nothing is. Everything has to be taken on trust; truth is only that which is taken to be true. It's the currency of living. There may be nothing behind it, but it doesn't make any difference so long as it is honoured. One acts on assumptions. What do you assume?
ROS   Hamlet is not himself, outside or in. We have to glean what afflicts him.
GUIL   He doesn't give much away.
PLAYER   Who does, nowadays?
GUIL   He's—melancholy.
PLAYER   Melancholy?
ROS   Mad.
PLAYER   How is he mad?

ROS   Ah. [*To* GUIL] How is he mad?
GUIL   More morose than mad, perhaps.
PLAYER   Melancholy.
GUIL   Moody.
ROS   He has moods.
PLAYER   Of moroseness?
GUIL   Madness. And yet.
ROS   Quite.
GUIL   For instance.
ROS   He talks to himself, which might be madness.
GUIL   If he didn't talk sense, which he does.
ROS   Which suggests the opposite.
PLAYER   Of what?

Small pause.

GUIL   I think I have it. A man talking sense to himself is no madder than a man talking nonsense not to himself.
ROS   Or just as mad.
GUIL   Or just as mad.
ROS   And he does both.
GUIL   So there you are.
ROS   Stark raving sane.

Pause.

PLAYER   Why?
GUIL   Ah. [*to* ROS] Why?
ROS   Exactly.
GUIL   Exactly what?
ROS   Exactly why.
GUIL   Exactly why *what?*
ROS   What?
GUIL   *Why?*
ROS   Why what, exactly?
GUIL   Why is he mad?!
ROS   *I* don't know!

Beat.

PLAYER   The old man thinks he's in love with his daughter.
ROS [*appalled*]   Good God! We're out of our depth here.
PLAYER   No, no, no—*he* hasn't got a daughter—the old man thinks he's in love with *his* daughter.
ROS   The old man is?
PLAYER   Hamlet, in love with the old man's daughter, the old man thinks.
ROS   Ha! It's beginning to make sense! Unrequited passion!

The PLAYER *moves.*

GUIL [*fascist.*]   Nobody leaves this room! [*Pause, lamely*] Without a *very* good reason.

PLAYER   Why not?
GUIL   All this strolling about is getting too arbitrary by half—I'm rapidly losing my grip. From now on reason will prevail.
PLAYER   I have lines to learn.
GUIL   Pass!

The PLAYER *passes into one of the wings.* ROS *cups his hands and shouts into the opposite one.*

ROS   Next!

But no one comes.

GUIL   What do you expect?
ROS   Something . . . someone . . . nothing.

[*They sit facing front.*]

Are you hungry?
GUIL   No, are you?
ROS [*thinks*]   No. You remember that coin?
GUIL   No.
ROS   I think I lost it.
GUIL   What coin?
ROS   I don't remember exactly.

Pause.

GUIL   Oh, that coin . . . clever.
ROS   I can't remember how I did it.
GUIL   It probably comes natural to you.
ROS   Yes, I've got a show-stopper there.
GUIL   Do it again.

Slight pause.

ROS   We can't afford it.
GUIL   Yes, one must think of the future.
ROS   It's the normal thing.
GUIL   To have one. One is, after all, having it all the time . . . now . . . and now . . . and now. . . .
ROS   It could go on for ever. Well, not for *ever,* I suppose. [*Pause*] Do you ever think of yourself as actually *dead,* lying in a box with a lid on it?
GUIL   No.
ROS   Nor do I, really. . . . It's silly to be depressed by it. I mean one thinks of it like being *alive* in a box, one keeps forgetting to take into account the fact that one is *dead* . . . which should make all the difference . . . shouldn't it? I mean, you'd never *know* you were in a box, would you? It would be just like being *asleep* in a box. Not that I'd like to sleep in a box, mind you, not without any air—you'd wake up dead, for a start, and then where would you be? Apart from inside a box. That's the bit I don't like, frankly. That's why I don't think of it. . . .

GUIL *stirs restlessly, pulling his cloak round him.*

Because you'd be helpless, wouldn't you? Stuffed in a box like that, I mean you'd be in there for ever. Even taking into account the fact that you're dead, it isn't a pleasant thought. *Especially* if you're dead, really . . . *ask* yourself, if I asked you straight off—I'm going to stuff you in this box now, would you rather be alive or dead? Naturally, you'd prefer to be alive. Life in a box is better than no life at all. I expect. You'd have a chance at least. You could lie there thinking—well, at least I'm not dead! In a minute someone's going to bang on the lid and tell me to come out. [*Banging the floor with his fists.*] "Hey you, whatsyername! Come out of there!"
    GUIL [*jumps up savagely*]   You don't have to flog it to death!

Pause.

    ROS   I wouldn't think about it, if I were you. You'd only get depressed. [*Pause*] Eternity is a terrible thought. I mean, where's it going to end? [*Pause, then brightly*] Two early Christians chanced to meet in Heaven. "Saul of Tarsus yet!" cried one. "What are *you* doing here?!" . . . "Tarsus-Schmarsus," replied the other, "I'm Paul already." [*He stands up restlessly and flaps his arms.*] They don't care. We count for nothing. We could remain silent till we're green in the face, they wouldn't come.
    GUIL   Blue, red.
    ROS   A Christian, a Moslem and a Jew chanced to meet in a closed carriage. . . . "Silverstein!" cried the Jew. "Who's your friend?" . . . "His name's Abdullah," replied the Moslem, "but he's no friend of mine since he became a convert." [*He leaps up again, stamps his foot and shouts into the wings.*] All right, we know you're in there! Come out talking! [*Pause*] We have no control. None at all . . . [*He paces.*] Whatever became of the moment when one first knew about death? There must have been one, a moment, in childhood when it first occurred to you that you don't go on for ever. It must have been shattering—stamped into one's memory. And yet I can't remember it. It never occurred to me at all. What does one make of that? We must be born with an intuition of mortality. Before we know the words for it, before we know that there are words, out we come, bloodied and squalling with the knowledge that for all the compasses in the world, there's only one direction, and time is its only measure. [*He reflects, getting more desperate and rapid.*] A Hindu, a Buddhist and a lion-tamer chanced to meet, in a circus on the Indo-Chinese border. [*He breaks out.*] They're taking us for granted! Well, I won't stand for it! In future, notice will be taken. [*He wheels again to face into the wings.*] Keep out, then! I forbid anyone to enter! [*No one comes. Breathing heavily.*] That's better. . . .

Immediately, behind him a grand procession enters, principally CLAUDIUS, GER-
TRUDE, POLONIUS *and* OPHELIA. CLAUDIUS *takes* ROS's *elbow as he passes and is immediately deep in conversation: the context is Shakespeare Act III, scene i.* GUIL *still faces front as* CLAUDIUS, ROS, *etc., pass upstage and turn.*

    GUIL   Death followed by eternity . . . the worst of both worlds. It *is* a terrible thought.

He turns upstage in time to take over the conversation with CLAUDIUS. GERTRUDE *and* ROS *head downstage.*

GERTRUDE   Did he receive you well?

ROS   Most like a gentleman.

GUIL [*returning in time to take it up*]   But with much forcing of his disposition.

ROS [*a flat lie and he knows it and shows it, perhaps catching* GUIL's *eye*]
Niggard of question, but of our demands most free in his reply.

GERTRUDE   Did you assay him to any pastime?

ROS   Madam, it so fell out that certain players
We o'erraught on the way: of these we told him
And there did seem in him a kind of joy
To hear of it. They are here about the court,
And, as I think, they have already order
This night to play before him.

POLONIUS   'Tis most true
And he beseeched me to entreat your Majesties
To hear and see the matter.

CLAUDIUS   With all my heart, and it doth content me
To hear him so inclined.
Good gentlemen, give him a further edge
And drive his purpose into these delights.

ROS   We shall, my lord.

CLAUDIUS [*leading out procession*]:
Sweet Gertrude, leave us, too,
For we have closely sent for Hamlet hither,
That he, as t'were by accident, may here
Affront Ophelia. . . .

Exeunt CLAUDIUS *and* GERTRUDE.

ROS [*peevish*]   Never a moment's peace! In and out, on and off, they're coming
at us from all sides.

GUIL   You're never satisfied.

ROS   Catching us on the trot. . . . Why can't *we* go by *them*?

GUIL   What's the difference?

ROS   I'm going.

[ROS *pulls his cloak round him.* GUIL *ignores him. Without confidence* ROS *heads
upstage. He looks out and comes back quickly.*]

He's coming.

GUIL   What's he doing?

ROS   Nothing.

GUIL   He must be doing something.

ROS   Walking.

GUIL   On his hands?

ROS   No, on his feet.

GUIL   Stark naked?

ROS   Fully dressed.

GUIL   Selling toffee apples?

ROS   Not that I noticed.

GUIL   You could be wrong?

ROS   I don't think so.

Pause.

GUIL   I can't for the life of me see how we're going to get into conversation.

HAMLET *enters upstage, and pauses, weighing up the pros and cons of making his quietus.*

ROS *and* GUIL *watch him.*

ROS   Nevertheless, I suppose one might say that this was a chance. . . . One might well . . . accost him. . . . Yes, it definitely looks like a chance to me. . . . Something on the lines of a direct informal approach . . . man to man . . . straight from the shoulder. . . . Now look here, what's it all about . . . sort of thing. Yes. Yes, this looks like one to be grabbed with both hands, I should say . . . if I were asked. . . . No point in looking at a gift horse till you see the whites of its eyes, etcetera. [*He has moved towards* HAMLET *but his nerve fails. He returns.*] We're overawed, that's our trouble. When it comes to the point we succumb to their personality. . . .

OPHELIA *enters, with prayerbook, a religious procession of one.*

HAMLET   Nymph, in thy orisons be all my sins remembered.

At his voice she has stopped for him, he catches her up.

OPHELIA   Good my lord, how does your honour for this many a day?
HAMLET   I humbly thank you—well, well, well.

They disappear talking into the wing.

ROS   It's like living in a public park!
GUIL   Very impressive. Yes, I thought your direct informal approach was going to stop this thing dead in its tracks there. If I might make a suggestion—shut up and sit down. Stop being perverse.
ROS [*near tears*]   I'm not going to stand for it!

A FEMALE FIGURE, *ostensibly the* QUEEN, *enters.* ROS *marches up behind her, puts his hands over her eyes and says with a desperate frivolity.*

ROS   Guess who?!
PLAYER [*having appeared in a downstage corner*]   Alfred!

ROS *lets go, spins around. He has been holding* ALFRED, *in his robe and blond wig.* PLAYER *is in the downstage corner still.* ROS *comes down to that exit. The* PLAYER *does not budge. He and* ROS *stand toe to toe.*

ROS   Excuse me.

The PLAYER *lifts his downstage foot.* ROS *bends to put his hand on the floor. The* PLAYER *lowers his foot.* ROS *screams and leaps away.*

PLAYER [*gravely*]   I beg your pardon.
GUIL [*to* ROS]   What did he do?
PLAYER   I put my foot down.
ROS   My hand was on the floor!
GUIL   You put your hand under his foot?
ROS   I——
GUIL   What for?
ROS   I thought——[*Grabs* GUIL] Don't leave me!

He makes a break for an exit. A TRAGEDIAN *dressed as a* KING *enters.* ROS *recoils, breaks for the opposite wing. Two cloaked* TRAGEDIANS *enter.* ROS *tries again but another* TRAGEDIAN *enters, and* ROS *retires to midstage. The* PLAYER *claps his hands matter-of-factly.*

PLAYER   Right! We haven't got much time.
GUIL   What are you doing?
PLAYER   Dress rehearsal. Now if you two wouldn't mind just moving back . . . there . . . good. . . . [*To* TRAGEDIANS] Everyone ready? And for goodness' sake, remember what we're doing. [*To* ROS *and* GUIL] We always use the same costumes more or less, and they forget what they are supposed to be *in* you see. . . . Stop picking your nose, Alfred. When Queens have to they do it by a cerebral process passed down in the blood. . . . Good. Silence! Off we go!
PLAYER-KING   Full thirty times hath Phoebus' cart——

PLAYER *jumps up angrily.*

PLAYER   No, no, no! Dumbshow first, your confounded majesty! [*To* ROS *and* GUIL] They're a bit out of practice, but they always pick up wonderfully for the deaths—it brings out the poetry in them.
GUIL   How nice.
PLAYER   There's nothing more unconvincing than an unconvincing death.
GUIL   I'm sure.

PLAYER *claps his hands.*

PLAYER   Act One—moves now.

The mime. Soft music from a recorder. PLAYER-KING *and* PLAYER-QUEEN *embrace. She kneels and makes a show of protestation to him. He takes her up, declining his head upon her neck. He lies down. She, seeing him asleep, leaves him.*

GUIL   What is the dumbshow for?
PLAYER   Well, it's a device, really—it makes the action that follows more or less comprehensible; you understand, we are tied down to a language which makes up in obscurity what it lacks in style.

The mime (continued)—enter another. He takes off the SLEEPER's *crown, kisses it. He has brought in a small bottle of liquid. He pours the poison in the* SLEEPER's *ear, and leaves him. The* SLEEPER *convulses heroically, dying.*

ROS   Who was that?
PLAYER   The King's brother and uncle to the Prince.
GUIL   Not exactly fraternal.
PLAYER   Not exactly avuncular, as time goes on.

The QUEEN *returns, makes passionate action, finding the* KING *dead. The* POI-
SONER *comes in again, attended by two others (the two in cloaks). The* POISONER
seems to console with her. The dead body is carried away. The POISONER *woos
the* QUEEN *with gifts. She seems harsh awhile but in the end accepts his love. End
of mime, at which point, the wail of a woman in torment and* OPHELIA *appears,
wailing, closely followed by* HAMLET *in a hysterical state, shouting at her, circling
her, both midstage.*

HAMLET   Go to, I'll no more on't; it hath made me mad!

[*She falls on her knees weeping.*]

I say we will have no more marriage! [*His voice drops to include the* TRAGEDIANS,
who have frozen.] Those that are married already [*he leans close to the* PLAYER-
QUEEN *and* POISONER, *speaking with quiet edge*] all but one shall live. [*He smiles
briefly at them without mirth, and starts to back out, his parting shot rising
again.*] The rest shall keep as they are. [*As he leaves,* OPHELIA *tottering upstage,
he speaks into her ear a quick clipped sentence.*] To a nunnery, go.

He goes out. OPHELIA *falls on to her knees upstage, her sobs barely audible. A
slight silence.*

PLAYER-KING   Full thirty times hath Phoebus' cart——

CLAUDIUS *enters with* POLONIUS *and goes over to* OPHELIA *and lifts her to her
feet. The* TRAGEDIANS *jump back with heads inclined.*

CLAUDIUS   Love? His affections do not that way tend,
Or what he spake, though it lacked form a little,
Was not like madness. There's something
In his soul o'er which his melancholy sits on
Brood, and I do doubt the hatch and the
Disclose will be some danger; which for to
Prevent I have in quick determination thus set
It down: he shall with speed to England . . .

*Which carries the three of them—*CLAUDIUS, POLONIUS, OPHELIA—*out of sight.
The* PLAYER *moves, clapping his hands for attention.*
PLAYER   Gentlemen! [*They look at him.*] It doesn't seem to be coming. We are
not getting it at all. [*To* GUIL] What did you think?
GUIL   What was I supposed to think?
PLAYER [*to* TRAGEDIANS]   You're not getting across!

ROS *had gone halfway up to* OPHELIA; *he returns.*

ROS   That didn't look like love to me.

GUIL   Starting from scratch again . . .

PLAYER [*to* TRAGEDIANS]   It was a *mess.*

ROS [*to* GUIL]   It's going to be chaos on the night.

GUIL   Keep back—we're spectators.

PLAYER   Act Two! Positions!

GUIL   Wasn't that the end?

PLAYER   Do you call that an ending?—with practically everyone on his feet? My goodness no—over your dead body.

GUIL   How am I supposed to take that?

PLAYER   Lying down. [*He laughs briefly and in a second has never laughed in his life.*] There's a design at work in all art—surely you know that? Events must play themselves out to aesthetic, moral and logical conclusion.

GUIL   And what's that, in this case?

PLAYER   It never varies—we aim at the point where everyone who is marked for death dies.

GUIL   Marked?

PLAYER   Between "just desserts" and "tragic irony" we are given quite a lot of scope for our particular talent. Generally speaking, things have gone about as far as they can possibly go when things have got about as bad as they reasonably get. [*He switches on a smile.*]

GUIL   Who decides?

PLAYER [*switching off his smile*]   Decides? It is *written.*

[*He turns away.* GUIL *grabs him and spins him back violently.*]

[*Unflustered.*] Now if you're going to be subtle, we'll miss each other in the dark. I'm referring to oral tradition. So to speak.

[GUIL *releases him.*]

We're tragedians, you see. We follow directions—there is no *choice* involved. The bad end unhappily, the good unluckily. That is what tragedy means. [*Calling*] Positions!

The TRAGEDIANS *have taken up positions for the continuation of the mime: which in this case means a love scene, sexual and passionate, between the* QUEEN *and the* POISONER/KING.

PLAYER   Go!

[*The lovers begin. The* PLAYER *contributes a breathless commentary for* ROS *and* GUIL.]

Having murdered his brother and wooed the widow—the poisoner mounts the throne! Here we see him and his queen give rein to their unbridled passion! She little knowing that the man she holds in her arms——!

ROS   Oh, I say—here—really! You can't do that!

PLAYER   Why not?

ROS   Well, really—I mean, people want to be *entertained*—they don't come expecting sordid and gratuitous filth.

PLAYER   You're wrong—they do! Murder, seduction and incest—what do you want—*jokes?*

ROS   I want a good story, with a beginning, middle and end.

PLAYER [*to* GUIL]   And you?

GUIL   I'd prefer art to mirror life, if it's all the same to you.

PLAYER   It's all the same to me, sir. [*To the grappling* LOVERS] All right, no need to indulge yourselves. [*They get up. To* GUIL] I come on in a minute. Lucianus, nephew to the king! [*Turns his attention to the* TRAGEDIANS.] Next!

They disport themselves to accommodate the next piece of mime, which consists of the PLAYER *himself exhibiting an excitable anguish* [*choreographed, stylized*] *leading to an impassioned scene with the* QUEEN [*cf. "The Closet Scene," Shakespeare Act III, scene iv*] *and a very stylized reconstruction of a* POLONIUS *figure being stabbed behind the arras* [*the murdered* KING *to stand in for* POLONIUS] *while the* PLAYER *himself continues his breathless commentary for the benefit of* ROS *and* GUIL.

PLAYER   Lucianus, nephew to the king . . . usurped by his uncle and shattered by his mother's incestuous marriage . . . loses his reason . . . throwing the court into turmoil and disarray as he alternates between bitter melancholy and unrestricted lunacy . . . staggering from the suicidal [*a pose*] to the homicidal [*here he kills* "POLONIUS"] . . . he at last confronts his mother and in a scene of provocative ambiguity—[*a somewhat oedipal embrace*] begs her to repent and recant——[*He springs up, still talking.*] The King—[*he pushes forward the* POISONER/KING] tormented by guilt—haunted by fear—decides to despatch his nephew to England—and entrusts this undertaking to two smiling accomplices—friends—courtiers—to two spies——

[*He has swung round to bring together the* POISONER/KING *and the two cloaked* TRAGEDIANS; *the latter kneel and accept a scroll from the* KING.]

—giving them a letter to present to the English court——!
And so they depart—on board ship——

[*The two* SPIES *position themselves on either side of the* PLAYER, *and the three of them sway gently in unison, the motion of a boat; and then the* PLAYER *detaches himself.*]

—and they arrive——

[*One* SPY *shades his eyes at the horizon.*]

—and disembark—and present themselves before the English king——[*He wheels round.*] The English king——

[*An exchange of headgear creates the* ENGLISH KING *from the remaining player—that is, the* PLAYER *who played the original murdered king.*]

But where is the Prince? Where indeed? The plot has thickened—a twist of fate and cunning has put into their hands a letter that seals their deaths!

[*The two* SPIES *present their letter; the* ENGLISH KING *reads it and orders their deaths. They stand up as the* PLAYER *whips off their cloaks preparatory to execution.*]

Traitors hoist by their own petard?—or victims of the gods?—we shall never know!

The whole mime has been fluid and continuous but now ROS *moves forward and brings it to a pause. What brings* ROS *forward is the fact that under their cloaks the two* SPIES *are wearing coats identical to those worn by* ROS *and* GUIL, *whose coats are now covered by their cloaks.* ROS *approaches "his"* SPY *doubtfully. He does not quite understand why the coats are familiar.* ROS *stands close, touches the coat, thoughtfully.* . . .

ROS   Well, if it isn't——! No, wait a minute, don't tell me—it's a long time since—where was it? Ah, this is taking me back to—when was it? I know you, don't I? I never forget a face—[*he looks into the* SPY's *face*] . . . not that I know yours, that is. For a moment I thought—no, I don't know you, do I? Yes, I'm afraid you're quite wrong. You must have mistaken me for someone else.

GUIL *meanwhile has approached the other* SPY, *brow creased in thought.*

PLAYER [*to* GUIL]   Are you familiar with this play?
GUIL   No.
PLAYER   A slaughterhouse—eight corpses all told. It brings out the best in us.
GUIL [*tense, progressively rattled during the whole mime and commentary*]   You!—What do *you* know about *death?*
PLAYER   It's what the actors do best. They have to exploit whatever talent is given to them, and their talent is dying. They can die heroically, comically, ironically, slowly, suddenly, disgusting, charmingly, or from a great height. My own talent is more general. I extract significance from melodrama, a significance which it does not in fact contain; but occasionally, from out of this matter, there escapes a thin beam of light that, seen at the right angle, can crack the shell of mortality.
ROS   Is that all they can do—die?
PLAYER   No, no—they kill beautifully. In fact some of them kill even better than they die. The rest die better than they kill. They're a team.
ROS   Which ones are which?
PLAYER   There's not much in it.
GUIL [*fear, derision*]   Actors! The mechanics of cheap melodrama! That isn't death! [*More quietly*] You scream and choke and sink to your knees, but it doesn't bring death home to anyone—it doesn't catch them unawares and start the whisper in their skulls that says—"One day you are going to die." [*He straightens up.*] You die so many times; how can you expect them to believe in your death?
PLAYER   On the contrary, it's the only kind they do believe. They're conditioned to it. I had an actor once who was condemned to hang for stealing a sheep—or a lamb, I forget which—so I got permission to have him hanged in the middle of a play—had to change the plot a bit but I thought it would be effective, you know—and you wouldn't believe it, he just *wasn't* convincing! It was impossible to sus-

pend one's disbelief—and what with the audience jeering and throwing peanuts, the whole thing was a *disaster!*—he did nothing but cry all the time—right out of character—just stood there and cried. . . . Never again.

[*In good humour he has already turned back to the mime: the two* SPIES *awaiting execution at the hands of the* PLAYER, *who takes his dagger out of his belt.*]

Audiences know what to expect, and that is all that they are prepared to believe in. [*To the* SPIES] Show!

The SPIES *die at some length, rather well.*

The light has begun to go, and it fades as they die, and as GUIL *speaks.*

    GUIL   No, no, no . . . you've got it all wrong . . . you can't act death. The *fact* of it is nothing to do with seeing it happen—it's not gasps and blood and falling about—that isn't what makes it death. It's just a man failing to reappear, that's all—now you see him, now you don't, that's the only thing that's real: here one minute and gone the next and never coming back—an exit, unobtrusive and unannounced, a disappearance gathering weight as it goes on, until, finally, it is heavy with death.

The two SPIES *lie still, barely visible. The* PLAYER *comes forward and throws the* SPIES' *cloaks over their bodies.* ROS *starts to clap, slowly.*

BLACKOUT.

A second of silence, then much noise. Shouts . . . "The King rises!" . . . "Give o'er the play!" . . . and cries for "Lights, lights, lights!"

When the light comes, after a few seconds, it comes as a sunrise.

The stage is empty save for two cloaked figures sprawled on the ground in the approximate positions last held by the dead SPIES. *As the light grows, they are seen to be* ROS *and* GUIL, *and to be resting quite comfortably.* ROS *raises himself on his elbows and shades his eyes as he stares into the auditorium. Finally:*

    ROS   That must be east, then. I think we can assume that.
    GUIL   I'm assuming nothing.
    ROS   No, it's all right. That's the sun. East.
    GUIL [*looks up*]   Where?
    ROS   I watched it come up.
    GUIL   No . . . it was light all the time, you see, and you opened your eyes very, very slowly. If you'd been facing back there you'd be swearing *that* was east.
    ROS [*standing up*]   You're a mass of prejudice.
    GUIL   I've been taken in before.
    ROS [*looks out over the audience*]   Rings a bell.
    GUIL   They're waiting to see what we're going to do.
    ROS   Good old east.
    GUIL   As soon as we make a move they'll come pouring in from every side, shouting obscure instructions, confusing us with ridiculous remarks, messing us about from here to breakfast and getting our names wrong.

ROS *starts to protest but he has hardly opened his mouth before:*

CLAUDIUS [*off stage—with urgency*]   Ho, Guildenstern!

GUIL *is still prone. Small pause*

  ROS AND GUIL   You're wanted. . . .

GUIL *furiously leaps to his feet as* CLAUDIUS *and* GERTRUDE *enter. They are in some desperation.*

  CLAUDIUS   Friends both, go join you with some further aid: Hamlet in madness hath Polonius slain, and from his mother's closet hath he dragged him. Go seek him out; speak fair and bring the body into the chapel. I pray you haste in this. [*As he and* GERTRUDE *are hurrying out*] Come Gertrude, we'll call up our wisest friends and let them know both what we mean to do. . . .

They've gone. ROS *and* GUIL *remain quite still.*

  GUIL   Well . . .
  ROS   Quite . . .
  GUIL   Well, well.
  ROS   Quite, quite. [*Nods with spurious confidence*] Seek him out. [*Pause*] Etcetera.
  GUIL   Quite.
  ROS   Well. [*Small pause*] Well, that's a step in the right direction.
  GUIL   You didn't like him?
  ROS   Who?
  GUIL   Good God, I hope more tears are shed for *us!* . . .
  ROS   Well, it's *progress,* isn't it? Something positive. Seek him out. [*Looks round without moving his feet*] Where does one begin . . . ? [*Takes one step towards the wings and halts*]
  GUIL   Well, that's a step in the right direction.
  ROS   You think so? He could be anywhere.
  GUIL   All right—you go that way, I'll go this way.
  ROS   Right.

[*They walk towards opposite wings.* ROS *halts.*]

No.

[GUIL *halts.*]

You go this way—I'll go that way.
  GUIL   All right.

They march towards each other, cross. ROS *halts.*

  ROS   Wait a minute.

[GUIL *halts.*]

I think we should stick together. He might be violent.
   GUIL   Good point. I'll come with you.

   GUIL *marches across to* ROS. *They turn to leave.* ROS *halts.*

   ROS   No, I'll come with *you.*
   GUIL   Right.

They turn, march across to the opposite wing. ROS *halts.*

GUIL *halts.*

   ROS   I'll come with *you, my* way.
   GUIL   All right.

They turn again and march across. ROS *halts.* GUIL *halts.*

   ROS   I've just thought. If we both go, he could come *here.* That would be stupid, wouldn't it?
   GUIL   All right—I'll stay, you go.
   ROS   Right.

[GUIL *marches to midstage.*]

I say.

[GUIL *wheels and carries on marching back towards* ROS, *who starts marching downstage. They cross.* ROS *halts.*]

I've just thought.

[GUIL *halts.*]

We ought to stick together; he might be violent.
   GUIL   Good point.

[GUIL *marches down to join* ROS. *They stand still for a moment in their original positions.*]

Well, at last we're getting somewhere.

[*Pause*]

Of course, he might not come.
   ROS [*airily*]   Oh, he'll come.
   GUIL   We'd have some explaining to do.
   ROS   He'll come. [*Airily wanders upstage*] Don't worry—take my word for it—
[*Looks out—is appalled*] He's coming!
   GUIL   What's he doing?
   ROS   Walking.
   GUIL   Alone?

ROS   No.
GUIL   Not walking?
ROS   No.
GUIL   Who's with him?
ROS   The old man.
GUIL   Walking?
ROS   No.
GUIL   Ah. That's an opening if ever there was one. [*And is suddenly galvanized into action*] Let him walk into the trap!
ROS   What trap.
GUIL   You stand there! Don't let him pass!

He positions ROS *with his back to one wing, facing* HAMLET's *entrance.*

GUIL *positions himself next to* ROS, *a few feet away, so that they are covering one side of the stage, facing the opposite side.* GUIL *unfastens his belt.* ROS *does the same. They join the two belts, and hold them taut between them.* ROS's *trousers slide slowly down.*

HAMLET *enters opposite, slowly, dragging* POLONIUS's *body. He enters upstage, makes a small arc and leaves by the same side, a few feet downstage.*

ROS *and* GUIL, *holding the belts taut, stare at him in some bewilderment.*

HAMLET *leaves, dragging the body. They relax the strain on the belts.*

ROS   That was close.
GUIL   There's a limit to what two people can do.

They undo the belts: ROS *pulls up his trousers.*

ROS [*worriedly—he walks a few paces towards* HAMLET's *exit*]   He *was* dead.
GUIL   Of course he's dead!
ROS [*turns to* GUIL]   Properly.
GUIL [*angrily*]   Death's death, isn't it?

[ROS *falls silent. Pause.*]

Perhaps he'll come back this way.

[ROS *starts to take off his belt.*]

No, no, no!—if we can't learn by experience, what else have we got?

ROS *desists.*

Pause

ROS   Give him a shout.
GUIL   I thought we'd been into all that.
ROS [*shouts*]   Hamlet!
GUIL   Don't be absurd.
ROS [*shouts*]   Lord Hamlet!

[HAMLET *enters.* ROS *is a little dismayed.*]

What have you done, my lord, with the dead body?
    HAMLET Compounded it with dust, whereto 'tis kin.
    ROS Tell us where 'tis, that we may take it thence and bear it to the chapel.
    HAMLET Do not believe it.
    ROS Believe what?
    HAMLET That I can keep your counsel and not mine own. Besides, to be demanded of a sponge, what replication should be made by the son of a king?
    ROS Take you me for a sponge, my lord?
    HAMLET Ay, sir, that soaks up the King's countenance, his rewards, his authorities. But such officers do the King best service in the end. He keeps them, like an ape, in the corner of his jaw, first mouthed, to be last swallowed. When he needs what you have gleaned, it is but squeezing you and, sponge, you shall be dry again.
    ROS I understand you not, my lord.
    HAMLET I am glad of it: a knavish speech sleeps in a foolish ear.
    ROS My lord, you must tell us where the body is and go with us to the King.
    HAMLET The body is with the King, but the King is not with the body. The King is a thing——
    GUIL A thing, my lord——?
    HAMLET Of nothing. Bring me to him.

HAMLET *moves resolutely towards one wing. They move with him, shepherding. Just before they reach the exit,* HAMLET, *apparently seeing* CLAUDIUS *approaching from off stage, bends low in a sweeping bow.* ROS *and* GUIL, *cued by* HAMLET, *also bow deeply—a sweeping ceremonial bow with their cloaks swept round them.* HAMLET, *however, continues the movement into an about-turn and walks off in the opposite direction.* ROS *and* GUIL, *with their heads low, do not notice.*

No one comes on. ROS *and* GUIL *squint upwards and find that they are bowing to nothing.*

CLAUDIUS *enters behind them. At first words they leap up and do a double-take.*

    CLAUDIUS How now? What hath befallen?
    ROS Where the body is bestowed, my lord, we cannot get from him.
    CLAUDIUS But where is he?
    ROS [*fractional hesitation*] Without, my lord; guarded to know your pleasure.
    CLAUDIUS [*moves*] Bring him before us.

This hits ROS *between the eyes but only his eyes show it. Again his hesitation is fractional. And then with great deliberation he turns to* GUIL.

    ROS Ho! Bring in the lord.

Again there is a fractional moment in which ROS *is smug,* GUIL *is trapped and betrayed.* GUIL *opens his mouth and closes it.*

The situation is saved: HAMLET, *escorted, is marched in just as* CLAUDIUS *leaves.* HAMLET *and his* ESCORT *cross the stage and go out, following* CLAUDIUS.

Lighting changes to Exterior.

ROS [*moves to go*]   All right, then?

GUIL [*does not move; thoughtfully*]   And yet it doesn't seem enough; to have breathed such significance. Can that be all? And why us?—anybody would have done. And we have contributed nothing.

ROS   It was a trying episode while it lasted, but they've done with us now.

GUIL   Done what?

ROS   I don't pretend to have understood. Frankly, I'm not very interested. If they won't tell us, that's their affair. [*He wanders upstage towards the exit.*] For my part, I'm only glad that that's the last we've seen of him—[*and he glances off stage and turns front, his face betraying the fact that* HAMLET *is there.*]

GUIL   I knew it wasn't the end. . . .

ROS [*high*]   What else?!

GUIL   We're taking him to England. What's he doing?

ROS *goes upstage and returns.*

ROS   Talking.

GUIL   To himself?

[ROS *makes to go,* GUIL *cuts him off.*]

Is he alone?

ROS   No, he's with a soldier.

GUIL   Then he's not talking to himself, is he?

ROS   Not *by* himself. . . . Should we go?

GUIL   Where?

ROS   Anywhere.

GUIL   Why?

ROS *puts up his head listening.*

ROS   There it is again. [*In anguish*] All I ask is a change of ground!

GUIL [*coda*]   Give us this day our daily round. . . .

HAMLET *enters behind them, talking with a soldier in arms.* ROS *and* GUIL *don't look round.*

ROS   They'll have us hanging about till we're dead. At least. And the weather will change. [*Looks up*] The spring can't last for ever.

HAMLET   Good sir, whose powers are these?

SOLDIER   They are of Norway, sir.

HAMLET   How purposed sir, I pray you?

SOLDIER   Against some part of Poland.

HAMLET   Who commands them, sir?

SOLDIER   The nephew to old Norway, Fortinbras.

ROS   We'll be cold. The summer won't last.

GUIL   It's autumnal.

ROS [*examining the ground*]   No leaves.

GUIL   Autumnal—nothing to do with leaves. It is to do with a certain brown-ness at the edges of the day. . . . Brown is creeping up on us, take my word for it. . . . Russets and tangerine shades of old gold flushing the very outside edge of the senses . . . deep shining ochres, burnt umber and parchments of baked earth—reflecting on itself and through itself, filtering the light. At such times, perhaps, coincidentally, the leaves might fall, somewhere, by repute. Yesterday was blue, like smoke.

ROS [*head up, listening*]   I got it again then.

They listen—faintest sound of TRAGEDIANS' *band.*

HAMLET   I humbly thank you, sir.
SOLDIER   God by you, sir. [*Exit*]

ROS *gets up quickly and goes to* HAMLET.

ROS   Will it please you go, my lord?
HAMLET   I'll be with you straight. Go you a little before.

HAMLET *turns to face upstage.* ROS *returns down.* GUIL *faces front, doesn't turn.*

GUIL   Is he here?
ROS   Yes.
GUIL   What's he doing?

ROS *looks over his shoulder.*

ROS   Talking.
GUIL   To himself?
ROS   Yes.

Pause. ROS *makes to leave.*

ROS   He *said* we can go. Cross my heart.
GUIL   I like to know where I am. Even if I don't know where I am, I like to know *that*. If we go there's no knowing.
ROS   No knowing what?
GUIL   If we'll ever come back.
ROS   We don't want to come back.
GUIL   That may very well be true, but do we want to go?
ROS   We'll be free.
GUIL   I don't know. It's the same sky.
ROS   We've come this far.

[*He moves towards exit.* GUIL *follows him.*]

And besides, anything could happen yet.

They go.

BLACKOUT

Act III

Opens in pitch darkness.
Soft sea sounds.

After several seconds of nothing, a voice from the dark . . .

GUIL   Are you there?
ROS   Where?
GUIL [*bitterly*]   A flying start. . . .

Pause

ROS   Is that you?
GUIL   Yes.
ROS   How do you know?
GUIL [*explosion*]   Oh-for-God's-sake!
ROS   We're not finished, then?
GUIL   Well, we're here, aren't we?
ROS   Are we? I can't see a thing.
GUIL   You can still *think*, can't you?
ROS   I think so.
GUIL   You can still *talk*.
ROS   What should I say?
GUIL   Don't bother. You can *feel*, can't you?
ROS   Ah! There's life in me yet!
GUIL   What are you feeling?
ROS   A leg. Yes, it feels like my leg.
GUIL   How does it feel?
ROS   Dead.
GUIL   Dead?
ROS [*panic*]   I can't feel a thing!
GUIL   Give it a pinch! [*Immediately he yelps.*]
ROS   Sorry.
GUIL   Well, that's cleared that up.

[*Longer pause: the sound builds a little and identifies itself—the sea. Ship timbers, wind in the rigging, and then shouts of sailors calling obscure but inescapably nautical instructions from all directions, far and near: A short list:*]

Hard a larboard!
Let go the stays!
Reef down me hearties!
Is that you, cox'n?
Hel-llo! Is that you?
Hard a port!
Easy as she goes!
Keep her steady on the lee!
Haul away, lads!
[*Snatches of sea shanty maybe.*]
Fly the jib!
Tops'l up, me maties!

When the point has been well made and more so.

>   ROS We're on a boat. [*Pause.*] Dark, isn't?
>   GUIL Not for night.
>   ROS No, not for *night*.
>   GUIL Dark for day.

Pause

>   ROS Oh yes, it's dark for *day*.
>   GUIL We must have gone north, of course.
>   ROS Off course?
>   GUIL Land of the midnight sun, that is.
>   ROS Of course.

[*Some sailor sounds.*

A lantern is lit upstage—in fact by HAMLET.

The stage lightens disproportionately—

Enough to see:

ROS *and* GUIL *sitting downstage.*

Vague shapes of rigging, etc., behind.]

I think it's getting light.
>   GUIL Not for night.
>   ROS This far north.
>   GUIL Unless we're off course.
>   ROS [*small pause*] Of course.

A better light—Lantern? Moon? . . . Light.
Revealing, among other things, three large man-sized casks on deck, upended,
with lids. Spaced but in line. Behind and above—a gaudy striped umbrella, on a
pole stuck into the deck, tilted so that we do not see behind it—one of those huge
six-foot-diameter jobs. Still dim upstage. ROS *and* GUIL *still facing front.*

>   ROS Yes, it's lighter than it was. It'll be night soon. This far north. [*Dolefully.*]
> I suppose we'll have to go to sleep. [*He yawns and stretches.*]
>   GUIL Tired?
>   ROS No . . . I don't think I'd take to it. Sleep all night, can't see a thing all
> day. . . . Those eskimos must have a quiet life.
>   GUIL Where?
>   ROS What?
>   GUIL I thought you——[*Relapses*] I've lost all capacity for disbelief. I'm not
> sure that I could even rise to a little gentle scepticism.

Pause

ROS   Well, shall we stretch our legs?
GUIL   I don't feel like stretching my legs.
ROS   I'll stretch them for you, if you like.
GUIL   No.
ROSS   We could stretch each other's. That way we wouldn't have to go any-
where.
GUIL [*pause*]   No, somebody might come in.
ROS   In where?
GUIL   Out here.
ROS   In out here?
GUIL   On deck.

ROS *considers the floor: slaps it.*

ROS   Nice bit of planking, that.
GUIL   Yes, I'm very fond of boats myself. I like the way they're—contained. You
don't have to worry about which way to go, or whether to go at all—the question
doesn't arise, because you're on a *boat,* aren't you? Boats are safe areas in the
game of tag . . . the players will hold their positions until the music starts. . . . I
think I'll spend most of my life on boats.
ROS   Very healthy.

ROS *inhales with expectation, exhales with boredom.* GUIL *stands up and looks
over the audience.*

GUIL   One is free on a boat. For a time. Relatively.
ROS   What's it like?
GUIL   Rough.

ROS *joins him. They look out over the audience.*

ROS   I think I'm going to be sick.

GUIL *licks a finger, holds it up experimentally.*

GUIL   Other side, I think.

[ROS *goes upstage: Ideally a sort of upper deck joined to the downstage lower deck
by short steps. The umbrella being on the upper deck.* ROS *pauses by the umbrella
and looks behind it.* GUIL *meanwhile has been resuming his own theme—looking
out over the audience——*]

Free to move, speak, extemporise, and yet. We have not been cut loose. Our
truancy is defined by one fixed star, and our drift represents merely a slight change
of angle to it: we may seize the moment, toss it around while the moments pass,
a short dash here, an exploration there, but we are brought round full circle to
face again the single immutable fact—that we, Rosencrantz and Guildenstern,
bearing a letter from one king to another, are taking Hamlet to England.

By which time, ROS *has returned, tiptoeing with great import, teeth clenched for
secrecy, gets to* GUIL, *points surreptitiously behind him—and a tight whisper:*

ROS   I say—*he's there!*
GUIL [*unsurprised*]   What's he doing?
ROS   Sleeping.
GUIL   It's all right for him.
ROS   What is?
GUIL   He can sleep.
ROS   It's all right for him.
GUIL   He's got us now.
ROS   He can sleep.
GUIL   It's all done for him.
ROS   He's got us.
GUIL   And we've got nothing. [*A cry.*] All I ask is our common due!
ROS   For those in peril on the sea. . . .
GUIL   Give us this day our daily cue.

Beat, pause. Sit. Long pause.

ROS [*after shifting, looking around*]   What now?
GUIL   What do you mean?
ROS   Well, nothing is happening.
GUIL   We're on a boat.
ROS   I'm aware of that.
GUIL [*angrily*]   Then what do you expect? [*Unhappily.*] We act on scraps of information . . . sifting half-remembered directions that we can hardly separate from instinct.

ROS *puts a hand into his purse, then both hands behind his back, then holds his fists out.*

GUIL *taps one fist.*

ROS *opens it to show a coin.*

He gives it to GUIL.

He puts his hand back into his purse. Then both hands behind his back, then holds his fists out.

GUIL *taps one.*

ROS *opens it to show a coin. He gives it to* GUIL.

Repeat.

Repeat.

GUIL *getting tense. Desperate to lose.*

Repeat.

GUIL *taps a hand, changes his mind, taps the other, and* ROS *inadvertently reveals that he has a coin in both fists.*

GUIL   You had money in both hands.

ROS [*embarrassed*]   Yes.
GUIL   Every time?
ROS   Yes.
GUIL   What's the point of that?
ROS [*pathetic*]   I wanted to make you happy.

Beat.

GUIL   How much did he give you?
ROS   Who?
GUIL   The King. He gave us some money.
ROS   How much did he give you?
GUIL   I asked you first.
ROS   I got the same as you.
GUIL   He wouldn't discriminate between us.
ROS   How much did you get?
GUIL   The same.
ROS   How do you know?
GUIL   You just told me—how do *you* know?
ROS   He wouldn't discriminate between us.
GUIL   Even if he could.
ROS   Which he never could.
GUIL   He couldn't even be sure of mixing us up.
ROS   Without mixing us up.
GUIL [*turning on him furiously*]   Why don't you say something original! No wonder the whole thing is so stagnant! You don't take me up on anything—you just repeat it in a different order.
ROS   I can't think of anything original. I'm only good in support.
GUIL   I'm sick of making the running.
ROS [*humbly*]   It must be your dominant personality. [*Almost in tears*] Oh, what's going to become of us!

And GUIL *comforts him, all harshness gone.*

GUIL   Don't cry . . . it's all right . . . there . . . there, I'll see we're all right.
ROS   But we've got nothing to go on, we're out on our own.
GUIL   We're on our way to England—we're taking Hamlet there.
ROS   What for?
GUIL   What for? Where have you been?
ROS   When? [*Pause.*] We won't know what to do when we get there.
GUIL   We take him to the King.
ROS   Will *he* be there?
GUIL   No—the king of England.
ROS   He's expecting us?
GUIL   No.
ROS   He won't know what we're playing at. What are we going to *say*?
GUIL   We've got a letter. You remember the letter.
ROS   Do I?
GUIL   Everything is explained in the letter. We count on that.

ROS   Is that it, then?

GUIL   What?

ROS   We take Hamlet to the English king, we hand over the letter—what then?

GUIL   There may be something in the letter to keep us going a bit.

ROS   And if not?

GUIL   Then that's it—we're finished.

ROS   At a loose end?

GUIL   Yes.

Pause.

ROS   Are there likely to be loose ends? [*Pause.*] Who is the English king?

GUIL   That depends on when we get there.

ROS   What do you think it says?

GUIL   Oh . . . greetings. Expressions of loyalty. Asking of favours, calling in of debts. Obscure promises balanced by vague threats. . . . Diplomacy. Regards to the family.

ROS   And about Hamlet?

GUIL   Oh yes.

ROS   And us—the full background?

GUIL   I should say so.

Pause.

ROS   So we've got a letter which explains everything.

GUIL   You've got it.

[ROS *takes that literally. He starts to pat his pockets, etc.*]

What's the matter?

ROS   The letter.

GUIL   Have you got it?

ROS [*rising fear*]   Have I? [*Searches frantically.*] Where would I have put it?

GUIL   You can't have lost it.

ROS   I must have!

GUIL   That's odd—I thought he gave it to me.

ROS *looks at him hopefully.*

ROS   Perhaps he did.

GUIL   But you seemed so sure it was *you* who hadn't got it.

ROS [*high*]   It *was* me who hadn't got it!

GUIL   But if he gave it to me there's no reason why you should have had it in the first place, in which case I don't see what all the fuss is about you *not* having it.

ROS [*pause*]   I admit it's confusing.

GUIL   This is all getting rather undisciplined. . . . The boat, the night, the sense of isolation and uncertainty . . . all these induce a loosening of the concentration. We must not lose control. Tighten up. Now. Either you have lost the letter or you didn't have it to lose in the first place, in which case the King never gave it to you, in which case he gave it to me, in which case I would have put it into my inside top pocket, in which case [*calmly producing the letter*] . . . it will be . . . here. [*They smile at each other.*] We mustn't drop off like that again.

Pause. ROS *takes the letter gently from him.*

>   ROS   Now that we have found it, why were we looking for it?
>   GUIL [*thinks*]   We thought it was lost.
>   ROS   Something else?
>   GUIL   No.

Deflation.

>   ROS   Now we've lost the tension.
>   GUIL   What tension?
>   ROS   What was the last thing I said before we wandered off?
>   GUIL   When was that?
>   ROS [*helplessly*]   I can't remember.
>   GUIL [*leaping up*]   What a shambles! We're just not getting anywhere.
>   ROS [*mournfully*]   Not even England. I don't believe in it anyway.
>   GUIL   What?
>   ROS   England.
>   GUIL   Just a conspiracy of cartographers, you mean?
>   ROS   I mean I don't believe it! [*Calmer.*] I have no image. I try to picture us arriving, a little harbour perhaps . . . roads . . . inhabitants to point the way . . . horses on the road . . . riding for a day or a fortnight and then a palace and the English king. . . . That would be the logical kind of thing. . . . But my mind remains a blank. No. We're slipping off the map.
>   GUIL   Yes . . . yes. . . . [*Rallying.*] But you don't believe anything till it happens. And it *has* all happened. Hasn't it?
>   ROS   We drift down time, clutching at straws. But what good's a brick to a drowning man?
>   GUIL   Don't give up, we can't be long now.
>   ROS   We might as well be dead. Do you think death could possibly be a boat?
>   GUIL   No, no, no . . . Death is . . . not. Death isn't. You take my meaning. Death is the ultimate negative. Not-being. You can't not-be on a boat.
>   ROS   I've frequently not been on boats.
>   GUIL   No, no, no—what you've been is not on boats.
>   ROS   I wish I was dead. [*Considers the drop.*] I could jump over the side. That would put a spoke in their wheel.
>   GUIL   Unless they're counting on it.
>   ROS   I shall remain on board. That'll put a spoke in their wheel. [*The futility of it, fury.*] All right! We don't question, we don't doubt. We perform. But a line must be drawn somewhere, and I would like to put it on record that I have no confidence in England. Thank you. [*Thinks about this.*] And even if it's true, it'll just be another shambles.
>   GUIL   I don't see why.
>   ROS [*furious*]   He won't know what we're talking about.—What are we going to *say*?

GUIL We say—Your majesty, we have arrived!
ROS [*kingly*] And who are you?
GUIL We are Rosencrantz and Guildenstern.
ROS [*barks*] Never heard of you!
GUIL Well, we're nobody special——
ROS [*regal and nasty*] What's your game?
GUIL We've got our instructions——
ROS First I've heard of it——
GUIL [*angry*] Let me finish——[*Humble.*] We've come from Denmark.
ROS What do you want?
GUIL Nothing—we're delivering Hamlet——
ROS Who's he?
GUIL [*irritated*] You've heard of *him*——
ROS Oh, I've heard of him all right and I want nothing to do with it.
GUIL But——
ROS You march in here without so much as a by-your-leave and expect me to
take in every lunatic you try to pass off with a lot of unsubstantiated——
GUIL We've got a letter——

ROS *snatches it and tears it open.*

ROS [*efficiently*] I see . . . I see . . . well, this seems to support your story
such as it is—it is an exact command from the king of Denmark, for several
different reasons, importing Denmark's health and England's too, that on the reading of this letter, without delay, I should have Hamlet's head cut off——!

GUIL *snatches the letter.* ROS, *double-taking, snatches it back.* GUIL *snatches it
half back. They read it together, and separate.*

Pause.

They are well downstage looking front.

ROS The sun's going down. It will be dark soon.
GUIL Do you think so?
ROS I was just making conversation. [*Pause.*] We're his *friends.*
GUIL How do you know?
ROS From our young days brought up with him.
GUIL You've only got their word for it.
ROS But that's what we depend on.
GUIL Well, yes, and then again no. [*Airily.*] Let us keep things in proportion.
Assume, if you like, that they're going to kill him. Well, he is a man, he is mortal,
death comes to us all, etcetera, and consequently he would have died anyway,
sooner or later. Or to look at it from the social point of view—he's just one man
among many, the loss would be well within reason and convenience. And then
again, what is so terrible about death? As Socrates so philosophically put it, since
we don't know what death is, it is illogical to fear it. It might be . . . very nice.
Certainly it is a release from the burden of life, and, for the godly, a haven and a
reward. Or to look at it another way—we are little men, we don't know the ins
and outs of the matter, there are wheels within wheels, etcetera—it would be
presumptuous of us to interfere with the designs of fate or even of kings. All in

all, I think we'd be well advised to leave well alone. Tie up the letter—there—neatly—like that.—They won't notice the broken seal, assuming you were in character.

    ROS   But what's the point?

    GUIL   Don't apply logic.

    ROS   He's done nothing to us.

    GUIL   Or justice.

    ROS   It's awful.

    GUIL   But it could have been worse. I was beginning to think it was. [*And his relief comes out in a laugh.*]

Behind them HAMLET *appears from behind the umbrella. The light has been going. Slightly.* HAMLET *is going to the lantern.*

    ROS   The position as I see it, then. We, Rosencrantz and Guildenstern, from our young days brought up with him, awakened by a man standing on his saddle, are summoned, and arrive, and are instructed to glean what afflicts him and draw him on to pleasures, such as a play, which unfortunately, as it turns out, is abandoned in some confusion owing to certain nuances outside our appreciation—which, among other causes, results in, among other effects, a high, not to say, homicidal, excitement in Hamlet, whom we, in consequence, are escorting, for his own good, to England. Good. We're on top of it now.

HAMLET *blows out the lantern. The stage goes pitch black. The black resolves itself to moonlight, by which* HAMLET *approaches the sleeping* ROS *and* GUIL. *He extracts the letter and takes it behind his umbrella; the light of his lantern shines through the fabric,* HAMLET *emerges again with a letter, and replaces it, and retires, blowing out his lantern.*

Morning comes.

ROS *watches it coming—from the auditorium. Behind him is a gay sight. Beneath the re-tilted umbrella, reclining in a deck-chair, wrapped in a rug, reading a book, possibly smoking, sits* HAMLET.

ROS *watches the morning come, and brighten to high noon.*

    ROS   I'm assuming nothing. [*He stands up.* GUIL *wakes.*] The position as I see it, then. That's west unless we're off course, in which case it's night; the King gave me the same as you, the King gave you the same as me; the King never gave me the letter, the King gave you the letter, we don't know what's in the letter; we take Hamlet to the English king, it depending on when we get there who he is, and we hand over the letter, which may or may not have something in it to keep us going, and if not, we are finished and at a loose end, if they have loose ends. We could have done worse. I don't think we missed any chances. . . . Not that we're getting much help. [*He sits down again. They lie down—prone.*] If we stopped breathing we'd vanish.

The muffled sound of a recorder. They sit up with disproportionate interest.

    GUIL   Here we go.

ROS   Yes, but what?

They listen to the music.

GUIL [*excitedly*]   Out of the void, finally, a sound; while on a boat [admittedly] outside the action [admittedly] the perfect and absolute silence of the wet lazy slap of water against water and the rolling creak of timber—breaks; giving rise at once to the speculation or the assumption or the hope that something is about to happen; a pipe is heard. One of the sailors has pursed his lips against a woodwind, his fingers and thumb governing, shall we say, the ventages, whereupon, giving it breath, let us say, with his mouth, it, the pipe, discourses, as the saying goes, most eloquent music. A thing like that, it could change the course of events. [*Pause.*] Go and see what it is.
  ROS   It's someone playing on a pipe.
  GUIL   Go and find him.
  ROS   And then what?
  GUIL   I don't know—request a tune.
  ROS   What for?
  GUIL   Quick—before we lose our momentum.
  ROS   Why!—something is happening. It had quite escaped my attention!

He listens: Makes a stab at an exit. Listens more carefully: Changes direction.

GUIL *takes no notice.*

ROS *wanders about trying to decide where the music comes from. Finally he tracks it down—unwillingly—to the middle barrel. There is no getting away from it. He turns to* GUIL *who takes no notice.* ROS, *during this whole business, never quite breaks into articulate speech. His face and his hands indicate his incredulity. He stands gazing at the middle barrel. The pipe plays on within. He kicks the barrel. The pipe stops. He leaps back toward* GUIL. *The pipe starts up again. He approaches the barrel cautiously. He lifts the lid. The music is louder. He slams down the lid. The music is softer. He goes back towards* GUIL. *But a drum starts, muffled. He freezes. He turns. Considers the left-hand barrel. The drumming goes on within, in time to the flute. He walks back to* GUIL. *He opens his mouth to speak. Doesn't make it. A lute is heard. He spins round at the third barrel. More instruments join in. Until it is quite inescapable that inside the three barrels, distributed, playing together a familiar tune which has been heard three times before, are the* TRAGEDIANS.

They play on.

ROS *sits beside* GUIL. *They stare ahead.*

The tune comes to an end.

Pause.

  ROS   I thought I heard a band. [*In anguish.*] Plausibility is all I presume!
  GUIL [*coda*]   Call us this day our daily tune. . . .

The lid of the middle barrel flies open and the PLAYER's *head pops out.*

PLAYER   Aha! All in the same boat, then! [*He climbs out. He goes round banging on the barrels.*]

Everybody out!

[*Impossibly, the* TRAGEDIANS *climb out of the barrels. With their instruments, but not their cart. A few bundles. Except* ALFRED. *The* PLAYER *is cheerful.*]

[*To* ROS] Where are we?
ROS   Travelling.
PLAYER   Of course, we haven't got there yet.
ROS   Are we all right for England?
PLAYER   You look all right to me. I don't think they've very particular in England. Al-l-fred!

ALFRED *emerges from the* PLAYER's *barrel.*

GUIL   What are you doing here?
PLAYER   Travelling. [*To* TRAGEDIANS:] Right—blend into the background!

[*The* TRAGEDIANS *are in costume (from the mime): A king with crown,* ALFRED *as Queen, Poisoner and the two cloaked figures.*

They blend.]

[*To* GUIL] Pleased to see us? [*Pause*] You've come out of it very well, so far.
GUIL   And you?
PLAYER   In disfavour. Our play offended the King.
GUIL   Yes.
PLAYER   Well, he's a second husband himself. Tactless, really.
ROS   It was quite a good play nevertheless.
PLAYER   We never really got going—it was getting quite interesting when they stopped it.

[*Looks up at* HAMLET]

That's the way to travel. . . .
GUIL   What were you doing in there?
PLAYER   Hiding. [*Indicating costumes.*] We had to run for it just as we were.
ROS   Stowaways.
PLAYER   Naturally—we didn't get paid, owing to circumstances ever so slightly beyond our control, and all the money we had we lost betting on certainties. Life is a gamble, at terrible odds—if it was a bet you wouldn't take it. Did you know that any number doubled is even?
ROS   Is it?
PLAYER   We learn something every day, to our cost. But we troupers just go on and on. Do you know what happens to old actors?
ROS   What?
PLAYER   Nothing. They're still acting. Surprised, then?
GUIL   What?
PLAYER   Surprised to see us?

GUIL   I knew it wasn't the end.
PLAYER   With practically everyone on his feet. What do you make of it, so far?
GUIL   We haven't got much to go on.
PLAYER   You speak to him?
ROS   It's possible.
GUIL   But it wouldn't make any difference.
ROS   But it's possible.
GUIL   Pointless.
ROS   It's allowed.
GUIL   Allowed, yes. We are not restricted. No boundaries have been defined, no inhibitions imposed. We have, for the while, secured, or blundered into, our release, for the while. Spontaneity and whim are the order of the day. Other wheels are turning but they are not our concern. We can breathe. We can relax. We can do what we like and say what we like to whomever we like, without restriction.
ROS   Within limits, of course.
GUIL   Certainly within limits.

HAMLET *comes down to footlights and regards the audience. The others watch but don't speak.* HAMLET *clears his throat noisily and spits into the audience. A split second later he claps his hand to his eye and wipes himself. He goes back upstage.*

ROS   A compulsion towards philosophical introspection is his chief characteristic, if I may put it like that. It does not mean he is mad. It does not mean he isn't. Very often, it does not mean anything at all. Which may or may not be a kind of madness.
GUIL   It really boils down to symptoms. Pregnant replies, mystic allusions, mistaken identities, arguing his father is his mother, that sort of thing; intimations of suicide, forgoing of exercise, loss of mirth, hints of claustrophobia not to say delusions of imprisonment; invocations of camels, chameleons, capons, whales, weasels, hawks, handsaws—riddles, quibbles and evasions; amnesia, paranoia, myopia; day-dreaming, hallucinations; stabbing his elders, abusing his parents, insulting his lover, and appearing hatless in public—knock-kneed, droop-stockinged and sighing like a love-sick schoolboy, which at his age is coming on a bit strong.
ROS   And talking to himself.
GUIL   And talking to himself.

[ROS *and* GUIL *move apart together.*]

Well, where has that got us?
ROS   He's the Player.
GUIL   His play offended the King——
ROS   —offended the King——
GUIL   —who orders his arrest——
ROS   —orders his arrest——
GUIL   —so he escapes to England——
ROS   On the boat to which he meets——
GUIL   Guildenstern and Rosencrantz taking Hamlet——
ROS   —who also offended the King——
GUIL   —and killed Polonius——

ROS   —offended the King in a variety of ways——
GUIL   —to England. [*Pause.*] That seems to be it.

ROS *jumps up.*

ROS   Incidents! All we get is incidents! Dear God, is it too much to expect a little sustained action?!

And on the word, the PIRATES *attack. That is to say: Noise and shouts and rushing about. "Pirates. "*

Everyone visible goes frantic. HAMLET *draws his sword and rushes downstage.* GUIL, ROS *and* PLAYER *draw swords and rush upstage. Collision.* HAMLET *turns back up. They turn back down. Collision. By which time there is general panic right upstage. All four charge upstage with* ROS, GUIL *and* PLAYER *shouting:*

At last!
To arms!
Pirates!
Up there!
Down there!
To my sword's length!
Action!

All four reach the top, see something they don't like, waver, run for their lives downstage:

HAMLET, *in the lead, leaps into the left barrel.* PLAYER *leaps into the right barrel.* ROS *and* GUIL *leap into the middle barrel. All closing the lids after them.*

The lights dim to nothing while the sound of fighting continues. The sound fades to nothing. The lights come up. The middle barrel [ROS's *and* GUIL's] *is missing.*

The lid of the right-hand barrel is raised cautiously, the heads of ROS *and* GUIL *appear.*

The lid of the other barrel [HAMLET's] *is raised. The head of the* PLAYER *appears.*

All catch sight of each other and slam down lids.

Pause.

Lids raised cautiously.
ROS [*relief*]   They've gone. [*He starts to climb out.*] That was close. I've never thought quicker.

They are all three out of barrels. GUIL *is wary and nervous.* ROS *is light-headed. The* PLAYER *is phlegmatic. They note the missing barrel.*

ROS *looks round.*

ROS   Where's——?

The PLAYER *takes off his hat in mourning.*

PLAYER   Once more, alone—on our own resources.
GUIL [*worried*]   What do you mean? Where is he?
PLAYER   Gone.
GUIL   Gone where?
PLAYER   Yes, we were dead lucky there. If that's the word I'm after.
ROS [*not a pick up*]   Dead?
PLAYER   Lucky.
ROS [*he means*]   Is he dead?
PLAYER   Who knows?
GUIL [*rattled*]   He's not coming back?
PLAYER   Hardly.
ROS   He's dead then. He's dead as far as we're concerned.
PLAYER   Or we are as far as he is. [*He goes and sits on the floor to one side.*] Not too bad, is it?
GUIL [*rattled*]   But he can't—we're supposed to be—we've got a *letter*—we're going to England with a letter for the King——
PLAYER   Yes, that much seems certain. I congratulate you on the unambiguity of your situation.
GUIL   But you don't understand—it contains—we've had our instructions—— the whole thing's pointless without him.
PLAYER   Pirates could happen to anyone. Just deliver the letter. They'll send ambassadors from England to explain. . . .
GUIL [*worked up*]   Can't you see—the pirates left us home and high—dry and home—drome——[*Furiously.*] The pirates left us high and dry!
PLAYER [*comforting*]   There . . .
GUIL [*near tears*]   Nothing will be resolved without him. . . .
PLAYER   There . . . !
GUIL   We need Hamlet for our release!
PLAYER   There!
GUIL   What are we supposed to do?
PLAYER   This.

He turns away, lies down if he likes. ROS *and* GUIL *apart.*

ROS   Saved again.
GUIL   Saved for what?

ROS *sighs.*

ROS   The sun's going down. [*Pause.*] It'll be night soon. [*Pause.*] If that's west. [*Pause.*] Unless we've——
GUIL [*shouts*]   Shut up! I'm sick of it! Do you think conversation is going to help us now?
ROS [*hurt, desperately ingratiating*]   I—I bet you all the money I've got the year of my birth doubled is an odd number.
GUIL [*moan*]   No-o.
ROS   *Your* birth!

GUIL *smashes him down.*

GUIL [*broken*]   We've travelled too far, and our momentum has taken over; we move idly towards eternity, without possibility of reprieve or hope of explanation.

ROS   Be happy—if you're not even *happy* what's so good about surviving? [*He picks himself up.*] We'll be all right. I suppose we just go on.

GUIL   Go where?

ROS   To England.

GUIL   England! *That's* a dead end. I never believed in it anyway.

ROS   All we've got to do is make our report and that'll be that. Surely.

GUIL   I don't *believe* it—a shore, a harbour, say—and we get off and we stop someone and say—Where's the King?—And he says, Oh, you follow that road there and take the first left and——[*Furiously.*] I don't believe any of it!

ROS   It doesn't sound very plausible.

GUIL   And even if we came face to face, what do we say?

ROS   We say—We've arrived!

GUIL [*kingly*]   And who are you?

ROS   We are Guildenstern and Rosencrantz.

GUIL   Which is which?

ROS   Well, I'm—You're——

GUIL   What's it all about?——

ROS   Well, we were bringing Hamlet—but then some pirates——

GUIL   I don't begin to understand. Who are all these people, what's it got to do with me? You turn up out of the blue with some cock and bull story——

ROS [*with letter*]   We have a letter——

GUIL [*snatches it, opens it*]   A letter—yes—that's true. That's something . . . a letter . . . [*Reads.*] "As England is Denmark's faithful tributary . . . as love between them like the palm might flourish, etcetera . . . that on the knowing of this contents, without delay of any kind, should those bearers, Rosencrantz and Guildenstern, put to sudden death——"

He double-takes. ROS *snatches the letter.* GUIL *snatches it back.* ROS *snatches it half back. They read it again and look up.*

The PLAYER *gets to his feet and walks over to his barrel and kicks it and shouts into it.*

PLAYER   They've gone! It's all over!

One by one the PLAYERS *emerge, impossibly, from the barrel, and form a casually menacing circle round* ROS *and* GUIL, *who are still appalled and mesmerised.*

GUIL [*quietly*]   Where we went wrong was getting on a boat. We can move, of course, change direction, rattle about, but our movement is contained within a larger one that carries us along as inexorably as the wind and current. . . .

ROS   They had it in for us, didn't they? Right from the beginning. Who'd have thought that we were so important?

GUIL   But why? Was it all for this? Who are we that so much should converge on our little deaths? [*In anguish to the* PLAYER] Who are *we*?

PLAYER   You are Rosencrantz and Guildenstern. That's enough.

GUIL   No—it is not enough. To be told so little—to such an end—and still, finally, to be denied an explanation——

PLAYER   In our experience, most things end in death.
GUIL [*fear, vengeance, scorn*]   Your experience!—*Actors!*

[*He snatches a dagger from the* PLAYER's *belt and holds the point at the* PLAYER's *throat: the* PLAYER *backs and* GUIL *advances, speaking more quietly.*]

I'm talking about death—and you've never experienced *that*. And you cannot *act* it. You die a thousand casual deaths—with none of that intensity which squeezes out life . . . and no blood runs cold anywhere. Because even as you die you know that you will come back in a different hat. But no one gets up after *death*—there is no applause—there is only silence and some second-hand clothes, and that's— *death*——

[*And he pushes the blade in up to the hilt. The* PLAYER *stands with huge, terrible eyes, clutches at the wound as the blade withdraws: he makes small weeping sounds and falls to his knees, and then right down.*

While he is dying, GUIL, *nervous, high, almost hysterical, wheels on the* TRAGE-DIANS—]

If we have a destiny, then so had he—and if this is ours, then that was his—and if there are no explanations for us, then let there be none for him——

The TRAGEDIANS *watch the* PLAYER *die: they watch with some interest. The* PLAYER *finally lies still. A short moment of silence. Then the* TRAGEDIANS *start to applaud with genuine admiration. The* PLAYER *stands up, brushing himself down.*

PLAYER [*modestly*]   Oh, come, come, gentlemen—no flattery—it was merely competent——

The TRAGEDIANS *are still congratulating him. The* PLAYER *approaches* GUIL, *who stands rooted, holding the dagger.*

PLAYER   What did you think? [*Pause.*] You see, it *is* the kind they do believe in—it's what is expected.

[*He holds his hand out for the dagger.* GUIL *slowly puts the point of the dagger on to the* PLAYER's *hand, and pushes . . . the blade slides back into the handle. The* PLAYER *smiles, reclaims the dagger.*]

For a moment you thought I'd—cheated.

ROS *relieves his own tension with loud nervy laughter.*

ROS   Oh, very good! *Very* good! Took me in completely—didn't he take you in completely—[*claps his hands.*] Encore! Encore!
PLAYER [*activated, arms spread, the professional*]   Deaths for all ages and oc-casions! Deaths by suspension, convulsion, consumption, incision, execution, asphyxiation and malnutrition—! Climactic carnage, by poison and by steel—! Double deaths by duel!—! Show!—

[ALFRED, *still in his* Queen's *costume, dies by poison: the* PLAYER, *with rapier, kills the* "KING" *and duels with a fourth* TRAGEDIAN, *inflicting and receiving a wound. The two remaining* TRAGEDIANS, *the two* "SPIES" *dressed in the same coats as* ROS *and* GUIL, *are stabbed, as before. And the light is fading over the deaths which take place right upstage.*]

[*Dying amid the dying—tragically; romantically.*] So there's an end to that—it's commonplace: light goes with life, and in the winter of your years the dark comes early. . . .
    GUIL [*tired, drained, but still an edge of impatience; over the mime*] No . . . no . . . not for *us,* not like that. Dying is not romantic, and death is not a game which will soon be over . . . Death is not anything . . . death is not . . . It's the absence of presence, nothing more . . . the endless time of never coming back . . . a gap you can't see, and when the wind blows through it, it makes no sound. . . .

The light has gone upstage. Only GUIL *and* ROS *are visible as* ROS's *clapping falters to silence.*

Small pause.

    ROS   That's it, then, is it?

[*No answer. He looks out front.*]

The sun's going down. Or the earth's coming up, as the fashionable theory has it.

[*Small pause.*]

Not that it makes any difference.

[*Pause.*]

What was it all about? When did it begin?

[*Pause. No answer.*]

Couldn't we just stay put? I mean no one is going to come on and drag us off. . . . They'll just have to wait. We're still young . . . fit . . . we've got years. . . .

[*Pause. No answer.*]

[*A cry.*] We've done nothing wrong! We didn't harm anyone. Did we?
    GUIL   I can't remember.

ROS *pulls himself together.*

    ROS   All right, then. I don't care. I've had enough. To tell you the truth, I'm relieved.

And he disappears from view. GUIL *does not notice.*

GUIL   Our names shouted in a certain dawn . . . a message . . . a summons . . . There must have been a moment, at the beginning, where we could have said—no. But somehow we missed it. [*He looks round and sees he is alone.*]

Rosen—?
Guil—?

[*He gathers himself.*]

Well, we'll know better next time. Now you see me, now you—[*and disappears*].

Immediately the whole stage is lit up, revealing, upstage, arranged in the approximate positions last held by the dead TRAGEDIANS, *the tableau of court and corpses which is the last scene of* Hamlet.

That is: The KING, QUEEN, LAERTES *and* HAMLET *all dead.* HORATIO *holds* HAMLET, FORTINBRAS *is there.*

So are two AMBASSADORS *from England.*

AMBASSADOR   The sight is dismal;
and our affairs from England come too late.
The ears are senseless that should give us hearing
to tell him his commandment is fulfilled,
that Rosencrantz and Guildenstern are dead.
Where should we have our thanks?
    HORATIO   Not from his mouth,
had it the ability of life to thank you:
He never gave commandment for their death.
But since, so jump upon this bloody question,
you from the Polack wars, and you from England,
are here arrived, give order that these bodies
high on a stage be placed to the view;
and let me speak to the yet unknowing world
how these things came about: so shall you hear
of carnal, bloody and unnatural acts,
of accidental judgments, casual slaughters,
of deaths put on by cunning and forced cause,
and, in this upshot, purposes mistook
fallen on the inventors' heads: all this can I
truly deliver.

But during the above speech, the play fades out, overtaken by dark and music.

Questions

1. Guildenstern has several alternate explanations for the behavior of the coins. Relate each explanation to the play as a whole.

2. Look at the end of the first act. What does the playwright do just before the curtain to make his dramatic actions suitable for interruption?
3. A messenger who is offstage, whom we never see, is responsible for the action of the play. Do messengers in earlier plays perform a similar function? Are there other characters, not precisely messengers, whose function resembles a messenger's function?
4. In stage directions, Hamlet spits at the audience and then wipes his own eye. What has happened? What does this farcical bit of stage business imply?
5. When Rosencrantz cannot remember his own name, he repeats an old moment of theatrical farce. Why is this joke a staple of low comedy? Does Stoppard's use of it mean anything more profound?
6. Why do Hamlet and Ophelia not speak in their first scene in this play? When Stoppard writes stage directions for this scene, he uses an archaic language. Is the language appropriate to the dumb show described? Can the prose style of this stage direction be interpreted by a director in his direction?
7. When the player greets Rosencrantz and Guildenstern as *fellow artists,* does his mistake seem significant? If so, why?
8. Comment on these lines:

   a. We didn't come all this way for a christening.
   b. Give us this day our daily . . .
   c. Words, words. That's all we have to go on.

9. Guildenstern plays Hamlet when he and Rosencrantz are rehearsing for their meeting with the prince. Could you argue that this play proposes that everybody is Hamlet? Explain.
10. In an interview, Stoppard once said: "I write plays because dialogue is the most respectable way of contradicting myself." Is there anything inherently dramatic about contradicting oneself?
11. On page 1006, the player describes theater. Look at what he says. Does Rosencrantz use the theater as a symbol or an analogy to all human life? Is there a consistent view of theater in this play? Give your reasons.
12. The player tells us about an actor who was really hanged onstage but the hanging was theatrically unconvincing. Comment.
13. On learning that they are delivering Hamlet to his death, Guildenstern improvises a series of excuses for continuing on the murderous errand. Does this moral equivocation remind you of *Tartuffe?* Why? Does it make the play a satire? Why?
14. How does this play differ in its script from a realistic play? Do stage directions make nonrealistic suggestions? Is the dialogue nonrealistic?
15. Find two or three pages to stage—indicating costumes, makeup, lighting, blocking, sound effects—in a nonrealistic fashion.
16. In several speeches, Claudius mixes up Shakespeare's language. How do you know without looking back at the original?
17. In *Rosencrantz and Guildenstern Are Dead* the play within a play—which we watch in rehearsal and hear in the Players' summary—differs from the play within a play in Shakespeare's *Hamlet.* How does it differ and why?
18. The critic Clive James wrote: "The mainstream of *Rosencrantz and Guildenstern Are Dead* is the perception—surely a compassionate one—that the fact of their deaths mattering so little to Hamlet was something that ought to have mattered to Shakespeare." When people do not like *Rosencrantz and Guilden-*

stern Are Dead, they call it cold, artificial, shallow, without feeling. Do you agree with these critics or with Clive James? Why?

19. Compare the final scenes in Shakespeare and Stoppard.
20. Do Rosencrantz and Guildenstern have a chance to avoid their fate? If so, how?
21. Critics have noticed a connection between this play and T. S. Eliot's "The Love Song of J. Alfred Prufrock" (pages 625–628). Read the poem and comment.

Plays for Further Reading

William Shakespeare and *Othello*

After Shakespeare finished *Hamlet* he probably next wrote his dark comedy *Measure for Measure*. Then his tragic imagination traveled south, and he wrote about the Moor of Venice in *Othello*—the tale of a heroic black soldier who loves and marries a Venetian maiden. (To review the background of Elizabethan theater and Shakespearean tragedy, see pages 800–803.) The two tragedies differ greatly. Prince Hamlet is inward, a brooding young man given to self-analysis; the stage is dark with ghosts and portents. General Othello is vigorous, outward, generous, brave, apparently less complex than the Dane, and the play turns on real objects in a clear light—like a lady's handkerchief. Yet both plays are tragedies of love and jealousy, and readers have found similarities in the murderous poison that starts the action of *Hamlet* and the figurative poison of Iago's malice in *Othello*.

William Shakespeare
Othello, The Moor of Venice

Dramatis Personae

OTHELLO, the Moor
BRABANTIO, father to Desdemona
CASSIO, an honorable lieutenant
IAGO, a villain
RODERIGO, a gulled gentleman
DUKE OF VENICE
SENATORS
MONTANO, Governor of Cyprus
GENTLEMEN OF CYPRUS

LODOVICO and GRATIANO, two noble
  Venetians
SAILORS
CLOWN
DESDEMONA, wife to Othello
EMILIA, wife to Iago
BIANCA, a courtesan
[MESSENGER, HERALD, OFFICERS,
  GENTLEMEN, MUSICIANS,
  ATTENDANTS]

Scene: Venice and Cyprus

Act I,   Scene I. [*Venice. A street.*]

RODERIGO Tush! Never tell me? I take it much unkindly
  That thou, Iago, who hast had my purse
  As if the strings were thine, shouldst know of this.
IAGO Sblood, but you'll not hear me! If ever I did dream
  Of such a matter, abhor me.
5 RODERIGO   Thou told'st me
  Thou didst hold him in thy hate.
IAGO   Despise me
  If I do not. Three great ones of the city,
  In personal suit to make me his lieutenant,
  Off-capped[1] to him; and, by the faith of man,
10 I know my price; I am worth no worse a place.
  But he, as loving his own pride and purposes,
  Evades them with a bombast circumstance,[2]
  Horribly stuffed with epithets of war;
  Nonsuits[3] my mediators. For, "Certes," says he,
15 "I have already chose my officer." And what was he?

This text of *Othello,* edited by Alvin Kernan, is based on that of the First Folio, or large collection, of Shakespeare's plays (1623). However, there are many differences between the Folio text and that of the play's first printing in the Quarto, or small volume, of 1621 (eighteen or nineteen years after the play's first performance). Some readings from the Quarto are included. Some material has been added by the editor (some indications of scene, some stage directions). Such additions are enclosed in brackets. Alvin Kernan's text and notes were prepared for the edition of *Othello* in the Signet Classic Shakespeare series (New York: New American Library, 1963), under the general editorship of Sylvan Barnet.

Footnotes that gloss or translate a single word are in roman type. When the explanation covers more than one word, the relevant passage in Shakespeare precedes the explanation, in *italic* type.

[1]doffed their caps—as a mark of respect   [2]*bombast circumstance* stuffed, roundabout speech
[3]rejects

Forsooth, a great arithmetician,[1]
One Michael Cassio, a Florentine,
(A fellow almost damned in a fair wife)[2]
That never set a squadron in the field,
20   Nor the division of a battle knows
More than a spinster; unless the bookish theoric,
Wherein the tonguèd[3] consuls can propose
As masterly as he. Mere prattle without practice
Is all his soldiership. But he, sir, had th' election;
25   And I, of whom his eyes had seen the proof
At Rhodes, at Cyprus, and on other grounds
Christian and heathen, must be belee'd and calmed
By debitor and creditor. This counter-caster,[4]
He, in good time, must his lieutenant be,
30   And I—God bless the mark!—his Moorship's ancient.[5]
RODERIGO   By heaven, I rather would have been his hangman.
IAGO   Why, there's no remedy. 'Tis the curse of service:
Preferment goes by letter and affection,[6]
And not by old gradation,[7] where each second
35   Stood heir to th' first. Now, sir, be judge yourself,
Whether I in any just term am affined[8]
To love the Moor.
RODERIGO   I would not follow him then.
IAGO   O, sir, content you.
I follow him to serve my turn upon him.
40   We cannot all be masters, nor all masters
Cannot be truly followed. You shall mark
Many a duteous and knee-crooking[9] knave
That, doting on his own obsequious bondage,
Wears out his time, much like his master's ass,
45   For naught but provender; and when he's old, cashiered.
Whip me such honest knaves! Others there are
Who, trimmed in forms and visages of duty,
Keep yet their hearts attending on themselves,
And, throwing but shows of service on their lords,
50   Do well thrive by them, and when they have lined their coats,
Do themselves homage. These fellows have some soul;
And such a one do I profess myself. For, sir,
It is as sure as you are Roderigo,
Were I the Moor, I would not be Iago.
55   In following him, I follow but myself.
Heaven is my judge, not I for love and duty,

---

[1]theorist (rather than practical)   [2]*A . . . wife* (a much-disputed passage, probably best taken as a general sneer at Cassio as a dandy and a ladies' man. But in the story from which Shakespeare took his plot the counterpart of Cassio is married, and it may be that at the beginning of the play Shakespeare had decided to keep him married but later changed his mind)   [3]eloquent   [4]*counter-caster* i.e., a bookkeeper who casts (reckons up) figures on a *counter* (abacus)   [5]standard-bearer; an under-officer   [6]*letter and affection* recommendations (from men of power) and personal preference   [7]*old gradation* seniority   [8]bound   [9]bowing

But seeming so, for my peculiar[1] end;
For when my outward action doth demonstrate
The native[2] act and figure of my heart
60 In complement extern,[3] 'tis not long after
But I will wear my heart upon my sleeve
For daws to peck at; I am not what I am.
RODERIGO What a full fortune does the thick-lips owe[4]
If he can carry't thus!
IAGO   Call up her father,
65 Rouse him. Make after him, poison his delight,
Proclaim him in the streets, incense her kinsmen,
And though he in a fertile climate dwell,
Plague him with flies; though that his joy be joy,
Yet throw such chances of vexation on't
70 As it may lose some color.
RODERIGO Here is her father's house. I'll call aloud.
IAGO Do, with like timorous[5] accent and dire yell
As when, by night and negligence, the fire
Is spied in populous cities.
75 RODERIGO What, ho, Brabantio! Signior Brabantio, ho!
IAGO Awake! What, ho, Brabantio! Thieves! Thieves!
Look to your house, your daughter, and your bags!
Thieves! Thieves!

BRABANTIO *above*[6] [*at a window*].

BRABANTIO What is the reason of this terrible summons?
80 What is the matter there?
RODERIGO Signior, is all your family within?
IAGO Are your doors locked?
BRABANTIO   Why, wherefore ask you this?
IAGO Zounds, sir, y'are robbed! For shame. Put on your gown!
Your heart is burst, you have lost half your soul.
85 Even now, now, very now, an old black ram
Is tupping your white ewe. Arise, arise!
Awake the snorting citizens with the bell,
Or else the devil will make a grandsire of you.
Arise, I say!
BRABANTIO   What, have you lost your wits?
90 RODERIGO Most reverend signior, do you know my voice?
BRABANTIO Not I. What are you?
RODERIGO My name is Roderigo.
BRABANTIO   The worser welcome!
I have charged thee not to haunt about my doors.
In honest plainness thou hast heard me say
95 My daughter is not for thee; and now, in madness,
Being full of supper and distemp'ring draughts,[7]

---

[1]personal   [2]natural, innate   [3]*complement extern* outward appearance   [4]own   [5]frightening
[6](i.e., on the small upper stage above and to the rear of the main platform stage, which resembled
the projecting upper story of an Elizabethan house)   [7]*distemp'ring draughts* unsettling drinks

           Upon malicious knavery dost thou come
           To start[1] my quiet.
    RODERIGO   Sir, sir, sir—
    BRABANTIO   But thou must needs be sure
100   My spirits and my place[2] have in their power
           To make this bitter to thee.
    RODERIGO   Patience, good sir.
    BRABANTIO   What tell'st thou me of robbing? This is Venice,
           My house is not a grange.[3]
    RODERIGO   Most grave Brabantio,
           In simple and pure soul I come to you.
105   IAGO   Zounds, sir, you are one of those that will not serve God if the devil bid
           you. Because we come to do you service and you think we are ruffians, you'll
           have your daughter covered with a Barbary[4] horse, you'll have your nephews[5]
           neigh to you, you'll have coursers for cousins,[6] and gennets for germans.[7]
    BRABANTIO   What profane wretch art thou?
110   IAGO   I am one, sir, that comes to tell you your daughter and the Moor are making
           the beast with two backs.
    BRABANTIO   Thou art a villain.
    IAGO   You are—a senator.
    BRABANTIO   This thou shalt answer. I know thee, Roderigo.
    RODERIGO   Sir, I will answer anything. But I beseech you,
115   If't be your pleasure and most wise consent,
           As partly I find it is, that your fair daughter,
           At this odd-even[8] and dull watch o' th' night,
           Transported, with no worse nor better guard
           But with a knave of common hire, a gondolier,
120   To the gross clasps of a lascivious Moor—
           If this be known to you, and your allowance,
           We then have done you bold and saucy wrongs;
           But if you know not this, my manners tell me
           We have your wrong rebuke. Do not believe
125   That from the sense of all civility[9]
           I thus would play and trifle with your reverence.
           Your daughter, if you have not given her leave,
           I say again, hath made a gross revolt,
           Tying her duty, beauty, wit, and fortunes
130   In an extravagant[10] and wheeling stranger
           Of here and everywhere. Straight satisfy yourself.
           If she be in her chamber, or your house,
           Let loose on me the justice of the state
           For thus deluding you.
    BRABANTIO   Strike on the tinder, ho!
135   Give me a taper! Call up all my people!

---

[1]disrupt   [2]rank, i.e., of senator   [3]isolated house   [4]Arabian, i.e., Moorish   [5]i.e., grandsons   [6]relations   [7]*gennets for germans* Spanish horses for blood relatives   [8]between night
and morning   [9]*sense of all civility* feeling of what is proper   [10]vagrant, wandering (Othello is
not Venetian and thus may be considered a wandering soldier of fortune)

This accident[1] is not unlike my dream.
Belief of it oppresses me already.
Light, I say! Light!   *Exit [above]*
IAGO   Farewell, for I must leave you.
It seems not meet, nor wholesome to my place,
140   To be produced—as, if I stay, I shall—
Against the Moor. For I do know the State,
However this may gall him with some check,[2]
Cannot with safety cast[3] him; for he's embarked
With such loud reason to the Cyprus wars,
145   Which even now stands in act,[4] that for their souls
Another of his fathom[5] they have none
To lead their business; in which regard,
Though I do hate him as I do hell-pains,
Yet, for necessity of present life,
150   I must show out a flag and sign of love,
Which is indeed but sign. That you shall surely find him,
Lead to the Sagittary[6] that raisèd search:
And there will I be with him. So farewell.   *[Exit.]*

Enter BRABANTIO *[in his nightgown], with Servants and torches.*

BRABANTIO It is too true an evil. Gone she is;
155   And what's to come of my despisèd time
Is naught but bitterness. Now, Roderigo,
Where didst thou see her?—O unhappy girl!—
With the Moor, say'st thou?—Who would be a father?—
How didst thou know 'twas she?—O, she deceives me
160   Past thought!—What said she to you? Get moe[7] tapers!
Raise all my kindred!—Are they married, think you?
RODERIGO Truly I think they are.
BRABANTIO O heaven! How got she out? O treason of the blood!
Fathers, from hence trust not your daughters' minds
165   By what you see them act.[8] Is there not charms
By which the property[9] of youth and maidhood
May be abused? Have you not read, Roderigo,
Of some such thing?
RODERIGO   Yes, sir, I have indeed.
BRABANTIO Call up my brother.—O, would you had had her!—
170   Some one way, some another.—Do you know
Where we may apprehend her and the Moor?
RODERIGO I think I can discover him, if you please
To get good guard and go along with me.
BRABANTIO Pray you lead on. At every house I'll call;
175   I may command at most.—Get weapons, ho!
And raise some special officers of night.—
On, good Roderigo; I will deserve your pains.[10]   *[Exeunt.]*

[1]happening   [2]restraint   [3]dismiss   [4]*stands in act* takes place   [5]ability   [6](probably the
name of an inn)   [7]more   [8]do   [9]true nature   [10]*deserve your pains* be worthy of (and reward)
your efforts

Scene II. [*A street.*]

Enter OTHELLO, IAGO, ATTENDANTS *with torches.*

IAGO Though in the trade of war I have slain men,
　　Yet do I hold it very stuff¹ o' th' conscience
　　To do no contrived murder. I lack iniquity
　　Sometime to do me service. Nine or ten times
5　　I had thought t' have yerked² him here, under the ribs.
OTHELLO 'Tis better as it is.
IAGO　　　　　　　　　　　　Nay, but he prated,
　　And spoke such scurvy and provoking terms
　　Against your honor, that with the little godliness I have
　　I did full hard forbear him. But I pray you, sir,
10　　Are you fast married? Be assured of this,
　　That the magnifico³ is much beloved,
　　And hath in his effect a voice potential
　　As double as the Duke's.⁴ He will divorce you,
　　Or put upon you what restraint or grievance
15　　The law, with all his might to enforce it on,
　　Will give him cable.⁵
OTHELLO　　　　　　　　Let him do his spite.
　　My services which I have done the Signiory⁶
　　Shall out-tongue his complaints. 'Tis yet to know⁷—
　　Which when I know that boasting is an honor
20　　I shall promulgate—I fetch my life and being
　　From men of royal siege,⁸ and my demerits⁹
　　May speak unbonneted to as proud a fortune
　　As this that I have reached.¹⁰ For know, Iago,
　　But that I love the gentle Desdemona,
25　　I would not my unhousèd¹¹ free condition
　　Put into circumscription and confine
　　For the seas' worth. But look, what lights come yond?

Enter CASSIO, *with* [OFFICERS *and*] *torches.*

IAGO Those are the raisèd father and his friends.
　　You were best go in.
OTHELLO　　　　　　　　Not I. I must be found.
30　　My parts, my title, and my perfect soul¹²
　　Shall manifest me rightly. Is it they?
IAGO By Janus, I think no:
OTHELLO The servants of the Duke? And my lieutenant?
　　The goodness of the night upon you, friends.
　　What is the news?
35　　CASSIO　　　　　　　The Duke does greet you, general;

---

¹essence ²stabbed ³nobleman ⁴*hath ... Duke's* i.e., can be as effective as the Duke
⁵range, scope ⁶the rulers of Venice ⁷*yet to know* unknown as yet ⁸rank ⁹deserts ¹⁰*May
... reached* i.e., are the equal of the family I have married into ¹¹unconfined ¹²*perfect
soul* clear, unflawed conscience

And he requires your haste-posthaste appearance
Even on the instant.
OTHELLO   What is the matter, think you?
CASSIO Something from Cyprus, as I may divine
   It is a business of some heat. The galleys
40   Have sent a dozen sequent[1] messengers
   This very night at one another's heels,
   And many of the consuls, raised and met,
   Are at the Duke's already. You have been hotly called for.
   When, being not at your lodging to be found,
45   The Senate hath sent about three several[2] quests
   To search you out.
OTHELLO   'Tis well I am found by you.
   I will but spend a word here in the house,
   And go with you.   [*Exit.*]
CASSIO   Ancient, what makes he here?
IAGO Faith, he tonight hath boarded a land carack.[3]
50   If it prove lawful prize, he's made forever.
CASSIO I do not understand.
IAGO   He's married.
CASSIO   To who?

   [*Enter* OTHELLO.]

IAGO Marry,[4] to—Come captain, will you go?
OTHELLO   Have with you.
CASSIO Here comes another troop to seek for you.

   Enter BRABANTIO, RODERIGO, *with* OFFICERS *and torches.*

IAGO It is Brabantio. General, be advised.
   He comes to bad intent.
55   OTHELLO   Holla! Stand there!
RODERIGO Signior, it is the Moor.
BRABANTIO   Down with him, thief! [*They draw swords.*]
IAGO You, Roderigo? Come, sir, I am for you.
OTHELLO Keep up your bright swords, for the dew will rust them.
   Good signior, you shall more command with years
60   Than with your weapons.
BRABANTIO O thou foul thief, where hast thou stowed my daughter?
   Damned as thou art, thou hast enchanted her!
   For I'll refer me to all things of sense,[5]
   If she in chains of magic were not bound,
65   Whether a maid so tender, fair, and happy,
   So opposite to marriage that she shunned
   The wealthy, curlied darlings of our nation,
   Would ever have, t'incur a general mock,[6]
   Run from her guardage to the sooty bosom

---

[1]successive [2]separate [3]treasure ship [4]By Mary (an interjection) [5]*refer . . . sense* i.e.,
base (my argument) on all ordinary understanding of nature   [6]*general mock* public shame

70   Of such a thing as thou—to fear, not to delight.
         Judge me the world if 'tis not gross in sense[1]
         That thou hast practiced[2] on her with foul charms,
         Abused her delicate youth with drugs or minerals
         That weaken motion.[3] I'll have 't disputed on;
75   'Tis probable, and palpable to thinking.
         I therefore apprehend and do attach[4] thee
         For an abuser of the world, a practicer
         Of arts inhibited and out of warrant.[5]
         Lay hold upon him. If he do resist,
         Subdue him at his peril.
80   OTHELLO   Hold your hands,
         Both you of my inclining and the rest.
         Were it my cue to fight, I should have known it
         Without a prompter. Whither will you that I go
         To answer this your charge?
     BRABANTIO   To prison, till fit time
85   Of law and course of direct session
         Call thee to answer.
     OTHELLO   What if I do obey?
         How may the Duke be therewith satisfied,
         Whose messengers are here about my side
         Upon some present[6] business of the state
         To bring me to him?
90   OFFICER   'Tis true, most worthy signior.
         The Duke's in council, and your noble self
         I am sure is sent for.
     BRABANTIO   How? The Duke in council?
         In this time of the night? Bring him away.
         Mine's not an idle cause. The Duke himself,
95   Or any of my brothers[7] of the state,
         Cannot but feel this wrong as 'twere their own;
         For if such actions may have passage free,
         Bondslaves and pagans shall our statesmen be.   *Exeunt.*

Scene III. [*A council chamber.*]

Enter DUKE, SENATORS, *and* OFFICERS [*set at a table, with lights and* ATTEND-ANTS].

DUKE   There's no composition[8] in this news
       That gives them credit.[9]
FIRST SENATOR   Indeed, they are disproportioned.
       My letters say a hundred and seven galleys.
DUKE   And mine a hundred forty.
SECOND SENATOR   And mine two hundred.

---

[1]*gross in sense* obvious   [2]used tricks   [3]thought, i.e., reason   [4]arrest   [5]*inhibited . . . warrant* prohibited and illegal (black magic)   [6]immediate   [7]i.e., the other senators   [8]agreement
[9]*gives them credit* makes them believable

5   But though they jump[1] not on a just accompt[2]—
       As in these cases where the aim[3] reports
       'Tis oft with difference—yet do they all confirm
       A Turkish fleet, and bearing up to Cyprus.
       DUKE Nay, it is possible enough to judgment.[4]
10   I do not so secure me in the error,
       But the main article I do approve
       In fearful sense.[5]
       SAILOR [*Within*] What, ho! What, ho! What, ho!

       Enter SAILOR.

       OFFICER A messenger from the galleys.
       DUKE   Now? What's the business?
       SAILOR The Turkish preparation makes for Rhodes.
15   So was I bid report here to the State
       By Signior Angelo.
       DUKE How say you by this change?
       FIRST SENATOR   This cannot be
       By no assay of reason. 'Tis a pageant[6]
       To keep us in false gaze.[7] When we consider
20   Th' importancy of Cyprus to the Turk,
       And let ourselves again but understand
       That, as it more concerns the Turk than Rhodes,
       So may he with more facile question[8] bear it,
       For that it stands not in such warlike brace,[9]
25   But altogether lacks th' abilities
       That Rhodes is dressed in. If we make thought of this,
       We must not think the Turk is so unskillful
       To leave that latest which concerns him first,
       Neglecting an attempt of ease and gain
30   To wake and wage a danger profitless.
       DUKE Nay, in all confidence he's not for Rhodes.
       OFFICER Here is more news.

       Enter a MESSENGER.

       MESSENGER The Ottomites, reverend and gracious,
       Steering with due course toward the isle of Rhodes,
35   Have there injointed them with an after[10] fleet
       FIRST SENATOR Ay, so I thought. How many, as you guess?
       MESSENGER Of thirty sail; and now they do restem
       Their backward course, bearing with frank appearance
       Their purposes toward Cyprus. Signior Montano,
40   Your trusty and most valiant servitor,
       With his free duty[11] recommends[12] you thus,

---

[1]agree   [2]*just accompt* exact counting   [3]approximation   [4]*to judgment* when carefully considered   [5]*I do . . . sense* i.e., just because the numbers disagree in the reports, I do not doubt that the principal information (that the Turkish fleet is out) is fearfully true   [6]show, pretense   [7]*in false gaze* looking the wrong way   [8]*facile question* easy struggle   [9]*warlike brace* "military posture"   [10]following   [11]*free duty* unlimited respect   [12]informs.

And prays you to believe him.
DUKE   'Tis certain then for Cyprus.
    Marcus Luccicos, is not he in town?
45   FIRST SENATOR   He's now in Florence.
DUKE   Write from us to him; post-posthaste dispatch.
FIRST SENATOR   Here comes Brabantio and the valiant Moor.

    Enter BRABANTIO, OTHELLO, CASSIO, IAGO, RODERIGO, *and* OFFICERS.

DUKE   Valiant Othello, we must straight[1] employ you
    Against the general[2] enemy Ottoman.
50   [*To* BRABANTIO] I did not see you. Welcome, gentle signior.
    We lacked your counsel and your help tonight.
BRABANTIO   So did I yours. Good your grace, pardon me.
    Neither my place, nor aught I heard of business,
    Hath raised me from my bed; nor doth the general care
55   Take hold on me; for my particular grief
    Is of so floodgate and o'erbearing nature
    That it engluts and swallows other sorrows,
    And it is still itself.
DUKE   Why, what's the matter?
BRABANTIO   My daughter! O, my daughter!
SENATORS   Dead?
BRABANTIO   Ay, to me.
60   She is abused, stol'n from me, and corrupted
    By spells and medicines bought of mountebanks;
    For nature so prepost'rously to err,
    Being not deficient, blind, or lame of sense,
    Sans[3] witchcraft could not.
65   DUKE   Whoe'er he be that in this foul proceeding
    Hath thus beguiled your daughter of herself,
    And you of her, the bloody book of law
    You shall yourself read in the bitter letter
    After your own sense; yea, though our proper[4] son
    Stood in your action.[5]
70   BRABANTIO   Humbly I thank your Grace.
    Here is the man—this Moor, whom now, it seems,
    Your special mandate for the state affairs
    Hath hither brought.
ALL   We are very sorry for't.
DUKE [*To* OTHELLO]   What in your own part can you say to this?
75   BRABANTIO   Nothing, but this is so.
OTHELLO   Most potent, grave, and reverend signiors,
    My very noble and approved[6] good masters,
    That I have ta'en away this old man's daughter,
    It is most true; true I have married her.
80   The very head and front[7] of my offending

---

[1]at once   [2]universal   [3]without   [4]own   [5]*Stood in your action* were the accused in your
suit   [6]tested, proven by past performance   [7]*head and front* extreme form (*front* = forehead)

Hath this extent, no more. Rude am I in my speech,
And little blessed with the soft phrase of peace.
For since these arms of mine had seven years' pith[1]
Till now some nine moons wasted,[2] they have used
85　　Their dearest[3] action in the tented field;
And little of this great world can I speak
More than pertains to feats of broils and battle;
And therefore little shall I grace my cause
In speaking for myself. Yet, by your gracious patience,
90　　I will a round[4] unvarnished tale deliver
Of my whole course of love—what drugs, what charms,
What conjuration, and what mighty magic,
For such proceeding I am charged withal,
I won his daughter—
　　BRABANTIO　　　　　　　A maiden never bold,
95　　Of spirit so still and quiet that her motion
Blushed at herself,[5] and she, in spite of nature,
Of years, of country, credit, everything,
To fall in love with what she feared to look on!
It is a judgment maimed and most imperfect
100　　That will confess perfection so could err
Against all rules of nature, and must be driven
To find out practices of cunning hell
Why this should be. I therefore vouch again
That with some mixtures pow'rful o'er the blood,
105　　Or with some dram, conjured to this effect,
He wrought upon her.
　　DUKE　　　　　　　　　　To vouch this is no proof,
Without more wider and more overt test
Than these thin habits[6] and poor likelihoods
Of modern[7] seeming do prefer against him.
110　　FIRST SENATOR　But, Othello, speak.
Did you by indirect and forcèd courses
Subdue and poison this young maid's affections?
Or came it by request, and such fair question[8]
As soul to soul affordeth?
　　OTHELLO　　　　　　　　　I do beseech you,
115　　Send for the lady to the Sagittary
And let her speak of me before her father.
If you do find me foul in her report,
The trust, the office, I do hold of you
Not only take away, but let your sentence
Even fall upon my life.
120　　DUKE　　　　　　　　Fetch Desdemona hither.
　　OTHELLO　Ancient, conduct them; you best know the place.

[*Exit* IAGO, *with two or three* ATTENDANTS.]

---

[1]strength　[2]past　[3]most important　[4]blunt　[5]*her motion/Blushed at herself* i.e., she was
so modest that she blushed at every thought (and movement)　[6]clothing　[7]trivial　[8]discussion

And till she come, as truly as to heaven
I do confess the vices of my blood,
So justly to your grave ears I'll present
125 How I did thrive in this fair lady's love,
And she in mine.
DUKE   Say it, Othello.
OTHELLO Her father loved me; oft invited me;
Still[1] questioned me the story of my life
From year to year, the battle, sieges, fortune
130 That I have passed.
I ran it through, even from my boyish days
To th' very moment that he bade me tell it.
Wherein I spoke of most disastrous chances,
Of moving accidents by flood and field,
135 Of hairbreadth scapes i' th' imminent[2] deadly breach,
Of being taken by the insolent foe
And sold to slavery, of my redemption thence
And portance[3] in my travel's history,
Wherein of anters[4] vast and deserts idle,[5]
140 Rough quarries, rocks, and hills whose heads touch heaven,
It was my hint to speak. Such was my process.
And of the Cannibals that each other eat,
The Anthropophagi,[6] and men whose heads
Grew beneath their shoulders. These things to hear
145 Would Desdemona seriously incline;
But still the house affairs would draw her thence;
Which ever as she could with haste dispatch,
She'd come again, and with a greedy ear
Devour up my discourse. Which I observing,
150 Took once a pliant hour, and found good means
To draw from her a prayer of earnest heart
That I would all my pilgrimage dilate,[7]
Whereof by parcels she had something heard,
But not intentively.[8] I did consent,
155 And often did beguile her of her tears
When I did speak of some distressful stroke
That my youth suffered. My story being done,
She gave me for my pains a world of kisses.
She swore in faith 'twas strange, 'twas passing[9] strange;
160 'Twas pitiful, 'twas wondrous pitiful.
She wished she had not heard it; yet she wished
That heaven had made her such a man. She thanked me,
And bade me, if I had a friend that loved her,
I should but teach him how to tell my story,
165 And that would woo her. Upon this hint I spake.
She loved me for the dangers I had passed,
And I loved her that she did pity them.

---

[1]regularly [2]threatening [3]manner of acting [4]caves [5]empty, sterile [6]maneaters
[7]relate in full [8]at length and in sequence [9]surpassing

This only is the witchcraft I have used.
Here comes the lady. Let her witness it.

Enter DESDEMONA, IAGO, ATTENDANTS.

170 DUKE I think this tale would win my daughter too.
Good Brabantio, take up this mangled matter at the best.[1]
Men do their broken weapons rather use
Than their bare hands.
BRABANTIO I pray you hear her speak.
If she confess that she was half the wooer,
175 Destruction on my head if my bad blame
Light on the man. Come hither, gentle mistress.
Do you perceive in all this noble company
Where most you owe obedience?
DESDEMONA My noble father,
I do perceive here a divided duty.
180 To you I am bound for life and education;
My life and education both do learn me
How to respect you. You are the lord of duty,
I am hitherto your daughter. But here's my husband,
And so much duty as my mother showed
185 To you, preferring you before her father,
So much I challenge[2] that I may profess
Due to the Moor my lord.
BRABANTIO God be with you. I have done.
Please it your Grace, on to the state affairs.
I had rather to adopt a child than get[3] it.
190 Come hither, Moor.
I here do give thee that with all my heart
Which, but thou hast already, with all my heart
I would keep from thee. For your sake,[4] jewel,
I am glad at soul I have no other child,
195 For thy escape would teach me tyranny,
To hang clogs on them. I have done, my lord.
DUKE Let me speak like yourself and lay a sentence[5]
Which, as a grise[6] or step, may help these lovers.
When remedies are past, the griefs are ended
200 By seeing the worst, which late on hopes depended.[7]
To mourn a mischief that is past and gone
Is the next[8] way to draw new mischief on.
What cannot be preserved when fortune takes,
Patience her injury a mock'ry makes.
205 The robbed that smiles, steals something from the thief;
He robs himself that spends a bootless[9] grief.
BRABANTIO So let the Turk of Cyprus us beguile:
We lose it not so long as we can smile.

---

[1]*take ... best* i.e., make the best of this disaster [2]claim as right [3]beget [4]*For your sake* because of you [5]*lay a sentence* provide a maxim [6]step [7]*late on hopes depended* was supported by hope (of a better outcome) until lately [8]closest, surest [9]valueless

He bears the sentence well that nothing bears
210   But the free comfort which from thence he hears;
But he bears both the sentence and the sorrow
That to pay grief must of poor patience borrow.
These sentences, to sugar, or to gall,
Being strong on both sides, are equivocal.
215   But words are words. I never yet did hear
That the bruisèd heart was piercèd[1] through the ear.
I humbly beseech you, proceed to th' affairs of state.
DUKE   The Turk with a most mighty preparation makes for Cyprus. Othello, the
fortitude[2] of the place is best known to you; and though we have there a sub-
220   stitute[3] of most allowed sufficiency,[4] yet opinion, a more sovereign mistress of
effects, throws a more safer voice on you.[5] You must therefore be content to
slubber[6] the gloss of your new fortunes with this more stubborn and boisterous[7]
expedition.
OTHELLO   The tyrant Custom, most grave senators,
225   Hath made the flinty and steel couch of war
My thrice-driven[8] bed of down. I do agnize[9]
A natural and prompt alacrity
I find in hardness and do undertake
These present wars against the Ottomites.
230   Most humbly, therefore, bending to your state,
I crave fit disposition for my wife,
Due reference of place, and exhibition,[10]
With such accommodation and besort
As levels with[11] her breeding.
DUKE   Why, at her father's.
BRABANTIO   I will not have it so.
235   OTHELLO   Nor I.
DESDEMONA   Nor would I there reside,
To put my father in impatient thoughts
By being in his eye. Most gracious Duke,
To my unfolding[12] lend your prosperous[13] ear,
240   And let me find a charter[14] in your voice,
T' assist my simpleness.
DUKE   What would you, Desdemona?
DESDEMONA   That I love the Moor to live with him,
My downright violence, and storm of fortunes,
May trumpet to the world. My heart's subdued
245   Even to the very quality of my lord.[15]

---

[1](some editors emend to *piecèd,* i.e., "healed." But *piercèd* makes good sense: Brabantio is saying
in effect that his heart cannot be further hurt [pierced] by the indignity of the useless, conventional
advice the Duke offers him. *Pierced* can also mean, however, "lanced" in the medical sense, and
would then mean "treated")   [2]fortification   [3]viceroy   [4]*most allowed sufficiency* generally acknowledged capability   [5]*opinion . . . you* i.e., the general opinion, which finally controls affairs,
is that you would be the best man in this situation   [6]besmear   [7]*stubborn and boisterous* rough
and violent   [8]i.e., softest   [9]know in myself   [10]grant of funds   [11]*levels with* is suitable to
[12]explanation   [13]favoring   [14]permission   [15]*My . . . lord* i.e., I have become one in nature and
being with the man I married (therefore, I too would go to the wars like a soldier)

I saw Othello's visage in his mind,
And to his honors and his valiant parts
Did I my soul and fortunes consecrate.
So that, dear lords, if I be left behind,
250   A moth of peace, and he go to the war,
The rites[1] for why I love him are bereft me,
And I a heavy interim shall support
By his dear absence. Let me go with him.
OTHELLO   Let her have your voice.[2]
255   Vouch with me, heaven, I therefore beg it not
To please the palate of my appetite,
Nor to comply with heat[3]—the young affects[4]
In me defunct—and proper satisfaction;[5]
But to be free and bounteous to her mind;
260   And heaven defend[6] your good souls that you think
I will your serious and great business scant
When she is with me. No, when light-winged toys
Of feathered Cupid seel[7] with wanton[8] dullness
My speculative and officed instrument,[9]
265   That my disports corrupt and taint my business,
Let housewives make a skillet of my helm,
And all indign[10] and base adversities
Make head[11] against my estimation![12]—
DUKE   Be it as you shall privately determine,
270   Either for her stay or going. Th' affair cries haste,
And speed must answer it.
FIRST SENATOR   You must away tonight.
OTHELLO   With all my heart.
DUKE   At nine i' th' morning here we'll meet again.
Othello, leave some officer behind,
275   And he shall our commission bring to you,
And such things else of quality and respect
As doth import you.
OTHELLO   So please your grace, my ancient;
A man he is of honesty and trust.
To his conveyance I assign my wife,
280   With what else needful your good grace shall think
To be sent after me.
DUKE   Let it be so.
Good night to every one. [*To* BRABANTIO] And, noble signior,
If virtue no delighted[13] beauty lack,
Your son-in-law is far more fair than black.
285   FIRST SENATOR   Adieu, brave Moor. Use Desdemona well.
BRABANTIO   Look to her, Moor, if thou hast eyes to see:
She has deceived her father, and may thee.

---

[1](may refer either to the marriage rites or to the rites, formalities, of war)   [2]consent   [3]lust
[4]passions   [5]*proper satisfaction* i.e., consummation of the marriage   [6]forbid   [7]sew up
[8]lascivious   [9]*speculative . . . instrument* i.e., sight (and, by extension, the mind)   [10]unworthy
[11]*Make head* form an army, i.e., attack   [12]reputation   [13]delightful

[*Exeunt* DUKE, SENATORS, OFFICERS, *etc.*]

OTHELLO My life upon her faith! Honest Iago,
My Desdemona must I leave to thee.
290 I prithee let thy wife attend on her,
And bring them after in the best advantage.[1]
Come, Desdemona, I have but an hour
Of love, of worldly matter, and direction
To spend with thee. We must obey the time.

Exit [MOOR *with* DESDEMONA].

295 RODERIGO Iago?
IAGO What say'st thou, noble heart?
RODERIGO What will I do, think'st thou?
IAGO Why, go to bed and sleep.
RODERIGO I will incontinently[2] drown myself.
300 IAGO If thou dost, I shall never love thee after. Why, thou silly gentleman?
RODERIGO It is silliness to live when to live is torment; and then have we a
prescription to die when death is our physician.
IAGO O villainous! I have looked upon the world for four times seven years, and
since I could distinguish betwixt a benefit and an injury, I never found man that
305 knew how to love himself. Ere I would say I would drown myself for the love
of a guinea hen, I would change my humanity with a baboon.
RODERIGO What should I do? I confess it is my shame to be so fond, but it is
not in my virtue[3] to amend it.
IAGO Virtue? A fig! 'Tis in ourselves that we are thus, or thus. Our bodies are
310 our gardens, to the which our wills are gardeners; so that if we will plant nettles
or sow lettuce, set hyssop and weed up thyme, supply it with one gender of
herbs or distract[4] it with many—either to have it sterile with idleness or manured
with industry—why, the power and corrigible[5] authority of this lies in our wills.
If the balance of our lives had not one scale of reason to poise another of sen-
315 suality, the blood and baseness of our natures would conduct us to most pre-
post'rous conclusions.[6] But we have reason to cool our raging motions, our
carnal sting or unbitted[7] lusts, whereof I take this that you call love to be a sect
or scion.[8]
RODERIGO It cannot be.
320 IAGO It is merely a lust of the blood and a permission of the will. Come, be a
man! Drown thyself? Drown cats and blind puppies! I have professed me thy
friend, and I confess me knit to thy deserving with cables of perdurable toughness. I could never better stead[9] thee than now. Put money in thy purse. Follow
thou the wars; defeat thy favor[10] with an usurped[11] beard. I say, put money in
325 thy purse. It cannot be long that Desdemona should continue her love to the
Moor. Put money in thy purse. Nor he his to her. It was a violent commencement in her and thou shalt see an answerable[12] sequestration—put but money
in thy purse. These Moors are changeable in their wills—fill thy purse with

---

[1]opportunity   [2]at once   [3]strength (Roderigo is saying that his nature controls him)   [4]vary
[5]corrective   [6]ends   [7]i.e., uncontrolled   [8]*sect or scion* off-shoot   [9]serve   [10]*defeat thy favor* disguise your face   [11]assumed   [12]similar

330

money. The food that to him now is as luscious as locusts[1] shall be to him
shortly as bitter as coloquintida.[2] She must change for youth; when she is sated
with his body, she will find the errors of her choice. Therefore, put money in
thy purse. If thou wilt needs damn thyself, do it a more delicate way than
drowning. Make all the money thou canst. If sanctimony[3] and a frail vow betwixt
an erring[4] barbarian and supersubtle Venetian be not too hard for my wits, and

335

all the tribe of hell, thou shalt enjoy her. Therefore, make money. A pox of
drowning thyself, it is clean out of the way. Seek thou rather to be hanged in
compassing[5] thy joy than to be drowned and go without her.

RODERIGO Wilt thou be fast to my hopes, if I depend on the issue?

IAGO Thou art sure of me. Go, make money. I have told thee often, and I retell

340

thee again and again, I hate the Moor. My cause is hearted;[6] thine hath no less
reason. Let us be conjunctive[7] in our revenge against him. If thou canst cuckold
him, thou dost thyself a pleasure, me a sport. There are many events in the
womb of time, which will be delivered. Traverse, go, provide thy money! We will
have more of this tomorrow. Adieu.

345

RODERIGO Where shall we meet i' th' morning?

IAGO At my lodging.

RODERIGO I'll be with thee betimes.

IAGO Go to, farewell. Do you hear, Roderigo?

RODERIGO I'll sell all my land.   *Exit.*

350

IAGO Thus do I ever make my fool my purse;
For I mine own gained knowledge[8] should profane
If I would time expend with such snipe
But for my sport and profit. I hate the Moor,
And it is thought abroad that 'twixt my sheets

355

H'as done my office. I know not if't be true,
But I, for mere suspicion in that kind,
Will do, as if for surety.[9] He holds me well;
The better shall my purpose work on him.
Cassio's a proper[10] man. Let me see now:

360

To get his place, and to plume up my will[11]
In double knavery. How? How? Let's see.
After some time, to abuse Othello's ears
That he is too familiar with his wife.
He hath a person and a smooth dispose[12]

365

To be suspected—framed[13] to make women false.
The Moor is of a free and open nature
That thinks men honest that but seem to be so;
And will as tenderly be led by th' nose
As asses are.

370

I have't! It is engendered! Hell and night
Must bring this monstrous birth to the world's light.   [*Exit.*]

---

[1]a sweet fruit   [2]a purgative derived from a bitter apple   [3]sacred bond (of marriage)
[4]wandering   [5]encompassing, achieving   [6]deepseated in the heart   [7]joined   [8]*gained knowledge* i.e., practical, worldly wisdom   [9]certainty   [10]handsome   [11]*plume up my will* (many
explanations have been offered for this crucial line, which in Q[1] reads "make up my will." The
general sense is something like "to make more proud and gratify my ego")   [12]manner   [13]designed

Act II, Scene I. [*Cyprus.*]

> *Enter* MONTANO *and two* GENTLEMEN [*one above*].[1]

MONTANO What from the cape can you discern at sea?
FIRST GENTLEMAN Nothing at all, it is a high-wrought flood.
    I cannot 'twixt the heaven and the main
    Descry a sail.
5   MONTANO Methinks the wind hath spoke aloud at land;
    A fuller blast ne'er shook our battlements.
    If it hath ruffianed so upon the sea,
    What ribs of oak, when mountains melt on them,
    Can hold the mortise? What shall we hear of this?
10   SECOND GENTLEMAN A segregation[2] of the Turkish fleet.
    For do but stand upon the foaming shore,
    The chidden billow seems to pelt the clouds;
    The wind-shaked surge, with high and monstrous main,[3]
    Seems to cast water on the burning Bear
15   And quench the guards of th' ever-fixèd pole.[4]
    I never did like molestation view
    On the enchafèd flood.
    MONTANO   If that the Turkish fleet
    Be not ensheltered and embayed, they are drowned;
    It is impossible to bear it out.

> *Enter a* [*third*] GENTLEMAN.

20   THIRD GENTLEMAN News, lads! Our wars are done.
    The desperate tempest hath so banged the Turks
    That their designment halts. A noble ship of Venice
    Hath seen a grievous wrack and sufferance[5]
    On most part of their fleet.
    MONTANO How? Is this true?
25   THIRD GENTLEMAN   The ship is here put in,
    A Veronesa; Michael Cassio,
    Lieutenant to the warlike Moor Othello,
    Is come on shore; the Moor himself at sea,
    And is in full commission here for Cyprus.
30   MONTANO I am glad on't. 'Tis a worthy governor.
    THIRD GENTLEMAN But this same Cassio, though he speak of comfort
    Touching the Turkish loss, yet he looks sadly
    And prays the Moor be safe, for they were parted
    With foul and violent tempest.
    MONTANO   Pray heavens he be;
35   For I have served him, and the man commands
    Like a full soldier. Let's to the seaside, ho!

---

[1](the Folio arrangement of this scene requires that the First Gentleman stand above—on the upper stage—and act as a lookout reporting sights which cannot be seen by Montano standing below on the main stage)   [2]separation   [3]both "ocean" and "strength"   [4]*Seems . . . pole* (the constellation Ursa Minor contains two stars which are the *guards,* or companions, of the *pole,* or North Star)   [5]damage

As well to see the vessel that's come in
As to throw out our eyes for brave Othello,
Even till we make the main and th' aerial blue
An indistinct regard.[1]

40 THIRD GENTLEMAN   Come, let's do so;
For every minute is expectancy
Of more arrivancie.[2]

Enter CASSIO.

CASSIO Thanks, you the valiant of the warlike isle,
That so approve[3] the Moor. O, let the heavens
45   Give him defense against the elements,
For I have lost him on a dangerous sea.
MONTANO Is he well shipped?
CASSIO His bark is stoutly timbered, and his pilot
Of very expert and approved allowance;[4]
50   Therefore my hopes, not surfeited to death,[5]
Stand in bold cure.[6] (*Within:* A sail, a sail, a sail!)
CASSIO What noise?
FIRST GENTLEMAN The town is empty; on the brow o' th' sea
Stand ranks of people, and they cry, "A sail!"
55 CASSIO My hopes do shape him for the governor.   [*A shot.*]
SECOND GENTLEMAN They do discharge their shot of courtesy:
Our friends at least.
CASSIO   I pray you, sir, go forth
And give us truth who 'tis that is arrived.
SECOND GENTLEMAN I shall.   [*Exit.*]
60 MONTANO But, good lieutenant, is your general wived?
CASSIO Most fortunately. He hath achieved a maid.
That paragons[7] description and wild fame;[8]
One that excels the quirks of blazoning pens,[9]
And in th' essential vesture of creation[10]
Does tire the ingener.[11]

Enter [*Second*] GENTLEMAN.

65   How now? Who has put in?
SECOND GENTLEMAN 'Tis one Iago, ancient to the general.
CASSIO H'as had most favorable and happy speed:
Tempests themselves, high seas, and howling winds,
The guttered[12] rocks and congregated[13] sands,
70   Traitors ensteeped[14] to enclog the guiltless keel,
As having sense[15] of beauty, do omit

[1]*the main . . . regard* i.e., the sea and sky become indistinguishable   [2]*arrivals*   [3]"honor" or,
perhaps, "are as warlike and valiant as your governor"   [4]*approved allowance* known and tested
[5]*not surfeited to death* i.e., not so great as to be in danger   [6]*Stand in bold cure* i.e., are likely
to be restored   [7]*exceeds*   [8]*wild fame* extravagant report   [9]*quirks of blazoning pens* ingenuities
of praising pens   [10]*essential vesture of creation* essential human nature as given by the Creator
[11]*tire the ingener* a difficult line that probably means something like "outdo the human ability to
imagine and picture"   [12]*jagged*   [13]*gathered*   [14]*submerged*   [15]*awareness*

Their mortal[1] natures, letting go safely by
The divine Desdemona.
MONTANO   What is she?
CASSIO She that I spake of, our great captain's captain,
75   Left in the conduct of the bold Iago,
Whose footing[2] here anticipates our thoughts
A se'nnight's[3] speed. Great Jove, Othello guard,
And swell his sail with thine own pow'rful breath,
That he may bless this bay with his tall[4] ship,
80   Make love's quick pants in Desdemona's arms,
Give renewed fire to our extincted spirits.

Enter DESDEMONA, IAGO, RODERIGO, *and* EMILIA.

O, behold! The riches of the ship is come on shore!
You men of Cyprus, let her have your knees.   [*Kneeling.*]
Hail to thee, lady! and the grace of heaven,
85   Before, behind thee, and on every hand,
Enwheel thee round.
DESDEMONA   I thank you, valiant Cassio.
What tidings can you tell of my lord?
CASSIO He is not yet arrived, nor know I aught
But that he's well and will be shortly here.
90   DESDEMONA O but I fear. How lost you company?
CASSIO The great contention of sea and skies
Parted our fellowship. (*Within:* A sail, a sail!)   [*A shot.*]
But hark. A sail!
SECOND GENTLEMAN They give this greeting to the citadel;
This likewise is a friend.
95   CASSIO   See for the news.   [*Exit* GENTLEMAN.]
Good ancient, you are welcome. [*To* EMILIA] Welcome, mistress.
Let it not gall your patience, good Iago,
That I extend[5] my manners. 'Tis my breeding[6]
That gives me this bold show of courtesy.   [*Kisses* EMILIA.]
100   IAGO Sir, would she give you so much of her lips
As of her tongue she oft bestows on me,
You would have enough.
DESDEMONA   Alas, she has no speech.
IAGO In faith, too much.
I find it still when I have leave to sleep.[7]
105   Marry, before your ladyship,[8] I grant.
She puts her tongue a little in her heart
And chides with thinking.
EMILIA   You have little cause to say so.

---

[1]deadly   [2]landing   [3]week's   [4]brave   [5]stretch   [6]careful training in manners (Cassio is
considerably more the polished gentleman than Iago, and aware of it)   [7]*still . . . sleep* i.e., even
when she allows me to sleep she continues to scold   [8]*before your ladyship* in your presence
[9]models (of virtue)

IAGO Come on, come on! You are pictures⁹ out of door,
    Bells in your parlors, wildcats in your kitchens,
110   Saints in your injuries,¹ devils being offended,
    Players in your housewifery,² and housewives in your beds.
DESDEMONA O, fie upon thee, slanderer!
IAGO Nay, it is true, or else I am a Turk:
    You rise to play, and go to bed to work.
EMILIA You shall not write my praise.
115 IAGO   No, let me not.
DESDEMONA What wouldst write of me, if thou shouldst praise me?
IAGO O gentle lady, do not put me to't.
    For I am nothing if not critical.
DESDEMONA Come on, assay. There's one gone to the harbor?
IAGO Ay, madam.
120 DESDEMONA [*Aside*] I am not merry; but I do beguile
    The thing I am by seeming otherwise.—
    Come, how wouldst thou praise me?
IAGO I am about it; but indeed my invention
    Comes from my pate as birdlime³ does from frieze⁴—
125   It plucks out brains and all. But my Muse labors,
    And thus she is delivered:
    If she be fair⁵ and wise: fairness and wit,
    The one's for use, the other useth it.
DESDEMONA Well praised. How if she be black⁶ and witty?
130 IAGO If she be black, and thereto have a wit,
    She'll find a white that shall her blackness fit.
DESDEMONA Worse and worse!
EMILIA How if fair and foolish?
IAGO She never yet was foolish that was fair,
135   For even her folly helped her to an heir.
DESDEMONA Those are old fond⁷ paradoxes to make fools laugh i' th' alehouse.
    What miserable praise hast thou for her that's foul and foolish?
IAGO There's none so foul, and foolish thereunto,
    But does foul pranks which fair and wise ones do.
140 DESDEMONA O heavy ignorance. Thou praisest the worst best. But what praise
    couldst thou bestow on a deserving woman indeed—one that in the authority
    of her merit did justly put on the vouch of very malice itself?⁸
IAGO She that was ever fair, and never proud;
    Had tongue at will, and yet was never loud;
145   Never lacked gold, and yet went never gay;
    Fled from her wish, and yet said "Now I may";
    She that being angered, her revenge being nigh,
    Bade her wrong stay, and her displeasure fly;

---

¹*in your injuries* when you injure others   ²this word can mean "careful, economical household management," and Iago would then be accusing women of only pretending to be good housekeepers, while in bed they are either [1] economical of their favors, or more likely [2] serious and dedicated workers   ³a sticky substance put on branches to catch birds   ⁴rough cloth   ⁵light-complexioned   ⁶brunette   ⁷foolish   ⁸*one ... itself* i.e., a woman so honest and deserving that even malice would be forced to approve of her

She that in wisdom never was so frail
150   To change the cod's head for the salmon's tail;[1]
She that could think, and nev'r disclose her mind;
See suitors following, and not look behind:
She was a wight[2] (if ever such wights were)—
DESDEMONA To do what?
155 IAGO To suckle fools and chronicle small beer.[3]
DESDEMONA O most lame and impotent conclusion. Do not learn of him, Emilia,
    though he be thy husband. How say you, Cassio? Is he not a most profane and
    liberal[4] counselor?
CASSIO He speaks home,[5] madam. You may relish him more in[6] the soldier than
160   in the scholar. [*Takes* DESDEMONA's *hand.*]
IAGO [*Aside*] He takes her by the palm. Ay, well said, whisper! With as little a
    web as this will I ensnare as great a fly as Cassio. Ay, smile upon her, do! I will
    gyve[7] thee in thine own courtship.—You say true; 'tis so, indeed!—If such tricks
    as these strip you out of your lieutenantry, it had been better you had not kissed
165   your three fingers so oft—which now again you are most apt to play the sir[8] in.
    Very good! Well kissed! An excellent curtsy![9] 'Tis so, indeed. Yet again your
    fingers to your lips? Would they were clyster pipes[10] for your sake! [*Trumpets
    within.*] The Moor! I know his trumpet.[11]
CASSIO 'Tis truly so.
170 DESDEMONA Let's meet him and receive him.
CASSIO Lo, where he comes.
OTHELLO O my fair warrior!
DESDEMONA   My dear Othello.
OTHELLO It gives me wonder great as my content
    To see you here before me. O my soul's joy!
175   If after every tempest come such calms,
    May the winds blow till they have wakened death.
    And let the laboring bark climb hills of seas
    Olympus-high, and duck again as low
    As hell's from heaven. If it were now to die,
180   'Twere now to be most happy; for I fear
    My soul hath her content so absolute
    That not another comfort like to this
    Succeeds in unknown fate.
DESDEMONA   The heavens forbid
    But that our loves and comforts should increase
185   Even as our days do grow.
OTHELLO   Amen to that, sweet powers!
    I cannot speak enough of this content:
    It stops me here [*touches his heart*]; it is too much of joy.
    And this, and this, the greatest discords be   [*They kiss.*]
    That e'er our hearts shall make!

---

[1]*To . . . tail* i.e., to exchange something valuable for something useless   [2]*person*   [3]*chronicle
small beer* i.e., keep household accounts (the most trivial of occupations in Iago's opinion)
[4]*licentious*   [5]*speaks home* thrusts deeply with his speech   [6]*relish him more in* enjoy him more
as   [7]*bind*   [8]*the sir* the fashionable gentleman   [9]courtesy, i.e., bow   [10]*clyster pipes* enema
tubes   [11]*his trumpet* (great men had their own distinctive calls)

IAGO [*Aside*]   O, you are well tuned now!
190   But I'll set down the pegs[1] that make this music,
As honest as I am.
OTHELLO   Come, let us to the castle.
News, friends! Our wars are done; the Turks are drowned.
How does my old acquaintance of this isle?
Honey, you shall be well desired in Cyprus;
195   I have found great love amongst them. O my sweet,
I prattle out of fashion, and I dote
In mine own comforts. I prithee, good Iago,
Go to the bay and disembark my coffers.
Bring thou the master to the citadel;
200   He is a good one and his worthiness
Does challenge[2] much respect. Come, Desdemona,
Once more well met at Cyprus.

Exit OTHELLO *and* DESDEMONA [*and all but* IAGO *and* RODERIGO].

IAGO [*To an* ATTENDANT] Do thou meet me presently at the harbor. [*To* ROD-
ERIGO] Come hither. If thou be'st valiant (as they say base men being in love
205   have then a nobility in their natures more than is native to them), list me. The
lieutenant tonight watches on the court of guard.[3] First, I must tell thee this:
Desdemona is directly in love with him.
RODERIGO With him? Why, 'tis not possible.
IAGO Lay thy finger thus [*puts his finger to his lips*], and let thy soul be in-
210   structed. Mark me with what violence she first loved the Moor but for bragging
and telling her fantastical lies. To love him still for prating? Let not thy discreet
heart think it. Her eye must be fed. And what delight shall she have to look on
the devil? When the blood is made dull with the act of sport, there should be a
game[4] to inflame it and to give satiety a fresh appetite, loveliness in favor,[5]
215   sympathy in years,[6] manners, and beauties; all which the Moor is defective in.
Now for want of these required conveniences,[7] her delicate tenderness will find
itself abused, begin to heave the gorge,[8] disrelish and abhor the Moor. Very
nature will instruct her in it and compel her to some second choice. Now sir,
this granted—as it is a most pregnant[9] and unforced position—who stands so
220   eminent in the degree of this fortune as Cassio does? A knave very voluble; no
further conscionable[10] than in putting on the mere form of civil and humane[11]
seeming for the better compass of his salt[12] and most hidden loose[13] affection.
Why, none! Why, none! A slipper[14] and subtle knave, a finder of occasion, that
has an eye can stamp and counterfeit advantages, though true advantage never
225   present itself. A devilish knave. Besides, the knave is handsome, young, and
hath all those requisites in him that folly and green minds look after. A pestilent
complete knave, and the woman hath found him already.
RODERIGO I cannot believe that in her; she's full of most blessed condition.
IAGO Blessed fig's-end! The wine she drinks is made of grapes. If she had been

---

[1]*set down the pegs* loosen the strings (to produce discord)   [2]require, exact   [3]*court of
guard* guardhouse   [4]sport (with the added sense of "gamey," "rank")   [5]countenance, appearance   [6]*sympathy in years* sameness of age   [7]advantages   [8]*heave the gorge* vomit   [9]likely
[10]*no further conscionable* having no more conscience   [11]polite   [12]lecherous   [13]immoral
[14]slippery

230   blessed, she would never have loved the Moor. Blessed pudding! Didst thou not
       see her paddle with the palm of his hand? Didst not mark that?
       RODERIGO   Yes, that I did; but that was but courtesy.
       IAGO   Lechery, by this hand! [*Extends his index finger*] An index[1] and obscure
       prologue to the history of lust and foul thoughts. They met so near with their
235   lips that their breaths embraced together. Villainous thoughts, Roderigo. When
       these mutualities so marshal the way, hard at hand comes the master and main
       exercise, th' incorporate[2] conclusion: Pish! But, sir, be you ruled by me. I have
       brought you from Venice. Watch you tonight; for the command, I'll lay't upon
       you. Cassio knows you not. I'll not be far from you. Do you find some occasion
240   to anger Cassio, either by speaking too loud, or tainting[3] his discipline, or from
       what other course you please which the time shall more favorably minister.
       RODERIGO   Well.
       IAGO   Sir, he's rash and very sudden in choler,[4] and haply may strike at you.
       Provoke him that he may; for even out of that will I cause these of Cyprus to
245   mutiny, whose qualification shall come into no true taste[5] again but by the
       displanting of Cassio. So shall you have a shorter journey to your desires by the
       means I shall then have to prefer them; and the impediment most profitably
       removed without the which there were no expectation of our prosperity.
       RODERIGO   I will do this if you can bring it to any opportunity.
250   IAGO   I warrant thee. Meet me by and by at the citadel. I must fetch his neces-
       saries ashore. Farewell.
       RODERIGO   Adieu.   *Exit.*
       IAGO   That Cassio loves her, I do well believe't;
       That she loves him, 'tis apt and of great credit.
255   The Moor, howbeit that I endure him not,
       Is of a constant, loving, noble nature,
       And I dare think he'll prove to Desdemona
       A most dear[6] husband. Now I do love her too;
       Not out of absolute[7] lust, though peradventure[8]
260   I stand accountant for as great a sin,
       But partly led to diet[9] my revenge,
       For that I do suspect the lusty Moor
       Hath leaped into my seat; the thought whereof
       Doth, like a poisonous mineral, gnaw my inwards;
265   And nothing can or shall content my soul
       Till I am evened with him, wife for wife.
       Or failing so, yet that I put the Moor
       At least into a jealousy so strong
       That judgment cannot cure. Which thing to do,
270   If this poor trash of Venice, whom I trace[10]
       For his quick hunting, stand the putting on,
       I'll have our Michael Cassio on the hip,
       Abuse him to the Moor in the right garb[11]

---

[1]pointer   [2]carnal   [3]discrediting   [4]anger   [5]*qualification . . . taste* i.e., appeasement will not
be brought about (wine was "qualified" by adding water)   [6]expensive   [7]*out of absolute*
absolutely out of   [8]perchance   [9]feed   [10](most editors emend to "trash," meaning to hang
weights on a dog to slow his hunting: but "trace" clearly means something like "put on the trace"
or "set on the track"   [11]*right garb* i.e., "proper fashion"

·

(For I fear Cassio with my nightcap too),
275 Make the Moor thank me, love me, and reward me
For making him egregiously an ass
And practicing upon¹ his peace and quiet,
Even to madness. 'Tis here, but yet confused:
Knavery's plain face is never seen till used.   *Exit.*

Scene II. [*A street.*]

Enter OTHELLO'S HERALD, *with a proclamation.*

HERALD It is Othello's pleasure, our noble and valiant general, that upon certain
tidings now arrived importing the mere perdition² of the Turkish fleet, every
man put himself into triumph. Some to dance, some to make bonfires, each
man to what sport and revels his addition³ leads him. For, besides these ben-
5 eficial news, it is the celebration of his nuptial. So much was his pleasure should
be proclaimed. All offices⁴ are open, and there is full liberty of feasting from this
present hour of five till the bell have told eleven. Bless the isle of Cyprus and
our noble general Othello!   *Exit.*

Scene III. [*The citadel of Cyprus.*]

Enter OTHELLO, DESDEMONA, CASSIO, *and* ATTENDANTS.

OTHELLO Good Michael, look you to the guard tonight.
Let's teach ourselves that honorable stop,
Not to outsport direction.
CASSIO Iago hath discretion what to do;
5 But notwithstanding, with my personal eye
Will I look to't.
OTHELLO   Iago is most honest.
Michael, good night. Tomorrow with your earliest
Let me have speech with you. [*To* DESDEMONA] Come, my dear love,
The purchase made, the fruits are to ensue.
10 That profit's yet to come 'tween me and you.
Good night.   *Exit* [OTHELLO *with* DESDEMONA *and* ATTENDANTS].

Enter IAGO.

CASSIO Welcome, Iago. We must to the watch.
IAGO Not this hour, lieutenant; 'tis not yet ten o' th' clock. Our general cast⁵ us
thus early for the love of his Desdemona; who let us not therefore blame. He
15 hath not yet made wanton the night with her, and she is sport for Jove.
CASSIO She's a most exquisite lady.
IAGO And, I'll warrant her, full of game.
CASSIO Indeed, she's a most fresh and delicate creature.
IAGO What an eye she has! Methinks it sounds a parley to provocation.
20 CASSIO An inviting eye; and yet methinks right modest.

---

¹*practicing upon* scheming to destroy.   ²*mere perdition* absolute destruction   ³rank
⁴kitchens and storerooms of food   ⁵dismissed

IAGO And when she speaks, is it not an alarum[1] to love?

CASSIO She is indeed perfection.

IAGO Well, happiness to their sheets! Come, lieutenant, I have a stoup[2] of wine, and here without are a brace of Cyprus gallants that would fain have a measure
25   to the health of black Othello.

CASSIO Not tonight, good Iago. I have very poor and unhappy brains for drinking; I could well wish courtesy would invent some other custom of entertainment.

IAGO O they are our friends. But one cup! I'll drink for you.

CASSIO I have drunk but one tonight, and that was craftily qualified[3] too; and
30   behold what innovation it makes here. I am unfortunate in the infirmity and dare not task my weakness with any more.

IAGO What, man! 'Tis a night of revels, the gallants desire it.

CASSIO Where are they?

IAGO Here, at the door. I pray you call them in.

35 CASSIO I'll do't, but it dislikes me.   *Exit.*

IAGO If I can fasten but one cup upon him
With that which he hath drunk tonight already,
He'll be as full of quarrel and offense
As my young mistress' dog. Now, my sick fool Roderigo,
40   Whom love hath turned almost the wrong side out,
To Desdemona hath tonight caroused
Potations pottle-deep;[4] and he's to watch.
Three else[5] of Cyprus, noble swelling spirits,
That hold their honors in a wary distance,[6]
45   The very elements of this warlike isle,
Have I tonight flustered with flowing cups,
And they watch too. Now, 'mongst this flock of drunkards
And I to put our Cassio in some action
That may offend the isle. But here they come.

Enter CASSIO, MONTANO, *and* GENTLEMEN.

50   If consequence do but approve my dream
My boat sails freely, both with wind and stream.

CASSIO 'Fore God, they have given me a rouse[7] already.

MONTANO Good faith, a little one; not past a pint, as I am a soldier.

IAGO Some wine, ho!
55   [*Sings*] And let me the canakin clink, clink;
            And let me the canakin clink.
              A soldier's a man;
              O man's life's but a span.
              Why then, let a soldier drink.
60   Some wine, boys!

CASSIO 'Fore God, an excellent song!

IAGO I learned it in England, where indeed they are most potent in potting. Your Dane, your German, and your swag-bellied[8] Hollander—Drink, ho!—are nothing to your English.

---

[1]the call to action, "general quarters"   [2]two-quart tankard   [3]diluted   [4]to the bottom of the cup   [5]others   [6]*hold ... distance* are scrupulous in maintaining their honor   [7]drink   [8]pendulous-bellied

65   CASSIO Is your Englishman so exquisite[1] in his drinking?

      IAGO Why, he drinks you with facility your Dane dead drunk; he sweats not to overthrow your Almain; he gives your Hollander a vomit ere the next pottle can be filled.

      CASSIO To the health of our general!

70   MONTANO I am for it, lieutenant, and I'll do you justice.

      IAGO O sweet England!

      [*Sings*] King Stephen was and a worthy peer;
                      His breeches cost him but a crown;
                      He held them sixpence all too dear,
75   With that he called the tailor lown.[2]
                      He was a wight of high renown,
                      And thou art but of low degree:
                      'Tis pride that pulls the country down;
                      And take thine auld cloak about thee.

80   Some wine, ho!

      CASSIO 'Fore God, this is a more exquisite song than the other.

      IAGO Will you hear't again?

      CASSIO No, for I hold him to be unworthy of his place that does those things. Well, God's above all; and there be souls must be saved, and there be souls

85   must not be saved.

      IAGO It's true, good lieutenant.

      CASSIO For mine own part—no offense to the general, nor any man of quality—I hope to be saved.

      IAGO And so do I too, lieutenant.

90   CASSIO Ay, but, by your leave, not before me. The lieutenant is to be saved before the ancient. Let's have no more of this; let's to our affairs.—God forgive us our sins!—Gentlemen, let's look to our business. Do not think, gentlemen, I am drunk. This is my ancient; this is my right hand, and this is my left. I am not drunk now. I can stand well enough, and I speak well enough.

95   GENTLEMEN Excellent well!

      CASSIO Why, very well then. You must not think then that I am drunk.

                                                                            Exit.

      MONTANO To th' platform, masters. Come, let's set the watch.

      IAGO You see this fellow that is gone before.
      He's a soldier fit to stand by Caesar
100   And give direction; and do but see his vice.
      'Tis to his virtue a just equinox,[3]
      The one as long as th' other. 'Tis pity of him.
      I fear the trust Othello puts him in,
      On some odd time of his infirmity,
      Will shake this island.

105   MONTANO   But is he often thus?

      IAGO 'Tis evermore his prologue to his sleep:
      He'll watch the horologe a double set[4]
      If drink rock not his cradle.

---

[1]superb   [2]lout   [3]*just equinox* exact balance (of dark and light)   [4]*watch . . . set* stay awake twice around the clock

MONTANO   It were well
The general were put in mind of it.
110   Perhaps he sees it not, or his good nature
Prizes the virtue that appears in Cassio
And looks not on his evils. Is not this true?

Enter RODERIGO.

IAGO [*Aside*] How now, Roderigo?
I pray you after the lieutenant, go!   [*Exit* RODERIGO.]
115   MONTANO And 'tis great pity that the noble Moor
Should hazard such a place as his own second
With one of an ingraft[1] infirmity.
It were an honest action to say so
To the Moor.
IAGO   Not I, for this fair island!
120   I do love Cassio well and would do much
To cure him of this evil.   (Help! Help! *Within.*)
But hark! What noise?

Enter CASSIO, *pursuing* RODERIGO.

CASSIO Zounds, you rogue! You rascal!
MONTANO What's the matter, lieutenant?
CASSIO A knave teach me my duty? I'll beat the knave into a twiggen[2] bottle.
125   RODERIGO Beat me?
CASSIO Dost thou prate, rogue?   [*Strikes him.*]
MONTANO Nay, good lieutenant! I pray you, sir, hold your hand.

                                                    [*Stays him.*]

CASSIO Let me go, sir, or I'll knock you o'er the mazzard.[3]
MONTANO Come, come, you're drunk!
130   CASSIO Drunk?   [*They fight.*]
IAGO [*Aside to* RODERIGO] Away, I say! Go out and cry a mutiny!

                                                    [*Exit* RODERIGO]

Nay, good lieutenant. God's will, gentlemen!
Help, ho! Lieutenant. Sir. Montano.
Help, masters! Here's a goodly watch indeed!   [*A bell rung.*]
135   Who's that which rings the bell? Diablo, ho!
The town will rise. God's will, lieutenant,
You'll be ashamed forever.

Enter OTHELLO *and* ATTENDANTS.

OTHELLO   What is the matter here?
MONTANO Zounds, I bleed still. I am hurt to the death.
He dies.   [*He and* CASSIO *fight again.*]
140   OTHELLO Hold for your lives!
IAGO Hold, ho! Lieutenant. Sir. Montano. Gentlemen!

[1]ingrained   [2]wicker-covered   [3]head

Have you forgot all place of sense and duty?
Hold! The general speaks to you. Hold, for shame!
OTHELLO　Why, how now, ho? From whence ariseth this?
145　Are we turned Turks, and to ourselves do that
Which heaven hath forbid the Ottomites?[1]
For Christian shame put by this barbarous brawl!
He that stirs next to carve for his own rage
Holds his soul light;[2] he dies upon his motion.
150　Silence that dreadful bell! It frights the isle
From her propriety.[3] What is the matter, masters?
Honest Iago, that looks dead with grieving,
Speak. Who began this? On thy love, I charge thee.
IAGO　I do not know. Friends all, but now, even now,
155　In quarter[4] and in terms like bride and groom
Devesting them for bed; and then, but now—
As if some planet had unwitted men—
Swords out, and tilting one at other's breasts
In opposition bloody. I cannot speak
160　Any beginning to this peevish odds,[5]
And would in action glorious I had lost
These legs that brought me to a part of it!
OTHELLO　How comes it, Michael, you are thus forgot?
CASSIO　I pray you pardon me; I cannot speak.
165　OTHELLO　Worthy Montano, you were wont to be civil;
Thy gravity and stillness of your youth
The world hath noted, and your name is great
In mouths of wisest censure.[6] What's the matter
That you unlace[7] your reputation thus
170　And spend your rich opinion[8] for the name
Of a night-brawler? Give me answer to it.
MONTANO　Worthy Othello, I am hurt to danger.
Your officer, Iago, can inform you.
While I spare speech, which something now offends[9] me,
175　Of all that I do know; nor know I aught
By me that's said or done amiss this night,
Unless self-charity be sometimes a vice,
And to defend ourselves it be a sin
When violence assails us.
OTHELLO　　　　　　　　　　Now, by heaven,
180　My blood begins my safer guides to rule,
And passion, having my best judgment collied,[10]
Assays to lead the way. If I once stir
Or do but lift this arm, the best of you
Shall sink in my rebuke. Give me to know
185　How this foul rout began, who set it on;

---

[1]*heaven . . . Ottomites* i.e., by sending the storm which dispersed the Turks　　[2]*Holds his soul light* values his soul lightly　　[3]proper order　　[4]*In quarter* on duty　　[5]quarrel　　[6]judgment　　[7]undo (the term refers specifically to the dressing of a wild boar killed in the hunt)　　[8]reputation　　[9]harms, hurts　　[10]darkened

      And he that is approved in this offense,
      Though he had twinned with me, both at a birth,
      Shall lose me. What? In a town of war
      Yet wild, the people's hearts brimful of fear,
190   To manage[1] private and domestic quarrel?
      In night, and on the count and guard of safety?
      'Tis monstrous. Iago, who began't?
    MONTANO If partially affined, or leagued in office,[2]
      Thou dost deliver more or less than truth,
      Thou art no soldier.
195   IAGO   Touch me not so near.
      I had rather have this tongue cut from my mouth
      Than it should do offense to Michael Cassio.
      Yet I persuade myself to speak the truth
      Shall nothing wrong him. This it is, general.
200   Montano and myself being in speech,
      There comes a fellow crying out for help,
      And Cassio following him with determined sword
      To execute upon him. Sir, this gentleman
      Steps in to Cassio and entreats his pause.
205   Myself the crying fellow did pursue,
      Lest by his clamor—as it so fell out—
      The town might fall in fright. He, swift of foot,
      Outran my purpose; and I returned then rather
      For that I heard the clink and fall of swords,
210   And Cassio high in oath; which till tonight
      I ne'er might say before. When I came back—
      For this was brief—I found them close together
      At blow and thrust, even as again they were
      When you yourself did part them.
215   More of this matter cannot I report;
      But men are men; the best sometimes forget.
      Though Cassio did some little wrong to him,
      As men in rage strike those that wish them best,
      Yet surely Cassio I believe received
220   From him that fled some strange indignity,
      Which patience could not pass.[3]
    OTHELLO   I know, Iago,
      Thy honesty and love doth mince[4] this matter,
      Making it light to Cassio. Cassio, I love thee;
      But never more be officer of mine.

     Enter DESDEMONA, *attended.*

225   Look if my gentle love be not raised up.
      I'll make thee an example.
    DESDEMONA   What is the matter, dear?
    OTHELLO All's well, sweeting; come away to bed.

---

[1]conduct
(of Cassio)   [2]*If . . . office* if you are partial because you are related ("affined") or the brother officer   [3]allow to pass   [4]cut up (i.e., tell only part of).

[*To* MONTANO] Sir, for your hurts, myself will be your surgeon.
Lead him off.

                                                 [MONTANO *led off.*]

230 Iago, look with care about the town
     And silence those whom this vile brawl distracted.
     Come, Desdemona: 'tis the soldiers' life
     To have their balmy slumbers waked with strife.

                          Exit [*with all but* IAGO *and* CASSIO].

     IAGO What, are you hurt, lieutenant?
235 CASSIO Ay, past all surgery.
     IAGO Marry, God forbid!
     CASSIO Reputation, reputation, reputation! O, I have lost my reputation! I have
        lost the immortal part of myself, and what remains is bestial. My reputation,
        Iago, my reputation.
240 IAGO As I am an honest man, I had thought you had received some bodily wound.
        There is more sense[1] in that than in reputation. Reputation is an idle and most
        false imposition,[2] oft got without merit and lost without deserving. You have
        lost no reputation at all unless you repute yourself such a loser. What, man,
        there are more ways to recover the general again. You are but now cast in his
245   mood[3]—a punishment more in policy[4] than in malice—even so as one would
        beat his offenseless dog to affright an imperious lion. Sue to him again, and he's
        yours.
     CASSIO I will rather sue to be despised than to deceive so good a commander
        with so slight, so drunken, and so indiscreet an officer. Drunk! And speak
250   parrot![5] And squabble! Swagger! Sweat! and discourse fustian[6] with one's own
        shadow! O thou invisible spirit of wine, if thou hast no name to be known by,
        let us call thee devil!
     IAGO What was he that you followed with your sword?
        What had he done to you?
255 CASSIO I know not.
     IAGO Is't possible?
     CASSIO I remember a mass of things, but nothing distinctly: a quarrel, but noth-
        ing wherefore. O God, that men should put an enemy in their mouths to steal
        away their brains! that we should with joy, pleasance, revel, and applause trans-
260   form ourselves into beasts!
     IAGO Why, but you are now well enough. How came you thus recovered?
     CASSIO It hath pleased the devil drunkenness to give place to the devil wrath.
        One unperfectness shows me another, to make me frankly despise myself.
     IAGO Come, you are too severe a moraler. As the time, the place, and the con-
265   dition of this country stands, I could heartily wish this had not befall'n; but
        since it is as it is, mend it for your own good.
     CASSIO I will ask him for my place again: he shall tell me I am a drunkard. Had
        I as many mouths as Hydra, such an answer would stop them all. To be now
        a sensible man, by and by a fool, and presently a beast! O strange! Every inor-
270   dinate cup is unblest, and the ingredient is a devil.

---

[1]*physical feeling*   [2]*external thing*   [3]*cast in his mood* dismissed because of his anger   [4]*in
policy* politically necessary   [5]*speak parrot* gabble without sense   [6]*discourse fustian* speak
nonsense ("fustian" was a coarse cotton cloth used for stuffing)

IAGO Come, come, good wine is a good familiar creature if it be well used. Exclaim no more against it. And, good lieutenant, I think you think I love you.

CASSIO I have well approved it, sir. I drunk?

IAGO You or any man living may be drunk at a time, man. I tell you what you

275   shall do. Our general's wife is now the general. I may say so in this respect, for all he hath devoted and given up himself to the contemplation, mark, and devotement of her parts[1] and graces. Confess yourself freely to her; importune her help to put you in your place again. She is of so free, so kind, so apt, so blessed a disposition she holds it a vice in her goodness not to do more than she is

280   requested. This broken joint between you and her husband entreat her to splinter;[2] and my fortunes against any lay[3] worth naming, this crack of your love shall grow stronger than it was before.

CASSIO You advise me well.

IAGO I protest, in the sincerity of love and honest kindness.

285 CASSIO I think it freely; and betimes in the morning I will beseech the virtuous Desdemona to undertake for me. I am desperate of my fortunes if they check[4] me.

IAGO You are in the right. Good night, lieutenant; I must to the watch.

CASSIO Good night, honest Iago.

                                                            Exit CASSIO.

290 IAGO And what's he then that says I play the villain,
     When this advice is free[5] I give, and honest,
     Probal to[6] thinking, and indeed the course
     To win the Moor again? For 'tis most easy
     Th' inclining[7] Desdemona to subdue

295   In any honest suit; she's framed as fruitful[8]
     As the free elements.[9] And then for her
     To win the Moor—were't to renounce his baptism,
     All seals and symbols of redeemèd sin—
     His soul is so enfettered to her love

300   That she may make, unmake, do what she list,
     Even as her appetite[10] shall play the god
     With his weak function.[11] How am I then a villain
     To counsel Cassio to this parallel course,
     Directly to his good? Divinity of hell!

305   When devils will the blackest sins put on,[12]
     They do suggest at first with heavenly shows,[13]
     As I do now. For whiles this honest fool
     Plies Desdemona to repair his fortune,
     And she for him pleads strongly to the Moor,

310   I'll pour this pestilence into his ear:
     That she repeals him[14] for her body's lust;
     And by how much she strives to do him good,
     She shall undo her credit with the Moor.
     So will I turn her virtue into pitch,

---

[1]*devotement of her parts* devotion to her qualities   [2]splint   [3]wager   [4]repulse   [5]generous and open   [6]*Probal to* provable by   [7]inclined (to be helpful)   [8]*framed as fruitful* made as generous   [9]i.e., basic nature   [10]liking   [11]thought   [12]*put on* advance, further   [13]appearances   [14]*repeals him* asks for (Cassio's reinstatement)

315 And out of her own goodness make the net
  That shall enmesh them all. How now, Roderigo?   *Enter* RODERIGO.
  RODERIGO I do not follow here in the chase, not like a hound that hunts, but
  one that fills up the cry.[1] My money is almost spent; I have been tonight ex-
  ceedingly well cudgeled; and I think the issue will be, I shall have so much
320 experience for my pains; and so, with no money at all, and a little more wit,
  return again to Venice.
  IAGO How poor are they that have not patience!
  What wound did ever heal but by degrees?
  Thou know'st we work by wit, and not by witchcraft;
325 And wit depends on dilatory time.
  Does't not go well? Cassio hath beaten thee,
  And thou by that small hurt hath cashiered Cassio.
  Though other things grow fair against the sun,
  Yet fruits that blossom first will first be ripe.
330 Content thyself awhile. By the mass, 'tis morning!
  Pleasure and action make the hours seem short.
  Retire thee, go where thou art billeted.
  Away, I say! Thou shalt know more hereafter.
  Nay, get thee gone!   *Exit* RODERIGO.

335 Two things are to be done:
  My wife must move[2] for Cassio to her mistress;
  I'll set her on;
  Myself awhile[3] to draw the Moor apart
  And bring him jump[4] when he may Cassio find
340 Soliciting his wife. Ay, that's the way!
  Dull not device by coldness and delay.   *Exit.*

Act III, Scene I. [*A street.*]

  Enter CASSIO [*and*] MUSICIANS.

  CASSIO Masters, play here. I will content your pains.[5]
  Something that's brief; and bid "Good morrow, general." [*They play.*]

  [*Enter* CLOWN.[6]]

  CLOWN Why, masters, have your instruments been in Naples[7] that they speak i'
  th' nose thus?
5 MUSICIAN How, sir, how?
  CLOWN Are these, I pray you, wind instruments?
  MUSICIAN Ay, marry, are they, sir.
  CLOWN O, thereby hangs a tale.
  MUSICIAN Whereby hangs a tale, sir?
10 CLOWN Marry, sir, by many a wind instrument that I know. But, masters, here's

---

[1]*fills up the cry* makes up one of the hunting pack, adding to the noise but not actually tracking [2]petition [3]at the same time [4]at the precise moment and place [5]*content your pains* reward your efforts [6]fool [7]this may refer either to the Neapolitan nasal tone, or to syphilis—rife in Naples—which breaks down the nose

money for you; and the general so likes your music that he desires you, for
love's sake, to make no more noise with it.

MUSICIAN Well, sir, we will not.

CLOWN If you have any music that may not be heard, to't again. But, as they say,
15   to hear music the general does not greatly care.

MUSICIAN We have none such, sir.

CLOWN Then put up your pipes in your bag, for I'll away. Go, vanish into air,
away!   *Exit* MUSICIANS.

CASSIO Dost thou hear me, mine honest friend?

20   CLOWN No. I hear not your honest friend. I hear you.

CASSIO Prithee keep up thy quillets.[1] There's a poor piece of gold for thee. If the
gentlewoman that attends the general's wife be stirring, tell her there's one
Cassio entreats her a little favor of speech. Wilt thou do this?

CLOWN She is stirring, sir. If she will stir hither, I shall seem to notify unto
25   her.[2]   *Exit* CLOWN.

Enter IAGO.

CASSIO In happy time, Iago.

IAGO   You have not been abed then?

CASSIO Why no, the day had broke before we parted.
I have made bold, Iago, to send in to your wife;
My suit to her is that she will to virtuous Desdemona
Procure me some access.

30   IAGO   I'll send her to you presently,
And I'll devise a mean to draw the Moor
Out of the way, that your converse and business
May be more free.

CASSIO I humbly thank you for't.   *Exit* [IAGO].

35   I never knew
A Florentine[3] more kind and honest.

Enter EMILIA.

EMILIA Good morrow, good lieutenant. I am sorry
For your displeasure;[4] but all will sure be well.
The general and his wife are talking of it,
40   And she speaks for you stoutly. The Moor replies
That he you hurt is of great fame in Cyprus
And great affinity,[5] and that in wholesome wisdom
He might not but refuse you. But he protests he loves you.
And needs no other suitor but his likings
To bring you in again.

45   CASSIO   Yet I beseech you,
If you think fit, or that it may be done,
Give me advantage of some brief discourse
With Desdemona alone.

EMILIA   Pray you come in.

---

[1]puns   [2]*seem . . . her* (the Clown is mocking Cassio's overly elegant manner of speaking)
[3]i.e., Iago is as kind as if he were from Cassio's home town, Florence   [4]discomforting   [5]family

50
I will bestow you where you shall have time
To speak your bosom[1] freely.
CASSIO   I am much bound to you.   *Exeunt.*

Scene II. [*The citadel.*]

Enter OTHELLO, IAGO, *and* GENTLEMEN.

OTHELLO   These letters give, Iago, to the pilot
And by him do my duties to the Senate.
That done, I will be walking on the works;
Repair[2] there to me.
IAGO   Well, my good lord, I'll do't.
5   OTHELLO   This fortification, gentlemen, shall we see't?
GENTLEMEN   We'll wait upon your lordship.   *Exeunt.*

Scene III. [*The citadel.*]

Enter DESDEMONA, CASSIO, *and* EMILIA.

DESDEMONA   Be thou assured, good Cassio, I will do
All my abilities in thy behalf.
EMILIA   Good madam, do. I warrant it grieves my husband
As if the cause were his.
5   DESDEMONA   O, that's an honest fellow. Do not doubt, Cassio,
But I will have my lord and you again
As friendly as you were.
CASSIO   Bounteous madam,
Whatever shall become of Michael Cassio,
He's never anything but your true servant.
10   DESDEMONA   I know't; I thank you. You do love my lord.
You have known him long, and be you well assured
He shall in strangeness stand no farther off
Than in a politic distance.[3]
CASSIO   Ay, but, lady,
That policy may either last so long,
15   Or feed upon such nice[4] and waterish diet,
Or breed itself so out of circumstances,[5]
That, I being absent, and my place supplied,[6]
My general will forget my love and service.
DESDEMONA   Do not doubt[7] that; before Emilia here
20   I give thee warrant of thy place. Assure thee,
If I do vow a friendship, I'll perform it
To the last article. My lord shall never rest;
I'll watch him tame[8] and talk him out of patience;

---

[1]inmost thoughts   [2]go   [3]*He . . . distance* i.e., he shall act no more distant to you than is necessary for political reasons   [4]trivial   [5]*Or . . . circumstances* i.e., or grow so on the basis of accidental happenings and political needs   [6]filled   [7]imagine   [8]*watch him tame* (animals were tamed by being kept awake)

His bed shall seem a school, his board a shrift;[1]
25 I'll intermingle everything he does
With Cassio's suit. Therefore be merry, Cassio,
For thy solicitor shall rather die
Than give thy cause away.

Enter OTHELLO *and* IAGO [*at a distance*].

EMILIA Madam, here comes my lord.
30 CASSIO Madam, I'll take my leave.
DESDEMONA Why, stay, and hear me speak.
CASSIO Madam, not now. I am very ill at ease,
    Unfit for mine own purposes.
DESDEMONA Well, do your discretion.   *Exit* CASSIO.
IAGO Ha! I like not that.
35 OTHELLO   What dost thou say?
IAGO Nothing, my lord; or if—I know not what.
OTHELLO Was not that Cassio parted from my wife?
IAGO Cassio, my lord? No, sure, I cannot think it
    That he would steal away so guilty-like,
    Seeing you coming.
40 OTHELLO   I do believe 'twas he.
DESDEMONA [*Coming to them*] How now, my lord?
    I have been talking with a suitor here,
    A man that languishes in your displeasure.
OTHELLO Who is't you mean?
45 DESDEMONA Why, your lieutenant, Cassio. Good my lord,
    If I have any grace or power to move you,
    His present[2] reconciliation take.
    For if he be not one that truly loves you,
    That errs in ignorance, and not in cunning,
50 I have no judgment in an honest face.
    I prithee call him back.
OTHELLO   Went he hence now?
DESDEMONA I' sooth so humbled
    That he hath left part of his grief with me
    To suffer with him. Good love, call him back.
55 OTHELLO Not now, sweet Desdemon; some other time.
DESDEMONA But shall't be shortly?
OTHELLO   The sooner, sweet, for you.
DESDEMONA Shall't be tonight at supper?
OTHELLO   No, not tonight.
DESDEMONA Tomorrow dinner then?
OTHELLO   I shall not dine at home;
    I meet the captains at the citadel.
60 DESDEMONA Why then, tomorrow night, on Tuesday morn,
    On Tuesday noon, or night, on Wednesday morn.
    I prithee name the time, but let it not
    Exceed three days. In faith, he's penitent;

---

[1]*board a shrift* table (seem) a confessional   [2]immediate

And yet his trespass, in our common reason
65 (Save that, they say, the wars must make example
Out of her best), is not almost a fault
T' incur a private check.[1] When shall he come?
Tell me, Othello. I wonder in my soul
What you would ask me that I should deny
70 Or stand so mamm'ring[2] on. What? Michael Cassio,
That came awooing with you, and so many a time,
When I have spoke of you dispraisingly,
Hath ta'en your part—to have so much to do
To bring him in? By'r Lady, I could do much—
75 OTHELLO Prithee no more. Let him come when he will!
I will deny thee nothing.
DESDEMONA   Why, this is not a boon;
'Tis as I should entreat you wear your gloves,
Or feed on nourishing dishes, or keep you warm,
Or sue to you to do a peculiar profit[3]
80 To your own person. Nay, when I have a suit
Wherein I mean to touch your love indeed,
It shall be full of poise[4] and difficult weight,
And fearful to be granted.
OTHELLO   I will deny thee nothing!
Whereon I do beseech thee grant me this,
85 To leave me but a little to myself.
DESDEMONA Shall I deny you? No. Farewell, my lord.
OTHELLO Farewell, my Desdemona: I'll come to thee straight.[5]
DESDEMONA Emilia, come. Be as your fancies teach you;
Whate'er you be, I am obedient.   *Exit [with* EMILIA *]*.
90 OTHELLO Excellent wretch! Perdition catch my soul
But I do love thee! And when I love thee not,
Chaos is come again.
IAGO My noble lord—
OTHELLO   What dost thou say, Iago?
IAGO Did Michael Cassio, when you wooed my lady,
95 Know of your love?
OTHELLO He did, from first to last. Why dost thou ask?
IAGO But for a satisfaction of my thought,
No further harm.
OTHELLO   Why of thy thought, Iago?
IAGO I did not think he had been acquainted with her.
100 OTHELLO O, yes, and went between us[6] very oft.
IAGO Indeed?
OTHELLO Indeed? Ay, indeed! Discern'st thou aught in that?
Is he not honest?
IAGO   Honest, my lord?
OTHELLO   Honest? Ay, honest.

---

[1]*is . . . check* is almost not serious enough for a private rebuke (let alone a public disgrace)
[2]hesitating   [3]*peculiar profit* particularly personal good   [4]weight   [5]at once   [6]*between us* i.e.,
as messenger

IAGO My lord, for aught I know.

OTHELLO What dost thou think?

IAGO   Think, my lord?

105 OTHELLO   Think, my lord?
By heaven, thou echoest me,
As if there were some monster in thy thought
Too hideous to be shown. Thou dost mean something.
I heard thee say even now, thou lik'st not that,
110 When Cassio left my wife. What didst not like?
And when I told thee he was of my counsel[1]
Of my whole course of wooing, thou cried'st "Indeed?"
And didst contract and purse thy brow together,
As if thou then hadst shut up in thy brain
115 Some horrible conceit.[2] If thou dost love me,
Show me thy thought.

IAGO My lord, you know I love you.

OTHELLO   I think thou dost;
And, for I know thou'rt full of love and honesty
And weigh'st thy words before thou giv'st them breath,
120 Therefore these stops[3] of thine fright me the more;
For such things in a false disloyal knave
Are tricks of custom;[4] but in a man that's just
They're close dilations,[5] working from the heart
That passion cannot rule.

IAGO   For Michael Cassio,
125 I dare be sworn, I think that he is honest.

OTHELLO I think so too.

IAGO   Men should be what they seem;
Or those that be not, would they might seem none!

OTHELLO Certain, men should be what they seem.

IAGO Why then; I think Cassio's an honest man.

130 OTHELLO Nay, yet there's more in this?
I prithee speak to me as to thy thinkings,
As thou dost ruminate, and give thy worst of thoughts
The worst of words.

IAGO   Good my lord, pardon me:
Though I am bound to every act of duty,
135 I am not bound to that all slaves are free to.
Utter my thoughts? Why, say they are vile and false,
As where's that place whereinto foul things
Sometimes intrude not? Who has that breast so pure
But some uncleanly apprehensions
140 Keep leets and law days,[6] and in sessions sit
With meditations lawful?

OTHELLO Thou dost conspire against thy friend, Iago,
If thou but think'st him wronged, and mak'st this ear
A stranger to thy thoughts.

---

[1]*of my counsel* in my confidence   [2]*thought*   [3]*interruptions*   [4]*of custom* customary   [5]*close*
dilations expressions of hidden thoughts   [6]*leets and law days* meetings of local courts

IAGO   I do beseech you—
145   Though I perchance am vicious in my guess
       (As I confess it is my nature's plague
       To spy into abuses, and of my jealousy
       Shape faults that are not), that your wisdom
       From one that so imperfectly conceits
150   Would take no notice, nor build yourself a trouble
       Out of his scattering and unsure observance.
       It were not for your quiet nor your good,
       Nor for my manhood, honesty, and wisdom,
       To let you know my thoughts.
       OTHELLO   What dost thou mean?
155   IAGO Good name in man and woman, dear my lord,
       Is the immediate jewel of their souls.
       Who steals my purse steals trash; 'tis something, nothing;
       'Twas mine, 'tis his, and has been slave to thousands;
       But he that filches from me my good name
160   Robs me of that which not enriches him
       And makes me poor indeed.
       OTHELLO By heaven, I'll know thy thoughts!
       IAGO You cannot, if my heart were in your hand;
       Nor shall not whilst 'tis in my custody.
       OTHELLO Ha!
165   IAGO   O, beware, my lord, of jealousy!
       It is the green-eyed monster, which doth mock
       The meat it feeds on. That cuckold lives in bliss
       Who, certain of his fate, loves not his wronger;
       But O, what damnèd minutes tells[1] he o'er
170   Who dotes, yet doubts—suspects, yet fondly[2] loves!
       OTHELLO O misery.
       IAGO Poor and content is rich, and rich enough;
       But riches fineless[3] is as poor as winter
       To him that ever fears he shall be poor.
175   Good God the souls of all my tribe defend.
       From jealousy!
       OTHELLO   Why? Why is this?
       Think'st thou I'd make a life of jealousy,
       To follow still[4] the changes of the moon
       With fresh suspicions? No! To be once in doubt
180   Is to be resolved. Exchange me for a goat
       When I shall turn the business of my soul
       To such exsufflicate and blown[5] surmises,
       Matching thy inference. 'Tis not to make me jealous
       To say my wife is fair, feeds well, loves company,
185   Is free of speech, sings, plays, and dances;
       Where virtue is, these are more virtuous.
       Nor from mine own weak merits will I draw

---

[1]counts   [2]foolishly   [3]infinite   [4]*To follow still* to change always (as the phases of the moon)   [5]*exsufflicate and blown* inflated and flyblown

The smallest fear or doubt of her revolt,
For she had eyes, and chose me. No, Iago;
190   I'll see before I doubt; when I doubt, prove;
And on the proof there is no more but this:
Away at once with love or jealousy!

IAGO I am glad of this; for now I shall have reason
To show the love and duty that I bear you
195   With franker spirit. Therefore, as I am bound,
Receive it from me. I speak not yet of proof.
Look to your wife; observe her well with Cassio;
Wear your eyes thus: not jealous nor secure.
I would not have your free and noble nature
200   Out of self-bounty[1] be abused. Look to't.
I know our country disposition well:
In Venice they do let heaven see the pranks
They dare not show their husbands; their best conscience
Is not to leave't undone, but kept unknown.[2]
205   OTHELLO Dost thou say so?

IAGO She did deceive her father, marrying you;
And when she seemed to shake and fear your looks,
She loved them most.

OTHELLO   And so she did.

IAGO   Why, go to then!
She that so young could give out such a seeming
210   To seel[3] her father's eyes up close as oak[4]—
He thought 'twas witchcraft. But I am much to blame.
I humbly do beseech you of your pardon
For too much loving you.

OTHELLO   I am bound to thee forever.

IAGO I see this hath a little dashed your spirits.

OTHELLO Not a jot, not a jot.

215   IAGO   Trust me, I fear it has.
I hope you will consider what is spoke
Comes from my love. But I do see y' are moved.
I am to pray you not to strain[5] my speech
To grosser issues nor to larger reach[6]
220   Than to suspicion.

OTHELLO I will not.

IAGO   Should you do so, my lord,
My speech should fall into such vile success
Which my thoughts aimed not. Cassio's my worthy friend—
My lord, I see y' are moved.

OTHELLO   No, not much moved.
225   I do not think but Desdemona's honest.

IAGO Long live she so. And long live you to think so.

OTHELLO And yet, how nature erring from itself—

---

[1]innate kindness (which attributes his own motives to others)   [2]*their . . . unknown* i.e., their morality does not forbid adultery, but it does forbid being found out   [3]hoodwink   [4]a close-grained wood   [5]enlarge the meaning   [6]meaning

IAGO Ay, there's the point, as (to be bold with you)
　　　　Not to affect many proposèd matches
230　　　Of her own clime, complexion, and degree,[1]
　　　　Whereto we see in all things nature tends[2]—
　　　　Foh! One may smell in such a will most rank,
　　　　Foul disproportions, thoughts unnatural.
　　　　But, pardon me, I do not in position[3]
235　　　Distinctly[4] speak of her; though I may fear
　　　　Her will, recoiling to her better judgment,
　　　　May fall to match[5] you with her country forms,[6]
　　　　And happily[7] repent.
OTHELLO　　　　　　　　Farewell, farewell!
　　　　If more thou dost perceive, let me know more.
240　　　Set on thy wife to observe. Leave me, Iago.
IAGO My lord, I take my leave.　　　　　　　　　　　　　　*Going.*
OTHELLO Why did I marry? This honest creature doubtless
　　　　Sees and knows more, much more, than he unfolds.
IAGO [*Returns*] My lord, I would I might entreat your honor
245　　　To scan this thing no farther. Leave it to time.
　　　　Although 'tis fit that Cassio have his place,
　　　　For sure he fills it up with great ability,
　　　　Yet, if you please to hold him off awhile,
　　　　You shall by that perceive him and his means.
250　　　Note if your lady strains his entertainment[8]
　　　　With any strong or vehement importunity;
　　　　Much will be seen in that. In the meantime
　　　　Let me be thought too busy in my fears
　　　　(As worthy cause I have to fear I am)
255　　　And hold her free, I do beseech your honor.
OTHELLO Fear not my government.[9]
IAGO　　　　　　　　　　　I once more take my leave.　　　　*Exit.*
OTHELLO This fellow's of exceeding honesty,
　　　　And knows all qualities,[10] with a learnèd spirit
　　　　Of human dealings. If I do prove her haggard,[11]
260　　　Though that her jesses[12] were my dear heartstrings,
　　　　I'd whistle her off and let her down the wind[13]
　　　　To prey at fortune. Haply for[14] I am black
　　　　And have not those soft parts[15] of conversation
　　　　That chamberers[16] have, or for I am declined
265　　　Into the vale of years—yet that's not much—
　　　　She's gone. I am abused, and my relief
　　　　Must be to loathe her. O curse of marriage,

---

[1]social station　[2]*in . . . tends* i.e., all things in nature seek out their own kind　[3]general argument　[4]specifically　[5]*fall to match* happen to compare　[6]*country forms* i.e., the familiar appearance of her countrymen　[7]by chance　[8]*strains his entertainment* urge strongly that he be reinstated　[9]self-control　[10]natures, types of people　[11]a partly trained hawk which has gone wild again　[12]straps which held the hawk's legs to the trainer's wrist　[13]*I'd . . . wind* I would release her (like an untamable hawk) and let her fly free　[14]*Haply for* it may be because　[15]*soft parts* gentle qualities and manners　[16]courtiers—or, perhaps, accomplished seducers

That we can call these delicate creatures ours,
And not their appetites! I had rather be a toad
270 And live upon the vapor of a dungeon
Than keep a corner in the thing I love
For others' uses. Yet 'tis the plague to great ones;
Prerogatived are they less than the base.
'Tis destiny unshunnable, like death.
275 Even then this forkèd[1] plague is fated to us
When we do quicken.[2] Look where she comes.

Enter DESDEMONA *and* EMILIA.

If she be false, heaven mocked itself!
I'll not believe't.
DESDEMONA   How now, my dear Othello?
Your dinner, and the generous islanders
280 By you invited, do attend[3] your presence.
OTHELLO I am to blame.
DESDEMONA   Why do you speak so faintly?
Are you not well?
OTHELLO I have a pain upon my forehead, here.[4]
DESDEMONA Why, that's with watching; 'twill away again,
285 Let me but bind it hard, within this hour
It will be well.
OTHELLO   Your napkin[5] is too little;

[*He pushes the handkerchief away, and it falls.*]

Let it[6] alone. Come, I'll go in with you.
DESDEMONA I am very sorry that you are not well.   *Exit* [*with* OTHELLO].
EMILIA I am glad I have found this napkin;
290 This was her first remembrance from the Moor.
My wayward husband hath a hundred times
Wooed me to steal it; but she so loves the token
(For he conjured her she should ever keep it)
That she reserves it evermore about her
295 To kiss and talk to. I'll have the work ta'en out[7]
And give't Iago. What he will do with it,
Heaven knows, not I; I nothing[8] but to please his fantasy.[9]

Enter IAGO.

IAGO How now? What do you here alone?
EMILIA Do not you chide; I have a thing for you.
300 IAGO You have a thing for me? It is a common thing—
EMILIA Ha?
IAGO To have a foolish wife.

---

[1]horned (the skin of the cuckold was horns)   [2]*do quicken* are born   [3]wait   [4](he points to his imaginary horns)   [5]elaborately worked handkerchief   [6](it makes a considerable difference in the interpretation of later events whether this "it" refers to Othello's forehead or to the handkerchief; nothing in the text makes the reference clear)   [7]*work ta'en out* needlework copied   [8]*I nothing* I wish nothing   [9]fancy, whim

EMILIA   O, is that all? What will you give me now
　　For that same handkerchief?
IAGO 　　　　　　　　　　　What handkerchief?
305   EMILIA   What handkerchief!
　　Why, that the Moor first gave to Desdemona,
　　That which so often you did bid me steal.
IAGO   Hast stol'n it from her?
EMILIA   No, but she let it drop by negligence,
310   And to th' advantage,[1] I, being here, took't up.
　　Look, here 't is.
IAGO 　　　　　　A good wench. Give it me.
EMILIA   What will you do with't, that you have been so earnest
　　To have me filch it?
IAGO 　　　　　　　Why, what is that to you?   [*Takes it.*]
EMILIA   If it be not for some purpose of import,[2]
315   Give't me again. Poor lady, she'll run mad
　　When she shall lack[3] it.
IAGO 　　　　　　　Be not acknown on't.[4]
　　I have use for it. Go, leave me.   *Exit* EMILIA.
　　I will in Cassio's lodging lose this napkin
　　And let him find it. Trifles light as air
320   Are to the jealous confirmations strong
　　As proofs of Holy Writ. This may do something.
　　The Moor already changes with my poison:
　　Dangerous conceits are in their natures poisons,
　　Which at the first are scarce found to distaste,[5]
325   But with a little,[6] act upon the blood,
　　Burn like the mines of sulfur. I did say so.

Enter OTHELLO.

　　Look where he comes! Not poppy nor mandragora,[7]
　　Nor all the drowsy syrups of the world,
　　Shall ever medicine thee to that sweet sleep
　　Which thou owedst[8] yesterday.
330   OTHELLO 　　　　　　　Ha! ha! False to me?
IAGO   Why, how now, general? No more of that.
OTHELLO   Avaunt! be gone! Thou hast set me on the rack.
　　I swear 'tis better to be much abused
　　Than but to know't a little.
IAGO 　　　　　　　How now, my lord?
335   OTHELLO   What sense had I of her stol'n hours of lust?
　　I saw't not, thought it not, it harmed not me;
　　I slept the next night well, fed well, was free and merry;
　　I found not Cassio's kisses on her lips.
　　He that is robbed, not wanting[9] what is stol'n,
340   Let him not know't, and he's not robbed at all.

---

[1]*to th' advantage* being lucky   [2]*importance*   [3]*miss*   [4]*Be not acknown on't* forget you ever
saw it   [5]*are scarce found to distaste* scarcely can be tasted   [6]*with a little* in a short time
[7]*poppy nor mandragora* soporifics   [8]*possessed*   [9]*missing*

IAGO I am sorry to hear this.

OTHELLO I had been happy if the general camp,
Pioners[1] and all, had tasted her sweet body,
So I had nothing known. O now, forever
345 Farewell the tranquil mind! Farewell content!
Farewell the plumèd troops, and the big wars
That make ambition virtue! O, farewell!
Farewell the neighing steed and the shrill trump,
The spirit-stirring drum, th' ear-piercing fife,
350 The royal banner, and all quality,
Pride, pomp, and circumstance[2] of glorious war!
And O you mortal engines[3] whose rude throats
Th' immortal Jove's dread clamors[4] counterfeit,
Farewell! Othello's occupation's gone!

355 IAGO Is't possible, my lord?

OTHELLO Villain, be sure thou prove my love a whore!
Be sure of it; give me the ocular proof;
Or, by the worth of mine eternal soul,
Thou hadst been better have been born a dog
Than answer my waked wrath!

360 IAGO   Is't come to this?

OTHELLO Make me to see't; or at the least so prove it
That the probation[5] bear no hinge nor loop
To hang a doubt on—or woe upon thy life!

IAGO My noble lord—

365 OTHELLO If thou dost slander her and torture me,
Never pray more; abandon all remorse;
On horror's head horrors accumulate;
Do deeds to make heaven weep, all earth amazed;
For nothing canst thou to damnation add
Greater than that.

370 IAGO   O grace! O heaven forgive me!
Are you a man? Have you a soul or sense?
God b' wi' you! Take mine office. O wretched fool,
That lov'st to make thine honesty a vice!
O monstrous world! Take note, take note, O world,
375 To be direct and honest is not safe.
I thank you for this profit, and from hence
I'll love no friend, sith[6] love breeds such offense.

OTHELLO Nay, stay. Thou shouldst be honest.

IAGO I should be wise; for honesty's a fool
And loses that it works for.

380 OTHELLO   By the world,
I think my wife be honest, and think she is not;
I think that thou art just, and think thou are not.
I'll have some proof. My name, that was as fresh
As Dian's[7] visage, is now begrimed and black

[1]the basest manual laborers in the army, who dug trenches and mines   [2]pageantry   [3]*mortal
engines* lethal weapons, i.e., cannon   [4]i.e., thunder   [5]proof   [6]since   [7]Diana's (goddess of
the moon and of chastity)

385   As mine own face. If there be cords, or knives,
         Poison, or fire, or suffocating streams,
         I'll not endure it. Would I were satisfied!
     IAGO   I see you are eaten up with passion.
         I do repent me that I put it to you.
         You would be satisfied?
390 OTHELLO   Would? Nay, and I will.
     IAGO   And may; but how? How satisfied, my lord?
         Would you, the supervisor,[1] grossly gape on?
         Behold her topped?
     OTHELLO   Death and damnation! O!
     IAGO   It were a tedious[2] difficulty, I think,
395   To bring them to that prospect.[3] Damn them then,
         If ever mortal eyes do see them bolster[4]
         More than their own! What then? How then?
         What shall I say? Where's satisfaction?
         It is impossible you should see this,
400   Were they as prime[5] as goats, as hot as monkeys,
         As salt[6] as wolves in pride,[7] and fools as gross
         As ignorance made drunk. But yet, I say,
         If imputation and strong circumstances
         Which lead directly to the door of truth
405   Will give you satisfaction, you might hav't.
     OTHELLO   Give me a living reason she's disloyal.
     IAGO   I do not like the office.[8]
         But sith I am entered in this cause so far,
         Pricked[9] to't by foolish honesty and love,
410   I will go on. I lay with Cassio lately,
         And being troubled with a raging tooth,
         I could not sleep.
         There are a kind of men so loose of soul
         That in their sleeps will mutter their affairs.
415   One of this kind is Cassio.
         In sleep I heard him say, "Sweet Desdemona,
         Let us be wary, let us hide our loves!"
         And then, sir, would he gripe[10] and wring my hand,
         Cry "O sweet creature!" Then kiss me hard,
420   As if he plucked up kisses by the roots
         That grew upon my lips; laid his leg o'er my thigh,
         And sigh, and kiss, and then cry, "Cursèd fate
         That gave thee to the Moor!"
     OTHELLO   O monstrous! monstrous!
     IAGO   Nay, this was but his dream.
425 OTHELLO   But this denoted a foregone conclusion,[11]
         'Tis a shrewd doubt,[12] though it be but a dream.
     IAGO   And this may help to thicken other proofs
         That do demonstrate[13] thinly.

[1]onlooker   [2]hard to arrange   [3]sight (where they can be seen)   [4]go to bed with   [5,6]*prime,
salt* lustful   [7]heat   [8]duty   [9]spurred   [10]seize   [11]*foregone conclusion* consummated fact
[12]*shrewd doubt* penetrating guess   [13]show, appear

OTHELLO   I'll tear her all to pieces!
IAGO   Nay, yet be wise. Yet we see nothing done;
430   She may be honest yet. Tell me but this:
           Have you not sometimes seen a handkerchief
           Spotted with strawberries in your wife's hand?
OTHELLO   I gave her such a one; 'twas my first gift.
IAGO   I know not that; but such a handkerchief—
435   I am sure it was your wife's—did I today
           See Cassio wipe his beard with.
OTHELLO   If it be that—
IAGO   If it be that or any that was hers,
           It speaks against her with the other proofs.
OTHELLO   O, that the slave had forty thousand lives!
440   One is too poor, too weak for my revenge.
           Now do I see 'tis true. Look here, Iago:
           All my fond love thus do I blow to heaven.
           'Tis gone.
           Arise, black vengeance, from the hollow hell!
445   Yield up, O love, thy crown and hearted[1] throne
           To tyrannous hate! Swell, bosom, with thy fraught,[2]
           For 'tis of aspics'[3] tongues.
IAGO   Yet be content.[4]
OTHELLO   O, blood, blood, blood!
IAGO   Patience, I say. Your mind may change.
450   OTHELLO   Never, Iago. Like to the Pontic Sea,[5]
           Whose icy current and compulsive course
           Nev'r keeps retiring ebb, but keeps due on
           To the Propontic and the Hellespont,
           Even so my bloody thoughts, with violent pace,
455   Shall nev'r look back, nev'r ebb to humble love,
           Till that a capable and wide[6] revenge
           Swallow them up. [*He kneels.*] Now, by yond marble heaven,
           In the due reverence of a sacred vow
           I here engage my words.
IAGO   Do not rise yet.   [IAGO *kneels.*]
460   Witness, you ever-burning lights above,
           You elements that clip[7] us round about,
           Witness that here Iago doth give up
           The execution[8] of his wit, hands, heart
           To wronged Othello's service! Let him command,
465   And to obey shall be in me remorse,[9]
           What bloody business ever.[10]   [*They rise.*]
OTHELLO   I greet thy love,
           Not with vain thanks but with acceptance bounteous,[11]
           And will upon the instant put thee to 't.[12]

[1]seated in the heart   [2]burden   [3]asps   [4]patient, quiet   [5]*Pontic Sea* the Black Sea (famous
for the strong and constant current with which it flows through the Bosporus into the Mediterranean, where the water level is lower)   [6]*capable and wide* sufficient and far-reaching   [7]enfold
[8]workings, action   [9]pity   [10]soever   [11]absolute   [12]i.e., to the work you have said you are
prepared to do

Within these three days let me hear thee say

470   That Cassio's not alive.

IAGO   My friend is dead. 'Tis done at your request.
    But let her live.

OTHELLO   Damn her, lewd minx! O, damn her! Damn her!
    Come, go with me apart. I will withdraw
    To furnish me with some swift means of death

475   For the fair devil. Now art thou my lieutenant.

IAGO   I am your own forever.   *Exeunt.*

Scene IV. [*A street.*]

Enter DESDEMONA, EMILIA, *and* CLOWN.

DESDEMONA   Do you know, sirrah, where Lieutenant Cassio lies?[1]

CLOWN   I dare not say he lies anywhere.

DESDEMONA   Why, man?

CLOWN   He's a soldier, and for me to say a soldier lies, 'tis stabbing.

5   DESDEMONA   Go to. Where lodges he?

CLOWN   To tell you where he lodges is to tell you where I lie.

DESDEMONA   Can anything be made of this?

CLOWN   I know not where he lodges, and for me to devise a lodging, and say he
lies here or he lies there, were to lie in mine own throat.[2]

10   DESDEMONA   Can you enquire him out, and be edified[3] by report?

CLOWN   I will catechize the world for him; that is, make questions, and by them
answer.

DESDEMONA   Seek him, bid him come hither. Tell him I have moved[4] my lord on
his behalf and hope all will be well.

15   CLOWN   To do this is within the compass[5] of man's wit, and therefore I will
attempt the doing it.   *Exit* CLOWN.

DESDEMONA   Where should[6] I lose the handkerchief, Emilia?

EMILIA   I know not, madam.

DESDEMONA   Believe me, I had rather have lost my purse

20   Full of crusadoes.[7] And but my noble Moor
    Is true of mind, and made of no such baseness
    As jealous creatures are, it were enough
    To put him to ill thinking.

EMILIA   Is he not jealous?

DESDEMONA   Who? He? I think the sun where he was born
    Drew all such humors[8] from him.

25   EMILIA   Look where he comes.

Enter OTHELLO.

DESDEMONA   I will not leave him now till Cassio
    Be called to him. How is't with you, my lord?

---

[1]lodges   [2]*lie in mine own throat* (to lie in the throat is to lie absolutely and completely)
[3]enlightened (Desdemona mocks the Clown's overly elaborate diction)   [4]pleaded with   [5]reach
[6]might   [7]Portuguese gold coins   [8]characteristics

OTHELLO Well, my good lady. [*Aside*] O, hardness to
    dissemble![1]—
  How do you, Desdemona?
30 DESDEMONA   Well, my good lord.
  OTHELLO Give me your hand. This hand is moist,[2] my lady.
  DESDEMONA It hath felt no age nor known no sorrow.
  OTHELLO This argues[3] fruitfulness and liberal[4] heart.
    Hot, hot, and moist. This hand of yours requires
35 A sequester[5] from liberty; fasting and prayer,
    Much castigation; exercise devout;
    For here's a young and sweating devil here
    That commonly rebels. 'Tis a good hand,
    A frank one.
40 DESDEMONA You may, indeed, say so;
    For 'twas that hand that gave away my heart.
  OTHELLO A liberal hand! The hearts of old gave hands,
    But our new heraldry[6] is hands, not hearts.
  DESDEMONA I cannot speak of this. Come now, your promise!
45 OTHELLO What promise, chuck?
  DESDEMONA I have sent to bid Cassio come speak with you.
  OTHELLO I have a salt and sorry rheum[7] offends me
    Lend me thy handkerchief.
  DESDEMONA   Here, my lord.
  OTHELLO That which I gave you.
  DESDEMONA   I have it not about me.
50 OTHELLO Not?
  DESDEMONA No, indeed, my lord.
  OTHELLO   That's a fault.
    That handkerchief
    Did an Egyptian to my mother give.
    She was a charmer,[8] and could almost read
55 The thoughts of people. She told her, while she kept it
    'Twould make her amiable[9] and subdue my father
    Entirely to her love; but if she lost it
    Or made a gift of it, my father's eye
    Should hold her loathèd, and his spirits should hunt
60 After new fancies. She, dying, gave it me,
    And bid me, when my fate would have me wived,
    To give it her. I did so; and take heed on't;
    Make a darling like your precious eye.
    To lose't or give't away were such perdition
    As nothing else could match.
65 DESDEMONA   Is't possible?

---

[1]*hardness to dissemble* (Othello may refer here either to the difficulty he has in maintaining his appearance of composure, or to what he believes to be Desdemona's hardened hypocrisy)   [2](a moist, hot hand was taken as a sign of a lustful nature)   [3]suggests   [4]free, open (but also with a suggestion of "licentious"; from here on in this scene Othello's words bear a double meaning, seeming to be normal but accusing Desdemona of being unfaithful)   [5]separation   [6]heraldic symbolism   [7]*a salt and sorry rheum* a heavy, running head cold   [8]magician   [9]desirable

OTHELLO 'Tis true. There's magic in the web[1] of it.
A sibyl that had numbered in the world
The sun to course two hundred compasses,
In her prophetic fury[2] sewed the work;
70   The worms were hallowed that did breed the silk,
And it was dyed in mummy[3] which the skillful
Conserved of maidens' hearts.
DESDEMONA   Indeed? Is't true?
OTHELLO Most veritable. Therefore look to't well.
DESDEMONA Then would to God that I had never seen't!
75   OTHELLO Ha! Wherefore?
DESDEMONA Why do you speak so startingly and rash?
OTHELLO Is't lost? Is't gone? Speak, is it out o' th' way?
DESDEMONA Heaven bless us!
OTHELLO Say you?
80   DESDEMONA It is not lost. But what an if it were?
OTHELLO How?
DESDEMONA I say it is not lost.
OTHELLO Fetch't, let me see't!
DESDEMONA Why, so I can; but I will not now.
85   This is a trick to put me from my suit:
Pray you let Cassio be received again.
OTHELLO Fetch me the handkerchief! My mind misgives.
DESDEMONA Come, come!
You'll never meet a more sufficient[4] man—
OTHELLO The handkerchief!
90   DESDEMONA   A man that all his time
Hath founded his good fortunes on your love,
Shared dangers with you—
OTHELLO The handkerchief!
DESDEMONA I'faith, you are to blame.
95   OTHELLO Away!   *Exit* OTHELLO.
EMILIA Is not this man jealous?
DESDEMONA I nev'r saw this before.
Sure there's some wonder in this handkerchief;
I am most unhappy in the loss of it.
100   EMILIA 'Tis not a year or two shows us a man.
They are all but stomachs, and we all but food;
They eat us hungerly, and when they are full,
They belch us.

Enter IAGO *and* CASSIO.

Look you, Cassio and my husband.
IAGO There is no other way; 'tis she must do't.
105   And lo the happiness! Go and importune her.
DESDEMONA How now, good Cassio? What's the news with you?

---

[1]*weaving*   [2]*prophetic fury* seized by the spirit and able to prophesy   [3]liquid drained from embalmed bodies   [4]complete, with all proper qualities

CASSIO   Madam, my former suit. I do beseech you
    That by your virtuous means I may again
    Exist, and be a member of his love
110   Whom I with all the office[1] of my heart
    Entirely honor. I would not be delayed.
    If my offense be of such mortal kind
    That nor my service past, nor present sorrows,
    Nor purposed merit in futurity,
115   Can ransom me into his love again,
    But to know so must be my benefit.[2]
    So shall I clothe me in a forced content,
    And shut myself up in some other course
    To fortune's alms.
DESDEMONA   Alas, thrice-gentle Cassio,
120   My advocation[3] is not now in tune.
    My lord is not my lord; nor should I know him
    Were he in favor[4] as in humor altered.
    So help me every spirit sanctified
    As I have spoken for you all my best
125   And stood within the blank[5] of his displeasure
    For my free speech. You must awhile be patient.
    What I can do I will; and more I will
    Than for myself I dare. Let that suffice you.
IAGO   Is my lord angry?
EMILIA   He went hence but now,
130   And certainly in strange unquietness.
IAGO   Can he be angry? I have seen the cannon
    When it hath blown his ranks into the air
    And, like the devil, from his very arm
    Puffed his own brother. And is he angry?
135   Something of moment[6] then. I will go meet him.
    There's matter in't indeed if he be angry.
DESDEMONA   I prithee do so.   *Exit* [IAGO.]
                    Something sure of state,[7]
    Either from Venice or some unhatched practice[8]
    Made demonstrable here in Cyprus to him,
140   Hath puddled[9] his clear spirit; and in such cases
    Men's natures wrangle with inferior things,
    Though great ones are their object. 'Tis even so.
    For let our finger ache, and it endues[10]
    Our other, healthful members even to a sense
145   Of pain. Nay, we must think men are not gods,
    Nor of them look for such observancy
    As fits the bridal. Beshrew me much, Emilia,
    I was, unhandsome warrior as I am,
    Arraigning his unkindness with my soul;

---

[1]duty   [2]good   [3]advocacy   [4]countenance   [5]bull's-eye of a target   [6]importance   [7]*of state* state affairs   [8]*unhatched practice* undisclosed plot   [9]muddied   [10]leads

150   But now I find I had suborned the witness,
          And he's indicted falsely.
          EMILIA   Pray heaven it be
          State matters, as you think, and no conception
          Nor no jealous toy[1] concerning you.
          DESDEMONA   Alas the day! I never gave him cause.
155   EMILIA   But jealous souls will not be answered so;
          They are not ever jealous for the cause,
          But jealous for they're jealous. It is a monster
          Begot upon itself, born on itself.
          DESDEMONA   Heaven keep the monster from Othello's mind!
160   EMILIA   Lady, amen.
          DESDEMONA   I will go seek him. Cassio, walk here about.
          If I do find him fit,[2] I'll move your suit
          And seek to effect it to my uttermost.
          CASSIO   I humbly thank your ladyship.   *Exit* [DESDEMONA *with* EMILIA].

          Enter BIANCA.

          BIANCA   Save you, friend Cassio!
165   CASSIO   What make you from home?
          How is't with you, my most fair Bianca?
          I'faith, sweet love, I was coming to your house.
          BIANCA   And I was going to your lodging, Cassio.
          What, keep a week away? Seven days and nights?
170   Eightscore eight hours? And lovers' absent hours
          More tedious than the dial eightscore times?
          O weary reck'ning.[3]
          CASSIO   Pardon me, Bianca.
          I have this while with leaden thoughts been pressed,
          But I shall in a more continuate[4] time
175   Strike off this score[5] of absence. Sweet Bianca,

                              [*Gives her* DESDEMONA's *handkerchief.*]

          Take me this work out.
          BIANCA   O Cassio, whence came this?
          This is some token from a newer friend.
          To the felt absence now I feel a cause.
          Is't come to this? Well, well.
          CASSIO   Go to, woman!
180   Throw your vile guesses in the devil's teeth,
          From whence you have them. You are jealous now
          That this is from some mistress, some remembrance.
          No, by my faith, Bianca.
          BIANCA   Why, whose is it?
          CASSIO   I know not neither; I found it in my chamber.
185   I like the work well; ere it be demanded,[6]

[1]trifle   [2]receptive   [3]addition   [4]uninterrupted   [5]*Strike off this score*   i.e., pay this bill (the
score being the account of drinks kept in a tavern)   [6]asked for (by the person who lost it)

As like enough it will, I would have it copied.
Take it and do't, and leave me for this time.
BIANCA Leave you? Wherefore?
CASSIO I do attend here on the general
190   And think it no addition, nor my wish,
To have him see me womaned.
BIANCA   Why, I pray you?
CASSIO Not that I love you not.
BIANCA   But that you do not love me!
I pray you bring[1] me on the way a little,
And say if I shall see you soon at night.
195 CASSIO 'Tis but a little way that I can bring you,
For I attend here; but I'll see you soon.
BIANCA 'Tis very good. I must be circumstanced.[2]   *Exeunt omnes.*

Act IV,   Scene I. [*A street.*]

    Enter OTHELLO *and* IAGO.

IAGO Will you think so?
OTHELLO   Think so, Iago?
IAGO   What,
To kiss in private?
OTHELLO   An unauthorized[3] kiss?
IAGO Or to be naked with her friend in bed
An hour or more, not meaning any harm?
5 OTHELLO Naked in bed, Iago, and not mean harm?
It is hypocrisy against the devil.
They that mean virtuously, and yet do so,
The devil their virtue tempts, and they tempt heaven.
IAGO If they do nothing, 'tis a venial slip.
10   But if I give my wife a handkerchief—
OTHELLO What then?
IAGO Why, then 'tis hers, my lord; and being hers,
She may, I think, bestow't on any man.
OTHELLO She is protectress of her honor too.
15   May she give that?
IAGO Her honor is an essence that's not seen;
They have it very oft that have it not.
But for the handkerchief—
OTHELLO By heaven, I would most gladly have forgot it!
20   Thou said'st—O, it comes o'er my memory
As doth the raven[4] o'er the infected house,
Boding to all—he had my handkerchief.
IAGO Ay, what of that?
OTHELLO   That's not so good now.
IAGO What if I had said I had seen him do you wrong?

---

[1]accompany   [2]*be circumstanced* accept things as they are   [3]illicit   [4](a harbinger of death)

25   Or heard him say—as knaves be such abroad[1]
        Who having, by their own importunate suit,
        Or voluntary dotage[2] of some mistress,
        Convincèd or supplied[3] them, cannot choose
        But they must blab—
OTHELLO   Hath he said anything?
30   IAGO   He hath, my lord; but be you well assured,
        No more than he'll unswear.
OTHELLO   What hath he said?
IAGO   Why, that he did—I know not what he did.
OTHELLO   What? what?
IAGO   Lie—
OTHELLO   With her?
35   IAGO   With her, on her; what you will.
OTHELLO   Lie with her? Lie on her?—We say lie on her when they belie her.—
        Lie with her! Zounds, that's fulsome.[4]—Handkerchief—confessions—handker-
        chief!—To confess, and be hanged for his labor—first to be hanged, and then to
        confess! I tremble at it. Nature would not invest herself in such shadow-
40   ing passion without some instruction.[5] It is not words that shakes me thus.—
        Pish! Noses, ears, and lips? Is't possible?—Confess?—Handkerchief?—O
        devil!   *Falls in a trance.*
IAGO   Work on.
        My med'cine works! Thus credulous fools are caught,
45   And many worthy and chaste dames even thus,
        All guiltless, meet reproach.[6] What, ho! My lord!
        My lord, I say! Othello!

        Enter CASSIO.

                          How now, Cassio?
CASSIO   What's the matter?
IAGO   My lord is fall'n into an epilepsy.
50   This is his second fit; he had one yesterday.
CASSIO   Rub him about the temples.
IAGO   The lethargy[7] must have his quiet course.
        If not, he foams at mouth, and by and by
        Breaks out to savage madness. Look, he stirs.
55   Do you withdraw yourself a little while.
        He will recover straight. When he is gone,
        I would on great occasion[8] speak with you.   [*Exit* CASSIO.]
        How is it, general? Have you not hurt your head?
OTHELLO   Dost thou mock[9] me?
IAGO   I mock you not, by heaven.
60   Would you would bear your fortune like a man.

---

[1] i.e., in the world   [2] *voluntary dotage* weakness of the will   [3] *Convincèd or supplied* persuaded or gratified (the mistress)   [4] foul, repulsive   [5] *Nature . . . instruction* i.e., my mind would not become so darkened (with anger) unless there were something in this (accusation); (it should be remembered that Othello believes in the workings of magic and supernatural forces)   [6] shame   [7] coma   [8] *great occasion* very important matter   [9] (Othello takes Iago's comment as a reference to his horns—which it is)

OTHELLO A hornèd man's a monster and a beast.

IAGO There's many a beast then in a populous city,
  And many a civil[1] monster.

OTHELLO Did he confess it?

IAGO   Good, sir, be a man.
65 Think every bearded fellow that's but yoked
  May draw[2] with you. There's millions now alive
  That nightly lie in those unproper[3] beds
  Which they dare swear peculiar.[4] Your case is better.
  O, 'tis the spite of hell, the fiend's arch-mock,
70 To lip a wanton in a secure couch,
  And to suppose her chaste. No, let me know;
  And knowing what I am, I know what she shall be.

OTHELLO O, thou art wise! 'Tis certain.

IAGO   Stand you awhile apart;
  Confine yourself but in a patient list.[5]
75 Whilst you were here, o'erwhelmèd with your grief—
  A passion most unsuiting such a man—
  Cassio came hither. I shifted him away[6]
  And laid good 'scuses upon your ecstasy,[7]
  Bade him anon return, and here speak with me;
80 The which he promised. Do but encave[8] yourself
  And mark the fleers,[9] the gibes, and notable[10] scorns
  That dwell in every region of his face.
  For I will make him tell the tale anew:
  Where, how, how oft, how long ago, and when
85 He hath, and is again to cope your wife.
  I say, but mark his gesture. Marry patience,
  Or I shall say you're all in all in spleen,[11]
  And nothing of a man.

OTHELLO   Dost thou hear, Iago?
  I will be found most cunning in my patience;
  But—dost thou hear?—most bloody.

90 IAGO   That's not amiss;
  But yet keep time in all. Will you withdraw?

[OTHELLO *moves to one side, where his remarks are not audible to* CASSIO *and* IAGO.]

  Now will I question Cassio of Bianca,
  A huswife[12] that by selling her desires
  Buys herself bread and cloth. It is a creature
95 That dotes on Cassio, as 'tis the strumpet's plague
  To beguile many and be beguiled by one.

---

[1]city-dwelling [2]i.e., like the horned ox [3]i.e., not exclusively the husband's [4]their own alone [5]*a patient list* the bounds of patience [6]*shifted him away* got rid of him by a strategem [7]trance (the literal meaning, "outside oneself," bears on the meaning of the change Othello is undergoing) [8]hide [9]mocking looks or speeches [10]obvious [11]passion, particularly anger [12]housewife (but with the special meaning here of "prostitute")

He, when he hears of her, cannot restrain
From the excess of laughter. Here he comes.

Enter CASSIO.

As he shall smile, Othello shall go mad:
100 And his unbookish[1] jealousy must conster[2]
Poor Cassio's smiles, gestures, and light behaviors
Quite in the wrong. How do you, lieutenant?
CASSIO The worser that you give me the addition[3]
Whose want even kills me.
105 IAGO Ply Desdemona well, and you are sure on't.
Now, if this suit lay in Bianca's power,
How quickly should you speed!
CASSIO   Alas, poor caitiff![4]
OTHELLO Look how he laughs already!
IAGO I never knew woman love man so.
110 CASSIO Alas, poor rogue! I think, i' faith, she loves me.
OTHELLO Now he denies it faintly, and laughs it out.
IAGO Do you hear, Cassio?
OTHELLO   Now he importunes him
To tell it o'er. Go to! Well said, well said!
IAGO She gives it out that you shall marry her.
115 Do you intend it?
CASSIO Ha, ha, ha!
OTHELLO Do ye triumph, Roman? Do you triumph?
CASSIO I marry? What, a customer?[5] Prithee bear some charity to my wit; do not
think it so unwholesome. Ha, ha, ha!
120 OTHELLO So, so, so, so. They laugh that win.
IAGO Why, the cry goes that you marry her.
CASSIO Prithee, say true.
IAGO I am a very villain else.
OTHELLO Have you scored[6] me? Well.
125 CASSIO This is the monkey's own giving out. She is persuaded I will marry her
out of her own love and flattery, not out of my promise.
OTHELLO Iago beckons me; now he begins the story.

[OTHELLO *moves close enough to hear.*]

CASSIO She was here even now; she haunts me in every place. I was the other
day talking on the sea bank with certain Venetians, and thither comes the bau-
130 ble,[7] and falls me thus about my neck——
OTHELLO Crying "O dear Cassio!" as it were. His gesture imports it.
CASSIO So, hangs, and lolls, and weaps upon me; so shakes and pulls me! Ha,
ha, ha!
OTHELLO Now he tells how she plucked him to my chamber. O, I see that nose
135 of yours, but not that dog I shall throw it to.
CASSIO Well, I must leave her company.
IAGO Before me![8] Look where she comes.

[1]ignorant   [2]construe   [3]title   [4]wretch   [5]one who sells, a merchant (here, a prostitute)
[6]marked, defaced   [7]plaything   [8]*Before me!* (an exclamation of surprise)

Enter BIANCA.

CASSIO   'Tis such another fitchew![1] Marry a perfumed one? What do you mean
    by this haunting of me?

140   BIANCA   Let the devil and his dam haunt you! What did you mean by that same
    handkerchief you gave me even now? I was a fine fool to take it. I must take out
    the work? A likely piece of work that you should find it in your chamber and
    know not who left it there! This is some minx's token, and I must take out the
    work? There! [*She throws down the handkerchief.*] Give it your hobbyhorse.[2]

145   Wheresoever you had it I'll take out no work on't.

CASSIO   How now, my sweet Bianca? How now? how now?

OTHELLO   By heaven, that should be my handkerchief!

BIANCA   If you'll come to supper tonight, you may; if you will not, come when
    you are next prepared for.[3]   *Exit.*

150   IAGO   After her, after her!

CASSIO   Faith, I must; she'll rail in the streets else.

IAGO   Will you sup there?

CASSIO   Yes, I intend so.

IAGO   Well, I may chance to see you, for I would very fain speak with you.

155   CASSIO   Prithee come. Will you?

IAGO   Go to, say no more.   [*Exit* CASSIO.]

OTHELLO [*Comes forward*]   How shall I murder him, Iago?

IAGO   Did you perceive how he laughed at his vice?

OTHELLO   O Iago!

160   IAGO   And did you see the handkerchief?

OTHELLO   Was that mine?

IAGO   Yours, by this hand! And to see how he prizes the foolish woman your wife!
    She gave it him, and he hath giv'n it his whore.

OTHELLO   I would have him nine years a-killing!—A fine woman, a fair woman,

165   a sweet woman?

IAGO   Nay, you must forget that.

OTHELLO   Ay, let her rot, and perish, and be damned tonight; for she shall not
    live. No, my heart is turned to stone; I strike it, and it hurts my hand. O, the
    world hath not a sweeter creature! She might lie by an emperor's side and com-

170   mand him tasks.

IAGO   Nay, that's not your way.[4]

OTHELLO   Hang her! I do but say what she is. So delicate with her needle. An
    admirable musician. O, she will sing the savageness out of a bear! Of so high
    and plenteous wit and invention[5]——

175   IAGO   She's the worse for all this.

OTHELLO   O, a thousand, a thousand times. And then, of so gentle a condition?[6]

IAGO   Ay, too gentle.

OTHELLO   Nay, that's certain. But yet the pity of it, Iago. O Iago, the pity of it,
    Iago.

180   IAGO   If you are so fond over her iniquity, give her patent to offend; for if it touch[7]
    not you, it comes near nobody.

---

[1]polecat, i.e., strong-smelling creature   [2]prostitute   [3]*next prepared for* next expected—i.e.,
never   [4]proper course   [5]imagination   [6]*gentle a condition* (1) well born (2) of a gentle nature   [7]affects

OTHELLO I will chop her into messes![1] Cuckold me!

IAGO O, 'tis foul in her.

OTHELLO With mine officer!

185 IAGO That's fouler.

OTHELLO Get me some poison, Iago, this night. I'll not expostulate with her, lest her body and beauty unprovide my mind[2] again. This night, Iago!

IAGO Do it not with poison. Strangle her in her bed, even the bed she hath contaminated.

190 OTHELLO Good, good! The justice of it pleases. Very good!

IAGO And for Cassio, let me be his undertaker.[3] You shall hear more by midnight.

OTHELLO Excellent good!

[*A trumpet.*]

What trumpet is that same?

IAGO I warrant something from Venice.

Enter LODOVICO, DESDEMONA, *and* ATTENDANTS.

'Tis Lodovico.
This comes from the Duke. See, your wife's with him.

LODOVICO God save you, worthy general.

195 OTHELLO   With[4] all my heart, sir.

LODOVICO The Duke and the senators of Venice greet you.

[*Gives him a letter.*]

OTHELLO I kiss the instrument of their pleasures.

[*Opens the letter and reads.*]

DESDEMONA And what's the news, good cousin Lodovico?

IAGO I am very glad to see you, signior.

200 Welcome to Cyprus.

LODOVICO Thank you. How does Lieutenant Cassio?

IAGO   Lives, sir.

DESDEMONA Cousin, there's fall'n between him and my lord
An unkind[5] breach; but you shall make all well.

OTHELLO Are you sure of that?

205 DESDEMONA My lord?

OTHELLO [*Reads*] "This fail you not to do, as you will—"

LODOVICO He did not call; he's busy in the paper.
Is there division 'twixt my lord and Cassio?

DESDEMONA A most unhappy one. I would do much

210 T' atone[6] them, for the love I bear to Cassio.

OTHELLO Fire and brimstone!

DESDEMONA   My lord?

OTHELLO   Are you wise?

DESDEMONA What, is he angry?

LODOVICO   May be th' letter moved him;
For, as I think, they do command him home,
Deputing Cassio in his government.[7]

---

[1]bits   [2]*unprovide my mind* undo my resolution   [3](not "burier" but "one who undertakes to do something")   [4]i.e., I greet you with   [5]unnatural   [6]reconcile   [7]office

DESDEMONA Trust me, I am glad on't.
OTHELLO   Indeed?
215 DESDEMONA   My lord?
OTHELLO I am glad to see you mad.
DESDEMONA   Why, sweet Othello——
OTHELLO Devil!   [*Strikes her.*]
DESDEMONA I have not deserved this.
LODOVICO My lord, this would not be believed in Venice,
220   Though I should swear I saw't. 'Tis very much.
        Make her amends; she weeps.
OTHELLO   O devil, devil!
        If that the earth could teem[1] with woman's tears,
        Each drop she falls[2] would prove a crocodile.[3]
        Out of my sight!
225 DESDEMONA   I will not stay to offend you.   [*Going.*]
LODOVICO Truly, an obedient lady.
        I do beseech your lordship call her back.
OTHELLO Mistress!
DESDEMONA   My lord?
OTHELLO   What would you with her, sir?
LODOVICO Who? I, my lord?
230 OTHELLO Ay! You did wish that I would make her turn
        Sir, she can turn, and turn, and yet go on
        And turn again; and she can weep, sir, weep;
        And she's obedient; as you say, obedient.
        Very obedient. Proceed you in your tears.
235   Concerning this, sir—O Well-painted passion!
        I am commanded home.—Get you away;
        I'll send for you anon.—Sir, I obey the mandate
        And will return to Venice.—Hence, avaunt!   [*Exit* DESDEMONA.]
        Cassio shall have my place. And, sir, tonight
240   I do entreat that we may sup together.
        You are welcome, sir, to Cyprus.—Goats and monkeys!   *Exit.*
LODOVICH Is this the noble Moor whom our full Senate
        Call all in all sufficient? Is this the nature
        Whom passion could not shake? whose solid virtue
245   The shot of accident nor dart of chance
        Could neither graze nor pierce?
IAGO   He is much changed.
LODOVICO Are his wits safe? Is he not light of brain?
IAGO He's that he is; I may not breathe my censure.
        What he might be (if, what he might, he is not)
        I would to heaven he were!
250 LODOVICO   What, strike his wife?
IAGO Faith, that was not so well; yet would I knew
        That stroke would prove the worst.
LODOVICO   Is it his use?[4]

---

[1]conceive   [2]drops   [3](the crocodile was supposed to shed false tears to lure its victims)   [4]habit

Or did the letters work upon his blood[1]
And new-create his fault?
IAGO   Alas, alas!
255 It is not honesty in me to speak
What I have seen and known. You shall observe him,
And his own courses[2] will denote him so
That I may save my speech. Do but go after
And mark how he continues.
260 LODOVICO I am sorry that I am deceived in him.   *Exeunt.*

Scene II. [*The citadel.*]

Enter OTHELLO *and* EMILIA.

OTHELLO You have seen nothing then?
EMILIA Nor ever heard, nor ever did suspect.
OTHELLO Yes, you have seen Cassio and she together.
EMILIA But then I saw no harm, and then I heard
5 Each syllable that breath made up[3] between them.
OTHELLO What, did they never whisper?
EMILIA   Never, my lord.
OTHELLO Nor send you out o' th' way?
EMILIA Never.
OTHELLO To fetch her fan, her gloves, her mask, nor nothing?
10 EMILIA Never, my lord.
OTHELLO That's strange.
EMILIA I durst, my lord, to wager she is honest,
Lay down my soul at stake.[4] If you think other,
Remove your thought. It doth abuse your bosom.
15 If any wretch have put this in your head,
Let heaven requite it with the serpent's curse,[5]
For if she be not honest,[6] chaste, and true,
There's no man happy. The purest of their wives
Is foul as slander.
OTHELLO   Bid her come hither. Go.   *Exit* EMILIA.
20 She says enough; yet she's a simple bawd[7]
That cannot say as much. This is a subtle whore,
A closet lock and key of villainous secrets,
And yet she'll kneel and pray; I have seen her do't.

Enter DESDEMONA *and* EMILIA.

DESDEMONA My lord, what is your will?
OTHELLO   Pray you, chuck, come hither.
DESDEMONA What is your pleasure?
25 OTHELLO   Let me see your eyes.
Look in my face.
DESDEMONA   What horrible fancy's this?

---

[1]passion [2]actions [3]*that breath made up* spoken [4]*at stake* as the wager [5]*serpent's curse* (God's curse on the serpent after the fall in Eden) [6]chaste [7]procuress

OTHELLO [*To* EMILIA] Some of your function,[1] mistress:
Leave procreants alone and shut the door;
Cough or cry hem if anybody come.
30 Your mystery,[2] your mystery! Nay, dispatch!   *Exit* EMILIA
DESDEMONA Upon my knee, what doth your speech import?
I understand a fury in your words.[3]
OTHELLO Why, what art thou?
DESDEMONA   Your wife, my lord; your true
And loyal wife.
OTHELLO   Come, swear it, damn thyself;
35 Lest, being like one of heaven, the devils themselves
Should fear to seize thee. Therefore be doubledamned:
Swear thou art honest.
DESDEMONA   Heaven doth truly know it.
OTHELLO Heaven truly knows that thou art false as hell.
DESDEMONA To whom, my lord? With whom? How am I false?
40 OTHELLO Ah, Desdemon! Away! Away! Away!
DESDEMONA Alas the heavy day! Why do you weep?
Am I the motive[4] of these tears, my lord?
If haply[5] you my father do suspect
An instrument of this your calling back,
45 Lay not your blame on me. If you have lost him,
I have lost him too.
OTHELLO   Had it pleased heaven
To try me with affliction, had they rained
All kinds of sores and shames on my bare head,
Steeped[6] me in poverty to the very lips,
50 Given to captivity me and my utmost hopes,
I should have found in some place of my soul
A drop of patience. But alas, to make me
The fixèd figure for the time of scorn[7]
To point his slow and moving finger at.
55 Yet could I bear that too, well, very well.
But there where I have garnered up my heart,
Where either I must live or bear no life,
The fountain from the which my current runs
Or else dries up—to be discarded thence,
60 Or keep it as a cistern for foul toads
To knot and gender[8] in—turn thy complexion there,
Patience, thou young and rose-lipped cherubin!
I here look grim as hell![9]
DESDEMONA I hope my noble lord esteems me honest.
65 OTHELLO O, ay, as summer flies are in the shambles,[10]
That quicken even with blowing.[11] O thou weed,

---

[1]*Some of your function* do your proper work (as the operator of a brothel)   [2]*trade*   [3](Q1 adds to this line, "But not the words")   [4]*cause*   [5]*by chance*   [6]*submerged*   [7]*The . . . scorn* the very image of scorn in our time   [8]*knot and gender* twist in bunches and procreate   [9]*turn . . . hell* (the rough sense would seem to be "even Patience would grow pale, turn complexion, at Desdemona's perfidy, but that Othello looks grimly on")   [10]*abattoirs*   [11]*quicken even with blowing* become impregnated as soon as they lay their eggs

Who art so lovely fair, and smell'st so sweet,
That the sense aches at thee, would thou hadst never been born!
DESDEMONA Alas, what ignorant[1] sin have I committed?
70   OTHELLO Was this fair paper, this most goodly book,
Made to write "whore" upon? What committed?
Committed? O thou public commoner,[2]
I should make very forges of my cheeks
That would to cinders burn up modesty,
75   Did I but speak thy deeds. What committed?
Heaven stops the nose at it, and the moon winks;[3]
The bawdy wind that kisses all it meets
Is hushed within the hollow mine of earth
And will not hear't. What committed?
80   DESDEMONA By heaven, you do me wrong!
OTHELLO Are not you a strumpet?
DESDEMONA   No, as I am a Christian!
If to preserve this vessel for my lord
From any other foul unlawful touch
Be not to be a strumpet, I am none.
OTHELLO What, not a whore?
85   DESDEMONA   No, as I shall be saved!
OTHELLO Is't possible?
DESDEMONA O, heaven forgive us!
OTHELLO   I cry you mercy[4] then
I took you for that cunning whore of Venice
That married with Othello. [*Calling*] You, mistress,

Enter EMILIA.

90   That have the office opposite to Saint Peter
And keep the gate of hell! You, you, ay, you!
We have done our course; there's money for your pains.

[*Throws her some coins.*]

I pray you turn the key and keep our counsel.   *Exit.*
EMILIA Alas, what does this gentleman conceive?
95   How do you, madam? How do you, my good lady?
DESDEMONA Faith, half asleep.
EMILIA Good madam, what's the matter with my lord?
DESDEMONA With who?
EMILIA Why, with my lord, madam.
DESDEMONA Who is thy lord?
100   EMILIA   He that is yours, sweet lady.
DESDEMONA I have none. Do not talk to me, Emilia.
I cannot weep, nor answers have I none
But what should go by water.[5] Prithee tonight
Lay on my bed my wedding sheets, remember;
And call thy husband hither.

---

[1]unknowing   [2]prostitute   [3]closes its eyes (the moon was the symbol of chastity)   [4]*cry you mercy* ask your pardon   [5]tears

105 EMILIA   Here's a change indeed!   *Exit.*
DESDEMONA 'Tis meet I should be used so, very meet.
   How have I been behaved, that he might stick
   The small'st opinion on my least misuse?[1]

   Enter IAGO *and* EMILIA.

IAGO What is your pleasure, madam? How is't with you?
110 DESDEMONA I cannot tell. Those that do teach young babes
   Do it with gentle means and easy tasks.
   He might have chid me so; for, in good faith,
   I am a child to chiding.
IAGO   What is the matter, lady?
EMILIA Alas, Iago, my lord hath so bewhored her,
115   Thrown such despite[2] and heavy terms upon her
   That true hearts cannot bear it.
DESDEMONA Am I that name, Iago?
IAGO   What name, fair lady?
DESDEMONA Such as she said my lord did say I was.
EMILIA He called her whore. A beggar in his drink
120   Could not have laid such terms upon his callet.[3]
IAGO Why did he so?
DESDEMONA I do not know; I am sure I am none such.
IAGO Do not weep, do not weep. Alas the day.
EMILIA Hath she forsook so many noble matches,
125   Her father and her country, and her friends,
   To be called whore? Would it not make one weep?
DESDEMONA It is my wretched fortune.
IAGO   Beshrew[4] him for't!
   How comes this trick upon him?
DESDEMONA   Nay, heaven doth know.
EMILIA I will be hanged if some eternal villain,
130   Some busy and insinuating rogue,
   Some cogging,[5] cozening slave, to get some office,
   Have not devised this slander. I will be hanged else.
IAGO Fie, there is no such man! It is impossible.
DESDEMONA If any such there be, heaven pardon him.
135 EMILIA A halter pardon him! And hell gnaw his bones!
   Why should he call her whore? Who keeps her company?
   What place? What time? What form? What likelihood?
   The Moor's abused by some most villainous knave,
   Some base notorious knave, some scurvy fellow.
140   O heavens, that such companions[6] thou'dst unfold,[7]
   And put in every honest hand a whip
   To lash the rascals naked through the world
   Even from the east to th' west!
IAGO   Speak within door.[8]
EMILIA O, fie upon them! Some such squire[9] he was

---

[1]*stick . . . misuse* base any doubt on my smallest fault   [2]abuse   [3]slut   [4]curse   [5]cheating
[6]fellows, rogues   [7]disclose   [8]*within door* more quietly and moderately   [9]a term of contempt

145   That turned your wit the seamy side without
        And made you to suspect me with the Moor.
        IAGO   You are a fool. Go to.
        DESDEMONA   Alas, Iago,
        What shall I do to win my lord again?
        Good friend, go to him, for, by this light of heaven,
150   I know not how I lost him. Here I kneel:
        If e'er my will did trespass 'gainst his love
        Either in discourse of thought[1] or actual deed,
        Or that mine eyes, mine ears, or any sense .
        Delighted them in any other form;
155   Or that I do not yet, and ever did,
        And ever will (though he do shake me off
        To beggarly divorcement) love him dearly,
        Comfort forswear me. Unkindness may do much,
        And his unkindness may defeat[2] my life,
160   But never taint my love. I cannot say "whore."
        It does abhor me now I speak the word;
        To do the act that might the addition earn
        Not the world's mass of vanity could make me.
        IAGO   I pray you be content. 'Tis but his humor.[3]
165   The business of the state does him offense.
        DESDEMONA   If 'twere no other.
        IAGO   It is but so, I warrant.   [*Trumpets within.*]
        Hark how these instruments summon to supper.
        The messengers of Venice stay the meat.[4]
        Go in, and weep not. All things shall be well.

                                      [*Exeunt* DESDEMONA *and* EMILIA.]

        Enter RODERIGO.

170   How now, Roderigo?
        RODERIGO   I do not find that thou deal'st justly with me.
        IAGO   What in the contrary?
        RODERIGO   Every day thou daff'st[5] me with some device,[6] Iago, and rather, as it
        seems to me now, keep'st from me all conveniency[7] than suppliest me with the
175   least advantage of hope. I will indeed no longer endure it; nor am I yet
        persuaded to put up[8] in peace what already I have foolishly suffered.
        IAGO   Will you hear me, Roderigo?
        RODERIGO   I have heard too much, and your words and performances are no kin
        together.
180   IAGO   You charge me most unjustly.
        RODERIGO   With naught but truth. I have wasted myself out of my means. The
        jewels you have had from me to deliver Desdemona would half have corrupted
        a votarist.[9] You have told me she hath received them, and returned me expec-
        tations and comforts of sudden respect[10] and acquaintance; but I find none.
185   IAGO   Well, go to; very well.

---

[1]*discourse of thought* thinking   [2]destroy   [3]mood   [4]*stay the meat* await the meal   [5]put
off   [6]scheme   [7] what is needful   [8]*put up* accept   [9]nun   [10]*sudden respect* immediate consideration

RODERIGO   Very well? Go to? I cannot go to, man; nor 'tis not very well. Nay, I
think it is scurvy, and begin to find myself fopped[1] in it.

IAGO   Very well.

RODERIGO   I tell you 'tis not very well. I will make myself known to Desdemona.
190   If she will return me my jewels, I will give over my suit and repent my unlawful
solicitation. If not, assure yourself I will seek satisfaction of you.

IAGO   You have said now?

RODERIGO   Ay, and said nothing but what I protest[2] intendment of doing.

IAGO   Why, now I see there's mettle[3] in thee, and even from this instant do build
195   on thee a better opinion than ever before. Give me thy hand, Roderigo. Thou
hast taken against me a most just exception,[4] but yet I protest I have dealt most
directly[5] in thy affair.

RODERIGO   It hath not appeared.

IAGO   I grant indeed it hath not appeared, and your suspicion is not without wit
200   and judgment. But, Roderigo, if thou hast that in thee indeed which I have
greater reason to believe now than ever—I mean purpose, courage, and valor—
this night show it. If thou the next night following enjoy not Desdemona, take
me from this world with treachery and devise engines for[6] my life.

RODERIGO   Well, what is it? Is it within reason and compass?[7]

205   IAGO   Sir, there is especial commission come from Venice to depute Cassio in
Othello's place.

RODERIGO   Is that true? Why, then Othello and Desdemona return again to
Venice.

IAGO   O, no; he goes into Mauritania and taketh away with him the fair Desde-
210   mona, unless his abode be lingered here by some accident; wherein none can
be so determinate[8] as the removing of Cassio.

RODERIGO   How do you mean, removing him?

IAGO   Why, by making him uncapable of Othello's place—knocking out his brains.

RODERIGO   And that you would have me to do?

215   IAGO   Ay, if you dare do yourself a profit and a right. He sups tonight with a
harlotry,[9] and thither will I go to him. He knows not yet of his honorable fortune.
If you will watch his going thence, which I will fashion to fall out[10] between
twelve and one, you may take him at your pleasure. I will be near to second[11]
your attempt, and he shall fall between us. Come, stand not amazed at it, but
220   go along with me. I will show you such a necessity in his death that
you shall think yourself bound to put it on him. It is now high supper time, and
the night grows to waste. About it.

RODERIGO   I will hear further reason for this.

IAGO   And you shall be satisfied.   *Exeunt.*

Scene III. [*The citadel.*]

Enter OTHELLO, LODOVICO, DESDEMONA, EMILIA, *and* ATTENDANTS.

LODOVICO   I do beseech you, sir, trouble yourself no further.

OTHELLO   O, pardon me; 'twill do me good to walk.

LODOVICO   Madam, good night. I humbly thank your ladyship.

---

[1]duped   [2]aver   [3]spirit   [4]objective   [5]straightforwardly   [6]*engines for* schemes against
[7]possibility   [8]effective   [9]female   [10]*fall, out* occur   [11]support

DESDEMONA Your honor is most welcome.

5 OTHELLO Will you walk, sir? O, Desdemona.

DESDEMONA My lord?

OTHELLO Get you to bed on th' instant; I will be returned forthwith.
   Dismiss your attendant there. Look't be done.

DESDEMONA I will, my lord.

                          Exit [OTHELLO, *with* LODOVICO *and* ATTENDANTS].

10 EMILIA How goes it now? He looks gentler than he did.

DESDEMONA He says he will return incontinent,[1]
   And hath commanded me to go to bed.
   And bade me to dismiss you.

EMILIA   Dismiss me?

DESDEMONA It was his bidding; therefore, good Emilia,
15   Give me my nightly wearing, and adieu.
   We must not now displease him.

EMILIA I would you had never seen him!

DESDEMONA So would not I. My love doth so approve him
   That even his stubbornness, his checks,[2] his frowns—
20   Prithee unpin me—have grace and favor.

EMILIA I have laid these sheets you bade me on the bed.

DESDEMONA All's one.[3] Good Father, how foolish are our minds!
   If I do die before, prithee shroud me
   In one of these same sheets.

25 EMILIA   Come, come! You talk.

DESDEMONA My mother had a maid called Barbary.
   She was in love; and he she loved proved mad
   And did forsake her. She had a song of "Willow";
   An old thing 'twas, but it expressed her fortune,
30   And she died singing it. That song tonight
   Will not go from my mind; I have much to do
   But to go hang my head all at one side
   And sing it like poor Barbary. Prithee dispatch.

EMILIA Shall I go fetch your nightgown?

35 DESDEMONA No, unpin me here.
   This Lodovico is a proper man.

EMILIA A very handsome man.

DESDEMONA He speaks well.

EMILIA I know a lady in Venice would have walked barefoot to Palestine for a
40   touch of his nether lip.

DESDEMONA [*Sings*]
   "The poor soul sat singing by a sycamore tree,
      Sing all a green willow;
   Her hand on her bosom, her head on her knee,
45   Sing willow, willow, willow.
   The fresh streams ran by her and murmured her moans;
      Sing willow, willow, willow;
   Her salt tears fell from her, and soft'ned the stones—
      Sing, willow, willow, willow—"

[1]at once   [2]rebukes   [3]*All's one* no matter

50   Lay by these.   [*Gives* EMILIA *her clothes.*]
            "Willow, Willow"——
            Prithee hie[1] thee; he'll come anon.[2]
            "Sing all a green willow must be my garland
            Let nobody blame him; his scorn I approve"——
55   Nay, that's not next. Hark! Who is't that knocks?
            EMILIA It is the wind.
            DESDEMONA [*Sings*]
            "I called my love false love; but what said he then?
                Sing willow, willow, willow:
            If I court moe[3] women, you'll couch with moe men."
60   So, get thee gone; good night. Mine eyes do itch.
            Doth that bode weeping?
            EMILIA   'Tis neither here nor there.
            DESDEMONA I have heard it said so. O, these men, these men
            Dost thou in conscience think, tell me, Emilia,
            That there be women do abuse their husbands
            In such gross kind?
65   EMILIA   There be some such, no question.
            DESDEMONA Wouldst thou do such a deed for all the world?
            EMILIA Why, would not you?
            DESDEMONA   No, by this heavenly light!
            EMILIA Nor I neither by this heavenly light.
            I might do't as well i' th' dark.
70   DESDEMONA Wouldst thou do such a deed for all the world?
            EMILIA The world's a huge thing; it is a great price for a small vice.
            DESDEMONA In troth, I think thou wouldst not.
            EMILIA In troth, I think I should; and undo't when I had done. Marry, I would
                not do such a thing for a joint-ring,[4] nor for measures of lawn,[5] nor for gowns,
75   petticoats, nor caps, nor any pretty exhibition,[6] but for all the whole world?
            Why, who would not make her husband a cuckold to make him a monarch? I
            should venture purgatory for't.
            DESDEMONA Beshrew me if I would do such a wrong for the whole world.
            EMILIA Why, the wrong is but a wrong i' th' world; and having the world for your
80   labor, 'tis a wrong in your own world, and you might quickly make it right.
            DESDEMONA I do not think there is any such woman.
            EMILIA Yes, a dozen; and as many to th' vantage as would store[7] the world they
                played for.
            But I do think it is their husbands' faults
85   If wives do fall. Say that they slack their duties
            And pour our treasures into foreign[8] laps;
            Or else break out in peevish jealousies,
            Throwing restraint upon us; or stay they strike us,
            Or scant our former having in despite[9]—
90   Why, we have galls; and though we have some grace,
            Yet have we some revenge. Let husbands know

___

[1]hurry   [2]at once   [3]more   [4]a ring with two interlocking halves   [5]fine linen   [6]payment
[7]*to . . . store* in addition as would fill   [8]alien, i.e., other than the wife   [9]*scant . . . despite* reduce,
in spite, our household allowance (?)

Their wives have sense like them. They see, and smell,
And have their palates both for sweet and sour,
As husbands have. What is it that they do
95 When they change[1] us for others? Is it sport?
I think it is. And doth affection[2] breed it?
I think it doth. Is't frailty that thus errs?
It is so too. And have not we affections?
Desires for sport? and frailty? as men have?
100 Then let them use us well; else let them know,
The ills we do, their ills instruct us so.[3]
    DESDEMONA   Good night, good night. Heaven me such uses[4] send,
    Not to pick bad from bad, but by bad mend.   *Exeunt.*

Act V, Scene I. [*A street.*]

Enter IAGO *and* RODERIGO.

IAGO   Here, stand behind this bulk;[5] straight will he come.
Wear thy good rapier bare, and put it home.
Quick, quick! Fear nothing; I'll be at thy elbow.
It makes us, or it mars us, think on that,
5 And fix most firm thy resolution.
RODERIGO   Be near at hand; I may miscarry in't.
IAGO   Here, at thy hand. Be bold, and take thy stand.   [*Moves to one side.*]
RODERIGO   I have no great devotion to the deed,
And yet he hath given me satisfying reasons.
10 'Tis but a man gone. Forth my sword! He dies!
IAGO   I have rubbed this young quat[6] almost to the sense,[7]
And he grows angry. Now, whether he kill Cassio,
Or Cassio him, or each do kill the other,
Every way makes my gain. Live Roderigo,
15 He calls me to a restitution large
Of gold and jewels that I bobbed[8] from him
As gifts to Desdemona.
It must not be. If Cassio do remain,
He hath a daily beauty in his life
20 That makes me ugly; and besides, the Moor
May unfold me to him; there stand I in much peril.
No, he must die. But so, I hear him coming.

Enter CASSIO.

RODERIGO   I know his gait. 'Tis he. Villain, thou diest!   [*Thrusts at* CASSIO.]
CASSIO   That thrust had been mine enemy indeed
25 But that my coat[9] is better than thou know'st.
I will make proof of thine.   [*Fights with* RODERIGO.]

---

[1]exchange   [2]strong feeling, desire   [3]*instruct us so* teach us to do likewise   [4]practices
[5]projecting stall of a shop   [6]pimple   [7]*to the sense* raw   [8]swindled   [9]i.e., a mail shirt or
bulletproof vest

RODERIGO   O, I am slain![1]
CASSIO   I am maimed forever. Help, ho! Murder! Murder!

Enter OTHELLO [*to one side*].

OTHELLO   The voice of Cassio, Iago keeps his word.
RODERIGO   O, villain that I am!
OTHELLO   It is even so.
30   CASSIO   O help, ho! Light! A surgeon!
OTHELLO   'Tis he. O brave Iago, honest and just,
    That hast such noble sense of thy friend's wrong!
    Thou teachest me, Minion,[2] your dear lies dead,
    And your unblest[3] fate hies.[4] Strumpet, I come.
35   Forth of my heart those charms, thine eyes, are blotted.
    Thy bed, lust-strained, shall with lust's blood be spotted.

                                 Exit OTHELLO.

Enter LODOVICO *and* GRATIANO.

CASSIO   What, ho? No watch? No passage?[5] Murder! Murder!
GRATIANO   'Tis some mischance. The voice is very direful.
CASSIO   O, help!
40   LODOVICO   Hark!
RODERIGO   O wretched villain!
LODOVICO   Two or three groan. 'Tis heavy night.
    These may be counterfeits. Let's think't unsafe
    To come into the cry without more help.
45   RODERIGO   Nobody come? Then shall I bleed to death.
LODOVICO   Hark!

Enter IAGO [*with a light*].

GRATIANO   Here's one comes in his shirt, with light and weapons.
IAGO   Who's there? Whose noise is this that cries on murder?
LODOVICO   We do not know.
IAGO   Do not you hear a cry?
CASSIO   Here, here! For heaven's sake, help me!
50   IAGO   What's the matter?
GRATIANO   This is Othello's ancient, as I take it.
LODOVICO   The same indeed, a very valiant fellow.
IAGO   What are you here that cry so grievously?
CASSIO   Iago? O, I am spoiled, undone by villains.
55   Give me some help.
IAGO   O me, lieutenant! What villains have done this?
CASSIO   I think that one of them is hereabout
    And cannot make away.
IAGO   O treacherous villains!

---

[1]Most editors add here a stage direction that has Iago wounding Cassio in the leg from behind, but remaining unseen. However, nothing in the text requires this, and Cassio's wound can be given him in the fight with Roderigo, for presumably when Cassio attacks Roderigo the latter would not simply accept the thrust but would parry. Since Iago enters again at line 46, he must exit at some point after line 22   [2]hussy, i.e., Desdemona   [3]unsanctified   [4]approaches swiftly   [5]passersby

[*To* LODOVICO *and* GRATIANO] What are you there?
60   Come in, and give some help.
     RODERIGO   O, help me here!
     CASSIO   That's one of them.
     IAGO   O murd'rous slave! O villain!   [*Stabs* RODERIGO.]
     RODERIGO   O damned Iago! O inhuman dog!
     IAGO   Kill men i' th' dark?—Where be these blood thieves?—
65   How silent is this town!—Ho! Murder! Murder!—
     What may you be? Are you of good or evil?
     LODOVICO   As you shall prove us, praise us.
     IAGO   Signior Lodovico?
     LODOVICO   He, sir.
70   IAGO   I cry you mercy. Here's Cassio hurt by villains.
     GRATIANO   Cassio?
     IAGO   How is't, brother?
     CASSIO   My leg is cut in two.
     IAGO   Marry, heaven forbid!
     Light, gentlemen. I'll bind it with my shirt.

     Enter BIANCA.

75   BIANCA   What is the matter, ho? Who is't that cried?
     IAGO   Who is't that cried?
     BIANCA   O my dear Cassio! My sweet Cassio!
     O Cassio, Cassio, Cassio!
     IAGO   O notable strumpet!—Cassio, may you suspect
     Who they should be that have thus mangled you?
80   CASSIO   No.
     GRATIANO   I am sorry to find you thus. I have been to seek you.
     IAGO   Lend me a garter. So. O for a chair
     To bear him easily hence.
     BIANCA   Alas, he faints! O Cassio, Cassio, Cassio!
85   IAGO   Gentlemen all, I do suspect this trash
     To be a party in this injury.—
     Patience awhile, good Cassio.—Come, come.
     Lend me a light. Know we this face or no?
     Alas, my friend and my dear countryman
90   Roderigo? No.—Yes, sure.—Yes, 'tis Roderigo!
     GRATIANO   What, of Venice?
     IAGO   Even he, sir. Did you know him?
     GRATIANO   Know him? Ay.
     IAGO   Signior Gratiano? I cry your gentle pardon.
     These bloody accidents must excuse my manners
     That so neglected you.
95   GRATIANO   I am glad to see you.
     IAGO   How do you, Cassio?—O, a chair, a chair!
     GRATIANO   Roderigo?
     IAGO   He, he, 'tis he! [*A chair brought in.*] O, that's well said;[1] the chair.
     Some good man bear him carefully from hence.

---

[1]*well said*   well done

100 I'll fetch the general's surgeon. [*To* BIANCA] For you, mistress,
Save you your labor. [*To* CASSIO] He that lies slain here, Cassio,
Was my dear friend. What malice was between you?
CASSIO None in the world; nor do I know the man.
IAGO What, look you pale?—O, bear him out o' th' air.

[CASSIO *is carried off.*]

105 Stay you, good gentlemen.—Look you pale, mistress?
Do you perceive the gastness[1] of her eye?
Nay, if you stare, we shall hear more anon.
Behold her well; I pray you look upon her.
Do you see, gentlemen? Nay, guiltiness will speak,
110 Though tongues were out of use.[2]

[*Enter* EMILIA.]

EMILIA Alas, what is the matter? What is the matter, husband?
IAGO Cassio hath here been set on in the dark
By Roderigo and fellows that are scaped.
He's almost slain, and Roderigo quite dead.
115 EMILIA Alas, good gentleman! Alas, good Cassio!
IAGO This is the fruits of whoring. Prithee, Emilia,
Go know of Cassio where he supped tonight.
[*To* BIANCA] What, do you shake at that?
BIANCA He supped at my house; but I therefore shake not.
120 IAGO O, did he so? I charge[3] you go with me.
EMILIA Oh fie upon thee, strumpet!
BIANCA I am no strumpet, but of life as honest
As you that thus abuse me.
EMILIA   As I? Fie upon thee!
IAGO Kind gentlemen, let's go see poor Cassio dressed.[4]
125 [*To* BIANCA] Come, mistress, you must tell's another tale.
Emilia, run you to the citadel
And tell my lord and lady what hath happed   [*Exit* EMILIA.]
Will you go on afore?   *Exeunt* [*all but* IAGO].
                         This is the night
That either makes me or fordoes me quite.[5]   [*Exit.*]

Scene II. [DESDEMONA's *chamber.*]

Enter OTHELLO [*with a light*]; *and* DESDEMONA *in her bed.*

OTHELLO It is the cause, it is the cause, my soul.
Let me not name it to you, you chaste stars.
It is the cause. Yet I'll not shed her blood,
Nor scar that whiter skin of hers than snow
5 And smooth as monumental alabaster.
Yet she must die, else she'll betray more men.

[1]terror   [2]*tongues were out of use* men no longer spoke   [3]command   [4]bandaged   [5]*fordoes me quite* completely ruins me

Put out the light, and then put out the light
If I quench thee, thou flaming minister,[1]
I can again thy former light restore,
10   Should I repent me; but once put out thy light,
Thou cunning'st[2] pattern of excelling nature,
I know not where is that Promethean heat[3]
That can thy light relume.[4] When I have plucked the rose,
I cannot give it vital[5] growth again;
15   It needs must wither. I'll smell thee on the tree   [*He kisses her.*]
O balmy breath, that dost almost persuade
Justice to break her sword. One more, one more!
Be thus when thou art dead, and I will kill thee,
And love thee after. One more, and that's the last!
20   So sweet was ne'er so fatal. I must weep,
But they are cruel tears. This sorrow's heavenly;
It strikes where it doth love. She wakes.
DESDEMONA   Who's there? Othello?
OTHELLO   Ay, Desdemona.
DESDEMONA   Will you come to bed, my lord?
OTHELLO   Have you prayed tonight, Desdemon?
25   DESDEMONA   Ay, my lord.
OTHELLO   If you bethink yourself of any crime
Unreconciled as yet to heaven and grace,
Solicit for it straight.
DESDEMONA   Alack, my lord, what may you mean by that?
30   OTHELLO   Well, do it, and be brief; I will walk by.[6]
I would not kill thy unpreparèd spirit.
No, heavens forfend! I would not kill thy soul.
DESDEMONA   Talk you of killing?
OTHELLO   Ay, I do.
DESDEMONA   Then heaven
Have mercy on me!
OTHELLO   Amen, with all my heart.
35   DESDEMONA   If you say so, I hope you will not kill me.
OTHELLO   Humh.
DESDEMONA   And yet I fear you; for you're fatal then
When your eyes roll so. Why I should fear I know not,
Since guiltiness I know not; but yet I feel I fear.
OTHELLO   Think on thy sins.
40   DESDEMONA   They are loves I bear to you.
OTHELLO   Ay, and for that thou diest.
DESDEMONA   That death's unnatural that kills for loving.
Alas, why gnaw you so your nether lip?
Some bloody passion shakes your very frame.
45   These are portents; but yet I hope, I hope,
They do not point on me.

---

[1]worker, servant   [2]most intricate and skillfully wrought (by nature excelling itself)   [3]*Promethean
heat* divine fire (Prometheus is the Titan who stole fire from heaven and gave it to man)   [4]relight
[5]living   [6]nearby

OTHELLO   Peace and be still.

DESDEMONA   I will so. What's the matter?

OTHELLO   That handkerchief which I so loved and gave thee,
    Thou gav'st to Cassio.

DESDEMONA   No, by my life and soul!
    Send for the man and ask him.

50   OTHELLO   Sweet soul, take heed,
    Take heed of perjury; thou art on thy deathbed.

DESDEMONA   Ay, but not yet to die.

OTHELLO   Presently.[1]
    Therefore confess thee freely of thy sin,
    For to deny each article[2] with oath

55   Cannot remove nor choke the strong conception
    That I do groan withal. Thou art to die.

DESDEMONA   Then Lord have mercy on me.

OTHELLO   I say, amen.

DESDEMONA   And have you mercy too. I never did
    Offend you in my life; never loved Cassio

60   But with such general warranty[3] of heaven
    As I might love. I never gave him token.

OTHELLO   By heaven, I saw my handkerchief in's hand!
    O perjured woman! thou dost stone[4] my heart,
    And mak'st me call what I intend to do

65   A murder, which I thought a sacrifice.
    I saw the handkerchief.

DESDEMONA   He found it then.
    I never gave it him. Send for him hither.
    Let him confess a truth.

OTHELLO   He hath confessed.

DESDEMONA   What, my lord?

OTHELLO   That he hath used thee.

DESDEMONA   How? Unlawfully?

70   OTHELLO   Ay.

DESDEMONA   He will not say so.

OTHELLO   No, his mouth is stopped.
    Honest Iago hath ta'en order for't.[5]

DESDEMONA   O, my fear interprets. What, is he dead?

OTHELLO   Had all his hairs been lives, my great revenge

75   Had stomach[6] for them all.

DESDEMONA   Alas, he is betrayed, and I undone!

OTHELLO   Out, strumpet! Weep'st thou for him to my face?

DESDEMONA   O, banish me, my lord, but kill me not!

OTHELLO   Down, strumpet!

80   DESDEMONA   Kill me tomorrow; let me live tonight!

OTHELLO   Nay, if you strive—

DESDEMONA   But half an hour!

OTHELLO   Being done, there is no pause.

---

[1]immediately   [2]item (of the charge of adultery. Othello makes heavy use of legal terms in this scene)   [3]allowance   [4]turn to stone   [5]*ta'en order for't* made sure of it   [6]appetite

DESDEMONA But while I say one prayer!
OTHELLO   It is too late.   *Smothers her.*

EMILIA *at the door.*

EMILIA [*Calls within*] My lord, my lord! What, ho, my lord, my lord!
85   OTHELLO What noise is this? Not dead? Not yet quite dead?
      I that am cruel am yet merciful;
      I would not have thee linger in thy pain.
      EMILIA [*Within*] What, ho! My lord, my lord!
      OTHELLO   So, so. Who's there?
      EMILIA [*Within*] O, good my lord, I would speak a word with you.
90   OTHELLO Yes, 'tis Emilia.—By and by.—She's dead.—
      'Tis like she comes to speak of Cassio's death.
      The noise was high.[1] Ha! No more moving?
      Still as the grave.—Shall she come in? Were't good?—
      I think she stirs again. No.—What's best to do?
95   If she come in, she'll sure speak to my wife.
      My wife! My wife! What wife? I have no wife.
      O, insupportable! O heavy hour!
      Methinks[2] it should be now a huge eclipse
      Of sun and moon, and that th' affrighted globe
      Should yawn[3] at alteration.
100   EMILIA [*Within*]   I do beseech you
      That I may speak with you, O good my lord!
      OTHELLO I had forgot thee. O, come in, Emilia.
      Soft, by and by.—Let me the curtains draw.—

                [*Draws the bed hangings and then opens the door.*]

      Where art thou?

      Enter EMILIA.

                What's the matter with thee now?
105   EMILIA O my good lord, yonder's foul murders done!
      OTHELLO What? Now?
      EMILIA But now, my lord.
      OTHELLO It is the very error[4] of the moon.
      She comes more nearer earth than she was wont
110   And makes men mad.
      EMILIA Cassio, my lord, hath killed a young Venetian
      Called Roderigo.
      OTHELLO   Roderigo killed?
      And Cassio killed?
      EMILIA   No, Cassio is not killed.
      OTHELLO Not Cassio killed? Then murder's out of tune,
115   And sweet revenge grows harsh.

---

[1]loud (Q1 reads "here")   [2]*Methinks . . . alteration* (the Elizabethans believed that great changes in human affairs were reflected by disorders in nature)   [3]gape open (as in an earthquake) [4]wandering out of regular course (disorders in the heavens were believed by some to cause disorders on earth, as well as vice versa)

DESDEMONA O, falsely, falsely murdered!

EMILIA   O Lord! What cry is that?

OTHELLO That? What?

EMILIA Out and alas! that was my lady's voice.
   Help! Help, ho! Help! O lady, speak again!

120   Sweet Desdemona! O sweet mistress, speak!

DESDEMONA A guiltless death I die.

EMILIA O, who hath done this deed?

DESDEMONA Nobody—I myself. Farewell.
   Commend me to my kind lord. O, farewell!   [*She dies.*]

OTHELLO Why, how should she be murd'red?

125 EMILIA   Alas, who knows?

OTHELLO You heard her say herself, it was not I.

EMILIA She said so. I must needs report the truth.

OTHELLO She's like a liar gone to burning hell!
   'Twas I that killed her.

EMILIA   O, the more angel she,

130 And you the blacker devil!

OTHELLO She turned to folly, and she was a whore.

EMILIA Thou dost belie her, and thou art a devil.

OTHELLO She was false as water.

EMILIA   Thou art rash as fire to say
   That she was false. O, she was heavenly true!

135 OTHELLO Cassio did top her. Ask thy husband else.
   O, I were damned beneath all depth in hell
   But that I did proceed upon just grounds
   To this extremity. Thy husband knew it all.

EMILIA My husband?

OTHELLO   Thy husband.

EMILIA   That she was false to wedlock?

140 OTHELLO Ah, with Cassio. Had she been true,
   If heaven would make me such another world
   Of one entire and perfect chrysolite,[1]
   I'd not have sold her for it.

EMILIA   My husband?

OTHELLO Ay, 'twas he that told me on her first.

145 An honest man he is, and hates the slime
   That sticks on filthy deeds.

EMILIA   My husband?

OTHELLO What needs this iterance? Woman, I say thy husband.

EMILIA O mistress, villainy hath made mocks with love!
   My husband say she was false?

OTHELLO   He, woman.

150 I say, thy husband. Dost understand the word?
   My friend, thy husband; honest, honest Iago.

EMILIA If he say so, may his pernicious soul
   Rot half a grain a day! He lies to th' heart.
   She was too fond of her most filthy bargain.

---

[1]topaz

155   OTHELLO Hah?
    EMILIA Do thy worst.
      This deed of thine is no more worthy heaven
      Than thou wast worthy her.
    OTHELLO   Peace, you were best.[1]
    EMILIA Thou hast not half that pow'r to do me harm
160   As I have to be hurt. O gull! O dolt!
      As ignorant as dirt! Thou hast done a deed—

                           [OTHELLO *moves to draw his sword.*]

      I care not for thy sword; I'll make thee known,
      Though I lost twenty lives. Help! Help! Ho! Help!
      The Moor hath killed my mistress! Murder! murder!

    Enter MONTANO, GRATIANO, *and* IAGO [*and* OTHERS].

165   MONTANO What is the matter? How now, general?
    EMILIA O, are you come, Iago? You have done well,
      That men must lay their murders on your neck.
    GRATIANO What is the matter?
    EMILIA Disprove this villain, if thou be'st a man.
170   He says thou told'st him that his wife was false.
      I know thou didst not; thou'rt not such a villain.
      Speak, for my heart is full.
    IAGO I told him what I thought, and told no more
      Than what he found himself was apt and true.
175   EMILIA But did you ever tell him she was false?
    IAGO I did.
    EMILIA You told a lie, an odious damnèd lie!
      Upon my soul, a lie! A wicked lie!
      She false with Cassio? Did you say with Cassio?
180   IAGO With Cassio, mistress. Go to, charm[2] your tongue.
    EMILIA I will not charm my tongue; I am bound to speak:
      My mistress here lies murdered in her bed.
    ALL O heavens forfend!
    EMILIA And your reports have set the murder on.
185   OTHELLO Nay, stare not, masters. It is true indeed.
    GRATIANO 'Tis a strange truth.
    MONTANO O monstrous act!
    EMILIA   Villainy, villainy, villainy!
      I think upon't—I think I smell't!—O villainy!
      I thought so then.—I'll kill myself for grief.—
190   O villainy, villainy!
    IAGO What, are you mad? I charge you get you home.
    EMILIA Good gentlemen, let me have leave to speak.
      'Tis proper I obey him, but not now.
      Perchance, Iago, I will ne'er go home.
    OTHELLO O! O! O!   [*Falls on the bed.*]

---

[1]*Peace, you were best* i.e., you had better be silent   [2]control

195   EMILIA   Nay, lay thee down and roar,
         For thou hast killed the sweetest innocent
         That e'er did lift up eye.
       OTHELLO   O, she was foul!   [*Rises.*]
         I scarce did know you, uncle. There lies your niece,
         Whose breath, indeed, these hands have newly stopped.
200   I know this act shows horrible and grim.
       GRATIANO Poor Desdemon! I am glad thy father's dead.
         Thy match was mortal to him, and pure grief
         Shore his old thread in twain. Did he live now,
         This sight would make him do a desperate turn;
205   Yea, curse his better angel from his side,
         And fall to reprobation.[1]
       OTHELLO 'Tis pitiful; but yet Iago knows
         That she with Cassio hath the act of shame
         A thousand times committed. Cassio confessed it;
210   And she did gratify his amorous works
         With that recognizance and pledge of love,
         Which I first gave her. I saw it in his hand.
         It was a handkerchief, an antique token
         My father gave my mother.
215   EMILIA O God! O heavenly God!
       IAGO Zounds, hold your peace!
       EMILIA   'Twill out, 'twill out! I peace?
         No, I will speak as liberal as the north.[2]
         Let heaven and men and devils, let them all,
         All, all, cry shame against me, yet I'll speak.
       IAGO Be wise, and get you home.
220   EMILIA   I will not.

                                [IAGO *draws and threatens* EMILIA.]

       GRATIANO Fie! Your sword upon a woman?
       EMILIA O thou dull Moor, that handkerchief thou speak'st of
         I found by fortune, and did give my husband;
         For often with a solemn earnestness—
225   More than indeed belonged to such a trifle—
         He begged of me to steal't.
       IAGO   Villainous whore!
       EMILIA She give it Cassio? No, alas, I found it,
         And I did give't my husband.
       IAGO   Filth, thou liest!
       EMILIA By heaven, I do not, gentlemen.
230   O murd'rous coxcomb! What should such a fool
         Do with so good a wife?
       OTHELLO   Are there no stones[3] in heaven
         But what serves for the thunder? Precious villain!

         [*The* MOOR *runs at* IAGO, *but is disarmed by* MONTANO. IAGO *kills his wife.*]

[1]damnation   [2]*liberal as the north* freely (and bitingly) as the north wind blows   [3]thunderbolts

GRATIANO The woman falls. Sure he hath killed his wife.

EMILIA Ay, ay. O, lay me by my mistress' side.   [*Exit* IAGO.]

235   GRATIANO He's gone, but his wife's killed.

MONTANO 'Tis a notorious[1] villain. Take you this weapon,
     Which I have recovered from the Moor.
     Come, guard the door without. Let him not pass,
     But kill him rather. I'll after that same villain,
     For 'tis a damnèd slave.   *Exit* [*with all but* OTHELLO *and* EMILIA].

240   OTHELLO   I am not valiant neither;
     But every puny whipster[2] gets my sword.
     But why should honor outlive honesty?
     Let it go all.

EMILIA   What did thy song bode, lady?
     Hark, canst thou hear me? I will play the swan,

245   And die in music. [*Sings*] "Willow, willow, willow."
     Moor, she was chaste. She loved thee, cruel Moor,
     So come my soul to bliss as I speak true.
     So speaking as I think, alas, I die.   [*She dies.*]

OTHELLO I have another weapon in this chamber;

250   It was a sword of Spain, the ice-brook's temper.
     O, here it is.—Uncle, I must come forth.

GRATIANO [*Within*] If thou attempt it, it will cost thee dear.
     Thou hast no weapon, and perforce must suffer.

OTHELLO Look in upon me then and speak with me,

255   Or, naked as I am, I will assault thee.

     [*Enter* GRATIANO.]

GRATIANO What is the matter?

OTHELLO   Behold, I have a weapon;
     A better never did itself sustain
     Upon a soldier's thigh. I have seen the day
     That with this little arm and this good sword

260   I have made my way through more impediments
     Than twenty times your stop. But O vain boast!
     Who can control his fate? 'Tis not so now.
     Be not afraid, though you do see me weaponed.
     Here is my journey's end, here is my butt,[3]

265   And very seamark of my utmost sail.[4]
     Do you go back dismayed? 'Tis a lost fear.
     Man but a rush[5] against Othello's breast.
     And he retires. Where should Othello go?
     Now, how dost thou look now? O ill-starred wench!

270   Pale as thy smock! When we shall meet at compt,[6]
     This look of thine will hurl my soul from heaven,
     And fiends will snatch at it. Cold, cold, my girl?
     Even like thy chastity.

---

[1]out-and-out   [2]*puny whipster* small top-whipping boy (?)   [3]target, stopping place   [4]*seamark of my utmost sail* maker of my furthest journey   [5]*Man but a rush* attack with only a reed
[6]Judgment Day

O cursèd, cursèd slave! Whip me, ye devils,
275   From the possession of¹ this heavenly sight!
Blow me about in winds! roast me in sulfur!
Wash me in steep-down gulfs of liquid fire!
O Desdemon! Dead Desdemon; dead. O! O!

Enter LODOVICO, CASSIO, MONTANO, *and* IAGO [*as prisoner,*] *with* OFFICERS.

LODOVICO Where is this rash and most unfortunate man?
280   OTHELLO That's he that was Othello? Here I am.
LODOVICO Where is that viper? Bring the villain forth.
OTHELLO I look down towards his feet²—but that's a fable.
    If that thou be'st a devil, I cannot kill thee.   [*Wounds* IAGO.]
LODOVICO Wrench his sword from him.   [OTHELLO *is disarmed.*]
IAGO   I bleed, sir, but not killed.
285   OTHELLO I am not sorry neither. I'd have thee live;
    For in my sense, 'tis happiness to die.
LODOVICO O thou Othello that was once so good,
    Fall'n in the practice³ of a cursèd slave,
    What shall be said to thee?
OTHELLO   Why, anything:
290   An honorable murderer, if you will;
    For naught I did in hate, but all in honor.
LODOVICO This wretch hath part confessed his villainy.
    Did you and he consent in Cassio's death?
OTHELLO Ay.
295   CASSIO Dear general, I never gave you cause.
OTHELLO I do believe it, and I ask your pardon.
    Will you, I pray, demand that demi-devil
    Why he hath thus ensnared my soul and body?
IAGO Demand me nothing. What you know, you know.
300   From this time forth I never will speak word.
LODOVICO What, not to pray?
GRATIANO   Torments will ope your lips.
OTHELLO Well, thou dost best.
LODOVICO Sir, you shall understand what hath befall'n,
    Which, as I think, you know not. Here is a letter
305   Found in the pocket of the slain Roderigo;
    And here another. The one of them imports
    The death of Cassio to be undertook
    By Roderigo.
OTHELLO O villain!
CASSIO   Most heathenish and most gross!
310   LODOVICO Now here's another discontented paper
    Found in his pocket too; and this, it seems,
    Roderigo meant t' have sent this damnèd villain;
    But that, belike, Iago in the interim
    Came in and satisfied him.

---

¹*the possession of* being possessed by   ²*towards his feet* i.e., for his cloven hoofs   ³plotting

OTHELLO   O thou pernicious caitiff!
315   How came you, Cassio, by that handkerchief
       That was my wife's?
CASSIO   I found it in my chamber;
       And he himself confessed it but even now
       That there he dropped it for a special purpose
       Which wrought to his desire.
OTHELLO   O fool! Fool! Fool!
320 CASSIO There is besides in Roderigo's letter,
       How he upbraids Iago that he made him
       Brave me upon the watch; whereon it came
       That I was cast; and even but now he spake,
       After long seeming dead—Iago hurt him,
325   Iago set him on.
LODOVICO You must forsake this room and go with us.
       Your power and your command is taken off,
       And Cassio rules in Cyprus. For this slave,
       If there be any cunning cruelty
330   That can torment him much and hold him long,
       It shall be his. You shall close prisoner rest
       Till that the nature of your fault be known
       To the Venetian state. Come, bring away.
OTHELLO Soft you, a word or two before you go.
335   I have done the state some service and they know't.
       No more of that. I pray you, in your letters,
       When you shall these unlucky deeds relate,
       Speak of me as I am. Nothing extenuate,
       Nor set down aught in malice. Then must you speak
340   Of one that loved not wisely, but too well;
       Of one not easily jealous, but, being wrought,
       Perplexed in the extreme; of one whose hand,
       Like the base Judean,[1] threw a pearl away
       Richer than all his tribe; of one whose subdued eyes,
345   Albeit unusèd to the melting mood,
       Drops tears as fast as the Arabian trees
       Their med'cinable gum. Set you down this.
       And say besides that in Aleppo once,
       Where a malignant and a turbaned Turk
350   Beat a Venetian and traduced the state,
       I took by th' throat the circumcisèd dog
       And smote him—thus.   [*He stabs himself.*]
LODOVICO O bloody period![2]
GRATIANO   All that is spoke is marred.
OTHELLO I kissed thee ere I killed thee. No way but this,
355   Killing myself, to die upon a kiss.   [*He falls over* DESDEMONA *and dies.*]
CASSIO This did I fear, but thought he had no weapon;
       For he was great of heart.

---

[1]Most editors use the Q1 reading, "Indian," here, but F is clear: both readings point toward the infidel, the unbeliever.   [2]end

LODOVICO [*To* IAGO]   O Spartan dog,
    More fell[1] than anguish, hunger, or the sea!
    Look on the tragic loading of this bed.
360   This is thy work. The object poisons sight;
    Let it be hid.   [*Bed curtains drawn.*]
            Gratiano, keep[2] the house,
    And seize upon the fortunes of the Moor,
    For they succeed on you. To you, lord governor,
    Remains the censure of this hellish villain,
365   The time, the place, the torture. O, enforce it!
    Myself will straight aboard, and to the state
    This heavy act with heavy heart relate.   *Exeunt.*

[1]cruel   [2]remain in

Henrik Ibsen and *Hedda Gabler*

The work of Henrik Ibsen (1828–1906) anticipates the variety of modern theater. His best-known plays are realistic, but he began as a poet and ended as a symbolist. Ibsen started young, writing his first play in 1850, and continued his apprenticeship with a series of romantic and historical plays. At the same time, he learned stagecraft by working as a resident with several theatrical companies. In 1866 he wrote the dramatic poem *Brand,* and followed it two years later with the poetic drama *Peer Gynt.*

In his great middle period, from about 1875 to 1890, Ibsen wrote his most famous plays, in the style of dramatic realism. *Pillars of Society* (1877) attacked bourgeois conventions. A series of plays like *A Doll's House* (1879) explored the hazards of domestic life. *Ghosts* (1883) was shocking because the plot turned on the subject of venereal disease. *An Enemy of the People* (1883), *The Wild Duck* (1885), and *Rosmersholm* (1887) all dealt with contemporary society; all were tightly constructed, informed by passion and compassion. Toward the end of his life, Ibsen returned to a symbolic, less realistic theater—with considerable success—in *The Master Builder* (1893), *John Gabriel Borkman* (1897), and in *When We Dead Awaken* (1900).

The realistic drama *Hedda Gabler* was first performed in Munich in 1861. The protagonist is an unusual woman married to a conventional man; she is fierce, proud, neurotic, unable to direct her intelligence and energy toward an acceptable goal. *Hedda Gabler* shows affinities with feminist thinking, for Ibsen understood the anger and despair of his heroine, denied power by a patriarchal society. Yet the play has dramatic power separate from its political morality, and its conclusion remains ambiguous.

Henrik Ibsen
Hedda Gabler

Translated by Edmund Gosse and William Archer

Cast

GEORGE TESMAN
HEDDA TESMAN, his wife
MISS JULIANA TESMAN, his aunt
MRS. ELVSTED

JUDGE BRACK
EILERT LÖVBORG
BERTA, servant at the Tesmans'

SCENE: *The action is at Tesman's villa, in the west end of Christiania*

Act I

SCENE: *A spacious, handsome, and tastefully furnished drawing room, decorated in dark colors. In the back, a wide doorway with curtains drawn back, leading into a smaller room decorated in the same style as the drawing room. In the right-hand wall of the front room, a folding door leading out to the hall. In the opposite wall, on the left, a glass door, also with curtains drawn back. Through the panes can be seen part of a veranda outside, and trees covered with autumn foliage. An oval table, with a cover on it, and surrounded by chairs, stands well forward. In front, by the wall on the right, a wide stove of dark porcelain, a high-backed armchair, a cushioned footrest, and two footstools. A settee, with a small round table in front of it, fills the upper right-hand corner. In front, on the left, a little way from the wall, a sofa. Farther back than the glass door, a piano. On either side of the doorway at the back a whatnot with terra-cotta and majolica orna-ments. Against the back wall of the inner room a sofa, with a table, and one or two chairs. Over the sofa hangs the portrait of a handsome elderly man in a General's uniform. Over the table a hanging lamp, with an opal glass shade. A number of bouquets are arranged about the drawing room, in vases and glasses. Others lie upon the tables. The floors in both rooms are covered with thick carpets. Morning light. The sun shines in through the glass door.*

.MISS JULIANA TESMAN, *with her bonnet on and carrying a parasol, comes in from the hall, followed by* BERTA, *who carries a bouquet wrapped in paper.* MISS TESMAN *is a comely and pleasant-looking lady of about sixty-five. She is nicely but simply dressed in a gray walking costume.* BERTA *is a middle-aged woman of plain and rather countrified appearance.*

MISS TESMAN [*stops close to the door, listens, and says softly*] Upon my word, I don't believe they are stirring yet!

BERTA [*also softly*] I told you so, Miss. Remember how late the steamboat got in last night. And then, when they got home!—good Lord, what a lot the young mistress had to unpack before she could get to bed.

MISS TESMAN Well, well—let them have their sleep out. But let us see that they get a good breath of the fresh morning air when they do appear. [*She goes to the glass door and throws it open.*]

BERTA [*beside the table, at a loss what to do with the bouquet in her hand*] I declare, there isn't a bit of room left. I think I'll put it down here, Miss. [*She places it on the piano.*]

MISS TESMAN So you've got a new mistress now, my dear Berta. Heaven knows it was a wrench to me to part with you.

BERTA [*on the point of weeping*] And do you think it wasn't hard for me, too, Miss? After all the blessed years I've been with you and Miss Rina.

MISS TESMAN We must make the best of it, Berta. There was nothing else to be done. George can't do without you, you see—he absolutely can't. He has had you to look after him ever since he was a little boy.

BERTA Ah, but, Miss Julia, I can't help thinking of Miss Rina lying helpless at home there, poor thing. And with only that new girl, too! She'll never learn to take proper care of an invalid.

MISS TESMAN Oh, I shall manage to train her. And, of course, you know I shall take most of it upon myself. You needn't be uneasy about my poor sister, my dear Berta.

BERTA Well, but there's another thing, Miss. I'm so mortally afraid I shan't be able to suit the young mistress.

MISS TESMAN Oh, well—just at first there may be one or two things . . .

BERTA Most like she'll be terrible grand in her ways.

MISS TESMAN Well, you can't wonder at that—General Gabler's daughter! Think of the sort of life she was accustomed to in her father's time. Don't you remember how we used to see her riding down the road along with the General? In that long black habit—and with feathers in her hat?

BERTA Yes, indeed—I remember well enough!—But, good Lord, I should never have dreamt in those days that she and Master George would make a match of it.

MISS TESMAN Nor I. But by the by, Berta—while I think of it: in future you mustn't say Master George. You must say Dr. Tesman.

BERTA Yes, the young mistress spoke of that, too—last night—the moment they set foot in the house. Is it true then, Miss?

MISS TESMAN Yes, indeed it is. Only think, Berta—some foreign university has made him a doctor—while he has been abroad, you understand. I hadn't heard a word about it, until he told me himself upon the pier.

BERTA Well, well, he's clever enough for anything, he is. But I didn't think he'd have gone in for doctoring people, too.

MISS TESMAN No, no, it's not that sort of doctor he is. [*Nods significantly*] But let me tell you, we may have to call him something still grander before long.

BERTA You don't say so! What can that be, Miss?

MISS TESMAN [*smiling*] H'm—wouldn't you like to know! [*With emotion*] Ah, dear, dear—if my poor brother could only look up from his grave now, and see what his little boy has grown into! [*Looks around*] But bless me, Berta—why have you done this? Taken the chintz covers off all the furniture?

BERTA The mistress told me to. She can't abide covers on the chairs, she says.

MISS TESMAN Are they going to make this their everyday sitting room then?

BERTA Yes, that's what I understood—from the mistress. Master George—the doctor—he said nothing.

GEORGE TESMAN *comes from the right into the inner room, humming to himself, and carrying an unstrapped empty portmanteau. He is a middle-sized, young-looking man of thirty-three, rather stout, with a round, open, cheerful face, fair hair and beard. He wears spectacles, and is somewhat carelessly dressed in comfortable indoor clothes.*

MISS TESMAN Good morning, good morning, George.

TESMAN [*in the doorway between the rooms*] Aunt Julia! Dear Aunt Julia! [*Goes up to her and shakes hands warmly*] Come all this way—so early! Eh?

MISS TESMAN   Why, of course I had to come and see how you were getting on.

TESMAN   In spite of your having had no proper night's rest?

MISS TESMAN   Oh, that makes no difference to me.

TESMAN   Well, I suppose you got home all right from the pier? Eh?

MISS TESMAN   Yes, quite safely, thank goodness. Judge Brack was good enough to see me right to my door.

TESMAN   We were so sorry we couldn't give you a seat in the carriage. But you saw what a pile of boxes Hedda had to bring with her.

MISS TESMAN   Yes, she had certainly plenty of boxes.

BERTA [*to* TESMAN]   Shall I go in and see if there's anything I can do for the mistress?

TESMAN   No thank you, Berta—you needn't. She said she would ring if she wanted anything.

BERTA [*going towards the right*]   Very well.

TESMAN   But look here—take this portmanteau with you.

BERTA [*taking it*]   I'll put it in the attic. [*She goes out by the hall door.*]

TESMAN   Fancy, Auntie—I had the whole of that portmanteau chock full of copies of documents. You wouldn't believe how much I have picked up from all the archives I have been examining—curious old details that no one has had any idea of . . .

MISS TESMAN   Yes, you don't seem to have wasted your time on your wedding trip, George.

TESMAN   No, that I haven't. But do take off your bonnet, Auntie. Look here! Let me untie the strings—eh?

MISS TESMAN [*while he does so*]   Well, well—this is just as if you were still at home with us.

TESMAN [*with the bonnet in his hand, looks at it from all sides*]   Why, what a gorgeous bonnet you've been investing in!

MISS TESMAN   I bought it on Hedda's account.

TESMAN   On Hedda's account? Eh?

MISS TESMAN   Yes, so that Hedda needn't be ashamed of me if we happened to go out together.

TESMAN [*patting her cheek*]   You always think of everything, Aunt Julia. [*Lays the bonnet on a chair beside the table.*] And now, look here—suppose we sit comfortably on the sofa and have a little chat, till Hedda comes. [*They seat themselves. She places her parasol in the corner of the sofa.*]

MISS TESMAN [*takes both his hands and looks at him*]   What a delight it is to have you again, as large as life, before my very eyes, George! My George—my poor brother's own boy!

TESMAN   And it's a delight for me, too, to see you again, Aunt Julia! You, who have been father and mother in one to me.

MISS TESMAN   Oh yes, I know you will always keep a place in your heart for your old aunts.

TESMAN   And what about Aunt Rina? No improvement—eh?

MISS TESMAN   Oh no—we can scarcely look for any improvement in her case, poor thing. There she lies, helpless, as she has lain for all these years. But heaven grant I may not lose her yet awhile. For if I did, I don't know what I should make of my life, George—especially now that I haven't you to look after any more.

TESMAN [*patting her back*] There, there, there . . . !

MISS TESMAN [*suddenly changing her tone*] And to think that here you are a married man, George! And that you should be the one to carry off Hedda Gabler—the beautiful Hedda Gabler! Only think of it—she, that was so beset with admirers!

TESMAN [*hums a little and smiles complacently*] Yes, I fancy I have several good friends about town who would like to stand in my shoes—eh?

MISS TESMAN And then this fine long wedding tour you have had! More than five—nearly six months . . .

TESMAN Well, for me it has been a sort of tour of research as well. I have had to do so much grubbing among old records—and to read no end of books too, Auntie.

MISS TESMAN Oh yes, I suppose so. [*More confidentially, and lowering her voice a little*] But listen now, George—have you nothing—nothing special to tell me?

TESMAN As to our journey?

MISS TESMAN Yes.

TESMAN No, I don't know of anything except what I have told you in my letters. I had a doctor's degree conferred on me—but that I told you yesterday.

MISS TESMAN Yes, yes, you did. But what I mean is—haven't you any—any—expectations . . . ?

TESMAN Expectations?

MISS TESMAN Why you know, George—I'm your old auntie!

TESMAN Why, of course I have expectations.

MISS TESMAN Ah!

TESMAN I have every expectation of being a professor one of these days.

MISS TESMAN Oh yes, a professor . . .

TESMAN Indeed, I may say I am certain of it. But my dear Auntie—you know all about that already!

MISS TESMAN [*laughing to herself*] Yes, of course I do. You are quite right there. [*Changing the subject*] But we were talking about your journey. It must have cost a great deal of money, George?

TESMAN Well, you see—my handsome traveling scholarship went a good way.

MISS TESMAN But I can't understand how you can have made it go far enough for two.

TESMAN No, that's not so easy to understand—eh?

MISS TESMAN And especially traveling with a lady—they tell me that makes it ever so much more expensive.

TESMAN Yes, of course—it makes it a little more expensive. But Hedda had to have this trip, Auntie! She really had to. Nothing else would have done.

MISS TESMAN No, no, I suppose not. A wedding tour seems to be quite indispensable nowadays. But tell me now—have you gone thoroughly over the house yet.

TESMAN Yes, you may be sure I have. I have been afoot ever since daylight.

MISS TESMAN And what do you think of it all?

TESMAN I'm delighted! Quite delighted! Only I can't think what we are to do with the two empty rooms between this inner parlor and Hedda's bedroom.

MISS TESMAN [*laughing*] Oh my dear George, I daresay you may find some use for them—in the course of time.

TESMAN   Why of course you are quite right, Aunt Julia! You mean as my library increases—eh?

MISS TESMAN   Yes, quite so, my dear boy. It was your library I was thinking of.

TESMAN   I am specially pleased on Hedda's account. Often and often, before we were engaged, she said that she would never care to live anywhere but in Secretary Falk's villa.

MISS TESMAN   Yes, it was lucky that this very house should come into the market, just after you had started.

TESMAN   Yes, Aunt Julia, the luck was on our side, wasn't it—eh?

MISS TESMAN   But the expense, my dear George! You will find it very expensive, all this.

TESMAN [*looks at her, a little cast down*]   Yes, I suppose I shall, Aunt!

MISS TESMAN   Oh, frightfully!

TESMAN   How much do you think? In round numbers?—Eh?

MISS TESMAN   Oh, I can't even guess until all the accounts come in.

TESMAN   Well, fortunately, Judge Brack has secured the most favorable terms for me—so he said in a letter to Hedda.

MISS TESMAN   Yes, don't be uneasy, my dear boy. Besides, I have given security for the furniture and all the carpets.

TESMAN   Security? You? My dear Aunt Julia—what sort of security could you give?

MISS TESMAN   I have given a mortgage on our annuity.

TESMAN [*jumps up*]   What! On your—and Aunt Rina's annuity!

MISS TESMAN   Yes, I knew of no other plan, you see.

TESMAN [*placing himself before her*]   Have you gone out of your senses, Auntie! Your annuity—it's all that you and Aunt Rina have to live upon.

MISS TESMAN   Well, well—don't get so excited about it. It's only a matter of form you know—Judge Brack assured me of that. It was he that was kind enough to arrange the whole affair for me. A mere matter of form, he said.

TESMAN   Yes, that may be all very well. But nevertheless . . .

MISS TESMAN   You will have your own salary to depend upon now. And, good heavens, even if we did have to pay up a little . . . ! To eke things out a bit at the start . . . ! Why, it would be nothing but a pleasure to us.

TESMAN   Oh Auntie—will you never be tired of making sacrifices for me!

MISS TESMAN [*rises and lays her hands on his shoulders*]   Have I any other happiness in this world except to smooth your way for you, my dear boy? You, who have had neither father nor mother to depend on. And now we have reached the goal, George! Things have looked black enough for us, sometimes; but, thank heaven, now you have nothing to fear.

TESMAN   Yes, it is really marvelous how everything has turned out for the best

MISS TESMAN   And the people who opposed you—who wanted to bar the way for you—now you have them at your feet. They have fallen, George. Your most dangerous rival—his fall was the worst. And now he has to lie on the bed he has made for himself—poor misguided creature.

TESMAN   Have you heard anything of Eilert? Since I went away, I mean.

MISS TESMAN   Only that he is said to have published a new book.

TESMAN   What! Eilert Lövborg! Recently—eh?

MISS TESMAN   Yes, so they say. Heaven knows whether it can be worth any-thing! Ah, when your new book appears—that will be another story, George! What is it to be about?

TESMAN   It will deal with the domestic industries of Brabant during the Middle Ages.

MISS TESMAN   Fancy—to be able to write on such a subject as that!

TESMAN   However, it may be some time before the book is ready. I have all these collections to arrange first, you see.

MISS TESMAN   Yes, collecting and arranging—no one can beat you at that. There you are my poor brother's own son.

TESMAN   I am looking forward eagerly to setting to work at it; especially now that I have my own delightful home to work in.

MISS TESMAN   And, most of all, now that you have got a wife of your heart, my dear George.

TESMAN [*embracing her*]   Oh yes, yes, Aunt Julia. Hedda—she is the best part of it all! [*Looks towards the doorway*] I believe I hear her coming—eh?

HEDDA *enters from the left through the inner room. She is a woman of nine-and-twenty. Her face and figure show refinement and distinction. Her complexion is pale and opaque. Her steel-gray eyes express a cold, unruffled repose. Her hair is of an agreeable medium brown, but not particularly abundant. She is dressed in a tasteful, somewhat loose-fitting morning gown.*

MISS TESMAN [*going to meet* HEDDA]   Good morning, my dear Hedda! Good morning, and a hearty welcome!

HEDDA [*holds out her hand*]   Good morning, dear Miss Tesman! So early a call! That is kind of you.

MISS TESMAN [*with some embarrassment*]   Well—has the bride slept well in her new home?

HEDDA   Oh yes, thanks. Passably.

TESMAN [*laughing*]   Passably! Come, that's good, Hedda! You were sleeping like a stone when I got up.

HEDDA   Fortunately. Of course one has always to accustom one's self to new surroundings, Miss Tesman—little by little. [*Looking towards the left*] Oh—there the servant has gone and opened the veranda door, and let in a whole flood of sunshine.

MISS TESMAN [*going towards the door*]   Well, then we will shut it.

HEDDA   No, no, not that! Tesman, please draw the curtains. That will give a softer light.

TESMAN [*at the door*]   All right—all right. There now, Hedda, now you have both shade and fresh air.

HEDDA   Yes, fresh air we certainly must have, with all these stacks of flowers . . . But—won't you sit down, Miss Tesman?

MISS TESMAN   No, thank you. Now that I have seen that everything is all right here—thank heaven!—I must be getting home again. My sister is lying longing for me, poor thing.

TESMAN   Give her my very best love, Auntie; and say I shall look in and see her later in the day.

MISS TESMAN   Yes, yes, I'll be sure to tell her. But by the by, George—[*feeling *in her dress pocket*]—I had almost forgotten—I have something for you here.

TESMAN   What is it, Auntie? Eh?

MISS TESMAN [*produces a flat parcel wrapped in newspaper and hands it to him*]   Look here, my dear boy.

TESMAN [*opening the parcel*]   Well, I declare! Have you really saved them for me, Aunt Julia! Hedda! Isn't this touching—eh?

HEDDA [*beside the whatnot on the right*]   Well, what is it?

TESMAN   My old morning shoes! My slippers.

HEDDA   Indeed. I remember you often spoke of them while we were abroad.

TESMAN   Yes, I missed them terribly. [*Goes up to her*] Now you shall see them, Hedda!

HEDDA [*going towards the stove*]   Thanks, I really don't care about it.

TESMAN [*following her*]   Only think—ill as she was, Aunt Rina embroidered these for me. Oh you can't think how many associations cling to them.

HEDDA [*at the table*]   Scarcely for me.

MISS TESMAN   Of course not for Hedda, George.

TESMAN   Well, but now that she belongs to the family, I thought . . .

HEDDA [*interrupting*]   We shall never get on with this servant, Tesman.

MISS TESMAN   Not get on with Berta?

TESMAN   Why, dear, what puts that in your head? Eh?

HEDDA [*pointing*]   Look there! She has left her old bonnet lying about on a chair.

TESMAN [*in consternation, drops the slippers on the floor*]   Why, Hedda . . .

HEDDA   Just fancy, if any one should come in and see it!

TESMAN   But Hedda—that's Aunt Julia's bonnet.

HEDDA   Is it!

MISS TESMAN [*taking up the bonnet*]   Yes, indeed it's mine. And, what's more, it's not old, Madam Hedda.

HEDDA   I really did not look closely at it, Miss Tesman.

MISS TESMAN [*trying on the bonnet*]   Let me tell you it's the first time I have worn it—the very first time.

TESMAN   And a very nice bonnet it is too—quite a beauty!

MISS TESMAN   Oh, it's no such great thing, George. [*Looks around her*] My parasol . . . ? Ah, here. [*Takes it*] For this is mine too—[*mutters*] —not Berta's.

TESMAN   A new bonnet and a new parasol! Only think, Hedda!

HEDDA   Very handsome indeed.

TESMAN   Yes, isn't it? Eh? But Auntie, take a good look at Hedda before you go! See how handsome she is!

MISS TESMAN   Oh, my dear boy, there's nothing new in that. Hedda was always lovely. [*She nods and goes towards the right.*]

TESMAN [*following*]   Yes, but have you noticed what splendid condition she is in? How she has filled out on the journey?

HEDDA [*crossing the room*]   Oh, do be quiet . . . !

MISS TESMAN [*who has stopped and turned*]   Filled out?

TESMAN   Of course you don't notice it so much now that she has that dress on. But I, who can see . . .

HEDDA [*at the glass door, impatiently*]   Oh, you can't see anything.

TESMAN   It must be the mountain air in the Tyrol . . .

HEDDA [*curtly, interrupting*]   I am exactly as I was when I started.

TESMAN   So you insist; but I'm quite certain you are not. Don't you agree with me, Auntie?

MISS TESMAN [*who has been gazing at her with folded hands*]   Hedda is lovely—lovely—lovely. [*Goes up to her, takes her head between both hands, draws it downwards, and kisses her hair.*] God bless and preserve Hedda Tesman—for George's sake.

HEDDA [*gently freeing herself*]   Oh—! Let me go.

MISS TESMAN [*in quiet emotion*]   I shall not let a day pass without coming to see you.

TESMAN   No you won't, will you, Auntie? Eh?

MISS TESMAN   Good-bye—good-bye!

She goes out by the hall door. TESMAN *accompanies her. The door remains half open.* TESMAN *can be heard repeating his message to* AUNT RINA *and his thanks for the slippers. In the meantime,* HEDDA *walks about the room, raising her arms and clenching her hands as if in desperation. Then she flings back the curtains from the glass door, and stands there looking out. Presently* TESMAN *returns and closes the door behind him.*

TESMAN [*picks up the slippers from the floor*]   What are you looking at, Hedda?

HEDDA [*once more calm and mistress of herself*]   I am only looking at the leaves. They are so yellow—so withered.

TESMAN [*wraps up the slippers and lays them on the table*]   Well you see, we are well into September now.

HEDDA [*again restless*]   Yes, to think of it! Already in—in September.

TESMAN   Don't you think Aunt Julia's manner was strange, dear? Almost solemn? Can you imagine what was the matter with her? Eh?

HEDDA   I scarcely know her, you see. Is she not often like that?

TESMAN   No, not as she was today.

HEDDA [*leaving the glass door*]   Do you think she was annoyed about the bonnet?

TESMAN   Oh, scarcely at all. Perhaps a little, just at the moment . . .

HEDDA   But what an idea, to pitch her bonnet about in the drawing room! No one does that sort of thing.

TESMAN   Well you may be sure Aunt Julia won't do it again.

HEDDA   In any case, I shall manage to make my peace with her.

TESMAN   Yes, my dear, good Hedda, if you only would.

HEDDA   When you call this afternoon, you might invite her to spend the evening here.

TESMAN   Yes, that I will. And there's one thing more you could do that would delight her heart.

HEDDA   What is it?

TESMAN   If you could only prevail on yourself to say *du*[1] to her. For my sake, Hedda? Eh?

HEDDA   No, no, Tesman—you really mustn't ask that of me. I have told you so already. I shall try to call her "Aunt"; and you must be satisfied with that.

TESMAN   Well, well. Only I think now that you belong to the family, you . . .

[1]*Du*, the second person singular, implies intimacy.

HEDDA   H'm—I can't in the least see why . . . [*She goes up towards the middle doorway*]

TESMAN [*after a pause*]   Is there anything the matter with you, Hedda? Eh?

HEDDA   I'm only looking at my old piano. It doesn't go at all well with all the other things.

TESMAN   The first time I draw my salary, we'll see about exchanging it.

HEDDA   No, no—no exchanging. I don't want to part with it. Suppose we put it there in the inner room, and then get another here in its place. When it's convenient, I mean.

TESMAN [*a little taken aback*]   Yes—of course we could do that.

HEDDA [*takes up the bouquet from the piano*]   These flowers were not here last night when we arrived.

TESMAN   Aunt Julia must have brought them for you.

HEDDA [*examining the bouquet*]   A visiting card. [*Takes it out and reads*] "Shall return later in the day." Can you guess whose card it is?

TESMAN   No. Whose? Eh?

HEDDA   The name is "Mrs. Elvsted."

TESMAN   Is it really? Sheriff Elvsted's wife? Miss Rysing that was.

HEDDA   Exactly. The girl with the irritating hair, that she was always showing off. An old flame of yours I've been told.

TESMAN [*laughing*]   Oh, that didn't last long; and it was before I knew you, Hedda. But fancy her being in town!

HEDDA   It's odd that she should call upon us. I have scarcely seen her since we left school.

TESMAN   I haven't seen her either for—heaven knows how long. I wonder how she can endure to live in such an out-of-the-way hole—eh?

HEDDA [*after a moment's thought, says suddenly*]   Tell me, Tesman—isn't it somewhere near there that he—that—Eilert Lövborg is living?

TESMAN   Yes, he is somewhere in that part of the country.

BERTA *enters by the hall door.*

BERTA   That lady, ma'am, that brought some flowers a little while ago, is here again. [*Pointing*] The flowers you have in your hand, ma'am.

HEDDA   Ah, is she? Well, please show her in.

BERTA *opens the door for* MRS. ELVSTED, *and goes out herself.*—MRS. ELVSTED *is a woman of fragile figure, with pretty, soft features. Her eyes are light blue, large, round, and somewhat prominent, with a startled, inquiring expression. Her hair is remarkably light, almost flaxen, and unusually abundant and wavy. She is a couple of years younger than* HEDDA. *She wears a dark visiting dress, tasteful, but not quite in the lastest fashion.*

HEDDA [*receives her warmly*]   How do you do, my dear Mrs. Elvsted? It's delightful to see you again.

MRS. ELVSTED [*nervously, struggling for self-control*]   Yes, it's a very long time since we met.

TESMAN [*gives her his hand*]   And we too—eh?

HEDDA   Thanks for your lovely flowers . . .

MRS. ELVSTED   Oh, not at all . . . I would have come straight here yesterday afternoon; but I heard that you were away . . .

TESMAN   Have you just come to town? Eh?

MRS. ELVSTED   I arrived yesterday, about midday. Oh, I was quite in despair when I heard that you were not at home.

HEDDA   In despair! How so?

TESMAN   Why, my dear Mrs. Rysing—I mean Mrs. Elvsted . . .

HEDDA   I hope that you are not in any trouble?

MRS. ELVSTED.   Yes, I am. And I don't know another living creature here that I can turn to.

HEDDA [*laying the bouquet on the table*]   Come—let us sit here on the sofa . . .

MRS. ELVSTED   Oh, I am too restless to sit down.

HEDDA   Oh no, you're not. Come here. [*She draws* MRS. ELVSTED *down upon the sofa and sits at her side.*]

TESMAN   Well? What is it, Mrs. Elvsted . . . ?

HEDDA   Has anything particular happened to you at home?

MRS. ELVSTED   Yes—and no. Oh—I am so anxious you should not misunderstand me . . .

HEDDA   Then your best plan is to tell us the whole story, Mrs. Elvsted.

TESMAN   I suppose that's what you have come for—eh?

MRS. ELVSTED   Yes, yes—of course it is. Well then, I must tell you, if you don't already know, that Eilert Lövborg is in town, too.

HEDDA   Lövborg . . . !

TESMAN   What! Has Eilert Lövborg come back? Fancy that, Hedda!

HEDDA   Well, well—I hear it.

MRS. ELVSTED   He has been here a week already. Just fancy—a whole week! In this terrible town, alone! With so many temptations on all sides.

HEDDA   But, my dear Mrs. Elvsted—how does he concern you so much?

MRS. ELVSTED [*looks at her with a startled air, and says rapidly*]   He was the children's tutor.

HEDDA   Your children's?

MRS. ELVSTED   My husband's. I have none.

HEDDA   Your stepchildren's, then?

MRS. ELVSTED   Yes.

TESMAN [*somewhat hesitatingly*]   Then was he—I don't know how to express it—was he—regular enough in his habits to be fit for the post? Eh?

MRS. ELVSTED   For the last two years his conduct has been irreproachable.

TESMAN   Has it indeed? Fancy that, Hedda!

HEDDA   I hear it.

MRS. ELVSTED   Perfectly irreproachable, I assure you! In every respect. But all the same—now that I know he is here—in this great town—and with a large sum of money in his hands—I can't help being in mortal fear for him.

TESMAN   Why did he not remain where he was? With you and your husband? Eh?

MRS. ELVSTED   After his book was published he was too restless and unsettled to remain with us.

TESMAN   Yes, by the by, Aunt Julia told me he had published a new book.

MRS. ELVSTED   Yes, a big book, dealing with the march of civilization—in broad outline, as it were. It came out about a fortnight ago. And since it has sold so well, and been so much read—and made such a sensation . . .

TESMAN   Has it indeed? It must be something he has had lying by since his better days.

MRS. ELVSTED   Long ago, you mean?

TESMAN   Yes.

MRS. ELVSTED   No, he has written it all since he has been with us—within the last year.

TESMAN   Isn't that good news, Hedda? Think of that.

MRS. ELVSTED   Ah yes, if only it would last!

HEDDA   Have you seen him here in town?

MRS. ELVSTED   No, not yet. I have had the greatest difficulty in finding out his address. But this morning I discovered it at last.

HEDDA [*looks searchingly at her*]   Do you know, it seems to me a little odd of your husband—h'm . . .

MRS. ELVSTED [*starting nervously*]   Of my husband! What?

HEDDA   That he should send you to town on such an errand—that he does not come himself and look after his friend.

MRS. ELVSTED   Oh no, no—my husband has no time. And besides, I—I had some shopping to do.

HEDDA [*with a slight smile*]   Ah, that is a different matter.

MRS. ELVSTED [*rising quickly and uneasily*]   And now I beg and implore you, Mr. Tesman—receive Eilert Lövborg kindly if he comes to you! And that he is sure to do. You see you were such great friends in the old days. And then you are interested in the same studies—the same branch of science—so far as I can understand.

TESMAN   We used to be, at any rate.

MRS. ELVSTED   That is why I beg so earnestly that you—you too—will keep a sharp eye upon him. Oh, you will promise me that, Mr. Tesman—won't you?

TESMAN   With the greatest of pleasure, Mrs. Rysing . . .

HEDDA   Elvsted.

TESMAN   I assure you I shall do all I possibly can for Eilert. You may rely upon me.

MRS. ELVSTED   Oh, how very, very kind of you! [*Presses his hands*] Thanks, thanks, thanks! [*Frightened*] You see, my husband is so very fond of him!

HEDDA [*rising*]   You ought to write to him, Tesman. Perhaps he may not care to come to you of his own accord.

TESMAN   Well, perhaps it would be the right thing to do, Hedda? Eh?

HEDDA   And the sooner the better. Why not at once?

MRS. ELVSTED [*imploringly*]   Oh, if you only would!

TESMAN   I'll write this moment. Have you his address, Mrs.—Mrs. Elvsted?

MRS. ELVSTED   Yes. [*Takes a slip of paper from her pocket, and hands it to him*] Here it is.

TESMAN   Good, good. Then I'll go in . . . [*Looks about him*] By the by—my slippers? Oh, here. [*Takes the packet, and is about to go*]

HEDDA   Be sure you write him a cordial, friendly letter. And a good long one too.

TESMAN   Yes, I will.

MRS. ELVSTED   But please, please don't say a word to show that I have suggested it.

TESMAN   No, how could you think I would? Eh? [*He goes out to the right, through the inner room.*]

HEDDA [*goes up to* MRS. ELVSTED, *smiles and says in a low voice*]   There! We have killed two birds with one stone.

MRS. ELVSTED   What do you mean?

HEDDA   Could you not see that I wanted him to go?

MRS. ELVSTED   Yes, to write the letter . . .

HEDDA   And that I might speak to you alone.

MRS. ELVSTED [*confused*]   About the same thing?

HEDDA   Precisely.

MRS. ELVSTED [*apprehensively*]   But there is nothing more, Mrs. Tesman! Absolutely nothing!

HEDDA   Oh yes, but there is. There is a great deal more—I can see that. Sit here—and we'll have a cozy, confidential chat. [*She forces* MRS. ELVSTED *to sit in the easy-chair beside the stove, and seats herself on one of the footstools.*]

MRS. ELVSTED [*anxiously, looking at her watch*]   But, my dear Mrs. Tesman—I was really on the point of going.

HEDDA   Oh, you can't be in such a hurry. Well? Now tell me something about your life at home.

MRS. ELVSTED   Oh, that is just what I care least to speak about.

HEDDA   But to me, dear . . . ? Why, weren't we schoolfellows?

MRS. ELVSTED   Yes, but you were in the class above me. Oh, how dreadfully afraid of you I was then!

HEDDA   Afraid of me?

MRS. ELVSTED   Yes, dreadfully. For when we met on the stairs you used always to pull my hair.

HEDDA   Did I, really?

MRS. ELVSTED   Yes, and once you said you would burn it off my head.

HEDDA   Oh, that was all nonsense, of course.

MRS. ELVSTED   Yes, but I was so silly in those days. And since then, too—we have drifted so far—far apart from each other. Our circles have been so entirely different.

HEDDA   Well then, we must try to drift together again. Now listen! At school we said *du* to each other; and we called each other by our Christian names . . .

MRS. ELVSTED   No, I am sure you must be mistaken.

HEDDA   No, not at all! I can remember quite distinctly. So now we are going to renew our old friendship. [*Draws the footstool closer to* MRS. ELVSTED.] There now! [*Kisses her cheek.*] You must say *du* to me and call me Hedda.

MRS. ELVSTED [*presses and pats her hands*]   Oh, how good and kind you are! I am not used to such kindness.

HEDDA   There, there, there! And I shall say *du* to you, as in the old days, and call you my dear Thora.

MRS. ELVSTED   My name is Thea.

HEDDA   Why, of course! I meant Thea. [*Looks at her compassionately*] So you are not accustomed to goodness and kindness, Thea? Not in your own home?

MRS. ELVSTED   Oh, if I only had a home! But I haven't any; I have never had a home.

HEDDA [*looks at her for a moment*]   I almost suspected as much.

MRS. ELVSTED [*gazing helplessly before her*]   Yes—yes—yes.

HEDDA   I don't quite remember—was it not as housekeeper that you first went to Mr. Elvsted's?

MRS. ELVSTED   I really went as governess. But his wife—his late wife—was an invalid, and rarely left her room. So I had to look after the housekeeping as well.

HEDDA   And then—at last—you became mistress of the house.

MRS. ELVSTED [*sadly*]   Yes, I did.

HEDDA   Let me see—about how long ago was that?

MRS. ELVSTED   My marriage?

HEDDA   Yes.

MRS. ELVSTED   Five years ago.

HEDDA   To be sure; it must be that.

MRS. ELVSTED   Oh those five years . . . ! Or at all events the last two or three of them! Oh, if you[1] could only imagine . . .

HEDDA [*giving her a little slap on the hand*]   De? Fie, Thea!

MRS. ELVSTED   Yes, yes, I will try . . . Well, if—you could only imagine and understand . . .

HEDDA [*lightly*]   Eilert Lövborg has been in your neighborhood about three years, hasn't he?

MRS. ELVSTED [*looks at her doubtfully*]   Eilert Lövborg? Yes—he has.

HEDDA   Had you known him before, in town here?

MRS. ELVSTED   Scarcely at all. I mean—I knew him by name of course.

HEDDA   But you saw a good deal of him in the country?

MRS. ELVSTED   Yes, he came to us every day. You see, he gave the children lessons; for in the long run I couldn't manage it all myself.

HEDDA   No, that's clear.—And your husband—? I suppose he is often away from home?

MRS. ELVSTED   Yes. Being sheriff, you know, he has to travel about a good deal in his district.

HEDDA [*leaning against the arm of the chair*]   Thea—my poor, sweet Thea—now you must tell me everything—exactly as it stands.

MRS. ELVSTED   Well then, you must question me.

HEDDA   What sort of a man is your husband, Thea? I mean—you know—in everyday life. Is he kind to you?

MRS. ELVSTED [*evasively*]   I am sure he means well in everything.

HEDDA   I should think he must be altogether too old for you. There is at least twenty years' difference between you, is there not?

MRS. ELVSTED [*irritably*]   Yes, that is true, too. Everything about him is repellent to me! We have not a thought in common. We have no single point of sympathy—he and I.

HEDDA   But is he not fond of you all the same? In his own way?

MRS. ELVSTED   Oh I really don't know. I think he regards me simply as a useful property. And then it doesn't cost much to keep me. I am not expensive.

HEDDA   That is stupid of you.

MRS. ELVSTED [*shakes her head*]   It cannot be otherwise—not with him. I don't think he really cares for any one but himself—and perhaps a little for the children.

HEDDA   And for Eilert Lövborg, Thea.

MRS. ELVSTED [*looking at her*]   For Eilert Lövborg? What puts that into your head?

HEDDA   Well, my dear—I should say, when he sends you after him all the way to town . . . [*Smiling almost imperceptibly.*] And besides, you said so yourself, to Tesman.

MRS. ELVSTED [*with a little nervous twitch*]   Did I? Yes, I suppose I did. [*Vehemently, but not loudly.*] No—I may just as well make a clean breast of it at once!

---

[1]Mrs. Elvsted uses the formal *de* (for *you*) instead of the intimate *du*.

For it must all come out in any case.

HEDDA Why, my dear Thea . . . ?

MRS. ELVSTED Well, to make a long story short: My husband did not know that I was coming.

HEDDA What! Your husband didn't know it!

MRS. ELVSTED No, of course not. For that matter, he was away from home himself—he was traveling. Oh, I could bear it no longer, Hedda! I couldn't in- deed—so utterly alone as I should have been in future.

HEDDA Well? And then?

MRS. ELVSTED So I put together some of my things—what I needed most—as quietly as possible. And then I left the house.

HEDDA Without a word?

MRS. ELVSTED Yes—and took the train straight to town.

HEDDA Why, my dear, good Thea—to think of you daring to do it!

MRS. ELVSTED [*rises and moves about the room*] What else could I possibly do?

HEDDA But what do you think your husband will say when you go home again?

MRS. ELVSTED [*at the table, looks at her*] Back to him?

HEDDA Of course.

MRS. ELVSTED I shall never go back to him again.

HEDDA [*rising and going towards her*] Then you have left your home—for good and all?

MRS. ELVSTED Yes. There was nothing else to be done.

HEDDA But then—to take flight so openly.

MRS. ELVSTED Oh, it's impossible to keep things of that sort secret.

HEDDA But what do you think people will say of you, Thea?

MRS. ELVSTED They may say what they like, for aught *I* care. [*Seats herself wearily and sadly on the sofa.*] I have done nothing but what I had to do.

HEDDA [*after a short silence*] And what are your plans now? What do you think of doing?

MRS. ELVSTED I don't know yet. I only know this, that I must live here, where Eilert Lövborg is—if I am to live at all.

HEDDA [*takes a chair from the table, seats herself beside her, and strokes her hands*] My dear Thea—how did this—this friendship—between you and Eilert Lövborg come about?

MRS. ELVSTED Oh it grew up gradually. I gained a sort of influence over him.

HEDDA Indeed?

MRS. ELVSTED He gave up his old habits. Not because I asked him to, for I never dared do that. But of course he saw how repulsive they were to me; and so he dropped them.

HEDDA [*concealing an involuntary smile of scorn*] Then you have reclaimed him—as the saying goes—my little Thea.

MRS. ELVSTED So he says himself, at any rate. And he, on his side, has made a real human being of me—taught me to think, and to understand so many things.

HEDDA Did he give you lessons too, then?

MRS. ELVSTED No, not exactly lessons. But he talked to me—talked about such an infinity of things. And then came the lovely, happy time when I began to share in his work—when he allowed me to help him!

HEDDA Oh he did, did he?

MRS. ELVSTED Yes! He never wrote anything without my assistance.

HEDDA   You were two good comrades, in fact?

MRS. ELVSTED [*eagerly*]   Comrades! Yes, fancy, Hedda—that is the very word he used! Oh, I ought to feel perfectly happy; and yet I cannot; for I don't know how long it will last.

HEDDA   Are you no surer of him than that?

MRS. ELVSTED [*gloomily*]   A woman's shadow stands between Eilert Lövborg and me.

HEDDA [*looks at her anxiously*]   Who can that be?

MRS. ELVSTED   I don't know. Some one he knew in his—in his past. Some one he has never been able wholly to forget.

HEDDA   What has he told you—about this?

MRS. ELVSTED   He has only once—quite vaguely—alluded to it.

HEDDA   Well! And what did he say?

MRS. ELVSTED   He said that when they parted, she threatened to shoot him with a pistol.

HEDDA [*with cold composure*]   Oh, nonsense! No one does that sort of thing here.

MRS. ELVSTED   No. And that is why I think it must have been that red-haired singing woman whom he once . . .

HEDDA   Yes, very likely.

MRS. ELVSTED   For I remember they used to say of her that she carried loaded firearms.

HEDDA   Oh—then of course it must have been she.

MRS. ELVSTED [*wringing her hands*]   And now just fancy, Hedda—I hear that this singing woman—that she is in town again! Oh, I don't know what to do . . .

HEDDA [*glancing towards the inner room*]   Hush! Here comes Tesman. [*Rises and whispers.*] Thea—all this must remain between you and me.

MRS. ELVSTED [*springing up*]   Oh yes—yes! For heaven's sake . . . !

GEORGE TESMAN, *with a letter in his hand, comes from the right through the inner room.*

TESMAN   There now—the epistle is finished.

HEDDA   That's right. And now Mrs. Elvsted is just going. Wait a moment—I'll go with you to the garden gate.

TESMAN   Do you think Berta could post the letter, Hedda dear?

HEDDA [*takes it*]   I will tell her to.

[BERTA *enters from the hall.*]

BERTA   Judge Brack wishes to know if Mrs. Tesman will receive him.

HEDDA   Yes, ask Judge Brack to come in. And look here—put this letter in the post.

BERTA [*taking the letter*]   Yes, Ma'am.

She opens the door for JUDGE BRACK *and goes out herself.* BRACK *is a man of forty-five; thickset, but well built and elastic in his movements. His face is round-ish with an aristocratic profile. His hair is short, still almost black, and carefully dressed. His eyes are lively and sparkling. His eyebrows thick. His mustaches are also thick, with short-cut ends. He wears a well-cut walking suit, a little too youthful for his age. He uses an eyeglass, which he now and then lets drop.*

JUDGE BRACK [*with his hat in his hand, bowing*]   May one venture to call so early in the day?

HEDDA   Of course one may.

TESMAN [*presses his hand*]   You are welcome at any time. [*Introducing him.*] Judge Brack—Miss Rysing . . .

HEDDA   Oh . . .!

BRACK [*bowing*]   Ah—delighted . . .

HEDDA [*looks at him and laughs*]   It's nice to have a look at you by daylight, Judge!

BRACK   Do you find me—altered?

HEDDA   A little younger, I think.

BRACK   Thank you so much.

TESMAN   But what do you think of Hedda—eh? Doesn't she look flourishing? She has actually . . .

HEDDA   Oh, do leave me alone. You haven't thanked Judge Brack for all the trouble he has taken . . .

BRACK   Oh, nonsense—it was a pleasure to me . . .

HEDDA   Yes, you are a friend indeed. But here stands Thea all impatience to be off—so *au revoir*, Judge. I shall be back again presently.

Mutual salutations. MRS. ELVSTED *and* HEDDA *go out by the hall door.*

BRACK   Well, is your wife tolerably satisfied . . .

TESMAN   Yes, we can't thank you sufficiently. Of course she talks of a little rearrangement here and there; and one or two things are still wanting. We shall have to buy some additional trifles.

BRACK   Indeed!

TESMAN   But we won't trouble you about these things. Hedda says she herself will look after what is wanting. Shan't we sit down? Eh?

BRACK   Thanks, for a moment. [*Seats himself beside the table.*] There is something I wanted to speak to you about, my dear Tesman.

TESMAN   Indeed? Ah, I understand! [*Seating himself*] I suppose it's the serious part of the frolic that is coming now. Eh?

BRACK   Oh, the money question is not so very pressing; though, for that matter, I wish we had gone a little more economically to work.

TESMAN   But that would never have done, you know! Think of Hedda, my dear fellow! You, who know her so well . . . I couldn't possibly ask her to put up with a shabby style of living!

BRACK   No, no—that is just the difficulty.

TESMAN   And then—fortunately—it can't be long before I receive my appointment.

BRACK   Well, you see—such things are often apt to hang fire for a time.

TESMAN   Have you heard anything definite? Eh?

BRACK   Nothing exactly definite . . . [*Interrupting himself*] But by the by—I have one piece of news for you.

TESMAN   Well?

BRACK   Your old friend, Eilert Lövborg, has returned to town.

TESMAN   I know that already.

BRACK   Indeed! How did you learn it?

TESMAN   From that lady who went out with Hedda.

BRACK   Really? What was her name? I didn't quite catch it.

TESMAN   Mrs. Elvsted.

BRACK   Aha—Sheriff Elvsted's wife? Of course—he has been living up in their regions.

TESMAN   And fancy—I'm delighted to hear that he is quite a reformed character!

BRACK   So they say.

TESMAN   And then he has published a new book—eh?

BRACK   Yes, indeed he has.

TESMAN   And I hear it has made some sensation!

BRACK   Quite an unusual sensation.

TESMAN   Fancy—isn't that good news! A man of such extraordinary talents . . .I felt so grieved to think that he had gone irretrievably to ruin.

BRACK   That was what everybody thought.

TESMAN   But I cannot imagine what he will take to now! How in the world will he be able to make his living? Eh?

During the last words, HEDDA *has entered by the hall door.*

HEDDA [*to* BRACK, *laughing with a touch of scorn*]   Tesman is for every worrying about how people are to make their living.

TESMAN   Well you see, dear—we were talking about poor Eilert Lövborg.

HEDDA [*glancing at him rapidly*]   Oh, indeed? [*Seats herself in the armchair beside the stove and asks indifferently.*] What is the matter with him?

TESMAN   Well—no doubt he has run through all his property long ago; and he can scarcely write a new book every year—eh? So I really can't see what is to become of him.

BRACK   Perhaps I can give you some information on that point.

TESMAN   Indeed!

BRACK   You must remember that his relations have a good deal of influence.

TESMAN   Oh, his relations, unfortunately, have entirely washed their hands of him.

BRACK   At one time they called him the hope of the family.

TESMAN   At one time, yes! But he has put an end to all that.

HEDDA   Who knows? [*With a slight smile*] I hear they have reclaimed him up at Sheriff Elvsted's . . .

BRACK   And then this book that he has published . . .

TESMAN   Well, well, I hope to goodness they may find something for him to do. I have just written to him. I asked him to come and see us this evening, Hedda dear.

BRACK   But my dear fellow, you are booked for my bachelors' party this evening. You promised on the pier last night.

HEDDA   Had you forgotten, Tesman?

TESMAN   Yes, I had utterly forgotten.

BRACK   But it doesn't matter, for you may be sure he won't come.

TESMAN   What makes you think that? Eh?

BRACK [*with a little hesitation, rising and resting his hands on the back of his chair*]   My dear Tesman—and you too, Mrs. Tesman—I think I ought not to keep you in the dark about something that—that . . .

TESMAN   That concerns Eilert . . . ?

BRACK   Both you and him.

TESMAN   Well, my dear Judge, out with it.

BRACK   You must be prepared to find your appointment deferred longer than you desired or expected.

TESMAN [*jumping up uneasily*]   Is there some hitch about it? Eh?

BRACK   The nomination may perhaps be made conditional on the result of a competition . . .

TESMAN   Competition! Think of that, Hedda!

HEDDA [*leans further back in the chair*]   Aha—aha!

TESMAN   But who can my competitor be? Surely not . . . ?

BRACK   Yes, precisely—Eilert Lövborg.

TESMAN [*clasping his hands*]   No, no—it's quite inconceivable! Quite impossible! Eh?

BRACK   H'm—that is what it may come to, all the same.

TESMAN   Well but, Judge Brack—it would show the most incredible lack of consideration for me. [*Gesticulates with his arms*] For—just think—I'm a married man! We have married on the strength of these prospects, Hedda and I; and run deep into debt; and borrowed money from Aunt Julia too. Good heavens, they had as good as promised me the appointment. Eh?

BRACK   Well, well, well—no doubt you will get it in the end; only after a contest.

HEDDA [*immovable in her armchair*]   Fancy, Tesman, there will be a sort of sporting interest in that.

TESMAN   Why, my dearest Hedda, how can you be so indifferent about it?

HEDDA [*As before*]   I am not at all indifferent. I am most eager to see who wins.

BRACK   In any case, Mrs. Tesman, it is best that you should know how matters stand. I mean—before you set about the little purchases I hear you are threatening.

HEDDA   This can make no difference.

BRACK   Indeed! Then I have no more to say. Good-bye! [*To* TESMAN] I shall look in on my way back from my afternoon walk, and take you home with me.

TESMAN   Oh yes, yes—your news has quite upset me.

HEDDA [*reclining, holds out her hand*]   Good-bye, Judge; and be sure you call in the afternoon.

BRACK   Many thanks. Good-bye, good-bye!

TESMAN [*accompanying him to the door*]   Good-bye, my dear Judge! You must really excuse me . . .

JUDGE BRACK *goes out by the hall door.*

TESMAN [*crosses the room*]   Oh Hedda—one should never rush into adventures. Eh?

HEDDA [*looks at him, smiling*]   Do you do that?

TESMAN   Yes, dear—there is no denying—it was adventurous to go and marry and set up house upon mere expectations.

HEDDA   Perhaps you are right there.

TESMAN   Well—at all events, we have our delightful home, Hedda! Fancy, the home we both dreamed of—the home we were in love with, I may almost say. Eh?

HEDDA [*rising slowly and wearily*]   It was part of our compact that we were to go into society—to keep open house.

TESMAN   Yes, if you only knew how I had been looking forward to it! Fancy—to see you as hostess—in a select circle! Eh? Well, well, well—for the present we shall have to get on without society, Hedda—only to invite Aunt Julia now and then. Oh, I intended you to lead such an utterly different life, dear . . . !

HEDDA   Of course I cannot have my man in livery just yet.

TESMAN   Oh no, unfortunately. It would be out of the question for us to keep a footman, you know.

HEDDA   And the saddle horse I was to have had . . .

TESMAN [*aghast*]   The saddle horse!

HEDDA   . . . I suppose I must not think of that now.

TESMAN   Good heavens, no!—that's as clear as daylight.

HEDDA [*goes up the room*]   Well, I shall have one thing at least to kill time with in the meanwhile.

TESMAN [*beaming*]   Oh thank heaven for that! What is it, Hedda? Eh?

HEDDA [*in the middle doorway, looks at him with covert scorn*]   My pistols, George.

TESMAN [*in alarm*]   Your pistols!

HEDDA [*with cold eyes*]   General Gabler's pistols. [*She goes out through the inner room, to the left.*]

TESMAN [*rushes up to the middle doorway and calls after her*]   No, for heaven's sake, Hedda darling—don't touch those dangerous things! For my sake, Hedda! Eh?

Act II

SCENE: *The room at the* TESMANS' *as in the first act, except that the piano has been removed, and an elegant little writing table with bookshelves put in its place. A smaller table stands near the sofa on the left. Most of the bouquets have been taken away.* MRS. ELVSTED'S *bouquet is upon the large table in front. It is afternoon.* HEDDA, *dressed to receive callers, is alone in the room. She stands by the open glass door, loading a revolver. The fellow to it lies in an open pistol case on the writing table.*

HEDDA [*looks down the garden, and calls*]   So you are here again, Judge!

BRACK [*is heard calling from a distance*]   As you see, Mrs. Tesman!

HEDDA [*raises the pistol and points*]   Now I'll shoot you, Judge Brack!

BRACK [*calling unseen*]   No, no, no! Don't stand aiming at me!

HEDDA   This is what comes of sneaking in by the back way. [*She fires.*]

BRACK [*nearer*]   Are you out of your senses! . . .

HEDDA   Dear me—did I happen to hit you?

BRACK [*still outside*]   I wish you would let these pranks alone!

HEDDA   Come in then, Judge.

JUDGE BRACK, *dressed as though for a men's party, enters by the glass door. He carries a light overcoat over his arm.*

BRACK   What the deuce—haven't you tired of that sport, yet? What are you shooting at?

HEDDA   Oh, I am only firing in the air.

BRACK [*gently takes the pistol out of her hand*]   Allow me, Madam! [*Looks at it*] Ah—I know this pistol well! [*Looks around*] Where is the case? Ah, here it is.

[*Lays the pistol in it, and shuts it*] Now we won't play at that game any more today.

HEDDA   Then what in heaven's name would you have me do with myself?

BRACK   Have you had no visitors?

HEDDA [*closing the glass door*]   Not one. I suppose all our set are still out of town.

BRACK   And is Tesman not at home either?

HEDDA [*at the writing table, putting the pistol case in a drawer which she shuts*]   No. He rushed off to his aunt's directly after lunch; he didn't expect you so early.

BRACK   H'm—how stupid of me not to have thought of that!

HEDDA [*turning her head to look at him*]   Why stupid?

BRACK   Because if I had thought of it I should have come a little—earlier.

HEDDA [*Crossing the room*]   Then you would have found no one to receive you; for I have been in my room changing my dress ever since lunch.

BRACK   And is there no sort of little chink that we could hold a parley through?

HEDDA   You have forgotten to arrange one.

BRACK   That was another piece of stupidity.

HEDDA   Well, we must just settle down here—and wait. Tesman is not likely to be back for some time yet.

BRACK   Never mind; I shall not be impatient.

HEDDA *seats herself in the corner of the sofa.* BRACK *lays his overcoat over the back of the nearest chair, and sits down, but keeps his hat in his hand. A short silence. They look at each other.*

HEDDA   Well?

BRACK [*in the same tone*]   Well?

HEDDA   I spoke first.

BRACK [*bending a little forward*]   Come, let us have a cozy little chat, Mrs. Hedda.

HEDDA [*leaning further back in the sofa*]   Does it not seem like a whole eternity since our last talk? Of course I don't count those few words yesterday evening and this morning.

BRACK   You mean since our last confidential talk? Our last *tête-à-tête*?

HEDDA   Well, yes—since you put it so.

BRACK   Not a day has passed but I have wished that you were home again.

HEDDA   And I have done nothing but wish the same thing.

BRACK   You? Really, Mrs. Hedda? And I thought you had been enjoying your tour so much!

HEDDA   Oh, yes, you may be sure of that!

BRACK   But Tesman's letters spoke of nothing but happiness.

HEDDA   Oh, Tesman! You see, he thinks nothing so delightful as grubbing in libraries and making copies of old parchments, or whatever you call them.

BRACK [*with a spice of malice*]   Well, that is his vocation in life—or part of it at any rate.

HEDDA   Yes, of course; and no doubt when it's your vocation . . . But *I*! Oh, my dear Mr. Brack, how mortally bored I have been.

BRACK [*sympathetically*]   Do you really say so? In downright earnest?

HEDDA   Yes, you can surely understand it . . . ! To go for six whole months without meeting a soul that knew anything of our circle, or could talk about the things we are interested in.

BRACK   Yes, yes—I, too, should feel that a deprivation.

HEDDA   And then, what I found most intolerable of all . . .

BRACK   Well?

HEDDA   . . . was being everlastingly in the company of—one and the same person . . .

BRACK [*with a nod of assent*]   Morning, noon, and night, yes—at all possible times and seasons.

HEDDA   I said "everlastingly."

BRACK   Just so. But I should have thought, with our excellent Tesman, one could . . .

HEDDA   Tesman is—a specialist, my dear Judge.

BRACK   Undeniably.

HEDDA   And specialists are not at all amusing to travel with. Not in the long run at any rate.

BRACK   Not even—the specialist one happens to love?

HEDDA   Faugh—don't use that sickening word!

BRACK [*taken aback*]   What do you say, Mrs. Hedda?

HEDDA [*half laughingly, half irritated*]   You should just try it! To hear of nothing but the history of civilization morning, noon, and night . . .

BRACK   Everlastingly.

HEDDA   Yes, yes, yes! And then all this about the domestic industry of the Middle Ages . . . ! That's the most disgusting part of it!

BRACK [*looks searchingly at her*]   But tell me—in that case, how am I to understand your . . . ? H'm . . .

HEDDA   My accepting George Tesman, you mean?

BRACK   Well, let us put it so.

HEDDA   Good heavens, do you see anything so wonderful in that?

BRACK   Yes and no—Mrs. Hedda.

HEDDA   I had positively danced myself tired, my dear Judge. My day was done . . . [*With a slight shudder*] Oh, no—I won't say that; nor think it, either!

BRACK   You have assuredly no reason to.

HEDDA   Oh, reasons . . . [*Watching him closely*] And George Tesman—after all, you must admit that he is correctness itself.

BRACK   His correctness and respectability are beyond all question.

HEDDA   And I don't see anything absolutely ridiculous about him. Do you?

BRACK   Ridiculous? N—no—I shouldn't exactly say so . . .

HEDDA   Well—and his powers of research, at all events, are untiring. I see no reason why he should not one day come to the front, after all.

BRACK [*looks at her hesitatingly*]   I thought that you, like every one else, expected him to attain the highest distinction.

HEDDA [*with an expression of fatigue*]   Yes, so I did—And then, since he was bent, at all hazards, on being allowed to provide for me—I really don't know why I should not have accepted his offer.

BRACK   No—if you look at it in that light . . .

HEDDA   It was more than my other adorers were prepared to do for me, my dear Judge.

BRACK [*laughing*] Well, I can't answer for all the rest; but as for myself, you know quite well that I have always entertained a—a certain respect for the marriage tie—for marriage as an institution, Mrs. Hedda.

HEDDA [*jestingly*] Oh, I assure you I have never cherished any hopes with respect to you.

BRACK All I require is a pleasant and intimate interior, where I can make myself useful in every way, and am free to come and go as—as a trusted friend . . .

HEDDA Of the master of the house, do you mean?

BRACK [*bowing*] Frankly—of the mistress first of all; but, of course, of the master, too, in the second place. Such a triangular friendship—if I may call it so— is really a great convenience for all parties, let me tell you.

HEDDA Yes, I have many a time longed for some one to make a third on our travels. Oh—those railway-carriage *tête-à-têtes* . . . !

BRACK Fortunately your wedding journey is over now.

HEDDA [*shaking her head*] Not by a long—long way. I have only arrived at a station on the line.

BRACK Well, then the passengers jump out and move about a little, Mrs. Hedda.

HEDDA I never jump out.

BRACK Really?

HEDDA No—because there is always some one standing by to . . .

BRACK [*laughing*] To look at your legs, do you mean?

HEDDA Precisely.

BRACK Well, but, dear me . . .

HEDDA [*with a gesture of repulsion*] I won't have it. I would rather keep my seat where I happen to be—and continue the *tête-à-tête*.

BRACK But suppose a third person were to jump in and join the couple.

HEDDA Ah—that is quite another matter!

BRACK A trusted, sympathetic friend . . .

HEDDA . . . with a fund of conversation on all sorts of lively topics . . .

BRACK . . . and not the least bit of a specialist!

HEDDA [*with an audible sigh*] Yes, that would be a relief, indeed.

BRACK [*hears the front door open, and glances in that direction*] The triangle is completed.

HEDDA [*half aloud*] And on goes the train.

GEORGE TESMAN, *in a gray walking suit, with a soft felt hat, enters from the hall. He has a number of unbound books under his arm and in his pockets.*

TESMAN [*goes up to the table beside the corner settee*] Ouf—what a load for a warm day—all these books. [*Lays them on the table*] I'm positively perspiring, Hedda. Hallo—are you there already, my dear Judge? Eh? Berta didn't tell me.

BRACK [*rising*] I came in through the garden.

HEDDA What books have you got there?

TESMAN [*stands looking them through*] Some new books on my special sub-jects—quite indispensable to me.

HEDDA Your special subjects?

BRACK Yes, books on his special subjects, Mrs. Tesman.

BRACK *and* HEDDA *exchange a confidential smile.*

HEDDA   Do you need still more books on your special subjects?

TESMAN   Yes, my dear Hedda, one can never have too many of them. Of course, one must keep up with all that is written and published.

HEDDA   Yes, I suppose one must.

TESMAN [*searching among his books*]   And look here—I have got hold of Eilert Lövborg's new book, too. [*Offering it to her*] Perhaps you would like to glance through it, Hedda? Eh?

HEDDA   No, thank you. Or rather—afterwards perhaps.

TESMAN   I looked into it a little on the way home.

BRACK   Well, what do you think of it—as a specialist?

TESMAN   I think it shows quite remarkable soundness of judgment. He never wrote like that before. [*Putting the books together*] Now I shall take all these into my study. I'm longing to cut the leaves . . . ! And then I must change my clothes. [*To* BRACK] I suppose we needn't start just yet? Eh?

BRACK   Oh, dear, no—there is not the slightest hurry.

TESMAN   Well, then, I will take my time. [*Is going with his books, but stops in the doorway and turns*] By the by, Hedda—Aunt Julia is not coming this evening.

HEDDA   Not coming? Is it that affair of the bonnet that keeps her away?

TESMAN   Oh, not at all. How could you think such a thing of Aunt Julia? Just fancy . . . ! The fact is, Aunt Rina is very ill.

HEDDA   She always is.

TESMAN   Yes, but today she is much worse than usual, poor dear.

HEDDA   Oh, then it's only natural that her sister should remain with her. I must bear my disappointment.

TESMAN   And you can't imagine, dear, how delighted Aunt Julia seemed to be—because you had come home looking so flourishing!

HEDDA [*half aloud, rising*]   Oh, those everlasting aunts!

TESMAN   What?

HEDDA [*going to the glass door*]   Nothing.

TESMAN   Oh, all right. [*He goes through the inner room, out to the right.*]

BRACK   What bonnet were you talking about?

HEDDA   Oh, it was a little episode with Miss Tesman this morning. She had laid down her bonnet on the chair there—[*looks at him and smiles*] —and I pretended to think it was the servant's.

BRACK [*shaking his head*]   Now, my dear Mrs. Hedda, how could you do such a thing? To that excellent old lady, too!

HEDDA [*nervously crossing the room*]   Well, you see—these impulses come over me all of a sudden; and I cannot resist them. [*Throws herself down in the easy-chair by the stove*] Oh, I don't know how to explain it.

BRACK [*behind the easy-chair*]   You are not really happy—that is at the bottom of it.

HEDDA [*Looking straight before her*]   I know of no reason why I should be—happy. Perhaps you can give me one?

BRACK   Well—amongst other things, because you have got exactly the home you had set your heart on.

HEDDA [*looks up at him and laughs*]   Do you, too, believe in that legend?

BRACK   Is there nothing in it, then?

HEDDA   Oh, yes, there is something in it.

BRACK   Well?

HEDDA   There is this in it, that I made use of Tesman to see me home from evening parties last summer . . .

BRACK   I, unfortunately, had to go quite a different way.

HEDDA   That's true. I know you were going a different way last summer.

BRACK [*laughing*]   Oh fie, Mrs. Hedda! Well, then—you and Tesman . . . ?

HEDDA   Well, we happened to pass here one evening; Tesman, poor fellow, was writhing in the agony of having to find conversation; so I took pity on the learned man . . .

BRACK [*smiles doubtfully*]   You took pity? H'm . . .

HEDDA   Yes, I really did. And so—to help him out of his torment—I happened to say, in pure thoughtlessness, that I should like to live in this villa.

BRACK   No more than that?

HEDDA   Not that evening.

BRACK   But afterwards?

HEDDA   Yes, my thoughtlessness had consequences, my dear Judge.

BRACK   Unfortunately that too often happens, Mrs. Hedda.

HEDDA   Thanks! So you see it was this enthusiasm for Secretary Falk's villa that first constituted a bond of sympathy between George Tesman and me. From that came our engagement and our marriage, and our wedding journey, and all the rest of it. Well, well, my dear Judge—as you make your bed so you must lie, I could almost say.

BRACK   This is exquisite! And you really cared not a rap about it all the time?

HEDDA   No, heaven knows I didn't.

BRACK   But now? Now that we have made it so homelike for you?

HEDDA   Ugh—the rooms all seem to smell of lavender and dried roseleaves. But perhaps it's Aunt Julia that has brought that scent with her.

BRACK [*laughing*]   No, I think it must be a legacy from the late Mrs. Secretary Falk.

HEDDA   Yes, there is an odor of mortality about it. It reminds me of a bouquet— the day after the ball. [*Clasps her hands behind her head, leans back in her chair and looks at him*]   Oh, my dear Judge—you cannot imagine how horribly I shall bore myself here.

BRACK   Why should not you, too, find some sort of vocation in life, Mrs. Hedda?

HEDDA   A vocation—that should attract me?

BRACK   If possible, of course.

HEDDA   Heaven knows what sort of a vocation that could be. I often wonder whether . . . [*Breaking off*] But that would never do, either.

BRACK   Who can tell? Let me hear what it is.

HEDDA   Whether I might not get Tesman to go into politics, I mean.

BRACK [*laughing*]   Tesman? No, really now, political life is not the thing for him—not at all in his line.

HEDDA   No, I daresay not. But if I could get him into it all the same?

BRACK   Why—what satisfaction could you find in that? If he is not fitted for that sort of thing, why should you want to drive him into it?

HEDDA   Because I am bored, I tell you! [*After a pause*] So you think it quite out of the question that Tesman should ever get into the ministry?

BRACK   H'm—you see, my dear Mrs. Hedda—to get into the ministry, he would have to be a tolerably rich man.

HEDDA [*rising impatiently*]   Yes, there we have it! It is this genteel poverty I have managed to drop into . . . ! [*Crosses the room*] That is what makes life so pitiable! So utterly ludicrous!—For that's what it is.

BRACK   Now I should say the fault lay elsewhere.

HEDDA   Where, then?

BRACK   You have never gone through any really stimulating experience.

HEDDA   Anything serious, you mean?

BRACK   Yes, you may call it so. But now you may perhaps have one in store.

HEDDA [*tossing her head*]   Oh, you're thinking of the annoyances about this wretched professorship! But that must be Tesman's own affair. I assure you I shall not waste a thought upon it.

BRACK   No, no, I daresay not. But suppose now that what people call—in elegant language—a solemn responsibility were to come upon you? [*Smiling*] A new responsibility, Mrs. Hedda?

HEDDA [*angrily*]   Be quiet! Nothing of that sort will ever happen!

BRACK [*warily*]   We will speak of this again a year hence—at the very outside.

HEDDA [*curtly*]   I have no turn for anything of the sort, Judge Brack. No responsibilities for me!

BRACK   Are you so unlike the generality of women as to have no turn for duties which . . . ?

HEDDA [*beside the glass door*]   Oh, be quiet, I tell you! I often think there is only one thing in the world I have any turn for.

BRACK [*drawing near to her*]   And what is that, if I may ask?

HEDDA [*stands looking out*]   Boring myself to death. Now you know it. [*Turns, looks towards the inner room, and laughs*] Yes, as I thought! Here comes the Professor.

BRACK [*softly, in a tone of warning*]   Come, come, come, Mrs. Hedda!

GEORGE TESMAN, *dressed for the party, with his gloves and hat in his hand, enters from the right through the inner room.*

TESMAN   Hedda, has no message come from Eilert Lövborg? Eh?

HEDDA   No.

TESMAN   Then you'll see he'll be here presently.

BRACK   Do you really think he will come?

TESMAN   Yes, I am almost sure of it. For what you were telling us this morning must have been a mere floating rumor.

BRACK   You think so?

TESMAN   At any rate, Aunt Julia said she did not believe for a moment that he would ever stand in my way again. Fancy that!

BRACK   Well, then, that's all right.

TESMAN [*placing his hat and gloves on a chair on the right*]   Yes, but you must really let me wait for him as long as possible.

BRACK   We have plenty of time yet. None of my guests will arrive before seven or half-past.

TESMAN   Then meanwhile we can keep Hedda company, and see what happens. Eh?

HEDDA [*placing* BRACK's *hat and overcoat upon the corner settee*] And at the worst Mr. Lövborg can remain here with me.

BRACK [*offering to take his things*] Oh, allow me, Mrs. Tesman! What do you mean by "at the worst"?

HEDDA If he won't go with you and Tesman.

TESMAN [*looks dubiously at her*] But, Hedda, dear—do you think it would quite do for him to remain with you? Eh? Remember, Aunt Julia can't come.

HEDDA No, but Mrs. Elvsted is coming. We three can have a cup of tea together.

TESMAN Oh, yes, that will be all right.

BRACK [*smiling*] And that would perhaps be the safest plan for him.

HEDDA Why so?

BRACK Well, you know, Mrs. Tesman, how you used to jeer at my little bachelor parties. You declared they were adapted only for men of the strictest principles.

HEDDA But no doubt Mr. Lövborg's principles are strict enough now. A converted sinner . . .

BERTA *appears at the hall door.*

BERTA There's a gentleman asking if you are at home, ma'am . . .

HEDDA Well, show him in.

TESMAN [*softly*] I'm sure it is he! Fancy that!

EILERT LÖVBORG *enters the hall. He is slim and lean; of the same age as* TESMAN, *but looks older and somewhat worn-out. His hair and beard are of a blackish brown, his face long and pale, but with patches of color on the cheekbones. He is dressed in a well-cut black visiting suit, quite new. He has dark gloves and a silk hat. He stops near the door, and makes a rapid bow, seeming somewhat embarrassed.*

TESMAN [*goes up to him and shakes him warmly by the hand*] Well, my dear Eilert—so at last we meet again!

EILERT LÖVBORG [*speaks in a subdued voice*] Thanks for your letter, Tesman. [*Approaching* HEDDA] Will you, too, shake hands with me, Mrs. Tesman?

HEDDA [*taking his hand*] I am glad to see you, Mr. Lövborg. [*With a motion of her hand.*] I don't know whether you two gentlemen . . . ?

LÖVBORG [*bowing slightly*] Judge Brack, I think.

BRACK [*doing likewise*] Oh, yes—in the old days . . .

TESMAN [*to* LÖVBORG, *with his hands on his shoulders*] And now you must make yourself entirely at home, Eilert! Mustn't he, Hedda?—For I hear you are going to settle in town again? Eh?

LÖVBORG Yes, I am.

TESMAN Quite right, quite right. Let me tell you, I have got hold of your new book; but I haven't had time to read it yet.

LÖVBORG You may spare yourself the trouble.

TESMAN Why so?

LÖVBORG Because there is very little in it.

TESMAN Just fancy—how can you say so?

BRACK But it has been very much praised, I hear.

LÖVBORG   That was what I wanted; so I put nothing into the book but what every one would agree with.

BRACK   Very wise of you.

TESMAN   Well, but, my dear Eilert . . . !

LÖVBORG   For now I mean to win myself a position again—to make a fresh start.

TESMAN [*a little embarrassed*]   Ah, that is what you wish to do? Eh?

LÖVBORG [*smiling, lays down his hat, and draws a packet, wrapped in paper, from his coat pocket*]   But when this one appears, George Tesman, you will have to read it. For this is the real book—the book I have put my true self into.

TESMAN   Indeed? And what is it?

LÖVBORG   It is the continuation.

TESMAN   The continuation? Of what?

LÖVBORG   Of the book.

TESMAN   Of the new book?

LÖVBORG   Of course.

TESMAN   Why, my dear Eilert—does it not come down to our own days?

LÖVBORG   Yes, it does; and this one deals with the future.

TESMAN   With the future! But, good heavens, we know nothing of the future!

LÖVBORG   No; but there is a thing or two to be said about it all the same. [*Opens the packet*] Look here . . .

TESMAN   Why, that's not your handwriting.

LÖVBORG   I dictated it. [*Turning over the pages*] It falls into two sections. The first deals with the civilizing forces of the future. And here is the second—[*running through the pages towards the end*]—forecasting the probable line of development.

TESMAN   How odd now! I should never have thought of writing anything of that sort.

HEDDA [*at the glass door, drumming on the pane*]   H'm . . . I daresay not.

LÖVBORG [*replacing the manuscript in its paper and laying the packet on the table*]   I brought it, thinking I might read you a little of it this evening.

TESMAN   That was very good of you, Eilert. But this evening . . . ? [*Looking at* BRACK]   I don't quite see how we can manage it . . .

LÖVBORG   Well, then, some other time. There is no hurry.

BRACK   I must tell you, Mr. Lövborg—there is a little gathering at my house this evening—mainly in honor of Tesman, you know . . .

LÖVBORG [*looking for his hat*]   Oh—then I won't detain you . . .

BRACK   No, but listen—will you not do me the favor of joining us?

LÖVBORG [*curtly and decidedly*]   No, I can't—thank you very much.

BRACK   Oh, nonsense—do! We shall be quite a select little circle. And I assure you we shall have a "lively time," as Mrs. Hed—as Mrs. Tesman says.

LÖVBORG   I have no doubt of it. But nevertheless . . .

BRACK   And then you might bring your manuscript with you, and read it to Tesman at my house. I could give you a room to yourselves.

TESMAN   Yes, think of that, Eilert—why shouldn't you? Eh?

HEDDA [*interposing*]   But, Tesman, if Mr. Lövborg would really rather not! I am sure Mr. Lövborg is much more inclined to remain here and have supper with me.

LÖVBORG [*looking at her*]   With you, Mrs. Tesman?

HEDDA   And with Mrs. Elvsted.

LÖVBORG   Ah . . .[*lightly*] I saw her for a moment this morning.

HEDDA   Did you? Well, she is coming this evening. So you see you are almost bound to remain, Mr. Lövborg, or she will have no one to see her home.

LÖVBORG   That's true. Many thanks, Mrs. Tesman—in that case I will remain.

HEDDA   Then I have one or two orders to give the servant . . .

She goes to the hall door and rings. BERTA *enters.* HEDDA *talks to her in a whisper, and points towards the inner room.* BERTA *nods and goes out again.*

TESMAN [*at the same time, to* LÖVBORG]   Tell me, Eilert—is it this new subject—the future—that you are going to lecture about?

LÖVBORG   Yes.

TESMAN   They told me at the bookseller's that you are going to deliver a course of lectures this autumn.

LÖVBORG   That is my intention. I hope you won't take it ill, Tesman.

TESMAN   Oh no, not in the least! But . . . ?

LÖVBORG   I can quite understand that it must be disagreeable to you.

TESMAN [*cast down*]   Oh, I can't expect you, out of consideration for me, to . . .

LÖVBORG   But I shall wait till you have received your appointment.

TESMAN   Will you wait? Yes, but—yes, but—are you not going to compete with me? Eh?

LÖVBORG   No; it is only the moral victory I care for.

TESMAN   Why, bless me—then Aunt Julia was right after all! Oh, yes—I knew it! Hedda! Just fancy—Eilert Lövborg is not going to stand in our way!

HEDDA [*curtly*]   Our way? Pray leave me out of the question.

She goes up towards the inner room, where BERTA *is placing a tray with decanters and glasses on the table.* HEDDA *nods approval, and comes forward again.* BERTA *goes out.*

TESMAN [*at the same time*]   And you, Judge Brack—what do you say to this? Eh?

BRACK   Well, I say that a moral victory—h'm—may be all very fine . . .

TESMAN   Yes, certainly. But all the same . . .

HEDDA [*looking at* TESMAN *with a cold smile*]   You stand there looking as if you were thunderstruck . . .

TESMAN   Yes—so I am—I almost think . . .

BRACK   Don't you see, Mrs. Tesman, a thunderstorm has just passed over?

HEDDA [*pointing towards the inner room*]   Will you not take a glass of cold punch, gentlemen?

BRACK [*looking at his watch*]   A stirrup cup? Yes, it wouldn't come amiss.

TESMAN   A capital idea, Hedda! Just the thing! Now that the weight has been taken off my mind . . .

HEDDA   Will you not join them, Mr. Lövborg?

LÖVBORG [*with a gesture of refusal*]   No, thank you. Nothing for me.

BRACK   Why bless me—cold punch is surely not poison.

LÖVBORG   Perhaps not for every one.

HEDDA   I will keep Mr. Lövborg company in the meantime.

TESMAN   Yes, yes, Hedda dear, do.

He and BRACK *go into the inner room, seat themselves, drink punch, smoke cig-arettes, and carry on a lively conversation during what follows.* EILERT LÖVBORG *remains standing beside the stove.* HEDDA *goes to the writing table.*

HEDDA [*raising her voice a little*] Do you care to look at some photographs, Mr. Lövborg? You know Tesman and I made a tour in the Tyrol on our way home?

She takes up an album, and places it on the table beside the sofa, in the further corner of which she seats herself. EILERT LÖVBORG *approaches, stops, and looks at her. Then he takes a chair and seats himself to her left, with his back towards the inner room.*

HEDDA [*opening the album*] Do you see this range of mountains, Mr. Lövborg? It's the Ortler group. Tesman has written the name underneath. Here it is: "The Ortler group near Meram."
LÖVBORG [*who has never taken his eyes off her, says softly and slowly*] Hedda—Gabler!
HEDDA [*glancing hastily at him*] Ah! Hush!
LÖVBORG [*repeats softly*] Hedda Gabler!
HEDDA [*looking at the album*] That was my name in the old days—when we two knew each other.
LÖVBORG And I must teach myself never to say Hedda Gabler again—never, as long as I live.
HEDDA [*still turning over the pages*] Yes, you must. And I think you ought to practice in time. The sooner the better, I should say.
LÖVBORG [*in a tone of indignation*] Hedda Gabler married? And married to—George Tesman!
HEDDA Yes—so the world goes.
LÖVBORG Oh, Hedda, Hedda—how could you[1] throw yourself away!
HEDDA [*looks sharply at him*] What? I can't allow this!
LÖVBORG What do you mean?

TESMAN *comes into the room and goes towards the sofa.*

HEDDA [*hears him coming and says in an indifferent tone*] And this is a view from the Val d'Ampezzo, Mr. Lövborg. Just look at these peaks! [*Looks affection-ately up at* TESMAN] What's the name of these curious peaks, dear?
TESMAN Let me see. Oh, those are the Dolomites.
HEDDA Yes, that's it! Those are the Dolomites, Mr. Lövborg.
TESMAN Hedda, dear, I only wanted to ask whether I shouldn't bring you a little punch after all? For yourself, at any rate—eh?
HEDDA Yes, do, please; and perhaps a few biscuits.
TESMAN No cigarettes?
HEDDA No.
TESMAN Very well.

He goes into the inner room and out to the right. BRACK *sits in the inner room, and keeps an eye from time to time on* HEDDA *and* LÖVBORG.

[1]*du*

LÖVBORG [*softly, as before*] Answer me, Hedda—how could you go and do this?

HEDDA [*apparently absorbed in the album*] If you continue to say *du* to me I won't talk to you.

LÖVBORG May I not say *du* even when we are alone?

HEDDA No. You may think it; but you mustn't say it.

LÖVBORG Ah, I understand. It is an offense against George Tesman, whom you[1] love.

HEDDA [*glances at him and smiles*] Love? What an idea!

LÖVBORG You don't love him then!

HEDDA But I won't hear of any sort of unfaithfulness! Remember that.

LÖVBORG Hedda—answer me one thing . . .

HEDDA Hush!

TESMAN *enters with a small tray from the inner room.*

TESMAN Here you are! Isn't this tempting?

He puts the tray on the table.

HEDDA Why do you bring it yourself?

TESMAN [*filling the glasses*] Because I think it's such fun to wait upon you, Hedda.

HEDDA But you have poured out two glasses. Mr. Lövborg said he wouldn't have any . . .

TESMAN No, but Mrs. Elvsted will soon be here, won't she?

HEDDA Yes, by the by—Mrs. Elvsted . . .

TESMAN Had you forgotten her? Eh?

HEDDA We were so absorbed in these photographs. [*Shows him a picture*] Do you remember this little village?

TESMAN Oh, it's that one just below the Brenner Pass. It was there we passed the night . . .

HEDDA . . . and met that lively party of tourists.

TESMAN Yes, that was the place. Fancy—if we could only have had you with us, Eilert! Eh?

He returns to the inner room and sits beside BRACK.

LÖVBORG Answer me this one thing, Hedda . . .

HEDDA Well?

LÖVBORG Was there no love in your friendship for me, either? Not a spark—not a tinge of love in it?

HEDDA I wonder if there was? To me it seems as though we were two good comrades—two thoroughly intimate friends. [*Smilingly*] You especially were frankness itself.

LÖVBORG It was you that made me so.

HEDDA As I look back upon it all, I think there was really something beautiful,

[1]*du*

something fascinating—something daring—in—in that secret intimacy—that comradeship which no living creature so much as dreamed of.

LÖVBORG   Yes, yes, Hedda! Was there not?—When I used to come to your father's in the afternoon—and the General sat over at the window reading his papers—with his back towards us . . .

HEDDA   And we two on the corner sofa . . .

LÖVBORG   Always with the same illustrated paper before us . . .

HEDDA   For want of an album, yes.

LÖVBORG   Yes, Hedda, and when I made my confessions to you—told you about myself, things that at that time no one else knew! There I would sit and tell you of my escapades—my days and nights of devilment. Oh, Hedda—what was the power in you that forced me to confess these things?

HEDDA   Do you think it was any power in me?

LÖVBORG   How else can I explain it? And all those—those roundabout questions you used to put to me . . .

HEDDA   Which you understood so particularly well . . .

LÖVBORG   How could you sit and question me like that? Question me quite frankly . . .

HEDDA   In roundabout terms, please observe.

LÖVBORG   Yes, but frankly nevertheless. Cross-question me about—all that sort of thing?

HEDDA   And how could you answer, Mr. Lövborg?

LÖVBORG   Yes, that is just what I can't understand—in looking back upon it. But tell me now, Hedda—was there not love at the bottom of our friendship? On your side, did you not feel as though you might purge my stains away—if I made you my confessor? Was it not so?

HEDDA   No, not quite.

LÖVBORG   What was your motive, then?

HEDDA   Do you think it quite incomprehensible that a young girl—when it can be done—without any one knowing . . .

LÖVBORG   Well?

HEDDA   . . . should be glad to have a peep, now and then, into a world which . . .

LÖVBORG   Which . . . ?

HEDDA   . . . which she is forbidden to know anything about?

LÖVBORG   So that was it?

HEDDA   Partly. Partly—I almost think.

LÖVBORG   Comradeship is the thirst for life. But why should not that, at any rate, have continued?

HEDDA   The fault was yours.

LÖVBORG   It was you that broke with me.

HEDDA   Yes, when our friendship threatened to develop into something more serious. Shame upon you, Eilert Lövborg! How could you think of wronging your—your frank comrade?

LÖVBORG [clenching his hands]   Oh, why did you not carry out your threat? Why did you not shoot me down?

HEDDA   Because I have such a dread of scandal.

LÖVBORG   Yes, Hedda, you are a coward at heart.

HEDDA   A terrible coward. [Changing her tone] But it was a lucky thing for you. And now you have found ample consolation at the Elvsteds'.

LÖVBORG   I know what Thea has confided to you.

HEDDA   And perhaps you have confided to her something about us?

LÖVBORG   Not a word. She is too stupid to understand anything of that sort.

HEDDA   Stupid?

LÖVBORG   She is stupid about matters of that sort.

HEDDA   And I am cowardly. [*Bends over towards him, without looking him in the face, and says more softly*] But now I will confide something to you.

LÖVBORG [*eagerly*]   Well?

HEDDA   The fact that I dared not shoot you down . . .

LÖVBORG   Yes!

HEDDA   . . . that was not my most arrant cowardice—that evening.

LÖVBORG [*looks at her a moment, understands and whispers passionately*]   Oh, Hedda! Hedda Gabler! Now I begin to see a hidden reason beneath our comradeship! You[1] and I . . . ! After all, then, it was your craving for life . . .

HEDDA [*softly, with a sharp glance*]   Take care! Believe nothing of the sort!

Twilight has begun to fall. The hall door is opened from without by BERTA.

HEDDA [*closes the album with a bang and calls smilingly*]   Ah, at last! My darling Thea—come along!

MRS. ELVSTED *enters from the hall. She is in evening dress. The door is closed behind her.*

HEDDA [*on the sofa, stretches out her arms towards her*]   My sweet Thea—you can't think how I have been longing for you!

MRS. ELVSTED, *in passing, exchanges slight salutations with the gentlemen in the inner room, then goes up to the table and gives* HEDDA *her hand.* EILERT LÖVBORG *has risen. He and* MRS. ELVSTED *greet each other with a silent nod.*

MRS. ELVSTED   Ought I to go in and talk to your husband for a moment?

HEDDA   Oh, not at all. Leave those two alone. They will soon be going.

MRS. ELVSTED   Are they going out?

HEDDA   Yes, to a supper party.

MRS. ELVSTED [*quickly, to* LÖVBORG]   Not you?

LÖVBORG   No.

HEDDA   Mr. Lövborg remains with us.

MRS. ELVSTED [*takes a chair and is about to seat herself at his side*]   Oh, how nice it is here!

HEDDA   No, thank you, my little Thea! Not there! You'll be good enough to come over here to me. I will sit between you.

MRS. ELVSTED   Yes, just as you please.

She goes round the table and seats herself on the sofa on HEDDA's *right.* LÖVBORG *reseats himself on his chair.*

LÖVBORG [*after a short pause, to* HEDDA]   Is not she lovely to look at?

[1]Back to *du*; Hedda continues to say *de*.

HEDDA [*lightly stroking her hair*] Only to look at?

LÖVBORG Yes. For we two—she and I—we are two real comrades. We have absolute faith in each other; so we can sit and talk with perfect frankness . . .

HEDDA Not roundabout, Mr. Lövborg?

LÖVBORG Well . . .

MRS. ELVSTED [*softly clinging close to* HEDDA] Oh, how happy I am, Hedda! For, only think, he says I have inspired him, too.

HEDDA [*looks at her with a smile*] Ah! Does he say that, dear?

LÖVBORG And then she is so brave, Mrs. Tesman!

MRS. ELVSTED Good heavens—am I brave?

LÖVBORG Exceedingly—where your comrade is concerned.

HEDDA Ah, yes—courage! If one only had that!

LÖVBORG What then? What do you mean?

HEDDA Then life would perhaps be livable, after all. [*With a sudden change of tone*] But now, my dearest Thea, you really must have a glass of cold punch.

MRS. ELVSTED No, thanks—I never take anything of that kind.

HEDDA Well, then, you, Mr. Lövborg.

LÖVBORG Nor I, thank you.

MRS. ELVSTED No, he doesn't, either.

HEDDA [*looks fixedly at him*] But if I say you shall?

LÖVBORG It would be no use.

HEDDA [*laughing*] Then I, poor creature, have no sort of power over you?

LÖVBORG Not in that respect.

HEDDA But seriously, I think you ought to—for your own sake.

MRS. ELVSTED Why, Hedda . . . !

LÖVBORG How so?

HEDDA Or rather on account of other people.

LÖVBORG Indeed?

HEDDA Otherwise people might be apt to suspect that—in your heart of hearts—you did not feel quite secure—quite confident in yourself.

MRS. ELVSTED [*softly*] Oh, please, Hedda . . . !

LÖVBORG People may suspect what they like—for the present.

MRS. ELVSTED [*joyfully*] Yes, let them!

HEDDA I saw it plainly in Judge Brack's face a moment ago.

LÖVBORG What did you see?

HEDDA His contemptuous smile, when you dared not go with them into the inner room.

LÖVBORG Dared not? Of course I preferred to stop here and talk to you.

MRS. ELVSTED What could be more natural, Hedda?

HEDDA But the Judge could not guess that. And I saw, too, the way he smiled and glanced at Tesman when you dared not accept his invitation to this wretched little supper party of his.

LÖVBORG Dared not? Do you say I dared not?

HEDDA *I* don't say so. But that was how Judge Brack understood it.

LÖVBORG Well, let him.

HEDDA Then you are not going with them?

LÖVBORG I will stay here with you and Thea.

MRS. ELVSTED Yes, Hedda—how can you doubt that?

HEDDA [*smiles and nods approvingly to* LÖVBORG] Firm as a rock! Faithful to your principles, now and forever! Ah, that is how a man should be! [*Turns to*

MRS. ELVSTED *and caresses her*] Well, now, what did I tell you, when you came to us this morning in such a state of distraction . . .

· LÖVBORG [*surprised*] Distraction!

MRS. ELVSTED [*terrified*] Hedda—oh, Hedda . . . !

HEDDA You can see for yourself! You haven't the slightest reason to be in such mortal terror . . . [*Interrupting herself*] There! Now we can all three enjoy ourselves!

LÖVBORG [*who has given a start*] Ah—what is all this, Mrs. Tesman?

MRS. ELVSTED Oh, my God, Hedda! What are you saying? What are you doing?

HEDDA Don't get excited! That horrid Judge Brack is sitting watching you.

LÖVBORG So she was in mortal terror! On my account!

MRS. ELVSTED [*softly and piteously*] Oh, Hedda—now you have ruined everything!

LÖVBORG [*looks fixedly at her for a moment. His face is distorted.*] So that was my comrade's frank confidence in me?

MRS. ELVSTED [*imploringly*] Oh, my dearest friend—only let me tell you . . .

LÖVBORG [*takes one of the glasses of punch, raises it to his lips, and says in a low, husky voice*] Your health, Thea!

He empties the glass, puts it down, and takes the second.

MRS. ELVSTED [*softly*] Oh, Hedda, Hedda—how could you do this?

HEDDA *I* do it? *I?* Are you crazy?

LÖVBORG Here's to your health, too, Mrs. Tesman. Thanks for the truth. Hurrah for the truth!

He empties the glass and is about to refill it.

HEDDA [*lays her hand on his arm*] Come, come—no more for the present. Remember you are going out to supper.

MRS. ELVSTED No, no, no!

HEDDA Hush! They are sitting watching you.

LÖVBORG [*putting down the glass*] Now, Thea—tell me the truth . . .

MRS. ELVSTED Yes.

LÖVBORG Did your husband know that you had come after me?

MRS. ELVSTED [*wringing her hands*] Oh, Hedda—do you hear what he is asking?

LÖVBORG Was it arranged between you and him that you were to come to town and look after me? Perhaps it was the Sheriff himself that urged you to come? Aha, my dear—no doubt he wanted my help in his office. Or was it at the card table that he missed me?

MRS. ELVSTED [*softly, in agony*] Oh, Lövborg, Lövborg . . . !

LÖVBORG [*seizes a glass and is on the point of filling it*] Here's a glass for the old Sheriff, too!

HEDDA [*preventing him*] No more just now. Remember, you have to read your manuscript to Tesman.

LÖVBORG [*calmly, putting down the glass*] It was stupid of me all this, Thea—to take it in this way, I mean. Don't be angry with me, my dear, dear comrade. You shall see—both you and the others—that if I was fallen once—now I have risen again! Thanks to you, Thea.

MRS. ELVSTED [*radiant with joy*]   Oh, heaven be praised . . . !

BRACK *has in the meantime looked at his watch. He and* TESMAN *rise and come into the drawing room.*

BRACK [*takes his hat and overcoat*]   Well, Mrs. Tesman, our time has come.
HEDDA   I suppose it has.
LÖVBORG [*rising*]   Mine too, Judge Brack.
MRS. ELVSTED [*softly and imploringly*]   Oh, Lövborg, don't do it!
HEDDA [*pinching her arm*]   They can hear you!
MRS. ELVSTED [*with a suppressed shriek*]   Ow!
LÖVBORG [*to* BRACK]   You were good enough to invite me.
BRACK   Well, are you coming after all?
LÖVBORG   Yes, many thanks.
BRACK   I'm delighted . . .
LÖVBORG [*to* TESMAN, *putting the parcel of MS. in his pocket*]   I should like to show you one or two things before I send it to the printers.
TESMAN   Fancy—that will be delightful. But, Hedda dear, how is Mrs. Elvsted to get home? Eh?
HEDDA   Oh, that can be managed somehow.
LÖVBORG [*looking towards the ladies*]   Mrs. Elvsted? Of course, I'll come again and fetch her.[*approaching*] At ten or thereabouts, Mrs. Tesman? Will that do?
HEDDA   Certainly. That will do capitally.
TESMAN   Well, then, that's all right. But you must not expect me so early, Hedda.
HEDDA   Oh, you may stop as long—as long as ever you please.
MRS. ELVSTED [*trying to conceal her anxiety*]   Well, then, Mr. Lövborg—I shall remain here until you come.
LÖVBORG [*with his hat in his hand*]   Pray do, Mrs. Elvsted.
BRACK   And now off goes the excursion train, gentlemen! I hope we shall have a lively time, as a certain fair lady puts it.
HEDDA   Ah, if only the fair lady could be present unseen . . . !
BRACK   Why unseen?
HEDDA   In order to hear a little of your liveliness at first hand, Judge Brack.
BRACK [*laughing*]   I should not advise the fair lady to try it.
TESMAN [*also laughing*]   Come, you're a nice one, Hedda! Fancy that!
BRACK   Well, good-bye, good-bye, ladies.
LÖVBORG [*bowing*]   About ten o'clock, then.

BRACK, LÖVBORG, *and* TESMAN *go out by the hall door. At the same time,* BERTA *enters from the inner room with a lighted lamp, which she places on the drawing room table; she goes out by the way she came.*

MRS. ELVSTED [*who has risen and is wandering restlessly about the room*]   Hedda—Hedda—what will come of all this?
HEDDA   At ten o'clock—he will be here. I can see him already—with vine leaves[1] in his hair—flushed and fearless . . .

---

[1]In classical mythology the Roman god Bacchus—the Greek Dionysus—was pictured with a wreath of bay (vine) leaves in his hair.

MRS. ELVSTED Oh, I hope he may.

HEDDA And then, you see—then he will have regained control over himself. Then he will be a free man for all his days.

MRS. ELVSTED Oh, God!—if he would only come as you see him now!

HEDDA He will come as I see him—so, and not otherwise! [*Rises and approaches* THEA] You may doubt him as long as you please; *I* believe in him. And now we will try . . .

MRS. ELVSTED You have some hidden motive in this, Hedda!

HEDDA Yes, I have. I want for once in my life to have power to mold a human destiny.

MRS. ELVSTED Have you not the power?

HEDDA I have not—and have never had it.

MRS. ELVSTED. Not your husband's?

HEDDA Do you think that is worth the trouble? Oh, if you could only understand how poor I am. And fate has made you so rich! [*Clasps her passionately in her arms*] I think I must burn your hair off, after all.

MRS. ELVSTED Let me go! Let me go! I am afraid of you, Hedda!

BERTA [*in the middle doorway*] Tea is laid in the dining room, ma'am.

HEDDA Very well. We are coming.

MRS. ELVSTED No, no, no! I would rather go home alone! At once!

HEDDA Nonsense? First you shall have a cup of tea, you little stupid. And then—at ten o'clock—Eilert Lövborg will be here—with vine-leaves in his hair.

She drags MRS. ELVSTED *almost by force towards the middle doorway.*

Act III

SCENE: *The room at the* TESMANS'. *The curtains are drawn over the middle doorway, and also over the glass door. The lamp, half turned down, and with a shade over it, is burning on the table. In the stove, the door of which stands open, there has been a fire, which is now nearly burnt out.* MRS. ELVSTED, *wrapped in a large shawl, and with her feet upon a foot-rest, sits close to the stove, sunk back in the armchair.* HEDDA, *fully dressed, lies sleeping upon the sofa, with a sofa-blanket over her.*

MRS. ELVSTED [*after a pause, suddenly sits up in her chair, and listens eagerly. Then she sinks back again wearily, moaning to herself*] Not yet!—Oh God—oh God—not yet!

BERTA *slips in by the hall door. She has a letter in her hand.*

MRS. ELVSTED [*turns and whispers eagerly*] Well—has anyone come?

BERTA [*softly*] Yes, a girl has just brought this letter.

MRS. ELVSTED [*quickly, holding out her hand*] A letter! Give it to me!

BERTA No, it's for Dr. Tesman, ma'am.

MRS. ELVSTED Oh, indeed.

BERTA It was Miss Tesman's servant that brought it. I'll lay it here on the table.

MRS. ELVSTED Yes, do.

BERTA [*laying down the letter*] I think I had better put out the lamp. It's smoking.

MRS. ELVSTED   Yes, put it out. It must soon be daylight now.

BERTA [*putting out the lamp*]   It is daylight already, ma'am.

MRS. ELVSTED   Yes, broad day! And no one come back yet . . . !

BERTA   Lord bless you, ma'am—I guessed how it would be.

MRS. ELVSTED   You guessed?

BERTA   Yes, when I saw that a certain person had come back to town—and that he went off with them. For we've heard enough about that gentleman before now.

MRS. ELVSTED   Don't speak so loud. You will waken Mrs. Tesman.

BERTA [*looks towards the sofa and sighs*]   No, no—let her sleep, poor thing. Shan't I put some wood on the fire?

MRS. ELVSTED   Thanks, not for me.

BERTA   Oh, very well.

She goes softly out by the hall door.

HEDDA [*is awakened by the shutting of the door, and looks up*]   What's that . . . ?

MRS. ELVSTED   It was only the servant . . .

HEDDA [*looking about her*]   Oh, we're here . . . ! Yes, now I remember. [*Sits erect upon the sofa, stretches herself, and rubs her eyes*] What o'clock is it, Thea?

MRS. ELVSTED [*looks at her watch*]   It's past seven.

HEDDA   When did Tesman come home?

MRS. ELVSTED   He has not come.

HEDDA   Not come home yet?

MRS. ELVSTED [*rising*]   No one has come.

HEDDA   Think of our watching and waiting here till four in the morning . . .

MRS. ELVSTED [*wringing her hands*]   And how I watched and waited for him!

HEDDA [*yawns, and says with her hand before her mouth*]   Well, well—we might have spared ourselves the trouble.

MRS. ELVSTED   Did you get a little sleep?

HEDDA   Oh, yes; I believe I have slept pretty well. Have you not?

MRS. ELVSTED   Not for a moment. I couldn't, Hedda!—not to save my life.

HEDDA [*rises and goes towards her*]   There, there, there! There's nothing to be so alarmed about. I understand quite well what has happened.

MRS. ELVSTED   Well, what do you think? Won't you tell me?

HEDDA   Why, of course, it has been a very late affair at Judge Brack's . . .

MRS. ELVSTED   Yes, yes—that is clear enough. But all the same . . .

HEDDA   And then, you see, Tesman hasn't cared to come home and ring us up in the middle of the night. [*Laughing*] Perhaps he wasn't inclined to show himself either—immediately after a jollification.

MRS. ELVSTED   But in that case—where can he have gone?

HEDDA   Of course, he has gone to his aunts' and slept there. They have his old room ready for him.

MRS. ELVSTED   No, he can't be with them; for a letter has just come for him from Miss Tesman. There it lies.

HEDDA   Indeed? [*Looks at the address*] Why, yes, it's addressed in Aunt Julia's own hand. Well, then, he has remained at Judge Brack's. And as for Eilert Lövborg—he is sitting, with vine leaves in his hair, reading his manuscript.

MRS. ELVSTED   Oh, Hedda, you are just saying things you don't believe a bit.

HEDDA   You really are a little blockhead, Thea.

MRS. ELVSTED   Oh, yes, I suppose I am.

HEDDA   And how mortally tired you look.

MRS. ELVSTED   Yes, I am mortally tired.

HEDDA   Well, then, you must do as I tell you. You must go into my room and lie down for a little while.

MRS. ELVSTED   Oh, no, no—I shouldn't be able to sleep.

HEDDA   I am sure you would.

MRS. ELVSTED   Well, but your husband is certain to come soon now; and then I want to know at once . . .

HEDDA   I shall take care to let you know when he comes.

MRS. ELVSTED   Do you promise me, Hedda?

HEDDA   Yes, rely upon me. Just you go in and have a sleep in the meantime.

MRS. ELVSTED   Thanks; then I'll try to.

She goes off through the inner room. HEDDA *goes up to the glass door and draws back the curtains. The broad daylight streams into the room. Then she takes a little hand glass from the writing table, looks at herself in it and arranges her hair. Next she goes to the hall door and presses the bell button.* BERTA *presently appears at the hall door.*

BERTA   Did you want anything, ma'am?

HEDDA   Yes; you must put some more wood in the stove. I am shivering.

BERTA   Bless me—I'll make up the fire at once. [*She rakes the embers together and lays a piece of wood upon them; then stops and listens*] That was a ring at the front door, ma'am.

HEDDA   Then go to the door. I will look after the fire.

BERTA   It'll soon burn up.

She goes out by the hall door. HEDDA *kneels on the footrest and lays some more pieces of wood in the stove. After a short pause,* GEORGE TESMAN *enters from the hall. He looks tired and rather serious. He steals on tiptoe towards the middle doorway and is about to slip through the curtains.*

HEDDA [*at the stove, without looking up*]   Good morning.

TESMAN [*turns*]   Hedda! [*Approaching her*] Good heavens—are you up so early? Eh?

HEDDA   Yes, I am up very early this morning.

TESMAN   And I never doubted you were still sound asleep! Fancy that, Hedda!

HEDDA   Don't speak so loud. Mrs. Elvsted is resting in my room.

TESMAN   Has Mrs. Elvsted been here all night?

HEDDA   Yes, since no one came to fetch her.

TESMAN   Ah, to be sure.

HEDDA [*closes the door of the stove and rises*]   Well, did you enjoy yourselves at Judge Brack's?

TESMAN   Have you been anxious about me? Eh?

HEDDA   No, I should never think of being anxious. But I asked if you had enjoyed yourself.

TESMAN   Oh, yes—for once in a way. Especially the beginning of the evening; for then Eilert read me part of his book. We arrived more than an hour too early—fancy that! And Brack had all sorts of arrangements to make—so Eilert read to me.

HEDDA [*seating herself by the table on the right*]   Well? Tell me, then . . .

TESMAN [*sitting on a footstool near the stove*]   Oh, Hedda, you can't conceive what a book that is going to be! I believe it is one of the most remarkable things that have ever been written. Fancy that!

HEDDA   Yes, yes; I don't care about that . . .

TESMAN   I must make a confession to you, Hedda. When he had finished reading—a horrid feeling came over me.

HEDDA   A horrid feeling?

TESMAN   I felt jealous of Eilert for having had it in him to write such a book. Only think, Hedda!

HEDDA   Yes, yes, I am thinking!

TESMAN   And then how pitiful to think that he—with all his gifts—should be irreclaimable, after all.

HEDDA   I suppose you mean that he has more courage than the rest?

TESMAN   No, not at all—I mean that he is incapable of taking his pleasures in moderation.

HEDDA   And what came of it all—in the end?

TESMAN   Well, to tell the truth, I think it might best be described as an orgy, Hedda.

HEDDA   Had he vine leaves in his hair?

TESMAN   Vine leaves? No, I saw nothing of the sort. But he made a long, rambling speech in honor of the woman who had inspired him in his work—that was the phrase he used.

HEDDA   Did he name her?

TESMAN   No, he didn't; but I can't help thinking he meant Mrs. Elvsted. You may be sure he did.

HEDDA   Well—where did you part from him?

TESMAN   On the way to town. We broke up—the last of us at any rate—all together; and Brack came with us to get a breath of fresh air. And then, you see, we agreed to take Eilert home; for he had had far more than was good for him.

HEDDA   I daresay.

TESMAN   But now comes the strange part of it, Hedda; or, I should rather say, the melancholy part of it. I declare I am almost ashamed—on Eilert's account—to tell you . . .

HEDDA   Oh, go on . . . !

TESMAN   Well, as we were getting near town, you see, I happened to drop a little behind the others. Only for a minute or two—fancy that!

HEDDA   Yes, yes, yes, but . . . ?

TESMAN   And then, as I hurried after them—what do you think I found by the wayside? Eh?

HEDDA   Oh, how should I know!

TESMAN   You mustn't speak of it to a soul, Hedda! Do you hear? Promise me, for Eilert's sake. [*Draws a parcel, wrapped in paper, from his coat pocket*] Fancy, dear—I found this.

HEDDA   Is not that the parcel he had with him yesterday?

TESMAN   Yes, it is the whole of his precious, irreplaceable manuscript! And he had gone and lost it, and knew nothing about it. Only fancy, Hedda! So deplorably . . .

HEDDA   But why did you not give him back the parcel at once?

TESMAN   I didn't dare to—in the state he was then in . . .

HEDDA   Did you not tell any of the others that you had found it?

TESMAN   Oh, far from it! You can surely understand that, for Eilert's sake, I wouldn't do that.

HEDDA   So no one knows that Eilert Lövborg's manuscript is in your possession?

TESMAN   No. And no one must know it.

HEDDA   Then what did you say to him afterwards?

TESMAN   I didn't talk to him again at all; for when we got in among the streets, he and two or three of the others gave us the slip and disappeared. Fancy that!

HEDDA   Indeed! They must have taken him home then.

TESMAN   Yes, so it would appear. And Brack, too, left us.

HEDDA   And what have you been doing with yourself since?

TESMAN   Well, I and some of the others went home with one of the party, a jolly fellow, and took our morning coffee with him; or perhaps I should rather call it our night coffee—eh? But now, when I have rested a little, and given Eilert, poor fellow, time to have his sleep out, I must take this back to him.

HEDDA [holds out her hand for the packet]   No—don't give it to him! Not in such a hurry, I mean. Let me read it first.

TESMAN   No, my dearest Hedda, I mustn't, I really mustn't.

HEDDA   You must not?

TESMAN   No—for you can imagine what a state of despair he will be in when he wakens and misses the manuscript. He has no copy of it, you must know! He told me so.

HEDDA [looking searchingly at him]   Can such a thing not be reproduced? Written over again?

TESMAN   No, I don't think that would be possible. For the inspiration, you see . . .

HEDDA   Yes, yes—I suppose it depends on that . . . [Lightly.] But, by the by— here is a letter for you.

TESMAN   Fancy . . . !

HEDDA [handing it to him]   It came early this morning.

TESMAN   It's from Aunt Julia! What can it be? [He lays the packet on the other footstool, opens the letter, runs his eye through it, and jumps up] Oh, Hedda— she says that poor Aunt Rina is dying!

HEDDA   Well, we were prepared for that.

TESMAN   And that if I want to see her again, I must make haste. I'll run in to them at once.

HEDDA [suppressing a smile]   Will you run?

TESMAN   Oh, my dearest Hedda—if you could only make up your mind to come with me! Just think!

HEDDA [rises and says wearily, repelling the idea]   No, no, don't ask me. I will not look upon sickness and death. I loathe all sorts of ugliness.

TESMAN   Well, well, then . . . ! [Bustling around] My hat . . . ? My overcoat . . . ? Oh, in the hall . . . I do hope I mayn't come too late, Hedda! Eh?

HEDDA   Oh, if you run . . .

BERTA *appears at the hall door.*

    BERTA   Judge Brack is at the door, and wishes to know if he may come in.
    TESMAN   At this time! No, I can't possibly see him.
    HEDDA   But I can. [*To* BERTA] Ask Judge Brack to come in.

BERTA *goes out.*

    HEDDA [*quickly, whispering*]   The parcel, Tesman!

She snatches it up from the stool.

    TESMAN   Yes, give it to me!
    HEDDA   No, no, I will keep it till you come back.

She goes to the writing table and places it in the bookcase. TESMAN *stands in a flurry of haste, and cannot get his gloves on.* JUDGE BRACK *enters from the hall.*

    HEDDA [*nodding to him*]   You are an early bird, I must say.
    BRACK   Yes, don't you think so? [*To* TESMAN] Are you on the move, too?
    TESMAN   Yes, I must rush off to my aunts'. Fancy—the invalid one is lying at death's door, poor creature.
    BRACK   Dear me, is she indeed? Then on no account let me detain you. At such a critical moment . . .
    TESMAN   Yes, I must really rush . . . Good-bye! Good-bye!

He hastens out by the hall door.

    HEDDA [*approaching*]   You seem to have made a particularly lively night of it at your rooms, Judge Brack.
    BRACK   I assure you I have not had my clothes off, Mrs. Hedda.
    HEDDA   Not you, either?
    BRACK   No, as you may see. But what has Tesman been telling you of the night's adventures?
    HEDDA   Oh, some tiresome story. Only that they went and had coffee somewhere or other.
    BRACK   I have heard about that coffee party already. Eilert Lövborg was not with them, I fancy?
    HEDDA   No, they had taken him home before that.
    BRACK   Tesman too?
    HEDDA   No, but some of the others, he said.
    BRACK [*smiling*]   George Tesman is really an ingenuous creature, Mrs. Hedda.
    HEDDA   Yes, heaven knows he is. Then is there something behind all this?
    BRACK   Yes, perhaps there may be.
    HEDDA   Well then, sit down, my dear Judge, and tell your story in comfort.

She seats herself to the left of the table. BRACK *sits near her, at the long side of the table.*

HEDDA   Now then?

BRACK   I had special reasons for keeping track of my guests—or rather of some of my guests—last night.

HEDDA   Of Eilert Lövborg among the rest, perhaps?

BRACK   Frankly—yes.

HEDDA   Now you make me really curious . . .

BRACK   Do you know where he and one or two of the others finished the night, Mrs. Hedda?

HEDDA   If it is not quite unmentionable, tell me.

BRACK   Oh no, it's not at all unmentionable. Well, they put in an appearance at a particularly animated *soirée*.

HEDDA   Of the lively kind?

BRACK   Of the very liveliest . . .

HEDDA   Tell me more of this, Judge Brack . . .

BRACK   Lövborg, as well as the others, had been invited in advance. I knew all about it. But he had declined the invitation; for now, as you know, he has become a new man.

HEDDA   Up at the Elvsteds', yes. But he went after all, then?

BRACK   He seems to have made a violent resistance—to have hit one of the constables on the head and torn the coat off his back. So they had to march him off to the police station with the rest.

HEDDA   How have you learnt all this?

BRACK   From the police themselves.

HEDDA [*gazing straight before her*]   So that is what happened. Then he had no vine leaves in his hair.

BRACK   Vine leaves, Mrs. Hedda?

HEDDA [*changing her tone*]   But tell me now, Judge—what is your real reason for tracking out Eilert Lövborg's movements so carefully?

BRACK   In the first place, it could not be entirely indifferent to me if it should appear in the police court that he came straight from my house.

HEDDA   Will the matter come into court then?

BRACK   Of course. However, I should scarcely have troubled so much about that. But I thought that, as a friend of the family, it was my duty to supply you and Tesman with a full account of his nocturnal exploits.

HEDDA   Why so, Judge Brack?

BRACK   Why, because I have a shrewd suspicion that he intends to use you as a sort of blind.

HEDDA   Oh, how can you think such a thing!

BRACK   Good heavens, Mrs. Hedda—we have eyes in our head. Mark my words! This Mrs. Elvsted will be in no hurry to leave town again.

HEDDA   Well, even if there should be anything between them, I suppose there are plenty of other places where they could meet.

BRACK   Not a single home. Henceforth, as before, every respectable house will be closed against Eilert Lövborg.

HEDDA   And so ought mine to be, you mean?

BRACK   Yes. I confess it would be more than painful to me if this personage were to be made free of your house. How superfluous, how intrusive, he would be, if he were to force his way into . . .

HEDDA   . . . into the triangle?

BRACK   Precisely. It would simply mean that I should find myself homeless.

HEDDA [*looks at him with a smile*] So you want to be the one cock in the basket—that is your aim.

BRACK [*nods slowly and lowers his voice*] Yes, that is my aim. And for that I will fight—with every weapon I can command.

HEDDA [*her smile vanishing*] I see you are a dangerous person—when it comes to the point.

BRACK Do you think so?

HEDDA I am beginning to think so. And I am exceedingly glad to think—that you have no sort of hold over me.

BRACK [*laughing equivocally*] Well, well, Mrs. Hedda—perhaps you are right there. If I had, who knows what I might be capable of?

HEDDA Come, come now, Judge Brack! That sounds almost like a threat.

BRACK [*rising*] Oh, not at all! The triangle, you know, ought, if possible, to be spontaneously constructed.

HEDDA There I agree with you.

BRACK Well, now I have said all I had to say; and I had better be getting back to town. Good-bye, Mrs. Hedda. [*He goes towards the glass door.*]

HEDDA [*rising*] Are you going through the garden?

BRACK Yes, it's a short cut for me.

HEDDA And then it is a back way, too.

BRACK Quite so. I have no objection to back ways. They may be piquant enough at times.

HEDDA When there is shooting practice going on, you mean?

BRACK [*in the doorway, laughing to her*] Oh, people don't shoot their tame poultry, I fancy.

HEDDA [*also laughing*] Oh no, when there is only one cock in the basket . . .

They exchange laughing nods of farewell. He goes. She closes the door behind him. HEDDA, *who has become quite serious, stands for a moment looking out. Presently she goes and peeps through the curtain over the middle doorway. Then she goes to the writing table, takes* LÖVBORG'S *packet out of the bookcase, and is on the point of looking through its contents.* BERTA *is heard speaking loudly in the hall.* HEDDA *turns and listens. Then she hastily locks up the packet in the drawer, and lays the key on the inkstand.* EILERT LÖVBORG, *with his greatcoat on and his hat in his hand, tears open the hall door. He looks somewhat confused and irritated.*

LÖVBORG [*looking towards the hall*] And I tell you I must and will come in! There!

He closes the door, turns, sees HEDDA, *at once regains his self-control, and bows.*

HEDDA [*at the writing table*] Well, Mr. Lövborg, this is rather a late hour to call for Thea.

LÖVBORG You mean rather an early hour to call on you. Pray pardon me.

HEDDA How do you know that she is still here?

LÖVBORG They told me at her lodgings that she had been out all night.

HEDDA [*going to the oval table*] Did you notice anything about the people of the house when they said that?

LÖVBORG [*looks inquiringly at her*] Notice anything about them?

HEDDA   I mean, did they seem to think it odd?

LÖVBORG [*suddenly understanding*]   Oh yes, of course! I am dragging her down with me! However, I didn't notice anything.—I suppose Tesman is not up yet?

HEDDA   No—I think not. . .

LÖVBORG   When did he come home?

HEDDA   Very late.

LÖVBORG   Did he tell you anything?

HEDDA   Yes, I gathered that you had had an exceedingly jolly evening at Judge Brack's.

LÖVBORG   Nothing more?

HEDDA   I don't think so. However, I was so dreadfully sleepy . . .

MRS.ELVSTED *enters through the curtains of the middle doorway.*

MRS. ELVSTED [*going towards him*]   Ah, Lövborg! At last . . . !

LÖVBORG   Yes, at last. And too late!

MRS. ELVSTED [*looks anxiously at him*]   What is too late?

LÖVBORG   Everything is too late now. It is all over with me.

MRS. ELVSTED   Oh no, no—don't say that!

LÖVBORG   You will say the same when you hear . . .

MRS. ELVSTED   I won't hear anything!

HEDDA   Perhaps you would prefer to talk to her alone? If so, I will leave you.

LÖVBORG   No, stay—you too. I beg you to stay.

MRS.ELVSTED   Yes, but I won't hear anything, I tell you.

LÖVBORG   It is not last night's adventures that I want to talk about.

MRS. ELVSTED   What is it then . . . ?

LÖVBORG   I want to say that now our ways must part.

MRS. ELVSTED   Part!

HEDDA [*involuntarily*]   I knew it!

LÖVBORG   You can be of no more service to me, Thea.

MRS. ELVSTED   How can you stand there and say that! No more service to you! Am I not to help you now, as before? Are we not to go on working together?

LÖVBORG   Henceforward I shall do no work.

MRS. ELVSTED [*despairingly*]   Then what am I to do with my life?

LÖVBORG   You must try to live your life as if you had never known me.

MRS. ELVSTED   But you know I cannot do that!

LÖVBORG   Try if you cannot, Thea. You must go home again . . .

MRS. ELVSTED [*in vehement protest*]   Never in this world! Where you are, there will I be also! I will not let myself be driven away like this! I will remain here! I will be with you when the book appears.

HEDDA [*half aloud, in suspense*]   Ah yes—the book!

LÖVBORG [*looks at her*]   My book and Thea's; for that is what it is.

MRS. ELVSTED   Yes, I feel that it is. And that is why I have a right to be with you when it appears! I will see with my own eyes how respect and honor pour in upon you afresh. And the happiness—the happiness—oh, I must share it with you!

LÖVBORG   Thea—our book will never appear.

HEDDA   Ah!

MRS. ELVSTED   Never appear!

LÖVBORG   Can never appear.

MRS. ELVSTED [*in agonized foreboding*]   Lövborg—what have you done with the manuscript?

HEDDA [*looks anxiously at him*]   Yes, the manuscript . . .

MRS. ELVSTED   Where is it?

LÖVBORG   Oh, Thea—don't ask me about it!

MRS. ELVSTED   Yes, yes, I will know. I demand to be told at once.

LÖVBORG   The manuscript . . . Well then—I have torn the manuscript into a thousand pieces.

MRS. ELVSTED [*shrieks*]   Oh no, no . . . !

HEDDA [*involuntarily*]   But that's not . . .

LÖVBORG [*looks at her*]   Not true, you think?

HEDDA [*collecting herself*]   Oh well, of course—since you say so. But it sounded so improbable . . .

LÖVBORG   It is true, all the same.

MRS. ELVSTED [*wringing her hands*]   Oh God—oh God, Hedda—torn his own work to pieces!

LÖVBORG   I have torn my own life to pieces. So why should I not tear my lifework too . . . ?

MRS. ELVSTED   And you did this last night?

LÖVBORG   Yes, I tell you! Tore it into a thousand pieces—and scattered them on the fjord—far out. There there is a cool sea water at any rate—let them drift upon it—drift with the current and the wind. And then presently they will sink—deeper and deeper—as I shall, Thea.

MRS. ELVSTED   Do you know, Lövborg, that what you have done with the book—I shall think of it to my dying day as though you had killed a little child.

LÖVBORG   Yes, you are right. It is a sort of child murder.

MRS. ELVSTED   How could you, then . . . ! Did not the child belong to me too?

HEDDA [*almost inaudibly*]   Ah, the child . . .

MRS. ELVSTED [*breathing heavily*]   It is all over then. Well, well, now I will go, Hedda.

HEDDA   But you are not going away from town?

MRS. ELVSTED   Oh, I don't know what I shall do. I see nothing but darkness before me. [*She goes out by the hall door.*]

HEDDA [*stands waiting for a moment*]   So you are not going to see her home, Mr. Lövborg?

LÖVBORG   I? Through the streets? Would you have people see her walking with me?

HEDDA   Of course I don't know what else may have happened last night. But is it so utterly irretrievable?

LÖVBORG   It will not end with last night—I know that perfectly well. And the thing is that now I have no taste for that sort of life either. I won't begin it anew. She has broken my courage and my power of braving life out.

HEDDA [*looking straight before her*]   So that pretty little fool has had her fingers in a man's destiny. [*Looks at him*] But all the same, how could you treat her so heartlessly?

LÖVBORG   Oh, don't say that it was heartless!

HEDDA   To go and destroy what has filled her whole soul for months and years! You do not call that heartless!

LÖVBORG   To you I can tell the truth, Hedda.

HEDDA The truth?

LÖVBORG First promise me—give me your word—that what I now confide to you Thea shall never know.

HEDDA I give you my word.

LÖVBORG Good. Then let me tell you that what I said just now was untrue.

HEDDA About the manuscript?

LÖVBORG Yes. I have not torn it to pieces—nor thrown it into the fjord.

HEDDA No, no . . . But—where is it then?

LÖVBORG I have destroyed it none the less—utterly destroyed it, Hedda!

HEDDA I don't understand.

LÖVBORG Thea said that what I had done seemed to her like a child murder.

HEDDA Yes, so she said.

LÖVBORG But to kill his child—that is not the worst thing a father can do to it.

HEDDA Not the worst?

LÖVBORG No. I wanted to spare Thea from hearing the worst.

HEDDA Then what is the worst?

LÖVBORG Suppose now, Hedda, that a man—in the small hours of the morning—came home to his child's mother after a night of riot and debauchery, and said: "Listen—I have been here and there—in this place and in that. And I have taken our child with me—to this place and to that. And I have lost the child—utterly lost it. The devil knows into what hands it may have fallen—who may have had their clutches on it."

HEDDA Well—but when all is said and done, you know—this was only a book . . .

LÖVBORG Thea's pure soul was in that book.

HEDDA Yes, so I understand.

LÖVBORG And you can understand, too, that for her and me together no future is possible.

HEDDA What path do you mean to take then?

LÖVBORG None. I will only try to make an end of it all—the sooner the better.

HEDDA [*a step nearer him*] Eilert Lövborg—listen to me. Will you not try to—to do it beautifully?

LÖVBORG Beautifully? [*Smiling*] With vine leaves in my hair, as you used to dream in the old days . . . ?

HEDDA No, no. I have lost my faith in the vine leaves. But beautifully nevertheless! For once in a way! Good-bye! You must go now—and do not come here any more.

LÖVBORG Good-bye, Mrs. Tesman. And give George Tesman my love. [*He is on the point of going.*]

HEDDA No, wait! I must give you a memento to take with you.

She goes to the writing table and opens the drawer and the pistol case; then returns to LÖVBORG *with one of the pistols.*

LÖVBORG [*looks at her*] This? Is this the memento?

HEDDA [*nodding slowly*] Do you recognize it? It was aimed at you once.

LÖVBORG You should have used it then.

HEDDA Take it—and do you use it now.

LÖVBORG [*puts the pistol in his breast pocket*] Thanks!

HEDDA   And beautifully, Eilert Lövborg. Promise me that!
LÖVBORG   Good-bye, Hedda Gabler.

He goes out by the hall door. HEDDA *listens for a moment at the door. Then she goes up to the writing table, takes out the packet of manuscript, peeps under the cover, draws a few of the sheets half out, and looks at them. Next she goes over and seats herself in the armchair beside the stove, with the packet in her lap. Presently she opens the stove door, and then the packet.*

HEDDA [*throws one of the quires into the fire and whispers to herself*]   Now I am burning your child, Thea!—Burning it, curly-locks! [*Throwing one or two more quires into the stove*] Your child and Eilert Lövborg's. [*Throws the rest in*] I am burning—I am burning your child.

Act IV

SCENE: *The same rooms at the* TESMANS'. *It is evening. The drawing room is in darkness. The back room is lighted by the hanging lamp over the table. The curtains over the glass door are drawn close.* HEDDA, *dressed in black, walks to and fro in the dark room. Then she goes into the back room and disappears for a moment to the left. She is heard to strike a few chords on the piano. Presently she comes in sight again, and returns to the drawing room.* BERTA *enters from the right, through the inner room, with a lighted lamp, which she places on the table in front of the corner settee in the drawing room. Her eyes are red with weeping, and she has black ribbon in her cap. She goes quietly and circumspectly out to the right.* HEDDA *goes up to the glass door, lifts the curtain a little aside, and looks out into the darkness. Shortly afterwards,* MISS TESMAN, *in mourning, with a bonnet and veil on, comes in from the hall.* HEDDA *goes towards her and holds out her hand.*

MISS TESMAN   Yes, Hedda, here I am, in mourning and forlorn; for now my poor sister has at last found peace.
HEDDA   I have heard the news already, as you see. Tesman sent me a card.
MISS TESMAN   Yes, he promised me he would. But nevertheless I thought that to Hedda—here in the house of life—I ought myself to bring the tidings of death.
HEDDA   That was very kind of you.
MISS TESMAN   Ah, Rina ought not to have left us just now. This is not the time for Hedda's house to be a house of mourning.
HEDDA [*changing the subject*]   She died quite peacefully, did she not, Miss Tesman?
MISS TESMAN   Oh, her end was so calm, so beautiful. And then she had the unspeakable happiness of seeing George once more—and bidding him good-bye. Has he not come home yet?
HEDDA   No. He wrote that he might be detained. But won't you sit down?
MISS TESMAN   No thank you, my dear, dear Hedda. I should like to, but I have so much to do. I must prepare my dear one for her rest as well as I can. She shall go to her grave looking her best.
HEDDA   Can I not help you in any way?
MISS TESMAN   Oh, you must not think of it! Hedda Tesman must have no hand in such mournful work. Nor let her thoughts dwell on it either—not at this time.
HEDDA   One is not always mistress of one's thoughts . . .

MISS TESMAN [*continuing*]   Ah, yes, it is the way of the world. At home we shall be sewing a shroud; and here there will soon be sewing too, I suppose—but of another sort, thank God!

GEORGE TESMAN *enters by the hall door.*

HEDDA   Ah, you have come at last!

TESMAN   You here, Aunt Julia? With Hedda? Fancy that!

MISS TESMAN   I was just going, my dear boy. Well, have you done all you promised?

TESMAN   No; I'm really afraid I have forgotten half of it. I must come to you again tomorrow. Today my brain is all in a whirl. I can't keep my thoughts together.

MISS TESMAN   Why, my dear George, you mustn't take it in this way.

TESMAN   Mustn't . . . ? How do you mean?

MISS TESMAN   Even in your sorrow you must rejoice, as I do—rejoice that she is at rest.

TESMAN   Oh yes, yes—you are thinking of Aunt Rina.

HEDDA   You will feel lonely now, Miss Tesman.

MISS TESMAN   Just at first, yes. But that will not last very long, I hope. I daresay I shall soon find an occupant for poor Rina's little room.

TESMAN   Indeed? Who do you think will take it? Eh?

MISS TESMAN   Oh, there's always some poor invalid or other in want of nursing, unfortunately.

HEDDA   Would you really take such a burden upon you again?

MISS TESMAN   A burden! Heaven forgive you, child—it has been no burden to me.

HEDDA   But suppose you had a total stranger on your hands . . .

MISS TESMAN   Oh, one soon makes friends with sick folk; and it's such an absolute necessity for me to have some one to live for. Well, heaven be praised, there may soon be something in *this* house, too, to keep an old aunt busy.

HEDDA   Oh, don't trouble about anything here.

TESMAN   Yes, just fancy what a nice time we three might have together, if . . . ?

HEDDA   If . . .?

TESMAN [*uneasily*]   Oh, nothing. It will all come right. Let us hope so—eh?

MISS TESMAN   Well, well, I daresay you two want to talk to each other. [*Smiling*] And perhaps Hedda may have something to tell you too, George. Good-bye! I must go home to Rina. [*Turning at the door*] How strange it is to think that now Rina is with me and with my poor brother as well!

TESMAN   Yes, fancy that, Aunt Julia! Eh? [MISS TESMAN *goes out by the hall door.*]

HEDDA [*follows* TESMAN *coldly and searchingly with her eyes*]   I almost believe your Aunt Rina's death affects you more than it does your Aunt Julia.

TESMAN   Oh, it's not that alone. It's Eilert I am so terribly uneasy about.

HEDDA [*quickly*]   Is there anything new about him?

TESMAN   I looked in at his rooms this afternoon, intending to tell him the manuscript was in safe keeping.

HEDDA   Well, did you not find him?

TESMAN   No. He wasn't at home. But afterwards I met Mrs. Elvsted, and she told me that he had been here early this morning.

HEDDA   Yes, directly after you had gone.

TESMAN   And he said that he had torn his manuscript to pieces—eh?

HEDDA   Yes, so he declared.

TESMAN   Why, good heavens, he must have been completely out of his mind! And I suppose you thought it best not to give it back to him, Hedda?

HEDDA   No, he did not get it.

TESMAN   But of course you told him that we had it?

HEDDA   No. [*Quickly*] Did you tell Mrs. Elvsted?

TESMAN   No; I thought I had better not. But you ought to have told him. Fancy, if, in desperation, he should go and do himself some injury! Let me have the manuscript, Hedda! I will take it to him at once. Where is it?

HEDDA [*cold and immovable, leaning on the armchair*]   I have not got it.

TESMAN   Have not got it? What in the world do you mean?

HEDDA   I have burnt it—every line of it.

TESMAN [*with a violent movement of terror*]   Burnt! Burnt Eilert's manuscript!

HEDDA   Don't scream so. The servant might hear you.

TESMAN   Burnt! Why, good God . . . ! No, no, no! It's impossible!

HEDDA   It is so, nevertheless.

TESMAN   Do you know what you have done, Hedda? It's unlawful appropriation of lost property. Fancy that! Just ask Judge Brack, and he'll tell you what it is.

HEDDA   I advise you not to speak of it—either to Judge Brack, or to any one else.

TESMAN   But how could you do anything so unheard of? What put it into your head? What possessed you? Answer me that—eh?

HEDDA [*suppressing an almost imperceptible smile*]   I did it for your sake, George.

TESMAN   For my sake!

HEDDA   This morning, when you told me about what he had read to you . . .

TESMAN   Yes, yes—what then?

HEDDA   You acknowledged that you envied him his work.

TESMAN   Oh, of course I didn't mean that literally.

HEDDA   No matter—I could not bear the idea that any one should throw you into the shade.

TESMAN [*in an outburst of mingled doubt and joy*]   Hedda! Oh, is this true? But—but—I never knew you to show your love like that before. Fancy that!

HEDDA   Well, I may as well tell you that—just at this time . . . [*Impatiently, breaking off*] No, no; you can ask Aunt Julia. She will tell you, fast enough.

TESMAN   Oh, I almost think I understand you, Hedda! [*Clasps his hands together*] Great heavens! do you really mean it? Eh?

HEDDA   Don't shout so. The servant might hear.

TESMAN [*laughing in irrepressible glee*]   The servant! Why, how absurd you are, Hedda. It's only my old Berta! Why, I'll tell Berta myself.

HEDDA [*clenching her hands together in desperation*]   Oh, it is killing me—it is killing me, all this!

TESMAN   What is, Hedda? Eh?

HEDDA [*coldly, controlling herself*]   All this—absurdity—George.

TESMAN   Absurdity! Do you see anything absurd in my being overjoyed at the news! But after all—perhaps I had better not say anything to Berta.

HEDDA   Oh . . . why not that too?

TESMAN   No, no, not yet! But I must certainly tell Aunt Julia. And then that you have begun to call me George too! Fancy that! Oh, Aunt Julia will be so happy—so happy!

HEDDA   When she hears that I have burnt Eilert Lövborg's manuscript—for your sake?

TESMAN   No, by the by—that affair of the manuscript—of course nobody must know about that. But that you love me so much, Hedda—Aunt Julia must really share my joy in that! I wonder, now, whether this sort of thing is usual in young wives? Eh?

HEDDA   I think you had better ask Aunt Julia that question too.

TESMAN   I will indeed, some time or other. [*Looks uneasy and downcast again*] And yet the manuscript—the manuscript! Good God! It is terrible to think what will become of poor Eilert now.

MRS. ELVSTED, *dressed as in the first act, with hat and cloak, enters by the hall door.*

MRS. ELVSTED [*greets them hurriedly, and says in evident agitation*]   Oh, dear Hedda, forgive my coming again.

HEDDA   What is the matter with you, Thea?

TESMAN   Something about Eilert Lövborg again—eh?

MRS. ELVSTED   Yes! I am dreadfully afraid some misfortune has happened to him.

HEDDA [*seizes her arm*]   Ah—do you think so?

TESMAN   Why, good Lord—what makes you think that, Mrs. Elvsted?

MRS. ELVSTED   I heard them talking at my boardinghouse—just as I came in. Oh, the most incredible rumors are afloat about him today.

TESMAN   Yes, fancy, so I heard too! And I can bear witness that he went straight home to bed last night. Fancy that!

HEDDA   Well, what did they say at the boardinghouse?

MRS. ELVSTED   Oh, I couldn't make out anything clearly. Either they knew nothing definite, or else . . . They stopped talking when they saw me; and I did not dare to ask.

TESMAN [*moving about uneasily*]   We must hope—we must hope that you misunderstood them, Mrs. Elvsted.

MRS. ELVSTED   No, no; I am sure it was of him they were talking. And I heard something about the hospital or . . .

TESMAN   The hospital?

HEDDA   No—surely that cannot be!

MRS. ELVSTED   Oh, I was in such mortal terror! I went to his lodgings and asked for him there.

HEDDA   You could make up your mind to that, Thea!

MRS. ELVSTED   What else could I do? I really could bear the suspense no longer.

TESMAN   But you didn't find him either—eh?

MRS. ELVSTED   No. And the people knew nothing about him. He hadn't been home since yesterday afternoon, they said.

TESMAN   Yesterday! Fancy, how could they say that?

MRS. ELVSTED   Oh, I am sure something terrible must have happened to him.

TESMAN   Hedda dear—how would it be if I were to go and make inquiries . . . ?

HEDDA   No, no—don't mix yourself up in this affair.

JUDGE BRACK, *with his hat in his hand, enters by the hall door, which* BERTA *opens, and closes behind him. He looks grave and bows in silence.*

TESMAN   Oh, is that you, my dear Judge? Eh?

BRACK   Yes. It was imperative I should see you this evening.

TESMAN   I can see you have heard the news about Aunt Rina?

BRACK   Yes, that among other things.

TESMAN   Isn't it sad—eh?

BRACK   Well, my dear Tesman, that depends on how you look at it.

TESMAN [*looks doubtfully at him*]   Has anything else happened?

BRACK   Yes.

HEDDA [*in suspense*]   Anything sad, Judge Brack?

BRACK   That too, depends on how you look at it, Mrs. Tesman.

MRS. ELVSTED [*unable to restrain her anxiety*]   Oh! it is something about Eilert Lövborg!

BRACK [*with a glance at her*]   What makes you think that, Madam? Perhaps you have already heard something . . . ?

MRS. ELVSTED [*in confusion*]   No, nothing at all, but . . .

TESMAN   Oh, for heaven's sake, tell us!

BRACK [*shrugging his shoulders*]   Well, I regret to say Eilert Lövborg has been taken to the hospital. He is lying at the point of death.

MRS. ELVSTED [*shrieks*]   Oh God! oh God . . . !

TESMAN   To the hospital! And at the point of death!

HEDDA [*involuntarily*]   So soon then . . .

MRS. ELVSTED [*wailing*]   And we parted in anger, Hedda!

HEDDA [*whispers*]   Thea—Thea—be careful!

MRS. ELVSTED [*not heeding her*]   I must go to him! I must see him alive!

BRACK   It is useless, Madam. No one will be admitted.

MRS. ELVSTED   Oh, at least tell me what has happened to him? What is it?

TESMAN   You don't mean to say that he has himself . . . Eh?

HEDDA   Yes, I am sure he has.

TESMAN   Hedda, how can you . . . ?

BRACK [*keeping his eyes fixed upon her*]   Unfortunately you have guessed quite correctly, Mrs. Tesman.

MRS. ELVSTED   Oh, how horrible!

TESMAN   Himself, then! Fancy that!

HEDDA   Shot himself!

BRACK   Rightly guessed again, Mrs. Tesman.

MRS. ELVSTED [*with an effort at self-control*]   When did it happen, Mr. Brack?

BRACK   This afternoon—between three and four.

TESMAN   But, good Lord, where did he do it? Eh?

BRACK [*with some hesitation*]   Where? Well—I suppose at his lodgings.

MRS. ELVSTED   No, that cannot be; for I was there between six and seven.

BRACK   Well then, somewhere else. I don't know exactly. I only know that he was found . . . He had shot himself—in the breast.

MRS. ELVSTED   Oh, how terrible! That he should die like that!

HEDDA [*to* BRACK]   Was it in the breast?

BRACK   Yes—as I told you.

HEDDA   Not in the temple?

BRACK   In the breast, Mrs. Tesman.

HEDDA   Well, well—the breast is a good place, too.

BRACK   How do you mean, Mrs. Tesman?

HEDDA [*evasively*]   Oh, nothing—nothing.

TESMAN   And the wound is dangerous, you say—eh?

BRACK   Absolutely mortal. The end has probably come by this time.

MRS. ELVSTED   Yes, yes, I feel it. The end! The end! Oh, Hedda . . . !

TESMAN   But tell me, how have you learnt all this?

BRACK [*curtly*]   Through one of the police. A man I had some business with.

HEDDA [*in a clear voice*]   At last a deed worth doing!

TESMAN [*terrified*]   Good heavens, Hedda! what are you saying?

HEDDA   I say there is beauty in this.

BRACK   H'm, Mrs. Tesman . . .

TESMAN   Beauty! Fancy that!

MRS. ELVSTED   Oh, Hedda, how can you talk of beauty in such an act!

HEDDA   Eilert Lövborg has himself made up his account with life. He has had
the courage to do—the one right thing.

MRS. ELVSTED   No, you must never think that was how it happened! It must
have been in delirium that he did it.

TESMAN   In despair!

HEDDA   That he did not. I am certain of that.

MRS. ELVSTED   Yes, yes! In delirium! Just as when he tore up our manuscript.

BRACK [*starting*]   The manuscript? Has he torn that up?

MRS. ELVSTED   Yes, last night.

TESMAN [*whispers softly*]   Oh, Hedda, we shall never get over this.

BRACK   H'm, very extraordinary.

TESMAN [*moving about the room*]   To think of Eilert going out of the world in
this way! And not leaving behind him the book that would have immortalized his
name . . .

MRS. ELVSTED   Oh, if only it could be put together again!

TESMAN   Yes, if it only could! I don't know what I would not give . . .

MRS. ELVSTED   Perhaps it can, Mr. Tesman.

TESMAN   What do you mean?

MRS. ELVSTED [*searches in the pocket of her dress*]   Look here. I have kept all
the loose notes he used to dictate from.

HEDDA [*a step forward*]   Ah . . . !

TESMAN   You have kept them, Mrs. Elvsted! Eh?

MRS. ELVSTED   Yes, I have them here. I put them in my pocket when I left
home. Here they still are . . .

TESMAN   Oh, do let me see them!

MRS. ELVSTED [*hands him a bundle of papers*]   But they are in such disorder—
all mixed up.

TESMAN   Fancy, if we could make something out of them, after all! Perhaps if
we two put our heads together . . .

MRS. ELVSTED   Oh yes, at least let us try . . .

TESMAN   We will manage it! We must! I will dedicate my life to this task.

HEDDA   You, George? Your life?

TESMAN   Yes, or rather all the time I can spare. My own collections must wait
in the meantime. Hedda—you understand, eh? I owe this to Eilert's memory.

HEDDA   Perhaps.

TESMAN   And so, my dear Mrs. Elvsted, we will give our whole minds to it.

There is no use in brooding over what can't be undone—eh? We must try to control our grief as much as possible, and . . .

MRS. ELVSTED   Yes, yes, Mr. Tesman, I will do the best I can.

TESMAN   Well then, come here. I can't rest until we have looked through the notes. Where shall we sit? Here? No, in there, in the back room. Excuse me, my dear Judge. Come with me, Mrs. Elvsted.

MRS. ELVSTED   Oh, if only it were possible!

TESMAN *and* MRS. ELVSTED *go into the back room. She takes off her hat and cloak. They both sit at the table under the hanging lamp, and are soon deep in an eager examination of the papers.* HEDDA *crosses to the stove and sits in the armchair. Presently* BRACK *goes up to her.*

HEDDA [*in a low voice*]   Oh, what a sense of freedom it gives one, this act of Eilert Lövborg's.

BRACK   Freedom, Mrs. Hedda? Well, of course, it is a release for him . . .

HEDDA   I mean for me. It gives me a sense of freedom to know that a deed of deliberate courage is still possible in this world—a deed of spontaneous beauty.

BRACK [*smiling*]   H'm—my dear Mrs. Hedda . . .

HEDDA   Oh, I know what you are going to say. For you are a kind of specialist, too, like—you know!

BRACK [*looking hard at her*]   Eilert Lövborg was more to you than perhaps you are willing to admit to yourself. Am I wrong?

HEDDA   I don't answer such questions. I only know that Eilert Lövborg has had the courage to live his life after his own fashion. And then—the last great act, with its beauty! Ah! that he should have the will and the strength to turn away from the banquet of life—so early.

BRACK   I am sorry, Mrs. Hedda, but I fear I must dispel an amiable illusion.

HEDDA   Illusion?

BRACK   Which could not have lasted long in any case.

HEDDA   What do you mean?

BRACK   Eilert Lövborg did not shoot himself—voluntarily.

HEDDA   Not voluntarily!

BRACK   No. The thing did not happen exactly as I told it.

HEDDA [*in suspense*]   Have you concealed something? What is it?

BRACK   For poor Mrs. Elvsted's sake I idealized the facts a little.

HEDDA   What are the facts?

BRACK   First, that he is already dead.

HEDDA   At the hospital?

BRACK   Yes—without regaining consciousness.

HEDDA   What more have you concealed?

BRACK   This—the event did not happen at his lodgings.

HEDDA   Oh, that can make no difference.

BRACK   Perhaps it may. For I must tell you—Eilert Lövborg was found shot in—in Mademoiselle Diana's boudoir.

HEDDA [*makes a motion as if to rise, but sinks back again*]   That is impossible, Judge Brack! He cannot have been there again today.

BRACK   He was there this afternoon. He went there, he said, to demand the return of something, which they had taken from him. Talked wildly about a lost child . . .

HEDDA Ah—so that was why . . .

BRACK I thought probably he meant his manuscript; but now I hear he destroyed that himself. So I suppose it must have been his pocketbook.

HEDDA Yes, no doubt. And there—there he was found?

BRACK Yes, there. With a pistol in his breast pocket, discharged. The ball had lodged in a vital part.

HEDDA In the breast—yes.

BRACK No—in the bowels.

HEDDA [looks up at him with an expression of loathing] That, too! Oh, what a curse is it that makes everything I touch turn ludicrous and mean?

BRACK There is one point more, Mrs. Hedda—another disagreeable feature in the affair.

HEDDA And what is that?

BRACK The pistol he carried . . .

HEDDA [breathless] Well? What of it?

BRACK He must have stolen it.

HEDDA [leaps up] Stolen it! That is not true! He did not steal it!

BRACK No other explanation is possible. He must have stolen it . . . Hush!

TESMAN and MRS. ELVSTED have risen from the table in the back room, and come into the drawing room.

TESMAN [with the papers in both his hands] Hedda, dear, it is almost impossible to see under that lamp. Think of that!

HEDDA Yes, I am thinking.

TESMAN Would you mind our sitting at your writing table—eh?

HEDDA If you like. [Quickly] No, wait! Let me clear it first!

TESMAN Oh, you needn't trouble, Hedda. There is plenty of room.

HEDDA No, no, let me clear it, I say! I will take these things in and put them on the piano. There!

She has drawn out an object, covered with sheet music, from under the bookcase, places several other pieces of music upon it, and carries the whole into the inner room, to the left. TESMAN lays the scraps of paper on the writing table, and moves the lamp there from the corner table. He and MRS ELVSTED sit down and proceed with their work. HEDDA returns.

HEDDA [behind MRS. ELVSTED's chair, gently ruffing her hair] Well, my sweet Thea, how goes it with Eilert Lövborg's monument?

MRS. ELVSTED [looks dispiritedly up at her] Oh, it will be terribly hard to put in order.

TESMAN We must manage it. I am determined. And arranging other people's papers is just the work for me.

HEDDA goes over to the stove, and seats herself on one of the footstools. BRACK stands over her, leaning on the armchair.

HEDDA [whispers] What did you say about the pistol?

BRACK [softly] That he must have stolen it.

HEDDA Why stolen it?

BRACK   Because every other explanation ought to be impossible, Mrs. Hedda.

HEDDA   Indeed?

BRACK [*glances at her*]   Of course, Eilert Lövborg was here this morning. Was he not?

HEDDA   Yes.

BRACK   Were you alone with him?

HEDDA   Part of the time.

BRACK   Did you not leave the room whilst he was here?

HEDDA   No.

BRACK   Try to recollect. Were you not out of the room a moment?

HEDDA   Yes, perhaps just a moment—out in the hall.

BRACK   And where was your pistol case during that time?

HEDDA   I had it locked up in . . .

BRACK   Well, Mrs. Hedda?

HEDDA   The case stood there on the writing table.

BRACK   Have you looked since, to see whether both the pistols are there?

HEDDA   No.

BRACK   Well, you need not. I saw the pistol found in Lövborg's pocket, and I knew it at once as the one I had seen yesterday—and before, too.

HEDDA   Have you it with you?

BRACK   No, the police have it.

HEDDA   What will the police do with it?

BRACK   Search till they find the owner.

HEDDA   Do you think they will succeed?

BRACK [*bends over her and whispers*]   No, Hedda Gabler—not so long as I say nothing.

HEDDA [*looks frightened at him*]   And if you do not say nothing—what then?

BRACK [*shrugs his shoulders*]   There is always the possibility that pistol was stolen.

HEDDA [*firmly*]   Death rather than that.

BRACK [*smiling*]   People say such things—but they don't do them.

HEDDA [*without replying*]   And supposing the pistol was not stolen, and the owner is discovered? What then?

BRACK   Well, Hedda—then comes the scandal.

HEDDA   The scandal!

BRACK   Yes, the scandal—of which you are so mortally afraid. You will, of course, be brought before the court—both you and Mademoiselle Diana. She will have to explain how the thing happened—whether it was an accidental shot or murder. Did the pistol go off as he was trying to take it out of his pocket, to threaten her with? Or did she tear the pistol out of his hand, shoot him, and push it back into his pocket? That would be quite like her; for she is an able-bodied young person, this same Mademoiselle Diana.

HEDDA   But *I* have nothing to do with all this repulsive business.

BRACK   No. But you will have to answer the question: Why did you give Eilert Lövborg the pistol? And what conclusions will people draw from the fact that you did give it to him?

HEDDA [*lets her head sink*]   That is true. I did not think of that.

BRACK   Well, fortunately, there is no danger, so long as I say nothing.

HEDDA [*looks up at him*]   So I am in your power, Judge Brack. You have me at your beck and call, from this time forward.

BRACK [*whispers softly*]   Dearest Hedda—believe me—I shall not abuse my advantage.

HEDDA   I am in your power none the less. Subject to your will and your demands. A slave, a slave then! [*Rises impetuously*] No, I cannot endure the thought of that! Never!

BRACK [*looks half-mockingly at her*]   People generally get used to the inevitable.

HEDDA [*returns his look*]   Yes, perhaps. [*She crosses to the writing table. Suppressing an involuntary smile, she imitates* TESMAN's *intonations.*] Well? Are you getting on, George? Eh?

TESMAN   Heaven knows, dear. In any case it will be the work of months.

HEDDA [*as before*]   Fancy that! [*Passes her hands softly through* MRS. ELVSTED's *hair*] Doesn't it seem strange to you, Thea? Here you are sitting with Tesman—just as you used to sit with Eilert Lövborg?

MRS. ELVSTED   Ah, if I could only inspire your husband in the same way!

HEDDA   Oh, that will come, too—in time.

TESMAN   Yes, do you know, Hedda—I really think I begin to feel something of the sort. But won't you go and sit with Brack again?

HEDDA   Is there nothing I can do to help you two?

TESMAN   No, nothing in the world. [*Turning his head*] I trust to you to keep Hedda company, my dear Brack.

BRACK [*with a glance at* HEDDA]   With the very greatest of pleasure.

HEDDA   Thanks. But I am tired this evening. I will go in and lie down a little on the sofa.

TESMAN   Yes, do, dear—eh?

HEDDA *goes into the back room and draws the curtains. A short pause. Suddenly she is heard playing a wild dance on the piano.*

MRS. ELVSTED [*starts from her chair*]   Oh—what is that?

TESMAN [*runs to the doorway*]   Why, my dearest Hedda—don't play dance music tonight! Just think of Aunt Rina! And of Eilert, too!

HEDDA [*puts her head out between the curtains*]   And of Aunt Julia. And of all the rest of them. After this, I will be quiet. [*Closes the curtains again*]

TESMAN [*at the writing table*]   It's not good for her to see us at this distressing work. I'll tell you what, Mrs. Elvsted—you shall take the empty room at Aunt Julia's, and then I will come over in the evenings, and we can sit and work there—eh?

HEDDA [*in the inner room*]   I hear what you are saying, Tesman. But how am *I* to get through the evenings out here?

TESMAN [*turning over the papers*]   Oh, I daresay Judge Brack will be so kind as to look in now and then, even though I am out.

BRACK [*in the armchair, calls out gaily*]   Every blessed evening, with all the pleasure in life, Mrs. Tesman! We shall get on capitally together, we two!

HEDDA [*speaking loud and clear*]   Yes, don't you flatter yourself we will, Judge Brack? Now that you are the one cock in the basket . . .

A shot is heard within. TESMAN, MRS. ELVSTED, *and* BRACK *leap to their feet.*

TESMAN   Oh, now she is playing with those pistols again.

He throws back the curtains and runs in, followed by MRS. ELVSTED. HEDDA *lies stretched on the sofa, lifeless. Confusion and cries.* BERTA *enters in alarm from the right.*

TESMAN [*shrieks to* BRACK]   Shot herself! Shot herself in the temple! Fancy that!

BRACK [*half-fainting in the armchair*]   Good God!—people don't do such things.

George Bernard Shaw and *Saint Joan*

George Bernard Shaw (1856–1950) wrote novels and criticism before he became a playwright. Music critic, socialist lecturer, moral essayist, he promoted the social theater of Ibsen and then wrote his own. His plays propose ideas and argue with wit and paradox but owe their success to his inventive and entertaining theatricality.

His first play was *Widower's Houses* (1892), followed by his first considerable success, *Arms and the Man* (1894). *Mrs. Warren's Profession* was written earlier, in 1893, but because the shocking profession was prostitution, the play was not staged in London until 1925. Other plays include *Candida* (1895), *The Devil's Disciple* (1897), *Caesar and Cleopatra* (1898), *Major Barbara* (1905), *Man and Superman* (1901–1903), and *Pygmalion* (1913, in 1956 adapted as the musical *My Fair Lady*).

Saint Joan (1923) is comparatively late, one of his best plays, combining an historical figure with Shaw's invention. The sharpness and wit of its dialogue and its intelligent skepticism do not preclude an appropriate compassion for the play's heroine. Shaw was awarded the Nobel Prize for Literature in 1925.

George Bernard Shaw
Saint Joan

Characters

BERTRAND DE POULENGY	DUNOIS' PAGE
STEWARD	RICHARD DE BEAUCHAMP, EARL OF WARWICK
JOAN	CHAPLAIN DE STOGUMBER
ROBERT DE BAUDRICOURT	PETER CAUCHON, BISHOP OF BEAUVAIS
THE ARCHBISHOP OF RHEIMS	WARWICK'S PAGE
MGR DE LA TRÉMOUILLE	THE INQUISITOR
COURT PAGE	D'ESTIVET
GILLES DE RAIS	DE COURCELLES
CAPTAIN LA HIRE	BROTHER MARTIN LADVENU
THE DAUPHIN (later CHARLES VII)	THE EXECUTIONER
DUCHESS DE LA TRÉMOUILLE	AN ENGLISH SOLDIER
DUNOIS, BASTARD OF ORLEANS	A GENTLEMAN OF 1920

Scene 1

A fine spring morning on the river Meuse, between Lorraine and Champagne, in the year 1429 A.D. *in the castle of Vaucouleurs.*

Captain ROBERT DE BAUDRICOURT *a military squire, handsome and physically energetic, but with no will of his own, is disguising that defect in his usual fashion by storming terribly at his steward, a trodden worm, scanty of flesh, scanty of hair, who might be any age from 18 to 55, being the sort of man whom age cannot wither because he has never bloomed.*

The two are in a sunny stone chamber on the first floor of the castle. At a plain strong oak table, seated in chair to match, the captain presents his left profile. The steward stands facing him at the other side of the table, if so deprecatory a stance as his can be called standing. The mullioned thirteenth-century window is open behind him. Near it in the corner is a turret with a narrow arched doorway leading to a winding stair which descends to the courtyard. There is a stout fourlegged stool under the table, and a wooden chest under the window.

ROBERT   No eggs! No eggs!! Thousand thunders, man, what do you mean by no eggs?

STEWARD   Sir: it is not my fault. It is the act of God.

ROBERT   Blasphemy. You tell me there are no eggs; and you blame your Maker for it.

STEWARD   Sir: what can I do? I cannot lay eggs.

ROBERT [*sarcastic*]   Ha! You jest about it.

STEWARD   No, sir, God knows. We all have to go without eggs just as you have, sir. The hens will not lay.

ROBERT   Indeed! [*Rising*] Now listen to me, you.

STEWARD [*humbly*]   Yes, sir.

ROBERT   What am I?

STEWARD   What are you, sir?

ROBERT [*coming at him*]   Yes: what am I? Am I Robert, squire of Baudricourt and captain of this castle of Vaucouleurs; or am I a cowboy?

STEWARD   Oh, sir, you know you are a greater man here than the king himself.

ROBERT   Precisely. And now, do you know what you are?

STEWARD   I am nobody, sir, except that I have the honor to be your steward.

ROBERT [*driving him to the wall, adjective by adjective*]   You have not only the honor of being my steward, but the privilege of being the worst, most incompetent, drivelling snivelling jibbering jabbering idiot of a steward in France. [*He strides back to the table.*]

STEWARD [*cowering on the chest*]   Yes, sir: to a great man like you I must seem like that.

ROBERT [*turning*]   My fault, I suppose. Eh?

STEWARD [*coming to him deprecatingly*]   Oh, sir: you always give my most innocent words such a turn!

ROBERT   I will give your neck a turn if you dare tell me, when I ask you how many eggs there are, that you cannot lay any.

STEWARD [*protesting*]   Oh sir, oh sir—

ROBERT   No: not oh sir, oh sir, but no sir, no sir. My three Barbary hens and the black are the best layers in Champagne. And you come and tell me that there are no eggs! Who stole them? Tell me that, before I kick you out through the castle gate for a liar and a seller of my goods to thieves. The milk was short yesterday, too: do not forget that.

STEWARD [*desperate*]   I know, sir. I know only too well. There is no milk: there are no eggs: tomorrow there will be nothing.

ROBERT   Nothing! You will steal the lot: eh?

STEWARD   No, sir: nobody will steal anything. But there is a spell on us: we are bewitched.

ROBERT   That story is not good enough for me. Robert de Baudricourt burns witches and hangs thieves. Go. Bring me four dozen eggs and two gallons of milk here in this room before noon, or Heaven have mercy on your bones! I will teach you to make a fool of me. [*He resumes his seat with an air of finality.*]

STEWARD   Sir: I tell you there are no eggs. There will be none—not if you were to kill me for it—as long as The Maid is at the door.

ROBERT   The Maid! What maid? What are you talking about?

STEWARD   The girl from Lorraine, sir. From Domrémy.

ROBERT [*rising in fearful wrath*]   Thirty thousand thunders! Fifty thousand devils! Do you mean to say that that girl, who had the impudence to ask to see me two days ago, and whom I told you to send back to her father with my orders that he was to give her a good hiding, is here still?

STEWARD   I have told her to go, sir. She wont.

ROBERT   I did not tell you to tell her to go: I told you to throw her out. You have fifty men-at-arms and a dozen lumps of able-bodied servants to carry out my orders. Are they afraid of her?

STEWARD   She is so positive, sir.

ROBERT [*seizing him by the scruff of the neck*]   Positive! Now see here. I am going to throw you downstairs.

STEWARD   No, sir. Please.

ROBERT   Well, stop me by being positive. It's quite easy: any slut of a girl can do it.

STEWARD [*hanging limp in his hands*]   Sir, sir: you cannot get rid of her by throwing me out. [ROBERT *has to let him drop. He squats on his knees on the floor, contemplating his master resignedly.*] You see, sir, you are much more positive than I am. But so is she.

ROBERT   I am stronger than you are, you fool.

STEWARD   No, sir: it isnt that: it's your strong character, sir. She is weaker than we are: she is only a slip of a girl; but we cannot make her go.

ROBERT   You parcel of curs: you are afraid of her.

STEWARD [*rising cautiously*]   No sir: we are afraid of you; but she puts courage into us. She really doesnt seem to be afraid of anything. Perhaps you could frighten her, sir.

ROBERT [*grimly*]   Perhaps. Where is she now?

STEWARD   Down in the courtyard, sir, talking to the soldiers as usual. She is always talking to the soldiers except when she is praying.

ROBERT   Praying! Ha! You believe she prays, you idiot. I know the sort of girl that is always talking to soldiers. She shall talk to me a bit. [*He goes to the window and shouts fiercely through it.*] Hallo, you there!

A GIRL'S VOICE [*bright, strong and rough*]   Is it me, sir?

ROBERT   Yes, you.

THE VOICE   Be you captain?

ROBERT   Yes, damn your impudence, I be captain. Come up here. [*To the soldiers in the yard*] Shew her the way, you. And shove her along quick. [*He leaves the window, and returns to his place at the table, where he sits magisterially.*]

STEWARD [*whispering*]   She wants to go and be a soldier herself. She wants you to give her soldier's clothes. Armor, sir! And a sword! Actually! [*He steals behind* ROBERT.]

JOAN *appears in the turret doorway. She is an ablebodied country girl of 17 or 18, respectably dressed in red, with an uncommon face; eyes very wide apart and bulging as they often do in very imaginative people, a long well-shaped nose with wide nostrils, a short upper lip, resolute but full-lipped mouth, and handsome fighting chin. She comes eagerly to the table, delighted at having penetrated to* BAUDRICOURT's *presence at last, and full of hope as to the results. His scowl does not check or frighten her in the least. Her voice is normally a hearty coaxing voice, very confident, very appealing, very hard to resist.*

JOAN [*bobbing a curtsey*]   Good morning, captain squire. Captain: you are to give me a horse and armor and some soldiers, and send me to the Dauphin. Those are your orders from my Lord.

ROBERT [*outraged*]   Orders from your lord! And who the devil may your lord be? Go back to him, and tell him that I am neither duke nor peer at his orders: I am squire of Baudricourt; and I take no orders except from the king.

JOAN [*reassuringly*]   Yes, squire: that is all right. My Lord is the King of Heaven.

ROBERT   Why, the girl's mad. [*To the steward*] Why didnt you tell me so, you blockhead?

STEWARD   Sir: do not anger her: give her what she wants.

JOAN [*impatient, but friendly*]   They all say I am mad until I talk to them, squire. But you see that it is the will of God that you are to do what He has put into my mind.

ROBERT   It is the will of God that I shall send you back to your father with orders to put you under lock and key and thrash the madness out of you. What have you to say to that?

JOAN   You think you will, squire; but you will find it all coming quite different. You said you would not see me; but here I am.

STEWARD [*appealing*]   Yes, sir. You see, sir.

ROBERT   Hold your tongue, you.

STEWARD [*abjectly*]   Yes, sir.

ROBERT [*to* JOAN, *with a sour loss of confidence*]   So you are presuming on my seeing you, are you?

JOAN [*sweetly*]   Yes, squire.

ROBERT [*feeling that he has lost ground, brings down his two fists squarely on the table, and inflates his chest imposingly to cure the unwelcome and only too familiar sensation*]   Now listen to me. I am going to assert myself.

JOAN [*busily*]   Please do, squire. The horse will cost sixteen francs. It is a good deal of money: but I can save it on the armor. I can find a soldier's armor that will fit me well enough: I am very hardy; and I do not need beautiful armor made to my measure like you wear. I shall not want many soldiers: the Dauphin will give me all I need to raise the siege of Orleans.

ROBERT [*flabbergasted*]   To raise the siege of Orleans!

JOAN [*simply*]   Yes, squire: that is what God is sending me to do. Three men will be enough for you to send with me if they are good men and gentle to me. They have promised to come with me. Polly and Jack and—

ROBERT   Polly!! You impudent baggage, do you dare call squire Bertrand de Poulengey Polly to my face?

JOAN   His friends call him so, squire: I did not know he had any other name. Jack—

ROBERT   That is Monsieur John of Metz, I suppose?

JOAN   Yes, squire. Jack will come willingly: he is a very kind gentleman, and gives me money to give to the poor. I think John Godsave will come, and Dick the Archer, and their servants John of Honecourt and Julian. There will be no trouble for you, squire: I have arranged it all: you have only to give the order.

ROBERT [*contemplating her in a stupor of amazement*]   Well, I am damned!

JOAN [*with unruffled sweetness*]   No, squire: God is very merciful; and the blessed saints Catherine and Margaret, who speak to me every day [*he gapes*], will intercede for you. You will go to paradise; and your name will be remembered for ever as my first helper.

ROBERT [*to the* STEWARD, *still much bothered, but changing his tone as he pursues a new clue*]   Is this true about Monsieur de Poulengey?

STEWARD [*eagerly*]   Yes, sir, and about Monsieur de Metz too. They both want to go with her.

ROBERT [*thoughtful*]   Mf! [*He goes to the window, and shouts into the court-yard.*] Hallo! You there: send Monsieur de Poulengey to me, will you? [*He turns to* JOAN.] Get out; and wait in the yard.

JOAN [*smiling brightly at him*]   Right, squire. [*She goes out.*]

ROBERT [*to the steward*]   Go with her, you, you dithering imbecile. Stay within call; and keep your eye on her. I shall have her up here again.

STEWARD   Do so in God's name, sir. Think of those hens, the best layers in Champagne; and—

ROBERT   Think of my boot; and take your backside out of reach of it.

The STEWARD *retreats hastily and finds himself confronted in the doorway by* BERTRAND DE POULENGEY, *a lymphatic French gentleman-at-arms, aged 36 or thereabout, employed in the department of the provost-marshal, dreamily absent-minded, seldom speaking unless spoken to, and then slow and obstinate in reply; altogether in contrast to the self-assertive, loud-mouthed, superficially energetic, fundamentally will-less* ROBERT. *The* STEWARD *makes way for him, and vanishes.* POULENGEY *salutes, and stands awaiting orders.*

ROBERT [*genially*] It isnt service, Polly. A friendly talk. Sit down. [*He hooks the stool from under the table with his instep.*]

POULENGEY, *relaxing, comes into the room; places the stool between the table and the window; and sits down ruminatively.* ROBERT, *half sitting on the end of the table, begins the friendly talk.*

ROBERT Now listen to me, Polly. I must talk to you like a father.

POULENGEY *looks up at him gravely for a moment, but says nothing.*

ROBERT It's about this girl you are interested in. Now, I have seen her. I have talked to her. First, she's mad. That doesnt matter. Second, she's not a farm wench. She's a bourgeoise. That matters a good deal. I know her class exactly. Her father came here last year to represent his village in a lawsuit: he is one of their notables. A farmer. Not a gentleman farmer: he makes money by it, and lives by it. Still, not a laborer. Not a mechanic. He might have a cousin a lawyer, or in the Church. People of this sort may be of no account socially; but they can give a lot of bother to the authorities. That is to say, to me. Now no doubt it seems to you a very simple thing to take this girl away, humbugging her into the belief that you are taking her to the Dauphin. But if you get her into trouble, you may get me into no end of a mess, as I am her father's lord, and responsible for her protection. So friends or no friends, Polly, hands off her.

POULENGEY [*with deliberate impressiveness*] I should as soon think of the Blessed Virgin herself in that way, as of this girl.

ROBERT [*coming off the table*] But she says you and Jack and Dick have offered to go with her. What for? You are not going to tell me that you take her crazy notion of going to the Dauphin seriously, are you?

POULENGEY [*slowly*] There is something about her. They are pretty foul-mouthed and foulminded down there in the guardroom, some of them. But there hasnt been a word that has anything to do with her being a woman. They have stopped swearing before her. There is something. Something. It may be worth trying.

ROBERT Oh, come, Polly! pull yourself together. Commonsense was never your strong point; but this is a little too much. [*He retreats disgustedly.*]

POULENGEY [*unmoved*] What is the good of commonsense? If we had any commonsense we should join the Duke of Burgundy and the English king. They hold half the country, right down to the Loire. They have Paris. They have this castle: you know very well that we had to surrender it to the Duke of Bedford, and that you are only holding it on parole. The Dauphin is in Chinon, like a rat in a corner, except that he wont fight. We dont even know that he is the Dauphin: his mother says he isnt; and she ought to know. Think of that! the queen denying the legitimacy of her own son!

ROBERT   Well, she married her daughter to the English king. Can you blame the woman?

POULENGEY   I blame nobody. But thanks to her, the Dauphin is down and out; and we may as well face it. The English will take Orleans: the Bastard will not be able to stop them.

ROBERT   He beat the English the year before last at Montargis. I was with him.

POULENGEY   No matter: his men are cowed now; and he cant work miracles. And I tell you that nothing can save our side now but a miracle.

ROBERT   Miracles are all right, Polly. The only difficulty about them is that they dont happen nowadays.

POULENGEY   I used to think so. I am not so sure now. [*Rising, and moving ruminatively towards the window*] At all events this is not a time to leave any stone unturned. There is something about the girl.

ROBERT   Oh! You think the girl can work miracles, do you?

POULENGEY   I think the girl herself is a bit of a miracle. Anyhow, she is the last card left in our hand. Better play her than throw up the game. [*He wanders to the turret.*]

ROBERT [*wavering*]   You really think that?

POULENGEY [*turning*]   Is there anything else left for us to think?

ROBERT [*going to him*]   Look here, Polly. If you were in my place would you let a girl like that do you out of sixteen francs for a horse?

POULENGEY   I will pay for the horse.

ROBERT   You will!

POULENGEY   Yes: I will back my opinion.

ROBERT   You will really gamble on a forlorn hope to the tune of sixteen francs?

POULENGEY   It is not a gamble.

ROBERT   What else is it?

POULENGEY   It is a certainty. Her words and her ardent faith in God have put fire into me.

ROBERT [*giving him up*]   Whew! You are as mad as she is.

POULENGEY [*obstinately*]   We want a few mad people now. See where the sane ones have landed us!

ROBERT [*his irresoluteness now openly swamping his affected decisiveness*]   I shall feel like a precious fool. Still, if you feel sure—?

POULENGEY   I feel sure enough to take her to Chinon—unless you stop me.

ROBERT   This is not fair. You are putting the responsibility on me.

POULENGEY   It is on you whichever way you decide.

ROBERT   Yes: thats just it. Which way am I to decide? You dont see how awkward this is for me. [*Snatching at a dilatory step with an unconscious hope that* JOAN *will make up his mind for him*] Do you think I ought to have another talk to her?

POULENGEY [*rising*]   Yes. [*He goes to the window and calls.*] Joan!

JOAN'S VOICE   Will he let us go, Polly?

POULENGEY   Come up. Come in. [*Turning to* ROBERT] Shall I leave you with her?

ROBERT   No: stay here; and back me up.

POULENGEY *sits down on the chest.* ROBERT *goes back to his magisterial chair, but remains standing to inflate himself more imposingly.* JOAN *comes in, full of good news.*

JOAN   Jack will go halves for the horse.
ROBERT   Well!! [*He sits, deflated.*]
POULENGEY [*gravely*]   Sit down, Joan.
JOAN [*checked a little, and looking to* ROBERT]   May I?
ROBERT   Do what you are told.

JOAN *curtsies and sits down on the stool between them.* ROBERT *outfaces his perplexity with his most peremptory air.*

ROBERT   What is your name?
JOAN [*chattily*]   They always call me Jenny in Lorraine. Here in France I am Joan. The soldiers call me The Maid.
ROBERT   What is your surname?
JOAN   Surname? What is that? My father sometimes calls himself d'Arc; but I know nothing about it. You met my father. He—
ROBERT   Yes, yes; I remember. You come from Domrémy in Lorraine, I think.
JOAN   Yes; but what does it matter? we all speak French.
ROBERT   Dont ask questions: answer them. How old are you?
JOAN   Seventeen: so they tell me. It might be nineteen. I dont remember.
ROBERT   What did you mean when you said that St Catherine and St Margaret talked to you every day?
JOAN   They do.
ROBERT   What are they like?
JOAN [*suddenly obstinate*]   I will tell you nothing about that: they have not given me leave.
ROBERT   But you actually see them; and they talk to you just as I am talking to you?
JOAN   No: it is quite different. I cannot tell you: you must not talk to me about my voices.
ROBERT   How do you mean? voices?
JOAN   I hear voices telling me what to do. They come from God.
ROBERT   They come from your imagination.
JOAN   Of course. That is how the messages of God come to us.
POULENGEY   Checkmate.
ROBERT   No fear! [*To* JOAN] So God says you are to raise the siege of Orleans?
JOAN   And to crown the Dauphin in Rheims Cathedral.
ROBERT [*gasping*]   Crown the D—! Gosh!
JOAN   And to make the English leave France.
ROBERT [*sarcastic*]   Anything else?
JOAN [*charming*]   Not just at present, thank you, squire.
ROBERT   I suppose you think raising a siege is as easy as chasing a cow out of a meadow. You think soldiering is anybody's job?
JOAN   I do not think it can be very difficult if God is on your side, and you are willing to put your life in His hand. But many soldiers are very simple.
ROBERT [*grimly*]   Simple! Did you ever see English soldiers fighting?
JOAN   They are only men. God made them just like us; but He gave them their own country and their own language; and it is not His will that they should come into our country and try to speak our language.
ROBERT   Who has been putting such nonsense into your head? Dont you know

that soldiers are subject to their feudal lord, and that it is nothing to them or to you whether he is the duke of Burgundy or the king of England or the king of France? What has their language to do with it?

JOAN   I do not understand that a bit. We are all subject to the King of Heaven; and He gave us our countries and our languages, and meant us to keep to them. If it were not so it would be murder to kill an Englishman in battle; and you, squire, would be in great danger of hell fire. You must not think about your duty to your feudal lord, but about your duty to God.

POULENGEY   It's no use, Robert: she can choke you like that every time.

ROBERT   Can she, by Saint Dennis! We shall see. [*To* JOAN] We are not talking about God: we are talking about practical affairs. I ask you again, girl, have you ever seen English soldiers fighting? Have you ever seen them plundering, burning, turning the countryside into a desert? Have you heard no tales of their Black Prince who was blacker than the devil himself, or of the English king's father?

JOAN   You must not be afraid, Robert—

ROBERT   Damn you, I am not afraid. And who gave you leave to call me Robert?

JOAN   You were called so in church in the name of our Lord. All the other names are your father's or your brother's or anybody's.

ROBERT   Tcha!

JOAN   Listen to me, squire. At Domrémy we had to fly to the next village to escape from the English soldiers. Three of them were left behind, wounded. I came to know these three poor goddams quite well. They had not half my strength.

ROBERT   Do you know why they are called goddams?

JOAN   No. Everyone calls them goddams.

ROBERT   It is because they are always calling on their God to condemn their souls to perdition. That is what goddam means in their language. How do you like it?

JOAN   God will be merciful to them; and they will act like His good children when they go back to the country He made for them, and made them for. I have heard the tales of the Black Prince. The moment he touched the soil of our country the devil entered into him, and made him a black fiend. But at home, in the place made for him by God, he was good. It is always so. If I went into England against the will of God to conquer England, and tried to live there and speak its language, the devil would enter into me; and when I was old I should shudder to remember the wickednesses I did.

ROBERT   Perhaps. But the more devil you were the better you might fight. That is why the goddams will take Orleans. And you cannot stop them, nor ten thousand like you.

JOAN   One thousand like me can stop them. Ten like me can stop them with God on our side. [*She rises impetuously, and goes at him, unable to sit quiet any longer.*] You do not understand, squire. Our soldiers are always beaten because they are fighting only to save their skins; and the shortest way to save your skin is to run away. Our knights are thinking only of the money they will make in ransoms: it is not kill or be killed with them, but pay or be paid. But I will teach them all to fight that the will of God may be done in France; and then they will drive the poor goddams before them like sheep. You and Polly will live to see the day when there will not be an English soldier on the soil of France; and there will be but one king there: not the feudal English king, but God's French one.

ROBERT [*to* POULENGEY]   This may be all rot, Polly; but the troops might swallow it, though nothing that we can say seems able to put any fight into them. Even the Dauphin might swallow it. And if she can put fight into him, she can put it into anybody.

POULENGEY   I can see no harm in trying. Can you? And there is something about the girl—

ROBERT [*turning to* JOAN]   Now listen you to me; and [*desperately*] dont cut in before I have time to think.

JOAN [*plumping down on the stool again, like an obedient schoolgirl*]   Yes, squire.

ROBERT   Your orders are, that you are to go to Chinon under the escort of this gentleman and three of his friends.

JOAN [*radiant, clasping her hands*]   Oh, squire! Your head is all circled with light, like a saint's.

POULENGEY   How is she to get into the royal presence?

ROBERT [*who has looked up for his halo rather apprehensively*]   I dont know: how did she get into my presence? If the Dauphin can keep her out he is a better man than I take him for. [*Rising*] I will send her to Chinon; and she can say I sent her. Then let come what may: I can do no more.

JOAN   And the dress? I may have a soldier's dress, maynt I, squire?

ROBERT   Have what you please. I wash my hands of it.

JOAN [*wildly excited by her success*]   Come, Polly. [*She dashes out.*]

ROBERT [*shaking* POULENGEY's *hand*]   Goodbye, old man, I am taking a big chance. Few other men would have done it. But as you say, there is something about her.

POULENGEY   Yes: there is something about her. Goodbye. [*He goes out.*]

ROBERT, *still very doubtful whether he has not been made a fool of by a crazy female, and a social inferior to boot, scratches his head and slowly comes back from the door.*

The STEWARD *runs in with a basket.*

STEWARD   Sir, sir—

ROBERT   What now?

STEWARD   The hens are laying like mad, sir. Five dozen eggs!

ROBERT [*stiffens convulsively: crosses himself: and forms with his pale lips the words*]   Christ in heaven! [*Aloud but breathless*] She did come from God.

Scene 2

Chinon, in Touraine. An end of the throne room in the castle, curtained off to make an antechamber. The ARCHBISHOP OF RHEIMS, *close on 50, a full-fed prelate with nothing of the ecclesiastic about him except his imposing bearing, and the Lord Chamberlain,* MONSEIGNEUR DE LA TRÉMOUILLE, *a monstrous arrogant wineskin of a man, are waiting for the* DAUPHIN. *There is a door in the wall to the right of the two men. It is late in the afternoon on the 8th of March, 1429. The* ARCHBISHOP *stands with dignity whilst the* CHAMBERLAIN, *on his left, fumes about in the worst of tempers.*

LA TRÉMOUILLE   What the devil does the Dauphin mean by keeping us waiting like this? I dont know how you have the patience to stand there like a stone idol.

THE ARCHBISHOP   You see, I am an archbishop; and an archbishop is a sort of idol. At any rate he has to learn to keep still and suffer fools patiently. Besides, my dear Lord Chamberlain, it is the Dauphin's royal privilege to keep you waiting, is it not?

LA TRÉMOUILLE   Dauphin be damned! saving your reverence. Do you know how much money he owes me?

THE ARCHBISHOP   Much more than he owes me, I have no doubt, because you are a much richer man. But I take it he owes you all you could afford to lend him. That is what he owes me.

LA TRÉMOUILLE   Twenty-seven thousand: that was his last haul. A cool twenty-seven thousand!

THE ARCHBISHOP   What becomes of it all? He never has a suit of clothes that I would throw to a curate.

LA TRÉMOUILLE   He dines on a chicken or a scrap of mutton. He borrows my last penny; and there is nothing to shew for it. [*A page appears in the doorway.*] At last!

THE PAGE   No, my lord: it is not His Majesty. Monsieur de Rais is approaching.

LA TRÉMOUILLE   Young Bluebeard! Why announce him?

THE PAGE   Captain La Hire is with him. Something has happened, I think.

GILLES DE RAIS, *a young man of 25, very smart and self-possessed, and sporting the extravagance of a little curled beard dyed blue at a clean-shaven court, comes in. He is determined to make himself agreeable, but lacks natural joyousness, and is not really pleasant. In fact when he defies the Church some eleven years later he is accused of trying to extract pleasure from horrible cruelties, and hanged. So far, however, there is no shadow of the gallows on him. He advances gaily to the* ARCHBISHOP. *The* PAGE *withdraws.*

BLUEBEARD   Your faithful lamb, Archbishop. Good day, my lord. Do you know what has happened to La Hire?

LA TRÉMOUILLE   He has sworn himself into a fit, perhaps.

BLUEBEARD   No: just he opposite. Foul Mouthed Frank, the only man in Touraine who could beat him at swearing, was told by a soldier that he shouldnt use such language when he was at the point of death.

THE ARCHBISHOP   Nor at any other point. But was Foul Mouthed Frank on the point of death?

BLUEBEARD   Yes: he has just fallen into a well and been drowned. La Hire is frightened out of his wits.

CAPTAIN LA HIRE *comes in: a war dog with no court manners and pronounced camp ones.*

BLUEBEARD   I have just been telling the Chamberlain and the Archbishop. The Archbishop says you are a lost man.

LA HIRE [*striding past* BLUEBEARD, *and planting himself between the* ARCHBISHOP *and* LA TRÉMOUILLE]   This is nothing to joke about. It is worse than we thought. It was not a soldier, but an angel dressed as a soldier.

THE ARCHBISHOP
THE CHAMBERLAIN } [*exclaiming all together*] An angel!
BLUEBEARD

LA HIRE   Yes, an angel. She has made her way from Champagne with half a dozen men through the thick of everything: Burgundians, Goddams, deserters, robbers, and Lord knows who; and they never met a soul except the country folk. I know one of them: de Poulengey. He says she's an angel. If ever I utter an oath again may my soul be blasted to eternal damnation!

THE ARCHBISHOP   A very pious beginning, Captain.

BLUEBEARD *and* LA TRÉMOUILLE *laughs at him. The* PAGE *returns.*

THE PAGE   His Majesty.

They stand perfunctorily at court attention. The DAUPHIN, *aged 26, really King Charles the Seventh since the death of his father, but as yet uncrowned, comes in through the curtains with a paper in his hands. He is a poor creature physically; and the current fashion of shaving closely, and hiding every scrap of hair under the headcovering or headdress, both by women and men, makes the worst of his appearance. He has little narrow eyes, near together, a long pendulous nose that droops over his thick short upper lip, and the expression of a young dog accustomed to be kicked, yet incorrigible and irrepressible. But he is neither vulgar nor stupid; and he has a cheeky humor which enables him to hold his own in conversation. Just at present he is excited, like a child with a new toy. He comes to the* ARCH-BISHOP's *left hand.* BLUEBEARD *and* LA HIRE *retire towards the curtains.*

CHARLES   Oh, Archbishop, do you know what Robert de Baudricourt is sending me from Vaucouleurs?

THE ARCHBISHOP [*contemptuously*]   I am not interested in the newest toys.

CHARLES [*indignantly*]   It isnt a toy. [*Sulkily*] However, I can get on very well without your interest.

THE ARCHBISHOP   Your Highness is taking offence very unnecessarily.

CHARLES   Thank you. You are always ready with a lecture, arnt you?

LA TRÉMOUILLE [*roughly*]   Enough grumbling. What have you got there?

CHARLES   What is that to you?

LA TRÉMOUILLE   It is my business to know what is passing between you and the garrison at Vaucouleurs. [*He snatches the paper from the* DAUPHIN's *hand, and begins reading it with some difficulty, following the words with his finger and spelling them out syllable by syllable.*]

CHARLES [*mortified*]   You all think you can treat me as you please because I owe you money, and because I am no good at fighting. But I have the blood royal in my veins.

THE ARCHBISHOP   Even that has been questioned, your Highness. One hardly recognizes in you the grandson of Charles the Wise.

CHARLES   I want to hear no more of my grandfather. He was so wise that he used up the whole family stock of wisdom for five generations, and left me the poor fool I am, bullied and insulted by all of you.

THE ARCHBISHOP   Control yourself, sir. These outbursts of petulance are not seemly.

CHARLES   Another lecture! Thank you. What a pity it is that though you are an archbishop saints and angels dont come to see you!

THE ARCHBISHOP   What do you mean?

CHARLES   Aha! Ask that bully there [*Pointing to* LA TRÉMOUILLE.]

LA TRÉMOUILLE [*furious*]   Hold your tongue. Do you hear?

CHARLES   Oh, I hear. You neednt shout. The whole castle can hear. Why dont you go and shout at the English, and beat them for me?

LA TRÉMOUILLE [*raising his fist*]   You young—

CHARLES [*running behind the* ARCHBISHOP]   Dont you raise your hand to me. It's high treason.

LA HIRE   Steady, Duke! Steady!

THE ARCHBISHOP [*resolutely*]   Come, come! this will not do. My Lord Chamberlain: please! please! we must keep some sort of order. [*To the* DAUPHIN] And you, sir: if you cannot rule your kingdom, at least try to rule yourself.

CHARLES   Another lecture! Thank you.

LA TRÉMOUILLE [*handing over the paper to the* ARCHBISHOP]   Here: read the accursed thing for me. He has sent the blood boiling into my head: I cant distinguish the letters.

CHARLES [*coming back and peering round* LA TRÉMOUILLE's *left shoulder*]   I will read it for you if you like. I can read, you know.

LA TRÉMOUILLE [*with intense contempt, not at all stung by the taunt*]   Yes: reading is about all you are fit for. Can you make it out, Archbishop?

THE ARCHBISHOP   I should have expected more commonsense from De Baudricourt. He is sending some cracked country lass here—

CHARLES [*interrupting*]   No: he is sending a saint: an angel. And she is coming to me: to me, the king, and not to you, Archbishop, holy as you are. She knows the blood royal if you dont. [*He struts up to the curtains between* BLUEBEARD *and* LA HIRE.]

THE ARCHBISHOP   You cannot be allowed to see this crazy wench.

CHARLES [*turning*]   But I am the king; and I will.

LA TRÉMOUILLE [*brutally*]   Then she cannot be allowed to see you. Now!

CHARLES   I tell you I will. I am going to put my foot down—

BLUEBEARD [*laughing at him*]   Naughty! What would your wise grandfather say?

CHARLES   That just shews your ignorance, Bluebeard. My grandfather had a saint who used to float in the air when she was praying, and told him everything he wanted to know. My poor father had two saints, Marie de Maillé and the Gasque of Avignon. It is in our family; and I dont care what you say: I will have my saint too.

THE ARCHBISHOP   This creature is not a saint. She is not even a respectable woman. She does not wear women's clothes. She is dressed like a soldier, and rides round the country with soldiers. Do you suppose such a person can be admitted to your Highness's court?

LA HIRE   Stop. [*Going to the* ARCHBISHOP] Did you say a girl in armor, like a soldier?

THE ARCHBISHOP   So De Baudricourt describes her.

LA HIRE   But by all the devils in hell—Oh, God forgive me, what am I saying?— by Our Lady and all the saints, this must be the angel that struck Foul Mouthed Frank dead for swearing.

CHARLES [*triumphant*]   You see! A miracle!

LA HIRE   She may strike the lot of us dead if we cross her. For Heaven's sake, Archbishop, be careful what you are doing.

THE ARCHBISHOP [*severely*] Rubbish! Nobody has been struck dead. A drunken blackguard who has been rebuked a hundred times for swearing has fallen into a well, and been drowned. A mere coincidence.

LA HIRE I do not know what a coincidence is. I do know that the man is dead, and that she told him he was going to die.

THE ARCHBISHOP We are all going to die, Captain.

LA HIRE [*crossing himself*] I hope not. [*He backs out of the conversation.*]

BLUEBEARD We can easily find out whether she is an angel or not. Let us arrange when she comes that I shall be the Dauphin, and see whether she will find me out.

CHARLES Yes: I agree to that. If she cannot find the blood royal I will have nothing to do with her.

THE ARCHBISHOP It is for the Church to make saints: let de Baudricourt mind his own business, and not dare usurp the function of his priest. I say the girl shall not be admitted.

BLUEBEARD But, Archbishop—

THE ARCHBISHOP [*sternly*] I speak in the Church's name. [*To the* DAUPHIN] Do you dare say she shall?

CHARLES [*intimidated but sulky*] Oh, if you make it an excommunication matter, I have nothing more to say, of course. But you havnt read the end of the letter. De Baudricourt says she will raise the siege of Orleans, and beat the English for us.

LA TRÉMOUILLE Rot!

CHARLES Well, will you save Orleans for us, with all your bullying?

LA TRÉMOUILLE [*savagely*] Do not throw that in my face again: do you hear? I have done more fighting than you ever did or ever will. But I cannot be everywhere.

THE DAUPHIN Well, thats something.

BLUEBEARD [*coming between the* ARCHBISHOP *and* CHARLES] You have Jack Dunois at the head of your troops in Orleans: the brave Dunois, the handsome Dunois, the wonderful invincible Dunois, the darling of all the ladies, the beautiful bastard. Is it likely that the country lass can do what he cannot do?

CHARLES Why doesnt he raise the siege, then?

LA HIRE The wind is against him.

BLUEBEARD How can the wind hurt him at Orleans? It is not on the Channel.

LA HIRE It is on the river Loire; and the English hold the bridgehead. He must ship his men across the river and upstream, if he is to take them in the rear. Well, he cannot, because there is a devil of a wind blowing the other way. He is tired of paying the priests to pray for a west wind. What he needs is a miracle. You tell me that what the girl did to Foul Mouthed Frank was no miracle. No matter: it finished Frank. If she changes the wind for Dunois, that may not be a miracle either; but it may finish the English. What harm is there in trying?

THE ARCHBISHOP [*who has read the end of the letter and become more thoughtful*] It is true that de Baudricourt seems extraordinarily impressed.

LA HIRE De Baudricourt is a blazing ass; but he is a soldier; and if he thinks she can beat the English, all the rest of the army will think so too.

LA TRÉMOUILLE [*to the* ARCHBISHOP, *who is hesitating*] Oh, let them have their way. Dunois' men will give up the town in spite of him if somebody does not put some fresh spunk into them.

THE ARCHBISHOP   The Church must examine the girl before anything decisive is done about her. However, since his Highness desires it, let her attend the Court.

LA HIRE   I will find her and tell her. [*He goes out.*]

CHARLES   Come with me, Bluebeard; and let us arrange so that she will not know who I am. You will pretend to be me. [*He goes out through the curtains.*]

BLUEBEARD   Pretend to be that thing! Holy Michael! [*He follows the* DAUPHIN.]

LA TRÉMOUILLE   I wonder will she pick him out!

THE ARCHBISHOP   Of course she will.

LA TRÉMOUILLE   Why? How is she to know?

THE ARCHBISHOP   She will know what everybody in Chinon knows: that the Dauphin is the meanest-looking and worst-dressed figure in the Court, and that the man with the blue beard is Gilles de Rais.

LA TRÉMOUILLE   I never thought of that

THE ARCHBISHOP   You are not so accustomed to miracles as I am. It is part of my profession.

LA TRÉMOUILLE [*puzzled and a little scandalized*]   But that would not be a miracle at all.

THE ARCHBISHOP [*calmly*]   Why not?

LA TRÉMOUILLE   Well, come! what is a miracle?

THE ARCHBISHOP   A miracle, my friend, is an event which creates faith. That is the purpose and nature of miracles. They may seem very wonderful to the people who witness them, and very simple to those who perform them. That does not matter: if they confirm or create faith they are true miracles.

LA TRÉMOUILLE   Even when they are frauds, do you mean?

THE ARCHBISHOP   Frauds deceive. An event which creates faith does not deceive: therefore it is not a fraud, but a miracle.

LA TRÉMOUILLE [*scratching his neck in his perplexity*]   Well, I suppose as you are an archbishop you must be right. It seems a bit fishy to me. But I am no churchman, and dont understand these matters.

THE ARCHBISHOP   You are not a churchman; but you are a diplomatist and a soldier. Could you make our citizens pay war taxes, or our soldiers sacrifice their lives, if they knew what is really happening instead of what seems to them to be happening?

LA TRÉMOUILLE   No, by Saint Dennis: the fat would be in the fire before sundown.

THE ARCHBISHOP   Would it not be quite easy to tell them the truth?

LA TRÉMOUILLE   Man alive, they wouldnt believe it.

THE ARCHBISHOP   Just so. Well, the Church has to rule men for the good of their souls as you have to rule them for the good of their bodies. To do that, the Church must do as you do: nourish their faith by poetry.

LA TRÉMOUILLE   Poetry! I should call it humbug.

THE ARCHBISHOP   You would be wrong, my friend. Parables are not lies because they describe events that have never happened. Miracles are not frauds because they are often—I do not say always—very simple and innocent contrivances by which the priest fortifies the faith of his flock. When this girl picks out the Dauphin among his courtiers, it will not be a miracle for me, because I shall know how it has been done, and my faith will not be increased. But as for the others, if they feel the thrill of the supernatural, and forget their sinful clay in a sudden sense of the glory of God, it will be a miracle and a blessed one. And you will find that the girl herself will be more affected than anyone else. She will forget how she really picked him out. So, perhaps, will you,

LA TRÉMOUILLE   Well, I wish I were clever enough to know how much of you is God's archbishop and how much the most artful fox in Touraine. Come on, or we shall be late for the fun; and I want to see it, miracle or no miracle.

THE ARCHBISHOP [*detaining him a moment*]   Do not think that I am a lover of crooked ways. There is a new spirit rising in men: we are at the dawning of a wider epoch. If I were a simple monk, and had not to rule men, I should seek peace for my spirit with Aristotle and Pythagoras rather than with the saints and their miracles.

LA TRÉMOUILLE   And who the deuce was Pythagoras?

THE ARCHBISHOP   A sage who held that the earth is round, and that it moves round the sun.

LA TRÉMOUILLE   What an utter fool! Couldnt he use his eyes?

They go out together through the curtains, which are presently withdrawn, revealing the full depth of the throne room with the Court assembled. On the right are two Chairs of State on a dais. BLUEBEARD *is standing theatrically on the dais, playing the king, and, like the courtiers, enjoying the joke rather obviously. There is a curtained arch in the wall behind the dais; but the main door, guarded by men-at-arms, is at the other side of the room; and a clear path across is kept and lined by the courtiers.* CHARLES *is in this path in the middle of the room.* LA HIRE *is on his right. The* ARCHBISHOP, *on his left, has taken his place by the dais:* LA TRÉMOUILLE *at the other side of it. The* DUCHESS DE LA TRÉMOUILLE, *pretending to be the Queen, sits in the Consort's chair, with a group of ladies in waiting close by, behind the* ARCHBISHOP.*

The chatter of the courtiers makes such a noise that nobody notices the appearance of the page at the door.

THE PAGE   The Duke of—[*Nobody listens.*] The Duke of—[*The chatter continues. Indignant at his failure to command a hearing, he snatches the halberd of the nearest man-at-arms, and thumps the floor with it. The chatter ceases; and everybody looks at him in silence.*] Attention! [*He restores the halberd to the man-at-arms.*] The Duke of Vendôme presents Joan the Maid to his Majesty.

CHARLES [*putting his finger on his lip*]   Ssh! [*He hides behind the nearest courtier, peering out to see what happens.*]

BLUEBEARD [*majestically*]   Let her approach the throne.

JOAN, *dressed as a soldier, with her hair bobbed and hanging thickly round her face, is led in by a bashful and speechless nobleman, from whom she detaches herself to stop and look round eagerly for the* DAUPHIN.

THE DUCHESS [*to the nearest lady in waiting*]   My dear! Her hair!

All the ladies explode in uncontrollable laughter.

BLUEBEARD [*trying not to laugh, and waving his hand in deprecation of their merriment*]   Ssh—ssh! Ladies! Ladies!!

JOAN [*not at all embarrassed*] I wear it like this because I am a soldier. Where be Dauphin?

A titter runs through the Court as she walks to the dais.

BLUEBEARD [*condescendingly*] You are in the presence of the Dauphin.

Joan looks at him sceptically for a moment, scanning him hard up and down to make sure. Dead silence, all watching her. Fun dawns in her face.

JOAN Coom, Bluebeard! Thou canst not fool me. Where be Dauphin?

A roar of laughter breaks out as GILLES, *with a gesture of surrender, joins in the laugh, and jumps down from the dais beside* LA TRÉMOUILLE. JOAN, *also on the broad grin, turns back, searching along the row of courtiers, and presently makes a dive, and drags out* CHARLES *by the arm.*

JOAN [*releasing him and bobbing him a little curtsey*] Gentle little Dauphin, I am sent to you to drive the English away from Orleans and from France, and to crown you king in the cathedral at Rheims, where all true kings of France are crowned.
CHARLES [*triumphant, to the Court*] You see, all of you: she knew the blood royal. Who dare say now that I am not my father's son? [*To* JOAN] But if you want me to be crowned at Rheims you must talk to the Archbishop, not to me. There he is [*he is standing behind her*]!
JOAN [*turning quickly, overwhelmed with emotion*] Oh, my lord! [*She falls on both knees before him, with bowed head, not daring to look up.*] My lord: I am only a poor country girl; and you are filled with the blessedness and glory of God Himself; but you will touch me with your hands, and give me your blessing, wont you?
BLUEBEARD [*whispering to* LA TRÉMOUILLE] The old fox blushes.
LA TRÉMOUILLE Another miracle!
THE ARCHBISHOP [*touched, putting his hand on her head*] Child: you are in love with religion.
JOAN [*startled: looking up at him*] Am I? I never thought of that. Is there any harm in it?
THE ARCHBISHOP There is no harm in it, my child. But there is danger.
JOAN [*rising, with a sunflush of reckless happiness irradiating her face*] There is always danger, except in heaven. Oh, my lord, you have given me such strength, such courage. It must be a most wonderful thing to be Archbishop.

The Court smiles broadly: even titters a little

THE ARCHBISHOP [*drawing himself up sensitively*] Gentlemen: your levity is rebuked by this maid's faith. I am, God help me, all unworthy; but your mirth is a deadly sin.

Their faces fall. Dead silence.

BLUEBEARD   My lord: we were laughing at her, not at you.

THE ARCHBISHOP   What? Not at my unworthiness but at her faith! Gilles de Rais: this maid prophesied that the blasphemer should be drowned in his sin—

JOAN [*distressed*]   No!

THE ARCHBISHOP [*silencing her by a gesture*]   I prophesy now that you will be hanged in yours if you do not learn when to laugh and when to pray.

BLUEBEARD   My lord: I stand rebuked. I am sorry: I can say no more. But if you prophesy that I shall be hanged, I shall never be able to resist temptation, because I shall always be telling myself that I may as well be hanged for a sheep as a lamb.

The courtiers take heart at this. There is more tittering.

JOAN [*scandalized*]   You are an idle fellow, Bluebeard; and you have great impudence to answer the Archbishop.

LA HIRE [*with a huge chuckle*]   Well said, lass! Well said!

JOAN [*impatiently to the* ARCHBISHOP]   Oh, my lord, will you send all these silly folks away so that I may speak to the Dauphin alone?

LA HIRE [*goodhumoredly*]   I can take a hint. [*He salutes; turns on his heel; and goes out.*]

THE ARCHBISHOP   Come, gentlemen. The Maid comes with God's blessing, and must be obeyed.

The courtiers withdraw, some through the arch, others at the opposite side. The Archbishop marches across to the door, followed by the DUCHESS *and* LA TRÉMOUILLE. *As the* ARCHBISHOP *passes* JOAN, *she falls on her knees, and kisses the hem of his robe fervently. He shakes his head in instinctive remonstrance; gathers the robe from her; and goes out. She is left kneeling directly in the* DUCHESS's *way.*

THE DUCHESS [*coldly*]   Will you allow me to pass, please?

JOAN [*hastily rising, and standing back*]   Beg pardon, maam, I am sure.

The DUCHESS *passes on.* JOAN *stares after her; then whispers to the* DAUPHIN.

JOAN   Be that Queen?

CHARLES   No. She thinks she is.

JOAN [*again staring after the* DUCHESS]   Oo-oo-ooh! [*Her awestruck amazement at the figure cut by the magnificently dressed lady is not wholly complimentary.*]

LA TRÉMOUILLE [*very surly*]   I'll trouble your Highness not to gibe at my wife. [*He goes out. The others have already gone.*]

JOAN [*to the* DAUPHIN]   Who be old Gruff-and-Grum?

CHARLES   He is the Duke de la Trémouille.

JOAN   What be his job?

CHARLES   He pretends to command the army. And whenever I find a friend I can care for, he kills him.

JOAN   Why dost let him?

CHARLES [*petulantly moving to the throne side of the room to escape from her magnetic field*]   How can I prevent him? He bullies me. They all bully me.

JOAN   Art afraid?

CHARLES   Yes: I am afraid. It's no use preaching to me about it. It's all very well for these big men with their armor that is too heavy for me, and their swords that I can hardly lift, and their muscle and their shouting and their bad tempers. They like fighting: most of them are making fools of themselves all the time they are not fighting; but I am quiet and sensible; and I dont want to kill people: I only want to be left alone to enjoy myself in my own way. I never asked to be a king: it was pushed on me. So if you are going to say 'Son of St Louis: gird on the sword of your ancestors, and lead us to victory' you may spare your breath to cool your porridge; for I cannot do it. I am not built that way; and there is an end of it.

JOAN [*trenchant and masterful*]   Blethers! We are all like that to begin with. I shall put courage into thee.

CHARLES   But I dont want to have courage put into me. I want to sleep in a comfortable bed, and not live in continual terror of being killed or wounded. Put courage into the others, and let them have their bellyful of fighting; but let me alone.

JOAN   It's no use, Charlie: thou must face what God puts on thee. If thou fail to make thyself king, thoult be a beggar: what else art fit for? Come! Let me see thee sitting on the throne. I have looked forward to that.

CHARLES   What is the good of sitting on the throne when the other fellows give all the orders? However! [*He sits enthroned, a piteous figure.*] here is the king for you! Look your fill at the poor devil.

JOAN   Thourt not king yet, lad: thourt but Dauphin. Be not led away by them around thee. Dressing up dont fill empty noddle. I know the people: the real people that make thy bread for thee; and I tell thee they count no man king of France until the holy oil has been poured on his hair, and himself consecrated and crowned in Rheims Cathedral. And thou needs new clothes, Charlie. Why does not Queen look after thee properly?

CHARLES   We're too poor. She wants all the money we can spare to put on her own back. Besides, I like to see her beautifully dressed; and I dont care what I wear myself: I should look ugly anyhow.

JOAN   There is some good in thee, Charlie; but it is not yet a king's good.

CHARLES   We shall see. I am not such a fool as I look. I have my eyes open; and I can tell you that one good treaty is worth ten good fights. These fighting fellows lose all on the treaties that they gain on the fights. If we can only have a treaty, the English are sure to have the worst of it, because they are better at fighting than at thinking.

JOAN   If the English win, it is they that will make the treaty; and then God help poor France! Thou must fight, Charlie, whether thou will or no. I will go first to hearten thee. We must take our courage in both hands: aye, and pray for it with both hands too.

CHARLES [*descending from his throne and again crossing the room to escape from her dominating urgency*]   Oh do stop talking about God and praying. I cant bear people who are always praying. Isnt it bad enough to have to do it at the proper times?

JOAN [*pitying him*]   Thou poor child, thou hast never prayed in thy life. I must teach thee from the beginning.

CHARLES   I am not a child: I am a grown man and a father; and I will not be taught any more.

JOAN   Aye, you have a little son. He that will be Louis the Eleventh when you die. Would you not fight for him?

CHARLES No: a horrid boy. He hates me. He hates everybody, selfish little beast! I dont want to be bothered with children. I dont want to be a father; and I dont want to be a son: especially a son of St Louis. I dont want to be any of these fine things you all have your heads full of: I want to be just what I am. Why cant you mind your own business, and let me mind mine?

JOAN [*again contemptuous*] Minding your own business is like minding your own body: it's the shortest way to make yourself sick. What is my business? Helping mother at home. What is thine? Petting lapdogs and sucking sugarsticks. I call that muck. I tell thee it is God's business we are here to do: not our own. I have a message to thee from God; and thou must listen to it, though thy heart break with the terror of it.

CHARLES I dont want a message; but can you tell me any secrets? Can you do any cures? Can you turn lead into gold, or anything of that sort?

JOAN I can turn thee into a king, in Rheims Cathedral; and that is a miracle that will take some doing, it seems.

CHARLES If we go to Rheims, and have a coronation, Anne will want new dresses. We cant afford them. I am all right as I am.

JOAN As you are! And what is that? Less than my father's poorest shepherd. Thourt not lawful owner of thy own land of France till thou be consecrated.

CHARLES But I shall not be lawful owner of my own land anyhow. Will the consecration pay off my mortgages? I have pledged my last acre to the Archbishop and that fat bully. I owe money even to Bluebeard.

JOAN [*earnestly*] Charlie: I come from the land, and have gotten my strength working on the land; and I tell thee that the land is thine to rule righteously and keep God's peace in, and not to pledge at the pawnshop as a drunken woman pledges her children's clothes. And I come from God to tell thee to kneel in the cathedral and solemnly give thy kingdom to Him for ever and ever, and become the greatest king in the world as His steward and His bailiff, His soldier and His servant. The very clay of France will become holy: her soldiers will be the soldiers of God: the rebel dukes will be rebels against God: the English will fall on their knees and beg thee let them return to their lawful homes in peace. Wilt be a poor little Judas, and betray me and Him that sent me?

CHARLES [*tempted at last*] Oh, if I only dare!

JOAN I shall dare, dare, and dare again, in God's name! Art for or against me?

CHARLES [*excited*] I'll risk it, I warn you I shant be able to keep it up; but I'll risk it. You shall see. [*Running to the main door and shouting*] Hallo! Come back, everybody. [*To* JOAN, *as he runs back to the arch opposite*] Mind you stand by and dont let me be bullied. [*Through the arch*] Come along, will you: the whole Court. [*He sits down in the royal chair as they all hurry in to their former places, chattering and wondering.*] Now I'm in for it; but no matter: here goes! [*To the* PAGE] Call for silence, you little beast, will you?

THE PAGE [*snatching a halberd as before and thumping with it repeatedly*] Silence for His Majesty the King. The King speaks. [*Peremptorily*] Will you be silent there? [*Silence*]

CHARLES [*rising*] I have given the command of the army to The Maid. The Maid is to do as she likes with it. [*He descends from the dais.*]

General amazement. LA HIRE, *delighted, slaps his steel thighpiece with his gauntlet.*

LA TREMOUILLE [*turning threateningly towards* CHARLES] What is this? *I* command the army.

Joan quickly puts her hand on CHARLES's *shoulder as he instinctively recoils.* CHARLES, *with a grotesque effort culminating in an extravagant gesture, snaps his fingers in the* CHAMBERLAIN's *face.*

JOAN Thou't answered, old Gruff-and-Grum. [*Suddenly flashing out her sword as she divines that her moment has come*] Who is for God and His Maid? Who is for Orleans with me?

LA HIRE [*carried away, drawing also*] For God and His Maid! To Orleans!

ALL THE KNIGHTS [*following his lead with enthusiasm*] To Orleans!

Joan, radiant, falls on her knees in thanksgiving to God. They all kneel, except the ARCHBISHOP, *who gives his benediction with a sigh, and* LA TRÉMOUILLE, *who collapses, cursing.*

Scene 3

Orleans, April 29th, 1429. DUNOIS, *aged 26, is pacing up and down a patch of ground on the south bank of the silver Loire, commanding a long view of the river in both directions. He has had his lance stuck up with a pennon, which streams in a strong east wind. His shield with its bend sinister lies beside it. He has his commander's baton in his hand. He is well built, carrying his armor easily. His broad brow and pointed chin give him an equilaterally triangular face, already marked by active service and responsibility, with the expression of a goodnatured and capable man who has no affectations and no foolish illusions. His page is sitting on the ground, elbows on knees, cheeks on fists, idly watching the water. It is evening; and both man and boy are affected by the loveliness of the Loire.*

DUNOIS [*halting for a moment to glance up at the streaming pennon and shake his head wearily before he resumes his pacing*] West wind, west wind, west wind. Strumpet: steadfast when you should be wanton, wanton when you should be steadfast. West wind on the silver Loire: what rhymes to Loire? [*He looks again at the pennon, and shakes his fist at it.*] Change, curse you, change, English harlot of a wind, change. West, west, I tell you. [*With a growl he resumes his march in silence, but soon begins again.*] West wind, wanton wind, wilful wind, womanish wind, false wind from over the water, will you never blow again?

THE PAGE [*bounding to his feet*] See! There! There she goes!

DUNOIS [*startled from his reverie: eagerly*] Where? Who? The Maid?

THE PAGE No: the kingfisher. Like blue lightning. She went into that bush.

DUNOIS [*furiously disappointed*] Is that all? You infernal young idiot: I have a mind to pitch you into the river.

THE PAGE [*not afraid, knowing his man*] It looked frightfully jolly, that flash of blue. Look! There goes the other!

DUNOIS [*running eagerly to the river brim*] Where? Where?

THE PAGE [*pointing*] Passing the reeds.

DUNOIS [*delighted*] I see.

They follow the flight till the bird takes cover.

THE PAGE   You blew me up because you were not in time to see them yesterday.

DUNOIS   You knew I was expecting The Maid when you set up your yelping. I will give you something to yelp for next time.

THE PAGE   Arnt they lovely? I wish I could catch them.

DUNOIS   Let me catch you trying to trap them, and I will put you in the iron cage for a month to teach you what a cage feels like. You are an abominable boy.

THE PAGE [*laughs, and squats down as before*]!

DUNOIS [*pacing*]   Blue bird, blue bird, since I am friend to thee, change thou the wind for me. No: it does not rhyme. He who has sinned for thee: thats better. No sense in it, though. [*He finds himself close to the* PAGE] You abominable boy! [*He turns away from him*] Mary in the blue snood, kingfisher color: will you grudge me a west wind?

A SENTRY'S VOICE WESTWARD   Halt! Who goes there?

JOAN'S VOICE   The Maid.

DUNOIS   Let her pass. Hither, Maid! To me!

JOAN, *in splendid armor, rushes in in a blazing rage. The wind drops; and the pennon flaps idly down the lance; but* DUNOIS *is too much occupied with* JOAN *to notice it.*

JOAN [*bluntly*]   Be you Bastard of Orleans?

DUNOIS [*cool and stern, pointing to his shield*]   You see the bend sinister. Are you Joan the Maid?

JOAN   Sure.

DUNOIS   Where are your troops?

JOAN   Miles behind. They have cheated me. They have brought me to the wrong side of the river.

DUNOIS   I told them to.

JOAN   Why did you? The English are on the other side!

DUNOIS   The English are on both sides.

JOAN   But Orleans is on the other side. We must fight the English there. How can we cross the river?

DUNOIS [*grimly*]   There is a bridge.

JOAN   In God's name, then, let us cross the bridge, and fall on them.

DUNOIS   It seems simple; but it cannot be done.

JOAN   Who says so?

DUNOIS   I say so; and older and wiser heads than mine are of the same opinion.

JOAN [*roundly*]   Then your older and wiser heads are fatheads: they have made a fool of you; and now they want to make a fool of me too, bringing me to the wrong side of the river. Do you not know that I bring you better help than ever came to any general or any town?

DUNOIS [*smiling patiently*]   Your own?

JOAN   No: the help and counsel of the King of Heaven. Which is the way to the bridge?

DUNOIS   You are impatient, Maid.

JOAN   Is this a time for patience? Our enemy is at our gates; and here we stand doing nothing. Oh, why are you not fighting? Listen to me: I will deliver you from fear. I—

DUNOIS [*laughing heartily, and waving her off*]   No, no, my girl: if you delivered me from fear I should be a good knight for a story book, but a very bad commander of the army. Come! let me begin to make a soldier of you. [*He takes her to the water's edge.*] Do you see those two forts at this end of the bridge? the big ones?

JOAN   Yes. Are they ours or the goddams'?

DUNOIS   Be quiet, and listen to me. If I were in either of those forts with only ten men I could hold it against an army. The English have more than ten times ten goddams in those forts to hold them against us.

JOAN   They cannot hold them against God. God did not give them the land under those forts: they stole it from Him. He gave it to us. I will take those forts.

DUNOIS   Single-handed?

JOAN   Our men will take them. I will lead them.

DUNOIS   Not a man will follow you.

JOAN   I will not look back to see whether anyone is following me.

DUNOIS [*recognizing her mettle, and clapping her heartily on the shoulder*]   Good. You have the makings of a soldier in you. You are in love with war.

JOAN [*startled*]   Oh! And the Archbishop said I was in love with religion.

DUNOIS   I, God forgive me, am a little in love with war myself, the ugly devil! I am like a man with two wives. Do you want to be like a woman with two husbands?

JOAN [*matter-of-fact*]   I will never take a husband. A man in Toul took an action against me for breach of promise; but I never promised him. I am a soldier: I do not want to be thought of as a woman. I will not dress as a woman. I do not care for the things women care for. They dream of lovers, and of money. I dream of leading a charge, and of placing the big guns. You soldiers do not know how to use the big guns: you think you can win battles with a great noise and smoke.

DUNOIS [*with a shrug*]   True. Half the time the artillery is more trouble than it is worth.

JOAN   Aye, lad; but you cannot fight stone walls with horses: you must have guns, and much bigger guns too.

DUNOIS [*grinning at her familiarity, and echoing it*]   Aye, lass; but a good heart and a stout ladder will get over the stoniest wall.

JOAN   I will be first up the ladder when we reach the fort, Bastard. I dare you to follow me.

DUNOIS   You must not dare a staff officer, Joan: only company officers are allowed to indulge in displays of personal courage. Besides, you must know that I welcome you as a saint, not as a soldier. I have daredevils enough at my call, if they could help me.

JOAN   I am not a daredevil: I am a servant of God. My sword is sacred: I found it behind the altar in the church of St Catherine, where God hid it for me; and I may not strike a blow with it. My heart is full of courage, not of anger. I will lead; and your men will follow: that is all I can do. But I must do it: you shall not stop me.

DUNOIS   All in good time. Our men cannot take those forts by a sally across the bridge. They must come by water, and take the English in the rear on this side.

JOAN [*her military sense asserting itself*]   Then make rafts and put big guns on them; and let your men cross to us.

DUNOIS   The rafts are ready; and the men are embarked. But they must wait for God.

JOAN   What do you mean? God is waiting for them.

DUNOIS   Let Him send us a wind then. My boats are downstream: they cannot come up against both wind and current. We must wait until God changes the wind. Come: let me take you to the church.

JOAN   No. I love church; but the English will not yield to prayers: they understand nothing but hard knocks and slashes. I will not go to church until we have beaten them.

DUNOIS   You must: I have business for you there.

JOAN   What business?

DUNOIS   To pray for a west wind. I have prayed; and I have given two silver candlesticks; but my prayers are not answered. Yours may be: you are young and innocent.

JOAN   Oh yes: you are right. I will pray: I will tell St Catherine: she will make God give me a west wind. Quick: shew me the way to the church.

THE PAGE [*sneezes violently*]   At-cha!!!

JOAN   God bless you, child! Coom, Bastard.

They go out. The PAGE *rises to follow. He picks up the shield, and is taking the spear as well when he notices the pennon, which is now streaming eastward.*

THE PAGE [*dropping the shield and calling excitedly after them*]   Seigneur! Seigneur! Mademoiselle!

DUNOIS [*running back*]   What is it? The kingfisher? [*He looks eagerly for it up the river.*]

JOAN [*joining them*]   Oh, a kingfisher! Where?

THE PAGE   No: the wind, the wind, the wind [*pointing to the pennon*]: that is what made me sneeze

DUNOIS [*looking at the pennon*]   The wind has changed. [*He crosses himself*] God has spoken. [*Kneeling and handing his baton to* JOAN] You command the king's army. I am your soldier.

THE PAGE [*looking down the river*]   The boats have put off. They are ripping upstream like anything.

DUNOIS [*rising*]   Now for the forts. You dared me to follow. Dare you lead?

JOAN [*bursting into tears and flinging her arms around* DUNOIS, *kissing him on both cheeks*]   Dunois, dear comrade in arms, help me. My eyes are blinded with tears. Set my foot on the ladder, and say 'Up, Joan.'

DUNOIS [*dragging her out*]   Never mind the tears: make for the flash of the guns.

JOAN [*in a blaze of courage*]   Ah!

DUNOIS [*dragging her along with him*]   For God and Saint Dennis!

THE PAGE [*shrilly*]   The Maid! The Maid! God and The Maid! Hurray-ay-ay! [*He snatches up the shield and lance, and capers out after them, mad with excitement.*]

Scene 4

A tent in the English camp. A bullnecked English CHAPLAIN *of 50 is sitting on a stool at a table, hard at work writing. At the other side of the table an imposing* NOBLEMAN, *aged 46, is seated in a handsome chair turning over the leaves of an illuminated Book of Hours. The* NOBLEMAN *is enjoying himself: the* CHAPLAIN *is struggling with suppressed wrath. There is an unoccupied leather stool on the* NOBLEMAN's *left. The table is on his right.*

THE NOBLEMAN   Now this is what I call workmanship. There is nothing on earth more exquisite than a bonny book, with well-placed columns of rich black writing in beautiful borders, and illuminated pictures cunningly inset. But nowadays, instead of looking at books, people read them. A book might as well be one of those orders for bacon and bran that you are scribbling.

THE CHAPLAIN   I must say, my lord, you take our situation very coolly. Very coolly indeed.

THE NOBLEMAN [*supercilious*]   What is the matter?

THE CHAPLAIN   The matter, my lord, is that we English have been defeated.

THE NOBLEMAN   That happens, you know. It is only in history books and ballads that the enemy is always defeated.

THE CHAPLAIN   But we are being defeated over and over again. First, Orleans—

THE NOBLEMAN [*poohpoohing*]   Oh, Orleans!

THE CHAPLAIN   I know what you are going to say, my lord: that was a clear case of witchcraft and sorcery. But we are still being defeated. Jargeau, Meung, Beaugency, just like Orleans. And now we have been butchered at Patay, and Sir John Talbot taken prisoner. [*He throws down his pen, almost in tears.*] I feel it, my lord: I feel it very deeply. I cannot bear to see my countrymen defeated by a parcel of foreigners.

THE NOBLEMAN   Oh! you are an Englishman, are you?

THE CHAPLAIN   Certainly not, my lord: I am a gentleman. Still, like your lordship, I was born in England; and it makes a difference.

THE NOBLEMAN   You are attached to the soil, eh?

THE CHAPLAIN   It pleases your lordship to be satirical at my expense: your greatness privileges you to be so with impunity. But your lordship knows very well that I am not attached to the soil in a vulgar manner, like a serf. Still, I have a feeling about it; [*with growing agitation*] and I am not ashamed of it; and [*rising wildly*] by God, if this goes on any longer I will fling my cassock to the devil, and take arms myself, and strangle the accursed witch with my own hands.

THE NOBLEMAN [*laughing at him goodnaturedly*]   So you shall, chaplain: so you shall, if we can do nothing better. But not yet, not quite yet.

The CHAPLAIN *resumes his seat very sulkily.*

THE NOBLEMAN [*airily*]   I should not care very much about the witch—you see, I have made my pilgrimage to the Holy Land; and the Heavenly Powers, for their own credit, can hardly allow me to be worsted by a village sorceress—but the Bastard of Orleans is a harder nut to crack; and as he has been to the Holy Land too, honors are easy between us as far as that goes.

THE CHAPLAIN   He is only a Frenchman, my lord.

THE NOBLEMAN   A Frenchman! Where did you pick up that expression? Are these Burgundians and Bretons and Picards and Gascons beginning to call themselves Frenchmen, just as our fellows are beginning to call themselves Englishmen? They actually talk of France and England as their countries. Theirs, if you please! What is to become of me and you if that way of thinking comes into fashion?

THE CHAPLAIN   Why, my lord? Can it hurt us?

THE NOBLEMAN   Men cannot serve two masters. If this cant of serving their country once takes hold of them, good-bye to the authority of their feudal lords, and goodbye to the authority of the Church. That is, goodbye to you and me.

THE CHAPLAIN   I hope I am a faithful servant of the Church; and there are only six cousins between me and the barony of Stogumber, which was created by the Conqueror. But is that any reason why I should stand by and see Englishmen beaten by a French bastard and a witch from Lousy Champagne?

THE NOBLEMAN   Easy, man, easy: we shall burn the witch and beat the bastard all in good time. Indeed I am waiting at present for the Bishop of Beauvais, to arrange the burning with him. He has been turned out of his diocese by her faction.

THE CHAPLAIN   You have first to catch her, my lord.

THE NOBLEMAN   Or buy her. I will offer a king's ransom.

THE CHAPLAIN   A king's ransom! For that slut!

THE NOBLEMAN   One has to leave a margin. Some of Charles's people will sell her to the Burgundians; the Burgundians will sell her to us; and there will probably be three or four middlemen who will expect their little commissions.

THE CHAPLAIN   Monstrous. It is all those scoundrels of Jews: they get in every time money changes hands. I would not leave a Jew alive in Christendom if I had my way.

THE NOBLEMAN   Why not? The Jews generally give value. They make you pay; but they deliver the goods. In my experience the men who want something for nothing are invariably Christians.

A PAGE *appears.*

THE PAGE   The Right Reverend the Bishop of Beauvais: Monseigneur Cauchon.

CAUCHON, *aged about 60, comes in. The* PAGE *withdraws. The two Englishmen rise.*

THE NOBLEMAN [*with effusive courtesy*]   My dear Bishop, how good of you to come! Allow me to introduce myself: Richard de Beauchamp, Earl of Warwick, at your service.

CAUCHON   Your lordship's fame is well known to me.

WARWICK   This reverend cleric is Master John de Stogumber.

THE CHAPLAIN [*glibly*]   John Bowyer Spenser Neville de Stogumber, at your service, my lord: Bachelor of Theology, and Keeper of the Private Seal to His Eminence the Cardinal of Winchester.

WARWICK [*to* CAUCHON]   You call him the Cardinal of England, I believe. Our king's uncle.

CAUCHON   Messire John de Stogumber: I am always the very good friend of His Eminence. [*He extends his hand to the chaplain, who kisses his ring.*]

WARWICK   Do me the honor to be seated. [*He gives* CAUCHON *his chair, placing it at the head of the table.*]

CAUCHON *accepts the place of honor with a grave inclination.* WARWICK *fetches the leather stool carelessly, and sits in his former place. The* CHAPLAIN *goes back to his chair.*

Though WARWICK *has taken second place in calculated deference to the Bishop, he assumes the lead in opening the proceedings as a matter of course. He is still cordial and expansive; but there is a new note in his voice which means that he is coming to business.*

WARWICK   Well, my Lord Bishop, you find us in one of our unlucky moments.

Charles is to be crowned at Rheims, practically by the young woman from Lorraine; and—I must not deceive you, nor flatter your hopes—we cannot prevent it. I suppose it will make a great difference to Charles's position.

CAUCHON Undoubtedly. It is a masterstroke of The Maid's.

THE CHAPLAIN [*again agitated*] We were not fairly beaten, my lord. No Englishman is ever fairly beaten.

CAUCHON *raises his eyebrow slightly, then quickly composes his face.*

WARWICK Our friend here takes the view that the young woman is a sorceress. It would, I presume, be the duty of your reverend lordship to denounce her to the Inquisition, and have her burnt for that offence.

CAUCHON If she were captured in my diocese: yes.

WARWICK [*feeling that they are getting on capitally*] Just so. Now I suppose there can be no reasonable doubt that she is a sorceress.

THE CHAPLAIN Not the least. An arrant witch.

WARWICK [*gently reproving the interruption*] We are asking for the Bishop's opinion, Messire John.

CAUCHON We shall have to consider not merely our own opinions here, but the opinions—the prejudices, if you like—of a French court.

WARWICK [*correcting*] A Catholic court, my lord.

CAUCHON Catholic courts are composed of mortal men, like other courts, however sacred their function and inspiration may be. And if the men are Frenchmen, as the modern fashion calls them, I am afraid the bare fact that an English army has been defeated by a French one will not convince them that there is any sorcery in the matter.

THE CHAPLAIN What! Not when the famous Sir John Talbot himself has been defeated and actually taken prisoner by a drab from the ditches of Lorraine!

CAUCHON Sir John Talbot, we all know, is a fierce and formidable soldier, Messire; but I have yet to learn that he is an able general. And though it pleases you to say that he has been defeated by this girl, some of us may be disposed to give a little of the credit to Dunois.

THE CHAPLAIN [*contemptuously*] The Bastard of Orleans!

CAUCHON Let me remind—

WARWICK [*interposing*] I know what you are going to say, my lord. Dunois defeated me at Montargis.

CAUCHON [*bowing*] I take that as evidence that the Seigneur Dunois is a very able commander indeed.

WARWICK Your lordship is the flower of courtesy. I admit, on our side, that Talbot is a mere fighting animal, and that it probably served him right to be taken at Patay.

THE CHAPLAIN [*chafing*] My lord: at Orleans this woman had her throat pierced by an English arrow, and was seen to cry like a child from the pain of it. It was a death wound; yet she fought all day; and when our men had repulsed all her attacks like true Englishmen, she walked alone to the wall of our fort with a white banner in her hand; and our men were paralyzed, and could neither shoot nor strike whilst the French fell on them and drove them on to the bridge, which immediately burst into flames and crumbled under them, letting them down into the river, where they were drowned in heaps. Was this your bastard's generalship? or were those flames the flames of hell, conjured up by witchcraft?

WARWICK   You will forgive Messire John's vehemence, my lord; but he has put our case. Dunois is a great captain, we admit; but why could he do nothing until the witch came?

CAUCHON   I do not say that there were no supernatural powers on her side. But the names on that white banner were not the names of Satan and Beelzebub, but the blessed names of our Lord and His holy mother. And your commander who was drowned—Clahz-da I think you call him—

WARWICK   Glasdale. Sir William Glasdale.

CAUCHON   Glass-dell, thank you. He was no saint; and many of our people think that he was drowned for his blasphemies against The Maid.

WARWICK [*beginning to look very dubious*]   Well, what are we to infer from all this, my lord? Has The Maid converted you?

CAUCHON   If she had, my lord, I should have known better than to have trusted myself here within your grasp.

WARWICK [*blandly deprecating*]   Oh! oh! My lord!

CAUCHON   If the devil is making use of this girl—and I believe he is—

WARWICK [*reassured*]   Ah! You hear, Messire John? I knew your lordship would not fail us. Pardon my interruption. Proceed.

CAUCHON   If it be so, the devil has longer views than you give him credit for.

WARWICK   Indeed? In what way? Listen to this, Messire John.

CAUCHON   If the devil wanted to damn a country girl, do you think so easy a task cost him the winning of half a dozen battles? No, my lord: any trumpery imp could do that much if the girl could be damned at all. The Prince of Darkness does not condescend to such cheap drudgery. When he strikes, he strikes at the Catholic Church, whose realm is the whole spiritual world. When he damns, he damns the souls of the entire human race. Against that dreadful design The Church stands ever on guard. And it is as one of the instruments of that design that I see this girl. She is inspired, but diabolically inspired.

THE CHAPLAIN   I told you she was a witch.

CAUCHON [*fiercely*]   She is not a witch. She is a heretic.

THE CHAPLAIN   What difference does that make?

CAUCHON   You, a priest, ask me that! You English are strangely blunt in the mind. All these things that you call witchcraft are capable of a natural explanation. The woman's miracles would not impose on a rabbit: she does not claim them as miracles herself. What do her victories prove but that she has a better head on her shoulders than your swearing Glass-dells and mad bull Talbots, and that the courage of faith, even though it be a false faith, will always outstay the courage of wrath?

THE CHAPLAIN [*hardly able to believe his ears*]   Does your lordship compare Sir John Talbot, three times Governor of Ireland, to a mad bull?!!!

WARWICK   It would not be seemly for you to do so, Messire John, as you are still six removes from a barony. But as I am an earl, and Talbot is only a knight, I may make bold to accept the comparison. [*To the* BISHOP] My lord: I wipe the slate as far as the witchcraft goes. None the less, we must burn the woman.

CAUCHON   I cannot burn her. The Church cannot take life. And my first duty is to seek this girl's salvation.

WARWICK   No doubt. But you do burn people occasionally.

CAUCHON   No. When The Church cuts off an obstinate heretic as a dead branch from the tree of life, the heretic is handed over to the secular arm. The Church has no part in what the secular arm may see fit to do.

WARWICK   Precisely. And I shall be the secular arm in this case. Well, my lord, hand over your dead branch; and I will see that the fire is ready for it. If you will answer for The Church's part, I will answer for the secular part.

CAUCHON [*with smouldering anger*]   I can answer for nothing. You great lords are too prone to treat The Church as a mere political convenience.

WARWICK [*smiling and propitiatory*]   Not in England, I assure you.

CAUCHON   In England more than anywhere else. No, my lord: the soul of this village girl is of equal value with yours or your king's before the throne of God; and my first duty is to save it. I will not suffer your lordship to smile at me as if I were repeating a meaningless form of words, and it were well understood between us that I should betray the girl to you. I am no mere political bishop: my faith is to me what your honor is to you; and if there be a loophole through which this baptized child of God can creep to her salvation, I shall guide her to it.

THE CHAPLAIN [*rising in a fury*]   You are a traitor.

CAUCHON [*springing up*]   You lie, priest. [*Trembling with rage*] If you dare do what this woman has done—set your country above the holy Catholic Church— you shall go to the fire with her.

THE CHAPLAIN   My lord: I—I went too far. I—[*He sits down with a submissive gesture.*]

WARWICK [*who has risen apprehensively*]   My lord: I apologize to you for the word used by Messire John de Stogumber. It does not mean in England what it does in France. In your language traitor means betrayer: one who is perfidious, treacherous, unfaithful, disloyal. In our country it means simply one who is not wholly devoted to our English interests.

CAUCHON   I am sorry: I did not understand. [*He subsides into his chair with dignity.*]

WARWICK [*resuming his seat, much relieved*]   I must apologize on my own account if I have seemed to take the burning of this poor girl too lightly. When one has seen whole countrysides burnt over and over again as mere items in military routine, one has to grow a very thick skin. Otherwise one might go mad: at all events, I should. May I venture to assume that your lordship also, having to see so many heretics burned from time to time, is compelled to take—shall I say a professional view of what would otherwise be a very horrible incident?

CAUCHON   Yes: it is a painful duty: even, as you say, a horrible one. But in comparison with the horror of heresy it is less than nothing. I am not thinking of this girl's body, which will suffer for a few moments only, and which must in any event die in some more or less painful manner, but of her soul, which may suffer to all eternity.

WARWICK   Just so; and God grant that her soul may be saved! But the practical problem would seem to be how to save her soul without saving her body. For we must face it, my lord: if this cult of The Maid goes on, our cause is lost.

THE CHAPLAIN [*his voice broken like that of a man who has been crying*]   May I speak, my lord?

WARWICK   Really, Messire John, I had rather you did not, unless you can keep your temper.

THE CHAPLAIN   It is only this. I speak under correction; but The Maid is full of deceit: she pretends to be devout. Her prayers and confessions are endless. How can she be accused of heresy when she neglects no observance of a faithful daughter of The Church?

CAUCHON [*flaming up*]   A faithful daughter of The Church! The Pope himself at his proudest dare not presume as this woman presumes. She acts as if she herself were The Church. She brings the message of God to Charles; and The Church must stand aside. She will crown him in the cathedral of Rheims: she, not The Church! She sends letters to the king of England giving him God's command through her to return to his island on pain of God's vengeance, which she will execute. Let me tell you that the writing of such letters was the practice of the accursed Mahomet, the anti-Christ. Has she ever in all her utterances said one word of The Church? Never. It is always God and herself.

WARWICK   What can you expect? A beggar on horseback! Her head is turned.

CAUCHON   Who has turned it? The devil. And for a mighty purpose. He is spreading this heresy everywhere. The man Hus, burnt only thirteen years ago at Constance, infected all Bohemia with it. A man named WcLeef, himself an anointed priest, spread the pestilence in England; and to your shame you let him die in his bed. We have such people here in France too: I know the breed. It is cancerous: if it be not cut out, stamped out, burnt out, it will not stop until it has brought the whole body of human society into sin and corruption, into waste and ruin. By it an Arab camel driver drove Christ and His Church out of Jerusalem, and ravaged his way west like a wild beast until at last there stood only the Pyrenees and God's mercy between France and damnation. Yet what did the camel driver do at the beginning more than this shepherd girl is doing? He had his voices from the angel Gabriel: she has her voices from St Catherine and St Margaret and the Blessed Michael. He declared himself the messenger of God, and wrote in God's name to the kings of the earth. Her letters to them are going forth daily. It is not the Mother of God now to whom we must look for intercession, but to Joan the Maid. What will the world be like when The Church's accumulated wisdom and knowledge and experience, its councils of learned, venerable pious men, are thrust into the kennel by every ignorant laborer or dairymaid whom the devil can puff up with the monstrous self-conceit of being directly inspired from heaven? It will be a world of blood, of fury, of devastation, of each man striving for his own hand: in the end a world wrecked back into barbarism. For now you have only Mahomet and his dupes, and the Maid and her dupes; but what will it be when every girl thinks herself a Joan and every man a Mahomet? I shudder to the very marrow of my bones when I think of it. I have fought it all my life; and I will fight it to the end. Let all this woman's sins be forgiven her except only this sin; for it is the sin against the Holy Ghost; and if she does not recant in the dust before the world, and submit herself to the last inch of her soul to her Church, to the fire she shall go if she once falls into my hand.

WARWICK [*unimpressed*]   You feel strongly about it, naturally.

CAUCHON   Do not you?

WARWICK   I am a soldier, not a churchman. As a pilgrim I saw something of the Mahometans. They were not so illbred as I had been led to believe. In some respects their conduct compared favorably with ours.

CAUCHON [*displeased*]   I have noticed this before. Men go to the East to convert the infidels. And the infidels pervert them. The Crusader comes back more than half a Saracen. Not to mention that all Englishmen are born heretics.

THE CHAPLAIN   Englishmen heretics!!! [*Appealing to* WARWICK] My lord: must we endure this? His lordship is beside himself. How can what an Englishman believes be heresy? It is a contradiction in terms.

CAUCHON   I absolve you, Messire de Stogumber, on the ground of invincible ignorance. The thick air of your country does not breed theologians.

WARWICK   You would not say so if you heard us quarrelling about religion, my lord! I am sorry you think I must be either a heretic or a blockhead because, as a travelled man, I know that the followers of Mahomet profess great respect for our Lord, and are more ready to forgive St Peter for being a fisherman than your lordship is to forgive Mahomet for being a camel driver. But at least we can proceed in this matter without bigotry.

CAUCHON   When men call the zeal of the Christian Church bigotry I know what to think.

WARWICK   They are only east and west views of the same thing.

CAUCHON [*bitterly ironical*]   Only east and west! Only!!

WARWICK   Oh, my Lord Bishop, I am not gainsaying you. You will carry The Church with you; but you have to carry the nobles also. To my mind there is a stronger case against The Maid than the one you have so forcibly put. Frankly, I am not afraid of this girl becoming another Mahomet, and superseding The Church by a great heresy. I think you exaggerate that risk. But have you noticed that in these letters of hers, she proposes to all the kings of Europe, as she has already pressed on Charles, a transaction which would wreck the whole social structure of Christendom?

CAUCHON   Wreck The Church. I tell you so.

WARWICK [*whose patience is wearing out*]   My lord: pray get The Church out of your head for a moment; and remember that there are temporal institutions in the world as well as spiritual ones. I and my peers represent the feudal aristocracy as you represent The Church. We are the temporal power. Well, do you not see how this girl's idea strikes at us?

CAUCHON   How does her idea strike at you, except as it strikes at all of us, through The Church?

WARWICK   Her idea is that the kings should give their realms to God, and then reign as God's bailiffs.

CAUCHON [*not interested*]   Quite sound theologically, my lord. But the king will hardly care, provided he reign. It is an abstract idea: a mere form of words.

WARWICK   By no means. It is a cunning device to supersede the aristocracy, and make the king sole and absolute autocrat. Instead of the king being merely the first among his peers, he becomes their master. That we cannot suffer: we call no man master. Nominally we hold our lands and dignities from the king, because there must be a keystone to the arch of human society; but we hold our lands in our own hands, and defend them with our own swords and those of our own tenants. Now by The Maid's doctrine the king will take our lands—our lands!— and make them a present to God; and God will then vest them wholly in the king.

CAUCHON   Need you fear that? You are the makers of kings after all. York or Lancaster in England, Lancaster or Valois in France: they reign according to your pleasure.

WARWICK   Yes; but only as long as the people follow their feudal lords, and know the king only as a travelling show, owning nothing but the highway that belongs to everybody. If the people's thoughts and hearts were turned to the king, and their lords became only the king's servants in their eyes, the king could break us across his knee one by one; and then what should we be but liveried courtiers in his halls?

CAUCHON   Still you need not fear, my lord. Some men are born kings; and some are born statesmen. The two are seldom the same. Where would the king find counsellors to plan and carry out such a policy for him?

WARWICK [*with a not too friendly smile*] Perhaps in the Church, my lord.

CAUCHON, *with an equally sour smile, shrugs his shoulders, and does not contradict him.*

WARWICK Strike down the barons; and the cardinals will have it all their own way.

CAUCHON [*conciliatory, dropping his polemical tone*] My lord: we shall not defeat The Maid if we strive against one another. I know well that there is a Will to Power in the world. I know that while it lasts there will be a struggle between the Emperor and the Pope, between the dukes and the political cardinals, between the barons and the kings. The devil divides us and governs. I see you are no friend to The Church: you are an earl first and last, as I am a churchman first and last. But can we not sink our differences in the face of a common enemy? I see now that what is in your mind is not that this girl has never once mentioned The Church, and thinks only of God and herself, but that she has never once mentioned the peerage, and thinks only of the king and herself.

WARWICK Quite so. These two ideas of hers are the same idea at bottom. It goes deep, my lord. It is the protest of the individual soul against the interference of priest or peer between the private man and his God. I should call it Protestantism if I had to find a name for it.

CAUCHON [*looking hard at him*] You understand it wonderfully well, my lord. Scratch an Englishman, and find a Protestant.

WARWICK [*playing the pink of courtesy*] I think you are not entirely void of sympathy with The Maid's secular heresy, my lord. I leave you to find a name for it.

CAUCHON You mistake me, my lord. I have no sympathy with her political presumptions. But as a priest I have gained a knowledge of the minds of the common people; and there you will find yet another most dangerous idea. I can express it only by such phrases as France for the French, England for the English, Italy for the Italians, Spain for the Spanish, and so forth. It is sometimes so narrow and bitter in country folk that it surprises me that this country girl can rise above the idea of her village for its villagers. But she can. She does. When she threatens to drive the English from the soil of France she is undoubtedly thinking of the whole extent of country in which French is spoken. To her the French-speaking people are what the Holy Scriptures describe as a nation. Call this side of her heresy Nationalism if you will: I can find you no better name for it. I can only tell you that it is essentially anti-Catholic and anti-Christian; for the Catholic Church knows only one realm, and that is the realm of Christ's kingdom. Divide that kingdom into nations, and you dethrone Christ. Dethrone Christ, and who will stand between our throats and the sword? The world will perish in a welter of war.

WARWICK Well, if you will burn the Protestant, I will burn the Nationalist, though perhaps I shall not carry Messire John with me there. England for the English will appeal to him.

THE CHAPLAIN Certainly England for the English goes without saying: it is the simple law of nature. But this woman denies to England her legitimate conquests, given her by God because of her peculiar fitness to rule over less civilized races for their own good. I do not understand what your lordships mean by Protestant and Nationalist: you are too learned and subtle for a poor clerk like myself. But I know as a matter of plain commonsense that the woman is a rebel; and that is enough for me. She rebels against Nature by wearing man's clothes, and fighting. She rebels against The Church by usurping the divine authority of the Pope. She rebels against God by her damnable league with Satan and his evil spirits against our army. And all these rebellions are only excuses for her great rebellion against England. That is not to be endured. Let her perish. Let her burn. Let her not infect the whole flock. It is expedient that one woman die for the people.

WARWICK [*rising*]   My lord: we seem to be agreed.

CAUCHON [*rising also, but in protest*]   I will not imperil my soul. I will uphold the justice of the Church. I will strive to the utmost for this woman's salvation.

WARWICK   I am sorry for the poor girl. I hate these severities. I will spare her if I can.

THE CHAPLAIN [*implacably*]   I would burn her with my own hands.

CAUCHON [*blessing him*]   Sancta simplicitas!

Scene 5

The ambulatory in the cathedral of Rheims, near the door of the vestry. A pillar bears one of the stations of the cross. The organ is playing the people out of the nave after the coronation. JOAN *is kneeling in prayer before the station. She is beautifully dressed, but still in male attire. The organ ceases as* DUNOIS, *also splendidly arrayed, comes into the ambulatory from the vestry.*

DUNOIS   Come, Joan! you have had enough praying. After that fit of crying you will catch a chill if you stay here any longer. It is all over: the cathedral is empty; and the streets are full. They are calling for The Maid. We have told them you are staying here alone to pray; but they want to see you again.

JOAN   No: let the king have all the glory.

DUNOIS   He only spoils the show, poor devil. No, Joan: you have crowned him; and you must go through with it.

JOAN [*shakes her head reluctantly.*]

DUNOIS [*raising her*]   Come come! it will be over in a couple of hours. It's better than the bridge at Orleans: eh?

JOAN   Oh, dear Dunois, how I wish it were the bridge at Orleans again! We lived at that bridge.

DUNOIS   Yes, faith, and died too: some of us.

JOAN   Isnt it strange, Jack? I am such a coward: I am frightened beyond words before a battle; but it is so dull afterwards when there is no danger: oh, so dull! dull! dull!

DUNOIS   You must learn to be abstemious in war, just as you are in your food and drink, my little saint.

JOAN   Dear Jack: I think you like me as a soldier likes his comrade.

DUNOIS   You need it, poor innocent child of God. You have not many friends at court.

JOAN   Why do all these courtiers and knights and churchmen hate me? What have I done to them? I have asked nothing for myself except that my village shall not be taxed; for we cannot afford war taxes. I have brought them luck and victory: I have set them right when they were doing all sorts of stupid things: I have crowned Charles and made him a real king; and all the honors he is handing out have gone to them. Then why do they not love me?

DUNOIS [*rallying her*]   Sim-ple-ton! Do you expect stupid people to love you for shewing them up? Do blundering old military dug-outs love the successful young captains who supersede them? Do ambitious politicians love the climbers who take the front seats from them? Do archbishops enjoy being played off their own altars, even by saints? Why, I should be jealous of you myself if I were ambitious enough.

JOAN You are the pick of the basket here, Jack: the only friend I have among all these nobles. I'll wager your mother was from the country. I will go back to the farm when I have taken Paris.

DUNOIS I am not so sure that they will let you take Paris.

JOAN [*startled*] What!

DUNOIS I should have taken it myself before this if they had all been sound about it. Some of them would rather Paris took you, I think. So take care.

JOAN Jack: the world is too wicked for me. If the goddams and the Burgundians do not make an end of me, the French will. Only for my voices I should lose all heart. That is why I had to steal away to pray here alone after the coronation. I'll tell you something, Jack. It is in the bells I hear my voices. Not to-day, when they all rang: that was nothing but jangling. But here in this corner, where the bells come down from heaven, and the echoes linger, or in the fields, where they come from a distance through the quiet of the countryside, my voices are in them. [*The cathedral clock chimes the quarter.*] Hark! [*She becomes rapt.*] Do you hear? 'Dear-child-of-God': just what you said. At the half-hour they will say 'Be-brave-go-on'. At the three-quarters they will say 'I-am-thy-Help'. But it is at the hour, when the great bell goes after 'God-will-save-France': it is then that St Margaret and St Catherine and sometimes even the blessed Michael will say things that I cannot tell beforehand. Then, oh then—

DUNOIS [*interrupting her kindly but not sympathetically*] Then, Joan, we shall hear whatever we fancy in the booming of the bell. You make me uneasy when you talk about your voices: I should think you were a bit cracked if I hadnt noticed that you give me very sensible reasons for what you do, though I hear you telling others you are only obeying Madame Saint Catherine.

JOAN [*crossly*] Well, I have to find reasons for you, because you do not believe in my voices. But the voices come first; and I find the reasons after: whatever you may choose to believe.

DUNOIS Are you angry, Joan?

JOAN Yes. [*Smiling*] No: not with you. I wish you were one of the village babies.

DUNOIS Why?

JOAN I could nurse you for awhile.

DUNOIS You are a bit of a woman after all.

JOAN No: not a bit: I am a soldier and nothing else. Soldiers always nurse children when they get a chance.

DUNOIS That is true. [*He laughs.*]

KING CHARLES, *with* BLUEBEARD *on his left and* LA HIRE *on his right, comes from the vestry, where he has been disrobing.* JOAN *shrinks away behind the pillar.* DUNOIS *is left between* CHARLES *and* LA HIRE.

DUNOIS Well, your Majesty is an anointed king at last. How do you like it?

CHARLES I would not go through it again to be emperor of the sun and moon. The weight of those robes! I thought I should have dropped when they loaded that crown on to me. And the famous holy oil they talked so much about was rancid:

phew! The Archbishop must be nearly dead: his robes must have weighed a ton: they are stripping him still in the vestry.

DUNOIS [*drily*] Your majesty should wear armor oftener. That would accustom you to heavy dressing.

CHARLES Yes: the old jibe! Well, I am not going to wear armor: fighting is not my job. Where is The Maid?

JOAN [*coming forward between* CHARLES *and* BLUEBEARD, *and falling on her knee*] Sire: I have made you king: my work is done. I am going back to my father's farm.

CHARLES [*surprised, but relieved*] Oh, are you? Well, that will be very nice.

JOAN *rises, deeply discouraged.*

CHARLES [*continuing heedlessly*] A healthy life, you know.

DUNOIS But a dull one.

BLUEBEARD You will find the petticoats tripping you up after leaving them off for so long.

LA HIRE You will miss the fighting. It's a bad habit, but a grand one, and the hardest of all to break yourself of.

CHARLES [*anxiously*] Still, we dont want you to stay if you would really rather go home.

JOAN [*bitterly*] I know well that none of you will be sorry to see me go. [*She turns her shoulder to* CHARLES *and walks past him to the more congenial neighborhood of* DUNOIS *and* LA HIRE.]

LA HIRE Well, I shall be able to swear when I want to. But I shall miss you at times.

JOAN La Hire: in spite of all your sins and swears we shall meet in heaven; for I love you as I love Pitou, my old sheep dog. Pitou could kill a wolf. You will kill the English wolves until they go back to their country and become good dogs of God, will you not?

LA HIRE You and I together: yes.

JOAN · No: I shall last only a year from the beginning.

ALL THE OTHERS What!

JOAN I know it somehow.

DUNOIS Nonsense!

JOAN Jack: do you think you will be able to drive them out?

DUNOIS [*with quiet conviction*] Yes: I shall drive them out. They beat us because we thought battles were tournaments and ransom markets. We played the fool while the goddams took war seriously. But I have learnt my lesson, and taken their measure. They have no roots here. I have beaten them before; and I shall beat them again.

JOAN You will not be cruel to them, Jack?

DUNOIS The goddams will not yield to tender handling. We did not begin it.

JOAN [*suddenly*] Jack: before I go home, let us take Paris.

CHARLES [*terrified*] Oh no no. We shall lose everything we have gained. Oh dont let us have any more fighting. We can make a very good treaty with the Duke of Burgundy.

JOAN Treaty! [*She stamps with impatience.*]

CHARLES Well, why not, now that I am crowned and anointed? Oh, that oil!

The ARCHBISHOP *comes from the vestry, and joins the group between* CHARLES *and* BLUEBEARD.

CHARLES   Archbishop: The Maid wants to start fighting again.

THE ARCHBISHOP   Have we ceased fighting, then? Are we at peace?

CHARLES   No: I suppose not; but let us be content with what we have done. Let us make a treaty. Our luck is too good to last; and now is our chance to stop before it turns.

JOAN   Luck! God has fought for us; and you call it luck! And you would stop while there are still Englishmen on this holy earth of dear France!

THE ARCHBISHOP [*sternly*]   Maid: the king addressed himself to me, not to you. You forget yourself. You very often forget yourself.

JOAN [*unabashed, and rather roughly*]   Then speak, you; and tell him that it is not God's will that he should take his hand from the plough.

THE ARCHBISHOP   If I am not so glib with the name of God as you are, it is because I interpret His will with the authority of the Church and of my sacred office. When you first came you respected it, and would not have dared to speak as you are now speaking. You came clothed with the virtue of humility; and because God blessed your enterprises accordingly, you have stained yourself with the sin of pride. The old Greek tragedy is rising among us. It is the chastisement of hubris.

CHARLES   Yes: she thinks she knows better than everyone else.

JOAN [*distressed, but naïvely incapable of seeing the effect she is producing*]   But I do know better than any of you seem to. And I am not proud: I never speak unless I know I am right.

BLUEBEARD ⎱ [*exclaiming* ⎰ Ha Ha!
CHARLES   ⎰   *together*] ⎱ Just so.

THE ARCHBISHOP   How do you know you are right?

JOAN   I always know. My voices—

CHARLES   Oh, your voices, your voices. Why dont the voices come to me? I am king, not you.

JOAN   They do come to you; but you do not hear them. You have not sat in the field in the evening listening for them. When the angelus rings you cross yourself and have done with it; but if you prayed from your heart, and listened to the thrilling of the bells in the air after they stop ringing, you would hear the voices as well as I do. [*Turning brusquely from him*] But what voices do you need to tell you what the blacksmith can tell you: that you must strike while the iron is hot? I tell you we must make a dash at Compiègne and relieve it as we relieved Orleans. Then Paris will open its gates; or if not, we will break through them. What is your crown worth without your capital?

LA HIRE   That is what I say too. We shall go through them like a red hot shot through a pound of butter. What do you say, Bastard?

DUNOIS   If our cannon balls were all as hot as your head, and we had enough of them, we should conquer the earth, no doubt. Pluck and impetuosity are good servants in war, but bad masters: they have delivered us into the hands of the English every time we have trusted to them. We never know when we are beaten: that is our great fault.

JOAN   You never know when you are victorious: that is a worse fault. I shall have to make you carry looking-glasses in battle to convince you that the English have not cut off all your noses. You would have been besieged in Orleans still, you and your councils of war, if I had not made you attack. You should always attack; and if you only hold on long enough the enemy will stop first. You dont know how to begin a battle; and you dont know how to use your cannons. And I do.

She squats down on the flags with crossed ankles, pouting.

DUNOIS   I know what you think of us, General Joan.

JOAN   Never mind that, Jack. Tell them what you think of me.

DUNOIS   I think that God was on your side; for I have not forgotten how the wind changed, and how our hearts changed when you came; and by my faith I shall never deny that it was in your sign that we conquered. But I tell you as a soldier that God is no man's daily drudge, and no maid's either. If you are worthy of it He will sometimes snatch you out of the jaws of death and set you on your feet again; but that is all: once on your feet you must fight with all your might and all your craft. For He has to be fair to your enemy too: dont forget that. Well, He set us on our feet through you at Orleans; and the glory of it has carried us through a few good battles here to the coronation. But if we presume on it further, and trust to God to do the work we should do ourselves, we shall be defeated; and serve us right!

JOAN   But—

DUNOIS   Sh! I have not finished. Do not think, any of you, that these victories of ours were won without generalship. King Charles: you have said no word in your proclamations of my part in this campaign; and I make no complaint of that; for the people will run after The Maid and her miracles and not after the Bastard's hard work finding troops for her and feeding them. But I know exactly how much God did for us through The Maid, and how much He left me to do by my own wits; and I tell you that your little hour of miracles is over, and that from this time on he who plays the war game best will win—if the luck is on his side.

JOAN   Ah! if, if, if, if! If ifs and ans were pots and pans there'd be no need of tinkers. [*Rising impetuously*] I tell you, Bastard, your art of war is no use, because your knights are no good for real fighting. War is only a game to them, like tennis and all their other games: they make rules as to what is fair and what is not fair, and heap armor on themselves and on their poor horses to keep out the arrows; and when they fall they cant get up, and have to wait for their squires to come and lift them to arrange about the ransom with the man that has poked them off their horse. Cant you see that all the like of that is gone by and done with? What use is armor against gunpowder? And if it was, do you think men that are fighting for France and for God will stop to bargain about ransoms, as half your knights live by doing? No: they will fight to win; and they will give up their lives out of their own hand into the hand of God when they go into battle, as I do. Common folks understand this. They cannot afford armor and cannot pay ransoms; but they followed me half naked into the moat and up the ladder and over the wall. With them it is my life or thine, and God defend the right! You may shake your head, Jack; and Bluebeard may twirl his billygoat's beard and cock his nose at me; but remember the day your knights and captains refused to follow me to attack the English at Orleans! You locked the gates to keep me in; and it was the townsfolk and the common people that followed me, and forced the gate, and shewed you the way to fight in earnest.

BLUEBEARD [*offended*]   Not content with being Pope Joan, you must be Caesar and Alexander as well.

THE ARCHBISHOP Pride will have a fall, Joan.

JOAN Oh, never mind whether it is pride or not: is it true? is it commonsense?

LA HIRE It is true. Half of us are afraid of having our handsome noses broken; and the other half are out for paying off their mortgages. Let her have her way, Dunois: she does not know everything; but she has got hold of the right end of the stick. Fighting is not what it was; and those who know least about it often make the best job of it.

DUNOIS I know all that. I do not fight in the old way: I have learnt the lesson of Agincourt, of Poitiers and Crecy. I know how many lives any move of mine will cost; and if the move is worth the cost I make it and pay the cost. But Joan never counts the cost at all: she goes ahead and trusts to God: she thinks she has God in her pocket. Up to now she has had the numbers on her side; and she has won. But I know Joan; and I see that some day she will go ahead when she has only ten men to do the work of a hundred. And then she will find that God is on the side of the big battalions. She will be taken by the enemy. And the lucky man that makes the capture will receive sixteen thousand pounds from the Earl of Ouareek.

JOAN [*flattered*] Sixteen thousand pounds! Eh, laddie, have they offered that for me? There cannot be so much money in the world.

DUNOIS There is, in England. And now tell me, all of you, which of you will lift a finger to save Joan once the English have got her? I speak first, for the army. The day after she has been dragged from her horse by a goddam or a Burgundian, and he is not struck dead: the day after she is locked in a dungeon, and the bars and bolts do not fly open at the touch of St Peter's angel: the day when the enemy finds out that she is as vulnerable as I am and not a bit more invincible, she will not be worth the life of a single soldier to us; and I will not risk that life, much as I cherish her as a companion-in-arms.

JOAN I dont blame you, Jack: you are right. I am not worth one soldier's life if God lets me be beaten; but France may think me worth my ransom after what God has done for her through me.

CHARLES I tell you I have no money; and this coronation, which is all your fault, has cost me the last farthing I can borrow.

JOAN The Church is richer than you. I put my trust in the Church.

THE ARCHBISHOP Woman: they will drag you through the streets, and burn you as a witch.

JOAN [*running to him*] Oh, my lord, do not say that. It is impossible. I a witch!

THE ARCHBISHOP Peter Cauchon knows his business. The University of Paris has burnt a woman for saying that what you have done was well done, and according to God.

JOAN [*bewildered*] But why? What sense is there in it? What I have done is according to God. They could not burn a woman for speaking the truth.

THE ARCHBISHOP They did.

JOAN But you know that she was speaking the truth. You would not let them burn me.

THE ARCHBISHOP How could I prevent them?

JOAN You would speak in the name of the Church. You are a great prince of the Church. I would go anywhere with your blessing to protect me.

THE ARCHBISHOP I have no blessing for you while you are proud and disobedient.

JOAN Oh, why will you go on saying things like that? I am not proud and disobedient. I am a poor girl, and so ignorant that I do not know A from B. How could I be proud? And how can you say that I am disobedient when I always obey my voices, because they come from God.

THE ARCHBISHOP   The voice of God on earth is the voice of the Church Militant; and all the voices that come to you are the echoes of your own wilfulness.

JOAN   It is not true.

THE ARCHBISHOP [*flushing angrily*]   You tell the Archbishop in his cathedral that he lies; and yet you say you are not proud and disobedient.

JOAN   I never said you lied. It was you that as good as said my voices lied. When have they ever lied? If you will not believe in them: even if they are only the echoes of my own commonsense, are they not always right? and are not your earthly counsels always wrong?

THE ARCHBISHOP [*indignantly*]   It is waste of time admonishing you.

CHARLES   It always comes back to the same thing. She is right; and everyone else is wrong.

THE ARCHBISHOP   Take this as your last warning. If you perish through setting your private judgment above the instructions of your spiritual directors, the Church disowns you, and leaves you to whatever fate your presumption may bring upon you. The Bastard has told you that if you persist in setting up your military conceit above the counsels of your commanders—

DUNOIS [*interposing*]   To put it quite exactly, if you attempt to relieve the garrison in Compiègne without the same superiority in numbers you had at Orleans—

THE ARCHBISHOP   The army will disown you, and will not rescue you. And His Majesty the King has told you that the throne has not the means of ransoming you.

CHARLES   Not a penny.

THE ARCHBISHOP   You stand alone: absolutely alone, trusting to your own conceit, your own ignorance, your own headstrong presumption, your own impiety in hiding all these sins under the cloak of a trust in God. When you pass through these doors into the sunlight, the crowd will cheer you. They will bring you their little children and their invalids to heal: they will kiss your hands and feet, and do what they can, poor simple souls, to turn your head, and madden you with the self-confidence that is leading you to your destruction. But you will be none the less alone: they cannot save you. We and we only can stand between you and the stake at which our enemies have burnt that wretched woman in Paris.

JOAN [*her eyes skyward*]   I have better friends and better counsel than yours.

THE ARCHBISHOP   I see that I am speaking in vain to a hardened heart. You reject our protection, and are determined to turn us all against you. In future, then, fend for yourself; and if you fail, God have mercy on your soul.

DUNOIS   That is the truth, Joan. Heed it.

JOAN   Where would you all have been now if I had heeded that sort of truth? There is no help, no counsel, in any of you. Yes: I am alone on earth: I have always been alone. My father told my brothers to drown me if I would not stay to mind his sheep while France was bleeding to death: France might perish if only our lambs were safe. I thought France would have friends at the court of the king of France; and I find only wolves fighting for pieces of her poor torn body. I thought God would have friends everywhere, because He is the friend of everyone; and in my innocence I believed that you who now cast me out would be like strong towers to keep harm from me. But I am wiser now; and nobody is any the worse for being wiser. Do not think you can frighten me by telling me that I am alone. France is alone; and God is alone; and what is my loneliness before the loneliness of my country and my God? I see now that the loneliness of God is His strength: what would He be if He listened to your jealous little counsels? Well, my loneliness shall be my strength too; it is better to be alone with God: His friendship will not fail me, nor His counsel, nor His love. In His strength I will dare, and dare, and dare, until I die. I will go out now to the common people, and let the love in their eyes comfort me for the hate in yours. You will all be glad to see me burnt; but if I go through the fire I shall go through it to their hearts for ever and ever. And so, God be with me!

She goes from them. They stare after her in glum silence for a moment. Then GILLES DE RAIS *twirls his beard.*

BLUEBEARD   You know, the woman is quite impossible. I dont dislike her, really; but what are you to do with such a character?

DUNOIS   As God is my judge, if she fell into the Loire I would jump in in full armor to fish her out. But if she plays the fool at Compiègne, and gets caught, I must leave her to her doom.

LA HIRE   Then you had better chain me up; for I could follow her to hell when the spirit rises in her like that.

THE ARCHBISHOP   She disturbs my judgment too: there is a dangerous power in her outbursts. But the pit is open at her feet; and for good or evil we cannot turn her from it.

CHARLES   If only she would keep quiet, or go home!

They follow her dispiritedly.

Scene 6

Rouen, 30th May 1431. A great stone hall in the castle, arranged for a trial-at-law, but not a trial-by-jury, the court being the Bishop's court with the Inquisition participating: hence there are two raised chairs side by side for the Bishop and the Inquisitor as judges. Rows of chairs radiating from them at an obtuse angle are for the canons, the doctors of law and theology, and the Dominican monks, who act as assessors. In the angle is a table for the scribes, with stools. There is also a heavy rough wooden stool for the prisoner. All these are at the inner end of the hall. The further end is open to the courtyard through a row of arches. The court is shielded from the weather by screens and curtains.

Looking down the great hall from the middle of the inner end, the judicial chairs and scribes' table are to the right. The prisoner's stool is to the left. There are arched doors right and left. It is a fine sunshiny May morning.

WARWICK *comes in through the arched doorway on the judges' side, followed by his* PAGE.

THE PAGE [*pertly*]   I suppose your lordship is aware that we have no business here. This is an ecclesiastical court; and we are only the secular arm.

WARWICK   I am aware of that fact. Will it please your impudence to find the Bishop of Beauvais for me, and give him a hint that he can have a word with me here before the trial, if he wishes?

THE PAGE [*going*]   Yes, my lord.

WARWICK   And mind you behave yourself. Do not address him as Pious Peter.

THE PAGE   No, my lord. I shall be kind to him, because, when The Maid is brought in, Pious Peter will have to pick a peck of pickled pepper.

CAUCHON *enters through the same door with a Dominican monk and a canon, the latter carrying a brief.*

THE PAGE   The Right Reverend his lordship the Bishop of Beauvais. And two other reverend gentlemen.
WARWICK   Get out; and see that we are not interrupted.
THE PAGE   Right, my lord [*he vanishes airily.*]
CAUCHON   I wish your lordship good-morrow.
WARWICK   Good-morrow to your lordship. Have I had the pleasure of meeting your friends before? I think not.
CAUCHON [*introducing the monk, who is on his right*]   This, my lord, is Brother John Lemaître, of the order of St Dominic. He is acting as deputy for the Chief Inquisitor into the evil of heresy in France. Brother John: the Earl of Warwick.
WARWICK   Your Reverence is most welcome. We have no Inquisitor in England, unfortunately; though we miss him greatly, especially on occasions like the present.

The INQUISITOR *smiles patiently, and bows. He is a mild elderly gentleman, but has evident reserves of authority and firmness.*

CAUCHON [*introducing the Canon, who is on his left*]   This gentleman is Canon John D'Estivet, of the Chapter of Bayeux. He is acting as Promoter.
WARWICK   Promoter?
CAUCHON   Prosecutor, you would call him in civil law.
WARWICK   Ah! prosecutor. Quite, quite. I am very glad to make your acquaintance, Canon D'Estivet.

D'ESTIVET *bows.* [*He is on the young side of middle age, well mannered, but vulpine beneath his veneer.*]

WARWICK   May I ask what stage the proceedings have reached? It is now more than nine months since The Maid was captured at Compiègne by the Burgundians. It is fully four months since I bought her from the Burgundians for a very handsome sum, solely that she might be brought to justice. It is very nearly three months since I delivered her up to you, my Lord Bishop, as a person suspected of heresy. May I suggest that you are taking a rather unconscionable time to make up your minds about a very plain case? Is this trial never going to end?
THE INQUISITOR [*smiling*]   It has not yet begun, my lord.
WARWICK   Not yet begun! Why, you have been at it eleven weeks!
CAUCHON   We have not been idle, my lord. We have held fifteen examinations of The Maid: six public and nine private.
THE INQUISITOR [*always patiently smiling*]   You see, my lord, I have been present at only two of these examinations. They were proceedings of the Bishop's court solely, and not of the Holy Office. I have only just decided to associate myself—that is, to associate the Holy Inquisition—with the Bishop's court. I did not at first think that this was a case of heresy at all. I regarded it as a political

case, and The Maid as a prisoner of war. But having now been present at two of the examinations, I must admit that this seems to be one of the gravest cases of heresy within my experience. Therefore everything is now in order, and we proceed to trial this morning. [*He moves towards the judicial chairs.*]

CAUCHON   This moment, if your lordship's convenience allows.

WARWICK [*graciously*]   Well, that is good news, gentlemen. I will not attempt to conceal from you that our patience was becoming strained.

CAUCHON   So I gathered from the threats of your soldiers to drown those of our people who favor The Maid.

WARWICK   Dear me! At all events their intentions were friendly to you, my lord.

CAUCHON [*sternly*]   I hope not. I am determined that the woman shall have a fair hearing. The justice of the Church is not a mockery, my lord.

THE INQUISITOR [*returning*]   Never has there been a fairer examination within my experience, my lord. The Maid needs no lawyers to take her part: she will be tried by her most faithful friends, all ardently desirous to save her soul from perdition.

D'ESTIVET   Sir: I am the Promoter; and it has been my painful duty to present the case against the girl; but believe me, I would throw up my case today and hasten to her defence if I did not know that men far my superiors in learning and piety, in eloquence and persuasiveness, have been sent to reason with her, to explain to her the danger she is running, and the ease with which she may avoid it. [*Suddenly bursting into forensic eloquence, to the disgust of* CAUCHON *and the* INQUISITOR, *who have listened to him so far with patronizing approval*] Men have dared to say that we are acting from hate; but God is our witness that they lie. Have we tortured her? No. Have we ceased to exhort her; to implore her to have pity on herself; to come to the bosom of her Church as an erring but beloved child? Have we—

CAUCHON [*interrupting drily*]   Take care, Canon. All that you say is true; but if you make his lordship believe it I will not answer for your life, and hardly for my own.

WARWICK [*deprecating, but by no means denying*]   Oh, my lord, you are very hard on us poor English. But we certainly do not share your pious desire to save The Maid: in fact I tell you now plainly that her death is a political necessity which I regret but cannot help. If the Church lets her go—

CAUCHON [*with fierce and menacing pride*]   If the Church lets her go, woe to the man, were he the Emperor himself, who dares lay a finger on her! The Church is not subject to political necessity, my lord.

THE INQUISITOR [*interposing smoothly*]   You need have no anxiety about the result, my lord. You have an invincible ally in the matter: one who is far more determined than you that she shall burn.

WARWICK   And who is this very convenient partisan, may I ask?

THE INQUISITOR   The Maid herself. Unless you put a gag in her mouth you cannot prevent her from convicting herself ten times over every time she opens it.

D'ESTIVET   That is perfectly true, my lord. My hair bristles on my head when I hear so young a creature utter such blasphemies.

WARWICK   Well, by all means do your best for her if you are quite sure it will be of no avail. [*Looking hard at* CAUCHON] I should be sorry to have to act without the blessing of the Church.

CAUCHON [*with a mixture of cynical admiration and contempt*]   And yet they say Englishmen are hypocrites! You play for your side, my lord, even at the peril of your soul. I cannot but admire such devotion; but I dare not go so far myself. I fear damnation.

WARWICK   If we feared anything we could never govern England, my lord. Shall I send your people in to you?

CAUCHON   Yes: it will be very good of your lordship to withdraw and allow the court to assemble.

WARWICK *turns on his heel, and goes out through the courtyard.* CAUCHON *takes one of the judicial seats; and* D'ESTIVET *sits at the scribes' table, studying his brief.*

CAUCHON [*casually, as he makes himself comfortable*]   What scoundrels these English nobles are!

THE INQUISITOR [*taking the other judicial chair on* CAUCHON's *left*]   All secular power makes men scoundrels. They are not trained for the work; and they have not the Apostolic Succession. Our own nobles are just as bad.

The BISHOP's *assessors hurry into the hall, headed by* CHAPLAIN DE STOGUMBER *and* CANON DE COURCELLES, *a young priest of 30. The scribes sit at the table, leaving a chair vacant opposite* D'ESTIVET. *Some of the assessors take their seats: others stand chatting, waiting for the proceedings to begin formally.* DE STOGUM-BER, *aggrieved and obstinate, will not take his seat: neither will the* CANON, *who stands on his right.*

CAUCHON   Good morning, Master de Stogumber. [*To the* INQUISITOR] Chaplain to the Cardinal of England.

THE CHAPLAIN [*correcting him*]   Of Winchester, my lord. I have to make a protest, my lord.

CAUCHON   You make a great many.

THE CHAPLAIN   I am not without support, my lord. Here is Master de Cour-celles, Canon of Paris, who associates himself with me in my protest.

CAUCHON   Well, what is the matter?

THE CHAPLAIN [*sulkily*]   Speak you, Master de Courcelles, since I do not seem to enjoy his lordship's confidence. [*He sits down in dudgeon next to* CAUCHON, *on his right.*]

COURCELLES   My lord: we have been at great pains to draw up an indictment of The Maid on sixty-four counts. We are now told that they have been reduced, without consulting us.

THE INQUISITOR   Master de Courcelles: I am the culprit. I am overwhelmed with admiration for the zeal displayed in your sixty-four counts; but in accusing a heretic, as in other things, enough is enough. Also you must remember that all the members of the court are not so subtle and profound as you, and that some of your very great learning might appear to them to be very great nonsense. There-fore I have thought it well to have your sixty-four articles cut down to twelve—

COURCELLES [*thunderstruck*]   Twelve!!!

THE INQUISITOR   Twelve will, believe me, be quite enough for your purpose.

THE CHAPLAIN   But some of the most important points have been reduced almost to nothing. For instance, The Maid has actually declared that the blessed saints Margaret and Catherine, and the holy Archangel Michael, spoke to her in French. That is a vital point.

THE INQUISITOR   You think, doubtless, that they should have spoken in Latin?

CAUCHON   No: he thinks they should have spoken in English.

THE CHAPLAIN   Naturally, my lord.

THE INQUISITOR   Well, as we are all here agreed, I think, that these voices of The Maid are the voices of evil spirits tempting her to her damnation, it would not be very courteous to you, Master de Stogumber, or to the King of England, to assume that English is the devil's native language. So let it pass. The matter is not wholly omitted from the twelve articles. Pray take your places, gentlemen; and let us proceed to business.

All who have not taken their seats, do so.

THE CHAPLAIN   Well I protest. That is all.

COURCELLES   I think it hard that all our work should go for nothing. It is only another example of the diabolical influence which this woman exercises over the court. [*He takes his chair, which is on the* CHAPLAIN's *right.*]

CAUCHON   Do you suggest that I am under diabolical influence?

COURCELLES   I suggest nothing, my lord. But it seems to me that there is a conspiracy here to hush up the fact that The Maid stole the Bishop of Senlis's horse.

CAUCHON [*keeping his temper with difficulty*]   This is not a police court. Are we to waste our time on such rubbish?

COURCELLES [*rising, shocked*]   My lord: do you call the Bishop's horse rubbish?

THE INQUISITOR [*blandly*]   Master de Courcelles: The Maid alleges that she paid handsomely for the Bishop's horse, and that if he did not get the money the fault was not hers. As that may be true, the point is one on which The Maid may well be acquitted.

COURCELLES   Yes, if it were an ordinary horse. But the Bishop's horse! how can she be acquitted for that? [*He sits down again, bewildered and discouraged.*]

THE INQUISITOR   I submit to you, with great respect, that if we persist in trying The Maid on trumpery issues on which we may have to declare her innocent, she may escape us on the great main issue of heresy, on which she seems so far to insist on her own guilt. I will ask you, therefore, to say nothing, when The Maid is brought before us, of these stealings of horses, and dancings round fairy trees with the village children, and prayings at haunted wells, and a dozen other things which you were diligently inquiring into until my arrival. There is not a village girl in France against whom you could not prove such things: they all dance round haunted trees, and pray at magic wells. Some of them would steal the Pope's horse if they got the chance. Heresy, gentlemen, heresy is the charge we have to try. The detection and suppression of heresy is my peculiar business: I am here as an inquisitor, not as an ordinary magistrate. Stick to the heresy, gentlemen, and leave the other matters alone.

CAUCHON   I may say that we have sent to the girl's village to make inquiries about her, and there is practically nothing serious against her.

THE CHAPLAIN	[*rising and clamoring together*]	Nothing serious, may lord—
COURCELLES		What! The fairy tree not—

CAUCHON [*out of patience*]   Be silent, gentlemen; or speak one at a time.

COURCELLES *collapses into his chair, intimidated.*

THE CHAPLAIN [*sulkily resuming his seat*] That is what The Maid said to us last Friday.

CAUCHON I wish you had followed her counsel, sir. When I say nothing serious, I mean nothing that men of sufficiently large mind to conduct an inquiry like this would consider serious. I agree with my colleague the Inquisitor that it is on the count of heresy that we must proceed.

LADVENU [*a young but ascetically fine-drawn Dominican who is sitting next* COURCELLES, *on his right*] But is there any great harm in the girl's heresy? Is it not merely her simplicity? Many saints have said as much as Joan.

THE INQUISITOR [*dropping his blandness and speaking very gravely*] Brother Martin: if you had seen what I have seen of heresy, you would not think it a light thing even in its most apparently harmless and even lovable and pious origins. Heresy begins with people who are to all appearance better than their neighbors. A gentle and pious girl, or a young man who has obeyed the command of our Lord by giving all his riches to the poor, and putting on the garb of poverty, the life of austerity, and the rule of humility and charity, may be the founder of a heresy that will wreck both Church and Empire if not ruthlessly stamped out in time. The records of the holy Inquisition are full of histories we dare not give to the world, because they are beyond the belief of honest men and innocent women; yet they all began with saintly simpletons. I have seen this again and again. Mark what I say: the woman who quarrels with her clothes, and puts on the dress of a man, is like the man who throws off his fur gown and dresses like John the Baptist: they are followed, as surely as the night follows the day, by bands of wild women and men who refuse to wear any clothes at all. When maids will neither marry nor take regular vows, and men reject marriage and exalt their lusts into divine inspirations, then, as surely as the summer follows the spring, they begin with polygamy, and end by incest. Heresy at first seems innocent and even laudable; but it ends in such a monstrous horror of unnatural wickedness that the most tenderhearted among you, if you saw it at work as I have seen it, would clamor against the mercy of the Church in dealing with it. For two hundred years the Holy Office has striven with these diabolical madnesses; and it knows that they begin always by vain and ignorant persons setting up their own judgment against the Church, and taking it upon themselves to be the interpreters of God's will. You must not fall into the common error of mistaking these simpletons for liars and hypocrites. They believe honestly and sincerely that their diabolical inspiration is divine. Therefore you must be on your guard against your natural compassion. You are all, I hope, merciful men: how else could you have devoted your lives to the service of our gentle Savior? You are going to see before you a young girl, pious and chaste; for I must tell you, gentlemen, that the things said of her by our English friends are supported by no evidence, whilst there is abundant testimony that her excesses have been excesses of religion and charity and not of worldliness and wantonness. This girl is not one of those whose hard features are the sign of hard hearts, and whose brazen looks and lewd demeanor condemn them before they are accused. The devilish pride that has led her into her present peril has left no mark on her countenance. Strange as it may seem to you, it has even left no mark on her character outside those special matters in which she is proud; so that you will see a diabolical pride and a natural humility seated side by side in the selfsame soul. Therefore be on your guard. God forbid that I should tell you to harden your hearts; for her punishment if we condemn her will be so cruel that we should forfeit our own hope of divine mercy were there one grain of malice against her in our hearts. But if you hate cruelty—and if any man here does not hate it I command him on his soul's salvation to quit this holy court—I say, if you hate cruelty, remember that nothing is so cruel in its consequences as the toleration of heresy. Remember also that no court of law can be so cruel as the common people are to those whom they suspect of heresy. The heretic in the hands of the Holy Office is safe from violence, is assured of a fair trial, and cannot suffer death, even when guilty, if repentance follows sin. Innumerable lives of heretics have been saved because the Holy Office has taken them out of the hands of the people, and because the people have yielded them up, knowing that the Holy Office would deal with them. Before the Holy Inquisition existed, and even now when its officers are not within reach, the unfortunate wretch suspected of heresy, perhaps quite ignorantly and unjustly, is stoned, torn in pieces, drowned, burned in his house with all his innocent children, without a trial, unshriven, unburied save as a dog is buried: all of them deeds hateful to God and most cruel to man. Gentlemen: I am compassionate by nature as well as by my profession; and though the work I have to do may seem cruel to those who do not know how much more cruel it would be to leave it undone, I would go to the stake myself sooner than do it if I did not know its righteousness, its necessity, its essential mercy. I ask you to address yourself to this trial in that conviction. Anger is a bad counsellor: cast out anger. Pity is sometimes worse: cast out pity. But do not cast out mercy. Remember only that justice comes first. Have you anything to say, my lord, before we proceed to trial?

CAUCHON   You have spoken for me, and spoken better than I could. I do not see how any sane man could disagree with a word that has fallen from you. But this I will add. The crude heresies of which you have told us are horrible; but their horror is like that of the black death: they rage for a while and then die out, because sound and sensible men will not under any incitement be reconciled to nakedness and incest and polygamy and the like. But we are confronted today throughout Europe with a heresy that is spreading among men not weak in mind nor diseased in brain: nay, the stronger the mind, the more obstinate the heretic. It is neither discredited by fantastic extremes nor corrupted by the common lusts of the flesh; but it, too, sets up the private judgment of the single erring mortal against the considered wisdom and experience of the Church. The mighty structure of Catholic Christendom will never be shaken by naked madmen or by the sins of Moab and Ammon. But it may be betrayed from within, and brought to barbarous ruin and desolation, by this arch heresy which the English Commander calls Protestantism.

THE ASSESSORS [*whispering*]   Protestantism! What was that? What does the Bishop mean? Is it a new heresy? The English Commander, he said. Did you ever hear of Protestantism? etc., etc.

CAUCHON [*continuing*]   And that reminds me. What provision has the Earl of Warwick made for the defence of the secular arm should The Maid prove obdurate, and the people be moved to pity her?

THE CHAPLAIN   Have no fear on that score, my lord. The noble earl has eight hundred men-at-arms at the gates. She will not slip through our English fingers even if the whole city be on her side.

CAUCHON [*revolted*] Will you not add, God grant that she repent and purge her sin?

THE CHAPLAIN   That does not seem to me to be consistent; but of course I agree with your lordship.

CAUCHON [*giving him up with a shrug of contempt*]   The court sits.

THE INQUISITOR   Let the accused be brought in.

LADVENU [*calling*]   The accused. Let her be brought in.

JOAN, *chained by the ankles, is brought in through the arched door behind the prisoner's stool by a guard of English soldiers. With them is the* EXECUTIONER *and his assistants. They lead her to the prisoner's stool, and place themselves behind it after taking off her chain. She wears a page's black suit. Her long imprisonment and the strain of the examinations which have preceded the trial have left their mark on her; but her vitality still holds: she confronts the court unabashed, without a trace of the awe which their formal solemnity seems to require for the complete success of its impressiveness.*

THE INQUISITOR [*kindly*]   Sit down, Joan. [*She sits on the prisoner's stool.*] You look very pale today. Are you not well?

JOAN   Thank you kindly: I am well enough. But the Bishop sent me some carp; and it made me ill.

CAUCHON   I am sorry. I told them to see that it was fresh.

JOAN   You meant to be good to me, I know; but it is a fish that does not agree with me. The English thought you were trying to poison me—

CAUCHON } [*together*] { What!
THE CHAPLAIN }   { No, my lord.

JOAN [*continuing*]   They are determined that I shall be burnt as a witch; and they sent their doctor to cure me; but he was forbidden to bleed me because the silly people believe that a witch's witchery leaves her if she is bled; so he only called me filthy names. Why do you leave me in the hands of the English? I should be in the hands of the Church. And why must I be chained by the feet to a log of wood? Are you afraid I will fly away?

D'ESTIVET [*harshly*]   Woman: it is not for you to question the court: it is for us to question you.

COURCELLES   When you were left unchained, did you not try to escape by jumping from a tower sixty feet high? If you cannot fly like a witch, how is it that you are still alive?

JOAN   I suppose because the tower was not so high then. It has grown higher every day since you began asking me questions about it.

D'ESTIVET   Why did you jump from the tower?

JOAN   How do you know that I jumped?

D'ESTIVET   You were found lying in the moat. Why did you leave the tower?

JOAN   Why would anybody leave a prison if they could get out?

D'ESTIVET   You tried to escape?

JOAN   Of course I did; and not for the first time either. If you leave the door of the cage open the bird will fly out.

D'ESTIVET [*rising*]   That is a confession of heresy. I call the attention of the court to it.

JOAN   Heresy, he calls it! Am I a heretic because I try to escape from prison?

D'ESTIVET   Assuredly, if you are in the hands of the Church, and you wilfully take yourself out of its hands, you are deserting the Church; and that is heresy.

JOAN   It is great nonsense. Nobody could be such a fool as to think that.

D'ESTIVET   You hear, my lord, how I am reviled in the execution of my duty by this woman. [*He sits down indignantly.*]

CAUCHON   I have warned you before, Joan, that you are doing yourself no good by these pert answers.

JOAN   But you will not talk sense to me. I am reasonable if you will be reasonable.

THE INQUISITOR [*interposing*]   This is not yet in order. You forget, Master Promoter, that the proceedings have not been formally opened. The time for questions is after she has sworn on the Gospels to tell us the whole truth.

JOAN   You say this to me every time. I have said again and again that I will tell you all that concerns this trial. But I cannot tell you the whole truth: God does not allow the whole truth to be told. You do not understand it when I tell it. It is an old saying that he who tells too much truth is sure to be hanged. I am weary of this argument: we have been over it nine times already. I have sworn as much as I will swear; and I will swear no more.

COURCELLES   My lord: she should be put to the torture.

THE INQUISITOR   You hear, Joan? That is what happens to the obdurate. Think before you answer. Has she been shewn the instruments?

THE EXECUTIONER   They are ready, my lord. She has seen them.

JOAN   If you tear me limb from limb until you separate my soul from my body you will get nothing out of me beyond what I have told you. What more is there to tell that you could understand? Besides, I cannot bear to be hurt; and if you hurt me I will say anything you like to stop the pain. But I will take it all back afterwards; so what is the use of it?

LADVENU   There is much in that. We should proceed mercifully.

COURCELLES   But the torture is customary.

THE INQUISITOR   It must not be applied wantonly. If the accused will confess voluntarily, then its use cannot be justified.

COURCELLES   But this is unusual and irregular. She refuses to take the oath.

LADVENU [*disgusted*]   Do you want to torture the girl for the mere pleasure of it?

COURCELLES [*bewildered*]   But it is not a pleasure. It is the law. It is customary. It is always done.

THE INQUISITOR   That is not so, Master, except when the inquiries are carried on by people who do not know their legal business.

COURCELLES   But the woman is a heretic. I assure you it is always done.

CAUCHON [*decisively*]   It will not be done today if it is not necessary. Let there be an end of this. I will not have it said that we proceeded on forced confessions. We have sent our best preachers and doctors to this woman to exhort and implore her to save her soul and body from the fire: we shall not now send the executioner to thrust her into it.

COURCELLES   Your lordship is merciful, of course. But it is a great responsibility to depart from the usual practice.

JOAN   Thou art a rare noodle, Master. Do what was done last time is thy rule, eh?

COURCELLES [*rising*]   Thou wanton: dost thou dare call me noodle?

THE INQUISITOR   Patience, Master, patience: I fear you will soon be only too terribly avenged.

COURCELLES [*mutters*]   Noodle indeed! [*He sits down, much discontented.*]

THE INQUISITOR   Meanwhile, let us not be moved by the rough side of a shepherd lass's tongue.

JOAN   Nay: I am no shepherd lass, though I have helped with the sheep like anyone else. I will do a lady's work in the house—spin or weave—against any woman in Rouen.

THE INQUISITOR   This is not a time for vanity, Joan. You stand in great peril.

JOAN   I know it: have I not been punished for my vanity? If I had not worn my cloth of gold surcoat in battle like a fool, that Burgundian soldier would never have pulled me backwards off my horse; and I should not have been here.

THE CHAPLAIN   If you are so clever at woman's work why do you not stay at home and do it?

JOAN   There are plenty of other women to do it; but there is nobody to do my work.

CAUCHON   Come! we are wasting time on trifles. Joan: I am going to put a most solemn question to you. Take care how you answer; for your life and salvation are at stake on it. Will you for all you have said and done, be it good or bad, accept the judgment of God's Church on earth? More especially as to the acts and words that are imputed to you in this trial by the Promoter here, will you submit your case to the inspired interpretation of the Church Militant?

JOAN   I am a faithful child of the Church. I will obey the Church—

CAUCHON [*hopefully leaning forward*]   You will?

JOAN   —provided it does not command anything impossible.

CAUCHON *sinks back in his chair with a heavy sigh.* THE INQUISITOR *purses his lips and frowns.* LADVENU *shakes his head pitifully.*

D'ESTIVET   She imputes to the Church the error and folly of commanding the impossible.

JOAN   If you command me to declare that all that I have done and said, and all the visions and revelations I have had, were not from God, then that is impossible: I will not declare it for anything in the world. What God made me do I will never go back on; and what He has commanded or shall command I will not fail to do in spite of any man alive. That is what I mean by impossible. And in case the Church should bid me do anything contrary to the command I have from God, I will not consent to it, no matter what it may be.

THE ASSESSORS [*shocked and indignant*]   Oh! The Church contrary to God! What do you say now? Flat heresy. This is beyond everything, etc., etc.

D'ESTIVET [*throwing down his brief*]   My lord: do you need anything more than this?

CAUCHON   Woman: you have said enough to burn ten heretics. Will you not be warned? Will you not understand?

THE INQUISITOR   If the Church Militant tells you that your revelations and visions are sent by the devil to tempt you to your damnation, will you not believe that the Church is wiser than you?

JOAN   I believe that God is wiser than I; and it is His commands that I will do. All the things that you call my crimes have come to me by the command of God.

I say that I have done them by the order of God: it is impossible for me to say anything else. If any Churchman says the contrary I shall not mind him: I shall mind God alone, whose command I always follow.

LADVENU [*pleading with her urgently*] You do not know what you are saying, child. Do you want to kill yourself? Listen. Do you not believe that you are subject to the Church of God on earth?

JOAN   Yes. When have I ever denied it?

LADVENU   Good. That means, does it not, that you are subject to our Lord the Pope, to the cardinals, the archbishops, and the bishops for whom his lordship stands here today?

JOAN   God must be served first.

D'ESTIVET   Then your voices command you not to submit yourself to the Church Militant?

JOAN   My voices do not tell me to disobey the Church; but God must be served first.

CAUCHON   And you, and not the Church, are to be the judge?

JOAN   What other judgment can I judge by but my own?

THE ASSESSORS [*scandalized*] Oh! [*They cannot find words.*]

CAUCHON   Out of your own mouth you have condemned yourself. We have striven for your salvation to the verge of sinning ourselves: we have opened the door to you again and again; and you have shut it in our faces and in the face of God. Dare you pretend, after what you have said, that you are in a state of grace?

JOAN   If I am not, may God bring me to it: if I am, may God keep me in it!

LADVENU   That is a very good reply, my lord.

COURCELLES   Were you in a state of grace when you stole the Bishop's horse?

CAUCHON [*rising in a fury*] Oh, devil take the Bishop's horse and you too! We are here to try a case of heresy; and no sooner do we come to the root of the matter than we are thrown back by idiots who understand nothing but horses. [*Trembling with rage, he forces himself to sit down.*]

THE INQUISITOR   Gentlemen, gentlemen: in clinging to these small issues you are The Maid's best advocates. I am not surprised that his lordship has lost patience with you. What does the Promoter say? Does he press these trumpery matters?

D'ESTIVET   I am bound by my office to press everything; but when the woman confesses a heresy that must bring upon her the doom of excommunication, of what consequence is it that she has been guilty also of offences which expose her to minor penances? I share the impatience of his lordship as to these minor charges. Only, with great respect, I must emphasize the gravity of two very horrible and blasphemous crimes which she does not deny. First, she has intercourse with evil spirits, and is therefore a sorceress. Second, she wears men's clothes, which is indecent, unnatural, and abominable; and in spite of our most earnest remonstrances and entreaties, she will not change them even to receive the sacrament.

JOAN   Is the blessed St Catherine an evil spirit? Is St Margaret? Is Michael the Archangel?

COURCELLES   How do you know that the spirit which appears to you is an archangel? Does he not appear to you as a naked man?

JOAN   Do you think God cannot afford clothes for him?

The assessors cannot help smiling, especially as the joke is against COURCELLES.

LADVENU   Well answered, Joan.

THE INQUISITOR   It is, in effect, well answered. But no evil spirit would be so simple as to appear to a young girl in a guise that would scandalize her when he meant her to take him for a messenger from the Most High. Joan: the Church instructs you that these apparitions are demons seeking your soul's perdition. Do you accept the instruction of the Church?

JOAN   I accept the messenger of God. How could any faithful believer in the Church refuse him?

CAUCHON   Wretched woman: again I ask you, do you know what you are saying?

THE INQUISITOR   You wrestle in vain with the devil for her soul, my lord: she will not be saved. Now as to this matter of the man's dress. For the last time, will you put off that impudent attire, and dress as becomes your sex?

JOAN   I will not.

D'ESTIVET [*pouncing*]   The sin of disobedience, my lord.

JOAN [*distressed*]   But my voices tell me I must dress as a soldier.

LADVENU   Joan, Joan: does not that prove to you that the voices are the voices of evil spirits? Can you suggest to us one good reason why an angel of God should give you such shameless advice?

JOAN   Why, yes: what can be plainer commonsense? I was a soldier living among soldiers. I am a prisoner guarded by soldiers. If I were to dress as a woman they would think of me as a woman; and then what would become of me? If I dress as a soldier they think of me as a soldier, and I can live with them as I do at home with my brothers. That is why St Catherine tells me I must not dress as a woman until she gives me leave.

COURCELLES   When will she give you leave?

JOAN   When you take me out of the hands of the English soldiers. I have told you that I should be in the hands of the Church, and not left night and day with four soldiers of the Earl of Warwick. Do you want me to live with them in petticoats?

LADVENU   My lord: what she says is, God knows, very wrong and shocking; but there is a grain of worldly sense in it such as might impose on a simple village maiden.

JOAN   If we were as simple in the village as you are in your courts and palaces, there would soon be no wheat to make bread for you.

CAUCHON   That is the thanks you get for trying to save her, Brother Martin.

LADVENU   Joan: we are all trying to save you. His lordship is trying to save you. The Inquisitor could not be more just to you if you were his own daughter. But you are blinded by a terrible pride and self-sufficiency.

JOAN   Why do you say that? I have said nothing wrong. I cannot understand.

THE INQUISITOR   The blessed St Athanasius has laid it down in his creed that those who cannot understand are damned. It is not enough to be simple. It is not enough even to be what simple people call good. The simplicity of a darkened mind is no better than the simplicity of a beast.

JOAN   There is great wisdom in the simplicity of a beast, let me tell you; and sometimes great foolishness in the wisdom of scholars.

LADVENU   We know that, Joan: we are not so foolish as you think us. Try to resist the temptation to make pert replies to us. Do you see that man who stands behind you [*he indicates the* EXECUTIONER]?

JOAN [*turning and looking at the man*]   Your torturer? But the Bishop said I was not to be tortured.

LADVENU   You are not to be tortured because you have confessed everything that is necessary to your condemnation. That man is not only the torturer: he is also the Executioner. Executioner: let The Maid hear your answers to my questions. Are you prepared for the burning of a heretic this day?

THE EXECUTIONER   Yes, Master.

LADVENU   Is the stake ready?

THE EXECUTIONER   It is. In the market-place. The English have built it too high for me to get near her and make the death easier. It will be a cruel death.

JOAN [*horrified*]   But you are not going to burn me now?

THE INQUISITOR   You realize it at last.

LADVENU   There are eight hundred English soldiers waiting to take you to the market-place the moment the sentence of excommunication has passed the lips of your judges. You are within a few short moments of that doom.

JOAN [*looking round desperately for rescue*]   Oh God!

LADVENU   Do not despair Joan. The Church is merciful. You can save yourself.

JOAN [*hopefully*]   Yes: my voices promised me I should not be burnt. St Catherine bade me be bold.

CAUCHON   Woman: are you quite mad? Do you not yet see that your voices have deceived you?

JOAN   Oh no: that is impossible.

CAUCHON   Impossible! They have led you straight to your excommunication, and to the stake which is there waiting for you.

LADVENU [*pressing the point hard*]   Have they kept a single promise to you since you were taken at Compiègne? The devil has betrayed you. The Church holds out its arms to you.

JOAN [*despairing*]   Oh, it is true: it is true: my voices have deceived me. I have been mocked by devils: my faith is broken. I have dared and dared; but only a fool will walk into a fire: God, who gave me my commonsense, cannot will me to do that.

LADVENU   Now God be praised that He has saved you at the eleventh hour! [*He hurries to the vacant seat at the scribes' table, and snatches a sheet of paper, on which he sets to work writing eagerly.*]

CAUCHON   Amen!

JOAN   What must I do?

CAUCHON   You must sign a solemn recantation of your heresy.

JOAN   Sign? That means to write my name. I cannot write.

CAUCHON   You have signed many letters before.

JOAN   Yes; but someone held my hand and guided the pen. I can make my mark.

THE CHAPLAIN [*who has been listening with growing alarm and indignation*]   My lord: do you mean that you are going to allow this woman to escape us?

THE INQUISITOR   The law must take its course, Master de Stogumber. And you know the law.

THE CHAPLAIN [*rising, purple with fury*]   I know that there is no faith in a Frenchman. [*Tumult, which he shouts down.*] I know what my lord the Cardinal of Winchester will say when he hears of this. I know what the Earl of Warwick will do when he learns that you intend to betray him. There are eight hundred men at the gate who will see that this abominable witch is burnt in spite of your teeth.

THE ASSESSORS [*meanwhile*]   What is this? What did he say? He accuses us of treachery! This is past bearing. No faith in a Frenchman! Did you hear that? This is an intolerable fellow. Who is he? Is this what English Churchmen are like? He must be mad or drunk, etc., etc.

THE INQUISITOR [*rising*]   Silence, pray! Gentlemen: pray silence! Master Chaplain: bethink you a moment of your holy office: of what you are, and where you are. I direct you to sit down.

THE CHAPLAIN [*folding his arms doggedly, his face working convulsively*]   I will NOT sit down.

CAUCHON   Master Inquisitor: this man has called me a traitor to my face before now.

THE CHAPLAIN   So you are a traitor. You are all traitors. You have been doing nothing but begging this damnable witch on your knees to recant all through this trial.

THE INQUISITOR [*placidly resuming his seat*]   If you will not sit, you must stand: that is all.

THE CHAPLAIN   I will NOT stand [*He flings himself back into his chair.*]

LADVENU [*rising with the paper in his hand*]   My lord: here is the form of recantation for The Maid to sign.

CAUCHON   Read it to her.

JOAN   Do not trouble. I will sign it.

THE INQUISITOR   Woman: you must know what you are putting your hand to. Read it to her, Brother Martin. And let all be silent.

LADVENU [*reading quietly*]   'I, Joan, commonly called The Maid, a miserable sinner, do confess that I have most grievously sinned in the following articles. I have pretended to have revelations from God and the angels and the blessed saints, and perversely rejected the Church's warnings that these were temptations by demons. I have blasphemed abominably by wearing an immodest dress, contrary to the Holy Scripture and the canons of the Church. Also I have clipped my hair in the style of a man, and, against all the duties which have made my sex specially acceptable in heaven, have taken up the sword, even to the shedding of human blood, inciting men to slay each other, invoking evil spirits to delude them, and stubbornly and most blasphemously imputing these sins to Almighty God. I confess to the sin of sedition, to the sin of idolatry, to the sin of disobedience, to the sin of pride, and to the sin of heresy. All of which sins I now renounce and abjure and depart from, humbly thanking you Doctors and Masters who have brought me back to the truth and into the grace of our Lord. And I will never return to my errors, but will remain in communion with our Holy Church and in obedience to our Holy Father the Pope of Rome. All this I swear by God Almighty and the Holy Gospels, in witness whereof I sign my name to this recantation.'

THE INQUISITOR   You understand this, Joan?

JOAN [*listless*]   It is plain enough, sir.

THE INQUISITOR   And it is true?

JOAN   It may be true. If it were not true, the fire would not be ready for me in the market-place.

LADVENU [*taking up his pen and a book, and going to her quickly lest she should compromise herself again*]   Come, child: let me guide your hand. Take

the pen. [*She does so; and they begin to write, using the book as a desk*]
J.E.H.A.N.E. So. Now make your mark by youself.

JOAN [*makes her mark, and gives him back the pen, tormented by the rebellion of her soul against her mind and body*]   There!

LADVENU [*replacing the pen on the table, and handing the recantation to* CAU-CHON *with a reverence*]   Praise be to God, my brothers, the lamb has returned to the flock; and the shepherd rejoices in her more than in ninety and nine just persons. [*He returns to his seat.*]

THE INQUISITOR [*taking the paper from* CAUCHON]   We declare thee by this act set free from the danger of excommunication in which thou stoodest. [*He throws the paper down to the table.*]

JOAN   I thank you.

THE INQUISITOR   But because thou has sinned most presumptuously against God and the Holy Church, and that thou mayst repent thy errors in solitary contemplation, and be shielded from all temptation to return to them, we, for the good of thy soul, and for a penance that may wipe out thy sins and bring thee finally unspotted to the throne of grace, do condemn thee to eat the bread of sorrow and drink the water of affliction to the end of thy earthly days in perpetual imprisonment.

JOAN [*rising in consternation and terrible anger*]   Perpetual imprisonment! Am I not then to be set free?

LADVENU [*mildly shocked*]   Set free, child, after such wickedness as yours! What are you dreaming of?

JOAN   Give me that writing. [*She rushes to the table; snatches up the paper; and tears it into fragments.*] Light your fire: do you think I dread it as much as the life of a rat in a hole? My voices were right.

LADVENU   Joan! Joan!

JOAN   Yes: they told me you were fools [*the word gives great offence*], and that I was not to listen to your fine words nor trust your charity. You promised me my life; but you lied [*indignant exclamations*]. You think that life is nothing but not being stone dead. It is not the bread and water I fear: I can live on bread: when have I asked for more? It is no hardship to drink water if the water be clean. Bread has no sorrow for me, and water no affliction. But to shut me from the light of the sky and the sight of the fields and flowers; to chain my feet so that I can never again ride with the soldiers nor climb the hills; to make me breathe foul damp darkness, and keep from me everything that brings me back to the love of God when your wickedness and foolishness tempt me to hate Him: all this is worse than the furnace in the Bible that was heated seven times. I could do without my warhorse; I could drag about in a skirt; I could let the banners and the trumpets and the knights and soldiers pass me and leave me behind as they leave the other women, if only I could still hear the wind in the trees, the larks in the sunshine, the young lambs crying through the healthy frost, and the blessed blessed church bells that send my angel voices floating to me on the wind. But without these things I cannot live; and by your wanting to take them away from me, or from any human creature, I know that your counsel is of the devil, and that mine is of God.

THE ASSESSORS [*in great commotion*]   Blasphemy! blasphemy! She is possessed. She said our counsel was of the devil. And hers of God. Monstrous! The devil is in our midst, etc., etc.

D'ESTIVET [*shouting above the din*]   She is a relapsed heretic, obstinate, incorrigible, and altogether unworthy of the mercy we have shewn her. I call for her excommunication.

    THE CHAPLAIN [*to the* EXECUTIONER] Light your fire, man. To the stake with her.

The EXECUTIONER *and his assistants hurry out through the courtyard.*

    LADVENU You wicked girl: if your counsel were of God would He not deliver you?

    JOAN His ways are not your ways. He wills that I go through the fire to His bosom; for I am His child, and you are not fit that I should live among you. That is my last word to you.

The soldiers seize her.

    CAUCHON [*rising*] Not yet.

They wait. There is a dead silence. CAUCHON *turns to the* INQUISITOR *with an inquiring look. The* INQUISITOR *nods affirmatively. They rise solemnly, and intone the sentence antiphonally.*

    CAUCHON We decree that thou art a relapsed heretic.

    THE INQUISITOR Cast out from the unity of the Church.

    CAUCHON Sundered from her body.

    THE INQUISITOR Infected with the leprosy of heresy.

    CAUCHON A member of Satan.

    THE INQUISITOR We declare that thou must be excommunicate.

    CAUCHON And now we do cast thee out, segregate thee, and abandon thee to the secular power.

    THE INQUISITOR Admonishing the same secular power that it moderate its judgment of thee in respect of death and division of the limbs. [*He resumes his seat.*]

    CAUCHON And if any true sign of penitence appear in thee, to permit our Brother Martin to administer to thee the sacrament of penance.

    THE CHAPLAIN Into the fire with the witch [*he rushes at her, and helps the soldiers to push her out*].

JOAN *is taken away through the courtyard. The assessors rise in disorder, and follow the soldiers, except* LADVENU, *who has hidden his face in his hands.*

    CAUCHON [*rising again in the the act of sitting down*] No, no: this is irregular. The representative of the secular arm should be here to receive her from us.

    THE INQUISITOR [*also on his feet again*] That man is an incorrigible fool.

    CAUCHON Brother Martin: see that everything is done in order.

    LADVENU My place is at her side, my Lord. You must exercise your own authority. [*He hurries out.*]

    CAUCHON These English are impossible: they will thrust her straight into the fire. Look!

He points to the courtyard, in which the glow and flicker of fire can now be seen reddening the May daylight. Only the BISHOP *and the* INQUISITOR *are left in the court.*

CAUCHON [*turning to go*] We must stop that.

THE INQUISITOR [*calmly*] Yes; but not too fast, my lord.

CAUCHON [*halting*] But there is not a moment to lose.

THE INQUISITOR We have proceeded in perfect order. If the English choose to put themselves in the wrong, it is not our business to put them in the right. A flaw in the procedure may be useful later on: one never knows. And the sooner it is over, the better for that poor girl.

CAUCHON [*relaxing*] That is true. But I suppose we must see this dreadful thing through.

THE INQUISITOR One gets used to it. Habit is everything. I am accustomed to the fire: it is soon over. But it is a terrible thing to see a young and innocent creature crushed between these mighty forces, the Church and the Law.

CAUCHON You call her innocent!

THE INQUISITOR Oh, quite innocent. What does she know of the Church and the Law? She did not understand a word we were saying. It is the ignorant who suffer. Come, or we shall be late for the end.

CAUCHON [*going with him*] I shall not be sorry if we are: I am not so accustomed as you.

They are going out when WARWICK *comes in, meeting them.*

WARWICK Oh, I am intruding. I thought it was all over. [*He makes a feint of retiring.*]

CAUCHON Do not go, my lord. It is all over.

THE INQUISITOR The execution is not in our hands, my lord; but it is desirable that we should witness the end. So by your leave—[*He bows, and goes out through the courtyard.*]

CAUCHON There is some doubt whether your people have observed the forms of law, my lord.

WARWICK I am told that there is some doubt whether your authority runs in this city, my lord. It is not in your diocese. However, if you will answer for that I will answer for the rest.

CAUCHON It is to God that we both must answer. Good morning, my lord.

WARWICK My lord: good morning.

They look at one another for a moment with unconcealed hostility. Then CAUCHON *follows the* INQUISITOR *out.* WARWICK *looks round. Finding himself alone, he calls for attendance.*

WARWICK Hallo: some attendance here! [*Silence*] Hallo, there! [*Silence*] Hallo! Brian, you young blackguard, where are you? [*Silence*] Guard! [*Silence*] They have all gone to see the burning: even that child.

The silence is broken by someone frantically howling and sobbing.

WARWICK What in the devil's name—?

THE CHAPLAIN *staggers in from the courtyard like a demented creature, his face streaming with tears, making the piteous sounds that* WARWICK *has heard. He stumbles to the prisoner's stool, and throws himself upon it with heartrending sobs.*

WARWICK [*going to him and patting him on the shoulder*]   What is it, Master John? What is the matter?

THE CHAPLAIN [*clutching at his hand*]   My lord, my lord: for Christ's sake pray for my wretched guilty soul.

WARWICK [*soothing him*]   Yes, yes: of course I will. Calmly, gently—

THE CHAPLAIN [*blubbering miserably*]   I am not a bad man, my lord.

WARWICK   No, no: not at all.

THE CHAPLAIN   I meant no harm. I did not know what it would be like.

WARWICK [*hardening*]   Oh! You saw it, then?

THE CHAPLAIN   I did not know what I was doing. I am a hotheaded fool; and I shall be damned to all eternity for it.

WARWICK   Nonsense! Very distressing, no doubt; but it was not your doing.

THE CHAPLAIN [*lamentably*]   I let them do it. If I had known, I would have torn her from their hands. You dont know: you havnt seen: it is so easy to talk when you dont know. You madden yourself with words: you damn yourself because it feels grand to throw oil on the flaming hell of your own temper. But when it is brought home to you; when you see the thing you have done; when it is blinding your eyes, stifling your nostrils, tearing your heart, then—then—[*Falling on his knees*] O God, take away this sight from me! O Christ, deliver me from this fire that is consuming me! She cried to Thee in the midst of it: Jesus! Jesus! Jesus! She is in Thy bosom; and I am in hell for evermore.

WARWICK [*summarily hauling him to his feet*]   Come come, man! you must pull yourself together. We shall have the whole town talking of this. [*He throws him not too gently into a chair at the table.*] If you have not the nerve to see these things, why do you not do as I do, and stay away?

THE CHAPLAIN [*bewildered and submissive*] She asked for a cross. A soldier gave her two sticks tied together. Thank God he was an Englishman! I might have done it; but I did not: I am a coward, a mad dog, a fool. But he was an Englishman too.

WARWICK   The fool! they will burn him too if the priests get hold of him.

THE CHAPLAIN [*shaken with a convulsion*]   Some of the people laughed at her. They would have laughed at Christ. They were French people, my lord: I know they were French.

WARWICK   Hush! someone is coming. Control yourself.

LADVENU *comes back through the courtyard to* WARWICK's *right hand, carrying a bishop's cross which he has taken from a church. He is very grave and composed.*

WARWICK   I am informed that it is all over, Brother Martin.

LADVENU [*enigmatically*]   We do not know, my lord. It may have only just begun.

WARWICK   What does that mean, exactly?

LADVENU   I took this cross from the church for her that she might see it to the last: she had only two sticks that she put into her bosom. When the fire crept round us, and she saw that if I held the cross before her I should be burnt myself, she warned me to get down and save myself. My lord: a girl who could think of another's danger in such a moment was not inspired by the devil. When I had to snatch the cross from her sight, she looked up to heaven. And I do not believe that the heavens were empty. I firmly believe that her Savior appeared to her then in His tenderest glory. She called to Him and died. This is not the end for her, but the beginning.

WARWICK   I am afraid it will have a bad effect on the people.

LADVENU   It had, my lord, on some of them. I heard laughter. Forgive me for saying that I hope and believe it was English laughter.

THE CHAPLAIN [*rising frantically*]   No: it was not. There was only one Eng-lishman there that disgraced his country; and that was the mad dog, de Stogumber. [*He rushes wildly out, shrieking.*] Let them torture him. Let them burn him. I will go pray among her ashes. I am no better than Judas: I will hang myself.

WARWICK   Quick, Brother Martin: follow him: he will do himself some mis-chief. After him, quick.

LADVENU *hurries out,* WARWICK *urging him. The* EXECUTIONER *comes in by the door behind the judges' chairs; and* WARWICK, *returning, finds himself face to face with him.*

WARWICK   Well, fellow: who are you?

THE EXECUTIONER [*with dignity*]   I am not addressed as fellow, my lord. I am the Master Executioner of Rouen: it is a highly skilled mystery. I am come to tell your lordship that your orders have been obeyed.

WARWICK   I crave you pardon, Master Executioner; and I will see that you lose nothing by having no relics to sell. I have your word, have I, that nothing remains, not a bone, not a nail, not a hair?

THE EXECUTIONER   Her heart would not burn, my lord; but everything that was left is at the bottom of the river. You have heard the last of her.

WARWICK [*with a wry smile, thinking of what* LADVENU *said*]   The last of her? Hm! I wonder!

Epilogue

A restless fitfully windy night in June 1456, full of summer lightning after many days of heat. KING CHARLES THE SEVENTH *of France, formerly Joan's Dauphin, now Charles the Victorious, aged 51, is in bed in one of his royal chateaux. The bed, raised on a dais of two steps, is towards the side of the room so as to avoid blocking a tall lancet window in the middle. Its canopy bears the royal arms in embroidery. Except for the canopy and the huge pillows there is nothing to distin-guish it from a broad settee with bed-clothes and a valance. Thus its occupant is in full view from the foot.*

CHARLES *is not asleep: he is reading in bed, or rather looking at the pictures in Fouquet's Boccaccio with his knees doubled up to make a reading desk. Beside the bed on his left is a little table with a picture of the Virgin, lighted by candles of painted wax. The walls are hung from ceiling to floor with painted curtains which stir at times in the draughts. At first glance the prevailing yellow and red in these hanging pictures is somewhat flamelike when the folds breathe in the wind.*

The door is on CHARLES's *left, but in front of him close to the corner farthest from him. A large watchman's rattle, handsomely designed and gaily painted, is in the bed under his hand.*

CHARLES *turns a leaf. A distant clock strikes the half-hour softly.* CHARLES *shuts the book with a clap; throws it aside; snatches up the rattle; and whirls it energetically, making a deafening clatter.* LADVENU *enters, 25 years older, strange and stark in bearing, and still carrying the cross from Rouen.* CHARLES *evidently does not expect him; for he springs out of bed on the farther side from the door.*

CHARLES   Who are you? Where is my gentleman of the bedchamber? What do you want?

LADVENU [*solemnly*]   I bring you glad tidings of great joy. Rejoice, O king; for the taint is removed from your blood, and the stain from your crown. Justice, long delayed, is at last triumphant.

CHARLES   What are you talking about? Who are you?

LADVENU   I am Brother Martin.

CHARLES   And who, saving your reverence, may Brother Martin be?

LADVENU   I held this cross when The Maid perished in the fire. Twenty-five years have passed since then: nearly ten thousand days. And on every one of those days I have prayed God to justify His daughter on earth as she is justified in heaven.

CHARLES [*reassured, sitting down on the foot of the bed*]   Oh, I remember now. I have heard of you. You have a bee in your bonnet about The Maid. Have you been at the inquiry?

LADVENU   I have given my testimony.

CHARLES   Is it over?

LADVENU   It is over.

CHARLES   Satisfactorily?

LADVENU   The ways of God are very strange.

CHARLES   How so?

LADVENU   At the trial which sent a saint to the stake as a heretic and a sorceress, the truth was told; the law was upheld; mercy was shewn beyond all custom; no wrong was done but the final and dreadful wrong of the lying sentence and the pitiless fire. At this inquiry from which I have just come, there was shameless perjury, courtly corruption, calumny of the dead who did their duty according to their lights, cowardly evasion of the issue, testimony made of idle tales that could not impose on a ploughboy. Yet out of this insult to justice, this defamation of the Church, this orgy of lying and foolishness, the truth is set in the noonday sun on the hilltop; the white robe of innocence is cleansed from the smirch of the burning faggots; the holy life is sanctified; the true heart that lived through the flame is consecrated; a great lie is silenced for ever; and a great wrong is set right before all men.

CHARLES   My friend: provided they can no longer say that I was crowned by a witch and a heretic, I shall not fuss about how the trick has been done. Joan would not have fussed about it if it came all right in the end: she was not that sort: I knew her. Is her rehabilitation complete? I made it pretty clear that there was to be no nonsense about it.

LADVENU   It is solemnly declared that her judges were full of corruption, cozenage, fraud, and malice. Four falsehoods.

CHARLES   Never mind the falsehoods: her judges are dead.

LADVENU   The sentence on her is broken, annulled, annihilated, set aside as non-existent, without value or effect.

CHARLES   Good. Nobody can challenge my consecration now, can they?

LADVENU   Not Charlemagne nor King David himself was more sacredly crowned.

CHARLES [*rising*]   Excellent. Think of what that means to me!

LADVENU   I think of what it means to her!

CHARLES   You cannot. None of us ever knew what anything meant to her. She was like nobody else; and she must take care of herself wherever she is; for *I* cannot take care of her; and neither can you, whatever you may think: you are not big enough. But I will tell you this about her. If you could bring her back to life, they would burn her again within six months, for all their present adoration of her. And you would hold up the cross, too, just the same. So [*Crossing himself*] let her rest; and let you and I mind our own business, and not meddle with hers.

LADVENU   God forbid that I should have no share in her, nor she in me! [*He turns and strides out as he came, saying*] Henceforth my path will not lie through palaces, nor my conversation be with kings.

CHARLES [*following him towards the door, and shouting after him*]   Much good may it do you, holy man! [*He returns to the middle of the chamber, where he halts, and says quizzically to himself*] That was a funny chap. How did he get in? Where are my people? [*He goes impatiently to the bed, and swings the rattle. A rush of wind through the open door sets the walls swaying agitatedly. The candles go out. He calls in the darkness*] Hallo! Someone come and shut the windows: everything is being blown all over the place. [*A flash of summer lightning shews up the lancet window. A figure is seen in silhouette against it.*] Who is there? Who is that? Help! Murder! [*Thunder. He jumps into bed, and hides under the clothes.*]

JOAN'S VOICE   Easy, Charlie, easy. What art making all that noise for? No one can hear thee. Thou'rt asleep. [*She is dimly seen in a pallid greenish light by the bedside.*]

CHARLES [*peeping out*]   Joan! Are you a ghost, Joan?

JOAN   Hardly even that, lad. Can a poor burnt-up lass have a ghost? I am but a dream that thou'rt dreaming. [*The light increases: they become plainly visible as he sits up.*] Thou looks older, lad.

CHARLES   I am older. Am I really asleep?

JOAN   Fallen asleep over thy silly book.

CHARLES   That's funny.

JOAN   Not so funny as that I am dead, is it?

CHARLES   Are you really dead?

JOAN   As dead as anybody ever is, laddie. I am out of the body.

CHARLES   Just fancy! Did it hurt much?

JOAN   Did what hurt much?

CHARLES   Being burnt.

JOAN   Oh, that! I cannot remember very well. I think it did at first; but then it all got mixed up; and I was not in my right mind until I was free of the body. But do not thou go handling fire and thinking it will not hurt thee. How hast been ever since?

CHARLES   Oh, not so bad. Do you know, I actually lead my army out and win battles? Down into the moat up to my waist in mud and blood. Up the ladders with the stones and hot pitch raining down. Like you.

JOAN   No! Did I make a man of thee after all, Charlie?

CHARLES   I am Charles the Victorious now. I had to be brave because you were. Agnes put a little pluck into me too.

JOAN   Agnes! Who was Agnes?

CHARLES   Agnes Sorel. A woman I fell in love with. I dream of her often. I never dreamed of you before.

JOAN   Is she dead, like me?

CHARLES.   Yes. But she was not like you. She was very beautiful.

JOAN [*laughing heartily*]   Ha Ha! I was no beauty: I was always a rough one: a regular soldier. I might almost as well have been a man. Pity I wasnt: I should not have bothered you all so much then. But my head was in the skies; and the glory of God was upon me; and, man or woman, I should have bothered you as long as your noses were in the mud. Now tell me what has happened since you wise men knew no better than to make a heap of cinders of me?

CHARLES   Your mother and brothers have sued the courts to have your case tried over again. And the courts have declared that your judges were full of corruption and cozenage, fraud and malice.

JOAN   Not they. They were as honest a lot of poor fools as ever burned their betters.

CHARLES   The sentence on you is broken, annihilated, annulled: null, nonexistent, without value or effect.

JOAN   I was burned, all the same. Can they unburn me?

CHARLES   If they could, they would think twice before they did it. But they have decreed that a beautiful cross be placed where the stake stood, for your perpetual memory and for your salvation.

JOAN   It is the memory and the salvation that sanctify the cross, not the cross that sanctifies the memory and the salvation. [*She turns away, forgetting him.*] I shall outlast that cross. I shall be remembered when men will have forgotten where Rouen stood.

CHARLES   There you go with your self-conceit, the same as ever! I think you might say a word of thanks to me for having had justice done at last.

CAUCHON [*appearing at the window between them*]   Liar!

CHARLES   Thank you.

JOAN   Why, if it isnt Peter Cauchon! How are you, Peter? What luck have you had since you burned me?

CAUCHON   None. I arraign the justice of Man. It is not the justice of God.

JOAN   Still dreaming of justice, Peter? See what justice came to with me! But what has happened to thee? Art dead or alive?

CAUCHON   Dead. Dishonored. They pursued me beyond the grave. They excommunicated my dead body: they dug it up and flung it into the common sewer.

JOAN   Your dead body did not feel the spade and the sewer as my live body felt the fire.

CAUCHON   But this thing that they have done against me hurts justice; destroys faith; saps the foundation of the Church. The solid earth sways like the treacherous sea beneath the feet of men and spirits alike when the innocent are slain in the name of law, and their wrongs are undone by slandering the pure of heart.

JOAN   Well, well, Peter, I hope men will be the better for remembering me; and they would not remember me so well if you had not burned me.

CAUCHON   They will be the worse for remembering me: they will see in me evil triumphing over good, falsehood over truth, cruelty over mercy, hell over heaven. Their courage will rise as they think of you, only to faint as they think of me. Yet

God is my witness I was just: I was merciful: I was faithful to my light: I could do no other than I did.

CHARLES [*scrambling out of the sheets and enthroning himself on the side of the bed*] Yes: it is always you good men that do the big mischiefs. Look at me! I am not Charles the Good, nor Charles the Wise, nor Charles the Bold. Joan's worshippers may even call me Charles the Coward because I did not pull her out of the fire. But I have done less harm than any of you. You people with your heads in the sky spend all your time trying to turn the world upside down; but I take the world as it is, and say that top-side-up is right-side-up; and I keep my nose pretty close to the ground. And I ask you, what king of France has done better, or been a better fellow in his little way?

JOAN Art really king of France, Charlie? Be the English gone?

DUNOIS [*coming through the tapestry on* JOAN's *left, the candles relighting themselves at the same moment, and illuminating his armor and surcoat cheerfully*] I have kept my word: the English are gone.

JOAN Praised be God! now is fair France a province in heaven. Tell me all about the fighting, Jack. Was it thou that led them? Wert thou God's captain to thy death?

DUNOIS I am not dead. My body is very comfortably asleep in my bed at Chateaudun; but my spirit is called here by yours.

JOAN And you fought them my way, Jack: eh? Not the old way, chaffering for ransoms; but The Maid's way: staking life against death, with the heart high and humble and void of malice, and nothing counting under God but France free and French. Was it my way, Jack?

DUNOIS Faith, it was anyway that would win. But the way that won was always your way. I give you best, lassie. I wrote a fine letter to set you right at the new trial. Perhaps I should never have let the priests burn you; but I was busy fighting; and it was the Church's business, not mine. There was no use in both of us being burned, was there?

CAUCHON Ay! put the blame on the priests. But I, who am beyond praise and blame, tell you that the world is saved neither by its priests nor its soldiers, but by God and His Saints. The Church Militant sent this woman to the fire; but even as she burned, the flames whitened into the radiance of the Church Triumphant.

The clock strikes the third quarter. A rough male voice is heard trolling an improvised tune.

Rum tum trumpledum,
Bacon fat and rumpledum,
Old Saint mumpledum,
Pull his tail and stumpledum
O my Ma—ry Ann!

A ruffianly English soldier comes through the curtains and marches between DUNOIS *and* JOAN.

DUNOIS   What villainous troubadour taught you that doggrel?

THE SOLDIER   No troubadour. We made it up ourselves as we marched. We were not gentlefolks and troubadours. Music straight out of the heart of the people, as you might say. Rum tum trumpledum, Bacon fat and rumpledum, Old Saint mumpledum, Pull his tail and stumpledum: that dont mean anything, you know; but it keeps you marching. Your servant, ladies and gentlemen. Who asked for a saint?

JOAN   Be you a saint?

THE SOLDIER   Yes, lady, straight from hell.

DUNOIS   A saint, and from hell!

THE SOLDIER   Yes, noble captain: I have a day off. Every year, you know. Thats my allowance for my one good action.

CAUCHON   Wretch! In all the years of your life did you do only one good action?

THE SOLDIER   I never thought about it: it came natural like. But they scored it up for me.

CHARLES   What was it?

THE SOLDIER   Why, the silliest thing you ever heard of. I—

JOAN [*interrupting him by strolling across to the bed, where she sits beside* CHARLES]   He tied two sticks together, and gave them to a poor lass that was going to be burned.

THE SOLDIER   Right. Who told you that?

JOAN   Never mind. Would you know her if you saw her again?

THE SOLDIER   Not I. There are so many girls! and they all expect you to remember them as if there was only one in the world. This one must have been a prime sort; for I have a day off every year for her; and so, until twelve o'clock punctually, I am a saint, at your service, noble lords and lovely ladies.

CHARLES   And after twelve?

THE SOLDIER   After twelve, back to the only place fit for the likes of me.

JOAN [*rising*]   Back there! You! that gave the lass the cross!

THE SOLDIER [*excusing his unsoldierly conduct*]   Well, she asked for it; and they were going to burn her. She had as good a right to a cross as they had; and they had dozens of them. It was her funeral, not theirs. Where was the harm in it?

JOAN   Man: I am not reproaching you. But I cannot bear to think of you in torment.

THE SOLDIER [*cheerfully*]   No great torment, lady. You see I was used to worse.

CHARLES   What! worse than hell?

THE SOLDIER   Fifteen years' service in the French wars. Hell was a treat after that.

JOAN *throws up her arms, and takes refuge from despair of humanity before the picture of the Virgin.*

THE SOLDIER [*continuing*]   —Suits me somehow. The day off was dull at first, like a wet Sunday. I dont mind it so much now. They tell me I can have as many as I like as soon as I want them.

CHARLES   What is hell like?

THE SOLDIER   You wont find it so bad, sir. Jolly. Like as if you were always drunk without the trouble and expense of drinking. Tip top company too: emperors and popes and kings and all sorts. They chip me about giving that young judy the cross; but I dont care: I stand up to them proper, and tell them that if she hadnt a better right to it than they, she'd be where they are. That dumbfounds them, that does. All they can do is gnash their teeth, hell fashion; and I just laugh, and go off singing the old chanty: Rum tum trumple—Hullo! Who's that knocking at the door?

They listen. A long gentle knocking is heard.

CHARLES Come in.

The door opens; and an old priest, white-haired, bent, with a silly but benevolent smile, comes in and trots over to JOAN.

THE NEWCOMER Excuse me, gentle lords and ladies. Do not let me disturb you. Only a poor old harmless English rector. Formerly chaplain to the cardinal: to my lord of Winchester. John de Stogumber, at your service. [*He looks at them inquiringly.*] Did you say anything? I am a little deaf, unfortunately. Also a little— well, not always in my right mind, perhaps; but still, it is a small village with a few simple people. I suffice: I suffice: they love me there; and I am able to do a little good. I am well connected, you see; and they indulge me.

JOAN Poor old John! What brought thee to this state?

DE STOGUMBER I tell my folks they must be very careful. I say to them, 'If you only saw what you think about you would think quite differently about it. It would give you a great shock. Oh, a great shock.' And they all say 'Yes, parson: we all know you are a kind man, and would not harm a fly.' That is a great comfort to me. For I am not cruel by nature, you know.

THE SOLDIER Who said you were?

DE STOGUMBER Well, you see, I did a very cruel thing once because I did not know what cruelty was like. I had not seen it, you know. That is the great thing: you must see it. And then you are redeemed and saved.

CAUCHON Were not the sufferings of our Lord Christ enough for you?

DE STOGUMBER No. Oh no: not at all. I had seen them in pictures, and read of them in books, and been greatly moved by them, as I thought. But it was no use: it was not our Lord that redeemed me, but a young woman whom I saw actually burned to death. It was dreadful: oh, most dreadful. But it saved me. I have been a different man ever since, though a little astray in my wits sometimes.

CAUCHON Must then a Christ perish in torment in every age to save those that have no imagination?

JOAN Well, if I saved all those he would have been cruel to if he had not been cruel to me, I was not burnt for nothing, was I?

DE STOGUMBER Oh no; it was not you. My sight is bad: I cannot distinguish your features: but you are not she: oh no: she was burned to a cinder: dead and gone, dead and gone.

THE EXECUTIONER [*stepping from behind the bed curtains on* CHARLES's *right, the bed being between them*] She is more alive than you, old man. Her heart would not burn; and it would not drown. I was a master at my craft: better than the master of Paris, better than the master of Toulouse; but I could not kill The Maid. She is up and alive everywhere.

THE EARL OF WARWICK [*sallying from the bed curtains on the other side, and coming to* JOAN's *left hand*] Madam: my congratulations on your rehabilitation. I feel that I owe you an apology.

JOAN   Oh, please dont mention it.

WARWICK[*pleasantly*]   The burning was purely political. There was no personal feeling against you, I assure you.

JOAN   I bear no malice, my lord.

WARWICK   Just so. Very kind of you to meet me in that way: a touch of true breeding. But I must insist on apologizing very amply. The truth is, these political necessities sometimes turn out to be political mistakes; and this one was a veritable howler; for your spirit conquered us, madam, in spite of our faggots. History will remember me for your sake, though the incidents of the connection were perhaps a little unfortunate.

JOAN   Ay, perhaps just a little, you funny man.

WARWICK   Still, when they make you a saint, you will owe your halo to me, just as this lucky monarch owes his crown to you.

JOAN [*turning from him*]   I shall owe nothing to any man: I owe everything to the spirit of God that was within me. But fancy me a saint! What would St Catherine and St Margaret say if the farm girl was cocked up beside them!

A clerical-looking gentleman in black frockcoat and trousers, and tall hat, in the fashion of the year 1920, suddenly appears before them in the corner on their right. They all stare at him. Then they burst into uncontrollable laughter.

THE GENTLEMAN   Why this mirth, gentlemen?

WARWICK   I congratulate you on having invented a most extraordinarily comic dress.

THE GENTLEMAN   I do not understand. You are all in fancy dress: I am properly dressed.

DUNOIS   All dress is fancy dress, is it not, except our natural skins?

THE GENTLEMAN   Pardon me: I am here on serious business, and cannot engage in frivolous discussions. [*He takes out a paper, and assumes a dry official manner.*] I am sent to announce to you that Joan of Arc, formerly known as The Maid, having been the subject of an inquiry instituted by the Bishop of Orleans—

JOAN [*interrupting*]   Ah! They remember me still in Orleans.

THE GENTLEMAN [*emphatically, to mark his indignation at the interruption*]   — by the Bishop of Orleans into the claim of the said Joan of Arc to be canonized as a saint—

JOAN [*again interrupting*]   But I never made any such claim.

THE GENTLEMAN [*as before*]   —the Church has examined the claim exhaustively in the usual course, and, having admitted the said Joan successively to the ranks of Venerable and Blessed,—

JOAN [*chuckling*]   Me venerable!

THE GENTLEMAN   —has finally declared her to have been endowed with heroic virtues and favored with private revelations, and calls the said Venerable and Blessed Joan to the communion of the Church Triumphant as Saint Joan.

JOAN [*rapt*]   Saint Joan!

THE GENTLEMAN   On every thirtieth day of May, being the anniversary of the death of the said most blessed daughter of God, there shall be in every Catholic church to the end of time be celebrated a special office in commemoration of her;

and it shall be lawful to dedicate a special chapel to her, and to place her image on its altar in every such church. And it shall be lawful and laudable for the faithful to kneel and address their prayers through her to the Mercy Seat.

JOAN   Oh no. It is for the saint to kneel. [*She falls on her knees, still rapt.*]

THE GENTLEMAN [*putting up his paper, and retiring beside the* EXECU-
TIONER]   In Basilica Vaticana, the sixteenth day of May, nineteen hundred and twenty.

DUNOIS [*raising* JOAN]   Half an hour to burn you, dear Saint: and four centuries to find out the truth about you!

DE STOGUMBER   Sir: I was chaplain to the Cardinal of Winchester once. They always would call him the Cardinal of England. It would be a great comfort to me and to my master to see a fair statue to The Maid in Winchester Cathedral. Will they put one there, do you think?

THE GENTLEMAN   As the building is temporarily in the hands of the Anglican heresy, I cannot answer for that.

A vision of the statue in Winchester Cathedral is seen through the window.

DE STOGUMBER   Oh look! look! that is Winchester.

JOAN   Is that meant to be me? I was stiffer on my feet.

The vision fades.

THE GENTLEMAN   I have been requested by the temporal authorities of France to mention that the multiplication of public statues to The Maid threatens to become an obstruction to traffic. I do so as a matter of courtesy to the said authorities, but must point out on behalf of the Church that The Maid's horse is no greater obstruction to traffic than any other horse.

JOAN   Eh! I am glad they have not forgotten my horse.

A vision of the statue before Rheims Cathedral appears.

JOAN   Is that funny little thing me too?

CHARLES   That is Rheims Cathedral where you had me crowned. It must be you.

JOAN   Who has broken my sword? My sword was never broken. It is the sword of France.

DUNOIS   Never mind. Swords can be mended. Your soul is unbroken; and you are the soul of France.

The vision fades. The ARCHBISHOP *and the* INQUISITOR *are now seen on the right and left of* CAUCHON.

JOAN   My sword shall conquer yet: the sword that never struck a blow. Though men destroyed my body, yet in my soul I have seen God.

CAUCHON [*kneeling to her*]   The girls in the field praise thee; for thou hast raised their eyes; and they see that there is nothing between them and heaven.

DUNOIS [*kneeling to her*]   The dying soldiers praise thee, because thou art a shield of glory between them and the judgment.

THE ARCHBISHOP [*kneeling to her*] The princes of the Church praise thee, because thou hast redeemed the faith their worldlinesses have dragged through the mire.

WARWICK [*kneeling to her*] The cunning counsellors praise thee, because thou hast cut the knots in which they have tied their own souls.

DE STOGUMBER [*kneeling to her*] The foolish old men on their deathbeds praise thee, because their sins against thee are turned into blessings.

THE INQUISITOR [*kneeling to her*] The judges in the blindness and bondage of the law praise thee, because thou hast vindicated the vision and the freedom of the living soul.

THE SOLDIER [*kneeling to her*] The wicked out of hell praise thee, because thou hast shewn them that the fire that is not quenched is a holy fire.

THE EXECUTIONER [*kneeling to her*] The tormentors and executioners praise thee, because thou hast shewn that their hands are guiltless of the death of the soul.

CHARLES [*kneeling to her*] The unpretending praise thee, because thou hast taken upon thyself the heroic burdens that are too heavy for them.

JOAN Woe unto me when all men praise me! I bid you remember that I am a saint, and that saints can work miracles. And now tell me: shall I rise from the dead, and come back to you a living woman?

A sudden darkness blots out the walls of the room as they all spring to their feet in consternation. Only the figures and the bed remain visible.

JOAN What! Must I burn again? Are none of you ready to receive me?

CAUCHON The heretic is always better dead. And mortal eyes cannot distinguish the saint from the heretic. Spare them. [*He goes out as he came.*]

DUNOIS Forgive us, Joan: we are not yet good enough for you. I shall go back to my bed. [*He also goes.*]

WARWICK We sincerely regret our little mistake; but political necessities, though occasionally erroneous, are still imperative; so if you will be good enough to excuse me—[*He steals discreetly away.*]

THE ARCHBISHOP Your return would not make me the man you once thought me. The utmost I can say is that though I dare not bless you, I hope I may one day enter into your blessedness. Meanwhile, however—[*He goes.*]

THE INQUISITOR I who am of the dead, testified that day that you were innocent. But I do not see how The Inquisition could possibly be dispensed with under existing circumstances. Therefore—[*He goes.*]

DE STOGUMBER Oh, do not come back: you must not come back. I must die in peace. Give us peace in our time, O Lord! [*He goes.*]

THE GENTLEMAN The possibility of your resurrection was not contemplated in the recent proceedings for your canonization. I must return to Rome for fresh instructions. [*He bows formally, and withdraws.*]

THE EXECUTIONER As a master in my profession I have to consider its interests. And, after all, my first duty is to my wife and children. I must have time to think over this. [*He goes.*]

CHARLES Poor old Joan! They have all run away from you except this blackguard who has to go back to hell at twelve o'clock. And what can I do but follow Jack Dunois' example, and go back to bed too? [*He does so.*]

JOAN [*sadly*] Goodnight, Charlie.

CHARLES [*mumbling in his pillows*] Goo ni. [*He sleeps. The darkness envelops the bed.*]

JOAN [*to the soldier*] And you, my one faithful? What comfort have you for Saint Joan?

THE SOLDIERS Well, what do they all amount to, these kings and captains and bishops and lawyers and such like? They just leave you in the ditch to bleed to death; and the next thing is, you meet them down there, for all the airs they give themselves. What I say is, you have as good a right to your notions as they have to theirs, and perhaps better. [*Settling himself for a lecture on the subject*] You see, it's like this. If—[*the first stroke of midnight is heard softly from a distant bell.*] Excuse me: a pressing appointment—[*He goes on tiptoe.*]

The last remaining rays of light gather into a white radiance descending on JOAN. *The hour continues to strike.*

JOAN O God that madest this beautiful earth, when will it be ready to receive Thy saints? How long, O Lord, how long?

William Butler Yeats and *The Cat and the Moon*

William Butler Yeats (1865–1939) was a great poet and a leader of the Irish literary renaissance who co-founded the Abbey Theatre in Dublin with the playwright Lady Gregory. Yeats was best known for his poetry (he was awarded a Nobel Prize in 1923) but spent much of his life as a man of the theater.

He wrote many plays, in prose and in verse; originals, adaptations, and translations. Most of them, like *The Cat and the Moon* (1926), run contrary to the conventions of realistic theater. Dancers dance, musicians play, and characters speak to each other in poetry or in a prose that is poetical and ritualistic. Most of his life Yeats despised art that catered to the mass of people; he made his theater for an artistic elite. He was influenced by translations of the Noh dramas of Japan, ancient and hierarchical plays with dancers and musicians.

To appreciate Yeats's theater, we must approach it without expecting it to resemble Ibsen's realism, which Yeats disliked. We will not find characters with a reality like Hedda Gabler's; instead we will more likely find types like The Fool or The Blind Man or creatures of myth like Cuchulain. We will find no realism of speech, costume, or scenery; instead, we will find screens unrolled, actors wearing masks and speaking in rhyme.

If we allow it, the effect can be spellbinding. Yeats's drama resembles liturgy and reminds us of the theater's ritual origins. We will not precisely identify ourselves with characters in their struggle; we will not find ourselves moved by empathy or by dread; instead, our senses and our minds will be captured by language that wins us by dazzling us.

The Cat and the Moon begins and ends with a sung poem. The time and the setting are unhistorical and mythic, the characters unspecified and archetypal.

William Butler Yeats
The Cat and the Moon

Persons in the Play

A BLIND BEGGAR
A LAME BEGGAR
THREE MUSICIANS

SCENE: *The scene is any bare place before a wall against which stands a patterned screen, or hangs a patterned curtain suggesting Saint Colman's Well.* THREE MU-SICIANS *are sitting close to the wall, with zither, drum, and flute. Their faces are made up to resemble masks.*

FIRST MUSICIAN [*singing*]
    The cat went here and there
    And the moon spun round like a top,
    And the nearest kin of the moon,
    The creeping cat, looked up.
    Black Minnaloushe stared at the moon,
    For, wander and wail as he would,
    The pure cold light in the sky
    Troubled his animal blood.

Two BEGGARS *enter—a blind man with a lame man on his back. They wear grotesque masks. The* BLIND BEGGAR *is counting the paces.*

BLIND BEGGAR   One thousand and six, one thousand and seven, one thousand and nine. Look well now, for we should be in sight of the holy well of Saint Colman. The beggar at the cross-roads said it was one thousand paces from where he stood and a few paces over. Look well now, can you see the big ash-tree that's above it?

LAME BEGGAR [*getting down*]   No, not yet.

BLIND BEGGAR   Then we must have taken a wrong turn; flighty you always were, and maybe before the day is over you will have me drowned in Kiltartan River or maybe in the sea itself.

LAME BEGGAR   I have brought you the right way, but you are a lazy man, Blind Man, and you make very short strides.

BLIND BEGGAR   It's great daring you have, and how could I make a long stride and you on my back from the peep o' day?

LAME BEGGAR   And maybe the beggar of the cross-roads was only making it up when he said a thousand paces and a few paces more. You and I, being beggars, know the way of beggars, and maybe he never paced it at all, being a lazy man.

BLIND BEGGAR   Get up. It's too much talk you have.

LAME BEGGAR [*getting up*]   But as I was saying, he being a lazy man—O, O, O, stop pinching the calf of my leg and I'll not say another word till I'm spoken to.

They go round the stage once, moving to drum-taps, and as they move the follow-ing song is sung.

FIRST MUSICIAN [*singing*]
> Minnaloushe runs in the grass
> Lifting his delicate feet.
> Do you dance, Minnaloushe, do you dance?
> When two close kindred meet
> What better than call a dance?
> Maybe the moon may learn,
> Tired of that courtly fashion,
> A new dance turn.

BLIND BEGGAR   Do you see the big ash-tree?

LAME BEGGAR   I do then, and the wall under it, and the flat stone, and the things upon the stone; and here is a good dry place to kneel in.

BLIND BEGGAR   You may get down so. [LAME BEGGAR *gets down*] I begin to have it in my mind that I am a great fool, and it was you who egged me on with your flighty talk.

LAME BEGGAR   How should you be a great fool to ask the saint to give you back your two eyes?

BLIND BEGGAR   There is many gives money to a blind man and would give nothing but a curse to a whole man, and if it was not for one thing—but no matter anyway.

LAME BEGGAR   If I speak out all that's in my mind you won't take a blow at me at all?

BLIND BEGGAR   I will not this time.

LAME BEGGAR   Then I'll tell you why you are not a great fool. When you go out to pick up a chicken, or maybe a stray goose on the road, or a cabbage from a neighbour's garden, I have to go riding on your back; and if I want a goose, or a chicken, or a cabbage, I must have your two legs under me.

BLIND BEGGAR   That's true now, and if we were whole men and went different ways, there'd be as much again between us.

LAME BEGGAR   And your own goods keep going from you because you are blind.

BLIND BEGGAR   Rogues and thieves ye all are, but there are some I may have my eyes on yet.

LAME BEGGAR   Because there's no one to see a man slipping in at the door, or throwing a leg over the wall of a yard, you are a bitter temptation to many a poor man, and I say it's not right, it's not right at all. There are poor men that because you are blind will be delayed in Purgatory.

BLIND BEGGAR   Though you are a rogue, Lame Man, maybe you are in the right.

LAME BEGGAR   And maybe we'll see the blessed saint this day, for there's an odd one sees him, and maybe that will be a grander thing than having my two legs, though legs are a grand thing.

BLIND BEGGAR   You're getting flighty again, Lame Man; what could be better for you than to have your two legs?

LAME BEGGAR   Do you think now will the saint put an ear on him at all, and we without an Ave or a Paternoster to put before the prayer or after the prayer?

BLIND BEGGAR   Wise though you are and flighty though you are, and you throwing eyes to the right of you and eyes to the left of you, there's many a thing you don't know about the heart of man.

LAME BEGGAR   But it stands to reason that he'd be put out and he maybe with a great liking for the Latin.

BLIND BEGGAR   I have it in mind that the saint will be better pleased at us not knowing a prayer at all, and that we had best say what we want in plain language. What pleasure can he have in all that holy company kneeling at his well on holidays and Sundays, and they as innocent maybe as himself?

LAME BEGGAR   That's a strange thing to say, and do you say it as I or another might say it, or as a blind man?

BLIND BEGGAR   I say it as a blind man, I say it because since I went blind in the tenth year of my age, I have been hearing and remembering the knowledges of the world.

LAME BEGGAR   And you who are a blind man say that a saint, and he living in a pure well of water, would soonest be talking with a sinful man.

BLIND BEGGAR   Do you mind what the beggar told you about the holy man in the big house at Laban?

LAME BEGGAR   Nothing stays in my head, Blind Man.

BLIND BEGGAR   What does he do but go knocking about the roads with an old lecher from the county of Mayo, and he a woman-hater from the day of his birth! And what do they talk of by candle-light and by daylight? The old lecher does be telling over all the sins he committed, or maybe never committed at all, and the man of Laban does be trying to head him off and quiet him down that he may quit telling them.

LAME BEGGAR   Maybe it is converting him he is.

BLIND BEGGAR   If you were a blind man you wouldn't say a foolish thing the like of that. He wouldn't have him different, no, not if he was to get all Ireland. If he was different, what would they find to talk about, will you answer me that now?

LAME BEGGAR   We have great wisdom between us, that's certain.

BLIND BEGGAR   Now the Church says that it is a good thought, and a sweet thought, and a comfortable thought, that every man may have a saint to look after him, and I, being blind, give it out to all the world that the bigger the sinner the better pleased is the saint. I am sure and certain that Saint Colman would not have us two different from what we are.

LAME BEGGAR   I'll not give in to that, for, as I was saying, he has a great liking maybe for the Latin.

BLIND BEGGAR   Is it contradicting me you are? Are you in reach of my arm? [*Swinging stick*]

LAME BEGGAR   I'm not, Blind Man, you couldn't touch me at all; but as I was saying—

FIRST MUSICIAN [*speaking*]   Will you be cured or will you be blessed?

LAME BEGGAR   Lord save us, that is the saint's voice and we not on our knees.   [*They kneel*

BLIND BEGGAR   Is he standing before us, Lame Man?

LAME BEGGAR   I cannot see him at all. It is in the ash-tree he is, or up in the air.

FIRST MUSICIAN   Will you be cured or will you be blessed?

LAME BEGGAR   There he is again.

BLIND BEGGAR   I'll be cured of my blindness.

FIRST MUSICIAN   I am a saint and lonely. Will you become blessed and stay blind and we will be together always?

BLIND BEGGAR   No, no, your Reverence, if I have to choose, I'll have the sight of my two eyes, for those that have their sight are always stealing my things and telling me lies, and some maybe that are near me. So don't take it bad of me, Holy Man, that I ask the sight of my two eyes.

LAME BEGGAR   No one robs him and no one tells him lies; it's all in his head, it is. He's had his tongue on me all day because he thinks I stole a sheep of his.

BLIND BEGGAR   It was the feel of his sheepskin coat put it into my head, but my sheep was black, they say, and he tells me, Holy Man, that his sheepskin is of the most lovely white wool so that it is a joy to be looking at it.

FIRST MUSICIAN   Lame Man, will you be cured or will you be blessed?

LAME BEGGAR   What would it be like to be blessed?

FIRST MUSICIAN   You would be of the kin of the blessed saints and of the martyrs.

LAME BEGGAR   Is it true now that they have a book and that they write the names of the blessed in that book?

FIRST MUSICIAN   Many a time I have seen the book, and your name would be in it.

LAME BEGGAR   It would be a grand thing to have two legs under me, but I have it in my mind that it would be a grander thing to have my name in that book.

FIRST MUSICIAN   It would be a grander thing.

LAME BEGGAR   I will stay lame, Holy Man, and I will be blessed.

FIRST MUSICIAN   In the name of the Father, the Son and the Holy Spirit I give this Blind Man sight and I make this Lame Man blessed.

BLIND BEGGAR   I see it all now, the blue sky and the big ash-tree and the well and the flat stone,—all as I have heard the people say—and the things the praying people put on the stone, the beads and the candles and the leaves torn out of prayer-books, and the hairpins and the buttons. It is a great sight and a blessed sight, but I don't see yourself, Holy Man—is it up in the big tree you are?

LAME BEGGAR   Why, there he is in front of you and he laughing out of his wrinkled face.

BLIND BEGGAR   Where, where?

LAME BEGGAR   Why, there, between you and the ash-tree.

BLIND BEGGAR   There's nobody there—you're at your lies again.

LAME BEGGAR   I am blessed, and that is why I can see the holy saint.

BLIND BEGGAR   But if I don't see the saint, there's something else I can see.

LAME BEGGAR   The blue sky and green leaves are a great sight, and a strange sight to one that has been long blind.

BLIND BEGGAR   There is a stranger sight than that, and that is the skin of my own black sheep on your back.

LAME BEGGAR   Haven't I been telling you from the peep o' day that my sheep-skin is that white it would dazzle you?

BLIND BEGGAR   Are you so swept with the words that you've never thought that when I had my own two eyes, I'd see what colour was on it?

LAME BEGGAR [*very dejected*]   I never thought of that.

BLIND BEGGAR   Are you that flighty?

LAME BEGGAR   I am that flighty. [*Cheering up*] But am I not blessed, and it's a sin to speak against the blessed?

BLIND BEGGAR   Well, I'll speak against the blessed, and I'll tell you something more that I'll do. All the while you were telling me how, if I had my two eyes, I could pick up a chicken here and a goose there, while my neighbours were in bed, do you know what I was thinking?

LAME BEGGAR   Some wicked blind man's thought.

BLIND BEGGAR   It was, and it's not gone from me yet. I was saying to myself, I have a long arm and a strong arm and a very weighty arm, and when I get my own two eyes I shall know where to hit.

LAME BEGGAR   Don't lay a hand on me. Forty years we've been knocking about the roads together, and I wouldn't have you bring your soul into mortal peril.

BLIND BEGGAR   I have been saying to myself, I shall know where to hit and how to hit and who to hit.

LAME BEGGAR   Do you not know that I am blessed? Would you be as bad as Caesar and as Herod and Nero and the other wicked emperors of antiquity?

BLIND BEGGAR   Where'll I hit him, for the love of God, where'll I hit him?

BLIND BEGGAR *beats* LAME BEGGAR. *The beating takes the form of a dance and is accompanied on drum and flute. The* BLIND BEGGAR *goes out.*

LAME BEGGAR   That is a soul lost, Holy Man.

FIRST MUSICIAN   Maybe so.

LAME BEGGAR   I'd better be going, Holy Man, for he'll rouse the whole country against me.

FIRST MUSICIAN   He'll do that.

LAME BEGGAR   And I have it in my mind not to even myself again with the martyrs, and the holy confessors, till I am more used to being blessed.

FIRST MUSICIAN   Bend down your back.

LAME BEGGAR   What for, Holy Man?

FIRST MUSICIAN   That I may get up on it.

LAME BEGGAR   But my lame legs would never bear the weight of you.

FIRST MUSICIAN   I'm up now.

LAME BEGGAR   I don't feel you at all.

FIRST MUSICIAN   I don't weigh more than a grasshopper.

LAME BEGGAR   You do not.

FIRST MUSICIAN   Are you happy?

LAME BEGGAR   I would be if I was right sure I was blessed.

FIRST MUSICIAN   Haven't you got me for a friend?

LAME BEGGAR   I have so.

FIRST MUSICIAN   Then you're blessed.

LAME BEGGAR   Will you see that they put my name in the book?

FIRST MUSICIAN   I will then.

LAME BEGGAR   Let us be going, Holy Man.

FIRST MUSICIAN   But you must bless the road.

LAME BEGGAR   I haven't the right words.

FIRST MUSICIAN   What do you want words for? Bow to what is before you, bow to what is behind you, bow to what is to the left of you, bow to what is to the right of you. [*The* LAME BEGGAR *begins to bow.*]

FIRST MUSICIAN   That's no good.

LAME BEGGAR   No good, Holy Man?

FIRST MUSICIAN   No good at all. You must dance.

LAME BEGGAR   But how can I dance? Ain't I a lame man?

FIRST MUSICIAN   Aren't you blessed?

LAME BEGGAR   Maybe so.

FIRST MUSICIAN   Aren't you a miracle?

LAME BEGGAR   I am, Holy Man.

FIRST MUSICIAN   Then dance, and that'll be a miracle.

The LAME BEGGAR *begins to dance, at first clumsily, moving about with his stick, then he throws away the stick and dances more and more quickly. Whenever he strikes the ground strongly with his lame foot the cymbals clash. He goes out dancing, after which follows the* FIRST MUSICIAN's *song.*

FIRST MUSICIAN [*singing*]
    Minnaloushe creeps through the grass
    From moonlit place to place.
    The sacred moon overhead
    Has taken a new phase.
    Does Minnaloushe know that his pupils
    Will pass from change to change,
    And that from round to crescent,
    From crescent to round they range?
    Minnaloushe creeps through the grass
    Alone, important and wise,
    And lifts to the changing moon
    His changing eyes.

THE END

Arthur Miller and *Death of a Salesman*

Arthur Miller (1915–   ) is an American playwright whose tragic vision remains unreconciled to the inevitability of doom. Finding human nature alterable, he looks at society with a prophet's fierceness, analyzing with compassion, denouncing with energy, deploring, and understanding. His first successful play, *All My Sons* (1947), attacked war profiteering. *Death of a Salesman* followed a year later, an attempt to write the tragedy not of a king but of a traveling salesman, a relatively low man named Willy Loman. Miller has written, "I believe that the common man is as apt a subject for tragedy . . . as kings were. . . ." This protagonist experiences tragic recognition when he is able to see with clarity the implications of his past life. In the Salesman's recognition he does not discover that he killed his father and married his mother; nevertheless what he recognizes shatters him as much as Oedipus is shattered. ". . . the tragic feeling," wrote Miller, "is evoked in us when we are in the presence of a character who is ready to lay down his life . . . to secure . . . his sense of personal dignity."

In 1952 Miller wrote *The Crucible,* based upon the Salem witch trials of the seventeenth century. The play was courageous; it took the metaphor of witch hunts, used to describe the political activities of Senator Joseph McCarthy, and let the analogy work itself out on the stage. He has followed with *A View from the Bridge* (1955), *After the Fall* (1964), *Incident at Vichy* (1964), and *The Price* (1968.)

Arthur Miller
Death of a Salesman

Certain Private Conversations in Two Acts and a Requiem

Characters

WILLY LOMAN	THE WOMAN
LINDA, his wife	HOWARD WAGNER
BIFF ⎤ his sons	JENNY
HAPPY ⎦	STANLEY
UNCLE BEN	MISS FORSYTHE
CHARLEY	LETTA
BERNARD	

The action takes place in WILLY LOMAN'S *house and yard and in various places he visits in the New York and Boston of today.*

Act I

A melody is heard, played upon a flute. It is small and fine, telling of grass and trees and the horizon. The curtain rises.

Before us is the Salesman's house. We are aware of towering, angular shapes behind it, surrounding it on all sides. Only the blue light of the sky falls upon the house and forestage; the surrounding area shows an angry glow of orange. As more light appears, we see a solid vault of apartment houses around the small, fragile-seeming home. An air of the dream clings to the place, a dream rising out of reality. The kitchen at center seems actual enough, for there is a kitchen table with three chairs, and a refrigerator. But no other fixtures are seen. At the back of the kitchen there is a draped entrance, which leads to the living-room. To the right of the kitchen, on a level raised two feet, is a bedroom furnished only with a brass bedstead and a straight chair. On a shelf over the bed a silver athletic trophy stands. A window opens onto the apartment house at the side.

Behind the kitchen, on a level raised six and a half feet, is the boys' bedroom, at present barely visible. Two beds are dimly seen, and at the back of the room a dormer window. (This bedroom is above the unseen living-room.) At the left a stairway curves up to it from the kitchen.

The entire setting is wholly or, in some places, partially transparent. The roof-line of the house is one-dimensional; under and over it we see the apartment buildings. Before the house lies an apron, curving beyond the forestage into the orchestra. This forward area serves as the back yard as well as the locale of all WILLY's *imaginings and of his city scenes. Whenever the action is in the present the actors observe the imaginary wall-lines, entering the house only through its door at the left. But in the scenes of the past these boundaries are broken, and characters enter or leave a room by stepping "through" a wall onto the forestage.*

[*From the right,* WILLY LOMAN, *the Salesman, enters, carrying two large sample cases. The flute plays on. He hears but is not aware of it. He is past sixty years of age, dressed quietly. Even as he crosses the stage to the doorway of the house, his exhaustion is apparent. He unlocks the door, comes into the kitchen, and thankfully lets his burden down, feeling the soreness of his palms. A word-sigh escapes his lips—it might be "Oh, boy, oh, boy." He closes the door, then carries his cases out into the living-room, through the draped kitchen doorway.*]

[LINDA, *his wife, has stirred in her bed at the right. She gets out and puts on a robe, listening. Most often jovial, she has developed an iron repression of her exceptions to* WILLY's *behavior—she more than loves him, she admires him, as though his mercurial nature, his temper, his massive dreams and little cruelties, served her only as sharp reminders of the turbulent longings within him, longings which she shares but lacks the temperament to utter and follow to their end.*]

LINDA [*hearing* WILLY *outside the bedroom, calls with some trepidation*] Willy!
WILLY   It's all right. I came back.
LINDA   Why? What happened? [*Slight pause*] Did something happen, Willy?
WILLY   No, nothing happened.
LINDA   You didn't smash the car, did you?
WILLY [*with casual irritation*]   I said nothing happened. Didn't you hear me?
LINDA   Don't you feel well?
WILLY   I'm tired to the death. [*The flute has faded away. He sits on the bed beside her, a little numb.*] I couldn't make it. I just couldn't make it, Linda.
LINDA [*very carefully, delicately*]   Where were you all day? You look terrible.
WILLY   I got as far as a little above Yonkers. I stopped for a cup of coffee. Maybe it was the coffee.
LINDA   What?
WILLY [*after a pause*]   I suddenly couldn't drive any more. The car kept going off onto the shoulder, y'know?
LINDA [*helpfully*]   Oh. Maybe it was the steering again. I don't think Angelo knows the Studebaker.
WILLY   No, it's me, it's me. Suddenly I realize I'm goin' sixty miles an hour and I don't remember the last five minutes. I'm—I can't seem to—keep my mind to it.
LINDA   Maybe it's your glasses. You never went for your new glasses.
WILLY   No, I see everything. I came back ten miles an hour. It took me nearly four hours from Yonkers.
LINDA [*resigned*]   Well, you'll just have to take a rest, Willy, you can't continue this way.
WILLY   I just got back from Florida.
LINDA   But you didn't rest your mind. Your mind is overactive, and the mind is what counts, dear.
WILLY   I'll start out in the morning. Maybe I'll feel better in the morning. [*She is taking off his shoes.*] These goddam arch supports are killing me.
LINDA   Take an aspirin. Should I get you an aspirin? It'll soothe you.
WILLY [*with wonder*]   I was driving along, you understand? And I was fine. I was even observing the scenery. You can imagine, me looking at scenery, on the road every week of my life. But it's so beautiful up there, Linda, the trees are so

thick, and the sun is warm. I opened the windshield and just let the warm air bathe over me. And then all of a sudden I'm goin' off the road! I'm tellin' ya, I absolutely forgot I was driving. If I'd've gone the other way over the white line I might've killed somebody. So I went on again—and five minutes later I'm dreamin' again, and I nearly— [*He presses two fingers against his eyes.*] I have such thoughts, I have such strange thoughts.

LINDA   Willy, dear. Talk to them again. There's no reason why you can't work in New York.

WILLY   They don't need me in New York. I'm the New England man. I'm vital in New England.

LINDA   But you're sixty years old. They can't expect you to keep traveling every week.

WILLY   I'll have to send a wire to Portland. I'm supposed to see Brown and Morrison tomorrow morning at ten o'clock to show the line. Goddammit, I could sell them! [*He starts putting on his jacket.*]

LINDA [*taking the jacket from him*]   Why don't you go down to the place tomorrow and tell Howard you've simply got to work in New York? You're too accommodating, dear.

WILLY   If old man Wagner was alive I'd a been in charge of New York now! That man was a prince, he was a masterful man. But that boy of his, that Howard, he don't appreciate. When I went north the first time, the Wagner Company didn't know where New England was!

LINDA   Why don't you tell those things to Howard, dear?

WILLY [*encouraged*]   I will, I definitely will. Is there any cheese?

LINDA   I'll make you a sandwich.

WILLY   No, go to sleep. I'll take some milk. I'll be up right away. The boys in?

LINDA   They're sleeping. Happy took Biff on a date tonight.

WILLY [*interested*]   That so?

LINDA   It was so nice to see them shaving together, one behind the other, in the bathroom. And going out together. You notice? The whole house smells of shaving lotion.

WILLY   Figure it out. Work a lifetime to pay off a house. You finally own it, and there's nobody to live in it.

LINDA   Well, dear, life is a casting off. It's always that way.

WILLY   No, no, some people—some people accomplish something. Did Biff say anything after I went this morning?

LINDA   You shouldn't have criticized him, Willy, especially after he just got off the train. You mustn't lose your temper with him.

WILLY   When the hell did I lose my temper? I simply asked him if he was making any money. Is that a criticism?

LINDA   But, dear, how could he make any money?

WILLY [*worried and angered*]   There's such an undercurrent in him. He became a moody man. Did he apologize when I left this morning?

LINDA   He was crestfallen, Willy. You know how he admires you. I think if he finds himself, then you'll both be happier and not fight any more.

WILLY   How can he find himself on a farm? Is that a life? A farmhand? In the beginning, when he was young, I thought, well, a young man, it's good for him to tramp around, take a lot of different jobs. But it's more than ten years now and he has yet to make thirty-five dollars a week!

LINDA   He's finding himself, Willy.

WILLY   Not finding yourself at the age of thirty-four is a disgrace!

LINDA   Shh!

WILLY   The trouble is he's lazy, goddammit!

LINDA   Willy, please!

WILLY   Biff is a lazy bum!

LINDA   They're sleeping. Get something to eat. Go on down.

WILLY   Why did he come home? I would like to know what brought him home.

LINDA   I don't know. I think he's still lost, Willy. I think he's very lost.

WILLY   Biff Loman is lost. In the greatest country in the world a young man with such—personal attractiveness, gets lost. And such a hard worker. There's one thing about Biff—he's not lazy.

LINDA   Never.

WILLY [with pity and resolve]   I'll see him in the morning; I'll have a nice talk with him. I'll get him a job selling. He could be big in no time. My God! Remember how they used to follow him around in high school? When he smiled at one of them their faces lit up. When he walked down the street . . . [He loses himself in reminiscences.]

LINDA [trying to bring him out of it]   Willy, dear, I got a new kind of American-type cheese today. It's whipped.

WILLY   Why do you get American when I like Swiss?

LINDA   I just thought you'd like a change—

WILLY   I don't want a change! I want Swiss cheese. Why am I always being contradicted?

LINDA [with a covering laugh]   I thought it would be a surprise.

WILLY   Why don't you open a window in here, for God's sake?

LINDA [with infinite patience]   They're all open, dear.

WILLY   The way they boxed us in here. Bricks and windows, windows and bricks.

LINDA   We should've bought the land next door.

WILLY   The street is lined with cars. There's not a breath of fresh air in the neighborhood. The grass don't grow any more, you can't raise a carrot in the back yard. They should've had a law against apartment houses. Remember those two beautiful elm trees out there? When I and Biff hung the swing between them?

LINDA   Yeah, like being a million miles from the city.

WILLY   They should've arrested the builder for cutting those down. They massacred the neighborhood. [lost] More and more I think of those days, Linda. This time of year it was lilac and wisteria. And then the peonies would come out, and the daffodils. What fragrance in this room!

LINDA   Well, after all, people had to move somewhere.

WILLY   No, there's more people now.

LINDA   I don't think there's more people. I think—

WILLY   There's more people! That's what's ruining this country! Population is getting out of control. The competition is maddening! Smell the stink from that apartment house! And another one on the other side . . . How can they whip cheese?

On WILLY's last line, BIFF and HAPPY raise themselves up in their beds, listening.

LINDA   Go down, try it. And be quiet.

WILLY [turning to LINDA, guiltily]   You're not worried about me, are you, sweetheart?

BIFF What's the matter?

HAPPY Listen!

LINDA You've got too much on the ball to worry about.

WILLY You're my foundation and my support, Linda.

LINDA Just try to relax, dear. You make mountains out of molehills.

WILLY I won't fight with him any more. If he wants to go back to Texas, let him go.

LINDA He'll find his way.

WILLY Sure. Certain men just don't get started till later in life. Like Thomas Edison, I think. Or B. F. Goodrich. One of them was deaf. [*He starts for the bedroom doorway.*] I'll put my money on Biff.

LINDA And Willy—if it's warm Sunday we'll drive in the country. And we'll open the windshield, and take lunch.

WILLY No, the windshields don't open on the new cars.

LINDA But you opened it today.

WILLY Me? I didn't. [*He stops.*] Now isn't that peculiar! Isn't that a remarkable— [*He breaks off in amazement and fright as the flute is heard distantly.*]

LINDA What, darling?

WILLY That is the most remarkable thing.

LINDA What, dear?

WILLY I was thinking of the Chevvy. [*Slight pause*] Nineteen twenty-eight . . . when I had that red Chevvy— [*Breaks off*] That funny? I coulda sworn I was driving that Chevvy today.

LINDA Well, that's nothing. Something must've reminded you.

WILLY Remarkable. Ts. Remember those days? The way Biff used to simonize that car? The dealer refused to believe there was eighty thousand miles on it. [*He shakes his head.*] Heh! [*To* LINDA] Close your eyes, I'll be right up. [*He walks out of the bedroom.*]

HAPPY [*to* BIFF] Jesus, maybe he smashed up the car again!

LINDA [*calling after* WILLY] Be careful on the stairs, dear! The cheese is on the middle shelf! [*She turns, goes over to the bed, takes his jacket, and goes out of the bedroom.*]

Light has risen on the boys' room. Unseen, WILLY *is heard talking to himself, "Eighty thousand miles," and a little laugh.* BIFF *gets out of bed, comes downstage a bit, and stands attentively.* BIFF *is two years older than his brother* HAPPY, *well built, but in these days bears a worn air and seems less self-assured. He has succeeded less, and his dreams are stronger and less acceptable than* HAPPY's. HAPPY *is tall, powerfully made. Sexuality is like a visible color on him, or a scent that many women have discovered. He, like his brother, is lost, but in a different way, for he has never allowed himself to turn his face toward defeat and is thus more confused and hard-skinned, although seemingly more content.*

HAPPY [*getting out of bed*] He's going to get his license taken away if he keeps that up. I'm getting nervous about him, y'know, Biff?

BIFF His eyes are going.

HAPPY No, I've driven with him. He sees all right. He just doesn't keep his mind on it. I drove into the city with him last week. He stops at a green light and then it turns red and he goes. [*He laughs.*]

BIFF Maybe he's color-blind.

HAPPY   Pop? Why he's got the finest eye for color in the business. You know that.

BIFF [*sitting down on his bed*]   I'm going to sleep.

HAPPY   You're not still sour on Dad, are you, Biff?

BIFF   He's all right, I guess.

WILLY [*underneath them, in the living-room*]   Yes, sir, eighty thousand miles—eighty-two thousand!

BIFF   You smoking?

HAPPY [*holding out a pack of cigarettes*]   Want one?

BIFF [*taking a cigarette*]   I can never sleep when I smell it.

WILLY   What a simonizing job, heh!

HAPPY [*with deep sentiment*]   Funny, Biff, y'know? Us sleeping in here again? The old beds. [*He pats his bed affectionately*] All the talk that went across those two beds, huh? Our whole lives.

BIFF   Yeah. Lotta dreams and plans.

HAPPY [*with a deep and masculine laugh*]   About five hundred women would like to know what was said in this room.

They share a soft laugh.

BIFF   Remember that big Betsy something—what the hell was her name—over on Bushwick Avenue?

HAPPY [*combing his hair*]   With the collie dog!

BIFF   That's the one. I got you in there, remember?

HAPPY   Yeah, that was my first time—I think. Boy, there was a pig! [*They laugh, almost crudely.*] You taught me everything I know about women. Don't forget that.

BIFF   I bet you forgot how bashful you used to be. Especially with girls.

HAPPY   Oh, I still am, Biff.

BIFF   Oh, go on.

HAPPY   I just control it, that's all. I think I got less bashful and you got more so. What happened, Biff? Where's the old humor, the old confidence? [*He shakes* BIFF's *knee.* BIFF *gets up and moves restlessly about the room.*] What's the matter?

BIFF   Why does Dad mock me all the time?

HAPPY   He's not mocking you, he—

BIFF   Everything I say there's a twist of mockery on his face. I can't get near him.

HAPPY   He just wants you to make good, that's all. I wanted to talk to you about Dad for a long time, Biff. Something's—happening to him. He—talks to himself.

BIFF   I noticed that this morning. But he always mumbled.

HAPPY   But not so noticeable. It got so embarrassing I sent him to Florida. And you know something? Most of the time he's talking to you.

BIFF   What's he say about me?

HAPPY   I can't make it out.

BIFF   What's he say about me?

HAPPY   I think the fact that you're not settled, that you're still kind of up in the air . . .

BIFF   There's one or two other things depressing him, Happy.

HAPPY   What do you mean?

BIFF   Never mind. Just don't lay it all to me.

HAPPY   But I think if you just got started—I mean—is there any future for you out there?

BIFF   I tell ya, Hap, I don't know what the future is. I don't know—what I'm supposed to want.

HAPPY   What do you mean?

BIFF   Well, I spent six or seven years after high school trying to work myself up. Shipping clerk, salesman, business of one kind or another. And it's a measly manner of existence. To get on that subway on the hot mornings in summer. To devote your whole life to keeping stock, or making phone calls, or selling or buying. To suffer fifty weeks of the year for the sake of a two-week vacation, when all you really desire is to be outdoors, with your shirt off. And always to have to get ahead of the next fella. And still—that's how you build a future.

HAPPY   Well, you really enjoy it on a farm? Are you content out there?

BIFF [*with rising agitation*]   Hap, I've had twenty or thirty different kinds of jobs since I left home before the war, and it always turns out the same. I just realized it lately. In Nebraska when I herded cattle, and the Dakotas, and Arizona, and now in Texas. It's why I came home now, I guess, because I realized it. This farm I work on, it's spring there now, see? And they've got about fifteen new colts. There's nothing more inspiring or—beautiful than the sight of a mare and a new colt. And it's cool there now, see? Texas is cool now, and it's spring. And whenever spring comes to where I am, I suddenly get the feeling, my God, I'm not gettin' anywhere! What the hell am I doing, playing around with horses, twenty-eight dollars a week! I'm thirty-four years old, I oughta be makin' my future. That's when I come running home. And now, I get here, and I don't know what to do with myself. [*after a pause*] I've always made a point of not wasting my life, and everytime I come back here I know that all I've done is to waste my life.

HAPPY   You're a poet, you know that, Biff? You're a—you're an idealist!

BIFF   No, I'm mixed up very bad. Maybe I oughta get married. Maybe I oughta get stuck into something. Maybe that's my trouble. I'm like a boy. I'm not married, I'm not in business, I just—I'm like a boy. Are you content, Hap? You're a success, aren't you? Are you content?

HAPPY   Hell, no!

BIFF   Why? You're making money, aren't you?

HAPPY [*moving about with energy, expressiveness*]   All I can do now is wait for the merchandise manager to die. And suppose I get to be merchandise manager? He's a good friend of mine, and he just built a terrific estate on Long Island. And he lived there about two months and sold it, and now he's building another one. He can't enjoy it once it's finished. And I know that's just what I would do. I don't know what the hell I'm workin' for. Sometimes I sit in my apartment—all alone. And I think of the rent I'm paying. And it's crazy. But then, it's what I always wanted. My own apartment, a car, and plenty of women. And still, goddammit, I'm lonely.

BIFF [*with enthusiasm*]   Listen, why don't you come out West with me?

HAPPY   You and I, heh?

BIFF   Sure, maybe we could buy a ranch. Raise cattle, use our muscles. Men built like we are should be working out in the open.

HAPPY [*avidly*]   The Loman Brothers, heh?

BIFF [*with vast affection*]   Sure, we'd be known all over the counties!

HAPPY [*enthralled*]   That's what I dream about, Biff. Sometimes I want to just rip my clothes off in the middle of the store and outbox that goddam merchandise manager. I mean I can outbox, outrun, and outlift anybody in that store, and I have to take orders from those common, petty sons-of-bitches till I can't stand it any more.

BIFF I'm tellin' you, kid, if you were with me I'd be happy out there.

HAPPY [*enthused*] See, Biff, everybody around me is so false that I'm constantly lowering my ideals . . .

BIFF Baby, together we'd stand up for one another, we'd have someone to trust.

HAPPY If I were around you—

BIFF Hap, the trouble is we weren't brought up to grub for money. I don't know how to do it.

HAPPY Neither can I!

BIFF Then let's go!

HAPPY The only thing is—what can you make out there?

BIFF But look at your friend. Builds an estate and then hasn't the peace of mind to live in it.

HAPPY Yeah, but when he walks into the store the waves part in front of him. That's fifty-two thousand dollars a year coming through the revolving door, and I got more in my pinky finger than he's got in his head.

BIFF Yeah, but you just said—

HAPPY I gotta show some of those pompous, self-important executives over there that Hap Loman can make the grade. I want to walk into the store the way he walks in. Then I'll go with you, Biff. We'll be together yet, I swear. But take those two we had tonight. Now weren't they gorgeous creatures?

BIFF Yeah, yeah, most gorgeous I've had in years.

HAPPY I get that any time I want, Biff. Whenever I feel disgusted. The only trouble is, it gets like bowling or something. I just keep knockin' them over and it doesn't mean anything. You still run around a lot?

BIFF Naa. I'd like to find a girl—steady, somebody with substance.

HAPPY That's what I long for.

BIFF Go on! You'd never come home.

HAPPY I would! Somebody with character, with resistance! Like Mom, y'know? You're gonna call me a bastard when I tell you this. That girl Charlotte I was with tonight is engaged to be married in five weeks. [*He tries on his new hat.*]

BIFF No kiddin'!

HAPPY Sure, the guy's in line for the vice-presidency of the store. I don't know what gets into me, maybe I just have an overdeveloped sense of competition or something, but I went and ruined her, and furthermore I can't get rid of her. And he's the third executive I've done that to. Isn't that a crummy characteristic? And to top it all, I go to their weddings! [*Indignantly, but laughing*] Like I'm not supposed to take bribes. Manufacturers offer me a hundred-dollar bill now and then to throw an order their way. You know how honest I am, but it's like this girl, see. I hate myself for it. Because I don't want the girl, and, still, I take it and—I love it!

BIFF Let's go to sleep.

HAPPY I guess we didn't settle anything, heh?

BIFF I just got one idea that I think I'm going to try.

HAPPY What's that?

BIFF Remember Bill Oliver?

HAPPY   Sure, Oliver is very big now. You want to work for him again?

BIFF   No, but when I quit he said something to me. He put his arm on my shoulder, and he said, "Biff, if you ever need anything, come to me."

HAPPY   I remember that. That sounds good.

BIFF   I think I'll go to see him. If I could get ten thousand or even seven or eight thousand dollars I could buy a beautiful ranch.

HAPPY   I bet he'd back you. 'Cause he thought highly of you, Biff. I mean, they all do. You're well liked, Biff. That's why I say to come back here, and we both have the apartment. And I'm tellin' you, Biff, any babe you want . . .

BIFF   No, with a ranch I could do the work I like and still be something. I just wonder though. I wonder if Oliver still thinks I stole that carton of basketballs.

HAPPY   Oh, he probably forgot that long ago. It's almost ten years. You're too sensitive. Anyway, he didn't really fire you.

BIFF   Well, I think he was going to. I think that's why I quit. I was never sure whether he knew or not. I know he thought the world of me, though. I was the only one he'd let lock up the place.

WILLY [*below*]   You gonna wash the engine, Biff?

HAPPY   Shh!

BIFF *looks at* HAPPY, *who is gazing down, listening.* WILLY *is mumbling in the parlor.*

HAPPY   You hear that?

They listen. WILLY *laughs warmly.*

BIFF [*growing angry*]   Doesn't he know Mom can hear that?

WILLY   Don't get your sweater dirty, Biff!

A look of pain crosses BIFF'S *face.*

HAPPY   Isn't that terrible! Don't leave again, will you? You'll find a job here. You gotta stick around. I don't know what to do about him, it's getting embarrassing.

WILLY   What a simonizing job!

BIFF   Mom's hearing that!

WILLY   No kiddin', Biff, you got a date? Wonderful!

HAPPY   Go on to sleep. But talk to him in the morning, will you?

BIFF [*reluctantly getting into bed*]   With her in the house. Brother!

HAPPY [*getting into bed*]   I wish you'd have a good talk with him.

The light on their room begins to fade.

BIFF [*to himself in bed*]   That selfish, stupid . . .

HAPPY   Sh . . . Sleep, Biff.

Their light is out. Well before they have finished speaking, WILLY's *form is dimly seen below in the darkened kitchen. He opens the refrigerator, searches in there, and takes out a bottle of milk. The apartment houses are fading out, and the entire house and surroundings become covered with leaves. Music insinuates itself as the leaves appear.*

WILLY   Just wanna be careful with those girls, Biff, that's all. Don't make any promises. No promises of any kind. Because a girl, y'know, they always believe what you tell 'em, and you're very young, Biff, you're too young to be talking seriously to girls.

Light rises on the kitchen. WILLY, *talking, shuts the refrigerator door and comes downstage to the kitchen table. He pours milk into a glass. He is totally immersed in himself, smiling faintly.*

WILLY   Too young entirely, Biff. You want to watch your schooling first. Then when you're all set, there'll be plenty of girls for a boy like you. [*He smiles broadly at a kitchen chair.*] That so? The girls pay for you? [*He laughs.*] Boy, you must really be makin' a hit.

WILLY *is gradually addressing—physically—a point offstage, speaking through the wall of the kitchen, and his voice has been rising in volume to that of a normal conversation.*

WILLY   I been wondering why you polish the car so careful. Ha! Don't leave the hubcaps, boys. Get the chamois to the hubcaps. Happy, use newspaper on the windows, it's the easiest thing. Show him how to do it, Biff! You see, Happy? Pad it up, use it like a pad. That's it, that's it, good work. You're doin' all right, Hap. [*He pauses, then nods in approbation for a few seconds, then looks upward.*] Biff, first thing we gotta do when we get time is clip that big branch over the house. Afraid it's gonna fall in a storm and hit the roof. Tell you what. We get a rope and sling her around, and then we climb up there with a couple of saws and take her down. Soon as you finish the car, boys, I wanna see ya. I got a surprise for you, boys.
    BIFF [*offstage*]   Whatta ya got, Dad?
    WILLY   No, you finish first. Never leave a job till you're finished—remember that. [*Looking toward the "big trees"*] Biff, up in Albany I saw a beautiful hammock. I think I'll buy it next trip, and we'll hang it right between those two elms. Wouldn't that be something? Just swingin' there under those branches. Boy, that would be . . .

YOUNG BIFF *and* YOUNG HAPPY *appear from the direction* WILLY *was addressing.* HAPPY *carries rags and a pail of water.* BIFF, *wearing a sweater with a block "S," carries a football.*

    BIFF [*pointing in the direction of the car offstage*]   How's that, Pop, professional?
    WILLY   Terrific. Terrific job, boys. Good work, Biff.
    HAPPY   Where's the surprise, Pop?
    WILLY   In the back seat of the car.
    HAPPY   Boy! [*He runs off.*]
    BIFF   What is it, Dad? Tell me, what'd you buy?
    WILLY [*laughing, cuffs him*]   Never mind, something I want you to have.
    BIFF [*turns and starts off*]   What is it, Hap?
    HAPPY [*offstage*]   It's a punching bag!
    BIFF   Oh, Pop!
    WILLY   It's got Gene Tunney's signature on it!

HAPPY *runs onstage with a punching bag.*

BIFF   Gee, how'd you know we wanted a punching bag?

WILLY   Well, it's the finest thing for the timing.

HAPPY [*lies down on his back and pedals with his feet*]   I'm losing weight, you notice, Pop?

WILLY [*to* HAPPY]   Jumping rope is good too.

BIFF   Did you see the new football I got?

WILLY [*examining the ball*]   Where'd you get a new ball?

BIFF   The coach told me to practice my passing.

WILLY   That so? And he gave you the ball, heh?

BIFF   Well, I borrowed it from the locker room. [*He laughs confidentially.*]

WILLY [*laughing with him at the theft*]   I want you to return that.

HAPPY   I told you he wouldn't like it!

BIFF [*angrily*]   Well, I'm bringing it back!

WILLY [*stopping the incipient argument, to* HAPPY]   Sure, he's gotta practice with a regulation ball, doesn't he? [*To* BIFF] Coach'll probably congratulate you on your initiative!

BIFF   Oh, he keeps congratulating my initiative all the time, Pop.

WILLY   That's because he likes you. If somebody else took that ball there'd be an uproar. So what's the report, boys, what's the report?

BIFF   Where'd you go this time, Dad? Gee we were lonesome for you.

WILLY [*pleased, puts an arm around each boy and they come down to the apron*]   Lonesome, heh?

BIFF   Missed you every minute.

WILLY   Don't say? Tell you a secret, boys. Don't breathe it to a soul. Someday I'll have my own business, and I'll never have to leave home any more.

HAPPY   Like Uncle Charley, heh?

WILLY   Bigger than Uncle Charley! Because Charley is not—liked. He's liked, but he's not—well liked.

BIFF   Where'd you go this time, Dad?

WILLY   Well, I got on the road, and I went north to Providence. Met the Mayor.

BIFF   The Mayor of Providence!

WILLY   He was sitting in the hotel lobby.

BIFF   What'd he say?

WILLY   He said, "Morning!" And I said, "You got a fine city here, Mayor." And then he had coffee with me. And then I went to Waterbury. Waterbury is a fine city. Big clock city, the famous Waterbury clock. Sold a nice bill there. And then Boston—Boston is the cradle of the Revolution. A fine city. And a couple of other towns in Mass., and on to Portland and Bangor and straight home!

BIFF   Gee, I'd love to go with you sometime, Dad.

WILLY   Soon as summer comes.

HAPPY   Promise?

WILLY   You and Hap and I, and I'll show you all the towns. America is full of beautiful towns and fine, upstanding people. And they know me, boys, they know me up and down New England. The finest people. And when I bring you fellas up, there'll be open sesame for all of us, 'cause one thing, boys: I have friends. I can park my car in any street in New England, and the cops protect it like their own. This summer, heh?

BIFF and HAPPY [*together*]   Yeah! You bet!

WILLY   We'll take our bathing suits.

HAPPY   We'll carry your bags, Pop!

WILLY   Oh, won't that be something! Me comin' into the Boston stores with you boys carryin' my bags. What a sensation!

BIFF *is prancing around, practicing passing the ball.*

WILLY   You nervous, Biff, about the game?

BIFF   Not if you're gonna be there.

WILLY   What do they say about you in school, now that they made you captain?

HAPPY   There's a crowd of girls behind him everytime the classes change.

BIFF [*taking* WILLY's *hand*]   This Saturday, Pop, this Saturday—just for you, I'm going to break through for a touchdown.

HAPPY   You're supposed to pass.

BIFF   I'm takin' one play for Pop. You watch me, Pop, and when I take off my helmet, that means I'm breakin' out. Then you watch me crash through that line!

WILLY [*kisses* BIFF]   Oh, wait'll I tell this in Boston!

BERNARD *enters in knickers. He is younger than* BIFF, *earnest and loyal, a worried boy.*

BERNARD   Biff, where are you? You're supposed to study with me today.

WILLY   Hey, looka Bernard. What're you lookin' so anemic about, Bernard?

BERNARD   He's gotta study, Uncle Willy. He's got Regents next week.

HAPPY [*tauntingly, spinning* BERNARD *around*]   Let's box, Bernard!

BERNARD   Biff! [*He gets away from* HAPPY.] Listen, Biff, I heard Mr. Birnbaum say that if you don't start studyin' math he's gonna flunk you, and you won't graduate. I heard him!

WILLY   You better study with him, Biff. Go ahead now.

BERNARD   I heard him!

BIFF   Oh, Pop, you didn't see my sneakers! [*He holds up a foot for* WILLY *to look at.*]

WILLY   Hey, that's a beautiful job of printing!

BERNARD [*wiping his glasses*]   Just because he printed University of Virginia on his sneakers doesn't mean they've got to graduate him, Uncle Willy!

WILLY [*angrily*]   What're you talking about? With scholarships to three universities they're gonna flunk him?

BERNARD   But I heard Mr. Birnbaum say—

WILLY   Don't be a pest, Bernard! [*To his boys*] What an anemic!

BERNARD   Okay, I'm waiting for you in my house, Biff.

BERNARD *goes off. The* LOMANS *laugh.*

WILLY   Bernard is not well liked, is he?

BIFF   He's liked, but he's not well liked.

HAPPY   That's right, Pop.

WILLY   That's just what I mean. Bernard can get the best marks in school, y'understand, but when he gets out in the business world, y'understand, you are going to be five times ahead of him. That's why I thank Almighty God you're both built like Adonises. Because the man who makes an appearance in the business world, the man who creates personal interest, is the man who gets ahead. Be liked and you will never want. You take me, for instance. I never have to wait in line to see a buyer. "Willy Loman is here!" That's all they have to know, and I go right through.

BIFF   Did you knock them dead, Pop?

WILLY   Knocked 'em cold in Providence, slaughtered 'em in Boston.

HAPPY [*on his back, pedaling again*]   I'm losing weight, you notice, Pop?

LINDA *enters, as of old, a ribbon in her hair, carrying a basket of washing.*

LINDA [*with youthful energy*]   Hello, dear!

WILLY   Sweetheart!

LINDA   How'd the Chevvy run?

WILLY   Chevrolet, Linda, is the greatest car ever built. [*to the boys*] Since when do you let your mother carry wash up the stairs?

BIFF   Grab hold there, boy!

HAPPY   Where to, Mom?

LINDA   Hang them up on the line. And you better go down to your friends, Biff. The cellar is full of boys. They don't know what to do with themselves.

BIFF   Ah, when Pop comes home they can wait!

WILLY [*laughs appreciatively*]   You better go down and tell them what to do, Biff.

BIFF   I think I'll have them sweep out the furnace room.

WILLY   Good work, Biff.

BIFF [*goes through wall-line of kitchen to doorway at back and calls down*]   Fellas! Everybody sweep out the furnace room! I'll be right down!

VOICES   All right! Okay, Biff.

BIFF   George and Sam and Frank, come out back! We're hangin' up the wash! Come on, Hap, on the double! [*He and* HAPPY *carry out the basket.*]

LINDA   The way they obey him!

WILLY   Well, that's training, the training. I'm tellin' you, I was sellin' thousands and thousands, but I had to come home.

LINDA   Oh, the whole block'll be at that game. Did you sell anything?

WILLY   I did five hundred gross in Providence and seven hundred gross in Boston.

LINDA   No! Wait a minute, I've got a pencil. [*She pulls pencil and paper out of her apron pocket.*] That makes your commission . . . Two hundred—my God! Two hundred and twelve dollars!

WILLY   Well, I didn't figure it yet, but . . .

LINDA   How much did you do?

WILLY   Well, I—I did—about a hundred and eighty gross in Providence. Well, no—it came to—roughly two hundred gross on the whole trip.

LINDA [*without hesitation*]   Two hundred gross. That's . . . [*She figures.*]

WILLY   The trouble was that three of the stores were half closed for inventory in Boston. Otherwise I woulda broke records.

LINDA   Well, it makes seventy dollars and some pennies. That's very good.

WILLY   What do we owe?

LINA   Well, on the first there's sixteen dollars on the refrigerator—

WILLY   Why sixteen?

LINDA   Well, the fan belt broke, so it was a dollar eighty.

WILLY   But it's brand new.

LINDA   Well, the man said that's the way it is. Till they work themselves in, y'know.

They move through the wall-line into the kitchen.

WILLY   I hope we didn't get stuck on that machine.

LINDA   They got the biggest ads of any of them!

WILLY   I know, it's a fine machine. What else?

LINDA   Well, there's nine-sixty for the washing machine. And for the vacuum cleaner there's three and a half due on the fifteenth. Then the roof, you got twenty-one dollars remaining.

WILLY   It don't leak, does it?

LINDA   No, they did a wonderful job. Then you owe Frank for the carburetor.

WILLY   I'm not going to pay that man! That goddam Chevrolet, they ought to prohibit the manufacture of that car!

LINDA   Well, you owe him three and a half. And odds and ends, comes to around a hundred and twenty dollars by the fifteenth.

WILLY   A hundred and twenty dollars! My God, if business don't pick up I don't know what I'm gonna do!

LINDA   Well, next week you'll do better.

WILLY   Oh, I'll knock 'em dead next week. I'll go to Hartford. I'm very well liked in Hartford. You know, the trouble is, Linda, people don't seem to take to me.

They move onto the forestage.

LINDA   Oh, don't be foolish.

WILLY   I know it when I walk in. They seem to laugh at me.

LINDA   Why? Why would they laugh at you? Don't talk that way, Willy.

WILLY *moves to the edge of the stage.* LINDA *goes into the kitchen and starts to darn stockings.*

WILLY   I don't know the reason for it, but they just pass me by. I'm not noticed.

LINDA   But you're doing wonderful, dear. You're making seventy to a hundred dollars a week.

WILLY   But I gotta be at it ten, twelve hours a day. Other men—I don't know—they do it easier. I don't know why—I can't stop myself—I talk too much. A man oughta come in with a few words. One thing about Charley. He's a man of few words, and they respect him.

LINDA   You don't talk too much, you're just lively.

WILLY [*smiling*]   Well, I figure, what the hell, life is short, a couple of jokes. [*to himself*] I joke too much! [*The smile goes.*]

LINDA   Why? You're—

WILLY   I'm fat. I'm very—foolish to look at, Linda. I didn't tell you, but Christmas time I happened to be calling on F. H. Stewarts, and a salesman I know, as I was going in to see the buyer I heard him say something about—walrus. And I—I cracked him right across the face. I won't take that. I simply will not take that. But they do laugh at me. I know that.

LINDA   Darling . . .
WILLY   I gotta overcome it. I know I gotta overcome it. I'm not dressing to
advantage, maybe.
LINDA   Willy, darling, you're the handsomest man in the world—
WILLY   Oh, no, Linda.
LINDA   To me you are. [*Slight pause*] The handsomest.

From the darkness is heard the laughter of a woman. WILLY *doesn't turn to it, but
it continues through* LINDA's *lines.*

LINDA   And the boys, Willy. Few men are idolized by their children the way you
are.

Music is heard as behind a scrim, to the left of the house, THE WOMAN, *dimly
seen, is dressing.*

WILLY [*with great feeling*]   You're the best there is, Linda, you're a pal, you
know that? On the road—on the road I want to grab you sometimes and just kiss
the life outa you.

The laughter is loud now, and he moves into a brightening area at the left, where
THE WOMAN *has come from behind the scrim and is standing, putting on her hat,
looking into a "mirror" and laughing.*

WILLY   'Cause I get so lonely—especially when business is bad and there's
nobody to talk to. I get the feeling that I'll never sell anything again, that I won't
make a living for you, or a business, a business for the boys. [*He talks through*
THE WOMAN's *subsiding laughter;* THE WOMAN *primps at the "mirror."*] There's
so such I want to make for—
THE WOMAN   Me? You didn't make me, Willy. I picked you.
WILLY [*pleased*]   You picked me?
THE WOMAN [*who is quite proper-looking,* WILLY's *age*]   I did. I've been sitting
at that desk watching all the salesmen go by, day in, day out. But you've got such
a sense of humor, and we do have such a good time together, don't we?
WILLY   Sure, sure. [*He takes her in his arms.*] Why do you have to go now?
THE WOMAN   It's two o'clock . . .
WILLY   No, come on in! [*He pulls her.*]
THE WOMAN   . . . my sisters'll be scandalized. When'll you be back?
WILLY   Oh, two weeks about. Will you come up again?
THE WOMAN   Sure thing. You do make me laugh. It's good for me. [*She squeezes
his arm, kisses him.*] And I think you're a wonderful man.
WILLY   You picked me, heh?
THE WOMAN   Sure. Because you're so sweet. And such a kidder.
WILLY   Well, I'll see you next time I'm in Boston.
THE WOMAN   I'll put you right through to the buyers.
WILLY [*slapping her bottom*]   Right. Well, bottoms up!
THE WOMEN [*slaps him gently and laughs*]   You just kill me, Willy. [*He sud-
denly grabs her and kisses her roughly.*] You kill me. And thanks for the stockings.
I love a lot of stockings. Well, good night.
WILLY   Good night. And keep your pores open!

THE WOMAN   Oh, Willy!

THE WOMAN *bursts out laughing, and* LINDA's *laughter blends in.* THE WOMAN *disappears into the dark. Now the area at the kitchen table brightens.* LINDA *is sitting where she was at the kitchen table, but now is mending a pair of her silk stockings.*

LINDA   You are, Willy. The handsomest man. You've got no reason to feel that—

WILLY [*coming out of* THE WOMAN's *dimming area and going over to* LINDA]   I'll make it all up to you, Linda, I'll—

LINDA   There's nothing to make up, dear. You're doing fine, better than—

WILLY [*noticing her mending*]   What's that?

LINDA   Just mending my stockings. They're so expensive—

WILLY [*angrily, taking them from her*]   I won't have you mending stockings in this house! Now throw them out!

LINDA *puts the stockings in her pocket.*

BERNARD [*entering on the run*]   Where is he? If he doesn't study!

WILLY [*moving to the forestage, with great agitation*]   You'll give him the answers!

BERNARD   I do, but I can't on a Regents! That's a state exam! They're liable to arrest me!

WILLY   Where is he? I'll whip him, I'll whip him!

LINDA   And he'd better give back that football, Willy, it's not nice.

WILLY   Biff! Where is he? Why is he taking everything?

LINDA   He's too rough with the girls, Willy. All the mothers are afraid of him!

WILLY   I'll whip him!

BERNARD   He's driving the car without a license!

THE WOMAN's *laugh is heard.*

WILLY   Shut up!

LINDA   All the mothers—

WILLY   Shut up!

BERNARD [*backing quietly away and out*]   Mr. Birnbaum says he's stuck up.

WILLY   Get outa here!

BERNARD   If he doesn't buckle down he'll flunk math! [*He goes off.*]

LINDA   He's right, Willy, you've gotta—

WILLY [*exploding at her*]   There's nothing the matter with him! You want him to be a worm like Bernard? He's got spirit, personality . . .

As he speaks, LINDA, *almost in tears, exits into the living-room.* WILLY *is alone in the kitchen, wilting and staring. The leaves are gone. It is night again, and the apartment houses look down from behind.*

WILLY   Loaded with it. Loaded! What is he stealing? He's giving it back, isn't he? Why is he stealing? What did I tell him? I never in my life told him anything but decent things.

HAPPY *in pajamas has come down the stairs;* WILLY *suddenly becomes aware of* HAPPY's *presence.*

HAPPY   Let's go now, come on.

WILLY [*sitting down at the kitchen table*]   Huh! Why did she have to wax the floors herself? Everytime she waxes the floors she keels over. She knows that!

HAPPY   Shh! Take it easy. What brought you back tonight?

WILLY   I got an awful scare. Nearly hit a kid in Yonkers. God! Why didn't I go to Alaska with my brother Ben that time! Ben! That man was a genius, that man was success incarnate! What a mistake! He begged me to go.

HAPPY   Well, there's no use in—

WILLY   You guys! There was a man started with the clothes on his back and ended up with diamond mines!

HAPPY   Boy, someday I'd like to know how he did it.

WILLY   What's the mystery? The man knew what he wanted and went out and got it! Walked into a jungle, and comes out, the age of twenty-one, and he's rich! The world is an oyster, but you don't crack it open on a mattress!

HAPPY   Pop, I told you I'm gonna retire you for life.

WILLY   You'll retire me for life on seventy goddam dollars a week? And your women and your car and your apartment, and you'll retire me for life! Christ's sake, I couldn't get past Yonkers' today! Where are you guys, where are you? The woods are burning! I can't drive a car!

CHARLEY *has appeared in the doorway. He is a large man, slow of speech, laconic, immovable. In all he says, despite what he says, there is pity, and, now, trepidation. He has a robe over pajamas, slippers on his feet. He enters the kitchen.*

CHARLEY   Everything all right?

HAPPY   Yeah, Charley, everything's . . .

WILLY   What's the matter?

CHARLEY   I heard some noise. I thought something happened. Can't we do something about the walls? You sneeze in here, and in my house hats blow off.

HAPPY   Let's go to bed, Dad. Come on.

CHARLEY *signals to* HAPPY *to go.*

WILLY   You go ahead, I'm not tired at the moment.

HAPPY [*to* WILLY]   Take it easy, huh? [*He exits.*]

WILLY   What're you doin' up?

CHARLEY [*sitting down at the kitchen table opposite* WILLY]   Couldn't sleep good. I had a heartburn.

WILLY   Well, you don't know how to eat.

CHARLEY   I eat with my mouth.

WILLY   No, you're ignorant. You gotta know about vitamins and things like that.

CHARLEY   Come on, let's shoot. Tire you out a little.

WILLY [*hesitantly*]   All right. You got cards?

CHARLEY [*taking a deck from his pocket*]   Yeah, I got them. Someplace. What is it with those vitamins?

WILLY [*dealing*]   They build up your bones. Chemistry.

CHARLEY   Yeah, but there's no bones in a heartburn.
WILLY   What are you talkin' about? Do you know the first thing about it?
CHARLEY   Don't get insulted.
WILLY   Don't talk about something you don't know anything about.

They are playing. Pause.

CHARLEY   What're you doin' home?
WILLY   A little trouble with the car.
CHARLEY   Oh. [*Pause*] I'd like to take a trip to California.
WILLY   Don't say.
CHARLEY   You want a job?
WILLY   I got a job, I told you that. [*After a slight pause*] What the hell are you offering me a job for?
CHARLEY   Don't get insulted.
WILLY   Don't insult me.
CHARLEY   I don't see no sense in it. You don't have to go on this way.
WILLY   I got a good job. [*Slight pause*] What do you keep comin' in here for?
CHARLEY   You want me to go?
WILLY [*after a pause, withering*]   I can't understand it. He's going back to Texas again. What the hell is that?
CHARLEY   Let him go.
WILLY   I got nothin' to give him, Charley, I'm clean, I'm clean.
CHARLEY   He won't starve. None a them starve. Forget about him.
WILLY   Then what have I got to remember?
CHARLEY   You take it too hard. To hell with it. When a deposit bottle is broken you don't get your nickel back.
WILLY   That's easy enough for you to say.
CHARLEY   That ain't easy for me to say.
WILLY   Did you see the ceiling I put up in the living-room?
CHARLEY   Yeah, that's a piece of work. To put up a ceiling is a mystery to me. How do you do it?
WILLY   What's the difference?
CHARLEY   Well, talk about it.
WILLY   You gonna put up a ceiling?
CHARLEY   How could I put up a ceiling?
WILLY   Then what the hell are you bothering me for?
CHARLEY   You're insulted again.
WILLY   A man who can't handle tools is not a man. You're disgusting.
CHARLEY   Don't call me disgusting, Willy.

UNCLE BEN, *carrying a valise and an umbrella, enters the forestage from around the right corner of the house. He is a stolid man, in his sixties, with a mustache and an authoritative air. He is utterly certain of his destiny, and there is an aura of far places about him. He enters exactly as* WILLY *speaks.*

WILLY   I'm getting awfully tired, Ben.

BEN'S *music is heard.* BEN *looks around at everything.*

CHARLEY   Good, keep playing; you'll sleep better. Did you call me Ben?

BEN *looks at his watch.*

WILLY   That's funny. For a second there you reminded me of my brother Ben.

BEN   I only have a few minutes. [*He strolls, inspecting the place.* WILLY *and* CHARLEY *continue playing.*]

CHARLEY   You never heard from him again, heh? Since that time?

WILLY   Didn't Linda tell you? Couple of weeks ago we got a letter from his wife in Africa. He died.

CHARLEY   That so.

BEN [*chuckling*]   So this is Brooklyn, eh?

CHARLEY   Maybe you're in for some of his money.

WILLY   Naa, he had seven sons. There's just one opportunity I had with that man . . .

BEN   I must make a train, William. There are several properties I'm looking at in Alaska.

WILLY   Sure, sure! If I'd gone with him to Alaska that time, everything would've been totally different.

CHARLEY   Go on, you'd froze to death up there.

WILLY   What're you talking about?

BEN   Opportunity is tremendous in Alaska, William. Surprised you're not up there.

WILLY   Sure, tremendous.

CHARLEY   Heh?

WILLY   There was the only man I ever met who knew the answers.

CHARLEY   Who?

BEN   How are you all?

WILLY [*taking a pot, smiling*]   Fine, fine.

CHARLEY   Pretty sharp tonight.

BEN   Is Mother living with you?

WILLY   No, she died a long time ago.

CHARLEY   Who?

BEN   That's too bad. Fine specimen of a lady, Mother.

WILLY [*to* CHARLEY]   Heh?

BEN   I'd hoped to see the old girl.

CHARLEY   Who died?

BEN   Heard anything from Father, have you?

WILLY [*unnerved*]   What do you mean, who died?

CHARLEY [*taking a pot*]   What're you talkin' about?

BEN [*looking at his watch*]   William, it's half-past eight!

WILLY [*as though to dispel his confusion he angrily stops* CHARLEY's *hand*] That's my build!

CHARLEY   I put the ace—

WILLY   If you don't know how to play the game I'm not gonna throw my money away on you!

CHARLEY [*rising*]   It was my ace, for God's sake!

WILLY   I'm through, I'm through!

BEN   When did Mother die?

WILLY   Long ago. Since the beginning you never knew how to play cards.

CHARLEY [*picks up the cards and goes to the door*]   All right! Next time I'll bring a deck with five aces.

WILLY   I don't play that kind of game!

CHARLEY [*turning to him*]   You ought to be ashamed of yourself!

WILLY   Yeah?

CHARLEY   Yeah! [*He goes out.*]

WILLY [*slamming the door after him*]   Ignoramus!

BEN [*as WILLY comes toward him through the wall-line of the kitchen*]   So you're William.

WILLY [*shaking BEN's hand*]   Ben! I've been waiting for you so long! What's the answer? How did you do it?

BEN   Oh, there's a story in that.

LINDA *enters the forestage, as of old, carrying the wash basket.*

LINDA   Is this Ben?

BEN [*gallantly*]   How do you do, my dear.

LINDA   Where've you been all these years? Willy's always wondered why you—

WILLY [*pulling BEN away from her impatiently*]   Where is Dad? Didn't you follow him? How did you get started?

BEN   Well, I don't know how much you remember.

WILLY   Well, I was just a baby, of course, only three or four years old—

BEN   Three years and eleven months.

WILLY   What a memory, Ben!

BEN   I have many enterprises, William, and I have never kept books.

WILLY   I remember I was sitting under the wagon in—was it Nebraska?

BEN   It was South Dakota, and I gave you a bunch of wild flowers.

WILLY   I remember you walking away down some open road.

BEN [*laughing*]   I was going to find Father in Alaska.

WILLY   Where is he?

BEN   At that age I had a very faulty view of geography, William. I discovered after a few days that I was heading due south, so instead of Alaska, I ended up in Africa.

LINDA   Africa!

WILLY   The Gold Coast!

BEN   Principally diamond mines.

LINDA   Diamond mines!

BEN   Yes, my dear. But I've only a few minutes—

WILLY   No! Boys! Boys! [YOUNG BIFF *and* HAPPY *appear.*] Listen to this. This is your Uncle Ben, a great man! Tell my boys, Ben!

BEN   Why, boys, when I was seventeen I walked into the jungle, and when I was twenty-one I walked out. [*He laughs.*] And by God I was rich.

WILLY [*to the boys*]   You see what I been talking about? The greatest things can happen!

BEN [*glancing at his watch*]   I have an appointment in Ketchikan Tuesday week.

WILLY   No, Ben! Please tell about Dad. I want my boys to hear. I want them to know the kind of stock they spring from. All I remember is a man with a big beard, and I was in Mamma's lap, sitting around a fire, and some kind of high music.

BEN   His flute. He played the flute.

WILLY   Sure, the flute, that's right!

New music is heard, a high, rollicking tune.

BEN   Father was a very great and a very wild-hearted man. We would start in Boston, and he'd toss the whole family into the wagon, and then he'd drive the team right across the country; through Ohio, and Indiana, Michigan, Illinois, and all the Western states. And we'd stop in the towns and sell the flutes that he'd made on the way. Great inventor, Father. With one gadget he made more in a week than a man like you could make in a lifetime.

WILLY   That's just the way I'm bringing them up, Ben—rugged, well liked, all-around.

BEN   Yeah? [*to* BIFF] Hit that, boy—hard as you can. [*He pounds his stomach.*]

BIFF   Oh, no, sir!

BEN [*taking boxing stance*]   Come on, get to me! [*He laughs.*]

BIFF   Okay! [*He cocks his fists and starts in.*]

LINDA [*to* WILLY]   Why must he fight, dear?

BEN [*sparring with* BIFF]   Good boy! Good boy!

WILLY   How's that, Ben, heh?

HAPPY   Give him the left, Biff!

LINDA   Why are you fighting?

BEN   Good boy! [*Suddenly comes in, trips* BIFF, *and stands over him, the point of his umbrella poised over* BIFF's *eye.*]

LINDA   Look out, Biff!

BIFF   Gee!

BEN [*patting* BIFF's *knee*]   Never fight fair with a stranger, boy. You'll never get out of the jungle that way. [*Taking* LINDA's *hand and bowing*] It was an honor and a pleasure to meet you, Linda.

LINDA [*withdrawing her hand coldly, frightened*]   Have a nice—trip.

BEN [*to* WILLY]   And good luck with your—what do you do?

WILLY   Selling.

BEN   Yes. Well . . . [*He raises his hand in farewell to all.*]

WILLY   No, Ben, I don't want you to think . . . [*He takes* BEN's *arm to show him.*] It's Brooklyn, I know, but we hunt too.

BEN   Really, now.

WILLY   Oh, sure, there's snakes and rabbits and—that's why I moved out here. Why, Biff can fell any one of these trees in no time! Boys! Go right over to where they're building the apartment house and get some sand. We're gonna rebuild the entire front stoop right now! Watch this, Ben!

BIFF   Yes, sir! On the double, Hap!

HAPPY [*as he and* BIFF *run off*]   I lost weight, Pop, you notice?

CHARLEY *enters in knickers, even before the boys are gone.*

CHARLEY   Listen, if they steal any more from that building the watchman'll put the cops on them!

LINDA [*to* WILLY]   Don't let Biff . . .

BEN *laughs lustily.*

WILLY   You shoulda seen the lumber they brought home last week. At least a dozen six-by-tens worth all kinds a money.

CHARLEY Listen, if that watchman—

WILLY I gave them hell, understand. But I got a couple of fearless characters there.

CHARLEY Willy, the jails are full of fearless characters.

BEN [*clapping* WILLY *on the back, with a laugh at* CHARLEY] And the stock exchange, friend!

WILLY [*joining in* BEN's *laughter*] Where are the rest of your pants?

CHARLEY My wife bought them.

WILLY Now all you need is a golf club and you can go upstairs and go to sleep. [*To* BEN] Great athlete! Between him and his son Bernard they can't hammer a nail!

BERNARD [*rushing in*] The watchman's chasing Biff!

WILLY [*angrily*] Shut up! He's not stealing anything!

LINDA [*alarmed, hurrying off left*] Where is he? Biff, dear! [*She exits.*]

WILLY [*moving toward the left, away from* BEN] There's nothing wrong. What's the matter with you?

BEN Nervy boy. Good!

WILLY [*laughing*] Oh, nerves of iron, that Biff!

CHARLEY Don't know what it is. My New England man comes back and he's bleedin', they murdered him up there.

WILLY It's contacts, Charley, I got important contacts!

CHARLEY [*sarcastically*] Glad to hear it, Willy. Come in later, we'll shoot a little casino. I'll take some of your Portland money. [*He laughs at* WILLY *and exits.*]

WILLY [*turning to* BEN] Business is bad, it's murderous. But not for me, of course.

BEN I'll stop by on my way back to Africa.

WILLY [*longingly.*] Can't you stay a few days? You're just what I need, Ben, because I—I have a fine position here, but I—well, Dad left when I was such a baby and I never had a chance to talk to him and I still feel—kind of temporary about myself.

BEN I'll be late for my train.

They are at opposite ends of the stage.

WILLY Ben, my boys—can't we talk? They'd go into the jaws of hell for me, see, but I—

BEN William, you're being first-rate with your boys. Outstanding, manly chaps!

WILLY [*hanging on to his words*] Oh, Ben, that's good to hear! Because sometimes I'm afraid that I'm not teaching them the right kind of— Ben, how should I teach them?

BEN [*giving great weight to each word, and with a certain vicious audacity*] William, when I walked into the jungle, I was seventeen. When I walked out I was twenty-one. And, by God, I was rich! [*He goes off into darkness around the right corner of the house.*]

WILLY . . . was rich! That's just the spirit I want to imbue them with! To walk into a jungle! I was right! I was right! I was right!

BEN *is gone, but* WILLY *is still speaking to him as* LINDA, *in nightgown and robe, enters the kitchen, glances around for* WILLY, *then goes to the door of the house, looks out and sees him. Comes down to his left. He looks at her.*

LINDA   Willy, dear? Willy?

WILLY   I was right!

LINDA   Did you have some cheese? [*He can't answer.*] It's very late, darling. Come to bed, heh?

WILLY [*looking straight up*]   Gotta break your neck to see a star in this yard.

LINDA   You coming in?

WILLY   Whatever happened to that diamond watch fob? Remember? When Ben came from Africa that time? Didn't he give me a watch fob with a diamond in it?

LINDA   You pawned it, dear. Twelve, thirteen years ago. For Biff's radio correspondence course.

WILLY   Gee, that was a beautiful thing. I'll take a walk.

LINDA   But you're in your slippers.

WILLY [*starting to go around the house at the left*]   I was right! I was! [*Half to* LINDA, *as he goes, shaking his head*] What a man! There was a man worth talking to. I was right!

LINDA [*calling after* WILLY]   But in your slippers, Willy!

WILLY *is almost gone when* BIFF, *in his pajamas, comes down the stairs and enters the kitchen.*

BIFF   What is he doing out there?

LINDA   Sh!

BIFF   God Almighty, Mom, how long has he been doing this?

LINDA   Don't, he'll hear you.

BIFF   What the hell is the matter with him?

LINDA   It'll pass by morning.

BIFF   Shouldn't we do anything?

LINDA   Oh, my dear, you should do a lot of things, but there's nothing to do, so go to sleep.

HAPPY *comes down the stairs and sits on the steps.*

HAPPY   I never heard him so loud, Mom.

LINDA   Well, come around more often; you'll hear him. [*She sits down at the table and mends the lining of* WILLY's *jacket.*]

BIFF   Why didn't you ever write me about this, Mom?

LINDA   How would I write to you? For over three months you had no address.

BIFF   I was on the move. But you know I thought of you all the time. You know that, don't you, pal?

LINDA   I know, dear, I know. But he likes to have a letter. Just to know that there's still a possibility for better things.

BIFF   He's not like this all the time, is he?

LINDA   It's when you come home he's always the worst.

BIFF   When I come home?

LINDA   When you write you're coming, he's all smiles, and talks about the future, and—he's just wonderful. And then the closer you seem to come, the more shaky he gets, and then, by the time you get here, he's arguing, and he seems angry at you. I think it's just that maybe he can't bring himself to—to open up to you. Why are you so hateful to each other? Why is that?

BIFF [*evasively*]   I'm not hateful, Mom.

LINDA   But you no sooner come in the door than you're fighting!

BIFF   I don't know why. I mean to change. I'm tryin', Mom, you understand?

LINDA   Are you home to stay now?

BIFF   I don't know. I want to look around see what's doin'.

LINDA   Biff, you can't look around all your life, can you?

BIFF   I just can't take hold, Mom. I can't take hold of some kind of a life.

LINDA   Biff, a man is not a bird, to come and go with the springtime.

BIFF   Your hair . . . [*He touches her hair.*] Your hair got so gray.

LINDA   Oh, it's been gray since you were in high school. I just stopped dyeing it, that's all.

BIFF   Dye it again, will ya? I don't want my pal looking old. [*He smiles.*]

LINDA   You're such a boy! You think you can go away for a year and . . . You've got to get it into your head now that one day you'll knock on this door and there'll be strange people here—

BIFF   What are you talking about? You're not even sixty, Mom.

LINDA   But what about your father?

BIFF [*lamely*]   Well, I meant him too.

HAPPY   He admires Pop.

LINDA   Biff, dear, if you don't have any feeling for him, then you can't have any feeling for me.

BIFF   Sure I can, Mom.

LINDA   No. You can't just come to see me, because I love him. [*With a threat, but only a threat, of tears*] He's the dearest man in the world to me, and I won't have anyone making him feel unwanted and low and blue. You've got to make up your mind now, darling, there's no leeway any more. Either he's your father and you pay him that respect, or else you're not to come here. I know he's not easy to get along with—nobody knows that better than me—but . . .

WILLY [*from the left, with a laugh*]   Hey, hey, Biffo!

BIFF [*starting to go out after* WILLY]   What the hell is the matter with him? [HAPPY *stops him.*]

LINDA   Don't—don't go near him!

BIFF   Stop making excuses for him! He always, always wiped the floor with you. Never had an ounce of respect for you.

HAPPY   He's always had respect for—

BIFF   What the hell do you know about it?

HAPPY [*surlily*]   Just don't call him crazy!

BIFF   He's got no character—Charley wouldn't do this. Not in his own house— spewing out that vomit from his mind.

HAPPY   Charley never had to cope with what he's got to.

BIFF   People are worse off than Willy Loman. Believe me, I've seen them!

LINDA   Then make Charley your father, Biff. You can't do that, can you? I don't say he's a great man. Willy Loman never made a lot of money. His name was never in the paper. He's not the finest character that ever lived. But he's a human being, and a terrible thing is happening to him. So attention must be paid. He's not to be allowed to fall into his grave like an old dog. Attention, attention must be finally paid to such a person. You called him crazy—

BIFF   I didn't mean—

LINDA   No, a lot of people think he's lost his—balance. But you don't have to be very smart to know what his trouble is. The man is exhausted.

HAPPY   Sure!

LINDA   A small man can be just as exhausted as a great man. He works for a company thirty-six years this March, opens up unheard-of territories to their trademark, and now in his old age they take his salary away.

HAPPY [*indignantly*]   I didn't know that, Mom.

LINDA   You never asked, my dear! Now that you get your spending money someplace else you don't trouble your mind with him.

HAPPY   But I gave you money last—

LINDA   Christmas time, fifty dollars! To fix the hot water it cost ninety-seven fifty! For five weeks he's been on straight commission, like a beginner, an unknown!

BIFF   Those ungrateful bastards!

LINDA   Are they any worse than his sons? When he brought them business, when he was young, they were glad to see him. But now his old friends, the old buyers that loved him so and always found some order to hand him in a pinch—they're all dead, retired. He used to be able to make six, seven calls a day in Boston. Now he takes his valises out of the car and puts them back and takes them out again and he's exhausted. Instead of walking he talks now. He drives seven hundred miles, and when he gets there no one knows him any more, no one welcomes him. And what goes through a man's mind, driving seven hundred miles home without having earned a cent? Why shouldn't he talk to himself? Why? When he has to go to Charley and borrow fifty dollars a week and pretend to me that it's his pay? How long can that go on? How long? You see what I'm sitting here and waiting for? And you tell me he has no character? The man who never worked a day but for your benefit? When does he get the medal for that? Is this his reward—to turn around at the age of sixty-three and find his sons, who he loved better than his life, one a philandering bum—

HAPPY   Mom!

LINDA   That's all you are, my baby! [*To* BIFF] And you! What happened to the love you had for him? You were such pals! How you used to talk to him on the phone every night! How lonely he was till he could come home to you!

BIFF   All right, Mom. I'll live here in my room, and I'll get a job. I'll keep away from him, that's all.

LINDA   No, Biff. You can't stay here and fight all the time.

BIFF   He threw me out of this house, remember that.

LINDA   Why did he do that? I never knew why.

BIFF   Because I know he's a fake and he doesn't like anybody around who knows!

LINDA   Why a fake? In what way? What do you mean?

BIFF   Just don't lay it all at my feet. It's between me and him—that's all I have to say. I'll chip in from now on. He'll settle for half my pay check. He'll be all right. I'm going to bed. [*He starts for the stairs.*]

LINDA   He won't be all right.

BIFF [*turning on the stairs, furiously*]   I hate this city and I'll stay here. Now what do you want?

LINDA   He's dying, Biff.

HAPPY *turns quickly to her, shocked.*

BIFF [*after a pause*]   Why is he dying?

LINDA   He's been trying to kill himself.

BIFF [*with great horror*] How?

LINDA I live from day to day.

BIFF What're you talking about?

LINDA Remember I wrote you that he smashed up the car again? In February?

BIFF Well?

LINDA The insurance inspector came. He said that they have evidence. That all these accidents in the last year—weren't—weren't—accidents.

HAPPY How can they tell that? That's a lie.

LINDA It seems there's a woman . . . [*She takes a breath as*]

⎰ BIFF [*sharply but contained*] What woman?

⎱ LINDA [*simultaneously*] . . . and this woman . . .

LINDA What?

BIFF Nothing. Go ahead.

LINDA What did you say?

BIFF Nothing. I just said what woman?

HAPPY What about her?

LINDA Well, it seems she was walking down the road and saw his car. She says that he wasn't driving fast at all, and that he didn't skid. She says he came to that little bridge, and then deliberately smashed into the railing, and it was only the shallowness of the water that saved him.

BIFF Oh, no, he probably just fell asleep again.

LINDA I don't think he fell asleep.

BIFF Why not?

LINDA Last month . . . [*With great difficulty*] Oh, boys, it's so hard to say a thing like this! He's just a big stupid man to you, but I tell you there's more good in him than in many other people. [*She chokes, wipes her eyes.*] I was looking for a fuse. The lights blew out, and I went down the cellar. And behind the fuse box— it happened to fall out—was a length of rubber pipe—just short.

HAPPY No kidding?

LINDA There's a little attachment on the end of it. I knew right away. And sure enough, on the bottom of the water heater there's a new little nipple on the gas pipe.

HAPPY [*angrily*] That—jerk.

BIFF Did you have it taken off?

LINDA I'm—I'm ashamed to. How can I mention it to him? Every day I go down and take away that little rubber pipe. But, when he comes home, I put it back where it was. How can I insult him that way? I don't know what to do. I live from day to day, boys. I tell you, I know every thought in his mind. It sounds so old-fashioned and silly, but I tell you he put his whole life into you and you've turned your backs on him. [*She is bent over in the chair, weeping, her face in her hands.*] Biff, I swear to God! Biff, his life is in your hands!

HAPPY [*to* BIFF] How do you like that damned fool!

BIFF [*kissing her*] All right, pal, all right. It's all settled now. I've been remiss. I know that, Mom. But now I'll stay, and I swear to you, I'll apply myself. [*Kneeling in front of her, in a fever of self-reproach.*] It's just—you see, Mom, I don't fit in business. Not that I won't try. I'll try, and I'll make good.

HAPPY Sure you will. The trouble with you in business was you never tried to please people.

BIFF I know, I—

HAPPY Like when you worked for Harrison's. Bob Harrison said you were tops, and then you go and do some damn fool thing like whistling whole songs in the elevator like a comedian.

BIFF [*against* HAPPY]   So what? I like to whistle sometimes.

HAPPY   You don't raise a guy to a responsible job who whistles in the elevator!

LINDA   Well, don't argue about it now.

HAPPY   Like when you'd go off and swim in the middle of the day instead of taking the line around.

BIFF [*his resentment rising*]   Well, don't you run off? You take off sometimes, don't you? On a nice summer day?

HAPPY   Yeah, but I cover myself!

LINDA   Boys!

HAPPY   If I'm going to take a fade the boss can call any number where I'm supposed to be and they'll swear to him that I just left. I'll tell you something that I hate to say, Biff, but in the business world some of them think you're crazy.

BIFF [*angered*]   Screw the business world!

HAPPY   All right, screw it! Great, but cover yourself!

LINDA   Hap, Hap!

BIFF   I don't care what they think! They've laughed at Dad for years, and you know why? Because we don't belong in this nuthouse of a city! We should be mixing cement on some open plain, or—or carpenters. A carpenter is allowed to whistle!

WILLY *walks in from the entrance of the house, at left.*

WILLY   Even your grandfather was better than a carpenter. [*Pause. They watch him.*] You never grew up. Bernard does not whistle in the elevator, I assure you.

BIFF [*as though to laugh* WILLY *out of it*]   Yeah, but you do, Pop.

WILLY   I never in my life whistled in an elevator! And who in the business world thinks I'm crazy?

BIFF   I didn't mean it like that, Pop. Now don't make a whole thing out of it, will ya?

WILLY   Go back to the West! Be a carpenter, a cowboy, enjoy yourself!

LINDA   Willy, he was just saying—

WILLY   I heard what he said!

HAPPY [*trying to quiet* WILLY]   Hey, Pop, come on now . . .

WILLY [*continuing over* HAPPY'*s line*]   They laugh at me, heh? Go to Filene's, go to the Hub, go to Slattery's, Boston. Call out the name Willy Loman and see what happens! Big shot!

BIFF   All right, Pop.

WILLY   Big!

BIFF   All right!

WILLY   Why do you always insult me?

BIFF   I didn't say a word. [*To* LINDA] Did I say a word?

LINDA   He didn't say anything, Willy.

WILLY [*going to the doorway of the living-room*]   All right, good night, good night.

LINDA   Willy, dear, he just decided . . .

WILLY [*to* BIFF]   If you get tired hanging around tomorrow, paint the ceiling I put up in the living-room.

BIFF   I'm leaving early tomorrow.

HAPPY   He's going to see Bill Oliver, Pop.

WILLY [*interestedly*]   Oliver? For what?

BIFF [*with reserve, but trying, trying*]   He always said he'd stake me. I'd like to go into business, so maybe I can take him up on it.

LINDA   Isn't that wonderful?

WILLY   Don't interrupt. What's wonderful about it? There's fifty men in the City of New York who'd stake him. [*To* BIFF] Sporting goods?

BIFF   I guess so. I know something about it and—

WILLY   He knows something about it! You know sporting goods better than Spalding, for God's sake! How much is he giving you?

BIFF   I don't know, I didn't even see him yet, but—

WILLY   Then what're you talkin' about?

BIFF [*getting angry*]   Well, all I said was I'm gonna see him, that's all!

WILLY [*turning away*]   Ah, you're counting your chickens again.

BIFF [*starting left for the stairs*]   Oh, Jesus, I'm going to sleep!

WILLY [*calling after him*]   Don't curse in this house!

BIFF [*turning*]   Since when did you get so clean?

HAPPY [*trying to stop them*]   Wait a . . .

WILLY   Don't use that language to me! I won't have it!

HAPPY [*grabbing* BIFF, *shouts*]   Wait a minute! I got an idea. I got a feasible idea. Come here, Biff, let's talk this over now, let's talk some sense here. When I was down in Florida last time, I thought of a great idea to sell sporting goods. It just came back to me. You and I, Biff—we have a line, the Loman Line. We train a couple of weeks, and put on a couple of exhibitions, see?

WILLY   That's an idea!

HAPPY   Wait! We form two basketball teams, see? Two waterpolo teams. We play each other. It's a million dollars' worth of publicity. Two brothers, see? The Loman Brothers. Displays in the Royal Palms—all the hotels. And banners over the ring and the basketball court: "Loman Brothers." Baby, we could sell sporting goods!

WILLY   That is a one-million-dollar idea!

LINDA   Marvelous!

BIFF   I'm in great shape as far as that's concerned.

HAPPY   And the beauty of it is, Biff, it wouldn't be like a business. We'd be out playin' ball again . . .

BIFF [*enthused*]   Yeah, that's . . .

WILLY   Million-dollar . . .

HAPPY   And you wouldn't get fed up with it, Biff. It'd be the family again. There'd be the old honor, and comradeship, and if you wanted to go off for a swim or somethin'—well, you'd do it! Without some smart cooky gettin' up ahead of you!

WILLY   Lick the world! You guys together could absolutely lick the civilized world.

BIFF   I'll see Oliver tomorrow. Hap, if we could work that out . . .

LINDA   Maybe things are beginning to—

WILLY [*wildly enthused, to* LINDA]   Stop interrupting! [*To* BIFF] But don't wear sport jacket and slacks when you see Oliver.

BIFF   No, I'll—

WILLY   A business suit, and talk as little as possible, and don't crack any jokes.

BIFF   He did like me. Always liked me.

LINDA   He loved you!

WILLY [*to* LINDA]   Will you stop! [*To* BIFF] Walk in very serious. You are not applying for a boy's job. Money is to pass. Be quiet, fine, and serious. Everybody likes a kidder, but nobody lends him money.

HAPPY   I'll try to get some myself, Biff. I'm sure I can.

WILLY   I see great things for you kids, I think your troubles are over. But remember, start big and you'll end big. Ask for fifteen. How much you gonna ask for?

BIFF   Gee, I don't know—

WILLY   And don't say "Gee." "Gee" is a boy's word. A man walking in for fifteen thousand dollars does not say "Gee!"

BIFF   Ten, I think, would be top though.

WILLY   Don't be so modest. You always started too low. Walk in with a big laugh. Don't look worried. Start off with a couple of your good stories to lighten things up. It's not what you say, it's how you say it—because personality always wins the day.

LINDA   Oliver always thought the highest of him—

WILLY   Will you let me talk?

BIFF   Don't yell at her, Pop, will ya?

WILLY [*angrily*]   I was talking, wasn't I?

BIFF   I don't like you yelling at her all the time, and I'm tellin' you, that's all.

WILLY   What're you, takin' over this house?

LINDA   Willy—

WILLY [*turning on her*]   Don't take his side all the time, goddammit!

BIFF [*furiously*]   Stop yelling at her!

WILLY [*suddenly pulling on his cheek, beaten down, guilt ridden*]   Give my best to Bill Oliver—he may remember me.

He exits through the living-room doorway.

LINDA [*her voice subdued*]   What'd you have to start that for? [BIFF *turns away.*] You see how sweet he was as soon as you talked hopefully? [*She goes over to* BIFF.] Come up and say good night to him. Don't let him go to bed that way.

HAPPY   Come on, Biff, let's buck him up.

LINDA   Please, dear. Just say good night. It takes so little to make him happy. Come. [*She goes through the living-room doorway, calling upstairs from within the living-room.*] Your pajamas are hanging in the bathroom, Willy!

HAPPY [*looking toward where* LINDA *went out*]   What a woman! They broke the mold when they made her. You know that, Biff?

BIFF   He's off salary. My God, working on commission!

HAPPY   Well, let's face it: he's no hot-shot selling man. Except that sometimes, you have to admit, he's a sweet personality.

BIFF [*deciding*]   Lend me ten bucks, will ya? I want to buy some new ties.

HAPPY   I'll take you to a place I know. Beautiful stuff. Wear one of my striped shirts tomorrow.

BIFF   She got gray. Mom got awful old. Gee, I'm gonna go in to Oliver tomorrow and knock him for a—

HAPPY   Come on up. Tell that to Dad. Let's give him a whirl. Come on.

BIFF [*steamed up*]   You know, with ten thousand bucks, boy!

HAPPY [*as they go into the living-room*]   That's the talk, Biff, that's the first time I've heard the old confidence out of you! [*From within the living-room, fading off*] You're gonna live with me, kid, and any babe you want just say the word . . . [*The last lines are hardly heard. They are mounting the stairs to their parents' bedroom.*]

LINDA [*entering her bedroom and addressing* WILLY, *who is in the bathroom. She is straightening the bed for him.*] Can you do anything about the shower? It drips.

WILLY [*from the bathroom*] All of a sudden everything falls to pieces! Goddam plumbing, oughta be sued, those people. I hardly finished putting it in and the thing . . . [*His words rumble off.*]

LINDA I'm just wondering if Oliver will remember him. You think he might?

WILLY [*coming out of the bathroom in his pajamas*] Remember him? What's the matter with you, you crazy? If he'd've stayed with Oliver he'd be on top by now! Wait'll Oliver gets a look at him. You don't know the average caliber any more. The average young man today—[*He is getting into bed*]—is got a caliber of zero. Greatest thing in the world for him was to bum around.

BIFF *and* HAPPY *enter the bedroom. Slight pause.*

WILLY [*stops short, looking at* BIFF] Glad to hear it, boy.

HAPPY He wanted to say good night to you, sport.

WILLY [*to* BIFF] Yeah. Knock him dead, boy. What'd you want to tell me?

BIFF Just take it easy, Pop. Good night. [*He turns to go.*]

WILLY [*unable to resist*] And if anything falls off the desk while you're talking to him—like a package or something—don't you pick it up. They have office boys for that.

LINDA I'll make a big breakfast—

WILLY Will you let me finish? [*To* BIFF] Tell him you were in the business in the West. Not farm work.

BIFF All right, Dad.

LINDA I think everything—

WILLY [*going right through her speech*] And don't undersell yourself. No less than fifteen thousand dollars.

BIFF [*unable to bear him*] Okay. Good night, Mom. [*He starts moving.*]

WILLY Because you got a greatness in you, Biff, remember that. You got all kinds a greatness . . . [*He lies back, exhausted.*]

BIFF *walks out.*

LINDA [*calling after* BIFF] Sleep well, darling!

HAPPY I'm gonna get married, Mom. I wanted to tell you.

LINDA Go to sleep, dear.

HAPPY [*going*] I just wanted to tell you.

WILLY Keep up the good work. [HAPPY *exits.*] God . . . remember that Ebbets Field game? The championship of the city?

LINDA Just rest. Should I sing to you?

WILLY Yeah. Sing to me. [LINDA *hums a soft lullaby.*] When that team came out—he was the tallest, remember?

LINDA Oh, yes. And in gold.

BIFF *enters the darkened kitchen, takes a cigarette, and leaves the house. He comes downstage into a golden pool of light. He smokes, staring at the night.*

WILLY   Like a young god. Hercules—something like that. And the sun, the sun all around him. Remember how he waved to me? Right up from the field, with the representatives of three colleges standing by? And the buyers I brought, and the cheers when he came out—Loman, Loman, Loman! God Almighty, he'll be great yet. A star like that, magnificent, can never really fade away!

The light on WILLY *is fading. The gas heater begins to glow through the kitchen wall, near the stairs, a blue flame beneath red coils.*

LINDA [*timidly*]   Willy dear, what has he got against you?
WILLY   I'm so tired. Don't talk any more.

BIFF *slowly returns to the kitchen. He stops, stares toward the heater.*

LINDA   Will you ask Howard to let you work in New York?
WILLY   First thing in the morning. Everything'll be all right.

BIFF *reaches behind the heater and draws out a length of rubber tubing. He is horrified and turns his head toward* WILLY's *room, still dimly lit, from which the strains of* LINDA's *desperate but monotonous humming rise.*

WILLY [*staring through the window into the moonlight*]   Gee, look at the moon moving between the buildings!

BIFF *wraps the tubing around his hand and quickly goes up the stairs.*

Act II

Music is heard, gay and bright. The curtain rises as the music fades away. WILLY, *in shirt sleeves, is sitting at the kitchen table, sipping coffee, his hat in his lap.* LINDA *is filling his cup when she can.*

WILLY   Wonderful coffee. Meal in itself.
LINDA   Can I make you some eggs?
WILLY   No. Take a breath.
LINDA   You look so rested, dear.
WILLY   I slept like a dead one. First time in months. Imagine, sleeping till ten on a Tuesday morning. Boys left nice and early, heh?
LINDA   They were out of here by eight o'clock.
WILLY   Good work!
LINDA   It was so thrilling to see them leaving together. I can't get over the shaving lotion in this house!
WILLY [*smiling*]   Mmm—
LINDA   Biff was very changed this morning. His whole attitude seemed to be hopeful. He couldn't wait to get downtown to see Oliver.
WILLY   He's heading for a change. There's no question, there simply are certain men that take longer to get—solidified. How did he dress?

LINDA His blue suit. He's so handsome in that suit. He could be a—anything in that suit!

WILLY *gets up from the table.* LINDA *holds his jacket for him.*

WILLY There's no question, no question at all. Gee, on the way home tonight I'd like to buy some seeds.

LINDA [*laughing*] That'd be wonderful. But not enough sun gets back there. Nothing'll grow any more.

WILLY You wait, kid, before it's all over we're gonna get a little place out in the country, and I'll raise some vegetables, a couple of chickens . . .

LINDA You'll do it yet, dear.

WILLY *walks out of his jacket.* LINDA *follows him.*

WILLY And they'll get married, and come for a weekend. I'd build a little guest house. 'Cause I got so many fine tools, all I'd need would be a little lumber and some peace of mind.

LINDA [*joyfully*] I sewed the lining . . .

WILLY I could build two guest houses, so they'd both come. Did he decide how much he's going to ask Oliver for?

LINDA [*getting him into the jacket*] He didn't mention it, but I imagine ten or fifteen thousand. You going to talk to Howard today?

WILLY Yeah. I'll put it to him straight and simple. He'll just have to take me off the road.

LINDA And Willy, don't forget to ask for a little advance, because we've got the insurance premium. It's the grace period now.

WILLY That's a hundred . . . ?

LINDA A hundred and eight, sixty-eight. Because we're a little short again.

WILLY Why are we short?

LINDA Well, you had the motor job on the car . . .

WILLY That goddam Studebaker!

LINDA And you got one more payment on the refrigerator . . .

WILLY But it just broke again!

LINDA Well, it's old, dear.

WILLY I told you we should've bought a well-advertised machine. Charley bought a General Electric and it's twenty years old and it's still good, that son-of-a-bitch.

LINDA But, Willy—

WILLY Whoever heard of a Hastings refrigerator? Once in my life I would like to own something outright before it's broken! I'm always in a race with the junk-yard! I just finished paying for the car and it's on its last legs. The refrigerator consumes belts like a goddam maniac. They time those things. They time them so when you finally paid for them, they're used up.

LINDA [*buttoning up his jacket as he unbuttons it*] All told, about two hundred dollars would carry us, dear. But that includes the last payment on the mortgage. After this payment, Willy, the house belongs to us.

WILLY It's twenty-five years!

LINDA Biff was nine years old when we bought it.

WILLY Well, that's a great thing. To weather a twenty-five year mortgage is—

LINDA   It's an accomplishment.

WILLY   All the cement, the lumber, the reconstruction I put in this house! There ain't a crack to be found in it any more.

LINDA   Well, it served its purpose.

WILLY   What purpose? Some stranger'll come along, move in, and that's that. If only Biff would take this house, and raise a family . . . [*He starts to go.*] Good-by, I'm late.

LINDA [*suddenly remembering*]   Oh, I forgot! You're supposed to meet them for dinner.

WILLY   Me?

LINDA   At Frank's Chop House on Forty-eighth near Sixth Avenue.

WILLY   Is that so! How about you?

LINDA   No, just the three of you. They're gonna blow you to a big meal!

WILLY   Don't say! Who thought of that?

LINDA   Biff came to me this morning, Willy, and he said, "Tell Dad, we want to blow him to a big meal." Be there six o'clock. You and your two boys are going to have dinner.

WILLY   Gee whiz! That's really somethin'. I'm gonna knock Howard for a loop, kid. I'll get an advance, and I'll come home with a New York job. Goddammit, now I'm gonna do it!

LINDA   Oh, that's the spirit, Willy!

WILLY   I will never get behind a wheel the rest of my life!

LINDA   It's changing, Willy, I can feel it changing!

WILLY   Beyond a question. G'by, I'm late. [*He starts to go again.*]

LINDA [*calling after him as she runs to the kitchen table for a handkerchief*]   You got your glasses?

WILLY [*feels for them, then comes back in*]   Yeah, yeah, got my glasses.

LINDA [*giving him the handkerchief*]   And a handkerchief.

WILLY   Yeah, handkerchief.

LINDA   And your saccharine?

WILLY   Yeah, my saccharine.

LINDA   Be careful on the subway stairs.

She kisses him, and a silk stocking is seen hanging from her hand. WILLY *notices it.*

WILLY   Will you stop mending stockings? At least while I'm in the house. It gets me nervous. I can't tell you. Please.

LINDA *hides the stocking in her hand as she follows* WILLY *across the forestage in front of the house.*

LINDA   Remember, Frank's Chop House.

WILLY [*passing the apron*]   Maybe beets would grow out there.

LINDA [*laughing*]   But you tried so many times.

WILLY   Yeah. Well, don't work hard today. [*He disappears around the right corner of the house.*]

LINDA   Be careful!

As WILLY *vanishes,* LINDA *waves to him. Suddenly the phone rings. She runs across the stage and into the kitchen and lifts it.*

LINDA   Hello? Oh, Biff! I'm so glad you called, I just . . . Yes, sure, I just told him. Yes, he'll be there for dinner at six o'clock, I didn't forget. Listen, I was just dying to tell you. You know that little rubber pipe I told you about? That he connected to the gas heater? I finally decided to go down the cellar this morning and take it away and destroy it. But it's gone! Imagine? He took it away himself, it isn't there! [*She listens.*] When? Oh, then you took it. Oh—nothing, it's just that I'd hoped he'd taken it away himself. Oh, I'm not worried, darling, because this morning he left in such high spirits, it was like the old days! I'm not afraid any more. Did Mr. Oliver see you? . . . Well, you wait there then. And make a nice impression on him, darling. Just don't perspire too much before you see him. And have a nice time with Dad. He may have big news too! . . . That's right, a New York job. And be sweet to him tonight, dear. Be loving to him. Because he's only a little boat looking for a harbor. [*She is trembling with sorrow and joy.*] Oh, that's wonderful, Biff, you'll save his life. Thanks, darling. Just put your arm around him when he comes into the restaurant. Give him a smile. That's the boy . . . Good-by, dear. . . . You got your comb? . . . That's fine. Good-by, Biff dear.

In the middle of her speech, HOWARD WAGNER, *thirty-six, wheels on a small typewriter table on which is a wire-recording machine and proceeds to plug it in. This is on the left forestage. Light slowly fades on* LINDA *as it rises on* HOWARD. HOWARD *is intent on threading the machine and only glances over his shoulder as* WILLY *appears.*

WILLY   Pst! Pst!
HOWARD   Hello, Willy, come in.
WILLY   Like to have a little talk with you, Howard.
HOWARD   Sorry to keep you waiting. I'll be with you in a minute.
WILLY   What's that, Howard?
HOWARD   Didn't you ever see one of these? Wire recorder.
WILLY   Oh. Can we talk a minute?
HOWARD   Records things. Just got delivery yesterday. Been driving me crazy, the most terrific machine I ever saw in my life. I was up all night with it.
WILLY   What do you do with it?
HOWARD   I bought it for dictation, but you can do anything with it. Listen to this. I had it home last night. Listen to what I picked up. The first one is my daughter. Get this. [*He flicks the switch and "Roll out the Barrel" is heard being whistled.*] Listen to that kid whistle.
WILLY   That is lifelike, isn't it?
HOWARD   Seven years old. Get that tone.
WILLY   Ts, ts. Like to ask a little favor if you . . .

The whistling breaks off, and the voice of HOWARD'S DAUGHTER *is heard.*

HIS DAUGHTER   "Now you, Daddy."
HOWARD   She's crazy for me! [*Again the same song is whistled.*] That's me! Ha! [*He winks.*]
WILLY   You're very good!

The whistling breaks off again. The machine runs silent for a moment.

HOWARD   Sh! Get this now, this is my son.

HIS SON   "The capital of Alabama is Montgomery; the capital of Arizona is Phoenix; the capital of Arkansas is Little Rock; the capital of California is Sacramento . . ." [*And on, and on*]

HOWARD [*holding up five fingers*]   Five years old, Willy!

WILLY   He'll make an announcer some day!

HIS SON [*continuing*]   "The capital . . ."

HOWARD   Get that—alphabetical order! [*The machine breaks off suddenly.*] Wait a minute. The maid kicked the plug out.

WILLY   It certainly is a—

HOWARD   Sh, for God's sake!

IIIS SON   "It's nine o'clock, Bulova watch time. So I have to go to sleep."

WILLY   That really is—

HOWARD   Wait a minute! The next is my wife.

They wait.

HOWARD'S VOICE   "Go on, say something." [*Pause*] "Well, you gonna talk?"

HIS WIFE   "I can't think of anything."

HOWARD'S VOICE   "Well, talk—it's turning."

HIS WIFE [*shyly, beaten*]   "Hello." [*Silence*] "Oh, Howard, I can't talk into this . . ."

HOWARD [*snapping the machine off*]   That was my wife.

WILLY   That is a wonderful machine. Can we—

HOWARD   I tell you, Willy, I'm gonna take my camera, and my bandsaw, and all my hobbies, and out they go. This is the most fascinating relaxation I ever found.

WILLY   I think I'll get one myself.

HOWARD   Sure, they're only a hundred and a half. You can't do without it. Supposing you wanna hear Jack Benny, see? But you can't be at home at that hour. So you tell the maid to turn the radio on when Jack Benny comes on, and this automatically goes on with the radio . . .

WILLY   And when you come home you . . .

HOWARD   You can come home twelve o'clock, one o'clock, any time you like, and you get yourself a Coke and sit yourself down, throw the switch, and there's Jack Benny's program in the middle of the night!

WILLY   I'm definitely going to get one. Because lots of time I'm on the road, and I think to myself, what I must be missing on the radio!

HOWARD   Don't you have a radio in the car?

WILLY   Yeah, but who ever thinks of turning it on?

HOWARD   Say, aren't you supposed to be in Boston?

WILLY   That's what I want to talk to you about, Howard. You got a minute?

He draws a chair in from the wing.

HOWARD   What happened? What're you doing here?

WILLY   Well . . .

HOWARD   You didn't crack up again, did you?

WILLY   Oh, no. No . . .

HOWARD   Geez, you had me worried there for a minute. What's the trouble?

WILLY   Well, tell you the truth, Howard. I've come to the conclusion that I'd rather not travel any more.

HOWARD   Not travel! Well, what'll you do?

WILLY   Remember, Christmas time, when you had the party here? You said you'd try to think of some spot for me here in town.

HOWARD   With us?

WILLY   Well, sure.

HOWARD   Oh, yeah, yeah. I remember. Well, I couldn't think of anything for you, Willy.

WILLY   I tell ya, Howard. The kids are all grown up, y'know. I don't need much any more. If I could take home—well, sixty-five dollars a week, I could swing it.

HOWARD   Yeah, but Willy, see I—

WILLY   I tell ya why, Howard. Speaking frankly and between the two of us, y'know—I'm just a little tired.

HOWARD   Oh, I could understand that, Willy. But you're a road man, Willy, and we do a road business. We've only got a half-dozen salesmen on the floor here.

WILLY   God knows, Howard, I never asked a favor of any man. But I was with the firm when your father used to carry you up here in his arms.

HOWARD   I know that, Willy, but—

WILLY   Your father came to me the day you were born and asked me what I thought of the name of Howard, may he rest in peace.

HOWARD   I appreciate that, Willy, but there just is no spot here for you. If I had a spot I'd slam you right in, but I just don't have a single solitary spot.

He looks for his lighter. WILLY *has picked it up and gives it to him. Pause.*

WILLY [*with increasing anger*]   Howard, all I need to set my table is fifty dollars a week.

HOWARD   But where am I going to put you, kid?

WILLY   Look, it isn't a question of whether I can sell merchandise, is it?

HOWARD   No, but it's a business, kid, and everybody's gotta pull his own weight.

WILLY [*desperately*]   Just let me tell you a story, Howard—

HOWARD   'Cause you gotta admit, business is business.

WILLY [*angrily*]   Business is definitely business, but just listen for a minute. You don't understand this. When I was a boy—eighteen, nineteen—I was already on the road. And there was a question in my mind as to whether selling had a future for me. Because in those days I had a yearning to go to Alaska. See, there were three gold strikes in one month in Alaska, and I felt like going out. Just for the ride, you might say.

HOWARD [*barely interested*]   Don't say.

WILLY   Oh, yeah, my father lived many years in Alaska. He was an adventurous man. We've got quite a little streak of self-reliance in our family. I thought I'd go out with my older brother and try to locate him, and maybe settle in the North with the old man. And I was almost decided to go, when I met a salesman in the Parker House. His name was Dave Singleman. And he was eighty-four years old, and he'd drummed merchandise in thirty-one states. And old Dave, he'd go up to his room, y'understand, put on his green velvet slippers—I'll never forget—and pick up his phone and call the buyers, and without ever leaving his room, at the age of eighty-four, he made his living. And when I saw that, I realized that selling was the greatest career a man could want. 'Cause what could be more satisfying than to be able to go, at the age of eighty-four, into twenty or thirty different cities, and pick up a phone, and be remembered and loved and helped by so many different people? Do you know? when he died—and by the way he died the death of a salesman, in his green velvet slippers in the smoker of the New York, New Haven and Hartford, going into Boston—when he died, hundreds of salesmen and buyers were at his funeral. Things were sad on a lotta trains for months after that. [*He stands up.* HOWARD *has not looked at him.*] In those days there was personality in it, Howard. There was respect, and comradeship, and gratitude in it. Today, it's all cut and dried, and there's no chance for bringing friendship to bear—or personality. You see what I mean? They don't know me any more.

HOWARD [*moving away, to the right*]   That's just the thing, Willy.

WILLY   If I had forty dollars a week—that's all I'd need. Forty dollars, Howard.

HOWARD   Kid, I can't take blood from a stone, I—

WILLY [*desperation is on him now*]   Howard, the year Al Smith was nominated, your father came to me and—

HOWARD [*starting to go off*]   I've got to see some people, kid.

WILLY [*stopping him*]   I'm talking about your father! There were promises made across this desk! You mustn't tell me you've got people to see—I put thirty-four years into this firm, Howard, and now I can't pay my insurance! You can't eat the orange and throw the peel away—a man is not a piece of fruit! [*After a pause*] Now pay attention. Your father—in 1928 I had a big year. I averaged a hundred and seventy dollars a week in commissions.

HOWARD [*impatiently*]   Now, Willy, you never averaged—

WILLY [*banging his hand on the desk*]   I averaged a hundred and seventy dollars a week in the year of 1928! And your father came to me—or rather, I was in the office here—it was right over this desk—and he put his hand on my shoulder—

HOWARD [*getting up*]   You'll have to excuse me, Willy, I gotta see some people. Pull yourself together. [*Going out*] I'll be back in a little while.

On HOWARD's *exit, the light on his chair grows very bright and strange.*

WILLY   Pull myself together! What the hell did I say to him? My God, I was yelling at him! How could I! [WILLY *breaks off, staring at the light, which occupies the chair, animating it.*] Frank, Frank, don't you remember what you told me that time? How you put your hand on my shoulder, and Frank . . . [*He leans on the desk and as he speaks the dead man's name he accidentally switches on the recorder, and instantly*]

HOWARD's SON   ". . . of New York is Albany. The capital of Ohio is Cincinnati, the capital of Rhode Island is . . ." [*The recitation continues.*]

WILLY [*leaping way with fright, shouting*]   Ha! Howard! Howard! Howard!

HOWARD [*rushing in*]   What happened?

WILLY [*pointing at the machine, which continues nasally, childishly, with the capital cites*]   Shut it off! Shut it off!

HOWARD [*pulling the plug out*]   Look, Willy . . .

WILLY [*pressing his hands to his eyes*]   I gotta get myself some coffee. I'll get some coffee . . .

WILLY *starts to walk out.* HOWARD *stops him.*

HOWARD [*rolling up the cord*] Willy, look . . .

WILLY I'll go to Boston.

HOWARD Willy, you can't go to Boston for us.

WILLY Why can't I go?

HOWARD I don't want you to represent us. I've been meaning to tell you for a long time now.

WILLY Howard, are you firing me?

HOWARD I think you need a good long rest, Willy.

WILLY Howard—

HOWARD And when you feel better, come back, and we'll see if we can work something out.

WILLY But I gotta earn money, Howard. I'm in no position to—

HOWARD Where are your sons? Why don't your sons give you a hand?

WILLY They're working on a very big deal.

HOWARD This is no time for false pride, Willy. You go to your sons and you tell them that you're tired. You've got two great boys, haven't you?

WILLY Oh, no question, no question, but in the meantime . . .

HOWARD Then that's that, heh?

WILLY All right, I'll go to Boston tomorrow.

HOWARD No, no.

WILLY I can't throw myself on my sons. I'm not a cripple!

HOWARD Look, kid, I'm busy this morning.

WILLY [*grasping* HOWARD's *arm*] Howard, you've got to let me go to Boston!

HOWARD [*hard, keeping himself under control*] I've got a line of people to see this morning. Sit down, take five minutes, and pull yourself together, and then go home, will ya? I need the office, Willy. [*He starts to go, turns, remembering the recorder, starts to push off the table holding the recorder.*] Oh, yeah. Whenever you can this week, stop by and drop off the samples. You'll feel better, Willy, and then come back and we'll talk. Pull yourself together, kid, there's people outside.

HOWARD *exits, pushing the table off left.* WILLY *stares into space, exhausted. Now the music is heard—*BEN's *music—first distantly, then closer. As* WILLY *speaks,* BEN *enters from the right. He carries valise and umbrella.*

WILLY Oh, Ben, how did you do it? What is the answer? Did you wind up the Alaska deal already?

BEN Doesn't take much time if you know what you're doing. Just a short business trip. Boarding ship in an hour. Wanted to say good-by.

WILLY Ben, I've got to talk to you.

BEN [*glancing at his watch*] Haven't much time, William.

WILLY [*crossing the apron to* BEN] Ben, nothing's working out. I don't know what to do.

BEN Now, look here, William. I've bought timberland in Alaska and I need a man to look after things for me.

WILLY God, timberland! Me and my boys in those grand outdoors!

BEN You've a new continent at your doorstep, William. Get out of these cities, they're full of talk and time payments and courts of law. Screw on your fists and you can fight for a fortune up there.

WILLY Yes, yes! Linda, Linda!

LINDA *enters as of old, with the wash.*

LINDA Oh, you're back?
BEN I haven't much time.
WILLY No, wait! Linda, he's got a proposition for me in Alaska.
LINDA But you've got—[*To* BEN] He's got a beautiful job here.
WILLY But in Alaska, kid, I could—
LINDA You're doing well enough, Willy!
BEN [*to* LINDA] Enough for what, my dear?
LINDA [*frightened of* BEN *and angry at him*] Don't say those things to him!
Enough to be happy right here, right now. [*To* WILLY, *while* BEN *laughs*] Why
must everybody conquer the world? You're well liked, and the boys love you, and
someday—[*To* BEN]—why old man Wagner told him just the other day that if he
keeps it up he'll be a member of the firm, didn't he, Willy?
WILLY Sure, sure. I am building something with this firm, Ben, and if a man
is building something he must be on the right track, mustn't he?
BEN What are you building? Lay your hand on it. Where is it?
WILLY [*hesitantly*] That's true, Linda, there's nothing.
LINDA Why? [*To* BEN] There's a man eighty-four years old—
WILLY That's right, Ben, that's right. When I look at that man I say, what is
there to worry about?
BEN Bah!
WILLY It's true, Ben. All he has to do is go into any city, pick up the phone,
and he's making his living and you know why?
BEN [*picking up his valise*] I've got to go.
WILLY [*holding* BEN *back*] Look at this boy!

BIFF, *in his high school sweater, enters carrying suitcase.* HAPPY *carries* BIFF's
shoulder guards, gold helmet, and football pants.

WILLY Without a penny to his name, three great universities are begging for
him, and from there the sky's the limit, because it's not what you do, Ben. It's
who you know and the smile on your face! It's contacts, Ben, contacts! The whole
wealth of Alaska passes over the lunch table at the Commodore Hotel, and that's
the wonder, the wonder of this country, that a man can end with diamonds here
on the basis of being liked! [*He turns to* BIFF] And that's why when you get out
on that field today it's important. Because thousands of people will be rooting for
you and loving you. [*To* BEN, *who has again begun to leave*] And Ben! when he
walks into a business office his name will sound out like a bell and all the doors
will open to him! I've seen it, Ben, I've seen it a thousand times! You can't feel it
with your hand like timber, but it's there!
BEN Good-by, William.
WILLY Ben, am I right? Don't you think I'm right? I value your advice.
BEN There's a new continent at your doorstep, William. You could walk out
rich. Rich! [*He is gone.*]
WILLY We'll do it here, Ben! You hear me? We're gonna do it here!

YOUNG BERNARD *rushes in. The gay music of the Boys is heard.*

BERNARD Oh, gee, I was afraid you left already!

WILLY   Why? What time is it?

BERNARD   It's half-past one!

WILLY   Well, come on, everybody! Ebbets Field next stop! Where's the pennants? [*He rushes through the wall-line of the kitchen and out into the living-room.*]

LINDA [*to* BIFF]   Did you pack fresh underwear?

BIFF [*who has been limbering up*]   I want to go!

BERNARD   Biff, I'm carrying your helmet, ain't I?

HAPPY   No, I'm carrying the helmet.

BERNARD   Oh, Biff, you promised me.

HAPPY   I'm carrying the helmet.

BERNARD   How am I going to get in the locker room?

LINDA   Let him carry the shoulder guards. [*She puts her coat and hat on in the kitchen.*]

BERNARD   Can I, Biff? 'Cause I told everybody I'm going to be in the locker room.

HAPPY   In Ebbets Field it's the clubhouse.

BERNARD   I meant the clubhouse. Biff!

HAPPY   Biff!

BIFF [*grandly, after a slight pause*]   Let him carry the shoulder guards.

HAPPY [*as he gives* BERNARD *the shoulder guards*]   Stay close to us now.

WILLY *rushes in with the pennants.*

WILLY [*handing them out*]   Everybody wave when Biff comes out on the field. [HAPPY *and* BERNARD *run off.*] You set now, boy?

The music has died away.

BIFF   Ready to go, Pop. Every muscle is ready.

WILLY [*at the edge of the apron*]   You realize what this means?

BIFF   That's right, Pop.

WILLY [*feeling* BIFF's *muscles*]   You're comin' home this afternoon captain of the All-Scholastic Championship Team of the City of New York.

BIFF   I got it, Pop. And remember, pal, when I take off my helmet, that touchdown is for you.

WILLY   Let's go! [*He is starting out, with his arm around* BIFF, *when* CHARLEY *enters, as of old, in knickers.*] I got no room for you, Charley.

CHARLEY   Room? For what?

WILLY   In the car.

CHARLEY   You goin' for a ride? I wanted to shoot some casino.

WILLY [*furiously*]   Casino! [*Incredulously*] Don't you realize what today is?

LINDA   Oh, he knows, Willy. He's just kidding you.

WILLY   That's nothing to kid about!

CHARLEY   No, Linda, what's goin' on?

LINDA   He's playing in Ebbets Field.

CHARLEY   Baseball in this weather?

WILLY   Don't talk to him. Come on, come on! [*He is pushing them out.*]

CHARLEY   Wait a minute, didn't you hear the news?

WILLY   What?

CHARLEY   Don't you listen to the radio? Ebbets Field just blew up.

WILLY   You go to hell! [CHARLEY *laughs. Pushing them out.*] Come on, come on! We're late.

CHARLEY [*as they go*]   Knock a homer, Biff, knock a homer!

WILLY [*the last to leave, turning to* CHARLEY]   I don't think that was funny, Charley. This is the greatest day of his life.

CHARLEY   Willy, when are you going to grow up?

WILLY   Yeah, heh? When this game is over, Charley, you'll be laughing out the other side of your face. They'll be calling him another Red Grange. Twenty-five thousand a year.

CHARLEY [*kidding*]   Is that so?

WILLY   Yeah, that's so.

CHARLEY   Well, then, I'm sorry, Willy. But tell me something.

WILLY   What?

CHARLEY   Who is Red Grange?

WILLY   Put up your hands. Goddam you, put up your hands!

CHARLEY, *chuckling, shakes his head and walks away, around the left corner of the stage.* WILLY *follows him. The music rises to a mocking frenzy.*

WILLY   Who the hell do you think you are, better than everybody else? You don't know everything, you big, ignorant, stupid. . . . Put up your hands!

Light rises, on the right side of the forestage, on a small table in the reception room of CHARLEY's *office. Traffic sounds are heard.* BERNARD, *now mature, sits whistling to himself. A pair of tennis rackets and an overnight bag are on the floor beside him.*

WILLY [*offstage*]   What are you walking away for? Don't walk away! If you're going to say something say it to my face! I know you laugh at me behind my back. You'll laugh out of the other side of your goddam face after this game. Touchdown! Touchdown! Eighty thousand people! Touchdown. Right between the goal posts.

BERNARD *is a quiet, earnest, but self-assured young man.* WILLY's *voice is coming from right upstage now.* BERNARD *lowers his feet off the table and listens.* JENNY, *his father's secretary, enters.*

JENNY [*distressed*]   Say, Bernard, will you go out in the hall?

BERNARD   What is that noise? Who is it?

JENNY   Mr. Loman. He just got off the elevator.

BERNARD [*getting up*]   Who's he arguing with?

JENNY   Nobody. There's nobody with him. I can't deal with him any more, and your father gets all upset everytime he comes. I've got a lot of typing to do, and your father's waiting to sign it. Will you see him?

WILLY [*entering*]   Touchdown! Touch—[*He sees* JENNY.] Jenny, Jenny, good to see you. How're ya? Workin'? Or still honest?

JENNY   Fine. How've you been feeling?

WILLY   Not much any more, Jenny. Ha, ha! [*He is surprised to see the rackets.*]

BERNARD Hello, Uncle Willy.

WILLY [*almost shocked*] Bernard! Well, look who's here! [*He comes quickly, guiltily, to* BERNARD *and warmly shakes his hand.*]

BERNARD How are you? Good to see you.

WILLY What are you doing here?

BERNARD Oh, just stopped off to see Pop. Get off my feet till my train leaves. I'm going to Washington in a few minutes.

WILLY Is he in?

BERNARD Yes, he's in his office with the accountants. Sit down.

WILLY [*sitting down*] What're you going to do in Washington?

BERNARD Oh, just a case I've got there, Willy.

WILLY That so? [*Indicating the rackets*] You going to play tennis there?

BERNARD I'm staying with a friend who's got a court.

WILLY Don't say. His own tennis court. Must be fine people, I bet.

BERNARD They are, very nice. Dad tells me Biff's in town.

WILLY [*with a big smile*] Yeah, Biff's in. Working on a very big deal, Bernard.

BERNARD What's Biff doing?

WILLY Well, he's been doing very big things in the West. But he decided to establish himself here. Very big. We're having dinner. Did I hear your wife had a boy?

BERNARD That's right. Our second.

WILLY Two boys! What do you know!

BERNARD What kind of a deal has Biff got?

WILLY Well, Bill Oliver—very big sporting-goods man—he wants Biff very badly. Called him in from the West. Long distance, carte blanche, special deliveries. Your friends have their own private tennis court?

BERNARD You still with the old firm, Willy?

WILLY [*after a pause*] I'm—I'm overjoyed to see how you made the grade, Bernard, overjoyed. It's an encouraging thing to see a young man really—really— Looks very good for Biff—very—[*He breaks off, then*] Bernard— [*He is so full of emotion, he breaks off again.*]

BERNARD What is it, Willy?

WILLY [*small and alone*] What—what's the secret?

BERNARD What secret?

WILLY How—how did you? Why didn't he ever catch on?

BERNARD I wouldn't know that, Willy.

WILLY [*confidentially, desperately*] You were his friend, his boyhood friend. There's something I don't understand about it. His life ended after that Ebbets Field game. From the age of seventeen nothing good ever happened to him.

BERNARD He never trained himself for anything.

WILLY But he did, he did. After high school he took so many correspondence courses. Radio mechanics; television; God knows what, and never made the slightest mark.

BERNARD [*taking off his glasses*] Willy, do you want to talk candidly?

WILLY [*rising, faces* BERNARD] I regard you as a very brilliant man, Bernard. I value your advice.

BERNARD Oh, the hell with the advice, Willy. I couldn't advise you. There's just one thing I've always wanted to ask you. When he was supposed to graduate, and the math teacher flunked him—

WILLY Oh, that son-of-a-bitch ruined his life.

BERNARD   Yeah, but, Willy, all he had to do was go to summer school and make up that subject.

WILLY   That's right, that's right.

BERNARD   Did you tell him not to go to summer school?

WILLY   Me? I begged him to go. I ordered him to go!

BERNARD   Then why wouldn't he go?

WILLY   Why? Why! Bernard, that question has been trailing me like a ghost for the last fifteen years. He flunked the subject, and laid down and died like a hammer hit him!

BERNARD   Take it easy, kid.

WILLY   Let me talk to you—I got nobody to talk to. Bernard, Bernard, was it my fault? Y'see? It keeps going around in my mind, maybe I did something to him. I got nothing to give him.

BERNARD   Don't take it so hard.

WILLY   Why did he lay down? What is the story there? You were his friend!

BERNARD   Willy, I remember, it was June, and our grades came out. And he'd flunked math.

WILLY   That son-of-a-bitch!

BERNARD   No, it wasn't right then. Biff just got very angry, I remember, and he was ready to enroll in summer school.

WILLY [*surprised*]   He was?

BERNARD   He wasn't beaten by it at all. But then, Willy, he disappeared from the block for almost a month. And I got the idea that he'd gone up to New England to see you. Did he have a talk with you then?

WILLY *stares in silence.*

BERNARD   Willy?

WILLY [*with a strong edge of resentment in his voice*]   Yeah, he came to Boston. What about it?

BERNARD   Well, just that when he came back—I'll never forget this, it always mystifies me. Because I'd thought so well of Biff, even though he'd always taken advantage of me. I loved him, Willy, y'know? And he came back after that month and took his sneakers—remember the sneakers with "University of Virginia" printed on them? He was so proud of those, wore them every day. And he took them down in the cellar, and burned them up in the furnace. We had a fist fight. It lasted at least half an hour. Just the two of us, punching each other down the cellar, and crying right through it. I've often thought of how strange it was that I knew he'd given up his life. What happened in Boston, Willy?

WILLY *looks at him as at an intruder.*

BERNARD   I just bring it up because you asked me.

WILLY [*angrily*]   Nothing. What do you mean, "What happened?" What's that got to do with anything?

BERNARD   Well don't get sore.

WILLY   What are you trying to do, blame it on me? If a boy lays down is that my fault?

BERNARD   Now, Willy, don't get—

WILLY Well, don't—don't talk to me that way! What does that mean, "What happened?"

CHARLEY *enters. He is in his vest, and he carries a bottle of bourbon.*

CHARLEY Hey, you're going to miss that train. [*He waves the bottle.*]
BERNARD Yeah, I'm going. [*He takes the bottle.*] Thanks, Pop. [*He picks up his rackets and bag.*] Good-by, Willy, and don't worry about it. You know, "If at first you don't succeed . . ."
WILLY Yes, I believe in that.
BERNARD But sometimes, Willy, it's better for a man just to walk away.
WILLY Walk away?
BERNARD That's right.
WILLY But if you can't walk away?
BERNARD [*after a slight pause*] I guess that's when it's tough. [*Extending his hand*] Good-by, Willy.
WILLY [*shaking* BERNARD's *hand*] Good-by, boy
CHARLEY [*an arm on* BERNARD's *shoulder*] How do you like this kid? Gonna argue a case in front of the Supreme Court.
BERNARD [*protesting*] Pop!
WILLY [*genuinely shocked, pained, and happy*] No! The Supreme Court!
BERNARD I gotta run. 'By, Dad!
CHARLEY Knock 'em dead, Bernard!

BERNARD *goes off.*

WILLY [*as* CHARLEY *takes out his wallet*] The Supreme Court! And he didn't even mention it!
CHARLEY [*counting out money on the desk*] He don't have to—he's gonna do it.
WILLY And you never told him what to do, did you? You never took any interest in him.
CHARLEY My salvation is that I never took any interest in anything. There's some money—fifty dollars. I got an accountant inside.
WILLY Charley, look . . . [*With difficulty*] I got my insurance to pay. If you can manage it—I need a hundred and ten dollars.

CHARLEY *doesn't reply for a moment; merely stops moving.*

WILLY I'd draw it from my bank but Linda would know, and I . . .
CHARLEY Sit down, Willy.
WILLY [*moving toward the chair*] I'm keeping an account of everything, remember. I'll pay every penny back. [*He sits.*]
CHARLEY Now listen to me, Willy.
WILLY I want you to know I appreciate . . .
CHARLEY [*sitting down on the table*] Willy, what're you doin'? What the hell is goin' on in your head?
WILLY Why? I'm simply . . .
CHARLEY I offered you a job. You can make fifty dollars a week. And I won't send you on the road.

WILLY   I've got a job.

CHARLEY   Without pay? What kind of a job is a job without pay? [*He rises.*] Now, look, kid, enough is enough. I'm no genius but I know when I'm being insulted.

WILLY   Insulted!

CHARLEY   Why don't you want to work for me?

WILLY   What's the matter with you? I've got a job.

CHARLEY   Then what're you walkin' in here every week for?

WILLY [*getting up*]   Well, if you don't want me to walk in here—

CHARLEY   I am offering you a job.

WILLY   I don't want your goddam job!

CHARLEY   When the hell are you going to grow up?

WILLY [*furiously*]   You big ignoramus, if you say that to me again I'll rap you one! I don't care how big you are! [*He's ready to fight.*]

Pause.

CHARLEY [*kindly, going to him*]   How much do you need, Willy?

WILLY   Charley, I'm strapped. I'm strapped. I don't know what to do. I was just fired.

CHARLEY   Howard fired you?

WILLY   That snotnose. Imagine that? I named him. I named him Howard.

CHARLEY   Willy, when're you gonna realize that them things don't mean anything? You named him Howard, but you can't sell that. The only thing you got in this world is what you can sell. And the funny thing is that you're a salesman, and you don't know that.

WILLY   I've tried to think otherwise, I guess. I always felt that if a man was impressive, and well liked, that nothing—

CHARLEY   Why must everybody like you? Who liked J. P. Morgan? Was he impressive? In a Turkish bath he'd look like a butcher. But with his pockets on he was very well liked. Now listen, Willy, I know you don't like me, and nobody can say I'm in love with you, but I'll give you a job because—just for the hell of it, put it that way. Now what do you say?

WILLY   I—I just can't work for you, Charley.

CHARLEY   What're you, jealous of me?

WILLY   I can't work for you, that's all, don't ask me why.

CHARLEY [*angered, takes out more bills*]   You been jealous of me all your life, you damned fool! Here, pay your insurance. [*He puts the money in* WILLY's *hand.*]

WILLY   I'm keeping strict accounts.

CHARLEY   I've got some work to do. Take care of yourself. And pay your insurance.

WILLY [*moving to the right*]   Funny, y'know? After all the highways, and the trains, and the appointments, and the years, you end up worth more dead than alive.

CHARLEY   Willy, nobody's worth nothin' dead. [*After a slight pause*] Did you hear what I said?

WILLY *stands still, dreaming.*

CHARLEY   Willy!

WILLY   Apologize to Bernard for me when you see him. I didn't mean to argue with him. He's a fine boy. They're all fine boys, and they'll end up big—all of them. Someday they'll all play tennis together. Wish me luck, Charley. He saw Bill Oliver today.

CHARLEY   Good luck.

WILLY [*on the verge of tears*]   Charley, you're the only friend I got. Isn't that a remarkable thing? [*He goes out.*]

CHARLEY   Jesus!

CHARLEY *stares after him a moment and follows. All light blacks out. Suddenly raucous music is heard, and a red glow rises behind the screen at right.* STANLEY, *a young waiter, appears, carrying a table, followed by* HAPPY, *who is carrying two chairs.*

STANLEY [*putting the table down*]   That's all right, Mr. Loman, I can handle it myself. [*He turns and takes the chairs from* HAPPY *and places them at the table.*]

HAPPY [*glancing around*]   Oh, this is better.

STANLEY   Sure, in the front there you're in the middle of all kinds of noise. Whenever you got a party, Mr. Loman, you just tell me and I'll put you back here. Y'know, there's a lotta people they don't like it private, because when they go out they like to see a lotta action around them because they're sick and tired to stay in the house by theirself. But I know you, you ain't from Hackensack. You know what I mean?

HAPPY [*sitting down*]   So how's it coming, Stanley?

STANLEY   Ah, it's a dog's life. I only wish during the war they'd a took me in the Army. I coulda been dead by now.

HAPPY   My brother's back, Stanley.

STANLEY   Oh, he come back, heh? From the Far West.

HAPPY   Yeah, big cattle man, my brother, so treat him right. And my father's coming too.

STANLEY   Oh, your father too!

HAPPY   You got a couple of nice lobsters?

STANLEY   Hundred per cent, big.

HAPPY   I want them with claws.

STANLEY   Don't worry, I don't give you no mice. [HAPPY *laughs.*] How about some wine? It'll put a head on the meal.

HAPPY   No. You remember, Stanley, that recipe I brought you from overseas? With the champagne in it?

STANLEY   Oh, yeah, sure. I still got it tacked up yet in the kitchen. But that'll have to cost a buck apiece anyways.

HAPPY   That's all right.

STANLEY   What'd you, hit a number or somethin'?

HAPPY   No, it's a little celebration. My brother is—I think he pulled off a big deal today. I think we're going into business together.

STANLEY   Great! That's the best for you. Because a family business, you know what I mean?—that's the best.

HAPPY   That's what I think.

STANLEY   'Cause what's the difference? Somebody steals? It's in the family. Know what I mean? [*Sotto voce*] Like this bartender here. The boss is goin' crazy what kinda leak he's got in the cash register. You put it in but it don't come out.

HAPPY [*raising his head*] Sh!
STANLEY What?
HAPPY You notice I wasn't lookin' right or left, was I?
STANLEY No.
HAPPY And my eyes are closed.
STANLEY So what's the—?
HAPPY Strudel's comin'.
STANLEY [*catching on, looks around*] Ah, no, there's no—

He breaks off as a furred, lavishly dressed GIRL *enters and sits at the next table. Both follow her with their eyes.*

STANLEY Geez, how'd ya know?
HAPPY I got radar or something. [*Staring directly at her profile*] Oooooooo . . . Stanley.
STANLEY I think that's for you, Mr. Loman.
HAPPY Look at that mouth. Oh God. And the binoculars.
STANLEY Geez, you got a life, Mr. Loman.
HAPPY Wait on her.
STANLEY [*going to the* GIRL*'s table*] Would you like a menu, ma'am?
GIRL I'm expecting someone, but I'd like a—
HAPPY Why don't you bring her—excuse me, miss, do you mind? I sell champagne, and I'd like you to try my brand. Bring her a champagne, Stanley.
GIRL That's awfully nice of you.
HAPPY Don't mention it. It's all company money. [*He laughs.*]
GIRL That's a charming product to be selling, isn't it?
HAPPY Oh, gets to be like everything else. Selling is selling, y'know.
GIRL I suppose.
HAPPY You don't happen to sell, do you?
GIRL No, I don't sell.
HAPPY Would you object to a compliment from a stranger? You ought to be on a magazine cover.
GIRL [*looking at him a little archly*] I have been.

STANLEY *comes in with a glass of champagne.*

HAPPY What'd I say before, Stanley? You see? She's a cover girl.
STANLEY Oh, I could see, I could see.
HAPPY [*to the* GIRL] What magazine?
GIRL Oh, a lot of them. [*She takes the drink.*] Thank you.
HAPPY You know what they say in France, don't you? "Champagne is the drink of the complexion"—Hya, Biff!

BIFF *has entered and sits with* HAPPY.

BIFF Hello, kid. Sorry I'm late.
HAPPY I just got here. Uh, Miss—?
GIRL Forsythe.
HAPPY Miss Forsythe, this is my brother.
BIFF Is Dad here?

HAPPY   His name is Biff. You might've heard of him. Great football player.

GIRL   Really? What team?

HAPPY   Are you familiar with football?

GIRL   No, I'm afraid I'm not.

HAPPY   Biff is quarterback with the New York Giants.

GIRL   Well, that is nice, isn't it? [*She drinks.*]

HAPPY   Good health.

GIRL   I'm happy to meet you.

HAPPY   That's my name. Hap. It's really Harold, but at West Point they called me Happy.

GIRL [*now really impressed*]   Oh, I see. How do you do? [*She turns her profile.*]

BIFF   Isn't Dad coming?

HAPPY   You want her?

BIFF   Oh, I could never make that.

HAPPY   I remember the time that idea would never come into your head. Where's the old confidence, Biff?

BIFF   I just saw Oliver—

HAPPY   Wait a minute. I've got to see that old confidence again. Do you want her? She's on call.

BIFF   Oh, no. [*He turns to look at the* GIRL.]

HAPPY   I'm telling you. Watch this. [*Turning to the* GIRL] Honey? [*She turns to him*] Are you busy?

GIRL   Well, I am . . . but I could make a phone call.

HAPPY   Do that, will you, honey? And see if you can get a friend. We'll be here for a while. Biff is one of the greatest football players in the country.

GIRL [*standing up*]   Well, I'm certainly happy to meet you.

HAPPY   Come back soon.

GIRL   I'll try.

HAPPY   Don't try, honey, try hard.

The GIRL *exits.* STANLEY *follows, shaking his head in bewildered admiration.*

HAPPY   Isn't that a shame now? A beautiful girl like that? That's why I can't get married. There's not a good woman in a thousand. New York is loaded with them, kid!

BIFF   Hap, look—

HAPPY   I told you she was on call!

BIFF [*strangely unnerved*]   Cut it out, will ya? I want to say something to you.

HAPPY   Did you see Oliver?

BIFF   I saw him all right. Now look, I want to tell Dad a couple of things and I want you to help me.

HAPPY   What? Is he going to back you?

BIFF   Are you crazy? You're out of your goddam head, you know that?

HAPPY   Why? What happened?

BIFF [*breathlessly*]   I did a terrible thing today, Hap. It's been the strangest day I ever went through. I'm all numb, I swear.

HAPPY   You mean he wouldn't see you?

BIFF   Well, I waited six hours for him, see? All day. Kept sending my name in. Even tried to date his secretary so she'd get me to him, but no soap.

HAPPY   Because you're not showin' the old confidence, Biff. He remembered you, didn't he?

BIFF [*stopping* HAPPY *with a gesture*]   Finally, about five o'clock, he comes out. Didn't remember who I was or anything. I felt like such an idiot, Hap.

HAPPY   Did you tell him my Florida idea?

BIFF   He walked away. I saw him for one minute. I got so mad I could've torn the walls down! How the hell did I ever get the idea I was a salesman there? I even believed myself that I'd been a salesman for him! And then he gave me one look and—I realized what a ridiculous lie my whole life has been! We've been talking in a dream for fifteen years. I was a shipping clerk.

HAPPY   What'd you do?

BIFF [*with great tension and wonder*]   Well, he left, see. And the secretary went out. I was all alone in the waiting-room. I don't know what came over me, Hap. The next thing I know I'm in his office—paneled walls, everything. I can't explain it. I—Hap, I took his fountain pen.

HAPPY   Geez, did he catch you?

BIFF   I ran out. I ran down all eleven flights. I ran and ran and ran.

HAPPY   That was an awful dumb—what'd you do that for?

BIFF [*agonized*]   I don't know, I just—wanted to take something, I don't know. You gotta help me, Hap, I'm gonna tell Pop.

HAPPY   You crazy? What for?

BIFF   Hap, he's got to understand that I'm not the man somebody lends that kind of money to. He thinks I've been spiting him all these years and it's eating him up.

HAPPY   That's just it. You tell him something nice.

BIFF   I can't.

HAPPY   Say you got a lunch date with Oliver tomorrow.

BIFF   So what do I do tomorrow?

HAPPY   You leave the house tomorrow and come back at night and say Oliver is thinking it over. And he thinks it over for a couple of weeks, and gradually it fades away and nobody's the worse.

BIFF   But it'll go on forever!

HAPPY   Dad is never so happy as when he's looking forward to something!

WILLY *enters.*

HAPPY   Hello, scout!

WILLY   Gee, I haven't been here in years!

STANLEY *has followed* WILLY *in and sets a chair for him.* STANLEY *starts off but* HAPPY *stops him.*

HAPPY   Stanley!

STANLEY *stands by, waiting for an order.*

BIFF [*going to* WILLY *with guilt, as to an invalid*]   Sit down, Pop. You want a drink?

WILLY   Sure, I don't mind.

BIFF   Let's get a load on.

WILLY   You look worried.

BIFF   N-no. [*To* STANLEY] Scotch all around. Make it doubles.

STANLEY   Doubles, right. [*He goes.*]

WILLY   You had a couple already, didn't you?

BIFF   Just a couple, yeah.

WILLY   Well, what happened, boy? [*Nodding affirmatively, with a smile*] Everything go all right?

BIFF [*takes a breath, then reaches out and grasps* WILLY's *hand*]   Pal . . . [*He is smiling bravely, and* WILLY *is smiling too.*] I had an experience today.

HAPPY   Terrific, Pop.

WILLY   That so? What happened?

BIFF [*high, slightly alcoholic, above the earth*]   I'm going to tell you everything from first to last. It's been a strange day. [*Silence. He looks around, composes himself as best he can, but his breath keeps breaking the rhythm of his voice.*] I had to wait quite a while for him, and—

WILLY   Oliver?

BIFF   Yeah, Oliver. All day, as a matter of cold fact. And a lot of—instances—facts, Pop, facts about my life came back to me. Who was it, Pop? Who ever said I was a salesman with Oliver?

WILLY   Well, you were.

BIFF   No, Dad, I was a shipping clerk.

WILLY   But you were practically—

BIFF [*with determination*]   Dad, I don't know who said it first, but I was never a salesman for Bill Oliver.

WILLY   What're you talking about?

BIFF   Let's hold on to the facts tonight, Pop. We're not going to get anywhere bullin' around. I was a shipping clerk.

WILLY [*angrily*]   All right, now listen to me—

BIFF   Why don't you let me finish?

WILLY   I'm not interested in stories about the past or any crap of that kind because the woods are burning, boys, you understand? There's a big blaze going on all around. I was fired today.

BIFF [*shocked*]   How could you be?

WILLY   I was fired, and I'm looking for a little good news to tell your mother, because the woman has waited and the woman has suffered. The gist of it is that I haven't got a story left in my head, Biff. So don't give me a lecture about facts and aspects. I am not interested. Now what've you got to say to me?

STANLEY *enters with three drinks. They wait until he leaves.*

WILLY   Did you see Oliver?

BIFF   Jesus, Dad!

WILLY   You mean you didn't go up there?

HAPPY   Sure he went up there.

BIFF   I did.—I saw him. How could they fire you?

WILLY [*on the edge of his chair*]   What kind of a welcome did he give you?

BIFF   He won't even let you work on commission?

WILLY   I'm out! [*Driving*] So tell me, he gave you a warm welcome?

HAPPY   Sure, Pop, sure!

BIFF [*driven*]   Well, it was kind of—

WILLY   I was wondering if he'd remember you. [*To* HAPPY] Imagine, man doesn't see him for ten, twelve years and gives him that kind of a welcome!

HAPPY   Damn right!

BIFF [*trying to return to the offensive*]   Pop, look—

WILLY   You know why he remembered you, don't you? Because you impressed him in those days.

BIFF   Let's talk quietly and get this down to the facts, huh?

WILLY [*as though* BIFF *had been interrupting*]   Well, what happened? It's great news, Biff. Did he take you into his office or'd you talk in the waiting-room?

BIFF   Well, he came in, see, and—

WILLY [*with a big smile*]   What'd he say? Betcha he threw his arm around you.

BIFF   Well, he kinda—

WILLY   He's a fine man. [*To* HAPPY] Very hard man to see, y'know.

HAPPY [*agreeing*]   Oh, I know.

WILLY [*to* BIFF]   Is that where you had the drinks?

BIFF   Yeah, he gave me a couple of—no, no!

HAPPY [*cutting in*]   He told him my Florida idea.

WILLY   Don't interrupt. [*To* BIFF] How'd he react to the Florida idea?

BIFF   Dad, will you give me a minute to explain?

WILLY   I've been waiting for you to explain since I sat down here! What happened? He took you into his office and what?

BIFF   Well—I talked. And—and he listened, see.

WILLY   Famous for the way he listens, y'know. What was his answer?

BIFF   His answer was—[*He breaks off, suddenly angry.*] Dad, you're not letting me tell you what I want to tell you!

WILLY [*accusing, angered*]   You didn't see him, did you?

BIFF   I did see him!

WILLY   What'd you insult him or something? You insulted him, didn't you?

BIFF   Listen, will you let me out of it, will you just let me out of it!

HAPPY   What the hell!

WILLY   Tell me what happened!

BIFF [*to* HAPPY]   I can't talk to him!

A single trumpet note jars the ear. The light of green leaves stains the house, which holds the air of night and a dream. YOUNG BERNARD *enters and knocks on the door of the house.*

YOUNG BERNARD [*frantically*]   Mrs. Loman, Mrs. Loman!

HAPPY   Tell him what happened!

BIFF [*to* HAPPY]   Shut up and leave me alone!

WILLY   No, no! You had to go and flunk math!

BIFF   What math? What're you talking about?

YOUNG BERNARD   Mrs. Loman, Mrs. Loman!

LINDA *appears in the house, as of old.*

WILLY [*wildly*]   Math, math, math!

BIFF   Take it easy, Pop!

YOUNG BERNARD   Mrs. Loman!

WILLY [*furiously*]   If you hadn't flunked you'd've been set by now!

BIFF   Now, look, I'm gonna tell you what happened, and you're going to listen to me.

YOUNG BERNARD   Mrs. Loman!

BIFF   I waited six hours—

HAPPY   What the hell are you saying?

BIFF   I kept sending in my name but he wouldn't see me. So finally he . . .

He continues unheard as light fades low on the restaurant.

YOUNG BERNARD   Biff flunked math!

LINDA   No!

YOUNG BERNARD   Birnbaum flunked him! They won't graduate him!

LINDA   But they have to. He's gotta go to the university. Where is he? Biff! Biff!

YOUNG BERNARD   No, he left. He went to Grand Central.

LINDA   Grand—You mean he went to Boston!

YOUNG BERNARD   Is Uncle Willy in Boston?

LINDA   Oh, maybe Willy can talk to the teacher. Oh, the poor, poor boy!

Light on house area snaps out.

BIFF [*at the table, now audible, holding up a gold fountain pen*]   . . .so I'm washed up with Oliver, you understand? Are you listening to me?

WILLY [*at a loss*]   Yeah, sure. If you hadn't flunked—

BIFF   Flunked what? What're you talking about?

WILLY   Don't blame everything on me! I didn't flunk math—you did! What pen?

HAPPY   That was awful dumb, Biff, a pen like that is worth—

WILLY [*seeing the pen for the first time*]   You took Oliver's pen?

BIFF [*weakening*]   Dad, I just explained it to you.

WILLY   You stole Bill Oliver's fountain pen!

BIFF   I didn't exactly steal it! That's just what I've been explaining to you!

HAPPY   He had it in his hand and just then Oliver walked in, so he got nervous and stuck it in his pocket!

WILLY   My God, Biff!

BIFF   I never intended to do it, Dad!

OPERATOR'S VOICE   Standish Arms, good evening!

WILLY [*shouting*]   I'm not in my room!

BIFF [*frightened*]   Dad, what's the matter? [*He and* HAPPY *stand up.*]

OPERATOR   Ringing Mr. Loman for you!

WILLY   I'm not there, stop it!

BIFF [*horrified, gets down on one knee before* WILLY]   Dad, I'll make good, I'll make good. [WILLY *tries to get to his feet.* BIFF *holds him down.*] Sit down now.

WILLY   No, you're no good, you're no good for anything.

BIFF   I am, Dad, I'll find something else, you understand? Now don't worry about anything. [*He holds up* WILLY's *face.*] Talk to me, Dad.

OPERATOR   Mr. Loman does not answer. Shall I page him ?

WILLY [*attempting to stand, as though to rush and silence the* OPERATOR]   No, no, no!

HAPPY   He'll strike something, Pop.

WILLY   No, no . . .

BIFF [*desperately, standing over* WILLY]   Pop, listen! Listen to me! I'm telling you something good. Oliver talked to his partner about the Florida idea. You listening? He—he talked to his partner, and he came to me . . . I'm going to be all right, you hear? Dad, listen to me, he said it was just a question of the amount!

WILLY Then you . . . got it?

HAPPY He's gonna be terrific, Pop!

WILLY [*trying to stand*] Then you got it, haven't you? You got it! You got it!

BIFF [*agonized, holds* WILLY *down*] No, no. Look, Pop. I'm supposed to have lunch with them tomorrow. I'm just telling you this so you'll know that I can still make an impression, Pop. And I'll make good somewhere, but I can't go tomorrow, see?

WILLY Why not? You simply—

BIFF But the pen, Pop!

WILLY You give it to him and tell him it was an oversight!

HAPPY Sure, have lunch tomorrow!

BIFF I can't say that—

WILLY You were doing a crossword puzzle and accidentally used his pen!

BIFF Listen, kid, I took those balls years ago, now I walk in with his fountain pen? That clinches it, don't you see? I can't face him like that! I'll try elsewhere.

PAGE'S VOICE Paging Mr. Loman!

WILLY Don't you want to be anything?

BIFF Pop, how can I go back?

WILLY You don't want to be anything, is that what's behind it?

BIFF [*now angry at* WILLY *for not crediting his sympathy*] Don't take it that way! You think it was easy walking into that office after what I'd done to him? A team of horses couldn't have dragged me back to Bill Oliver!

WILLY Then why'd you go?

BIFF Why did I go? Why did I go! Look at you! Look at what's become of you!

Off left, THE WOMAN *laughs.*

WILLY Biff, you're going to go to that lunch tomorrow, or—

BIFF I can't go. I've got no appointment!

HAPPY Biff, for . . . !

WILLY Are you spiting me?

BIFF Don't take it that way! Goddammit!

WILLY [*strikes* BIFF *and falters away from the table*] You rotten little louse! Are you spiting me?

THE WOMAN Someone's at the door, Willy!

BIFF I'm no good, can't you see what I am?

HAPPY [*separating them*] Hey, you're in a restaurant! Now cut it out, both of you! [*The girls enter.*] Hello, girls, sit down.

THE WOMAN *laughs, off left.*

MISS FORSYTHE I guess we might as well. This is Letta.

THE WOMAN Willy, are you going to wake up?

BIFF [*ignoring* WILLY] How're ya, miss, sit down. What do you drink?

MISS FORSYTHE Letta might not be able to stay long.

LETTA I gotta get up very early tomorrow. I got jury duty. I'm so excited! Were you fellows ever on a jury?

BIFF   No, but I been in front of them! [*The girls laugh.*] This is my father.

LETTA   Isn't he cute? Sit down with us, Pop.

HAPPY   Sit him down, Biff!

BIFF [*going to him*]   Come on, slugger, drink us under the table. To hell with it! Come on, sit down, pal.

On BIFF's *last insistence,* WILLY *is about to sit.*

The WOMAN [*now urgently*]   Willy, are you going to answer the door!

THE WOMAN's *call pulls* WILLY *back. He starts right, befuddled.*

BIFF   Hey, where are you going?

WILLY   Open the door.

BIFF   The door?

WILLY   The washroom . . . the door . . . where's the door?

BIFF [*leading* WILLY *to the left*]   Just go straight down.

WILLY *moves left.*

THE WOMAN   Willy, Willy, are you going to get up, get up, get up, get up?

WILLY *exits left.*

LETTA   I think it's sweet you bring your daddy along.

MISS FORSYTHE   Oh, he isn't really your father!

BIFF [*at left, turning to her resentfully*]   Miss Forsythe, you've just seen a prince walk by. A fine, troubled prince. A hard-working, unappreciated prince. A pal, you understand? A good companion. Always for his boys.

LETTA   That's so sweet.

HAPPY   Well, girls, what's the program? We're wasting time. Come on, Biff. Gather round. Where would you like to go?

BIFF   Why don't you do something for him?

HAPPY   Me!

BIFF   Don't you give a damn for him, Hap?

HAPPY   What're you talking about? I'm the one who—

BIFF   I sense it, you don't give a good goddam about him. [*He takes the rolled-up hose from his pocket and puts it on the table in front of* HAPPY.] Look what I found in the cellar, for Christ's sake. How can you bear to let it go on?

HAPPY   Me? Who goes away? Who runs off and—

BIFF   Yeah, but he doesn't mean anything to you. You could help him—I can't! Don't you understand what I'm talking about? He's going to kill himself, don't you know that?

HAPPY   Don't I know it! Me!

BIFF   Hap, help him! Jesus . . . help him . . . Help me, help me, I can't bear to look at his face! [*Ready to weep, he hurries out, up right.*]

HAPPY [*starting after him*]   Where are you going?

MISS FORSYTHE   What's he so mad about?

HAPPY   Come on, girls, we'll catch up with him.

MISS FORSYTHE [*as* HAPPY *pushes her out*]   Say, I don't like that temper of his!

HAPPY   He's just a little overstrung, he'll be all right!

WILLY [*off left, as* THE WOMAN *laughs*]   Don't answer! Don't answer!

LETTA   Don't you want to tell your father—

HAPPY   No, that's not my father. He's just a guy. Come on, we'll catch Biff, and, honey, we're going to paint this town! Stanley, where's the check! Hey, Stanley!

They exit. STANLEY *looks toward left.*

STANLEY [*calling to* HAPPY *indignantly*]   Mr. Loman! Mr. Loman!

STANLEY *picks up a chair and follows them off. Knocking is heard off left.* THE WOMAN *enters, laughing.* WILLY *follows her. She is in a black slip; he is buttoning his shirt. Raw, sensuous music accompanies their speech.*

WILLY   Will you stop laughing? Will you stop?

THE WOMAN   Aren't you going to answer the door? He'll wake the whole hotel.

WILLY   I'm not expecting anybody.

THE WOMAN   Whyn't you have another drink, honey, and stop being so damn self-centered?

WILLY   I'm so lonely.

THE WOMAN   You know you ruined me, Willy? From now on, whenever you come to the office, I'll see that you go right through to the buyers. No waiting at my desk any more, Willy. You ruined me.

WILLY   That's nice of you to say that.

THE WOMAN   Gee, you are self-centered! Why so sad? You are the saddest, self-centeredest soul I ever did see-saw. [*She laughs.*] [*He kisses her.*] Come on inside, drummer boy. It's silly to be dressing in the middle of the night. [*As knocking is heard*] Aren't you going to answer the door?

WILLY   They're knocking on the wrong door.

THE WOMAN   But I felt the knocking. And he heard us talking in here. Maybe the hotel's on fire!

WILLY [*his terror rising*]   It's a mistake.

THE WOMAN   Then tell him to go away!

WILLY   There's nobody there.

THE WOMAN   It's getting on my nerves, Willy. There's somebody standing out there and it's getting on my nerves!

WILLY [*pushing her away from him*]   All right, stay in the bathroom here, and don't come out. I think there's a law in Massachusetts about it, so don't come out. It may be that new room clerk. He looked very mean. So don't come out. It's a mistake, there's no fire.

The knocking is heard again. He takes a few steps away from her, and she vanishes into the wing. The light follows him, and now he is facing YOUNG BIFF, *who carries a suitcase.* BIFF *steps toward him. The music is gone.*

BIFF   Why didn't you answer?

WILLY   Biff! What are you doing in Boston?

BIFF   Why didn't you answer? I've been knocking for five minutes, I called you on the phone—

WILLY I just heard you. I was in the bathroom and had the door shut. Did anything happen home?

BIFF Dad—I let you down.

WILLY What do you mean?

BIFF Dad . . .

WILLY Biffo, what's this about? [*Putting his arm around* BIFF] Come on, let's go downstairs and get you a malted.

BIFF Dad, I flunked math.

WILLY Not for the term?

BIFF The term. I haven't got enough credits to graduate.

WILLY You mean to say Bernard wouldn't give you the answers?

BIFF He did, he tried, but I only got a sixty-one.

WILLY And they wouldn't give you four points?

BIFF Birnbaum refused absolutely. I begged him, Pop, but he won't give me those points. You gotta talk to him before they close the school. Because if he saw the kind of man you are, and you just talked to him in your way, I'm sure he'd come through for me. The class came right before practice, see, and I didn't go enough. Would you talk to him? He'd like you, Pop. You know the way you could talk.

WILLY You're on. We'll drive right back.

BIFF Oh, Dad, good work! I'm sure he'll change it for you!

WILLY Go downstairs and tell the clerk I'm checkin' out. Go right down.

BIFF Yes, sir! See, the reason he hates me, Pop—one day he was late for class so I got up at the blackboard and imitated him. I crossed my eyes and talked with a lithp.

WILLY [*laughing*] You did? The kids like it?

BIFF They nearly died laughing!

WILLY Yeah? What'd you do?

BIFF The thquare root of thixthy twee is . . . [WILLY *bursts out laughing;* BIFF *joins him.*] And in the middle of it he walked in!

WILLY *laughs and* THE WOMAN *joins in offstage.*

WILLY [*without hesitation*] Hurry downstairs and—

BIFF Somebody in there?

WILLY No, that was next door.

BIFF Somebody got in your bathroom!

THE WOMAN *laughs offstage.*

WILLY No, it's the next room, there's a party—

THE WOMAN [*enters, laughing. She lisps this*] Can I come in? There's something in the bathtub, Willy, and it's moving!

WILLY *looks at* BIFF, *who is staring open-mouthed and horrified at* THE WOMAN.

WILLY Ah—you better go back to your room. They must be finished painting by now. They're painting her room so I let her take a shower here. Go back, go back . . . [*He pushes her.*]

THE WOMAN [*resisting*] But I've got to get dressed, Willy, I can't—

WILLY   Get out of here! Go back, go back . . . [*Suddenly striving for the ordinary*] This is Miss Francis, Biff, she's a buyer. They're painting her room. Go back, Miss Francis, go back . . .

THE WOMAN   But my clothes, I can't go out naked in the hall!

WILLY [*pushing her offstage*]   Get outa here! Go back, go back!

BIFF *slowly sits down on his suitcase as the argument continues offstage.*

THE WOMAN   Where's my stockings? You promised me stockings, Willy!

WILLY   I have no stockings here!

THE WOMAN   You had two boxes of size nine sheers for me, and I want them!

WILLY   Here, for God's sake, will you get outa here!

THE WOMAN [*enters holding a box of stockings*]   I just hope there's nobody in the hall. That's all I hope. [*To* BIFF] Are you football or baseball?

BIFF   Football.

THE WOMAN [*angry, humiliated*]   That's me too. G'night. [*She snatches her clothes from* WILLY, *and walks out.*]

WILLY [*after a pause*]   Well, better get going. I want to get to the school first thing in the morning. Get my suits out of the closet. I'll get my valise. [BIFF *doesn't move.*] What's the matter? [BIFF *remains motionless, tears falling*] She's a buyer. Buys for J. H. Simmons. She lives down the hall—they're painting. You don't imagine—[*He breaks off. After a pause*] Now listen, pal, she's just a buyer. She sees merchandise in her room and they have to keep it looking just so . . . [*Pause. Assuming command*] All right, get my suits. [BIFF *doesn't move.*] Now stop crying and do as I say. I gave you an order. Biff, I gave you an order! Is that what you do when I give you an order? How dare you cry! [*Putting his arm around* BIFF] Now look, Biff, when you grow up you'll understand about these things. You mustn't—you mustn't overemphasize a thing like this. I'll see Birnbaum first thing in the morning.

BIFF   Never mind.

WILLY [*getting down beside* BIFF]   Never mind! He's going to give you those points. I'll see to it.

BIFF   He wouldn't listen to you.

WILLY   He certainly will listen to me. You need those points for the U. of Virginia.

BIFF   I'm not going there.

WILLY   Heh? If I can't get him to change that mark you'll make it up in summer school. You've got all summer to—

BIFF [*his weeping breaking from him*]   Dad . . .

WILLY [*infected by it*]   Oh, my boy . . .

BIFF   Dad . . .

WILLY   She's nothing to me, Biff. I was lonely, I was terribly lonely.

BIFF   You—you gave her Mama's stockings! [*His tears break through and he rises to go.*]

WILLY [*grabbing for* BIFF]   I gave you an order!

BIFF   Don't touch me, you—liar!

WILLY   Apologize for that!

BIFF   You fake! You phony little fake! You fake! [*Overcome, he turns quickly and weeping fully goes out with his suitcase.* WILLY *is left on the floor on his knees.*]

WILLY I gave you an order! Biff, come back here or I'll beat you! Come back here! I'll whip you!

STANLEY *comes quickly in from the right and stands in front of* WILLY.

WILLY [*shouts at* STANLEY] I gave you an order . . .
STANLEY Hey, let's pick it up, pick it up, Mr. Loman. [*He helps* WILLY *to his feet*] Your boys left with the chippies. They said they'll see you home.

A SECOND WAITER *watches some distance away.*

WILLY But we were supposed to have dinner together.

Music is heard, WILLY's *theme.*

STANLEY Can you make it?
WILLY I'll—sure, I can make it. [*Suddenly concerned about his clothes*] Do I— I look all right?
STANLEY Sure, you look all right. [*He flicks a speck off* WILLY's *lapel.*]
WILLY Here—here's a dollar.
STANLEY Oh, your son paid me. It's all right.
WILLY [*putting it in* STANLEY's *hand*] No, take it. You're a good boy.
STANLEY Oh, no, you don't have to . . .
WILLY Here—here's some more, I don't need it any more. [*After a slight pause*] Tell me—is there a seed store in the neighborhood?
STANLEY Seeds? You mean like to plant?

As WILLY *turns,* STANLEY *slips the money back into his jacket pocket.*

WILLY Yes. Carrots, peas . . .
STANLEY Well, there's hardware stores on Sixth Avenue, but it may be too late now.
WILLY [*anxiously*] Oh, I'd better hurry. I've got to get some seeds. [*He starts off to the right.*] I've got to get some seeds, right away. Nothing's planted. I don't have a thing in the ground.

WILLY *hurries out as the light goes down.* STANLEY *moves over to the right after him, watches him off. The other waiter has been staring at* WILLY.

STANLEY [*to the* WAITER] Well, whatta you looking at?

The WAITER *picks up the chairs and moves off right.* STANLEY *takes the table and follows him. The light fades on this area. There is a long pause, the sound of the flute coming over. The light gradually rises on the kitchen, which is empty.* HAPPY *appears at the door of the house, followed by* BIFF. HAPPY *is carrying a large bunch of long-stemmed roses. He enters the kitchen, looks around for* LINDA. *Not seeing her, he turns to* BIFF, *who is just outside the house door, and makes a gesture with his hands, indicating "Not here, I guess." He looks into the living-room and freezes. Inside,* LINDA, *unseen, is seated,* WILLY's *coat on her lap. She rises ominously and quietly and moves toward* HAPPY, *who backs up into the kitchen, afraid.*

HAPPY   Hey, what're you doing up? [LINDA *says nothing but moves toward him implacably.*] Where's Pop? [*He keeps backing to the right, and now* LINDA *is in full view in the doorway to the living-room.*] Is he sleeping?

LINDA   Where were you?

HAPPY [*trying to laugh it off*]   We met two girls, Mom, very fine types. Here, we brought you some flowers. [*Offering them to her*] Put them in your room, Ma.

She knocks them to the floor at BIFF's *feet. He has now come inside and closed the door behind him. She stares at* BIFF, *silent.*

HAPPY   Now what'd you do that for? Mom, I want you to have some flowers—

LINDA [*cutting* HAPPY *off, violently to* BIFF]   Don't you care whether he lives or dies?

HAPPY [*going to the stairs*]   Come upstairs, Biff.

BIFF [*with a flare of disgust, to* HAPPY]   Go away from me! [*To* LINDA] What do you mean, lives or dies? Nobody's dying around here, pal.

LINDA   Get out of my sight! Get out of here!

BIFF   I wanna see the boss.

LINDA   You're not going near him!

BIFF   Where is he? [*He moves into the living-room and* LINDA *follows.*]

LINDA [*shouting after* BIFF]   You invite him for dinner. He looks forward to it all day—[BIFF *appears in his parents' bedroom, looks around, and exits.*]—and then you desert him there. There's no stranger you'd do that to!

HAPPY   Why? He had a swell time with us. Listen, when I—[LINDA *comes back into the kitchen.*]—desert him I hope I don't outlive the day!

LINDA   Get out of here!

HAPPY   Now look, Mom . . .

LINDA   Did you have to go to women tonight? You and your lousy rotten whores!

BIFF *re-enters the kitchen.*

HAPPY   Mom, all we did was follow Biff around trying to cheer him up! [*To* BIFF] Boy, what a night you gave me!

LINDA   Get out of here, both of you, and don't come back! I don't want you tormenting him any more. Go on now, get your things together! [*To* BIFF] You can sleep in his apartment. [*She starts to pick up the flowers and stops herself.*] Pick up this stuff, I'm not your maid any more. Pick it up, you bum, you!

HAPPY *turns his back to her in refusal.* BIFF *slowly moves over and gets down on his knees, picking up the flowers.*

LINDA   You're a pair of animals! Not one, not another living soul would have had the cruelty to walk out on that man in a restaurant!

BIFF [*not looking at her*]   Is that what he said?

LINDA   He didn't have to say anything. He was so humiliated he nearly limped when he came in.

HAPPY   But, Mom, he had a great time with us—

BIFF [*cutting him off violently*]   Shut up!

Without another word, HAPPY *goes upstairs.*

LINDA   You! You didn't even go in to see if he was all right!

BIFF [*still on the floor in front of* LINDA, *the flowers in his hand; with self-loathing*]   No. Didn't. Didn't do a damned thing. How do you like that, heh? Left him babbling in a toilet.

LINDA   You louse. You . . .

BIFF   Now you hit it on the nose! [*He gets up, throws the flowers in the wastebasket.*] The scum of the earth, and you're looking at him!

LINDA   Get out of here!

BIFF   I gotta talk to the boss, Mom. Where is he?

LINDA   You're not going near him. Get out of this house!

BIFF [*with absolute assurance, determination*]   No. We're gonna have an abrupt conversation, him and me.

LINDA   You're not talking to him!

Hammering is heard from outside the house, off right. BIFF *turns toward the noise.*

LINDA [*suddenly pleading*]   Will you please leave him alone?

BIFF   What's he doing out there?

LINDA   He's planting the garden!

BIFF [*quietly*]   Now? Oh, my God!

BIFF *moves outside,* LINDA *following. The light dies down on them and comes up on the center of the apron as* WILLY *walks into it. He is carrying a flashlight, a hoe, and a handful of seed packets. He raps the top of the hoe sharply to fix it firmly, and then moves to the left, measuring off the distance with his foot. He holds the flashlight to look at the seed packets, reading off the instructions. He is in the blue of night.*

WILLY   Carrots . . . quarter-inch apart. Rows . . . one-foot rows. [*He measures it off.*] One foot. [*He puts down a package and measures off.*] Beets. [*He puts down another package and measures again.*] Lettuce. [*He reads the package, puts it down.*] One foot—[*He breaks off as* BEN *appears at the right and moves slowly down to him.*] What a proposition, ts, ts. Terrific, terrific. 'Cause she's suffered, Ben, the woman has suffered. You understand me? A man can't go out the way he came in, Ben, a man has got to add up to something. You can't, you can't— [BEN *moves toward him as though to interrupt.*] You gotta consider, now. Don't answer so quick. Remember, it's a guaranteed twenty-thousand-dollar proposition. Now look, Ben, I want you to go through the ins and outs of this thing with me. I've got nobody to talk to, Ben, and the woman has suffered, you hear me?

BEN [*standing still, considering*]   What's the proposition?

WILLY   It's twenty thousand dollars on the barrelhead. Guaranteed, gilt-edged, you understand?

BEN   You don't want to make a fool of yourself. They might not honor the policy.

WILLY   How can they dare refuse? Didn't I work like a coolie to meet every premium on the nose? And now they don't pay off? Impossible!

BEN   It's called a cowardly thing, William.

WILLY   Why? Does it take more guts to stand here the rest of my life ringing up a zero?

BEN [*yielding*] That's a point, William. [*He moves, thinking, turns.*] And twenty thousand—that *is* something one can feel with the hand, it is there.

WILLY [*now assured, with rising power*] Oh, Ben, that's the whole beauty of it! I see it like a diamond, shining in the dark, hard and rough, that I can pick up and touch in my hand. Not like—like an appointment! This would not be another damned-fool appointment, Ben, and it changes all the aspects. Because he thinks I'm nothing, see, and so he spites me. But the funeral—[*Straightening up*] Ben, that funeral will be massive! They'll come from Maine, Massachusetts, Vermont, New Hampshire! All the old-timers with the strange license plates—that boy will be thunder-struck, Ben, because he never realized—I am known! Rhode Island, New York, New Jersey—I am known, Ben, and he'll see it with his eyes once and for all. He'll see what I am, Ben! He's in for a shock, that boy!

BEN [*coming down to the edge of the garden*] He'll call you a coward.

WILLY [*suddenly fearful*] No, that would be terrible.

BEN   Yes. And a damned fool.

WILLY   No, no, he mustn't, I won't have that! [*He is broken and desperate.*]

BEN   He'll hate you, William.

The gay music of the Boys is heard.

WILLY   Oh, Ben, how do we get back to all the great times? Used to be so full of light, and comradeship, the sleigh-riding in winter, and the ruddiness on his cheeks. And always some kind of good news coming up, always something nice coming up ahead. And never even let me carry the valises in the house, and simonizing, simonizing that little red car! Why, why can't I give him something and not have him hate me?

BEN   Let me think about it. [*He glances at his watch.*] I still have a little time. Remarkable proposition, but you've got to be sure you're not making a fool of yourself.

BEN *drifts upstage and goes out of sight.* BIFF *comes down from the left.*

WILLY [*suddenly conscious of* BIFF, *turns and looks up at him, then begins picking up the packages of seeds in confusion*] Where the hell is that seed? [*Indignantly*] You can't see nothing out here! They boxed in the whole goddam neighborhood!

BIFF   There are people all around here. Don't you realize that?

WILLY   I'm busy. Don't bother me.

BIFF [*taking the hoe from* WILLY] I'm saying good-by to you, Pop. [WILLY *looks at him, silent, unable to move.*] I'm not coming back any more.

WILLY   You're not going to see Oliver tomorrow?

BIFF   I've got no appointment, Dad.

WILLY   He put his arm around you, and you've got no appointment?

BIFF   Pop, get this now, will you? Everytime I've left it's been a fight that sent me out of here. Today I realized something about myself and I tried to explain it to you and I—I think I'm just not smart enough to make any sense out of it for you. To hell with whose fault it is or anything like that. [*He takes* WILLY's *arm.*] Let's just wrap it up, heh? Come on in, we'll tell Mom. [*He gently tries to pull* WILLY *to left.*]

WILLY [*frozen, immobile, with guilt in his voice*] No, I don't want to see her.
BIFF Come on! [*He pulls again, and* WILLY *tries to pull away.*]
WILLY [*highly nervous*] No, no, I don't want to see her.
BIFF [*tries to look into* WILLY's *face, as if to find the answer there*] Why don't you want to see her?
WILLY [*more harshly now*] Don't bother me, will you?
BIFF What do you mean, you don't want to see her? You don't want them calling you yellow, do you? This isn't your fault; it's me, I'm a bum. Now come inside! [WILLY *strains to get away.*] Did you hear what I said to you?

WILLY *pulls away and quickly goes by himself into the house.* BIFF *follows.*

LINDA [*to* WILLY] Did you plant, dear?
BIFF [*at the door, to* LINDA] All right, we had it out. I'm going and I'm not writing any more.
LINDA [*going to* WILLY *in the kitchen*] I think that's the best way, dear. 'Cause there's no use drawing it out, you'll just never get along.

WILLY *doesn't respond.*

BIFF People ask where I am and what I'm doing, you don't know, and you don't care. That way it'll be off your mind and you can start brightening up again. All right? That clears it, doesn't it? [WILLY *is silent, and* BIFF *goes to him.*] You gonna wish me luck, scout? [*He extends his hand.*] What do you say?
LINDA Shake his hand, Willy.
WILLY [*turning to her, seething with hurt*] There's no necessity to mention the pen at all, y'know.
BIFF [*gently*] I've got no appointment, Dad.
WILLY [*erupting fiercely*] He put his arm around . . . ?
BIFF Dad, you're never going to see what I am, so what's the use of arguing? If I strike oil I'll send you a check. Meantime forget I'm alive.
WILLY [*to* LINDA] Spite, see?
BIFF Shake hands, Dad.
WILLY Not my hand.
BIFF I was hoping not to go this way.
WILLY Well, this is the way you're going. Good-by.

BIFF *looks at him a moment, then turns sharply and goes to the stairs.*

WILLY [*stops him with*] May you rot in hell if you leave this house!
BIFF [*turning*] Exactly what is it that you want from me?
WILLY I want you to know, on the train, in the mountains, in the valleys, wherever you go, that you cut down your life for spite!
BIFF No, no.
WILLY Spite, spite, is the word of your undoing! And when you're down and out, remember what did it. When you're rotting somewhere beside the railroad tracks, remember, and don't you dare blame it on me!
BIFF I'm not blaming it on you!
WILLY I won't take the rap for this, you hear?

HAPPY *comes down the stairs and stands on the bottom step, watching.*

BIFF   That's just what I'm telling you!

WILLY [*sinking into a chair at the table, with full accusation*]   You're trying to put a knife in me—don't think I don't know what you're doing!

BIFF   All right, phony! Then let's lay it on the line. [*He whips the rubber tube out of his pocket and puts it on the table.*]

HAPPY   You crazy—

LINDA   Biff! [*She moves to grab the hose, but* BIFF *holds it down with his hand.*]

BIFF   Leave it there! Don't move it!

WILLY [*not looking at it*]   What is that?

BIFF   You know goddam well what that is.

WILLY [*caged, wanting to escape*]   I never saw that.

BIFF   You saw it. The mice didn't bring it into the cellar! What is this supposed to do, make a hero out of you? This supposed to make me sorry for you?

WILLY   Never heard of it.

BIFF   There'll be no pity for you, you hear it? No pity!

WILLY [*to* LINDA]   You hear the spite!

BIFF   No, you're going to hear the truth—what you are and what I am!

LINDA   Stop it!

WILLY   Spite!

HAPPY [*coming down toward* BIFF]   You cut it now!

BIFF [*to* HAPPY]   The man don't know who we are! The man is gonna know! [*to* WILLY] We never told the truth for ten minutes in this house!

HAPPY   We always told the truth!

BIFF [*turning on him*]   You big blow, are you the assistant buyer? You're one of the two assistants to the assistant, aren't you?

HAPPY   Well, I'm practically—

BIFF   You're practically full of it! We all are! And I'm through with it. [*To* WILLY] Now hear this, Willy, this is me.

WILLY   I know you!

BIFF   You know why I had no address for three months? I stole a suit in Kansas City and I was in jail. [*To* LINDA, *who is sobbing*] Stop crying. I'm through with it.

LINDA *turns away from them, her hands covering her face.*

WILLY   I suppose that's my fault!

BIFF   I stole myself out of every good job since high school!

WILLY   And whose fault is that?

BIFF   And I never got anywhere because you blew me so full of hot air I could never stand taking orders from anybody! That's whose fault it is!

WILLY   I hear that!

LINDA   Don't, Biff!

BIFF   It's goddam time you heard that! I had to be boss big shot in two weeks, and I'm through with it!

WILLY   Than hang yourself! For spite, hang yourself!

BIFF   No! Nobody's hanging himself, Willy! I ran down eleven flights with a pen in my hand today. And suddenly I stopped, you hear me? And in the middle of that office building, do you hear this? I stopped in the middle of that building and I saw—the sky. I saw the things that I love in this world. The work and the food and time to sit and smoke. And I looked at the pen and said to myself, what the hell am I grabbing this for? Why am I trying to become what I don't want to be? What am I doing in an office, making a contemptuous, begging fool of myself, when all I want is out there, waiting for me the minute I say I know who I am! Why can't I say that, Willy?

He tries to make WILLY *face him, but* WILLY *pulls away and moves to the left.*

WILLY [*with hatred, threateningly.*]   The door of your life is wide open!
BIFF   Pop! I'm a dime a dozen, and so are you!
WILLY [*turning on him now in an uncontrolled outburst*]   I am not a dime a dozen! I am Willy Loman, and you are Biff Loman!

BIFF *starts for* WILLY, *but is blocked by* HAPPY. *In his fury,* BIFF *seems on the verge of attacking his father.*

BIFF   I am not a leader of men, Willy, and neither are you. You were never anything but a hard-working drummer who landed in the ash can like all the rest of them! I'm one dollar an hour, Willy! I tried seven states and couldn't raise it. A buck an hour! Do you gather my meaning? I'm not bringing home any prizes any more, and you're going to stop waiting for me to bring them home!
WILLY [*directly to* BIFF]   You vengeful, spiteful mut!

BIFF *breaks from* HAPPY. WILLY, *in fright, starts up the stairs.* BIFF *grabs him.*

BIFF [*at the peak of his fury*]   Pop, I'm nothing! I'm nothing, Pop. Can't you understand that? There's no spite in it any more. I'm just what I am, that's all.

BIFF's *fury has spent itself, and he breaks down, sobbing, holding on to* WILLY, *who dumbly fumbles for* BIFF's *face.*

WILLY [*astonished*]   What're you doing? What're you doing? [*To* LINDA] Why is he crying?
BIFF [*crying, broken*]   Will you let me go, for Christ's sake? Will you take that phony dream and burn it before something happens? [*Struggling to contain himself, he pulls away and moves to the stairs.*] I'll go in the morning. Put him—put him to bed. [*Exhausted,* BIFF *moves up the stairs to his room.*]
WILLY [*after a long pause, astonished, elevated*]   Isn't that—isn't that remarkable? Biff—he likes me!
LINDA   He loves you, Willy!
HAPPY [*deeply moved*]   Always did, Pop.
WILLY   Oh, Biff! [*Staring wildly*] He cried! Cried to me. [*He is choking with his love, and now cries out his promise.*] That boy—that boy is going to be magnificent!

BEN *appears in the light just outside the kitchen.*

BEN   Yes, outstanding, with twenty thousand behind him.

LINDA [*sensing the racing of his mind, fearfully, carefully*] Now come to bed, Willy. It's all settled now.

WILLY [*finding it difficult not to rush out of the house*] Yes, we'll sleep. Come on. Go to sleep, Hap.

BEN And it does take a great kind of a man to crack the jungle.

In accents of dread, BEN's *idyllic music starts up.*

HAPPY [*his arm around* LINDA] I'm getting married, Pop, don't forget it. I'm changing everything. I'm gonna run that department before the year is up. You'll see, Mom. [*He kisses her.*]

BEN The jungle is dark but full of diamonds, Willy.

WILLY *turns, moves, listening to* BEN.

LINDA Be good. You're both good boys, just act that way, that's all.

HAPPY 'Night, Pop. [*He goes upstairs.*]

LINDA [*to* WILLY] Come, dear.

BEN [*with greater force*] One must go in to fetch a diamond out.

WILLY [*to* LINDA, *as he moves slowly along the edge of the kitchen, toward the door*] I just want to get settled down, Linda. Let me sit alone for a little.

LINDA [*almost uttering her fear*] I want you upstairs.

WILLY [*taking her in his arms*] In a few minutes, Linda. I couldn't sleep right now. Go on, you look awful tired. [*He kisses her.*]

BEN Not like an appointment at all. A diamond is rough and hard to the touch.

WILLY Go on now. I'll be right up.

LINDA I think this is the only way, Willy.

WILLY Sure, it's the best thing.

BEN Best thing!

WILLY The only way. Everything is gonna be—go on, kid, get to bed. You look so tired.

LINDA Come right up.

WILLY Two minutes.

LINDA *goes into the living-room, then reappears in her bedroom.* WILLY *moves just outside the kitchen door.*

WILLY Loves me. [*wonderingly*] Always loved me. Isn't that a remarkable thing? Ben, he'll worship me for it!

BEN [*with promise*] It's dark there, but full of diamonds.

WILLY Can you imagine that magnificence with twenty thousand dollars in his pocket?

LINDA [*calling from her room*] Willy! Come up!

WILLY [*calling into the kitchen*] Yes! Yes. Coming! It's very smart, you realize that, don't you, sweetheart? Even Ben sees it. I gotta go, baby. 'By! 'By! [*Going over to* BEN, *almost dancing*] Imagine? When the mail comes he'll be ahead of Bernard again!

BEN A perfect proposition all around.

WILLY Did you see how he cried to me? Oh, if I could kiss him, Ben!

BEN Time, William, time!

WILLY   Oh, Ben, I always knew one way or another we were gonna make it, Biff and I!

BEN [*looking at his watch*]   The boat. We'll be late. [*He moves slowly off into the darkness.*]

WILLY [*elegiacally, turning to the house*]   Now when you kick off, boy, I want a seventy-yard boot, and get right down the field under the ball, and when you hit, hit low and hit hard, because it's important, boy. [*He swings around and faces the audience.*] There's all kinds of important people in the stands, and the first thing you know . . . [*Suddenly realizing he is alone*] Ben! Ben, where do I . . . ? [*He makes a sudden movement of search.*] Ben, how do I . . . ?

LINDA [*calling*]   Willy, you coming up?

WILLY [*uttering a gasp of fear, whirling about as if to quiet her*]   Sh! [*He turns around as if to find his way; sounds, faces, voices, seem to be swarming in upon him and he flicks at them, crying*] Sh! Sh! [*Suddenly music, faint and high, stops him. It rises in intensity, almost to an unbearable scream. He goes up and down on his toes, and rushes off around the house.*] Shhh!

LINDA   Willy?

There is no answer. LINDA *waits.* BIFF *gets up off his bed. He is still in his clothes.* HAPPY *sits up.* BIFF *stands listening.*

LINDA [*with real fear*]   Willy, answer me! Willy!

There is the sound of a car starting and moving away at full speed.

LINDA   No!

BIFF [*rushing down the stairs*]   Pop!

As the car speeds off, the music crashes down in a frenzy of sound, which becomes the soft pulsation of a single cello string. BIFF *slowly returns to his bedroom. He and* HAPPY *gravely don their jackets.* LINDA *slowly walks out of her room. The music has developed into a dead march. The leaves of day are appearing over everything.* CHARLEY *and* BERNARD, *somberly dressed, appear and knock on the kitchen door.* BIFF *and* HAPPY *slowly descend the stairs to the kitchen as* CHARLEY *and* BERNARD *enter. All stop a moment when* LINDA, *in clothes of mourning, bearing a little bunch of roses, comes through the draped doorway into the kitchen. She goes to* CHARLEY *and takes his arm. Now all move toward the audience, through the wall-line of the kitchen. At the limit of the apron,* LINDA *lays down the flowers, kneels, and sits back on her heels. All stare down at the grave.*

Requiem

CHARLEY   It's getting dark, Linda.

LINDA *doesn't react. She stares at the grave.*

BIFF   How about it, Mom? Better get some rest, heh? They'll be closing the gate soon.

LINDA *makes no move. Pause.*

HAPPY [*deeply angered*] He had no right to do that. There was no necessity for it. We would've helped him.

CHARLEY [*grunting*] Hmmm.

BIFF Come along, Mom.

LINDA Why didn't anybody come?

CHARLEY It was a very nice funeral.

LINDA But where are all the people he knew? Maybe they blame him.

CHARLEY Naa. It's a rough world, Linda. They wouldn't blame him.

LINDA I can't understand it. At this time especially. First time in thirty-five years we were just about free and clear. He only needed a little salary. He was even finished with the dentist.

CHARLEY No man only needs a little salary.

LINDA I can't understand it.

BIFF There were a lot of nice days. When he'd come home from a trip; or on Sundays, making the stoop; finishing the cellar; putting on the new porch; when he built the extra bathroom; and put up the garage. You know something, Charley, there's more of him in that front stoop than in all the sales he ever made.

CHARLEY Yeah. He was a happy man with a batch of cement.

LINDA He was so wonderful with his hands.

BIFF He had all the wrong dreams. All, all, wrong.

HAPPY [*almost ready to fight* BIFF] Don't say that!

BIFF He never knew who he was.

CHARLEY [*stopping* HAPPY's *movement and reply. To* BIFF] Nobody dast blame this man. You don't understand. Willy was a salesman. And for a salesman, there is no rock bottom to the life. He don't put a bolt to a nut, he don't tell you the law or give you medicine. He's a man way out there in the blue, riding on a smile and a shoeshine. And when they start not smiling back—that's an earthquake. And then you get yourself a couple of spots on your hat, and you're finished. Nobody dast blame this man. A salesman is got to dream, boy. It comes with the territory.

BIFF Charley, the man didn't know who he was.

HAPPY [*infuriated*] Don't say that!

BIFF Why don't you come with me, Happy?

HAPPY I'm not licked that easily. I'm staying right in this city, and I'm gonna beat this racket! [*He looks at* BIFF, *his chin set.*] The Loman Brothers!

BIFF I know who I am, kid.

HAPPY All right, boy. I'm gonna show you and everybody else that Willy Loman did not die in vain. He had a good dream. It's the only dream you can have—to come out number-one man. He fought it out here, and this is where I'm gonna win it for him.

BIFF [*with a hopeless glance at* HAPPY, *bends toward his mother*] Let's go, Mom.

LINDA I'll be with you in a minute. Go on, Charley. [*He hesitates*] I want to, just for a minute. I never had a chance to say good-by.

CHARLEY *moves away, followed by* HAPPY. BIFF *remains a slight distance up and left of* LINDA. *She sits there, summoning herself. The flute begins, not far away, playing behind her speech.*

LINDA Forgive me, dear. I can't cry. I don't know what it is, but I can't cry. I don't understand it. Why did you ever do that? Help me, Willy, I can't cry. It seems to me that you're just on another trip. I keep expecting you. Willy, dear, I can't cry. Why did you do it? I search and search and I search, and I can't understand it, Willy. I made the last payment on the house today. Today, dear. And there'll be nobody home. [*A sob rises in her throat.*] We're free and clear. [*Sobbing more fully, released*] We're free. [BIFF *comes slowly toward her.*] We're free . . . We're free . . .

BIFF *lifts her to her feet and moves out up right with her in his arms.* LINDA *sobs quietly.* BERNARD *and* CHARLEY *come together and follow them, followed by* HAPPY. *Only the music of the flute is left on the darkening stage as over the house the hard towers of the apartment buildings rise into sharp focus, and*

THE CURTAIN FALLS

Edward Albee and *The Zoo Story*

Edward Albee (1928–   ) is a leading American playwright of the generation after Arthur Miller and Tennessee Williams. His work includes elements of the absurd—see pages 997–998—and elements that remind us of Ibsen's realism. His most famous play, *Who's Afraid of Virginia Woolf?* (1962), centers on a husband and wife who have learned to torture each other. His other plays include *The Death of Bessie Smith* (1960), *The American Dream* (1961), *Tiny Alice* (1965), *A Delicate Balance* (1966), *All Over* (1971), *Seascape* (1975), and *The Lady from Dubuque* (1980). *The Zoo Story* (1959) is Albee's first play, a one-act confrontation between a character representing conventional life and a hectoring, fantastic, neurotic, sensitive antagonist.

Edward Albee

The Zoo Story

The Players

PETER A man in his early forties, neither fat not gaunt, neither handsome nor homely. He wears tweeds, smokes a pipe, carries horn-rimmed glasses. Although he is moving into middle age, his dress and his manner would suggest a man younger.

JERRY A man in his late thirties, not poorly dressed, but carelessly. What was once a trim and lightly muscled body has begun to go to fat; and while he is no longer handsome, it is evident that he once was. His fall from physical grace should not suggest debauchery; he has, to come closest to it, a great weariness.

THE SCENE *It is Central Park; a Sunday afternoon in summer; the present. There are two park benches, one toward either side of the stage; they both face the audience. Behind them: foliage, trees, sky. At the beginning, Peter is seated on one of the benches.*

As the curtain rises, PETER *is seated on the bench stage-right. He is reading a book. He stops reading, cleans his glasses, goes back to reading. Jerry enters.*

JERRY   I've been to the zoo. [PETER *doesn't notice*] I said, I've been to the zoo.
MISTER, I'VE BEEN TO THE ZOO!

PETER   Hm? . . . What? . . . I'm sorry, were you talking to me?

JERRY   I went to the zoo, and then I walked until I came here. Have I been walking north?

PETER [*puzzled*]   North? Why . . . I . . . think so. Let me see.

JERRY [*pointing past the audience*]   Is that Fifth Avenue?

PETER   Why yes; yes, it is.

JERRY   And what is that cross street there; that one, to the right?

PETER   That? Oh, that's Seventy-fourth Street.

JERRY   And the zoo is around Sixty-fifth Street; so, I've been walking north.

PETER [*anxious to get back to his reading*]   Yes, it would seem so.

JERRY   Good old north.

PETER [*lightly, by reflex*]   Ha, ha.

JERRY [*after a slight pause*]   But not due north.

PETER   I . . . well, no, not due north; but, we . . . call it north. It's northerly.

JERRY [*watches as PETER, anxious to dismiss him, prepares his pipe*]   Well, boy; you're not going to get lung cancer, are you?

PETER [*looks up a little annoyed; then smiles*]   No, sir. Not from this.

JERRY   No, sir. What you'll probably get is cancer of the mouth, and then you'll have to wear one of those things Freud wore after they took one whole side of his jaw away. What do they call those things?

PETER [*uncomfortable*]   A prosthesis?

JERRY   The very thing! A prosthesis. You're an educated man, aren't you? Are you a doctor?

PETER   Oh, no; no. I read about it somewhere; *Time* magazine, I think. [*He turns to his book.*]

JERRY   Well, *Time* magazine isn't for blockheads.

PETER   No, I suppose not.

JERRY [*after a pause*]   Boy, I'm glad that's Fifth Avenue there.

PETER [*vaguely*]   Yes.

JERRY   I don't like the west side of the park much.

PETER   Oh? [*Then, slightly wary, but interested*] Why?

JERRY [*offhand*]   I don't know.

PETER   Oh. [*He returns to his book.*]

JERRY [*He stands for a few seconds, looking at PETER, who finally looks up again, puzzled.*]   Do you mind if we talk?

PETER [*obviously minding*]   Why . . . no, no.

JERRY   Yes you do; you do.

PETER [*puts his book down, his pipe out and away, smiling*]   No, really; I don't mind.

JERRY   Yes you do.

PETER [*finally decided*]   No; I don't mind at all, really.

JERRY   It's . . . it's a nice day.

PETER [*stares unnecessarily at the sky*]   Yes. Yes, it is; lovely.

JERRY   I've been to the zoo.

PETER   Yes, I think you said so . . . didn't you?

JERRY   You'll read about it in the papers tomorrow, if you don't see it on your TV tonight. You have TV, haven't you?

PETER   Why yes, we have two; one for the children.

JERRY You're married!

PETER [*with pleased emphasis*] Why, certainly.

JERRY It isn't a law, for God's sake.

PETER No . . . no, of course not.

JERRY And you have a wife.

PETER [*bewildered by the seeming lack of communication*] Yes!

JERRY And you have children.

PETER Yes; two.

JERRY Boys?

PETER No, girls . . . both girls.

JERRY But you wanted boys.

PETER Well . . . naturally, every man wants a son, but . . .

JERRY [*lightly mocking*] But that's the way the cookie crumbles?

PETER [*annoyed*] I wasn't going to say that.

JERRY And you're not going to have any more kids, are you?

PETER [*a bit distantly*] No. No more. [*Then back, and irksome*] Why did you say that? How would you know about that?

JERRY The way you cross your legs, perhaps; something in the voice. Or maybe I'm just guessing. Is it your wife?

PETER [*furious*] That's none of your business! [*A silence*] Do you understand? [JERRY *nods.* PETER *is quiet now.*] Well, you're right. We'll have no more children.

JERRY [*softly*] That *is* the way the cookie crumbles.

PETER [*forgiving*] Yes . . . I guess so.

JERRY Well, now; what else?

PETER What were you saying about the zoo . . . that I'd read about it, or see. . . ?

JERRY I'll tell you about it, soon. Do you mind if I ask you questions?

PETER Oh, not really.

JERRY I'll tell you why I do it; I don't talk to many people—except to say like: give me a beer, or where's the john, or what time does the feature go on, or keep your hands to yourself, buddy. You know—things like that.

PETER I must say I don't . . .

JERRY But every once in a while I like to talk to somebody, really *talk;* like to get to know somebody, know all about him.

PETER [*lightly laughing, still a little uncomfortable*] And am I the guinea pig for today?

JERRY On a sun-drenched Sunday afternoon like this? Who better than a nice married man with two daughters and . . . uh . . . a dog? [PETER *shakes his head, sadly.*] Oh, that's a shame. But you look like an animal man. CATS? [PETER *nods his head, ruefully.*] Cats! But, that can't be your idea. No, sir. Your wife and daughters? [PETER *nods his head.*] Is there anything else I should know?

PETER [*He has to clear his throat.*] There are . . . there are two parakeets. One . . . uh . . . one for each of my daughters.

JERRY Birds.

PETER My daughters keep them in a cage in their bedroom.

JERRY Do they carry disease? The birds.

PETER I don't believe so.

JERRY That's too bad. If they did you could set them loose in the house and the cats could eat them and die, maybe. [PETER *looks blank for a moment, then laughs.*] And what else? What do you do to support your enormous household?

PETER   I . . . uh . . . I have an executive position with a . . . small publishing house. We . . . uh . . . we publish textbooks.

JERRY   That sounds nice; very nice. What do you make?

PETER [*still cheerful*]   Now look here!

JERRY   Oh, come on.

PETER   Well, I make around eighteen thousand a year, but I don't carry more than forty dollars at any one time . . . in case you're a . . . holdup man . . . ha, ha, ha.

JERRY [*ignoring the above*]   Where do you live? [PETER *is reluctant.*] Oh, look; I'm not going to rob you, and I'm not going to kidnap your parakeets, your cats, or your daughters.

PETER [*too loud*]   I live between Lexington and Third Avenue, on Seventy-fourth Street.

JERRY   That wasn't so hard, was it?

PETER   I didn't mean to seem . . . ah . . . it's that you don't really carry on a conversation; you just ask questions, and I'm . . . I'm normally . . . uh . . . reticent. Why do you just stand there?

JERRY   I'll start walking around in a little while, and eventually I'll sit down. [*Recalling*] Wait until you see the expression on his face.

PETER   What? Whose face? Look here; is this something about the zoo?

JERRY [*distantly*]   The what?

PETER   The zoo; the zoo. Something about the zoo.

JERRY   The zoo?

PETER   You've mentioned it several times.

JERRY [*still distant, but returning abruptly*]   The zoo? Oh, yes; the zoo. I was there before I came here. I told you that. Say, what's the dividing line between upper-middle-middle-class and lower-upper-middle-class?

PETER   My dear fellow, I . . .

JERRY   Don't my dear fellow me.

PETER [*unhappily*]   Was I patronizing? I believe I was; I'm sorry. But, you see, your question about the classes bewildered me.

JERRY   And when you're bewildered you become patronizing?

PETER   I . . . I don't express myself too well, sometimes. [*He attempts a joke on himself.*] I'm in publishing, not writing.

JERRY [*amused, but not at the humor*]   So be it. The truth *is: I* was being patronizing.

PETER   Oh, now; you needn't say that.

It is at this point that JERRY *may begin to move about the stage with slowly increasing determination and authority, but pacing himself, so that the long speech about the dog comes at the high point of the arc.*

JERRY   All right. Who are your favorite writers? Baudelaire and J. P. Marquand?

PETER [*wary*]   Well, I like a great many writers; I have a considerable . . . catholicity of taste, if I may say so. Those two men are fine; each in his way. [*Warming up*] Baudelaire, of course . . . uh . . . is by far the finer of the two, but Marquand has a place . . . in our . . . uh . . . national . . .

JERRY   Skip it.

PETER   I . . . sorry.

JERRY   Do you know what I did before I went to the zoo today? I walked all the way up Fifth Avenue from Washington Square; all the way.

PETER   Oh; you live in the Village! [*This seems to enlighten* PETER.]

JERRY   No, I don't. I took the subway down to the Village so I could walk all the way up Fifth Avenue to the zoo. It's one of those things a person has to do; sometimes a person has to go a very long distance out of his way to come back a short distance correctly.

PETER [*almost pouting*]   Oh, I thought you lived in the Village.

JERRY   What were you trying to do? Make sense out of things? Bring order? The old pigeonhole bit? Well, that's easy; I'll tell you. I live in a four-story brownstone roominghouse on the upper West Side between Columbus Avenue and Central Park West. I live on the top floor; rear; west. It's a laughably small room, and one of my walls is made of beaverboard; this beaverboard separates my room from another laughably small room, so I assume that the two rooms were once one room, a small room, but not necessarily laughable. The room beyond my beaverboard wall is occupied by a colored queen who always keeps his door open; well, not always, but *always* when he's plucking his eyebrows, which he does with Buddhist concentration. This colored queen has rotten teeth, which is rare, and he has a Japanese kimono, which is also pretty rare; and he wears this kimono to and from the john in the hall, which is pretty frequent. I mean, he goes to the john a lot. He never bothers me, and he never brings anyone up to his room. All he does is pluck his eyebrows, wear his kimono and go to the john. Now, the two front rooms on my floor are a little larger, I guess; but they're pretty small, too. There's a Puerto Rican family in one of them, a husband, a wife, and some kids; I don't know how many. These people entertain a lot. And in the other front room, there's somebody living there, but I don't know who it is. I've never seen who it is. Never. Never ever.

PETER [*embarrassed*]   Why . . . why do you live there?

JERRY [*from a distance again*]   I don't know.

PETER   It doesn't sound like a very nice place . . . where you live.

JERRY   Well, no; it isn't an apartment in the East Seventies. But, then again, I don't have one wife, two daughters, two cats and two parakeets. What I do have, I have toilet articles, a few clothes, a hot plate that I'm not supposed to have, a can opener, one that works with a key, you know; a knife, two forks, and two spoons, one small, one large; three plates, a cup, a saucer, a drinking glass, two picture frames, both empty, eight or nine books, a pack of pornographic playing cards, regular deck, an old Western Union typewriter that prints nothing but capital letters, and a small strongbox without a lock which has in it . . . what? Rocks! Some rocks . . . sea-rounded rocks I picked up on the beach when I was a kid. Under which . . . weighed down . . . are some letters . . . please letters . . . please why don't you do this, and please when will you do that letters. And when letters, too. When will you write? When will you come? When? These letters are from more recent years.

PETER [*stares glumly at his shoes, then*]   About those two empty picture frames . . . ?

JERRY   I don't see why they need any explanation at all. Isn't it clear? I don't have pictures of anyone to put in them.

PETER   Your parents . . . perhaps . . . a girl friend . . .

JERRY   You're a very sweet man, and you're possessed of a truly enviable innocence. But good old Mom and good old Pop are dead . . . you know? . . . I'm broken up about it, too . . . I mean really. BUT. That particular vaudeville act is playing the cloud circuit now, so I don't see how I can look at them, all neat and framed. Besides, or, rather, to be pointed about it, good old Mom walked out on good old Pop when I was ten and a half years old; she embarked on an adulterous turn of our southern states . . . a journey of a year's duration . . . and her most constant companion . . . among others, among many others . . . was a Mr. Barleycorn. At least, that's what good old Pop told me after he went down . . . came back . . . brought her body north. We'd received the news between Christmas and New Year's, you see, that good old Mom had parted with the ghost in some dump in Alabama. And, without the ghost . . . she was less welcome. I mean, what was she? A stiff . . . a northern stiff. At any rate, good old Pop celebrated the New Year for an even two weeks and then slapped into the front of a somewhat moving city omnibus, which sort of cleaned things out family-wise. Well no; then there was Mom's sister, who was given neither to sin nor the consolations of the bottle. I moved in on her, and my memory of her is slight excepting I remember still that she did all things dourly: sleeping, eating, working, praying. She dropped dead on the stairs to her apartment, my apartment then, too, on the afternoon of my high school graduation. A terribly middle-European joke, if you ask me.

PETER   Oh, my; oh, my.

JERRY   Oh, your what? But that was a long time ago, and I have no feeling about any of it that I care to admit to myself. Perhaps you can see, though, why good old Mom and good old Pop are frameless. What's your name? Your first name?

PETER   I'm Peter.

JERRY   I'd forgotten to ask you. I'm Jerry.

PETER [*with a slight, nervous laugh*]   Hello, Jerry.

JERRY [*nods his hello*]   And let's see now; what's the point of having a girl's picture, especially in two frames? I have two picture frames, you remember. I never see the pretty little ladies more than once, and most of them wouldn't be caught in the same room with a camera. It's odd, and I wonder if it's sad.

PETER   The girls?

JERRY   No. I wonder if it's sad that I never see the little ladies more than once. I've never been able to have sex with, or, how is it put? . . . make love to anybody more than once. Once; that's it . . . Oh, wait; for a week and a half, when I was fifteen . . . and I hang my head in shame that puberty was late . . . I was a h-o-m-o-s-e-x-u-a-l. I mean, I was queer . . . [*very fast*] . . . queer, queer, queer . . . with bells ringing, banners snapping in the wind. And for those eleven days, I met at least twice a day with the park superintendent's son . . . a Greek boy, whose birthday was the same as mine, except he was a year older. I think I was very much in love . . . maybe just with sex. But that was the jazz of a very special hotel, wasn't it? And now; oh, do I love the little ladies; really, I love them. For about an hour.

PETER   Well, it seems perfectly simple to me. . . .

JERRY [*angry*]   Look! Are you going to tell me to get married and have parakeets?

PETER [*angry himself*]   Forget the parakeets! And stay single if you want to. It's no business of mine. I didn't start this conversation in the . . .

JERRY   All right, all right. I'm sorry. All right? You're not angry?

PETER [*laughing*]   No, I'm not angry.

JERRY [*relieved*]   Good. [*Now back to his previous tone*] Interesting that you asked me about the picture frames. I would have thought that you would have asked me about the pornographic playing cards.

PETER [*with a knowing smile*] Oh, I've seen those cards.

JERRY That's not the point. [*Laughs*] I suppose when you were a kid you and your pals passed them around, or you had a pack of your own.

PETER Well, I guess a lot of us did.

JERRY And you threw them away just before you got married.

PETER Oh, now; look here. I didn't *need* anything like that when I got older.

JERRY No?

PETER [*embarrassed*] I'd rather not talk about these things.

JERRY So? Don't. Besides, I wasn't trying to plumb your postadolescent sexual life and hard times; what I wanted to get at is the value difference between pornographic playing cards when you're a kid, and pornographic playing cards when you're older. It's that when you're a kid you use the cards as a substitute for a real experience, and when you're older you use real experience as a substitute for the fantasy. But I imagine you'd rather hear about what happened at the zoo.

PETER [*enthusiastic*] Oh, yes; the zoo. [*Then, awkward*] That is . . . if you . . .

JERRY Let me tell you about why I went . . . well, let me tell you some things. I've told you about the fourth floor of the roominghouse where I live. I think the rooms are better as you go down, floor by floor. I guess they are; I don't know. I don't know any of the people on the third and second floors. Oh, wait! I do know that there's a lady living on the third floor, in the front. I know because she cries all the time. Whenever I go out or come back in, whenever I pass her door, I always hear her crying, muffled, but . . . very determined. Very determined indeed. But the one I'm getting to, and all about the dog, is the landlady. I don't like to use words that are too harsh in describing people. I don't like to. But the landlady is a fat, ugly, mean, stupid, unwashed, misanthropic, cheap, drunken bag of garbage. And you may have noticed that I very seldom use profanity, so I can't describe her as well as I might.

PETER You describe her . . . vividly.

JERRY Well, thanks. Anyway, she has a dog, and I will tell you about the dog, and she and her dog are the gatekeepers of my dwelling. The woman is bad enough; she leans around in the entrance hall, spying to see that I don't bring in things or people, and when she's had her midafternoon point of lemon-flavored gin she always stops me in the hall, and grabs ahold of my coat or my arm, and she presses her disgusting body up against me to keep me in a corner so she can talk to me. The smell of her body and her breath . . . you can't imagine it . . . and somewhere, somewhere in the back of that pea-sized brain of hers, an organ developed just enough to let her eat, drink, and emit, she has some foul parody of sexual desire. And I, Peter, I am the object of her sweaty lust.

PETER That's disgusting. That's . . . horrible.

JERRY But I have found a way to keep her off. When she talks to me, when she presses herself to my body and mumbles about her room and how I should come there, I merely say: but, Love; wasn't yesterday enough for you, and the day before? Then she puzzles, she makes slits of her tiny eyes, she sways a little, and then, Peter . . . and it is at this moment that I think I might be doing some good in that tormented house . . . a simple-minded smile begins to form on her unthinkable face, and she giggles and groans as she thinks about yesterday and the day before; as she believes and relives what never happened. Then, she motions to that black monster of a dog she has, and she goes back to her room. And I am safe until our next meeting.

PETER   It's so . . . unthinkable. I find it hard to believe that people such as that really *are*.

JERRY [*lightly mocking*]   It's for reading about, isn't it?

PETER [*seriously*]   Yes.

JERRY   And fact is better left to fiction. You're right, Peter. Well, what I have been meaning to tell you about is the dog; I shall, now.

PETER [*nervously*]   Oh, yes; the dog.

JERRY   Don't go. You're not thinking of going, are you?

PETER   Well . . . no, I don't think so.

JERRY [*as if to a child*]   Because after I tell you about the dog, do you know what then? Then . . . then I'll tell you about what happened at the zoo.

PETER [*laughing faintly*]   You're . . . you're full of stories, aren't you?

JERRY   You don't *have* to listen. Nobody is holding you here; remember that. Keep that in your mind.

PETER [*irritably*]   I know that.

JERRY   You do? Good.

The following long speech, it seems to me, should be done with a great deal of action, to achieve a hypnotic effect on PETER, *and on the audience, too. Some specific actions have been suggested, but the director and the actor playing* JERRY *might best work it out for themselves.*

ALL RIGHT. [*As if reading from a huge billboard*] THE STORY OF JERRY AND THE DOG! [*Natural again*] What I am going to tell you has something to do with how sometimes it's necessary to go a long distance out of the way in order to come back a short distance correctly; or, maybe I only think that it has something to do with that. But, it's why I went to the zoo today, and why I walked north . . . northerly, rather . . . until I came here. All right. The dog, I think I told you, is a black monster of a beast: an oversized head, tiny, tiny ears, and eyes . . . bloodshot, infected, maybe; and a body you can see the ribs through the skin. The dog is black, all black; all black except for the bloodshot eyes, and . . . yes . . . and an open sore on its . . . *right* forepaw; that is red, too. And, oh yes; the poor monster, and I do believe it's an old dog . . . it's certainly a misused one . . . almost always has an erection . . . of sorts. That's red, too. And . . . what else? . . . oh, yes; there's a gray-yellow-white color, too, when he bares his fangs. Like this: Grrrrrrr! Which is what he did when he saw me for the first time . . . the day I moved in. I worried about that animal the very first minute I met him. Now, animals don't take to me like Saint Francis had birds hanging off him all the time. What I mean is: animals are indifferent to me . . . like people [*he smiles slightly*] . . . most of the time. But this dog wasn't indifferent. From the very beginning he'd snarl and then go for me, to get one of my legs. Not like he was rabid, you know; he was sort of a stumbly dog, but he wasn't half-assed, either. It was a good, stumbly run; but I always got away. He got a piece of my trouser leg, look, you can see right here, where it's mended; he got that the second day I lived there; but, I kicked free and got upstairs fast, so that was that. [*Puzzles*] I still don't know to this day how the other roomers manage it, but you know what I *think*: I think it had to do only with me. Cozy. So. Anyway, this went on for over a week, whenever I came in; but never when I went out. That's funny. Or, it *was* funny. I could pack up and live in the street for all the dog cared. Well, I thought about it up in my room one day, one of the times after I'd bolted upstairs, and I made up my mind. I decided: First, I'll kill the dog with kindness, and if that doesn't work . . . I'll just kill him. [PETER *winces.*] Don't react, Peter, just listen. So, the next day I went out and bought a bag of hamburgers, medium rare, no catsup, no onion; and on the way home I threw away all the rolls and kept just the meat.

Action for the following, perhaps.

When I got back to the roominghouse the dog was waiting for me. I half opened the door that led into the entrance hall, and there he was; waiting for me. It figured. I went in, very cautiously, and I had the hamburgers, you remember; I opened the bag, and I set the meat down about twelve feet from where the dog was snarling at me. Like so! He snarled; stopped snarling; sniffed; moved slowly; then faster; then faster toward the meat. Well, when he got to it he stopped, and he looked at me. I smiled; but tentatively, you understand. He turned his face back to the hamburgers, smelled, sniffed some more, and then . . . RRRAAAAGGGGGHHHH, like that . . . he tore into them. It was as if he had never eaten anything in his life before, except like garbage. Which might very well have been the truth. I don't think the landlady ever eats anything but garbage. But. He ate all the hamburgers, almost all at once, making sounds in his throat like a woman. *Then,* when he'd finished the meat, the hamburger, and tried to eat the paper, too, he sat down and smiled. I think he smiled; I know cats do. It was a very gratifying few moments. Then, BAM, he snarled and made for me again. He didn't get me this time, either. So, I got upstairs, and I lay down on my bed and started to think about the dog again. To be truthful, I was offended, and I was damn mad, too. It was six perfectly good hamburgers with not enough pork in them to make it disgusting. I was offended. But, after a while, I decided to try it for a few more days. If you think about it, this dog had what amounted to an antipathy toward me; really. And, I wondered if I mightn't overcome this antipathy. So, I tried it for five more days, but it was always the same: snarl, sniff; move; faster; stare; gobble; RAAGGGHHH; smile; snarl; BAM. Well, now; by this time Columbus Avenue was strewn with hamburger rolls and I was less offended than disgusted. So, I decided to kill the dog.

PETER *raises a hand in protest.*

Oh, don't be so alarmed, Peter; I didn't succeed. The day I tried to kill the dog I bought only one hamburger and what I thought was a murderous portion of rat poison. When I bought the hamburger I asked the man not to bother with the roll, all I wanted was the meat. I expected some reaction from him, like: we don't sell no hamburgers without rolls; or, wha' d'ya wanna do, eat it out'a ya han's? But no; he smiled benignly, wrapped up the hamburger in waxed paper, and said: A bite for ya pussy-cat? I wanted to say: No, not really; it's part of a plan to poison a dog I know. But, you can't say "a dog I know" without sounding funny; so I said, a little too loud, I'm afraid, and too formally: YES, A BITE FOR MY PUSSY-CAT. People looked up. It always happens when I try to simplify things; people look up. But that's neither hither nor thither. So. On my way back to the room-inghouse, I kneaded the hamburger and the rat poison together between my hands, at that point feeling as much sadness as disgust. I opened the door to the entrance hall, and there the monster was, waiting to take the offering and then jump me. Poor bastard; he never learned that the moment he took to smile before he went for me gave me time enough to get out of range. BUT, there he was; malevolence with an erection, waiting. I put the poison patty down, moved toward the stairs and watched. The poor animal gobbled the food down as usual, smiled, which made me almost sick, and then BAM. But, I sprinted up the stairs, as usual, and the dog didn't get me, as usual. AND IT CAME TO PASS THAT THE BEAST WAS DEATHLY ILL. I knew this because he no longer attended me, and because the landlady sobered up. She stopped me in the hall the same evening of the attempted murder and confided the information that God had struck her puppy-dog a surely fatal blow. She had forgotten her bewildered lust, and her eyes were wide open for the first time. They looked like the dog's eyes. She sniveled and implored me to pray for the animal. I wanted to say to her: Madam, I have myself to pray for, the colored queen, the Puerto Rican family, the person in the front room whom I've never seen, the woman who cries deliberately behind her closed door, and the rest of the people in all roominghouses, everywhere; besides, Madam, I don't understand how to pray. But . . . to simplify things . . . I told her I would pray. She looked up. She said that I was a liar, and that I probably wanted the dog to die. I told her, and there was so much truth here, that I didn't want the dog to die. I didn't, and not just because I'd poisoned him. I'm afraid that I must tell you I wanted the dog to live so that I could see what our new relationship might come to.

PETER *indicates his increasing displeasure and slowly growing antagonism.*

Please understand, Peter; that sort of thing is important. You must believe me; it *is* important. We have to know the effect of our actions. [*Another deep sigh*] Well, anyway; the dog recovered. I have no idea why, unless he was a descendant of the puppy that guarded the gates of hell or some such resort. I'm not up on my mythology. [*He pronounces the word myth-o-*logy.] Are you?

PETER *sets to thinking, but* JERRY *goes on.*

At any rate, and you've missed the eight-thousand-dollar question, Peter; at any rate, the dog recovered his health and the landlady recovered her thirst, in no way altered by the bow-wow's deliverance. When I came home from a movie that was playing on Forty-second street, a movie I'd seen, or one that was very much like one or several I'd seen, after the landlady told me puppykins was better, I was so hoping for the dog to be waiting for me. I was . . . well, how would you put it . . . enticed? . . . fascinated? . . . no, I don't think so . . . heart-shatteringly anxious, that's it; I was heart-shatteringly anxious to confront my friend again.

PETER *reacts scoffingly.*

Yes, Peter; friend. That's the only word for it. I was heart-shatteringly et cetera to confront my doggy friend again. I came in the door and advanced, unafraid, to the center of the entrance hall. The beast was there . . . looking at me. And, you know, he looked better for his scrape with the nevermind. I stopped; I looked at him; he looked at me. I think . . . I think we stayed a long time that way . . . still, stone-statue . . . just looking at one another. I looked more into his face than he looked into mine. I mean, I can concentrate longer at looking into a dog's face than a dog can concentrate at looking into mine, or into anybody else's face, for that matter. But during that twenty seconds or two hours that we looked into each other's face, we made contact. Now, here is what I had wanted to happen: I loved the dog now, and I wanted him to love me. I had tried to love, and I had tried to kill, and both had been unsuccessful by themselves. I hoped . . . and I don't really know why I expected the dog to understand anything, much less my motivations : . . I hoped that the dog would understand.

PETER *seems to be hypnotized.*

It's just . . . it's just that . . . [JERRY *is abnormally tense, now.*] . . . it's just that if you can't deal with people, you have to make a start somewhere. WITH ANI-MALS! [*Much faster now, and like a conspirator*] Don't you see? A person has to have some way of dealing with SOMETHING. If not with people . . . if not with people . . . SOMETHING. With a bed, with a cockroach, with a mirror . . . no, that's too hard, that's one of the last steps. With a cockroach, with a . . . with a carpet, a roll of toilet paper . . . no, not that, either . . . that's a mirror, too; always check bleeding. You see how hard it is to find things? With a street corner, and too many lights, all colors reflecting on the oily-wet streets . . . with a wisp of smoke, a wisp . . . of smoke . . . with . . . with pornographic playing cards, with a strongbox . . . WITHOUT A LOCK . . . with love, with vomiting, with crying, with fury because the pretty little ladies aren't pretty little ladies, with making money with your body which is an act of love and I could prove it, with howling because you're alive; with God. How about that? WITH GOD WHO IS A COL-ORED QUEEN WHO WEARS A KIMONO AND PLUCKS HIS EYEBROWS, WHO IS A WOMAN WHO CRIES WITH DETERMINATION BEHIND HER CLOSED DOOR . . . with God who, I'm told, turned his back on the whole thing some time ago . . . with . . . some day, with people. [JERRY *sighs the next word heavily.*] People. With an idea; a concept. And where better, where ever better in this humiliating excuse for a jail, where better to communicate one single, sim-pleminded idea than in an entrance hall? Where? It would be A START! Where better to make a beginning . . . to understand and just possibly be understood . . . a beginning of an understanding, than with . . .

Here JERRY *seems to fall into almost grotesque fatigue.*

. . . than with A DOG. Just that; a dog.

Here there is a silence that might be prolonged for a moment or so; then JERRY *wearily finishes his story.*

A dog. It seemed like a perfectly sensible idea. Man is a dog's best friend, remem-ber. So: the dog and I looked at each other. I longer than the dog. And what I saw then has been the same ever since. Whenever the dog and I see each other we both stop where we are. We regard each other with a mixture of sadness and suspicion, and then we feign indifference. We walk past each other safely; we have an understanding. It's very sad, but you'll have to admit that it is an understanding. We had made many attempts at contact, and we had failed. The dog has returned to garbage, and I to solitary but free passage. I have not returned. I mean to say, I have *gained* solitary free passage, if that much further loss can be said to be gain. I have learned that neither kindness nor cruelty by themselves, independent of each other, creates any effect beyond themselves; and I have learned that the two combined, together, at the same time, are the teaching emotion. And what is gained is loss. And what has been the result: the dog and I have attained a compromise; more of a bargain, really. We neither love nor hurt because we do not try to reach each other. And, *was* trying to feed the dog an act of love? And, perhaps, was the dog's attempt to bite me *not* an act of love? If we can so misunderstand, well then, why have we invented the word love in the first place?

There is silence. JERRY *moves to* PETER's *bench and sits down beside him. This is first time* JERRY *has sat down during the play.*

The Story of Jerry and the Dog: the end.

PETER *is silent.*

Well, Peter? [JERRY *is suddenly cheerful.*] Well, Peter? Do you think I could sell that story to the *Reader's Digest* and make a couple of hundred bucks for *The Most Unforgettable Character I've Ever Met?* Huh?

JERRY *is animated, but* PETER *is disturbed.*

Oh, come on now, Peter, tell me what you think.
    PETER [*numb*] I . . . I don't understand what . . . I don't think I . . . [*Now, almost tearfully*] Why did you tell me all of this?
    JERRY Why not?
    PETER I DON'T UNDERSTAND!
    JERRY [*furious, but whispering*] That's a lie.
    PETER No. No, it's not.
    JERRY [*quietly*] I tried to explain it to you as I went along. I went slowly; it all has to do with . . .
    PETER I DON'T WANT TO HEAR ANY MORE. I don't understand you, or your landlady, or her dog. . . .
    JERRY Her dog! I thought it was my . . . No. No, you're right. It *is* her dog. [*Looks at* PETER *intently, shaking his head*] I don't know what I was thinking about; of course you don't understand. [*In a monotone, wearily*] I don't live in your block; I'm not married to two parakeets, or whatever your setup is. I am a *permanent transient*, and my home is the sickening roominghouses on the West Side of New York City, which is the greatest city in the world. Amen.
    PETER I'm . . . I'm sorry; I didn't mean to . . .
    JERRY Forget it. I suppose you don't quite know what to make of me, eh?
    PETER [*a joke*] We get all kinds in publishing. [*Chuckles*]
    JERRY You're a funny man. [*He forces a laugh.*] You know that? You're a very . . . a richly comic person.
    PETER [*modestly, but amused*] Oh, now, not really. [*Still chuckling*]
    JERRY Peter, do I annoy you, or confuse you?
    PETER [*lightly*] Well, I must confess that this wasn't the kind of afternoon I'd anticipated.

JERRY You mean, I'm not the gentleman you were expecting.

PETER I wasn't expecting anybody.

JERRY No, I don't imagine you were. But I'm here, and I'm not leaving.

PETER [*consulting his watch*] Well, you may not be, but I must be getting home soon.

JERRY Oh, come on; stay a while longer.

PETER I really should get home; you see . . .

JERRY [*tickles* PETER's *ribs with his fingers*] Oh, come on.

PETER [*he is very ticklish; as Jerry continues to tickle him his voice becomes falsetto.*] No, I . . . OHHHHH! Don't do that. Stop, stop. Ohhh, no, no.

JERRY Oh, come on.

PETER [*as* JERRY *tickles*] Oh, hee, hee, hee. I must go. I . . . hee, hee, hee. After all, stop, stop, hee, hee, hee, after all, the parakeets will be getting dinner ready soon. Hee, hee. And the cats are setting the table. Stop, stop, and, and . . . [PETER *is beside himself now.*] . . . and we've having . . . hee, hee . . . uh . . . ho, ho, ho.

JERRY *stops tickling* PETER, *but the combination of the tickling and his own mad whimsy has* PETER *laughing almost hysterically. As his laughter continues, then subsides,* JERRY *watches him; with a curious fixed smile.*

JERRY Peter?

PETER Oh, ha, ha, ha, ha, ha. What? What?

JERRY Listen, now.

PETER Oh, ho, ho. What . . . what is it, Jerry? Oh, my.

JERRY [*mysteriously*] Peter, do you want to know what happened at the zoo?

PETER Ah, ha, ha. The what? Oh, yes; the zoo. Oh, ho, ho. Well, I had my own zoo there for a moment with . . . hee, hee, the parakeets getting dinner ready, and the . . . ha, ha, whatever it was, the . . .

JERRY [*calmly*] Yes, that was very funny, Peter. I wouldn't have expected it. But do you want to hear about what happened at the zoo, or not?

PETER Yes. Yes, by all means; tell me what happened at the zoo. Oh, my. I don't know what happened to me.

JERRY Now I'll let you in on what happened at the zoo; but first, I should tell you why I went to the zoo. I went to the zoo to find out more about the way people exist with animals, and the way animals exist with each other, and with people too. It probably wasn't a fair test, what with everyone separated by bars from everyone else, the animals for the most part from each other, and always the people from the animals. But, if it's a zoo, that's the way it is. [*He pokes* PETER *on the arm.*] Move over.

PETER [*friendly*] I'm sorry, haven't you enough room? [*He shifts a little.*]

JERRY [*smiling slightly*] Well, all the animals are there, and all the people are there, and it's Sunday and all the children are there. [*He pokes* PETER *again.*] Move over.

PETER [*patiently, still friendly*] All right.

He moves some more, and JERRY *has all the room he might need.*

JERRY And it's a hot day, so all the stench is there, too, and all the balloon sellers, and all the ice cream sellers, and all the seals are barking, and all the birds are screaming. [*Pokes* PETER *harder*] Move over!

PETER [*beginning to be annoyed*]   Look here, you have more than enough room! [*But he moves more, and is now fairly cramped at one end of the bench.*]

JERRY   And I am there, and it's feeding time at the lions' house, and the lion keeper comes into the lion cage, one of the lion cages, to feed one of the lions. [*Punches* PETER *on the arm, hard*] MOVE OVER!

PETER [*very annoyed*]   I can't move over any more, and stop hitting me. What's the matter with you?

JERRY   Do you want to hear the story? [*Punches* PETER's *arm again*]

PETER [*flabbergasted*]   I'm not so sure! I certainly don't want to be punched in the arm.

JERRY [*punches* PETER's *arm again*]   Like that?

PETER   Stop it! What's the matter with you?

JERRY   I'm crazy, you bastard.

PETER   That isn't funny.

JERRY   Listen to me, Peter. I want this bench. You go sit on the bench over there, and if you're good I'll tell you the rest of the story.

PETER [*flustered*]   But . . . whatever for? What *is* the matter with you? Besides, I see no reason why I should give up this bench. I sit on this bench almost every Sunday afternoon, in good weather. It's secluded here; there's never anyone sitting here, so I have it all to myself.

JERRY [*softly*]   Get off this bench, Peter; I want it.

PETER [*almost whining*]   No.

JERRY   I said I want this bench, and I'm going to have it. Now get over there.

PETER   People can't have everything they want. You should know that; it's a rule; people can have some of the things they want, but they can't have everything.

JERRY [*laughs*]   Imbecile! You're slow-witted!

PETER   Stop that!

JERRY   You're a vegetable! Go lie down on the ground.

PETER [*intense*]   Now *you* listen to me. I've put up with you all afternoon.

JERRY   Not really.

PETER   LONG ENOUGH. I've put up with you long enough. I've listened to you because you seemed . . . well, because I thought you wanted to talk to somebody.

JERRY   You put things well; economically, and, yet . . . oh, what is the word I want to put justice to your . . . JESUS, you make me sick . . . get off here and give me my bench.

PETER   MY BENCH!

JERRY [*pushes* PETER *almost, but not quite, off the bench*]   Get out of my sight.

PETER [*regaining his position*]   God da . . . mn you. That's enough! I've had enough of you. I will not give up this bench; you can't have it, and that's that. Now, go away.

JERRY *snorts but does not move.*

Go away, I said.

JERRY *does not move.*

Get away from here. If you don't move on . . . you're a bum . . . that's what you are. . . . If you don't move on, I'll get a policeman here and make you go.

JERRY *laughs, stays.*

I warn you, I'll call a policeman.

JERRY [*softly*] You won't find a policeman around here; they're all over on the west side of the park chasing fairies down from trees or out of the bushes. That's all they do. That's their function. So scream your head off; it won't do you any good.

PETER POLICE! I warn you, I'll have you arrested. POLICE! [*Pause*] I said POLICE! [*Pause*] I feel ridiculous.

JERRY You look ridiculous: a grown man screaming for the police on a bright Sunday afternoon in the park with nobody harming you. If a policeman *did* fill his quota and come sludging over this way he'd probably take you in as a nut.

PETER [*with disgust and impotence*] Great God, I just came here to read, and now you want me to give up the bench. You're mad.

JERRY Hey, I got news for you, as they say. I'm on your precious bench, and you're never going to have it for yourself again.

PETER [*furiously*] Look, you; get off my bench. I don't care if it makes any sense or not. I want this bench to myself; I want you OFF IT!

JERRY [*mockingly*] Aw . . . look who's mad.

PETER GET OUT!

JERRY No.

PETER I WARN YOU!

JERRY Do you know how ridiculous you look *now?*

PETER [*his fury and self-consciousness have possessed him*] It doesn't matter. [*He is almost crying.*] GET AWAY FROM MY BENCH!

JERRY Why? You have everything in the world you want; you've told me about your home, and your family, and *your own* little zoo. You have everything, and now you want this bench. Are these the things men fight for? Tell me, Peter, is this bench, this iron and this wood, is this your honor? Is this the thing in the world you'd fight for? Can you think of anything more absurd?

PETER Absurd? Look, I'm not going to talk to you about honor, or even try to explain it to you, Besides, it isn't a question of honor; but even if it were, you wouldn't understand.

JERRY [*contemptuously*] You don't even know what you're saying, do you? This is probably the first time in your life you've had anything more trying to face than changing your cats' toilet box. Stupid! Don't you have any idea, not even the slightest, what other people *need?*

PETER Oh, boy, listen to you; well, you don't need this bench. That's for sure.

JERRY Yes; yes, I do.

PETER [*quivering*] I've come here for years; I have hours of great pleasure, great satisfaction, right here. And that's important to a man. I'm a responsible person, and I'm GROWNUP. This is my bench, and you have no right to take it away from me.

JERRY Fight for it, then. Defend yourself; defend your bench.

PETER You've *pushed* me to it. Get up and fight.

JERRY Like a man?

PETER [*still angry*] Yes, like a man, if you insist on mocking me even further.

JERRY I'll have to give you credit for one thing: you *are* a vegetable, and a slightly nearsighted one, I think . . .

PETER THAT'S ENOUGH. . . .

JERRY   . . . but, you know, as they say on TV all the time—you know—and I mean this, Peter, you have a certain dignity; it surprises me. . . .

PETER   STOP!

JERRY [*rises lazily*] Very well, Peter, we'll battle for the bench, but we're not evenly matched.

He takes out and clicks open an ugly-looking knife.

PETER [*suddenly awakening to the reality of the situation*]   You are mad! You're stark raving mad! YOU'RE GOING TO KILL ME!

But before PETER *has time to think what to do,* JERRY *tosses the knife at* PETER's *feet.*

JERRY   There you go. Pick it up. You have the knife and we'll be more evenly matched.

PETER [*horrified*] No!

JERRY [*rushes over to* PETER, *grabs him by the collar;* PETER *rises; their faces almost touch*] Now you pick up that knife and you fight with me. You fight for your self-respect; you fight for that goddamned bench.

PETER [*struggling*] No! Let . . . let go of me! He . . . Help!

JERRY [*slaps* PETER *on each "fight"*] You fight, you miserable bastard; fight for that bench; fight for your parakeets; fight for your cats, fight for your two daughters; fight for your wife; fight for your manhood, you pathetic little vegetable. [*Spits in* PETER's *face*] You couldn't even get your wife with a male child.

PETER [*breaks away, enraged*] It's a matter of genetics, not manhood, you . . . you monster.

He darts down, picks up the knife and backs off a little; he is breathing heavily.

I'll give you one last chance; get out of here and leave me alone!

He holds the knife with a firm arm, but far in front of him, not to attack, but to defend.

JERRY [*sighs heavily*] So be it!

With a rush he charges PETER *and impales himself on the knife. Tableau: For just a moment, complete silence,* JERRY *impaled on the knife at the end of* PETER's *still firm arm. Then* PETER *screams, pulls away, leaving the knife in* JERRY. JERRY *is motionless, on point. Then he, too, screams, and it must be the sound of an infuriated and fatally wounded animal. With the knife in him, he stumbles back to the bench that* PETER *had vacated. He crumbles there, sitting, facing* PETER, *his eyes wide in agony, his mouth open.*

Film

Film and the stage

Even a brief treatment of film as literature must begin by distinguishing cinema from drama. We need to distinguish these art forms—although we need not distinguish film from fiction or poetry—because they are superficially similar; each tells a story using actors' speech and gesture. But film and drama are at least as different as painting and sculpture. When Leonardo da Vinci praised painting over sculpture, he praised its self-reliance: painting includes its own light and shadow and does not depend like sculpture on an external light source. On the other hand, when the contemporary English sculptor Henry Moore prefers sculpture to painting, he praises its present reality; painting's light and painting's volume are illusory, while sculpture is obdurate and three-dimensional.

We need not choose sides; we may take the dispute as suggestive: arts that are superficially similar may be profoundly different.

Drama is more like sculpture and film more like painting. Film can create on its two-dimensional screen the illusion of *anything:* a thirty-foot shark, a gorilla towering over Manhattan, a galaxy exploding. But film remains illusion: its audience understands that it watches not real gorillas or galaxies but insubstantial images of them. In contrast, drama employs actual bodies that occupy space, limited by physical reality, which also provides drama's power. Drama's audience is aware not only of the stage's reality but of its own dynamic connection with living actors on the stage. In drama actors and audience make a community—interrelated, interactive, reciprocal. In films the audience is passive to the huge images reeling above; the audience knows that the film unwinds as it will, whatever the audience's response on this Wednesday night or that Saturday afternoon.

In remarking differences we should not reach a conclusion about superiority and inferiority. We compare the incomparable, like apples and oranges: after all, drama—like fiction and poetry—begins in prehistory; film is a product of modern technology. Because film depends more on spectacle and less on language, it is less literature than drama is. Yet, because it remains partly dependent on language, it remains literature at least partly. And because film derives in part from the stage play, the study of film reality grows out of the study of dramatic literature.

Reading a film script, most Americans can construct a mental cinema more easily than they construct a mental theater when reading a play, because most of them have seen more movies than plays. Reading the script of *Citizen Kane* will recall the film for many of us, because this classic is frequently shown on American campuses and on television. But many of us, though experienced in watching film, lack the vocabulary to discuss what we have seen.

A note on television

If most of us see more film than drama, it is equally true that most of us have seen more television than film. We need here to distinguish film from television, in order not to confuse them. Confusion is likely, of course, because much of the film we see we see on television. For the purposes of definition, let us define as **film** those moving pictures created for projection on a large screen before a large audience; let us define as **television** the visual materials created for small screens watched by small groups in domestic rooms.

The difference between movie theater and living room is crucial. Watching a film in a theater, we become part of a community of watchers self-convened to see a movie; in many living rooms the television set is an extra, often ignored member of the family, a continually jabbering presence that laughs a lot, that alters when we ask it to, and that generally tries not to give offense. Film is public and communal, television familial and domestic. Television has a potential for intimacy that has scarcely been exploited. The central image of television is the full face that looks directly at us and chats with us as if it were our cousin; television works best when the speaker seems to address a single person. Yet there is a strange loneliness to the medium, an electronic community of two: Walter Cronkite addresses *me*. Paradoxically, this loneliness is most apparent in the laugh track, by which producers of situation comedies try to glue American living rooms together coast to coast. But the disembodied laugh track, as Aristotle might have put it, does not imitate nature.

Yet, at its best, television often does. Its size may limit its artistic range for dramatic expression (seeing a good film on the small set, we miss detail in scenes that include a broad image and we miss the power of the huge face in a close-up) but television finds its legitimate place in intimate objectivity, in reporting and documentary, in news and sports. Tense performances seem to enter the living room—and actuality becomes in turn a kind of drama, as in the network cliché *real-life drama*.

The language of film

Films are collaborative efforts, requiring many skills. A **producer** retains overall coordinating power, integrating financing and style, marketing, casting, and scheduling. A **director** is usually most important to the film, especially to its esthetic success or failure. The director with assistants rehearses actors and controls the shooting of the film. The original script is usually assembled by a number of screenwriters. Then the cameraman contributes his expertise to produce the images the director requires. Other technicians handle makeup, costuming. One or more assistant directors may control second units, even third units, to photograph background scenery in Utah, while the director works indoors with actors on Hollywood sets constructed to look like Utah. The editor who assembles the film may be independent or assisted by the director—or may even *be* the director. The editing or assembly of the film is of central importance. A film is composed of thousands upon thousands of different shots, all spliced together in a particular organization. A shot may last a split second to fifteen seconds.

In the **long shot**, the screen shows a wide sweep from a long distance. We may see a city from the air or a distant mountain; we may look toward a settlement from such a distance that the houses are little bumps on the horizon; or we may look at a gathering and see thirty or forty people in a single image. Obviously in a long shot we can have much detail, much expanse, but little intimate imagery. In a **medium shot**, we move much closer to a main subject, perhaps isolating two or three people, or the detail of a house, or several objects in relation to each other. In a medium shot faces are large and memorable, but in a **close-up** an entire face can fill a huge screen. For that matter, we may isolate lips or one eye—or we may make a close-up of a flower or an insect or a bullet. The close-up makes use of the camera's enormous ability to alter scale, to turn the tiny into the huge. In all these shots of varying distances the camera determines our point of view; it can watch something from miles away or from half an inch. In the camera's point of view we find an enormous distinction between film and staged drama. When we watch stage drama, our point of view is fixed—the seat our ticket gives us. Blocking and lighting can emphasize certain movements and even actor's faces, but neither blocking nor lighting can approach what the camera's eye can do to isolate and emphasize by altering size and scale.

We have so far merely described shots in terms of their distance—or apparent distance—from the subject; there is also the angle of vision to consider. We can shoot from near the ground, in a **low-angle shot**, from a child's point of view, for instance. A single camera angle may express different feelings according to the director's intentions. A low-angle shot may impart a quality of menace, if the tall creature carries a gun; on the other hand, if the elongated character carries a Bible against a background of blue sky, the low-angle shot may express nobility or high purpose. Thus the shot's angle is not its meaning, but the shot's angle has connotations that can contribute an established context. A **high-angle shot**—say, a character seen from above—will often minimize that character, but not always: there is a famous shot in *Citizen Kane,* taken from above, in which Kane casts a shadow over his wife; the high-angle shot shows him dominating someone else.

In a **zoom shot** an adjustable lens moves from any distance and proceeds to any other, depending on the lens's capabilities; for instance, a long shot can zoom close, even into a close-up, suddenly focusing attention on detail. And the camera itself can move, following action on a crane, in a **crane shot**; or it can swivel on its base in panorama, a **pan shot**, even turning full circle: in a western the camera may pan in a complete circle to reveal that the hero is surrounded. A **tilt shot** moves the camera vertically, up or down instead of side to side; thus the camera may express the height of a building, a tree, or a village by starting at dirt level and tilting up to the top. Or a camera may move on wheels toward or away from an object in a **traveling shot**. A cameraman may put gauze over the lens to cut down the wrinkles in an old actor's face; a recent, aging ingénue of Hollywood, in the gossip of the trade, was always "photographed through linoleum." The kind of film, its emulsion, its method of development, may blur or mellow an image or create bright contrast, hard angles, and sharp edges. In an episode in *Bonnie and Clyde,* when the outlaws visit Bonnie's mother in a Depression campsite, the softness of the image creates a momentary relief, a brief relaxation in a generally hard and brittle film.

Whatever the shots, from whatever camera angle, with whatever emulsion or lens, the cutting room brings them together into sequences and scenes. The manner of assemblage is at least as important as what is assembled. Russian filmmakers and theorists—Serge Eisenstein foremost as a director—assembled brief shots into what they called **montage**, quick sequences of image that could tell a story or embody a feeling or emphasize a thought, or all three. At its simplest, montage can juxtapose images for satiric effect: we watch a talkative drunk become a braying donkey. Yet in a dense and resourceful sequence montage can be eloquently expressive. In Eisenstein's famous silent film *Potemkin,* a montage embodies the results of an anti-Tzarist mutiny. This montage is composed of many brief images, among them a long shot of a crowd cheering the successful mutineers, a middle shot of the Tzar's Cossacks shooting into the cheering multitude, another long shot of bodies littered and people fleeing the massacre, a close-up of a student-onlooker screaming, marching legs of the Cossacks, and the face of a crying mother who holds in her arms a dead baby.

Technical terms describe transitions from one shot to another. A **straight cut** is the most common, simply replacing one image with another. An **intercut** usually moves from one place to another within a sequence where one shot relates to another or comments on it. **Cross cuts** play two actions against each other, through intercutting, toward an eventual convergence—the fort is being attacked, the cavalry is coming! Either an intercut or a cross cut can be used for ironic commentary. A scene may end by a **fade-in** to another, as one image replaces another—a coin on a plate transforms into the sun rising the next morning. Such effects may be visual play, or they may be meaningful. In *2001*, when a gorilla hurls up a bone he has used as a weapon and that bone turns into a space ship, we are watching a message. Sounds can also create transitions—as when an invalid's moan at the end of one scene turns into the whistle of a train at the beginning of the next, a train bringing a doctor.

If Aristotle were to write a *Poetics* of film, perhaps he would list plot first, but he would need to insist that plot in film is often narrated by spectacle. The best directors delight in telling storis without words, plot as a sequence of images. Sometimes the rapid sequence of image seems the essence of film, as when a movie earns its name by concluding with a typical chase scene. Character, like plot, is revealed by image, as when we understand a character's thought by observing a **reaction shot** in close-up; someone says or does something, and without words we observe the effect. Of course language reveals character too; sometimes we hear a **voice over** a close-up, and soliloquy returns to our dramatic literature. But we are still more apt to *see* a character's thoughts in a montage than to *hear* a sequence of spoken words. Sometimes we see **flashback**, as characters remember the past; sometimes we see a film strip of fantasy, as they imagine the future or a present which they cannot observe.

Perhaps because of the size of the image, acting in films must be less obvious than stage acting. A flicker of an eyelash—maybe two yards across in a close-up—makes a bigger gesture than a stage actor swooping both arms over his head. Classic screen actors and actresses seem to be themselves: if screen actors appear to be acting at all, they appear to overact. Actors who have excelled at appearing to be themselves include Gary Cooper, Spencer Tracy, and Marilyn Monroe.

Orson Welles and *Citizen Kane*

Orson Welles (1915–   ) began his theatrical career as an actor and started directing at an early age. He founded the Mercury Theater in 1937 and in 1938 began a series of innovative radio plays. (One of them, a fictitious account of Martians landing in New Jersey, frightened listeners who took it as fact.) He went to Hollywood in 1939 and made *Citizen Kane* in 1941. His subsequent films have included *The Magnificent Ambersons* (1942), *Macbeth* (1947), *The Lady from Shanghai* (1948), *Othello* (1955), *Touch of Evil* (1958), and *Falstaff* (1967), but Welles never made another film as fine as *Citizen Kane,* for reasons that are chiefly the film industry's fault. *Citizen Kane* was a lightly disguised attack upon the famous newspaper publisher William Randolph Hearst, whose syndicated columnists subsequently set out to destroy Welles. Hollywood has never been known for its bravery in the face of criticism.

Welles not only directed and edited the film but also played the lead role of Kane, and played it magnificently, revealing with compassion the cold, empty, loveless center of a rich and powerful character. Although the credits list Welles as co-author of this script, Pauline Kael has argued convincingly that the principal screenwriter was Herman J. Mankiewicz (1897–1953). Mankiewicz was a brilliant, witty *New Yorker* writer who went to Hollywood for the large salary, drank, gambled his money away, wrote excellent screenplays, and died too young. Welles is the center of *Citizen Kane,* as actor and director, and doubtless he contributed to the script and revised it during shooting. But Mankiewicz not only wrote the script—he suggested the subject.

At least one other contributor needs special mention: cinematographer or cameraman Greg Toland created the stark and moving visual effects of the film, partly innovative, partly derived from German expressionist film. Earlier, we mentioned a particular high-angle shot, and many of Toland's shots used extreme angles, low as well as high. Some shots emphasized shadowy, indistinct detail; many others were brightly lighted, which allowed Toland to use a high f-stop on his camera and achieve depth of field. A wide-angle lens also maintained depth of field, and exaggerated distances in some shots. In turn, this depth of field allowed the audience to see, without distortion, something close to the camera at the same time as something far away: almost a close-up and a long shot in the same frame.

Ideally, we should see the film, then read the script—and then see the film again. But even reading the dialogue and stage directions alone, with the help of a few still photographs, we can experience the literature of film, distinct from drama written for the stage. For those who would like to continue the investigation, many books and articles have been written about this film. The place to begin is *The Citizen Kane Book* by Pauline Kael, which includes lengthy essays on Welles and on Mankiewicz, as well as a narrative of the film's conception and execution and of its problems in distribution.

When we read the text of this screenplay, the descriptions of camera shots and notes on the actors' expressions help us make a mental cinema.

Herman J. Mankiewicz
Orson Welles
Citizen Kane

Prologue

Fade In

1 Ext. Xanadu—Faint Dawn—1940 (Miniature)

Window, very small in the distance, illuminated. All around this an almost totally black screen. Now, as the camera moves slowly towards this window, which is almost a postage stamp in the frame, other forms appear; barbed wire, cyclone fencing, and now, looming up against an early morning sky, enormous iron grill-work. Camera travels up what is now shown to be a gateway of gigantic proportions and holds on the top of it—a huge initial "K" showing darker and darker against the dawn sky. Through this and beyond we see the fairy-tale mountaintop of Xanadu, the great castle a silhouette at its summit, the little window a distant accent in the darkness.

Dissolve

(A series of setups, each closer to the great window, all telling something of:)

2 The Literally Incredible Domain of Charles Foster Kane

Its right flank resting for nearly forty miles on the Gulf Coast, it truly extends in all directions farther than the eye can see. Designed by nature to be almost completely bare and flat—it was, as will develop, practically all marshland when Kane acquired and changed its face—it is now pleasantly uneven, with its fair share of rolling hills and one very good-sized mountain, all man-made. Almost all the land is improved, either through cultivation for farming purposes or through careful landscaping in the shape of parks and lakes. The castle itself, an enormous pile, compounded of several genuine castles, of European origin, of varying architecture—dominates the scene, from the very peak of the mountain.

Dissolve

3 Golf Links (Miniature)

Past which we move. The greens are straggly and overgrown, the fairways wild with tropical weeds, the links unused and not seriously tended for a long time.

Dissolve Out

Dissolve In

4 What Was Once a Good-Sized Zoo (Miniature)

Of the Hagenbeck type. All that now remains, with one exception, are the individual plots, surrounded by moats, on which the animals are kept, free and yet safe from each other and the landscape at large. (Signs on several of the plots indicate that here there were once tigers, lions, giraffes.)

Dissolve

5 The Monkey Terrace (Miniature)

In the f.g.,[1] a great obscene ape is outlined against the dawn murk. He is scratching himself slowly, thoughtfully, looking out across the estates of Charles Foster Kane, to the distant light glowing in the castle on the hill.

Dissolve

6 The Alligator Pit (Miniature)

The idiot pile of sleepy dragons. Reflected in the muddy water—the lighted window.

7 The Lagoon (Miniature)

The boat landing sags. An old newspaper floats on the surface of the water—a copy of the New York "Inquirer." As it moves across the frame, it discloses again the reflection of the window in the castle, closer than before.

8 The Great Swimming Pool (Miniature)

It is empty. A newspaper blows across the cracked floor of the tank.

Dissolve

9 The Cottages (Miniature)

In the shadows, literally the shadows, of the castle. As we move by, we see that their doors and windows are boarded up and locked, with heavy bars as further protection and sealing.

Dissolve Out

Dissolve In

10 A Drawbridge (Miniature)

Over a wide moat, now stagnant and choked with weeds. We move across it and through a huge solid gateway into a formal garden, perhaps thirty yards wide and one hundred yards deep, which extends right up to the very wall of the castle. The landscaping surrounding it has been sloppy and casual for a long time, but this particular garden has been kept up in perfect shape. As the camera makes its way through it, towards the lighted window of the castle, there are revealed rare and exotic blooms of all kinds. The dominating note is one of almost exaggerated tropical lushness, hanging limp and despairing—Moss, moss, moss. Angkor Wat, the night the last king died.

Dissolve

11 The Window (Miniature)

Camera moves in until the frame of the window fills the frame of the screen. Suddenly the light within goes out. This stops the action of the camera and cuts the music which has been accompanying the sequence. In the glass panes of the window we see reflected the ripe, dreary landscape of Mr. Kane's estate behind and the dawn sky.

Dissolve

[1]foreground

12 Int.[1] Kane's Bedroom—Faint Dawn—1940

A very long shot of Kane's enormous bed, silhouetted against the enormous window.

Dissolve

13 Int. Kane's Bedroom—Faint Dawn—1940

A snow scene. An incredible one. Big impossible flakes of snow, a too picturesque farmhouse and a snowman. The jingling of sleigh bells in the musical score now makes an ironic reference to Indian temple bells—the music freezes—

KANE'S OLD OLD VOICE   Rosebud!

The camera pulls back, showing the whole scene to be contained in one of those glass balls which are sold in novelty stores all over the world. A hand—Kane's hand, which has been holding the ball, relaxes. The ball falls out of his hand and bounds down two carpeted steps leading to the bed, the camera following. The ball falls off the last step onto the marble floor where it breaks, the fragments glittering in the first ray of the morning sun. This ray cuts an angular pattern across the floor, suddenly crossed with a thousand bars of light as the blinds are pulled across the window.

14 The Foot of Kane's Bed

The camera very close. Outlined against the shuttered window, we can see a form—the form of a nurse, as she pulls the sheet up over his head. The camera follows this action up the length of the bed and arrives at the face after the sheet has covered it.

Fade Out

Fade In

15 Int. of a Motion Picture Projection Room

On the screen as the camera moves in are the words:

MAIN TITLE

Stirring brassy music is heard on the sound track (which, of course, sounds more like a sound track than ours).

The screen in the projection room fills our screen as the second title appears:

CREDITS

(NOTE: Here follows a typical news digest short, one of the regular monthly or bimonthly features based on public events or personalities. These are distinguished from ordinary newsreels and short subjects in that they have a fully developed editorial or story line. Some of the more obvious characteristics of the "March of Time," for example, as well as other documentary shorts, will be combined to give an authentic impression of this now familiar type of short subject. As is the accepted procedure in these short subjects, a narrator is used as well as explanatory titles.)

Fade Out

[1]Interior

NARRATOR

Legendary was the Xanadu where Kubla Khan decreed his stately pleasure dome (With quotes in his voice):

"Where twice five miles of fertile ground With walls and towers were girdled round."

(Dropping the quotes) Today, almost as legendary is Florida's Xanadu—world's largest private pleasure ground. Here, on the deserts of the Gulf Coast, a private mountain was commissioned, successfully built for its landlord. . . . Here for Xanadu's landlord will be held 1940's biggest, strangest funeral; here this week is laid to rest a potent figure of our century—America's Kubla Khan—Charles Foster Kane.

U.S.A.
Xanadu's Landlord
CHARLES FOSTER KANE
Opening shot of great desolate expanse of Florida coastline. (Day—1940)

Dissolve

TITLE:
TO FORTY-FOUR MILLION U.S. NEWSBUYERS, MORE NEWSWORTHY THAN THE NAMES IN HIS OWN HEADLINES WAS KANE HIMSELF, GREATEST NEWSPAPER TYCOON OF THIS OR ANY OTHER GENERATION.

Shot of a huge, screen-filling picture of Kane.

Pull back to show that it is a picture on the front page of the "Inquirer," surrounded by the reversed rules of mourning, with masthead and headlines. (1940)

Dissolve

In journalism's history other names are honored more than Charles Foster Kane's, more justly revered. Among publishers, second only to James Gordon Bennett the First: his dashing expatriate son; England's Northcliffe and Beaverbrook; Chicago's Patterson and McCormick; Denver's Bonfils and Sommes; New York's late great Joseph Pulitzer; America's emperor of

A great number of headlines, set in different types and different styles, obviously from different papers, all announcing Kane's death, all appearing over photographs of Kane himself. (Perhaps a fifth of the headlines are in foreign languages.) An important item in connection with the headlines is that many of them—positively not all—reveal passionately conflicting opinions about Kane.

the news syndicate, another editorialist and landlord, the still mighty and once mightier Hearst. Great names all of them—but none of these so loved—hated—feared, so often spoken—as Charles Foster Kane.

Thus, they contain variously the words, "patriot," "Democrat," "pacifist," "warmonger," "traitor," "idealist," "American," etc.

TITLE:

1895 TO 1940
ALL OF THESE YEARS HE COVERED,
MANY OF THESE YEARS HE WAS.

The San Francisco earthquake. First with the news were the Kane Papers. First with relief of the sufferers, first with the news of their relief of the sufferers.

Newsreel Shots of San Francisco during and after the fire, followed by shots of special trains with large streamers: "Kane Relief Organization." Over these shots superimpose the date—1906.

Kane Papers scoop the world on the Armistice—publish, eight hours before competitors, complete details of the Armistice terms granted the Germans by Marshall Foch from his railroad car in the Forest of Compiègne.

Artist's painting of Foch's railroad car and peace negotiators, if actual newsreel shot unavailable. Over this shot superimpose the date—1918.

Shots with the date—1898—(to be supplied).

Shots with the date—1910—

(to be supplied).

Shots with the date—1922—(to be supplied).

For forty years appeared in Kane newsprint no public issue on which Kane Papers took no stand.

Headlines, cartoons, contemporary newsreels or stills of the following:

1. Woman suffrage. (The celebrated newsreel shot of about 1914.)
2. Prohibition. (Breaking up of a speakeasy and such.)
3. T.V.A.
4. Labor riots.

No public man whom Kane himself did not support or denounce—often support, then denounce.

Brief clips of old newsreel shots of William Jennings Bryan, Theodore Roosevelt, Stalin, Walter P. Thatcher, Al Smith, McKinley, Landon, Franklin D. Roosevelt and such. (Also recent newsreels of the elderly Kane with such Nazis as Hitler, Goering and England's Chamberlain and Churchill.)

Its humble beginnings a dying daily—	Shot of a ramshackle building with old-fashioned presses showing through plate-glass windows and the name "Inquirer" in old-fashioned gold letters. (1892)
	Dissolve
Kane's empire, in its glory, held dominion over thirty-seven newspapers, thirteen magazines, a radio network. An empire upon an empire. The first of grocery stores, paper mills, apartment buildings, factories, forests, ocean liners—	The magnificent Inquirer Building of to-day.
	A map of the U.S.A., *1891–1911,* covering the entire screen, which an animated diagram shows the Kane publications spreading from city to city. Starting from New York, miniature newsboys speed madly to Chicago, Detroit, St. Louis, Los Angeles, San Francisco, Washington, Atlanta, El Paso, etc., screaming, "Wuxtry, Kane Papers, Wuxtry."
An empire through which for fifty years flowed, in an unending stream, the wealth of the earth's third richest gold mine. . . .	Shot of a large mine going full blast, chimneys belching smoke, trains moving in and out, etc. A large sign reads "Colorado Lode Mining Co." (1940) Sign reading: "Little Salem, Colo., 25 Miles."
	Dissolve
	An old still shot of Little Salem as it was seventy years ago. (Identified by copper-plate caption beneath the still.) (1870)
Famed in American legend is the origin of the Kane fortune. . . . How, to boarding-house-keeper Mary Kane, by a defaulting boarder, in 1868, was left the supposedly worthless deed to an abandoned mine shaft: the Colorado Lode.	Shot of early tintype stills of Thomas Foster Kane and his wife Mary on their wedding day. A similar picture of Mary Kane some four or five years later with her little boy, Charles Foster Kane.
	Shot of Capitol in Washington, D.C.
Fifty-seven years later, before a congressional investigation, Walter P. Thatcher, grand old man of Wall Street, for years chief target of Kane Papers' attacks on "trusts," recalls a journey he made as a youth. . . .	Shot of congressional investigating committee. (Reproduction of existing J. P. Morgan newsreel.) This runs silent under narration. Walter P. Thatcher is on the stand. He is flanked by his son, Walter P. Thatcher, Jr., and other partners. He is being questioned by some Merry-Andrew congressmen. At this moment a baby alligator has just been placed in his lap, causing considerable confusion and embarrassment.

Newsreel closeup of Thatcher, the sound track of which now fades in.

THATCHER   . . . because of that trivial incident . . .

INVESTIGATOR   It is a fact, however, is it not, that in 1870 you did go to Colorado?

THATCHER   I did.

INVESTIGATOR   In connection with the Kane affairs?

THATCHER   Yes. My firm had been appointed trustee by Mrs. Kane for the fortune, which she had recently acquired. It was her wish that I should take charge of this boy, Charles Foster Kane.

INVESTIGATOR   Is it not a fact that on that occasion the boy personally attacked you after striking you in the stomach with a sled?

Loud laughter and confusion

THATCHER   Mr. Chairman, I will read to this committee a prepared statement I have brought with me—and I will then refuse to answer any further questions. Mr. Johnson, please!

A young assistant hands him a sheet of paper from a brief-case.

THATCHER (*reading it*)   "With full awareness of the meaning of my words and the responsibility of what I am about to say, it is my considered belief that Mr. Charles Foster Kane, in every essence of his social beliefs and by the dangerous manner in which he has persistently attacked the American traditions of private property, initiative and opportunity for advancement, is—in fact—nothing more or less than a Communist."

NARRATOR

That same month in Union Square—

Newsreel of Union Square meeting, section of crowd carrying banners urging boycott of Kane Papers. A speaker is on the platform above the crowd.

SPEAKER (*fading in on sound track*) . . . till the words "Charles Foster Kane" are a menace to every workingman in this land. He is today what he has always been and always will be—*a Fascist!*

And yet another opinion—Kane's own.

Silent newsreel on a windy platform, flag-draped, in front of the magnificent Inquirer Building. On platform, in full ceremonial dress, is Charles Foster Kane. He orates silently.

TITLE:
"I AM, HAVE BEEN, AND WILL BE ONLY ONE THING—AN AMERICAN."
CHARLES FOSTER KANE

Same locale, Kane shaking hands out of frame.

Deck of boat—Authentic newsreel interview on arrival in New York Harbor. Kane is posing for photographers (in his early seventies).

REPORTER This is a microphone, Mr. Kane.

KANE I know it's a microphone. You people still able to afford microphones with all that new income tax?

An embarrassed smile from the radio interviewer

REPORTER The transatlantic broadcast says you're bringing back ten million dollars worth of art objects. Is that correct?

KANE Don't believe everything you hear on the radio. Read the "Inquirer"!

NARRATOR

REPORTER   How'd you find business conditions abroad, Mr. Kane?

KANE   How did I find business conditions, Mr. Bones? With great difficulty? (*Laughs heartily*)

REPORTER   Glad to be back, Mr. Kane?

KANE   I'm always glad to get back, young man. I'm an American. (*Sharply*) Anything else? Come, young man— when I was a reporter we asked them faster than that.

REPORTER   What do you think of the chances for a war in Europe?

KANE   Young man, there'll be no war. I have talked with all the responsible leaders of the Great Powers, and I can assure you that England, France, Germany and Italy are too intelligent to embark upon a project that must mean the end of civilization as we now know it. There will be no war!

Dissolve

TITLE:

FEW PRIVATE LIVES WERE
MORE PUBLIC

Period still of Emily Norton. (1900)

Dissolve

Reconstruction of very old silent newsreel of wedding party on the back lawn of **Twice married—twice divorced—first** the White House. Many notables, including **to a President's niece, Emily Norton—** ing Kane, Emily, Thatcher Sr., Thatcher **who left him in 1916—died 1918 in a** Jr., and recognizably Bernstein, Leland, **motor accident with their son.** et al., among the guests. Also seen in this group are period newspaper photographers and newsreel cameramen. (1900)

Period still of Susan Alexander.

Dissolve

NARRATOR

Two weeks after his divorce from Emily Norton, Kane married Susan Alexander, singer, at the town hall in Trenton, New Jersey.

Reconstructed silent newsreel. Kane, Susan and Bernstein emerging from side doorway of town hall into a ring of press photographers, reporters, etc. Kane looks startled, recoils for an instant, then charges down upon the photographers, laying about him with his stick, smashing whatever he can hit. (1917)

For Wife Two, onetime opera-singing Susan Alexander, Kane built Chicago's Municipal Opera House. Cost: Three million dollars.

Still of architect's sketch with typically glorified "rendering" of the Chicago Municipal Opera House. (1919)

Dissolve

Conceived for Susan Alexander Kane, half finished before she divorced him, the still unfinished Xanadu. Cost: No man can say.

A glamorous shot of the almost finished Xanadu, a magnificent fairy-tale estate built on a mountain. (1927–1929)

Shots of its preparation. (1920–1929)

Shots of truck after truck, train after train, flashing by with tremendous noise.

Shots of vast dredges, steam shovels.

Shot of ships standing offshore unloading into lighters.

NARRATOR

In quick succession shots follow each other, some reconstructed, some in miniature, some real shots (maybe from the dam projects) of building, digging, pouring concrete, etc.

More shots as before, only this time we see (in miniature) a large mountain—at different periods in its development—rising out of the sands.

One hundred thousand trees, twenty thousand tons of marble, are the ingredients of Xanadu's mountain.

Xanadu's livestock: the fowl of the air, the fish of the sea, the beast of the field and jungle—two of each; the biggest private zoo since Noah.

Shots of elephants, apes, zebras, etc., being herded, unloaded, shipped, etc. in various ways.

Contents of Xanadu's palace: paintings, pictures, statues, and more statues, the very stones of many another palace, shipped to Florida from every corner of the earth. Enough for ten museums—The loot of the world.

Shots of packing cases being unloaded from ships, from trains, from trucks, with various kinds of lettering on them (Italian, Arabian, Chinese, etc.) but all consigned to Charles Foster Kane, Xanadu, Florida.

A reconstructed still of Xanadu—the main terrace. A group of persons in clothes of the period of 1929. In their midst, clearly recognizable, are Kane and Susan.

TITLE:
FROM XANADU, FOR THE PAST TWENTY-FIVE YEARS, ALL KANE ENTERPRISES HAVE BEEN DIRECTED, MANY OF THE NATION'S DESTINIES SHAPED.

Kane urged his country's entry into one war—

Shots of various authentically worded headlines of American papers since 1895.

—Opposed participation in another—

Spanish-American War shots. (1898)

A graveyard in France of the world war and hundreds of crosses. (1919)

—Swung the election to one American President at least—so furiously attacked another as to be blamed for his death—called his assassin—burned in effigy.

Old newsreels of a political campaign.

Night shot of crowd burning Charles Fos-

NARRATOR

Kane, molder of mass opinion though he was, in all his life was never granted elective office by the voters of his country. Few U.S. news publishers have been. Few, like one-time Congressman Hearst, have ever run for any office—most know better—conclude with other political observers that no man's press has power enough for himself. But Kane Papers were once strong indeed, and once the prize seemed almost his. In 1916, as independent candidate for governor, the best elements of the state behind him—the White House seemingly the next easy step in a lightning political career—

Then, suddenly—less than one week before election—defeat! Shameful, ignominious—Defeat that set back for twenty years the cause of reform in the U.S., forever canceled political chances for Charles Foster Kane.

Then in the third year of the Great Depression . . . as to all publishers it sometimes must—to Bennett, to Munsey and Hearst it did—a paper closes! For Kane, in four short years: collapse. Eleven Kane Papers, four Kane magazines merged, more sold, scrapped—

ter Kane in effigy. The dummy bears a grotesque, comic resemblance to Kane. It is tossed into the flames, which burn up . . . and then down. . . . (1916)

Fade Out

TITLE:
IN POLITICS—ALWAYS A BRIDESMAID, NEVER A BRIDE

Newsreel shots of great crowds streaming into a building—Madison Square Garden—then

Shots inside the vast auditorium, at one end of which is a huge picture of Kane. (1916)

Shot of box containing the first Mrs. Kane and young Charles Foster Kane aged nine and a half. They are acknowledging the cheers of the crowd. (Silent shot) (1916)

Newsreel shot of dignitaries on platform, with Kane alongside of speaker's table, beaming, hand upraised to silence the crowd. (Silent shot) (1916)

Newsreel shot—close-up of Kane delivering speech. (1916)

The front page of a contemporary paper— a screaming headline—twin photos of Kane and Susan. (1916) Headline reads:

CANDIDATE KANE CAUGHT
IN LOVE NEST WITH "SINGER"

Printed title about depression.

Once more repeat the map of the U.S.A., *1932–1939*. Suddenly the cartoon goes into reverse, the empire begins to shrink, illustrating the narrator's words.

The door of a newspaper office with the sign: "Closed."

Then four long years more—alone in his never finished, already decaying, pleasure palace, aloof, seldom visited, never photographed, Charles Foster Kane continued to direct his failing empire . . . vainly attempted to sway, as he once did, the destinies of a nation that had ceased to listen to him . . . ceased to trust him. . . .

Shots of Xanadu. (1940)

Series of shots, entirely modern, but rather jumpy and obviously bootlegged, showing Kane in a bath chair, swathed in steamer rugs, being perambulated through his rose garden, a desolate figure in the sunshine. (1935)

Then, last week, as it must to all men, death came to Charles Foster Kane.

Ext.[1] The new Inquirer Building, New York—night (1940) (Painting and Double Printing)

A moving electric sign, similar to the one on the Times Building—spells out the words:

CHARLES FOSTER KANE—DEAD

INSERT: Door with the sign PROJECTION ROOM on it.

16 Int. Projection Room—Day—1940

(A fairly large one, with a long throw to the screen.) It is dark. Present are the editors of a news digest short, and of the Rawlston magazines. Rawlston himself is also present. During this scene, nobody's face is really seen. Sections of their bodies are picked out by a table light, a silhouette is thrown on the screen, and their faces and bodies are themselves thrown into silhouette against the brilliant slanting rays of light from the projection booth.

THOMPSON That's it.

He rises, lighting a cigarette, and sits on corner of table. There is movement of men shifting in seats and lighting cigarettes

FIRST MAN (*into phone*) Stand by. I'll tell you if we want to run it again.

(*Hangs up*)

[1]Exterior

THOMPSON   Well?—How about it, Mr. Rawlston?
RAWLSTON (*has risen*)   How do you like it, boys?

A short silence

Almost together	{ SECOND MAN Well . . . er . . . THIRD MAN Seventy years of a man's life . . . FOURTH MAN That's a lot to try to get into a newsreel . . .

Thompson turns on the table lamp

RAWLSTON (*as he walks to Thompson*)   It's a good short, Thompson, but what it needs is an angle—All that picture tells us is that Charles Foster Kane is dead. I know that—I read the papers—

Laughter greets this

RAWLSTON [*Cont'd*]   What do you think, boys?
RAWLSTON [*Cont'd*] (*walks toward Thompson*)   I tell you, Thompson—a man's dying words—
SECOND MAN   What were they?
THOMPSON (*to Second Man*)   You don't read the papers.

Laughter

RAWLSTON   When Mr. Charles Foster Kane died he said just one word—
THOMPSON   Rosebud!

Almost together	{ FIRST MAN Is that what he said? Just Rosebud? SECOND MAN Umhum—Rosebud—

FOURTH MAN   Tough guy, huh? (*Derisively*) Dies calling for Rosebud!

Laughter

RAWLSTON (*riding over them*)   Yes, Rosebud!—Just that one word!—But who was she—
SECOND MAN   Or what was it?

Tittering

RAWLSTON   Here's a man who might have been President. He's been loved and hated and talked about as much as any man in our time—but when he comes to die, he's got something on his mind called Rosebud. What does that mean?
THIRD MAN   A race horse he bet on once, probably—
FOURTH MAN   Yeh—that didn't come in—

RAWLSTON   All right—(*Strides toward Third and Fourth Men*) But what was the race?

There is a short silence

RAWLSTON [*Cont'd*] Thompson!

THOMPSON Yes, Mr. Rawlston.

RAWLSTON Hold the picture up a week—two weeks if you have to—

THOMPSON (*feebly*) Don't you think, right after his death, if we release it now—it might be better than—

RAWLSTON (*decisively; cutting in on above speech*) Find out about Rosebud!—Go after everybody that knew him—that manager of his—(*Snaps fingers*)—Bernstein—his second wife—she's still living—

THOMPSON Susan Alexander Kane—

SECOND MAN She's running a nightclub in Atlantic City—

RAWLSTON (*crosses to Thompson*) See 'em all—all the people who worked for him—who loved him—who hated his guts—(*Pause*) I don't mean go through the city directory, of course.

The Third Man gives a hearty "Yes-man" laugh. Others titter

THOMPSON (*rising*) I'll get to it right away, Mr. Rawlston.

RAWLSTON (*pats his arm*) Good! Rosebud dead or alive! It'll probably turn out to be a very simple thing.

Fade Out

(NOTE: Now begins the story proper—the search by Thompson for the facts about Kane—his researches—his interviews with the people who knew Kane.)

Fade In

17 Ext. Cheap Cabaret—"El Rancho"—Atlantic City—Rain—Night—1940 (Miniature)

The first image to register is a sign:

"EL RANCHO"
Floor Show
Susan Alexander Kane
Twice Nightly

These words, spelled out in neon, glow out of the darkness. Then there is lightning which reveals a squalid rooftop on which the sign stands. Camera moves close to the skylight. We see through the skylight down into the cabaret. Directly below at a table sits the lone figure of a woman, drinking by herself.

Dissolve

18 Int. "El Rancho" Cabaret—Night—1940

The lone figure at the table is Susan. She is fifty, trying to look much younger, cheaply blonded, in a cheap, enormously generous evening dress. The shadows of Thompson and the Captain are seen moving toward the table from direction of doorway. The Captain appears, crosses to Susan, and stands behind her. Thompson moves into the picture in close f.g., his back to camera.

CAPTAIN (*to Susan*) Miss Alexander—this is Mr. Thompson, Miss Alexander.
SUSAN (*without looking up*) I want another drink, John.

Low thunder from outside

CAPTAIN Right away. Will you have something, Mr. Thompson?
THOMPSON (*starting to sit down*) I'll have a highball.
SUSAN (*looks at Thompson*) Who told you you could sit down here?
THOMPSON I thought maybe we could have a drink together.
SUSAN Think again!

There is an awkward pause

SUSAN [*Cont'd*] Why don't you people let me alone? I'm minding my own business. You mind yours.
THOMPSON If you'd just let me talk to you for a little while, Miss Alexander. All I want to ask you—
SUSAN Get out of here! (*Almost hysterical*) Get out!
THOMPSON (*rising*) I'm sorry.
SUSAN Get out.
THOMPSON Maybe some other time—
SUSAN Get out.

Thompson looks up at the Captain. The Captain indicates the door with a slight jerk of his head, then walks away from the table toward a waiter who is leaning against the wall in front of the door. Thompson follows

CAPTAIN Gino—get her another highball. (*To Thompson as he passes them*) She's just not talking to anybody, Mr. Thompson.
THOMPSON Okay.

Walks to phone booth

WAITER Another double?
CAPTAIN Yeh—

During above Thompson has dropped coin into phone slot and dialed long distance operator (112). The waiter exits for the drink

THOMPSON (*into phone*) Hello—I want New York City—Courtland 7-9970. . . .

The Captain steps closer to the phone booth

THOMPSON [*Cont'd*] This is Atlantic City 4-6827—All right—(*Puts coins into slot; turns to Captain*) Hey—do you think she ought to have another drink?
CAPTAIN Yeh. She'll snap out of it. Why, until he died, she'd just as soon talk about Mr. Kane as about anybody. Sooner—
THOMPSON (*into phone*) Hello—this is Thompson. Let me talk to the Chief, will you? (*Closes booth door*) Hello, Mr. Rawlston. She won't talk—

During above, waiter enters and sets highball in front of Susan. She drinks thirstily

RAWLSTON'S VOICE Who—?

THOMPSON The second Mrs. Kane—about Rosebud or anything else! I'm calling from Atlantic City.

RAWLSTON'S VOICE Make her talk!

THOMPSON All right—I'm going over to Philadelphia in the morning—to the Thatcher Library, to take a look at that diary of his—they're expecting me. Then I've got an appointment in New York with Kane's general manager—what's his name—Bernstein. Then I'll come back here.

RAWLSTON'S VOICE See everybody.

THOMPSON Yes, I'll see everybody—that's still alive. Good-bye, Mr. Rawlston. (*Hangs up; opens door*) Hey—er—

CAPTAIN John—

THOMPSON John—you just might be able to help me. When she used to talk about Kane—did she ever happen to say anything—about Rosebud?

CAPTAIN (*looks over at Susan*) Rosebud?

Thompson slips him a bill

CAPTAIN [*Cont'd*] (*pocketing it*) Oh, thank you, Mr. Thompson. Thanks. As a matter of fact, just the other day, when all that stuff was in the papers—I asked her—she never heard of Rosebud.

Fade Out

Fade

19 Int. Thatcher Memorial Library—Day—1940

A noble interpretation of Mr. Thatcher himself, executed in expensive marble, his stone eyes fixed on the camera. We move down off of this, showing the pedestal on which the words "Walter Parks Thatcher" are engraved. Immediately below the inscription we encounter, in a medium shot, Bertha Anderson, an elderly, mannish spinster, seated behind her desk. Thompson, his hat in his hand, is standing before her.

BERTHA (*into a phone*) Yes. I'll take him now. (*Hangs up and looks at Thompson*) The directors of the Thatcher Memorial Library have asked me to remind you again of the condition under which you may inspect certain portions of Mr. Thatcher's unpublished memoirs. Under no circumstances are direct quotations from his manuscript to be used by you.

THOMPSON That's all right.

BERTHA You may come with me.

She rises and starts towards a distant door. Thompson follows

Dissolve

20 Int. The Vault Room—Thatcher Memorial Library—Day—1940

A room with all the warmth and charm of Napoleon's tomb. As we dissolve in, the door opens in and we see past Thompson's shoulders the length of the room. The floor is marble. There is a gigantic, mahogany table in the center of everything. Beyond this is a safe from which a guard, with a revolver holster at his hip, is extracting the journal of Walter P. Thatcher. He brings it to Bertha.

BERTHA (*to the guard*)   Pages eighty-three to one hundred and forty-two, Jennings.

GUARD   Yes, Miss Anderson.

BERTHA (*to Thompson*)   You will confine yourself, it is our understanding, to the chapter dealing with Mr. Kane.

THOMPSON   That's all I'm interested in.

BERTHA   You will be required to leave this room at four-thirty promptly.

She leaves. Thompson starts to light a cigarette. The guard shakes his head. With a sigh, Thompson bends over to read the manuscript. Camera moves down over his shoulder onto page of manuscript

INSERT: MANUSCRIPT, neatly and precisely written:

CHARLES FOSTER KANE

When these lines appear in print, fifty years after my death, I am confident that the whole world will agree with my opinion of Charles Foster Kane, assuming that he is not then completely forgotten, which I regard as extremely likely. A good deal of nonsense has appeared about my first meeting with Kane, when he was six years old. . . The facts are simple. In the winter of 1870 . . .

Dissolve

21 Ext. Mrs. Kane's Boardinghouse—Day—1870

The white of a great field of snow. In the same position as the last word in above insert, appears the tiny figure of Charles Foster Kane, aged five. He throws a snowball at the camera. It sails toward us and out of scene.

22 Reverse Angle—on the house, featuring a large sign reading:

MRS. KANE'S BOARDINGHOUSE
HIGH CLASS MEALS AND LODGING
INQUIRE WITHIN

Charles Kane's snowball hits the sign.

23 Int. Parlor—Mrs. Kane's Boardinghouse—Day—1870

Camera is angling through the window, but the window frame is not cut into scene. We see only the field of snow again. Charles is manufacturing another snowball. Now—

Camera pulls back, the frame of the window appearing, and we are inside the

parlor of the boardinghouse. Mrs. Kane, aged about twenty-eight, is looking out towards her son.

MRS. KANE (*calling out*)   Be careful, Charles!
THATCHER'S VOICE   Mrs. Kane—
MRS. KANE (*calling out the window*)   Pull your muffler around your neck, Charles—

But Charles runs away. Mrs. Kane turns into camera and we see her face—a strong face, worn and kind

THATCHER'S VOICE   I think we'll have to tell him now—

Camera now pulls back further, showing Thatcher standing before a table on which is his stovepipe hat and documents. He is twenty-six and a very stuffy young man

MRS. KANE   I'll sign those papers now, Mr. Thatcher.
KANE SR.   You people seem to forget that I'm the boy's father.

At the sound of Kane Sr's. voice, both have turned to him and camera pulls back still further, taking him in

MRS. KANE   It's going to be done exactly the way I've told Mr. Thatcher—
KANE SR.   If I want to, I can go to court. A father has the right to—A boarder that beats his bill and leaves worthless stock behind—that property is just as much my property as anybody's if it turns out to be valuable. I knew Fred Graves

and if he'd had any idea this was going to happen—he'd have made out those certificates in both our names—

THATCHER   However, they were made out in Mrs. Kane's name.

KANE   He owed the money for the board to both of us. Besides, I don't hold with signing my boy away to any bank as guardeen just because—

MRS. KANE (*quietly*)   I want you to stop all this nonsense, Jim.

THATCHER   The bank's decision in all matters concerning his education, his places of residence and similar subjects are to be final.

KANE SR.   The idea of a bank being the guardeen . . .

Mrs. Kane has met his eye. Her triumph over him finds expression in his failure to finish his sentence

MRS. KANE (*even more quietly*)   I want you to stop all this nonsense, Jim.

THATCHER   We will assume full management of the Colorado Lode—of which you, Mrs. Kane, I repeat, are the sole owner.

Kane Sr. opens his mouth once or twice, as if to say something, but chokes down his opinion

MRS. KANE   Where do I sign, Mr. Thatcher?

THATCHER   Right here, Mrs. Kane.

KANE SR. (*sulkily*)   Don't say I didn't warn you—Mary, I'm asking you for the last time—anyone'd think I hadn't been a good husband and a—

Mrs. Kane looks at him slowly. He stops his speech

THATCHER   The sum of fifty thousand dollars a year is to be paid to yourself and Mr. Kane as long as you both live, and thereafter the survivor—

Mrs. Kane signs

KANE SR.   Well, let's hope it's all for the best.

MRS. KANE   It is—Go on, Mr. Thatcher—

Mrs. Kane, listening to Thatcher, of course, has had her other ear bent in the direction of the boy's voice. Kane Sr. walks over to close the window

24 *Ext. Mrs. Kane's Boardinghouse—Day—1870*

Kane Jr., seen from the window. He is advancing on the snowman, snowballs in his hands. He drops to one knee.

KANE   If the rebels want a fight, boys, let's give it to 'em! The terms are unconditional surrender. Up and at 'em! The Union forever!

25 *Int. Parlor—Mrs. Kane's Boardinghouse—Day—1870*

Kane Sr. closes the window.

THATCHER Everything else—the principal as well as all monies earned—is to be administered by the bank in trust for your son, Charles Foster Kane, until his twenty-fifth birthday, at which time he is to come into complete possession.

Mrs. Kane rises and goes to the window, opening it

MRS. KANE Go on, Mr. Thatcher.

26 Ext. Mrs. Kane's Boardinghouse—Day—1870

Kane Jr. seen from the window.

KANE You can't lick Andy Jackson! Old Hickory, that's me!

He fires his snowball, well wide of the mark and falls flat on his stomach, starting to crawl carefully toward the snowman

THATCHER'S VOICE It's nearly five, Mrs. Kane—don't you think I'd better meet the boy—

27 Int. Parlor—Mrs. Kane's Boardinghouse—Day—1870

Mrs. Kane at the window. Thatcher is now standing at her side.

MRS. KANE I've got his trunk all packed—(*She chokes a little*) I've had it packed for a couple of weeks—

She can't say any more. She starts for the hall door

THATCHER I've arranged for a tutor to meet us in Chicago. I'd have brought him along with me, but you were so anxious to keep everything secret—

He stops. Mrs. Kane is already well into the hall. He looks at Kane Sr., tightens his lips, and follows Mrs. Kane. Kane follows him

28 Ext. Mrs. Kane's Boardinghouse—Day—1870

Kane, in the snow-covered field. He holds the sled in his hand. The Kane house, in the b.g.,[1] is a dilapidated, shabby, two-story frame building, with a wooden outhouse. Kane looks up as he sees the procession, Mrs. Kane at its head, coming toward him.

KANE H'ya, Mom. (*Gesturing at the snowman*) See, Mom? I took the pipe out of his mouth. If it keeps on snowin', maybe I'll make some teeth and—

MRS. KANE You better come inside, son. You and I have got to get you all ready for—for—

THATCHER Charles, my name is Mr. Thatcher—

MRS. KANE This is Mr. Thatcher, Charles.

[1]background

THATCHER   How do you do, Charles.

KANE SR.   He comes from the East—

KANE   Hello. Hello, Pop.

KANE SR.   Hello, Charlie!

MRS. KANE   Mr. Thatcher is going to take you on a trip with him tonight, Charles.
You'll be leaving on Number Ten.

KANE SR.   That's the train with all the lights.

KANE   You goin', Mom?

THATCHER   Your mother won't be going right away, Charles—

KANE   Where'm I going?

KANE SR.   You're going to see Chicago and New York—and Washington, maybe
. . . isn't he, Mr. Thatcher?

THATCHER (*heartily*)   He certainly is. I wish I were a little boy and going to make
a trip like that for the first time.

KANE   Why aren't you comin' with us, Mom?

MRS. KANE   We have to stay here, Charles.

KANE SR.   You're going to live with Mr. Thatcher from now on, Charlie! You're
going to be rich. Your Ma figures—that is—er—she and I have decided that
this isn't the place for you to grow up in. You'll probably be the richest man
in America someday and you ought to—

MRS. KANE   You won't be lonely, Charles . . .

THATCHER   We're going to have a lot of good times together, Charles . . . really
we are.

Kane stares at him

THATCHER [*Cont'd*]   Come on, Charles. Let's shake hands. (*Kane continues to
look at him*) Now, now! I'm not as frightening as all that! Let's shake, what
do you say?

*He reaches out for Charles's hand. Without a word, Charles hits him in the stom-
ach with the sled. Thatcher stumbles back a few feet, gasping*

THATCHER [*Cont'd*]   (*with a sickly grin*)   You almost hurt me, Charles. Sleds
aren't to hit people with. Sleds are to—to sleigh on. When we get to New
York, Charles, we'll get you a sled that will—

*He's near enough to try to put a hand on Kane's shoulder. As he does, Kane kicks
him in the ankle*

MRS. KANE   Charles!

*He throws himself on her, his arms around her. Slowly Mrs. Kane puts her arms
around him.*

KANE (*frightened*)   Mom! Mom!

MRS. KANE   It's all right, Charles, it's all right.

KANE SR.   Sorry, Mr. Thatcher! What that kid needs is a good thrashing!

MRS. KANE   That's what you think, is it, Jim?

KANE SR.   Yes.

MRS. KANE (*looks at Mr. Kane; slowly*) That's why he's going to be brought up
  where you can't get at him.

Dissolve

INSERT: (NIGHT—1870) (STOCK OR MINIATURE) OLD-FASHIONED RAILROAD
WHEELS underneath a sleeper, spinning along the track.

Dissolve

29 *Int. Train—Old-Fashioned Drawing Room—Night—1870*

Thatcher, with a look of mingled exasperation, annoyance, sympathy and inability
to handle the situation, is standing alongside a berth, looking at Kane. Kane, his
face in the pillow, is crying with heartbreaking sobs.

KANE Mom! Mom!

Dissolve

INSERT: THE THATCHER MANUSCRIPT, which fills the screen. It reads:

*. . . nothing but a lucky scoundrel, spoiled, unscrupulous, irresponsible. He
acquired his first newspaper through a caprice. His whole attitude as a publisher . . .*

Dissolve Out

Dissolve In

30 *Int. Kane's Office—"Inquirer"—Day—1898*

Close-up on printed headline, which reads:

GALLEONS OF SPAIN OFF JERSEY COAST

Camera pulls back to reveal Thatcher, holding the "Inquirer" with its headline,
standing in front of Kane's desk. Kane is seated behind the desk.

THATCHER Is this really your idea of how to run a newspaper?
KANE I don't know how to run a newspaper, Mr. Thatcher. I just try everything
  I can think of.
THATCHER (*reading the headline*) Galleons of Spain off Jersey coast. You know
  you haven't the slightest proof that this—this armada is off the Jersey coast.
KANE Can you prove that it isn't?

Bernstein rushes in, a cable in his hand. He stops when he sees Thatcher

KANE [*Cont'd*] (*genially)* Mr. Bernstein, Mr. Thatcher.
BERNSTEIN How are you, Mr. Thatcher?

Thatcher gives him the briefest of nods

BERNSTEIN [*Cont'd*] We just had a wire from Cuba, Mr. Kane.

He stops, embarrassed

KANE That's all right. We have no secrets from our readers. Mr. Thatcher is one of our most devoted readers, Mr. Bernstein. He knows what's wrong with every copy of the "Inquirer" since I took charge. Read the cable.

BERNSTEIN (*Reading)* Food marvelous in Cuba—girls delightful stop could send you prose poems about scenery but don't feel right spending your money stop there's no war in Cuba signed Wheeler. Any answer?

KANE Yes. Dear Wheeler—(*Pauses a moment)*—you provide the prose poems— I'll provide the war.

BERNSTEIN That's fine, Mr. Kane.

Thatcher, bursting with indignation, sits down.

KANE I kinda like it myself. Send it right away.

BERNSTEIN Right away.

Bernstein leaves. After a moment of indecision, Thatcher decides to make one last try

THATCHER Charles, I came to see you about this—campaign of yours . . . er . . . the "Inquirer's" campaign—against the Metropolitan Transfer Company.

KANE Good. You got some material we can use against them?

THATCHER You're still a college boy, aren't you, Charles?

KANE Oh, no, I was expelled from college—several colleges. Don't you remember?

Thatcher glares at him

KANE [*Cont'd*] *I* remember. I think that's when I first lost my belief that you were omnipotent, Mr. Thatcher—when you told me that the dean's decision at

Harvard, despite all your efforts, was irrevocable—(*He thinks, and looks at Thatcher inquiringly*)—irrevocable—

Thatcher stares at him angrily, tight-lipped

KANE [*Cont'd*]   I can't tell you how often I've learned the correct pronunciation of that word, but I always forget.

THATCHER (*not interested, coming out with it*)   I think I should remind you, Charles, of a fact you seem to have forgotten. You are yourself one of the company's largest individual stockholders.

KANE   The trouble is, Mr. Thatcher, you don't realize you're talking to two people. As Charles Foster Kane, who has eighty-two thousand, six hundred and thirty-one shares of Metropolitan Transfer—you see, I do have a rough idea of my holdings—I sympathize with you. Charles Foster Kane is a dangerous scoundrel, his paper should be run out of town and a committee should be formed to boycott him. You may, if you can form such a committee, put me down for a contribution of one thousand dollars.

THATCHER (*angrily*)   Charles, my time is too valuable for me—

KANE   On the other hand—(*His manner becomes serious*) I am the publisher of the "Inquirer." As such, it is my duty—I'll let you in on a little secret, it is also my pleasure—to see to it that the decent, hardworking people of this city are not robbed blind by a group of money-mad pirates because, God help them, they have no one to look after their interests!

Thatcher has risen. He now puts on his hat and walks away

KANE [*Cont'd*]   —I'll let you in on another little secret, Mr. Thatcher.

Thatcher stops. Kane walks up to him

KANE [*Cont'd*]   I think I'm the man to do it. You see I have money and property. If I don't defend the interests of the underprivileged, somebody else will— maybe somebody *without* any money or any property—and that would be too bad.

THATCHER (*puts on his hat*)   I happened to see your consolidated statement this morning, Charles. Don't you think it's rather unwise to continue this philanthropic enterprise—this "Inquirer"—that's costing you one million dollars a year?

KANE   You're right. We did lose a million dollars last year. We expect to lose a million next year, too. You know, Mr. Thatcher—at the rate of a million a year—we'll have to close this place—in sixty years.

Dissolve

31 Int. The Vault Room—Thatcher Memorial Library—Day

THE MANUSCRIPT:
The ordinary decencies of human life were, I repeat, unknown to him. His incredible vulgarity, his utter disregard . . .

Before the audience has had a chance to read this, Thompson, with a gesture of annoyance, has closed the manuscript. He turns to confront Miss Anderson, who has come to shoo him out

MISS ANDERSON   You have enjoyed a very rare privilege, young man. Did you find what you were looking for?

THOMPSON   No. Tell me something, Miss Anderson. You're not Rosebud, are you?

MISS ANDERSON   What?

THOMPSON   I didn't think you were. Well, thanks for the use of the hall.

He puts his hat on his head and starts out, lighting a cigarette as he goes. Miss Anderson, scandalized, watches him

Dissolve

32   Int. Bernstein's Office—Inquirer Skyscraper—Day—1940

Close-up of a still of Kane, aged about sixty-five. Camera pulls back, showing it is a framed photograph on the wall. Under it sits Bernstein, back of his desk. Bernstein, always an undersized Jew, now seems even smaller than in his youth. He is bald as an egg, spry, with remarkably intense eyes. As camera continues to travel back, the back of Thompson's head and his shoulders come into the picture.

BERNSTEIN (*wryly*)   Who's a busy man? Me? I'm chairman of the board. I got nothing but time. . . . What do you want to know?

THOMPSON   Well, we thought maybe—(*slowly*) if we could find out what he meant by his last words—as he was dying—

BERNSTEIN   That Rosebud, huh? (*Thinks*) Maybe some girl? There were a lot of them back in the early days and—

THOMPSON (*amused*)   It's hardly likely, Mr. Bernstein, that Mr. Kane could have met some girl casually and then, fifty years later, on his deathbed—

BERNSTEIN   You're pretty young, Mr.—(*Remembers the name*)—Mr. Thompson. A fellow will remember things you wouldn't think he'd remember. You take me. One day, back in 1896, I was crossing over to Jersey on a ferry and as we pulled out there was another ferry pulling in—(*Slowly*)—and on it there was a girl waiting to get off. A white dress she had on—and she was carrying a white parasol—and I only saw her for one second and she didn't see me at all—but I'll bet a month hasn't gone by since that I haven't thought of that girl. (*Triumphantly*) See what I mean? (*Smiles*)

THOMPSON   Yes. (*A near sigh*) But about Rosebud. I wonder—

BERNSTEIN   Who else you been to see?

THOMPSON   Well, I went down to Atlantic City—

BERNSTEIN   Susie? I called her myself the day after he died. I thought maybe somebody ought to—(*Sadly*) She couldn't even come to the phone.

THOMPSON (*ruefully*)   She wasn't exactly in a condition to talk to me either. I'm going down to see her again in a couple of days. (*Pauses*) About Rosebud, Mr. Bernstein—

BERNSTEIN   If I had any idea who it was, believe me, I'd tell you.

THOMPSON   If you'd kind of just talk, Mr. Bernstein—about anything connected with Mr. Kane that you can remember—After all, you were with him from the beginning.

BERNSTEIN   From *before* the beginning, young fellow—(*Not too maudlinly*) And now it's after the end. (*After a pause*) Have you tried to see anybody else except Susie?

THOMPSON   I haven't *seen* anybody else, but I've been through that stuff of Walter Thatcher's. That journal of his—

BERNSTEIN   Thatcher! That man was the biggest darned fool I ever met.

THOMPSON   He made an awful lot of money.

BERNSTEIN   It's no trick to make a lot of money, if all you want is to make a lot of money. You take Mr. Kane—it wasn't money he wanted. Mr. Thatcher never did figure him out. Sometimes, even, I couldn't—(*Suddenly*) You know who you ought to talk to? Mr. Jed Leland. That is, if—he was Mr. Kane's closest friend, you know. They went to school together.

THOMPSON   Harvard, wasn't it?

BERNSTEIN   Harvard—Yale—Cornell—Princeton—Switzerland. Mr. Leland—he never had a nickel—one of those old families where the father is worth ten million, then one day he shoots himself and it turns out there's nothing but debts. (*Reflectively*) He was with Mr. Kane and me the first day Mr. Kane took over the "Inquirer."

Dissolve

33 *Ext. The Old Inquirer Building—Day—1890*

(The same shot as in news digest but this is the real thing, not a still.) A hansom cab comes into the scene. In it are Kane and Leland. They are both dressed like New York dandies. It is a warm summer day. Kane jumps from the cab, as Leland follows more slowly.

KANE (*pointing with his stick*)   Take a look at it, Jed. It's going to look a lot different one of these days.

He is boisterously radiant. Jed agrees with a thoughtful smile. As they start across the sidewalk toward the building, which they then enter, a delivery wagon draws up and takes the place vacated by the cab. In its open back, almost buried by a bed, bedding, trunks, framed pictures, etc., is Bernstein, who climbs out with difficulty

BERNSTEIN (*to the driver*)   Come on! I'll give you a hand with this stuff.

DRIVER   There ain't no bedrooms in this joint. That's a newspaper building.

BERNSTEIN   You're getting paid, mister, for opinions—or for hauling?

Dissolve

34 *Int. City Room—Inquirer Building—Day—1890*

The front half of the second floor constitutes one large city room. Despite the brilliant sunshine outside, very little of it is actually getting into the room because the windows are small and narrow. There are about a dozen tables and desks, of the old-fashioned type, not flat, available for reporters. Two tables, on a raised platform at the end of the room, obviously serve the city room executives. To the left of the platform is an open door which leads into the sanctum.

As Kane and Leland enter the room an elderly, stout gent on the raised platform strikes a bell and the other eight occupants of the room—all men—rise and face the new arrivals. Carter, the elderly gent, in formal clothes, rises and starts toward them.

CARTER   Welcome, Mr. Kane, to the "Inquirer." I am Herbert Carter.

KANE   Thank you, Mr. Carter. This is Mr. Leland.

CARTER (*bowing*)   How do you do, Mr. Leland?

KANE   Mr. Leland is your new dramatic critic, Mr. Carter. I hope I haven't made a mistake, Jedediah. It is dramatic critic you want to be, isn't it? (*Pointing to the reporters*) Are they standing for me?

CARTER   I thought it would be a nice gesture—the new publisher—

KANE (*grinning*)   Ask them to sit down.

CARTER   You may resume your work, gentlemen. (*To Kane*) I didn't know your plans and so I was unable to make any preparations.

KANE   I don't know my plans myself. As a matter of fact, I haven't got any. Except to get out a newspaper.

There is a terrific crash at the doorway. They all turn to see Bernstein sprawled at the entrance. A roll of bedding, a suitcase and two framed pictures were too much for him

KANE [*Cont'd*]   Oh, Mr. Bernstein! If you would come here a moment please, Mr. Bernstein?

Bernstein rises and comes over

KANE [*Cont'd*]   Mr. Carter, this is Mr. Bernstein. Mr. Bernstein is my general manager.

CARTER (*frigidly*)   How do you do, Mr. Bernstein?

KANE   You've got a private office here, haven't you?

The delivery-wagon driver has now appeared in the entrance with parts of the bedstead and other furniture

CARTER   My little sanctum is at your disposal. But I don't think I understand—

KANE   I'm going to live right here. (*Reflectively*) As long as I have to.

CARTER   But a morning newspaper, Mr. Kane—After all, we're practically closed for twelve hours a day—except for the business offices—

KANE   That's one of the things I think must be changed, Mr. Carter. The news goes on for twenty-four hours a day.

Dissolve

35 Int. Kane's Office—Late Day—1890

Kane, in his shirt-sleeves, at a rolltop desk, is working feverishly on copy and eating a very sizable meal at the same time. Carter, still formally coated, is seated alongside him. Leland, seated in a corner, is looking on, detached, amused. On a corner of the desk, Bernstein is writing down figures.

KANE I'm not criticizing, Mr. Carter, but here's what I mean. There's a front-page story in the "Chronicle" (*Points to it*) and a picture—of a woman in Brooklyn who is missing. Probably murdered. A Mrs. Harry Silverstone. Why didn't the "Inquirer" have that this morning?

CARTER (*stiffly*) Because we're running a newspaper, Mr. Kane, not a scandal sheet.

Kane has finished eating. He pushes away his plates

KANE I'm still hungry, Jed.

LELAND We'll go over to Rector's later and get something decent.

KANE (*pointing to the "Chronicle"*) The "Chronicle" has a two-column headline, Mr. Carter. Why haven't we?

CARTER The news wasn't big enough.

KANE If the headline is big enough, it *makes* the news big enough. The murder of this Mrs. Harry Silverstone—

CARTER There's no proof that the woman was murdered—or even that she's dead.

KANE (*smiling a bit*) The "Chronicle" doesn't say she's murdered, Mr. Carter. It says she's missing; the neighbors are getting suspicious.

CARTER It's not our function to report the gossip of housewives. If we were interested in that kind of thing, Mr. Kane, we could fill the paper twice over daily—

KANE (*gently*) That's the kind of thing we *are* going to be interested in from now on, Mr. Carter. I wish you'd send your best man up to see Mr. Silverstone. Have him tell Mr. Silverstone if he doesn't produce his wife at once, the "Inquirer" will have him arrested. (*Gets an idea*) Have him tell Mr. Silverstone he's a detective from the Central Office. If Mr. Silverstone asks to see his badge, your man is to get indignant and call Mr. Silverstone an anarchist. Loudly, so that the neighbors can hear.

CARTER Really, Mr. Kane, I can't see that the function of a respectable newspaper—

KANE Mr. Carter, you've been most understanding. Good day.

Carter leaves the room, closing the door behind him

LELAND Poor Mr. Carter!

KANE What makes these fellows think that a newspaper is something rigid, something inflexible, that people are supposed to pay two cents for—

BERNSTEIN Three cents.

KANE (*calmly*) Two cents.

Bernstein lifts his head and looks at Kane

BERNSTEIN (*tapping on the paper*) This is all figured at three cents a copy.

KANE Refigure it, Mr. Bernstein, at two cents. Ready for dinner, Jed?

BERNSTEIN Mr. Leland, if Mr. Kane he should decide at dinner to cut the price to one cent, or maybe even he should make up his mind to give the paper away with a half-pound of tea—

LELAND You people work too fast for me! Talk about new brooms!

BERNSTEIN Who said anything about brooms?
KANE It's a saying, Mr. Bernstein. A new broom sweeps clean.
BERNSTEIN Oh!

Dissolve

36 Int. Primitive Composing and Pressroom—New York "Inquirer"—Night—1890

The ground floor with the windows on the street. It is almost midnight. Grouped around a large table, on which are several locked forms of type, are Kane and Leland in elegant evening clothes, Bernstein, unchanged from the afternoon, Carter and Smathers, the composing room foreman, nervous and harassed.

KANE Mr. Carter, front pages don't look like this any more. Have you seen the "Chronicle"?
CARTER The "Inquirer" is not in competition with a rag like the "Chronicle."
BERNSTEIN We should be publishing such a rag. The "Inquirer"—I wouldn't wrap up the liver for the cat in the "Inquirer"—
CARTER Mr. Kane, I must ask you to see to it that this—this person learns to control his tongue. I don't think he's ever been in a newspaper office before.
KANE You're right. Mr. Bernstein is in the wholesale jewelry business.
BERNSTEIN *Was* in the wholesale jewelry business.
KANE His talents seemed to be what I was looking for.
CARTER (*sputtering; he's really sore*) I warn you, Mr. Kane, it would go against my grain to desert you when you need me so badly—but I would feel obliged to ask that my resignation be accepted.
KANE It *is* accepted, Mr. Carter, with assurances of my deepest regret.
CARTER But Mr. Kane, I meant—
KANE (*turning to Smathers; quietly*) Let's do these pages over again.
SMATHERS (*as though Kane were talking Greek*) We can't remake them, Mr. Kane.
KANE Remake? Is that the right word?
SMATHERS We go to press in five minutes.
KANE (*quietly*) Well, let's remake these pages, Mr. Smathers.
SMATHERS We go to press in five minutes, Mr. Kane.
KANE We'll have to publish half an hour late, that's all.
SMATHERS You don't understand, Mr. Kane. We go to press in five minutes. We can't remake them, Mr. Kane.

Kane reaches out and shoves the forms onto the floor, where they scatter into hundreds of bits

KANE You can remake them now, can't you, Mr. Smathers? After the type's been reset and the pages remade according to the way I told you before, Mr. Smathers, kindly have proofs pulled—is that right, Jed—proofs pulled?—and bring them to me. Then, if I can't find any way to improve them again—I suppose we'll have to go to press.

He starts out of the room, followed by Leland

BERNSTEIN In case you don't understand, Mr. Smathers—he's a new broom.

Dissolve Out

Dissolve In

37 Ext. New York Street—Very Early Dawn—1890

The picture is mainly occupied by the Inquirer Building, identified by sign. Over this newsboys are heard selling the "Chronicle." As the dissolve completes itself, camera moves toward the one lighted window—the window of Kane's office.

Dissolve

38 Int. Kane's Office—Very Early Dawn—1890

The newsboys are still heard from the street below. Kane, in his shirt-sleeves, stands at the open window looking out. On the bed is seated Bernstein. Leland is in a chair.

NEWSBOYS' VOICES "Chronicle"!—"Chronicle"!—H'ya—the "Chronicle"!—Get ya' "Chronicle"!

Kane closes the window and turns to the others

LELAND We'll be on the street soon, Charlie—another ten minutes.
BERNSTEIN It's three hours and fifty minutes late—but we did it—

Leland rises from the chair, stretching painfully

KANE Tired?
LELAND It's been a tough day.
KANE A wasted day.
BERNSTEIN Wasted?
LELAND Charlie?
BERNSTEIN You just made the paper over four times tonight, Mr. Kane—that's all—
KANE I've changed the front page a little, Mr. Bernstein. That's not enough— There's something I've got to get into this paper besides pictures and print— I've got to make the New York "Inquirer" as important to New York as the gas in that light.
LELAND What're you going to do, Charlie?
KANE My Declaration of Principles—don't smile, Jed—(*Getting the idea*) Take dictation, Mr. Bernstein—
BERNSTEIN I can't write shorthand, Mr. Kane—
KANE I'll write it myself.

Kane grabs a piece of rough paper and a grease crayon. Sitting down on the bed next to Bernstein, he starts to write

BERNSTEIN (*looking over his shoulder*)   You don't wanta make any promises, Mr. Kane, you don't wanta keep.

KANE (*as he writes*)   These'll be kept. (*Stops and reads what he has written*) I'll provide the people of this city with a daily paper that will tell all the news honestly. (*Starts to write again; reading as he writes*) I will also provide them—

LELAND   That's the second sentence you've started with "I"—

KANE (*looking up*)   People are going to know who's responsible. And they're going to get the news—the true news—quickly and simply and entertainingly. (*With real conviction*) And no special interests will be allowed to interfere with the truth of that news. (*Writes again; reading as he writes*) I will also provide them with a fighting and tireless champion of their rights as citizens and human beings—Signed—Charles Foster Kane.

LELAND   Charlie—

Kane looks up

LELAND [*Cont'd*]   Can I have that?

KANE   I'm going to print it—(*Calls*) Mike!

MIKE   Yes, Mr. Kane.

KANE   Here's an editorial. I want to run it in a box on the front page.

MIKE (*very wearily*)   Today's front page, Mr. Kane?

KANE   That's right. We'll have to remake again—better go down and let them know.

MIKE   All right, Mr. Kane

He starts away

Mike turns

LELAND   Just a minute, Mike.

LELAND [*Cont'd*]   When you're done with that, I'd like to have it back.

Mike registers that this, in his opinion, is another screwball and leaves. Kane looks at Leland

LELAND [*Cont'd*]   —I'd just like to keep that particular piece of paper myself. I've got a hunch it might turn out to be one of the important papers—of our time. (*A little ashamed of his ardor*) A document—like the Declaration of Independence—and the Constitution—and my first report card at school.

Kane smiles back at him, but they are both serious. The voices of the newsboys fill the air

VOICES OF NEWSBOYS   "Chronicle"!—H'ya, the "Chronicle"! Get ya' "Chronicle"!—the "Chronicle"!

Dissolve Out

Dissolve In

39 Ext. "Inquirer" Windows on Street Level—Day—1890

Close-up—front page of the "Inquirer" shows big boxed editorial with heading:

MY PRINCIPLES—A DECLARATION
By Charles Foster Kane

Camera continues pulling back and shows newspaper to be on the top of a pile of newspapers. As we draw further back, we see four piles—then six piles—until we see finally a big field of piles of "Inquirers." Hands come into the frame and start picking up the piles.

Camera pans to glass window on the street level of the "Inquirer." Painted on the glass are the words NEW YORK DAILY INQUIRER—CIRCULATION 26,000—this very prominent. Through the glass we can see Kane, Leland and Bernstein, leaning on the little velvet-draped rail at the back of the window, peering out through the glass to the street, where "Inquirer" newsboys are seen to be moving. During this, camera tightens on window until CIRCULATION 26,000 fills frame. Then—

Dissolve

40 Ext. "Chronicle" Window—On Street Level—Day—1890

Close-up of sign which reads: CIRCULATION 495,000

Camera pulls back to show this is a similar window on the street level of the Chronicle Building. The words NEW YORK DAILY CHRONICLE are prominently painted above this and through the glass we can see a framed photograph of some nine men. A sign over this reads: EDITORIAL AND EXECUTIVE STAFF OF THE NEW YORK CHRONICLE. A sign beneath it reads: GREATEST NEWSPAPER STAFF IN THE WORLD. Then camera continues pulling back to show Kane, Leland and Bernstein standing in front of the window, looking in. They look very tired and cold.

KANE   I know you're tired, gentlemen, but I brought you here for a reason. I think this little pilgrimage will do us good.

LELAND (*wearily*)   The "Chronicle" is a good newspaper.

KANE   It's a good idea for a newspaper. Notice the circulation?

BERNSTEIN (*sullenly*)   Four hundred ninety-five thousand.

KANE   Well, as the rooster said to his hens when they looked at the ostrich eggs— I am not criticizing, ladies—I am merely trying to show you what is being done in the same line by your competitors.

BERNSTEIN   Ah, Mr. Kane—with them fellows on the "Chronicle"—(*Indicates photograph*) it's no trick to get circulation.

KANE   You're right, Mr. Bernstein.

BERNSTEIN (*sighs*)   You know how long it took the "Chronicle" to get that staff together? Twenty years.

KANE   I know.

Kane smiling, lights a cigarette, looking into the window. Camera moves in to hold on the photograph of the nine men

Dissolve

41 Int. City Room—The "Inquirer"—Night—1898

The same nine men, arrayed as in the photograph but with Kane in the center of the first row.

Camera pulls back, revealing that they are being photographed in a corner of the room. It is 1:30 at night. Desks, etc., have been pushed against the wall. Running down the center of the room is a long banquet table.

PHOTOGRAPHER   That's all. Thank you.

The photographic subjects rise

KANE (*a sudden thought*)   Make up an extra copy and mail it to the "Chronicle."

Kane makes his way to the head of the table

KANE [*Cont'd*]   Gentlemen of the "Inquirer"! Eight years ago—eight long very busy years ago—I stood in front of the "Chronicle" window and looked at a picture of the nine greatest newspapermen in the world. I felt like a kid in front of a candy shop. Tonight I got my candy. Welcome, gentlemen, to the "Inquirer." It will make you happy to learn that our circulation this morning was the greatest in New York—six hundred and eighty-four thousand.

BERNSTEIN   Six hundred eighty-four thousand one hundred and thirty-two.

General applause

KANE All of you—new and old—you're all getting the best salaries in town. Not one of you has been hired because of his loyalty. It's your talent I'm interested in—I like talent. Talent has made the "Inquirer" the kind of paper I want—the best newspaper in the world.

Applause

KANE [*Cont'd*] Having thus welcomed you, perhaps you'll forgive my rudeness in taking leave of you. I'm going abroad next week for a vacation.

Murmurs

KANE [*Cont'd*] I have promised my doctor for some time that I would leave when I could. I now realize that I can. This decision is in every way the best compliment that I could pay you.

Gratified murmurs

KANE [*Cont'd*] I have promised Mr. Bernstein, and I herewith repeat that promise publicly, for the next three months to forget all about the new feature sections—the Sunday supplement—and not to try to think up any ideas for comic sections—and not to—
BERNSTEIN (*interrupting*) Say, Mr. Kane, so long as you're promising—there's a lot of statues in Europe you ain't bought yet—
KANE (*interrupting*) You can't blame me, Mr. Bernstein. They've been making statues for two thousand years, and I've only been buying for five.
BERNSTEIN Nine Venuses already we got, twenty-six Virgins—two whole warehouses full of stuff—promise me, Mr. Kane.
KANE I promise you, Mr. Bernstein.
BERNSTEIN Thank you.
KANE Oh, Mr. Bernstein—
BERNSTEIN Yes?
KANE You don't expect me to keep *any* of my promises, do you, Mr. Bernstein?

Terrific laughter

KANE [*Cont'd*] Do you, Mr. Leland?
LELAND Certainly not.

Laughter and applause

KANE And now, gentlemen, your complete attention, please!

Kane puts his two fingers in his mouth and whistles. This is a signal. A band strikes up and enters in advance of a regiment of very magnificent maidens. As some of the girls are detached from the line and made into partners for individual dancing—

BERNSTEIN   Isn't it wonderful? Such a party!

LELAND   Yes.

BERNSTEIN (*to Leland*)   What's the matter?

LELAND   —Bernstein, these men who are now with the "Inquirer"—who were with the "Chronicle" until yesterday—weren't they just as devoted to the "Chronicle" kind of paper as they are now to—our kind of paper?

BERNSTEIN   Sure. They're like anybody else. They got work to do. They do it. (*Proudly*) Only they happen to be the best men in the business.

LELAND (*after a minute*)   Do we stand for the same things the "Chronicle" stands for, Bernstein?

BERNSTEIN (*indignantly*)   Certainly not. What of it? Mr. Kane he'll have them changed to his kind of newspapermen in a week.

LELAND   There's always a chance, of course, that they'll change Mr. Kane—without his knowing it.

KANE (*lightly*)   Well, gentlemen, are we going to declare war on Spain?

LELAND   The "Inquirer" already has.

KANE   You long-faced, overdressed anarchist.

LELAND   I am not overdressed.

KANE   You are, too. Look at that necktie, Mr. Bernstein.

Bernstein embarrassed, beams from one to the other

LELAND   Charlie, I wish—

KANE   Are you trying to be serious?

LELAND (*holding the look for a minute and recognizing there isn't a chance*)   No. (*Out of the corner of his mouth—almost as an afterthought*) Only I'm not going to Cuba.

KANE (*to Bernstein*)   He drives me crazy. Mr. Bernstein, we get two hundred applications a day from newspapermen all over the country who want to go to Cuba—don't we, Mr. Bernstein?

Bernstein is unable to answer

LELAND   Bernstein, don't you like my necktie?

KANE (*ignoring him*)   I offer him his own byline—(*Pompously*) By Jed Leland— The "Inquirer's" Special Correspondent at the Front—I guarantee him— (*Turns to Leland*) Richard Harding Davis is doing all right. They just named a cigar after him.

LELAND   It's hardly what you'd call a cigar.

KANE   A man of very high standards, Mr. Bernstein.

LELAND   And it's hardly what you'd call a war either.

KANE   It's the best I can do. (*Looking up*) Hello, Georgie.

Georgie, a very handsome madam, has walked into the picture. She leans over and speaks quietly in his ear

GEORGIE   Hello, Charlo.

LELAND   You're doing very well.

GEORGIE   Is everything the way you want it, dear?

KANE (*looking around*)   If everybody's having fun, that's the way I want it.

GEORGIE I've got some other little girls coming over—

LELAND (*interrupting*) If you want to know what you're doing—you're dragging your country into a war. Do you know what a war is, Charlie?

KANE I've told you about Jed, Georgie. He needs to relax.

LELAND There's a condition in Cuba that needs to be remedied maybe—but between that and a war.

KANE You know Georgie, Jed, don't you?

GEORGIE Glad to meet you, Jed.

KANE Jed, how would the "Inquirer" look with no news about this nonexistent war with Pulitzer and Hearst devoting twenty columns a day to it.

LELAND They only do it because you do.

KANE And I only do it because they do it—and they only do it—it's a vicious circle, isn't it? (*Rises*) I'm going over to Georgie's, Jed—You know Georgie, don't you, Mr. Bernstein?

Bernstein shakes hands with Georgie

KANE Georgie knows a young lady whom I'm sure you'd adore, Jed—Wouldn't he, Georgie?

LELAND The first paper that had the courage to tell the actual truth about Cuba—

KANE Why only the other evening I said to myself, if Jedediah were only here to adore this young lady—this—(*Snaps his fingers*) What's her name again?

Dissolve Out

Dissolve In

42 *Int. Georgie's Place—Night—1898*

Georgie is introducing a young lady to Leland. On sound track we hear piano music.

GEORGIE (*right on cue from preceding scene*) Ethel—this gentleman has been very anxious to meet you—Mr. Leland, this is Ethel.

ETHEL Hello, Mr. Leland.

Camera pans to include Kane, seated at piano, with Bernstein and girls gathered around him

ONE OF THE GIRLS Charlie! Play the song about you.

ANOTHER GIRL Is there a song about Charlie?

KANE You buy a bag of peanuts in this town and you get a song written about you.

Kane has broken into "Oh, Mr. Kane!" and he and the girls start to sing. Ethel leads the unhappy Leland over to the group. Kane, seeing Leland and taking his eye, motions to the professor who has been standing next to him to take over. The professor does so. The singing continues. Kane rises and crosses to Leland.

KANE [*Cont'd*] Say, Jed—you don't have to go to Cuba if you don't want to. You don't have to be a war correspondent if you don't want to. I'd want to be a war correspondent. (*Silence*) I've got an idea.

LELAND Pay close attention, Bernstein. The hand is quicker than the eye.

KANE I mean I've got a job for you.

LELAND (*suspiciously*) What is it?

KANE The "Inquirer" is probably too one-sided about this Cuban thing—me being a warmonger and all. How's about your writing a piece every day—while I'm away—saying exactly what you think—(*Ruefully*) Just the way you say it to me, unless I see you coming.

LELAND Do you mean that?

Kane nods

LELAND [*Cont'd*] No editing of my copy?

KANE (*no one will ever be able to know what he means*) No-o.

Leland keeps looking at him with loving perplexity, knowing he will never solve the riddle of this face

KANE [*Cont'd*] We'll talk some more about it at dinner tomorrow night. We've only got about ten more nights before I go to Europe. Richard Carl's opening in *The Spring Chicken*. I'll get the girls. You get the tickets. A drama critic gets them free.

LELAND Charlie—

KANE It's the best I can do.

LELAND (*still smiling*) It doesn't make any difference about me, but one of these days you're going to find out that all this charm of yours won't be enough—

KANE You're wrong. It does make a difference about you—Come to think of it, Mr. Bernstein, I don't blame Mr. Leland for not wanting to be a war correspondent. It isn't much of a war. Besides, they tell me there isn't a decent restaurant on the whole island.

Dissolve

43 Int. Kane's office—Day—1898

The shot begins on a close-up of a label. The words "From C. F. Kane, Paris, France," fill the screen. This registers as camera pulls back to show remainder of label in larger letters, which read: "To Charles Foster Kane, New York—HOLD FOR ARRIVAL." Camera continues pulling back, showing the entire sanctum piled to the ceiling with packing boxes, crated statues and art objects. One-third of the statues have been uncrated. Leland is in his shirt-sleeves; clearly he has been opening boxes, with claw hammer in one hand. Bernstein has come to the door.

BERNSTEIN I got here a cable from Mr. Kane—Mr. Leland, why didn't you go to Europe with him? He wanted you to.

LELAND I wanted him to have fun—and with me along—

This stops Bernstein. Bernstein looks at him

LELAND [*Cont'd*] Bernstein, I wish you'd let me ask you a few questions—and answer me truthfully.

BERNSTEIN Don't I always? Most of the time?

LELAND Bernstein, am I a stuffed shirt? Am I a horse-faced hypocrite? Am I a New England schoolmarm?

BERNSTEIN Yes.

Leland is surprised

BERNSTEIN [*Cont'd*] If you thought I'd answer you different from what Mr. Kane tells you—well, I wouldn't.

Pause as Bernstein looks around the room

BERNSTEIN [*Cont'd*] Mr. Leland, it's good he promised not to send back any statues.

LELAND I don't think you understand, Bernstein. This is one of the rarest Venuses in existence.

BERNSTEIN (*studying the statue carefully*) Not so rare like you think, Mr. Leland. (*Handing cable to Leland*) Here's the cable from Mr. Kane.

Leland takes it, reads it, smiles

BERNSTEIN [*Cont'd*] (*as Leland reads cable*) He wants to buy the world's biggest diamond.

LELAND I didn't know Charles was collecting diamonds.

BERNSTEIN He ain't. He's collecting somebody that's collecting diamonds. Anyway—(*Taking his eye*) he ain't only collecting statues.

Dissolve

44 Int. City Room—Day—1898

Dissolve to elaborate loving cup on which is engraved:

WELCOME HOME, MR. KANE—*From 730 employees of the New York "Inquirer."*

As camera pulls back, it reveals that this cup is on a little table at the far end of the "Inquirer" city room. Next to the table stands Bernstein, rubbing his hands, Hillman and a few other executives. Throughout the entire city room, there is a feeling of cleanliness and anticipation.

COPY BOY (*at stairway*) Here he comes!

Bernstein and Hillman start toward the door. All the others rise. Just as Bernstein gets to the door, it bursts open and Kane, an envelope in his hand, storms in

KANE Hello, Mr. Bernstein!

Kane continues at the same rate of speed with which he entered, Bernstein following behind him, at the head of a train which includes Hillman and others. The race stops a couple of steps beyond the society editor's desk by Kane, who moves back to the desk, making something of a traffic jam. (A plaque on the desk which reads "Society Editor" is what caught Kane's eye)

KANE [*Cont'd*] Excuse me, I've been away so long, I don't know your routine. Miss—

BERNSTEIN (*proudly*) Miss Townsend, Mr. Charles Foster Kane!

KANE Miss Townsend, I'd—(*He's pretty embarrassed by his audience*) I—have a little social announcement here. (*He puts it on the desk*) I wish you wouldn't treat this any differently than you would—you would—any other—anything else.

He looks around at the others with some embarrassment. At that moment, Hillman hands Bernstein the cup

BERNSTEIN (*holding the cup*) Mr. Kane, on behalf of all the employees of the "Inquirer"—

KANE (*interrupting*) Mr. Bernstein, I can't tell you how much I appreciate—(*He takes the cup and starts to take a few steps—realizes that he is being a little boorish—turns around and hands the cup back to Bernstein*) Look, Mr. Bernstein—everybody—I'm sorry—I—I can't take it now.

Murmurs

KANE [*Cont'd*] I'm busy. I mean—please—give it to me tomorrow.

He starts to run out. There is surprised confusion among the rest

BERNSTEIN Say, he's in an awful hurry!

SAME COPY BOY (*at window*) Hey, everybody! Lookee out here!

The whole staff rushes to the window

45 Ext. Street in Front of Inquirer Building—Day—1898

Angle down from window—shot of Emily sitting in a barouche.

46 Ext. Window of "Inquirer" City Room—Day—1898

Up shot of faces in the window, reacting and grinning.

47 Int. City Room—Day—1898

Miss Townsend stands frozen at her desk. She is reading and rereading with trembling hands the piece of flimsy which Kane gave her.

TOWNSEND Mr. Bernstein!

Mr. Bernstein, at window, turns around

BERNSTEIN Yes, Miss Townsend.

TOWNSEND This—this announcement—(*She reads shakily*) Mr. and Mrs. Thomas Monroe Norton announce the engagement of their daughter, Emily Monroe Norton, to Mr. Charles Foster Kane.

Bernstein reacts

TOWNSEND [*Cont'd*] Emily Monroe Norton—she's the niece of the President of the United States.

Bernstein nods his head proudly and turns back to look out the window

48 *Ext. Street in Front of Inquirer Building—Day—1898*

Down shot of Kane, crossing the curb to the barouche. He looks up in this shot, sees the people in the window, waves gaily, steps into the barouche. Emily looks at him smilingly. He kisses her full on the lips before he sits down. She acts a bit taken aback because of the public nature of the scene, but she isn't really annoyed.

Dissolve

49 *Int. City Room—"Inquirer"—Day—1898*

Bernstein and group at window.

BERNSTEIN A girl like that, believe me, she's lucky! President's niece, huh! Say, before he's through, she'll be a President's wife!

Dissolve

INSERT: FRONT PAGE "INQUIRER" (1898–1900)

Large picture of the young couple—Kane and Emily—occupying four columns— very happy.

INSERT: NEWSPAPER—KANE'S MARRIAGE TO EMILY WITH STILL OF GROUP ON WHITE HOUSE LAWN (1900)

(Same setup as early newsreel in news digest.)

Dissolve

50 *Int. Bernstein's Office—"Inquirer"—Day—1940*

Bernstein and Thompson. As the dissolve comes, Bernstein's voice is heard.

BERNSTEIN The way things turned out, I don't need to tell you—Miss Emily Norton was no rosebud!
THOMPSON It didn't end very well, did it?
BERNSTEIN It ended—Then there was Susie—That ended too. (*Shrugs, a pause*) I guess he didn't make her very happy—You know, I was thinking—that Rosebud you're trying to find out about—
THOMPSON Yes—
BERNSTEIN Maybe that was something he lost. Mr. Kane was a man that lost— almost everything he had. You ought to talk to Mr. Leland. Of course, he and Mr. Kane didn't exactly see eye to eye. You take the Spanish-American War. I guess Mr. Leland was right. That was Mr. Kane's war. We didn't really have anything to fight about—(*Chuckles*) But do you think if it hadn't been for that war of Mr. Kane's, we'd have the Panama Canal? I wish I knew where Mr. Leland was—(*Slowly*) Maybe even he's—a lot of the time now they don't tell me those things—maybe even he's dead.

THOMPSON In case you'd like to know, Mr. Bernstein, he's at the Huntington Memorial Hospital on 180th Street.

BERNSTEIN You don't say! Why I had no idea—

THOMPSON Nothing particular the matter with him, they tell me. Just—

BERNSTEIN Just old age. (*Smiles sadly*) It's the only disease, Mr. Thompson, you don't look forward to being cured of.

Dissolve Out

Dissolve In

51 Ext. Hospital Roof—Day—1940

Close shot—Thompson. He is tilted back in a chair, leaning against a chimney. Leland's voice is heard for a few moments before Leland is seen.

LELAND'S VOICE When you get to my age, young man, you don't miss anything. Unless maybe it's a good drink of bourbon. Even that doesn't make much difference, if you remember there hasn't been any good bourbon in this country for twenty years.

Camera has pulled back, revealing that Leland, wrapped in a blanket, is in a wheelchair, talking to Thompson. They are on the flat roof of a hospital

THOMPSON Mr. Leland, you were—

LELAND You don't happen to have a cigar, do you? I've got a young physician who thinks I'm going to stop smoking. . . . I changed the subject, didn't I? Dear, dear! What a disagreeable old man I've become. You want to know what I think of Charlie Kane?—Well—I suppose he had some private sort of greatness. But he kept it to himself. (*Grinning*) He never . . . gave himself away . . . He never gave anything away. He just . . . left you a tip. He had a generous mind. I don't suppose anybody ever had so many opinions. That was because he had the power to express them, and Charlie lived on power and the excitement of using it—But he didn't believe in anything except Charlie Kane. He never had a conviction except Charlie Kane in his life. I guess he died without one—That must have been pretty unpleasant. Of course, a lot of us check out with no special conviction about death. But we do know what we're leaving . . . we believe in something. (*Looks sharply at Thompson*) You're absolutely sure you haven't got a cigar?

THOMPSON Sorry, Mr. Leland.

LELAND Never mind—Bernstein told you about the first days at the office, didn't he?—Well, Charlie was a bad newspaperman even then. He entertained his readers but he never told them the truth.

THOMPSON Maybe you could remember something that—

LELAND I can remember everything. That's my curse, young man. It's the greatest curse that's ever been inflicted on the human race. Memory . . . I was his oldest friend. (*Slowly*) As far as I was concerned, he behaved like a swine. Not that Charlie ever was brutal. He just did brutal things. Maybe I wasn't his friend. If *I* wasn't, he never had one. Maybe I was what nowadays you call a stooge.

THOMPSON Mr. Leland, what do you know about Rosebud?

LELAND Rosebud? Oh! His dying words—Rosebud—Yeh. I saw that in the "Inquirer." Well, I've never believed anything I saw in the "Inquirer." Anything else?

Thompson is taken aback

LELAND [*Cont'd*]   I'll tell you about Emily. I used to go to dancing school with her. I was very graceful. Oh!—we were talking about the first Mrs. Kane—
THOMPSON   What was she like?
LELAND   She was like all the other girls I knew in dancing school. They were nice girls. Emily was a little nicer. She did her best—Charlie did his best—well, after the first couple of months they never saw much of each other except at breakfast. It was a marriage just like any other marriage.

Dissolve

(NOTE: The following scenes cover a period of nine years—are played in the same set with only changes in lighting, special effects outside the window, and wardrobe.)

52 Int. Kane's Home—Breakfast Room—Day—1901

Kane, in white tie and tails, and Emily formally attired. Kane is pouring a glass of milk for Emily out of a milk bottle. As he finishes, he leans over and playfully nips the back of her neck.

EMILY (*flustered*)   Charles! (*She's loving it*) Go sit down where you belong.
KANE (*on the way to his own place*)   You're beautiful.
EMILY   I can't be. I've never been to six parties in one night before. I've never been up this late.
KANE   It's just a matter of habit.
EMILY   What do you suppose the servants will think?
KANE   They'll think we enjoyed ourselves. Didn't we?
EMILY (*she gives him a purring smile. Then—*)   Dearest—I don't see why you have to go straight off to the newspaper.
KANE   You never should have married a newspaperman. They're worse than sailors. I absolutely love you.

They look at each other

EMILY   Charles, even newspapermen have to sleep.
KANE (*still looking at her*)   I'll call up Bernstein and tell him to put off my appointments till noon—What time is it?
EMILY   I don't know—it's late.
KANE   It's early.

Dissolve Out

Dissolve In

53 Int. Kane's Home—Breakfast Room—Day—1902

Kane and Emily—different clothes—different food.

EMILY Do you know how long you kept me waiting while you went to the office last night for ten minutes? Really, Charles, we were dinner guests at the Boardman's—we weren't invited for the weekend.

KANE You're the nicest girl I ever married.

EMILY Charles, if I didn't trust you—What do you do on a newspaper in the middle of the night?

KANE My dear, your only corespondent is the "Inquirer."

Dissolve

54 Int. Kane Home—Breakfast Room—1904

Kane and Emily—change of costume and food. Emily is dressed for the street.

EMILY (*kidding on the level*) Sometimes I think I'd prefer a rival of flesh and blood.

KANE Ah, Emily—I don't spend that much time—

EMILY It isn't just time—it's what you print—attacking the President—

KANE You mean Uncle John.

EMILY I mean the President of the United States.

KANE He's still Uncle John, and he's still a well-meaning fathead—

EMILY (*interrupting*) Charles—

KANE (*continuing on top of her*)—who's letting a pack of high-pressure crooks run his administration. This whole oil scandal—

EMILY He happens to be the President, Charles—not you.

KANE That's a mistake that will be corrected one of these days.

Dissolve

55 Int. Kane's Home—Breakfast Room—1905

Kane and Emily—change of costume and food.

EMILY Charles, when people make a point of not having the "Inquirer" in their homes—Margaret English says that the reading room at the Assembly already has more than forty names that have agreed to cancel the paper—

KANE That's wonderful. Mr. Bernstein will be delighted. You see, Emily, when your friends cancel the paper, that just takes another name off our deadbeat list. You know, don't you, it's practically a point of honor among the rich not to pay the newsdealer.

Dissolve Out

Dissolve In

56 Int. Kane's Home—Breakfast Room—1906

Kane and Emily—change of costume and food.

EMILY Your Mr. Bernstein sent Junior the most incredible atrocity yesterday. I simply can't have it in the nursery.

KANE Mr. Bernstein is apt to pay a visit to the nursery now and then.

EMILY Does he have to?
KANE (*shortly*) Yes.

Dissolve

57 Int. Kane's Home—Breakfast Room—1908

Kane and Emily—change of costume and food.

EMILY Really, Charles—people have a right to expect—
KANE What I care to give them.

Dissolve

58 Int. Kane's Home—Breakfast Room—1909

Kane and Emily—change of costume and food. They are both silent, reading news-papers. Kane is reading his "Inquirer." Emily is reading a copy of the "Chronicle."

Dissolve Out

Dissolve In

59 Ext. Hospital Roof—Day—1940

Leland and Thompson

THOMPSON Wasn't he ever in love with her?
LELAND He married for love—(*A little laugh*) That's why he did everything.
   That's why he went into politics. It seems we weren't enough. He wanted all
   the voters to love him, too. All he really wanted out of life was love—That's
   Charlie's story—how he lost it. You see, he just didn't have any to give. He
   loved Charlie Kane, of course, very dearly—and his mother, I guess he always
   loved her.
THOMPSON How about his second wife?
LELAND Susan Alexander? (*He chuckles*) You know what Charlie called her?—
   The day after he'd met her he told me about her—he said she was a cross-
   section of the American public—I guess he couldn't help it—she must have
   had something for him. (*With a smile*) That first night, according to Charlie—
   all she had was a toothache.

Dissolve Out

Dissolve In

60 Ext. Corner Drugstore and Street on the West Side of New York—Night—1915

Susan, aged twenty-two, neatly but cheaply dressed, is leaving the drugstore. (It's
about eight o'clock at night.) With a large, man-sized handkerchief pressed to her
cheek, she is in considerable pain. A carriage crosses in front of the camera—
passes—Susan continues down the street—Camera following her—encounters
Kane—very indignant, standing near the edge of the sidewalk, covered with mud.
She looks at him and smiles. He glares at her. She starts on down the street;
turns, looks at him again, and starts to laugh.

KANE (*glowering*)   It's not funny.
SUSAN   I'm sorry, mister—but you *do* look awful funny.

Suddenly the pain returns and she claps her hand to her jaw

SUSAN [*Cont'd*]   Ow!
KANE   What's the matter with you?
SUSAN   Toothache.
KANE   Hmmm!

He has been rubbing his clothes with his handkerchief

SUSAN   You've got some on your face. (*Starts to laugh again*)
KANE   What's funny now?
SUSAN   You are. (*The pain returns*) Oh!
KANE   Ah ha!
SUSAN   If you want to come in and wash your face—I can get you some hot water
   to get that dirt off your trousers—
KANE   Thanks.

Susan starts, with Kane following her

Dissolve

61 *Int. Susan's Room–Night—1915*

Susan comes into the room, carrying a basin, with towels over her arm. Kane is
waiting for her. She doesn't close the door.

SUSAN (*by way of explanation*)   My landlady prefers me to keep this door open
   when I have a gentleman caller. She's a very decent woman. (*Making a face*)
   Ow!

*Kane rushes to take the basin from her, putting it on the chiffonier. To do this, he
has to shove the photograph to one side with the basin. Susan grabs the photograph
as it is about to fall over*

SUSAN [*Cont'd*]   Hey, you should be more careful. That's my Ma and Pa.
KANE   I'm sorry. They live here too?
SUSAN   No. They've passed on.

Again she puts her hand to her jaw.

KANE   You poor kid, you are in pain, aren't you?

*Susan can't stand it any more and sits down in a chair, bent over, whimpering
a bit*

KANE [*Cont'd*]   Look at me.

She looks at him.

KANE [*Cont'd*] Why don't you laugh? I'm just as funny in here as I was on the street.

SUSAN I know, but you don't like me to laugh at you.

KANE I don't like your tooth to hurt, either.

SUSAN I can't help it.

KANE Come on, laugh at me.

SUSAN I can't—what are you doing?

KANE I'm wiggling both my ears at the same time. (*He does so*) It took me two solid years at the finest boys' school in the world to learn that trick. The fellow who taught me is now president of Venezuela. (*He wiggles his ears again*)

Susan starts to smile

KANE [*Cont'd*] That's it.

Susan smiles very broadly—then starts to laugh

.
Dissolve

62 *Int. Susan's Room—Night—1915*

Close-up of a duck, camera pulls back, showing it to be a shadowgraph on the wall, made by Kane, who is now in his shirt-sleeves.

SUSAN (*hesitatingly*) A chicken?

KANE No. But you're close.

SUSAN A rooster?

KANE You're getting further away all the time. It's a duck.

SUSAN A duck. You're not a professional magician, are you?

KANE No. I've told you. My name is Kane—Charles Foster Kane.

SUSAN I know. Charles Foster Kane. Gee—I'm pretty ignorant, I guess you caught on to that—

KANE You really don't know who I am?

SUSAN No. That is, I bet it turns out I've heard your name a million times, only you know how it is—

KANE But you like me, don't you? Even though you don't know who I am?

SUSAN You've been wonderful! I can't tell you how glad I am you're here, I don't know many people and—(*She stops*)

KANE And I know too many people. Obviously, we're both lonely. (*He smiles*) Would you like to know where I was going tonight—when you ran into me and ruined my Sunday clothes?

SUSAN I didn't run into you and I bet they're not your Sunday clothes. You've probably got a lot of clothes.

KANE I was only joking! (*Pauses*) I was on my way to the Western Manhattan Warehouse—in search of my youth.

Susan is bewildered

KANE [*Cont'd*] You see, my mother died too—a long time ago. Her things were put into storage out West because I had no place to put them then. I still haven't. But now I've sent for them just the same. And tonight I'd planned to make a sort of sentimental journey—and now—

Kane doesn't finish. He looks at Susan. Silence

KANE [*Cont'd*] Who am I? Well, let's see. Charles Foster Kane was born in New Salem, Colorado, in eighteen six—(*He stops on the word "sixty"—obviously a little embarrassed*) I run a couple of newspapers. How about you?
SUSAN Me?
KANE How old did you say you were?
SUSAN (*very bright*) I didn't say.
KANE I didn't think you did. If you had, I wouldn't have asked you again, because I'd have remembered. How old?
SUSAN Pretty old. I'll be twenty-two in August.
KANE That's a ripe old age—What do you do?
SUSAN I work at Seligman's.
KANE Is that what you want to do?
SUSAN I wanted to be a singer. I mean, I didn't. Mother did for me.
KANE What happened to the singing?
SUSAN Mother always thought—she used to talk about grand opera for me. Imagine!—Anyway, my voice isn't that kind. It's just—you know what mothers are like.
KANE Yes.
SUSAN As a matter of fact, I do sing a little.
KANE Would you sing for me?
SUSAN Oh, you wouldn't want to hear me sing.
KANE Yes, I would. That's why I asked.
SUSAN Well, I—
KANE Don't tell me your toothache is bothering you again?
SUSAN Oh, no, that's all gone.
KANE Then you haven't any alibi at all. Please sing.

Susan, with a tiny ladylike hesitancy, goes to the piano and sings a polite song. Sweetly, nicely, she sings with a small, untrained voice. Kane listens. He is relaxed, at ease with the world.

Dissolve Out

Dissolve In

INSERT: "INQUIRER" HEADLINE. (1916)
> BOSS ROGERS PICKS DEMOCRATIC NOMINEE

Dissolve

INSERT: "INQUIRER" HEADLINE (1916)
> BOSS ROGERS PICKS REPUBLICAN NOMINEE

Dissolve

INSERT: FOUR COLUMN CARTOON ON BACK PAGE OF "INQUIRER." (1916)

This shows Boss Rogers, labeled as such, in convict stripes, dangling little marionette figures—labeled Democratic Candidate and Republican Candidate—from each hand. As camera pans to remaining four columns it reveals box. This is headed:

Put this man in jail, people of New York.

It is signed, in bold type, "Charles Foster Kane." The text between headline and signature, little of which need be read, tells of the boss-ridden situation.

Dissolve Out

Dissolve In

63 Int. Madison Square Garden—Night—1916

The evening of the final great rally. Emily and Junior are to be seen in the front of a box. Emily is tired and wears a forced smile on her face. Junior, now aged nine and a half, is eager, bright-eyed and excited. Kane is just finishing his speech.

KANE It is no secret that I entered upon this campaign with no thought that I could be elected governor of this state! It is no secret that my only purpose was to bring as wide publicity as I could to the domination of this state—of its every resource—of its every income—of literally the lives and deaths of its citizens by Boss Edward G. Rogers! It is now no secret that every straw vote, every independent poll, shows that I will be elected. And I repeat to you—my first official act as governor will be to appoint a special district attorney to arrange for the indictment, prosecution and conviction of Boss Edward G. Rogers!

Terrific screaming and cheering from the audience

Dissolve

65 Int. Madison Square Garden—Night—1916

The speaker's platform. Numerous officials and civic leaders are crowding around Kane. Cameramen take flash photographs.

FIRST CIVIC LEADER Great speech, Mr. Kane.
SECOND LEADER (*pompous*) One of the most notable public utterances ever made by a candidate in this state—
KANE Thank you, gentlemen. Thank you.

He looks up and notices that the box in which Emily and Junior were sitting is now empty. He starts toward rear of the platform, through the press of people. Hillman approaches him

HILLMAN A wonderful speech, Mr. Kane.

Kane pats him on the shoulder as he walks along

HILLMAN [*Cont'd*] If the election were held *today,* you'd be elected by a hundred thousand votes—on an Independent ticket there's never been anything like it!

Kane is very pleased. He continues with Hillman slowly through the crowd—a band playing off

KANE It does seem too good to be true.

HILLMAN   Rogers isn't even pretending. He isn't just scared any more. He's sick. Frank Norris told me last night he hasn't known Rogers to be that worried in twenty-five years.

KANE   I think it's beginning to dawn on Mr. Rogers that I mean what I say. With Mr. Rogers out of the way, Hillman, I think we may really begin to hope for a good government in this state. (*Stopping*)

A WELL-WISHER   Great speech, Mr. Kane!

ANOTHER WELL-WISHER   Wonderful, Mr. Kane!

Ad libs from other well-wishers

Dissolve Out

Dissolve In

65   Ext. One of the Exits—Madison Square Garden—Night—1916

Emily and Junior are standing, waiting for Kane.

JUNIOR   Is Pop governor yet, Mom?

Kane appears with Hillman and several other men. He rushes toward Emily and Junior. The men politely greet Emily

KANE   Hello, Butch! Did you like your old man's speech?

JUNIOR   I was in a box, Father. I could hear every word.

KANE   I saw you! Good night, gentlemen.

There are good-nights. Kane's car is at the curb and he starts to walk toward it with Junior and Emily

EMILY   I'm sending Junior home in the car, Charles—with Oliver—

KANE   But I'd arranged to go home with you myself.

EMILY   There's a call I want you to make with me, Charles.

KANE   It can wait.

EMILY   No, it can't. (*Kisses Junior*) Good night, darling.

JUNIOR   Good night, Mom.

KANE   (*as car drives off*)   What's this all about, Emily? I've had a very tiring day and—

EMILY   It may not be about anything at all. (*Starting to a cab at curb*) I intend to find out.

KANE   I insist on being told exactly what you have in mind.

EMILY   I'm going to—(*She looks at a slip of paper*) 185 West 74th Street.

Kane's reaction indicates that the address definitely means something to him

EMILY [*Cont'd*]   If you wish, you can come with me . . .

KANE (*nods*)   I'll come with you.

He opens the door and she enters the cab. He follows her

Dissolve

66 Int. Cab—Night—1916

Kane and Emily. He looks at her in search of some kind of enlightenment. Her face is set and impassive.

Dissolve Out

Dissolve In

67 Ext. Susan's Apartment House Door—Night—1916

Kane and Emily, in front of an apartment door. Emily is pressing the bell.

KANE I had no idea you had this flair for melodrama, Emily.

Emily does not answer. The door is opened by a maid, who recognizes Kane

THE MAID Come in, Mr. Kane, come in.

She stands to one side for Kane and Emily to enter. This they start to do. Beyond them we see into the room

68 Int. Susan's Apartment—Night—1916

As Kane and Emily enter, Susan rises from a chair. The other person in the room—a big, heavyset man, a little past middle age—stays where he is, leaning back in his chair, regarding Kane intently.

SUSAN It wasn't my fault, Charlie. He made me send your wife a note. He said I'd—oh, he's been saying the most terrible things, I didn't know what to do . . . I—(*She stops*)
ROGERS Good evening, Mr. Kane. (*He rises*) I don't suppose anybody would introduce us. Mrs. Kane, I'm Edward Rogers.
EMILY How do you do?
ROGERS I made Miss—Miss Alexander send you the note. She was a little unwilling at first—(*Smiles grimly*) but she did it.
SUSAN I can't tell you the things he said, Charlie. You haven't got any idea—
KANE (*turning on Rogers*) Rogers, I don't think I *will* postpone doing something about you until I'm elected. (*Starts toward him*) To start with, I'll break your neck.
ROGERS (*not giving way an inch*) Maybe you can do it and maybe you can't, Mr. Kane.
EMILY Charles! (*He stops to look at her*) Your—your breaking this man's neck—(*She is clearly disgusted*) would scarcely explain this note—(*Glancing at the note*) Serious consequences for Mr. Kane—(*Slowly*) for myself, and for my son. What does this note mean, Miss—
SUSAN (*stiffly*) I'm Susan Alexander. (*Pauses*) I know what you think, Mrs. Kane, but—
EMILY (*ignoring this*) What does this note mean, Miss Alexander?
SUSAN It's like this, Mrs. Kane. I happened to be studying singing—I always wanted to be an opera singer—and Mr. Kane happened—I mean, he's been helping me—
EMILY What does this note mean, Miss Alexander?

ROGERS   She doesn't know, Mrs. Kane. She just sent it—because I made her see it wouldn't be smart for her not to send it.

KANE   In case you don't know, Emily, this—this gentleman—is—

ROGERS   I'm not a gentleman, Mrs. Kane, and your husband is just trying to be funny, calling me one. I don't even know what a gentleman is. You see, my idea of a gentleman, Mrs. Kane—well, if I owned a newspaper and if I didn't like the way somebody else was doing things—some politician, say—I'd fight them with everything I had. Only I wouldn't show him in a convict suit with stripes—so his children could see the picture in the paper. Or his mother.

EMILY   Oh!!

KANE   You're a cheap, crooked grafter—and your concern for your children and your mother—

ROGERS   Anything you say, Mr. Kane. Only we're talking now about what *you* are. That's what that note is about, Mrs. Kane. I'm going to lay all my cards on the table. I'm fighting for my life. Not just my political life. My life. If your husband is elected governor—

KANE   I'm *going* to be elected governor. And the first thing I'm going to do—

EMILY   Let him finish, Charles.

ROGERS   I'm protecting myself every way I know how, Mrs. Kane. This last week, I finally found out how I can stop your husband from being elected. If the people of this state learn what I found out this week, he wouldn't have a chance to—he couldn't be elected dog catcher.

KANE   You can't blackmail me, Rogers. You can't—

SUSAN (*excitedly*)   Charlie, he said, unless you withdrew your name—

ROGERS   That's the chance I'm willing to give you, Mr. Kane. More of a chance than you'd give me. Unless you make up your mind by tomorrow that you're so sick that you've got to go away for a year or two—Monday morning every paper in this state—except yours—will carry the story I'm going to give them.

EMILY   What story, Mr. Rogers?

ROGERS   The story about him and Miss Alexander, Mrs. Kane.

Emily looks at Kane

SUSAN   There *is* no story. It's all lies. Mr. Kane is just—

ROGERS (*to Susan*)   Shut up! (*To Kane*) We've got evidence that would stand up in any court of law. You want me to give you the evidence, Mr. Kane?

KANE   You do anything you want to do.

ROGERS   Mrs. Kane, I'm not asking *you* to believe me. I'd like to show you—

EMILY   I believe you, Mr. Rogers.

ROGERS   I'd rather Mr. Kane withdrew without having to get the story published. Not that I care about him. But I'd be better off that way—and so would you, Mrs. Kane.

SUSAN   What about me? (*To Kane*) He said my name'd be dragged through the mud. He said everywhere I'd go from now on—

EMILY   There seems to me to be only one decision you can make, Charles. I'd say that it has been made for you.

KANE   Have you gone completely mad, Emily? You don't think I'm going to let this blackmailer intimidate me, do you?

EMILY   I don't see what else you can do, Charles. If he's right—and the papers publish this story he has—

KANE Oh, they'll publish it all right. I'm not afraid of the story. You can't tell me that the voters of this state—

EMILY I'm not interested in the voters of this state right now. I am interested in—well, Junior, for one thing.

SUSAN Charlie! If they publish this story—

EMILY They won't. Good night, Mr. Rogers. There's nothing more to be said. Are you coming, Charles?

KANE No.

She looks at him. He starts to work himself into a rage

KANE [*Cont'd*] There's only one person in the world to decide what I'm going to do—and that's me. And if you think—if any of you think—

EMILY You decided what you were going to do, Charles—some time ago. Come on, Charles.

KANE Go on! Get out! I can fight this all alone! Get out!

ROGERS You're making a bigger fool of yourself than I thought you would, Mr. Kane. You're licked. Why don't you—

KANE (*turning on him*) Get out! I've got nothing to talk to you about. If you want to see me, have the warden write me a letter.

Rogers nods, with a look that says "So you say"

SUSAN (*starting to cry*) Charlie, you're just excited. You don't realize—

KANE I know exactly what I'm doing. (*He is screaming*) Get out!

EMILY (*quietly*) Charles, if you don't listen to reason, it may be too late—

KANE Too late for what? Too late for you and this—this public thief to take the love of the people of this state away from me? Well, you won't do it, I tell you. You won't do it!

SUSAN Charlie, there are other things to think of. (*A sly look comes into her eyes*) Your son—you don't want him to read in the papers—

EMILY It *is* too late now, Charles.

KANE (*rushes to the door and opens it*) Get out, both of you!

SUSAN (*rushes to him*) Charlie, please don't—

KANE What are you waiting for? Why don't you go?

EMILY Good night, Charles.

She walks out. Rogers stops directly in front of Kane

ROGERS You're the greatest fool I've ever known, Kane. If it was anybody else, I'd say what's going to happen to you would be a lesson to you. Only you're going to need more than one lesson. And you're going to get more than one lesson.

KANE Don't worry about me. I'm Charles Foster Kane. I'm no cheap, crooked politician, trying to save himself from the consequences of his crimes—

69 Int. Apt. House Hallway—Night—1916

Camera angling toward Kane from other end of the hall. Rogers and Emily are already down the hall, moving toward f. g. Kane in apartment doorway b. g.

KANE (*screams louder*) I'm going to send you to Sing Sing, Rogers. Sing Sing!

Kane is trembling with rage as he shakes his fist at Rogers's back. Susan, quieter now, has snuggled into the hollow of his shoulder as they stand in the doorway

Dissolve

INSERT: The "Chronicle" front page with photograph (as in the news digest) revealing Kane's relations with Susan. Headline reads:

CANDIDATE KANE FOUND IN
LOVE NEST WITH "SINGER"

Dissolve

70 Int. Composing Room—"Inquirer"—Night—1916

Camera angles down on enormous headline in type with proof on top. In back of this headline lies complete front page, except for headline. Headline reads:

KANE GOVERNOR

Camera tilts up showing Bernstein, actually crying, standing with composing room foreman, Jenkins.

BERNSTEIN (*to foreman*) With a million majority already against him, and the church counties still to be heard from—I'm afraid we got no choice. This one.

Camera pans to where he is pointing; shows enormous headline, the proof of which in small type reads:

KANE DEFEATED

and in large type screams:

FRAUD AT POLLS!

Dissolve Out

Dissolve In

71 Int. Kane's Office—"Inquirer"—Night—1916

Kane looks up from his desk as there is a knock on the door.

KANE Come in.

Leland enters

KANE (*surprised*) I thought I heard somebody knock.
LELAND (*a bit drunk*) I knocked. (*He looks at him defiantly*)
KANE (*trying to laugh it off*) Oh! An official visit of state, eh? (*Waves his hand*) Sit down, Jedediah.
LELAND (*sitting down angrily*) I'm drunk.
KANE Good! It's high time—

LELAND You don't have to be amusing.

KANE All right. Tell you what I'll do. I'll get drunk, too.

LELAND (*thinks this over*) No. That wouldn't help. Besides, you never get drunk. (*Pauses*) I want to talk to you—about—about—(*He can't get it out*)

KANE (*looks at him sharply a moment*) If you've got yourself drunk to talk to me about Susan Alexander—I'm not interested.

LELAND She's not important. What's much more important—(*He keeps glaring at Kane*)

KANE (*as if genuinely surprised*) Oh! (*He gets up*) I frankly didn't think I'd have to listen to that lecture from you. (*Pauses*) I've betrayed the sacred cause of reform, is that it? I've set back the sacred cause of reform in this state twenty years. Don't tell me, Jed, *you—*

Despite his load, Leland manages to achieve a dignity about the silent contempt with which he looks at Kane.

KANE (*an outburst*) What makes the sacred cause of reform so sacred? Why does the sacred cause of reform have to be exempt from all the other facts of life? Why do the laws of this state have to be executed by a man on a white charger?

Leland lets the storm ride over his head

KANE [*Cont'd*] (*calming down*) But, if that's the way they want it—they've made their choice. The people of this state obviously prefer Mr. Rogers to me. (*His lips tighten*) So be it.

LELAND You talk about the people as though they belong to you. As long as I can remember you've talked about giving the people their rights as though you could make them a present of liberty—in reward for services rendered. You remember the workingman? You used to write an awful lot about the workingman. Well, he's turning into something called organized labor, and you're not going to like that a bit when you find out it means that he thinks he's entitled to something as his right and not your gift. (*He pauses*) And listen, Charles. When your precious underprivileged really do get together—that's going to add up to something bigger—than your privilege—and then I don't know what you'll do. Sail away to a desert island, probably, and lord it over the monkeys.

KANE Don't worry about it too much, Jed. There's sure to be a few of them there to tell me where I'm wrong.

LELAND You may not always be that lucky. (*Pauses*) Charlie, why can't you get to look at things less personally? Everything doesn't have to be between you and—the personal note doesn't always—

KANE (*violently*) The personal note is all there is to it. It's all there ever is to it. It's all there ever is to anything! Stupidity in our government—crookedness— even just complacency and self-satisfaction and an unwillingness to believe that anything done by a certain class of people can be wrong—you can't fight those things impersonally. They're not impersonal crimes against the people. They're being done by actual persons—with actual names and positions and— the right of the American people to their own country is not an academic issue, Jed, that you debate—and then the judges retire to return a verdict— and the winners give a dinner for the losers.

LELAND   You almost convince me, almost. The truth is, Charlie, you just don't care about anything except you. You just want to convince people that you love them so much that they should love you back. Only you want love on your own terms. It's something to be played your way—according to your rules. And if anything goes wrong and you're hurt—then the game stops, and you've got to be soothed and nursed, no matter what else is happening—and no matter who else is hurt!

They look at each other

KANE (*trying to kid him into a better humor*)   Hey, Jedediah!

Leland is not to be seduced

LELAND   Charlie, I wish you'd let me work on the Chicago paper—you said your-self you were looking for someone to do dramatic criticism there—
KANE   You're more valuable here.

There is silence

LELAND   Well, Charlie, then I'm afraid there's nothing I can do but to ask you to accept—
KANE (*harshly*)   All right. You can go to Chicago.
LELAND   Thank you.

There is an awkward pause. Kane opens a drawer of his desk and takes out a bottle and two glasses

KANE   I guess I'd better *try* to get drunk, anyway.

Kane hands Jed a glass, which he makes no move to take

KANE [*Cont'd*]   But I warn you, Jedediah, you're not going to like it in Chicago. The wind comes howling in off the lake, and the Lord only knows if they've ever heard of lobster Newburg.
LELAND   Will a week from Saturday be all right?
KANE (*wearily*)   Anytime you say.
LELAND   Thank you.

Kane looks at him intently and lifts the glass

KANE   A toast, Jedediah—to love on *my* terms. Those are the only terms anybody knows—his own.

Dissolve

72 *Ext. Town Hall in Trenton (as in News Digest)—Day—1917*

Kane (as in news digest) is just emerging with Susan. He smashes one camera and before he begins on a second, a cop removes a newsreel cameraman. He smashes a second camera, and is just about to start on a third.

PHOTOGRAPHER Mr. Kane! Mr. Kane! It's the "Inquirer"!

Kane sees the "Inquirer" painted on the side of the camera and stops

REPORTER (*quickly*) How about a statement, Mr. Kane?
ANOTHER REPORTER On the level, Mr. Kane, are you through with politics?
KANE I would say vice versa, young man. (*Smiles*) We're going to be a great opera
  star.
REPORTER Are you going to sing at the Metropolitan, Mrs. Kane?
KANE We certainly are.
SUSAN Charlie said if I didn't, he'd build me an opera house.
KANE That won't be necessary.

Dissolve

INSERT: FRONT PAGE CHICAGO "INQUIRER," with photograph proclaiming that Susan Alexander opens at new Chicago Opera House in *Thaïs* (as in news digest).
(1919)

On sound track during above we hear the big expectant murmur of an opening
night audience and the noodling of the orchestra.

Dissolve

73 Int. Chicago Opera House—Night—Set for Thaïs—1919

The camera is just inside the curtain, angling upstage. We see the set for *Thaïs*—
and in the center of all this, in an elaborate costume, looking very small and very
lost, is Susan. She is almost hysterical with fright. Applause is heard, and the
orchestra starts thunderously. The curtain starts to rise—the camera with it. Susan squints and starts to sing. Camera continues on up with the curtain the full
height of the proscenium arch and then on up into the gridiron. Susan's voice still
heard but faintly. Two typical stagehands fill the frame, looking down on the stage
below. They look at each other. One of them puts his hand to his nose.

Dissolve

74 Int. City Room—Chicago "Inquirer"—Night—1919

It is late. The room is almost empty. Nobody is at work at the desks. Bernstein
is waiting anxiously with a little group of Kane's hirelings, most of them in evening
dress with overcoats and hats. Everybody is tense and expectant.

CITY EDITOR (*turns to a young hireling; quietly*) What about Jed Leland? Has
  he got in his copy?
HIRELING Not yet.
BERNSTEIN Go in and ask him to hurry.
CITY EDITOR Well, why don't you, Mr. Bernstein? You know Mr. Leland.
BERNSTEIN (*slowly*) I might make him nervous. Mr. Leland, he's writing it from
  the dramatic angle?
CITY EDITOR Yes, I thought it was a good idea. We've covered it from the news
  end, of course.
BERNSTEIN And the social. How about the music notice? You got that in?

CITY EDITOR Oh, yes, it's already made up. Our Mr. Mervin wrote a swell review.
BERNSTEIN Enthusiastic?
CITY EDITOR Yes, very! (*Quietly*) Naturally.
BERNSTEIN Well, well—isn't that nice?
KANE'S VOICE Mr. Bernstein—

Bernstein turns

74A Med. Long Shot of Kane

He is in white tie, wearing his overcoat and carrying a folded opera hat.

BERNSTEIN Hello, Mr. Kane.

The hirelings rush, with Bernstein, to Kane's side. Widespread half-suppressed sensation

CITY EDITOR Mr. Kane, this *is* a surprise!
KANE We've got a nice plant here.

Everybody falls silent. There isn't anything to say

CITY EDITOR Everything has been done exactly to your instructions, Mr. Kane.
    We've got two spreads of pictures and—
KANE The music notice on the first page?
CITY EDITOR Yes, Mr. Kane. (*Hesitatingly*) There's still one notice to come. The
    dramatic.
KANE That's Leland, isn't it?
CITY EDITOR Yes, Mr. Kane.
KANE Has he said when he'll finish?
CITY EDITOR We haven't heard from him.
KANE He used to work fast—didn't he, Mr. Bernstein?
BERNSTEIN He sure did, Mr. Kane.
KANE Where is he?
ANOTHER HIRELING Right in there, Mr. Kane.

The hireling indicates the closed glass door of a little office at the other end of the city room. Kane takes it in

BERNSTEIN (*helpless but very concerned*) Mr. Kane—
KANE That's all right, Mr. Bernstein.

Kane crosses the length of the long city room to the glass door indicated before by the hireling. The city editor looks at Bernstein. Kane opens the door and goes into the office, closing the door behind him

BERNSTEIN Mr. Leland and Mr. Kane—they haven't spoken together for four
    years—
CITY EDITOR You don't suppose—

BERNSTEIN There's nothing to suppose. (*A long pause; finally . . .*) Excuse me. (*Starts toward the door*)

Dissolve Out

Dissolve In

75 Int. Leland's Office—Chicago "Inquirer"—Night—1919

Bernstein comes in. An empty bottle is standing on Leland's desk. He has fallen asleep over his typewriter, his face on the keys. A sheet of paper is in the machine. A paragraph has been typed. Kane is standing at the other side of the desk looking down at him. This is the first time we see murder in Kane's face. Bernstein looks at Kane, then crosses to Leland. He shakes him.

BERNSTEIN (*straightens, looks at Kane; a pause*) He ain't been drinking before, Mr. Kane. Never. We would have heard.
KANE (*finally, after a pause*) What does it say there?

Bernstein stares at him

KANE [*Cont'd*] What's he written?

Bernstein leans over near-sightedly, painfully reading the paragraph written on the page

BERNSTEIN (*reading*) "Miss Susan Alexander, a pretty but hopelessly incompetent amateur—(*Waits for a minute to catch his breath; doesn't like it*) last night opened the new Chicago Opera House in a performance of—of—" (*Looks up miserably*) I still can't pronounce that name, Mr. Kane.

Kane doesn't answer. Bernstein looks at Kane for a moment, then looks back, tortured

BERNSTEIN [*Cont'd*] (*Reading again*) "Her singing, happily, is no concern of this department. Of her acting, it is absolutely impossible to—" (*Continues to stare at the page*)
KANE (*after a short silence*) Go on!
BERNSTEIN (*without looking up*) That's all there is.

Kane snatches the paper from the roller and reads it for himself. Slowly a queer look comes into his face. Then he speaks, very quietly

KANE Of her acting, it is absolutely impossible to say anything except that it represents in the opinion of this reviewer a new low—(*Then sharply*) Have you got that, Mr. Bernstein? In the opinion of this reviewer—
BERNSTEIN (*miserably*) I didn't see that.
KANE It isn't there, Mr. Bernstein. I'm dictating it.
BERNSTEIN But Mr. Kane, I can't—I mean—I—
KANE Get me a typewriter. I'll finish this notice.

Bernstein retreats from the room

Dissolve Out

Dissolve In

76 *Int. Leland's Office—Chicago "Inquirer"—Night—1919*

Long shot—of Kane in his shirt-sleeves, illuminated by a desk light, typing furiously. As the camera starts to pull even further away from this . . .

Dissolve

77 *Int. Leland's Office—Chicago "Inquirer"—Night—1919*

Leland, sprawled across his typewriter. He stirs and looks up drunkenly, his eyes encountering Bernstein, who stands beside him.

BERNSTEIN Hello, Mr. Leland.
LELAND Hello, Bernstein. Where is it—where's my notice—I've got to finish it!
BERNSTEIN (*quietly*) Mr. Kane is finishing it.
LELAND Kane?—Charlie?—(*Painfully rises*) Where is he?

During all this, the sound of a busy typewriter has been heard. Leland's eyes follow the sound. Slowly he registers Kane out in the city room

78 *Int. City Room—Chicago "Inquirer"—Night—1919*

Kane, in white tie and shirt-sleeves, is typing away at a machine, his face, seen by the desk light before him, set in a strange half-smile. Leland stands in the door of his office, staring across at him.

LELAND I suppose he's fixing it up—I knew I'd never get that through.
BERNSTEIN (*moving to his side*) Mr. Kane is finishing your piece the way you
    started it.

Leland turns incredulously to Bernstein

BERNSTEIN [*Cont'd*] He's writing a bad notice like you wanted it to be—(*Then
    with a kind of quiet passion, rather than triumph*) I guess that'll show you.

*Leland picks his way across to Kane's side. Kane goes on typing, without looking
up*

KANE (*after pause*) Hello, Jedediah.
LELAND Hello, Charlie—I didn't know we were speaking.

Kane stops typing, but doesn't turn

KANE Sure, we're speaking, Jed—You're fired.

He starts typing again, the expression on his face doesn't change

                                                              Dissolve

79 *Ext. Hospital Roof—Day—1940*

Thompson and Leland. It is getting late. The roof is now deserted.

THOMPSON Everybody knows that story, Mr. Leland, but—why did he do it?
    How could he write a notice like that when—
LELAND You just don't know Charlie. He thought that by finishing that piece he
    could show me he was an honest man. He was always trying to prove some-
    thing. That whole thing about Susie being an opera singer—that was trying
    to prove something. Do you know what the headline was the day before the
    election? Candidate Kane found in love nest with quote singer unquote. He
    was going to take the quotes off the singer. (*Pauses*) Hey, nurse! Five years
    ago he wrote from that place of his down South—(*As if trying to think*) you
    know. Shangri-La? El Dorado? (*Pauses*) Sloppy Joe's? What's the name of
    that place? . . . All right. Xanadu. I knew what it was all the time. You caught
    on, didn't you?
THOMPSON Yes.
LELAND I guess maybe I'm not as hard to see through as I think. Anyway, I never
    even answered his letter. Maybe I should have. He must have been pretty
    lonely down there in that coliseum those last years. He hadn't finished it
    when she left him—he never finished it—he never finished anything, except
    my notice. Of course, he built the joint for her.
THOMPSON That must have been love.
LELAND I don't know. He was disappointed in the world. So he built one of his
    own—an absolute monarchy—It was something bigger than an opera house
    anyway—(*Calls*) Nurse! (*Lowers his voice*) Say, I'll tell you one thing you can
    do for me, young fellow.
THOMPSON Sure.

LELAND   On your way out, stop at a cigar store, will you, and send me up a couple of cigars?

THOMPSON   Sure, Mr. Leland. I'll be glad to.

LELAND   Hey, nurse!

A nurse has already appeared and stands behind him

NURSE   Yes, Mr. Leland.

LELAND   I'm ready to go in now. You know when I was a young man, there was an impression around that nurses were pretty. It was no truer then than it is now.

NURSE   Here, let me take your arm, Mr. Leland.

LELAND (*testily*)   All right, all right. You won't forget, will you, about the cigars? And tell them to wrap them up to look like toothpaste, or something, or they'll stop them at the desk. That young doctor I was telling you about, he's got an idea he wants to keep me alive.

Fade Out

Fade In

80 Ext. "El Rancho" Cabaret in Atlantic City—Early Dawn—1940

Neon sign on the roof:

"EL RANCHO"
Floor Show
Susan Alexander Kane
Twice Nightly

Camera, as before, moves through the lights of the sign and down on the skylight, through which is seen Susan at her regular table, Thompson seated across from her. Very faintly during this, idle piano music playing.

Dissolve

81 Int. "El Rancho" Cabaret—Early Dawn—1940

Susan and Thompson are facing each other. The place is almost deserted. Susan is sober. On the other side of the room somebody is playing a piano.

THOMPSON   I'd rather you just talked. Anything that comes into your mind—about yourself and Mr. Kane.

SUSAN   You wouldn't want to hear a lot of what comes into my mind about myself and Mr. Charlie Kane. (*She tosses down a drink*) You know—maybe I shouldn't ever have sung for Charlie that first time. Hah!—I did a lot of singing after that. To start with, I sang for teachers at a hundred bucks an hour. The teachers got that, I didn't.

THOMPSON   What did you get?

SUSAN   What do you mean?

Thompson doesn't answer

SUSAN [*Cont'd*]   I didn't get a thing. Just the music lessons. That's all there was
to it.

THOMPSON   He married you, didn't he?

SUSAN   He never said anything about marriage until it all came out in the papers
about us—and he lost the election and that Norton woman divorced him.
What are you smiling about? I tell you he was really interested in my voice.
(*Sharply*) What do you think he built that opera house for? I didn't want it.
I didn't want to sing. It was his idea—everything was his idea—except my
leaving him.

Dissolve

82 Int. Living Room—Kane's Home in New York—Day—1917–1918

Susan is singing. Matisti, her voice teacher, is playing the piano. Kane is seated
nearby. Matisti stops.

MATISTI   Impossible! Impossible!

KANE   It is not your job to give Mrs. Kane your opinion of her talents. You're
supposed to train her voice. Nothing more.

MATISTI (*sweating*)   But, it is impossible. I will be the laughing stock of the
musical world! People will say—

KANE   If you're interested in what people will say, Signor Matisti, I may be able
to enlighten you a bit. The newspapers, for instance. I'm an authority on what
the papers will say, Signor Matisti, because I own eight of them between here
and San Francisco. . . . It's all right, dear. Signor Matisti is going to listen to
reason. Aren't you, maestro?

MATISTI   Mr. Kane, how can I persuade you—

KANE   You can't.

There is a silence. Matisti rises

KANE [*Cont'd*]   I knew you'd see it my way.

Dissolve

83 Int. Chicago Opera House—Night—1919

It is the same opening night—it is the same moment as before—except that the
camera is now upstage angling toward the audience. The curtain is down. We see
the same tableau as before. As the dissolve commences, there is the sound of
applause and now, as the dissolve completes itself, the orchestra begins—the stage
is cleared—Susan is left alone. The curtain rises. Susan starts to sing. Beyond
her, we see the prompter's box, containing the anxious face of the prompter.
Beyond that, an apprehensive conductor.

84 Close-up

Kane's face—he is seated in the audience—listening. A sudden but perfectly correct lull in the music reveals a voice from the audience—a few words from a
sentence.

THE VOICE —really pathetic.

Music crashes in and drowns out the rest of the sentence, but hundreds of people around the voice have heard it (as well as Kane) and there are titters which grow in volume.

85 *Close-up*

Susan's face—singing.

86 *Close-up*

Kane's face—listening.

There is the ghastly sound of three thousand people applauding as little as possible. Kane still looks. Then, near the camera, there is the sound of about a dozen people applauding very, very loudly. Camera moves back, revealing Bernstein and Hillman and other Kane stooges, seated around him, beating their palms together.

87 *The Stage from Kane's Angle*

The curtain is down—Still the polite applause, dying fast. Nobody comes out for a bow.

88 *Close-up*

Kane—breathing heavily. Suddenly he starts to applaud furiously.

89 *The Stage from the Audience Again*

Susan appears for her bow. She can hardly walk. There is a little polite crescendo of applause, but it is sickly.

90 *Close-up*

Kane—still applauding very, very hard, his eyes on Susan.

91 *The Stage Again*

Susan, finishing her bow, goes out through the curtains. The light on the curtain goes out and the houselights go up.

92 *Close-up*

Kane—still applauding very, very hard.

Dissolve Out

Dissolve In

93 *Int. Hotel Room—Chicago—Day—1919*

Kane—Susan in a negligee. The floor is littered with newspapers.

SUSAN Stop telling me he's your friend. (*She points at the paper*) A friend don't

write that kind of an article. Anyway, not the kind of friends I know. Of course,
  I'm not high-class like you and I didn't go to any swell schools—
KANE That's enough, Susan.

*A look at him convinces Susan that he really means it's enough. There's a knock
at the door.*

SUSAN (*screeching*) Come in!

A copy boy enters

COPY BOY Mr. Leland said I was to come right up—He was very anxious—
KANE (*interrupting*) Thanks, son.

He shoves the kid out. He opens the envelope as Susan returns to the attack

SUSAN The idea of him trying to spoil my debut!

*Kane has taken a folded piece of paper out of the envelope and is holding it—
looking into the envelope*

KANE He won't spoil anything else, Susan.
SUSAN And you—you ought to have your head examined! Sending him a letter
  he's fired with a twenty-five thousand dollar check! What kind of firing do you
  call that? You did send him a twenty-five thousand dollar check, *didn't* you?
KANE (*slowly tipping over the envelope as pieces of torn papers fall to the
  floor*) Yes, I sent him a twenty-five thousand dollar check.

Kane now unfolds the piece of paper and looks at it

INSERT: Kane's original grease pencil copy of his Declaration of Principles.

SUSAN'S VOICE What's that?
KANE'S VOICE An antique.

BACK TO SCENE:

SUSAN You're awful funny, aren't you? Well, I can tell you one thing you're not
  going to keep on being funny about—my singing. I'm through. I never wanted
  to—
KANE (*without looking up*) You are continuing your singing, Susan. (*He starts
  tearing the paper*) I'm not going to have myself made ridiculous.
SUSAN *You* don't propose to have *yourself* made ridiculous? What about me? I'm
  the one that has to do the singing. I'm the one that gets the razzberries. Why
  can't you—
KANE (*looking up—still tearing the paper*) My reasons satisfy me, Susan. You
  seem to be unable to understand them. I will not tell them to you again. (*He
  has started to walk menacingly toward her, tearing the paper as he walks*)
  You are to continue with your singing.

His eyes are relentlessly upon her. She sees something that frightens her. She nods slowly; indicating surrender

Dissolve

INSERT: FRONT PAGE of the San Francisco "Inquirer" (1919) containing a large portrait of Susan as Thaïs. It is announced that Susan will open an independent season in San Francisco in *Thaïs*. The picture remains constant but the names of the papers change from New York to St. Louis, to Los Angeles to Cleveland, to Denver to Philadelphia—all "Inquirers."

During all this, on the sound track, Susan's voice is heard singing her aria very faintly.

Dissolve

94 *Int. Susan's Bedroom—Kane's N.Y. Home—Late Night—1920*

Camera angles across the bed and Susan's form towards the door, from the other side of which comes loud knocking and Kane's voice calling Susan's name. Then:

KANE'S VOICE   Joseph!
JOSEPH'S VOICE   Yes, sir.
KANE'S VOICE   Do you have the keys to Mrs. Kane's bedroom?
JOSEPH'S VOICE   No, Mr. Kane. They must be on the inside.
KANE'S VOICE   We'll have to break down the door.
JOSEPH'S VOICE   Yes, sir.

The door crashes open. Light floods the room, revealing Susan, fully dressed, stretched out on the bed. She is breathing, but heavily. Kane rushes to her, kneels at the bed, and feels her forehead. Joseph has followed him in

KANE   Get Dr. Corey.

Joseph rushes out

Dissolve

95 *Int. Susan's Bedroom—Kane's N.Y. Home—Late Night—1920*

A little later. All the lights are lit. At start of scene, Dr. Corey removes his doctor's bag from in front of camera lens, revealing Susan, in a nightgown, is in bed. She is breathing heavily. A nurse is bending over the bed, straightening the sheets.

DR. COREY'S VOICE   She'll be perfectly all right in a day or two, Mr. Kane.

The nurse walks away from the bed toward b.g. We now see Kane, who was hidden by the nurse's body, seated beyond the bed. He is holding an empty medicine bottle. Dr. Corey walks to him

KANE   I can't imagine how Mrs. Kane came to make such a foolish mistake. (*Susan turns her head away from Kane*) The sedative Dr. Wagner gave her

is in a somewhat larger bottle—I suppose the strain of preparing for the new opera has excited and confused her. (*Looks sharply up at Dr. Corey*)
DR. COREY Yes, yes—I'm sure that's it.

Dr. Corey turns and walks toward the nurse

KANE There are no objections to my staying here with her, are there?
DR. COREY No—not at all. But I'd like the nurse to be here, too. Good night, Mr. Kane.

Dr. Corey hurries out the door

Dissolve

96 *Int. Susan's Bedroom—Kane's N.Y. Home—Very Early Dawn—1920*

The lights are out. Camera pans from nurse, who is seated stiffly in a chair, toward Kane, seated beside the bed staring at Susan, to Susan who is asleep.

Dissolve

97 *Int. Susan's Bedroom—Kane's N.Y. Home—Day—1920*

Sunlight is streaming into the room. A hurdy-gurdy is heard. Kane is still seated beside the bed, looking at Susan, who is asleep. After a moment Susan gasps and opens her eyes. She looks toward the window, Kane leans toward her. She looks up at him, then away.

SUSAN (*painfully*) Charlie—I couldn't make you see how I felt—I just couldn't go through with the singing again—You don't know what it's like to feel that people—that a whole audience doesn't want you.
KANE (*angrily*) That's when you've got to fight them!

She looks up at him silently with pathetic eyes

KANE [*Cont'd*] (*after a moment; gently*) All right. You won't have to fight them any more—It's their loss.

She continues to look at him, but now gratefully

Dissolve

98 *Ext. Establishing Shot of Xanadu—Half Built—1925*

Dissolve

99 *Int. Great Hall—Xanadu—1929*

Close-up of an enormous jigsaw puzzle. A hand is putting in the last piece. Camera moves back to reveal jigsaw puzzle spread out on the floor.

Susan is on the floor before her jigsaw puzzle. Kane is in an easy chair. Candelabra illuminates the scene.

SUSAN What time is it?

There is no answer

SUSAN [*Cont'd*]   Charlie! I said, what time is it?
KANE (*looks up—consults his watch*)   Eleven-thirty.
SUSAN I mean in New York. (*No answer*) I said what time is it in New York!
KANE Eleven-thirty.
SUSAN At night?
KANE Umhmm. The bulldog's just gone to press.
SUSAN (*sarcastically*)   Hurray for the bulldog! (*Sighs*) Eleven-thirty! The shows're
    just getting out. People are going to nightclubs and restaurants. Of course,
    we're different because we live in a palace.
KANE You always said you wanted to live in a palace.
SUSAN A person could go nuts in this dump.

Kane doesn't answer

SUSAN [*Cont'd*]   Nobody to talk to—nobody to have any fun with.
KANE Susan—
SUSAN Forty-nine thousand acres of nothing but scenery and—statues. I'm lone-
    some.
KANE I thought you were tired of house guests. Till yesterday morning, we've
    had no less than fifty of your friends at any one time. As a matter of fact,
    Susan, if you'll look carefully in the west wing, you'll probably find a dozen
    vacationists still in residence.
SUSAN You make a joke out of everything! Charlie, I want to go back to New
    York. I'm tired of being a hostess. I wanta have fun. Please, Charlie, please!
KANE Our home is here, Susan. I don't care to visit New York.

Dissolve

100 Another Picture Puzzle

Susan's hands fitting in a missing piece. (1930)

Dissolve

101 Another Picture Puzzle

Susan's hands fitting in a missing piece. (1931)

Dissolve

102 Int. Great Hall—Xanadu—Day—1932

Close-up of another jigsaw puzzle. Camera pulls back to show Kane and Susan in
much the same positions as before, except that they are older.

KANE One thing I've never been able to understand, Susan. How do you know
    that you haven't done them before?

Susan shoots him an angry glance. She isn't amused

SUSAN It makes a whole lot more sense than collecting Venuses.

KANE You may be right—I sometimes wonder—but you get into the habit—

SUSAN (*snapping*) It's not a habit. I do it because I like it.

KANE I was referring to myself. (*Pauses*) I thought we might have a picnic tomorrow—Invite everybody to go to the Everglades—

SUSAN *Invite* everybody!—Order everybody, you mean, and make them sleep in
tents! Who wants to sleep in tents when they have a nice room of their own—
with their own bath, where they know where everything is?

Kane has looked at her steadily, not hostilely

KANE I thought we might invite everybody to go on a picnic tomorrow. Stay at
Everglades overnight.

Dissolve

103 Ext. Xanadu—Road—Day—1932

Tight two-shot—Kane and Susan seated in an automobile, silent, glum, staring
before them. Camera pulls back revealing that there are twenty cars full of pic-
nickers following them, on their way through the Xanadu estate.

SUSAN You never give me anything I really care about.

Dissolve Out

Dissolve In

104 Ext. The Everglades Camp—Night—1932

Long shot—of a number of classy tents.

Dissolve

105 Int. Large Tent—Everglades Camp—Night—1932

Two real beds have been set up on each side of the tent. A rather classy dressing
table is in the rear, at which Susan is preparing for bed. Kane, in his shirt-sleeves,
is in an easy chair, reading. Susan is very sullen.

SUSAN I'm not going to put up with it.

Kane turns to look at her

SUSAN [*Cont'd*] I mean it. Oh, I know I always say I mean it, and then I don't—
or *you* get me so I don't do what I say I'm going to—but—

KANE (*interrupting*) You're in a tent, darling. You're not at home. And I can hear
you very well if you just talk in a normal tone of voice.

SUSAN I'm not going to have my guests insulted, just because you—(*In a rage*)
if people want to bring a drink or two along on a picnic, that's their business.
You've got no right—

KANE (*quickly*) I've got more than a right as far as you're concerned, Susan.

SUSAN I'm sick and tired of your telling me what I mustn't do! And what I—

KANE   We can discuss all this some other time, Susan. Right now—

SUSAN   I'll discuss what's on my mind when *I* want to. I'm sick of having you run my life the way you want it.

KANE   Susan, as far as you're concerned, I've never wanted anything—I don't want anything now—except what you want.

SUSAN   What *you* want me to want, you mean. What you've decided I ought to have—what you'd want if you were me. Never what I want—

KANE   Susan!

SUSAN   You've never given me anything that—

KANE   I really think—

SUSAN   Oh sure, you give me things—that don't mean anything to you—What's the difference between giving me a bracelet or giving somebody else a hundred thousand dollars for a statue you're going to keep crated up and never look at? It's only money.

KANE (*he has risen*)   Susan, I want you to stop this.

SUSAN   I'm not going to stop it!

KANE   Right now!

SUSAN (*screams*)   You never gave me anything in your life! You just tried to—to buy me into giving *you* something. You're—it's like you were bribing me!

KANE   Susan!

SUSAN   That's all you ever done—no matter how much it cost you—your time, your money—that's all you've done with everybody. Tried to bribe them!

KANE   *Susan!*

She looks at him, with no lessening of her passion

KANE [*Cont'd*] (*quietly*)   Whatever I do—I do—because I love you.

SUSAN   You don't love me! You just want me to love you—sure—I'm Charles Foster Kane. Whatever you want—just name it and it's yours. But you gotta love me!

Without a word, Kane slaps her across the face. He continues to look at her

SUSAN [*Cont'd*]   You'll never get a chance to do that again.

SUSAN   Don't tell me you're sorry.

KANE   I'm not sorry.

Dissolve

106 Int. Great Hall—Xanadu—Day—1932

Kane is at the window looking out. He turns as he hears Raymond enter.

RAYMOND   Mrs. Kane would like to see you, Mr. Kane.

KANE   All right.

Raymond waits as Kane hesitates

KANE [*Cont'd*]   Is Mrs. Kane—(*He can't finish*)

RAYMOND   Marie has been packing her since morning, Mr. Kane.

Kane impetuously walks past him out of the room

107 Int. Susan's Room—Xanadu—Day—1932

Packed suitcases are on the floor. Susan is completely dressed for traveling. Kane bursts into the room.

SUSAN   Tell Arnold I'm ready, Marie. He can get the bags.
MARIE   Yes, Mrs. Kane.

She leaves. Kane closes the door behind her

KANE   Have you gone completely crazy?

Susan looks at him

KANE [*Cont'd*]   Don't you realize that everybody here is going to know about this? That you've packed your bags and ordered the car and—
SUSAN   —And left? Of course they'll hear. I'm not saying good-bye—except to you—but I never imagined that people wouldn't know.

Kane is standing against the door as if physically barring her way

KANE   I won't let you go.
SUSAN (*reaches out her hand*)   Good-bye, Charlie.
KANE (*suddenly*)   Don't go, Susan.

Susan just looks at him

KANE [*Cont'd*]   Susan, don't go! Susan, please!

He has lost all pride. Susan stops. She is affected by this

KANE [*Cont'd*]   You mustn't go, Susan. Everything'll be exactly the way you want it. Not the way *I* think you want it—but your way. Please, Susan—Susan!

She is staring at him. She might weaken

KANE [*Cont'd*]   Don't go, Susan! You mustn't go! (*Almost blubbering*) You—you can't do this to me, Susan—

It's as if he had thrown ice water into her face. She freezes

SUSAN   I see—it's *you* that this is being done to! It's not me at all. Not how I feel. Not what it means to me. Not—(*She laughs*) I can't do this to *you!* (*She looks at him*) Oh yes I can.

She walks out, past Kane, who turns to watch her go, like a very tired old man

Dissolve

108 Int. "El Rancho" Cabaret—Night—1940

Susan and Thompson at table. There is silence between them for a moment as she accepts a cigarette from Thompson and he lights it for her.

SUSAN In case you've never heard of how I lost all my money—and it was plenty, believe me—
THOMPSON The last ten years have been tough on a lot of people—
SUSAN Aw, they haven't been tough on me. I just lost my money— (*Takes a deep puff*) So you're going down to Xanadu.
THOMPSON Monday, with some of the boys from the office. Mr. Rawlston wants the whole place photographed carefully—all that art stuff. We run a picture magazine, you know—
SUSAN Yeah, I know. If you're smart, you'll talk to Raymond—(*Nervously douses out the cigarette*) That's the butler. You can learn a lot from him. He knows where the bodies are buried.

She grabs a glass and holds it tensely in both hands

THOMPSON You know, all the same I feel kind of sorry for Mr. Kane.
SUSAN (*Harshly*) Don't you think I do?

She lifts the glass, and as she drinks it she notices the dawn light coming through the skylight. She shivers and pulls her coat over her shoulders

SUSAN [*Cont'd*] Well, what do you know? It's morning already. (*Looks at him for a moment*) You must come around and tell me the story of your life sometime.

Dissolve Out

Dissolve In

109 Ext. Xanadu—Late Dusk—1940

The distant castle on the hill, seen through the great iron "K" as in the opening shot of the picture. Several lights are on.

Dissolve

110 Int. Great Hall—Xanadu—Late Dusk—1940

Camera is in close on Thompson and Raymond—will subsequently reveal surrounding scene.

RAYMOND Rosebud? I'll tell you about Rosebud—how much is it worth to you? A thousand dollars?
THOMPSON Okay.
RAYMOND He was a little gone in the head sometimes, you know.
THOMPSON No, I didn't.
RAYMOND He did crazy things sometimes—I've been working for him eleven years now—the last years of his life and I ought to know. Yes, sir, the old man was kind of queer, but I knew how to handle him.

THOMPSON   Need a lot of service?
RAYMOND   Yeah. But I knew how to handle him.

Dissolve Out

Dissolve In

111 Int. Corridor and Telegraph Office—Xanadu—Night—1932

Raymond walking rapidly along corridor. He pushes open a door. At a desk sits a wireless operator. Near him at a telephone switchboard sits a female operator.

RAYMOND (*Reading*)   Mr. Charles Foster Kane announced today that Mrs. Charles Foster Kane has left Xanadu, his Florida home, under the terms of a peaceful and friendly agreement with the intention of filing suit for divorce at an early date. Mrs. Kane said that she does not intend to return to the operatic career which she gave up a few years after her marriage, at Mr. Kane's request. Signed, Charles Foster Kane.

Fred finishes typing and then looks up

RAYMOND [*Cont'd*]   Exclusive for immediate transmission. Urgent priority all Kane Papers.
FRED   Okay.

There is the sound of the buzzer on the switchboard

KATHERINE   Yes . . . Yes . . . Mrs. Tinsdall. Very well. (*Turns to Raymond*) It's the housekeeper.
RAYMOND   Yes?
KATHERINE   She says there's some sort of disturbance up in Miss Alexander's room. She's afraid to go in.

Dissolve Out

112 Int. Corridor Outside Susan's Bedroom—Xanadu—Night—1932

The housekeeper, Mrs. Tinsdall, and a couple of maids are near the door but too afraid to be in front of it. From inside can be heard a terrible banging and crashing. Raymond hurries into scene, opens the door, and goes in.

113 Int. Susan's Bedroom—Xanadu—1932

Kane, in a truly terrible and absolutely silent rage, is literally breaking up the room—yanking pictures, hooks and all off the wall, smashing them to bits—ugly, gaudy pictures—Susie's pictures in Susie's bad taste. Off of tabletops, off of dressing tables, occasional tables, bureaus, he sweeps Susie's whorish accumulation of bric-a-brac.
  Raymond stands in the doorway watching him. Kane says nothing. He continues with tremendous speed and surprising strength, still wordlessly, tearing the room to bits. The curtains (too frilly—overly pretty) are pulled off the windows in a single gesture, and from the bookshelves he pulls down double armloads of

cheap novels—discovers a half-empty bottle of liquor and dashes it across the room. Finally he stops. Susie's cozy little chamber is an incredible shambles all around him. He stands for a minute breathing heavily, and his eye lights on a hanging whatnot in a corner which had escaped his notice. Prominent on its center shelf is the little glass ball with the snowstorm in it. He yanks it down. Something made of china breaks, but not the glass ball, It bounces on the carpet and rolls to his feet, the snow in a flurry. His eye follows it. He stoops to pick it up—can't make it. Raymond picks it up for him; hands it to him. Kane takes it sheepishly—looks at it—moves painfully out of the room into the corridor.

114 Int. Corridor Outside Susan's Bedroom—Xanadu—1932

Kane comes out of the door. Mrs. Tinsdall has been joined now by a fairly sizable turnout of servants. They move back away from Kane, staring at him. Raymond is in the doorway behind Kane. Kane still looks at the glass ball.

KANE (*without turning*)   Close the door, Raymond.
RAYMOND   Yes, sir. (*Closes it*)
KANE   Lock it—and keep it locked.

Raymond locks the door and comes to his side. There is a long pause—servants staring in silence. Kane gives the glass ball a gentle shake and starts another snowstorm

KANE (*almost in a trance*)   Rosebud.
RAYMOND   What's that, sir?

One of the younger servants giggles and is hushed up. Kane shakes the ball again. Another flurry of snow. He watches the flakes settle—then looks up. Finally, taking in the pack of servants and something of the situation, he puts the glass ball in his coat pocket. He speaks very quietly to Raymond, so quietly it only seems he's talking to himself

KANE   Keep it locked.

He slowly walks off down the corridor, the servants giving way to let him pass, and watching him as he goes. The mirrors which line the hall reflect his image as he moves. He is an old, old man!

Kane turns into a second corridor—sees himself reflected in the mirror—stops. His image is reflected again in the mirror behind him—multiplied again and again and again in long perspectives—Kane looks. We see a thousand Kanes

Dissolve

115 Int. Great Hall—Xanadu—Night—1940

Thompson and Raymond.

RAYMOND (*callously*)   That's the whole works, right up to date.
THOMPSON   Sentimental fellow, aren't you?
RAYMOND   Yes and no.
THOMPSON   And that's what you know about Rosebud?

RAYMOND That's more than anybody knows. I tell you, he was a little gone in the head—the last couple of years anyway—but I knew how to handle him. That Rosebud—I heard him say it that other time too. He just said Rosebud, then he dropped that glass ball and it broke on the floor. He didn't say anything after that, so I knew he was dead. He said all kinds of things that didn't mean anything.

THOMPSON That isn't worth anything.

RAYMOND You can go on asking questions if you want to.

THOMPSON (*coldly*) We're leaving tonight. As soon as they're through photo-graphing the stuff—

Thompson has risen. Raymond gets to his feet

RAYMOND Allow yourself plenty of time. The train stops at the junction on sig-nal—but they don't like to wait. Not now. I can remember when they'd wait all day . . . if Mr. Kane said so.

Camera has pulled back to show long shot of the great hall, revealing the magnif-icent tapestries, candelabra, etc., are still there, but now several large packing cases are piled against the walls, some broken open, some shut, and a number of objects, great and small, are piled pell-mell all over the place. Furniture, statues, paintings, bric-a-brac—things of obviously enormous value are standing beside a kitchen stove, an old rocking chair and other junk, among which is also an old sled, the self-same story.

In the center of the hall a photographer and his assistant are busy photographing the sundry objects. In addition there are a girl and two newspapermen—also Thompson and Raymond.

The girl and the second man, who wears a hat, are dancing somewhere in the back of the hall to the music of a phonograph playing "Oh, Mr. Kane!"

116 Int. Great Hall—Xanadu—Night—1940

The photographer has just photographed a picture, obviously of great value, an Italian primitive. The assistant consults a label on the back of it.

ASSISTANT No. 9182.

The third newspaperman jots this information down

ASSISTANT [*Cont'd*] *Nativity*—attributed to Donatello, acquired Florence, 1921, cost: 45,000 lire. Got that?

THIRD NEWSPAPERMAN Yeh.

PHOTOGRAPHER All right! Next! Better get that statue over there.

ASSISTANT Okay.

RAYMOND What do you think all this is worth, Mr. Thompson?

THOMPSON Millions—if anybody wants it.

RAYMOND The banks are out of luck, eh?

THOMPSON Oh, I don't know. They'll clear all right.

ASSISTANT *Venus,* fourth century. Acquired 1911. Cost: twenty-three thousand. Got it?

THIRD NEWSPAPERMAN Okay.

ASSISTANT (*patting the statue on the fanny*) That's a lot of money to pay for a dame without a head.

SECOND ASSISTANT (*reading a label*) No. 483. One desk from the estate of Mary Kane, Little Salem, Colorado. Value: $6.00. We're supposed to get everything. The junk as well as the art.

THIRD NEWSPAPERMAN Okay.

A flashlight bulb goes off. Thompson has opened a box and is idly playing with a handful of little pieces of cardboard

THIRD NEWSPAPERMAN [*Cont'd*] What's that?

RAYMOND It's a jigsaw puzzle.

THIRD NEWSPAPERMAN We got a lot of those. There's a Burmese temple and three Spanish ceilings down the hall.

Raymond laughs

PHOTOGRAPHER Yeh, all in crates.

THIRD NEWSPAPERMAN There's a part of a Scotch castle over there, but we haven't bothered to unwrap it.

PHOTOGRAPHER I wonder how they put all those pieces together?

ASSISTANT (*reading a label*) Iron stove. Estate of Mary Kane. Value: $2.00.

PHOTOGRAPHER Put it over by that statue. It'll make a good setup.

GIRL (*calling out*) Who is she anyway?

SECOND NEWSPAPERMAN Venus. She always is.

THIRD NEWSPAPERMAN He sure liked to collect things, didn't he?

PHOTOGRAPHER Anything and everything—he was a regular crow.

THIRD NEWSPAPERMAN I wonder—You put all this together—the palaces and the paintings and the toys and everything—what would it spell?

Thompson has turned around. He is facing the camera for the first time

THOMPSON Charles Foster Kane.

PHOTOGRAPHER Or Rosebud? How about it, Jerry?

THIRD NEWSPAPERMAN (*to the dancers*) Turn that thing off, will you? It's driving me nuts!—What's Rosebud?

PHOTOGRAPHER Kane's last words, aren't they, Jerry? (*To the third newspaperman*) That was Jerry's angle, wasn't it. Did you ever find out what it means?

THOMPSON No, I didn't.

The music has stopped. The dancers have come over to Thompson

SECOND NEWSPAPERMAN Say, what did you find out about him anyway?

THOMPSON Not much.

SECOND NEWSPAPERMAN Well, what have you been doing?

THOMPSON Playing with a jigsaw puzzle—I talked to a lot of people who knew him.

GIRL What do they say?

THOMPSON   Well—it's become a very clear picture. He was the most honest man who ever lived, with a streak of crookedness a yard wide. He was a liberal and a reactionary. He was a loving husband—and both his wives left him. He had a gift for friendship such as few men have—and he broke his oldest friend's heart like you'd throw away a cigarette you were through with. Outside of that—

THIRD NEWSPAPERMAN   Okay, okay.

GIRL   If you could have found out what that Rosebud meant, I bet that would've explained everything.

THOMPSON   No, I don't. Not much anyway. Charles Foster Kane was a man who got everything he wanted, and then lost it. Maybe Rosebud was something he couldn't get or something he lost, but it wouldn't have explained anything. I don't think any word explains a man's life. No—I guess Rosebud is just a piece in a jigsaw puzzle—a missing piece.

He drops the jigsaw pieces back into the box, looking at his watch

THOMPSON [*Cont'd*]   We'd better get along. We'll miss the train.

He picks up his overcoat—it has been resting on a little sled—the little sled young Charles Foster Kane hit Thatcher with at the opening of the picture. Camera doesn't close in on this. It just registers the sled as the newspaper people, picking up their clothes and equipment, move out of the great hall

Dissolve Out

Dissolve In

117 Int. Cellar—Xanadu—Night—1940

A large furnace, with an open door, dominates the scene. Two laborers, with shovels, are shoveling things into the furnace. Raymond is about ten feet away.

RAYMOND   Throw that junk in, too.

Camera travels to the pile that he has indicated. It is mostly bits of broken packing cases, excelsior, etc. The sled is on top of the pile. As camera comes close, it shows the faded rosebud and, through the letters are faded, unmistakably the word "Rosebud" across it. The laborer drops his shovel, takes the sled in his hand and throws it into the furnace. The flames start to devour it.

118 Ext. Xanadu—Night—1940

No lights are to be seen. Smoke is coming from a chimney. Camera reverses the path it took at the beginning of the picture, perhaps omitting some of the stages. It moves finally through the gates, which close behind it. As camera pauses for a moment, the letter "K" is prominent in the moonlight.

Just before we fade out, there comes again into the picture the pattern of barbed wire and cyclone fencing. On the fence is a sign which reads:

PRIVATE—NO TRESPASSING

Fade Out

Appendix: Writing on Writing

Writing on Writing

1. General advice

One way to learn about anything is to write about it. Thus it is important in studying literature to test our experience of literature by writing essays that explain or argue or compare or describe or discover or evaluate. Writing a paper we clarify our ideas to ourselves, explain to ourselves how we arrive at judgment. If our goal in studying literature is to arrive at sound taste and just discrimination, the purpose of paper-writing is to examine and clarify the means by which we arrive at judgment.

For general advice, there is none better at the start than *use your intelligence.* Many people beginning to write about literature feel that they should show themselves responding ("I cried when I finished this story") instead of applying their brains and looking closely at the words in front of them. Second, *be forthright* in stating an opinion; we learn by making a thesis and defending it, even if later we discover that we have erred. A noncommital paper usually has less to say than a paper that is vigorous but mistaken. Third, while writing and revising a paper, continually *question whether it serves the work* written about. Do not digress into subjects that lead away from the work itself. Writing about Richard Wilbur's short story "A Game of Catch," one student departed from the story to talk about problems of growing up as a boy in the suburbs; writing about Molière's *Tartuffe,* another made a spirited defense of the church's role in history; writing about Theodore Roethke's poem "Orchids," another displayed only botanic research into the flower. None of these students served the literary work itself, but something else the work suggested.

A. Ways of writing about writing

1. Concentration on the text

Most teachers, when they assign papers, ask their students to concentrate on the texts themselves—not on the lives of the authors, or the authors' historical eras, or the context of literary history or influence. Most assignments ask for an explication, an analysis, or a comparison and contrast.

a. Explication

The word *explication* originally means "unfolding." When we explicate a literary work we unfold its intricate layers of theme and form, showing its construction as if we spread it out upon a table. We use the tool of explication to explain work that is dense and concentrated, taking it word by word or line by line. Some passages of fiction and drama lend themselves to explication also: one speech of Hamlet may reflect in miniature the complexity of the whole play; or a paragraph of Flannery O'Connor may illuminate the author's methods of characterization. Most often, we explicate a brief poem or a portion of a longer poem—literature at its most concentrated. Remember that the goal of explication is not merely close paraphrase of theme or content. Pay attention not only to the meanings of words but also to rhythm, sound, tone, point of view, symbolism, and form. Explication's goal is to lay out in critical prose everything that the author has done in a brief passage or short poem; the best explication goes the furthest toward that goal.

Explication does not concern itself with the author's life or times; it treats the work of art almost as if it were anonymous. The author's historical period, however, may determine the definitions of words. If the work is a century or more old, some of its words will have changed in their meanings. Because the explicator's task is to make explicit what the author *may* have put into the work—not assuming conscious intentions, but aware of possibilities—the explicator must keep in mind the time when the work was written and the altering definitions of words. Thus when an eighteenth-century writer like Alexander Pope speaks of "science," we must notice that the word meant something like "general knowledge" and not that branch of knowledge we study as chemistry, physics, and biology. In order to determine the meaning of a word in a particular era, it is useful to consult the *Oxford English Dictionary* (see page 403).

Use common sense when explicating. It is tempting to go too far, to follow particular words down rabbit holes into Wonderland, using ingenuity more than intelligence. One student explicated a couplet of Robert Frost:

> The old dog barks backward without getting up.
> I can remember when he was a pup.

Desperate to write four hundred words about two lines—having chosen the wrong poem to write four hundred words about—the student noticed that Frost had elsewhere written about Sirius the Dog Star, and that *dog* was "God" spelled backward, and wrote four hundred words to confuse astrology and theology into a pair of lines about aging and the passage of time. The general advice must govern the explicator as well as all other critics: write so that you make sense of the whole work considered; do not entertain fascinating improbabilities.

A student's explication of a poem is printed in "Writing about Poems," pages 1471–1473, and "To Read a Poem" begins with a chapter explicating poems by Robert Frost and William Carlos Williams.

b. Analysis

To analyze something is to separate it into parts in order to understand it. Explication deals exhaustively with something small; analysis deals with a part of something—perhaps the use of offstage noises throughout Chekhov's *The Cherry Orchard* or the repetition of certain phrases in D. H. Lawrence's "The Rocking Horse Winner" or Robert Frost's characterization in "The Death of the Hired Man." Attending to one part of a play, story, or poem, the analyst must relate that part to the work as a whole. In analysis we thus use summary or paraphrase to establish the whole of which we analyze a part. If an analysis fails to relate part to whole, the paper will seem pointless. We want to know not only that the poet repeats the word *blue* twenty-seven times in thirty-nine lines but as well what this repetition accomplishes in the poem.

When we write about literary works of any length, analysis allows us to limit our topic. Never try to analyze a whole long work, any more than you would try to explicate a whole long work. Find ways to limit your topic by analysis—by the isolation of parts. No one can write a decent six-hundred-word theme on the whole of *The Death of Ivan Ilych*. Nor would an analysis of the characterization in that short novel be possible unless we wrote several thousand words. Analysis discovers part within part. It would be possible to analyze the characterization of Gerasim and relate Gerasim's character to the rest of the story.

When we consider writing an analytical paper, we begin by thinking analytically about what we have read. Perhaps we have read Flannery O'Connor's "A Good Man Is Hard to Find" and find ourselves fascinated and horrified by the character of The Misfit. Thinking analytically, we can separate the many ways in which we learned about The Misfit: we learn of him by his actions as reported by others; we learn of him by implication, through the responses of other people to him; we learn of him through his own speech; we learn of him by his actions as we watch him. As an example, we might find a disparity between our expectations before we meet him and the character we meet. We might write a paper that analyzes "The Misfit: Rumor and Reality." Looking at several poems by Robert Frost, fascinated by "Design" with its white flower that should have been blue, we might analyze "Color in Three Poems by Robert Frost."

For an analytical paper to hold together, it will assert and defend a *thesis* that can usually be reduced to a single sentence. A thesis is not the same as a topic. While the topic might be Gerasim's characterization, the thesis would make a statement about it, generally summarizing the relationship of analyzed part to story as a whole: "The character of Gerasim, as presented in his actions and dialogue by the author, relieves the dying Ivan Ilych by simple goodness." "For Robert Frost, in these poems, color disguises reality and suggests a malignancy of matter or maker." "Showing The Misfit from afar and up close, Flannery O'Connor indicates the difference between a public terror and a private one."

When beginning an analytic paper, we move from the general to the particular, then to the more particular, a series of concentric circles; the biggest circle is the work itself, *The Death of Ivan Ilych;* then the topic narrows but remains broad: characterization, and the relation of character to theme; then it narrows to Gerasim's character and its function in the story.

A student's analysis appears in "A Paper from Start to Finish," pages 1464–1468.

c. Comparison and Contrast

A third kind of paper is the comparison and contrast of two texts, usually in connection with a specific theme, a formal device, or a technical element of the genre. A teacher might invite a comparison of Shakespeare's use of the sonnet form with Robert Frost's, for instance. (When we compare two objects, we make notes of likeness and unlikeness; henceforth we will speak only of comparing, implying contrast.) Or a teacher might ask for a comparison of two short stories in their symbolism, or of two plays in their use of flashback. The process of comparison requires analysis of each work, with notice of similarities and differences in the matters analyzed.

Structure can be a problem in writing comparison and contrast. Here is a passage from a student's draft:

> In the sonnet by Shakespeare every four lines is a whole separate idea, then the last two lines is another unit that is complete to itself. In Milton's the first part is eight lines and the second is six, without further subdivision. Shakespeare's rhyming separates the parts, not just the ideas. Milton's rhyming is more difficult, using just two rhymes in the octave (ABBAABBA) but therefore making the eight lines a smooth whole. Shakespeare . . .

These rapid oscillations are nervous; the reader's head snaps back and forth, as if watching a ping-pong game; after a while we forget which poet is which, and who has the serve.

To be subjects for comparison and contrast, two works must share common ground. We would lack the basis to compare, say, a Keats poem with a Tolstoy novel, or a play with a sonnet sequence. Usually we compare works within the same genre, of similar length and quality. There are exceptions: sometimes we compare two works by one author in different genres, perhaps a play and a short story by Chekhov. Sometimes we compare good and bad to illuminate criteria for judgment. Sometimes we compare long and short, or genre with genre, to reveal strengths and weaknesses of different shapes and genres.

Mostly, we find the differences between two works with obvious similarities: the two sonnets are each fourteen lines long, each within iambic pentameter, each rhymed throughout—and then the differences begin: structure of thought, rhyme, rhythm, metaphor, diction. One paper might end by asserting that despite all the differences between them these two sonnets will share many qualities. Another might with equal justice argue that the differences outweighed the similarities. The conclusions will supply the writers' theses.

In a short paper of comparison, a writer may be able to write a paragraph or two of similarities, a paragraph or two of dissimilarities, and reach a conclusion in the final paragraph. But such simplicity of structure is rare. More likely, we will need to make a structure something like this:

1. Statement of comparability
2. First similarity
   Work A
   Work B
3. Second similarity
   Work A
   Work B
4. First dissimilarity
   Work A
   Work B
5. Second dissimilarity
   Work A
   Work B
6. Conclusion based on evidence: thesis

Sometimes the grammar of the complex sentence can avoid the ping-pong monotony of compounds that flick our heads and back and forth on our necks. Instead of saying "Work A is seven chapters which makes 110 pages and Work B is nine chapters which makes 131 pages," we can sound more various: "While Work A compacts its seven chapters into 110 pages, Work B finds 131 pages sufficient for its nine."

A different structure takes a topic and then looks at each work two ways:

First item (like the use of a symbolic protagonist)
   Similarities between Works A and B
   Dissimilarities between Works A and B
Second item (like the means used for indicating symbolism)
   Similarities between Works A and B
   Dissimilarities between Works A and B

The material we collect for a paper determines its best form. Always decide on a thesis before writing. If we start writing in the sweet hope that a thesis will solidify from the air of our prose, we write a disorganized paper.

3. Concentration on Context

Sometimes in studying literature, and in writing papers about it, we concentrate not so much on the text as on the context of the work of art—the historical, personal, or literary backgrounds out of which the work came. This kind of criticism usually suggests cause and effect. We argue that the work has characteristics that derive from causes or sources in the author's society, personal life, or reading. To establish these characteristics the critic must usually analyze or explicate; but then, having described these characteristics, the writer will shift emphasis from text to context.

a. History and Society

Whatever we do, we express the times we live in. When authors write, they reflect their own era by deploring it, by celebrating it, or even by writing to escape it. Social criticism sometimes supports philosophical positions. Some critics find literary form and content dominated and determined by economics; this criticism draws a line of causation from economic force to literary result. Other social criticism relates literature to theories of nationality and national history. Often the social or historical critic tries to illuminate meaning by understanding the social and historical conditions under which older work was written, helping the modern reader to understand how it seemed to its contemporaries. When we read ancient literature, we would be ignorant if we identified a queen as a figure resembling Queen Elizabeth II. Historical information can supply us with some notion of what it meant for Oedipus to be a king and for the somewhat different thing it meant for Hamlet's father and Hamlet's uncle to be kings.

Because this sort of criticism requires historical knowledge, a student writing about the historical sources of a text must do research. In the library we can find what critics and historians have discovered about the relationship of Greek society to Greek drama or of Elizabethan culture to the sonnet sequence. Often we can find books that give backgrounds to different literary periods, setting forth the dominating philosophical, political, and religious ideas of an era. Basil Willy's *Eighteenth Century Background* is an example.

We need not write about remote times when we write social or historical papers. Donald Barthelme's "The Indian Uprising" appeared at the height of the Vietnam war; a paper could investigate and illuminate the connection between Barthelme's fantasy and the war itself. Or, receding just a little further in time, a student could connect some poems by William Butler Yeats with the political situation of Yeats's Ireland by reading in the history of modern Ireland.

b. Biography

If a work of art cannot help but reflect its era, equally it cannot help but reflect the life of the man or woman who wrote it.

This statement is easy enough to make, but it is often difficult to demonstrate the connection between life and work. Things are subtler than they seem. For instance, a poet may speak of himself overtly—Yeats wrote the line "I, the poet William Yeats . . ."—yet make statements that are not historically true. If we take the poet's word, we are often deceived. Writers frequently make up a self to speak from, and make great literature out of this fabrication. Walt Whitman constructed a character called "Walt Whitman" who was rough, manly, vigorous brave, noisy; apparently the man himself was shy, and when he read his poems aloud spoke so softly that no one could hear him past the first row. On the other hand, T. S. Eliot proclaimed the impersonality of the artist, said that literature was a flight from personality, and proclaimed these doctrines when he had written "The Waste Land," which critics have begun to understand as the most personal of poems. By noticing disparities between the poets' proclamations and realities we begin to investigate the biographical context.

The student who undertakes biographical criticism should therefore take warning. Perhaps no other approach to literature requires more sophistication. Like historical criticism it requires research as well as subtlety, psychological acumen, and modesty. The last quality may be the most urgent; we may suspect a biographical connection and suggest it by inference, but we seldom *know*. We know only the obvious: reading a biography of Joseph Conrad, we can derive his writing about the sea from his experience as a sailor; but if we derive his ideas of evil from a childhood experience, we must be very careful.

c. The Literary History

If a literary work is a big river, we know the names of many of the tributaries that go to form it. There is the language an author grows up among, the common speech; there are the politics, economics, and social structure of an author's historical period and social class; there are an author's personal psyche, upbringing, relationships with parents and siblings, even inheritance of characteristics. Another large tributary is the literature that the author has learned from.

Everything a writer has read—like everything that has happened in the life—can contribute to the work done. As athletes learn their moves from watching other athletes, as a guitar player learns chords from another musician, writers learn their craft from observing, analyzing, and loving earlier literary work. For this reason literature has a history, a sequence if not a progress. Progress would imply that literature was getting better all the time, a proposition difficult to support.

To write a paper in literary history, the critic must know earlier literature. Reading Conan Doyle's short stories about Sherlock Holmes, we may look for the influence of Edgar Allan Poe, who in "The Murders in the Rue Morgue" and other stories invented the modern detective story. Looking at Shaw's *Saint Joan,* hearing Shaw described as a follower of Ibsen, we may try to discover what the younger playwright learned from the elder. Sometimes we do the same thing in reverse; focusing on Ibsen, we write about his influence on playwrights who followed him.

Although we have separated these approaches to literature's context in order to describe them, they are not mutually exclusive. To write about influence on Keats, we read his letters and consult his biographers. We need to use explication and analysis, within the historical or biographical or literary methods, to establish claims about the text discussed. It is most important to know what we are doing when we are doing it, and not to confuse our methods.

3. Common Pitfalls in Writing about Literature

A few common errors of method occur again and again.

a. The Personal Error

Many of the pitfalls that threaten us when we write about literature take one shape: we do not regard the work itself or its context, but some irrelevant matter from the outside. One of the most frequent irrelevancies is our personal histories and beliefs.

To write a theme about one's personal experience can be a fine thing, but such a theme is *not* about literature. Perhaps because it seems easier to write out of personal experience, many people fall into the personal error. Taking the subject of D. H. Lawrence's "The Rocking Horse Winner," they tell about their own experience as a child with a rocking horse. Writing about Robert Frost's "Stopping by Woods on a Snowy Evening," they confide that they respond to this poem with special pleasure because they are are so fond of horses. Writing about Tom Stoppard's *Rosencrantz and Guildenstern Are Dead,* they describe their experience of acting *Hamlet* in high school and what the local newspaper said in its review.

Even without personal narrative, there is danger of sanctifying personal response. It is a commonly held notion in the modern world that one person's opinion is as good as anybody else's. The defense of misreading is usually a smug "That is how *I* see it, and everyone is entitled to their own opinion." Democratic and egalitarian as the idea appears, it is an idea we hold to only so long as it conveniences us. The same student who holds that his opinion of Plato is as worthy as his philosophy professor's is unlikely to consider his professor's opinion of automobile repair as good as his own. Although there are many possible ways to understand a piece of literature, it is demonstrable that some interpretations are wrong; the text denies them. No one should go to jail for having a wrong opinion—but *opinions can be wrong.* Literature is not a series of cloud shapes into which we can imagine all sorts of castles. Be governed by the text. Learn to submit to the text, to test all ideas and interpretations to the scrutiny of the text, and discard ideas that do not fit. This attitude requires humility before the fact of literature and expels or denies that conceit which says "Whatever *I* discover in the text is right for *me.*" There is more of I/me in such reading than there is of literature.

b. The Historical Error

A less egotistical fallacy equally an impediment to good reading is the biographical and historical error that looks past an imaginary work to find events in the author's life or times of which the work is a representation or to which it responds. This error uses the text as a pretext for discourse, not about the work of art but about history or biography. I do not mean to attack the good criticism that legitimately connects the work and the life, and the work to the times. Too often, readers pick on some portion of a story or a poem or a play, trust it as a piece of reality, and run away from literature to speak of history or biography. Yeats's poem "The Second Coming" (page 603) speaks of a time of chaos and turbulence, when "the center does not hold. / Mere anarchy is loosed upon the world. . . ." One student, noticing Yeats's dates (1865–1939) decided that Yeats was referring to the Great War of 1914–1918, and wrote:

> As Yeats predicted, the great empires came apart, the German and especially the Austro-Hungarian, but really it was not "mere anarchy" because out of parts of these empires Czechoslovakia was created, and the Treaty of Versailles which followed the war determined exactly who had authority over what territory. It is true that the League of Nations . . .

Here the historical error has run away with the paper, and the student has taken a few lines from the poem as a text for a summary of world history. Information is used not to illuminate the poem but to escape from it. As a matter of fact, this poem was written after World War I at the time of the Civil War in Ireland.

A similar error, biographical rather than historical, hurt a student's paper on Tillie Olsen's "I Stand Here Ironing." In the story, a mother ruminates about a daughter, the mother a single parent who had lived through the Depression of the thirties. In a biographical note before the story, the student learned that Tillie Olsen was of an age to live through the thirties, that she had children, that she had been divorced. The student wrote:

> Tillie Olsen thinks these thoughts as she is ironing, remembering how her husband left her and she brought up her daughter and other kids by herself. Probably the sad experiences led her to becoming a writer, because she had so much to say about single parenting . . .

This student confuses the *I* of the short story with the author who wrote it, confuses the art of fiction with the facts of biography. It is tempting to make such a mishmash, when what we know of an author fits with the author's work—but we must avoid it. Our uninformed guesses are as likely to be wrong as right. When a writer undertakes a work, some of the material doubtless comes from the author's experience and observation, as true as a photograph or a verbatim account; and doubtless some of the material is imagined, made up in the services of a truth-telling broader than representation. For the most part, we cannot determine what is imagined and what is reported, and it does not matter. Our job as readers is not to determine the one from the other but to read the whole as a work of art.

c. The Error of Influence

The error of influence blights some papers in literary history. There is a logical fallacy for which there is a Latin phrase, *post hoc ergo propter hoc:* "after the fact, therefore on account of the fact," describing the human tendency to mistake sequence for cause and effect. Many poor themes assume an influence on tenuous evidence. But even when the influence is genuine, it is not always important. It may be useful to notice that Hemingway's prose style derives from earlier authors, or to claim that without Ibsen's realistic theater we would not have the different, realistic theater of George Bernard Shaw. In each case the causes are clear and the effects significant. But it does not follow that every literary phenomenon can usefully be discussed in terms of literary genealogy. Walt Whitman's style was a shock to the literary world it assaulted. We have learned that it derives partly from old Hebrew poetry translated by the scholars of the King James version of the Bible. Yet for the most part Whitman's style remains Whitman's invention. Anyone asserting literary influence ought to ask the question: If what I assert is true, what of it? It seems true enough, for instance, that the style of D. H. Lawrence's poetry altered after he had read Walt Whitman . . . but what of it? One student, noticing not only the influence but the background suggested by Whitman's style, came up with a notion of connection:

> Lawrence's rhythm and his use of parallel constructions changed only after he had studied Whitman in order to write his celebrated essay upon him. Such a fact, true enough, is merely a detail of influence. Whitman's rhythms apparently unleashed something in Lawrence, but what did they unleash? I want to suggest a connection which I cannot demonstrate. We know that much of Whitman's grammar, and therefore rhythm, came from the translations of Hebrew poetry, in its parallel syntactic structures, as rendered by the King James translators of the seventeenth century. We know from Lawrence's fiction and essays that he grew up listening to Bible readings and biblical oratory. Especially in his late work about the Book of Revelation, he reveals how essential to his emotional youth were the accents of prophecy. I suggest that Whitman affected Lawrence's poetry by way of the Bible. Whitman's rhythms showed Lawrence how to tap a source of feeling in himself.

Notice that this student takes a subject which has a factual base, and that he uses biographical information and inference. We know that Lawrence read Whitman with great attention because Lawrence wrote a famous essay about him. Sometimes, influence-hunters have argued the influence of X on Y where it has been virtually certain that Y was wholly unaware of X, or could not possibly have read more than a story or two. Even more embarrassing, on occasion a critic has described the influence of A on B—when B died before A was born.

4. Reading the Critics

If students are asked to write about history, biography, or literary influence, they are expected to use the library, to read historians, biographers, critics, and scholars.

Here we must address a question: If we explicate or analyze only—not requiring background information—how much do we use the library, how much do we refer to critics who have published analyses and explications of the works we write about?

Some teachers find it useful to ask their students to check out the critics, to test their own notions against the published work of professionals. Other teachers ask their students *not* to consult critics; some even forbid the practice. Many teachers feel that reading professional criticism inhibits their students and keeps them from developing their own ideas, from making mistakes and learning to correct their mistakes, from finding their own ways to evaluate and interpret. With an exaggerated respect for the printed word, these teachers argue, students become passive when they read critics; they assume that published work must be correct and parrot it back in their own papers. On the other hand, students doing their own work without help or interference from professional critics, knowing that fellow students also work alone, do their best work.

B. Writing the theme

1. Before Writing: Getting Ideas

Whether the topic is assigned or free, we need to gather ideas as the first stage of the paper-writing process, long before beginning a first draft.

Generally we will know which works we are to write about. If we have a choice, we should pick the work that fascinates us most, even if we feel we do not understand it thoroughly. It is a deadly mistake to pick something uninteresting because we think it is simple or easy. If we are not interested we will never write well about it. The story, poem, or play chosen, we must then undertake a series of thorough readings, pencil in hand. If the book is our own, we can write in the margins or underline. (If the book belongs to a library or someone else, do not make a mark on it.) Some notes will spill over the page, and we should keep a notebook beside the chair we read in. At first, we should not look for anything in particular, but take note of everything that strikes us— a pun, a piece of wit, a gesture that makes character, a rhyme, an ambiguity, a curious tone, a word to look up, a striking image, a puzzling repetition. We should make note not only of what we enjoy but of what puzzles or annoys us. We should read aggressively, demanding of each word or sentence that it reveal its function and usefulness. We should note big and note little, note outside and inside. If a short story occurs entirely in dialogue, or without dialogue, we should not neglect the fact. If a poem is fourteen lines long, we should remember that it can be embarrassing to write five pages on a brief poem without having mentioned that it is a sonnet.

We should read, taking notes, for one long session, then put the theme out of our minds for a day before we return to read again. It is astonishing how much thinking we do when we do not know we are thinking.

The next stage is to assemble notes toward a conclusion. If we are writing an explication, we may use all the notes that continue to look sensible, that contribute to understanding and elucidating the meaning and form of the text. If we are writing analysis, we will need to narrow the topic, which will probably mean discarding many notes. Look for a topic large enough to be worth the time and effort, small enough to be handled in the space assigned. Analyzing the use of games in *Rosencrantz and Guildenstern Are Dead,* we can discard many notes on characterization, on the use of names, on parallels and divergences from Shakespeare's *Hamlet.*

2. Writing and Revising

Notes make a blueprint for constructing the paper. It helps to make an informal outline, a recognition of what needs to follow what in order to demonstrate a thesis. These notes can be numbered in a notebook, or transferred to three-by-five-inch cards and stacked in order, or cut from long sheets and piled in appropriate piles. Probably many notes will refer to pages and lines of the text, for the heart of literary criticism is intelligent quotation. No amount of good argument—about characterization in Chekhov, or dialogue in Katherine Anne Porter—will persuade the reader so much as the brief, accurate example. Any paper will need to assert a thesis, list occasions, and exemplify.

We should always try to spend at least one day away from our paper, between a draft and a revision. Revising, we should check for good, complete sentences, fresh language, logic, accurate quotation, and correct spelling. Revising, we should try for conciseness. We all use too many adjectives, and for that matter we may find that we can drop a whole paragraph here and there. If we leave big margins in typing a first draft, or type it triple-space, we will be grateful for the correcting space. Revising, we fill out paragraphs that remain thin; we find more reasons, more examples, and bolster our points. We examine the order of ideas, arguments, and examples.

3. Manuscript Form

Teachers sometimes require particular form for papers. In the absence of other directions, the notes that follow should serve in most circumstances.

a. Paper, Margins, etc.

Use 8½-by-11-inch-paper.

Type if you can, double space. Avoid erasable typing paper, which smudges. If you write by hand, use paper with deep lines, or write every other line on narrow-lined paper. Use only one side of a piece of paper.

Put your name, your teacher's name, class and section number, and date in the upper right-hand corner of your paper.

Leave margins of 1¼ inches at top, bottom, and sides. Always make a copy—a carbon or a photocopy—before you hand your paper in.

Number your pages.

Staple your pages together in the upper left-hand corner.

b. Titles

Underline the titles of books and plays (<u>The Old Man and the Sea</u>, <u>Hamlet</u>). Put quotation marks around titles of short stories ("A Worn Path") and poems shorter than book length ("Stopping by Woods on a Snowy Evening"). A book-length poem's title is underlined (<u>The Iliad</u>). Note that titles underlined in papers will be *italicized* in print.

c. Quotations

Use quotation marks around excerpts from literature that you quote within sentence and paragraph:

> When William Carlos Williams looked at a primitive piece of farm machinery, he saw something which he made important through the power of his seeing; he saw it "glazed with rain / water . . ." He saw it "beside the white / chickens . . ." But seeing was not the only sense the doctor . . .

(We use a / , when quoting a poem, to indicate a line break.) But when we separate a quotation from sentence and paragraph—indenting it and typing it single space—we do not use quotation marks because we have indicated quotation by the spacings of the typography:

> When William Carlos Williams looked at a primitive piece of farm machinery, he saw something important because of the power of his seeing:
>
> > glazed with rain
> > water
> >
> > beside the white
> > chickens
>
> But seeing was not the only sense that the doctor employed in making his poems. . . .

These two ways of quoting are appropriate to different lengths of quotation. When we are quoting only a few words, we include the quotation within the paragraph, and put quotation marks around it. When we quote more than a few words, we indent the quotation, single-space it, and omit quotation marks— except when the quoted passage itself has already used quotation marks.

d. Footnotes

When we clearly quote from the text under discussion, as in an explication, there is no point in footnoting.

Often we can note the source of a quotation, without a footnote, in the text of the paper: "About halfway through the fourth scene, Guildenstern says to Rosencrantz . . ." Or: "Not until the fifth line does Frost use an image of sight . . ." When we find it awkward to include such information in the flow of sentences, a parenthesis can be used: "Early in *Hamlet* (I, ii, 14–19), we discover that . . ." Sometimes it is easiest, if there is likely to be any confusion, simply to footnote a reference. Always be certain that the reader knows what he is reading.

When we quote or paraphrase from a critic, scholar, biographer, or historian—or even from the *Encyclopaedia Britannica—we must always footnote our sources.* If we take full notes when we read and remain scrupulous in noting the sources of our ideas or words, no one will ever accuse us of plagiarism; plagiarism is stealing, borrowing, or otherwise appropriating other people's ideas or sentences.

To quote from a book, copy the quotation accurately, put quotation marks around it, and put a number slightly higher than the line of words:[1]. Number sequentially throughout your paper; i.e., do not begin a new series of numbers on each page. Footnoting from a book, give this information in this order: author's name, book's title, edition number if any, city and publisher, date, and the number of the page quoted from. Here is one example:

[1]X. J. Kennedy, *Literature,* 2nd ed. (Boston: Little, Brown, 1979), pp. 1386–1387.

When quoting from a magazine article, use the volume number and date in place of the edition number, city, publisher, and date. Here is an example:

> [12]Howard Norman, "Dry Tomb," *Westigan Review,* vol. 3, no. 4 (Fall 1978), 10.

When we refer again, later in the paper, to a source quoted earlier, we can shorten the reference to the writer's name and give the different page number:

> Kennedy, 1385.

But if we refer to two different books by Kennedy, or poems by Norman, we would need to use full footnote form, and in further references distinguish between the two sources by quoting title as well as author.

e. Bibliography

When we have consulted books or magazines in order to write a paper, we should list everything consulted on a separate sheet at the end of the paper, in a *bibliography*. We should list material consulted even if we have not footnoted the source as a quote or a paraphrase. Arrange the list alphabetically by the author's last name. We list anonymous works alphabetically by title, using the first words after an article.

A book:

> Newman, Edwin. *Strictly Speaking.* New York: Warner Books, 1975.

An article in a book:

> Hamill, Pete. "The Language of the New Politics." In *Language in America.* Ed. Neil Postman, Charles Weingartner, and Terence P. Moran. New York: Pegasus, 1969.

An article in a magazine:

> Middleton, Christopher. "Notes on a Viking Prow," *PN Review,* 10, Vol. 6, No. 2, 6–8.

An anonymous article from an encyclopedia:

> "Geisha." *The Columbia Encyclopedia.* 1963.

C. A paper from start to finish

In a course introducing literature, an instructor assigned a paper on fiction, asking students to write on one of three stories: James Baldwin's "This Morning, This Evening, So Soon," Carson McCullers' "A Tree, A Rock, A Cloud," or Kurt Vonnegut, Jr.'s "Harrison Bergeron." A student named Ralph Giannello chose to write about "Harrison Bergeron." The assignment called for an analysis in five hundred words: find a topic, elaborate it into a thesis, and prove the thesis.

Ralph liked the story, but at first had no notion of what to say about it. He reread the story, making checks in the margin when something caught his attention, not searching for a particular topic. Then he read it again, more slowly, and took notes in his notebook naming the points of interest. Here is the first page of notes he took:

> unusual name? Harrison President of U.S.? (Two)—Bergeron?
> 2081—sig. to date?
> "finally equal" first sentence starts theme of story?
> "equal" in first *three* sentences
> Handicapper—look up
> brains equal unfair advantage
> buzzer
> ballerinas with weights—horses—"handicap"
> milk bottle/hammer
> Diana Moon Glompers—?name
> gunfire
> 47 lbs bird shot
> all talk is clichés
> siren
> ANTI-UTOPIA
> Harrison's "handicaps," appearance
> auto-collision
> "I am the Emperor"? crazy?
> dance/music/art
> law-land/gravity
> suspended in air? fantasy?
> sadness/"forget sad things"
> rivetting gun
> say that again—old joke

When Ralph looked up "handicap," he confirmed his suspicion that the word meant first a forced or assumed disadvantage, as in a horse race; the dictionary listed "physical disability"—a meaning with which Ralph was more familiar— as secondary. In a horse race, he read, a horse may be handicapped by weights added to its saddle, making it equal to horses normally less swift.

Looking over his list, thinking of the story, Ralph decided that the author's topic was equality. "But"—he wrote in a note—"it's not equality like people being born with equal rights before the law. It's a kind of equality which makes everybody exactly the same. Not equal but average ability and achievement. Bright and beautiful handicapped down to average brains and average looks." He had noted that Vonnegut's story was an "anti-utopia," set in a future which exaggerated a social idea into a horrid reality.

Trying to formulate a thesis, Ralph wrote at the bottom of his notes, "Vonnegut imagines a future where everybody is forced to be average regardless of ability." True enough, he thought, but this thesis was obvious, uninteresting, and omitted much of the story. He tried again: "George and Helen Bergeron have a genius son named Harrison, driven crazy by . . ." He stopped, reminding himself that a thesis was not a plot summary.

He looked back over his notes. He drew lines through some of them, because they led nowhere, and put additional question marks where he was unsure. Then he put letters beside items that seemed to go together.

~~unusual name? Harrison President of U.S.? (Two)—Bergeron?~~

~~2081—sig. to date?~~

A "Finally equal" first sentence starts theme of story?

A "equal" in first *three* sentences

C Handicapper—look up

A brains equal unfair advantage

B buzzer

C ballerinas with weights—horses—"handicap"

B milk bottle/hammer

C Diana Moon Glompers—?name

B gunfire

C 47 lbs bird shot

D all talk is clichés

B siren

!!! ANTI-UTOPIA

C Harrison's "handicaps," appearance

B auto-collision

~~E "I am the Emperor"? crazy?~~

~~dance/music/art~~

A? law-land/gravity

~~E suspended in air? fantasy?~~

D sadness/"forget sad things"

B rivetting gun

D say that again—old joke

Then he noticed something about the notes he had labeled B. All of the noises that entered George's head are noises that we live with today; we needn't wait until 2081 for them. Ralph had heard the phrase "noise pollution" to describe the racket of daily life in cities and highways, shopping centers and college campuses. George's intelligence and concentration span is limited by things that we all live with: buzzers, hammering, gunfire, sirens, collisions, and riveting guns. This anti-utopia, Ralph saw, was not just Vonnegut's vision of a bad future; it was also his satire of a bad present.

This notion added something to his thesis: "Although Kurt Vonnegut, Jr.'s science-fiction story 'Harrison Bergeron' is an anti-utopia attacking the idea that equality means being the same, it is also a satire of present conditions which prevent individuals from exercising their brains and talents." It was too long a thesis sentence, he decided, but he used it tentatively, as a map, when he read the story again, underlining and making check marks.

He wrote a draft, let it sit overnight, and rewrote it; he omitted a discussion of whether Harrison was crazy or pretending to be crazy when he declared himself emperor, and whether he really floated in the air or the author exaggerated to show how graceful the dancing was. These speculations did not advance his thesis, nor was it essential to deal with them in order to construct his paper. (If he had talked about everything he thought of, his paper would have lacked focus.) He expanded his remarks on the nature of the handicapping, which he felt was needed for his critical argument. He rewrote the paper, corrected it again for spelling, paragraphing, and sentence structure, typed a fresh copy, and handed it in. The last thing he thought of was a title.

Ralph Giannello
English 102, sect. 4
Dr. Carmichael
February 10, 1980.

The Future Now

Kurt Vonnegut, Jr.'s "Harrison Bergeron" is science fiction because it is set in the future, but it is not a future of space travel, time warps, or little people with green brains. It is a future of political oppression, in the name of equality, enforced by gadgets. The story's theme is philosophical or political, and by making an anti-utopia in the future Vonnegut criticizes present-day society.

In the world of 2081 which Vonnegut imagines, the United States has made it illegal, by "the 211th, 212th, and 213th Amendments to the Constitution," to be anything but average. Being average is called being equal. The author makes his premise clear at the very beginning of the story, when he writes that now

> . . . everybody was finally equal. They weren't only equal before God and the law, they were equal every which way. Nobody was smarter than anybody else. Nobody was better looking than anybody else.

The author shows us how the government enforces equality by means of handicaps. The strong carry weights, like a fast horse handicapped in a race to make it average in strength and speed. Beauty is disguised to look ordinary, and brains are befuddled by the constant interruption of noise.

The story's events hold up to ridicule this idea of equality as sameness. We watch graceful dancers made to dance badly, and musicians prevented from making beautiful music. Because he shows us good things prevented, the author clearly indicates that he disagrees with an interpretation of equality which hinders excellence. When the author says, in the passage quoted, "They weren't only equal before God and the law," I think that he shows us the true ideal of equality, the ideal from the old Constitution before these amendments.

At the story's end the author gives us no hope for the future. The revolution attempted by Harrison Bergeron, seven-foot genius and son of the story's main characters, fails when he is killed by the United States Handicapper General, who is in charge of enforcing equality-as-averageness. But I feel that the story is not so much a prediction of the future as a criticism of the present world.

First, George and Hazel Bergeron talk exactly like ordinary people right now. Hazel talks in clichés and bad grammar that make her sound like a character in a television show. "You been so tired lately—kind of wore out." "He tried to do the best he could with what God gave him." The story ends with Hazel repeating one of the oldest jokes in the world. George says, "You can say that again," and so she says it again. Either she repeats an old joke or she is dumb enough to think he actually wants her to repeat herself.

George talks in clichés too, and seems to believe in enforced mediocrity, but Vonnegut shows him struggling more than Hazel does. George keeps starting to have a thought, but his chief handicap-gadget is a radio in his ear which keeps blasting noise in his ear so that he cannot think consistently. As Vonnegut tells it, George's attention span is destroyed, not by futuristic noises of 2081, but by things which blast our eardrums every day right now—by the noises of a buzzer, for instance, or of an automobile collision, or of a rivetting gun. Vonnegut shows us that his dreaded world of the future, where noise pollution prevents us from thinking consecutive thoughts, is already here—or at least beginning. He suggests that noise pollution has the effect of making us all average in our brains, and suggests that maybe some people like it that way.

II. Writing on each of the genres

The nature of each genre suggests special advice, to which the first part of this appendix is a general prologue.

A. Writing about fiction

1. Explicating Fiction

Because explication is line-by-line explanation, it would take us too long to explicate a whole work of fiction. Sometimes, however, we explicate a paragraph or a few lines of a work of fiction, relating it to the whole. In teaching James Joyce's huge novel *Ulysses,* some teachers have found it useful to assign one paragraph, asking students to explain everything in it and relate it to the rest of the novel. In a less demanding version of that assignment, a teacher may assign explication of one significant passage from a short story. Sometimes a passage of description or setting may relate to a protagonist's character, the way Faulkner's description of the town's architecture in "A Rose for Emily" applies to Miss Emily herself. Or a writer may explicate the last few lines of a story—including perhaps dialogue, narrative, and description—word by word, and reveal the whole story by explaining its conclusion.

2. Analyzing Fiction

In the analysis of fiction, we separate it into parts and examine one part. In analyzing "Harrison Bergeron," Ralph isolated elements of theme. For a reminder of the elements of fiction, look again at the chapter headings of "To

Read a Story"—plot, character, setting, and the rest. Remember that not every story contains all elements; many stories, for instance, do not deal in symbols.

For an analysis of plot, look at the first chapter of "To Read a Story," where several pages about "A Rose for Emily" analyze Faulkner's manipulation of plot. Because these pages intend to describe the story as a whole, they also include remarks on characterization, setting, and other elements. Analyzing plot in particular, the writer will want to understand the plot function of everything reported; if an episode seems out of place, what in fact is its use to the story, and why does it seem out of place? If sequence is other than chronological—if there is a flashback, for instance—what purpose does the sequence serve? Does the plot's action surprise? How? And why? Is there foreshadowing? What is the climax and the dénouement? In analyzing any element of fiction, the writer will do well to reread the chapter about the element he analyzes before writing the paper.

Often a useful subject for analysis in fiction is the characterization of one important character. Writing an analysis of characterization, the student should try to note *everything* in the story that gives an impression of the character chosen. Such impressions may derive from the character's major actions, from minor gestures of hands and eyebrows, from the character's speech or dialogue and other characters' response to it, from others' speech and actions in the character's absence, from the setting if it is described to suggest something about the character, sometimes from the author's outright statements, from tone and from point of view.

Point of view is itself subject to analysis, especially when it undergoes subtle change as it does in Chekhov's "Gooseberries," or when it is especially important to theme. Any of fiction's elements may be subject to analysis.

3. Comparison and Contrast in Writing about Fiction

When we use comparison and contrast for papers in fiction, we are often comparing thematic matters, usually not the entire theme of stories but parts of themes. For instance, Eudora Welty in "A Worn Path" and Flannery O'Connor in "A Good Man Is Hard to Find" write about old women. A comparison and contrast might be "The Aging of Opposites." Or a theme about two sorts of female endurance might combine "A Worn Path" with Tillie Olsen's "I Stand Here Ironing."

On the other hand, comparisons and contrasts of fiction's technical elements can provide excellent subjects. Compare, for instance, the use of the first-person narrator in "I Stand Here Ironing" and John Cheever's "The Chaste Clarissa." Compare the use of setting in Mary Lavin's "The Green Grave and the Black Grave" and Joseph Conrad's "Youth."

4. Things to Avoid when Writing about Fiction

A pitfall in writing about fiction is plot summary. We have all grown up listening to friends make forty-five-minute summaries of thirty-minute television shows. Unless instructed otherwise, assume that the reader knows what happens in the story, and refer only to those events that are germane to the thesis of the paper. Do not summarize except in the service of explanation. Anything else is padding.

Remember as well to avoid both the personal and the biographical errors. If we write about stories by Joyce or Lavin, it is irrelevant that our grandfather is Irish, or that we spent a summer in Dublin. If we write about Barthelme's "The Indian Uprising," it is irrelevant to speak of an uncle's protest against the Vietnam war. Of course if we are assigned contextual analysis, the history of the war protests would not be irrelevant. We must never drift unconsciously from one kind of criticism to another.

B. Writing about poetry

At first glance, it may seem easier or harder to write about poems than about stories—easier because poems tend to be shorter, harder because poems have the reputation of being difficult to understand. Although they are usually short, poems are complex and require a dense and attentive reading. Yet if we write about a poem that we respond to, that pleases us in its sound and its wisdom, we can find writing about it a pleasure as compact and shapely as the poem itself. With a short poem, we can have the pleasure of saying everything we know about it, as we cannot do with a story or a play. Writing about poems tests our ability, most of all, to respond to the words writers use, to their associations and connections, to their connotations and denotations, to their rhythms and their sounds.

1. Explicating Poems

For an example of explication, look again at the poems explained in the first chapter of "To Read a Poem"—Frost's "Stopping by Woods on a Snowy Evening" and Williams's "so much depends." These explications are longer and more detailed than most teachers will expect from students beginning a study of literature, but they give notions of method and range. Remember that when we explain a poem or a passage in poetry, we should attend to form as well as to content; we must not simply indicate intellectual understanding by paraphrase, but account for the shape and sound of a poem as well as its paraphrasable content.

Paraphrase is a necessary *part* of explication; it is not the whole thing. Many critics beginning an explication find it useful to summarize the action and theme of the poem as a prelude, giving a brief account of the whole before concentrating on the parts. This summary is like the beginning of a speech in a debate, which tells us the general conclusion the argument will lead to. With explication as with argument, the proof is in the pudding. The step-by-step explanation of the use and function of particular words is the pudding of explication.

To write a paper of explication, we should always pick a poem which pleases us and which we find fascinating. It will not serve to choose something we do not respond to, or something about which we find little intriguing. It is all right (it is possibly even good tactics) if something in the poem either displeases us or remains puzzling. When we have chosen a poem to write about, or narrowed choice down to a few, we should read and reread and reread. Read with a pencil or pen in hand, taking notes both of observations about the poem and about puzzlements. After many readings, with note-taking, it is wise to refresh the mind about the elements of poetry and reread again to notice matters possibly ignored. Everyone is naturally more sensitive to certain elements than to others. Perhaps we find ourselves sensitive to the poem's structure as argument, if it is a poem that structures an argument. Perhaps we need to look harder to pick up the poem's images and their connections. Use the elements of poetry, as noted in the chapters of this text, as a checklist suggesting what to look for. Not all poems will satisfy all items on the checklist of chapters. But it is our task as explicators to make ourselves aware of everything that is there.

Here is a paper by a student named Mary Lois Goldberg, who picked a short poem by Robert Frost for explication.

Mistaking Snow

Only eight lines long, Robert Frost's "A Patch of Old Snow" appears as slight as it is brief. Close reading of the poem, however, reveals that its off-hand manner or tone conceals something more serious than first appears. In this disparity between appearance and reality, between apparent lightness and real seriousness, we see a poem typical of Frost.

The title gives us no problem, because the poem's primary subject is simply "a patch of old snow." Somebody might try to work something out of the dictionary definition of "patch" as a "piece of material . . . to conceal or reinforce. . ."[1] Perhaps the poem in its playful tone acts as a concealment of its own seriousness— but really I don't think the title expresses an idea of hiding. The snow is "a patch" because it is smaller than the earth it lies on.

One of the first things I noticed about this poem was its rhyme, which is really good! They are rhymes which you would never expect. First, a verb with a -ed ending—"guessed," which we pronounce the same as "guest" really—is rhymed with the noun "rest." Just because they are spelled differently, and maybe because they are different parts of speech, they seem as if they should not go together, but they do. Then the second rhyme is a rhyme of two syllables, which is unusual in itself: "overspread it" and "read it." Although the parts of speech are the same— a verb followed by a pronoun object—the first of the verbs has three syllables and the second has one. This difference contributes to the surprise of the rhyme, and the surprise gives part of the poem's pleasure.

The poem is written not only in rhyme but in meter. The first and third lines of each stanza have three feet and the second and fourth have two. (Trimeter and dimeter). Some of the feet are three-syllable ($\smile\smile\prime$) and some are two-syllable ($\smile\prime$). I don't know whether to call the meter anapestic or iambic. Here is my scansion:

[1] *American Heritage Dictionary,* William Morris, ed., American Heritage Publishing Co. Inc. & Houghton Mifflin Co.: Boston, 1969.

> There's a patch | of old snow | in a corner
>   That I should | have guessed
> Was a blow | away pap | er the rain
>   Had brought | to rest.
> It is speck | led with grime | as if
>   Small print | overspread it
> The news | of a day | I've forgotten—
>   If I ev | er read it.

Thirteen of the twenty feet are anapestic and seven are iambic; maybe we should call the meter anapestic with iambic tendencies. Of the eight lines, *half* have feminine endings, including the last line of the poem.

Having written all this about meter, I am not sure what to say about it. I wonder if the tentativeness or uncertainty of the meter—all those extra syllables, or all those syllables cut away—might combine with the surprise of the rhyme to pull you along feeling that you are not just sure where you are going. But with the direct (if surprising) rhyme, and the foot-numbers staying the same, when you come to the end you know that this is the only place you could have come to.

Each stanza is composed of one sentence, and each sentence also seems tentative or uncertain at first, and finally conclusive. Frost built the sentences so that they stick together (which is like the direct rhyme and count of feet) but so that it's hard to see how they stick together (which is like the witty rhymes and mixed feet). The "I should have guessed" in the second line is an interruption to "that . . . was"—except that without the interruption the sentence would not make any sense because it would mix present and past tenses. Therefore the sentence looks at first as if it were careless or off-hand, but when you put it together, you see that all the parts fit and are necessary.

Finally I want to talk about the meaning or theme in the poem, and I come to it only now because I think that the poem needs its own sound-shape and sentence-shape to say what it has to say. The statement of the poem is easy enough to paraphrase: I see a piece of snow and at first I think it is a piece of newspaper because it looks like one, but it is a small matter anyhow. But the poem seems to me to imply something more.

There are two things I want to notice, one in each stanza. First is "paper," which could be wrapping paper or waxpaper but turns out to be newspaper. I think that the delay in discovering the kind of paper is a teasing which is like the surprise of the rhymes. Then in the second stanza, "speckled with grime" is an accurate image for old snow—and when I notice this I suddenly realize that this poem about something visible has hardly any images in it. The title, "A Patch of Old Snow," is an image, but not a vivid one. If this poem does not end in description, then what does it end in?

I think this poem is about a casual, unremarkable visual mistake—and then it says, "So what; it doesn't matter." At first the poet reports that he "would have guessed" that a clump of old snow was a piece of paper. We give easy assent to the comparison: yes, in April a piece of dirty snow does look like a newspaper. Then in the second stanza Frost explains that grime is speckled on snow *as* print overspreads paper, almost as if he needs to say: look; this mistake was easy to make! Then, as if he felt that he had protested too much, he says that the newspaper (which does not exist except as a mental error) probably did not have any news important to him anyway, because he would have forgotten it. As his withdrawal seems complete, he withdraws further: "If I ever read it." He has made a mistake and explained, and then said it's not worth worrying about, but at the same time he has shown himself worrying about it—a lot!

Another student in the same class decided that *patch* was a key word, that it implied diminishment, concealment, and repair in the poem—and wrote a good paper to defend her ideas.

2. Analyzing Poems

Analysis of a poem isolates a part, identifies it, and relates part to whole. Where explication unfolds a whole poem or passage, analysis deals with one element, usually in a longer poem or part of a poem. In the text of "To Read a Poem," many poems or passages are analyzed for one element—for the use of language, imagery, metaphor, for allusion, symbolism, rhythm, assonance and alliteration, and meter. For examples, look at the metaphorical analysis of a Shakespearean sonnet on pages 422–423, or the analysis of allusion in Louise Bogan's epigram on pages 439–440.

Students writing analytical papers often limit their topics by concentrating on one part of an element. Theodore Roethke's "The Meadow Mouse" (pages 533–534) includes so many images that "Imagery in 'The Meadow Mouse' " would make a long paper; we could narrow it to " 'My Thumb of a Child': Images of Infancy in Roethke's 'Meadow Mouse.' " Writing about Frost's "Stopping by Woods on a Snowy Evening," a student might analyze "The Tone of Frost's Speaker," or "Frost's Smart Horse in 'Stopping by Woods . . . ,' " or "Images of Cold and Comfort." Dealing with a longer poem, a writer might isolate one character: "The Characterization of the Hired Man in Frost's 'Death of the Hired Man' "; or analyze a part of theme: "Definitions of 'Home' in Frost's 'Death of the Hired Man.' "

Writing analysis, we remain aware that everything is related to everything else. If we speak of images, it is hard not to mention metaphor, because many images make metaphors. Discussing the metaphorical structure of a sonnet, we will notice that some of the linkage among metaphors is accomplished by images. Sometimes we can lose track of our topic by noticing too closely the interrelationships of many elements. We need, sometimes, to mention a rhyme when we are discussing characterization, if the rhyme makes a point of character. But we should not be sidetracked into a discussion of rhyme just because the subject comes up. We must keep watch of ourselves, as we write, that we do not lose track. A clear thesis can be the North Star to guide us through the wilderness of analysis.

In making a thesis, it is best to look for an element that has relevance to the whole poem. Sometimes we can fall into an analysis which records accurately some facts about a poem but stops short of showing the relevance of these facts. A formal analysis of a sonnet that only disclosed the existence of sonnet form would be trivial, too elementary for the name of analysis. However, a good analytical paper could be written which showed how sonnet form reflected itself in the poem's shapely argument, sorting itself out into the quatrains (if the sonnet is Shakespearean) and into octave and sestet.

3. Comparison and Contrast in Writing about Poems

We illustrate analyzed elements of poems by comparing and contrasting them. Sometimes we find within one poet's work a habit of writing or thinking: "Emily Dickinson's Imagery of Animals." Such a paper might compare and contrast parts of three or four Dickinson poems to investigate her use of animal images. Not only images, but structural devices, recurrent symbols, and themes may provide material for comparative analysis.

On the other hand, sometimes we contrast two or more poets. "Poets and Flowers: Two Strategies in Roethke and Frost" compares Frost's "Design" with Roethke's "Orchids." Any comparison and contrast, within one poet's work or among different poets, will require separate analyses or small explications, and judgment on likeness or difference. Note the remarks on the structure of such papers, pages 1452–1454.

4. Things to Avoid when Writing about Poems

In writing about poetry, we frequently fail by becoming too personal, by emphasizing our response or our connections with the poet's subject matter. For some reason, we tend to commit this kind of error more often in writing about poems than in writing about the other genres.

Do not confuse the speaker of the poem with the poet in his own skin. Stick to your thesis. Do not let the interrelatedness of a poem's elements lead you into a disorganized paper.

C. Writing about drama

Usually we are asked to write about a play we have read rather than a performance which we have witnessed. Reviewing a performance is different; for notes on reviewing, see page 1476.

Writing about modern plays, remember that the author provides stage directions, and often interpretations of characters' feelings; these indicators are as much the play as the dialogue is, and help us to stage our mental theater.

In older plays we supply the scene and understand the characters from the spoken words of dialogue, sometimes with the help of modern editors and commentators. Because the historical context of older dramas supplies the limits of mental theater, even in the shape of the physical stages, we should consult background information while studying the play we write about.

1. Explicating Drama

Explication of a whole play, or even of an act, is out of the question. We might explicate a brief scene, no longer than a page, or better still a key speech by a key character. Writing about a sufficiently important speech, however, the student is apt to feel that in order to explain it thoroughly everything in the play must be accounted for. As with fiction, we must be careful to stick to our topic, and to avoid plot summary. Refer to other acts and scenes by using a Roman numeral capital for the act, lower-case Roman numerals for the scene: II, iii or V, iv.

2. Analyzing Drama

Analysis is our most common method in writing about drama. By analysis we limit our topic. Noticing the importance of stage business in Chekhov's *The Cherry Orchard,* we may be tempted to isolate this element as "Stage Directions in *The Cherry Orchard,*" but unless we are called upon for a long term paper, we need to narrow our topic. "Fiers's Business: The Servant on Chekhov's Stage" would make a manageable topic. We would need to spend most of our time seeing what Chekhov's stage directions tell Fiers to do, and deciding what we can learn of Fiers's physical actions from dialogue. Then as part of our topic we would briefly relate Fiers's business to the play as a whole.

The theme of a play is too large a subject, but we may analyze theme into parts. Defining all the uses to which the play puts the cherry orchard would be too much; we could define the orchard's meaning to one or two characters. By analyzing the use of trains in that play (references in dialogue, offstage whistles) we could touch on the play's structure and the play's theme. Whatever element attracts us, as we reread the play with an eye to writing about it, we must be alert to subdivide it into smaller parts for analysis.

Many of the elements discussed when we read fiction or poetry can sustain analysis in writing about drama, if we narrow them sufficiently; plot, character, setting, tone, symbolism, imagery, metaphor. Aristotle's six elements provide another way to look at a play's components. It might be wise to glance again at the headings of "To Read a Play."

3. Comparison and Contrast in Writing about Drama

Different playwrights may be contrasted for any elements, for construction and characterization and dialogue. But focus must narrow. Do not attempt to compare and contrast the characters of Hamlet and Oedipus. It would be possible, nevertheless, to compare and contrast recognition scenes in which each protagonist recognizes an inevitable horror. It is possible to contrast scenes of comic and tragic unmasking.

In this book, the most rewarding pair of works for comparison and contrast is *Hamlet* and *Rosencrantz and Guildenstern Are Dead.* The richness of these contrasts makes it difficult to narrow the topic, but it can be done.

4. A Paper on Staging

Another kind of paper, which some instructors assign, asks the student to write imagining how to stage a small segment of a play. Taking one scene of *Hamlet,* for instance, a student might stage it as it might have been played at Shakespeare's Globe Theater, using the possibilities and limitations of the Elizabethan stage, indicating props, blocking, and the use of different areas of the stage. On the other hand, a student might write an account of the same scene produced on a modern stage. Such a paper, depending on the instructor's wishes, may include indications of spectacle from lighting to make-up to costuming, down to the director's indications for actors' interpretation.

5. Reviewing a Performance

When we review a new performance of an old play, we should reread the play's text before attending the performance, establishing in our minds a range of possibilities for production. We should be ready to be surprised by a director's original, valid interpretation. We should be ready as well to indicate in our review the nature of that interpretation, to estimate its validity, and to evaluate specifics of the production. It helps if we have seen other productions of the same play, to make comparison and contrast.

When we review a new play, we set ourselves the considerable task of making an intellectual separation between the play's text, which we have experienced only as a performance, and the performance of that text. We want to report on the value of the play at the same time we evaluate the jobs done by director, scene designer, costumer, and actors. In practice such a separation may prove more than difficult, but we should attempt it. It will help to consult some reviews of recent openings, usually in New York, in the pages of *The New York Times, The New Yorker, Time, Newsweek,* and other publications. Often critics attempt this separation, telling us that a new play is thin and trite, but that one or two superb performances almost save the evening; or that despite a promising script, miscasting or poor direction has left the performance a shambles.

Reviewing sounds like an impossible task; it is not an easy one. However, writing a play review is an excellent exercise in trying to investigate the complexities of theater, the play itself as well as the variable particulars of performance.

Writing a review, we must keep our readers in mind. If we write for a newspaper, we may need to summarize the play's plot even if it is *Hamlet,* to teach readers whom we cannot assume to have read the text. We must account for the play's text, and for the director's interpretation. We must list actors by name, and report on their competence; we must judge stage design, and even costuming and lighting if they are remarkable.

6. Things to Avoid when Writing about Drama

When we write about drama, we need especially to concentrate on narrowing our focus, because the length and variety of good drama tempt us to wander, to lose track, to write diffusely.

Beware of plot summary except when it is essential to the particulars of statement.

This advice and these rules of thumb—whether they apply to a four-line poem or a five-act tragedy—should serve one purpose: to clarify our thinking about literature in the act of writing about it.

Acknowledgments

Edward Albee. *The Zoo Story* by Edward Albee, copyright © 1960 by Edward Albee. Reprinted by permission of Coward, McCann & Geoghegan, Inc. *The Zoo Story* is the sole property of the author and is fully protected by copyright. It may not be acted by either professionals or amateurs without written consent. Public readings, radio and television broadcasts are likewise forbidden. All inquiries concerning these rights should be addressed to the William Morris Agency, 1350 Avenue of the Americas, New York, N.Y. 10019.

Woody Allen. "The Whore of Mensa" from *Without Feathers* by Woody Allen, copyright © 1974 by Woody Allen, is reprinted by permission of Random House, Inc. This story first appeared in *The New Yorker*.

A. R. Ammons. "Working with Tools" from *Briefings: Poems Small and Easy* by A. R. Ammons is reprinted by permission of W. W. Norton & Company, Inc. Copyright © 1971 by A. R. Ammons.

Max Apple. "The Oranging of America" from *The Oranging of America* by Max Apple; copyright © 1974, 1975, 1976 by Max Apple. Reprinted by permission of Viking Penguin Inc.

John Ashbery. "Rivers and Mountains" from *Rivers and Mountains* by John Ashbery; copyright © 1962, 1963, 1964, 1966 by John Ashbery. Reprinted by permission of Georges Borchardt, Inc.

W. H. Auden. "In Memory of W. B. Yeats" and "Musée des Beaux Arts" from *W. H. Auden: Collected Poems* by W. H. Auden, edited by Edward Mendelson; copyright 1940 and renewed 1968 by W. H. Auden; reprinted by permission of Random House, Inc., and from *Collected Shorter Poems 1927–1957* by W. H. Auden, reprinted by permission of Faber and Faber Limited.

Amiri Baraka (LeRoi Jones). "Watergate" and "Careers" from *Selected Poetry of Amiri Baraka/LeRoi Jones*; copyright © 1979 by Imamu Amiri Baraka. Reprinted by permission of William Morrow & Company.

Donald Barthleme. "Indian Uprising" from *Unspeakable Practices, Unnatural Acts* by Donald Barthleme; copyright © 1965 by Donald Barthleme. Reprinted by permission of Farrar, Straus & Giroux, Inc. This story originally appeared in *The New Yorker*.

Stephen Berg and Diskin Clay. *Oedipus the King* by Sophocles, translated by Stephen Berg and Diskin Clay; copyright © 1978 by Stephen Berg and Diskin Clay. Reprinted by permission of Oxford University Press, Inc.

Wendell Berry. "The Wild Geese" from *The Country of Marriage* by Wendell Berry; copyright © 1971 by Wendell Berry. Reprinted by permission of Harcourt Brace Jovanovich, Inc.

John Berryman. "Dream Song #14," "Dream Song #16," and "Dream Song #312," from *The Dream Songs* by John Berryman; copyright © 1959, 1962, 1963, 1964, 1965, 1966, 1967, 1968, 1969 by John Berryman. Reprinted by permission of Farrar, Straus & Giroux, Inc.

Elizabeth Bishop. "The Pink Dog" by Elizabeth Bishop; copyright © 1979 by Alice Methfessel, Executrix of the Estate of Elizabeth Bishop. This poem originally appeared in *The New Yorker*. "The Monument" from *Complete Poems* by Elizabeth Bishop; copyright © 1939, 1969 by Elizabeth Bishop, copyright renewed © 1967 by Elizabeth Bishop. Both reprinted by permission of Farrar, Straus & Giroux, Inc.

Robert Bly. "Taking the Hands . . . ," "Hunting Pheasants in a Cornfield," and "A Man Writes to a Part of Himself" from *Silence in the Snowy Fields,* Wesleyan University Press, Middletown, Conn., 1962; copyright © 1960, 1961, 1962 by Robert Bly and reprinted with his permission. "The Dead Seal Near McClure's Beach" from *The Morning Glory* by Robert Bly; copyright © 1975 by Robert Bly and reprinted with his permission.

Louise Bogan. "Cartography" and "To An Artist, to Take Heart" from *The Blue Estuaries* by Louise Bogan; copyright © 1964, 1965 by Louise Bogan. Reprinted by permission of Farrar, Straus & Giroux, Inc.

Jorge Luis Borges. "The Secret Miracle" from *Labyrinths* by Jorge Luis Borges, translated by Harriet de Onís; copyright © 1962 by New Directions Publishing Corporation. Reprinted by permission of New Directions.

Gwendolyn Brooks. "The Bean Eaters" and "We Real Cool. The Pool Players. Seven at the Golden Shovel" from *The World of Gwendolyn Brooks* by Gwendolyn Brooks; copyright © 1959 by Gwendolyn Brooks. Reprinted by permission of Harper & Row, Publishers.

Raymond Carver. "The Father" from *Will You Please Be Quiet Please* by Raymond Carver. Reprinted by permission of McGraw-Hill Book Company.

John Cheever. "The Chaste Clarissa" from *The Stories of John Cheever* by John Cheever; copyright 1952 by John Cheever. Reprinted by permission of Alfred A. Knopf, Inc.

Anton Chekhov. "Gooseberries" from *The Portable Chekhov,* edited by Avrahm Yarmolinsky; copyright © 1947 by the Viking Press, Inc. Reprinted by permission of Viking Penguin Inc.

Tom Clark. "Stones" from *Stones*; © Tom Clark. Reprinted by permission of the author.

Joseph Conrad. "Youth" by Joseph Conrad; reprinted by permission of the Trustees of the Joseph Conrad Estate.

Gregory Corso. "Marriage" from *The Happy Birthday of Death* by Gregory Corso; copyright © 1960 by New Directions Publishing Corporation. Reprinted by permission of New Directions.

Hart Crane. "Voyages, I and II" and lines from "The Bridge" from *The Complete Poems and Selected Prose and Poetry of Hart Crane*; copyright 1933, 1958, 1966 by Liveright Publishing Corporation. Reprinted by permission of Liveright Publishing Corporation.

Robert Creeley. "The Rain" and "The Hill" from *For Love: Poems 1950–1960* by Robert Creeley; copyright © 1962 by Robert Creeley. "For My Mother: Genevieve Jules Creeley" from *Selected Poems* by Robert Creeley; copyright © 1976 by Robert Creeley. Reprinted by permission of Charles Scribner's Sons.

E. E. Cummings. "1(a" from *Complete Poems 1913–1962* by E. E. Cummings; copyright © 1958 by E. E. Cummings. Reprinted by permission of Harcourt Brace Jovanovich, Inc. "next to of course god america i" and "Poem, or Beauty Hurts Mr. Vinal" from *IS 5, poems by E. E. Cummings*; copyright 1926 by Boni & Liveright; copyright renewed 1953 by E. E. Cummings. Reprinted by permission of Liveright Publishing Corporation.

J. V. Cunningham. Two epigrams by J. V. Cunningham, reprinted by permission of the Ohio University Press.

H. D. "Heat" and "The Sea Rose" from *Selected Poems* by Hilda Doolittle; copyright © 1925, 1953, 1957 by Norman Holmes Pearson. Reprinted by permission of New Directions.

James Dickey. "The Heaven of Animals" from *Poems 1957–1967*; copyright © 1961 by James Dickey. Reprinted by permission of Wesleyan University Press. "The Heaven of Animals" first appeared in *The New Yorker*.

Emily Dickinson. "After great pain, a formal feeling comes—," "The first Day's Night had come—," "Me from Myself—to banish—," "My Life had stood—a Loaded Gun—," "The Province of the Saved," and "A still—Volcano—Life—" from *The Complete Poems of Emily Dickinson,* edited by Thomas H. Johnson. Reprinted by permission of Little, Brown and Company. "Because I could not stop for Death—," "I cannot live with You—," "I'm ceded—I've stopped being Theirs—," "I felt a Cleaving in my Mind—," "He fumbles at your Soul—," "I heard a Fly buzz—when I died—," "Much Madness is divinest Sense—," "A narrow Fellow in the Grass," "He put a Belt around my life—," "Severer Service of myself—," "The Soul has Bandaged moments," and "I would not paint—a picture—" reprinted by permission of the publishers and the Trustees of Amherst College from *The Poems of Emily Dickinson,* edited by Thomas H. Johnson, Cambridge, Mass.: The Belknap Press of Harvard University Press; copyright © 1951, 1955 by the President and Fellows of Harvard College.

Edward Dorn. "On the Debt My Mother Owed to Sears Roebuck"; reprinted by permission of the author.

Robert Duncan. "Poetry, A Natural Thing" from *The Opening of the Field* by Robert Duncan; copyright © 1960 by Robert Duncan. Reprinted by permission of New Directions.

Richard Eberhart. "The Groundhog" from *Collected Poems 1930–1976* by Richard Eberhart; copyright © 1960, 1976 by Richard Eberhart. Reprinted by permission of Oxford University Press, Inc. and of Chatto & Windus Ltd.

Russell Edson. "Bringing a Dead Man Back to Life" from *The Intuitive Journey and Other Works* by Russell Edson; copyright © 1976 by Russell Edson. Reprinted by permission of Harper & Row, Publishers.

T. S. Eliot. "The Love Song of J. Alfred Prufrock" and "Journey of the Magi" from *Collected Poems 1909–1962* by T. S. Eliot; copyright 1936 by Harcourt Brace Jovanovich, Inc.; copyright © 1963, 1964 by T. S. Eliot. Reprinted by permission of Harcourt Brace Jovanovich and of Faber and Faber Limited.

Ralph Ellison. "Battle Royal" from *Invisible Man* by Ralph Ellison; copyright 1952 by Ralph Ellison. Reprinted by permission of Random House, Inc.

William Empson. "Villanelle" from *Collected Poems of William Empson*; copyright 1949, 1977 by William Empson. Reprinted by permission of Harcourt Brace Jovanovich, Inc. and of Chatto & Windus Ltd.

William Faulkner. "A Rose for Emily" from *Collected Stories of William Faulkner* by William Faulkner; copyright 1930 and renewed 1958 by William Faulkner. Reprinted by permission of Random House, Inc.

Ian Hamilton Finlay. "Homage to Malevich" from *Poems to Hear and See* by Ian Hamilton Finlay; copyright © 1971 by Ian Hamilton Finlay. Reprinted by permission of Macmillan Publishing Co., Inc.

Robert Francis. "Hogwash," copyright © 1965 by Robert Francis, and "Three Woodchoppers," copyright © 1944, 1972 by Robert Francis, from *Robert Francis: Collected Poems, 1936–1976,* University of Massachusetts Press, 1976.

Robert Frost. "Acquainted with the Night," "After Apple-Picking," "Birches," "Come In," "Desert Places," "Design," "The Draft Horse," "To Earthward," "Ends," "The Gift Outright," "Home Burial," "The Most of It," "Mowing," "The Need of Being Versed in Country Things," "Neither Out Far Nor In Deep," "Once by the Pacific," "Out, Out—," "The Pasture," "The Road Not Taken," "The Silken Tent," and "Stopping by Woods on a Snowy Evening" from *The Poetry of Robert Frost,* edited by Edward Connery Lathem. Copyright 1916, 1923, 1928, 1930, 1934, 1939, © 1967, 1969 by Holt, Rinehart and Winston; copyright 1936, 1942, 1944, 1951, © 1956, 1958, 1962 by Robert Frost; copyright © 1964, 1967, 1970 by Lesley Frost Ballantine. Reprinted by permission of Holt, Rinehart and Winston. "In White" from *The Dimensions of Robert Frost* by Reginald L. Cook; copyright © 1958 by Reginald L. Cook. Reprinted by permission of Holt, Rinehart and Winston.

Allen Ginsberg. "America," copyright © 1956, 1959 by Allen Ginsberg, and "First Party at Ken Kesey's with Hell's Angels," copyright © 1968 by Allen Ginsberg. Reprinted by permission of City Lights Books.

Louise Glück. "Gratitude" from *The House on the Marshland* by Louise Glück; copyright © 1975 by Louise Glück. Reprinted by permission of The Ecco Press.

Edward Gorey. Excerpt from "The Listing Attic" from *Amphigory* by Edward Gorey; copyright © 1954, 1972 by Edward Gorey. Reprinted by permission of Candida Donadio & Associates, Inc. "The Listing Attic" was first published by Duell, Sloan, & Pearce–Little, Brown.

Robert Graves. "In Broken Images" from *Poems 1929*, copyright 1929 by Robert Graves, published by the Seizin Press, and "To Juan at the Winter Solstice" from *Poems 1938–1945,* copyright 1945 by Robert Graves, published by Cassell and Company, Ltd. Reprinted by permission of Curtis Brown, Ltd., and from *Collected Poems* by permission of A. P. Watt Ltd.

Edgar A. Guest. "The Rough Little Rascal" from *Collected Verse of Edgar A. Guest,* copyright 1934. Reprinted by permission of Contemporary Books, Inc., Chicago.

Thom Gunn. "On the Move" from *The Sense of Movement* by Thom Gunn. Reprinted by permission of Faber and Faber Ltd.

John Haines. "To Turn Back" from *Winter News* by John Haines; copyright © 1964 by John Haines. Reprinted by permission of Wesleyan University Press.

Thomas Hardy. "During Wind and Rain," "Epitaph on a Pessimist," "The Man He Killed," "The Oxen," "The Ruined Maid," and "Transformations" from *Collected Poems of Thomas Hardy,* published by the Macmillan Publishing Co., Inc., New York, 1953.

Robert Hayden. "Middle Passage" from *Angle of Ascent, New and Selected Poems* by Robert Hayden; copyright © 1975, 1972, 1970 by Robert Hayden. Reprinted by permission of Liveright Publishing Corporation.

Anthony Hecht. "The Dover Bitch," copyright © 1960 by Anthony E. Hecht, and "Samuel Sewall" from *The Hard Hours* by Anthony Hecht, copyright 1954 by Anthony E. Hecht. Reprinted by permission of Atheneum Publishers.

Ernest Hemingway. "In Another Country" from *Men Without Women* by Ernest Hemingway; copyright 1927 Charles Scribner's Sons; renewed copyright © 1955 Ernest Hemingway. Reprinted by permission of Charles Scribner's Sons.

Geoffrey Hill. "Merlin" and "Orpheus and Eurydice" from *Somewhere Is Such a Kingdom* by Geoffrey Hill; copyright © 1975 by Geoffrey Hill. Reprinted by permission of Houghton Mifflin Company.

Spencer Holst. "The Case of the Giant Rat of Sumatra" from *Spencer Holst Stories* by Spencer Holst; copyright © 1976. Reprinted by permission of Horizon Press.

A. E. Housman. "To an Athlete Dying Young" from *A Shropshire Lad,* Authorized Edition, from *The Collected Poems of A. E. Housman* by A. E. Housman; copyright 1939, 1940, © 1965 by Holt, Rinehart and Winston. Copyright © 1967, 1968 by Robert E. Symons. "Eight O'Clock" from *The Collected Poems of A. E. Housman* by A. E. Housman; copyright 1922 by Holt, Rinehart and Winston. Copyright 1950 by Barclays Bank Ltd. Reprinted by permission of Holt, Rinehart and Winston; The Society of Authors as the literary representative of A. E. Housman; and Jonathan Cape Ltd., publishers of A. E. Housman's *Collected Poems.*

Langston Hughes. "Bad Luck Card" from *Selected Poems of Langston Hughes* by Langston Hughes; copyright 1927 by Alfred A. Knopf, Inc. renewed 1955 by Langston Hughes. "Homecoming" from *Selected Poems of Langston Hughes* by Langston Hughes; copyright © 1959 by Langston Hughes. "Hope" from *Selected Poems of Langston Hughes* by Langston Hughes; copyright 1942 by Alfred A. Knopf, Inc., renewed 1970 by Arna Bontemps and George Houston Bass. Reprinted by permission of Alfred A. Knopf, Inc. "On the Road" by Langston Hughes; copyright © 1934, 1952, 1962 by Langston Hughes. Reprinted by permission of Harold Ober Associates. "On the Road" first appeared in *Esquire* magazine.

Ted Hughes. "Thrushes" from *Selected Poems* by Ted Hughes; copyright © 1959 by Ted Hughes. Reprinted by permission of Harper & Row, Publishers.

David Ignatow. "Rescue the Dead" from *Rescue the Dead* by David Ignatow; copyright © 1966 by David Ignatow. Reprinted by permission of Wesleyan University Press. "Rescue the Dead" first appeared in *Poetry.*

Randall Jarrell. "Eighth Air Force" from *The Complete Poems* by Randall Jarrell; copyright © 1947 by Mrs. Randall Jarrell; copyright © 1969 by Mrs. Randall Jarrell.

Robinson Jeffers. "Hurt Hawks" from *The Selected Poetry of Robinson Jeffers* by Robinson Jeffers; copyright 1928 and renewed 1956 by Robinson Jeffers. Reprinted by permission of Random House, Inc.

Gayl Jones. "White Rat" from *White Rat: Short Stories* by Gayl Jones; copyright © 1977 by Gayl Jones. Reprinted by permission of Random House, Inc.

James Joyce. "Counterparts" from *Dubliners* by James Joyce; copyright © 1967 by the Estate of James Joyce. Originally published by B. W. Huebsch in 1916. Reprinted by permission of Viking Penguin Inc.

Donald Justice "Counting the Mad" from *The Summer Anniversaries* by Donald Justice; copyright © 1957 by Donald Justice. Reprinted by permission of Wesleyan University Press.

Franz Kafka. "A Hunger Artist" from *The Penal Colony* by Franz Kafka; copyright © 1948 by

Schocken Books Inc., renewed © 1975 by Schocken Books Inc. Reprinted by permission of Schocken Books Inc.

X. J. Kennedy. "In a Prominent Bar in Secaucus One Day" by X. J. Kennedy. Published by Doubleday & Company, Inc.

Galway Kinnell. "The Bear" from *Body Rags* by Galway Kinnell; copyright © 1967 by Galway Kinnell. Reprinted by permission of Houghton Mifflin Company.

Etheridge Knight. "Hard Rock Returns to Prison from the Hospital for the Criminal Insane" and "2 Poems for Black Relocation Centers" from *Poems from Prison* by Etheridge Knight; copyright © 1968 by Etheridge Knight; Broadside/Crummell Press, Detroit, Michigan. Reprinted by permission of the publisher.

Philip Larkin. "Aubade" reprinted by permission of the author. "Mr. Bleaney" from *The Whitsun Weddings* by Philip Larkin, reprinted by permission of Faber and Faber Ltd.

Mary Lavin. "The Green Grave and the Black Grave" from *Collected Stories* by Mary Lavin; copyright © 1971 by Mary Lavin. Reprinted by permission of Houghton Mifflin Company.

D. H. Lawrence. "The Song of a Man Who Has Come Through" and "Bavarian Gentians" from *The Complete Poems of D. H. Lawrence,* collected and edited by Vivian de Sola Pinto and F. Warren Roberts; copyright © 1964, 1971 by Angelo Ravagli and C. Montague Weekley, Executors of the Estate of Frieda Lawrence Ravagli. Reprinted by permission of Viking Penguin Inc. "The Rocking Horse Winner" from *The Complete Stories of D. H. Lawrence*; copyright © 1934 by Frieda Lawrence, © renewed 1962 by Angelo Ravagli and C. Montague Weekley, Executors of the Estate of Frieda Lawrence Ravagli. Reprinted by permission of Viking Penguin Inc.

Stanislaw Lem. "How Erg the Self-Inducting Slew a Paleface" from *Mortal Engines* by Stanislaw Lem. English translation copyright © 1977 by The Seabury Press, Inc. Reprinted by permission of the publisher.

Denise Levertov. "October" from *O Taste and See* by Denise Levertov; copyright © 1964 by Denise Levertov Goodman. Reprinted by permission of New Directions. "The World Outside" from *The Jacob's Ladder*; copyright © 1961 by Denise Levertov Goodman. Reprinted by permission of New Directions.

Philip Levine. "Salami" from *They Feed They Lion* by Philip Levine; copyright © 1968, 1969, 1970, 1971, 1972 by Philip Levine. Reprinted by permission of Atheneum Publishers.

Vachel Lindsay. "The Flower-Fed Buffaloes" from *Going to the Stars* by Vachel Lindsay; copyright © 1926, renewed 1954 by Elizabeth C. Lindsay. Reprinted by permission of Hawthorn Books, Inc. All rights reserved.

John Logan. "Picnic" from *Ghosts of the Heart* by John Logan, University of Chicago Press, 1960. Reprinted by permission of the author.

Robert Lowell. "After the Surprising Conversions" and "New Year's Day" from *Lord Weary's Castle* by Robert Lowell; copyright 1946, 1974 by Robert Lowell. Reprinted by permission of Harcourt Brace Jovanovich, Inc. "For the Union Dead" from *For the Union Dead* by Robert Lowell; copyright © 1960 by Robert Lowell. Reprinted by permission of Farrar, Straus & Giroux, Inc.

Rod McKuen. "One" from *Listen to the Warm* by Rod McKuen; copyright 1967 by Rod McKuen and Anita Kerr. Reprinted by permission of Random House, Inc.

Archibald MacLeish. "You, Andrew Marvell" from *New and Collected Poems, 1917–1976* by Archibald MacLeish; copyright © 1976 by Archibald MacLeish. Reprinted by permission of Houghton Mifflin Company.

Louis MacNeice. "The Sunlight in the Garden" from *The Collected Poems of Louis MacNeice.* Reprinted by permission of Faber and Faber Ltd.

Bernard Malamud. "The Magic Barrel" from *The Magic Barrel* by Bernard Malamud; copyright © 1954, 1958 by Bernard Malamud. Reprinted by permission of Farrar, Straus & Giroux, Inc.

Herman J. Mankiewicz *and* Orson Welles. Script of *Citizen Kane.* From *The Citizen Kane Book* by Pauline Kael and The Shooting Script by Herman J. Mankiewicz and Orson Welles. Copyright © 1971 by Bantam Books, Inc. Reprinted by arrangement with the publishers. All rights reserved.

Reprinted by permission of Olwyn Hughes. "Johnny Panic and the Bible of Dreams" from *Johnny Panic and the Bible of Dreams* by Sylvia Plath; copyright © 1958 by Sylvia Plath, copyright © 1979 by Ted Hughes. Reprinted by permission of Harper & Row, Publishers.

Katherine Anne Porter. "Rope" from *Flowering Judas and Other Stories* by Katherine Anne Porter; copyright © 1930, 1958 by Katherine Anne Porter. Reprinted by permission of Harcourt Brace Jovanovich, Inc.

Ezra Pound. "Hugh Selwyn Mauberly IV," "Hugh Selwyn Mauberly V," "In a Station of the Metro," "The Bath Tub," "The Return," and "The River-Merchant's Wife: A Letter" from *Personae*; copyright 1926 by Ezra Pound. Reprinted by permission of New Directions.

John Crowe Ransom. "Captain Carpenter" from *Selected Poems, Third Edition,* revised and enlarged, by John Crowe Ransom; copyright © 1924 by Alfred A. Knopf, Inc., and renewed 1952 by John Crowe Ransom. Reprinted by permission of Alfred A. Knopf, Inc.

Kenneth Rexroth. "Proust's Madeleine" from *Collected Shorter Poems* by Kenneth Rexroth; copyright © 1963, 1966 by Kenneth Rexroth. "The Signature of All Things" from *Collected Shorter Poems* by Kenneth Rexroth; copyright © 1949 by Kenneth Rexroth. Reprinted by permission of New Directions.

Charles Reznikoff. "A Deserter" from *By the Well of Living and Seeing* by Charles Reznikoff. Reprinted by permission of Black Sparrow Press.

Adrienne Rich. "From an Old House in America" from *Poems, Selected and New, 1950–1974* by Adrienne Rich; copyright © 1975, 1974, 1973, 1971, 1969, 1966 by W. W. Norton & Company, Inc. Copyright © 1967, 1963, 1962, 1961, 1960, 1959, 1958, 1957, 1956, 1955, 1954, 1953, 1952, 1951 by Adrienne Rich. Reprinted by permission of W. W. Norton & Company, Inc.

Edwin Arlington Robinson. "Eros Turannos" from *Collected Poems* by Edwin Arlington Robinson; copyright 1916 by Edwin Arlington Robinson, renewed 1944 by Ruth Nivison. Reprinted by permission of Macmillan Publishing Co., Inc.

Theodore Roethke. "Cuttings," copyright 1948 by Theodore Roethke; "Big Wind," copyright 1947 by The United Chapter of Phi Beta Kappa; "Dolor," copyright 1943 by Modern Poetry Association, Inc.; "Elegy for Jane," copyright 1950 by Theodore Roethke; "I Knew a Woman," copyright 1954 by Theodore Roethke; "Journey to the Interior," copyright © 1961 by Beatrice Roethke as Administratrix of the Estate of Theodore Roethke; "The Lost Son," copyright 1947 by Theodore Roethke; "The Meadow Mouse," copyright © 1963 by Beatrice Roethke as Administratrix of the Estate of Theodore Roethke; "My Papa's Waltz," copyright 1942 by Hearst Magazines, Inc.; "Orchids," copyright 1948 by Theodore Roethke; "The Rose," copyright © 1963 by Beatrice Roethke as Administratrix of the Estate of Theodore Roethke; "The Sloth," copyright 1950 by Theodore Roethke; "The Visitant," copyright 1950 by Theodore Roethke. All from *The Collected Poems of Theodore Roethke.* Reprinted by permission of Doubleday & Company, Inc.

Milton Rugoff. "Paul Bunyan's Big Griddle" from *A Harvest of World Folk Tales,* edited by Milton Rugoff; copyright 1949 by The Viking Press, Inc., © renewed 1977 by The Viking Press, Inc. Reprinted by permission of Viking Penguin Inc.

Carl Sandberg. "Chicago" from *Chicago Poems* by Carl Sandberg; copyright 1916 by Holt, Rinehart and Winston; copyright 1944 by Carl Sandberg. Reprinted by permission of Harcourt Brace Jovanovich, Inc.

Delmore Schwartz. "In the Naked Bed, in Plato's Cave" from *Selected Poems: Summer Knowledge* by Delmore Schwartz; copyright 1938 by New Directions. Reprinted by permission of New Directions.

Anne Sexton. "Wanting to Die" from *Live or Die* by Anne Sexton; copyright © 1966 by Anne Sexton. Reprinted by permission of Houghton Mifflin Company.

William Shakespeare. *The Tragedy of Hamlet* by William Shakespeare, edited by Edward Hubler, copyright © 1963 by Edward Hubler, and *The Tragedy of Othello* by William Shakespeare, edited by Alvin Kernan, copyright © 1963 by Alvin Kernan. Reprinted by permission of The New American Library, Inc.

George Bernard Shaw. *Saint Joan* by George Bernard Shaw; copyright 1924, 1930, by George

Leo Tolstoy. "The Death of Ivan Ilych" from *The Death of Ivan Ilych and Other Stories* by Leo Tolstoy, translated by Louise and Aylmer Maude (1935). Reprinted by permission of Oxford University Press.

Charles Tomlinson. "Paring the Apple"; reprinted by permission of the author.

Jean Toomer. "Reapers" from *Cane* by Jean Toomer; copyright 1923 by Boni & Liveright, renewed 1951 by Jean Toomer. Reprinted by permission of Liveright Publishing Corporation.

John Updike. "Ace in the Hole" from *The Same Door* by John Updike; copyright 1955 by John Updike. Reprinted by permission of Alfred A. Knopf, Inc. First appeared in *The New Yorker*.

Kurt Vonnegut, Jr. "Harrison Bergeron" from *Welcome to the Monkey House* by Kurt Vonnegut, Jr.; copyright © 1961 by Kurt Vonnegut, Jr. Reprinted by permission of Delacorte Press/Seymour Lawrence. Originally appeared in *Fantasy and Science Fiction*.

Eudora Welty. "A Worn Path" from *A Curtain of Green and Other Stories* by Eudora Welty; copyright 1941, 1969 by Eudora Welty. Reprinted by permission of Harcourt Brace Jovanovich, Inc.

Richard Wilbur. "Museum Piece" and "Still, Citizen Sparrow" from *Ceremony and Other Poems* by Richard Wilbur; copyright 1950, 1978 by Richard Wilbur. "Mind" from *Things of This World* by Richard Wilbur; copyright 1956 by Richard Wilbur. "Tywater" from *The Beautiful Changes and Other Poems* by Richard Wilbur; copyright 1947, 1975 by Richard Wilbur. Reprinted by permission of Harcourt Brace Jovanovich, Inc. "A Game of Catch" reprinted by permission of the author. *Tartuffe* by Molière, translated by Richard Wilbur, copyright © 1961, 1962, 1963 by Richard Wilbur. Reprinted by permission of Harcourt Brace Jovanovich, Inc. *Caution:* Professionals and amateurs are hereby warned that this translation of *Tartuffe*, being fully protected under the copyright laws of the United States of America, the British Empire, including the Dominion of Canada, and all other countries which are signatories to the Universal Copyright Convention and the International Copyright Union, is subject to royalty. All rights, including professional, amateur, motion picture, recitation, lecturing, public reading, radio broadcasting, and television, are strictly reserved. Inquiries on professional and amateur rights should be addressed to Mr. Gilbert Parker, Curtis Brown, Ltd., 575 Madison Avenue, New York, New York 10022; inquiries on translation rights should be addressed to Harcourt Brace Jovanovich, Inc., 757 Third Avenue, New York, New York 10017.

William Carlos Williams. "Nantucket," "Poem," "The Red Wheelbarrow," "Spring and All," and "This Is Just to Say" from *Collected Earlier Poems* by William Carlos Williams; copyright 1938 by New Directions Publishing Corporation. Reprinted by permission of New Directions.

Virginia Woolf. "A Haunted House" from *A Haunted House and Other Stories* by Virginia Woolf; copyright 1944, 1972 by Harcourt Brace Jovanovich, Inc. Reprinted by permission of the publisher.

Charles Wright. "Virgo Descending" from *Bloodlines* by Charles Wright; copyright © 1975 by Charles Wright. Reprinted by permission of Wesleyan University Press.

James Wright. "The First Days" from *To a Blossoming Pear Tree* by James Wright; copyright © 1974, 1979 by James Wright. Reprinted by permission of Farrar, Straus & Giroux, Inc. "A Blessing" and "Lying in a Hammock at William Duffy's Farm in Pine Island, Minnesota" from *Collected Poems* by James Wright; copyright © 1961 by James Wright. Reprinted by permission of Wesleyan University Press. "A Blessing" first appeared in *Poetry*.

William Butler Yeats. The following poems from *Collected Poems* by William Butler Yeats are reprinted by permission of Macmillan Publishing Co., Inc., A. P. Watt Ltd., The Macmillan Company of Canada, and Michael and Anne Yeats: "Among School Children," "Leda and the Swan," "Sailing to Byzantium" (copyright 1928 by Macmillan Publishing Co., Inc., renewed 1956 by Georgia Yeats); "The Apparitions" (copyright 1940 by Georgia Yeats, renewed 1968 by Bertha Georgia Yeats, Michael Butler Yeats, and Anne Yeats); "Crazy Jane Talks with the Bishop" (copyright 1933 by Macmillan Publishing Co., Inc., renewed 1961 by Bertha Georgia Yeats); "The Lamentation of the Old Pensioner," two lines from "When You Are Old," "Who Goes With Fergus?", four lines from the fourth version of "Cradle Song" (copyright 1906 by Macmillan Publishing Co., Inc., renewed 1934 by William Butler Yeats); "The Magi" (copyright 1916 by Macmillan Publishing Co., Inc., renewed 1944 by Bertha Georgia Yeats); "The Second Coming" (copyright 1924 by Macmillan Publishing Co., Inc., renewed 1952 by Bertha Georgia Yeats); 1890 text of "The Old Pensioner" and Versions 2 and 3 of the last stanza of "Cradle Song" from *The Variorum Edition of the Poems of W. B. Yeats,* edited by Peter Allt and Russell K. Alspach (copyright 1957 by Macmillan Publishing Co., Inc.). *The Cat and the Moon* from *Collected Plays* by W. B. Yeats; copyright 1934, 1952 by Macmillan Publishing Co., Inc. Reprinted by permission of Macmillan Publishing Co., Inc., A. P. Watt Ltd., Michael and Anne Yeats, and Macmillan London Limited.

Stark Young. *The Cherry Orchard* by Anton Chekhov, translated from the Russian by Stark Young.

Louis Zukofsky. "In Arizona" from *Collected Short Poems, 1923–1964* by Louis Zukofsky; copyright © 1971, 1966, 1965 by Louis Zukofsky. Reprinted by permission of W. W. Norton & Company, Inc.

Photo Credits

The Bettmann Archive: pages 4, 221, 500, 509, 804, 956, 1280

Chris Corpus: page 335

The Citizen Kane Book: pages 1370, 1380, 1389, 1394, 1402, 1430, 1448

Dimitrios Harissiadis: page 748

Jay: Leviton-Atlanta: page 35

Gloria Karlson/Portogallo Photographic Services: pages 1, 383

Wendell Kilmer: page 801; courtesy The Folger Shakespeare Library and John Cranford Adams

The New York Times: page 958

James O. Sneddon: page 520; from Roethke, *Selected Letters,* University of Washington Press

Brett Weston/Photo Researchers: page 731

Marilynn K. Yee/*The New York Times:* page 57

Index

Index

Page numbers in italic type show location of biographical information

A Guide to Literary Terms

These are basic literary terms and important words from the genres of fiction, poetry, drama, and film. The page numbers will guide you quickly to definitions. To find these words elsewhere in the text, check the index. When more than two citations appear, the term is used in connection with more than one sort of literature: *conflict,* for example, is discussed in relation to fiction on page 27 and to drama on page 736.